lonely planet

USA

WA
Pacific Northwest p1020
OR
ID
MT
Rocky Mountains p733
ND
SD
MN
WI
MI
New York, New Jersey & Pennsylvania p60
ME
VT
NH
MA
CT RI
NY
New England p170
WY
NE
IA
Great Lakes p514
OH
PA
NJ
DE
NV
UT
CO
Great Plains p612
IL
IN
WV
VA
MD
CA
Southwest p801
KS
MO
KY
California p901
AZ
NM
OK
AR
TN
NC
SC
Washington, DC & the Capital Region p254
TX
Texas p666
LA
MS
AL
The South p330
GA
Florida p456
FL

AK
Alaska p1082
HI
Hawaii p1101

THIS EDITION WRITTEN AND RESEARCHED BY
Regis St Louis,

Amy C Balfour, Sandra Bao, Michael Benanav, Greg Benchwick, Sara Benson, Alison Bing, Catherine Bodry, Celeste Brash, Gregor Clark, Lisa Dunford, Ned Friary, Michael Grosberg, Paula Hardy, Adam Karlin, Mariella Krause, Carolyn McCarthy, Christopher Pitts, Brendan Sainsbury, Caroline Sieg, Adam Skolnick, Ryan Ver Berkmoes, Mara Vorhees, Karla Zimmerman

PAUL E TESSIER /GETTY IMAGES ©

GREAT SMOKY MOUNTAINS
NATIONAL PARK P349

GEORGE OSTERTAG /GETTY IMAGES ©

COLUMBIA RIVER GORGE
P1068

Contents

ON THE ROAD

SANTA MONICA P918

ZION NATIONAL PARK P874

STEVE COLE /GETTY IMAGES ©

BLEND IMAGES - MICHAEL DEYOUNG /GETTY IMAGES ©

Contents

The Parks Today

Welcome to the USA

The great American experience is about so many things: bluegrass and beaches, snow-covered peaks and redwood forests, restaurant-loving cities and big open skies.

Bright Lights, Big Cities

America is the birthplace of LA, Las Vegas, Chicago, Miami, Boston and New York City – each a brimming metropolis whose name alone conjures a million different notions of culture, cuisine and entertainment. Look more closely, and the American quilt unfurls in all its surprising variety: the eclectic music scene of Austin, the easygoing charms of antebellum Savannah, the ecoconsciousness of free-spirited Portland, the magnificent waterfront of San Francisco, and the captivating old quarters of New Orleans, still rising up from its waterlogged ashes.

On the Road Again

This is a country of road trips and great open skies, where four million miles of highways lead past red-rock deserts, below towering mountain peaks, and across fertile wheat fields that roll off toward the horizon. The sun-bleached hillsides of the Great Plains, the lush rainforests of the Pacific Northwest and the scenic country lanes of New England are a few fine starting points for the great American road trip.

Food-Loving Nation

On one evening in the US, thick barbecue ribs and smoked brisket come piping hot at a Texas roadhouse, while talented chefs blend organic produce with Asian accents at award-winning West Coast restaurants. Locals get their fix of bagels and lox at a deli in Manhattan's Upper West Side and, several states away, pancakes and fried eggs disappear under the clatter of cutlery at a 1950s-style diner. Steaming plates of lobster served off a Maine pier, oysters and champagne in a fashion-forward wine bar in California, beer and pizza at a Midwestern pub – these are just a few ways to dine à la Americana.

Cultural Behemoth

The USA has made tremendous contributions to the arts. Georgia O'Keeffe's wild landscapes, Robert Rauschenberg's surreal collages and Jackson Pollock's drip paintings have entered the vernacular of 20th-century art. Chicago and New York have become veritable drawing boards for the great architects of the modern era. And from the soulful blues born in the Mississippi Delta to the bluegrass of Appalachia and Detroit's Motown sound – plus jazz, funk, hip-hop, country, and rock and roll – America has invented sounds integral to modern music.

Why I Love the USA

By Regis St Louis, Author

When it comes to travel, America has always floored me with its staggering range of possibilities. Not many other countries have so much natural beauty – mountains, beaches, rainforest, deserts, canyons, glaciers – coupled with fascinating cities to explore, an unrivaled music scene and all the things that make travel so rewarding (friendly locals, great restaurants and farmers markets, and a burgeoning microbrewery scene). I love living in a place where I don't need a car (Brooklyn), but there's nothing quite like getting out on the open road and exploring the unsung wonders and hidden corners of this inspiring country.

For more about our authors, see page 1224

Above: Route 66, p38

USA

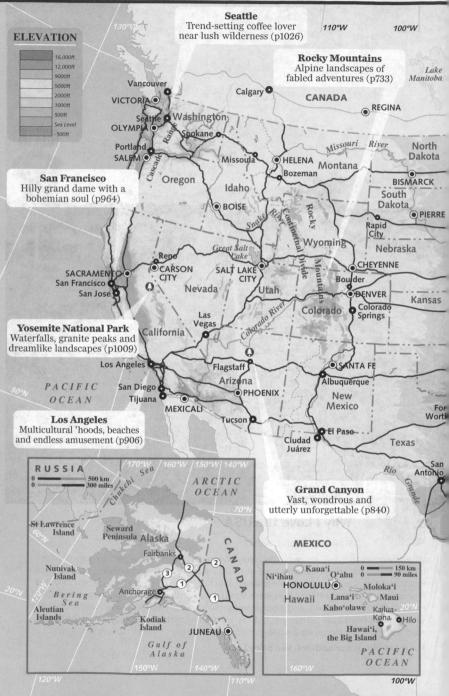

ELEVATION

16,000ft
12,000ft
9000ft
5000ft
2000ft
1000ft
500ft
Sea Level
-500ft

Seattle
Trend-setting coffee lover
near lush wilderness (p1026)

Rocky Mountains
Alpine landscapes of
fabled adventures (p733)

San Francisco
Hilly grand dame with a
bohemian soul (p964)

Yosemite National Park
Waterfalls, granite peaks and
dreamlike landscapes (p1009)

Los Angeles
Multicultural 'hoods, beaches
and endless amusement (p906)

Grand Canyon
Vast, wondrous and
utterly unforgettable (p840)

CANADA

Vancouver
VICTORIA
Seattle   Washington
OLYMPIA
Portland   Spokane
SALEM
Cascade Range
Oregon
Calgary
REGINA
Missoula   HELENA
Bozeman   Montana
Missouri River
North
Dakota
BISMARCK
South
Dakota
PIERRE
Idaho
BOISE
Snake River
Rocky
Mountains
Wyoming
Rapid
City
Nebraska
CHEYENNE
Reno
SACRAMENTO   CARSON
CITY
San Francisco
San Jose
Great Salt
Lake
SALT LAKE
CITY
Continental Divide
Boulder
DENVER
Colorado
Springs
Kansas
Nevada   Utah
California
Las
Vegas
Colorado River
Colorado
Los Angeles
San Diego
Tijuana
MEXICALI
Flagstaff
Arizona
PHOENIX
Tucson
SANTA FE
Albuquerque
New
Mexico
El Paso
Ciudad
Juárez
Texas
For
Wort
San
Antonio
Rio   Grande
MEXICO

PACIFIC
OCEAN

RUSSIA
Chukchi Sea
ARCTIC
OCEAN
St Lawrence
Island
Seward
Peninsula   Alaska
Fairbanks
Nunivak
Island
CANADA
Anchorage
Bering
Sea
Aleutian
Islands
Kodiak
Island
JUNEAU
Gulf of
Alaska

0   500 km
0   300 miles

Kaua'i
Ni'ihau   O'ahu
HONOLULU
Moloka'i
Hawaii   Lana'i   Maui
Kaho'olawe
Kailua-
Kona   Hilo
Hawai'i,
the Big Island
PACIFIC
OCEAN

0   150 km
0   90 miles

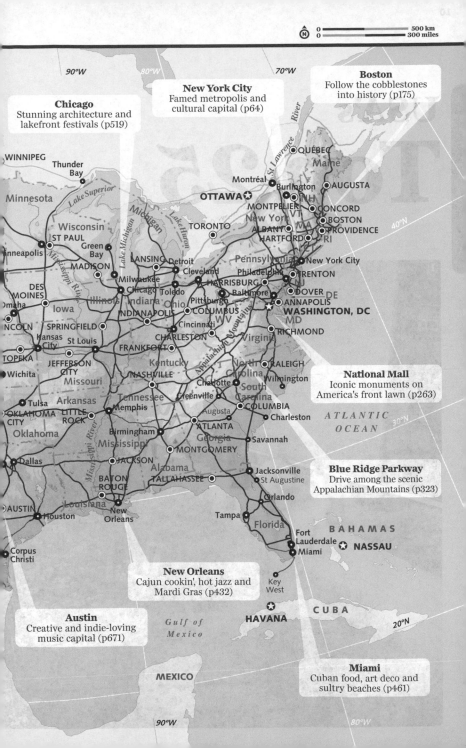

0 | 500 km
0 | 300 miles

Chicago
Stunning architecture and
lakefront festivals (p519)

New York City
Famed metropolis and
cultural capital (p64)

Boston
Follow the cobblestones
into history (p175)

90°W
80°W
70°W

WINNIPEG

Thunder
Bay

QUÉBEC
Maine

Montréal
Burlington
AUGUSTA

Minnesota

Lake Superior

OTTAWA

MONTPELIER
NH
CONCORD

Wisconsin
ST PAUL

New York
ALBANY
MA
BOSTON
HARTFORD
PROVIDENCE
RI

40°N

Green
Bay

Lake Michigan

Lake Huron

TORONTO

nneapolis

MADISON

LANSING
Detroit

Pennsylvania
New York City

inneapolis

Milwaukee
Cleveland

Philadelphia
TRENTON

DES
MOINES

Illinois
Indiana
Ohio

Chicago
Toledo

HARRISBURG

Baltimore
DOVER
DE

Omaha
Iowa

INDIANAPOLIS

Pittsburgh
COLUMBUS

ANNAPOLIS

NCOLN

SPRINGFIELD

Cincinnati

WV

WASHINGTON, DC
MD

Kansas
City
St Louis

CHARLESTON

Virginia
RICHMOND

TOPEKA

FRANKFORT

JEFFERSON
CITY

Appalachian Mountains

Wichita
Kentucky

North
Carolina
RALEIGH

Missouri
NASHVILLE

Wilmington

Tulsa
Arkansas
Tennessee
Charlotte

Greenville
South
Carolina
COLUMBIA

Mississippi River

OKLAHOMA
CITY
LITTLE
ROCK
Memphis

Augusta
Charleston

ATLANTIC
OCEAN

30°N

Oklahoma

Birmingham
ATLANTA

Dallas
Mississippi
Georgia
Savannah

JACKSON
MONTGOMERY

Alabama

BATON
ROUGE
TALLAHASSEE
Jacksonville
St Augustine

AUSTIN
Houston

Louisiana
New
Orleans

Orlando

Corpus
Christi

Tampa
Florida

BAHAMAS

Fort
Lauderdale
Miami
NASSAU

National Mall
Iconic monuments on
America's front lawn (p263)

Blue Ridge Parkway
Drive among the scenic
Appalachian Mountains (p323)

New Orleans
Cajun cookin', hot jazz and
Mardi Gras (p432)

Key
West

Austin
Creative and indie-loving
music capital (p671)

Gulf of
Mexico

HAVANA

CUBA

20°N

MEXICO

Miami
Cuban food, art deco and
sultry beaches (p461)

90°W
80°W

USA's
Top 25

New York City

1 Home to striving artists, hedge fund moguls and immigrants from every corner of the globe, New York City (p64) is constantly reinventing itself. It remains one of the world centers of fashion, theater, food, music, publishing, advertising and finance. A staggering number of museums, parks and ethnic neighborhoods are scattered through the five boroughs. Do as every New Yorker does: hit the streets. Every block reflects the character and history of this dizzying kaleidoscope, and on even a short walk you can cross continents. The High Line (p75)

Grand Canyon

2 You've seen it on film, heard about it from all and sundry who've made the trip. Is it worth the hype? The answer is a resounding yes. The Grand Canyon (p840) is vast and nearly incomprehensible in age – it took 6 million years for the canyon to form and some rocks exposed along its walls are 2 billion years old. Peer over the edge and you'll confront the great power and mystery of this earth we live on. Once you see it, no other natural phenomenon quite compares.

CLAIRE TAKACS / GETTY IMAGES ©

MICHELE FALZONE / GETTY IMAGES ©

Route 66

3 This ribbon of concrete was the USA's original road trip, connecting Chicago with Los Angeles in 1926. You'll find neon signs, motor courts, pie-filled diners and drive-in theaters along the way. The route (p38) was bypassed by the I-40 in 1984, but many original sites remain and tracing Route 66 today is a journey through small-town America. Whether you do the whole length or just a stretch, you'll come face to face with classic, nostalgic Americana.

New Orleans

4 Reborn after devastating Hurricane Katrina in 2005, New Orleans (p432) is back. Caribbean-colonial architecture, Creole cuisine and a riotous air of celebration seem more alluring than ever in the Big Easy. Nights out are spent catching Dixieland jazz, blues and rock amid bouncing live music joints, and the city's riotous annual Mardi Gras and Jazz Fest are famous the world over. 'Nola' is a food-loving town that celebrates its myriad culinary influences. Feast on lip-smacking jambalaya, soft-shelled crab and Louisiana *cochon* (pulled pork) before hitting the bar scene on Frenchman St.

Yellowstone National Park

5 Stunning natural beauty, amazing geology and some of the best wildlife watching in North America: these are just a few reasons why Yellowstone (p777) has such star power among the world's national parks. Divided into five distinct regions, this place is huge – almost 3500 sq miles – and you could spend many days exploring the park's wonders. Highlights include massive geysers, waterfalls, fossil forests, rugged mountains, scenic overlooks and gurgling mud pools – with some 1100 miles of hiking trails providing the best way to take it all in.
Morning Glory Pool, Upper Geyser Basin (p777)

New England in Fall

6 It's an event approaching epic proportions in New England (p170): watching the leaves change color. You can do it just about anywhere – all you need is one brilliant tree. But if you're most people, you'll want lots of trees. From the Litchfield Hills (p221) in Connecticut and the Berkshires (p208) in Massachusetts to the Green Mountains (p227) in Vermont, entire hillsides blaze in brilliant crimsons, oranges and yellows. Bridges and white-steeple churches with abundant maple trees put Vermont and New Hampshire at the forefront of leaf-peeping heaven. New Hampshire (p232)

Yosemite National Park

7 Yosemite's iconic glacier-carved valley never fails to get the heart racing, even when it's bumper-to-bumper in summer. In springtime, get drenched by the spray of its thundering snowmelt waterfalls and twirl singing to the *Sound of Music* in high-country meadows awash with wildflowers. The scenery of Yosemite (p1009) is intoxicating, with dizzying rock walls and formations, and ancient giant sequoia trees. If you look for it, you'll find solitude and space in the 1169 sq miles of development-free wilderness.

Walt Disney World

8 Want to set the bar high? Call yourself 'the happiest place on earth'. Walt Disney World (p506) does, and then pulls out all the stops to deliver the exhilarating sensation that you are the most important character in the show. Despite all the frantic rides, entertainment and nostalgia, the magic is watching your own child swell with belief after they have made Goofy laugh, been curtsied to by Cinderella, guarded the galaxy with Buzz Lightyear and battled Darth Maul like your very own Jedi knight.

7

PAWEL GAUL / GETTY IMAGES ©

GARRY GAY / GETTY IMAGES ©

Chicago

9 The Windy City (p519) will blow you away with its cloud-scraping architecture, lakefront beaches and world-class museums. But its true mojo is its blend of high culture and earthy pleasures. Is there another city that dresses its Picasso sculpture in local sports team gear? Where residents queue for hot dogs in equal measure to North America's top restaurant? Winters are brutal, but come summer, Chicago fetes the warm days with food and music festivals.

San Francisco & Wine Country

10 Amid the clatter of trams and thick fog that sweeps in by night, the diverse hill and valley neighborhoods of San Francisco (p964) invite long days of wandering, with great indie shops, world-class restaurants and bohemian nightlife. Round a corner to waterfront views and you'll be hooked. If you can tear yourself away, the vineyards of Napa, Sonoma and the Russian River Valley lie just north (p994). Touring vineyards, drinking great wine and lingering over farm-to-table meals is all part of the Wine Country experience. Sonoma County (p997)

DOUG MCKINLAY / GETTY IMAGES ©

Las Vegas

11 Sin City (p806) is a neon-fueled ride through the nerve center of American strike-it-rich fantasies. See billionaires' names gleam from the marquees of luxury hotels. Hear a raucous soundscape of slot machines, clinking martini glasses and the hypnotic beats of DJs spinning till dawn. Sip cocktails under palm trees and play blackjack by the pool. Visit Paris, the Wild West and a tropical island, all in one night. It's all here and it's open 24 hours, all for the price of a poker chip (and a little luck).

The Deep South

12 Steeped in history and complex regional pride, the Deep South (p351) is America at its weirdest and most fascinating, from the moss-draped South Carolina swamps to the cinder block juke joints of the steamy Mississippi Delta and the isolated French-speaking enclaves of the Louisiana bayou. Famous for its slow pace, the Deep South is all about enjoying life's small pleasures: sucking down fresh Gulf oysters at an Alabama seafood shack, strolling Savannah's antebellum alleys, or sipping sweet tea on the porch with new friends. Oak Alley Plantation (p449), Louisiana

National Mall

13 Nearly 2 miles long and lined with iconic monuments and hallowed marble buildings, the National Mall (p263) is the epicenter of Washington, DC's political and cultural life. In the summer, massive music and food festivals are staged here, while year-round visitors wander the halls of America's finest museums lining the green. For exploring American history, there's no better place to ruminate, whether tracing your hand along the Vietnam War Memorial or ascending the steps of Lincoln Memorial, where Martin Luther King Jr gave his famous 'I Have a Dream' speech. Lincoln Memorial (p267)

Pacific Coast Highways

14 Stunning coastal highways wind their way down the US West Coast from Canada all the way to the Mexican border and offer dramatic scenery. Clifftop views over crashing waves, rolling hills, fragrant eucalyptus forests and lush redwoods. There are wild and remote beaches, idyllic towns and fishing villages, and primeval rainforest. Amid the remote natural beauty you can mix things up with big-city adventures, dipping into Seattle, Portland, San Francisco and Los Angeles. Bixby Creek Bridge, Big Sur (p957)

Boston & Cape Cod

15 Start by tracing the footsteps of early Tea Partiers like Paul Revere and Sam Adams on Boston's famed Freedom Trail (p185). After following the road through American revolutionary history, go romp around the campus of Harvard University (p184) and do a little rabble-rousing yourself at one of the city's historic pubs. Then cool off by hitting the beaches of the Cape Cod National Seashore (p199), hopping on a whale-watching cruise or getting lost in the wild dunes of Provincetown (p200). Humpback whale, off Provincetown

Rocky Mountains

16 The Rockies (p733) are home to the highest peaks in the lower 48 states. Craggy peaks, raging rivers, age-old canyons and national parks set the scene. Go skiing and snowboarding down pristine, powdery slopes in the winter, hike and mountain bike amid spring wildflowers or feel the rush of white water on sun-drenched summer afternoons. After a good dose of the fine fresh air, recharge at microbreweries, farm-to-table restaurants and invigorating hot springs. Bison, Grand Teton National Park (p782)

Miami

17 How does one city get so lucky? Most content themselves with one or two attributes, but Miami (p461) seems to have it all. Beyond the stunning beaches and Art Deco Historic District, there's culture at every turn. In cigar-filled dance halls, Havana expats dance to *son* and boleros, in exclusive nightclubs stiletto-heeled, fiery-eyed Brazilian models shake to Latin hip-hop, and in the park old men clack dominoes. To top it off, street vendors and restaurants dish out flavors from the Caribbean, Cuba, Argentina and Spain. South Beach, Miami

STEPHEN SAKS / GETTY IMAGES ©

SHELLY PERRY / GETTY IMAGES ©

Native American Sites

18 The Southwest (p801) is Native American country with a fantastic array of sites covering both the distant past and the present. In Colorado and Arizona, you can visit the ancient clifftop homes of Ancestral Puebloans, who lived among this dramatic and rocky landscape before mysteriously abandoning it. For living cultures, visit the Navajo Nation. Amid spectacular scenery, you can trek to the bottom of the sacred Canyon de Chelly (p848), overnight on the reservation land and purchase handicrafts directly from the artisans. Puebloan cliff dwellings, Mesa Verde National Park (p769)

Blue Ridge Parkway

19 In the southern Appalachian Mountains of Virginia and North Carolina (p331), you can take in sublime sunsets, watch for wildlife and lose all sense of the present while staring off at the vast wilderness surrounding this 469-mile roadway. Dozens of great hikes take you deeper into nature, from easy trails along lakes and streams to challenging scrambles up to eagles' nest heights. Camp or spend the night at forest lodges and don't miss the great bluegrass and mountain music scene of nearby towns such as Asheville in North Carolina, and Floyd and Galax in Virginia.

Austin & San Antonio

20 One of Texas' brightest stars, eco-friendly Austin (p671) is a great dining, drinking and shopping city, with a creative, bohemian vibe courtesy of its university and renegade subculture. Austin is one of America's music capitals with a dizzying variety of sounds playing out on stages nightly. Two major music fests showcase the best of the best. Southwest of Austin, San Antonio (p682) beguiles visitors with its pretty Riverwalk, lively festivals (including the 10-day Fiesta San Antonio) and rich history (from serene Spanish missions to the battle-scarred Alamo). Musicians, Austin

SAPNA REDDY PHOTOGRAPHY / GETTY IMAGES ©

Columbia River Gorge

21 Carved out by the mighty Columbia as the Cascades uplifted, the Columbia River Gorge (p1068) is a geologic marvel. With Washington State on its north side and Oregon at its south, the state-dividing gorge offers countless waterfalls and spectacular hikes, as well as agricultural bounties of apples, pears and cherries. And if you're into windsurfing or kite-boarding, then head straight to the sporty town of Hood River, ground zero for these adventure sports. Whether you're a hiker, fruit-lover or adrenaline junkie, the gorge delivers. Multnomah Falls

Great Lakes

22 This watery region is prime for off-the-beaten path touring. Intrepid outdoors folk can wet a paddle in Minnesota's Boundary Waters (p609), where nighttime brings a blanket of stars and the lullaby of wolf howls. Or trek to Michigan's Upper Peninsula (p582), a remote landscape of rugged forests and wave-bashed cliffs. If that seems too far flung, there's always dairy-farm hopping in Wisconsin to test the cheeses. And unsung but rockin' towns such as Minneapolis, Milwaukee and Detroit offer groovy neighborhoods where local beers and bands thrive. Boundary Waters

Seattle

23 A cutting-edge Pacific Rim city with an uncanny habit of turning locally hatched ideas into global brands, Seattle (p1026) has earned its place in the pantheon of 'great' US metropolises, with a world-renowned music scene, a mercurial coffee culture, and a penchant for internet-driven innovation. But, while Seattle's trendsetters rush to unearth the next big thing, city traditionalists guard its soul with distinct urban neighborhoods, a homegrown food culture and what is arguably the nation's finest public market, Pike Place (p1026). Pike Place Market

Los Angeles

24 Although it's the entertainment capital of the world, Los Angeles (p906) is more than silver-screen stars. This is the city of odd-loving Venice Beach, art galleries and dining in Santa Monica, indie-loving neighborhoods such as Los Feliz and Silverlake, surf-loving beaches like Malibu, and rugged and wild Griffith Park. And this is just the beginning. Dig deeper and you'll find an assortment of museums displaying every kind of ephemera, a cultural renaissance happening downtown and vibrant multiethnic 'hoods with great food. Venice Beach (p918)

Middle Americana

25 Endless open roads, stunning parks like the Badlands and great food in Kansas City are just some of the myriad allures of the Great Plains (p612). Surprises abound: Nebraska's Carhenge (p653), South Dakota's Corn Palace (p640), just down the road from the huckster mecca of Wall Drug, and Kansas' fantabulous space museum (p657) plus its wild art in Lucas (p657) are but a few. Start down iconic old roads like US50 and you'll find so many diversions that the journey is the point of the trip. Carhenge (artist: Jim Reinders)

24

25

Need to Know

For more information, see Survival Guide (p1172)

Currency
US dollar ($)

Language
English

Money
ATMs widely available. Credit cards accepted at most hotels, restaurants and shops.

Visas
Visitors from Canada, the UK, Australia, New Zealand, Japan and many EU countries don't need visas for less than 90-day stays. Other nations see http://travel.state.gov.

Cell Phones
Foreign phones that operate on tri- or quad-band frequencies will work in the USA. Or purchase inexpensive cell phones with a pay-as-you-go plan here.

Driving
Drive on the right; steering wheel is on the left side of the car.

When to Go

- Tropical climate
- Dry climate
- Warm to hot summers, mild winters
- Mild to hot summers, cold winters
- Polar climate

Seattle
GO May–Sep

New York City
GO May–Sep

Chicago
GO Jun–Sep

Los Angeles
GO Apr–Oct

New Orleans
GO Dec–May

Miami
GO Dec–Apr

High Season
(Jun–Aug)

➡ Warm days across the country, with generally high temperatures.

➡ Busiest season, with big crowds and higher prices.

➡ In ski resort areas, January to March is high season.

Shoulder Season
(Oct & Apr–May)

➡ Milder temps, fewer crowds.

➡ Spring flowers (April); fiery autumn colors (October) in many parts.

Low Season
(Nov–Mar)

➡ Wintery days, with snowfall in the north, and heavier rains in some regions.

➡ Lowest prices for accommodations (aside from ski resorts and warmer getaway destinations).

23

Websites

Lonely Planet (www.lonely-planet.com/usa) Destination information, hotel bookings, travel forum and photos.

National Park Service (NPS; www.nps.gov) Gateway to America's greatest natural treasures, its national parks.

Festivals.com (www.festivals.com) Find America's best celebrations; live music, food, drink and dance.

New York Times Travel (http://travel.nytimes.com) Travel news, practical advice and engaging features.

Roadside America (www.roadsideamerica.com) For all things weird and wacky.

Important Numbers

To call any regular number, dial the area code, followed by the seven-digit number.

Emergency	911
USA Country Code	1
Directory Assistance	411
International directory assistance	00
International access code from the USA	011

Exchange Rates

Australia	A$1	US$0.94
Canada	C$1	US$0.96
Europe	€1	US$1.36
Japan	¥100	US$1.02
New Zealand	NZ$1	US$0.83
UK	UK£1	US$1.60

For current exchange rates see www.xe.com

Daily Costs

Budget: Less than $100

➡ Dorm beds: $20–30; campgrounds: $15–30; budget motels: $60

➡ Travel on buses, subways and other mass transit: $2–3

➡ Lunch from a cafe or food truck: $5–9

Midrange: $150–$250

➡ Double room in midrange hotel: $100–200

➡ Decent-restaurant dinner: $50–80 for two

➡ Car hire: from $30 per day

Top End: More than $250

➡ Lodging in a resort: from $250

➡ Dining in top restaurants: $60–100 per person

➡ Big nights out (plays, concerts, nightclubs): $60–200

Opening Hours

Bars 5pm to midnight Sunday to Thursday, to 2am Friday and Saturday

Banks 8:30am–4:30pm Monday to Friday

Nightclubs 10pm–3am Thursday to Saturday

Post offices 9am–5pm Monday to Friday

Shopping malls 9am–9pm

Stores 9am–6pm Monday to Saturday, noon to 5pm Sunday

Supermarkets 8am–8pm, some open 24 hours

Arriving in the USA

JFK (New York; p117) From JFK take the AirTrain to Jamaica Station and then LIRR to Penn Station, which costs $12 to $15 (45 minutes). A taxi to Manhattan costs $52, plus toll and tip (45 to 90 minutes).

Los Angeles International (LAX; p928) LAX Flyaway Bus to Union Station costs $7 (30 to 50 minutes); door-to-door Prime Time & SuperShuttle costs $16 to $28 (35 to 90 minutes); and a taxi to Downtown costs $47 (25 to 50 minutes).

Miami International (p472) SuperShuttle to South Beach for $21 (50 to 90 minutes); taxi to Miami Beach for $34 (40 to 60 minutes); or take the Metrorail to downtown (Government Center) for $2 (15 minutes).

Time Zones in the USA

There are four time zones in the continental US:

EST Eastern (GMT -5 hours): NYC, New England and Atlanta

CST Central (GMT -6 hours): Chicago, New Orleans and Houston

MST Mountain (GMT -7 hours): Denver, Santa Fe and Phoenix

PST Pacific (GMT -8 hours): Seattle, San Francisco and Las Vegas

Most of Alaska is one hour behind Pacific time (GMT -9 hours), while Hawaii is two hours behind Pacific time. So if it's 9pm in New York, it's 8pm in Chicago, 7pm in Denver, 6pm in Los Angeles, 4pm in Anchorage and 3pm in Honolulu.

For much more on **getting around**, see p1189

If You Like...

Beaches

Coastlines on two oceans and the Gulf of Mexico make tough choices for beach-lovers, from the rugged and wild shores of Maine to the surf-loving beauties of Southern California.

Point Reyes National Seashore The water is cold but the scenery is magical along this beautiful stretch of untamed coastline in Northern California. (p992)

South Beach This world-famous strand is less about wave frolicking than taking in the parade of passing people on Miami's favorite playground. (p461)

Cape Cod National Seashore Massive sand dunes, picturesque lighthouses and cool forests invite endless exploring on the Massachusetts cape. (p199)

Montauk At the eastern tip of Long Island, windswept Montauk has pretty shoreline, beach camping and a still-functioning 18th-century lighthouse. (p121)

Santa Monica Hit the shore, then go celeb-spotting at edgy art galleries and high-end bistros. (p918)

Grayton Beach State Park This pristine coastal park on the Florida panhandle has beautiful beaches. (p511)

Theme Parks

America's theme parks come in many varieties – from old-fashioned cotton candy and roller-coaster fun to multiday immersions in pure Peter Pan–style make-believe.

Disney With one on either coast, Disney makes things easy when you're ready to delve into this enchanting fairy-tale world. (p930; p506)

Dollywood A paean to the much-loved country singer Dolly Parton, with Appalachian-themed rides and attractions in the hills of Tennessee. (p385)

Legoland Everyone's favorite building block gets its due in this creative hands-on park for the younger set outside of San Diego. (p944)

Cedar Park Masochists line up for the frightening, corkscrewing GateKeeper (new in 2013) at this legendary park in Ohio. (p560)

Universal Orlando Resort Famed home of Universal Studios and the new Wizarding World of Harry Potter. (p503)

Wine

Visiting wineries isn't just about tasting first-rate drops, but drinking in the pretty countryside and sampling the enticing farm stands and delectable bistros that often sprout alongside vineyards.

Napa Valley Home to more than 200 vineyards, Napa is synonymous with world-class winemaking. You'll find superb varietals, gourmet bites and beautiful scenery. (p994)

Willamette Valley Outside of Portland, OR, this fertile region produces some of the tastiest Pinot Noir on the planet. (p1065)

Finger Lakes Upstate New York is a prime growing region. After a few quaffs, you can walk it off at nearby state parks. (p124)

Virginia Wine Country There's much history in this up-and-coming wine district. You can even sample the wines grown on Thomas Jefferson's old estate. (p307)

IF YOU LIKE... OLD-SCHOOL DINERS

Tuck into thick pancakes at Arcade, a Memphis classic diner where Elvis used to eat. (p369)

Verde Valley If you think Arizona is all desert, guess again. Take a winery tour in this lush setting near Sedona. (p834)

Yakima Valley Sample velvety reds in Washington State's biggest and oldest wine region. (p1052)

Great Food

The classic American dining experience: making a mess at a Maine lobster shack; plowing through BBQ in Texas Hill Country; feasting at world-famous restaurants in New York, Los Angeles and beyond.

New York City Whatever you crave, the world's great restaurant capital has you covered. (p100)

New England Lobsters, clambakes, oysters and fresh fish galore – the Northeast is a paradise for seafood lovers. (p205)

Chicago The city that earns rave reviews for its Greek, Thai and molecular gastronomy, famously deep-dish pizzas and much more. (p534)

San Francisco Real-deal taquerias and trattorias, world-class Vietnamese, magnificent farmers markets and acclaimed chefs all fire up world-class California cuisine. (p981)

Hill Country Texas smokes them all – at least when it comes to barbecue. Carnivores shouldn't miss the legendary capital of mouth-watering brisket. (p679)

Portland Bridgetown boasts a cutting-edge food scene; its food trucks serve imaginative dishes from every corner of the globe. (p1060)

New Orleans French, Spanish, Filipinos, Haitians and other nationalities have contributed to the gastro-amalgamation, making Nola one of America's most food-centric cities. (p442)

(Top) Nashville (p372)
(Bottom) Race Point Lighthouse (p201), Cape Cod

Hiking

The stage is set: soaring mountains, mist-covered rainforests, red-rock canyons and craggy clifftops overlooking wild, windswept seas. These are just a few places where you can hike the great American wilderness.

Appalachian Trail Even if you chose not to walk all 2178 miles, the AT is well worth visiting. Fourteen states provide access. (p327)

Marin County Hike amid towering redwoods at Muir Woods, then head to the nearby headlands for a scenic walk overlooking the Pacific. (p991)

North Cascades Glaciers, jagged peaks and alpine lakes are all part of the scenery at this wild and remote wilderness. (p1047)

Acadia National Park Hiking trails through this dramatic park pass along sea cliffs, though forests and near boulder-strewn peaks. (p249)

Rocky Mountain National Park This Colorado stunner has snowcapped peaks, wildflower-filled valleys and picturesque mountain lakes. (p751)

Off-Beat America

When you tire of traipsing through museums and ticking off well-known sights, unbuckle your safety belt and throw yourself into the strange world of American kitsch and nonesuch.

Carhenge A cheeky homage to Stonehenge, made of old cars assembled in a Nebraska field. (p653)

Emma Crawford Coffin Races Paint your coffin, add wheels and join the races at this spirited free-for-all in Colorado Springs. (p762)

NashTrash Tours Nashville's tall-haired 'Jugg Sisters' take visitors on a deliciously tacky journey through Nashville's spicier side. (p376)

Key West Cemetery Gothic labyrinth full of colorful epitaphs, such as 'I told you I was sick.' (p484)

American Visionary Art Museum See outsider art (including pieces created by the clinically insane) at this Baltimore curiosity. (p289)

Loneliest Road Take the empty highway through Nevada, and don't forget to stop at the Shoe Tree. (p824)

Mini Time Machine Museum of Miniatures This whimsical new museum in Tucson is devoted to tiny things. (p851)

Architecture

Whether you're a devotee of Frank Lloyd Wright or simply enjoy gazing at beautifully designed buildings, the US has a treasure chest of architectural wonders.

Chicago Birthplace of the skyscraper, Chicago has magnificent works by many of the great 20th-century architects. (p519)

Fallingwater This Frank Lloyd Wright masterpiece seamlessly blends into the forested landscape and the waterfall over which the house is built. (p168)

New York City Much photographed classics include the art-deco Chrysler Building, the spiraling Guggenheim and the majestic Brooklyn Bridge. (p64)

Miami Miami's art-deco district is a Technicolor dream come to life. (p461)

San Francisco See elegant Victorians and cutting-edge 21st-century masterpieces in perhaps America's most European city. (p964)

Savannah This Southern belle never fails to turn heads with her striking antebellum architecture. (p406)

Native American Culture

The continent's first peoples have a connection to the land and its animals, which stretches back many generations, and is most evident in sites of the southwest.

National Museum of the American Indian Appropriately, the capital holds America's finest museum dedicated to Native American peoples. (p266)

Mesa Verde Carved into the mountains of Southern Colorado, this fascinating site was mysteriously abandoned by Ancestral Puebloans. (p769)

Pine Ridge Indian Reservation Visit the tragic site where Lakotas were massacred by US Cavalry, then visit nearby Red Cloud, to learn more about the Lakota. (p642)

IF YOU LIKE... MOUNTAIN CLIMBING

Sign up for a challenging five-day guided climb to the summit of 14,411ft Mt Rainier. (p1050)

Alamo Square (p974), San Francisco

Navajo Nation Take in the stunning scenery and learn more about this proud people in Arizona. (p848)

Zuni Pueblo Purchase beautifully wrought silver jewelry and overnight at a tribally licensed inn. (p882)

Historical Sights

The East Coast is where you'll find the original 13 colonies. To delve into the past, head south and west, where Spanish explorers and indigenous peoples left their mark.

Philadelphia The nation's first capital is where the idea of America as an independent nation first coalesced. Excellent museums tell the story. (p142)

Boston Visit Paul Revere's former home, an 18th-century graveyard and the decks of the 1797 USS *Constitution*. (p175)

Williamsburg Step back into the 1700s in the preserved town of Williamsburg, the largest living history museum on the planet. (p311)

Washington, DC Visit the sites where Lincoln was assassinated, Martin Luther King Jr gave his most famous speech and Nixon's presidency was undone. (p259)

Harpers Ferry A fascinating open-air museum of 19th-century village life beautifully

framed by mountains and rivers. (p326)

St Augustine Cobblestone streets, 300-year-old forts and a youthful fountain at this Spanish Colonial town founded in the 1500s. (p491)

Beer & Microbreweries

Microbreweries have exploded in popularity, and you'll never be far from a finely crafted pint. Colorado, Washington and Oregon are particularly famed for their breweries.

IF YOU LIKE...
OLD-FASHIONED AMERICANA

Flash back to the 1950s at the Wellfleet Drive-In movie theater in Cape Cod. (p200)

IF YOU LIKE... OUTDOOR MUSIC

Red Rocks Park has a 9000-seat amphitheater dramatically set between 400ft-high red sandstone rocks. The acoustics are phenomenal, which is why many artists record live albums here. (p745)

Magic Hat Brewery Vermont, one of America's microbrewery capitals, deserves special mention – and Magic Hat makes for a refreshing and entertaining beer outing. (p230)

Mountain Sun Pub & Brewery Boulder's favorite microbrewery serves an array of excellent drafts, plus good food and regular music jams. (p750)

Portland Valhalla for beer lovers, Portland has over 30 microbreweries within city limits. (p1061)

Mammoth Brewing Company Head to the laid-back California mountain town of Mammoth Lakes for a dazzling tasting. (p1017)

Asheville Home to more than 20 microbreweries and brewpubs, Asheville is leading North Carolina's beer renaissance. (p347)

Geologic Wonders

With red-rock deserts, petrified forests, blasting geysers and one massive hole in the ground, you might feel like you've stepped onto another planet.

Grand Canyon Needing little introduction, this mile-deep, 10-mile wide hole was carved over 6 million years. Take your time when you go. (p840)

Yellowstone Massive geysers, rainbow-colored thermal pools and the supervolcano it all sits on: this national park certainly puts on a show. (p777)

Hawai'i Volcanoes National Park Glimpse lava deserts, smoldering craters and, with luck, the sight of molten lava rolling into the ocean. (p1113)

Carlsbad Caverns Take a two-mile walk along a subterranean passage to arrive in the great room – a veritable underground cathedral. (p900)

Southern Utah National Parks See 3000ft-tall slot canyons, eroding pinacles and spires in the seven national parks and monuments of Utah's red-rock country. (p871)

Live Music

Americans know where to catch a good live band – whether they're after Memphis blues, Appalachian bluegrass, New Orleans jazz, fist-pumping rock, sultry salsa, country crooning or much, much more.

Austin Home to more than 200 venues and the country's biggest music fest, Austin proudly wears the music crown. (p676)

New Orleans The Big Easy has a soundtrack as intoxicating as the city itself – from room-filling big-band jazz to indie rock. (p446)

Nashville This river city is a showcase for country, bluegrass, blues, folk and plenty of rough-and-tumble honky-tonks. (p380)

Los Angeles LA is a magnet for aspiring stars and draws serious talent. Don't miss the legendary Sunset Strip for A-list artists. (p926)

Memphis Juke joints and dive bars host blazing live bands. (p370)

Kansas City This barbecue-loving Missouri city has a venerable live-music scene, especially when it comes to jazz. (p630)

Month by Month

TOP EVENTS

Mardi Gras, February or March

South by Southwest, March

National Cherry Blossom Festival, March

Chicago Blues Festival, June

Independence Day, July

January

The New Year starts off with a shiver, as snowfall blankets large swaths of the country. Ski resorts kick into high gear, while sun-lovers seek refuge in warmer climes (especially Florida).

✈️ Mummers Parade

Philadelphia's biggest event is this brilliant parade (www.mummers.com), where local clubs spend months creating costumes and mobile scenery in order to win top honors on New Year's Day.

✈️ Sundance Film Festival

The legendary Sundance Film Festival (www.sundance.org) brings Hollywood stars, indie directors and avid film-goers to Park City, UT, for a 10-day indie extravaganza in late January. Plan well in advance, as passes sell out fast.

February

Aside from mountain getaways, many Americans dread February with its long dark nights and frozen days. For foreign visitors, this can be the cheapest time to travel, with ultradiscount rates for flights and hotels.

✈️ Mardi Gras

Held in late February or early March, on the day before Ash Wednesday, Mardi Gras (Fat Tuesday) is the finale of Carnival. New Orleans' celebrations (www.mardigrasneworleans.com) are legendary as colorful parades, masquerade balls, feasting and plenty of hedonism rule the day.

March

The first blossoms of spring arrive (at least in the south – the north still shivers in the chill). In the mountains, it's still high season for skiing. Meanwhile, drunken spring-breakers descend on Florida.

✈️ St Patricks Day

On the 17th, the patron saint of Ireland is honored with brass bands and ever-flowing pints of Guinness; huge parades occur in New York, Boston and Chicago (which goes all-out by dyeing the Chicago River green).

✈️ South by Southwest

Each year Austin, TX, becomes ground zero for one of the biggest music fests in North America. More than 2000 performers play at nearly 100 venues. SXSW is also a major film festival and interactive fest – a platform for groundbreaking ideas. (p673)

April

The weather is warming up, but April can still be unpredictable with chilly weather mixed with a few, teasingly warm days up north. Down south, it's a fine time to travel.

✈️ Fiesta San Antonio

Mid-April is the liveliest time to visit this pretty

river town in Texas, as you'll find 10 days of fiesta (www.fiesta-sa.org) with carnivals, parades, dancing and lots of great eating.

☆ Jazz Fest

On the last weekend in April, New Orleans hosts the country's best jazz jam (www.nojazzfest.com), with top-notch acts and plenty of good cheer. In addition to world-class jazz, there's also great food and crafts.

☆ Patriot's Day

Massachusetts' big day out falls on the third Monday in April and features Revolutionary War re-enactments and parades in Lexington and Concord, plus the running of the Boston Marathon and a much-watched Red Sox game at home.

☆ Gathering of Nations

For an immersion in indigenous culture, head to Albuquerque for the Gathering of Nations (www.gatheringofnations.com), the largest Native American powwow in the world. You'll find traditional dance, music, food, crafts and the crowning of Miss Indian World.

May

May is true spring and one of the loveliest times to travel, with blooming wildflowers and generally mild sunny weather. Summer crowds and high prices have yet to arrive.

☆ Beale Street Music Festival

Blues lovers descend on Memphis for this venerable music fest held over three days in early May. (p367)

☆ Cinco de Mayo

Celebrate Mexico's victory over the French with salsa music and pitchers of margaritas across the country. LA, San Francisco and Denver all throw some of the biggest bashes.

June

Summer is here. Americans spend more time at outdoor cafes and restaurants, and head to the shore or to national parks. School is out; vacationers fill the highways and resorts, bringing higher prices.

☆ Bonnaroo Music & Arts Festival

In the heartland of Tennessee, this sprawling music fest (p383) showcases big-name rock, soul, country and more over four days in mid-June.

☆ Gay Pride

In some cities, gay pride celebrations last a week, but in San Francisco, it's a month-long party, where the last weekend in June sees giant parades. You'll find other great pride events at major cities across the country.

☆ Chicago Blues Festival

It's the globe's biggest free blues fest (www.chicagobluesfestival.us), with three days of the music that made Chicago famous. More than 640,000 people unfurl blankets by the multiple stages that take over Grant Park in early June.

☆ CMA Music Festival

This legendary country-music fest (www.cmaworld.com) has more than 400 artists performing at stages on Riverfront Park and LP Field.

☆ Telluride Bluegrass Festival

The banjo gets its due at this festive, boot-stomping music jam (www.planetbluegrass.com) in Colorado mountain country. You'll find nonstop performances, excellent regional food stalls and great locally crafted microbrews. It's good all-comers entertainment and many folks even camp.

☆ Tanglewood Musical Festival

Open-air concerts run all summer long (late June to early September) in an enchanting setting in western Massachusetts.

July

With summer in full swing, Americans break out the backyard barbecues or head for the beach. The prices are high and the crowds can be fierce, but it's one of the liveliest times to visit.

☆ Independence Day

The nation celebrates its birthday with a bang, as nearly every town and city stages a massive fireworks show. Quick to the draw, Chicago goes off on the 3rd.

Washington, DC and New York, Philadelphia and Boston are all great spots.

Oregon Brewers Festival

The beer-loving city of Portland pulls out the stops and pours a heady array of handcrafted perfection (www.oregonbrewfest.com). Featuring 80 different beers from around the country, there are plenty of choices; and it's nicely set along the banks of the Willamette River.

Pageant of the Masters

This eight-week arts fest (www.lagunafestivalofarts.org) brings a touch of the surreal to Laguna Beach, CA. On stage, meticulously costumed actors create living pictures – imitations of famous works of art – which is accompanied by narration and an orchestra.

Newport Folk Festival

Newport, RI, a summer haunt of the well-heeled, hosts a world-class music fest (www.newportfolkfest.com) in late July. Top folk artists take to the stage at this fun, all-welcoming event.

August

Expect blasting heat in August, with temperatures and humidity less bearable the further south you go. You'll find people-packed beaches, high prices and empty cities on weekends, when residents escape to the nearest waterfront.

(Top) Mardi Gras parade, New Orleans (p432)

(Bottom) Halloween jack o'-lanterns

☆ Lollapalooza

This mondo rock (www.lollapalooza.com) fest sees more than 100 bands spilling off eight stages in Grant Park, Chicago, on the first Friday-to-Sunday in August.

☆ Iowa State Fair

If you've never been to a state fair, now's your chance. This event (www.iowastatefair.org) is where you'll find country crooning, wondrous carvings (in butter), livestock shows, sprawling food stalls and a down-home good time in America's heartland.

September

With the end of summer, cooler days arrive, making for pleasant outings nationwide. The kids are back in school, and concert halls, gallery spaces and performing arts venues kick off a new season.

☆ Santa Fe Fiesta

Santa Fe hosts the nation's longest-running festival (www.santafefiesta.org), a spirited two-week-long event with parades, concerts and the burning of Old Man Gloom.

☆ Burning Man Festival

Over one week, some 50,000 revelers, artists and assorted free spirits descend on Nevada's Black Rock Desert to create a temporary metropolis of art installations, theme camps and environmental curiosities. It culminates in the burning of a giant stick figure (www.burningman.com).

☆ New York Film Festival

Just one of many big film fests (www.filmlinc.com) in New York City – Tribeca Film Fest in late April is another goodie; this one features world premieres from across the globe.

October

Temperatures are falling, as autumn brings fiery colors to northern climes. It's high season where the leaves are most brilliant (New England); elsewhere expect lower prices and fewer crowds.

☆ Fantasy Fest

Key West's answer to Mardi Gras brings more than 100,000 revelers to the subtropical enclave in the week leading up to Halloween. Expect parades, colorful floats, costume parties, the selecting of a conch king and queen and plenty of alcohol-fueled merriment (www.fantasyfest.net).

☆ Halloween

In NYC, you can don a costume and join the Halloween parade up Sixth Ave. West Hollywood in Los Angeles and San Francisco's Castro district are great places to see outrageous outfits. Salem also hosts spirited events throughout October.

November

No matter where you go, this is generally low season, with cold winds discouraging visitors despite lower prices (although airfares skyrocket around Thanksgiving). There's much happening culturally in the cities.

☆ Thanksgiving

On the fourth Thursday of November, Americans gather with family and friends over day-long feasts – roast turkey, sweet potatoes, cranberry sauce, wine, pumpkin pie and loads of other dishes. New York City hosts a huge parade, and there's pro football on TV.

December

Winter arrives as ski season kicks off in the Rockies (out east conditions aren't usually ideal until January). Aside from winter sports, December means heading inside and curling up by the fire.

☆ Art Basel

This massive arts fest (www.artbaselmiamibeach.com) is four days of cutting-edge art, film, architecture and design. More than 250 major galleries from across the globe come to the event, with works by some 2000 artists; plus much hobnobbing with a glitterati crowd in Miami Beach.

☆ New Year's Eve

Americans are of two minds when it comes to ringing in the New Year. Some join festive crowds to celebrate; others plot a getaway to escape the mayhem. Whichever you choose, plan well in advance. Expect high prices (especially in New York City).

Itineraries

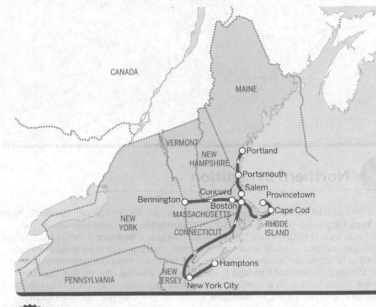

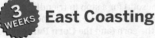 **East Coasting**

The great dynamo of art, fashion and culture, **New York City** is America at her most urbane. Spend four days exploring the metropolis, visiting memorable people-watching hoods such as the West and East Villages, the Lower East Side, Soho, Nolita and the Upper West Side, with a museum-hop down the Upper East Side. Have a ramble in Central Park, stroll the High Line and take a detour to Brooklyn. After big-city culture, catch your breath at the pretty beaches and enticing charms of the **Hamptons** on Long Island. Back in NYC, catch the train to **Boston**, for two days of visiting historic sights, dining in the North End and pub-hopping in Cambridge. Strike out for **Cape Cod**, with its idyllic dunes, forests and pretty shores. Leave time for **Provincetown**, the Cape's liveliest settlement. Back in Boston, hire a car and take a three-day jaunt taking in New England's back roads, covered bridges, picturesque towns and beautiful scenery, staying at heritage B&Bs en route. Highlights include **Salem** and **Concord** in Massachusetts; **Bennington**, VT; and **Portsmouth**, NH. If time allows, head all the way up to **Maine** for lobster feasts amid beautifully rugged coastline. Portland is a great place to stay for a few days.

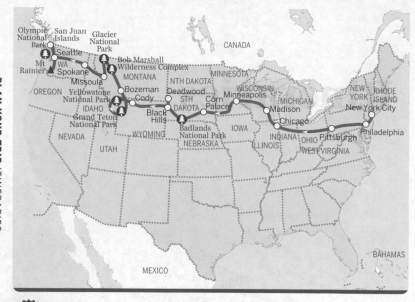

Northern Expedition

3 WEEKS

For a different take on the transcontinental journey, plan a route through the north. From **New York City**, head southwest to historic **Philadelphia**, then continue west to the idyllic backroads of Pennsylvania Dutch Country. Next is **Pittsburg**, a surprising town of picturesque bridges and green spaces, cutting-edge museums and lively neighborhoods. Enter Ohio by interstate, but quickly step back in time on a drive through old-fashioned Amish Country. Big-hearted **Chicago** is the Midwest's greatest city. Stroll or bike the lakefront, marvel at famous artwork, and take a culinary journey amid the celebrated restaurant scene. Head north to **Madison**, a youthful green-loving university town.

Detour north to the land of 10,000 lakes (aka Minnesota) for a stop in friendly, arty **Minneapolis**, followed by a visit to its quieter historic twin, St Paul, across the river. Return to I-90 and activate cruise control, admiring the corn (and the **Corn Palace**) and the flat, flat South Dakota plains. Hit the brakes for the **Badlands National Park** and plunge into the Wild West. In the **Black Hills**, contemplate the nation's complex history at the massive monuments of Mt Rushmore and Crazy Horse, then make a northern detour to watch mythic gunfights in **Deadwood**.

Halfway across Wyoming, cruise into **Cody** to catch a summer rodeo. Then take in the wonders of **Yellowstone National Park**, home to geysers, alpine lakes, waterfalls and abundant wildlife. Next, detour south for hikes past jewel-like lakes and soaring peaks in **Grand Teton National Park**. Drive back north, and continue west through rural Montana. The outdoorsy towns of **Bozeman** and **Missoula** make fun stops. Hit the boutique and cafe scene, enjoy a meal, then head off again into the alpine beauty of **Glacier National Park** followed by a trek through the **Bob Marshall Wilderness Complex**.

After a few days in the wild, **Spokane** is a great place to recharge, with a pleasant riverfront and historic district sprinkled with enticing eating and drinking spots. For more cosmopolitan flavor, keep heading west to **Seattle**, a forward-thinking, eco-minded city with cafe culture, abundant nightlife and speedy island escapes on Puget Sound. If you still have time, the region has some great places to explore, including **Mt Rainier**, **Olympic National Park**, and the **San Juan Islands**.

Above: Rio Grande, Big
Bend National Park
(p708)

Right: Weisman Art
Museum (p597;
architect: Frank
Gehry), Minneapolis

PAUL SOUDERS / GETTY IMAGES ©

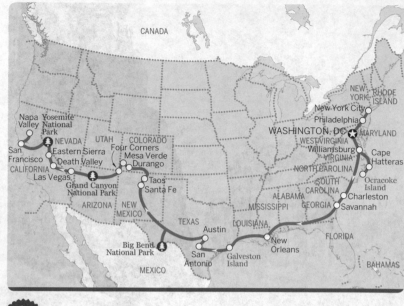

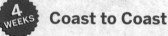

4 WEEKS Coast to Coast

The Great American road trip: it's been mythologized hundreds of ways. Now live the dream, driving the length and breadth of the USA. Start in **New York City** (but hire a car in cheaper New Jersey) and hit the road. First stop: **Philadelphia**, a historic city with a burgeoning food, art and music scene. Continue on to **Washington, DC**. The nation's capital has a dizzying array of sights, plus great dining (crab feasts, global fare) and revelry, after the museums close. Continue south through Virginia, taking a detour to visit the fantastic historic settlement of colonial **Williamsburg**. Stick to the coast as you drive south, visiting **Cape Hatteras** with its pristine dunes, marshes and woodlands. Catch the ferry to remote **Ocracoke Island,** where the wild ponies run. Further down, take in the antebellum allure of **Charleston** and **Savannah**, two of the south's most captivating destinations. Next it's on to jazz-loving **New Orleans**, with a soundtrack of smokin' hot funk brass bands, and succulent Cajun and Creole food.

The big open skies of Texas are next. Hit the beach at **Galveston** outside Houston. Follow the Mission Trail and stroll the tree-lined riverwalk in thriving **San Antonio**, then revel in the great music and drinking scene in **Austin**. Afterwards, eat your way through barbecue-loving Hill Country, then walk it off in jaw-dropping **Big Bend National Park**. Head north to New Mexico, following the Turquoise Trail up to artsy **Santa Fe** and far-out **Taos**. Roll up through Colorado and into mountain-beauty **Durango**, continuing to the Ancestral Puebloan clifftop marvel of **Mesa Verde** and the curious four-state intersection of the **Four Corners**. The awe-inspiring **Grand Canyon** is next. Stay in the area to maximize time near this great wonder. Try your luck amid the bright lights of (luck be a lady tonight?) **Las Vegas**, then take in the stunning desert landscapes at **Death Valley** on your ride into California. From there, head up into the majestic forests of the **Eastern Sierra**, followed by hiking and wildlife watching in **Yosemite**, California's most revered national park. The last stop is in hilly **San Francisco**, an enchanting city spread between ocean and bay with beautiful vistas, world-class dining and bohemian-loving nightlife. If there's time, tack on a grand finale, enjoying the vineyards and gourmet produce of **Napa Valley**.

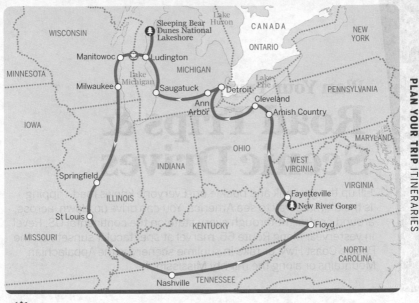

 ## Off the Beaten Path

Underdog cities, lakeside islands and boot-scooting mountain music are just a few of the things you'll encounter on this off-the-beaten-path ramble around the central US. Start off in **Detroit**, which isn't quite the apocalyptic landscape it's sometimes made out to be. Stroll the riverwalk, explore recent history (Motown, automobiles) and take in the River City's underground nightlife scene. Next head to nearby **Ann Arbor** with its easy-going college-town charm (coffee shops, farmers markets, pub-style bars), before continuing west to Lake Michigan. Drive up through waterfront towns (stopping perhaps in **Saugatuck** for gallery hopping) and continue all the way to **Sleeping Bear Dunes National Lakeshore**, with its dramatic sandscapes, scenic drives and wilderness-covered islands.

From there back-track to **Ludington** and take the ferry across Lake Michigan to **Manitowoc** in Wisconsin. Continue south to **Milwaukee**, one of the best little cities in America, with great art and architecture, abundant microbreweries, summer festivals and memorable riverfront cycling. From there, it's a four-and-a-half-hour drive south to **Springfield**, where you can delve into the fascinating past of hometown hero (and America's favorite president) Abraham Lincoln. Two hours south is **St Louis** with walkable neighborhoods and green spaces (including a park that dwarfs Central Park), plus blues, barbecue and bumping music joints. Speaking of music, up next is **Nashville**, a mecca for lovers of country and blues. Head towards Appalachia (start in **Floyd**, Virginia) for an authentic music scene – a frenzy of fiddles, banjos and boot-stompin' – in the idyllic scenery of southeastern Virginia. Continue north to **Fayetteville** in West Virginia, gateway to the breathtaking **New River Gorge**, which has superb hiking, climbing, mountain biking and whitewater rafting.

A five-hour-drive takes you to the epicenter of America's largest Amish community in **Amish Country**, near Kidron in Ohio. Step back in time at antique shops, old-fashioned farms and bakeries, and quaint 19th-century inns. Afterwards, fast-forward into **Cleveland**, a city on the cusp of reinvention with up-and-coming gastropubs, newly expanded art museums, green markets and the massive Rock and Roll Hall of Fame. It's less than three hours back to Detroit.

Plan Your Trip

Road Trips & Scenic Drives

Fill up the gas tank and buckle up. Everyone knows road-tripping is the ultimate way to see America. You can drive up, down, across, around or straight through every state on the continental US. Revel in yesteryear along Route 66, marvel at spectacular sunsets on the Pacific Coast Hwy, or take in sublime scenery in the Appalachian Mountains or along the mighty Mississippi.

Road-Tripping Tips

For more road-tripping ideas, see the Itineraries chapter (p33). For practical information about driving in the USA, see the Driving in the USA chapter (p1185).

Best Experiences

Dazzling coastal scenery on the Pacific Coast Hwy; the charming, rarely visited destinations on Route 66; dramatic sunsets over the Appalachian Mountains on the Blue Ridge Parkway; listening to Memphis blues at a jumping music-joint off the Great River Rd.

Key Starting Points

Chicago or Los Angeles for Route 66; Seattle or San Diego for the Pacific Coast Hwy; Waynesboro, VA, or Cherokee, NC, for Blue Ridge Parkway; Itasca State Park, MN, or Venice, LA, for Great River Rd.

Major Sights

Grand Canyon on Route 66; Point Reyes National Seashore on the Pacific Coast Hwy; Peaks of Otter on Blue Ridge Parkway; Shawnee National Park on Great River Road.

Route 66

For a classic American road trip, nothing beats good ol' Route 66. Nicknamed the nation's 'Mother Road' by novelist John Steinbeck, this string of small-town main streets and country byways first connected big-shouldered Chicago with the waving palm trees of Los Angeles in 1926.

Why Go?

Whether you seek to explore retro Americana or simply want to experience big horizons and captivating scenery far from the maddening crowd, Route 66 will take you there. The winding journey passes some of the USA's greatest outdoor attractions – not just the Grand Canyon, but also the Mississippi River, Arizona's Painted Desert and Petrified Forest National Park, and, at road's end, the Pacific beaches of sun-kissed Southern California.

Other highlights along the way: old-fashioned museums stocked with strange and wondrous objects from the past, Norman Rockwell-ish soda fountains, classic mom-and-pop diners, working gas stations that seem to have fallen right out of an old James Dean film clip and ghost towns (or soon-to-be ghost towns) hunkering on the edge of the desert.

Culturally speaking, Route 66 can be an eye-opener. Discard your preconceptions of small-town American life and unearth the joys of what bicoastal types dismissively term 'flyover' states. Mingle with farmers in Illinois and country-and-western stars in Missouri. Hear the legends of cowboys and Indians in Oklahoma. Visit Native American tribal nations and contemporary pueblos across the Southwest, all the while discovering the traditions of the USA's indigenous peoples. Then follow the trails of miners and desperados deep into the Old West.

When to Go

The best time to travel Route 66 is May to September, when the weather is warm and you can take advantage of open-air activities. Take care if you travel in the height of summer (July and August) as the heat can be unbearable – particularly in desert areas. Avoid traveling in the winter (December to March), when snow can lead to perilous driving conditions or outright road closures.

The Route

The journey starts in Chicago, just west of Michigan Ave, and runs for some 2400 miles across eight states before terminating in Los Angeles near the Santa Monica pier. The road remains a never-ending work in progress as old sections get resurrected or disappear owing to the rerouting of other major roads.

History of the Mother Road

Route 66 didn't really hit its stride until the Great Depression, when migrant farmers followed it as they fled the Dust Bowl across the Great Plains. Later, during the post-WWII baby boom, newfound prosperity encouraged many Americans to hit the road and 'get their kicks' on Route 66.

Almost as soon as it came of age, however, Route 66 began to lose steam. The shiny blacktop of an ambitious new interstate system started systematically paving over Route 66, bypassing its mom-and-pop diners, drugstore soda fountains and once-stylish motor courts. Railway towns were forgotten and way stations for travelers became dusty. Even entire towns began to disappear.

By the time Route 66 was officially decommissioned in 1984, preservation associations of Mother Road fans had sprung up. Today you can still get your kicks on Route 66, following gravel frontage roads and blue-line highways across the belly of America. It's like a time warp – connecting places where the 1950s seem to have stopped just yesterday.

Getting Lost

You need to be an amateur sleuth to follow Route 66 these days. Historical realignments of the route, dead-ends in farm fields and tumbleweed-filled desert patches, and rough, rutted driving conditions are par for the course. Remember that getting lost every now and then is

---

ROADSIDE ODDITIES: ROUTE 66

Kitschy, time-warped and just plain weird roadside attractions? Route 66 has got 'em in spades. Here are a few beloved Mother Road landmarks to make your own scavenger hunt:

➡ A massive statue of legendary lumberjack Paul Bunyan clutching a hotdog in Illinois

➡ Pacific's Black Madonna Shrine and Red Oak II outside Carthage in Missouri

➡ The 80ft-long Blue Whale in Catoosa, Oklahoma

➡ Devil's Rope Museum, Cadillac Ranch and Bug Ranch in Texas

➡ Seligman's Snow Cap Drive-In and Holbrook's WigWam Motel and Meteor Crater in Arizona

➡ Roy's Motel & Cafe in Amboy, in the middle of California's Mojave Desert

inevitable. But never mind; the road offers a leap back through time to see what America once was, and still sometimes is. Nostalgia never tasted so sweet.

Resources

Before you hit the road, arm yourself with useful maps and key insider tips to help you make the most of your trip.

Here It Is: Route 66 Maps with directions (traveling both east-to-west and west-to-east) that you'll definitely want to take along for the ride; available from booksellers.

Historic Route 66 (www.historic66.com) Excellent website, with turn-by-turn directions for each state.

Route 66: EZ66 Guide for Travelers By Jerry McClanahan; earns high marks for its glossy easy-to-follow maps.

Route 66: The Mother Road This book by Michael Wallis is a fascinating look at the history and lore of the great road with old photographs bringing it all to life.

Pacific Coast Highway

The classic west coast journey through California, Oregon and Washington takes in cosmopolitan cities, surf towns and charming coastal enclaves ripe for exploration. For many travelers, the real appeal of the Pacific Coast Hwy (PCH) is the magnificent scenery – wild and remote beaches, clifftop views overlooking crashing waves, rolling hills and lush forests (redwoods, eucalyptus trees) – that sometimes lies just beyond a city's outskirts.

Why Go?

The Pacific Coast Hwy is an epic adventure for water babies, surfers, kayakers, scuba divers and every other kind of outdoor enthusiast, including landlubbers. Or if you're a more laid-back road-tripper, who just dreams of cruising alongside the ocean in a cherry-red convertible, drifting from sunrise to sunset, the insanely scenic PCH can deliver that, too.

The PCH is a road trip for lovers, nomadic ramblers, bohemians, beatniks and curiosity seekers keen to search out every nook and cranny of forgotten beachside hamlets and pastoral farm towns along the way.

The Route

Technically 'the PCH' is one of several coastal highways, including Hwy 101, stretching nearly 2000 miles from Tijuana, Mexico to British Columbia, Canada. The route connects the dots between some of the West Coast's most striking cities, starting from surf-style San Diego, through hedonistic Los Angeles and offbeat San Francisco in California, then moving north

---

BEFORE YOU HIT THE ROAD

A few things to remember to ensure your road trip is as happy-go-lucky as possible:

➡ Join an automobile club that provides members with 24-hour emergency roadside assistance and discounts on lodging and attractions; some international clubs have reciprocal agreements with US automobile associations, so check first and bring your member card from home.

➡ Check the spare tire, tool kit (eg jack, jumper cables, ice scraper, tire pressure gauge) and emergency equipment (eg flashers) in your car; if you're renting a vehicle and these essential safety items are not provided, consider buying them.

➡ Bring good maps, especially if you're touring off-road or away from highways; don't rely on a GPS unit – they can malfunction, and in remote areas such as deep canyons or thick forests they may not even work.

➡ Always carry your driver's license and proof of insurance.

➡ If you're an international traveler, review the USA's road rules and common road hazards.

➡ Fill up the tank often, because gas stations can be few and far between on the USA's scenic byways.

USA – Scenic Drives

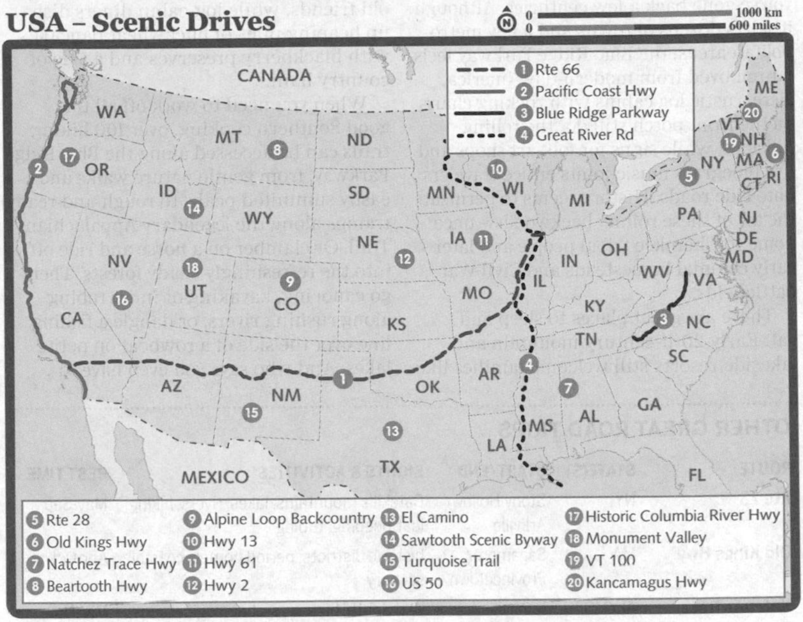
0 1000 km
0 600 miles
1 Rte 66
2 Pacific Coast Hwy
3 Blue Ridge Parkway
4 Great River Rd
CANADA
MEXICO
WA
OR
CA
NV
ID
MT
WY
UT
AZ
CO
NM
ND
SD
NE
KS
OK
TX
MN
IA
MO
AR
LA
WI
IL
MS
MI
IN
KY
TN
AL
OH
WV
VA
NC
SC
GA
FL
PA
NY
VT
NH
ME
MA
CT
RI
NJ
DE
MD
5 Rte 28
6 Old Kings Hwy
7 Natchez Trace Hwy
8 Beartooth Hwy
9 Alpine Loop Backcountry
10 Hwy 13
11 Hwy 61
12 Hwy 2
13 El Camino
14 Sawtooth Scenic Byway
15 Turquoise Trail
16 US 50
17 Historic Columbia River Hwy
18 Monument Valley
19 VT 100
20 Kancamagus Hwy

to equally alternative-minded and arty Seattle, WA.

When the urban streets start to make you feel claustrophobic, just head out back on the open road and hit the coast again, heading north or south. The direction doesn't really matter – the views and hidden places you find along the way make for rewarding exploring.

You could bypass metro areas and just stick to the places in between, like the almost too-perfect beaches of California's Orange County ('the OC') and Santa Barbara (the 'American Riviera'); wacky Santa Cruz, a university town and surfers' paradise; redwood forests along the Big Sur coast and north of Mendocino; the sand dunes, seaside resorts and fishing villages of coastal Oregon; and finally, the wild lands of Washington's Olympic Peninsula, with its primeval rainforest, and bucolic San Juan Islands, served by coastal ferries.

When to Go

There's no very bad time of year to drive the PCH, although northern climes will be rainier and snowier during winter. Peak travel season is June through August, which isn't always the best time to see the road – as thick fog blankets many stretches of the coast during early summer (locals call it 'June Gloom'). The shoulder seasons before Memorial Day (ie April and May) and after Labor Day (ie September and October) can be ideal, with sunny days, crisply cool nights and fewer crowds.

Blue Ridge Parkway

Snaking for some 469 miles through the southern Appalachian Mountains, the Blue Ridge Parkway is the land of great hiking and wildlife watching, old-fashioned music and captivating mountainous scenery – all of which make for a memorable and easily accessible road trip.

Construction on the parkway began in 1935 under President Franklin D Roosevelt and it was one of the great New Deal projects that helped put people back to work. It was a huge effort that took over 52 years to complete, with the final section laid in 1987.

Why Go?

Watch the sunset over this wilderness of forest and mountain, tranquil streams and blissful silence – and you might feel like you've gone back a few centuries. Although it skirts dozens of towns and a few metropolitan areas, the Blue Ridge Parkway feels far removed from modern-day America. Here, rustic log cabins with rocking chairs on the front porch still dot the rolling hillsides, while signs for folk-art shops and live bluegrass music-joints entice travelers onto side roads. History seems to permeate the air of these rolling backwoods – once home to Cherokee tribal people and later early colonial homesteads and Civil War battlefields.

There are great places to sleep and eat. Early-20th-century mountain and lakeside resorts still welcome families like old friends, while log-cabin diners dish up heaping piles of buckwheat pancakes with blackberry preserves and a side of country ham.

When you need to work off all that good Southern cooking, over 100 hiking trails can be accessed along the Blue Ridge Parkway, from gentle nature walks and easily summited peaks to rough-and-ready tramps along the legendary Appalachian Trail. Or clamber on a horse and ride off into the refreshingly shady forests. Then go canoeing, kayaking or inner tubing along rushing rivers, or dangle a fishing line over the side of a rowboat on petite lakes. And who says you even have to

OTHER GREAT ROAD TRIPS

ROUTE	STATE(S)	START/END	SIGHTS & ACTIVITIES	BEST TIME
Rte 28	NY	Stony Hollow/ Arkville	Catskills mountains, lakes, rivers, hiking, leaf-peeping, tubing	May-Sep
Old Kings Hwy	MA	Sagamore/ Provincetown	historic districts, period homes, coastal scenery	Apr-Oct
Natchez Trace Hwy	AL/MS/ TN	Nashville/ Natchez	'Old South' history, archaeological sites, scenic waterways, biking, camping, hiking	Mar-Nov
Beartooth Hwy	MT	Red Lodge/ Yellowstone	wildflowers, mountains, alpine scenery, camping	Jun-Sep
Alpine Loop Backcountry Byway	CO	Ouray/Lake City	mountains, views, valleys, abandoned mines	Jun-Sep
Hwy 13	WI	Bayfield/ Superior	lakeside beaches, forests, farmlands, nature walks	May-Sep
Hwy 61	IA	Duluth/Canadian Border	state parks, waterfalls, quaint towns, hiking	May-Sep
Hwy 2	NE	I-80/Alliance	grass-covered sand-dunes, open vistas	May-Sep
El Camino Real	TX	Lajitas/ Presidio	vast desert & mountain landscapes, hot springs, hiking, horseback riding	Feb-Apr & Oct-Nov
Sawtooth Scenic Byway	ID	Ketchum/ Stanley	jagged mountains, verdant forests, backpacking, hiking, wildlife watching	May-Sep
Turquoise Trail	NM	Albuquerque/ Santa Fe	mining towns, quirky museums & folk art, cycling, hiking	Mar-May & Sep-Nov
US 50	NV	Fernley/Baker	'Loneliest Road in America', epic wilderness, biking, hiking, spelunking	May-Sep
Historic Columbia River Hwy	OR	Portland	scenery, waterfalls, wildflowers, cycling, hiking	Apr-Sep
Monument Valley	UT	Monument Valley	iconic buttes, movie-set locations, 4WD tours, horseback riding	year-round
VT 100	VT	Stamford/ Newport	rolling pastures, green mountains, hiking, skiing	Jun-Sep
Kancamagus Hwy	NH	Conway/ Lincoln	craggy mountains, streams & waterfalls, camping, hiking, swimming	May-Sep

Blue Ridge Parkway (p41)

drive? The parkway makes an epic trip for long-distance cyclists, too.

The Route

This rolling, scenic byway still connects Virginia's Shenandoah National Park with Great Smoky Mountains National Park, straddling the North Carolina–Tennessee border. Towns include Boone and Asheville in North Carolina, and Galax and Roanoke in Virginia, with Charlottesville, VA, also within a short drive of the park. Cities within range of the parkway are Washington, DC, (140 miles) and Richmond, VA, (95 miles).

Detour: Skyline Drive

If you want to extend your journey through this scenic region, you can do so by hooking up with Skyline Dr. The northern terminus of the Blue Ridge Parkway meets up with this 105-mile road (which continues northeast) around Rockfish Gap.

Travel along the road is slow (speed limit 35mph), but that forces you to take in the amazing scenery (wildflowers on the hillsides in spring, blazing colors in fall and gorgeous blue skies in summer). Shenandoah National Park surrounds Skyline Dr, and has an excellent range of hikes, some of which scramble up mountain peaks and offer panoramic views. There are campgrounds in the park as well as nicely set lodges – all of which add up to worthwhile reasons not to rush through the area. Nearby attractions include the lively mountain town of Staunton (with its Shakespearean theater and farm-to-table restaurants), and an elaborate cave system at Luray Caverns.

There's just one caveat: you will have to pay to travel along Skyline Dr ($10 for a seven-day pass in the winter, $15 in the summer). This is not a toll, but rather an admission charge for visiting Shenandoah National Park. Expect heavy traffic on weekends.

When to Go

Keep in mind that the weather can vary greatly, depending on your elevation. While mountain peaks are snowed in during winter, the valleys can still be invitingly warm. Most visitor services along the parkway are only open from April through October. May is best for wildflowers, although most people come for leaf-peeping during fall. Spring and fall are good times for birdwatching, with nearly 160 species having been spotted in the skies over the parkway. Expect big crowds if you go during the summer or early autumn.

Resources

Blue Ridge Parkway (www.blueridgeparkway. org) Maps, activities and places to stay along the way. You can also download the free *Blue Ridge Parkway Travel Planner*.

Hiking the Blue Ridge Parkway By Randy Johnson; has in-depth trail descriptions, topographic trail maps and other essential info for hikes both short and long (including overnight treks).

Recreation.gov (www.recreation.gov) You can reserve some campsites through this site.

Skyline Drive (www.visitskylinedrive.org) Lodging, hiking, wildlife and more: the complete overview of the national park surrounding this picturesque drive.

Great River Road

Established in the late 1930s, the Great River Rd is an epic journey from the Mississippi's headwaters in the northern lakes of Minnesota, floating downstream all the way to the river's mouth on the Gulf of Mexico near New Orleans. For a look at America across cultural divides – north and south, urban and rural, Baptist and bohemian – this is the road trip to make.

Why Go?

You'll be awed by the sweeping scenery as you meander alongside North America's second-longest river, from the rolling plains of Iowa down to the sunbaked cotton fields of the Mississippi Delta. Limestone cliffs, dense forests, flower-filled meadows and steamy swamps are all part of the backdrop – along with smokestacks,

riverboat casinos and urban sprawl: this is the good, the bad and the ugly of life on the Mississippi. The portrait isn't complete without mentioning the great music, lip-smacking food and down-home welcome at towns well off the beaten path on this waterfront itinerary.

Small towns provide a glimpse into American culture: there's Hibbing, MN, where folk rocker Bob Dylan grew up; Brainerd, MN, as seen in the Coen Brothers' film *Fargo;* Spring Green, WI, where architect Frank Lloyd Wright cut his teeth; pastoral Hannibal, MO, boyhood home of Mark Twain; and Metropolis, IL, where you'll find Superman's quick-change phone booth.

The southern section of this route traces American musical history, from rock and roll in St Louis to Memphis blues and New Orleans jazz. And you won't go hungry either, with retro Midwestern diners, Southern barbecue joints and smokehouses, and Cajun taverns and dance halls in Louisiana.

The Route

The Great River Rd is not really one road at all, but rather a collection of roads that follow the 2300-mile-long Mississippi River, and takes travelers through 10 different states. Major urban areas that provide easy access to the road include New Orleans, Memphis, St Louis and Minneapolis.

When to Go

The best time to travel is from May to October, when the weather is warmest. Avoid going in the winter (or else stick to the deep south) when you'll have to contend with snowstorms.

Resources

Mississippi River Travel (www.experiencemis-sissippiriver.com) 'Ten states, one river' is the slogan for this official site, which is a great resource for history, outdoor recreation, live music and more.

Plan Your Trip
USA Outdoors

Towering redwoods, red-rock canyons, snow-covered peaks and a dramatic coastline of unrivaled beauty: the USA has no shortage of spectacular settings for a bit of adventure. No matter your weakness – hiking, biking, kayaking, rafting, surfing, horseback riding, rock climbing – you'll find world-class places to commune with the great outdoors.

Hiking & Trekking

Fitness-focused Americans take great pride in their formidable network of trails – literally tens of thousands of miles – and there's no better way to experience the countryside up close and at your own pace.

The wilderness is amazingly accessible, making for easy exploration. National parks are ideal for short and long hikes, and if you're hankering for nights in the wilderness beneath star-filled skies, plan on securing a backcountry permit in advance, especially in places like the Grand Canyon – spaces are limited, particularly during summer.

Beyond the parks, you'll find troves of trails in every state. There's no limit to the places you can explore, from sun-blasted hoodoos and red spires in Arizona's Chiricahua Mountains to dripping trees and mossy nooks in Washington's Hoh River Rainforest; from the dogwood-choked Wild Azalea Trail in Louisiana to the tropical paradise of Kaua'i's Na Pali Coast. Almost anywhere you go, great hiking and backpacking is within easy striking distance. All you need is a sturdy pair of shoes (sneakers or hiking boots) and a water bottle.

Best Outdoor Adventures

Best Wildlife Watching

Bears in Glacier National Park, MT; elk, bison and gray wolves in Yellowstone National Park, WY; alligators, manatees and sea turtles in the Florida Everglades; whales and dolphins on Monterey Bay, CA.

Top Aquatic Activities

White-water rafting on the New River, WV; surfing perfect waves in Oahu, HI; diving and snorkeling off the Florida Keys; kayaking pristine Penobscot Bay, ME.

Best Multiday Adventures

Hiking the Appalachian Trail; mountain-biking Kokopelli's Trail, UT; climbing 13,770ft Grand Teton in Grand Teton National Park, WY; canoeing, portaging and camping in the vast Boundary Waters, MN.

Best Winter Activities

Downhill skiing in Vail, CO; snowboarding in Stowe, VT; cross-country skiing off Lake Placid, NY.

Hiking Resources

➡ **Survive Outdoors** (www.surviveoutdoors.com) Dispenses safety and first-aid tips, plus helpful photos of dangerous critters.

➡ **Wilderness Survival** Gregory Davenport has written what is easily the best book on surviving nearly every contingency.

➡ **American Hiking Society** (www.americanhiking.org) Links to 'volunteer vacations' building trails.

➡ **Backpacker** (www.backpacker.com) Premier national magazine for backpackers, from novices to experts.

➡ **Rails-to-Trails Conservancy** (www.railstotrails.org) Converts abandoned railroad corridors into hiking and biking trails; publishes free trail reviews at www.traillink.com.

Cycling

Cycling's popularity increases by the day, with cities (including New York) adding more cycle lanes and becoming more cycle-friendly, and a growing number of greenways dotting the countryside. You'll find die-hards in every town, and out-fitters offering guided trips for all levels and durations. For the best advice on rides and rentals, stop by a local bike shop or do an internet search of the area you plan to visit.

Many states offer social multiday rides, such as Ride the Rockies (www.ridethe-rockies.com) in Colorado. For a modest fee, you can join the peloton on a scenic, well-supported route; your gear is ferried ahead to that night's camping spot. Other standout rides include Arizona's Mt Lemmon, a thigh-zinging 28-mile climb from the Sonoran Desert floor to the 9157ft summit, and Tennessee's Cherohala Skyway, 51 glorious miles of undulating road and Great Smoky Mountain views.

Top Cycling Towns

➡ **San Francisco, CA** A pedal over the Golden Gate Bridge lands you in the stunningly beautiful, and stunningly hilly, Marin Headlands.

➡ **Madison, WI** More than 120 miles of cycle paths, taking in the city's pretty lakes, parks and university campus.

➡ **Boulder, CO** Outdoors-loving town with loads of great cycling paths, including the 16-mile Boulder Creek Trail.

➡ **Austin, TX** Indie-rock-loving town with nearly 200 miles of trails and great year-round weather.

➡ **Burlington, VT** Bike haven in the Northeast, with great rides, the best-known along Lake Champlain.

➡ **Portland, OR** A trove of great cycling (on- and off-road) in the Pacific Northwest.

Surfing

Hawaii

Blessed is the state that started it all, where the best swells generally arrive between November and March.

➡ **Waikiki (South Shore of Oahu)** Hawaii's ancient kings rode waves on wooden boards well before 19th-century missionaries deemed the sport a godless activity. With warm water and gentle rolling waves, Waikiki is perfect for novices, offering long and sudsy rides.

➡ **Pipeline & Sunset Beach (North Shore of Oahu)** Home to the classic tubing wave, which form as deep-water swells break over reefs into shallows; these are expert-only spots but well worth an ogle.

West Coast/California

➡ **Huntington Beach, CA (aka Surf City, USA)** The quintessential surf capital, with perpetual sun and a 'perfect' break, particularly during winter when the winds are calm.

➡ **Black's Beach, San Diego, CA** This 2-mile sandy strip at the base of 300ft cliffs in La Jolla is known as one of the most powerful beach breaks in SoCal, thanks to an underwater canyon just offshore.

➡ **Oceanside Beach, Oceanside, CA** One of SoCal's prettiest beaches boasts one of the world's most consistent surf breaks come summer. It's a family-friendly spot.

➡ **Rincon, Santa Barbara, CA** Arguably one of the planet's top surfing spots; nearly every major surf champion on the globe has taken Rincon for a ride.

➡ **Steamer Lane & Pleasure Point, Santa Cruz, CA** There are 11 world-class breaks,

TOP HIKING TRAILS IN THE USA

Ask 10 people for their top trail recommendations and it's possible that no two answers will be alike. The country is varied and distances enormous, so there's little consensus. That said, you can't go wrong with the following all-star sampler.

➡ **Appalachian Trail** (www.appalachiantrail.org) Completed in 1937, the country's longest footpath is more than 2100 miles, crossing six national parks, traversing eight national forests and hitting 14 states from Georgia to Maine.

➡ **Pacific Crest Trail** (PCT; www.pcta.org) Follows the spines of the Cascades and Sierra Nevada, traipsing 2650 miles from Canada to Mexico, passing through six of North America's seven ecozones.

➡ **John Muir Trail in Yosemite National Park, CA** (http://johnmuirtrail.org) Find 222 miles of scenic bliss, from Yosemite Valley up to Mt Whitney.

➡ **Enchanted Valley, Olympic National Park, WA** Magnificent mountain views, roaming wildlife and lush rainforests – all on a 13-mile out-and-back trail. (p1042)

➡ **Great Northern Traverse, Glacier National Park, MT** A 58-mile haul that cuts through the heart of grizzly country and crosses the Continental Divide; check out the Lonely Planet *Banff, Jasper & Glacier National Parks* guide for more information.

➡ **Kalalau Trail, Na Pali Coast, Kaua'i, HI** Wild Hawaii at its finest – 11 miles of lush waterfalls, hidden beaches, verdant valleys and crashing surf. (p1119)

➡ **Mount Katahdin, Baxter State Park, ME** A 9.5-mile hike over the 5267ft summit, with panoramic views of the park's 46 peaks. (p253)

➡ **South Kaibab/North Kaibab Trail, Grand Canyon, AZ** A multiday cross-canyon tramp down to the Colorado River and back up to the rim. (p841)

➡ **South Rim, Big Bend National Park, TX** A 13-mile loop through the ruddy 7000ft Chisos Mountains, with views into Mexico. (p708)

➡ **Tahoe Rim Trail, Lake Tahoe, CA** (www.tahorimtrail.org) This 165-mile all-purpose trail circumnavigates the lake from high above, affording glistening Sierra views.

including the point breaks over rock bottoms at these two sweet spots.

➡ **Swami's, Encinitas, CA** Located below Seacliff Roadside Park, this popular surfing beach has multiple breaks guaranteeing you some fantastic waves.

East Coast

The Atlantic seaboard states harbor some terrific and unexpected surfing spots – especially if you're after more moderate swells. You'll find the warmest waters off Florida's Gulf Coast.

➡ **Cocoa Beach, Melbourne Beach, FL** Small crowds and mellow waves make it a paradise for beginners and longboarders. Just south is the Inlet, known for consistent surf and crowds to match.

➡ **Reef Rd, Palm Beach, FL** This stellar spot features exposed beach and reef breaks with consistent surf, especially at low tide; winter is best.

➡ **Cape Hatteras Lighthouse, NC** This very popular area has several quality spots and infinitely rideable breaks that gracefully handle swells of all sizes and winds from any direction.

➡ **Long Island, Montauk, NY** More than a dozen surfing areas dot the length of Long Island from Montauk's oft-packed Ditch Plains to Nassau County's Long Beach, with its 3-mile stretch of curling waves.

➡ **Casino Pier, Seaside Heights, NJ** Both sides of the pier offer arguably the longest tube rides in NJ – just be prepared to compete with the crowds and entitled locals.

➡ **Point Judith, Narragansett, RI** Rhode Island has premier surfing, with 40 miles of coastline and more than 30 surf spots, including this rocky point break offering long rollers as well as hollow barrels. Not for beginners.

➡ **Coast Guard Beach, Eastham, MA** Part of the Cape Cod National Seashore, this family-friendly beach is known for its consistent shortboard/longboard swell all summer long.

White-Water Rafting

East of the Mississippi, West Virginia has an arsenal of legendary white water. First, there's the New River Gorge National River (p329), which, despite its name, is one of the oldest rivers in the world. Slicing from North Carolina into West Virginia, it cuts a deep gorge, known as the Grand Canyon of the East, producing frothy rapids in its wake. Then there's the Gauley, arguably among the world's finest white water. Revered for its ultrasteep and turbulent chutes, this venerable Appalachian river is a watery roller coaster, dropping more than 668ft and churning up 100-plus rapids in a mere 28 miles. Six more rivers, all in the same neighborhood, offer training grounds for less-experienced river rats.

Out west there's no shortage of scenic and spectacular rafting, from Utah's Cataract Canyon, a thrilling romp through the red rocks of Canyonlands National Park (p870), to the Rio Grande in Texas, a lazy run through limestone canyons. The North Fork of the Owyhee – which snakes from the high plateau of southwest Oregon to the rangelands of Idaho – is rightfully popular and features towering hoodoos. In California, both the Tuolumne and American Rivers surge with moderate-to-extreme rapids while in Idaho, the Middle Fork of the Salmon River has it all: abundant wildlife, thrilling rapids, a rich homesteader history, waterfalls and hot springs. If you're organized enough to plan a few years in advance, book a spot on the Colorado River, the quintessential river trip. And if you're not after white-knuckle rapids, fret not – many rivers have sections suitable for peaceful float trips or inner-tube drifts that you can traverse with a cold beer in hand.

MAD FOR MOUNTAIN BIKING

Mountain-biking enthusiasts will find trail nirvana in Boulder, CO, Moab, UT, Bend, OR, Ketchum, ID, as well as Marin, CA, where Gary Fisher and Co bunny-hopped the sport forward by careening down the rocky flanks of Mt Tamalpais on home-rigged bikes. There are many other great destinations. For info on trails, tips and gear, check out **Bicycling magazine** (www.bicycling.com/mountainbike) or **IMBA** (www.imba.com/destinations).

➡ **Kokopelli's Trail, UT** One of the premier mountain-biking trails in the Southwest stretches 140 miles on mountainous terrain between Loma, CO, and Moab, UT. Other nearby options include the 206-mile, hut-to-hut ride between Telluride, CO, and Moab, UT, and the shorter but very challenging 38-mile ride from Aspen to Crested Butte – an equally stunning ride.

➡ **Maah Daah Hey Trail, ND** A 96-mile jaunt over rolling buttes along the Little Missouri River.

➡ **Sun Top Loop, WA** A 22-mile ride with challenging climbs that rewards with superb views of Mt Rainier and surrounding peaks on the western slopes of Washington's Cascade Mountains.

➡ **Downieville Downhill, Downieville, CA** Not for the faint of heart, this piney trail, located near its namesake Sierra foothill town in Tahoe's National Forest, skirts river-hugging cliffs, passes through old-growth forest and drops 4200ft in under 14 miles.

➡ **Finger Lakes Trail, Letchworth State Park, NY** A little-known treasure, 35 miles south of Rochester in upstate New York, featuring more than 20 miles of singletrack along the rim of the 'Grand Canyon of the East'.

➡ **McKenzie River Trail, Willamette National Forest, OR** (www.mckenzierivertrail.com) Twenty-two miles of blissful singletrack winding through deep forests and volcanic formations. The town of McKenzie is located about 50 miles east of Eugene.

➡ **Porcupine Rim, Moab, UT** A 30-mile loop from town, this venerable high-desert romp features stunning views and hairy downhills.

Kayaking & Canoeing

For exploring flatwater (no rapids or surf), opt for a kayak or canoe. While kayaks are seaworthy, they are not always suited for carrying bulky gear. For big lakes and the seacoast (including the San Juan Islands), use a sea kayak. For month-long wilderness trips – including the 12,000 miles of watery routes in Minnesota's Boundary Waters or Alabama's Bartram Canoe Trail, with 300,000 acres of marshy delta bayous, lakes and rivers – use a canoe.

You can kayak or canoe almost anywhere in the USA. Rentals and instruction are yours for the asking, from Wisconsin's Apostle Islands National Seashore and Utah's celebrated Green River to Hawaii's Na Pali Coast. Hire kayaks in Maine's Penobscot Bay to poke around the briny waters and spruce-fringed islets, or join a full-moon paddle in Sausalito's Richardson Bay, CA.

Skiing & Winter Sports

You can hit the slopes in 40 states, making for tremendous variety in terrain and ski-town vibe. Colorado has some of the best skiing in the nation, though California, Vermont and Utah are also top-notch destinations. Ski season typically runs from mid-December to April, though some resorts run longer. In summer, many resorts are great for mountain biking and hiking, courtesy of chair lifts. Ski packages (including airfare, hotel and lift tickets) are easy to find through resorts, travel agencies and online travel booking sites.

Wherever you ski, though, it won't come cheap. Find the best deals by going midweek, purchasing multiday tickets, heading to lesser-known 'sibling' resorts (like Alpine Meadows near Lake Tahoe) or checking out mountains that cater to locals, including Vermont's Mad River Glen (p228), Santa Fe Ski Area and Colorado's Wolf Grade.

Top Ski & Snowboard Resorts

Vermont's first-rate Stowe (p228) draws seasoned souls – freeze your tail off on the lifts, but thaw out nicely après-ski in timbered bars with local brews. Find more snow, altitude and attitude out west at Vail, CO, Squaw Valley, CA, and high-glitz Aspen, CO. For an unfussy scene and steep vertical chutes, try Alta, UT, Telluride, CO, Jackson, WY, and Taos, NM. In Alaska, slopes slice through spectacular terrain outside Juneau, Anchorage and Fairbanks. Mt Aurora SkiLand has the most northerly chairlift in North America and, from spring to summer, the shimmering green-blue aurora borealis.

Rock Climbing

Scads of climbers flock to Joshua Tree National Park, an otherworldly shrine in southern California. There, amid craggy monoliths and the country's oldest trees, they pay pilgrimage on more than 8000 routes, tackling sheer verticals, sharp edges and bountiful cracks. A top-notch climbing school offers classes for all levels. In Zion National Park, UT, multiday canyoneering classes teach the fine art of going *down:* rappelling off sheer sandstone cliffs into glorious, red-rock canyons filled with trees. Some of the sportier pitches are made in dry suits, down the flanks of roaring waterfalls into ice-cold pools. Other great spots abound.

➡ **Grand Teton National Park, WY** A great spot for climbers of all levels: beginners can take basic climbing courses (p782); the more experienced can join two-day expeditions to the top of Grand Teton itself: a 13,770ft peak with majestic views.

➡ **City of Rocks National Reserve, ID** More than 500 routes up wind-scoured granite and pinnacles 60 stories tall.

➡ **Yosemite National Park, CA** A hallowed shrine for rock climbers with superb climbing courses (p1011) for first timers as well as for those craving a night in a hammock 1000ft above terra firma.

➡ **Bishop, CA** South of the park and favored by many top climbers, this sleepy town in the Eastern Sierra is the gateway to excellent climbing in nearby Owens River Gorge and Buttermilk Hills.

➡ **Red Rock Canyon, NV** Ten miles west of Las Vegas, it has some of the world's finest sandstone climbing.

➡ **Enchanted Rock State Natural Area, TX** Located 70 miles west of Austin, this national park (p680) with its huge pink granite dome has hundreds of routes and stellar views of the Texas Hill Country.

→ **Rocky Mountain National Park, CO** Offers alpine climbing near Boulder.

→ **Flatirons, CO** Also near Boulder, has fine multipitch ascents.

→ **Shawangunk Ridge, NY** Located within a two-hour drive north of NYC, this ridge stretches some 50 miles, and the 'Gunks' are where many East Coast climbers tied their first billets.

→ **Hueco Tanks, TX** From October to early April Hueco Tanks ranks among the world's top rock-climbing destinations when other prime climbs become inaccessible (although in summer, the desert sun generally makes the rocks too hot to handle).

Climbing & Canyoneering Resources

→ **American Canyoneering Association** (www.canyoneering.net) An online canyons database and links to courses and local climbing groups.

→ **Climbing** (www.climbing.com) Cutting-edge rock-climbing news and information since 1970.

→ **SuperTopo** (www.supertopo.com) One-stop shop for rock-climbing guidebooks, free topographic maps and route descriptions.

Scuba Diving & Snorkeling

The most exotic underwater destination in the USA is Hawaii. There, in shimmering aquamarine waters that stay warm year-round, you'll be treated to a psychedelic display of surreal colors and shapes. Swim alongside sea turtles, octopuses and fiesta-colored parrot-fish – not to mention lava tubes and black coral. Back on shore, cap off the reverie with *poke* made from just-caught 'ahi tuna.

The best diving is off the coast or between the islands, so liveaboards are the way to go for scuba buffs. From the green turtles and WWII wrecks off the shores of Oahu to the undersea lava sculptures near little Lana'i, the Aloha State offers endless underwater bliss – but plan ahead, as dive sites change with the seasons.

On the continental USA, Florida has the lion's share of great diving, with more than 1000 miles of coastline subdivided into 20 unique undersea areas. There are hundreds of sites and countless dive shops

offering equipment and guided excursions. South of West Palm Beach, you'll find clear waters and fantastic year-round diving with ample reefs. In the Panhandle, or northern part of the state, you can scuba in the calm and balmy waters of the Gulf of Mexico; off Pensacola and Destin, there are fabulous wreck dives; and you can dive with manatees near Crystal River.

The Florida Keys, a curving string of 31 islets, are the crown jewel; expect a brilliant mix of marine habitats, North America's only living coral garden and the occasional shipwreck. Key Largo is home to the John Pennekamp Coral Reef State Park and more than 200 miles of underwater idyll.

There's terrific diving and snorkeling (and much warmer water) beyond the mangrove swamps of the Florida Keys, boasting the world's third-largest coral system. Look for manatees off Islamorada or take an expedition to Dry Tortugas, where the reef swarms with barracuda, sea turtles and a couple hundred sunken ships.

Other Underwater Destinations

For the latest on diving destinations in the US and abroad, visit **Scuba Diving** (www.scubadiving.com), or check out **DT Mag's USA overview** (http://www.dtmag.com/dive-usa/divingusa.html).

→ **Hanauma Bay Nature Preserve, Oahu, HI** Despite the crowds, this is still one of the world's great spots for snorkeling, with more than 450 resident species of reef fish.

→ **Point Lobos State Reserve, CA** Some of best shore-diving in California, with shallow reefs, caves, pinnacles, sea stars, torpedo rays, sea lions, seals and otters. The Monterey Bay Dive Company (www.montereyscubadiving.com) is a handy resource for sites and guides.

→ **The Channel Islands, CA** Lying between Santa Barbara and Los Angeles, these harbor spiny lobsters, angel sharks and numerous dive sites best accessed by liveaboard charter.

→ **Jade Cove** About 10 miles south of Lucia on Hwy 1, this aptly named spot has the world's only underwater concentration of jade, making for an unforgettable dive.

→ **Cape Hatteras National Seashore, NC** Along the northern coast of North Carolina, divers can explore historical wrecks from the Civil War (and encounter tiger sand sharks); there are also numerous options for dive

HONE YOUR SKILLS (OR LEARN SOME NEW ONES)

Whether you're eager to catch a wave or dangle from a cliff, learn some new outdoor tricks in these high-thrill programs.

→ **Club Ed Surf Camp** (www.club-ed.com) Learn to ride the waves from Manresa Beach to Santa Cruz, CA, with field trips to the surfing museum and surfboard companies included.

→ **Craftsbury Outdoor Center** (www.craftsbury.com) Come here for sculling, cross-country skiing and running amid the forests and hills of Vermont.

→ **Joshua Tree Rock Climbing School** (www.joshuatreerockclimbing.com) Local guides lead beginners to experts on 7000 different climbs in Joshua Tree National Park, CA.

→ **Nantahala Outdoor Center** (www.noc.com) Learn to paddle like a pro at this North Carolina–based school, which offers world-class instruction in canoeing and kayaking in the Great Smoky Mountains.

→ **Otter Bar Lodge Kayak School** (www.otterbar.com) Top-notch white-water kayaking instruction is complemented by saunas, hot tubs, salmon dinners and a woodsy lodge on California's north coast.

→ **Steep & Deep Ski Camp** (www.jacksonhole.com/steep-ski-camp.html) Finesse skiing extreme terrain (and snagging first tracks), then wind down over dinner parties. You can also ski with Olympian Tommy Moe.

→ **Chicks with Picks** (www.chickswithpicks.net) Based in Ridgway, CO, this group gives women's workshops across the country in mountaineering, climbing and ice-climbing.

→ **LL Bean Discovery Schools** (www.llbean.com) The famous Maine retailer offers instruction in kayaking, snowshoeing, cross-country skiing, wilderness first-aid, fly-fishing and more.

charters within the Outer Banks and the Cape Lookout areas.

→ **Lake Ouachita, AR** The largest lake in Arkansas is ringed by forested mountains, and is known for its pristine waters and some 30 distinct dive spots. Camp along the lakeshore and, quite literally, dive in. It's also the site of a 16-mile water-based trail, the first of its kind in the country.

→ **Great Lakes, MI** The USA's most unexpected dive spot? Michigan's Lake Superior and Lake Huron, with thousands of shipwrecks lying strewn on the sandy bottoms – just don't expect to see any angelfish!

Horseback Riding

Cowboy wannabes will be happy to learn that horseback riding of every style, from Western to bareback, is available across the USA. Out west, you'll find truly memorable experiences - everything from week-long expeditions through the canyons of southern Utah and cattle wrangling in

Wyoming, to pony rides along the Oregon coast. Finding horses is easy; rental stables and riding schools are located around and in many of the national parks. Experienced equestrians can explore alone or in the company of guides familiar with local flora, fauna and history. Half- and full-day group trail rides, which usually include lunch in a wildflower-speckled meadow, are popular and plentiful.

California is terrific for riding, with fog-swept trails leading along the cliffs of Point Reyes National Seashore, longer excursions through the high-altitude lakes of the Ansel Adams Wilderness, and multiday pack trips in Yosemite and Kings Canyon. Utah's Capitol Reef and Canyonlands also provide spectacular four-hoofed outings, as do the mountains, arroyos and plains of Colorado, Arizona, New Mexico, Montana and Texas.

Dude ranches come in all varieties, from down-duvet luxurious to barn-duty authentic on working cattle ranches. They're found in most of the western states, and even some eastern ones (such as Tennessee and North Carolina). Real-life cowboys are included.

Plan Your Trip

Travel with Children

From coast to coast, you'll find superb attractions for all ages: bucket-and-spade fun at the beach, amusement parks, zoos, eye-popping aquariums and natural history exhibits, hands-on science museums, camping adventures, battlefields, hikes in wilderness reserves, leisurely bike rides through countryside, and plenty of other activities likely to wow young ones.

Best Regions for Kids

New York City
The Big Apple has many kid-friendly museums, plus carriage rides and row-boating in Central Park, cruises on the Hudson and theme restaurants in Times Square.

California
Get behind the movie magic at Universal Studios, hit the beaches then head south to Disneyland and the San Diego Zoo. In Northern California, see redwoods and the Golden Gate Bridge.

Washington, DC
Washington has unrivaled allure for families with free museums, a panda-loving zoo, and boundless green spaces. Nearby, Virginia's Williamsburg is a slice of 18th-century America with costumed interpreters and fanciful activities.

Florida
Orlando's Walt Disney World is well worth planning a vacation around. Then hit the beautiful beaches.

Colorado
Ski resorts go full throttle in summer with camps, mountain biking, slides and zip lines.

The USA for Kids

Traveling with children can bring a whole new dimension to the American experience. You may make deeper connections, as locals, especially those with their own children, coo and embrace your family like long-lost cousins. From the city to the country, most facilities are ready to accommodate a child's needs.

To find family-oriented sights and activities, accommodations, restaurants and entertainment, just look for the child-friendly icon (⚐).

Dining with Children

The US restaurant industry seems built on family-style service: children are not just accepted almost everywhere, but usually are encouraged by special children's menus with smaller portions and lower prices. In some restaurants children under a certain age even eat for free. Restaurants usually provide high chairs and booster seats. Some restaurants may also offer children crayons and puzzles, and occasionally live performances by cartoon-like characters.

Restaurants without children's menus don't necessarily discourage kids, though higher-end restaurants might; however, even at the nicer places, if you show up early enough (right on dinner time opening hours, often 5pm or 6pm), you can usually eat without too much stress – and you'll likely be joined by other foodies with kids. You can ask if the kitchen will make a smaller order of a dish (also ask how much it will cost), or if they will split a normal-size main dish between two plates for the kids. Chinese, Mexican and Italian restaurants seem to be the best bet for finicky young eaters.

Farmers markets are growing in popularity in the USA, and every sizable town has at least one a week. This is a good place to assemble a first-rate picnic, sample local specialties and support independent growers in the process. After getting your stash, head to the nearest park or waterfront.

Accommodations

Motels and hotels typically have rooms with two beds, which are ideal for families. Some also have roll-away beds or cribs that can be brought into the room for an extra charge – but keep in mind these are usually Pack 'n Plays (portable cots), which not all children sleep well in. Some hotels offer 'kids stay free' programs for children up to 12 or sometimes 18 years old. Be wary of B&Bs, as most don't allow children; inquire before reserving.

Babysitting

Resort hotels may have on-call babysitting services; otherwise, ask the front-desk staff or concierge to help you make arrangements. Always ask if babysitters are licensed and bonded (ie they are qualified and insured), what they charge per hour per child, whether there's a minimum fee, and if they charge extra for transportation or meals. Most tourist bureaus list local resources for childcare and recreation facilities, medical services and so on.

Necessities, Driving & Flying

Many public toilets have a baby-changing table (sometimes in men's toilets too), and gender-neutral 'family' facilities appear in airports.

Medical services and facilities in America are of a high standard, and items such as baby food, formula and disposable diapers (nappies) are widely available

---

DISCOUNTS FOR CHILDREN

Child concessions often apply for tours, admission fees and transport, with some discounts as high as 50% off the adult rate. However, the definition of 'child' can vary from under 12 to under 16 years. Unlike in Europe, very few popular sights have discount rates for families; those that do will help you save a few dollars compared to buying individual tickets. Most sights give free admission to children under two years.

(including organic options) in supermarkets across the country.

Every car-rental agency should be able to provide an appropriate child seat, since these are required in every state, but you need to request it when booking and expect to pay around $13 more per day.

Domestic airlines don't charge for children under two. Those two and up must have a seat, and discounts are unlikely. Rarely, some resorts (eg Disneyland) offer a 'kids fly free' promotion. Amtrak and other train operators run similar deals (with kids up to age 15 riding free) on various routes.

Children's Highlights

Outdoor Adventure

All national parks have Junior Ranger programs that include activity booklets and badges upon completion.

➡ **Florida Everglades, FL** Kayak, canoe or take guided walks. (p476)

➡ **Yellowstone National Park, WY** Watch powerful geysers, spy on wildlife and take magnificent hikes. (p777)

➡ **Grand Canyon National Park, AZ** Gaze across one of earth's great wonders. (p840)

➡ **Olympic National Park, WA** Explore the wild and pristine wilderness of one of the world's only temperate rainforests. (p1041)

➡ **New River Gorge National River, WV** Go white-water rafting. (p329)

➡ **Zion National Park, UT** Wade in the Virgin River and hike to the Emerald Pools beneath the crimson canyon walls. (p874)

Theme Parks & Zoos

➡ **Bronx Wildlife Conservation Park, NY** One of the nation's biggest and best zoos is just a subway ride from Manhattan. (p92)

➡ **Walt Disney World, FL** With four action-packed parks spread across 20,000 acres, this is a place your children will long remember. (p506)

➡ **Disneyland, CA** Kids four and up appreciate the original Disneyland, while teenagers go nuts next door at **California Adventure**. (p930)

➡ **San Diego Zoo, CA** A fantastic place to see creatures great and small, it has more than 4000 animals (880 species). (p936)

➡ **Six Flags** One of America's favourite amusement parks, with 16 locations across the country. (p275)

➡ **Cedar Point, OH** Has some of the planet's most terrifying roller coasters, plus a mile-long beachfront, a water park and live entertainment. (p560)

Traveling in Time

➡ **Plimoth Plantation, Williamsburg, Yorktown and Jamestown** Don 18th-century garb and mingle with costumed interpreters in these history-rich settings. (p194, p311 & p313)

➡ **Fort Mackinac, MI** Plug your ears as soldiers in 19th-century garb fire muskets and cannons. (p582)

➡ **Freedom Trail, Boston** Go on a walking tour with Ben Franklin (or at least his 21st-century lookalike). (p185)

➡ **Lincoln Home, Springfield, IL** (www.nps.gov/liho) Stroll in the footsteps of one of America's greatest presidents. (p546)

➡ **St Augustine, FL** Rattle along in a horse-drawn carriage through the historic streets. (p491)

Rainy-Day Activities

➡ **National Air & Space Museum, Washington, DC** Rockets, spacecraft, old-fashioned biplanes and ride simulators to inspire any budding aviator. (p263)

➡ **American Museum of Natural History, NYC** Kids of all ages will enjoy a massive planetarium, immense dinosaur skeletons and 30 million other artifacts. (p83)

➡ **City Museum, St Louis** There's a packed funhouse of unusual exhibits here, plus a Ferris wheel on the roof. (p619)

➡ **Port Discovery, Baltimore** Three stories of adventure and (cleverly disguised) learning, including an Egyptian tomb, farmers market, train, art studio and physics stations. (p290)

➡ **Pacific Science Center, Seattle** Fascinating, hands-on exhibits, plus an IMAX theater, planetarium and laser shows. (p1033)

Planning

Weather and crowds are all-important considerations when planning a US family getaway. The peak travel season is from June to August, when schools are out and the weather is warmest. Expect high prices and abundant crowds – meaning long lines at amusement and water parks, fully booked resort areas and heavy traffic on the roads; you'll need to reserve well in advance for popular destinations. The same holds true for winter resorts (in the Rockies, Tahoe and the Catskills) during its high season of January to March.

For all-around information and advice, check out Lonely Planet's *Travel with Children*. For outdoor advice, read *Kids in the Wild: A Family Guide to Outdoor Recreation* by Cindy Ross and Todd Gladfelter, and Alice Cary's *Parents' Guide to Hiking & Camping*.

Baby's Away (www.babysaway.com) Rents cribs, high chairs, car seats, strollers and even toys at locations across the country.

Babies Travel Lite (www.babiestravellite.com) Delivers diapers, formula, travel beds, booster seats, baby-proofing gear, swim floats and more. Ships by FedEx to any US destination.

Family Travel Files (www.thefamilytravelfiles.com) Ready-made vacation ideas, destination profiles and travel tips.

Go City Kids (www.gocitykids.com) Excellent coverage of kid-centric activities and entertainment in more than 50 US cities.

Kids.gov (www.kids.gov) Eclectic, enormous national resource; download songs and activities, or even link to the CIA Kids' Page.

Travel Babees (www.travelbabees.com) Another reputable baby-gear rental outfit, with locations nationwide.

Regions at a Glance

Deciding where to go can be daunting in the massive USA. The East Coast has big-city allure, picturesque towns (especially New England), historic attractions, bountiful feasts (Maine lobsters, Maryland crabs) and outdoor beauty (beaches, islands, mountains).

The West Coast has memorable urban exploring (San Francisco, LA, Seattle), stunning scenery (dramatic coastline, redwoods, high Sierra) and feasting aplenty (wineries, award-winning restaurants).

In between, there's much more: soulful music and belly-pleasing fare in the South; big skies and Native American culture in the Rockies, Southwest and Great Plains; live music and barbecue in Texas; and off-the-beaten path adventures in the Great Lakes.

New York, New Jersey & Pennsylvania

Arts
History
Outdoors

Culture Spot

Home to the MET, MOMA and Broadway – and that's just NYC. Buffalo, Philadelphia and Pittsburgh also have a share of world-renowned cultural institutions.

A Living Past

From preserved Gilded Age mansions in the Hudson Valley to Independence National Historic Park in Philadelphia and sites dedicated to formative moments in the nation's founding, the region gives an interactive education.

Wild Outdoors

The outdoors lurks beyond the city's gaze, with hiking in the Adirondack wilderness and Catskills, rafting down the Delaware River and Atlantic Ocean, and frolics along the Jersey Shore and Hamptons.

p60

New England

Seafood
History
Beaches

Land of Lobsters

New England is justifiably famous for its fresh seafood. The coast is peppered with seaside eateries where you can feast on fresh oysters, lobster and fish as you watch the day-boats haul in their catch.

Legends of the Past

From the Pilgrims landing in Plymouth and the witch hysteria in Salem to Paul Revere's revolutionary ride, New England has shaped American history.

Along the Coast

Cape Cod, Martha's Vineyard and Block Island – New England is a summer mecca for sand- and sea-worshippers. The region's scores of beaches run the gamut from kid-friendly tidal flats to gnarly open ocean surf.

p170

DC & the Capital Region

Arts
History
Food

Top-Notch Arts

Washington has a superb collection of museums and galleries. You'll also find down-home mountain music on Virginia's Crooked Road, famous theaters and edgy art in Baltimore.

Early America

For historical lore, Jamestown, Williamsburg and Yorktown offer windows into Colonial America, while Civil War battlefields litter the Virginia countryside. There are fascinating presidential estates such as Mount Vernon and Monticello.

Culinary Feasts

Maryland blue crabs, oysters and seafood platters; international restaurants in DC and farm-to-table dining rooms in Baltimore, Charlottesville, Staunton and Rehoboth.

p254

The South

Food
Music
Charm

Southern Cookin'

From Georgia BBQ to Mississippi soul food to the Cajun-Creole smorgasbord in Louisiana, the South is a diverse and magnificent place to eat.

Country, Jazz & Blues

Nowhere on earth has a soundtrack as influential as the South. Head to music meccas for the authentic experience: country in Nashville, blues in Memphis and big-band jazz in New Orleans.

Southern Belles

Picture-book towns such as Charleston and Savannah, among others, have captivated visitors with their historic tree-lined streets, antebellum architecture and down-home welcome.

p330

Florida

Fun
Wildlife
Beaches

Good Times

Florida has a complicated soul: it's the home of Miami's art-deco district and Little Havana, plus historical attractions in St Augustine, theme parks in Orlando, and museums and island heritage in Key West.

Whales, Birds & Gators

Immerse yourself in aquatic life on a snorkeling or diving trip. For bigger beasts, head off on a whale-watching cruise, or spy alligators – along with egrets, eagles, manatees and other wildlife – on the Everglades.

Head in the Sand

You'll find an array of sandy shores from steamy South Beach to upscale Palm Beach, island allure on Sanibel and Captiva, and panhandle rowdiness in Pensacola.

p456

Great Lakes

Food
Music
Attractions

Heartland Cuisine

From James Beard Award–winning restaurants in Chicago and Minneapolis to fresh-from-the-dairy milkshakes, the Midwest's farms, orchards and breweries satisfy the palate.

Rock & Roll

Home to the Rock and Roll Hall of Fame, blowout fests like Lollapalooza and thrashing clubs in all the cities, the Midwest rocks, baby.

Quirky Sights

A big ball of twine, a mustard museum, a cow-doo throwing contest: the quirks rise from the Midwest's backyards and back roads, wherever there are folks with a passion, imagination and maybe a little too much time on their hands.

p514

Great Plains

Scenery
Geology
Nightlife

The Open Road

Beneath big open skies, a two-lane highway passes sunlit fields, rolling river valleys and dramatic peaks on its journey to the horizon – all par for the course (along with oddball museums and cozy cafes) on the great American road trip.

Nature Unbound

The Badlands are b-a-a-a-d in every good sense. These geologic wonders are matched by the wildlife-filled beauty of the Black Hills and Theodore Roosevelt National Park.

Big-City Soundtrack

Out in the wilds, streets roll up at sunset but in St Louis and Kansas City, that's when the fun begins. Legendary jazz, blues and rock are played in clubs and bars, big and small.

p612

Texas

Barbecue
Live Music
Outdoors

BBQ Delight

Meat lovers, you've died and gone to heaven (vegetarians, you're somewhere else). Some of the best barbecue on earth is served up in Lockhart near Austin, although you can dig in to brisket, ribs and sausage all across the state.

Tap to the Beat

Austin has proclaimed itself (and no one's arguing) the 'Live Music Capital of the World.' Two-step to live bands on worn wooden floors at honky-tonks and dance halls all around the state.

Big-Sky Scenery

Canyons, mountains and natural springs set the scene for memorable outings in Texas. Go rafting on the Big Bend River or get a beach fix along the prctty Southern Gulf Coast.

p666

Rocky Mountains

Outdoors
Culture
Landscapes

Mountain High

Skiing, hiking and boating make the Rockies a playground for adrenaline junkies, with hundreds of races and group rides, and an incredible infrastructure of parks, trails and cabins.

Old Meets New

Once a people of Stetsons and prairie dresses, today's Rocky folk are more often spotted in lycra, mountain bike nearby, sipping a microbrew or latte at a cafe. Hard playing and slow living still rule.

Perfect Views

The snow-covered Rocky Mountains are pure majesty. With chiseled peaks, clear rivers and red-rock contours, the Rockies contain some of the world's most famous parks and bucketloads of clean mountain air.

p733

Southwest

Scenery
Outdoors
Cultures

Natural Beauty

Home to spectacular national parks, the Southwest is famous for the jaw-dropping Grand Canyon, the dramatic red buttes of Monument Valley and the vast Carlsbad Caverns.

Hiking & Skiing

Ski powdery slopes at Park City, splash and frolic in Slide Rock State Park, skitter down dunes at White Sands, and hike to your heart's content at Bryce, Zion and countless other spots.

Indigenous Peoples

This is Native American country, and visiting the Hopi and Navajo Nations provides a fine introduction to America's first peoples. For a journey back in time, explore clifftop dwellings abandoned by Ancestral Puebloans.

p801

California

Beaches
Outdoors
Eating

Sunny Shores

With more than 1100 miles of coast, California rules the sands: rugged, pristine beaches in the north and people-packed beauties in the south, with great surfing, sea kayaking and beach-walking all along the coast.

Captivating Vistas

Snow-covered mountains, glittering sea and old-growth forests set the stage for skiing, hiking, biking, wave frolicking, wildlife-watching and more.

California Cooking

Fertile fields, talented chefs and an insatiable appetite for the new make California a major culinary destination. Browse food markets, sample the produce at lush vineyards and eat well in many celebrated dining rooms.

p901

Pacific Northwest

Food & Wine
Skiing
Parks

Culinary Bounty

Portland and Seattle have celebrated food scenes with wild-caught fish, superb wines and locally sourced vegetables among the Northwest bounty.

Powdery Allure

Year-round ski areas, rustic cross-country and snowboarding heaven at Mt Baker: the region with the highest snowfalls in North America delivers unparalleled winter sports. Cross-country skiing in the Methow Valley is world renowned.

Vast Nature

The northwest has four national parks: three Teddy Roosevelt–era classics – Olympic, Mt Rainier and Crater Lake – each bequeathed with historic lodges; and a wilder addition – the North Cascades.

p1020

Alaska

Wildlife
Glaciers
Food & Drink

Creatures Great & (Not So) Small

Alaska offers some of the best wildlife-viewing opportunities in the country. The sight of breaching whales and foraging bears in Southeast Alaska is unforgettable. Denali National Park is home to caribou, dall sheep, moose and yet more bears.

Cinematic Landscapes

If you want to explore glaciers in the USA, Alaska is the place. Glacier Bay National Park is the crown jewel for the cruise ships and a favorite for kayakers looking for an icy wilderness.

Eating Well

Alaska's restaurant scene is not Manhattan, but the seafood is magnificent and you may make a friend or two – Alaskans are always up for a drink.

p1082

Hawaii

Beaches
Adventure
Scenery

Tropical Shores

There's great sunning and people-watching on Waikiki (among dozens of other spots); stunning black-sand beaches on the Kona Coast, and world-class surfing all over Hawaii.

Outdoor Highs

You can trek through rain forest, kayak the Na Pali coast, go ziplining on the four biggest islands and go eye-to-eye with aquatic life in marvelous Hanauma Bay.

Unrivaled Landscapes

Hawaii has its head-turners, and we're not just talking people: volcanoes, ancient rainforests, picturesque waterfalls, clifftop vistas and jungle-lined valleys – not to mention the sparkling seas surrounding the islands.

p1101

On the Road

New York, New Jersey & Pennsylvania

Why Go?

Where else could you visit an Amish family's farm, camp on a mountaintop, read the Declaration of Independence and view New York, New York from the 86th floor of an art-deco landmark – all in a few days? Even though it's the most densely populated part of the US, it's full of places where jaded city dwellers escape to seek simple lives, where artists retreat for inspiration, and where pretty houses line main streets in small towns set amid stunning scenery.

Urban adventures in NYC, historic and lively Philadelphia and river-rich Pittsburgh are a must. Miles and miles of glorious beaches are within reach, from glamorous Long Island to the Jersey Shore – the latter ranges from stately to kitschy. The mountain wilderness of the Adirondacks reaches skyward just a day's drive north of New York City, a journey that perfectly encapsulates this region's heady character.

Best Places to Eat

➡ Blue Hill at Stone Barns (p122)

➡ Hazelnut Kitchen (p127)

➡ Il Buco (p103)

➡ Anchor Bar (p132)

➡ Reading Terminal Market (p153)

Best Places to Stay

➡ Roxbury Motel (p125)

➡ Yotel (p98)

➡ Giacomo (p134)

➡ White Pine Camp (p128)

➡ Congress Hall (p145)

When to Go
New York City

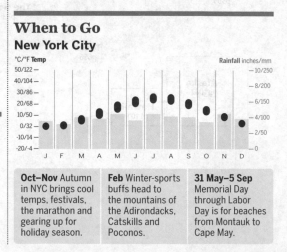

Oct–Nov Autumn in NYC brings cool temps, festivals, the marathon and gearing up for holiday season.

Feb Winter-sports buffs head to the mountains of the Adirondacks, Catskills and Poconos.

31 May–5 Sep Memorial Day through Labor Day is for beaches from Montauk to Cape May.

Transportation

The big cities all have airports, but New York's John F Kennedy is the region's major international gateway. Alternatives include Newark Liberty International Airport and LaGuardia, in Queens, with mostly domestic flights. Philadelphia and Pittsburgh also have international airports.

Greyhound buses serve main cities and towns, while Peter Pan Bus Lines and Adirondack Trailways are two regional bus lines. Amtrak provides rail services linking New York with much of New Jersey, as well as Philadelphia and Pittsburgh. Most popular day trips, at least from New York City, are easily accessible by one of the three commuter-rail lines. If you're driving, the main north–south highway is I-95.

NATIONAL & STATE PARKS

Parklands and recreation areas are in big supply here, as is wildlife, which is at first surprising to many who associate these states only with large urban areas. Black bears, bobcats and even elk can be found in forested parts of the states; more common are various species of deer. Falcons, eagles, hawks and migrating species of birds stop over in the region, some within only a few miles of New York City.

In New York alone, you'll find hundreds of state parks, ranging from waterfalls around Ithaca to wilderness in the Adirondacks. In New Jersey, float down the Delaware River, grab some sun at the Cape May beach and hike the forested Kittatinny Valley in the north. Pennsylvania includes a huge array of thick forests, rolling parklands and a significant portion of the Appalachian National Scenic Trail, a 2175-mile path that snakes its way from Maine to Georgia.

Top Five Scenic Drives

➔ **Catskills, New York – Platte Clove Rd to 214 to 28** This takes you past forested hills, rushing rivers and spectacular falls.

➔ **North Central, Pennsylvania – Rte 6** A drive through this rugged stretch of mountains and woodlands includes gushing creeks, wildlife and state forests.

➔ **Lake Cayuga, New York – Rte 80** Head north from Ithaca above the lake past dozens of wineries.

➔ **Delaware Water Gap, New Jersey – Old Mine Rd** One of the oldest roads in the US past beautiful vistas of the Delaware River and rural countryside.

➔ **PA Dutch Country – S Ronks Rd** This country lane takes you past bucolic farmland scenery between Strasburg and Bird-in-the-Hand.

THE WILD CENTER

Located in Tupper Lake, NY, the Wild Center (p130) is a jewel of a museum dedicated to the ecology of the Adirondacks. Interactive exhibits include a digitally rendered earth that displays thousands of science-related issues.

Fast Facts

➔ **Hub cities** New York City (population 8,245,000), Philadelphia (population 1,536,000)

➔ **Time zone** Eastern Standard

➔ **New York City subways** 24 hours a day

➔ **First oil well drilled** 1859, Titusville, PA

Did You Know?

From November to April harbor seals, as well as other seal species, migrate to the waters of the Jersey Shore, Long Island Sound and NYC, from Staten Island to beaches in the Bronx.

Resources

➔ **New York State Tourism** (www.iloveny.com) Info and maps available by phone.

➔ **New Jersey Travel & Tourism** (www.visitnj.org) Statewide tourism tips.

➔ **Pennsylvania Travel and Tourism** (www.visitpa.com) Maps, videos and suggested itineraries.

➔ **Gas Buddy** (www. gasbuddy.com) Find the cheapest places to grab gas.

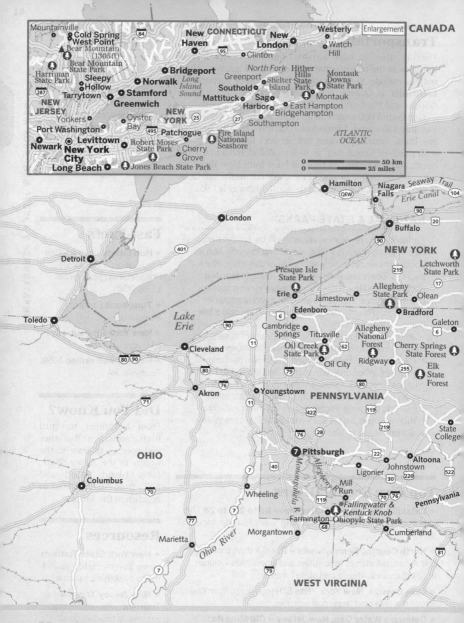

New York, New Jersey & Pennsylvania Highlights

1 Traveling round the world without ever leaving the kaleidoscope of neighborhoods and cultures that is **New York City** (p64).

2 Enjoying the kitsch and calm of the **Jersey Shore** (p136).

3 Absorbing the story of the birth of the nation in Philadelphia's **Independence** **National Historic Park** (p144).

4 Walking the densely forested paths of the unspoiled **Catskills** (p124).

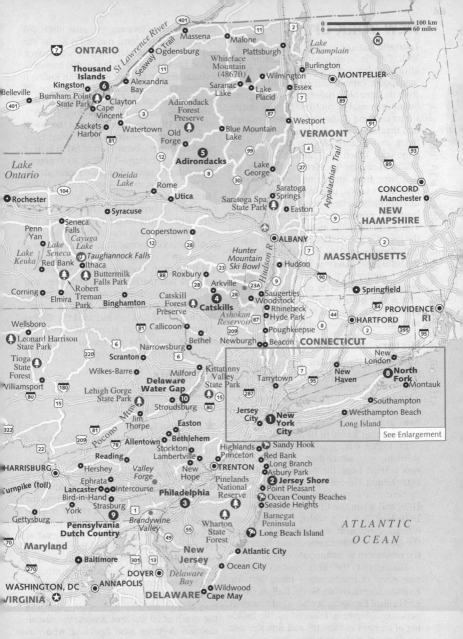

NEW YORK CITY

Loud and fast and pulsing with energy, New York City is symphonic, exhausting and always evolving. Maybe only a Walt Whitman poem cataloguing typical city scenes, from the humblest hole-in-the-wall to grand buildings, could begin to do the city justice. It remains one of the world centers of fashion, theater, food, music, publishing, advertising and finance. And as Groucho Marx once said, 'When it's 9:30 in New York, it's 1937 in Los Angeles.' Coming here for the first time from anywhere else is like stepping into a movie, one you've probably been unknowingly writing, one that contains all imagined possibilities. From the middle of Times Square to the most obscure corner of the Bronx, you'll find extremes. From Brooklyn's Russian enclave in Brighton Beach to the mini South America in Queens, virtually every country in the world has a bustling proxy community in the city. You can experience a little bit of everything on a visit here, as long as you take care to travel with a loose itinerary and an open mind.

History

After Henry Hudson first claimed this land in 1609 for his Dutch East India Company sponsors, he reported it to be 'as beautiful a land as one can hope to tread upon.' Soon after it was named 'Manhattan,' derived from local Munsee Native American words and meaning 'Island of Hills.'

By 1625 a colony, soon called New Amsterdam, was established, and the island was bought from the Munsee Indians by Peter Minuit. George Washington was sworn in here as the republic's first president in 1789, and when the Civil War broke out in 1861, New York City, which supplied a significant contingent of volunteers to defend the Union, became an organizing center for the movement to emancipate slaves.

Throughout the 19th century successive waves of immigrants – Irish, German, English, Scandinavian, Slavic, Italian, Greek and central European Jewish – led to a swift population increase, followed by the building of empires in industry and finance, and a golden age of skyscrapers.

After WWII New York City was the premier city in the world, but it suffered from a new phenomenon: 'white flight' to the suburbs. By the 1970s the graffiti-ridden subway system had become a symbol of New York's civic and economic decline. But NYC regained much of its swagger in the 1980s, led by colorful three-term mayor Ed Koch. The city elected its first African American mayor, David Dinkins, in 1989, but ousted him after a single term in favor of Republican Rudolph Giuliani (a 2008 primary candidate for US president). It was during Giuliani's reign that catastrophe struck on September 11, 2001, when the 110-story twin towers of the World Trade Center were struck by hijacked commercial airliners, became engulfed in balls of fire and then collapsed, killing 3000 people, the result of a now-infamous terrorist attack.

The billionaire Republican Mayor Michael Bloomberg, first elected in an atmosphere of turmoil and grief, came under early fire for his severe fiscal policies and draconian moves as head of the beleaguered public school system. Still, Bloomberg was elected to a second and a very controversial third term. Considered an independent political pragmatist, he's earned raves and criticism for his dual pursuit of environmental and development goals through a challenging period that has included the 'Global Financial Crisis' and Hurricane Sandy. It's anyone's guess who will rise to power once the Bloomberg days are over.

⊙ Sights

⊙ Lower Manhattan

★ **Brooklyn Bridge**   BRIDGE
(Map p68) Marianne Moore's description of the world's first suspension bridge – which inspired poets from Walt Whitman to Jack Kerouac even before its completion – as a 'climatic ornament, a double rainbow' is perhaps most evocative. Walking across the grand Brooklyn Bridge is a rite of passage for New Yorkers and visitors alike – with this in mind, walk no more than two abreast or else you're in danger of colliding with runners and speeding cyclists. With a span of 1596ft, it remains a compelling symbol of US achievement and a superbly graceful structure, despite the fact that its construction was plagued by budget overruns and the death of 20 workers. Among the casualties was designer John Roebling, who was knocked off a pier in 1869 while scouting a site for the western bridge tower and later died of tetanus poisoning. The bridge and the smooth pedestrian/cyclist path, beginning just east of City Hall, afford wonderful views of Lower Manhattan and Brooklyn

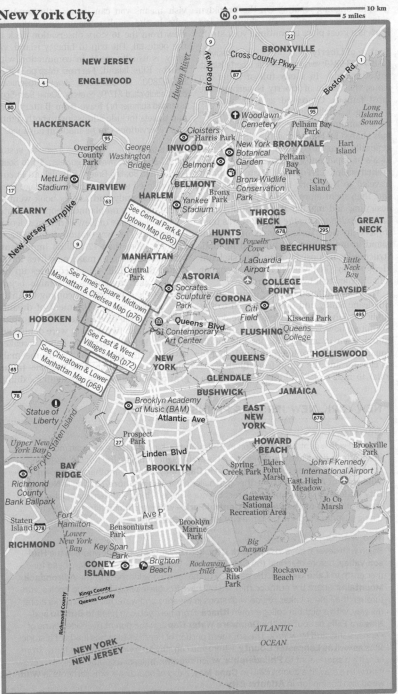

New York City

See Central Park & Uptown Map (p86)

See Times Square, Midtown Manhattan & Chelsea Map (p76)

See East & West Villages Map (p72)

See Chinatown & Lower Manhattan Map (p68)

(despite ongoing repairs). On the Brooklyn side, the ever-expanding **Brooklyn Bridge Park** is a great place to continue your stroll.

Statue of Liberty
MONUMENT

(☑ 877-523-9849; www.nps.gov/stli; Liberty Island; ⊙ 9:30am-5pm) In a city full of American icons, the Statue of Liberty is perhaps the most famous. Conceived as early as 1865 by French intellectual Edouard Laboulaye as a monument to the republican principals shared by France and the USA, it's still generally recognized as a symbol for the ideals of opportunity and freedom to many. French sculptor Frédéric-Auguste Bartholdi traveled to New York in 1871 to select the site, then spent more than 10 years in Paris designing and making the 151ft-tall figure *Liberty Enlightening the World*. It was then shipped to New York, erected on a small island in the harbor and unveiled in 1886. Structurally, it consists of an iron skeleton (designed by Gustave Eiffel) with a copper skin attached to it by metal bars.

The island suffered massive damage from Hurricane Sandy and only reopened to the public on July 4, 2013. Access to the crown is limited, however, so reservations are required as far in advance as possible (additional $3 admission). Keep in mind, there's no elevator and the climb from the base is equal to a 22-story building. Otherwise, a visit means you can wander the grounds, take in the small museum and enjoy the view from the 16-story observation deck in the pedestal. The trip to Liberty island, via ferry, is usually made in conjunction with nearby Ellis Island. **Ferries** (Map p68; ☑ 20 1-604-2800, 877-523-9849; www.statuecruises.com; adult/child $17/9; ⊙ every 30min 9am-5pm, extended summer hr) leave from Battery Park and tickets include admission to both sights, and reservations can be made in advance.

Ellis Island
LANDMARK, MUSEUM

(☑ 212-363-3200; www.nps.gov/elis; Ⓢ 1 to South Ferry, 4/5 to Bowling Green) Ellis Island is currently closed to visitors due to damage from Hurricane Sandy and as this book went to print there was no planned reopening date. Yet it remains one of New York's most iconic landmarks. The way-station from 1892 to 1954 for more than 12 million immigrants who were hoping to make new lives in the United States, Ellis Island conjures up the humble and sometimes miserable beginnings of the experience of coming to America – as well as the fulfillment of dreams. More than 3000 died in the island's hospital and more than two percent were denied admission. Before Hurricane Sandy wreaked havoc on the island, the handsome main building had been restored as the **Immigration Museum**, with fascinating exhibits

---

NEW YORK, NEW JERSEY & PENNSYLVANIA IN...

One Week

Start off with a gentle introduction in **Philadelphia**, birthplace of American independence. After a day touring the historic sites and a night sampling the hoppin' nightlife, head into New Jersey for a bucolic night in **Cape May**. Sample another beachtown like **Wildwood** or **Atlantic City** further north along the **Jersey Shore**, landing in **New York City** the following day. Spend the rest of your visit here, blending touristy must-dos – such as the **Top of the Rock** and **Central Park** – with vibrant nightlife and eclectic dining adventures, perhaps in the city's bustling **East Village**.

Two Weeks

Begin with several days in **New York City**, then a night or two somewhere in the **Hudson Valley**, before reaching the **Catskills**. After touring this bucolic region, head further north to **Lake George**, the gateway to the forested wilderness of the **Adirondack Mountains** where the outdoor-minded will have trouble leaving. Then loop back south through the Finger Lakes region with stops in wineries and waterfall-laden parks along the way, with a night in college-town **Ithaca**. From here you can head to **Buffalo** and **Niagara Falls** or south to the **Delaware Water Gap** and the quaint riverside towns of Pennsylvania and New York. The southern portion of Pennsylvania has loads of historic sites as well as **Lancaster County**, where you can stay on a working Amish farm. From here it's a short jaunt to **Philadelphia**, which deserves at least a couple of nights. Follow it up with a stay at a quaint B&B in **Cape May**, a day of boardwalk amusements in **Wildwood** and casino fun in **Atlantic City**.

and a film about immigrant experiences, the processing of immigrants and how the influx changed the USA.

National September 11 Memorial MEMORIAL (Map p68; ☎212-266-5211; www.911memorial.org; 🕘daily; [S] R to Cortlandt St) [FREE] After more than a decade of cost overruns, delays and politicking, the redevelopment of the World Trade Center site destroyed by the attacks of September 11, 2001, is finally coming to fruition. Half of the area's 16 acres is dedicated to honoring victims and preserving history, while the remaining space is occupied by office towers, a Santiago Calatrava–designed transport hub, museum and performing arts center – the last three not yet open. The focus of the moving memorial, which opened to the public on September 12, 2011, are the two large pools with cascading waterfalls set in the footprints of the north and south towers. Bronze parapets surrounding the pools are inscribed with the names of those killed in the attacks, and hundreds of swamp whitewood trees provide shade to the site. Visitor passes with a $2 service fee can be reserved through the memorial's website. The $3.2 billion One World Trade Center, formerly known as the Freedom Tower, has reached the 104th floor and the 408ft steel spire has been installed, making it at 1776ft the tallest building in the US. You can check progress on the site or reserve passes by visiting the **9/11 Memorial Preview Site** (Map p68; www.911memorial.org; 20 Vesey St; 🕘9am-7pm Mon-Fri, 8am-7pm Sat & Sun) [FREE], which has exhibits and information on the rebuilding or go to www.wtcprogress.com.

Nearby is the **Tribute WTC Visitor Center** (Map p68; ☎866-737-1184; www.tributewtc.org; 120 Liberty St; adult/child $17/5; 🕘10am-6pm Mon-Sat, to 5pm Sun; [S] E to World Trade Center, R/W to Cortland St), which provides exhibits, first-person testimony and **walking tours** of the site (adult/child $22/7, includes gallery admission, several tours from 11am to 3pm Sunday to Friday, and to 4pm Saturday).

Governor's Island National Monument PARK (www.govisland.com; 🕘10am-7pm Sat & Sun May 25-Sep 29) [FREE] Most New Yorkers have gazed out over this mysterious path of green in the harbor, less than half a mile from the southern tip of Manhattan, without a clue as to its purpose. Although it was once reserved only for the army or coast guard personnel who were based here, these days the general public can visit. The 22-acre Governor's Island National Monument is accessible by riding the **ferry** (Map p68; 🕘10am, 11am, then every 30min) leaving from the Battery Marine Terminal next to the Staten Island Ferry Whitehall Terminal in lower Manhattan. Guided **walking tours**, 90 minutes long, are run by the park service; tickets are available first-come, first-served an hour in advance at the Battery Marine Terminal. Highlights include two 19th-century fortifications – Fort Jay and the three-tiered, sandstone Castle Williams – plus open lawns, massive shade trees and unsurpassed city views.

South Street Seaport NEIGHBORHOOD (Map p68; ☎212-732-7678; www.southstreetseaport.com; 🕘10am-9pm Mon-Sat, 11am-8pm Sun; [S] 2/3, 4/5, J/M/Z to Fulton St) This 11-block enclave of shops, piers and sights combines the best and worst in historic preservation. It's not on the radar for most New Yorkers, but tourists are drawn to the sea air, the nautical feel, the frequent street performers and the mobbed restaurants. Pier 17, a fairly mundane waterfront mall that was home to several floors of shops and restaurants, was slated to be demolished in October 2013 and replaced with a more contemporary light-filled shopping and entertainment complex. Preliminary plans call for the reopening some time in 2015.

The pedestrian malls, historic tall ships and riverside locale of this neighborhood create a lovely backdrop if you happen to be standing in line for discounted Broadway tickets at the downtown TKTS Booth.

Bowling Green Park PARK (Map p68; cnr State & Whitehall Sts; [S] 4/5 to Bowling Green) At Bowling Green Park, British residents relaxed with quiet games in the late 17th century. The large **bronze bull** (Map p68) here is a tourist photo stop. The **National Museum of the American Indian** (Map p68; www.nmai.si.edu; 1 Bowling Green; 🕘10am-5pm Fri-Wed, to 8pm Thu; [S] 4/5 to Bowling Green) [FREE], housed in the gorgeous and historic Alexander Hamilton US Customs House, has quite an extensive collection of Native American arts, crafts and exhibits, plus a library and a great gift shop.

👁 Wall Street & The Financial District

Despite the worldwide economic crash of late 2007/early 2008 and the subsequent protests of Occupy Wall Street, the

Chinatown & Lower Manhattan

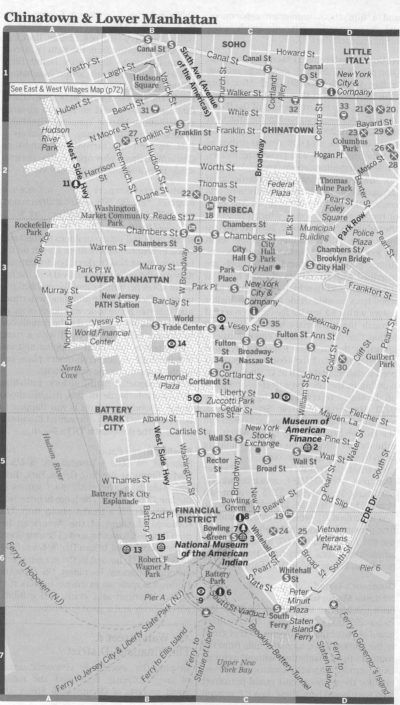

neighborhood and financial industry have rebounded. The etymological origin of **Wall Street**, both an actual street and the metaphorical home of US commerce, is the wooden barrier built by Dutch settlers in 1653 to protect Nieuw Amsterdam from Native Americans and the British. A comprehensive overview, warts and all, of the US economy is explained in fascinating up-to-date exhibits at the **Museum of American Finance** (Map p68; www.moaf.org; 48 Wall St btwn Pearl & William Sts; adult/child $8/free; ⊙10am-4pm Tue-Sat; S 2/3, 4/5 to Wall St), housed in the venerable former home of the Bank of New York. To get an up-close-and-personal view of what makes the world go round, sign up for an hour-plus tour of the **Federal Reserve** (Map p68; ☑ 212-825-6990; www.nps.gov/feha; 26 Wall St; ⊙9am-5pm) FREE.

Battery Park & Around NEIGHBORHOOD
The southwestern tip of Manhattan Island has been extended with landfill over the years to form **Battery Park** (Map p68; www.nycgovparks.org; Broadway at Battery Pl; ⊙sunrise-1am; S 4/5 to Bowling Green, 1 to South Ferry), so named for the gun batteries that used to be housed at the bulkheads. **Castle Clinton** (Map p68; www.nps.gov/cacl; Battery Park; ⊙8:30am-5pm; S 1 to South Ferry; 4/5 to Bowling Green), a fortification built in 1811 to protect Manhattan from the British, was originally 900ft offshore but is now at the edge of Battery Park, with only its walls remaining. Come summertime, it's transformed into a gorgeous outdoor concert arena. The **Museum of Jewish Heritage** (Map p68; www.mjhnyc.org; 36 Battery Pl; adult/child $12/free, 4-8pm Wed free; ⊙10am-5:45pm Sun-Tue & Thu, to 8pm Wed, to 5pm Fri; S 4/5 to Bowling Green) depicts aspects of New York Jewish history and culture, and includes a holocaust memorial. Also worth a look, the **Skyscraper Museum** (Map p68; www.skyscraper.org; 39 Battery Pl; admission $5; ⊙noon-6pm Wed-Sun; S 4/5 to Bowling Green) housed in a ground-floor space of the Ritz-Carlton Hotel features rotating exhibits plus a permanent study of high-rise history. Finally, Battery Place is the start of the stunning **Hudson River Park** (Map p68; www.hudsonriverpark.org; Manhattan's west side from Battery Park to 59th St; S 1 to Franklin St, 1 to Canal St), which incorporates renovated piers, grassy spaces, gardens, basketball courts, a trapeze school, food concessions and, best of all, a ribbon of a cycle/skate/running path that stretches 5 miles up to 59th St.

Chinatown & Lower Manhattan

⊙ Tribeca & SoHo

The 'TRIangle BElow CAnal St,' bordered roughly by Broadway to the east and Chambers St to the south, is the more downtown of these two sister 'hoods. It has old warehouses, very expensive loft apartments and chichi restaurants.

SoHo has nothing to do with its London counterpart, but instead, like Tribeca, takes its name from its geographical placement: SOuth of HOuston St. SoHo is filled with block upon block of cast-iron industrial buildings that date to the period just after the Civil War, when this was the city's leading commercial district. It had a Bohemian/artsy heyday that had ended by the 1980s, and now this super-gentrified area is a major shopping destination, home to chain stores and boutiques alike and to hordes of consumers, especially on weekends.

SoHo's hip cup overfloweth to the northern side of Houston St and the east side of Lafayette St, where two small areas, NoHo ('north of Houston') and NoLita ('north of Little Italy'), respectively, are known for excellent shopping – lots of small, independent and stylish clothing boutiques for women – and dining. Add them to SoHo and Tribeca for a great experience of strolling, window-shopping and cafe-hopping, and you'll have quite a lovely afternoon.

⊙ Chinatown & Little Italy

More than 150,000 Chinese-speaking residents live in cramped tenements and crowded apartments in **Chinatown**, the largest Chinese community that exists outside of Asia (though there are two other major Chinatowns in the city – Sunset Park in Brooklyn, and Flushing in Queens). In the 1990s, the neighborhood also attracted a growing number of Vietnamese immigrants, who set up their own shops and opened inexpensive restaurants; depending on what street you're on, you'll often notice more of a Vietnamese than Chinese presence.

The best reason to visit Chinatown is to experience a feast for the senses – it's the only spot in the city where you can simultaneously see whole roasted pigs hanging in butcher-shop windows, get whiffs of fresh fish and hear the twangs of Cantonese and Vietnamese rise over the calls of knock-off-Prada-bag hawkers on Canal St.

Whereas **Little Italy**, once a truly authentic pocket of Italian people, culture and eateries, is constantly shrinking (Chinatown keeps encroaching). Still, loyal Italian Americans, mostly from the suburbs, flock here to gather around red-and-white-checked tablecloths at one of a handful of longtime red-sauce restaurants. Join them for a stroll along Mulberry Street, and take a peek at the **Old St Patrick's Cathedral** (263 Mulberry St), which became the city's first Roman Catholic cathedral in 1809 and remained so until 1878, when its more famous uptown successor was completed. The former Ravenite Social Club, now a fancy shoe shop, is a reminder of the not-so-long-ago days when mobsters ran the neighborhood. Originally known as the Alto Knights Social Club, where big hitters like Lucky Luciano spent time, the Ravenite was a favorite hangout of John Gotti (and the FBI) before his arrest and life sentencing in 1992.

Museum of Chinese in America MUSEUM
(Map p72; ☎212-619-4785; www.mocanyc.org; 211-215 Centre St near Grand St; adult/child $10/free; ⏲11am-6pm Tue-Wed & Fri-Sun, to 9pm Thu; [S] N/Q/R/W, J/M/Z, 6 to Canal St) Strikingly designed and cutting-edge interactive exhibits trace the history and cultural impact of Chinese communities in the US. Lectures, film series and walking tours as well.

Lower East Side

First came the Jews, then the Latinos, followed by the hipsters and accompanying posers, frat boy bros, and the bridge and tunnel contingent. Today, this neighborhood, once the densest in the world, is focused on being cool – offering low-lit lounges, live-music clubs and trendy bistros. Luxury high-rise condominiums and boutique hotels coexist with public-housing projects (read Richard Price's novel *Lush Life* for entertaining insight into this class conflict). Nevertheless, 40% of residents are still immigrants and two-thirds speak a language other than English at home.

★Lower East Side Tenement Museum MUSEUM
(Map p72; ☎212-982-8420; www.tenement.org; 103 Orchard St; tours from $22; ⏲visitor center 10am-5:30pm, tours 10:15am-5pm) There's no museum in New York that humanizes the city's colorful past quite like this one. The neighborhood's heartbreaking but inspiring heritage is on full display in several recreations of turn-of-the-20th-century tenements. Always evolving and expanding, the museum has a variety of tours and talks. And while the main portion of your visit is the tenement tour, during which you'll have the opportunity to interact with a guide, don't forget to check out the one-of-a-kind visitor center unveiled at the end of 2011. The expansion has allowed for the addition of gallery space, an enlarged museum shop, a screening room that plays an original film and plenty of seminar space.

Museum at Eldridge Street Synagogue MUSEUM
(Map p68; ☎212-219-0302; www.eldridgestreet.org; 12 Eldridge St btwn Canal & Division Sts; adult/child $10/6; ⏲10am-5pm Sun-Thu, to 3pm Fri; [S] F to East Broadway) Built in 1887 with Moorish and Romanesque ornamental work, this synagogue attracted as many as 1000 worshippers on the High Holidays at the turn of the 20th century. But membership dwindled in the 1920s with restricted immigration laws, and by the 1950s the temple closed altogether. A 20-year restoration project was completed in 2007 and now the synagogue holds Friday-evening and Saturday-morning worship services, hosts weddings and offers **tours** (on the half-hour) of the building. Check out the massive circular **stained-glass window** above the ark (space where torahs are kept).

New Museum of Contemporary Art MUSEUM
(Map p72; ☎212-219-1222; www.newmuseum.org; 235 Bowery btwn Stanton & Rivington Sts; adult/child $14/free, 7-9pm Thu free; ⏲11am-6pm Wed & Fri-Sun, to 9pm Thu; [S] N/R to Prince St, F to 2nd Ave, J/Z to Bowery, 6 to Spring St) Housed in an architecturally ambitious building on a formerly gritty Bowery strip, this is the city's sole museum dedicated to contemporary art. There's the added treat of a city viewing platform, which provides a unique perspective on the constantly changing neighborhood landscape.

East Village

If you've been dreaming of those quintessential New York City moments – graffiti on crimson brick, punks and grannies walking side by side, and cute cafes with rickety tables spilling out onto the sidewalks – then the East Village is your Holy Grail. Stick to the area around Tompkins Square Park, and the lettered avenues (known as Alphabet City) to its east, for interesting little nooks

East & West Villages

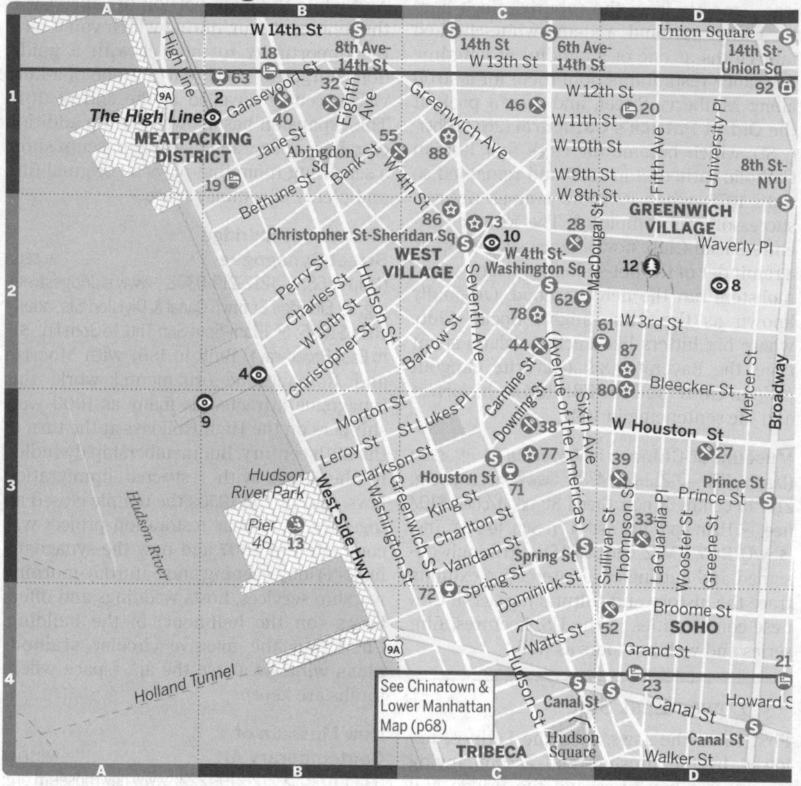

in which to imbibe and ingest – as well as a collection of great little community gardens that provide leafy respites and sometimes even live performances.

Tompkins Square Park PARK

(Map p72; www.nycgovparks.org; E 7th & 10th Sts btwn Aves A & B; ⏰6am-midnight; [S] 6 to Astor Pl) [FREE] This 10.5-acre park is like a friendly town square for locals, who gather for chess at concrete tables, picnics on the lawn on warm days and spontaneous guitar or drum jams on various grassy knolls. It's also the site of basketball courts, a fun-to-watch dog run (a fenced-in area where humans can unleash their canines), frequent summer concerts and an always-lively kids' playground. The annual Howl! Festival of East Village Arts brings Allen Ginsberg–inspired theater, music, film, dance and spoken-word events to the park and various neighborhood venues each September.

Astor Place & Around NEIGHBORHOOD

This **square** (Map p72; 8th St btwn Third & Fourth Aves; [S] R/W to 8th St-NYU, 6 to Astor Pl) is named after the Astor family, who built an early New York fortune on beaver pelts and lived on Colonnade Row, just south of the square. The large, brownstone Cooper Union, the public college founded in 1859 by glue millionaire Peter Cooper, dominates the square – now more than ever – as the school now has its first new academic building in over 50 years, a striking, twisting, nine-story sculpture of glazed glass wrapped in perforated stainless steel (and LEED-certified, too) by architect Thom Mayne of Morphosis.

Russian & Turkish Baths BATHHOUSE

(Map p72; ☎212-674-9250; www.russianturkishbaths.com; 268 E 10th St btwn First Ave & Ave A; per visit $35; ⏰noon-10pm Mon-Tue & Thu-Fri, 10am-10pm Wed, 9am-10pm Sat, 8am-10pm Sun; [S] L to 1st Ave; 6 to Astor Pl) The historic bathhouse is a great place to work out your stress in one

of the four hot rooms; traditional massages are also offered. It's authentic and somewhat grungy, and you're as likely to share a sauna with a downtown couple on a date, a well-known actor looking for a time-out or an actual Russian.

⊙ West Village & Greenwich Village

Once a symbol for all things artistic, outlandish and Bohemian, this storied and popular neighborhood – the birthplace of the gay-rights movement as well as former home of Beat poets and important artists – feels worlds away from busy Broadway and, in fact, almost European. Known by most visitors as 'Greenwich Village,' although that term is not used by locals (West Village encompasses Greenwich Village, which is the area immediately around Washington Square Park), it has narrow streets lined with well-groomed and high-priced real estate, as well as cafes and restaurants, making it an ideal place to wander.

Washington Square Park & Around PARK
This **park** (Map p72; Fifth Ave at Washington Sq N; ⓢA/C/E, B/D/F/V to W 4th St-Washington Sq, N/R/W to 8th St-NYU) began as a 'potter's field' – a burial ground for the penniless – and its status as a cemetery protected it from development. It is now a completely renovated and incredibly well-used park, especially on the weekend. Children use the playground, NYU students catch some rays and friends meet 'under the arch,' the renovated landmark on the park's northern edge, designed in 1889 by society architect Stanford White. Dominating a huge swath of property in the middle of the Village, New York University, one of the largest in the country, defines the area around the park and beyond, architecturally and demographically.

East & West Villages

Christopher Street Piers/Hudson River Park
PIER, PARK

(Map p72; Christopher St & West Side Hwy; §1 to Christopher St-Sheridan Sq) Like so many places in the Village, the extreme west side was once a derelict eyesore used mostly as a cruising ground for quick, anonymous sex. Now it's a pretty waterside hangout, bisected by the Hudson River Park's slender bike and jogging paths. It's still a place to cruise, just much less dangerous.

Sheridan Square & Around NEIGHBORHOOD

The western edge of the Village is home to **Sheridan Square** (Map p72; Christopher St & Seventh Ave; [S] 1 to Christopher St-Sheridan Sq), a small, triangular park where life-sized white statues by George Segal honor the gay community and gay pride movement that began in the nearby renovated **Stonewall Inn**, sitting just across the street from the square. A block further east, an appropriately bent street is officially named Gay St. Although gay social scenes have in many ways moved further uptown to Chelsea, **Christopher Street** is still the center of gay life in the Village.

Meatpacking District

Nestled between the far West Village and the southern border of Chelsea is the gentrified and now inappropriately named Meatpacking District. The neighborhood was once home to 250 slaughterhouses and was best known for its groups of tranny hookers, racy S&M sex clubs and, of course, its sides of beef. These days the hugely popular High Line park has only intensified an ever-increasing proliferation of trendy wine bars, eateries, nightclubs, high-end designer clothing stores, chic hotels and high-rent condos.

★ **The High Line** OUTDOORS

(Map p72; ☎ 212-500-6035; www.thehighline.org; Gansevoort St; 🕑 7am-7pm; 🚌 M11 to Washington St; M11, M14 to 9th Ave M23, M34 to 10th Ave, [S] L or A/C/E to 14th St-8th Ave, C/E to 23rd St-8th Ave)

[FREE] With the completion of the High Line, a 30ft-high abandoned stretch of elevated railroad track has been transformed into a long ribbon of parkland. Spanning from Gansevoort St to W 34th St, there's finally some greenery amid the asphalt jungle. Only three stories above the streetscape, this thoughtfully and carefully designed mix of contemporary, industrial and natural elements is nevertheless a refuge and escape from the ordinary. A glass-front **amphitheater** with bleacher-like seating sits just above 10th Ave – bring some food and join local workers on their lunch break. Entrances are at Gansevoort, 14th, 16th, 18th, 20th and 30th Sts; elevator access at all but 18th St) The third and final phase will bend closer to the Hudson at 34th St but it's final status is dependent on the ongoing massive redevelopment of the adjoining Hudson Rail Yards. The **Whitney Museum of American Art** (long located on the Upper East Side), will relocate to its Renzo Piano–designed home situated between the High Line and the Hudson River in 2015.

Chelsea

This 'hood is popular for two main attractions: one, the parade of gorgeous gay men (known affectionately as 'Chelsea boys') who roam Eighth Ave, darting from gyms to trendy happy hours; and two, it's one of the hubs of the city's art-gallery scene – it's currently home to nearly 200 modern-art exhibition spaces, most of which are clustered west of Tenth Ave. Find specific galleries at www.westchelseaarts.com.

Rubin Museum of Art MUSEUM

(Map p76; ☎ 212-620-5000; www.rmanyc.org; 150 W 17th St at Seventh Ave; adult/child $10/free, 6-10pm Fri free; 🕑 11am-5pm Mon & Thu, to 7pm Wed, to 10pm Fri, to 6pm Sat & Sun; [S] 1 to 18th St)

Dedicated to the art of the Himalayas and surrounding regions, this museum's impressive collections include embroidered textiles from China, metal sculptures from Tibet, intricate Bhutanese paintings, as well as ritual objects and dance masks from various Tibetan regions, spanning from the 2nd to the 19th centuries.

Chelsea Piers Complex SPORTS

(Map p76; ☎ 212-336-6666; www.chelseapiers.com; Hudson River at end of W 23rd St; [S] C/E to 23rd St)

A waterfront sports center that caters to the athlete in everyone. It's got a four-level driving range, indoor ice rink, jazzy bowling alley, Hoop City for basketball, a sailing school for kids, batting cages, a huge gym, indoor rock-climbing walls – the works.

Flatiron District

The famous (and absolutely gorgeous) 1902 **Flatiron Building** (Map p76; Broadway cnr Fifth Ave & 23rd St; [S] N/R, 6 to 23rd St) has a distinctive triangular shape to match its site. New York's first iron-frame high-rise, and the world's tallest building until 1909. Its surrounding district is a fashionable area of boutiques, loft apartments and a burgeoning high-tech corridor, the city's answer to Silicon Valley. Peaceful **Madison Square Park** bordered by 23rd and 26th Sts, and Fifth and Madison Aves, has an active dog run, rotating outdoor sculptures, shaded

Times Square, Midtown Manhattan & Chelsea

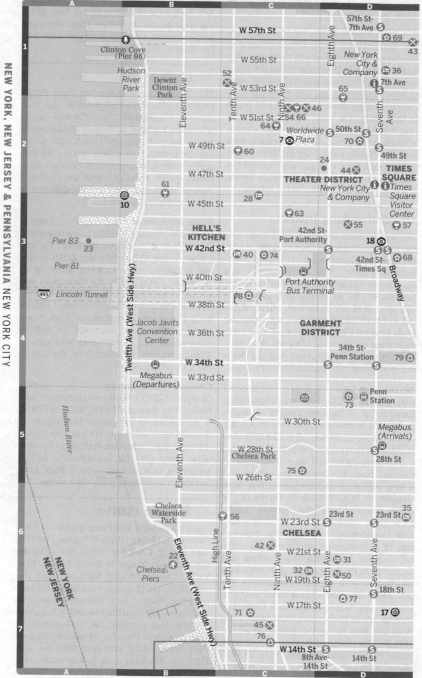

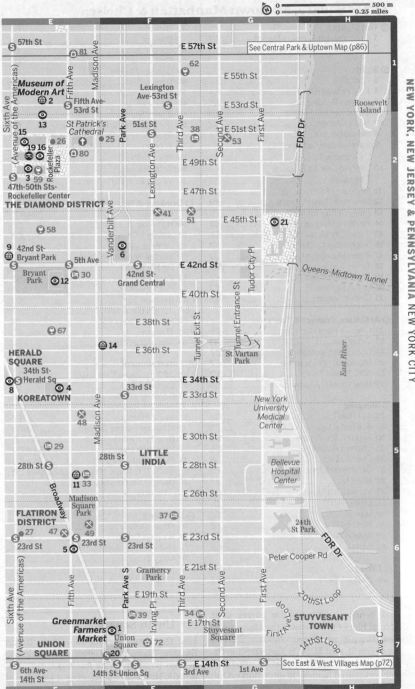

Times Square, Midtown Manhattan & Chelsea

Top Sights
1 Greenmarket Farmers Market.......F7
2 Museum of Modern Art.......E1

Sights
3 Christie's.......E2
4 Empire State Building.......E4
5 Flatiron Building.......E6
6 Grand Central Station.......F3
7 Hell's Kitchen.......C2
8 Herald Square.......E4
9 International Center of Photography.......E3
10 Intrepid Sea, Air & Space Museum.......B3
11 Museum of Sex.......E5
12 New York Public Library.......E3
13 Paley Center for Media.......E2
14 Pierpont Morgan Library.......F4
15 Radio City Music Hall.......E2
16 Rockefeller Center.......E2
17 Rubin Museum of Art.......D7
18 Times Square.......D3
19 Top of the Rock.......E2
20 Union Square.......F7
21 United Nations.......G3

Activities, Courses & Tours
22 Chelsea Piers Complex.......B6
23 Circle Line.......A3
24 Gray Line Sightseeing.......D2
25 Municipal Art Society.......F2
26 NBC Studio Tours.......E2
27 New York City Audubon.......E6

Sleeping
28 414 Hotel.......C3
29 Ace Hotel New York City.......E5
30 Andaz Fifth Avenue.......E3
31 Chelsea Hostel.......D6
32 Chelsea Lodge.......C6
33 Gershwin Hotel.......E5
34 Hotel 17.......F7
35 Inn on 23rd St.......D6
36 London NYC.......D1
37 Marcel.......F6
38 Pod Hotel.......F2
39 W New York Union Square.......F7
40 Yotel.......C3

Eating
41 99 Cent Pizza.......F3
42 Blossom.......C6
Breslin.......(see 29)
43 Burger Joint.......D1
44 Café Edison.......D2
45 Chelsea Market.......C7
46 Danji.......C2
47 Eataly.......E6
48 Hangawi.......E5
49 Shake Shack.......E6
50 Soccarat Paella Bar.......D6
51 Sparks.......F3
52 Taboon.......C1
53 The Smith.......G2
54 Totto Ramen.......C2
55 Virgil's Real Barbecue.......D3

Drinking & Nightlife
Birreria.......(see 47)
56 Half King.......C6
57 Jimmy's Corner.......D3
58 Lantern's Keep.......E3
59 Morrell Wine Bar & Café.......E2
60 On the Rocks.......C2
61 Pacha.......B2
62 PJ Clarke's.......F1
63 Réunion Surf.......C3
64 Rudy's Bar & Grill.......C2
65 Russian Vodka Room.......D1
66 Therapy.......C2
67 Top of the Strand.......E4

Entertainment
68 BB King Blues Club & Grill.......D3
69 Carnegie Hall.......D1
70 Caroline's on Broadway.......D2
71 Highline Ballroom.......C7
72 Irving Plaza.......F7
73 Madison Square Garden.......D5
New York Knicks.......(see 73)
New York Liberty.......(see 73)
74 Playwrights Horizons.......C3
Radio City Music Hall.......(see 15)
75 Upright Citizens Brigade Theatre.......C5

Shopping
76 Apple Store.......C7
77 Barneys Co-op.......D7
78 Hell's Kitchen Flea Market.......C4
79 Macy's.......D4
80 Saks Fifth Ave.......E2
81 Tiffany & Co.......E1

park benches and a popular burger joint. Several blocks to the east is the **Museum of Sex** (Map p76; www.museumofsex.com; 233 Fifth Ave at 27th St; adult $17.50; ⏰10am-8pm Sun-Thu, to 9pm Fri & Sat; [S]N/R to 23rd St), a somewhat intellectualized homage to intercourse. Only 18 and over admitted.

Union Square

Like the Noah's Ark of New York, **Union Square** (Map p76; www.unionsquarenyc.org; 17th St btwn Broadway & Park Ave S; [S]L, N/Q/R/W, 4/5/6 to 14th St-Union Sq) rescues at least two of every kind from the curling seas of concrete.

In fact, one would be hard-pressed to find a more eclectic cross-section of locals gathered in one public place. Here, amid the tapestry of stone steps and fenced-in foliage, it's not uncommon to find denizens of every ilk: suited businessfolk gulping fresh air during their lunch breaks, dreadlocked loiterers tapping beats on their tabla, skateboarding punks flipping tricks on the southeastern stairs, rowdy college kids guzzling student-priced eats, and throngs of protesting masses chanting fervently for various causes.

Gramercy Park, just to the northeast, is named after one of New York's loveliest parks; for residents only, though, and you need a key to get in!

★ Greenmarket Farmers Market FOOD MARKET

(Map p76; ☎ 212-788-7476; www.grownyc.org; 17th St, btwn Broadway & Park Ave S; ⏲ 8am-6pm Mon, Wed, Fri & Sat) 🍃 On most days, Union Square's north end hosts the most popular of the nearly 50 greenmarkets throughout the five boroughs, where even celebrity chefs come for just-picked rarities including fiddlehead ferns, heirloom tomatoes and fresh curry leaves.

👁 Midtown

The classic NYC fantasy – shiny skyscrapers, teeming mobs of worker bees, Fifth Ave store windows, taxi traffic – and some of the city's most popular attractions can be found here. Long ago when print ruled and newspaper and magazines were the cultural currency of the day, Midtown was actually also the literary district – the prime movers and shakers used to meet at the Algonquin Hotel. Major media companies such as the *New York Times* are still based here.

★ Museum of Modern Art MUSEUM

(MoMA; Map p76; www.moma.org; 11 W 53rd St btwn Fifth & Sixth Aves, Midtown West; adult/child $25/free, 4-8pm Fri free; ⏲ 10:30am-5:30pm Sat-Thu, to 8pm Fri; [S] E/M to 5th Ave-53rd St) Superstar of the modern art scene, MoMA's booty makes many other collections look, well, endearing. You'll find more A-listers here than at an Oscars after party: Van Gogh, Matisse, Picasso, Warhol, Lichtenstein, Rothko, Pollock and Bourgeois. Since its founding in 1929, the museum has amassed over 150,000 artworks, documenting the emerging creative ideas and movements of the late 19th century through to those that dominate today. For art buffs, it's Valhalla. For the uninitiated, it's a thrilling crash course in all that is beautiful and addictive about art.

Times Square & Theater District NEIGHBORHOOD

There are few images more universally iconic than the glittering orb dropping from **Times Square** (Map p76; www.timessquare.com; Broadway at Seventh Ave; [S] N/Q/R, S, 1/2/3, 7 to Times Sq-42nd St) on New Year's Eve – the first one descended 100 years ago. Smack in the middle of Midtown Manhattan, this area around the intersection of Broadway and Seventh Ave, with its gaudy billboards, glittery marquees and massive video screens, has become so intertwined with New York City in the minds of non–New Yorkers that regardless of how Disneyfied it has become, it's still considered quintessential New York. Once again 'the Crossroads of the World,' and unrecognizable from its '70s-era seediness of strip clubs, hookers and pickpockets, the square draws 35 million visitors annually. Massive chain and themed stores pull in folks, and multiplex theaters draw crowds with large screens and stadium seating. In an effort to make the area more pedestrian-friendly and diminish the perpetual gridlock, Broadway from 47th to 42nd St was turned into a vehicle-free zone.

The Times Square area is at least as famous as New York's official **Theater District**, with dozens of Broadway and off-Broadway theaters located in an area that stretches from 41st to 54th Sts, between Sixth and Ninth Aves. The Times Square branch of New York City & Company (p116) sits smack in the middle of this famous crossroads. Broadway, the road, once ran all the way to the state capitol in Albany.

Rockefeller Center NOTABLE BUILDING

(Map p76; www.rockefellercenter.com; Fifth to Sixth Aves & 48th to 51st Sts; ⏲ 24hr, times vary for individual businesses; [S] B/D/F/M to 47th-50th Sts-Rockefeller Center) It was built during the height of the Great Depression in the 1930s, and construction of the 22-acre Rockefeller Center, including the landmark art-deco skyscraper gave jobs to 70,000 workers over nine years and was the first project to combine retail, entertainment and office space in what is often referred to as a 'city within a city.' The 360-degree views from the tri-level observation deck of the **Top of the Rock** (Map p76; www.topoftherocknyc.com; 30 Rockefeller Plaza at 49th St, entrance on W 50th St btwn Fifth

& Sixth Aves; adult/child $27/17, sunrise & sunset $40/22; ☺ 8:00am-midnight, last elevator at 11pm; S B/D/F/M to 47th-50th Sts-Rockefeller Center) are absolutely stunning and should not be missed; on a clear day you can see quite a distance across the river into New Jersey. In winter the ground floor outdoor space is abuzz with ice-skaters and Christmas-tree gawkers. Within the complex is the 1932, 6000-seat **Radio City Music Hall** (Map p76; www.radiocity.com; 1260 Sixth Ave at 51st St; tours adult/child $22.50/16; ☺ tours 11am-3pm; S B/D/F/M to 47th-50th Sts-Rockefeller Center). To get an inside look at this former movie palace and protected landmark, which has been gorgeously restored in all its art-deco grandeur, join one of the frequent guided tours that leave the lobby every half-hour. Fans of the NBC TV show *30 Rock* will recognize the 70-story GE Building as the network headquarters. Tours of the **NBC studios** (Map p76; ☑ reservations 212-664-6298; www.nbcstudiotour. com; 30 Rockefeller Plaza at 49th St; tours adult/child $24/20, children under 6yr not admitted; ☺ tours every 15mins 8:30am-5:30pm Mon-Thu, to 6:30pm Fri & Sat, to 4.30pm Sun; S B/D/F/M to 47th-50th Sts-Rockefeller Center) leave from the lobby of the GE Building every 15 minutes; note that children under six are not admitted. *The Today Show* broadcasts live 7am to 11am daily from a glass-enclosed street-level studio near the fountain.

New York Public Library CULTURAL BUILDING
(Stephen A Schwarzman Building; Map p76; www. nypl.org; Fifth Ave at 42nd St; ☺ 10am-6pm Mon & Thu-Sat, to 8pm Tue & Wed, 1-5pm Sun, guided tours 11am & 2pm Mon-Sat, 2pm Sun; S B/D/F/M to 42nd St-Bryant Park, 7 to 5th Ave) Flanked by two huge marble lions nicknamed 'Patience' and 'Fortitude' by former mayor Fiorello La-Guardia, the stairway leading up to the New York Public Library is a grand entrance. The massive, superb beaux-arts building stands as testament to the value of learning and culture in the city, as well as to the wealth of the philanthropists who made its founding possible. A magnificent 3rd-floor reading room has a painted ceiling and bountiful natural light – rows of long wooden tables are occupied by students, writers and the general public working away at laptops. This, the main branch of the entire city library system, has galleries of manuscripts on display, as well as fascinating temporary exhibits. A controversial redesign of the building has been proposed. Immediately behind the library is beautifully maintained **Bryant Park**, a grassy expanse furnished with tables and chairs, and even a lending library, chessboards and Ping Pong tables in warm weather, as well as an ice-skating rink in winter.

Empire State Building
NOTABLE BUILDING, LOOKOUT
(Map p76; www.esbnyc.com; 350 Fifth Ave at 34th St; 86th-floor observation deck adult/child $25/19, incl 102nd-floor observation deck $42/36; ☺ 8am-2am, last elevators up 1:15am; S B/D/F/M, N/Q/R to 34th St-Herald Sq) Catapulted to Hollywood stardom both as the planned meeting spot for Cary Grant and Deborah Kerr in *An Affair to Remember,* and the vertical perch that helped to topple King Kong, the classic Empire State Building is one of the most famous members of New York's skyline. It's a limestone classic built in just 410 days, or seven million man-hours, during the depths of the Depression at a cost of $41 million. On the site of the original Waldorf-Astoria Hotel, the 102-story, 1472ft (to the top of the antenna) Empire State Building opened in 1931 after 10 million bricks were laid, 6400 windows installed and 328,000 sq ft of marble laid. Today you can ride the elevator to observatories on the 86th and 102nd floors, but be prepared for crowds; try to come very early or very late (and purchase your tickets ahead of time, online or pony up for $50 'express passes') for an optimal experience.

Grand Central Station
NOTABLE BUILDING
(Map p76; www.grandcentralterminal.com; 42nd St at Park Ave) Built in 1913 as a prestigious terminal by New York Central and Hudson River Railroad, Grand Central Station is no longer a romantic place to begin a cross-country journey, as it's now the terminus for Metro North commuter trains to the northern suburbs and Connecticut. But even if you're not boarding a train to the 'burbs, it's worth exploring the grand, vaulted main concourse and gazing up at the restored ceiling, decorated with a star map that is actually a 'God's-eye' image of the night sky. There's a high-end food market and the lower level houses a truly excellent array of eateries, while the balcony has a cozy '20s-era salon kind of bar called the **Campbell Apartment**.

Fifth Avenue & Around
NEIGHBORHOOD
(725 Fifth Ave, at 56th St) Immortalized in both film and song, Fifth Ave first developed its high-class reputation in the early 20th century, when it was considered desirable for its 'country' air and open spaces. A series of mansions called **Millionaire's Row** extended

right up to 130th St, though most of the heirs to the millionaire mansions on Fifth Ave above 59th St sold them for demolition or converted them to the cultural institutions that now make up Museum Mile.

The avenue's Midtown stretch still boasts upmarket shops and hotels, including Trump Tower and the Plaza (cnr Fifth Ave and Central Park South). While a number of the more exclusive boutiques have migrated to Madison Ave – leaving outposts of Gap and H&M in their wake – several superstars still reign over Fifth Ave above 50th St, including the famous Tiffany & Co.

Pierpont Morgan Library MUSEUM
(Map p76; www.morganlibrary.org; 29 E 36th St at Madison Ave; adult/child $18/12; 🕘10:30am-5pm Tue-Thu, to 9pm Fri, 10am-6pm Sat, 11am-6pm Sun; [S] 6 to 33rd St) The beautifully renovated library is part of the 45-room mansion once owned by steel magnate JP Morgan. His collection features a phenomenal array of manuscripts, tapestries and books, a study filled with Italian Renaissance artwork, a marble rotunda and the three-tiered East Room main library.

United Nations NOTABLE BUILDING
(Map p76; ☎212-963-7539; www.un.org/tours; visitors' gate First Ave at 47th St; guided tour adult/child $16/9, children under 5yr not admitted; 🕘9:15am-4:15pm; [S] S, 4/5/6, 7 to Grand Central-42nd St) The UN is technically on a section of international territory overlooking the East River. Take a guided 45-minute tour (English language tours are frequent; limited tours in several other languages) of the facility and you'll get to see the General Assembly, where the annual fall convocation of member nations takes place, the Security Council Chamber (depending on schedules) and also the Economic & Social Council Chamber. There is a park to the south of the complex which is home to several sculptures with a peace theme. The visitors' gate entrance is at a temporary location until 2015, while the UN headquarters is undergoing renovation works; guided tours are slated to continue, but expect changes to access and tour availability.

Paley Center for Media CULTURAL BUILDING
(Map p76; www.paleycenter.org; 25 W 52nd St btwn Fifth & Sixth Aves; adult/child $10/5; 🕘noon-6pm Wed & Fri-Sun, to 8pm Thu; [S] E/M to 5th Ave-53rd St) TV fanatics who spent their childhood glued to the tube and proudly claim instant recall of all of Fonzi's *Happy Days* exploits can hold their heads high. This is the 'museum' for them. Search through a catalogue of more than 100,000 US TV and radio programs and advertisements and a click of the mouse will play your selection on one of the library's computer screens. A comfy theater shows some great specials on broadcasting history, and there are frequent events and screenings.

Intrepid Sea, Air & Space Museum MUSEUM
(Map p76; www.intrepidmuseum.org; Pier 86, Twelfth Ave at 46th St; adult/child $24/12; 🕘10am-5pm; 👪; 🚌M42 bus westbound, [S] A/C/E to 42nd St-Port Authority Bus Terminal) The USS *Intrepid,* a hulking aircraft carrier that survived both a WWII bomb and kamikaze attacks has been transformed into a military museum with high-tech exhibits and fighter planes and helicopters for view on the outdoor flight deck. The pier area contains the guided-missile submarine *Growler,* a decommissioned Concorde and, as of 2012, the *Enterprise* space shuttle.

International Center of Photography GALLERY
(ICP; Map p76; www.icp.org; 1133 Sixth Ave at 43rd St; adult/child $14/free, by donation Fri 5-8pm; 🕘10am-6pm Tue-Thu & Sat-Sun, to 8pm Fri; [S] B/D/F/M to 42nd St-Bryant Park) The city's most important showcase for major photographers, especially photojournalists. Its past exhibitions have included work by Henri Cartier-Bresson, Matthew Brady and Robert Capa.

Herald Square SQUARE
(Map p76; cnr Broadway, Sixth Ave & 34th St; [S] B/D/F/M, N/Q/R to 34th St-Herald Sq) This crowded convergence of Broadway, Sixth Ave and 34th St is best known as the home of **Macy's** department store, where you can still ride some of the remaining original wooden elevators to floors ranging from home furnishings to lingerie. But the busy square gets its name from a long-defunct newspaper, the *Herald,* and the small, leafy park here bustles during business hours. In order to cut down on some of the area gridlock, Broadway, from 33rd to 35th Sts has been turned into a pedestrian plaza.

West of Herald Sq, the **Garment District** has most of New York's fashion design offices, and while not much clothing is actually made here anymore, for anyone into pawing through dreamy selections of fabrics, buttons, sequins, lace and zippers it is the place to shop.

From 31st St to 36th St, between Broadway and Fifth Ave, **Koreatown** is an interesting and lively neighborhood with an ever-expanding number of good restaurants and authentic karaoke spots.

Hell's Kitchen
NEIGHBORHOOD

(Clinton; Map p76) For years, the far west side of Midtown was a working-class district of tenements and food warehouses known as Hell's Kitchen – supposedly its name was muttered by a cop in reaction to a riot in the neighborhood in 1881. A 1990s economic boom seriously altered the character and developers reverted to using the cleaned-up name, Clinton, a moniker originating from the 1950s; locals are split on usage. New, primarily inexpensive ethnic restaurants exploded along Ninth and Tenth Aves between about 37th and 55th Sts. Thrift-store lovers should visit the **Hell's Kitchen Flea Market** (Map p76; 212-243-5343; 39th St btwn Ninth & Tenth Aves; 7am-4pm Sat & Sun; A/C/E to 42nd St), boasting 170 vendors of vintage clothing, antique jewelry, period furniture and more.

Museum of Arts & Design
MUSEUM

(MAD; Map p86; www.madmuseum.org; 2 Columbus Circle btwn Eighth Ave & Broadway; adult/child $16/free; 10am-6pm Tue-Wed & Sat-Sun, to 9pm Thu & Fri; A/C, B/D, 1 to 59th St-Columbus Circle) On the southern side of the circle, exhibiting a diverse international collection of modern, folk, craft and fine-art pieces. The plush and trippy design of **Robert**, the 9th floor restaurant, complements fantastic views of Central Park.

SOLD!

Even if your idea of a significant art purchase is a Van Gogh postcard, the adrenalin-pumping thrill of an art auction combines the best of museum-going and high-end shopping. Both **Christie's** (Map p76; 212-636-2000; www.christies.com; 20 Rockefeller Plaza; B/D/F/M to 47-50th Sts-Rockefeller Ctr) and **Sotheby's** (Map p86; 212-606-7000; www.sothebys.com; 1334 York Ave, at 72nd St; 6 to 68th St-Hunter College), two of the city's and world's most prominent auction houses are open to the public. Whether it's a collection of Warhol canvases or old European masterworks, the prices remain generally stratospheric – keep your hands down or else your casual twitch will be taken for a bid and you could be on the hook for tens of millions of dollars.

Upper West Side

Shorthand for liberal, progressive and intellectual New York – think Woody Allen movies (although he lives on the Upper East Side) and *Seinfeld* – this neighborhood comprising the west side of Manhattan from Central Park to the Hudson River, and from Columbus Circle to 110th St, is no longer as colorful as it once was. Upper Broadway has been taken over by banks, pharmacies and national retail chain stores and many of the mom-and-pop shops and bookstores are long gone. You'll still find massive, ornate apartments and a diverse mix of stable, upwardly mobile folks (with many actors and classical musicians sprinkled throughout), and some lovely green spaces – **Riverside Park** stretches for 4 miles between W 72nd St and W 158th St along the Hudson River, and is a great place for strolling, running, cycling or simply gazing at the sun as it sets over the Hudson River.

★ Central Park
PARK

(Map p86; www.centralparknyc.org; 59th & 110th Sts btwn Central Park West & Fifth Ave; 6am-1am;) It's hard to imagine what the city would be like without this refuge from the claustrophobia, from the teeming sidewalks and clogged roadways. This enormous wonderland of a park, sitting right in the middle of Manhattan, provides oxygen, both metaphorical and actual, to its residents. The park's 843 acres were set aside in 1856 on the marshy northern fringe of the city. The landscaping (the first in a US public park), by Frederick Law Olmsted and Calvert Vaux, was innovative in its naturalistic style, with forested groves, meandering paths and informal ponds. Highlights include **Sheep Meadow** (mid-park from 66th to 69th Sts), where tens of thousands of people lounge and play on warm weather weekends; **Central Park Zoo** (Map p86; 212-861-6030; www.centralparkzoo.com; Central Park, 64th St at Fifth Ave; adult/child $12/7; 10am-5:30pm Apr-Nov, to 4:30pm Nov-Apr; ; N/Q/R to 5th Ave-59th St); and the **Ramble**, a rest stop for nearly 250 migratory species of birdlife – early morning is best for sightings. A favorite tourist activity is to rent a **horse-drawn carriage** (Map p86; at 59th St, Central Park South; 30min tour $50 plus generous tip) or hop in a pedicab (one hour tours $45); the latter congregate at Central Park West and 72nd St. For more information while you're strolling, visit the **Dairy Building visitor center** (Map p86; 212-794-6564; www.centralpark.org) in the southern section of the park.

★**Lincoln Center**   CULTURAL CENTER
(Map p86; ☑212-875-5456; www.lincolncenter.org; Columbus Ave btwn 62nd & 66th Sts; public plazas free, tours adults/child $15/8; ♿; Ⓢ1 to 66th St-Lincoln Center) The billion-dollar-plus redevelopment of the world's largest performing-arts center includes the dramatically redesigned Alice Tully Hall and other stunning venues surrounding a massive fountain; public spaces, including the roof lawn of the North Plaza (an upscale restaurant is underneath), have been upgraded. The lavishly designed **Metropolitan Opera House** (MET), the largest opera house in the world, seats 3900 people. Fascinating one-hour **tours** of the complex leave from the lobby of Avery Fisher Hall from 10:30am to 4:30pm daily; these vary from architectural to backstage tours. Free wi-fi is available on the property as well as at the **David Rubenstein Atrium** (Map p86; Broadway btwn 62nd & 63rd Sts; Ⓢ1 to 66th St-Lincoln Center), a modern public space featuring a lounge area, cafe, information desk, and ticket center offering day-of discounts to Lincoln Center performances.

★**American Museum of Natural History**   MUSEUM
(Map p86; ☑212-769-5100; www.amnh.org; Central Park West at 79th St; adult/child $19/10.50; ⊙10am-5:45pm, Rose Center to 8:45pm Fri, Butterfly Conservancy Oct-May; ♿; Ⓢ B, C to 81st St-Museum of Natural History, 1 to 79th St) Founded in 1869, this museum includes more than 30 million artifacts, interactive exhibits and loads of taxidermy. It's most famous for its three large dinosaur halls, an enormous (fake) blue whale that hangs from the ceiling above the Hall of Ocean Life and the elaborate **Rose Center for Earth & Space**. Just gazing at its facade – a massive glass box that contains a silver globe, home to space-show theaters and the planetarium – is mesmerizing, especially at night, when all of its otherworldly features are aglow.

New-York Historical Society   MUSEUM
(Map p86; www.nyhistory.org; 2 W 77th St at Central Park West; adult/child $15/5, by donation 6-8pm, library free; ⊙10am-6pm Tue-Thu & Sat, to 8pm Fri, 11am-5pm Sun; Ⓢ B, C to 81st St-Museum of Natural History) This museum, founded in 1804 and widely credited with being the city's oldest, received a full-scale makeover in 2011. The quirky and wide-ranging collection, including a leg brace worn by President Franklin D Roosevelt and a 19th-century mechanical bank in which a political figure slips coins into his pocket, is now housed in a spruced-up contemporary exhibition space; there's an auditorium, a library and a restaurant as well.

◉ **Upper East Side**

The Upper East Side (UES) is home to New York's greatest concentration of cultural centers, including the Metropolitan Museum of Art, and many refer to Fifth Ave above 57th St as Museum Mile. The real estate, at least along Fifth, Madison and Park Aves, is some of the most expensive in the world. Home to ladies who lunch as well as frat boys who drink, the neighborhood becomes decidedly less chichi the further east you go.

★**Metropolitan Museum of Art**   MUSEUM
(Map p86; ☑212-535-7710; www.metmuseum.org; 1000 Fifth Ave at 82nd St; suggested donation adult/child $25/free; ⊙10am-5:30pm Sun-Thu, to 9pm Fri & Sat; ♿; Ⓢ4/5/6 to 86th St) With more than five million visitors a year, the Met is New York's most popular single-site tourist attraction, with one of the richest coffers in the arts world. The Met is a self-contained cultural city-state, with two million individual objects in its collection and an annual budget of over $120 million; the revamped American galleries include everything from colonial portraiture to Hudson River School masterpieces. Other highlight rooms include ancient Egyptian Art, Arms and Armor, Modern Art, Greek and Roman Art, European Paintings and the gorgeous rooftop, which offers bar service and spectacular views throughout the summer. Note that the suggested donation (which is, truly, a *suggestion*) includes same-day admission to the Cloisters.

★**Frick Collection**   GALLERY
(Map p86; ☑212-288-0700; www.frick.org; 1 E 70th St at Fifth Ave; admission $18, by donation 11am-1pm Sun, children under 10 not admitted; ⊙10am-6pm Tue-Sat, 11am-5pm Sun; Ⓢ6 to 68th St-Hunter College) This spectacular art collection sits in a mansion built by Henry Clay Frick in 1914; it's a shame that the 2nd floor of the residence isn't open for viewing. The 12 richly furnished rooms on the ground floor display paintings by Titian, Vermeer, El Greco, Goya and other masters. Perhaps the best asset here is that it's rarely crowded, providing a welcome break from the swarms of gawkers at larger museums, especially on weekends.

Central Park

THE LUNGS OF NEW YORK

The rectangular patch of green that occupies Manhattan's heart began life in the mid-19th century as a swampy piece of land that was carefully bulldozed into the idyllic naturescape you see today. Since officially becoming Central Park, it has brought New Yorkers of all stripes together in interesting and unexpected ways. The park has served as a place for the rich to show off their fancy carriages (1860s), for the poor to enjoy free Sunday concerts (1880s) and for activists to hold be-ins against the Vietnam War (1960s). Since then, legions of locals – not to mention travelers from all kinds of faraway places – have poured in to stroll, picnic, sunbathe, play ball and catch free concerts and performances of works by Shakespeare.

The park's varied terrain offers a wonderland of experiences. There are quiet, woodsy knolls in the north. To the south is the

Loeb Boathouse
Perched on the shores of the Lake, the historic Loeb Boathouse is one of the city's best settings for an idyllic meal. You can also rent rowboats and bicycles and ride on a Venetian gondola.

Duke Ellington Circle

Harlem Meer

The Blockhouse

North Woods

97th St Transverse

Fifth Ave

86th St Transverse

The Great Lawn

Central Park West

Conservatory Garden
The only formal garden in Central Park is perhaps the most tranquil. On the northern end, chrysanthemums bloom in late October. To the south, the park's largest crab apple tree grows by the Burnett Fountain.

STEVEN GREAVES / GETTY IMAGES ©

Jacqueline Kennedy Onassis Reservoir
This 106-acre body of water covers roughly an eighth of the park's territory. Its original purpose was to provide clean water for the city. Now it's a good spot to catch a glimpse of waterbirds.

ANGUS OSBORN / GETTY IMAGES ©

Belvedere Castle
A so-called 'Victorian folly,' this Gothic-Romanesque castle serves no other purpose than to be a very dramatic lookout point. It was built by Central Park co-designer Calvert Vaux in 1869.

reservoir, crowded with joggers. There are European gardens, a zoo and various bodies of water. For maximum flamboyance, hit the Sheep Meadow on a sunny day, when all of New York shows up to lounge.

Central Park is more than just a green space. It is New York City's backyard.

FACTS & FIGURES

» **Landscape architects** Frederick Law Olmsted and Calvert Vaux

» **Year that construction began** 1858

» **Acres** 843

» **On film** Hundreds of movies have been shot on location, from Depression-era blockbusters such as *Gold Diggers* (1933) to the monster-attack flick *Cloverfield*.

Conservatory Water
This pond is popular in the warmer months, when children sail their model boats across its surface. Conservatory Water was inspired by 19th-century Parisian model-boat ponds and figured prominently in EB White's classic book, *Stuart Little*.

Bethesda Fountain
This neoclassical fountain is one of New York's largest. It's capped by the *Angel of the Waters*, who is supported by four cherubim. The fountain was created by bohemian-feminist sculptor Emma Stebbins in 1868.

Metropolitan Museum of Art

Alice in Wonderland Statue

79th St Transverse

The Ramble

Delacorte Theater

The Lake

Fifth Ave

Central Park Zoo

65th St Transverse

Sheep Meadow

Strawberry Fields
A simple mosaic memorial pays tribute to musician John Lennon, who was killed across the street outside the Dakota Building. Funded by Yoko Ono, its name is inspired by the Beatles song 'Strawberry Fields Forever.'

The Mall / Literary Walk
A Parisian-style promenade – the only straight line in the park – is flanked by statues of literati on the southern end, including Robert Burns and Shakespeare. It is lined with rare North American elms.

Columbus Center

Central Park & Uptown

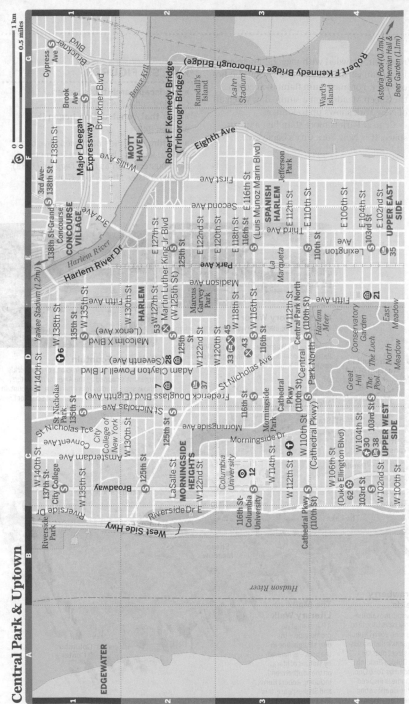

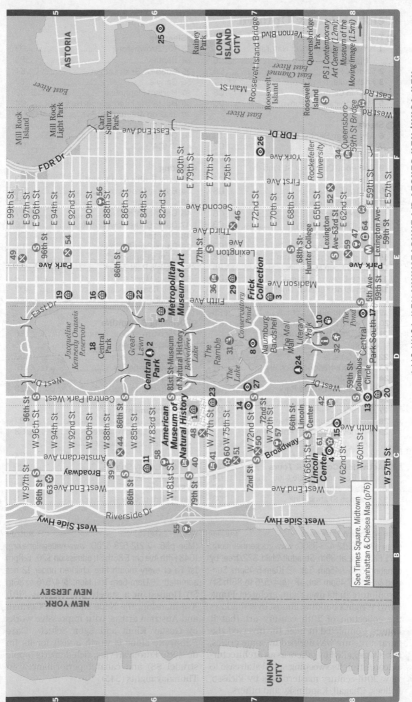

See Times Square, Midtown Manhattan & Chelsea Map (p76)

Central Park & Uptown

Top Sights

1 American Museum of Natural History ... C6
2 Central Park ... D6
3 Frick Collection ... E7
4 Lincoln Center ... C8
5 Metropolitan Museum of Art ... D6

Sights

6 Abyssinian Baptist Church ... D1
7 Apollo Theater ... D2
8 Bethesda Fountain ... D7
9 Cathedral Church of St John the Divine ... C3
10 Central Park Zoo ... D8
11 Children's Museum of Manhattan ... C6
12 Columbia University ... C3
13 Columbus Circle ... D8
14 Dakota Building ... C7
15 David Rubenstein Atrium ... C8
16 Guggenheim Museum ... E5
17 Horse-Drawn Carriages ... D8
18 Jacqueline Kennedy Onassis Reservoir ... D5
19 Jewish Museum ... E5
20 Museum of Arts & Design ... D8
21 Museum of the City of New York ... E4
22 Neue Galerie ... E6
23 New-York Historical Society ... D7
24 Sheep Meadow ... D7
25 Socrates Sculpture Park ... G6
26 Sotheby's ... F7
27 Strawberry Fields ... D7
28 Studio Museum in Harlem ... D2
29 Whitney Museum of American Art ... E7

Activities, Courses & Tours

30 Five Borough Bicycle Club ... C4
31 Loeb Boathouse ... D7
32 Wollman Skating Rink ... D8

Sleeping

33 102 Brownstone ... D3
34 Bentley ... F8
35 Bubba & Bean Lodges ... E4
36 Carlyle ... E7
37 Harlem Flophouse ... D2
38 Hostelling International New York ... C4
39 Jazz on Amsterdam Ave ... C6
40 Lucerne ... C6
41 On the Ave ... C7
42 YMCA ... D8

Eating

43 Amy Ruth's Restaurant ... D3
44 Barney Greengrass ... C6
45 Caffe Latte ... D3
46 Candle Cafe ... E7
47 David Burke Townhouse ... E8
48 Dovetail ... C6
49 Earl's Beer & Cheese ... E5
50 Gray's Papaya ... C7
51 Josie's Restaurant ... C7
52 Maya Mexican ... F8
53 Red Rooster ... D2
54 Sfoglia ... E5

Drinking & Nightlife

55 79th Street Boat Basin ... B6
56 Auction House ... F5
57 Barcibo Enoteca ... C7
Bemelmans Bar ... (see 36)
58 Dead Poet ... C6
59 Subway Inn ... E8

Entertainment

60 Beacon Theatre ... C7
61 Jazz at Lincoln Center ... C8
62 Smoke Jazz & Supper Club-Lounge ... C4
63 Symphony Space ... C5

Shopping

64 Bloomingdale's ... E8

Guggenheim Museum MUSEUM

(Map p86; ☎212-423-3500; www.guggenheim.org; 1071 Fifth Ave at 89th St; adult/child $22/free, by donation 5:45-7:45pm Sat; 🕐10am-5:45pm Sun-Wed & Fri, to 7:45pm Sat; 👪; [S] 4/5/6 to 86th St) A sculpture in its own right, architect Frank Lloyd Wright's building almost overshadows the collection of 20th century art that it houses. Completed in 1959, the inverted ziggurat structure was derided by some critics, but it was hailed by others as an architectural icon. Stroll its sweeping spiral staircase to view 20th-century masterpieces by Picasso, Pollock, Chagall, Kandinsky and others.

Neue Galerie MUSEUM

(Map p86; ☎212-628-6200; www.neuegalerie.org; 1048 Fifth Ave cnr E 86th St; admission $20, 6-8pm 1st Fri of every month free, children under 12 not admitted; 🕐11am-6pm Thu-Mon; [S] 4/5/6 to 86th St) Housed in a stately and elegant Fifth Ave mansion, the Neue showcases German and Austrian artists, with impressive works by Gustav Klimt and Egon Schiele. **Café Sabarsky** alone is worth a visit for its fin de siècle European vibe, rich desserts (apple strudel $8) and cabaret performances on Thursday nights ($45).

Whitney Museum of American Art MUSEUM
(Map p86; 212-570-3600; www.whitney.org; 945 Madison Ave cnr 75th St; adult/child $20/free; 11am-6pm Wed, Thu, Sat & Sun, 1-9pm Fri; 6 to 77th St) One of the few museums that concentrates on American works of art, specializing in 20th-century and contemporary art, with works by Hopper, Pollock and Rothko, as well as special shows, such as the much-ballyhooed Biennial. In 2015, the Whitney is moving to Gansevoort St in the Meatpacking District.

Jewish Museum MUSEUM
(Map p86; 212-423-3200; www.jewishmuseum. org; 1109 Fifth Ave at 92nd St; adult/child $12/free, Sat free; 11am-5:45pm Fri-Tue, to 8pm Thu; ; 6 to 96th St) This homage to Judaism primarily features artwork examining 4000 years of Jewish ceremony and culture; it also has a wide array of children's activities. The building, a gorgeous banker's mansion from 1908, houses more than 30,000 items of Judaica, as well as works of sculpture, paintings, decorative arts and photography.

Museum of the City of New York MUSEUM
(Map p86; 212-534-1672; www.mcny.org; 1220 Fifth Ave btwn 103rd & 104th Sts; suggested admission adult/child $10/free; 10am-6pm; 6 to 103rd St) Traces the city's history from beaver trading to futures trading with various cultural exhibitions. An excellent bookstore for every NYC obsession.

Morningside Heights

The Upper West Side's northern neighbor, comprises the area of Broadway and west up to about 125th St. Dominating the neighborhood is **Columbia University** (Map p86; www. columbia.edu; Broadway at 116th St, Morningside Heights; 1 to 116th St-Columbia University) FREE, the highly regarded Ivy League college, which features a spacious, grassy central quadrangle.

Cathedral Church of
St John the Divine CHURCH
(Map p86; tours 212-932-7347; www.stjohndivine. org; 1047 Amsterdam Ave at W 112th St, Morningside Heights; admission by donation, tours $6, vertical tours $15; 7:30am-6pm; ; B, C, 1 to 110th St-Cathedral Pkwy) This storied Episcopal cathedral, the largest place of worship in the United States, commands attention with its ornate Byzantine-style facade, booming vintage organ and extravagantly scaled nave – twice as wide as Westminster Abbey in London. High Mass, held at 11am Sunday, often comes with sermons by well-known intellectuals.

Harlem

The heart of African American culture has been beating in Harlem since its emergence as a black enclave in the 1920s. This neighborhood north of Central Park has been the setting for extraordinary accomplishments in art, music, dance, education and letters from the likes of Frederick Douglass, Paul Robeson, Thurgood Marshall, James Baldwin, Alvin Ailey, Billie Holiday, Jessie Jackson and many other African American luminaries. After steady decline from the 1960s to early '90s, Harlem is experiencing something of a second renaissance in the form of million-dollar brownstones and condos for sale next door to neglected tenement buildings and the presence of big box national chain stores all along 125th St.

For a traditional view of Harlem, visit on Sunday morning, when well-dressed locals flock to neighborhood churches. Just be respectful of the fact that these people are attending a religious service (rather than being on display for tourists). Unless you're invited by a member of a small congregation, stick to the bigger churches.

Apollo Theater HISTORIC BUILDING
(Map p86; 212-531-5305, tours 212-531-5337; www.apollotheater.org; 253 W 125th St at Frederick Douglass Blvd, Harlem; A/C, B/D to 125th St) Not just a mythical legend but a living theater. Head here for high-profile concerts and its famous long-running amateur night, 'where stars are born and legends are made,' which takes place every Wednesday night.

Abyssinian Baptist Church CHURCH
(Map p86; www.abyssinian.org; 132 W 138th St btwn Adam Clayton Powell Jr & Malcolm X Blvds; ; 2/3 to 135th St) Has a superb choir and a charismatic pastor, Calvin O Butts, who welcomes tourists and prays for them. Sunday services start at 9am and 11am – the later one is *very* well attended.

Studio Museum in Harlem MUSEUM
(Map p86; 212-864-4500; www.studiomuseum. org; 144 W 125th St at Adam Clayton Powell Jr Blvd, Harlem; suggested donation $7; noon-9pm Thu & Fri, 10am-6pm Sat, noon-6pm Sun; ; 2/3 to 125th St) One of the premier showcases for African American artists; look for rotating exhibits from painters, sculptors, illustrators and other installation artists.

Washington Heights

Near the northern tip of Manhattan (above 155th St), Washington Heights takes its name from the first US president, who set up a Continental Army fort here during the Revolutionary War. An isolated spot until the end of the 19th century, it attracted New Yorkers sniffing out affordable rents. Still, this neighborhood manages to retain its Latino – mainly Dominican – flavor, and is an interesting mix of blocks that alternate between former downtowners and longtime residents who operate within a tight, warm community.

★**Cloisters** MUSEUM
(☎212-923-3700; www.metmuseum.org/cloisters; Fort Tryon Park, at 190th St; suggested admission adult/child $25/free; ⏲10am-5:30pm Sun-Thu, to 9pm Fri & Sat; [S] A to 190th St) Constructed in the 1930s using stones and fragments from several French and Spanish medieval monasteries, the romantic, castle-like creation houses medieval frescoes, tapestries, courtyards, gardens and paintings, and has commanding views of the Hudson. The walk from the subway stop to the museum through Fort Tryon Park offers stupendous **views** of the Hudson River; rock climbers head here for practice.

Brooklyn

Brooklyn is a world in and of itself; residents sometimes don't go into Manhattan for days or even weeks at a time. With 2.5 million people and growing, from well-to-do new parents seeking stately brownstones in Carroll Gardens to young band members wanting cheap rents near gigs in Williamsburg, this outer borough has long surpassed Manhattan in the cool and livability factors in many people's minds. From sandy beaches and breezy boardwalks at one end to foodie destinations at the other, and with a massive range of ethnic enclaves, world-class entertainment, stately architecture and endless shopping strips in between, Brooklyn is a rival to Manhattan's attractions. The **Brooklyn Tourism & Visitors Center** (☎718-802-3846; www.visitbrooklyn.org; 209 Joralemon St btwn Court St & Brooklyn Bridge Blvd; ⏲10am-6pm Mon-Fri; [S] 2/3, 4/5 to Borough Hall) 🍃, in Brooklyn Heights, is an informative place to begin.

★**Coney Island & Brighton Beach** NEIGHBORHOOD
About 50 minutes by subway from Midtown, this popular pair of beach neighborhoods makes for a great day trip. The wide sandy beach of **Coney Island** has retained its nostalgic and kitschy wood-plank boardwalk (partly destroyed and replaced after Hurricane Sandy) and famous 1927 Cyclone roller coaster, despite a sanitized makeover of the amusement park area including a handful of new adrenalin-pumping thrill rides. For better or worse, its slightly sleazy charm is a thing of the past and developers plan to transform the area into a sleek residential city complete with high-rise hotels. The **New York Aquarium** (www.nyaquarium.com; Surf Ave & W 8th St; adult/child $15/11, with 4-D theater show $19/15; ⏲10am-6pm Mon-Fri, to 7pm Sat & Sun May-Sep; 👪; [S] F, Q to W 8th St-NY Aquarium) is a big hit with kids, as is taking in an early evening baseball game at **Key Span Park**, the waterfront stadium for the minor league **Brooklyn Cyclones** (www.brooklyncyclones.com).

A five-minute stroll north along the boardwalk past handball courts where some of the best in the world compete brings you to **Brighton Beach** ('Little Odessa'), where old-timers play chess and locals enjoy pierogies (boiled dumplings filled with meat or vegetables) and vodka shots at several boardwalk eateries. Then head into the heart of the 'hood, busy Brighton Beach Ave, to hit the many Russian shops, bakeries and restaurants.

Williamsburg, Greenpoint & Bushwick NEIGHBORHOOD
There is a definite Williamsburg look: skinny jeans, multiple tattoos, a discreet body piercing, shaggy hair for men, maybe some kind of retro head covering for women. Denizens of this raggedy and rowdy neighborhood across the East River seem to have the time and money to slouch in cafes and party all night in bars; a fair share of older – early 30s – transplants from Manhattan and Europe qualify as elders. The main artery is **Bedford Ave** between N 10th St and Metropolitan Ave, where there are boutiques, cafes, bars and cheap eateries. But cool spots have also sprouted along N 6th St and Berry St, and perhaps a sign of the times is that the uber-hip consider Williamsburg over and have long-since moved on to colonizing next door **Greenpoint**, a traditionally Polish neighborhood as well as the former warehouse buildings further out in **Bushwick**. The **Brooklyn Brewery** (☎718-486-7422; www.brooklynbrewery.com; 79 N 11th St btwn Berry St & Wythe Ave; ⏲free tours on the hr 1-4pm Sat & Sun; [S] L to Bedford Ave) hosts weekend tours, special events and pub nights.

Park Slope & Prospect Heights NEIGHBORHOOD
The Park Slope neighborhood is known for its classic brownstones, tons of great eateries and boutiques and liberal-minded stroller-pushing couples who resemble those on the Upper West Side (but have a backyard attached to their apartment). The 585-acre **Prospect Park**, created in 1866, is considered the greatest achievement of landscape designers Olmsted and Vaux, who also designed Central Park. Next door is the excellent 52-acre **Brooklyn Botanic Garden** (www.bbg.org; 1000 Washington Ave at Crown St; adult/child $10/free, Tue & 10am-noon Sat free; ⏲8am-6pm Tue-Fri, 10am-6pm Sat & Sun mid-March–Oct, 8am-4:30pm Tue-Fri, 10am-4:30pm Sat & Sun Nov-Mar; 👪; [S]2/3 to Eastern Pkwy-Brooklyn Museum), which features impressive cherry-tree blossoms in spring. Beside the garden is the **Brooklyn Museum** (☎718-638-5000; www.brooklynmuseum.org; 200 Eastern Pkwy; suggested admission $10; ⏲11am-6pm Wed, Sat & Sun, to 10pm Thu & Fri; [S]2/3 to Eastern Pkwy-Brooklyn Museum) with comprehensive collections of African, Islamic and Asian art, plus the Elizabeth A Sackler Center for Feminist Art.

Brooklyn Heights & Downtown Brooklyn NEIGHBORHOOD
When Robert Fulton's steam ferries started regular services across the East River in the early 19th century, well-to-do Manhattanites began building stellar houses – Victorian Gothic, Romanesque, neo-Greco, Italianate and others – in Brooklyn Heights. Strolling along the tree-lined streets to gaze at them now is a lovely afternoon activity.

Follow **Montague St**, the Heights' main commercial avenue, down to the waterfront until you hit the **Brooklyn Heights Promenade**, which juts out over the Brooklyn–Queens Expwy to offer stunning views of Lower Manhattan. Underneath the expressway is the **Brooklyn Bridge Park**, an 85-acre development of landscaped green space and pathways, built on piers stretching from the Brooklyn Bridge south to Atlantic Ave.

The small but fascinating **New York Transit Museum** (☎718-694-1600; www.mta.info/mta/museum; Schermerhorn St at Boerum Pl; adult/child $7/5; ⏲10am-4pm Tue-Fri, 11am-5pm Sat & Sun; 👪; [S]2/3, 4/5 to Borough Hall, R to Court St) has an amazing collection of original subway cars and transit memorabilia dating back more than a century. **Barclay's Center**, home to the NBA's New Jersey Nets, finally opened for the inaugural season in 2012, across the street from the Atlantic Center shopping mall in downtown Brooklyn.

Boerum Hill, Cobble Hill, Carroll Gardens & Red Hook NEIGHBORHOOD
These neighborhoods, home to a mix of families, mostly Italian, who have lived here for generations, and former Manhattanites looking for a real life after the city, are full of tree-lined streets with rows of attractively restored brownstones. **Smith St** and **Court St** are the two main arteries connecting to the most southerly area of the three, Carroll Gardens. The former is known as 'restaurant row,' while the latter has more of the

NEW YORK FOR CHILDREN

Contrary to popular belief, New York can be a pretty child-friendly city. Cutting-edge playgrounds have proliferated from Union Square to Battery Park and, of course, the city's major parks, including Central Park (check out Heckscher, Adventure and Ancient playgrounds), have them in abundance. There are at least as many attractions that will appeal to toddlers and tweens as there are for adults, from the two children's museums – **Children's Museum of Manhattan** (Map p86; www.cmom.org; 212 W 83rd St btwn Amsterdam Ave & Broadway; admission $11; ⏲10am-5pm Sun-Fri, to 7pm Sat; 👪; [S]B, C to 81st St-Museum of Natural History; 1 to 86th St) and the **Brooklyn Children's Museum** (www.brooklynkids.org; 145 Brooklyn Ave at St Marks Ave, Crown Heights; admission $9; ⏲10am-5pm, closed Mon; 👪; [S]C to Kingston-Throop Aves, 3 to Kingston Ave) – to the Central Park and Bronx zoos to the Coney Island aquarium. The boat ride to Lady Liberty or a Circle Line cruise offers the opportunity to chug around New York Harbor and the riverside Intrepid, Sea, Air & Space Museum has kid-friendly exhibits. Vintage carousels can be found in Bryant Park, Central Park and Brooklyn Bridge Park. Times Square's themed megastores and their neighboring kid-friendly restaurants are easy options. And of course delis and diners with quick sandwiches and extensive menus are everywhere. Check out the weekend Arts section of the *New York Times* for kid-themed events and performances.

old-school groceries, bakeries and red-sauce restaurants. Further west is Red Hook, a waterfront area with cobblestone streets and hulking industrial buildings. Though it's a bit of a hike from the subway line, the formerly gritty area is now home to a handful of bars and eateries, as well as a massive waterfront branch of Fairway (⏲718-694-6868; 480-500 Van Brunt St, Red Hook; ⏾8am-10pm; ⏾; ⏾B61 to cnr Coffey & Van Brunt Sts, ⏿F, G to Carroll St), a beloved gourmet grocery with breathtaking views of NY harbor.

Dumbo   NEIGHBORHOOD

Dumbo's nickname is an acronym for its location: 'Down Under the Manhattan–Brooklyn Bridge Overpass,' and while this north Brooklyn slice of waterfront used to be strictly for industry, it's now the domain of high-end condos, furniture shops and art galleries. Several highly regarded performing arts spaces are located in the cobblestone streets and the Empire-Fulton Ferry State Park hugs the waterfront and offers picture-postcard Manhattan views.

◉ The Bronx

This 42-sq-mile borough to the north of Manhattan has several claims to fame: the Yankees, fondly known as the Bronx Bombers, who can be seen in all their pinstriped glory at the new Yankee Stadium (⏲718-508-3917, 718-293-6000; www.yankees.com; E 161st St at River Ave; tours $20; ⏾call for hrs; ⏿B/D, 4 to 161st St-Yankee Stadium) in spring and summer; the 'real' Little Italy, namely Belmont (www.arthuravenuebronx.com), where bustling stretches of Arthur and Belmont Aves burst with Italian gourmet markets and eateries; and a super-sized attitude that's been mythologized in Hollywood movies from *The Godfather* to *Rumble in the Bronx*. But it's also got some cool surprises up its sleeve: a quarter of the Bronx is parkland, including the city beach of Pelham Bay Park. Also up in these parts is the magical City Island, a little slice of New England in the Bronx.

New York Botanical Garden   GARDENS

(www.nybg.org; Bronx River Pkwy & Fordham Rd; adult/child/senior & student $20/8/18, Wed & 10am-noon Sat free; ⏾10am-6pm Tue-Sun; ⏾; ⏾Metro-North to Botanical Garden) There are 250 acres, with old-growth forest, a wetlands trail, nearly 3000 roses and tens of thousands of newly planted azalea plants.

Bronx Wildlife Conservation Park   ZOO

(⏲718-220-5100; www.bronxzoo.com; Bronx River Pkwy, at Fordham Rd; adult/child $15/11; ⏾10am-5pm Apr-Oct; ⏿2 to Pelham Pkwy) Otherwise known as the Bronx Zoo, this is one of the biggest, best and most progressive zoos anywhere.

Woodlawn Cemetery   CEMETERY

(⏲718-920-0500; www.thewoodlawncemetery.org; Webster Ave at E 233rd St; ⏾8:30am-5pm; ⏿4 to Woodlawn) Famous, historic and fascinating, this 400-acre burial ground is the resting place of many notable Americans, including Irving Berlin and Herman Melville.

◉ Queens

There is no longer any typical Queens accent– think Archie and Edith Bunker in *All in the Family*. You're as likely to hear Bengali and Spanish – 170 languages are spoken – in this, the largest (282 sq miles) and most ethnically diverse county in the country. There are few of the tree-lined brownstone streets you find in Brooklyn, and the majority of the neighborhoods, architecturally speaking at least, do not befit this borough's grand name. However, because close to half its 2.3 million residents were born abroad, parts of Queens are endlessly reconstituting themselves, creating a vibrant and heady alternative universe to Manhattan. It's also home to two major airports, the Mets, a hip modern-art scene, miles of excellent beaches in the Rockaways and walking trails in the Gateway National Recreation Area (www.nps.gov/gate), and a wildlife refuge in Jamaica Bay, only minutes from JFK airport. The Queens Historical Society (⏲718-939-0647; www.queenshistoricalsociety.org) offers tours through many areas of the massive borough.

Long Island City   NEIGHBORHOOD

(admission $15, open 2pm to 9pm; ⏿G to 21st St) Neighboring Long Island City has several high-rise condominiums lining the riverfront with fantastic views of Manhattan. The area has also become a hub of art museums. PS 1 Contemporary Art Center (⏲718-784-2084; www.ps1.org; 22-25 Jackson Ave, at 46th Ave; suggested donation $10; ⏾noon-6pm Thu-Mon) is dedicated solely to new, cutting-edge works. On Saturdays from early July through September, the center's outdoor courtyard is transformed into an installation art space and crammed with the highest concentration of hipsters this side of the Mississippi. If the weather is pleasant, don't miss the waterside **Socrates Sculpture Park** (Map p86; www.socratessculpturepark.org; Broadway at Vernon Blvd; ⏱10am-dusk; [S] N/Q to Broadway) [FREE] with its outdoor exhibits of massive, climbable sculptures by greats including Mark di Suvero, who founded the space.

Astoria NEIGHBORHOOD

Home to the largest Greek community outside of Greece, this is obviously the place to find amazing Greek bakeries, restaurants and gourmet shops, mainly along **Broadway**. An influx of Eastern European, Middle Eastern (Steinway Ave, known as 'Little Egypt,' is the place for falafel, kabobs and hookah pipes) and Latino immigrants have created a rich and diverse mix. Young Bohemian types have also migrated here, making the area Queens' answer to Williamsburg. A reminder that movie-making started in Astoria in the 1920s, the renovated **American Museum of the Moving Image** (www.movingimage.us; 35th Ave at 36th St, Astoria; adult/child $12/6, admission 4-8pm Fri free; ⏱10.30am-5pm Tue-Thu, to 8pm Fri, to 7pm Sat & Sun; [S] M/R to Steinway St) exposes some of the mysteries of the craft with amazing exhibits and screenings in its ornate theater. In summer, cool off at the **Astoria Pool** (www.nycgovparks.org/parks/astoriapark; Astoria Park, cnr 19th St & 23rd Dr, Astoria; ⏱11am-7pm late Jun-early Sep; [S] N/Q to Astoria Blvd), the city's largest and oldest. Much of the neighborhood, as well as curious Manhattanites, can be found at the **Bohemian Hall & Beer Garden** (www.bohemianhall.com; 29-19 24th Ave btwn 29th & 31st Sts, Astoria; [S] N/Q to Astoria Blvd) during warm afternoons and evenings.

Flushing & Corona NEIGHBORHOOD

The intersection of Main St and Roosevelt Ave, downtown Flushing, can feel like the Times Square of a city a world away from NYC. Immigrants from all over Asia, primarily Chinese and Korean, make up this neighborhood bursting at the seams with markets and restaurants filled with delicious and cheap delicacies. **Flushing Meadows Corona Park**, meanwhile, is the home of **Citi Field**, the **USTA National Tennis Center** (the US Open is held here every August) and many lakes, ball fields, bike paths and grassy expanses, and was used for the 1939 and 1964 World's Fairs, of which there are quite a few faded leftovers. Kids can learn about science and technology through fun hands-on exhibits at the **New York Hall of Science** (☎718-699-0005; www.nyhallsci.org; 47-01 111th St; adult/child $11/8, 2-5pm Fri Sep-Jun free; ⏱daily Apr-Aug, closed Mon Sep-Mar; [S] 7 to 111th St); a quirky mini-golf course is on the site. Also within this massive park is the **Queens Museum of Art** (QMA; www.queensmuseum.org; Flushing Meadows Corona Park, Queens; suggested donation adult/child $5/free; ⏱noon-6pm Wed-Sun, to 8pm Fri Jul & Aug; [S] 7 to 111th St).

Jackson Heights Historic District NEIGHBOURHOOD

(btwn Roosevelt & 34th Aves, from 70th to 90th Sts; [S] E, F/V, R to Jackson Heights-Roosevelt Ave) A fascinating mix of Indian and South American (Roosevelt Ave) cultures, this is the place to purchase saris and 22-karat gold, dine on South Indian *masala dosas* – huge, paper-thin rice crepes folded around flavorful mixtures of masala potatoes, peas, cilantro and other earthy treats – and continue on with a plate of Colombian arepas (corn pancakes), a bite of Argentine empanadas and a cocktail at one of several Latin gay and lesbian bars, several of which line the main drag of Broadway.

Staten Island

While many New Yorkers will say that Staten Island has more in common with its neighbor, New Jersey, because of its suburban house and car cultures, there are compelling reasons to include this borough in your urban explorations. First and foremost is the **Staten Island Ferry** (Map p68; www.siferry.com; Whitehall Terminal at Whitehall & South Sts; ⏱24hr; [S] 1 to South Ferry) [FREE], which shuttles blasé commuters to work, while offering breathtaking views of the Statue of Liberty and the Manhattan skyline (the worlds' largest Ferris wheel is to be built amid a large shopping and retail complex near the ferry terminal). Not far from the ferry station on the Staten Island side is the **Richmond County Bank Ballpark** (75 Richmond Terrace, Staten Island), home to the minor-league Staten Island Yankees, as well as the hipper-than-ever neighborhood of St George.

Activities

Cycling

Hundreds of miles of designated cycling lanes have been added throughout the city by Mayor Bloomberg's very pro-cycling City Hall. And even more potentially momentous, the Bloomberg administration launched **Citi Bike** (www.citibikenyc.com; 24hr/7 days $11/27), its long awaited and semi-contentious bike-sharing program – the largest in the country – in the summer of 2013. Hundreds of kiosks in Manhattan and parts of Brooklyn house the almost instantly iconic bright blue and very sturdy bicycles available for rides of 30-minutes or less. However, unless you're an experienced urban cyclist, pedaling through the streets can be a risky activity, as bike lanes are often blocked by trucks, taxis and double-parked cars. More than 28-miles, mostly riverfront, have been integrated into the **Manhattan Waterfront Greenway**, a patchwork of park pathways, overpasses and a few city streets that circle the entire island of Manhattan. The mostly uninterrupted 10-mile stretch from the GW Bridge to Battery Park, including **Hudson River Park**, is perhaps the most spectacular. Of course **Central Park** and Brooklyn's **Prospect Park** have lovely cycling paths.

For cycling tips and weekend trips, contact **Five Borough Bicycle Club** (Map p86; www.5bbc.org; 891 Amsterdam Ave at 103rd St; [S] 1 to 103rd St). **Transportation Alternatives** (www.transalt.org), a nonprofit bicycle-lobbying group, is also a good source of information. Gay cycling enthusiasts should check the website of **Fast & Fabulous** (www.fastnfab.org), a gay cycling club that organizes long weekend rides. For bike rentals (other than Citi Bike), try Central Park's **Loeb Boathouse** or locate a rental shop on the comprehensive website **Bike New York** (www.bikenewyork.org).

Water Sports

This is an island, after all, and as such there are plenty of opportunities for boating and kayaking. The **Downtown Boathouse** (Map p72; www.downtownboathouse.org; Pier 40, near Houston St; tours free; ⏲10am-6pm Sat & Sun, 5-7pm Thu Jun-Sep; [S] 1 to Houston St) offers free 20-minute kayaking (including equipment) in the protected embayment of the Hudson River. Other locations include Pier 96 and 72nd St.

In Central Park, **Loeb Boathouse** (Map p86; ☎212-517-2233; www.thecentralparkboathouse.com; Central Park btwn 74th & 75th Sts; boating per hr $12, bike rentals per hr $9-15; ⏲10am-dusk Apr-Nov; 👪; [S] B, C to 72nd St, 6 to 77th St) rents rowboats for romantic trysts, and even fills Venice-style gondolas in summer ($30 for 30 minutes). For a sailing adventure, hop aboard the *Schooner Adirondack* at **Chelsea Piers**.

Surfers may be surprised to find a tight group of wave worshippers within city limits, at Queens' **Rockaway Beach** at 90th St, where you can hang ten after only a 45-minute ride on the A train from Midtown.

☞ Tours

The following is a small sample:

Big Onion Walking Tours WALKING TOUR
(☎888-606-9255; www.bigonion.com; tours $20) Popular and quirky guided tours specializing in ethnic and neighborhood tours.

Circle Line BOAT TOUR
(Map p76; ☎212-563-3200; www.circleline42.com; Pier 83, W 42nd St; tickets from $29; [S] A/C/E to 42nd St-Port Authority Bus Terminal) Ferry boat tours, from semicircle to a full island cruise with guided commentary, as well as powerful speedboat trips (adult/child $27/21).

Gray Line Sightseeing BUS TOUR
(Map p76; www.newyorksightseeing.com; 777 8th Ave; adult/child from $42/$32) Hop-on, hop-off double-decker multilingual guided bus tours of all the boroughs (except Staten Island).

Municipal Art Society WALKING TOUR
(Map p76; ☎212-935-3960; www.mas.org; 111 W 57th St; tours $20; [S] F to 57th St) Various scheduled tours focusing on architecture and history, including daily 12:30pm tours of Grand Central Terminal.

New York City Audubon WALKING TOUR
(Map p76; ☎212-691-7483; www.nycaudubon.org; 71 W 23rd St, Ste 1523; tours $8-100; [S] F/M to 23rd St) Expert instructors and guides lead trips including birding in Central Park and the Bronx and ecology cruises of the Jamaica Bay Wildlife Refuge.

NYC Gangster Tours WALKING TOUR
(www.nycgangstertours.com; tours $25) Sure, it's a little schticky, but colorful and knowledgeable guides make these walking tours focusing on NYC's Italian, Chinese and Jewish mafia interesting and fun.

On Location Tours TOUR
(☎212-209-3370; www.screentours.com; tours $15-45) *Gossip Girl* and *How I Met Your Mother* are on the list of tours as well as long-running ones that allow you to flesh out your Carrie Bradshaw or Tony Soprano fantasies.

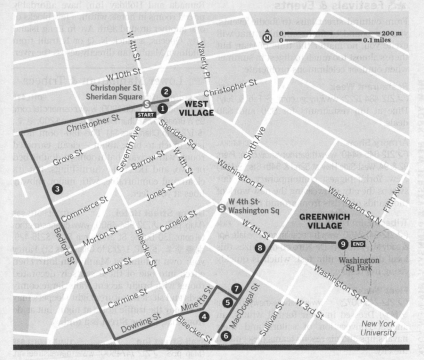

City Walk
Village Radicals

START CHRISTOPHER ST
END FIFTH AVE
LENGTH ½ MILE; 30 MINUTES

Greenwich Village has historically been a hotbed for upstarts, radicals, Bohemians, poets, folk singers, feminists and freedom-seeking gays and lesbians. Disembark the subway at Christopher St and stop at tiny **1 Christopher Park**, where two life-sized statues of same-sex couples (Gay Liberation, 1992) stand guard. On its north side is the legendary **2 Stonewall Inn**, where fed-up drag queens rioted for their civil rights in 1969, signaling the start of the gay revolution. Cross Seventh Ave South and continue west along Christopher St. Turn left onto quaint Bedford St; stop and peer into **3 Chumley's**, the site of a prohibition-dodging socialist-run speakeasy (closed since 2007 but hopes to reopen in the future). Continue along Bedford St for several blocks, make a left on Downing St and cross Sixth Ave. Continue east on the crooked

Minetta St, home to the unremarkable Panchito's Mexican Restaurant, which painted over the faded sign for the **4 Fat Black Pussycat** – called the Commons in 1962, when a young Bob Dylan wrote and first performed 'Blowin' in the Wind' here. Turn right on Minetta Lane and right on MacDougal St to find the historic **5 Minetta Tavern**, which opened as a speakeasy in 1922. Also on this block is the former site of the **6 Folklore Center**, where Izzy Young established a hangout for folk artists including Dylan, who found his first audience at the music venue **7 Cafe Wha?**. Continue back along MacDougal to the current Research Fellows & Scholars Office of the NYU School of Law, the former site of the **8 Liberal Club**, a meeting place for free thinkers, including Jack London and Upton Sinclair, founded in 1913. Beyond here is the southwest entrance to **9 Washington Square Park** (p73), which has a long history as a magnet for radicals. Wrap up the tour by leaving the park at the iconic arch and head up Fifth Ave.

✱ Festivals & Events

From cultural street fairs to foodie events, you are bound to find something that will excite you, no matter the time of year, but there's almost too much to digest in summer when outdoor celebrations proliferate.

Restaurant Week   FOOD
(☎212-484-1222; www.nycgo.com; ☺Feb & July) Dine at top restaurants for $20 and $30 deals.

Armory Show   CULTURAL
(☎212-645-6440; www.thearmoryshow.com; Piers 92 & 94, West Side Hwy at 52nd & 54th Sts; ☺Mar) New York's biggest contemporary art fair sweeps the city, showcasing the new work of thousands of artists from around the world.

Tribeca Film Festival   FILM
(☎212-941-2400; www.tribecafilm.com; ☺late Apr & early May) Robert De Niro co-organizes this local downtown film fest, which is quickly rising in prestige.

Fleet Week   NAVAL
(☎212-245-0072; www.fleetweeknewyork.com; ☺May) Dressed in their formal whites, an annual convocation of sailors and their naval ships and air rescue teams descend on the city.

**Lesbian, Gay, Bisexual
& Transgender Pride**   CULTURAL
(☎212-807-7433; www.nycpride.org; ☺Jun) Pride month, with a packed calendar of parties and events, culminates with a major march down Fifth Ave on the last Sunday of June.

Mermaid Parade   CULTURAL
(www.coneyisland.com; ☺late Jun) Something of Mardi Gras on the boardwalk, this parade turns Surf Ave on Coney Island in Brooklyn into a free-expression zone that's fun, crazy and artistic.

New York Film Festival   FILM
(www.filmlinc.com; ☺late Sep) Major world premieres from prominent directors at this Lincoln Center event.

🛏 Sleeping

Keep in mind that prices change depending on the value of the euro, yen and other worldwide currencies, as well as the general drift of the global economic climate, not to mention the day of the week and the season, with spring and fall being most expensive. Tax adds an additional 13.25% per night. A cluster of national chains, including Sheraton, Ramada and Holiday Inn, have affordably priced rooms in hotels within a few blocks of one another around 39th Ave in Long Island City, Queens, a quick N, Q or R train from midtown Manhattan directly across the river.

🛏 Lower Manhattan & Tribeca

Cosmopolitan Hotel   HOTEL $$$
(Map p68; ☎212-566-1900; www.cosmohotel.com; 95 W Broadway, at Chambers St; d from $200; ✸ 🛜; 🚇1/2/3 to Chambers St) The 130-room hotel isn't much to brag about – clean, carpeted rooms with private bathrooms, a double bed or two, and IKEA-like furnishings. But it's clean and comfortable, with major subway lines at your feet.

Duane Street Hotel   BOUTIQUE HOTEL $$$
(Map p68; ☎212-964-4600; www.duanestreethotel.com; 130 Duane St at Church St; r $215-429; ✸ @ 🛜 🐾; 🚇A/C, 1/2/3 to Chambers St) Fancy your own minimalist Manhattan loft? Then check into one of these sparsely decorated rooms with bright accent walls, large comfy beds and sleek furniture. Light sleepers may not enjoy the traffic noise at night, but aside from that, Duane Street is a find.

Wall Street Inn   LUXURY HOTEL $$$
(Map p68; ☎212-747-1500; www.thewallstreetinn.com; 9 S William St; r incl breakfast from $275; ✸ @ 🛜; 🚇2/3 to Wall St) Lehman Brothers, the failed bank, once occupied this classic limestone building and, while the mood of the hotel is very early American banker, there's little risk in a stay here. Old-fashioned and warm rather than stuffy, the rooms, with luxurious marble baths, are slightly over-furnished for their size.

🛏 SoHo

Mondrian SoHo   HOTEL $$$
(Map p72; ☎212-389-1000; www.mondriansoho.com; 9 Crosby St btwn Howard & Grand Sts; r from $249; ✸ @ 🛜 🐾; 🚇4/6, N/Q/R, J/Z to Canal St) The trademark Mondrian playfulness now inhabits over 250 rooms at this beautiful downtown property. The designs have dabbled with fairy-tale color schemes while tricking the senses with an eclectic assortment of oddly textured *objets d'art*.

Soho Grand Hotel   BOUTIQUE HOTEL $$$
(Map p72; ☎212-965-3000; www.sohogrand.com; 310 W Broadway; d $195-450; ✸ @ 🛜 🐾; 🚇6, N/Q/R, J to Canal St) The original boutique hotel of the 'hood still reigns, with its strik-

ing glass-and-cast-iron lobby stairway, and 367 rooms with cool, clean lines plus Frette linens, plasma flat-screen TVs and Kiehl's grooming products. The lobby's Grand Lounge buzzes with action.

Solita SoHo   HOTEL $$$
(Map p72; ☎212-925-3600; www.solitasohohotel. com; 159 Grand St, at Lafayette St; r from $220; ❀ 🛜; 🟥 6, N/Q/R, J to Canal St) Part of the Clarion chain, the Solita is a clean, functional alternative with boutique-style furnishings close to Little Italy, Chinatown, Soho and the Lower East Side. Lower winter rates.

🛏 Lower East Side, East Village & NoLita

Nolitan Hotel   HOTEL $$
(Map p72; ☎212-925-2555; www.nolitanhotel.com; 30 Kenmare St btwn Elizabeth & Mott Sts; r from $143; ❀🛜🞕; 🟥 J to Bowery, 4/6 to Spring St, B/D to Grand St) Set behind a memorable facade of floating postive-negative Tetris bricks, the Nolitan is a great find. Tuck into a good book in the inviting lobby lounge, or head upstairs to your stylish pad, which feels like it's waiting to be photographed in the next CB2 catalog.

East Village Bed & Coffee   B&B $$
(Map p72; ☎212-533-4175; www.bedandcoffee.com; 110 Ave C btwn 7th & 8th Sts; s/d with shared bath from $125/130; ❀🛜; 🟥 F/V to Lower East Side-2nd Ave) This family home has been transformed into a quirky, arty, offbeat B&B with colorful, themed private rooms (one shared bathroom and kitchen per floor) and even free bikes. Dogs roam the 1st floor, but the upper ones are pet free and the owner can supply wonderful insider neighborhood tips.

Blue Moon Hotel   BOUTIQUE HOTEL $$$
(Map p72; ☎212-533-9080; www.bluemoon-nyc. com; 100 Orchard St btwn Broome & Delancey Sts; r from $250; ❀🛜; 🟥 F/V to Lower East Side-2nd Ave) You'd never guess that this quaint, welcoming brick guesthouse – full of festive colors – was once a foul tenement back in the day (the day being 1879). Except for a few ornate touches, like wrought-iron bed frames and detailed molding, Blue Moon's clean, spare rooms are entirely modern and comfortable.

Bowery Hotel   BOUTIQUE HOTEL $$$
(Map p72; ☎212-505-9100; www.theboweryhotel. com; 335 Bowery btwn 2nd & 3rd Sts; r from $325; ❀@🛜; 🟥 F/V to Lower East Side-2nd Ave; 6 to Bleecker St) Perhaps as far as you can get from the Bowery's gritty flophouse history, this

stunningly stylish hotel is all 19th-century elegance. Rooms come equipped with lots of light and sleek furnishings mixed with antiques. The baroque-style lobby bar attracts the young and chic and on-site restaurant Gemma serves upscale Italian.

🛏 Chelsea, Meatpacking District & West (Greenwich) Village

Chelsea Hostel   HOSTEL $
(Map p76; ☎212-647-0010; www.chelseahostel. com; 251 W 20th St btwn Seventh & Eighth Aves; dm $38-68, s $70-95, d from $95; ❀@🛜; 🟥 A/C/E, 1/2 to 23 St; 1/2 to 18 St) Walkable to the Village and Midtown, Chelsea Hostel capitalizes on its convenient location with somewhat steep prices, but it's kept clean (even a tad sterile at times) and there's access to common rooms and kitchens where other budget travelers often meet and hang.

Jane Hotel   HOTEL $
(Map p72; ☎212-924-6700; www.thejanenyc.com; 113 Jane St btwn Washington St & West Side Hwy; r with shared bath from $99; ℗❀🛜; 🟥 L to 8th Ave, A/C/E to 14th St; 1/2 to Christopher St-Sheridan Sq) Originally built for sailors (obvious after one look at the cabin-sized rooms), the Jane became a temporary refuge for survivors of the *Titanic*, then a YMCA and a rock-and-roll venue. The single-bunk rooms feature flat-screen TVs and the communal showers are more than adequate.

Chelsea Lodge   HOTEL $$
(Map p76; ☎212-243-4499; www.chelsealodge. com; 318 W 20th St btwn Eighth & Ninth Aves; s/d from $118/128; ❀; 🟥 A/C/E to 14th St; 1 to 18th St) Housed in a landmark brownstone in Chelsea, the European-style, 20-room Chelsea Lodge is a super deal. Space is tight, so you won't get more than a bed, with a TV plopped on an old wooden cabinet. There are showers and sinks in rooms, but toilets are down the hall. Six suite rooms have private bathrooms, and two come with private garden access.

Inn on 23rd St   B&B $$
(Map p76; ☎212-463-0330; www.innon23rd.com; 131 W 23rd St btwn Sixth & Seventh Aves; r incl breakfast from $179; ❀🛜; 🟥 F/V, 1 to 23rd St) Housed in a lone 19th-century, five-story townhouse on busy 23rd St, this 14-room B&B is a Chelsea gem. The rooms are big and welcoming, with fanciful fabrics on big brass or poster beds and an ol' piano for you to play boogie-woogie on in the lounge, and a 2nd-floor, all-Victorian library that doubles as a breakfast room.

Larchmont Hotel HOTEL $$

(Map p72; ☎212-989-9333; www.larchmonthotel.com; 27 W 11th St, btwn Fifth & Sixth Aves; s/d with shared bath & breakfast from $90/119; ✴; Ⓢ4/5/6, N/Q/R to 14th St-Union Sq) Housed in a prewar building that blends in with the other fine brownstones on the block, a stay at the Larchmont is about location. The carpeted rooms are basic and in need of updating, as are the communal baths, but it's not a bad deal for the price.

Ace Hotel New York City BOUTIQUE HOTEL $$$

(Map p76; ☎212-679-2222; www.acehotel.com/newyork; 20 W 29th St btwn Broadway & Fifth Ave; r from $249-549; ✴ⓦ✴; Ⓢ N/R to 28th St) This outpost of a hip Pacific northwest chain is on the northern edge of Chelsea. Clever touches such as vintage turntables and handwritten welcome notes elevate the Ace beyond the standard. However, prison-issued bunk beds in one of the room styles are missteps. Juice, coffee and croissants are available in the morning.

Hotel Gansevoort LUXURY HOTEL $$$

(Map p72; ☎212-206-6700; www.hotelgansevoort.com; 18 Ninth Ave at 13th St; r from $325; ✴✴ⓦ✴; ⓈA/C/E, 1/2/3 to 14th St; L to 8th Ave) This 187-room luxury hotel in the trendy Meatpacking District has been a hit for its 400-thread-count linens, hypoallergenic down duvets, plasma TVs, chic basement spa and rooftop bar with fabulous views. Down-to-earth types, beware: it's on the nauseatingly trendy side of things.

🛏 Union Square, Flatiron District & Gramercy Park

Hotel 17 BUDGET HOTEL $$

(Map p76; ☎212-475-2845; www.hotel17ny.com; 225 E 17th St btwn Second & Third Aves; r $89-150; ✴ⓦ; ⓈN/Q/R/W, 4/5/6 to 14th St-Union Sq; L to 3rd Ave) Right off Stuyvesant Sq on a leafy residential block, this no-frills, eight-floor townhouse has relatively affordable prices. Rooms are small, with traditional, basic furnishings (gray carpet, chintzy bedspreads, burgundy blinds) and lack much natural light.

Gershwin Hotel HOTEL $$$

(Map p76; ☎212-545-8000; www.gershwinhotel.com; 7 E 27th St at Fifth Ave; r from $215; ✴ⓦⓦ; ⓈN/R, 6 to 28th St) This popular and funky spot is half youth hostel, half hotel, and buzzes with original pop art, touring bands and a young and artsy European clientele.

W New York Union Square HOTEL $$$

(Map p76; ☎888-625-5144, 212-253-9119; www.whotels.com; 201 Park Ave S at 17th St; r $389, ste from $625; ✴ⓦ@ⓦ✴; ⓈL, N/Q/R/W, 4/5/6 to 14th St-Union Sq) The ultra-hip W demands a black wardrobe and credit card. The standard rooms aren't big, but – set in a 1911, one-time insurance building – benefit from high ceilings, and are decked out with all the modern bells and whistles. The suites are spectacular.

Marcel BOUTIQUE HOTEL $$$

(Map p76; ☎212-696-3800; www.nychotels.com; 201 E 24th St, at Third Ave; d from $210; ✴@ⓦ; Ⓢ6 to 23rd St) Minimalist with earth-tone touches, this 97-room inn is a poor-man's chic boutique and that's not a bad thing. Modernist rooms on the avenue have great views, and the sleek lounge is a great place to unwind after a day of touring.

🛏 Midtown

★ Yotel HOTEL $$

(Map p76; ☎646-449-7700; www.yotel.com; 570 Tenth Ave at 41st St; r from $150; ✴ⓦ; ⓈA/C/E to 42nd St-Port Authority Bus Terminal; 1/2/3, N/Q/R, S, 7 to Times Sq-42nd St) Part futuristic spaceport, part Austin Powers set, this uber-cool 669-room option bases its rooms on airplane classes. Small but cleverly configured, Premium cabins include automated adjustable beds, while all cabins feature floor-to-ceiling windows with killer views, slick bathrooms and iPod connectivity.

Pod Hotel HOTEL $$

(Map p76; ☎866-414-4617; www.thepodhotel.com; 230 E 51st St btwn Second & Third Aves; r from $145; ✴ⓦ; Ⓢ6 to 51st St; E, V to Lexington Ave-53rd St) A dream come true for folks who'd like to live inside their iPod – or at least curl up and sleep with it – this affordable hot spot has a range of room types, most barely big enough for the bed. 'Pods' have bright bedding, tight workspaces, flat-screen TVs, iPod docking stations and 'rain' showerheads.

Andaz Fifth Avenue BOUTIQUE HOTEL $$$

(Map p76; ☎212-601-1234; http://andaz.hyatt.com; 485 Fifth Ave at 41st St; d $355-595; ✴ⓦ; ⓈS, 4/5/6 to Grand Central-42nd St, 7 to 5th Ave) Uber-chic yet youthful and relaxed, the Andaz ditches stuffy reception desks for hip, mobile staff who check you in on tablets in the art-laced lobby. The hotel's 184 rooms are contemporary and sleek, with NYC-inspired details like 'Fashion District' rolling racks and subway-inspired lamps.

London NYC LUXURY HOTEL $$$
(Map p76; ☎212-307-5000, 866-690-2029; www.thelondonnyc.com; 151 W 54th St btwn Sixth & Seventh Aves; ste from $389; ❄ 📶; Ⓢ B/D, E to 7th Ave) This luxe hotel salutes the British capital in sophisticated ways, including a Michelin-starred restaurant by Gordon Ramsay. But the real draw is the huge, plush rooms – all called suites, and all with separate bedroom and living area. In winter, online prices drop to the high $200s.

414 Hotel HOTEL $$$
(Map p76; ☎212-399-0006; www.414hotel.com; 414 W 46th St btwn Ninth & Tenth Aves; r incl breakfast from $200; ❄ 📶; Ⓢ C/E to 50th St) Set up like a guesthouse, this affordable, friendly option offers 22 tidy and tastefully decorated rooms a couple of blocks west of Times Square. Rooms facing the leafy inner courtyard, which is a perfect spot to enjoy your complimentary breakfast, are the quietest.

Upper West Side

Hostelling International New York HOSTEL $
(HI; Map p86; ☎212-932-2300; www.hinewyork.org; 891 Amsterdam Ave at 103rd St; dm $32-40, d from $135; ❄ 📶; Ⓢ 1 to 103rd St) It's got clean, safe and air-conditioned dorm rooms in a gorgeous landmark building, with a sprawling and shady patio and a super-friendly vibe.

Jazz on Amsterdam Ave HOSTEL $
(Map p86; ☎646-490-7348; www.jazzhostels.com; 201 W 87th St at Amsterdam Ave; dm $44, r $100; ❄ 📶; Ⓢ 1 to 86th St) Only a short walk to Central Park, this hostel chain's Upper West Side branch has clean rooms, both private rooms and two- to six-bed dorms. Free wi-fi in the lobby. Other branches in Harlem and Chelsea.

YMCA HOSTEL $$
(Map p86; ☎212-912-2600; www.ymca.com; 5 W 63rd St at Central Park West; r from $100; ❄ @; Ⓢ A/B/C/D to 59th St-Columbus Circle) Just steps from Central Park, this grand art-deco building has several floors – 8th to the 13th – of basic, but clean, rooms. Guests have access to extensive, but old-school gym, racquet ball courts, pool and sauna. Wi-fi on the ground floor. Other locations on the Upper East Side and Harlem.

Lucerne HOTEL $$$
(Map p86; ☎212-875-1000; www.thelucernehotel.com; 201 W 79th St cnr Amsterdam Ave; d $200-425, ste $400-625; ❄ 📶 👪; Ⓢ B, C to 81st St) This unusual 1903 structure breaks away from beaux arts in favor of the baroque, with an ornately carved terracotta-colored facade. Inside is a stately 197-room hotel with nine types of guest rooms evoking a contemporary Victorian look. Think: flowered bedspreads, scrolled headboards and plush pillows with fringe.

On the Ave BOUTIQUE HOTEL $$$
(Map p86; ☎212-362-1100; www.ontheave.com; 2178 Broadway at 77th St; r from $225; ❄ 📶; Ⓢ 1 to 77th St) A more welcoming feel and larger rooms make On the Ave a cut above the average sleek boutique hotel. And it's a good deal considering the high-concept design, stainless steel and marble baths, featherbeds, flat-screen TVs and original artwork.

Upper East Side

Bubba & Bean Lodges B&B $$
(Map p86; ☎917-345-7914; www.bblodges.com; 1598 Lexington Ave btwn 101st & 102nd Sts; r from $180; ❄ 📶; Ⓢ 6 to 103rd St) Hardwood floors, crisp white walls and pretty navy bedspreads make the rooms at this nifty B&B feel spacious, modern and youthful. The rooms are really more like full apartments (some fit up to six people). Good winter rates.

Bentley BOUTIQUE HOTEL $$$
(Map p86; ☎888-664-6835; www.nychotels.com; 500 E 62nd St, at York Ave; r from $200; ❄ 📶; Ⓢ N/Q/R to Lexington Ave/59th St) Featuring great East River views, the Bentley overlooks FDR Dr, as far east as you can go. Formerly an office building, the hotel has shed its utilitarian past in the form of chic boutique-hotel styling, a swanky lobby and sleek rooms.

★ **Carlyle** LUXURY HOTEL $$$
(Map p86; ☎212-744-1600; www.thecarlyle.com; 35 E 76th St btwn Madison & Park Aves; r from $450; ❄ 📶; Ⓢ 6 to 77th St) This legendary New York classic, the epitome of old-fashioned luxury hosts foreign dignitaries and celebrities alike. Opulence reigns from the hushed lobby with glossy marble floors to framed English country scenes or Audubon prints in the rooms; some have terraces and baby grand pianos.

Harlem

102 Brownstone HOTEL $$
(Map p86; ☎212-662-4223; www.102brownstone.com; 102 W 118th St btwn Malcolm X & Adam Clayton Powell Jr Blvds; r from $120; ❄ 📶; Ⓢ A/C, B, 2/3 to 116th St) A wonderfully redone Greek Revival

row house on a beautiful residential street; room styles, all with plush bedding, range from Zen to classy boudoir.

710 Guest Suites
APARTMENT $$

(☏ 212-491-5622; www.710guestsuites.com; 710 St Nicholas Ave at 146th St; ste from $174; ❄ 🛜; Ⓢ A/B/C/D to 145th St) Three fabulously chic suites with high ceilings, contemporary furnishings and wood floors in a brownstone. Three-night minimum and lower rates from January through March make this exceptionally good value. Located north of Central Park.

Harlem Flophouse
GUESTHOUSE $$

(Map p86; ☏ 347-632-1960; www.harlemflophouse. com; 242 W 123rd St btwn Adam Clayton Powell Jr & Frederick Douglass Blvds, Harlem; r with shared bath from $125; ❄ 🛜; Ⓢ A/C, B/D, 2/3 to 124th St) The four attractive bedrooms have antique light fixtures, glossed-wood floors and big beds, plus classic tin-ceilings and wooden shutters. Cat on the premises.

📷 Brooklyn

⭐ New York Loft Hostel
HOSTEL $

(☏ 718-366-1351; www.nylofthostel.com; 249 Varet St btwn Bogart & White Sts, Bushwick; dm $50, r with/without bath $70/65; ❄ @ 🛜; Ⓢ L to Morgan Ave) Live like a Williamsburg or more accurately Bushwick hipster in this renovated loft building. Brick walls, high ceilings, a beautiful kitchen and rooftop Jacuzzi make Manhattan hostels seem like tenements.

3B
B&B $

(☏ 347-762-2632; www.3bbrooklyn.com; 136 Lawrence St; dm/r incl breakfast $60/150; ❄ 🛜; Ⓢ A/C/F/N/R to Jay St-Metro Tech) The 3rd floor of this downtown Brooklyn brownstone has been turned into a bright and contemporary four-room B&B.

Nu Hotel
HOTEL $$$

(☏ 718-852-8585; www.nuhotelbrooklyn.com; 85 Smith St, Downtown Brooklyn; d incl breakfast from $300; ❄ @ 🛜; Ⓢ F, G to Bergen St) This location, only blocks from Brooklyn Heights and a nexus of attractive brownstone neighborhoods, is absolutely ideal – except for the fact that it's across the street from the Brooklyn House of Detention. It has a chic minimalist vibe and the clean, all-white rooms are comfortable.

🍴 Eating

In a city with nearly 19,000 restaurants, and new ones opening every single day, where are you supposed to begin? From Little Albania to Little Uzbekistan, your choice of ethnic eats is only a short subway ride away. A hotbed of buzz-worthy culinary invention and trends like artisanal doughnuts, farm-to-table pork sandwiches and *haute cuisine* reinterpretations of fried chicken, pizza and good ol' burgers and fries, NYC's restaurant scene, like the city, is constantly reinventing itself. The latest foodie obsession is the flotilla of roving, tweeting food trucks, the 21st-century equivalent of the classic pushcart, selling gourmet cupcakes, dumplings and Jamaican curry goat and everything in between.

🍴 Lower Manhattan & Tribeca

Ruben's Empanadas
ARGENTINE, FAST FOOD $

(Map p68; 64 Fulton St; empanadas $4; ⏱ 9am-7pm) Refuel with one of this Argentine chain's filling, greaseless empanadas in endless varieties, from chicken to apple or spicy tofu. Two other locations in the neighborhood.

Financier Patisserie
BAKERY, SANDWICHES $

(Map p68; ☏ 212-334-5600; 62 Stone St at Mill Lane; mains $8; ⏱ 7am-8pm Mon-Fri, 8:30am-6:30pm Sat; 🖐; Ⓢ 2/3, 4/5 to Wall St, J/Z to Broad St) There are now three Patisserie outposts in Lower Manhattan because nobody can get enough of the flaky, buttery croissants, almond, apricot and pear tarts, homemade soups and creamy quiches on the regular menu.

Fraunces Tavern
AMERICAN $$

(Map p68; ☏ 212-968-1776; www.frauncestavern. com; 54 Pearl St; mains $15-24; ⏱ noon-5pm; Ⓢ N/R to Whitehall) Can you really pass up a chance to eat where George Washington supped in 1762? Expect heaping portions of tavern stew, clam chowder and beef Wellington and, for dessert, bread pudding, spiked fig and apple tart or strawberry shortcake.

Blaue Gans
GERMAN-AUSTRIAN $$$

(Map p68; ☏ 212-571-8880; www.kg-ny.com; 139 Duane St; mains $15-30; ⏱ 11am-midnight; 🖐; Ⓢ A/C, 1/2/3 to Chambers St) Step inside this homage to minimalist Austrian cuisine and dive into some delectable *kavalierspitz* (boiled beef with horseradish), various wursts and yummy fried schnitzels. Kids get their own menu, and non-Austrian foodies can try delicate fish dishes, spicy soups and pastas.

Kutsher's Tribeca JEWISH $$$
(Map p68; ☎212-431-0606; www.kutsherstribeca.com; 186 Franklin St btwn Greenwich & Hudson Sts; mains $19-29; ⏰11:45am-10pm Mon-Wed, to 11pm Thu-Sat, 10am-3pm Sun; [S] A/C/E to Canal St, 1 to Franklin St) Jewish comfort food gets a refreshing makeover here. Forget the starch and stodge: here you'll be grazing on crispy artichokes with lemon, garlic and Parmesan; borscht salad with marinated goat cheese; or latkes with local apple compote.

🍴 Chinatown, Little Italy & NoLita

Lovely Day PAN-ASIAN $
(Map p72; ☎212-925-3310; 196 Elizabeth St, btwn Prince & Spring Sts; mains $9; ⏰11am-11pm; [S] J/M/Z to Bowery St, 6 to Spring St) Everything is just precious inside this affordable and funky nook that serves lovingly prepared Thai-inflected food. Coconut-rich curries, noodle dishes, papaya salad and spicy tofu squares create a fascinating harmony with the soda shop–inspired decor.

Pinche Taqueria MEXICAN $
(Map p72; ☎212-625-0090; www.pinchetaqueria.us; 227 Mott St, btwn Prince & Spring Sts; mains $4-9; ⏰10:30am-11pm Sun-Thu, to 1am Fri & Sat; 👪; [S] 6 to Spring St) Dig into authentic Mexican tacos, tostadas, burritos, quesadillas and more, topped with fresh yuca (cassava)fries and guacamole, and wash it all down with *horchata* (a beverage made with rice, flavored with lime and cinnamon and sweetened with sugar). Crowded and upbeat, Pinche is a great find on a hot, hungry afternoon.

BarBossa SOUTH AMERICAN $$
(Map p72; ☎212-625-2340; 232 Elizabeth St; mains $14; ⏰11am-midnight; [S] 6 to Spring St) A breezy, wide-open front window and low-level bossa nova in the background give this cafe a sultry and jazzy feel that's complemented by a light, tropical cuisine, heavy on salads, delicious soups and a few hearty mains.

Café Gitane MOROCCAN $$
(Map p72; ☎212-334-9552; www.cafegitanenyc.com; 242 Mott St; mains $12-18; ⏰9am-midnight Sun-Thu, to 12:30am Fri & Sat; [S] N/R/W to Prince St) Clear the Gauloise smoke from your eyes and blink twice if you think you're in Paris. Label-conscious shoppers love this authentic bistro, with its dark, aromatic coffee and dishes such as yellowfin tuna seviche and spicy meatballs in tomato turmeric sauce.

> **[i] A, B, C**
>
> Those letter grades you see posted in the windows of every NYC restaurant aren't the report cards of the owner's kids. They're issued by the NYC health department after an inspection of each establishment's hygiene standards. A is best and C worst – anything lower, well, you probably wouldn't want to eat there anyway.

Lombardi's PIZZA $$
(Map p72; ☎212-941-7994; 32 Spring St btwn Mulberry & Mott Sts; 6-slice pizza $16.50; ⏰11:30am-11pm Mon-Thu & Sun, to midnight Fri & Sat; [S] 6 to Spring St) The very first pizzeria in America was Lombardi's which opened here in 1905. It's justifiably proud of its New York style: thin crust and an even thinner layer of sauce – and slices that are triangular (unless they're Sicilian-style, in which case they're rectangular).

Da Nico ITALIAN $$$
(Map p72; ☎212-343-1212; www.danicoristorante.com; 164 Mulberry St; mains $18-40; ⏰noon-11pm Sun-Thu, to midnight Fri & Sat; [S] J/M/Z N/Q/R/W, 6 to Canal St) If you're hell-bent on having a Little Italy dinner, Da Nico is a classic. It's family-run and traditional in feel and the extensive menu highlights both northern and southern Italian cuisine that's red-sauce predictable but delicious.

★**Torrisi Italian Specialties** ITALIAN $$$
(Map p72; ☎212-965-0955; www.torrisinyc.com; 250 Mulberry St btwn Spring & Prince Sts; prix fixe menu $65; ⏰5:30-11pm Mon-Thu, from noon Fri-Sun; [S] N/R to Prince St; B/D/F, M to Broadway-Lafayette St; 4/6 to Spring St) Torrisi's tasting menu reads like an ode to Italy, with changes each week reflecting the whim of the owners (who also run popular Parm next door) and the seasonal rotation of fresh ingredients. Expect market produce and less-common items (such as rabbit and goat) spun into succulent platters.

🍴 Lower East Side

★**Katz's Delicatessen** DELI $
(Map p72; ☎212-254-2246; www.katzsdelicatessen.com; 205 E Houston St at Ludlow St; pastrami on rye $15, knockwurst $6; ⏰8am-10:45pm Mon-Wed & Sun, to 2:45am Thu-Sat; [S] F/V to Lower East Side-2nd Ave) One of the few remaining

Jewish delicatessens in the city, Katz's attracts locals, tourists and celebrities whose photos line the walls. Massive pastrami, corned beef, brisket and tongue sandwiches are throwbacks, as is the payment system: hold on to the ticket you're handed when you walk in and pay cash only.

Yonah Schimmel Knishery
KNISHES $

(Map p72; ☎212-477-2858; 137 E Houston St, btwn Eldridge & Forsyth Sts; ⊗9:30am-7pm; ☑; ☑F/V to Lower East Side-2nd Ave) Originally selling from a pushcart on Coney Island c 1890, this family business sells potato, cheese, cabbage and kasha knishes from a mini storefront on the Lower East Side.

Meatball Shop
ITALIAN $

(Map p72; ☎212-982-8895; www.themeatballshop. com; 84 Stanton St btwn Allen & Orchard Sts; dishes from $9; ⊗noon-2am Mon-Wed, Sun, to 4am Thu-Sat; ☑F to 2nd Ave; F to Delancey St; J/M/Z to Essex St) Masterfully executed meatball sandwiches have suddenly spiked in popularity,

and the Meatball Shop is riding the wave of success with moist incarnations of the traditional hero. Three other branches in the city.

Georgia's East Side BBQ
BBQ $

(Map p72; ☎212-253-6280; www.georgiaseastsidebbq.com; 192 Orchard St btwn Houston & Stanton Sts; ⊗noon-11pm; ☑F/V, M to Lower East Side-2nd Ave) Bring a big appetite to this little joint where the ribs are slow-cooked in beer then sizzled on the grill, the fried chicken is crisp and tender and there's no way you can eat all that sweet cornbread and decadent mac 'n' cheese. Cash only, and the bathroom is in the bar across the street.

Alias
MODERN AMERICAN $$

(Map p72; ☎212-505-5011; 76 Clinton St; ⊗6-11pm Tue-Fri, 11am-11:30pm Sat, 10:30am-10:30pm Sun; ☑F to Delancey St) Alias continues to deliver delicious, fresh food, heavy on seasonal ingredients, with dishes like Wild Alaskan black cod, maple syrup-drenched pears with ricotta and tomato-braised brisket.

EATING NYC: CHINATOWN

With hundreds of restaurants, from holes-in-the-wall to banquet-sized dining rooms, Chinatown is wonderful for exploring cheap eats on an empty stomach.

Amazing 66 (Map p68; 66 Mott St, at Canal St; mains $7; ⊗11am-11pm; ☑6, J, N/Q to Canal St) Terrific Cantonese lunches.

Prosperity Dumpling (Map p72; ☎212-343-0683; 46 Eldridge St btwn Hester & Canal Sts; dumplings $1-5; ⊗Mon-Sun 7:30am-10pm; ☑B/D to Grand St; F to East Broadway; J to Bowery) Among the best dumpling joints.

Vanessa's Dumpling House (Map p72; ☎212-625-8008; 118 Eldridge St btwn Grand & Broome Sts; dumplings $1-5; ⊗7:30am-10:30pm; ☑B/D to Grand St, J to Bowery, F to Delancey St) Great dumplings.

Big Wong King (Map p68; 67 Mott St, at Canal; mains $5-20; ⊗7am-9:30pm; ☑6, J, N/Q to Canal St) Chopped meat over rice and reliable congee (sweet or savory soft rice soup).

Bo Ky Restaurant (Map p68; ☎212-406-2292; 80 Bayard St, btwn Mott & Mulberry Sts; ⊗breakfast, lunch & dinner; ☑; ☑J, M, N, Q, R, W, Z, 6 to Canal St) Meat-studded soups, fish-infused flat noodles and curried rice dishes.

Banh Mi Saigon Bakery (Map p72; ☎212-941-1514; 198 Grand St btwn Mulberry & Mott Sts; mains $4-6; ⊗10am-7pm Tue-Sun; ☑J/M/Z, N/Q/R/W, 6 to Canal St) Some of the best Vietnamese sandwiches in town.

Joe's Shanghai (Map p68; ☎212-233-8888; www.joeshangairestaurants.com; 9 Pell St btwn Bowery & Doyers St; mains $5-16; ⊗11am-11pm Mon-Sun; ☑J/Z, N/Q, 4/6 to Canal St, B/D to Grand St) Always busy and tourist-friendly. Does good noodle and soup dishes.

Nom Wah Tea Parlor (Map p68; 13 Doyers St; mains $4-9; ⊗10:30am-9pm; ☑6, J, N/Q to Canal St) Looks like an old-school American diner, but is the oldest dim sum place in the city.

Original Chinatown Ice Cream Factory (Map p68; ☎212-608-4170; www.chinatown-icecreamfactory.com; 65 Bayard St; scoop $4; ⊗11am-10pm; ☑; ☑J/M, N/Q/R/W, 6 to Canal St) Overshadows the nearby Häagen-Dazs with its scoops of tea, ginger, passion fruit and lychee flavored sorbets.

'Inoteca ITALIAN $$
(Map p72; ☎ 212-614-0473; 98 Rivington St at Ludlow St; dishes $7-17; 🕘 noon-1am; [S] F/V to Lower East Side-2nd Ave) It's worth joining the crowd waiting at the cramped bar of this airy, dark-wood-paneled corner haven to choose from *tramezzini* (small sandwiches on white or whole-wheat bread), panini and bruschetta options, all delicious and moderately priced. There's also a list of 200 wines, 25 by the glass.

🍴 SoHo & NoHo

Mooncake Foods ASIAN, SANDWICHES $
(Map p72; 28 Watts St, btwn Sullivan & Thompson Sts; mains $8; 🕘 10am-11pm Mon-Fri, 9am-11pm Sat & Sun; [S] 1 to Canal St) This unpretentious family-run restaurant serves some of the best sandwiches in the neighborhood. Try the smoked white-fish salad sandwich or Vietnamese pork meatball hero. Another location in Chelsea and uptown in Hell's Kitchen.

Aroma Espresso Bar CAFE $
(Map p72; ☎ 212-533-1094; 145 Greene St, at Houston St; sandwiches $8.50; 🕘 7am-11pm; [S] B/D/F/V to Broadway-Lafayette St) An Israeli import to NYC, this sleek cafe chain has comfy and stylish seating and a menu bursting with fresh, tasty, affordable fare.

Boqueria Soho SPANISH TAPAS $$
(Map p72; ☎ 212-343-4255; 171 Spring St, btwn West Broadway & Thompson St; mains $13.50; 🕘 lunch & dinner daily, brunch Sat & Sun; [S] C/E to Spring St) This expansive, welcoming tapas joint features classics as well as new twists on the expected, and you can watch them being assembled as you sip your unique beer-and-pear sangria and peer into the open kitchen.

Dutch AMERICAN $$$
(Map p72; ☎ 212-677-6200; www.thedutchnyc.com; 131 Sullivan St btwn Prince & Houston Sts; mains $16-48; 🕘 11:30am-3pm Mon-Fri, 5:30pm-midnight Mon-Thu & Sun, 5:30pm-1am Fri & Sat, 10am-3pm Sat & Sun ; [S] A/C/E to Spring St, N/R to Prince St, 1/2 to Houston St) Oysters on ice and freshly baked homemade pies are the notable bookends of a meal – in the middle is fresh-from-the-farm cuisine, served in casseroles with the perfect amount of ceremony.

★ **Il Buco** ITALIAN $$$
(Map p72; ☎ 212-533-1932; www.ilbuco.com; 47 Bond St btwn Bowery & Lafayette St; mains $21-32; 🕘 noon-11pm Mon-Thu, to midnight Fri & Sat, 5-10:30pm Sun; [S] B/D/F/V to Broadway-Lafayette St; 6 to Bleecker St) This charming nook boasts hanging copper pots, kerosene lamps and antique furniture, plus a stunning menu and wine list. Sink your teeth into seasonal and ever-changing highlights like white polenta with braised broccoli rabe and anchovies.

🍴 East Village

Every cuisine and style is represented in the East Village, though even the very best places are certainly more casual than stuffy. St Marks Place and around, from Third to Second Ave, has turned into a little Tokyo with loads of Japanese sushi and grill restaurants. Cookie-cutter Indian restaurants line Sixth St between First and Second Ave.

★ **Xi'an Famous Foods** CHINESE $
(Map p72; 81 St Mark's Pl, at First Ave; mains $6; 🕘 24hr; [S] 6 to Astor Pl) This sliver of a restaurant, originally hailing from Flushing, Queens, has an interesting menu specializing in spicy noodle and soup dishes. Two other locations in Chinatown.

Veselka UKRAINIAN $
(Map p72; ☎ 212-228-9682; www.veselka.com; 144 Second Ave at 9th St; mains $6-14; 🕘 24hr; [S] L to 3rd Ave, 6 to Astor Pl) Generations of East Villagers have been coming to this bustling institution for blintzes and breakfast regardless of the hour.

Caracas Arepa Bar SOUTH AMERICAN $
(Map p72; ☎ 212-529-2314; www.caracasarepabar.com; 93 1/2 E 7th St btwn First Ave & Ave A; dishes $6-16; 🕘 noon-11pm; 🌿; [S] 6 to Astor Pl) Cram into this tiny joint and choose from 17 types of crispy, hot arepa (corn tortilla stuffed with veggies and meat), plus empanadas and daily specials like oxtail soup.

Luzzo's PIZZERIA $$
(Map p72; ☎ 212-473-7447; 211-213 First Ave btwn 12th & 13th Sts; pizzas $14-17; 🕘 noon-11pm Tue-Sun, 5-11pm Mon; [S] L to 1st Ave) Fan-favorite Luzzo's occupies a thin sliver of real estate, which gets stuffed to the gills each evening as discerning diners feast on thin-crust pies, kissed with ripe tomatoes and cooked in a coal-fired oven.

Banjara INDIAN $$
(Map p72; ☎ 212-477-5956; 97 First Ave at 6th St; mains $12-18; 🕘 noon-midnight; [S] L to 1st Ave) A little more upscale than some of the other options on the Indian restaurant row, Banjara has delicious, well-prepared Indian food without the headache-inducing Christmas lights that festoon many.

Angelica Kitchen VEGAN, CAFE **$$**
(Map p72; ☎ 212-228-2909; www.angelicakitchen.com; 300 E 12th St btwn First & Second Aves; dishes $14-20; ⏰ 11:30am-10:30pm; 🌿; [S] L to 1st Ave) This enduring herbivore classic has a calming vibe and enough creative options to make your head spin. Some dishes get too-cute names, but all do wonders with tofu, seitan (wheat gluten), spices and soy products, and sometimes an array of raw ingredients.

★ **Momofuku Noodle Bar** NOODLES **$$**
(Map p72; ☎ 212-777-7773; www.momofuku.com/noodle-bar/; 171 First Ave btwn 10th & 11th Sts; mains $16-25; ⏰ noon-11pm Mon-Thu & Sun, to 2am Fri & Sat; [S] L to 1st Ave, 6 to Astor Pl) Ramen and steamed buns are the name of the game at this infinitely creative Japanese eatery, part of the growing David Chang empire. Seating is on stools at a long bar or at communal tables. Momofuku's famous steamed chicken and pork buns ($9 for two) are recommended.

🍴 Chelsea, Meatpacking District & West (Greenwich) Village

★ **Chelsea Market** MARKET **$**
(Map p76; www.chelseamarket.com; 75 9th Ave; ⏰ 7am-9pm Mon-Sat, 8am-8pm Sun; [S] A/C/E to 14th St) This former cookie factory has been turned into an 800ft-long shopping concourse that caters to foodies with boutique bakeries, gelato shops, ethnic eats and a food court for gourmands.

Joe's Pizza PIZZA **$**
(Map p72; ☎ 212-366-1182; www.joespizzanyc.com; 7 Carmine St btwn Sixth Ave & Bleecker St; slices from $2.75; ⏰ 10am-4:30am Mon-Sun; [S] A/C/E, B/D/F, M to W 4th St, 1/2 to Christopher St-Sheridan Sq, 1/2 to Houston St) Joe's is the Meryl Streep of pizza parlors, collecting dozens of awards and accolades over the last three decades. No-frills pies are served up indiscriminately to students, tourists and celebrities alike.

Bonsignour SANDWICHES **$**
(Map p72; ☎ 212-229-9700; 35 Jane St at Eighth Ave; mains $7-12; ⏰ 7:30am-10pm, to 8pm Sun; [S] L to 8th Ave; A/C/E, 1/2/3 to 14th St) Nestled on a quiet Village street, this sandwich shop offers dozens of delicious choices as well as salads, frittatas and a wonderful beef chili. Get a sandwich or a chicken curry salad to go and wander down the street to Abingdon Sq for al fresco dining.

Ditch Plains SEAFOOD **$$**
(Map p72; ☎ 212-633-0202; www.ditch-plains.com; 29 Bedford St; ⏰ 11am-midnight; 👪; [S] A/C/E, B/D/F to W 4th St, 1 to Houston St) The sleek, metallic interior with wood booths is an inviting place to inhale celeb chef Marc Murphy's glammed-up seafood-shack food: oysters, mussels, fish tacos, fried clams, po' boys and more feed the masses until 2am daily.

Fatty Crab ASIAN **$$**
(Map p72; ☎ 212-352-3590; www.fattycrab.com; 643 Hudson St btwn Gansevoort & Horatio Sts; mains $16-28; ⏰ noon-midnight Mon-Wed, to 2am Thu & Fri, 11am-2am Sat, 11am-midnight Sun; [S] L to 8th Ave; A/C/E, 1/2/3 to 14th St) The Fatty folks have done it again with their small Malaysian-inspired joint. It's super hip and always teeming with locals who swing by in droves to devour fish curries and pork belly accompanied by a signature selection of cocktails.

Tartine FRENCH **$$**
(Map p72; ☎ 212-229-2611; www.tartinecafenyc.com; 253 W 11th St btwn 4th St & Waverly Pl; mains $10-24; ⏰ 9am-10:30pm Mon-Sat, to 10pm Sun; [S] 1/2/3 to 14th St, 1/2 to Christopher St-Sheridan Sq, L to 8th Ave) Tartine is the corner bistro of your Frenchified dreams: wobbly stacks of chairs and tables, pink steaks and escargot and a good-cop-bad-cop duo of waitresses who indiscriminately bounce dishes and diners around the teeny-tiny room. It's BYOB.

Kin Shop THAI **$$**
(Map p72; ☎ 212-675-4295; www.kinshopnyc.com; 469 Sixth Ave; mains $9-28; ⏰ 11:30am-3pm Mon-Sun, 5:30-11pm Mon-Thu, 5:30-11:30pm Fri & Sat, 5-10pm Sun; [S] L to 6th Ave; 1/2/3, F/M to 14th St) The second avatar of Top Chef winner Harold Dieterle (the first being Perilla – also a great find – nearby) is this Thai-inspired joint. Curry pastes are crushed in-house – a testament to the from-scratch methods used to craft every item on the colorful menu.

Soccarat Paella Bar SPANISH **$$**
(Map p76; ☎ 212-462-1000; www.soccaratpaellabar.com; 259 W 19th St, near Eighth Ave; mains $22; ⏰ noon-11pm, to 4pm Sun; 🌿; [S] 1 to 18th St) A cozy, narrow room dominated by a glass-topped communal table, Soccarat is famous for its heavenly, saffron-scented paellas filled with veggies, seafood and/or meat. Tapas are served too, but nothing compares to the rice.

Babbo ITALIAN **$$$**
(Map p72; ☎212-777-0303; www.babbonyc.com; 110 Waverly Pl; mains $19-29; 🕐11:30am-11:15pm, from 5pm Sun; [S]C/E, B/D/F to W 4th St; 1 to Christopher St-Sheridan Sq) This two-level split townhouse might be the best in celebrity chef Mario Batali's empire. Whether you order mint love letters, lamb's brain *francobolli* (small, stuffed ravioli) or pig's foot *milanese,* you'll find Batali at the top of his innovative, eclectic game. Reservations are in order.

🍴 Union Square & Flatiron District & Gramercy Park

Shake Shack BURGERS **$**
(Map p76; ☎212-989-6600; www.shakeshack.com; cnr 23rd St & Madison Ave; hamburger from $4.50; 🕐11am-11pm; [S]R/W to 23rd St) Tourists line up in droves for the hamburgers and shakes at this Madison Square Park counter-window-serving institution.

★**Eataly** ITALIAN **$$**
(Map p76; www.eatalyny.com; 200 Fifth Ave at 23rd St; 🕐hours vary; [S]F, N/R, 6 to 23rd St) The Macy's of food courts, celebrity-chef Mario Batali's NYC empire now has a footprint to match his ambitions. A number of specialty dining halls, all with a different focus (pizza, fish, vegetables, meat, pasta) and the *pièce de résistance,* a rooftop beer garden, not to mention a coffee shop, gelateria and grocery, would overwhelm even a blogging gourmand.

Breslin MODERN AMERICAN **$$**
(Map p76; 16 West 29th St; mains $18; 🕐7am-midnight; [S]N/R to 28th St) It might be hard to hear yourself think and the hipster overflow from the attached uber-trendy Ace Hotel can rub some the wrong way... However, what really matters is that the pub-influenced meat-heavy menu by widely celebrated chef April Bloomfield doesn't disappoint. No reservations, so expect a wait.

🍴 Midtown

99 Cent Pizza PIZZERIA **$**
(Map p76; 473 Lexington Ave; pizza slice $1; 🕐9:30am-4:30am; [S]S, 4/5/6, 7 to Grand Central-42nd St) It's not gourmet and doesn't claim to be, but if you're craving a good slice with a nice balance of tangy tomato sauce and creamy cheese, this barebones joint won't disappoint.

★**Burger Joint** BURGERS **$**
(Map p76; www.parkermeridien.com/eat4.php; Le Parker Meridien, 119 W 56th St; burgers $7; 🕐11am-11:30pm; [S]F to 57th St) With only a small neon burger as your clue, this speakeasy burger hut loiters behind the curtain in the lobby of the Le Parker Meridien hotel. You'll find graffiti-strewn walls, retro booths and attitude-loaded staff slapping up beef-n-patty brilliance.

Totto Ramen JAPANESE **$**
(Map p76; www.tottoramen.com; 366 W 52nd St; ramen $9.50-12.50; 🕐noon-midnight Mon-Sat, 4-11pm Sun; [S]C/E to 50th St) Write your name and number of guests on the clipboard by the door and wait for your (cash-only) ramen revelation. Skip the chicken and go for the pork, which sings in dishes like miso ramen (with fermented soybean paste, egg, scallion, bean sprouts, onion and homemade chili paste).

Café Edison DINER **$**
(Map p76; ☎212-840-5000; 228 W 47th St, btwn Broadway & Eighth Ave; mains from $6; 🕐6am-9:30pm Mon-Sat, to 7:30pm Sun; [S]N/Q/R to 49th St) Where else can you get a bologna sandwich? This landmark New York spot has been in business since the 1930s, serving up American diner classics like grilled cheese, hot corned beef, open-faced turkey sandwiches and cheese blintzes. Cash only.

Hangawi KOREAN **$$**
(Map p76; ☎212-213-0077; www.hangawirestaurant.com; 12 E 32nd St btwn Fifth & Madison Aves; mains $17-25; 🕐noon-10:15pm Mon-Sat, 5-9:30pm Sun; [S]B/D/F/M, N/Q/R to 34th St-Herald Sq) Sublime, flesh-free Korean is the draw at high-achieving Hangawi. Leave your shoes at the entrance and slip into a soothing, zen-like space of meditative music, soft low seating and clean, complexly flavored dishes.

Virgil's Real Barbecue AMERICAN **$$**
(Map p76; ☎212-921-9494; 152 W 44th St btwn Broadway & Eighth Ave; mains $14-25; 🕐11:30am-midnight; [S]N/R, S, W, 1/2/3, 7 to Times Sq-42nd St) Menu items cover the entire BBQ map, with Oklahoma State Fair corndogs, pulled Carolina pork and smoked Maryland ham sandwiches, and platters of sliced Texas beef brisket and Georgia chicken-fried steak.

Danji KOREAN **$$**
(Map p76; www.danjinyc.com; 346 W 52nd St; plates $7-20; 🕐noon-10:30pm Mon-Thu, to 11:30pm Fri, 5:30-11:30pm Sat; [S]C/E to 50th St) Young-gun chef Hooni Kim has captured tastebuds with

his Michelin-starred Korean 'tapas' served in a snug-and-slinky contemporary space. The celebrity dish on the menu (divided into 'traditional' and 'modern' options) are the sliders, a duo of *bulgogi* beef and spiced pork belly served on butter-grilled buns.

The Smith
AMERICAN **$$**

(Map p76; www.thesmithnyc.com; 956 Second Ave at 51st St; mains $17-29; ⊙Mon-Wed 7:30am-midnight, Thu & Fri to 1am, Sat 10am-1am, Sun to midnight; S 6 to 51st St) The Smith has sexed-up dining in the far eastern throws of Midtown with its industrial-chic interior, buzzing bar and well-executed brasserie grub. The emphasis is on regional produce, retro American and Italian-inspired flavors and slick, personable service.

Sparks
STEAKHOUSE **$$$**

(Map p76; www.sparkssteakhouse.com; 210 E 46th St btwn Second & Third Aves, Midtown East; mains $40; ⊙noon-midnight Mon-Fri, 5-11:30pm Sat; S S, 4/5/6, 7 to Grand Central-42nd St) Get an honest-to-goodness New York steakhouse experience at this classic joint, a former mob hangout that's been around for nearly 50 years and still packs 'em in for a juicy carnivorous feed.

Taboon
MEDITERRANEAN **$$$**

(Map p76; ☑ 212-713-0271; 773 Tenth Ave; mains $25-32; ⊙5-11pm Mon-Sat, 11am-10pm Sun; S C/E to 50th St) A white-domed oven grabs the eye as you enter this airy, stone-floored and brick-walled eatery. The food is a fusion from both sides of the Mediterranean: shrimp in shredded pastry, haloumi salad, lamb kabobs and various grilled-fish dishes.

✕ Upper West Side

★ Gray's Papaya
HOT DOGS **$**

(Map p86; ☑ 212-799-0243; 2090 Broadway at 72nd St; hot dog $2; ⊙24hr; S A/B/C, 1/2/3 to 72nd St) It doesn't get more New York than bellying up to this classic stand-up joint in the wake of a beer bender. The lights are bright, the color palette is 1970s and the hot dogs are unpretentiously good.

Barney Greengrass
DELI **$$**

(Map p86; www.barneygreengrass.com; 541 Amsterdam Ave at 86th St; bagel with cream cheese $5; ⊙8:30am-4pm Tue-Fri, to 5pm Sat & Sun; ⓦ; S 1 to 86th St) Old-school Upper Westsiders and pilgrims from other neighborhoods crowd this century-old 'sturgeon king' on weekends. It serves a long list of

traditional if pricey Jewish delicacies, from bagels and lox to sturgeon scrambled with eggs and onions.

Josie's Restaurant
HEALTH FOOD **$$**

(Map p86; ☑ 212-769-1212; 300 Amsterdam Ave; mains $14-22; ⊙11:30am-10pm Mon-Fri, 4-10:30pm Sat & Sun; ☑; S 1/2/3 to 72nd St) Organic fare (with its provenance listed on the menu) that satisfies vegans, vegetarians and meat eaters alike has kept Josie's around for more than a decade.

Dovetail
MODERN AMERICAN **$$$**

(Map p86; ☑ 212-362-3800; www.dovetailnyc.com; 103 W 77th St cnr Columbus Ave; tasting menu $85, mains $36-58; ⊙5:30-10pm Mon-Sat, 11:30am-10pm Sun; ☑; S A/C, B to 81st St-Museum of Natural History, 1 to 79th St) Everything about this Michelin-starred restaurant is simple, from the decor (exposed brick, bare tables) to the uncomplicated seasonal menus focused on bracingly fresh produce and quality meats (think: pistachio-crusted duck with sunchokes, dates and spinach).

✕ Upper East Side

★ Earl's Beer & Cheese
AMERICAN **$**

(Map p86; www.earlsny.com; 1259 Park Ave btwn 97th & 98th Sts; grilled cheese $6-8, mains $8-17; ⊙4pm-midnight Tue-Fri, 11am-midnight Sat & Sun; S 6 to 96th St) Chef Corey Cova's comfort food outpost channels a hipster hunting vibe. Basic grilled cheese is a paradigm shifter, served with pork belly, fried egg and kimchi. There is also mac 'n' cheese and waffles (with foie gras), none of it like anything you've ever eaten.

Maya Mexican
MEXICAN **$$**

(Map p86; www.modernmexican.com; 1191 First Ave; mains $13-28; ⊙11:30am-10pm Mon-Fri, from 10:30am Sat & Sun; S 4/5/6 to 59th St) Renovated Maya's looks something akin to an 18th-century Mexican hacienda, and the decor complements the powerful, mole-infused dishes as well as corn masa with *oaxaca* cheese and *chile poblano rajas* and seviche halibut.

Candle Cafe
VEGAN **$$**

(Map p86; ☑ 212-472-0970; www.candlecafe.com; 1307 Third Ave btwn 74th & 75th Sts; mains $15-20; ⊙11:30am-10:30pm Mon-Sat, to 9:30pm Sun; ☑; S 6 to 77th St) The moneyed, yoga set piles into this attractive vegan cafe, which serves a long list of sandwiches, salads, comfort food and market-driven specials. The specialty here is the house-made seitan.

★ Sfoglia ITALIAN $$$
(Map p86; ☎212-831-1402; 1402 Lexington Ave at E 92nd St; mains $26; 🕒noon-10pm Mon-Sat, from 5:30pm Sun; [S]6 to 96th St) A darling of the critics, Sfoglia brought its winning combo of fresh seafood and homemade Italian from Nantucket to New York. Innovative pairings like wild mussels with tomato, garlic, salami and fennel pollen.

David Burke Townhouse MODERN AMERICAN $$$
(Map p86; ☎212-813-2121; www.davidburketownhouse.com; 133 E 61St; mains $20-55; 🕒11:45am-10:30pm Mon-Sat, 10:30am-9pm Sun; [S]F to Lexington Ave-63rd St; N/R, W to Lexington Ave-59th St) Restaurateur Donatella Arpaia and partner David Burke have created a fashionable and stylish scene in an upper East Side townhouse. Food however is the focus, like salmon with warm potato knish, pretzel-crusted crabcake and yellowfin tuna on saltrock.

🍴 Harlem

Caffe Latte CAFE $
(Map p86; ☎212-222-2241; www.ilcaffelatte.com; 189 Malcolm X Blvd, near 119th St; 🕒8am-10pm Mon-Fri; 📶👪; [S]2/3 to 116th St) Full of students, seniors, old Harlem and new Harlem, Caffe Latte is fast becoming the place to meet and hang in the 'hood. Breakfasts feature deep rich coffee, omelettes, granola, pancakes and more.

Amy Ruth's Restaurant SOUTHERN $$
(Map p86; www.amyruthsharlem.com; 113 W 116th St near Malcolm X Blvd, Harlem; chicken & waffles $10, mains $12-20; 🕒11:30am-11pm Mon, 8:30am-11pm Tue-Thu, 8:30am-5:30pm Fri-Sat, 7:30am-11pm Sun; [S]B, C, 2/3 to 116th St) Tourists flock here for the specialty waffles: choose from sweet (chocolate, strawberry, blueberry, smothered in sautéed apples) or savory (paired with fried chicken, rib-eye or catfish). Smoked ham, chicken and dumplings are favorites as well.

★ Red Rooster MODERN AMERICAN $$$
(Map p86; www.redroosterharlem.com; 310 Malcolm X Blvd btwn 125th & 126th Sts, Harlem; dinner mains $16-35; 🕒11:30am-10:30pm Mon-Fri, 10am-11pm Sat & Sun; [S]2/3 to 125th St) Something of a pioneer, chef Marcus Samuelson's sophisticated uptown venture has a downtown bistro vibe, with a variety of Southern, soul and new American cooking such as blackened catfish and creative sandwiches. The front bar area and breakfast nook has pastries, biscuits and coffee.

🍴 Brooklyn

Of course it's impossible to begin to do justice to Brooklyn's eating options – it's as much a foodie's paradise as Manhattan. Virtually every ethnic cuisine has a significant presence somewhere in this borough. As far as neighborhoods close to Manhattan go: Williamsburg is chockablock with eateries, as are Fifth and Seventh Aves in Park Slope. Smith St is 'Restaurant Row' in the Carroll Gardens and Cobble Hill neighborhoods. Atlantic Ave, near Court St, has a number of excellent Middle Eastern restaurants and grocery stores.

Tom's Restaurant DINER $
(☎718-636-9738; 782 Washington Ave at Sterling Pl, Prospect Heights; 🕒6am-4pm; [S]2/3 to Eastern Pkwy-Brooklyn Museum) Inspiration for the eponymously named Suzanne Vega song, this old-school soda fountain diner's specialty is its variety of pancakes (eg mango walnut). Coffee and cookies are served to those waiting in the line that invariably snakes out the door on weekend mornings.

Sahadi's SELF-CATERING $
(www.sahadis.com; 187 Atlantic Ave btwn Court & Clinton Sts, Boerum Hill; 🕒9am-7pm Mon-Sat; 📶; [S]2/3, 4/5 to Borough Hall) The smell of fresh-roasted coffee and spices greets you as you enter this beloved Middle Eastern delicacies shop. The olive bar boasts two-dozen options and enough breads, cheeses, nuts and hummus to fulfill the self-catering needs of a whole battalion.

Mile End DELI $
(www.mileendbrooklyn.com; 97A Hoyt St, Boerum Hill; sandwiches $8-12; 🕒8am-4pm Mon & Tue, 8am-11pm Wed-Sat, 10am-10pm Sun; [S]A/C/G to Hoyt Schermerhorn Sts) Mile End is small, like its portions, but big on flavors. Try a smoked beef brisket on rye with mustard ($12) – the bread is sticky soft and the meat will melt in your mouth. The only buzzkill is the extra $1.50 charge for a pickle.

Café Glechik RUSSIAN $$
(☎718-616-0766; 3159 Coney Island Ave, Brighton Beach; cabbage rolls $11, kabobs $11-15, dumplings $7-9; 🕒11am-11pm; [S]B, Q to Brighton Beach) The dishes to get are the dumplings: *pelmeni* and *vareniki* with a wide assortment of stuffings. (Sour-cherry *vareniki* are the jam!) You'll also find classics like borscht, kabobs and hyper-sweet compote drinks. Cash only.

Al Di Là Trattoria ITALIAN $$

(www.aldilatrattoria.com; 248 5th Ave cnr Carroll St, Park Slope; ⊙noon-10:30pm Mon-Fri, 5:30-11pm Sat & Sun; [S]R to Union St) Run by a husband-and-wife team from northern Italy, this cheery Park Slope trattoria serves handmade pastas and belly-warming classics (braised rabbit with buttery polenta). There's an excellent brunch (duck confit hash!) and a long list of Italian wines.

Roberta's PIZZA $$

(www.robertaspizza.com; 261 Moore St near Bogart St, Bushwick; individual pizza $9-17, mains $13-28; ⊙11am-midnight; [🅿]; [S]L to Morgan Ave) This warehouse restaurant in Bushwick consistently produces some of the best pizza in New York. Service can be lackadaisical and the waits long, but the brick-oven pies are the right combination of chewy and fresh.

Prime Meats GERMAN $$

(www.frankspm.com; 465 Court St cnr Luquer St, Carroll Gardens; mains $17-32; ⊙10am-midnight Mon-Wed, to 1am Thu & Fri, 8am-1am Sat, to midnight Sun; [S]F, G to Carroll St) A pre-fab vintage spot in Carroll Gardens comes with lots of old-world flavor. The menu is all late-19th-century German, focusing on house-cured butchered meats and items like slow-braised beef sauerbraten with red cabbage.

🍸 Drinking & Nightlife

Watering holes come in many forms in this city: sleek lounges, pumping clubs, cozy pubs and booze-soaked dives – no smoke, though, thanks to city law. The majority are open to 4am, though closing (and opening) times do vary; most nightclubs are open from 10pm. Here's a highly selective sampling.

🍷 Downtown

★ Birreria BEER GARDEN

(Map p76; www.eatalyny.com; 200 Fifth Ave at 23rd St; ⊙11:30am-midnight Sun-Wed, to 1am Thu-Sat; [S]F, N/R, 6 to 23rd St) The crown jewel of Italian gourmet market Eataly is its rooftop beer garden tucked betwixt the Flatiron's corporate towers. A beer menu of encyclopedic proportions offers drinkers some of the best brews on the planet. The signature pork shoulder is your frosty one's soul mate.

Brandy Library BAR

(Map p68; www.brandylibrary.com; 25 N Moore St at Varick St; ⊙5pm-1am Sun-Wed, 4pm-2am Thu, 4pm-4am Fri & Sat; [S]1 to Franklin St) When sipping means serious business, settle into this uber-luxe library, with soothing reading lamps and club chairs facing backlit, floor-to-ceiling, bottle-filled shelves. Go for top-shelf cognac, malt scotch or 90-year-old brandies (prices range from $9 to $340).

Pravda COCKTAIL BAR

(Map p72; ☎212-226-4944; 281 Lafayette St btwn Prince & Houston Sts; [S]B/D/F/V to Broadway-Lafayette St) This subterranean bar heavy with Soviet-era nostalgia has red-leather banquettes and inviting armchairs. Enjoy blinis, handsomely made cocktails and a bit of eavesdropping on neighboring apparatchiks from the fashion or banking industry.

DBA BAR

(Map p72; ☎212-475-5097; www.drinkgoodstuff.com; 41 First Ave btwn 2nd & 3rd Sts; ⊙1pm-4am; [S]F/V to Lower East Side-2nd Ave) There are over 200 beers here, plus 130 single-malt scotches and a few dozen tequilas. There's a tiny plastic-chair patio in back, but most action is near the taps.

SOBs CLUB

(Map p72; ☎212-243-4940; www.sobs.com; 204 Varick St btwn King & Houston Sts; cover charge $10-20; ⊙6:30pm-3am; [S]1 to Houston St) Brazilian bossa nova, samba and other Latin vibes draw a mix of those who know how to move smoothly and sensually and those who like to watch.

Whiskey Tavern COCKTAIL BAR

(Map p68; ☎212-374-9119; 79 Baxter St btwn Bayard & Walker Sts; [S]J/M/Z, N/Q/R/W, 6 to Canal St) An odd interloper in the Chinatown scene, Whiskey Tavern nevertheless has earned many fans for its uber-friendly bartenders, casual ambience free of pretension, reasonably priced drinks and outdoor rear patio in warm weather.

Louis 649 BAR

(Map p72; ☎212-673-1190; www.louis649.com; 649 E 9th St, near Ave C; ⊙6pm-4am; [S]L to 1st Ave) Beloved by its patrons for the affordable prices and down-home, no-frills decor. Tuesday nights are free tasting nights, when the owner brings in a liquor specialist to talk about their brew and liberally pours free shots.

Jimmy's No 43 BAR

(Map p72; ☎212-982-3006; www.jimmysno43.com; 43 E 7th St btwn Third & Second Aves; ⊙noon-2am Mon-Thu & Sun, to 4am Fri & Sat; [S]N/R to 8th St-NYU, F to 2nd Ave, 4/6 to Astor Pl) Barrels and stag antlers line the walls of this basement beer hall. Select from over 50 imported favorites, to go with a round of delectable bar nibbles.

124 Old Rabbit Club BAR
(Map p72; ☎ 212-254-0575; 124 MacDougal St; [S] A/C/E, B/D/F, M to W 4th St, 1/2 to Christopher St-Sheridan Sq, 1/2 to Houston St) You'll wanna pat yourself on the back when you find this speakeasy-style joint (hint: look for the '124' and ring the buzzer). Reward yourself with a quenching stout or one of the dozens of imported brews.

Half King PUB
(Map p76; ☎ 212-462-4300; www.thehalfking.com; 505 W 23rd St at Tenth Ave; ⏲ 11am-4am Mon-Fri, 9am-4am Sat & Sun; [S] C/E to 23rd St) A unique marriage of cozy pub and sophisticated writers' lair, you'll often experience top-notch literary readings in this wood-accented, candlelit watering hole. During warm weather, there's also a front sidewalk cafe and backyard patio.

Bar Next Door BAR
(Map p72; ☎ 212-529-5945; 129 MacDougal St btwn W 3rd & W 4th Sts; ⏲ 6pm-2am Sun-Thu, to 3am Fri & Sat; [S] A/C/E, B/D/F/V to W 4th St) The basement of this restored townhouse is all low ceilings, exposed brick and romantic lighting. You'll find mellow, live jazz nightly, as well as a tasty Italian menu at the restaurant next door, La Lanterna di Vittorio.

Pyramid Club CLUB
(Map p72; ☎ 212-228-4888; www.thepyramidclub.com; 101 Ave A; cover charge $5-10; ⏲ 11pm-4am Mon, 8:30pm-1am Tue & Sun, 9pm-4am Thu & Sat, 10pm-4am Fri; [S] F/V to Lower East Side-2nd Ave) You'll find rather beat-up stools and sticky wooden floors, and if you like cheap drinks and sweaty, unselfconscious dancing to '80s tunes, then Thursdays are for you. Gay night is on Friday.

Sway Lounge CLUB
(Map p72; ☎ 212-620-5220; www.swaylounge.com; 305 Spring St; ⏲ 9pm-3am Mon & Thu; [S] C/E to Spring St) Small, seductive and sleek with an elegant Moroccan decor, Sway's got a tough door policy, but there's room to dance to '80s on Thursday nights, rock and hip-hop Fridays, and DJs like Mark Ronson and DJ Herschel other nights.

Mehanata CLUB
(Map p72; ☎ 212-625-0981; www.mehanata.com; 113 Ludlow St; [S] F, J/M/Z to Delancey St-Essex St) The 'Bulgarian Bar' is still gypsy heaven for East Euro–chic and indie-popsters. East Euro DJs spin some nights, and belly dancers and 'gypsy bands' take the small stage for jumping-in-place dancers.

Sapphire CLUB
(Map p72; ☎ 212-777-5153; www.sapphirenyc.com; 249 Eldridge St at E Houston St; admission $5; ⏲ 7pm-4am; [S] F/V to Lower East Side-2nd Ave) This tiny, hoppin' venue has survived the crowds of the mid-'90s Ludlow St boom with its hip factor intact, and its $5 cover keeps snootiness at a minimum. The tightly packed dance floor gets lit with a mix of R&B, rap, disco and funk.

Santos Party House CLUB
(Map p68; ☎ 212-584-5492; www.santospartyhouse.com; 96 Lafayette St; cover $5-15; ⏲ 10pm-4am) Shaggy rocker Andrew WK created this bi-level 8000-sq-ft cavernous bare-bones dance club. Devoted to good times and good vibes, this place requires that you check your attitude at the door – funk to electronica, and WK spins some nights.

Cielo CLUB
(Map p72; ☎ 212-645-5700; www.cieloclub.com; 18 Little W 12th St; cover charge $15-25; ⏲ 10:30pm-5am Mon-Sat; [S] A/C/E, L to 8th Ave-14th St) Known for its intimate space and kick-ass sound system, this space-age-looking Meatpacking District staple packs in a fashionable, multiculti crowd nightly for its blend of tribal, old-school house and soulful grooves.

🍷 Midtown

★ Russian Vodka Room BAR
(Map p76; ☎ 212-307-5835; 265 W 52nd St, btwn Eighth Ave & Broadway; [S] C/E to 50th St) Actual Russians aren't uncommon at this swanky and welcoming bar. The lighting is dark and the corner booths intimate, but more importantly the dozens of flavored vodkas, from cranberry to horseradish, are fun to experiment with.

Rudy's Bar & Grill BAR
(Map p76; 627 Ninth Ave; ⏲ 8am-4am; [S] A/C/E to 42nd St-Port Authority Bus Terminal) This semi-dive bar – neighborhood newcomers and professional types rub beer-soaked shoulders with hard-core drinkers – is a good place for cheap beer and even greasy hot dogs, if you don't mind not being able to hear yourself think.

Lantern's Keep COCKTAIL BAR
(Map p76; ☎ 212-453-4287; www.thelanternskeep.com; Iroquois Hotel, 49 W 44th St; ⏲ 5pm-midnight Tue-Sat; [S] B/D/F/M to 42nd St-Bryant Park) Cross the lobby of the Iroquois Hotel and slip into this dark, intimate cocktail salon. Its

specialty is pre-Prohibition libations, shaken and stirred by passionate, personable mixologists. Reservations recommended.

Top of the Strand COCKTAIL BAR
(Map p76; www.topofthestrand.com; Strand Hotel, 33 W 37th St btwn Fifth & Sixth Aves; 👪; [S] B/D/F/M to 34th St) For that 'Oh my God, I'm in New York' feeling, head to the Strand hotel's rooftop bar, order a martini (extra dirty) and drop your jaw (discreetly). Sporting slinky cabanas and a sliding glass roof, its view of the Empire State Building is unforgettable.

Pacha CLUB
(Map p76; ☎212-209-7500; www.pachanyc.com; 618 W 46th St btwn Eleventh Ave & West Side Hwy; admission $20-40; [S] A/C/E to 42nd St-Port Authority) A massive and spectacular place, this is 30,000 sq ft and four levels of glowing, sleek spaces and cozy seating nooks that rise up to surround the main dance-floor atrium. Big-name DJs are always on tap.

Morrell Wine Bar & Café BAR, CAFE
(Map p76; ☎212-262-7700; 1 Rockefeller Plaza, W 48th St btwn Fifth & Sixth Aves; 🕒11:30am-11pm Mon-Sat, noon-6pm Sun; [S] B/D/F/M to 47th-50th Sts-Rockefeller Center) The list of vinos at this pioneering wine bar is over 2000 long, with a whopping 150 available by the glass. And the airy, split-level room, right across from the famous skating rink, is equally as intoxicating.

Jimmy's Corner BAR
(Map p76; 140 W 44th St btwn Sixth & Seventh Aves, Midtown West; 🕒10am-4am; [S] N/Q/R, 1/2/3, 7 to 42nd St-Times Sq; B/D/F/M to 42nd St-Bryant Park) This skinny, welcoming, completely unpretentious dive off Times Square is run by an old boxing trainer – as if you wouldn't guess by all the framed photos of boxing greats. The jukebox covers Stax to Miles Davis.

PJ Clarke's BAR
(Map p76; www.pjclarkes.com; 915 Third Ave at 55th St, Midtown East; [S] E/M to Lexington Ave-53rd St) A bastion of old New York, this lovingly worn wooden saloon has been straddling the scene since 1884. Choose a jukebox tune, order a round of crab cakes, and settle in with a come-one-and-all crowd.

Réunion Surf BAR
(Map p76; 357 W 44th St at Ninth Ave; 🕒5:30pm-2am, to 4am Thu-Sat) Swanky Tiki-themed bar and restaurant serving delicious French South Pacific cuisine, such as banana-leaf-steamed mahi mahi.

On the Rocks COCKTAIL BAR
(Map p76; 696 Tenth Ave, btwn 48th & 49th Sts; 🕒5pm-4am) Whiskey nerds will delight at this cubbyhole-sized space.

Therapy GAY
(Map p76; www.therapy-nyc.com; 348 W 52nd St btwn Eighth & Ninth Aves; [S] C/E, 1 to 50th St) Multileveled, airy and sleekly contemporary, Therapy is a longstanding gay Hell's Kitchen hot spot. Theme nights abound, from stand-up comedy to musical shows.

🍷 Uptown

79th Street Boat Basin BAR
(Map p86; W 79th St, in Riverside Park; 🕒noon-11pm) A covered, open-sided party spot under the ancient arches of a park overpass, this is an Upper West Side favorite once spring hits. Order a pitcher, some snacks and enjoy the sunset view over the Hudson River.

Bemelmans Bar LOUNGE
(Map p86; www.thecarlyle.com/dining/bemelmans_bar; Carlyle Hotel, 35 E 76th St at Madison Ave; 🕒noon-2am Mon-Sat, to 12:30am Sun; [S] 6 to 77th St) Waiters wear white jackets, a baby grand piano is always being played and Ludwig Bemelman's *Madeline* murals surround you. It's a classic spot for a serious cocktail.

Barcibo Enoteca WINE BAR
(Map p86; www.barciboenoteca.com; 2020 Broadway cnr 69th St; 🕒4:30pm-2am; [S] 1/2/3 to 72nd St) Just north of Lincoln Center, this casual chic marble-table spot is ideal for sipping, with a long list of vintages from all over Italy, including 40 different varieties sold by the glass.

Auction House BAR
(Map p86; ☎212-427-4458; 300 E 89th St; 🕒7:30pm-4am; [S] 4/5/6 to 86th St) Dark maroon doors lead into a sexy, candlelit hangout that's perfect for a relaxing drink. Victorian-style couches and fat, overstuffed easy chairs are strewn about the wood-floored rooms.

Subway Inn BAR
(Map p86; 143 E 60th St btwn Lexington & Third Aves; [S] 4/5/6 to 59th St; N/Q/R to Lexington Ave-59th St) An old-geezer watering hole with cheap drinks and loads of authenticity. The entire scene – from the vintage neon sign to the well-worn red booths – is truly reminiscent of bygone days.

Dead Poet BAR
(Map p86; www.thedeadpoet.com; 450 Amsterdam Ave btwn 81st & 82nd Sts; ⏲9am-4am Mon-Sat, noon-4am Sun; [S] 1 to 79th St) This mahogany-paneled pub has been a neighborhood favorite for over a decade, with a mix of locals and students nursing pints of Guinness and cocktails named after dead poets.

Brooklyn

★Commodore BAR
(366 Metropolitan Ave cnr Havenmeyer St, Williamsburg; ⏲4pm-midnight Sun-Thu, to 1am Fri & Sat; [S] L to Lorimer St) This corner bar is a faux '70s recreation room with plenty of wood paneling and a few big booths to spread out in. Order a mint julep or a sloe gin fizz and play vintage arcade games for free.

61 Local BEER GARDEN
(www.61local.com; 61 Bergen St btwn Smith St & Boerum Pl, Cobble Hill; snacks $1-7, sandwiches $4-8; ⏲11am-midnight Sun-Thu, to 1am Fri & Sat; [S] F, G to Bergen) A roomy brick-and-wood hall in Cobble Hill manages to be both chic and warm, with large communal tables, a mellow vibe and a good selection of craft beers. There's a simple menu of charcuterie and other snacks.

Maison Premiere COCKTAIL BAR
(www.maisonpremiere.com; 298 Bedford Ave btwn 1st & Grand Sts, Williamsburg; ⏲4pm-4am Mon-Fri, noon-4am Sat & Sun; [S] L to Bedford Ave) This old-timey place features a chemistry lab–style bar full of syrups and essences and suspendered bartenders to mix them all up. The epic cocktail list includes more than 20 absinthe drinks and a raw bar provides a long list of snacks on the half shell.

Zabloski's BAR
(☎718-384-1903; 107 N 6th St btwn Berry St & Wythe Ave, Williamsburg; ⏲2pm-4am; [S] L to Bedford Ave) This welcoming brick-lined spot in Williamsburg has cheap beer, chill bartenders, a pinball machine, a dart board and a pool table. Snag the table by the roll-down gate during happy hour and watch the street come alive at night.

Union Hall BAR
(☎718-638-4400; 702 Union St btwn Fifth & Sixth Aves; ⏲4pm-4am Mon-Fri, noon-4am Sat & Sun; [S] M, R to Union St; 2/3 to Bergen St; F to 7th Ave) In Park Slope, head to this creatively idiosyncratic bar – leather chairs à la a snooty London social club, walls lined with bookshelves and two bocce courts, plus live music downstairs and an outdoor patio.

Weather Up COCKTAIL BAR
(589 Vanderbilt Ave btwn Bergen & Dean Sts; ⏲Tue-Sun; [S] 2/3 to Bergen St; B, Q to 7th Ave) No signage marks the exterior of this dark and shadowy Prospect Heights cocktail-centric speakeasy-like neighborhood favorite.

Radegast Hall & Biergarten BEER GARDEN
(www.radegasthall.com; 113 N 3rd St at Berry St, Williamsburg; ⏲4pm-4am Mon-Fri, noon-4am Sat & Sun; [S] L to Bedford Ave) Rowdy Williamsburg spot with excellent veal schnitzel.

☆ Entertainment

Those with unlimited fuel and appetites can gorge themselves on a seemingly infinite number of entertainments – from Broadway shows to performance art in someone's Brooklyn living room, and everything in between. *New York* magazine and the weekend editions of the *New York Times* are great guides for what's on once you arrive.

Live Music

★Joe's Pub LIVE MUSIC
(Map p72; ☎212-539-8778; www.joespub.com; Public Theater, 425 Lafayette St btwn Astor Pl & 4th St; [S] R/W to 8th St-NYU; 6 to Astor Pl) Part cabaret theater, part rock and new-indie venue, this small and lovely supper club hosts a wonderful variety of styles, voices and talent.

Rockwood Music Hall LIVE MUSIC
(Map p72; ☎212-477-4155; www.rockwoodmusichall.com; 196 Allen St btwn Houston & Stanton Sts; [S] F/V to Lower East Side-2nd Ave) This breadbox-sized two-room concert space features a rapid-fire flow of bands and singer-songwriters, no cover, and a max of one hour per band.

55 Bar LIVE MUSIC
(Map p72; ☎212-929-9883; www.55bar.com; 55 Christopher St at Seventh Ave; cover charge $3-15, 2-drink minimum; ⏲1pm-4am; [S] 1 to Christopher St-Sheridan Sq) This friendly basement dive is great for low-key shows without high cover. Regular performances twice nightly by quality artists-in-residence and some blues bands.

Bowery Ballroom LIVE MUSIC
(Map p72; ☎212-533-2111; www.boweryballroom.com; 6 Delancey St at Bowery St; ⏲performance times vary; [S] J/M/Z to Bowery St) This terrific, medium-sized venue has the perfect sound and feel for more blown-up indie-rock acts (The Shins, Stephen Malkmus, Patti Smith).

Le Poisson Rouge LIVE MUSIC
(Map p72; ☎ 212-505-3474; www.lepoissonrouge.com; 158 Bleecker St; [S] A/C/E, B/D/F/V to W 4th St-Washington Sq) This Bleecker St basement club is one of the premier venues for experimental contemporary, from classical to indie rock to electro-acoustic.

Mercury Lounge LIVE MUSIC
(Map p72; ☎ 212-260-4700; www.mercuryloungenyc.com; 217 E Houston St btwn Essex & Ludlow Sts; cover charge $8-15; ⏲ 4pm-4am; [S] F/V to Lower East Side-2nd Ave) The Mercury dependably pulls in a cool new or cool comeback band everyone downtown wants to see.

Music Hall of Williamsburg LIVE MUSIC
(www.musichallofwilliamsburg.com; 66 N 6th St btwn Wythe & Kent Aves, Williamsburg; [S] L to Bedford Ave) This popular Williamsburg music venue is *the* place to see indie bands in Brooklyn. (For many groups traveling through New York, this is their one and only spot.)

BB King Blues Club & Grill BLUES, JAZZ
(Map p76; ☎ 212-997-4144; www.bbkingblues.com; 237 W 42nd St btwn Seventh & Eighth Aves; [S] N/R/W, 1/2/3, 7 to 42nd St-Times Sq) In the heart of Times Square offers old-school blues along with rock, folk and reggae acts.

Bargemusic CLASSICAL MUSIC
(www.bargemusic.org; Fulton Ferry Landing, Brooklyn Heights; tickets $35; 👪; [S] A/C to High St) Exceptionally talented classical musicians perform in this intimate space, a decommissioned barge docked under the Brooklyn Bridge.

Highline Ballroom LIVE MUSIC
(Map p76; ☎ 212-414-5994; 431 W 16th St, btwn Ninth & Tenth Aves) A classy Chelsea venue with an eclectic lineup, from Mandy Moore to Moby.

Beacon Theatre LIVE MUSIC
(Map p86; www.beacontheatre.com; 2124 Broadway btwn 74th & 75th Sts; [S] 1/2/3 to 72nd St) This Upper West Side venue hosts big acts in an environment that's more intimate than a big concert arena.

Radio City Music Hall CONCERT VENUE
(Map p76; ☎ 212-247-4777; www.radiocity.com; Sixth Ave, at W 50th St) The architecturally grand concert hall in Midtown hosts the likes of Barry Manilow and Cirque de Soleil and of course the famous Christmas spectacular.

Delancey LIVE MUSIC
(Map p72; ☎ 212-254-9920; www.thedelancey.com; 168 Delancey St at Clinton St; [S] F, J/M/Z to Delancey-Essex Sts) Great indie-band bookings.

Irving Plaza LIVE MUSIC
(Map p76; www.irvingplaza.com; 17 Irving Pl at 15th St; [S] L, N/Q/R/W, 4/5/6 to 14th St-Union Sq) A great in-between stage for quirky mainstream acts. There's a cozy floor around the stage, and good views from the mezzanine.

JAZZ

Second only to New Orleans, Harlem was an early home to a flourishing jazz scene and one of its principal beating hearts. The neighborhood fostered greats like Duke Ellington, Charlie Parker, John Coltrane and Thelonius Monk. From bebop to free improvisation, in classic art-deco clubs and at intimate jam sessions, Harlem and other important venues scattered throughout the city, especially around the Village, continue to foster old-timers and talented newcomers alike. Tune in to **WKCR** (89.9 FM) for jazz and especially from 8:20am to 9:30am Monday through Friday for Phil Schaap's 30-plus-year-old program in which he dazzles listeners with his encyclopedic knowledge and appreciation for the art form.

Smalls (Map p72; ☎ 212-252-5091; www.smallsjazzclub.com; 183 W 4th St; cover $20) is a subterranean jazz dungeon that rivals the world-famous **Village Vanguard** (Map p72; ☎ 212-255-4037; www.villagevanguard.com; 178 Seventh Ave at 11th St; [S] 1/2/3 to 14th St) in terms of sheer talent. Of course, the latter has hosted every major star of the past 50 years; there's a two-drink minimum and a serious no-talking policy.

Heading uptown, **Dizzy's Club Coca-Cola: Jazz at the Lincoln Center** (Map p86; ☎ t212-258-9595; www.jazzatlincolncenter.org; Time Warner Center, Broadway at 60th St; [S] A/C, B/D, 1 to 59th St-Columbus Circle), one of Lincoln Center's three jazz venues, has stunning views overlooking Central Park and nightly shows featuring top lineups. Further north on the Upper West Side, check out the **Smoke Jazz & Supper Club-Lounge** (Map p86; ☎ 212-864-6662; www.smokejazz.com; 2751 Broadway, btwn W 105th & 106th Sts), which gets crowded on weekends.

Webster Hall
CLUB

(Map p72; ☑ 212-353-1600; www.websterhall.com; 125 E 11th St, near Third Ave; ☺ 10pm-4am Thu-Sat; Ⓢ L, N/Q/R/W, 4/5/6 to 14th St-Union Sq) The granddaddy of dancehalls. You'll get cheap drinks, eager young things ready to dance and enough room to really work up a sweat.

Theater

In general, 'Broadway' productions are staged in the lavish, early-20th-century theaters surrounding Times Square. You'll choose your theater based on its production – *The Book of Mormon, Spider-Man: Turn off the Dark, Lion King.* Evening performances begin at 8pm.

'Off Broadway' simply refers to shows performed in smaller spaces (500 seats or fewer), which is why you'll find many just around the corner from Broadway venues, as well as elsewhere in town. 'Off-off Broadway' events include readings, experimental and cutting-edge performances and improvisations held in spaces with fewer than 100 seats; these venues are primarily downtown. Some of the world's best theater happens in these more intimate venues before moving to Broadway.

Choose from current shows by checking print publications, or a website such as **Theater Mania** (☑ 212-352-3101; www.theatermania.com). You can purchase tickets through **Telecharge** (☑ 212-239-6200; www.telecharge.com) and **Ticketmaster** (☑ 800-448-7849, 800-745-3000; www.ticketmaster.com) for standard ticket sales, or **TKTS ticket booths** (www.tdf.org/tkts; cnr Front & John Sts; ☺ 11am-6pm Mon-Sat, to 4pm Sun; Ⓢ A/C to Broadway-Nassau; 2/3, 4/5, J/Z to Fulton St) for same-day tickets to a selection of Broadway and off-Broadway musicals at up to 50% off regular prices.

★ Public Theater
THEATER

(Map p72; ☑ 212-539-8500; www.publictheater.org; 425 Lafayette St, btwn Astor Pl & E 4th St; Ⓢ R/N to 8th Street, 6 to Astor Place)

St Ann's Warehouse
THEATER

(☑ 718-254-8779; www.stannswarehouse.org; 29 Jay St, Dumbo; Ⓢ A/C to High St)

PS 122
THEATER

(Map p72; ☑ 212-477-5288; www.ps122.org; 150 First Ave, at E 9th St)

Playwrights Horizons
THEATER

(Map p76; ☑ tickets 212-279-4200; www.playwrightshorizons.org; 416 W 42nd St btwn Ninth & Tenth Aves; Ⓢ A/C/E to 42nd St-Port Authority Bus Terminal)

New York Theater Workshop
THEATER

(Map p72; ☑ 212-460-5475; www.nytw.org; 79 E 4th St btwn Second & Third Aves; Ⓢ F/V to Lower East Side-2nd Ave)

Comedy

From lowbrow prop comics to experimental conceptual humor, there's a venue for every taste and budget. More-established ones push the alcohol with drink minimums.

★ Upright Citizens Brigade Theatre
COMEDY

(Map p76; ☑ 212-366-9176; www.ucbtheatre.com; 307 W 26th St btwn Eighth & Ninth Aves; cover charge $5-8; Ⓢ C/E to 23rd St) Improv venue featuring well-known, emerging and probably-won't-emerge comedians in a small basement theater nightly.

Village Lantern
COMEDY

(Map p72; ☑ 212-260-7993; www.villagelantern.com; 167 Bleecker St; Ⓢ A/B/C/D/F/M to W 4th St) Nightly alternative comedy underneath a bar of the same name.

Caroline's on Broadway
COMEDY

(Map p76; ☑ 212-757-4100; www.carolines.com; 1626 Broadway at 50th St; Ⓢ N/Q/R to 49th St, 1 to 50th St) One of the best-known places in the city, and host to the biggest names on the circuit.

Cinemas

Long lines in the evenings and on weekends are the norm. It's recommended that you call and buy your tickets in advance (unless it's midweek, midday or for a film that's been out for months already). Most cinemas are handled either through **Movie Fone** (☑ 212-777-3456; www.moviefone.com) or **Fandango** (www.fandango.com). You'll have to pay an extra $1.50 per ticket, but it's worth it. Large chain theaters with stadium seating are scattered throughout the city, including several in the Times Square and Union Sq areas. In summer free outdoor screenings blossom throughout the city on rooftops and in park spaces.

Film Forum
CINEMA

(Map p72; ☑ 212-727-8110; www.filmforum.com; 209 W Houston St btwn Varick St & Sixth Ave; ☺ daily; 🛈; Ⓢ 1 to Houston St) The long and narrow theaters can't dent cineasts love for this institution showing revivals, classics and documentaries.

IFC Center
CINEMA

(Map p72; ☑ 212-924-7771; www.ifccenter.com; 323 Sixth Ave at 3rd St; Ⓢ A/C/E, B/D/F/V to W 4th St-Washington Sq) Formerly the Waverly, this three-screen art-house cinema shows new indies, cult classics and foreign films – and the popcorn is organic.

Landmark Sunshine Cinema CINEMA
(Map p72; ☎ 212-358-7709; www.landmarktheatres.com; 143 E Houston St at Forsyth St; [S] F/V to Lower East Side-2nd Ave) Housed in a former Yiddish theater; shows first-run indies.

Anthology Film Archives CINEMA
(Map p72; ☎ 212-505-5181; www.anthologyfilmarchives.org; 32 Second Ave at 2nd St; [S] F/V to Lower East Side-2nd Ave) Film studies majors head to this schoolhouse-like building for independent and avant-garde cinema.

Performing Arts

World-class performers and venues mean the city is a year-round mecca for arts lovers.

Every top-end genre has a stage at the massive Lincoln Center (p83) complex. Its Avery Fisher Hall is the showplace of the New York Philharmonic, while Alice Tully Hall houses the Chamber Music Society of Lincoln Center, and the New York State Theater is home to the New York City Ballet. Great drama is found at both the Mitzi E Newhouse and Vivian Beaumont theaters; and frequent concerts at the Juilliard School. But the biggest draw is the Metropolitan Opera House, home to the Metropolitan Opera and American Ballet Theater.

★ **Carnegie Hall** LIVE MUSIC
(Map p76; ☎ 212-247-7800; www.carnegiehall.org; W 57th St & Seventh Ave; [S] N/Q/R to 57th St-7th Ave) Since 1891, the historic Carnegie Hall has hosted performances by the likes of Tchaikovsky, Mahler and Prokofiev, as well as Stevie Wonder, Sting and Tony Bennett. Today its three halls host visiting philharmonics, the New York Pops orchestra and various world-class musicians (mostly closed in July and August). Before or after a performance, check out the **Rose Museum** for a history of the institution.

★ **Brooklyn Academy of Music** PERFORMING ARTS
(BAM; www.bam.org; 30 Lafayette Ave at Ashland Pl, Fort Greene; [S] D, N/R to Pacific St, B, Q, 2/3, 4/5 to Atlantic Ave) Sort of a Brooklyn version of the Lincoln Center – in its all-inclusiveness rather than its vibe, which is much edgier – the spectacular academy also hosts everything from modern dance to opera, cutting-edge theater and music concerts.

Symphony Space LIVE MUSIC
(Map p86; ☎ 212-864-5400; www.symphonyspace.org; 2537 Broadway btwn 94th & 95th Sts; 👪; [S] 1/2/3 to 96th St) A multigenre space with several facilities in one. This Upper West Side gem is home to many performance series as well as theater, cabaret, comedy, dance and world-music concerts throughout the week.

Sports

The uber-successful **New York Yankees** (☎ 718-293-6000, tickets 877-469-9849; www.yankees.com; tickets $20-300) play at **Yankee Stadium** (☎ 718-293-6000, tickets 877-469-9849; www.yankees.com; E 161st St at River Ave; tours $20; 👪; [S] B, D, 4 to 161st St-Yankee Stadium), while the more historically beleaguered **New York Mets** (www.mets.com; tickets $12-102) play at **Citi Field** (126th St, at Roosevelt Ave, Flushing, Queens; [S] 7 to Mets-Willets Pt).

For less-grand settings but no-less-pleasant outings, check out the minor-league **Staten Island Yankees** (☎ 718-720-9265; www.siyanks.com; tickets $12; ⏲ ticket office 9am-5pm Mon-Fri, 10am-3pm Sat) at **Richmond County Bank Ballpark** (75 Richmond Terrace, Staten Island; ⛴ Staten Island Ferry) or the **Brooklyn Cyclones** (☎ 718-449-8497; www.brooklyncyclones.com; tickets $8-16) at **MCU Park** (1904 Surf Ave & W 17th St, Coney Island; [S] D/F, N/Q to Coney Island-Stillwell Ave).

For basketball, you can get courtside with the NBA's **New York Knicks** (Map p76; ☎ 212-465-6073, tickets 866-858-0008; www.nyknicks.com; tickets $13-330) at **Madison Square Garden** (Map p76; www.thegarden.com; Seventh Ave btwn 31st & 33rd Sts; [S] 1/2/3 to 34th St-Penn Station), called the 'mecca of basketball.' Or check out the rejuvenated franchise of the **Brooklyn Nets** (www.nba.com/nets; tickets from $15), previously the New Jersey Nets, who played their inaugural season at the **Barclays Center** (www.barclayscenter.com; cnr Flatbush & Atlantic Aves, Prospect Heights; [S] B/D, N/Q/R, 2/3, 4/5 to Atlantic Ave) in downtown Brooklyn in 2012. Also playing at Madison Square Garden, the women's WNBA league team **New York Liberty** (Map p76; ☎ 212-564-9622, tickets 212-465-6073; www.nyliberty.com; tickets $10-85) provides a more laid-back time.

New York City's NFL (pro-football) teams, the **Giants** (www.giants.com) and **Jets** (www.newyorkjets.com), share **MetLife Stadium** in East Rutherford, New Jersey.

Shopping

While chain stores have proliferated, turning once-idiosyncratic blocks into versions of generic strip malls, NYC is still the best American city for shopping. It's not unusual for shops – especially downtown boutiques – to stay open until 10pm or 11pm.

Downtown

Lower Manhattan is where you'll find across-the-board bargains, as well as more of the small, stylish boutiques. Downtown's coolest offerings are in NoLita (just east of SoHo), the East Village and the Lower East Side. SoHo has more expensive and equally fashionable stores, while Broadway from Union Sq to Canal St is lined with big retailers like H&M and Urban Outfitters, as well as dozens of jeans and shoe stores. The streets of Chinatown are filled with knock-off designer handbags, jewelry, perfume and watches. For coveted designer labels stroll through the Meatpacking District around 14th St and Ninth Ave.

★Strand Book Store BOOKS
(Map p72; ☎212-473-1452; www.strandbooks.com; 828 Broadway at 12th St; 🕒9:30am-10:30pm Mon-Sat, 11am-10:30pm Sun; [S] L, N/Q/R/W, 4/5/6 to 14th St-Union Sq) The city's preeminent bibliophile warehouse, selling new and used books.

★Century 21 FASHION
(Map p68; www.c21stores.com; 22 Cortlandt St btwn Church St & Broadway; 🕒7:45am-9pm Mon-Wed, to 9:30pm Thu & Fri, 10am-9pm Sat, 11am-8pm Sun; [S] A/C, J/Z, 2/3, 4/5 to Fulton St) A four-level department store loved by New Yorkers of every income. It's shorthand for designer bargains.

J&R Music & Computer World MUSIC
(Map p68; www.jr.com; 15-23 Park Row; [S] A/C, J/Z, M, 2/3, 4/5 to Fulton St-Broadway-Nassau St) Every electronic need, especially computer and camera related, can be satisfied here.

A-1 Records MUSIC
(Map p72; ☎212-473-2870; 439 E 6th St btwn First Ave & Ave A; 🕒1-9pm; [S] F/V to Lower East Side-2nd Ave) The East Village is home to New York's best selection of vinyl.

Economy Candy CANDY
(Map p72; ☎212-254-1531; www.economycandy.com; 108 Rivington St at Essex St; 🕒9am-6pm Sun-Fri, 10am-5pm Sat; [S] F, J/M/Z to Delancey St-Essex St) Bringing sweetness to the 'hood since 1937, this candy shop is stocked with floor-to-ceiling goods in package and bulk.

Trash & Vaudeville CLOTHING
(Map p72; 4 St Marks Pl; [S] 6 to Astor Pl) The capital of punk-rockerdom, Trash & Vaudeville was the veritable costume closet for singing celebs when the East Village played host to a much grittier scene.

Philip Williams Posters VINTAGE
(Map p68; www.postermuseum.com; 122 Chambers St btwn Church St & W Broadway; 🕒11am-7pm Tue-Sat; [S] A/C, 1/2/3 to Chambers St) You'll find over half a million posters in this cavernous treasure trove, from oversized French advertisements for perfume and cognac to Soviet film posters.

Apple Store COMPUTERS, ELECTRONICS
(Map p76; ☎212-444-3400; www.apple.com; 401 W 14th St at Ninth Ave; 🕒11am-8pm Mon-Fri, noon-7pm Sat & Sun; [S] A/C/E to 14th St, L to 8th Ave) Pilgrims flock here for shiny new gadgets.

Midtown & Uptown

Midtown's Fifth Ave and the Upper East Side's Madison Ave have the famous high-end fashion and clothing by international designers. Times Square has supersized chain stores. Chelsea has more unique boutiques, though like the Upper West Side it too has been colonized by banks, drugstores and big-box retailers.

Tiffany & Co JEWELRY, HOMEWARES
(Map p76; www.tiffany.com; 727 Fifth Ave; [S] F to 57th St) This famous jeweler, with the trademark clock-hoisting Atlas over the door, carries fine diamond rings, watches, necklaces etc, as well as crystal and glassware.

Saks Fifth Ave DEPARTMENT STORE
(Map p76; www.saksfifthavenue.com; 611 Fifth Ave at 50th St; [S] B/D/F/M to 47th-50th Sts-Rockefeller Center, E/M to 5th Ave-53rd St) Complete with beautiful vintage elevators, Saks' 10-floor flagship store fuses old-world glamour with solid service and must-have labels.

Macy's DEPARTMENT STORE
(Map p76; www.macys.com; 151 W 34th St at Broadway; [S] B/D/F/M, N/Q/R to 34th St-Herald Sq) The grande dame of Midtown department stores sells everything from jeans to kitchen appliances.

Bloomingdale's DEPARTMENT STORE
(Map p86; www.bloomingdales.com; 1000 Third Ave at E 59th St; 🕒10am-8:30pm Mon-Fri, to 7pm Sat, 11am-7pm Sun; 📶; [S] 4/5/6 to 59th St, N/Q/R to Lexington Ave-59th St) Uptown, the sprawling,

overwhelming Bloomingdale's is akin to the Metropolitan Museum of Art for shoppers.

Barneys Co-op FASHION, ACCESSORIES
(Map p76; ☎212-593-7800; 236 W 18th St; ⏲11am-8pm Mon-Fri, to 7pm Sat, noon-6pm Sun; [S]1 to 18th St) Offers hipper, less-expensive versions of high-end fashion.

Information

INTERNET ACCESS

It is rare to find accommodations in New York City that do not offer a way for guests to connect to the internet – a log-in fee is often required.

New York Public Library (☎212-930-0800; www.nypl.org/branch/local; E 42nd St, at Fifth Ave; [S]B, D, F or M to 42nd St-Bryant Park) offers free internet access for laptop toters and half-hour internet access via public terminals at almost all of its locations around the city.

Free wi-fi hotspots include Bryant Park, Battery Park, Tompkins Square Park and Union Square Park; other public areas with free wi-fi include Lincoln Center, Columbia University, South Street Seaport and Dumbo in Brooklyn and of course nearly 200 Starbucks scattered around the city.

Internet kiosks can also be found at **Staples** (www.staples.com) and **FedEx Kinko** (www.fedexkinkos.com) locations around the city.

MEDIA

Daily News (www.nydailynews.com) A daily tabloid, leans toward the sensational – archrival of the *New York Post*.

New York (www.newyorkmagazine.com) Weekly featuring nationally oriented reporting as well as NYC-centric news and listings for the arts and culture-oriented reader.

New York Post (www.nypost.com) Famous for spicy headlines, celebrity scandal-laden Page Six and good sports coverage.

New York Times (www.nytimes.com) The 'Gray Lady' is the newspaper of record for readers throughout the US.

NY1 (Time Warner Cable, Channel 1; www.ny1.com) This is the city's all-day news station on Time Warner cable's Channel 1.

Village Voice (www.villagevoice.com) The weekly tabloid is still a good resource for events, clubs and music listings.

WFUV-90.7FM The area's best alternative-music radio station is run by the Bronx's Fordham University.

WNYC 820am or 93.9FM National Public Radio's local affiliate.

MEDICAL SERVICES

Big retail pharmacies are everywhere, some with walk-in medical care; many stay open late.

New York County Medical Society (☎212-684-4670; www.nycms.org) Makes doctor referrals by phone, based on type of problem and language spoken.

New York University Langone Medical Center (☎212-263-7300; 550 First Ave; ⏲24hr)

Travel MD (☎212-737-1212; www.travelmd.com) A 24-hour house-call service for travelers and residents.

TELEPHONE

There are thousands of pay telephones lining the streets, but many are out of order. Manhattan's telephone area codes are ☎212, ☎646 and ☎917; in the four other boroughs they're ☎718, ☎347 and ☎929. You must dial ☎1 + the area code, even if you're calling from a borough that uses the same one you're calling to.

The city's ☎311 service allows you to dial from anywhere within the city for info or help with any city agency, from the parking-ticket bureau to the noise complaint department.

TOURIST INFORMATION

New York City & Company (Map p76; ☎212-484-1222; www.nycgo.com; 810 Seventh Ave, at 53rd St; ⏲8:30am-6pm Mon-Fri, 9am-5pm Sat & Sun; [S]B/D/E to 7th Ave) The official information service of the Convention & Visitors Bureau, it has helpful multilingual staff. Other branches include Chinatown (Map p68; cnr Canal, Walker & Baxter Sts; ⏲10am-6pm Mon-Fri, to 7pm Sat; [S]6/J/N/Q to Canal St); Lower Manhattan (Map p68; City Hall Park at Broadway; ⏲9am-6pm Mon-Fri, 10am-5pm Sat & Sun; [S]4/5/A/C to Fulton St); Times Square (Map p76; 1560 Broadway, btwn 46th & 47th Sts, Times Square; ⏲8am-8pm Mon-Sun; [S]N/Q/R to 49th St).

Getting There & Away

AIR

Three major airports serve New York City. The biggest is **John F Kennedy International Airport** (JFK; ☎718-244-4444; www.panynj.gov), in the borough of Queens, which is also home to **LaGuardia Airport** (LGA; www.panynj.gov/aviation/lgaframe). **Newark Liberty International Airport** (EWR; ☎973-961-6000; www.panynj.gov), across the Hudson River in Newark, NJ, is another option. When using online booking websites, search 'NYC' rather than a specific airport, which will allow most sites to search all three spots at once. **Long Island MacArthur Airport** (ISP; ☎631-467-3210; www.macarthurairport.com), in Islip, is a money-saving (though time-consuming) alternative, but may make sense if a visit to the Hamptons or other parts of Long Island are in your plans.

BUS

The massive and confusing **Port Authority Bus Terminal** (Map p76; ☎212-564-8484; www.

panynj.gov; 41st St at Eighth Ave; [S] A, C, E, N, Q, R, 1, 2, 3, & 7) is the gateway for buses into and out of Manhattan. Short Line (p124) runs numerous buses to towns in northern New Jersey and upstate New York, while **New Jersey Transit** (www.njtransit.state.nj.us) buses serve all of New Jersey.

A number of comfortable and reliably safe bus companies with Midtown locations, including **BoltBus** (☎ 877-265-8287; www.boltbus.com) and **Megabus** (☎ 877-462-6342; us.megabus.com), link NYC to Philadelphia ($10, two hours), Boston ($25, 4¼ hours) and Washington, DC ($25, 4½ hours); free wi-fi on board.

CAR & MOTORCYCLE

Note that renting a car in the city is expensive, starting at about $75 a day for a midsized car – before extra charges like the 13.25% tax and various insurance costs.

FERRY

Seastreak (www.seastreak.com) goes to Sandy Hook (return $45) in New Jersey and Martha's Vineyard (summer only; return $220) in Massachusetts from Pier 11 on the East River near Wall St and E 35th St. New York Waterway (p135) ferries leave from Pier 11 and the World Financial Center on the Hudson for Hoboken (one-way $7), Jersey City and other destinations.

TRAIN

Penn Station (33rd St, btwn Seventh & Eighth Aves; [S] 1/2/3/A/C/E to 34th St-Penn Station), not to be confused with the Penn Station in Newark, NJ, is the departure point for all **Amtrak** (☎ 800-872-7245; www.amtrak.com) trains, including the speedy Acela Express service to Boston (3¾ hours) and Washington, DC (two hours 52 minutes). Fares and durations vary based on the day and time you want to travel. Also arriving into Penn Station (NYC), as well as points in Brooklyn and Queens, is the **Long Island Rail Road** (LIRR; www.mta.nyc.ny.us/lirr), which serves several hundred-thousand commuters each day. New Jersey Transit (p135) also operates trains from Penn Station (NYC), with services to the suburbs and the Jersey Shore. Another option for getting into New Jersey, but strictly to points north of the city such as Hoboken and Newark, is the **New Jersey PATH** (☎ 800-234-7284; www.panynj.gov/path), which runs trains on a separate-fare system ($2.25) along the length of Sixth Ave, with stops at 34th, 23rd, 14th, 9th, and Christopher Sts and the World Trade Center station.

The only train line that departs from Grand Central Station, Park Ave at 42nd St, is the **Metro-North Railroad** (☎ 212-532-4900; www.mta.info/mnr), which serves the northern city suburbs, Connecticut and locations throughout the Hudson Valley.

ℹ Getting Around

TO/FROM THE AIRPORT

All major airports have on-site car-rental agencies. It's a hassle to drive into NYC, though, and many folks take taxis, shelling out the $52 taxi flat rate (plus toll and tip) from JFK and Newark or a metered fare of about $25 to Midtown from LaGuardia.

A cheaper and pretty easy option to/from JFK is the AirTrain ($5 one way), which connects to subway lines into the city ($2.50; coming from the city, take the Far Rockaway-bound A train) or to the LIRR ($9.50 one way) at Jamaica Station in Queens (this is probably the quickest route to Penn Station in the city).

To/from Newark, the AirTrain links all terminals to a New Jersey Transit train station, which connects to Penn Station in NYC ($12.50 one way combined NJ Transit/Airtrain ticket).

For LaGuardia, a reliable option to consider if you allow plenty of time is the M60 bus ($2.50), which heads to/from Manhattan across 125th St in Harlem and makes stops along Broadway on the Upper West Side.

All three airports are also served by express buses ($16) and shuttle vans ($23); such companies include the **New York Airport Service Express Bus** (☎ 718-560-3915; www.nyairportservice.com; ⏲ every 20 or so min), which leaves every 20 or so minutes for Port Authority, Penn Station (NYC) and Grand Central Station; and **Super Shuttle Manhattan** (www.supershuttle.com), which picks you (and others) up anywhere, on demand, with a reservation.

BICYCLE

NYC has a new bike-sharing program, called Citi Bike (p94).

CAR & MOTORCYCLE

Even for the most spiritually centered, road rage is an inevitable by-product of driving within the city. Traffic and parking are always problematic and anxiety-provoking.

If you are driving out or in, however, know that the worst part is joining the masses as they try to squeeze through tunnels and over bridges to traverse the various waterways that surround Manhattan. Be aware of local laws, such as the fact that you can't make a right on red (like you can in the rest of the state) and also the fact that every other street is one way.

FERRY

The **East River Ferry** (www.eastriverferry.com) service (one way $4, every 20 minutes) connects spots in Brooklyn (Greenpoint, North and South Williamsburg and Dumbo) and Queens (Long Island City) with Manhattan (Pier 11 at Wall St and E 35th St). And **New York Water Taxi** (☎ 212-742-1969; www.nywatertaxi.com;

hop-on, hop-off service 1-day $26) has a fleet of zippy yellow boats that run along several different routes, including a hop-on, hop-off weekend service around Manhattan and Brooklyn.

PUBLIC TRANSPORTATION

The **Metropolitan Transport Authority** (MTA; ☑ 718-330-1234; www.mta.info) runs both the subway and bus systems. Depending on the train line, time of day and whether the door slams in your face or not, New York City's 100-year-old round-the-clock subway system (per ride $2.50) is your best friend or worst enemy. The 656-mile system can be intimidating at first, but regardless of its faults it's an incredible resource and achievement, linking the most disparate neighborhoods in a continually pulsating network. Maps should be available for the taking at every stop. To board, you must purchase a MetroCard, available at windows and self-serve machines, which accept change, dollars or credit/debit cards; purchasing many rides at once works out cheaper per trip.

If you're not in a big hurry, consider taking the bus (per ride $2.50). You get to see the world go by, they run 24/7 and they're easy to navigate – going crosstown at all the major street byways (14th, 23rd, 34th, 42nd, 72nd Sts and all the others that are two-way roads) and uptown or downtown, depending which avenue they serve. You can pay with a MetroCard or exact change but not bills. Transfers from one line to another are free, as are transfers to or from the subway.

TAXI

The classic NYC yellow cab is no longer a boxy gas-guzzling behemoth but rather a streamlined hybrid model, outfitted with mini-TVs and credit-card machines. No matter the make or year of the car, however, expect a herky-jerky, somewhat out-of-control ride. Current fares are $2.50 for the initial charge (first one-fifth mile), 50¢ each additional one-fifth mile, as well as per 60 seconds of being stopped in traffic, $1 peak surcharge (weekdays 4pm to 8pm), and 50¢ night surcharge (8pm to 6am daily). Tips are expected to be 10% to 15%; minivan cabs can hold five passengers. You can only hail a cab that has a lit light on its roof. Also know that it can be difficult to score a taxi in the rain, at rush hour and at around 4pm, when many drivers end their shifts.

NEW YORK STATE

There's upstate and downstate and never the twain shall meet. The two have about as much in common as NYC's Upper East Side and the Bronx. And yet everyone shares the same governor and dysfunctional legislature in the capital, Albany. While this incompatibility produces legislative gridlock and downright operatic drama, it's a blessing for those who cherish quiet and pastoral idylls as much as Lower East Side bars and the subway. Defined largely by its inland waterways – the Hudson River, the 524-mile Erie Canal connecting Albany to Buffalo, and the St Lawrence River – New York stretches to the Canadian border at world-famous Niagara Falls and under-the-radar Thousand Islands. Buffalo is a cheap foodies' paradise and wine aficionados can pick their favorite vintage from around the state, but especially in the Finger Lakes region close to the college town of Ithaca. From wilderness trails with backcountry camping to small-town Americana and miles and miles of sandy beaches, from the historic, grand estates and artists colonies in the Hudson Valley and Catskills to the rugged and remote Adirondacks, it's easy to understand why so many people leave the city, never to return.

ℹ Information

New York State Office of Parks, Recreation and Historic Preservation (☑ 800-456-2267, 518-474-0456; www.nysparks.com) Camping, lodging and general info on all state parks. Reservations can be made up to nine months in advance.

511 New York: Traffic, Travel & Transit Info (www.511ny.org) Weather advisories, road information and more.

Uncork New York (☑ 585-394-3620; www.newyorkwines.org) One-stop shop for statewide wine info.

Long Island

Private-school blazers, nightmare commutes, strip malls colonized by national chains, cookie-cutter suburbia, moneyed resorts, windswept dunes and magnificent beaches – and those accents. Long Island, which accommodates the boroughs of Brooklyn and Queens, has all of these things, and that explains its somewhat complicated reputation. The site of small European whaling and fishing ports from as early as 1640, Levittown, just 25 miles east of Manhattan in Nassau County, is where builders first perfected the art of mass-producing homes. But visions of suburban dystopia aside, Long Island has wide ocean and bay beaches, important historic sites, renowned vineyards, rural regions and of course the Hamptons, in all their luxuriously sunbaked glory.

NEW YORK STATE FACTS

Nicknames Empire State, Excelsior State, Knickerbocker State

Population 19.6 million

Area 47,214 sq miles

Capital city Albany (population 98,000)

Other cities New York City (population 8,245,000)

Sales tax 4%, plus additional county and state taxes (total approximately 8%)

Birthplace of Poet Walt Whitman (1819–92), President Theodore Roosevelt (1858–1919), President Franklin D Roosevelt (1882–1945), first lady Eleanor Roosevelt (1884–1962), painter Edward Hopper (1882–1967), movie star Humphrey Bogart (1899–1957), comic Lucille Ball (1911–89), filmmaker Woody Allen (b 1935), actor Tom Cruise (b 1962), pro athlete Michael Jordan (b 1963), pop star Jennifer Lopez (b 1969)

Home of Six Nations of the Iroquois Confederacy, first US cattle ranch (1747, in Montauk, Long Island), US women's suffrage movement (1872), Erie Canal (1825)

Politics Popular Democratic governor Andrew Cuomo, NYC overwhelmingly Democratic, upstate more conservative

Famous for Niagara Falls (half of it), the Hamptons, wineries, Hudson River

Unusual river Genesee River is one of the few rivers in the world that flows south–north, from south central New York into Lake Ontario at Rochester

Driving distances NYC to Albany 160 miles, NYC to Buffalo 375 miles

❶ Getting There & Around

The most direct driving route is along the I-495, aka the LIE (Long Island Expwy), though be sure to avoid rush hour, when it's commuter hell. Once in the Hamptons, there is one main road to the end, Montauk Hwy. The **Long Island Rail Road** (LIRR; ☑ 718-217-5477; www.mta.info/lirr; one-way off-peak/peak $19.75/27) serves all regions of Long Island, including the Hamptons ($25 one way, two hours 45 minutes), from Penn Station (NYC), Brooklyn and Queens. The **Hampton Jitney** (☑ 212-362-8400; www.hamptonjitney.com; 1-way $25) and **Hampton Luxury Liner** (☑ 631-537-5800; www.hamptonluxuryliner.com; 1-way $40) bus services connect Manhattan's midtown and Upper East Side to various Hamptons villages; the former also has services to/from various spots in Brooklyn.

North Shore

Long Island's Gold Coast of the roaring 20s, of the Vanderbilts, Chryslers and Guggenheims, not to mention Gatsby, begins outside the suburban town of Port Washington. Castle Gould, the enormous turreted stable at the entrance to **Sands Point Preserve** (☑ 516-571-7900; www.sandspointpreserve.org; 127 Middleneck Rd; admission per car/walk-in $5/$2; ⊘ 9am-4:30pm) and now a visitor center, was once owned by Howard Gould, the heir to a railroad fortune. The preserve's forested trails and beautiful sandy bayfront beach are worth a stroll and the 1923 mansion **Falaise** (www.sandspointpreserve.org; admission $10; ⊘ tours hourly noon-3pm Thu-Sun Jun-Oct) is intact and furnished and open to guided tours (hourly from noon to 3pm). Eastward is the bucolic town of Oyster Bay, home to **Sagamore Hill** (☑ 516-922-4788; www.nps.gov/sahi; adult/child $5/free; ⊘ 9am-5pm Wed-Sun), a 23-room Victorian where Theodore Roosevelt and his wife raised six children and vacationed during his presidency. Spring and summer months mean long waits for guided tours. A nature trail leading from behind the excellent **museum** (admission free) ends at a picturesque waterfront beach. As of the summer of 2013, the guided tours of the home were suspended until a renovation and rehabilitation project is completed

South Shore

Despite the periodic roar of jets overhead, **Long Beach**, the closest beach to the city and most accessible by train, has a main town strip with ice-cream shops, bars and eateries, a lively surfers' scene and pale trendy city types mixing with suntanned locals.

On summer weekends the 6-mile stretch of pretty **Jones Beach** is a microcosm of the city's diversity, attracting surfers, wild city folk, local teens, nudists, staid families, gay and lesbian people and plenty of old-timers. The **Long Island Rail Road** (LIRR; ☑ 718-217-5477; www.mta.info/lirr) service to Wantagh has a bus connection to Jones Beach.

Further east, just off the southern shore, is a separate barrier island. **Fire Island** includes **Fire Island National Seashore** (☑ 631-289-4810; www.nps.gov/fiis) and several summer-only villages accessible by ferry from Long Island. The Fire Island Pines and Cherry Grove (both car-free) comprise a historic, gay bacchanalia that attracts men and women in droves from NYC, while villages on the west end cater to straight singles and families. There are limited places to stay, and booking in advance is strongly advised (check www.fireisland.com for accommodations information). **Madison Fire Island** (☑ 631-597-6061; www.themadisonfi.com; The Pines; r $200-775; ❄☎☎), the first and only boutique hotel here, rivals anything Manhattan has to offer in terms of amenities, but also has killer views from a rooftop deck and a gorgeous pool. At the eastern end of the island, the 1300-acre preserve of **Otis Pike Fire Island High Dune Wilderness** is a protected oasis of sand dunes that includes beach camping at **Watch Hill** (☑ 631-567-6664; www.watchhillfi.com; campsites $25; ☻early May-late Oct), though mosquitoes can be fierce and reservations are a must (Hurricane Sandy breached a nearby inlet so check on access routes). At the western end of Fire Island, **Robert Moses State Park** is the only spot accessible by car. **Fire Island Ferries** (☑ 631-665-3600; Bay Shore) runs services to Fire Island beaches and the national seashore; the terminals are close to LIRR stations at Bayshore, Sayville and Patchogue (round-trip adult/child $17/7.50, May to November).

The Hamptons

Attitudes about the Hamptons are as varied as the number of Maseratis and Land Rovers cruising the perfectly landscaped streets; however, no amount of attitudinizing can detract from the sheer beauty of the beaches and what's left of the picturesque farms and woodland. If you can bury the envy, a pleasurable day of sightseeing can be had simply driving past the homes of the extravagantly wealthy, ranging from cutting-edge modern-

ist to faux-castle monstrosities. However, many summertime residents are partying the weekends away in much more modest group rentals and at the revolving doors of clubs. While each Hampton is not geographically far from every other, traffic can be a nightmare.

SOUTHAMPTON
Though the village of Southampton appears blemish-free, as if it has been Botoxed, it gets a face-lift at night when raucous clubgoers let their hair down. Its beaches are sweeping and gorgeous (only Coopers Beach (per day $40) and Road D (free) offer parking to non-residents May 31 to September 15). The **Parrish Art Museum** (☑ 631-283-2118; www.parrishart.org; 279 Montauk Hwy, Water Mill; adult/child $10/free; ☻11am-6pm Wed-Mon, to 8pm Fri) is an impressive regional institution. The town's colonial-era roots as a whaling and seafaring community are evident at Halsey House, the oldest residence in the Hamptons, and the nearby **Southampton Historical Museum** (☑ 631-283-2494; www.southamptonhistoricalmuseum.org; 17 Meeting House Ln; adult/child $4/free; ☻11am-4pm Tue-Sat). To learn more about an even earlier age of Long Island's history, head to the **Shinnecock Nation Cultural Center & Museum** (☑ 631-287-4923; www.shinnecock.com; 100 Montauk Hwy, Southampton; adult/child under 5 $10/free; ☻11am-5pm Thu-Sun) at the edge of the village. Run by the Native American group who live on an 800-acre peninsula that juts into the bay, the recently opened site allows Shinnecock members and visitors alike to experience a recreated Wikun (village) c 1640–1750 with guided tours, singing, dancing and demonstrations of traditional skills. For a quick and reasonable meal try **Golden Pear** (☑ 631-283-8900; www.goldenpear.com; 99 Main St; snacks & meals $6-18; ☻7:30am-5pm), which serves delicious soups, salads and wraps.

BRIDGEHAMPTON & SAG HARBOR
Moving east, Bridgehampton has a more modest-looking drag, but has its fair share of trendy boutiques and fine restaurants. The modest, low-slung **Enclave Inn** (☑ 631-537-2900; www.enclaveinn.com; 2668 Montauk Hwy, Bridgehampton; r from $199; ❄☎), just a few blocks from the heart of the village, is one of the better value accommodations options; there are four other locations elsewhere in the Hamptons. Old-fashioned diner **Candy Kitchen** (☑ 646-537-9885; 2391 Montauk, Hwy, Bridgehampton; mains $5-12; ☻7am-9:30pm; ⊕)

has a luncheonette counter serving filling breakfasts, burgers and sandwiches.

Seven miles north, on Peconic Bay, is the lovely old whaling town of Sag Harbor; ferries to Shelter Island leave a few miles north of here. Check out Sag Harbor's **Whaling & Historical Museum** (☑631-725-0770; www.sagharborwhalingmuseum.org; 200 Main St; adult/child $6/2; ☺10am-5pm Mon-Sat, from 1pm Sun May 15-Oct 1), or simply stroll up and down its narrow, Cape Cod–like streets. Get gourmet sustenance at **Provisions** (☑631-725-3636; cnr Bay & Division Sts; sandwiches $9; ☺8am-6pm), a natural foods market with delicious take-out wraps, burritos and sandwiches.

EAST HAMPTON

Don't be fooled by the oh-so-casual-looking summer attire, heavy on pastels and sweaters tied around the neck – the sunglasses alone are probably equal to a month's rent. Some of the highest-profile celebrities have homes here. Catch readings, theater and art exhibits at **Guild Hall** (☑631-324-0806; www.guildhall.org; 158 Main St). West of town on the way to Bridgehampton is the **Townline BBQ** (www.townlinebbq.com; 3593 Montauk Hwy; mains $9; ☺11:30am-10pm), a down-to-earth roadside restaurant churning out smoky ribs and barbecue sandwiches. Just to the east toward Amagansett is **La Fondita** (74 Montauk Hwy, Amagansett; mains $9; ☺11:30am-8pm Thu & Sun, to 9pm Fri & Sat), the place to go for reasonably priced Mexican fare. Nightclubs come and go with the seasons.

MONTAUK & AROUND

Once a sleepy and humble stepsister to the Hamptons, these days Montauk, at the far eastern end of Long Island, draws a fashionable, younger crowd and even a hipster subset to its beautiful beaches. Longtime residents, fishermen and territorial surfers round out a motley mix that makes the dining and bar scene more democratic compared to other Hamptons villages. At the very eastern, wind-whipped tip of the South Fork is **Montauk Point State Park**, with its impressive, 1796 **Montauk Point Lighthouse** (☑631-668-2544; www.montauklighthouse.com; adult/child $9/4; ☺10:30am-5:30pm, hours vary), the fourth oldest still-active lighthouse in the US. You can camp a few miles west of town at the dune-swept **Hither Hills State Park** (☑631-668-2554; www.nysparks.com; 164 Old Montauk Hwy), right on the beach; just reserve early during summer months. Several miles to the north is the Montauk

harbor, with dockside restaurants and hundreds of boats in the marinas.

You'll find a string of standard motels near the entrance to the town beach, including the **Ocean Resort Inn** (☑631-668-2300; www.oceanresortinn.com; 96 S Emerson Ave; r from $135, ste from $185; ❈ 🕾). A few miles west, just across the street from the beach, is **Sunrise Guesthouse** (☑631-668-7286; www.sunrisebnb.com; 681 Old Montauk Hwy; r $125-185; ❈ 🕾), a modest and comfortable B&B.

Two great places to wind down the day (from May to October) with drinks and hearty, fresh seafood are the roadside restaurants **Clam Bar** (☑631-267-6348; 2025 Montauk Hwy; mains $7-14; ☺noon-8pm, weather permitting) and **Lobster Roll** (☑631-267-3740; 1980 Montauk Hwy; mains $10-12; ☺11:30am-10pm summer) aka 'Lunch,' now in its fifth decade, both on the highway between Amagansett and Montauk.

North Fork & Shelter Island

Mainly, the North Fork is known for its unspoiled farmland and wineries – there are close to 30 vineyards, clustered chiefly around the towns of Jamesport, Cutchogue and Southold – and the **Long Island Wine Council** (☑631-722-2220; www.liwines.com) provides details of the local wine trail, which runs along Rte 25 north of Peconic Bay. One of the nicer outdoor settings for a tasting is the **Peconic Bay Winery** (☑631-734-7361; www.peconicbaywinery.com; 31320 Main Rd, Cutchogue); this also means it's popular with bus and limo-loads of partiers. Beforehand, stop at popular **Love Lane Kitchen** (240 Love Lane; mains $9-28; ☺7am-9:30pm, Thu-Mon, 7am-4pm Tue & Wed) in Matituck for a meal, especially weekend brunch.

The main North Fork town and the place for ferries to Shelter Island, **Greenport** is a charming, laid-back place lined with restaurants and cafes, including family-owned **Claudio's Clam Bar** (www.claudios.com; 111 Main St; mains $15; ☺11:30am-9pm, closed Wed) with a wraparound deck perched over the marina. Or grab sandwiches for a picnic at the **Harbor Front Park**, where you can take a spin on the historic carousel.

Between the North and South Forks, **Shelter Island**, accessible by ferry from North Haven to the south and Greenport to the north (vehicle and driver $10, 10 minutes, every 15 to 20 minutes), is a low-key microcosm of beautiful Hamptons real estate with more of a traditional maritime New England atmosphere. And the **Mashomack Nature Preserve** (☑ 631-749-1001; www.nature.org; Rte 114; ⊘ 9am-5pm Mar-Sep, to 4pm Oct-Feb), covering over 2000 acres of the southern part of the island is a great spot for hiking or kayaking (no cycling).

On Shelter Island, just down the road from **Crescent Beach** and nestled on a prime piece of property surrounded by woods fronting the bay, **Pridwin Beach Hotel & Cottages** (☑ 631-749-0476; www.pridwin. com; 81 Shore Rd, Shelter Island; r & cottages from $165-315; ⚙ 🎧) has standard hotel rooms as well as private water-view cottages, some in high-designer style.

Hudson Valley

Immediately north of New York City, green becomes the dominant color and the vistas of the Hudson River and the mountains breathe life into your urban-weary body. The region was home to the Hudson River School of painting in the 19th century and its history is preserved in the many grand estates and picturesque villages. The Lower Valley and Middle Valley are more populated and suburban, while the Upper Valley has a rural feel, with hills leading into the Catskills mountain region. For area-wide information, check out the **Hudson Valley Network** (www.hvnet.com).

Lower Hudson Valley

Several magnificent homes and gardens can be found near Tarrytown and Sleepy Hollow, on the east side of the Hudson. **Kykuit**, one of the properties of the Rockefeller family, has an impressive array of Asian and European artwork and immaculately kept gardens with breathtaking views. **Lyndhurst** is the estate of railroad tycoon Jay Gould and **Sunnyside** is the home of author Washington Irving. Go to the **Historic Hudson Valley** (www.hudsonvalley.org) website for info on these and other historic attractions. Nearby is the elegant country restaurant **Blue Hill at Stone Barns** (☑ 914-366-9600; www.bluehillfarm.com; 630 Bedford Rd, Pocantico Hills; 5-course meal $108, 8-courses $148; ⊘ 5-10pm Wed-Thu, to 11pm Fri & Sat, 1-10pm Sun) 🍴, a pillar of the farm-to-table movement and a locavore's dream.

A pristine forested wilderness with miles of hiking trails is just 40 miles north of New York City on the west side of the Hudson:

Harriman State Park (☑ 845-786-5003; http://nysparks.state.ny.us/parks) covers 72 sq miles and offers swimming, hiking and camping; adjacent **Bear Mountain State Park** (☑ 845-786-2701; http://nysparks.state. ny.us/parks; ⊘ 8am-dusk) offers great views from its 1305ft peak, with the Manhattan skyline looming beyond the river and surrounding greenery; and there's a restaurant and lodging at the inn on Hessian Lake. In both parks there are several scenic roads snaking their way past secluded lakes with gorgeous vistas.

Not far to the north in Highland Falls and occupying one of the most breathtaking bends in the Hudson is **West Point US Military Academy**, open to visitors on **guided tours** (☑ 845-446-4724; www.westpointtours.com; adult/child $12/9). Next to the visitor center is a fascinating **museum** (open 10:30am-4:15pm; free admission) that traces the role of war and the military throughout human history. Nearby and west of Rte 9W, the **Storm King Art Center** (☑ 845-534-3115; www.stormking.org; Old Pleasant Hill Rd; admission $10; ⊘ Apr-Nov) is a 500-acre outdoor sculpture park with rolling hills that showcases stunning avant-garde sculpture by well-known artists; a free tram gives tours of the grounds.

At Beacon, a fairly nondescript town north of here, fashionable regulars of the international art scene stop for **Dia Beacon** (Beacon; ☑ 845-440-0100; www.diaart.org; adult $10; ⊘ 11am-6pm Thu-Mon mid-Apr–mid-Oct, 11am-4pm Fri-Mon mid-Oct–mid-Apr), a gallery featuring a renowned collection from 1960 to the present, and huge sculptures and installation pieces. Stop by **Hudson Beach Glass** (www.hudsonbeachglass.com; 162 Main St, Beacon), a boutique-gallery where you can buy artfully designed, hand-crafted pieces or sign up for a class to learn how to do it yourself.

Middle & Upper Hudson Valley

On the western side of the Hudson is **New Paltz**, home of a campus of the State University of New York, natural food stores and a liberal ecofriendly vibe. In the distance behind the town, the ridge of the Shawangunk (Shon-gum or just the 'Gunks') mountains rises more than 2000ft above sea level. More than two-dozen miles of nature trails and some of the best rock climbing in the Eastern US is found in the **Mohonk Mountain Preserve** (☑ 845-255-0919; www.mohonk-preserve.org; day pass for hikers/climbers & cyclists $12/17). Nearby **Minnewaska State Park Preserve** has 12,000 acres of wild landscape, the centerpiece of which is a usually ice-cold mountain lake. Contact **Alpine Endeavors** (☑877-486-5769; www.alpineendeavors.com) for climbing instruction and equipment.

The iconic **Mohonk Mountain House** (☑845-255-1000; www.mohonk.com; 1000 Mountain Rest Rd; r $320-2500; ❋ ❂ ▨ 🛉) looks like it's straight out of a fairy tale: a rustic castle perched magnificently over a dark lake. It's an all-inclusive resort where guests can gorge on elaborate five-course meals, stroll through gardens, hike miles of trails, canoe, swim etc. A luxury spa center is there to work out the kinks. Nonovernight guests can visit the grounds. (adult/child per day $25/20, less on weekdays) – well worth the price of admission.

On the eastern side of the Hudson is Poughkeepsie (puh-kip-see), the largest town on the east bank. It's famous for Vassar, a private liberal-arts college that until 1969 only admitted women. Worth a stroll for its breathtaking views is the **Walkway Over the Hudson** (www.walkway.org; ⊘7am-sunset); formerly the Highland-Poughkeepsie railroad bridge, and since 2009 the world's longest pedestrian bridge and the state's newest park.

Just north of here is Hyde Park, long associated with the Roosevelts, a prominent family since the 19th century. The estate of 1520 acres, formerly a working farm, includes the newly renovated and expanded **Franklin D Roosevelt Library & Museum** (☑845-229-8114; www.fdrlibrary.marist.edu; 511 Albany Post Rd/Rte 9, Hyde Park; admission museum $7, museum & house $14; ⊘9am-5pm), which details important achievements in FDR's presidency; a visit usually includes a guided tour of FDR's lifelong home where he delivered his fireside chats. First Lady Eleanor Roosevelt's peaceful cottage, **Val-Kill** (☑845-229-9115; www.nps.gov/elro; Albany Post Rd, Hyde Park; admission $8; ⊘9am-5pm daily May-Oct, Thu-Mon Nov-Apr), was her retreat from Hyde Park, FDR's mother and FDR himself. Just north of here is the 54-room **Vanderbilt Mansion** (☑877-444-6777; www.nps.gov/vama; Rte 9, Hyde Park; adult/child $8/free; ⊘9am-5pm), a Gilded Age spectacle of lavish beaux-arts design; nearly all of the original furnishings imported from European castles and villas remain in this country house – the smallest of any of the Vanderbilt mansions!

Hyde Park's famous **Culinary Institute of America** (☑845-471-6608; www.ciarestaurants. com; Hyde Park; ⊘most restaurants 11:30am-1pm & 6-8pm) trains future chefs and can satisfy absolutely anyone's gastronomic cravings; the **Apple Pie Café** (mains $10; ⊘7:30am-5pm), one of the five student-staffed eateries, looks out onto a tranquil courtyard and serves up gourmet sandwiches as well as specialty pastries. Tuck in for a good night's sleep at **Journey Inn** (☑845-229-8972; www. journeyinn.com; One Sherwood Pl, Poughkeepsie; r $130-190), a six-room B&B – including a Roosevelt Room, of course – right in the middle of Hyde Park's big estates.

Further north is **Rhinebeck**, with a charming main street, inns, farms and wineries. Three miles to the north, the **Aerodrome Museum** (☑845-752-3200; www.oldrhinebeck.org; 9 Norton Rd; adult/child Sat & Sun $20/5, Mon-Fri $10/3; ⊘10am-5pm mid-Jun–mid-Oct) has a collection of pre-1930s planes and automobiles and air shows on weekends in the summer. The **Bread Alone Bakery** (45 E Market St; mains $9; ⊘7am-7pm, 8am-3pm) serves lunch specialties such as brisket panini and spinach and feta quiche.

Continuing along 9G N you reach **Hudson** – a beautiful town with a hip, gay-friendly community of artists, writers and performers who fled the city. Warren St, the main road through town, is lined with antiques shops, high-end furniture stores, galleries and cafes. A few miles south of town is **Olana** (☑518-828-0135; www.olana.org; Rte 9G, Hudson; tour adult/child $12/free; ⊘grounds 8am-sunset daily, tours 10am-5pm Tue-Sun), the fish-out-of-water Moorish-style home of Frederic Church, one of the primary artists of the Hudson River School of Painting. On a house tour you can appreciate the totality of Church's aesthetic vision, and view paintings from his collection. At the riverside end of Hudson, the whitewashed, cozy and affordable **Front St Guesthouse** (☑518-828-1635; www.frontstreetguesthouse. com; 20 S Front St, Hudson; r from $140; ❋ 🛜) has polished wood floors, high-end bedding and an accommodating owner who will quickly meet guests' needs. **Helsinki** (☑518-828-4800; www.helsinkihudson.com; 405 Columbia St, Hudson; mains $13-25), in a restored carriage house, has a restaurant serving locally sourced cuisine and a popular music venue showcasing rock, jazz and indie performers.

NEW YORK, NEW JERSEY & PENNSYLVANIA HUDSON VALLEY

Catskills

American painters discovered this mountainous region rising west of the Hudson Valley in the mid-19th century. They celebrated its hidden mossy gorges and waterfalls as examples of sublime wilderness rivaling the Alps in Europe. Though the height and profile of its rounded peaks might have been exaggerated and romanticized, traveling through the Catskills it's still possible to glimpse the landscapes that beguiled these artists and inspires others today.

Despite the introduction of fine cuisine and cute boutiques in charming small towns, for some this bucolic region is still synonymous with Borscht-belt family resorts and the wise-cracking Jewish comedians and dance instructors *a la* Patrick Swayze in *Dirty Dancing* who entertained generations. While that era is long past, the Catskills have become a popular choice for sophisticated city dwellers seeking second-home getaways.

Having a car is near essential in these parts. **Adirondack Trailways** (⌨800-776-7548; www.trailwaysny.com) operates daily buses from NYC to Kingston (one way $25.50, two hours), the Catskills' gateway town, as well as to Catskills and Woodstock (one way $28, 2½ hours). **Shortline** (⌨201-529-3666, 800-631-8405; www.coachusa.com) has regular trips between NYC and Monticello (one way $30, two hours), the gateway to the southern Catskills. Buses leave from NYC's Port Authority. The commuter rail line **Metro-North** (⌨212-532-4900, 800-638-7646; http://mta.info; one-way off-peak $9-16) makes stops through the Lower and Middle Hudson Valleys.

Woodstock & Around

Shorthand for free love, free expression and the political ferment of the 1960s, world-famous **Woodstock** today still wears its counterculture tie-dye in the form of healing centers, art galleries, cafes and an eclectic mix of aging hippies and young Phish-fan types. The famous 1969 Woodstock music festival, though, actually occurred in Bethel. Overlooking Woodstock's town square, actually in front of the bus stop, is the **Village Green B&B** (⌨845-679-0313; www.villagegreenbb.com; 12 Tinker St; r incl breakfast $135; ✷✸🐾), a three-story Victorian with comfortable rooms. Housed in an elegantly restored farmhouse half a mile southeast of the town

square, **Cucina** (⌨845-679-9800; 109 Mill Hill Rd; mains $18; ⊘5am-late, from 11am Sat & Sun) does sophisticated seasonal Italian fare and thin-crust pizzas.

Saugerties, just 7 miles east of Woodstock, is not nearly as quaint and feels by comparison like the big city, but the **Saugerties Lighthouse** (⌨845-247-0656; www.saugertieslighthouse.com; r $165-180) offers a truly romantic and unique place to lay your head. The picturesque 1869 landmark is located on a small island in the Esopus Creek, accessible by boat or more commonly by a half-mile trail from the parking lot. Rooms are booked far in advance, but a walk to the lighthouse is highly recommended regardless.

Finger Lakes Region

A bird's-eye view of this region of rolling hills and 11 long narrow lakes – the eponymous fingers – reveals an outdoor paradise stretching all the way from Albany to far western New York. Of course there's boating, fishing, cycling, hiking and cross-country skiing, but this is also the state's premier wine-growing region, with more than 65 vineyards, enough for the most discerning oenophile.

Ithaca & Around

An idyllic home for college students and older generations of hippies who cherish elements of the traditional collegiate lifestyle – laid-back vibe, cafe poetry readings, art-house cinemas, green quads, good eats – Ithaca is perched above Cayuga Lake. Besides being a destination in itself, it is also a convenient halfway point between New York City and Niagara Falls. For tourist information, head to the **Visit Ithaca Information Center** (⌨607-272-1313; www.visitithaca.com; 904 E Shore Dr).

Founded in 1865, **Cornell University** boasts a lovely campus, mixing traditional and contemporary architecture, and sits high on a hill overlooking the picturesque town below. The modern **Johnson Museum of Art** (⌨607-255-6464; www.museum.cornell.edu; University Ave; ⊘10am-5pm Tue- Sun) FREE, designed by IM Pei, has a major Asian collection, plus pre-Columbian, American and European exhibits. Just east of the center of the campus is **Cornell Plantations** (⌨607-255-2400; www.cornellplantations.org; Plantations

SCENIC DRIVE: ROUTE 28 & AROUND

One sign that you've crossed into the Catskills is when the unending asphalt gives way to dense greenery crowding the snaking roadway as you exit the I-87 and turn onto Rte 28. As you drive through the heart of the region, the vistas open up and the mountains (around 35 peaks are above 3500ft) take on stunning coloring depending on the season and time of day. Esopus Creek winds its way through the area and **Ashokan Reservoir** is a nice place for a walk or drive. To the south of Rte 28, several roads wind their way up and over the high peaks in Catskill Park.

Emerson Spa Resort (☑877-688-2828; www.emersonresort.com; 5340 Rte 28, Mt Tremper; r at lodge/inn from $159/199; ❁@🔊📶❁) ✐ offers a full-service base for Catskills adventures whatever time of year. From luxurious Asian-inspired suites to rustic-chic rooms in the log-cabin-style lodge, Emerson aims to please; staff can help arrange trips from skiing to kayaking. The Phoenix restaurant (mains $15 to $30) is probably the best in the region and the Catamount, popular with locals, has pub fare (mains $10) including burgers and BBQ ribs, and live music and dancing Monday nights. The world's largest kaleidoscope and kaleidoscope boutique, selling sculpture-quality pieces, is attached, as well as a coffee-sandwich shop.

Only a few miles further west is the one-lane town of **Phoenicia**. It's a pleasant place to stop for a meal and a tube – **Town Tinker Tube Rental** (☑845-688-5553; www.towntinker.com; 10 Bridge St; tubes per day $15; ♿) can hook you up for repeated forays down the Esopus rapids. The refreshing water of Pine Hill Lake at nearby **Belleayre Beach** (☑845-254-5600; www.belleayre.com; ♿) is the summertime place to cool off (or ski in the winter). In nearby Arkville, you can take a scenic ride on the historic **Delaware & Ulster Rail Line** (☑845-586-3877; www.durr.org; Hwy 28; adult/child $12/7; ⊙11am & 2pm, Sat & Sun Jun-Nov, additional trips Thu & Fri Jul-Sep; ♿). Less than a mile west of Phoenicia is the **Phoenecia Lodge** (☑845-688-7772; www.phoenicialodge.com; Rte 28; r from $80, ste from $130; ❁📶❁), a classic and affordable roadside motel.

From here you can carry on north on Rte 30 to the **Roxbury Motel** (☑607-326-7200; www.theroxburymotel.com; 2258 County Hwy 41; r incl breakfast Mon-Fri Jun-Oct $100-300; ❁📶), in the tiny village of the same name, a wonderfully creative gem of a place with luxuriously designed and whimsically named rooms, each inspired by a particular '60s or '70s TV show or film – think *The Jetsons* and *Wizard of Oz*. Wintertime (lower room rates) means huddling around the fire pit whereas warm weather means sunbathing and lounging near the gazebo and the small stream that runs along the property; any time is good for relaxing at the full-service spa.

In winter, skiers should head further north, where Rtes 23 and 23A lead you to **Hunter Mountain Ski Bowl** (☑518-263-4223; www.huntermtn.com), a year-round resort with challenging runs and a 1600ft vertical drop. Nearby is **Kaaterskill Falls**, the highest falls in New York and once popularized and idealized in paintings by Thomas Cole and Asher Durand. The most traveled trail starts near a horseshoe curve in Rte 23A; park the car in a turnout just up the road, cross to the other side and walk back down behind a guardrail. What you see from here is only Bastion Falls; it's a not very strenuous hike a little more than three-quarters of a mile up to the lower falls. **Hotel Mountain Brook** (☑518-589-6740; www.hotelmountainbrook.com; 57 Hill St; r Mon-Fri $150, Sat & Sun $200, all incl breakfast; ❁📶❁) in Tannersville is set on a hill and evokes an Adirondack 'great camp.' Check out **Last Chance Cheese** (6009 Main St, Tannersville; mains $9-20; ⊙11am-midnight Fri-Sun), an independently minded Tannersville institution with an overstuffed counter displaying gourmet cheeses, chocolates, candies and three hundred varieties of beer.

Perhaps the most scenic drive in the region is the 7-mile stretch of Platte Clove Rd/Rte 16 (also signposted as 'Plattecove Mtn Rd') between Tannersville and Woodstock. It's white-knuckle driving through a narrow and steep valley with a 1200ft elevation change (sometimes no guardrail; no trucks or buses allowed; closed November to April).

Rd; ⊙10am-5pm, closed Mon) 🏷FREE, an expertly curated herb and flower garden. Kids can go interactive-wild at the extremely hands-on **Sciencenter** (☑607-272-0600; www.sciencecenter.org; 601 First St; adult/child $8/6; ⊙10am-5pm Tue-Sat, from noon Sun; ♿).

The area around Ithaca is known for its waterfalls, gorges and gorgeous parks. However, downtown has its very own natural feature: **Cascadilla Gorge**, which starts several blocks from Ithaca Commons and ends, after a steep and stunning vertical climb, at the Performing Arts Center of Cornell. **Buttermilk Falls Park** (☑607-273-5761; Rte 13) has something for everyone: a beach, cabins, fishing, hiking, recreational fields and camping. The big draw, however, is the waterfalls – more than 10 – some sending water tumbling as far as 500ft below into clear swimming pools. **Robert Treman Park** (☑607-273-3440; 105 Enfield Falls Rd), a few miles further out of town, has a gorge trail passing a stunning 12 waterfalls in under 3 miles. The two biggies you don't want to miss are Devil's Kitchen and Lucifer Falls. Eight miles north on Rte 89, the spectacular **Taughannock Falls** spills 215ft into the steep gorge below; **Taughannock Falls State Park** (☑607-387-6739; www.nysparks.com; 2221 Taughannock Rd, Trumansburg) has two major hiking trails, craggy gorges, tent-trailer sites and cabins.

A little further along on Rte 89 near the village of Interlaken is the **Creamery** (⊙11am-8pm), a roadside eatery that in addition to conventional ice cream sundaes serves buzz-inducing wine-infused sorbets. Just past here is **Lucas Vineyards** (☑607-532-4825; www.lucasvineyards.com; 3862 Cty Rd 150, Interlaken; ⊙10:30am-5:30pm Mon-Sat, from 11am Sun Mar-Oct; 10:30am-6pm Mon-Sun Memorial Day-Labor Day), one of the pioneers of Cayuga wineries, and a little further north down by the lake shore is **Sheldrake Point** (☑607-532-9401; www.sheldrakepoint.com; 7448 County Rd; ⊙11am-5pm Fri-Mon Jan-Mar, 10am-5:30pm daily Apr-Dec), which has lake views and award-winning whites.

The small, sleepy town of **Seneca Falls** is where the country's organized women's rights movement was born. After being excluded from an anti-slavery meeting, Elizabeth Cady Stanton and her friends drafted an 1848 declaration asserting that 'all men and women are created equal.' The inspirational **Women's Rights National Historical Park** (☑315-568-2991; www.nps.gov/wori; 136 Fall St; ⊙9am-5pm) FREE has a small but impressive museum with an informative film, plus a visitor center offering tours of Cady Stanton's house.

Seneca & Keuka Lakes

Geneva, at the northern tip of Seneca Lake, has an architecturally historic exterior and a lively vibe with both Hobart and William Smith colleges calling it home. South Main St is lined with an impressive number of immaculate turn-of-the-century homes. The restored 1894 **Smith Opera House** (☑315-781-5483; www.thesmith.org; 82 Seneca St, Geneva) is the place to go for performing arts. Stop by **Microclimate** (38 Linden St, Geneva; ⊙6pm-midnight Mon, 4:30pm-1am Thu-Sun), a cool little wine bar with wine flights where you can compare locally produced varietals with their international counterparts.

Y-shaped Keuka Lake is surrounded by two small state parks that keep it relatively pristine. One of its old canals has been converted into a rustic bike path and it's a favorite lake for trout fishing. Just south of **Penn Yan**, the largest village on the lake's shores, you come to **Keuka Spring Vineyards** (☑315-536-3147; www.keukaspringwinery.com; 54 E Lake Rd, Penn Yan; ⊙10am-5pm Mon-Sat, from 11am Sun summer, mostly weekends other months) and then **Rooster Hill Vineyards** (☑315-536-4773; www.roosterhill.com; 489 Rte 54, Penn Yan; ⊙10am-5pm Mon-Sat, from 11am Sun) – two local favorites that offer tastings and tours in pastoral settings.

🛏 Sleeping

⭐**William Henry Miller Inn**   B&B $$
(☑607-256-4553; www.millerinn.com; 303 N Aurora St, Ithaca; r incl breakfast $115-215; ❉🌐❉) Gracious and grand, and only a few steps from the commons, this is a completely restored historic home with luxuriously designed rooms – three have Jacuzzis – and a gourmet breakfast.

Inn on Columbia   INN $$
(☑607-272-0204; www.columbiabb.com; 228 Columbia St, Ithaca; r incl breakfast $175-225; ❉🌐❉) Also recommended; a modern, contemporary home on a quiet residential street.

Gone with the Wind B&B   B&B $$
(☑607-868-4603; www.gonewiththewindonkeukalake.com; 14905 West Lake Rd, Branchport; r incl breakfast $110-200; ❉) This lakeside B&B has

WORTH A TRIP

CORNING

Around 44 miles to the southwest is the charming town of Corning, home to Corning Glass Works and the hugely popular **Corning Museum of Glass** (☎800-732-6845; www.cmog.org; One Museum Way; adult/child $15/free; ⊙9am-5pm, to 8pm Memorial Day-Labor Day; ♿). The massive complex is home to fascinating exhibits on glassmaking arts, complete with demonstrations and interactive items for kids. After visiting the museum, stop by **Vitrix Hot Glass Studio** (www.vitrixhotglass.com; 77 W Market St; ⊙9am-8pm Mon-Fri, from 10am Sat, noon-5pm Sun) in the charming Market Street district to take a gander at museum-quality glass pieces.

The **Rockwell Museum of Western Art** (☎607-937-5386; www.rockwellmuseum. org; 111 Cedar St; adult/child $8/free; ⊙9am-5pm, to 8pm summer; ♿), housed in the former City Hall, has a large collection of art of the American West, including great works by Bierstadt, Russell and Remington.

two accommodation choices: the original stone mansion and a log lodge annex – both have generally homey furnishings.

Hotel Clarence   BOUTIQUE HOTEL **$$**
(☎315-712-4000; www.hotelclarence.com; 108 Fall St, Seneca Falls; r $140; ❄🛜🐾) Originally a 1920s-era hotel, the downtown building housing the Clarence has undergone a stylish renovation with a nod to the past. The standard rooms are small and the upscale restaurant called the Kitchen is the best in town.

Buttonwood Grove Winery   CABIN **$$**
(☎607-869-9760; www.buttonwoodgrove.com; 5986 Rte 89; r $135; 🐾) Has four fully furnished log cabins nestled in the hills above Lake Cayuga (open April to December); free wine tasting included.

Belhurst Castle   INN **$$$**
(☎315-781-0201; www.belhurst.com; 4069 Rte 14 S, Geneva; r from $160-415; ❄🛜) Even if you're not planning a wedding, this fairybook castle overlooking Lake Seneca might inspire you to take the plunge. Check out the three separate properties with a variety of room types. Two restaurants, the more casual Stone Cutters with live music on weekends and the more formal Edgar's.

Eating

A half-dozen restaurants with outdoor seating, including Japanese, Middle Eastern, Mexican and Spanish tapas, line North Aurora St between East State and East Seneca Sts at the east end of the Ithaca Commons. Upscale **Mercato** (www.mercatobarandkitchen. com; 108 N Aurora St, Ithaca; mains $25; ⊙5:30-

10pm Mon-Sat) is one of the best. **Ithaca's Farmers Market** (www.ithacamarket.com; Third St; ⊙Apr-Dec) is considered one of the region's standouts; local wines and cheeses are highlights; check the website for operating hours.

Glenwood Pines   BURGERS **$**
(1213 Taughannock Blvd; burgers $6; ⊙11am-10pm) According to locals in the know, this modest roadside restaurant, overlooking Lake Cayuga on Rte 89 and 4 miles north of Ithaca, serves the best burgers.

Yerba Maté Factor Café
& Juice Bar   SANDWICHES **$**
(143 The Commons, Ithaca; mains $8; ⊙9am-9pm Mon-Thu, to 3pm Fri, from noon Sun) Run by members of a fairly obscure religious organization, this large restaurant, housed in a converted historic building on the Ithaca Commons, is good for Belgian waffles, sandwiches and coffee.

★Hazelnut Kitchen   MODERN AMERICAN **$$**
(☎607-387-4433; 53 East Main St, Trumansburg; mains $14-23; ⊙5-9pm Thu-Mon) 🍃 The new owners, a young couple from Chicago interested in collaborating with area farmers, have maintained Hazelnut's status as arguably the finest restaurant in the region. Local ingredients, of course, seasonally inspired menu and au courant meat dishes such as pig face torchon.

Moosewood Restaurant   VEGETARIAN **$$**
(www.moosewoodcooks.com; 215 N Cayuga St, Ithaca; mains $8-18; ⊙11:30am-8:30pm, 5:30-9pm Sun; 🍴) Famous for its creative and constantly changing vegetarian menu and recipe books by founder Mollie Katzen.

❶ Getting There & Away

Shortline Bus (www.coachusa.com) has frequent departures to New York City ($53, four hours). Delta Airlines has direct flights from the **Ithaca Tompkins Regional Airport** (ITH; www.flyithaca.com) to Detroit, Newark and Philadelphia.

The Adirondacks

Majestic and wild, the Adirondacks, a mountain range with 42 peaks over 4000ft high, rival any of the nation's wilderness areas for sheer awe-inspiring beauty. The 9375 sq miles of park and forest preserve that climb from central New York State to the Canadian border include towns, mountains, lakes, rivers and more than 2000 miles of hiking trails. There's good trout, salmon and pike fishing, along with excellent camping spots. The Adirondack Forest Preserve covers 40% of the park, preserving the area's pristine integrity. In colonial times settlers exploited the forests for beaver fur, timber and hemlock bark, but by the 19th century 'log cabin' wilderness retreats, both in the form of hotels and grand estates, became fashionable.

Lake George

Maybe it's a blessing that the primary gateway to the Adirondacks, the village of **Lake George**, is a kitsch tourist town full of cotton candy, arcades and cheap souvenirs. The real reason for coming is the 32-mile-long lake itself, with its crystalline waters and forested shoreline, and once you leave the town behind the contrast is only more striking. Paddlewheel boat cruises, parasailing, kayaking and fishing trips are popular.

The state maintains wonderfully remote **campgrounds** (☑ 800-456-2267; www.dec.ny.gov/outdoor; tent sites $25) on Lake George's islands, and small motels line the main street of Lake George toward the northern end of town with dozens more on Rte 9 all the way to the village of **Bolton Landing**. Two with lake views that can be recommended are **Georgian Lakeside Resort** (☑ 518-668-5401; www.georgianresort.com; r incl breakfast from $99; ✴ 🎅 🏊) and renovated **Surfside on the Lake** (☑ 800-342-9795; www.surfsideonthelake.com; 400 Canada St; r from $60; ✴ 🎅 🏊).

Lake Placid & Saranac Lake

It's something of a stretch to imagine that this small mountain resort was once the center

of the world's attention – well, twice. In 1932 and 1980, **Lake Placid** hosted the Winter Olympics, and the facilities and infrastructure remain; elite athletes still train here. Hockey fans will recognize the **Olympic Center** (☑ 518-302-5326; www.whiteface.com; 2634 Main St; adult/child $7/5; ⏱ 10am-5pm; ♿) on Main St as the location of the 1980 'Miracle on Ice' when the upstart US hockey team managed to defeat the seemingly unstoppable Soviets. Not far from town on Rte 73 is the **Olympic Jumping Complex** (☑ 518-523-2202; www.whiteface.com; 5486 Cascade Rd ; adult/child $11/8; ⏱ hours vary seasonally) where you can take the elevator 20 stories up for impressive views. Seven miles to the south is **Mt Van Hoevenberg** (☑ 518-523-4436; 8 John Brown Rd, Rte 73, Lake Placid; adult/child $10/8, bobsled rides $30; ⏱ hr vary seasonally; ♿), home to Olympic 'sliding sports' where you can sign up for a bone-rattling, adrenalin-pumping ride on a bobsled, skeleton or luge during certain times of the year. Skiers should head to nearby **Whiteface Mountain** (www.whiteface.com), with 80 trails and a serious 3400ft vertical drop. Hotels, restaurants, bookstores and shops line the frontier-like main street in town, which actually fronts Mirror Lake. **Golden Arrow Lakeside Resort** (☑ 800-582-5540; www.golden-arrow.com; 2559 Main St, Lake Placid; r from $130; 🅿 ⏱ ✴ 🎅 🏊 ♿) 🍴, the only accommodation directly on the lake, has a variety of room types for families and couples alike.

South of Lake Placid town, **Adirondack Loj** (☑ 518-523-3441; www.adk.org; dm/r incl breakfast $50/155), run by the Adirondack Mountain Club (ADK), is a rustic retreat surrounded by mountains on the shore of peaceful Heart Lake. Wilderness campsites, lean-tos and cabins are also available.

Further north is the Saranac Lake region, where you'll find even more secluded wilderness areas – small lakes and ponds, ancient forests and wetlands. The town of **Saranac Lake** itself, once a center for tuberculosis treatments, feels a little down on its luck. Fourteen miles to the north is **White Pine Camp** (☑ 518-327-3030; www.whitepinecamp.com; 432 White Pine Rd, Paul Smiths; 2-person cottage from $105 late Oct-late Jun; weekly from $1085 mid-May–late Oct), one of the few remaining Adirondack 'great camps' where you can spend a night. Far from ostentatious or grand, White Pine is a collection of rustically cozy cabins set on scenic Osgood Pond.

WORTH A TRIP

THE THOUSAND ISLANDS

Virtually unknown to downstate New Yorkers, in part because of its relative inaccessibility, this region of over 1800 islands – from tiny outcroppings just large enough to lie down on to larger islands with roads and towns – is a scenic wonderland separating the US from Canada. From its source in the Atlantic Ocean far to the north, the wide and deceptively fast-moving St Lawrence River East empties into Lake Ontario at Cape Vincent. This portion of the river was once a summer playground for the very rich, who built large, stately homes here. It is still a popular vacation area known for its boating, camping and even shipwreck scuba diving.

The site of a major battle during the War of 1812, Sackets Harbor is on Lake Ontario but isn't technically part of the Thousand Islands. Still, it is a convenient starting point for touring the region. Several inviting restaurants with waterside patio seating line the street that runs down to the harbor front.

The relaxing, French-heritage village of **Cape Vincent** is at the western end of the river where it meets the lake. Drive out to the **Tibbetts Point Lighthouse** for stunning lake views; an attractive hostel (☎315-654-3450; www.hihostels.com; 33439 Co Rte 6; dm $25; ☺ Jul 1-Sep 15) shares the property. Nearby **Burnham Point State Park** (☎315-654-2522; Rte 12E; campsites $25) has wooded, lakeside campsites.

Fifteen miles to the east along the Seaway Trail (Rte 12), **Clayton** has more than a dozen marinas and a few good eating choices in an area generally bereft of them. The **Antique Boat Museum** (☎315-686-4104; www.abm.org; 750 Mary St, Clayton; adult/child $13/free; ☺9am-5pm mid-May–mid-Oct; ⓜ) actually lets you sail or row the old vessels as you learn about them. **TI Adventures** (☎315-686-2500; www.tiadventures.com; 1011 State St; half-day kayak rental $30) rents kayaks and runs white-water-rafting trips down the Black River. Similar activities are also organized by several companies in Watertown, a sizable city half an hour's drive to the south.

Lyric Coffee House (☎315-686-4700; 246 James St, Clayton; mains $7-24; ☺8am-8pm; ⓐ), surprisingly contemporary for Clayton, serves specialty coffee drinks, gelato and pastries. as well as meat, fish and pasta mains.

Further east, **Alexandria Bay** (Alex Bay), an early-20th-century resort town, is still the center of tourism on the American side – its sister city is Gananoque in Canada. While it is run-down and tacky, there's enough around to keep you occupied: go-karts, mini-golf and a **drive-in movie theater** (www.baydrivein.com; adult/child $5/2; ⓜ) are only minutes away. It's also the departure point for ferries to Heart Island, where **Boldt Castle** (☎315-482-9724; www.boldtcastle.com; adult/child $8/5.50; ☺10am-6:30pm mid-May–mid-Oct) marks the love story of a rags-to-riches New York hotelier who built the castle for his beloved wife, who died before its completion. The same hotelier once asked his chef to create a new salad dressing, which was popularized as 'Thousand Island' – an unfortunate blend of ketchup, mayonnaise and relish. **Uncle Sam's Boat Tours** (☎315-482-2611; www.usboattours.com; 45 James St; 2-nation tour adult/child $20/10) has several departures daily for its recommended two-nation cruise (visiting both the US and Canadian sides of the river), which allows you to stop at Boldt Castle and ride back on one of its half-hourly ferries for free.

Wellesley Island State Park (☎518-482-2722; www.nysparks.com; campsites from $15) offers camping, which is probably the best accommodations option even for the raccoon-averse. Many sites are almost directly on the riverfront and some have their own 'private' beaches. The island is only accessible by crossing a toll portion ($2.50) of the Thousand Islands Bridge.

There are several supposedly upscale resorts around Alex Bay, though none is especially good value. Probably the best midrange choice is **Capt Thomson's Resort** (☎315-482-9961; www.captthomsons.com; 45 James St; r $130-200; ⓟⓜⓜ) on the waterfront next to the office for Uncle Sam's Boat Tours.

Jet Blue (p1191) has regular daily flights to Hancock International Airport (SYR) in Syracuse, 90 minutes south. Several major car-rental agencies have offices in the airport. Cyclists will enjoy the mostly flat Scenic Byway Trail.

Around Lake Champlain

Since it was taken from the British in 1775 by the 'Green Mountain Boys,' **Fort Ticonderoga** (☑518-585-2821; www.fortticonderoga.org; 100 Fort Ti Rd; adult/child $17.50/8; ⊙9:30am-5pm May 17-Oct 20) has been synonymous with the American Revolution. Nowadays its buckling stone walls afford stellar views of Lake Champlain, and every summer the carefully preserved fort opens its museum and grounds for tours and reenactments.

Further north is **Crown Point State Historic Site** (☑518-597-4666; www.nysparks.com; 21 Grandview Dr, Crown Point; ⊙grounds 9am-6pm), the remains of two major 18th-century forts on a strategic promontory where Lake Champlain narrows between New York and Vermont.

Ausable Chasm (☑518-834-9990; www.ausablechasm.com; 2144 Rte 9; adult/child $17/10; ⊙9am-5pm summer, to 4pm rest of yr; ⊞) is a dramatically beautiful 2-mile long fissure carved from the sandstone by a gushing river over thousands of years. There are trails and walkways and rafting in summertime. **Essex Inn** (☑518-963-4400; www.essexinnessex.com; 2297 Main St, Essex; r from $225; ⊞⊛) in the town of Essex has beautifully renovated rooms in a 200-year old landmark building.

❶ Getting There & Around

Both **Greyhound** (www.greyhound.com) and **Adirondack Trailways** (www.trailwaysny.com) serve various towns in the region. A car is essential for exploring the area.

Western New York

Still trying to find their feet after hemorrhaging industries and population for over a decade, most of the cities in this region live in the shadow of Niagara Falls, a natural wonder that attracts upward of 12 million visitors from around the world per year. Buffalo was once a booming industrial center and the terminus of the Erie Canal, which used to serve as the transportation lifeline connecting the Great Lakes and the Atlantic Ocean; it now boasts an indigenous culinary scene and Bohemian enclaves. Syracuse and Rochester are both home to big universities.

Buffalo

This often maligned working-class city does have long, cold winters and its fair share of abandoned industrial buildings, but Buffalo also has a vibrant community of college students and thirty-somethings living well in cheap real estate and gorging on the city's affordable and tasty cuisine. Settled by the French in 1758 – its name is believed to derive from *beau fleuve* (beautiful river) – the city's illustrious past as a former trading post and later a booming manufacturing center and terminus of the Erie Canal means there's a certain nostalgia and hopefulness to ambitious revitalization plans (one calls for a massive expansion and relocation of the University of Buffalo medical school to downtown). Buffalo is about an eight-hour trip from New York City through the Finger

---

DON'T MISS

TUPPER & BLUE MOUNTAIN LAKES

Only a few miles east of Tupper Lake, an otherwise nondescript town, is the **Wild Center** (☑518-359-7800; www.wildcenter.org; 45 Museum Dr, Tupper Lake; adult/child $17/10, under 3 free; ⊙10am-6pm daily late May-early Sep, 10am-5pm Fri-Sun Sep-Mar, closed Apr; ⊞) ✐, a jewel of a museum dedicated to the ecology and conservation of the Adirondacks. Interactive exhibits make it great for kids, and walking trails lead to an oxbow overlook and the Raquette River. Don't miss the back-of-the-house tour, where you see the nuts and bolts of the operation such as freezers full of dead mice to feed the center's snakes, owls, skunks and other animals.

A wonderful more-than-a-full-day pairing with the Wild Center is the **Adirondack Museum** (☑518-352-7311; www.adkmuseum.org; 9097 Rte 30; adult/child $18/6; ⊙10am-5pm May 24-Oct 14; ⊞), which occupies a 30-acre compound overlooking Blue Mountain Lake. Lots of hands-on exhibits explore the human-centered story of the mountains, from the history of mining, logging and boat building to the role of tourism in the region's development.

Lakes region and only a half hour or so south of Niagara Falls.

The very helpful **Buffalo Niagara Convention & Visitors Bureau** (☑800-283-3256; www.visitbuffaloniagara.org; 617 Main St; ☉10am-4pm Mon-Fri, 10am-2pm Sat) located in a light-filled beaux arts–style shopping arcade (c 1892) has good walking-tour pamphlets and a small gift shop.

◉ Sights & Activities

Architecture buffs will enjoy a stroll around downtown – you can't miss City Hall – and the 'theater district,' which has several late-19th-century buildings with baroque, Italianate and art nouveau facades (for details check out www.walkbuffalo.com).

Once derelict, the city's redeveloped waterfront, now called **Canalside** (www.canalsidebuffalo.com), includes an attractive park space where you can board boat cruises and rent kayaks. Also check out the **Naval & Military Park** (www.buffalonavalpark.org; 1 Naval Park Cove; adult/child $10/6; ☉10am-5pm Apr-Oct, Sat & Sun Nov, closed Dec-Mar), a small museum with maritime war-related exhibits but more impressive are the two huge WWII-era ships and submarine (museum admission includes access to the ships). North of downtown, sprawling **Delaware Park** was designed by Frederick Law Olmsted. The **Elmwood** neighborhood is dotted with hip cafes, restaurants, boutiques and bookstores.

This is a hard-core sports town and locals live and die with the **NFL Buffalo Bills** (www.buffalobills.com) football team who play in Ralph Wilson Stadium in the suburb of Orchard Park and the **Buffalo Sabres** (www.sabres.com), the city's NHL ice-hockey team. In 2014 the Sabres are moving from the waterfront First Niagara Center to the **HARBORcenter**, a new development next door. A no less recommended option is to catch the **Buffalo Bisons** (www.bisons.com), the AAA affiliate of the major-league baseball team, the New York Mets, in their trendy-traditional downtown ballpark.

★**Albright-Knox Art Gallery** MUSEUM
(☑716-882-8700; www.albrightknox.org; 1285 Elmwood Ave; adult/child $12/5; ☉10am-5pm, closed Mon; car 198 West to Elmwood Ave S/Art Gallery) This low slung and sizable museum with a neoclassical facade includes some of the best of French Impressionists and American masters.

Darwin Martin House ARCHITECTURAL TOUR
(☑716-856-3858; www.darwinmartinhouse.org; 125 Jewett Pkwy; basic tour $15; in-depth tour incl Barton House $30; ☉guided tours by reservation only, closed Tue) One of Frank Lloyd Wright's most elaborate or fully realized Prairie-style homes, with especially remarkable designed glass, can be toured by appointment. The modernist visitor center next door provides historical context for Wright and the home.

Theodore Roosevelt Inaugural National Historic Site MUSEUM
(☑716-884-0095; www.nps.gov/thri; 641 Delaware Ave; adult/child $10/5; ☉tours hourly 9:30am-3:30pm Mon-Fri, from 12:30pm Sat & Sun) Guided tours of the Ansley-Wilcox house examine the tale of Teddy's emergency swearing-in here following the assassination of William McKinley in 1901 at the Pan American Exposition in Buffalo.

Burchfield Penney Art Center MUSEUM
(☑716-878-6011; www.burchfieldpenney.org; 1300 Elmwood Ave; adult/child $10/free; ☉10am-5pm Tue, Wed, Fri & Sat, to 9pm Thu, 1-5pm Sun) This modern museum exhibits mostly American art, from the late 19th century to contemporary.

🛏 Sleeping

Standard chains line the highways around the city and downtown has several large ones that cater mainly to business travelers like the Hyatt Regency and the affordable and recommended Hampton Inn & Suites Buffalo Downtown (rooms from $159).

Hostelling International – Buffalo Niagara HOSTEL $
(☑716-852-5222; www.hostelbuffalo.com; 667 Main St; dm/r $25/65; ✳@🛜) Budget travelers should head to this hostel conveniently located in Buffalo's downtown 'theater district' on the street where the light rail train runs. Though the furnishings could use an update – the basement and 2nd-floor lounges resemble suburban rec rooms c 1970 – it's a homey and secure place to bed down. Free coffee, tea, oatmeal and even complimentary bicycles available.

★**Hotel @ the Lafayette** BOUTIQUE HOTEL $$
(☑716-853-1505; www.thehotellafayette.com; 391 Washington St; r $169, ste from $200; P✳🛜) This grand seven-story French Renaissance building of the early 1900s, now restored and open for business in 2012, stands

impressively intact. The cool and stylish furnishings in the rooms and suites can't compete with the art-deco lobby and marble hallway; several recommended restaurants and a bar on the premises.

★ **Mansion on Delaware Avenue** HOTEL $$$
(☑716-886-3300; www.mansionondelaware.com; 414 Delaware Ave; r/ste incl breakfast from $190/390; P✳@⊜) For truly special and classy accommodations and flawless service, head to this hotel housed in a grand and regal home c 1862. Ask for room 200 – it has a fireplace and floor-to-ceiling windows. Noteworthy complimentary perks are two daily self-serve drinks from the light-filled lounge area and car service within a range of 3 miles of the hotel.

✗ Eating

Buffalo has an abundance of eateries serving unique, tasty and cheap dishes. Stylish and quality restaurants are scattered around downtown, Allentown, Elmwood and the suburbs. Chef-cum-restaurateur Mike Andrzejewski has a burgeoning mini-empire that includes Seabar (Japanese), Tappo (Italian), Mike A's (steakhouse) and Cantina Loco (Mexican); all are recommended for both their food and ambience.

★ **Anchor Bar** AMERICAN $
(☑716-886-8920; 1047 Main St; 10/20 wings $13/20; ◷10am-11pm Mon-Thu, 10am-1am Fri & Sat) For the famous deep-fried chicken wings covered in a spicy sauce (as well as pizza, pasta, sandwiches, burgers, etc), head to this landmark, which claims credit for inventing the delicacy. Walls are covered with license plates and other roadside memorabilia, and the whole place, including the central bar, has a honky-tonk vibe.

Cantina Loco MEXICAN $
(www.cantinaloco.com; 191 Allen St; mains $7; ◷4-10pm Mon-Thu, to 11pm Fri & Sat, 4-8pm Sun) Hip and lively, even on summertime Monday nights when the backyard patio also fills up, this Allentown restaurant serves up tacos, burritos and quesadillas. Some come with a twist like the Koreatown (Kalbi short ribs, kimchee and soy sauce). The desserts are excellent and super-efficient bartenders really know their mescals.

Ted's FAST FOOD $
(www.tedsonline.com; 7018 Transit Rd; hot dog $2; ◷10:30am-11pm Mon-Sun) Ted's fast-food specialty is hot dogs, foot-longs, any way you like 'em.

Ulrich's Tavern GERMAN $$
(☑716-855-8409; 674 Ellicott St; mains $15; ◷11am-3pm Mon-Wed, 11am-10pm Thu & Fri, 3-9pm Sat) One of Buffalo's oldest taverns has warped floors, dark-wood walls and gut-busting German specialties like liverwurst and red onions on rye, and a fish fry that comes with red cabbage, sauerkraut, potatoes and vegetables.

Betty's MODERN AMERICAN $$
(☑716-362-0633; 370 Virginia St; mains $9-22; ◷8am-9pm Tue, 8am-10pm Wed-Fri, 9am-10pm Sat, 9am-3pm Sun) On a quiet Allentown corner, slightly funky and bohemian Betty's does healthy and flavorful interpretations of American comfort food like meatloaf. Brunch is deservedly popular.

⚲ Drinking & Entertainment

A handful of bars along Chippewa St (aka Chip Strip) are open until 4am and cater primarily to the frat-boy crowd. More eclectic neighborhoods such as Elmwood, Linwood and Allentown have more than their fair share of late-night options. Allen St has a few dive bars with live music clustered near one another, including Nietzches and Duke's Bohemian Grove Bar. Several gay bars are around the south end of Elmwood. From June through August a **summer concert series** (☑716-856-3150; www.buffaloplace.com) draws an eclectic mix of new and established artists to outdoor spaces in downtown.

Pan American Grill & Brewery BREWERY
(☑716-856-0062; 391 Washington St, Hotel Lafayette; mains $9-18; ◷11am-10pm Mon-Thu, to midnight Fri & Sat, noon-10pm Sun) Several rooms, including two massive old-school mahogany bars, a lounge themed on a Teddy Roosevelt hunting lodge, and a mural room with vaulted ceilings, make up this space, which occupies a good chunk of Hotel Lafayette's ground floor. Their own beer is brewed in the basement and an excellent kitchen does standards such as burgers ($13) and chops ($14), but also dishes like a flatbread duck confit and goat cheese ($8).

Founding Fathers BAR
(75 Edward St; ◷11:30am-1am Mon-Thu, to 2am Fri, to 4am Sat, 5-11pm Sun) The theme of this small, laid-back neighborhood bar just north of downtown is American presidents, and this, ironically or not, attracts a coterie of local po-

liticos. A small menu with good sandwiches ($9) and free popcorn and nachos.

Allen Street Hardware Cafe BAR
(☑ 716-882-8843; 245 Allen St) Amid a block of dive bars, this more sophisticated bar and restaurant (mains $14 to $25) hosts performances by the best local musicians.

ⓘ Getting There & Around

Buffalo Niagara International Airport (BUF; ☑ 716-630-6000; www.buffaloairport.com), about 10 miles east of downtown, is a regional hub. Jet Blue Airways offers affordable round-trip fares from New York City. Buses arrive and depart from the **Greyhound terminal** (181 Ellicott St) (aka Buffalo Transportation Center). **NFTA** (www.nfta.com) local bus 40 and express bus 60 go to the transit center on the American side of Niagara Falls ($2, one hour). From the downtown **Amtrak train station** (☑ 716-856-2075; 75 Exchange St), you can catch trains to major cities to NYC ($88, eight hours) and Albany ($48, six hours). The Exchange Street station can feel dodgy, especially at night; locals recommend the **Buffalo-Depew station** (55 Dick Rd), 6 miles east.

Niagara Falls & Around

It's a tale of two cities and two falls, though either side of this international border affords views of an undeniably dramatic natural wonder. There are honeymooners and heart-shaped Jacuzzis, arcades, tacky shops and kitsch boardwalk-style sights, but as long as your attention is focused nothing can detract from the majestic sight. The closer to the falls you get the more impressive they seem and the wetter you become. For good reason, the Canadian side is where almost everyone visits, though it's easy to stroll back and forth between the two (bring your passport). The New York side is dominated by the purple, glass-covered Seneca Niagara Casino & Hotel, which towers over the surrounding derelict blocks.

◉ Sights & Activities

The falls are in two separate towns: Niagara Falls, New York (USA) and Niagara Falls, Ontario (Canada). The towns face each other across the Niagara River, spanned by the Rainbow Bridge, which is accessible for cars and pedestrians. Famous landscape architect Frederick Law Olmstead helped rescue and preserve the New York side, which by the 1870s was dominated by industry and gaudy signs. You can see views of the **American Falls** and their western portion, the **Bridal Veil Falls**, which drop 180ft from the **Prospect Point Observation Tower** (☑ 716-278-1796; admission $1, free from 5pm; ⊙ 9:30am-7pm). Cross the small bridge to **Goat Island** for close-up viewpoints, including Terrapin Point, which has a fine view of Horseshoe Falls and pedestrian bridges to the Three Sisters Islands in the upper rapids. From the north corner of Goat Island, an elevator descends to the **Cave of the Winds** (☑ 716-278-1730; adult/child $11/8), where walkways go within 25ft of the cataracts (raincoats provided).

The **Maid of the Mist** (☑ 716-284-8897; www.maidofthemist.com; 151 Buffalo Ave; adult/child $15.50/9; ⊙ 9am-7pm summer, times vary so check website) boat trip around the bottom of the falls has been a major attraction since 1846 and is highly recommended. Boats leave from the base of the Prospect Park Observation Tower on the US side and from the bottom of Clifton Hill on the Canadian side.

For those seeking more of an adrenaline rush, check out **Whirlpool Jet Boat Tours**

BORDER CROSSING: CANADIAN NIAGARA FALLS

When people say they are visiting the falls they usually mean the Canadian side, which is naturally blessed with superior views. Canada's **Horseshoe Falls** are wider and especially photogenic from Queen Victoria Park; at night they're illuminated with a colored light show. The **Journey Behind the Falls** (☑ 905-354-1551; 6650 Niagara Pkwy; adult/child Apr-Dec $15.95/10.95, Dec-Apr $11.25/6.95; ⊙ 9am-6pm, opens later in summer) gives access to a spray-soaked viewing area beneath the falls. **Niagara on the Lake**, 15km to the north, is a small town full of elegant B&Bs and a famous summertime theater festival.

Virtually every major hotel chain has at least several locations on the Canadian side of the falls. Obvious tourist-trap restaurants are a dime a dozen in and around Clifton Hill. American fare and chains dominate the culinary scene. The Lundy's Lane area has tons of cheap eats.

(☑888-438-4444; www.whirlpooljet.com; 1hr adult/child $50/42), which leave from **Lewiston**, a charming town with several good eateries 8 miles north of Niagara Falls. Shoppers can head to the **Fashion Outlets of Niagara Falls**, a few miles west of town, for designer-wear discounts.

Northeast of Niagara Falls is the town of **Lockport**, the western terminus of the Erie Canal. There's an excellent visitors center and **museum** and **boat tours** during the summer months.

🛏 Sleeping & Eating

Most all of the national hotel chains are represented – Ramada Inn, Howard Johnson, Holiday Inn. However, the quality of the pickings are poor compared to the Canadian side. There are a few restaurants near the bridge area, including several Indian takeaway places.

★**Giacomo**　　　　　　BOUTIQUE HOTEL **$$**
(☑716-299-0200; www.thegiacomo.com; 220 First St; r from $150; P✱☀) The equal of any Canadian-side lodging in terms of stylish comfort, the Giacomo occupies a renovated 1929 art-deco office tower. While the majority of floors are taken up by high-end condos, the three-dozen spacious rooms are luxuriously appointed and the 19th-floor lounge offers spectacular falls views.

Buzzy's　　　　　　　　PIZZA **$**
(☑716-283-5333; 7617 Niagara Falls Blvd; mains $6-15; ⊙11am-11pm Sun-Thu, to midnight Fri & Sat) New York–style pizza, spicy buffalo wings, calzones, subs and hoagies for hungry crowds who like to drink beer and watch sports.

ⓘ Information

On the US side, the **Niagara Tourism & Convention Corporation** (☑716-282-8992; www.niagara-usa.com; 10 Rainbow Blvd; ⊙9am-7pm Jun-Sep 15, to 5pm Sep 16-May 31) has all sorts of guides; its Canadian counterpart is located near the base of the **Skylon Tower** (☑905-356-6061; www.niagarafallstourism.com; 5400 Robinson St, Skylon Tower; ⊙9am-5pm).

ⓘ Getting There & Around

NFTA (Niagara Frontier Transportation Authority; www.nfta.com) bus 40 and express bus 60 connect downtown Buffalo and Niagara Falls ($2, one hour). The stop in Niagara Falls is at First and Rainbow Blvd (there's no reason to go to the terminal at Main and Pine Sts). Taxis run

around $75. The **Amtrak train station** (27th St, at Lockport Rd) is about 2 miles northeast of downtown. From Niagara Falls, daily trains go to Buffalo (35 minutes), Toronto (three hours) and New York City (nine hours); fares vary depending on time and day. **Greyhound** (www.greyhound. com; 303 Rainbow Blvd) buses are run out of the Daredevil Museum.

Parking costs $8 to $10 a day on either side of the falls. Most of the midrange hotels offer complimentary parking to guests, while upscale hotels (on the Canadian side) tend to charge $15 to $20 a day for the privilege.

Crossing the Rainbow Bridge to Canada and returning costs US$3.25/1 per car/pedestrian. There are customs and immigration stations at each end – US citizens and overseas visitors are required to have their passport or an enhanced driver's license. Driving a rental car from the US over the border should not be a problem, but check with your rental company before you depart.

NEW JERSEY

There are McMansions, à la the *Real Housewives of New Jersey*, guys who speak with thick Jersey accents like characters from a TV crime drama, and guidos and guidettes who spend their days GTL'ing (gym, tan and laundry) on the Shore. However, the state is at least as well defined by high-tech and banking headquarters and sophisticated, progressive people living in charming towns. Get off the exits, flee the malls and you are privy to a beautiful side of the state: a quarter is farmland and it has 127 miles of beautiful beaches and charming and fun beachside towns, as well as two of New York City's greatest icons: the Statue of Liberty and Ellis Island.

ⓘ Information

NJ.com (www.nj.com) Statewide news from all the major dailies including the *Newark Star-Leger* and Hudson County's *Jersey Journal*.

New Jersey Monthly (www.njmonthly.com) Monthly glossy with features on attractions and other stories relevant to visitors.

New Jersey Department of Environmental Protection (www.state.nj.us/dep/parksandforests) Comprehensive information on all state parks, including camping and historic sites.

ⓘ Getting There & Away

Though NJ is made up of folks who love their cars, there are other transportation options:

New Jersey PATH Train (www.panynj.gov/path) Connects lower Manhattan to Hoboken, Jersey City and Newark.

New Jersey Transit (www.njtransit.com) Operates buses out of NYC's Port Authority and trains out of Penn Station, NYC.

New York Waterway (☑ 800-533-3779; www.nywaterway.com) Its ferries make runs up the Hudson River Valley and from Midtown to Yankee Stadium in the Bronx. A popular commuter route goes from the New Jersey Transit train station in Hoboken to the World Financial Center in Lower Manhattan.

Northern New Jersey

Stay east and you'll experience the Jersey urban jungle. Go west to find its opposite: the peaceful, refreshing landscape of the Delaware Water Gap and rolling Kittatinny Mountains.

Hoboken & Jersey City

A sort of TV-land version of a cityscape, Hoboken is a cute little urban pocket just across the Hudson River from NYC – and, because of cheaper rents that lured pioneers almost 15 years ago, a sort of sixth city borough, too. On weekends the bars and live-music venues come alive, but the town also has loads of restaurants lining commercial Washington St, some lovely residential lanes and a leafy, revitalized waterfront – a far cry from when the gritty *On the Waterfront* was filmed here.

High-rise buildings housing condominiums and the offices of financial firms seeking lower rents have transformed **Jersey City** for better or worse from a primarily blue-collar and immigrant neighborhood into a 'restored' area for the upwardly mobile. Its biggest draw is the 1200-acre **Liberty State Park** (☑ 201-915-3440; www.libertystatepark.org; ☺ 6am-10pm), which hosts outdoor concerts with the Manhattan skyline as a backdrop and has a great bike trail, and also operates **ferries** (☑ 201-604-2800, 877-523-9849; www.statuecruises.com; adult/child $17/9; ☺ every 30min 9am-5pm, extended summer hr) to Ellis Island and the Statue of Liberty. Also in the park and great for kids – virtually every exhibit is interactive – is the expansive and modern **Liberty Science Center** (☑ 201-200-1000; www.lsc.org; adult/child $19.75/14.75, extra for IMAX & special exhibits; ☺ 9am-4pm Mon-Fri, to 5:30pm Sat & Sun; ⓓ).

Delaware Water Gap

The Delaware River meanders in a tight S-curve through the ridge of NJ's Kittatinny Mountains, and its beauteous image turned this region into a resort area, beginning in the 19th century. The **Delaware Water Gap National Recreation Area** (☑ 570-426-2452; www.nps.gov), which comprises land in both New Jersey and Pennsylvania, was established as a protected area in 1965, and today it's still an unspoiled place to swim, boat, fish, camp, hike and see wildlife – just 70 miles east of New York City. The 30 mile stretch of good paved road on the Pennsylvania side has several worthwhile stops including **Raymondskill Falls** and the **Pocono Environmental Education Center** (☑ 570-828-2319; www.peec.org; 538 Emery Rd,

---

NEW JERSEY FACTS

Nickname Garden State

Population 8.8 million

Area 8722 sq miles

Capital city Trenton (population 85,000)

Other cities Newark (population 277,000)

Sales tax 7%

Birthplace of Musician Count Basie (1904–84), singer Frank Sinatra (1915–98), actor Meryl Streep (b 1949), musician Bruce Springsteen (b 1949), actor John Travolta (b 1954), musician Jon Bon Jovi (b 1962), rapper Queen Latifah (b 1970), pop band Jonas Brothers: Kevin (b 1987), Joseph (b 1989), Nicolas (b 1992)

Home of The first movie (1889), first professional baseball game (1896), first drive-in theater (1933), the Statue of Liberty

Politics Republican governor Chris Christie, though strong traditionally Democratic legislature

Famous for *The Jersey Shore* (the real thing and the MTV reality show), the setting for *The Sopranos*, Bruce Springsteen's musical beginnings

Number of wineries Thirty six

Driving distances Princeton to NYC 55 miles, Atlantic City to NYC 135 miles

Dingman's Ferry; 🏕) 🎣; the very developed but stunning **Bushkill Falls** (☑570-588-6682; Rte 209, Bushkill; adult/child $12.50/7; ⊗opens 9am, closing times vary, closed Dec-Mar) is several miles to the north. On the New Jersey side, take Old Mine Rd, one of the oldest continually operating commercial roads in the US, to trailheads for day hikes such as the one to the top of the 1574ft Mt Tammany in **Worthington State Forest** (☑908-841-9575; www.njparksandforests.org).

For river fun, contact **Adventure Sports** (☑570-223-0505, 800-487-2628; www.adventuresport.com; Rte 209; per day canoe/kayak $40/44; ⊗9am-6pm Mon-Fri, from 8am Sat & Sun May-Oct) in Marshalls Creek, Pennsylvania. There are several different put-in and take-out points that allow a variety of itineraries. Camping is allowed at many points along the way and is a great way to experience the beauty of the area.

Northeast of here, **High Point State Park** (☑973-875-4800; www.njparksandforests. org; 1480 Rte 23, Sussex; ⊗8am-8pm Apr-Oct, to 4:30pm other months), which is also great for camping and hiking, has a monument that, at 1803ft above sea level, affords wonderful views of surrounding lakes, hills and farmland.

The nearby town of **Milford** across the border in Pennsylvania is a charming place with several good restaurants and **Grey Towers** (☑570-296-9630; www.greytowers. org; Old Owego Turnpike; tours adult/child $8/ free; ⊗grounds dawn-dusk), once the gorgeous French chateau-style home of Gifford Pinchot, the first director of the US Forest Service and a two-term governor of Pennsylvania.

Princeton & Around

Settled by an English Quaker missionary, the tiny town of Princeton is filled with lovely architecture and several noteworthy sites, number one of which is its Ivy League **Princeton University** (www.princeton.edu), which was built in the mid-1700s and soon became one of the largest structures in the early colonies. The town's **Palmer Square**, built in 1936, is a lovely place to shop and stroll. The **Historical Society of Princeton** (☑609-921-6748; www.princetonhistory.org; 158 Nassau St; tours adult/child $7/4) leads historical walking tours of the town on Sundays at 2pm, and the **Orange Key Guide Service & Campus Information Office** (☑609-258-3060; www.princeton.edu/orangekey) offers free university tours. The **Princeton University Art Museum** (☑609-258-3788; www.princetonartmuseum.org; McCormack Hall, Princeton University Campus; ⊗10am-5pm, to 10pm Thu) **FREE** is akin to a mini-Metropolitan Museum of Art in terms of its variety and quality of works, which range from ancient Greek pottery to Andy Warhol.

Accommodations are expensive and hard to find during graduation time in May and June, but beyond that it should be easy to arrange for a stay at one of several atmospheric inns, including the traditionally furnished **Nassau Inn** (☑609-921-7500; www. nassauinn.com; 10 Palmer Sq; r incl breakfast from $169; ❇🖸🐾). For reasonably priced healthy Mediterranean-style food with a Greek emphasis stop by **Olives** (22 Witherspoon St, Princeton; sandwiches $7; ⊗7am-8pm) for lunchtime takeout.

It may not be the most beautiful place, but New Jersey's capital, **Trenton**, has several historic sites, a museum and a farmers market worth visiting – especially if you can pair it up with a trip to Philly or Atlantic City.

Jersey Shore

Perhaps the most famous and revered feature of New Jersey is its sparkling shore (www.visitthejerseyshore.com), stretching from Sandy Hook to Cape May and studded with resort towns ranging from tacky to classy. You'll find as many mothers pushing strollers as throngs proudly clutching souvenir beer bongs. Though it's mobbed during summer weekends, you could find yourself wonderfully alone on the sand come early fall. Beach access varies across communities, though the majority charge reasonably priced fees for the day. Putting up a tent in a state park or private campground is a low cost alternative during the summer months when finding good-value accommodations is nearly as difficult as locating un-tattooed skin.

Sandy Hook & Around

At the northernmost tip of the Jersey Shore is the **Sandy Hook Gateway National Recreation Area** (☑718-354-4606), a 7-mile sandy barrier beach at the entrance to New York Harbor. You can see the city skyline from your beach blanket on clear days, which only heightens the sense of pleasure and feeling of dislocation. The ocean side of the peninsula has wide, sandy beaches (including a nude beach, the only legal one in NJ, at Gunnison Beach) edged by an extensive system of bike trails, while the bay side is great for fishing or wading. The brick buildings of the abandoned coast-guard station, **Fort Hancock** (⊙1-5pm Sat & Sun) FREE, house a small museum. The **Sandy Hook Lighthouse**, which offers guided tours, is the oldest in the country. Bug spray is recommended as biting flies can be a nuisance at dusk.

A fast ferry service, **Seastreak** (📞800-262-8743; www.seastreak.com; 2 First Ave, Atlantic Highlands; return $45), runs between Sandy Hook (and the Highlands) and Pier 11 in downtown Manhattan or East 35th St, NYC.

Long Branch, Asbury Park & Ocean Grove

Sanitized and slightly generic compared to other shore locations, **Long Branch** is the first major beach town south of the Highlands. Just a bit inland from here is the famed **Monmouth Park Race Track** (📞732-222-5100; www.monmouthpark.com; grandstand/clubhouse $3/5; ⊙11:30am-6pm May-Aug), where you can see thoroughbred racing in a gracious, historic setting.

Just south of Long Branch, massive homes the size of museums in the community of **Deal** are worth gawking at. However, once you cross over Deal Lake into **Asbury Park**, luxury gives way to abandoned row houses and potholed streets. But the town, which experienced passing prominence in the 1970s when Bruce Springsteen 'arrived' at the **Stone Pony** (📞732-502-0600; 913 Ocean Ave) nightclub and then a major decline, has been revitalized. Led by wealthy gay men from NYC who snapped up blocks of forgotten Victorian homes and storefronts to refurbish, the downtown (the liveliest on the shore), which includes several blocks of Cookman and Bangs Aves, is lined with charming shops, restaurants, bars and a restored art-house cinema. The sprawling **Antique Emporium of Asbury Park** (📞732-774-8230; 646 Cookman Ave; ⊙11am-5pm Mon-Sat & noon-5pm Sun) has two levels of amazing finds.

The town immediately to the south, **Ocean Grove**, is a fascinating place to wander. Founded by Methodists in the 19th century, the place retains what's left of a post–Civil War revival camp called **Tent City** – now a historic site with 114 cottage-like canvas tents clustered together, which are used as summer homes. The town has dazzling well-preserved Victorian architecture and a 6500-seat wooden auditorium, and there are many beautiful, big-porched **Victorian inns** to choose from for a stay; visit www.oceangrovenj.com for guidance. A few miles inland just off the Garden State Pkwy is a very utilitarian-looking **Premium outlet mall**.

Bradley Beach to Spring Lake

Bradley Beach has row after row of adorable summer cottages and a beautiful stretch of shore. **Belmar Beach** is equally inviting and has a boardwalk with a few food shacks and a handful of restaurants and busy bars on the oceanfront road. The **New Jersey Sandcastle Contest** (www.njsandcastle.com) is held here in mid-July.

South of here is **Spring Lake**, a wealthy community once known as the 'Irish Riviera,' with manicured lawns, grand oceanfront Victorian houses, a gorgeous beach and elegant accommodations. This quiet low-key base is about as far from the typical shore boardwalk experience as you can get. Try the bright and airy **Grand Victorian at Spring Lake** (📞732-449-5237; www.grandvictorianspringlake.com; 1505 Ocean Ave; r with shared/private bath with breakfast from $100/150; ※ 🗢).

HURRICANE SANDY

In late October 2012 Hurricane Sandy devastated much of the New York and New Jersey coastline, destroying homes, breaching barrier islands, ripping away boardwalks and washing away entire waterfront communities. In New York the hardest hit were Staten Island, the Rockaways and Red Hook, while the Jersey Shore from Sandy Hook to Atlantic City suffered the brunt of the hurricane's impact. The dimensions and profiles of many beaches were diminished and it remains to be seen whether rebuilding efforts will add dunes and other storm surge impediments where none existed before. More than six months later, there are still significant pockets of desolation: piles of debris, houses with their sides ripped away and others that teeter at gravity-defying angles.

Only 5 miles inland from Spring Lake is quirky **Historic Village at Allaire** (☏732-919-3500; www.allairevillage.org; adult/child $3/2; ◷noon-4pm Wed-Sun late May-early Sep, noon-4pm Sat & Sun Nov-May), the remains of what was a thriving 19th-century village called Howell Works. You can still visit various 'shops,' all run by folks in period costume.

Ocean County Beaches

Just south of the Manasquan River is **Point Pleasant**. The northern end of the town boardwalk is backed by small, idiosyncratic vacation homes only feet from the beach-going hordes; the southern half, called **Jenkinson's Boardwalk**, has the usual salt-water taffy shops, eateries and amusement rides, as well as an aquarium good for kids and an enormous bar and restaurant for adults jutting out over the beach. A few sea-food restaurants with outdoor patios built over the water can be found on a marina and inlet of the river – try the **Shrimp Box** (75 Inlet Dr; sandwiches $10, mains $17; ◷noon-10:30pm). Just north of here in Manasquan, **Inlet Beach** has the Shore's most reliable year-round waves for surfers.

Just below there, the narrow **Barnegat Peninsula** barrier island extends some 22 miles south from Point Pleasant. In its center, **Seaside Heights** of MTV reality-show

Jersey Shore fame sucks in the raucous twenty-something summer crowds with two amusement piers (one of these was torn apart by Hurricane Sandy, leaving the *Star Jet* roller coaster stranded in the ocean until June 2013) and an above-average number of boardwalk bars. Because the beach is relatively narrow, this is not the place to go for privacy or quiet. Better yet, ride the **chair lift** running from the Casino Pier to the northern end of the boardwalk. If the ocean is not to your taste, beat the heat on the lazy river at the **Breakwater Beach Waterpark** (www.casinopiernj.com/breakwaterbeach; admission $25; ◷10am-7pm May-Aug; ⊞). There isn't much to recommend about a stay at one of the crash pads on the neglected sun-baked streets inland from the boardwalk. Camping at **Surf & Stream Campground** (☏732-349-8919; www.surfnstream.com; 1801 Ridgeway Rd/Rte 571, Toms River; campsites $45) in Tom's River about 6 miles to the west is a convenient option. Tucked away in the K-Mart shopping plaza in Tom's River is the silly and sarcastically named **Shut Up and Eat!** (☏732-349-4544; 213 Rte 37 East; mains $9), where wait-resses in pajamas adept at snappy repartee serve up stuffed French toast, pancakes and more. Just to the north of Seaside Heights in Lavallette is **Music Man** (☏732-854-2779; www.njmusicman.com; 2305 Grand Central Ave/Rte 35, Lavallette; ice cream $3-8; ◷takeout 6am-

PINE BARRENS

Locals call this region the Pinelands – and like to carry on the lore about the one million acres of pine forest being home to a mythical beast known as the 'Jersey Devil.' Containing several state parks and forests, the area is a haven for bird-watchers, hikers, campers, canoeists and all-round nature enthusiasts. Inland is the **Wharton State Forest** (☏609-561-0024), one of the good places to canoe – as well as hike and picnic. To understand the region's early history, begin at the well-preserved village of **Batsto** founded in 1766 to forge 'bog iron' for the Revolutionary War. The best-known trail is the epic 50-mile **Batona Trail**, which cuts through several state parks and forests and passes by the **Apple Pie Hill Fire Tower**, from which there are magnificent 360-degree views of hundreds of square miles of forest. A good outfitter is **Micks Pine Barrens Canoe and Kayak Rental** (☏609-726-1515; www.pinebarrenscanoe.com; 3107 Rte 563; per day kayak/canoe $37/48), which has maps and other details about boating trips in the area. Further south along the coast is the **Edwin B Forsythe National Wildlife Refuge** (☏609-652-1665), 40,000 acres of bays, coves, forests, marshes, swamps, and barrier beaches and a paradise for bird-watchers. A recommended camping spot is the lakeside **Atsion Family Campground** (☏609-268-0444; www.state.nj.us; 31 Batsto Rd; tent sites $20; ◷Apr 31-Oct 1) in Wharton State Forest; nearby, between Atsion and the town of Hammonton is **Penza's** (☏609-567-3412; 51 Myrtle St, Hammonton; mains 5-$10; ◷8am-5pm), an old-fashioned cafe in a red barn serving great omelets and homemade fruit pies.

midnight, shows 6pm-midnight; 🛗), an ice-cream shop where servers belt out Broadway show tunes tableside.

Occupying the southern third of Barnegat Peninsula is **Island Beach State Park** (📞 732-793-0506; www.islandbeachnj.org; per car weekday/weekend $6/10), a 10-mile barrier island that's pure, untouched dunes and wetlands. Although the very southern tip of the park is within throwing distance of **Long Beach Island**, just across a narrow inlet to the bay south of here, to reach this long sliver of an island with beautiful beaches and impressive summer homes you have to backtrack all the way to Seaside Heights and travel along Rte 9 or the Garden State Pkwy. The landmark **Barnegat Lighthouse State Park** (📞 609-494-2016; www.njparksand-forests.org; off Long Beach Blvd; ⊙ 8am-4pm), at the very northern tip of the island, offers panoramic views at the top while fishermen cast off from a jetty extending 2000ft along the Atlantic Ocean. Tucked down a residential street in North Beach Haven is **Hudson House** (13th St, Beach Haven; ⊙ 5pm-1am), a nearly locals-only dive bar about as worn and comfortable as an old pair of flip-flops. A few miles south of Rte 72, which bisects Long Beach Island, is **Daddy O** (📞 609-361-5100; www.daddyohotel.com; 4401 Long Beach Blvd; r $195-375), a sleek boutique hotel and restaurant near the ocean.

Atlantic City

It's not exactly Vegas, but for many a trip to AC conjures up *Hangover*-like scenes of debauchery. And inside the casinos, which never see the light of day, it's easy to forget there's a sandy beach just outside and boarded-up shop windows a few blocks in the other direction. The 'AC' that was known throughout the late 19th and early 20th century for its grand boardwalk and Oceanside amusement pier, and for the glamorous corruption depicted in the HBO series *Boardwalk Empire* set in 1920 Prohibition-era AC, has been thoroughly overturned. Gray-haired retirees and vacationing families are at least as common as bachelors and bachelorettes.

It's worth nothing that AC's famous boardwalk, 8 miles long and still the lifeline of the city, was the first in the world. Built in 1870 by local business owners who wanted to cut down on sand being tracked into hotel lobbies, it was named in honor of Alexander Boardman who came up with the idea – Boardman's Walk later became 'Boardwalk'.

The Steel Pier, directly in front of the Taj Mahal casino, was the site of the famous high-diving horse that plunged into the Atlantic before crowds of spectators. Today it's a collection of amusement rides, games of chance, candy stands and a go-kart track.

The small **Atlantic City Historical Museum** (📞 609-347-5839; www.acmuseum.org; Garden Pier; ⊙ 10am-5pm) `FREE` provides a quirky look at AC's past. At the time of research it was closed due to damage from Hurricane Sandy, but was expected to reopen.

🛏 Sleeping & Eating

A handful of motor inns and cheap motels line Pacific Ave, a block inland from the boardwalk. Most of the big boardwalk hotel casinos offer extremely reduced rates midweek out of season (September to May). Some of the best in-casino dining is to be had at the Borgata. Good (and more affordable) food can be found in the 'real' part of downtown and in nearby Ventnor and Margate.

Chelsea BOUTIQUE HOTEL $
(📞 800-548-3030; www.thechelsea-ac.com; 111 S Chelsea Ave; r from $80; 🅿✳@🛜🌊) Non-casino, trendy with art-deco-style furnishings. Rooms in the attached annex are less expensive. Also houses a retro diner, steakhouse and cabana club.

Revel AC RESORT $$
(📞 609-572-6488; www.revelresorts.com; 500 Boardwalk; r from $160; 🅿✳@🛜🌊🐕) This 47-story $2.4 billion newcomer occupies a relatively isolated spot at the far northern end of the AC boardwalk; with a big beach in front – all rooms have ocean views. The Revel has all the bells and whistles you'd expect plus a concert hall and 12 restaurants, including a Mexican food truck parked indoors.

Kelsey & Kim's Café BARBECUE $
(201 Melrose Ave; mains $9; ⊙ 7am-10pm) Excellent Southern comfort food like fried whiting, pulled BBQ beef brisket sandwich and fried chicken.

Angelo's Fairmount Tavern ITALIAN $
(2300 Fairmount Ave; mains $7; ⊙ 11:30am-3pm & 5-10pm) Angelo's Fairmount Tavern is a beloved family-owned Italian restaurant. The outdoor patio makes a nice spot to take in the sunset and have a pint and a burger.

ℹ️ Information

The **Atlantic City Convention & Visitors Bureau** (☑ 609-348-7100; www.atlanticcitynj. com; 2314 Pacific Ave; ☺ 9am-5pm) has a location in the middle of the Atlantic City Expwy and another right on the boardwalk at Mississippi Ave. **Atlantic City Weekly** (www.acweekly.com) has useful info on events, clubs and eateries.

ℹ️ Getting There & Away

Air Tran and Spirit Airlines fly into the small **Atlantic City International Airport** (ACY; ☑ 609-645-7895; www.acairport.com), a 20-minute drive from the center of Atlantic City and a great option for reaching any part of South Jersey or Philadelphia.

There are many bus options to AC, including NJ Transit (one way $36, 2½ hours) and Greyhound (one way $25, 2½ hours), both leaving from New York's Port Authority (p116). A casino will often refund much of the fare (in chips, coins or coupons) if you get a bus directly to its door. Take note that when leaving AC, buses first stop at various casinos and only stop at the bus station when not full.

New Jersey Transit (☑ 800-772-2287; www. njtransit.com) trains only go to Atlantic City from Philadelphia (one way $10, 1½ hours).

Ocean City & The Wildwoods

South of Atlantic City, **Ocean City** is an old-fashioned family-holiday spot, home to dune-swept beaches and a number of child-centric arcades, a small waterpark, mini-golf courses and themed playlands along its lively boardwalk. Motels are plentiful, relatively cheap and old-fashioned, as are the myriad crab shacks and seafood joints.

Further south on the way to Cape May, the three towns of **North Wildwood**, **Wildwood** and **Wildwood Crest** are an archaeological find – whitewashed motels with flashing neon signs, turquoise curtains and pink doors, especially in Wildwood Crest, a kitsch slice of 1950s Americana. Check out eye-catching motel signs like the **Lollipop** at 23rd and Atlantic Aves. Wildwood, a party town popular with teens, twenty-somethings and the young people who staff the restaurants and shops, is the main social focus. The width of the beach, more than 1000ft in parts, makes it the widest in NJ and means there's always space. Several massive piers are host to **water parks** and **amusement parks** – easily the rival of any Six Flags Great Adventure – with roller coasters and rides best suited to aspir-

ing astronauts anchoring the 2-mile-long Grand Daddy of Jersey Shore boardwalks. Glow-in-the-dark 3D mini-golf is a good example of the Wildwood boardwalk ethos – take it to the limit, then one step further. Maybe the best ride of all, and one that doesn't induce nausea, is the **tram** (one-way $2.50; ☺ 9am-1am) running the length of the boardwalk from Wildwood Crest to North Wildwood. There's always a line for a table at Jersey Shore staple pizzeria **Mack & Manco's** on the boardwalk (it has other shore boardwalk locations).

About 250 small motels – no corporate chains here – offer rooms for $50 to $250; however, it makes sense to narrow your search to the more salubrious area of Wildwood Crest. The sea-green and white **Starlux** (☑ 609-522-7412; www.thestarlux.com; Rio Grande & Atlantic Aves, Wildwood; r $130-310; 🖥) has a soaring profile, lava lamps, boomerang-decorated bedspreads and even two chrome-sided Airstream trailers. If you're here for waterslides and roller coasters, book a room at the **Heart of Wildwood** (☑ 609-522-4090; www.heartofwildwood.com; Ocean & Spencer Aves, Wildwood; r $125-245; 🖥), facing the amusement piers. It's not fancy but it gets high marks for cleanliness.

Cape May

Founded in 1620, Cape May – the only place in the state where the sun rises and sets over the water – is on the state's southern tip and is the country's oldest seashore resort. Its sweeping beaches get crowded in summer, but the stunning Victorian architecture is attractive year-round.

In addition to 600 gingerbread-style houses, the city boasts antique shops and the opportunity to watch dolphins, whales (May to December) and birds. It's just outside the **Cape May Point State Park** and its 157ft **Cape May Lighthouse** (adult/child $7/3); there's an excellent visitors center and museum with exhibits on wildlife in the area. A mile-long loop of the nearby **Cape May Bird Observatory** (☑ 609-861-0700, 609-898-2473; www.birdcapemay.org; 701 East Lake Dr; ☺ 9am-4:30pm) is a pleasant stroll through preserved wetlands. The wide sandy **beaches** at the park (free) and in the town are the main attraction in summer months. **Aqua Trails** (☑ 609-884-5600; www. aquatrails.com; single/double from $40/70) offers kayak tours of the coastal wetlands.

Cape May's B&B options are endless, though the majority lean toward overstuffed and chintzy; check out www.capemaytimes.com for up-to-date listings. The classic, sprawling **Congress Hall** (📞888-944-1816; www.caperesorts.com; 251 Beach Ave; r $100-465) has a range of beautiful quarters overlooking the ocean, plus it has a cool on-site restaurant and bar; the affiliated **Beach Shack** (📞877-7422-507; www.caperesorts.com; 205 Beach Ave; r from $120; 🛜) and **Star Inn** (📞800-297-3779; www.caperesorts.com; 29 Perry St; r from $150; 🛜) offer a variety of accommodations for various budgets (look for deep discounts out of summer season).

The flapjacks at **Uncle Bill's Pancake House** (Beach Ave at Perry St; mains $7; ⊘6:30am-2pm), which resembles a 1950s high-school cafeteria in its size and decor, have been drawing in crowds for 50 years. For unarguably fresh seafood – the restaurant's own boats haul in the day's catch – try the **Lobster House** (906 Schellengers Landing Rd, Fisherman's Wharf; mains $12-27; ⊘11:30am-3pm & 4:30-10pm Apr-Dec, to 9pm other times). No reservations mean long waits are the norm; in that case grab a seat at the dockside raw bar. Otherwise, head to the Washington Street Mall, a cobblestone street lined with shops and more than a half-dozen restaurants.

To continue your journey further south without having to backtrack north and far inland, the **Cape May-Lewes Ferry** (www.cmlf.com; car/passenger $44/8; ⊘hourly in summer 6am-9:30pm; check website out of season) crosses the bay to Lewes, Delaware, near Rehoboth Beach. The journey takes 1½ hours.

PENNSYLVANIA

In a state so large it's unsurprising that geography helps determine identity. The further west you go the closer you are to the rest of America. Philadelphia, once the heart of the British colonial empire and the intellectual and spiritual motor of its demise, is firmly ensconced culturally in the East Coast. Residents of Pittsburgh and western Pennsylvania (PA), on the other hand, are proud to identify themselves as part of the city or immediate region, relishing their blue-collar reputation and their distinctiveness from East Coasters. Moving east to west, the terrain becomes more rugged and you begin to appreciate

---

PENNSYLVANIA FACTS

Nicknames Keystone State, Quaker State

Population 12.7 million

Area 46,058 sq miles

Capital city Harrisburg (population 53,000)

Other cities Philadelphia (population 1.45 million), Pittsburgh (population 313,000), Erie (population 102,000)

Sales tax 6%

Birthplace of Writer Louisa May Alcott (1832–88), dancer Martha Graham (1878–1948), artist Andy Warhol (1928–87), movie star Grace Kelly (1929–82), comic Bill Cosby (b 1937)

Home of US Constitution, the Liberty Bell, first daily newspaper (1784), first auto service station (1913), first computer (1946)

Politics 'Swing state,' Republican governor, progressive Philly and blue-collar Democrats elsewhere

Famous for Soft pretzels, Amish people, Philadelphia cheesesteak, Pittsburgh steel mills

Wildlife Home of the largest herd of wild elk east of the Mississippi

Driving distances Philadelphia to NYC 100 miles, Philadelphia to Pittsburgh 306 miles

---

the sheer size and diversity of the state. Philly's Independence Park and historic district offer an ideal opportunity to come to some understanding of this nation's origins. Nearby, the battle sites of Gettysburg and Valley Forge provide another chance to travel back in time. But the city and state offer more than the clichés associated with school field trips. Stunning natural forests and mountain areas such as the Poconos and Allegheny National Forest provide endless outdoor adventures. Both Philly and Pittsburgh are vibrant university cities with thriving music, performance and art scenes. Frank Lloyd Wright's architectural masterpiece, Fallingwater, and Amish country, not to mention the region's small, artsy towns, are perfect for weekend getaways.

Philadelphia

Although it may seem like a little sibling to NYC, which is less than 90 miles away, Philadelphia is more representative of what East Coast city living is like. And in the minds of many, it offers every upside of urban life: burgeoning food, music and art scenes, neighborhoods with distinct personalities, copious parkland and, just as importantly, relatively affordable real estate. The older, preserved buildings in historic Philadelphia provide a picture of what colonial

Philadelphia

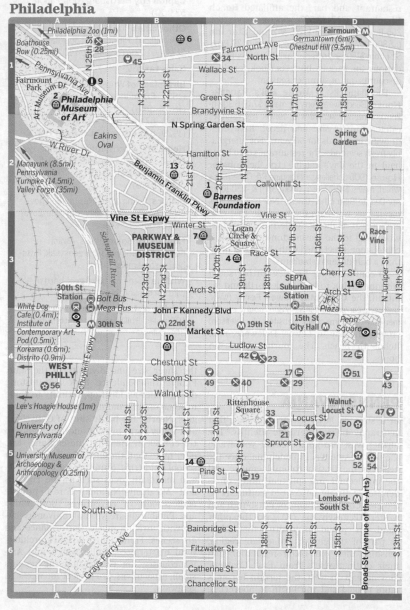

American cities once looked like – based on a grid with wide streets and public squares.

For a time the second-largest city in the British Empire (after London), Philadelphia became a center for opposition to British colonial policy. It was the new nation's capital at the start of the Revolutionary War and again after the war until 1790, when Washington, DC, took over. By the 19th century, NYC had superseded Philadelphia as the nation's cultural, commercial and industrial center. Though urban renewal has been going on for decades, parts of the city formerly populated by industrial workers are blighted

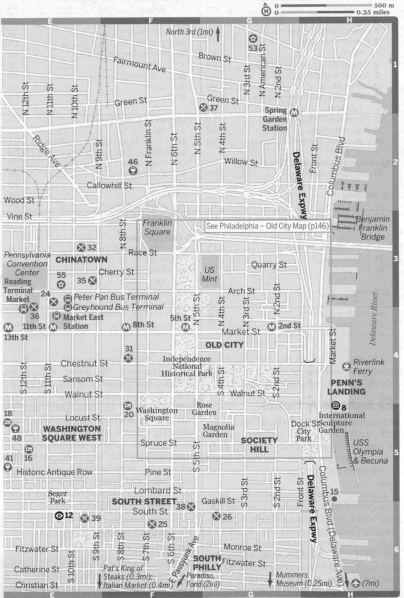

Philadelphia

and worlds away from the carefully manicured lawns and historic district around the Liberty Bell and Independence Hall.

◉ Sights & Activities

Philadelphia is easy to navigate. Most sights and hotels are within walking distance of each other, or a short bus ride away. East–west streets are named; north–south streets are numbered, except for Broad and Front Sts.

Historic Philadelphia includes Independence National Historic Park and Old City, which extends east to the waterfront. West of the historic district is Center City, home to Penn Sq and City Hall. The Delaware and Schuylkill (*skoo*-kill) Rivers border South Philadelphia, which features the colorful Italian Market, restaurants and bars. West of the Schuylkill, University City

has two important campuses as well as a major museum. Northwest Philadelphia includes the genteel suburbs of Chestnut Hill and Germantown, plus Manayunk, with plenty of bustling pubs and hip eateries. The South St area, between S 2nd, 10th, Pine and Fitzwater Sts, has grungy youthful bars, eateries and music venues. Northern Liberties and Fishtown are two burgeoning neighborhoods with eclectic bars, cafes and restaurants, a sort of Williamsburg and Greenpoint tandem for those who know Brooklyn.

◉ Independence National Historic Park

This L-shaped park, along with Old City, has been dubbed 'America's most historic square mile.' Once the backbone of the United States government, it has become the backbone of Philadelphia's tourist trade. Stroll around and you'll see storied buildings in which the seeds for the Revolutionary War were planted and the US government came into bloom. You'll also find beautiful, shaded urban lawns dotted with plenty of benches and costumed actors wandering about. Look for any of the 10 'Once Upon a Nation' signs for free dramatic historic storytelling sessions (11am to 4pm). Only the National Constitution Center charges admission; all other sites are free, though they may require reservations.

Liberty Bell Center
HISTORIC SITE

(Map p146; ✆215-597-8974; www.nps.gove/inde; 6th & Market Sts; ⊙9am-5pm) Philadelphia's top tourist attraction, the Liberty Bell was commissioned to commemorate the 50th anniversary of the Charter of Privileges (Pennsylvania's constitution, enacted in 1701 by William Penn). The 2080lb bronze bell was made in London's East End by the Whitechapel Bell Foundry in 1751. The bell's inscription, from Leviticus 25:10, reads: 'Proclaim liberty through all the land, to all the inhabitants thereof.' The bell was secured in the belfry of the Pennsylvania State House (now Independence Hall) and tolled on important occasions, most notably the first public reading of the Declaration of Independence in Independence Sq. The bell became badly cracked during the 19th century; despite initial repairs, it became unusable in 1846 after tolling for George Washington's birthday.

★National Constitution Center
MUSEUM

(Map p146; ✆215-409-6700; www.constitutioncenter.org; 525 Arch St; adult/child $14.50/8; ⊙9:30am-5pm Mon-Fri, to 6pm Sat, noon-5pm Sun; ⊕) This highly recommended museum makes the United States Constitution sexy and interesting for a general audience through theater-in-the-round reenactments. There are exhibits such as interactive voting booths and Signer's Hall, which contains lifelike bronze statues of the signers in action.

Independence Hall
HISTORIC BUILDING

(Map p146; ✆215-597-8974; Chestnut St, btwn 5th & 6th Sts) Independence Hall is the 'birthplace of American government,' where delegates from the 13 colonies met to approve the Declaration of Independence on July 4, 1776. An excellent example of Georgian architecture, it sports understated lines that reveal Philadelphia's Quaker heritage.

Other Attractions
HISTORIC BUILDINGS

Other attractions in this historic park include **Carpenters' Hall**, owned by the Carpenter Company, the USA's oldest trade guild (1724), which is the site of the First Continental Congress in 1774; **Library Hall** (Map p146), where you'll find a copy of the Declaration of Independence, handwritten in a letter by Thomas Jefferson, plus first editions of Darwin's *On the Origin of the Species* and Lewis and Clark's field notes; **Congress Hall** (Map p146; S 6th & Chestnut Sts), the meeting place for US Congress when Philly was the nation's capital; and **Old City Hall** (Map p146), finished in 1791, which was home to the US Supreme Court until 1800. The **Franklin Court** (Map p146) complex, a row of restored tenements, pays tribute to Benjamin Franklin with a clever underground museum displaying his inventions, and details his many other contributions (as statesman, author and journalist) to society. **Christ Church** (Map p146; ✆215-627-2750; N 2nd St), completed in 1744, is where George Washington and Franklin worshipped.

Philosophical Hall (Map p146; ✆215-440-3400; 104 S 5th St; admission $1; ⊙10am-4pm Thu–Sun Mar–Labor Day & Fri-Sun Labor Day–Feb), south of Old City Hall, is the headquarters of the American Philosophical Society, founded in 1743 by Benjamin Franklin. Past members have included Thomas Jefferson, Marie Curie, Thomas Edison, Charles Darwin and Albert Einstein.

Second Bank of the US (Map p146; Chestnut St, btwn 4th & 5th Sts), modeled after the Greek Parthenon, is an 1824 marble-faced Greek Revival masterpiece that was home to the world's most powerful financial institution until President Andrew Jackson dissolved its charter in 1836. The building then became the Philadelphia Customs House until 1935, when it became a museum. Today it's home to the **National Portrait Gallery** (Map p146; Chestnut St; ⊙11am-4pm Wed-Sun), housing many paintings by Charles Willson Peale, America's top portrait artist at the time of the American Revolution.

◉ Old City

Old City – the area bounded by Walnut, Vine, Front and 6th Sts – picks up where Independence National Historical Park leaves off. Along with Society Hill, Old City was early Philadelphia. The 1970s

Philadelphia – Old City

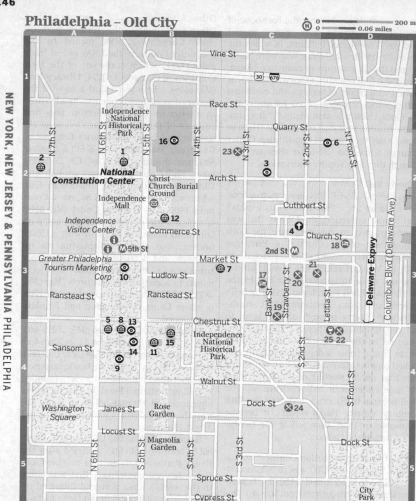

saw revitalization, with many warehouses converted into apartments, galleries and small businesses. Today it's a quaint and fascinating place for a stroll. Check out the 9ft-tall **Ben Franklin sculpture** at Fourth and Arch Sts.

Elfreth's Alley HISTORIC SITE
(Map p146; www.elfrethsalley.org; off 2nd St, btwn Arch & Race Sts; ⊙museum 10am-5pm Wed-Sat, from noon Sun) The tiny, cobblestone alleyway – a little slice of colonial America in miniature – is believed to be the oldest continuously occupied street in the USA. One

of the homes has been converted into a museum (tours $5, noon & 3pm). Its 32 well-preserved brick row houses are inhabited by real-live Philadelphians, so be considerate as you walk down the narrow space.

National Museum of American Jewish History MUSEUM
(Map p146; ☑215-923-3811; www.nmajh.org; 101 South Independence Mall E; adult/child $12/free; ⊙10am-5pm Tue-Fri, to 5:30pm Sat & Sun) The distinct translucent facade of this museum houses state-of-the-art exhibits that examine the historical role of Jews in the USA.

Philadelphia – Old City

Betsy Ross House   HISTORIC SITE

(Map p146; ☎ 215-686-1252; www.betsyross-house.org; 239 Arch St; suggested donation adult/child $3/2; ⊙ 10am-5pm daily Apr-Sep, closed Mon Oct-Mar) It's believed that Betsy Griscom Ross (1752–1836), upholsterer and seamstress, may have sewn the first US flag here.

United States Mint   TOUR

(Map p146; ☎ 215-408-0110; www.usmint.gov; 151 N Independence Mall E; ⊙ tours 9am-4:30pm Mon-Fri, incl Sat in summer) **FREE** Line up for same-day, self-guided tours that last about 45 minutes.

◎ Society Hill

Architecture from the 18th and 19th centuries dominates the lovely residential neighborhood of Society Hill, bounded by Front and 8th Sts from east to west, and Walnut and Lombard Sts north and south. Along the cobblestoned streets you'll see mainly 18th- and 19th-century brick row houses, mixed in with the occasional modern high-rise, such as the **Society Hill Towers** designed by IM Pei. **Washington Square** was conceived as part of William Penn's original city plan, and offers a peaceful respite from sightseeing. Two 18th-century brownstones, the **Physick House** and **Powel House** are open to the public for tours through the **Philadelphia Society for the Preservation of Landmarks** (☎ 215-925-2251; www.philalandmarks.org; 321 S 4th St; adult/child $5/free; ⊙ noon-4pm Thu-Sat, from 1pm Sun, by appt Jan & Feb).

◎ Center City, Rittenhouse Square & Around

Philadelphia's center of creativity, commerce, culture and just about everything else, this region is the engine that drives the city. It contains the city's tallest buildings, the financial district, big hotels, museums, concert halls, shops and restaurants.

The leafy **Rittenhouse Square**, with its wading pool and fine statues, is the best known of William Penn's city squares. Surrounded by upscale cafes, restaurants, condominiums and hotels, it feels like a little slice of European elegance.

City Hall   BUILDING

(Map p142; ☎ 215-686-2840; www.phila.gov; cnr Broad & Market Sts; ⊙ 9:30am-4:30pm Tue-Fri) **FREE** The majestic City Hall, completed in 1901, stands 548ft tall in Penn Sq. It's the world's tallest masonry construction (and larger than the US Capitol) without a steel frame, and it's topped by a 27-ton bronze statue of William Penn. A gentleman's agreement to keep City Hall the tallest building in the city lasted until 1987. Access to the tower observation deck and guided tours available.

Rosenbach Museum & Library   MUSEUM

(Map p142; ☎ 215-732-1600; www.rosenbach.org; 2008 Delancey Pl; adult/child $10/5; ⊙ noon-5pm Tue & Fri, Wed & Thu to 8pm, to 6pm Sat & Sun) This place is for bibliophiles, as it features rare books and manuscripts, including James Joyce's *Ulysses*, and incunabula, basically the earliest printed books from 1450 to 1500. Docent-led tours of the elegant home highlight period-furnished rooms, Thomas Sully portraits and the Marianne Moore room – essentially the modernist poet's Greenwich Village apartment lock, stock and barrel.

Mutter Museum MUSEUM
(Map p142; ☑215-563-3737; www.collphyphil.org; 19 S 22nd St; adult/child $14/10; ☺10am-5pm) Skip med school and visit this seriously twisted museum to learn all about the history of medicine in the US.

☉ Fairmount

Modeled after the Champs Elysées in Paris, the Benjamin Franklin Parkway is a center of museums and other landmarks.

★**Philadelphia Museum of Art** MUSEUM
(Map p142; ☑215-763-8100; www.philamuseum. org; 2600 Benjamin Franklin Pkwy; adult/child $20/ free; ☺10am-5pm Tue, Thu, Sat & Sun, to 8:45pm Wed & Fri) It's one of the nation's largest and most important museums, featuring excellent collections of Asian art, Renaissance masterpieces, post-impressionist works and modern pieces by Picasso, Duchamp and Matisse. The grand stairway at its entrance was immortalized when Sylvester Stallone ran up the steps in the 1976 flick *Rocky*. Music, food and wine Friday nights.

★**Barnes Foundation** MUSEUM
(Map p142; ☑866-849-7056; www.barnesfoundation.org; 2025 Benjamin Franklin Pkwy; adult/ child $18/10; ☺9:30am-6pm Wed-Mon, to 10pm Fri) The Barnes Foundation moved from it's original location in Merion, PA (the arboretum and archives are still there) to a strikingly contemporary building in May, 2012. An exceptionally fine collection of impressionist, post-impressionist and early French modern paintings, including works by Cézanne, Degas, Matisse, Monet, Picasso, Renoir and Van Gogh are displayed in the same idiosyncratic and unconventional arrangement as before; walls are cluttered in the 'gallery style' in accordance with Albert C Barnes' own particular 'objective method' to art education and appreciation.

Rodin Museum MUSEUM
(Map p142; ☑215-763-8100; www.rodinmuseum. org; 2154 Benjamin Franklin Pkwy; suggested admission $8; ☺10am-5pm Wed-Mon) The newly renovated museum has Rodin's great works *The Thinker* and *Burghers of Calais*.

Pennsylvania Academy of the Fine Arts MUSEUM
(Map p142; ☑215-972-7600; www.pafa.org; 118 N Broad St; adult/child $15/free; ☺10am-5pm Tue-Sat, from 11am Sun) A prestigious academy that has a museum with works by American painters, including Charles Willson Peale and Thomas Eakins.

Franklin Institute Science Museum MUSEUM
(Map p142; ☑215-448-1200; www.fi.edu; 222 N 20th St; adult/child $16.50/12.50; ☺9:30am-5pm; ⏹) This is where hands-on science displays were pioneered; a highlight is the Ben Franklin exhibit.

Academy of Natural Sciences Museum MUSEUM
(Map p142; ☑215-299-1000; www.ansp.org; 1900 Benjamin Franklin Pkwy; adult/child $15/13; ☺10am-4:30pm Mon-Fri, to 5pm Sat & Sun) The museum features a terrific dinosaur exhibition where you can dig for fossils on weekends.

Eastern State Penitentiary MUSEUM
(Map p142; www.easternstate.org; 2027 Fairmount Ave; adult/child $14/10; ☺10am-5pm) Take an audio or guided tour of this decomissioned medieval fortress-like prison where Al Capone once did time.

☉ Fairmount Park

The snaking Schuylkill River bisects this 9200-acre green space that's bigger than New York's Central Park and, in fact, the largest city park in the country. Scattered all throughout the park are some notable monuments, including one, at the far east end, of **Joan of Arc** (Map p142). From the earliest days of spring every corner is thrumming with activity – ball games, runners, picnickers, you name it. Runners will love the tree-lined, riverside trails, which range from 2 miles to 10 miles in length. Park trails are also great for cycling. Stop by **Fairmount Bicycles** (☑267-507-9370; www.fairmountbicycles. com; 2015 Fairmount Ave; full/half-day $18/30) for rentals and information.

Boathouse Row HOUSE
(www.boathouserow.org; 1 Boathouse Row; early American houses adult/child $5/2) On the east bank, Boathouse Row has Victorian-era rowing-club buildings that lend a lovely old-fashioned flavor to this stretch. Across the park are a number of **early American houses** that are open to the public.

Shofuso Japanese House and Garden
GARDEN

(☎ 215-878-5097; www.shofuso.com; Landsdowne & Horticultural Dr; adult/child $6/4; ⊙ 11am-5pm, check website) Check out the picturesque home and teahouse constructed in the traditional 16th-century style.

Philadelphia Zoo
ZOO

(☎ 215-243-1100; www.philadelphiazoo.org; 3400 W Girard Ave; adult/child $20/18; ⊙ 9:30am-5pm Mar-Oct, to 4pm Nov-Feb; ⊕) The country's oldest zoo has tigers, pumas, polar bears – you name it – in naturalistic habitats.

◉ South Street

Sort of an East Village or Williamsburg of Philly, slightly grungy Chinatown South Street is lined with tattoo parlors, art-supply stores, tiny cheapskate eateries and bars, and the teenage and college-age goth chicks and dudes who populate them.

Philadelphia's Magic Garden
GARDEN

(Map p142; ☎ 215-733-0390; www.phillymagicgardens.org; 1020 South St; adult/child $7/3; ⊙ 11am-6pm Sun-Thu, to 8pm Fri & Sat Apr-Oct, to 5pm Nov-Mar; ⊕) A hidden gem worth seeking out, the garden is a mystical, art-filled pocket of land that's the passion of mosaic muralist Isaiah Zager.

◉ South Philadelphia

★ Italian Market
MARKET

(S 9th St, btwn Wharton & Fitzwater Sts; ⊙ 9am-5pm Tue-Sat, 9am-2pm Sun) These days, the country's oldest outdoor market is as much Mexican as Italian and you'll probably find more taquiles than prosciutto; however, it's still a highlight of South Philadelphia. Butchers and artisans still hawk produce and cheese and a handful of authentic old-school Italian shops sell homemade pastas, pastries and freshly slaughtered fish and meats. Anthony's (915 S 9th St; gelato $3.50; ⊙ 7am-7pm), a small cafe, is a good place to take a break with an espresso or gelato.

Mummers Museum
MUSEUM

(☎ 215-336-3050; www.mummersmuseum.com; 1100 S 2nd St; adult/child $3.50/2.50; ⊙ 9:30am-4:30pm Wed-Sat) Amid all the foodie frenzy is the Mummers Museum, celebrating the tradition of disguise and masquerade. It has an integral role in the famed Mummers Parade, which takes place here every New Year's Day.

◉ Chinatown & Around

The fourth-largest Chinatown in the USA, Philly's version has existed since the 1860s. Chinese immigrants who built America's transcontinental railroads started out west and worked their way here. Now many of the neighborhood's residents come from Malaysia, Thailand and Vietnam, in addition to every province in China. The multicolored, four-story Chinese Friendship Gate is Chinatown's most conspicuous landmark.

African American Museum in Philadelphia
MUSEUM

(Map p146; ☎ 215-574-0380; www.aampmuseum.org; 701 Arch St; adult/child $14/10; ⊙ 10am-5pm Thu-Sat, from noon Sun) Housed in a foreboding concrete building, it contains excellent collections on African American history and culture.

◉ Penn's Landing

Back in its heyday Penn's Landing – the waterfront area along the Delaware River between Market and Lombard Sts – was a very active port area. Eventually those transactions moved further south down the Delaware, and today most of the excitement is about boarding boats, such as the Spirit of Philadelphia (Map p142; ☎ 866-455-3866; www.spiritofphiladelphia.com; tours from $40), for booze cruises, or simply strolling along the water's edge. The 1.8-mile Benjamin Franklin Bridge, the world's largest suspension bridge when completed in 1926, spans the Delaware River and dominates the view.

Independence Seaport Museum
MUSEUM

(Map p142; ☎ 215-413-8655; www.phillyseaport.org; 211 S Columbus Blvd; adult/child $13.50/10; ⊙ 10am-5pm, to 7pm Thu-Sat summer; ⊕) This interactive riverside museum highlights Philadelphia's maritime history (its shipyard closed in 1995 after 200 years). You can hop aboard two ships, an 1892 Cruiser and a WWII submarine.

◉ University City

This neighborhood, separated from downtown Philly by the Schuylkill River, feels like one big college town. That's because it's home to both Drexel University and the Ivy League University of Pennsylvania (commonly called 'U Penn'), founded in 1740. The leafy, bustling campus makes for a pleasant afternoon stroll, and it's got two museums definitely worth a visit.

University Museum of Archaeology & Anthropology MUSEUM

(215-898-4000; www.penn.museum; 3260 South St; adult/child $15/10; 10am-5pm Tue & Thu-Sun, to 8pm Wed; No 21, 30, 40) The University Museum of Archaeology & Anthropology is Penn's magical museum, containing archaeological treasures from ancient Egypt, Mesopotamia, the Mayan peninsula, Greece, Rome and North America.

Institute of Contemporary Art GALLERY

(215-898-7108; www.icaphila.org; 118 S 36th St; 11am-8pm Wed, to 6pm Thu & Fri, to 5pm Sat & Sun) FREE An excellent place to catch shows by folks making a big splash at the cutting edge of the art world.

30th Street Station LANDMARK

(Map p142; 215-349-2153; 30th St, at Market St) Whether you're catching a train or not, be sure to pop your head into this romantic, neoclassical station while you're in the 'hood.

Tours

Ed Mauger's Philadelphia on Foot TOUR

(215-627-8680; www.ushistory.org/more/mauger; tours per person $20) Historian and author Ed Mauger offers walking tours with a variety of themes, including Exercise Your Rights (Conservatives Tour), Exercise Your Lefts (Liberals Tour) and Women in the Colony.

Mural Tours TOUR

(215-389-8687; www.muralarts.org/tours; tours free to $30) Guided trolley tour of the city's diverse and colorful outdoor murals, the largest collection in the country.

Philadelphia Trolley Works & 76 Carriage Company TOUR

(215-389-8687; www.phillytour.com; adult/child from $25/10) Tour part of the city or just about every last corner, either on a narrated trolley ride or a quieter horse-drawn carriage.

Taste of Philly Food Tour TOUR

(215-545-8007; www.tasteofphillyfoodtour.com; adult/chid $16/9; 10am Wed & Sat) Explore the Reading Terminal Market with a knowledgeable food-obsessed expert.

Festivals & Events

Mummers' Parade PARADE

(www.mummers.com; Jan 1) A very Philly parade, this is an elaborate celebration of costumes every New Year's Day.

Manayunk Arts Festival CULTURE

(www.manayunk.com; Jun) It's the largest outdoor arts and crafts show in the Delaware Valley, with more than 250 artists from across the country.

Philadelphia Live Arts Festival & Philly Fringe PERFORMING ARTS

(www.livearts-fringe.org; Sep) Catch the latest in cutting-edge performance.

Sleeping

Though the majority of places are found in and around Center City, alternatives are sprinkled throughout other neighborhoods. There's certainly no shortage of places to stay, but it's primarily national chains. The Lowes, Sofitel and Westin can all be recommended. Note that most hotels offer some kind of parking service, usually costing about $20 to $45 per day, or in the very least have discounted arrangements with nearby garages.

Apple Hostels HOSTEL $

(Map p146; 215-922-0222; www.applehostels. com; 32 S Bank St; dm $38, r from $84;) This sparkling clean gem of a hostel is hidden down an alleyway, just a short walk from major sights. Everything, from the bunk beds to dishes in the spacious kitchen, looks like it's straight out of an Ikea catalogue – not a bad thing. And every need and desire has been accounted for: ear plugs, breath-rite strips for snorers, power outlets in lockers, USB ports at every bed, Nintendo Wii, free coffee and of course old-school amenities like laundry machines, Foosball, darts and even a guitar. Very friendly and helpful staff and nightly 'events' like walking tours, pasta nights (Wednesday) and free whiskey and bar crawl (Thursday).

Chamounix Mansion Hostel HOSTEL $

(215-878-3676; www.philahostel.org; 3250 Chamounix Dr, West Fairmount Park; dm $23; 8am-11am, 4:30-midnight, closed 15 Dec-15 Jan;) Looking more like a B&B than a hostel, Chamounix is in a lovely wooded area in Fairmount Park, north of the city, on the way to Manayunk; should only be considered by those with a car. Despite the 19th-century-style parlor and large communal rooms, the dorms themselves are basic but clean.

Morris House Hotel BOUTIQUE HOTEL **$$**

(Map p142; ✆215-922-2446; www.morrishouse-hotel.com; 225 S 8th St; r incl breakfast from $179; ✳🛜) If Benjamin Franklin were a hotelier, he would have designed a place like the Morris House Hotel. Upscale colonial-era boutique, this Federal-era building has the friendly charm and intimacy of an elegant B&B and the professionalism and good taste of a designer-run 21st-century establishment.

Penn's View Hotel BOUTIQUE HOTEL **$$**

(Map p146; ✆215-922-7600; www.pennsviewhotel.com; cnr Front & Market Sts; r from $149-329; ✳🛜) Housed in three early-19th-century buildings overlooking the Delaware waterfront, Penn's View is ideal for exploring the Old City. Quaint and full of character but not overly nostalgic or a prisoner to history, the rooms have marble bathrooms and modern conveniences. An authentic Italian trattoria and charming wine bar are part of the hotel.

Hotel Palomar BOUTIQUE HOTEL **$$**

(Map p142; ✆888-725-1778; www.hotelpalomar-philadelphia.com; 117 S 17th St; r from $149; P✳🛜✳) Part of the Kimpton chain, the Palomar occupies a former office building a few blocks from Rittenhouse Sq. Marble and

dark wood accents add warmth to the hip and stylish room furnishings. On offer are wine and snacks, hot chocolate (in winter), a gym and an attached restaurant. Valet parking $42 per night.

Independent Philadelphia BOUTIQUE HOTEL **$$**

(Map p142; ✆215-772-1440; www.theindependenthotel.com; 1234 Locust St; r incl breakfast from $150; ✳🛜) A good Center City option housed in a handsome brick Georgian-Revival building with a four-story atrium. The wood-floored rooms are cozy and bright and the complimentary off-site gym-pass and wine and cheese every evening sweeten the deal.

Alexander Inn BOUTIQUE HOTEL **$$**

(Map p142; ✆215-923-3535; www.alexanderinn.com; 12th & Spruce Sts; s/d incl breakfast from $120/130; ✳@🛜✳; 🚇12, 23) Though the outside is a weird combination of brick walls accented with vinyl-sided bay windows, the small rooms at this inn look and feel pretty good and the lobby boasts dark wood, a fireplace and some stained-glass windows. The hotel, because of its helpful, accepting staff and great location near Philly's gay neighbourhood, attracts lots of same-sex couples.

La Reserve B&B **$$**

(Map p142; ✆215-735 1137; www.lareservebandb.com; 1804 Pine St; r with shared/private bath incl breakfast from $80/125; ✳🛜✳) This lovely 1850s row house sits on a quiet stretch of

---

WORTH A TRIP

PHILLY'S OUTLYING 'HOODS

Manayunk

A compact residential neighborhood northwest of the city, with steep hills and Victorian row houses, Manayunk, from a Native American expression meaning 'where we go to drink,' is a lovely place for an afternoon and evening. Just be aware that thousands of others have the same idea on weekend nights, when this otherwise peaceful area overlooking the Schuylkill River has the feel of a raucous frat party. As well as drinking, visitors are also permitted to eat and shop (check out **Dalessandro's** and **Chubby's** for classic Philly sandwiches and cheesesteaks). Parking is near impossible to come by here on weekends, so cycling is a good option – there's a towpath that runs alongside the neighborhood.

Germantown & Chestnut Hill

An odd mix of blight and preserved grandeur, the Germantown historic district – a good 20-minute drive or ride north on the Septa 23 from central downtown Philly – has a handful of tiny museums and notable homes worth checking out. And just to the north is Chestnut Hill with its quaint, small-town-like main strip of shops and eateries and huge historic residential homes and mansions.

Pine Street a few blocks south of Rittenhouse Sq. The B&B's seven rooms come stocked with well-worn charm – often in the form of faded oriental rugs, plush draperies, tall ceilings, inoperative fireplaces and (it seems) the fragile furniture of a minor 19th-century French aristocrat.

Ritz-Carlton
HOTEL $$$

(Map p142; ☑ 215-523-8000; www.ritzcarlton.com/hotels/philadelphia; 10 Ave of the Arts; r from $300; P✳@🛜🏊✵) This Ritz possesses one of the most lavish lobbies in North America, modelled after the Pantheon. In the afternoon, a formal afternoon tea is held in the rotunda. The 331 rooms are contained in a pre–WWII adjoining tower. Spacious, marble-clad bathrooms feel about as clean as an operating room.

Rittenhouse 1715
HOTEL $$$

(Map p142; ☑ 215-546-6500; www.rittenhouse1715.com; 1715 Rittenhouse Square St; r $249-305, ste $309-699; ✳🛜) Just steps from Rittenhouse Sq, this is an elegant, top-notch choice. Housed in a 1911 mansion and infused with old-world sophistication, it's brimming with modern amenities: iPod docking stations, plasma TVs and rain showerheads. The friendly and efficient staff is also worth noting.

Eating

Philly is deservedly known for its cheesesteaks – local aficionados debate the relative merits of various shops as if they are biblical scholars parsing the meaning of Deuteronomy. The city's dining scene has grown exponentially, in part due to the contributions of the Starr and Garces groups, which have added a range of quality international eateries. Starr in particular has seemingly targeted every cuisine and theme known to humanity.

The locavore, farm-to-table modern American trend is going strong (even a single block, 20th St and Rittenhouse Sq has three) as are gastropubs, which obsess equally about the provenance of their brews and burgers (Fairmount neighborhood has a handful). Up-and-coming culinary hotspots inlcude Northern Liberties (Modomio for Northern Italian and Fette Sau for barbecue), Fishtown (Pickled Heron for creative French bistro) and East Passyunk in South Philadelphia (Le Virtu for locavore Italian). And food trucks, from gourmet, ethnic and everything in between, can be found in the City Hall area. Because of Pennsylvania's arcane liquor laws, many restaurants are Bring Your Own Bottle (BYOB).

Old City

★ Franklin Fountain
ICE CREAM $

(Map p146; ☑ 215-627-1899; 116 Market St; sundaes $10; ☉ noon-11pm Sun-Thu, to midnight Fri & Sat; ♿) One of the more romantic date spots in the city, especially on weekend nights, this old-timey ice-cream parlor features locally grown fruit and huge sundaes.

Amada
SPANISH $$

(Map p146; ☑ 215-625-2450; 217 Chestnut St; tapas $6-20; ☉ 11:30am-10pm Mon-Thu, to midnight Fri, 5pm-midnight Sat, 4-10pm Sun) Run by renowned restaurateur Jose Garces. The long communal tables foster a bustling, happening and loud atmosphere. The combination of bold and traditional dishes (try the crab-stuffed peppers) is phenomenal.

Cuba Libre
CARIBBEAN $$

(Map p146; ☑ 215-627-0666; www.cubalibrerestaurant.com; 10 S 2nd St; dinner $15-24; ☉ 11:30am-11pm Mon-Fri, from 10:30am Sat & Sun) Colonial America couldn't feel further away at this festive, multistoried Cuban eatery and rum bar. The creative and inspired menu includes Cuban sandwiches, guava-spiced BBQ, and savory black beans and salads tossed with smoked fish.

La Locanda del Ghiottone
ITALIAN $$

(Map p146; ☑ 215-829-1465; 130 N 3rd St; mains $16; ☉ 5-11pm Tue-Sun) The name means 'the Place of the Glutton,' and chef Giussepe and Joe the head waiter encourage overeating. Small and modestly designed, unlike other nearby trendy spots. Try the gnocchi, mushroom crepes and mussels. BYOB.

Silk City Diner
DINER $$

(Map p142; 435 Spring Garden St; mains $13; ☉ 4pm-1am, from 10am Sat & Sun) Cocktails have replaced milkshakes at this classic-looking diner on the edge of the Old City and Northern Liberties. It's worth noting Silk City is as much a late-night dance spot – Jerseyites come in for Saturday DJ nights. Outdoor beer garden in summer.

Zahav
MIDDLE EASTERN $$

(Map p146; ☑ 215-625-8800; 237 St James Pl, off Dock St; mains $11; ☉ 5-10pm Sun-Thu, to 11pm Fri & Sat) Small plates of sophisticated and modern Israeli and North African cuisine on Society Hill Towers' grounds.

Center City & Around

★ Reading Terminal Market   MARKET $
(Map p142; ☑ 215-922-2317; www.readingterminalmarket.org; 51 N 12th St; ☻ 8am-5:30pm Mon-Sat, 9am-4pm Sun) A wonderful one-stop shop for every appetite. Wander down the aisles past lines for famous Philly cheesesteaks, Amish food, lobster rolls, sushi, barbecue, and every cuisine and delicacy you can imagine.

Mama Palmas   PIZZERIA $
(Map p142; ☑ 215-735-7357; 2229 Spruce St; pizzas $10; ☻ 4-10pm Mon-Thu, 11am-11pm Fri & Sat, 2-10pm Sun) This small BYOB place serves up some of the best thin-slice brick-oven pizza in the city. It does have a reputation for not tolerating little tykes – if they're rowdy.

Philly Flavors   ICE CREAM $
(Map p142; ☑ 215-232-7748; 2004 Fairmount Ave, at 20th St; ☻ 11am-11pm Sun-Thu, to midnight Fri & Sat) The best place for Italian ices in the city; even the small kiddie size is large enough for most.

Lemon Hill Food & Drink   MODERN AMERICAN $$
(Map p142; www.lemonphilly.com; 747 N 25th St; mains $14; ☻ 5-10pm, from 10:30am Sat & Sun) If you're in hurry, do not ask for information about how the duck confit *poutine* is prepared or the type of rum in a cocktail. This Fairmount neighborhood gastropub takes the provenance of its ingredients seriously. Spiel or no spiel, food and drinks are worth the wait. Bar stays open till 1am.

La Viola   ITALIAN $$
(Map p142; ☑ 215-735-8630; 253 S 16th St, at Spruce St; mains $13; ☻ 11am-10pm Mon-Thu, to 11pm Fri & Sat, 4-10pm Sun) Facing off across the street from one another are two La Violas – both BYOB. The former is a cramped and unpretentious dining room, while the latter is larger and more modern; the cuisine at both, however, is fresh and reasonably priced.

Continental   DINER $$
(Map p142; www.continentalmidtown.com; 1801 Chestnut St; mains $10-20) A fashionably mod update on a diner, Continental boasts hip crowds, eclectic, fusiony tapas and specialty cocktails. Dishes are hit or miss, from a satisfying quinoa salad to a mediocre lunchtime Asian bento box. Another location on Market St.

Luke's Lobster   SEAFOOD $$
(Map p142; 130 S 17th St; sandwiches $10-17; ☻ 11am-9pm Sun-Thu, to 10pm Fri & Sat) For an authentic taste of a Maine lobster, crab or shrimp roll, head to this casual 'shack' in the Rittenhouse Sq area.

★ Morimoto   JAPANESE $$$
(Map p142; ☑ 215-413-9070; 723 Chestnut St; mains $25; ☻ 11:30am-10pm Mon-Fri, to midnight Fri & Sat) Morimoto is high concept and heavily stylized, from a dining room that looks like a futuristic aquarium to a menu of globe-spanning influence and eclectic combinations. A meal at this *Iron Chef* regular's restaurant is a theatrical experience.

Parc Brasserie   FRENCH $$$
(Map p142; ☑ 215-545-2262; 227 S 18th St; mains from $23; ☻ 7:30am-11pm, to midnight Fri & Sat) This enormous polished bistro is in a prime people-watching spot on Rittenhouse Sq. Brunch and lunch menus hit the right notes and are good value.

Zama   JAPANESE $$$
(Map p142; www.zamaphilly.com; 128 S 19th St; mains $20; ☻ 11:30am-10pm Mon-Fri, to 11pm Fri, 5-11pm Sat, 5-9pm Sun) This upscale place around the corner from Rittenhouse Sq is for sushi and sake connoissieurs. The 'sake sommelier' can guide you to interesting choices.

South Street

Jim's Steaks   STEAKHOUSE $
(Map p142; ☑ 877-313-5467; 400 South St, at 4th St; steak sandwiches $6-8; ☻ 10am-1am Mon-Thu, to 3am Fri & Sat, noon-10pm Sun) If you can brave the long lines – which bust out of the front door and snake around the side of building – you'll be in for a treat at this Philly institution, which serves mouthwatering cheesesteaks and hoagies (plus soups, salads and breakfasts).

South Street Souvlaki   GREEK $$
(Map p142; ☑ 215-925-3026; 507 South St; mains $13-18; ☻ noon-9:30pm Tue-Thu, to 10pm Fri & Sat, to 9pm Sun) A long-running and modest place that is still one of the best places for Greek food in the city. The very large Tom's special salad (Tom is the owner) is recommended.

Horizons   VEGAN $$
(Map p142; ☑ 215-923-6117; www.horizonsphiladelphia.com; 611 S 7th St; mains $15-20; ☻ 6-10pm Tue-Thu, 6-11pm Fri & Sat; ☑) Satisfying, healthy

and guilt-free dishes made of soy and veggies for the vegan gourmand.

Supper MODERN AMERICAN $$$
(Map p142; ✒215-592-8180; 926 South St; mains $24; ⊙6-11:30pm) Truly farm-to-table, supplied with fresh seasonal produce by its very own farm, Supper epitomizes the current culinary spirit, which weds the rural with the urban. Entrees are inventive and tasty creations like crispy confit duck leg with pecan waffles.

✗ Chinatown

Nan Zhou Hand Drawn Noodle House CHINESE $
(Map p142; ✒215-923-1550; 1022 Race St; mains $6-10; ⊙11am-10pm) Now in a relatively sleek and larger space a block away from the old hole-in-the-wall but still serving delicious and inexpensive meat noodle soups.

Rangoon BURMESE $
(Map p142; ✒215-829-8939; 112 N 9th St; mains $6-15; ⊙11:30am-9pm Sun-Thu, to 10pm Fri & Sat) This Burmese spot offers a huge array of tantalizing specialties from spicy red-bean shrimp and curried chicken with egg noodles to coconut tofu.

Dim Sum Garden CHINESE $
(Map p142; 59 N 11th St; mains $6; ⊙10:30am-10:30pm) Overall, not the most salubrious looking hole-in-the-wall near the bus station but some of the tastiest steamed buns in the city.

★Han Dynasty CHINESE $$
(Map p146; 108 Chestnut St; mains $15; ⊙11:30am-11:30pm) Innovative and burn-your-tongue spicy soups and noodle dishes in a more upscale dining room.

✗ South Philadelphia

The area around the corner of Washington and 11th Sts is chockablock with tasty family-owned Vietnamese restaurants, not to mention the Italian Market (p149).

Pat's King of Steaks FAST FOOD $
(✒215-468-1546; www.patskingofsteaks.com; cnr S 9th St & Passyunk Ave; sandwiches $7; ⊙24hr) An iconic Philly institution, Pat's is frequented by tourists and diehard locals, often inebriated patrons, possibly unaware of the level of grease they're ingesting. It's competitor Geno's is diagonally across the street.

Tony Luke's SANDWICHES $
(✒215-551-5725; www.tonylukes.com; 39 E Oregon Ave; sandwiches $7; ⊙6am-midnight Mon-Thu, to 2am Fri & Sat) A typical spot out by the sports stadiums with picnic tables and an ordering window, this place is famous for its roast pork and roast beef with hot peppers.

Paradiso ITALIAN $$
(✒215-271-2066; www.paradisophilly.com; 1627 E Passyunk Ave; mains $10-28; ⊙11:30am-3pm & 5-10pm Mon-Thu, to 11pm Fri & Sat, 4-9pm Sun) Elegantly airy, Paradiso turns out upscale Italian feasts such as pistachio-crusted lamb chops, homemade gnocchi and New York strip steak glazed with anchovy butter.

Fond AMERICAN $$$
(✒212-551-5000; 1617 E Passyunk Ave; mains $25; ⊙5:30-10pm) Tired of the neighborhood sandwich shops? Head to this upscale fine-dining restaurant whose young chefs turn out creatively conceived fish, meat and chicken dishes with French accents and seasonal ingredients.

✗ University City

Abyssinia Ethiopian Restaurant ETHIOPIAN $
(229 S 45th St; mains $9; ⊙10am-midnight) Excellent *foul madamas* (bean dip) and good brunch with a recommended bar upstairs.

Lee's Hoagie House SANDWICHES $
(✒215-387-0905; 4034 Walnut St; sandwiches $7; ⊙10am-10pm Mon-Sat, 11am-9pm Sun) For meat and chicken sandwiches, definitely the best in area.

Koreana KOREAN $
(✒215-222-2240; 3801 Chestnut St; mains $7; ⊙noon-10pm) Satisfying students and others interested in good, inexpensive Korean fare; enter from the parking lot in the back of the shopping plaza.

Distrito MEXICAN $$
(✒215-222-1657; 3945 Chestnut St; mains $9-30; ⊙11:30am-11pm Mon-Fri, 5-11pm Sat, to 10pm Sun) The vibrant pink and lime decor doesn't drown out the taste of the contemporary Mexican fare.

White Dog Cafe ORGANIC $$
(✒215-386-9224; 3420 Sansom St; dinner mains $12-29; ⊙11:30am-2:30pm Mon-Sat, 5-10pm Mon-Thu, to 11pm Fri & Sat, 10:30am-2:30pm & 5-10pm Sun) This neighborhood institution is the kind of funky-yet-upscale place that

college students get their visiting parents to take them to for special dinners or brunch. The local, largely organic menu offers creative interpretations of meat and fish dishes.

Pod ASIAN $$
(☑215-387-1803; 3636 Sansom St; dinner mains $14-29; ☺11:30am-11pm Mon-Thu, to midnight Fri, 5pm-midnight Sat, to 10pm Sun) Part of the restaurateur Stephen Starr's empire, this space-age-looking theme restaurant has pan-Asian treats including dumplings and some of the best sushi in Philly, plus plenty of quirky cocktails and original desserts.

🍸 Drinking & Entertainment

Judging Philly's bar scene by the over-the-top, raunchy TV series *It's Always Sunny in Philadelphia* is of course a mistake. Old-school dive bars are well represented but there's at least as many sophisticated cocktail lounges, wine bars and gastropubs intensely focused on local brews.

Apart from New Orleans, Old City boasts the highest concentration of liquor licenses in the US; to find a spot that appeals to your sensibilities, just stroll along S 2nd and S 3rd Sts. There are a fair number of spots where recently legal drinkers go for volume such as Lucy's Hat Shop, Drinker's Tavern and Buffalo Billiard's; South St can feel like an alternative fraternity row on weekend nights. Meanwhile, Center City hotels like the Le Meridien and the Bellevue have classy lounges and bars with popular happy hours. The area between Broad and 12th Sts and Walnut and Pine Sts has been dubbed Midtown Village and unofficially called 'gay'borhood and is permanently decked out with rainbow-flag-festooned street signs. Because nights and venues change frequently, check out www.phillygaycalendar.com. And finally, in the Fairmount neighborhood around the Eastern State Penitentiary there's a handful of recommended gastropubs.

Bars & Nightlife

⭐ **Paris Wine Bar** WINE BAR
(Map p142; 2301 Fairmount Ave; ☺5pm-midnight Thu Sat) Run by the duo behind the London Grill (an equally recommended gastropub next door to this bar and one of the first in the city), the owners have come up with another novel approach to satisfying sophisticated Philadelphians: Pennsylvania wines on tap! Kegs behind the bar are filled with two whites, three reds and a rose. There's

xcellent French-bistro-style food on the menu.

North 3rd GASTROPUB
(www.norththird.com; 801 N 3rd St; ☺4pm-2am) A Northern Liberties gem equally recommended for drinks like huge mojito martinis as for its tremendous food like steamed clams and pork chorizo in a tomato and cilantro broth. Expect extensively tattooed waitstaff and struggling conversations because of the noise level. Dinner served from 5pm to midnight and brunch on weekends, and every Tuesday night films are screened.

Mcgillin's Olde Ale House BAR
(Map p142; ☑215-735-5562; www.mcgillins.com; 1310 Drury St; ☺11am-2am Mon-Sat, to midnight Sun) Philadelphia's oldest continually operated tavern (since 1860) – it remained open as a speakeasy in the Prohibition years. Great buffalo wings (Tuesday is special wing night) and karaoke on Wednesdays and Fridays.

Dirty Frank's BAR
(Map p142; 347 S 13th St; ☺11am-2am) Recently discovered by hipsters, this has been a classic neighborhood dive bar since the 1970s. Expect sawdust on the floor and cheap shots and beer.

Shampoo CLUB
(Map p142; ☑215-922-7500; www.shampoooonline.com; on Willow St btwn N 7th & 8th Sts; cover $7-12; ☺9pm-2am) Home to foam parties, hot tubs and velvet seating, this giant nightclub's weekly repertoire includes an immensely popular gay night on Fridays, a long-standing Wednesday Goth night, and a conventional free-for-all on Saturdays.

Monk's Cafe BAR
(Map p142; www.monkscafe.com; 264 S 16th St; ☺11:30am-2am) A Belgian beer bar with a big bottle selection as well as a good selection of – what else? – Belgian and Belgian-style beers on tap as well as a bistro menu; the mussels and fries are recommended.

Brasil's CLUB
(Map p146; www.brasilsnightclub-philly.com; 112 Chestnut St; cover $10) The place to bump and grind to Latin, Brazilian and Caribbean sounds, with DJ John Rockwell.

Village Whiskey BAR
(Map p142; 118 S 20th St; ☺11:30am-midnight, to 1am Fri & Sat) Cool vibe, long whiskey menu and creative cuisine.

Franklin Mortgage & Investment Co

COCKTAIL BAR

(Map p142; 112 S 18th St; ⊗5pm-2am) Expertly made rye, whiskey and gin drinks in a classy setting.

Tavern on Camac

BAR, CLUB

(Map p142; ☑215-545-0900; www.tavernoncamac. com; 243 S Camac St; ⊗6pm-3am) One of the older gay bars in Philly, while a small upstairs dance floor gets packed with dance-happy folks.

Sisters

LESBIAN

(Map p142; ☑215-735-0735; www.sistersnightclub. com; 1320 Chancellor St; ⊗5pm-2am, closed Mon) A huge nightclub and restaurant for the ladies.

Dock Street Brewery & Restaurant

BREWERY

(701 S 50th St; ⊗3-11pm, to 1am Fri & Sat) Artisan beer and brick-oven pizza in West Philly.

Live Music

Chris' Jazz Club

BLUES, JAZZ

(Map p142; ☑215-568-3131; www.chrisjazzcafe. com; 1421 Sansom St; cover $10-20) Showcasing local talent along with national greats, this intimate space features a 4pm piano happy hour Tuesday through Friday and good bands Monday through Saturday nights.

Ortlieb's Jazzhaus

JAZZ

(Map p142; ☑267-324-3348; www.ortliebsphilly. com; 847 N 3rd St; cover Tue-Thu $3-10, Fri $10, Sat $15, Sun $3) A respectable jazz lineup with a house band jamming every Tuesday night and Cajun cuisine on the menu (mains $20).

World Cafe Live

LIVE MUSIC

(Map p142; ☑215-222-1400; www.worldcafelive. com; 3025 Walnut St; cover $10-40) Located on the eastern edge of University City, World Cafe Live has upstairs and downstairs performance spaces featuring a restaurant and bar and is home to the radio station WXPN. It hosts an eclectic variety of live acts.

Theater & Culture

Kimmel Center for the Performing Arts

PERFORMING ARTS

(Map p142; ☑215-790-5800; www.kimmelcenter. org; cnr Broad & Spruce Sts) Philadelphia's most active center for fine music, the Kimmel Center organizes a vast array of performances, including the **Philadelphia Dance Company** and the **Philadelphia Orchestra**.

Tours available at 1pm Tuesday through Saturday.

Philadelphia Theatre Company

THEATER

(Map p142; ☑215-985-0420; www.philadelphia theatrecompany.org; 480 S Broad St, at Lombard St, Suzanne Roberts Theatre; tickets $35-70) This company, which produces quality contemporary plays with regional actors, has a high-end home in the heart of the arts district.

Pennsylvania Ballet

DANCE

(☑215-551-7000; www.paballet.org; tickets $25-130) An excellent dance company that performs in the beautiful **Academy of Music** (Map p142; 240 S Broad St) and the next-door Merriam Theater, part of the Kimmel Center.

Trocadero Theater

PERFORMING ARTS

(Map p142; ☑215-922-6888; www.thetroc.com; 1003 Arch St; cover $10-40) A rock-and-roll showcase in Chinatown housed in a 19th-century Victorian theater. The calendar encompasses a hodgepodge of musicians, spoken-word artists and comedians; Monday night is movie night.

Sports

Football is all about the **Philadelphia Eagles** (www.philadelphiaeagles.com), who play at state-of-the-art Lincoln Financial Field from August through January, usually twice a month, on Sunday. The baseball team is the National League **Philadelphia Phillies** (www.phillies.mlb.com), who play 81 home games at Citizen's Bank Park from April to October. Finally, basketball comes courtesy of the **Philadelphia 76ers** (www.nba.com/sixers) at Wells Fargo Center.

ⓘ Information

MEDIA

Philadelphia Daily News (www.phillydailynews.com) A tabloid-style daily.

Philadelphia Magazine (www.phillymag.com) A monthly glossy.

Philadelphia Weekly (www.philadelphiaweekly. com) Free alternative newspaper available at street boxes around town.

Philly.com (www.philly.com) News, listings and more, courtesy of the *Philadelphia Inquirer*.

WHYY 91-FM (www.whyy.org) Local National Public Radio affiliate.

MEDICAL SERVICES

Pennsylvania Hospital (☑800-789-7366; www.pennmedicine.org; 800 Spruce St; ⊗24hr)

TOURIST INFORMATION

Greater Philadelphia Tourism Marketing Corp (Map p146; www.gophila.com; 6th St, at Market St) The highly developed, nonprofit visitors bureau has comprehensive visitor information. Its welcome center shares space with the Independence Visitor Center.

Independence Visitor Center (Map p146; ☑ 215-965-7676; www.independencevisitorcenter.com; 6th St btwn Market & Arch Sts; ☺ 8:30am-5pm) Run by the National Park Service, the center has maps and brochures for all of the sights in the city and around.

❶ Getting There & Away

AIR

Philadelphia International Airport (PHL; ☑ 215-937-6937; www.phl.org; 8000 Essington Ave), 7 miles south of Center City, is served by direct international flights; domestically, it has flights to over 100 destinations in the USA.

BUS

Greyhound (Map p142; ☑ 215-931-4075; www.greyhound.com; 1001 Filbert St) and **Peter Pan Bus Lines** (Map p142; www.peterpanbus.com; 1001 Filbert St) are the major bus carriers; **Bolt Bus** (Map p142; www.boltbus.com) and **Megabus** (Map p142; www.us.megabus.com) are popular and comfortable competitors. Greyhound connects Philadelphia with hundreds of cities nationwide, while Peter Pan and the others concentrate on the northeast. When booked online a round-trip ride to NYC can be as low as $18 (2½ hours one way), to Atlantic City it's $20 (1½ hours) and to Washington, DC, it's $28 (4½ hours). **NJ Transit** (www.njtransit.state.nj.us), based at the Greyhound terminal, carries you from Philly to various points in New Jersey.

CAR

From the north and south, the I-95 (Delaware Expwy) follows the eastern edge of the city beside the Delaware River, with several exits for Center City. The I-276 (Pennsylvania Turnpike) runs east across the northern part of the city and over the river to connect with the New Jersey Turnpike.

TRAIN

Beautiful **30th St Station** (☑ 215-349-2153; www.30thstreetstation.com; 30th St, at Market St) is one of the biggest train hubs in the country. **Amtrak** (www.amtrak.com) provides services from here to Boston (regional and Acela express service one way $87 to $206, five to 5¾ hours) and Pittsburgh (regional service from $55, seven to eight hours). A cheaper but longer and more complicated way to get to NYC is to take the Septa R7 suburban train to Trenton in New Jersey. From there you can connect with NJ Transit to Newark's Penn Station, then continue on NJ Transit to New York City's Penn Station.

❶ Getting Around

Downtown distances are short enough to let you see most places on foot, and a train, bus or taxi can get you to places further out with relative ease.

Septa (www.septa.org) operates Philadelphia's municipal buses, plus two subway lines and a trolley service. Though extensive and reliable, the web of bus lines (120 routes servicing 159 sq miles) is difficult to make sense of. The one-way fare on most routes is $2.25, for which you'll need exact change or a token. Many subway stations and transit stores sell discounted packages of two tokens for $3.60.

The fare for a taxi to Center City from the airport is a flat fee of $28.50. Septa's airport line ($6.50) will drop you off in University City or at numerous stops in Center City.

Cabs, especially around City Center, are easy to hail. The flag drop or fare upon entry is $2.70, then $2.30 per mile or portion thereof. All licensed taxis have GPS and most accept credit cards.

The **Phlash** (www.ridephillyphlash.com; ☺ 10am-6pm daily summer, 10am-6pm Fri-Sun May, Sep & Oct) shuttle bus looks like an old-school trolley and loops between Penn's Landing and the Philadelphia Museum of Art (one way/all day $2/12). It runs approximately every 15 minutes.

Around Philadelphia

Valley Forge

After the defeat at the Battle of Brandywine Creek and the British occupation of Philadelphia in 1777, General Washington and 12,000 Continental troops withdrew to Valley Forge. Today, Valley Forge symbolizes Washington's endurance and leadership. The **Valley Forge National Historic Park** (☑ 610-783-1099; www.nps.gov/vafo; cnr N Gulph Rd & Rte 23, park grounds; ☺ 6am-10pm, welcome center & Washington's Headquarters 9am-5pm) **FREE** contains 5½ sq miles of scenic beauty and open space 20 miles northwest of downtown Philadelphia – a remembrance of where 2000 of George Washington's 12,000 troops perished from freezing temperatures, hunger and disease, while many others returned home. A 22-mile cycling path along the Schuylkill River connects Valley Forge to Philadelphia.

New Hope & Lambertville

About 40 miles north of Philadelphia, New Hope and its sister town, Lambertville, across the Delaware River in NJ, sit equidistant from Philadelphia and NYC, and are a pair of quaint, artsy little towns. Both are edged with long and peaceful towpaths, perfect for runners, cyclists and strollers, and a bridge with a walking lane lets you crisscross between the two with ease. The towns draw a large number of gay folk; rainbow flags hanging outside various businesses demonstrate the town's gay-friendliness.

The **Golden Nugget Antique Market** (☑ 609-397-0811; www.gnmarket.com; 1850 River Rd; ◷ 6am-4pm), 1 mile south of Lambertville, has all sorts of finds, from furniture to clothing, from a variety of dealers. Or spend a few picturesque hours gliding downstream in a canoe, kayak, raft or tube, courtesy of **Bucks County River Country** (☑ 215-297-5000; www.rivercountry.net; 2 Walters Lane; tube $18-22, canoe $62; ◷ rental 9am-2:30pm, return by 5pm), about 8 miles north of New Hope, just off Rte 32.

Both towns have a plethora of cute B&Bs if you decide to make a weekend out of it. Try **Porches on the Towpath** (☑ 215-862-3277; www.porchesnewhope.com; 20 Fisher's Alley; r from $115 Mon-Fri, from $155 Sat & Sun), a quirky Victorian with porches and canal views.

For a meal in a divinely renovated former church try the **Marsha Brown Creole Kitchen and Lounge** (☑ 215-862-7044; 15 S Main St; mains $15-30; ◷ 11:30am-10pm Mon-Thu, to 11pm Fri & Sat, to 9pm Sun) in New Hope for catfish, steaks and lobster. Or head to **DeAnna's** (☑ 609-397-8957; 54 N Franklin St; mains $18-25; ◷ 5-9:30pm Tue-Thu, to 10pm Fri & Sat) in Lambertville for homemade pastas and delicious meat and fish dishes prepared by the owner/chef.

Pennsylvania Dutch Country

The core of Pennsylvania Dutch Country lies in the southeast region of Pennsylvania, in an area about 20 miles by 15 miles, east of Lancaster. The Amish (*ah*-mish), Mennonite and Brethren religious communities are collectively known as the 'Plain People.' All are Anabaptist sects (only those who choose the faith are baptized), who were persecuted in their native Switzerland, and from the early 1700s settled in tolerant Pennsylvania. Speaking German dialects, they became known as 'Dutch' (from 'Deutsch'). Most Pennsylvania Dutch live on farms and their beliefs vary from sect to sect. Many do not use electricity, and most opt for horse-drawn buggies – a delightful sight, and sound, in the area. The strictest believers, the Old Order Amish, wear dark, plain clothing, and live a simple, Bible-centered life – but have, ironically, become a major tourist attraction, thus bringing busloads of gawkers and the requisite strip malls, chain restaurants and hotels that lend this entire area an oxymoronic quality, to say the least. Because there is so much commercial development continually encroaching on multigenerational family farms, it takes some doing to appreciate the unique nature of the area. Try to find your way through a series of back roads snaking their way through rural countryside between Intercourse and Strasburg.

◉ Sights & Activities

On the western edge of Amish country, the city of **Lancaster** – a mix of art galleries, well-preserved brick row houses and somewhat derelict blocks – was briefly the US capital in September 1777, when Congress stopped here overnight. The monthly **First Friday** (www.lancasterarts.com) celebration brings out a friendly local crowd for gallery hops along artsy Prince St.

Probably named for its crossroads location, **Intercourse** includes Kitchen Kettle Village, which has touristy shops selling clothing, quilts, candles, furniture, fudge and, of course, souvenirs with off-color jokes. The **Tanger Outlet stores** on Rte 30 draw tourists with their 21st-century designer clothes.

★**Strasburg Railroad**　　　　　TRAIN
(☑ 717-687-7522;　www.strasburgrailroad.com; Rte 741, Strasburg; coach class adult/child $14/8; ◷ multiple trips daily, times vary by season; ☞) Since 1832 the Strasburg Railroad has run steam-driven trains along the same route to Paradise and back (at the same speed as well). The wooden train carriages are gorgeously restored with stained glass, shiny brass lamps and plush burgundy seats. The **Railroad Museum of Pennsylvania** (☑ 717-687-8628; www.rrmuseumpa.org; Rte 741, Strasburg; adult/child $10/8; ◷ 9am-5pm Mon-Sat, noon-5pm Sun, closed Sun Nov-Mar; ☞) across the street has 100 gigantic mechanical marvels to climb aboard and admire.

Landis Valley Museum
MUSEUM

(☑717-569-0401; www.landisvalleymuseum.org; 2451 Kissel Hill Rd, Lancaster; adult/child $12/8; ⊙9am-5pm, from noon Sun) In the 18th century, German immigrants flooded southeastern Pennsylvania and only some were Amish. Most lived like the costumed docents at this museum, a re-creation of village life that includes a working smithy, weavers, stables and more.

Ephrata Cloister
MUSEUM

(☑717-733-6600; www.ephratacloister.org; 632 W Main St, Ephrata; adult/child $10/6; ⊙9am-5pm Mon-Sat, from noon Sun) One of the country's earliest religious communities was founded here in 1732 by Conrad Beissel, a German emigre escaping persecution in his native land and dissatisfied with wordly ways and distractions. There's a small museum in the visitor center and you can walk or take a guided tour of its collection of medieval-style buildings.

Sturgis Pretzel House
FACTORY TOUR

(☑717-626-4354; www.juliussturgis.com; 219 E Main St, Lititz; admission $3; ⊙9am-5pm Mon-Sat; ♠) Try your hand at twisting and rolling dough at the USA's first pretzel factory.

Aaron & Jessica's Buggy Rides
TOUR

(☑717-768-8828; 3121 Old Philadelphia Pike, Bird-in-Hand; adult/child $10/6; ⊙9am-5pm Mon-Sat; ♠) A fun 2-mile tour narrated by an Amish driver.

🛏 Sleeping

There's a slew of inns and B&Bs in Amish country and virtually every national motel chain is represented along a strip-mall-filled stretch of Rte 30/Lincoln Hwy just east of Lancaster.

★General Sutter Inn
INN $

(☑717-626-2115; www.generalsutterinn.com; 14 East Main St, Lititz; r from $70; ❈🐾�🖥) The bones of this atmospheric and charming inn anchoring one end of Lititz's main street date to 1764. Ten wood-floored and cheerful rooms are tastefully furnished with antiques. A new top-floor annex called the Rock Lititz Penthouse has six, decidedly modern suites with a playful rock-and-roll theme. Attached is the extremely popular craft-beer-centric Bull's Head Pub.

A Farm Stay
ACCOMMODATION SERVICE $

(www.afarmstay.com; r from $60-180; ♠) If you like your vacations to be working ones,

check out this website which represents several dozen farm stays that range from stereotypical B&Bs to Amish farms. Most include breakfast, private bathrooms and some activity like milking cows or gathering eggs or simply petting a goat.

Fulton Steamboat Inn
HOTEL $$

(☑717-299-9999; 1 Hartman Bridge Rd, Lancaster; r from $100; ❈🐾🖥) A nautically themed hotel in landlocked Amish country seems like a gimmick even if the inventor of the steamboat was born nearby. The slight kitsch works, however. From shiny brass old-timey light fixtures to painterly wallpaper, the hotel's interior is rather elegant and its rooms are spacious and comfy.

Red Caboose Motel & Restaurant
MOTEL $$

(☑888-687-5005; www.redcaboosemotel.com; 312 Paradise Lane, Ronks; r from $120; ❈🐾🖥) There's nothing very hobo-esque about a night's sleep in one of these 25-ton cabooses – TVs and mini-fridges included – though the basic furnishings aren't the draw. Even if spaces are narrow – the width of a train car – the novelty appeals to adults as well as kids. Set on a beautiful rural lane surrounded by picturesque countryside.

Cork Factory
BOUTIQUE HOTEL $$

(☑717-735-2075; www.corkfactoryhotel.com; 480 New Holland Ave, Lancaster; r incl breakfast from $125; ❈🖥) An abandoned brick behemoth now houses a stylishly up-to-date hotel only a few miles northeast of the Lancaster city center. Sunday brunch at the hotel's restaurant is a fusion of seasonal new American and down-home comfort cooking.

🍴 Eating

To sample one of the famous family-style restaurants and hearty dishes of Amish country, get prepared to rub elbows with lots of tourists.

★Bird-in-Hand Farmers Market
MARKET

(☑717-393-9674; 2710 Old Philadelphia Pike, Bird-in-Hand; ⊙8:30am-5:30pm Wed-Sat Jul-Oct, call for other times of year) A one-stop shop of Dutch Country highlights. It has fudge, quilts and crafts but primarily great deals on tasty locally made jams, cheeses, pretzels, beef jerky and more specialties like scrapple (pork scraps mixed with cornmeal and wheat flour, shaped into a loaf and fried); two lunch counters serve meals.

Central Market
MARKET $

(www.centralmarketlancaster.com; 23 N Market St, Lancaster; ⊙ 6am-4pm Tue & Fri, to 2pm Sat) The bustling market offers local produce, cheese, meats, Amish baked goods and crafts and all the regional gastronomic delicacies – fresh horseradish, whoopie pies, soft pretzels, sub sandwiches stuffed with cured meats and dripping with oil – as well as ethnic eateries.

Tomato Pie Cafe
SANDWICHES $

(23 N Broad St, Lititz; mains $6; ⊙ 7am-9pm Mon-Sat; 🛜) Housed in a charming yellow and green home just around the corner from Main St, this cafe gets crowded especially at lunchtime on weekends. Besides the signature tomato pie, the menu has salads and sandwiches like a peanut butter, nutella and banana panini, excellent breakfasts and baristas who take their coffee seriously.

Dutch Haven
DESSERT $

(2857 Lincoln Hwy/Rte 30, Ronks; 6-inch pies $7) Stop by for a sticky-sweet shoofly pie.

Good 'N Plenty Restaurant
AMERICAN $$

(Rte 896, Smoketown; mains $11; ⊙ 11:30am-8pm Mon-Sat, closed Jan; 🍴) Sure, you'll be dining with busloads of tourists and your cardiologist might not approve, but hunkering down at one of the picnic tables for a family-style meal ($21) is a lot of fun. Besides the main dining room, which is the size of a football field, there are a couple of other mini-areas where you can order from an à la carte menu.

Bube's Brewery
EUROPEAN, BREWERY $$

(www.bubesbrewery.com; 102 North Market St, Mt Joy) This well-preserved 19th-century German brewery cum restaurant complex contains several atmospheric bars and four separate dining rooms (one underground), hosts costumed 'feasts' and, naturally, brews its own beer.

Lancaster Brewing Co
AMERICAN, BREWERY $$

(302 N Plum St, Lancaster; mains $9-22; ⊙ 11:30am-10pm) Just down the street from the Cork Factory Hotel in Lancaster, the bar here draws young neighborhood regulars. The menu is a big step up from standard pub fare – rack of wild boar and cranberry sausage is an example – but you can't beat specials like 35¢-wing night.

❶ Information

Use a map to navigate the back roads, avoiding main Rtes 30 and 340, or visit in winter when tourism is down. Even better, rent a bicycle from **Rails to Trail Bicycle Shop** (☎ 717-367-7000;

DON'T MISS

GETTYSBURG

This tranquil, compact and history-laden town, 145 miles west of Philadelphia, saw one of the Civil War's most decisive and bloody battles. It's also where Lincoln delivered his Gettysburg Address. Much of the ground where Robert E Lee's Army of Northern Virginia and Maj Gen Joseph Hooker's Union Army of the Potomac skirmished and fought can be explored either in your own car with a map and guide, on an audio CD tour, a bus tour or a two-hour guided ranger tour ($65 per vehicle) – the latter is most recommended, but if short on time, it's still worth driving the narrow lanes past fields with dozens of monuments marking significant sites and moments in the battle. The centerpiece of any visit (and where tours are booked) is the massive new **Gettysburg National Military Park Museum & Visitor Center** (☎ 717-334-1124; www.gettysburgfoundation.org; 1195 Baltimore Pike; adult/child $12.50/8.50; ⊙ 8am-5pm Nov-Mar, to 6pm Apr-Oct) several miles south of town. It houses an incredible museum filled with artifacts and displays exploring every nuance of the battle, a film explaining Gettsyburg's context, and Paul Philippoteaux's 377ft cyclorama painting of Pickett's Charge.

The annual **Civil War Heritage Days**, a festival held in the first weekend of July, features living-history encampments and battle reenactments drawing aficionados from near and far.

For accommodations, try the stately three-story Victorian **Brickhouse Inn** (☎ 717-338-9337; www.brickhouseinn.com; 452 Baltimore St; r with breakfast $119-189; 🅿 ❄ 🛜), built c 1898, a wonderful B&B with charming rooms and an outdoor patio. For a meal in Gettysburg's oldest home, built in 1776, head to **Dobbin House Tavern** (☎ 717-334-2100; 89 Steinwehr Ave; mains $8-30; ⊙ 11:30am-9pm), which serves heaping sandwiches and more elaborate meat and fish meals in kitschy themed dining rooms.

www.railstotrail.com; 1010 Hershey Rd; rental per day $25; ⊙10am-6pm) between Hershey and Lancaster, pack some food and hit the road. The **Dutch Country Visitors Center** (☑800-723-8824; www.padutchcountry.com; 501 Greenfield Rd; ⊙9am-5pm Mon-Sat, 10am-4pm Sun), off Rte 30 in Lancaster, offers comprehensive information.

❶ Getting There & Around

RRTA (www.redrosetransit.com) local buses link the main towns, but a car is much more convenient for sightseeing. The **Amtrak train station** (53 McGovern Ave) has trains to and from Philadelphia ($16, 70 minutes) and Pittsburgh ($51, six hours).

Pennsylvania Wilds

Interspersed throughout this rural region are regal buildings and grand mansions, remnants of a time when lumber, coal and oil brought great wealth and the world's attention to this corner of Pennsylvania. Several museums (oil ones in Titusville and Bradford and one on lumber in Galeton) tell the boom and bust industrial story. But natural resources of another kind remain – known as 'the Wilds' – roads (especially **scenic Rte 6**) and hundreds of miles of trails snake through vast national forests and state parks.

The Kinzua railroad viaduct, once the highest and one of the longest railroad suspension bridges in the world and partly destroyed by a tornado in 2011, has been converted into the **Kizua Bridge Skywalk** (www.visitanf.com). The walkway dead ends 600ft out in an overlook over the gorge; a small section has a glass floor so you can see directly to the valley floor 225ft below. The **Lodge at Glendorn** (☑800-843-8568; www.glendorn.com; 1000 Glendorn Dr, Bradford; r from $450) in Bradford to the north is a luxurious retreat with outdoor activities galore.

Ponder the immensity of the universe at **Cherry Springs State Park** (www.dcnr.state.pa.us/state parks/parks/cherrysprings), considered one of the best places for stargazing east of the Mississippi. Crowds of several hundred people are common on clear nights in July and August when the Milky Way is almost directly overhead. Camping is available here or nearby.

Often referred to as the 'Pennsylvania Grand Canyon,' Pine Creek Gorge in the Tioga State Forest has two access points

and parks on either side: the more visited and developed **Leonard Harrison State Park** (☑570-724-3061; www.visitpaparks.com) on the east rim and the more peaceful Colton Point State Park on the west rim. Both have trails to waterfalls and the canyon floor.

Pittsburgh

Famous as an industrial center during the 19th century, to many Americans Pittsburgh still conjures stark images of billowing clouds emanating from steel and coal factories. Today's city, however, has a well-earned reputation for being one of the more livable metropolitan areas in the country. The city sits at the point where the Monongahela (oft referred to as 'the Mon') and Allegheny Rivers join the Ohio River, spreads out over the waterways and has hilly neighborhoods connected by picturesque bridges all with footpaths (more than any other city in the US). Teeming with students from the many universities in town, it's a surprisingly hip and cultured city with top-notch museums, abundant greenery and several bustling neighborhoods with lively restaurant and bar scenes.

Scottish-born immigrant Andrew Carnegie made his fortune here by modernizing steel production, and his legacy is still synonymous with the city and its many cultural and educational institutions. Production dipped during the Great Depression but rose again because of mass-produced automobiles in the 1930s. When the economy and local steel industry took another major hit in the 1970s, the city's pride was buoyed by its local NFL football team: the Steelers achieved a remarkable run of four Super Bowl championships, a feat whose importance to the continuing psyche of some Pittsburghers can't be underestimated. After the steel industry's demise, Pittsburgh's economy refocused on health care, technology and education, and the city is home to several notable Fortune 500 companies, including Alcoa and Heinz.

◉ Sights & Activities

Points of interest in Pittsburgh are scattered everywhere, and the city's spread-out nature makes it a difficult place to cover thoroughly on foot. The Great Allegheny Passage, a 141-mile hiking and biking path between Cumberland, MD, and Pittsburgh was completed in the summer of 2013; from Cumberland, the C&O Canal Towpath carries on all the way to Washington, DC.

Pittsburgh Parks Conservancy   PARKS
(✅ 412-682-7275; www.pittsburghparks.org) For pretty much any outdoor pursuit, the best option is the elaborate 1700-acre system of the **Pittsburgh Parks Conservancy**, which comprises **Schenley Park** (with a public swimming pool and golf course), **Highland Park** (with swimming pool, tennis courts and bicycling track), **Riverview Park** (sporting ball fields and horseback riding trails) and **Frick Park** (with hiking trails, clay courts and a bowling green), all with beautiful running, cycling and in-line skating trails.

◉ Downtown

The mystical-sounding **Golden Triangle** (mostly only tourist brochures use this term), between the converging Monongahela and Allegheny Rivers, is Pittsburgh's renovated downtown containing the financial and business districts, as well as fourteen or so blocks filled with theaters, performance spaces and art galleries referred to as the 'Cultural District'. Every Thursday from May to November there's a farmers market in **Market Square**, a public piazza surrounded by restaurants – some fastfood chains – and tall office buildings (a large complex including a hotel, offices and parking garage was going up at the time of research). **CONSOL Energy Center** (www. consolenergycenter.com; 1001 Fifth Ave), just east of downtown, is where the NHL Pittsburgh Penguins drop the puck (major concerts held here as well). Just northeast of here, the **Strip** offers warehouses, ethnic food stores, cafes and nightclubs.

Point State Park   PARK
At the tip of the triangle formed by the meeting of the Monongahela and Allegheny Rivers is this park containing the **Fort Pitt Museum** (✅ 412-281-9284; www.heinzhistoryc-enter.org; 601 Commonwealth Pl; adult/child $6/3; ⊙ 10am-5pm), which commemorates the historic heritage of the French and Indian War. The renovated and beautified waterfront is popular during summer with strollers, cyclists, loungers and runners. For a longer run, head to the 11-mile gravel-paved **Montour Trail** (www.montourtrail.org), accessible by crossing the 6th St Bridge and catching the paved path at the Carnegie Science Center.

Senator John Heinz Pittsburgh Regional History Center   MUSEUM
(✅ 412-454-6000; www.heinzhistorycenter.org; 1212 Smallman St; adult/child incl Sports Museum $15/6; ⊙ 10am-5pm) This remodeled brick warehouse offers a good take on the region's past, with exhibits on the French and Indian War, early settlers, immigrants, steel and the glass industry. It's also home to the **Western Pennsylvania Sports Museum**, focusing on champs from Pittsburgh; fun interactive exhibits for kids and for adults who refuse to admit their shot at professional sports has passed them by.

August Wilson Center for African American Culture   ARTS CENTER
(✅ 412-258-2700; www.augustwilsoncenter.org; 980 Liberty Ave; special exhibitions adult/child $8/3; ⊙ 11am-6pm) Named for Pittsburgh native and award-winning playwright August Wilson, the strikingly contemporary building houses a museum, classrooms and performance spaces.

◉ North Side

This part of town across the Allegheny River feels lively when **Heinz Field** (✅ 412-323-1200; www.steelers.com; 100 Art Rooney Ave) or **PNC Park** (✅ 412-323-5000; www.pirateball.com; 115 Federal St) are filled with fans for a Steelers or Pirates game; bridges from downtown are closed to vehicular traffic at this time. One-hour tours of Heinz Field (a pivotal scene in the latest Batman, *The Dark Knight Rises,* film was shot here) are open to the public every Friday from April to the end of October (adult/child $7/3). Nearby in the northwest is the **Mexican War Streets** neighborhood, named after battles and soldiers of the 1846 Mexican War. The carefully restored row houses, with Greek Revival doorways and Gothic turrets lining the quiet streets, make for a peaceful, post-museum stroll. Keep in mind, non-fast-food restaurants are scarce around here.

★ Andy Warhol Museum   MUSEUM
(✅ 412-237-8300; www.warhol.org; 117 Sandusky St; adult/child $20/10; ⊙ 10am-5pm Tue-Thu, Sat & Sun, to 10pm Fri) This six-story musuem celebrates Pittsburgh's coolest native son, who became famous for his pop art, avant-garde movies, celebrity connections and Velvet Underground spectaculars. Exhibits include celebrity portraits, while the museum's theater hosts frequent film screenings and

quirky performers. Friday-night cocktails at the museum are popular with Pittsburgh's gay community.

Carnegie Science Center
MUSEUM

(☑412-237-3400; www.carnegiesciencecenter.org; 1 Allegheny Ave; adult/child $18/12, IMAX & special exhibits extra; ☺10am-5pm Sun-Fri, to 7pm Sat; ⚐) Great for kids and a cut above the average hands-on science museum, with innovative exhibits on subjects ranging from outer space to candy.

Children's Museum of Pittsburgh
MUSEUM

(☑412-322-5058; www.pittsburghkids.org; 10 Children's Way, Allegheny Sq; adult/child $13/12; ☺10am-5pm ; ⚐) Features loads of interactive exhibits, including a chance for kids to get under the hood of real cars and some child-friendly Warhol works.

National Aviary
WILDLIFE RESERVE

(☑412-323-7235; www.aviary.org; 700 Arch St; adult/child $13/11; ☺10am-5pm; ⚐) More than 600 exotic and endangered birds.

Mattress Factory
ARTS CENTER

(☑412-231-3169; www.mattress.org; 500 Sampsonia Way; adult $15; ☺10am-5pm Tue-Sat, 1-5pm Sun) Hosts avant-garde contemporary installation art and performances.

◉ South Side & Mt Washington

Across the Monongahela River is the South Side, whose Slopes rise up to Mt Washington; at the Flats, youthful and funky E Carson St bustles with clubs and restaurants. In the 10 blocks between the 10th St Bridge and Birmingham Bridge there are dozens of bars, including a bunch of hole-in-the-wall joints. Rising up from the bustling South Side valley is the neighborhood called the **South Side Slopes**, a fascinating community of houses that seem perilously perched on the edge of cliffs, accessible via steep, winding roads and hundreds of stairs.

★Monongahela & Duquesne Incline
CABLE CAR

(One-way adult/child $2.50/1.25; ☺5:30am-12:45am Mon-Sat, from 7am Sun) The historic funicular railroads (c 1877) that run up and down **Mt Washington's** steep slopes afford great city views, especially at night. At the start of the Monongahela Incline, which is just over the Smithfield St bridge, is **Station Square** (☑800-859-8959; www.stationsquare. com; Station Square Dr), a group of beautiful,

renovated railway buildings that now houses a few restaurants, nightclubs and bars. About halfway between the two inclines along the Monongahela River is **Highmark Stadium**, a new 3500 seat soccer stadium. Grandview Ave, at the top of the Duquesne Incline, has several excellent restaurants with romantic views including the five-star Le Mont.

◉ Oakland & Around

The University of Pittsburgh and Carnegie Mellon University are here, and the surrounding streets are packed with cheap eateries, cafes, shops and student homes.

Carnegie Museums
MUSEUM

(☑412-622-3131; www.carnegiemuseums. org; 4400 Forbes Ave; adult/child $18/12; ☺10am-5pm Tue-Sat, from noon Sun; ⚐) The **Carnegie Museum of Art**, has terrific exhibits of architecture, impressionist, postimpressionist and modern American paintings; and the **Carnegie Museum of Natural History** features a complete Tyrannosaurus skeleton and exhibits on Pennsylvania geology and Inuit prehistory.

Frick Art & Historical Center
MUSEUM

(☑412 371 0600; www.thefrickpittsburgh.org; 7227 Reynolds St; museum & grounds free, Clayton tours $12; ☺10am-5pm Tue-Sun) **FREE** East of Oakland, in Point Breeze, this museum displays some of Henry Clay Frick's Flemish, French and Italian paintings; assorted Frickmobiles like a 1914 Rolls Royce in the Car & Carriage Museum; more than 5 acres of grounds and gardens; and Clayton, the restored 1872 Frick mansion. Bus 71 C from downtown heads out this way.

Phipps Conservatory
GARDENS

(☑412-622-6914; www.phipps.conservatory.org; One Schenley Park; adult/child $15/11; ☺9:30am-5pm, to 10pm Fri; ⚐) ✎ An impressive steel-and-glass greenhouse with beautifully designed and curated gardens.

Cathedral of Learning
TOWER

(☑412-624-6000; 4200 Fifth Ave; tours $3; ☺9am-3pm Mon-Sat, from 11am Sun) **FREE** Rising up from the center of the University of Pittsburgh campus is this soaring grand, 42-story Gothic tower, which at 535ft is the second-tallest education building in the world. It houses the elegant **Nationality Classrooms**, each representing a different style and period; most are accessible only with a guided tour.

⊙ Squirrel Hill & Shadyside

These upscale neighborhoods feature wide streets, excellent restaurants, chain stores and independent boutiques and bakeries (try the burnt-almond tortes, a classic Pittsburgh dessert). Squirrel Hill is home to Pittsburgh's large Jewish community, the city's best kosher eateries, butchers and Judaica shops. Apartment buildings, duplexes and more modest housing are almost as common as the grand mansions the neighborhood is known for.

In Shadyside, Walnut St is the bustling main strip. The leafy campus of **Chatham University**, located between the two neighborhoods, is a nice place to stroll.

⊙ Greater Pittsburgh

Formerly gritty **Lawrenceville** has become the city's **Interior Design District**, comprising the stretch on and around Butler St from 16th to 62nd Sts. It's a long and spotty strip of shops, galleries, studios, bars and eateries that's on every hipster's radar, and runs into the gentrifying **Garfield** neighborhood, a good place for cheap ethnic eats.

Bloomfield, a really little Little Italy, is a strip of groceries, Italian eateries and, of all things, a landmark Polish restaurant, the Bloomfield Bridge Tavern. The Pittsburgh zoo and aquarium and a water park are nearby.

Kennywood Amusement Park AMUSEMENT PARK
(☑ 412-461-0500; www.kennywood.com; 4800 Kennywood Blvd, West Mifflin; adult/child $40/27; ☺ 10:30am-10pm Jun-Aug; 🖪) A nationally historic landmarked amusement park 12 miles southeast of downtown with four old wooden roller coasters.

☞ Tours

Rivers of Steel TOUR
(☑ 412-464-4020; www.riversofsteel.com) This organization is dedicated to preserving the physical heritage as well as the memories and stories of the region's industrial past. It's worth touring Carrie Furnace (Fridays & Saturdays April to end-October), the long ago decommissioned US Steel blast furnace that now stands like a decaying postapocalyptic memento mori. At its height in the late 1800s it produced 9000 tons of molten iron every day. Several films and music videos have been shot here.

Tour-Ed Mine TOUR
(☑ 724-224-4720; www.tour-edmine.com; 748 Bull Creek Rd, Tarentum; adult/child $10/9; ☺ 10am-4pm, closed Tue, Jun-Sep; 🖪) To experience something of the claustrophobia and learn about the working lives of coal miners, take this tour 160ft below the earth's surface.

Alan Irvine Storyteller Tours CULTURAL TOUR
(☑ 412-508-2077; www.alanirvine.com/walking_tour; tours $15) This historian brings the city's past to life in a journey through several neighborhoods.

'Burgh Bits & Bites Food Tour CULTURAL TOUR
(☑ 412-901-7150; www.burghfoodtour.com; tours $37) Wonderful way to discover the city's unique ethnic eats.

Pittsburgh History & Landmarks Foundation CULTURAL TOUR
(☑ 412-471-5808; www.phlf.org; Station Sq; some tours free, others from $5) Specialized historic, architectural or cultural tours by foot or motor coach.

🛏 Sleeping

Straight-up chain hotels, especially around Oakland, dominate the city's lodging options.

Inn on Negley INN $$
(☑ 412-661-0631; www.innonnegley.com; 703 Negley Ave; r $180-280; 🅿 ❄ 🛜) Formerly a pair of Shadyside inns, these two Victorian houses have been combined into one refurbished gem with a clean-line aesthetic that still bursts with romance. It features four-poster beds, handsome furniture and fireplaces, large windows and, in some rooms, hot tubs.

Priory INN $$
(☑ 412-231-3338; www.thepriory.com; 614 Pressley St; s/d/ste incl breakfast from $99/150/180; 🅿 ❄ 🛜) Housed in a former Catholic monastery on the North Side just over the Veterans Bridge, the Priory is a mix of old-fashioned furnishings with contemporary design touches. It has a parlor with a fireplace and an interior courtyard good for drinks in warm months. A wing with an additional 17 rooms was added in 2011. Attached is the magnificent Grand Hall, a former church, now host to weddings and events.

Inn on the Mexican War Streets
BOUTIQUE HOTEL $$

(☏412-231-6544; www.innonthemexicanwarstreets
.com; 604 W North Ave; r incl breakfast $139-199;
P❄🐾📶) This historic, gay-owned mansion on
the North Side is near the museums and right
on the bus line that takes you downtown. Ex-
pect hearty homemade breakfasts, charming
hosts, stunning antique furnishings and an
elegant porch, plus a martini lounge and the
four-star restaurant Acanthus.

Morning Glory Inn
B&B $$

(☏412-431-1707; www.gloryinn.com; 2119 Sarah St;
r incl breakfast $155-195, ste $190-450; P❄🐾📶)
An Italianate-style Victorian brick town
house popular for weddings, the Morning
Glory is in the heart of the busy South Side.
The overall decor is slightly chintzy – think
floral patterns, wicker furniture, four-poster
beds – but you can relax in the charming
backyard patio, and delicious breakfasts are
a major plus.

Parador Inn
B&B $$

(☏412-231-4800; www.theparadorinn.com; 939
Western Ave; r incl breakfast $150; P❄🐾📶) This
lovingly restored mansion on the North Side
not far from the National Aviary and Heinz
Field is a charming hodgepodge of aesthetic
influence – from Victorian to Caribbean
and everything in between. The owner is on
hand to answer any questions and there are
public rooms and a garden to relax in.

Sunnyledge
HOTEL $$

(☏412-683-5014; www.sunnyledge.com; 5124 Fifth
Ave; r/ste $189/275; P❄🐾📶) Though it refers
to itself as a 'boutique hotel,' it would be
more accurate to describe the Sunnyledge
as a 'historic' one. Housed in an 1886 mansion in Shadyside, the atmosphere is one of
traditional elegance, overwrought at times.
The restaurant on the premises gets mixed
reviews.

★ Omni William Penn Hotel
HOTEL $$$

(☏412-281-7100; www.omnihotels.com; 530 Wil-
liam Penn Place; r from $200; P❄🐾📶) Though
originally built by Henry Clay Frick nearly
100 years ago, his European inspiration is
alive and well in this elegant and stately
downtown behemoth. High tea is served
in the grand lobby, which is (surprisingly)
otherwise a welcoming meeting place for
nonguests. Above-average service, contem-
porary room furnishings, a spa, several din-
ing options and a newly opened basement
speakeasy bar round out the offerings.

✖ Eating

✖ Downtown & the Strip

For a taste of the city's ethnic texture, head
to the Strip district just east of downtown,
stretching from 14th St to 30th St between the
Allegheny River and Liberty Ave. A stroll along
Penn Ave from 17th to 23rd is the bustling
heart where local chefs go to shop at one-of-a-
kind food markets like **Stamoolis Brothers**,
Pennsylvania Macaroni and **Wholey**. The
best time to visit is between 10am and 3pm;
during the holiday season (parking close to
impossible), it's especially celebratory and in-
toxicating, literally, as homemade wine is typi-
cally passed out for free.

★ Original Oyster House
SEAFOOD $

(20 Market Sq; sandwich $6; ⊙10am-10pm Mon-
Sat) Operating in one form or another since
1870 and still drawing crowds of devotees
for its deep-fried fish sandwiches. Locals of
all stripes form a line out the door at lunch-
time but it's a strictly lowdown pretension-
free place with paper plates and plastic
silverware.

Primanti Bros
FAST FOOD $

(☏412-263-2142; www.primantibros.com; 18th
St, near Smallman St; sandwiches $6; ⊙24hr) A
Pittsburgh institution on the Strip, this al-
ways-packed place specializes in greasy and
delicious hot sandwiches, from knockwurst
and cheese to the 'Pitts-burger cheesesteak.'
Other outlets are in Oakland, Market Sq
downtown and South Side.

Pamela's
DINER $

(www.pamelasdiner.com; 60 21st St; mains $7;
⊙7am-3pm Mon-Sat, 8am-3pm Sun) Even Presi-
dent Obama liked this breakfast and sand-
wich joint in the Strip district. Several other
Pamela's throughout the city, all with a clas-
sic chrome diner look, are renowned for their
crepe-like crispy-around-the-edges pancakes.

★ Enrico Biscotti Company
ITALIAN $$

(www.enricobiscotti.com; 2022 Penn Ave; mains $10;
⊙11am-3pm Mon-Fri, from 8am Sat) The owner
Enrico, a charming raconteur, is as adept
at regaling customers with colorful neighborhood tales as he is at churning out delicious homemade bread and wood-burning-
oven pizzas. Housed in a former auto mechanic's garage in the Strip with high ceilings, brick walls and reclaimed furniture.
Check out the romantic comedy *The Bread,
My Sweet* for a version of Enrico's life. Bread,

wine and cheese-making classes ($65) are offered Sunday mornings.

Southside

Cafe du Jour
MEDITERRANEAN $$

(☑412-488-9695; 1107 E Carson St; mains $15-35; ☺11:30am-10pm Mon-Sat) A constantly changing menu of Mediterranean dishes includes especially good soups and salads for lunch; try to get a seat in the small outside courtyard. It's BYOB.

Dish Osteria Bar
MEDITERRANEAN $$

(☑412-390-2012; www.dishosteria.com; 128 S 17th St; mains $14-25; ☺5pm-2am Mon-Sat) A tuckedaway, intimate locals' fave. The simple wood tables and floors belie the at times extravagant Mediterranean creations, which range from fresh sardines with caramelized onions to fettuccine with lamb ragout.

Gypsy Café
MEDITERRANEAN $$

(☑412-381-4977; www.gypsycafe.net; 1330 Bingham St; mains $14-19; ☺11:30am-midnight) The purple floors and walls and brightly colored rugs make patrons here as happy as the fresh, seasonal fare. Menu items include a smoked trout plate and a stew of shrimp, scallop and feta. Hours are changeable so call ahead

Café Zenith
VEGETARIAN $$

(86 S 26th St; mains $10; ☺11am-9pm Thu-Sat, 11am-3pm Sun; ☑) A meal here is like eating in an antique shop, and everything from the formica tables and up is for sale. Regardless, the Sunday brunch ($10) and lengthy tea menu are up to date.

Other Neighborhoods

Original Hot Dog Shop
FAST FOOD $

(☑412-621-7388; 3901 Forbes Ave; sandwiches $3-7; ☺10am-3:30am) Affectionately nicknamed 'dirty Os' or 'the O' by locals, this is an Oakland favorite for its cheap dogs, subs, pizza, chicken wings, milk shakes and mounds of crispy fries – especially after a night at the bars. Inebriation isn't necessary for enjoyment, just very common.

Emil's Lounge
AMERICAN $

(414 Hawkins Ave, Braddock; mains $6; ☺10am-7pm Tue-Thu, to 8pm Fri, to 4pm Sat) Venture around 8.5 miles east of downtown to Braddock to experience a family-run survivor from the steel-mill era. Old, old, old school Emil's has been serving up artery-clogging portions of

chicken parm, catfish, burgers and other sandwiches for 60 years. Expect wood paneling, carpeting and a friendly welcome from the daughter of the original owners.

Ritter's Diner
DINER $

(5221 Baum Blvd; mains $7; ☺24hr) A classic greasy spoon where locals of the Bloomfield neighborhood head for a pierogi after a long night out. Each table has its own jukebox.

Quiet Storm Coffeehouse & Restaurant
CAFE $

(☑412-661-9355; www.qspgh.com; 5430 Penn Ave; mains $6-11; ☺8am-5pm Mon-Thu, to 10pm Fri, 9am-4pm Sat & Sun; ☑) This hipster-filled, multiuse cafe in Garfield specializes in veggie and vegan cuisine and hosts frequent readings and musical performances.

Dinette
PIZZERIA $$

(☑412-362-0202; www.dinette-pgh.com; 5996 Penn Circle South; pizzas $15; ☺5-10pm Tue-Thu, to 11pm Fri & Sat) Two time James Beard award semifinalist Sonja Finn has elevated this casual Shadyside eatery into a destination for local foodies. The individual gourmet thin-crust pizzas are topped with locally sourced meat and produce. Excellent wine selection.

Industry Public House
MODERN AMERICAN $$

(www.industrypgh.com; 4305 Butler St; mains $10; ☺11am-2am) Comfort food with a twist – eg lobster mac 'n' cheese, wild boar bacon burgers, artisanal cocktails and locally brewed beers – means this gastropub is prototypical Lawrenceville.

★Isabela on Grandview
MODERN AMERICAN $$$

(☑412-431-5882; www.isabelaongrandview.com; 1318 Grandview Ave; meals $70; ☺5-10pm Mon-Sat) Perched atop Mt Washington with gorgeous nighttime city views, this small romantic restaurant is worthy of anniversary or proposal dinners. The seven-course prixe-fixe meal might include lobster and duck and always fresh, seasonal ingredients.

Drinking & Entertainment

Bars & Nightclubs

Most nightlife is centered on the South Side and the Strip. Carson St is ground zero for bar-hopping. You'll find several big, frenzied dance clubs, known as 'meatmarkets,' clustered at the edge of the Strip district. Most gay bars are in a concentrated stretch of Liberty Ave downtown.

Wigle Whiskey DISTILLERY
(www.wiglewhiskey.com; 2401 Smallman St; ⊙10am-6pm Tue-Sun) Pittsburgh's one and only distillery is family owned (almost every member has made a dramatic career change) and uses organic and local ingredients to produce artisan batches of rye and wheat whiskey. Head to this renovated brick warehouse in the Strip for tours ($20) and $5 sample flights.

Bar Marco COCKTAIL BAR
(2216 Penn Ave; ⊙5-11pm Mon, to 2am Tue-Fri, 10am-2am Sat, to 10am-3pm Sun) Sample the top-flight wine menu and cocktails, expertly prepared by bartending pros, at this sophisticated space in a renovated fire house in the Strip. Excllent brunch on weekends.

Bloomfield Bridge Tavern PUB, LIVE MUSIC
(☑412-682-8611; 4412 Liberty Ave; ⊙5pm-2am Mon-Sat) 'The only Polish restaurant in Lil' Italy' is a gritty pub serving beers with excellent sides of pierogi, and indie-rock bands on the weekends.

Church Brew Works BREWERY
(☑412-688-8200; 3525 Liberty Ave) Serves handcrafted beers in a massive former church space. A standout in Lawrenceville.

Hofbräuhaus BEER HALL
(☑412-235-7065; 2705 S Water St) An imitation of the famous Munich beer hall and only a block off Carson.

Gooski BAR
(3117 Brereton St; ⊙3pm-2am) Hipster-cum-dive bar in Polish Hill neighborhood with cheap drinks and jukebox.

Brillo Box Bar BAR, LIVE MUSIC
(www.brillobox.net; 4104 Penn Ave; ⊙5pm-2am Tue-Sun) Live music, excellent menu and a good Sunday brunch at this popular spot in Lawrenceville.

Dee's Cafe BAR
(☑412-431-1314; www.deescafe.com; 1314 E Carson St; ⊙11am-2am) A notable punk bar with Pabst on tap and dirt-cheap bottles.

Live Music

AVA Bar & Lounge CLUB
(www.avapgh.net; 126 S Highland Ave; ⊙7pm-2am Mon-Sat, to midnight Sun) One of the coolest and most cutting-edge clubs in the city is ironically located in a generic strip in the East Liberty neighborhood (near Shadyside). The same owner and vibe from the recently closed Shadow Lounge, AVA has DJs and live hip-hop, jazz and other music.

Rex Theater LIVE MUSIC
(☑412-381-6811; www.rextheatre.com; 1602 E Carson St) A favorite South Side venue, a converted movie theater, for touring jazz, rock and indie bands, as well as a venue for the Moth Storyslam.

MCG Jazz LIVE MUSIC
(☑412-323-4000; www.mcgjazz.org; 1815 Metropolitan St) Live concerts/recordings of top jazz musicians are held at this venue on the north side of the city.

Club Café LIVE MUSIC
(☑412-431-4950; www.clubcafelive.com; 56-58 S 12th St) Live music nightly, mostly of the singer-songwriter type.

Theater & Culture

Pittsburgh Cultural Trust PERFORMING ARTS
(☑412-471-6070; www.pgharts.org; 803 Liberty Ave) Promotes all downtown arts, from the Pittsburgh Dance Council and PNC Broadway in Pittsburgh to visual art and opera. Go to the website for tickets to the Benedum Center, Byham Theater, Theater Square, Heinz Hall and other venues.

Gist Street Readings PERFORMING ARTS
(www.giststreet.org; 305 Gist St, 3rd fl; readings $10) Holds monthly readings from local and well-known national literary figures. Best to get there when doors open at 7:15pm, since turnout is typically large. Bring your own refreshments.

ℹ Information

MEDIA

Pittsburgh City Paper (www.pghcitypaper.com) Free alternative weekly with extensive arts listings.

Pittsburgh Post-Gazette (www.post-gazette.com) A major daily.

Pittsburgh Tribune-Review (www.triblive.com) Another major daily.

Pittsburgh's Out (www.outonline.com) Free monthly gay newspaper.

MEDICAL SERVICES

Allegheny County Health Department (☑412-687-2243; 3333 Forbes Ave) Has a walk-in medical center.

University of Pittsburgh Medical Center (☑412-647-8762; 200 Lothrop St; ⊙24hr) Emergency, high-ranking medical care.

DON'T MISS

THE LAUREL HIGHLANDS

A Frank Lloyd Wright masterpiece, **Fallingwater** (☎724-329-8501; www.fallingwater.org; 1491 Mill Run Rd; adult/child $23/17; ☺hours vary, closed Jan & Feb) is south of Pittsburgh on Rte 381. Completed in 1939 as a weekend retreat for the Kaufmanns, owners of the Pittsburgh department store, the building blends seamlessly with its natural setting. To see inside you must take one of the hourly guided tours, and reservations are recommended. A more intensive two-hour tour, with photography permitted, is offered ($55; times vary depending on day and month, reservations required). The rather attractive forested grounds open at 8:30am.

Much less visited is **Kentuck Knob** (☎724-329-1901; www.kentuckknob.com; 723 Kentuck Rd; adult/child $20/14; ☺hours vary, closed Jan 2-Mar 2), another Frank Lloyd Wright house (designed in 1953), built into the side of a rolling hill. It's noted for its natural materials, hexagonal design and honeycomb skylights. House tours last about an hour and include a jaunt through the onsite sculpture garden, with works by Andy Goldsworthy, Ray Smith and others.

From the end of May to the beginning of September the postage-stamp-sized town of Ohiopyle swells with visitors looking to ride the rapids of the Youghiogheny River (locals simply say 'the Yough' pronounced 'yawk') and explore **Ohiopyle State Park**. **Laurel Highlands River Tours** (☎800-472-3846; www.laurelhighlands.com) is a highly recommended operator and offers rock climbing and kayaking clinics if rafting is too tame. **Laurel Guesthouse** (☎724-329-8531; www.laurelhighlands.com/lodging; Grant St, Ohiopyle; s/d $80/90; ✽) has three bedrooms furnished like a comfortable suburban home.

Fort Ligonier (☎724-238-9701; www.fortligonier.org; 200 South Market St, Ligonier; adult/child $10/6; ☺10am-4:30pm Mon-Sat, noon-4:30pm Sun mid-Apr–mid-Nov), both a museum and a reconstructed fort with enthusiastic historical interpreters, does a great job of explaining the area's importance in the French and Indian War, as does the visitor center at the nearby **Fort Necessity** (www.nps.gov/fone; 1 Washington Pkwy/Rte 40, Farmington; ☺9am-5pm).

You can even spend a night in a Frank Lloyd Wright design at the **Duncan House** (☎877-833-7829; www.polymathpark.com; 187 Evergreen Ln, Acme; up to 3 people $400, per additional person $50, up to 6; ✽🛜), part of Polymath Park, a wooded property with three other homes designed by Wright apprentices. Don't expect Wright pyrotechnics – the house is a modest Eusonia-style and none of the furniture or interior pieces are Wright's but rather standard mid-century modern. Or try the swank **Nemacolin Woodlands Resort & Spa** (☎724-329-8555; www.nemacolin.com; 1001 Lafayette Dr, Farmington; r from $200; ✽@🛜🎿🐾✽) in Farmington with a spa, golf course and several restaurants.

TOURIST INFORMATION

Greater Pittsburgh Convention & Visitors Bureau Main Branch (☎412-281-7711; www.visitpittsburgh.com; Suite 2800, 120 Fifth Ave; ☺10am-6pm Mon-Fri, to 4pm Sat, to 3pm Sun) Publishes the *Official Visitors Guide* and provides maps and tourist advice.

WEBSITES

Citysearch (pittsburgh.citysearch.com) Nightlife, restaurant and shopping listings.

Pittsburgh.net (www.pittsburgh.net) Listings, neighborhoods and events.

Pop City (www.popcitymedia.com) Weekly e-magazine highlighting arts and cultural events.

ⓘ Getting There & Away

AIR

Pittsburgh International Airport (☎412-472-3525; www.pitairport.com), 18 miles west of downtown, has direct connections to Europe, Canada and major US cities via a slew of airlines.

BUS

From its station near the Strip, **Greyhound** (☎412-392-6500; www.greyhound.com; 55 11th St) has frequent buses to Philadelphia (from $30, six to seven hours), New York ($56, 8½ to 14 hours) and Chicago, IL ($68, 10 to 14 hours).

CAR

Pittsburgh is easily accessible via major highways, from the north or south on the I-76 or I-79, from the west on Rte 22 and from the east on the I-70. It's about an eight-hour drive from NYC and about three hours from Buffalo.

TRAIN

Amtrak (☎ 800-872-7245; www.amtrak.com; 1100 Liberty Ave) is behind the magnificent original train station, with trains heading to cities including Philadelphia (from $55, seven to eight hours) and NYC (from $73, nine to 11 hours).

❶ Getting Around

The excellent **28X Airport Flyer** (www.portauthority.org; One-way $3.75) public bus makes runs from the airport to Oakland and downtown every 20 minutes. Taxis are readily available and cost about $40 (not including tip) to downtown. Various shuttles also make downtown runs and cost $15 to $20 per person one way.

Driving around Pittsburgh can be extremely frustrating – roads end with no warning, one-way streets can take you in circles and there are various bridges to contend with.

Port Authority Transit (www.portauthority.org) operates an extensive bus system and a limited light-rail system, the 'T,' which is useful for going from downtown to the South Side. Bus and T fares range from free to $2.50, depending on the zones (traveling between the four downtown T stops is free).

For taxis, call **Yellow Cab Co of Pittsburgh** (☎ 412-321-8100), which charges by zone.

New England

Includes →

Best Places to Eat

→ Giacomo's Ristorante (p188)

→ Chatham Fish Pier Market (p198)

→ Nudel (p209)

→ Haven Brothers Diner (p212)

→ Hen of the Wood (p229)

Best Places to Stay

→ Harborside Inn (p186)

→ Carpe Diem (p201)

→ Hopkins Inn (p221)

→ Sea Breeze Inn (p215)

→ Inn at Shelburne Farms (p231)

Why Go?

Sure, you could drive from one end of New England to the other in a day, but why would you want to? Let the region's many diversions slow you down. The cities offer a vibrant mix of historical sites, chef-driven restaurants and Ivy League campuses. On the coast you'll find age-old fishing villages and sandy beaches begging a dip. Heading inland, the northern states are as rural and rugged as the mountains that run up their spines.

So take it easy. Crack open a lobster and let the sweet juices run down your fingers. Hike quiet trails. Or just get lost on a scenic back road and count the covered bridges. And if you're lucky enough to be here in autumn, you'll be rewarded with the most brilliant fall foliage you'll ever see.

When to Go

Boston

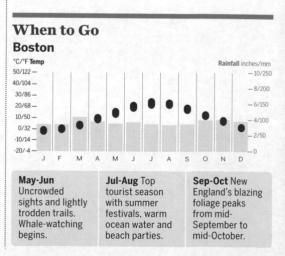

May-Jun Uncrowded sights and lightly trodden trails. Whale-watching begins.

Jul-Aug Top tourist season with summer festivals, warm ocean water and beach parties.

Sep-Oct New England's blazing foliage peaks from mid-September to mid-October.

Getting There & Around

Getting to New England is easy, but once you arrive you'll need a car if you want to explore the region thoroughly. The coastal I-95 and the inland I-91, the main north–south highways, transverse New England from Connecticut to Canada. Public transportation is fine between major cities but scarce in the countryside. **Greyhound** (www.greyhound.com) operates the most extensive bus service.

Amtrak (☐ 800-872-7245; www.amtrak.com) has a Northeast Corridor service that connects Boston, Providence, Hartford and New Haven with New York City; smaller regional services operate elsewhere in New England.

Boston's Logan International Airport (BOS) is New England's main hub. TF Green Airport (PVD) in Providence, RI, and Manchester Airport (MHT) in New Hampshire – both about an hour's drive from Boston – are growing 'minihubs' with less congestion and cheaper fares.

NEW ENGLAND PARKS

Acadia National Park (p249), on the rugged, northeastern coast of Maine, is the region's only national park but numerous other large tracts of New England's forest, mountains and shoreline are set aside for preservation and recreation.

The White Mountain National Forest (p235) is a vast 800,000-acre expanse of New Hampshire and Maine, offering a wonderland of scenic drives, hiking trails, campgrounds and ski slopes. Vermont's Green Mountain National Forest (p225) covers 400,000 acres of unspoiled forest. Both are crossed by the Appalachian Trail.

Another gem of federally protected land is the Cape Cod National Seashore (p199), a 44,600-acre stretch of rolling dunes and stunning beaches that's perfect for swimming, cycling and seaside hikes.

State parks are plentiful throughout New England, ranging from green niches in urban locations to the remote, untamed wilderness of Baxter State Park (p253) in northern Maine.

Seafood Specialties

➡ **Clam chowder** Or, as Bostonians say, *chow-dah;* combines chopped clams, potatoes and clam juice in a milk base

➡ **Oysters** Served raw on the half-shell or, for the less intrepid, broiled; sweetest are Wellfleet oysters from Cape Cod

➡ **Steamers** Soft-shelled clams steamed and served in a bucket of briny broth

➡ **Clambake** A meal of steamed lobster, clams and corn on the cob

DON'T MISS

Don't leave New England without cracking open a steamed lobster at a beachside seafood shack, such as the Lobster Dock (p247) in Boothbay Harbor.

Fast Facts

➡ **Hub cities** Boston (population 636,000), Providence (population 178,000)

➡ **Time zone** Eastern

➡ **Highest point** Mt Washington (6288ft)

➡ **Miles of coastline** 4965

Faux Pas

Don't mock, mimic or otherwise imitate a local's accent. New Englanders know they talk differently from other Americans, but they don't care.

Resources

➡ **Yankee Magazine** (www.yankeemagazine.com) Great destination profiles, recipes and events.

➡ **Mountain Summits** (www.mountainsummits.com) Everything you need to plan a hike in the New England hills.

➡ **Maine Lobster Council** (www.lobsterfrommaine.com) How to catch, order, buy, prepare and eat lobster.

New England Highlights

1 Following in the footsteps of Colonial rabble-rousers along **Boston's Freedom Trail** (p185).

2 Romping across the dunes at **Cape Cod National Seashore** (p199).

3 Ogling the mansions and basking in music at folk and jazz festivals in **Newport** (p213).

4 Wandering the cobbled Moby Dick–era streets of **Nantucket** (p203).

5 Anticipating your next black-diamond run from America's last surviving single chairlift at **Mad River Glen** (p228).

6 Befriending the pretty brown cows at **Billings Farm** (p226) in Woodstock.

7 Driving the **Kancamagus Highway** (p236) across the craggy White Mountains.

8 Hiking and cycling the carriage roads of **Acadia National Park** (p249).

9 Gawking at fall foliage in the **Berkshires** (p208) and **Litchfield Hills** (p221).

NEW ENGLAND IN...

One Week

Start in **Boston**, cruising the **Freedom Trail**, dining at a cozy **North End bistro** and exploring the city's highlights. Next, tramp through the mansions in **Newport**, then hit the beaches on **Cape Cod** and hop a ferry for a day trip to **Nantucket** or **Martha's Vineyard**. End the week with a jaunt north to New Hampshire's **White Mountains**, circling back down the **Maine coast**.

Two Weeks

Now you've got time for serious exploring. Use your second week to to take a leisurely drive through the **Litchfield Hills** and the **Berkshires**. Bookend the week with visits to the lively burgs of **Providence** and **Burlington**.

Alternatively, extend your stay on the Maine coast, with time to explore **Bar Harbor** and kayak along the shores of **Acadia National Park**. Wrap it up in Maine's vast wilderness, where you can work up a sweat on a hike up the northernmost peak of the **Appalachian Trail** or take an adrenaline-pumping ride down the **Kennebec River**.

History

When the first European settlers arrived, New England was inhabited by native Algonquians who lived in small tribes, raising corn and beans, hunting game and harvesting the rich coastal waters.

English captain Bartholomew Gosnold landed at Cape Cod and sailed north to Maine in 1602 but it wasn't until 1614 that Captain John Smith, who charted the region's coastline for King James I, christened the land 'New England.' With the arrival of the Pilgrims at Plymouth in 1620, European settlement began in earnest. Over the next century the colonies expanded, often at the expense of the indigenous people.

Although subjects of the British crown, New Englanders governed themselves with their own legislative councils and they came to view their affairs as separate from those of England. In the 1770s King George III imposed a series of costly taxes to pay for England's involvement in costly wars. The colonists, unrepresented in the English parliament, protested under the slogan 'no taxation without representation.' Attempts to squash the protests eventually led to battles at Lexington and Concord, setting off the War of Independence. The historic result was the birth of the USA in 1776.

Following independence, New England became an economic powerhouse, its harbors booming centers for shipbuilding, fishing and trade. New England's famed Yankee Clippers plied ports from China to South America. A thriving whaling industry brought unprecedented wealth to Nantucket and New Bedford. The USA's first water-powered cotton-spinning mill was established in Rhode Island in 1793. In the years that followed, New England's swift rivers became the engines of vast mills turning out clothing, shoes and machinery.

But no boom lasts forever. By the early 20th century many of the mills had moved south. Today education, finance, biotechnology and tourism are linchpins of the regional economy.

Local Culture

New Englanders tend to be reserved by nature, with the Yankee brusqueness standing in marked contrast to the casual outgoing nature of some other American regions. This taciturn quality shouldn't be confused with unfriendliness, as it's simply a more formal regional style.

Particularly in rural areas, folks take pride in their ingenuity and self-sufficient character. These New Englanders remain fiercely independent, from the fishing-boat crews who brave Atlantic storms to the Vermont small farmers who fight to keep operating independently within America's agribusiness economy.

Fortunately for the farmers and fishers, buy-local and go-organic movements have grown by leaps and bounds throughout New England. From bistros in Boston to small towns in the far north the menus are greening.

One place you won't find that ol' Yankee reserve is at the ball field. New Englanders are fanatical about sports. Attending a Red

Sox game is as close as you'll come to a modern-day gladiators-at-the-coliseum scene – wild cheers and nasty jeers galore.

Generally regarded as a liberal enclave, New England is in the forefront on progressive political issues from gay rights to health-care reform. Indeed, the universal health-insurance program in Massachusetts became the model for President Obama's national plan.

MASSACHUSETTS

From the woodsy hills of the Berkshires to the sandy beaches of Cape Cod, Massachusetts is filled with opportunities to explore the great outdoors. From Plymouth Rock to the Revolutionary War, the Commonwealth is rich with history. And from Boston's universities and museums to the Berkshires' summer theaters and Tanglewood, the cultural offerings are world-class. Your challenge lies in deciding: which Massachusetts will you discover?

ℹ Information

Massachusetts Department of Conservation and Recreation (☏617-626-1250; www.mass.gov/eea) Offers camping in 29 state parks.
Massachusetts Office of Travel & Tourism (☏617-973-8500; www.massvacation.com) Provides information on the entire state.

Boston

The winding streets and stately architecture recall a history of revolution and renewal; and still, today, Boston is among the country's most forward-looking and barrier-breaking cities.

For all intents and purposes, Boston is the oldest city in America. And you can hardly walk a step over its cobblestone streets without running into some historic site. But Boston has not been relegated to the past. The city's art and music scenes continue to charm and challenge contemporary audiences; cutting-edge urban planning projects are reshaping the city; and scores of universities guarantee an infusion of cultural energy every September.

History

When the Massachusetts Bay Colony was established by England in 1630, Boston became its capital. It's a city of firsts: Boston Latin School, the first public school in the USA, was founded in 1635, followed a year later by Harvard, the nation's first university. The first newspaper in the colonies was printed here in 1704, America's first labor union organized here in 1795 and the country's first subway system opened in Boston in 1897.

Not only were the first battles of the American Revolution fought nearby, but Boston was also home to the first African American regiment to fight in the US Civil War. Waves of immigrants, especially Irish in the mid-18th century and Italians in the early 20th, have infused the city with European influences.

Today Boston remains at the forefront of higher learning and its universities have spawned world-renowned industries in biotechnology, medicine and finance.

◉ Sights & Activities

Boston's small size means that it's easy to walk and difficult to drive. Most of Boston's

MASSACHUSETTS FACTS

Nickname Bay State
Population 6.5 million
Area 7840 sq miles
Capital city Boston (population 625,100)
Other cities Worcester (population 181,600), Springfield (population 153,200)
Sales tax 6.25%
Birthplace of Inventor Benjamin Franklin (1706–90), five presidents including John F Kennedy (1917–63), authors Jack Kerouac (1922–69) and Henry David Thoreau (1817–62)
Home of Harvard University, Boston Marathon, Plymouth Rock
Politics Lefty
Famous for Boston Tea Party, first state to legalize gay marriage
State Sweets Boston Cream Pie, Dunkin' Donuts, Fig Newtons
Driving distances Boston to Provincetown 145 miles, Boston to Northampton 98 miles, Boston to Acadia National Park 310 miles

Boston

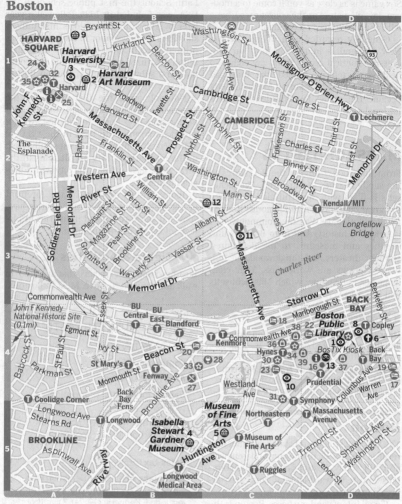

main attractions are found in or near the city center. Begin at Boston Common, where you'll find the tourist office and the start of the Freedom Trail.

👁 Boston Common & Public Garden

⭐ **Boston Common**   PARK

(Map p180; btwn Tremont, Charles, Beacon & Park Sts; ⏰6am-midnight; 👶; 🚆Park St) The Boston Common has served many purposes over the years, including as a campground

for British troops during the Revolutionary War and as green grass for cattle grazing until 1830. Although there is still a grazing ordinance on the books, the common today serves picnickers, sunbathers and people-watchers.

⭐ **Public Garden**   GARDENS

(Map p180; www.friendsofthepublicgarden.org; btwn Charles, Beacon, Boylston & Arlington Sts; ⏰6am-midnight; 👶; 🚆Arlington) Adjoining Boston Common, the 24-acre Public Garden provides an inviting oasis of bountiful flowers and shady trees. Its centerpiece, a tran-

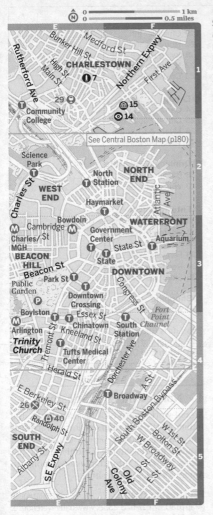

See Central Boston Map (p180)

NEW ENGLAND BOSTON

quil lagoon with old-fashioned pedal-powered **Swan Boats** (Map p180; www.swanboats. com; adult/child/senior $2.75/1.50/2; ⊙10am-4pm, to 5pm mid-Jun–Aug), has been delighting children for generations.

⊙ Beacon Hill & Downtown

Rising above Boston Common is Beacon Hill, one of the city's most historic and affluent neighborhoods. To the east is Downtown Boston, with a curious mix of Colonial sights and modern office buildings.

★**Massachusetts State House**   NOTABLE BUILDING

(Map p180; www.sec.state.ma.us; cnr Beacon & Bowdoin Sts; ⊙9am-5pm, tours 10am-4pm Mon-Fri; T Park St) **FREE** High atop Beacon Hill, Massachusetts' leaders and legislators attempt to turn their ideas into concrete policies and practices within the State House. Charles Bulfinch designed the commanding state capitol, but it was Oliver Wendell Holmes who called it 'the hub of the solar system' (thus earning Boston the nickname 'the Hub'). Knowledgeable 'Doric Docents' give free tours showcasing the building's history, artwork, architecture and political personalities.

Granary Burying Ground   CEMETERY

(Map p180; Tremont St; ⊙9am-5pm; T Park St) Dating to 1660, this atmospheric atoll is crammed with historic headstones, many with evocative (and creepy) carvings. This is the final resting place of all your favorite revolutionary heroes including Paul Revere, Samuel Adams, John Hancock and James Otis. Benjamin Franklin is buried in Philadelphia, but the Franklin family plot contains his parents.

Old South Meeting House   HISTORIC BUILDING

(Map p180; www.osmh.org; 310 Washington St; adult/child/senior & student $6/1/5; ⊙9:30am-5pm Apr-Oct, 10am-4pm Nov-Mar; 🖝; T Downtown Crossing) 'No tax on tea!' That was the decision on December 16, 1773, when 5000 angry colonists gathered here to protest British taxes, leading to the Boston Tea Party. Check out an exhibit about the history of the building and listen to an audio of the historic pre–Tea Party meeting.

Old State House   HISTORIC BUILDING

(Map p180; www.bostonhistory.org; 206 Washington St; adult/child $8.50/free; ⊙9am-5pm; 🖝; T State) Dating to 1713, the Old State House is Boston's oldest surviving public building, where the Massachusetts Assembly used to debate the issues of the day before the revolution. The building is best known for its balcony, where the Declaration of Independence was first read to Bostonians in 1776.

Faneuil Hall   HISTORIC BUILDING

(Map p180; www.faneuilhall.com; Congress St; ⊙9am-5pm; T Haymarket, Aquarium) **FREE** 'Those who cannot bear free speech had best go home,' said Wendell Phillips. 'Faneuil Hall

Boston

is no place for slavish hearts.' Indeed, this public meeting place was the site of so much rabble-rousing that it earned the nickname the 'Cradle of Liberty.' The 1st floor houses the National Park Service (NPS) Visitors Center, while the 2nd-floor meeting space is also open to the public.

★ **New England Aquarium**   AQUARIUM
(Map p180; www.neaq.org; Central Wharf; adult/child/senior $23/16/21; ⊘9am-5pm Mon-Fri, to 6pm Sat & Sun, 1hr later Jul & Aug; P ♿; T Aquarium) 🏊 The aquarium's main attraction is the newly renovated, three-story, cylindrical saltwater tank, which swirls with more than 600 creatures great and small, including turtles, sharks and eels. At the base of the tank the penguin pool is home to three species of fun-loving penguins. Other special features include the marine mammal exhibit and the shark-and-ray touch tank. The aquarium also organizes **whale-watching cruises** (Map p180; www.neaq. org; Central Wharf; adult/child/child under 3yr $40/32/15; ⊘10am Apr-Oct, additional cruises May-Sep; ♿; T Aquarium).

◎ North End & Charlestown

An old-world warren of narrow streets, the Italian North End offers visitors an irresistible mix of colorful period buildings and mouthwatering eateries. Colonial sights spill across the river into Charlestown, home to America's oldest battleship.

Paul Revere House   HISTORIC HOUSE
(Map p180; ☎617-523-2338; www.paulreverehouse. org; 19 North Sq; adult/child/senior & student $3.50/1/3; ⊘9:30am-5:15pm, shorter hours Nov-Apr; ♿; T Haymarket) When silversmith Paul Revere rode to warn patriots of the British march to Lexington and Concord, he set out from his home on North Sq. This small clapboard house was built in 1680, making it the oldest house in Boston. A self-guided tour through the house and courtyard gives a glimpse of what life was like for the Revere family (which included 16 children!).

Old North Church   CHURCH
(Map p180; www.oldnorth.com; 193 Salem St; donation $1, tour adult/child $5/4; ⊘9am-5pm Mar-Oct, 10am-4pm Tue-Sun Nov-Feb; T Haymarket or North

Station) Every American knows the line from Longfellow's poem 'Paul Revere's Ride': 'One if by land, Two if by sea...' It was here, on the night of April 18, 1775, that the sexton hung two lanterns from the steeple, as a signal that the British would march on Lexington and Concord via the sea route. Also called Christ Church, this 1723 place of worship is Boston's oldest church.

USS Constitution HISTORIC SITE
(Map p176; www.oldironsides.com; Charlestown Navy Yard; ☉10am-6pm Tue-Sun Apr-Oct, to 4pm Thu-Sun Nov-Mar; ♿; ☐93 from Haymarket, ⛴F4 from Long Wharf) **FREE** 'Her sides are made of iron!' So cried a crewman as he watched a shot bounce off the thick hull of the USS *Constitution* during the War of 1812. This bit of irony earned the legendary ship her nickname, Old Ironsides. The USS *Constitution* is still the oldest commissioned US Navy ship. Free 30-minute guided tours show off the top deck, gun deck and cramped quarters. The **museum** (Map p176; www.ussconstitutionmuseum. org; First Ave, Charlestown Navy Yard; adult/senior/child $5/3/2; ☉9am-6pm Apr-Oct, 10am-5pm Nov-Mar; ♿; ☐93 from Haymarket, ⛴F4 from Long Wharf) is great for history and activities for kids.

Bunker Hill Monument MONUMENT
(Map p176; www.nps.gov/bost; Monument Sq; ☉9am-5pm Sep-Jun, to 6pm Jul & Aug; ☐93 from Haymarket, ⊤Community College) **FREE** Remembering the eponymous battle of June 17, 1775, the 220ft granite obelisk monument is visible from across the harbor in the North End, from the expanse of the Zakim Bridge and from almost anywhere in Charlestown. Climb the 294 steps to the top of the monument and enjoy the 360° panorama.

⊙ Seaport District

Following the HarborWalk, it's a pleasant stroll across the Northern Ave Bridge and into the up-and-coming Seaport District.

Institute of Contemporary Art MUSEUM
(ICA; www.icaboston.org; 100 Northern Ave; adult/child/student/senior $15/free/10/13; ☉10am-5pm Tue, Wed, Sat & Sun, to 9pm Thu & Fri; ♿; ☐SL1 or SL2, ⊤South Station) The dramatic building of the ICA is a work of art in itself: a glass structure cantilevered over a waterside plaza. The light-filled interior allows for unique exhibitions and programs, including multimedia presentations and performance art. Most importantly, it allows for the development of the ICA's permanent collection, which has focused on artists featured in past exhibits.

★Boston Tea Party Ships & Museum MUSEUM
(Map p180; www.bostonteapartyship.com; Congress St Bridge; ♿; ⊤South Station) After years of anticipation and restoration, the Tea Party Ships are now moored at the reconstructed Griffin's Wharf, alongside a shiny new museum dedicated to the revolution's most catalytic event. Interactive exhibits allow visitors to meet reenactors in period costume, explore the ships, learn about contemporary popular perceptions through multimedia presentations and even participate in the protest.

⊙ Chinatown, Theater District & South End

Compact Chinatown offers enticing Asian eateries placed cheek by jowl, while the overlapping Theater District is clustered

NEW ENGLAND BOSTON

BOSTON IN...

Two Days
Spend one day reliving revolutionary history by following the **Freedom Trail**. Take time to lounge on **Boston Common**, peek in the **Old State House** and imbibe a little history at the **Union Oyster House**. Afterwards, stroll into the **North End** for an Italian dinner.

On your second day, rent a bicycle and ride along the Charles River. Go as far as **Harvard Square** to cruise the campus and browse the bookstores.

Four Days
On your third day, peruse the impressive American collection at the **Museum of Fine Arts**. In the evening, catch a performance of the world-famous **Boston Symphony Orchestra** or watch the Red Sox play at **Fenway Park**.

Spend your last day discovering Back Bay. Window-shop and gallery-hop on **Newbury St**, go to the top of the **Prudential Center** and browse the **Boston Public Library**.

Central Boston

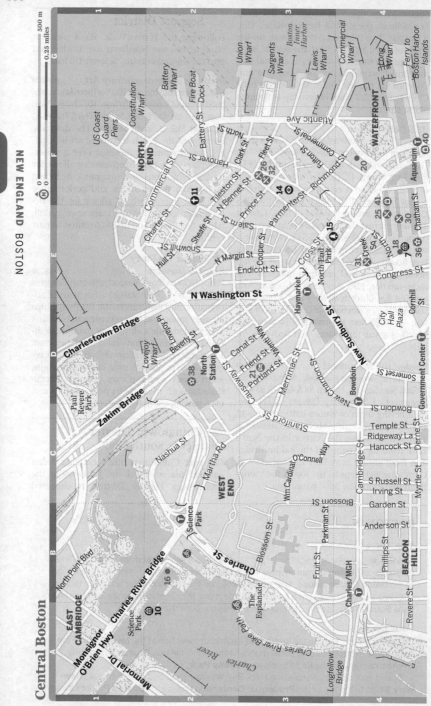

500 m
0.25 miles

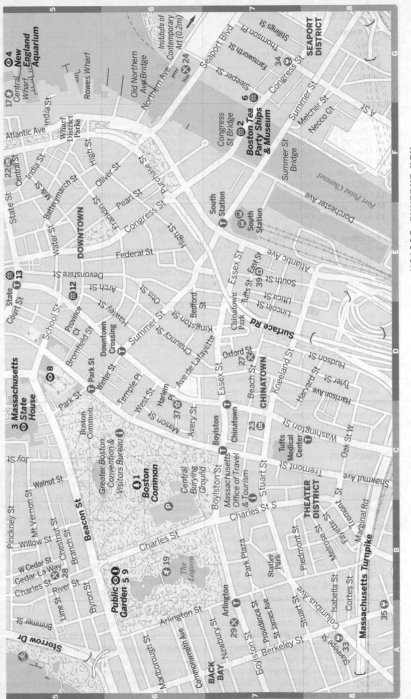

Central Boston

with performing-arts venues. To the west, the sprawling South End boasts one of America's largest concentrations of Victorian row houses, a burgeoning art community and a terrific restaurant scene.

◎ Back Bay

Extending west from Boston Common, this well-groomed neighborhood boasts graceful brownstone residences, grand edifices and the tony shopping mecca of Newbury St.

Copley Square   PLAZA
(Map p176; T Copley) Here you'll find a cluster of handsome historic buildings, including the masterwork of architect HH Richardson, the ornate neo-Romanesque **Trinity Church** (Map p176; www.trinitychurchboston.org; 206 Clarendon St; adult/child/senior & student $7/ free/5; ⊙10am-3:30pm Mon-Fri, 9am-4pm Sat, 1-5pm Sun). Across the street, the Renaissance Revival **Boston Public Library** (Map p176; www.bpl.org; 700 Boylston St; ⊙9am-9pm Mon-Thu, 9am-5pm Fri & Sat year-round, 1-5pm Sun Oct-May) **FREE** is America's first municipal library, lending credence to this city's reputation as the 'Athens of America.' Pick up a self-guided tour brochure and wander around, noting gems such as the murals by John Singer Sargent and sculpture by Augustus Saint-Gaudens.

Prudential Center
Skywalk Observatory   LOOKOUT
(Map p176; www.prudentialcenter.com; 800 Boylston St; adult/child/senior & student $15/10/13; ⊙10am-10pm Mar-Oct, to 8pm Nov-Feb; P ♿ T Prudential) Technically called the Shops at Prudential Center, this landmark city building is not much more than a fancy shopping mall. But it does provide a bird's-eye view of Boston from its 50th-floor Skywalk. Completely enclosed by glass, the Skywalk offers spectacular 360° views of Boston and Cambridge, accompanied by an entertaining audio tour (with a special version catering to kids).

Mary Baker Eddy
Library & Mapparium   LIBRARY
(Map p176; www.marybakereddylibrary.org; 200 Massachusetts Ave; adult/child/senior & student $6/ free/4; ⊙10am-4pm Tue-Sun; ♿; T Symphony) Ever had a hankering to walk across the entire planet? The Mary Baker Eddy Library contains a room-size stained-glass globe,

known as the Mapparium. Walk across the glass bridge and feel you're at the center of the world.

Fenway & Kenmore Square

Kenmore Sq is best for baseball and beer, while the southern part of the Fenway is dedicated to higher-minded cultural pursuits.

⭐ **Museum of Fine Arts** MUSEUM
(MFA; Map p176; www.mfa.org; 465 Huntington Ave; adult/child/senior & student $22/10/20; ⊙10am-5pm Sat-Tue, to 10pm Wed-Fri; 👶; Ⓣ Museum of Fine Arts or Ruggles) The Museum of Fine Arts collection encompasses all eras, from the ancient world to contemporary times, and all areas of the globe, making it truly encyclopedic in scope. The museum's latest addition is its new wings dedicated to the Art of the Americas and to Contemporary Art, which has significantly increased its exhibition space and broadened its focus, contributing to Boston's emergence as an art center in the 21st century.

⭐ **Isabella Stewart Gardner Museum** MUSEUM
(Map p176; www.gardnermuseum.org; 280 The Fenway; adult/child/student/senior $15/free/5/12; ⊙11am-5pm Wed-Mon, to 9pm Thu; 👶; Ⓣ Museum of Fine Arts) The Gardner is filled with almost 2000 priceless objects, primarily European, including outstanding tapestries and exquisit paintings from the Italian Renaissance and the Dutch Golden Age. The four-story greenhouse courtyard is a tranquil oasis that alone is worth the price of admission.

Cambridge

On the north side of the Charles River lies politically progressive Cambridge, home to academic heavyweights Harvard University and the Massachusetts Institute of Technology (MIT). Thousands of resident students guarantee a diverse, lively atmosphere. At its hub, **Harvard Square** overflows with cafes, bookstores and street performers.

BOSTON FOR CHILDREN

Boston is one giant history museum, the setting for many educational and lively field trips. Cobblestone streets and costume-clad tour guides can bring to life events from American history. Hands-on experimentation and interactive exhibits fuse education and entertainment.

Changing stations are ubiquitous in public restrooms and many restaurants offer children's menus and highchairs. You'll have no trouble taking your kid's stroller on the T.

Boston's small scale makes it easy for families to explore. A good place to start is the Public Garden (p176), where Swan Boats ply the lagoon and tiny tots climb on the bronze **statues** (Map p180) from Robert McCloskey's classic Boston tale *Make Way for Ducklings*. Across the street on Boston Common (p176), kids can cool their toes in the Frog Pond, ride the carousel and romp in the playground. At the New England Aquarium (p178), kids of all ages will enjoy face-to-face encounters with underwater creatures.

OTHER GREAT MUSEUMS FOR KIDS:

Boston Children's Museum (Map p180; www.bostonchildrensmuseum.org; 300 Congress St; admission $14, Fri evening $1; ⊙10am-5pm Sat-Thu, 10am-9pm Fri; 👶; Ⓣ South Station) 🧭 Oodles of fun for the youngest set.

Museum of Science (Map p180; www.mos.org; Charles River Dam; adult/child/senior $22/19/20, theater & planetarium $10/8/9; ⊙9am-5pm Sat-Thu Sep-Jun, to 7pm Jul & Aug, to 9pm Fri year-round; Ⓟ 👶; Ⓣ Science Park) 🧭 Hours of educational entertainment for all ages.

GREAT TOURS FOR KIDS:

Boston for Little Feet (p184) The only Freedom Trail walking tour designed especially for children aged six to 12.

Urban AdvenTours (p184) Rents kids' bicycles and helmets, as well as cycle trailers for toddlers.

Boston Duck Tours (p184) Quirky, quackiness is always a hit.

★**Harvard University** UNIVERSITY
(Map p176; www.harvard.edu; Massachusetts Ave; tours free; ☺ tours 10am, noon & 2pm Mon-Fri, 2pm Sat; ⊤ Harvard) Founded in 1636 to educate men for the ministry, Harvard is America's oldest college. (No other college came along until 1693.) The original Ivy League school has eight graduates who went on to be US presidents, not to mention dozens of Nobel laureates and Pulitzer Prize winners. The university's historic heart is **Harvard Yard**, its ancient oaks and redbrick buildings exuding an air of academia.

There are also several excellent museums on campus, including the **Harvard Art Museum** (Map p176; www.harvardartmuseum.org; 32 Quincy St), which is due to have completed a multiyear renovation and expansion by 2014, and the longstanding **Harvard Museum of Natural History** (Map p176; www.hmnh.harvard.edu; 26 Oxford St; adult/child & student $12/8/10; ☺ 9am-5pm; ⊕). Tours are more frequent in summer.

☞ Tours

Boston Duck Tours BOAT TOUR
(Map p176; ☎ 617-267-3825; www.bostonducktours.com; adult/child/senior $34/23/28; ⊕; ⊤ Aquarium, Science Park or Prudential) These wildly popular tours use WWII amphibious vehicles that cruise the downtown streets before splashing into the Charles River. Tours depart from the **Museum of Science** (Map p180; www.bostonducktours.com; Museum of Science, 1 Science Park; ⊤ Science Park) or from behind the Prudential Center, with more

---

WORTH A TRIP

MASSACHUSETTS INSTITUTE OF TECHNOLOGY

The **Massachusetts Institute of Technology** (MIT; Map p176; www.mit.edu; 77 Massachusetts Ave; ⊤ Kendall/MIT) offers a completely novel perspective on Cambridge academia: proudly nerdy, but not quite as tweedy as Harvard. The campus has an impressive collection of public art; and a recent frenzy of building has resulted in some of the most architecturally intriguing structures you'll find on either side of the river. The on-campus **MIT Museum** (Map p176; museum.mit.edu; 265 Massachusetts Ave; adult/child $8.50/4; ☺ 10am-5pm; Ⓟ ⊕; ⊤ Central) might be the city's quirkiest.

---

limited departures from the New England Aquarium. Reserve in advance.

Boston by Foot WALKING TOUR
(www.bostonbyfoot.com; adult/child $12/8; ⊕) This fantastic nonprofit offers 90-minute walking tours, with specialty themes such as Literary Landmarks, Boston Underfoot (with highlights from the Big Dig and the T) and Boston for Little Feet – a kid-friendly version of the Freedom Trail.

★**Urban AdvenTours** BICYCLE TOUR
(Map p180; ☎ 617-670-0637; www.urbanadventours.com; 103 Atlantic Ave; tours $50; ⊕; ⊤ Aquarium) ⌗ Founded by avid cyclists who believe the best views of Boston are from a bicycle. The City View Ride provides a great overview of how to get around by bike, but there are other specialty tours such as Bikes at Night and Bike & Brew Tour.

NPS Freedom Trail Tour WALKING TOUR
(Map p180; www.nps.gov/bost; Faneuil Hall; ☺ 10am & 2pm Apr-Nov; ⊕; ⊤ State) FREE Show up at least 30 minutes early to snag a spot on one of the free, ranger-led Freedom Trail tours provided by the National Park Service. Tours depart from the visitor center in Faneuil Hall and follow a portion of the Freedom Trail (not including Charlestown), for 90 minutes. Each tour is limited to 30 people.

✯✯ Festivals & Events

★**Boston Marathon** SPORTING EVENT
(www.baa.org; ☺ 3rd Mon Apr) One of the country's most prestigious marathons takes runners on a 26.2-mile course ending at Copley Sq on Patriots Day, a Massachusetts holiday.

Fourth of July HOLIDAY
(www.july4th.org) Boston hosts one of the biggest Independence Day bashes in the USA, with a free Boston Pops concert on the Esplanade and a nationally televised fireworks display.

🛏 Sleeping

Boston has a reputation for high hotel prices, but online discounts can lessen the sting at even high-end places. You'll typically find the best deals on weekends. The majority of hotels are in the downtown area and the Back Bay, both convenient to public transportation and sightseeing.

Try also **Bed & Breakfast Associates Bay Colony** (☎ 781-449-5302, 888-486-6018,

City Walk
Freedom Trail

START BOSTON COMMON
FINISH BUNKER HILL MONUMENT
LENGTH 2.5 MILES; THREE HOURS

Trace America's earliest history along the Freedom Trail, which covers Boston's key revolutionary sites. The well-trodden route is marked by a double row of red bricks, starting at the **1 Boston Common** (p176), America's oldest public park. Follow the trail north to the gold-domed **2 State House** (p177), designed by Charles Bulfinch, America's first homegrown architect. Rounding Park St onto Tremont St takes you past the Colonial-era **3 Park Street Church**; the **4 Granary Burying Ground** (p177), where victims of the Boston Massacre lie buried; and **5 King's Chapel**, topped with one of Paul Revere's bells. Continue down School St, past the site of **6 Boston's first public school** and the **7 Old Corner Bookstore**, a haunt of 19th-century literati.

Nearby, the **8 Old South Meeting House** (p177) tells the back story of the Boston Tea Party. There are more Revolutionary exhibits at the **9 Old State House** (p177). Outside, a ring of cobblestones at the intersection marks the **10 Boston Massacre Site**, the first violent conflict of the American Revolution. Next up is **11 Faneuil Hall** (p177), a public market since Colonial times.

Cross the Greenway to Hanover St, the main artery of Boston's Italian enclave. Treat yourself to lunch before continuing to North Sq, where you can tour the **12 Paul Revere House** (p178), the Revolutionary hero's former home. Follow the trail to the **13 Old North Church** (p178), where a lookout in the steeple signaled to Revere that the British were coming, setting off his famous midnight gallop.

Continue northwest on Hull St, where you'll find more Colonial graves at **14 Copp's Hill Burying Ground**. Then cross the Charlestown Bridge to reach the **15 USS Constitution** (p179), the world's oldest commissioned warship. To the north lies **16 Bunker Hill Monument** (p179), the site of the first battle fought in the American Revolution.

WORTH A TRIP

JFK SITES

The legacy of JFK is ubiquitous in Boston, but the official memorial to the 35th president is the **John F Kennedy Library & Museum** (www.jfklibrary.org; Columbia Point; adult/child/senior & student $12/9/10; ⊗ 9am-5pm; P; T JFK/UMass), a striking, modern, marble building designed by IM Pei. The museum is a fitting tribute to JFK's life and legacy. The effective use of video recreates history for visitors who may or may not remember the early 1960s.

In the streetcar suburb of Brookline, the **John F Kennedy National Historic Site** (www.nps.gov/jofi; 83 Beals St; ⊗ 9:30am-5pm Wed-Sun May-Oct; T Coolidge Corner) FREE occupies the modest three-story house that was JFK's birthplace and boyhood home. Guided tours allow visitors to see furnishings, photographs and mementos that have been preserved from the time the family lived here. Take the Green Line (C branch) to Coolidge Corner and walk north on Harvard St.

from UK 08-234-7113; www.bnbboston.com), which handles B&Bs, rooms and apartments.

HI Boston
HOSTEL $

(Map p180; ☑ 617-536-9455; www.bostonhostel.org; 19 Stuart St; dm $50-60, d $179; ❋ @ �fn; T Chinatown or Boylston) ⊘ Hostelling International (HI) Boston has a brand-new facility. The historic Dill Building has been completely revamped to allow for expanded capacity and community space, wheelchair access and – most impressively – state-of-the-art green amenities and energy efficiency. What stays the same? The reliably comfortable accommodations and excellent line-up of cultural activities that HI Boston has offered for the past three decades.

Friend Street Hostel
HOSTEL $

(Map p180; ☑ 617-934-2413; www.friendstreethostel.com; 234 Friend St; dm $48-54; @ �fn; T North Station) We believe them when they say it's the friendliest hostel in Boston. But there are other reasons to love this affable hostelry, such as the spic-and-span kitchen and the comfy common area with the huge flatscreen TV. Sleeping six to 10 people each, dorm rooms have painted brick walls, wide-plank wood floors and sturdy pine bunk beds.

Also: breakfast, bicycles and lots of free activities. What's not to love? Street noise.

★Oasis Guest House
GUESTHOUSE $$

(Map p176; ☑ 617-230-0105, 617-267-2262; www.oasisgh.com; 22 Edgerly Rd; r $136-228, without bath $114-148; P ❋ �fn; T Hynes or Symphony) True to its name, this homey guesthouse is a peaceful, pleasant oasis in the midst of Boston's chaotic city streets. Thirty-odd guest rooms occupy four attractive, brick, bow-front town houses on this tree-lined lane.

The modest, light-filled rooms are tastefully and traditionally decorated, most with queen beds, floral quilts and nondescript prints.

★Harborside Inn
BOUTIQUE HOTEL $$

(Map p180; ☑ 617-723-7500; www.harborsideinnboston.com; 185 State St; r from $169; P ❋ @ �fn; T Aquarium) Housed in a respectfully renovated 19th-century warehouse, this waterfront hostelry strikes just the right balance between historic digs and modern conveniences. Apparently, the architects who did the renovation cared about preserving historic details, as guest rooms have original exposed brick-and-granite walls and hardwood floors. They're offset perfectly by Oriental carpets, sleigh beds and reproduction Federal-era furnishings. Add $20 for a city view.

Irving House
GUESTHOUSE $$

(Map p176; ☑ 617-547-4600; www.irvinghouse.com; 24 Irving St; r $165-270, s without bath $135-160, d without bath $165-205; P ❋ @ �fn; T Harvard) ⊘ Call it a big inn or a homey hotel, this property welcomes the world-weariest travelers. The 44 rooms range in size, but every bed is covered with a quilt, and big windows let in plenty of light. Free continental breakfast.

Chandler Inn
HOTEL $$

(Map p176; ☑ 617-482-3450, 800-842-3450; www.chandlerinn.com; 26 Chandler St; r from $170; ❋ �fn; T Back Bay) The Chandler Inn is looking fine, after a complete overhaul. Small but sleek rooms have benefited from a designer's touch, giving them a sophisticated, urban glow. Modern travelers will appreciate the plasma TVs and iPod docks, all of which come at surprisingly affordable prices. As a bonus, congenial staff provide super service. On site is the South End drinking institution, Fritz.

Hotel Buckminster
HOTEL $$

(Map p176; ☑ 617-727-2825; www.bostonhotelbuckminster.com; 645 Beacon St; r $149-209, ste from $219; P✳☺☎; ⊤Kenmore) Designed by the architect of the Boston Public Library, the Buckminster is a convergence of Old Boston charm and affordable elegance. It offers nearly 100 rooms of varying shapes and sizes: economy rooms are small and stuffy, with slightly worn furniture (but still a great bargain); by contrast, the European-style suites are quite roomy, with all the tools and toys of comfort and convenience.

463 Beacon Street
Guest House
GUESTHOUSE $$

(Map p176; ☑ 617-536-1302; www.463beacon.com; 463 Beacon St; d with/without bath from $149/99; P✳☎; ⊤Hynes) What's more 'Boston' than a handsome, historic brownstone in Back Bay? This guesthouse lets you live the blue-blood fantasy – and save your cash for the boutiques and bars on Newbury St. Rooms vary in size and decor, but they all have the basics (except daily maid service, which is not offered). Bathrooms are cramped, but hopefully you won't be spending too much time in there.

40 Berkeley
HOSTEL $$

(Map p176; ☑ 617-375-2524; www.40berkeley.com; 40 Berkeley St; s/d/tr/q from $108/130/144/169; ☎; ⊤Back Bay) Straddling the South End and Back Bay, this safe, friendly Y rents over 200 small rooms (some overlooking the garden) to guests on a nightly and long-term basis. Bathrooms are shared, as are other useful facilities such as the telephone, library, TV room and laundry. All rates include a generous and delicious breakfast.

★Newbury Guest House
GUESTHOUSE $$$

(Map p176; ☑ 617-437-7666, 617-437-7668; www.newburyguesthouse.com; 261 Newbury St; r $219-249; P✳☎; ⊤Hynes or Copley) Dating to 1882, these three interconnected brick and brownstone buildings offer a prime location in the heart of Newbury St. A recent renovation has preserved charming features such as ceiling medallions and in-room fireplaces, but now the rooms feature clean lines, luxurious linens and modern amenities. Each morning, a complimentary continental breakfast is laid out next to the marble fireplace in the salon.

✕ Eating

New England cuisine is known for summertime clambakes and Thanksgiving turkey. But the Boston dining scene changes it up with wide-ranging international influences and contemporary interpretations. Indulge in affordable Asian fare in Chinatown and Italian feasts in the North End; or head to the South End for the city's trendiest foodie scene.

✕ Beacon Hill & Downtown

Quincy Market
FOOD COURT $

(Map p180; Congress St; ◷10am-9pm Mon-Sat, noon-6pm Sun; ☑♿; ⊤Haymarket) Northeast of the intersection of Congress and State Sts, this food hall offers a variety of places under one roof: the place is packed with about 20 restaurants and 40 food stalls. Choose from chowder, bagels, Indian, Greek, baked goods and ice cream, and take a seat at one of the tables in the central rotunda.

★Paramount
CAFETERIA $$

(Map p180; www.paramountboston.com; 44 Charles St; breakfast & lunch $8-12, dinner $15-30; ◷7am-10pm Mon-Thu, from 8am Sat-Sun, to 11pm Fri-Sat; ☑♿; ⊤Charles/MGH) This old-fashioned cafeteria is a neighborhood favorite. Basic diner fare includes pancakes, steak and eggs, burgers and sandwiches, and big, hearty salads. For dinner, add table service and candlelight, and the place goes upscale without losing its down-home charm. The menu is enhanced by homemade pastas, a selection of meat and fish dishes and an impressive roster of daily specials.

> ### BOSTON BOMBING
>
> On Patriot's Day 2013, the nation (and the world) turned their eyes to Boston when two bombs exploded near the finish line of the Boston Marathon, killing three and injuring hundreds. Several days later, an MIT police officer was shot dead and the entire city was locked down, as Boston became a battleground for the War on Terror. The tragedy was devastating, but Boston can claim countless heroes, especially the many victims that have inspired others with their courage and fortitude throughout their recoveries.

BOSTON GOES GREEN

Once there was a hulking highway that bisected the city center; now there is a ribbon of green parkland, reconnecting neighborhoods from the North End to Chinatown. Named for JFK's mother, the **Rose Kennedy Greenway** (Map p180; www.rosekennedygreenway.org; 🚇; T Aquarium or Haymarket) reclaims the land that was once obscured by the elevated section of I-93. The interconnecting parks offer shady respite from the city bustle, replete with water fountains, blooming gardens and – new in 2013 – a custom-designed Boston-themed carousel. If you're wondering what happened to the highway, it now runs through tunnels beneath the city, thanks to the 'Big Dig,' the costliest highway project in US history.

Durgin Park   AMERICAN $$
(Map p180; www.durgin-park.com; North Market, Faneuil Hall; lunch mains $9-15, dinner $15-30; ⊙11:30am-9pm; 🚇; T Haymarket) Known for no-nonsense service and sawdust on the floorboards, Durgin Park hasn't changed much since the restaurant opened in 1827. Nor has the menu, which features New England standards such as prime rib, fish chowder, chicken pot pie and Boston baked beans, with strawberry shortcake and Indian pudding for dessert. Be prepared to make friends with the other parties seated at your table.

Union Oyster House   SEAFOOD $$
(Map p180; www.unionoysterhouse.com; 41 Union St; mains $15-25; ⊙11am-9:30pm; T Haymarket) The oldest restaurant in Boston, ye olde Union Oyster House has been serving seafood in this historic redbrick building since 1826. Countless history-makers have propped themselves up at this bar, including Daniel Webster and John F Kennedy. Apparently JFK used to order the lobster bisque, but the raw bar is the real draw here. Order a dozen on the half-shell and watch the shucker work his magic.

✕ North End

Volle Nolle   SANDWICHES $
(Map p180; 351 Hanover St; sandwiches $8-12; ⊙11am-11pm; 🚇🚇; T Haymarket) Apparently, *volle nolle* is Latin for 'willy-nilly,' but there is nothing haphazard about this much-beloved North End sandwich shop. Black-slate tables and pressed-tin walls adorn the simple, small space. The chalkboard menu features fresh salads, delicious flatbread sandwiches and dark rich coffee. A perfect lunchtime stop along the Freedom Trail.

★**Giacomo's Ristorante**   ITALIAN $$
(Map p180; www.giacomosblog-boston.blogspot.com; 355 Hanover St; mains $14-19; ⊙4:30-10pm Mon-Sat, 4-9:30pm Sun; 🖋; T Haymarket) Customers line up before the doors open so they can guarantee themselves a spot in the first round of seating at this North End favorite. Enthusiastic and entertaining waiters, plus cramped quarters, ensure that you get to know your neighbors. The cuisine is no-frills southern Italian fare, served in unbelievable portions. Cash only.

✕ Seaport District

Barking Crab   SEAFOOD $$
(Map p180; www.barkingcrab.com; 88 Sleeper St; mains $12-30; ⊙11:30am-10pm Sun-Wed, to 11pm Thu-Sat; 🚢 SL1 or SL2, T South Station) Big buckets of crabs (Jonah, blue, snow, Alaskan etc), steamers dripping in lemon and butter, paper plates piled high with all things fried... The food is plentiful and cheap, and you eat it at communal picnic tables overlooking the water. Beer flows freely. Service is slack, but the atmosphere is jovial. Be prepared to wait for a table if the weather is warm.

✕ Chinatown, Theater District & South End

★**Gourmet Dumpling House**   CHINESE, TAIWANESE $
(Map p180; www.gourmetdumpling.com; 52 Beach St; lunch $8, dinner mains $10-15; ⊙11am-1am; 🖋; T Chinatown) *Xiao long bao.* That's all the Chinese you need to know to take advantage of the specialty at the Gourmet Dumpling House (or GDH, as it is fondly called). They are Shanghai soup dumplings, of course, and they are fresh, doughy and delicious. The menu offers plenty of other options, including scrumptious crispy scallion pancakes. Come early or be prepared to wait.

Myers & Chang   ASIAN $$$
(Map p176; ☎617-542-5200; www.myersand-chang.com; 1145 Washington St; small plates $10-18; ⊙11:30am-11pm Fri & Sat, to 10pm Sun-Thu;

⚲; 🚇 SL4 or SL5, T Tufts Medical Center) This super-hip Asian spot blends Thai, Chinese and Vietnamese cuisines, which means delicious dumplings, spicy stir-fries and oodles of noodles. The kitchen staff does amazing things with a wok and the menu of small plates allows you to sample a wide selection of dishes. The vibe is casual but cool, international and independent.

✕ Back Bay & Fenway

Tasty Burger   BURGERS $
(Map p176; www.tastyburger.com; 1301 Boylston St; burgers $4-6; ☺11am-2am; 🔒; T Fenway) Once a Mobile station, it's now a retro burger joint, with picnic tables outside and a pool table inside. The name of the place is a nod to *Pulp Fiction*, as is the poster of Samuel L Jackson on the wall. You won't find a half-pound of Kobe beef on your bun, but you will have to agree 'That's a tasty burger.'

Aside from the burgers, this is a fun place to drink cheap beer and watch sports on TV.

Parish Café   SANDWICHES $$
(Map p180; www.parishcafe.com; 361 Boylston St; sandwiches $12-15; ☺noon-2am; ⚲; T Arlington) Sample the creations of Boston's most famous chefs without exhausting your expense account. The menu at Parish features a rotating roster of salads and sandwiches, each designed by a local celebrity chef, including Lydia Shire, Ken Oringer and Barbara Lynch.

✕ Cambridge

★ Clover Food Lab   VEGETARIAN $
(Map p176; www.cloverfoodlab.com; 7 Holyoke St; mains $6-7; ☺7am-midnight; ⚲🔒; T Harvard)
⚲ Clover is on the cutting edge. It's all high-tech with its 'live' menu updates and electronic ordering system. But it's really about the food – local, seasonal, vegetarian food – which is cheap, delicious and fast. How fast? Check the menu. Interesting tidbit: Clover started as a food truck (and still has a few trucks making the rounds).

Cambridge, 1   PIZZERIA $$
(Map p176; www.cambridge1.us; 27 Church St; pizzas $17-22; ☺11:30am-midnight; ⚲; T Harvard) Set in the old fire station, this pizzeria's name comes from the sign chiseled into the stonework out front. The interior is sleek, sparse and industrial, with big windows overlooking the Old Burying Ground in the back. The menu is equally simple: pizza, soup, salad, dessert. These oddly-shaped pizzas are delectable, with crispy crusts and creative topping combos.

🍷 Drinking & Nightlife

★ Bleacher Bar   SPORTS BAR
(Map p176; www.bleacherbarboston.com; 82a Lansdowne St; T Kenmore) Tucked under the bleachers at Fenway Park, this classy bar offers a view onto center field (go Jacoby baby!). It's not the best place to watch the game, as the place gets packed, but it's an

---

GAY & LESBIAN BOSTON

Out and active gay communities are visible all around Boston and Cambridge, especially in the South End. **Calamus Bookstore** (Map p180; www.calamusbooks.com; 92 South St; ☺9am-7pm Mon-Sat, noon-6pm Sun; T South Station) is an excellent source of information about community events and organizations. Pick up a copy of the free weekly *Bay Windows* (www.baywindows.com).

There is no shortage of entertainment options catering to GLBT travelers. From drag shows to dyke nights, this sexually diverse community has something for everybody.

Club Cafe (Map p180; www.clubcafe.com; 209 Columbus Ave; ☺11am-2am; T Back Bay) Always hopping, it's a cool cafe by day and a crazy club by night. Aimed at men, open to all.

Diesel Cafe (www.diesel-cafe.com; 257 Elm St; ☺6am-11pm Mon-Sat, 7am-11am Sun; T Davis Sq) Shoot stick, drink coffee and swill beer in this industrial cafe popular with students and queers.

Fritz (Map p180; www.fritzboston.com; 26 Chandler St; ☺noon-2am; T Back Bay) Watch the boys playing sports on TV or watch the boys watching the boys playing sports on TV.

awesome way to experience America's oldest ballpark, even when the Sox are not playing.

If you want a seat in front of the window, get your name on the waiting list an hour or two before game time; once seated, diners have 45 minutes in the hot seat.

★ **Drink** COCKTAIL BAR

(Map p180; www.drinkfortpoint.com; 348 Congress St S; ⊙4pm-1am; 🚇SL1 or SL2, 🇹South Station) There is no cocktail menu at Drink. Instead you have a little chat with the bartender, and he or she will whip something up according to your specifications. The bar takes seriously the art of drink mixology – and you will too, after you sample one of its concoctions. The subterranean space creates a dark, sexy atmosphere, which makes for a great date destination.

Warren Tavern HISTORIC PUB

(Map p176; www.warrentavern.com; 2 Pleasant St; ⊙11am-1am; 🇹Community College) One of the oldest pubs in Boston, the Warren Tavern has been pouring pints for its customers since George Washington and Paul Revere drank here. It is named for General Joseph Warren, a fallen hero of the Battle of Bunker Hill (shortly after which – in 1780 – this pub was opened).

☆ Entertainment

Boston's entertainment scene offers something for everyone.

Live Music

★ **Club Passim** FOLK MUSIC

(Map p176; 🖉617-492-7679; www.clubpassim.org; 47 Palmer St; tickets $15-30; 🇹Harvard) Folk music in Boston seems to be endangered outside of Irish bars, but the legendary Club Passim does such a great job booking top-notch acts that it practically fills in the vacuum by itself. The colorful, intimate room is hidden off a side street in Harvard Sq, and those attending shows are welcome to order filling dinners from **Veggie**

ⓘ CHEAP SEATS

Half-price tickets to same-day theater and concerts in Boston are sold at by BosTix (www.bostix.org; ⊙10am-6pm Tue-Sat, 11am-4pm Sun) at Faneuil Hall and Copley Sq. No plastic – these deals are cash only.

Planet, an incredibly good restaurant that shares the space.

★ **Red Room @ Café 939** LIVE MUSIC

(Map p176; www.cafe939.com; 939 Boylston St; 🇹Hynes) Run by Berklee students, the Red Room @ 939 is emerging as one of Boston's best music venues. The place has an excellent sound system and a baby grand piano; most importantly, it books interesting, eclectic up-and-coming musicians. This is where you'll see that band that's about to make it big. Buy tickets in advance at the **Berklee Performance Center** (Map p176; www.berklee-bpc.com; 136 Massachusetts Ave; 🇹Hynes).

Sinclair LIVE MUSIC

(Map p176; www.sinclaircambridge.com; 52 Church St; tickets $15-18; ⊙11am-1am Tue-Sun, 5pm-1am Mon; 🇹Harvard) Great new small venue to see and hear live music. The acoustics are excellent and the mezzanine level allows you to escape the crowds on the floor. The club attracts a good range of local and regional bands and DJs. Bonus: under the direction of Michael Schlow, the attached kitchen puts out some delicious and downright classy food (though service seems to be a little spotty).

Classical Music & Theater

The big venues in the Theater District are lavish affairs, all restored to their early-20th-century glory.

★ **Boston Symphony Orchestra** CLASSICAL MUSIC

(BSO; Map p176; 🖉617-266-1200; www.bso.org; Symphony Hall, 301 Massachusetts Ave; tickets $30-115; 🇹Symphony) Near-perfect acoustics match the ambitious programs of the world-renowned Boston Symphony Orchestra. From September to April, the BSO performs in the beauteous Symphony Hall, featuring an ornamental high-relief ceiling and attracting a fancy-dress crowd. The building was designed in 1861 with the help of a Harvard physicist who pledged to make the building acoustically perfect (he succeeded).

Boston Ballet DANCE

(🖉617-695-6950; www.bostonballet.org; tickets $15-100) Boston's skillful ballet troupe performs both modern and classic works at the **Opera House** (Map p180; www.bostonoperahouse.com; 539 Washington St; 🇹Downtown Crossing). During the Christmas season, it puts on a wildly popular performance of the *Nutcracker*. Student and child 'rush' tickets are available for $20 two hours before the performance.

Sports

Boston loves its sports teams. And why not, with its professional teams bringing home the 'Grand Slam of American Sports' by winning the four major championships in recent years.

★ **Fenway Park**   SPORT
(Map p176; www.redsox.com; 4 Yawkey Way; tickets $25-125; T Kenmore) From April to September you can watch the Red Sox play at Fenway Park, the nation's oldest and most storied ballpark. Unfortunately, it is also the most expensive – not that this stops the Fenway faithful from scooping up the tickets. There are sometimes game-day tickets on sale starting two hours before the opening pitch.

TD Garden   BASKETBALL, HOCKEY
(Map p180; ☑ information 617-523-3030, tickets 617-931-2000; www.tdgarden.com; 150 Causeway St; T North Station) This reincarnation of the Boston Garden is still home to the Bruins, who play hockey here from September to June, and the Celtics, who play basketball from October to April.

🛍 Shopping

Newbury St in the Back Bay and Charles St on Beacon Hill are Boston's best shopping destinations for the biggest selection of shops, both traditional and trendy. Harvard Sq is famous for bookstores and the South End is the city's up-and-coming art district. **Copley Place** (Map p176; www.simon.com; 100 Huntington Ave; ☉10am-8pm Mon-Sat, noon-6pm Sun; T Back Bay) and the **Prudential Center** (Map p176; www.prudentialcenter.com; 800 Boylston St; ☉10am-9pm; 🛜; T Prudential), both in Back Bay, are big indoor malls.

Lucy's League   CLOTHING
(Map p180; www.thecolorstores.com; North Bldg, Faneuil Hall; T Government Center) We're not advocating those pink Red Sox caps. But sometimes a girl wants to look good while she's supporting the team. At Lucy's League, fashionable sports fans will find shirts, jackets and other gear sporting the local teams' logos – but in super-cute styles designed to flatter the female figure.

Life is Good   CLOTHING, GIFTS
(Map p176; www.lifeisgood.com; 285 Newbury St; T Hynes) Life *is* good for this locally designed brand of T-shirts, backpacks and other gear.

Styles depict the fun-loving stick figure Jake engaged in guitar playing, dog walking, coffee drinking, mountain climbing and just about every other good-vibe diversion you might enjoy. Jake's activity may vary, but his 'life is good' theme is constant.

Converse   SHOES, CLOTHING
(Map p176; www.converse.com; 348 Newbury St; T Hynes) Converse started making shoes right up the road in Malden, MA, way back in 1908. Chuck Taylor joined the 'team' in the 1920s and the rest is history. This retail store (one of three in the country) has an incredible selection of sneakers, denim and other gear.

The iconic shoes come in all colors and patterns; you can make them uniquely your own in the in-store customization area.

ℹ Information

INTERNET ACCESS

Aside from hotels, wireless access is common at cafes, on buses and even in public spaces such as Faneuil Hall and the Greenway. Many cafes charge a fee, though they may offer the first hour free.

Boston Public Library (www.bpl.org; 700 Boylston St; ⊙9am-9pm Mon-Thu, to 5pm Fri & Sat year-round, 1-5pm Sun Oct-May; ☏; ⊤Copley) Internet access free for 15-minute intervals. Or get a visitor courtesy card at the circulation desk and sign up for one hour of free terminal time. Arrive first thing in the morning to avoid long waits.

Wired Puppy (www.wiredpuppy.com; 250 Newbury St; ⊙6:30am-7:30pm; ☏; ⊤Hynes) Free wireless access and free computer use in case you don't have your own. This is also a comfortable, cozy place to just come and drink coffee.

MEDIA

Boston Globe (www.boston.com) One of two major daily newspapers, the *Globe* publishes an extensive Calendar section every Thursday and the daily Sidekick, both of which include entertainment options.

Improper Bostonian (www.improper.com) A sassy biweekly distributed free from sidewalk dispenser boxes.

MEDICAL SERVICES

CVS Pharmacy (www.cvs.com) Cambridge (www.cvs.com; 1426 Massachusetts Ave, Cambridge; ⊙24hr; ⊤Harvard); Back Bay (☎617-437-8414; 587 Boylston St; ⊙24hr; ⊤Copley)

Massachusetts General Hospital (☎617-726-2000; www.massgeneral.org; 55 Fruit St; ⊙24hr; ⊤Charles/MGH) Arguably the city's biggest and best. It can often refer you to smaller clinics and crisis hotlines.

POST

Main post office (www.usps.com; 25 Dorchester Ave; ⊙6am-midnight; ⊤South Station) One block southeast of South Station.

TOURIST INFORMATION

Cambridge Visitor Information Kiosk (Map p176; www.cambridge-usa.org; Harvard Sq; ⊙9am-5pm Mon-Fri, 1-5pm Sat & Sun; ⊤Harvard) Detailed information on current Cambridge happenings and self-guided walking tours.

Greater Boston Convention & Visitors Bureau (GBCVB; www.bostonusa.com) Boston

---

ⓘ GETTING TO NYC

The cheapest travel between Boston and NYC is by bus. **Yo! Bus** (www.yobus. com; one-way $12-28; ☏; ⊤South Station) runs six buses a day from South Station, while **Go Buses** (www.gobuses. com; one-way from $15; ☏; ⊤Alewife) depart from Cambridge.

Common (Map p180; ☎617-426-3115; 148 Tremont St, Boston Common; ⊙8:30am-5pm Mon-Fri, 9am-5pm Sat & Sun; ⊤Park St); Prudential Center (Map p176; www.bostonusa.com; 800 Boylston St, Prudential Center; ⊙9am-6pm; ⊤Prudential)

WEBSITES

Boston Central (www.bostoncentral.com) A solid resource for families, with listings for activities good for kids.

City of Boston (www.cityofboston.gov) Official website of Boston city government with links to visitor services.

ⓘ Getting There & Away

Getting in and out of Boston is easy. The train and bus stations are conveniently side by side, and the airport is a short subway ride away.

AIR

Logan International Airport (☎800-235-6426; www.massport.com/logan), just across Boston Harbor from the city center, is served by major US and foreign airlines and has full services.

BUS

South Station (Map p180; 700 Atlantic Ave) is the terminal for an extensive network of long-distance buses operated by Greyhound and regional bus companies.

TRAIN

MBTA Commuter Rail (☎800-392-6100, 617-222-3200; www.mbta.com) trains connect Boston's North Station with Concord and Salem and Boston's South Station with Plymouth and Providence.

The **Amtrak** (☎800-872-7245; www.amtrak. com; South Station) terminal is at South Station; trains to New York cost $73 to $126 (4¼ hours) or $147 on the speedier *Acela Express* (3½ hours).

ⓘ Getting Around

TO/FROM THE AIRPORT

Logan International Airport is just a few miles from downtown Boston: take the blue-line subway or the silver-line bus.

CAR

Driving in Boston is not for the faint of heart. It's best to stick to public transportation within the city. If you're traveling onward by rental car, pick up your car at the end of your Boston visit.

SUBWAY

The **MBTA** (☎800-392-6100, 617-222-3200; www.mbta.com; per ride $2-2.50; ⊙5:30am-

12:30am) operates the USA's oldest subway (known as the 'T'), built in 1897. Five color-coded lines – red, blue, green, orange and silver – radiate from the downtown stations of Park St, Downtown Crossing and Government Center. 'Inbound' trains are headed for one of these stations, 'outbound' trains away from them. Note that the silver line is actually a 'bus rapid transit service' that is useful for Logan airport and some other destinations.

TAXI

Taxis are plentiful; expect to pay between $15 and $25 between two points within the city limits. Flag taxis on the street, find them at major hotels or call **Metro Cab** (☑ 617-242-8000) or **Independent** (Map p176; ☑ 617-426-8700).

Around Boston

Up and down the coast, destinations with rich histories, vibrant cultural scenes and unique events merit a venture outside the city. Easily accessible from Boston by car or train, most of these are excellent day-trip destinations.

Lexington & Concord

In Lexington, 15 miles northwest of Boston, the historic **Battle Green** (Massachusetts Ave) is where a skirmish between patriots and British troops jump-started the War of Independence in 1775. Following the battle, the British Redcoats marched west to Concord, following a route now known as **Battle Road**. The Minutemen and the Redcoats faced off again at the **Old North Bridge** – the first American victory. This whole area is preserved as **Minute Man National Historic Park** (www.nps.gov/mima; 250 North Great Rd, Lincoln; ☺9am-5pm Apr-Oct, 9am-4pm Nov; ☷) **FREE**, with visitor centers at the east end of Battle Rd and near the bridge.

Aside from its revolutionary history, Concord also harbored a vibrant literary community in the 19th century. Next to the **Old North Bridge** is the **Old Manse** (www.thetrustees.org; 269 Monument St; adult/child/senior & student $8/5/7; ☺noon-5pm Tue-Sun May-Oct, Sat & Sun only Mar-Apr & Nov-Dec), former home of author Nathaniel Hawthorne. Within a mile of the town center are the **Ralph Waldo Emerson house** (www.rwe.org; 28 Cambridge Turnpike; adult/child/senior & student $7/free/5; ☺10am-4:30pm Thu-Sat, 1-4:30pm Sun mid-Apr–Oct) and Louisa May Alcott's **Orchard House** (www.louisamayalcott.org; 399 Lexington Rd; adult/child/senior & student

$10/5/8; ☺10am-4:30pm Mon-Sat, 1-4:30pm Sun Apr-Oct, 11am-3pm Mon-Fri, 10am-4:30pm Sat, 1-4:30pm Sun Nov-Mar).

Henry David Thoreau lived and wrote his most famous treatise at **Walden Pond** (www.mass.gov/dcr/parks/walden; 915 Walden St; ☺dawn-dusk) **FREE**, 3 miles south of the town center. Visit his cabin site and take an inspiring hike around the pond. All these authors are laid to rest in **Sleepy Hollow Cemetery** (www.friendsofsleepyhollow.org; Bedford St; ☺dawn-dusk) in the town center. The **Concord Chamber of Commerce** (www.concordchamberofcommerce.org; 58 Main St; ☺9:30am-4:30pm Apr-Oct) has full details on sites, including opening hours for the homes, which vary with the season.

Salem

Salem is renowned for the witch hysteria in 1692, when innocent folks were put to death for practicing witchcraft. Nowadays, the town embraces its role as 'Witch City' with witchy museums, spooky tours and Halloween madness.

These incidents obscure the city's true claim to fame: its glory days as a center for clipper-ship trade with the Far East. The **Salem Maritime National Historic Site** (www.nps.gov/sama; 193 Derby St; ☺9am-5pm) **FREE** comprises the custom house, the wharves and the other buildings along Derby St that are remnants of the shipping industry that

WITCH CITY

The city of Salem embraces its witchy past with a healthy dose of whimsy. But the history offers a valuable lesson about what can happen when fear and frenzy are allowed to trump common sense and compassion.

By the time the witch hysteria of 1692 had finally died down, a total of 156 people had been accused, 55 people had pleaded guilty and implicated others to save their own lives, and 14 women and five men had been hanged. Stop by at the **Witch Trials Memorial** (Charter St), a simple but dramatic monument that honors the innocent victims.

The most authentic of more than a score of witchy museums, the **Witch House** (Jonathan Corwin House; www.salemweb.com/witchhouse; 310 Essex St; adult/child/senior $8.25/4.25/6.25, tour add $2; ⊙10am-5pm May-Nov) was once the home of Jonathan Corwin, a local magistrate who investigated witchcraft claims.

For an informative, accurate overview of Salem's sordid past, sign up with **Hocus Pocus Tours** (www.hocuspocustours.com; adult/child $16/8), which is neither hokey nor pokey.

once thrived in Salem. Stroll out to the end of **Derby Wharf** and peek inside the 1871 **lighthouse** or climb aboard the tall ship **Friendship**. Get complete information from the **NPS Regional Visitor Center** (www.nps.gov/sama; 2 New Liberty St; ⊙9am-5pm).

This overview of Salem's maritime exploits is the perfect introduction to the exceptional **Peabody Essex Museum** (www.pem.org; 161 Essex St; adult/child $15/free; ⊙10am-5pm Tue-Sun; 🖈). The museum was founded upon the art, artifacts and curios collected by Salem traders during their early expeditions to the Far East. As the exhibits attest, they had deep pockets and refined taste. In addition to world-class Chinese and Pacific Island displays, the museum boasts an excellent Native American collection.

Plymouth

Plymouth calls itself 'America's Home Town.' It was here that the Pilgrims first settled in the winter of 1620, seeking a place where they could practice their religion without interference from government. An innocuous, weathered ball of granite – the famous **Plymouth Rock** – marks the spot where where they supposedly first stepped ashore in this foreign land. Nearby, **Mayflower II** (www.plimoth.org; State Pier, Water St; adult/child $10/7; ⊙9am-5pm Apr-Nov; 🖈) is a replica of the small ship in which they made the fateful voyage across the ocean.

Three miles south of Plymouth center, **Plimoth Plantation** (www.plimoth.org; MA 3A; adult/child $26/15; ⊙9am-5pm Apr-Nov; 🖈) authentically recreates the Pilgrims' settlement, in its primary exhibit entitled '1627

English Village.' Everything in the village – costumes, implements, vocabulary, artistry, recipes and crops – has been painstakingly researched and remade. The Wampanoag Homesite replicates the life of a Native American community in the same area during that time.

Cape Cod

Clambering across the National Seashore dunes, cycling the Cape Cod Rail Trail, eating oysters at Wellfleet Harbor – this sandy peninsula serves up a bounty of local flavor. Fringed with 400 miles of sparkling shoreline, 'the Cape,' as it's called by Cape Codders, rates as New England's top beach destination. But there's a lot more than just beaches here. When you've had your fill of sun and sand, get out and explore artist enclaves, take a cruise, or join the free-spirited street scene in Provincetown.

Cape Cod Chamber of Commerce (☑508-362-3225; www.capecodchamber.org; MA 132 at US 6, Hyannis; ⊙9am-5pm Mon-Sat, 10am-2pm Sun) has info.

Sandwich

The Cape's oldest village wraps its historic center around a picturesque swan pond with a gristmill (c 1654) and several small museums.

⊙ Sights

If you're ready for salt spray, head to **Sandy Neck Beach** (Sandy Neck Rd, West Barnstable), off MA 6A, a 6-mile dune-backed strand (parking $15–20) ideal for beachcombing and a bracing swim.

Sandwich Glass Museum
MUSEUM

(📞 508-888-0251; www.sandwichglassmuseum.org; 129 Main St; adult/child $6/1.25; ⏱ 9:30am-5pm) Artfully displayed here is the town's 19th-century glass-making heritage. Glass-blowing demonstrations are given hourly throughout the day.

Heritage Museums & Gardens
MUSEUM

(📞 508-888-3300; www.heritagemuseumsandgardens.org; 67 Grove St; adult/child $15/7; ⏱ 10am-5pm; 👶) Fun for kids and adults alike, this 76-acre site sports a superb vintage automobile collection in a Shaker-style round barn, a working 1912 carousel, folk-art collections and one of the finest rhododendron gardens in America.

Cape Cod Canal
CANAL

(www.capecodcanal.us; 👶🚲) FREE Cape Cod isn't connected by land to the mainland, but it's not exactly an island, or at least wasn't until the Cape Cod Canal was dug in 1914 to save ships from having to sail an extra 135 miles around the treacherous tip of the Cape. A 6 mile path ideal for walking, cycling and in-line skating runs along the south side of the canal from Sandwich Harbor.

🛏 Sleeping & Eating

Shawme-Crowell
State Forest
CAMPGROUND $

(📞 508-888-0351; www.reserveamerica.com; MA 130; tent sites $14) You'll find 285 shady campsites in this 760-acre woodland near MA 6A.

Belfry Inne & Bistro
B&B $$$

(📞 508-888-8550; www.belfryinn.com; 8 Jarves St; r incl breakfast $149-299; 🏴📶) Ever fall asleep in church? Then you'll love the rooms, some with stained-glass windows, in this creatively restored former church, now an upmarket B&B. If, however, you're uneasy about the angel Gabriel watching over you in bed, Belfry has two other nearby inns with conventional rooms.

Seafood Sam's
SEAFOOD $$

(www.seafoodsams.com; 6 Coast Guard Rd; mains $8-20; ⏱ 11am-9pm; 👶) Sam's is a good family choice for fish and chips, fried clams and lobster rolls. Dine at outdoor picnic tables overlooking Cape Cod Canal and watch the fishing boats sail by.

Falmouth

Fantastic beaches and a scenic seaside bike trail highlight the Cape's second-largest town.

◉ Sights & Activities

Old Silver Beach
BEACH

(off MA 28A; 👶) Deeply indented Falmouth has 70 miles of coastline, but none of it is finer than this long, sandy stretch of beach. A rock jetty, sandbars and tidal pools provide fun diversions for kids. Parking costs $20.

★ Shining Sea Bikeway
CYCLING

(👶) A bright star among the Cape's stellar bike trails, this 10.7-mile beaut runs along the entire west coast of Falmouth, offering unspoiled views of salt ponds, marsh and seascapes. Bike rentals are available at the north end of the trail.

🛏 Sleeping & Eating

Falmouth Heights Motor Lodge
MOTEL $$

(📞 508-548-3623; www.falmouthheightsresort.com; 146 Falmouth Heights Rd; r incl breakfast $129-259; 🏴📶) Don't be fooled by the name. This tidy operation is no drive-up motor lodge – it's not even on the highway. All 28 rooms are a cut above the competition. The beach and Vineyard ferry are minutes away.

Clam Shack
SEAFOOD $

(📞 508-540-7758; 227 Clinton Ave; light meals $6-15; ⏱ 11:30am-7:30pm) A classic of the genre, right on Falmouth Harbor. It's tiny, with picnic tables on the back deck and lots of fried seafood. The clams, huge juicy bellies cooked to a perfect crisp, are the place to start.

DON'T MISS

LOBSTER ICE CREAM, ANYONE?

Lobster mania takes a new twist at **Ben & Bill's Chocolate Emporium** (209 Main St, Falmouth; cones $5; ⏱ 9am-11pm) where the crustacean has crawled onto the ice-cream menu. Forget plain vanilla. Step up to the counter and order a scoop of lobster ice cream. Now there's one you won't find with the old 31-flavors folks.

Maison Villatte CAFE $

(☎ 774-255-1855; 267 Main St; snacks $3-10; ☉ 7am-7pm Wed-Sat, to 5pm Sun) A pair of French bakers work the ovens, creating crusty artisan breads, flaky croissants and sinful pastries at this bakery-cafe. Hearty sandwiches and robust coffee make it an ideal lunch spot.

Hyannis

Cape Cod's commercial hub, Hyannis is best known to visitors as the summer home of the Kennedy clan and a jumping-off point for ferries to Nantucket and Martha's Vineyard.

NEW ENGLAND CAPE COD

Cape Cod, Martha's Vineyard & Nantucket

0 — 10 km
0 — 5 miles

Hingham
Cohasset
Boston (25mi)
Hanover
Pembroke (14)
(53) (3A) Marshfield
(3)
(106)
Plymouth Bay
Plymouth
Plympton
(44)
(58) (3) (3A) Manomet
South Middleboro
Myles Standish State Forest
(495)
Cape Cod Canal
Rochester
(25) (6)
Buzzards Bay
(28) Bourne
North Falmouth
Old Silver Beach
East Falmouth
Buzzards Bay
Falmouth
Falmouth Heights
Woods Hole
Elizabeth Islands
Vineyard Sound
Vineyard Haven
Tisbury
Menemsha West Tisbury
Chilmark
Aquinnah
MARTHA'S VINEYARD
Oak Bluffs
Edgartown
Chappaquiddick Island
Katama Beach
Muskeget Island
ATLANTIC OCEAN

Ferry to Boston (seasonal)
Cedarville
Shawme-Crowell State Forest
Sagamore
Sandwich
(6A)
West Barnstable
(130) Mid-Cape Hwy
Marstons Mills
(28) Hyannis
Hyannisport
Mashpee
Vineyard Sound

Stellwagen Bank National Marine Sanctuary

Cape Cod Bay

Race Point Beach
Herring Cove Beach
Provincetown
North Truro
Truro
(6)
Wellfleet
Wellfleet Harbor
Wellfleet Beaches
Cape Cod National Seashore
Rock Harbor
Eastham
Orleans
Brewster Nickerson State Park
East Dennis
Dennis
Yarmouth (6A)
(6)
(134)
Harwich Port
South Yarmouth
(137)
(28) Chatham
Lighthouse Beach
Pleasant Bay
Monomoy National Wildlife Refuge
MONOMOY ISLAND

ATLANTIC OCEAN

Nantucket Sound

Great Point Light
Coskata
Wauwinet
Madaket
Cisco
Surfside
Nantucket
Siasconset
NANTUCKET

WORTH A TRIP

WOODS HOLE

The tiny village of Woods Hole is home to the largest oceanographic institution in the US. Research at the Woods Hole Oceanographic Institution (WHOI, pronounced 'hooey') has covered the gamut from exploring the sunken *Titanic* to global warming studies.

You can join one of the free tours departing from the **WHOI information office** (93 Water St). You'll also gain insights into scientists' work at the **WHOI Ocean Science Exhibit Center** (15 School St; ⊘10am-4:30pm Mon-Sat) FREE.

Woods Hole Science Aquarium (http://aquarium.nefsc.noaa.gov; 166 Water St; ⊘11am-4pm Tue-Sat; 🖔) FREE has little flash and dazzle, but you'll find unusual sea-life specimens, local fish and the *Homarus americanus* (aka lobster). Kids will enjoy the touch-tank creatures. Coolest time to come is at 11am or 4pm when the seals are fed.

Keeping with the nautical theme, head over to the drawbridge where you'll find **Fishmonger Café** (www.fishmongercafe.com; 56 Water St; mains $10-25; ⊘7am-9:30pm), with water views in every direction and an eclectic menu emphasizing fresh seafood.

To get to Woods Hole from Falmouth center take Woods Hole Rd south from MA28.

⊙ Sights

The town's mile-long Main St is fun to stroll and the place for dining, drinking and shopping. **Kalmus Beach** (Ocean St, Hyannis) is popular for windsurfing, while **Craigville Beach** (Craigville Beach Rd, Centerville) is where the college set goes; parking at either costs $15 to $20.

John F Kennedy
Hyannis Museum   MUSEUM
(☑508-790-3077; http://jfkhyannismuseum.org; 397 Main St, Hyannis; adult/child $8/3; ⊘9am-5pm Mon-Sat, noon-5pm Sun) This museum celebrates America's 35th president with photographs, videos and mementos. It also houses the **Cape Cod Baseball League Hall of Fame**.

🛏 Sleeping

HI-Hyannis   HOSTEL $
(☑508-775-7990; http://capecod.hiusa.org; 111 Ocean St, Hyannis; dm incl breakfast $32; @ 🛜) 🏊 For a million-dollar view on a backpacker's budget, book yourself a bed at this hostel overlooking the harbor and within walking distance of Main St, beaches and ferries. Just 37 beds, so book early.

SeaCoast Inn   MOTEL $$
(☑508-775-3828; www.seacoastcapecod.com; 33 Ocean St, Hyannis; r incl breakfast $128-168; ❄@🛜) This family-run motel is just a two-minute walk from the harbor in one direction and Main St restaurants in the other. There's no view or pool, but the rooms are thoroughly comfy, most have kitchenettes and the price is a deal for Hyannis.

✖ Eating

★ Bistrot de Soleil   MEDITERRANEAN $$
(www.bistrotdesoleil.com; 350 Stevens St, at Main St, Hyannis; mains $10-25; ⊘11:30am-9pm) Mediterranean influences meet fresh local ingredients in a menu that ranges from gourmet wood-fired pizzas to filet mignon. A smart setting, organic wine list and $20 prix fixe dinner specials round out the appeal.

Raw Bar   SEAFOOD $$
(www.therawbar.com; 230 Ocean St, Hyannis; lobster rolls $26; ⊘11am-7pm) Come here for the mother of all lobster rolls – it's like eating an entire lobster in a bun. The view overlooking Hyannis Harbor isn't hard to swallow either.

Brewster

Woodsy Brewster, on the Cape's bay side, makes a good base for outdoorsy types. The Cape Cod Rail Trail cuts clear across town and there are excellent options for camping, hiking and water activities.

⊙ Sights & Activities

Nickerson State Park   PARK
(☑508-896-3491; 3488 MA 6A; per car $5; ⊘dawn-dusk; 🖔) Miles of cycling and walking trails and eight ponds with sandy beaches highlight this 2000-acre oasis.

Jack's Boat Rental   BOATING
(☑508-349-9808; www.jacksboatrental.com; rentals per hr $25-45; ⊘10am-6pm) This operation, within Nickerson State Park, rents canoes, kayaks and sailboats.

DON'T MISS

CYCLING THE RAIL TRAIL

A poster child for the rails-to-trail movement, the **Cape Cod Rail Trail** follows a former railroad track for 22 glorious miles past cranberry bogs and along sandy ponds ideal for a dip. It's one of the finest cycling trails in all New England. There's a hefty dose of Olde Cape Cod scenery en route and you can detour into quiet villages for lunch or sightseeing. The path begins in Dennis on MA 134 and continues all the way to Wellfleet. If you have time to do only part of the trail, begin at Nickerson State Park in Brewster and head for the Cape Cod National Seashore in Eastham. Bicycle rentals are available at the trailhead in Dennis, at Nickerson State Park and opposite the National Seashore's Salt Pond Visitor Center (p199).

Barb's Bike Rental　　　　　　CYCLING
(📞 508-896-7231; www.barbsbikeshop.com; bicycles per half/full day $18/24; ⏱ 9am-6pm) Rents bicycles by the park entrance.

🛏 Sleeping

★Nickerson State Park　　CAMPGROUND **$**
(📞 877-422-6762; www.reserveamerica.com; campsites $17; yurts $30-40) Head here for Cape Cod's best camping with 418 wooded campsites. It often fills, so reserve early.

★Old Sea Pines Inn　　　　　B&B **$$**
(📞 508-896-6114; www.oldseapinesinn.com; 2553 MA 6A; r incl breakfast $85-195; @ 🛜) A former girls' boarding school dating to 1840, this inn retains an engaging yesteryear look. It's a bit like staying at grandma's house: antique fittings, sepia photographs, claw-foot bathtubs. No TV to spoil the mood, but rocking chairs await on the porch.

🍴 Eating

★Brewster Fish House　　　SEAFOOD **$$**
(www.brewsterfish.com; 2208 MA 6A; mains $14-32; ⏱ 11:30am-3pm & 5-9:30pm) A favorite of seafood lovers. Start with the lobster bisque, naturally sweet with chunks of fresh lobster. From there it's safe to cast your net in any direction. Just 11 tables, and no reservations, so think lunch or early dinner to avoid long waits.

Cobie's　　　　　　　　　　SEAFOOD **$$**
(www.cobies.com; 3256 MA 6A; mains $9-23; ⏱ 11am-9pm) Conveniently located near Nickerson State Park, this roadside clam shack dishes out fried seafood that you can crunch and munch at outdoor picnic tables.

Chatham

Upscale inns and tony shops are a hallmark of the Cape's most genteel town, but some of Chatham's finest pleasures come free for the taking. Start your exploring on Main St, with its old sea captains' houses and cool art galleries.

At **Chatham Fish Pier** (Shore Rd) watch fishermen unload their catch and spot seals basking on nearby shoals. A mile south on Shore Rd is **Lighthouse Beach**, an endless expanse of sea and sandbars that offers some of the finest beach strolling on Cape Cod. The 7600-acre **Monomoy National Wildlife Refuge** (www.fws.gov/northeast/monomoy) 🦆 covers two uninhabited islands thick with shorebirds; to see it up close take the 1½-hour boat tour with **Monomoy Island Excursions** (📞 508-430-7772; www.monomoysealcruise.com; 702 MA 28, Harwich Port; 1½hr tours adult/child $35/30).

🛏 Sleeping & Eating

Bow Roof House　　　　　　　B&B **$$**
(📞 508-945-1346; 59 Queen Anne Rd; r incl breakfast $115) This homey, six-room, c 1780 house is delightfully old-fashioned in price and offerings, and within easy walking distance of the town center and beach.

Chatham Cookware Café　　　CAFE **$**
(📞 508-945-1250; 524 Main St; sandwiches $8; ⏱ 6:30am-4pm) No, it's not a place to buy pots and pans, but rather *the* downtown spot for a coffee fix, homemade muffins and sandwiches.

★Chatham Fish Pier Market　SEAFOOD **$$**
(www.chathamfishpiermarket.com; 45 Barcliff Ave; mains $12-25; ⏱ 10am-7pm Mon-Thu, to 8pm Fri-Sun) If you like it fresh and local to the core, this salt-sprayed fish shack, with its own sushi chef and day boats, is for you. The chowder's incredible and the fish so fresh it was swimming earlier in the day. It's all takeout, but there are shady picnic tables nearby as well as a harbor full of sights.

Cape Cod National Seashore

Extending some 40 miles around the curve of the Outer Cape, **Cape Cod National Seashore** (www.nps.gov/caco) encompasses most of the shoreline from Eastham to Provincetown. It's a treasure-trove of unspoiled beaches, dunes, salt marshes and forests. Thanks to President John F Kennedy, this vast area was set aside for preservation in the 1960s, just before a building boom hit the rest of his native Cape Cod. The **Salt Pond Visitor Center** (508-255-3421; 50 Doane Rd, cnr US 6 & Nauset Rd, Eastham; 9am-5pm) FREE is the place to start and has a great view to boot. Here you will find exhibits and films about the area's ecology and the scoop on the park's numerous cycling and hiking trails, some of which begin right at the center.

You brought your board, didn't you? **Coast Guard Beach**, just down the road from the visitor center, is a stunner that attracts everyone from surfers to beachcombers. And the view of untouched Nauset Marsh from the dunes above the beach is nothing short of spectacular. **Nauset Light Beach**, running north from Coast Guard Beach, takes its name from the lighthouse perched above it; three other classic lighthouses are nearby. Summertime beach parking passes cost $15/45 per day/season and are valid at all Cape Cod National Seashore beaches including Provincetown.

Wellfleet

Art galleries, primo beaches and those famous Wellfleet oysters lure visitors to this little seaside town.

◉ Sights

Wellfleet Beaches BEACHES
backed by undulating dunes, **Marconi Beach** has a monument to Guglielmo Marconi, who sent the first wireless transmission across the Atlantic from this site. The adjacent **White Crest Beach** and **Cahoon Hollow Beach** offer high-octane surfing. **SickDay Surf Shop** (508-214-4158; www.sickdaysurf.com; 361 Main St; surfboards per day $25-30; 9am-9pm Mon-Sat) rents surfboards.

Wellfleet Bay Wildlife Sanctuary NATURE RESERVE
(508-349-2615; www.massaudubon.org; West Rd, off US 6; adult/child $5/3; 8:30am-dusk;) Birders flock to Mass Audubon's 1100-acre sanctuary, where trails cross tidal creeks, salt marshes and beaches.

★ Festivals & Events

Wellfleet OysterFest FOOD
(www.wellfleetoysterfest.org; mid-Oct) The town becomes a food fair for a weekend, with a beer garden, an oyster-shucking contest and, of course, belly-busters of the blessed bivalves.

🛏 Sleeping & Eating

Even'Tide Motel MOTEL $$
(508-349-3410; www.eventidemotel.com; 650 US 6; r from $135, cottages per week $1100-2800;) This 31-room motel, set back from the highway in a grove of pine trees, also has nine cottages. Pluses include a large indoor pool, picnic facilities and a playground.

PB Boulangerie & Bistro BAKERY $
(www.pbboulangeriebistro.com; 15 Lecount Hollow Rd; pastries from $3; 7am-7pm Tue-Sun) Incredible pastries, artisan breads and delicious sandwiches.

Mac's Seafood Market SEAFOOD $$
(www.macsseafood.com; 265 Commercial St, Wellfleet Town Pier; mains $7-20; 11am-3pm Mon-Fri, to 8pm Sat & Sun;) Head here for market-fresh seafood at bargain prices. Fried fish standards are paired with snappy-fresh oysters harvested from nearby flats. Order at a window and chow down at picnic tables overlooking Wellfleet Harbor.

☆ Entertainment

★ Beachcomber LIVE MUSIC
(508-349-6055; www.thebeachcomber.com; 1120 Cahoon Hollow Rd; 5pm-1am) 'Da Coma' is *the* place to rock the night away. It's a bar. It's a restaurant. It's a dance club. It's the

---

LOCAL KNOWLEDGE

SCENIC DRIVE: CAPE COD BAY

When exploring the Cape, eschew the speedy Mid-Cape Hwy (US 6) and follow instead the **Old King's Hwy (MA 6A)**, which snakes along Cape Cod Bay. The longest continuous stretch of historic district in the USA, it's lined with gracious period homes, antique shops and art galleries, all of which make for good browsing en route.

coolest summertime hangout on the entire Cape, set in a former lifesaving station right on Cahoon Hollow Beach. You can watch the surf action till the sun goes down, and after dark some really hot bands take the stage.

Wellfleet Harbor Actors Theater THEATER
(WHAT; ☑ 508-349-9428; www.what.org; 2357 US 6) This acclaimed theater produces edgy, contemporary plays.

Wellfleet Drive-In CINEMA
(☑ 508-349-7176; www.wellfleetcinemas.com; US 6; adult/child $9/6; ⊕) Enjoy an evening of nostalgia at this old-fashioned drive-in theater.

Truro

Squeezed between Cape Cod Bay on the west coast and the open Atlantic on the east, narrow Truro abounds with water views and beaches.

◎ Sights

Cape Cod Highland Light LIGHTHOUSE
(www.capecodlight.org; Light House Rd; admission $4; ⊙10am-5:30pm) Sitting on the Cape's highest elevation (a mere 120ft!), Cape Cod Highland Light casts the brightest beam on the New England coast and offers a sweeping view.

📙 Sleeping

Hostelling International Truro HOSTEL $
(☑ 508-349-3889; http://capecod.hiusa.org; N Pamet Rd; dm incl breakfast $39; @) Budget digs don't get more atmospheric than at this former coast-guard station perched amid undulating dunes. Book early.

Provincetown

This is it: as far as you can go on the Cape, and more than just geographically. The draw is irresistible. Fringe writers and artists began making a summer haven in Provincetown a century ago. Today this sandy outpost has morphed into the hottest gay

and lesbian destination in the Northeast. Flamboyant street scenes, brilliant art galleries and unbridled nightlife paint the town center. But that's only half the show. Provincetown's untamed coastline and vast beaches beg to be explored. Sail off on a whale watch, cruise the night away, get lost in the dunes – but whatever you do, don't miss this unique corner of New England.

◎ Sights & Activities

Province Lands Visitor Center BEACH
(☑ 508-487-1256; www.nps.gov/caco; Race Point Rd; ⊙9am-5pm; ℗) ✔ **FREE** Overlooking Race Point Beach, this Cape Cod National Seashore visitor center has displays on dune ecology and a rooftop observation deck with an eye-popping 360° view of the outermost reaches of Cape Cod.

Race Point Beach BEACH
(Race Point Rd) On the wild tip of the Cape, Race Point is a breathtaking stretch of sand, with crashing surf and undulating dunes as far as the eye can see.

Herring Cove Beach BEACH
(Province Lands Rd) This popular swimming beach faces west, making it a spectacular place to be at sunset.

★Pilgrim Monument & Provincetown Museum MUSEUM
(www.pilgrim-monument.org; High Pole Rd; adult/child $12/4; ⊙9am-7pm Jul & Aug, to 5pm Sep-Jun) Climb to the top of the USA's tallest all-granite structure (253ft) for a sweeping view of town and coast. At the base of the c 1910 tower an evocative museum depicts the landing of the *Mayflower* Pilgrims and other Provincetown history.

★Provincetown Art Association & Museum MUSEUM
(PAAM; www.paam.org; 460 Commercial St; adult/child $7/free; ⊙11am-8pm Mon-Thu, to 10pm Fri, to 5pm Sat & Sun) Founded in 1914 to celebrate the town's thriving art community, this vibrant museum showcases the works of artists who have found their inspiration in Provincetown. Chief among them is Edward Hopper, who had a home and gallery in the Truro dunes.

Whydah Pirate Museum MUSEUM
(www.whydah.com; MacMillan Wharf; adult/child $10/8; ⊙10am-5pm) See the salvaged booty from a pirate ship that sank off Cape Cod in 1717.

GALLERY BROWSING

Provincetown hosts scores of art galleries. For the best browsing begin at PAAM and walk southwest along waterfront Commercial St. Over the next few blocks every second storefront harbors a gallery worth a peek.

★ Dolphin Fleet
Whale Watch   WHALE-WATCHING
(☑508-240-3636; www.whalewatch.com; MacMillan Wharf; adult/child $44/29; ☺Apr-Oct; ⊞) ✦ Provincetown is the perfect launch point for whale-watching, since it's the closest port to Stellwagen Bank National Marine Sanctuary, a summer feeding ground for humpback whales. Dolphin offers as many as 12 whale-watch tours daily. Expect splashy fun. Humpback whales have a flair for acrobatic breaching and come surprisingly close to the boats, offering great photo ops.

Cape Cod National
Seashore Bike Trails   CYCLING
(www.nps.gov/caco) Eight exhilarating miles of paved bike trails crisscross the forest and undulating dunes of the Cape Cod National Seashore and lead to Herring Cove and Race Point beaches. There are several bike rental shops around town.

★⚐ Festivals & Events

Provincetown Carnival   CARNIVAL
(www.ptown.org/carnival.asp; ☺3rd week of August) Mardi Gras, drag queens, flowery floats – this is the ultimate gay party event in this gay party town, attracting tens of thousands of revelers.

🛏 Sleeping

Provincetown offers nearly 100 guesthouses, without a single chain hotel to mar the view. In summer it's wise to book ahead, doubly so on weekends. If you do arrive without a booking, the chamber of commerce keeps tabs on available rooms.

Dunes' Edge Campground   CAMPGROUND $
(☑508-487-9815; www.dunesedge.com; 386 US 6; tent/RV sites $42/54) Camp amid the dunes at this family-friendly campground.

Moffett House   GUESTHOUSE $$
(☑508-487-6615; www.moffetthouse.com; 296a Commercial St; r without bath $90-159; ⊞🔊🐾) Set back in a quiet alleyway, this guesthouse has a bonus: free bicycles. Rooms are basic – it's more like crashing with a friend than doing the B&B thing – but you get kitchen privileges and lots of ops to meet fellow travelers.

Race Point Lighthouse   INN $$
(☑508-487-9930; www.racepointlighthouse.net; Race Point; r $155-185) ✦ Want to *really* get away? If unspoiled sand dunes and a 19th-

PROVINCETOWN'S FIRST PORT OF CALL
In a town of quirky attractions the **Provincetown Public Library** (www.provincetownlibrary.org; 356 Commercial St; ☺10am-5pm Mon & Fri, to 8pm Tue-Thu, 1-5pm Sat & Sun) might be the last place you'd expect to find a hidden treasure. Erected in 1860 as a church, it was turned into a museum a century later, complete with a replica of Provincetown's race-winning schooner *Rose Dorothea*. When the museum went bust, the town converted the building to a library. One catch: the boat, which occupies the building's upper deck, was too big to remove. So it's still there, with bookshelves built around it. Pop upstairs and take a look.

century lighthouse sound like good company, book one of the three bedrooms in the old lighthouse-keeper's house. Cool place – powered by solar panels and a wind turbine, and literally on the outer tip of the Cape, miles from the nearest neighbor.

Ampersand Guesthouse   B&B $$
(☑508-487-0959; www.ampersandguesthouse.com; 6 Cottage St; r incl breakfast $130-200; ⊞🔊) It's not the fanciest place in town but it's friendly and cozy and its summer rates are good value.

Revere Guesthouse   B&B $$
(☑508-487-2292; www.reverehouse.com; 14 Court St; r incl breakfast $155-345; ⊞🔊) Tasteful rooms and a peaceful setting, yet just minutes from all the action.

★ Carpe Diem   BOUTIQUE HOTEL $$$
(☑508-487-4242; www.carpediemguesthouse.com; 12 Johnson St; r incl breakfast $229-419; ⊞@🔊) Sophisticated and relaxed, with smiling Buddhas, orchid sprays and a European-style spa. Each guest room is inspired by a different gay literary genius; the room themed on poet Raj Rao, for example, has sumptuous embroidered fabrics and hand-carved Indian furniture.

🍴 Eating

Every third building on Commercial St houses some sort of eatery, so that's the place to start.

Cafe Heaven CAFE $

(☑ 508-487-9639; 199 Commercial St; mains $7-12; ☺ 8am-3pm) Light and airy but small and crowded, this art-filled storefront is an easy-on-the-wallet lunch and breakfast place. The menu ranges from sinful croissant French toast to healthy salads. Don't be deterred by the wait – the tables turn over quickly.

Spiritus Pizza PIZZERIA $

(www.spirituspizza.com; 190 Commercial St; slices/pizzas $3/20; ☺ 11:30am-2am) A favorite place for a late-night bite and cruising after the clubs close.

Purple Feather Cafe & Treatery CAFE $

(www.thepurplefeather.com; 334 Commercial St; snacks $3-10; ☺ 11am-midnight; � ♦) Head to this stylish cafe for killer panini sandwiches, a rainbow of gelati and decadent desserts made from scratch. Lemon cupcakes never looked so lusty.

Fanizzi's by the Sea SEAFOOD $$

(☑ 508-487-1964; www.fanizzisrestaurant.com; 539 Commercial St; mains $10-25; ☺ 11:30am-9:30pm; ♦) An amazing water view and reasonable prices make Fanizzi's a local favorite. You'll find something for everyone, from fresh seafood and salads to comfort food and a kids' menu.

★ **Mews Restaurant & Cafe** MODERN AMERICAN $$$

(☑ 508-487-1500; www.mews.com; 429 Commercial St; mains $14-35; ☺ 5:30-10pm) Want affordable gourmet? Skip the excellent but pricey restaurant and go upstairs to the bar for a fab view, great martinis and scrumptious bistro fare.

Lobster Pot SEAFOOD $$$

(☑ 508-487-0842; www.ptownlobsterpot.com; 321 Commercial St; mains $22-37; ☺ 11:30am-9pm) True to its name, this bustling fish house is *the* place for lobster. Service can be s-l-o-w. Best way to beat the crowd is to come mid-afternoon.

♀ Drinking & Nightlife

Provincetown is awash with gay clubs, drag shows and cabarets. And don't be shy if you're straight – everyone's welcome.

Patio CAFE

(www.ptownpatio.com; 328 Commercial St; ☺ 11am-11pm) Grab yourself a sidewalk table and order up a ginger *mojito* at this umbrella-shaded cafe hugging the pulsating center of Commercial St.

Ross' Grill BAR

(www.rossgrille.com; 237 Commercial St; ☺ 11:30am-10pm) For an romantic place to have a drink with a water view, head to the bar at this smart bistro.

Pied Bar GAY & LESBIAN

(www.piedbar.com; 193 Commercial St) A popular waterfront lounge that attracts both lesbians and gay men. Particularly hot place to be around sunset.

A-House CLUB

(Atlantic House; www.ahouse.com; 4 Masonic Pl) A hot dance spot for the gay community.

☆ Entertainment

Provincetown boasts a rich theater history. Eugene O'Neill began his writing career here and several stars including Marlon Brando and Richard Gere performed on Provincetown stages before they hit the big screen.

Provincetown Theater THEATER

(☑ 508-487-7487; www.provincetowntheater.org; 238 Bradford St) There's almost always something of interest on here – anything from splashy Broadway musicals to offbeat local themes.

Crown & Anchor GAY & LESBIAN

(www.onlyatthecrown.com; 247 Commercial St) The queen of the gay scene, this multiwing complex has a nightclub, a leather bar and a steamy cabaret.

🛍 Shopping

Shops lining Commercial St sell everything from kitsch and tourist T-shirts to quality crafts and edgy clothing.

Shop Therapy ADULT

(www.shoptherapy.com; 346 Commercial St; ☺ 10am-10pm) Downstairs, it's patchouli and tie-dye clothing. But everyone gravitates upstairs, where the sex toys are wild enough to make an Amsterdam madam blush. Parents, you'll need to use discretion: your teenagers *will* want to go inside.

Womencrafts CRAFT

(www.womencrafts.com; 376 Commercial St; ☺ 11am-6pm) The name says it all: jewelry, pottery, books and music by female artists from across America.

❶ Information

Post office (www.usps.com; 219 Commercial St)
Provincetown Business Guild (www.ptown.
org) Oriented to the gay community.
Provincetown Chamber of Commerce (www.
ptownchamber.com; 307 Commercial St;
⊙9am-6pm) The town's helpful tourist office is
at MacMillan Wharf, where the ferries dock.
Provincetown on the Web (www.provincetown.
com) Online guide with the entertainment
scoop.
Seamen's Bank (221 Commercial St) Has a
24-hour ATM.
Wired Puppy (www.wiredpuppy.com; 379 Commercial St; ⊙6:30am-10pm; 🛜) Free online
computers for the price of an espresso.

❶ Getting There & Away

Plymouth & Brockton buses (www.p-b.com)
connect Boston and Provincetown ($35, 3½
hours). From mid-May to mid-October, **Bay
State Cruise Company** (📞877-783-3779; www.
boston-ptown.com; 200 Seaport Blvd, Boston;
round-trip adult/child fast ferry $85/62, slow
ferry $46/free; ⊙mid-May–mid-Oct) runs a
ferry between Boston's World Trade Center Pier
and MacMillan Wharf.

Nantucket

Once home port to the world's largest whaling fleet, Nantucket's storied past is reflected in its period homes and cobbled streets.
When whaling went bust in the mid-19th
century the town plunged from riches to
rags. The population dwindled and grand
old houses sat idle until wealthy urbanites
discovered Nantucket made a fine place to
spend summer. High-end tourism has been
Nantucket's mainstay ever since.

❍ Sights & Activities

Step off the boat and you're in the only place
in the USA where the entire town is a National Historic Landmark. It's a bit like stepping into a museum – wander around, soak
up the atmosphere. Start your explorations
by strolling up Main St, where you'll find the
grandest whaling-era mansions lined up in
a row.

★Nantucket Whaling Museum　MUSEUM
(13 Broad St; adult/child $20/5; ⊙10am-5pm mid-
May–Oct, 11am-4pm Nov–mid-May) A top sight is
this evocative museum in a former sperma-
ceti (whale-oil) candle factory.

Nantucket Beaches　BEACHES
If you have young 'uns head to **Children's
Beach**, right in Nantucket town, where the
water's calm and there's a playground. **Surfside Beach**, 2 miles to the south, is where
the college crowd heads for an active scene
and bodysurfing waves. The best place to
catch the sunset is **Madaket Beach**, 5.5
miles west of town.

Cycling　CYCLING
No destination on the island is more than
8 miles from town and thanks to Nantucket's relatively flat terrain and dedicated bike
trails, cycling is an easy way to explore. For
a fun outing, cycle to the picturesque village
of **Siasconset** ('Sconset), known for its rose-
covered cottages. A couple of companies rent
bikes ($30 a day) right at the ferry docks.

🛏 Sleeping

HI Nantucket　HOSTEL $
(📞508-228-0433; http://capecod.hiusa.org; 31
Western Ave; dm incl breakfast $35; ⊙mid-May–
mid-Sep; @) Known locally as Star of the Sea,
this atmospheric hostel in an 1873 lifesaving
station has a million-dollar setting near Surfside Beach. As Nantucket's sole nod to the
budget traveler, it's booked well in advance.

★Centerboard Inn　B&B $$$
(📞508-228-2811; www.centerboardinn.com; 8
Chestnut St; r incl breakfast $249-419; ❈@🛜) A
welcoming innkeeper who pampers guests
with extras, and loans iPads, gives this chic
B&B a leg up on the competition. Rooms
sport an upscale island decor, breakfast in-
cludes savory treats and the location is per-
fect for sightseeing. After a day on the town
slip back to relax over cheese and wine at
afternoon tea.

Barnacle Inn　B&B $$$
(📞508-228-0332; www.thebarnacleinn.com; 11
Fair St; r with/without bath incl breakfast from
$200/140) Folksy owners and simple, quaint
accommodations that hearken to earlier
times are in store at this turn-of-the-19th-
century inn.

🍴 Eating

Centre Street Bistro　CAFE $$
(www.nantucketbistro.com; 29 Centre St; mains $8-
30; ⊙11:30am-9:30pm Wed-Sat; 🛜🍴) Settle in
at a parasol-shaded sidewalk table and watch
the traffic trickle by at this relaxed cafe. The
chef-owners make everything from scratch,
including delicious warm goat's-cheese tarts.

Club Car
PUB $$

(www.theclubcar.com; 1 Main St; mains $12-30; ⊙11:30am-1am) This converted railroad car, a vestige of the actual railroad that sank in the sands of Nantucket, dishes up consistently good food, including the best lobster roll in town.

Black-Eyed Susan's
CAFE $$

(www.black-eyedsusans.com; 10 India St; mains $9-30; ⊙7am-1pm daily & 6-10pm Mon-Sat) Snag a seat on the back patio and try the sourdough French toast topped with caramelized pecans and Jack Daniel's butter. At dinner the fish of the day with black-eyed peas takes top honors. BYOB.

ⓘ Information

Visitor Services & Information Bureau
(☑508-228-0925; www.nantucket-ma.gov; 25 Federal St; ⊙9am-5pm) Maintains a summer-season kiosk at the ferry dock.

ⓘ Getting There & Around

AIR
Cape Air (www.flycapeair.com) flies from Boston, Hyannis and Martha's Vineyard to Nantucket Memorial Airport (ACK).

BOAT
The **Steamship Authority** (☑508-477-8600; www.steamshipauthority.com) runs ferries throughout the day between Hyannis and Nantucket. The fast ferry (round-trip adult/child $69/35) takes an hour; the slow ferry (round-trip adult/child $35/18) takes 2¼ hours.

BUS
Getting around Nantucket is a snap. The **NRTA Shuttle** (www.shuttlenantucket.com; rides $1-2, day pass $7; ⊙late May-Sep) operates buses around town and to 'Sconset, Madaket and the beaches. Buses have bike racks, so cyclists can bus one way and pedal back.

Martha's Vineyard

New England's largest island is a world unto itself. Home to 15,500 year-round residents, its population swells to 100,000 in summer. The towns are charming, the beaches good, the restaurants chef-driven. And there's something for every mood here – fine-dine in gentrified Edgartown one day and hit the cotton-candy and carousel scene in Oak Bluffs the next.

Martha's Vineyard Chamber of Commerce (☑508-693-0085; www.mvy.com; 24 Beach Rd, Vineyard Haven; ⊙9am-5pm Mon-Fri) has visitor information. There are also summertime visitor kiosks at the ferry terminals.

Oak Bluffs

Odds are this ferry-port town, where the lion's share of boats arrive, will be your introduction to the island. Welcome to the Vineyard's summer fun mecca – a place to wander with an ice-cream cone in hand, poke around honky-tonk sights and go clubbing into the night.

◉ Sights & Activities

Campgrounds & Tabernacle HISTORIC SITE
Oak Bluffs started out in the mid-19th century as a summer retreat for a revivalist church, whose members enjoyed a day at the beach as much as a gospel service. They built some 300 cottages, each adorned with whimsical gingerbread trim. These brightly painted cottages – known today as the Campgrounds – surround Trinity Park and its open-air Tabernacle (1879), a venue for festivals and concerts.

Flying Horses Carousel HISTORIC SITE
(www.mvpreservation.org; 15 Lake Ave, at Circuit Ave; rides $2.50; ⊙10am-10pm; ⊕) Take a nostalgic ride on the USA's oldest merry-go-round, which has been captivating kids of all ages since 1876. The antique horses have manes of real horse hair and, if you stare into their glass eyes, you'll see neat little silver animals inside.

Bike Trail CYCLING
A scenic bike trail runs along the coast connecting Oak Bluffs, Vineyard Haven and Edgartown – it's largely flat so makes a good pedal for families. Rent bicycles at **Anderson's Bike Rental** (☑508-693-9346; www.andersonsbikerentals.com; 1 Circuit Ave Extension; bicycles per day adult/child $18/10; ⊙9am-6pm) near the ferry terminal.

⌂ Sleeping

Nashua House INN $$
(☑508-693-0043; www.nashuahouse.com; 30 Kennebec Ave; r without bath $99-219; ✳ ☎) The Vineyard the way it used to be: no phones, no TV, no in-room bath. Instead you'll find suitably simple and spotlessly clean accommodations at this small inn right in the center of town.

IF YOU HAVE A FEW MORE DAYS

Known as **Up-Island**, the rural western half of Martha's Vineyard is a patchwork of rolling hills, small farms and open fields frequented by wild turkeys and deer. Feast your eyes and your belly at the picturesque fishing village of **Menemsha**, where you'll find seafood shacks with food so fresh the boats unload their catch at the back door. They'll shuck you an oyster and steam you a lobster while you watch and you can eat alfresco on a harborside bench.

The coastal **Aquinnah Cliffs**, also known as the Gay Head Cliffs, are so special they're a National Natural Landmark. These 150ft-high cliffs glow with an amazing array of colors that can be best appreciated in the late-afternoon light. You can hang out at **Aquinnah Public Beach** (parking $15), just below the multihued cliffs, or walk a mile north along the shore to an area that's popular with nude sunbathers.

Cedar Tree Neck Sanctuary (www.sheriffsmeadow.org; Indian Hill Rd; ⊙8:30am-5:30pm) FREE, off State Rd, has an inviting 2.5-mile hike across native bogs and forest to a coastal bluff with views of Cape Cod. The Massachusetts Audubon Society's **Felix Neck Wildlife Sanctuary** (www.massaudubon.org; Edgartown–Vineyard Haven Rd; adult/child $4/3; ⊙dawn-dusk; 🚻) is a birder's paradise with 4 miles of trails skirting marshes and ponds.

Narragansett House B&B $$
(☑508-693-3627; www.narragansetthouse.com; 46 Narragansett Ave; r incl breakfast $150-300; ❄️🖨️) On a quiet residential street, this B&B occupies two adjacent Victorian gingerbread-trimmed houses just a stroll from the town center. It's old-fashioned without being cloying and, unlike other places in this price range, all rooms have private baths.

✕ Eating

Linda Jean's DINER $
(www.lindajeansrestaurant.com; 25 Circuit Ave; mains $5-15; ⊙6am-10:30pm) The town's best all-around inexpensive eatery rakes in the locals with unbeatable blueberry pancakes, juicy burgers and simple but filling dinners.

MV Bakery BAKERY $
(www.mvbakery.com; 5 Post Office Sq; baked goods $1-3; ⊙7am-5pm) Inexpensive coffee, apple fritters and cannoli are served all day, but the best time to swing by is from 9pm to midnight, when folks line up at the back door to buy hot doughnuts straight from the baker.

Slice of Life CAFE $$
(www.sliceoflifemv.com; 50 Circuit Ave; mains $8-24; ⊙8am-9pm; 🖋️) The look is casual; the fare is gourmet. At breakfast, there's kick-ass coffee, portobello omelets and fab potato pancakes. At dinner the roasted cod with sun-dried tomatoes is a savory favorite. And the desserts – decadent crème brûlée and luscious lemon tarts – are as good as you'll find anywhere.

🍷 Drinking & Nightlife

Offshore Ale Co BREWERY
(www.offshoreale.com; 30 Kennebec Ave) This popular microbrewery is the place to enjoy a pint of Vineyard ale.

Lampost CLUB
(www.lampostmv.com; 6 Circuit Ave) Head to this combo bar and nightclub for the island's hottest dance scene. In the unlikely event you don't find what you're looking for here, keep cruising Circuit Ave where you'll stumble across several dive bars (one actually named the **Dive Bar**, another the **Ritz**), both dirty and nice.

Vineyard Haven

A harbor full of classic wooden sailboats and streets lined with eye-catching restaurants and shops, lure visitors to this appealing town.

🛏️ Sleeping & Eating

HI Martha's Vineyard HOSTEL $
(☑508-693-2665; http://capecod.hiusa.org; 525 Edgartown–West Tisbury Rd; dm $35; ⊙mid-May–mid-Oct; @🖨️) Reserve early for a bed at this popular purpose-built hostel in the center of the island. It has everything you'd expect of a top-notch hostel: a solid kitchen, bike delivery and no curfew. The public bus stops out front and it's right on the bike path.

★ Art Cliff Diner CAFE $$
(☑508-693-1224; 39 Beach Rd; mains $10-16; ⊙7am-2pm Thu-Tue) 🖋️ *The* place for

breakfast and lunch. Chef-owner Gina Stanley adds flair to everything she touches, from the almond-encrusted French toast to the fresh-fish tacos. The eclectic menu utilizes farm-fresh island ingredients. Expect a line – it's worth the wait.

Edgartown

Perched on a fine natural harbor, Edgartown has a rich maritime history and a patrician air. At the height of the whaling era it was home to more than 100 sea captains whose fortunes built the grand old homes that line the streets today.

Stroll along Main St where you'll find several historic buildings, some of which open to visitors during the summer.

◉ Sights

Katama Beach   BEACH
(Katama Rd) The Vineyard's best beach lies 4 miles south of Edgartown center. Also called South Beach, Katama stretches for three magnificent miles. Rugged surf will please surfers on the ocean side. Some swimmers prefer the protected salt ponds on the inland side.

⬛ Sleeping & Eating

Edgartown Inn   GUESTHOUSE $$
(☎508-627-4794; www.edgartowninn.com; 56 N Water St; r with /without bath from $175/125; ❄) The best bargain in town, with 20 straightforward rooms spread across three adjacent buildings. The oldest dates to 1798 and claims Nathaniel Hawthorne and Daniel Webster among its earliest guests! Ask about last-minute specials; you might score a discount if things are slow.

Among the Flowers Café   CAFE $$
(☎508-627-3233; 17 Mayhew Lane; mains $8-20; ☻8am-3:30pm; ☝) Join the in-the-know crowd on the garden patio for homemade soups, waffles, sandwiches, crepes and even lobster rolls. Although everything's served on paper or plastic, it's still kinda chichi. In July and August, they cafe adds on dinner as well and kicks it up a notch.

☆ Entertainment

★Flatbread Company   LIVE MUSIC
(www.flatbreadcompany.com; 17 Airport Rd; ☻3pm-late) Formerly the home of Carly Simon's legendary Hot Tin Roof, Flatbread continues the tradition, staging the best bands on the island. And it makes damn good organic pizzas too. It's adjacent to Martha's Vineyard Airport.

❶ Getting There & Around

BOAT

Frequent ferries operated by the **Steamship Authority** (☎508-477-8600; www.steamshipauthority.com) link Woods Hole to both Vineyard Haven and Oak Bluffs, a 45-minute voyage. If you're bringing a car, book well in advance.

From Falmouth Harbor, the passenger-only ferry **Island Queen** (☎508-548-4800; www.islandqueen.com; 75 Falmouth Heights Rd) sails to Oak Bluffs several times daily in summer.

From Hyannis, **Hy-Line Cruises** (☎508-778-2600; www.hylinecruises.com; Ocean St Dock; round-trip adult/child slow ferry $45/free, fast ferry $72/48) operates a slow ferry (1½ hours) once daily to Oak Bluffs and a high-speed ferry (55 minutes) five times daily.

BUS

Martha's Vineyard Regional Transit Authority (www.vineyardtransit.com; 1-/3-day pass $7/15) operates a bus network with frequent service between towns. It's a practical way to get around and you can even reach out-of-the-way destinations including the Aquinnah Cliffs.

Central Massachusetts

Poking around this central swath of Massachusetts, between big-city Boston and the fashionable Berkshires, provides a taste of the less-touristed stretch of the state. But it's no sleeper, thanks largely to a score of colleges that infuse a youthful spirit into the region.

The **Central Massachusetts Convention & Visitors Bureau** (☎508-755-7400; www.centralmass.org; 91 Prescott St, Worcester; ☻9am-5pm Mon-Fri) and the **Greater Springfield Convention & Visitors Bureau** (☎413-787-1548; www.valleyvisitor.com; 1441 Main St, Springfield; ☻8:30am-5pm Mon-Fri) provide regional visitor information.

Worcester

The state's second-largest city had its glory days in the 19th century. The industries that made the town rich went bust but the old barons left a legacy at the first-rate **Worcester Art Museum** (☎508-799-4406; www.worcesterart.org; 55 Salisbury St; adult/child $14/free; ☻11am-5pm Wed-Fri & Sun, 10am-5pm Sat; ☝), which showcases works by luminary French Impressionists and American masters such as Whistler.

Springfield

Workaday Springfield's top claim to fame is as the birthplace of the all-American game of basketball. The **Naismith Memorial Basketball Hall of Fame** (www.hoophall. com; 1000 W Columbus Ave; adult/child $19/14; ⊙10am-5pm; P⚑) celebrates the sport with exhibits and memorabilia from all the big hoop stars.

It's also the hometown of Theodor Seuss Geisel, aka children's author Dr Seuss. You'll find life-size bronze sculptures of the Cat in the Hat and other wonky characters at the **Dr Seuss National Memorial Sculpture Garden** (www.catinthehat.org; cnr State & Chestnut Sts; ⚑) FREE.

Northampton

The region's best dining, hottest nightlife and most interesting street scenes all await in this uber-hip burg known for its liberal politics and outspoken lesbian community. Easy to explore on foot, the eclectic town center is chockablock with cafes, funky shops and art galleries. **Greater Northampton Chamber of Commerce** (☎413-584-1900; www.explorenorthampton.com; 99 Pleasant St; ⊙9am-5pm Mon-Fri; 10am-2pm Sat & Sun) is information central.

◉ Sights

Smith College   COLLEGE CAMPUS
(www.smith.edu; Elm St; P) The Smith College campus, covering 127 acres with lovely gardens, is well worth a stroll.

Smith College Museum of Art   MUSEUM
(☎413-585-2760; www.smith.edu/artmuseum; Elm St, at Bedford Tce; adult/child $5/2; ⊙10am-4pm Tue-Sat, noon-4pm Sun; P) Don't miss the Smith College Museum of Art, which boasts an impressive collection of 19th- and 20th-century European and North American paintings, including works by John Singleton Copley, Picasso and Monet.

🛏 Sleeping

Autumn Inn   MOTEL $$
(☎413-584-7660; www.hampshirehospitality.com; 259 Elm St/MA 9; r incl breakfast $115-169; P@🛜⊠) Despite its motel-like layout, this two-story place near Smith campus sports an agreeable inn-style ambience and large, comfy rooms.

WORCESTER DINERS

Worcester nurtured a great American icon: the diner. Here, in this rust-belt city, you'll find a dozen of them tucked behind warehouses, underneath old train trestles, or steps from dicey bars. **Miss Worcester Diner** (☎508-753-5600; 300 Southbridge St; meals $5-9; ⊙6am-2pm Mon-Sat, 7am-2pm Sun) is a classic of the genre. Built in 1948, it was a showroom diner of the Worcester Lunch Car Company, which produced 650 diners at its factory right across the street. Harleys parked on the sidewalk and Red Sox paraphernalia on the walls set the tone. Enticing selections such as banana-bread French toast compete with the usual greasy-spoon menu of chili dogs and biscuits with gravy. It's one tasty slice of Americana.

Hotel Northampton   HISTORIC HOTEL $$$
(☎413-584-3100; www.hotelnorthampton.com; 36 King St; r $185-275; P🛜) Northampton's finest sleep since 1927, this 100-room hotel in the town center features period decor and well-appointed rooms.

🍴 Eating

Woodstar Cafe   CAFE $
(www.woodstarcafe.com; 60 Masonic St; mains $5-8; ⊙8am-8pm; 🛜✍) Students flock to this family-run bakery-cafe, just a stone's throw from Smith campus, for tasty sandwiches and luscious pastries at bargain prices. Perhaps the smoked salmon and chevre on an organic baguette?

Green Bean   CAFE $
(www.greenbeannorthampton.com; 241 Main St; mains $6-9; ⊙7am-3pm; 🛜) ✔ Pioneer Valley farmers stock the kitchen at this cute eatery that dishes up organic eggs at breakfast and juicy hormone-free beef burgers at lunch.

Haymarket Café   CAFE $
(www.haymarketcafe.com; 185 Main St; items $4-10; ⊙7am-10pm; 🛜✍) Northampton's coolest hangout for bohemians and caffeine addicts, the Haymarket serves up heady espresso, fresh juices and an extensive vegetarian menu.

♠ Drinking & Entertainment

Northampton Brewery BREWERY
(www.northamptonbrewery.com; 11 Brewster Ct; ⊙11:30am-2am Mon-Sat, noon-1am Sun) The oldest operating brewpub in New England enjoys a loyal summertime following thanks to its generously sized outdoor deck.

Calvin Theatre CONCERT VENUE
(☑413-584-0610; www.iheg.com; 19 King St) This gorgeously restored theater hosts big-name performances with everything from hot rock and indie bands to comedy shows.

Diva's LESBIAN
(www.divasofnoho.com; 492 Pleasant St; ⊙Wed-Sat) The city's main gay-centric dance club keeps its patrons sweaty thanks to a steady diet of thumping house music.

Iron Horse Music Hall CONCERT VENUE
(☑413-584-0610; www.iheg.com; 20 Center St) Nationally acclaimed folk and jazz artists line up to play in this intimate setting.

Amherst

This college town, a short drive from Northampton, is built around the mega **University of Massachusetts** (UMass; www.umass.edu) and two small colleges, the liberal **Hampshire College** (www.hampshire.edu) and the prestigious **Amherst College** (www.amherst.edu). Contact them for campus tours and event information; there's always something happening. If hunger strikes, you'll find the usual bevy of college-town eateries radiating out from Main St in the town center.

The lifelong home of poet Emily Dickinson (1830–86), the 'belle of Amherst,' is open to the public as the **Emily Dickinson Museum** (☑413-542-8161; www.emilydickinsonmuseum.org; 280 Main St; adult/child $10/5; ⊙10am-5pm Wed-Mon). Admission includes a 40-minute tour.

The Berkshires

Tranquil towns and a wealth of cultural attractions are nestled in these cool green hills. For more than a century the Berkshires have been a favored retreat for wealthy Bostonians and New Yorkers. And we're not just talking Rockefellers – the entire Boston symphony summers here as well. The **Berkshire Visitors Bureau** (☑413-743-4500; www.berkshires.org; 3 Hoosac St; ⊙10am-5pm) can provide information on the entire region.

Great Barrington

Hands-down the best place in the Berkshires to be at mealtime. Head straight to the intersection of Main (US 7) and Railroad Sts in the town center where you'll find an artful mix of galleries and eateries serving mouthwatering food – everything from bakeries to ethnic cuisines.

For wholesome Berkshire-grown meals on a budget, go to the **Berkshire Co-op Market Cafe** (www.berkshire.coop; 42 Bridge St; meals $6-10; ⊙8am-8pm Mon-Sat, 10am-8pm Sun; ☑) ✿ inside the local co-op. For fine dining, **Castle Street Cafe** (☑413-528-5244; www.castlestreetcafe.com; 10 Castle St; mains $21-29; ⊙5-9pm Wed-Mon; ☑) ✿ serves up an innovative menu that reads like a who's who of local farms: Ioka Valley Farm grass-fed natural beef, Rawson Brook chevre and more. For a little green with your suds, head to **Barrington Brewery** (www.barringtonbrewery.net; 420 Stockbridge Rd; mains $8-20; ⊙11:30am-9:30pm; 🐾) ✿, where the hoppy brews are created using solar power.

Stockbridge

This timeless New England town, sans even a single traffic light, looks like something straight out of a Norman Rockwell drawing. Oh wait...it is! Rockwell (1894–1978), the most popular illustrator in US history, lived on Main St and used the town and its residents as subjects. At the evocative **Norman Rockwell Museum** (☑413-298-4100; www.nrm.org; 9 Glendale Rd/MA 183; adult/child $16/5; ⊙10am-5pm), Rockwell's slice-of-Americana paintings come to life when examined up close.

Lenox

The cultural heart of the Berkshires, the refined village of Lenox hosts one of the country's premier musical events, the open-air **Tanglewood Music Festival** (☑888-266-1200; www.tanglewood.org; 297 West St/MA 183, Lenox; ⊙late Jun-early Sep), featuring the Boston Symphony Orchestra and guest artists such as James Taylor and Yo-Yo Ma. Buy a lawn ticket, spread a blanket, uncork a bottle of wine and enjoy the quintessential Berkshires experience.

Shakespeare & Company (☑413-637-1199; www.shakespeare.org; 70 Kemble St; ⊙Tue-Sun) gives performances of the Bard's work in evocative settings throughout the summer. The renowned **Jacob's Pillow Dance Festival** (☎413-243-0745; www.jacobspillow.org; 358 George Carter Rd, Becket; ☉mid-Jun–Aug), 10 miles east of Lenox in Becket, stages contemporary dance performances.

The **Mount** (www.edithwharton.org; 2 Plunkett St; adult/child $18/free; ☉10am-5pm May-Oct), the former estate of novelist Edith Wharton (1862–1937), offers tours of her mansion and inspirational gardens.

🛏 Sleeping & Eating

Birchwood Inn
INN $$$

(☎413-637-2600; www.birchwood-inn.com; 7 Hubbard St; r incl breakfast $200-375; ❀🐾🐕) Charming period inns abound in Lenox. The senior of them, Birchwood Inn, registered its first guest in 1767 and continues to offer warm hospitality today.

Cornell in Lenox
B&B $$$

(☎413-637-4800; www.cornellbb.com; 203 Main St; r incl breakfast $145-265; @ 🐕) Spread across three historic houses, this B&B provides good value in a high-priced town.

★Nudel
AMERICAN $$$

(☎413-551-7183; www.nudelrestaurant.com; 37 Church St; mains $22-25; ☉5:30-9:30pm Tue-Sat) Get a delicious taste of the area's sustainable food movement at Nudel, whose seasonally inspired menu takes a back-to-basics approach with the likes of heritage-bred pork chops and spaetzle pasta with rabbit.

Bistro Zinc
FRENCH $$$

(☎413-637-8800; www.bistrozinc.com; 56 Church St; mains $15-30; ☉11:30am-3pm & 5:30-10pm) You'll find stylish bistros along Church St in the town center, including Bistro Zinc with hot postmodern decor and French-inspired New American fare.

🍸 Drinking & Nightlife

Olde Heritage Tavern
PUB

(www.theheritagetavern.com; 12 Housatonic St; mains $7-15; ☉11:30am-12:30am Mon-Fri, 8am-12:30am Sat & Sun; 🖟) For family fare at honest prices visit Olde Heritage Tavern, an upbeat pub whose menu ranges from waffles to steaks.

Pittsfield

Just west of the town of Pittsfield is **Hancock Shaker Village** (☎413-443-0188; www.hancockshakervillage.org; US 20; adult/child $18/free; ☉10am-5pm mid-Apr–Oct; 🖟), a fascinating museum illustrating the lives of the Shakers, the religious sect that founded the village in 1783. The Shakers believed in communal ownership, the sanctity of work and celibacy, the latter of which proved to be their demise. Their handiwork – graceful in its simplicity – includes wooden furnishings and 20 buildings, the most famous of which is the round stone barn.

Williamstown & North Adams

Cradled by the Berkshire's rolling hills, Williamstown is a picture-perfect New England college town revolving around the leafy campus of Williams College. Williamstown and neighboring North Adams boast three outstanding art museums, each a worthy destination in itself.

◉ Sights & Activities

★Clark Art Institute
MUSEUM

(☎413-458-2303; www.clarkart.edu; 225 South St, Williamstown; adult/child Jun-Oct $15/free, Nov-May all free; ☉10am-5pm, closed Mon Sep-Jun) The Sterling & Francine Clark Art Institute is a gem among US art museums. Even if you're not an avid art lover, don't miss it. The collections are particularly strong in the impressionists, with significant works by Monet, Pissarro and Renoir. Mary Cassatt, Winslow Homer and John Singer Sargent represent contemporary American painting.

Williams College Museum of Art
MUSEUM

(☎413-597-2429; www.wcma.org; 15 Lawrence Hall Dr, Williamstown; ☉10am-5pm Tue-Sat, 1-5pm Sun) **FREE** This sister museum of the Clark Art Institute graces the center of town and has an incredible collection of its own. Around half of its 13,000 pieces comprise the American Collection, with substantial works by

> **WORTH A TRIP**
>
> ### SCENIC FOLIAGE DRIVE
>
> For the finest fall foliage drive in Massachusetts, head west on MA 2 from Greenfield to Williamstown on the 63-mile route known as the **Mohawk Trail**. The lively Deerfield River slides alongside, with roaring, bucking stretches of whitewater that turn leaf-peeping into an adrenaline sport for kayakers.

notables such as Edward Hopper (*Morning in a City*), Winslow Homer and Grant Wood, to name only a few.

MASS MoCA
MUSEUM

(☑413-662-2111; www.massmoca.org; 1040 Mass Moca Way, North Adams; adult/child $15/5; ☺10am-6pm Jul & Aug, 11am-5pm Wed-Mon Sep-Jun; ♿) The USA's largest contemporary art museum, MASS MoCA sprawls across an amazing 222,000 sq ft and includes art construction areas, performance centers and 19 galleries. One gallery is the size of a football field, giving installation artists the opportunity to take things into a whole new dimension. Bring your walking shoes!

Mt Greylock State Reservation
PARK

(☑413-499-4262; www.mass.gov/dcr/parks/mt-Greylock; ☺visitor center 9am-5pm) **FREE** Just south of North Adams, this park has both a road and trails up to Massachusetts' highest peak (3491ft), where there's a panoramic view of several mountain ranges and, on a clear day, five different states. Among the park's 45 miles of hiking trails is a portion of the Appalachian Trail. In addition, you'll find a rustic summit lodge.

🎉 Festivals & Events

Williamstown Theatre Festival
THEATER

(☑413-597-3400; www.wtfestival.org; 1000 Main St, Williamstown; ☺late Jun–late Aug) Stars of the theater world descend upon Williamstown every year. The festival mounts a mix of classics and contemporary works by up-and-coming playwrights. Bradley Cooper and Gwyneth Paltrow are just two of the well-known thespians who have performed here.

🛏 Sleeping & Eating

River Bend Farm B&B
B&B $$

(☑413-458-3121; www.riverbendfarmbb.com; 643 Simonds Rd/US 7, Williamstown; r without bath incl breakfast $120; ✳🤖) Step back to the 18th century in this Georgian Colonial B&B furnished with real-deal antiques and boasting five fireplaces. Four doubles share two bathrooms here. Despite the name it's not on a farm but along US 7 in Williamstown.

Maple Terrace Motel
MOTEL $$

(☑413-458-9677; www.mapleterrace.com; 555 Main St, Williamstown; r incl breakfast $121-157; 🤖🏊) On the eastern outskirts of Williamstown, the Swedish innkeepers here offer 15 simple, yet cozy rooms.

Porches
BOUTIQUE HOTEL $$$

(☑413-664-0400; www.porches.com; 231 River St, North Adams; r incl breakfast $189-285; ✳🤖🏊) Across the street from MASS MoCA in North Adams, the artsy rooms here combine well-considered color palettes, ample lighting and French doors into a pleasant sleeping experience.

Moonlight Diner & Grille
DINER $

(☑413-458-3305; 408 Main St, Williamstown; mains $6-10; ☺7am-8:30pm Mon-Thu, to 9:30pm Fri & Sat) This old-school diner on the east side of Williamstown dishes up all the classics at honest prices. Think retro '50s decor, huge burgers and cheesy omelets.

Public Eat & Drink
PUB $$

(www.publiceatanddrink.com; 34 Holden St, North Adams; mains $10-22; ☺5-9pm; 🍴) Come to this cozy North Adams pub for an excellent selection of craft beers and gourmet pub fare, including brie burgers, flatbread pizzas and bistro steak. Some decent vegetarian options as well.

★Mezze Bistro & Bar
FUSION $$$

(☑413-458-0123; www.mezzerestaurant.com; 777 Cold Spring Rd/US 7, Williamstown; mains $20-30; ☺5-9pm) East meets West at this chic restaurant that blends contemporary American cuisine with classic French and Japanese influences. Mezze's farm-to-table approach begins with an edible garden right on site. Much of the rest of the seasonal menu, from small-batch microbrews to organic meats, is locally sourced as well.

RHODE ISLAND

America's smallest state packs a lot into a compact package, more than making up for its lack of land with 400 miles of craggy coastline, deeply indented bays and lovely beaches. The state's engaging capital, Providence, is small enough to be friendly but big enough to offer top-notch dining and attractions. Newport, a summer haunt of the well-heeled, brims with opulent mansions, pretty yachts and world-class music festivals. Should you want to take it further afield, hopping on a ferry to Block Island makes a perfect day trip.

History

Ever since it was founded in 1636 by Roger Williams, a religious outcast from Boston,

Rhode Island's capital, Providence has enjoyed an independent frame of mind. Williams' guiding principle, the one that got him ostracized from Massachusetts, was that all people should have freedom of conscience. He put his liberal beliefs into practice when settling Providence, remaining on friendly terms with the local Narragansett Native Americans after purchasing from them the land for a bold experiment in tolerance and peaceful coexistence.

Williams' principles would not last long. As Providence and Newport grew and merged into a single colony, competition and conflict with area tribes sparked several wars, leading to the decimation of the Wampanoag, Pequot, Narragansett and Nipmuck peoples. Rhode Island was also a prolific slave trader and its merchants would control much of that industry in the years after the Revolutionary War.

The city of Pawtucket gave birth to the American industrial revolution with the establishment of the water-powered Slater Mill in 1790. Industrialism impacted the character of Providence and surrounds, particularly along the Blackstone River, creating urban density. As with many small east-coast cities, these urban areas went into a precipitous decline in the 1940s and '50s as manufacturing industries (textiles and costume jewelry) faltered. In the 1960s preservation efforts salvaged the historic architectural framework of Providence and Newport. The former has emerged as a lively place with a dynamic economy and the latter, equally lively, survives as a museum city.

❶ Information

Providence Journal (www.providencejournal.com) The state's largest daily newspaper.

Rhode Island Parks (www.riparks.com) Offers camping in five state parks.

Rhode Island Tourism Division (✆800-250-7384; www.visitrhodeisland.com) Distributes visitor information on the whole state.

Providence

Rhode Island's capital city, Providence presents its visitors with some of the finest urban strolling this side of the Connecticut River. In the crisp air and falling leaves of autumn, wander through Brown University's green campus on 18th-century College Hill and follow the Riverwalk into

---

RHODE ISLAND FACTS

Nicknames Ocean State, Little Rhody

Population 1,050,300

Area 1034 sq miles

Capital city Providence (population 178,400)

Other city Newport (population 24,000)

Sales tax 7%

Birthplace of Broadway composer George M Cohan (1878–1942) and toy icon Mr Potato Head (b 1952)

Home of The first US tennis championships

Politics Majority vote Democrat

Famous for Being the smallest state

Official state bird A chicken? Why not? The Rhode Island Red revolutionized the poultry industry

Driving distances Providence to Newport 37 miles, Providence to Boston 50 miles

---

downtown. Along the way you'll have opportunities to lounge in the sidewalk cafe of an art-house theater, dine in a stellar restaurant and knock back a few pints in a cool bar. At night, take in a play at the Trinity Repertory, squeeze into a club or eat some 3am burgers aboard the mobile Haven Brothers Diner.

◉ Sights

Exit 22 off I-95 deposits you downtown. The university area is a short walk to the east. The colorful Italian enclave of Federal Hill centers on Atwells Ave, a mile west of the city center.

College Hill   NEIGHBORHOOD
East of the Providence River, College Hill, headquarters of **Brown University** (www.brown.edu), contains over 100 Colonial, Federal and Revival houses dating from the 18th century. Stroll down **Benefit Street's** 'Mile of History' for the best of them. Amidst them you'll find the clean lines of William Strickland's 1838 **Providence Athenaeum** (✆401-421-6970; www.providenceathenaeum.org; 251 Benefit St; ⊘9am 7pm Mon-Thu, 9am-5pm Fri & Sat, 1-5pm Sun) FREE,

DON'T MISS

BONFIRES AFTER DARK

Move over, Christo. Providence has blazed onto the public-art installation scene with **WaterFire** (www.waterfire.org), set on the river that meanders through the city center. Nearly 100 braziers poke above the water, each supporting a bonfire that roars after dark. Flames dance off the water, music plays, black-clad gondoliers glide by, and party-goers pack the riverbanks. A captivating blend of art and entertainment, WaterFire takes place about a dozen times between May and September, mostly on a Saturday, from sunset to 1am.

inside which plaster busts of Greek gods and philosophers preside over a collection that dates from 1753.

Free tours of the campus begin from the **Brown University Admissions Office** (401-863-2378; Corliss Brackett House, 45 Prospect St). Call or drop by for times.

Museum of Art MUSEUM
(401-454-6500; www.risdmuseum.org; 224 Benefit St; adult/child $12/3; 10am-5pm Tue-Sun, to 9pm Thu;) Wonderfully eclectic, the Rhode Island School of Design's art museum showcases everything from ancient Greek art to 20th-century American paintings and decorative arts. Pop in before 1pm Sunday and admission is free.

State House HISTORIC BUILDING
(401-222-3983; 82 Smith St; 8:30am-4:30pm Mon-Fri, free tours 9am, 10am & 11am) FREE Providence's focal point is crowned with one of the world's largest self-supporting marble domes. Check out the Gilbert Stuart portrait of George Washington, then compare it to the $1 bill in your wallet.

Roger Williams Park PARK
(1000 Elmwood Ave) FREE In 1871 Betsey Williams, great-great-great-granddaughter of the founder of Providence, donated her farm to the city as a public park. Today this 430-acre expanse of greenery, only a short drive south of Providence, includes lakes and ponds, forest copses, broad lawns, picnic grounds and a **Planetarium and Museum of Natural History** (401-785-9457; museum $2, planetarium $4; 10am-4pm, planetarium shows 2pm Sat & Sun;).

Sleeping

Christopher Dodge House B&B $$
(401-351-6111; www.providence-hotel.com; 11 W Park St; r incl breakfast $120-180;) This 1858 Federal-style house is furnished with early American reproduction furniture and marble fireplaces. Austere on the outside, it has elegant proportions, large, shuttered windows and wooden floors.

Providence Biltmore HISTORIC HOTEL $$$
(401-421-0700; www.providencebiltmore.com; 11 Dorrance St; r/ste $146/279;) The grand-daddy of Providence's hotels, the Biltmore dates from the 1920s. The lobby, both intimate and regal, nicely combines dark wood, twisting staircases and chandeliers, while well-appointed rooms stretch many stories above the old city. Ask for one of the 292 rooms that are on a high floor.

Eating

Both the Rhode Island School of Design and Johnson & Wales University have top-notch culinary programs that annually turn out creative new chefs. The large student population on the East Side ensures that there are plenty of good places around College Hill and Fox Point. To experience old Providence, head over to Atwells Ave in Federal Hill.

East Side Pockets MEDITERRANEAN $
(www.eastsidepocket.com; 278 Thayer St; mains $4-7; 10am-1am Mon-Sat, 10am-10pm Sun;) Fabulous falafels and baklava at student-friendly prices.

★ **Haven Brothers Diner** DINER $
(Washington St; meals $5-10; 5pm-3am) As legend has it, the Haven Brothers started as a horse-drawn lunch wagon in 1893. Climb up a rickety ladder to get basic diner fare alongside everyone from prominent politicians, to college kids pulling an all-nighter, to drunks.

Flan y Ajo SPANISH $
(401-432-6656; 225a Westminster St; tapas $3-7; 6-11pm) This BYOB tapas bar serves lip-smacking *pintxos* (bites) such as single shell-on prawn with *salsa verde*, mussels in white wine and succulent *lomito* (pork tenderloin). Buy a bottle of wine from Eno Fine Wines next door.

Abyssinia ETHIOPIAN $$
(401-454-1412; www.abyssinia-restaurant.com; 333 Wickenden St; meals $20; 11am-10pm;) From the plum-colored banquettes to the

roaring (or is that smiling?) Lion of Judah on the wall, get ready to experience the heady flavors of Ethiopian cooking. Vegetarian lentils and split-pea curries tempt the taste buds before the spicy onslaught of *doro wat* (chicken stew) and beef *key wot*.

★ **birch**   MODERN AMERICAN $$$
(☑ 401-272-3105; www.birchrestaurant.com; 200 Washington St; meals $25-35; ☺ 5pm-midnight Thu-Tue) With a background at the fabulous Dorrance at the Biltmore, chef Benjamin Sukle and his wife, Heidi, now have their own place. Its intimate size and its style means attention to detail is exacting in both the decor and the food, which focuses on small-batch and hyper-seasonal produce.

🍷 Drinking & Entertainment

Trinity Brewhouse   BREWERY
(☑ 401-453-2337; www.trinitybrewhouse.com; 186 Fountain St; ☺ 11:30am-1am Sun-Thu, noon-2am Fri & Sat) This microbrewery in the entertainment district creates terrific British-style beers. Don't miss the stouts.

The Salon   BAR, CLUB
(www.thesalonpvd.com; 57 Eddy St; ☺ 5pm-1am Mon-Fri, 7pm-2am Sat) The Salon mixes ping-pong tables and pinball machines with '80s pop and pickleback shots (whiskey with a pickle juice chaser) upstairs, and live shows, open mic, DJs and dance parties downstairs.

Providence Performing Arts Center   PERFORMING ARTS
(☑ 401-421-2787; www.ppacri.org; 220 Weybosset St) This popular venue for touring Broadway musicals and other big-name performances is in a former Loew's Theater dating from 1928. It has a lavish art-deco interior.

AS220   CLUB
(☑ 401-831-9327; www.as220.org; 115 Empire St; ☺ 5pm-1am) A longstanding outlet for all forms of Rhode Island art, AS220 (say 'A-S-two-twenty') books experimental bands (Lightning Bolt, tuba and banjo duos), hosts readings and provides gallery space for a very active community. Hours given here are for the bar, but the gallery opens midday Wednesday through Saturday, and the cafe closes at 10pm.

🛍 Shopping

Providence Place (www.providenceplace.com; 1 Providence Place) in the city center is Rhode Island's largest mall. For more individual, quirky shops head to Westminster St, Thayer St and Wickenden St.

ℹ Information

Providence Visitor Information Center
(☑ 401-751-1177; www.goprovidence.com; Rhode Island Convention Center, 1 Sabin St; ☺ 9am-5pm Mon-Sat)

ℹ Getting There & Away

TF Green Airport (PVD; www.pvdairport.com; I-95, exit 13, Warwick), 20 minutes south of downtown Providence, is served by major US airlines and car-rental companies.

Peter Pan Bus Lines (www.peterpanbus.com) connects Providence with Boston ($8, one hour) and New York ($35, 3¾ hours). **Amtrak** (www.amtrak.com; 100 Gaspee St) trains also link cities in the Northeast with Providence.

Rhode Island Public Transit Authority (RIPTA; www.ripta.com; one way $2, day pass $6) runs city-wide bus services from downtown Kennedy Plaza; other RIPTA buses link Providence with Newport.

Newport

Established by religious moderates fleeing persecution from Massachusetts Puritans, 'new port' flourished to become the fourth richest city in the newly independent colony and the harbor remains one of the most active and important yachting centres in the country. Downtown the Colonial-era architecture is beautifully preserved, although it struggles to compete with the opulent 'summer cottages' built by latter-day industrialists on the back of shipping, railroad and mining fortunes. Modeled on Italianate *palazzi*, French *chateaux* and Elizabethan manor houses, these buildings remain the town's premier attraction alongside a series of summer music festivals, which are among the most important in the US.

⊙ Sights & Activities

★ **Preservation Society of Newport County**   HISTORIC BUILDINGS
(☑ 401-847-1000; www.newportmansions.org; 424 Bellevue Ave; 5-site ticket adult/child $49/19) Five of Newport's grandest mansions are managed by this society. Each mansion takes about 90 minutes to tour.

➡ **Breakers**
(44 Ochre Point Ave; adult/child $19.50/5.50; ☺ 9am-5pm Apr-mid-Oct, hours vary mid-Oct–Mar;

Ⓟ) If you have time for only one Newport mansion, make it this extravagant 70-room, 1895 Italian Renaissance mega-palace built for Cornelius Vanderbilt II, patriarch of America's then-richest family.

➡ Rosecliff
(548 Bellevue Ave; adult/child $14.50/5.50; ☺10am-5pm Apr-mid-Oct, hrs vary mid-Oct–Mar; Ⓟ) A 1902 masterpiece of architect Stanford White, Rosecliff resembles the Grand Trianon at Versailles. Its immense ballroom had a starring role in Robert Redford's *The Great Gatsby*.

➡ The Elms
(www.newportmansions.org; 367 Bellevue Ave; adult/child $14.50/5.50, servant-life tour adult/child $15/5; ☺10am-5pm Apr-mid-Oct, hours vary mid-Oct–Mar; Ⓟ🚲) Built in 1901, the Elms is a replica of Château d'Asnières, built near Paris in 1750. You can take a 'behind-the-scenes' tour which will have you snaking through the servants' quarters and up onto the roof.

★ Rough Point   HISTORIC BUILDING
(www.newportrestoration.com; 680 Bellevue Ave; adult/child $25/free; ☺10am-2pm Thu-Sat mid-Apr–mid-May, 10am-3.45pm Tue-Sat mid-May–mid-Nov; Ⓟ) Once called the 'richest little girl in the world,' Doris Duke (1912–93) was just 13 years old when she inherited this English manor estate from her father. Duke had a passion for travel and art collecting; Rough Point houses many of her holdings, from Ming dynasty ceramics to Renoir paintings.

International Tennis Hall of Fame   MUSEUM
(☎401-849-3990; www.tennisfame.com; 194 Bellevue Ave; adult/child $12/free; ☺9:30am-5pm) To experience something of the American aristocracy's approach to 19th-century leisure, visit this museum. It lies inside the historic Newport Casino building (1880), which served as a summer club for Newport's wealthiest residents. For $110 you can jump into your whites and play a game on the classic grass courts.

Touro Synagogue National Historic Site   SYNAGOGUE
(☎401-847-4794; www.tourosynagogue.org; 85 Touro St; adult/child $12/free; ☺10am-4pm Sun-Fri Jul-Sep, 10am-2pm Sun-Fri Sep-Oct, noon-1.30pm Sun-Fri May-Jun, noon-1.30pm Sun Nov-Apr) Tour the oldest synagogue (c 1763) in the USA, an architectural gem that treads the line between austere and lavish.

Cliff Walk   WALKING TRAIL
(www.cliffwalk.com) For a glorious hike take the 3.5-mile Cliff Walk, which hugs the coast behind the mansions. You will not only enjoy the same dramatic ocean views, but you will get to gawk at mansions along the way. The Cliff Walk stretches from Memorial Blvd to Bailey's Beach; a scenic place to start is at Ruggles Ave near the Breakers.

★ Fort Adams State Park   PARK
(www.fortadams.org; Harrison Ave; fort tours adult guided/self-guided $12/6, child $6/3; ☺sunrise-sunset) Fort Adams is America's largest coastal fortification and is the centerpiece of this gorgeous state park, which juts out into Narragansett Bay. It's the venue for the Newport Jazz and Folk Festivals. Swimming is OK at Fort Adams, but **Easton's Beach** (First Beach; Memorial Blvd) and **Sachuest (Second) Beach** (Purgatory Rd) are better.

★ Sail Newport   SAILING
(☎401-846-1983; www.sailnewport.org; 60 Fort Adams Dr; 1-/2-week sessions $365/475, sailboat rental per 3hr $73-138; ☺9am-7pm; 🚲) As you'd expect in the hometown of the prestigious America's Cup, the sailing in breezy Newport is phenomenal.

Adirondack II   CRUISE
(☎401-847-0000; www.sail-newport.com; Bowen's Wharf; 1½hr cruise $30-39; ☺11am-7pm) This schooner sails from Bowen's Wharf five times a day.

✯ Festivals & Events

For a full schedule of events, see www.gonewport.com.

Newport Folk Festival   MUSIC
(www.newportfolkfest.net; Fort Adams State Park; 1-/3-day pass $49/120, parking $12; ☺late Jul) Big-name stars and up-and-coming groups perform at Fort Adams State Park. Bring sunscreen.

Newport Jazz Festival   MUSIC
(www.newportjazzfest.net; Fort Adams State Park; tickets $47.50-100; ☺early Aug) The roster reads like a who's who of jazz, with the likes of Dave Brubeck and Wynton Marsalis.

Newport Music Festival   MUSIC
(www.newportmusic.org; tickets $20-42; ☺mid-Jul) This internationally regarded festival offers classical music concerts in many of the great mansions.

🛏 Sleeping

★ Newport International Hostel   HOSTEL $
(William Gyles Guesthouse; ☎ 401-369-0243; www.newporthostel.com; 16 Howard St; dm without bath incl breakfast $35-119; ⊙ Apr-Dec; 🐀) Welcome to Rhode Island's only hostel, run by an informal and knowledgeable host. Book as early as you can. The tiny guesthouse contains fixings for a simple breakfast, a laundry machine and spare, clean digs in a dormitory room. Private rooms are available but you need to enquire by email.

Stella Maris Inn   INN $$
(☎ 401-849-2862; www.stellamarisinn.com; 91 Washington St; r incl breakfast $125-225; 🅿) This quiet, stone-and-frame inn has numerous fireplaces, heaps of black-walnut furnishings, Victorian bric-a-brac and some floral upholstery. Rooms with garden views rent for less than those overlooking the water. The owner can be a bit gruff, but the prices are good (for Newport, that is). Oddly, it doesn't accept credit cards.

★ The Attwater   BOUTIQUE HOTEL $$$
(☎ 401-846-7444; www.theattwater.com; 22 Liberty St; r $180-309; 🅿 ❄ 🐀) Newport's newest hotel has the bold attire of a midsummer beach party with turquoise, lime-green and coral prints, ikat headboards and snazzily patterned geometric rugs. Picture windows and porches capture the summer light and rooms come furnished with thoughtful luxuries such as iPads, Apple TV and beach bags.

🍴 Eating

★ Rosemary & Thyme Cafe   BAKERY, CAFE $
(☎ 401-619-3338; www.rosemaryandthymecafe.com; 382 Spring St; baked goods $2-5, sandwiches & pizza $5.95-7.95; ⊙ 7.30am-3pm Tue-Sat, to 11.30am Sun; 📶) With a German baker in the kitchen, it is hardly surprising that the counter here is piled high with buttery croissants, apple and cherry tarts and plump muffins. At lunchtime gourmet sandwiches feature herbed goat's cheese and Tuscan dried tomatoes and an Alsatian cheese mix.

Franklin Spa   DINER $
(☎ 401-847-3540; 229 Spring St; meals $3-10; ⊙ 6am-2pm; 📶) This old-school joint slings hash, eggs and grease for cheap. It's locally loved and opens early. Enjoy freshly squeezed orange juice, homemade turkey noodle soup or coffee cabinet (milkshake with ice cream) at a Formica-topped table on a worn white-and-red-tiled floor.

Mamma Luisa   ITALIAN $$
(☎ 401-848-5257; www.mammaluisa.com; 673 Thames St; mains $14-25; ⊙ 5-10pm Thu-Tue) This cozy restaurant serves authentic Italian fare to its enthusiastic customers, who recommend this low-key pasta house as a place to escape the Newport crowds. There are classic pasta dishes (cheese ravioli with fava beans, spaghetti *alle vongole*), as well as meat and fish entrees.

OFF THE BEATEN TRACK

IF YOU HAVE A FEW MORE DAYS

Unspoiled **Block Island**, separated from the rest of Rhode Island by 12 miles of open ocean, offers simple pleasures: rolling farms, uncrowded beaches and miles of quiet hiking and cycling trails.

Ferries dock at **Old Harbor**, the main town, which has changed little since its gingerbread houses were built in the late 19th century. The beaches begin right at the north side of town. If you continue north 2 miles you'll come to the **Clay Head Nature Trail**, which follows high clay bluffs above the beach offering good bird-watching along the way. **Rodman Hollow**, a 100-acre wildlife refuge at the island's south end, is also laced with interesting trails.

A mere 7 miles long, Block Island begs to be explored by bicycle; several places near the ferry dock rent them for $25 a day. The **Block Island Chamber of Commerce** (☎ 800-383-2474; www.blockislandchamber.com), at the ferry dock, can help with accommodations, but be aware the island's four-dozen inns typically book out in summer and many require minimum stays. The **Sea Breeze Inn** (☎ 401-466-2275; www.seabreezeblockisland.com; Spring St, Old Harbor; r $230-310, with shared bath $150-180; 🅿) offers the cutest digs in seafront cottages sat above a wild meadow.

The **Block Island Ferry** (☎ 401-783-4613; www.blockislandferry.com; adult/child round-trip ferry $25.55/12.50, high-speed $35.85/19.50) operates high-speed (30 minutes) and traditional (55 minutes) ferries from Galilee State Pier in Point Judith.

The Mooring SEAFOOD $$$
(☑401-846-2260; www.mooringrestaurant.com; Sayer's Wharf; meals $15-40; ⊙11:30am-10pm) A harbor-front setting and a menu brimming with fresh seafood make this an unbeatable combination for seaside dining. Tip: if it's packed, take the side entrance to the bar, grab a stool and order the meaty clam chowder and a 'bag of doughnuts' (tangy lobster fritters).

🍷 Drinking & Entertainment

Fastnet BAR
(www.thefastnetpub.com; 1 Broadway; ⊙11am-1am) Named for a lighthouse off the coast of Cork, this pub serves classics such as bangers and mash and fish and chips, beside an ever-flowing river of Guinness. There's live Irish music every Sunday night.

Newport Blues Café CLUB
(☑401-841-5510; www.newportblues.com; 286 Thames St) This popular rhythm-and-blues bar and restaurant draws top acts to an old brownstone that was once a bank. It's an intimate space with many enjoying quahogs, house-smoked ribs or pork loins at tables adjoining the small stage. Dinner is offered 6pm to 10pm; the music starts at 9:30pm.

ℹ️ Information

Newport Visitor Center (☑401-845-9123; www.gonewport.com; 23 America's Cup Ave; ⊙9am-5pm) Offers maps, brochures, local bus information, tickets to major attractions, public restrooms and an ATM. There's free parking for 30 minutes adjacent to the center.

ℹ️ Getting There & Away

Peter Pan Bus Lines (www.peterpanbus.com) Has several buses daily to Boston ($27, 1¾ hours).

RIPTA (www.ripta.com) State-run RIPTA operates frequent buses (one way $2, day pass $6) from the visitor center to the mansions, beaches and Providence.

Scooter World (☑401-619-1349; www.scooterworldri.com; 11 Christie's Landing; bicycles per day $30; ⊙9am-7pm) Rents bicycles

Rhode Island Beaches

If you're up for a day at the beach, Rhode Island's southwestern coastal towns fit the bill. It is the Ocean State, after all.

The mile-long **Narragansett Town Beach** in Narragansett is the place to go for surfing. Nearby **Scarborough State Beach** is among Rhode Island's finest, with a wide sandy shore, a classic pavilion and inviting boardwalks. **Watch Hill** at the state's southwestern tip is a wonderful place to turn back the clock, with its Flying Horse Carousel and Victorian mansions. The **South County Tourism Council** (☑800-548-4662; www.southcountyri.com) has details on the entire area.

CONNECTICUT

Sandwiched between sexy New York City and northerly New England's quainter quarters, Connecticut typically gets short shrift from travelers. Sure, the brawny I-95 coastal corridor is largely industrial, but take a closer look and you're in for pleasant surprises. Seaside Mystic, with its nautical attractions, and the time-honored towns bordering the Connecticut River are a whole other world, and the Litchfield Hills, in the state's northwestern corner, are as charmingly rural as any place in New England.

History

A number of Native American tribes (notably the Pequot and the Mohegan, whose name for the river became the name of the state) were here when the first European explorers, primarily Dutch, appeared in the early 17th century. The first English settlement was at Old Saybrook in 1635, followed a year later by the Connecticut Colony, built by Massachusetts Puritans under Thomas Hooker. A third colony was founded in 1638 in New Haven. After the Pequot War (1637), the Native Americans were no longer a check to colonial expansion in New England, and Connecticut's English population grew. In 1686, Connecticut was brought into the Dominion of New England.

The American Revolution swept through Connecticut, leaving scars with major battles at Stonington (1775), Danbury (1777), New Haven (1779) and Groton (1781). Connecticut became the fifth state in 1788. It embarked on a period of prosperity, propelled by its whaling, shipbuilding, farming and manufacturing industries (from firearms to bicycles to household tools), which lasted well into the 19th century.

The 20th century brought world wars and the depression but, thanks in no small part to Connecticut's munitions industries, the state was able to fight back. Everything from planes to submarines was made in the state, and when the defense industry began to decline in the 1990s the growth of other businesses (such as insurance) helped pick up the slack.

ℹ️ Information

There are welcome centers at the Hartford airport and on I-95 and I-84 when entering the state by car.

Connecticut Tourism Division (www.ctvisit. com) Distributes visitor information for the entire state.

Hartford Courant (www.courant.com) The state's largest newspaper.

Connecticut Coast

The Connecticut Coast is not all of a piece. The western end is largely a bedroom community connected by commuter rail to New York City. By the time you get to New Haven, Connecticut's artsier side shines through. Mystic, at the eastern end of the state, is the location of the state's biggest attraction, Mystic Seaport, a recreated 19th-century whaling town spread across 17 acres.

New Haven

For visitors, New Haven is all about Yale. Head straight to New Haven Green, graced by old Colonial churches and Yale's hallowed ivy-covered walls. The oldest planned city in America (1638), New Haven is laid out in orderly blocks spreading out from the Green, making it a cinch to get around. **INFO New Haven** (📞203-773-9494; www.infonewhaven. com; 1000 Chapel St; ⊙10am-9pm Mon-Sat, noon-5pm Sun) is the city's helpful tourist office.

👁 Sights

★Yale University   UNIVERSITY
(www.yale.edu) Each year, thousands of high-school students make pilgrimages to Yale, nursing dreams of attending the country's third-oldest university, which boasts such notable alumni as Noah Webster, Eli Whitney, Samuel Morse, and Presidents William H Taft, George HW Bush, Bill Clinton and George W Bush. You don't need to share the students' ambitions in order to take a stroll around the campus, just pick up a map at the **visitors center** (www.yale.edu/visitor; cnr Elm & Temple Sts; ⊙9am-4:30pm Mon-Fri,

11am-4pm Sat & Sun) or join a free, one-hour guided tour.

★Yale University Art Gallery   MUSEUM
(📞203-432-0600; artgallery.yale.edu; 1111 Chapel St; ⊙10am-5pm Tue-Fri, 11am-5pm Sat & Sun) **FREE** America's oldest university art museum boasts American masterworks by Edward Hopper and Jackson Pollock, as well as a superb European collection that includes Vincent van Gogh's *The Night Café*.

Peabody Museum of Natural History   MUSEUM
(📞203-432-5050; www.yale.edu/peabody; 170 Whitney Ave; adult/child $9/5; ⊙10am-5pm Mon-Sat, noon-5pm Sun; 🅿🚼) Wannabe paleontologists will be thrilled by the dinosaurs here.

Yale Center for British Art   MUSEUM
(📞203-432-2800; ycba.yale.edu; 1080 Chapel St; ⊙10am-5pm Tue-Sat, noon-5pm Sun) **FREE** The most comprehensive British art collection outside the UK.

CONNECTICUT FACTS

Nicknames Constitution State, Nutmeg State

Population 3.6 million

Area 4845 sq miles

Capital city Hartford (population 124,890)

Other cities New Haven (population 129,585)

Sales tax 6.35%

Birthplace of Abolitionist John Brown (1800–59), circus man PT Barnum (1810–91), actress Katharine Hepburn (1909–2003)

Home of The first written constitution in the US; the first lollipop, Frisbee and helicopter

Politics Democrat-leaning

Famous for Starting the US insurance biz and building the first nuclear submarine

Quirkiest state song lyrics 'Yankee Doodle', which entwines patriotism with doodles, feathers and macaroni

Driving distances Hartford to New Haven 40 miles, Hartford to Providence 75 miles

🛏 Sleeping

Hotel Duncan HISTORIC HOTEL **$**
(📞 203-787-1273; www.hotelduncan.net; 1151 Chapel St; s/d $60/80; ❄) Though the shine has rubbed off this New Haven gem it's the enduring features that still make it worth a stay, including the handsome lobby and the hand-operated elevator. Check out the wall in the manager's office, filled with autographed pictures of celebrity guests such as Jodie Foster and Christopher Walken.

Study at Yale HOTEL **$$$**
(📞 203-503-3900; www.studyhotels.com; 1157 Chapel St; r $219-359; P 🛰) The Study at Yale manages to evoke 'Mad Men chic' without being over the top. Ultra-contemporary touches include in-room iPod docking stations and cardio machines with built-in televisions. There's also an in-house restaurant and cafe, into which you can stumble for morning snacks.

🍴 Eating

★ Frank Pepe PIZZERIA **$$**
(📞 203-865-5762; www.pepespizzeria.com; 157 Wooster St; pizza $7-20; ⊙11:30am-10pm) Pepe's serves immaculate pizza fired in a coal oven, just as it has since 1925, in frenetic white-walled surroundings. Prices vary depending on size and toppings; the large mozzarella pizza runs at $12. Try the white-clam pizza. No credit cards.

Caseus Fromagerie Bistro CHEESE SHOP **$$$**
(📞 203-624-3373; www.caseusnewhaven.com; 93 Whitney Ave; meals $10-30; ⊙11:30am-2:30pm Mon-Tue, 11:30am-2:30pm & 5:30-9pm Wed-Sat) With a boutique cheese counter piled with locally sourced labels and a concept menu devoted to *le grand fromage*, Caseus has hit upon a winning combination. After all, what's not to like about a perfectly executed mac 'n' cheese or the dangerously delicious poutine (pommes frites, cheese curds and velouté). There's also pavement seating.

Soul de Cuba CUBAN **$$$**
(📞 203-498-2822; www.souldecuba.com; 283 Crown St; meals $15-25; ⊙11:30am-10pm) With its peach-colored walls, Afro-Caribbean soundtrack and spirit-rousing cocktails, Soul de Cuba is warm and inviting. Aside from the enormous and excellent-value Cuban sandwiches the menu is packed with sunshine flavors from fried chicken with Spanish olives, to oxtail cooked in red wine.

☆ Entertainment

New Haven has a first-rate theatre scene. The free weekly *New Haven Advocate* (www.newhavenadvocate.com) has current entertainment listings.

Toad's Place MUSIC
(📞 203-624-8623; www.toadsplace.com; 300 York St) Toad's is arguably New England's premier music hall, having earned its rep hosting the likes of the Rolling Stones, U2 and Bob Dylan.

Shubert Theater THEATER
(📞 203-562-5666; www.shubert.com; 247 College St) Dubbed 'Birthplace of the Nation's Greatest Hits,' since 1914 the Shubert has been hosting ballet and Broadway musicals on their trial runs before heading off to New York City.

Yale Repertory Theatre THEATER
(📞 203-432-1234; www.yale.edu/yalerep; 1120 Chapel St) Performing classics and new works in a converted church.

ℹ Getting There & Away

By train from New York City skip Amtrak and take **Metro North** (www.mta.info; one way $14-19), which has near-hourly services and the lowest fares. **Greyhound Bus Lines** (www.greyhound.com) connects New Haven to scores of cities including Hartford ($12.75, one hour) and Boston ($33, four hours).

Mystic

A centuries-old seaport, Mystic boasts a top-notch nautical museum, a stellar aquarium and attractive period accommodations. Yes, it gets inundated with summer tourists, but there's a good reason why everyone stops here (including fans of the 1988 film *Mystic Pizza*), so get off the highway and check it out. The **Greater Mystic Chamber of Commerce** (📞 860-572-1102; www.mysticchamber.org; 2 Roosevelt Ave; ⊙9am-4:30pm), at the old train station, has visitor information.

⊙ Sights

★ Mystic Seaport Museum MUSEUM
(📞 860-572-5315; www.mysticseaport.org; 75 Greenmanville Ave/CT 27; adult/child $24/15; ⊙9am-5pm mid-Feb–Oct, to 4pm Nov-Dec; P) America's maritime history springs to life as costumed interpreters ply their trades at this sprawling re-created 19th-century seaport village. You can scurry aboard

several historic sailing vessels, including the *Charles W Morgan* (built in 1841), the last surviving wooden whaling ship in the world. If you want to experience a little voyage yourself, the **Sabino**, a 1908 steamboat, departs hourly (adult/child $5.50/4.50) on jaunts up the Mystic River.

★**Mystic Aquarium &**
Institute for Exploration AQUARIUM
(☑860-572-5955; www.mysticaquarium.org; 55 Coogan Blvd; adult/child 3-17 yr $29.95/21.95; ☺9am-5pm Apr-Oct, to 4pm Nov & Mar, 10am-4pm Dec-Feb; ♨) This state-of-the-art aquarium boasts more than 6000 species of sea creatures (including three beluga whales), an outdoor viewing area for watching seals and sea lions below the waterline, a penguin pavilion and the 1400-seat Marine Theater for dolphin shows.

🛏 **Sleeping**

★**Mermaid Inn** B&B $$
(☑860-536-6223; www.mermaidinnofmystic.com; 2 Broadway Ave; d incl breakfast $175-225; ℗) This quirky Italianate B&B sits on a quiet street within walking distance of the town center. Its three rooms each have special touches such as fresh flowers and Italian chocolates. In warm weather, guests enjoy breakfast on the porch.

★**Steamboat Inn** INN $$$
(☑860-536-8300; www.steamboatinnmystic.com; 73 Steamboat Wharf; d incl breakfast $160-295; ℗✴🛜) Located right in the heart of downtown Mystic, the 11 rooms of this historic inn have wraparound water views and luxurious amenities, including two-person whirlpool tubs. Antiques lend the interior a romantic atmosphere and service is top-notch with baked goods for breakfast, complimentary bikes, boat docks and gym facilities.

✕ **Eating**

Mystic Drawbridge Ice Cream ICE CREAM $
(www.mysticdrawbridgeicecream.com; 2 W Main St; cones $4, panini $7.50; ☺9am-11pm; ♨) Strolling through town is best done with an ice-cream cone in hand. Some of the more quirky flavors, such as pumpkin pie and southern peach, are seasonal, but on any given day there will be something innovative to try.

★**Captain Daniel Packer Inne** AMERICAN $$
(☑860-536-3555; www.danielpacker.com; 32 Water St; meals $14-24; ☺11am-10pm) This 1754 historic house has a low-beam ceiling,

creaky floorboards and a casual (and loud) pub downstairs. Upstairs, the dining room has river views and an imaginative American menu.

Oyster Club SEAFOOD $$$
(☑860-415-9266; www.oysterclubct.com; 13 Water St; Noank oysters $2, meals $12-35; ☺4-9pm Mon-Thu, 11am-2pm & 4-9pm Fri-Sun; ℗) A little off the main drag, this is the place locals come for oysters served grilled or raw on the deck out back. Classics such as chowder and cherrystone clams satisfy traditionalists, while mussels steamed in lemongrass and coconut milk tempt more adventurous palates.

Lower Connecticut River Valley

Several Colonial-era towns grace the banks of the Connecticut River, offering up their rural charm at an unhurried pace. The **River Valley Tourism District** (☑860-787-9640; www.visitctriver.com) provides information on the region.

Old Lyme

Set near the mouth of the Connecticut River, Old Lyme was home to some 60 sea captains in the 19th century. Today its claim to fame is its art community. In the early 1900s art patron Florence Griswold opened her estate to visiting artists, many of whom offered paintings in lieu of rent. Her Georgian mansion, now the **Florence Griswold Museum** (☑860-434-5542; www.flogris.org; 96 Lyme St; adult/child $10/free; ☺10am-5pm Tue-Sat, 1-5pm Sun; ℗) contains a fine selection of both impressionist and Barbizon paintings.

Nearby, the classy **Bee & Thistle Inn & Spa** (☑860-434-1667; www.beeandthistleinn.com; 100 Lyme St; r $180-280; ℗🛜), a 1756 Dutch Colonial farmhouse, has antique-filled rooms and a romantic dining room serving New American cuisine (meals $30 to $60).

Essex

Tree-lined Essex, established in 1635, stands as the chief town of the region and features well-preserved Federal-period houses, legacies of rum and tobacco fortunes made in the 19th century.

The **Connecticut River Museum** (☑860-767-8269; www.ctrivermuseum.org; 67 Main St; adult/child $8/5; ☺10am-5pm Tue-Sun; ℗), next to **Steamboat Dock**, recounts the region's history and includes a replica of the world's first submarine, built by Yale student David Bushnell in 1776. The museum runs summer river **cruises** (adult/child $26/16; ☺ Jun-Oct) and weekend **eagle-watch tours** Friday to Sunday between February and mid-March ($40 per person).

Alternatively, take the **Essex Steam Train & Riverboat Ride** (☑ 860-767-0103; www.essexsteamtrain.com; 1 Railroad Ave; adult/child $17/9, with cruise $26/17; ☝), an antique steam locomotive that runs 6 scenic miles to Deep River, where you can cruise on a Mississippi-style riverboat up to East Haddam before returning by train.

The landmark **Griswold Inn** (☑ 860-767-1776; www.griswoldinn.com; 36 Main St; r incl breakfast $110-190, ste $190-305; ℗ 🖤) has been Essex's physical and social centerpiece since 1776.

East Haddam

Two intriguing attractions mark this small town on the east bank of the Connecticut River. The medieval-style **Gillette Castle** (☑ 860-526-2336; www.ct.gov/dep/gillettecastle; 67 River Rd; adult/child $6/2; ☺ 10am-4:30pm late May–mid-Oct; ℗) is a wildly eccentric stone-turreted mansion built in 1919 by actor William Gillette, who made his fortune playing Sherlock Holmes.

With residents such as Gillette and banker William Goodspeed, East Haddam became a regular stopover on the summer circuit for New Yorkers, who travelled up on Goodspeed's steam ship to visit the **Goodspeed Opera House** (☑ 860-873-8668; www.goodspeed.org; 6 Main St; tickets $45-70; ☺ performances Wed-Sun Apr-Dec), an elegant 1876 Victorian music hall known as 'the birthplace of the American musical.'

Hartford

Despite its depressing reputation as the 'filing cabinet of America,' Connecticut's capital city, Hartford, is full of surprises. Settled in the 17th century by Dutch traders and, later, Puritans fleeing persecution in Massachusetts, it is one of New England's oldest cities and as such harbors a collection of impressive sights and museums. The **Greater Hartford Welcome Center** (☑ 860-244-0253; www.letsgoarts.org/welcomecenter; 100 Pearl St; ☺ 9am-5pm Mon-Fri) distributes tourist information.

◉ Sights

★ **Mark Twain House & Museum**　MUSEUM
(☑ 860-247-0998; www.marktwainhouse.org; 351 Farmington Ave; adult/child $16/10; ☺ 9:30am-5:30pm Mon-Sat, noon-5:30pm Sun) It was at this former home of Samuel Langhorne Clemens, aka Mark Twain, that the legendary author penned many of his greatest works, including *The Adventures of Huckleberry Finn* and *Tom Sawyer*. The house itself, a Victorian Gothic with fanciful turrets and gables, reflects Twain's quirky character.

Harriet Beecher Stowe House　MUSEUM
(☑ 860-522-9258; www.harrietbeecherstowe.org; 77 Forest St; adult/child $9/6; ☺ 9:30am-4:30pm Tue-Sat, noon-4:30pm Sun) Next door to the Twain house is the house of the woman who wrote the antislavery book *Uncle Tom's Cabin*. The book so rallied Americans against slavery that Abraham Lincoln once credited Stowe with starting the Civil War.

★ **Wadsworth Atheneum**　MUSEUM
(☑ 860-278-2670; www.thewadsworth.org; 600 Main St; adult/child $10/free; ☺ 11am-5pm Wed-Fri, 10am-5pm Sat & Sun) The nation's oldest public-art museum, the Wadsworth Atheneum houses nearly 50,000 pieces. On display are paintings by members of the Hudson River School, European old masters, 19th-century Impressionist works, sculptures by Connecticut artist Alexander Calder and a small yet outstanding array of surrealist works.

Old State House　HISTORIC BUILDING
(☑ 860-522-6766; www.ctoldstatehouse.org; 800 Main St; adult/child $6/3; ☺ 10am-5pm Tue-Sat Jul 4-Columbus Day, Mon-Fri Columbus Day-Jul 4; ☝) Connecticut's original capitol building (from 1797 to 1873) was designed by Charles Bulfinch, who also designed the Massachusetts State House in Boston, and was the site of the trial of the *Amistad* prisoners. Gilbert Stuart's famous 1801 portrait of George Washington hangs in the senate chamber.

🛏 Sleeping & Eating

Hartford Marriott Downtown　BUSINESS HOTEL $$
(☑ 866-373-9806, 860-249-8000; www.marriott.com; 200 Columbus Blvd; d/ste $159/299; ℗ @ 🖤 🏊) This colossal Marriott hotel is located in the Adriaen's Landing District overlooking the Connecticut River. There are 401 stylish rooms spread over 22-stories alongside an indoor rooftop pool and fitness

center. There's also an affiliated spa and an upscale Mediterranean restaurant.

Bin 228   ITALIAN $$
(☑860-244-9463; www.bin228winebar.com; 228 Pearl St; paninis & small plates $8-12; ⊘11:30am-10pm Mon-Thu, to midnight Fri, 4pm-midnight Sat) This wine bar serves Italian fare – paninis, cheese platters, salads – alongside its expansive all-Italian wine list. For those eager to avoid the louder late-night eateries, this is a good option on weekends, when the kitchen stays open to midnight (later for drinks).

🍷 Drinking & Nightlife

Vaughan's Public House   PUB
(☑860-882-1560; www.irishpublichouse.com; 59 Pratt St; pub fare $9-16; ⊘11:30am-1am) This popular Irish pub serves a full pub menu – including beer-battered cod and chips, Guinness lamb stew and farmhouse pie – at a long wooden bar. There are also two taps of Guinness, an excellent happy hour (3pm to 7pm, $3 for 16oz pints) and an amusing mural celebrating famous Irish.

❶ Getting There & Away

Central **Union Station** (☑860-247-5329; www.amtrak.com; 1 Union Pl) links Hartford to cities throughout the Northeast, including New Haven ($13, one hour) and New York City ($40 to $57, three hours).

Litchfield Hills

The rolling hills in the northwestern corner of Connecticut are sprinkled with lakes and carpeted with forests. Historic Litchfield is the hub of the region, but lesser-known villages such as Bethlehem, Washington, Preston, Warren and Kent boast similarly illustrious lineages and are just as photogenic. The **Western Connecticut Convention & Visitors Bureau** (☑800-663-1273; www.litchfieldhills.com) has information on the region.

Litchfield

Founded in 1719, Litchfield prospered from the commerce brought by stagecoaches en route between Hartford and Albany, and its many handsome period buildings are a testimony to that era. Stroll along North and South Sts to see the finest homes, including the 1773 **Tapping Reeve House & Law School** (☑860-567-4501; www.litchfieldhistoricalsociety.org; 82 South St; adult/child $5/free;

⊘11am-5pm Tue-Sat, 1-5pm Sun mid-Apr–Nov), the country's first law school, which trained 129 members of Congress.

Connecticut's largest wildlife preserve, the **White Memorial Conservation Center** (☑860-567-0857; www.whitememorialcc.org; US 202; park free, museum adult/child $6/3; ⊘park sunrise-sunset, museum 9am-5pm Mon-Sat, noon-5pm Sun) is 2.5 miles west of town and has 35 miles of walking trails and good bird-watching.

Lake Waramaug

The most beautiful of the dozens of lakes and ponds in the Litchfield Hills is Lake Waramaug. As you make your way around North Shore Rd, stop at Hopkins Vineyard (☑860-868-7954; www.hopkinsvineyard.com; 25 Hopkins Rd; ⊘10am-5pm Mon-Sat, 11am-5pm Sun May-Dec) for wine tastings. It's next to the 19th-century **Hopkins Inn** (☑860-868-7295; www.thehopkinsinn.com; 22 Hopkins Rd, Warren; r $120-135, apt $150; P❄🐾), which has lake-view accommodations and a restaurant with Austrian-influenced country fare. **Lake Waramaug State Park** (☑860-868-0220; www.ct.gov/deep; 30 Lake Waramaug Rd; tent sites $17-$27) has lakeside campsites, but book well in advance.

VERMONT

Artisanal cheeses, buckets of maple syrup, Ben & Jerry's ice cream...just try to get out of this state without gaining 10lb. Fortunately, there are plenty of ways to work it off: hike the trails of the Green Mountains, paddle a kayak on Lake Champlain or hit Vermont's snowy slopes.

Vermont gives true meaning to the word rural. Its capital would barely rate as a small town in other states and even its largest city, Burlington, has just 42,500 content souls. The countryside is a blanket of rolling green, with 80% of the state forested and most of the rest given over to some of the prettiest farms you'll ever see. So take your time, meander down quiet side roads, stop in those picturesque villages, and sample a taste of the good life.

History

Frenchman Samuel de Champlain explored Vermont in 1609, becoming the first European to visit these lands long inhabited by the native Abenaki.

Vermont & New Hampshire

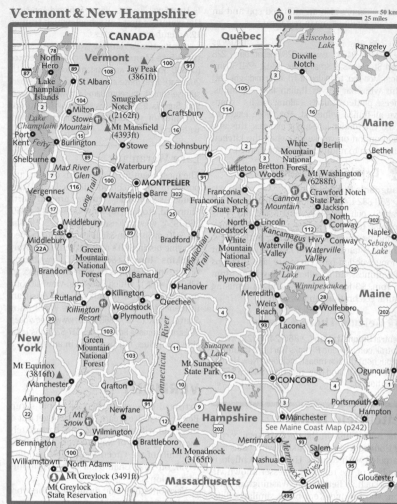

Vermont played a key role in the American Revolution in 1775 when Ethan Allen led a local militia, the Green Mountain Boys, to Fort Ticonderoga, capturing it from the British. In 1777 Vermont declared independence as the Vermont Republic, adopting the first New World constitution to abolish slavery and establish a public school system. In 1791 Vermont was admitted to the USA as the 14th state.

The state's independent streak is as long and deep as a vein of Vermont marble. Historically a land of dairy farmers, Vermont is still largely agricultural and has the lowest population of any New England state.

ℹ Information

Vermont Dept of Tourism (www.vermontvacation.com) Online information by region, season and other user-friendly categories.

Vermont Public Radio (VPR; www.vpr.net) Vermont's excellent statewide public radio station. The radio frequency varies depending on where you are in the state, but the following selection covers most areas: Burlington (northwestern Vermont) 107.9; Brattleboro (southeastern

Vermont) 94.5; Manchester (southwestern Vermont) 92.5; and St Johnsbury (north-eastern Vermont) 88.5.

Vermont State Parks (☑ 888-409-7579; www.vtstateparks.com) Complete camping and parks information.

Southern Vermont

The southern swath of Vermont holds the state's oldest towns and plenty of scenic back roads.

Brattleboro

Ever wondered where the 1960s counter-culture went? It's alive and well in this riverside burg overflowing with artsy types and more tie-dye per capita than any other place in New England.

◉ Sights

Paralleling the Connecticut River, Main St is lined with period buildings, including the handsome art-deco **Latchis Building**. The surrounding area boasts several **covered bridges**; pick up a driving guide at the Chamber of Commerce (p224).

Brattleboro Museum & Art Center   MUSEUM
(www.brattleboromuseum.org; 10 Vernon St; adult/child $8/4; ⊙ 11am-5pm Sun-Mon & Wed-Thu, 11am-7pm Fri, 10am-5pm Sat) Located in a 1915 railway station, this museum hosts rotating exhibitions of contemporary art, including multimedia works by local artists.

⊨ Sleeping

If all you're after is a cheap sleep, there are plenty of motels on Putney Rd north of town; take Exit 3 off I-91.

Latchis Hotel   HOTEL $$
(☑ 800-798-6301, 802-254-6300; http://hotel.latchis.com; 50 Main St; tw $80-100, d $105-180, ste $160-210; 🛜) You can't beat the prime downtown location of this art-deco hotel with a historic theater right next door.

★ Forty Putney Road B&B   B&B $$$
(☑ 800-941-2413, 802-254-6268; www.fortyputneyroad.com; 192 Putney Rd; r incl breakfast $159-329; @ 🛜) In a sweet riverside location just north of town, this 1930 B&B has a cheery pub, a glorious backyard, four rooms and a separate, self-contained cottage. On-site boat and bike rentals allow guests to explore the adjacent West River estuary.

✖ Eating

Amy's Bakery Arts Cafe   BAKERY, CAFE $
(113 Main St; sandwiches & salads $7-12; ⊙ 8am-6pm Mon-Sat, 9am-5pm Sun) Enjoy pastries and coffee, local artwork and Connecticut River views at this popular bakery. Lunchtime offerings include salads, soups and sandwiches.

Brattleboro Food Co-op   DELI $
(www.brattleborofoodcoop.com; 2 Main St; ⊙ 7am-9pm Mon-Sat, 9am-9pm Sun) 🍴 Load up your basket with wholefood groceries, organic produce and local cheeses at this thriving community co-op, or visit the juice bar and deli for healthy takeaway treats.

Whetstone Station   PUB $$
(www.whetstonestation.com; 36 Bridge St; mains $10-20; ⊙ 11:30am-10pm Sun-Thu, 11:30am-11pm Fri & Sat) Brattleboro's newest eatery has a dozen-plus craft brews on tap and excellent pub fare, but the real show-stopper is its outstanding roof deck with a bird's eye view of the Connecticut River. It's the ideal spot for a beer and a bite at sundown.

TJ Buckley's   AMERICAN $$$
(☑ 802-257-4922; www.tjbuckleys.com; 132 Elliot St; mains $40; ⊙ 5:30-9pm Thu-Sun) 🍴 Chef-owner Michael Fuller founded this exceptional, upscale 18-seat eatery in an authentic 1927

VERMONT FACTS

Nickname Green Mountain State

Population 626,000

Area 9217 sq miles

Capital city Montpelier (population 7860)

Other city Burlington (population 42,500)

Sales tax 6%

Birthplace of Mormon leader Brigham Young (1801–77), President Calvin Coolidge (1872–1933)

Home of More than 100 covered bridges

Politics Independent streak, leaning Democrat

Famous for Ben & Jerry's ice cream

Sudsiest state Most microbreweries per capita in the USA

Driving distances Burlington to Brattleboro 151 miles, Burlington to Boston 216 miles

diner over 30 years ago. The oral menu of four nightly changing items is sourced largely from local organic farms. Reserve ahead.

ℹ Information

Brattleboro Chamber of Commerce (☏877-254-4565, 802-254-4565; www.brattleborochamber.org; 180 Main St; ⊗9am-5pm Mon-Fri)

Mt Snow

Family-oriented **Mt Snow** (☏800-245-7669; www.mountsnow.com; VT 100, West Dover; adult lift ticket midweek/weekend $75/85) is the southernmost of Vermont's big ski resorts. When the snow melts, its lifts and trail system draw hikers and mountain bikers. The **Mt Snow Valley Chamber of Commerce** (☏877-887-6884, 802-464-8092; www.visitvermont.com; 21 W Main St; ⊗8:30am-4:30pm Mon-Wed, to 6pm Thu & Fri, 10am-4pm Sat & Sun) has information on accommodations and activities. Mt Snow is reached via Wilmington, midway between Brattleboro and Bennington.

Bennington

A measure of how rural southern Vermont really is, cozy Bennington, with just 15,000 inhabitants, ranks as the region's largest town. You'll find an interesting mix of cafes and shops downtown along Main St, while the adjacent Old Bennington historic district boasts age-old Colonial homes and a trio of covered bridges. A hilltop granite obelisk commemorating the 1777 Battle of Bennington towers above it all.

◉ Sights

Old First Church　　　　HISTORIC SITE
(cnr Monument Ave & VT 9) Gracing the center of Old Bennington, this early 19th-century church is best known for its churchyard, which holds the remains of five Vermont

VERMONT FRESH NETWORK

Finding locavore food in Vermont is a piece of cake. The farm-and-chef partnership **Vermont Fresh Network** (www.vermontfresh.net) 🖋 identifies restaurants that focus on sustainable, locally sourced produce, cheese and meats. Just look for the green-and-white square sticker with a plate and silverware, proudly displayed at farms and eateries throughout the state.

governors, numerous American Revolutionary soldiers and Vermont's beloved 20th-century poet Robert Frost (1874–1963).

Bennington Battle Monument　HISTORIC SITE
(www.benningtonbattlemonument.com; 15 Monument Circle; adult/child $3/1; ⊗9am-5pm mid-Apr–Oct) Vermont's loftiest structure offers an unbeatable 360-degree view of the surrounding countryside. An elevator whisks you painlessly to the top.

Bennington Museum　　　　MUSEUM
(☏802-447-1571; www.benningtonmuseum.org; 75 Main St; adult/child $10/free; ⊗10am-5pm daily, closed Jan, closed Wed Nov-Jun) Between downtown and Old Bennington, this museum's outstanding early Americana collection includes furniture, glassware, Bennington pottery, the world's oldest surviving American Revolutionary flag and works by American folk artist 'Grandma Moses.'

🛏 Sleeping & Eating

Greenwood Lodge & Campsites　HOSTEL, CAMPGROUND $
(☏802-442-2547; www.campvermont.com/greenwood; VT 9, Prospect Mountain; 2-person tent/RV site $27/35, dm/d from $29/70; ⊗mid-May–late Oct) Nestled in the Green Mountains 8 miles east of town, this 120-acre space with three ponds holds one of Vermont's best-sited hostels and campgrounds.

Henry House　　　　　　B&B $$
(☏802-442-7045; www.thehenryhouseinn.com; 1338 Murphy Rd, North Bennington; r incl breakfast $100-155; 🖥) Sit on the rocking chair and watch the traffic trickle across a covered bridge at this Colonial home on 25 peaceful acres, built in 1769 by American Revolution hero William Henry.

Blue Benn Diner　　　　　DINER $
(☏802-442-5140; 314 North St; mains $5-12; ⊗6am-4:45pm Mon-Fri, 7am-3:45pm Sat & Sun) This classic 1950s-era diner serves breakfast all day and a healthy mix of American and international fare. Enhancing the retro experience are little tabletop jukeboxes on which you can play Willie Nelson's 'Moonlight in Vermont' till your neighbors scream for mercy.

★Pangaea　　　　　INTERNATIONAL $$$
(☏802-442-7171; www.vermontfinedining.com; 1 Prospect St, North Bennington; lounge mains $11-23, restaurant mains $30-39; ⊗lounge 5-9pm daily, restaurant 5-9pm Tue-Sat) Offering fine dining for every budget, this top-end North Ben-

nington restaurant sits side-by-side with a more casual, intimate lounge. Opt for gourmet burgers served on the riverside terrace out back, or head to the tastefully decorated dining room next door for international specialties such as Provence-herbed Delmonico steak topped with gorgonzola.

Information

Bennington Area Chamber of Commerce (☎800-229-0252, 802-447-3311; www.bennington.com; 100 Veterans Memorial Dr; ⏲9am-5pm) One mile north of downtown.

Manchester

Sitting in the shadow of Mt Equinox, Manchester's been a fashionable summer retreat since the 19th century. The mountain scenery, the agreeable climate and the Batten Kill River – Vermont's best trout stream – continue to draw vacationers today.

Manchester Center, at the town's north end, sports cafes and upscale outlet stores. Further south lies dignified Manchester Village, lined with marble sidewalks, stately homes and the posh Equinox hotel.

Sights & Activities

The **Appalachian Trail**, which overlaps the Long Trail (p228) in southern Vermont, passes just east of Manchester. For trail maps and details on shorter day hikes, stop by the **Green Mountain National Forest office** (☎802-362-2307; 2538 Depot St, Manchester Center; ⏲8am-4:30pm Mon-Fri).

★Hildene HISTORIC SITE
(☎800-578-1788, 802-362-1788; www.hildene.org; 1005 Hildene Rd/VT 7A; adult/child $16/5, tours $5/2; ⏲9:30am-4:30pm) This stately 24-room Georgian Revival mansion was home to members of Abraham Lincoln's family from the 1800s until 1975, when it was converted into a museum. The collection of family heirlooms includes the hat Lincoln probably wore while delivering the Gettysburg Address. The gorgeous grounds offer 8 miles of walking and cross-country ski trails.

American Museum of Fly Fishing & Orvis MUSEUM
(www.amff.com; 4070 Main St; adult/child $5/3; ⏲10am-4pm Tue-Sun Jun-Oct, Tue-Sat Nov-May) This museum has perhaps the world's best display of fly-fishing equipment, including flies and rods used by Ernest Hemingway, Bing Crosby and US president Herbert Hoover.

BattenKill Canoe BOATING
(☎802-362-2800; www.battenkill.com; 6328 VT 7A, Arlington; ⏲9am-5:30pm daily May-Oct, Wed-Fri Nov-Apr) These outfitters 6 miles south of Manchester rent paddling equipment and organize trips on the lovely Battenkill River.

Skyline Drive SCENIC DRIVE
(☎802-362-1114; car & driver $15, extra passenger $5; ⏲9am-sunset May-Oct) For spectacular views, drive to the summit of **Mt Equinox** (3816ft) via Skyline Drive, a private 5-mile toll road off VT 7A.

Sleeping & Eating

Aspen Motel MOTEL $
(☎802-362-2450; www.theaspenatmanchester.com; 5669 Main St/VT 7A; r $85-150; ❄📶🏊) This family-run motel set back serenely from the road has 25 comfortable rooms and a convenient location within walking distance of Manchester Center.

Inn at Manchester INN $$
(☎800-273-1793, 802-362-1793; www.innatmanchester.com; 3967 Main St/VT 7A; r/ste incl breakfast from $155/205; ❄@📶🏊) In the heart of

> **WORTH A TRIP**
>
> **SCENIC DRIVE: COVERED BRIDGES**
>
> A 30-minute detour takes you across three picture-perfect covered bridges spanning the Wallomsac River at Bennington's rural north end. To get started turn west onto VT 67A just north of Bennington's tourist office and continue 3.5 miles, bearing left on Murphy Rd at the 117ft-long **Burt Henry Covered Bridge** (1840). Exhale, slow down: you're back in horse-and-buggy days. After curving to the left, Murphy Rd next loops through the **Paper Mill Bridge**, which takes its name from the 1790 mill whose gear works are still visible along the river below. Next turn right onto VT 67A, go half a mile and turn right onto Silk Rd where you'll soon cross the **Silk Road Bridge** (c 1840). Continue southeast for two more miles, bearing left at two T-intersections, to reach the Bennington Battle Monument (p224).

town, this delightful inn and carriage house offers comfy rooms with quilts and country furnishings, along with a big front porch, afternoon teas, an expansive backyard and a wee pub.

Spiral Press Café CAFE **$**
(cnr VT 11 & VT 7A; mains $6-10; ⊗7:30am-7pm; ☎) Attached to the fabulous Northshire Bookstore, Manchester Center's favorite cafe draws locals and tourists alike with good coffee, flaky croissants and delicious panini sandwiches.

Ye Olde Tavern AMERICAN **$$$**
(☎802-362-0611; www.yeoldetavern.net; 5183 Main St; mains $17-34; ⊗5-9pm) At this gracious roadside 1790s inn, hearthside dining at candlelit tables complementary the wide-ranging menu of 'Yankee favorites' that feature traditional pot roast (cooked in the tavern's own ale) or local venison (a regular Friday special).

ℹ Information

Manchester and the Mountains Regional Chamber of Commerce (☎802-362-6313, 800-362-4144; www.visitmanchestervt.com; 39 Bonnet St, Manchester Center; ⊗9am-5pm Mon-Fri, 10am-4pm Sat, 11am-3pm Sun; ☎) Spiffy new office with free wi-fi.

Central Vermont

Nestled in the Green Mountains, central Vermont is classic small-town, big-countryside New England. Its picturesque villages and venerable ski resorts have been luring travelers for generations.

Woodstock & Quechee

The archetypal Vermont town, Woodstock has streets lined with graceful Federal- and Georgian-style houses. The Ottauquechee River, spanned by a covered bridge, meanders right through the heart of town. Quechee (*kwee*-chee), 7 miles to the northeast, is famous for its dramatic gorge, dubbed 'Vermont's Little Grand Canyon.'

◉ Sights

★ **Quechee Gorge** CANYON
Quechee Gorge, an impressive 170ft-deep, 3000ft-long chasm cut by the Ottauquechee River, can be viewed from above or explored via nearby walking trails.

Marsh-Billings-Rockefeller National Historical Park PARK
(☎802-457-3368; www.nps.gov/mabi; Woodstock; mansion tours adult/child $8/free, trails free; ⊗10am-5pm late May-Oct) Encompassing the historic home and estate of early American conservationist George Perkins Marsh, Vermont's only national park offers mansion tours every 30 minutes, plus 20 miles of trails and carriage roads for walkers, cross-country skiers and snowshoers.

Billings Farm & Museum FARM
(☎802-457-2355; www.billingsfarm.org; 69 Old River Rd, Woodstock; adult/child $12/6; ⊗10am-5pm daily May-Oct, to 3:30pm Sat & Sun Nov-Feb; 👶) ♪ A mile north of the village green, this historic farm delights children with pretty Jersey cows and hands-on demonstrations of traditional farm life. The family-friendly seasonal events include wagon and sleigh rides, pumpkin and apple festivals and old-fashioned Halloween, Thanksgiving and Christmas celebrations.

VINS Nature Center WILDLIFE CENTER
(☎802-359-5000; www.vinsweb.org; US 4; adult/child $13/11; ⊗10am-5:30pm; 👶) ♪ Visit this nature center, a mile west of Quechee Gorge, for close-up looks at the magnificent bald eagles and other raptors that are rehabilitated here.

🛏 Sleeping

Quechee State Park CAMPGROUND **$**
(☎802-295-2990; www.vtstateparks.com/htm/quechee.htm; 5800 US 4, Quechee; tent & RV sites/lean-tos $20/27; ⊗mid-May-mid-Oct) Perched on the edge of Quechee Gorge, this 611-acre spot has 45 pine-shaded campsites and seven lean-tos.

Ardmore Inn B&B **$$**
(☎802-457-3887; www.ardmoreinn.com; 23 Pleasant St, Woodstock; r incl breakfast $155-230; ☎) Congenial owners and lavish breakfasts enhance the considerable appeal of this stately, centrally located 1867 Victorian-Greek Revival inn with five antique-laden rooms.

Shire Riverview Motel MOTEL **$$**
(☎802-457-2211; www.shiremotel.com; 46 Pleasant St/US 4, Woodstock; r $128-228; 🌐☎) Within walking distance of the town center, this 42-room motel features a wraparound porch overlooking the Ottauquechee River. Some rooms have fireplaces and most have river views.

✖ Eating

★ **Skunk Hollow Tavern** AMERICAN $$
(☑ 802-436-2139; www.skunkhollowtavern.com;
12 Brownsville Rd, Hartland Four Corners; mains
$13-25; ⊘5pm-late Wed-Sun) Exuding rustic
historic charm, this 200-year-old crossroads
tavern 8 miles south of Woodstock serves
burgers, fish and chips or rack of lamb
downstairs at the bar, or in the more inti-
mate space upstairs. There's live music on
Friday evenings.

Osteria Pane e Salute ITALIAN $$
(☑ 802-457-4882; www.osteriapaneesalute.com;
61 Central St, Woodstock; mains $16-23; ⊘6-10pm
Thu-Sun, closed Apr & Nov) This popular downtown bistro specializes in northern Italian
classics, plus thin-crust Tuscan pizza in
winter, complemented by an extensive list
of Italian wines from small boutique vineyards. Book ahead.

★ **Simon Pearce
Restaurant** NEW AMERICAN $$$
(☑ 802-295-1470; www.simonpearce.com; 1760
Main St, Quechee; lunch mains $13-18, dinner mains
$23-35; ⊘11:30am-2:45pm & 5:30-9pm) Reserve
ahead for a window table suspended over
the river in this converted brick mill, where
fresh-from-the-farm local ingredients are
used to inventive effect. The restaurant's
beautiful stemware is blown by hand in the
Simon Pearce Glass workshops next door.

ⓘ Information

**Woodstock Area Chamber of Commerce
Welcome Center** (☑ 802-432-1100; www.
woodstockvt.com; Mechanic St, Woodstock;
⊘10am-4pm Mon-Fri, 9am-5pm Sat & Sun)
On a riverside backstreet, two blocks from the
village green.

Killington

A half-hour's drive west of Woodstock, **Kil-
lington Resort** (☑ 802-422-6200; www.kil-
lington.com; adult/senior/youth lift ticket weekend
$88/75/68, midweek $80/68/62) is New Eng-
land's answer to Vail, boasting 200 runs on
seven mountains, a vertical drop of 3150ft
and more than 30 lifts. Thanks to the world's
most extensive snowmaking system, Killing-
ton has one of the East's longest ski seasons.
Come summer, mountain bikers and hikers
claim the slopes.

Killington is jam-packed with accom-
modations, from cozy ski lodges to chain
hotels. Most are along Killington Rd, the
6-mile road that heads up the mountain
from US 4. The **Killington Chamber of
Commerce** (☑ 800-337-1928, 802-773-4181;
www.killingtonchamber.com; 2046 US 4, Killington;
⊘10am-4:30pm Mon-Fri, 9am-1pm Sat) has all
the nitty-gritty.

Middlebury

Straddling the pretty falls of Otter Creek,
this former mill town nowadays revolves
around Middlebury College, whose Bread-
loaf School of English and summer language
programs lure writers and linguists from
around the world. The **Addison County
Chamber of Commerce** (☑ 802-388-7951;
www.addisoncounty.com; 93 Court St; ⊘9am-5pm
Mon-Fri) has area information.

There's excellent lakeside camping, just
10 miles south of town at **Branbury State
Park** (☑ 802-247-5925; www.vtstateparks.com/
htm/branbury.htm; VT 53; campsite/lean-to
$20/27; ⊘late May–mid-Oct). Back in Middle-
bury itself, the gracious 1803 Federal-style
Inn on the Green (☑ 888-244-7512, 802-388-
7512; www.innonthegreen.com; 71 S Pleasant St; r
incl breakfast $159-299; ✳@☎) has 11 attrac-
tive rooms that overlook the town green.

Go retro at **A&W Drive-In** (middaw.com;
1557 US 7; mains $3-10; ⊘11:30am-8:30pm),
where carhops deliver root-beer floats,
cheeseburgers and onion rings directly
to your car window. For dining with river
views, try the high-ceilinged, student-driven
51 Main (☑ 802-388-8209; www.go51main.com;

WORTH A TRIP

SCENIC DRIVE: VERMONT'S
GREEN MOUNTAINS

Following Vermont's Green Mountain
spine through the rural heart of the
state, the **VT 100** rambles past roll-
ing pastures speckled with cows,
tiny villages with country stores and
white-steepled churches, and verdant
mountains crisscrossed with hiking
trails and ski slopes. It's the quintes-
sential side trip for those who want to
slow down and experience Vermont's
bucolic essence. The road runs north to
south all the way from Massachusetts
to Canada. Even if your time is limited,
don't miss the scenic 45-mile stretch
between Waterbury and Stockbridge,
an easy detour off I-89.

51 Main St; mains $9-24; ⊙5pm-late Tue-Sat; 🛜), a restaurant-bar, or the outdoor terrace at **Storm Cafe** (✆802-388-1063; www.thestormcafe.com; 3 Mill St; mains $6-25; ⊙11:30am-2:30pm & 5-10pm Tue & Wed, 7:30am-2:30pm & 5-10pm Thu-Sat, 7:30am-2:30pm Sun), just below the waterfall.

Mad River Valley

The Mad River Valley, centered around the towns of Warren and Waitsfield, boasts two significant ski areas: **Sugarbush** (✆800-537-8427, 802-583-6300; www.sugarbush.com; 1840 Sugarbush Access Rd, Warren; adult lift ticket weekend/midweek $89/84; 10% discount if purchased online) and **Mad River Glen** (✆802-496-3551; www.madriverglen.com; VT 17; adult lift ticket weekend/midweek $71/55), in the mountains west of VT 100. Opportunities abound for cycling, canoeing, horseback riding, kayaking, gliding and other activities. Stop at the **Mad River Valley Chamber of Commerce** (✆800-828-4748, 802-496-3409; www.madrivervalley.com; 4061 Main St, Waitsfield; ⊙8am-5pm Mon-Fri) for a mountain of information.

Northern Vermont

Boasting some of New England's lushest and prettiest landscapes, northern Vermont cradles the fetching state capital of Montpelier, the ski mecca of Stowe, the vibrant college town of Burlington and the state's highest mountains.

Montpelier

America's smallest capital, Montpelier is a thoroughly likable town of period buildings backed by verdant hills and crowned by the gold-domed 19th-century **State House** (www.vtstatehouse.org; 115 State St; ⊙tours 10am-3:30pm Mon-Fri, 11am-2:30pm Sat Jul-Oct) FREE. Tours of the capitol building run on the half hour. Right across the street, the **Capitol Region Visitors Center** (✆802-828-5981; cri.center@state.vt.us; 134 State St; ⊙6am-5pm Mon-Fri, 9am-5pm Sat & Sun) has tourist information.

Bookstores, boutiques and restaurants throng the town's twin thoroughfares, State and Main Sts. Forget about junk food – Montpelier prides itself on being the only state capital in the USA without a McDonald's! The bakery-cafe **La Brioche** (www.neci.edu/labrioche; 89 Main St; pastries & sandwiches $2-8; ⊙7am-5pm Mon-Fri, to 3pm Sat), run by students from Montpelier's New England

Culinary Institute, gets an A-plus for its innovative sandwiches and flaky French pastries. Other terrific options include **Hunger Mountain Co-op** (✆802-223-8000; hungermountain.coop; 623 Stone Cutters Way; deli items $5-10; ⊙8am-8pm), a health-food store and deli with cafe tables perched above a river, and **Three-penny Taproom** (www.threepennytaproom.com; 108 Main St; mains $9-18; ⊙11am-late Mon-Fri, noon-late Sat, noon-5pm Sun), with 25 microbrews on tap and locally sourced bistro fare.

Stowe & Around

With Vermont's highest peak, **Mt Mansfield** (4393ft), as its backdrop, Stowe ranks as Vermont's classiest ski destination. It packs all the Alpine thrills you could ask for – both cross-country and downhill skiing, with gentle runs for novices and challenging drops for pros. Cycling, hiking and kayaking take center stage in the summer. Lodgings and eateries are thick along VT 108 (Mountain Rd), which continues northwest from Stowe village to the ski resorts.

◉ Sights & Activities

In warm weather, don't miss the drive through dramatic **Smugglers Notch**, northwest of Stowe on VT 108 (closed by heavy snows in winter). This narrow pass slices through mountains with 1000ft cliffs on either side. Roadside trails lead into the surrounding high country.

★**Ben & Jerry's Ice Cream Factory**   FACTORY
(✆802-882-1240; www.benjerrys.com; 1281 VT 100, Waterbury; adult/child $4/free; ⊙9am-9pm Jul–mid-Aug, 9am-7pm mid-Aug–Oct, 10am-6pm Nov-Jun; 🅿) A far cry from the abandoned Burlington gas station where ice-cream pioneers Ben Cohen and Jerry Greenfield first set up shop in 1978, this legendary factory, just north of I-89 in Waterbury, still draws crowds for tours that include a campy moovie and a taste tease of the latest flavor. Behind the factory, a mock cemetery holds 'graves' of Holy Cannoli and other long-forgotten flavors.

Long Trail   HIKING
Vermont's 300-mile Long Trail, which passes west of Stowe, follows the crest of the Green Mountains and runs the entire length of Vermont with rustic cabins, lean-tos and campsites along the way. Its caretaker, the **Green Mountain Club** (✆802-244-7037; www.

greenmountainclub.org; 4711 Waterbury-Stowe Rd/ VT 100) ☏, has full details on the Long Trail and shorter day hikes around Stowe.

★Stowe Recreation Path   OUTDOORS
(www.stowe-village.com/BikePath; 🖼) ☏ This flat to gently rolling 5.5-mile path offers a fabulous four-season escape for all ages, as it rambles through woods, meadows and outdoor sculpture gardens along the West Branch of the Little River, with sweeping views of Mt Mansfield unfolding in the distance. Bike, walk, skate, ski and/or swim in one of the swimming holes along the way.

Stowe Mountain Resort   SKIING
(☎888-253-4849, 802-253-3000; www.stowe. com; 5781 Mountain Rd) This venerable resort encompasses two major mountains, Mt Mansfield (vertical drop 2360ft) and Spruce Peak (1550ft). It offers 48 beautiful trails – 16% beginner, 59% intermediate and 25% for hard-core backcountry skiers.

Umiak Outdoor Outfitters   OUTDOORS
(☎802-253-2317; www.umiak.com; 849 S Main St; ⊙9am-6pm) Rents kayaks, snowshoes and telemark skis, offers boating lessons and leads boating and moonlight snowshoe tours.

AJ's Ski & Sports   EQUIPMENT RENTAL
(☎800-226-6257, 802-253-4593; www.stowe-sports.com; 350 Mountain Rd; ⊙10am-6pm) Rents bikes, kayaks, skiing and snowboarding equipment in the village center.

🛏 Sleeping

Smugglers Notch State Park   CAMPGROUND $
(☎802-253-4014; www.vtstateparks.com/htm/ smugglers.htm; 6443 Mountain Rd; tent & RV sites $20, lean-tos $27; ⊙mid-May–mid-Oct) This 35-acre park, 8 miles northwest of Stowe, is perched on the mountainside, with 20 tent and trailer sites and 14 lean-tos.

Fiddler's Green Inn   INN $
(☎800-882-5346, 802-253-8124; www.fiddlers-greeninn.com; 4859 Mountain Rd; r incl breakfast midweek/weekend $90/125; 🖼) A throwback to simpler times, this unembellished 1820s farmhouse a mile below the ski lifts has rustic pine walls, a fieldstone fireplace and seven humble guest rooms, the best of which overlook the river out back.

Stowe Motel & Snowdrift   MOTEL, APARTMENT $$
(☎800-829-7629, 802-253-7629; www.stowemo-tel.com; 2043 Mountain Rd; r $85-200, ste $182-240, apt $162-250; @ 🛰 🏊) With units ranging from simple to deluxe, this motel set on 16 acres comes complete with a tennis court, hot tubs, lawn games and free bicycles or snowshoes for use on the adjacent Stowe Recreation Path.

Trapp Family Lodge   LODGE $$$
(☎800-826-7000, 802-253-8511; www.trappfamily. com; 700 Trapp Hill Rd; r from $275; @ 🛰 🏊) Surrounded by wide-open fields and mountain vistas, this Austrian-style chalet, built by Maria von Trapp of *Sound of Music* fame, boasts Stowe's best setting. Traditional lodge rooms are complemented by guesthouses scattered across the 2700-acre property. A network of trails offers stupendous hiking, snowshoeing and cross-country skiing.

🍴 Eating

Harvest Market   MARKET $
(www.harvestatstowe.com; 1031 Mountain Rd; ⊙7am-7pm) Before heading for the hills, stop here for coffee, pastries, Vermont cheeses, sandwiches, gourmet deli items, wines and local microbrews.

Pie-casso   PIZZERIA $$
(☎802-253-4411; www.piecasso.com; 1899 Mountain Rd; mains $9-22; ⊙11am-9pm) Organic arugula chicken salad and portobello panini supplement the menu of excellent hand-tossed pizzas. There's a bar and live music too.

Gracie's Restaurant   BURGERS $$
(☎802-253-8741; www.gracies.com; 18 Edson Hill Rd; mains $11-35; ⊙5-9:30pm) Halfway between the village and the mountain, this animated, dog-themed eatery serves big burgers, hand-cut steaks, Waldorf salad and garlic-laden shrimp scampi.

★Hen of the Wood   AMERICAN $$$
(☎802-244-7300; www.henofthewood.com; 92 Stowe St, Waterbury; mains $18-32; ⊙5-10pm Mon-Sat) ☏ Arguably the finest dining in northern Vermont, this chef-driven restaurant in Waterbury gets rave reviews for its innovative farm-to-table cuisine. The setting in a historic grist mill rivals the extraordinary food, which features densely flavored dishes such as smoked duck breast and sheep's-milk gnocchi.

ℹ Information

Stowe Area Association (☎802-253-7321; www.gostowe.com; 51 Main St; ⊙9am-5pm Mon-Sat, to 8pm Jun-Oct & Jan-Mar) In the heart of the village.

Burlington

This hip college town on the shores of scenic Lake Champlain is one of those places that makes you think, wouldn't it be great to live here? The cafe and club scene is on par with a much bigger city, while the slow, friendly pace is pure small town. And where else can you walk to the end of Main St and paddle off in a kayak?

⊙ Sights

Burlington's shops, cafes and pubs are concentrated around Church St Marketplace, a bustling brick-lined pedestrian mall midway between the University of Vermont and Lake Champlain.

★ **Shelburne Museum**   MUSEUM
(☑ 802-985-3346; www.shelburnemuseum.org; US 7, Shelburne; adult/child $22/11, after 3pm $15/7; ⊙10am-5pm mid-May–Oct; ⊕) This extraordinary 45-acre museum, 9 miles south of Burlington, showcases a Smithsonian-caliber collection of Americana – 150,000 objects in all. The mix of folk art, decorative arts and more is housed in 39 historic buildings, most of them relocated here from other parts of New England to ensure their preservation.

Shelburne Farms   FARM
(☑ 802-985-8686; www.shelburnefarms.org; 1611 Harbor Rd, Shelburne; adult/child $8/5; ⊙9am-5:30pm mid-May–mid-Oct, 10am-5pm mid-Oct–mid-May; ⊕) ❧ This 1400-acre estate, designed by landscape architect Frederick Law Olmsted (who also designed New York's Central Park), was both a country house for the aristocratic Webb family and a working farm, with stunning lakefront perspectives.

LOCAL KNOWLEDGE

BURLINGTON'S SECRET GARDEN

Hidden away less than 2 miles from Burlington's city center is one of Vermont's most idyllic green spaces. Tucked among the lazy curves of the Winooski River, the **Intervale Center** (www.intervale.org; 180 Intervale Rd) FREE encompasses a dozen organic farms and a delightful trail network, open to the public 365 days a year for hiking, cycling, skiing, berry picking and more; check its website for details.

Sample the farm's superb Cheddar cheese, tour the magnificent barns, walk the network of trails, and enjoy afternoon tea or dinner at its award-winning inn (p231).

Echo Lake Aquarium & Science Center   SCIENCE CENTER
(☑ 802-864-1848; www.echovermont.org; 1 College St; adult/child $13.50/10.50; ⊙10am-5pm; ⊕) Examining the colorful past, present and future of Lake Champlain, this lakeside museum features a multitude of small aquariums and rotating science exhibits with plenty of hands-on, kid-friendly activities.

Magic Hat Brewery   BREWERY
(☑ 802-658-2739; www.magichat.net; 5 Bartlett Bay Rd, South Burlington; ⊙10am-6pm Mon-Sat, noon-5pm Sun) Drink in the history of one of Vermont's most dynamic microbreweries on the fun, free, self-guided tour. Afterwards, sample a few experimental brews from the four dozen taps in the on-site Growler Bar.

🏃 Activities

Ready for outdoor adventures? Head to the waterfront, where options include boating on **Lake Champlain** and cycling, in-line skating and walking on the 7.5-mile shorefront **Burlington Bike Path**. Jump-off points and equipment rentals for all these activities are within a block of each other near the waterfront end of Main St.

Local Motion   BICYCLE RENTAL
(☑ 802-652-2453; www.localmotion.org; 1 Steele St; bicycles per day $30; ⊙10am-6pm; ⊕) ❧ Rents quality bikes.

Whistling Man Schooner Company   SAILING
(☑ 802-598-6504; www.whistlingman.com; Boathouse, College St, at Lake Champlain; 2hr cruises adult/child $40/25; ⊙3 trips daily, late May–early Oct) Explore Lake Champlain on the *Friend Ship*, a 17-passenger, 43-ft sailboat.

🛏 Sleeping

Burlington's budget and midrange motels are on the outskirts of town, clustered along Shelburne Rd (US 7) in South Burlington, Williston Rd (US 2) east of I-89 exit 14, and US 7 north of Burlington in Colchester (I-89 exit 16).

North Beach Campground   CAMPGROUND $
(☑ 802-862-0942; www.enjoyburlington.com; 60 Institute Rd; tent/RV site $26/36; ⊙May–mid-Oct; 🛜) Two miles north of downtown, this wonderful spot on Lake Champlain offers 69

tent sites on 45 wooded acres, with picnic tables, fire rings, hot showers, a playground, beach and bike path.

Burlington Hostel   HOSTEL $
(☑ 802-540-3043; www.theburlingtonhostel.com; 53 Main St; dm incl breakfast midweek/weekend $35/40; ✳ @ ☎) Just minutes from Church St and Lake Champlain, Burlington's hostel accommodates up to 48 guests and offers both mixed and women-only dorms.

Lang House   B&B $$
(☑ 802-652-2500; www.langhouse.com; 360 Main St; r incl breakfast $145-245; ✳ ☎) Burlington's most elegant B&B occupies a centrally located, tastefully restored 19th-century Victorian home and carriage house. Reserve ahead for one of the 3rd-floor rooms with lake views.

Willard Street Inn   INN $$
(☑ 802-651-8710; www.willardstreetinn.com; 349 S Willard St; r incl breakfast $150-265; ☎) Perched on a hill within easy walking distance of the University of Vermont and the Church St Marketplace, this late-19th-century Queen Anne–Georgian Revival mansion has a fine-wood and cut-glass elegance, with several guest rooms overlooking Lake Champlain.

★ Inn at Shelburne Farms   INN $$$
(☑ 802-985-8498; www.shelburnefarms.org/stay dine; 1611 Harbor Rd, Shelburne; r with private/without bath from $289/169, cottage $289-430, guesthouse $436-926; ☎) At this historic 1400-acre lakefront estate (p230), 7 miles south of Burlington, guests stay in a gracious, welcoming country manor house, or in four independent, kitchen-equipped cottages and guesthouses scattered across the property. The attached farm-to-table restaurant is superb.

✕ Eating

On Saturday mornings, don't miss Burlington's thriving farmers market in City Hall Park.

★ Penny Cluse Cafe   CAFE $
(www.pennycluse.com; 169 Cherry St; mains $7-11; ☉ 6:45am-3pm Mon-Fri, 8am-3pm Sat & Sun) ☞ One of Burlington's most popular downtown eateries whips up pancakes, biscuits and gravy, omelets and tofu scrambles, along with sandwiches, fish tacos, salads and the best *chile relleno* you'll find east of the Mississippi. Expect long lines on weekends.

City Market   MARKET $
(www.citymarket.coop; 82 S Winooski Ave; ☉ 7am-11pm) ☞ If there's a natural-foods heaven, it must look something like this: chock-full of local produce and products (with over 1600 Vermont-based producers represented) and a huge takeout deli.

Stone Soup   VEGETARIAN $
(www.stonesoupvt.com; 211 College St; buffet per lb $9.75, light meals $5-10; ☉ 7am-9pm Mon-Fri, 9am-9pm Sat; ☎✕) Best known for its excellent vegetarian- and vegan-friendly buffet, this longtime local favorite also features homemade soups, sandwiches on home-baked bread, a salad bar and pastries.

★ American Flatbread   PIZZERIA $$
(www.americanflatbread.com/restaurants/burlington-vt; 115 St Paul St; flatbreads $14-23; ☉ restaurant 11:30am-2:30pm & 5-10pm, taproom 11:30am-late) ☞ Its central downtown location, great microbrews on tap, a back-alley outdoor terrace and scrumptious wood-fired flatbread (thin-crust pizza) topped with organic local ingredients make this a perennial local favorite.

Daily Planet   INTERNATIONAL $$
(☑ 802-862-9647; www.dailyplanet15.com; 15 Center St; mains $11-20; ☉ 4-11pm Mon-Sat, 10am-2pm & 4-11pm Sun; ☎✕) This stylish downtown haunt serves everything from burgers with exotic trimmings to barbecued duck confit to Prince Edward Island mussels to pecan-crusted rainbow trout. The bar stays open late nightly, and there's a good Sunday brunch.

Leunig's Bistro   FRENCH $$$
(☑ 802-863-3759; www.leunigsbistro.com; 115 Church St; lunch mains $10-17, dinner mains $21-32; ☉ 11am-10pm Mon-Fri, 9am-10pm Sat & Sun) With sidewalk seating and an elegant, tin-ceilinged dining room, this convivial Parisian-style brasserie is a longstanding Burlington staple. It's as much fun for the people-watching (windows face busy Church St Marketplace) as for the excellent wine list and food.

☕ Drinking & Entertainment

The free weekly *Seven Days* (www.7dvt.com) has event and entertainment listings.

Radio Bean   BAR, CAFE
(www.radiobean.com; 8 N Winooski Ave; ☉ 8am-2am; ☎) This funky cafe-bar features its own low-power FM radio station, a trendy attached

eatery serving international street food and live performances nightly that include jazz, acoustic music and poetry readings.

Vermont Pub & Brewery MICROBREWERY
(www.vermontbrewery.com; 144 College St;; ⊙11:30am-1am Sun-Wed, to 2am Thu-Sat) Specialty and seasonal brews, including weekly limited releases, are made on the premises, accompanied by British-style pub fare (mains $6 to $16).

Splash at the Boathouse BAR
(☑802-658-2244; www.splashattheboathouse. com; 0 College St; ⊙11:30am-2am) Perched atop Burlington's floating boathouse, this restaurant-bar with stellar views over Lake Champlain is perfect for kicking back with an evening cocktail or microbrew at sunset.

Nectar's LIVE MUSIC
(www.liveatnectars.com; 188 Main St; ⊙7pm-2am Sun-Tue, 5pm-2am Wed-Sat) Indie darlings Phish got their start here, and the joint still rocks out with a mix of theme nights and live acts.

Red Square LIVE MUSIC
(www.redsquarevt.com; 136 Church St; ⊙4pm-late Sun-Thu, 2pm-late Fri & Sat) With a stylish Soho-like ambience, this Church St institution is best in summertime when live bands play on its outdoor stage.

🛍 Shopping

You'll find boutiques and smart craft shops along Church St Marketplace. Don't miss the **Frog Hollow Craft Center** (www.froghollow. org; 85 Church St), a collective featuring some of the finest work in Burlington.

ⓘ Information

Fletcher Allen Health Care (☑802-847-0000; www.fletcherallen.org; 111 Colchester Ave; ⊙24hr) Vermont's largest hospital.
Lake Champlain Regional Chamber of Commerce (☑877-686-5253, 802-863-3489; www. vermont.org; 60 Main St; ⊙8am-5pm Mon-Fri, 9am-5pm Sat & Sun) Downtown tourist office.

ⓘ Getting There & Away

Greyhound (☑800-231-2222; www.greyhound. com; 219 S Winooski St) offers bus service to Boston and Montreal. **Amtrak's Vermonter train** (☑800-872-7245; www.amtrak.com/ vermonter-train) runs south to Brattleboro, New York City and Washington DC. **Lake Champlain Ferries** (☑802-864-9804; www.ferries.com; King St Dock; adult/child/car $8/3.10/30) runs summer-only ferries across the lake to Port Kent, NY (one hour).

NEW HAMPSHIRE

You're gonna like the scale of things in the Granite State: the towns are small and personable, the mountains majestic and rugged. The heart of New Hampshire is unquestionably the granite peaks of the White Mountain National Forest. Outdoor enthusiasts of all stripes flock to New England's highest range (6288ft at Mt Washington) for cold-weather skiing, summer hiking and the brilliant fall foliage scenery. Oh, and don't be fooled by that politically conservative label that people stick on the state. The state mantra, 'Live Free or Die,' indeed rings from every automobile license plate but, truth be told, residents here pride themselves on their independent spirit more than right-wing politics.

History

Named in 1629 after the English county of Hampshire, New Hampshire was one of the first American colonies to declare its independence from England in 1776. In the 19th century industrialization boom, the state's leading city, Manchester, became such a powerhouse that its textile mills were the world's largest.

New Hampshire played a high-profile role in 1944 when president Franklin D Roosevelt gathered leaders from 44 Allied nations at remote Bretton Woods for a conference to rebuild global capitalism. It was at the Bretton Woods Conference that the World Bank and the International Monetary Fund emerged.

In 1963 New Hampshire, long famed for its anti-tax sentiments, found another way to raise revenue – by becoming the first state in the USA to have a legal lottery.

ⓘ Information

Welcome centers are situated at major state border crossings, including one at the south end of I-93 that's open 24/7.

New Hampshire Division of Parks & Recreation (☑603-271-3556; www.nhstateparks. org) Offers information on a statewide bicycle route system and a very comprehensive camping guide.

New Hampshire Division of Travel & Tourism Development (☑603-271-2665; www.visitnh. gov) Information including ski conditions and fall foliage reports.

Union Leader (www.unionleader.com) The state's largest newspaper.

Portsmouth

America's third-oldest city (1623), Portsmouth wears its history on its sleeve. Its roots are in shipbuilding, but New Hampshire's sole coastal city also has a hip, youthful energy. The old maritime warehouses along the harbor now house cafes and boutiques. Elegant period homes built by shipbuilding tycoons have been converted into B&Bs.

⊙ Sights & Activities

Strawbery Banke Museum   MUSEUM
(☑ 603-433-1100; www.strawberybanke.org; cnr Hancock & Marcy Sts; adult/child $17.50/10; ⊙ 10am-5pm May-Oct) Spread across a 10-acre site, the Strawbery Banke Museum is an eclectic blend of period homes that date back to the 1690s. Costumed guides recount tales of events that took place among the 40 buildings (10 furnished). Strawbery Banke includes **Pitt Tavern** (1766), a hotbed of American revolutionary sentiment, **Goodwin Mansion** (a grand 19th-century house from Portsmouth's most prosperous time) and **Abbott's Little Corner Store** (1943). The admission ticket is good for two consecutive days.

USS Albacore   MUSEUM
(☑ 603-436-3680; http://ussalbacore.org; 600 Market St; adult/child $6/3; ⊙ 9:30am-5pm Jun-mid-Oct, to 4pm Thu-Mon mid-Oct–May) Like a fish out of water, this 205ft-long submarine is now a beached museum on a grassy lawn. Launched from Portsmouth Naval Shipyard in 1953, the *Albacore* was once the world's fastest submarine.

Isles of Shoals Steamship Co   CRUISE
(☑ 603-431-5500; www.islesofshoals.com; 315 Market St; adult/child $28/18; 🚻) From mid-June to October the company runs an excellent tour of the harbor and the historic Isles of Shoals aboard a replica 1900s ferry. Look into the all-day whale-watching and shorter sunset, hip-hop and dinner cruises.

🛏 Sleeping

Ale House Inn   INN $$
(☑ 603-431-7760; www.alehouseinn.com; 121 Bow St; r $150-280; ℗🛜) This brick warehouse for the Portsmouth Brewing Company is now Portsmouth's snazziest boutique, fusing contemporary design with comfort. Rooms are modern with clean lines of white and flatscreen TVs, plush tan sofas fill the suites, and deluxe rooms feature an in-room iPad. Rates include use of vintage cruising bikes.

Inn at Strawbery Banke   B&B $$
(☑ 603-436-7242; www.innatstrawberybanke.com; 314 Court St; r incl breakfast $170-190; ℗🛜) Set amid the historic buildings of Strawbery Banke, this colonial charmer has seven small but attractive rooms, each uniquely set with quilted bedspreads and brass or canopy beds.

🍴 Eating & Drinking

Head to the intersection of Market and Congress Sts, where restaurants and cafes are thick on the ground.

Friendly Toast   DINER $
(113 Congress St; mains $7-12; ⊙ 7am-10pm Sun-Thu, to 2am Fri & Sat; 🛜✍) Fun, whimsical furnishings set the scene for filling sandwiches, omelets, Tex-Mex and vegetarian fare at this retro diner. The breakfast menu is huge and is served around the clock – a good thing since weekend morning waits can be long.

NEW HAMPSHIRE FACTS

Nicknames Granite State, White Mountain State

Population 1.3 million

Area 8968 sq miles

Capital city Concord (population 42,800)

Other cities Manchester (population 109,800), Portsmouth (1.3 million)

Sales tax None

Birthplace of America's first astronaut Alan Shepard (1923–98), *The Da Vinci Code* author Dan Brown (b 1964)

Home of The highest mountains in northeastern USA

Politics New England's most Republican state

Famous for Being the first to vote in US presidential primaries, which gives the state enormous political influence for its size

Most extreme state motto Live Free or Die

Driving distances Boston to Portsmouth 60 miles, Portsmouth to Hanover 118 miles

★ **Black Trumpet Bistro**   INTERNATIONAL **$$$**
(☑603-431-0887; www.blacktrumpetbistro.com; 29 Ceres St; mains $17-38; ☺5:30-9pm) With brick walls and oozing sophisticated ambience, this bistro serves unique combinations (anything from housemade sausages infused with cocoa beans to seared haddock with yuzu and miso). The full menu is also available at its wine bar upstairs, which whips up equally inventive cocktails.

Jumpin' Jays Fish Cafe   SEAFOOD **$$$**
(☑603-766-3474; www.jumpinjays.com; 150 Congress St; mains $20-28; ☺5:30-10pm) This exceptional seafood cafe offers fresh catches of the day simply grilled or seared (with a choice of six sauces, such as 'tamarind and guava' or 'citrus and Dijon'), plus unconventional twists: bouillabaisse with lemongrass and coconut, or haddock Piccata. Add a raw bar and a huge warm and cold appetizer menu plus a buzzing modern space and Jumpin' Jays wins on all counts.

Portsmouth Brewery   MICROBREWERY
(www.portsmouthbrewery.com; 56 Market St; ☺11:30am-12:30am; ☏) Classically set with tin ceilings and exposed brick walls, this airy brewpub serves excellent homegrown pilsners, porters and ales. Come for the beer, not for the pub fare.

Thirsty Moose Taphouse   PUB
(www.thirstymoosetaphouse.com; 21 Congress St; bar snacks $3-11, brunch $10-17; ☺11:30-1am Mon-Sat, 10:30am-1pm Sun) More of a bar than a restaurant, this convivial spot pours more than 100 beers on tap, leaning heavily on New England brews (and a staff that can walk you through most – it's impressive). A fine spot to kick back and relax, bites include poutine (a Montreal fave: fries drenched in cheese and gravy), corn dogs and a handful of salads.

❶ Information

Greater Portsmouth Chamber of Commerce (☑603-436-3988; www.portsmouthchamber. org; 500 Market St; ☺8:30am-5pm Mon-Fri) Also operates an information kiosk in the city center at Market Sq.

Monadnock State Park

The 3165ft **Mt Monadnock** (www.nh-stateparks.org; NH 124; adult/child $4/2), in the southwestern corner of the state, is the most hiked summit in New England.

'Mountain That Stands Alone' in Algonquian, Monadnock is relatively isolated from other peaks, which means hikers who make the 5-mile round-trip to the summit are rewarded with unspoiled views of three states.

Lake Winnipesaukee

A popular summer retreat for families looking for a break from the city, New Hampshire's largest lake stretches 28 miles in length, contains 274 islands and offers abundant opportunities for swimming, boating and fishing.

Weirs Beach

This lakeside town dishes up a curious slice of honky-tonk Americana with its celebrated video arcades, mini-golf courses and go-cart tracks. The **Lakes Region Chamber of Commerce** (☑603-524-5531; www.lakesregion-chamber.org; 383 S Main St, Laconia ; ☺8:30am-4:30pm Mon-Fri) supplies information on the area.

Mount Washington Cruises (☑603-366-5531; www.cruisenh.com; cruises $27-43) operates scenic lake cruises, the pricier ones with champagne brunch, from Weirs Beach aboard the old-fashioned MS *Mount Washington*.

Winnipesaukee Scenic Railroad (☑603-279-5253; www.hoborr.com; adult/child $15/12) offers train rides along the shore of Lake Winnipesaukee.

Wolfeboro

On the opposite side of Lake Winnipesaukee, and a world away from the ticky-tacky commercialism of Weirs Beach, sits genteel Wolfeboro. Anointing itself 'the oldest summer resort in America,' the town is awash with graceful period buildings, including several that are open to the public. The **Wolfeboro Chamber of Commerce** (☑603-569-2200; www.wolfeborochamber.com; 32 Central Ave; ☺10am-3pm Mon-Fri, to noon Sat), in the old train station, has the scoop on everything from boat rentals to lakeside beaches.

Wolfeboro is home to the **Great Waters Music Festival** (☑603-569-7710; www.greatwaters.org; ☺Jul & Aug), featuring folk, jazz and blues artists at venues throughout town.

Off NH 28, about 4 miles north of town, is lakeside **Wolfeboro Campground** (✆603-569-9881; www.wolfeborocampground.com; 61 Haines Hill Rd; tent & RV sites $32; ☺ mid-May–mid-Oct) with 50 wooded campsites.

The classic stay is the **Wolfeboro Inn** (✆603-569-3016; www.wolfeboroinn.com; 90 N Main St; r incl breakfast $189-290; 🛜), the town's principal lodging since 1812. Some of the rooms have balconies overlooking the lake. The inn's cozy pub, **Wolfe's Tavern** (mains $10-26; ☺8am-10pm), offers a varied menu ranging from pizza to seafood. The old-school **Wolfeboro Diner** (5 N Main St; mains $5-12; ☺7am-2pm) hits the mark with juicy cheeseburgers and straightforward breakfast fare at honest prices.

White Mountains

What the Rockies are to Colorado the White Mountains are to New Hampshire. New England's loftiest mountain range is a magnet for adventurers, with boundless opportunities for everything from hiking and kayaking to skiing. Those who prefer to take it in from the comfort of a car seat won't be disappointed either, as scenic drives wind over rugged mountains rippling with waterfalls, sheer rock faces and sharply cut gorges.

You'll find information on the White Mountains at ranger stations throughout the **White Mountain National Forest** (www.fs.fed.us/r9/white) and chambers of commerce in the towns along the way.

Waterville Valley

In the shadow of Mt Tecumseh, Waterville Valley was developed as a resort community during the latter half of the 20th century, when hotels, condos, golf courses and ski trails were all laid out. It's very much a planned community and arguably a bit too groomed but there's plenty to do, including tennis, indoor ice skating, cycling and other family fun. The **Waterville Valley Region Chamber of Commerce** (✆603-726-3804; www.watervillevalleyregion.com; 12 Vintinner Rd, Campton; ☺9am-5pm), off I-93 exit 28, has all the details.

Like many New England ski mountains, the **Waterville Valley Ski Area** (www.waterville.com; lift ticket adult/student $63/53) is open in the summer for mountain biking and hiking.

Mt Washington Valley

Stretching north from the eastern terminus of the Kancamagus Hwy (p236), Mt Washington Valley includes the towns of Conway, North Conway, Intervale, Glen, Jackson and Bartlett. Every conceivable outdoor activity is available. The area's hub and biggest town, North Conway, is also a center for outlet shopping, including some earthy stores including LL Bean.

🏃 Activities

★**Conway Scenic Railroad**   TRAIN (✆603-356-5251; www.conwayscenic.com; NH 16, North Conway; Notch Train adult/child from $27/16, Valley Train from $14/10; ☺daily May-Oct, Sat & Sun Apr & Nov; 🚸) The **Notch Train**, built in 1874 and restored in 1974, offers New England's most scenic journey. The spectacular five- to 5½-hour trip passes through Crawford Notch. Accompanying live commentary recounts the railroad's history and folklore. Reservations required.

Alternatively, the same company operates the antique steam **Valley Train**, which makes a shorter journey south through the Mt Washington Valley, stopping in Conway and Bartlett. Sunset trains, dining trains and other special events are all available.

Echo Lake State Park   PARK (www.nhstateparks.org; River Rd; adult/child $4/2) Two miles west of North Conway via River Rd, this placid mountain lake lies at the foot of **White Horse Ledge**, a sheer rock wall. A scenic trail circles the lake. There is also a mile-long auto road and hiking trail leading to the 700ft-high

---

WORTH A TRIP

NEW HAMPSHIRE WINE & CHEESE TRAILS

Watch out, Vermont. New Hampshire's small cheese producers are multiplying and small wineries are popping up left and right. The tourism board has put together an excellent leaflet, *New Hampshire Wine & Cheese Trails*, detailing three itineraries across 21 farms and wineries, including a few cider producers. Pick it up from any tourist office or download it from the web (http://agriculture.nh.gov/publications/documents/winecheesepdf.pdf).

DON'T MISS

SCENIC DRIVE: WHITE MOUNTAIN NATIONAL FOREST

One of New England's finest, the 35-mile **Kancamagus Highway (NH 112)** is a beauty of a road cutting through the White Mountain National Forest (p235) between Conway and Lincoln. Laced with excellent hiking trails, scenic lookouts and swimmable streams, this is as natural as it gets. There's absolutely no development along the entire highway, which reaches its highest point at **Kancamagus Pass** (2868ft).

You can pick up brochures and hiking maps at the **Saco Ranger District Office** (☑ 603-447-5448; 33 Kancamagus Hwy; ☉ 8am-4:30pm) at the eastern end of the highway near Conway.

Coming from Conway, 6.5 miles west of the Saco ranger station, you'll see **Lower Falls** on the north side of the road – stop here for the view and a swim. No trip along this highway is complete without taking the 20-minute hike to the breathtaking cascade of **Sabbaday Falls**; the trail begins at Mile 15 on the south side of the road. The best place to spot moose is along the shores of **Lily Pond**; stop at the roadside overview at Mile 18. At the Lincoln Woods ranger station, which is near the Mile 29 marker, cross the suspension footbridge over the river and hike 3 miles to **Franconia Falls**, the finest swimming hole in the entire national forest, complete with a natural rock slide. Parking anywhere along the highway costs $3 per day (honor system) or $5 per week; just fill out an envelope at any of the parking areas.

The White Mountain National Forest is ideal for campers, and you'll find several campgrounds run by the forest service, accessible from the Kancamagus Hwy. Most are on a first-come, first-served basis; pick up a list at the Saco ranger station.

Cathedral Ledge, with panoramic White Mountains views. Both Cathedral Ledge and White Horse Ledge are excellent for rock climbing. This is also a fine spot for swimming and picnicking.

Saco Bound   CANOEING
(☑ 603-447-2177; www.sacobound.com; 2561 E Main/US 302, Conway; rentals per day $28) Saco Bound Inc rents out canoes and kayaks and organizes guided canoe trips, including the introductory trip to Weston's Bridge ($22) and overnight camping trips.

Attitash   SKIING
(☑ 603-374-2368; www.attitash.com; US 302, Bartlett; weekends & holidays lift ticket adult/child 13-18 yr/child 6-12 yr & seniors $70/55/50, weekdays $63/48/39) West of Glen, you can play and stay at Attitash. The resort includes two mountains, Attitash and Bear Peak, which offer a vertical drop of 1750ft, 12 lifts and 70 ski trails. Half the trails are intermediate level, while the other half are equally divided between expert and beginner level. From mid-June to mid-October the resort offers a slew of activities, including an alpine slide, horseback riding, mountain biking, bungy trampolines, a chair-lift ride, a water slide, a climbing wall and a mountain coaster (a roller coaster that barrels down the mountain).

Black Mountain Ski Area   SKIING
(☑ 603-383-4490; www.blackmt.com; NH 16B; weekends & holidays lift ticket adult/child $49/32, weekdays $35/25; ⊞) This smaller ski area has a vertical drop of 1100ft. Forty trails – about equally divided between beginner, intermediate and expert slopes – are served by four lifts. This is a good place for beginners and families with small children.

🛏 Sleeping

North Conway in particular is thick with sleeping options from resort hotels to cozy inns.

White Mountains Hostel   HOSTEL $
(☑ 603-447-1001; www.whitemountainshostel.com; 36 Washington St, Conway; dm/r $24/60; 🖙) Ⓟ Set in an early-1900s farmhouse, New Hampshire's only youth hostel is this cheery place off Main St (NH 16) in Conway. The environmentally conscientious hostel has five bedrooms with bunk beds, four family-size rooms and a communal lounge and kitchen. Excellent hiking and cycling opportunities are just outside the door, and canoeists can easily portage to two nearby rivers. Our only gripe is the location, which puts you 5 miles south of the action in North Conway. This place is smoke- and alcohol-free.

Saco River Camping Area   CAMPGROUND **$**
(☑ 603-356-3360; www.sacorivercampingarea.
com; 1550 NH 16; tent/RV sites $33/39; ☺ May–
mid-Oct; 🛜 ♨) A riverside campground, away
from the highway, with 140 wooded and
open sites as well as rustic huts (literally
walls and a roof; no electricity or kitchen).
Canoe and kayak rental available.

Cranmore Inn   B&B **$$**
(☑ 603-356-5502; www.cranmoreinn.com; 80 Kear-
sarge St; r incl breakfast $99-169; 🛜 ♨) The Cran-
more has been operating as a country inn
since 1863, and it has been known as reliably
good value for much of that time. Traditional
country decor predominates, meaning lots
of floral and frills. In addition to standard
rooms, there is one two-room suite and one
apartment with a kitchen, and there's a hot
tub on site, perfect for post-hike sore muscles.

🍴 Eating

Peach's   CAFE **$**
(www.peachesnorthconway.com; 2506 White Moun-
tain Hwy; mains $6-11; ☺ 7am-2:30pm) Away
from the in-town bustle, this perennially
popular little house is an excellent option for
soups, sandwiches and breakfast. Who can
resist fruit-smothered waffles and pancakes
and fresh-brewed coffee, served in some-
body's cozy living room?

★**Moat Mountain Smoke
House & Brewing Co**   PUB **$$**
(☑ 603-356-6381; www.moatmountain.com; 3378
White Mountain Hwy; mains $10-24; ☺ 11:30am-
11pm) Come here for a variety of American
with a nod to southern fare: BBQ Reuben
sandwiches, bowls of beefy chili, juicy burgers, luscious salads, wood-grilled pizzas and
cornmeal-crusted catfish. Wash it down with
one of the eight brews made on-site. The
friendly bar is also a popular local hangout.

ℹ Information

Mt Washington Valley Chamber of Commerce
(☑ 603-356-5701; www.mtwashingtonvalley.
org; 2617 White Mountain Hwy; ☺ 9am-5pm)
Tourist information just south of the town
center. Hours are notoriously unreliable.

North Woodstock & Lincoln

You'll pass right through the twin towns of
Lincoln and North Woodstock on your way
between the Kancamagus Hwy (p236) and
Franconia Notch State Park, so it's a handy
place to break for a bite or a bed. The towns

straddle the Pemigewasset River at the intersection of NH 112 and US 3. If you're ready
for some action, **Loon Mountain** (☑ 603-
745-8111; www.loonmtn.com; Kancamagus Hwy, Lincoln; tubing walk-up/lift $10/16, gondola adult/child
$17/11, lift ticket adult/child 13-18/child 6-12 & seniors
$79/69/59; ☺ tubing 6-9:40pm Wed-Sun, gondola
9:30am-5:30pm late Jun–mid-Oct) offers winter
skiing and snowboarding, and in summer
has mountain-bike trails, climbing walls and
New Hampshire's longest gondola ride. Or
ratchet the adrenaline up a notch by zipping
2000ft down a hillside while strapped to just
a cable with the treetop zip line at **Alpine Adventure** (☑ 603-745-9911; www.alpinezipline.com;
41 Main St, Lincoln; zips $92; ☺ 9am-4pm).

🛏 Sleeping & Eating

Woodstock Inn   INN **$$**
(☑ 603-745-3951; www.woodstockinnnh.com; US 3;
r incl breakfast with/without bath from $120/78; 🛜)
This Victorian country inn is North Wood-
stock's centerpiece. It features 33 individu-
ally appointed rooms across five separate
buildings (three in a cluster, two across the
street), each with modern amenities but old-
fashioned style. For dinner, you have your
choice of the on-site upscale restaurant and
microbrewery (Woodstock Station & Micro-
brewery), with outdoor seating on the lovely
flower-filled patio.

Woodstock Inn Station & Brewery   PUB **$$**
(☑ 603-745-3951; US 3; mains $12-28; ☺ 11:30am-
10pm) Formerly a railroad station, this eatery tries to be everything to everyone. In the
end, with more than 150 items, it can probably satisfy just about any food craving, but
pasta, sandwiches and burgers are the most
interesting. The beer-sodden rear tavern
here is one of the most happening places in
this neck of the woods.

ℹ Information

Lincoln/Woodstock Chamber of Commerce
(☑ 603-745-6621; www.lincolnwoodstock.com;
Main St/NH 112, Lincoln; ☺ 9am-5pm Mon-Fri)
Offers area information.

Franconia Notch State Park

Franconia Notch is the most celebrated
mountain pass in New England, a narrow
gorge shaped over the eons by a rushing
stream slicing through the craggy granite.
I-93, in places feeling more like a country
road than a highway, runs straight through
the state park. The **Franconia Notch State**

Park visitor center (☎603-745-8391; www.franconianotchstatepark.com; I-93, exit 34A), which is 4 miles north of North Woodstock, can give you details on hikes in the park, ranging from short nature walks to day-long treks.

◉ Sights & Activities

★ Frost Place   HISTORIC SITE
(☎603-823-5510; www.frostplace.org; 158 Ridge Rd, Franconia; adult/child $5/3; ☺1-5pm Sat & Sun late May-Jun, 1-5pm Wed-Mon Jul–mid-Oct) Robert Frost (1874–1963) was America's most renowned and best-loved poet in the mid-20th century. For several years he lived with his wife and children on a farm near Franconia, now known as the Frost Place. Many of his best and most famous poems describe life on this farm and the scenery surrounding it, including 'The Road Not Taken' and 'Stopping by Woods on a Snowy Evening.' The farmhouse has been kept as faithful to the period as possible, with numerous exhibits of Frost memorabilia.

Cannon Mountain
Aerial Tramway   CABLE CAR
(☎603-823-8800; www.cannonmt.com; I-93, exit 34B; round-trip adult/child $15/12; ☺9am-5pm late May–mid-Oct; ♿) This tramway shoots up the side of Cannon Mountain, offering a breathtaking view of Franconia Notch. In 1938 the first passenger aerial tramway in North America was installed on this slope. It was replaced in 1980 by the current, larger cable car, capable of carrying 80 passengers up to the summit of Cannon Mountain in five minutes – a 2022ft, 1-mile ride. Or, visitors can hike up the mountain and take the tramway down.

Flume Gorge   HIKING
(www.flumegorge.com; adult/child $14/11; ☺9am-5pm May-Oct) To see this natural wonder, take the 2-mile self-guided nature walk that includes the 800ft boardwalk through the Flume, a natural cleft (12ft to 20ft wide) in the granite bedrock. The granite walls tower 70ft to 90ft above you, with moss and plants growing from precarious niches and crevices. Signs along the way explain how nature formed this natural phenomenon. A nearby covered bridge is thought to be one of the oldest in the state, perhaps erected as early as the 1820s.

Echo Lake   BEACH
(☎603-823-8800; I-93, exit 34C; adult/child $4/2; ☺10am-5:30pm) Despite its proximity to the highway, this little lake at the foot of Cannon Mountain is a pleasant place to pass an afternoon swimming, kayaking or canoeing (rentals from $11 per hour) in the crystal-clear waters. And many people do. The small beach gets packed, especially on weekends.

⌴ Sleeping

Lafayette Place Campground   CAMPGROUND $
(☎603-271-3628; www.reserveamerica.com; campsites $21; ☺mid-May–early Oct) This popular campground has 97 wooded tent sites that are in heavy demand in summer. Reservations are accepted for 88 of the sites. For the others, arrive early in the day and hope for the best. Many of the state park's hiking trails start here.

Bretton Woods & Crawford Notch

Before 1944, Bretton Woods was known primarily as a low-key retreat for wealthy visitors who patronized the majestic Mt Washington Hotel. After President Roosevelt chose the hotel for the historic conference that established a new post-WWII economic order, the town's name gained worldwide recognition. The countryside, with Mt Washington looming above it, is as magnificent today as it was back then. The **Twin Mountain–Bretton Woods Chamber of Commerce** (☎800-245-8946; www.twinmountain.org; cnr US 302 & US 3) has details on the area.

The region's largest ski area, **Bretton Woods Ski Station** (☎603-278-3320; www.brettonwoods.com; US 302; weekends & holidays lift ticket adult/child 13-17/child 6-12 & seniors $79/64/49, weekdays $54/43/33) offers downhill and cross-country skiing as well as a zip line.

US 302 heads south from Bretton Woods to Crawford Notch (1773ft) through stunning mountain scenery ripe with towering cascades. **Crawford Notch State Park** (☎603-374-2272; www.nhstateparks.org; adult/child $4/2) maintains an extensive system of hiking trails, including short hikes around a pond and to a waterfall, and a longer trek up Mt Washington.

⌴ Sleeping

Dry River Campground   CAMPGROUND $
(☎603-271-3628; www.reserveamerica.org; US 302; campsites $25; ☺late May-early Oct) Near the southern end of Crawford Notch State Park, this quiet state-run campground has 36 tent sites with a nicely kept bathhouse, showers and laundry facilities. Thirty of the sites can be reserved in advance.

★ **Omni Mt Washington Hotel & Resort** HOTEL $$$
(📞 603-278-1000; www.brettonwoods.com; 310 Mt Washington Hotel Rd, Bretton Woods; r $299-480, ste $560; ✳@🐾🕏) Open since 1902, this grand hotel maintains a sense of fun – note the moose's head overlooking the lobby and the framed local wildflowers in many of the guest rooms. Also offers 27 holes of golf, red-clay tennis courts, an equestrian center and a spa. There's a $25 daily resort fee.

Mt Washington

From Pinkham Notch (2032ft), on NH 16 about 11 miles north of North Conway, a system of hiking trails provides access to the natural beauties of the Presidential Range, including lofty Mt Washington (6288ft), the highest mountain east of the Mississippi and north of the Smoky Mountains.

Hikers need to be prepared: Mt Washington's weather is notoriously severe and can turn on a dime. Dress warmly – not only does the mountain register New England's coldest temperatures (in summer, the average at the summit is 45°F/7°C) but unrelenting winds make it feel colder than the thermometer reading. In fact, Mt Washington holds the record for the USA's strongest wind gust – 231mph!

The **Pinkham Notch Visitor Center** (📞 603-466-2727; www.outdoors.org; NH 16; ⏲6:30am-10pm), run by the Appalachian Mountain Club (AMC), is the area's informational nexus for like-minded adventurers and a good place to buy hiking necessities, including topographic trail maps and the handy *AMC White Mountain Guide*.

One of the most popular trails up Mt Washington begins at the visitor center and runs 4.2 strenuous miles to the summit, taking four to five hours to reach the top and a bit less on the way down.

If your quads aren't up for a workout, the **Mt Washington Auto Road** (📞 603-466-3988; www.mountwashingtonautoroad.com; off NH 16; car & driver $26, extra adult/child $8/6; ⏲mid-May–mid-Oct), 2.5 miles north of Pinkham Notch Camp, offers easier summit access, weather permitting.

While purists walk and the out-of-shape drive, the quaintest way to reach the summit is to take the **Mt Washington Cog Railway** (📞 603-278-5404; www.thecog.com; adult/child $62/39; ⏲May-Oct). Since 1869, coal-fired steam-powered locomotives have followed a

3.5-mile track up a steep mountainside trestle for a jaw-dropping excursion.

Dolly Copp Campground (📞 603-466-2713; www.campsnh.com; NH 16; tent/RV sites $22/26; ⏲mid-May–mid-Oct), a USFS campground 6 miles north of the AMC's Pinkham Notch facilities, has 176 simple campsites.

Hanover

The archetypal New England college town, Hanover has a town green that is bordered on all four sides by the handsome brick edifices of Dartmouth College. Virtually the whole town is given over to this Ivy League school; chartered in 1769, Dartmouth is the nation's ninth-oldest college.

Main St, rolling down from the green, is surrounded by perky pubs, shops and cafes that cater to the collegian crowd.

⊙ Sights

Dartmouth College COLLEGE
(www.dartmouth.edu) Hanover is all about Dartmouth College, so hit the campus. Join a free student-guided **campus walking tour** (📞 603-646-2875) or just pick up a map at the admissions office and head off on your own. Don't miss the **Baker-Berry Library**, splashed with the grand *Epic of American Civilization,* painted by the outspoken Mexican muralist José Clemente Orozco (1883–1949), who taught at Dartmouth in the 1930s.

Hood Museum of Art MUSEUM
(📞 603-646-2808; E Wheelock St; ⏲10am-5pm Tue-Sat, to 9pm Wed, noon-5pm Sun) **FREE** Shortly after the university's founding in 1769 Dartmouth began to acquire artifacts of artistic or historical interest. Since then the collection has expanded to include nearly 70,000 items, which are housed at the Hood Museum of Art. The collection is particularly strong in American pieces, including Native American art. One of the highlights is a set of Assyrian reliefs from the Palace of Ashurnasirpal that date to the 9th century BC. Special exhibits often feature contemporary artists.

🛏 Sleeping & Eating

Storrs Pond Recreation Area CAMPGROUND $
(📞 603-643-2134; www.storrspond.com; NH 10; tent/RV sites $28/36; ⏲late May–early Sep; 🕏) In addition to 37 woodsy sites next to a 15-acre pond, this private campground has tennis courts and two sandy beaches for

swimming. From I-89 exit 13, take NH 10 north and look for signs.

Hanover Inn INN $$$
(☎800-443-7024, 603-643-4300; www.hanoverinn.com; cnr W Wheelock & S Main Sts; r from $280; ☎) Owned by Dartmouth College, Hanover's loveliest guesthouse has nicely appointed rooms with elegant wood furnishings. It has a wine bar and an award-winning restaurant on site.

Lou's DINER $
(www.lousrestaurant.net; 30 S Main St; mains $6-12; ☺6am-3pm Mon-Fri, 7am-3pm Sat & Sun) A Dartmouth institution since 1947, this is Hanover's oldest establishment, always packed with students meeting for a coffee or perusing their books. From the retro tables or the Formica-topped counter, order typical diner food: eggs, sandwiches and burgers. The bakery items are also highly recommended.

Canoe Club Bistro CAFE $$
(☎603-643-9660; www.canoeclub.us; 27 S Main St; mains $10-23; ☺11:30am-11:30pm) ✐ This smart cafe does a fine job with grilled food – not just burgers and steaks, but also tasty treats such as duck breast with fig port glaze. There's also live entertainment nightly – anything from acoustic to jazz.

☷ Drinking & Entertainment

Murphy's on the Green PUB
(☎603-643-4075; 11 S Main St; mains $8-18; ☺11am-12:30am) This classic collegiate tavern is where students and faculty meet over pints (it carries over 10 beers on tap, including local microbrews like Long Trail Ale) and satisfying pub fare (mains $8 to $18). Stained-glass windows and churchpew seating enhance the cozy atmosphere.

Hopkins Center for the Arts PERFORMING ARTS
(☎603-646-2422; www.hop.dartmouth.edu; 2 E Wheelock St) A long way from the big-city lights of New York and Boston, Dartmouth hosts its own entertainment at this outstanding performing arts venue. The season brings everything from movies to live performances by international companies.

❶ Information

Hanover Area Chamber of Commerce (☎603-643-3115; www.hanoverchamber.org; 53 S Main St, Suite 216; ☺9am-4pm Mon-Fri) For tourist information. It's inside the Nugget Building and also maintains an information booth on the village green, staffed July to mid-September.

MAINE

Maine is New England's frontier – a land so vast it could swallow the region's five other states with scarcely a gulp. The sea looms large with mile after mile of sandy beaches, craggy sea cliffs and quiet harbors. While time-honored fishing villages and seaside lobster joints are the fame of Maine, inland travel also offers ample reward. Maine's rugged interior is given over to rushing rivers, dense forests and lofty mountains aching to be explored.

As a traveler in Maine, your choices are as spectacularly varied as the landscape. You can opt to sail serenely along the coast on a graceful schooner or rip through whitewater rapids on a river raft, spend the night in an old sea captain's home-turned-B&B, or camp among the moose on a backwoods lake.

History

It's estimated that 20,000 Native Americans from tribes known collectively as Wabanaki ('People of the Dawn') inhabited Maine when the first Europeans arrived. The French and English vied to establish colonies in Maine during the 1600s but, deterred by the harsh winters, these settlements failed.

In 1652 Massachusetts annexed the territory of Maine to provide a front line of defense against potential attacks during the French and Indian War. And Maine at times did indeed become a battlefield between English colonists in New England and French forces in Canada. In the early 19th century, in an attempt to settle sparsely populated Maine, 100-acre homesteads were offered free to settlers willing to farm the land. In 1820 Maine broke from Massachusetts and entered the Union as a state.

In 1851 Maine became the first state to ban the sale of alcoholic beverages, the start of a temperance movement that eventually took hold throughout the United States. It wasn't until 1934 that Prohibition was finally lifted.

❶ Information

If you're entering the state on I-95 heading north, stop at the well-stocked visitor information center on the highway.

Maine Bureau of Parks and Land (☎800-332-1501; www.campwithme.com) Offers camping in 12 state parks.

Maine Office of Tourism (☎888-624-6345; www.visitmaine.com; 59 State House Station,

Augusta) These folks maintain information centers on the principal routes into the state: Calais, Fryeburg, Hampden, Houlton, Kittery and Yarmouth. Each facility is open 9am to 5pm, with extended hours in summer.

Southern Maine Coast

Maine's most touristed quarter, this seaside region lures visitors with its sandy beaches, resort towns and outlet shopping. The best place to stop for the latter is the southernmost town of Kittery, which is chockablock with outlet stores.

Ogunquit

Aptly named, Ogunquit means 'Beautiful Place by the Sea' in the native Abenaki tongue, and its 3-mile beach has long been a magnet for summer visitors. Ogunquit Beach, a sandy barrier beach, separates the Ogunquit River from the Atlantic Ocean, offering beachgoers the appealing option to swim in cool ocean surf or in the warmer, calmer cove.

As a New England beach destination, Ogunquit is second only to Provincetown for the number of gay travelers who vacation here. Most of the town lies along Main St (US 1), lined with restaurants, shops and motels. For waterfront dining and boating activities head to Perkins Cove at the south end of town.

◉ Sights & Activities

A highlight is walking the scenic 1.5-mile **Marginal Way**, the coastal footpath that skirts the 'margin' of the sea from Shore Rd, near the center of town, to Perkins Cove. A sublime stretch of family-friendly coastline, **Ogunquit Beach**, also called Main Beach by locals, begins right in the town center at the end of Beach St.

Finestkind Scenic Cruises CRUISES
(☎207-646-5227; www.finestkindcruises.com; Perkins Cove; adult/child from $17/9) Offers many popular trips, including a 50-minute lobstering trip, a sunset cocktail cruise and a two-hour cruise aboard the twin-sailed *Cricket*.

🛏 Sleeping

Pinederosa Camping CAMPGROUND $
(☎207-646-2492; www.pinederosa.com; 128 North Village Rd, Wells; campsites $30; ☒) This wholesome, wooded campground has 162 well-tended sites, some of which overlook the Ogunquit River. Amenities include a lovely in-ground pool, camp store and summer shuttle to Ogunquit Beach, about 3 miles away.

Gazebo Inn B&B $$
(☎207-646-3733; www.gazeboinnogt.com; 572 Main St; r incl breakfast $109-245; ☏☒) This stately 1847 farmhouse features 14 rooms that feel more like a private boutique hotel. Rustic-chic touches include heated wood floors, stone fireplaces in the bathrooms, and a media room with beamed ceilings and a wall-sized TV.

Ogunquit Beach Inn B&B $$
(☎207-646-1112; www.ogunquitbeachinn.com; 67 School St; r incl breakfast $139-179; @☏) In a tidy little arts-and-crafts-style bungalow, this gay-and-lesbian-friendly B&B has colorful, homey rooms and chatty owners who know all about the best new bistros and bars in town. The central location makes walking to dinner a breeze.

✖ Eating

You'll find Ogunquit's restaurants on the south side of town at Perkins Cove and in the town center along Main St.

MAINE FACTS

Nickname Pine Tree State

Population 1.3 million

Area 35,387 sq miles

Capital city Augusta (population 18,700)

Other cities Portland (population 66,400)

Sales tax 5%

Birthplace of Poet Henry Wadsworth Longfellow (1807–82)

Home of Horror novelist Stephen King

Politics Split between Democrats and Republicans

Famous for Lobster, moose, blueberries, LL Bean

State drink Maine gave the world Moxie, America's first (1884) and spunkiest soft drink

Driving distances Portland to Acadia National Park 160 miles, Portland to Boston 150 miles

Maine Coast

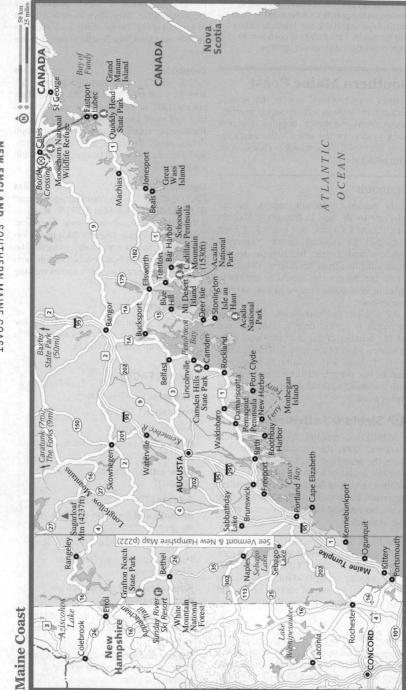

CANADA

Nova Scotia

Bay of Fundy

St George

Eastport
Lubec

Grand
Manan
Island

Quoddy Head
State Park

CANADA

Calais
Border
Crossing

Mooschorn National
Wildlife Refuge

Machias

Jonesport

Great
Wass
Island

Beals

ATLANTIC
OCEAN

Schoodic
Peninsula

Ellsworth

Trenton

Bar Harbor

Cadillac
Mountain
(1530ft)

Acadia
National
Park

Blue
Hill

Mt Desert
Island

Deer Isle

Stonington

Isle au
Haut

Bangor

Bucksport

Penobscot
Bay

Acadia
National
Park

Baxter
State Park
(50mi)

Belfast

Camden

Rockland

Lincolnville

Camden Hills
State Park

Port Clyde

New Harbor

Monhegan
Island

Damariscotta

Pemaquid
Peninsula

Boothbay
Harbor

Ferry

Ferry

Waldoboro

Waterville

AUGUSTA

Kennebec R

Skowhegan

Caratunk (7mi)
The Forks (9mi)

Longfellow Mountains

Sugarloaf
Mtn (4237ft)

Rangeley

Errol

Aziscohos
Lake

Colebrook

NEW
HAMPSHIRE

Grafton Notch
State Park

Bethel

Appalachian Trail

Sunday River
Ski Resort

White
Mountain
National
Forest

See Vermont & New Hampshire Map (p222)

Naples

Sebago
Lake

Sebago
Lake

Bath

Brunswick

Sabbathday
Lake

Freeport

Casco Bay

Portland

Cape Elizabeth

Kennebunkport

Ogunquit

Kittery

Portsmouth

Maine Turnpike

Rochester

Laconia

CONCORD

Lake
Winnipesaukee

50 km
25 miles

Bread & Roses
BAKERY $

(www.breadandrosesbakery.com; 246 Main St; snacks $3-9; ⊙7am-7pm; ⌨) 🍴 Get your coffee and blueberry-scone fix at this teeny slip of a bakery, in the heart of downtown Ogunquit. The cafe fare, such as veggie burritos and organic egg-salad sandwiches, is good for a quick lunch. No seating.

Lobster Shack
SEAFOOD $$

(110 Perkins Cove Rd; mains $10-25; ⊙11am-8pm) If you want good seafood and aren't particular about the view, this reliable joint serves lobster in all its various incarnations, from lobster rolls to lobster in the shell.

Barnacle Billy's
SEAFOOD $$$

(☑207-646-5575; www.barnbilly.com; 183 Shore Rd; mains $12-35; ⊙11am-9pm) This big, noisy barn of a restaurant overlooking Perkins Cove is a longtime favorite for casual seafood: steamers, crab rolls, clam chowder, and, of course, whole lobsters.

☆ Entertainment

Ogunquit Playhouse
THEATER

(☑207-646-5511; www.ogunquitplayhouse.org; 10 Main St; 🎭) First opened in 1933, presents both showy Broadway musicals and children's theater each summer.

ℹ Information

Ogunquit Chamber of Commerce (☑20
7-646-2939; www.ogunquit.org; 36 Main St; ⊙9am-5pm Mon-Fri, 10am-3pm Sat & Sun) Located on US 1, near the Ogunquit Playhouse and just south of the town's center.

Kennebunkport

On the Kennebunk River, Kennebunkport fills with tourists in summer who come to stroll the streets, admire the century-old mansions and get their fill of sea views. Be sure to take a drive along **Ocean Ave**, which runs along the east side of the Kennebunk River and then follows a scenic stretch of the Atlantic that holds some of Kennebunkport's finest estates, including the summer home of former president George Bush Snr.

Three public beaches extend along the west side of the Kennebunk River and are known collectively as **Kennebunk Beach**. The center of town spreads out from Dock Sq, which is along ME 9 (Western Ave) at the east side of the Kennebunk River bridge.

The **Kennebunk/Kennebunkport Chamber of Commerce** (☑207-967-0857; www.visit-thekennebunks.com; 17 Western Ave; ⊙10am-5pm Mon-Fri year-round, to 3pm Sat Jun-Sep) has tourist information.

🛏 Sleeping

Franciscan Guest House
GUESTHOUSE $$

(☑207-967-4865; www.franciscanguesthouse. com; 26 Beach Ave; r incl breakfast $89-159; 🛜 ❄) You can almost smell the blackboard chalk inside this high-school-turned-guesthouse, on the peaceful grounds of the St Anthony Monastery. Guest rooms, once classrooms, are basic and unstylish – acoustic tile, faux-wood paneling, motel beds. If you don't mind getting your own sheets out of the supply closet (there's no daily maid service), staying here's great value and a unique experience.

Colony Hotel
HOTEL $$

(☑207-967-3331; www.thecolonyhotel.com; 140 Ocean Ave; r incl breakfast $129-299; 🛜 ❄) Built in 1914, this grand dame of a summer resort evokes the splendor of bygone days. Inside, the 124 old-fashioned rooms have vintage cabbage-rose wallpaper and authentically creaky floors. Outside, ladies recline on Adirondack chairs on the manicured lawn, while young men in polo shirts play badminton nearby and children splash around at the private beach across the street.

Green Heron Inn
INN $$$

(☑207-967-3315; www.greenheroninn.com; 126 Ocean Ave; r incl breakfast $190-225; ❄@🛜) In a fine neighborhood, overlooking a picturesque cove, this engaging inn has 10 cozy rooms and is within walking distance of a sandy beach and several restaurants. Breakfast is a multicourse event.

🍴 Eating

Clam Shack
SEAFOOD $$

(2 Western Ave; mains $7-22; ⊙11am-9:30pm) Standing in line at this teeny gray hut that's perched on stilts above the river is a time-honored Kennebunkport summer tradition. Order a box of fat, succulent fried whole-belly clams or a 1lb lobster roll, which is served with your choice of mayo or melted butter. Outdoor seating only.

Bandaloop
BISTRO $$$

(☑207-967-4994; www.bandaloop.biz; 2 Dock Sq; mains $17-27; ⊙5-9:30pm; ⌨) 🍴 Local, organic and deliciously innovative, running the gamut from grilled rib-eye steak to baked tofu with hemp-seed crust. For the perfect starter, order the skillet-steamed Casco Bay mussels and a Peak's organic ale.

Hurricane
AMERICAN $$$

(✆207-967-9111; www.hurricanerestaurant.com; 29 Dock Sq; mains $12-45; ⊙11:30am-9:30pm) On Dock Sq, this popular fine-dining bistro specializes in the classics: crab-stuffed baked lobster, rack of lamb in a red wine reduction, bread pudding. Small plates are more modern and creative: tempura-fried spicy tuna rolls, duck-liver mousse with fig jam. Crowds tend to be middle-aged, well-heeled and high on wine.

Portland

The 18th-century poet Henry Wadsworth Longfellow referred to his childhood city as the 'jewel by the sea' and, thanks to a hefty revitalization effort, Portland once again sparkles. Its lively waterfront, burgeoning gallery scene and manageable size add up to great exploring. Foodies, rev up your taste buds: cutting-edge cafes and chef-driven restaurants have turned Portland into the hottest dining scene north of Boston.

Portland sits on a hilly peninsula surrounded on three sides by water: Back Cove, Casco Bay and the Fore River. It's easy to find your way around. Commercial St (US 1A) runs along the waterfront through the Old Port, while the parallel Congress St is the main thoroughfare through downtown.

◉ Sights

Old Port
NEIGHBORHOOD

Handsome 19th-century brick buildings line the streets of the Old Port. Portland's most enticing shops, pubs and restaurants are located within this five-square-block district. By night, flickering gas lanterns add to the atmosphere. What to do here? Eat some wicked fresh seafood, down a local microbrew, buy a nautical-themed T-shirt from an up-and-coming designer, peruse the many tiny local art galleries. Don't forget to wander the authentically stinky wharfs, ducking into a fishmongers to order some lobsters.

Portland Museum of Art
MUSEUM

(✆207-775-6148; www.portlandmuseum.org; 7 Congress Sq; adult/child $12/6, 5-9pm Fri free; ⊙10am-5pm Sat-Thu, to 9pm Fri, closed Mon mid-Oct–May) Founded in 1882, this well-respected museum houses an outstanding collection of American artists. Maine artists, including Winslow Homer, Edward Hopper, Louise Nevelson and Andrew Wyeth, are particularly well represented. You'll also find a few works by European masters, including Degas, Picasso and Renoir. The collections are spread across three separate buildings. The majority of works are found in the postmodern Charles Shipman Payson building, designed by the firm of famed architect IM Pei. The 1911 beaux-arts-style LDM Sweat Memorial Gallery and the 1801 Federal-style McLellan House hold the 19th-century American art collection.

Fort Williams Park
LIGHTHOUSE

(⊙sunrise-sunset) ⚑ FREE Four miles southeast of Portland on Cape Elizabeth, 90-acre Fort Williams Park is worth visiting simply for the panoramas and picnic possibilities. Stroll around the ruins of the fort, a late-19th-century artillery base, checking out the WWII bunkers and gun emplacements (a German U-boat was spotted in Casco Bay in 1942) that still dot the rolling lawns. Strange as it may seem, the fort actively guarded the entrance to Casco Bay until 1964.

Adjacent to the fort stands the **Portland Head Light**, the oldest of Maine's 52 functioning lighthouses. It was commissioned by George Washington in 1791 and staffed until 1989, when machines took over. The keeper's house has been passed into service as the **Museum at Portland Head Light** (✆207-799-2661; www.portlandheadlight.com; 1000 Shore Rd; adult/child $2/1; ⊙10am-4pm Jun-Oct), which traces the maritime and military history of the region.

Portland Observatory Museum
HISTORIC SITE

(✆207-774-5561; www.portlandlandmarks.org; 138 Congress St; adult/child $8/5; ⊙10am-5pm late May-early Oct) History buffs won't want to miss this hilltop museum, built in 1807 as a maritime signal station to direct ships entering the bustling harbor. Its function was roughly on a par with that of an airport traffic-control tower today. From the top of this observatory, the last of its kind remaining in the USA, you'll be rewarded with a sweeping view of Casco Bay.

Longfellow House
HISTORIC BUILDING

(✆207-879-0427; www.mainehistory.org; 489 Congress St; adult/child $12/3; ⊙10am-5pm Mon-Sat, noon-5pm Sun May-Oct) The revered American poet Henry Wadsworth Longfellow grew up in this Federal-style house, built in 1788 by his Revolutionary War hero grandfather. The house has been impeccably restored to look like it did in the 1800s, complete with original furniture and artifacts.

Children's Museum of Maine   MUSEUM
(☏207-828-1234; www.childrensmuseumofme.org; 142 Free St; admission $9; ☺10am-5pm Mon-Sat, noon-5pm Sun, closed Mon Sep-May; ♿) Kids aged zero to 10 shriek and squeal as they haul traps aboard a replica lobster boat, milk a fake cow on a model farm, or monkey around on an indoor rock-climbing wall. The highlight of this ultra-interactive museum might be the 3rd-floor camera obscura, where a single pinhole projects a panoramic view of downtown Portland.

🏃 Activities

For a whole different angle on Portland and Casco Bay, hop on one of the boats offering narrated scenic cruises out of Portland Harbor.

Casco Bay Lines   CRUISE
(☏207-774-7871; www.cascobaylines.com; 56 Commercial St; adult $13-24, child $7-11) This outfit cruises the Casco Bay islands delivering mail, freight and visitors. It also offers cruises to Bailey Island (adult/child $25/12).

Maine Island Kayak Company   KAYAKING
(☏207-766-2373; www.maineislandkayak.com; 70 Luther St, Peaks Island; tour $70; ☺May-Nov) On Peak Island, a 15-minute cruise from downtown on the Casco Bay Lines, this well-run outfitter offers fun day and overnight trips exploring the islands of Casco Bay.

Portland Schooner Company   CRUISE
(☏207-776-2500; www.portlandschooner.com; 56 Commercial St; adult/child $35/10; ☺May-Oct) Offers tours aboard an elegant, early-20th-century schooner. In addition to two-hour sails, you can book overnight tours ($240 per person, including dinner and breakfast).

Maine Narrow Gauge Railroad Co & Museum   RAILROAD
(☏207-828-0814; www.mngrr.org; 58 Fore St; adult/child $10/6; ☺10am-4pm mid-May–Oct, shorter hours off-season; ♿) Ride antique steam trains along Casco Bay; journeys depart on the hour.

🛌 Sleeping

Portland has a healthy selection of midrange and upscale B&Bs, though very little at the budget end. The most idyllic accommodations are in the old town houses and grand Victorians in the West End.

Inn at St John   INN $
(☏207-773-6481; www.innatstjohn.com; 939 Congress St; r incl breakfast $79-169; P🖨) This turn-of-the-century hotel has a stuck-in-time feel, from the old-fashioned pigeonhole mailboxes behind the lobby desk to the narrow, sweetly floral rooms. Ask for a room away from noisy Congress St.

Morrill Mansion   B&B $$
(☏207-774-6900; www.morrillmansion.com; 249 Vaughan St; r incl breakfast $149-239; 🖨) Charles Morrill, the original owner of this 19th-century West End town house, made his fortune by founding B&M baked beans, still a staple of Maine pantries. His home has been transformed into a handsome B&B, with seven guest rooms furnished in a trim, classic style. Think hardwood floors, lots of tasteful khaki and taupe shades. Some rooms are a bit cramped; if you need lots of space, try the two-room Morrill Suite.

La Quinta Inn   HOTEL $$
(☏207-871-0611; www.laquinta.com; 340 Park St; r incl breakfast $75-149; ♿@🖨☕) Best value among the chains, La Quinta has well-maintained rooms and a convenient location opposite the ballpark of the Portland Sea Dogs, a Boston Red Sox–affiliate team.

Portland Harbor Hotel   HOTEL $$$
(☏207-775-9090; www.portlandharborhotel.com; 468 Fore St; r from $269; P🖨) This independent hotel has a classically coiffed lobby, where guests relax on upholstered leather chairs surrounding the glowing fireplace. The rooms carry on the classicism, with sunny gold walls and pert blue toile bedspreads. The windows face Casco Bay, the interior garden or the street; garden rooms are quieter. Parking is $16.

🍴 Eating

Two Fat Cats Bakery   BAKERY $
(☏207-347-5144; www.twofatcatsbakery.com; 47 India St; treats $3-7; ☺8am-6pm Mon-Fri, to 5pm Sat, 10am-4pm Sun) Tiny bakery serving pastries, pies, melt-in-your-mouth chocolate-chip cookies and fabulous whoopie pies.

WHOOPIE!

Looking like steroid-pumped Oreos, these marshmallow-cream-filled chocolate snack cakes are a staple of bakeries and seafood-shack dessert menus across the state. Popular both in Maine and in Pennsylvania's Amish country, whoopie pies are said to be so named because Amish farmers would shout 'whoopie!' when they discovered one in their lunch pail. Don't leave the state without trying at least one. For our money, Portland's Two Fat Cats Bakery (p245) has the best.

★ **Green Elephant** VEGETARIAN $$
(☑ 207-347-3111; www.greenelephantmaine.com; 608 Congress St; mains $9-13; ⊘ 11:30am-2:30pm Tue-Sat & 5-9:30pm Tue-Sun; ♫) Even carnivores shouldn't miss the brilliant vegetarian fare at this Zen-chic, Thai-inspired cafe. Start with the crispy spinach wontons, then move on to one of the exotic soy creations, perhaps gingered 'duck' with shiitake mushrooms. Save room for the incredible chocolate-orange mousse pie.

Susan's Fish & Chips SEAFOOD $$
(www.susansfishnchips.com; 1135 Forest Ave/US 302; mains $7-19; ⊘ 11am-8pm) Pop in for fish and chips at this no-fuss eatery on US 302, where the tartar sauce comes in mason jars. Located in a former garage.

J's Oyster SEAFOOD $$
(www.jsoyster.com; 5 Portland Pier; mains $6-24; ⊘ 11:30am-11:30pm Mon-Sat, noon-10:30pm Sun) This well-loved dive has the cheapest raw oysters in town. Eat 'em on the deck overlooking the pier. The oyster-averse have plenty of sandwiches and seafood mains to choose from.

★ **Fore Street** MODERN AMERICAN $$$
(☑ 207-775-2717; www.forestreet.biz; 288 Fore St; mains $20-31; ⊘ 5:30-11pm) Chef-owner Sam Hayward has turned roasting into a high art at Fore Street, one of Maine's most lauded restaurants. Chickens turn on spits in the open kitchen as chefs slide iron kettles of mussels into the wood-burning oven. Local, seasonal eating is taken very seriously here and the menu changes daily to offer what's freshest. A recent dinner included a fresh pea salad, periwinkles (a local shell-

fish) in herbed cream, and roast bluefish with pancetta. The large, noisy dining room nods towards its warehouse past with exposed brick and pine paneling. It's also ecofriendly.

Hugo's FUSION $$$
(☑ 207-774-8538; www.hugos.net; 88 Middle St; mains $24-30; ⊘ 5:30-9pm Tue-Sat) James Beard Award–winning chef Rob Evans presides over this temple of molecular gastronomy. The menu, which changes regularly, might include such palate-challenging dishes as oxtail and monkfish dumplings, crispy fried pig ears, and bacon crème brûlée. The 'blind' tasting menu – diners only find out what they've eaten after they've eaten it – is the culinary equivalent of an avant-garde opera.

🍷 Drinking & Entertainment

Gritty McDuff's Brew Pub BREWPUB
(www.grittys.com; 396 Fore St; ⊘ 11am-1am) Gritty is an apt description for this party-happy Old Port pub. You'll find a generally raucous crowd here drinking excellent beers – Gritty brews its own award-winning ales downstairs.

Big Easy Blues Club CLUB
(www.bigeasyportland.com; 55 Market St; ⊘ 9pm-1am Tue-Sat, 4-9pm Sun, 6-10pm Mon) This small music club features a mostly local lineup of rock, jazz and blues bands, as well as open-mic hip-hop nights.

🛍 Shopping

Go to Exchange and Fore Sts for gallery row.

Portland Farmers Market FARMERS MARKET
(http://portlandmainefarmersmarket.org; ⊘ 7am-noon Sat, to 2pm Mon & Wed) On Saturdays in Deering Oak Park, vendors hawk everything from Maine blueberries to homemade pickles. On Monday and Wednesday the market is in Monument Sq.

Harbor Fish Market FOOD
(www.harborfish.com; 9 Custom House Wharf; ⊘ 7am-noon Mon-Sat) On Custom House Wharf, this iconic fishmonger packs lobsters to ship anywhere in the US.

Maine Potters Market CERAMICS
(www.mainepottersmarket.com; 376 Fore St; ⊘ 10am-8pm Mon-Fri, to 6pm Sat & Sun) A cooperatively owned gallery featuring the work of a dozen or so different Maine ceramists.

❶ Information

Greater Portland Convention & Visitors Bureau (www.visitportland.com; Ocean Gateway Bldg, 239 Park Ave; ⊙8am-5pm Mon-Fri, 10am-5pm Sat)

❶ Getting There & Around

Portland International Jetport (PWM; ☑20 7-874-8877; www.portlandjetport.org) has non-stop flights to cities in the eastern US.

Greyhound (www.greyhound.com) buses and **Amtrak** (☑800-872-7245; www.amtrak.com) trains connect Portland and Boston; both take about 2½ hours and charge $20 to $24 one way.

The local bus **Metro** (www.gpmetrobus.com; fares $1.50), which runs throughout the city, has its main terminus at Monument Sq, the intersection of Elm and Congress Sts.

Central Maine Coast

Midcoast Maine is where the mountains meet the sea. You'll find craggy peninsulas jutting deep into the Atlantic, alluring seaside villages and endless opportunities for hiking, sailing and kayaking.

Freeport

The fame and fortune of Freeport, 16 miles northeast of Portland, began a century ago when Leon Leonwood Bean opened a shop to sell equipment to hunters and fishers heading north into the Maine wilderness. Bean's good value earned him loyal customers. Over the years the **LL Bean store** (www.llbean.com; Main St; ⊙24hr) has expanded to add sportswear to its outdoor gear. Though a hundred other stores have joined the pack, the wildly popular LL Bean is still the epicenter of town.

The Victorian-era **White Cedar Inn** (☑20 7-865-9099; www.whitecedarinn.com; 178 Main St; r incl breakfast $150-185; ☎) is conveniently located within walking distance of the shops. The former home of Arctic explorer Donald MacMillan, it has seven atmospheric rooms, with brass beds and working fireplaces.

For the best atmosphere, head to the casual, harborside **Harraseeket Lunch & Lobster Co** (☑207-865-4888; www.harraseeketlunchandlobster.com; 36 Main St, South Freeport; mains $10-26; ⊙11am-7:45pm, to 8:45pm Jul & Aug; ☷), 3 miles south of Freeport center, for its popular lobster dinners, steamers and fried seafood. Feast at picnic tables within spitting distance of the bay.

Bath

Bath has been renowned for shipbuilding since Colonial times and that remains the raison d'être for the town today. **Bath Iron Works**, one of the largest shipyards in the USA, builds steel frigates and other ships for the US Navy. The substantial **Maine Maritime Museum** (☑207-443-1316; www.mainemaritimemuseum.org; 243 Washington St; adult/child $15/10; ⊙9:30am-5pm), south of the ironworks on the Kennebec River, showcases the town's centuries-old maritime history, which included construction of the six-mast schooner *Wyoming*, the largest wooden vessel ever built in the USA.

Boothbay Harbor

On a fjordlike harbor, this achingly picturesque fishing village with narrow, winding streets is thick with tourists in the summer. Other than eating lobster, the main activity here is hopping on boats. **Balmy Days Cruises** (☑207-633-2284; www.balmydayscruises.com; Pier 8; harbor tour adult/child $15/8, day trip cruise to Monhegan adult/child $32/18, sailing tour $24/18) runs one-hour harbor tour cruises, day trips to Monhegan Island and 1½-hour sailing trips around the scenic islands near Boothbay. The **Boothbay Harbor Region Chamber of Commerce** (☑207-633-2353; www.boothbayharbor.com; 192 Townsend Ave; ⊙8am-5pm Mon-Fri) provides visitor information.

🛏 Sleeping & Eating

Topside Inn　　　　　　　　　　B&B $$
(☑207-633-5404; www.topsideinn.com; 60 McKown St; r incl breakfast $165-275; ☎) Atop McKown Hill, this grand gray mansion has Boothbay's best harbor views. Rooms are elegantly turned out in crisp nautical prints and beachy shades of sage, sea glass and khaki. Main-house rooms have more historic charm, but rooms in the two adjacent modern guesthouses are sunny and lovely, too. Enjoy the sunset from an Adirondack chair on the inn's sloping manicured lawn.

Lobster Dock　　　　　　　　SEAFOOD $$
(www.thelobsterdock.com; 49 Atlantic Ave; mains $10-26; ⊙11:30am-8:30pm) Of all the many lobster joints in Boothbay Harbor, this sprawling wooden waterfront shack is one of the best and cheapest. It serves traditional

fried seafood platters, sandwiches and steamers, but whole, butter-dripping lobster is definitely the main event.

Monhegan Island

This small granite island with high cliffs and crashing surf, 9 miles off the Maine coast, attracts summer day-trippers, artists and nature-lovers who find inspiration in the dramatic views and agreeable isolation. Tidy and manageable, Monhegan is just 1.5 miles long and a half-mile wide. The online **Monhegan Island Visitor's Guide** (www. monheganwelcome.com) has information and accommodation links. Rooms typically book out in summer, so plan ahead if you're not just visiting on a day trip.

In addition to its 17 miles of walking trails, there's an 1824 **lighthouse** with a small museum in the former keeper's house and several **artists studios** that you can poke your head into.

Departing from Port Clyde, the **Monhegan Boat Line** (✆207-372-8848; www.monheganboat.com; round-trip adult/child $32/18) runs

OFF THE BEATEN TRACK

PEMAQUID PENINSULA

Adorning the southernmost tip of the Pemaquid Peninsula, **Pemaquid Point** is one of the most wildly beautiful places in Maine, with its tortured igneous rock formations pounded by treacherous seas. Perched atop the rocks in the 7-acre **Lighthouse Park** (✆207-677-2494; www.bristolparks.org; Pemaquid Point; adult/child $2/free; ☺sunrise-sunset) is the 11,000-candle-power Pemaquid Light, built in 1827, and a star of the 61 surviving lighthouses along the Maine coast, . A climb to the top will reward you with a fine coastal view. You may well be carrying an image of Pemaquid Light in your pocket without knowing it – it's the beauty featured on the back of the Maine state quarter. The keeper's house now serves as the **Fishermen's Museum** (☺9am-5:15pm mid-May–mid-Oct) displaying period photos, old fishing gear and lighthouse paraphernalia. Admission is included in the park fee. Pemaquid Peninsula is 15 miles south of US 1 via ME 130.

three trips daily to Monhegan from late May to mid-October, once a day for the rest of the year. The **MV Hardy III** (✆800-278-3346; www.hardyboat.com; round-trip adult/child $32/18; ☺mid-Jun–Sep) departs for Monhegan twice daily from New Harbor, on the east side of the Pemaquid Peninsula. Both boats take approximately one hour and both have early-morning departures and late-afternoon returns, perfect for day-tripping.

Camden & Around

With rolling hills as a backdrop and a harbor full of sailboats, Camden is a gem. Home to Maine's justly famed fleet of windjammers, it attracts nautical-minded souls. You can get a superb view of pretty Camden and its surroundings by taking the 45-minute climb up Mt Battie in **Camden Hills State Park** (✆207-236-3109; 280 Belfast Rd/US 1; adult/child $4.50/1; ☺7am-sunset) at the north side of Camden.

Lobster fanatics (and who isn't!) won't want to miss the **Maine Lobster Festival** (www.mainelobsterfestival.com; ☺early Aug), New England's ultimate homage to the crusty crustacean, held in nearby Rockland.

The **Camden-Rockport-Lincolnville Chamber of Commerce** (✆207-236-4404; www.camdenme.org; 2 Public Landing; ☺9am-5pm), near the harbor, provides visitor information on the region.

Two miles south of Camden, the sleepy harborside town of Rockport is a much smaller and more peaceful settlement that's known for the world-renowned **Maine Media Workshops** (www.mainemedia.edu; 70 Camden St, Rockport).

🛏 Sleeping & Eating

Whitehall Inn INN $$
(✆207-236-3391; www.whitehall-inn.com; 52 High St, Camden; r incl breakfast $119-230; ☺May-Oct; 🖥) Camden-raised poet Edna St Vincent Millay got her start reciting poetry to guests at this old-fashioned summer hotel. Read about her wild, often tragic life in the inn's Millay Room parlor, which still has the Steinway piano she once played. The 45 rooms have a vintage boarding-house character, some with Victorian striped wallpaper, in-room pedestal sinks and claw-foot tubs. Rocking chairs on the wide front porch are a nice place for evening socializing.

HOIST THE SAILS

Feel the wind in your hair and history at your side aboard the gracious, multimasted sailing ships known as windjammers. The sailing ships, both historic and replicas, gather in the harbors at Camden and neighboring Rockland to take passengers out on day trips and overnight sails.

Day sails cruise for two hours in Penobscot Bay from June to October for around $35 and you can usually book your place on the day. On the Camden waterfront, look for the 86ft wooden tall ship **Appledore** (☎207-236-8353; www.appledore2.com) and the two-masted schooner **Olad** (☎207-236-2323; www.maineschooners.com).

Other schooners make two- to six-day cruises, offer memorable wildlife viewing (seals, whales and puffins) and typically include stops at Acadia National Park, small coastal towns and offshore islands for a lobster picnic.

You can get full details on several glorious options in one fell swoop through the **Maine Windjammer Association** (☎800-807-9463; www.sailmainecoast.com), which represents 13 traditional tall ships, several of which have been designated National Historic Landmarks. Among them is the granddaddy of the schooner trade, the *Lewis R French*, America's oldest (1871) windjammer. Rates range from $400 for a two-day cruise to $1000 for a six-day voyage and are a bargain when you consider they include meals and accommodations. Reservations for the overnight sails are a must. Prices are highest in midsummer. June offers long days, uncrowded harbors and lower rates, though the weather can be cool. Late September, when the foliage takes on autumn colors, captures the scenery at its finest.

★**Shepherd's Pie**　　　　　　AMERICAN $$
(www.shepherdspierockport.com; 18 Central St, Rockport; mains $12-22; ☺5pm-late) Brian Hill, who runs successful restaurant Francine in neighbouring Camden, opened this more laid-back temple of food in a dark-wood pubby space with a tin ceiling. With a menu boasting four main sections – Bar Snacks, From the Grill, Plates and Sides –you can swing by for a bite or a full meal. Choose from usual suspects with a twist: seasonal pickles, smoked alewife (a fish) Caesar, grilled pork chop with apples sauce and salted caramel or buttermilk potatoes.

Cappy's　　　　　　　　　SEAFOOD $$
(www.cappyschowder.com; 1 Main St, Camden; mains $8-17; ☺11am-11pm; ☎) This friendly longtime favorite is better known for its bar and convivial atmosphere than for its food, though it does serve a decent bowl of chowder and other casual New England fare.

Acadia National Park

The only national park in New England, Acadia (www.nps.gov/acad) encompasses an unspoiled wilderness of undulating coastal mountains, towering cliffs, surf-pounded beaches and quiet ponds. The dramatic landscape offers a plethora of activities for both leisurely hikers and adrenaline junkies.

The park was established in 1919 on land that John D Rockefeller donated to the national parks system to save it from encroaching lumber interests. Today you can hike and cycle along the same carriage roads on which Rockefeller once rode his horse and buggy. The park covers over 62 sq miles, including most of mountainous Mt Desert Island and tracts of land on the Schoodic Peninsula and Isle au Haut, and has a wide diversity of wildlife including moose, puffins and bald eagles.

◉ Sights & Activities

◉ Park Loop Road

Park Loop Rd, the main sightseeing jaunt through the park, takes you to several of Acadia's highlights. If you're up for a bracing swim or just want to stroll Acadia's longest beach, stop at **Sand Beach**. About a mile beyond Sand Beach you'll come to **Thunder Hole**, where wild Atlantic waves crash into a deep, narrow chasm with such force that it creates a thundering boom, loudest during incoming tides. Look to the south to see **Otter Cliffs**, a favorite rock-climbing spot that rises vertically from the sea. At **Jordan Pond** choose from a 1-mile nature trail loop around the south side of the pond or a 3.5-mile trail that skirts the entire pond perimeter. After you've worked up an appetite, reward yourself with a relaxing afternoon tea on the lawn of Jordan Pond House (p250). Near the end of Park Loop Rd a side road leads up to Cadillac Mountain.

⊙ Cadillac Mountain

The majestic centerpiece of Acadia National Park is Cadillac Mountain (1530ft), the highest coastal peak in the eastern US, reached by a 3.5-mile spur road off Park Loop Rd. Four trails lead to the summit from four directions should you prefer hiking boots to rubber tires. The panoramic 360-degree view of ocean, islands and mountains is a winner any time of the day, but it's truly magical at dawn when hardy souls flock to the top to watch the sun rise over Frenchman Bay.

⊙ Other Activities

Some 125 miles of **hiking trails** crisscross Acadia National Park, from easy half-mile nature walks and level rambles to mountain treks up steep and rocky terrain. A standout is the 3-mile round-trip **Ocean Trail**, which runs between Sand Beach and Otter Cliffs and takes in the most interesting coastal scenery in the park. Pick up a guide describing all the trails at the visitor center.

The park's 45 miles of carriage roads are the prime attraction for **cycling**. You can rent quality mountain bikes, replaced new at the start of each season, at **Acadia Bike** (☑207-288-9605; www.acadiabike.com; 48 Cottage St; per day $22; ☺8am-8pm).

Rock climbing on the park's sea cliffs and mountains is breathtaking. Gear up with **Acadia Mountain Guides** (☑207-288-8186; www.acadiamountainguides.com; 228 Main St, Bar Harbor; half-day outing $75-140; ☺May–Oct); rates include a guide, instruction and equipment.

Scores of **ranger-led programs**, including nature walks, birding talks and kids' field trips, are available in the park. Check the schedule at the visitor center (p250).

For information on kayaking and other activities see Bar Harbor (p251)

🛏 Sleeping & Eating

The park has two campgrounds, both wooded and with running water, showers and barbecue pits.

There are scores of restaurants, inns and hotels in Bar Harbor, just a mile beyond the park.

Acadia National Park Campgrounds　　　　　CAMPGROUND $
(☑877-444-6777; www.nps.gov/acad; tent sites $14-24) Four miles south of Southwest Harbor, **Seawall** has both by-reservation and walk-up sites. Five miles south of Bar Harbor on ME 3, year-round **Blackwoods** requires reservations in summer. Both sites have restrooms and pay showers. Both are densely wooded but only a few minutes' walk to the ocean.

Jordan Pond House　　　　　AMERICAN $$
(☑207-276-3316; www.thejordanpondhouse.com; afternoon tea $9.50, mains $10-28; ☺11:30am-9pm mid-May–Oct) Afternoon tea at this lodge-like teahouse has been an Acadia tradition since the late 1800s. Steaming pots of Earl Grry come with hot popovers (hollow rolls made with egg batter) and strawberry jam. Eat outside on the broad lawn overlooking the lake. The park's only restaurant, Jordan Pond also does fancy but often mediocre lunches and dinners.

ℹ Information

Granite mountains and coastal vistas greet you upon entering Acadia National Park. The park is open year-round, though Park Loop Rd and most facilities are closed in winter. An admission fee is charged from May 1 to October 31. The fee, which is valid for seven consecutive days, is $22 per vehicle between mid-June and early October ($10 at other times) and $12 for cyclists or pedestrians.

Start your exploration at **Hulls Cove Visitor Center** (☑207-288-3338; ME 3; 7-day park admission per vehicle $22, walkers & cyclists $12; ☺8am-4:30pm mid-Apr–mid-Jun & Oct, to 6pm mid-Jun–Aug, to 5pm Sep), from where the 20-mile Park Loop Rd circumnavigates the eastern portion of the park.

ℹ Getting There & Around

The convenient **Island Explorer** (www.exploreacadia.com; ☺late Jun-early Oct) runs eight shuttle bus routes throughout Acadia National Park and to adjacent Bar Harbor, linking trailheads, campgrounds and accommodations.

Bar Harbor

Set on the doorstep of Acadia National Park, this alluring coastal town once rivaled Newport, RI, as a trendy summer destination for wealthy Americans. Today many of the old mansions have been turned into inviting inns and the town has become a magnet for outdoor enthusiasts. The **Bar Harbor Chamber of Commerce** (☑207-288-5103; www.barharbormaine.com; 1201 Bar Harbor Rd/ME 3, Trenton; ☺8am-6pm late May–mid-Oct, to 5pm Mon-Fri mid-Oct–late May) has a convenient welcome center just before the bridge onto Mt Desert Island.

⭐ Activities

Bar Harbor Whale Watch Co　CRUISE
(☑207-288-2386; www.barharborwhales.com; 1 West St; adult $34-64, child $22-34; ☺mid-May–Oct) Operates four-hour whale-watching and puffin-watching cruises, among other options.

Downeast Windjammer Cruises　CRUISE
(☑207-288-4585; www.downeastwindjammer.com; 27 Main St; adult/child $40/30) Offers two-hour cruises on the majestic 151ft, four-masted schooner *Margaret Todd*.

Acadian Nature Cruises　CRUISE
(☑207-288-2386; www.acadiannaturecruises.com; 1 West St; adult/child $28/17; ☺mid-May–Oct) See whales, porpoises, bald eagles, seals and more on these narrated two-hour nature cruises.

🛏 Sleeping

There's no shortage of sleeping options in Bar Harbor, ranging from period B&Bs to the usual chain hotels.

Bar Harbor Youth Hostel　HOSTEL $
(☑207-288-5587; www.barharborhostel.com; 321 Main St; dm/r $27/82; 🛜) In a converted home a few blocks south of the village green, this pleasant, friendly and very clean hostel has simple male and female dorm rooms, each sleeping 10, and a private room that sleeps four.

Holland Inn　B&B $$
(☑207-288-4804; www.hollandinn.com; 35 Holland Ave; r incl breakfast $95-185; 🛜) In a quiet residential neighborhood, walking distance from downtown, this restored 1895 house and adjacent cottage has nine homey, unfrilly rooms. Ambience is so low-key you'll feel like you're staying in a friend's private home.

Aysgarth Station Inn　B&B $$
(☑207-288-9655; www.aysgarth.com; 20 Roberts Ave; r incl breakfast $115-165; ▣) On a quiet side street, this 1895 B&B has six cozy rooms with homey touches. Request the Tan Hill room, which is on the 3rd floor, for a view of Cadillac Mountain.

🍴 Eating

Cafe This Way　AMERICAN $$
(☑207-288-4483; www.cafethisway.com; 14½ Mount Desert St; mains breakfast $6-9, dinner $15-25; ☺7-11:30am Mon-Sat, 8am-1pm Sun, 5:30-9pm nightly; 🖉) In a sprawling white cottage, this quirky eatery is *the* place for breakfast, with plump Maine blueberry pancakes and eggs Benedict with smoked salmon. It also serves eclectic, sophisticated dinners, such as roasted duck with blueberries, Moroccan-style squash and tuna tempura. Sit in the garden.

2 Cats　CAFE $$
(☑207-288-2808; www.2catsbarharbor.com; 130 Cottage St; mains $8-19; ☺7am-1pm; 🖉) On weekends crowds line up for smoked-trout omelets and homemade muffins at this sunny, arty little cafe. Lunch offerings include slightly heartier fare, like burritos and seafood dishes. Pick up a kitty-themed gift in the gift shop.

Mâche Bistro　FRENCH $$$
(☑207-288-0447; www.machebistro.com; 135 Cottage St; mains $18-28; ☺5-10:30pm Mon-Sat) Almost certainly Bar Harbor's best restaurant, Mâche serves contemporary French-inflected fare in a stylishly renovated cottage. The changing menu highlights the local riches: think pumpkin-seed-dusted scallops, lobster-and-brie flatbread, and wild-blueberry trifle. Specialty cocktails add to the appeal. Reservations are crucial.

Downeast Maine

The 900-plus miles of coastline running northeast from Bar Harbor are sparsely populated, slower-paced and foggier than southern and western Maine. Highlights include the **Schoodic Peninsula**, whose tip is a noncontiguous part of Acadia National Park; the lobster fishing villages of

Jonesport and Beals; and Great Wass Island, a nature preserve with walking paths and good bird-watching, including the chance to see puffins.

Machias, with a branch of the University of Maine, is the center of commerce along this stretch of coast. Lubec is about as far east as you can go and still be in the USA; folks like to watch the sun rise at nearby Quoddy Head State Park so they can say they were the first in the country to catch the sun's rays.

Interior Maine

Sparsely populated northern and western Maine is rugged outdoor country. River rafting, hiking trails up Maine's highest mountain and the ski town of Bethel make this region a magnet for adventurers.

Sabbathday Lake

The nation's only active Shaker community is at Sabbathday Lake, 25 miles north of Portland. It was founded in the early 18th century and a handful of devotees keep the Shaker tradition of simple living, hard work and fine artistry alive. You can tour several of their buildings on a visit to the **Shaker Museum** (☑207-926-4597; www.shaker.lib. me.us; adult/child $6.50/2; ☺10am-4:30pm Mon-Sat late May–mid-Oct). To get there, take exit 63 off the Maine Turnpike and continue north for 8 miles on ME 26.

Bethel

The rural community of Bethel, nestled in the rolling Maine woods 12 miles east of New Hampshire on ME 26, offers an engaging combination of mountain scenery, outdoor escapades and good-value accommodations. **Bethel Area Chamber of Commerce** (☑207-824-2282; www.bethelmaine.com; 8 Station Pl; ☺9am-5pm Mon-Fri) provides information for visitors.

🏃 Activities

Bethel Outdoor Adventure KAYAKING
(☑207-824-4224; www.betheloutdooradventure. com; 121 Mayville Rd/US 2; per day kayak/canoe $46/67; ☺8am-6pm) This downtown outfitter rents canoes, kayaks and bicycles, and it arranges lessons, guided trips and shuttles to and from the Androscoggin River.

Grafton Notch State Park HIKING
(☑207-824-2912; ME 26) If you're ready for a hike, head to this park north of Bethel for pretty mountain scenery, waterfalls and lots of trails of varying lengths.

Sunday River Ski Resort SKIING
(☑800-543-2754; www.sundayriver.com; ME 26; full-day lift ticket adult/child 13-18 yr/child under 12 yr& seniors $87/69/56, half-day $63/55/45; 🐾) Six miles north of Bethel along ME 5/26, Sunday River has eight mountain peaks and 132 trails, with 16 lifts. It's regarded as one of the region's best family ski destinations. It also offers summer activities, including chairlift rides, canoeing, ATV tours and a mountain-bike park. Two huge lodges have more than 400 rooms.

🛌 Sleeping

⭐ **Chapman Inn** B&B $
(☑207-824-2657; www.chapmaninn.com; 2 Church St; dm incl breakfast $35, r $89-129; 🐾) Run by a friendly globe-trotting retiree, this roomy downtown guesthouse has character in spades. The nine private rooms are done up in florals and antiques, with slightly sloping floors attesting to the home's age. The cozy common space is stocked with Monopoly and other rainy-day games. In winter, skiers bunk down in the snug dorm, complete with a wood-paneled game room presided over by a massive mounted moose head. Breakfast, a lavish spread of homemade pastries and made-to-order omelets, will keep you full for a day on the slopes. And, oh, if you feel a cold draft, it's probably just the ghost of little Abigail Chapman, the daughter of the home's 19th-century owner.

Sudbury Inn & Suds Pub INN $$
(☑207-824-2174; www.sudburyinn.com; 151 Main St; r incl breakfast $99-159; 🐾) The choice place to stay in downtown Bethel, this historic inn has 17 rooms, a pub with 29 beers on tap, pizza and live weekend entertainment. It also has an excellent dinner restaurant serving Maine-centric fare (mains $18 to $26).

Caratunk & The Forks

For white-water rafting at its best, head to the **Kennebec River**, below the Harris Dam, where the water shoots through a dramatic 12-mile gorge. With rapids with names like Whitewasher and Magic Falls, you know you're in for an adrenaline rush.

The adjoining villages of Caratunk and The Forks, on US 201 south of Jackman, are at the center of the Kennebec River rafting operations. The options range from rolling rapids and heart-stopping drops to calmer waters where children as young as seven can join in. Rates range from $75 to $130 per person for a day-long outing. Multiday packages, with camping or cabin accommodations, can also be arranged.

Reliable operators include **Crab Apple Whitewater** (☑800-553-7238; www.crabapplewhitewater.com) and **Three Rivers Whitewater** (☑877-846-7238; www.threeriverswhitewater.com).

Baxter State Park

Set in the remote forests of northern Maine, **Baxter State Park** (☑207-723-5140; www.baxterstateparkauthority.com; per car $14) cent-

ers on Mt Katahdin (5267ft), Maine's tallest mountain and the northern terminus of the 2175-mile **Appalachian Trail** (www.nps.gov/appa). This vast 209,500-acre park is maintained in a wilderness state – no electricity and no running water (bring your own or plan on purifying stream water) – and there's a good chance you'll see moose, deer and black bear. Baxter has extensive hiking trails, several leading to the top of Mt Katahdin, which can be hiked round-trip in a day as long as you're in good shape and get an early start.

At **Millinocket**, south of Baxter State Park, there are motels, campgrounds, restaurants and outfitters that specialize in white-water rafting and kayaking on the Penobscot River. Get information from the **Katahdin Area Chamber of Commerce** (☑207-723-4443; www.katahdinmaine.com; 1029 Central St, Millinocket).

Washington, DC & the Capital Region

Best Places to Eat

➡ Woodberry Kitchen (p291)

➡ Central Michel Richard (p280)

➡ Rasika (p279)

➡ Inn at Little Washington (p321)

➡ Julep's (p310)

Best Places to Stay

➡ Hay-Adams Hotel (p276)

➡ Jefferson Hotel (p310)

➡ Colonial Williamsburg Historic Lodging (p312)

➡ Cottages at Indian River Marina (p300)

➡ Inn at 2920 (p291)

Why Go?

No matter your politics, it's hard not to fall for the nation's capital. Iconic monuments, vast (and free) museums and venerable restaurants serving cuisine from around the globe are just the beginning of the great DC experience. There's much to discover: leafy, cobblestoned neighborhoods, sprawling markets and verdant parks – not to mention the corridors of power where visionaries and demagogues still roam.

Beyond the Beltway, the diverse landscapes of Maryland, Virginia, West Virginia and Delaware offer potent enticement to travel beyond the marble city. Craggy mountains, rushing rivers, vast nature reserves (including islands where wild horses run), sparkling beaches, historic villages and the magnificent Chesapeake Bay form the backdrop to memorable adventures: sail, hike, raft, camp or simply sit on a pretty stretch of shoreline, planning the next seafood feast. It's a region where traditions run deep, from the nation's birthplace to Virginia's still-thriving bluegrass scene.

When to Go
Washington DC

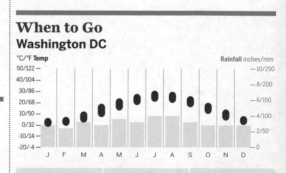

Mar-Apr Cherry blossoms bring crowds to the city during DC's most popular festival.

Jun-Aug Beaches and resorts heave; prices are high and accommodations scarce.

Sep-Oct Fewer crowds and lower prices, but pleasant temperatures and fiery fall scenery.

Transportation

The region is served by three major airports: Washington Dulles International Airport (IAD), Ronald Reagan Washington National Airport (DCA) and Baltimore/Washington International Thurgood Marshall Airport (BWI). Norfolk International Airport (ORF) and Richmond International Airport (RIC) are smaller regional hubs.

Train travel is possible in some areas, with service provided by Amtrak (www.amtrak.com). Key towns connected by rail to DC include Baltimore, MD; Wilmington, DE; Harpers Ferry, WV; and, in Virginia: Manassas, Fredericksburg, Richmond, Williamsburg, Newport News and Charlottesville.

TIPS ON VISITING WASHINGTON, DC

DC has a lot of great museums, but you'll be hard pressed to see them all – even if you spend two weeks in the capital. Some sights – including the Washington Monument, US Holocaust Memorial Museum and Ford's Theatre – have limited admittance; if they're high on your list, go early to ensure you get a spot.

Aside from the Museum of the American Indian, which has a great restaurant, dining is limited along the Mall. One strategy: hit Eastern Market first to assemble a picnic for later in the day (on the Mall or around the Tidal Basin).

If possible, leave the car at home. The Metro is excellent and driving in the city can get pricey, with overnight lots charging upward of $25 a night.

Best National Parks

→ The New River Gorge National River is utterly Edenlike and home to white-tailed deer and black bears. It also has world-class white-water rafting.

→ Shenandoah National Park provides spectacular scenery along the Blue Ridge Mountains, and great hiking and camping, including along the Appalachian Trail.

→ Assateague Island National Seashore and Chincoteague are beautiful coastal environments with great blue herons, ospreys, blue crabs and wild horses.

→ George Washington and Jefferson National Forests protect more than 1500 sq miles of forests and alpine scenery bordering the Shenandoah Valley.

→ Virginia's famous battlefields are also part of the park system. Good places to reconnect with America's darkest hours are Antietam and Manassas.

DON'T MISS

With Chesapeake Bay at its doorstep, this region is pure heaven for seafood-lovers. The Maine Avenue Fish Market (p278) in DC is legendary. In Baltimore, Annapolis and all along Maryland's Eastern Shore, you'll also find top-notch seafood.

Fast Facts

→ **Hub cities** Washington, DC (population 632,000), Baltimore (population 620,000), Virginia Beach (population 442,700)

→ **Distances from DC** Baltimore (40 miles), Williamsburg (152 miles), Abingdon (362 miles)

→ **Time zone** Eastern

Did You Know?

→ Thomas Jefferson was one of many Virginians to make wine in the state in the past 400 years. Now Virginia has more than 192 wineries and earns high marks at international awards shows.

Resources

→ **Washington** (www.washington.org) Lists upcoming events and loads of DC details.

→ **The Crooked Road** (www.thecrookedroad.org) Gateway to Virginia's heritage music trail.

→ **Virginia Wine** (www.virginiawine.org) Essential for planning a route through wine country.

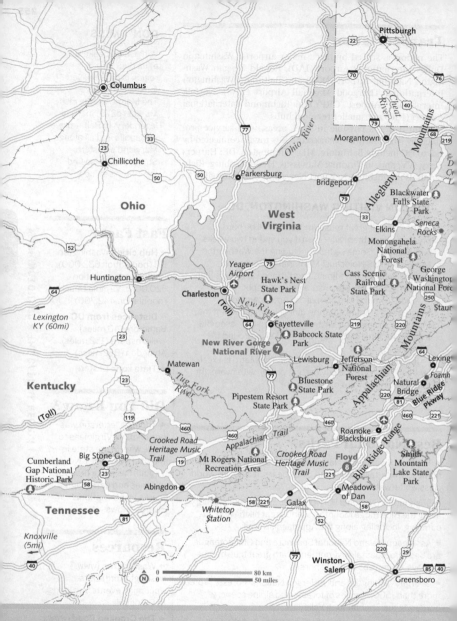

Washington, DC & the Capital Region Highlights

❶ Visiting Washington's **Smithsonian Institution museums** (p269), then watching the sunset over **Lincoln Memorial** (p267).

❷ Tracing America's roots at the living-history museum of **Colonial Williamsburg** (p312).

❸ Exploring the region's nautical past with a pub crawl through the cobblestoned port-town neighborhood of **Fells Point** (p290), Baltimore.

❹ Taking a Sunday drive along **Skyline Drive** (p320), followed by hiking and

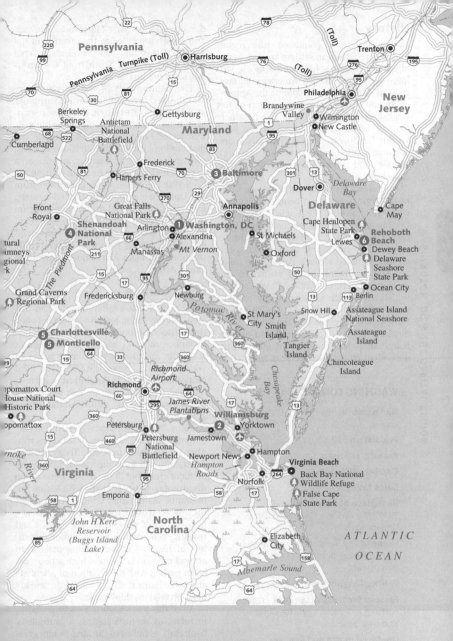

History

Native Americans populated this region long before European settlers arrived. Many of the area's geographic landmarks are still known by their Native American names, such as Chesapeake, Shenandoah, Appalachian and Potomac. In 1607 a group of 108 English colonists established the first permanent European settlement in the New World: Jamestown. During the early years, colonists battled harsh winters, starvation, disease and occasionally hostile Native Americans.

Jamestown survived, and the Royal Colony of Virginia came into being in 1624. Ten years later, fleeing the English Civil War, Lord Baltimore established the Catholic colony of Maryland at St Mary's City, where a Spanish Jewish doctor treated a town council that included a black Portuguese sailor and Margaret Brent, the first woman to vote in North American politics. Delaware was settled as a Dutch whaling colony in 1631, was practically wiped out by Native Americans, then later resettled by the British. Celts displaced from Britain filtered into the Appalachians, where they created a fiercely independent culture that persists today. Border disputes between Maryland, Delaware and Pennsylvania led to the creation of the Mason–Dixon line, which eventually separated the industrial North from the agrarian, slave-holding South.

The fighting part of the Revolutionary War finished here with the British surrender at Yorktown in 1781. Then, to diffuse regional tension, central, swampy Washington, District of Columbia (DC), was made the new nation's capital. But divisions of class, race and economy were strong, and this area in particular split along its seams during the Civil War (1861–65): Virginia seceded from the Union while its impoverished western farmers, long resentful of genteel plantation owners, seceded from Virginia. Maryland stayed in the Union but its white slave-owners rioted against Northern troops, while thousands of black Marylanders joined the Union Army.

Local Culture

The North–South tension long defined this area, but the region has also jerked between the aristocratic pretensions of upper-class Virginia, miners, watermen, immigrant boroughs and the ever-changing rulers of Washington, DC. Since the Civil War, local economies have made the shift from agriculture and manufacturing to high technology and the servicing and staffing of the federal government.

Many African Americans settled this border region, either as slaves or escapees running to Northern freedom. Today African Americans still form the visible underclass of major cities, but in the rough arena of the disadvantaged they compete with Latino immigrants, mainly from Central America. At the other end of the spectrum, ivory towers – in the form of world-class universities and research centers such as the National Institute of Health – attract intelligentsia from around the world. The local high schools are often packed with the children of scientists and consultants staffing some of the world's most prestigious think tanks.

All of this has spawned a culture that is, in turns, as sophisticated as a journalists' book club, as linked to the land as bluegrass festivals in Virginia and as hooked into the main vein of urban America as Tupac Shakur, go-go, Baltimore Club and DC Hardcore. And, of course, there's always politics, a subject continually simmering under the surface here.

WASHINGTON, DC, FACTS

Nickname DC, the District, Chocolate City

Population 632,300

Area 68.3 sq miles

Capital city Exactly!

Sales tax 5.75%

Birthplace of Duke Ellington (1899–1974), Marvin Gaye (1939–84), Dave Chappelle (b 1973)

Home of The Redskins, cherry blossoms, all three branches of American government

Politics Overwhelmingly Democrat

Famous for National symbols, crime, partying interns, struggle for Congressional recognition

Unofficial motto and license-plate slogan Taxation Without Representation

Driving distances Washington, DC, to Baltimore 40 miles, Washington, DC, to Virginia Beach 210 miles

THE CAPITAL REGION IN...

One Week

Follow a version of the two-day DC itinerary and spend a day exploring underrated **Baltimore** before heading to Maryland's gorgeous **Eastern Shore** and the **Delaware beaches**. Head south to cross over the Chesapeake Bay bridge-tunnel and time-warp through Virginia's history: visit the nation's birthplace at **Jamestown** and take a wander through the 18th century at **Williamsburg**, followed by the nation's post–Civil War reconciliation at **Appomattox Court House**. Swing north through **Richmond**, where students, Dixie aristocracy and African American neighborhoods combine to form a fascinating whole, before rolling back into DC.

Two Weeks

Head to **Charlottesville** to experience Virginia's aristocratic soul (and good dining and B&B scene), then drive down the mountainous backbone through **Staunton**, **Lexington** and **Roanoke**. Follow the **Crooked Road** on a weekend to hear some of the nation's best bluegrass. Truck through West Virginia, stopping to hike, mountain bike or ski in the **Monongahela National Forest**, then go rafting in **New River Gorge** before returning to Washington via the hallowed battlefields of **Antietam**.

WASHINGTON, DC

This is a terrifically exciting city. Whatever you think it may be, Washington, Dc is more. A workaholic capital? Absolutely; look at the interns scrabbling across Capitol Hill, the think-tank staff angling for a fellowship and the lobbyist on their smartphone. A study in monumental dignity? Yes; see the wide boulevards, iconic memorials, countless museums and idyllic vistas over the Potomac.

And then, DC is much more than a mere museum piece or marble backdrop to nightly news reports. It's home to tree-lined neighborhoods and a vibrant theater scene, with ethnically diverse restaurants, large numbers of immigrants and a dynamism percolating just beneath the surface. The city has a growing number of markets, historic cobblestoned streets and more overachieving and talented types than any city of this size deserves.

It also has an underclass, which lives in poverty and high crime (although these metrics have improved), and it has a high price tag. DC has undergone extensive gentrification since the late 1990s. With the exception of a few outlier years, crime has dropped as the cost of living has increased, although this has been accompanied by displacement of many area African Americans to the Maryland and Virginia suburbs. The cost of living in DC is among the highest in the nation, and coupled with waves of politically motivated transplants, thc city has a reputation as a place more geared towards transients than families. But it is nevertheless family-friendly if you're visiting with children, and DC's residential outer areas and Beltway suburbs provide a home base for those who want to live amid the capital's undeniable intellectual and cultural energy.

History

Like a lot of American history, the District of Columbia (DC) story is one of compromise. In this case, the balance was struck between Northern and Southern politicians who wanted to plant a federal city between their power bases. As potential capitals such as Boston, Philadelphia and Baltimore were rejected as too urban-industrial by Southern plantation owners, it was decided that a new city would be carved at the 13 colonies' midway point, along the banks of the Potomac River. Maryland and Virginia donated the land (which Virginia took back in the 19th century).

DC was originally run by Congress, was torched by the British during the War of 1812, and lost the south-bank slave port of Alexandria to Virginia in 1846 (when abolition talk was buzzing in the capital). Over the years, DC evolved along diverging tracks; as a marbled temple to federal government and residential city for federal employees on the one hand, and an urban ghetto for northbound African Americans and overseas immigrants on the other.

The city finally got its own mayor in 1973 (Walter Washington, among the first African

Washington, DC

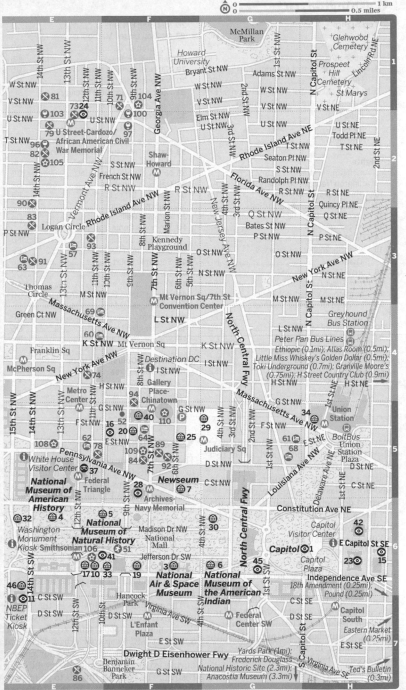

Washington, DC

American mayors of a major American city). DC was ever underfunded and today residents are taxed like other American citizens yet lack a voting seat in Congress. The educated upper class is leagues away from the neglected destitute; almost half the population has a university degree, yet a third is functionally illiterate.

With the election of Barack Obama in 2008, Washington, DC, gained a bit of cool cachet – New Yorkers are coming here now, instead of the other way around. Unfortunately, they've brought with them an NYC cost of living. DC remains quite divided between upwardly mobile transplants and long-term residents. The former possess wealth, while the latter are influential within local politics. In some places these two sectors coexist, but in other neighborhoods tensions can be palpable.

◎ Sights

The capital was designed by its two planners to be perfectly navigable. Unfortunately, their urban visions have mashed up against each other. Pierre L'Enfant's diagonal state-named streets share space with Andrew Ellicott's grid (remember: letters go east–west, numbers north–south). On top of that the city is divided into four quadrants with identical addresses in different divisions – F and 14th NW puts you near the White House, while F and 14th NE puts you near Rosedale Playground.

The majority of sights lie in the Northwest (NW) quadrant, while the most run-down neighborhoods tend to be in the Southeast (SE). Keep your urban wits about you at night, and be prepared for crowds during events such as the Cherry Blossom Festival. The Potomac River is to your south and west; Maryland lies to the north and

Sleeping

54	Akwaaba	D2
55	American Guest House	C1
56	Carlyle Suites	D2
57	Chester Arthur House	E3
58	Graham Georgetown	A3
59	Hay-Adams Hotel	D4
60	Hostelling International – Washington DC	E4
61	Hotel George	G5
62	Hotel Harrington	E5
63	Hotel Helix	E3
64	Hotel Monaco	F5
65	Hotel Palomar	C3
66	Inn at Dupont North	D2
67	Inn at Dupont South	C3
68	Liaison	G5
69	Morrison-Clark Inn	E4

Eating

70	Afterwords Cafe	C2
71	American Ice Company	F1
72	Baked & Wired	A4
73	Ben's Chili Bowl	E2
74	Bibiana	E4
75	Bistrot du Coin	C2
76	Blue Duck Tavern	C3
77	Cashion's Eat Place	C1
78	Central Michel Richard	E5
79	Desperados	E2
80	Diner	D1
81	Eatonville	E1
82	El Centro	E2
83	Estadio	E3
84	Hill Country Barbecue	F5
85	Komi	D3
	Little Serrow	(see 85)
86	Maine Avenue Fish Market	E7
87	Malaysia Kopitiam	C3
88	Martin's Tavern	A3
89	Merzi	F5
	Mitsitam Native Foods Cafe	(see 6)
90	Pearl Dive Oyster Palace	E2
91	Pig	E3
92	Rasika	F5
93	Veranda on P	E3
94	Zaytinya	F5

Drinking & Nightlife

95	18th Street Lounge	D3
96	Bar Pilar	E2
97	Brixton	F2
98	Ching Ching Cha	A3
99	Cobalt	D2
100	Dickson Wine Bar	F2
101	Filter	C2
102	JR's	D3
103	Marvin	E2
	Nellie's	(see 97)
	Patty Boom Boom	(see 103)

Entertainment

104	9:30 Club	F1
105	Black Cat	E2
106	Discovery Theater	E6
107	Kennedy Center	B5
108	National Theatre	E5
109	Shakespeare Theatre	F5
110	Verizon Center	F5

east; and the Beltway, the capital ring road, encircles the entire package.

◉ National Mall

When you imagine Washington, DC, you likely imagine this 1.9-mile-long lawn. Anchored at one end by the Lincoln Memorial and at the other by Capitol Hill, intersected by the Reflecting Pool and WWII Memorial, and centered on the Washington Monument, this is the heart of the city and, in some ways, the American experiment.

Perhaps no other symbol has housed the national ideal of massed voice affecting radical change – from Martin Luther King's 1963 'I Have a Dream' speech to marches for gay marriage in the 2000s. Hundreds of rallies occur here every year; the Mall, framed by great monuments and museums, and shot through with tourists, dog-walkers and idealists, acts as loudspeaker for any cause.

★ **National Air & Space Museum** MUSEUM
(http://airandspace.si.edu/; cnr 6th St & Independence Ave SW; ⊙10am-5:30pm daily, to 7:30pm Jun-Aug; Ⓜ Smithsonian, L'Enfant Plaza, Federal Center) **FREE** The Air & Space Museum is the most popular Smithsonian museum; everyone flocks to see the Wright brothers' flyer, Chuck Yeager's *Bell X-1*, Charles Lindbergh's *Spirit of St Louis* and the *Apollo 11* command module. There's also an IMAX theater, planetarium and simulator (adult/child $9/7.50 each).

★ **National Museum of Natural History** MUSEUM
(www.mnh.si.edu; cnr 10th St & Constitution Ave NW; ⊙10am-5:30pm, to 7:30pm Jun-Aug; Ⓘ; Ⓜ Smithsonian, Federal Triangle) **FREE** A favorite with the kids, the Museum of Natural History showcases dinosaur skeletons, an archaeology/anthropology collection, wonders from the ocean, and unusual gems and minerals, including the 45-carat Hope Diamond.

National Mall

Folks often call the Mall 'America's Front Yard,' and that's a pretty good analogy. It is indeed a lawn, unfurling scrubby green grass from the Capitol west to the Lincoln Memorial. It's also America's great public space, where citizens come to protest their government, go for scenic runs and connect with the nation's most cherished ideals writ large in stone, landscaping, monuments and memorials.

You can sample quite bit in a day, though it'll be a full one that requires roughly 4 miles of walking. Start at the **Vietnam Veterans Memorial 1**, then head counterclockwise around the Mall, swooping in on the **Lincoln Memorial 2**, **Martin Luther King Jr Memorial 3** and **Washington Monument 4**. You can also pause for the cause of the Korean War and WWII, among other monuments that dot the Mall's western portion.

Martin Luther King Jr Memorial

Walk all the way around the towering statue of Dr King by Lei Yixin and read the quotes. His likeness, incidentally, is 11ft taller than Lincoln and Jefferson in their memorials.

Tidal Basin

Smithsonian Castle

Seek out the tomb of James Smithson, the eccentric Englishman whose 1826 financial gift launched the Smithsonian Institution. His crypt is in a room by the Mall entrance.

Department of Agriculture

5

6

West Building

East Building

7

National Museum of the American Indian

National Air & Space Museum

Simply step inside and look up, and you'll be impressed. Lindbergh's *Spirit of St Louis* and Chuck Yeager's sound barrier–breaking Bell X-1 are among the machines hanging from the ceiling.

US Capitol

MARK WILLIAMSON / GETTY IMAGES ©

PETER GRIDLEY / GETTY IMAGES ©

RICHARD I'ANSON / GETTY IMAGES ©

Then it's onward to the museums, all fabulous and all free. Begin at the **Smithsonian Castle** 5 to get your bearings – and to say thanks to the guy making all this awesomeness possible – and commence browsing through the **National Air & Space Museum** 6, **National Gallery of Art & National Sculpture Garden** 7 and **National Museum of Natural History** 8.

Lincoln Memorial

Commune with Abe in his chair, then head down the steps to the marker where Martin Luther King Jr gave his 'Dream' speech. The view of the Reflecting Pool and Washington Monument is one of DC's best.

Vietnam Veterans Memorial

Check the symbol that's beside each name. A diamond indicates 'killed, body recovered.' A plus sign indicates 'missing and unaccounted for.' There are approximately 1200 of the latter.

Korean War Veterans Memorial

National WWII Memorial

Washington Monument

As you approach the obelisk, look a third of the way up. See how it's slightly lighter in color at the bottom? Builders had to use different marble after the first source dried up.

National Museum of American History

National Museum of Natural History

Wave to Henry, the elephant who guards the rotunda, then zip to the 2nd floor's Hope Diamond. The 45.52-carat bauble has cursed its owners, including Marie Antoinette, or so the story goes.

National Sculpture Garden

National Gallery of Art & National Sculpture Garden

Beeline to Gallery 6 (West Building) and ogle the Western Hemisphere's only Leonardo da Vinci painting. Outdoors, amble amid whimsical sculptures by Miró, Calder and Lichtenstein. Also check out IM Pei's design of the East Building.

★ **National Museum of American History** MUSEUM

(www.americanhistory.si.edu; cnr 14th St & Constitution Ave NW; ◷10am-5:30pm, to 7:30pm Jun-Aug; 🚼; Ⓜ Smithsonian, Federal Triangle) FREE The Museum of American History is accented with the daily bric-a-brac of the American experience – synagogue shawls, protest signs and cotton gins – plus an enormous display of the original Star-Spangled Banner and icons such as Dorothy's slippers and Kermit the Frog.

★ **National Museum of the American Indian** MUSEUM

(www.americanindian.si.edu; cnr 4th St & Independence Ave SW; ◷10am-5:30pm; 🚼; Ⓜ L'Enfant Plaza) FREE The Museum of the American Indian, ensconced in honey-colored sandstone, provides a good introduction to the indigenous people of the Americas, with an array of costumes, video and audio recordings, and cultural artifacts. Exhibits are largely organized and presented by individual tribes, which provides an extremely intimate, if sometimes disjointed, overall narrative. Don't miss the regionally specialized menu of Native-inspired dishes at **Mitsitam Native Foods Cafe** (www.mitsitamcafe.com; cnr 4th St & Independence Ave SW, National Museum of the American Indian; mains $8-18; ◷11am-5pm; Ⓜ L'Enfant Plaza) on the ground floor.

Hirshhorn Museum & Sculpture Garden MUSEUM

(www.hirshhorn.si.edu; cnr 7th St & Independence Ave SW; ◷10am-5:30pm, sculpture garden 7:30am-dusk; 🚼; Ⓜ Smithsonian) FREE The doughnut-shaped Hirshhorn Museum & Sculpture Garden houses a huge collection of modern sculpture, which is rotated regularly. It includes works by Rodin, Henry Moore and Ron Mueck, as well as paintings by O'Keeffe, Warhol, Man Ray and de Kooning.

National Museum of African Art MUSEUM

(www.nmafa.si.edu; 950 Independence Ave SW; ◷10am-5:30pm; 🚼; Ⓜ Smithsonian) FREE The National Museum of African Art showcases masks, textiles and ceramics from the sub-Sahara, as well as ancient and contemporary art from all over the continent.

Arthur M Sackler Gallery GALLERY

(www.asia.si.edu/; 1050 Independence Ave SW; ◷10am-5:30pm; Ⓜ Smithsonian, L'Enfant Plaza) FREE Poring over ancient manuscripts and Japanese silk screens is a peaceful way to spend an afternoon at this quiet gallery and the adjoining **Freer Gallery of Art** (http://www.asia.si.edu/; cnr 12 St & Jefferson Dr SW). Together they comprise the National Museum of Asian Art. The Freer, rather incongruously, also houses more than 1300 works by the American painter James Whistler.

WASHINGTON, DC, IN...

Two Days

Start your DC adventure at the Mall's much-loved **National Air & Space Museum** and **National Museum of Natural History**. Around lunchtime visit the **National Museum of the American Indian**, for aboriginal lore and a great meal. Wander down the **Mall** to the **Lincoln Memorial** and **Vietnam Veterans Memorial**. Before exhaustion creeps in, go to **U Street** for dining and drinks.

Next day, head to the **US Holocaust Memorial Museum**, **Arthur M Sackler Gallery** and **Freer Gallery of Art**. Catch the illuminated **White House** and the new **Martin Luther King Jr Memorial** at night. For dinner, browse the restaurant-lined **Penn Quarter**.

Four Days

On day three, go to **Georgetown** for a morning stroll along the Potomac, followed by window-shopping and lunch at **Martin's Tavern**. Afterwards, visit the lovely **Dumbarton Oaks** gardens, then take a hike in **Rock Creek Park**. Head to **Columbia Heights** for dinner, followed by drinks at **Meridian Pint**.

On the fourth day, visit the **Newseum**, **Capitol** and **Library of Congress**, then walk to **Eastern Market** for a meal. In the evening, try to catch a show a the **Kennedy Center**.

National Gallery of Art MUSEUM
(www.nga.gov; Constitution Ave NE, btwn 3rd & 4th Sts NW; ⊘10am-5pm Mon-Sat, 11am-6pm Sun) FREE Set in two massive buildings, the National Gallery of Art houses a staggering art collection (more than 100,000 objects), spanning the Middle Ages to the present. The neoclassical **west building** houses European art through the 1800s, with an excellent range of Italian Renaissance works (including the continent's only da Vinci); the geometric **east building**, designed by IM Pei, showcases modern art, with works by Picasso, Matisse, Pollock and a massive Calder mobile over the entrance lobby. An underground passage with a wonderful indoor waterfall ('Cascade') and cafe connects the two buildings.

Smithsonian Castle VISITOR CENTER
(☑202-633-1000; www.si.edu; 1000 Jefferson Dr SW; ⊘8:30am-5:30pm; Ⓜ Smithsonian) The red-turreted Smithsonian Castle is the visitor center for all museums, but is not that interesting in and of itself.

◉ Other Museums & Monuments

★ **Lincoln Memorial** MONUMENT
(2 Lincoln Memorial Cir NW) FREE Anchoring the Mall's west end is the hallowed shrine to Abraham Lincoln, who gazes peacefully across the Reflecting Pool beneath his neoclassical Doric-columned abode. To the left of Lincoln you can read the words of the Gettysburg Address, and the hall below highlights other great Lincoln-isms; on the steps, Martin Luther King Jr delivered his famed 'I Have a Dream' speech.

★ **Newseum** MUSEUM
(www.newseum.org; 555 Pennsylvania Ave NW; adult/child $22/13; ⊘9am-5pm; ☞; Ⓜ Archives-Navy Memorial, Judiciary Sq) Although you'll have to pay up, this massive, highly interactive news museum is well worth the admission price. You can delve inside the major events of recent years (the fall of the Berlin Wall, September 11, Hurricane Katrina), and spend hours watching moving film footage, perusing Pulitzer Prize–winning photographs and reading works by journalists killed in the line of duty.

US Holocaust Memorial Museum MUSEUM
(www.ushmm.org; 100 Raoul Wallenberg Pl; ⊘10am-5:20pm) FREE For a deep understanding of the Holocaust – its victims, perpetrators and bystanders – this harrowing museum is a must-see. The main exhibit (not recommended for under-11s, who can go to a separate on-site exhibit that's also free) gives visitors the identity card of a single Holocaust victim, whom visitors can ponder while taking a winding route into a hellish past amid footage of ghettos, rail cars and death camps where so many were murdered. Only a limited number of visitors are admitted each day, so go early.

Washington Monument MONUMENT
(☑202-426-6841; 2 15th St NW; ⊘9am-10pm Jun-Aug, to 5pm Sep-May) FREE Peaking at 555ft (and 5in), the Washington Monument is the tallest building in the district. It took two phases of construction to complete; note the different hues of the stone. Tickets are free but must be reserved from the **kiosk** (15th St, btwn Madison Dr NW & Jefferson Dr SW; ⊘8:30am-4:30pm), or you can order them in advance by calling the **National Park Service** (☑877-444-6777; www.recreation.gov; tickets $1.50).

Bureau of Engraving & Printing LANDMARK
(www.moneyfactory.gov; cnr 14th & C Sts SW; ⊘9am-3pm Mon-Fri, to 7:30pm summer; ☞; Ⓜ Smithsonian) FREE The Bureau of Engraving & Printing, aka the most glorified print shop in the world, is where all the US paper currency is designed. Some $32 million of it rolls off the presses daily. Get in line early at the **ticket kiosk** (Raoul Wallenberg Pl, aka 15th St) on Raoul Wallenberg Pl.

Vietnam Veterans Memorial MONUMENT
(Constitution Gardens) FREE The opposite of DC's white, gleaming marble is this black, low-lying 'V,' an expression of the psychic scar wrought by the Vietnam War. The monument follows a descent deeper into the earth, with the names of the 58,267 dead soldiers, listed in the order in which they died, chiseled into the dark wall. It's a subtle, but profound monument – and all the more surprising as it was designed by 21-year-old undergraduate student Maya Lin in 1981.

Korean War Veterans Memorial MONUMENT
(www.nps.gov/kwvm; 10 Daniel French Drive SW; Ⓜ Foggy Bottom-GWU) FREE The elaborate memorial depicts a patrol of ghostly steel soldiers marching by a wall of etched faces from that conflict; seen from a distance, the

images on the wall form the outline of the Korean mountains.

National WWII Memorial
MONUMENT

(www.wwiimemorial.com; 17th St; M Smithsonian) **FREE** Occupying one end of the Reflecting Pool (and, controversially, the center of the Mall – the only war memorial to have that distinction), the National WWII Memorial honors the 400,000 Americans who died in the war, along with the 16 million US soldiers who served during the conflict. Stirring quotes are sprinkled about the monument.

Corcoran Gallery
MUSEUM

(☏ 202-639-1704; www.corcoran.org; cnr 17th St & New York Ave NW; adult/child $10/free; ⊘ 10am-5pm Wed-Sun, to 9pm Thu; M Farragut West) DC's oldest art museum, the Corcoran Gallery has had a tough time standing up to the free, federal competition around the block, but this hasn't stopped it from maintaining one of the most eclectic exhibitions in the country.

⊙ Capitol Hill

The Capitol, appropriately, sits atop Capitol Hill (what Pierre L'Enfant called 'a pedestal waiting for a monument'; we'd say it's more of a stump, but hey), across a plaza from the dignified Supreme Court and Library of Congress. Congressional office buildings surround the plaza. A pleasant brownstone residential district stretches from E Capitol St to Lincoln Park. Union Station, Capitol South and Eastern Market Metro stations serve this area.

★ Capitol
LANDMARK

(East Capitol St NE & First St) Since 1800, this is where the legislative branch of American government – ie Congress – has met to write the country's laws. The lower House of Representatives (435 members) and upper Senate (100) meet respectively in the south and north wings of the building.

A **visitor center** (www.visitthecapitol.gov; 1st St NE & E Capitol St; ⊘ 8:30am-4:30pm Mon-Sat) showcases the exhaustive background of a building that fairly sweats history. If you book in advance (http://tours.visitthecapitol.gov), you can go on a free tour of the interior, which is as daunting as the exterior, cluttered with the busts, statues and personal mementos of generations of Congress members and a museum-worthy collection

of art. Note that it is also possible to queue for same-day tour passes at a walk-up line near an information desk of the visitor center; arrive early if you want a pass.

To watch Congress in action, US citizens can request visitor passes from their representatives or senators (☏ 202-224-3121); foreign visitors must show their passports at the House gallery. Congressional committee hearings are actually more interesting (and substantive) if you care about what's being debated; check for a schedule, locations and to see if they're open to the public (they often are) at www.house.gov and www.senate.gov.

Library of Congress
LANDMARK

(www.loc.gov; 1st St SE; ⊘ 8:30am-4:30pm Mon-Sat) **FREE** To prove to Europeans that America is cultured, John Adams plunked the world's largest library on Capitol Hill. The LOC's motivation is simple: 'universality' – the idea that all knowledge is useful. Stunning in scope and design, the building's baroque interior and neoclassical flourishes are set off by a main reading room that looks like an ant colony constantly harvesting 29 million books. The visitor center (p268) and tours of the reading rooms are both located in the **Jefferson Building**, just behind the Capitol building.

Supreme Court
LANDMARK

(☏ 202-479-3030; www.supremecourt.gov; 1 1st St NE; ⊘ 9am-4:30pm Mon-Fri; M Capitol South) **FREE** Even non-law students are impressed by the highest court in America. Arrive early to watch arguments (periodic Mondays through Wednesdays October to April). You can visit the permanent exhibits and the building's seven-spiral staircase year-round.

Folger Shakespeare
Library & Theatre
LIBRARY

(www.folger.edu; 201 E Capitol St SE; ⊘ 10am-5pm Mon-Sat, noon-5pm Sun; M Capitol South) **FREE** The Folger houses the world's largest collection of Shakespeare materials, and is open for both general visitation as well as ticketed performances and lectures.

National Postal Museum
MUSEUM

(www.postalmuseum.si.edu; 2 Massachusetts Ave NE; ⊘ 10am-5:30pm; ♿; M Union Station) **FREE** This museum has the planet's largest stamp collection, plus an antique mail plane and some moving war letters. A decent microbrewery sits above the museum.

SMITHSONIAN INSTITUTION MUSEUMS

Massive in size and ambition, the 19 **Smithsonian museums** (☑202-633-1000; www. si.edu; ☉10am to 5:30pm) **FREE**, galleries and zoo – all admission free – comprise the world's largest museum and research complex. You could spend weeks wandering endless corridors taking in the great treasures, artifacts and ephemera from America and beyond. Massive dinosaur skeletons, lunar modules and artworks from every corner of the globe are all part of the Smithsonian largesse. Thanks go to the curious Englishman James Smithson, who never visited the USA but willed the fledgling nation $500,000 to found an 'establishment for the increase and diffusion of knowledge' in 1826.

The Smithsonian's latest work-in-progress is the $500-million **National Museum of African American History and Culture** (www.nmaahc.si.edu; cnr Constitution Ave & 14th St NW), scheduled to open in 2015. Until then, you can peruse its temporary galleries on the 2nd floor of the National Museum of American History (p266).

Most museums are open daily (except Christmas Day). Some have extended hours in summer. Be prepared for lines and bag checks.

United States Botanic Garden   GARDENS

(www.usbg.gov; 100 Maryland Ave SW; ☉10am-5pm; ⚑; Ⓜ Federal Center SW) **FREE** This incongruous addition to the Hill is hot, sticky and green, with more than 4000 different plant species on display.

◉ Tidal Basin

It's magnificent to stroll around this constructed inlet and watch the monument lights wink across the Potomac. The blooms here are loveliest during the Cherry Blossom Festival, the city's annual spring rejuvenation, when the basin bursts into a pink-and-white floral collage. The original trees were a gift from the city of Tokyo, and planted in 1912.

Jefferson Memorial   MONUMENT

(900 Ohio Dr SW) **FREE** The domed memorial is etched with the Founding Father's most famous writings – although historians criticize some of the textual alterations (edited, allegedly, for space considerations). Regardless, there are wonderful views across the waterfront onto the Mall.

FDR Memorial   MONUMENT

(Memorial Park) **FREE** This 7.5-acre monument stands as tribute to the longest-serving president in US history and the era he governed. In a thoughtful, well-laid-out path, visitors are taken through the Depression, the New Deal era and WWII. It's best visited at night, when the interplay of rock, fountains and the lights of the Mall are enchanting.

Martin Luther King Jr Memorial   MONUMENT

(www.mlkmemorial.org) **FREE** The Martin Luther King Jr Memorial, which overlooks the banks of the Tidal Basin, is the Mall's first memorial dedicated to both a nonpresident and an African American, and pays moving tribute (through quotes taken from a dozen speeches) to one of the world's great peace advocates.

◉ Downtown

Downtown Washington began in what is now called Federal Triangle, but has since spread north and east, encompassing the area east of the White House to Judiciary Sq at 4th St, and from the Mall north to roughly M St.

Reynolds Center for American Art   MUSEUM

(cnr F & 8th Sts NW; ☉11:30am-7pm) **FREE** Don't miss the Reynolds Center for American Art, which combines the **National Portrait Gallery** (www.npg.si.edu) with the **American Art Museum** (http://americanart.si.edu) to create perhaps the most immersive, impressive collection of American art anywhere. From haunting depictions of both the inner city and rural heartland to the self-taught visions of itinerant wanderers, the center has dedicated itself to capturing the optimism and critical self-appraisal of American art, and it succeeds. The inner courtyard, roofed with slanting glass that filters the sunlight, is a lovely spot to relax in, while the impressive 3rd floor, once the model building of the national patent office, now serves as a stunning baroque great hall.

National Archives
LANDMARK

(www.archives.gov; 700 Constitution Ave NW; ⊙10am-7pm mid-Mar–early Sep, to 5:30pm early Sep–mid-Mar) FREE It's hard not to feel a little in awe of the big three documents in the National Archives: the Declaration of Independence, the Constitution and the Bill of Rights, plus one of four copies of the Magna Carta. Taken together, it becomes clear just how radical the American experiment was for its time. The Public Vaults, a bare scratching of archival bric-a-brac, make a flashy rejoinder to the main exhibit.

International Spy Museum
MUSEUM

(☑202-393-7798; www.spymuseum.org; 800 F St NW; adult/child $20/15; ⊙9am-7pm; ⦿; Ⓜ Gallery Place-Chinatown) You like those bits in the Bond movies with Q? Then you'll like the immensely popular International Spy Museum. All the undercover tools of the trade on display make this place great for (secret) history buffs. Get there early.

National Building Museum
MUSEUM

(www.nbm.org; 401 F St NW; adult/child $8/5; ⊙10am-5pm Mon-Sat, from 11am Sun, tours daily 11:30am, 12:30pm & 1:30pm; ⦿; Ⓜ Judiciary Sq) Devoted to architecture and urban design, this underappreciated museum is appropriately housed in a magnificent 19th-century edifice modeled after the Renaissance-era Palazzo Farnese in Rome. Four stories of ornamented balconies flank the dramatic 316ft-wide atrium, and the gold Corinthian columns rise 75ft high. Rotating exhibits on different aspects of the built environment are hidden in rooms off the atrium.

Renwick Gallery
MUSEUM

(www.americanart.si.edu/renwick; 1661 Pennsylvania Ave NW; ⊙10am-5:30pm; ⦿; Ⓜ Farragut West) FREE Near the White House, the Renwick Gallery is set in a stately 1859 mansion and exhibits a superb collection of American crafts and decorative-art pieces. Highlights include some over-the-top works such as Larry Fuente's extravagant kitsch *Game Fish* and Beth Lipman's ethereal *Bancketje (Banquet)*.

Old Post Office Pavilion
LOOKOUT

(www.oldpostofficedc.com; 1100 Pennsylvania Ave NW; ⊙10am-8pm Mon-Sat, to 7pm Sun; Ⓜ Federal Triangle) FREE If you don't want the hassle of the lines at the Washington Monument, head to this little-visited 1899 Romanesque Revival building, whose 315ft observation tower gives great downtown panoramas.

Down below, there's a floodlit atrium and international food court.

Ford's Theatre
HISTORIC SITE

(☑202-426-6924; www.fords.org; 511 10th St NW; tours $2.50; ⊙9am-4:30pm; Ⓜ Metro Center, Gallery Place-Chinatown) FREE On April 14, 1865, John Wilkes Booth assassinated Abraham Lincoln in his box seat here. The theater still operates today; you can also take a tour of the theater and learn about the events that transpired on that fateful April night. There's a restored **Lincoln Museum** devoted to Lincoln's presidency that you can see as part of the tour. Arrive early to get a ticket, as limited numbers are admitted each day. You can also use your ticket to explore the nearby **Petersen House** (516 10th St), where Lincoln eventually gave up the ghost.

Marian Koshland Science Museum of the National Academy of Sciences
MUSEUM

(www.koshland-science-museum.org; cnr 6th & E Sts NW; adult/child $7/4; ⊙10am-6pm Wed-Mon; ⦿; Ⓜ Judiciary Sq, Gallery Place-Chinatown) A big, kid-friendly complex of hands-on, educational fun with (as you would expect) a science-oriented focus.

◉ White House & Foggy Bottom

An expansive park called the Ellipse borders the Mall; on the east side is the powerbroker block of Pennsylvania Ave. Foggy Bottom was named for the mists that belched out of a local gasworks; now, as the home of the State Department and George Washington University, it's an upscale (if not terribly lively) neighborhood crawling with students and professionals.

★ White House
LANDMARK

(☑tours 202-456-7041; www.whitehouse.gov; ⊙tours 7:30am-11am Tue-Sat; Ⓜ Farragut West, Farragut North, McPherson Sq, Metro Center) The White House has survived both fire (the Brits torched it in 1814 – only a thunderstorm saved its complete destruction) and insults (Jefferson groused that it was 'big enough for two emperors, one Pope and the grand Lama'). Although its facade has changed little since 1924, its interior has seen frequent renovations. Franklin Roosevelt added a pool; Truman gutted the whole place (and simply discarded many of its historical features – today's rooms are replicas); Jacqueline Kennedy brought back antique furnishings and historic details; Nixon added a bowling alley; Carter installed solar roof panels, which Reagan then removed; Clinton added a jogging track; and George W Bush included a T-ball field. Cars can no longer pass the White House on Pennsylvania Ave, clearing the area for posing school groups and round-the-clock peace activists.

➡ Tours

A self-guided tour will lead you through the ground and 1st floors, but the 2nd and 3rd floors are off-limits, and we have to warn you: due to staffing reductions brought about by the government's inability to settle on a working budget, tours had been canceled until further notice at the time of writing. That said, the tours are so popular, we are confident (fingers crossed) they will resume.

If so, tours must be arranged (up to six months) in advance. Americans must apply via one of their state's members of Congress, and non-Americans must apply through either the US consulate in their home country or their country's consulate in DC. If that sounds like too much work, pop into the **White House Visitor Center** (www.whitehouse.gov; cnr 15th & E Sts NW; ⊙7:30am-4pm); it's not the real deal, but hey, there's executive paraphernalia scattered about.

➡ Watergate

The riverfront **Watergate complex** (www.watergatehotel.com; 2650 Virginia Ave NW; Ⓜ Foggy Bottom-GWU) encompasses apartments, boutiques and the office towers that made 'Watergate' a byword for political scandal after it broke that President Nixon's 'plumbers' had bugged the headquarters of the 1972 Democratic National Committee.

⊙ U Street, Logan Circle & Shaw

If you need proof that the District is a living, breathing, changing city as opposed to a calcified capital, look no further than U St. Through the 20th century, this road went from a center of African American commerce to a blighted drug-dealing corridor to possibly the most gentrified street in the city. Today the U St area (especially 14th St NW) is a center for dining, nightlife and shopping, The area's African American history is acknowledged by the presence of the **African American Civil War Memorial**, inscribed with the name of African American Civil War dead, at the U Street metro station. Nearby Shaw and Logan Circle are

STEVEN F UDVAR-HAZY CENTER

The Smithsonian National Air & Space Museum's **Steven F Udvar-Hazy Center** (www.nasm.si.edu/udvarhazy; 14390 Air & Space Museum Parkway; ⊙10am-5:30pm, to 6:30pm late May-early Sep; ▣) FREE, located in Chantilly near Dulles airport, is a huge hangar filled with surplus planes and spacecraft that wouldn't fit at the museum's DC location. Highlights include the space shuttle *Enterprise*, the B-29 *Enola Gay*, SR-71 *Blackbird* and a Concorde supersonic airliner. While the museum is free, parking costs $15.

some of the city's most pleasant residential neighborhoods.

Meridian Hill Park PARK
(www.nps.gov/mehi; btwn 15th, 16th, Euclid & W Sts NW; ⊙sunrise-sunset; Ⓜ U Street-Cardozo) This is an incredible bit of green space that gets short shrift in the list of America's great urban parks. What makes the park special is the way it emphasizes its distinctive geography. Lying on the fall line between the upland Piedmont Plateau and flat Atlantic Coastal Plain, the grounds are terraced like a hanging garden, replete with waterfalls, sandstone terraces and assorted embellishments that feel almost Tuscan. Many locals still call this Malcolm X Park.

Lincoln Theatre LANDMARK
(☑202-328-6000; www.thelincolntheatre.org; 1215 U St NW) The historic Lincoln Theatre was an early cornerstone of the nation's African American renaissance when it was founded in 1922. Luminaries such as DC-native Duke Ellington as well as Louis Armstrong, Ella Fitzgerald, Billie Holiday, Sarah Vaughan and many others have lit up the stage here.

⊙ Dupont Circle

A well-heeled splice of gay community and DC diplomatic scene, this is city life at its best. Great restaurants, bars, bookstores and cafes, captivating architecture and the electric energy of a lived-in, happening neighborhood make Dupont worth a linger. The historic mansions have largely been converted into embassies, and Embassy Row (on Massachusetts Ave) runs through DC's thumping gay heart.

Phillips Collection
MUSEUM

(www.phillipscollection.org; 1600 21st St NW; admission Mon-Fri free, Sat & Sun $10, ticketed exhibitions $12, chamber-music series per ticket $20; ⊙10am-5pm Tue & Wed, Fri & Sat, to 8:30pm Thu, 11am-6pm Sun, chamber-music series 4pm Sun Oct-May; Ⓜ Dupont Circle) The first modern-art museum in the country (opened in 1921) houses a small but exquisite collection of European and American works – including pieces by Gauguin, van Gogh, Matisse, Picasso, O'Keeffe, Hopper and many other greats. It's partially set in a beautifully restored Georgian Revival mansion.

Textile Museum
MUSEUM

(www.textilemuseum.org; 2320 S St NW; suggested donation $8; ⊙10am-5pm Tue-Sat, from 1pm Sun; Ⓜ Dupont Circle) Set in two historic mansions in the Kalorama neighborhood, the oft-overlooked Textile Museum showcases beautifully wrought creations from across the globe, including pre-Columbian weavings, American quilts and Ottoman embroidery.

National Geographic Society Museum
GALLERY

(🖉 202-857-7700; 1145 17 St NW; adult/child $11/7; ⊙10am-6pm; Ⓜ Farragut North) Rotating exhibits and lectures on the Society's worldwide expeditions are found here. Call ahead for details on what's offered.

⊙ Georgetown

Thousands of the bright and beautiful, from students to ivory-tower academics and diplomats, call this leafy, aristocratic neighborhood home. At night, shop-a-block M St becomes congested with traffic, turning into a weird mix of high-school cruising and high-street boutique.

The best way to explore the neighborhood is a stroll on the **C&O Canal Towpath** (🖉 20 2-653-5190; 1057 Thomas Jefferson St NW; ⊙9am-4:30pm Wed-Sun), which runs along a shaded path by a constructed waterway that once transported goods all the way to West Virginia. Also watch out for the **Exorcist Stairs** (3600 Prospect St NW), where Father Karras tumbled to his death in the eponymous 1973 horror movie.

Dumbarton Oaks
MUSEUM, GARDENS

(www.doaks.org; 1703 32nd St NW; museum free, gardens adult/child $8/5; ⊙museum 2-5pm Tue-Sun, gardens 2-6pm Tue-Sun) A museum featuring exquisite Byzantine and pre-Columbian art is housed within this historic mansion. More impressive are the 10 acres of beautifully designed formal gardens, which are simply stunning during the springtime blooms. Visit on weekdays to beat the crowds.

Mt Zion United Methodist Church
CHURCH

(www.mtzionumcdc.org; 1334 29th St NW) This church sits on one of the sites that recall the history of Georgetown's 19th-century free black community, who lived in an area known as Herring Hill. Founded in 1816, it claims DC's oldest black congregation. Its original site, on 27th St NW, was once a stop on the Underground Railroad.

Georgetown University
UNIVERSITY

(www.georgetown.edu; cnr 37th & O Sts NW) Bill Clinton went to school here, which should give you an idea of the student body: smart, hard-working party people.

Georgetown Waterfront Park
PARK

(www.georgetownwaterfrontpark.org; K St NW & Potomac River; 🖫) The Waterfront is a favorite with couples on first dates, singles hoping to hook up, families on an evening stroll and yuppies showing off their big yachts. The park begins at **Washington Harbour** (look for it east of 31st St NW), a modern complex of towers set around a circular terraced plaza filled with fountains (which light up like rainbows at night). Trees shade the pedestrian-friendly lanes, and benches dot the way, where you can sit and watch the rowing teams out on the water. Kids splash in the fountains at Wisconsin Ave's foot. At 33rd St there's a labyrinth in the grass; walk the circles and see if you feel more connected to the universe.

Oak Hill Cemetery
CEMETERY

(www.oakhillcemeterydc.org; cnr 30th & R Sts NW; ⊙9am-4:30pm Mon-Fri, 1-4pm Sun) This 24-acre, obelisk-studded cemetery contains winding walks and 19th-century gravestones set into the hillsides of Rock Creek. It's a fantastic spot for a quiet walk, especially in spring, when it seems as if every wildflower in existence blooms on the grounds. James Renwick designed the lovely gatehouse and charming gneiss-stone chapel.

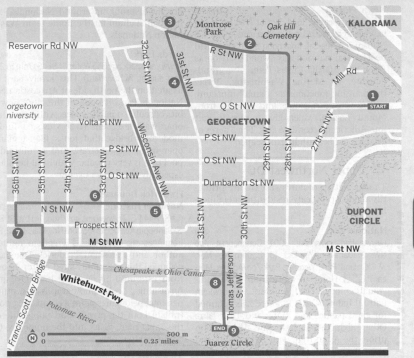

City Walk
Genteel Georgetown

START MT ZION CEMETERY
END GEORGETOWN WATERFRONT PARK
LENGTH 3 MILES; THREE HOURS

If ever a neighborhood was prime for ambling, it's Georgetown, in all its leafy, filigreed-
manor glory.

African American **1 Mt Zion Cemetery**,
near the intersection of 27th and Q Sts,
dates from the early 1800s. The nearby Mt
Zion church was a stop on the Underground
Railroad; escaping slaves hid in a vault in the
cemetery. The entrance to **2 Oak Hill Cemetery** (p272) is a few blocks away at 30th and
R Sts NW. Stroll the obelisk-studded grounds
and look for gravesites of prominent Washingtonians such as Edwin Stanton (Lincoln's war
secretary). Up the road **3 Dumbarton Oaks**
(p272) offers exquisite Byzantine art inside
and sprawling, fountain-dotted gardens outside. The blooms in springtime are stunning.

George Washington's step-granddaughter
Martha Custis Peter owned **4 Tudor Place**
(p274), the neoclassical mansion at 1644 31st
St. It has some of George's furnishings
from Mount Vernon on show.

Head over to Wisconsin Ave NW, and
stop in at **5 Martin's Tavern** (p282),
where John F Kennedy proposed to Jackie. Walk along N St and you'll pass several
Federal-style townhouses in the 3300
block. JFK and Jackie lived at **6 3307 N
St**, between 1958 and 1961.

At the corner of 36th St and Prospect
Ave, stare down the **7 Exorcist Stairs**
(p272). This is where demonically pos-
sessed Reagan of the *Exorcist* sent victims
to their screaming deaths. Joggers use the
stairs by day; at night the steps are legiti-
mately creepy as hell.

Head to M St NW and pop in to whichever boutiques your wallet permits. At
Jefferson St turn right and sniff your way to
8 Baked & Wired (p279) to replenish with
a monster cupcake and cappuccino. From
there you can stroll down to **9 Georgetown
Waterfront Park** (p272) to watch the boats
along the Potomac River.

Tudor Place   MUSEUM

(www.tudorplace.org; 1644 31st St NW; 1hr house tour adult/child $10/3, self-guided garden tour $3; ⊙10am-3pm Tue-Sat, from noon Sun) This 1816 neoclassical mansion was owned by Thomas Peter and Martha Custis Peter, the grand-daughter of Martha Washington. Today the mansion functions as a small museum, and features furnishings and artwork from Mount Vernon, which give a nice insight into American decorative arts. The 5 acres of grounds are beautifully landscaped.

👁 Upper Northwest DC

The far reaches of northwest DC are prima-rily made up of leafy residential neighbor-hoods.

National Zoo   ZOO

(www.nationalzoo.si.edu; 3001 Connecticut Ave NW; ⊙10am-6pm Apr-Oct, to 4:30pm Nov-Mar; Ⓜ Cleveland Park, Woodley Park-Zoo/Adams Morgan) FREE Home to more than 2000 indi-vidual animals (400 different species) in natural habitats, this 163-acre zoo is famed for giant pandas Mei Xiang and Tian Tian. Other highlights include: the African lion pride; the Asian trail, with red pandas and giant Japanese salamander; and dangling orangutans swinging 50ft overhead from steel cables and interconnected towers (the 'O Line').

Washington National Cathedral   CHURCH

(☏202-537-6200; www.nationalcathedral.org; 3101 Wisconsin Ave NW; suggested donation $5; ⊙10am-5:30pm Mon-Fri, to 4:30pm Sat, 8am-5pm Sun; 🚌32, 37) This Gothic cathedral, as dramatic as its European counterparts, blends both the spiritual and the profane in its architec-tural treasures. The stained-glass windows are stunning (check out the Space Window with its imbedded lunar rock), and you'll need binoculars to spy the Darth Vader gar-goyle on the exterior. Specialized tours delve deeper into the esoteric; call or go online for the schedule.

👁 Anacostia

The drive from Georgetown eastbound to Anacostia takes about 30 minutes – and the patience to endure a world of income dis-parity. The neighborhood's poverty in con-trast to the Mall, sitting mere miles away, forms one of DC's (and America's) great con-tradictory panoramas. Some high end con-

dos have sprung up around Nationals, the baseball stadium for the home team Wash-ington Nationals.

Yards Park   PARK

(www.yardspark.org; 355 Water St SE; ⊙7am to 2hr past sunset; Ⓜ Navy Yard) This lovely park is located on the north side of Anacostia near Nationals Park. It's one of the city's newer bits of sculpted public space, with a wooden boardwalk, excellent river views, a funky modernist bridge that looks like a giant, open-faced plastic straw, and a mini-tidal pool that is very popular with local families, especially on summer evenings.

Frederick Douglass
National Historic Site   HISTORIC SITE

(☏877-444-6777; www.nps.gov/frdo; 1411 W St SE; ⊙9am-5pm Apr-Oct, to 4:30pm Nov-Mar; 🚌B2, B4 from Anacostia Metro) FREE Freedom fighter, author and statesman Frederick Douglass occupied this beautifully sited hilltop house from 1878 until his death in 1895. Original furnishings, books, photographs and other personal belongings paint a compelling por-trait of both the private and public life of this great man. Visits into the home are by organized tour only.

Anacostia Museum   MUSEUM

(☏202-633-4820; www.anacostia.si.edu; 1901 Fort PI SE; ⊙10am-5pm; 🚌W2, W3 from Anacos-tia Metro) FREE This Smithsonian museum is surrounded by the community that is the subject of its educational mission, and houses good rotating exhibits on the African American experience in the USA. Call ahead, as the museum closes for about a month be-tween installations.

🏃 Activities

Under the auspices of the National Park Service (NPS), the 1754 acres of **Rock Creek Park** (www.nps.gov/rocr; ⊙sunrise-sunset; Ⓜ Cleveland Park, Woodley Park-Zoo/Adams Morga) follow Rock Creek as it winds through the northwest of the city. There are miles of bi-cycling, hiking and horseback-riding trails, and even a few coyotes. The C&O Canal of-fers cycling and hiking trails in canalside parks, and the lovely 11-mile **Capital Cres-cent Trail** (www.cctrail.org; Water St) connects Georgetown north to Silver Spring, MD, via splendid Potomac River views. Fifteen miles north of DC, Great Falls National Park (p304) is an outstanding slice of wilderness, great for rafting or rock climbing onthe beautiful cliffs that hang over the Potomac.

The **Potomac Heritage National Scenic Trail** (www.nps.gov/pohe) connects Chesapeake Bay to the Allegheny Highlands along an 830-mile network that includes DC's **C&O Canal Towpath** (adult/child $8/5; ⊙ Apr–mid-Aug), the 17-mile Mt Vernon Trail (Virginia) and the 75-mile Laurel Highlands Trail (Pennsylvania).

Paddleboat rentals (☑ 202-479-2426; www.tidalbasinpaddleboats.com/; 1501 Maine Ave SW; 2-person boat per hr $12) are available at the boathouse at Tidal Basin. At the Potomac River end of Rock Creek Park, **Thompson Boat Center** (www.thompsonboatcenter.com; 2900 Virginia Ave NW; per hr/day water craft from $10/24, bikes from $7/28; ⊙ 8am-5pm Mar-Oct) rents canoes, kayaks and bikes.

Big Wheel Bikes (www.bigwheelbikes.com; 1034 33rd St NW; per 3hr/day $21/35; ⊙ 11am-7pm Tue-Fri, 10am-6pm Sat & Sun) is a good bike-rental outfitter, or try **Capital Bikeshare** (☑ 877-430-2453; www.capitalbikeshare.com; membership 24hr/3 days $7/15), a scheme modeled on bike-sharing schemes in Europe. It has a network of 1000-plus bicycles scattered at 100-odd stations around DC. To check out a bike, select the membership, insert credit card and off you go. The first 30 minutes are free; after that, rates rise exponentially ($1.50/3/6 per extra 30/60/90 minutes). Call or go online for complete details.

☞ Tours

DC Metro Food Tours
WALKING TOUR

(☑ 800-979-3370; www.dcmetrofoodtours.com; per person $30-65) These walking tours take in the culinary riches of DC, exploring various neighborhoods and stopping for bites along the way. Offerings include Eastern Market, U St, Little Ethiopia, Georgetown and Alexandria, VA.

DC by Foot
WALKING TOUR

(www.dcbyfoot.com) Guides for this free, tip-based walking tour dispense intriguing stories and historical details on different walks covering the National Mall, Arlington Cemetery and Lincoln's assassination.

Bike & Roll
CYCLE TOUR

(www.bikethesites.com; adult/child from $40/30; ⊙ mid-Mar–Nov) Offers a handful of day and evening bike tours around the city (plus combo boat–bike trips to Mt Vernon).

WASHINGTON, DC, FOR CHILDREN

The top destination for families is undoubtedly the (free!) National Zoo, and museums around the city will entertain and educate children of all ages. But if you – or they – tire of indoor attractions, there are plenty of enticing green spaces, such as the excellent Yards Park.

The DC-area **Our Kids** (www.our-kids.com) website has listings for kid-centric shows and events, family-friendly restaurants and loads of activity ideas.

Many hotels offer babysitting services, but you can also book through the reputable organization **Mothers' Aides** (☑ 703-250-0700; www.mystaffingsolutions.com/).

The wide-open spaces of the Mall are perfect for outdoor family fun, whether you want to throw a Frisbee, have a picnic, ride the old-fashioned **carousel** (tickets $2.50) or stroll through museums.

Kids like things that go squish and/or make other things go squish; they can find both in the dinosaurs and insects of the National Museum of Natural History (p263). The Kennedy Center (p285) puts on entertaining shows for tots, and the National Air & Space Museum (p263) has moon rocks, IMAX films and a wild simulation ride.

The National Theatre (p285) offers free Saturday-morning performances, from puppet shows to tap dancers (reservations required); the **Discovery Theater** (www.discoverytheater.org; 1100 Jefferson Dr SW; ☑; Ⓜ Smithsonian) stages entertaining shows for young audiences; and the **Imagination Stage** (☑ 301-961-6060; www.imaginationstage.org; 4908 Auburn Ave, Bethesda, MD; ⊙ 301-961-6060; Ⓜ Bethedsda) is a wonderful children's theater in Bethesda, a Metro-accessible suburb just north of DC.

Located about 15 miles east of downtown in Largo, MD, **Six Flags America** (☑ 301-249-1500; www.sixflags.com/america; 13710 Central Avenue Upper Marlboro, MD ; adult/child $60/38; ⊙ May-Oct, hours vary) offers a full array of roller coasters and tamer kiddie rides. Take the Metro blue line to Largo, then take the C22 bus to the park.

City Segway Tours TOUR
(☑202-626-0017; http://citysegwaytours.com/
washington-dc; $70) Extremely popular and re-
laxing way of seeing the major sights along
the Mall and in Penn Quarter.

✯ Festivals & Events

National Cherry Blossom Festival CULTURE
(www.nationalcherryblossomfestival.org; ☺ late
Mar-early Apr) This festival marks DC at her
prettiest.

Smithsonian Folklife Festival CULTURE
(www.festival.si.edu; ☺ Jun & Jul) This fun family
event, held over two weekends in June and
July, features distinctive regional folk art,
crafts, food and music.

Independence Day CULTURE
(☺ Jul 4) Not surprisingly, Independence Day
is a big deal here, celebrated with a parade,
an open-air concert and fireworks over the
Mall.

🛏 Sleeping

For B&Bs and private apartments citywide,
contact **Bed & Breakfast Accommodations** (☑877-893-3233; www.bedandbreakfast-
dc.com).

If you bring a car to DC, plan on $20 up-
wards per day for in-and-out privileges (or
stay in Arlington or Alexandria, where some
hotels have free parking). Keep in mind that
accommodations prices in DC get hit with a
hefty 14.5% hotel tax on top of room rates.

🛏 Capitol Hill

Liaison HOTEL $$
(☑202-638-1616; www.affinia.com; 415 New Jersey
Ave NW; r from $200; P@✿✖; MUnion Sta-
tion) The Liason has jazzed up the accom-
modation options in Capitol Hill. Modernist
rooms come in a stately slate-and-earth-
tones color palette, which creates a feeling
that's the right mix of corporate business
and playful fun times. That said, the rooftop
is all about the latter; there's trippy house
music and a rooftop pool that seems perpet-
ually occupied by attractive folks. It's within
spitting distance of the Capitol.

Hotel George BOUTIQUE HOTEL $$$
(☑202-347-4200; www.hotelgeorge.com; 15 E St
NW; r from $290; P✖@✿; MUnion Station)
George was the first DC hotel to take the
term 'boutique' to a daring, ultramodern
level. The stylish interior is framed by clean

lines, chrome-and-glass furniture and modern art. Rooms exude a cool creamy-white
Zen. The pop-art presidential accents (paintings of American currency, artfully rear-
ranged and diced up) are a little overdone,
but that's a minor complaint about what is
otherwise the hippest lodging on the Hill.

🛏 Downtown & White House Area

**Hostelling International –
Washington DC** HOSTEL $
(☑202-737-2333; www.hiwashingtondc.org; 1009
11th St NW; dm incl breakfast $30-55, r $120-150;
✖@✿; MMetro Center) Top of the budget
picks, this large, friendly hostel attracts a
laid-back international crowd and has loads
of amenities: loungerooms, a pool table,
free tours and movie nights, a kitchen and
a laundry.

Hotel Monaco HOTEL $$
(☑202-628-7177; www.monaco-dc.com; 700 F St
NW; r from $410, ste from $670; P☺✖@✿;
MGallery Place-Chinatown) The neoclassical
facade has aged with considerable grace at
this marble temple to stylish glamour. Free
goldfish on request and a geometric, deco-
inspired interior help polish the 1930s cool-
daddy-o vibe. All this is in the historic, grand
Corinthian-columned 1839 Tariff Building.
The location works well for families: it's
across the street from the Spy Museum,
Smithsonian American Art Museum and
Metro, and just four blocks from the Mall.

Hotel Harrington HOTEL $$
(☑800-424-8532, 202-628-8140; www.hotel-har-
rington.com; 436 11th St NW; r $130-200; P✖✿;
MFederal Triangle) One of the most affordable
options near the Mall, this aging, family-run
hotel has small, basic rooms that are clean
but in definite need of an update. Helpful
service and a great location make the Har-
rington great value for travelers who don't
mind a little lack of amenities.

★ Hay-Adams Hotel LUXURY HOTEL $$$
(☑202-638-6600; www.hayadams.com; 800 16th
St NW; r from $450; P✖@✿✖; MMcPherson
Sq) One of the city's great heritage hotels,
the Hay is a beautiful old building, where
'nothing is overlooked but the White House.'
It's named for two mansions that once stood
on the site (owned by secretary of state John
Hay and historian Henry Adams) that were
the nexus of Washington's political and in-
tellectual elite. Today the hotel has a palaz-

zo-style lobby and probably the best rooms of the old-school luxury genre in the city: puffy mattresses like clouds, four-poster canopies and gold-braid tassels.

Morrison-Clark Inn   HISTORIC HOTEL **$$**
(☎202-898-1200; www.morrisonclark.com; 1015 L St NW; r $200-350; P❋@⚆; ⓂMt Vernon Sq/7th St Convention Center) Listed on the Register of Historic Places, this elegant inn comprises two 1864 residences filled with fine antiques, chandeliers, richly hued drapes and other features evocative of the antebellum South. Some rooms come with private balconies or decorative marble fireplaces.

🛏 U Street, Shaw & Logan Circle

Chester Arthur House   B&B **$$**
(☎877-893-3233; www.chesterarthurhouse.com; 13th & P Sts NW; r incl breakfast $175-275; ❋⚆; ⓂU Street-Cardozo) Run by a delightful couple with serious travel experience under their belts – they both have National Geographic credentials – this is a good option for those wanting to explore beneath Washington's surface. Accommodations are in one of three rooms in a beautiful Logan Circle row house which is filled with antiques and collected ephemera from the hosts' global expeditions.

Hotel Helix   BOUTIQUE HOTEL **$$$**
(☎866-508-0658, 202-462-9001; www.hotelhelix.com; 1430 Rhode Island Ave NW; r from $220; P⊖❋@⚆; ⓂDupont Circle, U Street-Cardozo) Modish and highlighter bright, the Helix is playfully hip – the perfect hotel for the bouncy international set that makes up the surrounding neighborhood. Little touches suggest a youthful energy (Pez dispensers in the minibar) balanced with worldly cool, such as the pop-punk decor – just camp enough to be endearing. Specialty rooms include Bunk (that's right, bunk beds) and studios with kitchenettes; all rooms have comfy, crisp-sheet beds and flat-screen TVs.

🛏 Adams Morgan

American Guest House   B&B **$$**
(☎202-588-1180; www.americanguesthouse.com; 2005 Columbia Rd NW; r incl breakfast $160-220; ❋@⚆; ⓂDupont Circle) This 12-room bed-and-breakfast earns high marks for its warm, friendly service, good breakfasts and elegantly furnished rooms. Decor runs the gamut from Victorian vibe (room 203) to New England cottage (room 304) to colonial love nest (room 303). Some quarters are rather small.

Adam's Inn   B&B **$$**
(☎202-745-3600; www.adamsinn.com; 1746 Lanier Pl NW; r incl breakfast with bath $129-99, without bath $99-159; P❋⚆; ⓂWoodley Park-Zoo/Adams Morgan) On a pretty tree-lined street near Adams Morgan, this townhouse has small but nicely decorated rooms; thin walls mean you might hear your neighbor.

🛏 Dupont Circle

Hotel Palomar   HOTEL **$$**
(☎877-866-3070, 202-448-1800; www.hotelpalomar-dc.com; 2121 P St NW; r $260-380; P❋@ ⚆⚇☒; ⓂDupont Circle) The Palomar brings in a stylish business clientele, plus a whole lot of pooches. Room decor is bright, colorful and lashed with pop-art accents. The outdoor pool and deck go beyond the norm. Then there's the pet-friendly vibe, which the hotel does up big time. Not only does your dog get pampered each night with gourmet treats at turndown, it can also get a massage. Or drop your pooch off at the Dish, the hotel's pet lounging area.

Dupont Collection   B&B **$$**
(☎202-467-6777; http://thedupontcollection. com; r $120-260; P❋❋⚆) If you're craving a good range of B&B coziness in the heart of the capital, check out these three excellent heritage properties. Most-centrally located are the inns at **Dupont North** (☎202-467-6777; www.thedupontcollection.com; 1620 T St NW; r incl breakfast $115-270; ❋⚆; ⓂDupont Circle) and **Dupont South** (☎202-467-6777; www.thedupontcollection.com; 1312 19th St NW; r incl breakfast $115-230; ❋⚆; ⓂDupont Circle); the former feels like the modern home of a wealthy friend, while the latter evokes much more of a chintz-and-lacy-linen sensibility. The **Brookland** (http://thedupontcollection. com; 3742 12th St NE, Brookland Inn) is in the far northeast (but Metro accessible).

Akwaaba   B&B **$$$**
(☎866-466-3855; www.akwaaba.com; 1708 16th St NW; r $200-265; P❋⚆; ⓂDupont Circle) Part of a small chain of B&Bs that emphasize African American heritage in its properties, the well-located Dupont branch has uniquely furnished rooms set in a late-19th-century mansion. Expect a friendly welcome and excellent cooked breakfasts.

Carlyle Suites APARTMENT **$$$**
(☑202-234-3200; www.carlylesuites.com; 1731 New Hampshire Ave NW; apt $180-320; P✳@➿; Ⓜ Dupont Circle) Inside this all-suites art-deco gem, you'll find sizeable, handsomely furnished rooms with crisp white linens, luxury mattresses, 37in flat-screen TVs and full kitchens. The friendly staff is first rate, and the added extras include free use of laptops and complimentary access to the Washington Sports Club. Plus the on-site bar pours a mean martini. Parking is limited to 20 spaces (out of about 170 rooms), and it's first-come, first-served.

🛏 Georgetown

Graham Georgetown HOTEL **$$$**
(☑202-337-0900; http://thegrahamgeorgetown. com/; 1075 Thomas Jefferson St NW; r from $330; P✳@➿; Ⓜ Foggy Bottom-GWU to DC Circulator) Set smack in the heart of Georgetown, the Graham occupies the intersection between stately tradition and modernist hip. Rooms have tasteful floral prints and duochrome furnishings with geometric accents. Even the most basic rooms have linens by Liddell Ireland and Bvlgari White Tea bath amenities, which means you'll be as fresh, clean and beautiful as the surrounding Georgetown glitterati.

🍴 Eating

As you might expect of one of the world's most international cities, DC has an eclectic palate, with a superb array of restaurants serving Ethiopian, Indian, Southeast Asian, French, Italian and more, plus good old-fashioned Southern fare. Annoyingly, this is an expensive town to eat out in; cheap options are rare and midrange dining options can be poor value for money. Well, unless you follow our recommendations, that is.

🍴 Capitol Hill

H St NE forms a continuous stretch of restaurants and bars, and becomes a nightlife miracle mile come weekends. To get to H St, you can either walk from Union Station (H & 14th, which is the far end of the strip, is 1.3 miles away), or take a free H St shuttle from Gallery Place-Chinatown and Minnesota Ave Metro stops. The shuttle runs from 5pm until Metro rail closes (midnight on weekdays, 3am on weekends). And 8th St SE near Eastern Market – also known as Bar-racks Row – is also packed with restaurants and bars.

Eastern Market MARKET **$**
(225 7th St SE; ⊘7am-7pm Tue-Fri, to 6pm Sat, 9am-5pm Sun) One of the icons of Capitol Hill, this covered arcade sprawls with delectable produce and good cheer on the weekends. The crab cakes at the Market Lunch stall are divine.

Toki Underground ASIAN **$**
(☑202-388-3086; www.tokiunderground.com; 1234 H St NE; mains $10; ⊘5-10pm Mon-Wed, to 11pm Thu, to midnight Fri & Sat, closed Sun; 🚍 H Street shuttle) Spicy, belly-warming ramen noodles and dumplings sum up the menu in wee Toki. Steaming pots and pans obscure the busy chefs, while diners slurp and sigh contentedly. No reservations are taken and there's typically a long wait. Take the opportunity to explore surrounding bars; Toki will text when your table's ready. Despite the name, Toki Underground is on the 2nd floor. It's not marked; look for the Pug bar sign – the restaurant is above it.

Maine Avenue Fish Market SEAFOOD **$**
(1100 Maine Ave SW; meals from $7; ⊘8am-9pm; Ⓜ L'Enfant Plaza) In case you didn't know, Washington, DC, is basically in Maryland, and Maryland does the best seafood in America. You get it fresh here – still flopping, in fact – where locals will kill, strip, shell, gut, fry, broil or whatever your fish, crabs, oysters etc in front of your eyes.

Atlas Room AMERICAN **$$**
(☑202-388-4020; 1015 H St NE; mains $11-25; ⊘5:30-9:30pm Mon, to 10pm Tue-Thu, to 10:30pm Fri & Sat, 5-9:30pm Sun; 🚍 H Street shuttle) The Atlas Room takes some cues from classical French and Italian gastronomy, but blends them in uniquely American ways, while drawing from an entirely seasonal roster of ingredients; in summer you might enjoy crab fritters, while in winter a braised daube of beef will melt your tongue (in a good way!).

Granville Moore's BELGIAN **$$**
(☑202-399-2546; www.granvillemoores.com; 1238 H St NE; mains $11-16; ⊘5pm-midnight Sun-Thu, to 3am Fri & Sat; 🚍 H Street shuttle) One of the anchors of the bohemian Atlas District (which runs along H St NE), Granville Moore's bills itself as a gastropub with a Belgian fetish. Indeed you'll find more

TOP CAFES

★ **Baked & Wired** (☑202-333-2500; www.bakedandwired.com; 1052 Thomas Jefferson St NW; snacks $3-6; ⊙7am-8pm Mon-Thu, to 9pm Fri, 8am-9pm Sat, 9am-8pm Sun; 🛜) Baked & Wired is a cheery little Georgetown cafe that whips up beautifully made coffees and delectable desserts; it's a fine spot to join students in both real and virtual chatter (free wi-fi, of course).

Ching Ching Cha (1063 Wisconsin Ave NW; teas $6-12; ⊙11am-9pm) This airy, Zenlike tea-house feels a world away from the shopping mayhem of Georgetown's M St. Stop in for a pot of rare tea (more than 70 varieties). CCC also serves steamed dumplings, sweets and simple but flavorful three-course lunches ($30).

Pound (www.poundcoffee.com; 621 Pennsylvania Ave SE; mains $5-8; ⊙7am-9:30pm Mon-Sat, 8am-8pm Sun; 🛜; Ⓜ Eastern Market) In Capitol Hill, Pound serves high-quality coffees in an elegant rustic interior (exposed brick and timber, original plaster ceilings, wood floors and nicely lit artwork). Breakfast quesadillas, panini and daily lunch specials are tops – as is the Nutella latte.

Filter (www.filtercoffeehouse.com; 1726 20th St NW; ⊙7am-7pm Mon-Fri, 8am-7pm Sat & Sun; 🛜; Ⓜ Dupont Circle) On a quiet street in Dupont, Filter is a jewel-box-sized cafe with a tiny front patio, a hipsterish laptop-toting crowd and, most importantly, great coffee. Those who seek caffeinated perfection can get a decent flat white here.

than 70 Belgian beers, good pub fare and fun crowds most nights.

Ethiopic   ETHIOPIAN $$
(☑202-675-2066; 401 H St NE ; mains $12-17; ⊙5-10pm Tue-Thu, from noon Fri & Sun; 🚌 H Street shuttle) In a city with no shortage of Ethiopian joints, Ethiopic stands above the rest. We're big fans of the signature ho*t wat* (stews) and *tibs* (sauteed meat and veg), derived from tender lamb that's sat in a bath of herbs and satisfyingly hot spices. Pair with good spongy *injera* bread and simmered *gomen* (collard greens). Plenty of options for vegetarians and vegans.

Ted's Bulletin   AMERICAN $$
(☑202-544-8337; www.tedsbulletin.com; 505 8th St SE; mains $10-18; ⊙7am-10:30pm, to 11:30pm Fri & Sat; 📶; Ⓜ Eastern Market) Plop into a booth in the art-deco-meets-diner ambience, and loosen the belt. Beer biscuits and sausage gravy for breakfast, meatloaf with ketchup glaze for dinner and other hipster spins on comfort foods hit the table. You've got to admire a place that lets you substitute pop tarts for toast. Breakfast is available all day.

✗ Downtown & White House Area

Merzi   INDIAN $
(☑202-656-3794; 415 7th St NW; meals under $10; ⊙11am-10pm Mon-Sat, to 9pm Sun; 📶; Ⓜ Gallery Place-Chinatown, Archives-Navy Memorial) 🍴 If

you need cheap Indian – especially cheap vegetarian Indian – in downtown DC, this is where to be. Merzi's setup is simple: choose a base (roti, rice, salad etc), a protein (chicken, lamb etc) or veg, then add sauces, chutney and such. Your wallet will barely feel lighter for the visit.

★ **Rasika**   INDIAN $$
(☑202-637-1222; www.rasikarestaurant.com; 633 D St NW; mains $16-26; ⊙11:30am-2:30pm Mon-Fri, 5:30-10:30pm Mon-Thu, to 11pm Fri, 5-11pm Sun; 📶; Ⓜ Archives-Navy Memorial) Rasika is as cutting edge as Indian food gets, both in terms of menu and presentation. The latter resembles a Jaipur palace decorated by a flock of modernist art-gallery curators; the former... well, it's *good*. Narangi duck is juicy, almost unctuous, and pleasantly nutty thanks to the addition of cashews; the deceptively simple *dal* (lentils) have the right kiss of sharp fenugreek. Vegans and vegetarians will feel a lot of love here.

Hill Country Barbecue   BARBECUE $$
(☑202-556-2050; 410 7th St NW; mains $13-22; ⊙11:30am-2am; Ⓜ Archives-Navy Memorial, Gallery Place-Chinatown) Penn Quarter is frankly overflowing with overpriced, overrated eating establishments. Hill Country is none of those things. It's a total anomaly for DC – a Texas-themed joint filled with cowboy hats and boots that doesn't feel corny; a barbecue spot that serves excellent smoked meat;

a live-music venue that hosts great Texas honky-tonk shows.

Zaytinya
MEDITERRANEAN $$
(☎202-638-0800; 701 9th St NW; mezze $7-13; ⏰11:30am-11:30pm Tue-Sat, to 10pm Sun & Mon) One of the culinary crown jewels of chef José Andrés, ever-popular Zaytinya serves superb Greek, Turkish and Lebanese mezze (small plates) in a long, narrow dining room with soaring ceilings and all-glass walls. Stop in for $4 happy-hour specials from 4:30pm to 6:30pm.

★ Central Michel Richard
FUSION $$$
(☎202-626-0015; 1001 Pennsylvania Ave NW; mains $19-34; ⏰11:30am-2:30pm Mon-Fri, 5-10:30pm Mon-Thu, to 11pm Fri & Sat; ⏰; Ⓜ Federal Triangle, Archives-Navy Memorial) Michel Richard is known for high-end eating establishments in the District, but Central stands out. It's aimed at hitting a comfort-food sweet spot; you're dining in a four-star bistro where the food is old-school favorites with a twist: lobster burgers, a sinfully complex meatloaf and fried chicken that redefines what fried chicken can be. It's an awesome dining experience, well worth a splurge.

Bibiana
ITALIAN $$$
(☎202-216-9550; 1100 New York Ave NW; mains $18-34; ⏰11:30am-2:30pm Mon-Fri, 5:30-10:30pm Mon-Wed , to 11pm Thu-Sat; ⏰) Owned by Ashok Bajaj of Rasika, Bibiana pushes contemporary Italian just as its sister establishment does with Indian cuisine. Chiluluy-esque chandeliers and light fixtures hang over an ultramodern dining room, where diners enjoy tortellini with guinea fowl and foie gras, or poached halibut over green-tomato polenta. A meat-free tasting menu is a standout in DC's vegetarian repertoire.

🍴 U Street, Shaw & Logan Circle

American Ice Company
BARBECUE $
(☎202-758-3562; 917 V St NW; mains under $10; ⏰5pm-2am Mon-Thu, to 3am Fri, 1pm-3am Sat, 1pm-2am Sun; Ⓜ U Street-Cardozo) The usual U St/Columbia Heights crew of hipsters, policy wonks (people who aren't politicians who work in politics as researchers, lobbyists, legislative aides etc) and policy wonks who kind of look like hipsters packs the cluttered interior and much nicer outdoor patio of this casual eatery. The focus is on barbecue and canned beer, pretty much in that order.

Try the gooey pork-and-cheese sandwich or the delicious pork nachos (yes, pork nachos).

Desperados
BURGERS $
(☎202-299-0433; 1342 U St NW; mains under $10; ⏰11am-1:30am Mon-Thu & Sun, to 2:30am Fri & Sat; Ⓜ U-St/Cardozo) This little cowboy-themed spot is a U St standby when you're out and need a cheap, filling burger. These beef patties don't play; they're the size of your face and come in several variations, including a pleasingly spicy Cajun version. The bar churns out cocktails that will lay you on your back.

El Centro
MEXICAN $$
(☎202-328-3131; 1819 14th St NW; mains $9-20; ⏰11am-11pm daily, brunch 10:30am-3pm Sat & Sun; ⏰; Ⓜ U Street-Cardozo) El Centro is our favorite of Richard Sandoval's many outposts in DC. With sleek furniture, chic clientele and a sexy rooftop deck, it's often known as more nightlife spot than restaurant (the bar is open till 2am). For shame – this is excellent noveau-Mexican cuisine. The guacamole is the best in town, duck tacos are delicious and the slow-roasted carnitas (pork) met in your mouth.

Estadio
SPANISH $$
(☎202-319-1404; 1520 14th St NW; tapas $5-15; ⏰Mon-Thu 5-10pm, to 11pm Fri & Sat, to 9pm Sun, 11:30am-2pm Fri-Sun; ⏰; Ⓜ U Street-Cardozo) Estadio stands tall amid the Spanish cuisine purveyors of the capital. The tapas menu (which is the focus) is as deep as an ocean trench; there's three variations of *Iberico* ham and a delicious foie gras, scrambled egg and truffle open-faced sandwich. Wash it down with some traditional *calimocho* (red wine and coke).

Veranda on P
MEDITERRANEAN $$
(☎202-234-6870; 1100 P St NW; mains $12-25; ⏰5pm-12:30am Mon-Thu, later Sat & Sun; ⏰; Ⓜ U Street-Cardozo) The interior of this cozy little nook vaguely brings a Greek Island to mind, but we prefer the outdoor eponymous veranda, which sits amid the handsome red-brick townhouses of Logan Circle. The food is Mediterranean and quite good value; melted Kefalograviera cheese is an excellent appetizer to set up for a main event of silky moussaka.

Pig
AMERICAN $$
(☎202-290-2821; 1320 14th St NW; mains $12-21; ⏰noon-10:30pm Mon & Tue, to 11pm Wed & Thu, to 11:30pm Fri, 11am-11:30pm Sat, to 10pm Sun; Ⓜ U

THE BEAUTY OF BEN'S CHILI BOWL

Ben's Chili Bowl (www.benschilibowl.com; 1213 U St; mains $5-9; ⊙11am-2am Mon-Thu, to 4am Fri & Sat, to midnight Sun; Ⓜ U Street-Cardozo) is to DC dining what the White House and Capitol are to sightseeing: a must-visit. To take that analogy further, while the White House and Capitol are the most recognizably important symbols of DC as a capital, Ben's holds the same status as regards DC as a place where people live. Opened and operated by Ben and Virginia Ali and family (Ben died in 2009; the alley adjacent is named in his honor), the diner-style Bowl has been around since 1958. It's one of the few businesses on U St to have survived the 1968 riots and the disruption that accompanied construction of the U St Metro stop. The main stock in trade are half-smokes, DC's meatier, smokier version of the hot dog, usually slathered in mustard and the namesake chili. Until recently, Bill Cosby was the only person who ate here for free, but Michelle Obama and daughters Sasha and Malia get the nod, too – though, apparently, not their presidential dad. That's a short list, as a lot of famous faces have passed through these doors, from Bono to both Bushes. Cash only.

Street-Cardozo) The Pig lives up to its name, offering plenty of porcine-inspired treats from crispy shank to a decadent cutlet-and-gruyere sandwich that will leave you lost for words. There's nonporky goodness as well, including some wonderful cornmeal-dusted oysters and a surprisingly vegetarian-friendly chickpea hash (that said, this isn't the best spot for herbivores).

Eatonville SOUTHERN $$
(☎202-332-9672; www.eatonvillerestaurant.com; 2121 U St NW; mains $9-21; ⊙11am-11pm Mon-Thu, to midnight Fri, 3pm-midnight Sat, 3-11pm Sun; Ⓜ U Street-Cardozo) Novelist Zora Neal Hurston is the unconventional theme at this restaurant. The atmosphere is superb, a sort of bayou dripped through impressionist-style murals of the South, then resurrected upon a modernist, cavernous dining hall that looks like nothing less than a cathedral to black intelligentsia. Catfish come correct with cheese grits, and the andouille-and-sweet-potato hash...don't get us started. Wash it down with lavender lemonade, which, on hot summer days, is sort of like drinking sex.

Pearl Dive Oyster Palace SEAFOOD $$
(www.pearldivedc.com; 1612 14th St NW; mains $19-25; ⊙noon-3pm Fri & Sat, 11am-3pm Sun, 5-10pm daily; Ⓜ U Street-Cardozo) 🌿 Flashy Pearl Dive serves exceptional sustainable oysters from both coasts, along with braised duck and oyster gumbo, crab cakes and insanely rich peanut-butter chocolate pie. Fresh air from the front windows wafts through the open industrial space, done up in a nautical, weathered-wood motif. No reservations; you'll need to take a number (like a deli).

Adams Morgan

Adams Morgan, particularly the area around 18th St and Columbia Rd NW, is lined with ethnic eateries and funky diners.

Diner AMERICAN $$
(www.dinerdc.com; 2453 18th St NW; mains $8-16; ⊙24hr; 👶; Ⓜ Woodley Park-Zoo/Adams Morgan) This is the ideal spot for late-night breakfast, (crowded) weekend bloody Mary brunches or anytime you want unfussy, well-prepared American fare (omelets, stuffed pancakes, mac 'n' cheese, grilled Portobello sandwiches, burgers and the like). It's a good spot for kids, too (staff will even hang their Diner-made colorings on the wall).

Cashion's Eat Place AMERICAN $$$
(☎202-797-1819; www.cashionseatplace.com; 1819 Columbia Rd NW; mains $17-34; ⊙5:30-11pm Tue-Sun; Ⓜ Woodley Park-Zoo/Adams Morgan) With an original menu and inviting decor, this little bistro is lauded as one of the city's very best. The mismatched furniture and flower boxes create an unpretentious setting for enjoying rich dishes such as scallion-cream sauced crab and bison rib eye with wild mushroom *bordelaise* sauce. The bar serves fancy late-night fare, such as pork cheek and goat's cheese quesadillas, till 2am on Friday and Saturday.

Dupont Circle

★**Afterwords Cafe** AMERICAN $$
(☎202-387-3825; www.kramers.com; 1517 Connecticut Ave; mains $15-24; ⊙7:30am-1:30am Sun-Thu, 24hr Fri & Sat; Ⓜ Dupont Circle) Not your average bookstore cafe, this buzzing spot

overflows with good cheer at its packed cafe tables and outdoor patio. The menu features tasty bistro fare and an ample beer selection, making it a prime spot for happy hour or brunch and all hours on weekends.

Bistrot du Coin
FRENCH **$$**

(📞 202-234-6969; www.bistrotducoin.com; 1738 Connecticut Ave; mains $14-24; ⏱ 11:30am-11pm, to 1am Thu-Sat; Ⓜ Dupont Circle) For a quick culinary journey across the Atlantic, the lively and much-loved Bistro du Coin delivers the goods. You'll find consistently good onion soup, classic *steak-frites* (grilled steak and french fries), cassoulet, open-faced sandwiches and nine varieties of its famous *moules* (mussels).

Blue Duck Tavern
AMERICAN **$$**

(📞 202-419-6755; www.blueducktavern.com; 1201 24th St NW; mains $16-34; ⏱ 6:30am-2:30pm & 5:30-10:30pm Sun-Thu, till 11.30pm Fri & Sat; 🍴; Ⓜ Dupont Circle) The Blue Duck tries to create a rustic kitchen ambience in the midst of one of M St's uber-urbanized concrete corridors. The menu draws from farms across the country, mixing mains such as a pork terrine and trotter croquette made from pigs in Virginia, and crab cakes sourced from Louisiana.

Malaysia Kopitiam
MALAYSIAN **$$**

(📞 202-833-6232; www.malaysiakopitiam.com; 1827 M St NW; mains $9-15; ⏱ 11:30am-10pm Mon-Thu, to 11pm Fri & Sat, noon-10pm Sun; Ⓜ Dupont Circle) This hole-in-the-wall restaurant is a good spot to get your Malaysian fix. Standouts include the *laksas* (curry noodle soups), *roti canai* (flatbread served with chicken curry) and crispy squid salad.

★ Little Serrow
THAI **$$$**

(1511 17th St NW; fixed menu per person $45; ⏱ 5:30-10pm Tue-Thu, to 10:30 Fri & Sat) There' are a lot of annoying rules at Little Serrow. There's no phone, and no reservations. It only allows groups of four or less, and you'll be lining up around the block. And what for? Superlative Northern Thai cuisine. The single-option menu changes by the week; you might get chicken livers and long peppers, or shrimp paste, eggplant and chilies, or pig ears garnished with mint. Every dish comes with mountains of heaping fresh herbs.

Komi
FUSION **$$$**

(📞 202-332-9200; www.komirestaurant.com; 1509 17th St NW; set menu $135; ⏱ 5-11pm Tue-Sat; Ⓜ Dupont Circle) There's an admirable simplicity to Komi's changing menu, which is rooted in Greece and influenced by everything – primarily genius. Suckling pig for two; scallops and truffles; a roasted baby goat. Komi's fairytale of a dining space doesn't take groups larger than four, and you need to reserve way in advance – like, now.

✗ Georgetown

Et Voila
BELGIAN **$$**

(📞 202-237-2300; 5120 MacArthur Blvd NW; mains $16-29; ⏱ 11:30am-2:30pm & 5:30-10pm Tue-Fri & Sat, 11:30am-2:30pm Sat & Sun, 5-9:30pm Mon) A definite local gem, Et Voila sits in a beautiful corner of the Palisades, northwest of Georgetown. While the name suggests French, this spot leans a little north to Belgium. Dishes such as rib eye with *frites*, lobster risotto and roasted chicken have a hearty, rustic heft coupled with a refined execution. The atmosphere is supremely intimate.

Martin's Tavern
AMERICAN **$$**

(📞 202-333-7370; www.martins-tavern.com; 1264 Wisconsin Ave NW; mains $12-25; ⏱ 11am-1:30am Mon-Thu, to 2:30am Fri, 9am-2:30am Sat, 8am-1:30am Sun) Martin's is a favorite with Georgetown students and US presidents, who all enjoy the tavern's old-fashioned dining room and unfussy classics such as thick burgers, crab cakes and prime rib.

✗ Upper Northwest DC

2 Amys
PIZZA **$$**

(📞 202-885-5700; www.2amyspizza.com; 3715 Macomb St NW; mains $9-14; ⏱ 11am-10pm Tue-Thu, to 11pm Fri & Sat, noon-10pm Sun, 5-10pm Mon; 🍴; Ⓜ Tenleytown-AU then southbound 🚌 31, 32, 36, 37) A bit out of the way (but a stone's throw from Washington National Cathedral), 2 Amys serves some of DC's best thin-crust pizzas. Pies are sprinkled with market-fresh ingredients and baked to perfection in a wood-burning oven. Avoid the weekend crowds.

Palena
AMERICAN **$$$**

(📞 202-537-9250; www.palenarestaurant.com; 3529 Connecticut Ave NW; 3-/5-course menu $80/100; ⏱ 5:30-10:30pm Tue-Sat; Ⓜ Cleveland Park) Tucked away in Cleveland Park, northwest on the Red Line, Palena is one of DC's food-loving heavyweights. Red snapper with ramps (wild leeks) and oyster mushrooms; artichoke risotto; and celery root soup with shrimp and almonds are recent favorites. Reserve ahead or eat in the more casual cafe (mains from $17 to $30).

✖ Columbia Heights & Around

Pho 14   VIETNAMESE $
(☑ 202-986-2326; www.dcpho14.com; 1436 Park Rd NW; mains $8-13; ☺ 11:30am-9pm Sun-Wed, to 10pm Thu-Sat; Ⓜ Columbia Heights) Smart, solid Pho 14 ladles out steaming bowls of the namesake noodle soup, as well as stir-fry dishes and *banh mi* sandwiches (baguettes filled with meat and/or spicy veggies) to brisk lunchtime and dinner crowds.

Kangaroo Boxing Club   AMERICAN $
(KBC; ☑ 202-505-4522; 3410 11th St NW; mains $10-17; ☺ 5pm-2am Mon-Thu, to 3am Fri, 10am-3am Sat, to 2am Sun) The gastropub concept – but a hip, laid-back, Brooklyn-esque gastropub – is all the rage among DC's hip young things. Enter the KBC: it has a quirky theme (vintage boxing), delicious food (burgers, BBQ, sweet spoon bread, mac 'n' cheese and the like) and a deep beer menu.

El Chucho   MEXICAN $
(☑ 202-290-3313; 3313 11th St NW; tacos $6-12; ☺ 4pm-2am, to 3am Fri & Sat) There's a *Day of the Dead*–inspired interior, margaritas on tap, excellent *elote (corn)* smothered in white cheese and spices, and fresh guacamole. The tiny tacos leave us wanting more. Lots of cool tattooed staff members, and customers who love them.

🍷 Drinking & Nightlife

See the weekly *Washington City Paper* (p286) or *Washington Post* (p286) weekend section for comprehensive listings. Same-day concert and show tickets at half-price (no phone sales).

🍸 Capitol Hill & Downtown

Little Miss Whiskey's Golden Dollar   BAR
(www.littlemisswhiskeys.com; 1104 H St NE; ☺ from 5pm; 🚃 H Street shuttle) If Alice had got back from Wonderland so traumatized by a near-beheading that she needed to start engaging in heavy drinking, we imagine she'd often pop down to Little Miss Whiskey's. She'd love the decor: somewhere between whimsical and the dark nightmares of a lost drug addict. And she'd probably have fun with the club kids partying on the upstairs dance floor on weekends.

H Street Country Club   BAR
(www.thehstreetcountryclub.com; 1335 H St NE; ☺ from 5pm Mon-Thu, from 4pm Fri-Sun; 🚃 H Street shuttle) The Country Club is two levels of great. The bottom floor is packed with pool tables, skeeball and shuffleboard, while the top contains (seriously) its own mini-golf course ($7 to play) done up to resemble a tour of the city on a small scale.

18th Amendment   BAR
(www.18thdc.com; 613 Pennsylvania Ave SE; Ⓜ Eastern Market, Capitol South) The Amendment embraces a speakeasy theme – hence the name. Gangsters and bootleggers should head directly to the basement, where the furniture is made from beer barrels and whiskey crates, and there are pool tables on which to fight your duel.

🍸 U Street, Shaw & Logan Circle

Marvin   BAR
(www.marvindc.com; 2007 14th St NW; Ⓜ U Street-Cardozo) Stylish Marvin has a low-lit lounge with vaulted ceilings where DJs spin soul and rare grooves to a mixed 14th St crowd. The upstairs roof deck is a draw both on summer nights and in winter, when folks huddle under roaring heat lamps sipping cocktails and Belgian beers. Good bistro fare, too.

Patty Boom Boom   CLUB
(☑ 202-629-1712; 1359 U St NW; ☺ 8pm-midnight, to 3am Sat & Sun) A mixed crowd of policy wonks and Howard University undergrads pack this spot, either chilling to soft reggae during cool-down sets or getting freaky when the dancehall DJs get going. Either way the theme is Caribbean, as evinced by the eponymous beef and veg patties on sale for when you need something to soak up a rum punch.

Brixton   BAR
(☑ 202-560-5045; 901 U St NW; ☺ 5pm-2am, to 3am Sat, from 11am Sun) As the name implies, this is a slice of England in DC, although it's not corny Olde England. Rather, its high young folk in tight jeans and ethnic scarves, stiff drinks, London slang and East End pop art on the walls. Has a decent pub-grubby menu if such is your fancy, and a rooftop patio with great views over U St.

Bar Pilar   BAR

(www.barpilar.com; 1833 14th St NW; Ⓜ U Street-Cardozo) Friendly neighborhood favorite Bar Pilar serves seasonal organic tapas dishes and excellent cocktails in a small, nicely designed space. The mustard-colored walls and curious collections (hats, Hemingway regalia) give it an old-fashioned feel.

Dickson Wine Bar   WINE BAR

(www.dicksonwinebar.com; 903 U St NW; ⊘ from 6pm Mon-Sat; Ⓜ U Street-Cardozo) Cozy and candlelit, with walls covered in wine bottles, Dickson pours romantic, first-date ambience throughout a three-story row house. The entrance is not marked by name; look for 'Dickson Building 903' above the door. It's a cool spot to swing into before a show at the 9:30 Club.

🍸 Dupont Circle

18th Street Lounge   LOUNGE

(www.eighteenthstreetlounge.com; 1212 18th St NW; ⊘ from 5:30pm Tue-Fri, from 9:30pm Sat & Sun; Ⓜ Dupont Circle) Chandeliers, velvet sofas, antique wallpaper and an attractive dance-loving crowd adorn this multifloored mansion. The DJs here – spinning funk, soul and Brazilian beats – are phenomenal, which is not surprising given Eric Hilton (of Thievery Corporation) is co-owner.

🍸 Georgetown

Tombs   BAR

(www.tombs.com; 1226 36th St NW; ⊘ from 11:30am Mon-Sat, from 9:30am Sun) If it looks familiar, think back to the '80s; this was the setting for *St Elmo's Fire*. Today this cozy windowless bar is a favorite with Georgetown students and teaching assistants boozing under crew regalia.

🍷 Columbia Heights & Around

Red Derby   BAR

(www.redderby.com; 3718 14th St NW; Ⓜ Columbia Heights) The unsigned Derby packs 'em in with an open-air deck up top (with heat lamps), films screening on the wall and riotous crowds. Order the $5 shot-and-Schlitz combo to start the night with a bang.

Wonderland   BAR

(www.thewonderlandballroom.com; 1101 Kenyon St NW; Ⓜ Columbia Heights) Wonderland is friendly but divey, with a spacious patio in front with outsized wooden benches that are just right on warm evenings. The upstairs dance floor sees a mix of DJs and bands, and gets packed on weekends.

Looking Glass Lounge   BAR

(www.thelookingglasslounge.com; 3634 Georgia Ave NW; Ⓜ Georgia Ave-Petworth) Petworth's neighborhood nightspot is an artfully designed dive with a great jukebox, DJs on weekends and a fine outdoor patio.

Meridian Pint   BAR

(www.meridianpint.com; 3400 11th St NW; Ⓜ Columbia Heights) Staffed by locals from the neighborhood, Meridian Pint is the quintessential corner tavern for Columbia Heights. Sports flicker on TV, folks play pool and shuffleboard, and impressive American craft beers flow from the taps.

DC Reynolds   BAR

(☎ 202-506-7178; 3628 Georgia Ave NW; ⊘ 11am-2am, to 3am Fri & Sat; Ⓜ Georgia Ave-Petworth) Petworth is one of the edges of DC's gentrification, and some interesting bars are opening here. DC Reynolds is one of our favorites of the bunch, although you need to visit outside the winter months, as the main draw is an enormous outdoor patio that's perfect for a cool beer and a pickle back (whiskey followed by pickle juice).

☆ Entertainment

Live Music

Black Cat   LIVE MUSIC

(www.blackcatdc.com; 1811 14th St NW, U St; admission $5-15; Ⓜ U Street-Cardozo) A pillar of DC's music scene since the 1990s, the battered Black Cat has hosted all the greats of years past (White Stripes, the Strokes, Arcade Fire among others). If you don't want to pony up for $20-a-ticket bands on the upstairs main stage (or the smaller Backstage below), head to the Red Room for jukebox, pool and strong cocktails.

9:30 Club   LIVE MUSIC

(www.930.com; 815 V St NW, U St; admission from $10; Ⓜ U Street-Cardozo) The 9:30, which can pack 1200 people into a surprisingly intimate venue, is the granddaddy of the live-music scene in DC. Pretty much every big name that comes through town ends up on this stage, and a concert here is the first-gig memory of many a DC-area teenager. Headliners usually take the stage between 10:30pm and 11:30pm.

GAY & LESBIAN WASHINGTON, DC

One of Washington's gay-bar scenes is concentrated around Dupont Circle.

Cobalt (www.cobaltdc.com; 1639 R St NW; ⊘ 5pm-2am; Ⓜ Dupont Circle) Featuring lots of hair product and faux-tanned gym bodies, Cobalt tends to gather a better-dressed late-20s to 30-something crowd who come for fun (but loud!) dance parties throughout the week.

Nellie's (www.nelliessportsbar.com; 900 U St NW; Ⓜ U Street-Cardozo) The vibe here is low key, and Nellie's is a good place to hunker down among a friendly crowd for tasty bar bites, events nights (including drag bingo Tuesdays) or early drink specials.

JR's (www.jrsbardc.com; 1519 17th St NW; ⊘ from 4pm Mon-Fri, from 1pm Sat & Sun; Ⓜ Dupont Circle) This popular gay hangout is a great spot for happy hour, and is packed more often than not. Embarrassing show tunes karaoke is great fun on Monday nights.

Verizon Center   CONCERT VENUE
(✔ 202-628-3200; www.verizoncenter.com; 601 F St NW, Gallery Place-Chinatown) DC's great big sports-arena-cum-big-name-band venue.

Performing Arts

Kennedy Center   PERFORMING ARTS
(✔ 202-467-4600; www.kennedy-center.org; 2700 F St NW, Georgetown; Ⓜ Foggy Bottom-GWU) Perched on 17 acres along the Potomac, the magnificent Kennedy Center hosts a staggering array of performances – more than 2000 each year among its multiple venues including the Concert Hall (home to the National Symphony), the Opera House and Eisenhower Theater. The Millennium Stage puts on free performances at 6pm daily.

Wolf Trap Farm Park
for the Performing Arts   PERFORMING ARTS
(✔ 703-255-1900; www.wolftrap.org; 1645 Trap Rd, Northern Virginia) This outdoor park some 40 minutes from downtown DC hosts summer performances by the National Symphony and other highly regarded musical and theatrical troupes.

National Theatre   THEATER
(✔ 202-628-6161; www.nationaltheatre.org; 1321 Pennsylvania Ave NW; ⊘ box office 10am-9pm Mon-Sat, noon-8pm Sun; Ⓜ Federal Triangle) Washington's oldest continuously operating theater shows big Broadway musicals and similar big-name productions.

Shakespeare Theatre   THEATER
(✔ 202-547-1122; www.shakespearetheatre.org; 450 7th St NW; tickets from $30; ⊘ box office 10am-6pm Mon-Sat, noon-6pm Sun; Ⓜ Archives-Navy Memorial) The nation's foremost Shakespeare company presents masterfully staged pieces by the Bard as well as works by George

Bernard Shaw, Oscar Wilde, Ibsen, Eugene O'Neill and other greats.

Carter Barron Amphitheater   THEATER
(✔ 202-895-6000; www.nps.gov/rocr; 4850 Colorado Ave NW, near 16th St NW, Rock Creek Park; ⊘ box office noon-8pm show days; Ⓜ McPherson Sq, then ⬚ S2, S4) In a lovely wooded setting inside Rock Creek Park, you can catch a mix of theater, dance and music (jazz, salsa, classical and reggae). Some events are free.

Sports

Washington Redskins   FOOTBALL
(✔ 301-276-6800; www.redskins.com; 1600 Fedex Way, Landover, MD; tickets from $65) The city's football team plays at FedEx Field, east of DC in Maryland. The season runs from September to February.

Washington Nationals   BASEBALL
(www.nationals.com; 1500 S Capitol St SE; Ⓜ Navy Yard) DC's baseball team plays at Nationals Park, along the Anacostia riverfront in southeast DC. The season runs from April through October.

DC United   SOCCER
(www.dcunited.com; 2400 East Capitol St; Ⓜ Stadium-Armory) DC United play at Robert F Kennedy (RFK) Memorial Stadium. The season runs from March through October.

Washington Capitals   HOCKEY
(✔ 202-397-7328; http://capitals.nhl.com; 601 F St NW; Ⓜ Gallery Place-Chinatown) DC's rough-and-tumble hockey team plays from October through April at the Verizon Center.

Washington Wizards   BASKETBALL
(www.nba.com/wizards; 601 F St NW; ⊘ box office 10am-5:30pm Mon-Sat; Ⓜ Gallery Place-Chinatown) NBA season runs from October

through April, with home games played at the Verizon Center. DC's WNBA team, the **Washington Mystics** (www.wnba.com/mystics), also plays here May to September.

ℹ Information

Destination DC (☑ 202-789-7000; www.washington.org; 901 7th St NW, 4th fl) Doles out loads of information online, over the phone or in person at a handy downtown location.

George Washington University Hospital (☑ 202-715-4000; 900 23rd St NW; Ⓜ Foggy Bottom-GWU)

International Visitors Information Desk (◷ 9am-5pm Mon-Fri) You'll find helpful multilingual staff at this information desk run by the Meridian International Center. At the arrivals terminal at Washington Dulles Airport.

Kramerbooks (1517 Connecticut Ave NW; ◷ 7:30am-1am Sun-Thu, 24hr Fri & Sat) One computer with free access in the bar.

Online Visitor Information (www.washington.org)

Washington City Paper (www.washingtoncitypaper.com) Free edgy weekly with entertainment and dining listings.

Washington Post (www.washingtonpost.com) Respected daily city (and national) paper. Its tabloid-format daily *Express* is free. Check online for events listings.

ℹ Getting There & Away

AIR

Washington Dulles International Airport (IAD; www.metwashairports.com), 26 miles west of the city center, and **Ronald Reagan Washington National Airport** (DCA; ☑ 703-417-8000), 4.5 miles south, are the main airports serving DC, although **Baltimore/Washington International Thurgood Marshall Airport** (BWI; ☑ 410-859-7111; www.bwiairport.com), 30 miles to the northeast, is also an option. All three airports, particularly Dulles and National, are major hubs for flights from around the world.

BUS

In addition to Greyhound, there are numerous cheap bus services to New York, Philadelphia and Richmond. Most charge around $20 for a one-way trip to NYC (it takes four to five hours). Pick-up locations are scattered around town, but are always Metro-accessible. Tickets usually need to be bought online, but can also be purchased on the bus itself if there are still seats available.

BoltBus (☑ 877-265-8287; www.boltbus.com; 🛜) The best of the budget options, BoltBus leaves from the upper level of Union Station.

DC2NY (☑ 202-332-2691; www.dc2ny.com; 20th St & Massachusetts Ave NW; 🛜) Leaves from near Dupont Circle.

Greyhound (☑ 202-589-5141; www.greyhound.com; 1005 1st St NE) Provides nationwide service. The terminal is a few blocks north of Union Station; take a cab after dark.

Megabus (☑ 877-462-6342; us.megabus.com; 🛜) Leaves from Union Station.

Peter Pan Bus Lines (☑ 800-343-9999; www.peterpanbus.com) Travels to northeastern US; uses a terminal just opposite Greyhound's.

WashNY (☑ 866-287-6932; www.washny.com; 1320 19th St NW, Union Station; 🛜) Has two stops in the city.

TRAIN

Amtrak (☑ 800-872-7245; www.amtrak.com) Set inside the magnificent beaux-arts Union Station. Trains depart for nationwide destinations, including New York City (3½ hours), Chicago (18 hours), Miami (24 hours) and Richmond, VA (three hours).

MARC (Maryland Rail Commuter; mta.maryland.gov) This regional rail service for the Washington, DC–Baltimore metro area runs trains frequently to Baltimore ($7, 71 minutes) and other Maryland towns (from $4 to $12); and to Harpers Ferry, WV ($15, 80 minutes).

ℹ Getting Around

TO/FROM THE AIRPORT

If you're using Baltimore/Washington International Airport, you can travel between Union Station and the BWI terminal stop on either **MARC** ($7, 40 minutes) or **Amtrak** ($16, 40 minutes). Or consider the **B30 bus**, which runs to Greenbelt Metro ($6.30, 40 minutes)

Metrobus 5A (www.wmata.com) Runs from Dulles to Rosslyn Metro station (35 minutes) and central DC (L'Enfant Plaza, 48 minutes); it departs every 30 to 40 minutes. The combo bus/Metro fare is about $8.

Metrorail (www.wmata.com) National airport has its own Metro rail station, which is fast and cheap.

Supershuttle (☑ 800-258-3826; www.supershuttle.com; ◷ 5:30am-12:30am) A door-to-door shuttle that connects downtown DC with Dulles ($29), National ($14) and BWI ($37).

Washington Flyer (www.washfly.com) Runs every 30 minutes from Dulles to West Falls Church Metro ($10).

PUBLIC TRANSPORTATION

Circulator (www.dccirculator.com) Buses run along handy routes – including Union Station to/from Georgetown. One-way fare costs $1.

Metrobus (www.wmata.com) Operates buses throughout the city and suburbs; have exact change handy ($1.80).

Metrorail (☑ 202-637-7000; www.wmata. com) One of the best transportation systems in the country will get you to most sights, hotels and business districts, and the Maryland and Virginia suburbs. Trains start running at 5am Monday through Friday (from 7am on weekends); the last service is around midnight Sunday through Thursday and 3am on Fridays and Saturdays. Machines inside stations sell computerized fare cards; fares cost from $1.60 (children under five ride free). Unlimited travel passes are also available (one day/seven days from $14/57.50).

TAXI

For a cab, try **Capitol Cab** (☑ 202-636-1600), **Diamond** (☑ 202-387-6200) or **Yellow Cab** (☑ 202-544-1212).

MARYLAND

Maryland is often described as 'America in Miniature,' and for good reason. This small state possesses all of the best bits of the country, from the Appalachian Mountains in the west to sandy white beaches in the east. A blend of Northern streetwise and Southern down-home gives this most osmotic of border states an appealing identity crisis. Its main city, Baltimore, is a sharp, demanding port town; the Eastern Shore jumbles art-and-antique-minded city refugees and working fishermen; while the DC suburbs are packed with government and office workers seeking green space, and the poor seeking lower rents. Yet it all somehow works – scrumptious blue crabs, Natty Boh beer and lovely Chesapeake country being the glue that binds all. This is also an extremely diverse and progressive state, and was one of the first in the country to legalize gay marriage.

History

George Calvert established Maryland as a refuge for persecuted English Catholics in 1634 when he purchased St Mary's City from the local Piscataway, with whom he initially tried to coexist. Puritan refugees drove both Piscataway and Catholics from control and shifted power to Annapolis; their harassment of Catholics produced the Tolerance Act, a flawed but progressive law that allowed freedom of any (Christian) worship in Maryland – a North American first.

That commitment to diversity has always characterized this state, despite a mixed record on slavery. Although state loyalties were split during the Civil War, a Confederate invasion was halted here in 1862 at Antietam. Following the war, Maryland harnessed its black, white and immigrant work force, splitting the economy between Baltimore's industry and shipping, and the later need for services in Washington, DC. Today the answer to 'What makes a Marylander?' is 'all of the above': the state mixes rich, poor, the foreign-born, urban sophisticates and rural villages like few other states do.

Baltimore

Once one of the most important port towns in America, Baltimore – or 'Bawlmer' to locals – is a city of contradictions. On one hand it remains something of an ugly duckling – a defiant, working-class, gritty city still tied to its nautical past. But in recent years Baltimore has begun to grow into a swan or, more accurately, gotten better at showing the world the swan that was always there, in the form of world-class museums, trendy shops, ethnic restaurants, boutique hotels, culture and sports. 'B'more' (another nickname) does this all with a twinkle in the eye and a wisecrack on the lips; this quirky city spawned Billie Holiday and John Waters. Yet it remains intrinsically tied to the water, from the Disney-fied Inner Harbor and cobblestoned streets of portside Fells Point to the shores of Fort McHenry, birthplace of America's national anthem, 'The Star-Spangled Banner.' There's an intense, sincere friendliness to this 'burg, which is why Baltimore lives up to its final, most accurate nickname: 'Charm City.'

Sights & Activities

Harborplace & Inner Harbor

This is where most tourists start and, unfortunately, end their Baltimore sightseeing. The Inner Harbor is a big, gleaming waterfront renewal project of shiny glass, air-conditioned malls and flashy bars that manages to capture the maritime heart of this city, albeit in a safe-for-the-family kinda way. But it's also just the tip of Baltimore's iceberg.

★ **National Aquarium** AQUARIUM
(☑ 410-576-3800; www.aqua.org; 501 E Pratt St, Piers 3 & 4; adult/child $35/22; ☉9am-5pm Mon-Thu, to 8pm Fri, 8:30am-8pm Sat, to 6pm Sun) ✐ Standing seven stories high and capped by a glass pyramid, this is widely considered to be the best aquarium in America. It houses 16,500 specimens of 660 species, a rooftop rainforest, a central ray pool and a multistory shark tank. There's also a reconstruction of the Umbrawarra Gorge in Australia's Northern Territory, complete with a 35ft waterfall, rocky cliffs and free-roaming birds and lizards. Kids will love the dolphin show and 4-D Immersion Theater (together an additional $5). Go on weekdays to beat the crowds.

Baltimore Maritime Museum MUSEUM
(☑410-396-3453; www.historicships.org; 301 E Pratt St, Piers 3 & 5; 1/2/4 ships adult $11/14/18, child $5/6/7; ☉10am-4:30pm) Ship-lovers can take a tour through four historic ships: a Coast Guard cutter, lightship, submarine and the USS Constellation, one of the last

sail-powered warships built (in 1797) by the US Navy. Admission to the 1856 Seven Foot Knoll Lighthouse on Pier 5 is free.

Downtown & Little Italy

You can easily walk from downtown to Little Italy, but follow the delineated path as there's a rough housing project along the way.

National Great Blacks in Wax Museum MUSEUM
(☑410-563-3404; www.greatblacksinwax.org; 1601 E North Ave; adult/child $13/11; ☉9am-6pm Tue-Sat, noon-6pm Sun, to 5pm Oct-Jan) This excellent African American history museum has exhibits on Frederick Douglass, Jackie Robinson, Martin Luther King Jr and Barack Obama, as well as lesser-known figures such as explorer Matthew Henson. The museum also covers slavery, the Jim Crow era and African leaders – all told in surreal fashion through Madame Tussaud-style figures.

Star-Spangled Banner Flag House & 1812 Museum MUSEUM
(☑410-837-1793; www.flaghouse.org; 844 E Pratt St; adult/child $8/6; ☉10am-4pm Tue-Sat; ⊛) This historic home, built in 1793, is where Mary Pickersgill sewed the gigantic flag that inspired America's national anthem. Costumed interpreters and 19th-century artifacts transport visitors back in time to dark days during the War of 1812; there's also a hands-on discovery gallery for kids.

Jewish Museum of Maryland MUSEUM
(☑410-732-6400; www.jewishmuseummd.org; 15 Lloyd St; adult/student/child $8/4/3; ☉10am-5pm Tue-Thu & Sun) Maryland has traditionally been home to one of the largest, most active Jewish communities in the country, and this is a fine place to explore their experience in America. It also houses two wonderfully preserved historical synagogues.

Babe Ruth Museum MUSEUM
(☑410-727-1539; www.baberuthmuseum.com; 216 Emory St; adult/child $6/3; ☉10am-5pm) Celebrates the Baltimore native son who happens to be the greatest baseball player in history. Four blocks east, **Sports Legends at Camden Yards** (cnr Camden & Sharp Sts, Camden Station; adult/child $8/4) honors more Maryland athletes. The museums share hours; combo tickets cost $12/5.

SCENIC DRIVE: MARITIME MARYLAND

Maryland and Chesapeake Bay have always been inextricable, but there are some places where the old-fashioned way of life on the bay seems to have changed little over the passing centuries.

About 150 miles south of Baltimore, at the edge of the Eastern Shore, is **Crisfield**, the top working water town in Maryland. Get visiting details at the **J Millard Tawes Historical Museum** (☑410-968-2501; www.crisfieldheritagefoundation.org/museum; 3 Ninth St; adult/child $3/1; ☺10am-4pm Mon-Sat), which doubles as a visitor center. Any seafood you eat will be first-rate, but for a true Shore experience, **Watermen's Inn** (☑410-968-2119; 901 W Main St; mains $12-25; ☺11am-8pm Thu & Sun, to 9pm Fri & Sat, closed Mon-Wed) is legendary. In a simple, unpretentious setting, you can feast on local catch from an ever-changing menu. You can find local waterfolk at their favorite hangout, having 4am coffee at **Gordon's Confectionery** (831 W Main St) before shipping off to check and set traps.

From here you can leave your car and take a boat to **Smith Island** (www.visitsmithisland.com), the only offshore settlement in the state. Settled by fisherfolk from the English West Country some 400 years ago, the island's tiny population still speaks with what linguists reckon is the closest thing to a 17th-century Cornish accent.

We'll be frank: this is more of a dying fishing town than charming tourist attraction, although there are B&Bs and restaurants (check the website for details). But it is also a last link to the state's past, and if you approach Smith Island as such, you may appreciate the limited amenities on offer. These notably include paddling through miles of some of the most pristine marshland on the eastern seaboard. Ferries will take you back to the mainland and the present day at 3:45pm.

Edgar Allan Poe House & Museum MUSEUM
(☑410-396-7932; 203 N Amity St; adult/child $4/free; ☺noon-3:30pm Wed-Sat Apr-Nov) Home to Baltimore's most famous adopted son from 1832 to 1835, it was here that the macabre poet and writer first found fame after winning a $50 short-story contest. After moving around, Poe later returned to Baltimore in 1849, where he died in mysterious circumstances. His grave can be found in nearby Westminster Cemetery.

⊙ Mt Vernon

For the best views of Baltimore, climb the 228 steps of Baltimore's **Washington Monument** (699 Washington Pl; suggested donation $5; ☺10am-5pm Wed-Sun), a 178ft-tall Doric column that's only slightly less phallic than its DC counterpart.

★**Walters Art Museum** MUSEUM
(☑410-547-9000; www.thewalters.org; 600 N Charles St; ☺10am-5pm Wed-Sun, to 9pm Thu) **FREE** Don't pass up this excellent, eclectic gallery, which spans more than 55 centuries, from ancient to contemporary, with excellent displays of Asian treasures, rare and ornate manuscripts and books, and a comprehensive French paintings collection.

Maryland Historical Society MUSEUM
(www.mdhs.org; 201 W Monument St; adult/child $9/6; ☺10am-5pm Wed-Sat, noon-5pm Sun) With more than 5.4 million artifacts, this is one of the largest collections of Americana in the world, and it includes Francis Scott Key's original manuscript of the 'Star-Spangled Banner.' There are often excellent temporary exhibits, as well as a fascinating permanent one tracing Maryland's maritime history.

⊙ Federal Hill & Around

On a bluff overlooking the harbor, **Federal Hill Park** lends its name to the comfortable neighborhood that's set around Cross St Market and comes alive after sundown.

★**American Visionary Art Museum** MUSEUM
(☑410-244-1900; www.avam.org; 800 Key Hwy; adult/child $16/10; ☺10am-6pm Tue-Sun) AVAM is a showcase for self-taught (or 'outsider' art,) a celebration of unbridled creativity utterly free of arts-scene pretension. Some of the work comes from asylums, other pieces are created by self-inspired visionaries, but it's all fantastically captivating and well worth a long afternoon.

Fort McHenry National Monument & Historic Shrine   HISTORIC SITE

(☑410-962-4290; 2400 E Fort Ave; adult/child $7/free; ☺8am-5pm) On September 13 and 14, 1814, the star-shaped fort successfully repelled a British navy attack during the Battle of Baltimore. After a long night of bombs bursting in the air, prisoner Francis Scott Key saw, 'by dawn's early light,' the tattered flag still waving, inspiring him to pen 'The Star-Spangled Banner' (set to the tune of a popular drinking song).

⊙ Fell's Point & Canton

Once the center of Baltimore's shipbuilding industry, the historic cobblestoned neighborhood of Fell's Point is now a gentrified mix of 18th-century homes and restaurants, bars and shops. The neighborhood has been the setting for several films and TV series, most notably *Homicide: Life on the Street*. Further east, the slightly more sophisticated streets of Canton fan out, with its grassy square surrounded by great restaurants and bars.

⊙ North Baltimore

The 'Hon' expression of affection, an oft-imitated but never quite duplicated 'Bawlmerese' peculiarity, was born in **Hampden**, an area straddling the line between working class and hipster-creative class. Spend a lazy afternoon browsing kitsch, antiques and vintage clothing along the **Avenue** (aka W 36th St). To get to Hampden, take the I-83 N, merge onto Falls Rd (northbound) and take a right onto the Avenue. The prestigious **Johns Hopkins University** (3400 N Charles St) is nearby.

☞ Tours

Baltimore Ghost Tours   WALKING TOUR

(☑410-357-1186; www.baltimoreghosttours.com; adult/child $13/10; ☺7pm Fri & Sat Mar-Nov) Offers several walking tours exploring the spooky and bizarre side of Baltimore. The popular Fells Point ghost walk departs from Max's on Broadway, 731 S Broadway.

★ Festivals & Events

Preakness   SPORTS

(www.preakness.com; ☺May) Held on the third Sunday of every May, the 'Freakness' is the second leg of the Triple Crown horse race.

Honfest   CULTURE

(www.honfest.net; ☺Jun) Put on your best 'Bawlmerese' accent and head to Hampden for this celebration of kitsch, beehive hairdos, rhinestone glasses and other Baltimore eccentricities.

Artscape   CULTURE

(www.artscape.org; ☺mid-July) America's largest free arts festival features art displays, live music, theater and dance performances.

☐ Sleeping

Stylish and affordable B&Bs are mostly found in the downtown 'burbs of Canton, Fell's Point and Federal Hill.

Mount Vernon Hotel   HOTEL $

(☑410-727-2000; www.mountvernonbaltimore. com; 24 W Franklin St, Mt Vernon; d from $90, ste from $120; P❋☎) The historic 1907 Mount Vernon Hotel is good value for its comfortable, heritage-style rooms in a nice location near the restaurant scene along Charles St. Hearty cooked breakfasts sweeten the deal.

BALTIMORE FOR CHILDREN

Most attractions are centered on the Inner Harbor, including the National Aquarium (p288), perfect for pint-sized visitors. Kids can run wild o'er the ramparts of historic Fort McHenry National Monument & Historic Shrine, too.

Maryland Science Center (☑410-685-5225; www.mdsci.org; 601 Light St; adult/child $17/14; ☺10am-5pm Mon-Fri, to 6pm Sat, 11am-5pm Sun, longer hours in summer) is an awesome center featuring a three-story atrium, tons of interactive exhibits on dinosaurs, outer space and the human body, and the requisite IMAX theater ($4 extra).

Two blocks north, **Port Discovery** (☑410-727-8120; www.portdiscovery.org; 35 Market Pl; admission $14; ☺10am-5pm Mon-Sat, noon-5pm Sun, reduced hours in winter) is a converted fish market, which has a playhouse, a laboratory, a TV studio and even Pharaoh's tomb. Wear your kids out here.

At **Maryland Zoo in Baltimore** (www.marylandzoo.org; Druid Hill Park; adult/child $16/11; ☺10am-4pm), lily-pad hopping, adventures with Billy the Bog Turtle and grooming live animals are all in a day's play here. Prices are slightly cheaper on weekdays.

HI-Baltimore Hostel
HOSTEL $

(☑410-576-8880; www.hiusa.org/baltimore; 17 W Mulberry St, Mt Vernon; dm/d incl breakfast $25/65; ✺@📶) Located in a beautifully restored 1857 mansion, the HI-Baltimore has four-, dorms with eight and 12-beds, plus a private double room. Helpful management, nice location and a filigreed classical chic look make this one of the region's best hostels.

★ Inn at 2920
B&B $$

(☑410-342-4450; www.theinnat2920.com; 2920 Elliott St, Canton; r incl breakfast $175-235; ✺@📶) ✐ Housed in a former bordello, this boutique B&B offers five individual rooms: high-thread-count sheets, sleek avant-garde decor and the nightlife-charged neighborhood of Canton right outside your door. The Jacuzzi bathtubs and green sensibility of the owners add a nice touch.

Inn at Henderson's Wharf
HOTEL $$

(☑800-584-7065, 410-522-7777; www.hendersonswharf.com; 1000 Fell St; r from $175; P✺📶) A complimentary bottle of wine upon arrival sets the tone at this marvelously situated Fell's Point hotel, which began life as an 18th-century tobacco warehouse. Consistently rated one of the city's best lodges.

Blue Door on Baltimore
B&B $$

(☑410-732-0191; www.bluedoorbaltimore.com; 2023 E Baltimore St, Fell's Point; r $140-180; ✺@📶) In an early 1900s row house, this spotless inn has three elegantly furnished rooms, each with a king-sized bed, claw-foot bathtub (and separate shower), and thoughtful extras such as an in-room fountain and fresh flowers. It lies just north of Fells Point.

Peabody Court
HOTEL $$

(☑410-727-7101; www.peabodycourthotel.com; 612 Cathedral St, Mt Vernon; r from $120; P✺📶) Right in the middle of Mt Vernon, this upscale 104-room hotel has large, handsomely appointed guest rooms with all-marble bathrooms and top-notch service. Often has great deals online.

✖ Eating

Baltimore is an ethnically rich town that sits on top of the greatest seafood repository in the world, not to mention the fault line between the down-home South and cutting-edge innovation of the Northeast.

Lexington Market
FAST FOOD $

(www.lexingtonmarket.com; 400 W Lexington St, Mt Vernon; ⊗9am-5pm Mon-Sat) Around since 1782, Mt Vernon's Lexington Market is one of Baltimore's true old-school food markets. It's a bit shabby on the outside, but the food is great. Don't miss the crab cakes at Faidley's (☑410-727-4898; www.faidleyscrabcakes.com; mains $8-14; ⊗Mon-Sat 9am-5pm) seafood stall, because my goodness, they are truly amazing.

Vaccaro's Pastry
ITALIAN $

(www.vaccarospastry.com; 222 Albemarle St, Little Italy; desserts $7; ⊗9am-10pm Sun-Thu, to midnight Fri & Sat) Vaccaro's serves some of the best desserts and coffee in town. The cannolis are legendary.

LP Steamers
SEAFOOD $$

(☑410-576-9294; 1100 E Fort Ave, South Baltimore; mains $8-28; ⊗11:30am-10pm) LP is the best in Baltimore's seafood stakes: working class, teasing smiles and the freshest crabs on the southside.

PaperMoon Diner
DINER $$

(227 W 29th St; mains $7-16; ⊗7am-midnight Sun-Thu, to 2am Fri & Sat) This brightly colored, quintessential Baltimore diner is decorated with thousands of old toys, creepy mannequins and other quirky knickknacks. The real draw here is the anytime breakfast – fluffy French toast, crispy bacon and bagels with lox.

City Cafe
CAFE $$

(☑410-539-4252; www.citycafebaltimore.com; 1001 Cathedral St, Mt Vernon; mains lunch $10-14, dinner $15-29; ⊗7:30am-10pm Mon-Fri, 10am-10:30pm Sat, to 8pm Sun; 📶) A bright, inviting Mt Vernon cafe with floor-to-ceiling windows, desserts and gourmet sandwiches; the dining room in back serves high-end bistro fare.

Dukem
ETHIOPIAN $$

(☑410-385-0318; 1100 Maryland Ave, Mt Vernon; mains $13-22; ⊗11am-10:30pm) Baltimore hosts one of the largest Ethiopian expat populations in the world, and they've brought their home cuisine to 'Charm City.' Dukem in Mt Vernon is a standout. Delicious mains, including spicy chicken, lamb and vegetarian dishes, all sopped up with spongy flatbread.

★**Woodberry Kitchen** AMERICAN $$$
(☑410-464-8000; www.woodberrykitchen.com;
2010 Clipper Park Rd, Woodberry; mains $24-45;
☺5-10pm Mon-Thu to 11pm Fri & Sat, to 9pm Sun)
The Woodberry takes everything the Chesapeake region has to offer, plops it into an industrial barn and creates culinary magic. The entire menu is like a playful romp through the best of local produce, seafood and meats, from a 'nose-to-tail' approach to rockfish (Maryland's state fish) to local turkey sausage with pork-fat potatoes, and wood-roasted tomatoes and garlic plucked from nearby farms. The food is just stupidly delicious, the service is warm and the experience is top-notch.

Charleston SOUTHERN $$$
(☑410-332-7373; www.charlestonrestaurant.com;
1000 Lancaster St, Harbor East; 3-/6-courses
$79/114; ☺5:30-10pm Mon-Sat) One of Baltimore's most celebrated restaurants, Charleston serves beautifully prepared Southern-accented fare in a plush setting. Extensive wine list and superb desserts (always included).

Salt AMERICAN $$$
(☑410-276-5480; www.salttavern.com; 2127 E Pratt St, Fells Point; mains $18-27; ☺5pm-midnight Tue-Sat, from 4:30pm Sun; ☑) Salt is heavy on the lips of Baltimore foodies (the restaurant, not crystallized sodium). The food is nouveau American, but there's a lot of international influence bordering on the cutting edge; start the meal with some sea-urchin custard, then move on to duck breast served over date puree with Moroccan spices.

BALTIMORE BEEF

Everyone knows Baltimore does crab cakes, but barely anyone outside the city knows about pit beef – thinly sliced top round grilled over charcoal – Baltimore's take on barbecue. The place to grab the stuff is **Chaps** (☑410-483-2379; 5801 Pulaski Hwy; mains under $10; ☺10:30am-10pm Sun-Thu), out on Pulaski Hwy, about 4 miles east of downtown Baltimore. Park (next to a strip club) and follow your nose to smoky mouthwatering goodness, and get that beef like a local: shaved onto a kaiser roll with a raw onion slice on top, smothered in Tiger Sauce (a creamy blend of horseradish and mayonnaise).

🍷 **Drinking & Nightlife**

On weekends, Fell's Point and Canton turn into temples of alcoholic excess that would make a Roman emperor blush. Mt Vernon and North Baltimore are a little more civilized, but any one of Baltimore's neighborhoods houses a cozy local pub. Closing time is generally 2am.

Brewer's Art PUB
(☑410-547-6925; 1106 N Charles St, Mt Vernon;
☺4pm-2am Mon-Sat, 5pm-2am Sun) This subterranean cave mesmerizes the senses with an overwhelming selection of beers. Its upstairs embodiment serves respectable dinners (sandwiches $9 to $12, mains $19 to $26) in its classy dining room.

Club Charles BAR
(☑410-727-8815; 1724 N Charles St, Mt Vernon;
☺from 6pm) Hipsters adorned in the usual skinny jeans/vintage T-shirt uniform, as well as characters from other walks of life, flock to this 1940s art-deco cocktail lounge to enjoy good tunes and cheap drinks.

Idle Hour BAR
(☑410-276-5480; 201 E Fort Ave, Federal Hill;
☺5pm-2am) Slip past the door that's papered with bumper stickers into a dark bar lit by sexy red Christmas lights and a bartenders' smile. Or, as the case may be, a bartender's surliness (good-hearted surliness, though). A watercolor of Elvis looks down upon you customers, blessing your cheap beers.

Ale Mary's BAR
(☑410-276-2044; 1939 Fleet St, Fell's Point; ☺from 4pm Mon-Thu, from 11:30am Fri-Sun) Its name and decor pay homage to Maryland's Catholic roots, with crosses and rosaries scattered about.

One-Eyed Mike's PUB
(☑410-327-0445; 708 S Bond St, Fell's Point;
☺11am-2am) Handshakes and a hearty welcome will make you feel right at home at this popular pirate-themed spot. With tin ceilings and old-world details, it's one of Baltimore's oldest taverns.

Little Havana BAR
(☑410-837-9903; 1325 Key Hwy, Federal Hill;
☺from 11:30am) A good after-work spot and a great place to sip *mojitos* on the waterfront deck, this converted brick warehouse is a major draw on warm, sunny days (especially around weekend brunch time).

MARYLAND BLUE CRABS

Eating at a crab shack, where the dress code stops at shorts and flip-flops, is the quintessential Chesapeake Bay experience. Folks in these parts take their crabs seriously and can spend hours debating the intricacies of how to crack a crab, the proper way to prepare crabs and where to find the best ones. There is one thing Marylanders can agree on: they must be blue crabs (scientific name: *Callinectes sapidus*, or 'beautiful swimmers'). With all this said, blue crab numbers have suffered with the contiuning pollution of the Chesapeake Bay. Sadly, many crabs you eat here are imported from elsewhere. Steamed crabs are prepared very simply, using beer and Old Bay seasoning. One of the best crab shacks in the state is **Jimmy Cantler's Riverside Inn** (458 Forest Beach Rd; ⊙11am-11pm Sun-Thu, to midnight Fri & Sat), where eating a steamed crab has been elevated to an art form – a hands-on, messy endeavor, normally accompanied by corn on the cob and ice-cold beer. Another fine spot is across the bay at the Crab Claw (p296).

Hippo   GAY
(www.clubhippo.com; 1 W Eager St; ⊙from 4pm)
The Hippo has been around forever and is still one of the city's largest gay clubs (though some nights the dance floor is dead), with themed nights (gay bingo, karaoke and hip-hop).

Grand Central   GAY & LESBIAN
(www.centralstationpub.com; 1001 N Charles St, Mt Vernon; ⊙9pm-2am Wed-Sun) More of a complex than a club, Central spreads a fancy to suit all moods – dance floor, pub and Sappho's (free admission for the ladies). Probably boasts B's best dance floors.

☆ Entertainment

Baltimoreans *love* sports. The town plays hard and parties even harder, with tailgating parties in parking lots and games showing on numerous televisions.

Baltimore Orioles   BASEBALL
(☎888-848-2473; www.orioles.com) The Orioles play at **Oriole Park at Camden Yards** (333 W Camden St, Downtown), arguably the best ballpark in America. Daily tours (adult/child $9/6) of the stadium are offered during regular season (April to October).

Baltimore Ravens   FOOTBALL
(☎410-261-7283; www.baltimoreravens.com) The Ravens play at **M&T Bank Stadium** (1101 Russell St, Downtown) from September to January.

Homewood Field   STADIUM
(☎410-516-8000; www.hopkinssports.com; Homewood Field on University Pkwy) Maryland is lacrosse heartland, and is home to arguably the sport's most fanatic followers. The best

place to watch 'lax' is at Johns Hopkins University's Homewood Field.

Pimlico   HORSE RACING
(☎410-542-9400; www.pimlico.com; 5201 Park Heights Ave) Horse racing is huge from April to late May, especially at Pimlico, which hosts the Preakness (p290). The track is roughly 7 miles north of downtown.

ℹ Information

Baltimore Area Visitor Center (☎877-225-8466; http://baltimore.org; 401 Light St; ⊙9am-6pm) Located on the Inner Harbor. Sells the Harbor Pass (adult/child $50/40), which gives admission to five major area attractions.

Baltimore Sun (www.baltimoresun.com) Daily city newspaper.

City Paper (www.citypaper.com) Free alt-weekly.

Enoch Pratt Free Library (400 Cathedral St; ⊙10am-8pm Mon-Wed, to 5pm Thu-Sat, 1-5pm Sun; ☎) Has free wi-fi and some public access computers (also free).

University of Maryland Medical Center (☎410-328-8667; 22 S Greene St) Has a 24-hour emergency room.

ℹ Getting There & Away

The Baltimore/Washington International Thurgood Marshall Airport (p286) is 10 miles south of downtown via I-295.

Greyhound (www.greyhound.com) and **Peter Pan Bus Lines** (☎410-752-7682; 2110 Haines St) have numerous buses from Washington, DC, (roughly every 45 minutes, one hour); and from New York (12 to 15 per day, 4½ hours). The **BoltBus** (☎877-265-8287; www.boltbus.com; 1610 St Paul St; ☎) has seven buses a day to/from NYC.

Penn Station (1500 N Charles St) is in north Baltimore. MARC operates weekday commuter trains to/from Washington, DC ($7, 71 minutes). **Amtrak** (☑ 800-872-7245; www.amtrak.com) trains serve the East Coast and beyond.

ℹ Getting Around

Light Rail (☑ 866-743-3682; mta.maryland. gov/light-rail; tickets $1.60; ⊙ 6am-11pm) runs from BWI airport to Lexington Market and Penn Station. Train frequency is every five to 10 minutes. MARC trains run hourly between Penn Station and BWI airport on weekdays for $5. Supershuttle (p286) provides a BWI-van service to the Inner Harbor for $14. Check **Maryland Transit Administration** (MTA; www.mtamaryland.com) for all local transportation schedules and fares.

Baltimore Water Taxi (☑ 410-563-3900; www.baltimorewatertaxi.com; Inner Harbor; daily pass adult/child $12/6; ⊙ 10am-11pm, to 9pm Sun) docks at all harborside attractions and neighborhoods.

Annapolis

Annapolis is as charming as state capitals get. The Colonial architecture, cobblestones, flickering lamps and brick row houses are worthy of Dickens, but the effect isn't artificial; this city has preserved, rather than created, its heritage.

Perched on Chesapeake Bay, Annapolis revolves around the city's rich maritime traditions. It's home to the US Naval Academy, whose 'middies' (midshipmen students) stroll through town in their starched white uniforms. Sailing is not just a hobby, it's a way of life, and the city docks are crammed with vessels of all shapes and sizes.

◉ Sights & Activities

Annapolis has more 18th-century buildings than any other city in America, and they include the homes of all four Marylanders who signed the Declaration of Independence.

Think of the State House as a wheel hub from which most attractions fan out, leading to the City Dock and historic waterfront.

US Naval Academy   UNIVERSITY
(www.usnabsd.com/for-visitors) The undergraduate college of the US Navy is one of the most selective universities in America. The **Armel-Leftwich visitor center** (☑ 410-293-8687; tourinfo@usna.edu; Gate 1, City Dock entrance; tours adult/child $9.50/7.50; ⊙ 9am-5pm) is the place to book tours and immerse yourself in all things Academy. Come for the formation weekdays at 12:05pm sharp, when the 4000 midshipmen and midshipwomen conduct a 20-minute military marching display in the yard. Photo ID is required for entry. If you've got a thing for American naval history, go revel in the **Naval Academy Museum** (☑ 410-293-2108; www.usna.edu/museum; 118 Maryland Ave; ⊙ 9am-5pm Mon-Sat, 11am-5pm Sun) FREE.

Maryland State House   HISTORIC BUILDING
(☑ 410-974-3400; 91 State Circle; ⊙ 9am-5pm Mon-Fri, 10am-4pm Sat & Sun, tours 11am & 3pm) FREE The country's oldest state capitol in continuous legislative use, the stately (haha) 1772 State House also served as national capital from 1733 to 1734. The Maryland Senate is in action here from January to April. The upside-down giant acorn atop the dome stands for wisdom. Photo ID is required for entry.

Hammond Harwood House   MUSEUM
(☑ 410-263-4683; www.hammondharwoodhouse. org; 19 Maryland Ave; adult/child $7/6; ⊙ noon-5pm Tue-Sun Apr-Oct, to 4pm Nov-Dec) Of the many historical homes in town, the 1774 HHH is the one to visit. It has a superb collection of decorative arts, including furniture, paintings and ephemera dating to the 18th century, and is one of the finest existing British Colonial homes in America.

Kunta Kinte–Alex Haley Memorial   MONUMENT
At the City Dock, the Kunta Kinte–Alex Haley Memorial marks the spot where Kunta Kinte – ancestor of *Roots* author Alex Haley – was brought in chains from Africa.

☞ Tours

Four Centuries Walking Tour   WALKING TOUR
(http://annapolistours.com; adult/child $16/10) A costumed docent will lead you on this great introduction to all things Annapolis. The 10:30am tour leaves from the visitor center and the 1:30pm tour leaves from the information booth at the City Dock; there's a slight variation in sights visited by each, but both cover the country's largest concentration of 18th-century buildings, influential African Americans and colonial spirits who don't want to leave. The associated one-hour **Pirates of the Chesapeake Cruise** (☑ 410-263-0002; www.chesapeakepirates.com; adult/child $20/12; ⊙ late May-early Sep; ♦) is good 'yar'-worthy fun, especially for the kids.

Woodwind

CRUISE

(☎410-263-7837; www.schoonerwoodwind. com; 80 Compromise St; sunset cruise adult/child $42/27; ☺May-Oct) This beautiful 74ft schooner offers two-hour day and sunset cruises. Or splurge for the Woodwind 'boat & breakfast' package (rooms $300, including breakfast), one of the more unique lodging options in town.

🛏 Sleeping

ScotLaur Inn

GUESTHOUSE $

(☎410-268-5665; www.scotlaurinn.com; 165 Main St; r $95-140; P❋🛜) The folks from Chick & Ruth's Delly offer 10 simple pink-and-blue rooms with private bath at their B&B (bed and bagel) above the deli.

Historic Inns of Annapolis

HOTEL $$

(☎410-263-2641; www.historicinnsofannapolis. com; 58 State Circle; r $130-205; ❋🛜) The Historic Inns comprise three different boutique guesthouses, each set in a heritage building in the heart of old Annapolis: the Maryland Inn, the Governor Calvert House and the Robert Johnson House. Common areas are packed with period details, and the best rooms boast antiques, a fireplace and attractive views (the cheapest are small and could use an update).

🍴 Eating & Drinking

With the Chesapeake at its doorstep, Annapolis has superb seafood.

Chick & Ruth's Delly

DINER $

(☎410-269-6737; www.chickandruths.com; 165 Main St; mains $6-12; ☺6:30am-10pm Sun-Thu, to 11:30pm Fri & Sat; 🧒) A cornerstone of Annapolis, the Delly is bursting with affable quirkiness and a big menu, heavy on sandwiches and breakfast fare. Patriots can relive grade-school days reciting the Pledge of Allegiance, weekdays at 8:30am (9:30am on weekends).

★ Vin 909

AMERICAN $$

(☎410-990-1846; 909 Bay Ridge Ave; mains $12-18; ☺5:30-10:30pm Tue, noon-10:30pm Wed-Fri, 5-11pm Sat, to 9pm Sun) Perched on a little wooded hill and exuding intimate but enjoyably casual ambience, Vin is the best thing happening in Annapolis for food. Farm-sourced goodness comes at you in the form of tasty sliders and homemade pizzas (try the Rock Star, with foie gras, truffles and peaches), and there's a wine cellar as deep as a trench.

Galway Bay

PUB $$

(☎410-263-8333; 63 Maryland Ave; mains $8-15; ☺11am-midnight Mon-Sat, from 10:30am Sun) The epitome of a power-broker bar, this Irish-owned and -operated pub is the dark sort of hideaway where political deals go down over Jameson, stouts and mouthwatering seafood specials.

Rams Head Tavern

PUB $$$

(☎410-268-4545; www.ramsheadtavern.com; 33 West St; mains $10-30; ☺from 11am) Serves pub fare and refreshing microbrews in an attractive oak-paneled setting, with live bands (tickets $15 to $55) on stage.

ℹ Information

There's a **visitor center** (www.visitannapolis. org; 26 West St; ☺9am-5pm) and a seasonal information booth at City Dock. A **Maryland Welcome Center** (☎410-974-3400; 350 Rowe Blvd; ☺9am-5pm) is inside the State House, and runs free tours of the building.

ℹ Getting There & Around

Greyhound (www.greyhound.com) runs buses to Washington, DC (once daily). **Dillon's Bus** (www.dillonbus.com; tickets $5) has 26 weekday-only commuter buses between Annapolis and Washington, DC, connecting with various DC Metro lines.

Inexpensive **bicycles** (per day $5; ☺9am-8pm) are available for hire from the Harbormaster's office at the City Dock.

Eastern Shore

Just across the Chesapeake Bay Bridge, a short drive from the urban sprawl of the Baltimore–Washington corridor, Maryland's landscape makes a dramatic about-face. Nondescript suburbs give way to unbroken miles of bird-dotted wetlands, serene water-scapes, endless cornfields, sandy beaches and friendly little villages. The Eastern Shore retains its charm despite the growing influx of city-dwelling yuppies and day-trippers. This area revolves around the water: working waterfront communities still survive off Chesapeake Bay and its tributaries, and boating, fishing, crabbing and hunting are integral to local life.

St Michaels & Tilghman Island

The prettiest little village on the Eastern Shore, St Michaels lives up to its motto as the 'Heart and Soul of Chesapeake Bay.' It's a mix of old Victorian homes, quaint B&Bs, boutique shops and working docks, where escape artists from Washington mix with salty-dog watermen. During the War of 1812, inhabitants rigged up lanterns in a nearby forest and blacked out the town. British naval gunners shelled the trees, allowing St Michaels to escape destruction. The building now known as the **Cannonball House** (Mulberry St) was the only structure to have been hit. At the lighthouse, the **Chesapeake Bay Maritime Museum** (☑ 410-745-2916; www.cbmm.org; 213 N Talbot St; adult/child $13/6; ☻ 9am-6pm summer; ♿) delves into the deep ties between Shore folk and America's largest estuary.

The Victorian red-brick **Parsonage Inn** (☑ 410-745-8383; www.parsonage-inn.com; 210 N Talbot St; r incl breakfast $150-210; P ❋) offers floral decadence (curtains, duvets) and brass beds, plus a friendly welcome from its hospitable innkeepers.

Next door to the Maritime Museum, the **Crab Claw** (☑ 410-745-2900; 304 Burns St; mains $15-30; ☻ 11am-10pm) has a splendid open-air setting at the water's edge. Get messy eating delicious steamed crabs ($36 to $60 per dozen) at picnic tables.

At the end of the road over the Hwy 33 drawbridge, tiny **Tilghman Island** still runs a working waterfront where local captains take visitors out on graceful oyster skipjacks; the historic **Rebecca T Ruark** (☑ 410-829-3976; www.skipjack.org; 2hr cruise adult/child $30/15), built in 1886, is the oldest certified vessel of its kind.

Berlin & Snow Hill

Imagine 'small-town, main street Americana,' cute that vision up by a few points, and you've come close to these Eastern Shore villages. Most of the buildings here are preserved or renovated to look preserved. Antiquity hunters will have to budget extra time to browse the antique shops littering this area.

In Berlin, the **Globe Theater** (☑ 410-641-0784; www.globetheater.com; 12 Broad St; lunch mains $6-12, dinner $11-25; ☻ 11am-10pm; ☎) is a lovingly restored main stage that serves as a restaurant, bar, art gallery and theater for nightly live music; the kitchen serves eclectic American fare with global accents (seafood burritos, jerk chicken wraps).

There are B&Bs galore, but we prefer the **Atlantic Hotel** (☑ 410-641-3589; www.atlantichotel.com; 2 N Main St; r $115-245; P ❋),

a handsome, Gilded-era lodger that gives guests the time-warp experience with all the modern amenities.

A few miles from Berlin, Snow Hill has a splendid location along the idyllic Pocomoke River. Get on the water with the **Pocomoke River Canoe Company** (☑ 410-632-3971; www.pocomokerivercanoe.com; 312 N Washington St; canoe per hr/day $15/40). They'll even take you upriver so you can have a leisurely paddle downstream. Nearby **Furnace Town** (☑ 410-632-2032; www.furnacetown.com; Old Furnace Rd; adult/child $6/3; ☻ 10am-5pm Mon-Sat Apr-Oct, from noon Sun; P ♿), off Rte 12, is a living-history museum that marks the old location of a 19th-century iron-smelting town. In Snow Hill itself, while away an odd, rewarding half-hour in the **Julia A Purnell Museum** (☑ 410-632-0515; 208 W Market St; adult/child $2/0.50; ☻ 10am-4pm Tue-Sat, from 1pm Sun Apr-Oct), a tiny structure that feels like an attic for the entire Eastern Shore.

Staying in town? Check out Snow Hill's **River House Inn** (☑ 410-632-2722; www.riverhouseinn.com; 201 E Market St; r $160-190, cottage $250-300; P ❋ ☎ ☀), with a lush backyard that overlooks a scenic bend of the river. **Palette** (☑ 410-632-0055; 104 W Market St; mains $14-22; ☻ 11am-3pm Tue-Wed, to 9pm Thu-Sat, 10am-2pm Sun; ☎) ☙ serves a changing menu of contemporary American fare, using organic locally sourced ingredients.

Ocean City

'The OC' is where you'll experience the American seaside resort at its tackiest. Here you can take a spin on nausea-inducing thrill rides, buy a T-shirt with obscene slogans and drink to excess at cheesy theme bars. The center of action is the 2.5-mile-long boardwalk, which stretches from the inlet to 27th St. The beach is attractive, but you'll have to contend with horny teenagers and noisy crowds; the beaches north of the boardwalk are much quieter.

In summer, the town's tiny year-round population of 7100 swells to more than 150,000; traffic is jammed and parking scarce.

▐ Sleeping

The **visitor center** (☑ 800-626-2326; www.ococean.com; Coastal Hwy at 40th St; ☻ 9am-5pm), in the convention center on Coastal Hwy, can help you find lodging.

WORTH A TRIP

ASSATEAGUE ISLAND

Just 8 miles south but a world away from Ocean City is Assateague Island seashore, a perfectly barren landscape of sand dunes and beautiful, secluded beaches. This undeveloped barrier island is populated by the only herd of wild horses on the East Coast, made famous in the book *Misty of Chincoteague.*

The island is divided into three sections. In Maryland there's **Assateague State Park** (☑ 410-641-2918; Rte 611; admission/campsites $4/31; ☉ campground late Apr-Oct) and federally administered **Assateague Island National Seashore** (☑ 410-641-1441; www.nps.gov/asis; Rte 611; admission/vehicles/campsites per week $3/15/20; ☉ visitor center 9am-5pm). **Chincoteague National Wildlife Refuge** (www.fws.gov/northeast/chinco; 8231 Beach Road, Chincoteague Island; daily/weekly pass $8/15 ; ☉ 5am-10pm Mon-Sat May-Sep, 6am-6pm Nov-Feb, to 8pm Mar, Apr & Oct; P ⌨) ⌨ is in Virginia.

As well as swimming and sunbathing, recreational activities include birding, kayaking, canoeing, crabbing and fishing. There are no services on the Maryland side of the island, so you must bring all your own food and drink. Don't forget insect repellent; the mosquitoes and biting horseflies can be ferocious!

King Charles Hotel GUESTHOUSE $$
(☑ 410-289-6141; www.kingcharleshotel.com; cnr N Baltimore Ave & 12th St; r $115-190; P ✳ ⌨) This place could be a quaint summer cottage, except it happens to be a short stroll to the heart of the boardwalk action. It has aging but clean rooms with small porches attached, and it's quiet (owners discourage young partiers).

Inn on the Ocean B&B $$$
(☑ 410-289-8894; www.innontheocean.com; 1001 Atlantic Ave, at the Boardwalk; r incl breakfast $275-395) This six-roomed B&B is an elegant escape from the usual OC big-box lodging.

🍴 Eating & Drinking

Surf 'n' turf and all-you-can-eat deals are the order of the day. Dance clubs cluster around the boardwalk's southern tip.

Liquid Assets MODERN AMERICAN $$
(☑ 410-524-7037; cnr 94th St & Coastal Hwy; mains $10-28; ☉ 11:30am-11pm Sun-Thu, to midnight Fri & Sat) Like a diamond in the rough, this bistro and wine shop is hidden in a strip mall in north OC. The menu is a refreshing mix of innovative seafood, grilled meats and regional classics (such as Carolina pork BBQ and 'ahi tuna burger).

Fager's Island MODERN AMERICAN $$$
(☑ 410-524-5500; www.fagers.com; 60th St; mains $19-36; ☉ from 11am) The food can be hit-and-miss, but it's a great place for a drink, with enviable views over Isle of Wight Bay. Live bands and DJs keep the bachelorettes rolling on weekends.

Seacrets BAR
(www.seacrets.com; cnr W 49th St & the Bay; ☉ 8am-2am) A water-laced, Jamaican-themed, rum-soaked bar straight out of MTV's *Spring Break.* You can drift around in an inner tube while sipping a drink and people-watching at OC's most famous meat market.

ℹ Getting There & Around

Greyhound (☑ 410-289-9307; www.greyhound.com; 12848 Ocean Gateway) buses run daily to and from Washington, DC (four hours), and Baltimore (3½ hours).

Ocean City Coastal Highway Bus (day pass $3) runs up and down the length of the beach, from 6am to 3am. There's also a tram ($3 or $6 all-day pass) that runs 11am to midnight from memorial day to late September.

Western Maryland

The western spine of Maryland is mountain country. The Appalachian peaks soar to 3000ft above sea level, and the surrounding valleys are packed with rugged scenery and Civil War battlefields. This is Maryland's outdoor playground, where hiking, skiing, rock climbing and white-water rafting are just a short drive from Baltimore.

Frederick

Halfway between the battlefields of Gettysburg, PA, and Antietam, Frederick, with its handsome 50-square-block historic district, resembles an almost perfect cliche of a mid-sized city.

The **National Museum of Civil War Medicine** (www.civilwarmed.org; 48 E Patrick St; adult/child $6.50/4.50; ⊙10am-5pm Mon-Sat, from 11am Sun) gives a fascinating, sometimes gruesome look at the health conditions soldiers and doctors faced during the war, as well as important medical advances that resulted from the conflict.

Hollerstown Hill B&B (☑301-228-3630; www.hollerstownhill.com; 4 Clarke Pl; r $135-145; P❄🎧) has four pattern-heavy rooms, an elegant billiard room and friendly, knowledgeable hosts.

The bouncy **Brewer's Alley** (☑301-631-0089; 124 N Market St; burgers $9-13, mains $18-29; ⊙11:30am-11:30pm Mon & Tue, to midnight Wed & Thu, to 12:30am Fri & Sat, noon-11:30pm Sun; 🎧) is one of our favorite places in town, for several reasons. First, the beer: homemade, plenty of variety, delicious. Second, the burgers: enormous, half-pound monstrosities. Third, the rest of the menu: excellent Chesapeake seafood and Frederick county farm produce. Finally: the beer. Again

Frederick is accessible via **Greyhound** (☑301-663-3311; www.greyhound.com) and **MARC trains** (☑301-682-9716) located across from the visitor center at 100 S East St.

Antietam National Battlefield

The site of the bloodiest day in American history is, ironically, supremely peaceful, quiet and haunting, uncluttered save for plaques and statues. On September 17, 1862, General Robert E Lee's first invasion of the North was stalled here in a tactical stalemate that left more than 23,000 dead, wounded or missing – more casualties than America had suffered in all her previous wars combined. Poignantly, many of the battlefield graves are inscribed with German and Irish names, a roll call of immigrants who died fighting for their new homeland. The **visitor center** (☑301-432-5124; State Rd 65; 3-day pass per person/family $4/6; ⊙8:30am-6pm, to 5pm off-season) sells a range of books and materials, including self-guided driving and walking tours of the battlefield.

Cumberland

At the Potomac River, the frontier outpost of Fort Cumberland (not to be confused with the Cumberland Gap between Virginia and Kentucky) was the pioneer gateway across the Alleghenies to Pittsburgh and the Ohio River. Today Cumberland has expanded into the outdoor recreation trade to guide visitors to the region's rivers, forests and mountains. Sights are a short stroll from the pedestrian-friendly streets of downtown Cumberland.

◉ Sights & Activities

C&O Canal National Historic Park   HIKING, CYCLING

A marvel of engineering, the C&O Canal was designed to stretch alongside the Potomac River from Chesapeake Bay to the Ohio River. Construction on the canal began in 1828 but was halted here in 1850 by the Appalachian Mountains. The park's protected 185-mile corridor includes a 12ft-wide towpath, hiking and cycling trail, which goes all the way from here to Georgetown in DC. The **C&O Canal Museum** (☑301-722-8226; http://www.nps.gov/choh; 13 Canal Pl; ⊙9am-5pm Mon-Fri; P) ✎ has displays chronicling the importance of river trade in eastern seaboard history.

Western Maryland Scenic Railroad   TOUR
(☑800-872-4650; www.wmsr.com; 13 Canal St; adult/child $33/16; ⊙11:30am Fri-Sun May-Oct, Sat & Sun Nov-Dec) Outside the Allegheny County visitor center, near the start of the C&O Canal, passengers can catch steam-locomotive rides, traversing forests and steep ravines to Frostburg, a 3½-hour round-trip.

Cumberland Trail Connection   CYCLING
(☑301-777-8724; www.ctcbikes.com; 14 Howard St, Canal Pl; half-day/day/week from $15/25/120; ⊙10am-6pm) Conveniently located near the start of the C&O Canal, this outfit rents out bicycles (cruisers, touring bikes and mountain bikes), and also arranges shuttle service anywhere from Pittsburgh to DC. Canoe rentals are in the works.

Allegany Expeditions   ADVENTURE TOUR
(☑301-777-9313; www.alleganyexpeditions.com; 10310 Columbus Ave/Rte 2) Leads adventure tours, including rock-climbing, canoeing, cross-country skiing and fly-fishing.

✗ Eating

Queen City Creamery & Deli   DINER $
(☑301-777-0011; 108 Harrison St; mains $6-8; ⊙7am-9pm) This retro soda fountain is like a 1940s time warp, with creamy shakes and homemade frozen custard, thick sandwiches and belly-filling breakfasts.

Deep Creek Lake

In the extreme west of the panhandle, Maryland's largest freshwater lake is an all-seasons playground. The crimson and copper glow of the Alleghenies attracts thousands during the annual **Autumn Glory Festival** (www.autumngloryfestival.com; ⊘Oct), rivaling New England's leaf-turning backdrops.

DELAWARE

Wee Delaware, the nation's second-smallest state (96 miles long and less than 35 miles across at its widest point) is overshadowed by its neighbors and overlooked by visitors to the Capital Region. And that's too bad, because Delaware has a lot more on offer than just tax-free shopping and chicken farms.

Long white sandy beaches, cute colonial villages, a cozy countryside and small-town charm characterize the 'Small Wonder'. Ignore those tolls: there's a whole state just waiting to be explored, and (forgive us one more joke about Delaware's size), it doesn't take long to get around.

History

In colonial days Delaware was the subject of an aggressive land feud between Dutch, Swedish and British settlers. The former imported classically northern European middle-class concepts, the latter a plantation-based aristocracy, which is partly why Delaware remains a typically mid-Atlantic cultural hybrid today.

The little state's big moment came on December 7, 1787, when Delaware became the first state to ratify the US Constitution and thus the first state in the Union. It remained in that union throughout the Civil War, despite supporting slavery. During this period, as throughout much of the state's history, the economy drew on its chemical industry. DuPont, the world's second-largest chemical company, was founded here in 1802 as a gunpowder factory by French Immigrant Eleuthère Irénée du Pont. Low taxes drew other firms (particularly credit-card companies) in the 20th century, boosting the state's prosperity.

Delaware Beaches

Delaware's 28 miles of sandy Atlantic beaches are the best reason to linger. Most businesses and services are open year-round. Off-season (outside June to August) price bargains abound.

Lewes

In 1631 the Dutch gave this whaling settlement the pretty name of Zwaanendael, or valley of the swans, before promptly getting massacred by local Nanticokes. The name was changed to Lewes (pronounced Loo-iss) when William Penn gained control of the area. Today it's an attractive seaside gem with a mix of English and Dutch architecture.

The **visitor center** (www.leweschamber.com; 120 Kings Hwy; ⊘ 9am-5pm Mon-Fri) directs you to sights such as the **Zwaanendael Museum** (102 Kings Hwy; ⊘10am-4:30pm Tue-Sat, 1:30-4:30pm Sun) FREE, where the friendly staff explains the Dutch roots of this first-state settlement.

For aquatic action, **Quest Fitness Kayak** (☑302-644-7020; www.questfitnesskayak.com; Savannah Rd; kayak per 2/8hr $25/50) operates a kayak rental stand next to the Beacon Motel. It also runs scenic paddle tours around the Cape (adult/child $65/35).

> ### DELAWARE FACTS
>
> **Nickname** The First State
>
> **Population** 917,000
>
> **Area** 1982 sq miles
>
> **Capital city** Dover (population 36,000)
>
> **Sales tax** None
>
> **Birthplace of** Rock musician George Thorogood (b 1952), actress Valerie Bertinelli (b 1960), actor Ryan Phillippe (b 1974)
>
> **Home of** Vice President Joe Biden, the Du Pont family, DuPont chemicals, credit-card companies, lots of chickens
>
> **Politics** Democrat
>
> **Famous for** Tax-free shopping, beautiful beaches
>
> **State bird** Blue hen chicken
>
> **Driving distances** Wilmington to Dover 52 miles, Dover to Rehoboth Beach 43 miles

Restaurant and hotel options in the small historic downtown include **Hotel Rodney** (☑302-645-6466; www.hotelrodneydelaware.com; 142 2nd St; r $160-260; P✳☀☎), a charming boutique hotel with exquisite bedding and antique furniture. On the other side of the canal, the **Beacon Motel** (☑302-645-4888; www.beaconmotel.com; 514 Savannah Rd; r $95-190; P✳☀☎) has large, quiet (if a little boring) rooms within 10-minutes' walk to the beach.

There are charming restaurants and cafes sprinkled along 2nd St. Located by the drawbridge over the canal, the clapboard **Striper Bites Bistro** (☑302-645-4657; 107 Savannah Rd; lunch mains $10-12, dinner $16-24; ☉11:30am-late Mon-Sat) specializes in innovative seafood dishes such as Lewes rockfish and fish tacos. Across the drawbridge, the **Wharf** (☑302-645-7846; 7 Anglers Rd; mains $15-29; ☉7am-1am; P▮) has a relaxing waterfront location (facing the canal), and serves a big selection of seafood and pub grub. Live music throughout the week.

The **Cape May–Lewes Ferry** (☑800-643-3779; www.capemaylewesferry.com; 43 Cape Henlopen Dr; per motorcycle/car $36/44, per adult/child $10/5) runs daily 90-minute ferries across Delaware Bay to New Jersey from the terminal, 1 mile from downtown Lewes. For foot passengers, a seasonal shuttle bus ($4) operates between the ferry terminal and Lewes and Rehoboth Beach. Fares are lower Sunday through Thursday and during winter. Reservations recommended.

Cape Henlopen State Park

One mile east of Lewes, more than 4000 acres of dune bluffs, pine forests and wetlands are preserved at this lovely **state park** (☑302-645-8983; http://www.destateparks.com/park/cape-henlopen/; 15099 Cape Henlopen Dr; admission $4; ☉8am-sunset) that's popular with bird-watchers and beachgoers ($6 per out-of-state car). You can see clear to Cape May from the observation tower. **North Shores beach** draws many gay and lesbian couples. **Camping** (☑877-987-2757; campsites $33; ☉Mar-Nov) includes oceanfront or wooded sites.

Rehoboth Beach & Dewey Beach

As the closest beach to Washington, DC (121 miles), Rehoboth is often dubbed 'the Nation's Summer Capital.' Founded in 1873 as a Christian seaside resort camp, Rehoboth is today a shining example of tolerance. It is both a family-friendly and gay-friendly destination, and has a particularly large lesbian community. There's even a gay beach – aka Poodle Beach – located, appropriately, at the end of Queen St.

Downtown Rehoboth is a mixture of grand Victorian and gingerbread houses, tree-lined streets, boutique B&Bs and shops, posh restaurants, kiddie amusements and wide beaches fronted by a mile-long boardwalk. Rehoboth Ave, the main drag, is lined with restaurants and the usual tacky souvenir shops; it stretches from the **visitor center** (☑302-227-2233; www.beach-fun.com; 501 Rehoboth Ave; ☉9am-5pm Mon-Fri, to 1pm Sat & Sun) at the traffic circle to the boardwalk. Outside of town, Rte 1 is a busy highway crammed with chain restaurants, hotels and outlet malls, where bargain-hunters take advantage of Delaware's tax-free shopping.

Less than 2 miles south on Hwy 1 is the tiny hamlet of **Dewey Beach**. Unapologetically known as 'Do Me' beach for its hook-up scene (straight) and hedonistic nightlife, it's is a major party beach. Another 3 miles past Dewey is **Delaware Seashore State Park** (☑302-227-2800; http://www.destateparks.com/park/delaware-seashore/; 39415 Inlet Rd; admission $4; ☉8am-sunset), a windswept slice of preserved dunes and salty breezes possessed of a wild, lonely beauty.

🛏 Sleeping

As elsewhere on the coast, prices sky rocket in high season (June to August). Cheaper lodging options are located on Rte 1.

⭐**Cottages at
Indian River Marina** COTTAGES **$$$**
(☑302-227-3071; http://www.destateparks.com/camping/cottages/rates.asp; Inlet 838, Rehoboth Beach; weekly peak/shoulder/off-season $1800/1350/835, 2 days off-season $280 ; P✳) These cottages, located in Delaware Seashore State Park five miles south of town, are some of our favorite local vacation rentals. Not for the decor per se, but the patios and unadulterated views across the pristine beach to the ocean. Each cottage has two bedrooms and a loft. They must be rented out by the week during the summer, but they're available in two-day increments off-season.

Bellmoor Inn & Spa BOUTIQUE HOTEL **$$$**
(☑866-899-2779, 302-227-5800; www.thebellmoor.com; 6 Christian St; r $190-260; P✳@☀) If money were no object, we'd splurge for

a room at Rehoboth's most luxurious inn. With its English country decor, fireplaces, quiet garden and secluded setting, this is not your usual seaside resort. A full-service day spa caps the amenities.

Hotel Rehoboth BOUTIQUE HOTEL **$$$**
(📋302-227-4300; www.hotelrehoboth.com; 247 Rehoboth Ave; r $230-320; 🅿✳@📶⛲) This boutique hotel has a reputation for great service and luxurious amenities. It offers a free shuttle to the beach.

Crosswinds Motel MOTEL **$$$**
(📋302-227-7997; www.crosswindsmotel.com; 312 Rehoboth Ave; r $130-275; 🅿✳📶) Located in the heart of Rehoboth Ave, this simple motel offers great value for your dollar, with its welcome amenities (minifridge, coffeemaker, flat-screen TV). Walk to the beach in 12 minutes.

🍴 Eating & Drinking

Cheap eats are available on the boardwalk, with favorites such as Thrasher's fries, Grotto's pizza and Dolle's saltwater taffy. For classier dining, browse the inviting restaurants sprinkled along Wilmington Ave.

Ed's Chicken & Crabs AMERICAN **$**
(📋302- 227-9484; 2200 Coastal Highway, Dewey Beach; mains $7-18; ⊙11am-10pm) It's fried. What's fried? Just about everything at this outdoor dining shack: shrimp, jalapenos, crabs. But not the corn – the corn is boiled and sweet and delicious. Ed's ain't fine dining, but it's tasty and old-school and unhealthy and, in its way, perfect.

★ Planet X FUSION **$$$**
(📋302-226-1928; 35 Wilmington Ave; mains $16-33; ⊙from 5pm; 🍴) This stylish spot shows its Asian influence in menu and decor – red paper lanterns and Buddhas adorn the walls, while diners feast on red Thai curry with jumbo shrimp and crab cakes with spicy Asian sesame noodles. There's alfresco dining on the open-sided front porch.

Henlopen City Oyster House SEAFOOD **$$$**
(50 Wilmington Ave; mains $21-26; ⊙from 3pm) Oyster- and seafood-lovers won't want to miss this elegant spot, where an enticing raw bar and beautifully prepared plates (soft-shell crabs, bouillabaisse and lobster mac 'n' cheese) draw crowds (arrive early; no reservations). Good microbrews, cocktails

---

DON'T MISS

CYCLING THE JUNCTION & BREAKWATER TRAIL

For a fantastic ride between Rehoboth and Lewes, rent a bicycle and hit the 6-mile Junction and Breakwater Trail. Named after the former rail line, which operated here in the 1800s, this smooth, graded greenway travels through wooded and open terrain, over coastal marshes and past farmland. Pick up a map from the Rehoboth visitor center or from **Atlantic Cycles** (📋302-226-2543; www.atlanticcycles. net; 18 Wilmington Ave; half-day/day from $16/24), also in Rehoboth, which offers inexpensive rentals. In Lewes, try **Ocean Cycles** (📋302-537-1522; www. oceancycles.com; 526 E Savannah Rd) at the Beacon Motel.

---

and wine selections make it an ideal early-evening drink-and-eat spot.

Cultured Pearl JAPANESE **$$$**
(📋302-227-8493; 301 Rehoboth Ave; mains $16-33; ⊙4:30pm-late) A longtime locals' favorite, this Asian restaurant has a Zen feel, with a koi pond at the entrance and a pleasant rooftop deck. The sushi and appetizers are first-rate. Live music most nights.

Dogfish Head MICROBREWERY
(www.dogfish.com; 320 Rehoboth Ave; mains $9-25; ⊙noon-late) When a place mixes its own brewery with some of the best live music on the Eastern Shore, you know you've got a winning combination.

ⓘ Getting There & Around

The **Jolly Trolley** (one way/round-trip $3/5; ⊙8am-2am summer) connects Rehoboth and Dewey, and makes frequent stops along the way. Unfortunately, long-distance buses no longer serve Rehoboth.

Bethany Beach & Fenwick Island

Want to get away from it all? The seaside towns of Bethany and Fenwick, about halfway between Rehoboth and Ocean City, are known as 'the Quiet Resorts.' They share a tranquil, almost boring, family-friendly scene.

There are only a few restaurants and even fewer hotels here; most visitors stay in rented apartments and beach houses. For a nice change of pace from the usual seafood fare, **Bethany Blues BBQ** (☎302-537-1500; www.bethanyblues.com; 6 N Pennsylvania Ave; mains $14-24; ⏲4:30-9pm, to 10pm Fri & Sat) has falling-off-the-bone ribs and pulled-pork sandwiches.

Northern & Central Delaware

The grit of Wilmington is balanced by the rolling hills and palatial residences of the Brandywine Valley, particularly the soaring estate of Winterthur. Dover is cute, friendly and gets a little lively after hours.

Wilmington

A unique cultural milieu (African Americans, Jews and Caribbeans) and an energetic arts scene make this town worth a visit.

The **Delaware Art Museum** (☎302-571-9590; www.delart.org; 800 S Madison St; adult/child $12/6, Sun free; ⏲10am-4pm Wed-Sat, from noon Sun) exhibits work of the local Brandywine School, including Edward Hopper, John Sloan and three generations of Wyeths.

The **Wilmington Riverfront** (www.riverfrontwilm.com) consists of several blocks of redeveloped waterfront shops, restaurants and cafes; the most striking building is the **Delaware Center for the Contemporary Arts** (☎302-656-6466; www.thedcca.org; 200 S Madison St; ⏲10am-5pm Tue & Thu-Sat, from noon Wed & Sun) FREE, which consistently displays innovative exhibitions. In the art-deco Woolworth's building, the **Delaware History Museum** (☎302-656-0637; www.hsd.org/dhm; 200 S Madison St; adult/child $6/4; ⏲11am-4pm Wed-Fri, 10am-4pm Sat) proves the First State's past includes loads more than being head of the line to sign the Constitution.

The premier hotel in the state, the **Hotel du Pont** (☎302-594-3100; www.hoteldupont.com; cnr Market & 11th Sts; r $230-480; P ❄ 🛜) is luxurious enough to satisfy its namesake (one of America's most successful industrialist families). On the riverfront, **Iron Hill Brewery** (☎302-472-2739; 710 South Madison St; mains $10-24; ⏲11am-11pm) is a spacious and airy multilevel space set in a converted brick warehouse. Satisfying microbrews (try the seasonal Belgian ale) match nicely with hearty pub grub.

The **visitor center** (☎800-489-6664; www.visitwilmingtonde.com; 100 W 10th St; ⏲9am-5pm Mon-Thu, 8:30am-4:30pm Fri) is downtown. Wilmington is accessible by Greyhound or Peter Pan Bus Lines, which run to major East Coast cities. Both bus lines serve the **Wilmington Transportation Center** (101 N French St). **Amtrak** (www.amtrak.com; 100 S French St) trains connect Wilmington with DC (1½ hours), Baltimore (45 minutes) and New York (1¾ hours).

Brandywine Valley

After making their fortune, the French-descended Du Ponts turned the Brandywine Valley into a sort of American Loire Valley, and it remains a nesting ground for the wealthy and ostentatious to this day.

Six miles northwest of Wilmington is **Winterthur** (☎302-888-4600; www.winterthur.org; 5105 Kennett Pike (Rte 52) ; adult/child $18/5; ⏲10am-5pm Tue-Sun), the 175-room country estate of industrialist Henry Francis du Pont, housing his collection of antiques and American arts, one of the world's largest.

Brandywine Creek State Park (☎302-577-3534; http://www.destateparks.com/park/brandywine-creek/; 41 Adams Dam Road, Wilmington; admission $3; ⏲8am-sunset) is the gem of the area. This green space would be impressive anywhere, but is doubly so considering how close it is to prodigious urban development. Nature trails and shallow streams wend through the park; contact **Wilderness Canoe Trips** (☎302-654-2227; www.wildernesscanoetrips.com; 2111 Concord Pike; kayak/canoe trip from $46/56, per tube $18) for information on paddling or tubing down the dark-green Brandywine creek.

New Castle

As cute as a colonial kitten, New Castle is a web of cobblestoned streets and beautifully preserved 18th-century buildings lying near a riverfront (that said, the surrounding area, however, is a bit of an urban wasteland). Sights include the **Old Court House** (☎302-323-4453; 211 Delaware St, New Castle; ⏲10am-3:30pm Wed-Sat, 1:30-4:30pm Sun) FREE, the arsenal on the Green, churches and cemeteries dating back to the 17th century, and historic houses.

The five-room **Terry House B&B** (☎302-322-2505; www.terryhouse.com; 130 Delaware St; r $90-110; P 🛜) is idyllically set in the historic district. The owner will play the piano for you while you enjoy a full breakfast.

A few doors down, **Jessop's Tavern** ([✆]302-322-6111; 114 Delaware St; mains $12-24; ⊙11:30am-10pm Sun-Thu, to midnight Fri & Sat) serves up Dutch pot roast, Pilgrim's feast (oven-roasted turkey with all the fixings) plus fish and chips and other pub grub in a colonial atmosphere. Half the fun is watching the bored teenage staff chafe in their Colonial-era garb.

Outside of town, check out the **Dog House** ([✆]302-328-5380; 1200 Dupont Hwy, New Castle; mains under $10; ⊙10:30am-midnight). Don't be fooled by the name; while this unassuming diner does hot dogs and does them well (the chili dogs are a treat), it also whips out mean subs and cheese-steaks that could pass muster in Philly.

Dover

Dover's city center is quite attractive; the row-house-lined streets are peppered with restaurants and shops and, on prettier lanes, broadleaf trees spread their branches.

Learn about the first official state at **First State Heritage Park** ([✆]302-744-5055; 121 Martin Luther King Blvd North, Dover; ⊙8am-4:30pm Mon-Fri, from 9am Sat, 1:30-4:30pm Sun) **FREE**. Located in the local archives, the park serves as a welcome center for the city of Dover, the state of Delaware and the adjacent state house. Access the latter via the Georgian **Old State House** ([✆]302-744-5055; http://history.delaware.gov/museums/; 25 The Green; ⊙9am-4:30pm Mon-Sat, from 1:30pm Sun) **FREE**, built in 1791 and since restored, which contains art galleries and in-depth exhibits on the First State's history and politics.

The **State Street Inn** ([✆]302-734-2294; www.statestreetinn.com; 228 N State St; r $125-135) is well located near the State House, and has four bright rooms with wood floors and period furnishings.

A short stroll from the State House, **Golden Fleece** ([✆]302-674-1776; 132 W Lockerman St; mains under $10; ⊙4pm-midnight, to late on Sat & Sun, from noon Sun) is our favorite bar in Dover. There's decent food and the atmosphere of an old English pub, which meshes well with the surrounding red-brick historical center.

Bombay Hook National Wildlife Refuge

You're not the only person making a trip to **Bombay Hook National Wildlife Refuge** ([✆]302-653-9345; http://www.fws.gov/refuge/ Bombay_Hook; 2591 Whitehall Neck Rd, Smyrna; ⊙sunrise-sunset). Hundreds of thousands of waterfowl use this protected wetland as a stopping point along their migration routes.

A 12-mile wildlife driving trail through 16,251 acres of sweet-smelling saltwater marsh, cordgrass and tidal mud flats, which manages to encapsulate all of the soft beauty of the DelMarVa peninsula in one perfectly preserved ecosystem, is the highlight of the sanctuary.

There are also five walking trails, two of which are accessible to travelers with disabilities, as well as observation towers overlooking the entire affair. Across the water you may see the lights and factories of New Jersey, an industrial yin to this area's wilderness yang.

VIRGINIA

Beautiful Virginia is a state steeped in history. It's the birthplace of America, where English settlers established the first permanent colony in the New World in 1607. From there, the Commonwealth of Virginia has played a lead role in nearly every major American drama, from the Revolutionary and Civil Wars to the Civil Rights movement and September 11, 2001.

Virginia's natural beauty is as diverse as its history and people. Chesapeake Bay and the wide sandy beaches kiss the Atlantic Ocean. Pine forests, marshes and rolling green hills form the soft curves of the central Piedmont region, while the rugged Appalachian Mountains and stunning Shenandoah Valley line its back.

The nation's invisible line between North and South is drawn here, somewhere around Richmond; you'll know it as soon as you hear the sweet southern drawl offering plates of biscuits and Virginia ham. With something for everyone, it's easy to appreciate the state's motto: 'Virginia is for Lovers.'

History

Humans have occupied Virginia for at least 5000 years. Several thousand Native Americans were already here in May 1607 when Captain James Smith and his crew sailed up Chesapeake Bay and founded Jamestown, the first permanent English colony in the New World. Named for the 'Virgin Queen' Elizabeth I, the territory originally occupied most of America's eastern seaboard. By 1610 most of the colonists had died from starvation in their quest for gold, until colonist John Rolfe (husband of Pocahontas) discovered Virginia's real riches: tobacco.

A feudal aristocracy grew out of tobacco farming, and many gentry scions became Founding Fathers, including native son George Washington. In the 19th century the slave-based plantation system grew in size and incompatibility with the industrializing North; Virginia seceded in 1861 and became the epicenter of the Civil War. Following its defeat the state walked a tense cultural tightrope, accruing a layered identity that included older aristocrats, a rural and urban working class, waves of immigrants and, today, the burgeoning tech-heavy suburbs of DC. The state revels in its history, yet still wants to pioneer the American experiment; thus, while Virginia only reluctantly desegregated in the 1960s, today it houses one of the most ethnically diverse populations of the New South.

VIRGINIA FACTS

Nickname Old Dominion

Population 8.2 million

Area 42,774 sq miles

Capital city Richmond (population 205,000)

Other cities Virginia Beach (population 447,000), Norfolk (population 245,800), Chesapeake (population 228,400), Richmond (population 210,300), Newport News (population) 180,700

Sales tax 5.3%

Birthplace of Eight US presidents including George Washington (1732–99), Confederate General Robert E Lee (1807–70), tennis ace Arthur Ashe (1943–93), author Tom Wolfe (b 1931), actress Sandra Bullock (b 1964)

Home of The Pentagon, the CIA, more technology workers than any other state

Politics Republican

Famous for American history, tobacco, apples, Shenandoah National Park

State beverage Milk

Driving distances Arlington to Shenandoah 113 miles, Richmond to Virginia Beach 108 miles

Northern Virginia

Hidden within its suburban sprawl exterior, Northern Virginia (NOVA) mixes small-town charm with metropolitan chic. Colonial villages and battlefields bump up against skyscrapers, shopping malls and world-class arts venues.

You'll discover unexpected green spaces such as **Great Falls National Park** (☑ 703-285-2965; www.nps.gov/grfa; ☉ 7am-sunset) 🐾. It's a well-maintained forest cut through by the Potomac River, which surges over a series of white-water rapids.

Arlington

Just across the Potomac River from DC, Arlington County was once part of Washington until it was returned to Virginia in 1847. In recent years the gentrified neighborhoods of Arlington have spawned some tempting dining and nightlife options.

◎ Sights

Arlington National Cemetery   HISTORIC SITE (☑ 877-907-8585; www.arlingtoncemetery.mil; tour bus adult/child $8.75/4.50; ☉ 8am-7pm Apr-Sep, to 5pm Oct-Mar) FREE This immensely powerful destination is the somber final resting place for more than 300,000 military personnel and their dependents, with veterans of every US war from the Revolution to Iraq. The cemetery is spread over 612 hilly acres. You can travel around via a **tour bus**, which departs continuously from the visitor center from 8:30am to 4:30pm.

➡ **The Grounds**

Much of the cemetery was built on the grounds of **Arlington House**, the former home of Robert E Lee and his wife Mary Anna Custis Lee, a descendant of Martha Washington. When Lee left to lead Virginia's army in the Civil War, Union troops confiscated the property to bury their dead. The **Tomb of the Unknowns** contains the remains of unidentified American servicemen from both World Wars and the Korean War; military guards retain a round-the-clock vigil and the changing of the guard (every half-hour March to September, every hour October to February) is one of Arlington's most moving sights. An eternal flame marks the **grave of John F Kennedy**, next to those of Jacqueline Kennedy Onassis and two of her infant children.

→ Marine Corps Memorial

Just north of the cemetery, the **Marine Corps Memorial** (N Meade & 14th Sts) depicts six soldiers raising the American flag on Iwo Jima. The Felix de Weldon–designed sculpture is based on an iconic photo by Associated Press photographer Joe Rosenthal.

Artisphere ARTS CENTER

(☑ 703-875-1100; www.artisphere.com; 1101 Wilson Blvd; ⛎ ; Ⓜ Rosslyn) For something completely different than memorials and museums, check out the excellent exhibits at this sleek, modern, multistory arts complex. Its several theaters host live performances (many free), including world music, film and experimental theater. Nearby **Freedom Park**, an elevated greenway that rests in an old road overpass running by Artisphere, is a nice spot to sit for a while and contemplate.

Pentagon BUILDING

South of Arlington Cemetery is the Pentagon, the largest office building in the world. It's not open to the public, but outside you may visit the **Pentagon Memorial** (www.whs.mil/memorial; 1 N Rotary Rd, Arlington; ⓢ 24hr) **FREE**; 184 illuminated benches honor each person killed in the September 11, 2001, terrorist attack on the Pentagon. Nearby, the three soaring arcs of the **Air Force Memorial** (☑ 703-247-5805; www.airforcememorial.org; 1 Air Force Memorial Dr, Arlington) evoke the contrails of jets.

🛏 Sleeping & Eating

In addition to hotels, there are dozens of chic restaurants and bars located along Clarendon and Wilson Blvds, clustered near Rosslyn and Clarendon Metro stations.

★ Myanmar BURMESE $

(☑ 703-289-0013; 7810 Lee Hwy, Falls Church; mains under $10; ⓢ 11am-10pm) Myanmar's decor is bare bones; the service is slow; the portions are small; and the food is delicious. This is homemade Burmese: curries cooked with lots of garlic, turmeric and oil, plus chili fish, mango salads and chicken swimming in rich gravies.

Lyon Hall FRENCH $$

(☑ 703-741-7636; http://lyonhallarlington.com; 3100 N Washington Blvd; mains $14-25; ⓢ 11.30am-3pm Mon-Fri, from 10am Sat & Sun, 5pm-10:30pm Sun-Thu, to 11:30pm Fri & Sat; Ⓜ Clarendon) Enter this French-Alsatian bistro under a deco-style sign. Cassoulet is wonderfully rich thanks to its base of duck fat; a trout served over summer beans is enlivened by vanilla butter. Wash it down with a local cocktail from the popular bar.

Eden Center VIETNAMESE $$

(www.edencenter.com; 6571 Wilson Blvd, Falls Church; mains $9-15; ⓢ 9am-11pm; 🅿) One of Washington's most fascinating ethnic enclaves isn't technically in Washington but west of Arlington in Falls Church, VA. The Eden Center is, basically, a bit of Saigon that got lost in America. And we mean 'Saigon' – this is a shopping center/strip mall entirely occupied and operated by South Vietnamese refugees and their descendants. You can buy Vietnamese DVDs, shop for odd fruits and unusual medicines and, of course, eat – anywhere.

Whitlow's on Wilson AMERICAN $$

(☑ 703-276-9693; 2854 Clarendon Blvd; mains $8-21; ⓢ 11am-2am Mon-Fri, from 9am Sat & Sun) Arlington's best Sunday-brunch menu, plus weekday happy-hour specials and live bands on weekends.

☆ Entertainment

★ Iota LIVE MUSIC

(www.iotaclubandcafe.com; 2832 Wilson Blvd; tickets from $10; ⓢ from 8am; 🛜 ; Ⓜ Clarendon) Iota is the best venue for live music in the area. Bands span genres; folk, reggae, traditional Irish and Southern rock are all possibilities. Tickets are available at the door only (no advance sales). The free open-mic Wednesdays can be lots of fun or painfully self-important, as these things are wont to be.

Alexandria

The charming colonial village of Alexandria is just 5 miles and 250 years away from Washington. Once a salty port town, Alexandria – known as 'Old Town' to locals – is today a posh collection of red-brick colonial homes, cobblestone streets, flickering gas lamps and a waterfront promenade. King St is packed with boutiques, outdoor cafes, and neighborhood bars and restaurants.

◉ Sights

George Washington Masonic National Memorial MONUMENT, LOOKOUT

(www.gwmemorial.org; 101 Callahan Dr at King St; adult/child $8/free; ⓢ 9am-4pm Mon-Sat, noon-4pm Sun; Ⓜ King St) Alexandria's most prominent landmark features a fine view from its 333ft tower, where you can see the Capitol,

Mount Vernon and the Potomac River. It is modeled after Egypt's Lighthouse of Alexandria and honors the first president (who was initiated into the shadowy Masons in Fredericksburg in 1752 and later became Worshipful Master of Alexandria Lodge No 22). The only way up is via a guided tour; they depart at 10am, 11:30am, 1:30pm and 3pm (on Sunday the first one is at 12:30pm).

Gadsby's Tavern Museum
MUSEUM
(www.gadsbystavern.org; 134 N Royal St; adult/child $5/2; ⊙10am-5pm Tue-Sat, 1-5pm Sun & Mon; M King St then trolley) Once a real tavern (operated by John Gadsby from 1796 to 1808), this building now houses a museum demonstrating the prominent role of the tavern in Alexandria during the 18th century. As the center of local political, business and social life, the tavern was frequented by anybody who was anybody, including George Washington, Thomas Jefferson and the Marquis de Lafayette. The rooms are restored to their 18th-century appearance, and the tavern occasionally still hosts pricey balls. Guided tours take place at quarter to and quarter past the hour.

Torpedo Factory Art Center
ARTS CENTER
(www.torpedofactory.org; 105 N Union St; ⊙10am-6pm, to 7pm Thu; M King St then trolley) FREE What do you do with a former munitions dump and arms factory? How about turning it into one of the best art spaces in the region? Three floors of artists studios and free creativity are on offer in Old Town Alexandria, as well as the opportunity to buy paintings, sculptures, glassworks, textiles and jewelry direct from their creators. The Torpedo Factory anchors Alexandria's revamped waterfront with a marina, parks, walkways, residences and restaurants.

✕ Eating & Drinking

Misha's Coffee Roaster
CAFE $
(www.mishascoffee.com; 102 S Patrick St; pastries $3-4; ⊙6am-8pm; ☎) Sip a lovely latte next to jars of strong-smelling beans imported from Indonesia and Ethiopia, bang out your play on your laptop (or procrastinate with the free wi-fi), check out the cute nerds at the other tables and reach caffeinated nirvana at this very hip indie cafe. Croissants and cookies add to the buzz.

Hank's Oyster Bar
SEAFOOD $$
(1026 King St; mains $6-28; ⊙5:30-9:30pm Tue-Thu, 11:30am-midnight Fri & Sat, 11am-9:30pm Sun)

There are a fair few oyster bars in Washington (slurping raw boys is good for political puffery, apparently) and Hank's is our favorite of the bunch. It's got the right testosterone combination, a bit of power-player muscle mixed with good-old-boy ambiance, which isn't to say women won't love it here; just that guys really do. Needless to say, the oyster menu is extensive and excellent; there are always at least four varieties on hand. Quarters are cramped, and you often have to wait for a table – nothing a saki oyster bomb won't fix.

Restaurant Eve
AMERICAN $$$
(☎703-706-0450; www.restauranteve.com; 110 S Pitt St; 5-/7-course tasting menus $120/135; ⊙lunch Mon-Fri, dinner Mon-Sat; ☞) While 'fusion' may be an overused adjective when it comes to describing restaurants, the best kitchens always fuse. Innovation and tradition, regional and international influences, comfort and class. Eve contains everything we have described, a combination of great American ingredients, precise French technique and some of the highest levels of service we've encountered in the area. Splurge here on the tasting menus, which are simply on another level of gastronomic experience. This is one of the few vegan-friendly high-end restaurants in the DC metro area; just be sure to call a day ahead and chef-owner Cathal Armstrong's team will be happy to accommodate you.

☆ Entertainment

Birchmere
LIVE MUSIC
(www.birchmere.com; 3701 Mount Vernon Ave; tickets $15-35; ⊙box office 5-9pm, shows 7:30pm; M Pentagon City then ☒ 10A) Known as 'America's Legendary Music Hall,' this is the DC area's premier venue for folk, country, Celtic and bluegrass music. The talent that graces the stage is reason enough to come, but the venue is pretty great too: it sort of looks like a warehouse that collided with an army of LSD-savvy muralists. Located north of Old Town Alexandria off Glebe Rd.

Tiffany Tavern
LIVE MUSIC
(www.tiffanytavern.com; 1116 King St; M King St) FREE The food is kind of lame and the beer selection weak, but the live bluegrass (from 8:30pm Friday and Saturday) hits the spot at the well-worn Tiffany Tavern. It gets a little rough and a lot raucous on the best nights, when Yuengling on tap, mandolin and fiddle equal hours of roots-music magic.

VIRGINIA VINEYARDS

Now the fifth-biggest wine producer in the USA, Virginia has 192 vineyards around the state, many located in the pretty hills around Charlottesville. Particularly notable is the Virginia Viognier. For more information on Virginia wine, visit www.virginiawine.org.

Jefferson Vineyards (☑ 434-977-3042; www.jeffersonvineyards.com; 1353 Thomas Jefferson Pkwy) Known for consistent quality vintage, this winery harvests from its namesake's original 1774 vineyard site.

Keswick Vineyards (☑ 434-244-3341; www.keswickvineyards.com; 1575 Keswick Winery Dr) Keswick won a wave of awards for its first vintage and has since been distilling a big range of grapes. It's off Rte 231.

Kluge Estate (☑ 434-977-3895; www.klugeestateonline.com; 100 Grand Cru Dr) Oenophiles regularly rate Kluge wine as the best in the state.

ℹ Information

The **visitor center** (☑ 703-838-5005; www. visitalexandriava.com; 221 King St; ⊙ 9am-5pm) issues parking permits and discount tickets for historic sites.

ℹ Getting There & Away

To get to Alexandria from downtown DC, get off at the King St Metro station. A free trolley makes the 1-mile journey between the Metro station and the waterfront (every 20 minutes, from 11:30am to 10pm).

Mount Vernon

One of the most visited historic shrines in the nation, **Mount Vernon** (☑ 703-780-2000, 800-429-1520; www.mountvernon.org; 3200 Mount Vernon Memorial Hwy, Mt Vernon; adult/child $17/8; ⊙ 8am-5pm Apr-Aug, 9am-4pm Nov-Feb, to 5pm Mar, Sep & Oct) was the beloved home of George and Martha Washington, who lived here from the time of their marriage in 1759 until Washington's death in 1799. Now owned and operated by the Mount Vernon Ladies Association, the estate offers glimpses of 18th-century farm life and the first president's life as a country planter. Mount Vernon does not gloss over the Founding Father's slave ownership; visitors can tour the slave quarters and burial ground. Other sights include Washington's **distillery and grist mill** (www.tourmobile.com; adult/child $4/2, incl Mount Vernon adult/child $30/15), 3 miles south of the estate.

Mount Vernon is 16 miles south of DC off the Mount Vernon Memorial Hwy. By public transportation, take the Metro to Huntington, then switch to Fairfax Connector bus 101. **Grayline** (☑ 202-289-1995; www.grayline.

com; adult/child incl Mt Vernon admission from $55/20) tours depart daily from DC's Union Station year-round.

Several companies offer seasonal boat trips from DC and Alexandria; the cheapest is **Potomac Riverboat Company** (☑ 703-684-0580; www.potomacriverboatco.com; adult/child incl Mt Vernon admission $40/20). A healthy alternative is to take a lovely bike ride along the Potomac River from DC (18 miles from Roosevelt Island).

Manassas

On July 21, 1861, Union and Confederate soldiers clashed in the first major land battle of the Civil War. Expecting a quick victory, DC residents flocked here to picnic and watch the First Battle of Bull Run (known in the South as First Manassas). The surprise Southern victory erased any hopes of a quick end to the war. Union and Confederate soldiers again met on the same ground for the larger Second Battle of Manassas in August 1862; again the South was victorious. Today, **Manassas National Battlefield Park** is a curving green hillscape, sectioned into fuzzy fields of tall grass and wildflowers by split-rail wood fences. Start your tour at the **Henry Hill Visitor Center** (☑ 703-361-1339; www.nps.gov/mana; adult/child $3/free; ⊙ 8:30am-5pm) to watch the orientation film and pick up park and trail maps.

Daily **Amtrak** (www.amtrak.com; one way $16-28) and **Virginia Railway Express** (VRE; www.vre.org; one way $9.10; ⊙ Mon-Fri) trains make the 50-minute journey between DC's Union Station and the historic Old Town Manassas Railroad Station on 9451 West St; from there it's a 6-mile taxi ride to the park. There are several restaurants and bars around the Manassas train station, but the rest of the city is a mess of strip malls and suburban sprawl.

Fredericksburg

Fredericksburg is a pretty town with a historical district that is almost a cliché of small-town Americana. George Washington grew up here, and the Civil War exploded in the streets and surrounding fields. Today the main street is a pleasant amble of bookstores, gastropubs and cafes.

◉ Sights

The **visitor center** (☑ 540-373-1776; www.visitfred.com; 706 Caroline St; ☉ 9am-5pm, from 11am Sun) offers a Timeless Fredericksburg pass ($32), which includes admission to nine local sights.

Fredericksburg & Spotsylvania National Military Park   HISTORIC SITE
(adult/child $32/10) More than 13,000 Americans were killed during the Civil War in four battles fought in a 17-mile radius covered by this park that's maintained by the NPS. Don't miss the burial site of Stonewall Jackson's amputated arm near the **Fredericksburg Battlefield visitor center** (☑ 540-654-5535; www.nps.gov/frsp; 1013 Lafayette Blvd; film $2; ☉ 9am-5pm) FREE

James Monroe Museum & Memorial Library   HISTORIC SITE
(☑ 540-654-1043; http://jamesmonroemuseum.umw.edu; 908 Charles St; adult/child $5/1; ☉ 10am-5pm Mon-Sat, from 1pm Sun) The museum's namesake was the nation's fifth president.

Mary Washington House   HISTORIC SITE
(☑ 540-373-1569; www.apva.org; 1200 Charles St; adult/child $5/2; ☉ 11am-5pm Mon-Sat, noon-4pm Sun) The 18th-century home of George Washington's mother.

🛌 Sleeping & Eating

You'll find dozens of restaurants and cafes along historic Caroline and William Sts.

Richard Johnston Inn   B&B $$
(☑ 540-899-7606; www.therichardjohnstoninn.com; 711 Caroline St; r $125-200; P ❄ 🛜) In an 18th-century brick mansion, this cozy B&B scores points for location, comfort and friendliness (especially from the two resident Scottie dogs). Guests get full breakfast on weekends.

Sammy T's   AMERICAN $
(☑ 540-371-2008; 801 Caroline St; mains $6-14; ☉ 11:30am-9:30pm; 🛜 🍴) Located in a circa 1805 building in the heart of historic Fredericksburg, Sammy T's serves soups and sandwiches and pub-y fare, with an admirable mix of vegetarian options including a local take on lasagna and black-bean quesadillas.

Foode   AMERICAN $$
(☑ 540-479-1370; 1006 C Caroline St; mains $13-24; ☉ 11am–3pm & 4:30pm–8pm Tue-Thu, to 9pm Fri, 10am-2:30pm & 4:30-9pm Sat, 10am-2pm Sun; 🍴)
🍴 Foode takes all the feel-good restaurant trends of the late naughties/early teens — fresh, local, free range, organic and a casual-artsy-rustic-chic decor over white tablecloths and dark lighting — and runs with the above all the way to pretty delicious results.

❶ Getting There & Away

VRE ($11.10, 1½ hours) and **Amtrak** ($25 to $43, 1¼ hours) trains depart from the **Fredericksburg train station** (200 Lafayette Blvd) with service to DC. **Greyhound** has buses to/from DC (five per day, 1½ hours) and Richmond (three per day, one hour). The **Greyhound station** (☑ 540-373-2103; 1400 Jefferson Davis Hwy) is roughly 1.5 miles west of the historic district.

Richmond

Richmond has been the capital of the Commonwealth of Virginia since 1780. That's the stable part of its identity. What this town is constantly trying to define is its culture: a welcoming, warm Southern city on the one hand, and part of the international milieu of the Northeast Corridor on the other. Maybe it's better to throw away that dichotomy and say Richmond is the northernmost city of the New South: grounded in tradition yet international and well-educated on the one hand, but full of income disparities and social tensions on the other.

This is a handsome town, full of red-brick and brownstone row-houses that leave a softer impression than their sometimes-staid Northeastern counterparts. History is ubiquitous and, sometimes, uncomfortable; this was where patriot Patrick Henry gave his famous 'Give me Liberty, or give me Death!' speech, and where the slave-holding Southern Confederate States placed their capital. Today a population of students and young professionals makes the 'River City' a lot more fun than you might expect.

○ Sights

The James River bisects Richmond, with most attractions lying to its north. Uptown residential neighborhoods include the **Fan district**, south of Monument Ave, and **Carytown**, in the west end. Downtown, Court End holds the capitol and several museums.

On E Cary St between 12th and 15th Sts, converted warehouses in Shockoe Slip are home to shops and restaurants. Once you pass under the trestle-like freeway overpass, you're in Shockoe Bottom. Just north of Court End is the historic African American neighborhood of Jackson Ward. Keep in mind that Cary St is more than 5 miles long; E Cary St is downtown, while W Cary St is in Carytown.

Monument Avenue, a tree-lined boulevard in northeast Richmond, holds **statues** of such revered Southern heroes as JEB Stuart, Robert E Lee, Matthew Fontaine Maury, Jefferson Davis, Stonewall Jackson and, in a nod to diversity, African American tennis champion Arthur Ashe.

Jackson Ward, an African American neighborhood that was known as Little Africa in the late 19th century, is now a National Historic Landmark district. It comes off as a tough neighborhood (which it is), but there's a deep cultural legacy here as well.

The 1.25-mile waterfront **Canal Walk** between the James River and the Kanawha (ka-naw) and Haxall Canals is a lovely way of seeing a dozen highlights of Richmond history.

American Civil War Center at Historic Tredegar
MUSEUM
(www.tredegar.org; 500 Tredegar St; adult/child $8/2; ⊘9am-5pm) Located in an 1861 gun foundry, this fascinating site explores the causes and course of the Civil War from the perspectives of Union, Confederate and African American experiences. The center is one of 13 protected area sites that make up **Richmond National Battlefield Park** (www.nps.gov/rich).

Museum & White House of the Confederacy
HISTORIC SITE
(www.moc.org; cnr 12th & Clay Sts; adult/child $12/7; ⊘10am-5pm Mon-Sat, from noon Sun) While this was once a shrine to the Southern 'Lost Cause,' the Museum of the Confederacy has graduated into an educational institution, and its collection of Confederate artifacts is probably the best in the country. The optional tour of the Confederate White House is recommended for its quirky insights (did you know the second-most powerful man in the Confederacy may have been a gay Jew?).

Virginia State Capitol
BUILDING
(www.virginiacapitol.gov; cnr 9th & Grace Sts, Capitol Sq; ⊘9am-5pm Mon-Sat, 1-4pm Sun) FREE Designed by Thomas Jefferson, the capitol building was completed in 1788 and houses the oldest legislative body in the Western Hemisphere, the Virginia General Assembly, established in 1619. Free tours.

Virginia Historical Society
MUSEUM
(www.vahistorical.org; 428 N Blvd; adult/student $6/4; ⊘10am-5pm Mon-Sat, from 1pm Sun) Changing and permanent exhibits trace the history of the Commonwealth from prehistoric to present times.

St John's Episcopal Church
CHURCH
(www.historicstjohnschurch.org; 2401 E Broad St; tours adult/child $7/5; ⊘10am-4pm Mon-Sat, from 1pm Sun) It was here that firebrand Patrick Henry uttered his famous battle cry, 'Give me Liberty, or give me Death!' during the rebellious 1775 Second Virginia Convention. His speech is reenacted at 2pm on Sundays in summer.

Virginia Museum of Fine Arts
MUSEUM
(VMFA; ✆804-340-1400; www.vmfa.state.va.us; 2800 Grove Ave; ⊘10am-5pm Sat-Wed, to 9pm Thu & Fri) FREE Has a remarkable collection of European works, sacred Himalayan art and one of the largest Fabergé egg collections on display outside Russia. Also hosts excellent temporary exhibitions (admission from free of charge to $20).

Poe Museum
MUSEUM
(✆804-648-5523; www.poemuseum.org; 1914-16 E Main St; adult/student $6/5; ⊘10am-5pm Tue-Sat, from 11am Sun) Contains the world's largest collection of manuscripts and memorabilia of poet Edgar Allan Poe, who lived and worked in Richmond.

Hollywood Cemetery
CEMETERY
(hollywoodcemetery.org; entrance cnr Albemarle & Cherry Sts; ⊘8am-5pm, to 6pm summer) FREE This tranquil cemetery, perched above the James River rapids, contains the gravesites of two US presidents (James Monroe and John Tyler), the only Confederate president (Jefferson Davis) and 18,000 Confederate soldiers. Free walking tours are given at 10am, Monday through Saturday.

🛏 Sleeping

Massad House Hotel MOTEL $

(📞804-648-2893; www.massadhousehotel.com; 11 N 4th St; r $75-110) This is the cheapest in-city option and its location for exploring can't be beat. That said, you get what you pay for. The rooms are tiny but clean, but the hotel is in serious need of renovation.

Linden Row Inn BOUTIQUE HOTEL $$

(📞804-783-7000; www.lindenrowinn.com; 100 E Franklin St; r incl breakfast $120-170, ste $250; P 🅿️ @ 🛜) This antebellum gem has 70 attractive rooms (with period Victorian furnishings) spread among neighboring Greek Revival town houses in an excellent downtown location. Friendly southern hospitality and thoughtful extras (free passes to the YMCA, free around-town shuttle service) sweeten the deal.

Museum District B&B B&B $$

(📞804-359-2332; www.museumdistrictbb.com; 2811 Grove Ave; r $100-195; P 🅿️🛜) In a fine location near the dining and drinking of Carytown, this stately 1920s brick B&B has earned many admirers for its warm welcome. Rooms are comfortably set and guests can enjoy the wide front porch, cozy parlor with fireplace, and excellent cooked breakfasts – plus wine and cheese in the evenings.

★ Jefferson Hotel LUXURY HOTEL $$$

(📞804-788-8000; www.jeffersonhotel.com; 101 W Franklin St; r from $250; P 🅿️🛜🏊) The Jefferson is Richmond's grandest hotel and one of the finest in America. The vision of tobacco tycoon and Confederate major Lewis Ginter, the beaux-arts-style hotel was completed in 1895. Today it offers luxurious rooms, topnotch service and one of Richmond's finest restaurants. According to rumor, the magnificent grand staircase in the lobby served as the model for the famed stairs in *Gone with the Wind.*

🍴 Eating

You'll find dozens of restaurants along the cobbled streets of Shockoe Slip and Shockoe Bottom. Further west in Carytown (W Cary St between S Blvd and N Thompson St), you'll find even more dining options.

17th Street Farmers Market MARKET $

(cnr 17th & E Main Sts; ⏰8:30am-4pm Sat & Sun) For cheap eats and fresh produce, check out this bustling market, which runs from early May through October. On Sundays, the market sells antiques.

Burger Bach GASTROPUB $

(📞804-359-1305; 10 S Thompson St; mains $7-12; ⏰11am-10pm Sun-Mon, to 11pm Fri & Sat; 🅿️🛜🚻) 🍴 We give Burger Bach credit for being the only restaurant in the area that classifies itself as a New Zealand–inspired burger joint. And that said, why yes, they do serve excellent lamb burgers here, although the locally sourced beef (and vegetarian) options are awesome as well. Go crazy with the 14 different sauces available for the thick-cut fries.

Ipanema Café AMERICAN $$

(📞804-213-0190; 917 W Grace St; mains $8-13; ⏰11am-11pm Mon-Fri, from 5:30pm Sat & Sun; 🛜) This underground den is much loved by the bohemian and art-student crowd. It has a tempting selection of vegan and vegetarian fare (tempeh 'bacon' sandwich, curried vegetables, changing specials), plus *moules-frites,* tuna melts and a few other nonveg options. Vegan desserts are outstanding.

★ Julep's MODERN AMERICAN $$$

(📞804-377-3968; 1719 E Franklin St; mains $18-32; ⏰5:30-10pm Mon-Sat; P🅿️) One of Richmond's finest restaurants serves decadent New Southern cuisine in a classy old-fashioned dining room that's cinematically set inside a restored 1817 building. Start with a mint julep, fried green tomatoes or jumbo lump-crab soup, followed by Julep's signature shrimp and grits with grilled andouille sausage.

Edo's Squid ITALIAN $$$

(📞804-864-5488; 411 N Harrison St; mains $12-30) This is easily the best Italian restaurant in Richmond. Edo's serves up mouthwatering, authentic cuisine such as eggplant parmesan, spicy shrimp *diavolo* pasta, daily specials and, of course, squid. This place can get very crowded and noisy.

Millie's Diner MODERN AMERICAN $$$

(📞804-643-5512; 2603 E Main St; breakfast & lunch $7-12, dinner $20-32; ⏰11am-2:30pm & 5:30-10:30pm Tue-Fri, 10am-3pm & 5:30-10:30pm Sat & Sun) Breakfast, lunch or dinner, Millie's does it all, and docs it well. But where this Richmond icon really shines is Sunday brunch: the Devil's Mess – an open-faced omelet with spicy sausage, curry, veg, cheese and avocado – is quite legendary.

♥ Drinking & Entertainment

Lift CAFE
(218 W Broad St; ⊙7am-7pm Mon-Fri, 8am-8pm Sat, 9am-7pm Sun; 🛜) Part coffeehouse, part art gallery, Lift serves stiff lattes and tasty sandwiches and salads. Sidewalk seating.

Capital Ale House BAR
(623 E Main St; ⊙11am-1:30am) Popular with political wonks from the nearby state capitol, this downtown pub has a superb beer selection (more than 50 on tap and 250 bottled) and decent pub grub. The frozen trough on the bar keeps your drinks ice-cold.

Cary Street Cafe LIVE MUSIC
(📷804-353-7445; www.carystreetcafe.com; 2631 W Cary St; ⊙11am-2pm) Live music (or at least, karaoke) emanates from this excellent bar just about every night of the week. This spot is proudly pro-hippie, but doesn't just bust hippie tunes; the gigs juke from reggae to folk to alt-country.

Byrd Theater CINEMA
(📷804-353-9911; www.byrdtheatre.com; 2908 W Cary St; tickets $5) You can't beat the price at this classic 1928 cinema, which shows second-run films. Wurlitzer-organ concerts precede the Saturday-night shows.

ⓘ Information

Johnston-Willis Hospital (📷804-330-2000; 1401 Johnston-Willis Dr)
Post office (700 E Main St; ⊙7:30am-5pm Mon-Fri)
Richmond-Times Dispatch (www2.timesdispatch.com) Daily newspaper.
Richmond Visitor Center (📷804-783-7450; www.visitrichmondva.com; 405 N 3rd St; ⊙9am-5pm)

ⓘ Getting There & Around

The cab fare from **Richmond International Airport** (RIC; 📷804-226-3000), 10 miles east of town, costs about $30.

Amtrak (📷800-872-7245; www.amtrak.com) trains stop at the **main station** (7519 Staples Mill Rd), 7 miles north of town (connected to downtown by bus 27). More convenient but less frequent trains stop downtown at the **Main St Station** (1500 E Main St).
Greater Richmond Transit Company (GRTC; 📷804-358-4782; www.ridegrtc.com) Runs local buses (base fare $1.50; exact change only).
Greyhound/Trailways Bus Station (📷804-254-5910; www.greyhound.com; 2910 N Blvd)

Petersburg

About 25 miles south of Richmond, the little town of Petersburg played a big role in the Civil War; as a major railway junction, it provided Confederate troops and supplies. Union troops laid a 10-month siege of Petersburg in 1864–65, the longest on American soil. The **Siege Museum** (📷804-733-2404; 15 W Bank St; adult/child $5/4, incl Old Blandford Church $11/9; ⊙10am-5pm) relates the plight of civilians during the siege. Several miles east of town, the **Petersburg National Battlefield** (US 36; per vehicle/pedestrian $5/3; ⊙9am-5pm) is where Union soldiers planted explosives underneath a Confederate breastwork, leading to the Battle of the Crater (novelized and cinematized in *Cold Mountain*). West of downtown in Pamplin Historical Park, the excellent **National Museum of the Civil War Soldier** (📷804-861-2408; adult/child 6-12yr $10/5; ⊙9am-5pm) illustrates the hardships faced by soldiers on both sides of the conflict.

Historic Triangle

This is America's birthplace. Nowhere else in the country has such a small area played such a pivotal role in the course of the nation's history. The nation's roots were planted in Jamestown, the first permanent English settlement in the New World. The flames of the American Revolution were fanned at the colonial capital of Williamsburg, and America finally won its independence from Britain at Yorktown.

You'll need at least two days to do the Triangle any justice. A daily free shuttle travels between the Williamsburg visitor center, Yorktown and Jamestown.

Williamsburg

If you visit only one historical town in Virginia, make it Williamsburg, home to Colonial Williamsburg, one of the largest, most comprehensive living-history museums in the world. If any place is going to get kids into history, this is it, but it's plenty of fun for adults too.

The actual town of Williamsburg, Virginia's capital from 1699 to 1780, is a stately place. The prestigious campus of the College of William & Mary adds a decent dash of youth culture, with coffee shops, cheap pubs and fashion boutiques.

◎ Sights

Colonial Williamsburg HISTORIC SITE
(www.colonialwilliamsburg.org; adult/child $42/21;
⊙9am-5pm) The restored capital of England's largest colony in the New World is a
must-see attraction for visitors of all ages.
This is not some cheesy, fenced-in theme
park; Colonial Williamsburg is a living,
breathing, working history museum that
transports visitors to the 1700s.

➡ The Site

The 301-acre historic area contains 88
original 18th-century buildings and several
hundred faithful reproductions. Costumed
townsfolk and 'interpreters' in period dress
go about their Colonial jobs as blacksmiths,
apothecaries, printers, bartenders, soldiers
and patriots, breaking character only long
enough to pose for a snapshot.

Costumed patriots such as Patrick Henry
and Thomas Jefferson still deliver impas-
sioned speeches for freedom but, to its
credit, Colonial Williamsburg has grown up
a little. Where once it was all about project-
ing a rah-rah version of American-heck-yeah
in a powdered wig, today re-enactors debate
and question slavery, women's suffrage, the
rights of indigenous Americans and the very
moral right of revolution.

➡ Entrance

Walking around the historic district and pa-
tronizing the shops and taverns is free, but
entry to building tours and most exhibits is
restricted to ticket holders. Expect crowds,
lines and petulant children, especially in
summer.

To park and to purchase tickets, follow
the signs to the **visitor center** (☑757-220-
7645; 101 Visitor Center Drive; ⊙8:45am-5pm),
north of the historic district between
Hwy 132 and Colonial Pkwy, where kids
can hire out period costumes for $25 per
day. Start off with a 30-minute film about
Williamsburg, and peruse a copy of *Williamsburg This Week,* listing the day's programs and events.

Parking is free; shuttle buses run frequently to and from the historic district, or
you can walk along the tree-lined footpath.
You can also buy tickets at the **Merchants
Square information booth** (west end of Duke
of Gloucester St; ⊙9am-5pm).

College of William & Mary HISTORIC BUILDING
(www.wm.edu; 200 Stadium Dr) Chartered in
1693, the **College of William & Mary** is the

second-oldest college in the country and
retains the oldest academic building in continued use in the USA, the Sir Christopher
Wren Building. The school's alumni include
Thomas Jefferson, James Monroe and comedian Jon Stewart.

🛏 Sleeping

The **Williamsburg Hotel & Motel Association** (☑800-446-9244; www.gowilliamsburg.
com) at the visitor center will help find and
book accommodations at no cost. If you stay
in Colonial Williamsburg, guesthouses can
provide discount admission tickets (adult/
child $30/15).

Governor's Inn HOTEL $
(☑757-253-2277; www.colonialwilliamsburgresorts.
com; 506 N Henry St; r $70-120; P🅟🛜❄) Wil-
liamsburg's official 'economy' choice is a big
box by any other name, but rooms are clean,
and guests can use the pool and facilities of
the Woodlands Hotel. It's in a great location
three blocks from the historic district.

Williamsburg White House B&B $$
(☑757-229-8580; www.awilliamsburgwhitehouse.
com; 718 Jamestown Rd; r $160-200, ste $375;
P🅟🛜) This romantic, beautifully furnished
B&B decorated with red, white and blue
bunting is located across the campus of Wil-
liam & Mary, just a few blocks' walk from
Colonial Williamsburg. It's a favorite spot
of visiting politicos and bigwigs, but the
atmosphere and amicable management ex-
udes more stateliness than stuffiness. The
two-room FDR suite can accommodate up
to four guests.

**Colonial Williamsburg
Historic Lodging** GUESTHOUSE $$$
(☑757-253-2277; www.history.org; r $150-270) For
true 18th-century immersion, guests can
stay in one of 26 original Colonial houses
inside the historic district. Accommodations
range in size and style, though the best have
period furnishings, canopy beds and wood-
burning fireplaces.

Williamsburg Inn INN $$$
(☑757-253-2277; www.colonialwilliamsburg.com;
136 E Francis St; r from $320; P✳🛜❄) Queen
Elizabeth II has stayed here twice, so you
know this place is palatial. Williamsburg's
premier property has a not-so-colonial price
tag, but the pampering is nonstop at this
prestigious resort.

✗ Eating

You will find many restaurants, cafes and pubs in Merchants Sq, adjacent to Colonial Williamsburg.

Cheese Shop   DELI $
(410 Duke of Gloucester St, Merchants Sq; mains $6-7; ⊗ 10am-8pm Mon-Sat, 11am-6pm Sun) Adjoining Fat Canary, this gourmet deli showcases some flavorful sandwiches and antipasti, plus baguettes, pastries, wine, beer and wonderful cheeses.

King's Arms Tavern   MODERN AMERICAN $$
(☑ 757-229-2141; 416 E Duke of Gloucester St; lunch mains $13-15, dinner $31-37; ⊗ 11:30am-2:30pm & 5-9pm) Of the four restaurants located within Colonial Williamsburg, this is the most elegant, serving early-American cuisine such as game pie – venison, rabbit and duck braised in port-wine sauce.

Fat Canary   AMERICAN $$$
(☑ 757-229-3333; 410 Duke of Gloucester St, Merchants Sq; mains $28-39; ⊗ 5-10pm) For a splurge, there's no better place in the historic triangle. Top-notch service, excellent wines and heavenly desserts are only slightly upstaged by the magnificent seasonal cuisine (recent favorites: pan-seared sea scallops with oyster pork belly; wild rice stuffed quail; and seared foie gras and hazelnut toast).

ℹ Getting There & Around

Williamsburg Transportation Center (☑ 757-229-8750; cnr Boundary & Lafayette Sts) **Amtrak** (www.amtrak.com) trains run from here twice a day to Washington, DC ($43, four hours), Richmond ($33, 50 minutes) and New York ($84 to $152, eight hours). Greyhound buses run to Richmond ($18, one hour) five times daily. Buses to other destinations require a transfer in Richmond.

Triangle Theme Parks

Three miles east of Williamsburg on Hwy 60, **Busch Gardens** (☑ 800-343-7946; www.buschgardens.com; adult/child $70/60; ⊗ Apr-Oct; ⊞) is a European-themed park with some of the best roller coasters on the East Coast. Just down the road, off Hwy 199 east of Williamsburg, **Water Country USA** (☑ 800-343-7946; www.watercountryusa.com; adult/child $49/42; ⊗ May-Sep; ⊞) is a kids' paradise, with twisty slides, raging rapids and wave pools. A three-day combo ticket for both parks costs $75. Parking costs $13 at both places.

Jamestown

On May 14, 1607, a group of 104 English men and boys settled on this swampy island with a charter from the Virginia Company of London to search for gold and other riches. Instead, they found starvation and disease. By January of 1608, only about 40 colonists were still alive, and these had resorted to cannibalism to survive. The colony survived the 'Starving Time' with the leadership of Captain James Smith and help from Powhatan, a local king. In 1619 the elected House of Burgesses convened, forming the first democratic government in the Americas.

Historic Jamestowne (☑ 757-856-1200; www.historicjamestowne.org; 1368 Colonial Pkwy; adult/child $14/free; ⊗ 8:30am-4:30pm), run by the NPS, is the original Jamestown site. Start your visit at the on-site museum and check out the statues of John Smith and Pocahontas. The original Jamestown ruins were rediscovered in 1994; visitors can watch the ongoing archaeological work at the site.

More child-friendly, the state-run **Jamestown Settlement** (☑ 757-253-4838; www.historyisfun.org; 2110 Jamestown Rd; adult/child $16/7.50, incl Yorktown Victory Center $20.50/10.25; ⊗ 9am-5pm; P ⊞) reconstructs the 1607 James Fort, a Native American village and full-scale replicas of the first ships that brought the settlers to Jamestown, along with multimedia exhibits and costumed interpreters portraying life in the 17th century.

Yorktown

On October 19, 1781, British General Cornwallis surrendered to George Washington here, effectively ending the American Revolution. Overpowered by massive American guns on land and cut off from the sea by the French, the British were in a hopeless position. Although Washington anticipated a much longer siege, the devastating barrage quickly overwhelmed Cornwallis, who surrendered within days.

Yorktown Battlefield (☑ 757-898-3400; 1000 Colonial Pkwy; incl Historic Jamestowne adult/child $10/free; ⊗ 9am-5pm; P ⊞) ⚑, run by the NPS, is the site of the last major battle of the American Revolution. Start your tour at the visitor center and check out the orientation film and the display of Washington's original tent. The 7-mile Battlefield Rd Tour takes you past the major highlights. Don't miss a walk through the last British defensive sites, Redoubts 9 and 10.

The state-run **Yorktown Victory Center** (☑757-887-1776; www.historyisfun.org; 200 Water St; adult/child $9.75/5.50; ☺9am-5pm; P♿) ♪ is an interactive, living-history museum that focuses on reconstruction, reenactment and the Revolution's impact on the people who lived through it. At the re-created encampment, costumed Continental soldiers fire cannons and discuss food preparation and field medicine of the day.

The actual town of Yorktown is a pleasant waterfront village overlooking the York River with a nice range of shops, restaurants and pubs. Set in an atmospheric 1720 house, the **Carrot Tree** (☑757-988-1999; 411 Main St; mains $10-16; ☺11am-3:30pm daily, 5-8:30pm Thu-Sat) is a good, affordable spot serving playfully named dishes such as Lord Nelson's BBQ and Battlefield beef stroganoff.

James River Plantations

The grand homes of Virginia's slave-holding aristocracy were a clear sign of the era's class divisions. A string of them line scenic Hwy 5 on the north side of the river, though only a few are open to the public.

Sherwood Forest (☑804-829-5377; sherwoodforest.org; 14501 John Tyler Memorial Hwy), the longest frame house in the country, was the home of 10th US president John Tyler. Tours are available by appointment for $35 per person. The grounds (and a touching pet cemetery) are open to **self-guided tours** (adult/child $10/free; ☺9am-5pm).

Berkeley (☑804-829-6018; www.berkeleyplantation.com; 12602 Harrison Landing Rd; adult/child $11/7.50; ☺9:30am-4:30pm) was the site of the first official Thanksgiving in 1619. It was the birthplace and home of Benjamin Harrison V, a signatory to of the Declaration of Independence, and his son William Henry Harrison, the ninth US president.

Shirley (☑800-232-1613; www.shirleyplantation.com; 501 Shirley Plantation Rd; adult/child $11/7.50; ☺9am-5pm), situated picturesquely on the river, is Virginia's oldest plantation (1613) and perhaps the best example of how a British-model plantation actually appeared, with its tidy row of brick service and trade houses – tool barn, ice house, laundry etc – leading up to the big house.

Hampton Roads

The Hampton Roads (named not for asphalt, but the confluence of the James, Nansemond and Elizabeth Rivers and Chesapeake Bay) have always been prime real estate. The Powhatan Confederacy fished these waters and hunted the fingerlike protrusions of the Virginia coast for thousands of years before John Smith arrived in 1607. Today Hampton Roads is known for congestion and a cultural mishmash of history, the military and the arts.

Norfolk

Home to the world's largest naval base, it's not surprising that Norfolk had a reputation as a rowdy port town filled with drunken sailors. In recent years, the city has worked hard to clean up its image through development, gentrification and focusing on its burgeoning arts scene.

⊙ Sights

Naval Station Norfolk   NAVY BASE
(☑757-444-7955; www.cnic.navy.mil/norfolksta; 9079 Hampton Blvd; adult/child $10/5) The world's largest navy base, and one of the busiest airfields in the country, this is a must-see. The 45-minute bus tours are conducted by naval personnel and must be booked in advance (hours vary). Photo ID is required for adults.

Nauticus   MUSEUM
(☑757-664-1000; www.nauticus.org; 1 Waterside Dr; adult/child $16/11.50; ☺10am-5pm Tue-Sun) This massive interactive maritime-themed museum has exhibits on undersea exploration, aquatic life of the Chesapeake Bay and US Naval lore. The museum's highlight is clambering around the decks and inner corridors of the **USS Wisconsin**. Built in 1943, it was the largest (887ft long) and last battleship built by the US Navy.

Chrysler Museum of Art   MUSEUM
(☑757-664-6200; www.chrysler.org; 245 W Olney Rd; ☺10am-9pm Wed, to 5pm Thu-Sat, noon-5pm Sun) **FREE** A glorious setting for a spectacular and eclectic collection of artifacts from ancient Egypt to the present day, including works by Monet, Matisse, Renoir, Warhol and a world-class collection of Tiffany blown glass. Set to re-open with a brand new facade and interior in April 2014.

🛏 Sleeping

For waterfront digs, there are tons of budget to midrange options lining Ocean View Ave (which actually borders the bay).

Residence Inn HOTEL **$$**
(📞757-842-6216; www.marriott.com; 227 W Brambleton Ave; r $140, ste $210; P🤶🏠) A short stroll to the Granby St eating strip, this friendly chain hotel has a boutique feel, with stylish, spacious rooms featuring small kitchenettes and excellent amenities.

Page House Inn B&B **$$$**
(📞757-625-5033; www.pagehouseinn.com; 323 Fairfax Ave; r $155-230; P✳🏠) Opposite the Chrysler Museum of Art, this luxurious B&B is a cornerstone of Norfolk elegance.

🍴 Eating

Two of the best dining strips are downtown's Granby St and Ghent's Colley Ave.

Doumar's DINER **$**
(1919 Monticello Ave, at E 20th St; mains $2-4; ⊙8am-11pm Mon-Sat) Since 1904 this slice of Americana has been the drive-up home of the world's original ice-cream-cone machine, plus great BBQ.

Luna Maya LATIN AMERICAN **$$**
(📞757-622-6986; 2010 Colley Ave, Ghent; mains $13-19; ⊙4:30-10pm Tue-Sat; 🍴) On Ghent's restaurant-lined Colley Ave, Luna Maya serves up delectable pan-Latin fare and ever-flowing *mojitos* in a stylish, rustic open dining room. It's run by two Bolivian sisters, and standouts include the *pastel de choclo con chorizo,* a Bolivian corn casserole with spicy chicken sausage.

Press 626 Cafe & Wine Bar MODERN AMERICAN **$$$**
(📞757-282-6234; 150 W Main St; mains $19-35; ⊙11am-11pm Mon-Fri, from 5pm Sat, 10:30am-2:30pm Sun; 🍴) Embracing the Slow Food movement, Press 626 has a small high-end menu (pan-seared swordfish with sun-dried tomato polenta, for example), plus delectable cheeses and sharing plates.

🍸 Drinking & Entertainment

Elliot's Fair Grounds CAFE
(806 Baldwin Ave; ⊙7am-10pm Mon-Sat, from 8am Sun; 🏠) This tiny, funky coffeehouse attracts everyone from students to sailors. The menu also includes vegan and kosher items such as Boca burgers.

Taphouse Grill at Ghent PUB
(931 W 21st St) Good microbrews are served and good local bands jam at this warm little pub.

ℹ Getting There & Around

The region is served by **Norfolk International Airport** (NIA; 📞757-857-3351), 7 miles northeast of downtown Norfolk. **Greyhound** (📞757-625-7500; www.greyhound.com; 701 Monticello Ave) runs buses to Virginia Beach ($16, 35 minutes), Richmond ($32, 2¾ hours) and Washington, DC ($50, 6½ hours).

Hampton Roads Transit (📞757-222-6100; www.hrtransit.org) serves the entire Hampton Roads region. Buses ($1.50) run from downtown throughout the city and to Newport News and Virginia Beach. **Norfolk Electronic Transit** (NET; ⊙6:30am-11pm Mon-Fri, noon-midnight Sat, to 8pm Sun) is a free bus service that connects Norfolk's major downtown sites, including Nauticus and the Chrysler Museum.

Newport News

The city of Newport News comes off as a giant example of suburban sprawl, but there are several attractions here, notably the amazing **Mariners' Museum** (📞757-596-2222; www.marinersmuseum.org; 100 Museum Dr; adult/child $12/7; ⊙9am-5pm Wed-Sat, from 11am Sun), one of the biggest, most-comprehensive maritime museums in the world. The on-site **USS Monitor Center** houses the dredged carcass of the Civil War–era *Monitor,* one of the world's first ironclad warships, as well as a life-sized replica of the real deal.

The **Virginia Living Museum** (📞757-595-1900; thevlm.org; 524 J Clyde Morris Blvd; adult/child $17/13; ⊙9am-5pm, from noon Sun; P🚻) 🍃 is a fine introduction to Virginia's terrestrial and aquatic life set in naturalistic ecosystems. The complex comprises open-air animal enclosures, an aviary, gardens and a planetarium.

Virginia Beach

With 35 miles of sandy beaches, a 3-mile concrete oceanfront boardwalk and nearby outdoor activities, it's no surprise that Virginia Beach is a prime tourist destination. The city has worked hard to shed its reputation as a rowdy 'Redneck Riviera,' and, hey, the beach is wider and cleaner and there are fewer louts. But the town's appeal is limited: uninspiring high-rise hotels dominate the horizon, and the crowded beachfront and traffic-choked streets leave much to be desired.

Surfing is permitted at the beach's southern end near Rudee Inlet and alongside the 14th St pier.

◉ Sights

Virginia Aquarium & Marine Science Center
AQUARIUM

(☎ 757-385-3474; www.virginiaaquarium.com; 717 General Booth Blvd; adult/child $22/15; ⊙ 9am-5pm) If you want to see an aquarium done right, come here. You can get up close in a tidal pool with playful seals ($175) or observe the feeding and interact with the local sea turtles ($20).

Mt Trashmore
PARK

(310 Edwin Dr; ⊙ 7:30am-dusk) FREE Off I-64 exit 17B, Virginia Beach's only verticality was the creative solution to a landfill problem. Today the 165-acre park serves as a prime picnicking and kite-flying venue, with two lakes, playgrounds, a skate park and other recreational areas.

First Landing State Park
NATURE RESERVE

(☎ 800-933-7275; 2500 Shore Dr; per vehicle $4-5) Virginia's most-visited state park is a vast 2888-acre woodland with 20 miles of hiking trails, plus opportunities for camping, cycling, fishing, kayaking and swimming.

Contemporary Arts Center of Virginia
MUSEUM

(www.virginiamoca.org; 2200 Parks Ave; adult/child $7.70/5.50; ⊙ 10am-9pm Tue, to 5pm Wed-Fri, to 4pm Sat & Sun) Has excellent rotating exhibitions housed in a fresh, ultramodern building that lovingly focuses natural light onto an outstanding collection of local and international artwork.

Back Bay National Wildlife Refuge
NATURE RESERVE

(www.fws.gov/backbay; per vehicle/pedestrian $5/2 Apr-Oct, free Nov-Mar; ⊙ sunrise-sunset) This 9250-acre wildlife and migratory bird marshland habitat is most stunning during the December migration season.

Great Dismal Swamp National Wildlife Refuge
NATURE RESERVE

(☎ 757-986-3705; www.fws.gov/refuge/great_dismal_swamp; 3100 Desert Rd, Suffolk; GPS 36.631509,-76.559715; ⊙ sunrise-sunset; 🐾) 🐾 FREE Some 30 miles southwest of Virginia Beach, this 112,000-acre refuge, which straddles the North Carolina border, is rich in flora and fauna, including black bears, bobcats and more than 200 species of bird.

🛏 Sleeping

Angie's Guest Cottage & Hostel
GUESTHOUSE $

(☎ 757-491-1830; www.angiescottage.com; 302 24th St; dm $23-31, s/d $55/70; P ❄) Located just one block from the beach, Angie's HI-USA-affiliated hostel offers dormitories, two private rooms and a communal kitchen. It's as good value as you'll find in the area and, besides that, it has a communal, hostel-y feel that encourages hanging out with other budget travelers.

First Landing State Park
CAMPGROUND $

(☎ 800-933-7275; http://dcr.virginia.gov; Cape Henry; campsites $24-30, cabins from $75; P) 🐾 You couldn't ask for a prettier campground than the one at this bayfront state park, though cabins have no water view.

Cutty Sark Motel
MOTEL $$

(☎ 757-428-2116; www.cuttysarkvb.com; 3614 Atlantic Ave; r $140-160, apt per week from $1000; P ❄) Rooms at Cutty Sark have private balconies and kitchenettes, but check that the view you're promised doesn't look out onto a parking lot. Rates drop like a rock off-season.

Hilton Virginia Beach Oceanfront
HOTEL $$$

(☎ 757-213-3000; www.hiltonvb.com; 3001 Atlantic Ave; r $180-250, ste from $290; P ☎ ❄) The premier place to stay on the beach, this 21-story hotel is superluxurious. The oceanfront rooms are spacious, comfortable and packed with amenities including huge flat-screen TVs, dreamy bedding and large balconies that open out to the beach and Neptune Park below.

🍴 Eating

There is no shortage of restaurants along the boardwalk and Atlantic Ave, most geared toward local seafood. A bevy of interchangeable clubs and bars sits between 17th and 23rd Sts around Pacific and Atlantic Aves.

Jewish Mother
DELI $

(☎ 757-428-1515; 600 Nevan Rd; mains $5-14; ⊙ 10am-9pm Mon-Thu, 8am-2am Fri & Sat, to 9pm Sun) Get your nosh on here with packed deli sandwiches, 'penicillin soup' (chicken and matzo ball) and monster-sized pie. Excellent live music staged nightly.

Mary's Restaurant
DINER $

(☑757-428-1355; 616 Virginia Beach Blvd; mains $4-9; ☺6am-3pm) A local institution for more than 40 years, Mary's is a great place to start the day with a tasty, filling, cheap breakfast. Fluffy, gooey, chocolate-chip waffles have earned many fans.

Catch 31
SEAFOOD $$$

(☑757-213-3474; 3001 Atlantic Ave; mains $18-35; ☺7am-11pm) One of the top seafood restaurants on the boardwalk has a sleek interior and a popular deck that's great for people-watching and catching a bit of an ocean breeze. Find it in the Hilton.

ℹ Information

The I-264 runs straight to the **visitor center** (☑800-822-3224; www.visitvirginiabeach.com; 2100 Parks Ave; ☺9am-5pm) and the beach.

ℹ Getting There & Around

Greyhound (☑757-422-2998; www.greyhound. com; 971 Virginia Beach Blvd) has several buses a day to Richmond (3½ hours), which also stop in Norfolk and Newport News; transfer in Richmond for services to Washington, DC, Wilmington, NYC and beyond. Buses depart from Circle D Food Mart, 1 mile west of the boardwalk. **Hampton Roads Transit** runs the Virginia Beach Wave trolley (tickets $1), which plies Atlantic Ave in summer.

The Piedmont

Central Virginia's rolling central hills and plateaus separate the coastal lowlands from the mountainous frontier. The fertile valley gives way to dozens of wineries, country villages and grand Colonial estates.

Charlottesville

Set in the shadow of the Blue Ridge Mountains, Charlottesville is regularly ranked as one of the country's best places to live. This culturally rich town of 45,000 is home to the University of Virginia (UVA), which attracts Southern aristocracy and artsy lefties in equal proportion. With the UVA grounds and pedestrian downtown area overflowing with students, couples, professors and the occasional celebrity under a blanket of blue skies, 'C-ville' is practically perfect.

Charlottesville Visitor Center (☑877-386-1103; www.visitcharlottesville.org; 610 E Main St; ☺9am-5pm) is a helpful office in the heart of downtown.

◉ Sights

Blenheim Vineyards
WINERY

(☑434-293-5366; http://blenheimvineyards.com; 31 Blenheim Farm, Charlottesville; tastings $5; ☺11am-5:30pm) Blenheim is owned by Dave Matthews, who in some ways – what with his folkie-preppie vibe and eternal gap-year sunniness, and the fact that he owns a vineyard – is the Platonic ideal of a UVA student. The wines are great and the setting is sheer bucolic joy.

University of Virginia
UNIVERSITY

(☑434-924-0311; www.virginia.edu; 400 Ray C Hunt Dr, Charlottesville) Thomas Jefferson founded the University of Virginia, where the classically designed buildings and grounds embody the spirit of communal living and learning that Jefferson envisioned. The centerpiece is the Jefferson-designed **Rotunda** (☑434-924-7969; 1826 University Ave; ☺tours daily 10am, 11am, 2pm, 3pm & 4pm), a scale replica of Rome's Pantheon. Free, student-led tours of the Rotunda meet inside the main entrance. UVA's **Fralin Art Museum** (☑434-924-3592; 155 Rugby Rd; ☺noon-5pm Tue-Sun) **FREE** has an eclectic and interesting collection of American, European and Asian arts.

🛏 Sleeping

There's a good selection of budget and mid-range chain motels lining Emmet St/US 29 north of town. If you're after a reservation service, try **Guesthouses** (☑434-979-7264; www.va-guesthouses.com; r from $150), which provides cottages and B&B rooms in private homes. Two-night minimum stays are common on weekends.

White Pig
B&B $$

(☑434-831-1416; www.thewhitepig.com; 5120 Irish Rd; r $180-190; P ❄) ✔ It's worth the pilgrimage to the White Pig, about 22 miles southwest of Monticello. Rooms have pleasant meadow and garden views, and there's a hot tub for guests. Located on the 170-acre Briar Creek Farm, this B&B-cum–animal sanctuary has one of the most innovative vegan menus in the state.

English Inn
HOTEL $$

(☑434-971-9900; www.englishinncharlottesville. com; 2000 Morton Dr; r incl breakfast $100-160; P ☺❄) British hospitality and furnishings and a Tudor facade accent this unique hotel. It's 1.5 miles north of UVA. Cheaper rates on weekdays.

DON'T MISS

MONTICELLO & AROUND

Monticello (🖰 434-984-9800; www.monticello.org; 931 Thomas Jefferson Pkwy; adult/child $24/16; ⊙ 9am-6pm Mar-Oct, 10am-5pm Nov-Feb) is an architectural masterpiece designed and inhabited by Thomas Jefferson, Founding Father and third US president. 'I am as happy nowhere else and in no other society, and all my wishes end, where I hope my days will end, at Monticello,' wrote Jefferson, who spent 40 years building his dream home, finally completed in 1809. Today it is the only home in America designated a UN World Heritage site. Built in Roman neoclassical style, the house was the centerpiece of a 5000-acre plantation tended by 150 slaves. Monticello today does not gloss over the complicated past of the man who declared that 'all men are created equal' in the Declaration of Independence, while owning slaves and likely fathering children with slave Sally Hemings. Jefferson and his family are buried in a small wooded plot near the home.

Visits to the house are by guided tours only; you can take self-guided tours of the plantation grounds, gardens and cemetery. A high-tech exhibition center delves deeper into Jefferson's world – including exhibits on architecture, enlightenment through education, and the complicated idea of liberty. Frequent shuttles run from the visitor center to the hilltop house, or you can take the wooded footpath.

Tours are also offered of the nearby 1784 **Michie Tavern** (🖰 434-977-1234; www.michietavern.com; 683 Thomas Jefferson Pkwy; adult/child $5/2; ⊙ 9am-4:20pm) and James Monroe's estate **Ash Lawn-Highland** (🖰 434-293-8000; www.ashlawnhighland.org; adult/child $14/8; ⊙ 9am-6pm Apr-Oct, 11am-5pm Nov-Mar), 2.5 miles east of Monticello. A combo ticket for all three sites costs $36. Visit the Michie Tavern during lunchtime, when its dining room, the **Ordinary** (buffet $17; ⊙ 11:15am-3:30pm), serves lunch buffets of Southern delights such as fried chicken with biscuits.

Monticello is about 4.5 miles northwest of downtown Charlottesville.

South Street Inn B&B $$$
(🖰 434-979-0200; www.southstreetinn.com; 200 South St; r incl breakfast $150-255; P ❋) In the heart of downtown Charlottesville, this elegant 1856 building went through previous incarnations as a girl's finishing school, boarding house and brothel. Now it houses heritage-style rooms – a total of two dozen, which gives this place more depth and diversity than your average B&B.

🗙 Eating

The Downtown Mall, a pedestrian zone lined with dozens of shops and restaurants, is great for people-watching and outdoor dining on warm days. At night the bars along University Ave attract students and 20-somethings.

Whiskey Jar SOUTHERN $
(🖰 434-202-1549; 227 West Main St; mains $9-16; 🖈) The Whiskey Jar does neo-Southern comfort food in an affected rustic setting of wooden furniture where wait staff wear plaid and drinks are served out of Mason jars. We're tempted to say it's all a little too cute, but honestly, the Jar nails it – simple, fresh food, such as mustard-braised rabbit, is delicious and exceedingly good value.

Local MODERN AMERICAN $$
(🖰 434-984-9749; 824 Hinton Ave; mains $11-25; ⊙ 5:30-10pm Sun-Thu, to 11pm Fri & Sat) The Local has earned many fans for its locavore-loving menu (try black truffle mac 'n' cheese or roast duck with blood orange gastrique) and the elegant, warmly lit interior (exposed brick adorned with colorful oil paintings). There's sidewalk and rooftop dining in warmer months, plus great cocktails.

Blue Moon Diner AMERICAN $$
(512 W Main St; mains $10-20; ⊙ 8am-10pm Mon-Fri, from 9am Sat, 9am-3pm Sun) One of Charlottesville's best breakfast and weekend brunch spots is a festive retro-style diner that serves up delicious fare using locally sourced ingredients. You'll also find Virginia beers on tap, old-school rock on the radio and the occasional live band.

Continental Divide MEXICAN $$
(🖰 434-984-0143; 811 W Main St; mains $10-15; ⊙ 5-10:15pm, to 10:45pm Fri & Sat, to 9:45pm Sun) This fun, easy-going spot has no sign (look for the neon 'Get in Here' in the window) but is well worth seeking out for its Mexican fusion fare – tacos with slow-cooked pork, tuna tostadas, nachos with bison chili – and C-ville's best margaritas. Equally popular

with students on a budget and professors looking for a bargain night out.

South Street Brewery SOUTHERN $$
(106 W South St; mains $9-18; ⊙ from 5pm Mon-Sat) In a restored 1800s brick warehouse, you'll find tasty craft brews, good Southern bistro fare (barbecue pulled pork, crawfish-and-mushroom-stuffed trout) and occasional live bands (currently Wednesday nights from 10pm). It's a short stroll from the Downtown Mall.

Zocalo FUSION $$$
(☑434-977-4944; 201 E Main St; mains $19-26; ⊙5:30pm-2am Tue-Sun) This sleek and stylish restaurant-bar serves nicely turned out Latin-inspired dishes (spicy tuna tartar, chili-dusted sea scallops and achiote-rubbed grilled pork). There's an outdoor patio for warm nights and a crackling fireplace in winter.

ⓘ Getting There & Around

Amtrak (www.amtrak.com; 810 W Main St) Two daily trains to Washington, DC ($33, three hours).

Charlottesville Albemarle Airport (CHO; ☑434-973-8342; www.gocho.com) Ten miles north of downtown; offers regional flights.

Greyhound/Trailways Terminal (☑434-295-5131; 310 W Main St) Runs three daily buses to both Richmond ($20, 1¼ hours) and Washington, DC ($26, three hours).

Trolley (⊙6:40am-11:30pm Mon-Sat, 8am-5pm Sun) A free trolley connects W Main St with UVA.

Appomattox Court House & Around

At the McLean House in the town of Appomattox Court House, General Robert E Lee surrendered the Army of Northern Virginia to General Ulysses S Grant, in effect ending the Civil War. Instead of coming straight here, follow **Lee's retreat** (☑800-673-8732; www.varetreat.com) on a winding 25-stop tour that starts in Petersburg at Southside Railroad Station (River St and Cockade Alley) and cuts through some of the most attractive countryside in Virginia. Best take a detailed road map, as the trail is not always clearly marked. You'll finish at the 1700-acre **Appomattox Court House National Historic Park** (☑434-352-8987; www.nps.gov/apco; Jun-Aug $4, Sep-May $3; ⊙8:30am-5pm).

Most of the 27 restored buildings are open to visitors.

If you need a place to stay, consider **Longacre** (☑800-758-7730; www.longacreva.com; 1670 Church St; r from $105, ste $275; P❋), which looks as if it got lost somewhere in the English countryside and decided to set up shop in Virginia. Seriously, amid the six elegantly furnished rooms there could be children lost in magical kingdoms after slipping through wardrobes.

Shenandoah Valley

Local lore says Shenandoah was named for a Native American word meaning 'Daughter of the Stars.' True or not, there's no question this is God's country, one of the most beautiful places in America. The 200-mile-long valley and its Blue Ridge Mountains are packed with picturesque small towns, wineries, preserved battlefields and caverns. This was once the western border of colonial America, settled by Scotch–Irish frontiersmen who were Highland Clearance refugees. Outdoor activities – hiking, camping, fishing, horseback riding and canoeing – abound.

Shenandoah National Park

One of the most spectacular national parks in the country, **Shenandoah** (☑540-999-3500; www.nps.gov/shen; week pass per car Mar-Nov $15) is like a new smile from nature: in spring and summer the wildflowers explode, in fall the leaves burn bright red and orange, and in winter a cold, starkly beautiful hibernation period sets in. White-tailed deer are a common sight and, if you're lucky, you might spot a black bear, bobcat or wild turkey. The park lies just 75 miles west of Washington, DC.

🏃 Activities

There are two visitor centers in the park, **Dickey Ridge** (☑540-635-3566; Skyline Dr, Mile 4.6; ⊙9am-5pm Apr-Nov) in the north and **Harry F Byrd** (Mile 51; ⊙8:30am-5pm Mar 31-Oct 27) in the south. Both have maps, backcountry permits and information on horseback riding, hang gliding, cycling (only on public roads) and other wholesome goodness. Shenandoah has more than 500 miles of hiking trails, including 101 miles of the Appalachian Trail. The trails described in this section are listed from north to south.

DON'T MISS

SCENIC ROUTE: SKYLINE DRIVE

A 105-mile-long road running down the spine of the Blue Ridge Mountains, Shenandoah National Park's **Skyline Drive** redefines the definition of 'Scenic Route.' You're constantly treated to an impressive view, but keep in mind the road is bendy, slow-going (35mph limit) and (in peak season) congested. It's best to start this drive just south of Front Royal, VA; from here you'll snake over Virginia wine and hill country. Numbered mile posts mark the way and there's lots of pull-offs. Our favorite is around Mile 51.2, where you can take a moderately difficult 3.6 mile-loop hike to Lewis Spring Falls.

Old Rag Mountain   HIKING

This is a tough, 8-mile circuit trail that culminates in a rocky scramble only suitable for the physically fit. Your reward is the summit of Old Rag Mountain and, along the way, some of the best views in Virginia.

Big Meadows   HIKING

A very popular area with four easy to medium difficulty hikes. The Lewis Falls and Rose River trails run by the park's most spectacular waterfalls, and the former accesses the Appalachian Trail.

Bearfence Mountain   HIKING

A short trail leads to a spectacular 360-degree viewpoint. The circuit hike is only 1.2 miles, but it involves a strenuous scramble over rocks.

Riprap   HIKING

Three trails of varying difficulty. Blackrock Trail is an easy 1-mile loop that yields fantastic views. You can either hike the moderate 3.4-mile Riprap Trail to Chimney Rock, or detour and make a fairly strenuous 9.8-mile circuit that connects with the Appalachian Trail.

🛏 Sleeping & Eating

Camping is at four **NPS campgrounds** (☑877-444-6777; www.recreation.gov; $15-25): **Mathews Arm** (Mile 22.1; campsites $15), **Big Meadows** (Mile 51.3; campsites $20), **Lewis Mountain** (Mile 57.5; campsites $15, no reservations) and **Loft Mountain** (Mile 79.5; campsites $15). Most are open from mid-May to Oc-

tober. Camping elsewhere requires a free backcountry permit, available from any visitor center.

For not-so-rough lodging, stay at **Skyland Resort** (☑877-247-9261; www.goshenandoah.com/Skyland-Resort.aspx; Skyline Dr, Mile 41.7; r from $140, incl breakfast $150; ☺Apr-Oct; 🅿), **Big Meadows Lodge** (☑540-999-2255; www.goshenandoah.com/Big-Meadows-Lodge.aspx; Skyline Dr, Mile 51.2; r $130-210; ☺late May-Oct; 🛜) or **Lewis Mountain Cabins** (☑877-247-9261; www.goshenandoah.com/Lewis-Mountain-Cabins.aspx; Skyline Dr, Mile 57.6; cabins $90-100, campsites $16; ☺Apr-Oct; 🐾 🅿).

Skyland and Big Meadows both have restaurants and taverns with occasional live music. Big Meadows offers the most services, including gas, laundry and camp store. It's best to bring your own food into the park if you're going camping or on extended hikes.

❶ Getting There & Around

Amtrak (www.amtrak.com) trains run to Staunton, in the Shenandoah Valley, once a day from Washington, DC ($65, four hours). You'll really need your own wheels to explore the length and breadth of the park, which can be easily accessed from several exits off I-81.

Front Royal & Around

The northernmost tip of Skyline Dr looks like a drab strip of gas stations, but there's a friendly main street and some cool caverns nearby. Stop at the **visitor center** (☑800-338-2576; 414 E Main St; ☺9am-5pm) and the **Shenandoah Valley Travel Association** (☑800-847-4878; www.visitshenandoah.org; US 211 W, I-81 exit 264; ☺9am-5pm) before heading 'up' the valley.

Front Royal's claim to fame is **Skyline Caverns** (☑800-296-4545; www.skylinecaverns.com; entrance to Skyline Dr; adult/child $16/8; ☺9am-5pm), which boast rare white-spiked anthodites – delicate mineral formations that resemble sea urchins. Kids may enjoy mini-train rides ($3) and the mirror maze ($5).

Woodward House on Manor Grade (☑800-635-7011, 540-635-7010; www.acountry-home.com; 413 S Royal Ave/US 320; r $110-155, cottage $225; 🅿🛜) has seven cheerful rooms and two separate cottages (with wood-burning fireplaces). Sip your coffee from the deck and don't let the busy street below distract from the Blue Ridge Mountain vista.

Element (☑540-636-9293; jsgourmet.com; 206 S Royal Ave; mains $12-22; ☻11am-3pm & 5-10pm Tue-Sat; ☑) ✆ is a foodie favorite for quality bistro fare. The small dinner menu features changing specials such as horseradish-crusted red snapper; for lunch, come for gourmet sandwiches, soups and salads. Upstairs, **Apartment 2G** (☑540-636-9293; 206 S Royal Ave; 5 courses $50, tapas $6-14; ☻from 6:30pm Sat & 3rd Thur) ✆ serves decadent five-course dinners on Saturday evening in a cozy space (like dining at a friend's place). Reservations essential. Check the website for other culinary happenings. **Jalisco's** (☑540-635-7348; 1303 N Royal Ave; mains $8-15; ☻11am-10pm Mon-Thu, to 11pm Fri & Sat, to 9:30pm Sun) has surprisingly good Mexican; the chili *rellenos* (stuffed peppers) go down a treat.

Some 25 miles north, in the town of Winchester, the **Museum of the Shenandoah Valley** (☑540-662-1473, 888-556-5799; www.shenandoahmuseum.org; 901 Amherst St; adult/student $10/8; ☻10am-4pm Tue-Sun) comprises an 18th-century period-filled house museum, 6-acre garden and a multimedia museum that delves into the valley's history. There's also a cafe.

If you can only fit one cavern into your itinerary, head 25 miles south from Front Royal to the world-class **Luray Caverns** (☑540-743-6551; www.luraycaverns.com; Rte 211; adult/child $21/10; ☻9am-7pm Jun-Aug, to 6pm Sep-Nov, Apr & May, to 4pm Mon-Fri Dec-Mar) and hear the 'Stalacpipe Organ,' hyped as the largest musical instrument on earth.

Staunton & Around

You may want to end your trip and look into local real estate when you get here. There are some towns in the USA that just, for lack of a better term, nail it, and Staunton is one of those towns.

◉ Sights

The pedestrian-friendly, handsome center boasts more than 200 buildings designed by noted Victorian architect TJ Collins. There's an artsy yet unpretentious bohemian vibe thanks to the presence of Mary Baldwin, a small women's liberal-arts college, and the gem of the Shenandoah mountains: **Blackfriars Playhouse** (☑540-851-1733; www.americanshakespearecenter.com; 10 S Market St; tickets $20-42). This is the world's only re-creation of Shakespeare's original indoor theater. The facility hosts the immensely talented American Shakespeare Center company, which puts on performances throughout the year. See a show here. It will do you good.

SCENIC DRIVE: VIRGINIA'S HORSE COUNTRY

About 40 miles west of Washington, DC, suburban sprawl gives way to endless green farms, vineyards, quaint villages and palatial estates and ponies. This is 'Horse Country,' where wealthy Washingtonians pursue their equestrian pastimes.

The following route is the most scenic drive to Shenandoah National Park. From DC, take Rte 50 West to **Middleburg**, a too-cute-for-words town of B&Bs, taverns, wine shops and boutiques. The **National Sporting Library** (☑540-687-6542; www.nsl.org; 102 The Plains Rd; ☻10am-4pm Wed-Sat, from noon Sun) FREE is a museum and research center devoted to horse and field sports such as foxhunting, dressage, steeplechase and polo.

Griffin Tavern (☑540-675-3227; 659 Zachary Taylor Hwy; mains $9-18; ☻11:30am-9pm Mon-Fri, to 10pm Sat, 10:30am-9pm Sun) is a quintessential British pub with English and Irish food and beer. Head southwest on Rte 522 and 211 to Flint Hill.

Six miles down Rte 211 is **Little Washington**, another cute town that's home to one of the finest B&B restaurants in America, the **Inn at Little Washington** (☑540-675-3800; www.theinnatlittlewashington.com; cnr Middle & Main Sts, Washington, VA; dinner prix fixe $148-165; ☻5:30-11pm). The Inn at Little Washington has been perfecting locally sourced, seasonally selected menus since well before that practice became a culinary trend. The result is New American cuisine inspired by the best of the Piedmont and the Chesapeake, served in an atmosphere that puts one in mind of a romantic French country inn. Book early and eat well. Further down the road at the foothills of the Blue Ridge Mountains is **Sperryville**. Its many galleries and shops are a must-stop for antique-lovers. Continue 9 miles west to reach the Thornton Gap entrance of Skyline Dr in Shenandoah National Park.

History buffs should check out the **Woodrow Wilson Presidential Library** (www.woodrowwilson.org; 18-24 N Coalter St; adult/student/child $14/7/5; ⊘ 9am-5pm Mon-Sat, from noon Sun) across town. Stop by and tour the hilltop Greek Revival house where Wilson grew up, which has been faithfully restored to its original 1856 appearance.

The excellent **Frontier Culture Museum** (⊘ 540-332-7850; overlooking I-81 exit 222; adult/student/child $10/9/6; ⊘ 9am-5pm mid-Mar–Nov, 10am-4pm Dec–mid-Mar) has authentic historic buildings from Germany, Ireland and England, plus re-created West African dwellings and a separate area of American frontier dwellings on the site's 100-plus acres. Costumed interpreters (aided by bleating livestock) do an excellent job showing what life was like for the disparate ancestors of today's Virginians.

🛏 Sleeping

Frederick House   B&B $$
(⊘ 540-885-4220; www.frederickhouse.com; 28 N New St; r incl breakfast $130-240; P ❋ 🛜) To stay right downtown, the thoroughly mauve and immensely welcoming Frederick House consists of five historical residences with 25 varied rooms and suites, all with private bathrooms and some with antique furnishings and decks.

Anne Hathaway's Cottage   B&B $$
(⊘ 540-885-8885; www.anne-hathaways-cottage.com; 950 West Beverley St; r $150-170; P ❋ 🛜) Head out of town to Anne Hathaway's Cottage, named for Shakespeare's wife, who would have thoroughly enjoyed a night in one of the three rooms in this ridiculously romantic Tudor-style, thatched-roof cottage.

🍴 Eating

West Beverley St is sprinkled with restaurants and cafes.

Pompeii Lounge   ITALIAN $
(⊘ 540-885-5553; 23 East Beverley St; snacks $4-9; ⊘ 5pm-1am Tue-Thu, to 2am Fri & Sat; 🎵) The Pompeii is a three-story Italian restaurant that doubles as the nicest spot in Staunton to grab a drink. The jewel in the crown is the top-floor deck, from where you can stare out over the Staunton skyline and enjoy live music, antipasto-style small plates and some fine locally crafted cocktails.

Mugshots   CAFE $
(⊘ 540-887-0005; 32 S New St, Staunton; pastries under $5; ⊘ 7am-5:30pm Mon-Fri, 8am-5pm Sat, 8am-4pm Sun; 🛜) This simple cafe is a prime spot to sit down, catch up on your email, sip a coffee and enjoy a bagel or a muffin.

AVA Restaurant & Wine Bar   AMERICAN $$
(⊘ 540-886-2851; 103 W Beverley St, Staunton; mains $10-30; ⊘ 4-9:30pm Wed-Thu, noon-10pm Fri & Sat, 10:30am-2:30pm Sun; 🎵) 🍴 AVA offers fine dining with Creole-style catfish and roasted duck breast, plus the best vegetarian food in town – the vegetarian Beef Wellington uses beets in place of beef.

Lexington & Around

This is the place to see Southern gentry at their stately best, as cadets from the Virginia Military Institute jog past the prestigious academics of Washington & Lee University. The **visitor center** (⊘ 540-463-3777; 106 E Washington St; ⊘ 9am-5pm) has free parking.

👁 Sights & Activities

Founded in 1749, colonnaded Washington & Lee University is one of the top small colleges in America. The **Lee Chapel & Museum** (⊘ 540-458-8768; ⊘ 9am-4pm, from 1pm Sun) inters Robert E Lee, while his horse Traveller is buried outside. One of the four Confederate banners surrounding Lee's tomb is set in an original flagpole, a branch a rebel soldier turned into a makeshift standard.

Virginia Military Institute   UNIVERSITY
(VMI; Letcher Ave; ⊘ 9am-5pm when campus & museums open) You'll either be impressed or put off by the extreme discipline of the cadets at Virginia Military Institute, the only university to have sent its entire graduating class into combat (plaques to student war dead are touching and ubiquitous). A full-dress parade takes place most Fridays at 4:30pm during the school year. The school's **George C Marshall Museum** (⊘ 540-463-7103; http://www.marshallfoundation.org/museum/; adult/student $5/2; ⊘ 9am-5pm Tue-Sat, from 1pm Sun) honors the creator of the Marshall Plan for post-WWII European reconstruction. The **VMI Cadet Museum** (⊘ 540-464-7334; ⊘ 9am-5pm) **FREE** houses the stuffed carcass of Stonewall Jackson's horse, a homemade American flag made by an alumnus prisoner of war in Vietnam, and a tribute to VMI students killed in the War on Terror. Contact

the museum for a free guided tour of the campus offered at noon.

Natural Bridge & Foamhenge LANDMARK

Yes, it's a kitschy tourist trap, and yes, vocal creationists who insist it was made by the hand of God are dominating the site, but the 215ft-high **Natural Bridge** (www.naturalbridgeva.com; bridge adult/child $21/12, bridge & caverns $29/17; ⊙ 9am-dusk), 15 miles from Lexington, is still pretty cool. It was surveyed by 16-year-old George Washington, who supposedly carved his initials into the wall, and was once owned by Thomas Jefferson. You can also take a tour of some exceptionally deep caverns here. Just up the road, check out **Foamhenge** (Hwy 11) FREE, a marvelous full-sized replica of Stonehenge made entirely of Styrofoam. There are fine views – and even an on-site wizard. It's a mile north of Natural Bridge.

🛏 Sleeping

Historic Country Inns INN $$
(☎ 877-283-9680; 11 N Main St; r $110-145, ste $170-190; P ❄) Historic Country Inns operates two inns in downtown Lexington and one outside town. All of the buildings have some historical significance to Lexington, and most of the rooms are individually decorated with period antiques.

Applewood Inn & Llama Trekking INN $$
(☎ 800-463-1902; www.applewoodbb.com; 242 Tarn Beck Lane; r $155-165; P ❄) The charming, ecominded Applewood Inn & Llama Trekking offers accommdations and a slew of outdoorsy activities (including, yes, Llama trekking) on a farm a 10-minute drive away from downtown Lexington in a positively bucolic valley.

🍴 Eating

Red Hen SOUTHERN $$
(☎ 540-464-4401; 11 E Washington St; mains $17-26; ⊙ 5:30-9pm Tue-Sat; 🖉) 🌿 Reserve well ahead for a memorable meal at Red Hen, which features a creative menu showcasing the fine local produce. Try the roasted pork loin with savory beer bread pudding and oyster mushrooms.

Bistro On Main BISTRO $$
(8 N Main St; mains $9-24; ⊙ 11:30am-2:30pm & 5-9pm Tue-Sat) This is a bright, welcoming spot with big windows onto Lexington's main street, tasty bistro fare and a bar.

☆ Entertainment

Hull's Drive-in CINEMA
(☎ 540-463-2621; http://hullsdrivein.com; 2367 N Lee Hwy/US 11; per person $6; ⊙ 7pm Thu-Sun May-Oct) For old-fashioned amusement, catch a movie at Hull's Drive-in, 5.5 miles north of Lexington.

Blue Ridge Highlands & Southwest Virginia

The southwestern tip of Virginia is the most rugged part of the state. Turn onto the Blue Ridge Pkwy or any side road and you'll immediately plunge into dark strands of dogwood and fir, fast streams and white waterfalls. You're bound to see Confederate flags in the small towns, but will find there's a proud hospitality behind the fierce veneer of independence.

Blue Ridge Parkway

Where Skyline Dr ends, the **Blue Ridge Pkwy** (www.blueridgeparkway.org) picks up. The road is just as pretty and runs from the southern Appalachian ridge in Shenandoah National Park at Mile 0 to North Carolina's Great Smoky Mountains National Park at Mile 469. Wildflowers bloom in spring, and fall colors are spectacular, but watch out for foggy days; the lack of guardrails can make for hairy driving. There are a dozen visitor centers scattered over the Pkwy, and any of them make a good kick-off point to start your trip.

◉ Sights & Activities

There are all kinds of sights running along the Pkwy.

Mabry Mill HISTORIC SITE
(Mile 176) One of the most-photographed buildings in the state, the mill nests in such a fuzzy green vale you'll think you've entered the opening chapter of a Tolkien novel.

Humpback Rocks HIKING
(Mile 5.8) Tour 19th-century farm buildings or take the steep trail to Humpback Rocks, offering spectacular 360-degree views.

Sherando Lake Recreation Area SWIMMING
(☎ 540-291-2188; off Mile 16) In George Washington National Forest, you'll find two pretty lakes (one for swimming, one for fishing), with hiking trails and campsites. To get there, take Rte 664 W.

Peaks of Otter
HIKING

(Mile 86) There are trails to the tops of these mountains: Sharp Top, Flat Top and Harkening Hill. Shuttles run to the top of Sharp Top or you can try a fairly challenging hike (3 miles return) to the summit.

🛏 Sleeping

There are nine local **campgrounds** (🕿877-444-6777; www.recreation.gov; campsites $19; ⊘May-Oct), four in Virginia. Every year the staggered opening date of facilities changes, but sites are generally accessible from April to November. Two NPS-approved indoor facilities are on the Pkwy in Virginia.

Rocky Knob Cabins
CABIN $

(🕿540-593-3503; www.rockyknobcabins.com; 266 Mabry Mill Rd; cabin without bath $75; ⊘May-Oct; 🐾 P) Rustic cabins set in a secluded stretch of forest. Bring food, as eating options are limited along the Pkwy.

Peaks of Otter
LODGE $$

(🕿540-586-1081; www.peaksofotter.com; Mile 86, 85554 Blue Ridge Pkwy; r from $130; 🐾) A pretty, split-rail-surrounded lodge on a small lake that's nestled between two of its namesake mountains. There's a restaurant, but no public phones and no cellphone reception.

Roanoke & Around

Illuminated by the giant star atop Mill Mountain, Roanoke is the largest city in the valley and is the self-proclaimed 'Capital of the Blue Ridge.'

The striking **Taubman Museum of Art** (www.taubmanmuseum.org; 110 Salem Ave SE; ⊘10am-5pm Tue-Sat, to 9pm Thu & 1st Fri of month; P) FREE, opened in 2008, is set in a sculptural steel-and-glass edifice that's reminiscent of the Guggenheim Bilbao (it's no coincidence, as architect Randall Stout was a one-time associate of Frank Gehry). Inside, you'll find a superb collection of artworks spanning 3500 years (it's particularly strong in 19th- and 20th-century American works).

About 30 miles east of Roanoke, the tiny town of Bedford suffered the most casualties per capita during WWII, and hence was chosen to host the moving **National D-Day Memorial** (🕿540-586-3329; US 460 & Hwy 122; adult/child $7/5; ⊘10am-5pm). Among its towering arch and flower garden is a cast of bronze figures re-enacting the storming of the beach, complete with bursts of water symbolizing the hail of bullets the soldiers

faced. Walking tours ($3) leave hourly between 10:30am and 3:30pm.

Rose Hill (🕿540-400-7785; www.bandbrosehill.com; 521 Washington Ave; r $100-125) is a charming and welcoming three-room B&B in Roanoke's historic district.

For eats, head to **Wildflour** (🕿540-343-4543; 1212 4th St SW; sandwiches under $10, dinner mains $15-24; ⊘11am-9pm Mon-Sat; P) 🐾, which serves wonderful homemade sandwiches and a rustic fusion-meets-New-American menu, with entrees such as maple-soy-glazed salmon and a hearty meatloaf.

Mt Rogers National Recreation Area

This seriously beautiful district is well worth a visit for outdoor enthusiasts. Hike, fish or cross-country ski among ancient hardwood trees and the state's tallest peak. The **park headquarters** (🕿800-628-7202, 276-783-5196; www.fs.usda.gov/gwj; 3714 Hwy 16, Marion) offers maps and recreation directories. The NPS operates five campgrounds in the area; contact park headquarters for details.

Abingdon

One of the most photogenic towns in Virginia, Abingdon retains fine Federal and Victorian architecture in its historic district, and hosts the bluegrass **Virginia Highlands Festival** over the first half of August. The **visitor center** (🕿800-435-3440; 335 Cummings St; ⊘9am-5pm) has exhibits on local history.

Fields-Penn 1860 House Museum (208 W Main St; adult/child $3/2; ⊘11am-4pm Wed, from 1pm Thu-Sat) has exhibits on 19th-century life in southwest Virginia. Founded during the Depression, **Barter Theatre** (🕿276-628-3991; www.bartertheatre.com; 133 W Main St; performances from $20) earned its name from audiences trading food for performances. Actors Gregory Peck and Ernest Borgnine (and uh, Wayne Knight, *Seinfeld*'s 'Newman') cut their teeth on Barter's stage.

The **Virginia Creeper Trail** (www.vacreepertrail.org), named for the railroad that once ran this route, travels 33 miles between Whitetop Station near the North Carolina border and downtown Abingdon. Several outfitters rent bicycles, organize outings and run shuttles, including **Virginia**

WORTH A TRIP

CARTER FAMILY FOLD

In a tiny hamlet of SW Virginia, formerly known as Maces Spring (today part of Hiltons), you'll find one of the hallowed birthplaces of mountain music. The **Carter Family Fold** (☑276-386-6054; www.carterfamilyfold.org; 3449 AP Carter Hwy, Hiltons; adult/child $8/1; ⊙7:30pm Sat) continues the musical legacy begun by the talented Carter family back in 1927. Every Saturday night, the 900-person arena hosts first-rate bluegrass and gospel bands; there's also a museum with family memorabilia and the original mid-1800s log cabin where AP Carter was born. With no nearby lodging, your best bet is to stay in Abingdon (30 miles east), Kingsport, TN (12 miles southwest) or Bristol (25 miles southeast).

Creeper Trail Bike Shop (☑276-676-2552; www.vacreepertrailbikeshop.com; 201 Pecan St; bike hire 2hr/day $10/20; ⊙9am-6pm Sun-Fri, from 8am Sat) near the trailhead.

Martha Washington Inn (☑276-628-3161; www.marthawashingtoninn.com; 150 W Main St; r from $173; P❈@🖵❄) , opposite the Barter, is the region's premier historic hotel, a Victorian sprawl of elegant rooms and excellent amenities (wood-paneled library, outdoor Jacuzzi, saltwater pool and tennis courts).

Step back in time at **Pop Ellis Soda Shoppe** (217 W Main St; mains $8-11; ⊙11am-4pm Mon, to 9pm Tue-Sat) with a beautifully restored interior reminiscent of 1920s-era soda fountains. Thick burgers, wraps and nachos are a fine accompaniment to hand-jerked sodas and milkshakes.

Equal parts cafe and bookstore, **Zazzy'z** (380 E Main St; mains around $5; ⊙8am-6pm Mon-Sat, 9am-3pm Sun) serves inexpensive quiches, lasagnas and paninis, plus decent coffee.

The Crooked Road

When Scotch–Irish fiddle-and-reel married African American banjo-and-percussion, American mountain or 'old-time' music was born, with such genres as country and bluegrass. The latter genre still dominates the Blue Ridge, and Virginia's Heritage Music Trail, the 250-mile-long **Crooked Road** (www.thecrookedroad.org), takes you through nine sites associated with that history, along with some eye-stretching mountain scenery. It's well worth taking a detour and joining the music-loving fans of all ages who kick up their heels (many arrive with tap shoes) at these festive jamborees. During a live show you'll witness elders connecting to deep cultural roots and a new generation of musicians keeping that heritage alive and evolving.

FLOYD

Tiny, cute-as-a-postcard Floyd is nothing more than an intersection between Hwys 8 and 221, but life explodes on Friday nights at the **Floyd Country Store** (☑540-745-4563; www.floydcountrystore.com; 206 S Locust St; ⊙11am-5pm Tue-Thu, to 11pm Fri, to 5pm Sat, noon-5pm Sun). Every Friday starting at 6:30pm, $5 gets you four bluegrass bands in four hours and the chance to watch happy crowds jam along to regional heritage. No smokin', no drinkin', but there's plenty of dancin' (of the jig-and-tap style) and good cheer. On weekends, there's lots of live music happening nearby.

Built in 2007 with ecofriendly materials and furnishings, **Hotel Floyd** (☑540-745-6080; www.hotelfloyd.com; 120 Wilson St; r $85-145; P❈🖵❄) 🅿 is one of the most 'green' hotels in Virginia, and is a model of sustainability. Each of the 14 unique rooms were decorated by local artisans. Eight miles west of Floyd, **Miracle Farm B&B** (☑540-789-2214; www.miraclefarmbnb.com; 179 Ida Rose Lane; r $125-155; P❈🖵) has lovely ecofriendly cabins amid lush scenery.

When you're all jigged out, head for **Oddfella's** (☑540-745-3463; 110 N Locust St; lunch mains $7-14, dinner $8-21; ⊙11am-2:30pm Wed-Sat, 5-9pm Thu-Sun, 10am-3pm Sun; P🖉) 🅿, which has a woodsy, organic mostly Tex-Mex menu, and satisfying locally produced microbrews from the Shooting Creek Brewery.

Above the Harvest Moon health-food store, **Natasha's Market Cafe** (☑540-745-2450; 227 N Locust St; lunch/dinner mains from $8/16; ⊙11am-3pm Tue-Sat, 5:30-9pm Thu-Sat) is a bright and cheery spot serving organic local produce.

GALAX

Galax claims to be the world capital of mountain music, although it feels like anywhere-else-ville outside of the immediate downtown area, which is on the National Register of Historic Places. The main attraction is the **Rex Theater** (☑ 276-236-0329; www.rextheatergalax.com; 113 E Grayson St), a musty, red-curtained belle of yore. Frequent bluegrass acts cross its stage, but the easiest one to catch is the free Friday-night live WBRF 98.1 show, which pulls in crowds from across the mountains.

Tom Barr of **Barr's Fiddle Shop** (☑ 276-236-2411; http://barrsfiddleshop.com/; 105 S Main St; ☺ 9am-5pm Mon-Sat) is the Stradivarius of the mountains, a master craftsman sought out by fiddle and mandolin aficionados from across the world. The **Old Fiddler's Convention** (www.oldfiddlersconvention.com) is held on the second weekend in August in Galax; it's one of the premier mountain-music festivals in the world.

Doctor's Inn (☑ 276-238-9998; thedoctorsinnvirginia.com; 406 W Stuart Dr; r $140-150; P☀☎) is a welcoming guesthouse with antique-filled chambers and excellent breakfasts.

The **Galax Smokehouse** (☑ 276-236-1000; 101 N Main St; mains $7-18; ☺ 11am-9pm Mon-Sat, to 3pm Sun) serves platters of sweetly sauced Memphis-style BBQ.

WEST VIRGINIA

Wild and wonderful West Virginia is often overlooked by American and foreign travelers. It doesn't help that the state can't seem to shake its negative stereotypes. That's too bad, because West Virginia is one of the prettiest states in the Union. With its line of unbroken green mountains, raging whitewater rivers and snowcapped ski resorts, this is an outdoors-lovers' paradise.

Created by secessionists from secession, the people here still think of themselves as hardscrabble sons of miners, and that perception isn't entirely off. But the Mountain State is also gentrifying and, occasionally, that's a good thing: the arts are flourishing in the valleys, where some towns offer a welcome break from the state's constantly evolving outdoor activities.

History

Virginia was once the biggest state in America, divided between the plantation aristocracy of the Tidewater and the mountains of what is now West Virginia. The latter were settled by tough farmers who staked out independent freeholds across the Appalachians. Always resentful of their Eastern brethren and their reliance on cheap (ie slave) labor, the mountaineers of West Virginia declared their independence from Virginia when the latter tried to break off from America during the Civil War.

Yet the scrappy, independent-at-all-costs stereotype was challenged in the late 19th and early 20th centuries, when miners here formed into cooperative unions and fought employers in some of the bloodiest battles in American labor history. That mix of chip-on-the-shoulder resentment toward authority and look-out-for-your-neighbor community values continues to characterize West Virginia today.

❶ Information

West Virginia Division of Tourism (☑ 800-225-5982; www.wvtourism.com) operates welcome centers at interstate borders and in **Harpers Ferry** (☑ 304-535-2482). Check www.adventuresinwv.com for info on the state's myriad adventure-tourism opportunities.

Many hotels and motels tack on a $1 'safe' fee, refundable upon request at checkout. So if you didn't use that room safe, get your dollar back.

Eastern Panhandle

The most accessible part of the state has always been a mountain getaway for DC types.

Harpers Ferry

History lives on in this attractive town, set with steep cobblestoned streets, framed by the Shenandoah Mountains and the confluence of the rushing Potomac and Shenandoah Rivers. The lower town functions as an open-air museum, with more than a dozen buildings that you can wander through to get a taste of 19th-century life in the small town. Exhibits narrate the town's role at the forefront of westward expansion, American industry and, most famously, the slavery debate. In 1859 old John Brown tried to spark a slave uprising here and was hanged for his efforts; the incident rubbed friction between North and South into the fires of Civil War.

Pick up a pass to visit the historic buildings at the **Harpers Ferry National Historic Park Visitor Center** (☑ 304-535-6029; www.nps.gov/hafe; 171 Shoreline Dr; per person/

vehicle $5/10; ⊙8am-5pm; ⓘ) ⊘ off Hwy 340. You can also park and take a free shuttle from here. Parking is extremely limited in Harpers Ferry proper.

⊙ Sights & Activities

There are great hikes in the area, from three-hour scrambles to the scenic overlook from the Maryland Heights Trail, past Civil War fortifications on the Loudoun Heights Trail or along the Appalachian Trail. You can also cycle or walk along the C&O Canal towpath.

Master Armorer's House　HISTORIC SITE
(☑304-535-6029; www.nps.gov/hafe; 171 Shoreline Dr, Harpers Ferry) FREE Among the free sites in the historic district, this 1858 house explains how rifle technology developed here revolutionized the firearms industry.

Storer College Building　MUSEUM
(☑304-535-6029; www.nps.gov/hafe; 171 Shoreline Dr, Harpers Ferry) FREE Long ago a teachers' college for freed slaves, it now traces the town's African American history.

John Brown Wax Museum　MUSEUM
(☑304-535-6342; www.johnbrownwaxmuseum. com; 168 High St, Harpers Ferry; adult/child $7/5; ⊙9am-4:30pm winter, 10am-5:30pm summer) For those of you who appreciate kitsch, the ultimate, if overpriced, attraction to seek out in these parts is the John Brown Wax Museum. A somewhat imbalanced albeit brave zealot, Brown led an ill-conceived slave rebellion here that helped spark the Civil War. The museum dedicated to his life and the event is laughably old-school, and worth a visit for all that; nothing says historical accuracy like scratchy vocals, jerky animatronics and a light-and-sound show that sounds as if it was recorded some time around the late Cretaceous.

Appalachian Trail Conservancy　HIKING
(☑304-535-6331; www.appalachiantrail.org; 799 Washington Trail, cnr Washington & Jackson Sts; ⊙9am-5pm Mon-Fri Apr-Oct) The 2160-mile Appalachian Trail is headquartered here at this tremendous resource for hikers.

River Riders　ADVENTURE SPORTS
(☑800-326-7238; www.riverriders.com; 408 Alstadts Hill Rd) The go-to place for rafting, canoeing, tubing, kayaking and multiday cycling trips, plus cycle rental.

WEST VIRGINIA FACTS

Nickname Mountain State

Population 1.85 million

Area 24,230 sq miles

Capital city Charleston (population 52,000)

Other cities Huntington (population 49,000), Parkersburg (population 31,500), 4 Morgantown (population 29,500), Wheeling (population 28,500)

Sales tax 6%

Birthplace of Olympic gymnast Mary Lou Retton (b 1968), writer Pearl S Buck (1892–1973), pioneer aviator Chuck Yeager (b 1923), actor Don Knotts (1924–2006)

Home of The National Radio Astronomy Observatory, much of the American coal industry

Politics Republican

Famous for Mountains, John Denver's 'Take Me Home, Country Roads,' the Hatfield–McCoy feud

State slogan 'Wild and Wonderful'

Driving distances Harpers Ferry to Fayetteville 280 miles, Fayetteville to Morgantown 148 miles

🛏 Sleeping & Eating

HI-Harpers Ferry Hostel　HOSTEL $
(☑301-834-7652; www.hiusa.org; 19123 Sandy Hook Rd, Knoxville, MD; dm $20; ⊙mid-Apr–mid-Oct; Pⓧ@⊚) Located 2 miles from downtown on the Maryland side of the Potomac River, this friendly hostel has plenty of amenities including a kitchen, laundry and lounge area with games and books.

Jackson Rose　B&B $$
(☑304-535-1528; www.thejacksonrose.com; 1167 W Washington St; r weekday/weekend $135/150; ⓧ⊚) This marvelous brick 18th-century residence with stately gardens has three attractive guestrooms, including a room where Stonewall Jackson briefly lodged during the Civil War. Antique furnishings and vintage curios are sprinkled about the house, and the cooked breakfast is excellent. It's a 600m walk downhill to the historic district. No children under 12.

WORTH A TRIP

ROADSIDE MYSTERIES

See gravity and the known limits of tackiness defied at the **Mystery Hole** (☑ 304-658-9101; www.mysteryhole.com/; 16724 Midland Trail, Ansted; adult/child $6/5; ⊘ 10:30am-6pm), one of the great attractions of roadside America. Everything inside this madhouse *tilts at an angle!* It's located 1 mile west of Hawks Nest State Park. Call ahead to check open days.

Town's Inn

INN **$$**

(☑ 877-489-2447, 304-702-1872; www.thetownsinn.com; 175 & 179 High St; r $70-140; ✴) Spread between two neighboring pre–Civil War residences, the Town's Inn has rooms ranging from small and minimalist to charming heritage-style quarters. It's set in the middle of the historic district and has an indoor-outdoor restaurant as well.

Canal House

AMERICAN **$$**

(1226 Washington St; mains $7-14; ⊘ 11am-3pm Wed-Sat, 5:30-8:30pm Thu-Sat, noon-6pm Sun; ⊕) Roughly 1 mile west (and uphill) from the historic district, Canal House is a perennial favorite for delicious sandwiches and friendly service in a flower-trimmed stone house. Outdoor seating.

Anvil

AMERICAN **$$**

(☑ 304-535-2582; 1270 Washington St; lunch mains $8-12, dinner mains $15-24; ⊘ 11am-9pm Wed-Sun) Local trout melting in honey-pecan butter and an elegant Federal dining room equals excellence at Anvil, in next-door Bolivar.

Beans in the Belfry

AMERICAN **$$**

(☑ 301-834-7178; 122 W Potomac St, Brunswick, MD; mains under $10; ⊘ 9am-9pm Mon-Sat, to 7pm Sun; 🛜⊕) Across the river in Brunswick, MD (roughly 10 miles east), you'll find this converted red-brick church, sheltering mismatched couches and kitsch-laden walls, light fare (chili, sandwiches, quiche) and a tiny stage where live folk, blues and bluegrass bands strike up most nights. Sunday jazz brunch ($18) is a hit.

❶ Getting There & Around

Amtrak (www.amtrak.com) trains run to Washington's Union Station ($14, one daily, 71 minutes). **MARC trains** (mta.maryland.gov) run three times daily Monday to Friday.

Berkeley Springs

America's first spa town (George Washington relaxed here) is an odd jumble of spiritualism, artistic expression and pampering spa centers. Farmers in pickups, sporting Confederate flags, and acupuncturists in tie-dye smocks regard each other with bemusement on the roads of Bath (still the official name).

The Berkeley Springs State Park's **Roman Baths** (☑ 304-258-2711; www.berkeleyspringssp.com/spa.html; 2 S Washington St; bath $22; ⊘ 10am-6pm) are uninspiring soaks in dimly lit individual tile-lined rooms, but it's the cheapest spa deal in town. (Fill your water bottle with some of the magic stuff at the fountain outside the door.) For a more indulgent experience, book a treatment (massage, facial, aromatherapy) across the green at the **Bath House** (☑ 800-431-4698; www.bathhouse.com; 21 Fairfax St; 1hr massage $75; ⊘ 10am-5pm).

Cacapon State Park (☑ 304-258-1022; 818 Cacapon Lodge Dr; lodge/cabins from $85/91) has simple lodge accommodations plus modern and rustic cabins (with fireplaces) in a peaceful wooded setting, 9 miles south of Berkeley Springs (off US 522). There's hiking, lake swimming and a golf course.

Tari's (☑ 304-258-1196; 33 N Washington St; lunch $8-12, dinner $19-27; ⊘ 11am-9pm; 🚗) 🍴 is a very Berkeley Springs sort of spot, with fresh local food and good vegetarian options served in a laid-back atmosphere, where all the right hints of good karma abound.

Monongahela National Forest

Almost the entire eastern half of West Virginia is marked green parkland on the map, and all that goodness falls under the auspices of this stunning national forest. Within its 1400 sq miles are wild rivers, caves and the highest peak in the state (Spruce Knob). More than 850 miles of trails include the 124-mile **Allegheny Trail**, for hiking and backpacking, and the 75-mile rails-to-trails **Greenbrier River Trail**, popular with cyclists.

Elkins, at the forest's western boundary, is a good base of operations. The **National Forest Service Headquarters** (☑ 304-636-1800; 200 Sycamore St; campsites $5-30, primitive camping free) distributes recreation directories for hiking, cycling and camping. Stock up on trail mix, energy bars and hippie auras at **Good Energy Foods** (214 3rd St; ☉ 9am-5:30pm Mon-Sat).

In the southern end of the forest, **Cranberry Mountain Nature Center** (☏304-653-4826; cnr Hwys 150 & 39/55; ☉9am-4:30pm Thu-Mon May-Oct) has scientific information on the forest and the surrounding 750-acre bog ecosystem, the largest of its kind in the state.

The surreal landscapes at **Seneca Rocks**, 35 miles southeast of Elkins, attract rock climbers up the 900ft-tall sandstone strata. **Seneca Shadows Campground** (☏877-444-6777; campsites $11-30; ☉Apr-Oct) lies 1 mile east.

Southern West Virginia

This part of the state has carved out a viable stake as adventure-sports capital of the eastern seaboard.

New River Gorge National River

The New River is actually one of the oldest in the world, and the primeval forest gorge it runs through is one of the most breathtaking in the Appalachians. The NPS protects a stretch of the New River that falls 750ft over 50 miles, with a compact set of rapids up to Class V concentrated at the northernmost end.

Canyon Rim visitor center (☏304-574-2115; www.nps.gov/neri; 162 Visitor Center Road Lansing, WV , GPS 38.07003 N, 81.07583 W; ☉9am-5pm; ♿) ✐, just north of the impressive gorge bridge, is only one of five NPS visitor centers along the river. It has information on scenic drives, river outfitters, gorge climbing, hiking and mountain biking, as well as white-water rafting to the north on the Gauley River. Rim and gorge trails offer beautiful views. There are several free basic camping areas.

Nearby **Hawks Nest State Park** offers views from its rim-top **lodge** (☏304-658-5212; www.hawksnestsp.com; r $86-128; ❋ 🛜); from June through October it operates an aerial tram (closed Wednesdays) to the river, where you can catch a cruising boat ride.

Babcock State Park (☏304-438-3004; www.babcocksp.com; cabins $77-88, campsites $20-23) has hiking, canoeing, horseback riding, camping and cabin accommodations. The park's highlight is its photogenic Glade Creek Grist Mill.

Fayetteville & Around

Pint-sized Fayetteville acts as jumping-off point for New River thrill-seekers and is an artsy mountain enclave besides. On the third Saturday in October, hundreds of base jumpers parachute from the 876ft-high New River Gorge Bridge for the **Bridge Day Festival**.

Among the many state-licensed rafting outfitters in the area, **Cantrell Ultimate Rafting** (☏304-574-2500, 304-663-2762; www.cantrellultimaterafting.com/; 49 Cantrell Dr; packages from $60) stands out for its white-water rafting trips. **Hard Rock** (☏304-574-0735; www.hardrockclimbing.com; 131 South Court St; half-/full day from $75/140) offers trips and training courses for rock climbers

The **Beckley Exhibition Coal Mine** (☏304-256-1747; www.beckleymine.org; adult/child $20/12; ☉10am-6pm Apr-Oct) in nearby Beckley is a museum for the region's coal heritage. Visitors can descend 1500ft to a former coal mine. Bring a jacket, as it's cold underground!

River Rock Retreat Hostel (☏304-574-0394; www.riverrockretreatandhostel.com; Lansing-Edmond Rd; dm $23; 🅿❋), located less than 1 mile north of the New River Gorge Bridge, has basic, clean rooms and plenty of common space. Owner Joy Marr is a wealth of local information. Two miles south of the bridge, **Rifrafters Campground** (☏304-574-1065; www.rifrafters.com; Laurel Creek Rd; campsites per person $12, cabins d/q $40/80) has primitive campsites, comfy cabins and hot-shower and bathroom facilities.

Start the day with breakfast and coffee under stained-glass windows at **Cathedral Café & Bookstore** (☏304-574-0202; 134 S Court St; mains $5-8; ☉7:30am-4pm; 🛜✐) ✐.

WASHINGTON, DC & THE CAPITAL REGION SOUTHERN WEST VIRGINIA

The South

Includes ➡

Best Places to Stay

➡ 21c Museum Hotel (p387)

➡ Nashville Downtown Hostel (p376)

➡ Lodge on Little St Simons (p411)

➡ Shack Up Inn (p421)

➡ Mansion on Forsyth Park (p407)

Best Places to Eat

➡ Proof (p388)

➡ Prince's Hot Chicken (p377)

➡ Boucherie (p445)

➡ Octopus Bar (p401)

➡ Restaurant August (p444)

Why Go?

More than any other part of the country, the South has an identity all its own – a lyrical dialect, a complicated political history and a pride in a shared culture that cuts across state lines. Nurtured by deep roots yet shaped by hardship, the South has a rich legacy in politics and culture. Icons and leaders like Martin Luther King Jr, Rosa Parks, and Bill Clinton, novelists like William Faulkner, Eudora Welty and Flannery O'Connor are all Southern-born. So is barbecue, bourbon and Coca-Cola, and the blues. Which, of course, gave birth to rock and roll, soul and American popular music as a whole. The cities of the South are some of the country's most fascinating, from antebellum beauties like New Orleans and Savannah to New South powerhouses like Atlanta and Nashville.

But it's the legendary Southern hospitality that makes travel in the region such a pleasure. People round here love to talk. Stay long enough and you'll no doubt be invited for dinner.

When to Go
New Orleans

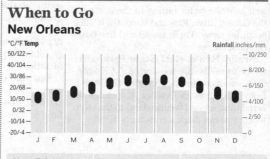

Nov–Feb Winter is generally mild here, and Christmas is a capital-E Event.

Apr–Jun Springs are lush and warm, abloom with fragrant jasmine, gardenia and tuberose.

Jul–Sep Summer is steamy, often unpleasantly so, and locals hit the beaches.

Understanding Southern Culture

Southerners have long been the butt of their fellow countrymen's jokes. They're slow-moving, hard-drinking, funny-talking and spend all their time fixing their pickup trucks and marrying their cousins. Or so the line goes. Well, while Southerners do tend to be relatively friendly and laid-back, the drawling country bumpkin is more the exception than the norm. Today's Southerner is just as likely to be a Mumbai-born motel owner in rural Arkansas, a fast-talking Atlanta investment banker with a glitzy high-rise condo, or a 20-something gay hipster in trendy Midtown Memphis.

Southerners do love sports, especially football, college basketball and Nascar, while fine arts thrive in historic cities like Charleston and Savannah, and college towns like Chapel Hill, Knoxville and Athens are famed for their indie-music scenes. Religion is hugely important here – the so-called Bible belt runs smack through the South, with about half of all Southerners identifying as Evangelical Christians.

THE SOUTH FOR MUSIC LOVERS

The history of American music is the history of Southern music: the blues, bluegrass, jazz, gospel, country and rock 'n' roll were all born here. Music hot spots include: Nashville, the birthplace of country music and home to more boot-stompin' honky-tonks than anywhere in the world; Memphis, where bluesmen still groove in the clubs of Beale St; and New Orleans, where you can hear world-class jazz, blues and zydeco every night of the week. Asheville, NC, is an emerging center of Appalachian revival music, while Kentucky claims bluegrass as its own.

Must-Eat Southern Foods

➡ **Barbecue** (region-wide, especially in North Carolina and Tennessee)

➡ **Fried chicken** (region-wide)

➡ **Cornbread** (region-wide)

➡ **Shrimp and grits** (South Carolina and Georgia coasts)

➡ **Boudin** (Cajun pork and rice sausage; Southern Louisiana)

➡ **Gumbo/jambalaya/étouffée** (rice and seafood or meat stew or a mixture; Southern Louisiana)

➡ **Po'boy** (sandwich, traditionally with fried seafood or meat; Southern Louisiana)

➡ **Hot tamales** (cornmeal stuffed with spiced beef or pork; Mississippi Delta)

➡ **Collards** (a leafy green, often cooked with ham; region-wide)

➡ **Pecan pie, coconut cake, red velvet cake, sweet-potato pie** (region-wide)

➡ **Bourbon** (Kentucky)

DID YOU KNOW?

The South is America's fastest-growing region, with 14.3% of the country's population.

Fast Facts

➡ **Nickname** Dixie

➡ **Biggest cities** Atlanta, Charlotte, Memphis

➡ **Time zones** Eastern, Central

Scenic Drives

➡ **Blue Ridge Parkway** North Carolina to Virginia (www.blueridgeparkway.org)

➡ **Natchez Trace** Tennessee to Mississippi (www.nps.gov/natr)

➡ **Hwy 12** North Carolina's Outer Banks

➡ **Kentucky Bourbon Trail** (p391) Sniff, taste and enjoy the locals' favorite liquor

➡ **Blues Highway** (p421) Take the mythic Hwy 61 from Memphis to the Crossroads

Resources

➡ **Visit South** (www.visitsouth.com) Sights and activities across the region

➡ **South Carolina** (www.discoversouthcarolina.com) This state's official tourism site; better than most

➡ **North Carolina** (www.visitnc.com) Roadtrips, Asheville and the coast

➡ **Tennessee** (www.tnvacation.com) Events, activities and sights

➡ **Louisiana** (www.louisianatravel.com) Info on the Cajun countryside

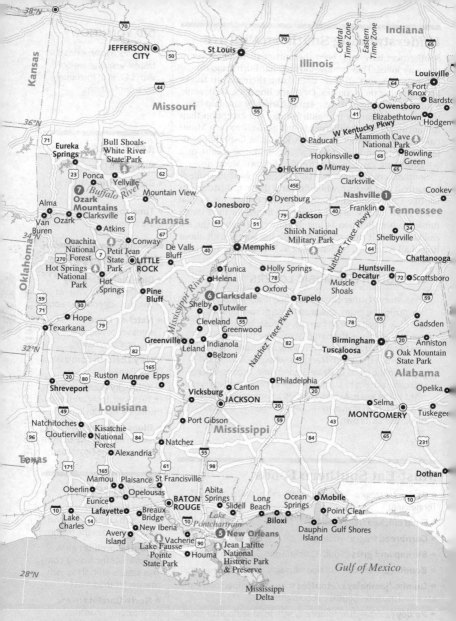

The South Highlights

❶ Stomping your boots at **Tootsie's Orchid Lounge** (p380) on Nashville's honky-tonk-lined Lower Broadway.

❷ Hiking and camping in the magnificent **Great Smoky Mountains National Park** (p349 and p384).

❸ Driving windswept Hwy 12 the length of North Carolina's **Outer Banks** (p335) and riding the ferry to Ocracoke Island.

❹ Touring the grand antebellum homes and cotton plantations of **Charleston** (p352).

❺ Putting yourself into a Cajun-Creole food-induced

coma in **New Orleans** (p432), one of America's most treasured foodie havens.

6 Immersing yourself in the soul, rhythm, history and perseverance of the **Delta Blues Museum** (p420) in Clarksdale, MS.

7 Exploring the caverns, mountains, rivers and forests of Arkansas' **Ozark Mountains** (p429), where folk music reigns.

8 Falling for the hauntings, murderous tales and Southern hospitality in Georgia's living romance novel, the architecturally pristine **Savannah** (p406).

NORTH CAROLINA

Hipsters, hog farmers and hi-tech wunder-kinds – all cross paths in fast-growing North Carolina, where the Old South and the New South stand shoulder to shoulder. From the ancient mountains in the west to the sandy barrier islands of the Atlantic you'll find a variety of cultures and communities not easy to stereotype.

Agriculture is North Carolina's leading moneymaker, with 50,400 farms, and the state is the second-largest producer of hogs and pigs in the nation. But new technologies are also an economic force, with more than with 170 global companies operating in Research Triangle Park alone. Other important industries include finance, nanotechnology, tobacco and Christmas trees.

Though the bulk of North Carolinians live in the business-oriented urban centers of the central Piedmont region, most travelers stick to the scenic routes along the coast and through the Appalachian Mountains.

So come on down, ya'll, grab a platter of barbecue and a hoppy microbrew, and watch the Duke Blue Devils battle the Carolina Tar Heels on the basketball court. College hoops rival Jesus for Carolinians' souls.

History

Native Americans have inhabited North Carolina for more than 10,000 years. Major tribes included the Cherokee, in the mountains, the Catawba in the Piedmont and the Waccamaw in the Coastal Plain.

North Carolina was the second territory to be colonized by the British, named in memory of King Charles I (Carolus in Latin), but the first colony to vote for independence from the Crown. Several important Revolutionary War battles were fought here.

The state was a sleepy agricultural backwater through the 1800s, earning it the nickname the 'Rip Van Winkle State.' Divided on slavery (most residents were too poor to own slaves), North Carolina was the last state to secede during the Civil War, but went on to provide more Confederate soldiers than any other state.

North Carolina was a civil rights hotbed in the mid-20th century, with highly publicized lunch-counter sit-ins in Greensboro and the formation of the influential Student Nonviolent Coordinating Committee (SNCC) in Raleigh. The later part of the century brought finance to Charlotte, and technology and medicine to the Raleigh-Durham area, driving a huge population boom and widening cultural diversity.

ℹ Information

North Carolina Division of Tourism (☏ 919-733-8372; www.visitnc.com; 301 N Wilmington St, Raleigh; ⊘ 8am-5pm Mon-Fri) Sends out good maps and information, including its annual *Official Travel Guide*.

North Carolina State Parks (www.ncparks. gov) Offers info on North Carolina's 38 state parks and recreation areas, some have camping (prices range from free to more than $20 a night).

THE SOUTH IN...

One Week

Fly into **New Orleans** and stretch your legs with a walking tour in the legendary **French Quarter** before devoting your remaining time to celebrating jazz history and partying the night away in a zydeco joint. Then wind your way upward through the languid Delta, stopping in **Clarksdale** for a sultry evening of blues at the juke joints before alighting in **Memphis** to walk in the footsteps of the King at **Graceland**. From here, head on down the Music Hwy to **Nashville** to see Elvis' gold Cadillac at the **Country Music Hall of Fame & Museum** and practice your line dancing at the honky-tonks (country-music clubs) of the **District**.

Two to Three Weeks

From Nashville, head east to hike amid the craggy peaks and waterfalls of **Great Smoky Mountains National Park** before a revitalizing overnight in the arty mountain town of **Asheville** and a tour of the scandalously opulent **Biltmore Estate**, America's largest private home. Plow straight through to the coast to loll on the sandy barrier islands of the isolated **Outer Banks**, then head down the coast to finish up in **Charleston**, with decadent food and postcard-pretty architecture.

North Carolina Coast

The coast of North Carolina remains remarkably under-developed. Yes, the wall of cottages stretching south from Corolla can seem endless, but for the most part the state's shores remain free of flashy, highly commercialized resort areas. Instead you'll find rugged, windswept barrier islands, Colonial villages once frequented by pirates, and laid-back beach towns full of locally owned ice-cream shops and mom 'n' pop motels. Even the most touristy beaches have a small-town vibe.

If it's solitude you seek, head to the isolated Outer Banks (OBX), where fishermen still make their living hauling in shrimp and the older locals speak in an archaic British-tinged brogue. The Hwy 158 bypass from Kitty Hawk to Nags Head gets congested in summer, but the beaches themselves still feel uncrowded. Further south, Wilmington is known as a center of film and TV production, and its surrounding beaches are popular with local spring breakers and tourists.

Outer Banks

These fragile ribbons of sand trace the coastline for 100 miles, cut off from the mainland by various sounds and waterways. From north to south, the barrier islands of Bodie (pronounced 'Body'), Roanoke, Hatteras and Ocracoke, essentially large sandbars, are linked by bridges and ferries. The far-northern communities of **Corolla** (pronounced kur-all-ah, not like the car), **Duck** and **Southern Shores** are former duck-hunting grounds for the northeastern rich, and are quiet and upscale. The nearly contiguous Bodie Island towns of **Kitty Hawk, Kill Devil Hills** and **Nags Head** are heavily developed and more populist in nature, with fried-fish joints, drive-thru beer shops, motels and dozens of sandals 'n' sunblock shops. **Roanoke Island**, west of Bodie Island, offers Colonial history and the quaint waterfront town of **Manteo**. Further south, **Hatteras Island** is a protected national seashore with a few teeny villages and a wild, windswept beauty. At the southern end of OBX, wild ponies run free and old salts shuck oysters and weave hammocks on **Ocracoke Island**, accessible only by ferry.

A meandering drive down Hwy 12, which connects much of the Outer Banks, is one of the truly great American road trips, whether

you come during the stunningly desolate winter months or the sunny summer.

◉ Sights

Corolla, the northernmost town on US 158, is famed for its wild horses. Descendants of Colonial Spanish mustangs, the horses roam the northern dunes, and numerous commercial outfitters go in search of them. The non-profit **Corolla Wild Horse Fund** (www.corollawildhorses.com; 1129 Corolla Village Rd; ⊙9:30am-5pm Mon-Fri, 10am-4pm Sat Jun-Aug, 10am-4pm Mon-Fri Sep-May) FREE runs a small museum and leads tours.

The following places are listed from north to south.

Currituck Heritage Park HISTORIC BUILDINGS
(Corolla; ⊙dawn-dusk) The sunflower-yellow, art-nouveau-style **Whalehead Club** (www.whaleheadclub.org; tours $10; ⊙tours 10am-5pm Mon-Sat mid-Mar–Dec, 11am-4pm Dec–mid-Mar),

NORTH CAROLINA FACTS

Nickname Tar Heel State

Population 9.7 million

Area 48,711 sq miles

Capital city Raleigh (population 416,000)

Other city Charlotte (population 751,000)

Sales tax 6.75%, plus an additional hotel-occupancy tax of up to 6%

Birthplace of President James K Polk (1795–1849), jazzman John Coltrane (1926–67), Nascar driver Richard Petty (b 1937), singer-songwriter Tori Amos (b 1963)

Home of America's first state university, the Biltmore House, Krispy Kreme doughnuts

Politics Conservative in rural areas, increasingly liberal in urban ones

Famous for The Andy Griffith Show, first airplane flight, college basketball

Pet name Natives are called 'tar heels,' a nickname of uncertain origin but said to be related to their pine tar production and their legendary stubbornness

Driving distances Asheville to Raleigh 247 miles, Raleigh to Wilmington 131 miles

built in the 1920s as a hunting 'cottage' for a Philadelphia industrialist, is the center-piece of this manicured park in the village of Corolla. You can also climb the **Currituck Beach Lighthouse** (www.currituckbeachlight.com; adult/child $7/free; ⊘9am-5pm Mar 23-Nov 23), or check out the modern **Outer Banks Center for Wildlife Education** (www.ncwild-life.org/obx; 1160 Village Ln; ⊘9am-4:30pm Mon-Sat) FREE for an interesting film about area history, info on local hiking trails and a life-size marsh diorama.

Wright Brothers National Memorial
PARK, MUSEUM

(www.nps.gov/wrbr; Mile 7.5, US 158 Bypass; adult/child $4/free; ⊘9am-5pm, to 6pm summer) Self-taught engineers Wilbur and Orville Wright launched the world's first successful airplane flight on December 17, 1903 (it lasted 12 seconds). A boulder now marks the take-off spot. Climb a nearby hill, where the brothers conducted earlier glider experiments, for fantastic views of sea and sound. The on-site **Wright Brothers Visitor Center** has a re-production of the 1903 flyer and exhibits.

The 30-minute 'Flight Room Talk,' a lecture about the brother's dedication and ingenuity, is excellent. For an up-close look at the plane's intricacies, check out the bronze-and-steel replica behind the hill; it's okay to scramble aboard.

Fort Raleigh National Historic Site
HISTORIC BUILDINGS

In the late 1580s, three decades before the Pilgrims landed at Plymouth Rock, a group of 116 British colonists disappeared with-out a trace from their Roanoke Island set-tlement. Were they killed off by drought? Did they run away with a Native American tribe? Did they try to sail home and capsize? The fate of the 'Lost Colony' remains one of America's greatest mysteries, and one of the site's star attractions is the beloved musical the **Lost Colony Outdoor Drama** (www.the-lostcolony.org; 1409 National Park Dr; adult/child $26.50/9.50; ⊘8pm Mon-Sat Jun-late Aug).

The play, from Pulitzer Prize–winning North Carolina playwright Paul Green, dramatizes the fate of the colonists and celebrated its 75th anniversary in 2012. It plays at the Waterside Theater throughout summer.

Other attractions include exhibits, arti-facts, maps and a free film to fuel the imagi-nation, hosted at the **visitor center** (www.nps.gov/fora; 1401 National Park Dr, Manteo; ⊘grounds dawn-dusk, visitor center 9am-5pm) FREE. The 16th-century-style **Elizabethan Gardens** (www.elizabethangardens.org; 1411 National Park Dr; adult/child $9/6; ⊘9am-7pm Jun-Aug, shorter hours Sep-May) include a Shakespearian herb garden and rows of beautifully manicured flower beds.

Cape Hatteras National Seashore
ISLANDS

(www.nps.gov/caha) Extending some 70 miles from south of Nags Head to the south end of Ocracoke Island, this fragile necklace of is-lands remains blissfully free of overdevelop-ment. Natural attractions include local and migratory water birds, marshes, woodlands, dunes and miles of empty beaches.

Bodie Island Lighthouse
LIGHTHOUSE

(☑252-441-5711, ticket reservations 255-475-9417; Bodie Island Lighthouse Rd, Bodie Island; museum free, tours adult/child $8/4; ⊘museum 9am-6pm Jun-Aug, to 5pm Sep-May, tours 9am-5:45pm late Apr-early Oct; 🛦) This photogenic light-house opened its doors to visitors in 2013. The 156ft-high structure still has its origi-nal Fresnel lens, a rarity. Entry is by guided tour. Tickets can be purchased by advance reservation by phone (☑255-475-9417), but not on the day of the tour. Tickets are also available on a first-come, first-served basis.

Pea Island National Wildlife Refuge
PRESERVE

(☑252-987-2394; www.fws.gov/peaisland; Hwy 12; ⊘visitor center 9am-4pm, trails dawn-dusk) At the northern end of Hatteras Island, this 5834-acre preserve is a birdwatcher's heaven, with two nature trails (one fully disabled-accessi-ble) and 13 miles of unspoiled beach.

Chicamacomico Lifesaving Station
MUSEUM

(www.chicamacomico.net; adult/child $6/4; ⊘10am-5pm Mon-Fri Apr-Nov) Built in 1874, this was the first lifesaving station in the state. It's now a museum filled with pre-Coast Guard artifacts.

Cape Hatteras Lighthouse
LIGHTHOUSE

(www.nps.gov/caha; climbing tours adult/child $8/4; ⊘visitor center 9am-5pm Sep-May, to 6pm Jun-Aug, lighthouse late Apr-early Oct) At 208ft, this striking black-and-white-striped edifice is the tallest brick lighthouse in the US and is one of North Carolina's most iconic im-ages. Climb the 248 steps and check out the visitor center.

WORTH A TRIP

OCRACOKE ISLAND

Crowded in summer and desolate in the winter, **Ocracoke Village** (www.ocracokevillage. com) is a funky little community that moves at a slower pace. The village is at the southern end of 14-mile-long Ocracoke Island and is accessed from Hatteras via the free Hatteras–Ocracoke ferry (p339). The ferry lands at the northeastern end of the island. With the exception of the village, the National Park Service owns the island.

The older residents still speak in the 17th-century British dialect known as 'Hoi Toide' (their pronunciation of 'high tide') and refer to non-islanders as 'dingbatters.' Edward Teach, aka Blackbeard the pirate, used to hide out in the area and was killed here in 1718. You can camp by the beach where wild ponies run, have a fish sandwich in a local pub, bike around the village's narrow streets or visit the 1823 **Ocracoke Lighthouse**, the oldest one still operating in North Carolina.

The island makes a terrific day trip from Hatteras Island, or you can stay the night. There are a handful of B&Bs, a park service campground and rental cottages.

For good eats, try the shrimp basket special on the patio of **Dajio** (dajiorestaurant.com; 305 Irvin Garrish Hwy) from 3pm to 5pm, followed by the to-die-for lemon berry marscapone. For drinks, savor a Grasshopper latte with chocolate mint and toffee at **Ocracoke Coffee** (www.ocracokecoffee.com; 226 Back Rd) or quaff a beer at **Howard's Pub** (mains $8-23; ☺11am-10pm early Mar-late Nov, may stay open later on Fri & Sat), a big old wooden pub that's been an island tradition for beer and fried seafood since the 1850s.

Want to get on the water? Take a kayaking tour with **Ride the Wind** (☎252-928-6311; www.surfocracoke.com; 2-2½ hr tours adult/child $35/15). The sunset tours are easy on the arms, and the guides are easy on the eyes.

Graveyard of the Atlantic Museum MUSEUM (☎252-986-2995; www.graveyardoftheatlantic. com; 59200 Museum Dr; donations appreciated; ☺10am-4pm Mon-Sat Apr-Oct, Mon-Fri Nov-Mar) **FREE** Exhibits about shipwrecks, piracy and salvaged cargo are highlights at this maritime museum at the end of the road. According to one exhibit, in 2006 a container washed ashore near Frisco, releasing thousands of Doritos bags.

🏃 Activities

The same strong wind that helped the Wright brothers launch their biplane today propels windsurfers, sailors and hang gliders. Other popular activities include kayaking, fishing, cycling, horse tours, stand-up paddleboarding and scuba diving. The coastal waters kick up between August and October, creating perfect conditions for bodysurfing.

Kitty Hawk Kites ADVENTURE SPORTS (☎877-359-2447, 252-441-2426; www.kittyhawk. com; 3933 S Croatan Hwy; hang gliding $99, bike rental per day $25, kayaks $39-49, stand-up paddleboards $59) Has locations all over OBX offering beginners' kiteboarding lessons (two hours $300) and hang-gliding lessons at Jockey's Ridge State Park (from $99). It also rents kayaks, sailboats, stand-up paddleboards, bikes and inline skates and offers a variety of tours and courses.

Corolla Outback Adventures DRIVING TOURS (☎252-453-4484; www.corollaoutback.com; 1150 Ocean Trail, Corolla; 2hr tour adult/child $50/25) Owner Jay Bender, whose family started Corolla's first guide service, knows his local history and his local horses. Tours bounce you down the beach and through the dunes to see the wild mustangs that roam the northern Outer Banks.

Outer Banks Dive Center DIVING (☎252-449-8349; www.obxdive.com; 3917 S Croatan Hwy; wreck dives $120) Has NAUI-certified instructors who run everything from basic classes to guided dives of the shipwrecks of the Graveyard of the Atlantic.

🛏 Sleeping

Crowds swarm the Outer Banks in summer, so reserve in advance. The area has few massive chain hotels, but hundreds of small motels, rental cottages and B&Bs; the visitor centers offer referrals. Also check www.outer-banks.com. For cottage rentals, try www.sunrealtync.com or www.southern shores.com.

THE SOUTH NORTH CAROLINA COAST

DON'T MISS

SCENIC DRIVE: BLUE RIDGE PARKWAY

Commissioned by President Franklin D Roosevelt as a Depression-era public-works project, the Blue Ridge Parkway traverses the southern Appalachians from Virginia's Shenandoah National Park at Mile 0 to the Great Smoky Mountains National Park at Mile 469.

North Carolina's piece of the parkway twists and turns for 262 miles of killer alpine vistas. The **National Park Service** (NPS; www.nps.gov/blri; ☉ May–Oct) runs campgrounds and visitor centers. Note that restrooms and gas stations are few and far between. For details about the Parkway in Virginia, see p323.

Parkway highlights and campgrounds include the following, from the Virginia border south:

Cumberland Knob (Mile 217.5) NPS visitor center, easy walk to the knob.

Doughton Park (Mile 241.1) Trails and camping.

Blowing Rock (Mile 291.8) Small town named for a craggy, commercialized cliff that offers great views, occasional updrafts and a Native American love story.

Moses H Cone Memorial Park (Mile 294.1) A lovely old estate with carriage trails and a craft shop.

Julian Price Memorial Park (Mile 296.9) Camping.

Grandfather Mountain (Mile 305.1) Hugely popular for its mile-high pedestrian 'swinging bridge.' Also has a nature center and small animal reserve.

Linville Falls (Mile 316.4) Short hiking trails to the falls, campsites.

Little Switzerland (Mile 334) Old-style mountain resort.

Mt Mitchell State Park (Mile 355.5) Highest peak east of the Mississippi (6684ft); hiking and camping.

Craggy Gardens (Mile 364) Hiking trails explode with rhododendron blossoms in summer.

Folk Art Center (Mile 382) High-end Appalachian crafts for sale.

Blue Ridge Parkway Visitor Center (Mile 384) Inspiring film, interactive map, trail information.

Mt Pisgah (Mile 408.8) Hiking, camping, restaurant, inn.

Graveyard Fields (Mile 418) Short hiking trails to waterfalls.

Campgrounds
CAMPGROUND **$**

(☎ 252-473-2111; www.nps.gov/caha; tent sites $20-23; ☉ late spring–early fall) The National Park Service runs four campgrounds on the islands which feature cold-water showers and flush toilets. They are located at Oregon Inlet (near Bodie Island Lighthouse), Cape Point and Frisco (near Cape Hatteras Lighthouse) and **Ocracoke** (☎ 800-365-2267; www.recreation.gov). Sites at Ocracoke can be reserved; the others are first-come, first-served.

Breakwater Inn
MOTEL **$$**

(☎ 252-986-2565; www.breakwaterhatteras.com; 57896 Hwy 12; r/ste inn $159/189, motel $104/134; P ❀ 🛜 🏊) The end of the road doesn't look so bad at this three-story inn. Rooms come with kitchenettes and private decks that have views of the sound. On a budget? Try one of the older 'Fisherman's Quarters' rooms, with microwave and refrigerator. The inn is near the Hatteras–Ocracoke ferry landing.

Shutters on the Banks
HOTEL **$$**

(☎ 800-848-3728; www.shuttersonthebanks.com; 405 S Virginia Dare Trail; r $149-289; P ❀ 🛜 🏊) Formerly Colony IV by the Sea, this welcoming beachfront hotel exudes a sassy, colorful style. The inviting rooms come with plantation windows and colorful bedspreads, as well as a flatscreen TV, refrigerator and microwave.

Sanderling Resort & Spa
RESORT **$$$**

(☎ 252-261-4111; www.sanderling-resort.com; 1461 Duck Rd; r/ste from $299/539; P ❀ 🛜 🏊) These posh digs have impeccably tasteful neutral-toned rooms with decks and flatscreen TVs, several restaurants and bars, and a spa offering luxe massage.

✖ Eating

The main tourist strip on Bodie Island has the most restaurants and nightlife, but many are only open Memorial Day (last Monday in May) through early fall.

John's Drive-In SEAFOOD, ICE CREAM $
(www.johnsdrivein.com; 3716 N Virginia Dare Trail; mains $2-13; ⊙11am-5pm Mon, Tue & Thu, to 6pm Fri-Sun May-Sep) A Kitty Hawk institution for perfectly fried baskets of 'dolphin' (mahi-mahi) and rockfish, to be eaten at outdoor picnic tables and washed down with one of hundreds of possible milkshake varieties. Some folks just come for the ice cream.

★ Kill Devil Grill SEAFOOD, AMERICAN $$
(⊉252-449-8181; www.thekilldevilgrill.com; Beach Rd, Mile 9¾; lunch $7-11, dinner $9-20; ⊙11:30am-10pm Tue-Sat) Yowza, this place is good. It's also a bit historic – the entrance is a 1939 diner that's listed in the National Registry of Historic Places. Pub grub and seafood arrive with tasty flair, and portions are generous. Check out the specials, where the kitchen can really shine.

Tortugas' Lie SEAFOOD $$
(www.tortugaslie.com; 3014 S Virginia Dare Trail/ Mile 11; lunch $9-18, dinner $12-24; ⊙11:30am-9:30pm Sun-Thu, to 10pm Fri & Sat) With its surfboards and license plates, the interior of this divey stand-by isn't dressed to impress, but who cares? The reliably good seafood, burritos and burgers go down well with the beer. Guy Fieri stopped by in 2012 and scrawled his signature on the wall. Fills up by 6:30pm. Kids are okay.

Mama Quan's OBX Grill & Tiki Bar CALIFORNIAN, SEAFOOD $$
(www.mamakwans.com; 1701 S Virginia Dare Trail; lunch $9-15, dinner $10-25; ⊙11:30am-2am Mon-Sat, to midnight Sat) Five words: Mama's World Famous Fish Tacos. Upon your first bite of these mahimahi-filled wonders, a baby angel earns its wings.

❶ Orientation

Hwy 12, also called Virginia Dare Trail or 'the coast road,' runs close to the Atlantic for the length of the Outer Banks. US 158, usually called 'the Bypass,' begins just north of Kitty Hawk and merges with US 64 as it crosses onto Roanoke Island. Locations are usually given in terms of 'mile posts' (Mile or MP), beginning with Mile 0 at the foot of the Wright Memorial Bridge at Kitty Hawk.

❶ Information

The best sources of information are at the main visitor centers. Many smaller centers are open seasonally. Also useful is www.outerbanks.org. The entire Manteo waterfront has free wi-fi.

Aycock Brown Visitor Center (⊉252-261-4644; www.outerbanks.org; Mile 1, US 158, Kitty Hawk; ⊙9am-5pm)

Corolla Public Library (1123 Ocean Trail/Hwy 12; 🛜) Free wi-fi and internet access.

Hatteras Island Visitor Center (⊉252-441-5711; www.nps.gov/caha; ⊙9am-6pm Jun-Aug, to 5pm Sep-May) Beside Cape Hatteras Lighthouse.

Ocracoke Island Visitor Center (⊉252-928-4531; www.nps.gov/caha; ⊙9am-5pm)

Outer Banks Welcome Center on Roanoke Island (⊉877-629-4386, 252-473-2138; www.outerbanks.org; 1 Visitors Center Cir, Manteo; ⊙9am-5pm)

❶ Getting There & Away

No public transportation exists to or on the Outer Banks. However, the **North Carolina Ferry System** (⊉800-293-3779; www.ncdot.gov/ferry) operates several routes, including the free 40-minute Hatteras–Ocracoke car ferry, which runs at least hourly from 5:15am to 11:45pm from Hatteras in high season; reservations aren't accepted. North Carolina ferries also run between Ocracoke and Cedar Island (one-way $15, 2¼ hours) and Ocracoke and Swan Quarter on the mainland ($15, 2½ hours) every two hours or so; reservations are recommended in summer for these two routes.

Crystal Coast

The southern Outer Banks are collectively called the 'Crystal Coast,' at least for tourist offices' promotional purposes. Less rugged than the northern beaches, they include several historic coastal towns, a number of sparsely populated islands, and some vacation-friendly beaches.

An industrial and commercial stretch of US 70 goes through **Morehead City**, with plenty of chain hotels and restaurants. Stop here for shrimp burgers at **El's Drive-In** (3706 Arendell St; mains $2-13; ⊙10:30am-10pm Sun-Thu, to 10:30pm Fri & Sat), a legendary seafood spot where your food is brought to you by carhop.

Down the road, postcard-pretty **Beaufort** (*bow*-fort), the third-oldest town in the state, has a charming boardwalk and lots of B&Bs. Nibble chili-lime shrimp tacos beside Taylor's Creek at stylish **Front Street Grill at Stillwater** (www.frontstreetgrillatstillwater.com; 300 Front St; brunch & lunch $11-17, dinner $19- 24; ◉ 11:30am-9pm Tue-Thu, to 10:30pm Sat & Sun), then rest your head at the homey **Beaufort Inn** (☑ 252-728-2600; www.beaufort-inn.com; 101 Ann St; r/ ste incl breakfast from $139/189). The pirate Blackbeard was a frequent visitor to the area in the early 1700s – in 1996 the wreckage of his flagship, the *Queen Anne's Revenge,* was discovered at the bottom of Beaufort Inlet. See artifacts from the ship at the **North Carolina Maritime Museum** (www.ncmaritimemuseum.org; 315 Front St; ◉ 9am-5pm Mon-Fri, 10am-5pm Sat, 1-5pm Sun) **FREE**. Blackbeard himself is said to have lived in the **Hammock House** off Front St. You can't go inside, but some claim you can still hear the screams of the pirate's murdered wife at night.

Currently, small commercial ferries leave regularly from the Beaufort boardwalk for the isolated islands of the **Cape Lookout National Seashore** (www.nps.gov/calo; ferries $10-16). Highlights include **Shackleford Banks,** an uninhabited sandbar with spectacular seashells and herds of wild ponies, and the diamond-patterned **Cape Lookout Lighthouse** (adult/child $8/4; ◉ mid-May–mid-Sep). Primitive camping is allowed in some areas – the coolest place to sleep is on **Portsmouth Island,** where you can wander an abandoned 18th-century settlement and sleep on the beach. Bring plenty of bug spray – the mosquitoes are notorious. There are also rustic multiroom **cabins** (☑ 877-444-6777; www.nps.gov/calo; www.reserve.com; from $76 Jun-Aug, from $101 fall & spring) popular with fishermen. At press time the park service was moving forward with plans to work with one ferry operator; check the park website for the latest details.

The **Bogue Banks,** across the Sound from Morehead City via the Atlantic Beach Causeway, have several well-trafficked beach communities – try Atlantic Beach if you like the smell of coconut suntan oil and doughnuts. Pine Knoll Shores is home to the **North Carolina Aquarium** (www.ncaquariums.com; 1 Roosevelt Blvd; adult/child $8/6; ◉ 9am-5pm; ♿), with fast-moving river otters and a cool exhibit re-creating the local shipwreck of a U-352 German submarine. In Atlantic Beach, **Fort Macon State Park** (www.ncparks.gov; ◉ 8am-9pm Jun-Aug, shorter hours Sep-May) **FREE** draws crowds to its reconstructed Civil War fort.

Wilmington

If you're driving down the coast, carve out a day or two for Wilmington. This seaside charmer may not have the name recognition of Charleston and Savannah, but eastern North Carolina's largest city has historic neighborhoods, azalea-choked gardens and cute cafes aplenty. All that plus reasonable hotel prices and a lack of crowds. At night the historic riverfront downtown becomes the playground for local college students, tourists and the occasional Hollywood type – there are so many movie studios here the town has earned the nickname 'Wilmywood.'

HOLLYWOOD EAST

North Carolina is one of the top states for TV and film production, and its scenery is known to millions.

Wilmington *Dawson's Creek* and *One Tree Hill* were both shot on sets at EUE/Screen Gem Studios. In 2012, stunts for *Iron Man III* were filmed over the Cape Fear River. Check www.visitnc.com for a list of *Iron Man III*–related sites or take a delightfully campy movie tour with **Hollywood Location Walk** (www.hollywoodnc.com; adult/child $13/11).

Asheville Pay homage to Katniss Everdeen with a stop by the visitor center (p349) where you can pick-up a list of *Hunger Games* film sites in the area. Henry River Mill Village, about an hour east of Asheville, doubled as District 12.

Blue Ridge Mountains and around The final 17 minutes of *The Last of the Mohicans* was filmed in Chimney Rock State Park, and Grandfather Mountain was a backdrop for *Forrest Gump*. The Cheoah Dam near the Nantahala Outdoor Center (p351) appears in *The Fugitive*.

WILMINGTON-AREA BEACHES

While riverfront Wilmington doesn't have its own beach, there are plenty of sandy stretches just a few minutes away. These are listed from north to south.

Topsail Beach A clean, white-sand beach, home to a sea-turtle rehab center.

Wrightsville Beach The closest to Wilmington, with plenty of fried-fish joints, sunglasses shops and summer crowds.

Carolina Beach Warm water and a boardwalk equal row upon row of beach umbrellas.

Kure Beach A popular fishing beach and home to the North Carolina Aquarium at Fort Fisher.

Southport Not a swimming beach, but a quaint town with antique stores and the famed **Provision Company** (www.provisioncompany.com) seafood shack.

◉ Sights

Wilmington sits at the mouth of the Cape Fear River, about 8 miles from the beach. The historic **riverfront** is perhaps the city's most important sight, abounding with boutiques and boardwalks.

A **free trolley** (www.wavetransit.com) runs through the historic district from morning through evening.

★**Cape Fear Serpentarium** SNAKE ZOO
(☎910-762-1669; www.capefearserpentarium.com; 20 Orange St; admission $8; ⊙11am-5pm Mon-Fri, to 6pm Sat & Sun) Herpetologist Dean Ripa's museum is fun and informative – if you don't mind standing in a building slithering with venomous snakes, giant constrictors and big-teethed crocodiles. They're all behind glass but...ssssssss. Just hope there's not an earthquake. One sign explains the effects of a bite from a bushmaster: 'It is better to just lie down under a tree and rest, for you will soon be dead.' Enjoy!

The Serpentarium may close on Monday and Tuesday in the off-season. Live feedings are held at 3pm on Saturdays and Sundays, but call ahead to confirm.

Battleship North Carolina HISTORIC SHIP
(www.battleshipnc.com; 1 Battleship Rd; adult/child $12/6; ⊙8am-5pm Sep-May, to 8pm Jun-Aug) Take a river taxi ($5 round-trip) or cross the Cape Fear Bridge to get here. Self-guided tours take you through the decks of this 45,000-ton megaship, which earned 15 battle stars in the Pacific theater in WWII before being decommissioned in 1947.

Airlie Gardens GARDEN
(www.airliegardens.org; 300 Airlie Rd; adult/child $8/3; ⊙9am-5pm, closed Mon winter) Wander beneath the wisteria, with 67 acres of bewitching formal flower beds, pine trees, lakes and trails. The Airlie Oak dates back to 1545.

⊨ Sleeping & Eating

There are numerous budget hotels on Market St, just north of downtown. Restaurants directly on the waterfront can be crowded and mediocre; head a block or two inland for the best eats and nightlife.

CW Worth House B&B $$
(☎910-762-8562; www.worthhouse.com; 412 S 3rd St; r $154-194; ✹@♠) Within a few blocks of downtown, this turreted 1893 home is dotted with antiques and Victorian touches, but still manages to feel kick-back and cozy. Breakfasts are top-notch.

Blockade Runner Beach Resort HOTEL $$$
(☎910-256-2251; www.blockade-runner.com; 275 Waynick Blvd, Wrightsville Beach; r from $204) It's not as glossy as most boutique hotels, with a little wear around the edges, but rooms have a spare, smart style, and the beach is just steps away. For the best sunset views, stay on the sound side.

Flaming Amy's Burrito Barn MEXICAN $
(☎910-799-2919; www.flamingamys.com; 4002 Oleander Dr; mains $5-9; ⊙11am-10pm) The burritos are big and tasty at Flaming Amy's, a scrappy barn filled with kitschy decor from Elvis to Route 66. Burritos include the Philly Phatboy, the Thai Mee Up and the jalapeno-and-pepper-loaded Flaming Amy itself. Everyone is here or on the way.

Manna NEW AMERICAN $$$
(☎910-763-5252; www.mannaavenue.com; 123 Princess St; ⊙5-10pm Tue-Thu, to 11pm Fri & Sat, to 9pm Sun) The menu changes daily at this stylish downtown dinner spot, where fresh and farm-to-table form the credo. Look for

intriguing, savory dishes like vanilla-seared tuna and sherry-brined duck breast. The carefully crafted cocktails are also a highlight.

🍷 Drinking & Nightlife

Front Street Brewery PUB
(www.frontstreetbrewery.com; 9 N Front St; mains $7-15; ⊙11am-midnight) This two-story downtown pub is madly popular for its simple grub, like drippy burgers and crab cakes, and its microbrews. There are free beer tastings and brewery tours daily from 3pm to 5pm.

ℹ️ Information

Visitor Center (📞877-406-2356, 910-341-4030; www.wilmingtonandbeaches.com; 505 Nutt St; ⊙8:30am-5pm Mon-Fri, 9am-4pm Sat, 1-4pm Sun) The visitor center, an 1800s freight warehouse, has a walking-tour map.

The Triangle

The central Piedmont region is home to the cities of Raleigh, Durham and Chapel Hill, which form a rough triangle. Three top research universities – Duke, University of North Carolina and North Carolina State – are located here, as is the 7000-acre computer and biotech-office campus known as Research Triangle Park. Swarming with egghead computer programmers, bearded peace activists and hip young families, each town has its own unique personality, despite being only a few miles apart. In March, everyone – we mean *everyone* – goes crazy for college basketball.

ℹ️ Getting There & Around

Raleigh-Durham International Airport (RDU; 📞919-840-2123; www.rdu.com), a significant hub, is a 25-minute (15 mile) drive northwest of downtown Raleigh. **Greyhound** (📞919-834-8275; 314 W Jones St) serves Raleigh and Durham. The **Triangle Transit Authority** (📞919-549-9999; www.triangletransit.org; adult $2) operates buses linking Raleigh, Durham and Chapel Hill to each other and the airport. Rte 100 runs from downtown Raleigh to the airport and the Regional Transit Center in Durham.

Raleigh

Founded in 1792 specifically to serve as the state capital, Raleigh remains a rather staid government town with major sprawl issues. Still, the handsome downtown has some neat (and free!) museums and galleries, and the food and music scene is on the upswing.

⊙ Sights

★**North Carolina Museum of Art** MUSEUM
(www.ncartmuseum.org; 2110 Blue Ridge Rd; ⊙10am-5pm Tue-Thu, Sat & Sun, 10am-9pm Fri) **FREE** The light-filled glass-and-anodized-steel West Building won praise from architecture critics nationwide when it opened in 2010. The fine and wide-ranging collection, with everything from ancient Roman sculpture to Raphael to graffiti artists, is worthy as well, as is the winding outdoor sculpture trail. A few miles west of downtown.

North Carolina Museum of Natural Sciences MUSEUM
(www.naturalsciences.org; 11 W Jones St; ⊙9am-5pm Mon-Wed, Fri & Sat, to 9pm Thu & 1st Fri of every month, noon-5pm Sun) **FREE** The museum was the state's most visited attraction in 2012, surpassing even the Biltmore. Thanks goes to the glossy **Nature Research Center**, a new wing that's fronted by a three-story multimedia globe. The research center spotlights scientists and their projects, and visitors can watch them at work. Skywalks lead to the main museum building, which holds habitat dioramas, taxidermy and the world's only dinosaur with a heart (it's fossilized).

There's also a scary exhibit about the Acrocanthosaurus dinosaur, a three-ton carnivore known as the Terror of the South. Its toothy skull is the stuff of nightmares.

North Carolina Museum of History MUSEUM
(www.ncmuseumofhistory.org; 5 E Edenton St; ⊙9am-5pm Mon-Sat, noon-5pm Sun) **FREE** This engaging museum is low on tech but high on straightforward information. Artifacts include a 3000-year-old canoe, Civil War photos, and a 1960s sit-in lunch counter. There's a special exhibit about stock-car racing.

Raleigh State Capitol HISTORIC BUILDING
(Edenton St) Check out the handsome 1840 state capitol, one of the best examples of Greek Revival architecture. It's open for visitors.

🛏️ Sleeping & Eating

Downtown is pretty quiet on nights and weekends, except for the City Market area at E Martin and S Person Sts. Just to the northwest, the Glenwood South neighborhood hops with cafes, bars and clubs. You'll find plenty of moderately priced chain hotels around exit 10 off I-440 and off I-40 near the airport.

Umstead Hotel & Spa HOTEL $$$
(☑919-447-4000; www.theumstead.com;
100 Woodland Pond Dr; r/ste from $279/369;
🅿❀🛜🏊) Computer chips embedded in
the silver room-service trays alert bellhops
to whisk away leftovers post haste at this
lavish boutique hotel. How's that for taking
care of details? In a wooded suburban office
park, the Umstead caters to visiting biotech
CEOs with simple, sumptuous rooms and a
Zen-like spa.

Raleigh Times PUB $
(14 E Hargett St; mains $10-12; ☺11:30am-2am)
Chase plates of BBQ nachos with pints of
North Carolina craft brews at this popular
downtown pub.

Poole's Downtown Diner MODERN AMERICAN $$
(www.ac-restaurants.com; 426 S McDowell St; mains
$18-22; ☺5:30pm-midnight) Chef Ashley Chris-
tensen sautés burgers in duck fat and bakes
the world's most exquisitely creamy mac 'n'
cheese at this Southern diner–meets–Parisian bistro, the toast of the local food scene.
Don't miss the haute takes on classic American pies like banana cream. No reservations.

ⓘ Information

Raleigh Visitor Information Center (☑919-
834-5900; www.visitraleigh.com; 500 Fayetteville St; ☺9am-5pm Mon Sat) Hands out maps
and other info.

Durham & Chapel Hill

Ten miles apart, these two university towns
are twinned by their rival basketball teams
and left-leaning attitudes. Chapel Hill is a
pretty Southern college town whose culture
revolves around the nearly 30,000 students
at the prestigious University of North Carolina, founded in 1789 as the nation's first
state university. A funky, forward-thinking
place, Chapel Hill is renowned for its indie
rock scene and loud 'n' proud hippie culture.
Down the road, Durham is a once-gritty
tobacco-and-railroad town whose fortunes
collapsed in the 1960s and have only recently begun to revive. Though still funda-
mentally a working-class Southern city, the
presence of top-ranking Duke University has
long drawn progressive types to the area and
Durham is now making its name as a hot
spot for gourmands, artists and gays and
lesbians.

The hip former mill town of **Carrboro** is
just west of downtown Chapel Hill. Here,

the big lawn at **Weaver Street Market**
(www.weaverstreetmarket.com) grocery co-op
serves as an informal town square, with live
music and free wi-fi.

In Durham, activity revolves around the
renovated brick tobacco warehouses of the
handsome downtown: check out Brightleaf
Sq and the American Tobacco Campus for
shopping and outdoor dining.

◎ Sights

★**Duke Lemur Center** ZOO
(☑919-489-3364; www.lemur.duke.edu; 3705 Erwin
Rd, Durham; adult/child $10/7; ♿) Perhaps the
coolest, least-known sight in Durham, the
Lemur Center has the largest collection of
endangered prosimian primates outside
their native Madagascar. Only a robot could
fail to melt at the sight of these big-eyed
fuzzy-wuzzies. Call well in advance for tours,
held Monday to Saturday by appointment
only.

Duke University UNIVERSITY, GALLERY
(www.duke.edu; Campus Dr, Durham) Endowed
by the Duke family's cigarette fortune, the
university has a Georgian-style East Campus and a neo-Gothic West Campus notable
for its towering 1930s chapel. The **Nasher
Museum of Art** (2001 Campus Dr; admission
$5; ☺10am-5pm Tue, Wed, Fri & Sat, to 9pm Thu,
noon-5pm Sun) is also worth a gander, as is
the heavenly 55-acre **Sarah P Duke Gardens** (420 Anderson St; ☺8am to dusk) FREE.
Metered parking at both sites is $2 per
hour.

University of North Carolina UNIVERSITY
(www.unc.edu; Chapel Hill) America's oldest
public university has a classic quad lined
with flowering pear trees and gracious antebellum buildings. Don't miss the Old Well,
said to give good luck to students who drink
from it. Pick up a map of the site at the **visitor center** (☑919-962-1630; 250 E Franklin St;
☺9am-5pm Mon-Fri) inside the Morehead
Planetarium and Science Center.

Durham Bulls Athletic Park SPECTATOR SPORT
(www.dbulls.com; 409 Blackwell St, Durham; tickets
$7-9; ♿) Have a quintessentially American
afternoon of beer and baseball watching the
minor-league Durham Bulls (of 1988 Kevin
Costner film *Bull Durham* fame), who play
from April to September.

🛏 Sleeping

There are plenty of cheap chain motels off I-85 in north Durham.

Duke Tower   HOTEL $

(☏ 866-385-3869, 919-687-4444; www.duketower.com; 807 W Trinity Ave, Durham; ste $88-98; P ❊ 🌐 📶) For less than most local hotel rooms you can enjoy a condo with hardwood floors, full kitchen, and a tempur-pedic mattress. Premium suites have flatscreen TVs. Located in Durham's historic downtown tobacco-mill district.

Inn at Celebrity Dairy   B&B $$

(☏ 919-742-5176; www.celebritydairy.com; 144 Celebrity Dairy Way, Siler City; r incl breakfast $100-165, ste $165; P ❊ 🌐) Thirty miles west of Chapel Hill in rural Chatham County, this working goat dairy offers B&B accommodations in a Greek Revival farmhouse. Savor goat's-cheese omelets for breakfast then head out to the barn to pet the goat who provided the milk.

Carolina Inn   HOTEL $$

(☏ 919-933-2001; www.carolinainn.com; 211 Pittsboro St, Chapel Hill; r from $179; P ❊ 🌐) Even if you're not a Tar Heel, this lovely on-campus inn will win you over with hospitality and historic touches. The charm starts in the bright lobby then continues through the hallways, lined with photos of alums and championship teams. At press time the inn had finished renovating some of the guestrooms, adding eco-friendly features.

🍴 Eating

Durham was named 'The South's Tastiest Town' by *Southern Living* in 2013, and for good reason. The area abounds with top-notch restaurants. Downtown Durham has scads of great eateries, coffee shops and bars. Most of Chapel Hill's better restaurants are found along Franklin St.

Neal's Deli   BREAKFAST, DELI $

(www.nealsdeli.com; 100 E Main St, Carrboro; breakfast $3-6, lunch $5-9; ⏰ 7:30am-7pmTue-Fri, 8am-4pm Sat & Sun) Before starting your day, chow down on a delicious buttermilk breakfast biscuit at this tiny deli in downtown Carrboro. The egg, cheese and bacon is some kind of good. For lunch, Neal's serves sandwiches and subs, from chicken salad to pastrami to a three-cheese pimiento with a splash of bourbon.

Toast   SANDWICHES $

(www.toast-fivepoints.com; 345 W Main St, Durham; sandwiches $7; ⏰ 11am-8pm Mon-Fri, to 3pm Sat) Families, couples, solos and the downtown lunch crowd – everybody loves this tiny Italian sandwich shop, one of the eateries at the forefront of downtown Durham's revitalization. Order your panini at the counter then grab a table by the window – if you can – for people watching.

Guglhupf Bakery & Cafe   BAKERY, CAFE $$

(www.guglhupf.com; 2706 Durham-Chapel Hill Blvd, Durham; lunch $8-11, dinner $15-24; ⏰ bakery 7am-5pm Tue-Sat, 8:30am-2pm Sun, cafe 8am-4:30pm Tue-Sat, 9am-3pm Sun) Mornings, a tart cherry Danish and a cappuccino are the way to go at this superior German-style bakery and cafe. In the afternoon, try a Westphalian ham sandwich and a pilsner on the sunny patio.

★ Lantern   ASIAN $$$

(☏ 919-969-8846; www.lanternrestaurant.com; 423 W Franklin St, Chapel Hill; mains $23-32; ⏰ 5:30-10pm Mon-Sat) If you only have time for one dinner in the Triangle, dine here. Tea-smoked chicken and roll-your-own bento boxes have earned this modern Asian spot a shower of James Beard Awards. For special occasions, the stylish front rooms are just right, but for a casual more convivial atmosphere try the bar and lounge in back. And the eat-the-shell salt and pepper shrimp? Excellent.

Watts Grocery   NEW SOUTHERN $$$

(☏ 919-416-5040; www.wattsgrocery.com; 1116 Broad St, Durham; lunch $8-13, dinner $18-23, brunch $7-13; ⏰ 11am-2:30pm Wed-Sun, 5:30-10pm Tue-Sun) Durham's hippest 'farm-to-table' joint serves upscale takes on local bounty in an airy renovated storefront. Sausage- and avocado-laden bowls of grits might be the best weekend brunch in town.

🍷 Drinking & Entertainment

Chapel Hill has an excellent music scene, with shows nearly every night of the week. For entertainment listings, pick up the free weekly *Independent* (www.indyweek.com).

★ Cocoa Cinnamon   COFFEE SHOP

(www.cocoacinnamon.com; 420 W Geer St, Durham; ⏰ 7:30am-10pm Mon-Thu, 7:30am-midnight Fri & Sat, 9am-9pm Sun) If someone tells you that you *must* order a hot chocolate at Cocoa Cinnamon, ask them to be more specific. This new, talk-of-the town coffee shop offers several cocoas, and newbies may be paralyzed by the plethora of chocolatey awesomeness. Come here to enjoy cocoa, teas, single-source coffee and the energetic vibe.

Fullsteam Brewery BREWPUB
(www.fullsteam.ag; 726 Rigsbee Ave, Durham; ⊙4pm-midnight Mon-Thu, to 2am Fri, noon-2am Sat, to midnight Sun) Calling itself a 'plow-to-pint' brewery, Fullsteam has gained national attention for pushing the boundaries of beer with wild, super-Southern concoctions like sweet-potato lager and persimmon ale. Mixed-age crowds.

Top of the Hill PUB
(www.thetopofthehill.com; 100 E Franklin St, Chapel Hill; ⊙11am-2am) The 3rd-story patio of this downtown restaurant and microbrewery is *the* place for the Chapel Hill preppy set to see and be seen after football games.

Cat's Cradle MUSIC
(☑919-967-9053; www.catscradle.com; 300 E Main St, Carrboro) Everyone from Nirvana to Arcade Fire has played the Cradle, hosting the cream of the indie-music world for three decades. Most shows are all-ages.

❶ Information

Chapel Hill Visitor Center (☑919-968-2060; www.visitchapelhill.org; 501 W Franklin St, Chapel Hill; ⊙8:30am-5pm Mon-Fri, 10am-2pm Sat)
Durham Visitor Center (☑800-446-8604, 919-687-0288; www.durham-nc.com; 101 E Morgan St, Durham; ⊙8:30am-5pm Mon-Fri, 10am-2pm Sat) The visitor center has information and maps.

Charlotte

The largest city in North Carolina and the biggest US banking center after New York, Charlotte has the sprawling, sometimes faceless look of many New South suburban megalopolises. But although the Queen City, as it's known, is primarily a business town, it's got a few good museums, stately old neighborhoods and lots of fine food.

Busy Tryon St cuts through skyscraper-filled 'uptown' Charlotte, home to banks, hotels, museums and restaurants. The renovated textile mills of the NoDa neighborhood (named for its location on N Davidson St) and the funky mix of boutiques and restaurants in the Plaza–Midwood area, just northeast of uptown, have a hipper vibe.

THE BARBECUE TRAIL

North Carolina pulled-pork BBQ is practically a religion in these parts, and the rivalry between Eastern Style (with a thin vinegar sauce) and Western Style (with a sweeter, tomato-based sauce) occasionally comes to blows. The North Carolina Barbecue Society has an interactive **Barbecue Trail Map** (www.ncbbqsociety.com), directing pilgrims to the best spots. So try both styles, then take sides (hint: Eastern style is better. Just kidding! Sort of.).

◉ Sights & Activities

Billy Graham Library RELIGIOUS
(www.billygrahamlibrary.org; 4330 Westmont Dr; ⊙9:30am-5pm Mon-Sat) FREE This multimedia 'library' is a tribute to the life of superstar evangelist and 'pastor to the presidents' Billy Graham, a Charlotte native. The 90-minute tour starts with a gospel-preaching animatronic cow and ends with a paper questionnaire asking whether or not you've been moved to accept Christ today.

Levine Museum of the New South MUSEUM
(www.museumofthenewsouth.org; 200 E 7th St; adult/child $8/5; ⊙10am-5pm Mon-Sat, noon-5pm Sun) This slick museum has an informative permanent exhibit on post–Civil War Southern history and culture, from sharecropping to sit-ins.

★US National Whitewater Center ADVENTURE SPORTS
(www.usnwc.org; 5000 Whitewater Center Pkwy; all-sport day pass adult/child $54/44, individual activities $20-25, 3hr canopy tour $89; ⊙dawn-dusk) A beyond-awesome hybrid of nature center and waterpark, this 400-acre facility is home to the largest artificial white-water river in the world, whose rapids serve as training grounds for Olympic canoe and kayak teams. Paddle it as part of a guided rafting trip, or try one of the center's other adventurous activities: ziplines, an outdoor rock-climbing wall, ropes courses, paddleboarding, aerial canopy tours of the surrounding forest, miles of hiking and mountain-biking trails. Parking is $5.

Charlotte Motor Speedway SPEEDWAY
(www.charlottemotorspeedway.com; tours $12; ⊙tours 9:30am-3:30pm Mon-Sat, 1:30-3:30pm Sun) Nascar races, a homegrown Southeastern

obsession, are held at the visible-from-outer-space speedway, 12 miles northeast of town. For the ultimate thrill/near-death experience, ride shotgun at up to 160 miles per hour in a real stock car with the **Richard Petty Driving Experience** (☑800-237-3889; www.drivepetty.com; rides from $59).

🍴 Sleeping & Eating

Many uptown hotels cater to business travelers, so rates are often lower on weekends. Cheaper chains cluster off I-85 and I-77. Uptown eating and drinking options cater to the preppy banker set; you'll see more tattoos at the laid-back pubs and bistros of NoDa.

Duke Mansion   B&B $$
(☑704-714-4400; www.dukemansion.com; 400 Hermitage Rd; r $99-219, ste $279; P❄@🐾) Tucked away in an oak-shaded residential neighborhood, this stately white-columned inn was the residence of 19th-century tobacco millionaire James B Duke and still retains the quiet, discreet feel of a posh private home. Most rooms have high ceilings and their own screened-in sleeping porches.

Hyatt House   HOTEL $$
(☑704-373-9700; www.charlottecentercity.house. hyatt.com; 435 E Trade St; r from $239; P❄@🐾) Formerly the Hotel Sierra, this chic hotel has a space-agey lime-and-charcoal color scheme and a gleaming lobby. Parking is $22 per night.

★Price's Chicken Coop   SOUTHERN $
(www.priceschickencoop.com; 1614 Camden Rd; mains $2-11; ☺10am-6pm Tue-Sat) A Charlotte institution, scruffy Price's regularly makes 'Best Fried Chicken in America' lists. Line up to order your 'dark quarter' or 'white half' from the army of white-jacketed cooks, then take your bounty outside – there's no seating. Cash only.

Mac's Speed Shop   SOUTHERN $$
(☑704-522-6227; www.macspeedshop.com; 2511 South Blvd; mains $8-16; ☺11am-midnight Sun-Tue, 11am-2am Wed-Sat) Rev it up for Mac's Speed Shop, a BBQ joint in an old service station that also dishes out local brews and live music. Sit inside or outside on the patio, where you might see a fine array of motorcycles.

Soul Gastrolounge Tapas   SUSHI $$
(☑704-348-1848; www.souldgastrolounge.com; 1500 Central Ave; mains $5-18; ☺5pm-2am Mon-Sat, 11am-3pm & 5pm-2am Sun) In Plaza Midtown, this sultry speakeasy serves a glo-bally inspired selection of small plates, from spanakopita to Korean BBQ, a Cuban panini and sushi rolls.

ℹ Information

Check out the alt-weekly *Creative Loafing* (charlotte.creativeloafting.com) for entertainment listings.

Public Library (College St) The public library-has 90 terminals with free internet.

Visitor Center (☑800-231-4636, 704-331-2700; www.charlottesgotalot.com; 330 S Tryon St; ☺8:30am-5pm Mon-Fri, 9am-3pm Sat) The downtown visitor center publishes maps and a visitors' guide.

ℹ Getting There & Around

Charlotte Douglas International Airport (CLT; ☑704-359-4027; www.charmeck.org/depart ments/airport; 5501 Josh Birmingham Pkwy) is a US Airways hub with direct flights from Europe and the UK. Both the **Greyhound station** (601 W Trade St) and **Amtrak** (1914 N Tryon St) are handy to Uptown. **Charlotte Area Transit** (www. charmeck.org; 310 E Trade St) runs local bus and light-rail services.

North Carolina Mountains

These ancient mountains have drawn seekers for generations. Cherokee came here to hunt, followed by 18th-century Scots-Irish immigrants looking for a better life. Lofty towns like Blowing Rock drew the sickly, who came for the fresh air. Today, scenic drives, leafy trails and roaring rivers draw outdoor adventurers.

The Appalachians in the western part of the state include the Great Smoky, Blue Ridge, Pisgah and Black Mountain subranges. Carpeted in blue-green hemlock, pine and oak trees, these cool hills are home to cougars, deer, black bears, wild turkeys and great horned owls. Hiking, camping, climbing and rafting adventures abound, and there's another jaw-dropping photo opportunity around every bend.

High Country

The northwestern corner of the state is known as 'High Country.' Its main towns are Boone, Blowing Rock and Banner Elk, all short drives from the Blue Ridge Pkwy. Boone is a lively college town, home to Appalachian State University (ASU). Blowing Rock and Banner Elk are quaint tourist centers near the winter ski areas.

◉ Sights & Activities

Hwy 321 from Blowing Rock to Boone is studded with **gem-panning mines** and other tourist traps. In Boone, check out the shops on King St and keep an eye out for the bronze **statue** of local bluegrass legend Doc Watson. He's strumming his guitar on the corner of King and Depot Sts.

Tweetsie Railroad   AMUSEMENT PARK
(✆ 877-893-3874; www.tweetsie.com; 300 Tweetsie Railroad Ln; adult/child $37/23; ⊙ 9am-6pm daily Jun-Aug, Fri-Sun mid-Apr–May, Sep & Oct; ⊕) A much-loved Wild West–themed amusement park. The highlight is a 1917 coal-fired steam train that chugs past marauding Indians and heroic cowboys.

Grandfather Mountain   HIKING
(✆ 828-733-4337; www.grandfather.com; Blue Ridge Pkwy Mile 305; adult/child 4-12yr $18/8; ⊙ 8am-7pm Jun-Aug) Tiptoe across a vertigo-inducing mile-high suspension bridge then lose the crowds on one of 11 hiking trails, the most difficult of which include steep hands-and-knees scrambles. In 2008 the family that owns the mountain sold the backcountry to the state park system, which opened **Grandfather Mountain State Park** (www.ncparks.gov) the following year.

River and Earth Adventures   OUTDOORS
(✆ 828-963-5491; www.raftcavehike.com; 1655 Hwy 105; half-/full-day rafting from $60/100; ⊕) Offers everything from family-friendly caving trips to rafting Class V rapids at Watauga Gorge. Eco-conscious guides even pack organic lunches. Canoe and kayak rentals.

🛏 Sleeping & Eating

Chain motels abound in Boone. You'll find private campgrounds and B&Bs scattered throughout the hills.

Mast Farm Inn   B&B $$
(✆ 828-963-5857; www.themastfarminn.com; 2543 Broadstone Rd, Vale Crucis; r/cottages incl breakfast from $209/349; ❰❉❈❭) In the beautiful hamlet of Valle Crucis, this restored farmhouse defines rustic chic with worn hardwood floors, claw-foot tubs and handmade toffees on your bedside table. The upscale mountain cuisine at the inn's restaurant, Simplicity, is worth a trip in itself.

Six Pence Pub   PUB $$
(www.sixpencepub.com; 1121 Main St, Blowing Rock; mains $9-18; ⊙ restaurant 11:30am-10:30pm Sun-Thu, to midnight Fri & Sat, bar to 2am) The bartenders keep a sharp but friendly eye on things at this lively British pub, where the shepherd's pie comes neat, not messy.

Hob Nob Farm Cafe   CAFE $$
(www.hobnobfarmcafe.com; 506 West King St, Boone; breakfast & lunch $3-12, dinner $8-15; ⊙ 10am-10pm Wed-Sun; ⊕) Gobble up avocado-tempeh melts, Thai curry bowls and sloppy burgers made from local beef at a wildly painted cottage near ASU. Brunch is served until 5pm.

ℹ Information

Visitor Center (✆ 800-438-7500, 828-264-1299; www.highcountryhost.com; 1700 Blowing Rock Rd; ⊙ 9am-5pm Mon-Sat, to 3pm Sun) The High Country visitor center has info on accommodations and outdoors outfitters.

Asheville

With its homegrown microbreweries, decadent chocolate shops and stylish New Southern eateries, Asheville is one of the trendiest small cities in the East. Glossy magazines swoon for the place. But don't be put off by the hipsters and the flash. At heart, Asheville is still an overgrown mountain town, and it holds tight to its traditional roots. Just look around. There's a busker fiddling a high lonesome tune on Biltmore Ave and hikers chowing down after climbing Mt Pisgah. Cars swoop on and off the Blue Ridge Parkway, which swings around the city. A huge artist population and a visible contingent of hardcore hippies also keep things real.

◉ Sights

Downtown is compact and easy to negotiate on foot. The art-deco buildings remain much as they were in 1930. The shopping's fantastic, with everything from hippie-dippy candle shops to vintage shops to high-end local art. West Ashville is an up-and-coming area, still gritty but very cool.

★ Biltmore Estate   HOUSE, GARDENS
(✆ 800-543-2961; www.biltmore.com; 1 Approach Rd; adult/child under 16yr from $59/30; ⊙ house 9am-4:30pm) The country's largest private home, and Asheville's number-one tourist attraction, the Biltmore was built in 1895 for shipping and railroad heir George Washington Vanderbilt II. He modeled it after the grand chateaux he'd seen on his various European jaunts. Viewing the estate and its 250 acres of gorgeously manicured grounds and gardens takes several hours.

Tours of the house are self-guided. To get the most out of your visit, pay an extra $10 for the audio tour. Also available are behind-the-scenes guided tours ($17) covering the architecture, the family or the servants.

Beyond the house, there are numerous cafes, a gift shop the size of a small supermarket, a hoity-toity hotel, and an award-winning winery that offers free tastings. In Antler Village, the new Biltmore Legacy exhibit, 'The Vanderbilts at Home and Abroad,' provides a more personal look at the family.

Chimney Rock Park   PARK

(www.chimneyrockpark.com; Hwy 64/74A; adult/child $15/7; ⊗ 8:30am-5:30pm late Mar-Oct, hours vary Nov-Feb) The American flag flaps in the breeze atop this popular park's namesake 315ft granite monolith. An elevator takes visitors up to the chimney, but the real draw is the exciting hike around the cliffs to a 404ft waterfall. The park, once privately owned, is now part of the state park system; access to the rock is still managed commercially. The park is a 20-mile drive southeast of Asheville.

Thomas Wolfe Memorial   HOUSE

(www.wolfememorial.com; 52 N Market St; museum free, house tour $5; ⊗ 9am-5pm Tue-Sat) FREE This downtown memorial, with a small museum and a separate house tour, honors *Look Homeward Angel* author Thomas Wolfe. The author grew up in Asheville, which was the inspiration for the novel's setting.

☞ Tours

Brews Cruise   MICROBREWERIES

(☑ 828-545-5181; www.ashevillebrewscruise.com; per person $50-55) Tour several of Asheville's microbreweries on the Brews Cruise.

Lazoom Comedy Tour   COMEDY

(☑ 828-225-6932; www.lazoomtours.com; per person $21-24) For a hysterically historical tour of the city, hop on the purple bus – and bring your own booze.

🛏 Sleeping

The **Asheville Bed & Breakfast Association** (☑ 877-262-6867; www.ashevillebba.com) handles bookings for numerous area B&Bs, from gingerbread cottages to alpine cabins.

Sweet Peas   HOSTEL $

(☑ 828-285-8488; www.sweetpeashostel.com; 23 Rankin Ave; dm/pod/r $28/35/60; P ❄ @ 🛜) This spic-and-span hostel gleams with IKEA-like style, with shipshape steel bunk

beds and blond wood sleeping 'pods.' The loftlike space is very open and can be noisy (a downstairs pub adds to the ruckus) – what you lose in privacy and quiet, you gain in style, cleanliness, sociability and an unbeatable downtown location.

Campfire Lodgings   CAMPGROUND $$

(☑ 828-658-8012; www.campfirelodgings.com; 116 Appalachian Village Rd; tent/RV sites $38/45, yurts from $115, cabins $160; P ❄ 🛜) All yurts should have flatscreen TVs, don't you think? Sleep like the world's most stylish Mongolian nomad in one of these furnished multi-room tents, on the side of a wooded hill. Cabins and tent sites are also available. Wi-fi access at RV sites, which have stunning valley views.

Grove Park Inn Resort & Spa   RESORT $$$

(☑ 828-252-2711; www.groveparkinn.com; 290 Macon Ave; r from $269; P ❄ @ 🛜 ❄ 🐾) This titanic arts-and-crafts-style stone lodge, which celebrates its centennial in 2013, has a hale-and-hearty look that sets the mood for adventure. But no worries all you modern mavens, the well-appointed rooms come with 21st-century amenities. The spa is an underground grotto with stone pools and an indoor waterfall. The Nantahala Outdoor Center (p351) just opened a 'basecamp' here, certified by Leadership in Energy and Environmental Design (LEED).

Aloft Asheville   HOTEL $$$

(☑ 828-232-2838; www.aloftasheville.com; 51 Biltmore Ave; r from $242; P ❄ @ 🛜 ❄ 🐾) At first glance this new downtown hotel looks like the 7th ring of hipster: giant chalkboard in the lobby, groovy young staff, a neon lounge with bright retro chairs. The only thing missing is a wool-cap-wearing bearded guy drinking a hoppy microwbr– oh, wait, over there. We jest. Once settled, you'll find the staff knowledgeable, the rooms spacious, and the vibe convivial. The hotel is close to downtown hotspots, including the Orange Peel (p349).

✗ Eating

Asheville is a great foodie town – many visitors come here just to eat!

★12 Bones   BARBECUE $

(www.12bones.com; 5 Riverside Dr; dishes $4-20; ⊗ 11am-4pm Mon-Fri) Soooooiieeee, this place is good. The slow-cooked meats are smoky tender, and the sides, from the jalapeño cheese grits to the buttery green beans, will have you kissing your mama and blessing the day you were born. Order at the counter, grab a picnic table, die happy.

Sunny Point Cafe   CAFE $
(www.sunnypointcafe.com; 626 Haywood Rd; breakfast & lunch $8-12, dinner $8-17; ☺8:30am-2:30pm Sun & Mon, to 9pm Tue-Sat) This bright West Asheville spot is beloved for its hearty, homemade fare. The huevos rancheros, with feta cheese and chorizo sausage, is deservedly popular. The cafe embraces the organic and fresh, and even has its own garden. The biscuits are divine.

French Broad Chocolate Lounge   BAKERY, DESSERTS $
(www.frenchbroadchocolates.com; 10 S Lexington; snacks $2-6; ☺11am-11pm Sun-Thu, to midnight Fri & Sat) Small-batch organic chocolates, a sippable 'liquid truffle,' pints of local stout served á la mode with vanilla ice cream... hey, where'd you go?

★**Admiral**   MODERN AMERICAN $$
(☑828-252-2541; www.theadmiralnc.com; 400 Haywood Rd; small plates $10-14, large plates $22-30; ☺5-10pm) This concrete bunker next to a car junkyard looks divey on the outside, but inside? That's where the magic happens. This low-key West Asheville spot is one of the state's finest New American restaurants serving wildly creative dishes – flat-iron steak with soy-sauce mashed potatoes and Vietnamese slaw – that taste divine. No reservation? Grab a seat at the bar.

Tupelo Honey   NEW SOUTHERN $$
(☑828-255-4863; www.tupelohoneycafe.com; 12 College St; breakfast $7-15, lunch & dinner $10-28; ☺9am-10pm) A longtime favorite for New Southern fare like shrimp and grits with goat cheese. Breakfasts are superb but no matter the meal, say yes to the biscuit. And add a drop of honey.

🍸 Drinking & Entertainment

Downtown Asheville has a range of bars and cafes, from frat-boy beer halls to hookah-n-sprout hippie holes-in-the-wall. West Asheville has a more laid-back townie vibe. For more about the region's 20-plus microbreweries and beer pubs, visit www.asheville-aletrail.com.

Wicked Weed   MICROBREWERY
(www.wickedweedbrewing.com; 91 Biltmore Ave) Henry VIII called hops 'a wicked and pernicious weed' that ruined the taste of beer. His subjects kept quaffing it anyway - just like the hordes at this new microbrewery, which overflows with hoppy brews. In a former gas station with a wide front patio, it's a big and breezy spot to chill.

Thirsty Monk   BREW PUB
(www.monkpub.com; 95 Patton Ave; ☺4pm-midnight Mon-Thu, noon-2am Fri & Sat, noon-10pm Sun) Try a variety of North Carolina craft beers and plenty of Belgian ales at this scruffy but lovable beer bar.

Jack of the Wood   PUB
(www.jackofthewood.com; 95 Patton Ave) This Celtic pub is a good place to bond with local 20- and 30-somethings over a bottle of organic ale.

Asheville Pizza & Brewing Company   BREWERY, CINEMA
(www.ashevillebrewing.com; 675 Merrimon Ave; movies $3; ☺movies 1pm, 4pm, 7pm & 10pm) Catch a flick at the small theater inside this one-of-a-kind spot.

Orange Peel   LIVE MUSIC
(www.theorangepeel.net; 101 Biltmore Ave; tickets $15-33) For live music, try this warehouse-sized place for big-name indie and punk.

Grey Eagle   LIVE MUSIC
(www.thegreyeagle.com; 185 Clingman Ave; tickets $5-20) For bluegrass and jazz.

ℹ Information

Public Library (67 Haywood Ave) Has computers with free internet.
Visitor Center (☑828-258-6129; www.exploreasheville.com; 36 Montford Ave; ☺9am-5:30pm Mon-Fri, 9am-5pm Sat & Sun) The shiny new visitor center is at I-240 exit 4C.

ℹ Getting There & Around

Asheville Transit (www.ashevilletransit.com; tickets $1) has 16 local bus routes, with most running from 6:30am to about 8pm Monday to Saturday. Twenty minutes south of town, **Asheville Regional Airport** (AVL; ☑828-684-2226; www.flyavl.com) has a handful of non-stop flights, including to/from Atlanta, Charlotte, Chicago and New York. **Greyhound** (2 Tunnel Rd) is just northeast of downtown.

Great Smoky Mountains National Park

The Great Smoky Mountains National Park is a moody, magical place. Covering 521,000-acres, it is one of the world's most diverse areas. Landscapes range from deep,

SMOKY MOUNTAINS DAY HIKES

These are a few of our favorite short hikes in the North Carolina side of the park.

Big Creek Trail Hike an easy 2 miles to Mouse Creek Falls or go another 3 miles to a backcountry campground; the trailhead's near I-40 on the park's northeastern edge.

Boogerman Trail Moderate 7-mile loop passing old farmsteads; accessible via Cove Creek Rd.

Chasteen Creek Falls From Smokemont campground, this 4-mile round-trip passes a small waterfall.

Shuckstack Tower Starting at massive Fontana Dam, climb 3.5 miles for killer views from an old fire tower.

dim spruce forest to sunny meadows carpeted with daisies and Queen Anne's lace to wide, coffee-brown rivers. There's ample hiking and camping, and opportunities for horseback riding, bike rental and fly-fishing. Unfortunately, with more than 9.6 million annual visitors – which is the highest of any national park in the US – the place can get annoyingly crowded. The North Carolina side has less traffic than the Tennessee side, however, so even at the height of summer tourist season you'll still have room to roam (p384).

Newfound Gap Rd/Hwy 441 is the only thoroughfare that crosses Great Smoky Mountains National Park, winding through the mountains from Gatlinburg, TN, to the town of Cherokee and the busy **Oconaluftee Visitor Center** (✍general information 865-436-1200, visitor center 865-436-1200; www.nps.gov/grsm; Hwy 441; ☉8am-7pm Jun-Aug, hours vary Sep-May) **FREE**, in the southeast. Pick up your backcountry camping permits here. The **Oconaluftee River Trail**, one of only two in the park that allows leashed pets, leaves from the visitor center and follows the river for 1.5 miles.

The on-site **Mountain Farm Museum** (✍423-436-1200; www.nps.gov/grsm; ☉dawn-dusk) is a restored 19th-century farmstead, complete with barn, blacksmith shop and smokehouse (with real pig heads!), assembled from original buildings from different parts of the park. Just north is the 1886 **Min-gus Mill** (self-guided tours free; ☉9am-5pm daily mid-Mar–mid-Nov, plus Thanksgiving weekend 9am-5pm), a turbine-powered mill that still grinds wheat and corn much as it always has. A few miles away the **Smokemont Campground** (www.nps.gov/grsm; tent & RV sites $20) is the only North Carolina campground open year-round.

To the east, remote **Cataloochee Valley** has several historic buildings to wander through and is a prime location for elk and black bears.

Around Great Smoky Mountains National Park

The state's westernmost tip is blanketed in parkland and sprinkled with tiny mountain towns. The area has a rich but sad Native American history – many of the original Cherokee inhabitants were forced off their lands during the 1830s and marched to Oklahoma on the Trail of Tears. Descendants of those who escaped are known as the Eastern Band of the Cherokee, about 12,000 of whom still live on the 56,000-acre Qualla Boundary territory at the edge of Great Smoky Mountains National Park.

The town of **Cherokee** anchors the Qualla Boundary with ersatz Native American souvenir shops, fast-food joints and **Harrah's Cherokee Casino** (www.harrahscherokee.com; 777 Casino Dr), which has an impressive water and video display, the Rotunda, in the lobby. The best sight is the modern and engaging **Museum of the Cherokee Indian** (✍828-497-3481; www.cherokeemuseum.org; 589 Tsali Blvd/Hwy 441, at Drama Rd; adult/child 6-12yr $10/6; ☉9am-5pm daily, to 7pm Mon-Sat Jun-Aug), with an informative exhibit about the Trail of Tears.

South of Cherokee, the contiguous Pisgah and Nantahala National Forests have more than a million acres of dense hardwood trees, windswept mountain balds and some of the country's best white water. Both contain portions of the Appalachian Trail. **Pisgah National Forest** highlights include the bubbling baths in the village of **Hot Springs** (www.hotspringsnc.org), the natural waterslide at **Sliding Rock**, and the 3.2-mile round-trip hike to the summit of 5721ft **Mt Pisgah**, which has a view of Cold Mountain of book and movie fame. **Nantahala National Forest** has several recreational lakes and dozens of roaring waterfalls.

Just north of Nantahala is quaint **Bryson City**, an ideal jumping-off point for outdoor adventures. It's home to the huge and highly recommended **Nantahala Outdoor Center** (NOC; ☑ 828-488-2176, 888-905-7238; www.noc.com; 13077 Hwy 19/74; kayak/canoe rental per day $30/50, guided trips $30-189), which specializes in wet and wild rafting trips down the Nantahala, French Broad, Pigeon and Ocoee Rivers. There's also a zipline and an alpine tower. It even has its own lodge and restaurant. The Appalachian Trail rolls across the property too. From the Bryson City depot, the **Great Smoky Mountains Railroad** (☑ 800-872-4681; www.gsmr.com; 226 Everett St, Bryson City; Nantahala Gorge trip adult/child 2-12yr from $55/31; ⊙ Mar-Dec) runs scenic train excursions through the dramatic river valley. For lodging and dining try the lofty **Fryemont Inn** (☑ 828-488-2159; www.fryemontinn.com; 245 Fryemont St; lodge/ste/cabins from $110/$180/245; nonguests breakfast $6-9, dinner $20-29 ; ⊙ restaurant 8am-10am & 6-8pm Sun-Tue, 6-9pm Fri & Sat mid-Apr–late Nov; P ⚏), a family-owned lodge and restaurant. The bark-covered inn has a front-porch view of the Smokies and downtown Bryson City.

SOUTH CAROLINA

The air is hotter, the accents thicker and the traditions more dear in South Carolina, where the Deep South begins. From its Revolutionary War patriots to its 1860s secessionist government to its current crop of feisty legislators, the Palmetto State has never shied away from a fight.

From the silvery sands of the Atlantic Coast, the state climbs westward from the Coastal Plain across the Piedmont and up into the Blue Ridge Mountains. Most travelers stick to the coast, with its splendid antebellum cities and palm-tree-studded beaches. But the interior has a wealth of sleepy old towns, wild and undeveloped state parks and spooky black-water swamps. Along the sea islands you hear the sweet songs of the Gullah, a culture and language created by former slaves who held onto many West African traditions through the ravages of time.

From genteel, gardenia-scented Charleston to bright, tacky Myrtle Beach, South Carolina is always an engaging destination.

History

More than 28 separate tribes of Native Americans have lived in what is now South Carolina, many of them Cherokee who were later forcibly removed during the Trail of Tears era.

The English founded the Carolina colony in 1670, with settlers pouring in from the royal outpost of Barbados, giving the port city known as Charles Towne a Caribbean flavor. West African slaves were brought over to turn the thick coastal swamps into rice paddies and by the mid-1700s the area was deeply divided between the slave-owning aristocrats of the Lowcountry and the poor Scots-Irish and German farmers of the rural backcountry.

South Carolina was the first state to secede from the Union, and the first battle of the Civil War occurred at Fort Sumter in Charleston Harbor. The end of the war left much of the state in ruins.

South Carolina traded in cotton and textiles for most of the 20th century. It remains a relatively poor agricultural state, though with a thriving coastal tourism business.

In recent years the Palmetto State has garnered headlines because of its politicians, from Nikki Haley, the state's first woman and first Indian American governor, to disgraced ex-governor and now Congressman, Mark Sanford. While governor, Sanford famously claimed that he was hiking the

---

GULLAH CULTURE

African slaves were transported from the region known as the Rice Coast (Sierra Leone, Senegal, the Gambia and Angola) to a landscape of remote islands that was shockingly similar – swampy coastlines, tropical vegetation and hot, humid summers.

These new African Americans were able to retain many of their homeland traditions, even after the fall of slavery and well into the 20th century. The resulting Gullah (also known as Geechee) culture has its own language, an English-based Creole with many African words and sentence structures, and many traditions, including fantastic storytelling, art, music and crafts. The Gullah culture is celebrated annually with the energetic **Gullah Festival** (www.gullahfestival.org; ⊙ late May) in Beaufort. For a Gullah-style meal, stop in Mt Pleasant for the lunch buffet at **Gullah Cuisine** (www.gullahcuisine.net; 1717 Hwy 17 N; buffet adult/child $8.25/4.50).

SOUTH CAROLINA FACTS

Nickname Palmetto State

Population 4.7 million

Area 30,109 sq miles

Capital city Columbia (population 130,500)

Other city Charleston (122,700)

Sales tax 6%, plus up to 10% extra tax on accommodations

Birthplace of Jazzman Dizzy Gillespie (1917–93), political activist Jesse Jackson (b 1941), boxer Joe Frazier (b 1944), *Wheel of Fortune* hostess Vanna White (b 1957)

Home of The first US public library (1698), museum (1773) and steam railroad (1833)

Politics Leans Republican

Famous for Firing the first shot of the Civil War, from Charleston's Fort Sumter

State dance The shag

Driving distances Columbia to Charleston 115 miles, Charleston to Myrtle Beach 97 miles

Appalachian Trail when he was in fact visiting his Argentinian honey.

ℹ Information

South Carolina Department of Parks, Recreation & Tourism (☏803-734-1700; www.discoversouthcarolina.com; 1205 Pendleton St, room 505; ☎) Sends out the state's official vacation guide. The state's nine highway welcome centers offer wi-fi. Ask inside for password.

South Carolina State Parks (☏camping reservations 866-345-7275, 803-734-0156; www.southcarolinaparks.com) The helpful website lists activities, hiking trails and allows online reservations for campsites (prices vary).

Charleston

This lovely city will embrace you with the warmth and hospitality of an old and dear friend – who died in the 1700s. We jest, but the cannons, cemeteries and carriage rides do conjure an earlier era. And that historic romanticism, along with the food and Southern graciousness, is what makes Charleston one of the world's favorite cities and one of the most popular tourist destinations in the South. In fact, Charleston was named the Best City to Visit in The World by readers of *Condé Nast Traveler* in 2012.

How best to enjoy its charms? Charleston is a city for savoring – stroll past the historic buildings, admire the antebellum architecture, stop to smell the blooming jasmine and enjoy long dinners on the verandah. It's also a place for romance, everywhere you turn another blushing bride is standing on the steps of yet another charming church.

In the high season the scent of gardenia and honeysuckle mixes with the tang of horse from the aforementioned carriage tours that clip-clop down the cobblestones. In winter the weather is milder and the crowds thinner, making Charleston a great bet for off-season travel.

History

Well before the Revolutionary War, Charles Towne (named for Charles II) was one of the busiest ports on the eastern seaboard, the center of a prosperous rice-growing and trading colony. With influences from the West Indies and Africa, France and other European countries, it became a cosmopolitan city, often compared to New Orleans.

The first shots of the Civil War rang out at Fort Sumter, in Charleston's harbor. After the war, as the labor-intensive rice plantations became uneconomical without slave labor, the city's importance declined. But much of the town's historic fabric remains, to the delight of more than four million tourists every year.

⊙ Sights

⊙ Historic District

The quarter south of Beaufain and Hasell Sts has the bulk of the antebellum mansions, shops, bars and cafes. At the southernmost tip of the peninsula are the antebellum mansions of the Battery.

Gateway Walk   CHURCHES
Long a culturally diverse city, Charleston gave refuge to persecuted French Protestants, Baptists and Jews over the years and earned the nickname the 'Holy City' for its abundance of houses of worship. The Gateway Walk, a little-known garden path between Archdale St and Philadelphia Alley,

connects four of the city's most beautiful historic churches: the white-columned **St John's Lutheran Church** (5 Clifford St), the Gothic Revival **Unitarian Church** (4 Archdale St), the striking Romanesque **Circular Congregational Church** (150 Meeting St) originally founded in 1681; and **St Philip's Church** (146 Church St), with its picturesque steeple and 17th-century graveyard, parts of which were once reserved for 'strangers and transient white persons.'

Gibbes Museum of Art   GALLERY
(www.gibbesmuseum.org; 135 Meeting St; adult/child $9/7; ☉10am-5pm Tue-Sat, 1-5pm Sun) Houses a decent collection of American and Southern works. The contemporary collection includes works by local artists, with Lowcountry life as a highlight.

Old Slave Mart Museum   MUSEUM
(www.nps.gov/nr/travel/charleston/osm.htm; 6 Chalmers St; adult/child $7/5; ☉9am-5pm Mon-Sat) African men, women and children were once auctioned off here, it's now a museum of South Carolina's shameful past. Text-heavy exhibits illuminate the slave experience; the few artifacts, such as leg shackles, are especially chilling. For first-hand stories, listen to the oral recollections of former slave Elijah Green.

Old Exchange & Provost Dungeon   HISTORIC BUILDING
(www.oldexchange.org; 122 E Bay St; adult/child $8/4; ☉9am-5pm; 🖝) Kids love the dungeon, used as a prison for pirates and for American patriots held by the British during the Revolutionary War. The cramped space sits beneath a stately Georgian Palladian customs house completed in 1771. Costumed guides lead the dungeon tours.

Kahal Kadosh Beth Elohim   SYNAGOGUE
(www.kkbe.org; 90 Hasell St; ☉tours 10am-noon & 1:30-3:30pm Mon-Thu, 10am-noon & 1-3pm Fri, 1-4pm Sun) The oldest continuously used synagogue in the country. There are free docent-led tours.

The Battery & White Point Gardens   GARDEN
The Battery is the southern tip of the Charleston Peninsula, buffered by a seawall. Stroll past cannons and statues of military heroes in the gardens then walk the promenade and look for Fort Sumter.

Rainbow Row   NEIGHBORHOOD
Around the corner from White Point Gardens, this stretch of lower E Bay St is one of the most photographed areas of town for its candy-colored houses.

Historic Homes

About half a dozen majestic historic homes are open to visitors. Discounted combination tickets may tempt you to see more, but one or two will be enough for most people. Guided tours run every half-hour.

Aiken-Rhett House   HISTORIC BUILDING
(www.historiccharleston.org; 48 Elizabeth St; admission $10; ☉10am-5pm Mon-Sat, 2-5pm Sun) The only surviving urban plantation, this house gives a fascinating glimpse into antebellum life. The role of slaves is also presented, and you can wander into the dorm-style quarters behind the main house. The Historic Charleston Foundation manages the house with a goal of preserving and conserving, but not restoring, the property, meaning there have been few alterations.

Joseph Manigault House   HISTORIC BUILDING
(www.charlestonmuseum.org; 350 Meeting St; admission $10; ☉10am-5pm Mon-Sat, 1-5pm Sun) The three-story Federal-style house was once the showpiece of a French Huguenot rice planter. Don't miss the tiny neoclassical temple in the garden.

Nathaniel Russell House   HISTORIC BUILDING
(www.historiccharleston.org; 51 Meeting St; adult/child $10/5; ☉10am-5pm Mon-Sat, 2-5pm Sun, last tour 4:15pm) Built by a Rhode Islander, known in Charleston as 'the king of the Yankees,' the 1808 Federal-style house is noted especially for its spectacular, self-supporting spiral staircase and lush English garden.

◉ Marion Square

Formerly home to the state weapons arsenal, this 10-acre park is Charleston's living room, with various monuments and an excellent Saturday farmers market.

Charleston Museum   MUSEUM
(www.charlestonmuseum.org; 360 Meeting St; adult/child $10/5; ☉9am-5pm Mon-Sat, 1-5pm Sun) Founded in 1773, this claims to be the country's oldest museum. It's informative if you're looking for more historic background after strolling through the Historic District. Exhibits

spotlight various periods of Charleston's long and storied history, and artifacts range from prehistoric whale skeletons to slave tags and Civil War weapons.

Aquarium Wharf

Aquarium Wharf surrounds pretty Liberty Sq and is a great place to stroll and watch the tugboats guiding ships into the fourth-largest container port in the US. The wharf is one of two embarkation points for tours to Fort Sumter, the other is at Patriot's Point (p357).

Fort Sumter
HISTORIC SITE

The first shots of the Civil War rang out at Fort Sumter, on a pentagon-shaped island in the harbor. A Confederate stronghold, the fort was shelled to bits by Union forces from 1863 to 1865. A few original guns and fortifications give a feel for the momentous history. The only way to get here is by **boat tours** (boat tour 843-722-2628, park 843-883-3123; www.nps.gov/fosu; adult/child $18/11), which depart from 340 Concord St at 9:30am, noon and 2:30pm in summer (less often in winter) and from Patriot's Point in Mt Pleasant, across the river, at 10:45am, 1:30pm and 4pm from mid-March to late August (less in winter).

South Carolina Aquarium
AQUARIUM

(www.scaquarium.org; 100 Aquarium Wharf; adult/child $25/15; ⊙9am-5pm Mar-Aug, to 4pm Sep-Feb; ⊛) Ticket prices are steep, so this riverside aquarium is best for a rainy day. Exhibits showcase the state's diverse aquatic life. The highlight is the 42ft Great Ocean Tank, which teems with sharks and alien-looking puffer fish.

Arthur Ravenel Jr Bridge
BRIDGE

Stretching across the Cooper River like some massive stringed instrument, the 3-mile-long Arthur Ravenel Jr Bridge is a triumph of contemporary engineering. Cycling or jogging across the protected no-car lane is one of active Charlestonians' go-to weekend activities. There are parking lots on either side of the bridge. Rent a cruiser at **Affordabike** (843-789-3281; www.affordabike.com; 534 King St; bikes per day from $20).

Tours

Listing all of Charleston's walking, horse-carriage, bus and boat tours could take up this entire book. Ask at the visitor center for the gamut.

Culinary Tours of Charleston
CULINARY

(843-722-8687; www.culinarytoursofcharleston.com; 2½hr tour $42) You'll likely sample grits, pralines, BBQ and more on this walking tour of Charleston's restaurants and markets.

Adventure Harbor Tours
BOAT

(843-442-9455; www.adventureharbortours.com; adult/child $55/30.) Runs fun trips to uninhabited Morris Island, great for shelling.

Charleston Footprints
WALKING

(843-478-4718; www.charlestonfootprints.com; 2hr tour $20) A highly rated walking tour of historical Charleston sights.

Olde Towne Carriage Company
CARRIAGE

(843-722-1315; www.oldetownecarriage.com; 20 Anson St; 1hr tour adult/child $22/12) Guides on this popular horse-drawn-carriage tour offer colorful commentary as you clip-clop around town.

Festivals & Events

Lowcountry Oyster Festival
OYSTER

(www.charlestonrestaurantassociation.com/lowcountry-oyster-festival; ⊙Jan) In January oyster-lovers in Mt Pleasant feast on 65,000lb of the salty bivalves.

Spoleto USA
PERFORMING ARTS

(www.spoletousa.org; ⊙May) This 17-day performing-arts festival is Charleston's biggest event, with operas, dramas and musicals staged across the city, and artisans and food vendors lining the streets.

MOJA Arts Festival
ARTS

(www.mojafestival.com; ⊙Sep) Spirited poetry jams and gospel concerts mark this two-week celebration of African American and Caribbean culture.

Sleeping

Staying in the historic downtown is the most attractive option, but it's also the most expensive, especially on weekends and in high season. The rates below are for high season (spring and early summer). The chain hotels on the highways and near the airport offer significantly lower rates. Hotel parking in central downtown is usually between $12 and $20 a night; accommodations on the fringes of downtown often have free parking.

The city is bursting with charming B&Bs serving Southern breakfasts and Southern hospitality. They fill up fast, so try using an agency such as **Historic Charleston B&B**

(📞 843-722-6606; www.historiccharlestonbedand-breakfast.com; 57 Broad St).

NotSo Hostel
HOSTEL $

(📞 843-722-8383; www.notsohostel.com; 156 Spring St; dm/r $26/62; P✳@🐾) On the north edge of downtown, three tottering old houses have been carved into dorms and private rooms. Get local tips from friendly staff members during the shared morning breakfast. A new nearby annex at 33 Cannon St offers private rooms with queen beds ($70) and a quieter vibe, good for couples.

James Island County Park
CAMPGROUND $

(📞 843-795-4386; www.ccprc.com; 871 Riverland Dr; tent sites from $25, 8-person cottages $169) Southwest of town, this 643-acre park has meadows, a marsh and a dog park. Rent bikes and kayaks or play the disc golf course. The park offers shuttle services downtown ($10). Reservations are highly recommended. Cottages require one-week rental June to August.

Indigo Inn
BOUTIQUE $$

(📞 843-577-5900; www.indigoinn.com; 1 Maiden Ln; r $171) Our favorite part? The tasty ham biscuits at breakfast. Other perks include a prime location in the middle of the historic district and an oasis-like private courtyard, where guests can enjoy free wine and cheese by the fountain. Decor gives a nod to the 18th century, and the beds are quite comfy. A good value.

1837 Bed & Breakfast
B&B $$

(📞 877-723-1837, 843-723-7166; www.1837bb.com; 126 Wentworth St; r incl breakfast $129-169; P✳🐾) Close to the College of Charleston, this B&B may bring to mind the home of your eccentric, antique-loving aunt. The 1837 has nine charmingly overdecorated rooms, including three in the old brick carriage house.

Anchorage Inn
INN $$

(📞 843-723-8300; www.anchoragecharleston.com; 26 Vendue Range; r from $159; ✳🐾) One of the best values of Charleston's intimate Historic District inns, its rooms have the dark and small feel of ship's quarters but they're plenty plush.

★ Ansonborough Inn
HOTEL $$$

(📞 800-522-2073; www.ansonboroughinn.com; 21 Hasell St; r incl breakfast $209-259; P✳@🐾) A central atrium done up with burnished pine, exposed beams and nautical-themed oil paintings makes this intimate Historic District hotel feel like an antique sailing ship. Droll neo-Victorian touches like the Persian-carpeted glass elevator, the closet-sized British pub and the formal portraits of dogs add a sense of fun. Huge guest rooms mix old and new, with worn leather couches, high ceilings and flatscreen TVs. Complimentary wine and cheese social from 5pm to 6pm.

Vendue Inn
INN $$$

(📞 843-577-7970; www.vendueinn.com; 19 Vendue Range; r incl breakfast $205-425, ste $395-465; P✳🐾) This boutique hotel, in the part of downtown known as the French Quarter, is decked out in a trendy mix of exposed brick and eccentric antiques. Rooms have cool amenities like deep soaking tubs and gas fireplaces. Even cooler is the aptly named Rooftop bar. Parking is $14 per night.

✖️ Eating

Charleston is one of America's finest eating cities, and there are enough fabulous restaurants here for a town three times its size. The 'classic' Charleston establishments stick to fancy seafood with a French flair, while many of the trendy up-and-comers are re-inventing Southern cuisine with a focus on the area's copious local bounty, from oysters to heirloom rice to heritage pork. On Saturday, stop by the terrific **farmers market** (Marion Sq; ⏰8am-1pm Sat Apr-Oct).

Sugar Bakeshop
BAKERY $

(www.sugarbake.com; 59 Cannon St; pastries $1-4; ⏰10am-6pm Mon-Fri, 11am-5pm Sat) The staff is as sweet as the cupcakes at Sugar, a teensy space north of downtown. Pop in on Thursdays for the Lady Baltimore cupcake, a retro Southern specialty with dried fruit and white frosting.

The Ordinary
SEAFOOD $$

(📞 843-414-7060; www.eattheordinary.com; 544 King St; small plates $5-25, large $24-28; ⏰from 3pm Tue-Sun) Stepping through the door you feel like you've arrived at the best party in town at the Ordinary, a buzzy seafood hall and oyster bar inside a cavernous 1927 bank building. The menu is short, but the savory dishes are prepared with finesse – from the oyster sliders to the lobster rolls to the nightly fish dishes. Efficient but welcoming bar works well for solos.

This is the latest venue from Chef Mike Lata, a James Beard winner and owner of beloved FIG.

Poe's Tavern

PUB $$

(www.poestavern.com; 2210 Middle St, Sullivan's Island; meals $9-13; ⊙ 11am-10pm, bar to midnight) On a sunny day the front porch of Poe's on Sullivan's Island is the place to be. The tavern's namesake, master of the macabre Edgar Allen Poe, was once stationed at nearby Fort Moultrie. The burgers, are superb, and the Amontillado comes with guacamole, jalapeño jack, pico de gallo and chipotle sour cream. Quoth the raven: 'Gimme more.'

Gaulart & Maliclet

FRENCH $$

(www.fastandfrenchcharleston.com; 98 Broad St; mains $5-16; ⊙ 8am-11pm Mon-Sat) Locals crowd around the shared tables at this tiny spot, known as 'Fast & French,' to nibble on Gallic cheeses and sausages or nightly specials ($16) that include bread, soup, a main dish and wine.

Monza

PIZZA $$

(www.monzapizza.com; 451 King St; mains $12-14; ⊙ 11am-10pm Sun-Thu, to 11pm Fri & Sat) Burnt out on shrimp and grits? We know, it happens. After shopping on King St, pop into this exposed-brick spot. Monza is an Italian raceway, and the names of the wood-fired pizzas are inspired by racing legends. The Volpini is topped with prosciutto and argula. Salads and pastas are also on the menu.

Hominy Grill

NEW SOUTHERN $$

(www.hominygrill.com; 207 Rutledge Ave; mains $8-18; ⊙ 7:30am-9pm Mon-Fri, 9am-9pm Sat, to 3pm Sun; 🖉) Slightly off the beaten path, this neighborhood cafe serves modern, vegetarian-friendly Lowcountry cuisine in an old barbershop. The shady patio is tops for brunch.

Husk

NEW SOUTHERN $$$

(☑ 843-577-2500; www.huskrestaurant.com; 76 Queen St; brunch & lunch $10-16, dinner $27-30; ⊙ 11:30am-2:30pm Mon-Sat, 10am-2:30pm Sun , 5:30-10pm Sun-Thu, 5:30-11pm Fri & Sat) Everything – *everything* – on the menu at this buzzed-about restaurant is grown or raised in the South, from the jalapeño marmalade-topped Georgia corn soup to the yuzu-scented Cooper River oysters, to the local lard featured in the 'pork butter' brought out with the restaurant's addictive sesame-seed rolls.

The setting, in a two-story mansion, is elegant but unfussy, and the adjacent speakeasy-style bar is near-close to perfect – if only they would expand the bar food menu.

FIG

NEW SOUTHERN $$$

(☑ 843-805-5900; www.eatatfig.com; 232 Meeting St; mains $28-31; ⊙ 5:30-10:30pm Mon-Thu, to 11pm Fri & Sat) Foodies swoon over inspired nouvelle-Southern fare like crispy pig's trotters (that means 'feet' – local and hormone-free, of course) with celery-root remoulade in this rustic-chic dining room. FIG stands for Food is Good. And the gourmands agree.

S.N.O.B.

NEW SOUTHERN $$$

(☑ 843-723-3424; www.mavericksouthernkitchens. com; 192 E Bay St; lunch $10-14, dinner $18-34; ⊙ 11:30am-3pm Mon-Fri, 5:30pm-late nightly) The cheeky name (it stands for 'slightly north of Broad,' as in Broad St) reflects the anything-goes spirit of this upscale-casual spot, which draws raves for its eclectic menu, filled with treats such as BBQ tuna with fried oysters and sautéed squab breast over South Carolina rice.

🍷 Drinking & Nightlife

Balmy Charleston evenings are perfect for lifting a cool cocktail or dancing to live blues. Check out the weekly *Charleston City Paper* and the 'Preview' section of Friday's *Post & Courier*.

Husk Bar

BAR

(www.huskrestaurant.com; 76 Queen St; ⊙ from 4pm) Adjacent to Husk restaurant, this intimate brick-and-worn-wood spot recalls a speakeasy, with historic cocktails such as the Monkey Gland (gin, OJ, raspberry syrup).

Rooftop at Vendue Inn

BAR

(www.vendueinn.com; 23 Vendue Range; ⊙ 11:30am-midnight) This rooftop bar has the best views of downtown, and the crowds to prove it. Enjoy afternoon nachos or late-night live blues.

Blind Tiger

PUB

(www.blindtigercharleston.com; 36-38 Broad St; ⊙ 11:30am-2am Mon-Sat, 11am-2am Sun) A cozy and atmospheric dive, with stamped-tin ceilings, a worn wood bar and good pub grub.

Closed for Business

PUB

(www.closed5business.com; 535 King St; ⊙ 11am-2am Mon-Sat, 10am-2pm Sun) Charleston's best beer selection and a raucous neighborhood pub vibe.

🔒 Shopping

The historic district is clogged with overpriced souvenir shops and junk markets. Head instead to King St: hit lower King for antiques, middle King for cool boutiques, and upper King for trendy design and gift shops. The main stretch of Broad St is known as 'Gallery Row' for its many art galleries.

**Shops of Historic
Charleston Foundation**   GIFTS
(www.historiccharleston.org; 108 Meeting St; ⊙9am-6pm Mon-Sat, noon-5pm Sun) This place showcases jewelry, home furnishings and furniture inspired by the city's historic homes, like earrings based on the cast-iron railings at the Aiken-Rhett House. Pick up a 'Charleston' candle, scented with hyacinth, white jasmine and tuberose.

Charleston Crafts Cooperative   CRAFT
(www.charlestoncrafts.org; 161 Church St; ⊙10am-6pm) A pricey, well-edited selection of contemporary South Carolina–made crafts such as sweetgrass baskets, hand-dyed silks and wood carvings.

Blue Bicycle Books   BOOKS
(www.bluebicyclebooks.com; 420 King St; ⊙10am-7:30pm Mon-Sat, 1-6pm Sun) Excellent new-and-used bookshop with a great selection of Southern history and culture.

ℹ Information

The City of Charleston maintains free public internet (wi-fi) access throughout the downtown area.

Charleston City Paper (www.charlestoncitypaper.com) Published each Wednesday, this alt-weekly has good entertainment and restaurant listings.

Main Police Station (☑non-emergencies 843-577-7434; 180 Lockwood Blvd)

Post & Courier (www.postandcourier.com) Charleston's daily newspaper.

Post Office (www.usps.com; 83 Broad St; ⊙11:30am-3:30pm)

Public Library (68 Calhoun St; ⊙9am-8pm Mon-Thu, to 6pm Fri & Sat, 2-5pm Sun) Free internet access.

University Hospital (Medical University of South Carolina; ☑843-792-1414; 171 Ashley Ave; ⊙24hr) Emergency room.

Visitor Center (☑843-853-8000; www.charlestoncvb.com; 375 Meeting St; ⊙8:30am-5pm) Find help with accommodations and tours or watch a half-hour video on Charleston history in this spacious renovated warehouse.

ℹ Getting There & Around

Charleston International Airport (CHS; ☑843-767-7000; www.chs-airport.com; 5500

MEXICAN HAT DANCE

Yes, that's a giant sombrero rising above I-95 on the North Carolina–South Carolina state line. *Bienvenidos* to **South of the Border** (www.thesouthoftheborder.com; 3346 Hwy 301 N Hamer), a Mexican-flavored monument to American kitsch. Begun in the 1950s as a fireworks stand – pyrotechnics are illegal in North Carolina – it's morphed into a combo rest stop, souvenir mall, motel and (mostly defunct) amusement park, promoted on hundreds of billboards by a wildly stereotypical Mexican cartoon character named Pedro. The place has been looking tired lately, but it's still worth a quick stop for a photo and some taffy.

International Blvd) is 12 miles outside of town in North Charleston, with 124 daily flights to 17 destinations.

The **Greyhound station** (3610 Dorchester Rd) and the **Amtrak train station** (4565 Gaynor Ave) are both in North Charleston.

CARTA (www.ridecarta.com; fare $1.75) runs city-wide buses; the free DASH streetcars do three loop routes from the visitor center.

Mt Pleasant

Across the Cooper River from Charleston is the residential and vacation community of Mt Pleasant, originally a summer retreat for early Charlestonians, along with the slim barrier resort islands of **Isle of Palms** and **Sullivan's Island**. Though increasingly glutted with traffic and strip malls, the area still has some charm, especially in the historic downtown, called the **Old Village**. Some good seafood restaurants sit overlooking the water at **Shem Creek**, where it's fun to dine creekside at sunset and watch the incoming fishing-boat crews unload their catch. This is also a good place to rent kayaks to tour the estuary.

◉ Sights

**Patriot's Point Naval
& Maritime Museum**   MUSEUM
(www.patriotspoint.org; 40 Patriots Point Rd; adult/child $18/11; ⊙9am-6:30pm) Patriot's Point Naval & Maritime Museum is home to the USS *Yorktown*, a giant aircraft carrier used extensively in WWII. You can tour the ship's

flight deck, bridge and ready rooms and get a glimpse of what life was like for its sailors. Also on site are a small museum, submarine, naval destroyer, Coast Guard cutter and a re-created 'fire base' from Vietnam. You can also catch the Fort Sumter boat tour from here.

Boone Hall Plantation HISTORIC BUILDING
(☑ 843-884-4371; www.boonehallplantation.com; 1235 Long Point Rd; adult/child $20/10; ☉ 8:30am-6:30pm Mon-Sat, noon-5pm Sun early Mar-Aug, shorter hours Sep-Feb, closed Jan) Just 11 miles from downtown Charleston on Hwy 17N, Boone Hall Plantation is famous for its magical Avenue of Oaks, planted by Thomas Boone in 1743. Boone Hall is still a working plantation, though strawberries, tomatoes and Christmas trees long ago replaced cotton as the primary crop. The main house, built in 1936, is the fourth house on the site. The most compelling buildings are the Slave Street cabins, built between 1790 and 1810 and now lined with exhibits.

Ashley River Plantations

Only a 20-minute drive northwest from Charleston, there are three spectacular plantations. You'll be hard-pressed for time to visit all three in one outing, but you could squeeze in two (allow at least a couple of hours for each). Ashley River Rd is also known as SC 61, which can be reached from downtown Charleston via Hwy 17.

◉ Sights

★**Middleton Place** HISTORIC BUILDING, GARDENS
(☑ 843-556-6020; www.middletonplace.org; 4300 Ashley River Rd; gardens adult/child $28/10, house museum tour adult & child extra $15; ☉ 9am-5pm) Designed in 1741, this plantation's vast gardens are the oldest in the US. One hundred slaves spent a decade terracing the land and digging the precise geometric canals for the owner, wealthy South Carolina politician Henry Middleton. The bewitching grounds are a mix of classic formal French gardens and romantic woodland, bounded by flooded rice paddies and rare-breed farm animals. Union soldiers burned the main house in 1865; a 1755 guest wing, now housing the house museum, still stands.

The on-site inn is a series of ecofriendly modernist glass boxes overlooking the Ashley River. Enjoy a traditional Lowcountry plantation lunch of she-crab soup and pole beans at the highly regarded cafe.

Magnolia Plantation HOUSE, GARDENS
(www.magnoliaplantation.com; 3550 Ashley River Rd; adult/child $15/10, tours $8; ☉ 8am-5:30pm) On 500 acres owned by the Drayton family since 1676, Magnolia Plantation is a veritable plantation theme park, complete with a tram tour, a swamp walk, a petting zoo, and a guided house tour. At the reconstructed slave cabins, the Slavery to Freedom Tour traces the African American experience at the plantation.

Drayton Hall PLANTATION
(☑ 843-769-2600; www.draytonhall.org; 3380 Ashley River Rd; adult/child $18/8; ☉ 9am-5pm Mon-Sat, 11am-5pm Sun, last tour 3:30pm) This 1738 Palladian brick mansion was the only plantation house on the Ashley River to survive the Revolutionary and Civil Wars and the great earthquake of 1886. Guided tours explore the unfurnished house, which has been preserved, but not restored. Walking trails wander along the river and a marsh.

Lowcountry

From just north of Charleston, the southern half of the South Carolina coast is a tangle of islands cut off from the mainland by inlets and tidal marshes. Here, descendants of West African slaves known as the Gullah maintain small communities in the face of resort and golf-course development. The landscape ranges from tidy stretches of shimmery, oyster-gray sand, to wild, moss-shrouded maritime forests.

Charleston County Sea Islands

The following islands are all within an hour's drive from Charleston.

About 8 miles south of Charleston, **Folly Beach** is good for a day of sun and sand. **Folly Beach County Park** (☑ 843-588-2426; www.ccprc.com; 1100 W Ashley Ave, Folly Beach; admission per vehicle $8, walk-in/bicycle free; ☉ 10am-6pm), on the west side, has public changing areas and beach-chair rentals. The other end of the island is popular with surfers.

Upscale rental homes and golf courses abound on **Kiawah Island**, just southeast of Charleston, while nearby **Edisto Island** (*ed*-is-tow) is a homespun family vacation spot without a single traffic light. At its southern tip, **Edisto Beach State Park** (☏843-869-2156; www.southcarolinaparks.com; adult/child $5/3, tent sites from $21, furnished cabins from $80) has a gorgeous, uncrowded beach and oak-shaded hiking trails and campgrounds.

Beaufort & Hilton Head

The southernmost stretch of South Carolina's coast is popular with a mostly up-scale set of golfers and B&B aficionados, but the area's got quirky charms aplenty for everyone.

On Port Royal Island, the darling colonial town of **Beaufort** (byoo-furt) is often used as a set for Hollywood films about the South. The streets of the historic district are lined with antebellum homes and magnolias dripping with Spanish moss, and the riverfront downtown has gobs of linger-worthy cafes and galleries. The most romantic of the city's handful of B&Bs is **Cuthbert House** (☏843-521-1315; www.cuthberthouseinn.com; 1203 Bay St; r incl breakfast $179-245; P✳️🛜), a sumptuously grand white-columned mansion straight out of *Gone With the Wind II*. Bay St has the bulk of the cute bistros, but for hardcore local flavor head inland to **Sgt White's** (1908 Boundary St; mains $7-12; ⊘11am-3pm Mon-Fri), where a retired Marine sergeant serves up juicy BBQ ribs, collards and cornbread.

South of Beaufort, some 20,000 young men and women go through boot camp each year at the **Marine Corps Recruit Depot** on Parris Island, made notorious by Stanley Kubrick's *Full Metal Jacket*. The fascinating **Parris Island Museum** (☏843-228-2951; www.mcrdpi.usmc.mil; 111 Panama St; ⊘10am-4:40pm) **FREE** has antique uniforms and weaponry, and covers marine corps history. Come for Friday graduations to see newly minted marines parade proudly for family and friends. You may be asked to show ID and car registration before driving onto the base.

East of Beaufort, the Sea Island Pkwy/Hwy 21 connects a series of marshy, rural islands, including **St Helena Island**, considered the heart of Gullah country. Once one of the nation's first schools for freed slaves, the **Penn Center** (☏843-838-2432; www.discoversouthcarolina.com; 16 Penn Center Circle W; adult/child $5/3; ⊘11am-4pm Mon-Sat) has a small museum that covers Gullah culture and traces the history of Penn School, which was one of the nation's first schools for freed slaves. Further down the road, **Hunting Island State Park** (☏843-838-2011; www.southcarolinaparks.com; 2555 Sea Island Pkwy; adult/child $5/3, tent sites $17-38, cabins $210; ⊘visitor center 9am-5pm Mon-Fri, 11am-5pm Sat & Sun) has acres of spooky maritime forest, tidal lagoons, and empty, bone-white beach. The Vietnam War scenes from *Forrest Gump* were filmed in the marsh, a nature-lover's dream. Campgrounds fill up quickly in summer.

Across Port Royal Sound, tony **Hilton Head Island** is South Carolina's largest barrier island and one of America's top golf spots. There are dozens of courses, many enclosed in posh private residential communities called 'plantations.' Though summer traffic and miles of stoplights make it hard to see the forest (or a tree) along Hwy 278,

THE SOUTH LOWCOUNTRY

LOWCOUNTRY CUISINE

The traditional cooking style of the South Carolina and Georgia coasts, Lowcountry cuisine is seafood-centric Southern fare with a heavy dash of West African influence. Dishes to look for:

Benne wafers Sesame-seed cookies.

Country Captain Curried chicken stew, brought to the city via India by British sea captains.

Hoppin' John A rice-and-bean dish, sometimes spicy.

Lowcountry boil/Frogmore stew Crabs, shrimp, oysters and other local seafood boiled in a pot with corn and potatoes, generally eaten at picnics.

Perlau A rice-and-meat dish, cousin to rice pilaf.

She-crab soup Cream-based crab soup fortified with sherry.

Shrimp and grits A classic Charleston fisherman's breakfast of shrimp and ground corn, now a ubiquitous main course.

DON'T MISS

BOWEN'S ISLAND RESTAURANT

Down a long dirt road through Low-country marshland near Folly Beach, this unpainted wooden **shack** (1870 Bowen's Island Rd; ☺5-10pm Tue-Sat) is one of the South's most venerable seafood dives – grab an oyster knife and start shucking! Cool beer and friendly locals give the place its soul.

there are some lush nature preserves and wide, white beaches hard enough to ride a bike on. Stop by the **visitor center** (☎800-523-3373; wwwhiltonheadisland.org; 1 Chamber of Commerce Dr; ☺8:30am-5pm), on the island, for information and brochures.

North Coast

The coastline from the North Carolina border to the city of Georgetown is known as the Grand Strand, with some 60 miles of fast-food joints, beach resorts and three-story souvenir shops. What was once a laid-back summer destination for working-class people from across the Southeast has become some of the most overdeveloped real estate in the country. Whether you're ensconced in a behemoth resort or sleeping in a tent at a state park, all you need to enjoy your stay is a pair of flip-flops, a margarita and some quarters for the pinball machine.

Myrtle Beach

Love it or hate it, Myrtle Beach means summer vacation, American-style.

Bikers take advantage of the lack of helmet laws to let their graying ponytails fly in the wind, bikini-clad teenagers play Pac-Man and eat hot dogs in smoky arcades, and whole families roast like chickens on the white sand.

North Myrtle Beach, actually a separate town, is slightly lower-key, with a thriving culture based on the 'shag' (no, not that kind of shag) – a jitterbug-like dance invented here in the 1940s.

It ain't for nature-lovers, but with enormous outlet malls and innumerable mini-golf courses, water parks, daiquiri bars and t-shirt shops, it's a rowdy good time.

☉ Sights & Activities

The beach itself is pleasant enough – wide, hot and crowded with umbrellas. Beachfront Ocean Blvd has the bulk of the hamburger stands and seedy gift shops. Hwy 17 is choked with mini-golf courses, boasting everything from animatronic dinosaurs to faux volcanoes spewing lurid-pink water.

Several amusement park–shopping mall hybrids teem with people at all hours.

Brookgreen Gardens GARDENS
(www.brookgreen.org; adult/child $14/7; ☺9:30am-5pm) These magical gardens, 16 miles south of town on Hwy 17S, are home to the largest collection of American sculpture in the country, set amid 9000 acres of rice plantation turned subtropical garden paradise. Seasonal blooms are listed on the website.

Wonderworks MUSEUM
(www.wonderworksonline.com; 1313 Celebrity Circle; adult/child from $23/15; ☺9am-9pm Sun-Thu, to 10pm Fri & Sat, hours vary; 🖼) The Inversion Tunnel, which 'flips' visitors as they enter, is pretty darn freaky. It's also just the start of the fun at this interactive museum/amusement zone, with ropes courses, laser tag, beeping and flashing 'science' exhibits and more. We dare you to lie on the bed of nails.

Broadway at the Beach MALL
(www.broadwayatthebeach.com; 1325 Celebrity Circle) With shops, restaurants, nightclubs, rides and an IMAX theater, this is Myrtle Beach's nerve center.

Family Kingdom AMUSEMENT PARK
(www.family-kingdom.com; combo pass $36; 🖼) An old-fashioned amusement-and-water-park combo overlooking the ocean. Hours vary by season. Closed in winter.

🛏 Sleeping

Hundreds of hotels, ranging from retro family-run motor inns to vast resort complexes, have prices that vary widely by season; a room might cost $30 in January and more than $150 in July. The following are high-season rates.

Myrtle Beach State Park CAMPGROUND $
(☎843-238-5325; www.southcarolinaparks.com; 4401 S Kings Hwy; tent & RV sites $21-52, cabins & apts $65-210; 🅿🐾📶♿) Sleep beneath the pines or rent a cabin, all just steps from the shore. The park is 3 miles south of central Myrtle Beach. Wi-fi available at the ranger station.

Serendipity Inn
INN $$

(☎800-762-3229; www.serendipityinn.com; 407 71st Ave N; r incl breakfast $99, ste $109-149; P❋☎☀) This intimate Spanish-style inn hides from the city's buzz on a quiet side street. Rooms, done up with florals and knickknacks, are comfy but not fancy.

Compass Cove
RESORT $$

(☎855-330-6258; www.compasscove.com; 2311 S Ocean Blvd; r from $172; P❋@☎☀) Got the kids? Go full Myrtle Beach at this three-towered resort with 23 water attractions, including eight pools and two waterslides.

✗ Eating

The hundreds of restaurants are mostly high-volume and middlebrow – think buffets longer than bowling alleys and 24-hour doughnut shops. Ironically, good seafood is hard to come by; locals go to the nearby fishing village of **Murrells Inlet**.

Prosser's BBQ
SOUTHERN $$

(3750 Business Hwy 17, Murrells Inlet; buffet breakfast/lunch $6/8.30, dinner $9.30-13 ; ☺6am-2pm Mon-Sat, plus 4-8pm Wed-Sat; ✋) The gut-busting lunch buffet is downhome delicious. It includes fried fish and chicken, sweet potatoes, mac 'n' cheese, green beans, and vinegary pulled pork. Hours vary by season. Your best bet on Murrells Inlet's 'restaurant row.' Worth the drive.

Duffy Street Seafood Shack
SEAFOOD $$

(www.duffyst.com; 202 Main St; mains $10-23; ☺noon-10pm) This place has a divey, peanut-shells-on-the-floor ambience and a raw bar 'happy hour' with 35¢ shrimp.

☆ Entertainment

★ Fat Harold's Beach Club
DANCE

(www.fatharolds.com; 212 Main St; ☺from 4pm Mon & Tue, from 11am Wed-Sun) Folks groove to doo-wop and old-time rock and roll at this North Myrtle institution, which calls itself 'Home of the Shag.' The dance, that is. Free shag lessons are offered at 7pm every Tuesday.

❶ Information

Chapin Memorial Library (www.chapinlibrary.org; 400 14th Ave N; ☎) Internet access.

Visitor Center (☎800-356-3016, 843-626-7444; www.myrtlebeachinfo.com; 1200 N Oak St; ☺8:30am-5pm Mon-Fri, 10am-2pm Sat) Has loads of maps and brochures.

❶ Getting There & Around

The traffic coming and going on Hwy 17 Business/Kings Hwy can be infuriating. To avoid 'the Strand' altogether, stay on the Hwy 17 bypass, or take Hwy 31/Carolina Bays Pkwy, which parallels Hwy 17 between Hwy 501 and Hwy 9.

Myrtle Beach International Airport (MYR; ☎843-448-1589; www.flymyrtlebeach.com; 1100 Jetport Rd) is located within the city limits, as is the **Greyhound** (☎843-448-2472; 511 7th Ave N) station.

Around Myrtle Beach

Fifteen minutes down I-17 is **Pawleys Island**, a narrow strip of pastel sea cottages that's worlds away from the neon of Myrtle Beach. There's not much to do here but kayak and fish, but that's just fine. Another 15 minutes will bring you to mellow **Georgetown**, South Carolina's third-oldest city. Have lunch on Front St, with photogenic 19th-century storefronts overlooking the water, or use it as a quiet jumping-off point for exploring the Francis Marion National Forest.

Greenville & The Upcountry

Cherokee Indians once roamed the state's mountain foothills, which they called 'The Great Blue Hills of God.' The region today is known as the Upcountry. Geographically, it's the spot where the Blue Ridge mountains drop dramatically into meet the Piedmont.

The region is anchored by Greenville, home to one of the most inviting downtowns in the South. The Reedy River twists through the city center, and its dramatic falls tumble beneath Main St at **Falls Park** (www.fallspark.com). Main St itself rolls past a lively array of indie shops, good restaurants and craft-beer pubs. Whimsical quotes, called 'Thoughts on a Walk' dot the sidewalk. Kids will get a kick out of **Mice on Main**, a find-the-bronze-mouse scavenger hunt inspired by the book *Goodnight Moon*. Nibble porchetta and sip wine beside the river at much-lauded **Lazy Goat** (☎864-679-5299; www.thelazygoat.com; 170 River Pl; lunch $5-15, dinner small plates $5-10, dinner mains $12-25; ☺11:30am-9pm Mon-Wed, to 10pm Thu-Sat), a stylish spot known for its Mediterranean small plates. For a welcoming B&B that's close to downtown, try **Pettigru Place** (☎864-242-4529; www.pettigruplace.

EXPLORING SOUTH CAROLINA SWAMPS

Inky-black water, dyed with tannic acid leached from decaying plant matter. Bone-white cypress stumps like the femurs of long-dead giants. Spanish moss as dry and gray as witches' hair. There's nothing like hiking or canoeing through one of South Carolina's unearthly swamps to make you feel like a character in a Southern Gothic novel.

Near Columbia, the 22,000-acre **Congaree National Park** (☑ 803-776-4396; www.nps.gov/cong; 100 National Park Rd, Hopkins; ⊙ visitor center 9am-5pm), America's largest contiguous, old-growth floodplain forest, has camping and free ranger-led canoe trips (reserve in advance). Casual day-trippers can wander the 2.4-mile elevated boardwalk. Look carefully at the cool Blue Sky mural in the visitor center – the scene seems to change as you move.

Between Charleston and Myrtle Beach, **Francis Marion National Forest** (☑ 843-928-3368; www.fs.usda.gov/scnfs; 5821 Hwy 17 N, Awendaw; ⊙ visitor center 9am-5pm Tue-Sat) has 259,000 acres of black-water creeks, camping, and hiking trails, including the 42-mile Palmetto Trail, which runs along old logging routes. Charleston-based **Nature Adventures Outfitters** (☑ 843-568-3222; www.kayakcharleston.com; adult/child half-day $55/39) leads kayak and canoe trips.

com; 302 Pettrigru St; r incl breakfast $145-225; P❋☎).

The region's marquee natural attraction is Table Rock Mountain, a 3124ft-high mountain with a striking granite face. The 7.2-mile round trip hike to its summit at **Table Rock State Park** (☑ 864-878-9813; www.southcarolinaparks.com; 158 Ellison Ln, Pickens; adult/child $2/free; ⊙ 7am-7pm Sun-Thu, to 9pm Fri & Sat, extended hours mid-May–early Nov) is a popular local challenge. For overnight stays, camping is available (campsites $16 to $21), as are cabins built by the Civilian Conservation Corps ($52 to $181).

TENNESSEE

Most states have one official state song. Tennessee has seven. And that's not just a random fact – Tennessee has music deep within its soul. Here, the folk music of the Scots-Irish in the eastern mountains combined with the bluesy rhythms of the African Americans in the western Delta to give birth to the modern country music that makes Nashville famous.

These three geographic regions, represented by the three stars on the Tennessee flag, have their own unique beauty: the heather-colored peaks of the Great Smoky Mountains descend into lush green valleys in the central plateau around Nashville and then onto the hot, sultry lowlands near Memphis.

In Tennessee you can hike shady mountain trails in the morning, and by evening whoop it up in a Nashville honky-tonk or walk the streets of Memphis with Elvis' ghost.

From country churches where snake handlers still speak in tongues, to modern cities where record execs wear their sunglasses at night, Tennesseans are a passionate, diverse lot.

ℹ Information

Department of Environment & Conservation (☑ 888-867-2757; www.state.tn.us/environment/parks) Check out the well-organized website for camping (prices range from free to $27 or more), hiking and fishing info for Tennessee's more than 50 state parks.

Department of Tourist Development (☑ 800-462-8366, 615-741-2159; www.tnvacation.com; 312 8th Ave N, Nashville) Has welcome centers at the state borders.

Memphis

Memphis doesn't just attract tourists. It draws pilgrims. Music-lovers lose themselves to the throb of blues guitar on Beale St. Barbecue connoisseurs descend to stuff themselves psychotic on smoky pulled pork and dry-rubbed ribs. Elvis fanatics fly in to worship at the altar of the King at Graceland. You could spend days hopping from one museum or historic site to another, stopping only for barbecue, and leave happy.

But once you get away from the lights and the tourist buses, Memphis is a different place entirely. Named after the capital of ancient Egypt, it has a certain baroque ruined quality that's both sad and beguiling. Poverty is rampant – Victorian mansions sit beside tumbledown shotgun shacks (a narrow style of house popular in the South), college campuses lie in the shadow of eerie abandoned factories, and whole neighborhoods seem to have been almost reclaimed by kudzu and honeysuckle vines. Memphis' wild river-town spirit reveals itself to visitors willing to look, and wherever you wander, you'll quickly feel the open-hearted warmth of the people.

◎ Sights

◎ Downtown

The pedestrian-only stretch of Beale St is a 24-hour carnival zone, where you'll find deep-fried funnel cakes, to-go beer counters, and music, music, music. Although locals don't hang out here much, visitors tend to get a kick out of it.

★ **National Civil Rights Museum** MUSEUM
(Map p366; www.civilrightsmuseum.org; 450 Mulberry St; adult/student & senior/child $10/9/8; ◎9am-5pm Mon & Wed-Sat, 1-5pm Sun Sep-May, to 6pm Jun-Aug) Housed across the street from the Lorraine Motel, where the Reverend Dr Martin Luther King Jr was fatally shot on April 4, 1968, is the gut-wrenching National Civil Rights Museum. Five blocks south of Beale St, this museum's extensive exhibits and detailed timeline chronicle the struggle for African American freedom and equality. Both Dr King's cultural contribution and his assassination serve as prisms for looking at the Civil Rights movement, its precursors and its continuing impact on American life. The turquoise exterior of the 1950s motel and two preserved interior rooms remain much as they were at the time of King's death, and serve as pilgrimage points in their own right.

Memphis Rock 'n' Soul Museum MUSEUM
(Map p366; ☑901-205-2533; www.memphisrocknsoul.org; cnr Lt George W Lee Ave & 3rd St; adult/child $11/8; ◎10am-7pm) The Smithsonian's museum, next to FedEx Forum, examines how African American and white music mingled in the Mississippi Delta to create the modern rock and soul sound. The audio tour has more than 100 songs.

Gibson Beale Street Showcase FACTORY TOUR
(Map p366; www.gibson.com; 145 Lt George W Lee Ave; admission $10, no children under 5 yr; ◎tours 11am-4pm Mon-Sat, noon-4pm Sun) Take the fascinating 45-minute tour of this enormous place to see master craftspeople transform solid blocks of wood into Stratocasters. Tours leave on the hour.

WC Handy House Museum MUSEUM
(Map p366; ☑901-522-1556; www.wchandymemphis.org; 352 Beale St; adult/child $6/4; ◎11am-4pm Tue-Sat winter, 10am-5pm Tue-Sat summer) On the corner of 4th St, this shotgun shack once belonging to the composer called the 'father of the blues.' He was the first to transpose the 12 bars and later wrote 'Beale Street Blues' in 1916.

Peabody Ducks MARCHING DUCKS
(Map p366; www.peabodymemphis.com; 149 Union Ave; ◎11am & 5pm; 🎔) FREE Every day at 11am sharp, five ducks file from the Peabody Hotel's gilded elevator, waddle across the red-carpeted lobby, and decamp in the marble lobby fountain for a day of happy splashing. The ducks make the reverse march at 5pm, when they retire to their penthouse

---

TENNESSEE FACTS

Nickname Volunteer State

Population 6.35 million

Area 41,217 sq miles

Capital city Nashville (population 641,000)

Other city Memphis (population 634,000)

Sales tax 7%, plus local taxes of up to about 15%

Birthplace of Frontiersman Davy Crockett (1786–1836), soul diva Aretha Franklin (b 1942), singer Dolly Parton (b 1946)

Home of Graceland, Grand Ole Opry, Jack Daniel's distillery

Politics Pretty darn conservative, with liberal hot spots in urban areas

Famous for 'Tennessee Waltz', country music, Tennessee walking horses, soul music

Odd law In Tennessee, it's illegal to fire a gun at any wild game, other than whales, from a moving vehicle

Driving distances Memphis to Nashville 213 miles, Nashville to Great Smoky Mountains National Park 223 miles

accompanied by their red-coated Duckmaster. The march of the ducks dates back to the 1930s and always draws major crowds – get here early to secure your spot (the mezzanine has the best views).

North of Downtown

Mud Island   PARK
(www.mudisland.com; 125 N Front St; ⊘10am-5pm Tue-Sun Apr-Oct, later Jun-Aug; ⊕) FREE A small peninsula jutting into the Mississippi, Mud Island is downtown Memphis' best-loved green space. Hop the monorail ($4, or free with Mississippi River Museum admission) or walk across the bridge to the park, where you can jog and rent bikes.

Mississippi River Museum   MUSEUM
(Map p366; www.mudisland.com/c-3-mississippi-river-museum.aspx; 350 East 3rd St; adult/child $15/10; ⊘10am-5pm Apr-Oct) Located on Mud Island, this place is part Aquarium, part geological and historical examination of America's greatest river. You'll find a full-size replica of a packet boat and a scale model of the lower Mississippi, which includes a Gulf of Mexico aquarium schooling with sharks and rays, where visitors tool around on pedal boats.

Slave Haven Underground
Railroad Museum/Burkle Estate   MUSEUM
(Map p365; ☏901-527-3427; www.slavehaven-undergroundrailroadmuseum.org; 826 N 2nd St; adult/child $10/8; ⊘10am-1pm Mon-Sat) An unimposing clapboard house, it's thought to have been a way station for runaway slaves on the Underground Railroad, complete with trapdoors and tunnels.

East of Downtown

★Sun Studio   STUDIO TOUR
(Map p365; ☏800-441-6249; www.sunstudio.com; 706 Union Ave; adult/child $12/free; ⊘10:30am-5:30pm) It doesn't look like much from outside, but this dusty storefront is ground zero for American rock and roll music. Starting in the early 1950s, Sun's Sam Phillips recorded blues artists such as Howlin' Wolf, BB King and Ike Turner, followed by the rockabilly dynasty of Jerry Lee Lewis, Johnny Cash, Roy Orbison and, of course, the King himself (who started here in 1953).

Packed 40-minute guided tours through the tiny studio offer a chance to hear original tapes of historic recording sessions. Guides are full of anecdotes; you can pose for photos on the 'X' where Elvis once stood,

or buy a CD of the 'Million Dollar Quartet,' Sun's spontaneous 1956 jam session between Elvis, Johnny Cash, Carl Perkins and Jerry Lee Lewis. From here, hop on the studio's free shuttle (hourly, starting at 11:15am), which does a loop between Sun Studio, Beale St and Graceland.

Children's Museum of Memphis   MUSEUM
(Map p365; www.cmom.com; 2525 Central Ave; admission $12; ⊘9am-5pm; ⊕) Gives the kids a chance to let loose and play in, on and with exhibits such as an airplane cockpit, tornado generator and waterwheel. For $5 extra you can maraud through the fun Splash Park, a plaza with over 40 spouts and sprayers that will keep the kids cool and smiling.

Overton Park

Off Poplar Ave in Midtown, stately homes surround this 342-acre rolling green oasis in the middle of this often gritty city. If Beale St is Memphis' heart, then Overton Park is its lungs.

Memphis Zoo   ZOO
(Map p365; www.memphiszoo.org; 2000 Prentiss Pl; adult/child $15/10; ⊘9am-5pm Mar-Oct, to 4pm Nov-Feb; ⊕) At the park's northwestern corner, this world-class zoo hosts two giant panda stars in a $16-million exhibit on native Chinese habitat. Other residents include the full gamut of monkeys, polar bears, penguins, eagles and sea lions.

Brooks Museum of Art   GALLERY
(Map p365; www.brooksmuseum.org; 1934 Poplar Ave; adult/child $7/3; ⊘10am-4pm Wed & Fri, to 8pm Thu, to 5pm Sat, from 11am Sun) A well-regarded art museum on the park's western fringe, the excellent permanent collection encompasses everything from Renaissance sculpture to Impressionists to abstract expressionists.

Levitt Shell   ARCHITECTURE
(Map p365; www.levittshell.org) A historic band shell and the site of Elvis' first concert, in 1954. Today the mod-looking white shell hosts free concerts all summer.

South of Downtown

★Graceland   HISTORIC BUILDING
(Map p365; ☏901-332-3322; www.elvis.com; Elvis Presley Blvd/US 51; tours house only adult/child $33/30, full tour $37/33; ⊘9am-5pm Mon-Sat, to 4pm Sun, shorter hour & closed Tue winter; ℗)

Greater Memphis

If you only make one stop in Memphis, it ought to be here: the sublimely kitschy, gloriously bizarre home of the King of Rock and Roll. Though born in Mississippi, Elvis Presley was a true son of Memphis, raised in the Lauderdale Courts public housing projects, inspired by blues clubs on Beale St, and discovered at Sun Studio. In the spring of 1957, the already-famous 22-year-old spent $100,000 on a Colonial-style mansion, named Graceland by its previous owners.

The King himself had the place, ahem, redecorated in 1974. With a 15ft couch, fake waterfall, yellow vinyl walls and green shag-carpet ceiling – it's a virtual textbook of ostentatious '70s style. You'll begin your tour at the visitor plaza on the other side of Elvis Presley Blvd. Book ahead in the busy season to ensure a prompt tour time. The basic self-guided mansion tour comes with an engaging headset audio narration. Pay just $4 extra to see the car museum, and

two custom planes (check out the blue-and-gold private bathroom on the *Lisa Marie*, a Convair 880 Jet).

Priscilla Presley (who divorced Elvis in 1973) opened Graceland to tours in 1982, and now millions come here to pay homage to the King who died here (in the upstairs bathroom) from heart failure in 1977. Throngs of fans still weep at his grave, next to the swimming pool out back. Graceland is 9 miles south of Downtown on US 51, also called 'Elvis Presley Blvd.' You can also hop on the free shuttle from Sun Studio. Parking costs $10.

★ Stax Museum of American Soul Music
MUSEUM

(Map p365; ☎ 901-942-7685; www.staxmuseum. com; 926 E McLemore Ave; adult/child $12/9; ⊙10am-5pm Tue-Sat, 1-5pm Sun Mar-Oct, closed Mon Nov-Mar) Wanna get funky? Head directly to Soulsville USA, where this 17,000-sq-ft museum sits on the site of the old Stax

Memphis

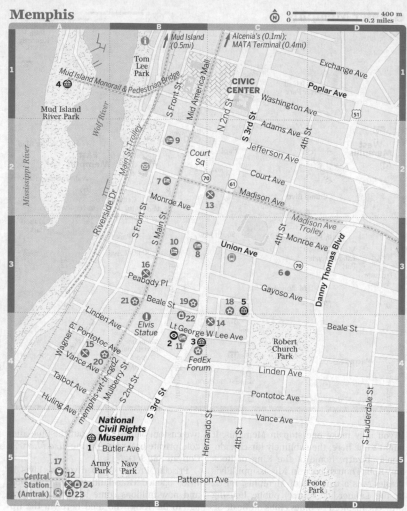

THE SOUTH MEMPHIS

recording studio. This venerable spot was soul music's epicenter in the 1960s, when Otis Redding, Booker T and the MGs and Wilson Pickett recorded here. Dive into soul music history with photos, displays of '60s and '70s peacock clothing and, above all, Isaac Hayes' 1972 Superfly Cadillac outfitted with shag-fur and 24-carat-gold exterior trim.

Full Gospel Tabernacle Church   CHURCH
(www.algreenmusic.com; 787 Hale Rd; ☺ services 11:30am & 4pm Sun) If you're in town on a Sunday, put on your smell goods and head to services in South Memphis, where soul

music legend turned reverend Al Green presides over a powerful choir. Visitors are welcome, and usually take up about half the pews. Join in the whooping 'hallelujahs,' but don't forget the tithe (a few bucks is fine). Green is not around every weekend, but services are a fascinating cultural experience nonetheless.

☞ Tours

★ **American Dream Safari**   CULTURE
(☎ 901-527-8870; www.americandreamsafari. com; walking tour per person $15, driving tours per vehicle from $200) Southern culture junkie

Memphis

Tad Pierson shows you the quirky, personal side of Memphis – juke joints, gospel churches, decaying buildings – on foot or in his pink Cadillac. Ask about day trips to the Delta and special photography tours.

Blues City Tours   BUS TOUR
(Map p366; 🖋 901-522-9229; www.bluescitytours.com; adult/child from $24/19) A variety of themed bus tours, including an Elvis tour and a Memphis Music Tour.

✯✯ Festivals & Events

Trolley Night   ART WALK
(www.southmainmemphis.net; S Main St; per person $10; ⊙6-9pm last Fri of month) On Trolley Night galleries on South Main stay open late, and pour wine for the people.

★ Beale Street Music Festival   MUSIC
(www.memphisinmay.org; Tom Lee Park; 3-day pass $85; ⊙1st weekend in May) You've heard of Coachella, New Orleans Jazz Fest and Bonnaroo, but Memphis' Beale Street Music Festival gets very little attention, though it offers one of the country's best line-ups of old school blues masters, up-and-coming rockers and gloriously past their prime pop and hip-hop artists.

It runs over three days and attracts 100,000 people.

International Blues Challenge   MUSIC
(www.blues.org; ⊙Jan/Feb) Sponsored by the Blues Foundation, blues acts do battle in front of a panel of judges.

Memphis in May   CULTURAL
(www.memphisinmay.org; ⊙May) Every Friday, Saturday and Sunday in May, something's cookin', whether it's the Beale Street Music Festival (p367), the barbecue contest or the grand-finale sunset symphony.

⊨ Sleeping

Chain motels lie off I-40, exit 279, across the river in West Memphis, AR. Prices jump during the Memphis in May festival.

⊨ Downtown

★ Talbot Heirs   GUESTHOUSE $$
(Map p366; 🖋 901-527-9772, 800-955-3956; www.talbothouse.com; 99 S 2nd St; ste from $130; ❁ 🛜) Inconspicuously located on the 2nd floor of a busy Downtown street, this cheerful guesthouse is one of Memphis' best kept and most unique secrets. Spacious suites are more like hip studio apartments than hotel rooms, with Asian rugs and funky local artwork, and kitchens stocked with snacks.

When big stars, like Harvey Keitel, Kathy Bates or Eric Clapton are in town, they nest here. Parking costs $10.

WORTH A TRIP

JACK DANIEL'S DISTILLERY

The irony of the **Jack Daniel's Distillery** (www.jackdaniels.com; Rte 1; ⊙ 9am-4:30pm) **FREE** being in a 'dry county' is lost on no one – local liquor laws dictate that no hard stuff can be sold within county lines, but they do give out small samples on their free hour-long tours. For $10 you can take a two-hour Distillery Tour (book in advance), where you'll get a more generous sample. The oldest registered distillery in the US, the folks at Jack Daniels have been dripping whiskey through layers of charcoal then aging it in oak barrels since 1866. It's located off Hwy 55 in tiny Lynchburg.

Sleep Inn at Court Square HOTEL **$$**
(Map p366; ☑ 901-522-9700; www.sleepinn.com; 400 N Front St; r from $114; P ❋ ❄) Our pick of the cheaper Downtown digs, this stubby stucco box, part of a jumble of corporate sleeps, has pleasant, airy rooms with flat-screen TVs. Parking is $12.

Madison Hotel BOUTIQUE **$$$**
(Map p366; ☑ 901-333-1200; www.madison-hotelmemphis.com; 79 Madison Ave; r from $264; P ❋ @ ❄ ☲) If you're looking for a sleek treat, check in to this swanky, boutique sleep. The rooftop garden is one of the best places in town to watch a sunset, and rooms have nice touches, like high ceilings, Italian linens and whirlpool tubs.

Peabody Hotel HOTEL **$$$**
(Map p366; ☑ 901-529-4000; www.peabodymemphis.com; 149 Union Ave; r from $229; ❋ ❄ ☲) The city's most storied hotel has been catering to a who's who of Southern gentry since the 1860s. The current incarnation, a 13-story Italian Renaissance Revival–style building, dates to the 1920s, and it remains a social center, with a spa, shops, various restaurants and an atmospheric marble-and-gold lobby bar. The daily march of the lobby fountain's resident ducks (p363) is a Memphis tradition.

Westin Memphis
Beale Street Hotel HOTEL **$$$**
(Map p366; ☑ 901-334-5900; www.westinmemphisbealestreet.com; 170 Lt George W Lee Ave; r from $189) Directly across from the FedEx Forum and the gateway to Beale St, this is Memphis' newest and flashiest hotel. Spacious rooms have all the four-star trimmings and excellent service.

🛏 East of Downtown

Pilgrim House Hostel HOSTEL **$**
(☑ 901-273-8341; www.pilgrimhouse.org; 1000 S Cooper St; dm $20, r $30-50; P ❋ @ ❄) Yes, it's in a church. No, no one will try to convert you. Dorms and private rooms are clean and spare. An international crowd plays cards and chats (no alcohol) in a sunny, open common area resembling an IKEA catalog, and all guests must do a brief daily chore, like taking out the trash.

🛏 South of Downtown

Memphis Graceland
RV Park & Campground CAMPGROUND **$**
(☑ 901-396-7125; www.elvis.com; 3691 Elvis Presley Blvd; tent sites/cabins from $27/51; P ❋ ❄) Keep Lisa Marie in business when you camp out or sleep in the no-frills log cabins (with shared bathrooms) next to Graceland.

Heartbreak Hotel HOTEL **$$**
(☑ 877-777-0606, 901-332-1000; www.elvis.com/epheartbreakhotel/; 3677 Elvis Presley Blvd; d from $120; ❋ @ ❄) At the end of Lonely St (seriously) across from Graceland, this basic hotel is tarted up with all things Elvis. Ramp up the already-palpable kitsch with one of the themed suites, such as the red-velvet Burnin' Love room.

Days Inn Graceland MOTEL **$$**
(☑ 901-346-5500; www.daysinn.com; 3839 Elvis Presley Blvd; r from $104; P ❋ ❄) With a guitar-shaped pool, gold records and Elvis memorabilia in the lobby and neon Cadillacs on the roof, the Days Inn manages to out-Elvis the neighboring Heartbreak Hotel. Guest rooms themselves are clean but nothing special. You'll need wheels or to depend upon the shuttle to get Downtown.

🍴 Eating

Locals come to blows over which of the city's chopped-pork sandwiches or dry-rubbed ribs are the best. Barbecue joints are scattered across the city; the ugliest exteriors often yield the tastiest goods. Hip young locals head to the South Main Arts District or Midtown's Cooper-Young neighborhood, a hip bloom of tasty restaurants and bars.

Downtown

Gus's World Famous Fried Chicken
CHICKEN $

(Map p366; ☑901-527-4877; 310 S Front St; mains $6-9; ⊙11am-9pm Sun-Thu, to 10pm Fri & Sat) Fried-chicken connoisseurs across the globe twitch in their sleep at night, dreaming about the gossamer-light fried chicken at this Downtown concrete bunker with the fun, neon-lit interior and vintage juke box. On busy nights, waits can top an hour.

Alcenia's
SOUTHERN $

(www.alcenias.com; 317 N Main St; mains $6-9; ⊙11am-5pm Tue-Fri, 9am-3pm Sat) The only thing sweeter than Alcenia's famous 'ghetto juice' (a diabetes-inducing fruit drink) is owner Betty-Joyce 'BJ' Chester-Tamayo – don't be surprised to receive a kiss on the top of the head as soon as you sit down. The lunch menu at this funky little gold- and purple-painted cafe rotates daily – look for killer fried chicken and catfish, melt-in-your-mouth spiced cabbage and an exquisite eggy custard pie.

Arcade
DINER $

(Map p366; www.arcaderestaurant.com; 540 S Main St; mains $8-10; ⊙7am-3pm, plus dinner Fri) Elvis used to eat at this ultra-retro diner, Memphis' oldest. Crowds still pack in for sublime sweet-potato pancakes – as fluffy, buttery and addictive as advertised. The rest of the dishes are standard greasy-spoon fare.

Dyer's
FAST FOOD $

(Map p366; www.dyersonbeale.com; 205 Beale St; burgers $4-7; ⊙11am-midnight Sun-Thu, to late Fri & Sat) Purportedly one of America's best burgers – annointed so by both *Esquire* and *Playboy* – the meat is smacked flat with a spatula at least 4in wide then submerged in bubbling grease, which is continuously filtered like it is a life-giving elixir when, well, it's probably the opposite.

Charlie Vergos' Rendezvous
BARBECUE $$

(Map p366; ☑901-523-2746; www.hogsfly.com; 52 S 2nd St; mains $10-20; ⊙4:30-10:30pm Tue-Thu, 11am-11pm Fri, from 11:30am Sat) Tucked in an alleyway off Union Ave, this subterranean institution sells an astonishing 5 tons of its exquisite dry-rubbed ribs weekly. The ribs don't come with any sauce, but the pork shoulder does, so try a combo and you'll have plenty of sauce to enjoy. The beef brisket is also tremendous. With a superb, no-nonsense wait staff, and walls plastered with historic memorabilia, eating here is an event. Expect a wait.

Majestic Grille
CONTINENTAL $$$

(Map p366; ☑901-522-8555; www.majesticgrille. com; 145 S Main St; mains $17-36; ⊙11am-10pm Mon-Thu, to 11pm Fri & Sat, to 9pm Sun) Set in an old silent-movie theater, with pre-talkie black and whites strobing in the handsome dark-wood dining room, here is classic continental fare, from roasted half chickens, to seared tuna and grilled pork tenderloin, and four varieties of hand-cut filet mignon. Just a stone's throw from Beale St.

East of Downtown

Bar DKDC
GASTROPUB $

(www.facebook.com/BARDKDC; 964 S Cooper St; dishes $3-8; ⊙5pm-3am Wed-Sun) It's all tapas here, and the food is cheap and flavorful. Per the menu's suggestions, 'begin' with sugarcane shrimp, 'continue' with an island jerk fish club sandwich, 'keep going' with jerk chicken or lamb chops or a guava-glazed pork chop. The space sports an eclectic decor, chalkboard wine list, and friendly bartenders.

Payne's Bar-B-Q
BARBECUE $

(1762 Lamar Ave; sandwihes $4-7, plates $7-9; ⊙11am-6:30pm Tue-Sat) We'd say this converted gas station has the best chopped-pork sandwich in town, but we don't want to have to fight anyone. Decide for yourself.

Neely's Interstate Bar-B-Q
BARBECUE $

(☑901-775-1045; www.interstatebarbecue.com; 2265 S 3rd St; mains $8-20; ⊙11am-11pm Sun-Thu, to midnight Fri & Sat; 👪) Two words: barbecued spaghetti. It's just as weird as it sounds, but not half bad. Jim Neely's ribs and chopped-shoulder sandwiches are superb, so is the smoked turkey, and the atmosphere is homey and family-friendly.

★ Cozy Corner
BARBECUE $$

(www.cozycornerbbq.com; 745 N Pkwy; mains $7-12; ⊙11am-9pm Tue-Sat) Slouch in a torn vinyl booth and devour an entire barbecued Cornish game hen, the house specialty at this pug-ugly cult favorite. Ribs and wings are spectacular too, and the fluffy, silken sweet-potato pie is an A-plus specimen of the classic Southern dessert.

Alchemy
SOUTHERN TAPAS $$

(☑901-726-4444; www.alchemymemphis.com; 940 S Cooper St; tapas $10-13, mains $23-28;

☺ 4pm-1am Mon-Sat, to 10pm Sun) A flash spot in the Cooper-Young district, serving tasty southern tapas like diver scallops with truffled cauliflower purée, roasted asparagus with Benton's bacon, and cornmeal dusted and flash-fried calamari. The kitchen stays open until 1am.

Soul Fish Cafe SEAFOOD **$$**
(☑ 901-755-6988; www.soulfishcafe.com; 862 S Cooper St; mains $10-13; ☺ 11am-10pm Mon-Sat, to 9pm Sun) A cute cinderblock cafe in the Cooper-Young neighborhood, known for delectable po'boys, fried fish plates and, in a departure, some rather indulgent cakes.

Restaurant Iris NEW SOUTHERN **$$$**
(☑ 901-590-2828; www.restaurantiris.com; 2146 Monroe Ave; mains $25-37; ☺ 5-10pm Mon-Sat) Chef Kelly English crafts special, avant-garde Southern fusion dishes that delight foodies, hence the James Beard noms. He's got a fried-oyster-stuffed steak, a sublime shrimp 'n' grits and an American Kobe beef garnished with aloo gobi and mint chutney. There's brunch on the third Sunday of each month.

Sweet Grass SOUTHERN **$$$**
(☑ 901-278-0278; www.sweetgrassmemphis.com; 937 S Cooper St; mains $21-27; ☺ 5:30pm-late Tue-Sun, 11am-2pm Sun) Contemporary Low Country cuisine (the seafood-heavy cooking of the South Carolina and Georgia coasts) wins raves at this sleek new Midtown bistro. Shrimp and grits, a classic fisherman's breakfast, is a crowd-pleaser. However, the vibe can be a bit stuffy.

⊕ Drinking & Nightlife

Last call for alcohol is 3am, but bars do close early on quiet nights.

★ **Earnestine & Hazel's** BAR
(Map p366; 531 S Main St) One of the great dive bars in Memphis has a 2nd floor full of rusty bedsprings and claw-foot tubs, remnants of its brothel past. The Soul Burger, the bar's only food, is the stuff of legend. Things heat up after midnight.

Cove BAR
(www.thecovememphis.com; 2559 Broad Ave) This hipsterish new dive rocks a nautical theme while serving retro cocktails and upscale bar snacks (oysters on the half shell, chips with fresh anchovies). A good place to meet locals.

☆ Entertainment

Beale St is the obvious spot for live blues, rock and jazz. There's no cover for most clubs, or it's only a few bucks, and the bars are open all day, while neighborhood clubs tend to start filling up around 10pm. To find out the latest, check the Memphis Flyer (p371) online calendar.

★ **FedEx Forum** SPORTS ARENA
(Map p366; ☑ box office 901-205-2640; www.fedexforum.com; 191 Beale St, Beale Street Entertainment District) A Downtown arena home to the Memphis Grizzlies, the city's only major professional sports team. Memphis does love their basketball squad, and this place gets electric loud when the team is rolling. It hosts big-name concerts too.

Wild Bill's BLUES
(1580 Vollentine Ave; ☺ 10pm-late Fri & Sat) Don't even think of showing up at this gritty, hole-in-the-wall before midnight. Order a 40oz beer and a basket of wings then sit back to watch some of the greatest blues acts in Memphis. Expect some stares from the locals; it's worth it for the kick-ass, ultra-authentic jams.

Hi-Tone Cafe LIVE MUSIC
(www.hitonememphis.com; 1913 Poplar Ave) Near Overton Park, this unassuming little dive is one of the city's best places to hear live local bands and touring indie acts.

Young Avenue Deli LIVE MUSIC
(www.youngavenuedeli.com; 2119 Young Ave; ☺ 11am-3pm Mon-Sat, from 11:30am Sun) This Midtown favorite has food, pool, occasional live music and a laid-back young crowd.

New Daisy Theater LIVE MUSIC
(Map p366; ☑ 901-525-8971, events hotline 901-525-8979; www.newdaisy.com; 330 Beale St; ☺ varies) Where popular indie acts like Minus the Bear, Gorilla, and Napalm Death (their band, their name) perform on Beale St.

Rum Boogie BLUES
(Map p366; ☑ 912-528-0150; www.rumboogie.com; 182 Beale St) Huge, popular and loud, this Cajun-themed Beale club hops every night to the tunes of a tight house blues band.

Rumba Room DANCE
(Map p366; www.memphisrumbaroom.com; 303 S Main St; ☺ 7:30-11:30pm Mon, 6pm-2am Thu, 6:30pm-3am Fri, 8pm-3am Sat, to 1am Sun) Crave something other than the blues? This arts district ballroom hosts DJs, swing and salsa

nights that will get you spinning and twirling like a pro after a few drinks.

The Orpheum
VENUE

(Map p366; ☑901-525-7800; www.orpheum-memphis.com; 203 S Main St; ☉times vary) Broadway shows and big-name concerts in historic, 1928 environs. Its walk of fame glitters out front, and beware the ghost of a pigtailed little girl named Mary, said to giggle eerily between acts.

🛍 Shopping

Beale St abounds with cheesy souvenir shops, while Cooper-Young is the place for boutiques and bookshops. The streets around South Main have been branded an arts district. That's where some of the most interesting shopping happens these days, and it has a monthly Trolley Night (p367) too.

★Hoot & Louise
VINTAGE

(Map p366; www.facebook.com/hootandlouise; 109 GE Patterson Ave; ☉10:30am-6:30pm Mon-Sat, noon-5pm Sun) This store combines new vintage-inspired design with affordable and classic vintage pieces, along with quirky jewelry. Brand new, the space is special in its own right.

A Schwab's
GIFTS

(Map p366; ☑901-523-9782; www.a-schwab.com; 163 Beale St; ☉noon-7pm Mon-Wed, to 9pm Thu, to 10pm Fri & Sat) It has everything from denim shirts to flasks to rubber duckies to fine hats to overalls. But the real attractions are the antiques upstairs. Think: vintage scales and irons, hat stretchers and a cast-iron anchor of a cash register.

D'Edge
GALLERY

(Map p366; www.dedgeart.com; 550 S Main St; ☉11am-5pm) A colorful art gallery with a whimsical, musical soul, combining classic Mississippi Delta–inspired, African American art with creative landscapes. Here is fun, exuberant art of the people for the people.

Lanksy Brothers
CLOTHING

(Map p366; ☑901-529-9070; www.lanskybros. com; 149 Union Ave; ☉9am-6pm Sun-Wed, to 9pm Thu-Sat) The 'Clothier to the King,' this mid-century men's shop once outfitted Elvis with his two-tone shirts. Today it has a retro line of menswear, plus gifts and women's clothes. It's located in the Peabody Hotel.

ℹ Information

Almost all hotels, and many restaurants, have free wi-fi.

Commercial Appeal (www.commercialappeal. com) Daily newspaper with local entertainment listings.

Main Post Office (Map p366; 555 S 3rd St)

Memphis Flyer (www.memphisflyer.com) Free weekly distributed on Thursday; has entertainment listings.

Police Station (☑901-545-2677; 545 S Main St)

Public Library (www.memphislibrary.org; 33 S Front St; ☉10am-5pm Mon-Fri) Computers with free internet access.

Regional Medical Center at Memphis (☑901-545-7100; www.the-med.org; 877 Jefferson Ave) Has the only level-one trauma center in the region.

Tennessee State Visitor Center (Map p366; ☑888-633-9099, 901-543-5333; www. memphistravel.com; 119 N Riverside Dr; ☉9am-5pm Nov-Mar, to 6pm Apr-Oct) Brochures for the whole state.

ℹ Getting There & Around

Memphis International Airport (MEM; ☑901-922-8000; www.memphisairport.org; 2491 Winchester Rd) is 12 miles southeast of Downtown via I-55; taxis to Downtown cost about $30.

Memphis Area Transit Authority (MATA; www. matatransit.com; 444 N Main St; fares $1.75) operates local buses; buses 2 and 32 go to the airport.

MATA's vintage **trolleys** ($1, every 12 minutes) ply Main St and Front St downtown. **Greyhound** (Map p366; www.greyhound.com; 203 Union Ave) is right downtown, as is **Central Station** (www.amtrak.com; 545 S Main St), the Amtrak terminal.

Shiloh National Military Park

'No soldier who took part in the two day Battle at Shiloh ever spoiled for a fight again,' said one veteran of the bloody 1862 clash, which took place among these lovely fields and forests. Ulysses S Grant, then a major general, led the Army of Tennessee. After a vicious Confederate assault on the first day that took Grant by surprise, his creative maneuver on the second day held Pittsburgh Landing, and turned the Confederates back. During the fight over 3500 soldiers died and nearly 24,000 were wounded. A relative unknown at the beginning of the war, Grant went on to lead the Union to victory and eventually became the 18th president of the United States.

The vast **Shiloh National Military Park** (www.nps.gov/shil; 1055 Pittsburg Landing Rd; ☺ park dawn-dusk, visitor center 8am-5pm) **FREE** is located just north of the Mississippi border near the town of Crump, TN, and can only be seen by car. Sights include the Shiloh National Cemetery, and an overlook of the Cumberland River where Union reinforcement troops arrived by ship. The visitor center gives out maps, shows a video about the battle, and sells an audio driving tour.

Nashville

Imagine you're an aspiring country singer arriving in downtown Nashville after days of hitchhiking, with nothing but your battered guitar on your back. Gaze up at the neon lights of Lower Broadway, take a deep breath of smoky, beer-perfumed air, feel the boot-stompin' rumble from deep inside the crowded honky-tonks, and say to yourself 'I've made it.'

For country-music fans and wannabe songwriters all over the world, a trip to Nashville is the ultimate pilgrimage. Since the 1920s the city has been attracting musicians who have taken the country genre from the 'hillbilly music' of the early 20th century to the slick 'Nashville sound' of the 1960s to the punk-tinged alt-country of the 1990s.

Its many musical attractions range from the Country Music Hall of Fame to the revered Grand Ole Opry to Jack White's niche of a record label. It also has a lively university community, some excellent down-home grub, and some seriously kitschy souvenirs.

◎ Sights

◎ Downtown

The historic 2nd Ave N business area was the center of the cotton trade in the 1870s and 1880s, when most of the Victorian warehouses were built; note the cast-iron and masonry facades. Today it's the heart of the **District**, with shops, restaurants, underground saloons and nightclubs. It's a bit like the French Quarter meets Hollywood Boulevard drenched in bourbon and country twang. Two blocks west, **Printers Alley** is a narrow cobblestoned lane known for its nightlife since the 1940s. Along the Cumber-

land River, **Riverfront Park** is a landscaped promenade, featuring Fort Nashborough, a replica of the city's original outpost. The brand-new **Music City Center** (www.nashvillemusiccitycenter.com; Broadway St btwn 5th & 8th Aves) convention and events complex looks up-to-the-nanosecond modern.

★ **Country Music Hall of Fame & Museum**   MUSEUM
(www.countrymusichalloffame.com; 222 5th Ave S; adult/child $22/14, audio tour additional $2, Studio B 1hr tour adult/child $13/11; ☺ 9am-5pm) 'Honor Thy Music' is the catchphrase of this monumental museum, reflecting the near-biblical importance of country music to Nashville's soul. Gaze at Patsy Cline's cocktail gown, Hank Williams' guitar, Elvis' gold Cadillac and Conway Twitty's yearbook picture (back when he was Harold Jenkins).

Written exhibits trace country's roots, computer touch screens access recordings and photos from the enormous archives, and the fact- and music-filled audio tour is narrated by contemporary stars. From here you can also take the Studio B Tour, which shuttles you to Radio Corporation of America's (RCA's) famed Music Row studio, where Elvis recorded 'Are You Lonesome Tonight?' and Dolly Parton cut 'I Will Always Love You.'

Ryman Auditorium   HISTORIC BUILDING
(www.ryman.com; 116 5th Ave N; self-guided tour adult/child $13/6.50, backstage tour $17/10.50; ☺ 9am-4pm) The so-called 'Mother Church of Country Music' has hosted a laundry list of 20th-century performers, from Martha Graham to Elvis to Katherine Hepburn to Bob Dylan. The soaring brick tabernacle was built in 1890 by wealthy riverboat captain Thomas Ryman to house religious revivals, and watching a show from one of its 2000 seats can still be described as a spiritual experience.

The Grand Ole Opry took place here for 31 years, until it moved out to the Opryland complex in Music Valley in 1974. Today the Opry returns to the Ryman during winter.

Tennessee State Capitol   HISTORIC BUILDING
(www.tnmuseum.org; Charlotte Ave; ☺ tours 9am-4pm Mon-Fri) **FREE** At the northeast edge of downtown, this 1845 Greek Revival building was built from local limestone and marble by slaves and prison inmates working alongside European artisans. Around back, steep stairs lead down to the **Tennessee Bicen-**

tennial Mall, whose outdoor walls are covered with historical facts about Tennessee's history, and the wonderful daily **Farmers Market**.

Tennessee State Museum   MUSEUM
(www.tnmuseum.org; 5th Ave, btwn Union & Deaderick Sts; ⊙10am-5pm Tue-Sat, 1-5pm Sun) FREE For history buffs, this engaging but not flashy museum on the ground floor of a massive office tower, offers a worthy look at the state's past, with Native American handicrafts, a life-size log cabin and quirky historical artifacts such as President Andrew Jackson's inaugural hat. Rotating exhibits pass through, as well.

Frist Center for the Visual Arts   GALLERY
(www.fristcenter.org; 919 Broadway; adult/senior/child $10/7/free; ⊙10am-5:30pm Mon-Wed & Sat, to 9pm Thu & Fri, 1-5pm Sun) A top-notch art museum and complex hosting traveling exhibitions of everything from American folk art to Picasso in the grand, refurbished post-office building. There was a Rembrandt show on when we passed through.

Fort Nashborough   FORT
(1st Ave) Down along the banks of the Cumberland River is a reconstruction of a late-18th-century wooden fort, the first flagpost of a pioneer settlement that later became Nashville.

⊙ West End

Along West End Ave, starting at 21st Ave, sits prestigious **Vanderbilt University**, founded in 1883 by railway magnate Cornelius Vanderbilt. The 330-acre campus buzzes with some 12,000 students, and student culture influences much of Midtown's vibe.

Parthenon   PARK, GALLERY
(www.parthenon.org; 2600 West End Ave; adult/child $6/4; ⊙9am-4:30pm Tue-Sat, plus Sun summer) Yes, that is indeed a reproduction Athenian Parthenon sitting in **Centennial Park**. Originally built in 1897 for Tennessee's Centennial Exposition and rebuilt in 1930 due to popular demand, the full-scale plaster copy of the 438 BC original now houses an art museum with a collection of American paintings and a 42ft statue of the Greek goddess Athena.

Music Row   NEIGHBORHOOD
(Music Sq West & Music Sq East) Just west of downtown, sections of 16th and 17th Aves, called Music Sq West and Music Sq East,

LOCAL KNOWLEDGE

FIVE POINTS

Five Points in East Nashville is the epicenter of a new hipster scene, and despite all appearances, this is actually the old part of town. Yes, Nashville originally developed east of the Cumberland River but after a great fire the folks moved across the river where downtown presently stands. These days, Five Points is sprinkled with cafes and restaurants, with most of the action focused on Woodlawn Ave between 10th and 11th.

are home to the production companies, agents, managers and promoters who run Nashville's country-music industry. There's not much to see, but you can pay to cut your own record at some of the smaller studios, and the famed RCA Studio B is here too.

RCA Studio B   LANDMARK
(www.countrymusichalloffame.org; 1611 Roy Acuff Pl; tours adult/child $35/26) One of Music Row's most historic studios, this is where Elvis, the Everly Brothers and Dolly Parton all recorded numerous hits. It's marked by the Heartbreak Hotel guitar sculpture emblazoned with a pelvis jutting image of the King. You can tour the studio via the Country Music Hall of Fame's (p372) Studio B Tour, included with the Platinum Package.

⊙ Music Valley

This suburban tourist zone is about 10 miles northeast of downtown at Hwy 155/Briley Pkwy, exits 11 and 12B, and reachable by bus.

Grand Ole Opry House   MUSEUM
(☏615-871-6779; www.opry.com; 2802 Opryland Dr; tours adult/child $18.50/13.50; ⊙museum 10:30am-6pm Mar-Dec) This unassuming modern brick building seats 4400 for the Grand Ole Opry (p380) on Friday and Saturday from March to November. Guided backstage tours are offered daily by reservation – book online up to two weeks ahead. Across the plaza, a small, free **museum** tells the story of the Opry with wax characters, colorful costumes and dioramas.

Nashville

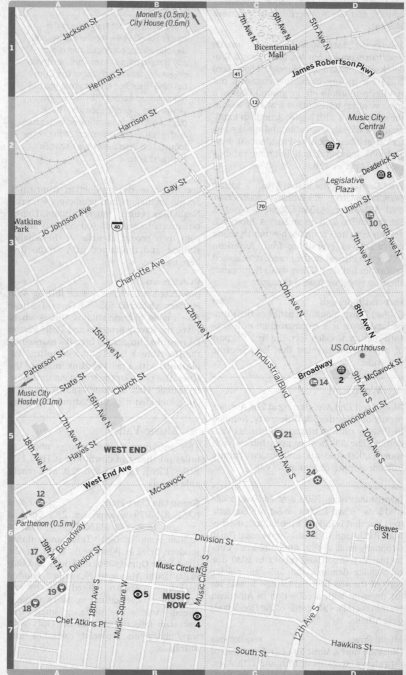

Monell's (0.5mi);
City House (0.6mi)

Jackson St

Herman St

Harrison St

Gay St

Watkins Park

Jo Johnson Ave

Charlotte Ave

Patterson St

State St

Music City Hostel (0.1mi)

Church St

Parthenon (0.5 mi)

WEST END

West End Ave

McGavock

Hayes St

Broadway

Division St

19th Ave N

Chet Atkins Pl

18th Ave S

Music Square W

MUSIC ROW

Music Circle N

Music Circle S

Division St

7th Ave N

6th Ave N

5th Ave N

Bicentennial Mall

James Robertson Pkwy

Music City Central

Legislative Plaza

Deaderick St

Union St

6th Ave N

7th Ave N

10th Ave N

8th Ave N

US Courthouse

9th McGavock St

Broadway

9th Ave S

Industrial Blvd

12th Ave N

15th Ave N

16th Ave N

17th Ave N

18th Ave N

12th Ave S

12th Ave S

Demonbreun St

10th Ave S

Gleaves St

Hawkins St

South St

12th Ave S

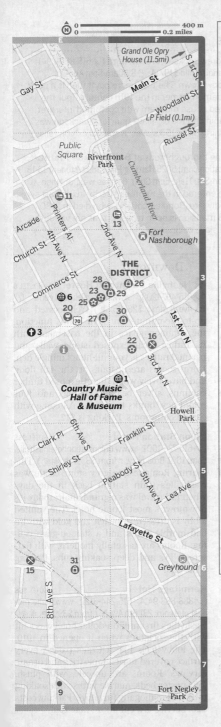

Nashville

◎ Top Sights
1 Country Music Hall of Fame & Museum F4

◎ Sights
2 Frist Center for the Visual Arts D4
3 Music City Center E4
4 Music Row.. B7
5 RCA Studio B..................................... B7
6 Ryman Auditorium E3
7 Tennessee State Capitol.................... D2
8 Tennessee State Museum.................. D2

⊕ Activities, Courses & Tours
9 NashTrash E7

⊜ Sleeping
10 Hermitage Hotel............................... D3
11 Hotel Indigo E2
12 Hutton Hotel A6
13 Nashville Downtown Hostel.............. F2
14 Union Station Hotel D4

⊗ Eating
15 Arnold's... E6
16 Southern F4
17 Tavern A6

⊖ Drinking & Nightlife
18 Rebar A7
19 Soulshine A7
20 Tootsie's Orchid Lounge................... E3
21 Whiskey Kitchen...............................C5

✪ Entertainment
22 Nashville Symphony.......................... F4
23 Robert's Western World E3
   Ryman Auditorium ....(see 6)
24 Station Inn D5
25 Tootsie's Orchid Lounge................... E3

⊟ Shopping
26 Boot Country F3
27 Ernest Tubb E3
28 Gruhn Guitars E3
29 Hatch Show Print F3
30 Johnny Cash Museum Store.............. F3
31 Third Man Records E6
32 Two Old Hippies D6

THE SOUTH NASHVILLE

WORTH A TRIP

PLANTATIONS NEAR NASHVILLE

The former home of seventh president Andrew Jackson, **Hermitage** (☑615-889-2941; www.thehermitage.com; 4580 Rachel's Lane; adult/child $19/14; ⊗8:30am-5pm Apr-Oct, 9am-4:30pm Oct-Mar), lies 15 miles east of downtown. The 1000-acre plantation is a peek into what life was like for a Mid-South gentleman farmer in the 19th century. Tour the Federal-style brick mansion, now a furnished house museum with costumed interpreters, and see Jackson's original 1804 log cabin and the old slave quarters (Jackson was a lifelong supporter of slavery, at times owning up to 150 slaves; a special exhibit tells their stories).

The Harding-Jackson family began raising thoroughbreds at **Belle Meade Plantation** (☑615-356-0501; www.bellemeadeplantation.com; 5025 Harding Pike; adult/student 13-18 yr/child under 13 yr $16/10/8; ⊗9am-5pm Mon-Sat, 11am-5pm Sun), 6 miles west of Nashville, in the early 1800s. Nearly every horse entered in the Kentucky Derby in the past six years is a descendant of Belle Meade's studly sire, Bonnie Scotland, who died in 1880. Yes, Bonnie can be a boy's name! The 1853 mansion is open to visitors, as are various interesting outbuildings, including a model slave cabin.

☞ Tours

★ NashTrash
BUS TOUR
(☑615-226-7300; www.nashtrash.com; 900 8th Ave N; 1½hr tours $35) The big-haired 'Jugg Sisters' lead a campy frolic through the risqué side of Nashville history while guests sip BYO booze on the big pink bus. Buy in advance: tours can sell out *months* in advance.

Tommy's Tours
BUS TOUR
(☑615-335-2863; www.tommystours.com; tours from $35) Wisecracking local Tommy Garmon leads highly entertaining three-hour tours of country-music sights.

General Jackson Showboat
BOAT TOUR
(☑615-458-3900; www.generaljackson.com; tours from $45) Paddleboat sightseeing cruises of varying length on the Cumberland River, some with music and food.

✰ Festivals & Events

CMA Music Festival
MUSIC
(www.cmafest.com; ⊗Jun) Draws tens of thousands of country-music fans to town.

Tennessee State Fair
FAIR
(www.tennesseestatefair.org; ⊗Sep) Nine days of racing pigs, mule-pulls and cake bake-offs.

🛏 Sleeping

Bargain-bin chain motels cluster on all sides of downtown, along I-40 and I-65. Music Valley has a glut of family-friendly midprice chains.

Downtown

★ Nashville Downtown Hostel
HOSTEL $
(☑615-497-1208; www.nashvillehostel.com; 177 1st Ave N; dm/r $28/85; ℗) Well located and up-to-the-minute in style and function, the common space in the basement with its rather regal exposed stone walls and beamed rafters is your all-hours mingle den. Dorm rooms are upstairs on the 4th floor, and have lovely wood floors, exposed timber columns, silver beamed ceilings and four brand new bunks to a room. All come with shared bathrooms. Parking is $12.

Union Station Hotel
HOTEL $$$
(☑615-726-1001; www.unionstationhotelnashville. com; 1001 Broadway; r from $359; ℗❋🛜) This soaring Romanesque grey stone castle was Nashville's train station back in the days when rail travel was a grand affair; today it's downtown's most iconic hotel. The vaulted lobby is dressed in peach and gold with inlaid marble floors and a stained-glass ceiling. Rooms are tastefully modern, with flatscreen TVs and deep soaking tubs. Parking costs $20.

Hermitage Hotel
HOTEL $$$
(☑888-888-9414, 615-244-3121; www.thehermitagehotel.com; 231 6th Ave N; r from $399; ℗❋🛜) Nashville's first million-dollar hotel was a hit with the socialites when it opened in 1910. The lobby feels like a Czar's palace, every surface covered in rich tapestries and ornate carvings. Rooms are upscale, with plush, four-poster beds, marble baths with soaking tubs, and mahogany furniture. Parking costs $20. Service is a cut above here too.

Hotel Indigo   BOUTIQUE $$$

(☑615-891-6000; www.ihg.com; 301 Union St; r from $299; P) Part of a smallish international chain, the Indigo has a fun, pop-art look, with 130 rooms, 24 of which were recently remodeled at research time. Those King Rooms are spacious, with brand new wood floors, high ceilings, flatscreens, leather headboards and office chairs, and the location, on Capitol Hill, walking distance to the honky tonks, is ideal. Parking is $20.

⌂ West End

Music City Hostel   HOSTEL $

(☑615-692-1277; www.musiccityhostel.com; 1809 Patterson St; dm/r $28/85; P✳@☎) These squat brick bungalows are less than scenic, but Nashville's West End hostel is lively and welcoming, with bike rental, and a common kitchen. The crowd is young, international and fun, and many hoppin' West End bars are within walking distance. Private rooms share showers but have their own toilet.

★Hutton Hotel   HOTEL $$$

(☑615-340-9333; www.huttonhotel.com; 1808 West End Ave; r from $289; P✳@☎) ✎ Our favorite Nashville boutique hotel riffs on mid-century-modern design with bamboo-paneled walls and grown-up beanbags in the lobby. Rust- and chocolate-colored rooms are sizable and well appointed with marble rain showers, glass wash basins, king beds, ample desk space, fat flatscreens, high-end carpet and linens, and top-level service.

⌂ Music Valley

Gaylord Opryland Hotel   RESORT $$

(☑866-972-6779, 615-889-1000; www.gaylordhotels.com; 2800 Opryland Dr; r from $149; P✳@☎☒)

This whopping 2881-room hotel is a universe unto itself. Why set foot outdoors when you could ride a paddleboat along an artificial river, eat sushi beneath a faux waterfall in an indoor garden, shop for bolo ties in a model 19th-century town, or sip scotch in an antebellum-style mansion, all *inside* the hotel's three massive glass atriums.

✖ Eating

The classic Nashville meal is the 'meat-and-three' – a heaping portion of meat, served with your choice of three home-style sides. Gentrifying Germantown offers a handful of cafes and restaurants, including two standouts. Five Points is worth exploring, and do not miss the best fried chicken of your life!

✖ Five Points

★Prince's Hot Chicken   FRIED CHICKEN $

(123 Ewing Dr; quarter/half/whole chicken $5/9/18; ⊙noon-10pm Tue-Thu, to 4am Fri, 2pm-4am Sat; P) Cayenne-rubbed 'hot chicken,' fried to succulent perfection and served on a piece of white bread with a side of pickles, is Nashville's unique contribution to the culinary universe.

Tiny, faded, family-owned Prince's, set in a gritty, northside strip mall, is a local legend that's gotten shout-outs everywhere from the *New York Times* to *Bon Appétit* and attracts everyone from hipsters to frat boys to entire immigrant families to local heads to hillbillies. Fried up mild (a total lie), medium (what a joke), hot (verging on insanity) and extra hot (extreme masochism), its chicken will burn a hole in your stomach, and take root in your soul. You may wait an hour for yours – time well spent. It's cash only.

VIVA NASHVEGAS!

Brash, glittery Nashville is proud to have earned the nickname NashVegas. So put on your rhinestone cowboy boots and explore its weird and wild side.

'Outlaw Country' star Willie Nelson sold all his worldly goods to pay off $16.7 million in unpaid taxes in the early 1990s. You can see them at the **Willie Nelson Museum** (www.willienelsongeneralstore.com; 2613 McGavock Pike; admission $8; ⊙8:30am-9pm).

The **Doyle and Debbie** show at **Zanies Comedy Club** (www.nashville.zanies.com; 2025 8th Ave S) is a cult-hit parody of a washed-up country-music duo.

The **Johnny Cash Museum Store** (www.facebook.com/johnnycashmuseum; 119 3rd Ave; ⊙11am-7pm) is less a museum and more a gift shop where fans of the Man In Black descend for all things Cash, from leather to books to CDs to vintage vinyl.

In the quirky 12th Ave S neighborhood, a former stylist to New York City's drag queens stocks bouffant wigs, vintage cowboy boots and handmade bolo ties at **Katy K's Ranch Dressing** (www.katyk.com; 2407 12th Ave S).

Pied Piper Creamery
ICE CREAM $

(www.thepiedpipercreamery.com; 114 S 11th St; scoops under $3; ⊙ noon-9pm Sun-Thu, to 10pm Fri & Sat) Thicker, smoother and more packed with goodness than any other ice-cream shop in town, we love the toffee lovers coffee flavor, but it does have two dozen varieties available to explore at any one time. It's in Five Points.

I Dream of Weenie
HOT DOGS $

(www.facebook.com/IDreamofWeenie; 113 S 11th St; hot dogs $3-5; ⊙ 11am-4pm Mon-Thu, to 6pm Fri, 10:30am-7pm Sat, to 4pm Sun) If you want something quick and easy hit this VW bus turned hot dog stand in Five Points, pick a tubular product made from beef, turkey or tofu and get yours creatively topped. Picnic In A Bun includes baked beans, coleslaw and BBQ sauce, or just go simple with a Kraut Weenie (sauerkraut and spicy mustard).

King Market Cafe
LAOTIAN, THAI $

(300 Church St, Antioch Pike; dishes $6-10; ⊙ 8:30am-7pm) An authentic Southeast Asian cafe set inside an Asian Grocer in the Antioch Pike area – an east Nashville suburb where this city suddenly seems much less homogenous. It does noodle dishes, soups, curries and stirfrys, a Thai-style country pork sausage, deep-fried mackerel, and adventurous eats like fried pork intestine. Food comes rapidly and in heaping portions.

Marché Artisan Foods
BISTRO $$

(www.marcheartisanfoods.com; 1000 Main St; mains $9-16; ⊙ 8am-9pm Tue-Sat, to 4pm Sun) In rapidly gentrifying Five Points, this lovely and bright glass box of a farm-to-table cafe offers a corned-beef Ruben on marble rye, a popular lamb burger and a delicious warm broccoli salad with brown rice at lunch. It hosts special beer and wine dinners too.

✗ Downtown

Arnold's
SOUTHERN $

(www.facebook.com/Arnoldsmeatand3; 605 8th Ave S; mains $5-8; ⊙ 10:30am-2:30pm Mon-Fri) Grab a tray and line up with college students, garbage collectors and country-music stars at Arnold's, king of the meat-and-three. Slabs of drippy roast beef are the house specialty, along with fried green tomatoes, cornbread two ways, and big gooey wedges of chocolate cream pie.

Monell's
SOUTHERN $$

(☎ 615-248-4747; www.monellstn.com; 1235 6th Ave N; all-you-can-eat $13-19; ⊙ 10:30am-2pm Mon, 10:30am-2pm & 5-8:30pm Tue-Fri, 8:30am-3pm & 5-8:30pm Sat, 8:30am-4pm Sun) In an old brick house just north of the District, Monell's is beloved for down-home Southern food served family style. This is not just a meal, it's an experience. Especially at breakfast when platter after platter of sausage, bacon, bone in ham, skillet-fried chicken, hominy, corn pudding, baked apples and potatoes are served along with baskets of biscuits and bowls of sugary cinnamon rolls.

City House
NEW SOUTHERN $$$

(☎ 615-736-5838; www.cityhousenashville.com; 1222 4th Ave N; mains $15-24; ⊙ 5-10pm Mon & Wed-Sat, to 9pm Sun) This signless brick building in Nashville's gentrifying Germantown hides one of the city's best restaurants. The food, cooked in an open kitchen in the warehouse-like space, is a crackling bang-up of Italy meets New South.

It does tangy kale salads, a tasty chickpea and octopus dish flavored with fennel, onion, lemon and garlic, and pastas featuring twists like rigatoni rabbit, or gnocchi in cauliflower ragu. It cures its own sausage and salamis, and takes pride in the cocktail and wine list. Save room for dessert. Sunday supper features a stripped-down menu.

Southern
BAR & GRILL $$$

(www.thesouthernnashville.com; 150 3rd Ave; lunch mains $11-15, dinner mains $14-48; ⊙ 7:30am-10pm Mon-Thu, to midnight Fri, 10am-midnight Sat, 10am-10pm Sun) A brand-new eatery in the heart of downtown with a nice oyster menu sourced from Cape Cod, the Pacific Northwest, and Gulf Coast. Craftsman draft beers are poured at the marble bar and an open kitchen serves up everything from gourmet burgers to fish tacos to double-smoked pork chops and a plethora of steaks.

It's part of the new, ahem, SoBro area. Their terminology. Not ours, bro.

✗ West End

Fido
CAFE $

(www.fidocafe.com; 1812 21st S; mains $6-12; ⊙ 7am-11pm; ☎) A Hillsboro institution, known for excellent coffees and breakfasts, as well as an affordable menu of salads and sandwiches, some creative entrees like green chile mac and cheese, a nice crispy tofu stirfry, and a kale and collard green salad.

FRANKLIN

About 20 miles south of Nashville off I-65, the historic town of **Franklin** (www.historic-franklin.com) has a charming downtown and beautiful B&Bs. It was also the site of one of the Civil War's bloodiest battlefields. On November 30, 1864, 37,000 men (20,000 Confederates and 17,000 Union soldiers) fought over a 2-mile stretch of Franklin's outskirts. Nashville's sprawl has turned much of that battlefield into suburbs, but the **Carter House** (☑ 615-791-1861; www.carter-house.org; 1140 Columbia Ave, Franklin; adult/senior/child $8/7/4; ☺ 9am-5pm Mon-Sat, 1-5pm Sun; ☗ ☏) property is a preserved 8-acre chunk of the Battle of Franklin. The house is still riddled with 1000-some bullet holes. Before leaving town stop off at **Puckett's Grocery** (www.puckettsgrocery.com; 120 4th Ave S, Franklin; mains $10-20; ☺ 7am-3pm Mon, to 9pm Tue-Sat, to 7pm Sun) for a fried catfish sandwich and some bluegrass.

It's generally packed, yet spacious enough to accomodate the rather appealing crowd.

Pancake Pantry   BREAKFAST $
(www.pancakepantry.com; 1796 21st Ave S; mains $7-11; ☺ 6am-3pm) For 50-plus years, crowds have been lining up around the block for tall stacks of pancakes done up every-which-way at this iconic breakfast joint. Try the sweet-potato kind.

Provence   BAKERY, CAFE $
(www.provencebreads.com; 1705 21st Ave S; mains $7-11; ☺ 7am-8pm Mon-Fri, to 8pm Sat, to 6pm Sun) A popular spot in the Hillsboro District, lovers of breads will want to stop here for a loaf or a ready-made turkey, chicken salad or tuna sandwich. It also does frittatas, salads, tasty pastries, and a French toast made with a peach compote. Order your flavor and grab a table in the bright dining area that's popular at lunch.

Tin Angel   NEW AMERICAN $$
(☑ 615-298-3444; www.tinangel.net; 3201 West End Ave; mains $14-22; ☺ 11am-10pm Mon-Fri, 5-10pm Sat, 11am-3pm Sun) This low-key West End bistro serves a business crowd some good New American grub. With a house-smoked pork loin, vegetarian moussaka, maple bourbon duck breast and tasty entree salads, there really is something for everyone in this darkwood, intimately lit dining room. The only issue we had was that 1980s smooth jazz soundtrack. Ain't this Nashville?!

Tavern   GASTROPUB $$
(www.mstreetnashville.com; 1904 Broadway; mains $9-22; ☺ 11am-1am Mon-Thu, to 3am Fri, 10am-3am Sat, to 1am Sun) This Music Row gatsropub does everything from a Thai Cobb salad to wood-grilled artichokes to Ozzie-style meat pies to steak and seafood. All afford-ably priced. It has a nice whiskey list, and a handsome minimalist interior of moulded concrete booths, brick walls and built-in book cases.

🍷 Drinking & Nightlife

Nashville has the nightlife of a city three times its size, and you'll be hard-pressed to find a place that *doesn't* have live music. College students, bachelor-party-goers, Danish backpackers and conventioneers all rock out downtown, where neon-lit Broadway looks like a country-fried Las Vegas. Bars and venues west and south of downtown tend to attract more locals, with many places clustered near Vanderbilt University. Last call is at 3am.

3 Crow Bar   BAR
(www.3crowbar.com; 1024 Woodland St; ☺ 11am-3am; ☏) Garage-door windows roll open onto this truly divey cinderblock cavern with ample table and bar space in Five Points. This is the kinda joint you can lay back and enjoy not for a few minutes, but a few hours. The crowd is young and local, and there isa great back patio, as well.

Whiskey Kitchen   PUB
(www.whiskeykitchen.com; 118 12th Ave S) In the Gulch, an up-and-coming patch of rehabbed warehouses adjacent to downtown, this neo-Southern gastropub with a mile-long whiskey menu attracts an upmarket crowd.

Bongo Java   COFFEE HOUSE
(www.bongojava.com; 107 S 11th St; ☺ 6:30am-6pm Mon-Fri, from 7:30am Sat & Sun) A low-key hipster habitat, pretty goth girls expose fishnets and melancholy on the shady porch, and more serious thinker/writers/(web)surfers hunch over laptops in the cavernous interior where the coffee is house-

roasted and sacked, and where Robert Plant has been known to grab a cup when he's in town.

Rebar
BAR

(www.rebarnashville.com; 1919 Division St; ⊙2pm-3am Mon-Fri, from 11am Sat & Sun) Set in an old brick-and-stone house with an attractive tiled bar and low ceilings, wide concrete patio and flatscreens strobing the ball game – any ball game – this is a popular day-drinking spot among locals in Midtown, thanks to its two-for-one drinks from 2pm to 7pm daily.

Soulshine
PUB

(www.soulshinepizza.com; 1907 Division St; ⊙11am-1am Sun-Thu, to 2am Fri & Sat) A two-story, concrete-floor, brickhouse pub and pizzeria in Midtown. Bands rock the wide rooftop patio on weekend nights.

☆ Entertainment

Nashville's opportunities for hearing live music are unparalleled. As well as the big venues, many talented country, folk, bluegrass, Southern-rock and blues performers play smoky honky-tonks, college bars, coffee shops and organic cafes for tips. Most places are free Monday to Friday.

★ Station Inn
BLUEGRASS

(☑615-255-3307; www.stationinn.com; 402 12th Ave S; ⊙open mic 7pm, live bands 9pm) Sit at one of the small cocktail tables, squeezed together on the worn-wood floor in this beer-only dive, illuminated with stage lights, and neon signs, and behold the lightning fingers of bluegrass savants. We are talking stand-up bass, banjo, mandolin, fiddle and a modicum of yodelling.

Bluebird Cafe
CLUB

(☑615-383-1461; www.bluebirdcafe.com; 4104 Hillsboro Rd; cover free-$15; ⊙shows 6:30pm & 9:30pm) It's in a strip mall in suburban South Nashville, but don't let that fool you: some of the best original singer-songwriters in country music have graced this tiny stage. Steve Earle, Emmylou Harris and the Cowboy Junkies have all played the Bluebird, which is the setting for the popular television series, *Nashville*. Try your luck at Monday open mic nights.

It's first-come, first-serve seating, and it's best to show up at least an hour before the show begins. No talking during the show or you will get bounced.

Tootsie's Orchid Lounge
HONKY-TONK

(☑615-726-7937; www.tootsies.net; 422 Broadway; ⊙10am-late) **FREE** The most venerated of the downtown honky-tonks, Tootsie's is a blessed dive oozing boot-stomping, hillbilly, beer-soaked grace. In the 1960s club owner and den mother 'Tootsie' Bess nurtured Willie Nelson, Kris Kristofferson and Waylon Jennings on the come up.

No-name country musicians still play her two tiny stages, but it's not unusual for big stars to stop by for an impromptu jam.

Grand Ole Opry
MUSICAL THEATER

(☑615-871-6779; www.opry.com; 2802 Opryland Dr; adult $28-88, child $18-53) Though you'll find a variety of country shows throughout the week, the performance to see is the *Grand Ole Opry*, a lavish tribute to classic Nashville country music, every Tuesday, Friday and Saturday night. Shows return to the Ryman from November to February.

Robert's Western World
HONKY-TONK

(www.robertswesternworld.com; 416 Broadway; ⊙11am-2am) **FREE** Buy a pair of boots, a beer or a burger at Robert's, a longtime favorite on the strip. Music starts at 11am and goes all night; Brazilbilly, the house band, rocks it after 10pm on weekends. All ages are welcome before 10pm, afterward it's strictly 21 and up.

Ryman Auditorium
CONCERT VENUE

(☑info 615-889-3060, tickets 615-458-8700; www.ryman.com; 116 5th Ave) The Ryman's excellent acoustics, historic charm and large seating capacity have kept it the premier venue in town, with big names frequently passing through. The *Opry* returns for winter runs.

Belcourt
CINEMA

(www.belcourt.org; 2012 Belcourt Ave; child/adult $7.25/9.25; ⊙hour vary) A sweet art-house cinema playing new indie releases and a lot of old classics in a historic cinema space. Occasional live concerts too.

Nashville Symphony
SYMPHONY

(☑615-687-6500; www.nashvillesymphony.org; 1 Symphony Pl) Hosts maestros, the local symphony and major pop stars from Randy Travis to Smokey Robinson, in the shiny new, yet beautifully antiquated, Schermerhorn Symphony Hall.

LP Field
FOOTBALL

(☑615-565-4200; www.titansonline.com; 1 Titans Way; ticket prices vary; ⊙games Sep-Dec) Home of Nashville's own Tennessee Titans, part of

SCENIC DRIVE: NASHVILLE'S COUNTRY TRACKS

About 25 miles southwest of Nashville off Hwy 100, drivers pick up the **Natchez Trace Pkwy**, which leads 444 miles southwest to Natchez, MS. This northern section is one of its most attractive stretches, with broad-leafed trees leaning together to form an arch over the winding road. There are three primitive campsites along the way, free and available on a first-come, first-served basis. Near the parkway entrance, stop at the landmark **Loveless Cafe** (☎ 615-646-9700; www.lovelesscafe.com; 8400 Hwy 100, Nashville, TN 37221), a 1950s roadhouse famous for its biscuits with homemade preserves, country ham and ample portions of Southern fried chicken.

the National Football League. It's linked to downtown by a pedestrian bridge that spans the Cumberland River.

🛍 Shopping

Lower Broadway has tons of record shops, boot stores and souvenir stalls. The 12th Ave South neighborhood is the spot for ultra-trendy boutiques and vintage stores.

★**Hatch Show Print**   ART, SOUVENIRS
(www.hatchshowprint.com; 316 Broadway; ⊘9am-5pm Mon-Fri, from 10am Sat) One of the oldest letterpress print shops in the US, Hatch has been using old-school, hand-cut blocks to print its bright, iconic posters since the early days of Vaudeville. The company has produced graphic ads and posters for almost every country star since, and they're still in business.

If you don't have a special order in mind, you can buy reproductions of original Louis Armstrong, Patsy Cline, Hank Williams and Bill Monroe publicity posters.

Third Man Records   MUSIC
(www.thirdmanrecords.com; 623 7th Ave S; ⊘10am-6pm Mon-Sat, 1-4pm Sun) In a still-industrial slice of downtown, you'll find Jack White's boutique record label and shop complete with its own vinyl press. It sells only Third Man recordings on vinyl and CD, collectible t-shirts, stickers, and headphones, and its own Spinerette record players. You'll also find old White Stripes records and White's more recent Raconteurs recordings.

Live shows go off in the studio's **Blue Room** once a month. They're typically open to the public, cost about $10, but are only announced a couple weeks in advance. Often those shows become limited-edition vinyl – such as Jerry Lee Lewis' performance – sold in store.

Boot Country   BOOTS
(www.facebook.com/bootcountrynashville; 304 Broadway; ⊘10am-10:30pm Mon-Thu, to 11pm Fri & Sat, 11am-7:30pm Sun) If you're into leather, or worn rawhide, or anything close, they do all manner of boot here. From sexy to staid, flamboyant to stern, worn and frayed to polished and glossy. Buy one, get two free. No joke!

Two Old Hippies   CLOTHING, MUSIC
(www.twooldhippies.com; 401 12th Ave S) Only in Nashville would an upscale retro-inspired clothing shop have a bandstand with regular live shows of high quality. And, yes, just like the threads, countrified hippie rock is the rule. The shop itself has special jewelry, fitted tees, excellent belts, and an unfortunate collection of man purses.

As well, it has, ahem, $2000 leather jackets (including a beaded rpelica of the one Jimmie wore at Woodstock), and superb guitars! It's part of the Gulch shopping center.

A Thousand Faces   GIFTS
(www.athousandfaces.com; 1720 21st Ave S; ⊘10am-6pm Mon-Thu, to 7pm Fri & Sat, to 5pm Sun) A lovely gift boutique specializing in handmade ceramics, exquisite silver jewelry and interesting art. We loved the intriguing guitar sculpture that you simply have to see.

Ernest Tubb   RECORDS
(www.etrecordshop.com; 417 Broadway) Marked by a giant neon guitar sign, this is the best place to shop for country and bluegrass records. Open late.

Parnassus Books   BOOKS
(www.parnassusbooks.net; 3900 Hillsboro Pike; ⊘10am-8pm Mon-Sat, noon-5pm Sun) Anne Patchett's Parnassus Books is arguably one of America's most famous indie booksellers. The bright space hosts special events, readings, and signings, promotes local authors and even sells e-books.

Gruhn Guitars
MUSIC

(www.gruhn.com; 400 Broadway; ⊙9:30am-5:30pm Mon-Fri, to 2:30pm Sat) This renowned vintage instrument store has expert staff, and at any minute some unassuming virtuoso may just walk in, grab a guitar, mandolin or banjo off the wall and jam.

Pangaea
GIFTS

(www.pangaeanashville.com; 1721 21st Ave S; ⊙10am-6pm Mon-Thu, to 9pm Fri & Sat, noon-5pm Sun) There are no groovier shops in town. What with the beaded belts and silly scarves, funky hats and summery dresses. Not to mention the triple milled soap, Frida Kahlo match holders, stunning mirrors and light fixtures all of which scream vintage, as do the worn wood floors. Welcome to your sweet-smelling, good-vibing blast of Nashville bohemia.

ℹ Information

Downtown Nashville and Centennial Park have free wi-fi, as do nearly all hotels and many restaurants and coffee shops.

InsideOut (www.insideoutnashville.com) A weekly covering the local gay and lesbian scene.

Main Police Station (☎615-862-8600; 310 1st Ave S)

Nashville Scene (www.nashvillescene.com) Free alternative weekly with entertainment listings.

Nashville Visitors Information Center (☎800-657-6910, 615-259-4747; www.visitmusiccity.com; 501 Broadway, Sommet Center; ⊙8:30am-5:30pm) Pick up free city maps here at the glass tower. Great online resource.

Post Office (1718 Church St)

Public Library (www.library.nashville.org; 615 Church St; 🕾) Free internet access.

Tennessean (www.tennessean.com) Nashville's daily newspaper.

Vanderbilt University Medical Center (☎615-322-5000; 1211 22nd Ave S)

ℹ Getting There & Around

Nashville International Airport (BNS; ☎615-275-1675; www.nashintl.com), 8 miles east of town, is not a major air hub. **Metropolitan Transit Authority** (MTA; www.nashvillemta.org; fares $1.70-2.25) bus 18 links the airport and downtown; the **Gray Line Airport Express** (www.graylinenashville.com; one-way/return $14/25; ⊙5am-11pm) serves major downtown and West End hotels. Taxis charge a flat rate of $25 to $27 to downtown or Opryland.

Greyhound (www.greyhound.com; 709 5th Ave S) is downtown. The MTA operates city bus services, based downtown at **Music City Central** (400 Charlotte Ave). Express buses go to Music Valley.

Eastern Tennessee

Dolly Parton, Eastern Tennessee's most famous native, loves her home region so much she has made a successful career out of singing about girls who leave the honeysuckle-scented embrace of the Smoky Mountains for the false glitter of the city. They're always sorry. Largely a rural region of small towns, rolling hills and river valleys, the eastern third of the state has friendly folks, hearty country food and pastoral charm. The lush, heather-tinted Great Smoky Mountains are great for hiking, camping and rafting, while the region's two main urban areas, Knoxville and Chattanooga, are easygoing riverside cities with lively student populations.

Chattanooga

Named 'the dirtiest city in America' in the 1960s, today the city is recognized as being one of the country's greenest, with miles of well-used waterfront trails, electric buses and pedestrian bridges crossing the Tennessee River. With world-class rock-climbing, hiking, biking and water-sports opportunities, it's one of the South's best cities for outdoorsy types.

The city was once a major railway hub throughout the 19th and 20th centuries, hence the 'Chattanooga Choo-Choo,' which was originally a reference to the Cincinnati Southern Railroad's passenger service from Cincinnati to Chattanooga and later the title of a 1941 Glen Miller tune. The eminently walkable downtown is an increasingly gentrified maze of historic stone and brick buildings and some tasty gourmet kitchens. There's a lot to love about Chattanooga.

⦿ Sights & Activities

Coolidge Park is a good place to start a riverfront stroll. There's a carousel, well-used playing fields and a 50ft climbing wall attached to one of the columns supporting the **Walnut Street Bridge**. Abutting that park, the city has installed gabions to restore the wetlands and attract more bird life. Check them out by strolling to the edge of the cool, floating decks that jut over the marsh. The much larger **Tennessee River Park** is an 8-mile, multi-use greenway that runs from downtown through Amincola Marsh and along South Chickamauga Creek. Plans are to expand its reach to a full 22 miles.

Tennessee Aquarium   AQUARIUM
(www.tnaqua.org; 1 Broad St; adult/child $25/15; ⊙10am-8pm, last entry 6pm; 🔊) That glass pyramid looming over the riverside bluffs is the world's largest freshwater aquarium. Climb aboard the aquarium's high-speed catamaran for two-hour excursions through the Tennessee River Gorge (adult/child $29/22).

Hunter Museum of American Art   GALLERY
(www.huntermuseum.org; 10 Bluff View; adult/child $10/5, 1st Sun of month free; ⊙10am-5pm Mon, Tue, Fri & Sat, to 8pm Thu, noon-5pm Wed & Sun) Set high on the river bluffs, east of the aquarium, is this equally striking melted-steel and glass edifice, easily the most singular architectural achivement in Tennessee. Oh, and the 19th- and 20th-century art collection is fantastic.

Lookout Mountain   OUTDOORS
(www.lookoutmountain.com; 827 East Brow Rd; adult/child $48/25; ⊙varies, 🔊) Some of Chattanooga's oldest and best-loved attractions are 6 miles outside the city. Admission price includes: the **Incline Railway**, which chugs up a steep incline to the top of the mountain; the world's longest underground waterfall, **Ruby Falls**; and **Rock City**, a garden with a dramatic clifftop overlook.

The mountain is also a popular hang-gliding location. The folks at **Lookout Mountain Flight Park** (📞800-688-5637; www.hanglide.com; 7201 Scenic Hwy; intro tandem flight $149) offer tandem flights.

Outdoor Chattanooga   OUTDOORS
(📞423-643-6888; www.outdoorchattanooga.com; 200 River St) A city-run agency promoting active recreation, the website is a good resource for outdoor information, river and trail suggestions, though walk-in visitors may be disappointed in the lack of spur-of-the-moment guidance. It occasionally runs guided trips.

🛏 Sleeping & Eating

You can find plenty of budget motels around I-24 and I-75.

★ Stone Fort Inn   BOUTIQUE HOTEL $$
(📞423-267-7866; www.stonefortinn.com; 120 E 10th St; r from $135-155; P🔊🔊) In the midst of a

refurbish at research time, rooms at this historic hotel have flatscreens and soaker Jacuzzi tubs and new fixtures in the bathrooms. Ceilings are high, the furnishings are vintage and service is phenomenal. The Appalachia-style, farm-to-table restaurant is the newest winner in town. Some beds do sag.

Sheraton Read House   HOTEL $$
(📞423-266-4121; www.sheratonreadhouse.com; 827 Broad St; r from $149; P🔊🔊) Set in a historic building dating to 1926, this is the nicest of Chattanooga's chain hotels, and the only one in the downtown center (most are on the northern edge near the river). Rooms are clean and good sized with high ceilings, crown mouldings, wood desks and flatscreens. It's within walking distance of the best restaurants and the riverside. Parking is $15

Chattanooga Choo-Choo   HOTEL $$
(📞423-308-2440; www.choochoo.com; 1400 Market St; r/railcars from $133; P🔊@🔊🔊) One hundred years old at research time, the city's grand old railway terminal has been transformed into a bustling hotel, complete with 48 authentic Victorian railcar rooms, a retro Gilded Age bar, and stunning grand portico in the lobby. Standard rooms and suites, in separate buildings, are ordinary.

★ Public House   NEW AMERICAN $$
(📞423-266-3366; www.publichousechattanooga.com; 1110 Market St; mains $9-22; ⊙5-9pm Mon-Thu, to 10pm Fri & Sat) A rather chic pub and restaurant in the refurbished warehouse district, the in-house bar, **Social**, is a dark

THE SOUTH EASTERN TENNESSEE

welcoming brick house, the dining room is draped, bright and homey, and both rooms serve a tasty upscale menu.

Think: duck confit with red cabbage, grilled pork tenderloin with green-apple chutney, or sautéed trout with cauliflower and tomato preserve.

St John's Meeting Place NEW AMERICAN $$$
(☏ 423-266-4400; www.stjohnsrestaurant.com; 1278 Market St; mains $28-36; ◷ 5-9:30pm Mon-Thu, to 10pm Fri & Sat) Set on the south end of downtown is another of Chattanooga's creative new culinary habitats, and it's widely considered the best. A black granite floor, black-glass chandeliers and drapes lend a mod elegance, and the menu is fine farm-to-table cuisine featuring roast pork, antelope, lamb, shortrib and duck mains.

ⓘ Getting There & Around

Chattanooga's modest **airport** (CHA; ☏ 423-855-2202; www.chattairport.com; 1001 Airport Rd) is just east of the city. The **Greyhound station** (960 Airport Rd) is just down the road. For access to most downtown sites, ride the free electric **shuttle buses** that ply the center. The **visitor center** (☏ 800-322-3344, 423-756-8687; www.chattanoogafun.com; 215 Broad St; ◷ 8:30am-5:30pm) has a route map. If you'd rather pedal, fill out an online application and take part in **Bike Chattanooga** (www.bikechattanooga.com), a city sponsored, bicycle-sharing program. Bikes are lined and locked up at 31 stations throughout the city. Rides under 60 minutes are free.

Knoxville

Once known as the 'underwear capital of the world' for its numerous textile mills, Knoxville is home to the University of Tennessee. Downtown's **Market Square** is full of ornate, 19th-century buildings and lovely outdoor cafes shaded by pear trees, while **Old Town**, an arty, renovated warehouse district centered on Gay St, is where the best nightlife blooms.

The city's visual centerpiece is the **Sunsphere** (☏ 865-251-6860; World's Fair Park, 810 Clinch Ave; ◷ 9am-10pm Apr-Oct, 11am-6pm Nov-Mar), a gold orb atop a tower that's the main remnant of the 1982 World Fair. You can take the elevator up to the (usually deserted) viewing deck to see the skyline and a dated exhibit on Knoxville's civic virtues. You can't miss the massive orange basketball that marks the **Women's Basketball Hall of Fame** (www.wbhof.com; 700 Hall of Fame Dr;

adult/child $8/6; ◷ 10am-5pm Mon-Sat summer, 11am-5pm Tue-Sat winter), a nifty look at the sport from the time when women competed in full-length dresses.

For dinner, find **Tupelo Honey Cafe** (www.tupelohoneycafe.com; 1 Market Sq; mains $9-19; ◷ 9am-10pm Mon-Thu, to 11pm Fri, 8am-11pm Sat, to 9pm Sun) a bustling, eclectic dining room on Market Sq serving chorizo-crusted sea scallops, pulled pork with jalapeño BBQ sauce, and shrimp and goat cheese grits. It does a handful of vegetarian dishes too. The **Oliver Hotel** (☏ 865-521-0050; www.theoliver-hotel.com; 407 Union Ave; r from $145) is the most stylish nest.

Great Smoky Mountains National Park

The Cherokee called this territory Shaconage (shah-*cone*-ah-jey), meaning roughly 'land of the blue smoke,' for the heather-colored mist that hangs over the ancient peaks. The Southern Appalachians are the world's oldest mountain range, with mile upon mile of cool, humid deciduous forest.

The 815-sq-mile **park** (www.nps.gov/grsm) **FREE** is the country's most visited and, while the main arteries and attractions can get crowded, 95% of visitors never venture further than 100 yards from their cars, so it's easy to leave the teeming masses behind. There are sections of the park in Tennessee and North Carolina.

Unlike most national parks, Great Smoky charges no admission fee. Stop by a visitor center to pick up a park map and the free *Smokies Guide*. The remains of the 19th-century settlement at **Cades Cove** are some of the park's most popular sights, as evidenced by the teeth-grinding summer traffic jams on the loop road.

Mt LeConte offers terrific hiking, as well as the only non-camping accommodations, **LeConte Lodge** (☏ 865-429-5704; www.lecontelodge.com; cabins per person adult/child 4-12yr $126/85). Though the only way to get to the lodge's rustic, electricity-free cabins is via an 8-mile uphill slog. It's so popular you need to reserve up to a year in advance. You can drive right up to the dizzying heights of **Clingmans Dome**, the third-highest mountain east of the Mississippi, with a futuristic observation tower.

With 10 developed campgrounds offering about 1000 campsites, you'd think finding a place to pitch would be easy. Not so in the busy summer season, so plan ahead. You can

make **reservations** (☎800-365-2267; www.
nps.gov/grsm; tent site per night $14-23) for some
sites; others are first-come, first-served.
Cades Cove and Smokemont campgrounds
are open year-round; others are open March
to October.

Backcountry camping (☎reservations
865-436-1231; www.nps.gov/grsm/planyourvisit/
backcountry-camping.htm; per night $4) is an ex-
cellent option. A permit is required; you can
make reservations and get permits at the
ranger stations or visitor centers.

ⓘ Information

The park's three interior visitor centers are
Sugarlands Visitor Center (☎865-436-1291;
www.nps.gov/grsm; ⊗8am-7pm Jun-Aug, hours
vary Sep-May), at the park's northern entrance
near Gatlinburg; **Cades Cove Visitor Center**
(☎877-444-6777; ⊗9am-7pm Apr-Aug, earlier
Sep-Mar), halfway up Cades Cove Loop Rd,
off Hwy 441 near the Gatlinburg entrance; and
Oconaluftee Visitor Center (p350), at the park's
southern entrance near Cherokee in North
Carolina.

Gatlinburg

Wildly kitschy Gatlinburg hunkers at the
entrance of the Great Smoky Mountains
National Park, waiting to stun hikers with
the scent of fudge and cotton candy. Amuse
yourself Gatlinburg-style at the city's various
Ripley's franchise attractions (a 'Believe it
or Not!' museum of oddities, a mirror maze,
a haunted house, a massive aquarium),
or by riding the scenic 2-mile aerial **tramway** (www.obergatlinburg.com; 1001 Parkway;
adult/child $11/8.50; ⊗7:30am-6:20pm Sun, to
10:40pm Mon, Fri & Sat, 9:30am-9:49pm Tue-Thu)
to the Bavarian-themed **Ober Gatlinburg
Ski Resort** (www.obergatlinburg.com; lift ticket
adult $35-54, child $25-44, equipment rental packages ski/snowboard $25/30). Afterwards, suck
down free samples of white lightnin' at the
Ole Smoky Moonshine Distillery (☎865-
436-6995; www.olesmokymoonshine.com; 903
Parkway; ⊗10am-10pm), the country's first
licensed moonshine maker (sounds like an
oxymoron to us!). If you plan on sleeping
it off in Gatlinburg, find homey and inviting **Bearskin Lodge** (☎877-795-7546; www.
thebearskinlodge.com; 840 River Rd; r from $110)
on the river. **Wild Boar Saloon & Howard's
Steakhouse** (☎865-436-3600; www.wildboar-
saloon.com; 976 Parkway; mains $9-30; ⊗10am-
10pm Sun-Thu, to 1:30am Fri & Sat) will make you
feel right at home, come dinner time.

DOLLYWOOD

Dollywood (☎865-428-9488; www.
dollywood.com; 2700 Dollywood Parks
Blvd; adult/child $57/45; ⊗Apr-Dec) is a
self-created ode to the patron saint of
East Tennessee, the big-haired, bigger-
bosomed country singer Dolly Parton.
The park features Appalachian-themed
rides and attractions, from the Mystery
Mine roller coaster to the faux one-
room chapel named after the doctor
who delivered Dolly. Find it looming
above the outlet mall mosh pit of
Pigeon Forge (www.mypigeonforge.
com), 9 miles north of Gatlinburg.

KENTUCKY

With an economy based on bourbon, horse
racing and tobacco, you might think Kentucky would rival Las Vegas as Sin Central.
Well, yes and no. For every whiskey-soaked
Louisville bar there's a dry county where
you can't get anything stronger than ginger
ale. For every racetrack there's a church.
Kentucky is made of such strange juxtaposi-
tions. A geographic and cultural crossroads,
the state combines the friendliness of the
South, the rural frontier history of the West,
the industry of the North and the aristocratic charm of the East. Every corner is easy
on the eye, but there are few sights more
heartbreakingly beautiful than the rolling
limestone hills of horse country, where thoroughbred breeding is a multimillion-dollar
industry. In spring the pastures bloom with
tiny azure buds, earning it the moniker
'Bluegrass State.'

ⓘ Information

The boundary between Eastern and Central time
goes through the middle of Kentucky.
Kentucky State Parks (☎800-255-7275; www.
parks.ky.gov) Offers info on hiking, caving, fishing, camping and more in Kentucky's 52 state
parks. So-called 'Resort Parks' have lodges.
'Recreation Parks' are for roughin' it.
Kentucky Travel (☎800-225-8747, 502-564-
4930; www.kentuckytourism.com) Sends out a
detailed booklet on the state's attractions.

Louisville

Best known as the home of the Kentucky
Derby, Louisville (or Louahvul, as the locals
say) is handsome and underrated. A major

KENTUCKY FACTS

Nickname Bluegrass State

Population 4.4 million

Area 39,728 sq miles

Capital city Frankfort (pop 28,000)

Other cities Louisville (pop 600,000), Lexington (pop 300,000)

Sales tax 6%

Birthplace of 16th US president Abraham Lincoln (1809–65), 'gonzo' journalist Hunter S Thompson (1937–2005), boxer Muhammad Ali (b 1942), actresses Ashley Judd (b 1968) and Jennifer Lawrence (b 1990)

Home of Kentucky Derby, Louisville Slugger, bourbon

Politics Generally to extremely conservative in rural areas

Famous for Horses, bluegrass music, basketball, bourbon, caves

Ongoing internal conflict North vs South allegiance during the Civil War

Driving distances Louisville to Lexington 77 miles, Lexington to Mammoth Cave National Park 135 miles

Ohio River shipping center during the days of westward expansion, Kentucky's largest city is on the come up, with hip bars, superb farm-to-table restaurants, and an engaging, young and increasingly progressive population. It's a fun place to spend a few days, checking out the museums, wandering the old neighborhoods, and sipping some bourbon.

⊙ Sights & Activities

The Victorian-era **Old Louisville** neighborhood, just south of downtown, is well worth a stroll. Don't miss **St James Court**, just off Magnolia Ave, with its utterly charming gas lamp–lit park. There are several wonderful **historic homes** (www.historichomes.org) in the area open for tours, including Thomas Edison's old shotgun cottage.

★ **Churchill Downs**   RACETRACK
(www.churchilldowns.com; 700 Central Ave) On the first Saturday in May, a who's who of upper-crust America puts on their searsucker suits and most flamboyant hats and descends for the 'greatest two minutes in sports,' the Ken-

tucky Derby. After the race, the crowd sings 'My Old Kentucky Home' and watches as the winning horse is covered in a blanket of roses. Then they party.

Actually, they've been partying for a while. The **Kentucky Derby Festival** (www.kdf.org), which includes a balloon race, a marathon, and the largest fireworks display in North America, starts two weeks before the big event. Most seats at the derby are by invitation only or have been reserved years in advance. On Derby Day, $50 gets you into the infield, which is a debaucherous rave with no seats. It's so crowded you won't see much of the race. Not that you'll mind. If you are a conniseur of the thoroughbreds, from April through to November, you can get a $3 seat at the Downs for exciting warm-up races leading up to the big event.

Kentucky Derby Museum   MUSEUM
(www.derbymuseum.org; Gate 1, Central Ave; adult/child $14/6; ⊙8am-5pm Mon-Sat, 11am-5pm Sun) On the racetrack grounds, the museum has exhibits on derby history, including a peek into the life of jockeys and a roundup of the most illustrious horses. There is a 360-degree audiovisual about the race, and admission includes a 30-minute walking tour of the horse staging area and the track, which includes some engaging yarns.

The 90-minute Inside the Gates Tour ($11) leads you through the jockey's quarters and posh VIP seating areas known as Millionaire's Row.

Muhammad Ali Center   MUSEUM
(www.alicenter.org; 144 N 6th St; adult/senior & student/child 4-12 yr $9/8/5; ⊙9:30am-5pm Tue-Sat, noon-5pm Sun) A love offering to the city from its most famous native, and an absolute must-see. Start on the 5th level where there is a wonderful orientation film. The video archives on the 4th floor enable you to watch every Ali fight!

'Confidence' is a wonderful exhibit about how Ali's supposed swaggering braggadocio more accurately signified rare self love and confidence. For a black man from the South during his era, to rejoice in his own greatness and beauty, was revolutionary and inspiring to behold.

Louisville Slugger Museum   MUSEUM
(www.sluggermuseum.org; 800 W Main St; adult/senior/child $11/10/6; ⊙9am-5pm Mon-Sat, 11am-5pm Sun; 🚹) Look for the 120ft baseball bat leaning against the museum. Hillerich & Bradsby Co have been making the famous

Louisville Slugger here since 1884. Admission includes a plant tour, a hall of baseball memorabilia including Babe Ruth's bat, a batting cage and a free mini slugger.

Frazier International History Museum
MUSEUM
(www.fraziermuseum.org; 829 W Main St; adult/student/child $10.50/7.50/6; ☉ 9am-5pm Mon-Sat, noon-5pm Sun) Surprisingly ambitious for a midsized city, this state-of-the-art museum covers 1000 years of history with grisly battle dioramas and costumed interpreters demonstrating swordplay and staging mock debates.

State Science Center of Kentucky
MUSEUM
(☎ 502-561-6100; www.kysciencecenter.org; 727 W Main St; adult/child $13/11; ☉ 9:30am-5:30pm Sun-Thu, to 9pm Fri & Sat; 🖐) Set in a historic building on Main St there are three floors of exhibits that illuminate biology, physiology, physics, computing and more for families (kids love it). For an extra $7 you can catch a film in the IMAX theatre.

Big Four Bridge
WALKING, CYCLING
(East River Rd) Town's latest attraction, is an old bridge fixed up new. Built between 1888 and 1895, the Big Four Bridge, which spans the Ohio River and reaches the Indiana shores, had been closed to vehicular traffic since 1969 and was reopened in 2013 as a pedestrian and cycling path, with excellent city and river views throughout.

Dogs are allowed. Skates and skateboards are not. Ample parking.

🛏 Sleeping

Chain hotels cluster near the airport off I-264.

Rocking Horse B&B
B&B $$
(☎ 888-467-7322, 502-583-0408; www.rocking-horse-bb.com; 1022 S 3rd St; r incl breakfast $125-215) On a stretch of 3rd St once known as Millionaire's Row, this 1888 Romanesque mansion has six guest rooms decorated with Victorian antiques and splendid stained glass. Guests can eat their two-course breakfast in the English country garden or sip complimentary port in the parlor.

★ 21c Museum Hotel
HOTEL $$$
(☎ 502-217-6300; www.21chotel.com; 700 W Main St; r from $269; 🅿✳🛜) This contemporary art museum–hotel would be edgy anywhere; in laid-back Louisville, it's mind expanding.

Video screens project your distorted image and falling language on the wall as you wait for the elevator. Chandeliers made from scissors dangle in the hallways. Urban loft-like rooms have iPod docks and mint julep kits in the mini-fridge.

The hotel restaurant, Proof (p388), is one of the city's hippest New Southern bistros, and service could not be finer. Parking is $18.

Brown Hotel
HOTEL $$$
(☎ 502-583-1234; www.brownhotel.com; 335 West Broadway; r from $250; 🅿🚬✳🛜) Opera stars, queens and prime ministers have trod the marble floors of this storied downtown hotel, now restored to all its 1920s gilded glamour with 293 comfy rooms and a swank bar. Parking is $18.

✕ Eating

The number of incredible kitchens multiplies every year, especially in the engaging NuLu area, where there are numerous galleries and boutiques to explore. The Highlands area around Bardstown and Baxter Rds is another popular nightlife and dining spot.

★ Hillbilly Tea
APPALACHIAN $$
(☎ 502-587-7350; 120 S First St; dishes $10-17; ☉ 10am-9pm Tue-Sat, to 4pm Sun) An excellent value cafe off Main St specializing in Appalachian food with a modern twist. You may find smoked catfish served over smashed potatoes or a smoked cornish hen over brussels and parsnips, and the grilled moonshine pork loin looks fantastic.

THE HAUNTED HOSPITAL

Towering over Louisville like a mad king's castle, the abandoned **Waverly Hills Sanatorium** once housed victims of an early 20th-century tuberculosis epidemic. When patients died, workers dumped their bodies down a chute into the basement. No wonder the place is said to be one of America's most haunted buildings. Search for spooks with a nighttime ghost-hunting **tour** (☎ 502-933-2142; www.therealwaverlyhills.com; 4400 Paralee Ln; 2hr tours/2hr ghost hunt/overnight $22/50/100; ☉ Mar-Aug); the genuinely fearless can even spend the night! Many claim it's the scariest place they've ever been.

THE SOUTH LOUISVILLE

Garage Bar
GASTROPUB $$
(www.garageonmarket.com; 700 E Market St; dishes $7-16) The best thing to do on a warm afternoon in Louisville is to make your way to this über-hip converted NuLu service station (accented by two kissing Camaros) and order a round of basil gimlets and the ham platter: a tasting of four regionally cured hams, served with fresh bread and preserves.

Then move onto the menu which ranges from the best brick-oven pizza in town, to pork meatballs and turkey wings, to rolled oysters that are divine.

Wiltshire on Market
NEW AMERICAN $$
(502-589-5224; www.wiltshirepantry.com; 636 Market St; mains $14-23; 5-10pm Thu & Sun, to 11pm Fri & Sat) The live music on Sunday nights and community-activist chef are appealing, sure, but the reasonably priced gourmet eats are why you're here. Choose from a half dozen oyster platters paired with a weekly charcuterie board, or go with the country sausage flatbread, the lamb bolognese, or the seriously good veggie burger.

Eiderdown
GASTROPUB $$
(502-290-2390; www.eiderdowngernantown.com; 983 Goss Ave; dishes $4-17; 4-10pm Tue-Thu, 11:30am-11pm Fri & Sat, noon-10pm Sun) When this Kentucky-born, 30-something, French-trained chef fled the corporate confines of a local Outback kitchen, he envisioned this exposed-brick, dark-wood destination pub suffused with the aroma of duck fat popcorn, cabbage, bacon, and *spaetzle* – a melange of root vegetables and sausage dripping with sage butter.

It's in the still-gritty, mostly residential corner of Louisville known as Germantown.

Ghyslain
MARKET CAFE $$
(502-690-8645; www.Ghyslain.com; 721 E Market St; dishes $10-13; 7am-9pm) An inviting market cafe with a menu of delectable baguettes stuffed with roast pork and broccoli, or pesto meatballs, and it does a nice chicken curry wrapped in naan. It also simmers some tasty gumbo (a roux-based stew) and chili. Grab a marble-table top, and finish with fine chocolates or gelato.

★ Proof
NEW SOUTHERN $$$
(502-217-6360; www.proofonmain.com; 702 W Main St; mains $17-36; 7-10am, 11am-2pm & 5:30-10pm Mon-Thu, to 11pm Fri & 7am-3pm, 5:30-11pm Sat, to 10pm Sun) Arguably Louisville's best, and certainly its most lauded restaurant. The cocktails are incredible, the wine and bourbon list (they're known to pour from exclusive and rare barrels of Woodford Reserve and Van Winkle) is long and satsifying, and mains range from a bone-in pork chop, to a succulent bison burger to a high-minded take on chicken and dumplings.

Did we mention they grow and raise some of the ingredients on their own farm? The art is loud and inspired, the servers hip and deadly serious, and the bar crowd is well dressed and festive.

🍷 Drinking & Entertainment

The free *Weekly Leo* (www.leoweekly.com) lists local gigs. You'll have no problem finding a watering hole in the Highlands area. Check out the many galleries, restaurants and cafes in NuLu and downtown on the **First Friday Trolley Hop** (www.ldmd.org/First-Friday-Trolley-Hop.html; Main & Market St; 5-11pm, 1st Fri of month) FREE.

Holy Grale
PUB
(www.holygralelouisville.com; 1034 Bardstown Rd; 4pm-late) One of Bardstown's best bars is housed in an old church, with a menu of funked-up pub grub (Scotch quail eggs, kimchee hot dogs) and a dozen rare German, Belgian and Japanese brews on tap. The most intense beers (up to 13% alcohol) can be found in the choir loft.

Please & Thank You
CAFE
(www.pleaseandthankyoulouisville.com/welcome; 800 E Market St; drinks $2-5; 7am-6pm Mon-Fri, 10am-2pm Sat & Sun) The kind of indie cafe that makes a neighborhood. It does tasty coffee drinks and home-baked bread pudding, creative scones and coffee cakes, zucchini bread and gooey chocolate-chip cookies. Oh, and it also sells vinyl, which only adds to the anti-Starbucks mystique.

Rudyard Kipling
BAR, MUSIC
(www.therudyardkipling.com; 422 W Oak St) In Old Louisville, this place is loved by arty locals for its intimate indie-bluegrass shows, way-off-broadway plays and Kentucky bar food (try the 'snappy cheese').

KFC Yum! Center
BASKETBALL
(502-690-9000; www.gocards.com; 1 Arena Plaza) A flood of Cardinal red floods into this downtown arena on game day. The University of Louisville Cardinals, National Collegiate Athletic Association national basketball champs at research time, are led by famed coach Rick Pitino, and the games are almost always sold out. If you love basket-

ball, you should definitely see a game here. The arena also lures the odd pop star.

🛍 Shopping

★ Joe Ley Antiques   ANTIQUES
(www.joeley.com; 615 E Market St; ⊙10am-5pm Tue-Sat) A massive, four-story brick-and-stained glass antique emporium crammed with collectibles from eight decades. Think homely dolls, freaky furniture and chunky jewelry.

Butchertown Market   BOUTIQUES
(www.thebutchertownmarket.com; 1201 Story Ave; ⊙10am-6pm Mon-Fri, to 5pm Sat) It's new and ambitious, and you simply have to see this converted slaughterhouse complex that's been turned into a grab bag of quirky, cute and artsy boutiques. Whether it's funky jewelry, kooky gifts, exquisite chocolates, craftsman metal fixtures, bath and body products or baby clothes, someone is selling it here.

Cellar Door Chocolates   CHOCOLATIER
(www.thebutchertownmarket.com; 1201 Story Ave, Butchertown Market; ⊙10am-6pm Mon-Fri, to 5pm Sat) The choclates are as creative as they are delcctable, and it has the awards to prove it. Green chili? Check. Coconut milk chocolate? Indeed. Wasabi truffles, white-chocolate bark, sea-salt caramel? Yes please. It hasespresso too.

Flea Off Market   FLEA MARKET
(www.facebook.com/thefleaoffmarket; 1007 E Jefferson St; ⊙2nd weekend of month) A monthly, weekend-long bazaar of 1980s-era Adidas, rockabilly vinyl, artful terrariums, local craftsman preserves and jerky, and jewelry. Not to mention plenty of vintage threads. The whole thing is catered by food trucks. Somewhere in Portlandia, Fred Armisted is smiling.

Taste   WINE
(☎502-409-4646; www.tastefinewinesandbourbons.com; 634 E Market Street; tastings $4-8; ⊙11am-8pm Tue-Wed, noon-late Thu & Fri, 10:30am-late Sat) A high-end wine shop that sells small-batch wines and bourbons, and offers sips of either (or both) to help you decide (or perhaps it muddles the whole process). The point is, come, sip, buy.

ℹ Information

Public Library (301 York St) Surf the web free, downtown.

Visitor Center (☎888-568-4784, 502-582-3732; www.gotolouisville.com; 301 S 4th St; ⊙10am-6pm Mon-Sat, noon-5pm Sun)

WORTH A TRIP

INTERNATIONAL BLUEGRASS MUSIC MUSEUM

Kentuckian Bill Monroe is considered the founding father of bluegrass music; his band, the Blue Grass Boys, gave the genre its name. Bluegrass has its roots in the old-time mountain music, mixed with the fast tempo of African songs and spiced with lashings of jazz. Any banjo picker or fiddle fan will appreciate the historic exhibits at the **International Bluegrass Music Museum** (www.bluegrassmuseum.org; 107 Daviess St; adult/student $5/2; ⊙10am-5pm Tue-Sat, 1-4pm Sun) in Owensboro, where you can stumble into a jam session on the first Thursday of the month. The pretty Ohio River town, about 100 miles west of Louisville, also hosts the **ROMP Bluegrass Festival** (www.rompfest.com; ⊙late Jun).

ℹ Getting There & Around

Louisville's International Airport (SDF; ☎502-367-4636; www.flylouisville.com) is 5 miles south of town on I-65. Get there by cab for a flat rate of $20 or by local bus 2. The **Greyhound station** (www.greyhound.com; 720 W Muhammad Ali Blvd) is just west of downtown. **TARC** (www.ridetarc.org; 1000 W Broadway) runs local buses ($1.75) from the Union Station depot.

Bluegrass Country

Drive through northeast Kentucky's Bluegrass Country on a sunny day and glimpse horses grazing in the brilliant-green hills dotted with ponds, poplar trees and handsome estate houses. These once-wild woodlands and meadows have been a center of horse breeding for almost 250 years – the region's natural limestone deposits, and you'll see limestone bluffs rise majestic from out of nowhere, are said to produce especially nutritious grass. The area's principal city, Lexington, is called the 'Horse Capital of the World.'

Lexington

Even the prison looks like a country club in Lexington, home of million-dollar houses and multimillion-dollar horses. Once the wealthiest and most cultured city west of the Allegheny Mountains, it was called 'the Athens of the West.' It's home to the University of

Kentucky and is the heart of the thoroughbred industry. The small downtown has some pretty Victorian neighborhoods, but most of the attractions are in the countryside.

🎯 Sights

Kentucky Horse Park   MUSEUM, PARK
(www.kyhorsepark.com; 4089 Iron Works Pkwy; adult/child $16/8, horseback riding $25; ⊙9am-5pm daily mid-Mar–Oct, Wed-Sun Nov–mid-Mar; ♿) An educational theme park and equestrian sports center sits on 1200 acres just north of Lexington. Horses representing 50 different breeds live in the park and participate in special live shows. Also included, the international **Museum of the Horse** has neat dioramas of the horse through history, from the tiny prehistoric 'eohippus' to Pony Express mail carriers. Guided 35 minute horseback rides are offered seasonally.

Thoroughbred Center   FARM
(www.thethoroughbredcenter.com; 3380 Paris Pike; adult/child $15/8; ⊙tours 9am Mon-Sat Apr-Oct, Mon-Fri Nov-Mar) Most farms are closed to the public, but you can see working racehorses up close here, with tours of the stables, practice tracks and paddocks.

Ashland   LANDMARK
(www.henryclay.org; 120 Sycamore Rd; adult/child $10/5; ⊙10am-4pm Tue-Sat, 1-4pm Sun) Just 1.5 miles east of downtown, part historic home of one of Kentucky's favorite sons, part public park, this was the Italianate estate of statesman Henry Clay (1777–1852) famed for his contribution to Abraham Lincoln's cabinet.

A gorgeous property set in the midst of a tony historic neighborhood, you'll need to pay to enter the home, but you can walk the property for free, peer into the carriage house where his coach is on display, and you can see the, ahem, privy too.

Mary Todd-Lincoln House   HISTORIC BUILDING
(www.mtlhouse.org; 578 W Main St; adult/child $10/5; ⊙10am-4pm Mon-Sat) Just behind Rupp Arena, this modest (compared to Ashland) 1806 house has articles from the first lady's childhood and her years as Abe's wife.

🛏 Sleeping

Kentucky Horse Park   CAMPGROUND $
(☏800-370-6416, 859-259-4257; www.kyhorsepark.com; 4089 Iron Works Pkwy; sites $20, powered sites $28-35; ⊙year-round; ♨) There are 260 paved sites and showers, laundry, a

grocery, playgrounds and more. Primitive camping is also available.

Gratz Park Inn   HOTEL $$
(☏800-752-4166; www.gratzparkinn.com; 120 W 2nd St; r from $179; P❄🐾) On a quiet downtown street, this 41-room hotel feels like a genteel hunt club, with mahogany furnishings and Old World oil paintings in heavy frames, and a baby grand in the lobby. It's the only boutique choice downtown.

🍴 Eating

There are several downtown cafes and bars with outdoor seating around Main and Limestone Sts.

Magee's   BAKERY $
(www.mageesbakery.com; 726 E Main St; donuts & pastries $1-3, mains $6-8; ⊙6:30am-2pm Mon & Sat, to 4pm Tue-Fri, 8am-2pm Sun; P) Lexington's guiltiest pleasure is this adorable brickhouse bakery with high-arced ceilings, and happy-making cinnamon and pecan rolls, hulking doughnuts and frosted cupcakes. It's especially popular on Sunday morns.

Village Idiot   GASTROPUB $$
(☏859-252-0099; www.lexingtonvillageidiot.com; 307 West Short St; dishes $7-17; ⊙5pm-midnight Sun-Wed, to 1am Thu-Sat) Hip young foodies descend for dishes comfy and familiar, but with a twist. Think: duck confit and waffles, or scallop and foie gras benedict. The baked brie is wrapped in phyllo dough, drizzled in fig vinegar, and is transcendent. There is a decent bourbon selection too.

⭐ Table Three Ten   NEW AMERICAN $$$
(☏859-309-3901; www.table-three-ten.com; 310 West Short St; dishes $8-32; ⊙4:30-11pm Mon-Fri, 11am-3pm Sat, 11am-9pm Sun) Everyday farmers pull up in old pick-ups hauling baskets of rabbits, hens, pork shoulder and veggies, the raw material from which Lexington's best chefs work. Mains are listed on the blackboard, and all the dishes are imganitive (think: lobster mac and cheese) and flavorful. Cocktails are tasty too.

A la Lucie   BISTRO $$$
(☏859-252-5277; www.alalucie.com; 159 N Limestone St; mains $19-30; ⊙11am-2pm Tue-Fri, 5-10pm Mon-Thu, to 11pm Fri & Sat) An intimate and whimsically decorated bistro serving the classics: a lamb shank here, steak frites there. Don't overlook the white-wine-and-herb-braised Kentucky rabbit. The local choice on date night.

☆ Entertainment

Keeneland Association RACETRACK
(☎859-254-3412; www.keeneland.com; 4201 Versailles Rd; general admission $5; ☺races Aug & Oct) Second only to Churchill Downs in terms of quality of competition, races run in April and October, when you can also glimpse champions training from sunrise to 10am. Frequent horse auctions lure sheiks, sultans, hedge fund princes and those who love (or serve) them.

Red Mile RACETRACK
(www.theredmile.com; 1200 Red Mile Rd; ☺races Aug-Oct) Head here to see harness racing, where jockeys are pulled behind horses in special two-wheeled carts. Live races are in the fall, but you can watch and wager on simulcasts year-round.

Rupp Arena ARENA
(www.rupparena.com; 430 W Vine St) The home court of perennial national title contender, University of Kentucky basketball. Set in the

THE BOURBON TRAIL

Silky, caramel-colored bourbon whiskey was likely first distilled in Bourbon County, north of Lexington, around 1789. Today 90% of all bourbon that comes out of the US is produced here in Kentucky, thanks to its pure, limestone-filtered water. Bourbon must contain at least 51% corn, and is stored in charred oak barrels for a minimum of two years. While connoisseurs drink it straight or with water, you must try a mint julep, the archetypal Southern drink made with bourbon, simple syrup and crushed mint.

The **Oscar Getz Museum of Whiskey History** (www.whiskeymuseum.com; 114 N 5th St; donations appreciated; ☺10am-4pm Tue-Sat, noon-4pm Sun), in Bardstown, tells the bourbon story with old moonshine stills and other artifacts.

Most of Kentucky's distilleries, which are centered on Bardstown and Frankfort, offer free tours. Check out Kentucky's official **Bourbon Trail website** (www.kybourbontrail.com). Note that it doesn't include every distillery.

Distilleries near Bardstown include:

Heaven Hill (www.bourbonheritagecenter.com; 1311 Gilkey Run Rd; tours $3-5) Distillery tours are offered, but you may also opt to explore the interactive Bourbon Heritage Center.

Jim Beam (www.jimbean.com; 149 Happy Hollow Rd; tours per person $8; ☺9am-5:30pm Mon-Sat, noon-4:30pm Sun) Watch a film about the Beam family and sample small-batch bourbons at the country's largest bourbon distillery. Beam makes Knob Creek (good), Knob Creek Single Barrel (better), Basil Hayden's (velvety) and the fabulous Booker's (high-proof enlightenment).

Maker's Mark (www.makersmark.com; 3350 Burks Spring Rd; tours $7; ☺10am-4:30pm Mon-Sat, 1-4:30pm Sun) This restored Victorian distillery is like a bourbon theme park, with an old gristmill and a gift shop where you can seal your own bottle in red wax.

Willet (☎502-348-0899; www.kentuckybourbonwhiskey.com; Loretto Rd, Bardstown; tours $7) A craftsman, family-owned distillery making small-batch bourbon in its own patented style. It's a gorgeous 120-acre property and one of our favorites. Tours run throughout the day.

Distilleries near Frankfort/Lawrenceburg:

Buffalo Trace (www.buffalotrace.com; 1001 Wilkinson Blvd) The nation's oldest continuously operating distillery has highly regarded tours and free tastings.

Four Roses (☎502-839-2655; www.fourrosesbourbon.com; 1224 Bonds Mills Rd; ☺9am-4pm Mon-Sat, noon-4pm Sun, closed summer) FREE One of the most scenic distilleries, in a riverside Spanish Mission–style building. Free tastings.

Woodford Reserve (www.woodfordreserve.com; 7855 McCracken Pike; tour per person $7; ☺10am-5pm) The historic site along a creek is restored to its 1800s glory; the distillery still uses old-fashioned copper pots. By far the most scenic of the lot.

middle of downtown, it also hosts conventions, concerts and other happenings.

❶ Information

Pick up maps and area information from the **visitor center** (☑ 800-845-3959, 859-233-7299; www.visitlex.com; 301 E Vine St; ⊙ 8:30am-5pm Mon-Fri, 10am-4pm Sat). The **public library** (140 E Main St; ⊙ 10am-5pm Tue-Fri, noon-5pm Sat & Sun; ☎) has free internet access and free wi-fi for laptop luggers.

❶ Getting There & Around

Blue Grass Airport (LEX; ☑ 859-425-3114; www.bluegrassairport.com; 4000 Terminal Dr) is west of town, with about a baker's dozen domestic nonstops. **Greyhound** (www.greyhound. com; 477 W New Circle Rd) is 2 miles from downtown. **Lex-Tran** (www.lextran.com) runs local buses (bus 6 goes to the Greyhound station).

Central Kentucky

The Bluegrass Pkwy runs from I-65 in the west to Rte 60 in the east, passing through some of the most luscious pasturelands in Kentucky.

About 40 miles south of Louisville is **Bardstown**, the 'Bourbon Capital of the World'. The historic downtown comes alive for the **Kentucky Bourbon Festival** (www. kybourbonfestival.com; Bardstown; ⊙ Sep). Have a meal, some bourbon and a good night's sleep in the dim limestone environs of Old **Talbott Tavern** (☑ 502-348-3494; www.talbotts.com; 107 W Stephen Foster Ave; r from $69-109, mains $8-11; ❷❊), which has been welcoming the likes of Abraham Lincoln and Daniel Boone since the late 1700s.

Follow Hwy 31 southwest to **Hodgenville** and the **Abraham Lincoln Birthplace** (www. nps.gov/abli; 2995 Lincoln Farm Road, Hodgenville; ⊙ 8am-4:45pm, to 6:45pm summer) **FREE**, a faux-Greek temple constructed around an old log cabin. Ten minutes away is Honest Abe's boyhood home at Knob Creek, with access to hiking trails.

About 25 miles (30 minutes) southwest of Lexington is **Shaker Village at Pleasant Hill** (www.shakervillageky.org; 3501 Lexington Rd; adult/child $15/5, riverboat rides $10/5; ⊙ 10am-5pm), home to a community of the Shaker religious sect until the early 1900s. Tour impeccably restored buildings, set amid buttercup meadows and winding stone paths. There's a charming **inn** (☑ 859-734-5611; www. shakervillageky.org; 3501 Lexington Rd; r from $100;

❷☎) and restaurant, a paddle-boat ride beneath the limestone bluffs along the Kentucky River, and a gift shop.

Daniel Boone National Forest

Over 700,000 acres of rugged ravines and gravity-defying sandstone arches cover much of the Appalachian foothills of eastern Kentucky. The main **ranger station** (☑ 859-745-3100; www.fs.fed.us/r8/boone; 1700 Bypass Rd) is in Winchester.

An hour southeast of Lexington is the **Red River Gorge**, whose cliffs and natural arches make for some of the best rock climbing in the country. **Red River Outdoors** (☑ 859-230-3567; www.redriveroutdoors. com; 415 Natural Bridge Rd; full-day guided climb from $115) offers guided climbing trips. **Red River Climbing** (www.redriverclimbing.com) offers detailed route information on its website. Climbers (only) can also pay $2 to camp out behind **Miguel's Pizza** (www.miguelspizza. com; 1890 Natural Bridge Rd; mains $10-14; ⊙ 7am-10pm Mon-Thu, to 11pm Fri & Sat) in the hamlet of Slade. Bordering Red River Gorge is the **Natural Bridge State Resort Park** (☑ 606-663-2214; www.parks.ky.gov; 2135 Natural Bridge Rd; r $70-150, cottages $100-170), notable for its sandstone arch. It's a family-friendly park, with camping, and some short hiking trails.

Mammoth Cave National Park

With the longest cave system on earth, **Mammoth Cave National Park** (www.nps. gov/maca; 1 Mammoth Cave Pkwy, exit 53, off I-65; tours adult $5-48, child $3.50-18; ⊙ 8:45am-5:15pm fall-spring, 8:15am-6:30pm summer) has some 400 miles of surveyed passageways. Mammoth is at least three times bigger than any other known cave, with vast interior cathedrals, bottomless pits and strange, undulating rock formations. The caves have been used for prehistoric mineral-gathering, as a source of saltpeter for gunpowder and as a tuberculosis hospital. Tourists started visiting around 1810 and guided tours have been offered since the 1830s. The area became a national park in 1926 and now brings nearly two million visitors each year.

The only way to see the caves is on the excellent **ranger-guided tours** (☑ 800-967-2283; adult $5-48, child $3-18) and it's wise to book ahead, especially in summer. Tours range from subterranean strolls to strenuous, day-long spelunking adventures (adults only). The history tour is especially interesting.

In addition to the caves, the park contains 70 miles of trails for hiking, horseback riding and mountain biking. There are also three **campsites** with restrooms, but no electricity or water hookups ($12 to $30), and 13 free backcountry campsites. Get your backcountry permit at the visitor center at the caves.

GEORGIA

The largest state east of the Mississippi River is a labyrinth of geographic and cultural extremes: right-leaning Republican politics rub against liberal idealism; small, conservative towns merge with sprawling, progressive, financially flush cities; northern mountains rise to the clouds and produce roaring rivers, while coastal marshlands teem with fiddler crabs and swaying cordgrass. Georgia's southern beaches and islands are a treat. And so are its kitchens.

ℹ Information

For statewide tourism information, contact **Discover Georgia** (📞 800-847-4842; www.exploregeorgia.org). For information on camping and activities in state parks, contact the **Georgia Department of Natural Resources** (📞 800-864-7275; www.gastateparks.org). Cars are the most convenient way to move around Georgia. I-75 bisects the state running north–south; I-20 runs east–west.

Atlanta

With five million residents in the metro and outlying areas, the so-called capital of the South continues to experience explosive growth thanks to southbound Yankees and international immigrants alike. It's also booming as a tourist destination. Beyond the big-ticket downtown attractions you'll find a constellation of superlative restaurants, a palpable Hollywood influence as Atlanta has become something of a production center, and iconic African American history.

Without natural boundaries to control development, Atlanta keeps growing, yet for all this suburbanization, Atlanta is a pretty city covered with trees and elegant homes. Distinct neighborhoods are like friendly small towns stitched together. The economy is robust, the population is young and creative, and racial tensions are minimal in 'the city too busy to hate.'

GEORGIA FACTS

Nickname Peach State

Population 9.9 million

Area 59,425 sq miles

Capital city Atlanta (population 5.3 million)

Other city Savannah (population 136,286)

Sales tax 7%, plus 6% extra on hotel accommodations

Birthplace of Baseball legend Ty Cobb (1886–1961), president Jimmy Carter (b 1924), civil rights leader Martin Luther King Jr (1929–68), singer Ray Charles (1930–2004)

Home of Coca-Cola, the world's busiest airport, the world's biggest aquarium

Politics Socially conservative as a whole, Atlanta has been known to swing both ways

Famous for Peaches

Odd law Donkeys may not be kept in bathtubs. Seriously, don't do it.

Driving distances Atlanta to St Marys 343 miles, Atlanta to Dahlonega 75 miles

👁 Sights & Activities

◉ Downtown

In recent years developers and politicians have been focusing on making the urban core more vibrant and livable. Big attractions in the city have contributed to the success.

World of Coca-Cola   MUSEUM
(www.woccatlanta.com; 121 Baker St; adult/senior/child $16/14/12; ⊙9am-7:30pm Mon-Fri, to 8:30pm Sat, 10am-7:30pm Sun) Next door to the Georgia Aquarium, this self-congratulatory museum might prove entertaining to fizzy beverage and rash commercialization fans. The climactic moment comes when guests sample Coke products from around the world – a taste-bud-twisting good time! But there are also Andy Warhol pieces on view, a 4D film to catch, company history to learn, and promotional materials aplenty.

Atlanta

MIDTOWN

Ponce de Leon Pl

Virginia Ave

Monroe Dr

Goin' Coastal;
Virginia-Highland (0.5mi)

Decatur (4mi)

Highland Inn (1mi)

City Hall East

Glen Iris Dr

Ave

Greenwood

Seal Pl

Charles Allen Dr

Monroe Dr

Ponce de Leon Ave

Linden Ave

North Ave

Boulevard Pl

Durant Pl

6th Pl

8th St

9th St

10th St

Glendale

5th St

3rd St

Argonne Ave

Penn Ave

Myrtle St

Piedmont Ave

12th St

8th St

Juniper St

6th St

5th St

4th St

3rd St

Crescent Ave

11th St

Old 10th St

Peachtree Pl

Peachtree St NE

Biltmore Pl

Cypress St

7th St

W Peachtree St

Spring St

Spring St NW

Williams St

Techwood Dr

Downtown Connector

Fowler St

8th St

6th St

4th St

Georgia Institute of Technology

Bobby Dodd Stadium

Techwood Dr

North Ave

Luckie St

10th St

5th St

Bobby Dodd Way

Tech Pkwy NW

Westside (1mi)

Atlanta Botanical Garden (0.4mi);
Fat Matt's Rib Shack (1.2mi)

High Museum of Art (0.1mi);
Hotel Artmore (0.2mi);
Woodruff Arts Center (0.2mi);
Amtrak Station (1mi)

Center for Puppetry Arts (0.3mi);
Westside Provisions District (0.7mi)

N4 Midtown

N3 North Ave

1 km
0.5 miles

THE SOUTH ATLANTA

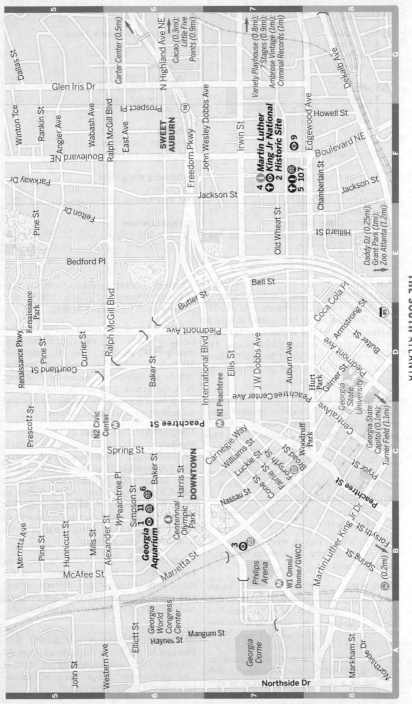

Carter Center (0.5mi)
Cacao (0.3mi);
Little Five
Points (0.9mi)

Variety Playhouse (0.8mi);
7 Stages (0.9mi);
Ambrose Vintage (1mi);
Criminal Records (1mi)

Dallas St
Glen Iris Dr
Winton Tce
Rankin St
N Angier Ave
Wabash Ave
Ralph McGill Blvd
Prospect Pl
East Ave
N Highland Ave NE

SWEET
AUBURN

Freedom Pkwy
John Wesley Dobbs Ave
Irwin St

Dekalb Ave
Howell St
Edgewood Ave
Boulevard NE

Martin Luther
King Jr National
Historic Site

Jackson St
Chamberlain St
Jackson St

Boulevard NE
Parkway Dr
Pine St
Felton Dr
Bedford Pl
Renaissance
Park
Renaissance Pkwy
Pine St
Courtland St
Currier St
Ralph McGill Blvd

Old Wheat St
Hilliard St

Daddy Dz (0.25mi);
Grant Park (1mi);
Zoo Atlanta (1.2mi)

Bell St
Butler St
Piedmont Ave

Coca Cola Pl
Armstrong St
Butler St

85

Prescott St
Pine St
Baker St
International Blvd
Ellis St
J W Dobbs Ave
Auburn Ave
Peachtree Center Ave

Hurt
Park
Gilmer St
Piedmont Ave
Central Ave
Georgia State
University

N2 Civic
Center
Spring St
Baker St
Harris St
Peachtree St

N1 Peachtree

Georgia State
Capitol (0.1mi);
Turner Field (1.1mi)

Merritts Ave
Pine St
Hunnicutt St
Mills St
W Peachtree St
Alexander St
Simpson St
Baker St

DOWNTOWN

Carnegie Way
Williams St
Luckie St
Cone St
Fairlie St
Forsyth St
Broad St
Woodruff
Park

Pryor St
Peachtree St

McAfee St
Georgia
Aquarium

Centennial
Olympic
Park
Nassau St
Marietta St

Philips
Arena

W1 Omni/
Dome/GWCC

Martin Luther King Jr Dr
Forsyth St
Spring St

(0.2mi)

Western Ave
Ellicott St
Georgia
World
Congress
Center
Haynes St
Mangum St

Georgia
Dome

Northside Dr

John St
Markham St
Northside Dr

Northside Dr

Atlanta

CNN Center   TV STUDIO
(☎404-827-2300; www.cnn.com/tour/atlanta; 1 CNN Center; tour adult/senior/child $15/14/12; ⊙9am-5pm) You might be tempted to take a 55-minute behind-the-scenes tour through the headquarters of the international, 24-hour news giant, but don't be heartbroken if you miss it. Visitors don't get very close to Wolf Blitzer (or his cronies).

Georgia State Capitol   LANDMARK
(☎404-463-4536; www.libs.uga.edu/capitol-museum; 214 State Capitol; ⊙8am-5pm Mon-Fri, tours 10am, 10:30am, 11am & 11:30am) FREE The gold-domed capitol is Atlanta's political hub. The free tours (choose to be guided or self-guided) include a film about the legislative process and a glance at the government's communications facility.

◉ Midtown

Midtown is like a hipper, second downtown, with plenty of great bars, restaurants and cultural venues.

★**High Museum of Art**   GALLERY
(www.high.org; 1280 Peachtree St NE; adult/child $19.50/12; ⊙10am-5pm Mon-Sat, noon-5pm Sun) Atlanta's modern High Museum was the first to ever exhibit art lent from Paris' Louvre, and is a destination as much for its architecture as its world-class exhibits. The striking whitewashed multilevel building houses a permanent collection of eye-catching late-19th-century furniture, early American modern canvases from the likes of George Morris and Albert Gallatin, and postwar work from Mark Rothko.

Atlanta Botanical Garden   GARDENS
(☎404-876-5859; www.atlantabotanicalgar-den.org; 1345 Piedmont Ave NE; adult/child $18.95/12.95; ⊙9am-5pm Tue-Sun, to 7pm Apr-Oct) In the northwest corner of Piedmont Park, the stunning 30-acre botanical garden has a Japanese garden, winding paths and the amazing Fuqua Orchid Center.

Margaret Mitchell House & Museum   LANDMARK
(☎404-249-7015; www.margaretmitchellhouse.com; 990 Peachtree St, at 10th St; adult/student/child $13/10/8.50; ⊙10am-5:30pm Mon-Sat, noon-5:30pm Sun) A shrine to the author of *Gone With the Wind*. Mitchell wrote her epic in a small apartment in the basement of this historic house, though nothing inside it actually belonged to her.

Piedmont Park   PARK
(www.piedmontpark.org) A glorious, rambling urban park and the setting of many cultural and music festivals. The park has fantastic bike paths, and a Saturday **Green Market**.

Skate Escape   CYCLING
(☎404-892-1292; www.skateescape.com; 1086 Piedmont Ave NE) Rents out bicycles (from $6 per hour) and in-line skates ($6 per hour). It also has tandems ($12 per hour) and mountain bikes ($25 for three hours).

◎ Sweet Auburn

Auburn Ave was the thumping commercial and cultural heart of African American culture in the 1900s. Today a collection of sights is associated with its most famous son, Martin Luther King Jr, who was born and preached here and whose grave now looks onto the street. All of the King sites are a few blocks' walk from the MARTA (p404) King Memorial station.

★ **Martin Luther King Jr**
National Historic Site   HISTORIC SITE
(☑ 404-331-5190, 404-331-6922; www.nps.gov/malu/index.htm; 450 Auburn Ave; ⊙9am-5pm) **FREE** The historic site commemorates the life, work and legacy of a civil rights leader and one of the great Americans. The center takes up several blocks. A stop by the excellent bustling **visitor center** (⊙9am-5pm, to 6pm summer) will help you get oriented with a map and brochure of area sites, and exhibits that elucidate the context – ie the segregation, systematic oppression and racial violence that inspired and fueled King's work. A 1.5-mile long, landscaped trail leads from here to the Carter Center (p398).

Martin Luther King Jr Birthplace   LANDMARK
(www.nps.gov/malu; 501 Auburn Ave; ⊙tours 10am, 11am, 2pm, 3pm, 4pm & 4:30pm) **FREE** Free guided tours of King's childhood home take about 30 minutes to complete and require reservations, which can be made at the National Historic Site visitor center.

King Center for Non-Violent
Social Change   MUSEUM
(www.thekingcenter.org; 449 Auburn Ave NE; ⊙9am-5pm, to 6pm summer) Across from the National Historic Site visitor center, this place has more information on King's life and work and a few of his personal effects, including his Nobel Peace Prize. His **gravesite** is surrounded by a long reflecting pool and can be viewed any time.

First Ebenezer Baptist Church   CHURCH
(www.historicebenezer.org; 407 Auburn Ave NE; ⊙tours 9am-6pm Mon-Sat, 1:30-6pm Sun) **FREE** Martin Luther King Jr, his father and grandfather were all pastors here, and King Jr's mother was the choir director. Sadly she was murdered here by a deranged gunwan while she sat at the organ in 1974. A multimillion-dollar restoration, completed in 2011, brought the church back to the 1960–68 period when King Jr served as co-pastor with his father.

THE SOUTH ATLANTA

ATLANTA FOR CHILDREN

Atlanta has plenty of activities to keep children entertained, delighted and educated.

Georgia Aquarium (www.georgiaaquarium.com; 225 Baker St; adult/child $35/29; ⊙10am-5pm Sun-Fri, 9am-6pm Sat; **P** 🚼) The world's largest aquarium is Atlanta's showstopper. Here are whale sharks (certified divers can swim with them), beluga whales and a, gulp, dolphin show, where human actors/trainers and majestic bottlenose dolphins perform together in a Vegas-meets-Broadway production of spectacle and cheese (think more *Pirates of the Caribbean* than underwater Cirque du Soleil).

Imagine It! Children's Museum of Atlanta (☑404-659-5437; www.childrensmuseum-atlanta.org; 275 Centennial Olympic Park Dr NW; admission $12.75; ⊙10am-4pm Mon-Fri, to 5pm Sat & Sun; 🚼) A hands-on museum geared toward kids aged eight and under. Adults aren't allowed in without a youngster in tow.

Center for Puppetry Arts (☑tickets 404-873-3391; www.puppet.org; 1404 Spring St NW; museum $8.25, performances $16.50-25; ⊙9am-3pm Tue-Fri, 10am-5pm Sat, noon-5pm Sun; 🚼) A wonderland for visitors of all ages and, hands-down, one of Atlanta's most unique attractions, the museum houses a treasury of puppets, some of which you get to operate yourself. Separate tickets are required for performances, which delight children and often sell out.

Grant Park (www.grantpark.org) A verdant oasis on the southeast edge of the city center, the park is home to **Zoo Atlanta** (www.zooatlanta.org; Grant Park; adult/child $22/17; ⊙9:30am-5:30pm Mon-Fri, to 6:30pm Sat & Sun; 🚼), which features flamingos, elephants, kangaroos and the odd tiger. But the zoo's pride and joy are the giant pandas. Their cubs will slaughter you with cuteness.

LOCAL KNOWLEDGE

LITTLE FIVE POINTS & EAST ATLANTA

While much of Atlanta keeps getting ever more hipster and hipsterer, Little Five Points (L5P) has always been Atlanta's bohemian home, though it is becoming more gentrified and touristy by the year. The epicenter is a three-way intersection with a mini plaza where drifters and hippies congregate and strum broke-down guitars and panhandle for smokes. As L5P becomes increasingly yuppified, East Atlanta has emerged as the new hot spot where the hip, gay and ghetto chic converge, conflict and party.

Both are dominated by a main drag – **Euclid Ave** in L5P and **Flat Shoals Ave** in East Atlanta – and anchored by popular music venues, Variety Playhouse (p403) and the EARL (p403), respectively.

You can sit in this time capsule, as his voice booms beautifully through the sanctuary. Sunday services are now held at a new Ebenezer across the street.

◎ Virginia-Highland

Leafy and bucolic, families enjoy the historic homes and quiet streets off North Highland Ave. The main focal point of the area is the triangular Virginia-Highland intersection-turned–commercial district, chockablock with restaurants cafes and boutiques – corporate and indie.

Carter Center   LIBRARY, MUSEUM
(✆ 404-865-7100; www.jimmycarterlibrary.org; 441 Freedom Pkwy; adult/senior/child $8/6/free; ◎ 9am-4:45pm Mon-Sat, noon-4:45pm Sun) Located on a hilltop overlooking downtown, it features exhibits highlighting Jimmy Carter's 1977–81 presidency, including a replica of the Oval Office. Carter's Nobel Prize is also on display. Don't miss the tranquil Japanese garden out back. The 1.5-mile long, landscaped, **Freedom Park Trail** leads from here to the Martin Luther King Jr National Historic Site (p397) through **Freedom Park**.

🎉 Festivals & Events

Atlanta Jazz Festival   MUSIC
(www.atlantafestivals.com; Piedmont Park; ◎ May) The month-long event culminates in live concerts in Piedmont Park on Memorial Day weekend.

Atlanta Pride Festival   GAY & LESBIAN
(www.atlantapride.org; ◎ Oct) Atlanta's annual GLBT festival.

National Black Arts Festival   CULTURAL
(✆ 404-730-7315; www.nbaf.org; ◎ Jul) Artists from across the country converge to celebrate African American music, theater, literature and film.

🛏 Sleeping

Rates at downtown hotels tend to fluctuate wildly depending on whether there is a large convention in town. The least expensive option is to stay in one of the many chain hotels along the MARTA line outside downtown and take the train into the city for sightseeing.

Hotel Artmore   BOUTIQUE HOTEL $$
(✆ 404-876-6100; www.artmorehotel.com; 1302 W Peachtree St; r $134-274; P ❀ @ 🕸) This funky art-deco gem wins all sorts of accolades: excellent service, a wonderful, wine-inviting courtyard with fire pit and a superb location across the street from Arts Center MARTA station. The 1924 Spanish-Mediterranean architectural landmark was completely revamped in 2009 resulting in an artistic boutique hotel that's become an urban sanctuary for those who appreciate their trendiness with a dollop of discretion. Parking is $18.

Hotel Indigo   BOUTIQUE $$
(✆ 404-874-9200; www.hotelindigo.com; 683 Peachtree St; r $129-179; P) A boutique-style hotel that's actually part of a chain, the Indigo has a boisterous blue color scheme and a sunny personality. More important is the outstanding Midtown location, across the street from restaurants and entertainment and within walking distance of MARTA. Parking costs $18.

Highland Inn   INN $$
(✆ 404-874-5756; www.thehighlandinn.com; 644 N Highland Ave; r from $81; P ❀ 🕸) This European-style inn, built in 1927, has appealed to touring musicians over the years. Rooms aren't huge, and that carpet is a bit threadbare, but it's as affordably comfy as Atlanta gets and is well located in the Virginia-Highland area. Paying $10 more gets you a much bigger room and a queen bed.

W Midtown HOTEL $$
(☎404-892-6000; www.watlantamidtown.com; 188 14th St NE; r from $190; ⓅⓍ@🛜🏊) A short stroll from Piedmont Park this iteration of the W offers the typical mod style you've come to expect. Rooms aren't huge but are plenty spacious with flatscreens, love seats and excellent views from top floors. The in-house **Whiskey Park** club attracts scenesters on the weekends.

This place caters mostly to a corporate crowd which means rates soar midweek but you can score great deals on the weekends.

★Stonehurst Place B&B $$$
(☎404-881-0722; www.stonehurstplace.com; 923 Piedmont Ave NE; r $159-399; ⓅⓍ@🛜) Built in 1896 by the Hinman family, this elegant B&B has all the modern amenities one could ask for, is fully updated with eco-friendly water treatment and heating systems, and has original Warhol illustrations on the wall. Well located, it's an exceptional choice if you have the budget.

Loews Atlanta HOTEL $$$
(☎404-745-5000; www.loewshotels.com; 1065 Peachtree St; r from $269; Ⓧ@🛜) Smart and modern, arguably Atlanta's finest luxury hotel is part of the Loews chain and offers all the over-the-top comforts in the heart of Midtown. The attached **Exhale Spa** will soothe your weary heart after board meetings and its art collection adds some flair.

✖ Eating

After New Orleans, Atlanta is the best city in the South to eat and food culture here is nothing short of obsessive.

✖ Downtown & Midtown

Fat Matt's Rib Shack BARBECUE $$
(www.fatmattsribshack.com; 1811 Piedmont Ave NE; mains $6-21; ⊙11:30am-11:30pm Mon-Fri, to 12:30am Sat, 1-11:30pm Sun) A classic shrine to two great Southern traditions: barbecue and the blues. Take special note of the Brunswick stew, a delicious side dish best described as barbecue soup.

Daddy Dz BARBECUE $$
(☎404-222-0206; www.daddydz.com; 264 Memorial Dr; sandwiches $6-12, plates $13-20; Ⓟ) This juke joint of a BBQ shack, consistently voted tops in town, has soul to spare. From the graffiti murals on the red, white and blue exterior to the all-powerful smoky essence to the reclaimed booths on the covered patio. Order the succulent ribs or a pulled-pork plate. You'll leave smiling.

Tamarind Seed THAI $$
(www.tamarindseed.com; 1197 Peach Tree St NE; mains $14-28; ⊙11am-10pm Mon-Thu, to 11pm Fri, 4-11pm Sat, noon-10pm Sun; Ⓟ) A bustling and sleek Thai eatery amidst the Midtown towers, serving the upwardly mobile business crowd. It does all the Thai staples and some intriguing departures like spicy lamb with

THE SOUTH ATLANTA

MARTIN LUTHER KING JR: A CIVIL RIGHTS GIANT

Martin Luther King Jr, the quintessential figure of the American Civil Rights movement and arguably America's greatest leader, was born in 1929, the son of an Atlanta preacher and choir leader. His lineage was significant not only because he followed his father to the pulpit of Ebenezer Baptist Church, but also because his political speeches rang out with a preacher's inflections.

In 1955 King led the year-long 'bus boycott' in Montgomery, AL, which resulted in the US Supreme Court removing laws that enforced segregated buses. From this successful beginning King emerged as an inspiring moral voice.

His nonviolent approach to racial equality and peace, which he borrowed from Gandhi and used as a potent weapon against hate, segregation and racially motivated violence – a Southern epidemic at the time – makes his death all the more tragic. He was assassinated on a Memphis hotel balcony in 1968, four years after receiving the Nobel Peace Prize and five years after giving his legendary 'I Have a Dream' speech in Washington, DC.

King remains one of the most recognized and respected figures of the 20th century. Over 10 years he led a movement that essentially ended a system of statutory discrimination in existence since the country's founding. The Martin Luther King Jr National Historic Site (p397) and the King Center for Non-Violent Social Change (p397) in Atlanta are testaments to his moral vision, his ability to inspire others and his lasting impact on the fundamental fabric of American society.

basil and baked scallops with Penang curry. It validates parking.

South City Kitchen SOUTHERN **$$$**
(☏404-873-7358; www.southcitykitchen.com; 1144 Crescent Ave; mains $17-36; ⊗11am-3:30pm, 5-10pm Sun-Thu, to 10:30pm Fri & Sat) An upscale Southern kitchen featuring tasty updated staples like buttermilk fried chicken served with sautéed collards and mash, and a Georgia trout, pan fried with lemon mascarpone. Start with flash fried oysters dipped in cornmeal, served with shellfish etoufee, grilled andouille and fried capers.

✗ Westside

The **Westside Provisions District** (www. westsidepd.com; 100-1210 Howell Mill Rd; [P]) is an inviting new complex of hip, farm-to-table-inspired restaurants sprinkled among upscale shops and lofts on Atlanta's Westside. There is a lot to choose from here.

★ West Egg Cafe DINER **$**
(www.westeggcafe.com; 1100 Howell Mill Rd; mains $6-12; ⊗9am-9pm Mon & Tue, to 10pm Wed-Fri, 8am-10pm Sat, to 9pm Sun; [P][✿]) Belly up to the marble breakfast counter or grab a table and dive into a salmon cake Benedict, eggs and grits, banana-bread french toast, a fried green tomato BLT, sugar bacon pancakes, or short rib hash. All the dishes are reimagined versions of old school classics, served in a stylish and spare dining room.

The tasty Irish coffees and cute wait staff don't hurt.

Star Provisions SELF-CATERING **$**
(☏404-365-0410; www.starprovisions.com; 1198 Howell Mill Rd; ⊗10am-midnight Mon-Sat) DIY gourmands will feel at home among the cheese shops and butcher cases, bakeries and kitchen hardware depots. The meat department has an exceptional array of house-cured meats, including pepperoni, bresaola, lonzino and prosciutto, if you have picnic on the brain.

Yeah! Burger BURGERS **$**
(www.yeahburger.com; 1168 Howell Mill Rd; burgers $6-11; ⊗11:30am-10pm Sun-Thu, to 11pm Fri & Sat; [P][✿][✿]) A creative, cheap-and-cheerful burger joint where you pick the patty: grass-fed beef, bison, turkey, veggie or chicken breast, tap a bun (including a gluten-free option), select one of nine cheeses and 22 toppings among rarities like jalapeños, ni-

trate-free bacon or fig jam, and add one of 18 sauces.

Kids love it, there's a full bar, and the plastic cups are compostable.

JCT Kitchen & Bar NEW AMERICAN **$$**
(☏404-355-2252; www.jctkitchen.com; 1198 Howell Mill Rd; mains $9-24; ⊗11am-2:30pm Mon-Sat, 5-10pm Mon-Thu, to 11pm Fri & Sat, 5-9pm Sun) Think: stylish wood floors and glass walls with bird-cage lighting, a knotty-wood bar and a tasty array of plates from chicken liver mousse on toast to shrimp and grits to slow-cooked rabbit to a tasty lump crab roll. It does a damn fine hanger steak too.

Abattoir CHOPHOUSE **$$$**
(☏404-892-3335; www.starprovisions.com/abattoir; 1170 Howell Mill Rd; mains $15-35; ⊗6-11pm Tue-Sat; [P]) An aptly named, upscale, carnivorous kitchen with a gorgeous bar area. The burger is top shelf, the fried quail comes with braised greens and a cornbread waffle, the shrimp and grits is curry spiced, and the hanger steak is a classic. This is a chophouse, pure and simple, complete with laid-back swank.

Bacchanalia FINE DINING **$$$**
(☏404-365-0410; www.starprovisions.com/bacchanalia; 1198 Howell Mill Rd; prix-fixe per person $85; ⊗from 6pm) Widely considered the top restaurant in the city at research time, the menu rotates daily and you may choose from six dishes for each of the five courses. Start with a Hawaiian hamachi with preserved lemon shoyu and raddish or perhaps a foie gras confit. Move into a Gulf crab fritter, a sweet-potato angilotti or poached halibut.

Then comes the lamb strip steak or quail or local Berkshire pork and winter kale, before the decadent cheese course and dessert. The atmosphere verges on chilly. Reserve ahead.

✗ Virginia-Highland & Around

Little Five has a fun vibe on weekends. Inman Park is a transitional neighborhood, set just east of downtown. And amidst the mayhem of East Atlanta, there is a lobster roll that will make you quiver.

Sevananda SELF-CATERING **$**
(www.sevananda.coop; 467 Moreland Ave NE, Little Five Points; ⊗8am-10pm) Voted Atlanta's best health-food store and a gold mine for self caterers, this co-op has a decent deli, hot soups, organic produce, natural health rem-

edies, and that unmistakable sniff of left-leaning food politics.

Cacao
CHOCOLATIER $

(www.cacaoatlanta.com; 312 N Highland Ave NE; sweets $4-6; ⊙11am-9pm Mon-Thu, 10am-10pm Fri & Sat, 11am-6pm Sun) Chocolate lovers should duck into this sleek boutique for sinful truffles and gelato (the dark choclate is absurdly good), an outrageous-looking, four-layer chocolate cake, and soul-warming mocha.

★ Fox Brothers
BARBECUE $$

(☑ 404-577-4030; www.foxbrosbbq.com; 1238 DeKalb Ave NE; dishes $8-25; ⊙11am-10pm Sun-Thu, to 11pm Fri & Sat) Another longtime Atlanta classic, set in Inman Park, ribs are scorched and smoked perfectly with a hint of charcoaled crust on the outside and tender on the inside. They're also known for their exceptional Texas-style brisket, and they bottle their own sauce.

Octopus Bar
ASIAN FUSION $$

(www.octopusbaratl.com; 560 Gresham Ave SE, East Atlanta; dishes $3-14; ⊙10:30pm-2:30am Mon-Sat) Do they keep odd hours? Is seating difficult to come by? Does it take so long to get your fusion grub because the chefs are maybe, sorta, getting high in the back alley? And, finally, is that bartender the handsomest man in Georgia? The answer, of course, is yes, to all of the above. So leave your hang-ups at the hotel and get to know what good is at this indoor-outdoor patio dive nuanced with graffed-up walls and ethereal electronica. Offerings include the best dish in the city: the lobster roll of enlightenment. No reservations, so line up early.

★ Goin' Coastal
SEAFOOD $$$

(www.goincoastalseafood.com; 1021 Virginia Ave NE; mains $18-26; ⊙5-10pm Sun-Thu, to 11pm Fri & Sat) ⊘ A casual neighborhood seafood kitchen in the heart of the Highlands lists fresh catch on the blackboard, supplemented by stunning staples such as lobster tacos ($18), coastal trout ($24) and a heap of delicious sides (creamy grits, jalapeño cornbread pudding). Whole Maine lobsters are just $20 on Monday nights.

✕ Decatur

Independent Decatur, 6 miles east of downtown, has grown into a countercultural enclave and a bonafide foodie destination. Like most traditional Southern towns, the gazebo-crowned **Courthouse Square** is the center of the action, with a number of restaurants, cafes and shops surrounding it.

Victory
SANDWICHES $

(www.vicsandwich.com; 340 Church St, Decatur; sandwiches $4; ⊙11am-2am) One of two area locations, the other is in Inman Park, this spare, converted Decatur brick house is a wonderful bargain gourmet sandwich counter where baguettes are stuffed with white anchovies and lemon mayo, or prosciutto, arugula and apples, among other intriguing options.

★ Leon's Full Service
FUSION $$

(☑ 404-687-0500; www.leonsfullservice.com; 131 E Ponce de Leon Ave; mains $11-24; ⊙5pm-1am Mon, 11:30am-1am Tue-Thu & Sun, to 2am Fri & Sat) No pretense, just a gorgeous concrete bar and an open floorplan that spills out of a former service station and onto a groovy heated deck with floating beams. Everything, from the beer, wine and cocktails (their spirits are all craftsman, small-batch creations) to the menu (think pan-roasted trout served with roasted cauliflower and an apple-curry broth or house-made chicken sausage in green curry with baby bok choi) show love and attention to detail. No wonder this place is packed. No reservations.

No. 246
ITALIAN $$

(☑ 678-399-8246; www.no246.com; 129 E Ponce de Leon Ave; mains $12-25; ⊙11am-3pm & 5-10pm Mon-Sat, to 9pm Sun) An upscale woodfired pizza and house-made pasta joint with gourmet gravitas. It does charcuterie and cheese to start, and the wonderful agnolotti is stuffed with goat cheese, roasted beets, radish and tarragon. The gnocchi with fennel sausage meatballs is worthy too. So are the pizzas. Service is superb.

Cake's & Ale
NEW AMERICAN $$$

(☑ 404-377-7994; www.cakesandalerestaurant. com; 155 Sycamore St; mains $24-36; ⊙6-11pm Tue-Thu, 5:30pm-midnight Fri & Sat) A recent Top Chef alum and pastry mastermind opened this hip and new eatery on the square. The bakery next door has life-affirming hot chocolate along with a case of delecatable pastries, but it closes early. Fear not, have a port at the molded-concrete bar and pair it with a ricotta cheesecake and blood-orange sorbet, or make that the pineapple fritters folded in brioche dough and topped with rum ice cream.

The dinner menu is spare, and rotates almost weekly, but usually offers oysters, a rib eye, and intriguing options like pork belly and shrimp served over fennel purée. That crispy rabbit leg looks good too.

Drinking & Nightlife

Brick Store Pub
BAR

(www.brickstorepub.com; 125 E Court Sq) Beer hounds geek out on Atlanta's best beer selection at this pub in Decatur, with some 17 meticulously chosen draughts, and a separate, and more intimate Belgian beer bar upstairs. In total, it serves nearly 200 beers by the bottle and draw a fun, young crowd every night.

Ormsby's
BAR

(www.ormsbysatlanta.com; 1170 Howell Mill Rd, Westside; ⊙11am-3am Mon-Fri, from noon Sat, noon-midnight Sun) Submerged beneath the Westside Provisions District (p400), this sprawling, well populated, underground pub not only has over a dozen craftsman beers on tap, and dozens more from Germany, Belgium, Sri Lanka and other exotic ports, it has games! Bocce ball, shuffleboard, billiards, ski ball and board games like Connect Four are yours to play until the wee smalls.

Rumor has it, this joint was originally a prohibition-era burlesque haunt with S&M proclivities.

Graveyard Tavern
BAR

(www.graveyardtavern.com; 1245 Glenwood Ave SE; ⊙5pm-2am Mon-Sat, 7pm-midnight Sun) Here the rafters are exposed along with the building's age, not out of high design impulse, but because this dive in East Atlanta is deliciously decrepit. The octagonal wood bar and vinyl booths host all kinds: hipsters, queers, hip-hoppers, gangsters and retirees.

Park Tavern
BAR

(www.parktavern.com; 500 10th Street NE; ⊙4:30pm-midnight Mon-Fri, from 11:30am Sat & Sun) This microbrewery-restaurant may not be all that hip, but its outdoor patio on the edge of Piedmont Park is one of the most beautiful spots in Atlanta to sit back and drink away a weekend afternoon. It pours $1 drafts on rainy days.

Blake's
GAY & LESBIAN

(www.blakesontheparkatlanta.com; 227 10th St NE) On Piedmont Park, Blake's bills itself as 'Atlanta's favorite gay bar since 1987.'

☆ Entertainment

Atlanta has big-city nightlife with lots of live music and cultural events. For listings, check out **Atlanta Coalition of Performing Arts** (www.atlantaperforms.com). The **Atlanta Music Guide** (www.atlantamusicguide.com) maintains a live-music schedule, plus a directory of local venues and links to online ticketing. Smartphone addicts should check into the **Bandsintown** app. It's especially useful in big-city America.

Theater

Woodruff Arts Center
ARTS CENTER

(www.woodruffcenter.org; 1280 Peachtree St NE, at 15th St) An arts campus hosting the High Museum, the Atlanta Symphony Orchestra and the Alliance Theatre.

Fox Theatre
THEATER

(☑855-285-8499; www.foxtheatre.org; 660 Peachtree St NE; ⊙box office 10am-6pm Mon-Fri, to 3pm Sat) A spectacular 1929 movie palace with fanciful Moorish and Egyptian designs. It hosts Broadway shows and concerts in an auditorium holding more than 4500 people.

14th Street Playhouse
THEATRE

(☑404-733-5000; www.14thstplayhouse.org; 173 14th St NE; admission from $25) If you crave a night at the Theatre, head here for professional productions of mainstream, and some avant-garde, plays and musical theatre.

7 Stages
THEATRE

(☑404-523-7647; www.7stages.org; 1105 Euclid Ave) An independently operated, nonprofit

---

GAY & LESBIAN ATLANTA

Atlanta – or 'Hotlanta' as some might call it – is one of the few places in Georgia with a noticeable and active gay and lesbian population. Midtown is the center of gay life; the epicenter is around Piedmont Park and the intersection of 10th St and Piedmont Ave. try Blake's (p402). The town of Decatur, east of downtown Atlanta, has a significant lesbian community. For news and information, grab a copy of *David Atlanta* (www.david-atlanta.com); also check out www.gayatlanta.com.

Atlanta Pride Festival (p398) is a massive annual celebration of the city's gay and lesbian community. Held in October in and around Piedmont Park.

theatre complex specializing in productions featuring local playwrights.

Live Music & Nightclubs

Cover charges at the following vary nightly. Check their respective websites for music calendars and ticket prices.

EARL   LIVE MUSIC
(www.badearl.com; 488 Flat Shoals Ave, East Atlanta) The indie rocker's pub of choice – with a busy live-music calendar and surprisingly good food.

Eddie's Attic   LIVE MUSIC
(404-377-4976; www.eddiesattic.com; 515b N McDonough St) One of the city's best venues to hear live folk and acoustic music, renowned for breaking local artists, in a nonsmoking atmosphere seven nights a week. In East Atlanta.

Variety Playhouse   LIVE MUSIC
(www.variety-playhouse.com; 1099 Euclid Ave NE) A smartly booked and well-run concert venue for a variety of touring artists. It's the anchor that keeps Little Five Points relevant.

Sports

Order tickets to sporting events through **Ticketmaster** (404-249-6400; www.ticketmaster.com).

Atlanta Braves   BASEBALL
(404-522-7630; www.atlantabraves.com; 755 Hank Aaron Dr SE; tickets $8-90) The Major League Baseball (MLB) team plays at **Turner Field**. The MARTA/Braves shuttles to the games leave from **Underground Atlanta** (www.underground-atlanta.com; cnr Peachtree & Alabama Sts; ⊙10am-9pm Mon-Sat, 11am-6pm Sun) at Steve Polk Plaza beginning 90 minutes before first pitch.

🔒 Shopping

Ambrose Vintage   VINTAGE
(www.facebook.com/AmbroseVintage; 1160 Euclid Ave; ⊙11am-7pm) By far the finest of Little Five's vintage boutiques. You'll find a nice selection of blazers and leathers for men, tweed jackets and slacks, ties and denim jackets, skirts, sweaters, blouses and hats for the ladies – all of it spanning four decades. It has tasty rock on the sound system too.

Criminal Records   MUSIC
(www.criminalatl.com; 1154 Euclid Ave; ⊙11am-9pm Mon-Sat, noon-7pm Sun) A throwback record store with used and new pop, soul, jazz, and metal, on CD or vinyl, here for your perusal. It has a fun music-related book section, and some decent comic books.

ℹ Information

EMERGENCY & MEDICAL SERVICES

Atlanta Medical Center (www.atlantamedcenter.com; 303 Pkwy Dr NE) A 460-bed tertiary care hospital operating since 1901.

Atlanta Police Department (404-614-6544; www.atlantapd.org)

Emory University Hospital (www.emoryhealthcare.org; 1364 Clifton Rd NE)

Piedmont Hospital (www.piedmonthospital.org; 1968 Peachtree Rd NW)

INTERNET ACCESS

Central Library (www.afpls.org; 1 Margaret Mitchell Sq; ⊙9am-9pm Mon-Sat, 2-6pm Sun; 🛜) Many branches of the public library offer two free 15-minute internet sessions daily, including this main branch.

MEDIA

Atlanta (www.atlantamagazine.com) A monthly general-interest magazine covering local issues, arts and dining.

Atlanta Daily World (www.atlantadailyworld.com) The nation's oldest continuously running African American newspaper (since 1928).

Atlanta Journal-Constitution (www.ajc.com) Atlanta's major daily newspaper, with a good travel section on Sunday.

Creative Loafing (www.clatl.com) For hip tips on music, arts and theater, this free alternative weekly comes out every Wednesday.

POST

For general postal information call 800-275-8777. There are post office branches at **CNN Center** (190 Marietta St NW, CNN Center); **Little Five Points** (455 Moreland Ave NE); **North Highland** (1190 N Highland Ave NE) and **Phoenix Station** (41 Marietta St NW).

Useful Websites

Scout Mob (www.scoutmob.com) Tips on what's new and hot in Atlanta.

Dixie Caviar (www.dixiecaviar.com) Recipes and restaurant recommendations from a young, brainy Atlanta-area foodie in the know.

Atlanta Travel Guide (www.atlanta.net) Official site of the Atlanta Convention & Visitors Bureau with excellent links to shops, restaurants, hotels and upcoming events. Its website also lets you buy a CityPass, a tremendous money saver that bundles admission to five of the city's attractions for a discounted price (see www.citypass.com/atlanta for more).

ℹ Getting There & Away

Atlanta's huge **Hartsfield-Jackson International Airport** (ATL; Atlanta; www.atlanta-airport.com), 12 miles north of downtown, is a major regional hub and an international gateway.

The **Greyhound terminal** (232 Forsyth St) is next to the MARTA Garnett station. Some destinations include Nashville, TN (five hours), New Orleans, LA (10½ hours), New York (20 hours), Miami, FL (16 hours) and Savannah, GA (4¾ hours).

The **Amtrak station** (1688 Peachtree St NW, at Deering Rd) is just north of downtown.

ℹ Getting Around

The **Metropolitan Atlanta Rapid Transit Authority** (MARTA; ☑ 404-848-5000; www.its-marta.com; fares $2.50) rail line travels to/from the airport to downtown, along with less useful commuter routes. Each customer must purchase a Breeze card ($1), which can be loaded and reloaded as necessary.

The shuttle and car-rental agencies have desks in the airport, situated at baggage claim.

Driving in Atlanta can be infuriating. You'll often find yourself sitting in traffic jams, and it's easy to get disoriented – Google Maps is invaluable. Some cyclists brave the city streets.

North Georgia

The southern end of the great Appalachian Range extends some 40 miles into Georgia's far north, providing superb mountain scenery, some damn decent wines, and frothing rivers. Fall colors emerge late here, peaking in October. A few days are warranted to see sites like the 1200ft-deep **Tallulah Gorge** (www.gastateparks.org/tallulahgorge), and the mountain scenery and hiking trails at **Vogel State Park** (www.gastateparks.org/vogel) and **Unicoi State Park** (www.gastateparks.org/unicoi).

Dahlonega

In 1828 Dahlonega was the site of the first gold rush in the USA. The boom these days, though, is in tourism, as it's an easy day excursion from Atlanta and is a fantastic mountain destination. The **visitor center** (☑ 706-864-3513; www.dahlonega.org; 13 S Park St; ☺ 9am-5:30pm Mon-Fri, 10am-5pm Sat), on Courthouse Sq has plenty of information on area sights and activities (including hiking, canoeing, kayaking, rafting and mountain biking). **Amicalola Falls State Park** (☑ 706-265-4703; www.amicalolafalls.com; entry per vehi-

cle $5), 18 miles west of Dahlonega on Hwy 52, features the 729ft **Amicalola Falls**, the highest waterfall in Georgia.

A dozen or so wineries on the town's outskirts produce tasty products. You can sip on the square at the **Naturally Georgia** (www.naturallygeorgia.com; 90 Public Sq N; ☺ noon-5pm Mon-Thu, to 8pm Fri-Sun) tasting room, but it's well worth seeking out **Frogtown Cellars** (☑ 706-878-5000; www.frogtownwine.com; 700 Ridge Point Dr; tastings $15; ☺ noon-5pm Mon-Fri, to 6pm Sat, 12:30-5pm Sun), a beautiful winery with a killer deck on which to sip libations, and behind it, **Three Sisters** (☑ 706-865-9463; www.threesistersvineyards.com; tastings $15; ☺ 1-5pm Thu-Sun). They pair their fine wine with bluegrass and Cheetos.

Crimson Moon Café (www.thecrimsonmoon.com; 24 N Park St; mains $8-15; ☺ 11am-3pm Mon, to 9pm Wed, to 9:30pm Thu-Sun) is an organic coffeehouse offering Southern comfort food and an intimate live-music venue. The seafood at **Back Porch Oyster Bar** (☑ 706-864-8623; www.facebook.com/backporchoysterbar; 19 North Chestatee St; mains $9-30; ☺ 11:30am-8pm) is delivered fresh daily.

★ **Hiker Hostel** (☑ 770-312-7342; www.hikerhostel.com; 7693 Hwy 19N; dm/r $18/42; ⓟ ✳ @ ⓢ), on Hwy 19N near the Three Gap Loop, is owned by avid outdoors enthusiasts and caters to those looking to explore the Appalachian Trail, which begins nearby. Each bunk room has its own bathroom and it is wonderfully neat and clean.

Central Georgia

Central Georgia is a mostly rural catch-all for everything that's not metro Atlanta, mountainous north Georgia or swampy Savannah. It feels rustic, real and definitively Southern.

Athens

A beery, artsy and laid-back college town roughly 70 miles east of Atlanta, Athens has an extremely popular football team (the University of Georgia Bulldogs), a world-famous music scene (which has launched artists including the B-52s, R.E.M. and Widespread Panic) and a burgeoning restaurant culture. The university drives the culture of Athens and ensures an ever-replenishing supply of young bar-hoppers and concert goers, some of whom stick around long after graduation and become 'townies.' The pleasant, walkable downtown offers a plethora of funky choices for eating, drinking and shopping.

◉ Sights

★ Georgia Museum of Art   MUSEUM
(www.georgiamuseum.org; 90 Carlton St; suggested donation $3; ⊗10am-5pm Tue-Wed, Fri & Sat, to 9pm Thu, 1-5pm Sun) A smart, modern gallery open to the public where brainy, arty types set up in the wired lobby for personal study and art hounds gawk at modern sculpture in the courtyard garden and a tremendous collection from American realists of the 1930s. Rotating exhibitions always inspire.

State Botanical Garden
of Georgia   GARDENS
(☑706-369-5884;   www.uga.edu/~botgarden; 2450 S Milledge Ave; ⊗8am-8pm) **FREE** Truly gorgeous, with winding outdoor paths and a socio-historical edge to boot, Athens' gardens rivals Atlanta's. Signs provide smart context for its amazing collection of plants, which runs the gamut from rare and threatened species to nearly 5 miles of top-notch woodland walking trails.

⊨ Sleeping & Eating

Athens does not have a great selection of lodging. There are standard chains just out of town on W Broad St.

★ Hotel Indigo   BOUTIQUE HOTEL $$
(☑706-546-0430; www.indigoathens.com; 500 College Ave; r weekend/weekday from $159/139; P❀@✿✵) Rooms are spacious, loft-like pods of cool at this eco-chic boutique hotel. Part of the Indigo chain, it's a Leadership in Energy and Environmental Design gold-certified sustainable standout. Green elements include regenerative elevators and priority parking for hybrid vehicles, and 30% of the building was constructed from recycled content.

Foundry Park Inn & Spa   INN $$
(☑706-549-7020; www.foundryparkinn.com; 295 E Dougherty St; r from $110; P❀@✿✵) A cute, indie choice on pleasant grounds that include a restored Confederate iron foundry. In addition to its on-site spa, the hotel campus includes a restaurant and a cozy music venue.

Ike & Jane   CAFE $
(www.ikeandjane.com; 1307 Prince Ave; mains $3.50-7; ⊗6:30am-5pm Mon-Fri) If your idea of a balanced breakfast is doughnuts and cof-fee, you might be a police officer, an 85-year-old man or a fan of this sunny little shingle in Normal Town, where the doughnuts involve creative ingredients like red velvet, caramel, peanut butter, banana and bacon.

The coffee is gourmet, and it does quiche, bagels, and gourmet soups, salads and sandwiches too.

Heirloom Cafe   CAFE $$
(☑706-354-7901; www.heirloomathens.com; 815 N Chase St; mains $10-15; ⊗11am-3pm & 5:30-9pm Mon-Thu, to 10pm Fri, 9:30am-2:30pm & 5:30-10pm Sat, 9:30am-2:30pm Sun; P) A new spot specializing in locally sourced ingredients folded into tasty dishes like shrimp and grits, a prosciutto, cheese and apple baguette, and a mean pulled-pork sandwich. Weekend brunch features a popular gruyere-and-fig omelet.

★ Five & Ten   AMERICAN $$$
(☑706-546-7300; www.fiveandten.com; 1653 S Lumpkin St; mains $18-29; ⊗10:30am-2:30pm Sun, 5:30-10pm Sun-Thu, to 11pm Fri & Sat) Driven by sustainable ingredients, Five & Ten ranks among the South's best restaurants. Its menu is earthy and slightly gamey: sweatbreads, hand-cut pasta and Frogmore stew (stewed corn, sausage and potato). Reservations mandatory.

National   NEW SOUTHERN $$$
(☑706-549-3450; www.thenationalrestaurant.com; 232 W Hancock Ave; mains $20-28; ⊗11:30am-10pm Mon-Thu, to late Fri & Sat, 5-10pm Sun) An effortlessly cool bistro on the downtown outskirts, favored for the kale Caesar, the peppery crawfish bisque, a nice pan-roasted trout, and mussels steamed in an orange-saffron-chili vinnegrette. The bar is one where you may want to sit and sip a while.

♟ Drinking & Entertainment

Nearly 100 bars and restaurants dot Athens' compact downtown area, so it's not hard to find a good time. Pick up a free *Flagpole* (www.flagpole.com) to find out what's on.

Normal Bar   BAR
(www.facebook.com/normal.bar.7; 1365 Prince Ave; ⊗4pm-2am Mon-Thu, from 3pm Fri & Sat) This lovable dark storefront bar, a bit out of the way in Normal Town, is very un-student but still very much Athens. The beer goes from PBR cheap to local craftsman IPA-sophiticati. It has a terrific wine list and the crowd is young, cute and doesn't care either way.

Grab a candlelit booth inside, belly up to the bar or hang on the back patio.

Flicker
BAR

(www.flickertheatreandbar.com; 263 W Washington St; ⊕4pm-2am Mon-Fri, from 1pm Sat) A happening hipster scene simmers. It hosts live bands and has a slender smoking patio populated with intellectual, self-confident hairdos and the occasional vaguely sexy fire twirler. It's always busy. Even on Monday nights.

Cutter's
SPORTS BAR

(www.facebook.com/cutterspub; 120 E Clayton St; ⊕2:30pm-2am Mon-Fri, from noon Sat) A popular sports bar with gargantuan flatscreens. If victory is grasped by the UGA Bulldogs, the interior becomes a sloshed dance hall of depravity. But in a good way.

Walker's Coffee & Pub
PUB

(www.walkerscoffee.com; 128 College Ave; ⊕7am-2am) Where grad students and a few sophisticated under grads stretch out in the built-in wooden booths that wrap around the room. It specializes in an array of liquored-up coffee drinks. But you can get a sensible coffee here too.

40 Watt Club
LIVE MUSIC

(☎706-549-7871; www.40watt.com; 285 W Washington St; admission $5-30) This legendary joint has lounges, a tiki bar, $2 PBRs, and has welcomed indie rock to its stage since R.E.M., the B-52s and Widespread Panic owned this town. It's still where the big hitters play when they visit.

Georgia Theatre
VENUE

(☎706-850-7670; www.georgiatheatre.com; 215 N Lumpkin St; ⊕11:30am-midnight Mon-Sat) When this historic movie theater burnt down it was rebuilt as a hip music venue. Only the facade and marquee remain from the original, and there is a brand-new bar on the rooftop with stunning views of uplit downtown.

Sanford Stadium
STADIUM

(☎706-542-9036; www.georgiadogs.com; 100 Sanford Dr) Home of the beloved University of Georgia Bulldogs football team.

ⓘ Information

The **Athens Welcome Center** (☎706-353-1820; www.athenswelcomecenter.com; 280 E Dougherty St; ⊕10am-5pm Mon-Sat, noon-5pm Sun), in a historic antebellum house at the corner of Thomas St, provides maps and information on local tours – these include a Civil War tour and the 'Walking Tour of Athens Music History.'

Savannah

Like a proper Southern belle with a an electric-blue streak in her hair, this grand historic town revolves around formal antebellum architecture and the revelry of local students from Savannah College of Art & Design (SCAD). It sits alongside the Savannah River, about 18 miles from the coast, amid Lowcountry swamps and mammoth live oak trees dripping with Spanish moss. With its colonial mansions, and beautiful squares, Savannah preserves its past with pride and grace. However, unlike its sister city of Charleston, SC, which retains its reputation as a dignified and refined cultural center, Savannah is a little gritty, lived in, and real.

⊙ Sights & Activities

The Central Park of Savannah is a sprawling rectangular green space called **Forsyth Park**. The park's beautiful fountain is a quintessential photo op. Savannah's **riverfront** is mostly populated with forgettable shops and cafes. But it's worth a short stroll. As is **Jones Street**, among Savannah's prettiest thanks to the mossy oaks that hold hands from either side.

A $20 multi-venue ticket gets you into the Jepson Center for the Arts, Telfair Academy and the Owen-Thomas House.

★ Wormsloe Plantation Historic Site
PLANTATION

(www.gastateparks.org; 7601 Skidaway Rd; adult/senior/youth 6-17yr/child 1-5yr $10/9/4.50/1; ⊕9am-5pm Tue-Sun) A short drive from downtown, on the beautiful **Isle of Hope**, this is one of the most photographed sites in town. The real draw is the dreamy entrance through a corridor of mossy, ancient oaks that runs for 1.5 miles, known as the **Avenue of the Oaks**.

But there are other draws, including an existing antebellum mansion still lived in by the descendants of the original owner, Noble Jones, some old colonial ruins, and a touristy site where you can see folks demonstrate blacksmithing and other bygone trades. There are two flat, wooded walking trails here too. The one-miler takes in the main sights. A 3-mile trail extends to the plantation boundary.

Owens-Thomas House HISTORIC BUILDING
(www.telfair.org; 124 Abercorn St; adult/child $15/5;
⊙noon-5pm Mon, 10am-5pm Tue-Sat, 1-5pm Sun)
Completed in 1819 by British architect William Jay, this gorgeous villa exemplifies English Regency-style architecture, which is known for its symmetry. The guided tour is fussy, but it delivers interesting trivia about the spooky 'haint blue' ceiling paint in the slaves' quarters (made from crushed indigo, buttermilk and crushed oyster shells) and the number of years by which this mansion preceded the White House in getting running water (nearly 20).

Jepson Center for the Arts GALLERY
(JCA; www.telfair.org; 207 W York St; adult/child
$12/5; ⊙10am-5pm Mon, Wed, Fri & Sat, to 8pm
Thu, noon-5pm Sun; ⊛) Looking pretty darn space-age by Savannah's standards, the JCA focuses on 20th- and 21st-century art. Its contents are modest in size but intriguing. There's also a neat interactive area for kids.

Mercer-Williams House HISTORIC BUILDING
(www.mercerhouse.com; 429 Bull St; adult/child
$12.50/8) Although Jim Williams, the Savannah art dealer portrayed by Kevin Spacey in the film version of *Midnight in the Garden of Good and Evil,* died back in 1990, his infamous mansion didn't become a museum until 2004. You're not allowed to see the upstairs, where Williams' family still lives, but the downstairs is an interior decorator's fantasy.

Telfair Academy of Arts & Sciences MUSEUM
(www.telfair.org; 121 Barnard St; adult/child $12/5;
⊙noon-5pm Mon, 10am-5pm Tue-Sat, 1-5pm Sun)
Considered Savannah's top art museum, the historic Telfair family mansion is filled with 19th-century American art, silver from that century, and a smattering of European pieces.

SCAD Museum of Art ART MUSEUM
(www.scadmoa.org; 601 Turner Blvd; adult/child under 14 yr $10/free; ⊙10am-5pm Tue, Wed & Fri, to 8pm Thu, noon-5pm Sat & Sun) Brand new and architecturally striking, this brick, steel, concrete and glass longhouse delivers your modern fix. With groovy, creative sitting areas inside and out, and fun rotating exhibitions.

Cathedral of St John the Baptist CHURCH
(222 E Harris St) If you like old churches, you will love it here. Completed in 1896 but destroyed by fire two years later, this impressive cathedral, reopened in 1912, features stunning stained-glass transept windows from Austria depicting Christ's ascension into heaven, as well as ornate Station of the Cross woodcarvings from Bavaria. The pipe organ is equally spectacular.

Ralph Mark Gilbert Civil Rights Museum MUSEUM
(460 Martin Luther King Jr Blvd; adult/senior/child
$8/6/4; ⊙9am-5pm Tue-Sat) Set in what was once the most successful black-owned bank in America, this private museum focuses on the local history of segregated schools, hotels, hospitals, jobs and lunch counters. Push the buttons at Levy's lunch counter for a stinging dramatization.

Savannah Bike Tours CYCLING
(☑912-704-4043; www.savannahbiketours.com; 41
Habersham St) Operating out of a cute little storefront on Habersham St, this outfit offers two-hour bike tours on its fleet of cruisers (with baskets of course).

🛏 Sleeping

Luckily for travelers, it's become stylish for Savannah hotels and B&Bs to serve hors d'oeuvres and wine to guests in the evening. Cheap sleeps are difficult to find and all accommodations should be booked in advance.

Azalea Inn INN $$
(☑912-236-2707; www.azaleainn.com; 217 E
Huntingdon St; r from $199; P❈🅿📶☀) A humble stunner on a quiet street, we love this sweet canary-yellow historic inn near Forsyth Park. The 10 rooms aren't huge, but are well done with varnished dark-wood floors, crown mouldings, four-post beds and a small dipping pool out back.

Bed & Breakfast Inn B&B $$
(☑912-238-0518; www.savannahbnb.com; 117
W Gordon St; r $179-229; P❈📶) Spittin' distance from Savannah's most architecturally diverse square (Monterrey), this is a well-loved, well-worn establishment. Meaning it does show its age. Easy to walk right by on a uniform street of 1850 row houses, the location is ideal.

Mansion on Forsyth Park HOTEL $$$
(☑912-238-5158; www.mansiononforsyth-park.com; 700 Drayton St; r weekend/weekday
$249/199; P❈@📶☀) A choice location and chic design highlight the luxe accommodations on offer at the 18,000-sq-ft Mansion – the sexy bathrooms alone are practically

Savannah

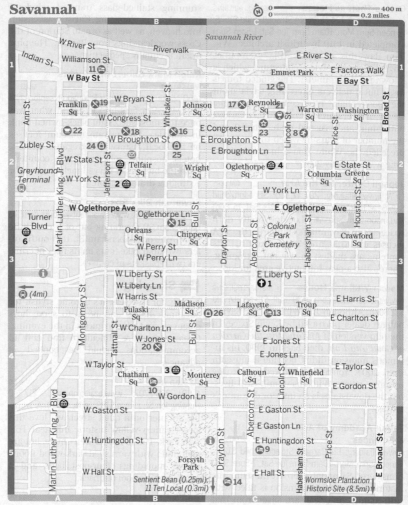

worth the money. The best part of the hotel-spa is the amazing local and international art that crowds its walls and hallways, over 400 pieces in all. Parking costs $20 per day.

Bohemian Hotel
BOUTIQUE HOTEL $$$
(☎ 912-721-3800; www.bohemianhotelsavannah.com; 102 West Bay St; r from $299; P❋@☎) Enjoy sleek, dark, Gothic hallways, a riverside perch and small touches like driftwood and oyster chandeliers. Rooms are stunning, though too low-lit for some. Personalized service makes it feel far more intimate than its 75 rooms indicate. Parking is $25

East Bay Inn
INN $$$
(☎ 912-238-1225; www.eastbayinn.com; 225 E Bay St; r from $235) Wedged between corporate rivals, this brick behemoth offers just 28 huge rooms all with original wood floors, exposed brick walls, soaring ceilings, slender support columns and fat flatscreens, along with much charm and warmth.

Hamilton Turner Inn
INN $$$
(☎ 912-233-1833; www.hamilton-turnerinn.com; 330 Abercorn St; d from $189; ❋☎) Set on picturesque Lafayette Sq and built in classic French style in 1873, all 17 rooms offer

Savannah

elegant antique decor that may make you swoon, though service is not one of the inn keepers' strong points.

✗ Eating

Angel's BBQ BARBECUE $
(www.angels-bbq.com; 21 West Oglethorpe Lane; sandwiches/plates $6/8; ⊙11:30am-3pm Tue, to 6pm Wed-Sat) Utterly low-brow and hidden down an uneventful lane, Angel's pulled-pork sandwich and sea-salted fries will leave you humbled and thoroughly satisfied – and that's before you tear through the impressive list of housemade sauces.

Vinnie Van GoGo's PIZZERIA $
(www.vinnievangogo.com; 317 W Bryan St; pizza slices from $2.50; ⊙4-11pm Mon-Thu, noon-midnight Fri & Sat, noon-11:30pm Sun) This locally owned pizzeria draws legions of locals for its Neapolitan brick-oven pies.

Wilkes' House SOUTHERN $$
(www.mrswilkes.com; 107 W Jones St; lunch $16; ⊙11am-2pm Mon-Fri) The line outside can begin as early as 8am at this first-come, first served, Southern comfort food institution. Once the lunch bell rings and you are seated family-style, the kitchen unloads on you: fried chicken, beef stew, meatloaf, cheese potatoes, collard greens, black-eyed peas, mac 'n' cheese, rutabaga, candied yams, squash casserole, creamed corn *and* biscuits.

It's like Thanksgiving and the Last Supper rolled into one massive feast chased with sweet tea.

Papillote CAFE $$
(www.papillote-savannah.com; 218 W Broughton St; mains $9-14; ⊙10:30am-7pm Wed-Fri, 9:30am-5pm Sat & Sun) One of our favorite new spots in town serves creative yet simple delights, like a chicken curry pot pie, and a baguette stuffed with braised pork, roasted red peppers and melted Swiss. The omelets and brioche French toast for brunch are popular too.

Circa 1875 BISTRO $$
(☏912-443-1875; www.circa1875.com; 48 Whitaker St; mains $12-28; ⊙bar 5pm-2am, dinner 6-11pm) A gorgeous little bistro downtown with high tin ceilings, turn-of-the-century tiled floors, and a dynamite burger drenched in peppercorn sauce and served with truffle fries. It also does frog legs, escargot, pâté, steak tartare and steak frites, of course.

★**11 Ten Local** NEW AMERICAN $$$
(☏912-790-9000; www.local11ten.com; 1110 Bull St; mains $24-32; ⊙6-10pm Mon-Sat) Upscale, sustainable, local, fresh: these elements help create an elegant, well-run restaurant, that's, hands down, the best in Savannah. Start with a spring roll salad, an unfurled spring roll speckled with ginger dressing, then move on to the fabulous big eye tuna,

seared perfectly fresh and plated with kim chi and green-pea purée.

Or just pick a grilled protein – fillet, fresh catch, scallops, or chicken breast – and one or three of their awesome sauces and sides like brussels with walnuts and sausage or a historically good mac and cheese.

Olde Pink House NEW SOUTHERN $$$
(912-232-4286; www.plantersinnsavannah.com/savannah-dining.htm; 23 Abercorn St; mains $25-31; 11am-10:30pm) Classic Southern food done upscale, our favorite appetizer is southern sushi – shrimp and grits rolled in a coconut-crusted nori roll. Dine in the slender digs upstairs, or go underground to the fabulous tavern where the piano player rumbles and the room is cozy, funky and perfect. The buidling is a 1771 landmark.

Drinking & Nightlife

Rocks on the Roof BAR
(www.bohemianhotelsavannah.com/dining/lounge; 102 West Bay St; from 11am;) The expansive rooftop bar at the Bohemian Hotel is breezy, fun and best when the weather is nice and the firepit is glowing. The views are sensational.

Lulu's Chocolate Bar CAFE
(www.luluschocolatebar.net; 42 Martin Luther King Jr Blvd) More a place to sink yourself into a sugar coma than catch a buzz, Lulu's is an adorable yet chic neighborhood martini and dessert bar. The heavenly signature Lulutini is pure chocolate decadence.

Sentient Bean CAFE
(www.sentientbean.com; 13 E Park Ave; 7am-10pm;) Everything you want from an indie coffee house: terrific brew, gourmet scones, spacious boho interior and hipster clientele and baristas. It's Savannah's favorite and just across from Forsyth Park.

Abe's on Lincoln BAR
(17 Lincoln St) Ditch the tourists – drink with the locals in dark, dank, all-wood environs. It hosts open-mic nights and occasional live performances.

Entertainment

Lucas Theatre for the Arts THEATER
(912-525-5040; www.lucastheatre.com; 32 Abercorn St) Hosting concerts (guitarist Jonny Lang), plays *(Guys and Dolls)* and films *(The Day the Earth Stood Still)* in a historic building dating from 1921.

Shopping

West Broughton St is Savannah's preeminent shopping district – with both corporate and indie entities shoulder to shoulder, and all of it punctuated with a distinctly SCAD flavor.

★**Satchel** HANDBAGS
(912-233-1008; www.shopsatchel.com; 311 W Broughton St) After graduating from SCAD, 29-year-old designer and owner, Elizabeth Seeger, didn't want to get a real job (or move away from Savannah), so she opened a store. She makes her all-leather goods in-house, and we're talking about an amazing collection of high-end bespoke hand bags that belong on a runway. Her men's wallets are terrific too.

Savannah Bee Company FOOD
(www.savannahbee.com; 104 W Broughton St; 10am-8pm Mon-Sat, 11am-5pm Sun) This internationally renowned honey dreamland is one of Savannah's must-stops. Expect artisanal honey of infinite variety and limitless free tastings.

ShopSCAD ARTS & CRAFTS
(www.shopscadonline.com; 340 Bull St; 9am-5:30pm Mon-Wed, to 8pm Thu & Fri, 10am-8pm Sat, noon-5pm Sun) All the wares at this funky, kitschy boutique were designed by students, faculty and alumni of Savannah's prestigious art college.

Information

Candler Hospital (www.sjchs.org; 5353 Reynolds St)
CVS Pharmacy (cnr Bull & W Broughton Sts)
Live Oak Public Library (www.liveoakpl.org; 2002 Bull St; 9am-8pm Mon-Tue, to 6pm Wed-Fri, 2-6pm Sun;) Offers free internet and wi-fi access.
Post Office Historic District (118 Barnard Street; 8am-5pm Mon-Fri); Main (1 E Bay St; 8am-5:30pm Mon-Fri, 9am-1pm Sat)
Savannah Chatham Metropolitan Police (912 651-6675; www.scmpd.com; cnr E Oglethorpe Ave & Habersham St)
Visitor Center (912-944-0455; www.savannahvisit.com; 301 Martin Luther King Jr Blvd; 8:30am-5pm Mon-Fri, 9am-5pm Sat & Sun) Excellent resources and services are available in this center, based in a restored 1860s train station. Many privately operated city tours start here. There is also a small interactive tourist-info kiosk in the new Visitor Center at Forsyth Park.

ⓘ Getting There & Around

The **Savannah/Hilton Head International Airport** (SAV; www.savannahairport.com) is about 5 miles west of downtown off I-16. Taxis from the airport to the Historic District cost a standard $28. **Greyhound** (www.greyhound.com; 610 W Oglethorpe Ave) has connections to Atlanta (about five hours), Charleston, SC (about two hours) and Jacksonville, FL (2½ hours). The **Amtrak station** (www.amtrak.com; 2611 Seaboard Coastline Dr) is just a few miles west of the Historic District.

You won't need a car. It's best to park and walk. **Chatham Area Transit** (CAT; www.catchacat.org; per ride $1.50) operates local buses that run on bio-diesel, including a free shuttle (the Dot) that makes its way around the Historic District and stops within a couple of blocks of nearly every major site.

Brunswick & the Golden Isles

Georgia has a coast? Oh yes, a righteously beautiful one, blessed with a string of picturesque islands ranging from rustic to kitschy to indulgent. With its large shrimp-boat fleet and downtown historic district shaded beneath lush live oaks, **Brunswick** dates from 1733 and has charms you might miss when sailing by on I-95 or the Golden Isle Pkwy (US Hwy 17). During WWII Brunswick shipyards constructed 99 Liberty transport ships for the navy. Today a 23ft scale model at **Mary Ross Waterfront Park** (Bay St) stands as a memorial to those ships and their builders. On the first Friday of the month quirky Brunswick opens up its fun antique and art galleries and pours wine for all comers.

St Simons Island

Famous for its golf courses, resorts and majestic live oaks, St Simons Island is the largest and most developed of the Golden Isles. It lies 75 miles south of Savannah and just 5 miles from Brunswick. The southern half of the island is a thickly settled residential and resort area. However the northern half and adjacent **Sea Island** (www.explorestsimonsisland.com) offer tracts of coastal wilderness amid a tide-water estuary. **East Beach**, the island's best, is accessible from **Massengale Park** (1350 Ocean Blvd). Much tasty seafood at **Crab Trap** (☑912-638-3552; www.thecrabtrapssi.com; 1209 Ocean Blvd; dishes $11-25). Bed down near the main downtown drag at **St Simons Inn by the Lighthouse** (☑912-

638-1101; www.saintsimonsinn.com; 609 Beachview Dr; r from $179; [P][✱][☎][≋]).

Little St Simons is an all-natural jewel, accessible by boat only to guests at the exclusive **Lodge on Little St Simons** (☑912-638-7472; www.littlessi.com; 1000 Hampton Pt, Little St Simons Island; all-inclusive d from $475; ⊙May-Sep) or to their **day trippers** (☑912-638-7472; www.littlestsimonsisland.com; Hampton Point Dr; ⊙trips 10:30am).

Jekyll Island

An exclusive refuge for millionaires in the late 19th and early 20th centuries, Jekyll is a 4000-year-old barrier island with 10 miles of beaches. Today it's an unusual clash of wilderness, historically preserved buildings, modern hotels and a massive campground. It's an easily navigable place – you can get around by car, horse or bicycle, but there's a $5 parking fee per day.

An endearing attraction is the **Georgia Sea Turtle Center** (☑912-635-4444; www.georgiaseaturtlecenter.org; 214 Stable Rd; adult/child $7/5; ⊙9am-5pm Sun-Tue, 10am-2pm Mon, tours 8:30pm & 9:30pm from Jun 1; [♿]), a conservation center and turtle hospital where patients are on view for the public. Come sunrise, you must find **Driftwood Beach**.

The posh yet antiquated **Jekyll Island Club Hotel** (☑800-535-9547; www.jekyllclub.com; 371 Riverview Dr; d/ste from $179/279; [P][✱][@][☎][≋]) is a great place for a drink after a sunset seafood dinner at its waterfront **Latitude 31 Restaurant & Rah Bar** (www.latitude31andrahbar.com; mains $14-23; ⊙from 11:30am Tue-Sun), located right on the wharf. For something closer to the best beaches, find **Villas By The Sea** (☑912-635-2521, 800-841-6262; www.villasbythesearesort.com; 1175 N Beachview Dr; condos from $149).

Cumberland Island & St Marys

An unspoiled paradise, a backpacker's fantasy, a site for day trips or extended stays – it's clear why the family of 19th-century industrialist and philanthropist Andrew Carnegie used Cumberland as a retreat long ago. Most of this southernmost barrier island is now occupied by the **Cumberland Island National Seashore** (www.nps.gov/cuis; admission $4). Almost half of its 36,415 acres consists of marsh, mudflats and tidal creeks. On the ocean side are 16 miles of wide, sandy beach that you might have all to yourself. The island's interior is characterized by maritime forest. Ruins from the Carnegie estate **Dungeness** are astounding, as are the wild turkeys, tiny fiddler crabs and beautiful butterflies. Feral horses roam the island and are a common sight.

The only public access to the island is via boat to/from the quirky, lazy town of **St Marys** (www.stmaryswelcome.com). Convenient and pleasant **ferries** (☑912-882-4335; www.nps.gov/cuis; round-trip adult/senior/child $20/18/14) leave from the mainland at the St Marys dock at 9am and 11:45am and return at 10:15am and 4:45pm. Reservations are staunchly recommended well before you arrive, and visitors are required to check in at the **visitor's center** (☑912-882-4336; www.nps.gov/cuis; ⊙8am-4:30pm) at the dock at least 30 minutes prior to departure. December through February, the ferry does not operate on Tuesday or Wednesday.

St Marys caters to tourists visiting Cumberland. This tiny, lush one-horse town has a number of comfortable B&Bs, including the lovely **Spencer House Inn** (☑912-882-1872; www.spencerhouseinn.com; 200 Osborne St; r $135-245), circa 1872. It's brushed-up pink, with 14 spacious rooms on three floors. The staff book reservations, pack lunches for day trippers and serve a full gourmet breakfast each morning. When you're hungry, find **Riverside Cafe** (www.riversidecafesaintmarys.com; 106 St Marys Rd; mains $8-18; ⊙11am-9pm Mon-Fri, from 8:30am Sat & Sun), a wonderful Greek diner with sea views.

On Cumberland Island, the only private accommodations are at the **Greyfield Inn** (☑904-261-6408; www.greyfieldinn.com; r incl meals $425-635), a mansion built in 1900, with a two-night minimum stay. Camping is available at **Sea Camp Beach** (☑912-882-4335; www.nps.gov/cuis; tent sites per person $4), a campground set among magnificent verdant oaks.

Note: there are no stores or waste bins on the island. Eat before arriving or bring lunch, and take your trash with you.

ALABAMA

Football and history are two things Southerners never stop discussing, and Alabama is the perfect prism for both. It was home to one of gridiron's most legendary coaches, Paul 'Bear' Bryant, and to Jefferson Davis, the first president of the Confederacy in 1861 (the year the Civil War began).

More significantly, in the 1950s and '60s, Alabama became a civil rights battleground pitting racial segregationists against nonviolent activists who demanded freedom. The ripple effects were felt in legislation that affected the entire country, and exploring this state provides powerful insight into uniquely American racial dynamics, and the United States' checkered history as a whole.

Geographically, Alabama has a surprising diversity of landscapes, from leafy foothills in the north to the subtropical Gulf Coast down south. And let's not forget endearing Birmingham, a shining light of progress in a state that all too often seems to be shadow boxing with its own demons.

ⓘ Information

Alabama Bureau of Tourism & Travel (www.alabama.travel) Sends out a vacation guide and has a website with extensive tourism options.

Alabama State Parks (☑800-252-7575; www.alapark.com) There are 23 parks statewide with camping facilities ranging from primitive ($12) to RV hookups ($26). Advanced reservations are suggested for weekends and holidays.

Birmingham

No one can ignore Birmingham's checkered past – civil rights violence earned it the nickname 'Bombingham.' Yet this midsize, blue-collar city will show you a good time, has a surprising amount of culture, and has integrated its civil rights struggle into the tourist experience. Such perspective, and a bustling economy – Mercedes Benz manufactures here – has allowed the city to look forward, and become modern, open and new.

⊙ Sights & Activities

Art-deco buildings in trendy **Five Points South** house shops, restaurants and nightspots. Equally noteworthy is the newer and more upscale **Homewood** community's quaint commercial drag on 18th St S, close to the Vulcan who looms illuminated above the city and is visible from nearly all angles, day and night.

★ Birmingham Civil Rights Institute
MUSEUM
(www.bcri.org; 520 16th St N; adult/senior/child $12/5/3, Sun free; ⊙10am-5pm Tue-Sat, 1-5pm Sun) A maze of moving audio, video and photography exhibits tell the story of racial segregation in America, and the Civil Rights

movement – with a focus on activities in and around Birmingham. There's an extensive exhibit on the 16th Street Baptist Church bombing in 1963, and it's the beginning of the city's new Civil Rights Memorial Trail.

16th Street Baptist Church
CHURCH
(www.16thstreetbaptist.org; cnr 16th St & 6th Ave N; donation $5; ⊙ministry tours 10am-4pm Tue-Fri, to 1pm Sat) This church became a gathering place for organizational meetings and a launch pad for protests in the 1950s and '60s. During a massive desegregation campaign directed at downtown merchants in 1963, Ku Klux Klan members bombed the church during Sunday school, killing four little girls. Today the rebuilt church is a memorial and a house of worship (services 10:45am Sunday).

Vulcan Park
PARK
(www.visitvulcan.com; 1701 Valley View Dr; observation tower adult/child $6/4; ⊙7am-10pm, observation tower 10am-6pm Mon-Sat, from 1pm Sun) Visible from all over the city thanks to the world's largest cast-iron statue, the park offers fantastic views for free, and an **observation tower**.

Birmingham Museum of Art
GALLERY
(www.artsbma.org; 2000 Rev Abraham Woods Jr Blvd; ⊙10am-5pm Tue-Sat, noon-5pm Sun) FREE Collects work from Asia, Africa, Europe and the Americas. Don't miss the work of Rodin, Botero and Dalí in the sculpture garden.

Birmingham Civil Rights Memorial Trail
WALKING TOUR
(www.bcri.org; 520 16th St N; ⊞) Seven blocks long, a poignant walk perfect for the whole family, and installed in 2013 for the 50th anniversary of the Civil Rights campaign, the walk depicts 22 moving scenes with statues and photography, and peels back yet another layer of the sweat and blood behind a campaign that changed America.

For instance, you'll learn that Martin Luther King Jr's strategy was to flood the city jails, but to spare families from losing their bread winners, they recruited high-school students who became known as 'foot soldiers' within the movement.

🛏 Sleeping

★Aloft
HOTEL $$
(205-874-8055; www.aloftbirminghamsohosquare.com; 1903 29th Ave S; r from $129; P✳🐾) Yes, it's a chain, but this W-conceived kid sister in the Homewood area is a steal with

new, modern interiors, king beds and high ceilings, up-to-the-minute electronics, ample light, and luscious bathrooms and linens. There's a fun bar with a pool table and a news ticker in the groovy lobby.

Redmont Hotel
HISTORIC HOTEL $$
(205-324-2101; 2101 5th Ave N; r/ste from $89/129; ✳@🐾) A historic hotel built in 1925, the piano and chandelier in the lobby lend a certain historical, old-world feel and all deluxe rooms are just renovated giving it modern edge. The spacious rooftop bar doesn't hurt, either. It's walking distance to the civil rights sights.

Hotel Highland
HOTEL $$
(205-271-5800; www.thehotelhighland.com; 1023 20th St S; r from $129; P✳@🐾) Nuzzled right up next to the lively Five Points district, this colorful, slightly trippy, modern hotel manages to be very comfortable and a good deal. The rooms are thankfully a bit less bright and funky than the lobby.

✗ Eating & Drinking

For such a small Southern city, student-tilted Birmingham has a wide variety of eateries and cafes, and plenty of free live music on weekends.

Garage Café   CAFE $
(www.garagecafe.us; 2304 10th Ter S; sandwiches $7; ⊙ 3pm-midnight Sun-Mon, 11am-2am Tue-Sat) By day it's a great soup and create-your-own-sandwich spot; by night eclectic crowds knock back myriad beer choices while tapping their toes to live music in a courtyard full of junk, antiques, ceramic statues *and* the kitchen sink.

★ Hot & Hot Fish Club   SEAFOOD $$$
(✆ 205-933-5474; www.hotandhotfishclub.com; 2180 11th Court South; mains $29-36; ⊙ 5:30-10:30pm Tue-Sat) This crazy-awesome Southside Birmingham restaurant – one of the South's best – will bring you to your knees hollerin' gastro-hallelujah's! Chef Chris Hastings was a James Beard Best Chef in the South finalist three years in a row – his daily-changing seasonal menu (including cocktails) is a knockout.

Bottega   ITALIAN $$$
(✆ 205-939-1000; www.bottegarestaurant.com; 2240 Highland Ave S; lunch mains $13-19, dinner $25-42; ℗) Enjoy a spot of Birmingham posh at this fine Italian bistro in the Highlands. It impresses with creative pizzas like fried oyster and pancetta or the Persian piadine with watercress, mint, dill, walnuts and raddish. It also does a nice pasta with pork meatballs and a popular hanger steak. Not to mention a pan-roasted venison.

Bottletree Cafe   BAR
(✆ 205-533-6288; www.thebottletree.com; 3719 3rd Ave S; ⊙ 5pm-2am Mon, 11am-2am Tue-Sat, 11am-3pm Sun) A bit out if the way, in an industrial area north of downtown, this funky dive with Delta-blues art and vintage decor is best for late-night mingling and indie bands. The food gets good reviews too.

Pale Eddie's   PUB
(✆ 205-297-0052; www.paleeddiespourhouse.com; 2308 2nd Ave N; ⊙ from 4pm Mon-Thu, from 2pm Fri, from 6pm Sat) On the groovy northern edge of downtown this pub wins for its brick house environs, the array of craftsman brews, including a gluten-free cider (et tu beer man?), and free live music every weekend.

ℹ Getting There & Around

The **Birmingham International Airport** (BHM; www.flybirmingham.com) is about 5 miles northeast of downtown.

Greyhound (✆ 205-253-7190; www.greyhound.com; 618 19th St N), north of downtown, serves cities including Huntsville, Montgomery, Atlanta, GA, Jackson, MS, and New Orleans, LA (10 hours). **Amtrak** (✆ 205-324-3033; www.amtrak.com; 1819 Morris Ave), downtown, has trains daily to New York and New Orleans.

Birmingham Transit Authority (www.bjcta.org; adult $1.25) runs local buses.

Around Birmingham

North of Birmingham, the aerospace community of Huntsville hosts the US space program that took off and attracted international aerospace-related companies. **US Space & Rocket Center** (www.spacecamp.com/museum; 1 Tranquility Base, I-565, exit 15; museum adult/child $25/20; ⊙ 9am-5pm; ♿) is a combination science museum and theme park. A great place to take a kid, or to become one again. Admission includes an IMAX film, exhibits, rides and video presentations.

East of Huntsville, in Scottsboro, you'll find the infamous **Unclaimed Baggage Center** (✆ 256-259-1525; www.unclaimedbaggage.com; 509 W Willow St; ⊙ 9am-6pm Mon-Thu, to 7pm Fri, 8am-7pm Sat), which draws pilgrims from far and wide who peruse the now-for-sale belongings of unfortunate air travelers who have lost their baggage irrevocably down the dark annals of fate. Finders keepers.

Fans of Ricky Bobby, or, you know, Nascar racing, should find **Talladega Superspeedway** (✆ 877-462-3342; ww.talladegasuperspeedway.com; 3366 Speedway Blvd; tickets $45-200), 48 miles east of Birmingham on the I-20. Pitched to absurd angles, it's the biggest and fastest oval in the circuit and an absolute adrenaline rush on race day.

Montgomery

In 1955 Rosa Parks refused to give up her seat to a white man on a city bus, launching a bus boycott and galvanizing the Civil Rights movement nationwide. The city has commemorated that incident with a museum, which along with a few other civil rights sights, is the main reason to visit. Alabama's capital, Montgomery is an otherwise pleasant but sleepy city.

◉ Sights

Montgomery's pleasant **Riverwalk** is accessed via a tunnel from downtown and is an extended plaza along a bend in the river with a natural amphitheater and a riverboat dock.

★**Rosa Parks Museum**   MUSEUM
(www.trojan.troy.edu/community/rosa-parks-museum; 251 Montgomery St; adult/child 4-12yr $7.50/5.50; ☺9am-5pm Mon-Fri, 9am-3pm Sat; ◉) A tribute to Mrs Parks (who died in October 2005), the museum, set in front of the bus stop where she took her stand, features a sophisticated video re-creation of that pivotal moment that launched the 1955 boycott. While it is true that she worked as a tailor, do not believe the myth that Parks was simply an ordinary woman pushed too far.

She was an activist with a sharp, strategic intellect who volunteered for the local National Association for the Advancement of Colored People chapter and was trained in the principles of nonviolent civil disobedience before her moment arrived.

Civil Rights Memorial Center   MEMORIAL
(www.civilrightsmemorialcenter.org; 400 Washington Ave; adult/child $2/free; ☺9am-4:30pm Mon-Fri, 10am-4pm Sat) With its circular design crafted by Maya Lin, this haunting memorial focuses on 40 martyrs of the Civil Rights movement, all murdered senselessly. Some cases remain unsolved. Martin Luther King Jr was the most famous, but there were many 'faceless' deaths along the way, white and African American alike.

The memorial is part of the Southern Poverty Law Center, a legal foundation committed to racial equality and equal opportunity for justice under the law. They are best known for their landmark victory in 1987 that found the Ku Klux Klan responsible for the death of a young black man, Michael Donald, in 1981. The judgment bankrupted the Klan nationwide.

Dexter Avenue King Memorial Church   CHURCH
(☏334-263-3970; www.dexterkingmemorial.org; 454 Dexter Ave; adult/child 3-12yr $10/6; ☺10am-4pm Tue-Fri, to 2pm Sat) Formerly known as Dexter Avenue Baptist Church, here a 26-year-old Atlanta minister began his long march toward freedom. Built in 1885, Martin Luther King was the minister here (he planned the Montgomery bus boycott from his office) from 1954 to 1960. The nearby **Dexter Parsonage Museum**, is the humble house where King lived with his family. It was bombed in 1956.

One-hour tours must be booked in advance.

Scott & Zelda Fitzgerald Museum   MUSEUM
(www.fitzgeraldmuseum.net; 919 Felder Ave; donation adult/child $5/2; ☺10am-2pm Wed-Fri, 1-5pm Sat & Sun) The writers' home from 1931 to 1932 now houses first editions, translations and original artwork including a mysterious self-portrait of Zelda. We loved the handwritten letters from Zelda to Scott, and the typed letters from Scott to his great foil and friend, Ernest Hemingway.

Hank Williams Museum   MUSEUM
(www.thehankwilliamsmuseum.com; 118 Commerce St; admission $10; ☺9am-4:30pm Mon-Fri, 10am-4pm Sat, 1-4pm Sun) Pays homage to the

---

ROLL TIDE!

Roll Tide! It's the call you'll hear, well pretty much everywhere in the town of Tuscaloosa, 60 miles southwest of Birmingham, but especially on Saturday afternoons in the fall. During football season, students and alumni gather in the **University of Alabama** (www.ua.edu) quad, hours before kickoff, for a pre-game party like none other. White tents, wired with satellite TV, fill the expansive lawn. Barbecue is smoked and devoured, cornhole (drunken bean-bag toss) is played. At game time all migrate to **Bryant-Denny Stadium** (☏205-348-3600; www.rolltide.com; 920 Paul W Bryant Dr), a 102,000 capacity football stadium that looks out onto the rolling hills and is always packed with rabid fans, and with good reason. The Alabama Crimson Tide have won 19 national championships, including the last two, and three of the last four. Get a full dose of Crimson Tide football history, at the **Paul W Bryant Museum** (☏205-348-4668; www.bryantmuseum.com; 300 Paul W Bryant Dr; adult/senior & child $2/1; ☺9am-4pm), named for the greatest coach of them all. Or so the legend goes...

ECHOES OF A KING

After the long march from Selma to Montgomery on March 25, 1965, Dr Martin Luther King Jr gave his speech 'Our God is Marching On!' on the steps of the state capitol. Here are some highlights:

There never was a moment in American history more honorable and more inspiring than the pilgrimage of clergymen and laymen of every race and faith pouring into Selma to face danger at the side of its embattled Negroes.

...Our aim must never be to defeat or humiliate the white man but to win his friendship and understanding. We must come to see that the end we seek is a society at peace with itself, a society that can live with its conscience. That will be a day not of the white man, not of the black man. That will be the day of man as man. I know you are asking today, 'How long will it take?' I come to say to you this afternoon however difficult the moment, however frustrating the hour, it will not be long, because truth pressed to earth will rise again.

How long? Not long, because no lie can live forever.

How long? Not long, because you still reap what you sow.

How long? Not long. Because the arm of the moral universe is long but it bends toward justice.

country-music giant and Alabama native, a pioneer who effortlessly fused hillbilly music with the blues.

🛏 Sleeping & Eating

Montgomery isn't known for its restaurants and accommodations, and can be done on a day trip, but there are a couple of finds. **The Alley**, a dining and entertainment district, has helped perk up a dormant downtown.

Renaissance Hotel　　　　　HOTEL $
(📞 334-481-5000; www.marriott.com; 201 Tallapoosa St; r from $189; 🅿❄@🛜🏊) Yes, it's a corporate monstrosity, but it is also well located and is easily Montgomery's nicest address.

Dreamland BBQ　　　　　BARBECUE $
(www.dreamlandbbq.com; 101 Tallapoosa St; mains $8-11; ⊙11am-9pm Sun-Thu, to 10pm Sat) It's an Alabama chain and the ribs, chopped-pork sandwich and traditional banana pudding are all solid. It's the culinary cradle of the Alley, the focal point of Montgomery's downtown makeover.

★ Central　　　　　CHOPHOUSE $$$
(www.central129coosa.com; 129 Coosa St; mains $18-33; ⊙11am-2pm Mon-Fri, 5:30pm-late Mon-Sat) The gourmand's choice, this stunner has a creative interior with a reclaimed-wood bar. The booths are sumptuous and it specializes in wood-fired fish, chicken, steaks and chops.

❶ Information

Montgomery Area Visitor Center (📞 334-262-0013; www.visitingmontgomery.com; 300 Water St; ⊙8:30am-5pm Mon-Sat) Has tourist information and a helpful website.

❶ Getting There & Around

Montgomery Regional Airport (MGM; www.montgomeryairport.org; 4445 Selma Hwy) is about 15 miles from downtown and is served by daily flights from Atlanta, Charlotte and Dallas. **Greyhound** (📞 334-286-0658; www.greyhound.com; 950 W South Blvd) also serves the city. The **Montgomery Area Transit System** (www.montgomerytransit.com; tickets $1) operates the infamous city buses.

Selma

On Bloody Sunday, March 7, 1965, the media captured state troopers and deputies beating and gassing African Americans and white sympathizers near the **Edmund Pettus Bridge** (Broad St & Walter Ave). The crowd was marching to the state capital (Montgomery) to demonstrate against the murder of a local black activist by police, during a demonstration for voting rights. When the scene was broadcast on every network later that night, it marked one of the first times Americans outside the South had witnessed the horrifying images of the struggle. Shock and outrage was widespread, and support for the movement grew. Martin

Luther King arrived swiftly to Selma and after another aborted attempt due to the threat of violence, helped lead what became 8000 people on a four-day, 54 mile march to Montgomery, culminating with a classic King speech on the capitol steps. Soon after, President Johnson signed the Voting Rights Act of 1965.

Selma's story is told at the **National Voting Rights Museum** (☎334-327-8218; www.nvrm.org; 1012 Water Ave; adult/senior & student $6/4; ◷10am-4pm Mon-Thu), near the Edmund Pettus Bridge, and in more detail at the **Lowndes County Interpretive Center** (www.nps.gov/semo; 7002 US Hwy 80; ◷9am-4:30pm) halfway between Selma and Montgomery. Oddly, as we are writing this, the US Supreme Court has ruled that the Voting Rights Act is unconstitutional – a controversial decision that has cut down party lines. The passage of that federal law was the key to victory during this phase of the Civil Rights movement. The ramifications of the decision are still unclear, though many observers fear it could potentially make access to the polls more difficult. Some states, like Florida, have been plagued by accusations of racial discrimination when it comes to voting rights.

Mobile

Wedged between Mississippi and Florida, the only real Alabama coastal city is Mobile (mo-*beel*), a busy industrial seaport with green spaces, shady boulevards and four historic districts. It's ablaze with azaleas in early spring, and festivities are held throughout February for **Mardi Gras** (www.mobilemardigras.com), which has been celebrated here for nearly 200 years. The Dauphin St historic district is where you'll find most bars and restaurants, and it's where much of the Mardi Gras action blooms.

USS Alabama (www.ussalabama.com; 2703 Battleship Pkwy; adult/child $15/6; ◷8am-6pm Apr-Sep, to 5pm Oct-Mar), a 690ft behemoth famous for escaping nine major WWII battles unscathed, is a worthwhile self-guided tour. Parking's $2.

Battle House (☎251-338-2000; www.marriott.com; 26 N Royal St; r from $159; P❄@🛜🐾) is the best address in downtown Mobile. You'll want to stay in the original historic wing with its ornate domed marble lobby, though the striking new tower is on the waterfront. Home to Mobile's best burg-

ers and consistently voted one of America's best bars, the ramshackle **Callaghan's Irish Social Club** (www.callaghansirishsocialclub.com; 916 Charleston St; burgers $7-9; ◷11am-9pm Mon, 11am-10pm Tue & Wed, 11am-11pm Thu-Sat) in a 1920s-era building that used to house a meat market in the Oakleigh District, is unmissable. Closer to the town center, **Wintzell's** (☎251-432-4605; www.wintzellsoysterhouse.com; 605 Dauphin St; mains $11-23; ◷11am-10pm Sun-Thu, to 11pm Fri & Sat), open since 1938, serves oysters raw, chargrilled or fried in brewhouse environs.

MISSISSIPPI

One of the USA's most misunderstood (and yet most mythologized) states, Mississippi is home to gorgeous country roads, shabby juke joints, crispy catfish, hallowed authors and acres of cotton. Most people feel content to malign Mississippi, long scorned for its lamentable civil rights history and low-ranking on the list of nearly every national marker of economy and education, without ever experiencing it. But unpack your bags for a moment and you'll feel its bottomless soul.

❶ Getting There & Away

There are three routes most folks take when traveling through Mississippi. I-55 and US-61 both run north–south from the state's northern to southern borders. US-61 goes through the delta, and I-55 flows in and out of Jackson. The gorgeous Natchez Trace Parkway, runs diagonally across the state from Tupelo to Natchez.

❶ Information

Mississippi Division of Tourism Development (☎601-359-3297; www.visitmississippi.org) Has a directory of visitor bureaus and thematic travel itineraries to choose from. Most are well thought out and run quite deep.

Mississippi Wildlife, Fisheries, & Parks (☎1-800-467-2757; www.mississippistateparks.reserveamerica.com) Camping costs $12 to $28, depending on the facilities, and some parks have cabins for rent.

Tupelo

Unless you want to pick up the Natchez Trace Pkwy, you probably won't plan to spend a long time here. But an afternoon pop-in is rewarding indeed for devotees of the King.

MISSISSIPPI FACTS

Nickname the Magnolia State

Population 3 million

Area 48,430 sq miles

Capital city Jackson (population 175,437)

Sales tax 7%

Birthplace of Author Eudora Welty (1909–2001), musicians Robert Johnson (1911–38), Muddy Waters (1913–83), BB King (b 1925) and Elvis Presley (1935–77), activist James Meredith (b 1933) and puppeteer Jim Henson (1936–90)

Home of The blues

Politics Traditionally conservative, but has voted for third-party candidates more than any other state since WWII

Famous for Cotton fields

Kitschiest souvenir Elvis lunchbox in Tupelo

Driving distances Jackson to Clarksdale 187 miles, Jackson to Ocean Springs 176 miles

Elvis Presley's Birthplace (☑662-841-1245; www.elvispresleybirthplace.com; 306 Elvis Presley Blvd; adult/senior/child $15/12/6; ⊙9am-5:30pm Mon-Sat, 1-5pm Sun) is east of downtown off Hwy 78. The 15-acre complex contains the two-room shack Elvis lived in as a boy, a museum displaying personal items, the modest chapel where a very young Elvis attended church with his mother, got bit by the music bug and danced in the aisles, and a massive gift shop.

Oxford

Oxford is one of those rare towns that seeps into your bones and never leaves. Local culture revolves around the quaint-yet-hip **Square**, where you'll find inviting bars, wonderful food and decent shopping, and the regal **University of Mississippi** (www.olemiss.edu), aka Ole Miss. All around and in between are quiet residential streets, sprinkled with antebellum homes, shaded by majestic oaks, including William Faulkner's old lair. Oxford has just 10,000 year-round residents, but the 18,000 students infuse the town with youth and life.

Oxford is best reached via Hwy 6, which runs between Clarksdale and Tupelo in Northern Mississippi.

⊙ Sights & Activities

The gorgeous, 0.6-miles long and rather painless **Bailee's Woods Trail** connects two of the town's most popular sights, Rowan Oak and the University of Mississippi Museum.

Rowan Oak   HISTORIC BUILDING
(www.rowanoak.com; Old Taylor Rd; adult/child $5/free; ⊙10am-4pm Tue-Sat, 1-4pm Sun) Literary pilgrims head directly here, to the graceful 1840s home of William Faulkner, who authored so many brilliant and dense novels set in Mississippi, and whose work is celebrated in Oxford with an annual conference in July. Tours of Rowan Oak – where Faulkner lived from 1930 until he died in 1962 – are self-guided. The staff can also provide directions to **Faulkner's grave**, which is located in St Peter's Cemetery, northeast of the Square.

University of Mississippi Museum MUSEUM
(www.museum.olemiss.edu; University Ave at 5th St; admission $5; ⊙10am-6pm Tue-Sat) This museum has fine and folk arts, a Confederate uniform and a plethora of science-related marvels, including a microscope and electromagnet from the 19th century.

⊨ Sleeping & Eating

The cheapest accommodations are chains on the outskirts of town. A number of high-quality restaurants dot the Square.

★ **(5) Twelve**   B&B $$
(☑662-234-8043; www.the5twelve.com; 512 Van Buren Ave; r from $115; 🅿❋🛜) This six-room B&B has an antebellum-style exterior and modern interior (think: tempurpedic beds and flatscreens). Room rates include full Southern breakfasts to order. It's an easy walk from shops and restaurants, and the inn keepers will make you feel like family.

Inn at Ole Miss   HOTEL $$
(☑662-234-2331; www.theinnatolemiss.com; 120 Alumni Dr; r from $129; 🅿❋@🛜🏊) Unless it's a football weekend, in which case, you'd be wise to book well ahead, you can usually find a nice room at this 180-room hotel and conference center right on the Ole Miss

Grove. Although less personal than the local inns, it's comfortable, well-located and walkable to downtown.

Bottletree Bakery BAKERY $
(www.bottletreebakery.net; 923 Van Buren; pastries $3-4, mains $6-9; ⊘7am-4pm Tue-Fri, 9am-4pm Sat, to 2pm Sun; 🛜) This place trades in exquisite pastries including saucer-sized cinnamon rolls, a brioche of the day, shortbread streusel, mammoth chocolate croissants, and a nice collection of sandwiches and salads.

★**Snackbar** NEW AMERICAN $$
(☑662-236-6363; www.citygroceryonline.com; 721 N Lamar Blvd; small plates $11-26; ⊘4pm-midnight Mon-Sat) A fabulous find in an otherwise nondescript mini-mall. It specializes in craftsman cocktails, and are also known for its exquisite raw bar (oysters, blue crab, Gulf shrimp) and small plates that wander from oysters and grits to a kale Caesar. The burger is legendary. All served in rather dark and groovy hardwood environs.

Taylor Grocery SEAFOOD $$
(www.taylorgrocery.com; 4 County Rd 338A; dishes $9-15; ⊘5-10pm Thu-Sat, to 9pm Sun) Be prepared to wait – and to tailgate in the parking lot – at this splendidly rusticated catfish haunt. Get yours fried or grilled, and bring a marker to sign your name on the wall. The joint is about 7 miles from downtown Oxford, south on Old Taylor Rd.

☆ **Entertainment**

On the last Tuesday of the month, an increasingly popular **Art Crawl**, connects galleries across town with free buses carrying well-lubricated art lovers. Nibbles and wine aplenty.

Proud Larry's LIVE MUSIC
(☑662-236-0050; www.proudlarrys.com; 211 S Lamar Blvd; ⊘shows 9:30pm) On the Square, this iconic music venue hosts consistently good bands, and it does a nice pub grub business at lunch and dinner before stage lights dim.

Rooster's Blues House BLUES
(www.roostersblueshouse.com; 114 Courthouse Sq) Enjoy soulful crooning on the weekends.

The Lyric VENUE
(☑662-234-5333; www.thelyricoxford.com; 1006 Van Buren St) This old brickhouse, and rather intimate theater with concrete floors, exposed rafters and a mezzanine, is where you come to see indie acts like Beach House or Band of Horses.

🔒 **Shopping**

Square Books BOOKSTORE
(☑662-236-2262; www.squarebooks.com; 160 Courthouse Sq; ⊘9am-9pm Mon-Thu, to 10pm Fri & Sat, to 6pm Sun) Square Books, one of America's great independent bookstores, is the epicenter of Oxford's lively literary scene and a frequent stop for traveling authors. There's a cafe and balcony upstairs, along with an immense section devoted to Faulkner. Nearby **Square Books Jr** is where you can find children's and young adult lit. **Off Square** trades in used fare.

JAMES MEREDITH'S MARCH

The Grove, the shady heart center of Ole Miss (the University of Mississippi), is generally peaceful, except on football Saturdays, when it buzzes with brass-band, pre-game anticipation.

Yet it was also the setting of one of the Civil Rights movement's most harrowing scenes. Here, on October 1, 1962, James Meredith, a young student,, accompanied by his advisor, National Association for the Advancement of Colored People state chair Medgar Evers, marched through a violent mob of segregationists to become the first African American student to register for classes at Ole Miss. He was supposed to have registered 10 days before, but riots ensued and the Kennedy administration had to call in 500 federal marshalls and the National Guard to ensure his safety.

Evers was eventually assasinated, and Meredith later walked across the state to raise awareness about racial violence in Mississippi. Some of Meredith's correspondence is on display at the **Center for Southern Culture** (☑662-915-5855; 1 Library Loop, University of Mississippi; ⊘8am-9pm Mon-Thu, to 4pm Fri, to 5pm Sat, 1-5pm Sun; 🐾) FREE, at the campus library.

Southside Gallery ART
(www.southsideartgallery.com; 150 Courthouse Sq; ☉10am-6pm Tue-Sat) The best of Oxford's downtown art galleries puts an emphasis on local, young, up-and-coming artists who create modern works from abstract to realist; from big format to smaller than seems reasonable.

Mississippi Delta

In the cultivated flood plain, along Hwy 61, American music took root. It arrived from Africa in the souls of slaves, morphed into field songs, and wormed into the brain of a sharecropping troubadour waiting for a train. In Tutweiler, WC Handy eavesdropped and wrote the rhythm down. In Clarksdale, at the crossroads, Robert Johnson made a deal with the devil and became America's first guitar hero. Yes, the Delta has soul food and a blood-soaked history, but its chief export, its white-hot legacy will always be the blues. There is no Beatles, no Stones, no Hendrix, Zeppelin, or even hip-hop without the music of the Mississippi Delta, which runs from Memphis all the way to Vicksburg.

Clarksdale

Clarksdale is the Delta's most useful base – with more comfortable hotel rooms and modern, tasteful kitchens here than the rest of the Delta combined. It's within a couple of hours from all the blues sights, and big-name blues acts honor Clarksdale on the weekends.

◉ Sights

The **Crossroads** of Hwys 61 and 49, is the intersection where the great Robert Johnson made his mythical deal with the devil, immortalized in his tune 'Cross Road Blues.'

Delta Blues Museum MUSEUM
(www.deltabluesmuseum.org; 1 Blues Alley; adult/senior & student $7/5; ☉9am-5pm Mon-Sat) A small but well-presented collection of memorabilia is on display. The shrine to Delta legend Muddy Waters includes the actual cabin where he grew up; local art exhibits and a gift shop round out the revelry.

**Rock N' Roll & Blues
Heritage Museum** MUSEUM
(☎901-605-8662; www.blues2rock.com; 113 E Second St; admission $5; ☉11am-5pm Tue-Sat) A jovial Dutch transplant and blues fanatic displays an impressive personal collection of records, memorabilia and artifacts that trace the roots of rock and roll from blues through the '70s.

✸ Festivals & Events

Clarksdale has two blues parties.

Juke Joint Festival MUSIC
(www.jukejointfestival.com; tickets $15; ☉Apr) There are more than 100 daytime and over 20 night venues at this three-day festival held in joints sprinkled in and around Clarksdale.

**Sunflower River
Blues & Gospel Festival** MUSIC
(www.sunflowerfest.org; ☉Aug) Draws bigger names than the Juke Joint Festival.

A WHOLE LOTTA JUKIN' GOING ON

It's believed that 'juke' is a West African word that survived in the Gullah language, the Creole−English hybrid spoken by isolated African Americans in the US. The Gullah 'juke' means 'wicked and disorderly.' Little wonder, then, that the term was applied to the roadside sweatboxes of the Mississippi Delta, where secular music, suggestive dancing, drinking and, in some cases, prostitution were the norm. The term 'jukebox' came into vogue when recorded music, spun on automated record-changing machines, began to supplant live musicians in such places, as well as in cafes and bars.

Most bona-fide juke joints are African American neighborhood clubs, and outside visitors can be a rarity. Many are mostly male hangouts. There are very few places that local women, even in groups, would turn up without a male chaperone. Otherwise, women can expect a lot of persistent, suggestive attention.

For a taste of the juke-joint scene, we recommend Red's, which is usually open on Friday and Saturday nights. It can be intimidating to first-timers, but it is one of Clarksdale's best jukes. If the pit's smoking, order whatever's cooking.

🛏 Sleeping & Eating

⭐ Shack Up Inn INN $

(📞 662-624-8329; www.shackupinn.com; Hwy 49; d $75-165; 🅿❄🛜) At the cheeky Hopson Plantation, this self-titled 'bed and beer' 2 miles south on the west side of Hwy 49 evokes the blues like no other. Guests stay in refurbished sharecropper cabins or the creatively renovated cotton gin. The cabins have covered porches and are filled with old furniture and musical instruments.

The old commissary, the Juke Joint Chapel (equipped with pews), is an atmospheric venue inside the cotton gin for live-music performances. The whole place reeks of down-home dirty blues and Deep South character – possibly the coolest place you'll ever stay.

Lofts at the Five & Dime LOFTS $$

(📞 888-510-9604; www.fiveanddimelofts.com; 211 Yazoo St; lofts $150-175) Set in a 1954 building are six plush, loft-style apartments with molded-concrete counters in the full kitchen, massive flatscreens in the living room and bedroom, terrazzo showers and free sodas and water throughout your stay. They sleep up to four comfortably.

Abe's BBQ $

(📞 662-624-9947; 616 State St; sandwiches $4-6, plates $6-14; ⊙10am-9pm Mon-Thu, to 10pm Fri & Sat, 11am-2pm Sun; 🍴) Abe's has served zesty pork sandwiches, vinegary slaw and slow-burning tamales at the Crossroads since 1924.

⭐ Yazoo Pass CAFE $$

(www.yazoopass.com; 207 Yazoo Ave; lunch mains $6-10, dinner $13-26; ⊙7am-9pm Mon-Sat; 🛜) A contemporary space where you can enjoy fresh scones and croissants in the mornings, salad bar, sandwiches and soups at lunch, and pan-seared ahi, filet mignon, burgers and pastas at dinner.

Rust SOUTHERN $$

(www.rustclarksdale.com; 218 Delta Ave; mains $12-36; ⊙6-9pm Tue-Thu, to 10pm Fri & Sat) The souped-up Southern comfort food served here (blackened rib eye with red chili mustard, crawfish cakes with grilled asparagus) amid junkyard-chic decor makes it a nice place for a bite before a show.

☆ Entertainment

Red's BLUES CLUB

(📞 662-627-3166; 395 Sunflower Ave; cover $10; ⊙live music 9pm Fri & Sat) Clarksdale's best juke joint, with its neon-red mood lighting, plastic-bag ceiling and general soulful disintegration is the best place to see blues men howl. Red runs the bar, and may have some moonshine hidden back there?

Ground Zero BLUES CLUB

(www.groundzerobluesclub.com; 0 Blues Alley; ⊙11am-2pm Mon-Tue, to 11pm Wed & Thu, to 1am Fri & Sat) For blues in more polished environs, we recommend Morgan Freeman's Ground Zero, a huge and friendly hall with a dancefloor surrounded by tables. Bands take the stage Wednesday to Saturday.

🛍 Shopping

Cat Head Delta Blues & Folk Art ARTS & CRAFTS

(www.cathead.biz; 252 Delta Ave; ⊙10am-5pm Mon-Sat) Friendly St Louis carpetbagger and author, Roger Stolle runs a colorful, all-purpose, blues emporium. The shelves are jammed with books, face jugs, local art and blues records. Stolle seems to be connected to everyone in the Delta, and knows when and where the bands will play.

Around Clarksdale

For such a poor, flat part of the country, the Delta has a surprisingly deep list of funky little towns to explore.

Down Hwy 49, **Tutwiler** is where the blues began its migration from oral tradition to popular art form. Here, WC Handy, known as the Father of the Blues, first heard a share cropper moan his 12-bar prayer while the two waited for a train in 1903. He transcribed it in 1912, but wasn't recognized as a blues pioneer until his 'Beale Street Blues' became a hit in 1916. That meeting is immortalized by a mural at the **Tutwiler Tracks** (off Hwy 49, Tutwiler; 🅿).

East of Greenville, Hwy 82 heads out of the Delta. The **Highway 61 Blues Museum** (www.highway61blues.com; 307 N Broad St; ⊙10am-4pm Tue-Sat Nov-Feb, 10am-5pm Mon-Sat Mar-Oct), at the start of the route known as the **Blues Highway'** packs a mighty wallop in a condensed, six-room space venerating local bluesman from the Delta. **Leland** (www.lelandms.org) hosts the **Highway 61 Blues Festival** in June.

Stopping in the tiny Delta town of **Indianola** is well worthwhile, to visit the incredible, modern **BB King Museum and Delta Interpretive Center** (www.bbkingmuseum.org; 400 Second St; adult/student/child $10/5/free;

10am-5pm Tue-Sat, noon-5pm Sun-Mon, closed Mon Nov-Mar). The best blues museum in the Delta is filled with interactive displays, video exhibits and an amazing array of BB King artifacts, effectively communicating the history and legacy of the blues while shedding light on the soul of the Delta.

Greenwood is a once-poor Delta town infused with a dose of opulence thanks to Viking Range Corporation's investment (its headquarters are here). Visitors are usually wealthy patrons or splurging travelers who want to take advantage of the Delta's most refined sleep, the **Alluvian** (☑662-453-2114; www.thealluvian.com; 318 Howard St; r $200-215; P🌣@☂), owned by Viking. The nearby **Delta Bistro** (☑662-455-9575; www.deltabistro. com; 117 Main St, Greenwood; mains $9-24; ☺11am-9pm Mon-Sat) is the best restaurant in the region.

Vicksburg

Vicksburg is famous for its strategic location in the Civil War, on a high bluff overlooking the Mississippi River. General Ulysses S Grant besieged the city for 47 days, until its surrender on July 4, 1863, at which point the North gained dominance over North America's greatest river, and the war was all but over.

◉ Sights & Activities

The major sights are readily accessible from I-20 exit 4B (Clay St).

National Military Park (www.nps.gov/vick; Clay St; per car/individual $8/4; ☺8am-5pm Oct-Mar, to 7pm Apr-Sep), north of I-20 is Vicksburg's main attraction. A 16-mile driving tour passes historic markers explaining battle scenarios and key events. You can buy an audio tour in the visitor center gift shop, or drive through on your own using the free map distributed on-site. Plan for at least two hours to do it justice. If you have your bike, cycling is a fantastic way to take it in. The cemetery contains some 17,000 Union graves. **Civil War re-enactments** are held in May and July.

Historic downtown stretches along several cobblestoned blocks of Washington St. Down by the water is a block of murals depicting the history of the area, and a **Children's Art Park**. The surprsingly interesting **Lower Mississippi River Museum** (☑601-638-9900; www.lmrm.org; 910 Washington St; ☺9am-5pm Tue-Sat year-round, 1-5pm

Sun Apr-Oct) **FREE** delves into such topics as the famed 1927 flood. Kids will dig the aquarium and clambering around the dry-docked research vessel, the **M/V Mississippi IV**. Don't leave town without stopping by the **Attic Gallery** (☑601-638-9221; www.atticgallery.net; 1101 Washington St; ☺10am-5pm Mon-Sat), a treasure trove of fine and folk art from across the Delta.

🛏 Sleeping & Eating

Corners Mansion   B&B $$
(☑601-636-7421; www.thecorners.com; 601 Klein St; r incl breakfast from $125; P🌣☂) The best part of this 1873 B&B is looking over the Ya-zoo and Mississippi Rivers from your porch-swing. The gardens and Southern breakfast don't hurt either.

Rusty's Riverfront Grill   SOUTHERN $$
(www.rustysriverfront.com; 901 Washington St; mains $17-29; ☺11am-2pm & 5-9:30pm Tue-Fri, 11am-9:30pm Sat) Set at the north end of downtown, this down-home grill is known for the terriffic rib eye, but it has a nice selection of Southern-style seafood too, including crab cakes, blackened redfish, and a nice New Orleans–style gumbo.

Jackson

Mississippi's capital and largest city is victim to the common car-culture phenomenon of a latent (though stately and gentrifying) downtown surrounded by plush suburbs. However, interesting areas like the funky Fondren District, along with a cluster of well-done museums, historic sites and bars and restaurants, give insight into the culture of Mississippi and are elevating Jackson to a good time.

◉ Sights

★**Mississippi Museum of Art**   GALLERY
(www.msmuseumart.org; 380 South Lamar St; permanent collections free, special exhibitions $5-12; ☺10am-5pm Tue-Sat, noon-5pm Sun) **FREE** This is the one fantastic attraction in Jackson. The collection of Mississippi art – a permanent exhibit dubbed 'The Mississippi Story' – is superb.

Old Capitol Museum   MUSEUM
(www.mdah.state.ms.us/museum; 100 State St; ☺9am-5pm Tue-Sat, 1-5pm Sun) **FREE** The state's Greek Revival capitol building from 1839 to 1903 now houses a Mississippi

history museum filled with films and exhibits. You'll learn that secession was far from unanimous, and how reconstruction brought some of the harshest, pre-segregation 'black codes' in the South.

Eudora Welty House LANDMARK
(☑601-353-7762; www.mdah.state.ms.us/welty; 1119 Pinehurst St; ☺tours 9am, 11am, 1pm & 3pm Tue-Fri) Literature buffs should make a reservation to tour the Pulitzer Prize–winning author's Tudor Revival house, where she lived for more than 75 years. It's now a true historical preservation down to the most minute details.

Smith Robertson Museum MUSEUM
(www.jacksonms.gov/visitors/museums/smith-robertson; 528 Bloom St; adult/child $4.50/1.50; ☺9am-5pm Mon-Fri, 10am-2pm Sat, 2-5pm Sun) Housed in Mississippi's first public school for African American kids is the alma mater of author Richard Wright. It offers insight and explanation into the pain and perseverance of the African American legacy in Mississippi.

🛏 Sleeping & Eating

Fondren District is the budding artsy, boho area of town, with fun restaurants, art galleries and cafes dotting the happening commercial strip.

Old Capitol Inn BOUTIQUE HOTEL $$
(☑601-359-9000; www.oldcapitolinn.com; 226 N State St; r incl breakfast from $135; P🅿@🛜♨) This 24-room, all-suite, boutique hotel, near museums and restaurants, is terrific. The rooftop garden includes a hot tub. A full Southern breakfast (and early-evening wine and cheese) are included and the rooms are all comfortable and uniquely furnished.

Fairview Inn INN $$
(☑601-948-3429; www.fairviewinn.com; 734 Fairview St; r incl breakfast $129-329; P🅿@🛜) For a colonial estate experience, the 18-room Fairview Inn, set in a converted historic mansion, will not let you down. The antique decor is stunning. It also has a full spa.

High Noon Cafe VEGETARIAN $
(www.rainbowcoop.org; 2807 Old Canton Rd; mains $7-10; ☺11:30am-2pm Mon-Fri; P🛜🍴) 🍴 Tired of fried, green, pulled-pork-covered catfish? This organic vegetarian grill, inside the Rainbow Co-op grocery store in the Fondren District does beet burgers, portabello Rebens and other healthy delights. Stock up on organic groceries too.

★ Walker's Drive-In SOUTHERN $$$
(☑601-982-2633; www.walkersdrivein.com; 3016 N State St; lunch mains $10-17, dinner $25-35; ☺11am-2pm Mon-Fri & from 5:30pm Tue-Sat) This retro diner has been restored with love and infused with new Southern foodie ethos. Lunch is diner 2.0 fare with grilled redfish sandwiches, tender burgers and grilled oyster po'boys, as well as an exceptional seared, chili-crusted tuna salad, which comes with spiced calamari and seaweed.

Things get even more gourmet at dinner. Think lamb porterhouse, wood-grilled octopus and miso-marinated seabass. There's an excellent wine list and service is impeccable.

Mayflower SEAFOOD $$$
(☑601-355-4122; 123 W Capitol St; mains $21-29; ☺11am-2:30pm & 4:30-9:15pm Mon-Fri, 4:30-9:30pm Sat) It looks like just another downtown dive, but it's a damn fine seafood house. Locals swear by the broiled redfish, and the Greek salad, which becomes a meal when you add pan-seared scallops (sensational!). Everything is obscenely fresh.

☆ Entertainment

★ F Jones Corner BLUES
(www.fjonescorner.com; 303 N Farish St; ☺11am-2pm Tue-Fri, 10am-late Thu-Sat) All shapes and sizes, colors and creeds descend on this down-home Farish St club when everywhere else closes. It hosts authentic Delta musicians who have been known to play until sunrise. Don't show up before 1am.

119 Underground BLUES
(www.underground119.com; 119 S President St; ☺5-11pm Tue, 4pm-midnight Wed-Thu, 4pm-2am Fri & Sat, 6pm-2am Sat) A funky, supremely cool supper club serving up blues, jazz and bluegrass alongside excellent eats (the chef's Southern fusion comes from his extended travels and backyard urban garden).

ℹ Information

Convention & Visitors Bureau (☑601-960-1891; www.visitjackson.com; 111 E Capitol St, suite 102; ☺8am-5pm Mon-Fri) Free information.

ⓘ Getting There & Away

At the junction of I-20 and I-55, it's easy to get in and out of Jackson. Its international **airport** (JAN; www.jmaa.com) is 10 miles east of downtown. **Greyhound** (☎ 601-353-6342; www.greyhound.com; 300 W Capitol St) buses serve Birmingham, AL, Memphis, TN, and New Orleans, LA. Amtrak's *City of New Orleans* stops at the station.

Natchez

A tiny dollop of cosmopolitan in Mississippi, adorable Natchez is home to gay log-cabin Republicans, intellectual liberals, and down-home folks, who've never left. Perched on a bluff overlooking the Mississippi, it's the oldest town on the river and attracts tourists in search of antebellum history and architecture – 668 antebellum homes pepper the oldest civilized settlement on the Mississippi River (beating New Orleans by two years). It's also the end (or the beginning!) of the scenic 444-mile Natchez Trace Pkwy, the state's cycling and recreational jewel.

The **visitor and welcome center** (☎601-446-6345; www.visitnatchez.org; 640 S Canal St; tours adult/child $12/8; ☉8:30am-5pm Mon-Sat, 9am-4pm Sun) is a large, well-organized tourist resource. Tours of the historic downtown and antebellum mansions leave from here. During the 'pilgrimage' seasons in spring and fall, local mansions are opened to visitors.

Ever wish you could sleep in one of those historic homes? At the **Historic Oak Hill Inn** (☎601-446-2500; www.historicoakhill.com; 409 S Rankin St; r incl breakfast from $125; P☀🖥), you can sleep in an original 1835 bed and dine

on pre–Civil War porcelain under 1850 Waterford crystal gasoliers – it's all about purist antebellum aristocratic living at this classic Natchez B&B. You can skip rocks into the Mississippi from the **Mark Twain Guesthouse** (☎601-446-8023; www.underthehillsaloon.com; 33 Silver St; r without bathroom $65-85; ☀🖥) where three rooms (two with views) sit on top of a classic local watering hole, **Under the Hill Saloon** (☎601-446-8023; 25 Silver St; ☉9am-late). (Check-in for the guesthouse is at the saloon).

To get your fill of Southern fusion eats, follow your nose to the **Magnolia Grill** (☎601-446-7670; www.magnoliagrill.com; 49 Silver St; mains $13-20; ☉11am-9pm, to 10pm Fri & Sat; 🖥). **Cotton Alley** (www.cottonalleycafe.com; 208 Main St; mains $10-15; ☉11am-10pm Mon-Sat) is a good place for lighter fare.

Gulf Coast

In the backyard of New Orleans, the Gulf Coast's economy, traditionally based on the seafood industry, got a shot of adrenaline in the 1990s when Vegas-style casinos muscled in alongside sleepy fishing villages. And then a double whammy of disasters: just when the casinos in Biloxi had been rebuilt following Hurricane Katrina in 2005, the Gulf's Deepwater Horizon oil spill in 2010 dealt the coast another unexpected blow. However, Mississippi's barrier islands helped divert much of the oil problems toward New Orleans and Alabama.

Through it all, **Ocean Springs** remains charming with a romantic line up of shrimp boats in the harbor alongside recreational sailing yachts, a historic downtown core, and a powdery fringe of white sand on the Gulf. The highlight is the **Walter Anderson Museum** (www.walterandersonmuseum.org; 510 Washington St; adult/child $10/5; ☉9:30am-4:30pm Mon-Sat, 12:30-4:30pm Sun). A consummate artist and lover of Gulf Coast nature, Anderson suffered from mental illness, which spurred his monastic existence and fuelled his life's work. After he died, the beachside shack where he lived on **Horn Island** was discovered to be painted in mind-blowing murals, which you'll see here.

Hotels line the highway as you approach downtown. Nice camping (and a visitor center) can be found at **Gulf Islands National Seashore Park** (www.nps.gov/guis; camping $16-20), just out of town.

PADDLING THE MISSISSIPPI

According to Keith Benoist, a photographer, landscaper and co-founder of the **Phatwater Challenge** (www.kayakmississippi.com) marathon kayak race, the Mississippi has more navigable river miles than any other state in the union. Natchez-born Benoist trains for his 42-mile race by paddling 10 miles of the Old River, an abandoned section of the Mississippi fringed with cypress and teeming with gators. If you're lucky enough to meet him at Under the Hill, he may just take you with him.

ARKANSAS

Hiding out between the Midwest and the Deep South, Arkansas (*ar*-kan-saw) is America's overlooked treasure. This is a nature lover's Shangri La, with the worn slopes of the Ozarks and the Ouachita (wash-*ee*-tah) mountains; clean, gushing rivers; and lakes bridged by crenelated granite and limestone outcrops. The entire state is dotted with exceptionally well-presented state parks and tiny, empty roads crisscrossing dense forests that let out onto breathtaking vistas and gentle pastures dotted with grazing horses. The rural towns of Mountain View and Eureka Springs hold quirky charm, and don't be fooled by talk of Wal-Mart or backwoods culture. As one local put it, 'Say what you want about Arkansas, but it's an outdoor paradise.'

❶ Information

Arkansas State Parks (☑ 888-287-2757; www. arkansasstateparks.com) Arkansas' well-reputed park system has 52 state parks, 30 offering camping (tent and RV sites are $12 to $55, depending on amenities). A number of the parks offer lodge and cabin accommodations. Due to popularity, reservations on weekends and holidays often require multiday stays.

Little Rock

It's tempting for those who zip in and out of this leafy, attractive state capital on the Arkansas River to dismiss it as quiet, maybe a little dull, certainly conservative. They're wrong. Little Rock is young, up-and-coming, gay- and immigrant-friendly, and just friendly in general. Downtown has perked up thanks to the burgeoning River Market district, and the Hillcrest neighborhood is a tiny epicenter of cafes and funky shops. If you know where to look, you'll enjoy this town.

◎ Sights

The best stroll is in the **River Market district** (www.rivermarket.info; W Markham St & President Clinton Ave), an area of shops, galleries, restaurants and pubs along the riverbank.

★ Little Rock Central High School
HISTORIC SITE
(www.nps.gov/chsc; 2125 Daisy Bates Dr; ⊙ 9:30am-4:30pm, tours 9am & 1:15pm Mon-Fri mid-Aug–early Jun) Little Rock's most riveting attraction is the site of the 1957 desegrega-

---

ARKANSAS FACTS

Nickname Natural State

Population 2.9 million

Area 52,068 sq miles

Capital city Little Rock (population 193,537)

Other cities Fayetteville (population 76,899), Bentonville (population 38,294)

Sales tax 6%, plus 2% visitors tax and local taxes

Birthplace of General Douglas MacArthur (1880–1964), musician Johnny Cash (1932–2003), former president Bill Clinton (b 1946), author John Grisham (b 1955), actor Billy Bob Thornton (b 1955)

Home of Wal-Mart

Politics Like most Southern states, opposition to civil rights turned the state Republican in the '60s

Famous for Football fans 'calling the Hogs' – Woooooooooo, Pig ! Sooie!

Official state instrument Fiddle

Driving distances Little Rock to Eureka Springs 182 miles, Eureka Springs to Mountain View 123 miles

---

tion crisis that changed the country forever. It was here that a group of African American students known as the Little Rock Nine were first denied entry inside the then all-white high school (despite a unanimous 1954 Supreme Court ruling forcing the integration of public schools).

Eventually, President Eisenhower commanded the 1200-man 101st Airborne Battle Group to keep the crowds at bay and escort the students inside, a pivotal moment in the American Civil Rights movement. Today it's both a National Historic Site and a working high school. There's a spiffy new visitor center airing all the dirty laundry and putting the crisis into perspective alongside the greater Civil Rights movement.

William J Clinton Presidential Center
LIBRARY
(☑ 501-748-0419; www.clintonlibrary.gov; 1200 President Clinton Ave; adult/student & senior/child $7/5/3, with audio $10/8/6; ⊙ 9am-5pm Mon-Sat, 1-5pm Sun) ✐ This library houses the largest

ARKANSAS DELTA

Roughly 120 miles east of Little Rock, and just 20 from Clarksdale, Hwy 49 crosses the Mississippi River into the Arkansas Delta. **Helena**, a formerly prosperous, currently depressed mill town with a blues tradition (Sonny Boy Williamson made his name here), awakens for its annual **Arkansas Blues & Heritage Festival** (www.kingbiscuitfestival. com; tickets $45; ☉ Oct) when blues musicians and their fans take over downtown for three days in early October. Year-round, blues fans and history buffs should visit the **Delta Cultural Center** (☏ 870-338-4350; www.deltaculturalcenter.com; 141 Cherry St; ☉ 9am-5pm Tue-Sat) **FREE**. The museum displays all manner of memorabilia such as Albert King's and Sister Rosetta Tharpe's guitars, and John Lee Hooker's signed handkerchief.

The world's longest-running blues radio program, *King Biscuit Time*, is broadcast here (12:15pm Monday to Friday), and *Delta Sounds* (1pm Monday to Friday) often hosts live musicians; both air on KFFA AM-1360. Before leaving town, make like Robert Plant and stop by the wonderfully cluttered **Bubba's Blues Corner** (☏ 870-995-1326; 105 Cherry St, Helena; ☉ 9am-5pm Tue-Sat; ⊛) **FREE**, to pick up a blues record. Bubba puts on the **Arkansas Delta Rockabilly Festival** (www.deltarockabillyfest.com; tickets $30; ☉ May).

archival collection in presidential history, including 80 million pages of documents and two million photographs. Peruse the full-scale replica of the Oval Office, the exhibits on all stages of Clinton's life or the gifts from visiting dignitaries. The entire complex is built to environmentally friendly 'green' standards.

Old State House Museum MUSEUM
(www.oldstatehouse.com; 300 W Markham St; ☉ 9am-5pm Mon-Sat, 1-5pm Sun) **FREE** The state capitol from 1836 to 1911 now holds restored legislative chambers and displays on Arkansas history and culture.

Riverfront Park PARK
Just northwest of downtown, Riverfront Park rolls pleasantly along the Arkansas River and both pedestrians and cyclists take advantage of this fantastic city park daily. You can't miss the **Big Dam Bridge** (www.bigdambridge.com; ⊛), which connects 17 miles of multiuse trails that form a complete loop thanks to the renovation of the recently renamed, **Clinton Presidential Park Bridge**.

For a proper perusal of Riverfront Park, rent a bike (or tandem) from **Fike's Bike** (☏ 501-374-5505; www.fikesbikes.com; 200 S Olive St; 4hr/day from $12/20; ☉ 3-8pm Tue-Fri, 7-11am & 3-8pm Sat & Sun) – outside opening hours you can call for a reservation. In the River Market area, saddle up at **Bobby's Bike Hike** (☏ 501-613-7001; www.bobbysbikehike.com/

littlerock; 400 President Clinton Ave; 4hr $17-30, day $28-55).

🛏 Sleeping & Eating

Because of government and convention-center traffic, it's difficult to find inexpensive hotels downtown, and rates fluctuate wildly. Budget motels lie off the interstates. The fun-loving pubs in the River Market district buzz at night. **Ottenheimer Market Hall** (btwn S Commerce & S Rock Sts; ☉ 7am-6pm Mon-Sat) houses an eclectic collection of inexpensive food stalls.

Capital Hotel BOUTIQUE HOTEL **$$**
(☏ 888-293-4121, 501-374-7474; www.capitalhotel. com; 111 W Markham St; r from $160; P ❄ @ ☎) This 1872 former bank building with a cast-iron facade – a near-extinct architectural feature – is the top digs in Little Rock. There is a wonderful outdoor mezzanine for cocktails (and, unfortunately, smokers).

Rooms are plush, and the chef at **Ashley's**, one of two restaurants on the premises, won the *Food & Wine* People's Choice Best New Chef for the Midwest in 2011 (except this ain't the Midwest, though it's no fault of the food).

Rosemont HISTORIC B&B **$$**
(☏ 501-374-7456; www.rosemontoflittlerock.com; 515 W 15th St; r incl breakfast from $99; P ❄ ☎) An 1880s restored farmhouse near the Governor's mansion that oozes cozy Southern charm. The proprietors have also opened a few historic cottages nearby (from $125).

River City CAFE $
(www.rivercityteacoffeeandcream.com; 2715 Kavanaugh Blvd; ⊙6am-9pm Mon-Fri, from 7am Sat & Sun; 🤝) A killer Hillcrest tea and coffeehouse, cozy and homey with cushy sofas and an excellent selection of loose leaf tea. It has good ice cream too.

House PUB $
(www.facebook.com/thehouseinhillcrest; 722 N Palm St; mains $8-11; ⊙11am-2pm, 5pm-late Mon-Sat; 🤝) Arkansas' first gastropub is really all about the excellent burgers. The jerk burger comes smothered in warm mango chutney and jerk spices, the mac and cheese burger comes with, well, mac and cheese and the black-apple bourbon burger is drizzled with bourbon glaze and topped with a slice of crisp Arkansas black apple and bacon.

Get yours with a turkey or veggie patty if you must.

Acadia SOUTHERN $$$
(www.acadiahillcrest.com; 3000 Kavanaugh Blvd; dinner mains $18-23; ⊙5:30-10pm Mon-Sat; 🤝) Another Hillcrest standout, Acadia's multilevel patio with twinkling lights is a fabulous place to enjoy fancy-shmancy Southern dishes like oven-roasted duck breast glazed with Guinness-honey mustard paired with white truffled portobello-mushroom jack-cheese grits.

❶ Getting There & Around

Bill & Hillary Clinton National Airport (LIT; ☑501-372-3439; www.lrn-airport.com) lies just east of downtown. The **Greyhound station** (☑501-372-3007; www.greyhound.com; 118 E Washington St), in North Little Rock, serves Hot Springs (one to two hours), Memphis, TN (2½ hours), and New Orleans (18 hours). Amtrak occupies **Union Station** (☑501-372-6841; 1400 W Markham St). **Central Arkansas Transit** (CAT; ☑501-375-6717; www.cat.org) runs local buses and the **River Rail Streetcar**, a trolley which makes a loop on W Markham and President Clinton Ave (adult/child $1/50¢).

Hot Springs

The little city of Hot Springs once hosted the vacationing organized-crime elite. At full throttle in the 1930s, the city was a hotbed of gambling, bootlegging, prostitution, opulence and dangerous thugs. Yet it was also a spot of truce between warring gangs, a place where it was decreed that all criminals could be gluttonous hedonists in peace.

When gambling was squelched, so was the city's economy.

Though it still hasn't recovered from that blow, the healing waters have always drawn people, everyone from Native Americans to present-day pilgrims. Elaborate restored bathhouses, where you can still get old-school spa treatments, line Bathhouse Row behind shady magnolias on the east side of Central Ave.

◉ Sights & Activities

A promenade runs through the park around the hillside behind Bathhouse Row, where some springs survive intact, and a network of trails covers Hot Springs' mountains. Only two of the historic bathhouses are in operation.

Gangster Museum of America MUSEUM
(www.tgmoa.com; 510 Central Ave; adult/child $12/free; ⊙10am-5pm Sun-Thu, to 6pm Fri & Sat) Learn about the sinful glory days of prohibition when this small town in the middle of nowhere turned into a pinpoint of lavish wealth thanks to Chicago bootleggers like Capone, and his NYC counterparts. Highlights include original slots and a tommy gun.

Hot Springs Museum of Contemporary Art ART
(☑501-608-9966; www.museumofcontemporaryart.org; 425 Central Ave; adult/child $5/free; ⊙9am-4pm Tue-Sat, noon-3pm Sun) The historic Ozark bathhouse is now home to 11,000 sq ft of gallery space housing rotating exhibits. Given Hot Springs' arts reputation, it is worth a look.

NPS Visitor Center MUSEUM
(☑501-620-6715; www.nps.gov/hosp; 369 Central Ave; ⊙9am-5pm) On Bathhouse Row, traditionally set up in the 1915 Fordyce bathhouse, the NPS visitor center and museum have exhibits about the park's history first as a Native American free-trade zone, and later as a turn-of-the-19th-century European spa. At research time, however, the Fordyce was under renovation and a temporary center was set up in the Lamar bathhouse down the street.

Hot Springs Mountain Tower OUTDOORS
(401 Hot Springs Mountain Rd; adult/child $7/4; ⊙9am-5pm Nov-Feb, to 6pm Mar-May 15 & Labor Day-Oct, to 9pm May 16-Labor Day) On top of Hot Springs Mountain, the 216ft tower has

spectacular views of the surrounding mountains covered with dogwood, hickory, oak and pine – lovely in the spring and fall.

★ **Buckstaff Bathhouse** SPA
(☑ 501-623-2308; www.buckstaffbaths.com; 509 Central Ave; thermal bath $30, with 20min massage $60; ⊙ 7-11:45am & 1:30-3pm Mon-Sat) Spa service Hot Springs style was never a 'foofy' experience. Buckstaff's no-nonsense staff whip you through the baths, treatments and massages, just as in the 1930s. And it is wonderful.

Quapaw Baths SPA
(www.quapawbaths.com; 413 Central Ave; thermal bath $18, massage $50-80; ⊙ 10am-6pm Mon & Wed-Sat, 10am-3pm Sun) 🗲 If the traditional 'wham, bam, thank you, ma'am' approach isn't your thing, the newly remodeled Quapaw offers a more 21st-century vibe, with lovely restored thermal baths and gentle treatments.

🛏 Sleeping & Eating

Restaurants congregate along the Central Ave tourist strip and offer ho-hum food.

★ **Alpine Inn** INN $
(☑ 501-624-9164; www.alpine-inn-hot-springs.com; 741 Park Ave/Hwy 7 N; r $55-90; P ✳ 🖺 🏊) The friendly Scottish owners of this inn, less than a mile from Bathhouse Row, have spent a few years upgrading an old motel to remarkable ends. The rooms are impeccable, comfortable and include new flatscreen TVs and sumptuous beds.

Arlington Resort Hotel & Spa HISTORIC HOTEL $
(☑ 501-623-7771; www.arlingtonhotel.com; 239 Central Ave; s/d from $88/98, with mineral bath $145; P ✳ 🖺 🏊) This imposing historic hotel tops Bathhouse Row and constantly references its glory days. The grand lobby buzzes at night when there might be a live band. There's an in-house spa, and rooms are well-maintained, if aging. There's even a half-hearted Starbucks! Corner rooms with a view are a steal.

Colonial Pancake House DINER $
(111 Central Ave; mains $6-10; ⊙ 7am-3pm) A Hot Springs classic, with turquoise booths and homey touches like quilts and doilies on the walls, it's almost like your grandma's kitchen. Except the pancakes, French toast (made with Texas toast) and malted or buckwheat

waffles are better'n grandma's. Get yours with pecans inside. It does burgers and other diner grub at lunch.

McClard's BARBECUE $$
(www.mcclards.com; 505 Albert Pike; mains $4-15; ⊙ 11am-8pm Tue-Sat) Southwest of the center, Bill Clinton's favorite boyhood BBQ is still popular for ribs, slow-cooked beans, chili and tamales. It's on the outskirts of downtown.

Central Park Fusion ASIAN FUSION $$$
(☑ 501-623-0202; www.centralparkfusion.com; 200 Park Ave; mains $19-33) The town favorite at research time, this east-meets-west kitchen grills steaks Hawaiian style, steams mussels in Thai curry, does an Asian duck salad, and glazes salmon in Thai chili. All served in a contemporary dining space accented with local art.

☆ Entertainment

Maxine's BAR
(☑ 501-321-0909; www.maxineslive.com; 700 Central Ave) If you're looking for some (loud) night music, head to this infamous cathouse turned live music venue. It hosts bands out of Austin regularly, and cater to a younger crowd.

ℹ Getting There & Away

Greyhound (☑ 501-623-5574; www.greyhound. com; 1001 Central Ave) has buses heading to Little Rock (1½ hours, three daily).

Around Hot Springs

The wild, pretty **Ouachita National Forest** (☑ 501-321-5202; www.fs.usda.gov/ouachita; welcome center 100 Reserve St; ⊙ 8am-4:30pm) is studded with lakes and draws hunters, fisherfolk, mountain-bike riders and boaters. The small roads through the mountains unfailingly bring hidden nooks and wonderful views. The Ouachita boasts two designated National Forest Scenic Byways: Arkansas Scenic Hwy 7 and Talimena Scenic Byway, navigating mountain ranges from Arkansas into Oklahoma.

Clinton buffs might stop at **Hope**, where the ex-pres spent his first seven years, but there's not much to see other than the spiffy **Hope Visitor Center & Museum** (www. hopearkansas.net; 100 E Division St; ⊙ 8:30am-5pm Mon-Fri, from 9am Sat, 1-4pm Sun), in the old depot, and the **President Bill Clinton**

First Home Museum (www.clintonchildhood-homemuseum.com; 117 S Hervey St; ⊘8:30am-4:30pm) FREE.

Arkansas River Valley

The Arkansas River cuts a swath across the state from Oklahoma to Mississippi. Folks come to fish, canoe and camp along its banks and tributaries. The excellently maintained trails of **Petit Jean State Park** (☑501-727-5441; www.petitjeanstatepark.com; ⊛), west of Morrilton, wind past a lush 95ft waterfall, romantic grottoes, expansive vistas and dense forests. There's a rustic stone lodge, reasonable **cabins** (per night $105-180) and campgrounds. Another stellar state park is **Mount Magazine** (☑479-963-8502; www.mountmagazinestatepark.com; 16878 Hwy 309 S), which maintains 14 miles of trails around Arkansas' highest point. Outdoor enthusiasts enjoy great hang gliding and rock climbing here as well as hiking.

The spectacular **Highway 23/Pig Trail Byway**, lined with wild echinacea and lilies, climbs through **Ozark National Forest** and into the mountains; an excellent way to reach Eureka Springs.

Ozark Mountains

Stretching from northwest and central Arkansas into Missouri, the **Ozark Mountains** (☑870-404-2741; www.ozarkmountainregion.com) are an ancient range, once surrounded by sea and now well worn by time. Verdant rolling mountains give way to misty fields, and dramatic karst formations line sparkling lakes, meandering rivers and scenic back roads. Though some of the towns bank on kitschy hillbilly culture, scratch below the surface to find unique cultural traditions, such as acoustic folk music and home-cooked hush puppies and catfish.

Mountain View

Detour east of US 65 or along Hwy 5 to this wacky Ozark town, known for its tradition of informal music-making at **Courtsquare**. Creeping commercialism is taking its toll, as the **Visitor Information Center** (☑870-269-8068; www.yourplaceinthemountains.com; 107 N Peabody Ave; ⊘9am-4:30pm Mon-Sat) promotes the place as the 'Folk Music Capital of the World,' but cutesy sandstone architecture downtown, and impromptu folk, gospel and bluegrass hootenannies (jam sessions) by the Stone County Courthouse (especially on Saturday night) – and on porches all around town anytime – make a visit here rather harmonious.

Ozark Folk Center State Park (☑800-264-3655; www.ozarkfolkcenter.com; 1032 Park Ave; auditorium adult/child $12/7; ⊘10am-5pm Tue-Sat Apr-Nov), just north of town, hosts ongoing craft demonstrations and a traditional herb garden, as well as frequent live music from 7pm that attracts an avid, older crowd. The zip and slack lines, free-fall and climbing wall at **LocoRopes** (☑870-269-6566; www. locoropes.com; 1025 Park Ave; per zip line $7.50; ⊘10am-5pm Mar 1-Nov 30) is strictly for the young and wild at heart.

The spectacular **Blanchard Springs Caverns** (☑870-757-2211; www.blanchardsprings.org; NF 54, Forest Rd, off Hwy 14; adult/child Drip Stone Tour $10.50/5.50, Wild Cave Tour $75; ⊘10:30am-4:30pm; ⊛), located 15 miles northwest of Mountain View, were carved by an underground river and rival those at Carlsbad Caverns National Park. Three Forest Service guided tours range from disabled-accessible to adventurous three- to four-hour spelunking sessions. The welcoming and historic 1918 **Wildflower B&B** (☑870-269-4383; www.wildflowerbb.com; 100 Washington; r incl breakfast from $89; ⊕❋☞) is right on the Courtsquare with a rocking chair–equipped, wrap-around porch, and cozy down-home trappings. **Tommy's Famous Pizza and BBQ** (cnr Carpenter & W Main Sts; pizza $7-26, mains $7-13; ⊘from 3pm) is run by the friendliest bunch of backwoods hippies you could ask for. The pulled-pork BBQ pizza marries Tommy's specialties perfectly.

Eureka Springs

Artsy, quirky and drop-dead gorgeous, Eureka Springs, near Arkansas' northwestern corner, perches in a steep valley and is one of the coolest towns in the South. Victorian buildings line crooked streets and a crunchy local population welcomes all – it's one of the most explicitly gay-friendly towns in the Ozarks and an island of Democratic blue in a sea of Republican red. On the surface, art galleries and kitschy shops compete with commercialized country music and the 70ft **Christ of the Ozarks** statue for your attention. But bend a local's ear and find out who's playing at the nearest pub, or the location of their favorite swimming hole, and this idiosyncratic village will take on new

DON'T MISS

A LOVELY LOOP

Downtown Eureka Springs is beautiful in and of itself, but the town's real coup is its easily overlooked **Historic Loop**, a 3.5-mile ring of history through downtown and neighboring residential neighborhoods. The route is dotted with over 300 Victorian homes, all built before 1910, each and every one of them a jaw-dropper and on par with any preserved historic district in the USA.

Pick up a *Six Scenic Walking Tours* brochure from the visitor center in Eureka Springs, rent a bike from **Adventure Mountain Outfitters** (☑479-253-0900; www. adventuremountainoutfitters.com; 151 Spring St, Eureka Springs; half day from $50; ☺9am-5pm Wed-Sat); or catch the Red Line of the **Eureka Trolley** (www.eurekatrolley.org; day pass adult/child $6/2; ☺9am-5pm Jan-Apr & Nov-Dec, to 8pm Sun May-Oct).

dimensions. Hiking, cycling, and horseback-riding opportunities abound. There are no red lights or perpendicular cross streets, so zipping around its historical beauty is a breeze. Well, except for those steep hills.

The **visitor center** (☑479-253-8737; www. eurekaspringschamber.com; 516 Village Circle, Hwy 62 E; ☺9am-5pm) has information about lodging, activities, tours and local attractions, such as the rockin' **Blues Festival** (www.eurekaspringsblues.com; ☺Jun). The old **ES & NA Railway** (☑479-253-9623; www. esnarailway.com; 299 N Main St; adult/child $14/7; ☺Tue-Sat Apr-Oct) puffs through the Ozark hills on an hour-long tour three times a day (four times on Saturday).

Thorncrown Chapel (☑479-253-7401; www.thorncrown.com; 12968 Hwy 62 W; donation suggested; ☺9am-5pm Apr-Nov, 11am-4pm Mar & Dec) is a magnificent sanctuary made of glass, with its 48ft-tall wooden skeleton holding 425 windows. There's not much between your prayers and God's green earth here. It's just outside of town in the woods.

You can nest downtown at the historic **New Orleans Hotel and Suchness Spa** (☑479-253-8630; www.neworleanshotelandspa.com; 63 Spring St; r from $89; P❄🕸), which would send you reeling back in time, except for the New Age, chakra balancing spa in the lobby. **Treehouse Cottages** (☑479-253-8667; www. treehousecottages.com; 165 W Van Buren St; cottages $149-169; P❄🕸) offers gorgeous sunlit, Jacuzzi-equipped tree houses (that are more like cottages on stilts) in the woods on the canyon rim.

At **Mud Street Café** (www.mudstreetcafe. com; 22G S Main St; mains $9-13; ☺8am-3pm Thu-Tue), downtown, the coffee drinks and breakfasts are renowned. After dark, find **Chelsea's Pizzeria** (☑479-253-8231; www. chelseascornercafe.com; 10 Mountain St; mains $10-20; ☺noon-10pm Sun-Thu, to midnight Fri &

Sat), for good pies and Mediterranean fare, and an excellent live music scene in the cavernous bar downstairs.

Buffalo National River

Yet another under-acknowledged Arkansas gem, and perhaps the best of them all, this 135-mile river flows beneath dramatic bluffs through unspoiled Ozark forest. The upriver section tends to have most of the white water, while the lower reaches ease lazily along – perfect for an easy paddle. The **Buffalo National River** (☑870-741-5443; www.nps.gov/ buff) has 10 campgrounds and three designated wilderness areas; the most accessible is through the **Tyler Bend visitor center** (☑870-439-2502; ☺8:30am-4:30pm), 11 miles north of Marshall on Hwy 65, where you can also pick up a list of approved outfitters for self-guided rafting or canoe trips, the best way to tour the park and see the gargantuan limestone bluffs. Or simply seek out **Buffalo Outdoor Center** (BOC; ☑800-221-5514; www. buffaloriver.com; cnr Hwys 43 & 74; kayak/canoe per day $58/60, car shuttle from $18, zipline tour $89; ☺8am-5pm; 🚼🐾) in Ponca. They will point you in the right direction and rent out attractive cabins in the woods too. Thanks to its National River designation in 1972, the Buffalo is one of the few remaining unpolluted, free-flowing rivers in America.

LOUISIANA

Southerners will often tell you they're different from other Americans. They say it's their intensely felt local traditions and connection to the land, though they might say this sitting on the porch of a cookie-cutter subdivision that could be Anywhere, America. But in Louisiana, that regional pride becomes actual regionalism, a palpable sense that you are somewhere different.

A French colony turned Spanish protectorate turned reluctant American purchase; a southern fringe of swampland, bayou and alligators dissolving into the Gulf of Mexico; a northern patchwork prairie of heartland farm country, and everywhere, a population tied together by a deep, unshakeable appreciation for the good things: food and music.

Louisiana's first city, New Orleans, lives and dies by these qualities, and her restaurants and music halls are second to none, but everywhere, the state shares a love for this joie de vivre. We're not dropping French for fun, by the way; while the language is not a cultural component of North Louisiana, near I-10 and below it is a generation removed from the household – if it has been removed at all.

History

The lower Mississippi River area was dominated by the Mississippian mound-building culture until around 1592 when Europeans arrived and decimated the Native Americans with the usual combination of disease, unfavorable treaties and outright hostility.

The land was then passed back and forth between France, Spain and England. Under the French 'Code Noir,' slaves were kept, but retained a somewhat greater degree of freedom, and thus native culture, than their counterparts in British North America.

After the American Revolution the whole area passed to the USA in the 1803 Louisiana Purchase, and Louisiana became a state in 1812. The resulting blend of American and Franco-Spanish traditions, plus the influence of Afro-Caribbean communities, gave Louisiana a unique culture she retains to this day.

Steamboats opened a vital trade network across the continent. New Orleans was a major port, and Louisiana's slave-based plantation economy kept up a flowing export of rice, tobacco, indigo, sugarcane and especially cotton. After the Civil War, Louisiana was readmitted to the Union in 1868, and the next 30 years saw political wrangling, economic stagnation and renewed discrimination against African Americans.

In the 1920s, industry and tourism developed, but so did a tradition of unorthodox and sometimes ruthless politics; in 1991, former Ku Klux Klan leader David Duke ran for Governor against Edwin Edwards; Edwards, a famously colorful and corrupt politician. Edwards won the race and was eventually convicted on racketeering charges.

Hurricane Katrina (2005) and the BP Gulf Coast Oil Spill (2010) significantly damaged the local economy and infrastructure. Louisiana remains a bottom-rung state in terms of per capita income and education levels, yet on the flip side, ranks high in national happiness scales.

ⓘ Information

Sixteen welcome centers dot freeways throughout the state, or contact the **Louisiana Office of Tourism** (☑ 800-993-7515, 225-342-8100; www.louisianatravel.com).

Louisiana State Parks (☑ 877-226-7652; www.crt.state.la.us/parks; primitive/premium sites $1/18) Louisiana has 22 state parks that offer camping. Some parks offer lodge accommodations and cabins. Reservations (☑ 877-226-7652; http://reservations2.usedirect.com/LAStateParksHome/) can be made online, by phone, or on a drop-in basis if there's availability.

New Orleans

New Orleans is very much of America, and extraordinarily removed from it as well. 'Nola' is something, and somewhere, else. Founded by the French and administered by the Spanish (and then the French again), she is, with her sidewalk cafes and iron balconies, the most European city in America, yes. But she is also, with her *vodoun* (voodoo), weekly second-line parades (essentially, neigborhood parades), Mardi Gras Indians, jazz and brass and gumbo, the most African and Caribbean city in the country as well. New Orleans celebrates; while America is on deadline, this city is getting a cocktail after a long lunch. But if you saw how people here rebuilt their homes after floods and storms, you'd be foolish to call the locals lazy.

Tolerating everything and learning from it is the soul of this city. When her citizens aspire to that great Creole ideal – a mix of all influences into something better – we get: jazz; Nouveau Louisiana cuisine; storytellers from African *griots* (West African bards) to Seventh Ward rappers to Tennessee Williams; French townhouses a few blocks from Foghorn Leghorn mansions groaning under sweet myrtle and bougainvillea; Mardi Gras celebrations that mix pagan mysticism with Catholic pageantry. Just don't forget the indulgence and immersion, because that Creole-ization gets watered down when folks don't live life to its intellectual and epicurean hilt.

New Orleans may take it easy, but it takes it. The whole hog. Stuffed with crawfish.

History

The town of Nouvelle Orléans was founded as a French outpost in 1718 by Jean-Baptiste Le Moyne de Bienville. Early settlers arrived from France, Canada and Germany, and the French imported thousands of African slaves. The city became a central port in the slave trade; due to local laws some slaves were allowed to earn their freedom and assume an established place in the Creole community as *les gens de couleur libres* (free people of color).

The Spanish were largely responsible for building the French Quarter as it still looks today because fires in 1788 and 1794 decimated the earlier French architecture. The influx of Anglo Americans after the Louisiana Purchase led to an expansion of the city into the Central Business District (CBD), Garden District and Uptown.

New Orleans survived the Civil War intact after an early surrender to Union forces, but the economy languished with the end of the slavery-based plantations. In the early 1900s, New Orleans was the birthplace of jazz music. Many of the speakeasies and homes of the jazz originators have been destroyed through neglect, but the cultural claim was canonized in 1994 when the National Park Service established the New Orleans Jazz National Historical Park to celebrate the origins and evolution of America's most widely recognized indigenous musical art form. Oil and petrochemical industries developed in the 1950s, and today tourism is the other lifeblood of the local economy.

In 2005 Katrina, a relatively weak Category 3 hurricane, overwhelmed New Orleans' federal flood protection system in over 50 places. Some 80% of the city was flooded, over 1800 people lost their lives and the entire city was evacuated. Today the population has largely returned (80% of pre-Katrina population levels), and cheap housing and the vibrant culture has attracted a whole generation of entrepreneurs.

◉ Sights

◉ French Quarter

Elegant, Caribbean-colonial architecture, lush gardens and wrought-iron accents are the visual norm in the French Quarter. But this is also the heart of New Orleans' tourism scene. Bourbon St generates a loutish membrane that sometimes makes the rest of the Quarter difficult to appreciate. Look past this. The Vieux Carré (Old Quarter; first laid out in 1722) is the focal point of much of this city's culture and in the quieter back lanes and alleyways there's a sense of faded time shaken and stirred with joie de vivre.

Jackson Square   SQUARE, PLAZA
(🗹504-568-6968; www.jackson-square.com; Decatur & St Peter Sts) Jackson Sq is the heart of the Quarter. Sprinkled with lazing loungers, surrounded by fortune-tellers, sketch artists and traveling showmen, and overlooked by cathedrals, offices and shops plucked from a fairy tale, this is one of America's great green spaces.

St Louis Cathedral CATHEDRAL
(☑ 504 525-9585; Jackson Sq; donations accepted; ⊙ 9am-5pm Mon-Sat, 1-5pm Sun) St Louis Cathedral is Jackson Sq's masterpiece. Designed by Gilberto Guillemard, this is one of the finest examples of French ecumenical (church) architecture in America.

Louisiana State Museum MUSEUM
(http://lsm.crt.state.la.us; per bldg adult/child $6/ free; ⊙ 10am-4:30pm Tue-Sun) This institution operates several buildings across the state. The standouts here include the 1911 **Cabildo** (701 Chartres St), on the left of the cathedral, a Louisiana history museum located in the old city hall where Plessy vs Ferguson (which legalized segregation) was argued. The huge number of exhibits inside can easily eat up half a day (don't miss the 1875 Upright Piano on the 3rd floor), the remainder of which can be spent in the Cabildo's sister building, on the right of the church, the 1813 **Presbytère** (751 Chartres St; ♿). Inside is an excellent **Mardi Gras museum**, with displays of costumes, parade floats and royal jewelry; and a poignant **Katrina & Beyond** exhibit,

chronicling the before and after of this devastating storm – a surefire don't-miss for understanding the effects of this disaster on the city.

Historic New Orleans Collection MUSEUM
(www.hnoc.org; 533 Royal St; tours $5; ⊙ 9:30am-4:30pm Tue-Sat, 10:30am-4:30pm Sun) FREE In several exquisitely restored buildings are thoughtfully curated exhibits with an emphasis on archival materials, such as the original transfer documents of the Louisiana Purchase. Separate home, architecture/ courtyard and history tours also run at 10am, 11am, 2pm and 3pm.

Old Ursuline Convent HISTORIC BUILDING
(1112 Chartres St; adult/child $5/3; ⊙ tours 10am-4pm Mon-Sat) In 1727, 12 Ursuline nuns arrived in New Orleans to care for the French garrison's 'miserable little hospital' and to educate the young girls of the colony. Between 1745 and 1752 the French colonial army built what is now the oldest structure in the Mississippi River Valley and the only remaining French building in the Quarter.

NEW ORLEANS IN...

Two Days

On the first day, wander Jackson Sq and the French Quarter's museums. The **Cabildo** and **Presbytere** are adjacent to each other and give a good grounding in Louisiana culture, as does the nearby **Historic New Orleans Collection**. Afterwards, stroll along the mighty Mississippi.

Grab dinner at **Bayona**, localvore base of hometown legend Susan Spicer. Enjoy drinks at **Tonique** and go see some live music at **Preservation Hall**.

Next morning, stroll along Magazine St in a state of shopping nirvana. Then walk north, pop into **Lafayette Cemetery No 1**, consider having a drink at **Commander's Palace** – it helps to be well-dressed – and hop onto the St Charles Avenue Streetcar. Have a haute Southern dinner at **Boucherie**.

Four Days

On day three, join the morning Creole Neighborhoods bike tour with **Confederacy of Cruisers**. This is exceptionally easy riding, and takes in all elements of the funky Marigny and Bywater, but if you don't fancy bikes, walk past Washington Sq Park and soak up the Marigny's vibe.

Have dinner at **Bacchanal** and enjoy great wine and cheese in this musical garden.

If you're feeling edgy, head to St Claude Avenue where the offerings range from punk to hip-hop to bounce to '60s mod. For more traditional Nola jazz and blues, head down Frenchmen St.

The next day drive, or consider renting a bicycle, and explore around the Tremé – don't miss the **Backstreet Cultural Museum** or **Willie Mae's** fried chicken.

Head up Esplanade Ave and gawk at all the gorgeous Creole mansions sitting pretty under the big live oaks. Take Esplanade all the way to **City Park** and wander around the **New Orleans Museum of Art**.

New Orleans

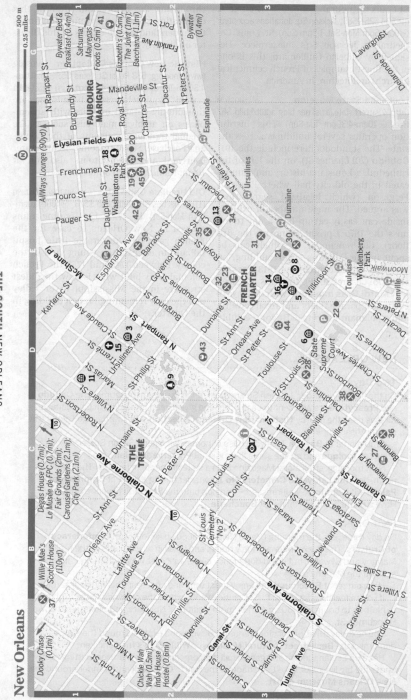

500 m
0.25 miles

FAUBOURG MARIGNY

Bywater Bed &
Breakfast (0.4mi);
Satsuma;
Maurepas
Foods (0.5mi) 41

Elizabeth's (0.5mi);
The Joint (1mi);
Bacchanal (1.1mi)

Franklin Ave
Port St

Bywater
(0.4mi)

N Rampart St
Burgundy St
N Rampart St
Mandeville St
Royal St
Chartres St
Decatur St
N Peters St

Lavergne St

Delaronde St

Elysian Fields Ave

AllWays Lounge (90yd)

18
Frenchmen St
Washington Sq
Park

19 45
20 46

47

Touro St
Dauphine St

Pauger St

42

13
34

Esplanade Ave
25
39
Barracks St

Chartres St
Royal St
35
N Peters St
Ursulines

Dumaine

Esplanade

Woldenberg
Park

Moonwalk

31

21
8

30

Kerlerec St
St Claude Ave
Governor Nicholls St
Bourbon St
Dauphine St
Burgundy St

32 23

14

FRENCH
QUARTER

16
5

Wilkinson St

Toulouse

Bienville

Ursulines Ave
15
3
N Rampart St
St Philip St
Dumaine St
St Ann St
Orleans Ave
St Peter St

22

Decatur St
N Peters St
Chartres St

11
Marais St
N Villere St
N Robertson St

THE TREMÉ
N Claiborne Ave

6
Dumaine St
St Peter St
43

44
St Louis St
Toulouse St
St Louis St
Bourbon St
Dauphine St
38

6
St Charles Ave
State
Supreme
Court
28

St Louis St
Conti St
Basin St
N Rampart St
Bienville St
Iberville St

36

7

27
University Pl
Barone St
S Rampart St

Degas House (0.7mi);
Le Musée de FPC (0.7mi);
Fair Grounds (2mi);
Carousel Gardens (2.1mi);
City Park (2.1mi)

10

10

St Louis
Cemetery
No 2

St Ann St
Orleans Ave
Lafitte Ave
Toulouse St
N Roman St
N Prieur St
N Johnson St
N Derbigny St
N Robertson St
S Villere St
Cleveland St

Canal St
Tulane Ave

Willie Mae's
Scotch House
(110yd)

Dooky Chase
(0.1mi)

37

N Tonti St
N Miro St
N Galvez St
Chickie Wah
Wah (0.5mi);
India House
Hostel (0.6mi)

N Johnson St
N Prieur St
Bienville St
Iberville St
S Roman St
S Prieur St
S Johnson St
Palmyra St
S Derbigny St
S Robertson St
S Claiborne Ave
Elk Pl
Saratoga St
Cleveland St
S Villere St
La Salle St
Gravier St
Perdido St
Crozat St
Treme St
Marais St
Basin St
Crozat St

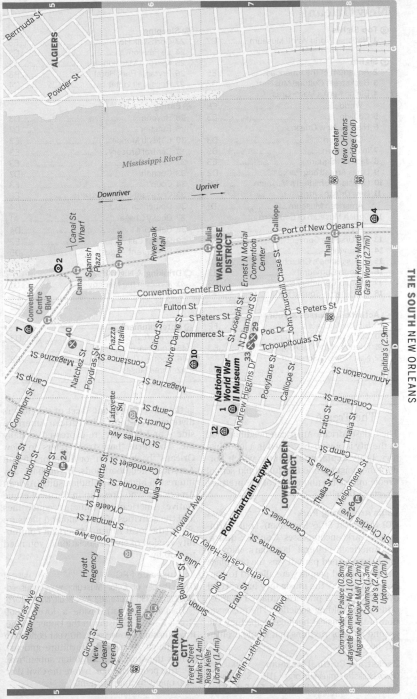

ALGIERS

Bermuda St

Powder St

Mississippi River

Downriver

Upriver

Greater New Orleans Bridge (toll)

WAREHOUSE DISTRICT

Canal St Wharf

Spanish Plaza

Poydras

Riverwalk Mall

Julia

Canal St

Port of New Orleans Pl

Calliope

Thalia

Blaine Kern's Mardi Gras World (2.7mi)

Convention Centre Blvd

Convention Center Blvd

Ernest N Morial Convention Center

John Churchill Chase St

S Peters St

Tipitina's (2.9mi)

Fulton St

S Peters St

Commerce St

Girod St

Notre Dame St

Magazine St

Constance St

Natchez St

Poydras St

Piazza D'Italia

Magazine St

St Joseph St

N Diamond St

Poe Dr

Tchoupitoulas St

Poeyfarre St

Calliope St

Annunciation St

National World War II Museum

Andrew Higgins Dr

Magazine St

Camp St

Church St

Lafayette Sq

St Charles Ave

Camp St

Common St

Gravier St

Union St

Perdido St

Carondelet St

Lafayette St

Julia St

Baronne St

O'Keefe St

S Rampart St

Loyola Ave

Howard Ave

Oretha Castle Haley Blvd

Pontchartrain Expwy

LOWER GARDEN DISTRICT

Erato St

Constance St

Camp St

Prytania St

Thalia St

Melpomene St

St Charles Ave

Thalia St

Hyatt Regency

Poydras Ave

Sugarbowl Dr

Girod St

New Orleans Arena

Union Passenger Terminal

CENTRAL CITY

Freret Street Market (1.4mi); Rosa Keller Library (1.4mi)

Bolivar St

Simon

Simon

Clio St

Erato St

Martin Luther King Jr Blvd

Commander's Palace (0.8mi);
Lafayette Cemetery No 1 (0.8mi);
Magazine Antique Mall (1.2mi);
Columns (1.3mi);
St Joe's (2.4mi);
Uptown (2mi)

2

4

7

40

10

29

33

1

12

24

26

New Orleans

◉ The Tremé

The oldest African American neighborhood in the city is obviously steeped in a lot of history. Leafy **Esplanade Avenue**, which borders the neighborhood, is full of old-school Creole mansions, and is one of the prettiest streets in the city.

Louis Armstrong Park   PARK
(701 N Rampart St; ◷ 9am-10pm) Louis Armstrong Park encompasses **Congo Square**, an American cultural landmark. Now a lovely landscaped park, it was the one place where enslaved people were allowed to congregate and play the music they had carried over the seas – a practice outlawed in most other slave-holding societies. The preservation of this musical heritage helped lay the groundwork for rhythms that would eventually become jazz.

Backstreet Cultural Museum   MUSEUM
(www.backstreetmuseum.org; 1116 St Claude Ave; admission $8; ◷10am-5pm Tue-Sat) This is the place to see one facet of this town's distinctive customs – its African American side – and how they're expressed in daily life. The term 'backstreet' refers to New Orleans' 'back o' town,' or the poor African American neighborhoods. If you have any interest in Mardi Gras Indian suits (African Americans who dress up in Carnival-esque Native American costume), second lines and the activities of social aid and pleasure clubs (the local African American community version of civic associations), you need to stop by.

Le Musée de FPC   MUSEUM
(Free People of Color Museum; www.lemuseedefpc.com; 2336 Esplanade Ave; adult/child $10/5; ◷11am-4pm Wed-Sat) Inside a lovely 1859 Greek Revival mansion in the Upper Tremé, this museum showcases a 30-year collection of artifacts, documents, furniture and art, telling the story of a forgotten subculture: the 'free people of color' before the Civil War. Also opens by appointment.

St Louis Cemetery No 1   CEMETERY
(Basin St; ☉ 9am-3pm Mon-Sat, to noon Sun; 👣)
This cemetery received the remains of most
early Creoles. The shallow water table ne-
cessitated above ground burials, with bodies
placed in the family tombs you see to this
day. The supposed grave of voodoo queen
Marie Laveau is here, scratched with XXXs
from spellbound devotees – this is graffiti
you shouldn't add to, per the request of the
family that owns the tomb. Do not come
here at night; the area can be dangerous.

**New Orleans African
American Museum**   MUSEUM
(www.thenoaam.org; 1418 Governor Nicholls St;
adult/student/child $7/5/3; ☉ 11am-4pm Wed-Sat)
This small museum features rotating displays of local artists and semi-permanent installations on slavery and African American
history in a series of tidy Creole homes.

St Augustine's Church   CHURCH
(☎ 504-525-5934;   www.staugustinecatholic-
church-neworleans.org; 1210 Governor Nicholls St)
The 1824 church is the second-oldest African American Catholic church in the US;
many jazz funeral processions originate
here. It has Sunday services but you'll need
to call ahead for a tour. Note the haunting
cross fashioned from chains on the side of
the building marking the **Tomb of the Unknown Slave.**

◉ Faubourg Marigny, the Bywater & the Ninth Ward

North of the French Quarter are the Creole
suburbs (faubourgs, which more accurately
means 'neighborhoods') of the Marigny
and the Bywater. The Marigny is the heart
of the local gay scene. **Frenchmen Street,**
which runs through the center of the 'hood,
is a fantastic strip of live-music goodness. It
used to be known as a locals' Bourbon, but
recently it's been inundated with tourists,
although it's still nowhere near as tacky as
Bourbon. Nearby **St Claude Avenue** now
boasts a collection of good live music venues that are fairly undiscovered by outsiders,
but don't expect Dixie-style jazz joints; folks
here rock out to punk and bounce (a local
style of frenetic dance music).

The Bywater is a collection of candy-
colored shotgun houses (local houses that
are laid out one room after another with
no hallway) and Creole cottages. It has the
heaviest concentration of transplants in

the city and an ever-expanding number of
sometimes awesome, sometimes cloyingly
hip new restaurant and bars.

Old New Orleans Rum Distillery   FACTORY
(☎ 504-945-9400;   www.oldneworleansrum.com;
2815 Frenchmen St; admission $10; ☉ tours noon,
2pm & 4pm Mon-Fri, 2pm & 4pm Sat) A short
drive north of the Marigny is the Old New
Orleans Rum distillery. Founded by local
artists James Michalopoulos and his artist-
musician friends, the distillery makes great
spirits you'll find in most local bars. You can
sample all of them, including a rare vintage
unavailable outside the factory, on an entertaining 45-minute distillery tour. The rum
distillery is in an industrial area 2 miles
north of Faubourg Marigny.

Washington Square Park   PARK
(cnr Frenchmen & Royal St) Also known as
'Marigny Green,' this park is a popular
spot for locals to play with their dogs, toss
Frisbees and, based on the frequent smell,
smoke things that aren't cigarettes. There's a
touching HIV/AIDS memorial on the north
side of the park.

◉ CBD & Warehouse District

★ **National World War II Museum**   MUSEUM
(☎ 504-528-1944;   www.ddaymuseum.org;   945
Magazine St; adult/child $22/13, with 1/2 films
add $5/10; ☉ 9am-5pm) The extensive, heart-
wrenching museum should satisfy the historical curiosity of anyone with even a passing interest in WWII. The museum presents
an admirably nuanced and thorough analy-
sis of the biggest war of the 20th century.
Of particular note is the **D-Day exhibition,**
arguably the most in-depth of its type in the
country. Beyond All Boundaries, a film narrated by Tom Hanks and shown on a 120ft-
wide immersive screen in the new **Solomon
Victory Theater,** is a loud, proud and awesome extravaganza. Final Mission places
27 audience members on the submarine
USS Tang during her final mission; you will
become a crew member with naval respon-
sibilities and learn the ultimate fate of the
ship's complement.

Ogden Museum of Southern Art   MUSEUM
(☎ 504-539-9600; www.ogdenmuseum.org; 925
Camp St; adult/student/child $10/8/5; ☉ 10am-
5pm Wed-Mon, 10am-5pm & 6-8pm Thu) New Orleans entrepreneur Roger Houston Ogden
has assembled one of the finest collections
of Southern art anywhere – far too large

ART FOR EVERY WEEKEND

Lindsay Glatz from the Arts Council of New Orleans fills us in on the places where you can discover local artists and meet local artists every weekend in New Orleans.

New Orleans Arts District Art Walk (www.neworleansartsdistrict.com; Julia St; ◷6-9pm 1st Sat of month) The fine-art galleries in New Orleans Art District celebrate the opening night of month-long feature artist exhibitions. In the Warehouse District/CBD.

Freret Street Market (www.freretmarket.org; cnr Freret St & Napoleon Ave; ◷noon-5pm 1st Sat of month Sep-Jun) A combination farmers market, flea market and art show in Uptown, this offers a great mix of local culture.

Saint Claude Arts District Gallery Openings (www.scadnola.com; ◷2nd Sat of month) New Orleans' newest arts district, this growing collective of art-exhibition spaces spans Faubourg Marigny and the Bywater, home to some of New Orleans' more eclectic artists. Ask locals for weekend recommendations and you may be rewarded with a fire-eating display or impromptu collective installations at a secret, hidden art space.

Art Market of New Orleans (www.artscouncilofneworleans.org; Palmer Park, cnr Carrolton & Claiborne Aves; ◷last Sat of month) Featuring hundreds of the area's most creative local artists, this monthly Uptown market is juried for quality and always features local food, music and kids' activities. Perfect on warm-weather days.

to keep to himself – which includes huge galleries ranging from Impressionist landscapes to outsider folk-art quirkiness, to contemporary installation work. There's live music from 6pm to 8pm Thursday with normal museum admission.

Blaine Kern's Mardi Gras World　MUSEUM
(◷504-655-9586; www.mardigrasworld.com; 1380 Port of New Orleans Pl; adult/child $19.95/12.95; ◷tours 9:30am-4:30pm; ◉) This garish and good-fun spot houses (and constructs) many of the greatest floats used in Mardi Gras parades. The tour takes you through the giant workshops where artists create elaborate floats for New Orleans *krewes* (marching clubs), Universal Studios and Disney World.

Aquarium of the Americas　AQUARIUM
(◷504-581-4629; www.auduboninstitute.org; 1 Canal St; adult/child $22.50/16, with IMAX $29/23, with Audubon Zoo $36/25; ◷10am-5pm; ◉) Simulates an eclectic selection of watery habitats – look for the rare white alligator. You can buy combination tickets to the IMAX theater next door, the nearby Insectarium, the Audubon Zoo in Uptown or all of the above (adult/child $44.50/27.50).

Insectarium　MUSEUM, GARDEN
(◷504-581-4629; www.auduboninstitute.org; 423 Canal St; adult/child $16.50/12; ◷10am-5pm; ◉) A supremely kid-friendly learning center that's a joy for budding entomologists. The Japanese garden dotted with whispering butterflies is particularly beautiful. Has a nice exhibit on New Orleans' notorious cockroaches.

◉ Garden District & Uptown

The main architectural division in New Orleans is between the elegant townhouses of the Creole and French northeast and the magnificent mansions of the American district, settled after the Louisiana Purchase. These huge structures, plantationesque in their appearance, are most commonly found in the Garden District and Uptown. Magnificent oak trees arch over St Charles Ave, which cuts through the heart of this sector and where the supremely picturesque **St Charles Avenue streetcar** (per ride $1.25; ◉) runs. The boutiques and galleries of **Magazine Street** form the best shopping strip in the city.

Lafayette Cemetery No 1　CEMETERY
(Washington Ave at Prytania St; ◷9am-2:30pm) This necropolis was established in 1833 by the former City of Lafayette. Sitting as it does just across from **Commander's Palace** and shaded by magnificent groves of lush greenery, the cemetery has a strong sense of Southern subtropical gothic about it. Some of the wealthier family tombs were built of marble, with elaborate detail rivaling the finest architecture in the district. You'll notice many German and Irish names on the above ground graves, testifying that immigrants were devastated by 19th-century yellow-fever epidemics. Take bus 11 or 12.

Audubon Zoological Gardens ZOO
(www.auduboninstitute.org; 6500 Magazine St; adult/child $17.50/12; ⊙10am-5pm Mon-Fri, to 6pm Sat & Sun; 🔾) This wonderful zoo is great for kids and adults. It contains the ultracool **Louisiana Swamp** exhibit, full of alligators, bobcats, foxes, bears and snapping turtles.

⊙ City Park & Mid-City

City Park PARK
(www.neworleanscitypark.com; City Park Ave) The Canal streetcar (p448) makes the run from the CBD to City Park. Three miles long, 1 mile wide, stroked by weeping willows and Spanish moss and dotted with museums, gardens, waterways, bridges, birds and the occasional alligator, City Park is the nation's fifth-largest urban park (bigger than Central Park in NYC) and New Orleans' prettiest green lung.

New Orleans Museum of Art MUSEUM
(www.noma.org; 1 Collins Diboll Circle; adult/child $10/6; ⊙10am-6pm Tue-Thu, to 9pm Fri, 11am-5pm Sat & Sun) Inside City Park, this elegant museum was opened in 1911 and is well worth a visit both for its special exhibitions and top-floor galleries of African, Native American, Oceanic and Asian art (don't miss the outstanding Qing-dynasty snuff-bottle collection). Its **sculpture garden** (⊙10am-4:30pm Sat-Thu, to 8:45pm Fri) **FREE** contains a cutting-edge collection in lush, meticulously planned grounds.

Fair Grounds PARK
(1751 Gentilly Blvd, btwn Gentilly Blvd & Fortin St; ⊙late April-early May) Besides hosting the reg-

ular horse-racing season, the fair grounds are also home to the huge springtime New Orleans Jazz & Heritage Festival.

🍴 Courses

New Orleans School of Cooking COOKING
(☑800-237-4841; www.neworleansschoolofcooking.com; 524 St Louis St; courses $24-29) Most open courses are food demonstrations. Menus rotate daily, but rest assured you'll be snacking on creations such as gumbo, jambalaya and pralines at the end of class, all the while learning about the history of the city as told by the charismatic chefs. A hands-on class in cooking Creole cuisine is offered as well ($125).

🧭 Tours

The Jean Lafitte National Historic Park and Preserve (p447) visitor center leads free walking tours of the French Quarter at 9:30am (get tickets at 9am).

Confederacy of Cruisers CYCLING
(☑504-400-5468; www.confederacyofcruisers.com; tours from $49) Get yourself out of the Quarter and on two wheels – this super-informative, laid-back bike tour takes you through Nola's non-Disneyland neighborhoods – Faubourg Marigny, Esplanade Ridge, the Tremé – often with a bar stop and the occasional jazz funeral pop-in along the way. Offers cocktail ($85) and culinary ($89) tours as well.

Friends of the Cabildo WALKING
(☑504-523-3939; 1850 House Museum Store, 523 St Ann St; adult/student $15/10; ⊙tours 10am

THE SOUTH NEW ORLEANS

SWAMP TOURS

Arrange swamp tours in New Orleans or go on your own and contract directly with a bayou-side company.

Louisiana Lost Land Tours (☑504-400-5920; http://lostlandstours.org) Wonderful tours that include kayak paddles into the wetlands and a motorboat tour of Barataria Bay. Excursions focus on land loss and wildlife threats, and are led by folks who genuinely love this land. Check out their blog on environemtnal issues in South Louisiana, http://lostlandstours.org/category/blog, maintained by Pulitzer Prize–winning journalist Bob Marshall.

Annie Miller's Son's Swamp & Marsh Tours (☑985-868-4758; www.annie-miller.com; 3718 Southdown Mandalay Rd, Houma; adult/child $15/10; 🔾) The son of legendary swamp guide Annie Miller has taken up his mom's tracks. The tours run about 50 miles outside New Orleans; call to arrange transportation.

Cajun Encounters (☑504-834-1770; www.cajunencounters.com; without/with pick-up from $25/50, night tours $40/70) Popular, well-run and offering a wide variety of tour options, including night tours.

& 1:30pm Tue-Sun) Volunteers lead the best available walking tours of the Quarter.

City Segway Tours SEGWAY
(☑504-619-4162; neworleans.citysegwaytours.com; 3-/2-/1-hr tours $75/65/45) Get on a Segway and glide around the French Quarter, the Tremé and the river front.

✨ Festivals & Events

New Orleans never needs an excuse to party. Just a few listings are included below; check www.neworleansonline.com for a good events calendar.

Mardi Gras CULTURAL
(www.mardigrasneworleans.com; ⊙ Feb or early Mar) Fat Tuesday marks the orgasmic finale of the Carnival season.

St Patrick's Day CULTURAL
(www.stpatricksdayneworleans.com; ⊙ Mar) March 17 and its closest weekend see parades of cabbage-wielding partiers all dressed in green.

St Joseph's Day – Super Sunday CULTURAL
(⊙ Mar) March 19 and its nearest Sunday bring the tribes of Mardi Gras Indians out into the streets in all their feathered, drumming glory. The Super Sunday parade usually begins around noon at Bayou St John and Orleans Ave, but follows no fixed route.

Tennessee Williams Literary Festival LITERARY
(www.tennesseewilliams.net; ⊙ Mar) Five days of literary panels, plays and parties celebrate the author's work.

French Quarter Festival MUSIC
(www.fqfi.org; ⊙ 2nd weekend Apr) Free music on multiple stages.

Jazz Fest MUSIC
(www.nojazzfest; ⊙ Apr-May) The last weekend of April and the first weekend of May; a world-renowned extravaganza of music, food, crafts and good living.

🛏 Sleeping

Rates peak during Mardi Gras and Jazz Fest, and fall in the hot summer months. Book early and call or check the internet for special deals. Parking in the Quarter costs $15 to $30 per day.

Bywater Bed & Breakfast B&B $
(☑504-944-8438; www.bywaterbnb.com; 1026 Clouet St, Bywater; r without bathroom $100) An artsy B&B, Bywater is particularly popular with the LGBT crowd (particularly lesbians), and is about as homey and laid-back as it gets. It's a restored double-shotgun, very colorful, with a kitchen and parlors in which guests can cook or loiter. The walls double as gallery space, showcasing a collection of vibrant outsider and folk art. The four guest rooms are simple and comfortable with more cheery paint and art.

Prytania Park Hotel HOTEL $
(☑504-524-0427; www.prytaniaparkhotel.com; 1525 Prytania St, Garden District; r from $75, ste from $100; P ❄ 🗔) This great-value complex of three separate hotels in the Garden District offers friendly, well-located bang-for-the-buck. The **Prytania Park** offers clean-cut, smallish rooms with flatscreen TVs for budget travelers. The **Prytania Oaks** (rooms from $110) is sleeker and the **Queen Anne** (rooms from $120) is an exquisite boutique hotel, nicely renovated and bedecked with antiques. It's a perfect spot for folks of all budgets bouncing between the Quarter and the Garden District and/or Uptown. Parking is free and so is access to St Charles Ave Athletic Club.

India House Hostel HOSTEL $
(☑504-821-1904; www.indiahousehostel.com; 124 S Lopez St, Mid-City; dm/d $20/55; @ 🗔 ❄) In Mid-City, this place has a free-spirited party atmosphere. A large aboveground swimming pool and cabana-like patio add ambience to the three well-used old houses that serve as sparse but nice dorms. Private rooms are so-so.

Columns HISTORIC HOTEL $$
(☑504-899-9308; www.thecolumns.com; 3811 St Charles Ave, Garden District; r incl breakfast weekend/weekday from $170/134; ❄ 🗔) A steal in low season (from $99), still a deal in high, this stately 1883 Italianate mansion in the Garden District is both elegant and relaxed, boasting all sorts of extraordinary original features: a stained-glass-topped staircase, elaborate marble fireplaces, richly carved woodwork throughout etc. To top it off, there's a lovely 2nd-floor porch overlooking oak-draped St Charles Ave and a damn inviting bar. It's everything that's wonderful about Nola.

Melrose Mansion B&B $$$
(☑504-944-2255, 800-650-3323; www.melrose-mansion.com; 937 Esplanade Ave, French Quarter; ste weekdays/weekends from $150/330; 🗔 ❄)

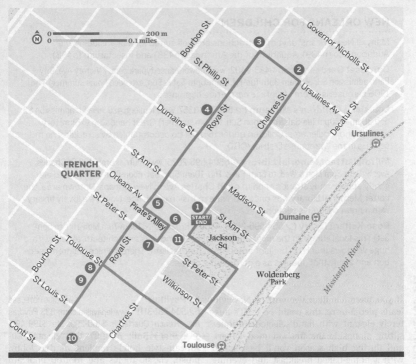

City Walk
French Quarter

START JACKSON SQ
END JACKSON SQ
LENGTH 1.1 MILE; 1 HOUR 30 MINUTES

Begin your walk at the ❶ **Presbytère** (p433) on Jackson Sq and head down Chartres St to the corner of Ursulines Ave. Directly across Chartres St, at No 1113, the 1826 ❷ **Beauregard-Keyes House** combines Creole and American styles of design. Walk along Ursulines Ave to Royal St – the soda fountain at the ❸ **Royal Pharmacy** is a preserved relic from halcyon malt-shop days.

When it comes to quintessential New Orleans postcard images, Royal St takes the prize. Cast-iron galleries grace the buildings and a profusion of flowers garland the facades.

At No 915 Royal, the ❹ **Cornstalk Hotel** (p442) stands behind one of the most frequently photographed fences anywhere. At Orleans Ave, stately magnolia trees and lush tropical plants fill ❺ **St Anthony's Garden**, behind ❻ **St Louis Cathedral** (p433).

Alongside the garden, take the inviting Pirate's Alley and turn right down Cabildo Alley and then right up St Peter St toward Royal St. Tennessee Williams shacked up at No 632 St Peter, the ❼ **Avart-Peretti House** in 1946–47, while he wrote *A Streetcar Named Desire*.

Turn left on Royal St. At the corner of Royal and Toulouse Sts stands a pair of houses built by Jean François Merieult in the 1790s. The building known as the ❽ **Court of Two Lions**, at 541 Royal St, opens onto Toulouse St and next door is the ❾ **Historic New Orleans Collection** (p433).

On the next block, the massive 1909 ❿ **State Supreme Court Building** was the setting for many scenes in director Oliver Stone's movie *JFK*.

Turn around and head right on Toulouse St to Decatur St and turn left. Cut across the road and walk the last stretch of this tour along the river. As Jackson Sq comes into view, cross back over to the Presbytère's near-identical twin, the ⓫ **Cabildo** (p433).

NEW ORLEANS FOR CHILDREN

Many of New Orleans' daytime attractions are well suited for kids, including the Audubon Zoo (p439), Aquarium of the Americas (p438) and Insectarium (p438).

Carousel Gardens (☑504-483-9402; www.neworleanscitypark.com; 7 Victory Ave, City Park; admission $3; ☉10am-3pm Tue-Fri, 11am-6pm Sat & Sun, extended hours summer) The 1906 carousel is a gem of vintage carny-ride happiness.

Louisiana Children's Museum (☑504-523-1357; www.lcm.org; 420 Julia St; admission $8; ☉9:30am-4:30pm Tue-Sat, from noon Sun, to 5pm summer) Great hands-on exploratory exhibits and toddler area. Children under 16 must be accompanied by an adult. The museum is in the Warehouse District/CBD.

Milton Latter Memorial Library (☑504-596-2625; www.nutrias.org; 5120 St Charles Ave; ☉9am-8pm Mon & Wed, to 6pm Tue & Thu, 10am-5pm Sat, noon-5pm Sun) Poised elegantly above shady strands of palm on St Charles Ave in New Orleans' Uptown area, the Latter Memorial Library was once a private mansion residence. Now it's a lovely library with a great children's section.

Rosa Keller Library (☑504-596-2660; 4300 S Broad St; ☉10am-7pm Mon-Thu, to 5pm Sat) This local library, in the neighborhood of Broadmoor, is an architectural gem with huge windows that let in brilliant amounts of natural light. There's a nice children's section and a cafe that doubles as a communtiy center.

If you were a millionaire with a New Orleans pied-à-terre, this could be it. It's austerely elegant with hand-selected antiques sitting alongside the freshest modern art, and during high season you'll be regaled with a home-baked breakfast and evening wine and cheese in the chic parlor. A chic studio option offers sleeker, more modern accommodations.

Roosevelt Hotel HOTEL $$$
(☑504-648-1200; www.therooseveltneworleans. com; 123 Baronne St, Warehouse District/CBD; r from $200, ste from $290; P @ 🕾) With its majestic, block-long lobby, this was the city's elite establishment when it opened in 1893. By the 1930s, its swanky bar was frequented by governor Huey Long. After a meticulous $145 million renovation, the Roosevelt reopened its doors in June 2009 as part of the Waldorf-Astoria Collection. Swish rooms have classical details, but the full spa, a John Besh restaurant and the storied Sazerac Bar are at least half the reason to stay.

Cornstalk Hotel B&B $$$
(☑504-523-1515; www.cornstalkhotel.com; 915 Royal St, French Quarter; r $125-250; ✳🕾) Pass through the famous cast-iron fence and into a plush, antiqued B&B where the serenity sweeps away the whirl of the busy streets outside. Gemlike rooms are all luxurious and clean – carpets are given the once-over monthly! Limited parking.

Le Pavillon HISTORIC HOTEL $$$
(☑504-581-3111; www.lepavillon.com; 833 Poydras Ave, French Quarter; r $160-299, ste $199-499; P ✳🕾🏊) Built in 1907, this elegant European-style hotel's opulent marble lobby, plush, classic rooms and rooftop pool are a steal. Decadent suites might prevent you from ever leaving the building. If booking a queen room, request a bay window. Parking costs $25.

Degas House HISTORIC HOTEL $$$
(☑504-821-5009; www.degashouse.com; 2306 Esplanade Ave; r incl breakfast from $199; P ✳🕾) Edgar Degas, the famed French Impressionist, lived in this 1852 Italianate house in Treme when visiting his mother's family in the early 1870s. Arty rooms recall the painter's stay with reproductions of his work and period furnishings. The suites have balconies and fireplaces, while the less-expensive garret rooms are the cramped top-floor quarters that once offered resident artists some much-need respite.

🍴 Eating

Louisiana may have the greatest native culinary tradition in the USA – not necessarily by dint of the quality of food (although quality is very high) but from the long history that lies behind dishes that are older than most American states. While the rest of us eat to live, New Orleanians live to eat.

French Quarter

Croissant D'Or Patisserie
CAFE $

(617 Ursulines Ave; items $1.50-5.75; ⊙6:30am-3pm Mon & Wed-Sun) This wonderful pastry shop is where many Quarter locals start their day. Bring a paper, order coffee and a croissant and bliss out. On your way in, check out the tiled sign on the threshold that says 'ladies entrance' – a holdover from pre-feminist days that is no longer enforced.

Clover Grill
DINER $

(900 Bourbon St; mains $3-8; ⊙24hr) Gay greasy spoon? Yup. It's all slightly surreal, given this place otherwise totally resembles a '50s diner, but nothing adds to the Americana like a prima-donna-style argument between an out-of-makeup drag queen and a drunk club kid, all likely set to blaring disco music.

Café du Monde
CAFE $

(800 Decatur St; beignets $2.14; ⊙24hr; ▣) Du Monde is overrated, but you're probably gonna go there, so here goes: the coffee is decent and the beignets (square, sugar-coated fritters) are inconsistent. The atmosphere is off-putting; you're a number forced through the wringer, trying to shout over Bob and Fran while they mispronounce 'jambalaya' and a street musician badly mangles John Lennon's 'Imagine.' At least it's open 24 hours.

Coop's
CAJUN, CREOLE $$

(1109 Decatur St; mains $8-17.50; ⊙11am-3am) For a cheap but thoroughly satisfying meal in the Quarter, this Cajun country shack disguised as a divey bar is as good as it gets: try the rabbit and sausage jambalaya or the red beans and rice for a taste of Cajun heaven.

Port of Call
BAR $$

(☑504 523-0120; 838 Esplanade Ave; mains $7-21; ⊙11am-late) The Port of Call burger is, simply put, one of the best we've had, anywhere. The meat is unadulterated and, well, meaty, and the burger is enormous – a half pound that easily looks the size, and we mean this, of your face. There are a lot of other menu items, but we can't get enough of that burger-y heaven, and neither can the locals, who willingly wait outside in long lines for a seat (no reservations).

Central Grocery
ITALIAN $$

(923 Decatur St; half/full muffuletta $7.50/14.50; ⊙9am-5pm Mon-Sat) Here, in 1906, a Sicilian immigrant invented the world-famous *muf-fuletta* sandwich – a round, seeded loaf of bread stuffed with ham, salami, provolone and marinated olive salad that's roughly the size of a manhole cover. This is still the best place in town to get one.

Bayona
MODERN AMERICAN $$$

(☑504-525-4455; www.bayona.com; 430 Dauphine St; mains $27-32; ⊙11:30am-2pm Mon-Fri, plus 6-10pm Mon-Thu, to 11pm Fri & Sat) Bayona is a great splurge in the Quarter. It's rich but not overwhelming, classy but unpretentious, innovative without being precocious. Expect fish, fowl and game on the daily-changing menu divided between long-time classics and daily specials (about four of each), all done up in a way that makes you raise an eyebrow, then smile like you've discovered comfort food gone classy.

Galatoire's
CREOLE $$$

(☑504 525 2021; 209 Bourbon St; mains $17-38; ⊙11:30am-10pm Tue-Sat, noon-10pm Sun) The century-plus history of this institution, which only accepted cash until quite recently, drips from the unchanged walls. Ask a tuxedo-ed waiter for what's fresh, don a jacket if you're a guy and treat yourself to the old-line masterpieces and mainstays: *pompano meunière,* liver with bacon and onions, and the signature chicken *clemenceau*. Friday lunch (which lasts all day) is a boozy affair that attracts many local aristocrats.

The Tremé

Willie Mae's Scotch House
SOUTHERN $$

(2401 St Ann St; fried chicken $10; ⊙11am-7pm Mon-Sat) The fried chicken at Willie Mae's is good. Very good. Some may claim it's the best in the world (we say: it's a contender for sure).

Dooky Chase
SOUTHERN $$

(☑504-821-0600; 2301 Orleans Ave; buffet $17.95; ⊙11am-3pm Tue-Fri, plus 5-9pm Fri) Ray Charles wrote 'Early in the Morning' about Dooky's, local civil rights leaders used the spot as an informal headquarters in the 1960s and Bush and Barack have tucked into the refined soul food at this overpriced Tremé backbone.

Bywater

The Joint
BARBEQUE $

(☑504-949-3232; 701 Mazant St; mains $7-17; ⊙11:30am-10pm Mon-Sat) The Joint's smoked pork has the olfactory effect of the Sirens' sweet song, pulling you, the proverbial traveling sailor, off course from your Ithaca into the gnashing rocks of savory meat-induced blissful death (classical Greek analogies ending now). Knock some ribs or pulled pork or brisket back with some sweet tea in the backyard garden and learn to love life.

Satsuma
HEALTH FOOD $

(☑ 504-304-5962; 3218 Dauphine St; breakfast & lunch under $10, dinner mains $8-16; ⊙ 7am-7pm) With its chalkboard menu of organic soups and sandwiches, Mediterranean-inspired salads, pasta, seafood and lamb, ginger limeade (seriously, the ginger limeade on a hot day – heaven), graphic/pop art-decorated walls – and lots of MacBooks – it's like the cute hipster girl with a frock, bangs and thick eyeglass frames you've secretly had a crush on, given restaurant form. The fact said girls are largely the clientele of this place confirms: the Bywater is becoming Brooklyn.

Bacchanal
CAFE $$

(www.bacchanalwine.com; 600 Poland Ave; cheese from $5, mains $8-16; ⊙ 11am-midnight) Grab a bottle of wine, let the folks behind the counter prep some *fromage* into a work of art, then kick back in an overgrown garden green scattered with rusted-out lawn chairs and tatty foldouts set to whoever showed up to play live music that day. Or order from the inventive full menu cooked out of the kitchen in the back (cash only).

Maurepas Foods
AMERICAN $$

(☑ 504-267-0072; 3200 Burgundy St; mains $7-16; ⊙ 11am-midnight, closed Wed; 🖉) Maurepas isn't your typical Bywater spot. It's got high ceilings, minimalist decor, polished floors and metal fixtures. And holy hell is the food good: the organic chicken, market greens, grits and a poached egg are delicious. Vegetarians should snack on the soba noodles, and everyone should get drunk on the craft cocktails.

Elizabeth's
CAJUN, CREOLE $$$

(www.elizabeths-restaurant.com; 601 Gallier St; mains $16-26; ⊙ 8am-2:30pm & 6-10pm Tue-Sat, 8am-2:30pm Sun) Elizabeth's is deceptively divey, mixing corner-shack ambiance, folk-art music gallery and damned excellent food. The food can be startlingly out-of-the-box and is rich as all get out. But it tastes as

good as the best haute New Orleans chefs can offer. Be sure to order praline bacon, no matter the time of day: fried up in brown sugar and, as far as we can tell, God's own cooking oil. If you're into steak, the smoked ribeye is heaven.

✕ CBD & Warehouse District

Domenica
ITALIAN $$

(☑ 504-648-6020; 123 Baronne St; mains $13-30; ⊙ 11am-11pm; 🖉) Domenica's rustic pies are loaded with nontraditional but savory toppings – spicy lamb meatballs, roast pork shoulder – and are big enough that solo diners should have a slice or two leftover. With its wooden refectory tables, white lights and soaring ceiling, Domenica feels like a village trattoria gone posh.

Butcher
CAJUN, SOUTHERN $$

(www.cochonbutcher.com; 930 Tchoupitoulas St; sandwiches $9-12; ⊙ 10am-10pm Mon-Thu, to 11pm Fri & Sat, to 4pm Sun) Around the corner from Cochon, chef Donald Link makes his in-house cured meat philosophy accessible to all budgets at this don't-miss butcher shop–deli and bar. Sandwich highlights here include milk-fed pork Cubans, Carolina-style pulled pork, the Cochon *muffaletta* and the Buckboard bacon melt.

★ Cochon
CONTEMPORARY CAJUN $$$

(☑ 504-588-2123; www.cochonrestaurant.com; 930 Tchoupitoulas St; mains $19-25; ⊙ 11am-10pm Mon-Fri, 5:30-10pm Sat) James Beard Award–winning chef Donald Link's fabulous brasserie serves up gourmet Southern comfort food in such curious and intriguing ways, you won't know what to do with yourself. The house-made Louisiana *cochon* – moist, pulled-pork heaven on the inside, crusty, pan-seared perfection on the outside – is probably the best swine you will ever have, unless you eat here twice. Reservations essential.

Restaurant August
CREOLE $$$

(☑ 504 299-9777; 301 Tchoupitoulas St; mains $24-45; ⊙ 5-9pm Tue-Thu & Sat, 11am-2pm & 5-9pm Fri; 🖉) August's converted 19th-century tobacco warehouse gets the nod for most aristocratic dining room in New Orleans. Candles flicker soft, warm shades over a meal that will, quite likely, blow your mind. If you're ready to splurge and eat like an emperor, consider arranging a private tasting menu dinner.

Garden District & Uptown

Dat Dog
HOT DOGS $

(☑504-899-6883; 5031 Freret St, Uptown; mains under $8; ☺11am-10pm Mon-Sat, to 9pm Sun; 🖶) Every part of your dog, from the steamed link to the toasted sourdough bun to the flavor-packed toppings, is produced with tasty exuberance at this outdoor joint. There's an enormous amount of sausages and toppings, from olive salad to crawfish etuofee, to pick from. If you like your dawgs spicy, try the Louisiana hot sausage from nearby Hanrahan.

★Boucherie
NEW SOUTHERN $$

(☑504-862-5514; www.boucherie-nola.com; 8115 Jeannette St, Uptown; large plates $13-18; ☺11am-3pm & 5:30-9pm Tue-Sat) Just when you thought a Krispy Kreme doughnut was already perfection personified, Boucherie comes along and turns it into a bread pudding. When married to a honey-glaze, drowning in syrup, that heavy bread pudding becomes airy yet drool-tastically unforgettable! For dinner, blackened shrimp-and-grits cakes are darkly sweet and savory, garlic Parmesan fries are gloriously stinky and gooey and the smoked Wagyu beef brisket melts in your mouth. Just amazing.

Domilise's Po-Boys
CREOLE $$

(5240 Annunciation St, Uptown; po'boys $9-15; ☺10am-7pm Mon-Wed & Fri, 10:30am-7pm Sat) A dilapidated white shack by the river serving Dixie beer (brewed in Wisconsin!), staffed

---

FROM THE MEKONG TO THE MISSISSIPPI

Following the Vietnam War, thousands of South Vietnamese fled to America, settling in Southern California, Boston, the Washington, DC, area and New Orleans. If the last choice seems odd, remember that many of these refugees were Catholic and the New Orleans Catholic community – one of the largest in the country – was helping to direct refugee resettlement. In addition, the subtropical climate, rice fields and flat wetlands must have been geographically reassuring. For a Southeast Asian far from home, the Mississippi delta may have borne at least a superficial resemblance to the Mekong delta.

Restaurants

Probably the most pleasant way to experience local Vietnamese culture is by eating its delicious food. The following are all in the suburbs of Gretna or New Orleans East.

Pho Tau Bay (☑504 368 9846; 113 Westbank Expwy, Gretna; mains under $10; ☺9am-8:30pm Mon-Wed, Fri & Sat) Fantastic executions of Vietnamese mains and some of the best *pho* (rice-noodle soup) we've tried in metropolitan New Orleans.

Dong Phuong Oriental Bakery (☑504 254 0214; 14207 Chef Menteur Hwy, New Orleans East; mains under $10) For the best *banh mi* (Vietnamese sandwiches of sliced pork, cucumber, cilantro and other lovelies, locally called a 'Vietnamese po'boy') around and some very fine durian cake.

Tan Dinh (☑504 361 8008; 2005 Belle Chasse Hwy, Gretna; mains $8-15; ☺9:30am-9pm Mon & Wed-Fri, 9am-9pm Sat, 8am-9pm Sun) We'd happily contend that Tan Dinh is one of the best restaurants in greater New Orleans. The garlic butter chicken wings could be served in heaven's pub, and the Korean short ribs are mouthwatering. Also contends with PhoTau Bay for some of that high quality *pho*.

Markets

Try not to miss the local markets either.

Hong Kong Food Market (☑394-7075; 925 Behrman Highway, Gretna; ☺8am-9pm) Hong Kong Food Market is a general Asian grocery store that serves plenty of Chinese and Filipinos, but the main customer base is Vietnamese.

Vietnamese Farmers' Market (☑394-7075; 14401 Alcee Fortier Blvd, New Orleans East; ☺6am-9am) The closest you'll come to witnessing Saigon on a Saturday morning (by the way, lots of local Vietnamese, being southern refugees, still call it 'Saigon') is the Vietnamese Farmers' Market, also known as the 'squat market' thanks to the ladies in *non la* (conical straw hats) squatting over their fresh, wonderful-smelling produce.

by folks who've worked here for decades and dressing one of the most legendary po'boys (traditional Louisiana submarine sandwich) in the city. It's cash-only and prepare to hurry up and wait on weekends.

Mat and Naddie's CONTEMPORARY CREOLE $$$
(☑ 504-861-9600; 937 Leonidas St, Uptown; mains $22-29; ☺ 5:30-9:30pm Thu-Sat, Mon & Tue) Set in a beautiful riverfront shotgun house with a Christmas-light-bedecked patio in the back, M&N's is rich, innovative, even outlandish: artichoke, sun-dried tomato and roasted garlic cheesecake (oh yes!), sherry-marinated grilled quail with waffles, pecan sweet-potato pie – all crazy delicious. High quality topped with quirkiness.

Commander's Palace CONTEMPORARY CREOLE $$$
(☑ 504-899-8221; 1403 Washington Ave, Garden District; dinner mains $28-45; ☺ 11:30am-2pm & 6:30-10pm Mon-Fri, 11:30am-1pm & 6:30-10pm Sat, 10:30am-1:30pm Sun) It's no small coincidence that some of the most famous Nola chefs – check that, US chefs – got their start in this kitchen (Paul Prudhomme, Emeril Lagasse); this New Orleans grand dame is outstanding across the board. It's an impeccable mainstay of Creole cooking and knowledgeable, friendly service, in the heart of the gorgeous Garden District. Pop in for the lunchtime 25¢ martinis and a cup of the signature turtle soup. No shorts allowed.

🍷 Drinking

New Orleans is a drinking town. Heads up: Bourbon St sucks. Get into the neighborhoods and experience some of the best bars in America.

Most bars open every day, often by noon, get hopping around 10pm, and can stay open all night. There's no cover charge unless there's live music. It's illegal to have open glass liquor containers in the street, so all bars dispense plastic 'go cups' when you're ready to wander.

Tonique BAR
(www.bartonique.com; 820 Rampart St, French Quarter) If you're going to drink in the Quarter (on the edge of it, anyway), this serious cocktail bar is the place, where cool folks who appreciate an excellent concoction gather over the best Sazerac we had in town. And we had many.

Mimi's in the Marigny BAR
(2601 Royal St, Faubourg Marigny; ☺ to 5am) Great bi-level bar (pool downstairs, music

upstairs) serving up excellent Spanish tapas ($5 to $8) and a casual neighborhood vibe.

St Joe's BAR
(5535 Magazine St, Uptown) Good-time Uptown pious-themed bar with great blueberry mojitos (praise the Lord!), a cool back courtyard and friendly ambience.

R Bar BAR
(1431 Royal St, Marigny) Somewhere between a dive and a neighborhood joint; a beer and a shot runs you $5.

☆ Entertainment

What's New Orleans without live local music? Almost any weekend night you can find something for every taste: jazz, blues, brass band, country, Dixieland, zydeco (Cajun dance music), rock or Cajun. Free shows in the daytime abound. Check *Gambit* (www.bestofneworleans.com), *Offbeat* (www.offbeat.com) or www.nolafunguide.com for schedules.

★ Spotted Cat LIVE MUSIC
(www.spottedcatmusicclub.com; 623 Frenchmen St, Faubourg Marigny) A throwback retro cool permeates through this excellent Frenchmen staple you might recognize from numerous episodes of *Tremé*. Hipster jazz is on nightly and there's never a cover unless a special event is on.

Three Muses JAZZ
(www.thethreemuses.com; 536 Frenchmen St, Marigny; ☺ 4-10pm Wed, Thu, Sun & Mon, to 2am Fri & Sat) Three Muses has managed to happily marry an excellent soundtrack with gourmet cuisine in a more intimate room than most on Frenchmen. There's loads of great local art to peruse between acts and courses. Start here.

AllWays Lounge THEATER
(☑ 504-218-5778; 2240 St Claude Ave, Marigny) In a city full of funky music venues, the AllWays stands out as one of the funkiest. On any given night of the week you may see experimental guitar, local theater, thrash-y rock or a '60s-inspired shagadelic dance party. Also: the drinks are super cheap.

Chickie Wah Wah LIVE MUSIC
(☑ 504-304-4714; www.chickiewahwah.com; 2828 Canal St, Mid-City; ☺ shows around 8pm) Despite the fact it lies on one of the most unremarkable stretches of Canal St as you please, Chickie Wah Wah is a great jazz club.

It hosts some good names such as John Mooney, Jolly House and Papa Mali in a cozy little setting where the French Quarter feels several universes away.

Tipitina's   LIVE MUSIC
(www.tipitinas.com; 501 Napoleon Ave, Uptown) Always drawing a lively crowd, this legendary Uptown club rocks out like the musical mecca it is: local jazz, blues, soul and funk acts stop in, as well as national touring bands.

Rock & Bowl   LIVE MUSIC
(☑504-861-1700; www.rockandbowl.com; 3000 S Carrollton Ave, Mid-City; ⊙5pm-late, live music Wed-Sat; ⊕) A night at the Rock & Bowl is a quintessential New Orleans experience. Come see a strange, wonderful combination of bowling alley, deli, and a huge live music and dance venue, where patrons get down to New Orleans roots music while trying to avoid that 7-10 split. Thursday night zydeco shows will knock your socks off.

Snug Harbor   JAZZ
(www.snugjazz.com; 626 Frenchmen St, Marigny) In the Marigny, the city's best contemporary jazz venue is all about world-class music and a good variety of acts. If you can't spring for the show (cover $15 to $25), sit downstairs at the bar and watch on closed-circuit.

Preservation Hall   JAZZ
(www.preservationhall.com; 726 St Peter St, French Quarter; cover $15; ⊙8-11pm) A veritable museum of traditional and Dixieland jazz, Preservation Hall is a pilgrimage. But like many religious obligations, it ain't necessarily easy, with no air-conditioning, limited seating and no refreshments (you can bring your own water, that's it).

🛍 Shopping

Magazine Antique Mall   ANTIQUES
(☑504 896 9994; www.magazineantiquemall.com; 3017 Magazine St; ⊙10:30am-5:30pm Mon-Sat, from noon Sun) Hard-core rummagers are likely to score items of interest in the dozen or so stalls here, where independent dealers peddle an intriguing and varied range of antique bric-a-brac.

Maple Street Book Shop   BOOKSHOP
(www.maplestreetbookshop.com; 7523 Maple St, Uptown; ⊙9am-7pm Mon-Sat, 11am-5pm Sun) A mainstay independent bookstore in Uptown, with a used bookstore affiliate next door.

❶ Information

DANGERS & ANNOYANCES

New Orleans has a high violent-crime rate, and neighborhoods go from good to ghetto very quickly. Be careful walking too far north of Faubourg Marigny and the Bywater (St Claude Ave is a good place to stop), south of Magazine St (things get dodgier past Laurel St) and too far north of Rampart St (Lakeside) from the French Quarter into Tremé without a specific destination in mind. Stick to places that are well peopled, particularly at night, and spring for a cab to avoid dark walks. In the Quarter, street hustlers frequently approach tourists – just walk away. With all that said, don't be paranoid. Crime here, as in most of America, tends to be between people who already know each other.

INTERNET ACCESS

There's pretty good wi-fi coverage in the CBD, French Quarter, Garden and Lower Garden Districts and Uptown. Almost every coffee shop in the city has wi-fi coverage. Libraries have free internet access for cardholders.

MEDIA

Gambit Weekly (www.bestofneworleans.com) Free weekly hot sheet of music, culture, politics and classifieds.

Offbeat Magazine (www.offbeat.com) Free monthly specializing in music.

WWOZ 90.7 FM (www.wwoz.org) Tune in here for Louisiana music and more.

MEDICAL SERVICES

Tulane University Medical Center (☑504-988-5800; http://tulanehealthcare.com; 1415 Tulane Ave; ⊙24hr) Has an emergency room; located in the CBD.

POST

Post Office Lafayette Sq (610 S Maestri Pl, Lafayette Sq; ⊙8:30am-4:30pm Mon-Fri); Main branch (701 Loyola Ave; ⊙7am-7pm Mon-Fri, 8am-4pm Sat) Mail sent General Delivery, New Orleans, LA 70112, goes to the main branch at 701 Loyola Ave. Postboxes in outlying areas are not necessarily reliable since Katrina.

TOURIST INFORMATION

The city's official visitor website is www.neworleansonline.com.

Jean Lafitte National Historic Park and Preserve Visitor Center (☑504-589-2133, 504-589-3822; www.nps.gov/jela; 419 Decatur St, French Quarter; ⊙9am-5pm) Operated by the NPS, with exhibits on local history, guided walks and daily live music.

Basin St Visitor's Center (☑504-293-2600; www.neworleanscvb.com; 501 Basin St, French Quarter; ⊙9am-5pm) This interactive tourist info center inside the former freight administration building of the Southern Railway has loads of helpful info and maps, as well as an historical overview film and a small rail museum component.

ℹ Getting There & Away

Louis Armstrong New Orleans International Airport (MSY; www.flymsy.com; 900 Airline Hwy), 11 miles west of the city, handles primarily domestic flights.

The **Union Passenger Terminal** (☎504-299-1880; 1001 Loyola Ave) is home to **Greyhound** (☎504-525-6075; ◷5:15am-1pm & 2:30-6pm), which has regular buses to Baton Rouge (two hours), Memphis, TN (11 hours) and Atlanta, GA ($84 to $106, 12 hours). **Amtrak** (☎504-528-1610; ◷ticketing 5:45am-10pm) trains also operate from the Union Passenger Terminal, running to Jackson, MS; Memphis, TN; Chicago, IL. Birmingham, AL; Atlanta, GA; Washington, DC; New York City; Los Angeles, CA; and Miami, FL.

ℹ Getting Around

TO/FROM THE AIRPORT

There's an information booth at the airport's A&B concourse. The **Airport Shuttle** (☎866-596-2699; www.airportshuttleneworleans.com; one way $20) runs to downtown hotels. The **Jefferson Transit** (☎504-364-3450; www.jeffersontransit.org; adult $2) airport route E2 picks up outside entrance 7 on the airport's upper level; it stops along Airline Hwy (Hwy 61) on its way into town (final stop Tulane and Loyola Aves). After 7pm it only goes to Tulane and Carrollton Aves in Mid-City; a solid 5 miles through a dreary neighborhood to get to the CBD, from here you must transfer to a Regional Transit Authority (RTA) bus – a haphazard transfer at best, especially with luggage.

Taxis downtown cost $34 for one or two people, $14 more for each additional passenger.

CAR & MOTORCYCLE

Bringing a car is a useful way of exploring beyond the Quarter; just be aware that parking in the Quarter is a hassle. Garages charge about $13 for the first three hours and $30 to $35 for 24 hours.

PUBLIC TRANSPORTATION

The **Regional Transit Authority** (RTA; www.norta.com) runs the local bus service. Bus and streetcar fares are $1.25, plus 25¢ for transfers; express buses cost $1.50. Exact change is required. RTA Visitor Passes for one/three days cost $5/12.

The RTA also operates three **streetcar** lines (one-way $1.25, day pass $3; have exact change). The historic St Charles streetcar is running only a short loop in the CBD due to hurricane damage to the Uptown tracks. The Canal streetcar makes a long journey up Canal St to City Park, with a spur on Carrollton Ave. The Riverfront line runs 2 miles along the levee from the Old US Mint, past Canal St, to the upriver convention center and back.

For a taxi, call **United Cabs** (☎504-522-9771; www.unitedcabs.com).

Rent bicycles at **Bicycle Michael's** (☎504-945-9505; www.bicyclemichaels.com; 622 Frenchmen St, Faubourg Marigny; per day $35; ◷10am-7pm Mon, Tue & Thu-Sat, to 5pm Sun).

Around New Orleans

Leaving gritty, colorful New Orleans quickly catapults you into a world of swamps, bayous, antebellum plantation homes, laid-back small communities and miles of bedroom suburbs and strip malls.

Barataria Preserve

This section of the **Jean Lafitte National Historical Park & Preserve**, south of New Orleans near the town of Marrero, provides the easiest access to the dense swamplands that ring New Orleans. The 8 miles of platform trails are a stunning way to tread lightly through the fecund, thriving swamp where you can check out gators and other fascinating plant life and creatures. The preserve is home to alligators, nutrias (read: big invasive rats), tree frogs and hundreds of species of birds. It is well worth taking a ranger-led walk to learn about the many ecosystems that make up what are often lumped together as 'wetlands.'

Start at the **NPS Visitors Center** (☎504-589-2330; www.nps.gov/jela; Hwy 3134; ◷9am-5pm; ♿) ᴳᴿᴱᴱ, 1 mile west of Hwy 45 off the Barataria Blvd exit, where you can pick up a map or join a guided walk or canoe trip (most Saturday mornings and monthly on full-moon nights; call to reserve a spot). To rent canoes or kayaks for a tour or an independent paddle, go to **Bayou Barn** (☎504-689-2663; http://bayoubarn.com; 7145 Barataria Blvd; canoes per person $20, 1-person kayak per day $25; ◷10am-6pm Thu-Sun) about 3 miles from the park entrance.

The North Shore

Bedroom communities sprawl along **Lake Pontchartrain's** north shore, but head north of Mandeville and you'll reach the bucolic village of **Abita Springs**, which was popular in the late 1800s for its curative waters. Today the spring water still flows from a fountain in the center of the village, but the primary liquid attraction here is the **Abita Brew Pub** (☑985-892-5837; www.abitabrewpub. com; 7201 Holly St; ☉11am-9pm Tue-Thu, to 10pm Fri & Sat, closed Mon), where you can choose from the many Abita beers on tap that are made a mile west of town at **Abita Brewery** (www.abita.com; 166 Barbee Rd; tours free; ☉tours 2pm Wed-Fri, 11am, noon, 1pm & 2pm Sat).

The 31-mile **Tammany Trace trail** (www. tammanytrace.org) connects north shore towns, beginning in Covington, passing through Abita Springs and **Fontainebleau State Park**, on the lakeshore near Mandeville, and terminating in Slidell. This converted railroad makes for a lovely bike ride that drops you into each town's center. In Lacombe, about 9 miles east of Mandeville, you can rent bicycles and kayaks at **Bayou Adventures** (☑985-882-9208; www.bayou-adventure.com; 27725 Main St, Lacombe; bicycles per hr/day $8/25, single/double kayaks per day $35/50; ☉5am-6pm).

River Road

Elaborate plantation homes dot the east and west banks of the Mississippi River between New Orleans and Baton Rouge. First indigo, then cotton and sugarcane, brought great wealth to these plantations, many of which are open to the public. Most tours focus on the lives of the plantation owners, the restored architecture and the ornate gardens of antebellum Louisiana.

◉ Sights

Laura Plantation   PLANTATION
(www.lauraplantation.com; 2247 Hwy 18, Vacherie; adult/child $20/6; ☉10am-4pm) Laura Plantation, in Vacherie on the west bank, offers the most dynamic and informative tour of the River Road plantations. This ever-evolving and popular tour teases out the distinctions between Creole, Anglo, free and enslaved African Americans via meticulous research and the written records of the Creole women who ran the place for generations. Laura is

also fascinating because it was a Creole mansion, founded and maintained by a continental European-descended elite, as opposed to Anglo-Americans; the cultural and architectural distinctions between this and other plantations is obvious and striking.

Oak Alley Plantation   PLANTATION
(www.oakalleyplantation.com; 3645 Hwy 18, Vacherie; adult/child $20/7.50; ☉9am-4:40pm) The most impressive aspect of Oak Alley Plantation is its canopy of 28 majestic live oaks lining the entry to the grandiose Greek Revival–style house – even better with a fresh mint julep. The tour is relatively staid, but there are guest cottages ($145 to $200) and a restaurant on-site.

River Road African American Museum   MUSEUM
(www.africanamericanmuseum.org; 406 Charles St, Donaldsonville; admission $5; ☉10am-5pm Wed-Sat, 1-5pm Sun) Be sure to flesh out any plantation tour with a visit to the River Road African American Museum, 25 miles beyond Vacherie in Donaldsonville. This excellent museum preserves the important history of African Americans in the rural communities along the Mississippi, and offers insight into the free people of color, a unique sociopolitical demographic within Louisiana that had huge bearing on the state's culture. Tours are by appointment only.

Baton Rouge

In 1699 French explorers named this area *baton rouge* (red stick) when they came upon a reddened cypress pole that Bayagoulas and Houma Native Americans had staked in the ground to mark the boundaries of their respective hunting territories. From one pole grew a lot of sprawl; Baton Rouge stretches out in an unplanned clutter in many directions. Visitors are mostly drawn to Baton Rouge for Louisiana State University (LSU) and Southern University; the latter is one of the largest historically African American universities in the country.

◉ Sights & Activities

Louisiana State Capitol   HISTORIC BUILDING
(☉9am-4pm Tue-Sat) **FREE** The art-deco skyscraper looming over town was built at the height of the Great Depression to the tune of $5 million. It's the most visible leftover legacy of populist governor 'Kingfish' Huey

Long. The 27th-floor **observation deck** offers stunning views and the ornate lobby is equally impressive. There are hourly free tours.

Louisiana Arts & Science Museum
MUSEUM

(www.lasm.org; 100 S River Rd; adult/child $7.25/6.25, with planetarium show $9/8; ☺10am-3pm Tue-Fri, to 5pm Sat, 1-4pm Sun; ⊞) Interesting arts and natural-history installations, and planetarium shows. If you just want a good stretch of the legs, there's a pleasant **pedestrian/bike path** along the Mississippi River, covering 2.5 miles from the downtown promenade to LSU.

Old State Capitol
HISTORIC BUILDING

(☑225-342-0500; www.louisianaoldstatecapitol. org; 100 North Blvd; ☺9am-4pm Tue-Sat) FREE The Gothic Revival, pink, fairytale castle is... well, look, it's a pink castle. Should tell you something about how eccentric the government of its resident state can be. Today the structure houses exhibits about the colorful political history of the state.

LSU Museum of Art
MUSEUM

(LSUMOA; www.lsumoa.com; 100 Lafayette St; adult/child $5/free; ☺10am-5pm Tue-Sat, to 8pm Thu, 1-5pm Sun) The physical space this museum is ensconced in, the clean, geometric lines of the Shaw Center, is as impressive as the on-site galleries, which include a permanent collection of over 5000 works and temporary, curated galleries exploring regional artistic heritage and contemporary trends.

Rural Life Museum
MUSEUM

(☑225-765-2437; 4560 Essen Ln; adult/child $7/6; ☺8am-5pm; ⊞⊞) This outdoor museum promises a trip into the architecture, occupations and folkways of rural Louisiana. Numerous rough-hewn buildings are scattered over the bucolic campus, and exhibits are refreshingly honest and informative, lacking any rose-colored romanticization of the hard country legacy that built Louisiana.

Dixie Landin & Blue Bayou
AMUSEMENT PARK

(☑225-753-3333; www.bluebayou.com; 18142 Perkins Rd; adult/child $37/30; ⊞) Just east of town at I-10 and Highland Rd. Kids will love the respective amusement and water parks; check the online calendar for opening hours.

🛏 Sleeping & Eating

Stockade Bed & Breakfast
B&B $$$

(☑888-900-5430, 225-769-7358; www.thestockade.com; 8860 Highland Rd; r incl breakfast $135-215; P⊞☎) Chain hotels line the sides of I-10, but for a more intimate stay, try this wonderful B&B with five spacious, comfortable and elegant rooms just 3.5 miles southeast of LSU and within earshot of several standout neighborhood restaurants. Book ahead on weekends, especially during football season.

Schlittz & Giggles
BAR, PIZZERIA $$

(www.schlittz.com; 301 3rd St; pizzas $10-22; ☺11am-midnight Mon-Thu, to 3am Fri-Sun; ☎) The food stands up to the awesomely named downtown late-night bar and pizzeria. Bubbly coeds serve up thin-as-black-ice pizza slices ($3 to $3.50) and fabulous paninis to a student crowd, while a gaggle of old-timer locals tend to belly up at the bar.

Buzz Café
CAFE $

(www.thebuzzcafe.org; 340 Florida St; meals $7-9; ☺7:30am-2pm Mon-Fri; ☎) For an awesome cup of joe and a plethora of creative wraps and sandwiches at a funky coffee shop in a historic building, try the Buzz.

☆ Entertainment

Varsity Theatre
LIVE MUSIC

(☑225-383-7018; www.varsitytheatre.com; 3353 Highland Rd; ☺8pm-2am) At the gates of LSU, you'll find live music here, often on weeknights. The attached restaurant boasts an extensive beer selection and a raucous college crowd.

Boudreaux and Thiboudeux
LIVE MUSIC

(☑225-636-2442; www.bandtlive.com; 214 3rd St) Try this place downtown for live music Thursday to Saturday and a great upstairs balcony bar. Named for the dumb and dumber duo of classic Cajun comedy.

ⓘ Information

Visitor Center (☑225-383-1825, 800-527-6843; www.visitbatonrouge.com; 359 3rd St; ☺8am-5pm) The downtown city branch has maps, brochures of local attractions and festival schedules.

Capital Park (☑225-219-1200; www.louisianatravel.com; 702 River Rd N; ☺8am-4:30pm) Near the visitor center, it's even more extensive.

ℹ️ Getting There & Around

Baton Rouge lies 80 miles west of New Orleans on I-10. **Baton Rouge Metropolitan Airport** (BTR; www.flybtr.com) is north of town off I-110; it's about 1½ hours from New Orleans, so it's a viable airport of entry if you're renting a car. **Greyhound** (✆ 225-383-3811; 1253 Florida Blvd, at N 12th St) has regular buses to New Orleans, Lafayette and Atlanta, GA. **Capitol Area Transit System** (CATS; ✆ 225-389-8282; www.brcats. com) operates buses around town.

St Francisville

Lush St Francisville is the quintessential Southern artsy small town, a blend of historical homes, bohemian shops and outdoors activities courtesy of the nearby Tunica Hills (you read that right – hills in Louisiana). During the antebellum decade this was home to plantation millionaires, and much of their architecture is still intact.

⊙ Sights & Activities

In town, stroll down historic **Royal St** to catch a glimpse of antebellum homes and buildings-turned-homes. The visitor center has pamphlets that lead you on self-guided tours.

Myrtles Plantation   HISTORIC BUILDING
(✆ 225-635-6277, 800-809-0565; www. myrtlesplantation.com; 7747 US Hwy 61 N; ☉ 9am-4:30pm, tours 6pm, 7pm & 8pm Fri & Sat) An especially notable B&B because supposedly it's haunted, and it has night mystery tours (by reservation) on the weekend. We heard secondhand corroboration of the supernatural presence, so it might be fun to stay overnight (rooms from $115) to commune with the other world.

Oakley Plantation & Audubon State Historic Site   HISTORIC SITE
(✆ 225 342 8111; www.crt.state.la.us; 11788 Hwy 965; admission $2; ☉ 9am-5pm) Outside of St Francisville is Oakley Plantation & Audubon State Historic Site, where John James Audubon spent his tenure, arriving in 1821 to tutor the owner's daughter. Though his assignment lasted only four months (and his room was pretty darn spartan), he and his assistant finished 32 paintings of birds found in the plantation's surrounding forest. Furnishing of the small West Indies–influenced house (1806) includes several original Audubon prints.

Mary Ann Brown Preserve   NATURE RESERVE
(✆ 225-338-1040; 13515 Hwy 965; ☉ sunrise-sunset) Operated by the Nature Conservancy, the Mary Ann Brown Preserve takes in some of the beech woodlands, dark wetlands and low, clay-soil hill country of the Tunica uplands. A 2-mile series of trails and boardwalks crosses the woods, the same trees that John James Audubon tramped around when he began work on *Birds of America*.

🛌 Sleeping & Eating

⭐ **Shadetree Inn**
Bed and Breakfast   B&B $$
(✆ 225-635-6116; www.shadetreeinn.com; cnr Royal & Ferdinand Sts; r from $165; P ❄ 📶) Sidled up against the historic district and a bird sanctuary, this super-cozy B&B has a gorgeous flower-strewn, hammock-hung courtyard and spacious, upscale rustic rooms. A deluxe continental breakfast can be served in your room and is included along with a bottle of wine or champagne.

3-V Tourist Court   HISTORIC INN $$
(✆ 225-721-7003; 5689 Commerce St; 1-/2-bed cabins $80/130; P ❄ 📶) One of the oldest motor inns in the United States (started in the 1930s and on the National Register of Historic Places), these five units bring you back to simpler times. Rooms have period decorations and fixtures, though a recent renovation upgraded the beds, hardwood floors and flatscreen TVs into borderline trendy territory.

Birdman Coffee and Books   CAFE $
(Commerce St; mains $5-6.50; ☉ 7-5pm Tue-Fri, 8am-5pm Sat, to 4pm Sun; 📶) Right in front of the Magnolia Café lies the Birdman, *the* spot for a local breakfast (old-fashioned yellow grits, sweet-potato pancakes etc) and local art.

Magnolia Café   CAFE $$
(✆ 225-635-2528; www.themagnoliacafe.com; 5687 Commerce St; mains $7-12; ☉ 10am-4pm Sun-Wed, to 9pm Thu & Sat, to 10pm Fri) The nucleus of what's happening in St Francisville, the Magnolia Café used to be a health-food store/VW bus repair shop. Now it's where people go to eat, socialize and dance to live music on Friday night. Try the cheesy shrimp po'boy.

ℹ️ Information

Tourist Information (📞225-635-4224; www. stfrancisville.us; 11757 Ferdinand St) Provides helpful information about the numerous plantations open for viewing in the area, many of which offer B&B services.

Cajun Country

When people think of 'Louisiana,' this (and New Orleans) is the image that comes to mind: miles of bayou, sawdust-strewn shacks, a unique take on French and lots of good food. Welcome to Cajun Country, also called Acadiana for French settlers exiled from L'Acadie (now Nova Scotia, Canada) by the British in 1755.

Cajuns are the largest French-speaking minority in the US – prepare to hear it on radios, in church services and in the sing-song lilt of local English accents. While Lafayette is the nexus of Acadiana, getting out and around the waterways, villages and ramshackle roadside taverns really drops you straight into Cajun living. This is largely a socially conservative region, but the Cajuns also a have well-deserved reputation for hedonism. It's hard to find a bad meal here; jambalaya (a rice-based dish with tomatoes, sausage and shrimp) and crawfish étouffée (a thick Cajun stew) are prepared slowly with pride (and cayenne!), and if folks aren't fishing, then they are probably dancing. Don't expect to sit on the sidelines...*allons danson* (let's dance).

Lafayette

The term 'undiscovered gem' gets thrown around too much in travel writing, but Lafayette really fits the bill. The bad first: this town is deader then a cemetery on Sundays. The rest: there's an entirely fantastic amount of good eating and lots of music venues here, plus one of the best free music festivals in the country. This is a university town; bands are rocking most any night. Heck, even those quiet Sundays have a saving grace: some famously delicious brunch options.

👁️ Sights

Vermilionville　　　　　CULTURAL BUILDING
(📞337-233-4077; www.vermilionville.org; 300 Fisher Rd; adult/student $8/6; ⊙10am-4pm Tue-Sun; 🅿️) A tranquil restored/re-created 19th-century Cajun village wends along the bayou near the airport. Friendly, enthusiastic costumed docents explain Cajun, Creole and Native American history, and local bands perform on Sundays. Also offers guided **boat tours** (📞337-233-4077; adult/student $12/8; ⊙10:30am Tue-Sat Mar-May & Sep-Nov) of Bayou Vermilion.

Acadiana Center for the Arts　　GALLERY
(📞337-233-7060; www.acadianacenterforthearts. org; 101 W Vermilion St; adult/student/child $5/3/2; ⊙9am-5pm Tue-Fri, to 6pm Sat) This arts center in the heart of downtown maintains three chic galleries and hosts dynamic theater, lectures and special events.

CAJUNS, CREOLES AND...CREOLES

A lot of tourists in Louisiana use the terms 'Cajun' and 'Creole' interchangeably, but the two cultures are different and distinct. 'Creole' refers to descendants of the original European settlers of Louisiana, a blended mix of mainly French and Spanish ancestry. The Creoles tend to have urban connections to New Orleans and considered their own culture refined and civilized. Many (but not all) were descended from aristocrats, merchants and skilled tradesmen.

The Cajuns can trace their lineage to the Acadians, colonists from rural France who settled Nova Scotia. After the British conquered Canada, the proud Acadians refused to kneel to the new crown, and were exiled in the mid-18th century – an act known as the Grand Dérangement. Many exiles settled in South Louisiana; they knew the area was French, but the Acadians ('Cajun' is an English bastardization of the word) were often treated as country bumpkins by the Creoles. The Acadians-cum-Cajuns settled in the bayous and prairies, and to this day self-conceptualize as a more rural, frontier-stye culture.

Adding confusion to all of the above is the practice, standard in many post-colonial French societies, of referring to mixed-race individuals as 'Creoles.' This happens in Louisiana, but there is a cultural difference between Franco-Spanish Creoles and mixed-race Creoles, even as these two communities very likely share actual blood ancestry.

Acadian Cultural Center MUSEUM
(www.nps.gov/jela; 501 Fisher Rd; ☉8am-5pm)
This National Parks Service museum has extensive exhibits on Cajun culture, next door to Vermilionville.

✵ Festivals & Events

Festival International de Louisiane MUSIC
(www.festivalinternational.com; ☉last weekend Apr) At the fabulous Festival International de Louisiane, hundreds of local and international artists rock out for five days – the largest free music festival of its caliber in the US. Although 'Festival' avowedly celebrates Francophone music and culture, the event's remit has grown to accommodate other music styles and languages.

🛏 Sleeping & Eating

Chain hotels clump near exits 101 and 103, off I-10 (doubles from $65). Head to Jefferson St mid-downtown to take your choice of bars and restaurants, from sushi to Mexican.

★ Blue Moon Guest House GUESTHOUSE $
(☑337-234-2422, 877-766-2583; www.bluemoonguesthouse.com; 215 E Convent St; dm $18, r $73-94; [P][❀][@][☎]) This tidy old home is one of Louisiana's travel gems, an upscale hostel-like hangout that's walking distance from downtown. Snag a bed and you'll be on the guest list for Lafayette's most popular down-home music venue, located in the backyard. The friendly owners, full kitchen and camaraderie among guests create a unique music-meets-migration environment catering to backpackers, flashpackers and those in transition (flashbackpackers?). Prices skyrocket during festival time. Decidedly not a quiet spot.

Buchanan Lofts BOUTIQUE APARTMENTS $$
(☑337-534-4922; www.buchananlofts.com; 403 S Buchanan; r per night/week from $110/600; [P][❀][@][☎]) These über-hip lofts could be in New York City if they weren't so big. Doused in contemporary-cool art and design – all fruits of the friendly owner's globetrotting – the extra spacious units all come with kitchenettes and are awash in exposed brick and hardwoods.

Johnson's Boucanière CAJUN $
(1111 St John St; mains under $10; ☉10am-6pm Tue-Thu, to 9pm Fri, 7am-9pm Sat) This resurrected 70-year-old family prairie smoker business

turns out detour-worthy *boudin* (Cajun-style pork and rice sausage) and an unstoppable smoked pork-brisket sandwich topped with smoked sausage.

Artmosphere AMERICAN $
(☑337-233-3331; 902 Johnston St; mains under $10; ☉11am-2am Mon-Sat, to midnight Sun; ✐) Your place if you're jonesing for vegan/vegetarian food, or even just a hookah, plus a lovely selection of beer on offer. Live music every night and a crowd that largely consists of the student and artist set.

★ French Press BREAKFAST $$$
(www.thefrenchpresslafayette.com; 214 E Vermillion; breakfast $6-$10.50, dinner mains $29-38; ☉7am-2pm Tue-Thu, 7am-2pm & 5:30-9pm Fri, 9am-2pm & 5:30-9pm Sat, 9am-2pm Sun; ☎) This French-Cajun hybrid is the best culinary thing going in Lafayette. Breakfast is mind blowing, with a sinful Cajun benedict (*boudin* instead of ham), cheddar grits (that will kill you dead) and organic granola (offset the grits). Dinner is wonderful as well; that rack of lamb with the truffled gratin is a special bit of gastronomic dreaminess.

☆ Entertainment

To find out what's playing around town, pick up the free weekly *Times* (www.theadvertiser.com – check under Times of Acadiana) or *Independent* (www.theind.com).

Besides the places below, Cajun restaurants like **Randol's** (☑337-981-7080; www.randols.com; 2320 Kaliste Saloom Rd; ☉5-10pm Sun-Thu, to 11pm Fri & Sat) and **Prejean's** (☑337-896-3247; www.prejeans.com; 3480 NE Evangeline Thruway/I-49) feature live music on weekends nights.

Blue Moon Saloon LIVE MUSIC
(www.bluemoonpresents.com; 215 E Convent St; cover $5-8) This intimate venue on the back porch of the accompanying guesthouse is what Louisiana is all about: good music, good people and good beer. What's not to love?

Artmosphere LIVE MUSIC
(902 Johnston St; ☉11am-2am Mon-Sat, to midnight Sun) Graffiti, hookahs, hipsters and an edgy line-up of acts; it's more CBGB's than Cajun dancehall, but it's a lot of fun, and there's good Mexican food to boot.

THE SOUTH CAJUN COUNTRY

WORTH A TRIP

THE TAO OF FRED'S

Deep in the heart of Cajun Country, Mamou is a typical South Louisiana small town six days of the week, worth a peek and a short stop before rolling to Eunice. But on Saturday mornings, Mamou's hometown hangout, little **Fred's Lounge** (420 6th St; ⊘8am-2pm Sat), becomes the apotheosis of a Cajun dancehall.

OK, to be fair: Fred's is more of a dance shack than hall. It's a little bar and it gets more than a little crowded from 8:30am to2ish in the afternoon, when owner 'Tante' (auntie) Sue and her staff host a Francophone-friendly music morning, with bands, beer, cigarettes and dancing (seriously, it gets smoky in here. Fair warning). Sue herself will often take to the stage to dispense wisdom and songs in Cajun French, all while taking pulls off a bottle of brown liquor she keeps in a pistol holster.

ⓘ Information

Visitor Center (⊘800-346-1958, 337-232-3737; www.lafayettetravel.com; 1400 NW Evangeline Thruway; ⊘8:30am-5pm Mon-Fri, 9am-5pm Sat & Sun)

ⓘ Getting There & Away

From I-10, exit 103A, the Evangeline Thruway (Hwy 167) goes to the center of town. **Greyhound** (⊘337-235-1541; 100 Lee Ave) operates from a hub beside the central commercial district, making several runs daily to New Orleans (3½ hours) and Baton Rouge (one hour). The **Amtrak** (100 Lee Ave) train *Sunset Limited* goes to New Orleans three times a week.

Cajun Wetlands

In 1755, the Grand Dérangement, the British expulsion of rural French settlers from Acadiana (now Nova Scotia, Canada), created a homeless population of Acadians who searched for decades for a place to settle. In 1785, seven boatloads of exiles arrived in New Orleans. By the early 19th century, 3000 to 4000 Acadians occupied the swamplands southwest of New Orleans. Native American tribes such as the Attakapas helped them learn to eke out a living based upon fishing

and trapping, and the aquatic way of life is still the backdrop to modern living.

East and south of Lafayette, the **Atchafalaya Basin** is the preternatural heart of the Cajun wetlands. Stop in to the **Atchafalaya Welcome Center** (⊘337-228-1094; www.louisianatravel.com/atchafalaya-welcome-center; I-10, exit 121; ⊘8:30am-5pm) to learn how to penetrate the dense jungle protecting these swamps, lakes and bayous from the casual visitor (incidentally, it also screens one of the most gloriously cheesy nature films in existence). They'll fill you in on camping in **Indian Bayou** and exploring the **Sherburne Wildlife Management Area**, as well as the exquisitely situated **Lake Fausse Pointe State Park**.

Eleven miles east of Lafayette in the compact, crawfish-lovin' town of **Breaux Bridge**, you'll find the utterly unexpected **Café des Amis** (www.cafedesamis.com; 140 E Bridge St; mains $17-26; ⊘11am-2pm Tue, to 9pm Wed & Thu, 7:30am-9:30pm Fri & Sat, 8am-2pm Sun), where you can relax amid funky local art as waiters trot out sumptuous weekend breakfasts, sometimes set to a zydeco jam. Just 3.5 miles south of Breaux Bridge, **Lake Martin** (Lake Martin Rd) is a wonderful introduction to bayou landscapes. This bird sanctuary hosts thousands of great and cattle egrets, blue heron and more than a few gators.

Check out the friendly **tourist center** (⊘337-332-8500; www.breauxbridgelive.com; 318 E Bridge St; ⊘8am-4pm Mon-Fri, to noon Sat), who can hook you up with one of numerous B&Bs in town, or the wonderful **Bayou Cabins** (⊘337-332-6158; www.bayoucabins.com; 100 W Mills Ave; cabins $60-125): 14 completely individualized cabins situated on Bayou Teche, some with 1950s retro furnishings, others decked out in regional folk art. The included breakfast is delicious, but the smoked meats may shave a few years off your lifespan. If you're in town the first week of May, don't miss the gluttony of music, dancing and Cajun food at the **Crawfish Festival** (www.bbcrawfest.com; ⊘May)

Cajun Prairie

Think: dancing cowboys! Cajun and African American settlers in the higher, drier terrain north of Lafayette developed a culture based around animal husbandry and farming, and the 10-gallon hat still rules. It's also the hotbed of Cajun and zydeco music (and thus accordions) and crawfish farming.

Opelousas squats sleepily alongside Hwy 49, and its historic downtown is home to the esoteric **Museum & Interpretive Center** (☑ 337-948-2589; 315 N Main St; ☉ 8am-4:30pm Mon-Fri, 10am-3pm Sat) **FREE**; check out the doll collection.

The top zydeco joints in Acadiana, **Slim's Y-Ki-Ki** (www.slimsykiki.com; cnr Main St & Park St, Opelousas), a few miles north on Main St, across from the Piggly Wiggly, and the **Zydeco Hall of Fame** (11154 Hwy 190), 4 miles west in Lawtell, strike it up most weekends. Wear your dancing shoes and don't be afraid to sweat!

Plaisance, northwest of Opelousas, hosts the grassroots, fun-for-the-family **Southwest Louisiana Zydeco Festival** (www.zydeco.org; ☉ late Aug).

In **Eunice** (www.eunice-la.com) there's the Saturday-night (6pm to 7:30pm) 'Rendez-Vous des Cajuns' at the **Liberty Theater** (☑ 337-457-7389; 200 Park Ave; admission $5), which is broadcast on local radio. In fact, visitors are welcome all day at **KBON** (www.kbon.com; 109 S 2nd St), 101.1FM. Browse the capacious Wall of Fame, signed by visiting musicians. Two blocks away, the **Cajun Music Hall of Fame & Museum** (☑ 337-457-6534; www.cajunfrenchmusic.org; 230 S CC Duson Dr; ☉ 9am-5pm Tue-Sat) **FREE** is a dusty colletion of instruments and cultural ephemera that caters to the die-hard music buff. The NPS runs the **Prairie Acadian Cultural Center** (☑ 337-457-8499; www.nps.gov/jela; 250 West Park Ave; ☉ 8am-5pm Tue-Fri, to 6pm Sat) **FREE**, which has exhibits on rural life and Cajun culture and shows a variety of documentaries explaining the history of the area.

If all this leaves you in need of a respite, try centrally located **Potier's Cajun Inn** (☑ 337-457-0440; 110 W Park Ave, Eunice; r from $55; P ❄) for spacious, down-home-Cajun-style cozy apartments with kitchenettes. **Ruby's Café** (☑ 337-550-7665; 123 S 2nd St, Eunice; meals under $10; ☉ 6am-2pm Mon-Fri, 5-9pm Wed & Thu, to 10pm Fri & Sat) does popular plate lunches in a 1950s diner setting and **Café Mosaic** (202 S 2nd St, Eunice; meals $3-4.50; ☉ 6am-10pm Mon-Fri, from 7am Sat, 7am-7pm Sun; ☎) is a smart coffeehouse with waffles and grilled sandwiches.

Northern Louisiana

Make no mistake: the rural, oil-industry towns along the Baptist Bible belt make northern Louisiana as far removed from New Orleans as Paris, TX, is from Paris, France. There's a lot of optimistic tourism development, but at the end of the day, most folks come here from states like Texas and Arkansas to gamble.

Captain Henry Shreve cleared a 165-mile logjam on the Red River and founded the river-port town of **Shreveport**, in 1839. The city boomed with oil discoveries in the early 1900s, but declined after WWII. Some revitalization came in the form of huge Vegas-sized casinos and a riverfront entertainment complex. The **visitor center** (☑ 888-458-4748; www.shreveport-bossier.org; 629 Spring St; ☉ 8am-5pm Mon-Fri, 10am-2pm Sat) is downtown. If you're a rose-lover, it would be a shame to miss the **Gardens of the American Rose Center** (☑ 318-938-5402, 800-637-6534; www.ars.org; 8877 Jefferson Paige Rd; admission by donation, tours $10; ☉ 9am-5pm Mon-Sat, 1-5pm Sun), which contains more than 65 individual gardens designed to show how roses can be grown in a home garden – take exit 5 off the I-20. If you're hungry, stop by **Strawn's Eat Shop** (☑ 318-868-0634; 125 E Kings Hwy; mains under $10; ☉ 6am-8pm Mon-Sat, to 3pm Sun). This basic diner serves good, hearty Americana fare with a lot of Southern charm – think chicken-fried steak and mustard greens – but it's most notable for its delicious pies.

About 50 miles northeast of Monroe on Hwy 557 near the town of Epps, the **Poverty Point State Historic Site** (☑ 888-926-5492, 318-926-5492; www.crt.state.la.us; 6859 Highway 577, Pioneer; adult/child $4/free; ☉ 9am-5pm) has a remarkable series of earthworks and mounds along what was once the Mississippi River. A two-story observation tower gives a view of the site's six concentric ridges, and a 2.6-mile hiking trail meanders through the grassy countryside. Around 1000 BC this was the hub of a civilization comprising hundreds of communities, with trading links as far north as the Great Lakes.

Florida

Includes ➡

Best Places to Eat

➡ Blue Heaven (p486)

➡ Floridian (p492)

➡ Michy's (p470)

➡ Broken Egg (p500)

➡ Ella's Folk Art Cafe (p497)

Best Places to Stay

➡ Pelican Hotel (p469)

➡ Biltmore Hotel (p469)

➡ Dickens House (p498)

➡ Pillars (p473)

➡ Everglades International Hostel (p477)

Why Go?

Juan Ponce de León came in search of the fountain of youth. Henry Flagler built a railroad for snowbirds looking for a little sunshine. And Walt Disney put Florida on many a bucket list when he chose it as the location of his legendary theme park.

For centuries, people have flocked to Florida in search of a little magic, and they seldom leave disappointed. The Sunshine State is built on tourism and it insists that everyone have a good time, packing an extraordinary amount into a narrow peninsula.

It's home to glitzy theme parks and campy roadside attractions, white-sand beaches and laid-back islands, and top-notch art museums and fascinating historical sites (including the oldest city in the US). It's nearly impossible to be bored here, and if you are, just hop on a roller coaster, kayak alongside some alligators or swim with a manatee. We're betting it will pass.

When to Go
Miami

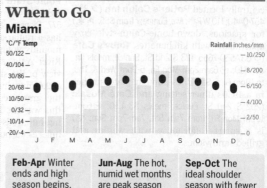

Feb-Apr Winter ends and high season begins, coinciding with spring break.

Jun-Aug The hot, humid wet months are peak season for northern Florida beaches and theme parks.

Sep-Oct The ideal shoulder season with fewer crowds, cooler temperatures and warm waters.

Spring Training

Forget daylight savings – for many Florida residents, the seasons are measured by the beginning and end of baseball spring training. Every March, 15 major league baseball teams hold their spring training in stadiums across central and south Florida, where sunshine is practically guaranteed. The intimate stadiums put you within spitting and signing distance of big leaguers and future hall of famers, making it a pilgrimage for fans of teams like the Boston Red Sox, the New York Yankees and the Philadelphia Phillies (not to mention several Florida-based teams). Around 240 exhibition games are held over 30 days, and fans have been known to camp out for prime seats. For information, visit www.floridagrapefruitleague.com.

AMERICA'S BEST STATE PARKS

Encountering Florida's bizarre, beautiful terrain and its wealth of ancient critters, migratory seabirds and imposing wildlife is unquestionably a highlight. Thankfully, Florida makes it easy for travelers with one of the nation's best state park systems. It is the first and only state to be a two-time recipient of the National Gold Medal Award for Excellence (in 1999 and 2005).

The state's 160 state parks span an overwhelming array of environments, home to epic coral reefs (John Pennekamp), thousands of alligators (Myakka River), otherworldly limestone karst terrain (Paynes Prairie) and crystal springs (Wakulla Springs). Of course, Florida is also legendary for the quality of its beaches, including such top beach parks as Grayton Beach, Fort DeSoto, Honeymoon Island and St Joseph Peninsula.

For the full list, visit **Florida State Parks** (www.floridastateparks.org). For advice on wildlife watching (what, when and how), visit the **Florida Fish & Wildlife Commission** (www.myfwc.com), which also facilitates boating, hunting and fishing.

Green Florida

Until recently, Florida wasn't known for conservation and ecotourism, but that's changing fast.

➡ **Department of Environmental Protection** (www.dep.state.fl.us) State-run agency tackles ecological and sustainability issues.

➡ **Green Lodging Program** (www.dep.state.fl.us/greenlodging) DEP-run program recognizes lodgings committed to conservation and sustainability.

➡ **Florida Sierra Club** (http://florida.sierraclub.org) Venerable outdoors and advocacy group.

➡ **Florida Surfrider** (http://florida.surfrider.org) Venerable outdoors and advocacy group.

➡ **Greenopia** (www.greenopia.com) Rates ecofriendly businesses in more than a dozen Florida cities.

HIAASEN'S FLORIDA

Writer Carl Hiaasen's unique, black-comic vision of Florida is a hilarious gumbo of misfits and murderous developers. Try *Skinny Dip* (for adults), *Hoot* (for kids) and *Paradise Screwed* (for his selected columns).

Fast Facts

➡ **Population** Miami (population 413,892), Miami-Dade County (2.5 million)

➡ **Distances from Miami** Key West (160 miles), Orlando (235 miles)

➡ **Time zones** Eastern (eastern Florida), Central Time Zone (western Panhandle)

FLORIDA

Best Beaches

You'll never want for shoreline in the Sunshine State. Here are a few of our favorites.

➡ Siesta Key (p499)

➡ South Beach (p461)

➡ Bahia Honda (p483)

➡ Apollo Beach (p488)

➡ St George Island (p511)

Resources

➡ **Visit Florida** (www.visitflorida.com) The official state tourism website.

➡ **My Florida** (www.myflorida.com) The official government portal.

➡ **Florida Smart** (www.floridasmart.com/news) Provides comprehensive Florida links.

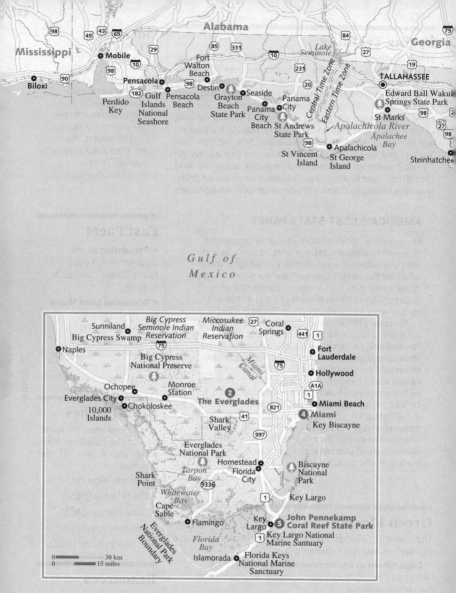

Florida Highlights

❶ Join Mallory Square's **sunset bacchanal** (p483) in Key West.

❷ Paddle among alligators and sawgrass in the **Everglades** (p476).

❸ Be swept up in nostalgia and thrill rides at **Walt Disney World** (p506).

❹ Marvel at the **murals** (p465) all around Wynwood in Miami.

❺ Snorkel the USA's most extensive coral reef at **John Pennekamp** (p479).

❻ Relax on the sugar-sand beaches of Sarasota's **Siesta Key** (p499).

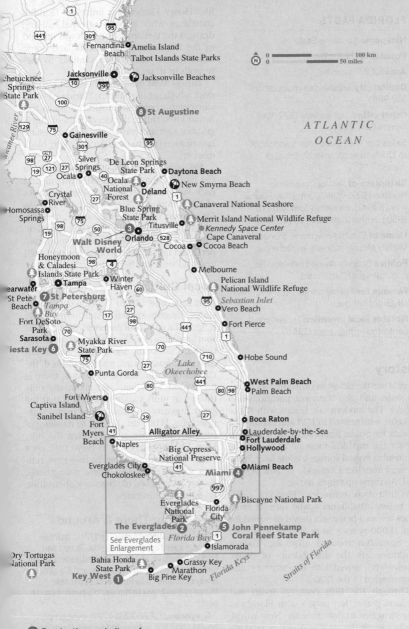

ATLANTIC
OCEAN

Fernandina
Beach
Amelia Island
Talbot Islands State Parks

Jacksonville
Jacksonville Beaches

tchetucknee
Springs
State Park

St Augustine

Gainesville

Silver
Springs
De Leon Springs
State Park
Daytona Beach
Ocala
Ocala
National
Forest
Deland
New Smyrna Beach
Crystal
River
Canaveral National Seashore
Homosassa
Springs
Blue Spring
State Park
Titusville
Merrit Island National Wildlife Refuge
Kennedy Space Center
Walt Disney
World
Orlando
Cape Canaveral
Cocoa Cocoa Beach

Honeymoon
& Caladesi
Islands State Park
Winter
Haven
Melbourne
Pelican Island
National Wildlife Refuge

earwater
Tampa
St Pete
Beach
St Petersburg
Tampa
Bay
Sebastian Inlet
Vero Beach
Fort DeSoto
Park
Sarasota
Fort Pierce
iesta Key
Myakka River
State Park
Lake
Okeechobee
Hobe Sound
Punta Gorda

Fort Myers
Captiva Island
Sanibel Island
Fort
Myers
Beach
Naples
West Palm Beach
Palm Beach
Boca Raton
Lauderdale-by-the-Sea
Fort Lauderdale
Hollywood
Alligator Alley
Big Cypress
National Preserve
Everglades City
Chokoloskee
Miami
Miami Beach

Everglades
National
Park
Florida
City
Biscayne National Park

The Everglades
Florida Bay
John Pennekamp
Coral Reef State Park
Islamorada

ry Tortugas
ational Park
Bahia Honda
State Park
Grassy Key
Marathon
Straits of Florida
Key West
Big Pine Key
Florida Keys

See Everglades
Enlargement

7 Ponder the symbolism of
The Hallucinogenic Toreador
at **Dalí Museum** (p499).

8 Growl like a pirate among
the historic Spanish buildings
of **St Augustine** (p491).

0   100 km
0   50 miles

FLORIDA FACTS

Nickname Sunshine State

Population 19.3 million

Area 53,927 sq miles

Capital city Tallahassee (population 182,965)

Other cities Jacksonville (827,908), Tampa (346,037)

Sales tax 6% (some towns add 9.5% to 11.5% to accommodations and meals)

Birthplace of Author Zora Neale Hurston (1891–1960), actor Faye Dunaway (b 1941), musician Tom Petty (b 1950), author Carl Hiaasen (b 1953)

Home of Cuban Americans, manatees, Mickey Mouse, retirees, key lime pie

Politics Sharply divided between Republicans and Democrats

Famous for Theme parks, beaches, alligators, art deco

Notable local invention Frozen concentrated orange juice (1946)

History

Florida has the oldest recorded history of any US state, and also the most notorious and bizarre. The modern tale begins with Ponce de León, who arrived in 1513 and claimed La Florida for Spain. Supposedly, he was hunting for the mythical fountain of youth (the peninsula's crystal springs), while later Spanish explorers like Hernando de Soto sought gold. All came up empty handed.

Within two centuries, Florida's original native inhabitants – who formed small tribes across a peninsula they'd occupied for over 11,000 years – were largely decimated by Spanish-introduced diseases. Today's Seminoles are the descendents of native groups who moved into the territory and intermingled in the 1700s.

Through the 18th century, Spain and England played hot potato with Florida as they struggled to dominate the New World, finally tossing the state to America, who admitted it to the Union in 1845. Meanwhile, developers and speculators were working hard to turn the swampy peninsula into a vacation and agricultural paradise. By the turn of the 20th century, railroad tycoons like Henry Flagler had unlocked Florida's coastlines, while a frenzy of canal-building drained the wetlands. The rush was on, and in the 1920s the South Florida land boom transformed Miami from sandbar to metropolis in 10 years.

Things went bust with the Great Depression, which set the pattern: Florida has ever since swung between intoxicating highs and brutal lows, riding the vicissitudes of immigration, tourism, hurricanes and real estate speculation (not to mention a thriving black market).

Following Castro's Cuban revolution in the 1960s, Cuban exiles flooded Miami, and each successive decade has seen the ranks of Latin immigrants grow and diversify. As for tourism, it was never the same after 1971, when Walt Disney built his Magic Kingdom, embodying the vision of eternal youth and perfected fantasy that Florida has packaged and sold since the beginning.

Local Culture

Florida is one of the USA's most diverse states. Broadly speaking, northern Florida reflects the culture of America's South, while southern Florida has welcomed so many Cuban, Caribbean, and Central and South American immigrants, it's been dubbed 'the Capital of Latin America.' As such, there is no 'typical Floridian,' and about the only thing that unifies state residents is that the great majority are transplants from someplace else. While this has led to its share of conflicts, tolerance is more often the rule. Most Floridians are left to carve their own self-defined communities, be they gays, retirees, Cubans, Haitians, bikers, evangelicals, Nascar-loving good old boys or globetrotting art-world sophisticates.

ⓘ Getting There & Around

Miami International Airport (p472) is an international gateway, as are Orlando, Tampa and Fort Lauderdale. The Fort Lauderdale and Miami airports are about 30 minutes apart; it's almost always cheaper to fly into Fort Lauderdale. Miami is also home to the world's busiest cruise port.

Greyhound (☑ 800-231-2222; www.greyhound.com) has widespread service throughout the state. **Amtrak** (www.amtrak.com) *Silver Meteor* and *Silver Star* trains run daily between New York and Miami.

Car-rental rates in Florida tend to fluctuate, but expect to pay at least $300 a week for a typical economy car.

SOUTH FLORIDA

Exemplifying the state's diversity, South Florida is a vivid pastiche of all that makes Florida wicked and wild. First is the multicultural entrepôt of Miami, and the sophisticated, rich beach communities stretching north from Fort Lauderdale to Palm Beach. In striking contrast, the beaches are bordered by the subtropical wilderness of the Everglades, while the tip of the state peters out in an ellipsis of fun-loving islands, culminating in anything-goes Key West.

Miami

Miami moves to a different rhythm from anywhere else in the USA. Pastel-hued, subtropical beauty and Latin sexiness are everywhere: from the cigar-filled dance halls where Havana expats dance to *son* and boleros to the exclusive nightclubs where stiletto-heeled Brazilian models shake to Latin hip-hop. Whether you're meeting avant-garde gallery hipsters or passing the buffed, perfect bodies recumbent along South Beach, everyone can seem oh-so-artfully posed. Meanwhile, street vendors and restaurants dish out flavors of the Caribbean, Cuba, Argentina and Haiti. For travelers, the city can be as intoxicating as a sweaty-glassed *mojito*.

Miami is its own world, an international city whose tempos, concerns and inspirations often arrive from distant shores. Over half the population is Latino and over 60% speak predominantly Spanish. In fact, many northern Floridians don't consider immigrant-rich Miami to be part of the state, and many Miamians, particularly Cubans, feel the same way.

◉ Sights

Greater Miami is a sprawling metropolis. Miami is on the mainland, while Miami Beach lies 4 miles east across Biscayne Bay. **South Beach** refers to the southern part of Miami Beach, extending from 5th St north to 21st St. Washington Ave is the main commercial artery. North of downtown (along NE 2nd Ave from about 17th St to 41st St), Wynwood and the Design District are focal points for art, food and nightlife. Just north again is Little Haiti. To reach Little Havana, head west on SW 8th St, or Calle Ocho, which pierces the heart of the neighborhood (and becomes the Tamiami Trail/Hwy

41). Just south of Little Havana are Coconut Grove and Coral Gables.

For more on South Florida, pick up a copy of Lonely Planet's guide to *Miami & the Keys.*

◉ Miami Beach

Miami Beach has some of the best beaches in the country, with white sand and warm aquamarine water. That movie in your head of art-deco hotels, in-line-skating models, preening young studs and cruising cars? That's **Ocean Drive** (from 1st to 11th Sts), with the beach merely a backdrop for strutting peacocks. This confluence of waves, sunshine and exhibitionist beauty is what made South Beach (or 'SoBe') world-famous.

Just a few blocks north, **Lincoln Road** (between Alton Rd and Washington Ave) becomes a pedestrian mall, or outdoor fashion runway, so all may admire SoBe's fabulously gorgeous creatures.

★ **Art Deco Historic District** NEIGHBORHOOD (Map p464) The well-preserved, pastel-hued Art Deco Historic District verily screams 'Miami.' It's the largest concentration of deco anywhere in the world, with approximately 1200 buildings lining the streets around Ocean Dr and Collins Ave. For tours and info, make your

---

FLORIDA IN...

One Week

Start in **Miami** and plan on spending three full days exploring museums and galleries, the art-deco district, Little Havana and the South Beach scene. Take a day to hike and kayak the **Everglades**, and don't miss **Coral Castle**. Then spend three days in the Keys: snorkel at **John Pennekamp Coral Reef State Park**, go tarpon fishing in **Islamorada** and let yourself get loose in **Key West**.

Two Weeks

Spend one or two days at the theme parks of **Orlando**, then scoot over to **Tampa** for fine cuisine and Ybor City nightlife. Get surreal in **St Petersburg** at the **Salvador Dalí Museum**, and visit a few **Tampa Bay Area beaches**. Finally, save a couple of days for **Sarasota**, with its jaw-dropping **Ringling Museum Complex** and the dreamy sands of **Siesta Key**.

Greater Miami

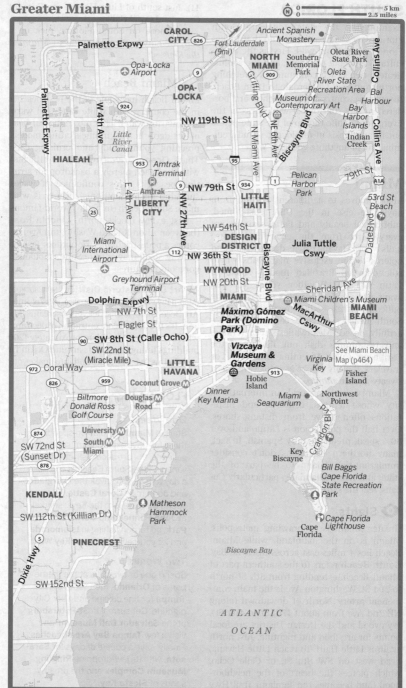

first stop the **Art Deco Welcome Center** (Map p464; ☑ 305-531-3484; 1001 Ocean Dr, South Beach; guided tour per adult/child/senior $20/free/15; ⊙ tours 10:30am Fri-Wed, 6:30pm Thu).

★**Wolfsonian-FIU** MUSEUM
(Map p464; www.wolfsonian.org; 1001 Washington Ave; adult/child 6-12 $7/5; ⊙ noon-6pm Thu-Tue, to 9pm Fri) A fascinating collection that spans transportation, urbanism, industrial design, advertising and political propaganda from the late 19th to mid-20th century.

Bass Museum of Art MUSEUM
(www.bassmuseum.org; 2121 Park Ave; adult/child $8/6; ⊙ noon-5pm Wed-Sun) The best art museum in Miami Beach has a playfully futurist facade, and the collection isn't shabby either, ranging from 16th-century European religious works to Renaissance paintings.

World Erotic Art Museum MUSEUM
(Map p464; www.weam.com; 1205 Washington Ave; adult over 18yr $15; ⊙ 11am-10pm Mon-Thu, to midnight Fri-Sun) Unfazed by SoBe's bare flesh? Something will get your attention here, with an amazingly extensive collection of naughty and erotic art, and even furniture depicting all sorts of parts and acts.

◉ Downtown Miami

Downtown isn't a tourist magnet, but it is home to a couple of worthwhile museums. Look for the brand new **Pérez Art Museum Miami** (MAM; www.miamiartmuseum.org), formerly Miami Art Museum, at its new location in **Bicentennial Park**.

History Miami MUSEUM
(www.historymiami.org; 101 W Flagler St; adult/child $8/5; ⊙ 10am-5pm Tue-Fri, from noon Sat & Sun) South Florida's complex, excitable history of Seminole warriors, rumrunners, pirates, land grabbers, tourists and Latin American immigrants is succinctly and vividly told. In a plaza just off W Flagler St.

◉ Little Havana

As SW 8th St heads away from downtown, it becomes **Calle Ocho** (pronounced *kah-yeh oh*-cho, Spanish for 'Eighth Street'). That's when you know you've arrived in Little Havana, the most prominent community of Cuban Americans in the US. Despite the cultural monuments, this is no Cuban theme park. The district remains a living, breathing immigrant enclave, though one whose residents have become, admittedly, more broadly Central American. One of the best times to come is the last Friday of the month during **Viernes Culturales** (www.viernesculturales.org), or 'Cultural Fridays,' a street fair showcasing Latino artists and musicians.

★**Máximo Gómez Park** PARK
(SW 8th St at SW 15th Ave; ⊙ 9am-6pm) Get a sensory-filled taste of old Cuba. It's also known as 'Domino Park,' and you'll understand why when you see the old-timers throwing bones.

El Crédito Cigars CIGARS
(☑ 305-858-4162; 1106 SW 8th St) One of Miami's most popular cigar stores; watch *tabaqueros* hand-roll them.

MIAMI IN...

Two Days

Focus your first day on South Beach. Bookend an afternoon of sunning and swimming with a walking tour through the **Art Deco Historic District** and a visit to **Wolfsonian-FIU**, which explains it all. That evening, sample some Haitian cuisine at **Tap Tap**, while away the evening with swanky cocktails at **Skybar** or, for a low-key brew, head to **Room**. For a late jolt, stop by the **World Erotic Art Museum**, open to midnight on weekends. Next morning, shop for Cuban music along Calle Ocho in **Little Havana**, followed by classic Cuban cuisine at **Versailles**. Go for a stroll at **Vizcaya Museum & Gardens**, cool off with a dip at the **Venetian Pool**, then end the day with dinner and cocktails at **Senora Martinez**.

Four Days

Follow the two-day itinerary, then head to the **Everglades** on day three and jump in a kayak. For your last day, immerse yourself in art and design in **Wynwood** and the **Design District**, followed by a visit to the **Miami Art Museum** or **Museum of Contemporary Art**. In the evening, party with the hipsters at the **Electric Pickle** or check out some live music: enjoy rock at **Tobacco Road** or Latin grooves at **Hoy Como Ayer**.

Miami Beach

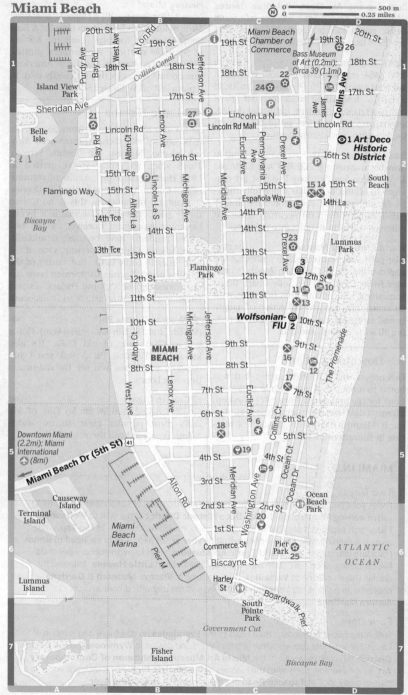

Miami Beach

Design District, Wynwood & Little Haiti

Proving that SoBe doesn't hold the lease on hip, these two trendy areas north of downtown – all but deserted 25 years ago – have ensconced themselves as bastions of art and design. The Design District is a mecca for interior designers, home to dozens of galleries and contemporary furniture, fixture and design showrooms. Just south of the Design District, **Wynwood** is a notable arts district, with myriad galleries and art studios housed in abandoned factories and warehouses.

The home of Miami's Haitian refugees, **Little Haiti** is defined by brightly painted homes, markets and *botanicas* (voodoo shops).

Wynwood Walls PUBLIC ART
(www.thewynwoodwalls.com; NW 2nd Ave btwn 25th & 26th St; ⊘noon-8pm Wed-Sat) Not a gallery per se, Wynwood Walls is a collection of murals and paintings laid out over an open courtyard in the heart of Wynwood. What's on offer tends to change with the coming and going of major arts events like Art Basel (one of the US's major annual art shows); when we visited the centerpiece was an enormous and fantastic piece by artist Shepard Fairey.

Coral Gables & Coconut Grove

For a slower pace and a more European feel, head inland. Designed as a 'model suburb' by George Merrick in the early 1920s, Coral Gables is a Mediterranean-style village that's centered around the shops and restaurants of the **Miracle Mile**, a four-block section of Coral Way between Douglas and LeJeune Rds.

★**Vizcaya Museum & Gardens** HISTORIC BUILDING
(www.vizcayamuseum.org; 3251 S Miami Ave; adult/child 6-12 $15/6; ⊘9:30am-4:30pm Wed-Mon) In Coconut Grove, this Italian Renaissance–style villa, the housing equivalent of a Fabergé egg, is Miami's most fairy-tale residence. The 70 rooms are stuffed with centuries-old furnishings and art, and the 30-acre grounds contain splendid formal gardens and Florentine gazebos.

Biltmore Hotel HISTORIC BUILDING
(☑855-311-6903; www.biltmorehotel.com; 1200 Anastasia Ave) Architecturally speaking, the crown jewel of Coral Gables is this magnificent edifice that once housed a speakeasy run by Al Capone. Even if you don't stay, drop by for a drink at the bar and gawk at the pool, or catch a free tour on Sunday afternoons.

🏃 City Walk
Art-Deco Magic

START ART DECO WELCOME CENTER
END EDISON HOTEL
LENGTH 1-2 MILES; 30 MINUTES

There are excellent walking tours available for the Art Deco Historic District – both guided and self-guided – but if you just want to hit the highlights, follow this quick and easy path.

Start at the **1 Art Deco Welcome Center** (p463) at the corner of Ocean Dr and 12th St, and head inside for a taste of deco style. Next, go north on Ocean Dr. Between 12th and 14th Sts, you'll see three classic examples of deco hotels: the **2 Leslie**, with classic 'eyebrows' and a typically boxy shape; the **3 Carlyle**, which was featured in the film *The Birdcage;* and the graceful **4 Cardozo Hotel**, with sleek, rounded edges. At 14th St, peek inside **5 Winter Haven** to see its fabulous terrazzo floors.

Turn left and head along 14th St to Washington Ave, and turn left again to find the **6 US Post Office** at 13th St. Step inside to admire the domed ceiling and marble stamp tables, and try whispering into the domed ceiling. Two blocks down on your left is the **7 11th St Diner** (p470), a gleaming aluminum deco-style Pullman car where you can also stop for lunch. At 10th St, you'll find the **8 Wolfsonian-FIU** (p463), an excellent museum with many deco-era treasures, and across the street is the beautifully restored **9 Hotel Astor**.

Turn left on 8th St and head east to Collins Ave. On the corner, you'll see **10 The Hotel** – originally the Tiffany Hotel and still topped by a deco-style neon spire bearing that name. Continue to Ocean Dr and turn right to see the **11 Colony Hotel** and its famous neon sign, then double back to find the 1935 **12 Edison Hotel**, another creation of deco legend Henry Hohauser, half a block past 9th St.

Venetian Pool SWIMMING
(www.coralgablesvenetianpool.com; 2701 De Soto Blvd; adult/child $11/7.35; ☺ hours vary; ♿) 'Swimming pool' doesn't even begin to describe it: with waterfalls, grottos and an Italianate feel, this spring-fed pool made by filling in the limestone quarry used to build Coral Gables looks like a vacation home for rich mermaids.

Lowe Art Museum MUSEUM
(www.lowemuseum.org; 1301 Stanford Dr; adult/student $10/5; ☺ 10am-4pm Tue-Sat, from noon Sun) The Lowe's tremendous collection satisfies a wide range of tastes, but it's particularly strong in Asian, African and South Pacific art and archaeology, and its pre-Columbian and Mesoamerican collection is stunning.

◉ Greater Miami

Museum of Contemporary Art MUSEUM
(MoCA; www.mocanomi.org; 770 NE 125th St; adult/student $5/3; ☺ 11am-5pm Tue & Thu-Sat, 1-9pm Wed, noon-5pm Sun) North of downtown, MoCA has frequently changing exhibitions focusing on international, national and emerging artists.

Ancient Spanish Monastery CHURCH
(☎ 305-945-1461; www.spanishmonastery.com; 16711 W Dixie Hwy; adult/child $8/4; ☺ 10am-4:30pm Mon-Sat, from 11am Sun) Said to be the oldest building in the Western Hemisphere, this monastery was built in Segovia, Spain, in 1141 and shipped here by William Randolph Hearst. Call to confirm hours.

◉ Key Biscayne

Bill Baggs Cape Florida State Park PARK
(www.floridastateparks.org/capeflorida; 1200 S Crandon Blvd; per car $8, pedestrian $2; ☺ 8am-sunset) If you don't make it to the Florida Keys, come to this park for a taste of their unique island ecosystems. The 494-acre space is a tangled clot of tropical fauna and dark mangroves, all interconnected by sandy trails and wooden boardwalks and surrounded by miles of pale ocean. A concession shack rents kayaks, bikes, in-line skates, beach chairs and umbrellas. At the southernmost tip, the 1825 brick **Cape Florida Lighthouse** offers free tours at 10am and 1pm Thursday through Monday.

> **DON'T MISS**
>
> ## WYNWOOD GALLERIES
>
> In Wynwood, Miami's hip proving ground for avant-garde art, 'Wypsters' (Wynwood hipsters) stock dozens of galleries with 'guerrilla' installations, new murals, graffiti and other inscrutableness. The neighborhood is roughly bound by NW 20th and NW 37th streets on the south and north, and N Miami Ave and NW 3rd Ave east and west. The best way to experience the scene is to attend the **Wynwood and Design District Arts Walks** (www.artcircuits. com; ☺ second Saturday of the month 7-10pm) FREE, with music, food and wine on the second Saturday of the month from 7pm to 10pm.

✦ Activities

Cycling & In-Line Skating

Skating or cycling the strip along Ocean Dr in South Beach is pure Miami; also try the Rickenbacker Causeway to Key Biscayne.

Fritz's Skate, Bike & Surf SPORTS RENTALS
(Map p464; ☎ 305-532-1954; www.fritzsmiamibeach.com; 1620 Washington Ave; hour/day/week bike & skate rentals $10/24/69; ☺ 10am-9pm Mon-Sat, to 8pm Sun) Sports equipment rentals and free in-line skate lessons (10:30am Sunday).

Miami Beach Bicycle Center CYCLING
(Map p464; www.bikemiamibeach.com; 601 5th St; per hr/day from $5/14; ☺ 10am-7pm Mon-Sat, to 5pm Sun) Convenient bike rentals in the heart of SoBe.

Water Sports

Boucher Brothers Watersports WATER SPORTS
(☎ 305-535-8177; www.boucherbrothers.com; ☺ 10:30am-4:30pm) Rentals and lessons for all sorts of water-related activities: kayaking, waterskiing, windsurfing, parasailing, waverunners and boats. You can find locations up and down the beach; your best bet is to call first to find out where to go for whatever it is you want to rent.

Sailboards Miami WATER SPORTS
(☎ 305-892-8992; www.sailboardsmiami.com; 1 Rickenbacker Causeway; ☺ 10am-6pm Fri-Tue) The waters off Key Biscayne are perfect for windsurfing, kayaking and kiteboarding; get your gear and lessons here.

⛟ Tours

Miami Design Preservation League
WALKING

(Map p464; ☑305-531-3484; guided tours adult/child $20/free, audio tours $15; ⊙10:30am Fri-Wed, 6:30pm Thu) Learn about art deco and its icons on a 90-minute walking tour departing from the Art Deco Welcome Center at 1200 Ocean Dr, Miami Beach.

History Miami Tours
WALKING, CYCLING

(☑305-375-1621; www.historymiami.org/tours; tours $20-54) Historian extraordinaire Dr Paul George leads fascinating bike, boat, coach and walking tours, including those that focus on Stiltsville. Get the full menu online.

South Beach Bike Tours
CYCLING

(☑305-673-2002; www.southbeachbiketours.com; half-day tour per person $59) Three-hour, two-wheel tours of South Beach.

✯ Festivals & Events

Calle Ocho Festival
CULTURAL

(www.carnavalmiami.com) This massive street party in March is the culmination of Carnaval Miami, a 10-day celebration of Latin culture.

Winter Music Conference
MUSIC

(www.wmcon.com) The SXSW of dance music and electronica takes place every March.

Art Basel Miami Beach
ART

(www.artbaselmiamibeach.com) An internationally known art show held each December.

🛏 Sleeping

Miami Beach is the well-hyped mecca for stylish boutique hotels in renovated art-deco buildings. To find them and other chic options, check out www.miamiboutiquehotels. com. Rates vary widely by season and all bets are off during spring break, when rates can quintuple; the summer months are slowest. For hotel parking, expect to pay $20 to $35 a night.

South Beach

Clay Hotel
HOTEL $$

(Map p464; ☑305-534-2988, 800-379-2529; www. clayhotel.com; 1438 Washington Ave; r $88-190; ❋@☎) Located in a 100-year-old Spanish-style villa – legend has it that Al Capone once slept here – the Clay has clean and comfortable rooms and is right on Espanola Way.

MIAMI FOR CHILDREN

The best beaches for kids are in Miami Beach north of 21st St, especially at 53rd St, which has a playground and public toilets, and the dune-packed beach around 73rd St. Also head south to Matheson Hammock Park, which has calm artificial lagoons.

Miami Seaquarium (www.miamiseaquarium.com; 4400 Rickenbacker Causeway; adult/child $40/30; ⊙9:30am-6pm, last entry 4:30pm) On the way to Key Biscayne, this 38-acre marine-life park is more extensive than the usual aquarium; it also rehabilitates dolphins, manatees and sea turtles, and presents great animal shows. You can swim with the dolphins.

Miami Children's Museum (www.miamichildrensmuseum.org; 980 MacArthur Causeway; admission $16; ⊙10am-6pm) On Watson Island, between downtown Miami and Miami Beach, this hands-on museum has fun music and art studios, as well as some branded 'work' experiences that make it feel a tad corporate.

Jungle Island (www.jungleisland.com; 1111 Parrot Jungle Trail, off MacArthur Causeway; adult/child $35/27; ⊙10am-5pm) Jungle Island is packed with tropical birds, alligators, orangutans, chimps and (to the delight of *Napoleon Dynamite* fans) a liger, a cross between a lion and a tiger.

Zoo Miami (Metrozoo; www.miamimetrozoo.com; 12400 SW 152nd St; adult/child $16/12; ⊙9:30am-5:30pm, last admission 4pm) Miami's tropical weather makes strolling around Zoo Miami almost feel like a day in the wild. For a quick overview (and because the zoo is so big), hop on the Safari Monorail; it departs every 20 minutes. There's a glut of grounds tours available, and kids will love feeding the Samburu giraffes ($2).

Monkey Jungle (www.monkeyjungle.com; 14805 SW 216th St; adult/child $30/24; ⊙9:30am-5pm, last entry 4pm) The tagline, 'Where humans are caged and monkeys run free,' tells you all you need to know – except for the fact that it's in far south Miami.

GUIDE TO MIAMI BEACHES

The beaches around Miami are some of the best in the country. The water is clear and warm. They're also informally zoned into areas with their own unique crowds so that everyone can enjoy them at their own speed.

Scantily-Clad Beaches In South Beach between 5th St and 21st St, modesty is in short supply.

Family-Fun Beaches North of 21st St is where you'll find the more family-friendly beaches, and the beach at 53rd St has a playground and public toilets.

Nude Beaches Nude bathing is legal at Haulover Beach Park in Sunny Isles. North of the lifeguard tower is predominantly gay; south is straight.

Gay Beaches All of South Beach is gay-friendly, but a special concentration seems to hover around 12th St.

Windsurfing Beaches Hobie Beach, along the Rickenbacker Causeway on the way to Key Biscayne, is actually known as 'Windsurfing Beach.'

★**Hotel St Augustine**   BOUTIQUE HOTEL $$
(Map p464; ☎305-532-0570; www.hotelstaugustine.com; 347 Washington Ave; r $126-289; P☀☎) Wood that's blonder than Barbie and a crisp-and-clean deco theme combine to create one of South Beach's most elegant yet stunningly modern sleeps. A hip-and-homey standout.

Lords Hotel   BOUTIQUE HOTEL $$
(Map p464; ☎877-448-4754; www.lordssouthbeach.com; 1120 Collins Ave; r $120-240, ste $330-540; P☀☎☒) The epicenter of South Beach's gay scene is this 'appropriately oriented' hotel, with rooms decked out in lemony yellow and offset by pop art. Lords is hip, yet doesn't affect an attitude.

Kent Hotel   BOUTIQUE HOTEL $$
(Map p464; ☎305-604-5068; www.thekenthotel.com; 1131 Collins Ave; r $69-199; P☀☎) The lobby is a kick, filled with fuchsia and electric-orange geometric furniture plus bright Lucite toy blocks. Rooms continue the playfulness. One of South Beach's better deals.

★**Pelican Hotel**   BOUTIQUE HOTEL $$$
(Map p464; ☎305-673-3373; www.pelicanhotel.com; 826 Ocean Dr; r $165-425, ste $295-555; ☀☎) The name and deco facade don't hint at anything unusual, but the decorators went wild inside with great themes such as 'Best Whorehouse,' 'Executive Zebra' and 'Me Tarzan, You Vain.'

Cadet Hotel   BOUTIQUE HOTEL $$$
(Map p464; ☎305-672-6688; www.cadethotel.com; 1701 James Ave; r $189-280; ☀☎☒) This unassuming little boutique hotel has the perfect deco aesthetic, with creative embellishments everywhere and a shaded verandah that's an oasis of calm.

Northern Miami Beach

★**Circa 39**   BOUTIQUE HOTEL $$
(☎305-538-4900; www.circa39.com; 3900 Collins Ave; r $85-144; P☀@☒) If you love South Beach style but loathe South Beach attitude, Circa has got your back. Combines one of the funkiest lobbies in Miami, hip icy-blue-and-white rooms and a welcoming attitude. Web rates are phenomenal.

Coral Gables

Hotel St Michel   HOTEL $$
(☎305-444-1666; www.hotelstmichel.com; 162 Alcazar Ave; r $85-225; P☀☎) You could conceivably think you're in Europe in this vaulted place at Coral Gables, with inlaid floors, old-world charm and just 28 rooms.

★**Biltmore Hotel**   HISTORIC HOTEL $$$
(☎855-311-6903; www.biltmorehotel.com; 1200 Anastasia Ave; r from $209; P☀☎☒) This 1926 hotel is a National Historic Landmark and an icon of luxury. Standard rooms may be small, but public spaces are palatial; its fabulous pool is the largest hotel pool in the country.

✕ Eating

Florida's most international city has an international-level food scene.

✕ South Beach

Walking up Ocean Ave, you'll find a veritable gauntlet of restaurants taking over the patios and sidewalks of almost every hotel facing the beach, all hawking lunch specials and happy hour deals. Competition is fierce, which means you can eat inexpensively. Stroll till you find something that suits, anywhere between 5th St and 14th Pl.

Puerto Sagua
CUBAN $

(Map p464; ☎ 305-673-1115; 700 Collins Ave; most mains $6-20; ☺ 7:30am-2am) Pull up to the counter for authentic, tasty and inexpensive *ropa vieja* (shredded beef), black beans and *arroz con pollo* (rice with chicken) – plus some of the best Cuban coffee in town – at this beloved Cuban diner.

11th St Diner
DINER $

(Map p464; www.eleventhstreetdiner.com; 1065 Washington Ave; mains $9-18; ☺ 24hr except midnight-7am Wed) This deco diner housed inside a gleaming Pullman train car sees round-the-clock activity and is especially popular with people staggering home from clubs.

Pizza Rustica
PIZZERIA $

(Map p464; www.pizza-rustica.com; 863 Washington Ave; slices $5, other mains $8-10; ☺ 11am-6pm) Big square slices that are a meal in themselves – when you're wandering around hungry, there's nothing better. Also at 667 Lincoln Rd.

★ Tap Tap
HAITIAN $$

(Map p464; ☎ 305-672-2898; www.taptaprestaurant.com; 819 5th St; mains $9-20; ☺ noon-11:30pm) In this tropi-psychedelic Haitian eatery, you dine under bright murals of Papa Legba, enjoying cuisine that's a happy marriage of West Africa, France and the Caribbean: try spicy pumpkin soup, curried goat and *mayi moulen,* a signature side of cornmeal.

Jerry's Famous Deli
DELI $$

(Map p464; ☎ 305-532-8030; www.jerrysfamousdeli.com; 1450 Collins Ave; most mains $9-18; ☺ 24hr) Jerry's does it all – from pastrami melts to Chinese chicken salad to fettuccine

Alfredo – and does it all day long. It also does it big, with huge portions served in a large, open, deco space or delivered to you.

★ Osteria del Teatro
ITALIAN $$$

(Map p464; ☎ 305-538-7850; http://osteriadelteatromiami.com; 1443 Washington Ave; mains $17-38; ☺ 6-11pm Mon-Thu, to 1am Fri-Sun) Stick to the specials of one of Miami's oldest and best Italian restaurants, and you can't go wrong. Better yet, let the gracious Italian waiters coddle and order for you. They never pick wrong.

Downtown Miami

Azul
FUSION $$$

(☎ 305-913-8288; 500 Brickell Key Dr; mains $35-65; ☺ 7-11pm Tue-Sat) Be pampered at this terrific restaurant on Brickell Key with a stellar Asian fusion menu. In addition to a massive wine list and waterfront views of downtown, Azul offers some of the best service in Miami.

Little Havana

Versailles
CUBAN $$

(☎ 305-444-0240; www.versaillesrestaurant. com; 3555 SW 8th St; mains $5-26; ☺ 8am-1am) *The* Cuban restaurant in town is not to be missed. It finds room for everybody in the large, cafeteria-style dining rooms.

Design District & Wynwood

Michy's
FUSION $$$

(☎ 305-759-2001; http://michysmiami.com; 6927 Biscayne Blvd; meals $29-38; ☺ 6-10:30pm Tue-Thu, to 11pm Fri-Sat, to 10pm Sun; ✐) Organic, locally sourced ingredients and a stylish, fantastical decor are what you'll find at Michelle 'Michy' Bernstein's place – one of the brightest stars in Miami's culinary constellation.

LATIN AMERICAN SPICE IN MIAMI

Thanks to its immigrant heritage, Miami is legendary for its authentic Cuban, Haitian, Brazilian and other Latin American cuisines. Cuban food is a mix of Caribbean, African and Latin American influences, and the fertile cross-pollination of these traditions has given rise to endlessly creative, tasty gourmet fusions, sometimes dubbed 'nuevo Latino,' 'nouvelle Floridian' or 'Floribbean' cuisine.

For a good introduction to Cuban food, sidle up to a Cuban *loncheria* (snack bar) and order a *pan cubano:* a buttered, grilled baguette stuffed with ham, roast pork, cheese, mustard and pickles. For dinner, order the classic *ropa vieja:* shredded flank steak cooked in tomatoes and peppers, and accompanied by fried plantains, black beans and yellow rice.

Other treats to look for include Haitian *griots* (marinated fried pork), Jamaican jerk chicken, Brazilian BBQ, Central American *gallo pinto* (red beans and rice) and *batidos,* a milky, refreshing Latin American fruit smoothie.

♀ Drinking & Entertainment

Miami truly comes alive at night. There is always something going on, and usually till the wee hours, with many bars staying open till 3am or 5am. For events calendars and gallery, bar and club reviews, check out www.cooljunkie.com and www.beachedmiami.com.

Bars

There are tons of bars along Ocean Dr; a meander at happy hour will get you half-price drinks.

★Room
BAR

(Map p464; www.theotheroom.com; 100 Collins Ave; ⊙7pm-5am) This dark, atmospheric, boutique beer bar in SoBe is a gem: hip and sexy as hell but with a low-key attitude. Per the name, it's small and gets crowded.

★Abraxas
BAR

(Map p464; 407 Meridian Ave; ⊙7pm-3am Sun-Mon, 5pm-5am Tue-Sat) In a classic deco building, Abraxas couldn't be friendlier. Uncrowded and serving fantastic beer from around the world, it's tucked away in a residential part of South Beach.

Electric Pickle
BAR

(www.electricpicklemiami.com; 2826 N Miami Ave; ⊙10pm-5am Wed-Sat) In Wynwood, arty hipsters become glamorous club kids in this two-story hepcat hot spot. The Pickle is sexy, gorgeous and literate.

Nightclubs

To increase your chances of getting into the major nightclubs, call ahead to get on the guest list. Having gorgeous, well-dressed females in your group doesn't hurt either (unless you're going to a gay bar). In South Beach clubs and live music venues, cover charges range from $20 to $25; elsewhere you'll get in for around half that.

Skybar
CLUB

(Map p464; ☑305-695-3100; Shore Club, 1901 Collins Ave; 4pm-2am Mon-Wed, to 3am Thu-Sat) Sip chic cocktails on the alfresco terrace – they're too expensive to guzzle. Or, if you're 'somebody,' head for the indoor A-list Red Room. Both have a luxurious Moroccan theme and beautiful-people-watching.

Twist
CLUB

(Map p464; ☑305-538-9478; www.twistsobe. com; 1057 Washington Ave; ⊙1pm-5am) This gay hangout has serious staying power and a

little bit of something for everyone, including dancing, drag shows and go-go dancers.

Nikki Beach Club
CLUB

(Map p464; ☑305-538-1111; www.nikkibeach.com; 1 Ocean Dr; cover from $25; ⊙11am-6pm Mon-Tue, to 11pm Wed-Sat, to 5pm Sun) Lounge on beds or inside your own tipi in this beach-chic outdoor space that's right on the sand.

Mansion
CLUB

(Map p464; ☑305-532-1525; www.mansionmiami.com; 1235 Washington Ave; cover from $20; ⊙11pm-5am Wed-Sat) Prepare for some quality time with the velvet rope and wear fly duds to enter this grandiose, exclusive megaclub, which lives up to its name.

Live Music

Hoy Como Ayer
LIVE MUSIC

(☑305-541-2631; www.hoycomoayer.us; 2212 SW 8th St; ⊙from 9pm Thu-Sat) Authentic Cuban music.

Tobacco Road
LIVE MUSIC

(☑305-374-1198; www.tobacco-road.com; 626 S Miami Ave; ⊙11:30am-5am) Old-school roadhouse around since 1912; blues, jazz and occasional impromptu jams by well-known rockers.

Jazid
LOUNGE

(Map p464; ☑305-673-9372; www.jazid.net; 1342 Washington Ave; ⊙10pm-5am) Jazz in a candlelit lounge; upstairs, DJ-fueled soul and hip-hop.

Theater & Culture

Adrienne Arsht Center for the Performing Arts
PERFORMING ARTS

(www.arshtcenter.org; 1300 Biscayne Blvd) Showcases jazz from around the world, as well as theater, dance, music, comedy and more.

New World Center
CLASSICAL MUSIC

(Map p464; www.newworldcenter.com; 500 17th St) The new home of the acclaimed New World Symphony is one of the most beautiful buildings in Miami.

Colony Theater
PERFORMING ARTS

(Map p464; www.mbculture.com; 1040 Lincoln Rd) Everything – from off-Broadway productions to ballet and movies – plays in this renovated 1934 art-deco showpiece.

Fillmore Miami Beach
PERFORMING ARTS

(Map p464; www.fillmoremb.com; 1700 Washington Ave) Miami Beach's premier showcase for Broadway shows and headliners.

Sports

Miami hosts pro teams in all four major US team sports.

Miami Dolphins FOOTBALL
(☎305-943-8000; www.miamidolphins.com; Sun Life Stadium, 2269 Dan Marino Blvd; tickets from $35) NFL football season runs from August to December.

Florida Marlins BASEBALL
(http://miami.marlins.mlb.com; Marlins Park, 501 Marlins Way; tickets from $15) MLB baseball season is May to September.

Miami Heat BASKETBALL
(☎786-777-1000; www.nba.com/heat; American Airlines Arena, 601 Biscayne Blvd; tickets from $20) NBA basketball season is November to April.

Florida Panthers HOCKEY
(☎954-835-7825; http://panthers.nhl.com; BB&T Center, 1 Panther Pkwy, Sunrise; tickets from $15) NHL hockey season runs mid-October to mid-April.

🛍 Shopping

Browse for one-of-a-kind and designer items at the South Beach boutiques around Collins Ave between 6th and 9th Sts and along Lincoln Rd mall. For unique items, try Little Havana and the Design District.

Bal Harbour Shops MALL
(www.balharbourshops.com; 9700 Collins Ave) Miami's most elegant mall.

Bayside Marketplace MALL
(www.baysidemarketplace.com; 401 Biscayne Blvd) Near the marina, a buzzy if touristy shopping and entertainment hub.

Books & Books BOOKS
(Map p464; ☎305-532-3222; www.booksandbooks.com; 927 Lincoln Rd) Best indie bookstore in South Florida; the original location is in Coral Gables at 265 Aragon Ave and there's another in Bal Harbour Shops.

ℹ Information

DANGERS & ANNOYANCES

Miami has a few areas considered dangerous at night: Little Haiti, stretches of the Miami riverfront and Biscayne Blvd, and areas below 5th St in South Beach. Downtown, use caution near the Greyhound station and shantytowns around causeways, bridges and overpasses.

EMERGENCY

Beach Patrol (☎305-673-7714)

INTERNET ACCESS

Most hotels offer wi-fi access (as do Starbucks), and libraries also have free internet terminals.

INTERNET RESOURCES

Art Circuits (www.artcircuits.com) Insider info on art events; neighborhood-by-neighborhood gallery maps.
Mango & Lime (www.mangoandlime.net) The best local food blog.
Miami Beach 411 (www.miamibeach411.com) A great general guide for Miami Beach visitors.

MEDIA

Miami Herald (www.miamiherald.com) The city's major English-language daily.
El Nuevo Herald (www.elnuevoherald.com) Spanish-language daily published by the *Miami Herald*.
Miami New Times (www.miaminewtimes.com) Edgy, alternative weekly.

MEDICAL SERVICES

Mount Sinai Medical Center (☎305-674-2121, 24hr visitors medical line 305-674-2222; 4300 Alton Rd) The area's best emergency room.

MONEY

Bank of America has branch offices all over Miami and Miami Beach.

TOURIST INFORMATION

Greater Miami & the Beaches Convention & Visitors Bureau (☎305-539-3000; www.miamiandbeaches.com; 701 Brickell Ave, 27th fl; ⊗8:30am-5pm Mon-Fri) Located in an oddly intimidating high-rise building.
Miami Beach Chamber of Commerce (Map p464; ☎305-674-1300; www.miamibeachchamber.com; 1920 Meridian Ave; ⊗9am-5pm Mon-Fri) You can purchase a Meter Card from the **Miami Beach Chamber of Commerce**. Denominations come in $10, $20 and $25 (and meters cost $1 per hour).

ℹ Getting There & Away

Miami International Airport (MIA; www.miami-airport.com) is about 6 miles west of downtown and is accessible by **SuperShuttle** (☎305-871-8210; www.supershuttle.com), which costs about $21 to South Beach.

Greyhound (☎800-231-2222; www.greyhound.com) serves all the major cities in Florida with four stations in Miami; check their website to see which location is best for you.

Amtrak (☎800-872-7245, 305-835-1222; www.amtrak.com; 8303 NW 37th Ave) has a main Miami terminal. The **Tri-Rail** (☎800-874-7245; www.tri-rail.com) commuter system serves Miami (with a free transfer to Miami's transit system) and MIA, Fort Lauderdale and its airport, and West Palm Beach and its airport ($11.55 round-trip).

ⓘ Getting Around

Metro-Dade Transit (📞 305-891-3131; www.mi-amidade.gov/transit/routes.asp; tickets $2) runs the local Metrobus and Metrorail ($2), as well as the free Metromover monorail serving downtown.

Fort Lauderdale

Fort Lauderdale was once known as spring-break party central, but like the drunken teens who once littered the beach, the town has grown up and moved on. It's now a stylish, sophisticated city known more for museums, Venice-style waterways, yachting and open-air cafes than wet T-shirt contests and beer bongs. It's also a very popular gay and lesbian destination, along with most of South Florida. And the beach is as lovely as always.

For local information, head to the **visitor bureau** (📞 800-227-8669, 954-765-4466; www.sunny.org; 100 E Broward Blvd, Suite 200; ⏱8:30-5pm Mon-Fri).

◎ Sights & Activities

Fort Lauderdale Beach & Promenade
BEACH

Fort Lauderdale's promenade – a wide, brick, palm-tree-dotted pathway swooping along the beach and A1A – is a magnet for runners, in-line skaters, walkers and cyclists. The white-sand beach is one of the nation's cleanest and best, stretching 7 miles to Lauderdale-by-the-Sea.

Museum of Art
MUSEUM

(www.moafl.org; 1 E Las Olas Blvd; adult/child 6-17 $10/5; ⏱10am-5pm Mon-Sat, noon-5pm Sun) A curvaceous Florida standout known for its William Glackens collection (among Glackens fans) and its exciting exhibitions (among everyone else).

Museum of Discovery & Science
MUSEUM

(www.mods.org; 401 SW 2nd St; adult/child 2-12 $14/12; ⏱10am-5pm Mon-Sat, noon-6pm Sun; 👶) A 52ft kinetic-energy sculpture greets you, and fun exhibits include Gizmo City and Runways to Rockets – where it actually *is* rocket science. Plus there's an Everglades exhibit and IMAX theater.

Bonnet House
HISTORIC HOME

(www.bonnethouse.org; 900 N Birch Rd; adult/child $20/16, grounds only $10; ⏱9am-4pm Tue-Sat, from 11am Sun) Wandering the 35 acres of lush, subtropical gardens, you might just spot the resident Brazilian squirrel monkeys. The art-filled house is open to guided tours only.

★ Carrie B
BOAT TOURS

(📞 954-642-1601, 888-238-9805; www.carriebcruises.com; tours adult/child $23/13) Hop aboard this replica 19th-century riverboat for a narrated 90-minute 'lifestyles of the rich and famous' tour of the ginormous mansions along the Intracoastal and New River.

Water Taxi
BOAT TOURS

(www.watertaxi.com; all-day pass adult/child $20/13) The fun, yellow **Water Taxi** travels the canals and waterways between 17th St to the south, Atlantic Blvd/Pompano Beach to the north, the Riverfront to the west and the Atlantic Ocean to the east. A daily pass entitles you to unlimited rides.

🛏 Sleeping

The area from Rio Mar St in the south to Vistamar St in the north, and from Hwy A1A in the east to Bayshore Dr in the west, offers the highest concentration of accommodations in all price ranges. Check out the CVB's list of **superior small lodgings** (www.sunny.org/ssl).

Shell Motel
MOTEL $

(📞 954-463-1723; www.sableresorts.com; 3030 Bayshore Dr; r/ste from $90/150; 🅿🐾🗚) One of six modest motels owned by the same company, this sweet Old Florida–style spot has bright, clean rooms surrounding a small pool. Splash out for a roomy suite.

Riverside Hotel
HOTEL $$

(📞 954-467-0671; www.riversidehotel.com; 620 E Las Olas Blvd; r $129-224; 🅿✳🗚🐾🗚) This Fort Lauderdale landmark – fabulously located downtown on Las Olas – has three room types: more modern rooms in the newer tower, restored rooms in the original property and the more old-fashioned 'classic' rooms.

★ Pillars
B&B $$$

(📞 954-467-9639; www.pillarshotel.com; 111 N Birch Rd; r $179-520; 🅿✳🗚🗚) From the harp in the sitting area to the private balconies and the intimate prearranged dinners for two, this tiny boutique B&B radiates hushed good taste. A block from the beach, facing one of the best sunsets in town.

🍴 Eating

★ Gran Forno
ITALIAN $

(www.gran-forno.com; 1235 E Las Olas Blvd; mains $6-12; ⏱7am-6pm Tue-Sun) The best lunch spot in downtown Fort Lauderdale is this delightfully old-school Milanese-style

FLORIDA FORT LAUDERDALE

GAY & LESBIAN FORT LAUDERDALE

Sure, Miami's South Beach is a mecca for gay travelers, but Fort Lauderdale has long been nipping at the high heels of its southern neighbor. For information on local gay life, visit www.gayftlauderdale. com. Other resources that cover South Florida include the glossy weekly **Hot Spots** (www.hotspotsmagazine.com), the insanely comprehensive www.jumponmarkslist.com, and www.sunny.org/glbt.

bakery and cafe: warm crusty pastries, bubbling pizzas, and fat golden loaves of ciabatta, sliced and stuffed with ham, roast peppers, pesto and other delicacies.

11th Street Annex AMERICAN $
(http://twouglysisters.com; 14 SW 11th St; lunch $9; ⊙11:30am-2pm Mon-Fri) In this off-the-beaten-path peach cottage, the owners serve whatever strikes their fancy: perhaps brie mac 'n' cheese, chicken confit, and sour cream chocolate cake. Most of the vegetables are grown from the cottage's garden.

★ **Le Tub** BURGERS, AMERICAN $$
(www.theletub.com; 1100 N Ocean Dr, Hollywood; mains $9-20; ⊙11am-1am Mon-Fri, noon-2am Sat & Sun; ●) Decorated exclusively with flotsam collected over four years of daybreak jogs along Hollywood Beach, this quirky intracoastal-side institution features multiple tiers of outdoor seating, plus bathtubs and toilet bowls (!) sprouting lush plants. The thing to order here is the sirloin burger – it's bigger than your head (seriously) and is routinely named 'Best in America' by the likes of *GQ*. Expect a wait, both for seating and for cooking time. It's worth it.

Casablanca Cafe MEDITERRANEAN $$$
(☑954-764-3500; www.casablancacafeonline .com; 3049 Alhambra St; mains $10-38; ⊙11:30am-2am) Try to score a seat on the upstairs balcony of this Moroccan-style home where Mediterranean-inspired food and Florida-style ocean views are served. Live music Wednesday through Sunday.

Rustic Inn SEAFOOD $$$
(☑954-584-1637; www.rusticinn.com; 4331 Anglers Ave; mains $14-30; ⊙11:30am-10:30pm Mon-Sat, noon-9:30pm Sun) Hungry locals at this messy, noisy crab-house use wooden mallets at

long, newspaper-covered tables to get at the Dungeness crab, blue crab and golden crab drenched in garlic.

Drinking & Entertainment

Bars generally stay open until 4am on weekends and 2am during the week. Meander the **Riverwalk** (www.goriverwalk.com) along the New River, where you'll find the alfresco mall **Las Olas Riverfront** (SW 1st Ave at Las Olas Blvd), with stores, restaurants, a movie theater and entertainment.

Elbo Room BAR
(www.elboroom.com; 241 S Fort Lauderdale Beach Blvd; ⊙10am-2am) Featured in the movie *Where the Boys Are,* Elbo Room hangs onto its somewhat seedy reputation as one of the oldest and diviest bars around.

Lulu's Bait Shack BAR
(www.lulusbaitshack.com; 17 S Atlantic Blvd; ⊙11am-1am) Get lured in by the buckets of beer, bowls of mussels and fishbowl drinks at the ocean's edge.

Getting There & Around

The **Fort Lauderdale-Hollywood International Airport** (☑866-435-9355, 954-359-6100; www.broward.org/airport; 320 Terminal Dr) is served by more than 35 airlines, some with nonstop flights from Europe. A taxi from the airport to downtown costs around $20.

The **Greyhound station** (www.greyhound. com; 515 NE 3rd St) is four blocks from Broward Central Terminal, with multiple daily services. The **train station** (200 SW 21st Tce) serves **Amtrak** (☑800-872-7245; www.amtrak.com; 200 SW 21st Tce), and the **Tri-Rail** (www.tri-rail. com; 6151 N Andrews Ave) has services to Miami and Palm Beach.

Hail a **Sun Trolley** (www.suntrolley.com; fare 50¢) for rides between downtown, the beach, Las Olas and the Riverfront.

Palm Beach & Around

Palm Beach isn't all yachts and mansions – but just about. This is where railroad baron Henry Flagler built his winter retreat, and it's also home to Donald Trump's **Mar-a-Lago** (1100 S Ocean Blvd). In other words, if you're looking for middle-class tourism or Florida kitsch, keep driving. Contact the Palm Beach County **Convention & Visitor Bureau** (☑800-554-7256; www.palmbeachfl. com; 1555 Palm Beach Lakes Blvd) in West Palm Beach for area information and maps.

Boca Raton

Halfway between Fort Lauderdale and Palm Beach is this largely residential stretch of picturesque coast that's been preserved from major development. For a great taste, hike the elevated boardwalks of the **Gumbo Limbo Nature Center** (☎561-544-8605; www.gumbolimbo.org; 1801 N Ocean Blvd; admission by donation; ⏲9am-4pm Mon-Sat, noon-4pm Sun; 👪), a beautiful wetlands preserve; also visit its sea turtle rehabilitation center. Another good reason to stop is the outstanding **Boca Raton Museum of Art** (☎561-392-2500; www.bocamuseum.org; 501 Plaza Real; adult/student $8/5; ⏲10am-5pm Tue-Fri, noon-5pm Sat & Sun), with a permanent collection of contemporary works by Picasso, Matisse, Warhol and more. The museum is in **Mizner Park** (www.miznerpark.org), a ritzy outdoor mall with stores, restaurants and regular free concerts.

Palm Beach

About 30 miles north of Boca Raton are Palm Beach and West Palm Beach. The two towns have flip-flopped the traditional coastal hierarchy: Palm Beach, the beach town, is more upscale, while West Palm Beach on the mainland is younger and livelier.

Palm Beach is an enclave of the ultra-wealthy, especially during its winter 'social season,' so the main tourist activities involve gawking at oceanfront mansions and window-shopping the boutiques along the aptly named **Worth Avenue** (www.worth-avenue.com). You can also visit one of the country's most fascinating museums, the resplendent **Flagler Museum** (www.flaglermuseum.us; 1 Whitehall Way; adult/child $18/10; ⏲10am-5pm Tue-Sat, noon-5pm Sun), housed in the railroad magnate's 1902 winter estate, Whitehall Mansion. The elaborate 55-room palace is an evocative immersion in Gilded Age opulence.

Flagler's opulent oceanfront 1896 hotel, the **Breakers** (☎888-273-2537, 561-655-6611; www.thebreakers.com; 1 S County Rd; r $270-1250, ste $510-5500; ❄@📶🏊), is a super-luxurious world unto itself, modeled after Rome's Villa Medici. It encompasses two golf courses, 10 tennis courts, a three-pool Mediterranean beach club and a trove of restaurants.

For a low-end treat, kick it Formica-style with an egg cream and a low-cal platter at the lunch counter in **Green's Pharmacy** (151 N County Rd; mains $4-11; ⏲8am-6pm Mon-Fri, to 4pm Sat).

West Palm Beach

Henry Flagler initially developed West Palm Beach as a working-class community to support Palm Beach. Today West Palm works harder, plays harder and is simply cooler and more relaxed. It's a groovy place to explore.

Florida's largest museum, the **Norton Museum of Art** (☎561-832-5196; www.norton.org; 1451 S Olive Ave; adult/child $12/5; ⏲10am-5pm Tue-Sat, to 9pm Thu, 11am-5pm Sun) houses an enormous collection of American and European modern masters and Impressionists, along with a large Buddha head presiding over an impressive Asian art collection. If you like that, you'll love the outdoor **Ann Norton Sculpture Garden** (www.ansg.org; 253 Barcelona Rd; admission adult/under 5 $7/free; ⏲10am-4pm Wed-Sun). This serene collection of sculptures sprinkled among verdant gardens is a real West Palm gem.

If you have children, take them to **Lion Country Safari** (www.lioncountrysafari.com; 2003 Lion Country Safari Rd; adult/child $28.50/21; ⏲9:30am-5:30pm; 👪), the country's first cageless drive-through safari, where around 900 creatures roam freely around 500 acres.

The coolest lodging in town is **Hotel Biba** (☎561-832-0094; www.hotelbiba.com; 320 Belvedere Rd; r $69-129; ❄📶🏊) 🌿. The retro-funky exterior looks like a cute 1950s motel, but the rooms have a modern, boutique style that would be right at home in Miami's SoBe.

Much of the action centers around **CityPlace** (www.cityplace.com; 700 S Rosemary Ave; ⏲10am-10pm Mon-Sat, noon-6pm Sun), a European village-style outdoor mall with splashing fountains and a slew of dining and entertainment options. Clematis St also has several worthy bars, live-music clubs and restaurants, and every Thursday **Clematis by Night** (www.clematisbynight.net) hosts friendly outdoor concerts. If you're hungry, try **Rocco's Tacos & Tequila Bar** (www.roccostacos.com; 224 Clematis St; mains $12-23; ⏲11:30am-11pm Sun-Wed, to midnight Thu-Sat), a saucy *nuevo* Mexican restaurant with funky decor, tableside guacamole and 175 different kinds of tequila – no wonder it's so loud in here!

Admirably servicing its migration of snowbirds is **Palm Beach International Airport** (PBI; ☎561-471-7420; www.pbia.org), 2.5 miles west of downtown West Palm Beach. The downtown **Tri-Rail station** (☎800-875-7245; www.tri-rail.com; 203 S Tamarind Ave) also serves as the **Amtrak station** (☎561-832-6169; www.amtrak.com; 209 S Tamarind Ave).

The Everglades

Contrary to what you may have heard, the Everglades isn't a swamp. Or at least, it's not *only* a swamp. It's most accurately characterized as a wet prairie – grasslands that happen to be flooded most of the year. Nor is it stagnant. In the wet season, a horizon-wide river creeps ever-so-slowly beneath the rustling saw grass and around the subtly raised cypress and hardwood hammocks toward the ocean. The Everglades are indeed filled with alligators – and perhaps a few dead bodies, as *CSI: Miami* would have it. Yet its beauty is not measured in fear or geological drama, but in the timeless, slow Jurassic flap of a great blue heron as it glides over its vast and shockingly gentle domain.

Which is one reason that exploring the Everglades by foot, bicycle, canoe and kayak (or camping) is so much more satisfying than by noisy, vibrating airboat. There is an incredible variety of wonderful creatures to see within this unique, subtropical wilderness, and there are accessible entrances that, at the cost of a few hours, get you easily into the Everglades' soft heart.

The Everglades has two seasons: the summer wet season and the winter dry season. Winter – from December to April – is the prime time to visit: the weather is mild and pleasant, and the wildlife is out in abundance. In summer – May through October – it's stiflingly hot, humid and buggy, with frequent afternoon thunderstorms. In addition, as water sources spread out, so the animals disperse.

Everglades National Park

While the Everglades has a history dating back to prehistoric times, the park wasn't founded until 1947. It's considered the most endangered national park in the USA, but the Comprehensive Everglades Restoration Plan (www.evergladesplan.org) has been enacted to undo some of the damage done by draining and development.

The park has three main entrances and areas: in the south along Rte 9336 through Homestead and Florida City to Ernest Coe Visitor Center and, at road's end, Flamingo; along the Tamiami Trail/Hwy 41 in the north to Shark Valley; and on the Gulf Coast near Everglades City.

The main park entry points have visitor centers where you can get maps, camping permits and ranger information. You only need to pay the entrance fee (per car/pedestrian $10/5 for seven days) once to access all points.

Even in winter it's almost impossible to avoid mosquitoes, but they're ferocious in summer: bring *strong* repellent. Alligators are also prevalent. As obvious as it sounds, never, ever feed them: it's illegal and is a sure way to provoke attacks. Four types of poisonous snakes call the Everglades home; avoid all snakes, just in case, and wear long, thick socks and lace-up boots.

◉ Sights & Activities

Shark Valley   PARK
(☑ 305-221-8776; www.nps.gov/ever/planyour-visit/svdirections.htm; 36000 SW 8th St; car/cyclist $10/5; ☺ 9:15am-5:15pm) One of the best places to dip your toe into the Everglades (figuratively speaking) is Shark Valley, where you can take an excellent two-hour **tram tour** (☑ 305-221-8455; www.sharkvalleytramtours.com; adult/child $20/12.75) along a 15-mile asphalt trail and see copious amounts of alligators in the winter months. Not only do you get to experience the park from the shady comfort of a breezy tram, but the tours are narrated by knowledgeable park rangers who give a fascinating overview of the Everglades. The pancake-flat trail is perfect for bicycles, which can be rented at the entrance for $7.50 per hour. Bring water with you.

Ernest Coe Visitor Center   PARK
(☑ 305-242-7700; www.nps.gov/ever; Hwy 9336; ☺ 9am-5pm) Those with a day to give the Glades could start with this visitor center in the south. It has excellent, museum-quality exhibits and tons of activity info: the road accesses numerous short trails and lots of top-drawer canoeing opportunities. Call for a schedule of fun ranger-led programs, such as the two-hour 'slough slog.' At the nearby **Royal Palm Area** (☑ 305-242-7700; Hwy 9336), you can catch two short trails: the **Anhinga Trail** is great for wildlife spotting, especially alligators in winter; and the **Gumbo-Limbo Trail** showcases plants and trees.

Flamingo Visitor Center   PARK
(☑ 239-695-2945; ☺ 8am-4:30pm) From Royal Palm, Hwy 9336 cuts through the belly of the park for 38 miles until it reaches the isolated Flamingo Visitor Center, which has maps of canoeing and hiking trails. Call ahead about the status of facilities: the former Flamingo Lodge was wiped out by hurricanes in 2005.

Flamingo Marina (☑239-695-3101; ☺store hours 7am-5:30pm Mon-Fri, from 6am Sat & Sun) has reopened and offers backcountry boat tours and kayak/canoe rentals for self-guided trips along the coast.

Gulf Coast Visitor Center PARK
(☑239-695-3311; 815 Oyster Bar Lane, off Hwy 29, Everglades City; ☺9am-4:30pm) Those with more time should also consider visiting the northwestern edge of the Everglades, where the mangroves and waterways of the **10,000 Islands** offer incredible canoeing and kayaking opportunities, and great boat tours with a chance to spot dolphins. The visitor center is next to the marina, with rentals (from $13 per hour) and various guided boat trips (from $25). Everglades City also has other private tour operators who can get you camping in the 10,000 Islands.

🛏 Sleeping

Everglades National Park has two developed campgrounds, both of which have water, toilets and grills. The best are the first-come, first-served sites at **Long Pine Key** (☑305-242-7873; campsite/RV site $16/30), just west of Royal Palm Visitor Center; reserve ahead for campsites at **Flamingo** (☑877-444-6777; www.recreation.gov; campsite/RV site $16/30), which have cold-water showers and electricity. **Backcountry camping** (permit $10, plus per person per night $2) is throughout the park and includes beach sites, ground sites and chickees (covered wooden platforms above the water). A permit from the visitor center is required.

ⓘ Getting There & Around

The largest subtropical wilderness in the continental USA is easily accessible from Miami. The Glades, which comprise the 80 southernmost miles of Florida, are bound by the Atlantic Ocean to the east and the Gulf of Mexico to the west. The Tamiami Trail (US Hwy 41) goes east–west, parallel to the more northern (and less interesting) Alligator Alley (I-75).

You need a car to properly enter the Everglades and once you're in, wearing a good pair of walking boots is essential to penetrate the interior. Having a canoe or kayak helps as well; these can be rented from outfits inside and outside of the park, or else you can seek out guided canoe and kayak tours. Bicycles are well suited to the flat roads of Everglades National Park, particularly in the area between Ernest Coe and Flamingo Point, but they're useless off the highway. In addition, the road shoulders in the park tend to be dangerously small.

Around the Everglades

Coming from Miami, the gateway town of Homestead on the east side of the park can make a good base, especially if you're headed for the Keys.

Biscayne National Park

Just south of Miami (and east of Homestead), this national park is only 5% land. The 95% that's water is **Biscayne National Underwater Park** (☑305-230-1100; www.nps.gov/bisc), containing a portion of the world's third-largest coral reef, where manatees, dolphins and sea turtles highlight a vibrant, diverse ecosystem. Get general park information from **Dante Fascell Visitor Center** (☑305-230-7275; www.nps.gov/bisc; 9700 SW 328th St; ☺8:30am-5pm). The park offers canoe/kayak rentals, snorkel and dive trips, and popular three-hour glass-bottom boat tours; all require reservations.

Homestead & Florida City

Homestead and Florida City don't look like much, but they have some true Everglades highlights. Don't miss **Robert Is Here** (www.robertishere.com; 19200 SW 344th St, Homestead; ☺8am-7pm Nov-Aug) – a kitschy Old Florida institution with a petting zoo, live music and crazy-good milk shakes.

The Homestead–Florida City area has no shortage of chain motels along Krome Ave. For a seriously good hostel experience, consider the **Everglades International Hostel**

CORAL CASTLE

'You will be seeing unusual accomplishment' reads the inscription on the rough-hewn quarried wall. That's an understatement. Exemplifying all that is weird and wacky about South Florida, **Coral Castle** (☑305-248-6345; www.coralcastle.com; 28655 S Dixie Hwy; adult/child $15/7; ☺8am-6pm Sun-Thu, to 8pm Fri & Sat) is a unique monument to unrequited love. Of course, what's an altar-jilted Latvian to do, except move to Florida and hand carve, unseen, in the dead of night, a rock compound that includes a 'throne room,' a sun dial, a stone stockade and a revolving boulder gate that engineers to this day cannot explain...

(☑800-372-3874, 305-248-1122; www.everglade-shostel.com; 20 SW 2nd Ave, Florida City; camping $18, dm $28, d $61-75, ste $125-225; P❄🛜🐾). Rooms are good value, the vibe is very friendly, but the back gardens – wow. It's a fantasia of natural delights, and the hostel conducts some of the best Everglades tours around. For a more personal touch than the chain hotels, book a room at the historic **Redland Hotel** (☑800-595-1904; www.hotel-redland.com; 5 S Flagler Ave, Homestead; r $100-140; P🛜). Homestead's modestly quaint main street, along Krome Ave, is the central restaurant and shopping district.

Tamiami Trail

The Tamiami Trail/Hwy 41 starts in Miami and beelines to Naples along the north edge of Everglades National Park. Just past the entrance to the Everglades' Shark Valley is **Miccosukee Village** (www.miccosukee.com; MM 70 Hwy 41; adult/child/5yr and under $10/6/free; ⊙9am-5pm), an informative, entertaining open-air museum showcasing Miccosukee culture. Tour traditional homes, attend performances (from dance to gator wrestling), take an airboat ride ($16) and peruse handmade crafts in the gift store.

About 20 miles west of Shark Valley, you reach the **Oasis Visitor Center** (☑941-695-1201; ⊙8am-4:30pm Mon-Fri; ♿) for 1139-sq-mile **Big Cypress National Preserve** (☑239-695-4758; 33000 Tamiami Trail E; ⊙8:30am-4:30pm). Good exhibits and

short trails bring the region's ecology to life, though the adventurous might consider tackling a portion of the **Florida National Scenic Trail** (www.nps.gov/bicy/planyourvisit/florida-trail.htm); 31 miles cut through Big Cypress.

Half a mile east of the visitor center, drop into the **Big Cypress Gallery** (☑941-695-2428; www.clydebutcher.com; Tamiami Trail; ⊙10am-5pm Wed-Mon) ✏, displaying Clyde Butcher's work; his large-scale B&W landscape photographs spotlight the region's unusual beauty.

The tiny town of **Ochopee** is home to the country's smallest post office. If that's not enough to make you pull over, then stop into the eccentric **Skunk Ape Research Headquarters** (☑239-695-2275; www.skunkape.info; 40904 Tamiami Trail E; ⊙7am-7pm, 'zoo' closes around 4pm), dedicated to tracking Bigfoot's legendary, if stinky, Everglades kin. It's goofy but sincere. Based out of Skunk Ape HQ, **Everglades Adventure Tours** (EAT; ☑800-504-6554; www.evergladesadventuretours.com; tours from $69) offers knowledgeable swamp hikes, 'safaris,' airboats and, best of all, trips being poled around in a canoe or skiff.

Finally, just west of Ochopee, is the quintessential 1950s-style swamp shack, **Joanie's Blue Crab Cafe** (joaniesbluecrab-cafe.com; Tamiami Trail; mains $9-17; ⊙9am-5pm), with open rafters, colorful, shellacked picnic tables and a swamp dinner of gator nuggets and fritters.

A KINDER, GENTLER WILDERNESS ENCOUNTER

As you explore Florida's outdoors and encounter its wildlife, keep in mind the following guidelines.

Airboats and swamp buggies For exploring wetlands, airboats are better than big-wheeled buggies, but nonmotorized (and silent) canoes and kayaks are least-damaging and disruptive.

Wild dolphins Captive dolphins are typically rescued animals already acclimated to humans. However, federal law makes it illegal to feed, pursue or touch wild dolphins in the ocean.

Manatee swims When swimming near manatees, a federally protected endangered species, look but don't touch. 'Passive observation' is the standard.

Feeding wild animals In a word, don't. Acclimating wild animals to humans usually leads to the animal's death, whether because of accidents or aggression.

Sea-turtle nesting sites It's a federal crime to approach nesting sea turtles or hatchling runs. Observe beach warning signs. If you encounter nesting turtles, keep your distance and no flash photos.

Coral-reef etiquette Never touch the coral reef. It's that simple. Coral polyps are living organisms. Touching or breaking coral creates openings for infection and disease.

Everglades City

This small town at the edge of the park makes a good base for exploring the **10,000 Islands** region. With large renovated rooms, **Everglades City Motel** (☎800-695-8353, 239-695-4244; www.evergladescitymotel.com; 310 Collier Ave; r from $80; ❇☀) is exceptionally good value, and the fantastically friendly staff can hook you up with any kind of tour. The same can be said for the **Ivey House Bed & Breakfast** (☎877-567-0679, 239-695-3299; www.iveyhouse.com; 107 Camellia St; lodge $74-120, inn $99-209; ❇☀). Choose between basic lodge accommodations or somewhat sprucer inn rooms, then book some of the region's best nature trips with the on-site **North American Canoe Tours** (NACT; ☎877-567-0679, 239-695-3299; www.evergladesadventures.com; 107 Camellia St, Ivey House Bed & Breakfast; tours $124, canoe rentals $25-35; ☺Nov–mid-Apr). Ask about room/tour packages. For dinner, try the **Seafood Depot** (102 Collier Ave; mains $6-20; ☺10:30am-9pm), a haven of fried seafood and a great place to sample gator and frog's legs; just douse with Tabasco and devour.

Florida Keys

Before Henry Flagler completed his railroad in 1912, which connected the Keys to the mainland, this 126-mile string of islands was just a series of untethered bumps of land accessible only by boat. (Little surprise, then, that their early economies were built on piracy, smuggling, ship salvaging and fishing.) Flagler's railroad was destroyed by a hurricane in 1935, but what remained of its bridges allowed the Overseas Hwy to be completed in 1938. Now, streams of travelers swarm down from the mainland to indulge in the alluring jade-green waters, laid-back island lifestyle, great fishing, and idyllic snorkeling and diving.

The islands are typically divided into the Upper Keys (Key Largo to Islamorada), Middle Keys and Lower Keys (from Little Duck Key). Yet far from petering out, they crescendo at highway's end, reaching their grand finale in Key West – the Keys' gloriously unkempt, bawdy, freak-loving exclamation point.

Many addresses in the Keys are noted by their proximity to mile markers (indicated as MM), which start at MM 126 in Florida City and count down to MM 0 in Key West.

They also might indicate whether they're 'oceanside' (the south side of the highway) or 'bayside' (which is north).

The **Florida Keys & Key West Visitors Bureau** (☎800-352-5397; www.fla-keys.com) has information; also check www.keysnews.com.

Key Largo

Stretching from Key Largo to Islamorada, the Upper Keys are cluttered with touristy shops and motels. At first you can't even see the water from the highway, then – bam – you're in Islamorada and water is everywhere.

Key Largo has long been romanticized in movies and song, so it can be a shock to arrive and find...no Bogart, no Bacall, no love-sick Sade. Yes, Key Largo is underwhelming, a sleepy island and town with middling views. That is, if all you do is stick to the highway and keep your head above water. On the side roads you can find some of those legendary island idiosyncrasies, and dive underwater for the most amazing coral reef in the continental US.

For maps and brochures, visit the **chamber of commerce** (☎305-451-1414; www.keylargo.org; MM 106 bayside; ☺9am-6pm), located in a yellow building just past Seashell World (not to be confused with the *other* yellow visitor center at 10624 that makes reservations and works on commission).

🏃 Activities

John Pennekamp Coral Reef State Park PARK
(www.pennekamppark.com; MM 102.6 oceanside; car/motorcycle/cyclist or pedestrian $8/4/2; ☺8am-sunset, aquarium 8am-5pm; ♿) The USA's first underwater park, Pennekamp contains the third largest coral barrier reef in the world – the only one in the US – and is home to a panoply of sea life and the oft-photographed statue *Christ of the Deep*. Your options for seeing the reef are many: take a 2½-hour **glass-bottom boat tour** (☎305-451-6300; adult/child $24/17; ☺9:15am, 12:15pm & 3:15pm) on a thoroughly modern 65ft catamaran. Dive in with a **snorkeling trip** (☎305-451-6300; adult/child $30/25) or two-tank **diving trip** (☎305-451-6322; $55); half-day trips leave twice daily, usually around 9am and 1pm. Or go DIY and rent a canoe or kayak (per hour single/double $12/17) and journey through a 3-mile network of water trails. Call the park for boat-rental information.

African Queen
BOAT TOUR

(📞305-451-8080; www.africanqueenflkeys.com; MM 100 oceanside at the Holiday Inn Marina; canal cruise $49, dinner cruise $89) For years, the African Queen – the steamboat used in the 1951 movie starring Humphrey Bogart and Katherine Hepburn – has been docked in Key Largo, but the owners have restored her to her former, er, splendor, and now offer canal and dinner cruises. Canal cruises are every two hours from 10am to 6pm; best to call for reservations: the tiny vessel only accommodates six.

Florida Bay Outfitters
KAYAKING

(📞305-451-3018; www.kayakfloridakeys.com; MM 104 bayside; kayak rental per half-day $40) See the keys from the water: rent a kayak or canoe or catch a guided trip.

Horizon Divers
DIVING

(📞305-453-3535; www.horizondivers.com; 100 Ocean Dr, off MM 100 oceanside; snorkel/scuba trips $50/80) Get beneath the surface on a scuba or snorkel trip with Horizon's friendly crew.

🛏 Sleeping

In addition to luxe resorts, Key Largo has loads of bright, cheery motels and camping.

John Pennekamp Coral Reef State Park
CAMPGROUND $

(📞800-326-3521; www.pennekamppark.com; campsite/RV site both $36; P) Sleep with–er, near the fishes at one of the 47 coral-reef-adjacent sites here. Camping's popular; reserve well in advance.

Largo Lodge
HOTEL $$

(📞305-451-0424; www.largolodge.com; MM 102 bayside; cottages $150-265; P) These six charming, sunny cottages with their own private beach are surrounded by palm trees, tropical flowers and lots of roaming birds, for a taste of Florida in the good old days.

Key Largo House Boatel
HOTEL $$

(📞305-766-0871; www.keylargohouseboatel.com; Shoreland Dr, MM 103.5 oceanside; houseboat small/medium/large from $75/100/150) These five houseboats are a steal. The largest is incredibly spacious, sleeping six people comfortably. The boats are right on the docks, so there's no possibility of being isolated from land (or booze). Call for directions.

Kona Kai Resort & Gallery
HOTEL $$$

(📞305-852-7200; www.konakairesort.com; MM 97.8 bayside; r $199-439; P❄🐾🏊) This intimate hideaway features 11 airy rooms and suites (with full kitchens). They're all bright and comfortable, though some feel a little old-fashioned. Tons of activities, plus its own beach.

🍴 Eating & Drinking

Mrs Mac's Kitchen
AMERICAN $

(📞305-451-3722; www.mrsmacskitchen.com; MM 99.4 bayside; breakfast & lunch $8-12, dinner $9-22; ☺7am-9:30pm Mon-Sat) This cute roadside diner bedecked with rusty license plates serves classic highway food such as burgers and fish baskets. Look for a second location just half a mile south on the opposite side of the road.

Alabama Jack's
SEAFOOD, BAR $

(http://alabamajacks.com; 58000 Card Sound Rd; mains $7-14; ☺11am-7pm) On the back road between Key Largo and Florida City (about 15 miles north of Key Largo), this funky open-air joint draws an eclectic booze-hungry crowd of genuine Keys characters. Try the rave-worthy conch fritters.

★ Key Largo Conch House
FUSION $$

(📞305-453-4844; www.keylargocoffeehouse.com; MM 100.2 oceanside; mains $8-26; ☺8am-10pm) Now *this* feels like the islands: Conch architecture, tropical foliage, and crab and conch dishes that ease you off the mainland.

Fish House
SEAFOOD $$

(📞305-451-4665; www.fishhouse.com; MM 102.4 oceanside; mains $9-24; ☺11:30am-10pm; 🚗) Delivers on its name, serving fish, fish and more fish that's as fresh as it gets. Your main decision: fried, broiled, jerked, blackened or grilled?

Islamorada

It sounds like an island, but Islamorada is actually a string of several islands, the epicenter of which is Upper Matecumbe Key. It's right around here that the view starts to open up, allowing you to fully appreciate the fact that you're surrounded by water. Several little nooks of beach are easily accessible, providing scenic rest stops. Housed in an old red caboose, the **chamber of commerce** (📞305-664-4503; www.islamoradachamber.com; MM 83.2 bayside; ☺9am-5pm Mon-Fri, to 4pm Sat, to 3pm Sun) has area information.

💿 Sights & Activities

Billed as 'the Sportfishing Capital of the World,' Islamorada is an angler's paradise.

Indeed, most of its highlights involve getting on or in the sea.

Indian Key Historic State Park   ISLAND
(☑305-664-2540; www.floridastateparks.org/indiankey; MM 78.5 oceanside; per person $2.50; ☺8am-sunset) A few hundred yards offshore, this peaceful island contains the crumbling foundations of a 19th-century settlement that was wiped out by Native Americans during the Second Seminole War. It's a moody ramble, accessible only by kayak or boat, which you can rent from Robbie's Marina.

Lignumvitae Key Botanical State Park   ISLAND
(☑305-664-2540; www.floridastateparks.org/lignumvitaekey; admission $2.50, tour $2; ☺tours 10am & 2pm Fri-Sun) It'll feel like just you and about a jillion mosquitoes on this bayside island park, with virgin tropical forests and the 1919 Matheson House. Come for the shipwrecked isolation. Robbie's Marina offers boat rentals and tours.

Florida Keys History of Diving Museum   MUSEUM
(☑305-664-9737; www.divingmuseum.org; MM 83; adult/child $12/6; ☺10am-5pm) Don't miss this collection of diving paraphernalia from around the world, including diving 'suits' and technology from the 19th century. This charmingly eccentric museum embodies the quirky Keys.

Windley Key Fossil Reef Geological State Site   PARK
(☑305-664-2540; www.floridastateparks.org/windleykey; MM 85.5 oceanside; admission $2.50, tour $2; ☺8am-5pm, closed Tue & Wed) Wander through layer after layer of geological history in the quarry, with 8ft walls of fossilized coral. Tours are offered Friday to Sunday at 10am and 2pm.

Anne's Beach   BEACH
(MM 73.5 oceanside) The area's best public beach; shaded picnic tables and a ribbon of sand.

★ Robbie's Marina   MARINA
(☑305-664-8070; www.robbies.com; MM 77.5 bayside; half-day kayak & canoe rentals $40-75; ☺9am-8pm) This marina/roadside attraction offers the buffet of boating options: fishing charters, jet skiing, party boats, ecotours, snorkeling trips, kayak rentals and more (come here to visit the area's island parks). At a minimum, stop to feed the freakishly large tarpon from the dock ($3 per bucket, $1 to watch), and sift the flea market/tourist shop for tacky seaside trinkets.

Theater of the Sea   DOLPHIN ENCOUNTER
(☑305-664-2431; www.theaterofthesea.com; MM 84.7 bayside; adult/child 3-10 $30/21; ☺9:30am-5pm) Dolphins and sea lions perform in an intimate, close-up setting, and for an extra fee you can meet or swim with them.

⌂ Sleeping

Long Key State Recreation Area   CAMPGROUND $
(☑305-664-4815, 305-326-3521; www.floridastateparks.org/longkey; MM 67.5; campsite/RV site both $38.50) Book as far ahead as possible for the 60 coveted oceanfront campsites in this shady 965-acre park.

Lime Tree Bay Resort Motel   MOTEL $$
(☑800-723-4519, 305-664-4740; www.limetreebayresort.com; MM 68.5 bayside; r $135-175, ste $185-395) A plethora of hammocks and lawn chairs provide front-row seats for the spectacular sunsets at this 2.5-acre waterfront hideaway.

Ragged Edge Resort   RESORT $$
(☑305-852-5389; www.ragged-edge.com; 243 Treasure Harbor Rd; apt $69-259; P✳☀) Swim off the docks at this happily unpretentious oceanfront complex off MM 86.5. It has 10 spotless and popular studios and apartments, and a happily comatose vibe.

Casa Morada   HOTEL $$$
(☑888-881-3030, 305-664-0044; www.casamorada.com; 136 Madeira Rd, off MM 82.2; ste incl breakfast $279-659; P✳☀) Come for a welcome dash of South Beach sophistication mixed with laid-back Keys style. The slick bar is a great oceanside sunset perch.

✗ Eating

★ Midway Cafe   CAFE $
(☑305-664-2622; 80499 Overseas Hwy; menu items $2-11; ☺7am-3pm Thu-Tue, to 2pm Sun; 🖋) Celebrate your Keys adventure with a friendly cup of joe, a smoothie or a treat from the overflowing bakery case. The lovely folks who run this art-filled cafe roast their own beans and make destination-worthy baked goods.

Hog Heaven   BAR $$
(☑305-664-9669; MM 83 oceanside; mains $10-18; ☺11am-4am) From sandwiches and salads to chicken wings and steaks, the diverse menu rocks. Come during happy hour (3pm to 7pm) and bring a designated driver; the drinks are cheap and plentiful.

Morada Bay
AMERICAN $$$

(☑305-664-0604; www.moradabay-restaurant.com; MM 81.6 bayside; mains $14-33; ⊙11:30am-10pm) Grab a table under a palm tree on the white-sand beach and sip a rum drink with your fresh seafood for a lovely, easy-going Caribbean experience. Don't miss the monthly full-moon party.

Grassy Key

To reach Grassy Key in the Middle Keys, you enjoy a vivid sensation of island-hopping, ending with the biggest hop, the **Seven Mile Bridge**, one of the world's longest causeways.

◉ Sights

Dolphin Research Center
WILDLIFE RESERVE

(☑305-289-1121; www.dolphins.org; MM 59 bayside; adult/child under 4yr/child 4-12yr/senior $20/free/15/17.50, swim program $180-650; ⊙9am-4pm) By far the most popular activity on Grassy Key is swimming with the descendants of Flipper. Of all the dolphin swimming spots in the Keys, this one stands out; the dolphins are free to leave the grounds and a lot of marine-biology research goes on behind the (still pretty commercial) tourist activities, such as getting a dolphin to paint your T-shirt or playing 'trainer for a day' ($650).

Marathon

Halfway between Key Largo and Key West, Marathon is the most sizable town; it's a good base and a hub for commercial fishing and lobster boats. Get local information at the **visitor center** (☑305-743-5417; www.floridakeys-marathon.com; MM 53.5 bayside; ⊙9am-5pm).

◉ Sights & Activities

Crane Point Museum
MUSEUM

(www.cranepoint.net; MM 50.5 bayside; adult/child $12.50/8.50; ⊙9am-5pm Mon-Sat, from noon Sun; 🖼) Escape all the development at this 63-acre reserve, where you'll find a vast system of nature trails and mangroves, a raised boardwalk and a rare early-20th-century Bahamian-style house. Kids will enjoy pirate and wreck exhibits, a walk-through coral reef tunnel and the bird hospital.

Pigeon Key National Historic District
ISLAND

(☑305-743-5999; www.pigeonkey.net; tours leave from MM 47 oceanside; adult/child/under 5yr $12/9/free; ⊙tours 10am, noon & 2pm) On the

Marathon side of Seven Mile Bridge, this tiny key served as a camp for the workers who toiled to build the Overseas Hwy in the 1930s. You can tour the historic structures or just sun and snorkel on the beach. Reach it by ferry, included in admission, or walk or bike your way there on the **Old Seven Mile Bridge**, which is closed to traffic but serves as the 'World's Longest Fishing Bridge.'

Sombrero Beach
BEACH

(Sombrero Beach Rd, off MM 50 oceanside) This beautiful little white-sand beach has a playscape, shady picnic spots and big clean bathrooms.

Marathon Kayak
KAYAKING

(☑305-395-0355; www.marathonkayak.com; 3hr tours $60) Kayak Dave is a reliable source for kayak instruction and excellent guided tours.

🛏 Sleeping & Eating

Siesta Motel
MOTEL $

(☑305-743-5671; www.siestamotel.net; MM 51 oceanside; r $75-105; P❋🗲) Head here for one of the cheapest, cleanest flops in the Keys, located in a friendly cluster of cute Marathon homes – with great service, to boot.

Seascape Motel & Marina
MOTEL $$

(☑305-743-6212; www.seascapemotelandmarina.com; 1275 76th St Ocean E, btwn MM 51 & 52; r from $99; P❋🗲🗲) Choose one of the nine crisp, clean rooms or an apartment that sleeps six at this oceanfront hideaway with a waterfront pool, boat dock and barbecue area.

★ Keys Fisheries
SEAFOOD $

(www.keysfisheries.com; 3502 Gulfview Ave; mains $7-16; ⊙11am-9pm) Shoo the seagulls from your picnic table on the deck and dig in to fresh seafood in a down-and-dirty dockside atmosphere. The lobster reuben is the stuff of legend.

Wooden Spoon
AMERICAN $

(7007 Overseas Hwy; menu items $2-10; ⊙5:30am-1:30pm) It's the best breakfast around, served by sweet Southern women who know their way around a diner. The biscuits are fluffy, the sausage gravy is delicious, and the grits buttery and creamy.

Hurricane
AMERICAN $$

(☑305-743-2200; MM 49.5 bayside; mains $9-19; ⊙11am-midnight) As well as being a favorite Marathon bar, the Hurricane also serves an excellent menu of creative South Florida–

inspired goodness, like snapper stuffed with crabmeat and conch sliders jerked in Caribbean seasoning.

Island Fish Co
SEAFOOD $$

(☎305-743-4191; www.islandfishco.com; MM 54 bayside; mains $8-22; ⊙8am-11pm) Grab a spicy bowl of conch chowder and a seat overlooking the water at this huge, open-air tiki hut that has a raw bar and copious fish specialties.

Lower Keys

The Lower Keys (MM 46 to MM 0) are fierce bastions of Conch culture in all its variety. The **chamber of commerce** (☎305-872-2411; www.lowerkeyschamber.com; MM 31 oceanside; ⊙9am-5pm Mon-Fri, 9am-3pm Sat) is on Big Pine Key.

One of Florida's most acclaimed beaches – and certainly the best in the Keys for its shallow, warm water – is at **Bahia Honda State Park** (☎305-872-3210; www.bahiahondapark.com; MM 36.8; per car/motorcycle/cyclist $5/4/2; ⊙8am-sunset; 🐾), a 524-acre park with nature trails, ranger-led programs, watersports rentals and some of the best coral reefs outside Key Largo.

Offshore from **Looe Key** is a marine sanctuary teeming with colorful tropical fish and coral; try **Looe Key Dive Center** (☎305-872-2215; www.diveflakeys.com; snorkel/dive $44/84) on Ramrod Key for snorkeling and diving day trips, including wreck drives.

Overnight camping at **Bahia Honda State Park** (☎305-872-2353; www.reservea-merica.com; MM 37, Bahia Honda Key; sites $36, cabins $160; ℗) is sublime; it'd be perfect except for the sandflies. There are also six popular waterfront cabins. Reserve far ahead for all. For a completely different experience, book one of the four cozily scrumptious rooms at **Deer Run Bed & Breakfast** (☎305-872-2015; www.deerrunfloridabb.com; 1997 Long Beach Dr, Big Pine Key, off MM 33 oceanside; r $235-355; ℗🐾). This state-certified green lodge and vegetarian B&B is a garden of quirky delights, and the owners are extremely helpful.

On Big Pine Key, stop in for a pizza, beer and ambience at **No Name Pub** (☎305-872-9115; N Watson Blvd, Big Pine Key, off MM 30.5 bayside; mains $7-18; ⊙11am-11pm) – if you can find it. The quirky hideout is right before the causeway that gets you to **No Name Key**. While you're there, staple a dollar bill to the wall to contribute to the collection of approximately $60,000 wallpapering the room.

Key West

Key West's funky, laid-back vibe has long attracted artists, renegades and free spirits. In the words of one local: 'It's like they shook the United States and all the nuts fell to the bottom.' Part of that independent streak is rooted in Key West's geography: it's barely connected to the USA, and it's closer to Cuba than to the rest of the States. There's only one road in, and it's not on the way to anywhere. In other words, it's an easy place to do your own thing.

Originally called 'Cayo Hueso' – Spanish for 'Bone Island' – Key West was named for all the skeletons early explorers found littering the beach. Since then, the island has enjoyed a long and colorful history that includes pirates, sunken treasures, literary legends and lots of ghosts.

These days, people flock to Key West to soak up the sun, the mellow atmosphere and more than a little booze. They listen to tales of the past. They snorkel the crystal clear water. And they find their internal clocks set to 'island time.'

⊙ Sights

Key West has more than its fair share of historic homes, buildings and districts (like the colorful Bahama Village); it's a walkable town that rewards exploring. Naturally, you'll snap a pic at the USA's much ballyhooed **Southernmost Point Marker**, even though it's not technically the southernmost point in the USA. (That distinction goes to a point about half a mile down the beach, but since it's part of a naval air station, it's hardly tourist-friendly.)

★ Mallory Square
SQUARE

Sunset at Mallory Sq, at the end of Duval St, is a bizzaro attraction of the highest order. It takes all those energies, subcultures and oddities of Keys life – the hippies, the rednecks, the foreigners and the tourists – and focuses them into one torchlit, playfully edgy (but family-friendly) street party. Come for the jugglers, fire-eaters, sassy acrobats and tightrope-walking dogs, and stay for the after-dark madness.

Duval Street
STREET

Key West locals have a love–hate relationship with their island's most famous road. Duval, Old Town Key West's main drag, is a miracle mile of booze, tacky everything and awful behavior that still manages, somehow, to be fun. At the end of the night, the 'Duval Crawl' is one of the best pub crawls in the country.

Hemingway House
HOUSE

(☎305-294-1136; www.hemingwayhome.com; 907 Whitehead St; adult/child $13/6; ☉9am-5pm) Ernest Hemingway lived in this Spanish-Colonial house from 1931 to 1940 – to write, drink and fish, if not always in that order. Tours run every half-hour, and as you listen to docent-spun yarns of Papa, you'll see his studio, his unusual pool, and the descendents of his six-toed cats languishing in the sun, on furniture and pretty much wherever they feel like.

Florida Keys
Eco-Discovery Center
MUSEUM

(☎305-809-4750; http://eco-discovery.com/ecokw.html; 35 East Quay Rd; ☉9am-4pm Tue-Sat; P⊛) FREE This excellent nature center pulls together all the plants, animals and habitats that make up the Keys' unique ecosystem and presents them in fresh, accessible ways. A great place for kids and the big picture.

Key West Cemetery
CEMETERY

(cnr Margaret & Angela Sts; ☉7am - 6pm; ⊛) This dark, alluring Gothic labyrinth is in the center of town. Livening up the mausoleums are famous epitaphs like 'I told you I was sick.'

Key West Butterfly &
Nature Conservatory
ANIMAL SANCTUARY

(☎305-296-2988; www.keywestbutterfly.com; 1316 Duval St; adult/child 4-12 $12/8.50; ☉9am-5pm; ⊛) Even if you have only the faintest interest in butterflies, you'll find yourself entranced by the sheer quantity flittering around you here.

Museum of Art & History
at the Custom House
MUSEUM

(☎305-295-6616; www.kwahs.com/customhouse; 281 Front St; adult/child $7/5; ☉9:30am-4:30pm) Offering a more low-key, less swashbuckling version of Key West history, this is an interesting collection of folklore, international art and historical exhibits housed in the impressive former Customs House.

Fort East Martello
Museum & Gardens
MUSEUM

(☎305-296-3913; www.kwahs.com/martello.htm; 3501 S Roosevelt Blvd; adult/child $7/5; ☉9:30am-4:30pm) This fortress preserves interesting historical artifacts and some fabulous folk art by Mario Sanchez and 'junk' sculptures

by Stanley Papio. But Martello's most famous resident is Robert the Doll – a genuinely creepy, supposedly haunted, 19th-century doll that's kept in a glass case to keep him from making mischief.

🏃 Activities

Seeing as how you're out in the middle of the ocean, getting out on or in the water is one of the top activities. Charters abound for everything from fishing to snorkeling to scuba diving, including dive trips to the USS Vandenberg, a 522-foot transport ship sunk off the coast to create the world's second largest artificial reef.

Fort Zachary Taylor
BEACH

(www.floridastateparks.org/forttaylor; 601 Howard England Way; per car/pedestrian $6/2; ☉8am-sunset) Key West has three city beaches, but they aren't special; most people head to Bahia Honda. That said, Fort Zachary Taylor has the best beach on Key West, with white sand, decent swimming and some nearshore snorkeling; it's great for sunsets and picnics.

Dive Key West
DIVING

(☎305-296-3823; www.divekeywest.com) Everything you need for wreck-diving trips, from equipment to charters.

★ Jolly Rover
CRUISE

(☎305-304-2235; www.schoonerjollyrover.com; cnr Greene & Elizabeth Sts, Schooner Wharf; cruise $45) Set sail on a pirate-esque schooner offering daytime and sunset cruises.

Reelax Charters
KAYAKING

(☎305-304-1392; www.keyskayaking.com; MM 17 Sugarloaf Key Marina; kayak trips $240) Take a guided kayak tour from nearby Sugarloaf Key.

Sunny Days Catamaran
SNORKELING

(☎866-878-2223; www.sunnydayskeywest.com; 201 Elizabeth St; adult/child $35/22) Our favorite for snorkel trips, water sports and other aquatic adventures.

Clearly Unique
KAYAKING

(☎877-282-5327; www.clearlyuniquecharters.com) Rents out glass-bottomed kayaks, providing a unique view of the water.

👉 Tours

Both the Conch Tour Train (☎305-294-5161; www.conchtourtrain.com; adult/child under 13yr/senior $29/free/26; ☉tours 9am-4:30pm; ⊛)

and **Old Town Trolley** (🖉 305-296-6688; www.
trolleytours.com/key-west; adult/child under 13yr/
senior $29/free/26; ⊙ tours 9am-4:30pm; 🐾)
offer tours leaving from Mallory Sq. The
train offers a 90-minute narrated tour in a
breezy, open car, while the hop-on, hop-off
trolley makes 12 stops around town.

Original Ghost Tours
GHOST

(🖉 305-294-9255; www.hauntedtours.com; adult/
child $15/10; ⊙ 8pm & 9pm) Is your guesthouse
haunted? Probably. Why should you fear
Robert the Doll in East Martello? You're
about to find out.

✹ Festivals & Events

Key West hosts a party every sunset, but
residents don't need an excuse to go crazy.

Conch Republic
Independence Celebration
CULTURE

(www.conchrepublic.com) A 10-day tribute to
Conch Independence, held every April; vie
for (made-up) public offices and watch a
drag queens footrace.

Hemingway Days Festival
CULTURE

(www.hemingwaydays.net) Includes a bull run,
marlin tournament and look-alike contest,
as well as literary events, in late July.

Fantasy Fest
CULTURE

(www.fantasyfest.net) Room rates get hiked to
the hilt for this raucous, 10-day Halloween-
meets-Carnivale event in late October.

🛏 Sleeping

Key West lodging is generally pretty expensive – especially in the wintertime and even
more especially during special events, when
room rates can triple. Book ahead, or you
may well end up joining the long traffic jam
headed back to the mainland.

You can find chain motels in New Town,
but you've got to stay in Old Town to truly
experience Key West. Visit the **Key West
Innkeepers Association** (www.keywestinns.
com) for more guesthouses; pretty much all
are gay-friendly.

Caribbean House
GUESTHOUSE $

(🖉 305-296-0999; www.caribbeanhousekw.com;
226 Petronia St; summer $89, winter $119-139;
🅿 ❄ @) In the heart of Bahama Village,
rooms are tiny, but they're clean, cozy and
cheery. Add free breakfast and welcoming
hosts and you get a rare find in Key West:
a bargain.

★ Key West Bed & Breakfast
B&B $$

(🖉 800-438-6155, 305-296-7274; www.keywest-
bandb.com; 415 William St; r summer $79-155,
winter $89-265; ❄ 🛜) Sunny, airy and full of
artistic touches: hand-painted pottery here,
a working loom there – is that a ship's mast-
head in the corner? There are also a range of
rooms to fit every budget.

L'Habitation
GUESTHOUSE $$

(🖉 305-293-9203; www.lhabitation.com; 408 Ea-
ton St; r $119-189; ❄ 🛜) At this beautiful clas-
sic Keys cottage, the friendly, bilingual owners welcome guests in English or French.
The cute rooms come kitted out in light
tropical shades, with lamps that look like
contemporary art pieces and skittles-bright
quilts.

Key Lime Inn
HOTEL $$

(🖉 800-549-4430; www.historickeywestinns.com;
725 Truman Ave; r $99-229; 🅿 🛜 ❄) These cozy
cottages are scattered around a tropical
hardwood backdrop. Inside, the blissfully
cool rooms are greener than a jade mine,
with wicker furniture and tiny flat-screens
to keep you from ever leaving.

Mermaid & the Alligator
GUESTHOUSE $$$

(🖉 305-294-1894; www.kwmermaid.com; 729 Truman Ave; r summer $168-228, winter $258-328,
🅿 ❄ @ 🛜 ❄) Book way ahead: with only
nine rooms, this place's charm exceeds its
capacity. It's chock-a-block with treasures
collected from the owners' travels, giving it a
worldly flair that's simultaneously European
and Zen.

Curry Mansion Inn
HOTEL $$$

(🖉 305-294-5349; www.currymansion.com; 511
Caroline St; r summer $195-285, winter $240-
365; 🅿 ❄ 🛜 ❄) In a city full of stately 19th-
century homes, the Curry Mansion is espe-
cially handsome. It's a pleasing mix of aris-
tocratic American elements, but especially
the bright Floridian rooms with canopied
beds. Enjoy bougainvillea and breezes on
the verandah.

Big Ruby's Guesthouse
HOTEL $$$

(🖉 305-296-2323; www.bigrubys.com; 409 Appelrouth Lane; r $179-499; 🅿 ❄ 🛜 ❄) Catering
exclusively to a gay clientele, the hotel's exterior is all refined Conch mansion, while
inside, the rooms are sleekly contemporary.
The capper is the clothing-optional lagoon
pool. Breakfast is included.

FLORIDA KEYS FLORIDA FLORIDA KEYS

GAY & LESBIAN KEY WEST

Gay and lesbian visitors can get information at the **Gay & Lesbian Community Center** (☑ 305-292-3223; www.glcckeywest.org; 513 Truman Ave). While you'll find the entire island extraordinarily welcoming, several bars and guesthouses cater specifically to a gay clientele. Toast your arrival in town at one of the following:

801 Bourbon Bar (www.801bourbon. com; 801 Duval St), where boys will be boys.

Aqua (☑ 305-294-0555; www.aquakeywest.com; 711 Duval St) caters to both gays and lesbians.

Pearl's Patio (☑ 305-292-1450; www. pearlsrainbow.com; 525 United St; ☺ noon-10pm Sun-Thu, to midnight Fri & Sat) is a lesbian bar at Pearl's Guesthouse.

✖ Eating

You aren't technically allowed to leave the island without sampling the conch fritters – like hushpuppies, but made with conch – or the key lime pie, made with key limes, sweetened condensed milk, eggs and sugar on a Graham-cracker crust.

Help Yourself Organic Foods   VEGETARIAN $
(☑ 315-296-7766; www.helpyourselfcafe.com; 829 Fleming St; dishes $5-12; ☺ 8am-6pm) Vegetarian, vegan and gluten-free options abound in this cute, colorful cafe that serves wraps, salads, smoothies and other hippified offerings – a nice break from fried fish and key lime pie.

Camille's   FUSION $$
(☑ 305-296-4811; www.camilleskeywest.com; 1202 Simonton St; breakfast & lunch $4-13, dinner $15-25; ☺ 8am-3pm & 6-10pm; ☑) Ditch Duval St and dine with the locals at Camille's; this healthy and tasty neighborhood joint is where local families go for a casual meal. Their inventive menu ranges from French toast with Godiva liqueur to tasty chicken salad.

El Siboney   CUBAN $$
(900 Catherine St; mains $8-16; ☺ 11am-9:30pm) Key West is only 90 miles from Cuba, so this awesome rough-and-ready corner establishment is quite literally the closest you can get to real Cuban food in the US. Cash only.

Mo's Restaurant   CARIBBEAN $$
(☑ 305-296-8955; 1116 White St; mains $6-17; ☺ 11am-10pm Mon-Sat) If the phrase 'Caribbean home cooking' causes drool to form in the corners of your mouth, don't hesitate. The dishes are mainly Haitian, and they're delicious.

BO's Fish Wagon   SEAFOOD $$
(☑ 305-294-9272; 801 Caroline St; mains $8-22; ☺ 11am-9pm) This looks like the backyard shed of a crazy old fisherman (but in a good way). Fried fish, conch fritters and cold beer – not to mention great prices – will win over any scaredy-cats in your group.

★**Blue Heaven**   AMERICAN $$$
(☑ 305-296-8666; http://blueheavenkw.homestead.com; 729 Thomas St; dinner $17-35; ☺ 8am-4pm, until 2pm Sun & 5-10:30pm daily) One of the island's quirkiest venues (and it's a high bar), where you dine in an outdoor courtyard with a flock of chickens. Customers gladly wait, bemusedly, for Blue Heaven's well-executed, Southern-fried interpretation of Keys cuisine.

★**Café Solé**   FRENCH $$$
(☑ 305-294-0230; www.cafesole.com; 1029 Southard St; dinner $20-34; ☺ 5:30-10pm) Conch carpaccio with capers? Yellowtail fillet and foie gras? Oh yes. This locally and critically acclaimed venue is known for its cozy backporch ambience and innovative menus, the result of a French-trained chef exploring island ingredients.

🍷 Drinking & Entertainment

Hopping (or staggering) from one bar to the next – also known as the 'Duval Crawl (p483)' – is a favorite pastime here in the Conch Republic, and there are plenty of options for your drinking pleasure.

★**Green Parrot**   BAR
(www.greenparrot.com; 601 Whitehead St; ☺ 10am-4am) This rogue's cantina has the longest tenure of any bar on the island (since 1890). It's a fabulous dive drawing a lively mix of locals and out-of-towners, with a century's worth of strange decor. Men, don't miss the urinal.

Captain Tony's Saloon   BAR
(www.capttonyssaloon.com; 428 Greene St) This former icehouse, morgue and Hemingway haunt is built around the town's old hanging tree. The eclectic decor includes emancipated bras and signed dollar bills.

Porch
BAR

(www.theporchkw.com; 429 Caroline St; ⊙10am-2am Mon-Sat, noon-2am Sun) Escape the Duval St frat boy bars at the Porch, where knowledgeable bartenders dispense artisan beers. It sounds civilized, and almost is, by Key West standards.

Garden of Eden
BAR

(224 Duval St) You can make like Adam and Eve at this clothing-optional rooftop bar; the fig leaf is also optional.

Virgilio's
JAZZ

(www.virgilioskeywest.com; 524 Duval St) Thank God for a little variety. This town needs a dark, candlelit martini lounge where you can chill to jazz and salsa. Enter on Appelrouth Lane.

La Te Da
CABARET

(www.lateda.com; 1125 Duval St) While the outside bar is where locals gather for mellow chats over beer, you can catch high-quality drag acts – big names come here from around the country – upstairs at the fabulous Crystal Room on weekends. More low-key cabaret acts grace the downstairs lounge.

ℹ Information

A great trip-planning resource is www.fla-keys. com/keywest. In town, get maps and brochures at **Key West Chamber of Commerce** (☑305-294-2587; www.keywestchamber.org; 510 Greene St; ⊙8:30am-6:30pm Mon-Sat, to 6pm Sun).

ℹ Getting There & Around

The easiest way to travel around Key West and the Keys is by car, though traffic along the one major route, US 1, can be maddening during the winter high season. **Greyhound** (☑305-296-9072; www.greyhound.com; 3535 S Roosevelt Blvd) serves the Keys along US Hwy 1 from downtown Miami.

You can fly into **Key West International Airport** (EYW; www.keywestinternationalairport. com) with frequent flights from major cities, most going through Miami. Or, take a fast catamaran from Fort Myers or Miami; call the **Key West Express** (☑888-539-2628; www. seakeywestexpress.com; adult/child round-trip $146/81, one-way $86/58) for schedules and fares; discounts apply for advance booking.

Within Key West, bicycles are the preferred mode of travel (rentals along Duval St run $10 to $25 per day). **City Transit** (☑305-600-1455; www.kwtransit.com; tickets $2) runs color-coded buses through downtown and the Lower Keys.

ATLANTIC COAST

Florida's Atlantic Coast isn't all beach volleyball, surfing and lazing in the sun. It offers travelers a remarkably well-rounded experience, with something for everyone from history buffs to thrill seekers to art lovers.

WORTH A TRIP

DRY TORTUGAS

Seventy miles west of the Keys in the middle of the Gulf, **Dry Tortugas National Park** (☑305-242-7700; www.nps.gov/drto; adult/15yr and under $5/free) is America's most inaccessible national park. Reachable only by boat or plane, it rewards your efforts to get there with amazing snorkeling, diving, bird-watching and stargazing.

Ponce de León christened the area Tortugas (tor-too-guzz) after the sea turtles he found here, and the 'Dry' part was added later to warn about the absence of fresh water on the island. But this is more than just a pretty cluster of islands with no drinking water. The never-completed Civil War-era **Fort Jefferson** provides a striking hexagonal centerpiece of red brick rising up from the emerald waters on **Garden Key**, meaning along with your bottled water, you should definitely bring your camera.

So how do you get there? **Yankee Freedom** (☑800-634-0939, 305-294-7009; www. yankeefreedom.com; Historic Seaport) is a fast ferry that leaves from the north end of Grinnell St in Key West; fare includes breakfast, a picnic lunch, snorkeling gear and tour of the fort. Or, you can hop on a **Key West Seaplane** (☑305-293-9300; www.keywestsea-planecharters.com/; half-day trip adult/child 3-12 $280/224) for a half-day or full-day trip. Whichever you choose, reserve at least a week ahead.

If you really want to enjoy the isolation, stay overnight at one of Garden Key's 13 **campsites** (per person $3). Reserve early through the park office, and bring everything you need, because once that boat leaves, you're on your own.

Space Coast

The Space Coast's main claim to fame (other than being the setting for the iconic 1960s TV series *I Dream of Jeannie*) is being the real-life home to the Kennedy Space Center and its massive visitor complex. Cocoa Beach is also a magnet for surfers, with Florida's best waves. Visitor information is available through **Florida's Space Coast Office of Tourism** (☑ 321-433-4470; www.visitspacecoast.com; 430 Brevard Ave, Cocoa Village; ⊙ 8am-5pm Mon-Sat).

◉ Sights

Kennedy Space Center Visitor Complex   MUSEUM

(☑ 321-449-4444; www.kennedyspacecenter.com; adult/child $50/40, parking $10; ⊙ 9am-5pm) Once a working space-flight facility, Kennedy Space Center is shifting from a living museum to a historical one since the end of NASA's space shuttle program in 2011. Devote most of your day to the new **Space Shuttle Atlantis** attraction, IMAX theaters and **Rocket Garden**, featuring replicas of classic rockets towering over the complex. And don't miss the **Shuttle Launch Simulator**, which reaches a top 'speed' of 17,500mph and feels just like a space-shuttle takeoff (but without the teary goodbyes). But first take the hop-on, hop-off bus tour of working NASA facilities that depart every 15 minutes from 10am to 2:45pm.

Add-on options abound, depending on how serious you are about your astronaut experience (they're popular – book in advance). Hungry space enthusiasts can have **Lunch with an Astronaut** (☑ 866-737-5235; adult/child $30/16), and the action-oriented **Astronaut Training Experience** (ticket $145) prepares you for space flight, should the opportunity arise.

★ **Merritt Island National Wildlife Refuge**   WILDLIFE RESERVE

(www.fws.gov/merrittisland; I-95 exit 80; ⊙ park dawn-dusk; visitor center 8am-4:30pm Mon-Fri, 9am-5pm Sat & Sun, closed Sun Apr-Oct) This unspoiled 140,000-acre refuge is one of the country's best birding spots, especially from October to May (early morning and after 4pm). More endangered and threatened species of wildlife inhabit the swamps, marshes and hardwood hammocks here than at any other site in the continental US. The best viewing is on Black Point Wildlife Dr.

Canaveral National Seashore   PARK

(☑ 321-267-1110; www.nps.gov/cana; car/bike $5/1; ⊙ dawn-dusk) The 24 miles of pristine, windswept beaches comprise the longest stretch of undeveloped beach on Florida's east coast. On the north end is family-friendly **Apollo Beach**, which shines in a class of its own with gentle surf and miles of solitude. On the south end, **Playalinda Beach** is surfer central. And in between the two is untrammeled **Klondike Beach**, a favorite of campers and nature lovers.

Mosquito Lagoon, with islands and mangroves teeming with wildlife, hugs the west side of the barrier island. Rent kayaks in Cocoa Beach. Rangers offer pontoon boat tours (per person $20) from the visitor information center on most Sundays. From June through August, rangers lead groups on nightly sea turtle nesting tours (adult/child 8-16yr $14/free; 7am-11:30pm); reservations required.

✴ Activities

Despite all the sunshine and shoreline, Florida is no *Endless Summer*. The water around Miami tends to stay flat, and much of the Gulf Coast is too protected to get much of a swell. But the 70 miles of beaches from New Smyrna to Sebastian Inlet are surfer central. Ten-time world champion surfer Kelly Slater was born in Cocoa Beach, which remains the epicenter of the surf community. For the local scene and surf reports, visit **Florida Surfing** (www.floridasurfing.com) and **Surf Guru** (www.surfguru.com).

Ron Jon's Surf Shop   WATER SPORTS

(☑ 321-799-8888; 4151 N Atlantic Ave; ⊙ 24 hrs) Rents just about anything water-related from fat-tired beach bikes ($15 daily) to surfboards ($30 daily).

Ron Jon Surf School   SURFING

(☑ 321-868-1980; www.cocoabeachsurfingschool.com; 150 E Columbia Lane, Cocoa Beach; per hr $50-65) The best surf school in Cocoa Beach for all ages and levels is the state's largest, Ron Jon Surf School run by ex-pro surfer and Kelly Slater coach, Craig Carroll.

Cocoa Beach Jetski Rentals   BOATING

(☑ 321-454-7661; http://cocoabeachjetskirentals.com; 1872 E 520 Causeway, Cocoa Beach; kayaks/jet skis per hr $20/90; ⊙ 8:45am-5pm) Rent boats, kayaks, surfboards – and of course jetskis. You can even buy live bait.

🛏 Sleeping

Charming Cocoa Beach has the most options, as well as the most chains. For a quieter stay, Vero Beach is also attractive.

Fawlty Towers   MOTEL $
(☑ 321-784-3870; www.fawltytowersresort.com; 100 E Cocoa Beach Causeway, Cocoa Beach; r $72-92; P ❋ 🎇 🛜 🌊) Beneath this motel's gloriously garish and extremely pink exterior lie fairly straightforward rooms with an unbeatable beachside location; quiet pool and tiki bar.

South Beach Place   MOTEL $$
(☑ 772-231-5366; www.southbeachplacevero.com; 1705 S Ocean Dr, Vero Beach; ste per day $125-175, per week $700-1100; 🛜 🌊) Old Florida with a facelift, this tasteful and bright two-story motel in Vero Beach sits in a particularly quiet stretch across from the beach. One-bedroom suites have a full kitchen.

Beach Place Guesthouses   APARTMENT $$$
(☑ 321-783-4045; www.beachplaceguesthouses.com; 1445 S Atlantic Ave, Cocoa Beach; ste $195-395; 🛜) A slice of heavenly relaxation in Cocoa Beach's partying beach scene, this laid-back two-story guesthouse in a residential neighborhood has roomy suites with hammocks and a lovely deck, all just steps from the dunes and beach.

🍴 Eating

Simply Delicious   CAFE $
(125 N Orlando Ave, Cocoa Beach; mains $6-12; ⊙ 8am-3pm Tue-Sat, to 2pm Sun) You can't miss this little yellow house on the southbound stretch of A1A. It's a homey Americana place – nothing fancy, nothing trendy, just simply delicious.

Slow and Low Barbecue   BARBECUE $$
(http://slowandlowbarbeque.com; 306 N Orlando Ave, Cocoa Beach; mains $7-15; ⊙ 11am-10pm Mon-Sat, from noon Sun) After a day on the beach, nothing satisfies better than a plate overflowing with barbecue ribs, fried okra, turnip greens and sweet fried potatoes. There's a daily happy hour and live music Thursday through Sunday.

Fat Snook   SEAFOOD $$$
(☑ 321-784-1190; http://thefatsnook.com; 2464 S Atlantic Ave, Cocoa Beach; mains $22-36; ⊙ 5:30-10pm) Hidden inside an uninspired building, yet sporting cool, minimalist decor, tiny Fat Snook stands out as an oasis of fine cooking. Yes, there's a distinct air of food snobbery here, but it's so tasty, no one seems to mind.

> **3-2-1...BLASTOFF**
> Along the Space Coast, even phone calls get a countdown, thanks to the local area code: 321. It's no coincidence; in 1999 residents led by Robert Osband petitioned to get the digits in honor of the rocket launches that took place at Cape Canaveral.

Maison Martinique   FRENCH $$$
(☑ 772-231-7299; Caribbean Court Hotel, 1603 S Ocean Dr, Vero Beach; mains $24-42; ⊙ 5-10pm Tue-Sat) In Vero Beach, outstanding French cuisine with first-rate service and intimate surrounds. On warm evenings, eat by the little pool; for something more casual, head to the piano bar upstairs.

ℹ Getting There & Away

From Orlando take Hwy 528 east, which connects with Hwy A1A. **Greyhound** (www.greyhound.com) has services from West Palm Beach and Orlando to Titusville. **Vero Beach Shuttle** (☑ 772-200-7427; www.verobeachshuttle.com) provides shuttle service from area airports.

Daytona Beach

With typical Floridian hype, Daytona Beach bills itself as 'The World's Most Famous Beach.' But its fame is less about quality than the size of the parties this expansive beach has witnessed during spring break, Speed-Weeks, and motorcycle events when half a million bikers roar into town. One Daytona title no one disputes is 'Birthplace of NASCAR,' which started here in 1947. Its origins go back as far as 1902 to drag races held on the beach's hard-packed sands.

The **Daytona Beach Convention & Visitors Bureau** (☑ 386-255-0415; www.daytonabeach.com; 126 E Orange Ave; ⊙ 9am-5pm Mon-Fri) has great lodging listings. Gay and lesbian travelers can visit www.gaydaytona.com.

⊙ Sights & Activities

Museum of Arts & Sciences   MUSEUM
(www.moas.org; 1040 Museum Blvd; adult/student $13/7; ⊙ 9am-5pm Tue-Sat, from 11am Sun) A wonderful mishmash of everything from Cuban art to Coca-Cola relics to a 13ft giant sloth skeleton.

FLORIDA DAYTONA BEACH

Ponce Inlet Lighthouse
& Museum
LIGHTHOUSE

(www.ponceinlet.org; 4931 S Peninsula Dr; adult/child $5/1.50; ☺ 10am-6pm winter, to 9pm summer) About 6 miles south of Daytona Beach, it's 203 steps to the top of Florida's tallest lighthouse.

Daytona Beach
BEACH

(per car $5) This stretch of sand was once the city's raceway. You can still drive sections at a strictly enforced top speed of 10mph. Or rent an ATV, fat-tired cruiser or recumbent trike. Water sports rentals are ubiquitous.

Daytona International
Speedway
RACETRACK

(☏ 800-748-7467; www.daytonaintlspeedway.com; 1801 W International Speedway Blvd; tickets from $20, adult tours $16-23, child 6-12 $10-17) The Holy Grail of raceways has a diverse race schedule. Ticket prices accelerate rapidly for the big races, headlined by the **Daytona 500** in February, but you can wander the massive stands for free on nonrace days. Two first-come, first-served **tram tours** take in the track, pits and behind-the-scenes areas. Real fanatics can indulge in the **Richard Petty Driving Experience** (☏ 800-237-3889; www.drivepetty.com), where you can either ride shotgun ($84 to $135) around the track or take a day to become the driver ($550 to $3200); check schedule online.

🛌 Sleeping

Daytona lodging is plentiful and spans all budgets and styles. Prices soar during events; book well ahead.

Shores
RESORT $$

(☏ 386-767-7350; www.shoresresort.com; 2637 N Atlantic Ave; r from $109; ⓟ❄️📶🏊) One of Daytona's most elegant offerings, this chic, beachfront boutique has hand-striped walls, a full-service spa and sophisticated color palette.

⭐ August Seven Inn
B&B $$

(☏ 386-248-8420; www.jpaugust.net; 1209 S Peninsula Dr; r $140-225; ⓟ❄️📶🏊) The friendly innkeepers of this gorgeous B&B have stocked it with period antiques and stylish deco, creating a soothing haven from Daytona's typical Nascar-and-spring-break carnival.

Tropical Manor
RESORT $$

(☏ 386-252-4920; www.tropicalmanor.com; 2237 S Atlantic Ave; r $80-315; ⓟ❄️📶🏊) This beachfront property is vintage Florida, with motel rooms, studios and cottages all blanketed in a frenzy of murals and bright pastels.

Sun Viking Lodge
RESORT $$

(☏ 800-815-2846; www.sunviking.com; 2411 S Atlantic Ave; r $79-259; ⓟ❄️📶🏊) Most rooms have kitchenettes, but they could stand a reno – oh never mind. For families, it's ideal: two pools, a 60ft waterslide, beach access, shuffleboard, endless activities and a Viking theme!

✗ Eating & Drinking

Dancing Avocado Kitchen
MEXICAN $

(110 S Beach St; mains $6-10; ☺ 8am-4pm Tue-Sat; ✈️) Fresh, healthful Mexican dishes like extreme burritos and quesadillas dominate the menu at this vegetarian-oriented cafe, but the signature Dancing Avocado Melt is tops.

Pasha
MIDDLE EASTERN $

(www.pashamideastcafe.com; 919 W International Speedway Blvd; mains $5-14; ☺ 11am-7:30pm Mon-Sat) Bread unchanged since it opened in the '70s, this place combines an Aladdin's cave deli of imported Middle Eastern goods and a cafe with authentic dishes like Armenian breaded cheese pie and platters served with the owner's grandma's pita bread.

Aunt Catfish's on the River
SOUTHERN $$

(☏ 386-767-4768; www.auntcatfishontheriver.com; 4009 Halifax Dr, Port Orange; mains $8-25; ☺ 11:30am-9pm Mon-Sat, from 9am Sun) Southern-style seafood lolling in butter and Cajun-spice catfish make this place insanely popular.

The Cellar
ITALIAN $$$

(☏ 386-258-0011; www.thecellarrestaurant.com; 220 Magnolia Ave; mains $19-37; ☺ 5-10pm Tue-Sun) Classic, upscale Italian fare and elegant ambience (located in the summer mansion of 29th US President Warren G Harding) has made this go-to spot for special-occasion dinners. Reservations recommended.

🍷 Drinking & Entertainment

Daytona's entertainment scene skews to rocking biker bars (mostly along Main St) and high-octane dance clubs (on or near Seabreeze Blvd).

Froggy's Saloon
BAR

(www.froggyssaloon.net; 800 Main St) Outside this train wreck of a bar, a bone chopper gleams in the window. Inside, a sign asks, 'Ain't drinking fun?' You better believe they mean it: opening at 7am, this is Party Central for bikers and others who want to go bonkers. Expect to see flashing chicks, smoky beards and more leather than on an African safari.

Razzles CLUB
(www.razzlesnightclub.com; 611 Seabreeze Blvd; ☺8pm-3am) The reigning dance club, permanently thumping.

ⓘ Getting There & Around

Daytona Beach International Airport (☑386-248-8030; www.flydaytonafirst.com; 700 Catalina Dr) is just east of the Speedway, and the **Greyhound bus station** (www.greyhound.com; 138 S Ridgewood Ave) is the starting point for services around Florida.

Daytona is close to the intersection of two of Florida's major interstates: I-95 is the quickest way to Jacksonville (about 90 miles) and Miami (260 miles), and I-4 leads to Orlando in an hour.

Votran (www.votran.org; fare $1.25) runs buses and trolleys throughout the city.

St Augustine

The first this, the oldest that... St Augustine was founded by the Spanish in 1565, which means it's chock-full of age-related superlatives. Tourists flock here to stroll the ancient streets, and horse-drawn carriages clip-clop past townsfolk dressed in period costume around the National Historic Landmark District, aka the oldest permanent settlement in the US.

At times St Augustine screams, 'Hey, everyone, look how quaint we are!' but it stops just short of feeling like a historic theme park because, well, the buildings and monuments are real, and the narrow, cafe-strewn lanes are genuinely charming. Walk the cobblestoned streets or stand where Juan Ponce de León landed in 1513, and the historical distance occasionally collapses into present-moment chills.

The main **visitor center** (☑904-825-1000; www.ci.st-augustine.fl.us; 10 Castillo Dr; ☺8:30am-5:30pm) screens a 45-minute film on the town's history.

⊙ Sights & Activities

The town's two Henry Flagler buildings shouldn't be missed.

★**Lightner Museum** MUSEUM
(☑904-824-2874; www.lightnermuseum.org; 75 King St; adult/child $10/5; ☺9am-5pm) Flagler's former Hotel Alcazar is now home to this wonderful museum, with a little bit of everything from ornate Gilded Age furnishings to collections of marbles and cigar-box labels.

Hotel Ponce de León HISTORIC BUILDING
(74 King St; tours adult/child $10/1; ☺tours hourly in summer 10am-3pm, 10am & 2pm during school year) This gorgeous former hotel was built in the 1880s and is now the world's most gorgeous dormitory, belonging to Flagler College. Take a guided tour – or at least step inside to gawk at the lobby for free.

Colonial Quarter HISTORIC BUILDINGS
(33 St George St; adult/child $13/7; ☺9am-6pm) See how they did things back in the 18th century at this re-creation of Spanish-Colonial St Augustine, complete with craftspeople demonstrating blacksmithing, leather working and other trades.

Pirate & Treasure Museum MUSEUM
(www.thepiratemuseum.com; 12 S Castillo Dr; adult/child $13/7; ☺9am-8pm; ⊛) A mash-up of theme park and museum, this celebration of all things pirate has real historical treasures (and genuine gold) as well as animatronic pirates, blasting cannons and a kid-friendly treasure hunt.

Castillo de San Marcos National Monument FORT
(☑904-829-6506; www.nps.gov/casa; 1 S Castillo Dr, St Augustine; adult/child under 16 $7/free; ☺8:45am-5:15pm; ⊛) This incredibly photogenic fort is another atmospheric monument to longevity: it's the country's oldest masonry fort, completed by the Spanish in 1695. Park rangers lead programs hourly and shoot off cannons most weekends.

Fountain of Youth HISTORIC SITE
(www.fountainofyouthflorida.com; 11 Magnolia Ave; adult/child 6-12 $12/8; ☺9am-5pm) Step right up for an acrid cup of eternal youth at this 'archaeological park.' As the story goes, Spanish explorer Juan Ponce de León came ashore here in 1513, and he considered this freshwater stream the possible legendary fountain of youth.

Anastasia State Recreation Area PARK
(☑904-461-2033; www.floridastateparks.org; 1340 Hwy A1A; car/bike $8/2; ☺8am-sundown) Locals escape the tourist hordes here, with a terrific beach, a campground (campsites $28) and rentals for all kinds of water sports.

FLORIDA ST AUGUSTINE

☞ Tours

St Augustine City Walks WALKING
(☎904-540-3476; www.staugustinecitywalks.com;
tours $12-49) Extremely fun walking tours of
all kinds, from silly to serious to spooky.

Old Town Trolley Tours TOUR
(☎888-910-8687; www.trolleytours.com; adult/
child 6-12 $23/10) Hop-on, hop-off narrated
trolley tours.

St Augustine Sightseeing Trains TRAIN
(☎904-829-6545; www.redtrains.com; 170 San
Marco Ave; tour adult/child $20/9) Hop-on, hop-
off narrated train tours or get creeped out on
the Ghost Train.

🛏 Sleeping

St Augustine is a popular weekend escape;
expect room rates to rise about 30% on
Friday and Saturday. Inexpensive motels
and chain hotels line San Marco Ave, near
where it meets US Hwy 1. More than two
dozen atmospheric B&Bs can be found at
www.staugustineinns.com.

Pirate Haus Inn HOSTEL $
(☎904-808-1999; www.piratehaus.com; 32 Treasury St; dm $20, r $65-109; P❀⦿) Yar, if ye
don't be needing anything fancy, this family-
friendly European-style guesthouse/hostel
has an unbeatable location and includes a
pirate pancake breakfast.

★ At Journey's End B&B $$
(☎904-829-0076; www.atjourneysend.com; 89 Ce-
dar St; r $149-199; P❀⦿) Free from the granny-
ish decor that haunts many St Augustine
B&Bs, this pet-friendly, kid-friendly and
gay-friendly spot is outfitted in a chic mix
of antiques and modern furniture, and run
by some affable hosts. Breakfast is included.

Casa de Solana B&B $$
(☎877-824-3555; www.casadesolana.com; 21 Aviles
St; r $149-279; P⦿) Just off pedestrian-only
Aviles St in the oldest part of town, this utterly charming little inn remains faithful to
its early-1800s period decor. Rooms are a bit
small, but price and location make it a good
deal.

Casa Monica HISTORIC HOTEL $$$
(☎904-827-1888; www.casamonica.com; 95 Cordova
St; r $179-379; P❀⦿≋) ⦿ Built in 1888, this
is *the* luxe hotel in town, with turrets and
fountains adding to the Spanish-Moorish cas-
tle atmosphere. Rooms are richly appointed,
with wrought-iron beds and every amenity.

✗ Eating & Drinking

St Augustine has a notable dining scene,
though it's also rife with overpriced tourist
traps.

★ Spanish Bakery BAKERY $
(www.thespanishbakery.com; 42½ St George St;
mains $3.50-5.50; ◷9:30am-3pm) Through an
arched gate in a table-filled courtyard, this
diminutive stucco bakeshop serves empana-
das, sausage rolls and other conquistador-era
favorites. Don't hesitate; they sell out quick.

★ Floridian MODERN AMERICAN $$
(☎904-829-0655; www.thefloridianstaug.com;
39 Cordova St; mains $12-20; ◷lunch 11am-3pm
Wed-Mon, dinner 5-9pm Mon-Thu, 5-10pm Fri &
Sat) Though it oozes with hipster-locavore
earnestness, this new farm-to-table restaurant is so friggin' fabulous you won't mind.
The chef-owners serve whimsical neo-
Southern creations in an oh-so-cool dining
room.

Collage INTERNATIONAL $$$
(☎904-829-0055; www.collagestaug.com; 60
Hypolita St; mains $28-38; ◷from 5:30pm) This
upscale spot feels a world away from the
bustling touristy downtown. The seafood-
heavy menu wins raves for its subtle touch
with global flavors.

Scarlett O'Hara's PUB
(www.scarlettoharas.net; 70 Hypolita St; ◷11am-
1am) Good luck grabbing a rocking chair:
the porch of this pine building is packed all
day, every day. Built in 1879, today Scarlett's
serves regulation pub grub, but it's got the
magic ingredients – hopping happy hour,
live entertainment nightly, hardworking
staff, funky bar – that draw folks like spirits
to a séance.

★ Taberna del Gallo BAR
(35 St George St; ◷noon-7pm Sun-Thu, to 11pm Fri
& Sat) Flickering candles provide the only
light at this 1736 stone tavern. Sing sea shan-
ties on weekends.

AlA Ale Works PUB
(www.a1aaleworks.com; 1 King St; ◷11am-11:30pm
Sun-Thu, to midnight Fri & Sat) Who needs histori-
cal ambience with fine-crafted beer like this?

ⓘ Getting There & Around

The **Greyhound bus station** (☎904-829-6401;
52 San Marcos Ave) is just a few blocks north of
the visitor's center. Once you're in Old Town, you
can get almost everywhere on foot.

Jacksonville

Are we there yet? Have we left yet? It's hard to tell, because Jacksonville sprawls out over a whopping 840 sq miles, making it the largest city by area in the continental US (eclipsed only by Anchorage, AK). Jacksonville Beach, known locally as 'Jax Beach,' is about 17 miles east of the city center and is where you'll find white sand and most of the action. For information, peruse www.visitjacksonville.com.

◉ Sights & Activities

★**Cummer Museum
of Art & Gardens** MUSEUM
(www.cummer.org; 829 Riverside Ave; adult/student $10/6; ⏱10am-9pm Tue, to 4pm Wed-Sat, noon-4pm Sun) This handsome museum, Jacksonville's premier cultural space, has a genuinely excellent collection of American and European paintings, Asian decorative art and antiquities.

Museum of Science & History MUSEUM
(www.themosh.org; 1025 Museum Circle; adult/child $10/8; ⏱10am-5pm Mon-Thu, to 8pm Fri, to 6pm Sat, noon-5pm Sun; 🖘) Packing kids? This museum offers dinosaurs, a planetarium and educational exhibits on Jacksonville's cultural and natural history.

**Jacksonville Museum of
Modern Art** MUSEUM
(www.mocajacksonville.org; 333 N Laura St; adult/child $8/5; ⏱11am-5pm Tue-Sat, to 9pm Thu, noon-5pm Sun) The focus of this ultramodern space extends beyond painting: get lost among contemporary sculpture, prints, photography and film.

Jacksonville Landing PROMENADE
(www.jacksonvillelanding.com; 2 Independent Dr) At the foot of the high-rise downtown, this prominent shopping and entertainment district has about 40 mostly touristy shops surrounding a tip-top food court with outdoor tables and regular, free live entertainment.

**Anheuser-Busch
Budweiser Brewery** BREWERY
(www.budweisertours.com; 111 Busch Dr; ⏱10am-4pm Mon-Sat) Enjoy a free tour (and free beer if you're over 21).

🛏 Sleeping & Eating

The cheapest rooms are along I-95 and I-10, where the lower-priced chains congregate. Beach lodging rates often rise in summer.

Riverdale Inn B&B $$
(☑904-354-5080; www.riverdaleinn.com; 1521 Riverside Ave; r $110-190, ste $200-220; P❋☎) In the early 1900s this was one of 50 or so mansions lining Riverside. Now there are only two left, and you're invited to enjoy its lovely rooms with full breakfast.

★**Clark's Fish Camp** SOUTHERN $$
(☑904-268-3474; www.clarksfishcamp.com; 12903 Hood Landing Rd; mains $13-22; ⏱4:30-9:30pm Mon-Thu, 4:30-10pm Fri, 11:30am-10pm Sat, 11:30am-9:30pm Sun) Sample Florida's Southern 'Cracker' cuisine of gator, snake, catfish and frog's legs while surrounded by the animal menagerie of 'America's largest private taxidermy collection.' This swamp shack is unforgettable. It's far south of downtown Jacksonville.

★**Aix** MEDITERRANEAN $$$
(☑904-398-1949; www.bistrox.com; 1440 San Marco Blvd; mains $10-28; ⏱11am-10pm Mon-Thu, to 11pm Fri, 5-11pm Sat, 5-9pm Sun) Dine with the fashionable food mavens at Aix, whose menu bursts with global flavors. Reservations recommended.

River City Brewing Company SEAFOOD $$$
(☑904-398-2299; www.rivercitybrew.com; 835 Museum Circle; mains $19-32; ⏱11am-4pm & 5-10pm Mon-Sat, 10:30am-2:30pm Sun) The perfect place to quaff a microbrew and enjoy some upscale seafood overlooking the water.

☆ Entertainment

Freebird Live LIVE MUSIC
(☑904-246-2473; www.freebirdlive.com; 200 N 1st St; ⏱8pm-2am on show nights) At the beach, a rocking music venue and home of the band Lynyrd Skynyrd.

❶ Getting There & Around

North of the city, **Jacksonville International Airport** (JAX; ☑904-741-4902; www.flyjax.com) has rental cars. **Greyhound** (www.greyhound.com; 10 N Pearl St) serves numerous cities, and **Amtrak** (☑904-766-5110; www.amtrak.com; 3570 Clifford Lane) has trains from the north and south. The **Jacksonville Transportation Authority** (www.jtafla.com) runs the free Skyway monorail and city buses (fare $1.50).

Amelia Island & Around

Residents are quick to tell you: Amelia Island is just as old as that braggart St Augustine – they just can't prove it. Unfortunately, no Ponce de León, no plaque, so they have to content themselves with being a pretty little island of moss-draped Southern charm and home to **Fernandina Beach**, a shrimping village with 40 blocks of historic buildings and romantic B&Bs. Pick up walking-tour maps and information at the **visitor center** (☑ 904-277-0717; www.ameliaisland.com/; 102 Centre St; ⊙ 10am-4pm).

Take a half-hour horse-drawn carriage tour with the **Old Towne Carriage Co** (☑ 904-277-1555; www.ameliacarriagetours.com; half-hour adult/child $15/7). If you'd rather a carriage didn't come between you and your horse, **Kelly's Seahorse Ranch** (☑ 904-491-5166; www.kellyranchinc.com; 1hr rides $60; ⊙ 10am, noon, 2pm & 4pm) offers beachfront trail rides for riders aged 13 and over .

⊙ Sights & Activities

Fort Clinch State Park PARK
(2601 Atlantic Ave; park pedestrian/car $2/6; ⊙ park 8am-sunset, fort 9am-5pm) Capping the north end of the island, the Spanish moss–draped Fort Clinch State Park has beaches, camping ($26), bike trails and a commanding Civil War–era fort, with re-enactments taking place the first full weekend of every month.

Amelia Island
Museum of History MUSEUM
(www.ameliamuseum.org; 233 S 3rd St; adult/student $7/4; ⊙ 10am-4pm Mon-Sat, 1-4pm Sun) Learn about Amelia Island's intricate history, which has seen it ruled under eight different flags starting with the French in 1562. Admission includes tours at 11am and 2pm.

Talbot Islands State Parks PARK
(☑ 904-251-2320; ⊙ 8am-dusk) Amelia Island is part of the Talbot Islands State Parks, which includes the pristine shoreline at Little Talbot Island and the 'boneyard beach' at Big Talbot Island State Park, where silvered tree skeletons create a dramatic landscape. Both are south of Amelia Island down the First Coast Hwy.

🛏 Sleeping

Florida House Inn HOTEL $$
(☑ 904-491-3322; www.floridahouseinn.com; 20 & 22 S 3rd St; r $140-160) Fernandina does beat out St Augustine with Florida's oldest hotel, Florida House Inn, which stays modern with beautifully restored rooms, wi-fi and free use of zippy, red scooters.

Hoyt House B&B $$$
(☑ 800-432-2085, 904-277-4300; www.hoythouse.com; 804 Atlantic Ave; r $239-359; ❋ 🤖 ❋) This tall Victorian, perched on the edge of downtown, boasts an enchanting gazebo that begs time with a cool drink. Ten rooms each have their own stylish mix of antiques and found treasures. Want a really unique stay? The owners will rent out their luxury yacht for overnights.

★ Elizabeth Pointe Lodge B&B $$$
(☑ 904-277-4851; www.elizabethpointelodge.com; 98 S Fletcher Ave; r $225-335, ste $385-470; ❋ 🤖) Located right on the ocean, this lodge looks like an old Nantucket-style sea captain's house with wraparound porches, gracious service and beautifully appointed rooms.

★ Fairbanks House B&B $$$
(☑ 904-277-0500; www.fairbankshouse.com; 227 S 7th St; r $185-240, ste $265-450; ❋ 🤖) This grand, Gothic Victorian is stuffed to the gills with silk carpets, heavy leather-bound books and global knickknacks. Guest rooms are so large they feel like suites; we especially like the downstairs room carved out of the house's original 1800s kitchen.

🍴 Eating & Drinking

Café Karibo & Karibrew FUSION, PUB $$
(☑ 904-277-5269; www.cafekaribo.com; 27 N 3rd St; mains $7-22; ⊙ 11am-9pm Tue-Sat, 11am-8pm Sun, 11am-3pm Mon) This funky side-street favorite serves a large and eclectic menu in a sprawling two-story space. The adjacent Karibrew brewpub has its own menu of global pub grub.

★ 29 South SOUTHERN $$$
(☑ 904-277-7919; www.29southrestaurant.com; 29 S 3rd St; mains lunch $8-13, dinner $18-28; ⊙ lunch 11:30am-2:30pm Wed-Sat, 10am-2pm Sun, dinner 5:30-9:30pm daily) Small plates and mains link arms happily at the tiny, stylish neo-Southern gourmet bistro.

Merge MODERN AMERICAN $$$
(☑ 904-277-8797; www.mergerestaurant.com; 510 S 8th St; meals $19-32; ⊙ from 5-9pm Sun-Thu, to 10pm Fri & Sat) Run by the former chef from the island's Ritz-Carlton resort, this new bistro is a bit off the beaten path on the side of busy 8th St. Local foodies rave about exquisite seafood dishes using local ingredients – think sea scallops over braised rhubarb, and cornmeal-breaded oysters in white cheddar cream.

★**Palace Saloon** BAR
(www.thepalacesaloon.com; 113-117 Centre St; ◷noon-2am daily) One more superlative for Fernandina: Florida's oldest bar, sporting swinging doors, draped velvet and a deadly Pirate's Punch.

WEST COAST

If Henry Flagler's railroad made the east coast of Florida what it is today, his non-attention to the rest of the state similarly affected the west coast. Things are calmer here, with fewer tourist hordes and more room for nature to amuse with shelling beaches, swamp lands and nature preserves. The west coast has front-row seats to flame-red sunsets emblazoned over the Gulf of Mexico, as well as adrenaline-pumping roller coasters, hand-rolled cigars and lip-synching mermaids.

Tampa

From the outside, Florida's third-largest city seems all business, even generically so. But Tampa surprises: its revitalized riverfront is a sparkling green swathe dotted with intriguing cultural institutions, and its historic Ybor City district preserves the city's Cuban cigar-industry past while, at night, transforming into the Gulf Coast's hottest bar and nightclub scene. South Tampa, meanwhile, has a cutting-edge dining scene that's drawing food mavens from Orlando and Miami.

◉ Sights

◉ Downtown Tampa

Aside from the zoo, downtown's sights are in or along Tampa's attractive green space, **Riverwalk** (www.thetampariverwalk.com).

★**Florida Aquarium** AQUARIUM
(☑813-273-4000; www.flaquarium.org; 701 Channelside Dr; adult/child $22/17; ◷9:30am-5pm) Tampa's excellent aquarium is among the state's best. Cleverly designed, the re-created swamp lets you walk among herons and ibis as they prowl the mangroves. Programs let you swim with the fishes (and the sharks) or take a catamaran ecotour in Tampa Bay.

★**Lowry Park Zoo** ZOO
(☑813-935-8552; www.lowryparkzoo.com; 1101 W Sligh Ave; adult/child $25/20; ◷9:30am-5pm; P♿) North of downtown, Tampa's zoo gets you as close to the animals as possible, with several free-flight aviaries, a camel ride, giraffe feeding, wallaby enclosure and rhino 'encounter.'

Tampa Museum of Art MUSEUM
(☑813-274-8130; www.tampamuseum.org; 120 W Gasparilla Plaza; adult/child $10/5; ◷11am-7pm Mon-Thu, to 8pm Fri, to 5pm Sat & Sun) In 2010 the museum christened its dramatically cantilevered new home. Six galleries balance Greek and Roman antiquities, contemporary photography and new media with major traveling exhibitions.

FLORIDA TAMPA

TAMPA BAY AREA BEACHES

The barrier islands of the Tampa Bay Area are graced with some of Florida's best beaches, whether you define 'best' as 'gorgeous untrammeled solitude' or 'family fun and thumping beach parties.' For more information, visit www.tampabaybeaches.com and www.visitstpeteclearwater.com. North to south, some highlights:

Honeymoon & Caladesi Islands Two of Florida's most beautiful beaches; unspoiled, lightly visited Caladesi Island is only reachable by ferry.

Clearwater Beach Idyllic soft white sand hosts raucous spring-break-style parties; huge resorts cater to the masses.

St Pete Beach Double-wide strand is an epicenter of activities and all-ages fun; packed with hotels, bars and restaurants.

Pass-a-Grille Beach Most popular with city-based day-trippers; extremely long and backed by houses (not resorts); cute-as-a-button village for eats.

Fort Desoto Park & Beach North Beach is one of Florida's finest white-sand beaches; ideal for families. Extensive park includes bike and kayak rentals, fishing piers and a cafe.

Tampa Bay History Center   MUSEUM
(☑813-228-0097; www.tampabayhistorycenter.org; 801 Old Water St; adult/child $13/8; ⊙10am-5pm) This first-rate history museum presents the region's Seminole people, Cracker pioneers and Tampa's Cuban community and cigar industry. The cartography collection dazzles.

Henry B Plant Museum   MUSEUM
(☑813-254-1891; www.plantmuseum.com; 401 W Kennedy Blvd; adult/child 4-12yrs $10/5; ⊙10am-5pm Tue-Sat, from noon Sun) The silver minarets of Henry B Plant's 1891 Tampa Bay Hotel glint majestically. Now part of the University of Tampa, one section re-creates the original hotel's luxurious, gilded late-Victorian world.

Glazer Children's Museum   MUSEUM
(☑813-443-3861; www.glazermuseum.org; 110 W Gasparilla Plaza; adult/child under 12 yr $15/9.50; ⊙10am-5pm Mon-Fri, to 6pm Sat, 1-6pm Sun; ⊞) Creative play spaces for kids don't get any better than this crayon-bright, inventive museum. Eager staff and tons of coolio fun; adjacent Curtis Hixon Park is picnic-and-playground friendly.

⊙ **Ybor City**

Like the illicit love child of Key West and Miami's Little Havana, Ybor City's cobblestoned 19th-century historic district is a redolent mix of wrought-iron balconies, globe streetlamps, immigrant history, ethnic cuisine, cigars and hip, happening nightlife. Diverse and youthful, Ybor (ee-bore) City oozes rakish, scruffy charm.

Get a great overview plus walking tour maps at the **visitor center** (☑813-241-8838; www.ybor.org; 1600 E 8th Ave; ⊙10am-5pm Mon-Sat, from noon Sun) – itself an excellent small museum. The main drag – along 7th Ave (La Septima) between 14th and 21st Sts – is packed with eats, drinks, shops and cigar stores.

Ybor City Museum State Park   MUSEUM
(☑813-247-6323; www.ybormuseum.org; 1818 E 9th Ave; adult/child under 5yr $4/free; ⊙9am-5pm) Join a **walking tour** (☑813-428-0854; tour $18 incl museum admission; ⊙by appt) run by a cigar-maker with a PhD, check out the cool museum store, or delve into the old-school history museum that preserves a bygone era, with cigar-worker houses and wonderful photos.

⊙ **Busch Gardens & Adventure Island**

No, it's not as thematically immersive as Orlando's Disney World or Universal, but Tampa's big theme park, **Busch Gardens** (☑813-987-5600; www.buschgardens.com; 10165 McKinley Dr; adult/child 3-9yr $85/77, discounts online; ⊙varies by day & season), will satisfy your adrenaline craving with epic roller coasters and flume rides that weave through an African-theme wildlife park. Music, performances and interactive 4D movies round out a full day. Check the website for opening hours, which vary seasonally.

Adjacent **Adventure Island** (☑813-987-5600; www.adventureisland.com; 10001 McKinley Dr; adult/child 3-9yr $46/42; ⊙hours vary; daily

---

MANATEES & MERMAIDS

Apparently, Florida's Spanish discoverers confused manatees with mermaids, but it's not hard to tell them apart. Mermaids are those beautiful long-haired women with the spangly tails swimming in the underwater theater at **Weeki Wachee Springs** (☑352-592-5656; www.weekiwachee.com; 6131 Commercial Way, Spring Hill; adult/child 6-12yr $13/8; ⊙9am-5:30pm). Their graceful adagios and *The Little Mermaid* show (three times daily) are Florida's most delightfully kitschy entertainment (just 45 minutes north of Tampa).

Lovable, ponderous, 1000lb manatees are the ones nibbling lettuce in the crystal bathtub of **Homosassa Springs Wildlife State Park** (☑352-628-5343; www.floridastateparks.org/homosassasprings; 4150 S Suncoast Blvd; adult/child 6-12yr $13/5; ⊙9am-5:30pm, last entrance 4pm), with its own underwater observatory (20 minutes north of Weeki Wachee).

Sadly, you can't swim with the mermaids, but you can with the manatees. Head a few miles north to King's Bay, within the **Crystal River National Wildlife Refuge** (☑352-563-2088; www.fws.gov/crystalriver; 1502 SE Kings Bay Dr; ⊙visitor center 8am-4pm Mon-Fri), where the visitor center can guide you to nearly 40 commercial operators that, had they existed, would have spared the Spaniards lots of heartache.

mid-Mar–Aug, weekends Sep-Oct) is a massive water park with slides and rides galore. Discounts and combination tickets are available online.

🛌 Sleeping

Chains abound along Fowler Ave and Busch Blvd (Hwy 580), near Busch Gardens.

Gram's Place   HOSTEL $
(☎813-221-0596; www.grams-inn-tampa.com; 3109 N Ola Ave; dm $23, r $25-70; ❇@) As charismatic as an aging rock star, Gram's is a tiny, welcoming hostel for international travelers who prefer personality over perfect linens. Dig the in-ground hot tub and Saturday night jams.

Tahitian Inn   HOTEL $$
(☎813-877-6721; www.tahitianinn.com; 601 S Dale Mabry Hwy; r $79-139, ste $149-199; P❇@🛜🏊) The name is reminiscent of a tiki-theme motel, but this family-owned, full-service hotel offers fresh, boutique stylings at midrange prices. Nice pool, and airport transportation.

Don Vicente de Ybor
Historic Inn   HISTORIC HOTEL $$
(☎813-241-4545; www.donvicenteinn.com; 1915 Republica de Cuba; r $139-219; P❇🛜) Slightly faded, the 1895 Don Vicente recalls Ybor City's glory days. Unfortunately, rooms are less warmly dramatic than the atmospheric Old World public spaces. Breakfast included.

🍴 Eating

At mealtime, focus on Ybor City, South Tampa's SoHo area (South Howard Ave) and up-and-coming Seminole Heights.

Wright's Gourmet House   SANDWICHES $
(1200 S Dale Mabry Hwy; sandwiches & salads $5-9; ⊙7am-6pm Mon-Fri, 8am-4pm Sat) It doesn't look like much from the outside. Heck, it doesn't look like much from the inside. But they've been slinging sandwiches since 1963, and their unique combinations and hearty portions win them plenty of fans.

★ Ella's Americana
Folk Art Cafe   AMERICAN $$
(www.ellasfolkartcafe.com; 5119 N Nebraska Ave; mains $11-22; ⊙5-11pm Tue-Thu, to midnight Fri & Sat, 11am-8pm Sun) Ten minutes from downtown in Seminole Heights, artsy Ella's aims to please with tasty flavor combinations, funky folk art, occasional live music, and pork ribs in their Bloody Marys during Soul Food Sundays.

Datz & Datz Dough   AMERICAN $$
(www.datztampa.com; 2616 S MacDill Ave; mains $10-19; ⊙7am-10pm Mon-Thu, to 11pm Fri, 8:30am-11pm Sat, 8:30am-3pm Sun) Perfect for a casual meal, this big, bustling place dishes out the humor, with menu items like Brie Bardot, Havana Hottie and When Pigs Fly. Next door, Datz Dough takes on the overflow, serving breakfast, lunch, baked goods and gelato.

Refinery   FUSION $$
(www.thetamparefinery.com; 5137 N Florida Ave; mains $12-18; ⊙5-10pm Sun-Thu, to 11pm Fri & Sat, brunch 11am-3pm Sun; ✏) 🍃 This blue-collar gourmet joint promises chipped plates and no pretensions, just playful, delicious hyperlocal cuisine that cleverly mixes a sustainability ethic with a punk attitude.

★ Columbia Restaurant   SPANISH $$$
(☎813-248-4961; www.columbiarestaurant.com; 2117 E 7th Ave; mains lunch $9-15, dinner $18-29; ⊙11am-10pm Mon-Thu, to 11pm Fri & Sat, noon-9pm Sun) Definitely reserve ahead for the exuberant, twice-nightly flamenco shows, and enjoy robust, classic Spanish cuisine and heady *mojitos* and sangria. It's an Old World Iberian time warp.

★ Bern's Steak House   STEAKHOUSE $$$
(☎813-251-2421; www.bernssteakhouse.com; 1208 S Howard Ave; mains $25-60; ⊙from 5pm) This legendary, nationally renowned steakhouse is an event as much as a meal. Dress up, order caviar and on-premises dry-aged beef, ask to tour the wine cellar and kitchens, and *don't* skip dessert.

🍷 Drinking & Entertainment

For nightlife, Ybor City is party central, though SoHo and Seminole Heights are also hip and happening. Tampa Bay's alternative weekly, **Creative Loafing** (www.cltampa.com), lists events and bars. Ybor City is also the center of Tampa's GLBT life; check out the **GaYBOR District Coalition** (www.gaybor.com) and **Tampa Bay Gay** (www.tampabaygay.com).

★ Skipper's Smokehouse   LIVE MUSIC
(☎813-971-0666; www.skipperssmokehouse.com; 910 Skipper Rd; cover $5-25; ⊙11am-midnight Tue-Fri, from noon Sat, from 1pm Sun) Feeling like it blew in from the Keys, Skipper's is a beloved, unpretentious open-air venue for blues, folk, reggae and gator-swamp rockabilly about ten miles north of downtown. Get directions online.

Straz Center for the Performing Arts

PERFORMING ARTS

(☑813-229-7827; www.strazcenter.org; 1010 MacInnes Pl) This enormous, multivenue complex draws the gamut of fine arts performances: touring Broadway shows, pop concerts, opera, ballet, drama and more.

ℹ Information

MEDIA

The area has two major daily newspapers, the **St Petersburg Times** (www.tampabay.com) and **Tampa Tribune** (www.tampatrib.com).

TOURIST INFORMATION

Tampa Bay Convention & Visitors Bureau (☑813-223-1111; www.visittampabay.com; 615 Channelside Dr; ☺10am-5:30pm Mon-Sat, 11am-5pm Sun) The visitor center has good free maps and lots of information. Book hotels directly through the website.

ℹ Getting There & Around

Tampa International Airport (TPA; www.tampaairport.com) has car-rental agencies. **Greyhound** (www.greyhound.com; 610 E Polk St) has numerous services. Trains run south to Miami and north through Jacksonville from the **Amtrak station** (☑813-221-7600; www.amtrak.com; 601 N Nebraska Ave). **Hillsborough Area Regional Transit** (HART; ☑813-254-4278; www.gohart.org; 1211 N Marion St; fare $2) connects downtown and Ybor City with buses, trolleys and old-style streetcars.

St Petersburg

In the bay area, St Petersburg is the more arty, youthful sibling. It also has a more compact and walkable tourist district along its attractive harbor. For a cultural city base within easy striking distance of the region's excellent beaches, St Pete is a great choice.

For maps and info, drop by the **chamber of commerce** (☑727-821-4069; www.stpete.com; 100 2nd Ave N; ☺9am-5pm Mon-Fri). For planning help, visit www.visitstpeteclearwater.com.

◎ Sights

Most of the action is around and along Central Ave, from 8th Ave to Bayshore Dr, which fronts the harbor and tourist pier.

St Petersburg Museum of Fine Arts

MUSEUM

(☑727-896-2667; www.fine-arts.org; 255 Beach Dr NE; adult/child $17/10; ☺10am-5pm Mon-Sat, to 8pm Thu, from noon Sun) The Museum of Fine Arts collection is as broad as the Dalí's deep, traversing the world's antiquities and following art's progression through nearly every era.

Florida Holocaust Museum

MUSEUM

(☑727-820-0100; www.flholocaustmuseum.org; 55 5th St S; adult/child $16/8; ☺10am-5pm) The understated exhibits of this Holocaust museum, one of the country's largest, present these mid-20th-century events with moving directness.

Chihuly Collection

GALLERY

(☑727-896-4527; www.chihulycollectionstpete.com; 400 Beach Dr; adult/child $15/11; ☺10am-5pm Mon-Sat, from noon Sun) A paean to Dale Chihuly's glass artistry, with galleries designed to hold the dramatic installations.

🛏 Sleeping

★Dickens House

B&B $$

(☑727-822-8622; www.dickenshouse.com; 335 8th Ave NE; r $119-245; P✳@🛜) Five lushly designed rooms await in this passionately restored arts-and-crafts-movement home. The gregarious, gay-friendly owner whips up a gourmet breakfast.

Ponce de Leon

BOUTIQUE HOTEL $$

(☑727-550-9300; www.poncedeleonhotel.com; 95 Central Ave; r $99-119, ste $169; P✳@🛜) A boutique hotel with Spanish flair in the heart of downtown. Splashy murals, designer-cool decor, and the hot restaurant and bar are highlights; off-site parking is not.

Renaissance Vinoy Resort

LUXURY HOTEL $$$

(☑727-894-1000; www.vinoyrenaissanceresort.com; 501 5th Ave NE; r $169-359; P✳@🛜⛵) St Pete's coral pink grande dame, the newly renovated 1925 Vinoy is a sumptuous concoction with standout off-season and online deals. It's worth it just for the gorgeous pool.

🍴 Eating & Drinking

At night, focus on Central Ave between 2nd and 3rd Sts, and along the harborfront. Many restaurants have lively, late bar scenes.

AnnaStella Cajun Bistro

CAJUN $

(☑727-498-8978; www.annastellacajunbistro.com; 300 Beach Dr N; dishes $6-16; ☺8am-10pm Sun-Thu, to 11pm Fri & Sat; 🛜) Enjoy a Cajun-spiced breakfast or lunch and harbor views; great gumbo and fresh beignets (French-style doughnuts).

SALVADOR DALÍ MUSEUM

Of course St Petersburg was the logical place to put a museum dedicated to Salvador Dalí, the eccentric Spanish artist who painted melting clocks, grew an exaggerated handlebar mustache to look like King Philip, and once filled a Rolls Royce with cauliflower. Right? In fact, **The Dalí Museum** (☑ 727-823-3767; www.thedali.org; 1 Dali Blvd; adult/child 6-12yr $21/7, after 5pm Thu $10; ⊙ 10am-5:30pm Mon-Sat, to 8pm Thu, noon-5:30pm Sun) is the largest Dalí collection outside of Spain. So how did that happen exactly?

In 1942, A. Reynolds Morse and his wife Eleanor began what would become the largest private Dalí collection in the world. When it came time to find a permanent home for the collection, they had one stipulation: that the collection had to stay together. Only three cities could agree to the terms, and St Petersburg won out for its waterfront location.

The museum now has a brand-new building with a theatrical exterior that, when seen from the bay side, looks like a geodesic atrium oozing out of a shoebox. It doesn't have *the* melting clocks, but it does have *some* melting clocks, as well as an impressive collection of paintings with titles such as *The Ghost of Vermeer of Delft Which Can Be Used as a Table*.

★ **Ceviche** TAPAS $$
(☑ 727-209-2299; www.ceviche.com; 10 Beach Dr; tapas $5-13, mains $15-23; ⊙ 11am-10pm) Panache counts and Ceviche has it in spades, with an upbeat Spanish atmosphere and flavorful, creative, generously portioned tapas. End the evening in the sexy, cavernlike Flamenco Room below, with live flamenco Thursday and Saturday nights.

Bella Brava ITALIAN $$
(☑ 727-895-5515; www.bellabrava.com; 204 Beach Dr NE; lunch $7-10, dinner $14-20; ⊙ 11:30am-10pm, to 11pm Fri & Sat, 3-9pm Sun) Anchoring the prime waterfront intersection, Bella Brava specializes in contemporary northern Italian cooking and breezy, sidewalk dining.

Garden MEDITERRANEAN $$
(☑ 727-896-3800; www.thegardendtsp.com; 217 Central Ave; lunch $7-12, dinner $15-24; ⊙ 11am-10pm Sun-Thu, to 11pm Fri & Sat) In a pretty hidden courtyard, Garden emphasizes Mediterranean-influenced salads and pastas. There's live jazz and DJs on weekends.

☆ **Entertainment**

★ **Jannus Live** CONCERT VENUE
(☑ 727-565-0551; www.jannuslive.com; 16 2nd St N) Well-loved outdoor concert venue inside an intimate courtyard; national and local bands reverberate downtown.

ⓘ Getting There & Around

St Petersburg-Clearwater International Airport (www.fly2pie.com; Roosevelt Blvd & Hwy 686, Clearwater) is served by several major carriers. **Greyhound** (☑ 727-898-1496;

www.greyhound.com; 180 Dr Martin Luther King Jr St N) services include Tampa.

Pinellas Suncoast Transit Authority (PSTA; www.psta.net; 340 2nd Ave N; fare $2; ⊙ 5am-9pm Mon-Sat, 7am-5pm Sun) operates buses citywide and the Suncoast Beach Trolley that links the beaches from Clearwater to Pass-a-Grille.

Sarasota

Artists, writers, musicians, entertainers – artsy types have flocked to Sarasota since the 1920s, with John Ringling leading the way. He set it on this course in 1911, when he made the town the winter home of his famous circus. Today the Ringling Museum Complex is a regional highlight, and Sarasota spills over with opera, theater and art. For arts and performance information, check out the **Arts and Cultural Alliance** (www.sarasotaarts.org). The all-encompassing **Van Wezel Performing Arts Hall** (☑ 800-826-9303, 941-953-3368; www.vanwezel.org; 777 N Tamiami Trail; tickets $25-80) showcases all types of performances, while the **Asolo Repertory Theatre** (☑ 941-351-8000; www.asolorep.org; 5555 N Tamiami Trail; tickets $15-50; ⊙ Nov-Jul) is a lauded regional theater company.

Another considerable boost to Sarasota's popularity is its luscious white-sand beaches. **Lido Beach** is closest and has free parking, but 5 miles away **Siesta Key** has sand like confectioner's sugar and is one of Florida's best and most popular strands; Siesta Village is also a lively, family-friendly beach town.

Want more nature? **Mote Aquarium** (☑ 941-388-4441; www.mote.org; 1600 Ken Thompson Pkwy, City Island; adult/child $17/14; ⊙ 10am-

RINGLING COMPLEX

Who doesn't love the circus? Well, people who are afraid of clowns, perhaps, but a little coulrophobia isn't necessarily a deal breaker at the **Ringling Museum Complex** (941-359-5700; www.ringling.org; 5401 Bay Shore Rd; adult/child 6-17yr $25/5; 10am-5pm daily, to 8pm Thu;). On the grounds of the 66-acre complex are three separate museums, all included in your admission and each one a worthy attraction on its own. Railroad, real-estate and circus baron John Ringling and his wife Mabel put down roots here, building a Venetian Gothic waterfront mansion called **Ca d'Zan**. You can wander the ground floor at your own pace, or take a guided tour – totally worth it – which grants you access to the upstairs bedrooms.

Also on the grounds, the **John & Mabel Museum of Art** is an excellent art museum with impressive high ceilings, intimidatingly large paintings and a re-created room from the Astor mansion. But the real standout here is the one-of-a-kind **Museum of the Circus**, with costumes, props, posters, antique circus wagons and an extensive miniature model that let you relive the excitement of the big-top era.

5pm) is a leading shark research center providing intimate encounters with sharks, manatees, sea turtles, rays and more, plus marine biologist-led sea-life cruises. Boasting the world's largest scientific collection of orchids and bromeliads, **Marie Selby Botanical Gardens** (941-366-5731; www.selby.org; 811 S Palm Ave; adult/child 6-11yr $17/6; 10am-5pm) is a relaxing yet fascinating botanical encounter. And about a half-hour from downtown, visit **Myakka River State Park** (www.myakkariver.org; 13208 State Road 72, Sarasota; car/bike $6/2; 8am-sunset) to kayak or airboat among hundreds of alligators, and for the area's best hiking and camping; get directions and tour times online.

Stop by the **Visitor Information Center** (941-706-1253; www.sarasotafl.org; 701 N Tamiami Trail; 10am-5pm Mon-Sat, 11am-2pm Sun;) for info and maps.

Sleeping & Eating

In addition to downtown Sarasota and Siesta Village, **St Armands Circle** on Lido Key is an evening social hub, with a proliferation of stylish shops and restaurants.

★ Hotel Ranola   BOUTIQUE HOTEL **$$**
(941-951-0111; www.hotelranola.com; 118 Indian Pl; r $109-149, ste $209;) The nine rooms feel like a designer's brownstone apartment: free-spirited and effortlessly artful, but with real working kitchens. It's urban funk, walkable to downtown Sarasota.

Sunsets on the Key   APARTMENT **$$$**
(941-312-9797; www.sunsetsonthekey.com; 5203 Avenida Navarre; apt in-season $230-340, off-season $149-209;) In Siesta

Village, eight well-kept, rigorously clean condo apartments are run like a hotel.

★ Broken Egg   BREAKFAST **$**
(www.thebrokenegg.com; 140 Avenida Messina; mains $7-14; 7:30am-2:30pm;) This diner-style breakfast institution on Siesta Key, known for huge pancakes and cheddary home fries, is a social hub each morning.

★ Owen's Fish Camp   SOUTHERN **$$**
(941-951-6936; www.owensfishcamp.com; 516 Burns Lane; mains $9-22; from 4pm) This ironically hip swamp-shack downtown serves upscale versions of Florida-style Southern cuisine with an emphasis on seafood.

Fort Myers

Workaday, sprawling Fort Myers is overshadowed by the region's pretty beaches and upscale, sophisticated towns. However, a recent facelift has spruced up the historic riverfront district (along 1st St between Broadway and Lee St) into an attractive, brick-lined collection of restaurants and bars. Visit www.fortmyers.org for information.

Fort Myers' main claim to fame is the **Edison & Ford Winter Estates** (239-334-7419; www.edisonfordwinterestates.org; 2350 McGregor Blvd; adult/child $20/11; 9am-5:30pm). Famous inventor Thomas Edison built a winter home and lab here in 1885, and automaker Henry Ford became his neighbor in 1916. The excellent museum focuses mainly on the overwhelming scope of Edison's genius, and their homes are genteel, landscaped delights.

From November through March, one of the easiest ways to encounter wintering manatees is at **Lee County Manatee Park** (☎239-690-5030; www.leeparks.org; 10901 State Rd 80; parking per hr/day $2/5; ☺8am-sunset daily) **FREE**, a warm-water power-plant discharge canal that's now a protected sanctuary. The park is signed off Hwy 80, about 6.5 miles from downtown.

For an easily accessible taste of South Florida wetlands, meander the 1.2-mile boardwalk trail of the **Six Mile Cypress Slough Preserve** (☎239-533-7550; www.leeparks.org/sixmile; 7791 Penzance Blvd; parking per hr/day $1/5; ☺dawn-dusk, nature center 10am-4pm Tue-Sat, to 2pm Sun) **FREE**.

Fort Myers Beach

Fifteen miles south of Fort Myers, Fort Myers Beach is 7 miles of talcum powder-fine sand along **Estero Island**, presided over by one of Florida's quintessential activity-and-party-fueled beach towns. Families often prefer Fort Myers Beach because it's more affordable than neighboring coastal towns, and coeds like it because its bars are louder and more raucous. For town information, visit www.fortmyersbeachchamber.org.

The only draw, and it's a good one, is the beachy fun, but nearby **Lovers Key State Park** (☎239-463-4588; www.floridastateparks.org; 8700 Estero Blvd; per car/bike $8/2; ☺8am-sunset) adds great shelling as well as hiking and kayaking among quiet islands and canals (frequented by manatees).

Impeccably clean and well maintained, **Edison Beach House** (☎239-463-1530; www.edisonbeachhouse.com; 830 Estero Blvd; r $145-415; ❈☎❄) is perfectly situated near action central (the so-called Times Sq area), yet soothingly comfortable, with full kitchens. For funky charm in a more low-key beach section, nab one of the six rooms at **Mango Street Inn** (☎239-233-8542; www.mangostreetinn.com; 126 Mango St; r $95-150; ❈☎❄), an idiosyncratic B&B serving delectable breakfasts by a Cajun-trained chef.

Sanibel & Captiva Islands

Shaped like a fish hook trying to lure Fort Myers, these two slivers of barrier island lie across a 2-mile causeway (toll $6). Upscale but unpretentious, with a carefully managed shoreline that feels remarkably lush and undeveloped, the islands are idyllic, cushy getaways, where bikes are the preferred mode of travel, the shelling is legendary and

romantic meals are a reservation away. The **Sanibel & Captiva Islands Chamber of Commerce** (☎239-472-1080; www.sanibel-captiva.org; 1159 Causeway Rd, Sanibel; ☺9am-5pm; ☎) is one of the most helpful visitors centers around and can help with accommodations.

In addition to its fabulous beaches, Sanibel's 6300-acre **JN 'Ding' Darling National Wildlife Refuge** (☎239-472-1100; www.fws.gov/dingdarling; 1 Wildlife Drive; per car/cyclist $5/1; ☺Wildlife Drive from 7am, closed Fri, visitor center 9am-5pm) is a splendid refuge that's home to an abundance of seabirds and wildlife. It has an excellent nature center, a 5-mile Wildlife Drive, narrated tram tours and easy kayaking in Tarpon Bay. For tours and boat rentals, contact **Tarpon Bay Explorers** (☎239-472-8900; www.tarponbayexplorers.com; 900 Tarpon Bay Rd, Sanibel; ☺8am-6pm).

Like a mermaid's jewel box, the **Bailey-Matthews Shell Museum** (☎239-395-2233; www.shellmuseum.org; 3075 Sanibel-Captiva Rd, Sanibel; adult/child 5-16yr $9/5; ☺10am-5pm) is a natural history of the sea, with covetous displays of shells worldwide. To rent bikes or any other wheeled contrivance, visit **Billy's Rentals** (☎239-472-5248; www.billysrentals.com; 1470 Periwinkle Way, Sanibel; bikes per 2hr/day from $5/15; ☺8:30am-5pm).

On Captiva, the **'Tween Waters Inn** (☎239-472-5161; www.tween-waters.com; 15951 Captiva Dr, Captiva; r $175-275, ste $265-390, cottages from $245; ❈@☎❄) is a full-service yet low-key resort with a variety of good-value lodging choices; ask for a renovated room. In addition to a big pool, tennis courts and spa, its marina offers various kayak rentals, guided trips and boat cruises. Or, for a more personal experience, stay in the five-room **Tarpon Tale Inn** (☎239-472-0939; www.tarpontale.com; 367 Periwinkle Way, Sanibel; r $80-219; ❈@☎❄), which does a nice imitation of a charming, hammock-strung B&B, but without breakfast.

Start your day at the **Over Easy Cafe** (www.overeasycafesanibel.com; 630 Tarpon Bay Rd at Periwinkle Way, Sanibel; mains $8-14; ☺7am-3pm daily; ❈), a social hub where everyone goes for a diner-style breakfast. **Island Cow** (☎239-472-0606; www.sanibelislandcow.com; 2163 Periwinkle Way; mains $8-19; ☺7am-10pm) has an extensive menu and a cheery interior, making it an easy choice any time of day. Or, for romantic gourmet, **Sweet Melissa's Cafe** (☎239-472-1956; www.sweetmelissascafe.net; 1625 Periwinkle Way, Sanibel; tapas $9-16, mains $26-34; ☺11:30am-2:30pm Mon-Fri, from 5pm Mon-Sat) offers creative, relaxed refinement.

Naples

The Gulf Coast's answer to Palm Beach, Naples is a perfectly manicured, rich town with an adult sense of self and one of the most pristine, relaxed city beaches in the state. While it is certainly family friendly, it appeals most to romance-minded travelers seeking fine art and fine dining, trendy cocktails, fashion-conscious shopping and luscious sunsets. Visit www.napleschamber. org for city information.

For contemporary art, the sophisticated **Naples Museum of Art** (☑ 239-597-1900; www.thephil.org; 5833 Pelican Bay Blvd; adult/child under 17 $10/free; ☉ 10am-4pm Tue-Sat, noon-4pm Sun) is a rewarding collection with cleverly designed exhibits. Meanwhile, one of the state's best nature conservancies and rehabilitation centers is **Naples Nature Center** (☑ 239-262-0304; www.conservancy.org; 1450 Merrihue Dr; adult/child 3-12 $13/9; ☉ 9:30am-4:30pm Mon-Sat), with a LEED-certified campus and fantastic exhibits.

For well-polished, Mediterranean-style luxury in the heart of downtown's 5th Ave corridor, stay at the historic **Inn on 5th** (☑ 239-403-8777; www.innonfifth.com; 699 5th Ave S; r $180-500; ✴@☎☎). For a well-located, good-value midrange motel, the **Lemon Tree Inn** (☑ 239-262-1414; www.lemontreeinn.com; 250 9th St S, at 3rd Ave S; r $89-169; ✴@☎☎) is a pretty, bright choice.

Good eats are abundant. Top choices for a special meal include **Cafe Lurcat** (☑ 239-213-3357; www.cafelurcat.com; 494 5th Ave; dinner $24-39; ☉ 5-10pm), a sexy, multilevel restaurant and lively bar (open to 11pm or midnight nightly), and the off-the-beaten-path **IM Tapas** (☑ 239-403-8272; http://imtapas.com; 965 4th Ave N; tapas $9-18; ☉ from 5:30pm Mon-Sat), where a mother-and-daughter team serves Madrid-worthy Spanish tapas.

CENTRAL FLORIDA

Before Disney – BD – most tourists came to Florida to see two things: the white-sand beaches and the alligator-infested Everglades. Walt Disney changed all that when he opened the Magic Kingdom in 1971. Today Orlando is the theme park capital of the world, and Walt Disney World is Florida's number one attraction.

Orlando

Like Las Vegas, Orlando is almost entirely given over to fantasy. It's a place to come when you want to imagine you're somewhere else: Hogwarts, perhaps, or Cinderella's Castle, or Dr Seuss' world, or an African safari. And like Vegas' casinos, Orlando's theme parks work hard to be constantly entertaining thrill rides where the only concern is your pleasure. Even outside the theme parks, Orlando can exhibit a hyper atmosphere of fiberglass-modeled, cartoon-costumed pop culture amusement.

Yet there is, in fact, a real city to explore, one with tree-shaded parks of the natural variety, art museums, orchestras, and dinners that don't involve high-fiving Goofy. And just outside the city, Florida's wilderness and wildlife, particularly its crystal springs, can be as memorably bizarre as anything Ripley ever dreamed up.

◉ Sights & Activities

◉ Downtown & Loch Haven Park

Fashionable Thornton Park has several good restaurants and bars, while Loch Haven Park is home to a cluster of cultural institutions.

★**Orlando Museum of Art**　MUSEUM
(☑ 407-896-4231; www.omart.org; 2416 N Mills Ave; adult/child $8/5; ☉ 10am-4pm Tue-Fri, from noon Sat & Sun) Spotlighting American and African art as well as unique traveling exhibits.

Mennello Museum of American Art　MUSEUM
(☑ 407-246-4278; www.mennellomuseum.com; 900 E Princeton St; adult/child 6-18yr $5/1; ☉ 10:30am-4:30pm Tue-Sat, from noon Sun) Features the bright folk art of Earl Cunningham, plus traveling exhibitions.

Orlando Science Center　MUSEUM
(☑ 407-514-2000; www.osc.org; 777 E Princeton St; adult/child 3-11yr $19/13; ☉ 10am-5pm Thu-Tue) Candy-coated hands-on science for the whole family.

Harry P Leu Gardens　PARK
(www.leugardens.org; 1920 N Forest Ave; adult/student $10/3; ☉ 9am-5pm) One mile east of Loch Haven Park is this 50-acre tranquil escape from all the gloss.

◎ International Drive

Like a theme park itself, International Dr (I-Dr) is shoulder to shoulder with high-energy amusements: sprinkled among the major theme, wildlife and water parks, smaller attractions shout for attention: Ripley's Believe It or Not, the upside-down WonderWorks and an indoor skydiving experience. Chain restaurants and hotels also crowd the thoroughfare.

Check online for combo tickets with Discovery Cove and Aquatica.

★**Universal Orlando Resort**   THEME PARK
(☑407-363-8000; www.universalorlando.com; 1000 Universal Studios Plaza; single/both parks $92/128, discounts on multiday; ☺daily, hours vary) Universal is giving Disney a run for its money with this mega-complex that features two theme parks, a water park, three hotels and Universal CityWalk, an entertainment district that connects the two parks. But where Disney World is all happy and magical, Universal Orlando gets your adrenaline pumping with revved-up rides and entertaining shows. The first of the two parks, Universal Studios, has a Hollywood backlot feel and simulation-heavy rides dedicated to television and the silver screen, from The Simpsons and Shrek to Revenge of the Mummy and Twister. Universal's Islands of Adventure is tops with coaster-lovers but also has plenty for the little ones in Toon Lagoon and Seuss Landing.

But the absolute highlight – and the hottest thing to hit Orlando since Cinderella's Castle – is the Wizarding World of Harry Potter. Located within Islands of Adventure, it's easily the most fantastically realized themed experience in Florida. Muggles are invited to poke along the cobbled streets and impossibly crooked buildings of Hogsmeade, sip frothy Butter Beer and mail a card via Owl Post, all in the shadow of Hogwarts Caste. The detail and authenticity tickle the fancy at every turn, from the screeches of the mandrakes in the shop windows to the groans of Moaning Myrtle in the bathroom; keep your eyes peeled for magical happenings.

Review multiple ticket options online, which can include add-ons like Express Plus line skipping and a dining plan; resort hotel guests also get nice park perks. Parking is $16.

SeaWorld   AMUSEMENT PARK
(☑407-351-3600; www.seaworld.com; 7007 Sea-World Dr; adult/child 3-9 $92/84; ☺from 9am) A peculiarly Floridian blend of marine animal shows and thrill rides, SeaWorld is home to both Shamu the killer whale and Kraken the floorless roller coaster. While the rides provide jolts of adrenaline, the real draws are the up-close sea life encounters (with manta rays, sharks, penguins, beluga whales) and the excellent dolphin, sea lion and killer whale shows. Look online for admission discounts and package deals. Make sure to check show and feeding times online before visiting, and plan your day accordingly.

Discovery Cove   WATER PARK
(☑877-557-7404; www.discoverycove.com; 6000 Discovery Cove Way; admission $169-269, incl dolphin swim $229-379; ☺8am-5:30pm) Attendance is limited, ensuring Discovery Cove retains the feel of an exclusive tropical resort, complete with beaches, a fish-filled reef and an aviary. No high-speed thrills or frantic screaming, just blessed relaxation and the chance to swim with dolphins. The price is steep, but everything is included: buffet lunch, beer, towels, parking, even a day pass to SeaWorld.

◎ Winter Park

On the northern edge of Orlando, Winter Park is a friendly college town with some outstanding museums and a relaxing downtown.

Charles Hosmer Morse Museum of American Art   MUSEUM
(www.morsemuseum.org; 445 N Park Ave; adult/child $5/free; ☺9:30am-4pm Tue-Sat, from 1pm Sun) Internationally famous, with the world's most comprehensive collection of Tiffany glass; its stunning centerpiece is a chapel interior.

Scenic Boat Tour   BOAT TOUR
(www.scenicboattours.com; 1 E Morse Blvd; adult/child $12/6; ☺hourly 10am-4pm) This recommended one-hour boat ride floats through 12 miles of tropical canals and lakes. The enthusiastic tour guide talks about the mansions, Rollins College and other sites along the way. Boats are small pontoons, holding about 10 people each.

◎ Greater Orlando

★**Gatorland**   AMUSEMENT PARK
(www.gatorland.com; 14501 S Orange Blossom Trail/Hwy 17; adult/child $25/17; ☺10am-6pm) This Old Florida throwback is small, silly and kitschy. It's all about alligators, with gator wrestling, gator jumping, feeding gators hot dogs and other great squeal-worthy moments.

Greater Orlando & Theme Parks

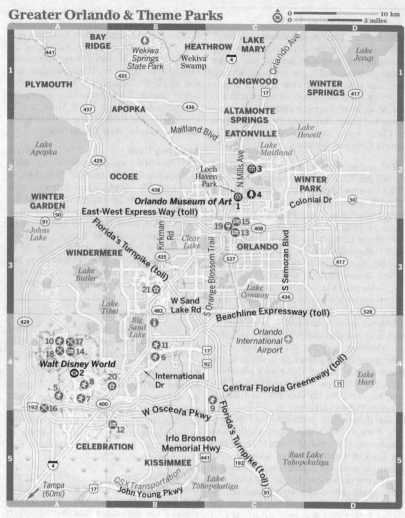

FLORIDA ORLANDO

🛏 Sleeping

In addition to the Walt Disney World resorts, Orlando has countless lodging options. Most are clustered around I-Dr, US 192 in Kissimmee and I-4. **Reserve Orlando** (www.reserveorlando.com) is a central booking agency. **Universal Orlando Resort** (☎407-363-8000; www.universalorlando.com; r & ste from $270) also has three recommended hotels.

★ EO Inn & Spa   BOUTIQUE HOTEL $$
(☎407-481-8485; www.eoinn.com; 227 N Eola Dr; r $129-229; P❄☎🐾) Sleek and understated, this downtown boutique inn overlooks Lake

Eola near Thornton Park, with neutral-toned rooms that are elegant in their simplicity.

Courtyard at Lake Lucerne   B&B $$
(☎407-648-5188; www.orlandohistoricinn.com; 211 N Lucerne Circle E; r $99-225; P❄☎) This lovely historic inn, with enchanting gardens and genteel breakfast, has roomy art-deco suites and handsome antiques throughout. Complimentary cocktails help you forgive its location under two highway overpasses.

Barefoot'n in the Keys   MOTEL $$
(☎877-978-3314; www.barefootn.com; 2754 Florida Plaza Blvd; ste $89-199; @🐾) Clean, bright

Greater Orlando & Theme Parks

and spacious suites in a yellow six-story building. Low-key, friendly and close to Disney, this makes an excellent alternative to generic chains.

✗ Eating

On and around I-Dr you'll find an explosion of chains; a half-mile stretch of Sand Lake Rd has been dubbed 'restaurant row' for its upscale dining.

Dandelion Communitea Café VEGETARIAN $
(http://dandelioncommunitea.com; 618 N Thornton Ave; mains $6-10; ⊙11am-10pm Mon-Sat, to 5pm Sun; ⚑⊛) ⚑ Unabashedly crunchy and definitively organic, this pillar of creative, sustainable, locavore vegetarianism is genuinely delicious, with tons of community spirit. Look for events.

**Graffiti Junktion
American Burger Bar** BURGERS $
(www.graffitijunktion.com; 900 E Washington St, Thornton Park; mains $6-13; ⊙11pm-2am) This neon graffiti-covered happenin' hangout is all about massive burgers with attitude. Top yours with a fried egg, artichoke hearts, chili, avocado and more.

Yellow Dog Eats BARBECUE $$
(☑407-296 0609; www.yellowdogeats.com; 1236 Hempel Ave, Windermere; mains $7-14; ⊙11am-9pm; ⚑) Housed in an old, tin-roof general store, and quirky to the extreme, it's not your typi-

cal barbecue. Try the excellent Cuban-style black beans and the Florida Cracker (pulled pork with gouda, bacon and fried onions). It's a drive; get directions online.

★Ravenous Pig AMERICAN $$$
(☑407-628-2333; www.theravenouspig.com; 1234 Orange Ave, Winter Park; mains $13-33; ⊙11:30am-2pm & 5:30-9:30pm Tue-Sat) One of Orlando's most talked-about foodie destinations, this bustling hot spot serves designer cocktails and creative, delicious versions of shrimp and grits, and lobster tacos. Reservations recommended.

☕ Drinking & Entertainment

Orlando Weekly (www.orlandoweekly.com) is the best source for entertainment listings. There's plenty to do downtown, where there's a happening bar district around Orange Ave between Church St and Jefferson St.

Universal Studio's **CityWalk** (www.city-walkorlando.com) has a concentration of cinemas, restaurants, clubs and big-name shows.

Latitudes BAR
(www.churchstreetbars.com; 33 W Church St; ⊙4:30pm-2am) Island-inspired rooftop bar, with two more bars below.

Wall Street Plaza BAR
(☑407 849-0471; www.wallstplaza.net; 25 Wall St Plaza) Eight theme bars, with live music, all in one plaza.

FLORIDA ORLANDO

The Social LIVE MUSIC
(☑ 407-246-1419; www.thesocial.org; 54 N Orange Ave) Check out great live music.

Parliament House GAY
(www.parliamenthouse.com; 410 N Orange Blossom Trail; ⊙ 10:30am-3am) Legendary gay resort and drag shows; six bars.

ℹ Information

For city information, discount tickets to attractions, and good multilingual guides and maps, visit Orlando's **Official Visitor Center** (☑ 407-363-5872; www.visitorlando.com; 8723 International Dr; ⊙ 8:30am-6pm). Gay travelers can peruse http://orlando.gaycities.com. For theme park advice, visit www.themeparkinsider.com.

ℹ Getting There & Around

Orlando International Airport (MCO; www.orlandoairports.net) has buses and taxis to major tourist areas. **Mears Transportation** (☑ 407-423-5566; www.mearstransportation.com) provides shuttles for $20 to $30 per person. **Greyhound** (www.greyhound.com; 555 N John Young Pkwy) serves numerous cities. **Amtrak** (www.amtrak.com; 1400 Sligh Blvd) has daily trains south to Miami and north to New York City.

Orlando's bus network is operated by **Lynx** (☑ route info 407-841-8240; www.golynx.com; single ride/day/week pass $2/4.50/16, transfers free). **I-Ride Trolley** (www.iridetrolley.com; rides adult/child under 12yr $1.50/free) buses run along I-Dr.

When driving, note that I-4 is the main north–south connector, though it's confusingly labeled east–west. To go north, take I-4 east (toward Daytona); to go south, get on I-4 west (toward Tampa). The main east–west roads are Hwy 50 and Hwy 528 (the Bee Line Expwy), which accesses Orlando International Airport.

Walt Disney World Resort

Covering 40 sq miles, **Walt Disney World** (WDW; ☑ 407-939-5277; http://disneyworld.disney.go.com) is the largest theme park resort in the world. It includes four separate theme parks, two water parks, a sports complex, five golf courses, two dozen hotels, 100 restaurants and two shopping and nightlife districts – proving that it's not such a small world, after all. At times it feels ridiculously crowded and corporate, but with or without kids, you won't be able to inoculate yourself against Disney's highly infectious enthusiasm and warm-hearted nostalgia. Naturally, expectations run high, and even the self-proclaimed 'happiest place on earth'

doesn't always live up to its billing. Still, it always happens: Cinderella curtsies to your little Belle, your own Jedi knight vanquishes Darth Maul, or you tear up on that corny ride about our tiny planet, and suddenly you're swept up in the magic.

⊙ Sights & Activities

Magic Kingdom THEME PARK
When most people think of WDW – especially kids – it's really the Magic Kingdom they're picturing. This is where you'll find all the classic Disney experiences, such as the iconic Cinderella's Castle, rides like Space Mountain and the nighttime fireworks and light parade illuminating **Main Street, USA**. For Disney mythology, it doesn't get better.

Cinderella's Castle is at the center of the park, and from there paths lead to the different 'lands':

Tomorrowland is where Space Mountain hurtles you through the darkness of outer space. This indoor roller coaster is the most popular ride in the Magic Kingdom, so come first thing and if the line is already excruciating, get a FastPass.

Fantasyland is the highlight of any Disney trip for the eight-and-under crowd. This is the land of Mickey and Minnie, Goofy and Donald Duck, Snow White and the Seven Dwarves, and many more big names.

Adventureland features pirates and jungles, magic carpets and tree houses, whimsical and silly representations of the exotic locales from storybooks and imagination.

Liberty Square is the home of the the Haunted Mansion, a rambling, 19th century mansion that's a Disney favorite, and **Frontierland** is Disney's answer to the Wild West.

Disney Hollywood Studios THEME PARK
Formerly Disney-MGM Studios, this is the least charming of Disney's parks. However, it does have two of WDW's most exciting rides: the unpredictable elevator in the **Twilight Zone Tower of Terror** and the Aerosmith-themed **Rock 'n' Roller Coaster**. Wannabe singers can audition for the American Idol Experience, kids can join the Jedi Training Academy, and various programs present Walt Disney himself and how Disney's movies are made.

Epcot THEME PARK
An acronym for 'Experimental Prototype Community of Tomorrow', Epcot was Disney's vision of a high-tech city when it opened in 1982. It's divided into two halves: **Future**

World, with rides and corporate-sponsored interactive exhibits, and **World Showcase**, providing an interesting toe-dip into the cultures of 11 countries. Epcot is much more soothingly low-key than other parks, and it has some of the best food and shopping. Plus, a few rides are WDW highlights, like Soarin' and Mission: Space. The interactive Turtle Talk with Crush is delightful.

Animal Kingdom   THEME PARK

This sometimes surreal blend of African safari, zoo, rides, costumed characters, shows and dinosaurs establishes its own distinct tone. It's best at animal encounters and shows, with the 110-acre **Kilimanjaro Safaris** as its centerpiece. The iconic **Tree of Life** houses the fun It's Tough to Be a Bug! show, and **Expedition Everest** and **Kali River Rapids** are the top thrill rides.

🛏 Sleeping

While it's tempting to save money by staying elsewhere, the value of staying at a Walt Disney World resort lies in the conveniences they offer. WDW has 24 family-friendly sleeping options, from camping to deluxe resorts, and Disney guests receive great perks (extended park hours, discount dining plans, free transportation, airport shuttles). Disney's thorough website outlines rates and amenities for every property. Don't expect the quality of the room and amenities to match the price: you're paying for Walt Disney World convenience, not for Ritz-like luxury.

One of our favorite deluxe resorts is the Yosemite-style **Wilderness Lodge** (☑ 407-824-3200; 901 Timberline Dr; r from $319; 🅿 ✳ 🛜 ☲); the 'rustic opulence' theme includes erupting geysers, a lakelike swimming area and bunk beds for the kids. And for wilderness on a budget, we love the **Fort Wilderness Resort & Campground** (☑ 407-824-2900; campsites $54-120, cabins from $325; ✳ 🛜 ☲ 🐾) with tent sites and cabins that sleep up to six people.

Disney's Value Resorts (https://disney-world.disney.go.com; r $90-150) are the least-expensive option (besides camping); quality is equivalent to basic chain hotels, and (fair warning) they are favored by school groups.

Disney's Art of Animation Resort   HOTEL

(☑ 407-938-7000; 1850 Animation Way; ✳ ☲) Inspired by animated Disney classics including *The Lion King, Cars, Finding Nemo* and *The Little Mermaid.*

Disney's All-Star Movies Resort   HOTEL

(☑ 407-939-7000; 1991 Buena Vista Dr; ✳ ☲) Icons from Disney movies including *Toy Story* and *101 Dalmatians.*

Disney's All-Star Music Resort   HOTEL

(☑ 407-939-6000; 1801 W Buena Vista Dr; ✳ ☲) Family suites and motel rooms surrounded by giant instruments.

Disney's All-Star Sports Resort   HOTEL

(☑ 407-939-5000; 1701 Buena Vista Dr; ✳ ☲) Five pairs of three-story buildings divided thematically by sport.

Disney's Pop Century Resort   HOTEL

(☑ 407-938-4000; 1050 Century Dr; ✳ ☲) Each section pays homage to a different decade of the late 20th century.

🍴 Eating

Theme park food ranges from OK to awful; the most interesting is served in Epcot's World Showcase. Sit-down meals are best, but *always* make reservations; seats can be impossible to get without one. For any dining, you can call **central reservations** (☑ 407-939-3463) up to 180 days in advance.

Disney has three dinner shows (a luau, country-style BBQ and vaudeville show) and about 15 character meals, and these

---

BEST OF MAGIC KINGDOM

With the exception of Space Mountain, Splash Mountain and the scary introduction to the Haunted Mansion, these are all Disney Perfect for children.

Mickey's Philharmagic 3D movie perfection.

Space Mountain Indoor roller coaster in the dark.

Pirates of the Caribbean Cruise through the world of pirates.

Haunted Mansion Slow-moving ride past lighthearted spooks.

Dumbo the Flying Elephant A favorite with toddlers.

Mad Tea Party Quintessential Disney spinning.

It's a Small World Boat ride through the world – you know the song.

Jungle Cruise Disney silliness at its best.

Splash Mountain Classic water ride.

TICKETS & TIPS

Tickets

Consider buying a ticket that covers more days in the parks than you think you'll need. It's less expensive per day, and it gives you the freedom to break up time at the theme parks with downtime in the pool or at low-key attractions beyond theme-park gates.

You can buy tickets for one park per day, or Park Hopper passes that allow entrance to all four parks. Check online for packages, and buy in advance to avoid lines at the gate. For discounts, check out www.mousesavers.com and www.undercovertourist.com.

When to Go

Anytime schools are out – during summer and holidays – WDW will be the most crowded. The least crowded times are January to February, mid-September through October and early December. Late fall tends to have the best weather; frequent downpours accompany the hot, humid summer months.

On the actual day you go, plan on arriving early so you can see as much of the park as possible before the midday peak. Consider going back to your hotel for to recharge around 2:00 or 3:00 pm when it's the hottest and most crowded, then come back a few hours later and stay till close.

Fast Pass

For the most popular attractions, WDW offers FastPass: a free paper ticket that assigns a time for you to return and skip (most of) the mind-numblingly long lines. Just swipe your park ticket at the automated ticket machine next to the ride (the park map will tell you which ones offer that option) and come back when it tells you to. FastPass waits are usually no more than 15 minutes.

The catch? You can only have one (sometimes two, depending on crowd levels) at a time. Check the bottom of your FastPass to find out when you are eligible to swipe your card for another FastPass. FastPasses for the most popular attractions can run out by midday; if you really want to see something, get your FastPass as early as possible.

are insanely popular (see website for details). Book them the minute your 180-day window opens. The most sought-after meal is **Cinderella's Royal Table** (adult $43-54, child $28-33) inside the Magic Kingdom's castle, where you dine with Disney princesses.

⭐ **Sci-Fi Dine-In Theater**   AMERICAN $$
(Hollywood Studios; mains $13-30; ⏱11am-10:30pm; 🖐) Dine in Cadillacs and watch classic sci-fi flicks.

O'Hana   HAWAIIAN $$$
(Polynesian Resort; adult $36-43, child $18-20; ⏱7:30-11am, 5-10pm) Great South Pacific decor and interactive Polynesian-themed luau shenanigans with all-you-care-to-eat meals served family style.

California Grill   AMERICAN $$$
(Disney's Contemporary Resort; mains $32-49; ⏱5-10pm; 🖐) Coveted seats with great views of the Magic Kingdom fireworks.

Boma   BUFFET $$$
(Animal Kingdom Lodge; adult/child breakfast $23/13, dinner $40/19; ⏱7:30-11am, 4:30-9:30pm; 🖐) African-inspired eatery with pleasant surroundings and a buffet several notches above the rest.

Victoria and Albert   AMERICAN $$$
(Grand Floridian; prix fixe $135) A true jacket-and-tie, crystal goblet romantic gourmet restaurant – no kidding, and no kids under 10.

☆ Entertainment

In addition to theme park events like Magic Kingdom parades and fireworks and Epcot's Illuminations, Disney has two entertainment districts – Downtown Disney and Disney's Boardwalk – with eats, bars, music, movies, shops and shows.

⭐ **Cirque du Soleil**
La Nouba   PERFORMING ARTS
(☎407-939-7600; www.cirquedusoleil.com; Downtown Disney's West Side; adult $61-144, child 3-9yr

$49-117; ☺6pm & 9pm Tue-Sat) This mind-blowing acrobatic extravaganza is one of the best shows at Disney.

House of Blues LIVE MUSIC

(☑407-934-2583; www.houseofblues.com; 1490 E Buena Vista Dr) Top acts visit this national chain; Sunday's Gospel Brunch truly rocks.

DisneyQuest ARCADE

(Downtown Disney; 1-day adult/child 3-9yr $48/41; ☺11:30am-10pm Sun-Thu, to 11pm Fri & Sat) Five floors of virtual reality and arcade games.

ⓘ Getting There & Around

Most hotels in Kissimmee and Orlando – and all Disney properties – offer free transportation to Walt Disney World. Disney-owned resorts also offer free transportation from the airport. Drivers can reach all four parks via I-4 and park for $14. The Magic Kingdom lot is huge; trams get you to the entrance.

Within Walt Disney World, a complex network of monorails, boats and buses get you between the parks, resorts and entertainment districts. Pick up a transportation map at your resort or at Guest Relations near the main entrance of all four parks.

Around Orlando

Just north of Orlando await some of Florida's best outdoor adventures, particularly swimming, snorkeling and kayaking in its crystal-clear, 72°F (22°C) natural springs. Closest is **Wekiwa Springs State Park** (☑407-884-2008; www.floridastateparks.org; 1800 Wekiwa Circle, Apopka; car $6, campsite $24; ☺8am-sundown), with 13 miles of hiking trails, a spring-fed swimming hole, nice campground and the tranquil 'Wild and Scenic' Wekiva River; rent kayaks from **Nature Adventures** (☑407-884-4311; www.canoewekiva.com; 2hr $18; ☺8am-8pm).

Blue Spring State Park (www.floridastateparks.org; 2100 W French Ave; car/bike $6/2; ☺8am-sundown) is a favorite of wintering manatees, and two-hour cruises ply the St John's River. Just north of Deland, **De Leon Springs State Park** (www.floridastateparks.org; 601 Ponce de Leon Blvd, Ponce de Leon; car/bike $6/2; ☺8am-sunset) has a huge swimming area, more kayaking and tours of Juan Ponce de León's alleged fountain of youth.

To really escape into raw wilderness, head for the **Ocala National Forest** (www.fs.usda.gov/ocala), which has dozens of campgrounds, hundreds of miles of trails and 600 lakes. The hiking, biking, canoeing and camping are some of the state's best. See the website for visitor centers and descriptions.

FLORIDA PANHANDLE

Take all the things that are great about the Deep South – friendly people, molasses-slow pace, oak-lined country roads, fried food galore – and then add several hundred miles of sugar-white beaches, dozens of gin-clear natural springs and all the fresh oysters you can suck down, and there you have it: the fantastic, highly underrated Florida Panhandle.

Tallahassee

Florida's capital, cradled between gently rising hills and beneath tree-canopied roadways, is a calm and gracious city. It's closer to Atlanta than it is to Miami – both geographically and culturally – and far more Southern than the majority of the state it administrates. Despite the city's two major universities (Florida State and Florida Agricultural and Mechanical University) and its status as a government center, there's not much to detain a visitor for more than a day or two.

Stop by the **visitor center** (☑800-628-2866, 850-606-2305; www.visittallahassee.com; 106 E Jefferson St; ☺8am-5pm Mon-Fri) for information.

◉ Sights & Activities

Mission San Luis HISTORIC SITE

(☑850-245-6406; www.missionsanluis.org; 2100 W Tennessee St; adult/child $5/2; ☺10am-4pm Tue-Sun) The 60-acre site of a 17th-century Spanish and Apalachee mission that's been wonderfully reconstructed, especially the soaring Council House. Good tours included with admission provide a fascinating taste of mission life 300 years ago.

Museum of Florida History MUSEUM

(www.museumoffloridahistory.com; 500 S Bronough St; ☺9am-4:30pm Mon-Fri, from 10am Sat, from noon Sun) **FREE** Here it is, Florida's history splayed out in fun, crisp exhibits: from mastodon skeletons to Florida's Paleo-Indians and Spanish shipwrecks, the Civil War to 'tin-can tourism.'

Florida Capitol Buildings HISTORIC BUILDING

FREE Old and new, side by side. The current **Florida State Capitol** (cnr Pensacola & Duval Sts; ☺8am-5pm Mon-Fri) is, in a word,

DON'T MISS

WAKULLA SPRINGS

Just 15 miles south of Tallahassee is the world's deepest freshwater spring at **Edward Ball Wakulla Springs State Park** (✆850-561-7276; www.floridastateparks.org; 465 Wakulla Park Dr; car/bike $6/2, boat tours adult/child $8/5; ⊙8am-dusk). The springs flow from massive underwater caves that are an archeologist's dream, with fossilized bones including a mastodon that was discovered around 1850. These days you can swim in the icy springs or enjoy them from a glass-bottom boat. You can also take a boat tour of the wildlife-filled Wakulla River, which was used as a movie set for several Tarzan movies, as well as *The Creature from the Black Lagoon*. Overnighters can stay in the park at the **Wakulla Springs Lodge** (✆850-926-0700; www.wakullaspringslodge.com; 465 Wakulla Park Dr; r $85-125), a grand Spanish-style lodge built in 1937 where an 11ft stuffed alligator named 'Old Joe' keeps an eye on things.

ugly, but its top-floor observation deck gives you a bird's-eye view of the city. Next door, the **Historic Capitol** (www.flhistoric-capitol.gov; 400 S Monroe St; ♿) FREE is the more charming 1902 predecessor. Inside, the **Florida Legislative Research Center and Museum** (www.flrcm.gov; free admission; ⊙9am-4:30pm Mon-Fri, from 10am Sat, from noon Sun) FREE has intriguing government and cultural exhibits, including one on the infamous 2000 US presidential election.

🛏 Sleeping & Eating

Chains are clumped at exits along I-10 and along Monroe St between I-10 and downtown.

Hotel Duval   HOTEL $$
(✆850-224-6000; www.hotelduval.com; 415 N Monroe St; r $109-179; P❄🛜🏊) Tallahassee's slickest digs. This new 117-room hotel goes in for a neo-mod look. A rooftop bar and lounge is open until 2am most nights, and Shula's, a fancy chain steakhouse, is off the lobby.

Governor's Inn   HOTEL $$
(✆850-681-6855; www.thegovinn.com; 209 S Adams St; r $149-209; P❄🛜) In a stellar downtown location, this warm, inviting inn has

everything from single rooms to two-level loft suites, plus a daily cocktail hour.

Catfish Pad   SEAFOOD $
(✆850-575-0053; www.catfishpad.com; 4229 W Pensacola St; mains $8-15; ⊙11am-3pm & 5-9pm Mon-Fri, 11am-9pm Sat) There's no doubt you're in the South at this home-style seafood joint. Go for a plate of cornmeal-battered catfish with a side of grits, chased down with a cup of sweet tea. Yum.

Reangthai   THAI $$
(reangthai.com; 2740 Capital Circle NE; lunch $9-12, mains $13-20; ⊙11am-2pm Tue-Fri, 5-10pm Mon-Sat) The real deal, and elegant despite its strip mall setting, Reangthai serves the kind of spicy, fish sauce-y, explode-in-your-mouth cuisine so many American Thai restaurants shy away from.

Andrew's   AMERICAN $$
(✆850-222-3444; www.andrewsdowntown.com; 228 S Adams St; mains $9-36; ⊙11:30am-10pm) Downtown's see-and-be-seen political hot spot. At this split-level place, the downstairs grill serves casual burgers and beer, while upstairs serves upscale neo-Tuscan dishes.

☆ Entertainment

Bradfordville Blues Club   LIVE MUSIC
(✆850-906-0766; www.bradfordvilleblues.com; 7152 Moses Lane, off Bradfordville Rd; tickets $5-25; ⊙10pm Fri & Sat, 8:30pm some Thu; check online) Down the end of a dirt road lit by tiki torches, you'll find a bonfire raging under the live oaks at this hidden-away juke joint that hosts excellent national blues acts.

❶ Getting There & Around

The **Tallahassee Regional Airport** (www.talgov.com/airport) is about 5 miles southwest of downtown, off Hwy 263. The **Greyhound station** (www.greyhound.com; 112 W Tennessee St) is right downtown. **Star Metro** (www.talgov.com/starmetro; single ride $1.25, unlimited 1/7 days $3/10) provides local bus service.

Apalachicola & Around

Slow, mellow and perfectly preserved, Apalachicola is one of the Panhandle's most irresistible, romantic villages. Perched on the edge of a broad bay famous for its oysters, the oak-shaded town is a hugely popular getaway, with a new wave of bistros, art galleries, eclectic boutiques and historic B&Bs.

For town information, visit www.apalachicolabay.org. For nature, the pristine **St Vincent Island** (www.fws.gov/saintvincent) holds pearly dunes, pine forests and wetlands teeming with wildlife. Neighboring **St George Island State Park** (☑850-927-2111; www.floridastateparks.org/stgeorgeisland; vehicle $6, camping $24; ⊙8am-dusk) offers 9 miles of glorious, undeveloped beaches. In town, seek out fishing charters and wildlife cruises.

Ensure romance with a night's stay at **Coombs House Inn** (☑850-653-9199; www.coombshouseinn.com; 80 6th St; r $129-169, ste $149-269; ❉🖤), a stunning Victorian home transformed into a luscious, luxury B&B. Sample the town's famous bivalve, freshly shucked, baked or fried, at **Papa Joe's Oyster Bar & Grill** (www.papajoesoysterbar.com; 301b Market St; mains $8-18; ⊙11am-10pm Mon-Tue, 11am-11pm Thu-Sat).

Panama City Beach

There's no mistaking Panama City Beach for anything other than it is: a quintessentially Floridian, carnival-esqe beach town. Spring breakers and summer vacationers flock here for the beautiful white-sand beaches and the hurdy-gurdy of amusements, while mile after mile of high-rise condos insist on disrupting the view. Stop by the **visitor bureau** (☑800-722-3224, 850-233-5070; www.visitpanamacitybeach.com; 17001 Panama City Beach Parkway; ⊙8am-5pm) for information.

A renowned wreck-diving site, the area around Panama City Beach has dozens of natural, historic and artificial reefs. **Dive Locker** (☑850-230-8006; www.divelocker.net; 106 Thomas Dr; ⊙8am-6pm Mon-Sat) has dives from $90, gear included.

St Andrews State Park (www.floridastateparks.org/standrews; car $8) is a peaceful escape with nature trails, swimming beaches and wildlife. Just offshore, **Shell Island** has fantastic snorkeling, and **shuttles** (☑850-233-0504; www.shellislandshuttle.com; adult/child $17/9; ⊙9am-5pm) depart every 30 minutes in summer.

🛏 Sleeping

Summer is the high season for Panhandle beaches. Panama City doesn't lack for choice; to avoid spring breakers, look for the code phrase 'family-friendly.'

Beachbreak by the Sea　　　　MOTEL **$**
(☑850-234-6644; www.beachbreakbythesea.com; 15405 Front Beach Rd; d $79-169; 🅿❉🐾) A refreshing four-story spot in a sea of high-rises, this place offers basic motel-style rooms, a central beachfront location and continental breakfast.

Wisteria Inn　　　　　　　　MOTEL **$$**
(☑850-234-0557; www.wisteria-inn.com; 20404 Front Beach Rd; d $89-149; 🅿❉🐾) This sweet little 15-room motel has a bright, Caribbean theme, poolside mimosa (champagne and orange juice drink) hours and an 'adults only' policy that discourages spring breakers.

DON'T MISS

SCENIC DRIVE: THE EMERALD COAST

Along the Panhandle coast between Panama City Beach and Destin, skip the main highway (Hwy 98) in favor of one of the most enchanting drives in Florida: **Scenic Hwy 30A**. This 18-mile stretch of road hugs what's referred to as the Emerald Coast for its almost fluorescent, gem-colored waters lapping brilliant white beaches of ground-quartz crystal.

Leading off Scenic Hwy 30A are pristine, wild parklands like **Grayton Beach State Park** (www.floridastateparks.org/graytonbeach; 357 Main Park Rd; car $5), considered one of Florida's prettiest, most pristine strands. About 15 quaint communities hug the coast, some arty and funky, and some master-planned resorts with matchy-matchy architectural perfection. Of these, the most intriguing and surreal is the little village of **Seaside** (www.seasidefl.com), a Necco Wafer–colored town that was hailed as a model of New Urbanism in the 1980s.

Seaside is such an idealized vision that, unaltered, it formed the setting for the 1998 film *The Truman Show*, about a man whose 'perfect life' is nothing but a TV show. Other variations on this theme are WaterColor, Alys Beach and Rosemary Beach.

Good online resources are www.30a.com and www.visitsouthwalton.com.

✖ Eating & Drinking

Pineapple Willy's   CARIBBEAN **$$**
(www.pwillys.com; 9875 S Thomas Dr; mains $10-26; ⊘11am-late) Ask for a table on the restaurant pier for breezy beachside dining. Famed for its signature drinks and its house special: Jack Daniels BBQ ribs.

Firefly   MODERN AMERICAN **$$$**
(☎850-249-3359; www.fireflypcb.com; 535 Richard Jackson Blvd; mains $23-42; ⊘5-10pm) This uber atmospheric, fine dining establishment beckons with clever seafood dishes and its cool Library Lounge. It's good enough for the US president – Obama ate here in 2010.

Tootsie's Orchid Lounge   HONKY TONK
(www.tootsies.net; 700 S Pier Park Dr; ⊘10am-late) Lacks the dusty character of the Nashville original, but the nonstop live country music is still plenty boot stompin'.

ⓘ Getting There & Around

The **Panama City International Airport** (PFN; www.iflybeaches.com) is served by a few major airlines. The **Greyhound Station** (www.greyhound.com; 917 Harrison Ave) is in Panama City, and the limited **Bay Town Trolley** (baytowntrolley.org; tickets $1.50) runs only weekdays from 6am to 8pm.

Pensacola & Pensacola Beach

Neighbors with Alabama, Pensacola and its adjacent beach town welcome visitors driving in from the west. Its gorgeous snow-white beaches and tolerance of the annual

---

GOODBYE, MULLET

Every April, locals gather along the Florida–Alabama state line on Perdido Key for a time-honored tradition: the **Interstate Mullet Toss**. The idea – apart from a great excuse for a party – is to see who can throw their (dead) mullet the furthest into Alabama (we're talking fish, not the unfortunate '80s hairstyle). The event is organized by the **Flora-Bama Lounge, Package and Oyster Bar** (www.florabama.com; 17401 Perdido Key Dr; ⊘11am-3am), a legendary roadhouse that's worth visiting even when the fish aren't flying.

---

spring break bacchanal ensure Pensacola's popularity. There is also a thrumming military culture and a sultry, Spanish-style downtown. The **visitor bureau** (☎800-874-1234, 850-434-1234; www.visitpensacola.com; 1401 E Gregory St; ⊘8am-5pm Mon-Fri, 9am-4pm Sat, 10am-4pm Sun) has maps.

The region has taken its licks in recent years. In 2004 Hurricane Ivan did its best to smash the place, and in 2010 the Deepwater Horizon oil spill in the Gulf of Mexico tainted beaches with tar balls. However, today, all Panhandle beaches are clean of oil, Pensacola's buildings and roads are repaired, and the region is eager to welcome travelers back.

◉ Sights & Activities

★ National Museum of Naval Aviation   MUSEUM
(☎850-452-3604; www.navalaviationmuseum.org; 1750 Radford Blvd; admission free; ⊘9am-5pm Mon-Fri, from 10am Sat & Sun; 🅿) FREE The Pensacola Naval Air Station (NAS) is home to both the museum – a don't-miss collection of jaw-dropping military aircraft – and the elite **Blue Angels** (www.blueangels.navy.mil) squadron.

Historic Pensacola Village   HISTORIC BUILDINGS
(www.historicpensacola.org; Zaragoza St, btwn Tarragona & Adams Sts; adult/child $6/3; ⊘10am-4pm Tue-Sat, tours 11am, 1pm & 2:30pm) Pensacola says 'take that, St Augustine!' with this village, a self-contained enclave of historic homes and museums. Admission is good for one week and includes a guided tour and entrance to each building.

TT Wentworth Museum   MUSEUM
(330 S Jefferson St; admission free; ⊘10am-4pm) FREE The TT Wentworth Museum has two floors of Florida history, including remnants of the Luna expedition and one floor of Wentworth's collection of oddities, including his famous petrified cat.

Pensacola Museum of Art   MUSEUM
(www.pensacolamuseumofart.org; 407 S Jefferson St; adult/student $5/3; ⊘10am-5pm Tue-Fri, from noon Sat) In the city's old jail (1908), this lovely art museum features an impressive, growing collection of major 20th- and 21st-century artists, spanning cubism, realism, pop art and folk art.

Gulf Islands National Seashore   PARK
(www.nps.gov/guis; 7-day pedestrian & cyclist/car
$3/8; ☉ sunrise-sunset) To enjoy the area's
lovely white sands, head to the easy-access
Pensacola Beach or the neighboring Gulf Islands National Seashore, part of a 150-mile
stretch of undeveloped beach. Aim for the
Naval Live Oaks section for a calm, family-
friendly beach, and drive out to **Fort Pickens** (☑850-934-2600; www.nps.gov/guis; Fort
Pickens Rd, Pensacola; ♿) to poke around this
crumbling wreck of a 19th-century fort.

🛏 Sleeping

Noble Inn   B&B $$
(☑850-434-9544; www.noblemanor.com; 110 W
Strong St; r $135-145, ste $160; P☉❄) This
B&B has the prettiest rooms in town; 'Bacall'
would be opulent enough for its namesake.

New World Inn   HOTEL $$
(☑850-432-4111; www.newworldlanding.com; 600
S Palafox St; r from $109; P❄☎) Peek under
the lid of this former box factory and you'll
find surprisingly lovely rooms with luxe
bedding and real carpeting (a beach-town
luxury).

Paradise Inn   MOTEL $$
(☑850-932-2319; www.paradiseinn-pb.com; 21 Via
de Luna Dr; r $80-200; P❄☎☰) Across from
the beach, this sherbet-colored motel is a
lively, cheery place thanks to its popular bar
and grill (for quiet, ask for rooms on the park-
ing lot's far side). Rooms are small and clean,
with tiled floors and brightly painted walls.

🍴 Eating & Drinking

★**Joe Patti's**   SEAFOOD MARKET $
(www.joepattis.com; 534 South B St, at Main St;
☉7:30am-7pm Mon-Sat, to 6pm Sun) At this be-
loved seafood emporium, get dock-fresh fish
and seafood, prepared picnic food and sushi.

Jerry's Drive-In   AMERICAN $
(2815 E Cervantes St; mains $7-12; ☉10am-10pm
Mon-Fri, from 7am Sat) No longer a drive-in
or owned by Jerry, but this greasy spoon is
always packed – possibly because you can
hardly eat for less. Cash only.

Dharma Blue   INTERNATIONAL $$
(☑850-433-1275; www.dharmablue.com; 300 S
Alcaniz St; mains $10-30; ☉11am-4pm & 5-9:30pm
Mon-Sat; ♿) Many locals consider this the
area's best restaurant. The eclectic menu
goes from fried green tomatoes to luscious
sushi rolls.

Peg Leg Pete's   SEAFOOD $$
(☑850-932-4139; 1010 Fort Pickens Rd; mains $8-
20; ☉11am-10pm; ♿) Raw? Rockefeller? Casi-
no? Get your oysters any way you like 'em at
this popular beach hangout with live music
and pirate decor.

McGuire's Irish Pub   PUB $$
(www.mcguiresirishpub.com; 600 E Gregory St;
mains $11-30; ☉11am-late) Promising 'feasting,
imbibery and debauchery,' this barnlike spot
delivers all three. Stick to steaks and burgers, and don't mind the animal heads or
dollar-bill-adorned walls. Stay late, and be
prepared to sing along.

★**Seville Quarter**   CLUB
(www.sevillequarter.com; 130 E Government St;
☉7am-2:30am) Taking up an entire city block,
this multi-venue complex always has something going on from breakfast through last
call in their seven separate eating, drinking
and music venues.

ℹ Getting There & Around

Five miles northeast of downtown, **Pensacola
Regional Airport** (www.flypensacola.com; 2430
Airport Blvd) is served by major airlines. The
Greyhound station (505 W Burgess Rd) is 9
miles north of downtown.

Great Lakes

Best Places to Eat

➡ Little Goat (p537)

➡ Tucker's (p567)

➡ Old Fashioned (p592)

➡ Zingerman's Roadhouse (p577)

➡ Bryant-Lake Bowl (p602)

Best Places to Stay

➡ Inn on Ferry Street (p573)

➡ Acme Hotel (p533)

➡ Brewhouse Inn & Suites (p588)

➡ Cleveland Hostel (p557)

➡ Lighthouse B&B (p609)

Why Go?

Don't be fooled by all the corn. Behind it lurk surfing beaches and Tibetan temples, car-free islands and the green-draped night-lights of the aurora borealis. The Midwest takes its knocks for being middle-of-nowhere boring; so consider the moose-filled national parks, urban five-ways and Hemingway, Dylan and Vonnegut sites to be its little secret.

Roll call for the Midwest's cities starts with Chicago, which unfurls what is arguably the country's mightiest skyline. Milwaukee keeps the beer-and-Harley flame burning, while Minneapolis shines a hipster beacon out over the fields. Detroit rocks, plain and simple.

The Great Lakes themselves are huge, like inland seas, offering beaches, dunes, resort towns and lots of lighthouse-dotted scenery. Dairy farms and fruit orchards blanket the region, meaning that fresh pie and ice cream await road trippers.

When to Go
Chicago

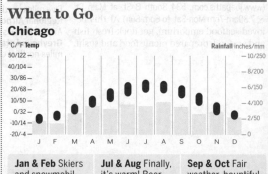

Jan & Feb Skiers and snowmobilers hit the trails.

Jul & Aug Finally, it's warm! Beer gardens hop, beaches splash, and festivals rock most weekends.

Sep & Oct Fair weather, bountiful farm and orchard harvests, and shoulder-season bargains.

Getting There & Around

Chicago's O'Hare International Airport (ORD) is the main air hub for the region. Detroit (DTW), Cleveland (CLE) and Minneapolis (MSP) also have busy airports.

A car is the easiest way to get around, especially if you want to head down Route 66 or dawdle on scenic backroads. Quarters and dollar bills are useful for tollways.

Greyhound (www.greyhound.com) connects many local cities and towns. Upstart **Megabus** (www.megabus.com/us) provides an efficient alternative between major Great Lakes cities; it has no terminals (drop-off and pick-up are at various street corners), and all purchases must be made in advance online (you cannot buy a ticket from the driver).

Amtrak's national rail network centers on Chicago. Trains depart at least once daily for San Francisco, Seattle, New York City, New Orleans and San Antonio. Regional trains chug to Milwaukee (seven daily) and Detroit (three daily).

The **Lake Express** (www.lake-express.com) car/passenger ferry provides a shortcut between Wisconsin and Michigan. It sails across Lake Michigan between Milwaukee and Muskegon.

PLANNING

A couple of things to know before you go: prebooking accommodation during summer is a good idea, especially in resort-orientated places such as Mackinac Island in Michigan, and the North Shore in Minnesota. It's also advised for festival-packed cities such as Milwaukee and Chicago.

Chowhounds who crave dinner at top-end restaurants such as Chicago's Alinea or Minneapolis' Butcher & the Boar should reserve in advance (for Alinea, start looking online a good two months prior).

Eyeing a nice beachfront campsite at one of the state parks? Better nab it early on; most parks take online reservations for a small fee.

Bring insect repellent, especially if you're heading to the Northwoods. The black flies in spring and mosquitoes in summer can be brutal.

Top Five Activity Hot Spots

→ **Boundary Waters** (p610) Canoe where wolves and moose roam

→ **Wisconsin's Rails to Trails** (p586) Pedal through cow-dotted farmland

→ **Apostle Islands** (p596) Kayak through sea caves

→ **New Buffalo** (p578) Learn to surf in Harbor Country

→ **Isle Royale** (p585) Hike and camp in pristine backcountry

DON'T MISS

Only in the Midwest can you fork into proper cheese curds (Wisconsin), deep-dish pizza (Chicago) and sugar cream pie (Indiana).

Fast Facts

→ **Hub cities** Chicago (population 2.7 million), Minneapolis (population 393,000), Detroit (population 701,000)

→ **Time zone** Eastern (IN, OH, MI), Central (IL, WI, MN)

→ **Amount of cheese Wisconsin produces annually** 2.5 billion pounds (25% of America's hunks)

Did You Know?

The Great Lakes hold about 20% of the earth's and 95% of America's fresh water.

Resources

→ **Chicago Reader** (www.chicagoreader.com) Arts and entertainment listings.

→ **Great Lakes Information Network** (www.great-lakes.net) Environmental news.

→ **Midwest Microbrews** (www.midwestmicrobrews.com) The sudsy lowdown.

Great Lakes Highlights

1 Absorbing the skyscrapers, museums, festivals and foodie bounty of **Chicago** (p519).

2 Beach lounging, berry eating on Michigan's **western shore** (p578).

3 Slowing down for clip-clopping horses and buggies in **Amish Country** (p555).

4 Polka dancing at a Friday-night fish fry in **Milwaukee** (p586).

5 Paddling the **Boundary Waters** (p610) and sleeping under a blanket of stars.

6 Cycling along the river against the urban backdrop of **Detroit** (p569).

7 Taking the slowpoke, pie-filled route through Illinois on **Route 66** (p544).

GREAT LAKES IN...

Five Days

Spend the first two days in **Chicago**. On your third day, make the 1½-hour trip to **Milwaukee** for culture, both high- and lowbrow. Take the ferry over to Michigan and spend your fourth day beaching in **Saugatuck**. Circle back via **Indiana Dunes** or **Indiana's Amish Country**.

Ten Days

After two days in **Chicago**, on day three make for **Madison** and its surrounding quirky sights. Spend your fourth and fifth days at the **Apostle Islands**, and then head into the Upper Peninsula to visit **Marquette** and **Pictured Rocks** for a few days, followed by **Sleeping Bear Dunes** and the wineries around **Traverse City**. Return via the galleries, pies and beaches of **Saugatuck**.

History

The region's first residents included the Hopewell (around 200 BC) and Mississippi River mound builders (around AD 700). Both left behind mysterious piles of earth that were tombs for their leaders and possibly tributes to their deities. You can see remnants at Cahokia in southern Illinois, and Mound City in southeastern Ohio.

French voyageurs (fur traders) arrived in the early 17th century and established missions and forts. The British turned up soon after that, with the rivalry spilling over into the French and Indian War (Seven Years' War, 1754–61), after which Britain took control of all of the land east of the Mississippi. Following the Revolutionary War, the Great Lakes area became the new USA's Northwest Territory, which was soon divided into states and locked to the region after it developed its impressive canal and railroad network. But conflicts erupted between the newcomers and the Native Americans, including the 1811 Battle of Tippecanoe in Indiana; the bloody 1832 Black Hawk War in Wisconsin, Illinois and around, which forced indigenous people to move west of the Mississippi; and the 1862 Sioux uprising in Minnesota.

Throughout the late 19th and early 20th centuries, industries sprang up and grew quickly, fueled by resources of coal and iron, and cheap transport on the lakes. The work available brought huge influxes of immigrants from Ireland, Germany, Scandinavia and southern and eastern Europe. For decades after the Civil War a great number of African Americans also migrated to the region's urban centers from the South.

The area prospered during WWII and throughout the 1950s, but this was followed by 20 years of social turmoil and economic stagnation. Manufacturing industries declined, which walloped Rust Belt cities such as Detroit and Cleveland with high unemployment and 'white flight' (ie white middle-class families who fled to the suburbs).

The 1980s and '90s brought urban revitalization. The region's population increased, notably with newcomers from Asia and Mexico. Growth in the service and high-tech sectors resulted in economic balance, although manufacturing industries such as car making and steel still played a big role, meaning that when the economic crisis hit in 2008, Great Lakes towns felt the pinch first and foremost.

Local Culture

The Great Lakes region – aka the Midwest – is the USA's solid, sensible heartland. It's no surprise that novelist Ernest Hemingway hailed from this part of the country, where words are seldom wasted.

If the Midwest had a mantra, it might be to work hard, go to church and stick to the straight and narrow...unless there's a sports game happening, and then it's OK to slather on the body paint and dye your hair purple (or whatever team colors dictate). Baseball, football, basketball and ice hockey are all hugely popular, with the big cities sponsoring pro teams for each sport.

Music has always been a big part of local culture. Muddy Waters and Chess Records spawned the electric blues in Chicago. Motown Records started the soul sound in Detroit. Alt rock shakes both cities (think Wilco in Chicago, White Stripes in Detroit) and has also come out of Minneapolis (the Replacements, Hüsker Dü) and Dayton, Ohio (Guided By Voices, the Breeders).

The region is more diverse than outsiders might expect. Immigrants from Mexico, Africa, the Middle East and Asia have established communities throughout the Midwest, mostly in the cities, where they are making welcomed contributions, especially to local dining scenes.

ILLINOIS

Chicago dominates the state with its sky-high architecture and superlative museums, restaurants and music clubs. But venturing further afield reveals Hemingway's hometown of 'wide lawns and narrow minds,' scattered shrines to local hero Abe Lincoln, and a trail of corn dogs, pies and drive-in movie theaters down Route 66. A cypress swamp and a prehistoric World Heritage site make appearances in Illinois too.

ℹ️ Information

Illinois Bureau of Tourism (www.enjoyillinois.com)

Illinois Highway Conditions (www.gettingaroundillinois.com)

Illinois State Park Information (www.dnr.illinois.gov) State parks are free to visit. Campsites cost $6 to $35; some accept reservations (www.reserveamerica.com; booking fee $5).

Chicago

Loving Chicago is 'like loving a woman with a broken nose: you may well find lovelier lovelies, but never a lovely so real.' Writer Nelson Algren summed it up well in *Chicago: City on the Make*. There's something about this cloud-scraping city that bewitches. Well, maybe not during the six-month winter, when the 'Windy City' gets slapped by snowy blasts; however, come May, when the weather warms and everyone dashes for the outdoor festivals, ballparks, lakefront beaches and beer gardens – ah, nowhere tops Chicago (literally: some of the world's tallest buildings are here).

Beyond its mighty architecture, Chicago is a city of Mexican, Polish, Vietnamese and other ethnic neighborhoods in which to wander. It's a city of blues, jazz and rock clubs any night of the week. And it's a chow-hound's town, where the queues for hot dogs equal those at North America's top restaurants.

Forgive us, but it has to be said: the Windy City will blow you away with its low-key, cultured awesomeness.

History

In the late 17th century the Potawatomi gave the name Checagou – meaning wild onions – to the once-swampy environs. The new city's pivotal moment happened on October 8, 1871, when (so the story goes) Mrs O'Leary's cow kicked over the lantern that started the Great Chicago Fire. It torched the entire inner city and left 90,000 people homeless.

'Damn,' said the city planners. 'Guess we shouldn't have built everything from wood. It's flammable.' So they rebuilt with steel and created space for bold new structures, such as the world's first skyscraper, which popped up in 1885.

Al Capone's gang more or less ran things during the 1920s and corrupted the city's political system. Local government has had issues ever since, with 31 city council members going to jail over the last four decades.

ILLINOIS FACTS

Nicknames Prairie State, Land of Lincoln

Population 12.9 million

Area 57,900 sq miles

Capital city Springfield (population 117,000)

Other cities Chicago (population 2.7 million)

Sales tax 6.25%

Birthplace of Author Ernest Hemingway (1899–1961), animator Walt Disney (1901–66), jazz musician Miles Davis (1926–91), actor Bill Murray (b 1950)

Home of Cornfields, Route 66 starting point

Politics Democratic in Chicago, Republican downstate

Famous for Skyscrapers, corn dogs, Abe Lincoln sights

Official snack food Popcorn

Driving distances Chicago to Milwaukee 92 miles, Chicago to Springfield 200 miles

Metro Chicago Area

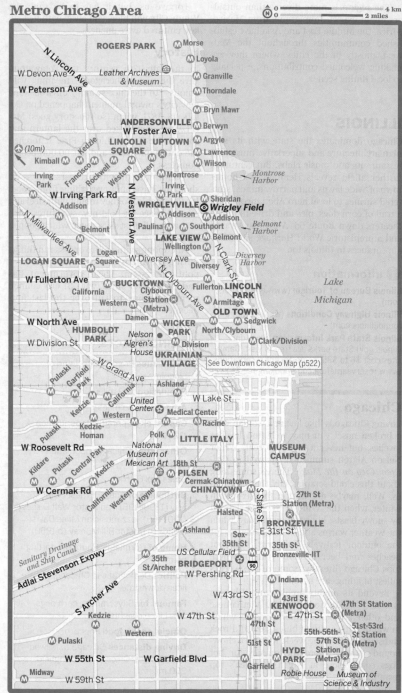

0   4 km
0   2 miles

ROGERS PARK

Morse
Loyola

Leather Archives
& Museum

W Devon Ave
W Peterson Ave

N Lincoln Ave

Granville
Thorndale
Bryn Mawr
Berwyn

ANDERSONVILLE
W Foster Ave

LINCOLN   UPTOWN
SQUARE

Argyle
Lawrence
Wilson

(10mi)

Kimball
Kedzie
Irving
Park
Francisco
Rockwell
Western
Damen

Montrose

Montrose
Harbor

Irving
Park

W Irving Park Rd
Addison

WRIGLEYVILLE

Sheridan

Wrigley Field

N Western Ave

Addison
Addison
Paulina   Southport

Belmont
Harbor

Belmont

LAKE VIEW   Belmont

Wellington

N Milwaukee Ave

Logan
Square

W Diversey Ave
Diversey

Diversey
Harbor

Logan
Square

LOGAN SQUARE

N Clybourn Ave

N Clark St

Lake
Michigan

W Fullerton Ave

California

BUCKTOWN
Clybourn
Station
(Metra)

Fullerton   LINCOLN
PARK

Armitage

OLD TOWN

Sedgwick

Western
Damen

W North Ave

HUMBOLDT
PARK

WICKER
PARK

North/Clybourn

Clark/Division

Nelson
Algren's
House

Division

W Division St

Pulaski
Garfield
Park
Kedzie
California

UKRAINIAN
VILLAGE

Ashland

W Grand Ave

See Downtown Chicago Map (p522)

W Lake St

United
Center

Medical Center
Racine

Western

Kedzie-
Homan

Polk
Kildare
Pulaski
Central Park
Kedzie

National
Museum of
Mexican Art

LITTLE ITALY

MUSEUM
CAMPUS

W Roosevelt Rd

18th St
PILSEN

W Cermak Rd

Cermak-Chinatown
CHINATOWN

California
Western
Hoyne

Halsted

Sanitary Drainage
and Ship Canal

Ashland

S State St

27th St
Station (Metra)

BRONZEVILLE
E 31st St

Adlai Stevenson Expwy

35th
St/Archer

Sox-
35th St

US Cellular Field

BRIDGEPORT

W Pershing Rd

35th St-
Bronzeville-IIT

90

Indiana

S Archer Ave

W 43rd St

43rd St
Station (Metra)

KENWOOD
E 47th St

47th St Station
(Metra)

Kedzie

W 47th St

47th St

51st St-53rd
St Station
(Metra)

Western

Pulaski

51st St

55th-56th-
57th St
Station
(Metra)

W 55th St   W Garfield Blvd

HYDE
PARK

Midway

W 59th St

Garfield

Robie House

Museum of
Science & Industry

⊙ Sights

Chicago's main attractions are found mostly in or near the city center, though visits to distant neighborhoods, such as Pilsen and Hyde Park, can also be rewarding. For more in-depth city explorations, pick up Lonely Planet's *Chicago* city guide.

⊙ The Loop

The city center and financial district is named for the elevated train tracks that lasso its streets. It's busy all day, though not much happens at night other than in Millennium Park and the Theater District, near the intersection of N State and W Randolph Sts.

★ Millennium Park PARK

(Map p522; ☑ 312-742-1168; www.millenniumpark. org; 201 E Randolph St; ⊙ 6am-11pm; ⊞; Ⓜ Brown, Orange, Green, Purple or Pink Line to Randolph) **FREE** The city's showpiece is a trove of free and arty sights. It includes **Pritzker Pavilion** (Map p522; 201 E Randolph St), Frank Gehry's swooping silver band shell, hosting free concerts nightly in summer; Anish Kapoor's beloved silvery sculpture **Cloud Gate** (Map p522) (aka 'The Bean'); and Jaume Plensa's **Crown Fountain** (Map p522), a de facto water park that projects video images of locals spitting water, gargoyle style.

The **McCormick Tribune Ice Rink** fills with skaters in winter (and alfresco diners in summer). The hidden **Lurie Garden** blooms with prairie flowers and tranquility. The Gehry-designed **BP Bridge** spans Columbus Dr and offers great skyline views. And the

Nichols Bridgeway arches from the park up to the Art Institute's 3rd-floor contemporary sculpture garden (free to view).

The pavilion concerts take place at lunchtime and at 6:30pm most nights. For the latter, bring a picnic and bottle of wine and tune in to indie rock and new music on Mondays, jazz and world music on Thursdays, and classical music on most other days. Each Saturday free exercise classes (yoga at 8am, Pilates at 9am and dance at 10am) take place on the Great Lawn. And the Family Fun Tent provides free kids' activities daily between 10am and 3pm. Free walking tours take place daily at 11:30am and 1pm; departure is from the Chicago Cultural Center Visitors Center, across the street from the park.

★ Art Institute of Chicago MUSEUM

(Map p522; ☑ 312-443-3600; www.artic.edu; 111 S Michigan Ave; adult/child $23/free; ⊙ 10:30am-5pm, to 8pm Thu; ⊞) The second-largest art museum in the country. The collection of impressionist and post-impressionist paintings is second only to those in France, and the number of surrealist works is tremendous. Download the free app for DIY tours. It offers 50 jaunts, everything from highlights (Grant Wood's *American Gothic*, Edward Hopper's *Nighthawks*) to a 'birthday-suit tour' of naked works.

Allow two hours to browse the museum's must-sees; art buffs should allocate much longer. The main entrance is on Michigan Ave, but you can also enter via the dazzling Modern Wing on Monroe St. Note that the 3rd-floor contemporary sculpture garden

---

CHICAGO IN...

Two Days

On your first day, take an **architectural tour** and gaze up at the city's skyscrapers. Look down from the **John Hancock Center**, one of the world's tallest buildings. See 'The Bean' reflect the skyline, and splash with Crown Fountain's human gargoyles at **Millennium Park**. Chow down on a deep-dish pizza at **Giordano's**.

Make the second day a cultural one: explore the **Art Institute of Chicago** or **Field Museum of Natural History**. Grab a stylish dinner in the **West Loop**. Or listen to blues at **Buddy Guy's Legends**.

Four Days

Follow the two-day itinerary. On your third day, dip your toes in Lake Michigan at **North Avenue Beach** and saunter through leafy **Lincoln Park**. If it's baseball season, head to **Wrigley Field** for a Cubs game. In the evening yuck it up at **Second City**.

Pick a neighborhood on your fourth day: vintage boutiques and rock 'n' roll in **Wicker Park**, murals and mole sauce in **Pilsen**, pagodas and Vietnamese sandwiches in **Uptown**, or Obama sights and the Nuclear Energy sculpture in **Hyde Park**.

Downtown Chicago

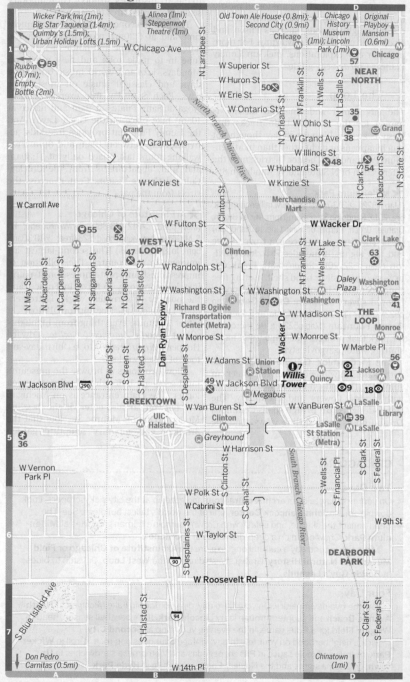

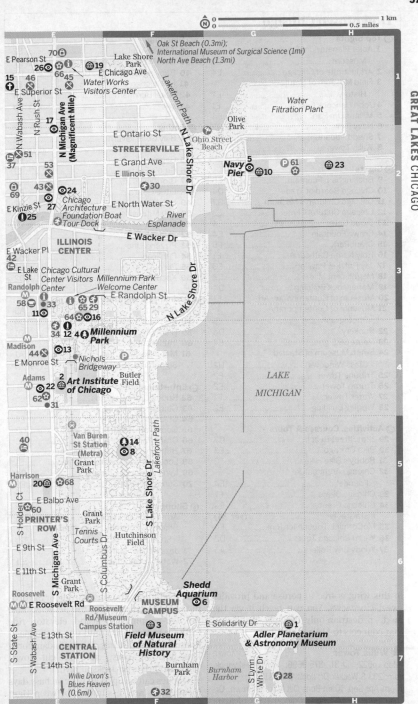

0 1 km
0 0.5 miles

E Pearson St 70
26
66 45
E Chicago Ave
19
Water Works
Visitors Center
15
46
E Superior St
17
N Michigan Ave (Magnificent Mile)
N Wabash Ave
N Rush St
E Ontario St
STREETERVILLE
Olive Park
Water
Filtration Plant
37
51
53
E Grand Ave
E Illinois St
Ohio Street Beach
Navy
Pier
5
10
61
23
69
43
24
27
Chicago
Architecture
Foundation Boat
Tour Dock
30
River
Esplanade
E North Water St
25
ILLINOIS
CENTER
E Wacker Dr
42
E Wacker Pl
E Lake
St
Chicago Cultural
Center Visitors
Center
Millennium Park
Welcome Center
LAKE
MICHIGAN
Randolph
58
11
33
65 29
E Randolph St
64
16
34
12
4
Millennium
Park
Madison
44
13
E Monroe St
Nichols
Bridgeway
2
Art Institute
of Chicago
22
Butler
Field
62
31

Oak St Beach (0.3mi);
International Museum of Surgical Science (1mi)
North Ave Beach (1.3mi)

Lake Shore
Park

E Kinzie St

N Lake Shore Dr

Lakefront Path

40

Van Buren
St Station
(Metra)
14
8
Grant
Park
Harrison
20
68
60
E Balbo Ave
S Holden Ct
PRINTER'S
ROW
Grant
Park
Tennis
Courts
Hutchinson
Field
Lakefront Path
E 9th St
E 11th St
Grant
Park
Roosevelt
E Roosevelt Rd
S State St
S Wabash Ave
S Michigan Ave
S Columbus Dr
Roosevelt
Rd/Museum
Campus Station
MUSEUM
CAMPUS
Shedd
Aquarium
6
3
E Solidarity Dr
1
E 13th St
Field Museum
of Natural
History
Adler Planetarium
& Astronomy Museum
CENTRAL
STATION
E 14th St
Burnham
Park
Burnham
Harbor
S Lynn White Dr
28
Willie Dixon's
Blues Heaven
(0.6mi)
32

Downtown Chicago

in this wing is free to peruse and provides sweet city views. You can reach it via the mod, pedestrian-only Nichols Bridgeway that connects to Millennium Park.

★ **Willis Tower**　　　　　　　　TOWER
(Map p522; ☏ 312-875-9696; www.the-skydeck. com; 233 S Wacker Dr; adult/child $18/12; ☺9am-10pm Apr-Sep, 10am-8pm Oct-Mar; Ⓜ Brown, Orange, Purple, Pink Line to Quincy) It's Chicago's

tallest building, and the 103rd-floor Skydeck puts you 1454ft up into the heavens. Take the ear-popping 70-second elevator ride to the top, then step onto one of the glass-floored ledges jutting out in midair for a knee-buckling perspective straight down. The entrance is on Jackson Blvd.

Queues can be up to an hour on busy days (peak times are in summer, between 11am and 4pm Friday through Sunday). A bit of history: it was the Sears Tower until insurance broker Willis Group Holdings bought the naming rights in 2009. And it was the USA's tallest building until New York's One World Trade Center shot past it in 2013.

For those who prefer a drink with their vista, the Gold Coast's John Hancock Center is a better choice.

Chicago Cultural Center CULTURAL BUILDING
(Map p522; ☎312-744-6630; www.chicagoculturalcenter.org; 78 E Washington St; ⏰8am-7pm Mon-Thu, to 6pm Fri, 9am-6pm Sat, 10am-6pm Sun; Ⓜ Brown, Orange, Green, Purple or Pink Line to Randolph) FREE The block-long building houses ongoing art exhibitions and foreign films, as well as jazz, classical and electronic dance music concerts at lunchtime (12:15pm Monday to Friday). It also contains the world's largest Tiffany stained-glass dome, Chicago's main visitor center and StoryCorps' recording studio (where folks tell their tale, get a CD of it, and have it preserved in the Library of Congress). All free!

Grant Park PARK
(Map p522; Michigan Ave btwn 12th & Randolph Sts; ⏰6am-11pm) Grant Park hosts the city's mega-events, such as Taste of Chicago, Blues Fest and Lollapalooza. **Buckingham Fountain** (Map p522; cnr E Congress Pkwy & S Columbus Dr; Ⓜ Red Line to Harrison) is Grant's centerpiece. The fountain is one of the world's largest, with a 1.5-million-gallon capacity. It lets loose on the hour every hour between 9am and 11pm mid-April to mid-October, accompanied at night by multicolored lights and music.

Route 66 Sign HISTORIC SITE
(Map p522; E Adams St btwn S Michigan & Wabash Aves; Ⓜ Brown, Orange, Green, Purple or Pink Line to Adams) Attention Route 66 buffs: the Mother Road's starting point is here. Look for the marker on Adams St's south side as you head west toward Wabash Ave.

South Loop

The South Loop, which includes the lower ends of downtown and Grant Park, bustles with the lakefront Museum Campus and gleaming new residential high-rises.

★ Field Museum of Natural History MUSEUM
(Map p522; ☎312-922-9410; www.fieldmuseum.org; 1400 S Lake Shore Dr; adult/child $15/10; ⏰9am-5pm; 👪; 🚌146, 130) This museum houses everything but the kitchen sink: beetles, mummies, gemstones, Bushman the stuffed ape. The collection's rockstar is Sue, the largest *Tyrannosaurus rex* yet discovered. She even gets her own gift shop. Special exhibits, like the 3D movie, cost extra.

★ Shedd Aquarium AQUARIUM
(Map p522; ☎312-939-2438; www.sheddaquarium.org; 1200 S Lake Shore Dr; adult/child $29/20; ⏰9am-6pm Jun-Aug, to 5pm Sep-May; 👪; 🚌146, 130) Top draws at the kiddie-mobbed Shedd Aquarium include the Oceanarium, with its beluga whales and frolicking white-sided

FAMOUS LOOP ARCHITECTURE

Ever since it presented the world with the first skyscraper, Chicago has thought big with its architecture and pushed the envelope of modern design. The Loop is a fantastic place to roam and gawk at these ambitious structures.

The Chicago Architecture Foundation (p532) runs tours that explain the following buildings and more:

Chicago Board of Trade (Map p522; 141 W Jackson Blvd; Ⓜ Brown, Orange, Purple, Pink Line to LaSalle) A 1930 art-deco gem. Inside, manic traders swap futures and options. Outside, check out the giant statue of Ceres, the goddess of agriculture, that tops the building.

Rookery (Map p522; www.gowright.org/rookery; 209 S LaSalle St; ⏰9:30am-5:30pm Mon-Fri; Ⓜ Brown, Orange, Purple, Pink Line to Quincy) The 1888 Rookery looks fortresslike outside, but the inside is light and airy thanks to Frank Lloyd Wright's atrium overhaul. Tours ($5 to $10) are available at noon weekdays. Pigeons used to roost here, hence the name.

Monadnock Building (Map p522; www.monadnockbuilding.com; 53 W Jackson Blvd; Ⓜ Blue Line to Jackson) Architectural pilgrims get weak-kneed when they see the Monadnock Building, which is two buildings in one. The north is the older, traditional design from 1891, while the south is the newer, mod half from 1893. See the difference? The Monadnock remains true to its original purpose as an office building.

dolphins, and the shark exhibit, where there's just 5in of Plexiglas between you and two dozen fierce-looking swimmers. The 4D theater, touch tanks and aquatic show cost extra (around $5 each).

★**Adler Planetarium & Astronomy Museum** MUSEUM
(Map p522; ☑312-922-7827; www.adlerplanetarium.org; 1300 S Lake Shore Dr; adult/child $12/8; ⊙9:30am-6pm Jun-Aug, 10am-4pm Sep-May; ⚑; ☐146, 130) Space enthusiasts will get a big bang (pun!) out of the Adler. There are public telescopes from which to view the stars, 3D lectures in which you can learn about supernovas, and the Planet Explorers exhibit where kids can 'launch' a rocket. The immersive digital films cost $10 extra. The Adler's front steps offer Chicago's primo skyline view.

Northerly Island PARK
(1400 S Lynn White Dr; ☐146 or 130) The prairie-grassed park has walking trails, fishing, bird-watching and an outdoor venue for big-name concerts (which you can hear from 12th Street Beach).

Museum of Contemporary Photography MUSEUM
(Map p522; ☑312-663-5554; www.mocp.org; Columbia College, 600 S Michigan Ave; ⊙10am-5pm Mon-Wed, Fri & Sat, 10am-8pm Thu, noon-5pm Sun; Ⓜ Red Line to Harrison) **FREE** The small museum has intriguing exhibits worth a quick browse.

⊙ Near North

The Loop may be where Chicago fortunes are made, but the Near North is where those fortunes are spent. Shops, restaurants and amusements abound.

★**Navy Pier** WATERFRONT
(Map p522; ☑312-595-7437; www.navypier.com; 600 E Grand Ave; ⊙10am-10pm Sun-Thu, to midnight Fri & Sat; ⚑; Ⓜ Red Line to Grand, then trolley) **FREE** Half-mile-long Navy Pier is Chicago's most-visited attraction, sporting a 150ft Ferris wheel and other carnival rides ($5 to $6 each), an IMAX theater, a beer garden and gimmicky chain restaurants. Locals groan over its commercialization, but its lakefront view and cool breezes can't be beat. The fireworks dis-

---

CHICAGO FOR CHILDREN

Chicago is a kid's kind of town. **Chicago Parent** (www.chicagoparent.com) is a dandy resource. Top choices for toddlin' times include the following:

Chicago Children's Museum (Map p522; ☑312-527-1000; www.chicagochildrensmuseum.org; 700 E Grand Ave; admission $14; ⊙10am-6pm Sun-Wed, to 8pm Thu-Sat; ⚑; Ⓜ Red Line to Grand, then trolley) Climb, dig and splash in this educational playland on Navy Pier; follow it with an expedition down the carnival-like wharf itself, including spins on the Ferris wheel and carousel.

Chicago Children's Theatre (☑773-227-0180; www.chicagochildrenstheatre.org) See a show by one the best kids' theater troupes in the country. Performances take place at venues around town.

American Girl Place (Map p522; www.americangirl.com; 835 N Michigan Ave; ⊙10am-8pm Mon-Thu, 9am-9pm Fri & Sat, 9am-6pm Sun; ⚑; Ⓜ Red Line to Chicago) Young ladies sip tea and get new hair-dos with their dolls at this multistory, girl-power palace.

Chic-A-Go-Go (p527) Groove at a taping of this cable-access TV show that's like a kiddie version of Soul Train. Check the website for dates and locations.

Other kid-friendly offerings:
➡ North Ave Beach (p532)
➡ Field Museum of Natural History (p525)
➡ Shedd Aquarium (p525)
➡ Lincoln Park Zoo (p528)
➡ Art Institute of Chicago (p521)
➡ Museum of Science & Industry (p530)

OFFBEAT CHICAGO

Sure, your friends will listen politely as you describe your trip to the Willis Tower's tip, but you'll stop them mid-yawn when you unleash stories of how you boozed with roller babes and saw an iron lung. Chicago has a fine collection of unusual sights and activities to supplement its standard attractions.

International Museum of Surgical Science (☑ 312-642-6502; www.imss.org; 1524 N Lake Shore Dr; adult/child $15/7, Tue free; ⊙ 10am-4pm Tue-Fri, to 5pm Sat & Sun; ☐ 151) Amputation saws, cadaver murals and a fine collection of 'stones' (as in kidney stones and gallstones) are among the offerings at this eerie museum. The antique hemorrhoid surgery toolkit serves as a reminder to eat lots of fiber. It's set in an old Gold Coast mansion, about a mile north of the Water Tower area.

Windy City Rollers (Map p522; www.windycityrollers.com; 525 S Racine Ave; tickets $20; Ⓜ Blue Line to Racine) The bang-'em-up sport of roller derby was born in Chicago in 1935, and the battlin' babes here will show you how it's played, bruises and all. Matches take place monthly at UIC Pavilion, west of the Loop.

Leather Archives & Museum (☑ 773-761-9200; www.leatherarchives.org; 6418 N Greenview Ave; admission $10; ⊙ 11am-7pm Thu & Fri, to 5pm Sat & Sun; ☐ 22) The kinky museum holds all sorts of fetish and S&M exhibits, from the Red Spanking Bench to info on famous foot fetishists. It's 8 miles north of the Loop, and 1.5 miles north of Andersonville.

Chic-A-Go-Go (www.roctober.com/chicagogo) The cable access show's live dance audience isn't just kids: adults, too, can shake it on the dance floor with Miss Mia and Ratso.

plays on summer Wednesdays (9:30pm) and Saturdays (10:15pm) are a treat too.

The Chicago Children's Museum and Smith Museum of Stained Glass Windows are also on the pier, as are several boat-cruise operators. Try the Shoreline water taxi for a fun ride to the Museum Campus (adult/child $8/5).

Smith Museum of
Stained Glass Windows   MUSEUM
(Map p522; ☑ 312-595-5024; 600 E Grand Ave; ⊙ 10am-10pm Sun-Thu, to midnight Fri & Sat; Ⓜ Red Line to Grand, then trolley) FREE More than 150 gorgeous windows – including stained-glass Michael Jordan – hide along the lower-level terraces of Navy Pier's Festival Hall.

Magnificent Mile   STREET
(Map p522; www.themagnificentmile.com; N Michigan Ave) Spanning Michigan Ave between the river and Oak St, the Mag Mile is the much-touted upscale shopping strip, where Bloomingdales, Neiman's and Saks will lighten your wallet.

Tribune Tower   ARCHITECTURE
(Map p522; 435 N Michigan Ave; Ⓜ Red Line to Grand) Take a close look when passing by the Gothic tower to see chunks of the Taj Mahal, Parthenon and other famous structures embedded in the lower walls.

Trump Tower   TOWER
(Map p522; 401 N Wabash Ave; Ⓜ Red Line to Grand) Donald's 1360ft tower is Chicago's second-tallest building, though architecture critics have mocked its 'toothpick' look.

Wrigley Building   ARCHITECTURE
(Map p522; 400 N Michigan Ave; Ⓜ Red Line to Grand) Built by the chewing-gum maker; the white exterior glows as white as the Doublemint Twins' teeth.

⊙ Gold Coast

The Gold Coast has been the address of Chicago's wealthiest residents for more than 125 years.

★ John Hancock Center   ARCHITECTURE
(☑ 888-875-8439; www.jhochicago.com; 875 N Michigan Ave; adult/child $18/12; ⊙ 9am-11pm; Ⓜ Red Line to Chicago) Get high in Chicago's third-tallest skyscraper. In many ways the view here surpasses the one at Willis Tower. Ascend to the 94th-floor observatory for the 'skywalk' (a screened-in porch that lets you feel the wind) and informative displays about the surrounding buildings. Or bypass the education and head up to the 96th-floor Signature Lounge, where the view is free if you buy a drink.

Museum of Contemporary Art   MUSEUM

(Map p522; 312-280-2660; www.mcachicago.org; 220 E Chicago Ave; adult/student $12/7; 10am-8pm Tue, to 5pm Wed-Sun; Red Line to Chicago) Consider it the Art Institute's brash, rebellious sibling, with especially strong minimalist, surrealist and arts collections, and permanent works by Franz Kline, René Magritte, Cindy Sherman and Andy Warhol.

Original Playboy Mansion   BUILDING

(1340 N State Pkwy; Red Line to Clark/Division) Hugh Hefner began wearing his all-day jammies here, when the rigors of magazine production and heavy partying prevented him from getting dressed. The building contains condos now, but a visit still allows you to boast that 'I've been to the Playboy Mansion.' Head east a block to Astor St and ogle other manors between the 1300 and 1500 blocks.

Water Tower   LANDMARK

(Map p522; 108 N Michigan Ave; Red Line to Chicago) The 154ft-tall turreted tower is a defining city landmark: it was the sole downtown survivor of the 1871 Great Fire.

Lincoln Park & Old Town

Lincoln Park is Chicago's largest green space, an urban oasis spanning 1200 leafy acres along the lakefront. 'Lincoln Park' is also the name of the abutting neighborhood. Both are alive day and night with people jogging, walking dogs, pushing strollers and driving in circles looking for a place to park.

Old Town rests at the southwest foot of Lincoln Park. The intersection of North Ave and Wells St is the epicenter, with saucy restaurants, bars and the Second City improv club fanning out from here.

Lincoln Park Zoo   ZOO

(312-742-2000; www.lpzoo.org; 2200 N Cannon Dr; 10am-4:30pm Nov-Mar, to 5pm Apr-Oct, to 6:30pm Sat & Sun Jun-Aug; ; 151) FREE A local family favorite, filled with gorillas, lions, tigers and other exotic creatures in the shadow of downtown. Check out the Regenstein African Journey, Ape House and Nature Boardwalk for the cream of the crop.

Lincoln Park Conservatory   GARDENS

(312-742-7736; www.lincolnparkconservancy.org; 2391 N Stockton Dr; 9am-5pm; 151) FREE Near the zoo's north entrance, the magnificent 1891 hothouse coaxes palms, ferns and orchids to flourish. In winter, it becomes a soothing, 75°F escape from the icy winds raging outside.

Chicago History Museum   MUSEUM

(312-642-4600; www.chicagohistory.org; 1601 N Clark St; adult/child $14/free; 9:30am-4:30pm Mon-Sat, noon-5pm Sun; ; 22) Multimedia displays cover it all, from the Great Fire to the 1968 Democratic Convention. President Lincoln's deathbed is here; so is the chance to 'become' a Chicago hot dog covered in condiments (in the kids' area, but adults are welcome for the photo op).

GANGSTER SITES

The city would rather not discuss its gangster past; consequently there are no brochures or exhibits about infamous sites. So you'll need to use your imagination when visiting the following as most are not designated as notorious.

Two murders took place near **Holy Name Cathedral** (Map p522; www.holynamecathedral.org; 735 N State St; 8:30am-8:30pm Mon-Sat, to 7pm Sun; Red Line to Chicago). In 1924 North Side boss Dion O'Banion was gunned down in his florist shop (738 N State St) after he crossed Al Capone. O'Banion's replacement, Hymie Weiss, fared no better. In 1926 he was killed on his way to church by bullets flying from a window at 740 N State St.

The **St Valentine's Day Massacre Site** (2122 N Clark St; 22) is where Capone's goons, dressed as cops, lined up seven members of Bugs Moran's gang against the garage wall that used to be here and sprayed them with bullets. The garage was torn down in 1967; the site is now a parking lot.

In 1934, the 'lady in red' betrayed 'public enemy number one' John Dillinger at the **Biograph Theater** (2433 N Lincoln Ave). Dillinger was shot dead by the FBI in the alley beside the venue.

The speakeasy in the basement of the glamorous jazz bar Green Mill (p539) was a Capone favorite.

LOCAL KNOWLEDGE

BLUES FANS' PILGRIMAGE

From 1957 to 1967, the humble building at 2120 S Michigan Ave was Chess Records, the seminal electric blues label. Muddy Waters, Howlin' Wolf and Bo Diddley cut tracks here, and paved the way for rock 'n' roll with their sick licks and amped-up sound. Chuck Berry and the Rolling Stones arrived soon after. The studio is now called **Willie Dixon's Blues Heaven** (312-808-1286; www.bluesheaven.com; 2120 S Michigan Ave; tours $5-10; 11am-4pm Mon-Fri, noon-2pm Sat; 1), named for the bassist who wrote most of the Chess hits. Staff give tours of the premises. It's pretty ramshackle, with few original artifacts on display. Still, when Willie's grandson hauls out the bluesman's well-worn standup bass and lets you take a pluck, it's pretty cool. Free blues concerts rock the side garden on summer Thursdays at 6pm. The building is near Chinatown and about a mile south of the Museum Campus.

Lake View & Wrigleyville

North of Lincoln Park, these neighborhoods can be enjoyed by ambling along Halsted St, Clark St, Belmont Ave or Southport Ave, which are well supplied with restaurants, bars and shops. The only real sight is ivy-covered **Wrigley Field** (www.cubs.com; 1060 W Addison St), named after the chewing-gum guy and home to the much-loved but perpetually losing Chicago Cubs. Ninety-minute tours ($25) of the iconic century-old ballpark are available. The area around the facility is getting a makeover with spiffed-up amenities for visitors.

Andersonville & Uptown

These northern neighborhoods are good for a delicious browse. Andersonville is an old Swedish enclave centered on Clark St, where timeworn European-tinged businesses mix with new foodie restaurants, funky boutiques, vintage shops and gay and lesbian bars. Take the CTA Red Line to the Berwyn stop, and walk west for six blocks.

A short distance south, Uptown is a whole different scene. Take the Red Line to the Argyle stop, and you're in the heart of 'Little Saigon' and its pho-serving storefronts.

Wicker Park, Bucktown & Ukrainian Village

West of Lincoln Park, these three neighborhoods – once havens for working-class central-European immigrants and bohemian writers – are hot property. Fashion boutiques, hipster record stores, thrift shops and cocktail lounges have shot up, especially near the intersection of Milwaukee and North Damen Aves. Division St is also prime wandering territory. It used to be called 'Polish Broadway' for all the polka bars that lined it, but now the requisite cafes and crafty businesses have taken over. There aren't many actual sights here, aside from **Nelson Algren's House** (1958 W Evergreen Ave; Blue Line to Damen), where he wrote several gritty, Chicago-based novels. Alas, it's a private residence, so you can only admire it from the sidewalk.

Logan Square & Humboldt Park

When artists and hipsters got priced out of Wicker Park, they moved west to the Latino communities of Logan Sq and Humboldt Park. For visitors, these are places for small, cool-cat eateries, brewpubs and music clubs. Take the CTA Blue Line to Logan Sq or California.

Near West Side & Pilsen

Just west of the Loop is, well, the **West Loop**. It's akin to New York City's Meatpacking District, with chic restaurants, clubs and galleries poking out between meat-processing plants. W Randolph St and W Fulton Market are the main veins. Nearby **Greektown** runs along S Halsted St near W Jackson Blvd. The areas are about 1.25 miles west of the Loop and easily reached by taxi.

Southwest lies the enclave of **Pilsen**, a festive mix of art galleries, Mexican bakeries, hipster cafes and murals on the buildings. The CTA Pink Line to 18th St drops you in the midst.

National Museum of Mexican Art MUSEUM (312-738-1503; www.nationalmuseumofmexicanart.org; 1852 W 19th St; 10am-5pm Tue-Sun; Pink Line to 18th St) FREE The largest Latino arts institution in the US. This museum's vivid permanent collection includes classical paintings, shining gold altars, skeleton-rich folk art and colorful beadwork.

Pilsen Mural Tours
WALKING TOUR

(☑773-342-4191; per group 1½hr tour $125) Local artist Jose Guerrero leads the highly recommended tours, during which you can learn more about this traditional art form; call to arrange an excursion.

◉ Chinatown

Chicago's small but busy Chinatown is an easy 10-minute train ride from the Loop. Take the Red Line to the Cermak-Chinatown stop, which puts you between the neighborhood's two distinct parts: Chinatown Sq (an enormous bilevel strip mall) unfurls to the north along Archer Ave, while Old Chinatown (the traditional retail area) stretches along Wentworth Ave to the south. Either zone allows you to graze through bakeries, dine on steaming bowls of noodles and shop for exotic wares.

◉ Hyde Park & South Side

The South Side is the generic term applied to Chicago's myriad neighborhoods, including some of its most impoverished, that lie south of 25th St. Hyde Park and abutting Kenwood are the South Side's stars, catapulted into the spotlight by local boy Barack Obama. To get here, take the Metra Electric Line trains from Millennium Station downtown, or bus 6 from State St in the Loop. Several bicycle tours also cruise by the highlights.

University of Chicago
UNIVERSITY

(www.uchicago.edu; 5801 S Ellis Ave; ☐6, ⓜMetra to 55th-56th-57th) The campus is worth a stroll, offering grand Gothic architecture and free art and antiquities museums. It's also where the nuclear age began: Enrico Fermi and his Manhattan Project cronies built a reactor and carried out the world's first controlled atomic reaction on December 2, 1942. The **Nuclear Energy sculpture** (S Ellis Ave btwn E 56th & E 57th Sts), by Henry Moore, marks the spot where it blew its stack.

Museum of Science & Industry
MUSEUM

(☑773-684-1414; www.msichicago.org; 5700 S Lake Shore Dr; adult/child $18/11; ⊗9:30am-5:30pm Jun-Aug, reduced hours Sep-May; 🅿; ☐6, ⓜMetra to 55th-56th-57th) Geek out at the largest science museum in the western hemisphere. Highlights include a WWII German U-boat nestled in an underground display ($8 extra

to tour it) and the 'Science Storms' exhibit with a mock tornado and tsunami. Kids will love the 'experiments' staff conduct in various galleries, like dropping things off the balcony and creating mini explosions.

Robie House
ARCHITECTURE

(☑312-994-4000; www.gowright.org; 5757 S Woodlawn Ave; adult/child $15/12; ⊗11am-3pm Thu-Mon; ☐6, ⓜMetra to 55th-56th-57th) Of the numerous buildings that Frank Lloyd Wright designed around Chicago, none is more famous or influential than Robie House. The resemblance of its horizontal lines to the flat landscape of the Midwestern prairie became known as the Prairie style. Inside are 174 stained-glass windows and doors, which you'll see on the hour-long tours (frequency varies by season).

Obama's House
BUILDING

(5046 S Greenwood Ave) Hefty security means you can't get close to the president's abode, but you can stand across the street on Hyde Park Blvd and glimpse over the barricades at the redbrick Georgian-style manor.

Hyde Park Hair Salon
BUILDING

(5234 S Blackstone Ave; ☐6, ⓜMetra to 51st-53rd) Visit Obama's barber Zariff and the bulletproof glass–encased presidential barber chair. Staff don't mind if you come in and take a look.

🏃 Activities

Tucked away among Chicago's 580 parks are public golf courses, ice rinks, swimming pools and more. Activities are free or low cost, and the necessary equipment is usually available for rent. The **Chicago Park District** (www.chicagoparkdistrict.com) runs the show.

Cycling

Riding along the 18-mile lakefront path is a fantastic way to see the city. Bike rental companies listed here also offer two- to four-hour tours ($35 to $60, including bikes) that cover themes like the lakefront, beer and pizza munching, or South Side sights (highly recommended). Booking online saves money. The **Active Transportation Alliance** (www.activetrans.org) lists groovy bike events around town.

Bike Chicago
CYCLING

(Map p522; ☑312-729-1000; www.bikechicago. com; 239 E Randolph St; bikes per hr/day from $10/35, tour adult/child from $39/25; ⊗6:30am-8pm Mon-Fri, from 8am Sat & Sun, closed Sat & Sun

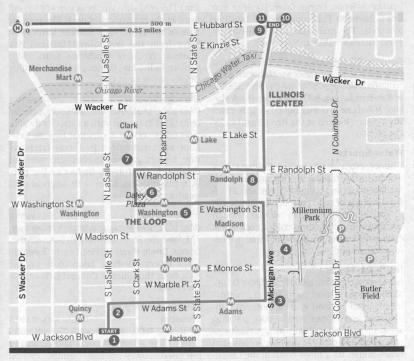

City Walk
The Loop

START CHICAGO BOARD OF TRADE
FINISH BILLY GOAT TAVERN
LENGTH 3 MILES; ABOUT TWO HOURS

This tour swoops through the Loop, highlighting Chicago's revered art and architecture, with a visit to Al Capone's dentist thrown in for good measure.

Start at the **1 Chicago Board of Trade** (p525), where guys in Technicolor coats swap corn (or something like that) inside a cool art-deco building. Step into the nearby **2 Rookery** (p525) to see Frank Lloyd Wright's handiwork in the atrium.

Head east on Adams St to the **3 Art Institute** (p521), one of the city's most-visited attractions. The lion statues out front make a classic keepsake photo. Walk a few blocks north to avant-garde **4 Millennium Park** (p521).

Leave the park and head west on Washington St to **5 Hotel Burnham** (p533). It's housed in the Reliance Building, which was the precursor to modern skyscraper design; Capone's dentist drilled teeth in what's now

room 809. Just west, Picasso's **6 Untitled** sculpture, created by Mr Abstract himself, is ensconced in Daley Plaza. Baboon, dog, woman? You decide. Then go north on Clark St to Jean Dubuffet's **7 Monument with Standing Beast**, another head-scratching sculpture.

Walk east on Randolph St through the theater district. Pop into the **8 Chicago Cultural Center** (p525) to see what free art exhibits or concerts are on. Now go north on Michigan Ave and cross the Chicago River. Just north of the bridge you'll pass the **9 Wrigley Building** (p527), shining bright and white, and the nearby Gothic, eye-popping **10 Tribune Tower** (p527).

To finish your tour, visit **11 Billy Goat Tavern** (p535), a vintage Chicago dive that spawned the Curse of the Cubs: the tavern's owner, Billy Sianis, once tried to enter Wrigley Field with his pet goat. The smelly creature was denied entry, so Sianis called down a mighty curse on the baseball team in retaliation. They've stunk ever since.

Nov-Mar; Ⓜ Brown, Orange, Green, Purple or Pink Line to Randolph) This company has multiple locations. The main one is at Millennium Park; there's another at Navy Pier.

Bobby's Bike Hike

CYCLING

(Map p522; ☑ 312-915-0995; www.bobbysbikehike. com; 465 N McClurg Ct; half/full day from $23/32; ☺ 8am-8pm Jun-Aug, 8:30am-7pm Sep-Nov & Mar-May; Ⓜ Red Line to Grand) Bobby's earns raves from riders; located at the River East Docks' Ogden Slip.

Water Sports

Visitors often don't realize Chicago is a beach town, thanks to mammoth Lake Michigan lapping its side. There are 24 official strands of sand patrolled by lifeguards in summer. Swimming is popular, though the water is pretty damn cold. Check www. cpdbeaches.com for water-quality advice before embarking.

North Ave Beach

BEACH

(www.cpdbeaches.com; 1600 N Lake Shore Dr; 🛗; 🚃 151) Chicago's most popular and amenity-laden stretch of sand wafts a southern California vibe. You can rent kayaks, jet skis, stand-up paddleboards and lounge chairs, as well as eat and drink at the party-orientated beach house. It's 2 miles north of the Loop.

Oak St Beach

BEACH

(www.cpdbeaches.com; 1000 N Lake Shore Dr; Ⓜ Red Line to Chicago) Packs in bodies beautiful at the edge of downtown.

12th Street Beach

BEACH

(Map p522; www.cpdbeaches.com; 1200 S Linn White Dr; 🚃 146, 130) A path runs from the Adler Planetarium to this handsome, secluded crescent of sand.

Ice Skating

Millennium Park's **McCormick Tribune Ice Rink** (Map p522; www.millenniumpark.org; 55 N Michigan Ave; skate rental $10; ☺ late Nov-late Feb) heats up when the temperature plummets.

🗣 Tours

Many companies offer discounts if you book online. Outdoors-oriented tours operate from April to November only, unless otherwise specified.

Chicago Architecture Foundation

BOAT, WALKING TOURS

(CAF; Map p522; ☑ 312-922-3432; www.architecture.org; 224 S Michigan Ave; tours $10-40; Ⓜ Brown, Orange, Green, Purple or Pink Line to Ad-

ams) The gold-standard boat tours ($40) sail from Michigan Ave's river dock. The popular Rise of the Skyscraper walking tours ($17) leave from the downtown Michigan Ave address. Weekday lunchtime tours ($10) explore individual landmark buildings. Buy tickets online or at CAF.

Chicago Greeter

WALKING TOUR

(Map p522; ☑ 312-945-4231; www.chicagogreeter. com) FREE Pairs you with a local city dweller who takes you on a personal tour customized by theme (architecture, history, gay and lesbian, and more) or neighborhood. Travel is by foot and/or public transportation. Reserve 10 business days in advance.

InstaGreeter

WALKING TOUR

(Map p522; www.chicagogreeter.com/instagreeter; 77 E Randolph St; ☺ 10am-3pm Fri-Sun; Ⓜ Brown, Orange, Green, Purple or Pink Line to Randolph) FREE Offers one-hour Loop tours on the spot from the Chicago Cultural Center visitor center.

Chicago History Museum

CYCLING, WALKING TOURS

(☑ 312-642-4600; www.chicagohistory.org; tours $20-55) The museum counts pub crawls, El (elevated/subway system) jaunts, cycling routes and cemetery walks among its excellent tour arsenal. Departure points and times vary.

Weird Chicago Tours

BUS TOUR

(Map p522; ☑ 888-446-7859; www.weirdchicago. com; 600 N Clark St; 3hr tours $30; ☺ 7pm Fri & Sat, 3pm Sat; Ⓜ Red Line to Grand) Drives by ghost, gangster and red-light sites. Departs across from the Hard Rock Cafe.

Chicago Food Planet Tours

WALKING TOUR

(☑ 212-209-3370; www.chicagofoodplanet.com; 3hr tours $47-60) Go on a walkabout in Wicker Park, the Gold Coast or Chinatown, where you'll graze through seven neighborhood eateries. Departure points and times vary.

🎊 Festivals & Events

Chicago has a full events calendar all year, but the biggies take place in the summer. The following events are held downtown on a weekend, unless noted otherwise.

St Patrick's Day Parade

CULTURAL

(www.chicagostpatsparade.com; ☺ mid-May) The local plumbers union dyes the Chicago River shamrock green; a big parade follows.

Blues Festival MUSIC
(www.chicagobluesfestival.us; ⊙ early Jul) The biggest free blues fest in the world, with four days of the music that made Chicago famous.

Taste of Chicago FOOD
(www.tasteofchicago.us; ⊙ mid-Jul) The free five-day bash in Grant Park includes bands and lots of food on a stick.

Pitchfork Music Festival MUSIC
(www.pitchforkmusicfestival.com; day pass $50; ⊙ mid-Jul) Indie bands strum for three days in Union Park.

Lollapalooza MUSIC
(www.lollapalooza.com; day pass $95; ⊙ early Aug) Around 130 bands spill off eight stages at Grant Park's three-day mega-gig.

Jazz Festival MUSIC
(www.chicagojazzfestival.us; ⊙ early Sep) Top names on the national jazz scene play over Labor Day weekend.

🛏 Sleeping

Chicago lodging doesn't come cheap. The best way to cut costs is to use a bidding site like Priceline or Hotwire (look for 'River North' or 'Mag Mile' locations). In summer and when the frequent big conventions trample through town, your options become much slimmer, so plan ahead to avoid unpleasant surprises. The prices we've listed are for the summer peak season. Taxes add 16.4%.

B&Bs give a nice bang for the midrange buck. Contact the **Chicago Bed & Breakfast Association** (www.chicago-bed-breakfast.com; r $125-250), which represents 18 guesthouses. Many properties have two- to three-night minimum stays. Vacation rentals in local apartments are also a good deal here. Try **Vacation Rental By Owner** (www.vrbo.com) or **AirBnB** (www.airbnb.com).

Hotels in the Loop are convenient to the museums, festival grounds and business district, but the area is pretty dead come nightfall. Accommodations in the Near North and Gold Coast are most popular, given their proximity to eating, shopping and entertainment venues. Rooms in Lincoln Park, Lake View and Wicker Park entice because they're often cheaper than rooms downtown; they are also near swingin' nightlife.

Wi-fi is free unless noted otherwise. You pay dearly for parking in Chicago; around $50 per night downtown, and $22 in outlying neighborhoods.

🛏 Loop & Near North

HI-Chicago HOSTEL $
(Map p522; ☏ 312-360-0300; www.hichicago.org; 24 E Congress Pkwy; dm incl breakfast $30-36; P ❀ @ 🛜; Ⓜ Brown, Orange, Purple or Pink Line to Library) Chicago's best hostel is immaculate, conveniently placed in the Loop, and offers bonuses like a staffed information desk, free volunteer-led tours and discount passes to museums and shows. The simple dorm rooms have six to 12 beds, and most have attached baths.

Buckingham Athletic Club Hotel BOUTIQUE HOTEL $$
(Map p522; ☏ 312-663-8910; www.bac-chicago.com; 440 S LaSalle St; r incl breakfast $169-209; P ❀ 🛜 🏊; Ⓜ Brown, Orange, Purple or Pink Line to LaSalle) Tucked into the 40th floor of the Chicago Stock Exchange building, this 21-room hotel is not easy to find. The benefit if you do? Elegant rooms so spacious they'd be considered suites elsewhere. There's also free access to the namesake gym with lap pool.

Best Western River North HOTEL $$
(Map p522; ☏ 800-780-7234, 312-467-0800; www.rivernorthhotel.com; 125 W Ohio St; r $169-249; P ❀ @ 🛜 🏊; Ⓜ Red Line to Grand) The well-maintained rooms with maple veneer beds and desks, together with free parking (!), an indoor pool and sundeck overlooking the city, make this good Near North value.

★ Acme Hotel BOUTIQUE HOTEL $$$
(Map p522; ☏ 312-894-0800; www.acmehotelcompany.com; 15 E Ohio St; r $179-309; P ❀ @ 🛜; Ⓜ Red Line to Grand) Urban bohemians are loving the Acme for its indie-cool style at (usually) affordable rates. The 130 rooms mix industrial fixtures with retro lamps, mid-century furniture and funky modern art. They're wired up with free wi-fi, good speakers, smart TVs and easy connections to stream your own music and movies. Graffiti, neon and lava lights decorate the common areas.

★ Hotel Burnham BOUTIQUE HOTEL $$$
(Map p522; ☏ 312-782-1111; www.burnhamhotel.com; 1 W Washington St; r $269-399; P ❀ @ 🛜 🍽; Ⓜ Blue Line to Washington) The proprietors brag that the Burnham has the highest guest return rates in Chicago; it's easy to see why. Housed in the landmark 1890s Reliance Building (precedent for the modern skyscraper), its slick decor woos architecture buffs. Mahogany writing desks and chaise lounges furnish the bright, butter-colored rooms. A free wine happy hour takes place each evening.

Wit
BOUTIQUE HOTEL $$$

(Map p522; ☏ 312-467-0200; www.thewithotel.com; 201 N State St; r $255-385; P ❋ @ ☎; M Brown, Orange, Green, Purple or Pink Line to State/Lake) Viewtastic rooms, a rooftop bar and an on-site movie theater draw holidaying hipsters and business travelers to the design-savvy, green-glass Wit. Wi-fi is free in the lobby, though there's a fee for in-room service.

Lake View & Wicker Park/Bucktown

★ Urban Holiday Lofts
HOSTEL $

(☏ 312-532-6949; www.urbanholidaylofts.com; 2014 W Wabansia Ave; dm incl breakfast $30-45; r from $100; ❋ @ ☎; M Blue Line to Damen) An international crowd fills the mix of dorms (with four to 10 beds) and private rooms in this building of converted loft condos. Exposed-brick walls, hardwood floors and bunks with plump bedding are common to all 25 rooms. It's close to the El (elevated/subway system) and in the thick of Wicker Park's nightlife.

Wrigley Hostel
HOSTEL $

(☏ 773-598-4471; www.wrigleyhostel.com; 3512 N Sheffield Ave; dm incl breakfast $30; P ❋ @ ☎; M Red Line to Addison) Opened in 2013, the hostel sits in a brick three-flat building within homerun distance of Wrigley Field and its rowdy bar scene. The homey blue-and-green rooms have an average of four beds (not necessarily bunks). Some bathrooms have vintage claw-foot tubs.

Willows Hotel
BOUTIQUE HOTEL $$

(☏ 773-528-8400; www.willowshotelchicago.com; 555 W Surf St; r incl breakfast $149-265; P ❋ ☎; ☐ 22) Small and stylish, the Willows wins an architectural gold star. The chic little lobby provides a swell refuge of overstuffed chairs by the fireplace, while the 55 rooms, done up in shades of peach, cream and soft green, evoke a 19th-century French countryside feel. It's a block north of the commercial hub where Broadway, Clark and Diversey Sts intersect.

Wicker Park Inn
B&B $$

(☏ 773-486-2743; www.wickerparkinn.com; 1329 N Wicker Park Ave; r incl breakfast $149-199; ❋ ☎; M Blue Line to Damen) This brick row house is steps away from rockin' restaurants and nightlife. The sunny rooms aren't huge, but have hardwood floors, pastel colors and small desk spaces. Across the street, two apartments with kitchens provide a self-contained experience. The inn is about a half-mile southeast of the El stop.

Longman & Eagle
INN $$

(☏ 773-276-7110; www.longmanandeagle.com; 2657 N Kedzie Ave; r $85-200; ❋ ☎; M Blue Line to Logan Square) Check in at the Michelin-starred gastropub downstairs, then head to your wood-floored, vintage-stylish accommodation on the floor above. The six rooms aren't particularly soundproofed, but after using your whiskey tokens in the bar you probably won't care. From the El stop, walk a block north on Kedzie Ave.

Days Inn Lincoln Park North
HOTEL $$

(☏ 773-525-7010; www.daysinnchicago.net; 644 W Diversey Pkwy; r incl breakfast $125-185; P ❋ @ ☎; ☐ 22) This well-maintained chain hotel in Lincoln Park is a favorite of both families and touring indie bands, providing good service and perks including free health-club access. It's an easy amble to the lakefront's parks and beaches, and a 15-minute bus ride to downtown. It's right at the hustle-bustle intersection of Broadway, Clark and Diversey streets.

✗ Eating

During the past decade Chicago has become a gastronome's paradise. The beauty here is that even the buzziest restaurants are accessible: they're visionary yet traditional, pubby at the core and decently priced. You can also fork into a superb range of ethnic eats, especially if you break out of downtown and head for neighborhoods such as Pilsen or Uptown.

Need help deciding where to eat? **LTH Forum** (www.lthforum.com) is a great local resource.

✗ The Loop & South Loop

Most Loop eateries are geared to lunch crowds of office workers.

★ Lou Mitchell's
BREAKFAST $

(Map p522; www.loumitchellsrestaurant.com; 565 W Jackson Blvd; mains $6-11; ⏲ 5:30am-3pm Mon-Sat, 7am-3pm Sun; ♿; M Blue Line to Clinton) A relic of Route 66; Lou's old-school waitresses deliver double-yoked eggs and thick-cut French toast just west of the Loop by Union Station. There's usually a queue, but free doughnut holes and Milk Duds help ease the wait.

Cafecito
CUBAN $

(Map p522; www.cafecitochicago.com; 26 E Congress Pkwy; sandwiches $5-7; ⊙7am-9pm Mon-Fri, 10am-6pm Sat & Sun; ☎; Ⓜ Brown, Orange, Purple or Pink Line to Library) Attached to the HI-Chicago hostel and perfect for the hungry, thrifty traveler, Cafecito serves killer Cuban sandwiches layered with citrus-garlic-marinated roasted pork and ham. Strong coffee and hearty egg sandwiches make a fine breakfast.

Gage
PUB $$$

(Map p522; ☑312-372-4243; www.thegagechicago.com; 24 S Michigan Ave; mains $17-36; ⊙11am-11pm, to midnight Fri; Ⓜ Brown, Orange, Green, Purple or Pink Line to Madison) This gastropub dishes up Irish-tinged grub with a fanciful twist, such as Guinness-battered fish and chips, and fries smothered in curry gravy. The booze rocks, too, including a solid whiskey list and small-batch beers that pair with the food.

✕ Near North

This is where you'll find Chicago's mother lode of restaurants.

★ Billy Goat Tavern
BURGERS $

(Map p522; www.billygoattavern.com; 430 N Michigan Ave; burgers $4-6; ⊙6am-2am Mon-Fri, 10am-2am Sat & Sun; Ⓜ Red Line to Grand) *Tribune* and *Sun-Times* reporters have guzzled in the subterranean Billy Goat for decades. Order a 'cheezborger' and Schlitz, then look around at the newspapered walls to get the scoop on infamous local stories, such as the Cubs Curse.

Mr Beef
SANDWICHES $

(Map p522; www.mrbeefonorleans.com; 666 N Orleans St; sandwiches $4-7; ⊙9am-5pm Mon-Fri, 10am-3pm Sat, plus 10:30pm-4am Fri & Sat; Ⓜ Brown or Purple Line to Chicago) A Chicago specialty, the Italian beef sandwich stacks up like this: thin-sliced, slow-cooked roast beef that's sopped in natural gravy and *giardiniera* (spicy, pickled vegetables), and then heaped on a hoagie roll. Mr Beef serves the best at its picnic-style tables.

Xoco
MEXICAN $$

(Map p522; www.rickbayless.com; 449 N Clark St; mains $9-13; ⊙8am-9pm Tue-Thu, to 10pm Fri & Sat; Ⓜ Red Line to Grand) 🍴 Crunch into warm *churros* (spiraled dough fritters) for breakfast,

---

CHICAGO'S HOLY TRINITY OF SPECIALTIES

Chicago cooks up three beloved specialties. Foremost is deep-dish pizza, a hulking mass of crust that rises two or three inches above the plate and cradles a molten pile of toppings. One gooey piece is practically a meal. A large pizza averages $20 at the following places:

Pizzeria Uno (Map p522; www.unos.com; 29 E Ohio St; small pizzas from $13; ⊙11am-1am Mon-Fri, to 2am Sat, to 11pm Sun; Ⓜ Red Line to Grand) The deep-dish concept supposedly originated here in 1943.

Gino's East (Map p522; www.ginoseast.com; 162 E Superior St; small pizzas from $15; ⊙11am-9:30pm Mon-Sat, from noon Sun; Ⓜ Red Line to Chicago) Write on the walls while you wait for your pie.

Lou Malnati's (Map p522; www.loumalnatis.com; 439 N Wells St; small pizzas from $7; ⊙11am-11pm Mon-Thu, 11am-midnight Fri & Sat, noon-11pm Sun; Ⓜ Brown or Purple Line to Merchandise Mart) Famous for its butter crust.

Giordano's (Map p522; www.giordanos.com; 730 N Rush St; small pizzas from $15; ⊙11am-10:30pm Sun-Thu, to 11:30pm Fri & Sat; Ⓜ Red Line to Chicago) Perfectly tangy tomato sauce.

Pizano's (www.pizanoschicago.com; 864 N State St; 10in pizzas from $14; ⊙11am-2am Sun-Fri, to 3am Sat; Ⓜ Red Line to Chicago) Oprah's favorite.

No less iconic is the Chicago hot dog – a wiener that's been 'dragged through the garden' (ie topped with onions, tomatoes, shredded lettuce, bell peppers, pepperoncini and sweet relish, or variations thereof, but *never* ketchup), and then cushioned on a poppy-seed bun. Hot Doug's (p537) does it right.

The city is also revered for its spicy, drippy, only-in-Chicago Italian beef sandwiches. Mr Beef (p535) serves the gold standard.

ROLLING WITH FOOD TRUCKS

Until 2012 it was illegal to cook on a food truck in Chicago. But now food trucks are rolling en masse. They generally prowl office-worker-rich hot spots such as the Loop and Near North around lunchtime, and then Wicker Park and Lake View toward evening. Most trucks tweet their location; *Chicago Magazine* (@ChicagoMag/chicago-food-trucks) amalgamates them. Keep an eye out for the Tamale Spaceship!

meaty *tortas* (sandwiches) for lunch and rich *caldos* (soups) for dinner at celeb chef Rick Bayless' Mexican street-food joint. His upscale restaurants Frontera Grill and Topolobampo are next door, but you'll need reservations or a whole lot of patience to get in.

Purple Pig MEDITERRANEAN $$
(Map p522; ☑312-464-1744; www.thepurplepigchicago.com; 500 N Michigan Ave; small plates $8-16; ☺11:30am-midnight Sun-Thu, to 1am Fri & Sat; ☑; Ⓜ Red Line to Grand) The Pig's Magnificent Mile location, wide-ranging meat and veggie menu, long list of affordable vinos and late-night serving hours make it a crowd pleaser. Milk-braised pork shoulder is the hamtastic specialty.

✖ Lincoln Park & Old Town

Halsted, Lincoln and Clark Sts are the main veins teeming with restaurants and bars.

Wiener's Circle AMERICAN $
(☑773-477-7444; 2622 N Clark St; hot dogs $3-6; ☺10:30am-4am Sun-Thu, to 5am Fri & Sat; Ⓜ Brown or Purple Line to Diversey) As famous for its unruly, foul-mouthed ambiance as for its char-dogs and cheddar fries, the Wiener Circle is *the* place for drunken, late-night munchies.

★ Alinea MODERN AMERICAN $$$
(☑312-867-0110; www.alinearestaurant.com; 1723 N Halsted St; multicourse menu $210-265; ☺5:30-9:30pm Wed-Sun; Ⓜ Red Line to North/Clybourn) Widely regarded as North America's best restaurant, Alinea brings on 20 courses of mind-bending molecular gastronomy. Dishes may emanate from a centrifuge or be pressed into a capsule, a la duck served with a 'pillow of lavender air.' There are no

reservations. Instead Alinea sells tickets two to three months in advance. Sign up at the website for details. Check the Twitter feed (@Alinea) for possible last-minute seats.

✖ Lake View & Wrigleyville

Clark, Halsted, Belmont and Southport are fertile grazing streets.

★ Crisp ASIAN $
(www.crisponline.com; 2940 N Broadway; mains $7-12; ☺11:30am-9pm; Ⓜ Brown Line to Wellington) Music pours from the stereo, and cheap, delicious Korean fusions arrive from the kitchen at this cheerful cafe. The 'Bad Boy Buddha' bowl, a variation on *bi bim bop* (mixed vegetables with rice), is one of the best cheap lunches in town.

Mia Francesca ITALIAN $$
(☑773-281-3310; www.miafrancesca.com; 3311 N Clark St; mains $13-25; ☺5-10pm Mon-Thu, 5-11pm Fri, 10am-11pm Sat, 10am-10pm Sun; Ⓜ Red, Brown or Purple Line to Belmont) Local chain Mia's buzzes with regulars who come for the trattoria's Italian standards, such as seafood linguine, spinach ravioli and mushroom-sauced veal medallions, all prepared with simple flair.

✖ Andersonville & Uptown

For 'Little Saigon' take the CTA Red Line to Argyle. For the European cafes in Andersonville, go one stop further to Berwyn.

★ Hopleaf EUROPEAN $$
(☑773-334-9851; www.hopleaf.com; 5148 N Clark St; mains $11-26; ☺noon-11pm Mon-Thu, to midnight Fri & Sat, to 10pm Sun; Ⓜ Red Line to Berwyn) A cozy, European-style tavern, Hopleaf draws crowds for its Montreal-style smoked brisket, cashew-butter-and-fig-jam sandwich and the house specialty – *frites* and ale-soaked mussels. It also pours 200 types of brew, heavy on the Belgian ales.

Tank Noodle VIETNAMESE $$
(☑773-878-2253; www.tank-noodle.com; 4953 N Broadway; mains $8-14; ☺8:30am-10pm Mon, Tue & Thu-Sat, to 9pm Sun; Ⓜ Red Line to Argyle) The official name is Pho Xe Tang, but everyone just calls it Tank Noodle. The crowds come for *banh mi*, served on crunchy fresh baguette rolls, and the pho, which is widely regarded as the city's best.

Wicker Park, Bucktown & Ukrainian Village

Trendy restaurants open almost every day in these 'hoods.

Big Star Taqueria   MEXICAN $
(www.bigstarchicago.com; 1531 N Damen Ave; tacos $3-4; ⊘11:30am-2am; Ⓜ Blue Line to Damen) This honky-tonk gets packed, but damn, the tacos are worth the wait – pork belly in tomato-*guajillo* (chili) sauce and lamb shoulder with *queso fresco* (white cheese) accompany the specialty whiskey list. Cash only.

★**Ruxbin**   MODERN AMERICAN $$$
(☑312-624-8509; www.ruxbinchicago.com; 851 N Ashland Ave; mains $25-30; ⊘5:30-10pm Tue-Sat, to 9pm Sun; Ⓜ Blue Line to Division) ∅ The passion of the brother-sister team who run Ruxbin is evident in everything from the warm decor made of found items to the artfully prepared flavors in dishes like the pork-belly salad with grapefruit, cornbread and blue cheese. It's a wee place of just 32 seats, and BYOB (bring your own bottle).

Logan Square & Humboldt Park

Logan Sq has become a mecca for inventive, no-pretense chefs. Eats and drinks ring the intersection of Milwaukee, Logan and Kedzie Blvds.

★**Hot Doug's**   AMERICAN $
(☑773-279-9550; www.hotdougs.com; 3324 N California Ave; mains $3-9; ⊘10:30am-4pm Mon-Sat; Ⓜ Blue Line to California or bus 52) Doug is the most famous weenie maker in town, and deservedly so. He serves multiple dog styles (Polish, bratwursts, Chicago) cooked multiple dog ways (char-grilled, deep-fried, steamed). Confused? He'll explain it all. Doug also makes gourmet 'haute dogs,' such as blue-cheese pork with cherry cream sauce. It's sublime, which is why there's always a queue. Cash only.

★**Longman & Eagle**   AMERICAN $$$
(☑773-276-7110; www.longmanandeagle.com; 2657 N Kedzie Ave; mains $17-29; ⊘9am-2am; Ⓜ Blue Line to Logan Sq) Hard to say whether this shabby-chic tavern is best for eating or drinking. Let's say eating, since it earned a Michelin star for its beautifully cooked comfort foods like vanilla brioche French toast

for breakfast, wild-boar sloppy joes for lunch and maple-braised pork shank for dinner. There's a whole menu of juicy small plates, too. Reservations not accepted.

Near West Side & Pilsen

The West Loop booms with hot-chef restaurants. Stroll along Randolph and Fulton Market Sts and take your pick. Greektown extends along S Halsted St (take the Blue Line to UIC-Halsted). The Mexican Pilsen enclave has loads of eateries around W 18th St.

Don Pedro Carnitas   MEXICAN $
(1113 W 18th St; tacos $1.50-2; ⊘6am-6pm Mon-Fri, 5am-5pm Sat, 5am-3pm Sun; Ⓜ Pink Line to 18th) At this no-frills Pilsen meat hive, a man with a machete salutes you at the front counter. He awaits your command to hack off pork pieces, and then wraps the thick chunks with onion and cilantro in a fresh tortilla. Cash only.

★**Little Goat**   DINER $$
(Map p522; www.littlegoatchicago.com; 820 W Randolph St; mains $8-12; ⊘7am-2am; 🛜✍; Ⓜ Green or Pink Line to Morgan) *Top Chef* winner Stephanie Izard opened this diner from her ever-booked main restaurant, Girl and the Goat. Sit on a vintage twirly stool and order from the all-day breakfast menu. Better yet, try lunchtime favorites like the goat sloppy joe with mashed potato tempura or the pork belly on scallion pancakes.

Publican   AMERICAN $$$
(Map p522; ☑312-733-9555; www.thepublicanrestaurant.com; 837 W Fulton Market; mains $19-25; ⊘3:30-10:30pm Mon-Thu, 3:30-11:30pm Fri, 10am-11:30pm Sat & Sun; Ⓜ Green or Pink Line to Morgan) ∅ Set up like a swanky beer hall, Publican specializes in oysters, hams and fine suds – all from small family farms and microbrewers.

🍷 Drinking & Nightlife

During the long winters, Chicagoans count on bars for warmth. The usual closing time is 2am, but some places stay open until 4am. In summer many bars boast beer gardens.

Clubs in the Near North and West Loop tend to be cavernous and luxurious (with dress codes). Clubs in Wicker Park and Ukrainian Village are usually more casual.

The Loop & Near North

Restaurants such as the Gage, Billy Goat Tavern and Purple Pig (see Eating) make fine drinking destinations, too.

★ Signature Lounge
LOUNGE
(www.signatureroom.com; 875 N Michigan Ave; drinks $6-16; ⊘ from 11am; ⓜ Red Line to Chicago) Have the Hancock Observatory view without the Hancock Observatory admission price. Grab the elevator up to the 96th floor and order a beverage while looking out over the city. Ladies: don't miss the bathroom view.

Berghoff
BAR
(Map p522; www.theberghoff.com; 17 W Adams St; ⊘ 11am-9pm Mon-Sat; ⓜ Blue or Red Line to Jackson) The Berghoff was the first spot in town to serve a legal drink after Prohibition (ask to see the liquor license stamped '#1'). Little has changed around the antique wood bar since then. Belly up for frosty mugs of the house-brand beer and order *sauerbraten* from the adjoining German restaurant.

★ Clark Street Ale House
BAR
(Map p522; www.clarkstreetalehouse.com; 742 N Clark St; ⊘ from 4pm; ⓜ Red Line to Chicago) Do as the retro sign advises and 'Stop & Drink Liquor.' Midwestern microbrews are the main draw; order a three-beer sampler for $6.

DON'T MISS

MIDWESTERN BEERS

The Midwest is ready to pour you a cold one thanks to its German heritage. Yes, Budweiser and Miller are based here, but that's not what we're talking about. Far more exciting is the region's cache of craft brewers. Keep an eye on the taps for these slurpable suds-makers, available throughout the area:

➡ Bell's (Kalamazoo, MI)

➡ Capital (Madison, WI)

➡ Founder's (Grand Rapids, MI)

➡ Great Lakes (Cleveland, OH)

➡ Lakefront (Milwaukee, WI)

➡ New Holland (Holland, MI)

➡ Summit (St Paul, MN)

➡ Surly (Minneapolis, MN)

➡ Three Floyds (Munster, IN)

➡ Two Brothers (Warrenville, IL)

Intelligentsia Coffee
CAFE
(Map p522; www.intelligentsiacoffee.com; 53 E Randolph St; ⊘ 6:30am-8pm Mon-Fri, 7am-9pm Sat, 7am-7pm Sun; ⓜ Brown, Orange, Green, Purple or Pink Line to Randolph) The local chain roasts its own beans and percolates strong stuff. Staff recently won the US Barista Championship.

Old Town & Wrigleyville

★ Old Town Ale House
BAR
(www.theoldtownalehouse.com; 219 W North Ave; ⊘ 3pm-4am Mon-Fri, from noon Sat & Sun; ⓜ Brown or Purple Line to Sedgwick) This unpretentious favorite lets you mingle with beautiful people and grizzled regulars, seated pint by pint under the nude-politician paintings. It's across the street from Second City.

★ Gingerman Tavern
BAR
(3740 N Clark St; ⊘ from 3pm Mon-Fri, from noon Sat & Sun; ⓜ Red Line to Addison) The pool tables, the good beer selection and the pierced-and-tattooed patrons make Gingerman wonderfully different from the surrounding Wrigleyville sports bars.

Smart Bar
CLUB
(www.smartbarchicago.com; 3730 N Clark St; ⊘ 10pm-4am Wed-Sat; ⓜ Red Line to Addison) A longstanding unpretentious favorite for dancing, attached to the Metro rock club.

Wicker Park, Bucktown & Ukrainian Village

Map Room
BAR
(www.maproom.com; 1949 N Hoyne Ave; ⊘ from 6:30am Mon-Fri, from 7:30am Sat, from 11am Sun; 🛜) At this map-and-globe-filled 'traveler tavern' artsy types sip coffee by day and suds from the 200-strong beer list by night.

Danny's
BAR
(1951 W Dickens Ave; ⊘ from 7pm; ⓜ Blue Line to Damen) Danny's comfortably dim and dog-eared ambience is perfect for conversations over a pint. A poetry-reading series and occasional DJs add to the scruffy artiness.

Matchbox
COCKTAIL BAR
(Map p522; 770 N Milwaukee Ave; ⊘ from 4pm; ⓜ Blue Line to Chicago) Lawyers, artists and bums all squeeze in for retro cocktails. It's small as – you got it – a matchbox, with about 10 barstools; everyone else stands against the back wall. Matchbox sits by its lonesome northwest of downtown.

Logan Square

Late Bar
CLUB

(www.latebarchicago.com; 3534 W Belmont Ave; ⊙from 10pm Tue-Sat; MⓂBlue Line to Belmont) Owned by a couple of DJs, Late Bar's weird, New Wave vibe draws fans of all stripes. It's off the beaten path in a forlorn stretch of Logan Sq, though easily reachable via the Blue Line train.

West Loop

Aviary
COCKTAIL BAR

(Map p522; www.theaviary.com; 955 W Fulton Market; ⊙from 6pm Tue-Sat; MⓂGreen or Pink Line to Morgan) The Aviary won the James Beard Award for best cocktails in the nation. The ethereal drinks are like nothing you've laid lips on before. Some arrive with Bunsen burners, others with a slingshot you use to break the ice. They taste terrific, whatever the science involved. It's wise to make reservations online.

☆ Entertainment

Check the **Reader** (www.chicagoreader.com) for listings.

Blues & Jazz
Blues and jazz have deep roots in Chicago.

★ Green Mill
JAZZ

(www.greenmilljazz.com; 4802 N Broadway; cover charge $5-15; ⊙noon-4am Mon-Sat, from 11am Sun; MⓂRed Line to Lawrence) The timeless Green Mill earned its notoriety as Al Capone's favorite speakeasy (the tunnels where he hid the booze are still underneath the bar). Sit in one of the curved leather booths and feel his ghost urging you on to another martini. Local and national jazz artists perform nightly; Green Mill also hosts the nationally acclaimed poetry slam on Sundays.

★ Buddy Guy's Legends
BLUES

(Map p522; www.buddyguys.com; 700 S Wabash Ave; tickets Sun-Thu $10, Fri & Sat $20; ⊙from 5pm Mon & Tue, from 11am Wed-Fri, from noon Sat & Sun; MⓂRed Line to Harrison) Top local and national acts wail on the stage of local icon Buddy Guy. The man himself usually plugs in his axe for a series of shows in January. The venue hosts free, all-ages acoustic performances from noon to 2pm Wednesday through Sunday.

Kingston Mines
BLUES

(www.kingstonmines.com; 2548 N Halsted St; tickets $12-15; ⊙8pm-4am Mon-Thu, from 7pm Fri & Sat, from 6pm Sun; MⓂBrown or Purple Line to

Fullerton) Two stages, seven nights a week, ensure somebody's always on. It's noisy, hot, sweaty, crowded and located in Lincoln Park.

BLUES
BLUES

(www.chicagobluesbar.com; 2519 N Halsted St; tickets $7-10; ⊙ from 8pm; MⓂBrown, Purple or Red Line to Fullerton) This veteran club draws a slightly older crowd that soaks up every crackling, electrified moment.

Rock & World Music

★ Hideout
LIVE MUSIC

(www.hideoutchicago.com; 1354 W Wabansia Ave; ⊙7pm-late Tue & Sat, from 4pm Wed-Fri, hours vary Sun & Mon; ᠍72) Hidden behind a factory at the edge of Bucktown, this two-room lodge of indie rock and alt-country is well worth seeking out. The owners have nursed an outsider, underground vibe, and the place feels like your grandma's downstairs rumpus room. Music and other events (bingo, literary readings etc) take place nightly.

SummerDance
MUSIC

(Map p522; ☑312-742-4007; www.chicagosummerdance.org; 601 S Michigan Ave; ⊙6pm Thu-Sat, 4pm Sun late Jun–mid-Sep; MⓂRed Line to Harrison) **FREE** Boogie at the Spirit of Music Garden in Grant Park with a multi-ethnic mash-up of locals. Bands play rumba, samba and other world beats preceded by fun dance lessons – all free.

Empty Bottle
LIVE MUSIC

(www.emptybottle.com; 1035 N Western Ave; ⊙5pm-late Mon-Wed, from 3pm Thu & Fri, from 11am Sat & Sun; ᠍49) The scruffy, go-to club

GAY & LESBIAN CHICAGO

Chicago has a flourishing gay and lesbian scene. The **Windy City Times** (www.windycitymediagroup.com) and **Pink magazine** (www.pinkmag.com) provide the local lowdown.

The **Chicago Area Gay & Lesbian Chamber of Commerce** (www.glchamber.org) has an online tourism directory. Chicago Greeter (p532) offers personalized sightseeing trips.

The biggest concentration of bars and clubs is in Wrigleyville on N Halsted St between Belmont Ave and Grace St, an area known as Boystown. Andersonville is the other main area for GLBT nightlife; it's a more relaxed, less party-oriented scene. Top picks:

Big Chicks (www.bigchicks.com; 5024 N Sheridan Rd; ⊙ from 4pm Mon-Fri, from 9am Sat, from 10am Sun; 🛜; M Red Line to Argyle) Despite the name, both men and women frequent Big Chicks, with its weekend DJs, art displays and next-door organic restaurant **Tweet** (www.tweet.biz; 5020 N Sheridan Rd; mains $7-12; ⊙ 9am-3pm; 🛜; M Red Line to Argyle) 🖋, where weekend brunch packs 'em in.

Sidetrack (www.sidetrackchicago.com; 3349 N Halsted St; ⊙ from 3pm Mon-Fri, from 1pm Sat & Sun; M Red, Brown or Purple Line to Belmont) Massive Sidetrack thumps dance music and show tunes and is prime for people-watching.

Hamburger Mary's (www.hamburgermarys.com/chicago; 5400 N Clark St; ⊙ from 11:30am Mon-Fri, from 10:30am Sat & Sun; M Red Line to Berwyn) Cabaret, karaoke, burgers and a booze-soaked outdoor patio make for good times at this hot spot.

Chance's Dances (www.chancesdances.org) Organizes queer dance parties at clubs around town.

Pride Parade (http://chicagopride.gopride.com; ⊙ late Jun) Pride winds through Boystown and attracts more than 800,000 revelers.

North Halsted Street Market Days (www.northalsted.com; ⊙ early Aug) Another raucous event on the Boystown calendar, featuring a street fair and wild costumes.

---

for edgy indie rock and jazz; Monday's show is usually free (and there's $1.50 Pabst).

★ **Metro**   LIVE MUSIC
(www.metrochicago.com; 3730 N Clark St; M Red Line to Addison) Local bands on the verge of stardom and national names looking for an 'intimate' venue turn up the volume at Metro.

Whistler   LIVE MUSIC
(☑773-227-3530; www.whistlerchicago.com; 2421 N Milwaukee Ave; ⊙ from 6pm Mon-Thu, from 5pm Fri-Sun; M Blue Line to California) **FREE** Indie bands and jazz trios brood at this artsy little club in Logan Sq. There's never a cover charge.

Theater

Chicago's reputation for stage drama is well deserved. Many productions export to Broadway. The Theater District is a cluster of big, neon-lit venues at State and Randolph Sts. **Broadway in Chicago** (☑800-775-2000; www.broadwayinchicago.com) handles tickets for most.

Steppenwolf Theatre   THEATER
(☑312-335-1650; www.steppenwolf.org; 1650 N Halsted St; M Red Line to North/Clybourn) Drama club of Malkovich, Sinise and other Hollywood stars; 2 miles north of the Loop in Lincoln Park.

Goodman Theatre   THEATER
(Map p522; ☑312-443-3800; www.goodmantheatre.org; 170 N Dearborn St; M Brown, Orange, Green, Purple, Pink or Blue Line to Clark/Lake) The city's other powerhouse, known for new and classic American works.

Chicago Shakespeare Theater   THEATER
(Map p522; ☑312-595-5600; www.chicagoshakes.com; 800 E Grand Ave; M Red Line to Grand, then trolley) The Bard's comedies and tragedies play at Navy Pier (and in local parks for free during summer).

Lookingglass Theatre Company   THEATER
(Map p522; ☑312-337-0665; www.lookingglasstheatre.org; 821 N Michigan Ave; M Red Line to Chicago) Dreamy and magical literary productions in the old Water Works building.

Neo-Futurists
THEATER

(☎773-275-5255; www.neofuturists.org; 5153 N Ashland Ave; Ⓜ Red Line to Berwyn) Presents original works that make you ponder and laugh simultaneously.

Comedy

Improv comedy began in Chicago, and the city still nurtures the best in the business.

Second City
COMEDY

(☎312-337-3992; www.secondcity.com; 1616 N Wells St; Ⓜ Brown or Purple Line to Sedgwick) It's the cream of the crop, where Bill Murray, Stephen Colbert, Tina Fey and many more honed their wit. Bargain: turn up after the evening's last show (Friday excluded) and watch the comics improv a performance for free.

iO Theater
COMEDY

(☎773-880-0199; www.ioimprov.com; 3541 N Clark St; Ⓜ Red Line to Addison) Chicago's other major improv house. It's scheduled to move to new, larger digs at 1501 N Kingsbury St (in Lincoln Park) in late 2014.

Sports

Chicago Cubs
BASEBALL

(www.cubs.com; 1060 W Addison St; Ⓜ Red Line to Addison) The Cubs last won the World Series in 1908, but that doesn't stop fans from coming out to see them. Part of the draw is atmospheric, ivy-walled Wrigley Field, which dates from 1914. The raucous bleacher seats are the most popular place to sit. No tickets? Peep through the 'knothole,' a garage-door-sized opening on Sheffield Ave, to watch the action for free.

Chicago White Sox
BASEBALL

(www.whitesox.com; 333 W 35th St; tickets $20-70; Ⓜ Red Line to Sox-35th) The Sox are the Cubs' South Side rivals and play in the more modern 'Cell,' aka US Cellular Field. Tickets are usually cheaper and easier to get than at Wrigley Field; Monday is half-price night.

Chicago Bears
FOOTBALL

(Map p522; www.chicagobears.com; 1410 S Museum Campus Dr; ☒146, 130) Da Bears, Chicago's NFL team, tackle at Soldier Field, recognizable by its classics-meets-flying-saucer architecture. Expect beery tailgate parties, sleet and snow.

Chicago Bulls
BASKETBALL

(www.nba.com/bulls; 1901 W Madison St; ☒19, 20) Is Derrick Rose the new Michael Jordan? Find out at the United Center, where the Bulls shoot hoops. It's about 2 miles west of the Loop. CTA runs special buses (No 19) on game days; it's best not to walk here.

Chicago Blackhawks
HOCKEY

(www.chicagoblackhawks.com; 1901 W Madison St; ☒19, 20) The 2010 and 2013 Stanley Cup winners skate in front of big crowds. They share the United Center with the Bulls.

Performing Arts

Grant Park Orchestra
CLASSICAL MUSIC

(Map p522; ☎312-742-7638; www.grantparkmusicfestival.com; Pritzker Pavilion, Millennium Park; ⏱6:30pm Wed & Fri, 7:30pm Sat mid-Jun–mid-Aug; Ⓜ Brown, Orange, Green, Purple or Pink Line to Randolph) 🆓 The beloved group puts on free classical concerts in Millennium Park throughout the summer.

Chicago Symphony Orchestra
CLASSICAL MUSIC

(Map p522; ☎312-294-3000; www.cso.org; 220 S Michigan Ave; Ⓜ Brown, Orange, Green, Purple or Pink Line to Adams) The CSO is one of America's best symphonies; it plays in the Daniel Burnham–designed Orchestra Hall.

Lyric Opera Of Chicago
OPERA

(Map p522; ☎312-332-2244; www.lyricopera.org; 20 N Wacker Dr; Ⓜ Brown, Orange, Purple or Pink Line to Washington) The renowned Lyric Opera hits high Cs in a chandeliered venue a few blocks west of the Loop.

Hubbard Street Dance Chicago
DANCE

(Map p522; ☎312-850-9744; www.hubbardstreetdance.com; 205 E Randolph St; Ⓜ Brown, Orange, Green, Purple or Pink Line to Randolph) Chicago's pre-eminent dance company performs at the Harris Theater for Music and Dance.

ℹ DISCOUNT TICKETS

National ticket broker **Goldstar** (www.goldstar.com) sells half-price tickets to all sorts of Chicago entertainment, including theater performances, sports events and concerts. You'll fare best if you sign up at least three weeks ahead of time, as Goldstar typically releases its seats well in advance of shows.

For same-week theater seats at half price, try **Hot Tix** (www.hottix.org). You can buy them online or in person at the three downtown booths. The selection is best early in the week.

🛍 Shopping

A siren song for shoppers emanates from N Michigan Ave, along the Magnificent Mile. **Water Tower Place** (Map p522; www.shopwatertower.com; 835 N Michigan Ave; ⊙10am-9pm Mon-Sat, 11am-6pm Sun; Ⓜ Red Line to Chicago) is among the large vertical malls here. Moving onward, boutiques fill Wicker Park/ Bucktown (indie and vintage), Lincoln Park (posh), Lake View (countercultural) and Andersonville (all of the above).

Chicago Architecture Foundation Shop   SOUVENIRS

(Map p522; www.architecture.org/shop; 224 S Michigan Ave; ⊙9:30am-6pm; Ⓜ Brown, Orange, Green, Purple or Pink Line to Adams) Skyline posters, Frank Lloyd Wright note cards, skyscraper models and more for those with an edifice complex.

Strange Cargo   CLOTHING

(www.strangecargo.com; 3448 N Clark St; ⊙11am-6:45pm Mon-Sat, to 5:30pm Sun; Ⓜ Red Line to Addison) This retro store stocks kitschy iron-on T-shirts featuring Ditka, Obama and other renowned Chicagoans.

Jazz Record Mart   MUSIC

(Map p522; www.jazzmart.com; 27 E Illinois St; ⊙10am-8pm Mon-Sat, noon-5pm Sun; Ⓜ Red Line to Grand) One-stop shop for Chicago jazz and blues CDs and vinyl.

Quimby's   BOOKS

(www.quimbys.com; 1854 W North Ave; ⊙noon-9pm Mon-Thu, to 10pm Fri & Sat, to 7pm Sun; Ⓜ Blue Line to Damen) Ground Zero for comics, zines and underground culture; in Wicker Park.

ℹ Information

INTERNET ACCESS

Many bars and restaurants have free wi-fi, as does the Chicago Cultural Center.

Harold Washington Library Center (www.chipublib.org; 400 S State St; ⊙9am-9pm Mon-Thu, 9am-5pm Fri & Sat, 1-5pm Sun) A grand, art-filled building with free wi-fi throughout and 3rd-floor internet terminals (get a day pass at the counter).

MEDIA

Chicago Reader (www.chicagoreader.com) Free alternative newspaper with comprehensive arts and entertainment listings.

Chicago Sun-Times (www.suntimes.com) The daily tabloid-style newspaper.

Chicago Tribune (www.chicagotribune.com) The stalwart daily newspaper; its younger, trimmed-down, freebie version is *RedEye*.

MEDICAL SERVICES

Northwestern Memorial Hospital (☎312-926-5188; www.nmh.org; 251 E Erie St) Well-respected hospital downtown.

Stroger Cook County Hospital (☎312-864-1300; www.cchil.org; 1969 W Ogden Ave) Public hospital serving low-income patients; 2.5 miles west of the Loop.

Walgreens (☎312-664-8686; 757 N Michigan Ave; ⊙24hr; Ⓜ Red Line to Chicago) On the Mag Mile.

MONEY

ATMs are plentiful downtown, with many near Chicago and Michigan Aves. To change money, try Terminal 5 at O'Hare International Airport or the following places in the Loop:

Travelex (☎312-807-4941; www.travelex.com; 19 S LaSalle St; ⊙8am-6pm Mon-Fri, to 1pm Sat; Ⓜ Blue Line to Monroe)

World's Money Exchange (☎312-641-2151; www.wmeinc.com; 203 N LaSalle St; ⊙8:45am-4:45pm Mon-Fri; Ⓜ Brown, Orange, Green, Purple, Pink or Blue Line to Clark/Lake)

POST

Post office (Map p522; 540 N Dearborn St)

TOURIST INFORMATION

Choose Chicago (www.choosechicago.com) is the city's tourism bureau. It operates two visitor centers, each with a staffed information desk, CTA transit-card kiosk and free wi-fi:

Chicago Cultural Center Visitors Center (Map p522; www.choosechicago.com; 77 E Randolph St; ⊙9am-7pm Mon-Thu, 9am-6pm Fri & Sat, 10am-6pm Sun; 🛜; Ⓜ Brown, Orange, Green, Purple or Pink Line to Randolph) InstaGreeter and Millennium Park tours also depart from here.

Water Works Visitors Center (Map p522; www.choosechicago.com; 163 E Pearson St; ⊙9am-7pm Mon-Thu, 9am-6pm Fri & Sat, 10am-6pm Sun; 🛜; Ⓜ Red Line to Chicago) There's a Hot Tix booth inside.

WEBSITES

Chicagoist (www.chicagoist.com) Quirky take on food, arts and events.

Gapers Block (www.gapersblock.com) News and events site with Chicago attitude.

Huffington Post Chicago (www.huffingtonpost.com/chicago) Amalgamates news from major local sources.

ℹ Getting There & Away

AIR

Chicago Midway Airport (MDW; www.flychicago.com) The smaller airport used mostly by domestic carriers, such as Southwest; often has cheaper flights than from O'Hare.

O'Hare International Airport (ORD; www.flychicago.com) Chicago's larger airport, and among the world's busiest. Headquarters for United Airlines and a hub for American. Most non-US airlines and international flights use Terminal 5 (except Lufthansa and flights from Canada).

BUS

Greyhound (Map p522; ✆312-408-5800; www.greyhound.com; 630 W Harrison St; M Blue Line to Clinton) Main station is two blocks southwest from the nearest CTA stop. Buses run frequently to Cleveland (7½ hours), Detroit (seven hours) and Minneapolis (nine hours), as well as to small towns throughout the USA.

Megabus (Map p522; www.megabus.com/us; Canal St & Jackson Blvd; ☏; M Blue Line to Clinton) Travels only to major Midwestern cities. Prices are often less, and quality and efficiency are better than Greyhound on these routes. The bus stop is adjacent to Union Station.

TRAIN

Chicago's classic **Union Station** (www.chicagounionstation.com; 225 S Canal St) is the hub for **Amtrak** (✆800-872-7245; www.amtrak.com) national and regional service. Routes include the following:

Detroit (5½ hours, three trains daily)
Milwaukee (1½ hours, seven trains daily)
Minneapolis/St Paul (eight hours, one train daily)
New York (20½ hours, one train daily)
San Francisco (Emeryville; 53 hours, one train daily)
St Louis (5½ hours, five trains daily)

ℹ Getting Around

TO/FROM THE AIRPORT

Chicago Midway Airport Eleven miles southwest of the Loop, connected via the CTA Orange Line ($3). Trains depart every 10 minutes or so; they reach downtown in 30 minutes. Shuttle vans cost $27, taxis cost $30 to $40.

O'Hare International Airport Seventeen miles northwest of the Loop. The CTA Blue Line train ($5) runs 24/7. Trains depart every 10 minutes or so; they reach downtown in 40 minutes. Airport Express shuttle vans cost $32, taxis around $50. They can take as long as the train, depending on traffic.

BICYCLE

Chicago is a cycling-savvy city with 200 miles of bike lanes and a bike-share program called **Divvy** (www.divvybikes.com). The **Department of Transportation** (www.chicagocompletestreets.org) provides free maps. Bike racks are plentiful; the biggest facility, with showers, is at the **McDonalds Cycle Center** (www.chicagobikestation.com; 239 E Randolph St) in Millennium Park.

CAR & MOTORCYCLE

Be warned: street and garage/lot parking is expensive. If you must, try **Millennium Park Garage** (www.millenniumgarages.com; 5 S Columbus Dr; per 3/24hr $23/30). Chicago's rush-hour traffic is abysmal.

PUBLIC TRANSPORTATION

The **Chicago Transit Authority** (CTA; www.transitchicago.com) operates the city's buses and the elevated/subway train system (aka the El).

➥ Two of the eight color-coded train lines – the Red Line, and the Blue Line to O'Hare airport – operate 24 hours a day. The other lines run from 4am to 1am daily. During the day, you shouldn't have to wait more than 15 minutes for a train. Get free maps at any station.

➥ CTA buses go everywhere from early morning until late evening.

➥ The standard fare per train is $3 (except from O'Hare, where it costs $5) and includes two transfers; per bus, it is $2.25.

➥ On the train, you must use a Ventra Ticket, which is sold from vending machines at train

---

ONLINE TICKETS & DISCOUNT CARDS

Most major sights, including the Art Institute of Chicago, Shedd Aquarium and Willis Tower, allow you to buy tickets online. The advantage is that you're assured entry and you get to skip the regular ticket lines. The disadvantage is that you have to pay a service fee of $1.50 to $4 per ticket (sometimes it's just per order), and at times the prepay line is almost as long as the regular one. Our suggestion: consider buying online in summer (especially for the Shedd Aquarium) and for big exhibits. Otherwise, there's no need.

Chicago offers a couple of discount cards that also let you skip the regular queues:

Go Chicago Card (www.gochicagocard.com) Allows you to visit an unlimited number of attractions for a flat fee; good for one, two, three, five or seven consecutive days.

CityPass (www.citypass.com) Gives access to five of the city's top draws, including Shedd Aquarium and Willis Tower, over nine days; a better option if you prefer a more leisurely sightseeing pace.

stations. You can also buy a Ventra Card, aka a rechargeable fare card, at stations. It has a one-time $5 fee that gets refunded once you register the card. It knocks 50¢ off the cost of each ride.

➡ On buses, you can use a Ventra Card or pay the driver with exact change.

➡ Unlimited ride passes (one-/three-day pass $10/20) are also available. Get them at rail stations and drug stores.

Metra commuter trains (www.metrarail.com; fares $2.75-$9.25, all-weekend pass $7) have 12 routes serving the suburbs from four terminals ringing the Loop: LaSalle St Station, Millennium Station, Union Station and Richard B Ogilvie Transportation Center (a few blocks north of Union Station).

PACE (www.pacebus.com) runs the suburban bus system that connects with city transport.

TAXI

Cabs are plentiful in the Loop, north to Andersonville and northwest to Wicker Park/Bucktown. Flagfall is $3.25, plus $1.80 per mile and $1 per extra passenger; a 15% tip is expected.

Flash Cab (☑773-561-1444; www.flashcab.com)

Yellow Cab (☑312-829-4222; www.yellowcab-chicago.com)

Around Chicago

Oak Park

Located 10 miles west of the Loop and easily reached via CTA train, Oak Park has two famous sons: novelist Ernest Hemingway was born here, and architect Frank Lloyd Wright lived and worked here from 1889 to 1909.

ROUTE 66: GET YOUR KICKS IN ILLINOIS

America's 'Mother Road' kicks off in Chicago on Adams St, just west of Michigan Ave. Before embarking, fuel up at Lou Mitchell's (p534) near Union Station. After all, it's 300 miles from here to the Missouri state line.

Sadly, most of the original Route 66 has been superseded by I-55 in Illinois, though the old road still exists in scattered sections, often paralleling the interstate. Keep an eye out for brown 'Historic Route 66' signs, which pop up at crucial junctions to mark the way.

Our first stop rises from the cornfields 60 miles south in Wilmington. Here the Gemini Giant – a 28ft fiberglass spaceman – stands guard outside the **Launching Pad Drive In** (810 E Baltimore St). The restaurant is now shuttered, but the statue remains a quintessential photo op. To reach it, exit I-55 at Joliet Rd, and follow it south as it becomes Hwy 53 into town.

Motor 45 miles onward to Pontiac and the tchotchke-and-photo-filled **Route 66 Hall of Fame** (☑815-844-4566; 110 W Howard St; ⊙9am-5pm Mon-Fri, 10am-4pm Sat & Sun) FREE. Cruise another 50 miles to Shirley and **Funk's Grove** (☑309-874-3360; www.funksmaplesirup.com; ⊙9am-5pm Mon-Fri, from 10am Sat, from noon Sun), a pretty 19th-century maple-syrup farm and nature preserve (exit 154 off I-55).

Ten miles later you'll reach the throwback hamlet of Atlanta. Pull up a chair at the **Palms Grill Cafe** (☑217-648-2233; www.thepalmsgrillcafe.com; 110 SW Arch St; pie slices $3; ⊙5am-8pm), where thick slabs of gooseberry, sour-cream raisin and other retro pies tempt from the glass case. Then walk across the street to snap a photo with **Tall Paul**, a sky-high statue of Paul Bunyan clutching a hot dog.

The state capital of Springfield, 50 miles further on, harbors a trio of sights: Shea's Gas Station Museum (p547), the Cozy Dog Drive In (p547) and Route 66 Drive In (p547).

Further south, a good section of old Route 66 parallels I-55 through Litchfield, where you can fork into chicken fried steak while chatting up locals at the 1924 **Ariston Cafe** (www.ariston-cafe.com; S Old Rte 66; mains $7-15; ⊙11am-9pm Tue-Fri, 4-10pm Sat, 11am-8pm Sun). Finally, before driving into Missouri, detour off I-270 at exit 3. Follow Hwy 3 (aka Lewis and Clark Blvd) south, turn right at the first stoplight and drive west to the 1929 **Chain of Rocks Bridge** (⊙9am-sunset). Only open to pedestrians and cyclists these days, the mile-long span over the Mississippi River has a 22-degree angled bend (cause of many a crash, hence the ban on cars).

For more information, visit the **Route 66 Association of Illinois** (www.il66assoc.org) or **Illinois Route 66 Scenic Byway** (www.illinoisroute66.org). Detailed driving directions are at www.historic66.com/illinois.

During Wright's 20 years in Oak Park, he designed many houses. Stop at the **visitor center** (🖉888-625-7275; www.visitoakpark. com; 1010 W Lake St; ☉10am-5pm) and buy an architectural site map ($4.25), which gives their locations. To actually get inside a Wright-designed dwelling, you'll need to visit the **Frank Lloyd Wright Home & Studio** (🖉312-994-4000; www.gowright.org; 951 Chicago Ave; adult/child/camera $15/12/5; ☉11am-4pm). Tour frequency varies, from every 20 minutes on summer weekends to every hour in winter. The studio also offers guided neighborhood walking tours, as well as a self-guided audio version.

Despite Hemingway calling Oak Park a 'village of wide lawns and narrow minds,' the town still pays homage to him at the **Ernest Hemingway Museum** (🖉708-848-2222; www.ehfop.org; 200 N Oak Park Ave; adult/child $10/8; ☉1-5pm Sun-Fri, from 10am Sat). Admission also includes access to **Hemingway's Birthplace** (339 N Oak Park Ave; ☉1-5pm Sun-Fri, from 10am Sat) across the street.

From downtown Chicago, take the CTA Green Line to its terminus at the Harlem stop, which lands you a quarter-mile from the visitor center. The train traverses some bleak neighborhoods before emerging into Oak Park's wide-lawn splendor.

Evanston & North Shore

Evanston, 14 miles north of the Loop and reached via the CTA Purple Line, combines sprawling old houses with a compact downtown. It's home to Northwestern University.

Beyond are Chicago's northern lakeshore suburbs, which became popular with the wealthy in the late 19th century. A classic 30-mile drive follows Sheridan Rd through various well-off towns to the socioeconomic apex of Lake Forest. Attractions include the **Baha'i House of Worship** (www.bahai.us/bahai-temple; 100 Linden Ave; admission free; ☉6am-10pm) **FREE**, a glistening white architectural marvel, and the **Chicago Botanic Garden** (🖉847-835-5440; www.chicagobotanic.org; 1000 Lake Cook Rd; admission free; ☉8am-sunset) **FREE**, with hiking trails, 255 bird species and weekend cooking demos by well-known chefs. Parking costs $20.

Inland lies the **Illinois Holocaust Museum** (🖉847-967-4800; www.ilholocaustmuseum. org; 9603 Woods Dr; adult/child $12/6; ☉10am-5pm Mon-Fri, to 8pm Thu, 11am-4pm Sat & Sun). Besides its excellent videos of survivors' stories from WWII, the museum contains thought-provoking art about genocides in Armenia, Rwanda, Cambodia and others.

Galena & Northern Illinois

The highlight of this region is the hilly northwest, where cottonwood trees, grazing horses and scenic byways fill the pocket around Galena.

En route is Union, where the **Illinois Railway Museum** (🖉815-923-4000; www.irm.org; US 20 to Union Rd; adult $10-14, child $7-10; ☉Apr-Oct, hours vary) sends trainspotters into fits of ecstasy with 200 acres of locomotives.

Galena

While it sometimes gets chided as a place for the 'newly wed and nearly dead,' thanks to all the tourist-oriented B&Bs, fudge and antique shops, there's no denying little Galena's beauty. It spreads across wooded hillsides near the Mississippi River, amid rolling, barn-dotted farmland. Red-brick mansions in Greek Revival, Gothic Revival and Queen Anne styles fill the streets, left over from the town's heyday in the mid-1800s, when local lead mines made it rich. Throw in cool kayak trips, horseback rides and winding backroad drives, and you've got a lovely slowpoke getaway.

👁 Sights & Activities

The **visitor center** (🖉877-464-2536; www. galena.org; 101 Bouthillier St; ☉9am-5pm), in the 1857 train depot as you enter from the east, is a good place to start. Get a map, leave your car in the lot ($5 per day) and explore on foot.

Elegant old Main St curves around the hillside and the historic heart of town. Among numerous sights is the **Ulysses S Grant Home** (🖉815-777-3310; www.granthome. com; 500 Bouthillier St; adult/child $5/3; ☉9am-4:45pm Wed-Sun Apr-Oct, reduced hours Nov-Mar), which was a gift from local Republicans to the victorious general at the Civil War's end. Grant lived here until he became the country's 18th president.

Outdoors enthusiasts should head to **Fever River Outfitters** (🖉815-776-9425; www.feverriveroutfitters.com; 525 S Main St; ☉10am-5pm, closed Tue-Thu early Sep-late May), which rents canoes, kayaks, stand-up paddleboards, bicycles and snowshoes. It also offers guided tours, such as two-hour kayak trips ($45 per person, equipment included) on the Mississippi River's backwaters. Or saddle up at **Shenandoah Riding Center** (☑ 815-777-2373; www.shenandoahridingcenter.com; 200 N Brodrecht Rd; 1hr ride $45). It leads trail rides through the valley for all levels of riders, including beginners. The stables are 8 miles east of town.

For a pretty drive mosey onto the **Stagecoach Trail**, a 26-mile ride on a narrow, twisty road en route to Warren. Pick it up by taking Main St northeast through downtown; at the second stop sign go right (you'll see a trail marker). And yes, it really was part of the old stagecoach route between Galena and Chicago

🛏 Sleeping & Eating

Galena brims with quilt-laden B&Bs. Most cost $100 to $200 nightly and fill up during weekends. The visitor center website provides contact information. Presidential types can be like Grant and Lincoln and stay in the well-furnished rooms at **DeSoto House Hotel** (☑ 815-777-0090; www.desotohouse.com; 230 S Main St; r $128-200; 🅿 🕸 🛜) 🐾, which dates from 1855. **Grant Hills Motel** (☑ 877-421-0924; www.granthills.com; 9372 US 20; r $70-100; 🅿 🛜 🏊) is a no-frills option 1.5 miles east of town, with countryside views and a horseshoe pitch.

111 Main (☑ 815-777-8030; www.oneelevenmain.com; 111 N Main St; mains $17-25; ⊘ 4-9pm Mon-Thu, 11am-10pm Fri & Sat, 11am-9pm Sun) makes meatloaf, pork-and-mashed-potatoes and other Midwestern favorites using ingredients sourced from local farms. Dig into mussels with champagne sauce or maybe a tender schnitzel, at cozy French-German bistro **Fritz and Frites** (☑ 815-777-2004; www.fritzandfrites.com; 317 N Main St; mains $17-22; ⊘ 4-9pm Tue & Wed, from 11:30am Thu-Sun). The **VFW Hall** (100 S Main St; ⊘ from 4pm) provides a sublime opportunity to sip cheap beers and watch TV alongside veterans of long-ago wars. Don't be shy: as the sign out front says, the public is welcome.

Quad Cities

South of Galena along a pretty stretch of the **Great River Road** (www.greatriverroad-illinois.org) is scenic **Mississippi Palisades State Park** (☑ 815-273-2731), a popular rock-climbing, hiking and camping area; pick up trail maps at the north entrance park office.

Further downstream, the **Quad Cities** (www.visitquadcities.com) – Moline and Rock

Island in Illinois, and Davenport and Bettendorf across the river in Iowa – make a surprisingly good stop. Rock Island has an appealing downtown (based at 2nd Ave and 18th St), with a couple of cafes and a lively pub and music scene. On the edge of town, **Black Hawk State Historic Site** (www.blackhawkpark.org; 1510 46th Ave; ⊘ sunrise-10pm) is a huge park with trails by the Rock River. Its **Hauberg Indian Museum** (☑ 309-788-9536; Watch Tower Lodge; ⊘ 9am-noon & 1-5pm Wed-Sun) FREE outlines the sorry story of Sauk leader Black Hawk and his people.

Out in the Mississippi River, the actual island of **Rock Island** once held a Civil War–era arsenal and POW camp. It now maintains the impressive **Rock Island Arsenal Museum** (⊘ noon-4pm Tue-Sat) FREE, Civil War cemetery, national cemetery and visitor center for barge viewing. All are free, but bring photo ID as the island is still an active army facility.

Moline is the home of John Deere, the international farm machinery manufacturer. Downtown holds the **John Deere Pavilion** (www.johndeerepavilion.com; 1400 River Dr; ⊘ 9am-5pm Mon-Fri, 10am-5pm Sat, noon-4pm Sun; 🚼) FREE, which is a kiddie-beloved museum/showroom. For Iowa-side attractions, see p633.

Springfield & Central Illinois

Abraham Lincoln and Route 66 sights are sprinkled liberally throughout central Illinois, which is otherwise farmland plain. East of Decatur, Arthur and Arcola are Amish centers.

Springfield

The small state capital has a serious obsession with Abraham Lincoln, who practiced law here from 1837 to 1861. Many of the attractions are walkable downtown and cost little or nothing.

◉ Sights & Activities

Lincoln Home & Visitor Center HISTORIC SITE (☑ 217-492-4150; www.nps.gov/liho; 426 S 7th St; ⊘ 8:30am-5pm) FREE Start at the National Park Service visitor center, where you must pick up a ticket to enter Lincoln's 12-room abode, located directly across the street. You can then walk through the house where Abe and Mary Lincoln lived from

1844 until they moved to the White House in 1861; rangers are stationed throughout to provide background information and answer questions.

Lincoln Presidential Library & Museum
MUSEUM
(📞217-558-8844; www.presidentlincoln.org; 212 N 6th St; adult/child $12/6; ⊙9am-5pm; 🎫) This museum contains the most complete Lincoln collection in the world. Real-deal artifacts like Abe's shaving mirror and briefcase join whiz-bang exhibits and Disneyesque holograms that keep the kids agog.

Lincoln's Tomb
CEMETERY
(www.lincolntomb.org; 1441 Monument Ave; ⊙9am-5pm, closed Sun & Mon Sep-May) FREE After his assassination, Lincoln's body was returned to Springfield, where it lies in an impressive tomb in Oak Ridge Cemetery, 1.5 miles north of downtown. The gleam on the nose of Lincoln's bust, created by visitors' light touches, indicates the numbers of those who pay their respects here. On summer Tuesdays at 7pm, infantry reenactors fire muskets and lower the flag.

Old State Capitol
HISTORIC SITE
(📞217-785-9363; cnr 6th & Adams Sts; ⊙9am-5pm, closed Sun & Mon Sep-May) Chatterbox docents will take you through the building and regale you with Lincoln stories, such as how he gave his famous 'House Divided' speech here in 1858. Suggested donation is $4.

Shea's Gas Station Museum
MUSEUM
(📞217-522-0475; 2075 Peoria Rd; ⊙by appointment) At the time of writing, the 91-year-old owner of this famed collection of Route 66 pumps and signs had finally stopped working. His family is trying to keep the museum afloat. Call for an appointment.

Route 66 Drive In
CINEMA
(📞217-698-0066; www.route66-drivein.com; 1700 Recreation Dr; adult/child $7/4; ⊙nightly Jun-Aug, Sat & Sun mid-Apr–May & Sep) Screens first-run flicks under the stars.

🛏 Sleeping & Eating

Statehouse Inn
HOTEL $$
(📞217-528-5100; www.thestatehouseinn.com; 101 E Adams St; r incl breakfast $95-155; 🅿❄@🛜) It looks concrete-drab outside, but inside the Statehouse shows its style. Comfy beds and large baths fill the rooms; a retro bar fills the lobby.

Inn at 835
B&B $$
(📞217-523-4466; www.innat835.com; 835 S 2nd St; r incl breakfast $130-200; 🅿❄🛜) The historic arts-and-crafts-style manor offers 11 rooms of the four-poster bed, claw-foot bathtub variety.

Cozy Dog Drive In
AMERICAN $
(www.cozydogdrivein.com; 2935 S 6th St; mains $2-4.50; ⊙8am-8pm Mon-Sat) This Route 66 legend – the reputed birthplace of the corn dog! – has memorabilia and souvenirs, and the deeply fried main course on a stick.

Norb Andy's Tabarin
PUB $
(www.norbandys.com; 518 E Capitol Ave; mains $7-10; ⊙from 11am Tue-Sat) A favorite with locals, Norb's is a dive bar-restaurant housed in the 1837 Hickox House downtown. It piles up Springfield's best 'horseshoe,' a local sandwich of fried meat on toasted bread, mounded with french fries and smothered in melted cheese.

ℹ Information

Springfield Convention & Visitors Bureau (www.visitspringfieldillinois.com) Produces a useful visitors' guide.

ℹ Getting There & Around

The downtown **Amtrak station** (📞217-753-2013; cnr 3rd & Washington Sts) has five trains daily to/from St Louis (two hours) and Chicago (3½ hours).

Petersburg

When Lincoln first arrived in Illinois in 1831, he worked variously as a clerk, storekeeper and postmaster in the frontier village of New Salem before studying law and moving to Springfield. In Petersburg, 20 miles northwest of Springfield, **Lincoln's New Salem State Historic Site** (📞217-632-4000; www.lincolnsnewsalem.com; Hwy 97; suggested donation adult/child $4/2; ⊙9am-5pm, closed Mon & Tue mid-Sep–mid-Apr) reconstructs the village with building replicas, historical displays and costumed performances – a pretty informative and entertaining package.

Southern Illinois

A surprise awaits near Collinsville, 8 miles east of East St Louis: classified as a Unesco World Heritage site with the likes of Stonehenge, the Acropolis and the Egyptian pyramids is **Cahokia Mounds State Historic**

Site (☎618-346-5160; www.cahokiamounds.org; Collinsville Rd; suggested donation adult/child $7/2; ☉visitor center 9am-5pm, grounds 8am-dusk). Cahokia protects the remnants of North America's largest prehistoric city (20,000 people, with suburbs), dating from AD 1200. While the 65 earthen mounds, including the enormous Monk's Mound and the 'Woodhenge' sun calendar, are not overwhelmingly impressive in themselves, the whole site is worth seeing. If you're approaching from the north, take exit 24 off I-255 S; if approaching from St Louis, take exit 6 off I-55/70.

A short distance north of St Louis, Hwy 100 between **Grafton** and **Alton** is perhaps the most scenic 15 miles of the entire Great River Rd. As you slip under windhewn bluffs, keep an eye out for the turnoff to ittybitty **Elsah** (www.elsah.org), a hidden hamlet of 19th-century stone cottages, wood buggy shops and farmhouses.

An exception to the state's flat farmland is the green southernmost section, punctuated by rolling **Shawnee National Forest** (☎618-253-7114; www.fs.usda.gov/shawnee) and its rocky outcroppings. The area has numerous state parks and recreation areas good for hiking, climbing, swimming, fishing and canoeing, particularly around **Little Grassy Lake** and **Devil's Kitchen**. And who would think that Florida-like swampland, complete with bald cypress trees and croaking bullfrogs, would be here? But it is, at **Cypress Creek National Wildlife Refuge** (☎618-634-2231; www.fws.gov/midwest/cypresscreek).

Union County, near the state's southern tip, has wineries and orchards. Sample the wares on the 35-mile **Shawnee Hills Wine Trail** (www.shawneewinetrail.com), which connects 12 vineyards.

INDIANA

The state revs up around the Indy 500 race, but otherwise it's about slow-paced pleasures in corn-stubbled Indiana: pie-eating in Amish Country, meditating in Bloomington's Tibetan temples and admiring the big architecture in small Columbus. For the record, folks have called Indianans 'Hoosiers' since the 1830s, but the word's origin is unknown. One theory is that early settlers knocking on a door were met with 'Who's here?' which soon became 'Hoosier.' It's certainly something to discuss with locals, perhaps over a traditional pork tenderloin sandwich.

ℹ️ Information

Indiana Highway Conditions (☎800-261-7623; www.trafficwise.in.gov)

Indiana State Park Information (☎800-622-4931; www.in.gov/dnr/parklake) Park entry costs $2 per day by foot or bicycle, $7 to $10 by vehicle. Campsites cost $10 to $40; reservations accepted (☎866-622-6746; www.camp.in.gov).

Indiana Tourism (☎888-365-6946; www.visitindiana.com)

Indianapolis

Clean-cut Indy is the state capital and a perfectly pleasant place to ogle racing cars and take a spin around the renowned speedway. The art museum and White River State Park have their merits, as do the Mass Ave and Broad Ripple 'hoods for eating and drinking. And Kurt Vonnegut fans are in for a treat.

◉ Sights & Activities

Downtown's bulls-eye is Monument Circle. White River State Park and its many attractions lie about three-quarters of a mile west.

Indianapolis Motor Speedway MUSEUM (☎317-492-6784; www.indianapolismotorspeedway.com; 4790 W 16th St; adult/child $5/3; ☉9am-5pm Mar-Oct, 10am-4pm Nov-Feb) The Speedway, home of the Indianapolis 500 motor race, is Indy's supersight. The Hall of Fame Museum features 75 racing cars (including former winners), a 500lb Tiffany trophy and a track tour ($5 extra). OK, so you're on a bus for the latter and not even beginning to burn rubber at 37mph, but it's still fun to pretend.

The big race itself is held on the Sunday of Memorial Day weekend (late May) and attended by 450,000 crazed fans. **Tickets** (☎800-822-4639; www.imstix.com; $30-150) can be hard to come by. Try the prerace trials and practices for easier access and cheaper prices. The track is about 6 miles northwest of downtown.

White River State Park PARK (http://inwhiteriver.wrsp.in.gov) The expansive park, located at downtown's edge, contains several worthwhile sights. The adobe **Eiteljorg Museum of American Indians & Western Art** (☎317-636-9378; www.eiteljorg.org; 500 W Washington St; adult/child $10/6; ☉10am-5pm Mon-Sat, from noon Sun) features Native American basketry, pots and masks, as well as several paintings by Frederic Remington and Georgia O'Keeffe. Other park highlights include an atmospheric **minor-league baseball stadium**, a zoo, a **canal walk, gardens** and a **science museum**.

The **NCAA Hall of Champions** (☑800-735-6222; www.ncaahallofchampions.org; 700 W Washington St; adult/child $5/3; ⊙10am-5pm Tue-Sat, from noon Sun) is also here, and reveals the country's fascination with college sports. Interactive exhibits let you shoot free throws or climb onto a swimming platform à la Michael Phelps.

Indianapolis
Museum of Art   MUSEUM, GARDENS

(☑317-920-2660; www.imamuseum.org; 4000 Michigan Rd; ⊙11am-5pm Tue-Sat, 11am-9pm Thu & Fri, noon-5pm Sun) [FREE] The museum has a terrific collection of European art (especially Turner and post-impressionists), African tribal art, South Pacific art and Chinese works. The complex also includes **Oldfields – Lilly House & Gardens**, where you can tour the 22-room mansion and flowery grounds of the Lilly pharmaceutical family, and **Fairbanks Art & Nature Park**, with eye-popping mod sculptures set amid 100 acres of woodlands.

Kurt Vonnegut Memorial Library   MUSEUM

(www.vonnegutlibrary.org; 340 N Senate Ave; ⊙noon-5pm Thu-Tue) [FREE] Author Kurt Vonnegut was born and raised in Indy, and this humble museum pays homage with displays including his Pall Mall cigarettes, Purple Heart medal and box of hilarious rejection letters from publishers. The library also replicates his office, complete with checkerboard carpet, red-rooster lamp and blue Coronamatic typewriter. You're welcome to sit at the desk and type Kurt a note.

Rhythm! Discovery Center   MUSEUM

(www.rhythmdiscoverycenter.org; 110 W Washington St; adult/child $9/6; ⊙10am-5pm Mon-Sat, from noon Sun) Bang drums, gongs, xylophones and exotic percussive instruments from around the globe at this hidden gem downtown. Kids love the interactive whomping. Adults appreciate the exhibits of famous drummers' gear and the soundproof, drumkitted studio where you can unleash (and record) your inner Neil Peart.

Monument Circle   MONUMENT, MUSEUM

(1 Monument Circle) At Monument Circle the city center is marked by the jaw-dropping 284ft **Soldiers & Sailors Monument**. For a

bizarre (and cramped) experience, take the elevator ($2) to the top. Beneath is the **Civil War Museum** (⊙10:30am-5:30pm Wed-Sun) [FREE], which neatly outlines the conflict and Indiana's abolition position. A few blocks north, the **World War Memorial** (cnr Vermont & Meridian Sts) is another impressively beefy monument.

Sun King Brewing   BREWERY

(www.sunkingbrewing.com; 135 N College Ave; ⊙4-7pm Thu, noon-7pm Fri, 1-5pm Sat) [FREE] Join Indy's young and hip, slurping free beers at Sun King's unvarnished downtown warehouse. You get six tastings (about the equivalent of a pint overall) in plastic cups, including year-round brews such as Osiris Pale Ale and seasonals like a pepper-spiced amber ale.

Indiana Medical
History Museum   MUSEUM

(☑317-635-7329; www.imhm.org; 3045 W Vermont St; adult/child $7/3; ⊙10am-3pm Thu-Sat) When you think 'horror movie insane asylum,' this century-old state psychiatric hospital is exactly what you envision. Guided tours roam the former pathology lab, from the cold-slabbed autopsy room to the eerie specimen room filled with brains in jars. It's a few miles west of White River park.

Bicycle Garage Indy
BICYCLE RENTAL

(www.bgindy.com; 222 E Market St; rental per hr/day $15/40) Cycling has really taken off in the city. Hop on the Cultural Trail in front of the shop; it eventually connects to the Monon Trail greenway. Rates include helmet, lock and map.

Festivals

The city celebrates the Indy 500 throughout May with the 500 Festival (www.500festival.com; tickets from $7). Events include a race-car drivers' parade and a community shindig at the racetrack.

Sleeping

Hotels cost more and are usually full during race weeks in May, July and August. Add 17% tax to the prices listed here. Look for low-cost motels off I-465, the freeway that circles Indianapolis.

Indy Hostel
HOSTEL $

(317-727-1696; www.indyhostel.us; 4903 Winthrop Ave; dm/r from $29/58; P ✳ @ 🛜) This small, friendly hostel has four dorm rooms in configurations from four to six beds. One room is for females only, while the others are mixed. There are also a couple of private rooms. The Monon Trail hiking/cycling path runs beside the property. It's located by Broad Ripple, so it's a bit of a haul from downtown (on bus 17).

Hilton Garden Inn
HOTEL $$

(317-955-9700; www.indianapolisdowntown.gardeninn.com; 10 E Market St; r incl breakfast $150-190; ✳ @ 🛜 ⛱) The century-old neoclassical architecture, plush beds, free omelet-laden breakfast and downtown location right by Monument Circle make this a fine chain-hotel choice. Parking is $25.

Stone Soup
B&B $$

(866-639-9550; www.stonesoupinn.com; 1304 N Central Ave; r incl breakfast $85-145; P ✳ 🛜) The nine rooms sprawl throughout a rambling,

> ### ⓘ INDIANA FOODWAYS
>
> Which restaurants serve the best pork tenderloin and sugar cream pie? Where are the local farmers markets and rib fests? What's the recipe for corn pudding? The Indiana Foodways Alliance (www.indianafoodways.com) is your one-stop shop for Hoosier cuisine info.

antique-filled house. It's a bit ramshackle, but it has its charm. The less-expensive rooms share a bath.

Alexander
HOTEL $$$

(317-624-8200; www.thealexander.com; 333 S Delaware St; r $160-280) Opened in 2013, the 209-room Alexander is all about art. Forty original works decorate the lobby; the Indianapolis Museum of Art curates the contemporary collection (the public is welcome to browse). The mod rooms have dark-wood floors and, of course, cool wall art. It's a block from the basketball arena, and it's where visiting teams typically stay. Parking is $27.

Eating

Massachusetts Ave (Mass Ave; www.discovermassave.com), by downtown, is bounteous when the stomach growls. Broad Ripple (www.discoverbroadripplevillage.com), 7 miles north, has pubs, cafes and ethnic eateries.

Mug 'N' Bun
AMERICAN $

(www.mug-n-bun.com; 5211 W 10th St; mains $3-5; ⊙10am-9pm Sun-Thu, to 10pm Fri & Sat) The mugs are frosted and filled with a wonderful home-brewed root beer. The buns contain burgers, chili dogs and juicy pork tenderloins. And don't forget the fried macaroni-and-cheese wedges. At this vintage drive-in near the Speedway, you are served – where else? – in your car.

City Market
MARKET $

(www.indycm.com; 222 E Market St; ⊙6am-9pm Mon-Fri, from 8am Sat; 🛜) A smattering of food stalls fill the city's old marketplace, which dates from 1886. The 2nd-floor bar pours 16 local brews; most other vendors close by 3pm.

Bazbeaux
PIZZERIA $$

(www.bazbeaux.com; 329 Massachusetts Ave; mains $8-12; ⊙11am-10pm Sun-Thu, to 11pm Fri & Sat) A local favorite, Bazbeaux offers an eclectic pizza selection, like the 'Tchoupitoulas,' topped with Cajun shrimp and andouille sausage. Muffaletta sandwiches, stromboli and Belgian beer are some of the other unusual offerings.

Shapiro's Deli
DELI $$

(317-631-4041; www.shapiros.com; 808 S Meridian St; mains $8-15; ⊙6am-8pm; 🛜) Chomp into a towering corned-beef or peppery pastrami sandwich on homemade bread, and then chase it with fat slices of chocolate cake or fruit pie.

🍸 Drinking & Entertainment

Downtown and Mass Ave have some good watering holes; Broad Ripple also has several.

Bars & Nightclubs

Slippery Noodle Inn   BAR
(www.slipperynoodle.com; 372 S Meridian St; ⊙from 11am Mon-Fri, from noon Sat, from 4pm Sun) Downtown's Noodle is the oldest bar in the state, and has seen action as a whorehouse, slaughterhouse, gangster hangout and Underground Railroad station; currently it's one of the best blues clubs in the country. There's live music nightly, and it's cheap.

Rathskeller   BEER HALL
(www.rathskeller.com; 401 E Michigan St; ⊙from 2pm Mon-Fri, from 11am Sat & Sun) Quaff German and local brews at the outdoor beer garden's picnic tables in summer, or at the deer-head-lined indoor beer hall once winter strikes. It is located in the historic Athenaeum building near Mass Ave.

Plump's Last Shot   BAR
(www.plumpslastshot.com; 6416 Cornell Ave; ⊙from 3pm Mon-Fri, from noon Sat & Sun; 🐾) Bobby Plump inspired the iconic movie *Hoosiers*. He's the kid who swished in the last-second shot, so his tiny school beat the 'big city' school in the 1950s state basketball championship. There's sports memorabilia everywhere. It's located in a big house in Broad Ripple – great for people-watching and sipping a cold one on the dog-friendly patio.

Sports

The motor races aren't the only coveted spectator events. The NFL's Colts win football games under a huge retractable roof at **Lucas Oil Stadium** (☎317-262-3389; www.colts.com; 500 S Capitol Ave). The NBA's Pacers shoot hoops at **Bankers Life Fieldhouse** (☎317-917-2500; www.pacers.com; 125 S Pennsylvania St).

🛍 Shopping

You could buy a speedway flag or Colts jersey as your Indy souvenir. Or you could purchase a bottle of mead made by a couple of enthusiastic former beekeepers at **New Day Meadery** (www.newdaymeadery.com; 1102 E Prospect St; ⊙2-9pm Tue-Fri, noon-9pm Sat, noon-6pm Sun). Sip the honeyed wares in the tasting room (six samples for $6) before making your selection.

WORTH A TRIP

GRAY BROTHERS CAFETERIA

Cafeterias are an Indiana tradition, but most have disappeared – except for **Gray Brothers** (www.graybrotherscatering.com; 555 S Indiana St; mains $4-8; ⊙11am-8:30pm Mon-Sat, from 10am Sun). Enter the time-warped dining room, grab a blue tray and behold a corridor of food that seems to stretch the length of a football field. Stack on plates of pan-fried chicken, meatloaf, mac 'n' cheese and sugar cream pie, then fork in with abandon. It's located in Mooresville, about 18 miles south of downtown Indianapolis en route to Bloomington.

ℹ Information

Gay Indy (www.gayindy.org) Gay and lesbian news and entertainment listings.

Indiana University Medical Center (☎317-274-4705; 550 N University Blvd)

Indianapolis Convention & Visitors Bureau (☎800-323-4639; www.visitindy.com) Download a free city app and print out coupons from the website.

Indianapolis Star (www.indystar.com) The city's daily newspaper.

Nuvo (www.nuvo.net) Free, weekly alternative paper with the arts and music low-down.

ℹ Getting There & Around

The fancy **Indianapolis International Airport** (IND; www.indianapolisairport.com; 7800 Col H Weir Cook Memorial Dr) is 16 miles southwest of town. The Washington bus (8) runs between the airport and downtown ($1.75, 50 minutes); the Go Green Airport van does it quicker ($10, 20 minutes). A cab to downtown costs about $35.

Greyhound (☎317-267-3076; www.greyhound.com) shares **Union Station** (350 S Illinois St) with Amtrak. Buses go frequently to Cincinnati (two hours) and Chicago (3½ hours). **Megabus** (www.megabus.com/us) stops at 200 E Washington St, and is often cheaper. Amtrak travels these routes but takes almost twice as long and (nonsensically) costs more.

IndyGo (www.indygo.net; fare $1.75) runs the local buses. Bus 17 goes to Broad Ripple. Service is minimal during weekends.

For a taxi, call **Yellow Cab** (☎317-487-7777).

Bloomington & Central Indiana

Bluegrass music, architectural hot spots, Tibetan temples and James Dean all furrow into the farmland around here.

Fairmount

This small town, north on Hwy 9, is the birthplace of James Dean, one of the original icons of cool. Fans should head directly to the **Fairmount Historical Museum** (☑765-948-4555; www.jamesdeanartifacts.com; 203 E Washington St; ⊙10am-5pm Mon-Sat, from noon Sun Apr-Oct) **FREE** to see Dean's bongo drums, among other artifacts. This is also the place to pick up a free map that will guide you to the farmhouse where Jimmy grew up and his lipstick-kissed grave site, among other sights. The museum sells Dean posters, zippo lighters and other memorabilia, and sponsors the annual **James Dean Festival** (⊙late Sep) **FREE**, when as many as 50,000 fans pour in for four days of music and revelry. The privately owned **James Dean Gallery** (☑765-948-3326; www.jamesdeangallery.com; 425 N Main St; ⊙9am-6pm) **FREE** has more memorabilia a few blocks away.

Columbus

When you think of the USA's great architectural cities – Chicago, New York, Washington, DC – Columbus, Indiana, doesn't quite leap to mind, but it should. Located 40 miles south of Indianapolis on I-65, Columbus is a remarkable gallery of physical design. Since the 1940s the city and its leading corporations have commissioned some of the world's best architects, including Eero Saarinen, Richard Meier and IM Pei, to create both public and private buildings. Stop at the **visitor center** (☑812-378-2622; www.columbus.in.us; 506 5th St; ⊙9am-5pm Mon-Sat year-round, noon-5pm Sun Mar-Nov, closed Sun Dec-Feb) to pick up a self-guided tour map ($3) or join a two-hour bus tour (adult/child $20/10) departing at 10am Monday to Friday, 10am and 2pm Saturday and 2:30pm Sunday. Over 70 notable buildings and pieces of public art are spread over a wide area (car required), but about 15 diverse works can be seen on foot downtown.

Hotel Indigo (☑812-375-9100; www.hotel-indigo.com; 400 Brown St; r $135-180; ✸🞱🗷🞱), downtown, offers the chain's trademark mod, cheery rooms, plus a fluffy white dog who works as the lobby ambassador (he even has his own email address). A few blocks away you can grab a counter stool, chat up the servers, and let the sugar buzz begin at retro, stained-glass-packed **Zaharakos** (www.zaharakos.com; 329 Washington St; ⊙11am-8pm), a 1909 soda fountain.

Nashville

Gentrified and antique-filled, this 19th-century town west of Columbus on Hwy 46 is now a bustling tourist center, at its busiest in fall when leaf-peepers pour in. The **visitor center** (☑800-753-3255; www.browncounty.com; 10 N Van Buren St; ⊙9am-6pm Mon-Thu, 9am-7pm Fri & Sat, 10am-5pm Sun; 🞱) provides maps and coupons.

Beyond gallery browsing, Nashville is the jump-off point to **Brown County State Park** (☑812-988-6406; tent & RV sites $12-36, cabins from $77), a 15,700-acre stand of oak, hickory and birch trees, where trails give hikers, mountain bikers and horseback riders access to the area's green hill country.

Among several B&Bs, central **Artists Colony Inn** (☑812-988-0600; www.artistscolonyinn.com; 105 S Van Buren St; r incl breakfast $112-180; 🞱) stands out for its spiffy Shaker-style rooms. The **dining room** (mains $9-17; ⊙7:30am-8pm Sun-Thu, to 9pm Fri & Sat) offers traditional Hoosier fare, such as catfish and pork tenderloins.

As with Nashville Tennessee, Nashville Indiana enjoys country music, and bands play regularly at several venues. To shake a leg, mosey into **Mike's Music & Dance Barn** (☑812-988-8636; www.mikesmusicbarn.com; 2277 Hwy 46; ⊙from 6:30pm Thu-Mon). The **Bill Monroe Museum** (☑812-988-6422; 5163 Rte 135 N; adult/child $4/free; ⊙9am-5pm, closed Tue & Wed Nov-Apr), 5 miles north of town, hails the bluegrass hero.

Bloomington

Lively and lovely Bloomington, 53 miles south of Indianapolis via Hwy 37, is the home of Indiana University. The town centers on Courthouse Sq, surrounded by restaurants, bars, bookshops and the historic facade of Fountain Sq Mall. Nearly everything is walkable. The **Bloomington CVB** (www.visitbloomington.com) has a downloadable guide.

On the expansive university campus, the **Art Museum** (☑812-855-5445; www.indiana.edu/~iuam; 1133 E 7th St; ⊙10am-5pm Tue-Sat, from noon Sun) FREE, designed by IM Pei, contains an excellent collection of African art, as well as European and US paintings.

The colorful, prayer-flag-covered **Tibetan Mongolian Buddhist Cultural Center** (☑ 812-336-6807; www.tmbcc.net; 3655 Snoddy Rd; ◎ sunrise-sunset) FREE – founded by the Dalai Lama's brother – as well as the **Dagom Gaden Tensung Ling Monastery** (☑ 812-339-0857; www.dgtlmonastery.org; 102 Clubhouse Dr; ◎ 9am-6pm) FREE, indicate Bloomington's significant Tibetan presence. Both have intriguing shops and offer free teachings and meditation sessions; check the websites for weekly schedules.

If you arrive in mid-April and wonder why an extra 20,000 people are hanging out in town, it's for the **Little 500** (www.iusf.indiana.edu; tickets $25; ◎ mid-Apr). It's one of the coolest bike races you'll see, in which amateurs ride one-speed Schwinns for 200 laps around a quarter-mile track.

Look for cheap lodgings along N Walnut St near Hwy 46. **Grant Street Inn** (☑ 800-328-4350; www.grantstinn.com; 310 N Grant St; r incl breakfast $159-239; @ ☎) has 24 rooms in a Victorian house and annex near campus.

For a town of its size, Bloomington offers a mind-blowing array of ethnic restaurants – everything from Burmese to Eritrean to Mexican. Browse Kirkwood Ave and E 4th St. **Anyetsang's Little Tibet** (☑ 812-331-0122; www.anyetsangs.com; 415 E 4th St; mains $9-13; ◎ 11am-9:30pm Wed-Mon) offers specialties from the Himalayan homeland. Pubs on Kirkwood Ave, close to the university, cater to the student crowd. **Nick's English Hut** (www.nicksenglishhut.com; 423 E Kirkwood Ave; ◎ from 11am) pours not only for students and professors, but has filled the cups of Kurt Vonnegut, Dylan Thomas and Barack Obama, as well.

Southern Indiana

The pretty hills, caves, rivers and utopian history of southern Indiana mark it as a completely different region from the flat and industrialized north.

Ohio River

The Indiana segment of the 981-mile Ohio River marks the state's southern border. From tiny Aurora, in the southeastern corner of the state, Hwys 56, 156, 62 and 66, known collectively as the **Ohio River Scenic Route**, wind through a varied landscape.

Coming from the east, a perfect place to stop is little **Madison**, a well-preserved river settlement from the mid-19th century where architectural beauties beckon genteelly from the streets. At the **visitor center** (☑ 812-265-2956; www.visitmadison.org; 601 W First St; ◎ 9am-5pm Mon-Fri, 9am-4pm Sat, 11am-5pm Sun), pick up a walking-tour brochure, which will lead you by notable landmarks.

Madison has motels around its edges, as well as several B&Bs. Main St lines up numerous places for a bite, interspersed with antique stores. Large, wooded **Clifty Falls State Park** (☑ 812-273-8885; tent & RV sites $12-36), off Hwy 56 and a couple of miles west of town, has camping, hiking trails, views and waterfalls.

In Clarksville, **Falls of the Ohio State Park** (☑ 812-280-9970; www.fallsoftheohio.org; 201 W Riverside Dr) has only rapids, no falls, but is of interest for its 386-million-year-old fossil beds. The **interpretive center** (adult/child $5/2; ◎ 9am-5pm Mon-Sat, from 1pm Sun) explains it all. Quench your thirst in adjacent New Albany, home to **New Albanian Brewing Company** (www.newalbanian.com; 3312 Plaza Dr; ◎ 11am-midnight Mon-Sat). Or cross the bridge to Louisville, Kentucky, where the tonsil-singeing native bourbon awaits...

Scenic Hwy 62 heads west and leads to the Lincoln Hills and southern Indiana's limestone caves. A plunge into **Marengo Cave** (☑ 812-365-2705; www.marengocave.com; ◎ 9am-6pm Jun-Aug, to 5pm Sep-May), north on Hwy 66, is highly recommended. It has a 40-minute tour (adult/child $14/8), 70-minute tour ($16/9) or combination tour ($24/13) walking past stalagmites and other ancient formations. The same group operates **Cave Country Canoes** (www.cavecountrycanoes.com; ◎ May-Oct) in nearby Milltown, with half-day ($25), full-day ($28) or longer trips on the scenic Blue River; keep an eye out for river otters and rare hellbender salamanders.

Four miles south of Dale, off I-64, is the **Lincoln Boyhood National Memorial** (☑ 812-937-4541; www.nps.gov/libo; adult/child/family $3/free/$5; ◎ 8am-5pm), where young Abe lived from age seven to 21. This isolated site also includes admission to a working **pioneer farm** (◎ 8am-5pm late May-Aug).

New Harmony

In southwest Indiana, the Wabash River forms the border with Illinois. Beside it, south of I-64, captivating New Harmony is the site of two early communal-living experiments and is worth a visit. In the early 19th century a German Christian sect, the Harmonists, developed a sophisticated town here while awaiting the Second Coming. Later, the British utopian Robert Owen acquired the town. Learn more and pick up a walking-tour map at the angular **Atheneum Visitors Center** (📞 812-682-4474; www.usi. edu/hnh; 401 N Arthur St; ⊘ 9:30am-5pm).

Today New Harmony retains an air of contemplation, if not otherworldliness, which you can experience at its newer attractions, such as the templelike Roofless Church and the Labyrinth, a maze symbolizing the spirit's quest. The town has a couple of guesthouses and camping at **Harmonie State Park** (📞 812-682-4821; campsites $12-29). Pop into **Main Cafe** (508 Main St; mains $4-7; ⊘ 5:30am-1pm Mon-Fri) for a ham, bean and cornbread lunch, but save room for the coconut cream pie.

Northern Indiana

The truck-laden I-80/I-90 tollways cut across Indiana's northern section. Parallel US 20 is slower and cheaper, but not much more attractive.

Indiana Dunes

Hugely popular on summer days with sunbathers from Chicago and South Bend, the **Indiana Dunes National Lakeshore** (📞 219-395-8914; www.nps.gov/indu; campsites $18; ⊘ Apr-Oct) stretches along 21 miles of Lake Michigan shoreline. In addition to its beaches, the area is noted for its plant variety: everything from cacti to pine trees sprouts here. Hiking trails crisscross the dunes and woodlands, winding by a peat bog, a still-operating 1870s farm and a blue-heron rookery, among other payoffs. Oddly, all this natural bounty lies smack-dab next to smoke-belching factories, which you'll also see at various vantage points. Stop at the **Dorothy Buell Visitor Center** (📞 219-926-7561; Hwy 49; ⊘ 8:30am-6:30pm Jun-Aug, to 4:30pm Sep-May) for beach details, a schedule of ranger-guided walks and activities, and to pick up hiking, biking and birding maps.

Or get guides in advance via the **Porter County Convention & Visitors Bureau** (www.indianadunes.com).

Indiana Dunes State Park (📞 219-926-1952; www.dnr.in.gov/parklake; per car $10) is a 2100-acre shoreside pocket within the national lakeshore; it's located at the end of Hwy 49, near Chesterton. It has more amenities than the National Foreshore, but also more regulation and more crowds (plus the vehicle entry fee). Wintertime brings out the cross-country skiers; summertime brings out the hikers. Seven trails zigzag over the landscape; Trail 4 up Mt Tom rewards with Chicago skyline views.

Other than a couple of beachfront snack bars, you won't find much to eat in the parks, so stop at **Great Lakes Cafe** (201 Mississippi St; mains $6-9; ⊘ 5am-3pm Mon-Fri, 6am-1pm Sat; 📶), the steelworkers' hearty favorite, at the Dunes' western edge in Gary.

The Dunes are an easy day trip from Chicago. Driving takes one hour. The **South Shore Metra train** (www.nictd.com) makes the journey from Millennium Station downtown, and it's about 1¼ hours to the Dune Park or Beverly Shores stops (both stations are a 1½-mile walk from the beach). Those who want to make a night of it can **camp** (national lakeshore campsites $18, state park tent & RV sites $19-36).

Near Illinois, the steel cities of **Gary** and **East Chicago** present some of the bleakest urban landscapes anywhere. Taking the train (Amtrak or South Shore line) through here will get you up close and personal with the industrial underbelly.

South Bend

South Bend is home to the **University of Notre Dame**. You know how some people say, 'football is a religion here'? They mean it at Notre Dame, where 'Touchdown Jesus' lords over the 80,000-capacity stadium (it's a mural of the resurrected Christ with arms raised, though the pose bears a striking resemblance to a referee signaling a touchdown).

Tours of the pretty campus, with its two lakes, Gothic-style architecture and iconic Golden Dome atop the main building, start at the **visitor center** (www.nd.edu/visitors; 111 Eck Center). Less visited but worth a stop is the **Studebaker National Museum** (📞 574-235-9714; www.studebakermuseum.org; 201 S Chapin St; adult/child $8/5; ⊘ 10am-5pm Mon-Sat, from noon Sun) near downtown, where you can gaze at a gorgeous 1956 Packard and other classic beauties that used to be built in South Bend.

Amish Country

East of South Bend, around **Shipshewana** and **Middlebury**, is the USA's third-largest Amish community. Horses and buggies clip-clop by, and long-bearded men hand-plow the tidy fields. Get situated with maps from the **Elkhart County CVB** (☎800-517-9739; www.amishcountry.org). Better yet, pick a back-road between the two towns and head down it. Often you'll see families selling beeswax candles, quilts and fresh produce on their porch, which beats the often-touristy shops and restaurants on the main roads. Note that most places close on Sunday.

Village Inn (☎574-825-2043; 105 S Main St; mains $3-7; ☺5am-8pm Mon-Fri, 6am-2pm Sat; ☎), in Middlebury, sells real-deal pies; bonneted women in pastel dresses come in at 4:30am to bake the flaky wares. Arrive before noon, or you'll be looking at crumbs.

Auburn

Just before reaching the Ohio border, classic car connoisseurs should dip south on I-69 to the town of Auburn, where the Cord Company produced the USA's favorite cars in the 1920s and '30s. The **Auburn Cord Duesenberg Museum** (☎260-925-1444; www.automobilemuseum.org; 1600 S Wayne St; adult/child $12.50/7.50; ☺10am-7pm Mon-Fri, to 5pm Sat & Sun) has a wonderful display of early roadsters in a beautiful art-deco setting. Next door are the vintage rigs of the **National Automotive and Truck Museum** (☎260-925-9100; www.natmus.org; 1000 Gordon Buehrig Pl; adult/child $7/4; ☺9am-5pm).

OHIO

All right, time for your Ohio quiz. In the Buckeye State you can 1) watch butter churn on an Amish farm; 2) lose your stomach on one of the world's fastest roller coasters; 3) suck down a dreamy creamy milkshake fresh from a working dairy; or 4) examine a massive, mysterious snake sculpture built into the earth. And the answer is...all of these. It hurts locals' feelings when visitors think the only thing to do here is tip over cows, so c'mon, give Ohio a chance. Besides these activities, you can partake in a five-way in Cincinnati and rock out in Cleveland.

❶ Information

Ohio Division of Travel and Tourism (☎800-282-5393; www.discoverohio.com)
Ohio Highway Conditions (www.ohgo.com)
Ohio State Park Information (☎614-265-6561; http://parks.ohiodnr.gov) State parks are free to visit; some have free wi-fi. Tent and RV sites cost $19 to $38; reservations accepted (☎866-644-6727; www.ohio.reserveworld.com; fee $8.25).

Cleveland

Does it or does it not rock? That is the question. Drawing from its roots as a working man's town, Cleveland has toiled hard in recent years to prove it does. Step one was to control the urban decay/river-on-fire thing – the Cuyahoga River was once so polluted that it actually burned. Check. Step two was to bring a worthy attraction to town, say the Rock and Roll Hall of Fame. Check. Step three was to get grub beyond steak-and-potatoes. Check. So can Cleveland finally wipe the sweat from its brow? More or less. Some of the downtown area remains bleak, though there are definite pockets of freshness.

OHIO FACTS

Nickname Buckeye State

Population 11.5 million

Area 44,825 sq miles

Capital city Columbus (population 810,000)

Other cities Cleveland (population 391,000), Cincinnati (population 297,000)

Sales tax 5.5%

Birthplace of Inventor Thomas Edison (1847–1931), author Toni Morrison (b 1931), entrepreneur Ted Turner (b 1938), filmmaker Steven Spielberg (b 1947)

Home of Cows, roller coasters, aviation pioneers the Wright Brothers

Politics Swing state

Famous for First airplane, first pro baseball team, birthplace of seven US presidents

State rock song 'Hang On Sloopy'

Driving distances Cleveland to Columbus 142 miles, Columbus to Cincinnati 108 miles

◉ Sights & Activities

Cleveland's center is Public Sq, dominated by the conspicuous Terminal Tower. It's bustling thanks to a ka-chinging new casino. Most attractions are downtown on the lakefront or at University Circle (the area around Case Western Reserve University, Cleveland Clinic and other institutions).

◎ Downtown

Rock and Roll Hall of Fame & Museum
MUSEUM

(☑ 216-781-7625; www.rockhall.com; 1 Key Plaza; adult/child $22/13; ◷ 10am-5:30pm, to 9pm Wed year-round, to 9pm Sat Jun-Aug) Cleveland's top attraction is like an overstuffed attic bursting with groovy finds: Jimi Hendrix's Stratocaster, Keith Moon's platform shoes, John Lennon's Sgt Pepper suit and a 1966 piece of hate mail to the Rolling Stones from a cursive-writing Fijian. It's more than memorabilia, though. Multimedia exhibits trace the history and social context of rock music and the performers who created it.

Why is the museum in Cleveland? Because this is the hometown of Alan Freed, the disk jockey who popularized the term 'rock 'n' roll' in the early 1950s, and because the city lobbied hard and paid big. Be prepared for crowds (especially thick until 1pm or so).

Great Lakes Science Center
MUSEUM

(☑ 216-694-2000; www.glsc.org; 601 Erieside Ave; adult/child $14/12; ◷ 10am-5pm; ⊞) One of 10 museums in the country with a NASA affiliation, Great Lakes goes deep in space with rockets, moon stones and the 1973 Apollo capsule, as well as exhibits on the lakes' environmental problems.

William G Mather
MUSEUM

(☑ 216-574-6262; www.glsc.org/mather_museum.php; 305 Mather Way; adult/child $8/6; ◷ 11am-5pm Tue-Sun Jun-Aug, Fri-Sun only May, Sep & Oct, closed Nov-Apr) Take a self-guided walk on this humungous freighter incarnated as a steamship museum. It's docked beside the Great Lakes Science Center, which manages it.

USS Cod
MUSEUM

(☑ 216-566-8770; www.usscod.org; 1089 E 9th St; adult/child $10/6; ◷ 10am-5pm May-Sep) The storied submarine USS *Cod* saw action in WWII. You're free to climb through it, tight spaces, ladders and all, while listening to audio stories about life on board.

The Flats
WATERFRONT

(www.flatseast.com) The Flats, an old industrial zone turned nightlife hub on the Cuyahoga River, has had a checkered life. After years of neglect, it's on the upswing once again. Developers poured $500 million into the East Bank for a waterfront boardwalk, restaurants, bars, an Aloft hotel and concert pavilion, all opened in 2013.

◎ Ohio City & Tremont

West Side Market
MARKET

(www.westsidemarket.org; cnr W 25th St & Lorain Ave; ◷ 7am-4pm Mon & Wed, to 6pm Fri & Sat) The European-style market overflows with greengrocers and their fruit and vegetable pyramids, as well as purveyors of Hungarian sausage, Mexican flat breads and Polish pierogi.

Christmas Story House & Museum
MUSEUM

(☑ 216-298-4919; www.achristmasstoryhouse.com; 3159 W 11th St; adult/child $10/6; ◷ 10am-5pm Thu-Sat, from noon Sun) Remember the beloved 1983 film *A Christmas Story,* in which Ralphie yearns for a Red Ryder BB gun? The original house sits in Tremont, complete with leg lamp. This attraction's for true fans only.

◎ University Circle

Several museums and attractions are within walking distance of each other at University Circle, 5 miles east of downtown. Carless? Take the HealthLine bus to Adelbert.

Cleveland Museum of Art
MUSEUM

(☑ 216-421-7340; www.clevelandart.org; 11150 East Blvd; ◷ 10am-5pm Tue-Sun, to 9pm Wed & Fri) FREE Fresh off a whopping expansion, the art museum houses an excellent collection of European paintings, as well as African, Asian and American art. Head to the 2nd floor for rock-star works from impressionists, Picasso and surrealists. Interactive touch screens are stationed throughout the galleries and provide fun ways to learn more. There's also a neat-o free iPad app.

Cleveland Botanical Garden
GARDENS

(☑ 216-721-1600; www.cbgarden.org; 11030 East Blvd; adult/child $9.50/4; ◷ 10am-5pm Tue-Sat, noon-5pm Sun, noon-9pm Wed) It has a Costa Rican cloud forest and Madagascan desert exhibits. An ice-skating rink opens nearby in winter; skate rentals cost $3. Parking costs $5 to $10 per day and gives access to all the museums here.

Museum of Contemporary Art Cleveland
MUSEUM

(MOCA; ☑ audio tours 216-453-3960; www.moca-cleveland.org; 11400 Euclid Ave; adult/child $8/5; ⊘11am-5pm Tue-Sun, to 9pm Thu) The shiny new building impresses, with four stories of geometric black steel, though there's not a lot to see inside. Floors 2 and 4 have the galleries; exhibits focus on an artist or two and change often. Call for an audio tour of the architecture and installations.

Lakeview Cemetery
CEMETERY

(☑216-421-2665; www.lakeviewcemetery.com; 12316 Euclid Ave; ⊘7:30am-7:30pm) Beyond the circle further east, don't forget this eclectic 'outdoor museum' where President Garfield and John Rockefeller rest, or, more intriguingly, local comic-book hero Harvey Pekar and crime-fighter Eliot Ness.

🛏 Sleeping

Prices listed here are for summer, which is high season, and do not include the 16.25% tax. Modest motels are southwest of Cleveland's center, near the airport. The W 150th exit off I-71 (exit 240) has several options for less than $100.

Cleveland Hostel
HOSTEL $

(☑216-394-0616; www.theclevelandhostel.com; 2090 W 25th St; dm/r from $25/65) This new hostel in Ohio City, steps from an RTA stop and the West Side Market, is fantastic. There are 15 rooms, a mix of dorms and private chambers. All have fluffy beds, fresh paint in soothing hues and nifty antique decor. Add in the rooftop deck, free parking lot and cheap bike rentals (per day $15), and no wonder it's packed.

Holiday Inn Express
HOTEL $$

(☑216-443-1000; www.hiexpress.com; 629 Euclid Ave; r incl breakfast $130-190; P✸@🛜) This goes way beyond the usual chain offering and is more like a true boutique hotel with large, nattily decorated rooms and lofty views. It's set in an old bank building that's conveniently located near the E 4th St entertainment strip. Parking costs $14.

Brownstone Inn
B&B $$

(☑216-426-1753; www.brownstoneinndowntown.com; 3649 Prospect Ave; r incl breakfast $89-139; P✸@🛜) This Victorian townhouse B&B has a whole lotta personality. All five rooms have a private bath, and each comes equipped with robes to lounge in and an invitation for evening aperitifs. It's between downtown and University Circle, though it's in a bit of a no-man's-land for walking to entertainment.

Hilton Garden Inn
HOTEL $$

(☑216-658-6400; www.hiltongardeninn.com; 1100 Carnegie Ave; r $110-169; P✸@🛜🏊) While it's nothing fancy, the Hilton's rooms are good value with comfy beds, wi-fi–rigged workstations and mini refrigerators. It's right by the baseball park. Parking costs $16.

🍴 Eating

There's more range than you might expect in a Rust Belt town.

🍴 Downtown

The Warehouse District, between W 6th and W 9th Sts, jumps with trendy restaurants. Off the beaten path and east of the city center, Asiatown (bounded by Payne and St Clair Aves, and E 30th and 40th Sts) has several Chinese, Vietnamese and Korean eateries.

Noodlecat
NOODLES $$

(www.noodlecat.com; 234 Euclid Ave; mains $9-13; ⊘11am-11pm) Hep-cat noodles fill bowls at this Japanese-American mash-up. Slurp mushroom udon, spicy octopus udon, beef-brisket ramen and fried-chicken ramen dishes. Lots of sake, craft beer and gluten-free options are available. There's another, smaller branch in the West Side Market.

Lola
MODERN AMERICAN $$$

(☑216-621-5652; www.lolabistro.com; 2058 E 4th St; mains $26-34; ⊘11:30am-2:30pm Mon-Fri, 5-10pm Mon-Thu, 5-11pm Fri & Sat) Famous for his piercings, Food Channel TV appearances and multiple national awards, local boy Michael Symon has put Cleveland on the foodie map with Lola. The lower-priced lunch dishes are the most fun; say, coconut-and-lime-tinged scallop ceviche, or the showstopper: an egg-and-cheese-topped fried bologna sandwich.

Pura Vida
MODERN AMERICAN $$$

(☑216-987-0100; www.puravidabybrandt.com; 170 Euclid Ave; mains $23-29; ⊘11:30am-2pm & 4-10pm Mon-Sat; ☑) Pura Vida serves creative, locally sourced comfort foods in a bright, ubermodern space fronting Public Sq. The trout po' boy and duck-leg confit with buttermilk waffles win praise. Small plates let you sample a couple of dishes, or you can load up on a main.

Ohio City & Tremont

Ohio City and Tremont, which straddle I-90 south of downtown, are areas that have lots of new establishments popping up.

West Side Market Cafe
CAFE $
(216-579-6800; 1995 W 25th St; mains $6-9; ☺7am-3pm Mon-Thu, 6am-6pm Fri & Sat, 9am-3pm Sun) This is a smart stop if you're craving well-made breakfast and lunch fare, and cheap fish and chicken mains. The cafe is inside West Side Market itself, which overflows with prepared foods that are handy for picnicking or road-tripping.

South Side
AMERICAN $$
(216-937-2288; www.southsidecleveland.com; 2207 W 11 St; mains $14-20; ☺11am-2am; ☺) Local athletes, blue-collar electricians and everyone in between piles into this sleek Tremont establishment to drink at the winding granite bar. They come for the late-night food too, like the grouper sandwich and bacon-cheddar burger.

Little Italy & Coventry

These two neighborhoods make prime stops for refueling after hanging out in University Circle. Little Italy is closest: it's along Mayfield Rd, near Lake View Cemetery (look out for the Rte 322 sign). Alternatively, relaxed Coventry Village is a bit further east off Mayfield Rd.

Presti's Bakery
BAKERY $
(www.prestisbakery.com; 12101 Mayfield Rd; items $2-6; ☺6am-9pm Mon-Thu, to 10pm Fri & Sat, to 6pm Sun) Try Presti's for its popular sandwiches, stromboli and divine pastries.

Tommy's
INTERNATIONAL $
(216-321-7757; www.tommyscoventry.com; 1823 Coventry Rd; mains $7-11; ☺9am-9pm Sun-Thu, 9am-10pm Fri, 7:30am-10pm Sat; ☺☺) Tofu, seitan and other old-school veggie dishes emerge from the kitchen, though carnivores have multiple options, too.

Drinking

The downtown action centers on the young, testosterone-fueled Warehouse District (around W 6th St), and around E 4th St's entertainment venues. Tremont is also chockablock with chic bars. Most places stay open until 2am.

Great Lakes Brewing Company
BREWERY
(www.greatlakesbrewing.com; 2516 Market Ave; ☺from 11:30am Mon-Sat) Great Lakes wins many prizes for its brewed-on-the-premises beers. Added historical bonus: Eliot Ness got into a shootout with criminals here; ask the bartender to show you the bullet holes.

Market Garden Brewery
BREWERY
(www.marketgardenbrewery.com; 1947 W 25th St; ☺4pm-2am Mon-Thu, 11am-2am Fri & Sat, 10am-3pm Sun) Since launching in 2011 this microbrewer has made a splash with its brown ale, though the other beers on tap are excellent, too. Sip indoors under the low-lit chandeliers, or outdoors at the communal wood tables striping the beer garden. It also distils small-batch whiskeys and rum, and shakes up beer cocktails.

Major Hoopples
BAR
(1930 Columbus Rd; ☺from 3pm Mon-Sat) Look over the bar for Cleveland's best skyline view from this friendly, eclectic watering hole. Films and sports games are projected on the bridge abutment out back.

☆ Entertainment

Gordon Square Arts District (www.gordonsquare.org) has a fun pocket of theaters, live-music venues and cafes along Detroit Ave between W 56th and W 69th Sts, a few miles west of downtown.

Live Music

Check Scene (www.clevescene.com) and Friday's Plain Dealer (www.cleveland.com) for listings.

★ Happy Dog
LIVE MUSIC
(www.happydogcleveland.com; 5801 Detroit Ave; ☺from 4pm Mon-Thu, from 11am Fri-Sun) Listen to scrappy bands while munching on a weenie, for which you can choose from among 50 toppings, from gourmet (black truffle) to, er, less gourmet (peanut butter and jelly); in the Gordon Sq district.

Grog Shop
LIVE MUSIC
(216-321-5588; www.grogshop.gs; 2785 Euclid Hts Blvd) Up-and-coming rockers thrash at Coventry's long-established music house.

Beachland Ballroom
LIVE MUSIC
(www.beachlandballroom.com; 15711 Waterloo Rd) Hip young bands play at this venue east of downtown.

Sports

Cleveland is a serious jock town with three modern downtown venues.

Progressive Field   BASEBALL

(www.indians.com; 2401 Ontario St) The Indians (aka 'the Tribe') hit here; great sightlines make it a good park to see a game.

Quicken Loans Arena   BASKETBALL

(www.nba.com/cavaliers; 1 Center Ct) The Cavaliers play basketball at 'the Q,' which doubles as an entertainment venue.

First Energy Stadium   FOOTBALL

(www.clevelandbrowns.com; 1085 W 3rd St) The NFL's Browns pass the football and score touchdowns on the lakefront.

Performing Arts

Severance Hall   CLASSICAL MUSIC

(☎216-231-1111; www.clevelandorchestra.com; 11001 Euclid Ave) The acclaimed Cleveland Symphony Orchestra holds its season (August to May) at Severance Hall, located by the University Circle museums. The orchestra's summer home is Blossom Music Center in Cuyahoga Valley National Park, about 22 miles south.

Playhouse Square Center   THEATER

(☎216-771-4444; www.playhousesquare.org; 1501 Euclid Ave) This elegant center hosts theater, opera and ballet. Check the website for $10 'Smart Seats.'

ℹ Information

INTERNET ACCESS

Many of Cleveland's public places have free wi-fi, such as Tower City and University Circle.

MEDIA

Gay People's Chronicle (www.gaypeople-schronicle.com) Free weekly publication with entertainment listings.

Plain Dealer (www.cleveland.com) The city's daily newspaper.

Scene (www.clevescene.com) A weekly entertainment paper.

MEDICAL SERVICES

MetroHealth Medical Center (☎216-778-7800; 2500 MetroHealth Dr)

TOURIST INFORMATION

Cleveland Convention & Visitors Bureau (www.positivelycleveland.com) Official website; the Twitter feed lists daily deals.

Visitor center (☎216-875-6680; 334 Euclid Ave; ☺8:30am-6:30pm Mon-Fri, from 10am Sat) Staff provide maps and reservation assistance.

WEBSITES

Cool Cleveland (www.coolcleveland.com) Hip arts and cultural happenings.

Ohio City (www.ohiocity.org) Eats and drinks in the neighborhood.

Tremont (www.tremontwest.org) Eats, drinks and gallery hops.

ℹ Getting There & Around

Eleven miles southwest of downtown, **Cleveland Hopkins International Airport** (CLE; www.clevelandairport.com; 5300 Riverside Dr) is linked by the Red Line train ($2.25). A cab to downtown costs about $30.

From downtown, **Greyhound** (☎216-781-0520; 1465 Chester Ave) offers frequent departures to Chicago (7½ hours) and New York City (13 hours). **Megabus** (www.megabus.com/us) also goes to Chicago, often for lower fares; check the website for the departure point.

Amtrak (☎216-696-5115; 200 Cleveland Memorial Shoreway) runs once daily to Chicago (seven hours) and New York City (13 hours).

The **Regional Transit Authority** (RTA; www.riderta.com; fare $2.25) operates the Red Line train that goes to both the airport and Ohio City. It also runs the HealthLine bus that motors along Euclid Ave from downtown to University Circle's museums. Day passes are $5.

For cab service, try phoning **Americab** (☎216-429-1111).

Around Cleveland

Sixty miles south of Cleveland, **Canton** is the birthplace of the NFL and home to the **Pro Football Hall of Fame** (☎330-456-8207; www.profootballhof.com; 2121 George Halas Dr; adult/child $22/16; ☺9am-8pm, to 5pm Sep-May). The shrine for the gridiron-obsessed sports sweet new interactive exhibits since the museum's expansion. Look for the football-shaped tower off I-77.

West of Cleveland, attractive **Oberlin** is an old-fashioned college town, with noteworthy architecture by Cass Gilbert, Frank Lloyd Wright and Robert Venturi. Further west, just south of I-90, the tiny town of **Milan** is the birthplace of Thomas Edison. His home has been restored to its 1847 likeness and is now a small **museum** (☎419-499-2135;

www.tomedison.org; 9 Edison Dr; adult/child $7/4; ⊙10am-5pm Tue-Sat, from 1pm Sun, reduced hours winter, closed Jan) outlining his inventions, including the light bulb and phonograph.

Still further west, on US 20 and surrounded by farmland, is **Clyde**, which bills itself as the USA's most famous small town. It got that way when native son Sherwood Anderson published *Winesburg, Ohio* in 1919. It didn't take long for the unimpressed residents to figure out where the fictitious town really was. Stop at the **Clyde Museum** (☑419-547-7946; www.clydeheritageleague. org; 124 W Buckeye St; ⊙1-4pm Thu Apr-Sep & by appointment) `FREE` in the old church for Anderson tidbits or at the library, a few doors down.

Erie Lakeshore & Islands

In summer this good-time resort area is one of the busiest – and most expensive – places in Ohio. The season lasts from mid-May to mid-September, and then just about everything shuts down. Make sure you prebook your accommodations.

DON'T MISS

CEDAR POINT'S RAGING ROLLER COASTERS

Cedar Point Amusement Park (☑419-627-2350; www.cedarpoint. com; adult/child $55/30; ⊙10am-10pm, closed Nov–mid-May) regularly wins the 'world's best amusement park' award, chosen each year by the public, which goes wild for the venue's 16 adrenaline-pumping roller coasters. Stomach-droppers include the Top Thrill Dragster, one of the globe's tallest and fastest rides. It climbs 420ft into the air before plunging and whipping around at 120mph. Meanwhile, the winglike GateKeeper loops, corkscrews and dangles riders from the world's highest inversion (meaning you're upside down a *lot*). If those and the 14 other coasters aren't enough to keep you occupied, the surrounding area has a nice beach, a water park and a slew of old-fashioned, cotton-candy-fueled attractions. It's about 6 miles from Sandusky. Buying tickets in advance online saves money. Parking costs $15.

Sandusky, long a port, now serves as the jump-off point to the Erie Islands and a mighty group of roller coasters. The **visitor center** (☑419-625-2984; www.shoresandislands. com; 4424 Milan Rd; ⊙8am-7pm Mon-Fri, 9am-6pm Sat, 9am-4pm Sun) provides lodging and ferry information. Loads of chain motels line the highways heading into town.

Bass Islands

In 1812's Battle of Lake Erie, Admiral Perry met the enemy English fleet near **South Bass Island**. His victory ensured that all the lands south of the Great Lakes became US, not Canadian, territory. But history is all but forgotten on a summer weekend in packed **Put In Bay**, the island's main town and a party place full of boaters, restaurants and shops. Move beyond it and you'll find a winery and opportunities for camping, fishing, kayaking and swimming.

A singular attraction is the 352ft Doric column known as **Perry's Victory and International Peace Memorial** (www.nps.gov/ pevi; admission $3; ⊙10am-7pm). Climb to the observation deck for views of the battle site and, on a good day, Canada.

The **Chamber of Commerce** (☑419-285-2832; www.visitputinbay.com; 148 Delaware Ave; ⊙10am-4pm Mon-Fri, to 5pm Sat & Sun) has information on activities and lodging. **Ashley's Island House** (☑419-285-2844; www. ashleysislandhouse.com; 557 Catawba Ave; r with/ without bath from $100/70; ❅ �🞄) is a 13-room B&B, where naval officers stayed in the late 1800s. The **Beer Barrel Saloon** (www. beerbarrelpib.com; Delaware Ave; ⊙11am-1am) has plenty of space for imbibing – its bar is 406ft long.

Cabs and tour buses serve the island, though cycling is a fine way to get around. Two ferry companies make the 20-minute trip regularly from the mainland. **Jet Express** (☑800-245-1538; www.jet-express.com) runs passenger-only boats direct to Put In Bay from Port Clinton (one way adult/child $15/2.50) almost hourly. It also departs from Sandusky ($19.50/5.50), stopping at Kelleys Island en route. Leave your car in the lot (per day $10) at either dock. **Miller Boatline** (☑800-500-2421; www.millerferry.com) operates a vehicle ferry that is the cheapest option, departing from further-flung Catawba (one way adult/child $7/1.50, car $15) every 30 minutes. It also cruises to **Middle Bass Island**, a good day trip from South Bass, offering nature and quiet.

Kelleys Island

Peaceful and green, Kelleys Island is a popular weekend escape, especially for families. It has pretty 19th-century buildings, Native American pictographs, a good beach and glacial grooves raked through its landscape. Even its old limestone quarries are scenic.

The **Chamber of Commerce** (☑419-746-2360; www.kelleysislandchamber.com; Seaway Marina Bldg; ⊙9:30am-4pm), by the ferry dock, has information on accommodations and activities – hiking, camping, kayaking and fishing are popular. The **Village**, the island's small commercial center, has places to eat, drink, shop and rent bicycles – the recommended way to sightsee.

Kelleys Island Ferry (☑419-798-9763; www.kelleysislandferry.com) departs from the wee village of Marblehead (one way adult/child $9.50/6, car $15). The crossing takes about 20 minutes and leaves hourly (more frequently in summer). **Jet Express** (☑800-245-1538; www.jet-express.com) departs from Sandusky (one way adult/child $15/4.50, no cars) and goes onward to Put In Bay on South Bass Island (island-hopping one way $22/6.50, no cars).

Pelee Island

Pelee, the largest Erie island, is a ridiculously green, quiet wine-producing and bird-watching destination that belongs to Canada. **Pelee Island Transportation** (☑800-661-2220; www.ontarioferries.com) runs a ferry (one way adult/child $13.75/6.75, car $30) from Sandusky to Pelee and onward to Ontario's mainland. Check www.pelee.org for lodging and trip-planning information.

Amish Country

Rural Wayne and Holmes counties are home to the USA's largest Amish community. They're only 80 miles south of Cleveland, but visiting here is like entering a pre-industrial time warp.

Descendants of conservative Dutch-Swiss religious factions who migrated to the USA during the 18th century, the Amish continue to follow the *ordnung* (way of life), in varying degrees. Many adhere to rules prohibiting the use of electricity, telephones and motorized vehicles. They wear traditional clothing, farm the land with plow and mule, and go to church in horse-drawn buggies. Others are not so strict.

Unfortunately, what would surely be a peaceful country scene is often disturbed by behemoth tour buses. Many Amish are happy to profit from this influx of outside dollars, but you shouldn't equate this with free photographic access – the Amish typically view photographs as taboo. Drive carefully as roads are narrow and curvy, and there's always the chance of pulling up on a slow-moving buggy just around the bend. Many places are closed Sunday.

◉ Sights & Activities

Kidron, on Rte 52, makes a good starting point. A short distance south, **Berlin** is the area's tchotchke-shop-filled core, while **Millersburg** is the region's largest town, more antique-y than Amish; US 62 connects these two 'busy' spots.

To get further off the beaten path, take Rte 557 or County Rd 70, both of which twist through the countryside to wee **Charm**, about 5 miles south of Berlin.

Lehman's   DEPARTMENT STORE
(www.lehmans.com; 4779 Kidron Rd, Kidron; ⊙8am-6pm Mon-Sat) Lehman's is an absolute must-see. It is the Amish community's main purveyor of modern-looking products that use no electricity, housed in a 32,000-sq-ft barn. Stroll through to ogle wind-up flashlights, wood-burning stoves and hand-cranked meat grinders.

Kidron Auction   MARKET
(www.kidronauction.com; 4885 Kidron Rd, Kidron; ⊙from 10am Thu) FREE If it's Thursday, follow the buggy line-up down the road from Lehman's to the livestock barn. Hay gets auctioned at 10am, cows at 11am and pigs at 1pm. A flea market rings the barn for folks seeking non-mooing merchandise. Similar auctions take place in Sugarcreek (Monday and Friday), Farmerstown (Tuesday) and Mt Hope (Wednesday).

Heini's Cheese Chalet   CHEESEMAKING FACTORY
(☑800-253-6636; www.heinis.com; 6005 Hwy 77, Berlin; tours free; ⊙8am-6pm Mon-Sat) Heini's whips up more than 70 cheeses. Learn how Amish farmers hand-milk their cows and spring-cool (versus machine-refrigerate) the output before delivering it each day. Then grab abundant samples and peruse the kitschy 'History of Cheesemaking' mural. To see the curd-cutting in action, come before 11am weekdays (except on Wednesday).

WORTH A TRIP

MALABAR FARM

What do Bogie, Bacall and Johnny Appleseed have in common? They've all spent time at **Malabar Farm State Park** (www.malabarfarm.org). There's a lot going on here: hiking and horse trails; pond fishing (ask for a free rod at the visitor center); tours of Pulitzer-winner Louis Bromfield's home (where Humphrey Bogart and Lauren Bacall got married); monthly barn dances; a farmhouse **hostel** (www.hiusa.org/lucas); and a fine **restaurant** (⊙11am-8pm Tue-Sun) that uses ingredients from the grounds. Malabar is 30 miles west of Millersburg via Hwy 39.

Hershberger's Farm & Bakery FARM
(☏330-674-6096; 5452 Hwy 557, Millersburg; ⊙bakery 8am-5pm Mon-Sat year-round, farm from 10am mid-Apr–Oct; 🖲) Gorge on 25 kinds of pie, homemade ice-cream cones and seasonal produce from the market inside. Pet the farmyard animals (free) and take pony rides ($3) outside.

Yoder's Amish Home FARM
(☏330-893-2541; www.yodersamishhome.com; 6050 Rte 515, Walnut Creek; tours adult/child $12/8; ⊙10am-5pm Mon-Sat mid-Apr–late Oct; 🖲) Peek into a local home and one-room schoolhouse, and take a buggy ride through a field at this Amish farm that's open to visitors.

🛏 Sleeping & Eating

Hotel Millersburg HISTORIC HOTEL $$
(☏330-674-1457; www.hotelmillersburg.com; 35 W Jackson St, Millersburg; r $79-149; ❄🐾) Built in 1847 as a stagecoach inn, the property still provides lodging in its 26 casual rooms, which sit above a modern dining room and tavern (one of the few places you can get a beer in Amish Country).

Guggisberg Swiss Inn HOTEL $$
(☏330-893-3600; www.guggisbergswissinn.com; 5025 Rte 557, Charm; r incl breakfast $110-160; ❄🐾) The 24 tidy, bright and compact rooms have quilts and light-wood furnishings. A cheesemaking facility and horseback riding stable are on the grounds, too.

Boyd & Wurthmann Restaurant AMERICAN $
(☏330-893-3287; www.boydandwurthmann.com; Main St, Berlin; mains $6-11; ⊙5:30am-8pm Mon-Sat) Hubcap-sized pancakes, 23 pie flavors, fat sandwiches and Amish specialties such as country-fried steak draw locals and tourists alike. Cash only.

ⓘ Information

Holmes County Chamber of Commerce (www.visitamishcountry.com)

Columbus

Ohio's capital city is like the blind date your mom arranges – average looking, restrained personality, but solid and affable. Better yet, she's easy on the wallet, an influence from Ohio State University's 55,000 students (the university is the nation's second largest). A substantial gay population has taken up residence in Columbus in recent years.

⊙ Sights & Activities

German Village NEIGHBORHOOD
(www.germanvillage.com) The remarkably large, all-brick German Village, a half-mile south of downtown, is a restored 19th-century neighborhood with beer halls, cobbled streets, arts-filled parks and Italianate and Queen Anne architecture.

Short North NEIGHBORHOOD
(www.shortnorth.org) Just north of downtown, the browseworthy Short North is a redeveloped strip of High St that holds contemporary art galleries, restaurants and jazz bars.

Wexner Center for the Arts ARTS CENTER
(☏614-292-3535; www.wexarts.org; cnr 15th & N High Sts; admission $8; ⊙11am-6pm Tue & Wed, 11am-8pm Thu & Fri, noon-7pm Sat, noon-4pm Sun) The campus arts center offers cutting-edge art exhibits, films and performances.

Columbus Food Tours GUIDED TOUR
(www.columbusfoodadventures.com; tours $40-80) Foodie guides lead tours by neighborhood or theme (ie taco trucks, desserts, coffee), some by foot and others by van.

🛏 Sleeping & Eating

German Village and the Short North provide fertile grazing and guzzling grounds. The **Arena District** (www.arenadistrict.com) bursts with midrange chains and brewpubs. Around the university and along N High St from 15th Ave onward, you'll find everything from Mexican to Ethiopian to sushi.

Marriott Residence Inn
HOTEL **$$**

(📞 614-222-2610; www.marriott.com; 36 E Gay St; r incl breakfast $129-199; P ❄ @ ➅) A great location downtown, close to everything. All rooms are suites with a full kitchen. The cute breakfast buffet is served in the old bank vault each morning. Wi-fi is free; parking is $20.

Short North B&B
B&B **$$**

(📞 614-299-5050; www.columbus-bed-breakfast. com; 50 E Lincoln St; r incl breakfast $129-149; P ❄ ➅) The seven well-maintained rooms are steps away from the eponymous neighborhood's scene.

North Market
MARKET **$**

(www.northmarket.com; 59 Spruce St; ⊙ 9am-5pm Mon, 9am-7pm Tue-Fri, 8am-5pm Sat, noon-5pm Sun) Local farmers' produce and prepared foods; renowned ice cream by Jeni.

Schmidt's
GERMAN **$$**

(📞 614-444-6808; www.schmidthaus.com; 240 E Kossuth St; mains $8-15; ⊙ 11am-9pm Sun & Mon, to 10pm Tue-Thu, to 11pm Fri & Sat) In German Village, shovel in Old Country staples like sausage and schnitzel, but save room for the whopping half-pound cream puffs. Oompah bands play Wednesday to Saturday.

Skillet
AMERICAN **$$**

(📞 614-443-2266; www.skilletruf.com; 410 E Whittier St; mains $12-16; ⊙ 11am-2:30pm & 5:30-9pm Wed-Fri, 8am-2pm Sat & Sun) 🍴 A teeny restaurant in German Village serving rustic, locally sourced fare.

☆ Entertainment

Spectator sports rule the city.

Ohio Stadium
FOOTBALL

(📞 800-462-8257; www.ohiostatebuckeyes.com; 411 Woody Hayes Dr) The Ohio State Buckeyes pack a rabid crowd into legendary, horseshoe-shaped Ohio Stadium for their games, held on Saturdays in the fall. Expect 102,000 extra partiers in town.

Nationwide Arena
HOCKEY

(📞 614-246-2000; www.bluejackets.com; 200 W Nationwide Blvd) The pro Columbus Blue Jackets slap the puck at downtown's big arena.

Crew Stadium
SOCCER

(📞 614-447-2739; www.thecrew.com) The popular Columbus Crew pro soccer team kicks north off I-71 and 17th Ave, from March to October.

🛈 Information

Alive (www.columbusalive.com) Free weekly entertainment newspaper.

Columbus Convention & Visitors Bureau (📞 866-397-2657; www.experiencecolumbus. com)

Columbus Dispatch (www.dispatch.com) The daily newspaper.

Outlook (www.outlookmedia.com) Monthly gay and lesbian publication.

🛈 Getting There & Away

The **Port Columbus Airport** (CMH; www.flycolumbus.com) is 10 miles east of town. A cab to downtown costs about $25.

Greyhound (📞 614-221-4642; www.greyhound.com; 111 E Town St) buses run at least six times daily to Cincinnati (two hours) and Cleveland (2½ hours). Often cheaper, **Megabus** (www. megabus.com/us) runs a couple times daily to Cincinnati and Chicago. Check the website for locations.

Athens & Southeastern Ohio

Ohio's southeastern corner cradles most of its forested areas, as well as the rolling foothills of the Appalachian Mountains and scattered farms.

Around Lancaster, southeast of Columbus, the hills lead gently into **Hocking County**, a region of streams and waterfalls, sandstone cliffs and cavelike formations. It's splendid to explore in any season, with miles of trails for hiking and rivers for canoeing, as well as abundant campgrounds and cabins at **Hocking Hills State Park** (📞 740-385-6165; www.hockinghills.com; 20160 Hwy 664; campsites/cottages from $24/130). **Old Man's Cave** is a scenic winner for hiking. **Hocking Valley Canoe Livery** (📞 740-385-8685; www.hockinghillscanoeing.com; 31251 Chieftain Dr; 2hr tours $44; ⊙ Apr-Oct) lets you paddle by moonlight and tiki torch from nearby Logan. **Earth-Water-Rock: Outdoor Adventures** (📞 740-664-5220; www.ewroutdoors. com; half-day tour $85-110) provides thrills with guided rock climbing and rappelling trips; beginners are welcome.

Athens (www.athensohio.com) makes a lovely base for seeing the region. Situated where US 50 crosses US 33, it's set among wooded hills and built around the Ohio University campus (which comprises half the town). Student cafes and pubs line Court St,

Athens' main road. The **Village Bakery & Cafe** (www.dellazona.com; 268 E State St; mains $4-8; ⊙7:30am-8pm Tue-Sat, 9am-2pm Sun) uses organic veggies, grass-fed meat and farmstead cheeses in its pizzas, soups and sandwiches.

The area south of Columbus was a center for the fascinating ancient Hopewell people, who left behind huge geometric earthworks and burial mounds from around 200 BC to AD 600. For a fine introduction visit the **Hopewell Culture National Historical Park** (📋740-774-1126; www.nps.gov/hocu; Hwy 104 north of I-35; ⊙8:30am-6pm Jun-Aug, to 5pm Sep-May) FREE, 3 miles north of Chillicothe. Stop in the visitor center, and then wander about the variously shaped ceremonial mounds spread over 13-acre **Mound City**, a mysterious town of the dead. **Serpent Mound** (📋937-587-2796; www.ohiohistory.org; 3850 Hwy 73; per vehicle $7; ⊙10:30am-4pm Mon-Fri, from 9:30am Sat & Sun, reduced hours in winter), southwest of Chillicothe and 4 miles northwest of Locust Grove, is perhaps the most captivating site of all. The giant uncoiling snake stretches over a quarter of a mile and is the largest effigy mound in the USA.

Dayton & Yellow Springs

Dayton has the aviation sights, but little Yellow Springs (18 miles northeast on US 68) has much more to offer in terms of accommodations and places to eat.

⊙ Sights & Activities

National Museum of the US Air Force   MUSEUM
(📋937-255-3286; www.nationalmuseum.af.mil; 1100 Spaatz St, Dayton; ⊙9am-5pm) FREE Located at the Wright-Patterson Air Force Base, 6 miles northeast of Dayton, the huuuuge museum has everything from a Wright Brothers 1909 Flyer to a Sopwith Camel (WWI biplane) and the 'Little Boy' atomic bomb dropped on Hiroshima. The hangars hold miles of planes, rockets and aviation machines. Download the audio tour from the website before arriving. Plan on three or more hours here.

Wright Cycle Company   HISTORIC SITE
(📋937-225-7705; www.nps.gov/daav; 16 S Williams St, Dayton; ⊙8:30am-5pm) FREE Browse exhibits in the original building where Wilbur and Orville developed bikes and aviation ideas.

Huffman Prairie Flying Field   HISTORIC SITE
(Gate 16A off Rte 444, Dayton; ⊙8am-6pm Thu-Tue) FREE This peaceful patch of grass looks much as it did in 1904 when the Wright Brothers tested aircraft here. A one-mile walking trail loops around, marked with history-explaining placards. It's a 15-minute drive from the Air Force museum.

Carillon Historical Park   HISTORIC SITE
(📋937-293-2841; www.daytonhistory.org; 1000 Carillon Blvd, Dayton; adult/child $8/5; ⊙9:30am-5pm Mon-Sat, from noon Sun) The many heritage attractions include the 1905 Wright Flyer III biplane and a replica of the Wright workshop.

🛏 Sleeping & Eating

The following are located in artsy, beatnik Yellow Springs.

Morgan House   B&B $$
(📋937-767-1761; www.arthurmorganhouse.com; 120 W Limestone St, Yellow Springs; r incl breakfast $105-125; ❀🏠) The six comfy rooms have super-soft linens and private baths. Breakfasts are organic. It's walkable to the main business district.

★ Young's Jersey Dairy   AMERICAN $$
(📋937-325-0629; www.youngsdairy.com; 6880 Springfield-Xenia Rd, Yellow Springs; 🏠) Young's is a working dairy farm with two restaurants: the **Golden Jersey Inn** (mains $9-15; ⊙11am-8pm Mon-Thu, 11am-9pm Fri, 8am-9pm Sat, 8am-8pm Sun), serving dishes like buttermilk chicken; and the **Dairy Store** (sandwiches $3.50-6.50; ⊙7am-11pm Sun-Thu, to midnight Fri & Sat), serving sandwiches, dreamy ice cream and Ohio's best milkshakes. There's also minigolf, batting cages, cheesemaking tours and opportunities to watch the cows get milked.

Winds Cafe   AMERICAN $$$
(📋937-767-1144; www.windscafe.com; 215 Xenia Ave, Yellow Springs; mains $18-25; ⊙11:30am-2pm & 5-10pm Tue-Sat, 10am-3pm Sun) A hippie co-op 30-plus years ago, the Winds has grown up to become a sophisticated foodie favorite plating seasonal dishes like fig-sauced asparagus crepes and rhubarb halibut.

Cincinnati

Cincinnati splashes up the Ohio River's banks. Its prettiness surprises, as do its neon troves, its twisting streets to hilltop Mt Adams, and the locals' unashamed ardor for a five-way. Amid all that action, don't forget to catch a baseball game, stroll the riverfront and visit the dummy museum.

◎ Sights & Activities

Many attractions are closed on Monday.

◎ Downtown

National Underground Railroad Freedom Center   MUSEUM
(☑ 513-333-7500; www.freedomcenter.org; 50 E Freedom Way; adult/child $12/8; ☺ 11am-5pm Tue-Sun) Cincinnati was a prominent stop on the Underground Railroad and a center for abolitionist activities led by residents such as Harriet Beecher Stowe. The Freedom Center tells their stories. Exhibits show how slaves escaped to the north, and the ways in which slavery still exists today. Download the free iPhone app for extra insight while touring.

Findlay Market   MARKET
(www.findlaymarket.org; 1801 Race St; ☺ 9am-6pm Tue-Fri, 8am-6pm Sat, 10am-4pm Sun) Indoor-outdoor Findlay Market greens the somewhat blighted area at downtown's northern edge. It's a good stop for fresh produce, meats, cheeses and baked goods. The Belgian waffle guy will wow your taste buds.

Rosenthal Center for Contemporary Arts   MUSEUM
(☑ 513-721-0390; www.contemporaryartscenter.org; 44 E 6th St; adult/child $7.50/5.50, Mon evening free; ☺ 10am-9pm Mon, 10am-6pm Wed-Fri, 11am-6pm Sat & Sun) This center displays modern art in an avant-garde building designed by Iraqi architect Zaha Hadid. The structure and its artworks are a pretty big deal for traditionalist Cincy.

Fountain Square   PLAZA
(www.myfountainsquare.com; cnr 5th & Vine Sts; ☎) Fountain Sq is the city's centerpiece, a public space with a seasonal ice rink, free wi-fi, concerts (7pm Tuesday to Saturday in summer), a Reds ticket kiosk and the fancy old 'Spirit of the Waters' fountain.

Roebling Suspension Bridge   BRIDGE
(www.roeblingbridge.org) The elegant 1876 spanner was a forerunner of John Roebling's famous Brooklyn Bridge in New York. It's cool to walk across while passing cars make it 'sing' around you. It links to Covington, Kentucky.

Purple People Bridge   BRIDGE
(www.purplepeoplebridge.com) This pedestrian-only bridge provides a unique crossing from Sawyer Point (a nifty park dotted by whimsical monuments and flying pigs) to Newport, Kentucky.

◎ Covington & Newport

Covington and Newport, Kentucky, are sort of suburbs of Cincinnati, just over the river from downtown. Newport is to the east and known for its massive **Newport on the Levee** (www.newportonthelevee.com) restaurant and shopping complex. Covington lies to the west and its **MainStrasse** (www.mainstrasse.org) quarter is filled with funky restaurants and bars in the neighborhood's 19th-century brick row houses. Antebellum mansions fringe Riverside Dr, and old paddle-wheel boats tie up along the water's edge.

Newport Aquarium   AQUARIUM
(☑ 859-491-3467; www.newportaquarium.com; 1 Aquarium Way; adult/child $23/15; ☺ 9am-7pm Jun-Aug, 10am-6pm Sep-May; ♿) Meet parading penguins, Sweet Pea the shark ray and lots of other razor-toothed fish at Newport's large, well-regarded facility.

OFF THE BEATEN TRACK

VENT HAVEN VENTRILOQUIST MUSEUM

Jeepers creepers! When you first glimpse the roomful of goggle-eyed wooden heads staring mutely into space, try not to run screaming for the door. (If you've seen the film *Magic*, you know what dummies are capable of.) Local William Shakespeare Berger started the **Vent Haven Museum** (☑ 859-341-0461; www.venthavenmuseum.com; 33 W Maple Ave; admission $5; ☺ by appointment May-Sep) after amassing a collection of some 700 dolls. Today Jacko the red-fezzed monkey, turtleneck-clad Woody DeForest and the rest of the crew sit silently throughout three buildings.

Lest you think this form of entertainment is history, stop by in July, when the annual conVENTion takes place and 400 ventriloquists arrive with their talkative wooden pals. The museum is located in Fort Mitchell, Kentucky, about 4 miles southwest of Covington off I-71/75.

Mt Adams

It might be a bit of a stretch to compare Mt Adams, immediately east of downtown, to Paris' Montmartre, but this hilly 19th-century enclave of narrow, twisting streets, Victorian town houses, galleries, bars and restaurants is certainly a pleasurable surprise. Most visitors ascend for a quick look around and a drink.

To get here, follow 7th St east of downtown to Gilbert Ave, bear northwest to Elsinore Ave, and head up the hill to reach the lakes, paths and cultural offerings in Eden Park. The yard at nearby **Immacula Church** (30 Guido St) is worth a stop for its killer views over the city.

Cincinnati Art Museum   MUSEUM
(✍ 513-721-2787; www.cincinnatiartmuseum.org; 953 Eden Park Dr; ⊙11am-5pm Tue-Sun) FREE
The collection spans 6000 years, with an emphasis on ancient Middle Eastern art and European old masters, plus a wing devoted to local works. Parking costs $4.

Krohn Conservatory   GARDENS
(✍ 513-421-4086; www.cincinnatiparks.com/krohn; 1501 Eden Park Dr; adult/child $3/2; ⊙10am-5pm Tue-Sun) The greenhouse sprouts a rainforest, desert flora and glorious seasonal flower shows. Special exhibits cost extra.

West End

Cincinnati Museum Center   MUSEUM
(✍ 513-287-7000; www.cincymuseum.org; 1301 Western Ave; adult/child $12.50/8.50; ⊙10am-5pm Mon-Sat, 11am-6pm Sun; 🚼) Two miles northwest of downtown, this museum complex occupies the 1933 Union Terminal, an art-deco jewel still used by Amtrak. The interior has fantastic murals made of Rookwood tiles. The **Museum of Natural History & Science** is mostly geared to kids, but it does have a limestone cave with real bats inside. A history museum, children's museum and Omnimax theater round out the offerings; the admission fee provides entry to all. Parking costs $6.

American Sign Museum   MUSEUM
(✍ 513-541-6366; www.signmuseum.org; 1330 Monmouth Ave; adult/child $15/10; ⊙10am-4pm Wed-Sat, from noon Sun) This museum stocks an awesome cache of flashing, lightbulb-studded beacons in an old parachute factory. You'll burn your retinas staring at vintage neon drive-in signs, hulking genies and the

Frisch's Big Boy, among other nostalgic novelties. Guides lead tours at 11am and 2pm that also visit the on-site neon-sign-making shop. It's located in the Camp Washington neighborhood (near Northside); take exit 3 off I-75.

Tours

American Legacy Tours   WALKING TOUR
(www.americanlegacytours.com; 1218 Vine St; 90min tours $20; ⊙Fri-Sun) Offers a variety of historical jaunts. The best is the Queen City Underground Tour that submerges into old lagering cellars deep beneath the Over-the-Rhine district.

Festivals & Events

Bunbury Music Festival   MUSIC
(www.bunburyfestival.com; ⊙mid-Jul) Big-name indie bands rock the riverfront for three days; a day pass costs $55.

Oktoberfest   FOOD
(www.oktoberfestzinzinnati.com; ⊙mid-Sep) German beer, brats and mania.

Sleeping

Hotel tax is cheaper on the Kentucky side at 11.3%, versus the 17% charged in Cincinnati. Tax is not included in the following prices.

Several midrange chain options line up on the Kentucky riverfront. You'll save money (less tax, free parking), but be prepared either to walk a few miles or take a short bus ride to reach downtown Cincy.

The **Greater Cincinnati B&B Network** (www.cincinnatibb.com) has links to Kentucky-side properties.

Holiday Inn Express   HOTEL $$
(✍ 859-957-2320; www.hiexpress.com; 109 Landmark Dr; r incl breakfast $125-180; P ❄ @ 🛜 ♨) A good pick among the riverfront chains; located about three-quarters of a mile east of Newport on the Levee.

Hotel 21c   HOTEL $$$
(✍ 513-578-6600; www.21cmuseumhotels.com/cincinnati; 609 Walnut St; r $189-299; P ❄ @ 🛜) The second outpost of Louisville's popular art hotel opened in 2013, next door to the Center for Contemporary Arts. The mod rooms have accoutrements such as a Nespresso machine, free wi-fi, plush bedding and, of course, original art. The lobby is a public gallery, so feel free to ogle the trippy videos and nude sculptures. The on-site restaurant and rooftop bar draw crowds. Parking costs $28.

Residence Inn Cincinnati Downtown
HOTEL $$$

(☎513-651-1234; www.marriott.com; 506 E 4th St; r incl breakfast $199-299; P☀@☎) All of the glistening rooms are suites with full kitchens. Parking costs $22.

✗ Eating

Vine St west of 12th St (in the Over-the-Rhine area) holds several hip new eateries. Restaurants also concentrate along the riverfront and in the Northside neighborhood (north of the intersection of I-74 and I-75, 5 miles north of downtown).

★ Tucker's
DINER $

(1637 Vine St; mains $4-9; ⏱9am-3pm Tue-Sat, 10am-2pm Sun; ✐) Located in a tough neighborhood a few blocks from Findlay Market, Tucker's has been feeding locals – black, white, foodies, penniless – since 1946. It's an archetypal diner, serving shrimp and grits, biscuits and gravy, and other hulking breakfast dishes, along with wildly inventive vegetarian fare (like beet sliders) using ingredients sourced from the market.

Son Joe Tucker cooks; Ma Tucker, age 90-plus, still peels the veggies. Try the goetta (pronounced *get-uh*), an herb-spiced, pork-and-oats breakfast sausage that's found only in Cincinnati.

Graeter's Ice Cream
ICE CREAM $

(www.graeters.com; 511 Walnut St; scoops $2.50-5; ⏱6:30am-9pm Mon-Fri, 7am-9pm Sat, 11am-7pm Sun) A local delicacy, with scoop shops around the city. The flavors that mix in the gargantuan, chunky chocolate chips top the list.

Terry's Turf Club
BURGERS $$

(☎513-533-4222; 4618 Eastern Ave; mains $10-15; ⏱11am-11pm Wed & Thu, to midnight Fri & Sat, to 9pm Sun) This 15-table beer-and-burger joint glows inside and out with owner Terry Carter's neon stash. A giant, waving Aunt Jemima beckons you in, where so many fluorescent beer and doughnut signs shine that no other interior lighting is needed. Terry grills a mean burgundy-mushroom-sauced burger to munch on while admiring the finery (the rosemary garlic and red curry ginger versions rock, too). Located 7 miles east of downtown via Columbia Pkwy.

Honey
AMERICAN $$

(☎513-541-4300; www.honeynorthside.com; 4034 Hamilton Ave; mains $15-23; ⏱5-9pm Tue-Thu, 5-10pm Fri & Sat, 11am-2pm Sun; ✐) Seasonal

CHILI FIVE-WAY

Don't worry – you can keep your clothes on for this experience, though you may want to loosen your belt. A 'five-way' in Cincinnati has to do with chili, which is a local specialty. It comprises meat sauce (spiced with chocolate and cinnamon) ladled over spaghetti and beans, then garnished with cheese and onions. Although you can get it three-way (minus onions and beans) or four-way (minus onions *or* beans), you should go the whole way – after all, life's an adventure. **Skyline Chili** (www.skylinechili.com; 643 Vine St; items $3.50-7.50; ⏱10:30am-8pm Mon-Fri, 11am-4pm Sat) has a cultlike following devoted to its version. There are outlets throughout town; this one is downtown near Fountain Sq.

comfort food – maybe Creole meatloaf or sweet pea ravioli – fills the plates on Honey's low-lit, sturdy wood tables. Brunch is a fan favorite, offering a special gift to herbivores: vegan goetta.

♟ Drinking

Mt Adams and Northside are busy nightspots. The Banks, the riverfront area between the baseball and football stadiums, has several new hot spots.

Moerlein Lager House
BREWERY

(www.moerleinlagerhouse.com; 115 Joe Nuxall Way; ⏱from 11am) Copper kettles cook up the house beers (Moerlein is an age-old Cincy brand that was defunct until the new brewhouse revitalized it). The patio unfurls awesome views of the riverfront and Roebling bridge. It's a busy spot pre or post a Reds game, as it sits across the street from the stadium.

Blind Lemon
BAR

(www.theblindlemon.com; 936 Hatch St; ⏱from 5:30pm Mon-Fri, from 3pm Sat & Sun) Head down the passageway to enter this atmospheric old speakeasy in Mt Adams. It has an outdoor courtyard in summer, with a fire pit added in winter, and there's live music nightly.

Motr Pub
BAR

(www.motrpub.com; 1345 Main St; ⏱from 5pm Mon-Fri, from 2pm Sat, from 10am Sun) Located in the on-again, off-again – currently on-again –

gritty Over-the-Rhine neighborhood on downtown's northern edge, Motr lets arty types congregate around Hudepohls (local beer) and live rock bands.

☆ Entertainment

Scope for free publications like *CityBeat* for current listings.

Sports

Great American Ballpark　　　BASEBALL
(☑ 513-765-7000; www.cincinnatireds.com; 100 Main St) Home to the Reds – pro baseball's first team – Cincy is a great place to catch a game thanks to its bells-and-whistles riverside ballpark.

Paul Brown Stadium　　　FOOTBALL
(☑ 513-621-3550; www.bengals.com; 1 Paul Brown Stadium) The Bengals pro football team scrimmages a few blocks west of the ballpark.

Performing Arts

Music Hall　　　CLASSICAL MUSIC
(☑ 513-721-8222; www.cincinnatiarts.org; 1241 Elm St) The acoustically pristine Music Hall is where the symphony orchestra, pops orchestra, opera and ballet hold their seasons. This is not the best neighborhood, so be cautious and park nearby.

Aronoff Center　　　THEATER
(☑ 513-621-2787; www.cincinnatiarts.org; 650 Walnut St) The mod Aronoff hosts touring shows.

ℹ Information

Cincinnati Enquirer (www.cincinnati.com) Daily newspaper.

Cincinnati USA Regional Tourism Network (☑ 800-344-3445; www.cincinnatiusa.com) There's a visitor center on Fountain Sq.

CityBeat (www.citybeat.com) Free alternative weekly paper with good entertainment listings.

Rainbow Cincinnati (www.gaycincinnati.com) GLBT news and business listings.

ℹ Getting There & Around

The **Cincinnati/Northern Kentucky International Airport** (CVG; www.cvgairport.com) is actually in Kentucky, 13 miles south. To get downtown, take the TANK bus ($2) from near Terminal 3; a cab costs about $30.

Greyhound (☑ 513-352-6012; www.greyhound.com; 1005 Gilbert Ave) buses travel daily to Indianapolis (2½ hours) and Columbus (two hours). Often cheaper and quicker, **Megabus** (www.megabus.com/us) travels the same routes, and goes to Chicago (six hours). It departs from downtown Cincy at 4th and Race Sts.

Amtrak (☑ 513-651-3337; www.amtrak.com) choo-choos into **Union Terminal** (1301 Western Ave) thrice weekly en route to Chicago (9½ hours) and Washington, DC (14½ hours), departing in the middle of the night.

Metro (www.go-metro.com; fare $1.75) runs the local buses and links with the **Transit Authority of Northern Kentucky** (TANK; www.tankbus.org; fare $1-2).

MICHIGAN

More, more, more – Michigan is the Midwest state that cranks it up. It sports more beaches than the Atlantic seaboard. More than half the state is covered by forests. And more cherries and berries get shoveled into pies here than anywhere else in the USA. Plus its gritty city Detroit is the Midwest's rawest of all – and we mean that in a good way.

Michigan occupies prime real estate, surrounded by four of the five Great Lakes (Superior, Michigan, Huron and Erie). Islands (Mackinac, Beaver and Isle Royale) freckle its coast and make top touring destinations. Surfing beaches, colored sandstone cliffs and trekkable sand dunes also woo visitors.

The state consists of two parts split by water: the larger Lower Peninsula, shaped like a mitten; and the smaller, lightly populated Upper Peninsula, shaped like a slipper. They are linked by the gasp-worthy Mackinac Bridge, which spans the Straits of Mackinac (pronounced *mac*-in-aw).

ℹ Information

Michigan Highway Conditions (☑ 800-381-8477; www.michigan.gov/mdot)

Michigan State Park Information (☑ 800-447-2757; www.michigan.gov/stateparks) Park entry requires a vehicle permit (per day/year $9/31). Campsites cost $16 to $33; reservations accepted (www.midnrreservations.com; fee $8). Some parks have wi-fi.

Travel Michigan (☑ 800-644-2489; www.michigan.org)

Detroit

Tell any American that you're planning to visit Detroit, and then watch their eyebrows shoot up quizzically. They'll ask 'Why?' and warn you that the city is bankrupt, and has off-the-chart homicide rates, nearly 80,000 abandoned buildings and whoppingly high foreclosure rates, a place where homes sell for $1. 'Detroit's a crap-hole. You'll get killed there.'

While the city does have a bombed-out, apocalyptic vibe, these same qualities fuel a raw urban energy you won't find anywhere else. Artists, entrepreneurs and young people are moving in, and a DIY spirit pervades. They're converting vacant lots into urban farms and abandoned buildings into hostels and museums. Plus, they shred a mean guitar in 'the D.' Very mean.

History

French explorer Antoine de La Mothe Cadillac founded Detroit in 1701. Sweet fortune arrived in the 1920s, when Henry Ford began churning out cars. He didn't invent the automobile, as so many mistakenly believe, but he did perfect assembly-line manufacturing and mass-production techniques. The result was the Model T, the first car the USA's middle class could afford to own.

Detroit quickly became the motor capital of the world. General Motors (GM), Chrysler and Ford were all headquartered in or near Detroit (and still are). The 1950s were the city's heyday, when the population exceeded two million and Motown music hit the airwaves. But racial tensions in 1967 and Japanese car competitors in the 1970s shook the city and its industry. Detroit entered an era of deep decline, losing about two-thirds of its population.

In July 2013 Detroit filed the largest municipal bankruptcy claim in US history: $18 billion. Stay tuned to see how it plays out.

⊙ Sights & Activities

Sights are commonly closed on Monday and Tuesday. And that's Canada across the Detroit River (Windsor, Canada, to be exact).

⊙ Midtown & Cultural Center

★ **Detroit Institute of Arts**　　MUSEUM
(☑ 313-833-7900; www.dia.org; 5200 Woodward Ave; adult/child $8/4; ⊙ 9am-4pm Tue-Thu, 9am-10pm Fri, 10am-5pm Sat & Sun) The cream of the museum crop. The centerpiece is Diego Rivera's mural *Detroit Industry,* which fills an entire room and reflects the city's blue-collar labor history. Beyond it are Picassos, suits of armor, mod African American paintings, puppets and troves more.

★ **Museum of Contemporary Art Detroit**　　MUSEUM
(MOCAD; ☑ 313-832-6622; www.mocadetroit. org; 4454 Woodward Ave; suggested donation $5; ⊙ 11am-5pm Wed-Sun, to 8pm Thu & Fri) MOCAD is set in an abandoned, graffiti-slathered auto dealership. Heat lamps hang from the ceiling over peculiar exhibits that change every few months. Music and literary events take place regularly. The cafe hosts pop-up restaurants for Wednesday lunch and Sunday brunch.

⊙ New Center

Motown Historical Museum　　MUSEUM
(☑ 313-875-2264; www.motownmuseum.org; 2648 W Grand Blvd; adult/child $10/8; ⊙ 10am-6pm Mon-Fri & 10am-8pm Sat Jul & Aug, 10am-6pm Tue-Sat Sep-Jun) In this row of modest houses Berry Gordy launched Motown Records – and the careers of Stevie Wonder, Diana Ross, Marvin Gaye and Michael Jackson – with an $800 loan in 1959. Gordy and Motown split for Los Angeles in 1972, but you can still step into humble Studio A and see where the famed names recorded their first hits.

MICHIGAN FACTS

Nicknames Great Lakes State, Wolverine State

Population 9.9 million

Area 96,720 sq miles

Capital city Lansing (population 114,000)

Other cities Detroit (population 701,000)

Sales tax 6%

Birthplace of Industrialist Henry Ford (1863–1947), filmmaker Francis Ford Coppola (b 1939), musician Stevie Wonder (b 1950), singer Madonna (b 1958), Google co-founder Larry Page (b 1973)

Home of Auto assembly plants, freshwater beaches

Politics Leans Democratic

Famous for Cars, cornflakes, tart cherries, Motown music

State reptile Painted turtle

Driving distances Detroit to Traverse City 255 miles, Detroit to Cleveland 168 miles

Detroit

0 — 500 m
0 — 0.25 miles

Merrick Ave

Wayne State University

Trumbull Ave

Ferry St

Kirby St

Frederick
Douglass Ave

Detroit Institute of Arts

Farnsworth St

Megabus

Warren Ave

Warren Ave

Hancock Ave

Hancock Ave

Forest Ave

Forest Ave

Prentis Ave

Carfield Ave

Canfield St

Museum of Contemporary Art Detroit

Canfield Ave

Willis St

Selden St

MIDTOWN & CULTURAL CENTER

Selden St

Selden St

Tolan Park

Brainard St

Parsens St

Martin Luther King Jr Blvd

Mack Ave

Rivard St

Ash St

Peterboro St

Erskine St

Elm St

Charlotte Ave

Watson St

Wilkins St

Wilkins St

Temple St

Temple Ave

Edmund Pl

Perry St

Cass Park

Alfred St

Alfred St

Spruce St

Ledyard St

Adelaide St

Eastern Market

Detroit Hostel (0.3mi)

Henry St

Winder St

Winder St

Fisher Fwy

Slows Bar BQ (0.5mi)

Montcalm St

Michigan Central (0.7mi)

Plum St

Gratiot Ave

Elizabeth St

Adams Ave

Beacon St

Beech St

Madison St

Bagley St

Plaza Dr

Broadway

Lafayette Plaisance

Labrosse St

Park Pl

Clinton St

Porter St

State St

Macomb St

Abbott St

Abbott St

Monroe St

GREEKTOWN

Howard St

Greyhound Bus Station

Lafayette Blvd

Lafayette Blvd

Green Dot Stables (0.5mi)

Fort St

Fort St

Congress St

Navarre Ple

Larned St

Jefferson Ave

Woodbridge St

Jefferson Ave

Franklin St

Cobo Center

Hart Plaza

Transit Windsor

Riverwalk

Detroit River

MICHIGAN (USA)

ONTARIO (CANADA)

Detroit Windsor Tunnel (toll)

Detroit

◎ Top Sights
1 Detroit Institute of Arts C1
2 Eastern Market D4
3 Museum of Contemporary Art
   Detroit C2

◎ Sights
4 Hart Plaza C6
5 People Mover B6
6 Renaissance Center C7

◎ Activities, Courses & Tours
7 Wheelhouse Bikes D7

◎ Sleeping
8 Ft Shelby Doubletree Hotel B6
9 Inn on Ferry Street................................... C1

◎ Eating
10 Cass Cafe.. B2
11 Foran's Grand Trunk Pub C6

A tour takes about 1½ hours, and consists mostly of looking at old photos and listening to guides' stories. The museum is 2 miles northwest of Midtown.

Model T Automotive Heritage
Complex   MUSEUM
(☑ 313-872-8759; www.tplex.org; 461 Piquette Ave; admission $10; ☺ 10am-4pm Wed-Fri, from 9am Sat, from noon Sun Apr-Oct) Henry Ford cranked out the first Model T in this landmark factory. Admission includes a detailed tour by enthusiastic docents, plus loads of shiny vehicles from 1904 onward. It's about 1 mile northeast of the Detroit Institute of Arts.

◎ Downtown & Around

Busy Greektown (centred on Monroe St) has restaurants, bakeries and a casino.

★ Eastern Market   MARKET
(www.detroiteasternmarket.com; Adelaide & Russell Sts) Produce, cheese, spice and flower vendors fill the large halls on Saturday, but you also can turn up Monday through Friday to browse the specialty shops (props to the peanut roaster), cafes, ethnic eats and occasional food trucks that flank the market on Russell and Market Sts.

Renaissance Center   BUILDING
(RenCen; www.gmrencen.com; 330 E Jefferson Ave) GM's glossy, cloud-poking headquarters is a fine place to mooch off the free wi-fi, take a free hour-long tour (Monday

through Friday at noon and 2pm) or embark on the riverfront walkway.

Hart Plaza   PLAZA
(cnr Jefferson & Woodward Aves) This is the site of many free summer weekend festivals and concerts. While there, check out the sculpture of Joe Louis' mighty fist.

People Mover   MONORAIL
(www.thepeoplemover.com; fare $0.75) As mass transit, the monorail's 3-mile loop on elevated tracks around downtown won't get you very far. As a tourist attraction, it's a sweet ride providing great views of the city and riverfront.

Heidelberg Project   ART INSTALLATION
(www.heidelberg.org; 3600 Heidelberg St; ☺ sunrise-sunset) FREE Polka-dotted streets, houses covered in Technicolor paint blobs, strange sculptures in yards – this is no acid trip, but rather a block-spanning neighborhood art installation. It's the brainchild of street artist Tyree Guyton, who wanted to beautify his run-down community. A 2013 fire burned much of the project, but Guyton has vowed to keep it open and turn what remains into art once again.

Get here by taking Gratiot Ave northwest to Heidelberg St; the project spans from Ellery to Mt Elliott Sts.

Riverwalk & Dequindre Cut WALKING, CYCLING
(www.detroitriverfront.org) The city's swell riverfront path runs for 3 miles along the churning Detroit River from Hart Plaza east to

DETROIT'S RUINS

More than 78,000 abandoned buildings blight Detroit's landscape. It has become popular among urban explorers to seek out the most spectacular 'ruins.' You can't go inside, obviously, but the exteriors make for striking photographs. Top of the list is **Michigan Central Station** (2405 W Vernor Hwy), the once-grand beaux-arts rail terminal now crumbling into oblivion within eyeshot of Corktown's main drag. The **Packard Auto Plant** (E Grand Blvd at Concord St) is another. Renowned architect Albert Kahn designed the 3.5-million-sq-ft factory, and it was a thing of beauty when it opened in 1903. Now it looks like something from a zombie movie. Stay tuned to see what happens to the structures. The city would like to demolish them, but it doesn't have the money. Detroiturbex (www.detroiturbex.com) provides good historical info on these and other ruins around town.

Mt Elliott St, passing several parks, outdoor theaters, riverboats and fishing spots en route. Eventually it will extend all the way to beachy **Belle Isle** (detour onto Jefferson Ave to get there now). About halfway along the Riverwalk, near Orleans St, the 1.5-mile Dequindre Cut Greenway path juts north, offering a convenient passageway to Eastern Market.

Wheelhouse Bikes   BICYCLE RENTAL
(☎313-656-2453; www.wheelhousedetroit.com; 1340 E Atwater St; per 2hr $15; ⊙10am-8pm Mon-Sat, 11am-5pm Sun Jun-Aug, reduced hours Sep-May) Cycling is a great way to explore the city. Wheelhouse rents sturdy two-wheelers (helmet and lock included) on the Riverwalk at Rivard Plaza. Tours ($35 including bike rental) on weekends roll by various neighborhoods and architectural sites.

☞ Tours

Preservation Detroit   WALKING
(☎313-577-7674; www.preservationdetroit.org; 2½hr tours $10-15; ⊙5:30pm Tue & 10am Sat May-Sep) Offers architectural walking tours through downtown, Midtown and other neighborhoods; departure points vary.

✷✷ Festivals & Events

North American International Auto Show   CARS
(www.naias.com; tickets $13; ⊙mid-Jan) It's autos galore for two weeks at the Cobo Center.

Movement Electronic Music Festival   MUSIC
(www.movement.us; day pass $50; ⊙late May) The world's largest electronic music festival congregates in Hart Plaza over Memorial Day weekend.

🛏 Sleeping

Add 9% to 15% tax (it varies by lodging size and location) to the rates listed here, unless stated otherwise.

Affordable motels abound in Detroit's suburbs. If you're arriving from Metro Airport, follow the signs for Merriman Rd when leaving the airport and take your pick.

Detroit Hostel   HOSTEL $
(☎313-451-0333; www.hosteldetroit.com; 2700 Vermont St; dm $27-30, r $40-60; ♈@☎) Volunteers rehabbed this old building, gathered up recycled materials and donations for the patchwork furnishings, and opened it to the public in 2011. There's a 10-bed dorm, a couple of smaller dorms and a handful of private rooms; everyone shares the four bathrooms and three kitchens. Bookings are taken online only (and must be done at least 24 hours in advance).

Bike rentals costs $10 per day. The hostel is located in Corktown on a desolate street, but near several good bars and restaurants.

★ Inn on Ferry Street   INN $$
(☎313-871-6000; www.innonferrystreet.com; 84 E Ferry St; r incl breakfast from $159; ♈✷@☎) Forty guest rooms fill a row of Victorian mansions right by the art museum. Lower-cost rooms are small but have deliciously soft bedding; the larger rooms feature plenty of antique wood furnishings. The healthy hot breakfast and shuttle to downtown are nice touches.

Ft Shelby Doubletree Hotel   HOTEL $$
(☎800-222-8733, 313-963-5600; http://doubletree1.hilton.com; 525 W Lafayette Blvd; ste $126-189; ♈✷@☎) This newish hotel fills a historic beaux-arts building downtown. All rooms are suites, with both the sitting area and bedroom equipped with HDTV and free wi-fi. Parking costs $23, and there's free shuttle service around downtown.

✗ Eating

Two nearby suburbs also have caches of hip restaurants and bars: walkable, gay-oriented Ferndale at 9 Mile Rd and Woodward Ave, and Royal Oak just north of Ferndale between 12 and 13 Mile Rds.

Midtown & Cultural Center

Good Girls Go to Paris Crepes   CREPERIE $
(📞877-727-4727; www.goodgirlsgotopariscrepes.com; 15 E Kirby St; mains $6-9; ⊙9am-4pm Mon-Wed, to 8pm Thu, to 10pm Fri & Sat, to 5pm Sun) This red-walled, French-style cafe transports diners across the pond via its sweet (Heath Bar and ricotta) and savory (goat's cheese and fig) pancakes.

Cass Cafe   CAFE $$
(📞313-831-1400; www.casscafe.com; 4620 Cass Ave; mains $8-15; ⊙11am-11pm Mon-Thu, 11am-1am Fri & Sat, 5-10pm Sun; 🛜🍴) The Cass is a bohemian art gallery fused with a bar and restaurant that serves soups, sandwiches and veggie beauties, like the lentil-walnut burger. Service can be fickle.

Downtown

Lafayette Coney Island   AMERICAN $
(📞313-964-8198; 118 Lafayette Blvd; items $2.50-4; ⊙8am-4am) The 'coney' – a hot dog smothered with chili and onions – is a Detroit specialty. When the craving strikes (and it will), take care of business at Lafayette. The minimalist menu consists of burgers, fries and beer, in addition to the signature item. Cash only.

Foran's Grand Trunk Pub   PUB $$
(📞313-961-3043; www.grandtrunkpub.com; 612 Woodward Ave; mains $8-13; ⊙11am-midnight) If the high vaulted ceiling and long narrow space make you feel like you're in an old railroad ticket station, that's because you are. The food is pub grub – sandwiches, burgers and shepherd's pie – but made with local ingredients such as Avalon bread and Eastern Market produce. The taps pour 18 Michigan craft brews.

Corktown & Mexicantown

Corktown, a bit west of downtown, shows the city's DIY spirit. Hipster joints slinging burgers, cocktails and artisanal coffee drinks line Michigan Ave. Mexicantown, along Bagley St 3 miles west of downtown, offers several inexpensive Mexican restaurants.

Green Dot Stables   BURGERS $
(www.greendotstables.com; 2200 W Lafayette Blvd; mains $2-3; ⊙11am-midnight Mon-Wed, 11am-1am Thu-Sat, noon-10pm Sun) It's a bit inconveniently located between downtown, Corktown and Mexicantown, but that doesn't deter young urbanites from flocking in to munch on 19 types of gourmet mini-burgers (say, wasabi-mayo tempeh or peanut-butter kimchi) with a side of poutine.

★Slows Bar BQ   BARBECUE $$
(📞313-962-9828; www.slowsbarbq.com; 2138 Michigan Ave; mains $10-19; ⊙11am-10pm Sun & Mon, to 11pm Tue-Thu, to midnight Fri & Sat; 🛜) Mmm, slow-cooked southern-style barbecue in Corktown. Carnivores can carve into the three-meat combo plate (brisket, pulled pork and chicken). Vegetarians have options from okra fritters to a faux-chicken sandwich. The taps yield 55 quality beers.

🍷 Drinking

★Bronx   BAR
(4476 2nd Ave; ⊙from noon; 🛜) There's not much inside Detroit's best boozer besides a pool table, dim lighting and a couple of jukeboxes filled with ballsy rock and soul. But that's the way the hipsters, slackers and rockers (the White Stripes used to hang here) like their dive bars. They're also fond of the beefy burgers served late at night and the cheap beer selection.

Great Lakes Coffee Bar   CAFE
(www.greatlakescoffee.com; 3965 Woodward Ave; ⊙7am-11pm Mon-Thu, 7am-midnight Fri & Sat, 10am-6pm Sun) Roasts its own beans and serves them pour-over style. Locally sourced brewskis, vinos, cheeses and charcuterie are available too. The hep furnishings are made of wood reclaimed from razed houses nearby.

☆ Entertainment

Live Music

Cover charges hover between $5 and $15.

Magic Stick & Majestic Theater   LIVE MUSIC
(www.majesticdetroit.com; 4120-4140 Woodward Ave) The White Stripes and Von Bondies are rockers who've risen from the beer-splattered ranks at the Magic Stick. The Majestic Theater next door hosts larger shows. There's bowling, billiards, a pizza joint and cafe. Something cool rocks here nightly.

FROM MOTOWN TO ROCK CITY

Motown Records and soul music put Detroit on the map in the 1960s, while the thrashing punk rock of the Stooges and MC5 was the 1970s response to that smooth sound. By 1976, Detroit was dubbed 'Rock City' by a Kiss song (though – just Detroit's luck – the tune was eclipsed by its B-side, 'Beth'). In recent years it has been hard-edged rock – aka whiplash rock 'n' roll – that has pushed the city to the music-scene forefront. Homegrown stars include the White Stripes, Von Bondies and Dirtbombs. Rap (thank you, Eminem) and techno are Detroit's other renowned genres. Many music aficionados say the city's blight is what produces such a beautifully angry explosion of sound, and who's to argue? Scope free publications like the *Metro Times* and blogs like Motor City Rocks (www.motorcityrocks.com) for current show and club listings.

PJ's Lager House   LIVE MUSIC
(www.pjslagerhouse.com; 1254 Michigan Ave; ☺ from 11am) Scrappy bands or DJs play most nights at this small Corktown club. By day it serves surprisingly good grub with a New Orleans/vegan twist (like the tempeh po' boy on gluten-free bread).

Cliff Bell's Jazz Club   LIVE MUSIC
(www.cliffbells.com; 2030 Park Ave) With its dark wood, candlelight and art-deco decor, Bell's evokes 1930s elegance. Local jazz bands and poetry readings attract a diverse young audience nightly.

Performing Arts
Puppet ART/Detroit
Puppet Theater   THEATER
(☎ 313-961-7777; www.puppetart.org; 25 E Grand River Ave; adult/child $10/5; ⊛) Soviet-trained puppeteers perform beautiful shows in this 70-person theater; a small museum displays puppets from different cultures. Shows are typically held on Saturday afternoon.

Detroit Opera House   OPERA
(☎ 313-237-7464; www.motopera.com; 1526 Broadway Ave) Gorgeous interior, top-tier company and nurturer of many renowned African American performers.

Sports
Comerica Park   BASEBALL
(www.detroittigers.com; 2100 Woodward Ave; ⊛) The Detroit Tigers play pro baseball at Comerica, one of the league's most decked-out stadiums. The park is particularly kid friendly, with a small Ferris wheel and carousel inside (per ride $2).

Joe Louis Arena   HOCKEY
(www.detroitredwings.com; 600 Civic Center Dr) The much-loved Red Wings play pro ice hockey at this arena where, if you can wrangle tickets, you might witness the strange octopus-throwing custom.

Ford Field   FOOTBALL
(www.detroitlions.com; 2000 Brush St) The Lions toss the pigskin at this indoor stadium next to Comerica Park.

Palace of Auburn Hills   BASKETBALL
(www.nba.com/pistons; 5 Championship Dr) The Palace hosts the Pistons pro basketball team. It's about 30 miles northwest of downtown; take I-75 to exit 81.

🛍 Shopping
Pure Detroit   SOUVENIRS
(www.puredetroit.com; 500 Griswold St; ☺ 10:30am-5:30pm Mon-Sat) Local artists create stylish products for Pure Detroit that celebrate the city's fast-cars-and-rock-music culture. Pick up handbags made from recycled seatbelts, groovy hoodies and local Pewabic pottery. Located in the landmark, mosaic-strewn Guardian Building (worth a peek in its own right).

People's Records   MUSIC
(3161 Woodward Ave; ☺ 10am-6pm Mon-Sat) Calling all crate-diggers: DJ-owned People's Records is your vinyl Valhalla. Used 45s are the specialty, with more than 80,000 jazz, soul and R&B titles filling bins.

ⓘ Information
The area between the sports arenas north to around Willis Rd is pretty deserted and best avoided on foot come nighttime.

EMERGENCY & MEDICAL SERVICES
Detroit Receiving Hospital (☎ 313-745-3000; 4201 St Antoine St)

INTERNET ACCESS
You'll find free wi-fi in many cafes and bars, as well as the Renaissance Center lobby.

MEDIA

Between the Lines (www.pridesource.com) Free weekly gay and lesbian paper.

Detroit Free Press (www.freep.com) Daily.

Detroit News (www.detnews.com) Daily.

Metro Times (www.metrotimes.com) Free alternative weekly that is the best guide to the entertainment scene.

TOURIST INFORMATION

Detroit Convention & Visitors Bureau (☑ 800-338-7648; www.visitdetroit.com)

WEBSITES

DetroitYES (www.detroityes.com) Images organized as 'tours' reveal the city's soul.

Model D (www.modeldmedia.com) Weekly e-zine about local developments and food/entertainment options, broken down by neighborhood.

❶ Getting There & Around

Detroit Metro Airport (DTW; www.metroairport.com), a Delta Airlines hub, is about 20 miles southwest of Detroit. Transport options from the airport to the city are few: you can take a cab for about $45; or there's the 125 SMART bus ($2), but it takes one to 1½ hours to get downtown.

Greyhound (☑ 313-961-8005; 1001 Howard St) runs to various cities in Michigan and beyond. **Megabus** (www.megabus.com/us) runs to/from Chicago (5½ hours) daily; departures are from downtown (corner of Cass and Michigan) and Wayne State University (corner of Cass and Warren Aves).

Amtrak (☑ 313-873-3442; 11 W Baltimore Ave) trains go three times daily to Chicago (5½ hours). You can also head east – to New York (16½ hours) or destinations en route – but you'll first be bused to Toledo.

Transit Windsor (☑ 519-944-4111; www.city-windsor.ca/transitwindsor) operates the Tunnel Bus to Windsor, Canada. It costs $4 (American or Canadian) and departs by Mariner's Church (corner of Randolph St and Jefferson Ave) near the Detroit-Windsor Tunnel entrance, as well as other spots downtown. Bring your passport.

For taxi service, call **Checker Cab** (☑ 313-963-7000).

Around Detroit

Stunning Americana and good eatin' lie just down the road from Detroit.

Dearborn

Dearborn is 10 miles west of downtown Detroit and home to two of the USA's finest museums. The indoor **Henry Ford Museum** (☑ 313-982-6001; www.thehenryford.org; 20900 Oakwood Blvd; adult/child $17/12.50; ⊙9:30am-5pm) contains a fascinating wealth of American culture, such as the chair Lincoln was sitting in when he was assassinated, the presidential limo in which Kennedy was killed, the hot-dog-shaped Oscar Mayer Wienermobile (photo op!) and the bus on which Rosa Parks refused to give up her seat. Don't worry: you'll get your vintage

---

CLASSIC CARS IN MICHIGAN

More than sand dunes, beaches and Mackinac Island fudge, Michigan is synonymous with cars. While the connection hasn't been so positive in recent years, the state commemorates its glory days via several auto museums. The following fleets are within a few hours' drive of the Motor City.

Henry Ford Museum (p576) This Dearborn museum is loaded with vintage cars, including the first one Henry Ford ever built. In adjacent Greenfield Village you can ride in a Model T that rolled off the assembly line in 1923.

Automotive Hall of Fame (☑ 313-240-4000; www.automotivehalloffame.org; 21400 Oakwood Blvd; adult/child $8/4; ⊙9am-5pm Wed-Sun) Next door to the Henry Ford Museum, the interactive Auto Hall focuses on the people behind famed cars, such as Mr Ferdinand Porsche and Mr Soichiro Honda.

Gilmore Car Museum (☑ 269-671-5089; www.gilmorecarmuseum.org; 6865 Hickory Rd; adult/child $12/9; ⊙9am-5pm Mon-Fri, to 6pm Sat & Sun) North of Kalamazoo along Hwy 43, this museum complex offers 22 barns filled with 120 vintage autos, including 15 Rolls Royces dating back to a 1910 Silver Ghost.

RE Olds Transportation Museum (p578) Twenty vintage cars sit in the old Lansing City Bus Garage, including the first Oldsmobile, which was built in 1897.

car fix here, too. Parking is $5. The adjacent outdoor **Greenfield Village** (adult/child $24/17.50; ⊘ 9:30am-5pm daily mid-Apr–Oct, Fri-Sun Nov & Dec) features historic buildings shipped in from all over the country, reconstructed and restored, such as Thomas Edison's laboratory from Menlo Park and the Wright Brothers' airplane workshop. Plus you can add on the **Rouge Factory Tour** (adult/child $15/11; ⊘ 9:30am-3pm Mon-Sat) and see F-150 trucks roll off the assembly line where Ford first perfected his self-sufficient mass-production techniques.

The three attractions are separate, but you can get a combination ticket (adult/child $35/25.50) for Henry Ford and Greenfield Village. Plan on at least one very full day at the complex.

Dearborn has the nation's greatest concentration of people of Arab descent, so it's no surprise that the **Arab American National Museum** (☑ 313-582-2266; www.arabamericanmuseum.org; 13624 Michigan Ave; adult/child $8/4; ⊘ 10am-6pm Wed-Sat, noon-5pm Sun) popped up here. It's a noble concept, located in a pretty, bright-tiled building, but it's not terribly exciting unless actor Jamie Farr's *M*A*S*H* TV-show script wows you. The Arabian eateries lining nearby Warren Ave provide a more engaging feel for the culture. Turquoise-roofed **Hamido** (www.hamidorestaurant.com; 13251 W Warren Ave; mains $5-12; ⊘ 11am-midnight) serves hummus, chicken shwarma and other staples. The number of birds roasting on the spit show its popularity.

Ann Arbor

Forty-odd miles west of Detroit, liberal and bookish Ann Arbor is home to the University of Michigan. The walkable downtown, which abuts the campus, is loaded with free-trade coffee shops, bookstores and brewpubs. It's also a mecca for chowhounds; follow the drool trail toward anything named 'Zingerman's.'

⊙ Sights & Activities

University of Michigan Museum of Art   MUSEUM
(☑ 734-764-0395; www.umma.umich.edu; 525 S State St; ⊘ 11am-5pm Tue-Sat, from noon Sun) FREE The campus' bold art museum impresses with its collections of Asian ceramics, Tiffany glass and modern abstract works.

Ann Arbor Farmers Market   MARKET
(www.a2gov.org/market; 315 Detroit St; ⊘ 7am-3pm Wed & Sat May-Dec, Sat only Jan-Apr) Given the surrounding bounty of orchards and farms, it's no surprise this place is stuffed to the rafters with everything from spicy pickles to cider to mushroom-growing kits; located downtown near Zingerman's Deli. On Sunday an artisan market with jewelry, ceramics and textiles takes over.

Zingerman's Bakehouse   COOKING COURSE
(www.bakewithzing.com; 3723 Plaza Dr) Part of Zingerman's epicurean empire, the Bakehouse offers popular 'bake-cations,' from two-hour cookie-making classes to week-long pastry courses.

✕ Eating & Drinking

Zingerman's Delicatessen   DELI $$
(☑ 734-663-3354; www.zingermansdeli.com; 422 Detroit St; sandwiches $11-17; ⊘ 7am-10pm; ♿) The shop that launched the foodie frenzy, Z's piles local, organic and specialty ingredients onto towering sandwiches in a sprawling downtown complex that also includes a coffee shop and bakery.

Frita Batidos   CUBAN $$
(www.fritabatidos.com; 117 W Washington St; mains $8-13; ⊘ 11am-11pm Sun-Wed, to midnight Thu-Sat) This mod take on Cuban street food is all the rage, offering burgers with tropical, citrusy toppings and booze-spiked milkshakes.

★ **Zingerman's Roadhouse**   AMERICAN $$$
(☑ 734-663-3663; www.zingermansroadhouse.com; 2501 Jackson Ave; mains $17-27; ⊘ 7am-10pm Mon-Thu, 7am-11pm Fri, 9am-11pm Sat, 9am-9pm Sun) Two words: doughnut sundae. The bourbon-caramel-sauced dessert is pure genius, as are the traditional American dishes like Carolina grits, Iowa pork chops and Massachusetts oysters, all using sustainably produced ingredients. It's 2 miles west of downtown.

Jolly Pumpkin   BREWERY
(www.jollypumpkin.com; 311 S Main St; ⊘ from 11am Mon-Fri, from 10am Sat & Sun) Known for its housemade sour beers (try the Bam Biere), rooftop patio, pizzas and truffle fries.

☆ Entertainment

If you happen to arrive on a fall weekend and wonder why 110,000 people – the size of Ann Arbor's entire population, more or less – are crowding into the school's stadium, the answer is football. Tickets are nearly impossible to purchase, especially when nemesis Ohio State is in town. You can try by contacting the **U of M Ticket Office** (☎734-764-0247; www.mgoblue.com/ticketoffice).

Blind Pig   LIVE MUSIC
(www.blindpigmusic.com; 208 S 1st St) Everyone from John Lennon to Nirvana to the Circle Jerks has rocked the storied stage.

Ark   LIVE MUSIC
(www.a2ark.org; 316 S Main St) The Ark hosts acoustic and folk-oriented tunesmiths.

ⓘ Information

There are several B&Bs within walking distance of downtown. Hotels tend to be about 5 miles out, with several clustered south on State St.

Ann Arbor Convention & Visitors Bureau (www.visitannarbor.org) Information on accommodations.

Lansing & Central Michigan

Michigan's heartland, plunked in the center of the Lower Peninsula, alternates between fertile farms and highway-crossed urban areas.

Lansing

Smallish Lansing is the state capital; a few miles east lies East Lansing, home of Michigan State University. The **Greater Lansing CVB** (www.lansing.org) has information on both.

Between Lansing's downtown and the university is the 8-mile **River Trail** (www.lansingrivertrail.org). The paved path is popular with cyclists and joggers, and links a number of attractions, including a children's museum, zoo and fish ladder.

On campus, the new **Broad Museum of Art** (www.broadmuseum.msu.edu; 547 E Circle Dr; ⊘10am-5pm Tue-Thu & Sat-Sun, noon-9pm Fri) FREE is a must-see. Renowned architect Zaha Hadid designed the wild-looking parallelogram of stainless steel and glass. It holds everything from Greek ceramics to Salvador Dali paintings. The **RE Olds Transportation Museum** (☎517-372-0529; www.reoldsmuseum.org; 240 Museum Dr; adult/child $6/4; ⊘10am-5pm Tue-Sat year-round, noon-5pm Sun Apr-Oct) will please car buffs.

Lansing's downtown hotels feed off politicians and lobbyists, so they're fairly expensive. It's best to head to East Lansing's **Wild Goose Inn** (☎517-333-3334; www.wildgooseinn.com; 512 Albert St; r incl breakfast $139-159; 🛜), a six-room B&B one block from Michigan State's campus. All rooms have fireplaces and most have Jacuzzis.

Golden Harvest (☎517-485-3663; 1625 Turner St; mains $7-9; ⊘7am-2:30pm Mon-Fri, from 8am Sat & Sun) is a loud, punk-rock-meets-hippie diner serving the sausage-and-French-toast Bubba Sandwich and hearty omelets; cash only. Abundant restaurants, pubs and nightclubs also fill Michigan State's northern campus area.

Grand Rapids

The second-largest city in Michigan, Grand Rapids is known for office-furniture manufacturing and, more recently, beer tourism. Twenty craft breweries operate in the area. The **Grand Rapids CVB** (www.experiencegr.com) has maps and self-guided tour information online.

Let's cut to the chase: if you've only got time for one brewery, make it rock-and-roll **Founders Brewing Company** (www.foundersbrewing.com; 235 Grandville Ave SW; ⊘11am-2am Mon-Sat, noon-midnight Sun). The ruby-tinged Dirty Bastard Ale is good swillin', and there's meaty (or vegetable-y, for vegetarians) deli sandwiches to soak it up. Want to try one more? Head to **Brewery Vivant** (www.breweryvivant.com; 925 Cherry St SE; ⊘from 3pm Mon-Fri, from 11am Sat, from noon Sun), which specializes in Belgian-style beers. Set in an old chapel with stained glass and a vaulted ceiling, the atmospheric brewpub also serves locally sourced cheese plates and burgers at farmhouse-style communal tables.

For intriguing non-beer sights, the downtown **Gerald R Ford Museum** (☎616-254-0400; www.fordlibrarymuseum.gov; 303 Pearl St NW; adult/child $7/3; ⊘9am-5pm) is dedicated to Michigan's only president. Ford stepped into the Oval Office after Richard Nixon and his vice president, Spiro Agnew, resigned in disgrace. It's an intriguing period in US history, and the museum does an excellent job of covering it, down to displaying the burglary tools used in the Watergate break-in. Ford and wife Betty are buried in the museum's grounds.

The 118-acre **Frederik Meijer Gardens** (☎616-957-1580; www.meijergardens.org; 1000 E Beltline NE; adult/child $12/6; ⊘9am-5pm Mon-Sat, 9am-9pm Tue, 11am-5pm Sun) features impressive blooms and sculptures by Auguste

Rodin, Henry Moore and others. It is 5 miles east of downtown via I-196. There's a good art museum downtown, too.

At night, tuck in under bamboo sheets at the **CityFlats Hotel** (☑ 866-609-2489; www. cityflatshotel.com/grandrapids; 83 Monroe Center St NW; r $169-239; ❄ ☎) downtown; it's gold-certified by the LEED (Leadership in Energy and Environmental Design) program.

Lake Michigan Shore

They don't call it the Gold Coast for nothing. Michigan's 300-mile western shoreline features seemingly endless stretches of beaches, dunes, wineries, orchards and B&B-filled towns that boom during the summer – and shiver during the snow-packed winter. Note all state parks listed here take **campsite reservations** (☑ 800-447-2757; www.midnrreservations.com; fee $8) and require a vehicle permit (day/year $9/31), unless specified otherwise.

Harbor Country

Harbor Country refers to a group of eight small, lake-hugging towns just over the Michigan border (an easy day trip from Chicago). Yep, they've got your requisite beaches, wineries and antique shops; they've got a couple of big surprises too. The **Harbor Country Chamber of Commerce** (www.harborcountry.org) has the basics.

First up, surfing. Believe it, people: you can surf Lake Michigan, and the VW-bus-driving dudes at **Third Coast Surf Shop** (☑ 269-932-4575; www.thirdcoastsurfshop.com; 110-C N Whittaker St; ⊙ 10am-6pm mid-May–late Sep) will show you how. They provide wetsuits and boards for surfing, skim boarding and paddleboarding (rentals per day $20 to $35). For novices, they offer 1½-hour lessons (including equipment $55 to $75) right on the public beach June through mid-September. The surf shop is in New Buffalo, Harbor Country's biggest town.

ⓘ WINE TRAIL

A dozen wineries cluster between New Buffalo and Saugatuck. The **Lake Michigan Shore Wine Trail** (www. lakemichiganshorewinetrail.com) provides a downloadable map of vineyards and tasting rooms. Most are signposted off the highway.

Three Oaks is the only Harbor community that's inland (6 miles in, via US 12). Here Green Acres meets Greenwich Village in a funky farm-and-arts blend. By day, rent bikes at **Dewey Cannon Trading Company** (☑ 269-756-3361; www.applecidercentury.com; 3 Dewey Cannon Ave; bike per day $20; ⊙ 9am-5pm) and cycle lightly used rural roads past orchards and wineries. By eve, catch a provocative play or arthouse flick at Three Oaks' theaters.

Hungry? Get a wax-paper-wrapped cheeseburger, spicy curly fries and cold beer at **Redamak's** (www.redamaks.com; 616 E Buffalo St; burgers $5-10; ⊙ noon-10:30pm Mar-Oct) in New Buffalo.

Saugatuck & Douglas

Saugatuck is one of the Gold Coast's most popular resort areas, known for its strong arts community, numerous B&Bs and gay-friendly vibe. Douglas is its twin city a mile or so south, and they've pretty much sprawled into one. The **Saugatuck/Douglas CVB** (www.saugatuck.com) provides maps and more.

The best thing to do in Saugatuck is also the most affordable. Jump aboard the clackety **Saugatuck Chain Ferry** (foot of Mary St; one way $1; ⊙ 9am-9pm late May-early Sep) and the operator will pull you across the Kalamazoo River. On the other side, walk to the dock's right and soon you'll come to **Mt Baldhead**, a 200ft-high sand dune. Huff up the stairs to see the grand view, and then race down the other side to beautiful **Oval Beach**.

Galleries and shops proliferate downtown on Water and Butler Sts. Antiquing prevails on the Blue Star Hwy running south for 20 miles. Blueberry U-pick farms share this stretch of road and make a juicy stop, too.

Several frilly B&Bs are tucked into the Saugatuck's century-old Victorian homes, with most ranging from $125 to $300 per night. Try the **Bayside Inn** (☑ 269-857-4321; www.baysideinn.net; 618 Water St; r incl breakfast $150-280; ☎), a 10-room former boathouse on Saugatuck's waterfront, or the retro-cool **Pines Motorlodge** (☑ 269-857-5211; www. thepinesmotorlodge.com; 56 Blue Star Hwy; r incl breakfast $139-199; ☎), with rooms amid the firs in Douglas.

For eats, **Wicks Park Bar & Grill** (☑ 269-857-2888; www.wickspark.com; 449 Water St; mains $11-25; ⊙ 11:30am-9pm), by the chain ferry, gets props for its lake perch and live music.

Locals like to hang out and sip the house-made suds at **Saugatuck Brewing Company** (www.saugatuckbrewing.com; 2948 Blue Star Hwy; ⊙ 11am-10pm Sun-Thu, to 11pm Fri & Sat). For dessert, buy a bulging slice at **Crane's Pie Pantry** (✔ 269-561-2297; www.cranespiepantry.com; 6054 124th Ave; pie slices $4; ⊙ 9am-8pm Mon-Sat, from 11am Sun May-Oct, reduced hours Nov-Apr), or pick apples and peaches in the surrounding orchards. Crane's is in Fennville, 3 miles south on the Blue Star Hwy, then 4 miles inland on Hwy 89.

Muskegon & Ludington

The **Lake Express ferry** (✔ 866-914-1010; www.lake-express.com; ⊙ May-Oct) crosses between Muskegon and Milwaukee (one way adult/child/car from $83/26/87, 2½ hours), providing a substantial shortcut over driving the Michigan-to-Wisconsin route. The town isn't much, but the **Muskegon Luge & Sports Complex** (✔ 231-744-9629; www.msports.org; 442 Scenic Dr) kicks butt with its full-on luge track (usable during summer, too) and cross-country ski trails. To the north, lakeside **Ludington State Park** (✔ 231-843-8671; tent & RV sites $16-29, cabins $45) is one of Michigan's largest and most popular playlots. It has a top-notch trail system, a renovated lighthouse to visit (or live in, as a volunteer lighthouse keeper) and miles of beach.

Sleeping Bear Dunes National Lakeshore

This national park stretches from north of Frankfort to just before Leland, on the Leelanau Peninsula. Stop at the park's **visitor center** (✔ 231-326-5134; www.nps.gov/slbe; 9922 Front St; ⊙ 8:30am-6pm Jun-Aug, to 4pm Sep-May) in Empire for information, trail maps and vehicle entry permits (week/year $10/20).

Attractions include the famous **dune climb** along Hwy 109, where you trudge up the 200ft-high dune and then run or roll down. Gluttons for leg-muscle punishment can keep slogging all the way to Lake Michigan, a strenuous 1½-hour trek one way; bring water. The **Sleeping Bear Heritage Trail** (www.sleepingbeartrail.org) paves 5 pretty miles from Glen Arbor to the Dune Climb; walkers and cyclists are all over it. It will stretch to Empire by summer 2014. Short on time or stamina? Take the 7-mile, one-lane, picnic-grove-studded **Pierce Stocking Sce-**

WORTH A TRIP

MANITOU ISLANDS

If you're looking for a wilderness adventure, the Manitou Islands – part of Sleeping Bear Dunes National Lakeshore – deliver. **Manitou Island Transit** (✔ 231-256-9061; www.manitoutransit.com) can help plan overnight camping trips on North Manitou, or day trips to South Manitou. Kayaking and hiking are popular activities, especially the 7-mile trek to the Valley of the Giants, a mystical stand of cedar trees on South Manitou. Ferries (round trip adult/child $35/20, 1½ hours) sail from Leland two to seven times per week from May to mid-October.

---

nic Drive, perhaps the best way to absorb the stunning lake vistas.

After you leave the park, swing into little **Leland** (www.lelandmi.com). Grab a bite at a waterfront restaurant downtown, and poke around atmospheric Fishtown with its weatherbeaten shacks-cum-shops. Boats depart from here for the Manitou Islands.

Onward near Suttons Bay, **Tandem Ciders** (www.tandemciders.com; 2055 Setterbo Rd; ⊙ noon-6pm Mon-Sat, to 5pm Sun) pours delicious hard ciders in its small tasting room on the family farm.

Traverse City

Michigan's 'cherry capital' is the largest city in the northern half of the Lower Peninsula. It's got a bit of urban sprawl, but it's still a happenin' base from which to see the Sleeping Bear Dunes, Mission Peninsula wineries, U-pick orchards and other area attractions.

Stop at the downtown **visitor center** (✔ 231-947-1120; www.traversecity.com; 101 W Grandview Pkwy; ⊙ 9am-6pm Mon-Sat, 11am-3pm Sun) for maps and the do-it-yourself foodie tour brochure (also available online; click 'Things to Do' on the website).

Road tripping out to the wineries is a must. Head north from Traverse City on Hwy 37 for 20 miles to the end of the grape-and cherry-planted Old Mission Peninsula. You'll be spoiled for choice: **Chateau Grand Traverse** (www.cgtwines.com; ⊙ 10am-7pm Mon-Sat, to 6pm Sun) and **Chateau Chantal** (www.chateauchantal.com; ⊙ 11am-8pm Mon-Sat, to 6pm Sun) pour crowd-pleasing Chardonnay and Pinot Noir. **Peninsula Cellars** (www.peninsulacellars.com; ◷ 10am-6pm), in an old schoolhouse, makes fine whites and is often less crowded. Whatever bottle you buy, take it out to Lighthouse Park beach, at the peninsula's tip, and enjoy it with the waves chilling your toes. The wineries stay open year-round, with reduced hours in winter.

The town goes all Hollywood during the **Traverse City Film Festival** (www.traversecityfilmfest.org; ◷ late Jul), when founder (and native Michigander) Michael Moore comes in and unspools a six-day slate of documentaries, international flicks and 'just great movies.'

Dozens of beaches, resorts, motels and water-sports operators line US 31 around Traverse City. On weekends, lodgings are often full, and more expensive; the visitor center website has contact details. Most resorts overlooking the bay cost $150 to $250 per night. The Chantal and Grand Traverse wineries also double as B&Bs and fit into this price range.

Guests can rent jet skis and enjoy nightly bonfires at **Park Shore Resort** (☑ 877-349-8898; www.parkshoreresort.com; 1401 US 31 N; r incl breakfast from $199; ✳ ☎ ✻). Motels on the other side of US 31 (away from the water) are more moderately priced, such as **Mitchell Creek Inn** (☑ 231-947-9330; www.mitchellcreek. com; 894 Munson Ave; r/cottages from $60/125; ☎), near the state park beach.

After a day of fun in the sun, refresh with sandwiches at gastronome favorite **Folgarelli's** (☑ 231-941-7651; www.folgarellis. net; 424 W Front St; sandwiches $7-11; ◷ 9:30am-6:30pm Mon-Fri, to 5:30pm Sat, 11am-4pm Sun) and Belgian and Michigan craft beers at **7 Monks Taproom** (www.7monkstap.com; 128 S Union St; ◷ noon-midnight).

ⓘ HIKING-TRAIL MAPS

Plot out your walk in the woods with **Michigan Trail Maps** (www.michigantrailmaps.com), a free resource with more than 100 trail guides. Search by county, trail length or activity (eg birding), then download and print the high-quality maps as pdfs. So far the trails covered are on the Lower Peninsula, but Upper Peninsula treks are reportedly in the works.

Charlevoix & Petoskey

These two towns hold several Hemingway sights. They're also where Michigan's upper-crusters maintain summer homes. The downtown areas of both places have gourmet restaurants and high-class shops, and the marinas are filled with yachts.

In Petoskey, **Stafford's Perry Hotel** (☑ 231-347-4000; www.staffords.com; Bay at Lewis St; r $149-269; ✳ @ ☎) is a grand historic place in which to stay. **Petoskey State Park** (☑ 231-347-2311; 2475 Hwy 119; tent & RV sites $27-29) is north along Hwy 119 and has a beautiful beach. Look for indigenous Petoskey stones, which are honeycomb-patterned fragments of ancient coral. From here, Hwy 119 (aka the **Tunnel of Trees scenic route**) dips and curves through thick forest as it rolls north along a sublime bluff, en route to the Straits of Mackinac.

Straits of Mackinac

This region, between the Upper and Lower Peninsulas, features a long history of forts and fudge shops. Car-free Mackinac Island is Michigan's premier tourist draw.

One of the most spectacular sights in the area is the 5-mile-long **Mackinac Bridge** (known locally as 'Big Mac'), which spans the Straits of Mackinac. The $4 toll is worth every penny as the views from the bridge, which include two Great Lakes, two peninsulas and hundreds of islands, are second to none in Michigan.

And remember: despite the spelling, it's pronounced *mac*-in-aw.

Mackinaw City

At the south end of Mackinac Bridge, bordering I-75, is touristy Mackinaw City. It serves mainly as a jump-off point to Mackinac Island, but it does have a couple of interesting sights.

Next to the bridge (its visitor center is actually beneath the bridge) is **Colonial Michilimackinac** (☑ 231-436-5564; www.mackinacparks.com; adult/child $11/6.50; ◷ 9:30am-7pm Jun-Aug, to 5pm May & Sep–mid-Oct). This National Historic Landmark features a reconstructed stockade first built in 1715 by the French. Some 3 miles southeast of the city on US 23 is **Historic Mill Creek** (☑ 231-436-4226; www.mackinacparks.com; adult/child

HEMINGWAY'S HAUNTS

A number of writers have ties to northwest Michigan, but none is as famous as Ernest Hemingway, who spent the summers of his youth at his family's cottage on Walloon Lake. Hemingway buffs often tour the area to view the places that made their way into his writing.

First up: Horton Bay. As you head north on US 31, past yacht-filled Charlevoix, look for Boyne City Rd veering off to the east. It skirts Lake Charlevoix and eventually arrives at the **Horton Bay General Store** (☑ 231-582-7827; www.hortonbaygeneralstore.com; 05115 Boyne City Rd; ⊙ 8am-2pm mid-May–mid-Oct). Hemingway fans will recognize the building, with its 'high false front,' from his short story 'Up in Michigan.' For the mother lode of Hemingway books and souvenirs, pop into the **Red Fox Inn Bookstore** (05156 Boyne City Rd; ⊙ late May–early Sep) next door.

Further up Hwy 31 in Petoskey, you can see the Hemingway collection at the **Little Traverse History Museum** (☑ 231-347-2620; www.petoskeymuseum.org; 100 Depot Ct; admission $3; ⊙ 10am-4pm Mon-Fri, from 1pm Sat late May–mid-Oct), including rare first-edition books that the author autographed for a friend when he visited in 1947. Afterward, toss back a drink at **City Park Grill** (☑ 231-347-0101; www.cityparkgrill.com; 432 E Lake St; ⊙ 11:30am-midnight), where Hemingway was a regular.

Tour Hemingway's Michigan (www.mihemingwaytour.org) provides further information for self-guided jaunts.

$8/4.75; ⊙ 9am-5pm Jun-Aug, to 4pm May & Sep–mid-Oct), which has an 18th-century sawmill, historic displays and nature trails. A combination ticket for both sights, along with Fort Mackinac, is available at a discount.

If you can't find lodging on Mackinac Island – which should be your first choice – motels line I-75 and US 23 in Mackinaw City. Most cost $100-plus per night. Try **Days Inn** (☑ 231-436-8961; www.daysinn.com; 206 N Nicolet St; r incl breakfast $115-170; ✳ 🖥 🞨).

St Ignace

At the north end of Mackinac Bridge is St Ignace, the other departure point for Mackinac Island and the second-oldest settlement in Michigan – Père Jacques Marquette founded a mission here in 1671. As soon as you've paid your bridge toll, you'll pass a huge **visitor center** (☑ 906-643-6979; I-75N; ⊙ 9am-5:30pm daily summer, Thu-Mon rest of year) which has racks of statewide information.

Mackinac Island

From either Mackinaw City or St Ignace you can catch a ferry to Mackinac Island. The island's location in the straits between Lake Michigan and Lake Huron made it a prized port in the North American fur trade, and a site the British and Americans battled over many times.

The most important date on this 3.8-sq-mile island was 1898 – the year cars were banned in order to encourage tourism. Today all travel is by horse or bicycle; even the police use bikes to patrol the town. The crowds of tourists – called Fudgies by the islanders – can be crushing at times, particularly during summer weekends. But when the last ferry leaves in the evening and clears out the day-trippers, Mackinac's real charm emerges and you drift back into another, slower era.

The **visitor center** (☑ 800-454-5227; www.mackinacisland.org; Main St; ⊙ 9am-5pm), by the Arnold Line ferry dock, has maps for hiking and cycling. Eighty percent of the island is state parkland. Not much stays open between November and April.

⊙ Sights & Activities

Edging the island's shoreline is Hwy 185, the only Michigan highway that doesn't permit cars. The best way to view the incredible scenery along this 8-mile road is by bicycle; bring your own or rent one in town for $8 per hour at one of the many businesses. You can loop around the flat road in about an hour.

The two best attractions – **Arch Rock** (a huge limestone arch that sits 150ft above Lake Huron) and **Fort Holmes** (the island's other fort) – are both free. You can also ride past the **Grand Hotel**, which boasts a porch stretching halfway to Detroit. Unfortunately, if you're not staying at the Grand (minimum $240 per night per person), it costs $10 to stroll its long porch. Best to admire from afar.

Fort Mackinac   HISTORIC SITE
(☑ 906-847-3328; www.mackinacparks.com; adult/child $11/6.50; ☺ 9:30am-6pm Jun-Aug, 9:30am-4:30pm May & Sep–mid-Oct; ☝) Fort Mackinac sits atop limestone cliffs near downtown. Built by the British in 1780, it's one of the best-preserved military forts in the country. Costumed interpreters and cannon and rifle firings (every half-hour) entertain the kids. Stop into the tearoom for a bite and million-dollar view of downtown and the Straits of Mackinac from the outdoor tables.

The fort admission price also allows you entry to five other museums in town along Market St, including the Dr Beaumont Museum (where the doctor performed his famous digestive tract experiments) and the Benjamin Blacksmith Shop. The **Mackinac Art Museum** (adult/child $5/3.50), housing Native American and other arts by the fort, is the newest member of the fold.

⌖ Sleeping

Rooms are booked far in advance during summer weekends; July to mid-August is peak season. The visitor center website has lodging contacts. Camping is not permitted anywhere on the island.

Most hotels and B&Bs charge at least $180 for two people. Exceptions (all are walkable from downtown) include the following.

Bogan Lane Inn   B&B $$
(☑ 906-847-3439; www.boganlaneinn.com; Bogan Lane; r incl breakfast $90-130) Four rooms, shared bath.

Cloghaun B&B   B&B $$
(☑ 906-847-3885; www.cloghaun.com; Market St; r incl breakfast $112-197; ☺ mid-May–late Oct; ☝) Eleven rooms, some with shared bath.

Hart's B&B   B&B $$
(☑ 906-847-3854; www.hartsmackinac.com; Market St; r incl breakfast $150-190; ☺ mid-May–late Oct; ☝) Eight rooms, all with private bath.

✖ Eating & Drinking

Fudge shops are the island's best-known eateries; resistance is futile when they use fans to blow the aroma out onto Huron St. Hamburger and sandwich shops abound downtown.

JL Beanery Coffeehouse   CAFE $
(☑ 906-847-6533; Huron St; mains $6-13; ☺ 7am-7pm; ☝) Read the newspaper, sip a steaming cup of joe and gaze at the lake at this waterside cafe. It serves dandy breakfasts, sandwiches and soups.

Horn's Bar   BURGERS, MEXICAN $$
(☑ 906-847-6154; www.hornsbar.com; Main St; mains $10-19; ☺ 11am-2am) Horn's saloon serves American burgers and south-of-the-border fare, and there's live entertainment nightly.

Cawthorne's Village Inn   AMERICAN $$$
(☑ 906-847-3542; www.grandhotel.com; Hoban St; mains $18-27; ☺ 11am-2am) Planked whitefish, pan-fried perch and other fresh-from-the-lake fish, meat and pasta dishes stuff diners at this year-round local hang-out with a bar and outdoor seating. Operated by the Grand Hotel.

❶ Getting There & Around

Three ferry companies – **Arnold Line** (☑ 800-542-8528; www.arnoldline.com), **Shepler's** (☑ 800-828-6157; www.sheplersferry.com) and **Star Line** (☑ 800-638-9892; www.mackinac-ferry.com) – operate out of Mackinaw City and St Ignace, and charge the same rates: round-trip adult/child/bicycle $25/13/8. Book online and you'll save a few bucks. The ferries run several times daily from May to October; Arnold Line runs longer, weather permitting. The trip takes about 15 minutes; once on the island, horse-drawn cabs will take you anywhere, or you can rent a bicycle.

Upper Peninsula

Rugged and isolated, with hardwood forests blanketing 90% of its land, the Upper Peninsula (UP) is a Midwest highlight. Only 45 miles of interstate highway slice through the trees, punctuated by a handful of cities, of which Marquette (population 20,000) is the largest. Between the small towns lie miles of undeveloped shoreline on Lakes Huron, Michigan and Superior; scenic two-lane roads; and pasties, the local meat-and-vegetable pot pies brought over by Cornish miners 150 years ago.

You'll find it's a different world up north. Residents of the UP, aka 'Yoopers,' consider themselves distinct from the rest of the state – they've even threatened to secede in the past.

Sault Ste Marie & Tahquamenon Falls

Founded in 1668, Sault Ste Marie (Sault is pronounced 'soo') is Michigan's oldest city and the third oldest in the USA. The town is best known for its locks that raise and lower 1000ft-long freighters between the different lake levels. **Soo Locks Park & Visitors Center** (⊙9am-9pm mid-May–mid-Oct) FREE is on Portage Ave downtown (take exit 394 off I-75 and go left). It features displays, videos and observation decks from which you can watch the boats leap 21ft from Lake Superior to Lake Huron. Pubs and cafes line Portage Ave. The **Sault CVB** (www.saultstemarie.com) has all the lowdown.

An hour's drive west of Sault Ste Marie, via Hwy 28 and Hwy 123, is eastern UP's top attraction: lovely **Tahquamenon Falls**, with tea-colored waters tinted by upstream hemlock leaves. The Upper Falls in **Tahquamenon Falls State Park** (✐906-492-3415; per vehicle $9), 200ft across with a 50ft drop, wow onlookers – including Henry Wadsworth Longfellow, who mentioned them in his *Song of Hiawatha*. The Lower Falls are a series of small cascades that swirl around an island; many visitors rent a rowboat and paddle out to it. The large state park also has **camping** (tent & RV sites $16-23), great hiking and – bonus – a brewpub near the park entrance.

North of the park, beyond the little town of Paradise, is the fascinating **Great Lakes Shipwreck Museum** (✐888-492-3747; www.shipwreckmuseum.com; 18335 N Whitefish Point Rd; adult/child $13/9; ⊙10am-6pm May-Oct), where the intriguing displays include items trawled up from sunken ships. Dozens of vessels – including the *Edmund Fitzgerald* that Gordon Lightfoot crooned about – have sunk in the area's congested sea lanes and storm-tossed weather, earning it such nicknames as the 'Shipwreck Coast' and 'Graveyard of the Great Lakes.' The grounds also include a lighthouse that President Lincoln commissioned and a bird observatory that 300 species fly by. To have the foggy place to yourself, spend the night at **Whitefish Point Light Station B&B** (✐888-492-3747; r $150; ⊙May–Oct), which offers five rooms in the old Coast Guard crew quarters on site.

Pictured Rocks National Lakeshore

Stretching along prime Lake Superior real estate, **Pictured Rocks National Lakeshore** (www.nps.gov/piro) is a series of wild cliffs and caves where blue and green minerals have streaked the red and yellow sandstone into a kaleidoscope of color. Rte 58 (Alger County Rd) spans the park for 52 slow miles from **Grand Marais** in the east to **Munising** in the west. Top sights (from east to west) include **Au Sable Point Lighthouse** (reached via a 3-mile round-trip walk beside shipwreck skeletons), agate-strewn **Twelvemile Beach**, hike-rich **Chapel Falls** and view-worthy **Miners Castle Overlook**.

Several boat tours launch from Munising. **Pictured Rock Cruises** (✐906-387-2379; www.picturedrocks.com; 100 W City Park Dr; 2½hr tours adult/child $36/10; ⊙mid-May–mid-Oct) departs from the city pier downtown and glides along the shore to Miners Castle. **Shipwreck Tours** (✐906-387-4477; www.shipwrecktours.com; 1204 Commercial St; 2hr tours adult/child $32/12; ⊙late May–mid-Oct) sails in glass-bottom boats to see sunken schooners.

Grand Island (www.grandislandmi.com), part of Hiawatha National Forest, is also a quick jaunt from Munising. Hop aboard the **Grand Island Ferry** (✐906-387-3503; round-trip adult/child $15/10; ⊙late May–mid-Oct) to get there and rent a mountain bike (per day $30) to zip around. There's also a ferry/bus tour package ($22). The ferry dock is on Hwy 28, which is about 4 miles west of Munising.

Munising has lots of motels, such as tidy **Alger Falls Motel** (✐906-387-3536; www.algerfallsmotel.com; E9427 Hwy 28; r $60-90; ✳🐾). **Falling Rock Cafe & Bookstore** (✐906-387-3008; www.fallingrockcafe.com; 104 E Munising Ave; mains $5-9; ⊙7am-10pm; 🐾) provides sandwiches and live music.

Staying in wee Grand Marais, on the park's east side, is also recommended. Turn in at **Hilltop Cabins and Motel** (✐906-494-2331; www.hilltopcabins.net; N14176 Ellen St; r & cabins $85-175; 🐾) after a meal of whitefish sandwiches and brewskis at rustic **Lake Superior Brewing Company** (✐906-494-2337; N14283 Lake Ave; mains $7-13; ⊙noon-11pm).

Marquette

From Munising, Hwy 28 heads west and hugs Lake Superior. This beautiful stretch of highway has lots of beaches, roadside parks and rest areas where you can pull over and enjoy the scenery. Within 45 miles you'll reach outdoorsy, oft-snowy Marquette.

Stop at the log-lodge **visitor center** (www.travelmarquettemichigan.com; 2201 US 41; ⊙9am-5pm) as you enter the city for brochures on local hiking trails and waterfalls.

The easy **Sugarloaf Mountain Trail** and the harder, wildernesslike **Hogsback Mountain Trail** offer panoramic views. Both are reached from County Rd 550, just north of Marquette. In the city, the high bluffs of **Presque Isle Park** make a great place to catch the sunset. The **Noquemanon Trail Network** (www.noquetrails.org) is highly recommended for mountain biking and cross-country skiing. Kayaking is awesome in the area; **Downwind Sports** (www.downwindsports.com; 514 N Third St ; ⊙10am-7pm Mon-Fri, 10am-5pm Sat, 11am-3pm Sun) has the lowdown on it, as well as fly fishing, surfing, ice climbing and other adventures.

Marquette is the perfect place to stay put for a few days to explore the central UP. Budgeteers can bunk at **Value Host Motor Inn** (☑906-225-5000; www.valuehostmotorinn.com; 1101 US 41 W; r incl breakfast $55-70; ❋🤶) a few miles west of town. Downtown's **Landmark Inn** (☑906-228-2580; www.thelandmarkinn.com; 230 N Front St; r $139-229; ❋🤶) fills a historic lakefront building and has a couple of resident ghosts.

Sample the local meat-and-veggie pie specialty at **Jean Kay's Pasties & Subs** (www.jeankayspasties.com; 1635 Presque Isle Ave; items $4-7.50; ⊙11am-9pm Mon-Fri, to 8pm Sat & Sun).

DA YOOPERS TOURIST TRAP

Behold Big Gus, the world's largest chainsaw. And Big Ernie, the world's largest rifle. Kitsch runs rampant at **Da Yoopers Tourist Trap and Museum** (☑800-628-9978; www.dayoopers.com; ⊙9am-9pm Mon-Fri, to 8pm Sat, to 7pm Sun) FREE, 15 miles west of Marquette on Hwy 28/41, past Ishpeming. Browse the store for only-in-the-UP gifts like a polyester moose tie or beer-can wind chimes.

In a quonset hut at Main St's foot, **Thill's Fish House** (☑906-226-9851; 250 E Main St; items $4-9; ⊙8am-5:30pm Mon-Fri, to 4pm Sat) is Marquette's last commercial fishing operation, and it hauls in fat catches daily; try the smoked whitefish sausage. Hop-heads and mountain bikers hang out at **Blackrocks Brewery** (www.blackrocksbrewery.com; 424 N Third St; ⊙from 4pm), set in an cool refurbished house downtown.

Isle Royale National Park

Totally free of vehicles and roads, **Isle Royale National Park** (www.nps.gov/isro; per day $4; ⊙mid-May–Oct), a 210-sq-mile island in Lake Superior, is certainly the place to go for peace and quiet. It gets fewer visitors in a year than Yellowstone National Park gets in a day, which means the packs of wolves and moose creeping through the forest are all yours.

The island is laced with 165 miles of hiking trails that connect dozens of campgrounds along Superior and inland lakes. You must be totally prepared for this wilderness adventure, with a tent, camping stove, sleeping bags, food and water filter. Otherwise, be a softie and bunk at the **Rock Harbor Lodge** (☑906-337-4993; www.isleroyaleresort.com; r & cottages $237-271; ⊙late May-early Sep)

From the dock outside the **park headquarters** (800 E Lakeshore Dr) in Houghton, the **Ranger III** (☑906-482-0984) departs at 9am on Tuesday and Friday for the six-hour boat trip (round-trip adult/child $126/46) to Rock Harbor, at the east end of the island. **Royale Air Service** (☑877-359-4753; www.royaleairservice.com) offers a quicker trip, flying from Houghton County Airport to Rock Harbor in 30 minutes (round-trip $299). Or head 50 miles up the Keweenaw Peninsula to Copper Harbor (a beautiful drive) and jump on the **Isle Royale Queen** (☑906-289-4437; www.isleroyale.com) for the 8am three-hour crossing (round-trip adult/child $130/65). It usually runs daily during peak season from late July to mid-August. Bringing a kayak or canoe on the ferries costs an additional $50 round-trip; ensure you make reservations well in advance. You can also access Isle Royale from Grand Portage, Minnesota.

Porcupine Mountains Wilderness State Park

Michigan's largest state park, with 90 miles of trails, is another UP winner, and it's a heck of a lot easier to reach than Isle Royale. 'The

Porkies,' as they're called, are so rugged that loggers bypassed most of the range in the early 19th century, leaving the park with the largest tract of virgin forest between the Rocky Mountains and Adirondacks.

From Silver City, head west on Hwy 107 to reach the **Porcupine Mountains Visitor Center** (☑ 906-885-5275; www.porcupinemountains.com; 412 S Boundary Rd; ☺ 10am-6pm mid-May–mid-Oct), where you buy vehicle entry permits (per day/year $9/31) and backcountry permits (one to four people per night $14). Continue to the end of Hwy 107 and climb 300ft for the stunning view of Lake of the Clouds.

Winter is also a busy time at the Porkies, with downhill skiing (a 787ft vertical drop) and 26 miles of cross-country trails on offer; check with the **ski area** (☑ 906-289-4105; www.skitheporkies.com) for conditions and costs.

The park rents **rustic cabins** (☑ 906-885-5275; www.mi.gov/porkies; cabins $60) perfect for wilderness adventurers, as you have to hike in for 1 to 4 miles, boil your own water and use a privy. **Sunshine Motel & Cabins** (☑ 906-884-2187; www.ontonagon.net/sunshinemotel; 24077 Hwy 64; r $60, cabins $68-120; ☎ 🐾), 3 miles west of Ontonagon, is another good base.

WISCONSIN

Wisconsin is cheesy and proud of it. The state pumps out 2.5 billion pounds of cheddar, Gouda and other smelly goodness – a quarter of America's hunks – from its cow-speckled farmland per year. Local license plates read 'The Dairy State' with udder dignity. Folks here even refer to themselves as 'cheeseheads' and emphasize it by wearing novelty foam-rubber cheese-wedge hats for special occasions (most notably during Green Bay Packers football games).

So embrace the cheese thing, because there's a good chance you'll be here for a while. Wisconsin has heaps to offer: exploring the craggy cliffs and lighthouses of Door County, kayaking through sea caves at Apostle Islands National Lakeshore, cow-chip throwing along US 12 and soaking up beer, art and festivals in Milwaukee and Madison.

❶ Information

Travel Green Wisconsin (www.travelgreenwisconsin.com) Certifies businesses as ecofriendly by grading them on waste reduction, energy efficiency and seven other categories.

WISCONSIN FACTS

Nicknames Badger State, America's Dairyland

Population 5.7 million

Area 65,500 sq miles

Capital city Madison (population 240,000)

Other cities Milwaukee (population 599,000)

Sales tax 5%

Birthplace of Author Laura Ingalls Wilder (1867–1957), architect Frank Lloyd Wright (1867–1959), painter Georgia O'Keeffe (1887–1986), actor Orson Welles (1915–85), guitar maker Les Paul (1915–2009)

Home of 'Cheesehead' Packer fans, dairy farms, water parks

Politics Leans Democratic

Famous for Breweries, artisanal cheese, first state to legislate gay rights

Official dance Polka

Driving distances Milwaukee to Minneapolis 336 miles, Milwaukee to Madison 80 miles

---

Wisconsin B&B Association (www.wbba.org)
Wisconsin Department of Tourism (☑ 800-432-8747; www.travelwisconsin.com) Produces loads of free guides on subjects like birdwatching, biking, golf and rustic roads; also a free app.
Wisconsin Highway Conditions (☑ 511; www.511wi.gov)
Wisconsin Milk Marketing Board (www.eatwisconsincheese.com) Provides a free statewide map of cheesemakers titled *A Traveler's Guide to America's Dairyland*.
Wisconsin State Park Information (☑ 608-266-2181; www.wiparks.net) Park entry requires a vehicle permit (per day/year $10/35). Campsites cost from $14 to $25; reservations (☑ 888-947-2757; www.wisconsinstateparks.reserveamerica.com; fee $10) accepted.

Milwaukee

Here's the thing about Milwaukee: it's cool, but for some reason everyone refuses to admit it. Yes, the reputation lingers as a working man's town of brewskis, bowling alleys and polka halls. But attractions like the Calatrava-designed art museum, bad-ass Harley-Davidson Museum and stylish eating and shopping 'hoods have turned Wisconsin's largest city into a surprisingly groovy place. In summertime, festivals let loose with revelry by the lake almost every weekend. And where else on the planet will you see racing sausages?

History

Milwaukee was first settled by Germans in the 1840s. Many started small breweries, but a few decades later the introduction of bulk brewing technology turned beer production into a major industry here. Milwaukee earned its 'Brew City' and 'Nation's Watering Hole' nicknames in the 1880s when Pabst, Schlitz, Blatz, Miller and 80 other breweries made suds here. Today, only Miller and a few microbreweries remain.

⊙ Sights & Activities

Lake Michigan sits to the east of the city, and is rimmed by parkland. The Riverwalk path runs along both sides of the Milwaukee River downtown.

Harley-Davidson Museum   MUSEUM
(☑ 877-436-8738; www.h-dmuseum.com; 400 W Canal St; adult/child $18/10; ⊙ 9am-6pm Fri-Wed, to 8pm Thu May-Oct, reduced hours Nov-Apr) Hundreds of motorcycles show the styles through the decades, including the flashy rides of Elvis and Evel Knievel. You can sit in the saddle of various bikes (on the bottom floor, behind the Design Lab), as well

---

TWO-WHEELING WISCONSIN

Wisconsin has converted an impressive number of abandoned railroad lines into paved, bike-only paths. They go up hills, through old tunnels, over bridges and alongside pastures. Wherever you are in the state, there's likely a sweet ride nearby; check the **Travel Wisconsin Bike Path Directory** (www.travelwisconsin.com/things-to-do/outdoor-fun/biking-/traffic-free-paved). The **400 State Trail** (www.400statetrail.org) and **Elroy-Sparta Trail** (www.elroy-spartatrail.com) top the list.

Bike rentals are available in gateway towns, and you can buy trail passes (per day/year $4/20) at area businesses or trailhead drop-boxes.

---

as get a mini lesson on how to ride (by the front entrance). Even nonbikers will enjoy the place.

It all started in 1903, when Milwaukee schoolmates William Harley and Arthur Davidson built and sold their first motorcycle. A century later the big bikes are a symbol of American manufacturing pride. The museum is located in a sprawling industrial building just south of downtown.

Harley-Davidson Plant   TOUR
(☑ 877-883-1450; www.harley-davidson.com/experience; W156 N9000 Pilgrim Rd; 30min tours free; ⊙ 9am-2pm Mon) Hog-heads can get a fix at the plant where engines are built, in suburban Menomonee Falls. In addition to Monday's free tour, longer tours take place on Wednesday, Thursday and Friday, but only as part of a package deal you buy from the museum (per person $32, including tour, museum admission, and transport between the two venues).

Milwaukee Art Museum   MUSEUM
(☑ 414-224-3200; www.mam.org; 700 N Art Museum Dr; adult/child $15/12; ⊙ 10am-5pm Tue, Wed & Fri-Sun, to 8pm Thu Sep-May) Even those who aren't usually museum-goers will be struck by this lakeside museum, which features a stunning winglike addition by Santiago Calatrava. It soars open and closed every day at 10am, noon and at closing time, which is wild to see. There are fabulous folk and outsider art galleries, and a sizeable collection of Georgia O'Keeffe paintings.

Miller Brewing Company   BREWERY
(☑ 414-931-2337; www.millercoors.com; 4251 W State St; ⊙ 10:30am-3:30pm Mon-Sat, to 4:30pm summer) FREE Pabst and Schlitz have moved on, but Miller preserves Milwaukee's beer legacy. Join the legions of drinkers lined up for the free tours. Though the mass-produced beer may not be your favorite, the factory impresses with its sheer scale: you'll visit the packaging plant where 2000 cans are filled each minute, and the warehouse where a half-million cases await shipment. And then there's the generous tasting session at the tour's end, where you can down three full-size samples. Don't forget your ID.

Lakefront Brewery   BREWERY
(☑ 414-372-8800; www.lakefrontbrewery.com; 1872 N Commerce St; 1hr tours $7; ⊙ 9am-4:30pm Mon-Thu, 9am-9pm Fri, 11am-4:30pm Sat, noon-4:30pm Sun) Well-loved Lakefront Brewery,

across the river from Brady St, has afternoon tours, but the swellest time to visit is on Friday nights when there's a fish fry, 16 beers to try and a polka band letting loose. Tour times vary throughout the week, but there's usually at least a 2pm and 3pm walkthrough.

Discovery World at Pier Wisconsin MUSEUM
(☏414-765-9966; www.discoveryworld.org; 500 N Harbor Dr; adult/child $17/13; ⊙9am-4pm Tue-Fri, 10am-5pm Sat & Sun; ⊕) The city's lakefront science and technology museum is primarily a kid-pleaser, with freshwater and saltwater aquariums (where you can touch sharks and sturgeon) and a dockside, triple-masted Great Lakes schooner to climb aboard ($2 extra). Adults will appreciate the Les Paul exhibit, showcasing the Wisconsin native's pioneering guitars and sound equipment.

Lakefront Park PARK
The parkland edging Lake Michigan is prime for walking, cycling and in-line skating. Also here is Bradford Beach, which is good for swimming and lounging.

✨ Festivals & Events

Summerfest MUSIC
(www.summerfest.com; day pass $17; ⊙late Jun-early Jul) It's dubbed 'the world's largest music festival,' and indeed hundreds of rock, blues, jazz, country and alternative bands swarm its 10 stages over 11 days. The scene totally rocks; it is held at downtown's lakefront festival grounds.

Other popular parties, held downtown during various summer weekends, include **PrideFest** (www.pridefest.com; ⊙mid-Jun), **Polish Fest** (www.polishfest.org; ⊙late Jun), **German Fest** (www.germanfest.com; ⊙late Jul) and **Irish Fest** (www.irishfest.com; ⊙mid-Aug).

🛏 Sleeping

Rates in this section are for summer, the peak season, when you should book in advance. Tax (15.1%) is not included. For cheap chain lodging, try Howell Ave, south near the airport.

County Clare Irish Inn INN $$
(☏414-272-5273; www.countyclare-inn.com; 1234 N Astor St; r incl breakfast $129-179; P❄☎) A winner near the lakefront. Rooms have that snug Irish-cottage feel, with four-poster beds, white wainscot walls and whirlpool baths. There's free parking and an on-site Guinness-pouring pub, of course.

THE BRONZE FONZ

Rumor has it the **Bronze Fonz** (east side of Riverwalk), just south of Wells St downtown, is the most photographed sight in Milwaukee. The Fonz, aka Arthur Fonzarelli, was a character from the 1970s TV show *Happy Days*, which was set in the city. What do you think – do the blue pants get an 'Aaay' or 'Whoa!'?

Aloft HOTEL $$
(☏414-226-0122; www.aloftmilwaukeedowntown. com; 1230 Old World 3rd St; r $129-179; P❄☎) The chain's Milwaukee property has the usual compact, industrial-looking tone. It's inland near Old World 3rd St and Water St's bar action (thus a bit noisy). Parking costs $23.

Brewhouse Inn & Suites HOTEL $$$
(☏414-810-3350; www.brewhousesuites.com; 1215 N 10th St; r incl breakfast $189-229; ❄@☎) This 90-room hotel opened in 2013 in the exquisitely renovated old Pabst Brewery complex. Each of the large chambers has steampunk decor, a kitchenette and free wi-fi. It's at downtown's far west edge, about a half-mile walk from sausagey Old World 3rd St and a good 2 miles from the festival grounds. Parking costs $26.

Iron Horse Hotel HOTEL $$$
(☏888-543-4766; www.theironhorsehotel.com; 500 W Florida St; r $189-259; P❄☎) This boutique hotel near the Harley museum is geared toward motorcycle enthusiasts, with covered parking for bikes. Most of the loft-style rooms retain the post-and-beam, exposed-brick interior of what was once a bedding factory. Parking costs $25.

🍴 Eating

Good places to scope for eats include Germanic Old World 3rd St downtown; hip, multi-ethnic Brady St by its intersection with N Farwell Ave; and the gastropub-filled Third Ward, anchored along N Milwaukee St south of I-94.

Milwaukee Public Market MARKET $
(www.milwaukeepublicmarket.org; 400 N Water St; ⊙10am-8pm Mon-Fri, 8am-7pm Sat, 10am-6pm Sun; ☎) Located in the Third Ward, it stocks mostly prepared foods – cheese, chocolate, beer, tacos, frozen custard. Take them upstairs where there are tables, free wi-fi and $1 used books.

Leon's   ICE CREAM **$**
(www.leonsfrozencustard.us; 3131 S 27th St; items $1.30-4; ⊙11am-midnight) This 1950s-era neon-lit drive-in specializes in frozen custard, a local concoction that's like ice cream but smoother and richer. Cash only.

★Comet Cafe   AMERICAN **$$**
(www.thecometcafe.com; 1947 N Farwell Ave; mains $8-12; ⊙10am-10pm Mon-Fri, from 9am Sat & Sun; 🍴) Students, young families, older couples and bearded, tattooed types pile in to the rock-and-roll Comet for gravy-smothered meatloaf, mac 'n' cheese, vegan gyros and hangover brunch dishes. It's a craft-beer-pouring bar on one side, and retro-boothed diner on the other. Be sure to try one of the giant cupcakes for dessert.

Distil   AMERICAN **$$**
(☑414-220-9411; www.distilmilwaukee.com; 722 N Milwaukee St; mains $10-20; ⊙from 5pm Mon-Sat) It's all about artisanal fare at dark, coppery Distil. The menu focuses on cheese and charcuterie (burgers, too). Heck, the beef comes from the owner's cow. Mixologists stir up Corpse Revivers and Sidecars to accompany the food.

🍷 Drinking & Entertainment

Bars

Milwaukee has the second most bars per capita in the country (a hair behind New Orleans). Several pour around N Water and E State Sts downtown and in the Third Ward. Drinkeries stay open to 2am.

Best Place   BAR
(www.bestplacemilwaukee.com; 901 W Juneau Ave; ⊙noon-midnight Thu-Sat, to 6pm Sun) Join the locals knocking back beers and mas-

sive whiskey pours at this small tavern in the former Pabst Brewery headquarters. A fireplace warms the cozy, dark-wood room; original murals depicting Pabst's history adorn the walls. Staff give daily tours ($8, including a 16oz Pabst or Schlitz tap brew) that explore the building.

Uber Tap Room   BAR
(www.ubertaproom.com; 1048 N Old 3rd St; ⊙11am-8pm Sun-Wed, to 10pm Thu, to 11pm Fri & Sat) It's touristy, in the thick of Old World 3rd St and attached to the Wisconsin Cheese Mart, but it's a great place to sample local fare. Thirty Wisconsin beers flow from the taps, and cheese from the state's dairy bounty accompanies. Themed plates (spicy cheeses, stinky cheeses etc) cost $8 to $12.

Palm Tavern   BAR
(2989 S Kinnickinnic Ave; ⊙from 5pm Mon-Sat, from 7pm Sun) Located in the fresh southside neighborhood of Bay View, this warm, jazzy little bar has a mammoth selection of beer (heavy on the Belgians) and single-malt Scotches.

Kochanski's Concertina Beer Hall   BAR
(www.beer-hall.com; 1920 S 37th St; ⊙from 6pm Wed-Fri, from 1pm Sat & Sun; 🛜) Live polka music rules at kitschy Kochanski's, with beers from Schlitz to Polish drafts to Wisconsin craft labels. It's 5 miles southwest of downtown.

Sports

Miller Park   BASEBALL
(www.brewers.com; 1 Brewers Way) The Brewers play baseball at fab Miller Park, which has a retractable roof, real grass and racing sausages. It's located near S 46th St.

Bradley Center   BASKETBALL
(www.nba.com/bucks; 1001 N 4th St) The NBA's Milwaukee Bucks dunk here.

ℹ Information

The East Side neighborhood near the University of Wisconsin-Milwaukee has several coffee shops with free wi-fi.

Froedtert Hospital (☑414-805-3000; 9200 W Wisconsin Ave)

Milwaukee Convention & Visitors Bureau (☑800-554-1448; www.visitmilwaukee.org) Tourist information.

Milwaukee Journal Sentinel (www.jsonline. com) The city's daily newspaper.

On Milwaukee (www.onmilwaukee.com) Traffic and weather updates, plus restaurant and entertainment reviews.

AMERICA'S BOWLING CAPITAL

You're in Milwaukee, so you probably should just do it: bowl. The city once had more than 200 bowling alleys, and many retro lanes still hide in timeworn dives. To get your game on try **Landmark Lanes** (www.landmarklanes.com; 2220 N Farwell Ave; per game $2.50-3.50; ⊙5pm-1:30am Mon-Thu, noon-1:30am Fri-Sun; 🛜), offering 16 beat-up alleys in the historic 1927 Oriental Theater. An arcade, three bars and butt-cheap beer round out the atmosphere.

Quest (www.quest-online.com) GLBT entertainment magazine.

Shepherd Express (www.expressmilwaukee.com) Free alternative weekly paper.

ℹ Getting There & Around

General Mitchell International Airport (MKE; www.mitchellairport.com) is 8 miles south of downtown. Take public bus 80 ($2.25) or a cab ($30).

The **Lake Express ferry** (📞 866-914-1010; www.lake-express.com) sails from downtown (the terminal is located a few miles south of the city center) to Muskegon, Michigan, providing easy access to Michigan's beach-lined Gold Coast.

Greyhound (📞 414-272-2156; 433 W St Paul Ave) runs frequent buses to Chicago (two hours) and Minneapolis (seven hours). **Badger Bus** (📞 414-276-7490; www.badgerbus.com; 635 N James Lovell St) goes to Madison ($19, two hours). **Megabus** (www.megabus.com/us; 446 N 4th St) runs express to Chicago (two hours) and Minneapolis (six hours), often for lower fares than Greyhound.

Amtrak (📞 414-271-0840; www.amtrakhiawatha.com; 433 W St Paul Ave) runs the *Hiawatha* train seven times a day to/from Chicago ($24, 1½ hours); catch it downtown (it shares the station with Greyhound) or at the airport.

The **Milwaukee County Transit System** (www.ridemcts.com; fare $2.25) provides the local bus service. Bus 31 goes to Miller Brewery; bus 90 goes to Miller Park.

For taxi service, try phoning **Yellow Cab** (📞 414-271-1800).

Madison

Madison reaps a lot of kudos: most walkable city, best road-biking city, most vegetarian-friendly, gay-friendly, environmentally friendly and just plain all-round friendliest city in the USA. Ensconced on a narrow isthmus between Mendota and Monona Lakes, it's a pretty combination of small, grassy state capital and liberal, bookish college town. An impressive foodie/locavore scene has been cooking here for years.

⊙ Sights & Activities

State St runs from the capitol west to the University of Wisconsin. The pedestrian-only avenue is lined with free-trade coffee shops, parked bicycles and incense-wafting stores selling hacky sacks and flowing Indian skirts.

DON'T MISS

RACING SAUSAGES

It's common to see strange things after too many stadium beers. But a group of giant sausages sprinting around Miller Park's perimeter – is that for *real*? It is if it's the middle of the 6th inning. That's when the famous 'Racing Sausages' (actually five people in costumes) waddle onto the field to give the fans a thrill. If you don't know your encased meats, that's Brat, Polish, Italian, Hot Dog and Chorizo vying for supremacy.

Chazen Museum of Art   MUSEUM
(www.chazen.wisc.edu; 750 University Ave; ⊙ 9am-5pm Tue-Fri, 9am-9pm Thu, 11am-5pm Sat & Sun) **FREE** The university's art museum is huge and fabulous, fresh off an expansion and way beyond the norm for a campus collection. The 3rd floor holds most of the genre-spanning trove: everything from the old Dutch masters to Qing Dynasty porcelein vases, Picasso sculptures and Andy Warhol pop art. Free chamber-music concerts and arthouse films take place on Sundays from September to mid-May.

Monona Terrace   ARCHITECTURE
(www.mononaterrace.com; 1 John Nolen Dr; ⊙ 8am-5pm) Frank Lloyd Wright designed the cool, white semicirclular structure in 1938, though it wasn't completed until 1997. The one-hour tours ($3) explain why; they're offered daily at 1pm. The building serves as a community center, offering free lunchtime yoga classes and evening concerts; check the events schedule online. The rooftop garden and cafe offer sweeping lake views.

Dane County Farmers Market   MARKET
(www.dcfm.org; Capitol Sq; ⊙ 6am-2pm Sat late Apr-early Nov) 🍴 On Saturdays, a food bazaar takes over Capitol Sq. It's one of the nation's most expansive markets, famed for its artisanal cheeses and breads. In winter it moves indoors to varying locations.

State Capitol   BUILDING
(📞 608-266-0382; ⊙ 8am-6pm Mon-Fri, to 4pm Sat & Sun) **FREE** The X-shaped capitol is the largest outside Washington, DC, and marks the heart of downtown. Tours are available on the hour most days, or you can go up to the observation deck on your own for a view.

Museum of Contemporary Art   MUSEUM
(☎608-257-0158; www.mmoca.org; 227 State St; ◷noon-5pm Tue-Thu, noon-8pm Fri, 10am-8pm Sat, noon-5pm Sun) FREE It's worth popping into the angular glass building to see what's on the walls. Diego Rivera? Claes Oldenburg? Exhibits change every three months or so. The museum connects to the **Overture Center for the Arts** (www.overturecenter.com; 201 State St), home to jazz, opera, dance and other performing arts.

Arboretum   GARDENS
(☎608-263-7888; http://uwarboretum.org; 1207 Seminole Hwy; ◷7am-10pm) FREE The campus' 1260-acre arboretum is dense with lilac.

Machinery Row   CYCLING
(☎608-442-5974; www.machineryrowbicycles.com; 601 Williamson St; rental per day $20; ◷9am-9pm Mon-Fri, 9am-7pm Sat, 10am-7pm Sun) It'd be a shame to leave town without taking advantage of the city's 120 miles of bike trails. Get wheels and maps at this shop, located by various trailheads.

✦ Festivals & Events

World's Largest Brat Fest   FOOD
(www.bratfest.com; ◷late May) FREE More than 209,000 bratwursts go down the hatch; carnival rides and bands provide the backdrop.

Great Taste of the Midwest Beer Festival   BEER
(www.greattaste.org; tickets $50; ◷early Aug) Tickets sell out fast for this festival where 120 craft brewers pour their elixirs.

🛏 Sleeping

Moderately priced motels can be found off I-90/I-94 (about 6 miles from the town center), off Hwy 12/18 and also along Washington Ave.

HI Madison Hostel   HOSTEL $
(☎608-441-0144; www.hiusa.org/madison; 141 S Butler St; dm $25-27, r $57-114; P @ 📶) The brightly painted, 33-bed brick house is located on a quiet street a short walk from the State Capitol. Dorms are gender segregated;

WORTH A TRIP

ODDBALL US 12

Unusual sights huddle around US 12, all within an easy northerly day trip from Madison.

Heading west out of town (take University Ave), stop first at the **National Mustard Museum** (☎800-438-6878; www.mustardmuseum.com; 7477 Hubbard Ave; ◷10am-5pm) FREE in suburban Middleton. Born of one man's ridiculously intense passion, the building houses 5200 mustards and kooky condiment memorabilia. Tongue-in-cheek humor abounds, especially if CMO (chief mustard officer) Barry Levenson is there to give you the shtick.

About 20 miles further on US 12 is the town of Prairie du Sac. It hosts the annual **Cow Chip Throw** (www.wiscowchip.com; ◷1st weekend Sep) FREE, where 800 competitors fling dried manure patties as far as the eye can see; the record is 248ft.

Seven miles onward is **Dr Evermor's Sculpture Park** (www.worldofdrevermor.com; ◷11am-5pm Thu-Mon) FREE. The doc welds old pipes, carburetors and other salvaged metal into a hallucinatory world of futuristic birds, dragons and other bizarre structures. The crowning glory is the giant, egg-domed Forevertron, once cited by *Guinness World Records* as the globe's largest scrap-metal sculpture. Finding the park entrance is tricky. Look for the Badger Army Ammunition Plant, and then a small sign leading you into a driveway across the street.

Baraboo, about 45 miles northwest of Madison, was once the winter home of the Ringling Brothers Circus. **Circus World Museum** (☎608-356-8341; circusworld.wisconsinhistory.org; 550 Water St; adult/child summer $18/8, winter $9/3.50; ◷9am-6pm summer, reduced hours winter; ♿) preserves a nostalgic collection of wagons, posters and equipment from the touring big-top heyday. In summer, admission includes clowns, animals and acrobats doing the three-ring thing.

Continue north another 12 miles to the **Wisconsin Dells** (☎800-223-3557; www.wisdells.com; ♿), a megacenter of kitschy diversions, including 21 water parks, water-skiing thrill shows and mini-golf courses. It's a jolting contrast to the natural appeal of the area, with its scenic limestone formations carved by the Wisconsin River. To appreciate the original attraction, take a boat tour or walk the trails at Mirror Lake or Devil's Lake state parks.

FISH FRIES & SUPPER CLUBS

Wisconsin has two dining traditions that you'll likely encounter when visiting the state:

Fish Fry Friday is the hallowed day of the 'fish fry.' This communal meal of beer-battered cod, French fries and coleslaw came about years ago, providing locals with a cheap meal to socialize around and celebrate the workweek's end. The convention is still going strong at many bars and restaurants, including Lakefront Brewery (p587) in Milwaukee.

Supper Club This is a type of time-warped restaurant common in the upper Midwest. Supper clubs started in the 1930s, and most retain a retro vibe. Hallmarks include a woodsy location, a radish- and carrot-laden relish tray on the table, a surf-and-turf menu and a mile-long, unironic cocktail list. See www.wisconsinsupperclub.com for more information. The Old Fashioned (p592) in Madison is a modern take on the venue (it's named after the quintessential brandy-laced supper-club drink).

linens are free. There's a kitchen and common room with DVDs. Parking is $7.

⭐ **Arbor House**   B&B $$
(☎608-238-2981; www.arbor-house.com; 3402 Monroe St; r incl breakfast $135-230; 🛜) Arbor House was a tavern back in the mid-1800s. Now it's a wind-powered, energy-efficient-appliance-using, vegetarian-breakfast-serving B&B. It's located about 3 miles southwest of the State Capitol but is accessible by public transportation. The owners will lend you mountain bikes, too.

University Inn   HOTEL $$
(☎800-279-4881, 608-285-8040; www.universityinn.org; 441 N Frances St; r $99-129; 🅿️✳️@🛜) The rooms are fine, though flowery-bedspread dowdy; the inn's greatest asset is its handy location right by State St and university action. Rates are highest at weekends.

✕ Eating & Drinking

A global smorgasbord of restaurants peppers State St amid the pizza, sandwich and cheap-beer joints; many places have inviting patios. Cruising Williamson ('Willy') St turns up cafes, dumpling bars and Lao and Thai joints. Bars stay open to 2am. Isthmus (www.thedailypage.com) is the free entertainment paper.

Food Trucks   INTERNATIONAL $
(mains $1-8; 🖊️) Madison's fleet impresses. The more traditional ones, serving barbecue, burritos, southwestern-style fare and Chinese food, ring the Capitol. Trucks ladling out more adventurous dishes – East African, Jamaican, Indonesian, vegan – huddle at the foot of State St by the campus.

⭐ **The Old Fashioned**   AMERICAN $$
(☎608-310-4545; www.theoldfashioned.com; 23 N Pinckney St; mains $8-16; ⊙7:30am-10:30pm Mon & Tue, 7:30am-2am Wed-Fri, 9am-2am Sat, 9am-10pm Sun) With its dark, woodsy decor, the Old Fashioned evokes a supper club, a type of retro eatery that's common in this state. The menu is all Wisconsin specialties, including walleye, cheese soup and sausages. It's hard to choose among the 150 types of state-brewed suds in bottles, so opt for a sampler (four or eight little glasses) from the 30 Wisconsin tap beers. The restaurant also serves $5 breakfast dishes (pancakes, eggs and bacon etc) on weekdays.

Graze   AMERICAN $$
(☎608-251-2700; www.grazemadison.com; 1 S Pinckney St; mains $11-21; ⊙7am-10pm Mon-Wed, 7am-11pm Thu-Sat, 9:30am-3pm Sun) 🖊️ Set in a glassy building with floor-to-ceiling windows and Capitol views, this green, cool-cat gastropub dishes up comfort foods such as fried chicken and waffles, mussels and *frites*, and burgers. Breakfast brings fresh-baked pastries, and lunch piles up fat sandwiches with vodka-battered cheese curds.

Himal Chuli   ASIAN $$
(☎608-251-9225; 318 State St; mains $8-15; ⊙11am-9pm Mon-Thu, 11am-10pm Fri & Sat, noon-8pm Sun; 🖊️) Cheerful and cozy Himal Chuli serves up homemade Nepali fare, including lots of vegetarian dishes.

L'Etoile   MODERN AMERICAN $$$
(☎608-251-0500; www.letoile-restaurant.com; 1 S Pinckney St; mains $36-44; ⊙from 5:30pm Mon-Fri, from 5pm Sat) 🖊️ L'Etoile started doing the farm-to-table thing more than three decades ago. It's still the best in the biz,

offering creative meat, fish and vegetable dishes, all sourced locally and served in a casually elegant room. Reserve in advance. The chef also runs Graze, the lower-priced, sustainably focused eatery that shares the building.

Memorial Union PUB
(www.union.wisc.edu/venue-muterrace.htm; 800 Langdon St; ⊘from 7am Mon-Fri, from 8am Sat & Sun; 🛜) The campus Union is Madison's gathering spot. The festive lakeside terrace pours microbrews and hosts free live music and free Monday-night films, while the indoor ice-cream shop scoops hulking cones from the university dairy.

🛍 Shopping

Fromagination FOOD
(☑608-255-2430; www.fromagination.com; 12 S Carroll St; ⊘10am-6pm Mon-Fri, 8am-5pm Sat, 11am-4pm Sun) The state's best cheese shop specializes in small-batch and hard-to-find local hunks. Browse the basket of 'orphans' by the cash register, where you can buy small quantities for $2 to $5. The shop also sells sandwiches, beer and wine.

ⓘ Information

Madison Convention & Visitors Bureau (www.visitmadison.com)

ⓘ Getting There & Around

Badger Bus (www.badgerbus.com) uses Memorial Union as its pick-up/drop-off point for trips to Milwaukee ($19, two hours), as does **Megabus** (www.megabus.com/us) for trips to Chicago (four hours) and Minneapolis (4½ hours).

Taliesin & Southern Wisconsin

This part of Wisconsin has some of the prettiest landscapes in the state, particularly the hilly southwest. Architecture fans can be unleashed at Taliesin, the Frank Lloyd Wright ubersight, and Racine, where two of his other works stand. Dairies around here cut a lot of cheese.

Racine

Racine is an unremarkable industrial town 30 miles south of Milwaukee, but it has two key Frank Lloyd Wright sights, both of which offer tours that must be prebooked. The first, the **Johnson Wax Company**

Administration Building (☑262-260-2154; www.scjohnson.com/visit; 1525 Howe St; ⊘Fri & Sat) FREE, dates from 1939 and is a magnificent space with tall, flared columns. There are three tour options, ranging from one hour to 3½ hours; departure times vary. The second is the lakeside **Wingspread** (☑262-681-3353; www.johnsonfdn.org; 33 E Four Mile Rd; ⊘9:30am-2:30pm Tue-Fri) FREE, the last and largest of Wright's Prairie houses. Tours take 45 minutes.

Green County

This pastoral area holds the nation's greatest concentration of cheesemakers, and **Green County Tourism** (www.greencounty.org) will introduce you to them. Monroe is a fine place to start sniffing. Follow your nose to **Roth Käse** (657 2nd St; ⊘9am-6pm Mon-Fri, 10am-5pm Sat & Sun), a store and factory where you can watch cheesemakers in action from the observation deck (weekday mornings only) and delve into the 'bargain bin' for hunks. Bite into a fresh limburger-and-raw-onion sandwich at **Baumgartner's** (www.baumgartnercheese.com; 1023 16th Ave; sandwiches $4-7; ⊘8am-11pm), an old Swiss tavern on the town square. At night, catch a flick at the local drive-in movie theater, and then climb into bed at **Inn Serendipity** (☑608-329-7056; www.innserendipity.com; 7843 County Rd P; r incl breakfast $110-125), a two-room, wind-and-solar-powered B&B on a 5-acre organic farm in Browntown, about 10 miles west of Monroe.

For more on local dairy producers and plant tours, pick up, or download, **A Traveler's Guide to America's Dairyland** (www.eatwisconsincheese.com) map.

Spring Green

Forty miles west of Madison and 3 miles south of the small town of Spring Green, **Taliesin** was the home of Frank Lloyd Wright for most of his life and is the site of his architectural school. It's now a major pilgrimage destination for fans and followers. The house was built in 1903, the Hillside Home School in 1932, and the **visitor center** (☑608-588-7900; www.taliesinpreservation.org; Hwy 23; ⊘9am-5:30pm May-Oct) in 1953. A wide range of guided tours ($16 to $80) cover various parts of the complex; reserve in advance for the lengthier ones. The one-hour Hillside Tour ($16) provides a nice introduction to Wright's work.

A few miles south of Taliesin is the **House on the Rock** (☑608-935-3639; www.thehouseontherock.com; 5754 Hwy 23; adult/child $12.50/7.50; ☉9am-6pm May-Aug, to 5pm Aug–mid-Nov & mid-Mar–May, closed mid-Nov–mid-Mar), one of Wisconsin's busiest attractions. Alex Jordan built the structure atop a rock column in 1959 (some say as an 'up yours' to neighbor Frank Lloyd Wright). He then stuffed the house to mind-blowing proportions with wonderments, including the world's largest carousel, whirring music machines, freaky dolls and crazed folk art. The house is broken into three parts, each with its own tour. Visitors with stamina (and about four hours to kill) can experience the whole shebang for adult/child $28.50/15.50.

Spring Green has a B&B in town and six motels strung along Hwy 14, north of town. Small **Usonian Inn** (☑877-876-6426; www.usonianinn.com; E 5116 Hwy 14; r $85-135; ✴🖂) was designed by a Wright student. Check www.springgreen.com for more options.

Chomp sandwiches or inventive specials like sweet-potato stew at **Spring Green General Store** (www.springgreengeneralstore.com; 137 S Albany St; mains $5-8; ☉9am-6pm Mon-Fri, 8am-6pm Sat, 8am-4pm Sun).

The **American Players Theatre** (☑608-588-2361; www.americanplayers.org) stages classical productions at an outdoor amphitheater by the Wisconsin River.

Along the Mississippi River

The Mississippi River forms most of Wisconsin's western border, and alongside it run some of the most scenic sections of the **Great River Road** (www.wigreatriverroad.org) – the designated route that follows Old Man River from Minnesota to the Gulf of Mexico.

From Madison, head west on US 18. You'll hit the River Rd (aka Hwy 35) at **Prairie du Chien**. North of town, the hilly riverside wends through the scene of the final battle in the bloody Black Hawk War. Historic markers tell part of the story, which finished at the Battle of Bad Ax when Native American men, women and children were massacred trying to flee across the Mississippi.

At Genoa, Hwy 56 leads inland for 20 miles to the trout-fishing mecca of **Viroqua** (www.viroquatourism.com), a pretty little town surrounded by organic farms and distinctive round barns. Pop into **Viroqua Food Cooperative** (www.viroquafood.coop; 609 Main

St; ☉7am-9pm) to meet farmers and munch their wares.

Back riverside and 18 miles upstream, **La Crosse** (www.explorelacrosse.com) has a historic center with restaurants and pubs. **Grandad Bluff** offers grand views of the river. It's east of town along Main St (which becomes Bliss Rd); follow Bliss Rd up the hill and then turn right on Grandad Bluff Rd. The **World's Largest Six-Pack** (3rd St S) is also in town. The 'cans' are actually storage tanks for City Brewery and hold enough beer to provide one person with a six-pack a day for 3351 years (or so the sign says).

Door County & Eastern Wisconsin

Rocky, lighthouse-dotted Door County draws crowds in summer, while Green Bay draws crazed football fans in the freakin' freezing winter.

Green Bay

Green Bay (www.greenbay.com) is a modest industrial town best known as the fabled 'frozen tundra' where the Green Bay Packers win Super Bowls. The franchise is unique as the only community-owned nonprofit team in the NFL; perhaps pride in ownership is what makes the fans so die-hard (and also makes them wear foam-rubber cheese wedges on their heads).

While tickets are nearly impossible to obtain, you can always get into the spirit by joining a pre-game tailgate party. The generous flow of alcohol has led to Green Bay's reputation as a 'drinking town with a football problem.' On nongame days, visit **Green Bay Packer Hall of Fame** (☑920-569-7512; www.lambeaufield.com; adult/child $10/5; ☉9am-6pm Mon-Sat, 10am-5pm Sun) at Lambeau Field, which is indeed packed with memorabilia and movies that'll intrigue any pigskin fan.

The **National Railroad Museum** (☑920-437-7623; www.nationalrrmuseum.org; 2285 S Broadway; adult/child $9/6.50; ☉9am-5pm Mon-Sat, 11am-5pm Sun, closed Mon Jan-Mar) features some of the biggest locomotives ever to haul freight into Green Bay's vast yards; train rides ($2) are offered in summer.

Bare-bones **Bay Motel** (☑920-494-3441; www.baymotelgreenbay.com; 1301 S Military Ave; r $52-75; 🖂) is located a mile from Lambeau Field. **Hinterland** (☑920-438-8050;

www.hinterlandbeer.com; 313 Dousman St; ⊘from 4pm Mon-Sat) gastropub brings a touch of rustic swankiness to beer drinkers.

Door County

With its rocky coastline, picturesque lighthouses, cherry orchards and small 19th-century villages, you have to admit that Door County is pretty damn lovely. The area spreads across a narrow peninsula jutting 75 miles into Lake Michigan, and visitors usually loop around on the county's two highways. Hwy 57 runs beside Lake Michigan and goes through Jacksonport and Baileys Harbor; this is known as the more scenic 'quiet side.' Hwy 42 borders Green Bay and passes through (from south to north) Egg Harbor, Fish Creek, Ephraim and Sister Bay; this side is more action oriented. Only about half the businesses stay open from November to April.

◉ Sights & Activities

Parkland blankets the county. Bayside **Peninsula State Park** is the largest, with bluffside hiking and biking trails and Nicolet Beach for swimming, kayaking and sailing (equipment rentals available on site). In winter, cross-country skiers and snowshoers take over the trails. On the lake side, secluded **Newport State Park** offers trails, backcountry camping and solitude. **Whitefish Dunes State Park** has sandscapes and

---

WORTH A TRIP

WASHINGTON ISLAND & ROCK ISLAND

From Door County's tip near Gills Rock, daily **ferries** (☑920-847-2546; www.wisferry.com; Northport Pier) go every half hour to **Washington Island** (round-trip adult/child/bike/car $13/7/4/26), which has 700 Scandinavian descendants, a couple of museums, beaches, bike rentals and carefree roads for cycling. Accommodations and camping are available. More remote is lovely **Rock Island**, a state park with no cars or bikes at all. It's a wonderful place for hiking, swimming and camping. Get there via the **Karfi ferry** (www.wisferry.com), which departs Jackson Harbor on Washington Island (round-trip adult/child $11/5).

---

a wide beach (beware of riptides). Adjacent **Cave Point Park** is known for its sea caves and kayaking.

Bay Shore Outfitters OUTDOORS
(☑920-854-9220; www.kayakdoorcounty.com; Sister Bay) Rents kayaks, stand-up paddleboards and winter gear and offers tours from locations in Sister Bay and Ephraim.

Nor Door Sport & Cyclery OUTDOORS
(☑920-868-2275; www.nordoorsports.com; Fish Creek) Nor Door rents bikes and snow shoes near the entrance to Peninsula State Park.

🛏 Sleeping & Eating

The bay side has the most lodgings. Prices listed are for July and August, the peak season; many places have minimum-stay requirements. Local restaurants often host a 'fish boil,' a regional specialty started by Scandinavian lumberjacks, in which whitefish, potatoes and onions are cooked in a fiery cauldron. Finish with Door's famous cherry pie.

Julie's Park Cafe and Motel MOTEL $
(☑920-868-2999; www.juliesmotel.com; Fish Creek; r $85-106; ▣ ☎) A great low-cost option located beside Peninsula State Park.

Peninsula State Park CAMPGROUND $
(☑920-868-3258; Fish Creek; tent & RV sites $15-17) Holds nearly 500 amenity-laden campsites.

Egg Harbor Lodge INN $$
(☑920-868-3115; www.eggharborlodge.com; Egg Harbor; r $160-200; ▣☎▧) All rooms have a water view and free bike use.

Village Cafe AMERICAN $
(☑920-868-3342; www.villagecafe-doorcounty.com; Egg Harbor; mains $7-10; ⊘7am-8pm; ▣) Delicious all-day breakfast dishes, plus sandwiches and burgers.

Wild Tomato PIZZERIA $$
(☑920-868-3095; www.wildtomatopizza.com; Fish Creek; mains $8-15; ⊘11am-10pm) Join the crowds indoors and out munching pizzas from the stone, wood-fired ovens. A lengthy list of craft beers help wash it down. It's extremely gluten-free friendly.

ℹ Information

Door County Visitors Bureau (☑800-527-3529; www.doorcounty.com) Special-interest brochures on art galleries, cycling and lighthouses.

Apostle Islands & Northern Wisconsin

The north is a thinly populated region of forests and lakes, where folks paddle and fish in summer, and ski and snowmobile in winter. The windswept Apostle Islands steal the show.

Northwoods & Lakelands

Nicolet National Forest is a vast wooded district ideal for outdoor activities. The simple crossroads of **Langlade** is a center for white-water river adventures. **Bear Paw Resort** (715-882-3502; www.bearpawoutdoors.com; cabins $72-85;) rents mountain bikes and kayaks, and provides full-day paddling lessons that include a trip on the river (per person $99). It also provides cozy cabins where you can dry off, get warm and celebrate your accomplishments in the on-site pub.

North on Hwy 13, folk artist and retired lumberjack Fred Smith's **Concrete Park** (www.friendsoffredsmith.org; sunrise-sunset) **FREE** in Phillips is extraordinary, with 200-plus whimsical life-size sculptures.

West on Hwy 70, **Chequamegon National Forest** offers exceptional mountain biking with 300 miles of off-road trails. The **Chequamegon Area Mountain Bike Association** (www.cambatrails.org) has trail maps and bike rental information. The season culminates in mid-September with the **Chequamegon Fat Tire Festival** (www.cheqfattire.com), when 1700 strong-legged men and women pedal 40 grueling miles through the woods. The town of **Hayward** (www.haywardareachamber.com) makes a good base.

Apostle Islands

The 21 rugged Apostle Islands, floating in Lake Superior and freckling Wisconsin's northern tip, are a state highlight. Jump off from **Bayfield** (www.bayfield.org), a humming resort town with hilly streets, Victorian-era buildings, apple orchards and nary a fast-food restaurant in sight.

The **Apostle Islands National Lakeshore visitors center** (715-779-3397; www.nps.gov/apis; 410 Washington Ave; 8am-4:30pm daily Jun-Sep, Mon-Fri Oct-May) has camping permits (per night $10) and paddling and hiking information. The forested islands have no facilities, and walking is the only way to get around.

SCENIC DRIVE: HIGHWAY 13

After departing Bayfield, Hwy 13 takes a fine route around the Lake Superior shore, past the Ojibwa community of **Red Cliff** and the Apostle Islands' mainland segment, which has a beach. Tiny **Cornucopia**, looking every bit like a seaside village, has great sunsets. The road runs on through a timeless countryside of forest and farm, reaching US 2 for the final miles back to civilization at Superior.

Various companies offer seasonal boat trips around the islands, and kayaking is very popular. Try **Living Adventure** (715-779-9503; www.livingadventure.com; Hwy 13; half/full-day tour $59/99; Jun-Sep) for a guided paddle through arches and sea caves; beginners are welcome. If you prefer a motor to power your explorations, climb aboard a vessel with **Apostle Islands Cruises** (715-779-3925; www.apostleisland.com; mid-May–mid-Oct). The 'grand tour' departs at 10am from Bayfield's City Dock for a three-hour narrated trip past sea caves and lighthouses (adult/child $40/24). A glass-bottom boat goes out to view shipwrecks at 2pm.

Inhabited **Madeline Island** (www.madelineisland.com), a fine day trip, is reached by a 20-minute **ferry** (715-747-2051; www.madferry.com) from Bayfield (round-trip adult/child/bicycle/car $13/7/7/24). Its walkable village of La Pointe has some mid-priced places to stay, and restaurants. Bus tours are available, and you can rent bikes and mopeds – everything is near the ferry dock. **Big Bay State Park** (715-747-6425; tent & RV sites $15-17, vehicle $10) has a beach and trails.

Back in Bayfield, there are loads of B&Bs and inns, but reserve ahead in summer; see www.bayfield.org for options. Most rooms at no-frills **Seagull Bay Motel** (715-779-5558; www.seagullbay.com; 325 S 7th St; r $75-105;) have decks; ask for a lake view. Going upscale, **Pinehurst Inn** (877-499-7651; www.pinehurstinn.com; 83645 Hwy 13; r incl breakfast $139-229;) is a carbon-neutral, solar-heated, eight-room B&B.

Ecoconscious **Big Water Cafe** (www.bigwatercoffee.com; 117 Rittenhouse Ave; mains $5-10; 6:30am-7pm summer, to 4pm winter) serves sandwiches, local farmstead cheeses and area microbrews. Kitschy, flamingo-themed

Maggie's (☑715-779-5641; www.maggies-bayfield.com; 257 Manypenny Ave; mains $7-16; ⊙11:30am-9pm Sun-Thu, to 10pm Fri & Sat) is the place to sample local lake trout and white-fish; there are pizza and burgers too.

The **Big Top Chautauqua** (☑888-244-8368; www.bigtop.org) is a major regional summer event that includes big-name concerts and musical theater.

MINNESOTA

Is Minnesota really the land of 10,000 lakes, as it's so often advertised? You betcha. Actually, in typically modest style, the state has undermarketed itself – there are 11,842 lakes. Which is great news for travelers. Intrepid outdoorsfolk can wet their paddles in the Boundary Waters, where nighttime brings a blanket of stars and the lullaby of wolf howls. Those wanting to get further off the beaten path can journey to Voyageurs National Park, where there's more water than roadway. If that all seems too far-flung, stick to the Twin Cities of Minneapolis and St Paul, where you can't swing a moose without hitting something cool or cultural. And for those looking for middle ground – a cross between the big city and big woods – the dramatic, freighter-filled port of Duluth beckons.

ℹ️ Information

Minnesota Highway Conditions (☑511; www.511mn.org)

Minnesota Office of Tourism (☑888-868-7476; www.exploreminnesota.com)

Minnesota State Park Information (☑888-646-6367; www.dnr.state.mn.us) Park entry requires a vehicle permit (per day/year $5/25). Campsites cost $12 to $28; reservations (☑866-857-2757; www.stayatmnparks.com; fee $8.50) accepted.

Minneapolis

Minneapolis is the biggest and artiest town on the prairie, with all the trimmings of progressive prosperity – swank art museums, rowdy rock clubs, organic and ethnic eateries and edgy theaters. It's always happenin', even in winter. But there's no attitude to go along with the abundance. It's the kind of place where homeless people are treated kindly at coffee shops, where the buses are kept immaculately clean, and where public workers tell everyone to 'Have a nice day' come rain or shine (or snow). The city is 'Minnesota Nice' in action.

History

Timber was the city's first boom industry, and water-powered sawmills rose along the Mississippi River in the mid-1800s. Wheat from the prairies also needed to be processed, so flour mills churned into the next big business. The population boomed in the late 19th century with mass immigration, especially from Scandinavia and Germany. Today Minneapolis' Nordic heritage is evident, whereas twin city St Paul is more German and Irish-Catholic.

⊙ Sights & Activities

The Mississippi River flows northeast of downtown. Despite the name, Uptown is actually southwest of downtown, with Hennepin Ave as its main axis. Minneapolis' twin city, St Paul, is 10 miles east.

Most attractions are closed Monday; many stay open late on Thursday.

MINNESOTA FACTS

Nicknames North Star State, Gopher State

Population 5.4 million

Area 86,940 sq miles

Capital city St Paul (population 291,000)

Other cities Minneapolis (population 393,000)

Sales tax 6.88%

Birthplace of Author F Scott Fitzgerald (1896–1940), songwriter Bob Dylan (b 1941), filmmakers Joel Coen (b 1954) and Ethan Coen (b 1957)

Home of Lumberjack legend Paul Bunyan, Spam, walleye fish, Hmong and Somali immigrants

Politics Leans Democratic

Famous for Niceness, funny accents, snowy weather, 10,000 lakes

Official muffin Blueberry

Driving distances Minneapolis to Duluth 153 miles, Minneapolis to Boundary Waters 245 miles

Downtown & Loring Park

Nicollet Mall STREET
Nicollet Mall is the pedestrian-friendly portion of Nicollet Ave in the heart of downtown, and is dense with stores, bars and restaurants. It's perhaps most famous as the spot where Mary Tyler Moore of '70s TV fame threw her hat into the air during the show's opening sequence. A cheesy **MTM statue** (7th St S & Nicollet Mall) depicts our girl doing just that. A **farmers market** (www.mplsfarmersmarket.com; ⊙6am-6pm) takes over the mall on Thursdays from May to November.

★**Minneapolis Sculpture Garden** GARDENS
(726 Vineland Pl; ⊙6am-midnight) FREE The 11-acre garden, studded with contemporary works such as the oft-photographed *Spoonbridge & Cherry* by Claes Oldenburg, sits beside the Walker Art Center. The Cowles Conservatory, abloom with exotic hothouse flowers, is also on the grounds. The garden connects to attractive Loring Park by a sculptural pedestrian bridge over I-94.

★**Walker Art Center** MUSEUM
(☑612-375-7622; www.walkerart.org; 725 Vineland Pl; adult/child $12/free, Thu evening & 1st Sat of month admission free; ⊙11am-5pm Tue, Wed & Fri-Sun, to 9pm Thu) The first-class center has a strong permanent collection of 20th-century art and photography, including big-name US painters and great US pop art.

Riverfront District

At the north edge of downtown at the foot of Portland Ave is the **St Anthony Falls Heritage Trail**, a recommended 2-mile path that provides both interesting history (placards dot the route) and the city's best access to the banks of the Mississippi River. View the cascading **St Anthony Falls** from the car-free **Stone Arch Bridge**. On the north side of the river, Main St SE has a stretch of redeveloped buildings housing restaurants and bars. From here you can walk down to **Water Power Park** and feel the river's frothy spray. Pick up a free trail map at the Mill City Museum.

Definitely head next door to the cobalt-blue Guthrie Theater (p603) and make your way up to its **Endless Bridge**, a cantilevered walkway overlooking the river. You don't need a theater ticket, as it's intended as a public space – though see a show if you can as the Guthrie is one of the Mid-west's finest companies. **Gold Medal Park** spirals next door.

Mill City Museum MUSEUM
(☑612-341-7555; www.millcitymuseum.org; 704 2nd St S; adult/child $11/6; ⊙10am-5pm Tue-Sat, noon-5pm Sun, open daily Jul & Aug) The building is indeed a former mill, and highlights include a ride inside an eight-story grain elevator (the 'Flour Tower'), Betty Crocker exhibits and a baking lab. It's not terribly exciting unless you're really into milling history. The **Mill City Farmer's Market** (www.millcityfarmersmarket.org; ⊙8am-1pm Sat mid-May–late Oct) takes place in the museum's attached train shed; cooking demos fire up at 10am.

Northeast

Once a working-class Eastern European neighborhood, Northeast (so named because of its position to the river) is where urbanites and artists now work and play. They appreciate the dive bars pouring microbrews along with Pabst, and the boutiques selling ecogifts next to companies grinding sausage. Hundreds of craftsfolk and galleries fill historic industrial buildings. They fling open their doors the first Thursday of each month when the **Northeast Minneapolis Arts Association** (www.nemaa.org) sponsors a gallery walk. Heady streets include 4th St NE and 13th Ave NE.

University Area

The **University of Minnesota**, by the river southeast of Minneapolis' center, is one of the USA's largest campuses, with over 50,000 students. Most of the campus is in the East Bank neighborhood. Dinkytown, based at 14th Ave SE and 4th St SE, is dense with student cafes and bookshops. A small part of the university is on the West Bank of the Mississippi River, near the intersection of 4th St S and Riverside Ave. This area has a few restaurants, some student hang-outs and a big Somali community.

★**Weisman Art Museum** MUSEUM
(☑612-625-9494; www.weisman.umn.edu; 333 E River Rd; ⊙10am-5pm Tue-Fri, to 8pm Wed, 11am-5pm Sat & Sun) FREE The Weisman, which occupies a swooping silver structure by architect Frank Gehry, is a uni (and city) highlight. It recently reopened with double the space and five new, airy galleries for American art, ceramics and works on paper.

Minneapolis

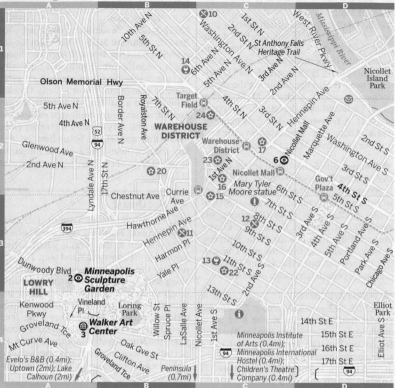

Minneapolis

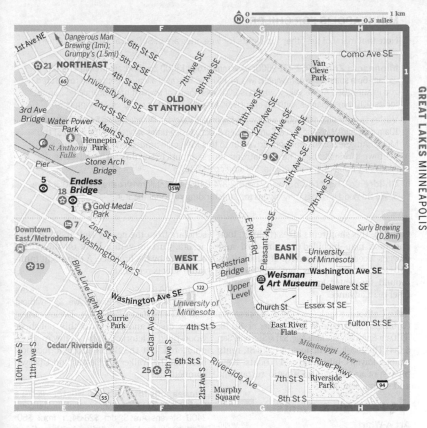

Uptown, Lyn-Lake & Whittier

These three neighborhoods are south of downtown.

Uptown, based around the intersection of Hennepin Ave and Lake St, is a punk-yuppie collision of shops and restaurants that stays lively until late. Lyn-Lake abuts Uptown to the east and sports a similar urban-cool vibe; it's centered on Lyndale and Lake Sts. (Get the name?)

Uptown is a convenient jump-off point to the 'Chain of Lakes' – Lake Calhoun, Lake of the Isles, Lake Harriet, Cedar Lake and Brownie Lake. Paved cycling paths (which double as cross-country ski trails in winter) meander around the five lakes, where you can go boating in summer or ice skating in winter.

Lake Calhoun sits at the foot of Lake St, where there are amenities galore. Further around Lake Calhoun, Thomas Beach is popular for swimming. Cedar Lake's freewheeling Hidden Beach (aka East Cedar Beach) used to bring out the nudists, though it's mostly clothed folks lolling about these days.

Minneapolis Institute of Arts MUSEUM
(📞612-870-3131; www.artsmia.org; 2400 3rd Ave S; ⊙10am-5pm Tue-Sat, 10am-9pm Thu, 11am-5pm Sun) FREE This museum is a huge treasure trove housing a veritable history of art. The modern and contemporary collections astonish, while the Prairie School and Asian galleries are also highlights. Brochures at the front desk can help you winnow it down to the must-sees if you're short on time. The museum is 1 mile due south of the convention center via 3rd Ave S.

Calhoun Rental CYCLING
(📞612-827-8231; www.calhounbikerental.com; 1622 W Lake St; per half/full day $25/35; ⊙10am-7pm Mon-Fri, 9am-8pm Sat, 10am-8pm Sun Apr-Oct) In Uptown, a couple blocks west of Lake

MINNEAPOLIS FOR CHILDREN

Note that many of the other top sights for wee ones are in St Paul, at the Mall of America and Fort Snelling.

Minnesota Zoo (☑ 952-431-9500; www.mnzoo.org; 13000 Zoo Blvd; adult/child $18/12; ☺ 9am-6pm summer, to 4pm winter; ⓘ) You'll have to travel a way to get to the respected zoo in suburban Apple Valley, which is 20 miles south of town. It has naturalistic habitats for its 400-plus species, with an emphasis on cold-climate creatures. Parking is $7.

Valleyfair (☑ 952-445-7600; www.valleyfair.com; 1 Valleyfair Dr; adult/child $44/30; ☺ from 10am daily mid-May–Aug, Sat & Sun only Sep & Oct, closing times vary; ⓘ) If the rides at the Mall of America aren't enough, drive out to this full-scale amusement park 25 miles southwest in Shakopee. The animatronic dinosaur park ($5 extra) is a big hit. Save money by booking tickets online. Parking costs $12.

Children's Theatre Company (☑ 612-874-0400; www.childrenstheatre.org; 2400 3rd Ave S; ⓘ) So good it won a Tony award for 'outstanding regional theater.'

Calhoun, this shop rents bikes (helmet, lock and bike map included); credit card and driver's license are required. It also offers two- to four-hour cycling tours ($39 to $49) around the water Friday through Sunday; reserve in advance.

Lake Calhoun Kiosk   WATER SPORTS
(☑ 612-823-5765; base of Lake St; per hr $11-18; ☺ 10am-8pm daily late May-Aug, Sat & Sun only Sep & Oct) The kiosk, at the foot of Lake St, rents canoes, kayaks, bikes and pedal boats. It's a busy spot as there's also a patio restaurant and sailing school here.

⭐ Festivals & Events

Art-A-Whirl   MUSIC
(www.nemaa.org; ☺ mid-May) The Northeast's weekend-long, rock-and-roll gallery crawl heralds the arrival of spring.

Minneapolis Aquatennial   CULTURAL
(www.aquatennial.com; ☺ mid-Jul) Ten days celebrating the ubiquitous lakes via parades, beach bashes and fireworks.

Holidazzle   CULTURAL
(www.holidazzle.com; ☺ Dec) Parades, lights and lots of good cheer downtown throughout December.

🛌 Sleeping

B&Bs offer the best value – they have budget prices but are solidly midrange in quality. Tax adds 13.4% to prices.

Wales House   B&B $
(☑ 612-331-3931; www.waleshouse.com; 1115 5th St SE; r incl breakfast $80, without bath $70; ⓟ❄☎) This cheery 10-bedroom B&B often houses

scholars from the nearby University of Minnesota. Curl up with a book on the porch, or lounge by the fireplace. A two-night minimum stay is required.

Evelo's B&B   B&B $
(☑ 612-374-9656; 2301 Bryant Ave S; r without bath incl breakfast $75-95; ☎) Evelo's three rooms creak and charm in this polished-wood-filled Victorian home. They're close quartered, but the B&B's strategic location between the Walker Art Center and Uptown compensates.

Minneapolis International Hostel   HOSTEL $
(☑ 612-522-5000; www.minneapolishostel.com; 2400 Stevens Ave S; dm $28-34, r from $60; ❄@☎) A cool old building with antique furniture and wood floors, and the location beside the Minneapolis Institute of Arts is excellent. But it's also not very well tended. The rooms come in a variety of configurations, from a 15-bed male dorm to private rooms with en suite bath.

Aloft   HOTEL $$
(☑ 612-455-8400; www.alofthotels.com/minneapolis; 900 Washington Ave S; r $139-189; ⓟ❄@ ☎✲) Aloft's compact, efficiently designed, industrial-toned rooms draw a younger clientele. The clubby lobby has board games, a cocktail lounge and 24-hour snacks. There's a tiny pool and decent fitness room. Parking costs $15.

🍴 Eating

Minneapolis has ripened into a rich dining scene known for its many restaurants that use local, sustainable ingredients.

✕ Downtown & Northeast

Nicollet Mall is loaded with eateries.

Hell's Kitchen
AMERICAN $$

(☑612-332-4700; www.hellskitcheninc.com; 80 9th St S; mains $10-20; ☺6:30am-10pm Mon-Fri, from 7:30am Sat & Sun; ☎) Descend the stairs to Hell's devilish lair, where spirited waitstaff bring you uniquely Minnesotan foods, like the walleye bacon-lettuce-tomato sandwich, bison burger and lemon-ricotta hotcakes. It morphs from a restaurant into a club with DJs late on weekend nights. Upstairs there's a delicious bakery and coffee shop.

Butcher & the Boar
AMERICAN $$$

(☑612-238-8887; www.butcherandtheboar.com; 1121 Hennepin Ave; mains $25-32; ☺5pm-midnight; ☎) The coppery, candlelit room is carnivore nirvana. Get your carving knife ready for wild-boar ham with country butter, rabbit pate with pickled cherries, chicken-fried veal sausage and many more house-crafted meats. Sampler plates are the way to go. The 30 taps flow with regional brews, backed up by a lengthy bourbon list. Reservations essential.

Bar La Grassa
ITALIAN $$$

(☑612-333-3837; www.barlagrassa.com; 800 Washington Ave N; pasta $12-24, mains $16-35; ☺5pm-midnight Mon-Thu, to 1am Fri & Sat, to 10pm Sun) Chef Isaac Becker won the 2011 James Beard award for 'best in the midwest,' so expect great things from the small plates menu of fresh pastas, bruschetta and *secondi*.

✕ University Area

Low-priced eateries cluster in the campus area by Washington Ave and Oak St.

Al's Breakfast
BREAKFAST $

(☑612-331-9991; 413 14th Ave SE; mains $4-8; ☺6am-1pm Mon-Sat, 9am-1pm Sun) The ultimate hole in the wall: 14 stools at a tiny counter. Whenever a customer comes in, everyone picks up their plates and scoots down to make room for the newcomer. Fruit-full pancakes are the big crowd-pleaser. Cash only.

✕ Uptown, Lyn-Lake & Whittier

Vietnamese, Greek, African and other ethnic restaurants line Nicollet Ave S between Franklin Ave (near the Minneapolis Institute of Arts) and 28th St – the stretch is known as 'Eat Street.' Lake St in Uptown is a rich vein for stylish bars and cafes.

★ Bryant-Lake Bowl
AMERICAN $$

(☑612-825-3737; www.bryantlakebowl.com; 810 W Lake St; mains $9-14; ☺8am-12:30am; ☎☑) A workingman's bowling alley meets epicurean food at the BLB. Biscuit-and-gravy breakfasts, artisanal cheese plates, mock-duck rolls and cornmeal-crusted walleye strips melt in the mouth. A long list of local beers washes it all down. The on-site theater always has something intriguing and odd going on too.

Peninsula
ASIAN $$

(☑612-871-8282; www.peninsulamalaysiancuisine.com; 2608 Nicollet Ave S; mains $9-15; ☺11am-10pm Sun-Thu, to 11pm Fri & Sat; ☑) Malaysian dishes – including *achat* (tangy vegetable salad in peanut dressing), red-curry hot pot, spicy crab and fish in banana leaves – rock the palate in this contemporary restaurant.

🍷 Drinking

Bars stay open until 2am. Happy hour typically lasts from 3pm to 6pm.

Brit's Pub
PUB

(www.britspub.com; 1110 Nicollet Mall; ☺from 11am) A lawn-bowling green on the roof, plus Brit's sweeping selection of Scotch, port and beer, are sure to unleash skills you never knew you had.

TAP ROOM BOOM

In 2011 Minnesota passed a law that allowed brewers to open tap rooms on site, and since then the concept has exploded throughout the Twin Cities. Excellent ones to try for beer fresh from the tank:

Fulton Beer (www.fultonbeer.com; 414 6th Ave N; ⊗3-10pm Wed-Fri, noon-10pm Sat) There's usually a fab pale ale and red ale among the selection that you sip at communal picnic tables in the warehouse. It's a few blocks from the baseball stadium and fills up on game days. Food trucks hang out in front.

Dangerous Man Brewing (www.dangerousmanbrewing.com; 1300 2nd St NE; ⊗4-10pm Tue-Thu, 3pm-midnight Fri, noon-midnight Sat) Pours strong, European-style beers. You're welcome to bring in your own food. It's one of many tap rooms colonizing the Northeast neighborhood.

Surly Brewing (www.surlybrewing.com; Malcolm Ave & 5th St SE) One of the biggest brewers, and it's not kidding around: it hired the architects who designed the Guthrie Theater to build a huge brewery and bar in southeast Minneapolis' Prospect Park neighborhood. It's scheduled to open in 2014.

Grumpy's   BAR
(www.grumpys-bar.com/nordeast; 2200 4th St NE; ⊗from 2pm Mon-Fri, from 11am Sat & Sun) Grumpy's is the Northeast's classic dive, with cheap (but good) beer and an outdoor patio. Sample the specialty 'hot dish' on Tuesdays for $1.

☆ Entertainment

With its large student population and thriving performing-arts scene, Minneapolis has an active nightlife. Check *Vita.MN* and *City Pages* for current goings on.

Live Music

Minneapolis rocks; everyone's in a band, it seems. Acts such as Prince and post-punkers Hüsker Dü and the Replacements cut their teeth here.

First Avenue & 7th St Entry   LIVE MUSIC
(www.first-avenue.com; 701 1st Ave N) This is the bedrock of Minneapolis' music scene, and it still pulls in top bands and big crowds. Check out the exterior stars; they're all bands that have graced the stage.

Nye's Polonaise Room   LIVE MUSIC
(www.nyespolonaise.com; 112 E Hennepin Ave) The World's Most Dangerous Polka Band lets loose Friday and Saturday. It's smashing fun, and enhanced if you find yourself an old-timer to twirl you around the room.

Triple Rock Social Club   LIVE MUSIC
(www.triplerocksocialclub.com; 629 Cedar Ave) Triple Rock is a popular punk-alternative club.

Lee's Liquor Lounge   LIVE MUSIC
(www.leesliquorlounge.com; 101 Glenwood Ave) Rockabilly and country-tinged alt bands twang here.

Theater & Performing Arts

The city hosts a vibrant theater scene. The neon-lit Hennepin Theater District (www.hennepintheatretrust.org) consists of several historic venues on Hennepin Ave between 6th and 10th Sts that host big touring shows.

Guthrie Theater   THEATER
(☑612-377-2224; www.guthrietheater.org; 818 2nd St S) This is Minneapolis' top-gun theater troupe, with the jumbo facility to prove it. Unsold 'rush' tickets go on sale 30 minutes before showtime for $15 to $35 (cash only). Download free audio tours from the website for self-guided jaunts around the funky building.

Brave New Workshop Theatre   THEATER
(☑612-332-6620; www.bravenewworkshop.com; 824 Hennepin Ave) An established venue for musical comedy, revue and satire.

Orchestra Hall   CLASSICAL
(☑612-371-5656; www.minnesotaorchestra.org; 1111 Nicollet Mall) Superb acoustics for concerts by the acclaimed Minnesota Symphony Orchestra.

Sports

Minnesotans love their sports teams. Note that ice hockey happens in St Paul.

Target Field   BASEBALL
(www.minnesotatwins.com; 3rd Ave N btwn 5th & 7th Sts N) The new stadium for the Twins pro baseball team is notable for its beyond-the-norm, locally focused food and drink.

Hubert H Humphrey Metrodome   FOOTBALL
(www.vikings.com; 900 5th St S) The Vikings pro football team passes in the marshmallow-like 'Dome.

Target Center   BASKETBALL
(www.nba.com/timberwolves; 600 1st Ave N) This is where the Timberwolves pro basketball team plays.

❶ Information

City Pages (www.citypages.com) Weekly entertainment freebie.

Fairview/University of Minnesota Medical Center (☑ 612-273-6402; 2450 Riverside Ave)

Minneapolis Convention & Visitors Association (www.minneapolis.org) Coupons, maps, guides and bike-route info online.

Minneapolis Public Library (www.hclib.org; 300 Nicollet Mall; ⊙10am-8pm Tue & Thu, 10am-6pm Wed, Fri & Sat, noon-5pm Sun; 🛜) Mod facility with free internet and wi-fi (plus a great used bookstore).

Pioneer Press (www.twincities.com) St Paul's daily.

Star Tribune (www.startribune.com) Minneapolis' daily.

Vita.mn (www.vita.mn) The *Star Tribune*'s weekly entertainment freebie.

❶ Getting There & Around

AIR

The **Minneapolis-St Paul International Airport** (MSP; www.mspairport.com) is between the two cities to the south. It's the home of Delta Airlines, which operates several direct flights to/from Europe.

The Blue Line light-rail service (regular/rush-hour fare $1.75/2.25, 25 minutes) is the cheapest way into Minneapolis. Bus 54 (regular/rush-hour fare $1.75/2.25, 25 minutes) goes to St Paul. Taxis cost around $45.

BICYCLE

Minneapolis hovers near the top of rankings for best bike city in the US. The bicycle-share program **Nice Ride** (www.niceridemn.org; ⊙Apr-Oct) has 1500 bikes in 170 self-serve kiosks around the Twin Cities. Users pay a subscription (per day/year $6/65) online or at the kiosk, plus a small fee per half-hour of use (with the first half-hour free). Bikes can be returned to any kiosk. Traditional rentals work better if you're

riding for recreation versus transportation purposes. See the **Minneapolis Bicycle Program** (www.ci.minneapolis.mn.us/bicycles) for rental shops and trail maps.

BUS

Greyhound (☑ 612-371-3325; 950 Hawthorne Ave) runs frequent buses to Milwaukee (seven hours), Chicago (nine hours) and Duluth (three hours).

Megabus (www.megabus.com/us) runs express to Milwaukee (six hours) and Chicago (eight hours), often for lower fares than Greyhound. It departs from both downtown and the university; check the website for exact locations.

PUBLIC TRANSPORTATION

Metro Transit (www.metrotransit.org; regular/rush-hour fare $1.75/2.25) runs the excellent Blue Line light-rail service between downtown and the Mall of America. The new Green Line is slated to begin running in mid-2014, connecting downtown Minneapolis to downtown St Paul. Until then, express bus 94 (regular/rush-hour fare $2.25/3) plies the route between cities; it departs from 6th St N's south side, just west of Hennepin Ave. A day pass ($6) is available from any rail station or bus driver.

TAXI

Call **Yellow Cab** (☑ 612-824-4444).

TRAIN

Amtrak chugs in to the newly restored **Union Depot** (www.uniondepot.org; 214 E 4th St; 🛜) in St Paul. Trains go daily to Chicago (eight hours) and Seattle (37 hours).

St Paul

Smaller and quieter than its twin city Minneapolis, St Paul has retained more of a historic character. Walk through F Scott Fitzgerald's old stomping grounds, trek the trails along the mighty Mississippi River, or slurp some Lao soup.

◉ Sights & Activities

Downtown and Cathedral Hill hold most of the action. The latter features eccentric shops, Gilded Age Victorian mansions and, of course, the hulking church that gives the area its name. Downtown has the museums. An insider's tip: there's a shortcut between the two areas, a footpath that starts on the Hill House's west side and drops into downtown.

Revitalized **Harriet Island**, running south off Wabasha St downtown, is a lovely place to meander; it has a park, river walk, concert stages and fishing dock.

F Scott Fitzgerald Sights & Summit Ave
STREET

The Great Gatsby author F Scott Fitzgerald is St Paul's most celebrated literary son. The Pullman-style apartment at **481 Laurel Ave** is his birthplace. Four blocks away, Fitzgerald lived in the brownstone at **599 Summit Ave** when he published *This Side of Paradise*. Both are private residences. From here stroll along Summit Ave toward the cathedral and gape at the Victorian homes rising from the street.

Literature buffs should grab the *Fitzgerald Homes and Haunts* map at the visitor center to see other footprints.

Landmark Center
MUSEUM

(www.landmarkcenter.org; 75 W 5th St; ☉8am-5pm Mon-Fri, 8am-8pm Thu, 10am-5pm Sat, noon-5pm Sun) Downtown's turreted 1902 Landmark Center used to be the federal courthouse, where gangsters such as Alvin 'Creepy' Karpis were tried; plaques by the various rooms show who was brought to justice here. In addition to the city's visitor center, the building also contains a couple of small museums.

On the 2nd floor the **Schubert Club Museum** (☏651-292-3267; www.schubert.org; ☉noon-4pm Sun-Fri) has a brilliant collection of old pianos and harpsichords – some tickled by the likes of Brahms and Mendelssohn – as well as old manuscripts and letters from famous composers. The club plays free chamber-music concerts Thursday at noon from October to April. A free wood-turning museum (it's a decorative form of woodworking) is also on the 2nd floor.

Mississippi River Visitors Center
INTERPRETIVE CENTER

(☏651-293-0200; www.nps.gov/miss; ☉9:30am-5pm Sun-Thu, to 9pm Fri & Sat) **FREE** The National Park Service visitor center occupies an alcove in the science museum's lobby. Stop by to pick up trail maps and see what sort of free ranger-guided activities are going on. Most take place at 10am on Wednesday, Thursday and Saturday in summer. In winter the center hosts ice-fishing and snowshoeing jaunts.

Science Museum of Minnesota
MUSEUM

(☏651-221-9444; www.smm.org; 120 W Kellogg Blvd; adult/child $13/10; ☉9:30am-9:30pm, reduced hours in winter) Has the usual hands-on kids' exhibits and Omnimax theater ($8 extra). Adults will be entertained by the wacky quackery of the 4th floor's 'questionable medical devices.'

Cathedral of St Paul
CHURCH

(www.cathedralsaintpaul.org; 239 Selby Ave; ☉7am-7pm Sun-Fri, to 9pm Sat) Modeled on St Peter's Basilica in Rome, the cathedral presides over the city from its hilltop perch. Tours ($2) are available at 1pm weekdays.

James J Hill House
HISTORIC BUILDING

(☏651-297-2555; www.mnhs.org/hillhouse; 240 Summit Ave; adult/child $9/6; ☉10am-3:30pm Wed-Sat, from 1pm Sun) Tour the palatial stone mansion of railroad magnate Hill. It's a Gilded Age beauty, with five floors and 22 fireplaces.

St Paul Curling Club
SNOW SPORTS

(www.stpaulcurlingclub.org; 470 Selby Ave; ☉from 11am Oct-May) For those uninitiated in northern ways, curling is a winter sport that involves sliding a hubcap-sized 'puck' down the ice toward a bull's-eye. The friendly folks here don't mind if you stop in to watch the action. Heck, they might invite you to share a Labatt's from the upstairs bar.

🍴 Tours

Down In History Tours
WALKING TOUR

(☏651-292-1220; www.wabashastreetcaves.com; 215 S Wabasha St; 45min tours $6; ☉5pm Thu, 11am Sat & Sun) Explore St Paul's underground caves, which gangsters once used as a speakeasy. The fun ratchets up on Thursday nights, when a swing band plays in the caverns (admission $7).

★✰ Festivals & Events

St Paul Winter Carnival
CULTURAL

(www.winter-carnival.com; ☉late Jan) Ten days of ice sculptures, ice skating and ice fishing.

🛏 Sleeping

You'll find a bigger selection of accommodations in Minneapolis.

Covington Inn
B&B $$

(☏651-292-1411; www.covingtoninn.com; 100 Harriet Island Rd; r incl breakfast $150-235; P❄) This four-room Harriet Island B&B is on a tugboat in the Mississippi River; watch the river traffic glide by while sipping your morning coffee.

Holiday Inn
HOTEL $$

(☏651-225-1515; www.holiday-inn.com/stpaulmn; 175 W 7th St; r $99-169; P❄🛜⛱) The rooms are the usual decent quality you expect from the Holiday Inn chain; the perks are the location adjacent to the RiverCentre (convention center), a small pool and an on-site Irish pub. Parking is $15.

✗ Eating & Drinking

Grand Ave between Dale St and Lexington Pkwy is a worthy browse, with cafes, foodie shops and ethnic eats in close proximity. Selby Ave by the intersection of Western Ave N also holds a quirky line-up.

Mickey's Dining Car   DINER $
(www.mickeysdiningcar.com; 36 W 7th St; mains $4-9; ⊘24hr) Mickey's is a downtown classic, the kind of place where the friendly waitress calls you 'honey' and satisfied regulars line the bar with their coffee cups and newspapers. The food has timeless appeal, too: burgers, malts and apple pie.

Hmongtown Marketplace   ASIAN $
(www.hmongtownmarketplace.com; 217 Como Ave; mains $5-8; ⊘8am-8pm) The nation's largest enclave of Hmong immigrants lives in the Twin Cities, and this market delivers their favorite Vietnamese, Lao and Thai dishes at its humble food court. Find the West Building and head to the back where vendors ladle hot-spiced papaya salad, beef ribs, sticky rice and curry noodle soup. Then stroll the market, where you can fix your dentures or buy a cockatoo or brass gong.

WA Frost & Company   AMERICAN $$$
(☎651-224-5715; www.wafrost.com; 374 Selby Ave; mains $18-28; ⊘11am-1:30pm Mon-Fri, 10:30am-2pm Sat & Sun, 5-10pm daily) Frost's tree-shaded, ivy-covered, twinkling-light patio is right out of a Fitzgerald novel, perfect for a glass of wine, beer or gin. The restaurant locally sources many ingredients for dishes like the artisanal cheese plate, Moroccan-spiced roasted chicken and heirloom bean cassoulet.

Happy Gnome   PUB
(www.thehappygnome.com; 498 Selby Ave; ⊘from 11:30am; 🔊) Seventy craft beers flow from the taps, best sipped on the fireplace-warmed outdoor patio. The pub sits across the parking lot from the St Paul Curling Club.

☆ Entertainment

Fitzgerald Theater   THEATER
(☎651-290-1221; www.fitzgeraldtheater.org; 10 E Exchange St) Where Garrison Keillor tapes his radio show *A Prairie Home Companion*.

Ordway Center for
Performing Arts   CLASSICAL MUSIC
(☎651-224-4222; www.ordway.org; 345 Washington St) Chamber music and the Minnesota Opera fill the hall here.

Xcel Energy Center   HOCKEY
(www.wild.com; 199 Kellogg Blvd) The Wild pro hockey team skates at Xcel.

🛍 Shopping

Common Good Books   BOOKS
(www.commongoodbooks.com; 38 S Snelling Ave; ⊘9am-9pm Mon-Sat, 10am-7pm Sun) Garrison Keillor owns this bright bookstore where statues of literary heroes stand guard over long shelves of tomes. It's west of downtown on the Macalester College campus.

ℹ Information

Visitor center (☎651-292-3225; www.visitsaintpaul.com; 75 W 5th St; ⊘10am-4pm Mon-Sat, from noon Sun) In the Landmark Center; makes a good first stop for maps and DIY walking tour info.

ℹ Getting There & Around

St Paul is served by the same transit systems as Minneapolis. See p604 for details. Union Depot (p604) is the hub for everything: Greyhound buses, city buses, the Green Line light-rail service and Amtrak trains.

Around Minneapolis–St Paul

◉ Sights

Mall of America   MALL, AMUSEMENT PARK
(www.mallofamerica.com; off I-494 at 24th Ave; ⊘10am-9:30pm Mon-Sat, 11am-7pm Sun; 🖈) The Mall of America, located in suburban Bloomington near the airport, is the USA's largest shopping center. Yes, it's just a mall, filled with the usual stores, movie theaters

---

DON'T MISS

BIG BALL O' TWINE

Behold the **World's Largest Ball of Twine** (1st St; admission free; ⊘24hr) **FREE** in Darwin, 62 miles west of Minneapolis on US 12. To be specific, it's the 'Largest Built by One Person' – Francis A Johnson wrapped the 17,400lb whopper on his farm over the course of 29 years. Gawk at it in the town gazebo. Better yet, visit the the **museum** (☎320-693-7544; ⊘by appointment) beside it and buy your own twine ball starter kit in the gift shop.

and eateries. But there's also a wedding chapel inside. And an 18-hole **mini-golf course** (☑952-883-8777; 3rd fl; admission $8). And an amusement park, aka **Nickelodeon Universe** (☑952-883-8600; www.nickelodeonuniverse.com), with 24 rides, including a couple of scream-inducing roller coasters. To walk through will cost you nothing; a one-day, unlimited-ride wristband is $30; or you can pay for rides individually ($3 to $6). What's more, the state's largest aquarium, **Minnesota Sea Life** (☑952-883-0202; www.visitsealife.com/minnesota; adult/child $24/16) – where children can touch sharks and stingrays – is in the mall too. Combination passes are available to save dough. The Blue Line light-rail runs to/from downtown Minneapolis. The mall is a 10-minute ride from the airport.

Fort Snelling   HISTORIC SITE
(☑612-726-1171; www.historicfortsnelling.org; cnr Hwys 5 & 55; adult/child $11/6; ☺10am-5pm Tue-Sat & noon-5pm Sun Jun-Aug, Sat only Sep & Oct; ⊕) East of the mall, Fort Snelling is the state's oldest structure, established in 1820 as a frontier outpost in the remote Northwest Territory. Guides in period dress show restored buildings and reenact pioneer life.

Southern Minnesota

Some of the scenic southeast can be seen on short drives from the Twin Cities. Better is a loop of a few days' duration, following the rivers and stopping in some of the historic towns and state parks.

SPAM MUSEUM

Sitting by its lonesome in Austin, near where I-35 and I-90 intersect in southern Minnesota, lies the **Spam Museum** (☑800-588-7726; www.spam.com; 1101 N Main St; ☺10am-5pm Mon-Sat, from noon Sun; ⊕) FREE, an entire institution devoted to the peculiar meat. It educates about how the blue tins have fed armies, become a Hawaiian food staple and inspired legions of haiku writers. What's more, you can chat up the staff (aka 'spambassadors'), indulge in free samples, and try your hand at canning the sweet pork magic.

Due east of St Paul, on Hwy 36, touristy **Stillwater** (www.discoverstillwater.com), on the lower St Croix River, is an old logging town with restored 19th-century buildings, river cruises and antique stores. It's also an official 'booktown,' an honor bestowed upon a few small towns worldwide that possess an extraordinary number of antiquarian bookshops. What's more, the town is filled with classy historic B&Bs.

Larger **Red Wing**, to the south on US 61, is a similar but less interesting restored town, though it does offer its famous Red Wing Shoes – actually more like sturdy boots – and salt-glaze pottery.

The prettiest part of the **Mississippi Valley** area begins south of here. To drive it and see the best bits, you'll need to flip-flop back and forth between Minnesota and Wisconsin on the Great River Road.

From Red Wing, cross the river on US 63. Before heading south along the water, though, make a cheesy detour. Go north on US 63 in Wisconsin for 12 miles until you hit US 10. Turn right and within a few miles you're in Ellsworth, the 'Cheese Curd Capital.' Pull into **Ellsworth Cooperative Creamery** (☑715-273-4311; www.ellsworthcheesecurds.com; 232 N Wallace St; ☺8am-6pm Mon-Fri, 9am-5pm Sat & Sun) – curd-maker for A&W and Dairy Queen – and savor squeaky goodness hot off the press (11am is prime time).

Back along the river on Wisconsin Hwy 35, a great stretch of road edges the bluffs beside **Maiden Rock**, **Stockholm** and **Pepin**. Follow your nose to local bakeries and cafes in the area.

Continuing south, cross back over the river to **Wabasha** in Minnesota, which has a historic downtown and large population of bald eagles that congregate in winter. To learn more, visit the **National Eagle Center** (☑651-565-4989; www.nationaleaglecenter.org; 50 Pembroke Ave; adult/child $8/5; ☺10am-5pm).

Inland and south, Bluff Country is dotted with limestone bluffs, southeast Minnesota's main geological feature. **Lanesboro** (www.lanesboro.com) is a gem for rails-to-trails cycling and canoeing. Seven miles westward on County Rd 8 (call for directions) is **Old Barn Resort** (☑507-467-2512; www.barnresort.com; dm/r/ tent site/RV site $25/50/30/44; ☺Apr-mid-Nov; ⊛), a pastoral hostel-campground-restaurant-outfitter. **Harmony**, south of Lanesboro, is the center of an Amish community and another welcoming town.

Duluth & Northern Minnesota

Northern Minnesota is where you come to 'do some fishing, do some drinking,' as one resident summed it up.

Duluth

At the Great Lakes' westernmost end, Duluth (with its neighbor, Superior, Wisconsin) is one of the busiest ports in the country. The town's dramatic location spliced into a cliff makes it a fab place to see changeable Lake Superior in action. The water, along with the area's trails and natural splendor, has earned Duluth a reputation as a hot spot for outdoors junkies.

◎ Sights & Activities

The waterfront area is distinctive. Mosey along the Lakewalk trail and around Canal Park, where most of the sights cluster. Look for the Aerial Lift Bridge, which rises to let ships into the port; about 1000 ships a year pass through here.

Maritime Visitors Center   MUSEUM
(☑ 218-720-5260; www.lsmma.com; 600 Lake Ave S; ⊙ 10am-9pm Jun-Aug, reduced hours Sep-May) **FREE** Check the computer screens inside to find out what time the big ships will be sailing through port. The first-rate center also has exhibits on Great Lakes shipping and shipwrecks.

William A Irvin   MUSEUM
(☑ 218-722-7876; www.williamairvin.com; 350 Harbor Dr; adult/child $10/8; ⊙ 9am-6pm Jun-Aug, 10am-4pm May, Sep & Oct) To continue the nautical theme, tour this mighty 610ft Great Lakes freighter.

Great Lakes Aquarium   AQUARIUM
(☑ 218-740-3474; www.glaquarium.org; 353 Harbor Dr; adult/child $16.50/10.50; ⊙ 10am-6pm; ⋔) One of the country's few freshwater aquariums; the highlights here include the daily stingray feedings at 2pm, and the otter tanks.

Leif Erikson Park   PARK
(cnr London Rd & 14th Ave E) This is a lakefront sweet spot with a rose garden, replica of Leif's Viking ship and free outdoor movies each Friday night in summer. Take the Lakewalk from Canal Park (about 1½ miles) and you can say you hiked the Superior Trail, which traverses this stretch.

DYLAN IN DULUTH

While Hibbing and the Iron Range are most often associated with Bob Dylan, he was born in Duluth. You'll see brown-and-white signs on Superior and London Sts for **Bob Dylan Way** (www.bobdylanway.com), pointing out places associated with the legend (like the armory where he saw Buddy Holly in concert, and decided to become a musician). But you're on your own to find **Dylan's birthplace** (519 N 3rd Ave E), up a hill a few blocks northeast of downtown. Dylan lived on the top floor until age six, when his family moved inland to Hibbing. It's a private residence (and unmarked), so all you can do is stare from the street.

Enger Park   PARK
(Skyline Pkwy) For a spectacular view of the city and harbor, climb the rock tower in Enger Park, located a couple miles southwest by the golf course.

Vista Fleet   BOAT TOUR
(☑ 218-722-6218; www.vistafleet.com; 323 Harbor Dr; adult/child $20/10; ⊙ mid-May–Oct) Ah, everyone loves a boat ride. Vista's two-hour harbor cruise is a favorite, departing from the dock beside the *William A Irvin* in Canal Park.

Spirit Mountain   SKIING
(☑ 218-628-2891; www.spiritmt.com; 9500 Spirit Mountain Pl; per day adult/child $35/28; ⊙ from 9am winter, from 10am summer) Skiing and snowboarding are big pastimes come winter; in summer there's a zip line, alpine slide and mini-golf. The mountain is 10 miles south of Duluth.

🛏 Sleeping

Duluth has several B&Bs; rooms cost at least $125 in the summer. Check **Duluth Historic Inns** (www.duluthbandb.com) for listings. The town's accommodations fill up fast in summer, which may mean you'll have to try your luck across the border in Superior, Wisconsin (where it's cheaper too).

Fitger's Inn   HOTEL $$
(☑ 218-722-8826; www.fitgers.com; 600 E Superior St; r incl breakfast $149-239; ❂ 🛜) Fitger's created its 62 large rooms, each with slightly varied decor, from an old brewery. Located

SCENIC DRIVE: HIGHWAY 61

Hwy 61 conjures a headful of images. Local boy Bob Dylan mythologized it in his angry 1965 album *Highway 61 Revisited*. It's the fabled 'Blues Hwy' clasping the Mississippi River en route to New Orleans. And in northern Minnesota it evokes red-tinged cliffs and forested beaches as it follows Lake Superior's shoreline.

But let's back up and get a few things straight. The Blues Hwy is actually US 61, and it starts just north of the Twin Cities. Hwy 61 is a state scenic road, and it starts in Duluth. To confuse matters more, there are two 61s between Duluth and Two Harbors: a four-lane expressway and a two-lane 'Old Hwy 61' (also called North Shore Scenic Drive, which morphs from London Rd in Duluth). Whatever the name, take it. After Two Harbors, it's one wondrous strip of pavement all the way to the Canadian border. For more information, check the North Shore Scenic Drive at www.superiorbyways.com.

on the Lakewalk, the pricier rooms have great water views. The free shuttle to local sights is handy.

Willard Munger Inn INN $$
(☎800-982-2453, 218-624-4814; www.mungerinn.com; 7408 Grand Ave; r incl breakfast $70-136; @🖤) Family-owned Munger Inn offers a fine variety of rooms (from budget to Jacuzzi suites), along with perks for outdoors enthusiasts, such as hiking and biking trails right outside the door, free use of bikes and canoes, and a fire pit. It's near Spirit Mountain.

🍴 Eating & Drinking

Most restaurants and bars reduce their hours in winter. The Canal Park waterfront area has eateries in all price ranges.

Duluth Grill AMERICAN $$
(www.duluthgrill.com; 118 S 27th Ave W; mains $8-16; ☉7am-9pm; 🖤🍴) 🍴 The garden in the parking lot is the tip-off that this is a sustainable, hippie-vibed place. The diner-esque menu is huge, ranging from eggy breakfast skillets to curried polenta stew to bison burgers, with plenty of vegan and gluten-free options to boot. It's a couple miles southwest of Canal Park, near the bridge to Superior, Wisconsin.

DeWitt-Seitz Marketplace ASIAN, AMERICAN $$
(www.dewittseitz.com; 394 Lake Ave S) This building in Canal Park holds several eateries, including vegetarian-friendly **Taste of Saigon** (☉11am-8:30pm Sun-Thu, to 9:30pm Fri & Sat; 🍴), hippie cafe **Amazing Grace** (☉7am-10pm; 🍴) and **Northern Waters Smokehaus** (☉10am-8pm Mon-Sat, to 6pm Sun), with sustainably harvested salmon and whitefish (primo for picnics).

Pizza Luce PIZZERIA $$
(☎218-727-7400; www.pizzaluce.com; 11 E Superior St; mains $10-20; ☉8am-1:30am Sun-Thu, to 2:30am Fri & Sat; 🍴) 🍴 Cooks locally sourced breakfasts and gourmet pizzas. It's also plugged into the local music scene and hosts bands. Fully licensed.

★**Thirsty Pagan** BREWERY
(www.thirstypaganbrewing.com; 1623 Broadway St; ☉from 11am) This one's a bit of a trek, over the bridge in Superior, Wisconsin (a 10-minute drive), but worth it for the aggressive, spicy beers to wash down hand-tossed pizzas.

Fitger's Brewhouse BREWERY
(www.fitgersbrewhouse.net; 600 E Superior St; ☉from 11am) In the hotel complex, the Brewhouse rocks with live music and fresh brews. Try them via the seven-beer sampler (3oz glasses $8).

🛍 Shopping

Electric Fetus MUSIC
(☎218-722-9970; www.electricfetus.com; 12 E Superior St; ☉9am-9pm Mon-Fri, 9am-8pm Sat, 11am-6pm Sun) Sells a whopping selection of CDs, vinyl and local arts and crafts, including Dylan tunes. It sits across the street from Pizza Luce.

ℹ Information

Duluth Visitors Center (☎800-438-5884; www.visitduluth.com; Harbor Dr; ☉9:30am-7:30pm summer) Seasonal center, opposite the Vista dock.

ℹ Getting There & Around

Greyhound (☎218-722-5591; 4426 Grand Ave) has a couple of buses daily to Minneapolis (three hours).

North Shore

Hwy 61 is the main vein through the North Shore. It edges Lake Superior and passes numerous state parks, waterfalls, hiking trails and mom-and-pop towns en route to Canada. Lots of weekend, summer and fall traffic makes reservations essential.

Two Harbors (www.twoharborschamber.com) has a museum, lighthouse and B&B. Actually, the latter two are one and the same; the **Lighthouse B&B** (☑ 888-832-5606; www.lighthousebb.org; r incl breakfast $135-155) is a unique place to spend the night if you can snag one of its four rooms. Nearby, **Betty's Pies** (www.bettyspies.com; 1633 Hwy 61; sandwiches $5-9; ☺ 7am-9pm, reduced hours Oct-May) has a five-layer chocolate tinful among its rackful of wares.

Route highlights north of Two Harbors are Gooseberry Falls, Split Rock Lighthouse and Palisade Head. About 110 miles from Duluth, artsy little **Grand Marais** (www.grandmarais.com) makes an excellent base for exploring the Boundary Waters and environs. For Boundary permits and information, visit the **Gunflint Ranger Station** (☑ 218-387-1750; ☺ 8am-4:30pm May-Sep), just south of town.

Do-it-yourself enthusiasts can learn to build boats, tie flies or brew beer at the **North House Folk School** (☑ 218-387-9762; www.northhouse.org; 500 Hwy 61). The course list is phenomenal – as is the school's two-hour sailing trip aboard the Viking schooner *Hjordis* (per person $45). Reserve in advance.

Grand Marais' lodging options include camping, resorts and motels, like the **Harbor Inn** (☑ 218-387-1191; www.harborinnhotel.com; 207 Wisconsin St; r $115-135; ☏) in town or rustic, trail-encircled **Naniboujou Lodge** (☑ 218-387-2688; www.naniboujou.com; 20 Naniboujou Trail; r $95-115; ☺ late May-late Oct), which is 14 miles northeast of town. **Sven and Ole's** (☑ 218-387-1713; www.svenandoles.com; 9 Wisconsin St; sandwiches $6-9; ☺ 11am-8pm, to 9pm Thu-Sat) is a classic for sandwiches and pizza; beer flows from the attached Pickled Herring Pub. Ecofriendly **Angry Trout Cafe** (☑ 218-387-1265; www.angrytroutcafe.com; 416 Hwy 61; mains $20-27; ☺ 11am-8:30pm May–mid-Oct) grills fresh-plucked lake fish in a converted fishing shanty.

Hwy 61 continues to **Grand Portage National Monument** (☑ 218-475-0123; www.nps.gov/grpo; ☺ 9am-5pm mid-May–mid-Oct) **FREE**, beside Canada, where the early voyageurs had to carry their canoes around the Pigeon River rapids. This was the center of a far-flung trading empire, and the reconstructed 1788 trading post and Ojibwe village is well worth seeing. **Isle Royale National Park** in Lake Superior is reached by daily **ferries** (☑ 218-475-0024; www.isleroyaleboats.com; day trip adult/child $58/32) from May to October. (The park is also accessible from Michigan.)

Boundary Waters

From Two Harbors, Hwy 2 runs inland to the legendary **Boundary Waters Canoe Area Wilderness** (BWCAW). This pristine region has more than 1000 lakes and streams in which to dip a paddle. It's possible to go just for the day, but most people opt for at least one night of camping. If you're willing to dig in and canoe for a while, you'll lose the crowds. Camping then becomes a wonderfully remote experience: just you, the howling wolves, the moose who's nuzzling the tent and the aurora borealis' greenish light filling the night sky. Beginners are welcome, and everyone can get set up with gear from local lodges and outfitters.

Permits for **camping** (☑ 877-550-6777; www.recreation.gov; adult/child $16/8, plus reservation fee $6) are required for overnight stays. Day permits, though free, are also required; get them at BWCAW entry-point kiosks or ranger stations. Call **Superior National Forest** (☑ 218-626-4300; www.fs.usda.gov/attmain/superior/specialplaces) for details; the website

---

SUPERIOR HIKING TRAIL

The 290-mile **Superior Hiking Trail** (www.shta.org) follows the lake-hugging ridgeline between Duluth and the Canadian border. Along the way it passes dramatic red-rock overlooks and the occasional moose and black bear. Trailheads with parking lots pop up every 5 to 10 miles, making it ideal for day hikes. The **Superior Shuttle** (☑ 218-834-5511; www.superiorhikingshuttle.com; from $15; ☺ Fri-Sun mid-May–mid-Oct) makes life even easier, picking up trekkers from 17 stops along the route. Overnight hikers will find 81 backcountry campsites and several lodges to cushion the body come nightfall; the trail website has details. The whole footpath is free, with no reservations or permits required.

has a useful trip planning guide. Try to plan ahead, as permits are quota restricted and sometimes run out.

Many argue the best BWCAW access is via the engaging town of **Ely** (www.ely.org), northeast of the Iron Range area, which has accommodations, restaurants and scores of outfitters. The **International Wolf Center** (218-365-4695; www.wolf.org; 1369 Hwy 169; adult/child $9.50/5.50; 10am-5pm daily mid-May–mid-Oct, Fri & Sat only mid-Oct–mid-May) offers intriguing exhibits and wolf-viewing trips. Across the highway from the center, **Kawishiwi Ranger Station** (218-365-7600; 1393 Hwy 169; 8am-4:30pm May-Sep) provides expert BWCAW camping and canoeing details, trip suggestions and required permits.

In winter, Ely gets mushy – it's a renowned dogsledding town. Outfitters such as **Wintergreen Dogsled Lodge** (218-365-6022; www.dogsledding.com; 4hr tour $125) offer numerous packages.

Iron Range District

An area of red-tinged scrubby hills rather than mountains, Minnesota's Iron Range District consists of the Mesabi and Vermilion Ranges, running north and south of Hwy 169 from roughly Grand Rapids northeast to Ely. Iron was discovered here in the 1850s, and at one time more than three-quarters of the nation's iron ore was extracted from these vast open-pit mines. Visitors can see working mines and the terrain's raw, sparse beauty all along Hwy 169.

In **Calumet**, a perfect introduction is the **Hill Annex Mine State Park** (218-247-7215; www.dnr.state.mn.us/hill_annex; 880 Gary St; tours adult/child $10/6; 12:30pm & 3pm Fri & Sat), with its open-pit tours and exhibit center. Tours are held in summertime only, on Friday and Saturday; there's also a fossil tour both days at 10am.

An even bigger pit sprawls in **Hibbing**, where a must-see **viewpoint** (9am-5pm mid-May–mid-Sep) FREE north of town overlooks the 3-mile Hull-Rust Mahoning Mine. Bob Dylan lived at 2425 E 7th Ave as a boy and teenager; the **Hibbing Public Library** (218-362-5959; www.hibbing.lib.mn.us; 2020 E 5th Ave; 10am-7pm Mon-Thu, to 5pm Fri) has well-done Dylan displays and a free walking-tour map (available online, too) that takes you past various sites, like the place where Bobby had his bar mitzvah. **Zimmy's** (www.zimmys.com; 531 E Howard St; mains $14-20; 11am-1am) has more memorabilia,

plus drinks and pub grub. For a bed, try **Hibbing Park Hotel** (218-262-3481; www.hibbingparkhotel.com; 1402 E Howard St; r $60-100; ❄ 🛜 ♿).

Soudan sports the area's only **underground mine** (www.dnr.state.mn.us/soudan; 1379 Stuntz Bay Rd; tours adult/child $12/7; 10am-4pm late May-early Sep); wear warm clothes.

Voyageurs National Park

In the 17th century, French-Canadian fur traders (voyageurs) began exploring the Great Lakes and northern rivers by canoe. **Voyageurs National Park** (www.nps.gov/voya) covers part of their customary waterway, which became the border between the USA and Canada.

It's all about water up here. Most of the park is accessible only by hiking or motorboat – the waters are mostly too wide and too rough for canoeing, though kayaks are becoming popular. A few access roads lead to campgrounds and lodges on or near Lake Superior, but these are mostly used by people putting in their own boats.

The visitor centers are car accessible and good places to begin your visit. Twelve miles east of International Falls on Hwy 11 is **Rainy Lake Visitors Center** (218-286-5258; 9am-5pm daily late May-Sep, Wed-Sun Sep-late May), the main park office. Ranger-guided walks and boat tours are available here. Seasonal visitor centers are at **Ash River** (218-374-3221; 9am-5pm late May-Sep) and **Kabetogama Lake** (218-875-2111; 9am-5pm late May-Sep). These areas have outfitters, rentals and services, plus some smaller bays for canoeing.

Houseboating is all the rage in the region. Outfitters such as **Ebel's** (888-883-2357; www.ebels.com; 10326 Ash River Trail) and **Voyagaire Houseboats** (800-882-6287; www.voyagaire.com; 7576 Gold Coast Rd) can set you up. Rentals range from $275 to $700 per day, depending on boat size. Novice boaters are welcome and receive instruction on how to operate the vessels.

Otherwise, for sleeping, your choices are pretty much camping or resorts. The 12-room, shared-bath **Kettle Falls Hotel** (218-240-1724; www.kettlefallshotel.com; r/cottage incl breakfast $80/180; May-mid-Oct) is an exception, located inside the park and accessible only by boat; make arrangements with the owners for pick-up (per person round-trip $45). **Nelson's Resort** (800-

433-0743; www.nelsonsresort.com; 7632 Nelson Rd; cabins from $180) at Crane Lake is a winner for hiking, fishing and relaxing under blue skies.

While this is certainly a remote and wild area, those seeking wildlife, canoeing and forest camping in all their glory are best off in the Boundary Waters.

Bemidji & Chippewa National Forest

This area is synonymous with outdoor activities and summer fun. Campsites and cottages abound, and almost everybody is fishing-crazy.

Itasca State Park (☑ 218-266-2100; www.dnr.state.mn.us/itasca; off Hwy 71 N; per vehicle $5, tent & RV sites $12-22) is an area highlight.

You can walk across the tiny headwaters of the mighty Mississippi River, rent canoes or bikes, hike the trails and camp. The log **HI Mississippi Headwaters Hostel** (☑ 218-266-3415; www.hiusa.org/parkrapids; dm $24-27, r $80-130; ❋ 🛜) is in the park; winter hours vary, so call ahead. Or if you want a little rustic luxury, try the venerable **Douglas Lodge** (☑ 866-857-2757; r $95-140; 🛜), run by the park, which also has cabins and a good restaurant.

On the western edge of the forest, about 30 miles from Itasca, tidy **Bemidji** is an old lumber town with a well-preserved downtown and a giant statue of logger Paul Bunyan and his faithful blue ox, Babe. The **visitor center** (www.visitbemidji.com; 300 Bemidji Ave N; ⊘8am-5pm, closed Sat & Sun Sep-May) displays Paul's toothbrush.

Great Plains

Includes ➡

Best Places to Eat

➡ Oklahoma Joe's (p629)

➡ Rieger Hotel Grill & Exchange (p629)

➡ Ted Drewes (p622)

➡ Cattlemen's Steakhouse (p660)

Best Places to Stay

➡ Hotel Fort Des Moines (p632)

➡ Magnolia Hotel (p651)

➡ Hotel Donaldson (p636)

➡ Hotel Alex Johnson (p644)

Why Go?

To best appreciate this vast and underappreciated region in the heart of the US, you need to split the name. The first word, 'great,' is easy. Great scenery, great tornadoes, great eats, great people all apply. The problem is with 'plains.' 'Humdrum' and 'flat' are two words that come to mind. Neither apply. Amid the endless horizons and raw natural drama are surprises such as St Louis and Kansas City, the Alpine beauty of the Black Hills and the legacy of Route 66.

Great distances across the beguiling wide-open spaces are the biggest impediment to enjoying this enormous region, which includes the states of Missouri, Iowa, North Dakota, South Dakota, Nebraska, Kansas and Oklahoma. Many sights lie near the interstates and the more intriguing two-laners, but other far-flung points of interest and scenic drives are also worth seeking out.

From miles of sand dunes to lushly forested countryside, small towns to great cities, the majestic sweep of the continent's center is yours to explore.

When to Go

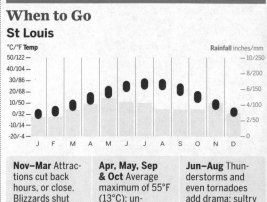

St Louis

Nov–Mar Attractions cut back hours, or close. Blizzards shut down roads and trains for days.

Apr, May, Sep & Oct Average maximum of 55°F (13°C); uncrowded seasons to visit.

Jun–Aug Thunderstorms and even tornadoes add drama; sultry days and wildflowers bloom.

Getting There & Around

The main airport is **Lambert-St Louis International** (www. flystl.com), but visitors from abroad will be better off flying to Chicago, Denver or Dallas and connecting to one of the region's myriad airports or hitting the open roads.

Greyhound buses only cover some interstates, but **Jefferson Lines** (www.jeffersonlines.com) and **Burlington Trailways** (www.burlingtontrailways.com) take up some of the slack. They both honor Greyhound's Discovery Pass.

Amtrak (www.amtrak.com) routes across the Plains make getting here by train easy, but getting around impractical. The main train services are:

California Zephyr Between Chicago and San Francisco via Iowa (including Osceola, south of Des Moines) and Nebraska (including Omaha and Lincoln).

Empire Builder Between Chicago and Seattle via North Dakota.

Heartland Flyer Between Fort Worth and Oklahoma City.

Lincoln Service Fast trains between Chicago and St Louis.

Missouri River Runner Between St Louis and Kansas City.

Southwest Chief Between Chicago and Los Angeles via Missouri (including Kansas City) and Kansas (including Topeka and Dodge City).

Texas Eagle Between Chicago and San Antonio via St Louis.

GET YOUR KICKS

Unlike elsewhere in the US, you can get somewhat of a feel for this region from the interstate, since the wide-open spaces know no bounds. But the real joy of the region is the many two-lane roads. Substantial stretches of Route 66 survive and are covered in the Missouri, Kansas and Oklahoma sections. And don't overlook other roads like US 2, US 20 and US 50.

Top Great Plains Parks

➡ **Theodore Roosevelt National Park** Buffalo roam amid stunning canyons carved by rivers after the ice age.

➡ **Badlands National Park** Bizarrely eroded rocks and canyons offer an unforgettable spectacle.

➡ **Wind Cave National Park** Below ground is one of the world's largest cave formations; above ground, deer, antelope and bison play.

➡ **Homestead National Monument** Farmland with hikes amid rivers and wildflowers.

➡ **Tallgrass Prairie National Preserve** Most of the prairie grasslands have gone the way of the farmer's plow; only 1% of the original tallgrass survives at places like this.

DON'T MISS

Local diners and cafes with fab home-cooked food are where locals gather to chew on all the news and gossip.

Fast Facts

➡ **Hub cities** Kansas City (population 460,000), Omaha (population 409,000)

➡ **Time zones** Central (one hour behind NYC), Mountain (two hours behind NYC)

➡ **Temperature** Enjoy balmy summer evenings when it stays light well past 8pm.

➡ **Driving** Check road conditions and forecasts in winter when even interstates can be closed.

Did You Know?

The population density in North Dakota is 9.9 people per sq mile. In NYC it's 26,800 people per sq mile.

Resources

➡ **National Scenic Byways** (www.byways.org) details scores of nationally designated scenic drives in the region.

➡ **National Park Service** (www.nps.gov) lists little-known sites.

➡ **Tornado HQ** (www.tornadohq.com) has maps and the latest official warnings.

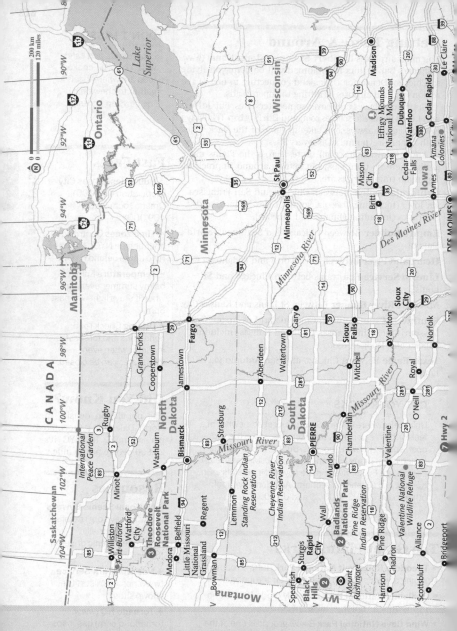

Great Plains Highlights

1 Immerse yourself in the blues rhythms of one of America's great old cities: **St Louis** (p617).

2 Go from mountain highs in the **Black Hills** to valley lows in **Badlands National Park** (p641).

3 Gape at the wildly striated, otherworldly landscapes of **Theodore Roosevelt National Park** (p637).

4 Eat yourself silly on the amazing barbecues in **Kansas City** (p627).

5 Find your own rhythms in quietly beautiful **Chase County** (p658), Kansas.

200 km
120 miles

N

Lake Superior

Ontario

Manitoba

CANADA

Saskatchewan

Minnesota

Wisconsin

North Dakota

South Dakota

Montana

WY

Iowa

Des Moines River

Missouri River

Minnesota River

Cheyenne River Indian Reservation

Standing Rock Indian Reservation

Pine Ridge Indian Reservation

Valentine National Wildlife Refuge

International Peace Garden

Little Missouri National Grassland

Effigy Mounds National Monument

Amana Colonies

St Paul
Minneapolis
Madison
Fargo
Grand Forks
Cooperstown
Jamestown
Bismarck
Washburn
Strasburg
Minot
Williston
Fort Buford
Watford City
Theodore Roosevelt National Park
Medora
Belfield
Regent
Bowman
Lemmon
Rugby

Mason City
Britt
Cedar Falls
Ames
Cedar Rapids
Dubuque
Waterloo
Le Claire
DES MOINES

Sioux City
Sioux Falls
Yankton
Norfolk
Royal
O'Neill
Valentine
Alliance
Bridgeport
Scottsbluff
Harrison
Chadron
Pine Ridge
Wall
Badlands National Park
Rapid City
Sturgis
Spearfish
Black Hills
Mount Rushmore
Murdo
PIERRE
Chamberlain
Mitchell
Watertown
Aberdeen
Gary

7 Hwy 2

6 Veer off the
interstates for
beguiling alternate
routes such as the old
Route 66 (p625, p656
and p663) through
Missouri, Kansas and
Oklahoma.

7 Put the pedal
to the metal and
your eyeballs on
high through the
entrancing rolling
hills and inland
dunes traversed
by Nebraska's
Hwy 2 (p654).

History

Spear-toting nomads hunted mammoths here 11,000 years ago, long before cannon-toting Spaniards introduced the horse around 1630. Fur-frenzied French explorers, following the Mississippi and Missouri Rivers, claimed most of the land between the Mississippi and the Rocky Mountains for France. The territory passed to Spain in 1763, the French got it back in 1800 and then sold it to the USA in the 1803 Louisiana Purchase.

Settlers' hunger for land pushed resident Native American tribes westward, often forcibly, as in the notorious relocation of the Five Civilized Tribes – Cherokee, Chickasaw, Choctaw, Creek and Seminole – along the 1838–39 'Trail of Tears,' which led to Oklahoma from back east. Pioneers blazed west on trails such as the Santa Fe across Kansas.

Earlier occupants, including the Osage and Sioux, had different, but often tragic, fates. Many resettled in pockets across the region, while others fought for lands once promised.

Railroads, barbed wire and oil all brought change as the 20th century hovered. The 1930s Dust Bowl ruined farms and spurred many residents to say: 'I've had enough of this crap – I'm heading west.' Even today, many regions remain eerily empty.

Local Culture

The people who settled the Great Plains usually faced difficult lives of scarcity, uncertainty and isolation; and it literally drove many of them crazy. Others gave up and got out (failed homesteads dot the region). Only fiercely independent people could thrive in those conditions and that born-and-bred rugged individualism is the core of Plains culture today. Quiet restraint is considered an important and polite trait here.

MISSOURI

The most populated state in the Plains, Missouri likes to mix things up, serving visitors ample portions of both sophisticated city life and down-home country sights. St Louis and Kansas City are the region's most interesting cities and each is a destination in its own right. But, with more forest and less farm field than neighboring states, Missouri also cradles plenty of wild places and wide-open spaces, most notably the rolling Ozark Mountains, where the winding valleys invite adventurous exploring or just some laid-back meandering behind the steering wheel. Maybe you'll find an adventure worthy of Hannibal native Mark Twain as you wander the state.

History

Claimed by France as part of the Louisiana Territory in 1682, Missouri had only a few small river towns by the start of the 19th century when the land passed to American hands and Lewis and Clark pushed up the Missouri River. Missouri was admitted to the Union as a slave state in 1821, per the

---

GREAT PLAINS IN...

One Week

Spend your first two or three days in either **St Louis** or **Kansas City** and the next two or three exploring the small-town standouts of Nebraska and Iowa, such as **Lincoln** or **Iowa City**. Try scenic routes such as **Nebraska's Hwy 2** or the **Great River Road** at either end of Iowa. Then head north to South Dakota where the gorgeous **Black Hills** and **Badlands National Park** will vie for your remaining time.

Two Weeks

With two weeks behind the wheel, you can take a big bite out of the Plains. Do the trip as above. Then head south from South Dakota along eastern Nebraska, stopping at fascinating, isolated sites such as the **Agate Fossil Beds National Monument**, **Carhenge** and **Scotts Bluff National Monument**.

Meander into Kansas and pick up **US 50** heading east. Stop at the amazing, astonishing **Cosmosphere & Space Center** in Hutchinson. Head south to Oklahoma and join historic **Route 66** going northeast for sights such as the **Will Rogers Memorial Museum**. Follow the road into Missouri and finish your trip at either of the major cities you skipped on the way out.

Missouri Compromise (which permitted slavery in Missouri but prohibited it in any other part of the Louisiana Territory above the 36°30′ parallel), but abolitionists never compromised their ideals, and bitter feelings were stoked along the Missouri–Kansas border by Civil War time.

The state's 'Show-Me' nickname is attributed to Congressman Willard Duncan Vandiver, who said in an 1899 speech, 'I come from a state that raises corn and cotton and cockleburs and Democrats, and frothy eloquence neither convinces nor satisfies me. I am from Missouri. You have got to show me.' The name now implies a stalwart, not-easily-impressed character.

ℹ Information

Bed & Breakfast Inns of Missouri (www.bbim.org)

Missouri Division of Tourism (www.visitmo.com)

Missouri State Parks (www.mostateparks.com) State parks are free to visit. Site fees range from $12 to $26 and some sites may be reserved in advance.

St Louis

Slide into St Louis and revel in the unique vibe of the largest city in the Great Plains. Beer, bowling and baseball are some of the top attractions, but history and culture, much of it linked to the Mississippi River, are a vital part of the fabric. And, of course, there's the iconic Gateway Arch that you have seen in a million pictures; it's even more impressive in reality. Many music legends, including Scott Joplin, Chuck Berry, Tina Turner and Miles Davis got their start here and the bouncy live-music venues keep the flame burning.

History

Fur-trapper Pierre Laclede knew prime real estate when he saw it, so he put down stakes at the junction of the Mississippi and Missouri Rivers in 1764. The hustle picked up considerably when prospectors discovered gold in California in 1848 and St Louis became the jump-off point (aka 'Gateway to the West') for get-rich-quick dreamers.

St Louis became known as a center of innovation after hosting the 1904 World's Fair. Aviator Charles Lindbergh furthered the reputation in 1927 when he flew the

---

MISSOURI FACTS

Nickname Show-Me State

Population 6 million

Area 69,710 sq miles

Capital city Jefferson City (population 43,000)

Other cities St Louis (population 319,000), Kansas City (population 460,000)

Sales tax 4.23-8.98%

Birthplace of Author Samuel Clemens (Mark Twain; 1835–1910), scientist George Washington Carver (1864–1943), author William S Burroughs (1914–97), author Maya Angelou (b 1928), singer Sheryl Crow (b 1962)

Home of Budweiser, Chuck Berry

Politics Split between Democrats and Republicans

Famous for Gateway Arch, Branson

Official dance Square dance

Driving distances St Louis to Kansas City 250 miles, St Louis to Chicago 300 miles

---

first nonstop, solo transatlantic flight in the 'Spirit of St Louis,' named for the far-sighted town that funded the aircraft.

◉ Sights

The landmark Gateway Arch rises right along the Mississippi River. Downtown runs west of the arch. Begin a visit here and wander for half a day. Then explore the rest of the city.

The neighborhoods of most interest radiate out from this core. These include the following:

Central West End Just east of Forest Park, a posh center for nightlife and shopping.

The Hill An Italian-American neighborhood with good delis and eateries.

Lafayette Square Historic, upscale and trendy.

The Loop Northwest of Forest Park, funky shops and nightlife line Delmar Blvd.

Soulard The city's oldest quarter, with good cafes, bars and blues.

Downtown St Louis

Downtown St Louis

◉ Top Sights

◉ Sights

✪ Activities, Courses & Tours

🛏 Sleeping

🍷 Drinking & Nightlife

✪ Entertainment

South Grand Bohemian and gentrifying, surrounds beautiful Tower Grove Park and has a slew of ethnic restaurants.

Cross the river to see Cahokia Mounds State Historic Site (p548).

★ **Jefferson National Expansion Memorial/Gateway Arch** MONUMENT (www.gatewayarch.com; tram ride adult/child $10/5; ⏰8am-10pm Jun-Aug, 9am-6pm Sep-May) As a symbol for St Louis, the arch has soared above any expectations its backers could have had in 1965 when it opened. The centerpiece of this National Park Service property, the silvery, shimmering Gateway Arch is the Great Plains' own Eiffel Tower. It stands 630ft high and symbolizes St Louis' historical role as 'Gateway to the West.' The **tram ride** takes you to the tight confines at the top.

The grounds around the arch are bucolic, but are something of an island. Unfortunately, well-founded fears of flooding mean that the arch site sits high atop levees and walls to the east while the west side is blocked by the noxious barriers of Memorial Dr and I-70. (Voters approved a tiny tax increase in 2013 to greatly improve the area; find out more at www.cityarchriver.org). Download downtown walking tours at www.gateway-arch.com/visit/walking-tours.

Museum of Westward Expansion   MUSEUM
(www.nps.gov/jeff; films adult/child $7/2.50; ⊙8am-10pm Jun-Aug, 9am-6pm Sep-May) FREE This subterranean museum, under the Arch, chronicles the Lewis and Clark expedition. Two theaters here show films throughout the day.

Old Courthouse & Museum   HISTORIC BUILDING
(11 N 4th St; ⊙8am-4:30pm) FREE Facing the Gateway Arch, this 1845 courthouse is where the famed Dred Scott slavery case was first tried. Galleries depict the trial's history, as well as that of the city.

★ City Museum   MUSEUM
(www.citymuseum.org; 701 N 15th St; admission $12, Ferris wheel $5; ⊙9am-5pm Mon-Thu, 9am-1am Fri & Sat, 11am-5pm Sun; ⊕) Possibly the wildest highlight to any visit to St Louis is this frivolous, frilly fun house in a vast old shoe factory. The Museum of Mirth, Mystery and Mayhem sets the tone. Run, jump and explore all manner of exhibits. The summer-only rooftop Ferris wheel offers grand views of the city.

Grant's Farm   AMUSEMENT PARK
(www.grantsfarm.com; 10501 Gravois Rd; ⊙9am-3:30pm Tue-Fri, 9am-4pm Sat, 9:30am-4pm Sun mid-May–mid-Aug, reduced hr spring & fall, closed Nov–mid-Apr; ⊕) FREE A small-time theme park on the beer-brewing Busch family's rural retreat, Grant's Farm thrills kids with its Clydesdale horses and 1000 other animals from six continents; a tram takes you through the preserve where the beasts roam free. Parking costs $12.

Missouri Botanical Garden   GARDENS
(www.mobot.org; 4344 Shaw Ave; adult/child $8/free; ⊙9am-5pm) These 150-year-old gardens hold a 14-acre Japanese garden, carnivorous plant bog and Victorian-style hedge maze.

Museum of Transportation   MUSEUM
(www.transportmuseumassociation.org; 3015 Barrett Station Rd, I-270, near exit 8; adult/child $8/5; ⊙9am-4pm) Huge railroad locomotives, historic cars cooler than your rental and more that moves.

Pulitzer Foundation for the Arts   MUSEUM
(www.pulitzerarts.org; 3716 Washington Blvd; ⊙noon-5pm Wed, from 10am Sat) FREE Grand

Center landmark, has programs and exhibits across disciplines including architecture.

Forest Park
New York City may have Central Park, but St Louis has the bigger (by 528 acres) Forest Park (www.stlouis.missouri.org/citygov/parks/forestpark; ⊙6am-10pm). The superb, 1371-acre spread was the setting of the 1904 World's Fair. It's a beautiful place to escape to and is dotted with attractions, many free. Two walkable neighborhoods, The Loop and Central West End, are close.

The Visitor & Education Center (www.forestparkforever.org; 5595 Grand Dr; ⊙8:30am-7pm Mon-Fri, 9am-4pm Sat & Sun) is in an old streetcar pavilion and has a cafe. Free walking tours leave from here, or you can borrow an iPod audio tour.

Missouri History Museum   MUSEUM
(www.mohistory.org; 5700 Lindell Blvd; ⊙10am-5pm, to 8pm Tue) FREE Presents the story of St Louis, starring such worthies as the World's Fair, Charles Lindbergh (look for the sales receipt for his first plane – he bought it at a variety store!) and a host of bluesmen. Oral histories from those who fought segregation are moving.

St Louis Art Museum   MUSEUM
(www.slam.org; 1 Fine Arts Dr; ⊙10am-5pm Tue-Sun, to 9pm Fri) FREE A grand beaux-arts palace originally built for the World's Fair. Now housing this storied institution, its collections span time and styles. A stunning new wing opened in 2013.

St Louis Zoo   ZOO
(www.stlzoo.org; 1 Government Dr; fee for some exhibits; ⊙8am-5pm daily, to 7pm Fri-Sun Jun-Aug; ⊕) FREE Divided into themed zones, this vast zoo includes a fascinating River's Edge area with African critters.

St Louis Science Center   MUSEUM
(www.slsc.org; 5050 Oakland Ave; ⊙9:30am-5:30pm Mon-Sat, from 11am Sun Jun-Aug, to 4:30pm rest of year; ⊕) FREE Live demonstrations, dinosaur exhibits, a planetarium and an IMAX theater (additional fee).

🏃 Activities
In warm weather head to Forest Park and sail over to the Boathouse (www.boathouseforestpark.com; 6101 Government Dr; boat rental per hr $15; ⊙10am-approx 1hr before sunset) to romp over Post-Dispatch Lake. In cooler

YOUR BELGIAN BUD

The world's largest beer plant, the historic **Anheuser-Busch Brewery** (www.budweisertours.com; cnr 12th & Lynch Sts; ⊙9am-4pm Mon-Sat, 11:30am-4pm Sun, to 5pm Jun-Aug, from 10am Sep-May) FREE , gives the sort of marketing-driven tours you'd expect from the company with nearly half of the US market. View the bottling plant and famous Clydesdale horses. One thing to note: the purchase of this St Louis icon by Belgium's InBev in 2008 is still a sore spot locally. And don't ask: 'How do you remove all the flavor?'

weather, make for the **Steinberg Ice Skating Rink** (www.steinbergskatingrink.com; off N Kingshighway Blvd; admission $6, skates rental $4; ⊙10am-9pm Sun-Thu, to midnight Fri & Sat mid-Nov–Feb) in the park. **City Cycling Tours** (www.citycyclingtours.com; 3hr tour $30; ⊙daily year-round, call for times) offers narrated rides through the park (bicycles and helmets included) starting at the visitor center. Bike rental from the visitor center costs $10/25 per hour/half day.

Gateway Arch Riverboats　　　　BOAT TOUR
(1hr tour adult/child $14/8; ⊙10:30am-6pm) Churn up the Big Muddy on replica 19th-century steamboats. A park ranger narrates the midday cruises and those after 3pm sail subject to availability. There are also numerous dinner and drinking cruises. Various combo tickets are available.

✷ Festivals & Events

Big Muddy Blues Festival　　　　MUSIC
(www.bigmuddybluesfestival.com; ⊙early Sep) FREE Five stages of riverfront blues at Laclede's Landing on the Labor Day weekend.

☐ Sleeping

Most midrange and upscale chains have a hotel near the Gateway Arch in downtown. Indie cheapies are thin on the ground in interesting areas but you'll find plenty near the airport and you can ride the MetroLink light-rail into the city. Upscale Clayton on I-170 (exit 1F) also has rail access and a cluster of chains.

Huckleberry Finn Hostel　　　　HOSTEL $
(☑314-241-0076; www.huckfinnhostel.com; 1908 S 12th St; dm from $25; ✸) In two old town houses, this independent hostel is basic, but it's a friendly gathering spot with a piano in the lounge/kitchen, and free lockers. Its Soulard location is ideal. Be sure to reserve ahead.

America's Best Value Downtown St Louis　　　　MOTEL $
(☑314-421-6556; www.americasbestvalueinn.com; 1100 N 3rd St; r $60-100; P✸❄✸) When you're sleeping in one of the bare bones but clean rooms here, you can't see just what a charmless place this is. But the Laclede's Landing location is good, as are the prices.

Water Tower Inn　　　　HOTEL $
(☑314-977-7500; www.watertowerinnstl.com; 3545 Lafayette Ave, St Louis University; r $80-120; P✸❄) Right in the middle of St Louis University and near the interesting Central West End, the 62 rooms over six floors here have corporate decor (some have views to the Arch). There's a laundry and free continental breakfast.

Parkway Hotel　　　　HOTEL $$
(☑314-256-7777; www.theparkwayhotel.com; 4550 Forest Park Ave; r $105-270; P✸@❄✸) Right in the midst of Central West End's upscale fun, this indie eight-story hotel contains 217 modern rooms inside a grand limestone building. Standards are high, hot breakfasts are included and you can't beat the location right across from Forest Park.

Napoleon's Retreat　　　　B&B $$
(☑314-772-6979; www.napoleonsretreat.com; 1815 Lafayette Ave; r $120-180, 2-night min weekends; ✸@❄) A lovely Second French Empire home in historic and leafy Lafayette Sq, this B&B has five bold and beautiful rooms, each with private bath and antique furnishings.

Moonrise Hotel　　　　BOUTIQUE HOTEL $$
(☑314-721-1111; www.moonrisehotel.com; 6177 Delmar Blvd; r $120-280; P✸@❄✸) The stylish eight-story Moonrise has a high profile amid the high energy of the Loop neighborhood. The 125 rooms sport a lunar motif but are grounded enough to slow things down to comfy.

✗ Eating

St Louis boasts the region's most diverse selection of food. The magazine and website **Sauce** (www.saucemagazine.com) is full of reviews.

Downtown & Midtown

Laclede's Landing, along the riverfront next to the historic Eads Railway Bridge, has several restaurants, though generally people pop down here for the atmosphere – cobblestoned streets, converted brick buildings and free-flowing beer – rather than the food.

★ Crown Candy Kitchen
CAFE $

(1401 St Louis Ave; mains $5-10; ⊙ 10:30am-9pm Mon-Sat, to 5pm Sun) An authentic family-run soda fountain that's been making families smile since 1913. Malts (try the butterscotch) come with spoons, the floats, well, float, and you can try the famous BLT. Homemade candies top it off. It's an oasis in the struggling North St Louis neighborhood.

Pappy's Smokehouse
BARBECUE $$

(☎ 314-535-4340; www.pappyssmokehouse.com; 3106 Olive St; mains from $9; ⊙ 11am-8pm Mon-Sat, to 4pm Sun) Named one of the nation's best joints for barbecue, Pappy's serves luscious ribs, pulled pork, brisket and smoked turkey. With fame, however, comes popularity, so be prepared for long lines and crowded communal dining. Ameliorate the wait with dreams of the sweet-potato fries.

Soulard & Lafayette Square

Restaurants and pubs occupy most corners in Soulard, with plenty of live blues and Irish music. Just wander. Historic Lafayette Sq, 1 mile northwest, has various stylish spots.

★ Soulard Farmers Market
MARKET $

(www.soulardmarket.com; 7th St; ⊙ 8am-5pm Wed-Sat) A local treasure with a range of vendors selling regional produce, baked goods and prepared foods. Picnic or nosh yourself silly. Dating to 1779, it's pretension-free.

Bogart's Smoke House
BARBECUE $$

(www.bogartssmokehouse.com; 1627 S 9th St; mains $7-15; ⊙ 10:30am-4pm Tue-Thu, to 8pm Fri & Sat) The soul of Soulard? The smoky meats here draw lines of people who tear into all the standards plus specialties like prime rib. Extras such as the searingly hot voodoo sauce and the 'fire and ice pickles' have creative flair.

Joanie's Pizzeria
PIZZERIA $$

(www.joanies.com; 2101 Menard St; mains $10-15; ⊙ 11am-11pm) Long a favorite before a Cardinals game, this unassuming neighborhood bar and grill turns out beloved local-style pizza (although this version isn't made with Provel, the locally beloved cheese concoction). The sauce wins kudos as does the toasted ravioli. Grab a table in the hidden courtyard.

Eleven Eleven Mississippi
MODERN AMERICAN $$

(☎ 314-241-9999; www.1111-m.com; 1111 Mississippi Ave; mains $9-22; ⊙ 11am-10pm Mon-Thu, to midnight Fri & Sat; 🖉) This popular bistro and wine bar fills an old shoe factory. Dinner mains draw on regional specialties with an Italian accent. Other options on the seasonal menu include sandwiches, pizzas, steaks and many veggie options. Excellent wine bar.

South Grand

Running along South Grand Blvd, this young, bohemian area near beautiful Tower Grove Park has a slew of excellent ethnic restaurants, many with outside terraces.

MoKaBe's Coffeehouse
CAFE $

(www.mokabes.com; 3606 Arsenal St; mains $5-7; ⊙ 8am-midnight; 🛜🖉) Overlooking Tower Grove Park, this hangout for neighborhood activists, hipsters and generally cool folk buzzes day and night. Grab a coffee, a baked treat, breakfast or a sandwich and ponder the views.

★ Local Harvest Cafe
CAFE $$

(www.localharvestcafe.com; 3137 Morganford Rd; mains $8-16; ⊙ 8am-9pm, to 2pm Mon) This small storefront place has a huge heart and a changing menu that's fresh and inventive, with lots of vegan and vegetarian options. Balance is provided by excellent mains such as the 'Locavore's Dream Burger.' Excellent Missouri-brewed beer list.

The Hill

This Italian neighborhood crammed with tortellini-sized houses has innumerable pasta joints. Stroll the tidy streets and stop for a coffee at an Italian cafe or deli.

Mama Toscano's
ITALIAN $

(www.mamatoscano.com; 2201 Macklind Ave; mains $5-8; ⊙ 7am-4pm Tue-Sat) More grocery than cafe, this corner Hill legend is renowned for its ravioli. Get an order toasted and enjoy outside at a picnic table (it's table-free inside). Other highlights include the sandwiches, especially the eggplant number; get it on garlic bread.

Adriana's

ITALIAN $

(www.adrianasonthehill.com; 5101 Shaw Ave; mains $5-10; ⊘10:30am-3pm Mon-Sat) Redolent of herbs, this Italian deli serves up fresh salads and sandwiches (get the meaty Hill Boy) to ravenous lunching crowds. There's also good pizza and pasta.

Milo's Bocce Garden

ITALIAN $$

(www.milosboccegarden.com; 5201 Wilson Ave; mains $6-14; ⊘11am-1am Mon-Sat) Enjoy sandwiches, pizzas and pastas in the vast outdoor courtyard or inside the old-world bar. Watch and join the regulars on the busy bocce ball courts.

Central West End & the Loop

Sidewalk cafes rule Euclid Ave in posh and trendy old Central West End. The Loop is near Washington University and runs along Delmar Blvd (embedded with the St Louis Walk of Fame); it has many bars and ethnic restaurants catering to a hipster crowd.

Pickles Deli

DELI $

(www.picklesdelistl.com; 22 N Euclid Ave; mains $5-10; ⊘9am-7pm Mon-Fri, 10am-3pm Sat) Top ingredients separate this slick deli from humdrum sandwich chains; for example, the French dip is laden with house-roasted beef. Options include excellent avocado spread and much more. Dine in or picnic in Forest Park.

Duff's

AMERICAN $$

(www.duffsrestaurant.com; 392 N Euclid Ave; mains $8-20; ⊘11:30am-10pm Sun-Thu, to 11pm Fri, 10am-11pm Sat) The hippies who once tossed back cheap Chablis here are now enjoying the many fine wines on the long list. Duff's has gentrified with the neighborhood and serves an eclectic fusion menu of sandwiches, salads and more ambitious fare. Score a sidewalk table outside under the trees.

🍷 Drinking & Nightlife

Schlafly, Civil Life and Urban Chestnut are excellent local microbrews that will let you forget that you're in the home of Bud. StL Hops (www.stlhops.com) is a guide to local beers and where to drink them.

Laclede's Landing, Soulard and the Loop are loaded with pubs and bars, many with live music. Most bars close at 1:30am, though some have 3am licenses.

★ Blueberry Hill

BAR

(www.blueberryhill.com; 6504 Delmar Blvd; ⊘11am-late) St Louis native Chuck Berry still rocks the small basement bar here at least one Wednesday a month. The $35 tickets sell out very quickly. The venue hosts smaller-tier bands on the other nights. It has good pub food, games, darts and more.

Bridge Tap House & Wine Bar

BAR

(www.thebridgestl.com; 1004 Locust St; ⊘11am-1am) Slip onto a sofa or rest your elbows on a table at this romantic bar where you can savor fine wines, the best local beers and a variety of exquisite little bites from a seasonal menu.

Schlafly Tap Room

BREWERY

(www.schlafly.com; 2100 Locust St; ⊘11am-10pm, to 1am Wed-Sat) The most famous local craft brewer runs this excellent pub just west of downtown. The menu has lots of pub classics like sandwiches and fish-and-chips, while the beer list comprises many of the 50 brews produced during the year. Nab a seat in the beer garden.

ST LOUIS: LOCAL SPECIALTIES

Try these local specialties:

Frozen custard Don't dare leave town without licking yourself silly on this super-creamy ice-cream-like treat at historic **Ted Drewes** (6726 Chippewa St; cones 50c to $2.50; ⊘11am-11pm Feb-Dec), west of the city center. There's a smaller summer-only branch south of the city center at 4224 S Grand Blvd. Rich and poor rub elbows enjoying a 'concrete,' a delectable stirred-up combination of flavors.

Toasted ravioli They're filled with meat, coated in breadcrumbs, then deep-fried. Practically every restaurant on the Hill serves them, most notably Mama Toscano's (p621).

St Louis pizza Its thin-crusted, square-cut pizzas are really addictive. They're made with Provel cheese, a locally beloved gooey concoction of processed cheddar, Swiss and provolone. Local chain **Imo's** (www.imospizza.com; large specials $16), with over 70 locations across the metro area, bakes 'the square beyond compare.'

☆ Entertainment

Check the **Riverfront Times** (www.riverfronttimes.com) for updates on entertainment options around town. Purchase tickets for most venues through **MetroTix** (http://metrotix.com).

Grand Center, west of downtown, is the heart of St Louis' theater scene and home of the **St Louis Symphony Orchestra** (www.stlsymphony.org; 718 N Grand Blvd), which has 50 free tickets for most performances (available online).

The **Muny** (www.muny.com; Forest Park; ⊘mid-Jun–mid-Aug), an outdoor theater, hosts nightly summer Broadway musicals outdoors in Forest Park; some of the 12,000 seats are free (check the website).

The Grove, a strip of Manchester Ave between Kingshighway Blvd and S Vandeventer Ave, is the gay-and-lesbian community's hub, but Soulard, the Central West End and South Grand also have hangouts. Peruse **Vital Voice** (www.thevitalvoice.com) for more.

Pageant   LIVE MUSIC
(☎314-726-6161; www.thepageant.com; 6161 Delmar Blvd) A big venue for touring bands.

BB's   BLUES
(www.bbsjazzbluessoups.com; ⊘6pm-3am) Part blues club, part blues museum, there's good music most nights in this glossy two-level joint. Good bar food includes legendary sweet-potato fries. **Beale** (www.bealeonbroadway.com; 701 S Broadway; ⊘7pm-3am), right across the street, is also a great blues venue.

Just John's Club   GAY
(www.justjohnsclub.com; 4112 Manchester Ave; ⊘3pm-3am) A Grove anchor, John's has a variety of bars inside and out and an ever-welcoming vibe.

Busch Stadium   BASEBALL
(www.stlcardinals.com; cnr Broadway & Clark Ave) The Cardinals play in this fun, retro stadium, opened in 2006. Second only to the New York Yankees in World Series wins, they last won the pennant in 2011.

🔒 Shopping

The Loop and Euclid Ave in the Central West End have the best mix of local shops.

Cherokee Antique Row   ANTIQUES
(www.cherokeeantiquerow.com; Cherokee St, east of Jefferson Ave to Indiana Ave) Six blocks of antique-filled stores in the appropriately historic Cherokee-Lemp neighborhood.

**MISSOURI:
DETOURS & EXTRAS**

Sixty-five miles south of St Louis, the petite, French-founded Mississippi River town of **Sainte Genevieve** oozes history. Many of the restored 18th- and 19th-century buildings are now B&Bs and gift shops.

The **George Washington Carver National Monument** (www.nps.gov/gwca; ⊘9am-5pm) FREE is at the birthplace of this African American scientist. Carver's experimentations with peanuts have been taught to generations of American school kids but, as the park makes clear, he was truly a renaissance man, with a vast range of interests and accomplishments. The museum is near Joplin. Take exit 11A off I-44, then follow US 71 4.5 miles south to Hwy V, then go east.

Left Bank Books   BOOKS
(www.left-bank.com; 399 N Euclid Ave; ⊘10am-10pm Mon-Sat, 11am-6pm Sun) A great indie bookstore stocking new and used titles. There are excellent recommendations of books by local authors and frequent author readings.

ℹ Information

MEDIA

KDHX FM 88.1 (www.kdhx.org) Community-run radio playing folk, blues, odd rock and local arts reports.

Riverfront Times (www.riverfronttimes.com) The city's alternative weekly.

St Louis Post-Dispatch (www.stltoday.com) St Louis' daily newspaper.

POST

Post Office (1720 Market St; ⊘8am-8pm Mon-Fri, 8am-1pm Sat)

TOURIST INFORMATION

Explore St Louis (www.explorestlouis.com; cnr 7th St & Washington Ave, America's Center; ⊘8:30am-5pm Mon-Sat, 11am-4pm Sun) An excellent resource, with other branches in Kiener Plaza (corner of 6th and Chestnut), and at the airport.

Missouri Welcome Center (☎314-869-7100; www.visitmo.com; I-270 exit 34; ⊘8am-5pm)

ℹ Getting There & Around

Lambert-St Louis International Airport (STL; www.flystl.com) is the hub of the Great Plains, with flights to many US cities. The airport is 12 miles northwest of downtown and is connected by the light-rail MetroLink ($4), taxi (about $40) and **Go Best Express** (☑ 314-222-5300; www.gobestexpress.com; one-way from $21) shuttles, which can drop you off in the main areas of town.

Amtrak (www.amtrak.com; 551 S 16th St) *Lincoln Service* travels five times daily to Chicago (from $26, 5½ hours). Two daily *Missouri River Runner* trains go to/from Kansas City (from $29, 5½ hours). The daily *Texas Eagle* goes to Dallas (16 hours; check website for prices as the fare range is vast).

Greyhound (430 S 15th St) Buses depart several times daily to Chicago ($25, six to seven hours), Memphis ($25, six hours), Kansas City ($25, 4½ hours) and many more cities. The station is near Amtrak downtown.

Megabus (www.megabus.com) Runs services to Chicago and Kansas City from as little as $15 one way; it stops next to Union Station on 20th St.

Metro (www.metrostlouis.org; single/day pass $2.25/7.50) Runs local buses and the MetroLink light-rail system (which connects the airport, the Loop, Central West End and downtown). Buses 30 and 40 serve Soulard from downtown.

St Louis County Cabs (☑ 314-993-8294; www.countycab.com) If you need a taxi, text or call this company.

Around St Louis

Several appealing and historic river towns north and south of St Louis on the Mississippi and just west on the Missouri make popular weekend trips for St Louisans, including the historic pair of St Charles and Hannibal. If you're looking for some grand meeting of the two rivers however, don't. The two muddies meet in a swirl of silt and are surrounded by square miles of – you guessed it – muddy and inaccessible floodplains.

St Charles

This Missouri River town, founded in 1769 by the French, is just 20 miles northwest of St Louis. The cobblestoned Main St anchors a well-preserved downtown where you can visit the **first state capitol** (200 S Main St; admission free, tours adult/child $4/2.50;

☺10am-4pm Mon-Sat, noon-4pm Sun, closed Mon Nov-Mar). Ask at the **visitor center** (☑ 800-366-2427; www.historicstcharles.com; 230 S Main St; ☺8am-5pm Mon-Fri, 10am-5pm Sat, noon-5pm Sun) about tours, which pass some rare French colonial architecture in the **Frenchtown neighborhood** just to the north.

Lewis and Clark began their epic journey in St Charles on May 21, 1804, and their encampment is reenacted annually on that date. The **Lewis & Clark Boathouse & Nature Center** (www.lewisandclarkcenter.org; 1050 Riverside Dr; adult/child $5/2; ☺10am-5pm Mon-Sat, noon-5pm Sun) has displays about the duo and replicas of their boats.

Hotels are spread along St Charles' four I-70 exits. St Charles also has several historic B&Bs, including **Boone's Colonial Inn** (☑ 888-377-0003; www.boonescolonialinn.com; 322 S Main St; r $165-370; ✳ 🐾 🛜). The three rooms in the 1820 stone row houses are posh.

Hannibal

When the air is sultry in this old river town, you almost expect to hear the whistle of a paddle steamer. Mark Twain's boyhood home, 100 miles northwest of St Louis, has some authentically vintage sections and plenty of sites where you can get a sense of the muse and his creations Tom Sawyer and Huck Finn.

The **Mark Twain Boyhood Home & Museum** (www.marktwainmuseum.org; 415 N Main St; adult/child $11/6; ☺9am-5pm) presents eight buildings, including two homes Twain lived in and that of Laura Hawkins, the real-life inspiration for Becky Thatcher. Afterward, float down the Mississippi on the **Mark Twain Riverboat** (www.marktwainriverboat.com; Center St; 1hr sightseeing cruise adult/child $16/11; ☺Apr-Nov, schedule varies). **National Tom Sawyer Days** (www.hannibaljaycees.org; ☺around Jul 4 weekend) features frog-jumping and fence-painting contests and much more.

Many of Hannibal's historic homes are now B&Bs. The **Hannibal Visitors Bureau** (☑ 573-221-2477; www.visithannibal.com; 505 N 3rd St; ☺9am-5pm) keeps contacts for all forms of lodging. **Reagan's Queen Anne** (☑ 573-221-0774; www.reagansqueenanne.com; 313 N 5th St; r $110-270) is a lavish B&B in a period house. Catch up on your Twain reading on the verandah.

ROUTE 66: GET YOUR KICKS IN MISSOURI

The Show-Me State will show you a long swath of the Mother Road. Meet the route in **St Louis**, where **Ted Drewes** (p622) has been serving frozen custard to generations of roadies from its Route 66 location on Chippewa St. There are a couple of well-signed historic routes through the city.

Follow I-44 (the interstate is built over most of Route 66 in Missouri) west to **Route 66 State Park** (www.mostateparks.com/route66.htm; I-44 exit 266; ☺7am-30min after sunset), with its visitor center and **museum** (☺9am-4:30pm Mar-Nov) FREE inside a 1935 roadhouse. Although the displays show vintage scenes from around St Louis, the real intrigue here concerns the town of Times Beach, which once stood on this very site. It was contaminated with dioxin and in the 1980s the government had to raze the entire area.

Head southwest on I-44 to Stanton, then follow the signs to family mobbed **Meramec Caverns** (www.americascave.com; Exit 230 off I-44; adult/child $20/10; ☺8:30am-7:30pm summer, reduced hours rest of year), as interesting for the Civil War history and hokey charm as for the stalactites; and the conspiracy-crazy **Jesse James Wax Museum** (www.jessejameswaxmuseum.com; adult/child $7/3; ☺9am-6pm Jun-Aug, reduced hr rest of yr), which posits that James faked his death and lived until 1951.

The **Route 66 Museum & Research Center** (www.lebanon-laclede.lib.mo.us; 915 S Jefferson St; ☺8am-8pm Mon-Thu, 8am-5pm Fri & Sat) FREE at the library in Lebanon has memorabilia past and present. Ready for a snooze? Head to the 1940s **Munger Moss Motel** (☎417-532-3111; www.mungermoss.com; 1336 E Rte 66; r from $50; ✸🖃⬚). It's got a monster of a neon sign and Mother Road–loving owners.

Ditch the interstate west of **Springfield**, taking Hwy 96 to Civil War–era **Carthage** with its historic town square and **66 Drive-In Theatre** (www.66drivein.com; 17231 Old 66 Blvd; adult/child $7/3; ☺Fri-Sun Apr-Oct). In **Joplin**, which is still recovering from its horrible 2011 tornado, get on State Hwy 66, turning onto old Route 66 (the pre-1940s route), before the Kansas state line.

The **Route 66 Association of Missouri** (www.missouri66.org) has loads of info. And don't miss the **Conway Welcome Center** (I-44 Mile 110, near Conway), which has an over-the-top Route 66 theme and scads of info on the historic road and Missouri in general.

Along I-70

The main highway artery between St Louis and Kansas City, I-70 is a congested dud (with a surprising number of porn and sex shops); whenever possible, leave the interstate.

You'll find much to engage with on **US 50**, which meanders on a parallel path south of I-70. From Jefferson City, **Hwy 94** follows the Missouri River east toward St Louis and passes through a beautiful region of wineries and forests.

There are a couple of good excuses to exit if you are on I-70. **Columbia** is home to the much-lauded University of Missouri. The downtown is easily walkable and is a very attractive collection of old brick buildings that feature thriving cafes, bars, bookstores and more. Try **Uprise Bakery** (10 Hitt St; meals $3-10; ☺7am-8pm Mon-Sat), renowned for its organic meals and baked goods.

Some 30 miles west of Columbia and 10 miles north of I-70, **Arrow Rock State Historic Site** (www.mostateparks.com/park/arrow-rock-state-historic-site; ☺visitor center 10am-4pm daily Mar-Nov, Fri-Sun Dec-Feb) is a small preserved town that feels little changed since the 1830s when it was on the main stagecoach route west.

The Ozarks

Ozark hill country spreads across southern Missouri and extends into northern Arkansas and eastern Oklahoma.

At lush and sprawling **Johnson's Shut-Ins State Park** (www.mostateparks.com/jshutins.htm), 8 miles north of Lesterville on Hwy N, the swift Black River swirls through canyon-like gorges (shut-ins). The swimming is some of the most exciting you'll find outside a water park.

North of US 60, in the state's south-central region, the **Ozark National Scenic Riverways** (www.nps.gov/ozar) – the Current and Jack's Fork Rivers – boast 134 miles of splendid canoeing and inner-tubing (rental agencies abound). Weekends often get busy and boisterous. The park headquarters, outfitters and motels are in **Van Buren**. **Eminence** also makes a good base. There are many campgrounds along the rivers. Sinuous Hwy E is a scenic gem.

Branson

Hokey Branson is a cheerfully shameless tourist resort. The main attractions are the more than 50 theaters hosting 100-plus country music, magic and comedy shows. The neon-lit '76 Strip' (Hwy 76) packs in miles of motels, restaurants, wax museums, shopping malls, fun parks and theaters. As Bart Simpson once said: 'It's like Vegas; if it were run by Ned Flanders.'

During the summer and again in November and December, the SUV-laden traffic often crawls. It's often faster to walk than drive, although few others have this idea.

The **Branson/Lakes Area Convention & Visitors Bureau** (☑800-296-0463; www.explorebranson.com; junction Hwy 248 & US 65; ☺8am-5pm Mon-Sat, 10am-4pm Sun), just west of the US 65 junction, has town and lodging information. The scores of 'Visitor Information' centers around town (even the 'official' ones) are fronts for time-share sales outfits. Sit through a pitch, however, and you can get free tickets to a show.

◉ Sights & Activities

While fudge is available in copious quantities, irony is not: when we drove by a much-hyped *Titanic* attraction, the sign implored people to come in and 'renew your wedding vows.' Expect every kind of hokey attraction along the main strips – yes there's even a giant ball of twine.

However, there is an actual **old town** of Branson, which has an authentic charm and a nice setting down by the White River (stroll the pretty walks). Drop into **Dick's 5 & 10** (www.dicksoldtime5and10.com; 103 West Main St; ☺8:30am-9pm), where 'I haven't seen that in years!' is heard up and down the aisles jammed with old-time candies, treats, toys, homewares and more. Could we say no to the BB Bats? No!

Silver Dollar City   AMUSEMENT PARK
(www.silverdollarcity.com; adult/child $58/48; ☺hrs vary) A Branson original, this huge amusement park west of town has thrilling roller coasters and water rides.

🛏 Sleeping & Eating

There are dozens of indie and chain motels (starting at around $35) along Hwy 76 on the strip. Nicer places are in quieter locales. **Table Rock Lake**, snaking through the hills southwest of town, is a deservedly popular destination for boating, fishing, camping and other outdoor activities, and it also has good-value lodging.

Branson cuisine consists mostly of fast food, junk food and all-you-can-eat buffets (most priced from $5 to $10).

Branson Hotel   B&B $$
(☑417-544-9814; www.thebransonhotel.com; 214 W Main St; r $120-150) Dating to 1903, this plush B&B has been remodelled into a fine nine-room boutique lodge right in the old town. It's away from the frenetic commercialism of the strips and anonymous chains.

Indian Trails Resort   RESORT $$
(☑417-338-2327; www.indiantrailsresort.com; Indian Point Rd; cabins $95-190; ❇❄) On Table Rock Lake 9 miles south of Branson, this low-key resort has cozy cabins.

Billy Bob's Dairyland   AMERICAN $
(1901 W 76 Country Blvd; mains $4-9; ☺10:30am-8pm) Excellent shakes and juicy, no-nonsense burgers are the stars at this always-busy diner.

☆ Entertainment

Popular **theater shows** feature performers you may have thought were dead (eg Andy Williams). However, Branson has been the salvation for scores of entertainers young and old whose careers were otherwise fading. Patriotic themes are a stock part of every show. Fundamentalist Christian themes are also common; expect dancers wearing enough fabric to outfit all of their counterparts in Vegas for a year.

Showtimes are geared for older travelers – you can catch a 'Red Skelton Tribute' at 10am (other tribute shows include John Denver, Neil Diamond, Journey et al), but most performances are in the afternoon and early evening. Prices range from about $25 to $50 a head, but you rarely need pay full price. Pick up any of the coupon books around town or stop by the myriad ticket outlets offering 'deals.'

Baldknobbers Jamboree VARIETY
(www.baldknobbers.com; 2835 W Hwy 76; adult/child $30/15) From the fake buck teeth in the comedy acts to the cornball country music, this show helped put Branson on the map back in 1959 and it hasn't let up since.

ℹ Getting There & Away

Tucked into the scenic southern corner of the state, Branson is surprisingly hard to reach, although this means you may end up driving some rural and lovely Ozark two-lane roads. **Branson Airport** (BKG; www.flybranson.com) has limited service from Southwest and Frontier airlines.

Kansas City

Wide open and inviting, Kansas City (KC) is famed for its barbecues (100-plus joints smoke it up), fountains (more than 200; on par with Rome) and jazz. Attractive neighborhoods jostle for your attention and you can easily run aground for several days as you enjoy the local vibe, among the hippest in the Plains.

History

Kansas City began life in 1821 as a trading post but really came into its own once westward expansion began. The Oregon, California and Santa Fe trails all met steamboats loaded with pioneers here.

Jazz exploded in the early 1930s under Mayor Tom Pendergast's Prohibition-era tenure, when he allowed alcohol to flow freely. At its peak, KC had more than 100 nightclubs, dance halls and vaudeville houses swinging to the beat (and booze). The roaring good times ended with Pendergast's indictment on tax evasion (the same way they got Capone) and the scene had largely faded by the mid-1940s.

◎ Sights & Activities

State Line Rd divides KC Missouri and KC Kansas (a conservative suburban sprawl with little to offer travelers). KC Missouri has some distinct areas, including the art deco-filled downtown, **Quality Hill**, around W 10th St and Broadway, has grand, restored buildings from the 1920s.

Interesting neighborhoods include the following:

39th St West KC's funkiest area is a strip of hemp shops, boutiques and lots of ethnic eateries; it's sometimes called 'Restaurant Row'.

Country Club Plaza Often shortened to 'the Plaza,' this 1920s shopping district is an attraction in itself.

Crossroads Arts District Around Baltimore and 20th Sts, it lives up to its name.

Crown Plaza South of downtown, this 1970s development is anchored by several major hotels and Hallmark (yes, the greeting card company is located right here).

Historic Jazz District On the upswing, this old African American neighborhood is at 18th and Vine Sts.

River Market Historic and still home to a large farmers market; immediately north of downtown.

Westport On Westport Rd just west of Main St and filled with alluring locally owned restaurants and bars.

★ National WWI Museum MUSEUM
(www.theworldwar.org; 100 W 26th St; adult/child $14/8; ◎10am-5pm, closed Mon Sep-May) You enter this impressive modern museum on a glass walkway over a field of red poppies, the symbol of the trench fighting. Through detailed and engaging displays you learn about a war that is almost forgotten by most Americans. The only quibble is that more effort is spent on the hardware and uniforms of the war as opposed to the actual horrific conditions. The museum is crowned by the historic **Liberty Memorial**, which has views over the city.

Museums at 18th & Vine MUSEUMS
(1616 E 18th St; one museum adult/child $10/6, both museums $15/8; ◎9am-6pm Tue-Sat, noon-6pm Sun) At the heart of KC's 1920s African

American neighborhood is this museum complex. You'll learn about different styles, rhythms, instruments and musicians – including KC native Charlie Parker – at the interactive **American Jazz Museum** (www.americanjazzmuseum.com). The **Negro Leagues Baseball Museum** (www.nlbm.com) covers African American teams (such as the KC Monarchs and New York Black Yankees) that flourished until baseball became fully integrated.

College Basketball Experience   MUSEUM
(www.collegebasketballexperience.com; 1401 Grand Blvd; adult/child $12/9; ⊙10am-6pm Wed-Sun) Really a gussied-up basketball hall of fame, this fun memorabilia-filled museum lets you try free throws or pretend you're an announcer calling them. It's connected to the glitzy **Sprint Center**, a vast arena in search of a major pro-sports franchise.

Country Club Plaza   NEIGHBORHOOD
(www.countryclubplaza.com) Built in the 1920s, this posh commercial district (centered on Broadway and 47th St) boasts finely detailed, sumptuous Spanish architecture. It's rich with public art and sculptures – look for the walking tour brochure and check out just two examples: the **Spanish Bullfight Mural** (Central St) and the **Fountain of Neptune** (47th St & Wornall Rd).

Nelson-Atkins Museum of Art   MUSEUM
(www.nelson-atkins.org; 4525 Oak St; ⊙10am-5pm Wed & Sat, 10am-9pm Thu & Fri, noon-5pm Sun) FREE Giant badminton shuttlecocks (the building represents the net) surround this encyclopedic museum, which has standout European painting, photography and Asian art collections. Its luminescent Bloch Building, designed by Steven Holl, has earned rave reviews.

Arabia Steamboat Museum   MUSEUM
(www.1856.com; 400 Grand Blvd; adult/child $16/6; ⊙10am-5:30pm Mon-Sat, noon-5:30pm Sun, last tour 90min before closing) In River Market, this museum displays 200 tons of salvaged 'treasure' from a riverboat that sank in 1856 (one of hundreds claimed by the river).

Kemper Museum of Contemporary Art   MUSEUM
(☎816-753-5784; www.kemperart.org; 4420 Warwick Blvd; ⊙10am-4pm Tue-Thu, 10am-9pm Fri & Sat, 11am-5pm Sun) FREE Near the Nelson-Atkins and Country Club Plaza, this museum is small and edgy.

Toy & Miniature Museum of Kansas City   MUSEUM
(www.toyandminiaturemuseum.org; 5235 Oak St; adult/child $7/5; ⊙10am-4pm Wed-Sat, from 1pm Sun; 🚼) Over 100 years of toys spread over 38 rooms.

★ Festivals & Events

American Royal World Series of Barbecue   FOOD
(www.americanroyal.com; ⊙first weekend in Oct) The world's largest barbecue contest (over 500 teams); it takes place in the old stockyards.

🛏 Sleeping

Downtown, Westport and the Plaza offer good lodging options near the action. For something cheap, you'll need to head out on the interstate: there are scores of chains north on I-35 and I-29, and east on I-70.

America's Best Value Inn   MOTEL $
(☎816-531-9250; www.americasbestvalueinn.com; 3240 Broadway; r $60-80; P❋@🛜🏊) Ideally located and convenient to everything, this basic 52-room motel has inside corridors and a pool big enough for a small family.

★ Q Hotel   HOTEL $$
(☎816-931-0001; www.theqhotel.com; 560 Westport Rd; r $110-140; P❋@🛜🏊) This environmentally conscious indie hotel is centrally located in Westport. All 123 rooms have a bright color scheme that seems as fresh as spring. Bounteous free breakfasts include fair-trade coffee. Extras include free local shuttles and evening drinks.

Southmoreland on the Plaza   B&B $$
(☎816-531-7979; www.southmoreland.com; 116 E 46th St, Country Club Plaza; r incl breakfast $120-200; P❋🛜) The 12 rooms at this posh B&B are furnished like the home of your rich country-club friends. It's a big old mansion between the art museums and the Plaza. Extras include Jacuzzis, decks, sherry, fresh flowers and more.

Aladdin   BOUTIQUE HOTEL $$
(☎816-421-8888; www.hialaddin.com; 1215 Wyandotte St; r $90-220; P❋🛜) Affiliated with Holiday Inn, this 16-story hotel dates from 1925. It has been restored to its Italian Romanesque splendor and has 193 compact yet daringly stylish rooms. It was a legendary haunt of mobsters and Greta Garbo.

BARBECUE JOINTS IN KANSAS CITY

Savoring hickory-smoked brisket, pork, chicken or ribs at one of the barbecue joints around town is a must for any visitor. The local style is pit-smoked and slathered with heavily seasoned vinegar-based sauces. You may well swoon for 'burnt ends,' the crispy ends of smoked pork or beef brisket. Amazing.

★ **Oklahoma Joe's** (www.oklahomajoesbbq.com; 3002 W 47th Ave; mains $6-15; ⊙ 11am-8:30pm Mon-Thu, to 9:30pm Fri & Sat) The best reason to cross the state border (it's not far from the Plaza), this legendary BBQ joint housed in a brightly lit old gas station makes grown men's voices crack with joyous emotion. The pulled pork is pleasure on a plate; expect lines.

★ **Arthur Bryant's** (www.arthurbryantsbbq.com; 1727 Brooklyn Ave; mains $8-15; ⊙ 10am-9:30pm Mon-Thu, to 10pm Fri & Sat, 11am-8pm Sun) Not far from the Jazz District, this famous institution serves up piles of superb BBQ in a somewhat slick setting. The sauce is silky and fiery; service is sweet.

★ **LC's Bar-B-Q** (5800 Blue Pkwy; mains $6-12; ⊙ 11am-9pm Mon-Sat) Just 4 miles east of the Plaza, this unadorned eatery does nothing to distract from KC's best burnt ends.

✗ Eating & Drinking

Westport and 39th St W are your best bets for clusters of atmospheric local food and drink places. Don't leave town without hitting several barbecue joints.

The heavily hyped **Power & Light District** (www.powerandlightdistrict.com) is a vast urban development centered on Grand Blvd and W 12th St. It has dozens of chain restaurants, formula bars and live-performance venues. When there's no sporting event or convention in town it can seem rather bleak.

Be sure to try a locally brewed Boulevard Beer; bars close between 1:30am and 3am.

City Market   MARKET $
(www.thecitymarket.org; cnr W 5th St & Grand Blvd; ⊙ hrs vary) City Market is a haven for small local businesses selling an idiosyncratic range of foods and other items. Ethnic groceries abound and there is a farmers market for regional producers on weekends. Little cafes and greasy spoons do big business from breakfast through to dinner.

Winstead's Steakburger   BURGERS $
(www.winsteadssteakburger.com; 101 Emanuel Cleaver III Blvd; mains $4-6; ⊙ 6am-midnight) Cheery waiters sling plates of excellent fresh burgers to families, hungover hipsters and more at this Country Club Plaza institution. Don't miss the onion rings and chili.

Room 39   AMERICAN $$
(☎ 816-753-3939; www.rm39.com; 1719 W 39th St; mains lunch $7-12, dinner $20-30; ⊙ 7am-3pm & 5-10pm Mon-Sat; ☎) The local provenance of the food at this excellent restaurant is listed at the top of the menu. Breakfast and lunch are casual with excellent eggs, burgers, salads and more. Dinner brings out white tablecloths and seasonal fare. The $39 tasting menu is a bargain.

★ **Rieger Hotel Grill & Exchange**   AMERICAN $$$
(☎ 816-471-2177; www.theriegerkc.com; 1924 Main St; mains $20-30; ⊙ 11am-2pm Mon-Fri, 5-10pm Mon-Sat) One of KC's most innovative restaurants is housed in what was once a humdrum 1915 vintage hotel in the Crossroads Arts District. Today it's been spiffed up to match the creative fare on Howard Hanna's seasonal menu. (Note the bathroom plaque pointing out where Al Capone once sought release.)

★ **Zoo Bar**   BAR
(1220 McGee St; ⊙ 11am-1:30am) The raw-edged antidote to the artifice of the nearby Power & Light District. Shoot some pool, shoot off your mouth, write something stronger than 'shoot' on the highly entertaining bathroom walls.

McCoy's Public House   BREWERY
(www.beerkc.com; 4057 Pennsylvania Ave; ⊙ 11am-3am, to midnight Sun) The patio at this Westport brewpub is the place to be on a balmy day. Beers are excellent and vary through the year. The food is strictly comfort and quite good: warm your cockles with mac 'n' cheese on a snowy night.

Westport Coffeehouse CAFE
(www.westportcoffeehouse.com; 4010 Pennsylvania St; mains $6-7; 7:30am-11pm Mon-Thu, to midnight Fri & Sat, 10am-10pm Sun;) This laid-back place off the main drag has good coffee and specialty teas. Look for live music, comedy, art films and more at night.

☆ Entertainment

The free weekly **Pitch** (www.pitch.com) has the best cultural calendar. Live-music venues are scattered across the city.

★ **Mutual Musicians Foundation** JAZZ
(www.thefoundationjamson.org; 1823 Highland Ave; midnight-6am Fri & Sat) Near 18th and Vine in the Historic Jazz District, this former union hall for African American musicians has hosted after-hours jams since 1930. Famous veteran musicians jam with young hotshots. It's friendly and pretension-free. A little bar serves cheap drinks in plastic cups.

Blue Room BLUES, JAZZ
(www.americanjazzmuseum.com; 1616 E 18th St; free Mon & Thu, cover varies Fri & Sat; 5-11pm Mon & Thu, to 1am Fri & Sat) This slick club, part of the American Jazz Museum, hosts local talent for free on Monday and Thursday. Touring acts perform weekends.

Riot Room LIVE MUSIC
(www.theriotroom.com; 4048 Broadway; cover varies; 5pm-3am) Part dive, part cutting-edge live-music venue, the Riot Room always rocks – and has many good beers.

**Kauffman Center for the
Performing Arts** PERFORMING ARTS
(www.kauffmancenter.org; 1601 Broadway) Twin venues headline this stunning new place designed by Moshe Safdie. There's a varied schedule of theater, opera, ballet, music and more through the year.

Truman Sports Complex STADIUM
(I-70 exit 9) Locals are passionate about Major League Baseball's **Royals** (www.kcroyals.com) and the NFL's **Chiefs** (www.kcchiefs.com). Both play at gleaming side-by-side stadiums east of the city near Independence.

🔒 Shopping

Historic Country Club Plaza is KC's most appealing shopping destination (its lavish architecture is modeled on Seville, Spain, and dates to 1923), though sadly it's mostly upscale national chains. Westport has more eclectic shops, as does 39th St. Over 60 galleries call Crossroads Arts District home.

Halls DEPARTMENT STORE
(www.halls.com; 211 Nichols Rd, Country Club Plaza; 10am-6pm, to 8pm Fri & Sat) Founded in 1913 by the same family behind, you guessed it, Hallmark, this high-end store is so gracious you may wish you were wearing gloves. There's top merchandise in KC's answer to Nordstroms.

Prospero's Books BOOKS
(www.prosperosbookstore.com; 1800 W 39th St; 10am-9pm) Funky used bookstore in a vibey part of town. Great recommendations, live poetry and even a few bands.

ℹ Information

Greater Kansas City Visitor Center (☑800-767-7700; www.visitkc.com; Union Station, 30 W Pershing Rd; 9:30am-4pm Tue-Sun) The National WWI Museum also has lots of local info.

Missouri Welcome Center (☑816-889-3330; www.visitmo.com; I-70 exit 9; 8am-5pm) Statewide maps and information near the Truman Sports Complex.

ℹ Getting There & Around

KC International Airport (MCI; www.flykci.com) is a confusing array of circular terminals 16 miles northwest of downtown. A taxi to downtown/Plaza costs about $40/45. Or take the cheaper **Super Shuttle** (☑800-258-3826; www.super-shuttle.com; downtown/Plaza $18/20).

Amtrak (www.amtrak.com) In majestic Union Station; has two daily *Missouri River Runner* trains to St Louis (from $29, 5½ hours). The *Southwest Chief* stops here on its daily runs between Chicago and LA.

Greyhound (www.greyhound.com; 1101 Troost St) Sends buses daily to St Louis ($25, 4½ hours) and Denver ($70, 11 hours) from the station poorly located east of downtown.

Jefferson Lines (www.jeffersonlines.com) Heads to Omaha ($45, three to five hours), Minneapolis ($75, eight to 10 hours) via Des Moines, and Oklahoma City ($75, seven hours) via Tulsa.

Megabus (www.megabus.com; cnr 3rd St & Grand Blvd) Serves St Louis and Chicago for as little as $15.

Metro (www.kcata.org; adult/child $1.50/75c) A one-day unlimited bus pass costs $3 on the bus. Bus 47 runs regularly between downtown, Westport and Country Club Plaza.

Yellow Cab (☑888-471-6050; www.kansas-city-taxi.com)

Around Kansas City

Independence

Just east of Kansas City, picture-perfect Independence is the perfect stereotype for an old Midwestern small town. It was the home of Harry S Truman, US president from 1945 to 1953.

◉ Sights & Activities

Independence's attractions can easily fill a day.

★ Truman Home   HISTORIC BUILDING
(www.nps.gov/hstr; 219 N Delaware St; tours adult/child $4/free; ⊘9am-4:30pm Tue-Sat) See the simple life Harry and Bess lived in this basic but charming wood house. It is furnished with their original belongings and you fully expect the couple to wander out and say hello. Truman lived here from 1919 to 1972 and in retirement entertained visiting dignitaries in his strictly pedestrian front room – he's said to have hoped none of the callers would linger more than 30 minutes.

Tour tickets are sold at the **visitor center** (223 N Main St; ⊘8:30am-5pm Tue-Sat). Ask for directions to the **Truman Family Farm**, where the future president 'got his common sense.'

Truman Presidential
Museum & Library   MUSEUM
(www.trumanlibrary.org; 500 W US 24; adult/child $8/3; ⊘9am-5pm Mon-Sat, noon-5pm Sun) Thousands of objects, including the famous 'The BUCK STOPS here!' sign, from the man who led the US through one of its most tumultuous eras, are displayed in this vast, modern building.

National Frontier Trails Museum   MUSEUM
(www.frontiertrailsmuseum.org; 318 W Pacific St; adult/child $6/3; ⊘9am-4:30pm Mon-Sat, 12:30-4:30pm Sun) Gives a good look at life for the pioneers along the Santa Fe, California and Oregon Trails; many began their journey in Independence.

★ Truman Historic
Walking Trail   WALKING TOUR
Starting at the Truman Home visitor center, this 2.7-mile self-guiding route leads to dozens of Truman-related sites, including the courthouse where he began his political career. On summer Saturdays at 9am rangers lead the walk.

🛏 Sleeping & Eating

Higher Ground Hotel   HOTEL $
(☑816-836-0292; www.highergroundhotel.com; 200 N Delaware St; r $75-100; ❄ 🐾 🛜) Stay across from the Truman House at this modern place that looks like a school. The 30 rooms are commodious and comfortable.

Clinton's Soda Fountain   ICE CREAM $
(www.clintonssodafountain.com; 100 W Maple Ave; mains $4-8; ⊘11am-8pm Mon-Sat) Little changed from when Truman got his first job here as a soda jerk.

St Joseph

The first Pony Express set out, carrying mail from 'St Jo' 2000 miles west to California, in 1860. The service, making the trip in as little as eight days, lasted just 18 months before telegraph lines made it redundant. The **Pony Express National Museum** (www.ponyexpress.org; 914 Penn St; adult/child $6/3; ⊘9am-5pm Mon-Sat, 11am-5pm Sun) tells the story of the Express and its riders, who were mostly orphans due to the dangers.

St Jo, 50 miles north of Kansas City, was also home to outlaw Jesse James. He was killed at what is now the **Jesse James Home Museum** (www.ponyexpressjessejames.com; cnr 12th & Penn Sts; adult/child $4/2; ⊘9am-4pm Mon-Sat, 1-4pm Sun, Sat & Sun only Nov-Mar). The fateful bullet hole is still in the wall.

Housed in the former 'State Lunatic Asylum No 2,' the **Glore Psychiatric Museum** (www.stjosephmuseum.org; 3406 Frederick Ave; adult/child $5/3; ⊘10am-5pm Mon-Sat, 1-5pm Sun) gives a frightening and fascinating look at lobotomies, the 'bath of surprise' and other discredited treatments. Tickets also include entrance to several other museums.

Get details on the town's many museums at the **visitor center** (☑816-232-1839; www.stjomo.com; 502 N Woodbine Rd; ⊘hrs vary) near I-29 exit 47, where most hotels are located.

IOWA

Instead of two girls for every boy, Iowa has eight pigs for every person. But there's a lot more to do here than roll in the mud. The towering bluffs on the Mississippi River and the soaring Loess Hills lining the Missouri River bookend the state; in between you'll find the writers' town of Iowa City, the commune-dwellers of the Amana Colonies and lots of little towns full of highlights.

In fact, Iowa surprises in many ways. It makes or breaks presidential hopefuls: the Iowa Caucus opens the national election battle, and wins by George W Bush in 2000 and Barack Obama in 2008 stunned many pundits and launched their victorious campaigns.

History

After the 1832 Black Hawk War pushed local Native Americans westward, immigrants flooded into Iowa from all parts of the world and hit the ground farming. Some established experimental communities such as the Germans of the Amana Colonies. Others spread out and kept coaxing the soil (95% of the land is fertile) until Iowa attained its current status as a leading grain producer (biofuel has caused a boomlet) and the US leader in hogs and corn (much of the latter ends up as syrup in junk food).

❶ Information

Iowa Bed & Breakfast Guild (📞 800-743-4692; www.ia-bednbreakfast-inns.com)

Iowa State Parks (www.iowadnr.gov) State parks are free to visit. Half of the park campsites are reservable; fees range from $6 to $20 per night.

Iowa Tourism Office (www.traveliowa.com)

IOWA FACTS

Nickname Hawkeye State

Population 3.1 million

Area 56,275 sq miles

Capital city Des Moines (population 206,600)

Sales tax 6-7%

Birthplace of Painter Grant Wood (1891–1942), actor John Wayne (1907–79), author Bill Bryson (b 1951)

Home of Madison County's bridges

Politics Center-right with flashes of liberalism

Famous for Iowa Caucus that opens the presidential election season

Official flower Wild rose

Driving distances Dubuque to Chicago 180 miles, Des Moines to Rapid City 625 miles

---

Iowa Wine & Beer (www.iowawineandbeer.com) Craft brewing and, yes, winemaking are booming in Iowa. Get the handy app.

Des Moines

Des Moines, meaning 'of the monks' not 'in the corn' as the surrounding fields might suggest, is Iowa's snoozy capital. The town really is rather dull, but does have a stately state capitol and one of the nation's best state fairs. Pause, but then get out and see the state.

◉ Sights & Activities

The Des Moines River slices through downtown. The Court Ave Entertainment District sits just west, while East Village, at the foot of the capitol, and east of the river, is home to galleries, eateries, clubs and a few gay bars.

State Capitol   HISTORIC BUILDING
(cnr E 9th St & Grand Ave; ⊙ 8am-4:30pm Mon-Fri, 9am-4pm Sat) FREE The bling-heavy capitol (1886) must have been Liberace's favorite government building. Every detail, from the sparkling gold dome to the spiral staircases and stained glass in the law library, seems to strive to outdo the other. Join a free tour and you can climb halfway up the dome.

✹ Festivals & Events

★ Iowa State Fair   FESTIVAL
(www.iowastatefair.org; cnr E 30th St & E University Ave; adult/child $11/5; ⊙ 9am-midnight mid-Aug; ⊕) Much more than just country music and butter sculpture, this festival draws a million visitors over its 10-day run. They enjoy the award-winning farm critters and just about every food imaginable that can be shoved on a stick. It's the setting for the Rodgers and Hammerstein musical *State Fair* and the 1945 film version.

🛏 Sleeping

Chains of all flavors congregate on I-80 at exits 121, 124, 131 and 136.

★ Hotel Fort Des Moines   HOTEL $$
(📞 515-243-1161; www.hotelfortdesmoines.com; 1000 Walnut St; r $90-200; 🅿 ❄ @ 🛜) Everyone from Mae West to JFK has spent the night in this locally owned old-school hotel. It retains its 1917 elegance and the 204 rooms spread across 11 floors are well equipped.

✕ Eating & Drinking

Downtown's Court Ave, Ingersoll Ave in the west, and East Village (Grand Ave and Locust St) are good for browsing restaurants.

B & B Grocery, Meat & Deli   AMERICAN $
(www.bbgrocerymeatdeli.com; 2001 SE 6th St; mains $4-9; ⊙ 8:30am-6pm Mon-Fri, to 3pm Sat) 'Keeping Iowans on top of the food chain since 1922!' is the slogan at this hole-in-the-wall store just south of downtown. Take your place in line for meaty sandwiches that include the 'killer pork tenderloin,' a bun-smothering creation.

Court Avenue Brewing Co   AMERICAN $$
(www.courtavebrew.com; 309 Court Ave; mains $7-20; ⊙food 11am-11pm, bar to 1am) Enjoy good microbrews in a vintage brick building downtown and select from various Iowa classics like a big burger, steak or pork chop.

House of Bricks   BAR
(www.thehouseofbricks.com; 525 E Grand Ave; meals $10-15; ⊙11am-late) A gritty live-music legend in the East Village, it serves up tasty, beer-absorbent chow and has a rooftop bar.

Madison County

This scenic county, about 30 miles southwest of Des Moines, slumbered for half a century until Robert James Waller's blockbuster, tear-jerking novel *The Bridges of Madison County* and its 1995 Clint Eastwood/Meryl Streep movie version brought in scores of fans to check out the **covered bridges** where Robert and Francesca fueled their affair. Pick up (or download) a map to all six surviving bridges and other movie sets at the **Chamber of Commerce** (☑800-298-6119; www.madisoncounty.com; 73 Jefferson St; ⊙9am-5pm Mon-Fri, 10am-4pm Sat, noon-4pm Sun) in Winterset.

The humble **birthplace of John Wayne** (www.johnwaynebirthplace.org; 216 S 2nd St, Winterset; adult/child $7/3; ⊙10am-4:30pm), aka Marion Robert Morrison, is now a small museum.

The farms and open land in this region are as bucolic as a painting. And that applies to the towns too. Besides **Winterset** and its silver-domed courthouse, **Adel**, 20 miles north on US 169, has its own beautiful courthouse square surrounded by shops and cafes.

WORTH A TRIP

GRANT WOOD'S ELDON

Grab a 'tool' out of your trunk and make your very own parody of Grant Wood's iconic painting *American Gothic* (1930) – the pitchfork painting – in tiny Eldon, about 90 miles southeast of Des Moines. The original house is across from the **American Gothic House Center** (www.americangothichouse.net; American Gothic St; ⊙10am-5pm Tue-Sat, 1-4pm Sun & Mon summer, 10am-4pm Tue-Fri, 1-4pm Sat-Mon rest of yr) **FREE**, which does a swell job of interpreting the artwork that sparked a million parodies. The actual painting is in the Art Institute of Chicago.

Wood spent much of his time in tiny **Stone City**, a cute little burg 14 miles north of Mt Vernon, off Hwy 1. It's on the 68-mile-long **Grant Wood Scenic Byway** (www.byways.org).

Along I-80

Many of Iowa's attractions are within an easy drive of bland I-80, which runs east–west across the state's center. Much more interesting alternatives are US 20 and US 30.

Quad Cities

Four cities straddle the Mississippi River by I-80: Davenport and Bettendorf in Iowa and Moline and Rock Island in Illinois. See p546 for the Illinois-side details. The **visitor center** (www.visitquadcities.com; 102 S Harrison St, Davenport; ⊙9am-5pm Mon-Sat, noon-5pm) has bike rentals ($10 per hour) for a ride along the Big Muddy.

Cruise the gorgeous Mississippi aboard the vintage-style riverboat **Twilight** (www.riverboattwilight.com; $380 per person incl hotel & meals; ⊙Jun-Oct), which runs two-day round trips to Dubuque from Le Claire, east of Davenport. Motels are found at I-74 exit 2 and I-780 exit 295A.

Iowa City

The youthful, artsy vibe here is courtesy of the **University of Iowa campus** (www.uiowa.edu), home to good art and natural history museums. It spills across both sides of the Iowa River (which has good **walks** on the banks); to the east it mingles with the charming **downtown**. In summer (when the student-to-townie ratio evens out) the city mellows somewhat. The school's writing programs are renowned and Iowa City was named a Unesco City of Literature in 2008. For a sharp parody of the town and school, read Jane Smiley's *Moo*.

The cute gold-domed building at the heart of campus is the **Old Capitol Museum** (www.uiowa.edu/oldcap; cnr Clinton St & Iowa Ave; ⊘10am-5pm Tue, Wed, Fri & Sat, to 8pm Thu, 1-5pm Sun) FREE. Built in 1840, it was the seat of government until 1857 when Des Moines grabbed the reins. It's now a museum with galleries and furnishings from back in its heyday.

🛏 Sleeping

Chain motels line 1st Ave in Coralville (I-80 exit 242) like hogs at the trough. Beer and cheap chow abound downtown.

Brown Street Inn   B&B **$$**
(☑319-338-0435; www.brownstreetinn.com; 430 Brown St; r $95-165; ❋@🛜) Four-poster beds and other antiques adorn this six-room 1913 Dutch Colonial place that's an easy walk from downtown.

Hotel Vetro   HOTEL **$$**
(☑319-337-4961; www.hotelvetro.com; 201 S Lynn St; r $120-300; ❋🛜🏊) Enjoy many of the comforts of home in the 56 studio apartments spread over six floors at this campus hotel. While your duds spin in the laundry, enjoy the indoor pool.

🍴 Eating & Drinking

This is a college town, which means lots of cheap ethnic eateries (and beer!).

★**Shorts Burger & Shine**   BURGERS **$**
(18 S Clinton St; mains $10; ⊘food 11am-10pm, bar to 2am; 🍴) A local legend, Shorts serves up all manner of gourmet burgers, including a fine selection of veggie burgers. The regional beer list is inspired.

Dave's Foxhead Tavern   BAR
(402 E Market St; ⊘5pm-2am Mon-Sat) Popular with the writers' workshop crowd, who debate gerunds while slouched in booths. Pool is also big in this tiny boozer, which boasts a wonderfully eclectic jukebox.

🛍 Shopping

Prairie Lights   BOOKS
(www.prairielights.com; 15 S Dubuque St; ⊘9am-9pm Mon-Sat, to 6pm Sun) A bookstore worthy

of a university that runs the famous Iowa Writers' Workshop.

ℹ Information

The **visitor center** (☑800-283-6592; www.iowacitycoralville.org; 900 1st Ave, at I-80 exit 242; ⊘8am-5pm Mon-Fri) is in neighboring Coralville, an unfortunate town with all the chains and urban sprawl missing from Iowa City.

Amana Colonies

These **seven villages**, just northwest of Iowa City, are stretched along a 17-mile loop. All were established as German religious communes between 1855 and 1861 by inspirationists who, until the Great Depression, lived a utopian life with no wages paid and all assets communally owned. Unlike the Amish and Mennonite religions, inspirationists embrace modern technology (and tourism).

Today the seven well-preserved (and discreetly tasteful) villages offer a glimpse of this unique culture, and there are lots of arts, crafts, cheeses, baked goods and wines to buy. However they are not immune to commercial pressures as evidenced by establishments such as a 'Man Cave' and gift shops selling the sorts of gewgaws that perplex the inspirationists' heirs.

Four **museums** are sprinkled throughout the villages, including the insightful **Amana Heritage Museum** (4310 220th Trail, Amana; ⊘10am-5pm Mon-Sat, noon-4pm Sun Apr-Oct, Sat only Mar & Nov-Dec). The others are open in summer only. A pass (adult/child $7/free) gets you into them all. Another popular stop is the privately owned **Barn Museum** (413 P St, South Amana; adult/child $3.50/1.25; ⊘9am-5pm Apr-Oct), which has miniature versions of the hay-filled buildings found across rural America.

The villages have many good-value B&Bs and historic inns, including **Zuber's Homestead Hotel** (☑319-622-3911; www.zubershomesteadhotel.com; 2206 44 Ave, Amana; r $85-120; ❋🛜), with 15 individually decorated rooms in an 1890s brick building.

One of the Amanas' top draws is the hefty-portioned, home-cooked German **cuisine** dished out at various humble dining spots. Pick up a picnic at **Amana Meat Shop & Smokehouse** (4513 F St, Amana; snacks from $3; ⊘9am-5pm), which even has coolers. **Millstream Brewing** (835 48th Ave, Amana; ⊘9am-7pm summer, reduced hr rest of yr) is an excellent microbrewery. It serves its own beer and brews from others in Iowa at its shop and beer garden.

Stop at the grain-elevator-shaped **visitor center** (☑800-579-2294; www.amana-colonies.com; 622 46th Ave, Amana; ⊙9am-5pm Mon-Sat, 10am-5pm Sun May-Oct, 9am-3pm rest of yr) for the essential guide-map. It offers bike rental ($15 per day), an ideal way to tour the area.

Along US 30

Like a clichéd needlepoint come to life, US 30 passes through fertile fields dotted with whitewashed farmhouses and red-hued barns. It parallels I-80 an average of 20 to 30 miles to the north before dropping down to Nebraska near Omaha.

The real attraction here is just enjoying the succession of small towns. In a state blessed with pretty places, **Mt Vernon** is one of the loveliest. It may be only two blocks long but there's much here, especially in the eating department. **Lincoln Cafe** (☑319-895-4041; www.foodisimportant.com; 17 1st St W; mains $7-25; ⊙11am-2pm & 5-9pm Tue-Sat, 10am-2pm Sun) is a foodie favorite; it cooks with fine local foods (try the burger with Maytag blue cheese).

Ames, 25 miles north of Des Moines, is home to Iowa State University and has lots of good motels and undergrad dives.

Along US 20

Stretching from Dubuque on the Mississippi River to Sioux City on the Missouri River, US 20 has offered up charms similar to those on US 30 to generations of travelers seeking new lives, adventure or just a new farm implement.

Dubuque

Dubuque makes a great entry into Iowa from Illinois: 19th-century Victorian homes line its narrow and lively streets between the Mississippi River and seven steep limestone hills.

The **4th Street Elevator** (www.dbq.com/fenplco; cnr 4th St & Fenelon; adult/child round-trip $3/1.50; ⊙8am-10pm Apr-Nov), built in 1882, climbs a steep hill for huge views. Ring the bell to begin the ride. Learn about life (of all sorts) on the Mississippi at the impressive **National Mississippi River Museum & Aquarium** (www.rivermuseum.com; 350 E 3rd St; adult/child $15/10; ⊙9am-6pm summer, 10am-

---

IOWA: DETOURS & EXTRAS

Effigy Mounds National Monument (www.nps.gov/efmo; ⊙8am-6pm summer, to 4:30pm rest of yr) **FREE** preserves hundreds of Native American burial mounds, which sit in the bluffs high above the Mississippi River in far northeast Iowa.

The only museum of its kind, **Hobo Museum** (☑641-843-9104; www.hobo.com; 51 Main Ave S; admission $3; ⊙10am-5pm Jun–mid-Aug), located in north-central Britt, hosts the National Hobo Convention on the second weekend in August. Confirm hours in advance.

Great River Road has an Iowa route that hugs the Mississippi and passes through some isolated towns (**Bellevue** is a gem and lives up to its name with good river views) and some verdant, rural scenery. **Burlington** has an excellent visitor center and is good for a break. Get info at www.byways.org and www.iowagreatriverroad.com.

5pm rest of year). Nearby, the **Spirit of Dubuque** (☑563-583-8093; www.dubuqueriverrides.com; 3rd St, at Ice Harbor; adult/child from $22/15; ⊙May-Oct) offers a variety of Mississippi sightseeing and dining cruises on a mock-paddleboat.

The historic eight-story **Hotel Julien** (☑563-556-4200; www.hoteljuliendubuque.com; 200 Main St; r $110-250; ✳ 🛜) was built in 1914 and was once a refuge for Al Capone. A lavish renovation has turned it upscale and it's a real antidote to chains.

Main St has eateries grand and humble.

Get information from the downtown **visitor center** (☑800-798-4748; www.traveldubuque.com; 300 Main St; ⊙9am-5pm Mon-Thu & Sat, to 6pm Fri, to 3pm Sun).

Waterloo & Around

Home to five **John Deere tractor factories**, Waterloo is the place to get one of those prized green-and-yellow caps you've seen across middle America. Fun tractor-driven **Tractor Assembly Tours** (☑800-765-9588; 3500 E Donald St; ⊙tours 8am, 10am & 1pm Mon-Fri) **FREE** show how these vehicles are made. The minimum age is 13 years and reservations are required.

NORTH DAKOTA

'Magnificent desolation.' Buzz Aldrin used it to describe the moon and it applies just as well in North Dakota. Fields of grain – green in the spring and summer, bronze in the fall and white in winter – stretch beyond every horizon. Except for the rugged 'badlands' of the far west, geographic relief is subtle. More often it is the collapsing remains of a failed homestead that breaks up the vista.

Isolated in the far US north, North Dakota is the least visited state. But that just means that there's less traffic as you whiz along at the usual legal limit of 75mph. This is a place to get lost on remote two-lane routes and to appreciate the magnificence of raw land.

But note that despite those seemingly endless summer fields of grain, the state's economy is tied to large oil deposits in the west. Soaring energy prices have turned once-moribund towns such as Williston and Watford City into boomtowns, with vast trailer encampments for oil-field workers and roads clogged – and battered – by huge trucks. Most are surprised to learn that North Dakota is the fastest growing state in the US.

History

During their epic journey, Lewis and Clark spent more time in what is now North Dakota than any other state, meeting up with Shoshone guide Sacagawea on their way west. In the mid-19th century, smallpox epidemics came up the Missouri River, decimating the Arikara, Mandan and Hidatsa tribes, who affiliated and established the Like-a-Fishhook Village around 1845. When the railroad arrived in North Dakota in the 1870s, thousands of settlers flocked in to take up allotments under the *Homestead Act*. By 1889 the state population was more than 250,000, half foreign-born (one in eight was from Norway).

Young Theodore Roosevelt came here to ditch his city-slicker image. As president, in-spired by his time in North Dakota, he earned the title 'The Father of Conservation' for his work creating national forests and parks.

❶ Information

North Dakota Bed & Breakfast Association (☑888-271-3380; www.ndbba.com)

North Dakota State Parks (☑800-807-4723; www.parkrec.nd.gov) Vehicle permits cost $5/25 per day/year. Nearly half of the park campsites are reservable; fees range from $10 to $20 per night.

North Dakota Tourism Division (☑800-435-5663; www.ndtourism.com)

Along I-94

Arrowing across North Dakota, I-94 provides easy access to most of the state's top attractions, although it would not be the road of scenic choice (US 2 is more atmospheric).

Fargo

Named for the Fargo of Wells Fargo Bank, North Dakota's biggest city has been a fur-trading post, a frontier town, a quick-divorce capital and a haven for folks in the Federal Witness Protection Program; not to mention the namesake of the Coen Brothers' film *Fargo* – though the movie was set across the Red River in Minnesota. Still, expect to hear a lot of accents similar to Frances McDormand's unforgettable version in the film. Film fame aside, there's not a lot in Fargo worth more than a quick stop off the highway.

The modern, ambitious **Plains Art Museum** (www.plainsart.org; 704 1st Ave N; adult/child $5/free; ◷11am-5pm Tue-Sat, noon-5pm Sun, to 8pm Tue & Thu) features sophisticated programing in a renovated warehouse. The permanent collection includes contemporary work by Native American artists.

🛏 Sleeping & Eating

Chain motels cluster at exits 64 on I-29 and 348 on I-94.

★ **Hotel Donaldson**   HOTEL $$$
(☑701-478-1000; www.hoteldonaldson.com; 101 Broadway; r from $190; ❉@☎) A stylish and swank revamp of a flophouse, the 17 luxurious suites here are each decorated by a local artist. Fargo's most chic restaurant and rooftop bar (and hot tub!) may lack competition but are still cool.

> ### ❶ MOUNTAIN TIME IN NORTH DAKOTA
>
> The southwest quarter of North Dakota, including Medora, uses Mountain Time, which is one hour earlier than the rest of the state's Central Time.

THE FARGO WOODCHIPPER

Fargo's embrace of its namesake film is on full display at the town's visitor center, which houses the actual woodchipper used for the scene where Gaear feeds the last of Carl's body into its maw and is discovered by Marge. And you can reenact the scene – although not the results – while wearing Fargo-style hats and jamming a fake leg in (both provided!).

ℹ️ Information

The grain-elevator-shaped **visitor center** (📞 800-235-7654; www.fargomoorhead.org; 2001 44th St; ⏱ 7:30am-8pm Mon-Fri, 10am-6pm Sat & Sun summer, 8am-5pm Mon-Fri, 10am-4pm Sat rest of yr) is off I-94 exit 348.

Bismarck

Like the surrounding plains of wheat, Bismarck, North Dakota's capital, has a quick and bountiful summer. Otherwise, it's a compact place that hunkers down for the long winters where the lows average -4°F (-20°C).

The stark 1930s **State Capitol** (📞 701-328-2480; N 7th St; ⏱ 8am-4pm Mon-Fri, tours hourly except noon, plus 9am-4pm Sat & 1-4pm Sun summer) **FREE** is often referred to as the 'skyscraper of the prairie' and looks something like a Stalinist school of dentistry from the outside, but has some art-deco flourishes inside. There's an observation deck on the 18th floor.

Behind the Sacagawea statue, the huge **North Dakota Heritage Center** (www.history.nd.gov; Capitol Hill; ⏱ 8am-5pm Mon-Fri, 10am-5pm Sat & Sun) **FREE** has details on everything from Norwegian bachelor farmers to the scores of nuclear bombs perched on missiles in silos across the state.

Fort Abraham Lincoln State Park (www.parkrec.nd.gov; per vehicle $5, plus adult/child to tour historical sites $6/4; ⏱ park 9am-5pm, tours May-Sep), 7 miles south of Mandan on SR 1806, is well worth the detour. Its **On-a-Slant Indian Village** has five re-created Mandan earth lodges, while the fort, with several replica buildings, was Custer's last stop before the Battle of Little Bighorn.

In Bismarck, chain motels congregate around I-94 exit 159. Get info at the **Bismarck-Mandan Visitor Center** (📞 800-767-3555; www.discoverbismarckmandan.com; 1600 Burnt Boat Dr; ⏱ 8am-7pm Mon-Fri, 8am-5pm Sat,

10am-4pm Sun summer, 8am-5pm Mon-Fri rest of yr), off I-94 exit 157.

West of Bismark

West on I-94, stop and see **Sue, the World's Largest Holstein Cow** at New Salem (exit 127). At exit 72, there's a unique detour south along the Enchanted Hwy (p638). In Dickinson, an hour west of Sue, the **Dakota Dinosaur Museum** (📞 701-225-3466; www.dakotadino.com; I-94 exit 61; adult/child $8/5; ⏱ 9am-5pm May-Aug) has oodles of dinosaur fossils and statues, most found in the state.

Theodore Roosevelt National Park

A tortured land known as the 'badlands', the colors of which seem to change with the moods of nature, **Theodore Roosevelt National Park** (www.nps.gov/thro; 7-day pass per vehicle $10) is the state's natural highlight. Bizarre rock formations, streaked with a rainbow of red, yellow, brown, black and silver minerals, are framed by green prairie.

Roosevelt described this area as 'a land of vast, silent spaces, of lonely rivers, and of plains where the wild game stared at the passing horsemen,' and it's hard to describe the place better even today. Wildlife is still

NORTH DAKOTA FACTS

Nickname Peace Garden State

Population 701,000

Area 70,705 sq miles

Capital city Bismarck (population 63,000)

Sales tax 5-8%

Birthplace of legendary Shoshone woman Sacagawea (1788–1812), cream of wheat (1893), bandleader Lawrence Welk (1903–92), singer-writer of westerns Louis L'Amour (1908–88)

Home of World's largest bison, turtle and Holstein statues

Politics Conservative Republican

Famous for The movie *Fargo*

Official fish Northern pike

Driving distances Fargo to Bismarck 193 miles

everywhere: mule deer, wild horses, bighorn sheep, elk, bison, around 200 bird species and, of course, sprawling subterranean prairie dog towns.

The park is divided into sections:

South Unit Most visitors opt for the 36-mile scenic drive that begins in Medora, an enjoyable town just off I-94. Prairie dogs are a highlight.

North Unit Gets few visitors but is well worth the journey for the 14-mile drive to the **Oxbow Overlook**, with its wide views into the vast and colorfully striated river canyon. The verdant surrounds are protected as the **Little Missouri National Grassland** and bison are everywhere. It is 68 miles north of I-94 on US 85.

The park has three visitor centers, including the **South Unit visitor center** (Medora; ☉ 8am-6pm summer, 8am-4:30pm rest of year), with Theodore Roosevelt's old cabin out back. The park has two simple **campgrounds** (campsites $10) and free backcountry camping (permit required).

Hikers can explore 85 miles of backcountry trails. For a good adventure, hike or cycle the 96-mile **Maah Daah Hey Trail** between the park units. Driving, continue north on US 85 to Fort Buford.

Medora

Medora (www.medora.com) is a somewhat re-created and restored pioneer town that is quite appealing and relatively uncommer-cialized. Accommodations include motels and B&Bs.

The most atmospheric choice is the **Rough Riders Hotel** (☏ 701-623-4444; www.medora.com; 301 3rd Ave; r $135-200; ❋ ☎ ✉), which dates back to 1885. Renovations made the eight original rooms dude-worthy and added 68 new ones.

Along US 2

US 2 is the more interesting alternative to I-94. The endless sky vistas stretch even further than the seas of golden grain. **Grand Forks** is a stolid city, while **Devils Lake** is one of the top waterfowl hunting destinations in the country. The entire area is subject to inundation by the flood-prone Red River.

Rugby

Rugby is about halfway down the highway, but its more notable location identity is as the **geographical center of North America**. The **Prairie Village Museum** (www.prairievillagemuseum.com; 102 US 2 SE; adult/child $7/3; ☉ 8:30am-5pm, from noon Sun mid-May–mid-Sep) re-creates Great Plains life through the decades.

Minot

North Dakota's fourth-largest city is home to military bases and not much else of note. But it does celebrate its Scandinavian roots during **Norsk Høstfest** (www.hostfest.com;

NORTH DAKOTA: DETOURS & EXTRAS

North Dakota still has underground nuclear missiles waiting for launch orders, however many more have been deactivated because of treaty agreements with the Russians. **Minuteman Missile Site** (www.history.nd.gov; adult/child $10/3; ☉ 10am-6pm mid-May–mid-Sep, reduced hours rest of year), near Cooperstown on Hwys 45 and 200, includes an **underground command center** from where missiles were launched. Visits are by tour. A nearby **missile silo** is actually more eerie. Often unattended, you can ponder the doors that hid a rocket with over 500 kilotons of nuclear explosive power (the Hiroshima bomb had 15 kilotons). It's surrounded by mundane farmland and a few distant farmhouses.

The **International Peace Garden** (www.peacegarden.com; per vehicle $10; ☉ 10am-5pm) provides a change of pace from nukes; some 150,000 flowers and several monuments sit symbolically on the North Dakota–Manitoba border on US 281.

The **Enchanted Highway** has huge whimsical metal sculptures of local folks and critters by local artist Gary Greff. It runs for 32 miles straight south to Regent from I-94 exit 72. Once there, you can stay in Greff's fun new motel, the **Enchanted Castle** (www.enchanted-castle.net; 607 Main St; r $90-125; ❋ ☎), which is an elementary school remodeled to look like just that.

LEWIS & CLARK IN NORTH DAKOTA

North of Bismarck are several worthwhile attractions near the spot where Lewis and Clark wintered with the Mandan in 1804–05. They offer an evocative look at the lives of the Native Americans and the explorers amid lands that even today seem little changed.

The **North Dakota Lewis & Clark Interpretive Center** (www.fortmandan.com; junction US 83 & ND Hwy 200A; adult/child $7.50/5; ⊘9am-5pm daily year-round, from noon Sun winter) is a newly renovated center where you can learn about the duo's epic expedition and the Native Americans who helped them. Check out the beautiful drawings from George Catlin's Portfolio.

The same ticket gets you into **Fort Mandan** (CR 17), a replica of the fort built by Lewis and Clark, 2.5 miles west (10 miles downstream from the flooded original site). It sits on a lonely stretch of the Missouri River marked by a monument to Seaman, the expedition's dog. Inside the small but worthwhile info building, look for the display on period medicine, including 'Thunderclappers.'

At **Knife River Indian Villages National Historical Site** (www.nps.gov/knri; off Hwy 200; ⊘8am-6pm, to 4:30pm winter) FREE you can still see the mounds left by three earthen villages of the Hidatsas, who lived on the Knife River, a narrow tributary of the Missouri, for more than 900 years. The National Park Service has re-created one of the earthen lodges. A stroll through the mostly wide-open and wild site leads to the village site where Lewis and Clark met Sacagawea. The historic site is just north of Stanton (22 miles west of Washburn) on Hwy 200, which runs through verdant rolling prairie for 110 miles between US 83 and US 85.

⊘early Oct), which is promoted as the world's largest Scandinavian festival.

Minot has a full range of modest chain motels along US 2, 52 and 83. However, North Dakota's oil boom means that it can be hard to find a motel room from Minot west to Montana. Vacancies are few and prices are very high.

West to Montana

West of Minot the land is dotted with forlorn little settlements slipping back into the prairie soil. However, the skyline is enlivened by the flames and bright lights of hundreds of oil drilling rigs. It's a huge boom fueled by the same high prices you curse when refilling your tank and the result is that small towns between Minot and Montana are swamped with workers.

Twenty-two miles southwest of Williston along SR 1804, **Fort Buford** (www.history.nd.gov; adult/child $5/2.50; ⊘10am-6pm mid-May–mid-Sep) is the bleak army outpost where Sitting Bull surrendered. The adjacent **Missouri-Yellowstone Confluence Interpretive Center** (⊘9am-7pm mid-May–mid-Sep, 9am-4pm Wed Sat, 1-5pm Sun rest of year) includes the fort's visitor center. Swing by the boat landing in May to see anglers reeling in paddlefish.

About 2 miles west, on the Montana–North Dakota border, the more evocative

Fort Union Trading Post (www.nps.gov/fous; SR 1804; ⊘8am-6:30pm Central Time summer, 9am-5:30pm rest of year) FREE is a reconstruction of the American Fur Company post built in 1828.

SOUTH DAKOTA

Gently rolling prairies through shallow fertile valleys mark much of this endlessly attractive state. But head southwest and hell breaks loose – in a good way. The Badlands National Park is the geologic equivalent of fireworks. The Black Hills are like opera: majestic, challenging, intriguing and even frustrating. Mt Rushmore matches the Statue of Liberty for five-star icon status. Throughout the state are important Native American sites and interesting towns big and small.

❶ Information

Bed & Breakfast Innkeepers of South Dakota (☏888-500-4667; www.southdakotabb.com)

South Dakota Department of Tourism (☏800-732 5682; www.travelsd.com)

South Dakota State Parks (☏800-710-2267; www.gfp.sd.gov) Vehicle permits cost $6/30 per day/year. Many park campsites are reservable; fees range from $8 to $25 per night. Cabins start at $35.

Sioux Falls

South Dakota's largest city (population 154,000) lives up to its name at **Falls Park** just north of downtown where the Big Sioux River plunges down a long series of rock faces. The park has an excellent **visitor center** (☑ 605-367-7430; www.siouxfallscvb.com; 900 N Phillips Ave; ☺ 10am-9pm daily Apr–mid-Oct, reduced hours other times) with citywide information and an observation tower.

The huge pink quartzite **Old Courthouse Museum** (www.siouxlandmuseums.com; 200 W 6th St; ☺ 8am-5pm Mon-Fri, 9am-5pm Sat, noon-5pm Sun, to 8pm Thu) **FREE**, a restored 1890s building, has three floors of well-curated changing exhibits on the region.

Sioux Falls has motels at I-29 exits 77 to 83. For diner fare, there are good choices on lively S Phillips Ave downtown, including **Minervas** (www.minervas.net; 301 S Phillips Ave; mains $10-25; ☺ 11am-10pm), a plush local fave with good bars (for drinks *and* salad).

Along I-90

Easily one of the least interesting stretches of interstate highway, I-90 across South Dakota fortunately has some worthy stops along the way.

SOUTH DAKOTA FACTS

Nickname Mt Rushmore State

Population 834,000

Area 77,125 sq miles

Capital city Pierre (population 13,900)

Sales tax 4-6%

Birthplace of Sitting Bull (c 1831–90), Crazy Horse (c 1840–77) and Black Elk (c 1863–1950), all of Battle of Little Bighorn fame, and genial broadcaster Tom Brokaw (b 1940)

Home of Mt Rushmore, the Sioux

Politics Increasingly Republican

Famous for HBO TV show *Deadwood*, Wounded Knee Massacre

Official animal Coyote

Driving distances Sioux Falls to Rapid City 341 miles, Sioux Falls to Des Moines 283 miles

Mitchell

Every year, half a million people pull off I-90 (exit 332) to see the Taj Mahal of agriculture, the all-time-ultimate roadside attraction, the **Corn Palace** (www.cornpalace.org; 604 N Main St; ☺ 8am-9pm summer, reduced hours rest of year) **FREE**. Close to 300,000 ears of corn are used each year to create a tableaux of murals on the outside of the building. Ponder the scenes and you may find a kernel of truth or just say 'aw shucks.'

Chamberlain

In a picturesque site where I-90 crosses the Missouri River, Chamberlain (exit 263) is home to the excellent **Akta Lakota Museum & Cultural Center** (www.aktalakota.org; 1301 N Main St; suggested donation $5; ☺ 8am-6pm Mon-Sat, 9am-5pm Sun summer, 8am-5pm Mon-Fri rest of year) at St Joseph's Indian School. It has Lakota cultural displays and contemporary art from numerous tribes.

History buffs should pop into the hilltop rest stop, between exits 263 and 265, where the **Lewis & Clark Information Center** (☺ 8:30am-4:30pm mid-May–Sep) **FREE** has exhibits on the intrepid band.

Pierre

Pierre (pronounced '*peer*') is just too small (population 14,100) and ordinary to feel like a seat of power. Small-town Victorian homes overlook the imposing 1910 **State Capitol** (500 E Capitol Ave; ☺ 8am-7pm Mon-Fri, to 5pm Sat & Sun) **FREE** with its black copper dome.

The best reason to detour off I-90 here is because it lies along the **Native American Scenic Byway** and lonely, stark **US 14** (for both, see p647).

Exhibits at the **South Dakota Cultural Heritage Center** (www.history.sd.gov; 900 Governor's Dr; adult/child $4/free; ☺ 9am-6:30pm Mon-Sat, 1-4:30pm Sun summer, to 4:30pm rest of year) include a bloody Ghost Dance shirt from Wounded Knee.

At a bend on the Missouri River, **Framboise Island** has several hiking trails and plentiful wildlife. It's across from where the Lewis and Clark expedition spent four days and was nearly derailed when they inadvertently offended members of the local Brule tribe.

Most hotels lie along US 83. The cute center of Pierre includes the excellent **Prairie Pages** (321 S Pierre St; ⊙9am-6pm Mon-Sat) bookstore.

Minuteman Missile National Historic Site

In the 1960s and 1970s, 450 Minutemen II intercontinental ballistic missiles, always at the ready in underground silos, were just 30 minutes from their targets in the Soviet Union. The missiles have since been retired (more modern ones still lurk in silos across the northern Great Plains). The first national park dedicated to the Cold War preserves a silo and its underground launch facility.

At the small temporary **visitor contact station** (605-433-5552; www.nps.gov/mimi; I-90 exit 131; ⊙8am-4:30pm) (a permanent spot to house it has yet to be built), you can get tickets for the free tours of the nearby launch complex where two people stood ready around the clock to turn keys launching missiles from this part of South Dakota. Tours are given daily and are first-come, first-served.

The **silo** (I-90 exit 116; ⊙8am-4pm) can be viewed without a tour through a glass cover.

Wall

Hyped for hundreds of miles, **Wall Drug** (www.walldrug.com; 510 Main St; ⊙6:30am-6pm, extended hours in summer;) is a surprisingly enjoyable stop. It really does have 5¢ coffee, free ice water, good doughnuts and enough diversions and come-ons to warm the heart of schlock-lovers everywhere. But amid the fudge in the faux frontier complex is a superb bookstore with a great selection of regional titles. Out back, ride the mythical **jackalope** and check out the historical photos.

Wall is a good place for an overnight pause. It's compact and walkable, there are tasty and cheap cafes and bars, and several good indie motels, including **Sunshine Inn** (605-279-2178; www.sunshineinnatwallsd.com; 608 Main St; r $50-80;), which has a genial owner and 22 basic and sparkling rooms.

Badlands National Park

This otherworldly landscape, oddly softened by its fantastic rainbow hues, is a spectacle of sheer walls and spikes stabbing the dry

ℹ MOUNTAIN TIME

Roughly the western one-third of South Dakota – including the Black Hills and everything west of I-90 exit 177 – uses Mountain Time, which is one hour earlier than Central Time in the rest of the state.

air. It was understandably named *mako sica* (badland) by Native Americans. Looking over the bizarre formations from the corrugated walls surrounding Badlands is like seeing an ocean someone boiled dry.

The park's north unit gets the most visitors; the **Hwy 240 Badlands Loop Rd** is easily reached from I-90 (exits 110 and 131) and you can drive it in an hour if you're in a hurry (and not stuck behind an RV). Lookouts and vistas abound.

Much less visited is the portion west of Hwy 240 along the gravel **Sage Creek Rim Rd**. There are stops at prairie dog towns and this is where most backcountry hikers and campers go. There is nearly no water or shade here, so don't strike out into the wilderness unprepared. The less-accessible south units are in the Pine Ridge Indian Reservation and see few visitors.

The **Ben Reifel Visitor Center** (www.nps.gov/badl; Hwy 240; ⊙7am-7pm summer, 8am-5pm Apr-May & Sep-Oct, 8am-4pm rest of year) has good exhibits and advice for ways to ditch your car to appreciate the geologic wonders. The **White River Visitor Center** (Hwy 27; ⊙10am-4pm Jun-Aug) is small. A seven-day pass costs $15 for cars and $7 for cyclists.

Neither the developed **Cedar Pass Campground** (campsites $10-28) or primitive **Sage Creek Campground** (campsites free) take reservations. Hotels can be found on I-90 in Kadoka and Wall, or stay at a cozy cabin inside the park at **Cedar Pass Lodge** (605-433-5460; www.cedarpasslodge.com; Hwy 240; cabins $130-140; ⊙mid-Apr–mid-Oct;). There is a restaurant and shops.

The national park, along with the surrounding **Buffalo Gap National Grassland**, protects the country's largest prairie grasslands, several species of Plains mammal (including bison and black-footed ferret), prairie falcons and lots of snakes. The **National Grasslands Visitors Center** (www.fs.fed.us/grasslands; 798 Main St, Wall; ⊙8am-4:30pm Mon-Fri) has good displays on the wealth of life in this complex ecosystem

LITTLE HOUSE(S) ON THE PRAIRIE

Fans of *Little House on the Prairie* should head to Laura Ingalls Wilder's former home, **De Smet**. The pint-sized author lived here from age 12 when her peripatetic Pa finally settled down (much of her famous book was based on her time in Independence, KS). The town is 40 miles west of I-29 (exit 133) on US 14.

Right in town, the fussy and frilly complex that's home to the **Laura Ingalls Wilder Memorial Society** (www.discoverlaura.org; 105 Olivet Ave; adult/child $10/5; ⊙9am-5pm Mon-Sat, 11am-5pm Sun summer, reduced hours rest of year; ⊞) has tours inside two original Wilder homes – the one where the Wilders spent the first winter in 1879 and the home Michael Landon, er, 'Pa', later built.

Just outside town and down a dirt road, the actual **Ingalls Homestead** (www.ingallshomestead.com; 20812 Homestead Rd; admission $10; ⊙9am-7pm summer; ⊞) has been much gussied up and includes all manner of attractions about 19th-century farm life and Laura herself. It's well done, with nary a fudge shop in sight.

Near the homestead, the long-running outdoor **Laura Ingalls Wilder Pageant** (www.desmetpageant.org; adult/child $10/7; ⊙weekends Jul) reenacts melodramatic scenes from Laura's books. Townfolk fill the roles, including one very lucky young girl.

For more info on the plethora of LHOTP-related sites across middle America, see www.liwfrontiergirl.com.

---

you've been whining about as 'boring' while you barrel down the freeway. Rangers can map out back-road routes that will let you do looping tours of Badlands National Park and the grasslands without ever touching I-90. **Hwy 44** to Rapid City is also a fine alternative to the interstate.

Pine Ridge Indian Reservation

Home to the Lakota Oglala Sioux, the Pine Ridge reservation south of Badlands National Park is one of the nation's poorest 'counties,' with over half the population living below the poverty line. Despite being at times a jarring dose of reality, it is also a place welcoming to visitors.

In 1890 the new Ghost Dance religion, which the Lakota followers believed would bring back their ancestors and eliminate the white man, became popular. This struck fear into the area's soldiers and settlers and the frenetic circle dances were outlawed. The 7th US Cavalry rounded up a band of Lakota under Chief Big Foot and brought them to the small village of Wounded Knee. On December 29, as the soldiers began to search for weapons, a shot was fired (nobody knows by whom), leading to the massacre of more than 250 men, women and children, most of them unarmed. It's one of the most infamous atrocities in US history. Twenty five soldiers also died.

The shabby **Wounded Knee Massacre Site**, 16 miles northeast of Pine Ridge town, is bisected by two-lane Hwy 27 and marked by a faded roadside sign. The mass grave, often frequented by people looking for handouts, sits atop the hill near a church. The nearby visitor center has little to offer. North of the site, Hwy 27 passes through some seldom-visited tracts of the Badlands.

Four miles north of Pine Ridge town at the Red Cloud Indian School is the **Red Cloud Heritage Center** (www.redcloudschool.org; Hwy 18; ⊙9am-7pm Mon-Fri, 11am-5pm Sat & Sun summer, 8am-5pm Tue-Fri, 11am-5pm Sat rest of year) FREE, a well-curated art museum with traditional and contemporary work and a craft shop. Look for photos taken after the massacre showing the frozen bodies of the dead with their expressions of shock locked in place.

Tune in to what's happening on KILI (90.1 FM), 'the voice of the Lakota nation,' which broadcasts community events and often plays traditional music.

Black Hills

This stunning region on the Wyoming–South Dakota border lures oodles of visitors with its winding canyons and wildly eroded 7000ft peaks. The region's name – the 'Black' comes from the dark Ponderosa pine-covered slopes – was conferred by the Lakota Sioux. In the 1868 Fort Laramie Treaty, they were assured that the hills would be theirs for eternity, but the discovery of gold changed that and the Sioux were shoved out to low-value flatlands only six years later. *Dances with Wolves* covers some of this period.

You'll need several days to explore the area. Throughout are bucolic back-road drives, caves, bison herds, forests, Mt Rushmore and Crazy Horse monuments, and outdoor activities (ballooning, cycling, rock climbing, boating, fishing, hiking, downhill skiing, gold-panning etc). Like fool's gold, gaudy tourist traps lurk in corners and keep things lively.

ℹ Information

There are hundreds of hotels and campgrounds across the hills; still, during summer, room rates shoot up like geysers and reservations are essential. Avoid visiting during the Sturgis Motorcycle Rally (early August), when motorbikes rule the roads and fill the rooms. Much is closed October to April.

Visitor centers and reservations:

Black Hills Central Reservations (☑866-601-5103; www.blackhillsvacations.com) Accommodation reservations and last-minute deals.

Black Hills Visitor Center (☑605-355-3700; www.blackhillsbadlands.com; I-90 exit 61; ⊘8am-8pm summer, to 5pm rest of year) Tons of info and apps.

Black Hills National Forest

The majority of the Black Hills lie within this 1875-sq-mile mixture of protected and logged forest, perforated by pockets of private land on most roads. The scenery is fantastic, whether you get deep into it on the 450 miles of hiking trails or drive the byways and gravel fire roads.

The 109-mile **George S Mickelson Trail** (www.mickelsontrail.com; daily/annual fee $3/15) cuts through much of the forest, running from Deadwood through Hill City and Custer to Edgemont on an abandoned railway line. There are bike rentals at various trailside towns.

The forest **headquarters** (☑605-673-9200; www.fs.fed.us/bhnf; 25041 US 16; ⊘9am-5pm Mon Fri) is in Custer and a modern **visitor center** (US 385, near Hwy 44; ⊘8:30am-5pm mid-May–mid-Sep) sits on the Pactola Reservoir between Hill City and Rapid City.

Good camping abounds in the forest. There are 30 basic (no showers or electricity) **campgrounds** (☑877-444-6777; www.recreation.gov; campsites free-$25); reserve in summer. Backcountry camping is allowed just about anywhere (free; no open fires).

Rapid City

A worthy capital to the region, 'Rapid' has an intriguing, lively and walkable downtown. Well-preserved brick buildings, filled with quality shopping and dining, make it a good urban base.

◉ Sights

Get a walking-tour brochure of Rapid's historic buildings and public art from the Black Hills Visitor Center (p643). Check out the watery fun on **Main St Square**.

Family friendly and delightfully hokey tourist attractions vie for dollars along Hwy 16 on the way to Mt Rushmore; these include Bear Country USA and Reptile Gardens.

★**Statues of Presidents**　　MONUMENT (www.cityofpresidents.com; 631 Main St; ⊘info center noon-9pm Mon-Sat Jun-Sep) From a shifty-eyed Nixon in repose to a triumphant Harry Truman, lifelike statues dot corners throughout the center. Collect all 42.

Museum of Geology　　MUSEUM (museum.sdsmt.edu; 501 E St Joseph St, O'Harra Bldg; ⊘9am-5pm Mon-Fri, to 6pm Sat, noon-5pm Sun summer, 9am-4pm Mon-Fri, 10am-4pm Sat rest of year) FREE All that drama underground has produced some spectacular rocks. See these plus dinosaur bones and some stellar fossils here, at the South Dakota School of Mines & Technology.

Bear Country USA　　WILDLIFE RESERVE (www.bearcountryusa.com; Hwy 16; adult/child $16/10; ⊘8am-6pm summer, reduced hours rest of year, closed winter; 🚼) Oodles of bears big and small in this drive-through park live off the land and hope you'll do something forbidden like offering them a Big Mac, or your hand. The reserve is 8 miles south of Rapid City.

Reptile Gardens　　WILDLIFE RESERVE (www.reptilegardens.com; Hwy 16; adult/child $16/11; ⊘8am-6pm summer, reduced hours rest of year, closed winter; 🚼) Reptiles, snakes, giant tortoises and many more critters inspire countless 'wows!'

Black Hills & Badlands National Park

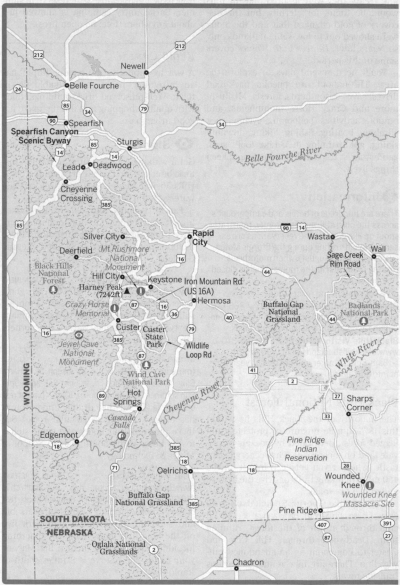

🛏 Sleeping & Eating

Motels, many indie, cluster at I-90 exits 57 and 60, downtown and US16 south of town. Downtown has scores of eateries and bars.

★**Hotel Alex Johnson**　　　HOTEL **$$**
(☎605-342-1210; www.alexjohnson.com; 523 6th St; r $60-200; ❄@☎) The design of this 1927 classic magically blends Germanic Tudor architecture and traditional Lakota Sioux symbols – note the lobby's painted ceiling

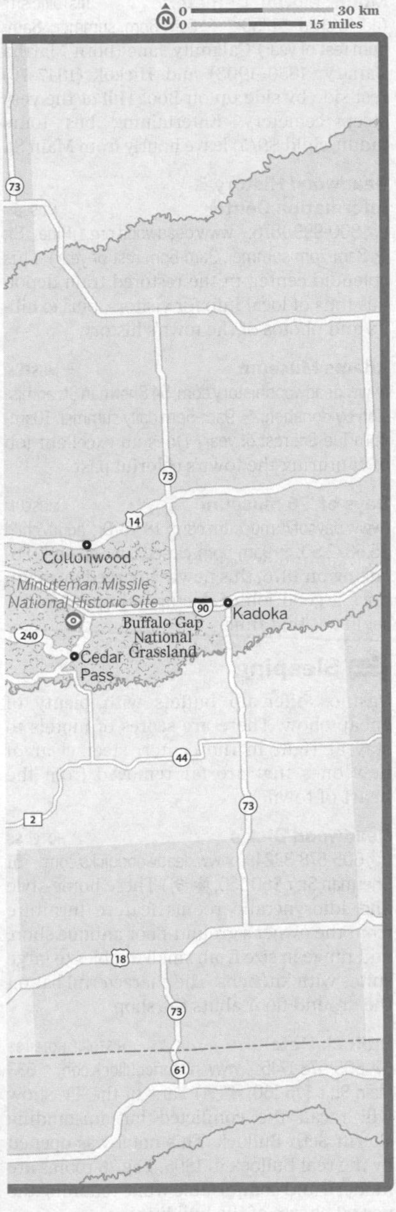

and the chandelier made of war lances. The 127 rooms are modern and slightly posh but the real appeal here is that it hasn't been turned into a boutique hotel. Its timeless qualities include a portrait of guest Al Capone near the front desk. The rooftop bar is a delight.

Adoba Eco Hotel HOTEL $$
(605-348-8300; www.adobahotelrapidcity.com; 445 Mt Rushmore Rd; r $80-200;) A former highrise Radisson has been reborn as a high-concept downtown hotel with green accents. Furniture is made from recycled materials yet there's no skimping on comfort. The marble floor in the lobby is a stunner.

Tally's AMERICAN $$
(530 6th St; mains $6-20; 7am-9pm Mon-Thu, to 10pm Fri & Sat) Carter or Reagan? Both statues are out front and you can ponder your preference while you savor the upscale diner fare at this stylish cafe and bar. Breakfasts are as good as ever; more creative regional fare is on offer at night.

Murphy's Pub & Grill AMERICAN $$
(www.murphyspubandgrill.com; 510 9th St; mains $6-20; food 11am-10pm, bar to 1am) Pub fare with creative flair makes this bustling downtown bar an excellent dining choice. Specials feature seasonal and local ingredients. The vast terrace is matched by the big interior.

Drinking

★**Independent Ale House** PUB
(www.independentalehouse.com; 625 St Joseph St; 3pm-late) Enjoy a fabulous (and changing) line-up of the best microbrews from the region in this vintage-style bar. There are chairs on the sidewalk and a short snack menu.

Sturgis

Fast food, Christian iconography and billboards for glitzy biker bars featuring dolled-up models unlikely to ever be found on the back of a Harley are just some of the cacophony of images of this tacky small town on I-90 (exits 30 and 32). Things get even louder for the annual **Sturgis Motorcycle Rally** (www.sturgismotorcyclerally.com; early Aug), when around 500,000 riders, fans and curious onlookers take over the town. Temporary campsites are set up and motels across the region unmuffle their rates. Check the rally website for vacancies.

The **Sturgis Motorcycle Museum** (www.sturgismuseum.com; 999 Main St; adult/child $10/free; 10am-4pm) houses dozens of bikes, including many classics. The 'freedom fighters' exhibit honors those who have fought for the rights of bikers.

Spearfish

Spearfish Canyon Scenic Byway (www.byways.org; US 14A) is a waterfall-lined, curvaceous 20-mile road that cleaves into the heart of the hills from Spearfish. There's a sight worth stopping for around every bend; pause for longer than a minute and you'll hear beavers hard at work.

The **chamber of commerce** (☏ 800-626-8013; www.spearfishchamber.org; 106 W Kansas St; ☺ 8am-5pm Mon-Fri, info available 24hr in lobby) has a self-guided tour of the byway and hiking trail maps.

Chain hotels cluster around I-90 exits 10 and 14, and aging indie motels are downtown. For a rural retreat, the **Spearfish Canyon Lodge** (☏ 605-584-3435; www.spfcanyon.com; US 14A; r $90-220; ✳ 🛜 🐾) is 13 miles south of Spearfish near trails and streams. The massive lobby fireplace adds charm and the 55 modern piney rooms are cozy.

Deadwood

'No law at all in Deadwood, is that true?' So began the iconic HBO TV series. Today things have changed, although the 80 gambling halls big and small would no doubt put a sly grin on the faces of the hard characters who founded the town.

Settled illegally by eager gold rushers in the 1870s, Deadwood is now a National Historic Landmark. Its atmospheric streets are lined with gold-rush-era buildings lavishly restored with gambling dollars. Its storied past is easy to find. There's eternal devotion to Wild Bill Hickok, who was shot in the back of the head here in 1876 while gambling.

👁 Sights

Actors reenact famous **shootouts** (☺ 2pm, 4pm & 6pm Jun-Aug) on Main St during summer. **Hickok's murder** (657 Main St; ☺ 1pm, 3pm, 5pm & 7pm Jun–mid-Sep) is acted out in Saloon No 10. A **trial** (cnr Main & Pine Sts; ☺ 8pm) of the killer takes place in the Masonic Temple.

Downtown is walkable, but the fake **trolley** (per ride $1) can be handy for getting between attractions, hotels and parking lots.

Mount Moriah Cemetery HISTORIC SITE (adult/child $1/50¢; ☺ 8am-8pm summer, 8am-5pm rest of year) Calamity Jane (born Martha Canary; 1850–1903) and Hickok (1847–76) rest side by side up on Boot Hill at the very steep cemetery. Entertaining bus tours (adult/child $9/5) leave hourly from Main St.

Deadwood History & Information Center MUSEUM (☏ 800-999-1876; www.deadwood.org; Pine St; ☺ 8am-7pm summer, 9am-5pm rest of year) This splendid center, in the restored train depot, has tons of local info for visitors, plus exhibits and photos of the town's history.

Adams Museum MUSEUM (www.deadwoodhistory.com; 54 Sherman St; admission by donation; ☺ 9am-5pm daily summer, 10am-4pm Tue-Sat rest of year) Does an excellent job of capturing the town's colorful past.

Days of '76 Museum MUSEUM (www.daysof76museum.com; 18 76 Dr; adult/child $5.50/2.50; ☺ 9am-5pm, closed Sun Sep-Apr) Focusing on 1876, this newly enlarged museum does a good job of documenting life in the region at that time.

🛏 Sleeping

Casinos offer up buffets with plenty of cheap chow. There are scores of motels to stay at right in the center; steer clear of new ones that are far removed from the heart of town.

Deadwood Dick's HOTEL $$ (☏ 605-578-3224; www.deadwooddicks.com; 51 Sherman St; r $60-160; ✳ 🛜) These home-style and idiosyncratic rooms feature furniture from the owner's ground-floor antique shop, and range in size from small doubles to large suites with kitchens. The characterful bar on the ground floor abuts the shop.

Bullock Hotel HISTORIC HOTEL $$ (☏ 605-578-1745; www.historicbullock.com; 633 Main St; r $75-160; ✳ 🛜) Fans of the TV show will recall the conflicted but upstanding sheriff Seth Bullock. This hotel was opened by the real Bullock in 1895. The 28 rooms are modern and comfortable while retaining the period charm of the building.

🍴 Eating & Drinking

Saloon No 10 BAR (www.saloon10.com; 657 Main St; mains $10-25; ☺ food noon-10pm, bar 8am-2am) Dark paneled walls and sawdust on the floor are

SOUTH DAKOTA: DETOURS & EXTRAS

Large swaths of South Dakota are unchanged since the 19th century when the Native Americans and the US Army clashed. See the land as it was then along the **Native American Scenic Byway** (www.byways.org), which begins in Chamberlain on Hwy 50 and meanders 100 crooked miles northwest to Pierre along Hwy 1806, following the Missouri River through rolling, rugged countryside. This stretch makes a good detour off I-90.

Highway 14 runs across the middle of the state, crossing I-29 at Brookings (exit 133), then traveling west through De Smet to Pierre and on to Wall. It meanders through a sea of grassland under big skies colored by long sunsets stretching across the broad horizon.

Way off in the northwest corner of the state, **Petrified Wood Park** (500 Main St; ⊙ park 24hr, museum 9am-5pm Jun-Aug) is a 1930s collection of geologic oddities covering an entire city block in the center of little **Lemmon**.

features of this storied bar. The original, where Hickok literally lost big time, stood across the street, but the building burned to the ground and the owners brought the bar over here. There's a rooftop bar and decent Italian-accented food.

Lead

Just uphill from Deadwood, Lead (pronounced *leed*) has an unrestored charm and still bears plenty of scars from the mining era. Gape at the 1250ft-deep **Homestake Gold Mine** (☑ 605-584-3110; www.homestaketour.com; 160 W Main St; viewing area free, tours adult/child $7.50/6.50; ⊙ tours 9am-4pm May-Sep) to see what open-pit mining can do to a mountain. Nearby are the same mine's shafts, which plunge more than 1.5 miles below the surface and are now being used for physics research.

The **Main Street Manor Hostel** (☑ 605-717-2044; www.mainstreetmanorhostel.com; 515 W Main St; per person/d $25/50; ⊙ closed Dec & Jan; ❋ 🛜) is a gem in its own right. Guests get use of the kitchen, garden and laundry at this very friendly place.

US 385

The scenic spine of the Black Hills, US 385 runs 90 miles from Deadwood to Hot Springs and beyond. Beautiful meadows and dark stands of conifers are interspersed with roadside attractions that include kangaroos, mistletoe and, of course, Elvis.

Hill City

One of the most appealing towns up in the hills, Hill City (www.hillcitysd.com) is less

frenzied than places such as Keystone. Its main drag has cafes and galleries.

★ **1880 Train** (www.1880train.com; 222 Railroad Ave; adult/child round-trip $28/12; ⊙ early May–mid-Oct) is a classic steam train running through rugged country to and from Keystone. A train museum is next door.

Right in the center, the **Alpine Inn** (☑ 605-574-2749; www.alpineinnhillcity.com; 133 Main St; r $80-160) dates to 1886 and has comfy rooms in bright red, and filling German fare. Dine amidst frontier charm at **Desperados** (301 Main St; mains $9-20; ⊙ 11:30am-9pm) (have the burger).

Mount Rushmore

Glimpses of Washington's nose from the roads leading to this hugely popular monument never cease to surprise and are but harbingers of the full impact of this mountainside sculpture once you're up close (and past the less impressive parking area and entrance walk). George Washington, Thomas Jefferson, Abraham Lincoln and Theodore Roosevelt each iconically stare into the distance in 60ft-tall granite glory.

Hugely popular, you can easily escape the crowds and fully appreciate the **Mount Rushmore National Memorial** (www.nps.gov/moru; off Hwy 244; parking $11; ⊙ 8am-10pm summer, 8am-5pm other times) while marveling at the artistry of sculptor Gutzon Borglum and the immense labor of the workers who created the memorial between 1927 and 1941.

The **Presidential Trail** loop passes right below the monument for some fine nostril views and accesses the worthwhile **Sculptor's Studio**. Start clockwise and you're right under Washington's nose in under five minutes. The nature trail to the right as you face the entrance connects the viewing and parking areas, passing through a pine forest and avoiding the crowds and commercialism.

The official Park Service information centers have excellent bookstores with proceeds going to the park. Avoid the schlocky Xanterra gift shop and the awful Carvers Cafe, which looked much better in the scene where Cary Grant gets plugged in *North by Northwest*. The main museum is spotty but the fascinating Sculptor's Studio conveys the drama of how the monument came to be.

Keystone

The nearest lodging and restaurants to Mt Rushmore are in Keystone, a one-time mining town now solely devoted to milking the monument. Gaudy motels vie with fudgeries for your attention, however you can get great sandwiches at Teddy's Deli (236 Winter St; mains from $5; ⊘9am-9pm summer, shorter hours other times).

⊙ Sights

Crazy Horse Memorial MONUMENT
(www.crazyhorsememorial.org; US 385; per person/car $10/27; ⊘8am-dusk summer, to 5pm rest of year) The world's largest monument is a 563ft-tall work-in-progress, with a lot of work to go. When finished it will depict the Sioux leader astride his horse, pointing to the horizon saying, 'My lands are where my dead lie buried.'

Never photographed or persuaded to sign a meaningless treaty, Crazy Horse was chosen for a monument that Lakota Sioux

---

MOUNT RUSHMORE'S FIFTH PRESIDENT

Only four presidents on Mt Rushmore right? Well, maybe not. Nature may have provided a fifth. Drive 1.3 miles northwest from the Mt Rushmore parking entrance (away from Keystone) on Hwy 244 and look for a sheer rock face that's the backside of Mt Rushmore. Pull over safely and then decide just which president might be honored by the rather lurid shape on the rock face. Which head of state it represents may depend on your politics.

---

elders hoped would balance the presidential focus of Mt Rushmore. In 1948 a Boston-born sculptor, the indefatigable Korczak Ziolkowski, started blasting granite. His family have continued the work since his death in 1982. (It should also be noted that many Native Americans oppose the monument as a desecration of sacred land.)

No one is predicting when the sculpture will be complete (the face was dedicated in 1998). A rather thrilling laser-light show tells the tales of the monument on summer evenings.

The visitor center complex includes a Native American museum, a cultural center where you can see artisans at work, cafes and Ziolkowski's studio. A bus takes you to the base of the mountain.

Custer State Park

The only reason 111-sq-mile Custer State Park (www.custerstatepark.info; 7-day pass per car $15) isn't a national park is that the state grabbed it first. It boasts one of the largest free-roaming bison herds in the world (about 1500), the famous 'begging burros' (donkeys seeking handouts) and more than 200 bird species. Other wildlife include elk, pronghorns, mountain goats, bighorn sheep, coyotes, prairie dogs, mountain lions and bobcats.

The Peter Norbeck Visitor Center (☑605-255-4464; www.custerstatepark.info; US 16A; ⊘8am-8pm summer, 9am-5pm rest of year), situated on the eastern side of the park, contains good exhibits and offers activities such as gold-panning demonstrations and guided nature walks. The nearby Black Hills Playhouse (www.blackhillsplayhouse.com; tickets adult/child $32/15; ⊘schedule varies Jun–mid-Aug) hosts summer theater.

Meandering over awesome stone bridges and across sublime Alpine meadows, the 18-mile Wildlife Loop Road and the incredible 14-mile Needles Highway (SD 87) are two superb drives in the park. The latter links with US 385 at either end.

However, the real road star is Iron Mountain Road (Hwy 16A). It's a 16-mile roller coaster of wooden bridges, virtual loop-the-loops, narrow tunnels and stunning vistas on the section between the park's west entrance and Keystone.

Hiking through the pine-covered hills and prairie grassland (keep an eye out for rattlesnakes) is a great way to see wildlife and rock formations. Trails through Sylvan

Lake Shore, Sunday Gulch, Cathedral Spires and French Creek Natural Area are all highly recommended.

You can pitch a tent in eight **campgrounds** (☑800-710-2267; www.campsd.com; tent sites $18-27) around the park. At four, you can rent a well-equipped camping cabin for $47 per night. Reservations are vital in summer.

Backcountry camping (per person per night $6) is allowed in the French Creek Natural Area. The park also has four impressive **resorts** (☑888-875-0001; www.custerresorts. com) with a mix of lodge rooms and cabins starting at $95 and going much higher. Book well ahead. The town of **Custer**, the main gateway into the park, has plenty of hotels and restaurants.

Wind Cave National Park

This park, protecting 44 sq miles of grassland and forest, sits just south of Custer State Park. The central feature is, of course, the cave, which contains 132 miles of mapped passages. The cave's foremost feature is its 'boxwork' calcite formations (95% of all that are known exist here), which look like honeycomb and date back 60 to 100 million years. The strong gusts, which are felt at the entrance, but not inside, give the cave its name. The **visitor center** (www.nps.gov/wica; ☽9am-6pm summer, reduced hours rest of year) has details on the variety of **tours** (☑reservations 605-745-4600; adult $7-23, child $3.50-4.50) that are offered. The four-hour Wild Cave Tour offers an orgy of spelunking.

Hiking is a popular activity in the park, where you'll find the southern end of the 111-mile **Centennial Trail** to Sturgis. The **campground** (campsites $12) usually has space; backcountry camping (free with permit) is allowed in limited areas.

Jewel Cave National Monument

Another of the Black Hills' many fascinating caves is Jewel Cave, 13 miles west of Custer on US 16, so named because calcite crystals line nearly all of its walls. Currently 145 miles have been surveyed, making it the second-longest known cave in the world, but it is presumed to be the longest. **Tours** (adult $4-27, child free–$4) range in length and difficulty and are offered on a first-come basis. Make arrangements at the **visitor center** (www. nps.gov/jeca; ☽8am-5:30pm summer, to 4:30pm

other times). If you'll only visit one Black Hills cave, this would be a good choice.

Hot Springs

This surprisingly attractive town, south of the main Black Hills circuit, boasts ornate 1890s red sandstone buildings and warm mineral springs feeding the Fall River.

You can fill your water bottles at **Kidney Springs**, just south of the **visitor center** (☑www.hotsprings-sd.com; 801 S 6th St; ☽9am-7pm summer) or swim at **Cascade Falls**, which is 71°F (22°C) all year, 11 miles south on US 71. The water at **Evans Plunge** (www.evansplunge.com; 1145 N River St; adult/child $12/10; ☽10am-9pm summer, reduced hours rest of year), a giant indoor geothermal springs waterpark, is always 87°F (30.5°C).

The remarkable **Mammoth Site** (www. mammothsite.com; 1800 US 18 bypass; adult/child $9/7; ☽8am-8pm May 15-Aug 15, reduced hours rest of year) is the country's largest left-as-found mammoth fossil display. Hundreds of animals perished in a sinkhole here about 26,000 years ago.

★**Red Rock River Resort** (☑605-745-4400; www.redrockriverresort.com; 603 N River St; r $85-170; ✻ 🛜) has cozy and stylish rooms in a beautiful 1891 downtown building, plus spa facilities (day passes for nonguests $25).

NEBRASKA

Those who just see Nebraska as 480 miles of blandness along I-80 are missing out on a lot. The Cornhusker State (they do grow a lot of ears) has beautiful river valleys and an often stark bleakness that is entrancing. Its links to the past – from vast fields of dinosaur remains to Native American culture to the toils of hardy settlers – provide a dramatic storyline. Dotted with cute little towns, Nebraska's two main cities, Omaha and Lincoln, are vibrant and artful.

The key to enjoying this long stoic stretch of country is to take the little roads, whether it's US 30 instead of I-80, US 20 to the Black Hills or the lonely and magnificent US 2.

ⓘ Information

Nebraska Association of Bed & Breakfasts (☑877-223-6222; www.nebraskabb.com)
Nebraska State Parks (☑reservations 402-471-1414; www.outdoornebraska.ne.gov) Vehicle permits cost $5/21 per day/year. Some

campsites at popular parks are reservable; fees are $7 to $26 per night.

Nebraska Tourism Commission (☎888-444-1867; www.visitnebraska.com)

Omaha

Be careful if you're planning a quick pit stop in Omaha. Home to the brick-and-cobblestoned Old Market neighborhood downtown, a lively music scene and several quality museums, this town can turn a few hours into a few days. After all, billionaire Warren Buffett lives here and when is he ever wrong?

Omaha grew to prominence as a transport hub. Its location on the Missouri River and proximity to the Platte made it an important stop on the Oregon, California and Mormon Trails, and later the Union Pacific Railroad stretched west from here. These days Omaha is in the nation's top 10 for billionaires and Fortune 500 companies per capita.

◉ Sights & Activities

It's easy to spend much of your Omaha visit in **Old Market** on the river edge of downtown. This revitalized warehouse district, full

NEBRASKA FACTS

Nickname Cornhusker State

Population 1.86 million

Area 77,360 sq miles

Capital city Lincoln (population 262,000)

Other cities Omaha (population 415,000)

Sales tax 5.5-7%

Birthplace of Dancer Fred Astaire (1899–1987), actors Marlon Brando (1924–2004) and Hilary Swank (b 1974), civil rights leader Malcolm X (1925–65)

Home of Air Force generals

Politics Solid Republican

Famous for Johnny Carson, corn

Official beverage Milk

Driving distances Omaha to the Wyoming border on I-80 480 miles, Omaha to Kansas City 186 miles

of nightclubs, restaurants and funky shops, easily holds its own when it comes to aesthetics, energy and sophistication. Nearby parks boast fountains and waterside walks.

★**Durham Museum** MUSEUM
(☎402-444-5071; www.durhammuseum.org; 801 S 10th St; adult/child $9/6; ⊙10am-8pm Tue, to 5pm Wed-Sat, 1-5pm Sun) The soaring art-deco Union Station train depot houses a remarkable museum. Covering local history from the Lewis and Clark expedition to the Omaha stockyards to the trains that once called here, the Durham makes the most of its beautiful surrounds. The soda fountain still serves hot dogs and phosphates.

The museum offers themed **history tours** of Omaha in summer several days per week ($20).

Riverfront LANDMARK
(8th St & Riverfront Dr) The riverfront along the Missouri River, downtown, has been massively spiffed up. Highlights include the architecturally stunning **Bob Kerry Pedestrian Bridge**, which soars over to Iowa; the **Heartland of America Park**, with fountains and lush botanical gardens; and **Lewis & Clark Landing**, where the explorers did just that in 1804. The riverfront is home to the **Lewis & Clark National Historic Trail Visitor Center** (www.nps.gov/lecl; 601 Riverfront Dr; ⊙9am-5pm summer, Mon-Fri only rest of the year).

Joslyn Art Museum MUSEUM
(www.joslyn.org; 2200 Dodge St; ⊙10am-4pm Tue-Sat, noon-4pm Sun, to 8pm Thu) FREE This admired and architecturally imposing museum has a great collection of 19th- and 20th-century European and American art. There's also a good selection of Western-themed works plus an exciting sculpture garden.

★**Union Pacific Railroad Museum** MUSEUM
(www.uprr.com; 200 Pearl St, Council Bluffs, IA; ⊙10am-4pm Tue-Sat) FREE Just across the river in the cute little downtown area of Council Bluffs, IA, this grand museum tells the story of the world's most profitable railroad, the company that rammed the transcontinental railroad west from here in the 1860s. Look for the pictures of Ronald Reagan and his chimp-pal Bonzo aboard a train.

🛏 Sleeping

There is a good mix of midrange and budget hotels along US 275 near 60th St, at I-80 exits 445 and 449, and across the river in Council Bluffs, IA, at I-29 exit 51. Old Market and downtown have several midrange chains.

★ **Magnolia Hotel**　　HISTORIC HOTEL $$
(☑402-341-2500; www.magnoliahotelomaha.com; 1615 Howard St; r $130-200; ❈@🛜🏊) Not far from Old Market, the Magnolia is a boutique hotel housed in a restored 1923 Italianate high-rise. The 145 rooms have a vibrant, modern style. Rates include a full buffet breakfast and bedtime milk and cookies.

✗ Eating & Drinking

The best thing you can do is just wander Old Market and see what you find.

Ted & Wally's Ice Cream　　ICE CREAM $
(www.tedandwallys.com; 1120 Jackson St; ice cream from $3; ◷11am-10pm) Ultra-creamy ice cream in myriad flavors made fresh daily.

Upstream Brewing Company　　AMERICAN $$
(☑402-344-0200; 514 S 11th St; mains $10-30; ◷11am-1am) In a big old firehouse, the beer here is also big on flavor. The Caesar salads have enough garlic to propel you over the Missouri to Iowa. Steaks are thick and up to local standards. There are sidewalk tables, a rooftop deck and a huge bar.

Spencer's　　STEAKHOUSE $$$
(☑402-280-8888; www.spencersforsteaksandchops.com; 102 S 10th St; mains $25-55; ◷5-10pm) Omaha's famous for steaks and this lavish restaurant is the current reigning champ for seared meat. Prices reflect its no-compromises philosophy, but you can enjoy excellent casual fare in the bar for a fraction of the price (the $14 burger is excellent).

Mister Toad's　　BAR
(1002 Howard St; ◷noon-1am) Sit out front on benches under big trees or nab a corner table inside while you work through the beer and cocktail list. It's woodsy, worn and flirting with dive-bar status. There's live jazz Sunday nights.

ℹ Information

Reader (www.thereader.com) Good entertainment listings.

Visitor Center (☑866-937-6624; www.visitomaha.com; 1001 Farnam St; ◷9am-6pm Mon-Sat, to 4pm Sun summer, reduced hours rest of year; 🛜) Near Old Market; has a good coffee bar and rents Trek bikes (from $10 per hour).

AMERICA'S FIRST HOMESTEAD

Homestead National Monument (www.nps.gov/home; Hwy 4; ◷heritage center 9am-5pm) FREE is on the site of the very first homestead granted under the landmark *Homestead Act of 1862*, which opened much of the US to settlers who received free land if they made it productive. The pioneering Freeman family is buried here and you can see their reconstructed log house and hike the site. The heritage center is a striking building with good displays. The site is 4 miles west of Beatrice, 35 miles south of Lincoln on Hwy 77. It's off Hwy 136, which is designated the 'Heritage Highway' scenic byway and passes through tumbledown yet evocative old towns such as Franklin.

ℹ Getting There & Away

Amtrak's *California Zephyr* stops in Omaha on its run between northern California and Chicago.

Around Omaha

If you see large military planes drifting across the sky slowly, they're likely headed for one of Omaha's large military air bases.

◉ Sights

Strategic Air & Space Museum　　MUSEUM
(www.strategicairandspace.com; I-80 exit 426; adult/child $12/6; ◷10am-5pm) After WWII Omaha's Offutt Air Force Base was home to the US Air Force Strategic Air Command, the force of nuclear bombers detailed in Stanley Kubrick's *Dr Strangelove*. This legacy is documented at this cavernous museum, which boasts a huge collection of bombers, from the B-17 to the B-52. Don't expect exhibits looking at the wider implications of bombing. It's 30 miles southwest of Omaha.

Lincoln

Home to the historic Haymarket District and a lively bar scene thanks to the huge downtown campus of the University of Nebraska, Lincoln makes a good overnight stop. Nebraska's capital city is a very livable place and has more parks per capita than any other similarly sized US city.

◉ Sights

The **University of Nebraska** (www.unl.edu) has its main campus in the middle of town. The complex is as practical as a farmer and lacks real highlights but is an interesting stroll. However, you'll have no end of excitement on one of the six fall Saturdays when the Cornhuskers football team plays at home; on these days passions run high and games are sold out.

State Capitol   LANDMARK
(www.capitol.org; 1445 K St; tours free; ⊙ 8am-5pm Mon-Fri, 10am-5pm Sat, 1-5pm Sun, tours hourly) From the outside, Nebraska's remarkable 1932 400ft-high state capitol represents the apex of phallic architecture (like many tall buildings in the Plains, it's often called 'the penis on the prairie'), while the symbolically rich interior curiously combines classical and art-deco motifs. Enjoy views from the 14th-floor observation decks.

Museum of Nebraska History   MUSEUM
(www.nebraskahistory.org; 131 Centennial Mall N; admission by donation; ⊙ 9am-4:30pm Mon-Fri, 1-4:30pm Sat & Sun) Follows the Cornhusker State's story, starting with a large First Nebraskans room.

⌂ Sleeping

Most hotels are near I-80. Those around exit 403 are mostly midrange, while there are budget motels aplenty at exit 399. There are some midrange chains downtown.

Rogers House   B&B $$
(☎ 402-476-6961; www.rogershouseinn.com; 2145 B St; r $90-170; ❋ �) Close to downtown, the 11 rooms here are spread out over two 100-year-old houses. Refreshingly, the decor eschews the froufrou silliness of many B&Bs.

✕ Eating & Drinking

Lincoln's **Haymarket District**, a strolling-friendly six-block warehouse area dating from the early 20th century, has numerous cafes, restaurants, coffeehouses and bars. If you're after falafel sandwiches followed by beer and body shots, follow the undergrads down O St to 14th St.

★**Indigo Bridge**   CAFE $
(701 P St; mains $0-5; ⊙ 8am-10pm; �) This fine cafe in a fantastic bookstore serves coffee

and snacks throughout the day. At lunch on Monday, Wednesday and Friday enjoy hearty organic soup and bread and pay what you can afford.

Yia Yia's Pizza   PIZZERIA $$
(1423 O St; mains $8-15; ⊙ 11am-1pm Mon-Sat, 11am-9pm Sun) Many a hangover has been chased away by the cheesy, gooey goodness at this Lincoln legend. The pizzas are cracker-thin, the regional beer list thick. Sit at a sidewalk table or inside amid the gregarious college crowd.

ⓘ Information

The **visitor center** (☎ 800-423-8212; www. lincoln.org; 201 N 7th St; ⊙ 9am-6pm Mon-Thu, to 8pm Fri, 8am-2pm Sat, reduced hours rest of year) is inside Lincoln Station, where Amtrak's *California Zephyr* stops.

Along I-80

Shortly after Lincoln, I-80 runs an almost razor-straight 83 miles before hugging the Platte River. Several towns along its route to Wyoming make up for its often monotonous stretches. Whenever possible, use parallel US 30, which bounces from one interesting burg to the next (**Gothenburg**, exit 211, is especially attractive). It follows the busy Union Pacific (UP) mainline the entire way.

Grand Island

★**Stuhr Museum of the Prairie Pioneer** (www.stuhrmuseum.org; I-80 exit 312, 3133 W Hwy 34; adult/child $8/6; ⊙ 9am-5pm Mon-Sat, noon-5pm Sun) is a remarkable combination of museum exhibits with a vast outdoor living museum. Note how conditions dramatically improved from the homes in 1860 to 1890 thanks to riches made possible by the railroad.

Upstream of Grand Island, the Platte hosts 500,000 sandhill cranes (80% of the world population) and 15 million waterfowl during the spring migration (mid-February to early April). The **Nebraska Nature & Visitor Center** (www.nebraskanature.org; I-80 exit 305; admission free, tours $25; ⊙ 9am-5pm Mon-Sat year-round, 8am-6pm daily Mar) is a good place to break out the binoculars.

Kearney

The **Great Platte River Road Archway Monument** (www.archway.org; adult/child $12/5;

⊙9am-6pm summer, reduced hours rest of year) arches unexpectedly over I-80 east of Kearney near exit 272. The multimedia exhibits tell an engaging story of the people who've passed this way, from those riding wagon trains to those zipping down the interstate.

Like all the I-80 towns, Kearney has no shortage of motels by the interstate. A good indie choice near downtown is **Midtown Western Inn** (☑308-237-3153; www.midtown-westerninn.com; 1401 2nd Ave; r $50-80; ❊⬛⬛), which has a vintage motel vibe with huge, clean rooms.

The compact downtown, near US 30 and the busy Union Pacific mainline, has good cafes and bars including **Thunderhead Brewing Co** (www.thunderheadbrewing.com; 18 E 21st St; mains $5-10; ⊙noon-1am), which makes a fine IPA and serves pizza.

North Platte

North Platte, a rail-fan mecca, is home to the **Buffalo Bill Ranch State Historical Park** (www.outdoornebraska.ne.gov; 2921 Scouts Rest Ranch Rd; house adult/child $2/1, vehicle permit $5; ⊙9am-5pm daily summer, to 4pm Mon-Fri mid-Mar–May & Sep–mid-Oct), 2 miles north of US 30. Once the home of Bill Cody, the father of rodeo and the famed Wild West Show, it has a fun museum that reflects his colorful life.

Enjoy sweeping views of Union Pacific's **Bailey Yard**, the world's largest railroad yard, from the **Golden Spike Tower** (www.goldenspiketower.com; 1249 N Homestead Rd; adult/child $7/5; ⊙9am-7pm Mon-Sat, from 1pm Sun summer, to 5pm rest of year), an eight-story observation tower with indoor and outdoor decks. From I-80, take exit 177.

Along US 20

The further west you go on US 20, the more space – and Sandhills – you'll see between towns, trees and pickup trucks. The western end of the road, known as the **Bridges to Buttes Byway**, traverses a Nebraska barely touched by time. Look for wild geologic features that pop out of the rolling green hills.

Royal

Watch paleontologists work at **Ashfall Fossil Beds** (www.ashfall.unl.edu; 86930 517th Ave; admission $5 plus vehicle permit $5; ⊙9am-5pm Mon-Sat, 11am-5pm Sun, reduced hours May & Sep–

mid-Oct), 8 miles northwest of town. You can see unearthed prehistoric skeletons of hundreds of animals, including rhinoceroses, buried 12 million years ago by ash from a Pompeii-like explosion in what is now Idaho.

Valentine

Fortunately, 'America's Heart City' doesn't milk the schtick. It sits on the edge of the Sandhills and is a great base for canoeing, kayaking and inner-tubing the winding canyons of the federally protected **Niobrara National Scenic River** (www.nps.gov/niob). The river crosses the **Fort Niobrara National Wildlife Refuge** (www.fws.gov/fortniobrara; Hwy 12; ⊙ visitor center 8am-4:30pm daily Jun-Aug, closed weekends rest of year). Driving tours here take you past bison, elk and more.

Floating down the river draws scores of people through the summer. Sheer limestone bluffs, lush forests and spring-fed waterfalls along the banks shatter any 'flat Nebraska' stereotypes. Most float tours are based in Valentine (www.visitvalentine.com).

Northern Panhandle

Get a feel for the tough lives led by early residents at the **Museum of the Fur Trade** (www.furtrade.org; off US 20; adult/child $5/free; ⊙8am-5pm May-Oct), 3 miles east of Chadron. It includes the restored sod-roofed Bordeaux

---

NEBRASKA: DETOURS & EXTRAS

Carhenge (www.carhenge.com) is a Stonehenge replica assembled from 38 discarded cars that lures 80,000 DeSoto druids a year. This artful reproduction rises out of a field 3 miles north of Alliance along Hwy 87, east of US 385, the road to the Black Hills.

Scotts Bluff National Monument has been a beacon to travelers for centuries. Rising 800ft above the flat plains of western Nebraska, it was an important waypoint on the Oregon Trail in the mid-19th century. You can still see wagon ruts today in the park. The **visitor center** (www.nps.gov/scbl; per vehicle $5; ⊙9am-5pm) has displays and can guide you to walks and drives. It's off US 26 south of Scottsbluff town.

SCENIC DRIVE: NEBRASKA'S SANDHILLS

Nebraska's **Hwy 2** branches northwest from I-80 and Grand Island through Broken Bow 272 miles to Alliance in the panhandle. It crosses the lonely and lovely **Sandhills** – 19,000 sq miles of sand dunes covered in grass – one of the country's most isolated areas. With the wind whistling in your ears, the distant call of a hawk and the biggest skies imaginable, this is pure iconic Great Plains travel.

Trading Post, which swapped pelts for guns, blankets and whiskey from 1837 to 1876.

Fort Robinson State Park (www.outdoornebraska.ne.gov; Hwy 20; admission per vehicle $5; ☉ sunrise-sunset), 4 miles west of Crawford, is where Crazy Horse was killed in 1877 while in captivity. It has a museum, camping and cabins.

At Harrison, detour 23 miles south on pastoral Hwy 29 to reach **Agate Fossil Beds National Monument** (☎ 308-668-2211; www.nps.gov/agfo; ☉ 9am-5pm summer, 8am-4pm rest of year) FREE, a rich source of unusual fossils dating back 20 million years. The Native American artifact display is small but excellent.

KANSAS

Wicked witches and yellow-brick roads, pitched battles over slavery and tornadoes powerful enough to pulverize entire towns are some of the more lurid images of Kansas. But the common image – amber waves of grain from north to south and east to west is closer to reality.

There's a simple beauty to the green rolling hills and limitless horizons. Places such as Chase County beguile those who value understatement. Gems abound, from the superb space museum in Hutchinson to the indie music clubs of Lawrence. Most importantly, follow the Great Plains credo of ditching the interstate for the two-laners and make your own discoveries. The website www.kansassampler.org is a brilliant resource for finding the best the state has to offer, as is the guidebook *8 Wonders of Kansas*.

ℹ Information

Kansas Bed & Breakfast Association (☎ 888-572-2632; www.kbba.com)

Kansas State Parks (www.kdwpt.state.ks.us) Per vehicle per day/year $5/25. Campsites cost $7 to $13.

Kansas Travel & Tourism (☎ 785-296-2009; www.travelks.com)

Wichita

From its early cow-town days at the head of the Chisholm Trail in the 1870s to its current claim as Air Capital of the World (thanks to about half the world's general aviation aircraft being built here by the likes of Cessna and others), Kansas' largest city has always been a busy place. It's a worthwhile stopover but not at the expense of the rest of the state.

◉ Sights

Wichita's historic, all-brick **Old Town**, good for shopping, eating and drinking, is on the east side of downtown.

The **Museums on the River** district includes the first three sights listed here, plus botanical gardens and a science museum aimed at kids. It fills a triangle of green space between the Big and Little Arkansas Rivers to the west of downtown.

★**Old Cowtown Museum**   MUSEUM
(www.oldcowtown.org; 1865 Museum Blvd; adult/child $8/5.50; ☉10am-5pm Tue-Sat; ⋒) An open-air museum that re-creates the Wild West (as seen on TV...). Pioneer-era buildings, staged gunfights and guides in cowboy costumes thrill kids. The river walks here are bucolic.

**Mid-America
All-Indian Center**   MUSEUM
(www.theindiancenter.org; 650 N Seneca St; adult/child $7/3; ☉10am-4pm Tue-Sat) Guarded by Wichita artist Blackbear Bosin's 44ft statue 'Keeper of the Plains,' this museum has exhibits of Native American art and artifacts, as well as a traditional Wichita-style grass lodge.

Exploration Place   MUSEUM
(www.exploration.org; 300 N McLean Blvd; adult/child from $10/6; ☉10am-5pm Mon-Sat, noon-5pm Sun; ⋒) Right on the river confluence, this striking modern museum has no end of cool exhibits, including a tornado chamber where you can feel 75mph winds and a sub-

lime erosion model where you can see water create a new little Kansas.

Museum of World Treasures MUSEUM
(www.worldtreasures.org; 835 E 1st St; adult/child $9/7; ⊙10am-5pm Mon-Sat, noon-5pm Sun; 🖼) With a complete T-Rex, Egyptian mummies, *Wizard of Oz* props, Abraham Lincoln's walking cane, military relics, a sports hall of fame and much more, this museum has something for everyone.

🛏 Sleeping

Hotbeds for chains include I-135 exit 1AB, I-35 exit 50 and the Hwy 96 Rock Rd and Webb Rd exits. Broadway north of the center offers a mixed bag of indie cheapies.

Hotel at Old Town HOTEL $$
(☎316-267-4800; www.hotelatoldtown.com; 830 1st St; r $100-200; P❊@🐾) In the midst of Old Town nightlife, this restored hotel is housed in the 1906 factory of the Keen Kutter Corp, a maker of household goods. Rooms have high ceilings, fridges and microwaves and there's a good breakfast buffet.

Hotel at Waterwalk HOTEL $$
(☎316-263-1061; www.hotelatwaterwalk.com; 711 S Main St; r $110-180; P❊🐾🖼) On the south edge of downtown, suites here range up to two-bedroom in size and have kitchens. It's modern and commodious, perfect for families or quarreling couples.

🍴 Eating & Drinking

Wichita is the home of Pizza Hut, but that's far from the pinnacle of the city's dining options. For some real-deal Mexican or Vietnamese, drive north on Broadway and take your pick. Old Town has a fruitful **farmers market** (www.oldtownfarmersmarket.com; 1st St & Mosley St; ⊙7am-noon Sat May-Oct).

★ Doo-Dah Diner DINER $
(www.doodahdiner.com; 206 E Kellogg Dr; mains $5-9; ⊙7am-2pm Wed-Sun) A model for diners everywhere. This bustling local fave has fabulous chow, including corned-beef hash, banana-bread French toast and eggs Benedict.

Nu Way Cafe BURGERS $
(1416 W Douglas Ave; mains $3-5; ⊙11am-9pm) Frosty glasses of homemade root beer are among the highlights at this west-of-downtown outlet of a beloved Wichita chain. Old-style Formica is a backdrop for delicate onion rings and loose-meat sandwiches.

KANSAS FACTS

Nickname Sunflower State

Population 2.9 million

Area 82,282 sq miles

Capital city Topeka (population 128,200)

Other cities Wichita (population 385,000)

Sales tax 6.3-9.8%

Birthplace of Aviator Amelia Earhart (1897–1937), temperance crusader Carrie Nation (1846–1911), TV talker Dr Phil (b 1950), Pizza Hut (established 1958), singer-songwriter Melissa Etheridge (b 1961)

Home of Dorothy and Toto (of *Wizard of Oz* fame)

Politics Very conservative

Famous for Wheat

Official state song 'Home on the Range'

Driving distances Wichita to Kansas City 200 miles, Dodge City to Abilene 188 miles

---

Anchor AMERICAN $$
(www.anchorwichita.com; 1109 E Douglas Ave; mains $7-12; ⊙11am-late) On the edge of Old Town, this vintage pub has high ceilings, a tiled floor, a great beer selection and tasty food. The sandwiches and burgers are fab, the specials sublime. It totally outclasses the nearby chain and theme bars.

Along I-70

What it lacks in glamour, Kansas' 420-mile 'Main Street' makes up for in efficiency, quickly shuttling you from Kansas City to the Colorado border. The scenery can be monotonous, but as always there are many interesting stops along the way. West of Salina, the landscape around I-70 stretches into rolling, wide-open plains, with small wind-blown towns like Hays, which did a desolate turn in many scenes in *Paper Moon*. US 50 and US 56 are intriguing alternatives.

ROUTE 66: GET YOUR KICKS IN KANSAS

Only 13 miles of Route 66 pass through the southeast corner of Kansas, but it's a good drive along Hwy 66 and US 69.

The first town you hit after Joplin, **Galena**, has been on the decline since even before the last of the area's lead and zinc mines closed in the 1970s.

Three miles down the road is **Riverton**, where you might consider a detour 20 miles north to Pittsburg for some famous fried chicken (p658).

Cross US 400 and stay on old Route 66 to the 1923 **Marsh Rainbow Arch Bridge**, the last of its kind.

From the bridge, it's less than 3 miles south to **Baxter Springs**, the site of a Civil War massacre and numerous bank robberies. The multifaceted **Baxter Springs Heritage Center** (www.baxterspringsmuseum.org; 740 East Ave; ⊙ 10am-4:30pm Mon-Sat, 1-4:30pm Sun Apr-Oct, closed Mon-Wed Nov-Mar) FREE has helped restore a 1939 Phillips 66 gas station into the **Kansas Route 66 Visitor Center** (cnr Military Ave & 10th St; ⊙ 10am-5pm Mon-Sat). Military Ave (US 69A) takes you into Oklahoma.

Lawrence

Lawrence, 40 miles west of Kansas City, has been an island of progressive politics from the start. Founded by abolitionists in 1854 and an important stop on the Underground Railroad, it became a battlefield in the clash between pro- and antislavery factions. In 1863, the Missouri 'Bushwhackers' of William Clarke Quantrill raided Lawrence, killing nearly 200 people and burning much of it to the ground. The city survived, however, and so did its free-thinking spirit, which is fitting for the home of the **University of Kansas** (KU; www.ku.edu).

⊙ Sights

The appealing downtown, where townies and students merge, centers on **Massachusetts St**, one of the most pleasant streets in this part of the country for a stroll.

Spencer Museum of Art   GALLERY
(www.spencerart.ku.edu; 1301 Mississippi St; ⊙ 10am-4pm Tue-Sat, noon-4pm Sun, to 8pm Wed & Thu) FREE It isn't large, but this museum has a collection encompassing work by Western artist Frederic Remington and many European masters.

🛏 Sleeping & Eating

Lawrence's motels cluster at the junction of US 40 and US 59 south of I-70. The choices downtown make Lawrence the state's best stop for the night.

Halcyon House B&B   B&B $$
(✆ 888-441-0314;   www.thehalcyonhouse.com; 1000 Ohio St; r $70-120; P❋ 🛜) The nine cute bedrooms here (some share bathrooms) have lots of natural light, and there's a landscaped garden and homemade baked goods for breakfast. Downtown is just a short walk away.

Eldridge Hotel   HISTORIC HOTEL $$
(✆ 785-749-5011;   www.eldridgehotel.com;   701 Massachusetts St; r from $140; P❋@🛜) The 56 modern two-room suites at this historic 1926 downtown hotel have antique-style furnishings. The bar and restaurant are stylish, the ghost misunderstood (rumors abound).

★ **Free State Brewing**   PUB $
(www.freestatebrewing.com; 636 Massachusetts St; mains $6-14; ⊙ 11am-late) One of many good places on Mass downtown, this was the first brewery to open in Kansas since Carrie Nation got one closed in 1880. A cut above brewpub standards, the beers are excellent. The food is creative with daily specials.

☆ Entertainment

Bottleneck   LIVE MUSIC
(www.bottlenecklive.com; 737 New Hampshire St) The music scene in town is up to collegetown standards and this joint usually has the best of the newest. Top bands often skip KC for the Bottleneck.

ℹ Information

Visitor Information Center (✆ 785-865-4499; www.visitlawrence.com; 402 N 2nd St; ⊙ 8:30am-5pm Mon-Sat, 1-5pm Sun) In the restored old Union Pacific depot, with trains still passing by constantly.

Topeka

Kansas and its vital role in America's race relations is symbolized in the otherwise humdrum state capital of Topeka.

◉ Sights

★ Brown vs Board of Education National Historic Site   MUSEUM
(www.nps.gov/brvb; 1515 SE Monroe St; ⊚9am-5pm) FREE It took real guts to challenge the segregationist laws common in the US in the 1950s and the stories of these courageous men and women are here. Set in Monroe Elementary School, one of Topeka's African American schools at the time of the landmark 1954 Supreme Court decision that banned segregation in US schools, the displays cover the whole Civil Rights movement.

State Capitol   LANDMARK
(300 SW 10th St; tours free; ⊚8am-5pm daily, tours 9am-3pm Mon-Fri) Under the huge green dome, don't miss the fiery John Steuart Curry mural of abolitionist John Brown.

Kansas History Center   MUSEUM
(www.kshs.org; 6425 SW 6th Ave; adult/child $8/6; ⊚9am-5pm Tue-Sat, 1-5pm Sun) From a Cheyenne war lance to Carrie Nation's hammer, this engaging center is packed with Kansas stories.

✕ Eating

Porubsky's Grocery   DELI $
(508 NE Sardou Ave; ⊚10am-7pm Mon-Sat) Hard by the old Santa Fe mainline close to downtown, this old Russian deli has been serving up simple sandwiches at its Formica counters since 1947. The chili (only Monday to Thursday) is best with piles of crackers. Try the housemade pickles, which burst with horseradishy goodness.

Abilene

In the late 19th century, Abilene was a rowdy cow town at the end of the Chisholm Trail. Today its compact core of historic brick buildings and well-preserved neighborhoods seems perfectly appropriate for the birthplace of Dwight D Eisenhower (1890–1969), president and WWII general.

Fittingly set against a backdrop of grain elevators, the rather regal **Eisenhower Center** (www.eisenhower.archives.gov; 200 SE 4th St; museum adult/child $10/2; ⊚8am-5:45pm summer, 9am-4:45pm rest of year) includes Ike's boyhood home, a museum and library, and his and Mamie's graves. Displays cover the Eisenhower presidential era (1953–61) and his role as allied commander in WWII. However, his ability to forge agreement between the squabbling allies is not fully covered. A highlight is the original text of his speech warning about the military-industrial complex.

The **Brookville Hotel** (www.brookvillehotel.com; 105 E Lafayette St; meals $15; ⊚11am-2pm & 4-7:30pm Wed-Sun) has been serving fried chicken since Ike graduated from West Point (1915). Cream-style corn, fresh biscuits and much more come with every meal.

Lucas

'Outsider art,' meaning works created outside the bounds of traditional culture, has blossomed in tiny Lucas. Samuel Dinsmoor began the trend in 1907 by filling his yard with enormous concrete sculptures reflecting his eccentric philosophies. His **Garden of Eden** (www.garden-of-eden-lucas-kansas.com; 301 2nd St; adult/child $6/1; ⊚10am-5pm May-Oct, 1-4pm Mar & Apr, 1-4pm Sat & Sun Nov-Feb) is visible from the sidewalk, but admission lets you hear some wonderful stories and see his remains in a glass-topped coffin (!).

> ### AMERICA'S BEST SPACE MUSEUM
>
> Possibly the most surprising sight in Kansas, the amazing **Cosmosphere & Space Center** (www.cosmo.org; 1100 N Plum St; all-attraction pass adult/child $18/16, museum only $12/10; ⊚9am-9pm Mon-Sat, noon-9pm Sun; ⊞) captures the race to the moon better than any museum on the planet. Absorbing displays and artifacts such as the Apollo 13 command module will enthrall you for hours. The museum is regularly called in to build props for Hollywood movies portraying the space race, including *Apollo 13*.
>
> All puns aside, the museum's isolated location in Hutchinson might as well be the moon, but it's an easy day trip from Wichita or diversion off I-70.

GREAT PLAINS ALONG US 50

Nicodemus is the only surviving town in the west built by emancipated slaves from the south after the Civil War. A national park **visitor center** (www.nps.gov/nico; ☺9am-4:30pm) **FREE** recounts the town's history and the experience of African Americans in the west. The town is on US 24 about 35 miles north of I-70 via US 183 or US 283.

Monument Rocks are 80ft-tall pyramid-shaped chalk formations that look like a Jawa hangout in *Star Wars*. Go 25 miles southeast of Oakley via US 83 off I-70 exit 76.

Norton, a burg up in the north, is the home of the **They Also Ran Gallery** (☎785-877-3341; First State Bank, 105 W Main St; ☺call for hours) **FREE**, which is devoted to people who ran for president and lost. The ignoble collection includes Aaron Burr, Thomas Dewey and many more.

Fort Scott (www.nps.gov/fosc; ☺8am-5pm) **FREE** is a restored fort near the Missouri border that dates to 1842. While the parade grounds and buildings in the heart of its namesake city are interesting, the real draw here is the story of the battles between pro- and antislavery forces that were fought here before the Civil War.

Legendary fried chicken is a hallmark of several restaurants in far southeastern Crawford County. In Pittsburg try **Chicken Mary's** (www.chickenmarys.us; 1133 E 600th Ave; meals from $6; ☺4-8:30pm Tue-Sat, 11am-8pm Sun), which isn't far from where Route 66 crosses into Kansas.

The phenomenal **Grassroots Art Center** (☎785-525-6118; www.grassrootsart.net; 213 S Main St; adult/child $6/2; ☺10am-5pm Mon-Sat, 1-5pm Sun May-Sep, 10am-4pm Mon & Thu-Sat, 1-4pm Sun Oct-Apr) has gathered works made of materials such as buttons, barbed wire, pull-tabs and strange machines by self-taught Kansas artists.

The best way to reach Lucas is along the **Post Rock Scenic Byway**, a picturesque 18-mile jaunt past Wilson Lake starting at I-70 exit 206.

Along US 50

Fabled US 50 splits off from I-35 at Emporia and follows the old Santa Fe mainline west through classic Kansas vistas.

Chase County

Nearly a perfect square, this is the county William Least Heat-Moon examined mile by mile in his best-selling *PrairyErth*.

The beautiful Flint Hills roll through here and are home to two thirds of the nation's remaining tallgrass prairie. The 10,894-acre **Tallgrass Prairie National Preserve** (www.nps.gov/tapr; Hwy 177; ☺buildings 8:30am-4:30pm, trails 24hr) **FREE**, 2 miles northwest of Strong City and US 50, is a perfect place to hike the prairie and revel in its ever-changing colorful flowers. Rang-

ers offer tours of the preserved ranch and **bus tours** (☎tour info 620-273-8494; ☺tour times vary) of the prairie from a beautiful new visitor center.

The rangers also have maps of some evocative remote drives in the county, as well as a tour of sights from Moon's book. Don't miss the showstopping **County Courthouse** in **Cottonwood Falls**, 2 miles south of Strong City. Completed in 1873, it is a fantasy of French Renaissance style.

Along US 56

US 56 follows the old Santa Fe Trail to Dodge City through the heart of the heartland. Most sights along here are also easily reached from US 50.

The large Mennonite communities around **Hillsboro** are descendants of Russian immigrants who brought the 'Turkey Red' strain of wheat to the Plains, where it thrived despite harsh conditions.

A further 110 miles west in **Larned**, the **Santa Fe Trail Center Museum** (www.santafetrailcenter.org; 1349 Hwy 156; adult/child $4/1.50; ☺9am-5pm Tue-Sat, also Sun Jun-Aug) details the vital route linking the US and Mexico for much of the 19th century. Six miles west of town on Hwy 156, **Fort Larned National Historic Site** (www.nps.gov/fols; ☺8:30am-4:30pm) **FREE** is a remarkably well-preserved Santa Fe Trail fort.

Dodge City

Dodge City, where famous lawmen Bat Masterson and Wyatt Earp tried, sometimes successfully, to keep law and order, had a notorious reputation during the 1870s and 1880s. The long-running TV series *Gunsmoke* (1955–75) spurred tourism and big crowds have got the heck *into* Dodge ever since. Geared toward families, historical authenticity here plays a distant third fiddle to fun and frolic.

Tours (adult/child $8/5; ⊘9:30am-3pm summer) on fake trolleys start at the **visitor center** (☑800-653-9378; www.visitdodgecity.org; 400 W Wyatt Earp Blvd; ⊗8am-6:30pm summer, 8:30am-5pm Mon-Fri Sep-Apr). Expect to hear a lot of well-spun apocryphal yarns. Self-guided audio tours and free maps let you visit on your own schedule.

The studio-backlot-like **Boot Hill Museum** (www.boothill.org; 500 W Wyatt Earp Blvd; adult/child from $10/8; ⊘8am-8pm Jun-Aug, 9am-5pm Sep-May; ⊞) includes a cemetery, jail and saloon, where gunslingers reenact high-noon shootouts while Miss Kitty and her dancing gals do the cancan.

Escape the schmaltz and view surviving **Santa Fe Trail wagon-wheel ruts** about 9 miles west of town on US 50. The site is well marked.

Chain and indie motels line Wyatt Earp Blvd.

OKLAHOMA

Oklahoma gets its name from the Choctaw name for 'Red People.' One look at the state's vividly red earth and you'll wonder if the name is really an ethnic comment. Still, with 39 tribes located here, it is a place with deep Native American significance. Museums, cultural displays and more abound.

The other side of the Old West coin, cowboys, also figure prominently in the Sooner State. Although pickups have replaced horses, there's still a great sense of the open range, interrupted only by urban Oklahoma City and Tulsa. Oklahoma's share of Route 66 links some of the Mother Road's iconic highlights and there are myriad atmospheric old towns. And just when it seems the vistas go on forever, mountains in the south and far west add texture.

ℹ Information

Oklahoma Bed & Breakfast Association (☑866-676-5522; www.okbba.com)

Oklahoma Department of Tourism (www.travelok.com)

Oklahoma State Parks (www.touroklahoma.com) Most parks are free for day use; campsites cost $12 to $28 per night, and some are reservable.

Oklahoma City

Often abbreviated to OKC, Oklahoma City is nearly dead-center in the state and is the cultural and political capital. It has worked hard over the years to become more than just a cow town, all without turning its back on its cowboy heritage. It makes a good pause on your Route 66 travels.

The city is forever linked to the 1995 bombing of the Alfred P Murrah Federal Building; the memorials to this tragedy are moving and worthy stops.

◎ Sights

You'll brush up against real cowboys in **Stockyards City** (www.stockyardscity.org; Agnew Ave & Exchange Ave), southwest of downtown, either in the shops and restaurants that cater to them or at the **Oklahoma National Stockyards** (www.onsy.com; ⊘auctions 8am Mon & Tue), the world's largest stocker and feeder cattle market.

★**Oklahoma City National Memorial Museum**   MUSEUM
(www.oklahomacitynationalmemorial.org; 620 N Harvey Ave; adult/student $12/10; ⊘9am-6pm Mon-Sat, noon-6pm Sun) The story of America's worst incident of domestic terrorism is told at this poignant museum, which avoids becoming mawkish and lets the horrible events speak for themselves. The outdoor **Symbolic Memorial** has 168 empty chair sculptures for each of the people killed in the attack (the 19 small ones are for the children who perished in the day-care center).

National Cowboy & Western Heritage Museum   MUSEUM
(www.nationalcowboymuseum.org; 1700 NE 63rd St; adult/child $12.50/6; ⊘10am-5pm) Only the smells are missing here, with both art and history covered. Even if you come for just one, you're sure to be enthralled by the other. The excellent collection of Western painting and sculpture features many works by Charles M Russell and Frederic Remington.

OKLAHOMA FACTS

Nickname Sooner State

Population 3.8 million

Area 69,900 sq miles

Capital city Oklahoma City (population 592,000)

Other cities Tulsa (population 397,000)

Sales tax 4.5-11%

Birthplace of Humorist Will Rogers (1879–1935), athlete Jim Thorpe (1888–1953), folk musician Woody Guthrie (1912–67), parking meters (invented 1935), actor Brad Pitt (b 1963)

Home of The band The Flaming Lips

Politics Deeply conservative

Famous for 1930s dust bowl, Carrie Underwood

Official state meal Okra, chicken fried steak and 10 more dishes

Driving distances Oklahoma City to Tulsa 104 miles, Kansas to Texas following historic Route 66 426 miles

Oklahoma History Center   MUSEUM
(www.okhistorycenter.org; 2401 N Laird Ave; adult/child $7/4; ⊙10am-5pm Mon-Sat) Makes people the focus as it tells the story of the Sooner State.

State Capitol   LANDMARK
(2300 N Lincoln Blvd; admission & tours free; ⊙8am-5pm Mon-Fri, 9am-4pm Sat & Sun, tours 9am-3pm Mon-Fri) Built in 1917, but only got its dome in 2002. Note the oil wells outside.

American Indian Cultural Center & Museum   MUSEUM
(www.theamericanindiancenter.org; junction I-40 & I-35) This center with its arresting design will be one of the premier Native American institutions in the world when it's completed. In the meantime, however, its construction has slowed due to state budget cuts.

✯✯ Festivals & Events

State Fair Park   CULTURE
(www.okstatefairpark.com; I-44 & NW 10th St) State Fair Park hosts frequent horse- or rodeo-related events. (The state fair itself is a dud.)

🛏 Sleeping

Many older motels line I-35 south of town; newer chain properties stack up along I-44, the NW Expwy/Hwy 3 and at Bricktown (which puts you near nightlife action).

Grandison Inn at Maney Park   B&B $$
(☑405-232-8778; www.grandisoninn.com; 1200 N Shartel St; r $110-190; P✳🐾) In a genteel quarter of OKC just northwest of downtown, this gracious 1904-vintage B&B welcomes guests to eight rooms with period charm and modern amenities such as DVD players. The house has amazing woodwork, including a showstopping staircase.

Colcord Hotel   BOUTIQUE HOTEL $$
(☑405-601-4300; www.colcordhotel.com; 15 N Robinson Ave; r $150-200; P✳@🐾) OKC's first skyscraper, built in 1910, is now a 12-story luxurious hotel. Many original flourishes, like the marble-clad lobby, survive, while the 108 rooms have a stylish, contemporary touch. It's within walking distance of Bricktown.

✗ Eating & Drinking

Bunches of eateries cluster in Bricktown, line Western Ave between 41st and 82nd Sts, and anchor the Asian district (around 23rd St and Classen Blvd).

Tucker's Onion Burgers   BURGERS $
(www.tuckersonionburgers.com; 324 NW 23rd St; mains from $4; ⊙11am-9pm) 🍴 A new kind of burger joint with an old-time Route 66 vibe, Tuckers has high-quality food (locally sourced) that includes iconic OK onion burgers, fresh-cut fries and shakes. It even has a green ethos and a fine patio.

★Cattlemen's Steakhouse   STEAKHOUSE $$
(www.cattlemensrestaurant.com; 1309 S Agnew Ave; mains $5-25; ⊙6am-10pm Sun-Thu, to midnight Fri & Sat) OKC's most storied restaurant, this Stockyards City institution has been feeding city slickers slabs of beef and lamb's fries (that's a polite way of saying gonads) since 1910. Deals are still cut at the counter (where you can jump the wait for tables) and back in the luxe booths.

Ann's Chicken Fry House   SOUTHERN $$
(4106 NW 39th St; mains $4-12; ⊙11am-8:30pm Tue-Sat) Part real diner, part tourist attraction, Ann's is a Route 66 veteran renowned for its – you guessed it – chicken fried steak. Okra and cream gravy also star, and the fried chicken lives up to the rep. Get the black-eyed peas.

Cheever's Cafe CAFE $$
(www.cheeverscafe.com; 2409 N Hudson Ave; mains $10-25; ⊙11am-9pm Sun-Thu, 11am-10:30pm Fri, 5-10:30pm Sat) This former art-deco flower shop is now an upscale cafe with excellent Southern- and Mexican-influenced fare. The menu changes seasonally and features foods drawn from the surrounding rich countryside.

Bricktown Brewery BREWERY
(www.bricktownbrewery.com; 1 N Oklahoma Ave; ⊙11am-1am) A large microbrewery in Bricktown, with revelers splayed out across large rooms enjoying pool, darts and just being spectators. Always hopping and has a decent food menu.

☆ **Entertainment**

For listings, check out the free weekly **Oklahoma Gazette** (www.okgazette.com) or just head to the renovated warehouses in the **Bricktown District**, which contain a vast array of bars, some good, some purely chain.

To make a complete night of it in the district, watch the **Triple A Redhawks** (www.oklahomaredhawks.com; 2 Mickey Mantle Dr; tickets $5-25) play at Bricktown Ballpark. The NBA's **Oklahoma City Thunder** (www.nba.com/thunder; 100 W Reno Ave; tickets from $30) play nearby at Chesapeake Energy Arena.

🛍 **Shopping**

The **Paseo Arts District** isn't much more than Paseo Dr itself, but there are several art galleries and boutiques in the Spanish colonial buildings. The **16th St Plaza District** is also a good bet for interesting shops.

You can buy all forms of Western wear and gear in **Stockyards City**, which is the real deal for cowboys. Start at **Langston's** (www.langstons.com; 2224 Exchange Ave; ⊙10am-6pm Mon-Sat), which has a vast selection.

ℹ **Information**

Oklahoma Welcome Center (☑405-478-4637; www.travelok.com; 1-35 exit 137; ⊙8:30am-5pm) Also has city info.

ℹ **Getting There & Around**

Will Rogers World Airport (OKC; www.flyokc.com) Will Rogers World Airport is 5 miles southwest of downtown; a cab costs about $25 to downtown.

Amtrak (www.amtrak.com; 100 S EK Gaylord Blvd) The *Heartland Flyer* goes from OKC to Fort Worth ($28, 4¼ hours). Buy your ticket on the train.

Go Metro (www.gometro.org; single fare/day pass $1.50/4) Runs city buses.

Greyhound (Union Bus Station, 427 W Sheridan Ave) Daily buses to Dallas ($58, five hours), Wichita ($46, 2¾ hours) and Tulsa

---

CHASING TORNADOES

Much of the Great Plains is prone to severe weather, including violent thunderstorms, hail the size of softballs, spectacular lightning storms and more. But the real stars of these meteorological nightmares are tornadoes. Far less benign than the cyclones that carried Dorothy off to Oz, tornadoes cause death and destruction from the Great Plains east across the central US. In 2013, two tornadoes in 11 days caused much havoc on the Oklahoma City area. With winds of 300mph or more, tornadoes are both awesome and terrifying. Still, each year many people visit the region hoping to spot a funnel cloud, drawn by the sheer spectacle and elemental drama.

Tour companies use gadget-filled vans to chase storms across multiple states, with no guarantee that you'll actually see a storm. Costs average $200 to $400 a day and April to July offer the best spotting. Operators include the following:

Cloud 9 Tours (☑405-323-1145; www.cloud9tours.com)

Extreme Tornado Tours (www.extremetornadotours.com)

Silver Lining Tours (☑832-717-4712; www.silverliningtours.com)

Tempest Tours (☑817-274-9313; www.tempesttours.com)

The book *Storm Kings: The Untold History of America's First Tornado Chasers* by Lee Sandlin, is an excellent and surprise-filled account of early tornado research. Read the recollections of veteran tornado chaser Roger Hill in *Hunting Nature's Fury*. For a completely overhyped look at the world of storm-spotters – in the best Hollywood tradition – check out the 1996 movie *Twister*.

ROUTE 66: GET YOUR KICKS IN OKLAHOMA

Oklahoma's connection with America's Main Street runs deep: the road's chief proponent, Cyrus Avery, was a Sooner; John Steinbeck's *Grapes of Wrath* told of the plight of Depression-era Okie farmers fleeing west on Route 66; and Oklahoma has more miles of the original alignment than any other state. The **Oklahoma Route 66 Association** (www.oklahomaroute66.com) puts out an excellent booklet that you can pick up from most visitor centers along the road. It's vital because so many of the brown-and-white Historic Route 66 signs have been stolen for souvenirs and the original road goes by a variety of monikers, including OK 66, US 69, US 270 etc.

Shortly after you enter the state from Kansas on US 69A you'll come to **Miami**. Continue south through town on Main St and 2.5 miles after crossing the Neosho River turn right at the T-intersection. This will take you to the first of two original and very rough 9ft-wide alignments. The second, E 140 Rd (turn west) comes soon after the first, just before I-44.

You'll cross I-44 twice before rolling into **Vinita**. **Clanton's** (www.clantonscafe.com; 319 E Illinois Ave; mains $4-10; ⊙6am-8pm Mon-Fri, to 2pm Sat & Sun) dates back to 1927 and is the place for chicken fried steak and calf fries (don't ask).

Thirty miles further on, **Foyil** is worth a 4-mile detour on Hwy 28A for the massive and colorful concrete sculptures of **Totem Pole Park** (www.rchs1.org; Hwy 28A) FREE. Another 10 miles brings you to **Claremore**, former home of Will Rogers. Next up at the port city of **Catoosa**, just before Tulsa, is one of the most photographed Route 66 landmarks, the 80ft-long **Blue Whale** (www.bluewhaleroute66.com; 2680 N Hwy 66).

East 11th St takes you into and right through art deco-rich **Tulsa**; be sure to look for the iconic neon wonder of the restored **Meadow Gold sign** at S Quaker Ave. Southwest Blvd takes you across the river and out of town.

The rural route from Tulsa to Oklahoma City is one of the longest continuous stretches of Mother Road remaining (110 miles), a fine alternative to the I-44 tollway. At **Chandler**, 60 miles southwest of Tulsa, the **Route 66 Interpretive Center** (www.route66interpretive-

($24, two hours, five daily), among other destinations.

Western Oklahoma

West of Oklahoma City toward Texas the land opens into expansive prairie fields, nowhere as beautifully as in the Wichita Mountains, which, along with some Route 66 attractions and Native American sites, make this prime road-trip country. US 281 passes through beautiful country.

Washita Battlefield National Historic Site

Washita Battlefield National Historic Site (www.nps.gov/waba; Hwy 47A, 2 miles west of Cheyenne; ⊙site dawn-dusk, visitor center 9am-5pm, talks & tours 10am-2pm Sat & Sun Jun-Aug) FREE is where George Custer's troops launched a dawn attack on November 27, 1868 on the peaceful village of Chief Black Kettle. It was a slaughter of men, women, children and domestic animals, an act some would say led to karmic revenge on Custer eight years later.

Self-guiding **trails** traverse the site of the killings, which is remarkably unchanged. A new visitor center 0.7 miles away contains a good **museum**. Seasonal tours and talks are very worthwhile. The site is near Cheyenne, 30 miles north of I-40 via US 283.

Tulsa

Self-billed as the 'Oil Capital of the World,' Tulsa has never dirtied its hands much on the black gold that oozes out elsewhere in the state. Rather, it is home to scores of energy companies that make their living drilling for oil, selling it or supplying those who do. The steady wealth this provides once helped create Tulsa's richly detailed art-deco downtown. But today Tulsa is not the most charming Great Plains town: suburban sprawl has dispersed its appeal, although the Brady Arts District downtown holds promise.

◉ Sights & Activities

Downtown Tulsa has so much art-deco architecture it was once known as the

center.org; 400 E Rte 66; adult/child $5/4; ⊙10am-5pm Tue-Sat, 1-5pm Sun) re-creates the experience of driving the road through the decades. It's housed in a magnificent 1936 armory.

Route 66 follows US 77 into **Oklahoma City** and beyond that, it's unmarked. Take Kelley Ave south, head over to Lincoln Blvd at 50th St and turn west on NW 23rd St at the capitol. You'll leave OKC by turning north on May Ave and west on NW 39th St past **Ann's Chicken Fry House** (p660). Beyond this, the route follows Business I-40.

El Reno, 20 miles west of OKC, is home to the fried onion burger, a road-food classic. Among several historic drive-ins and dives, try **Johnnie's Grill** (301 S Rock Island; ⊙9am-7pm) or **Sid's** (300 S Choctaw Ave; ⊙11am-7pm). Ground beef is combined with raw onions and then cooked and caramelized on the grill (Sid's has outdoor tables, Johnnie's the bigger dining area).

Some 17 miles west of El Reno, take a stretch of US 281 that runs on the north side of I-40 between exits 108 and 101. Where it crosses the Canadian River on the 38-truss-long **Pony Bridge**, stop at the west end. Here's the spot they had to ditch gramps in the 1939 movie version of the *Grapes of Wrath*.

Leave I-40 at exit 95 and follow a 1930s stretch of 66 that parallels the north side of the interstate. Just west of **Hydro** and Hwy 58, **Lucille's** is the atmospheric moldering remains of a legendary roadhouse. Some 4 miles further on as you approach **Weatherford**, the modern **Lucille's Roadhouse** (www.lucillesroadhouse.com; 1301 N Airport Rd, at I-40 exit 84; mains $4-10; ⊙6am-10pm) carries on the legacy with excellent food and a fine beer selection.

In **Clinton**, walk through six decades of history, memorabilia and music at the mid-sized **Route 66 Museum** (www.route66.org; 2229 W Gary Blvd; adult/child $5/1; ⊙9am-7pm Mon-Sat, 1-6pm Sun summer, reduced hours rest of year). Thirty miles further west in **Elk City**, the **National Route 66 Museum** (2717 W 3rd St/Hwy 66; adult/child $5/4; ⊙9am-5pm Mon-Sat, 2-5pm Sun summer, reduced hours rest of year) is three museums in one: old cars and photos, a re-created pioneer town and a farm museum. Route 66 spills into Texas at **Texola**, which is just a dust devil away from being a ghost town.

'Terra-Cotta City.' The **Philcade Building** (511 S Boston St), with its glorious T-shaped lobby, and **Boston Avenue United Methodist Church** (1301 S Boston St; ⊙8:30am-5pm Mon-Fri, 8am-5pm Sun, guided tours noon Sun), rising at the end of downtown, are two exceptional examples. A free walking guide from the visitor center will lead you to dozens more.

★**Woody Guthrie Center**   MUSEUM
(www.woodyguthriecenter.org; 102 E Brady St; adult/child $8/6; ⊙10am-6pm Tue-Sun) Woody Guthrie gained fame for his 1930s folk ballads that told stories of the Dust Bowl and the depression. His life and music are recalled in this impressive new museum, where you can listen to his music and explore his legacy via the works of Dylan and more.

★**Oklahoma Jazz Hall of Fame**   MUSEUM
(www.okjazz.org; 111 E 1st St; admission free, concerts $5; ⊙11am-5pm Mon-Sat, 1-7pm Sun, concerts 5pm Sun) Tulsa's beautiful Union Station is filled with sound again, but now it's melodious as opposed to cacophonous. During the first half of the 20th century, Tulsa was literally at the crossroads of American music with performers both homegrown and from afar. Learn about greats like Charlie Christian, Ernie Fields Senior and Wallace Willis in detailed exhibits. Sunday jazz concerts are played in the grand concourse.

Gilcrease Museum   MUSEUM
(www.gilcrease.org; 1400 Gilcrease Museum Rd; adult/child $8/free; ⊙10am-5pm Tue-Sun) Northwest of downtown, off Hwy 64, this superb American art museum sits on the manicured estate of a Native American who discovered oil on his allotment.

Philbrook Museum of Art   MUSEUM
(www.philbrook.org; 2727 S Rockford Rd, east of Peoria Ave; adult/child $9/free; ⊙10am-5pm Tue-Sun, to 8pm Thu) South of town, another oil magnate's converted Italianate villa, also ringed by fabulous foliage, houses some fine Native American works.

🛏 Sleeping

Chain motels aplenty line Hwy 244 and I-44, especially at the latter's exits 229 and 232. You can also recapture some of the adventure of Route 66 – but not the bugs that were once commonplace – at two restored places.

Desert Hills Motel
MOTEL $

(☎918-834-3311; www.deserthillstulsa.com; 5220 E 11th St; r from $40; ❇🐾📶) The glowing neon cactus out front beckons you in to this lovingly restored 1950s motor court with 50 rooms (with fridges and microwaves) arranged diagonally around the parking lot. It's 5 miles east of downtown, on historic Route 66.

Hotel Campbell
HOTEL $$

(☎918-744-5500; www.thecampbellhotel.com; 2636 E 11th St; r from $140; ❇🐾📶) Restored in 2011 to its 1927-era Route 66 splendor, this historic hotel east of downtown has 26 luxurious rooms with hardwood floors, and plush, period furniture. Ask for a tour.

✗ Eating & Drinking

Dining options are on Peoria Ave between 31st and 51st Sts; on Historic Cherry St (now 15th St) just east of Peoria Ave; and in the Brady Arts District, centered on Brady and Main Sts immediately north of downtown.

Ike's Chili House
DINER $

(5941 E Admiral Pl; mains under $7; ⊙10am-7pm Mon-Fri, to 3pm Sat) Ike's has been serving chili for over 100 years and its classic version is much-loved. You can get it straight or over Fritos, a hot dog, beans or spaghetti. Top with red peppers, onions, jalapeños, saltines and cheddar cheese for pure joy.

LEGACY OF A RIOT

On Memorial Day, May 30, 1921 an African American man and a white woman were alone on an elevator in downtown Tulsa and the woman screamed. The how and why have never been answered but it sparked three days of race riots in which 35 blocks of Tulsa's main African American neighborhood were destroyed by roving gangs and even by bombs lobbed from airplanes. Thousands were left homeless, hundreds injured and scores killed.

Near the center of the violence, the **John Hope Franklin Reconciliation Park** (www.jhfcenter.org; 415 N Detroit Ave; ⊙8am-8pm) tells the story of the riot.

Elmer's
BARBECUE $

(www.elmersbbq.com; 4130 S Peoria Ave; mains $5-10; ⊙11am-8pm Tue-Sat) A legendary barbecue joint where the star of the menu is the potentially deadly 'Badwich,' a bun-crushing combo of superbly smoked sausages, ham, beef, pork and more. The dining room is bright and has a house piano for the blues.

Tavern
AMERICAN $$

(www.taverntulsa.com; 201 N Main St; mains $10-30; ⊙11am-late) This beautiful pub anchors the Brady Arts District and serves excellent fare. The hamburgers are legendary or you can opt for steaks, salads or seasonal specials. The bartenders are true mixologists.

☆ Entertainment

Open-air **Guthrie Green** (www.guthriegreen.com; Boston Ave & Brady St) often hosts events. The **Urban Tulsa Weekly** (www.urbantulsa.com) has the scoop on what's going on.

★ Cain's Ballroom
LIVE MUSIC

(www.cainsballroom.com; 423 N Main St) Rising rockers grace the boards where Bob Wills played Western swing in the '30s and the Sex Pistols caused confusion in 1978 (check out the wall Sid Vicious punched a hole in).

➊ Information

Tulsa lacks a visitor center but the Tulsa website (www.visittulsa.com) is useful.

➊ Getting There & Around

Greyhound (317 S Detroit Ave) Buses include Oklahoma City ($24, two hours, five daily) and St Louis ($100, eight hours).

Tulsa Transit (www.tulsatransit.org; one-day pass $3.25) Buses originate downtown at 319 S Denver Ave.

Green Country

Subtle forested hills interspersed with iconic red dirt and lakes cover Oklahoma's northeast corner, aka Green Country (www.greencountryok.com), which includes Tulsa. The area has a strong Native American influence, as it is where several of the Five Civilized Tribes (Cherokee, Chickasaw, Choctaw, Creek and Seminole) were relocated in the 1820s and '30s.

Bartlesville

Oklahoma's first commercial oil well was dug in Bartlesville, 50 miles north of Tulsa, and soon after in 1905 Frank Phillips, of Phillips 66 fame, arrived to dig more. You can relive these rough-and-tumble days at the slick-as-a-lube-job **Phillips Petroleum Company Museum** (www.phillips66museum. com; 410 S Keeler Ave; ☉10am-4pm Mon-Sat) `FREE` right in town.

Phillips' country estate, the 1927 rustic-luxe **Woolaroc** (www.woolaroc.org; Rte 123, 12 miles southwest of Bartlesville; adult/child $10/ free; ☉10am-5pm Wed-Sun, open Tue summer), is now an excellent museum of southwestern art and culture, and a wildlife refuge with buffalo.

The only Frank Lloyd Wright–designed skyscraper ever built, the 1956, 221ft-tall **Price Tower** looms over the small downtown. Inside and out it's like *Architectural Digest* meets the *Jetsons*. Wright shopped the design around for 30 years before he found clients willing to build it here. The **Price Tower Arts Center** (www.pricetower.org; 510 Dewey Ave; art gallery adult/child $6/free, tours $12/10; ☉10am-5pm Tue-Sat, noon-5pm Sun, call for tour times) has rotating exhibits and original furniture from the building. Tours are a good way to fully appreciate the building's typically Wrightian idiosyncrasies. You can stay in one of 19 Wright-inspired rooms at the **Inn at Price Tower** (☏918-336-1000; www.pricetower. org; r from $135; ❀☎). The 15th-floor **Copper Bar** (☉4-9pm Tue-Thu, to 11pm Fri & Sat) has sweeping views of the surrounding oil fields.

Claremore

This was the setting for the 1931 play *Green Grow the Lilacs,* which became the hugely popular musical *Oklahoma!* The latter chronicles *highly* fictionalized events in 1906.

Born in a log cabin just north of town in 1879, Will Rogers was a cowboy, hilarious homespun philosopher, star of radio and movies, and part Cherokee. The hilltop **Will Rogers Memorial Museum** (www.willrogers. com; 1720 W Will Rogers Blvd; ☉8am-5pm) `FREE`, 30 miles northeast of Tulsa off Route 66, is an entertaining tribute to a man good for quotes such as 'We shouldn't elect a president. We should elect a magician' and 'No man is great if he thinks he is.'

OKLAHOMA: DETOURS & EXTRAS

Following Route 66 through Oklahoma can seem like one long detour and can offer days of exploration. But there are many more options in various corners of the state.

Brick-and-stone Victorian buildings line street after street of **Guthrie**, Oklahoma's first capital, 25 miles north of Oklahoma City. The well-preserved downtown contains shops, museums, B&Bs and eateries.

Pioneer Woman Museum (www. pioneerwomanmuseum.com; 701 Monument Rd; adult/child $4/1; ☉10am-5pm Tue-Sat) honors the people who did the real work in the Old West, while the men hung around towns waiting for shoot-outs or getting liquored up in saloons (at least that's how it seems in the movies). It segues to the modern age with a gallery of Oklahoma's female rock musicians. It's 15 miles east of I-35 in Ponca City.

Trail of Tears Country

The area southeast of present-day Tulsa was, and to some degree still is, Creek and Cherokee land. This is an excellent place to learn about Native American culture, especially before the 1800s.

Namesake of Merle Haggard's 1969 hit 'Okie from Muskogee?,' **Muskogee** ('where even squares can have a ball'), 49 miles southeast of Tulsa, is home to the **Five Civilized Tribes Museum** (www.fivetribes.org; Honor Heights Dr, Agency Hill; adult/student $4/2; ☉10am-5pm Mon-Fri, to 2pm Sat). It's inside an 1875 Union Indian Agency house and recalls the cultures of the Native Americans forcibly moved here from America's southeast.

Twenty miles east on Hwy 62 is **Tahlequah** (tal-*ah*-quaw), the Cherokee capital since 1839. The excellent **Cherokee Heritage Center** (www.cherokeeheritage.org; 21192 Keeler Rd; adult/child $8.50/5; ☉9am-5pm Jun-Aug, short hours rest of year) features Native American–led tours through a re-creation of a pre-European contact woodland village. The museum focuses on the Trail of Tears.

Texas

Best Places to Eat

➡ Cochineal (p712)

➡ Güero's Taco Bar (p676)

➡ Bread Winners (p701)

➡ Cove (p685)

➡ Hugo's (p691)

Best Places to Stay

➡ Gage Hotel (p713)

➡ Hotel San José (p674)

➡ Hotel Belmont (p701)

➡ Hotel ZaZa (p690)

➡ Stockyards Hotel (p706)

Why Go?

Cue the theme music, and make it something epic: Texas is as big and sweeping a state as can be imagined. If it were a country, it would be the 40th largest. And as big as it is geographically, it is equally large in people's imaginations.

Cattle ranches, pickup trucks, cowboy boots and thick Texas drawls – all of those are part of the culture, to be sure. But an Old West theme park it is not. With a state this big, there's room for Texas to be whatever you want it to be.

You can find beaches, amusement parks, citified shopping and nightlife, historical monuments and a vibrant music scene. And the nearly year-round warm weather makes it ideal for outdoor activities such as rock climbing, cycling, hiking and rowing. So saddle up for whatever adventure suits you best: the Lone Star state is ready to ride.

When to Go
Austin

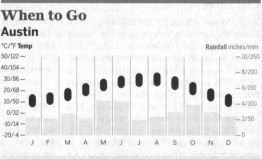

Mar Warm weather during spring break attracts college students and families with kids.

Apr–May Wildflowers line roadsides, festivals are in full swing and summer is yet to swelter.

Oct Crowds have thinned, the heat has broken, but it's still warm enough for shorts.

Getting Around

Texas is big, but it's easy to get around. The best way to travel is to rent a car or bring your own. Flying is another good option if time is short, especially with cut-rate carrier Southwest Airlines (p1191), which offers short hops within Texas for as little as $59 one way if you book ahead.

There's also limited train service within Texas. Amtrak's *Sunset Limited* (Florida–California) passes through Houston, San Antonio and El Paso, and the *Texas Eagle* (San Antonio–Chicago) stops in Dallas–Fort Worth and Austin. Note that trains often have late-night arrivals or departures in Texas.

Greyhound and its partner **Kerrville Bus Lines** (☑800-231-2222; www.iridekbc.com) serve all but the tiniest towns, though it may take several transfers and twice as long as by car.

TEXAS PARKS

In a state as big as Texas, there's plenty of exploring to be done, and packed into the wide, open spaces you'll find more than 125 state parks, historic sites and natural areas. You could seek out the unique ecosystem at swampy Caddo Lake, watch bats fly out of the Devil's Sinkhole, or descend into a 120-mile-long chasm at Palo Duro Canyon, just to name a few. Some parks are remote and rustic; others are downright fancy. Create your own adventure using the free guide from **Texas Parks & Wildlife** (☑800-792-1112; www.tpwd.state.tx.us), available both in print and online.

Texas Barbecue

Make no bones about it: Texas barbecue is an obsession. It's the subject of countless newspaper and magazine articles, from national press like the *New York Times* to regional favorite *Texas Monthly*, which publishes what many consider a definitive listing of the top barbecue joints in Texas.

Some of central Texas' smaller towns – Lockhart and Elgin, to name only two – maintain perennial reputations for their smokehouse cultures and routinely draw dedicated pilgrims from miles around. To find the best barbecue, you can either follow your nose or check out the **Texas Barbecue Trail** (www.texasbbqtrails.com), a list of some of the best family-owned joints in central Texas.

However you like it best – sliced thick onto butcher paper, slapped down on picnic plates, doused with a tangy sauce or eaten naturally flavorful right out of the smokehouse barbecue pit – be sure to savor it and then argue to the death that your way is the best way. Like a true Texan.

DID YOU KNOW?

Texas is unique in the USA as the only state that was once its own republic (1836–45). It still sometimes threatens to secede.

Fast Facts

➡ **Hub cities** Dallas (population 1.2 million), Houston (population 2.1 million)

➡ **Time zone** Central, except El Paso, which is Mountain

➡ **State flower** Bluebonnet (you'll see it everywhere in Texas)

Best Small Towns

➡ Marfa (p711) boasts minimalist art and mystery lights.

➡ Fredericksburg (p680) is lovely during wildflower season.

➡ Terlingua (p709) is a pretty happening ghost town.

➡ Under-the-radar Denton (p704) rocks.

➡ Find Texas' oldest dance hall in Gruene (p679).

Resources

➡ **Texas Tourism** (www.traveltex.com)

➡ **TX Department of Travel** (www.txdot.gov/travel)

➡ **State Parks** (www.tpwd.state.tx.us)

TEXAS

Texas Highlights

1 Scooting across a well-worn wooden floor at Texas' oldest dance hall in **Gruene** (p679).

2 Remembering **The Alamo** (p682), a historical shrine in San Antonio to the men who fought for Texas independence.

3 Getting your fill of live music and funky food trucks in beguiling **Austin** (p671).

4 Pondering JFK conspiracy theories at Dallas' one-of-a-kind **Sixth Floor Museum** (p699).

5 Immersing yourself in cowboy culture at the **Stockyards National Historic District** (p705) in Fort Worth.

6 Discovering the rugged natural beauty of **Big Bend National Park** (p708).

7 Getting a stellar view of the night sky at the **McDonald Observatory** (p711) star party.

8 Peeking at postmodern art at Houston's **Menil Collection** (p687).

9 Wandering the shady trails through fragrant piney woods at **Big Thicket National Preserve** (p695).

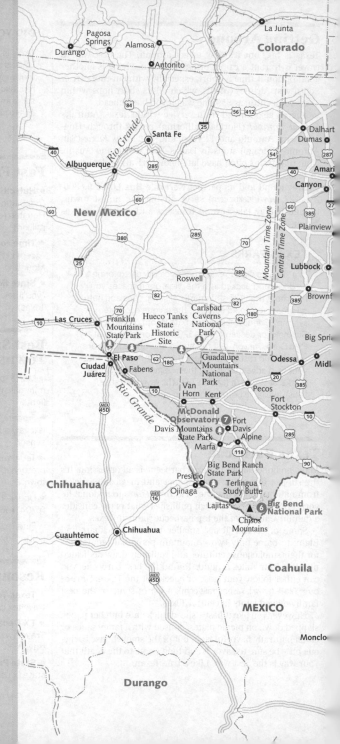

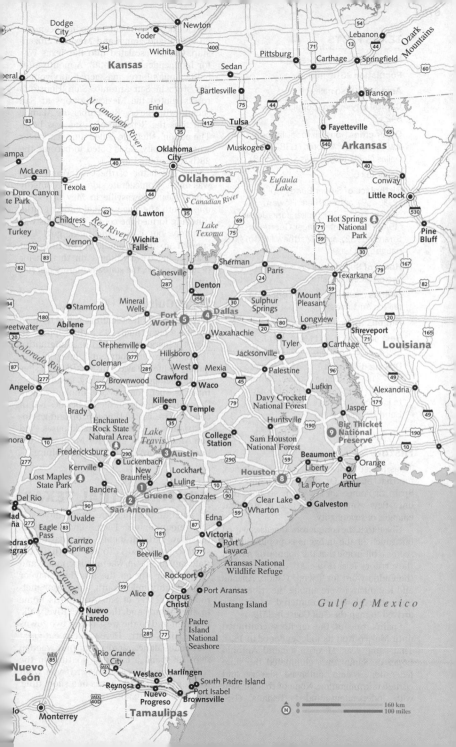

TEXAS FACTS

Nickname The Lone Star State

Population 26.06 million

Area 261,797 sq miles

Capital city Austin (population 842,592)

Other cities Houston (population 2,160,821), San Antonio (1,382,951), Dallas (1,241,162), El Paso (672,538)

Sales tax 6.25%

Birthplace of Singer Buddy Holly (1936–59), entrepreneur Howard Hughes (1905–76), rocker Janis Joplin (1943–70), country singer George Strait (b 1952), actor Matthew McConaughey (b 1969)

Home of Shiner Bock beer, Dr Pepper, two presidents Bush

Politics Leans Republican (but don't tell the Austinites)

Famous for Barbecue, cowboys

Best souvenir 'Don't Mess with Texas' items, from T-shirts to toilet paper

Driving distances Austin to San Antonio 78 miles, Austin to Dallas 196 miles, Dallas to Houston 242 miles, Houston to El Paso 745 miles, El Paso to Big Bend 291 miles

History

Texas hasn't always been Texas. Or Mexico, for that matter. Or the United States, or Spain, or France...or any of the six flags that once flew over this epic state in its eight changes of sovereignty.

Given that the conquerors' diseases wiped out much of the indigenous population, it seems a bit ironic that the Spaniards named the territory Tejas (*tay*-has) – a corruption of the Caddo word for 'friend.' Caddo, Apache and Karankawa were among the tribes that Spanish explorers encountered when they arrived to map the Gulf Coast in 1519.

Spain's rule of the territory continued until Mexico won its independence in 1821. That same year, Mexican general Antonio López de Santa Anna eliminated the state federation system, outlawed slavery and curtailed immigration. None of this sat well with independent-minded 'Texians' (US- and Mexico-born Texans) who had been given cheap land grants and Mexican citizenship. Clashes escalated into the Texas War for Independence (1835–36). A month after Santa Anna's forces massacred survivors of the siege in San Antonio, Sam Houston's rebels routed the Mexican troops at San Jacinto with the cry 'Remember the Alamo!' and thus the Republic of Texas was born. The nation's short life ended nine years later when, by treaty, Texas opted to become the 28th state of the Union.

The last battle of the Civil War (Texas was on the Confederate side) was reputedly fought near Brownsville in May of 1865 – one month after the war had ended. Cattle-ranching formed the core of Texas' postwar economy, but it was the black gold that spewed up from Spindletop in 1910 that really changed everything. From then on, for better or worse, the state's economy has run on oil.

Local Culture

Trying to typify Texas culture is like tryin' to wrestle a pig in mud – it's awful slippery. In a vast generalization, Austin is alternative Texas, where environmental integrity and quality of life are avidly discussed. Dallasites are the shoppers and society trendsetters; more is spent on silicone implants there than anywhere else in the US besides LA. In conservative, casual Houston, oil-and-gas industrialists dine at clubby steakhouses. And San Antonio is the most Tex-Mexican of the bunch – a showplace of Hispanic culture.

SOUTH-CENTRAL TEXAS

So what if the hills are more mole-size than mountainous? They – and the rivers that flow through them – are what define south-central Texas. To the north is the state capital, Austin, where music, music and more music are on the schedule, day or night. Eighty miles south, the major metropolitan center of San Antonio is home to the Alamo and the festive Riverwalk. Between and to the west of the two towns is the Hill Country. Here you can eat great barbecue, dance across an old wooden floor or spend a lazy day floating on the river in small Texas-y towns. If you want to get to the heart of Texas in a short time, this is the way to go.

Austin

You'll see it on bumper stickers and T-shirts throughout the city: 'Keep Austin Weird.' And while old-timers grumble that Austin has lost its funky charm, the city has still managed to hang on to its incredibly laid-back vibe. Though this former college town with a hippie soul has seen an influx of tech types and movie stars, it's still a town of artists with day jobs, where people try to focus on their music or write their novel or annoy their neighbors with crazy yard art.

Along the freeway and in the 'burbs, big-box stores and chain restaurants have proliferated at an alarming rate. But the neighborhoods still have an authentically Austin feel, with all sorts of locally owned businesses, including a flock of food trailers – a symbol of the low-key entrepreneurialism that represents Austin at its best.

The one thing everyone seems to know about Austin, whether they've been there or not, is that it's a music town, even if they don't actually use the words 'Live Music Capital of the World' (though that's a claim no one's disputing). The city now hosts two major music festivals, South by Southwest and the Austin City Limits festival, but you don't have to endure the crowds and exorbitant hotel prices to experience the scene, because Austin has live music all over town every night of the week.

◉ Sights

Don't limit yourself to the sights; Austin is about the experience. Bars, restaurants and even grocery stores and the airport have live music. And there are outdoor activities galore.

A full day might also include shopping for some groovy vintage clothes, sipping a margarita at a patio cafe and lounging on the shores of Barton Springs. But if your vacation isn't complete without a visit to a museum, there are some stops that are worth your while.

◉ Downtown

Bob Bullock Texas State History Museum
MUSEUM

(☑512-936-8746; www.thestoryoftexas.com; 1800 Congress Ave; adult/child 4-17yr $9/6, Texas Spirit film $5/4; ◉9am-6pm Mon-Sat, noon-6pm Sun) This is no dusty old historical museum. It's a big and glitzy ramble through the Lone Star State's history, all the way from when it used to be part of Mexico up to the present, with high-tech interactive exhibits and fun theatrics. Allow at least a few hours for your visit.

Blanton Museum of Art
MUSEUM

(☑512-471-5482; www.blantonmuseum.org; 200 E Martin Luther King Jr Blvd; adult/child $9/free; ◉10am-5pm Tue-Fri, 11am-5pm Sat, 1-5pm Sun) A big university with a big endowment is bound to have a big art collection and now, finally, it has a suitable building to show it off properly. With one of the best university art collections in the USA, the Blanton showcases a variety of styles. It doesn't go into any of them in great depth, but then again you're bound to find something of interest.

Texas State Capitol
HISTORIC BUILDING

(☑512-305-8402; cnr 11th St & Congress Ave; ◉7am-10pm Mon-Fri, 9am-8pm Sat & Sun) FREE Built in 1888 from sunset-red granite, this state capitol is the largest in the US, backing

TEXAS AUSTIN

TEXAS IN...

Five Days
Spend a day and a night enjoying San Antonio, sipping margaritas in the cafes along the **Riverwalk** and bargain-hunting for Mexico-made trinkets in **Market Square**. Then head 80 miles north: book two nights at the funky **Austin Motel** and arrange to listen to as much live music in the capital as you can, maybe catching a set at the **Continental Club** and taking a dip in frigid **Barton Springs Pool**. On days four and five, indulge in some shopping and dining in **Dallas** before moving on to see the Western art and sights in Cowtown, the apt nickname given to **Fort Worth**.

Ten Days
Follow the five-day itinerary in reverse, then drive west from San Antonio to west Texas – or fly, since driving takes the better part of a day. Stay a night at the Old West–era **Gage Hotel** before heading south to hike or raft among the deep canyons and craggy mountains of **Big Bend National Park**. You should also stop to see some stunning avant-garde art in **Marfa** and stargaze at the **McDonald Observatory** in Fort Davis.

Austin

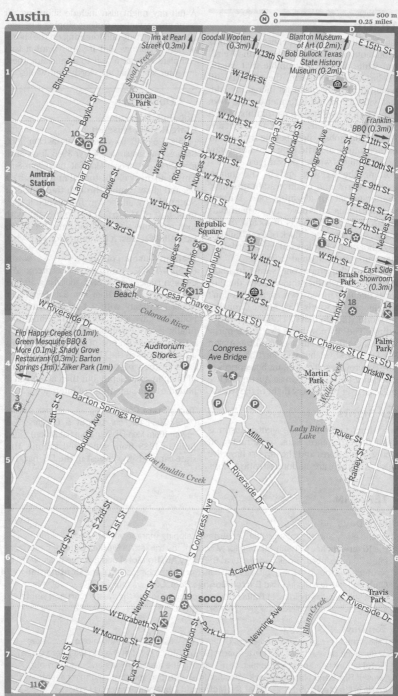

Austin

up the ubiquitous claim that everything is bigger in Texas. If nothing else, take a peek at the lovely rotunda and try out the whispering gallery created by its curved ceiling.

Austin Children's Museum MUSEUM
(☏ 512-472-2499; www.austinkids.org; 201 Colorado St; admission $6.50, child under 1yr free; ◷ 10am-5pm Tue-Sat, to 8pm Wed, noon-5pm Sun; ⊞) Kids can try their hand at running a ranch, ordering a meal at the Global Diner and hanging upside down beneath a bridge, just like the real Austin bats. At the time of research, construction had begun on a brand new facility at 1830 Simond Ave that will double the exhibition space, so check the website before you visit.

🏃 Activities

Barton Springs Pool SWIMMING
(☏ 512-867-3080; 2201 Barton Springs Rd; adult/child $3/2; ◷ 9am-10pm Fri-Wed mid-Apr–Sep) Hot? Not for long. Even when the temperature hits 100, you'll be shivering in a jiff after you jump into this icy-cold natural-spring pool. Draped with century-old pecan trees, the area around the pool is a social scene in itself, and the place gets packed on hot summer days.

Lady Bird Lake CANOEING
(☏ 512-459-0999; www.rowingdock.com; 2418 Stratford Dr; ◷ 6:30am-8pm) Named after former first lady Lady Bird Johnson, Lady Bird Lake kind of looks like a river. And no wonder: it's actually a dammed-off section of the Colorado River that divides Austin

into north and south. Get out on the water at the Rowing Dock, which rents kayaks, canoes and paddleboards for $10 to $20 per hour, and paddleboats for slightly more.

Zilker Park HIKING, CYCLING
(☏ 512-974-6700; www.austintexas.gov/department/zilker-metropolitan-park; 2100 Barton Springs Rd) This 350-acre park is a slice of green heaven, lined with hiking and biking trails. The park provides access to the famed Barton Springs natural swimming pool and Barton Creek Greenbelt. Find boat rentals, a miniature train and a botanical garden, too. During busy summer weekends admission is $5 per car.

Bicycle Sport Shop BICYCLE RENTAL
(☏ 512-477-3472; www.bicyclesportshop.com; 517 S Lamar Blvd; per 2hr from $16; ◷ 10am-7pm Mon-Fri, 9am-6pm Sat, 11am-5pm Sun) The cool thing about Bicycle Sport Shop is its proximity to Zilker Park, Barton Springs and the Lady Bird Lake bike paths, all of which are within a few blocks. Rentals range from $16 for a two-hour cruise on a standard bike to $62 for a full day on a top-end full-suspension model. On weekends and holidays, advance reservations are advised.

🎉 Festivals & Events

South by Southwest MUSIC, FILM
(SXSW; www.sxsw.com; single festival $625-1150, combo pass $900-1600; ◷ mid-Mar) One of the American music industry's biggest gatherings has now expanded to include film and interactive. The city is absolutely besieged

BY THE LIGHT OF THE MOON

Keep an eye out for Austin's **moonlight towers**. All the rage in the late 1800s, these 165ft-tall street lamps were designed to give off the light of a full moon. Austin is the only city in which these historic triangular metal towers topped by a halo of six large bulbs still operate. Fifteen burn bright around the city: how many can you spot?

with visitors during this two-week window, and many a new resident first came to Austin to hear a little live music.

Austin City Limits Music Festival MUSIC
(www.aclfestival.com; 3-day pass $200-225; ⊗Oct) Move over SXSW. This growing festival is a favorite with the locals and is gaining swiftly on the March event, with over 100 pretty impressive acts filling the eight stages in Zilker Park. Tickets usually sell out months in advance.

Formula 1 Grand Prix CAR RACING
(www.formula1.com; ⊗Nov) A brand-spanking-new racetrack means a city overtaken by F1 fans during this high-octane weekend.

🛏 Sleeping

South Congress (SoCo) has the coolest and quirkiest digs, and downtown has more high-rent options. For a complete list of choices, check with the Austin Visitor Information Center (p678).

Hotel rates soar and locals flee during SXSW and F1, so plan accordingly.

⭐ **Firehouse Hostel** HOSTEL $
(☎512-201-2522; www.firehousehostel.com; 605 Brazos St; dm $29-32, r $70-90, ste $120-145; ❄ 🤶) A hostel in downtown Austin? Finally! And a pretty darned spiffy one at that. Opened in January 2013 in a former firehouse, it's still fresh and new, and the downtown location right across from the historic Driskill Hotel is as perfect as you can get.

Goodall Wooten HOSTEL $
(☎512-472-1343; 2112 Guadalupe St; r $35; ❄ @) A private dorm near the University of Texas, 'the Woo' generally has rooms available mid-May to mid-August, and sometimes has space for travelers at other times of the year. Just the basics – expect sheets and toilet paper, but no decor – but each room has a small refrigerator. Cash only.

⭐ **Hotel San José** BOUTIQUE HOTEL $$
(☎512-444-7322; www.sanjosehotel.com; 1316 S Congress Ave; r without bath $95-145, with bath $165-285; P ❄ 🤶 ≋) Local hotelier Liz Lambert revamped a 1930s-vintage motel into a chic SoCo retreat with minimalist rooms in stucco bungalows, native Texas gardens and a very Austin-esque hotel bar in the courtyard that's known for its celebrity-spotting potential. South Congress has become quite the scene, and this hotel's location puts you right in the thick of it.

⭐ **Austin Motel** MOTEL $$
(☎512-441-1157; www.austinmotel.com; 1220 S Congress Ave; r $84-139, ste $163; P ❄ 🤶 ≋) 'Garage-sale chic' is the unifying factor at this wonderfully funky motel that embodies the spirit of the 'Keep Austin Weird' movement. Each room is individually decorated with whatever happened to be lying around at the time, with varying degrees of success.

Inn at Pearl Street B&B $$
(☎512-478-0051; www.innpearl.com; 1809 Pearl St; d $175-215, ste $225; P ❄ 🤶) This is a preservationist's dream come true. The owners picked up this run-down property, dusted it off and – well, they more than dusted it off. They completely restored it and decorated it in a plush European style.

⭐ **Driskill Hotel** HISTORIC HOTEL $$$
(☎800-252-9367, 512-474-5911; www.driskillhotel.com; 604 Brazos St; r $199-299, ste $300-900; P ❄ 🤶) Every city should have a beautiful historic hotel made of native stone, preferably built in the late 1800s by a wealthy cattle baron. No generic hotel decor here; this place is pure Texas, from the leather couches to the mounted longhorn head on the wall. (Not to worry: the elegant rooms are taxidermy-free.)

🍴 Eating

It's easy to find good, cheap food in Austin. South Congress provides a slew of options, but you'll be competing with lots of other hungry diners for a table. Those in the know go instead to S 1st St (1400 to 2100 blocks), where Mexican herbalists and tattoo parlors alternate with trailer-park food courts and organic cafes. Barton Springs Rd (east of Lamar Blvd) also has a number of interesting eateries, and Guadalupe St by UT is the place to look for cheap eats. Some great meat-market barbecue is available in nearby central Texas (p679).

Downtown

★ Franklin BBQ
BARBECUE **$**

(☑ 512-653-1187; www.franklinbarbecue.com; 900 E 11th St; mains $6-13; ☺ 11am-2pm Tue-Sun) It only serves lunch, and only till it runs out – usually well before 2pm. Don't wait till you're hungry to find out whether Franklin's is worth the insane amount of hype; there's usually a long line of people waiting before it even opens. When your moment of glory arrives, go for the two-meat plate, or nab all you can for a feast to enjoy later. (Just be quick about it. The people behind you are starving.)

★ Amy's Ice Cream
ICE CREAM **$**

(☑ 512-480-0673; www.amysicecreams.com; 1012 W Sixth St; ☺ 11am-midnight Sun-Thu, to 1am Fri & Sat) It's not just the ice cream we love; it's the toppings that get pounded and blended in, violently but lovingly, by the staff wielding a metal scoop in each hand. Look for other locations on Guadalupe St north of the UT campus, on South Congress near all the shops, or at the airport for a last-ditch fix.

Moonshine Patio Bar & Grill
AMERICAN **$$**

(☑ 512-236-9599; www.moonshinegrill.com; 303 Red River St; dinner mains $11-21; ☺ 11am-10pm Mon-Thu, to 11pm Fri & Sat, 9am-2pm & 5-10pm Sun) Dating from the mid-1850s, this historic building is a remarkably well preserved homage to Austin's early days. Within its exposed limestone walls you can enjoy upscale comfort food, half-price appetizers at happy hour or a lavish Sunday brunch buffet ($16.95). Or chill on the patio under the shade of pecan trees.

★ Lambert's
BARBECUE **$$$**

(☑ 512-494-1500; 401 W 2nd St; mains $14-42; ☺ 11am-2pm & 5:30-10pm) Torn between barbecue and fine dining? Lambert's serves intelligent updates of American comfort-food classics – some might call it 'uppity barbecue' – in a historic stone building run by Austin chef Lou Lambert. Sides are extra, so be prepared to spend. Or come early and nosh on half-price appetizers at happy hour (5pm till 7pm).

South Austin

Green Mesquite BBQ & More
BARBECUE **$**

(☑ 512-479-0485; www.greenmesquite.net; 1400 Barton Springs Rd; mains $6-11, kids' plates $5; ☺ 11am-10pm) As its T-shirts say, Green Mesquite has been 'horrifying vegetarians since 1988.' This inexpensive, low-key spot has lots of tasty meat, pecan pie, cold beer and a shady outdoor area that's lovely on cool days.

Bouldin Creek Coffee House
VEGETARIAN **$**

(☑ 512-416-1601; 1900 S 1st St; meals $5-9; ☺ 7am-midnight Mon-Fri, 8am-midnight Sat & Sun; 🛜🚲) You can get your veggie chorizo scrambler or organic oatmeal with apples all day long at this vegan-vegetarian eatery. It has an eclectic South Austin vibe and is a great place for people-watching, finishing your novel or joining a band.

TEXAS AUSTIN

DON'T MISS

MEALS ON WHEELS

Food trailers are here to stay – even if they can move around at whim. We haven't listed any of these rolling restaurants because of their transient nature, but instead invite you to explore some of the areas where they congregate. Wander from trailer to trailer till one strikes your fancy, or make a progressive dinner out of it. Look for clusters of airstreams and taco trucks in some of these likely spots:

South Austin Trailer Park & Eatery (1311 S 1st St) Seems to be a rather settled trailer community, with a fence, an official name, a sign and picnic tables.

1503 S 1st St Has a cluster of food trailers, and if you're lucky you'll find Gourdough's among them. The gourmet doughnuts here are expensive but provide a full dessert for two.

South Congress Between Elizabeth and Monroe, it yields lots of options, including the awesome Mighty Cone.

East Austin Has its own little enclave, conveniently located right among all the bars on the corner of E 6th and Waller Sts.

Flip Happy Crepes (☑ 512-552-9034; cnr Jessie St & Butler Rd; crepes $5-7; ☺ 10am-2pm Wed-Sun, plus 6:30-9pm Sat) Doesn't travel in a pack, but it was among the first (if not *the* first) so we thought it deserved a mention.

GAY & LESBIAN AUSTIN

With a thriving gay population – not to mention pretty mellow straight people – Austin is arguably the most gay-friendly city in Texas. The **Austin Gay & Lesbian Chamber of Commerce** (www.aglcc.org) sponsors the Pride Parade in June, as well as smaller events throughout the year. The **Austin Chronicle** (www.austinchronicle.com) runs a gay event column among the weekly listings, and the glossy **L Style/G Style** (www.lstylegstyle.com) magazine has a dual gal/guy focus.

★ **Güero's Taco Bar**   TEX-MEX **$$**
(☎ 512-447-7688; 1412 S Congress Ave; mains $6-15; ⏰ 11am-10pm) Oh Güero's, how we love you. Why must you make us wait? Well, clearly it's because of the three million other hungry people crammed into your bar area. Still, we'll try to be patient, because we love the atmosphere lent by the century-old former feed-and-seed store, and because we have an obsessive craving for your chicken tortilla soup.

✗ Around Town

Trudy's Texas Star   TEX-MEX **$$**
(☎ 512-477-2935; www.trudys.com; 409 W 30th St; mains $7-12; ⏰ 4pm-2am Mon-Thu, from 11am Fri, from 9am Sat & Sun) Get your Tex-Mex fix here; the menu is consistently good, with several healthier-than-usual options. But we'll let you in on a little secret: this place could serve nothing but beans and dirt and people would still line up for the margaritas, which might very well be the best in Austin.

Shady Grove Restaurant   AMERICAN **$$**
(☎ 512-474-9991; www.theshadygrove.com; 1624 Barton Springs Rd; mains $7-12; ⏰ 11am-10:30pm Sun-Thu, to 11pm Fri & Sat) 'Do you want inside or out?' What kind of question is that? We came for the shady patio, like everyone else. Outdoors under the pecan trees is prime real estate for enjoying everything from chili cheese fries to the vegetarian Hippie Sandwich.

★ **Salt Lick Bar-B-Que**   BARBECUE **$$**
(☎ 512-858-4959; www.saltlickbbq.com; 18300 FM 1826, Driftwood; mains $11-20; ⏰ 11am-10pm; 🚗) It's worth the 20-mile drive out of town just to see the massive outdoor barbecue pits at this parklike place off US 290. It's a bit of a tourist fave, but the crowd-filled experience

still gets our nod. BYOB. Hungry? Choose the family style all-you-can-eat option (adult/child $19.95/6.95).

🍷 Drinking

There are bejillions of bars in Austin, so what follows is only a very short list. The legendary 6th St bar scene has spilled onto nearby thoroughfares, especially on Red River St.

Many of the new places on 6th St are shot bars aimed at party-hardy college students and tourists, while the Red River establishments retain a harder local edge. The lounges around the Warehouse District (near the intersection of W 4th and Colorado Sts) are a bit more upscale, while SoCo caters to the more offbeat in eclectic Austin.

★ **Hotel San José**   BAR
(☎ 512-444-7322; 1316 S Congress Ave; ⏰ 5pm-midnight Mon-Thu, from noon Fri-Sun) Transcending the hotel-bar genre, this one is actually a cool, Zenlike outdoor patio that attracts a chill crowd. It's a nice place to hang if you want to actually have a conversation.

★ **East Side Showroom**   BAR
(☎ 512-467-4280; 1100 E 6th St; ⏰ 5pm-2am) With an ambience that would feel right at home in Brooklyn (in the late 1800s), this bar on the emerging east-side scene is full of hipsters soaking up the craft cocktails and bohemian atmosphere.

★ **Ginny's Little Longhorn Saloon**   BAR
(☎ 512-407-8557; 5434 Burnet Rd; ⏰ 5pm-midnight Tue, 5pm-1am Wed-Sat, 2-8pm Sun) This funky little cinder-block building is one of those dive bars that Austinites love so very much – and did even before it became nationally famous for chicken-shit bingo on Sunday night.

Contigo   BAR
(2027 Anchor Lane; ⏰ 5-11pm Mon-Thu, to midnight Fri & Sat) Big shade trees over a relaxed patio make this one of the nicest places in town to chill out with a cocktail.

☆ Entertainment
Live Music
On any given Friday night there are several hundred acts playing in the town's 200 or so venues, and even on an off night (Monday and Tuesday are usually the slowest) you'll typically have your pick of more than two dozen performances.

To plan your attack, check out the weekly *Austin Chronicle* or Thursday's *Austin American-Statesman*.

★ Continental Club   LIVE MUSIC
(☎512-441-0202; www.continentalclub.com; 1315 S Congress Ave; ◷4pm-2am) No passive toe-tapping here; this 1950s-era lounge has a dance floor that's always swinging with some of the city's best local acts.

Broken Spoke   LIVE MUSIC
(www.brokenspokeaustintx.com; 3201 S Lamar Blvd; ◷11am-midnight Tue-Thu, to 1am Fri & Sat) With sand-covered wood floors and wagonwheel chandeliers that George Strait once hung from, Broken Spoke is a true Texas honky-tonk.

Cactus Cafe   LIVE MUSIC
(www.utexas.edu/universityunions; Texas Union, cnr 24th & Guadalupe Sts; ◷varies by show) Listen to acoustic up close and personal at this intimate club on the UT campus.

Antone's   LIVE MUSIC
(www.antones.net; 213 W 5th St; ◷showtimes vary, check website) A key player in Austin's musical history, Antone's has attracted the best of the blues and other popular local acts since 1975. All ages, all the time.

Emo's East   LIVE MUSIC
(☎512-693-3667; www.emosaustin.com; 2015 E Riverside Dr; ◷showtimes vary, check website) For nearly 20 years, Emo's led the pack in the punk and indie scene in a crowded space on Red River St. Now it's got some shiny new digs (and a whole lot more space) out on Riverside.

Theater & Cinema

Long Center for the Performing Arts   PERFORMING ARTS
(☎512-474-5664; www.thelongcenter.org; 701 W Riverside Dr) This state-of-the-art theater opened in late 2008 as part of a waterfront redevelopment along Lady Bird Lake. The multistage venue hosts drama, dance, concerts and comedians.

Alamo Drafthouse Cinema   CINEMA
(☎512-476-1320; www.drafthouse.com; 320 E 6th St; admission $10) Easily the most fun you can have at the movies: sing along with *Grease,* quote along with *The Princess Bride,* or just enjoy food and drink delivered right to your seat during first-run films. Check the website for other locations.

Sports

TXRD Lonestar Rollergirls   SPECTATOR SPORT
(www.txrd.com) Get ready to rumble – it's roller-derby night and the Hellcat women skaters are expected to kick some Cherry Bomb ass. No matter who wins, the TXRD Lonestar Rollergirls league always puts on a good show, usually at the **Austin Convention Center** (☎512-404-4000; www.austinconventioncenter.com; 500 E Cesar Chavez St).

🛍 Shopping

Not many folks visit Austin just to shop. That said, music is a huge industry here and you'll find heaps of it in Austin's record stores. Vintage is a lifestyle, and the city's best hunting grounds for retro fashions and furnishings are South Austin and Guadalupe St near UT. Get a map at www.vintagaroundtownguide.com.

On the first Thursday of the month, S Congress Ave is definitely the place to be, when stores stay open until 10pm and there's live entertainment; visit www.firstthursday.info for upcoming events.

★ Uncommon Objects   VINTAGE
(☎512-912-1613; 1512 S Congress Ave; ◷11am-7pm Sun-Thu, to 8pm Fri & Sat) 'Curious oddities' is what they advertise at this quirky antique

TEXAS AUSTIN

MUSIC FESTIVALS

In mid-March tens of thousands of record-label reps, musicians, journalists and rabid fans descend on Austin for South by Southwest (p673), a musical extravaganza that attracts a couple of thousand groups and solo artists from around the world to 90 Austin venues.

Though SXSW started out as an opportunity for little-known bands and singers to catch the ear of a record-label rep, it has since become a wildly popular industry showcase for already-signed bands. Add to that a hugely popular interactive festival, as well as a more subdued but still well-attended film festival, and you've got a major international draw that takes over the city and sends most of the locals into hiding for two weeks every spring.

Too much hoopla? Come in October for a slightly more mellow experience at the Austin City Limits Music Festival (p674), an outdoor event at Zilker Park.

THE SWARM: AUSTIN'S BATS

Looking very much like a special effect from a B movie, a funnel cloud of up to 1.5 million Mexican free-tailed bats swarms from under the **Congress Avenue Bridge** nightly from late March to early November. Turns out, Austin isn't just the live-music capital of the world; it's also home to the largest urban bat population in North America.

Austinites have embraced the winged mammals – figuratively speaking of course – and gather to watch the bats' nightly exodus right around dusk as they leave for their evening meal. (Not to worry: they're looking for insects, and they mostly stay out of your hair.)

There's lots of standing around parking lots and on the bridge itself, but if you want a more leisurely bat-watching experience, try the TGI Friday's restaurant by the Radisson Hotel on Lady Bird Lake, or the **Lone Star Riverboat** (☑512-327-1388; www.lonestarriverboat.com; adult/child/senior 2-12yr $10/7/8) or **Capital Cruises** (☑512-480-9264; www.capitalcruises.com; adult/child/senior $10/5/8) for bat-watching tours.

store that sells a range of fabulous knick-knackery, all displayed with an artful eye. More than 20 vendors scour the state to stock their stalls, so there's plenty to look at.

Waterloo Records MUSIC
(☑512-474-2500; www.waterloorecords.com; 600 N Lamar Blvd; ⊘10am-11pm Mon-Sat, from 11am Sun) If you want to stock up on music, this is the record store to head to. There are sections reserved for local bands, and listening stations featuring Texas, indie and alt-country acts.

University Co-op SOUVENIRS
(☑512-476-7211; 2246 Guadalupe St; ⊘8:30am-7:30pm Mon-Fri, 9:30am-6pm Sat, 11am-5pm Sun) Stock up on souvenirs sporting the Longhorn logo at this store brimming with school spirit. The sheer quantity of objects that come in burnt orange and white is amazing.

Book People Inc BOOKS
(☑512-472-5050; 603 N Lamar Blvd; ⊘9am-11pm) Grab a coffee and browse the shelves of this lively independent bookstore across the street from Waterloo Records.

❶ Information

Austin indoors is nonsmoking, period (bars, too). A vast wi-fi network blankets downtown. For other hot spots check out www.austinwirelesscity.org. City of Austin libraries (www.ci.austin.tx.us) have free internet.
Austin American-Statesman (www.statesman.com) Daily newspaper.
Austin Chronicle (www.austinchronicle.com) Weekly newspaper, lots of entertainment info.
Austin Visitor Information Center (☑512-478-0098; www.austintexas.org; 209 E 6th St; ⊘9am-5pm) Helpful staff, free maps, extensive racks of brochures and a sample of local souvenirs for sale.

FedEx Office (327 Congress Ave; ⊘7am-11pm Mon-Fri, 9am-9pm Sat & Sun) Internet access for 30¢ a minute.
KLRU TV (www.klru.org) PBS affiliate with local programming that includes the popular music show *Austin City Limits*.

❶ Getting There & Around

Austin-Bergstrom International Airport (AUS; www.austintexas.gov/airport) is off Hwy 71, southeast of downtown. The Airport Flyer (bus 100, $1) runs to downtown (7th St and Congress Ave) and UT (Congress Ave and 18th St) every 40 minutes or so. **SuperShuttle** (☑512-258-3826; www.supershuttle.com) charges around $15 from the airport to downtown. A taxi between the airport and downtown costs from $25 to $30. Most of the national rental-car companies are represented at the airport.

The downtown **Amtrak station** (☑512-476-5684; www.amtrak.com; 250 N Lamar Blvd) is served by the *Texas Eagle* that extends from Chicago to Los Angeles. The **Greyhound Bus Station** (www.greyhound.com; 916 E Koenig Lane) is on the north side of town off I-35; take bus 7-Duval ($1) to downtown.

Austin's handy public transit system is run by **Capital Metro** (CapMetro; ☑512-474-1200; www.capmetro.org). Call for directions to anywhere or stop into the downtown **Capital Metro Transit Store** (323 Congress Ave; ⊘7:30am-5pm Mon-Fri) for information.

Around Austin

Northwest of Austin along the Colorado River are the six Highland Lakes. Though recent years have seen serious droughts, one of the most popular lakes for recreation – when there's water – is the 19,000-sq-acre **Lake Travis** off Hwy 71. Rent boats and Jet Skis at the associated marina, or overnight in the posh digs at **Lakeway Resort and Spa** (☎512-261-6600; www.lakewayresortandspa.com; 101 Lakeway Dr; r from $189; ❄@☎☒). **Lake Austin Spa Resort** (☎512-372-7300; www.lakeaustin.com; 1705 S Quinlan Park Rd, off FM 2222; 3-night packages from $1600; ❄@☒) is the premier place to be pampered in the state. And Lake Travis has Texas' only official nude beach, **Hippie Hollow** (www.hippiehollow.com; 7000 Comanche Trail; day pass car/bicycle $12/5; ☉9am-dusk Sep-May, 8am-dusk Jun-Aug). To get to Hippie Hollow from FM 2222, take Rte 620 south 1.5 miles to Comanche Trail and turn right. The entrance is 2 miles ahead on the left.

Hill Country

New York has the Hamptons, San Francisco has the wine country, and Texas has the Hill Country, whose natural beauty paired with its easygoing nature has inspired more than a few early retirements. Detour down dirt roads in search of fields of wildflowers, check into a dude ranch, float along the Guadalupe River or twirl around the floor of an old dance hall. Most of the small towns in the rolling hills and valleys west of Austin and San Antonio are easy day trips from either city.

Gruene

False-front wood buildings and old German homes make this the quintessential rustic Texas town. All of Gruene (pronounced *green*) is on the National Historic Register –

and boy, do day-trippers know it. You won't be alone wandering among the antiques, arts-and-crafts and knickknack shops.

◉ Sights & Activities

Gruene Hall DANCE HALL
(www.gruenehall.com; 1280 Gruene Rd; ☉11am-midnight Mon-Fri, 10am-1am Sat, 10am-9pm Sun) Folks have been congregating here since 1878, making it one of Texas' oldest dance halls and the oldest continually operating one. Toss back a longneck, two-step to live music on the well-worn wooden dance floor, or play horseshoes out in the yard.

Rockin' R River Rides WATER SPORTS
(☎830-629-9999; www.rockinr.com; 1405 Gruene Rd; tubes $17) Floating down the Guadalupe in an inner tube is a Texas summer tradition. This outfitter buses you upstream and you float the three to four hours back to base. Put a plastic cooler full of beverages (no bottles) in a bottom-fortified tube next to you and you have a day.

⌷ Sleeping & Eating

Gruene Mansion Inn INN $$$
(☎830-629-2641; www.gruenemansioninn.com; 1275 Gruene Rd; d $195-250) This cluster of buildings is practically its own village, with rooms in the mansion, a former carriage house and the old barns. Richly decorated in a style the owners call 'rustic Victorian elegance,' the rooms feature lots of wood, floral prints and pressed-tin ceiling tiles.

WORTH A TRIP

LOCKHART BARBECUE

In 1999 the Texas Legislature adopted a resolution naming Lockhart – 33 miles south of Austin – the barbecue capital of Texas. Of course, that means it's the barbecue capital of the *world*. You can eat very well for under $10 at these places:

Black's Barbecue (215 N Main St; sandwiches $4-6, brisket per pound $11; ☉10am-8pm Sun-Thu, to 8:30pm Fri & Sat) A longtime Lockhart favorite since 1932, with sausage so good Lyndon Johnson had Black's cater a party at the nation's capital.

Kreuz Market (☎512-398-2361; 619 N Colorado St; brisket per pound $11.90, sides extra; ☉10:30am-8pm Mon-Sat) Serving Lockhart since 1900, the barnlike Kreuz Market uses a dry rub. This means you shouldn't insult it by asking for barbecue sauce – Kreuz doesn't serve it, and the meat doesn't need it.

Chisholm Trail Bar-B-Q (☎512-398-6027; 1323 S Colorado St; lunch plates $6, brisket per pound $7.50; ☉8am-8:30pm) Like Black's and Kreuz Market, Chisholm Trail has been named one of the top 10 barbecue restaurants in the state by *Texas Monthly* magazine.

Smitty's Market (208 S Commerce St; lunch plates $6, brisket per pound $11.90; ☉7am-6pm Mon-Fri, 7am-6:30pm Sat, 9am-3pm Sun) The blackened pit room and homely dining room are all original (knives used to be chained to the tables). Ask to have the fat trimmed off the brisket if you're particular about that.

Gristmill Restaurant AMERICAN $$
(www.gristmillrestaurant.com; 1287 Gruene Rd;
mains $7-20; ◷11am-9pm Sun-Thu, to 10pm Fri &
Sat) Behind Gruene Hall and right under the
water tower, this restaurant is located within
the brick remnants of a long-gone gristmill.
Indoor seating affords a rustic ambience,
and outdoor tables get a view of the river.

❶ Getting There & Away

Gruene is just off I-10 and Rte 46, 45 miles south
of Austin and 25 miles northeast of San Antonio.

Fredericksburg

With fields full of wildflowers, shops full of
antiques and streets full of historic buildings
and B&Bs, Fredericksburg is the poster child
for 'quaint,' serving as the region's largest
old German-settled town (c 1870) and unof-
ficial capital of the Hill Country. It's more
cute than cool, but it's not a bad place to
linger a bit – especially during wildflower
season. It also makes a good base for explor-
ing the surrounding areas. Stop by the **Fred-
ericksburg Visitor Information Center**
(☑888-997-3600, 830-997-6523; www.visitfred-
ericksburgtx.com; 302 E Austin St; ◷8:30am-5pm
Mon-Fri, from 9am Sat, 11am-3pm Sun) to get your
bearings.

SCENIC DRIVE: WILDFLOWER TRAILS

You know spring has arrived in Texas
when you see cars pulling up roadside
and families climbing out to take the
requisite picture of their kids surround-
ed by bluebonnets – the state flower.
From March to April in Hill Country,
orange Indian paintbrushes, deep-
purple winecups and white-to-blue
bluebonnets are at their peak.

To see vast cultivated fields of color,
there's **Wildseed Farms** (www.wild-
seedfarms.com; 100 Legacy Dr; ◷9:30am-
6:30pm) FREE, which is 7 miles east
of Fredericksburg on US 290. Or for a
more do-it-yourself experience, check
with TXDOT's **Wildflower Hotline**
(☑800-452-9292) to find out what's
blooming where. Taking Rte 16 and FM
1323, north from Fredericksburg and
east to Willow City, is usually a good
route. Then again you might just set to
wandering – most backroads host their
own shows daily.

⦿ Sights & Activities

Spend an hour or two wandering Fredericks-
burg's historic district; despite having more
than its share of touristy shops, it's retained
the look (if not the feel) of 125 years ago.

Mid-May through June is peach-pickin'
season around town. You can get them
straight from the farm, and some will let you
pick your own. For a list of more than 20 local
peach farms, visit www.texaspeaches.com.

Thanks to its conducive *terroir*, the area
is also becoming known for its prolific win-
eries. If winery-hopping is on the agenda,
print a map at www.texaswinetrail.com or
www.wineroad290.com.

**National Museum of
the Pacific War** MUSEUM
(www.pacificwarmuseum.org; 340 E Main St; adult/
child $14/7, children 5yr & under free; ◷9am-5pm)
Three war-centric galleries comprise this
museum complex: the **Admiral Nimitz
Museum**, chronicling the life and career
of Fredericksburg's most famous son; the
George Bush Gallery of the Pacific War,
which houses big planes, big boats and big
artillery; and the **Pacific Combat Zone**, a
3-acre site that's been transformed into a
South Pacific battle zone. History buffs can
learn about (or refresh their memories on)
battles and campaigns, and kids will be
awed by the enormous vehicles.

Enchanted Rock State Natural Area PARK
(☑830-685-3636; www.tpwd.state.tx.us; 16710
Ranch Rd 965; adult/child 12yr & under $7/free;
◷8am-10pm) About 18 miles north of town is
a dome of pink granite dating from the Pro-
terozoic era that rises 425ft above ground –
one of the largest batholiths in the US. If you
want to climb it, go early; gates close when
the daily attendance quota is reached.

🛏 Sleeping & Eating

Fredericksburg is a popular weekend get-
away, especially during the spring, when
room rates are at their highest. Guesthouses
and B&Bs are a popular choice in Fredericks-
burg, and local reservation services can help
you find anything from a flowery guestroom
in a B&B to your own 19th-century limestone
cottage.

Gastehaus Schmidt ACCOMMODATION SERVICES
(☑830-997-5612, 866-427-8374; www.fbglodging.
com; 231 W Main St) Nearly 300 B&Bs do busi-
ness in this county; this reservation service
helps sort them out.

Fredericksburg Inn & Suites   MOTEL $$
(☑ 830-997-0202; www.fredericksburg-inn.com; 201 S Washington St; d $109-179, ste $139-209; 🛜❄🐾) Tops in the mid-priced-motel category, this place was built to look like the historic house it sits behind, and it succeeds. A fabulously inviting pool with a waterslide, all-day complimentary beverages and clean, updated rooms make it good value for the price.

Mahaley's Cafe   CAFE $
(☑ 830-997-4400; 341 E Main St; menu items $2-8; ⊙ 6:30am-3pm Mon-Sat, from 7:30am Sun; 🛜) Breakfast tacos are the big draw at this little cafe in a former gas station, but the cupcakes and coffee drinks are pretty tasty, too. It's also mighty generous with the wi-fi.

Hill Top Café   AMERICAN $$
(☑ 830-997-8922; mains $12-25; ⊙ 11am-2pm & 5-9pm Tue-Sun) Ten miles north of town inside a renovated 1950s gas station, this cozy roadhouse serves up satisfying meals and Hill Country ambience at its best. On weekends it has live blues from the owner, Johnny Nicholas, a former member of the west-coast swing band Asleep at the Wheel. Reservations recommended.

ℹ Getting There & Away

You can get a shuttle service from the San Antonio Airport through **Stagecoach Taxi and Shuttle** (☑ 830-385-7722; www.stagecoachtaxiandshuttle.com); the cost is $95 each way for up to four people. However, since driving around the Hill Country is half the fun, your best bet is to drive yourself.

Luckenbach

As small as Luckenbach is – three permanent residents, not counting the cat – it's big on Texas charm. You won't find a more laid-back place, where the main activity is sitting under an old oak tree with a bottle of Shiner Bock and listening to guitar pickers, who are often accompanied by roosters.

The heart of the, er, action is the old trading post established back in 1849 – now the **Luckenbach General Store** (⊙ 10am-9pm Mon-Sat, noon-9pm Sun), which also serves as the local post office, saloon and community center.

Check www.luckenbachtexas.com for the **music schedule**. Sometimes the guitar picking starts at 1pm, sometimes 5pm, and weekends usually see live-music events in the old **dance hall** – a Texas classic. The 4th

of July and Labor Day weekends are deluged with visitors for concerts.

We'd be remiss if we didn't mention that Luckenbach was made famous in a country song by Waylon Jennings – but we figured you either already knew that, or wouldn't really care.

From Fredericksburg, take US 290 east then take FM 1376 south for about 3 miles.

Bandera

It's not always easy finding real live cowboys in Texas, but it is in Bandera, which has branded itself the Cowboy Capital of Texas. In summer there are usually rodeos every weekend, and on Saturday afternoons gunslingers and cowboys roam the streets and entertain the crowds during **Cowboys on Main**. Check the **Bandera County Convention & Visitors Bureau** (CVB; ☑ 800-364-3833; www.banderacowboycapital.com; 126 Hwy 16; ⊙ 9am-5pm Mon-Fri, 10am-3pm Sat) website for the exact schedules and locations.

Ready to saddle up? The friendly folks at the visitors bureau also know nearly a dozen places in and around town where you can go **horseback riding**. For overnights, they can direct you to **dude ranch accommodations**, with packages that include lodging, meals and an equine excursion; plan on spending about $130 to $160 per adult per night ($45 to $90 for the young 'uns).

Another great reason to come to Bandera? Drinking beer and dancing in one of the many hole-in-the-wall cowboy bars and honky-tonks, where you'll find friendly locals, good live music and a rich atmosphere. Mosey over to the patio at **11th Street Cowboy Bar** (www.11thstreetcowboybar.com; 307 11th St; ⊙ 10am-2am Tue-Fri, from 9am Sat, from noon

TEXAS HILL COUNTRY

Sun) or **Arky Blue's Silver Dollar Saloon** (308 Main St; ⊙10am-2am). Both bars have live country crooners from Friday to Sunday.

San Antonio

In most large cities, downtown is bustling with businesspeople dressed for office work hurrying to their meetings and luncheons. Not so in San Antonio. Instead, downtown is filled with tourists in shorts consulting their maps. In fact, many people are surprised to find that two of the state's most popular destinations – the Riverwalk and the Alamo – are right smack dab in the middle of downtown, surrounded by historical hotels, tourist attractions and souvenir shops. The volume of visitors is daunting (as is the amount of commercial crap that's developed around the Alamo – Davy Crockett's wild amusement ride?), but the lively Tex-Mex culture is worth experiencing.

⊙ Sights & Activities

The intersection of Commerce and Losoya Sts is the very heart of downtown and the Riverwalk, which runs in a U shape below street level. Signs point out access stairways, but a 3D map bought at the info center is the best way to get oriented. The artsy **Southtown** neighborhood and the **King William Historic District** lie south along the river.

⊙ Downtown

★**The Alamo**   HISTORIC BUILDING
(☎210-225-1391; www.thealamo.org; 300 Alamo Plaza; ⊙9am-5:30pm Mon-Sat, from 10am Sun) **FREE** Find out why the story of the Alamo can rouse a Texan's sense of state pride like few other things. For many, it's not so much a tourist attraction as a pilgrimage. You might see visitors get dewy-eyed at the description of how a few hundred revolutionaries died defending the fort against thousands of Mexican troops.

★ **Riverwalk** WATERFRONT
(www.thesanantonioriverwalk.com) A little slice of Europe in the heart of downtown San Antonio, the Riverwalk is an essential part of experiencing this city. This is no ordinary riverfront, but a charming canal and pedestrian street that is the main artery at the heart of San Antonio's tourism efforts.

Buckhorn Saloon & Museum MUSEUM
(☑ 210-247-4000; www.buckhornmuseum.com; 318 E Houston St; adult/child 3-11yr $19/15; ⊙ 10am-5pm, to 8pm summer) An overpriced beverage is enough to buy your admission to the Saloon, which has an impressive number of mounted animals watching over you, including a giraffe, a bear and all manner of horn-wielding mammals. If that doesn't quench your thirst for taxidermy, pony up for a kitsch adventure that includes wildlife from all over the world, as well as oddities like a two-headed cow and an eight-legged lamb.

Rio San Antonio Cruises BOAT TOUR
(☑ 800-417-4139, 210-244-5700; www.riosanantonio.com; adult/child under 5yr $8.25/2; ⊙ 9am-9pm) One of the best ways to experience the Riverwalk is with these 40-minute narrated cruises that give you a good visual overview of the riv-er and a light history lesson. You can buy your tickets online, or get them on the waterfront at any of the stops. No reservations are necessary and tours leave every 15 to 20 minutes.

◉ Around Town

Brackenridge Park PARK
(3910 N St Mary's St; miniature train adult/child $3.25/2.70, carousel adult/child $2.50/2; ⊙ 5am-11pm) North of downtown near Trinity University, this 343-acre park is a great place to spend the day with your family. In addition to the **San Antonio Zoo** (☑ 210-734-7184; www.sazoo-aq.org; 3903 N St Mary's St; adult/child 3-11yr $12/9.50; ⊙ 9am-5pm), you'll find the *Brackenridge Eagle* **miniature train**, an old-fashioned **carousel** and the **Japanese Tea Gardens**.

San Antonio Museum of Art MUSEUM
(SAMA; www.samuseum.org; 200 W Jones Ave; adult/child $10/free, Tue free; ⊙ 10am-9pm Tue, Fri & Sat, 10am-5pm Wed & Thu, 10am-6pm Sun) Housed in the original 1880s Lone Star Brewery, which is a piece of art in itself, the San Antonio Museum of Art is off Broadway St just north of downtown. San Antonio's strong Latino influence is reflected in an impressive trove of Latin American art, including Spanish colonial, Mexican and pre-Columbian pieces; it's one of the most comprehensive collections in the US.

McNay Art Museum MUSEUM
(☑ 210-824-5368; www.mcnayart.org; 6000 N New Braunfels Ave; adult/12 & under $10/free, special exhibits extra; ⊙ 10am-4pm Tue, Wed & Fri, to 9pm Thu, to 5pm Sat, noon-5pm Sun, grounds 7am-6pm daily) In addition to seeing paintings by household names such as Van Gogh, Picasso, Matisse, Renoir, O'Keeffe and Cézanne, half the fun here is wandering the spectacular Spanish Colonial Revival–style mansion that was the private residence of Marion Koogler McNay.

Mission Trail HISTORIC SITE
(www.nps.gov/saan) Spain's missionary presence can best be felt at the ruins of the four missions south of town: Missions Concepción (1731), San José (1720), San Juan (1731) and Espada (1745–56) make up **San Antonio Missions National Historical Park**. Stop first at **Mission San José** (6701 San José Dr; ⊙ 9am-5pm) **FREE**, which is also the location of the main **visitor center**. Known in its time as the Queen of the Missions, it's certainly the largest and arguably the most beautiful.

TEXAS SAN ANTONIO

✿ Festivals & Events

San Antonio Stock Show & Rodeo   RODEO
(www.sarodeo.com; ⊘ mid-Feb) Big-name concerts follow each night's rodeo; 16 days in mid-February.

Fiesta San Antonio   CULTURE
(www.fiesta-sa.org; ⊘ mid-Apr) For over 10 days in mid-April there are river parades, carnivals, Tejano music, dancing and tons of food in a mammoth citywide party.

🛏 Sleeping

San Antonio has at least 10 gazillion-trillion hotel rooms, so you have plenty of choices right downtown. Because of the tourist trade, rates are higher on weekends. San Antonio also has its fair share of B&Bs, and generally speaking they're good value, ensconced in fine old homes in the more historic areas of the city.

Rodeway Inn Downtown   MOTEL $
(☑ 210-223-2951; www.rodewayinnsa.com; 900 N Main Ave; d $39-79; P ✳ ☎ ≈) You could walk to the Alamo and Riverwalk, which are just one mile away, but you don't even have to because the downtown trolley comes right to your door. Rooms are as basic as can be, but staying here will save you some dollars, especially when you factor in free parking and continental breakfast.

Hill Country Inn & Suites   HOTEL $
(☑ 800-314-3424, 210-599-4204; www.stayhci. com; 2383 NE Loop 410; d incl breakfast $65-99; P ✳ ☎ ≈) Just north of downtown, this anachronistic place feels like it belongs in the Hill Country more than off an interstate, with cabin-style rooms, ranch-style porches and country-style furnishings. With its playground and picnic tables, it's great for families.

★ King William Manor   B&B $$
(☑ 800-405-0367, 210-222-0144; www.kingwilliam-manor.com; 1037 S Alamo St; d incl breakfast $129-175; P ✳ ☎ ≈) In a neighborhood known for beautiful old houses and B&Bs, this grand Greek Revival mansion occupying a large corner lot still manages to jump out at you and say, 'Hey, look at me!' Maybe it's the columns, maybe it's the sprawling lawn or perhaps the wraparound porches. The inside lives up to the exterior, with understated elegant rooms, some of which are enormous.

★ Hotel Havana   HOTEL $$
(☑ 210-222-2008; www.havanasanantonio.com; 1015 Navarro St; d $106-189; P ✳ @ ☎ ≈) Texas design guru and hotelier Liz Lambert could make a radish look cool. Luckily she's turned her sights on fixing up a few lucky properties such as this one, judiciously adding eclectic touches – a retro pink refrigerator, for example – to her simple, clean designs. Check online for discounts for Texas residents or advance purchases.

Noble Inns   B&B $$
(☑ 800-242-2770, 210-223-2353; www.nobleinns. com; d incl breakfast from $139; P ✳ ☎ ≈) This collection of three inns has something for everyone – at least everyone who likes antiques and Victorian style. The Ogé House (209 Washington St; d $179-349) is the most elegant of the three, with lushly appointed rooms and a prime location on the residential end of the Riverwalk.

Omni La Mansion del Rio   HISTORIC HOTEL $$$
(☑ 210-518-1000; www.lamansion.com; 112 College St; d $199-399; P ✳ @ ≈) This fabulous downtown property was born out of 19th-century religious school buildings in the Spanish-Mexican hacienda style. It's

WORTH A TRIP

THE HOME OF SHINER BOCK

The highlight of any trip to Shiner, Texas, the self-proclaimed 'cleanest little city in Texas,' is a tour of the **Spoetzl Brewery** (www.shiner.com; 603 E Brewery St; tours free; ⊘ tours 11am & 1:30pm Mon-Fri year-round, plus 10am & 2:30pm Jun-Aug) FREE where Shiner Bock beer is brewed. Czech and German settlers who began making beer under brewmaster Kosmos Spoetzl founded the brewery 100 years ago. Today the brewery still produces several types using the same methods, including bock, blonde, honey wheat, summer stock and winter ale. You can sample the beers for free after the tour in the little bar.

Shiner is about an hour and a half (92 miles) east of San Antonio by car; to get there, take I-10 east 57 miles, head south on US-183, then east on US-90 at Gonzales. It's about the same distance from Austin; just take US-183 south and follow the same directions starting at Gonzales.

on a quiet stretch of the Riverwalk and its discreet oasis attracts stars and other notables. Enjoy in-room spa services, swim in the outdoor heated pool or unwind at the hotel's exceptional restaurant, **Las Canarias** (breakfast $12-16, mains $31-50; ◷ 6:30am-2pm & 5:30-10pm Mon-Sat, from 10am Sun).

Hotel Valencia BOUTIQUE HOTEL **$$$**
(☎210-227-9700; www.hotelvalencia-riverwalk. com; 150 E Houston St; d $159-459; P❋☎) Faux-mink throws, molded concrete, light shining through perforated metal – this place is all about texture. It could have been transported from New York City, both in its minimalist-chic style and in the size of some of the smaller rooms, but it's a hip option if you eschew chains and historic hotels.

✖ Eating

The Riverwalk offers easy pickings for dinner and drinks, but they're there for the tourists, so don't be surprised if there are busloads of the latter. South St Marys and S Alamo Sts in the Southtown–King William districts also host a good number of eateries. Look for hole-in-the-wall Mexican joints scattered the length of N Flores St.

★**Cove** AMERICAN **$**
(☎210-227-2683; www.thecove.us; 606 W Cypress St; mains $8-12; ◷ 11am-10pm Tue-Thu, to 11pm Fri & Sat, noon-6pm Sun; ▥) This weird, wonderful place northwest of downtown is a restaurant, bar, laundromat and car wash. As casual as the restaurant is, the food is top-notch, made from organic, sustainable meat and produce. Sure, it's just burgers, tacos and nachos, but they're made with love. There's even a playground for the kids so you can reward them for all their hard work washing your car.

Green Vegetarian Cuisine VEGETARIAN **$**
(☎210-320-5865; www.greensanantonio.com; 200 E Grayson St; meals $6-10; ◷ 7am-9pm Mon-Thu, to 8pm Fri, 9am-9pm Sun; ◪) ◉ Vegetarians rejoice: San Antonio's first vegetarian restaurant has a cool new location in the Pearl Brewery complex. With dishes like enchiladas, eggplant Parmesan and 'neatloaf,' it's the kind of place even a meat-eater can enjoy. Not only is it 100% vegetarian, it's 100% kosher and any meal can be made vegan.

★**Monterey** AMERICAN **$$**
(☎210-745-2581; www.themontereysa.com; 1127 S St Marys St; brunch $7-12, mains $10-17; ◷ 5-11pm Tue-Thu, to midnight Fri & Sat, 10am-2pm Sun) Extra style points to this King William gastro-

pub located in a former gas station with a big old patio. Despite the small number of options, the menu will please most foodies and you'll be dazzled by the choices available when it comes to its extensive selection of microbrews and wine. A great all-round place to hang out, day or night.

Paloma Blanca MEXICAN **$$**
(☎210-822-6151; 5800 Broadway St; lunch $8-10, mains $10-18; ◷ 11am-9pm Mon-Wed, to 10pm Thu & Fri, 10am-10pm Sat, 10am-9pm Sun) There are oodles of great Mexican choices around, but this place sets itself apart with a sleek and stylish ambience – think dim lighting, exposed brick walls and oversized artworks – and food that definitely lives up to the decor.

Mi Tierra Cafe & Bakery TEX-MEX **$$**
(☎210-225-1262; www.mitierracafe.com; 218 Produce Row; mains $12-16; ◷ 24hr) Dishing out traditional Mexican food since 1941, this 500-seat behemoth in Market Sq sprawls across several dining areas, giving the busy wait staff and strolling mariachis quite a workout. It's also open 24 hours, making it ideal for 3am enchilada cravings.

Boudro's TEX-MEX **$$$**
(☎210-224-8484; 421 E Commerce St, Riverwalk; lunch $8-12, dinner mains $20-32; ◷ 11am-11pm Sun-Thu, to midnight Fri & Sat) This brightly colored restaurant is hugely popular with locals. Fresh guacamole is made right at your table. The upscale Tex-Mex menu reveals some gourmet surprises, such as black-bean soup made with sherry and white cheddar, lobster-tail fajitas drizzled with pineapple *pico de gallo* (a type of salsa), and wines from Texas and California.

🍸 Drinking & Nightlife

The Riverwalk's many chain clubs blur together even before you've started drinking. Resist their glossy allure and opt for one of these San Antonio originals.

WORTH A TRIP

FLOORE'S COUNTRY STORE

This terrific old bar and dance hall first opened in 1942 as a store run by a friend of Willie Nelson. (Willie used to play here nightly; the sign still says so.) Visit **John T Floore's Country Store** (www. liveatfloores.com; 14492 Bandera Rd; tickets $10-30; ⊙11am-1am Fri & Sat, to 10pm Sun) today and you'll discover the true way to hear Texas country music, whether in the outdoor yard or by the fire in the rustic building. There are performances on Friday and Saturday nights; Sunday night is family dance night and there's no cover. Bandera Rd is off Hwy 16.

★**Friendly Spot Ice House** BAR
(☑210-224-2337; 943 S Alamo St; ⊙3pm-midnight Mon-Fri, from 11am Sat & Sun; 🚻🐾) What could be friendlier than a big pecan-tree-shaded yard filled with colorful metal lawn chairs? Friends (and their dogs) gather to knock back some longnecks, while the kids amuse themselves in the playground.

Brooklynite COCKTAIL BAR
(☑212-444-0707; www.thebrooklynitesa.com; 516 Brooklyn Ave; ⊙5pm-2am) Beer and wine are easy to come by in San Antonio, but this is where you head for a creative, handcrafted cocktail. Vintage wallpaper and wingback chairs give the place a dark, Victorian-esque decor, where you can sip your Boulvardier or Widow's Kiss in a fittingly dignified atmosphere.

Cove BEER HALL
(☑210-227-2683; www.thecove.us; 606 W Cypress St; ⊙11am-10pm Tue-Thu, to 11pm Fri & Sat, noon-6pm Sun; 🚻) Live music is just part of the reason to hang out at this chill beer hall. The Cove is a unique combo of food stand/cafe/Laundromat/car wash. It even has a kiddie playground.

Bonham Exchange BAR
(www.bonhamexchange.net; 411 Bonham St; ⊙7pm-2am Wed-Sun) There's plenty of room for everyone at the Bonham: although it's predominantly a gay bar, the sheer enormity of the place attracts a mixed crowd with drinking and dancing on their mind. Located in an imposing Victorian edifice built in 1892, it has huge dance floors and five bars spread over three floors.

☆ Entertainment

For listings of local music and cultural events, pick up the free weekly **San Antonio Current** (www.sacurrent.com).

Four-time NBA champions the **San Antonio Spurs** (www.nba.com/spurs) shoot hoops at the **AT&T Center** (☑tickets 800-745-3000; www.attcenter.com; 1 AT&T Center Pkwy) off I-35. Purchase tickets through **Ticketmaster** (☑210-525-1100; www.ticketmaster.com).

🔒 Shopping

A few artisan craft shops exist along the tourist-T-shirt-filled Riverwalk. The old buildings of the city's first neighborhood, **La Villita Historic Arts Village** (☑210-207-8610; www.lavillita.com; 418 Villita St; ⊙most shops 10am-6pm) ᴳᴿᴱᴱ, house the largest concentration of galleries and boutiques.

Pearl Complex MALL
(www.atpearl.com; 200 E Grayson St) The old Pearl Brewery has received a massive facelift as part of the new Pearl development north of downtown, including shops, cafes and restaurants.

Market Square MARKET
(www.marketsquaresa.com; 514 W Commerce St; ⊙10am-8pm Jun-Aug, to 6pm Sep-May) A little bit of Mexico in downtown San Antonio, Market Sq is a fair approximation of a trip south of the border, with Mexican food, mariachi bands, and store after store filled with Mexican wares.

Paris Hatters ACCESSORIES
(☑210-223-3453; www.parishatters.com; 119 Broadway St; ⊙9:30am-6:30pm Mon-Sat, noon-5pm Sun) Despite the name, this is no Parisian haberdashery but a purveyor of fine cowboy hats since 1917. You'll walk out looking like a real cowboy or girl with a hat that's been shaped and fitted to your very own noggin.

Southwest School of Art & Craft HANDICRAFTS
(☑210-224-1848; www.swschool.org; 300 Augusta St; ⊙10am-5pm Mon-Sat) The gallery shop exhibits and sells works by the school's artists and visiting artists, representing an eclectic mix of almost every medium imaginable.

ⓘ Information

Visitor center 'amigos' (in turquoise shirts and straw hats) roam the downtown core offering direction.

Downtown Visitors Center (📞 210-207-6875; www.visitsanantonio.com; 317 Alamo Plaza; ⏰ 9am-5pm, to 6pm Jun-Aug) Stop by the well-stocked visitors center, opposite the Alamo, for maps and brochures; its website also has loads of information useful for pre-planning. The staff can answer any questions you have, and also sell passes for tours or VIA buses and streetcars.

San Antonio Express-News (www.mysananto-nio.com) Daily news and travel info on the web.

San Antonio Public Library (www.mysapl.org; 600 Soledad St; ⏰ 9am-9pm Mon-Thu, to 5pm Fri & Sat, 11am-5pm Sun) Free internet. Other branch locations across the city also provide free access.

ℹ Getting There & Away

San Antonio is served by the **San Antonio International Airport** (SAT; 📞 210-207-3433; www.sanantonio.gov/sat; 9800 Airport Blvd), about 9 miles north of downtown. **VIA Metropolitan Transit** (📞 210-362-2020; www.viainfo.net; ride/day pass $1.20/4) city bus 2 runs from the airport to downtown. A taxicab ride will cost about $25. Major car-rental agencies all have offices at the airport.

From the **Greyhound Bus Station** (www.greyhound.com; 500 N St Marys St), you can get to all the big cities in the state (and lots of the small ones). The *Sunset Limited* (Florida–California) and *Texas Eagle* (San Antonio–Chicago) trains stop a few days a week (usually late at night) at the **Amtrak Station** (www.amtrak.com; 350 Hoefgen Ave).

The extremely tourist-friendly downtown trolleybus routes ($1.10 one way) are the best way to cover any distance around downtown. Buy a day pass ($4) at the **VIA Downtown Information Center** (📞 210-362-2020; www.viainfo.net; 211 W Commerce St; ⏰ 7am-6pm Mon-Fri, 9am-2pm Sat).

Houston

Concrete superhighways may blind you to Houston's good points when you first zoom into this sprawling city that covers a greater area than all of New Jersey. You'll miss out if you limit yourself to downtown: diverse residential neighborhoods and enclaves of restaurants and shops are spread far and wide.

The leafy Museum District is the city's cultural center; Upper Kirby and River Oaks have upscale shopping and dining; Montrose contains cute bungalows, quirky shops and eateries; Midtown has up-and-coming condos and some good restaurants; Washington Ave is nightlife central; and the Heights has historic homes and boutiques.

◉ Sights & Activities

Museum lovers will find plenty to love in the area north of Hermann Park. To get a full list of options or to plot your route, check out the map on the **Houston Museum District** (www.houstonmuseumdistrict.org) website.

A couple of the city's main attractions – NASA's Space Center Houston in Clear Lake and Galveston Island – are outside the city limits, requiring a 45-minute drive down I-45.

★**Menil Collection**   MUSEUM
(www.menil.org; 1515 Sul Ross St; ⏰ 11am-7pm Wed-Sun) 🆓 The late local philanthropists John and Dominique de Menil collected more than 17,000 works of painting, drawing, sculpture, archeological artifacts and more during their lives.The modernist building housing the main collection exhibits everything from 5000-year-old antiquities to avant-garde art, as well as rotating exhibits. Don't miss the Cy Twombly Gallery and Rothko Chapel, annexes of the collection.

Museum of Fine Arts Houston   MUSEUM
(www.mfah.org; 1001 Bissonnet St; adult/child $13/6; ⏰ 10am-5pm Tue & Wed, to 9pm Thu, to 7pm Fri & Sat, 12:15-7pm Sun; Metro Rail Museum District) French impressionism and post-1945 European and American painting really shine in this nationally renowned palace of art, which includes major works by Picasso

---

DON'T MISS

HOUSTON, WE HAVE AN ATTRACTION...

Dream of a landing on the moon? You can't get any closer (without years of training) than at **Space Center Houston** (📞 281-244-2100; http://space-center.org; 1601 NASA Pkwy 1; with audio guide adult/child $23.50/19.50; ⏰ 9am-7pm) off I-45 S, the official visitor center and museum of NASA's Johnson Space Center. Interactive exhibits let you try your hand at picking up an object in space or landing the shuttle. Be sure to enter the theater that shows short films, because you exit past *Apollo* capsules and history exhibits. The free tram tour covers the center at work – shuttle training facilities, zero-gravity labs and the original mission control, from which was uttered the famous words, 'Houston, we have a problem.'

Central Houston

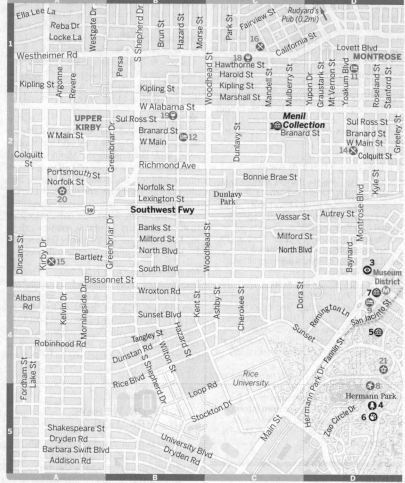

TEXAS HOUSTON

and Rembrandt. Across the street, admire the talents of luminaries such as Rodin and Matisse in the associated **Cullen Sculpture Garden** (cnr Montrose Blvd & Bissonnet St; ☉ dawn-dusk) FREE.

Art Car Museum
MUSEUM
(www.artcarmuseum.com; 140 Heights Blvd; ☉ 11am-6pm Wed-Sun) FREE The handful of art cars here are something to behold; some of them are straight out of *Mad Max*. But they're really just bait to lure you in to check out the quirky-cool rotating art exhibits, whose subjects have included road refuse and bone art.

Houston Museum of Natural Science
MUSEUM
(☏ 713-639-4629; www.hmns.org; 5555 Hermann Park Dr; adult/child $20/15; butterfly conservatory/special exhibits extra per person $5; ☉ 9am-6pm; ♿; Metro Rail Hermann Park/Rice) World-class traveling exhibits – on everything from Medici gems to Mayan civilization – have always been a big part of the attraction at this stellar museum. With the $30-million addition of an impressive dino-focused paleontology wing and the opening of an ancient Egyptian hall, there are now even more reasons to visit.

TEXAS HOUSTON

Art Car Parade & Festival PARADE
(www.orangeshow.org; ⊙ 2nd Sun May) Wacky,
arted-out vehicles (think *Mad Max* or giant
rabbits) hit the streets en masse. The parade
itself is complemented by weekend-long festivities, including concerts.

🛏 Sleeping

Chain motels line all the major freeways. If
you are visiting the Space Center and Galveston, consider staying on I-45 south.

Houston International Hostel HOSTEL **$**
(☏ 713-523-1009; www.houstonhostel.com; 5302
Crawford St; dm/d/q $16/50/110; P❋@🤶) A
mix of semipermanent residents and backpackers. A friendly, eccentric staff and worn
'70s furnishings lend the place a throwback
hippie feel. It's an easy walk to Houston's
major museums and light rail.

⭐ Festivals & Events

★ Houston Livestock
Show & Rodeo RODEO
(www.hlsr.com; ⊙ Feb-Mar) For three weeks
from February to March, rodeo fever takes
over Houston and everyone gets gussied up
in their Western best. The barbecue cook-off
is a hot seller but so are the nightly rodeos
followed by big-name concerts – starring
everyone from Bruno Mars to Blake Shelton.
Buy tickets way in advance. Fairgrounds-
only admission gets you access to midway
rides, livestock shows, shopping and nightly
dances.

QUIRKY HOUSTON

Conservative Houston has a wacky creative streak, especially when it comes to its quirkiest museums. Follow up a visit to the Art Car Museum with a pilgrimage to the **Orange Show Center for Visionary Art** (☑ 713-926-6368; www.orangeshow.org; per person $1), a mazelike junk-art tribute to one man's favorite citrus fruit. The center fosters the folk-art vision by offering children's art education and keeping up the 50,000-strong **Beer Can House** (www.beercanhouse.org; 222 Malone St, off Memorial Dr; admission $2; ☺ noon-5pm Sat & Sun).

★ Hotel ZaZa   BOUTIQUE HOTEL $$

(☑ 713-526-1991; www.hotelzaza.com; 5701 Main St; r $205-270; P ❋ @ 🛜 🌊; Metro Rail Hermann Park/Rice) Hip, flamboyant and fabulous. From the bordello-esque colors to the zebra-accent chairs, everything about Hotel ZaZa is good fun. Our favorite rooms are the concept suites, such as the eccentric Asian Geisha or the space-age 'Houston We Have a Problem.' You can't beat the location overlooking the Museum District's Hermann Park, near the light rail.

Modern B&B   B&B $$

(☑ 832-279-6367; http://modernbb.com; 4003 Hazard St; r incl breakfast $100-225; P ❋ @ 🛜) 🌿 An architect's dream, this mod solar-powered 11-room inn is rife with airy decks, spiral staircases and sunlight. Think organic mattresses, in-room Jacuzzis, private decks and iPod docking stations. The owners also rent two nearby apartments.

Sara's Inn on the Boulevard   INN $$

(☑ 713-868-1130; www.saras.com; 941 Heights Blvd; r incl breakfast $115-180; P ❋ @ 🛜) A Queen Anne Victorian feels right at home among the historic houses of the Heights. Eleven airy rooms say 'boutique hotel' more than 'frilly B&B,' but the inn still has the kind of sprawling Southern porch that makes you want to gossip over mint juleps.

La Colombe d'Or Hotel   LUXURY HOTEL $$$

(☑ 713-524-7999; www.lacolombedor.com; 3410 Montrose Blvd; ste $295-400; P ❋ 🛜) Each of the five exquisite one-bedroom suites here were inspired by the colors and styles of a painting master – Cézanne, Van Gogh, Re-

noir – and suitably so, as the rare oils and antiques decorating this 1923 Montrose mansion are museum quality. Standards at the intimate on-site French restaurant are in keeping with such refined tastes.

✖ Eating

Houston's restaurant scene is smokin' hot – and we don't just mean the salsa. In fact, Houstonians eat out more than residents of any other US city. To keep abreast of what's in and what isn't, we recommend the razor-tongued **Fearless Critic** (www.fearlesscritic.com). Twitterites can follow @eatdrinkhouston.

✖ Downtown

Treebeards   SOUTHERN $

(http://treebeards.com; 315 Travis St; specials $8-11; ☺ 11am-2pm Mon-Fri) Locals flock here at lunchtime to chow down on great Cajun gumbos and jambalaya, but don't discount the appeal of daily changing specials like jerk chicken and stuffed pork chops.

Grove Restaurant & Bar   AMERICAN $$

(☑ 713-337-7321; http://thegrovehouston.com; 1611 Lamar St; lunch & brunch mains $13-21, dinner mains $15-29; ☺ 11am-10pm Sun-Thu, to 11pm Fri & Sat; Metro Rail Main Street Sq) Free-range chicken pot pie, pork-belly sliders...the American classics get a metropolitan update at the Grove. The modern, glass-filled dining room overlooks Discovery Green park.

Original Ninfas   MEXICAN $$

(www.ninfas.com; 2704 Navigation Blvd; mains $10-21; ☺ 11am-10pm Mon-Fri, 10am-10pm Sat & Sun) Generations of Houstonians have come here since the 1970s for shrimp diablo, tacos *al carbon* (tacos cooked over charcoal) and handmade tamales crafted with pride. Hopefully the recent new ownership will not change anything vital.

✖ Midtown

Breakfast Klub   SOUTHERN $

(www.thebreakfastklub.com; 3711 Travis St; dishes $8-15; ☺ 7am-2pm Mon-Fri, 8am-2pm Sat; P 🛜) Come early: devotees line up around the block for down-home breakfast faves like fried wings 'n' waffles. Lunch hours are only slightly less crazy at this coffeehouse-like eatery favored by local girl Beyoncé and her boy, Jay-Z. Coffee is great and there's wi-fi.

Reef SEAFOOD $$

(713-526-8282; www.reefhouston.com; 2600 Travis St; lunch dishes $12-26, dinner mains $20-29; 11am-10pm Mon-Fri, 5-11pm Sat; Metro Rail McGowen) Gulf Coast seafood is creatively prepared and served in a sleek and sophisticated dining room – with a skyline-view raw bar. Chef Bryan Caswell has won oodles of national awards for himself and his restaurant.

Sparrow Bar & Cookshop MODERN AMERICAN $$$

(713-524-6922; http://sparrowhouston.com; 3701 Travis St; mains $16-32; 11am-3pm & 5-10pm Tue-Sat) Nationally renowned chef Monica Pope brings top-quality local and organic ingredients to life in her new American cuisine. Share plates might include shiitake dumplings with blue-cheese sauce, or wild boar. On a nice night, patio dining is a must.

Montrose

★**Eatsie Boys Cafe** CAFE $

(http://catsieboys.com; 4400 Montrose Blvd; dishes $6-12; 8am-10pm Mon-Sat, brunch 9am-3pm Sun;) The Eatsie Boys intergalactic food truck has landed. Its owners now operate out of a fun cafe, and we're all the better for it. Order your matzo-ball pho (trust us, it's good) or a Gulf shrimp po'boy with jalepeño tartar sauce, then side up to one of the shady picnic tables to enjoy. They brew their own craft beers, too. Mmmmmm...

Goode Co BBQ BARBECUE $$

(www.goodecompany.com; 5109 Kirby Dr; plates $10-16; 11am-10pm) Belly up to the beef brisket, smoked sausage and gallon ice teas in a big ol' barn or out back on picnic tables.

★**Hugo's** MEXICAN $$$

(713-524-7744; http://hugosrestaurant.net; 1600 Westheimer Rd; lunch & brunch $14-19, dinner mains $22-30; 11am-10pm Mon-Thu, 11am-11pm Fri & Sat, 10am-9pm Sun) Chef Hugo Ortega's inspired interior-Mexican regional cuisine tastes like nothing else in town. You might try squash-blossom crepes or Veracruz snapper with tomatoes, olives and capers. Brunch is not to be missed. Book ahead for any meal.

Drinking & Nightlife

To the youngish set, the stretch of Washington Ave bars and clubs defines all that is hip and happening in Houston nightlife (although lately downtown is none too shabby in that department). The corner of White Oak Dr and Studemont St in the Heights has a few funky little bars, including a roadhouse, a tiki bar and a live-music club in an old house.

★**Onion Creek Cafe** CAFE

(3106 White Oak Dr; 7am-midnight Sun-Wed, 7am-2am Thu-Sat) Open for early morning coffee and late-night cocktails, Onion Creek is the Heights' quintessential neighborhood hangout, just west of Studemont St. Every table on the sprawling ultrachill patio is taken on weekends. Great daily specials; Saturday morning farmers market.

La Carafe BAR

(813 Congress St; 1pm-2am) In an 1860 building, this intimate downtown place claims the title of the 'oldest bar in Houston.' Expect well-priced wines by the glass and an ancient wooden bar lit by candles.

TEXAS HOUSTON

HOUSTON FOR CHILDREN

Kids in tow? Don't miss downtown's **Discovery Green** (www.discoverygreen.com; 1500 McKinney St; 6am-11pm; ; Metro Rail Main St Sq). This 12-acre park has a lake, playground, fountains to splash in, outdoor art, restaurants and a performance space. The Green has become a hub for fun festivals and activities such as movies on the green, nighttime flea markets – even a Christmas-time ice rink. Check the online calendar for more.

Another great open space for kids is **Hermann Park** (www.hermannpark.org; Fannin St & Hermann Park Dr; 6am-11pm). This 445-acre park is home to playgrounds, a lake with paddleboats, the **Hermann Park Miniature Train** (713-529-5216; www.hermannpark. org/railroad.php; 6104 Hermann Park Dr, Kinder Station, Lake Plaza; per ride $3; 10am-5:30pm Mon Fri, 10am-6pm Sat & Sun;) and the **Houston Zoo** (www.houstonzoo.org; 6200 Hermann Park Dr; adult/child $14/10; 9am-6pm).

Within walking distance of Hermann Park is the activity-filled **Children's Museum of Houston** (www.cmhouston.org; 1500 Binz St; admission $9; 9am-6pm Tue-Sat, noon-6pm Sun), where kids can make tortillas in a Mexican village or draw in an open-air art studio.

WORTH A TRIP

SAN JACINTO MONUMENT

In the late afternoon on April 21, 1836, General Sam Houston and his ragtag Texan army caught up with the Mexican forces of General Antonio López de Santa Anna who were resting on the banks of the San Jacinto River. Fighting was fierce, as Houston's men 'remembered the Alamo' and the massacre at Goliad. Santa Anna's surrender came relatively quickly. The final tally: 630 Mexicans dead and hundreds more wounded, but only nine Texan casualties. Victory was total. The Mexican army retreated; Texas had won its independence.

More than 1100 acres of the battleground are now preserved as the **San Jacinto Battleground State Historical Site** (www.tpwd.state.tx.us; 3523 Hwy 134; park admission free, attractions vary; ⊘9am-6pm). Tour the museum, watch the movie, then ride up to the observation deck to look over the field. Also part of the historic site is the docked 1912 battleship, USS *Texas*, one of the first steel-plated ships of its era.

The park lies 22 miles east of downtown Houston, via I-10 E. Exit at Crosby-Lynchberg Rd, turn south and take the small car ferry across to the site.

West Alabama Ice House   BAR

(☑713-528-6874; 1919 W Alabama St; ⊘10am-midnight Mon-Fri, to 1am Sat, noon-midnight Sun) In Montrose, Texas' oldest 'ice house' (where people used to come to get their ice, now an open-air drinkery) draws the crowds, from bikers to lawyers. We think it's because of the cheap beer and huge dog-friendly yard with picnic tables.

Poison Girl   LOUNGE

(1641 Westheimer Rd; ⊘4pm-2am) Add a killer back patio with a Kool Aid–man statue to an arty interior with vintage pinball games and you get one very cool, divey bar. Nice eclectic crowd, too.

☆ Entertainment

There's a fair bit of nightlife around the Preston and Main Street Sq Metro Rail stops downtown. Montrose and Midtown have clubs, but they're spread around. Look for listings in the independent weekly **Houston Press** (www.houstonpress.com) and in the Thursday edition of the **Houston Chronicle** (www.chron.com).

Live Music

When it's time to rock out, visit www.spacecityrock.com, the online version of a local music mag.

Rudyard's Pub   LIVE MUSIC

(☑713-521-0521; www.rudyards.com; 2010 Waugh Dr; ⊘11:30am-2am) Host to eclectic – OK, sometimes downright kooky – theatrical fare, as well as good local-band concerts. Hipsters just love to hang at Rudyard's.

McGonigel's Mucky Duck   LIVE MUSIC

(☑713-528-5999; www.mcgonigels.com; 2425 Norfolk St; ⊘11am-11pm Mon-Thu, 11am-2am Fri & Sat, 5:30-9pm Sun) Acoustic, Irish, folk and country performers play nightly in pubby surrounds. Tickets are cash-only. Arrive early if you want supper before the show.

Last Concert Cafe   LIVE MUSIC

(☑713-226-8563; www.lastconcert.com; 1403 Nance St; ⊘11am-2am Tue-Sat, 10:30am-9pm Sun) For a real local original, find your way to the warehouse district northeast of downtown. After you knock on the red door (there's no sign), you can hang out drinking cheap suds at the bar or dig into cheap Tex-Mex and listen to live music evenings in the courtyard.

Theater & Performing Arts

The Houston Grand Opera, the Society of the Performing Arts, Houston Ballet, Da Camera chamber orchestra and the Houston Symphony all perform downtown in the **Theater District** (www.houstontheaterdistrict.org). From the district's website you can purchase tickets and view all schedules.

Miller Outdoor Theatre   THEATER

(☑281-373-3386; www.milleroutdoortheatre.com; 6000 Hermann Park Dr) Hermann Park's outdoor theater is a great place to spread a blanket on a summer night and enjoy a free play, musical or concert.

Alley Theatre   THEATER

(☑713-220-5700; www.alleytheatre.org; 615 Texas Ave) Houston's heavy-hitter theater is one of the last in the nation to keep a resident company of actors. From classics to modern plays, the magic of this ensemble is palpable.

Sports

While Houston teams don't get quite the rabid following of, say, the UT Longhorns or the San Antonio Spurs, there's plenty of sports action to be found.

Reliant Stadium   FOOTBALL

(www.reliantpark.com; 1 Reliant Park) The **Houston Texans** (www.houstontexans.com) play at this high-tech retractable-roof stadium.

Minute Maid Park   BASEBALL

(☎713-259-8000; 501 Crawford St) The **Houston Astros** (http://houston.astros.mlb.com) play pro baseball right downtown.

Toyota Center   BASKETBALL

(www.houstontoyotacenter.com; 1510 Polk St) Basketball fans can follow the NBA's **Houston Rockets** (www.nba.com/rockets/) here.

🔒 Shopping

For browsing in more eclectic and locally owned stores, hit the neighborhoods. Along 19th St (between Yale St and Shepherd Dr) in the **Heights** (www.houstonheights.org) you'll find unique antiques, clever crafts and cafes. On the first Saturday of every month the street takes on a carnival-like air with outdoor booths and entertainment.

In Montrose, **Westheimer St** is a dream for crafty fashionistas and antique-hunters alike. Start on Dunlavy Rd and work your way down the street, where you'll find a mix of used- and new-clothing stores running the gamut from vintage to punk rock to Tokyo mod, plus lots of funky old furniture.

For slightly less rebellious fashion terrain, stroll around **Rice Village** and let the window displays lure you in.

Galleria   MALL

(www.simon.com; 5075 Westheimer Rd; ⊘10am-9pm) Welcome to THE mall, Houston's Valhalla of shopping. The sprawling Galleria is Texas' biggest indoor shopping center, with 2.4 million sq ft, 400 stores, 30 restaurants, two hotels – oh, and an ice-skating rink.

Just about every upscale national department and chain store you can think of is represented here, plus exclusive design houses and boutiques. This place is so iconic to Houston that 'the Galleria' refers to the whole surrounding neighborhood, which has many more shopping and dining plazas.

ℹ Information

Chase Bank (www.chase.com; 712 Main St) Currency exchange and ATM.

Greater Houston Convention & Visitors Bureau (☎713-437-5200; www.visithoustontexas.com; City Hall, 901 Bagby St; ⊘9am-4pm Mon-Sat) As much a giant souvenir shop as an info center. Note that the office closes Saturdays during downtown events (festivals, marathons etc). Free parking on Walker St.

Houston Public Library (www.hpl.lib.tx.us; 500 McKinney St; ⊘10am-8pm Mon-Thu, 10am-5pm Fri & Sat, 1-5pm Sun; 🛜) Free internet computers and wi-fi.

Main post office (401 Franklin St; ⊘10am-5pm Mon-Fri) Plenty of parking; at the north edge of downtown.

ℹ Getting There & Away

Houston Airport System (www.fly2houston.com) has two airports. Twenty-two miles north of the city center, **George Bush Intercontinental** (IAH; www.fly2houston.com/iah; Will Clayton Parkway or JFK Blvd, off I-59, Beltway 8 or I-45) serves cities worldwide and is home base for Continental Airlines. Twelve miles southeast of town, **William P Hobby Airport** (HOU; www.fly2houston.com/hobby; Airport Blvd, off Broadway or Monroe Sts; 🛜) is a major hub for Southwest Airlines and domestic travel. Read your ticket closely: some airlines, like Delta, fly out of both airports. You can find every major car-rental agency at either airport.

If you're not renting a car, a shuttle is the most convenient and cost-effective way to get downtown. **SuperShuttle** (☎800-258-3826; www.supershuttle.com) provides regular service from both Bush ($25) and Hobby ($20) airports to hotels and addresses around town.

Cabs are readily available at both airports. Airport rates are determined by zone, and you'll pay either the flat zone rate or the meter rate, whatever's less. You'll shell out $50 to get from George Bush Intercontinental to downtown; from Hobby it's about $25.

The **Metropolitan Transit Authority** (METRO; ☎713-635-4000; www.ridemetro.org; one-way $1.25) runs bus 102 between George Bush Intercontinental and downtown from 5:30am to 8pm. Bus 88 operates between Hobby and downtown 6am to 11pm every day except Sunday.

Long-distance buses arrive at the **Greyhound Bus Terminal** (www.greyhound.com; 2121 Main St), which is located between downtown and the Museum District, and the *Sunset Limited* train stops at the **Amtrak Station** (☎800-872-7245; www.amtrak.com; 902 Washington Ave) three times a week.

❶ Getting Around

Houston's public transportation is run by the **Metropolitan Transit Authority**. Bus transit is geared toward weekday, downtown commuters. The light-rail train, Metro Rail, however, is exceptionally useful for travelers. It has only one simple line, but that line links most sights – and some restaurants – along its Downtown–Museum District–Reliant Park corridor. Look for maps, including downloadable smartphone ones, online. The Metro Rail operates from 5am until midnight Sunday through Thursday, and until 2:20am on Friday and Saturday.

Around Houston

Galveston

Don't think of Galveston as just another beach town. What makes it irresistible is that it's actually a historic town that happens to have some beaches. An easy day trip from Houston, it's also a very popular cruise-ship port, which has been a vital boost to the economy.

In 2008 Galveston was ravaged by a direct hit from Hurricane Ike. Many of the gingerbread-covered Victorian homes in the historic districts have been restored, but missing is the canopy of mature trees that once graced the island.

◉ Sights & Activities

Nothing more than a sandy barrier island, Galveston stretches 30 miles in length and is no more than 3 miles wide. The center of activity on the island, the historic 'Strand' district (around the intersection of 22nd and Mechanic Sts) is best covered on foot so you can check out the many attractions, shops, restaurants and bars. Find loads more dining and activity info at **Galveston Island Visitors Center** (☑409-797-5145; www.galveston.com; Ashton Villa, 2328 Broadway; ⊘10am-5pm Mon-Sat, 9am-4pm Sun).

For easy beach access, park anywhere along the seawall. Or, if you want more sand to spread out on, head to **East Beach** (1923 Boddecker Dr, off Seawall Blvd; per vehicle $16; ⊘dawn-dusk Mar-Oct) at the eastern end of the island.

Pier 21 Theatre   THEATRE
(☑409-763-8808; www.galveston.com/pier21theatre; cnr Pier 21 & Harborside Dr; adult/child $5/4; ⊘11am-6pm Sun-Thu, to 8pm Fri & Sat) The 30-minute multimedia documentary shown here avoids the maudlin as it recounts the 1900 hurricane through photos, special effects and eyewitness accounts of the deadliest natural disaster in US history.

Texas Seaport Museum & Tallship Elissa   MUSEUM
(www.galvestonhistory.org; cnr Harborside Dr & 21st St; adult/child $8/5; ⊘10am-4:30pm) This vast museum explains every facet of life around Galveston's port during its heyday in the 19th century. Outside, climb aboard to tour the *Elissa*, a beautiful 1877 Scottish tall ship that is still seaworthy.

Moody Gardens   AMUSEMENT PARK
(www.moodygardens.com; 1 Hope Blvd; day pass $50; ⊘10am-6pm; 🖼) Three colorful glass pyramids form the focus of one entertainment complex. The **Aquarium Pyramid** showcases king penguins, fur seals and the largest array of sea horses in the world. The 10-story **Rainforest Pyramid** is a lush tropical jungle full of plants, birds, butterflies and a wonderful creepy-crawly bug exhibit. The **Discovery Pyramid** hosts traveling exhibits and some so-so space-related stuff.

🛏 Sleeping & Eating

The sea is the primary food source in Galveston; fish restaurants (mostly chains) line the bayside piers near the Strand.

Beachcomber Inn   MOTEL $
(☑800-733-7133; www.galvestoninn.com; 2825 61st St; r $35-120; 🖼🖼🖼) A block removed from the beach, this basic two-story motel provides a neat-and-clean budget break. Minifridges and microwaves in every room.

Hotel Galvez   LUXURY HOTEL $$$
(☑409-765-7721; www.galveston.com/galvez; 2024 Seawall Blvd; r $160-400; 🖼🖼🖼) Bask in palm-fringed Spanish-colonial luxury at this 1911 historic hotel. The spa services – muscle-soaking milk bath or seaweed contour wraps, anyone? – are renowned, and the pool deck has a lovely gulf view. Ask about spa special package deals.

Shrimp N Stuff   SEAFOOD $
(3901 Ave O; mains $6-12; ⊘10:30am-8:30pm Mon-Thu, to 9:30pm Fri & Sat) Skip the big, expensive seafood emporiums and get your fried seafood fix at this beachy-casual fave.

★ Farley Girls   AMERICAN $$
(www.farleygirls.com; 901 Post Office St; dishes $9-13; ⊘10:30am-3:30pm Mon-Fri, from 8:30am Sat & Sun) The historic building may be elegant, with fern-studded colonnades and high wood

ceilings, but the tasty comfort food and counter service are down-home casual. Eclectic offerings include both Latin American–spiced *chimichurri* steak salad and mac 'n' cheese.

The Spot CAFE **$$**
(3204 Seawall Blvd; mains $11-21; ⊙11am-10pm Sun-Thu, to 11pm Sat & Sun) The three old houses containing this restaurant-tiki bar/ice-cream parlor are a favorite local hangout, with a great Gulf-view patio.

ⓘ Getting There & Away

From Houston, follow I-45 southeast for 51 miles.

Hurricane Ike knocked the Galveston Island Trolley off the rails. Until it's restored – at some far distant, undetermined date – you really need a car to get around. The island's bus service caters to local commuters, not tourists.

Piney Woods

In Piney Woods, northeast Texas, 100ft-plus-tall trees outnumber people. Nature is the attraction, but don't expect breathtaking vistas; here you'll find quiet trails and varied ecosystems. At **Big Thicket National Preserve** (www.nps.gov/bith), coastal plains meet desert sand dunes, and cypress swamps stand next to pine and hardwood forests. If you're lucky, you may run across one of 20 species of small wild orchids while hiking the 45 miles of trail. The eight disparate park units are 100 miles northwest of Houston.

SOUTHERN GULF COAST

Images of rowdy spring breakers aside, the Gulf Coast is known for its sparkling bays, small harbors filled with shrimp boats and more than 60 miles of protected beaches. Some parts of the Gulf Coast – like Port Arthur and Brazosport – have shunned the tourist trade and embraced the steady income that refineries and oil rigs can provide. But tiny coastal communities and wandering coastal back roads are reason enough to visit.

Aransas National Wildlife Refuge

For bird-watchers, the premier site on the Texas coast is the 115,000-acre **Aransas National Wildlife Refuge** (www.fws.gov/refuge/aransas; FM 2040; per person/carload $3/5; ⊙6am-dusk, visitor center 8:30am-4:30pm). The scenery alone is spectacular, and close to 400 bird species have been documented here.

None are more famous than the extremely rare whooping cranes that summer in Canada and spend their winters in the refuge. These endangered white birds – the tallest in North America – can stand 5ft tall with a 7ft wingspan.

From the observation tower you can usually spot one or two, but boats tour the estuaries from November to March, and this is easily the best way to get a good view of rare birds. Captain Tommy with **Rockport Birding & Kayak Adventures** (☑877-892-4737; www.whoopingcranetours.com; 202 N Fulton Beach Rd, Fulton Habor; 3½hr tours $50; ⊙7:30am & 1pm) has a relatively small, shallow-drafting boat, and so can get you into back bays that larger charters can't reach.

Corpus Christi & Around

The salt breezes and palm-tree-lined bay are quite pleasant in this 'city by the sea', with a population of just over 300,000. Downtown has a waterfront promenade and a few museums, but there's not too much in town to entice visitors. Trip out to Padre Island and the National Seashore for a beachy break, though don't expect the windblown surf to be azure. To the north, Port Aransas is a bustling little fishing town with tons of restaurants and boat charters.

Shoreline Dr, in downtown Corpus, has a small beach; the street continues south as Ocean Dr, which has bay-front playgrounds and parks, as well as some serious mansions lining it. **Corpus Christi Convention & Visitors Bureau** (☑800-766-2322; www.visitcorpuschristitx.org; 1823 N Chaparral St; ⊙10am-4pm Mon-Sat, plus noon-4pm Sun summer) has helpful coupons online.

◎ Sights & Activities

★**USS Lexington Museum** MUSEUM
(www.usslexington.com; 2914 N Shoreline Blvd; adult/child $14/9; ⊙9am-5pm, to 6pm Jun-Aug) The second sight you are likely to notice in Corpus (after the bay) is this 900ft-long aircraft carrier moored just north of the ship channel. The ship served in the Pacific during WWII and was finally retired in 1991. High-tech exhibits give visitors a chance to relive some wartime experiences. During the evening, the ship is eerily lit with blue lights that recall its WWII nickname, 'the Blue Ghost.'

> **WORTH A TRIP**
>
> ## PORT ARANSAS
>
> Driving north, Padre Island morphs into Mustang Island, at the tip of which (20 miles along) is **Port Aransas** (www.portaransas.org). This bustling fishing and vacation village is worth a stop. There are lots of places to eat seafood, from divey to divine. Gulf fishing charters depart from here; **Fisherman's Wharf** (www.wharfcat.com; 900 N Tarpon St; 5hr trip adult/child $60/30) has regular deep-sea excursions and runs jetty boats to outer islands (adult/child $12/6).

Museum of Science & History MUSEUM
(www.ccmuseum.com; 1900 N Chaparral St; adult/child $12.50/6; ⊙10am-5pm Tue-Sat, noon-5pm Sun; ⌖) Explore shipwrecks at this fun museum, right on the south side of the ship channel. See how Texas proved to be the doom of the French explorer La Salle and see the moldering remains of reproductions of two of Columbus' ships.

🛏 Sleeping & Eating

Bars and restaurants are clustered on the streets surrounding Chaparral and Water Sts downtown; there are few restaurants on the island.

George Blucher House B&B $$
(☎361-884-4884; www.georgeblucherhouse.com; 211 N Carrizo St; r $120-190; ⌖ @) A large wood-and-brick 1904 mansion near the center of town, the George Blucher House has six bedrooms, each with a bathroom. All are decorated in what could be described as 'period plush.' Sit on the covered porch and listen to the pecan trees grow.

V Boutique Hotel BOUTIQUE HOTEL $$$
(☎361-883-9200; www.vhotelcc.com; 701 N Water St; r $150-250; ⌖ ⌖) Adored by its guests, this small hotel in the heart of downtown offers a high level of service, including 24-hour concierge. Rooms come in eight styles, from studios to one-bedroom loft suites.

Executive Surf Club SOUTHERN $
(309 N Water St; mains $6-10; ⊙11am-11pm Sun-Wed, to midnight Thu-Sat) Eat a fried-shrimp po'boy from a surfboard table at this long-time fave, which has tables inside and out plus live music. It's just divey enough that you can forget you're downtown.

Brewster Street
Icehouse BURGERS, SEAFOOD $$
(1724 N Tancahua St; mains $7-16; ⊙11am-2am; ⌖) Has fried everything, cold brews, live music (Thursday to Saturday night) and a huge deck. This old warehouse really rocks after baseball games at nearby Whataburger Field. Kids love the playground.

Padre Island National Seashore

The 60 southern miles of 'North' Padre Island that lie outside Corpus Christi city limits are all a protected part of the **Padre Island National Seashore** (www.nps.gov/pais; Park Rd 22; 7-day pass per car $10; ⊙visitor center 9am-5pm). Four-wheel drive is necessary to see the extent of the park, but if you hike even a short distance from the visitor center, you'll be free of the crowds. The constant wind not only creates and moves dunes, it also attracts kitesurfers and windsurfers to the inland-side Bird Island Basin area.

Camping is available at the park's semi-developed, paved **Malaquite Campground** (campsites $8). Or go primitive: beach camping is free with the Padre Island National Seashore entrance permit.

Watch for the endangered Kemp Ridley sea turtles that nest in the park and are closely protected. If you're visiting in late summer, you might be able to take part in a turtle release; call the **Hatchling Hotline** (☎361-949-7163) for information.

South Padre Island

South Padre Island has discovered gold in spring break, the period in March when hordes of college students congregate at beaches for a week or more of completely pleasurable excess that's limited only by the capacity of their livers, loins and billfolds. To welcome this annual bacchanal, this condo-crammed island has beach activities and bars galore.

The website of the **South Padre Island Convention & Visitors Bureau** (☎956-761-4412; www.spichamber.com; 600 Padre Blvd; ⊙9am-5pm) has a comprehensive list of mini-golf courses, rowdy restaurants, condo rentals and beachfront hotels. You can settle right in at the **Tiki Condominium Hotel** (☎800-551-8454, 956-761-2694; www.thetiki.com; 6608 Padre Blvd; r $100-350; ⌖ ⌖ ⌖), which plays the tiki cliché to the max; it has units ranging in size from one to three bedrooms.

Stop in for a drink or a meal at the **Padre Island Brewing Company** (☎956-761-9585; www.pibrewingcompany.com; 3400 Padre Blvd; mains from $10; ☺11am-late), where you can wash down your burgers and seafood with a microbrew, or assemble a beach picnic at **Zeste Cafe & Market** (☎956-761-5555; 3508 Padre Blvd; meals from $8; ☺hours vary, usually 11am-8pm) (which will cause great envy among the hot-dog–scoffing masses).

For some refreshingly educational entertainment, try the tours and feeding presentations every 30 minutes at **Sea Turtle Inc** (www.seaturtleinc.com; 6617 Padre Blvd; suggested donation adult/child $3/2; ☺10am-4pm Tue-Sun) rescue facility.

The Valley

Way down here in the Rio Grande Valley (known simply as 'the Valley'), you're spittin' distance from Mexico. Citrus-tree plantations are gradually giving way to new subdivisions, but there are enough remaining to supply the roadside stands at which you can pick up fresh local grapefruits and oranges (harvested November through May).

Birders flock to the Valley's parks associated with the **World Birding Center** (www.worldbirdingcenter.org). Migrating avian masses, including thousands of hawks, pass through this natural corridor along the main north–south American fly route from March to April and September to October. Twenty miles or so west of Weslaco, the visitor and educational center at **Bentsen-Rio Grande Valley State Park** (www.tpwd.state.tx.us; 2800 S Bentsen Palm Dr; adult/child $5/free; ☺park 7am-10pm, center 8am-5pm) is a model of sustainable, green-driven architecture, including rainwater collection. Rent a bike (from $5 a day) or take the tram the 2 miles into the park. There, alligators and birds roam the wetlands, and you may spot a javelina (wild pig) or a horny toad on your way to the hawk-observation tower.

Twenty-seven miles southwest of South Padre is **Brownsville** (www.brownsville.org), the southernmost town in Texas, which has an authentic and slightly gritty culture that make it an excellent day trip. During the 19th century the fast-growing town was filled with ornate brick structures that drew architectural inspiration from Mexico and New Orleans. Many survive today and help make Brownsville an atmospheric stop.

DALLAS–FORT WORTH

Dallas and Fort Worth are as different as a Beemer-driving yuppie and a rancher in a Dodge dually pickup truck – the proverbial city slicker and his country cousin. Just 30 miles apart, the two towns anchor a giant megalopolis of six million people known as the Metroplex. Go see the excesses of the Big D and then day-trip to Fort Worth – the cowboy and Western sights and museums there might be the state's best-kept secret.

Dallas

Bright lights, big hair, shiny cars... In many ways, upscale Dallas is the belle of the Texas ball. From JR Ewing and the TV show *Dallas* to the Dallas Cowboys and their cheerleaders,

> ### ⓘ DAY TRIPS TO MEXICO: SHOULD YOU VISIT?
>
> Time was when no visit to the Rio Grande Valley was complete without a jaunt across the border. Good and cheap Mexican food (and tequila), mariachis and cheap souvenirs were just some of the lures. Plus there was the thrill of entering a dramatically different culture, just by strolling across a bridge spanning the Rio Grande.
>
> But several years of lurid headlines caused by the carnage of Mexico's drug wars have put a big question mark over day trips into Mexico. While Tex has always mixed well with Mex, the flow of Texans casually crossing into Mexican border towns has slowed to a trickle due to drug-cartel-related violence. Although tourists are not targets, fear of getting caught up in the violence is a real concern.
>
> Should you visit? The best answer is to ask locally on the Texas side of the border; conditions change constantly. No matter what, you'll probably be safest going during the day. You can also check with the **US State Department** (http://travel.state.gov/travel) for travel advisories. The state department urges caution when visiting all border towns in Mexico – as do we.

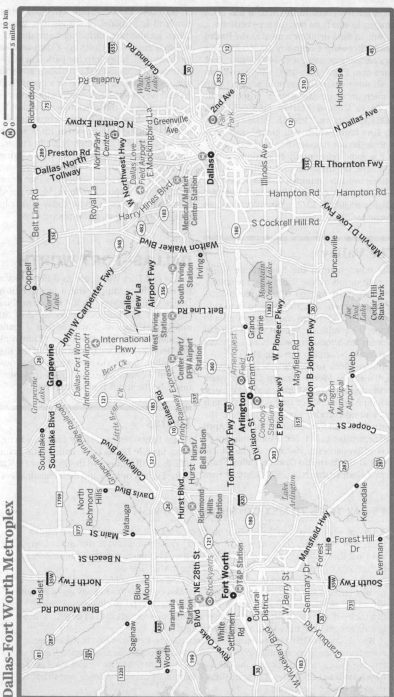

Dallas–Fort Worth Metroplex

Dallas has made a heavy mark on American popular culture, which seems fitting for a city whose ethos is image-consciousness and conspicuous consumption.

With all that money, it's no surprise that there's an amazing dining scene. (You can tell which place is hot by the caliber of cars the valet leaves out front.) And with more malls per capita than anywhere else in the US, shopping is definitely this city's guiltiest pleasure.

The museums are not only excellent, but unique – history buffs should not miss the memorials to former president John F Kennedy. The most impressive addition to Dallas' cultural landscape in recent years is the massive 68-acre Arts District, now the largest in the country.

North of downtown, uptown has smart, trendy bars, restaurants and hotels; follow Harwood St (or St Paul St, if you're taking the trolley) to McKinney Ave. Bars also line Greenville Ave, northeast of downtown off Ross Ave. Deep Ellum, at the eastern end of Elm St, is a bit gritty, but it's the nucleus of Dallas' small live-music scene.

◉ Sights

◉ Downtown

★ Sixth Floor Museum MUSEUM
(Map p700; www.jfk.org; Book Depository, 411 Elm St; adult/child $16/13; ⊙ 10am-6pm Tue-Sun, noon-6pm Mon; light rail West End) No city wants the distinction of being the site of a presidential assassination – especially if that president happens to be John F Kennedy. But rather than downplay the events that sent the city reeling in 1963, Dallas gives visitors a unique opportunity to delve into the shooting in this fascinating and memorable museum, located in the former Book Depository.

Dealey Plaza & the Grassy Knoll PARK
(Map p700; light rail West End) Conspiracy theorists, get your cameras out. Dealey Plaza became famous for all the wrong reasons as the location of the Kennedy assassination, and the 'grassy knoll' entered our collective vernacular as the place from which witnesses reported to have heard shots fired. (Look for the hillock that rises from the north side of Elm St to the edge of the picket fence.)

Dallas Museum of Art MUSEUM
(Map p700; www.dallasmuseumofart.org; 1717 N Harwood St; ⊙ 11am-5pm Tue-Sun, to 9pm Thu; ⚑; light rail St Paul) FREE This museum is a

high-caliber world tour of decorative and fine art. Highlights include Edward Hopper's enigmatic *Lighthouse Hill* and Rodin's *Sculptor and his Muse*. The Spanish Colonial art section is extraordinary. The museum's collection contains over 22,000 works of art spanning 5000 years. Kids (and parents) will appreciate the Young Learners' Gallery, with fun projects.

Nasher Sculpture Center MUSEUM
(Map p700; www.nashersculpturecenter.org; 2001 Flora St; adult/child $10/free; ⊙ 11am-5pm Tue-Sun; light rail St Paul) Modern-art installations shine at the fabulous glass-and-steel Nasher Sculpture Center. The Nashers accumulated what might be one of the greatest privately held sculpture collections in the world, with works by Calder, de Kooning, Rodin, Serra and Miró, and the divine sculpture garden is one of the best in the country.

Dallas World Aquarium AQUARIUM
(Map p700; www.dwazoo.com; 1801 N Griffin St; adult/child $21/13; ⊙ 9am-5pm; ⚑) The flora and fauna of 14 countries (think the watery Mayan cenote swimming with sharks and rays) come alive here.

☞ Tours

John Nagle WALKING TOUR
(⚑ 214-674-6295; www.jfktours.com; tours $20; ⊙ by appointment Sat & Sun) Dramatic and committed conspiracy-theorist historian guides 1¼-hour tours of JFK assassination sights.

✯ Festivals & Events

State Fair of Texas FAIR
(www.bigtex.com; Fair Park, 1300 Cullum Blvd; adult/child $17/13; ⊙ late-Sep–Oct) This massive fair is the fall highlight for many a Texan. Come ride one of the tallest Ferris wheels in North America, eat corn dogs (it's claimed that this is where they were invented) and browse among the prize-winning cows, sheep and quilts.

🛏 Sleeping

Staying uptown, you're closest to restaurants and nightlife, but hotels there can get pricey. The further you get from the center, the cheaper the highway chain motels get.

Abby Guest House GUESTHOUSE $
(⚑ 214-264-4804; www.abbyguesthouse.com; 5417 Goodwin Ave; cottage from $65; ⚑✿@🖘) This bright and cheerful garden cottage is within walking distance of great cafes and bars on

Downtown Dallas

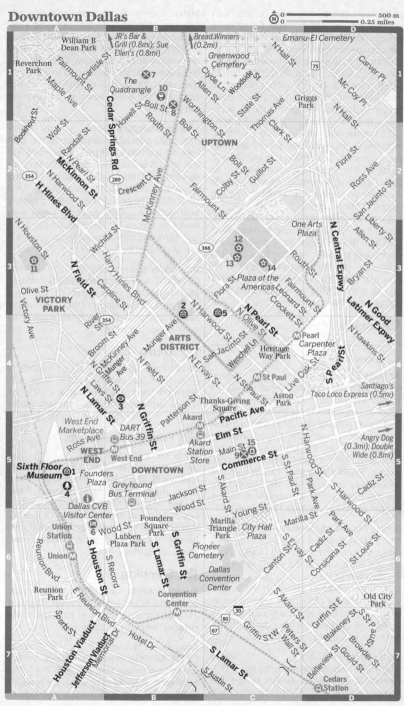

Downtown Dallas

◎ Top Sights
1 Sixth Floor Museum A5

◎ Sights
2 Dallas Museum of Art.........................B3
3 Dallas World Aquarium B4
4 Dealey Plaza & the Grassy Knoll.........A5
5 Nasher Sculpture Center....................C3

⊜ Sleeping
6 Hotel Lawrence A6

⊗ Eating
7 Dream Cafe...B1
8 S&D Oyster Company.........................B1
9 Zodiac..C5

◎ Drinking & Nightlife
10 Ginger Man B1

⊛ Entertainment
11 American Airlines Center....................A3
12 AT&T Performing Arts Center C3
13 Winspear Opera House......................C3
14 Wyly Theatre C3

⊜ Shopping
15 Neiman Marcus.................................C5

Upper Greenville Ave. With a full kitchen and sunny private patio, it's a great deal although often booked. Two-night minimum.

★ **Hotel Belmont**   BOUTIQUE HOTEL **$$**
(☏ 866-870-8010; www.belmontdallas.com; 901 Fort Worth Ave; r $100-200; ❄ @ ⊚ ☒) Just two miles west of downtown, this stylish 1940s bungalow-hotel is a fabulously low-key antidote to Dallas' flashier digs, with a touch of mid-century modern design and more than its share of soul. The garden rooms – with soaking tubs, Moroccan-blue tile work, kilim rugs and some city views – are tops.

Hotel Lawrence   HOTEL **$$**
(Map p700; ☏ 214-761-9090; www.hotellawrencedallas.com; 302 S Houston St; r $90-180; ❄ @ ⊚) One of the better deals among the midrange indie hotels, Hotel Lawrence has a convenient downtown location in a 1925 building. Rooms include a great buffet breakfast.

Hotel Palomar   HOTEL **$$**
(☏ 214-520-7969; www.hotelpalomar-dallas.com; 5300 E Mockingbird Lane; r from $169; P ❄ @ ⊚ ☒) The Palomar combines dramatic flair – like zebra robes, a Hollywood-esque infinity pool and a chichi spa – with eco-conscious

policies and enough freebies (eg the nightly wine-and-cheese happy hour) to make you feel good about being spoiled.

Rosewood Mansion on Turtle Creek   LUXURY HOTEL **$$$**
(☏ 214-559-2100; www.rosewoodhotels.com; 2821 Turtle Creek Blvd; r $275-600; ❄ @ ⊚ ☒ ☒) Step into a life of ease, where for every two guests there's one staff member attending. This is the definitive five-star Dallas hotel, and a worthy splurge. Rooms have fresh flowers and hand-carved European furnishings, and dinner is served in the original, marble-clad, 1925 Italianate villa.

✗ Eating

Deep Ellum, just east of downtown, is your choice for eclectic eats. Otherwise, head uptown for myriad choices. Bishop Ave, dotted with interesting places to eat and drink, merges hipster and funky – walk off your vittles by window-shopping the idiosyncratic boutiques.

✗ Uptown & Knox-Henderson

Highland Park Soda Shop   AMERICAN **$**
(☏ 214-521-2126; 3229 Knox St; mains $4-8; ⊙ 7am-6pm Mon-Sat, 10am-5pm Sun; ♿) Since 1912 this classic soda fountain has been serving up malts and comfort fare such as grilled-cheese sandwiches to generations of diners. When in doubt, get the root-beer float.

★ **Bread Winners**   AMERICAN **$$**
(www.breadwinnerscafe.com; 3301 McKinney Ave; mains $9-20; ⊙ 7am-10pm; ☏ ♿) If sipping a peach Bellini in a lush courtyard atrium is the reward for the agony of choosing what to order for brunch, then bring on the pain. Lunch and dinner offer similar, though less torturous, conundrums. In a pinch, at least stop in for something decadent from the bakery.

Dream Cafe   CAFE **$$**
(Map p700; www.thedreamcafe.com; 2800 Routh St; mains $8-20; ⊙ 7am-9pm Sun & Tue-Thu, to 10pm Fri & Sat, to 3pm Mon; ☏ ♿) Start your day early with a fabulous breakfast, or chill on the shady patio at lunchtime with some healthy, hearty fare. It has a playground plus on some nights it also has live jazz.

S&D Oyster Company   SEAFOOD **$$**
(Map p700; www.sdoyster.com; 2701 McKinney Ave; mains $12-20; ⊙ 11am-10pm Mon-Sat) An uptown staple for years – the simple Gulf Coast decor and great fried seafood keep 'em

coming back (especially gents of a certain age wearing bow ties). Try the BBQ shrimp and leave room for the bread pudding.

★ Javier's
MEXICAN $$$

(☎214-521-4211; www.javiers.net; 4912 Cole Ave; mains $20-30; ⊙5:30-10:30pm Mon-Sat) Discard any ideas you have about Tex-Mex at this deeply cultured restaurant that takes the gentrified food of old Mexico City to new levels. The setting is dark, leathery and quiet. The food meaty and piquant. Steaks come with a range of Mexican flavors that bring out the best in beef. Get a table under the stars.

Abacus
AMERICAN $$$

(☎214-559-3111; www.kentrathbun.com; 4511 McKinney Ave; mains $35-60, tasting menus from $65; ⊙6-10pm Mon-Sat) Too many steakhouses in Dallas are part of chains. For the real deal with a contemporary twist, Abacus delivers the beef. Start with sushi or the wildly popular lobster shooters and then make your way through a menu of small, seasonal plates. Then feast on simply superb steaks. The bar is excellent.

Downtown & Deep Ellum

★ Santiago's Taco Loco Express
MEXICAN $

(3014 Main St; mains $3-8; ⊙6am-10pm Mon-Thu, to 3am Fri & Sat) The breakfast tacos and tamales are addictive and draw locals who know how to start their day. At any time the fine range of tacos includes massive combos that make for an all-day meal. Service is from a window, with tables outside.

Angry Dog
AMERICAN $

(2726 Commerce St; mains $5-9; ⊙11am-midnight Mon-Thu, to 2am Fri & Sat, noon-10pm Sun) Nice, greasy, old-style burgers lure folks into this saloon at all hours. Other bar stalwarts, including wings, are good. The beer selection is tops.

★ Zodiac
AMERICAN $$

(Map p700; ☎214-573-5800; Neiman Marcus, 1618 Main St; mains $14-24; ⊙11am-3pm Mon-Sat; 📶) This classic lunch spot, which has been tucked into Neiman Marcus for more than 50 years, evokes old-school Dallas. Attentive waiters bustle about, soothing and pampering diners with hot chicken consommé, popovers with strawberry butter, and elegant salads.

🍷 Drinking

Numerous pubs with outdoor patios are to be found in uptown along not only McKinney Ave (in the 2500 to 2800 blocks especially) but also Knox St near Willis Ave. Note that bars and clubs in Dallas (at least mostly) have succumbed to the indoor smoking ban.

★ Ginger Man
PUB

(Map p700; ☎214-754-8771; www.dallas.gingermanpub.com; 2718 Boll St; ⊙noon-2am) An appropriately spice-colored house is home to this always-busy neighborhood pub. It has multilevel patios and porches, out front and back, as well as dartboards.

Old Monk Pub
PUB

(☎214-821-1880; www.oldmonkdallas.com; 2847 N Henderson Ave; ⊙4pm-2am Mon-Fri, 11am-2am Sat & Sun) The dimly lit patio on a starry night! The perfect cheese plate! The Belgian beers! Add in the upscale pub food and outdoor seating and you might not leave.

Double Wide
BAR

(☎214-887-6510; www.double-wide.com; 3510 Commerce St; ⊙6pm-2am) Are these rednecks pretending to be hipsters, or hipsters pretending to be rednecks? Live music keeps the irony from killing the fun. The two sides of the bar explain the name, with a fine patio in between.

TASTES BORN IN TEXAS

Corn dogs Cornbread-batter-dipped hot dogs on a stick were created in 1948 by Neil Fletcher for the State Fair of Texas; Fletcher's still sells 'em there. Now available with jalapeño cornbread, too.

Shiner Bock The state's favorite amber ale came to be when Kosmos Spoetzl brought Bavarian brewing to Shiner, Texas, in 1914. Available countrywide, Shiner Bock is still brewed at Spoetzl Brewery (p684).

Chicken-fried bacon You may have heard of steak coated and deep-fried like chicken, but the taste (and heart-attack factor) was taken to new heights when **Sodolak's**, in Somerville, started cooking bacon the same way in the early 1990s.

Dr Pepper A pharmacist in a Waco drugstore–soda shop invented this aromatic cola in the 1880s.

Reno's Chop Shop Saloon BAR

(☎214-742-7366; www.renoschopshop.com; 2210 N Crowdus St; ⊙6pm-2am Mon-Fri, 2pm-2am Sat & Sun) Slightly off Deep Ellum's Elm St artery, this is where you'll find Dallas' friendliest bikers. Hogs line the front while a delightfully jovial crowd parties inside. The rear patio, which hosts bands on Sundays, has great tables with umbrellas.

☆ Entertainment

For entertainment listings, check the weekly alternative newspaper **Dallas Observer** (www.dallasobserver.com) or **Guide Live** (www.guidelive.com), which appears in Friday's *Dallas Morning News*.

Live Music & Nightclubs

During lunch hour, office workers crowd into the bars and restaurants of downtown's **Deep Ellum** (www.deepellumtexas). The scene at night is definitely grittier, but this is still live-music central. Most of the clubs are hard-core, but you'll occasionally find country or jazz. The bars and clubs of Lower Greenville Ave (1500 to 2200 blocks) cater to a crowd temperament somewhere between the uptown yuppies and downtown grunge set.

Sports

Mesquite ProRodeo RODEO

(☎972-285-8777; www.mesquiterodeo.com; 1818 Rodeo Dr, Mesquite; ⊙7:30pm Fri & Sat Jun–late-Aug) The competition is fierce in classic rodeo events including bareback, steer wrestling and bull riding. The prize money attracts top talent to this series.

Dallas Cowboys Stadium FOOTBALL

(☎817-892-4467; http://stadium.dallascowboys.com; 1 Legends Way, off I-30 exits 28 & 29) The Dallas Cowboys gave themselves the nickname 'America's Team' after they had great success (with cheerleaders and otherwise) in the 1970s. Although the team's fortunes have been modest of late, they still have swagger, as shown in their enormous, retractable-roof home, which opened in 2009.

American Airlines Center STADIUM

(Map p700; www.americanairlinescenter.com; 2500 Victory Ave) Located in Victory Park, this stadium hosts mega-concerts and is home to the Dallas Stars ice-hockey team and the Dallas Mavericks pro basketball team.

GAY & LESBIAN DALLAS

You've got to love that the top gay and lesbian bars in Dallas are named JR's and Sue Ellen's, respectively, after the two lead (and presumably straight) characters in *Dallas*.

JR's Bar & Grill (www.jrsdallas.com; 3923 Cedar Springs Rd; ⊙11am-2am) One of the busiest bars in Texas, JR's serves lunch daily and boasts a variety of fun entertainment at night.

Sue Ellen's (www.sueellensdallas.com; 3014 Throckmorton St; ⊙4pm-2am) Chill out in the 'lipstick lounge' or on the dance floor at Dallas' favorite lesbian bar.

Theater & Culture

AT&T Performing Arts Center THEATER

(Map p700; www.attpac.org; 2403 Flora St) Four architecturally noteworthy performance venues are here, including the 2000-seat **Winspear Opera House** (Map p700; 2403 Flora St), home to the **Dallas Opera** (☎214-443-1000; www.dallasopera.org); the 1500-seat **Wyly Theatre** (Map p700; 2400 Flora St); and **Strauss Square**, an open-air stage.

🛍 Shopping

You can find some interesting gifts of arty homewares, like vintage Fiestaware plates, in the quirky, but small, **Bishop Arts District** (www.bishopartsdistrict.com). On the northern end of uptown (at Lemmon and McKinney Aves), the **West Village** (www.westvil.com) neighborhood has a collection of chain stores and individual boutiques, including Cowboy Cool.

Neiman Marcus DEPARTMENT STORE

(Map p700; ☎214-741-6911; www.neimanmarcus.com; 1618 Main St; ⊙10am-6pm Mon-Sat, to 8pm Thu; light rail Akard) A downtown landmark, this six-story veteran was the first Neiman Marcus store. Today it's still a wonderful place to enjoy a timeless shopping experience.

★ NorthPark Center MALL

(☎214-363-7441; www.northparkcenter.com; 8687 N Central Expwy; ⊙10am-9pm Mon-Sat, noon-6pm Sun) Almost 2 million sq ft of retail space, NorthPark's major stores include Neiman Marcus, Nordstrom and Macy's. It has hundreds of other retailers, including most upscale brands. Despite its size, it gets jammed and parking on a Saturday afternoon can be a pain.

Galleria MALL
(☑ 972-702-7100; www.galleriadallas.com; 13350 Dallas Pkwy; ⊙10am-9pm Mon-Sat, noon-6pm Sun) The Galleria defined Dallas and conspicuous consumption in the 1980s and 1990s. Its main anchors include Nordstrom, Saks Fifth Ave and Macy's, as well as an iconic ice-skating rink. But the last time we were there, we couldn't help wondering if it hadn't, well, peaked.

ℹ Information

Dallas CVB Visitor Center (Map p700; ☑ 214-571-1000; www.visitdallas.com; Old Red Courthouse, 100 S Houston St; ⊙9am-5pm) Vast amounts of material.

Dallas Morning News (www.dallasnews.com) The city's daily newspaper.

Police station (☑ 214-670-4413; 334 S Hall St)

Travelex (☑ 214-559-3564; www.travelex.com; 2911 Turtle Creek Blvd; ⊙9am-5pm Mon-Fri) Foreign-currency exchange.

ℹ Getting There & Away

American Airlines' main hub is **Dallas-Fort Worth International Airport** (DFW; www.dfwairport.com), 16 miles northwest of the city via I-35 E.

Southwest Airlines uses the smaller **Dallas Love Field** (DAL; www.dallas-lovefield.com), just northwest of downtown.

Greyhound buses make runs all over the country from the **Greyhound Bus Terminal** (Map p700; 205 S Lamar St).

The **Amtrak** (www.amtrak.com) San Antonio–Chicago *Texas Eagle* train stops at downtown's **Union Station** (401 S Houston St).

ℹ Getting Around

TO/FROM THE AIRPORT

From Monday to Saturday you can ride the **Trinity Railway Express** (www.trinityrailwayexpress.org; one way $2.50) between downtown's Union Station and the CenterPort/DFW Airport stop, which is actually in a parking lot; free shuttle buses then take you to the terminals. **DART Bus 39** (Map p700; 800 Pacific Ave; one way $2.50) travels between downtown's West End Transit Station and Dallas Love Field daily, but service is limited on weekends.

It's often easiest to take a shared-ride shuttle: **SuperShuttle** (☑ 817-329-2000; www.super-shuttle.com; fare from $17) runs from DFW or Dallas Love Field to downtown and major hotels in the region. A taxi between either airport and central Dallas should cost about $40 to $60.

BUS & LIGHT RAIL

Dallas Area Rapid Transit (DART; ☑ 214-979-1111; www.dart.org; 2hr ticket $2.50) operates buses and an extensive light-rail system that connects downtown with outlying areas. Day passes ($5) are available from the **store** (Map p700; 1401 Pacific Ave; ⊙7:30am-5:30pm Mon-Fri) at Akard Station.

Travel from downtown to uptown on the historic and free **M-Line Trolley** (☑ 214-855-0006; www.mata.org; ⊙7am-10pm Mon-Thu, to 11pm Fri, 10am-midnight Sat, to 10pm Sun), which runs from the corner of Ross Ave and St Paul St, near the Dallas Museum of Art, and up McKinney Ave to Blackburn St. An extension bringing the line into downtown should open by 2014.

WORTH A TRIP

DENTON

A bastion of college cool and indie cred, Denton has a great music scene. Home to the University of North Texas and its renowned arts programs, the fast-growing city rightfully claims the title as the most musical city in the region. The downtown, centered on **Courthouse Square**, boasts a plethora of music venues, music shops and instrument stores.

By day, pop into the **Courthouse on the Square Museum** (☑ 940-349-2850; 110 W Hickory St; ⊙10am-4:40pm Mon-Fri, 11am-3pm Sat) FREE for local lore and an amazing display of art created with pecans. Outside, check out the 1918 **Confederate War Memorial**, which has been modified with apologetic disclaimers. Nearby, **Recycled Books Records CDs** (☑ 940-566-5688; www.recycledbooks.com; 200 N Locust St; ⊙9am-9pm) has hard-to-find tunes.

For music, the top venue is **Dan's Silver Leaf** (☑ 940-320-2000; www.danssilverleaf.com; 103 Industrial St; ⊙7pm-2am), with a revered owner who books top bands but doesn't gouge on drink prices. Other clubs and bars are nearby.

Every March the city hosts **35 Denton** (www.35denton.com; ⊙Mar), a music festival featuring everything from rock to blues to jazz.

CAR & MOTORCYCLE

If you do rent a car, be warned that rush-hour freeway traffic is bad and there's little free parking downtown. Public garages cost from $12 per day.

Fort Worth

Often called 'Where the West Begins' – and more often referred to as 'Cowtown' – Fort Worth is one town that still has its twang.

The place first became famous during the great open-range cattle drives of the late 19th century, when more than 10 million head of cattle tramped through the city on the Chisholm Trail. Today you can see a mini cattle drive in the morning and a rodeo on Saturday night.

Down in the Cultural District, tour the Cowgirl Museum and others, including three amazing art collections. Then, after you've meditated on minimalism, Sundance Sq's restaurants and bars call you to the kick-up-your-heels downtown.

Whatever you do, don't mistake Fort Worth for being Dallas' sidekick. This city's got a headstrong spirit of its own, and it's more user-friendly than Dallas (and greener and cleaner). Bottom line? There's a lot to do here – without a lot of pretense.

◎ Sights

The area around the Stockyards is cowboy central; most area museums call the leafy Cultural District home.

◎ Stockyards National Historic District

Sure, you'll spot cowboys on horseback roaming around, but wander the dusty streets of the Stockyards and you'll soon be mingling with a mix of families, bikers, curious European tourists and novelty-seeking college kids. This place puts fun first, with equal parts authentic history and camera-ready tourism thrown into the pot.

Stockyards HISTORIC SITE
(www.fortworthstockyards.org; Exchange Ave) Western-wear stores and knickknack shops, saloons and steakhouses occupy the Old West-era buildings of the Stockyards. City-paid cowboys on horseback roam the district, answering questions and posing for photos.

◎ Cultural District

Five major museums and the Will Rogers Memorial Center are part of the parklike **Cultural District** (www.fwculture.com).

Kimbell Art Museum MUSEUM
(☑817-332-8451; www.kimbellart.org; 3333 Camp Bowie Blvd; ☉10am-5pm Tue-Thu & Sat, noon-8pm Fri, to 5pm Sun) FREE Some art aficionados say this is the country's best 'small' art museum, while others say it's one of the unqualified best. Take your time perusing: the stunning architecture lets in natural light that allows visitors to see paintings from antiquity to the 20th century the way the artists originally intended.

National Cowgirl Museum MUSEUM
(☑817-336-4475; www.cowgirl.net; 1721 Gendy St; adult/child $10/8; ☉10am-5pm Tue-Sat, noon-5pm Sun) This airy, impressive museum explores the myth and the reality of cowgirls in American culture. From rhinestone costumes to rare film footage, this is a fun and educational ride. By the time you walk out, you'll have a whole new appreciation for these tough workers.

Amon Carter Museum of American Art MUSEUM
(www.cartermuseum.org; 3501 Camp Bowie Blvd; ☉10am-5pm Tue-Sat, to 8pm Thu, noon-5pm Sun) FREE Pre-1945 American art shines at this museum, including iconic works by John Singer Sargent, Winslow Homer and Alexander Calder, as well as an impressive collection of works depicting the American West by artists Frederic Remington and Charles M Russell.

Modern Art Museum of Fort Worth MUSEUM
(www.themodern.org; 3200 Darnell St; adult/child $10/free; ☉10am-5pm Tue-Sun, to 8pm Thu) In a stunning, soaring space, this museum houses an incredible number of provocative and mind-expanding works by luminaries such as Mark Rothko and Picasso.

◎ Downtown

Sundance Square NEIGHBORHOOD
(www.sundancesquare.com) You can stroll yourself happy in the 14-block Sundance Sq, near Main and 3rd Sts. Colorful architecture, art galleries and a host of bars and restaurants make this one 'hood not to miss. New in 2013 was a big, spurting fountain and lots of surrounding condos.

THE WORLD'S LARGEST HONKY-TONK

Scoot on in to **Billy Bob's Texas** (☑817-624-7117; www.billybobstexas.com; 2520 Rodeo Plaza; cover $2-5 Sun-Thu, varies Fri & Sat; ☻11am-2am Mon-Sat, noon-2am Sun), the world's largest honky-tonk. The 100,000-sq-ft building was once a barn that housed prize cattle during the Fort Worth Stock Show. After the stock show moved to the Will Rogers Memorial Center, the barn became a department store so big that the stock keepers wore roller skates.

Now Billy Bob's can hold more than 6000 people and has 40 bars to serve the thirsty masses. The most bottled beer sold in one night was 16,000 bottles, during a 1985 Hank Williams Jr concert. Top country-and-western stars, house bands and country DJs play on two stages. On Friday and Saturday nights a live bull-riding competition takes place at an indoor arena. Pool tables and games help make this a family place; under 18s are welcome with a parent.

Sid Richardson Collection of Western Art
MUSEUM

(www.sidrichardsonmuseum.org; 309 Main St; ☻9am-5pm Mon-Thu, to 8pm Fri & Sat, noon-5pm Sun) **FREE** If the Stockyards didn't sate your hunger for all things Western, pop in here for some art. It's known for its Frederic Remington paintings and bronzes.

★ Festivals & Events

Fort Worth Stock Show & Rodeo
RODEO

(www.fwssr.com; ☻Jan) Catch the rodeo craze with nearly a million other people. Held in January for several weeks each year at **Will Rogers Memorial Center** (1 Amon Carter Sq) in the Cultural District.

🛏 Sleeping

Fort Worth is an easy day trip from Dallas, but if you're staying over, here are your best choices.

Miss Molly's Hotel
B&B $

(☑817-626-1522; www.missmollyshotel.com; 109 W Exchange Ave; r incl breakfast $100-175; ❋🛜) Set in the heart of the Stockyards, eight-room Miss Molly's occupies a former bordello. Its heavily atmospheric vibe will feel authentic to some (Miss Josie's room still looks like a bordello), eerie to others (they say it's haunted...), but probably at least a little charming either way. Look for cheap deals during the week – as low as $50.

Etta's Place
INN $$

(☑817-255-5760; www.ettas-place.com; 200 W 3rd St; r $150-240; ❋🛜) A grand piano, a comfy library and quilts galore are among the cozy pleasures at this Sundance Sq inn. Breakfast can be taken on the airy patio. The 10 rooms are large; suites have kitchenettes.

Texas White House
B&B $$

(☑817-923-3597; www.texaswhitehouse.com; 1417 Eighth Ave; r $150-250; ❋🛜) A large historic home with contemporary Texas style near downtown. The five rooms are well equipped; larger suites have fridges and microwaves.

★ Stockyards Hotel
HISTORIC HOTEL $$$

(☑817-625-6427; www.stockyardshotel.com; 109 E Exchange Ave; r $140-350; ❋🛜) First opened in 1907, this 52-room place clings to its cowboy past with Western-themed art, cowboy-inspired rooms and a grand Old West lobby with lots of leather. Hide out in the Bonnie and Clyde room, actually occupied by Clyde Barrow during his 1932 Fort Worth stay (the faux bullet holes and boot jacks only add to the mystique).

Ashton Hotel
BOUTIQUE HOTEL $$$

(☑866-327-4866; www.theashtonhotel.com; 610 Main St; r $208-290; ❋🛜🛋) This 39-room, six-story boutique hotel in a turn-of-the-century building off Sundance Sq offers hush-hush elegance without an ounce of snootiness. Parking is valet-only.

🍴 Eating

Put on the feed bag and grab some Texas-style fixins' in Sundance Sq and in the Stockyards. Head to West 7th for new-fangled additions to the dining scene, or just walk down Magnolia and breathe in the foodie revolution. Many of the museums, such as the Kimbell, also have excellent cafes. PS: You're in Fort Worth – have a steak.

★ Curly's Frozen Custard
ICE CREAM $

(☑817-763-8700; www.curlysfrozencustard.com; 4017 Camp Bowie Blvd; treats from $2; ☻11am-9pm) Creamy frozen custard that you can customize with all sorts of mix-ins to make a 'concrete.' Good any day the temp is above freezing.

⭐ **Kincaid's** BURGERS $
(🖂 817-732-2881; www.kincaidshamburgers.com; 4901 Camp Bowie Blvd; mains $4-7; ☺11am-8pm Mon-Sat, 11am-3pm Sun) Sit at picnic tables amid disused grocery shelves at this local institution (which unfortunately has an institutional shade of green on the walls) and wolf down some of the best burgers in the region. The burgers are thick, juicy and come covered in condiments.

Love Shack BURGERS $
(110 E Exchange Ave; mains from $6; ☺11am-10pm Sun-Thu, to 1am Fri & Sat) Enjoy a gourmet burger (the spicy Amore Caliente, yum!) at this joint owned by TV chef and Texas-born Tim Love. Don't miss the home-cut fries or Parmesan chips. There's live local music many nights.

⭐ **Zio Carlo Magnolia Brew Pub** PIZZERIA $$
(🖂 817-923-8000; www.gr8ale.com; 1001 Magnolia Ave; mains $12-16; ☺11:30am-midnight Mon-Fri, 11:30am-1am Sat, 10:30am-midnight Sun; 🖥) Pizza and beer: the perfect combo. Both are superb here. The pizza is thin-crust Italian and comes in 17 varieties. The beers are also fine and diverse. Enjoy some of both in the exposed-brick dining area or outside on the patio.

Esperanza's Bakery & Cafe MEXICAN $$
(🖂 817-626-5770; 2122 N Main St; mains $7-15; ☺6:30am-5:30pm) Breakfasts are spicy, plentiful and awfully tasty at this always-busy local fave. It even has a full bar so you can get a leg up on the day. Lunch items include Tex-Mex in fine form. Get *campanchanas* (crunchy sweet bread) from the bakery to go, or let the sun warm you on the terrace.

Joe T Garcia's MEXICAN $$
(www.joets.com; 2201 N Commerce St; mains $8-14; ☺11am-2:30pm & 5-10pm Mon-Thu, 11am-11pm Fri & Sat, to 10pm Sun) The most famous restaurant in Fort Worth, this fourth-generation place takes up a city block. Dinners in the candlelit walled courtyard are magical, as Mexican-tile fountains bubble among the acres of tropical foliage. On weekends the line (no reservations!) often stretches around the block.

⭐ **Lonesome Dove Western Bistro** SOUTHERN $$$
(🖂 817-740-8810; www.lonesomedovebistro.com; 2406 N Main St; mains $20-40; ☺11:30am-2:30pm & 5-10pm Tue-Sat, 5-10pm Mon) At Tim Love's mod-Western dining experience, even the chefs wear cowboy hats. It's Southern fusion, with the traditional flavors of the region enlivened by all manner of influences. The wine list is superb and the $9 lunch special is truly the best deal in town.

🍷 **Drinking**

All the restaurants in and around Sundance Sq have popular bars attached.

Usual Bar COCKTAIL BAR
(🖂 817-810-0114; www.theusualbar.com; 1408 W Magnolia Ave; ☺4pm-2am) Craft-cocktail lust packs hipsters in nightly at this bar that serves up debonair drinks such as 'Jimador's Revenge' and 'Taxation & Representation.' Of course you can be ironic and just have a well-poured Old Fashioned. Great terrace.

Flying Saucer Draught Emporium BAR
(🖂 817-336-7470; 111 E 3rd St; ☺11am-1am Mon-Thu, to 2am Fri & Sat, noon-midnight Sun) You definitely won't go thirsty: with 80 beers on tap, this downtown joint is made for craft-beer lovers. How can you not love a bar whose jam-packed patio is called 'Half-Acre Hell?'

Lola's Saloon BAR
(🖂 817-877-0666; www.lolasfortworth.com; 2736 W 6th St; ☺noon-2am) Dive into this dive bar for a fairly intimate music experience. Good bands many nights, otherwise a good local crowd more than happy to tell you where to go – in a nice, helpful way, of course.

☆ **Entertainment**

On weekend evenings, country music becomes common in the Stockyards District, and a variety of live bands play in and around Sundance Sq. Look for listings in **Fort Worth Weekly** (www.fwweekly.com).

Cowtown Coliseum Rodeo RODEO
(www.stockyardsrodeo.com; 121 E Exchange Ave; adult/child rodeo from $15/10, Wild West Show $12/8; ☺8pm Fri & Sat) See a real live rodeo at 8pm on Friday and Saturday nights year-round. From June to August, horses and

---

FREE RIDE

Fort Worth's coolest transportation option is the free **Molly the Trolley** (🖂 817-215-8600; www.mollythetrolley. com; ☺10am-10pm) **FREE**, a vintage trolley system that serves passengers traveling around downtown.

riders show off at Pawnee Bill's Wild West Show (2:30pm and 4:30pm on Saturday and Sunday).

★ **Pearls Dance Hall**   LIVE MUSIC
(www.pearlsdancehall.com; 302 W Exchange Ave; ☺7pm-2am) On the edge of the stockyards, this raucous old brothel once owned by Buffalo Bill Cody is an atmospheric place to hear traditional country music with an edge. Texas luminaries like Dale Watson are known to rock out here.

White Elephant Saloon   LIVE MUSIC
(www.whiteelephantsaloon.com; 106 E Exchange Ave; ☺noon-midnight Sun-Thu, to 2am Fri & Sat) Stockyards cowboys have been bellying up to this bar since 1887 (now owned by Tim Love). Local singers and songwriters are regularly showcased.

ℹ Information

Central Library (500 W 3rd St; ☺10am-6pm Mon, Wed, Fri & Sat, noon-8pm Tue & Thu, 1-5pm Sun) Free internet access.

Fort Worth Convention & Visitors Bureau (www.fortworth.com) The most together tourist board in the state, with three branches: Cultural District (☏817-882-8588; 3401 W Lancaster Ave; ☺9am-5pm Mon-Sat); Downtown (☏800-433-5747; 415 Throckmorton St; ☺8:30am-5pm Mon-Fri, 10am-4pm Sat); Stockyards (☏817-625-9715; www.stock-yardsstation.com/information; 130 E Exchange Ave; ☺8.30am-6pm Mon-Fri, 9am-6pm Sat, 11am-5pm Sun) Ask for the spiffy, free 3D maps.

ℹ Getting There & Away

Dallas–Fort Worth International Airport (p704) is 17 miles east of Fort Worth.

The **Amtrak** (www.amtrak.com; 1001 Jones St) *Texas Eagle* stops in Fort Worth en route to San Antonio and Chicago. The *Heartland Flyer* serves Oklahoma City.

Monday to Saturday the **Trinity Railway Express** (TRE; ☏817-215-8600; www.trinityrailwayexpress.org; 1001 Jones St) connects downtown Fort Worth with downtown Dallas ($5, 1¼ hours, roughly every 30 minutes).

Several **Greyhound** (www.greyhound.com; 1001 Jones St) buses a day make the one-hour trip from downtown Fort Worth to Dallas ($9). There's also service to other major Texas cities.

ℹ Getting Around

Fort Worth is fairly compact and easy to drive around: I-30 runs east–west through downtown, and I-35 W runs to the south.

The **Fort Worth Transit Authority** (The T; ☏817-215-8600; www.the-t.com; single ride/day pass $1.75/3.50) runs bus 1N to the Stockyards and bus 2 to the Cultural District. Stops include the Intermodal Transportation Center. Both of these lines run well into the evening.

WEST TEXAS

Welcome to the land of wide open spaces. Along I-10 there's not much to look at – just scrub brush and lots of sky – but dip below the interstate and you'll find vistas that are as captivating as they are endless. Sometimes the rugged terrain looks like the backdrop in an old Western movie; other times it looks like an alien landscape, with huge rock formations suddenly jutting out of the desert.

But what is there to do? Plenty. Exploring an enormous national park that's nearly the size of Rhode Island. Stopping in small towns that surprise you with minimalist art, planet-watching parties or fascinating ghost-town ruins. Chatting with friendly locals whenever the mood strikes you. And letting the slowness of west Texas get thoroughly under your skin.

Big Bend National Park

Everyone knows Texas is huge. But you can't really appreciate just how big it is until you visit this **national park** (www.nps.gov/bibe; 7-day pass per vehicle $20) that's almost the size of Rhode Island. Despite its sprawl, Big Bend is laced with enough well-placed roads and trails to permit short-term visitors to see a lot in two to three days.

Like many popular US parks, Big Bend has one area – the Chisos Basin – that absorbs the overwhelming crunch of traffic. But any visit should also include time in the **Chihuahuan Desert**, home to curious creatures and adaptable plants, and the **Rio Grande**, providing a watery border between the US and Mexico.

With over 200 miles of trails to explore, it's no wonder hiking is big in Big Bend. Get the scoop on the most popular hikes at the **Panther Junction Visitors Center** (☏915-477-2251; ☺8am-6pm) on the main park road, 29 miles south of the northern Persimmon Gap entrance and 26 miles east of the Maverick entrance at Study Butte. Or find a plethora of options in the park's booklet, *Hiker's Guide to Trails of Big Bend National Park* ($1.95 at park visitor centers).

In the heart of the park, **Chisos Mountain Lodge** (☎877-386-4383, 432-477-2291; www.chisosmountainslodge.com; lodge & motel r $123-127, cottages $150) offers lodging in the sought-after Roosevelt Stone Cottages or in one of two motel-style lodges. There's also a **dining room** (Lodge Dining Room; Chisos Mountain Lodge; mains $8-23; ☺7-10am, 11am-4pm & 5-8pm) within the complex, as well as a **camp store** (☺9am-9pm) with basic supplies.

For tent campers or smaller RVs that don't require hookups, there are three main campgrounds, some of which can be reserved, some of which are first-come, first-served. When everything's full, rangers direct tent campers to primitive sites throughout the Big Bend backcountry. Most popular – thanks to its mountain climate – is the **Chisos Basin Campground** (☎877-444-6777; www.recreation.gov; campsites $14).

West of Big Bend National Park

Small towns. Ghost towns. Towns that aren't even really towns. Throw in lots of dust and a scorching summer heat that dries out the stream of visitors until it's just a trickle. This isn't everyone's idea of a dream vacation. But if you can't relax out here, then you just plain can't relax. Whatever concerns you in your everyday life is likely to melt away along with anything you leave in your car. Speaking of cars, this is the land that public transportation forgot. You'll need a car out 'round these parts.

Terlingua

A former mining boomtown in the late 19th and early 20th centuries, Terlingua went bust when the mines were closed down in the 1940s. The town dried up and blew away like a tumbleweed, leaving buildings that fell into ruins and earning Terlingua a place in Texas folklore as a ghost town. But slowly the area has become repopulated, thanks in large part to the fact that it's only a few miles outside of Big Bend National Park. You'll hear people talk about Terlingua, Study Butte and Terlingua ghost town as if they're three different towns, but the only real town here is Terlingua; the other two are just areas of the town.

🛏 Sleeping & Eating

Chisos Mining Co Motel　　　MOTEL **$**
(☎432-371-2254; www.cmcm.cc; 23280 FM 170; s/d $60/78, cabins from $101; ✳) You'll recognize this quirky little place less than a mile west of Hwy 118 when you spot the oversized Easter eggs on the roof. The rooms are minimalist but as cheap as you'll find.

★ La Posada Milagro　　　INN **$$**
(☎432-371-3044; www.laposadamilagro.net; 100 Milagro Rd; d $185-210; ✳ 🛜) Built on top of and even incorporating some of the adobe ruins in the historic ghost town, this guesthouse pulls off the amazing feat of providing stylish rooms that blend in perfectly with the surroundings. The decor is west-Texas chic, and there's a nice patio for enjoying the cool evenings. Budget travelers can book a simpler room with four bunk beds for $145 a night.

ROUTE 66: GET YOUR KICKS IN TEXAS

The Texas Panhandle isn't exactly a hub of tourism, but it does get plenty of folks passing through as they pay homage to the Mother Road. If you find yourself up thataway, here are the top Texas stops on a Route 66 road trip, going from west to east:

Cadillac Ranch (I-40, btwn exits 60 & 62) This iconic roadside attraction features 10 Cadillacs buried headlights down and tailfins up.

Downtown Amarillo The San Jacinto District still has original Route 66 businesses, and W 6th St is a short, but entirely original, Mother Road segment.

★ Big Texan Steak Ranch (www.bigtexan.com; 7701 I-40 E, exit 74; mains $10-40; ☺7am-10:30pm; 🚆) A giant waving cowboy welcomes you to this roadside attraction/steakhouse that'll serve you a 72oz steak – free if you can eat it in under an hour.

Bug Ranch (Hwy 207 access road) In response to Cadillac Ranch, five stripped-down VW bugs have sprouted 18 miles east of Amarillo.

Devil's Rope Museum (www.barbwiremuseum.com; 100 Kingsley St, McLean; ☺9am-5pm Mon-Fri, 10am-4pm Sat Mar-Nov) **FREE** Learn more about barbed wire than you ever thought possible.

SCENIC DRIVE: RIVER ROAD

West of Lajitas, **Rte 170** (also known as River Rd, or *El Camino Del Rio* in Spanish) hugs the Rio Grande through some of the most spectacular and remote scenery in Big Bend country. Relatively few Big Bend visitors experience this driving adventure, even though it can be navigated in any vehicle with good brakes. Strap in and hold on: you have the Rio Grande on one side and fanciful geological formations all around, and at one point there's a 15% grade – the maximum allowable. When you reach Presidio, head north on US 67 to get to Marfa. Or, if you plan to go back the way you came, at least travel as far as Colorado Canyon (20 miles from Lajitas) for the best scenery.

Espresso...Y Poco Mas
CAFE **$**

(☑432-371-3044; 100 Milagro Rd; food $2.50-6.50; ◷8am-2pm, to 1pm summer; 🛜) We love this friendly little walk-up counter at La Posada Milagro, where you can find pastries, breakfast burritos, lunches and what might just be the best iced coffee in all of west Texas. Like the *casitas* (cottages), the cafe incorporates stone ruins for an authentic ghost-town feel, and the shady patio is a great place to soak up the ambience, make friends, fuel yourself up and use the wi-fi.

★ Starlight Theater
AMERICAN **$$**

(☑432-371-2326; www.thestarlighttheatre.com; 631 Ivey St; mains $9-25; ◷5pm-midnight) You'd think a ghost town would be dead at night (pardon the pun), but the Starlight Theater keeps things lively. This former movie theater had fallen into roofless disrepair (thus the 'starlight' name) before being converted into a restaurant. Monday nights are famous for two-for-one burgers.

🛍 Shopping

Terlingua Trading Co
GIFTS

(☑432-371-2234; 100 Ivey St; ◷11am-8pm) This store in the ghost town has great gifts, from hot sauces and wines to an impressive selection of books. Pick up a brochure on the walking tour of historic Terlingua, or buy a beer inside the store and hang out on the porch with locals at sunset.

Lajitas to Presidio

About half an hour west from the junction in Terlingua, you can trade funky and dusty for trendy and upscale (but still dusty) at **Lajitas Golf Resort & Spa** (☑432-424-5000; www.lajitasgolfresort.com; d from $169; ❄🛜🐾♨). What used to be small-town Texas got bought up and revamped into a swanky destination. The old Trading Post is gone and in its place is a new general store. (The former Trading Post was the stuff of folk legend, as it was the home of a beer-drinking goat who got elected mayor of the town. Alas, no more.)

The nine-hole golf course that included a shot over the river into Mexico has moved to drier ground to escape flooding, and now it's the 18-hole **Black Jack's Crossing. Lajitas Stables** (☑432-371-2212; www.lajitasstables.com; Rte 170; 2hr rides $70) offers short horseback trail rides as well as full-day rides to the Buena Suerte Mine and Ghost Town.

Lajitas is the eastern gateway of the massive **Big Bend Ranch State Park** (☑432-358-4444; www.tpwd.state.tx.us; off Rte 170; adult peak/nonpeak $5/3, child under 12yr free). At 433 sq miles, it's more than 11 times larger than Texas' next biggest state park (Franklin Mountains in El Paso). Taking up almost all the desert between Lajitas and Presidio, Big Bend Ranch reaches north from the Rio Grande into some of the wildest country in North America. It is full of notable features, most prominently the **Solitario**, formed 36 million years ago in a volcanic explosion. The resulting caldera measures 8 miles east to west and 9 miles north to south. As massive as it is, this former ranch is one of the best-kept secrets in Big Bend country.

Access to the park is limited and a permit is required, even if you're just passing through. Coming from Lajitas, stop at the **Barton Warnock Visitor Center** (☑432-424-3327; www.tpwd.state.tx.us; FM 170; ◷8am-4:30pm daily) for your day-use and camping permits (primitive campsites $8, backcountry $5). This education center is staffed by some of the most knowledgeable folks in the region. On the western edge of the park, you can pick up a permit at the **Fort Leaton State Historic Site** (☑432-229-3613; FM 170; ◷8am-4:30pm), a restored adobe fortress.

Central West Texas

The small towns of west Texas have become more than just the gateway to Big Bend National Park. Fort Davis, Marfa, Alpine and Marathon have a sprawling, easygoing charm and plenty of ways to keep a road-tripper entertained.

Fort Davis

False-front wooden buildings, an old fort and a stellar observatory make Texas' tallest town (elevation 5000ft) a Big Bend must-see. Its altitudinal advantage makes it a popular oasis during the summer, when west Texans head towards the mountains to escape the searing desert heat.

◉ Sights & Activities

★**McDonald Observatory** OBSERVATORY
(☏ 432-426-3640; www.mcdonaldobservatory.org; 3640 Dark Sky Dr; daytime pass adult/child 6-12yr/under 12yr $8/7/free, star parties adult/child $12/8; ☉ visitor center 10am-5:30pm; ♿) Away from all the light pollution of the big cities, the middle of west Texas has some of the clearest and darkest skies in North America, making it the perfect spot for an observatory. They have some of the biggest telescopes in the world here, perched on the peak of 6791ft Mt Locke and so enormous you can spot them from miles away.

Fort Davis National Historic Site HISTORIC SITE
(☏ 432-426-3224; www.nps.gov/foda; Hwy 17; adult/child $3/free; ☉ 8am-5pm) A remarkably well-preserved frontier military post with an impressive backdrop at the foot of **Sleeping Lion Mountain**, Fort Davis was established in 1854 and abandoned in 1891. More than 20 buildings remain – five of them restored with period furnishings – as well as 100 or so ruins.

Davis Mountains State Park PARK
(☏ 432-426-3337; http://www.tpwd.state.tx.us; Hwy 118; adult/child under 12yr $6/free) Hiking, mountain biking, horseback riding (BYO horse), bird-watching and stargazing are all big attractions here amid the most extensive mountain range in Texas.

🛏 Sleeping & Eating

Old Schoolhouse Bed & Breakfast B&B $
(☏ 432-426-2050; www.schoolhousebnb.com; 401 Front St; s incl breakfast $84-93, d $96-105; ❋ �) You can't really tell it used to be the town's

schoolhouse, but you can tell the owners put a lot of work into being great hosts, from the comfy rooms to the wonderful homemade breakfasts.

★**Indian Lodge** INN $$
(☏ lodge 432-426-3254, reservations 512-389-8982; Hwy 118; d $95-125, ste $135-150; ❋ �☃) Located in the Davis Mountains State Park, this historic 39-room inn has 18in-thick adobe walls, hand-carved cedar furniture and ceilings of pine viga and latilla that give it the look of a Southwestern pueblo – that is, one with swimming pool, gift shop and restaurant. The comfortable and surprisingly spacious guest rooms are a steal, so reserve early.

Fort Davis Drug Store AMERICAN $$
(☏ 432-426-3118; www.fortdavisdrugstore.net/; 113 N State St; mains $6-19; ☉ 7am-9pm; �I♿) Part diner, part old-fashioned soda fountain – but no 1950s nostalgia here. The theme is pure cowboy, with corrugated metal, big wooden chairs and lots of saddles providing the backdrop. Dine on country-style breakfasts, diner-style lunches and full mains at dinner. But, whatever you do, save room for a banana split (or at least a milkshake).

Murphy's Pizzeria & Café PIZZERIA $$
(107 Musquiz Dr; mains $7-13; ☉ 11am-9pm Mon & Wed-Sat) Plenty of choices, including thin-crust pizza, sandwiches and salads, make this casual cafe an easy sell.

Marfa

Founded in the 1880s Marfa got its first taste of fame when Rock Hudson, Elizabeth Taylor and James Dean came to town to film the

---

DON'T MISS

A STAR-STUDDED EVENT

On Tuesday, Friday and Saturday nights, about half an hour after sunset, **McDonald Observatory** shows off its favorite planets, galaxies and globular clusters at its popular **Star Parties**, where professional astronomers guide you in some heavy-duty stargazing. Using powerful laser pointers, they give you a tour of the night sky, and you'll get to use some of the telescopes to play planetary Peeping Tom. (It gets surprisingly brisk up there at night, so dress warmly and bring blankets.)

1956 Warner Brothers film *Giant*. It's also become a pilgrimage for art lovers, thanks to one of the world's largest installations of minimalist art. This, in turn, has attracted a disproportionate amount of art galleries, quirky lodging options and interesting restaurants.

Marfa is on its own schedule, which is pretty much made up according to whim. Plan on coming late in the week or on a weekend; half the town is closed early in the week.

◉ Sights & Activities

Marfa has all sorts of art to explore, and you can pick up a list of galleries at the **Marfa Visitors Center** (☑ 432-729-4942; www.visitmarfa.com; 302 S Highland Ave; ⊙ 9am-5pm Mon-Fri & event weekends).

Chinati Foundation Museum   MUSEUM
(☑ 432-729-4362; www.chinati.org; 1 Calvary Row; adult/student $25/10; ⊙ by guided tour only 10am & 2pm Wed-Sun) This is it. This is what all the fuss is about. Minimalist artist Donald Judd single-handedly put Marfa on the art-world map when he created the Chinati Foundation on the site of a former army post, using the abandoned buildings to create and display one of the world's largest permanent installations of minimalist art.

Marfa Lights   LOOKOUT
Ghost lights, mystery lights...call them what you want, but the real mystery of the lights that flicker on the horizon at night seems to be how many of the sightings are actually just car headlights. And because the Marfa Lights are one of west Texas' top tourist attractions, no one wants to be too specific about how to tell for sure. Decide for yourself at the **Marfa Lights Viewing Area** about 8 miles east of Marfa on Hwy 90/67.

ART IN THE MIDDLE OF NOWHERE

So you're driving along a two-lane highway in dusty west Texas, out in the middle of nowhere, when suddenly a small building appears up in the distance like a mirage. As you zip past it you glance over and see...a Prada store? Known as the **Marfa Prada** (although it's really more like Valentino), this art installation doesn't sell $1700 handbags, but it does get your attention as a tongue-in-cheek commentary on consumerism.

🛏 Sleeping & Eating

★ **El Cosmico**   CAMPGROUND **$$**
(☑ 432-729-1950; www.elcosmico.com; 802 S Highland Ave; tent camping per person $12, safari tents $65, tipis $80, trailers $110-180; ⊛) One of the funkiest choices in all of Texas, El Cosmico lets you sleep in a stylishly converted travel trailer, a tipi or a safari tent. It's not for everyone: the grounds are dry and dusty, you might have to shower outdoors, and there's no air-con (luckily, it's cool at night). But, hey, how often do you get to sleep in a Kozy Coach? The cool and colorful community lounge and the hammock grove make particularly pleasant common areas.

Thunderbird   BOUTIQUE HOTEL **$$**
(☑ 877-729-1984; www.thunderbirdmarfa.com; 601 W San Antonio St; d $120-150; ⊛⊛⊛⊛) This classic 1950s motel was reopened in 2005 as a small boutique with a spiffy new look. The rooms are hip and minimalist, and the grounds and common areas are as cool as the desert air at night.

Hotel Paisano   HOTEL **$$**
(☑ 432-729-3669; www.hotelpaisano.com; 207 N Highland Ave; d $99-149, ste $159-220; ⊛⊛⊛⊛) Marfa's historic hotel has a unique claim to fame: it's where the cast of the movie *Giant* stayed. Some of the rooms could stand a little updating, but the place does have a dignified charm, along with a snazzy indoor pool and a touch of taxidermy for good measure.

Food Shark   FOOD TRAILER **$**
(105 S Highland Ave; meals $5-8; ⊙ noon-3pm Thu-Sat) See that battered old food trailer pulled up under the open-air pavilion where the weekend farmers market is? If you do, that means Food Shark is open for business. If you're lucky enough to catch it, you'll find incredibly fresh food like pulled-pork tacos and the specialty, the Marfalafel. Daily specials are excellent, and sell out early.

★ **Cochineal**   AMERICAN **$$$**
(☑ 432-729-3300; 107 W San Antonio St; breakfast $4-10, small plates $5-15, dinner $24-28; ⊙ 9am-1pm Sat & Sun, 6-10pm Thu-Tue) This is where foodies get their fix at dinnertime, with a menu that changes regularly due to a focus on local, organic ingredients. Portions are generous, so don't be afraid to share a few small plates in lieu of a full dinner. Weekend brunch is also a treat. Reservations are recommended.

🍸 Drinking & Nightlife

★ Planet Marfa BAR

(☑432-386-5099; 200 S Abbott St; ⊘2pm-midnight Fri-Sun) Nightlife, Marfa style, is epitomized in this wonderful and funky open-air bar. There's usually live music at night, and shelters are scattered about to protect you from the elements. If you're lucky, someone will have saved you a spot inside the tipi.

Alpine

Primarily a pit stop, this university town has no real attractions of note. But it is the most sizable population (5700) in Big Bend – and the only place with big-name chain motels, numerous restaurants, grocery stores and more than one gas station.

You can get regionwide information at the **Alpine Chamber of Commerce** (☑432-837-2326; www.alpinetexas.com; 106 N 3rd St; ⊘8am-5pm Mon-Fri, to 4pm Sat).

🛏 Sleeping & Eating

Antelope Lodge CABIN $

(☑432-837-2451; www.antelopelodge.com; 2310 W Hwy 90; s $53-75, d $58-80, ste $105-120; ❄🖥) Rustic stucco cottages with Spanish-tile roofs – each one holding two guest rooms – sit sprinkled about a shady lawn. There's a casual, pleasant vibe, and the rooms have kitchenettes, making this great value for your money.

★ Holland Hotel HISTORIC HOTEL $$

(☑800-535-8040, 432-837-3844; www.thehollandhoteltexas.com; 209 W Holland Ave; d $99-120, ste $120-220; ❄🖥) Built in 1928 and beautifully renovated in 2009, the Holland is a Spanish Colonial building furnished in an understated hacienda-style decor that retains all of its 1930s charm, but with just the right contemporary touches.

Maverick Inn MOTEL $$

(☑432-837-0628; www.themaverickinn.com; 1200 E Holland Ave; r $96-117; ❄🖥) The maverick road-tripper will feel right at home at this retro motor court that's been smartly renovated to include luxury bedding and flat-screen TVs. We can't help but love this place, from the west Texas–style furnishings to the cool neon-art sign to the resident cat. Plus, the pool is mighty nice after a hot, dusty day.

Alicia's Burrito Place MEXICAN $

(☑432-837-2802; 708 E Ave G; mains $4-11; ⊘8am-8:30pm Mon, Tue & Thu-Sat, to 3pm Wed, to 4pm Sun) Alicia's is known for its quick and hot breakfast burritos, which, yes, is a Texas thing. Eggs, bacon and the like get rolled up in a portable meal you can eat with your hands (they've been known to cure a hangover or two in their time). The Mexican cheeseburger is also a favorite.

★ Reata STEAKHOUSE $$

(☑432-837-9232; www.reata.net; 203 N 5th St; lunch $9-14, dinner $10-25; ⊘11:30am-2pm & 5-10pm Mon-Sat, 11:30am-2pm Sun) Named after the ranch in the movie *Giant*, Reata does turn on the upscale ranch-style charm – at least in the front dining room, where the serious diners go. Step back into the lively bar area or onto the shady patio and it's a completely different vibe, where you can feel free to nibble your way around the menu and enjoy a margarita.

Marathon

The tiny town of Marathon (population 455) isn't much more than a main street with a few cafes and a historic hotel, but it does have two claims to fame: it's the closest town to Big Bend's north entrance, providing a last chance to fill up your car and your stomach before immersing yourself in the park. And it's got the **Gage Hotel** (☑432-386-4205; www.gagehotel.com; 102 NW 1st St/Hwy 90; d without bath $97, with bath $136-156; ❄🖥), a true Texas treasure.

Built in 1927, the Gage has a fabulous Old West style that's matched only by its love of taxidermy. Each room at this property is individually (though similarly) decorated with Native American blankets, cowboy gear and leather accents. The associated **12 Gage** (☑432-386-4205; 101 US 90 W; dinner mains $17-37; ⊘6-8:45pm Sun & Mon-Thu, to 9:45pm Fri & Sat) whips up gourmet renditions of Texas faves, and the **White Buffalo Bar** (☑432-386-4205; 101 US 90 W; ⊘5pm-midnight) invites you to enjoy a margarita while trying to ignore its namesake's glassy stare.

Before heading to Big Bend, stock up on picnic supplies at **French Co Grocer** (☑432-386-4522; www.frenchcogrocer.com; 206 N Ave D; ⊘7:30am-9pm Mon-Fri, from 8am Sat, from 9am Sun), or enjoy them at the tables outside at this charming little grocery – formerly the WM French General Merchandise store, established in 1900.

El Paso

Well, you've made it. You're just about as far west in Texas as you can go. Surrounded mostly by New Mexico and Mexico, El Paso seems to have more in common with its non-Texas neighbors than it does with Texas itself.

Sadly, El Paso and its sister city – Ciudad Juárez, Mexico, which is right across the river – have had a bit of a falling out. At one time the two cities were inextricably linked, with tourists streaming back and forth across the Good Neighbor International Bridge all day long. But with the rise in gang- and drug-related violence, Juárez has become so dangerous that there is now little traffic between the two sides.

◉ Sights & Activities

★ El Paso Museum of Art   MUSEUM

(☎ 915-532-1707; www.elpasoartmuseum.org; 1 Arts Festival Plaza; admission charge for special exhibits; ⊙ 9am-5pm Tue-Sat, to 9pm Thu, noon-5pm Sun) FREE This thoroughly enjoyable museum is in a former Greyhound bus station. They'd want us to brag about their *Madonna and Child* (c 1200), but the Southwestern art is terrific, and the engaging modern pieces round out the collection nicely. All this, and it's free?! Well done, El Paso, well done.

El Paso Holocaust Museum   MUSEUM

(www.elpasoholocaustmuseum.org; 715 N Oregon St; ⊙ 9am-4pm Tue-Fri, 1-5pm Sat & Sun) FREE This Holocaust Museum is as much a surprise inside as out for its thoughtful and moving exhibits that are imaginatively presented for maximum impact.

Franklin Mountains State Park   PARK

(www.tpwd.state.tx.us; Transmountain Rd; adult/child $5/free; ⊙ 8am-5pm Mon-Fri, 6:30am-8pm Sat & Sun) At 23,863 acres, this is the largest

---

WHAT TIME IS IT?

When it comes to time zones, El Paso sides with New Mexico, conforming to Mountain Time rather than Central Time like the rest of Texas. Confusing? Occasionally. If you're telling someone in neighboring Van Horn or Fort Stockton what time you'll meet them, be sure to add on the extra hour you'll lose just by leaving El Paso.

---

urban park in the US. Although it's in the middle of a city, it's home to ringtail cats, coyotes and a number of other smaller animals and reptiles, and it's capped by 7192ft North Franklin Peak.

Wyler Aerial Tramway   CABLE CAR

(☎ 915-566-6622; 1700 McKinley Ave; adult/child 12yr & under $8/4; ⊙ noon-7pm Fri & Sat, 10am-5pm Sun) Sure, you'd feel a sense of accomplishment if you hiked to the top of the Franklin Mountains. We're not suggesting you take the easy way out (or are we?), but it only takes about four minutes for a gondola ride to the top. After gliding 2400ft and gaining 940ft in elevation, you'll reach the viewing platform on top of Ranger Peak, where you'll enjoy spectacular views of Texas, New Mexico and Mexico.

⌷ Sleeping

In addition to the exceptions below, there are scads of characterless chain motels found along I-10.

★ El Paso Suites   HOTEL $

(☎ 915-779-6222; www.elpasosuiteshotel.com; 6100 Gateway Blvd E; ste $80-120; P ✻ 🕸 🛜 🏊) This is the only independent hotel in town – but it used to be an Embassy Suites, so the rooms still have that generic chain-hotel feel. Still, it's a bargain, especially considering you get two full rooms. Each suite opens onto an eight-story skylit atrium with iron balconies, which does actually make up for the rooms quite a bit.

Coral Motel   MOTEL $

(☎ 915-772-3263; fax 915-779-6053; 6420 Montana Ave; s/d $45/55; ✻) Anyone who loves 1950s roadside nostalgia will feel right at home at this funky little motel that mixes genres wildly, from the Spanish-style barrel-tile roof to the *Jetsons*-esque sign to the mishmash interiors.

Camino Real Hotel   HOTEL $$

(☎ 915-534-3000, 800-769-4300; www.caminorealelpaso.com; 101 S El Paso St; d $72-109, ste from $132; ✻ @ 🛜 🏊) The only US location of an upscale Mexican hotel chain, the historic Camino Real – which has been in operation for over 100 years – has a prime location, steps from the convention center and downtown museums. There's also a gorgeous bar with an art-glass dome; large, comfortable rooms; and pretty friendly service, even when it's swamped.

CUSTOM BOOTS

The ultimate west-Texas souvenir? A gorgeous pair of cowboy boots made just for you. As bootmaker to the stars, **Rocketbuster Boots** (☑915-541-1300; www.rocketbuster. com; 115 S Anthony St; ☺showroom 8am-4pm Mon-Fri, personalized service by appointment) has shod such celebrities as Julia Roberts, Dwight Yoakum, Emmylou Harris and Oprah Winfrey. Its over-the-top designs include everything from wild floral prints to 1950s-era pin-up cowgirls to Day of the Dead skeletons.

Sure, you could just pick up a pair of mass-produced boots somewhere else, like most people do – after all, these beauties start at $850 and go up to $3500 or more for a one-of-a-kind design – but it's not the same as having something created just for you. Your feet will know the difference, and besides, you'll be much more likely to get stopped on the street by awestruck admirers.

One visit to the showroom and you might be a little awestruck yourself. It's not a shop, per se, but there are lots of samples so you can get some inspiration. Call first if you'd like some personalized attention from owner-designer Nevena Christi. Otherwise, poke your head in for a visual treat, both from the boots and from the whimsical shop that's decorated with space-age gadgets and cowboy memorabilia.

✖ Eating

Mexican is the food of choice in El Paso; the town's known for a special bright-red chili-and-tomato sauce used on enchiladas. Tex-Mex in El Paso is cheap and abundant.

L&J Cafe   MEXICAN $
(☑915-566-8418; http://landjcafe.com; 3622 E Missouri Ave; mains $7-12; ☺10am-9pm) This El Paso staple is located next to the Concordia Cemetery. It's a great place to cure a hangover on Saturday morning, when it serves its famous *menudo* (tripe stew with chili). If the outside looks divey, it's because it's been open since 1927. Don't be scared; the inside is much more inviting.

Chicos Tacos   MEXICAN $
(5305 Montana Ave; tacos $1-4; ☺9am-1:30am Sun-Thu, to 3am Fri & Sat) With several locations, Chicos Tacos specializes in its namesake fare – with lots of garlic. Expect a crowd from about 10pm to midnight, when El Pasoans citywide experience a collective craving.

★ Tabla   TAPAS $$
(115 Durango St; small plates $6-15; ☺11am-10pm Mon-Thu, to midnight Fri, 5pm-midnight Sat, 9:30am-3pm Sun) Get ready to share all sorts of awesomeness. The small plates here are less Spanish-style tapas and more like an excuse to try a little bit of everything, like a big buffet of fun. The stylish warehouse space has tall ceilings, an open kitchen and the requisite pig motif sprinkled about (we're guessing you've spotted the mighty pig in many a trendy restaurant on your US travels), all making the vibe refreshingly current.

Crave   AMERICAN $$
(☑915-351-3677; www.cravekitchenandbar.com; 300 Cincinnati Ave; mains $9-30; ☺7am-11pm Mon-Sat, to 6pm Sun) Winning bonus points for style – from the cool sign to the forks hanging from the ceiling – this hip little eatery serves up comfort food and classics with extra flair. Although dinner goes up to $30, there's still plenty to munch on in the $15-and-under category. There's also a newer branch on the **east side** (☑915-594-7971; 11990 Rojas Dr; ☺7am-11pm Mon-Sat, to 6pm Sun).

★ Cattleman's Steakhouse STEAKHOUSE $$$
(☑915-544-3200; Indian Cliffs Ranch; mains $16-38; ☺5-10pm Mon-Fri, 12:30-10pm Sat, 12:30-9pm Sun; ▣) This place is 20 miles east of the city, but local folks would probably drive 200 miles to eat here. The food is good, and the scenery is even better. Portions are huge, and for just $6 extra you can share a main course and gain full access to the all-you-can-eat sides.

☆ Entertainment

Bars come and go quickly in El Paso. Your best bet is to head to the mini-entertainment district near the University of Texas El Paso (around Cincinnati St between Mesa and Stanton) to see what's happening in the bars and restaurants that are clustered there. For cultural and music listings, pick up the free weekly **El Paso Scene** (www.epscene.com) or the Friday 'Tiempo' supplement to the **El Paso Times** (www.elpasotimes.com).

🔒 Shopping

On I-10 east of town, several warehouselike shops sell all the goodies you can find in Mexico – pottery, blankets, silver – at similar prices.

El Paso Saddleblanket   SOUVENIRS
(☑915-544-1000; www.saddleblanket.com; 6926 Gateway Blvd E; ⊙9am-5pm Mon-Sat) 'Incredible 2-acre shopping adventure!' the billboards scream. This place is indeed huge, and it's chock-full of all things Southwestern. Stuff your suitcases with pottery, blankets, turquoise jewelry, even a sombrero if you must. They've got mounted steer horns, but we can tell you right now you're not going to be able to carry them onto the plane.

El Paso Connection   HOMEWARES
(☑915-852-0898; 14301 Gateway Blvd; ⊙9am-5pm Mon-Sun) Competing with El Paso Saddleblanket, this sprawling place east of town is made up of several showrooms and warehouses that are crowded with antique and imported goods, such as lampshades made from cowhide and large pieces of Southwestern-motif furniture.

ℹ️ Information

El Paso Public Library (☑915-543-5433; www.elpasolibrary.org; 501 N Oregon St; ⊙10am-7pm Mon-Thu, 11am-6pm Fri, 10am-6pm Sat, noon-6pm Sun) has free internet access.

The **El Paso Visitors Center** (☑800-351-6024, 915-534-0600; www.visitelpaso.com; 1 Civic Center Plaza; ⊙8am-5pm Mon-Fri, 10am-3pm Sat) stocks racks and racks of brochures, and the staff are quite helpful.

ℹ️ Getting There & Around

El Paso International Airport (ELP; www.elpasointernationalairport.com), 8 miles northeast of downtown off I-10, serves 16 US and two Mexican cities. Numerous chain rental-car companies are on site (you really need a car here).

ℹ️ HOT TOPIC: MEXICO BORDERLANDS

Tex has always mixed well with Mex. But the flow of Texans casually crossing from El Paso into Mexican border towns has slowed to a trickle due to drug cartel-related violence. The state department urges caution when visiting all border towns in Mexico – as do we.

Amtrak's Florida–California *Sunset Limited* stops at **Union Depot** (www.amtrak.com; 700 San Francisco Ave). The terminal for **Greyhound** (www.greyhound.com; 200 W San Antonio Ave) is four blocks from the center of downtown.

Hueco Tanks State Historical Park

About 32 miles east of El Paso is the 860-acre **Hueco Tanks State Historical Park** (☑park 915-857-1135, reservations 512-389-8900; www.tpwd.state.tx.us; 6900 Hueco Tanks Rd/FM 2775; adult/child $7/free; ⊙8am-6pm). Popular today among rock climbers, the area has attracted humans for as many as 10,000 years, and park staff estimate there are more than 2000 pictographs at the site, some dating back 5000 years.

To minimize human impact, a daily visitor quota is enforced; make reservations 24 hours in advance to gain entry. You can explore the North Mountain area by yourself, but to hike deeper into the park – where the more interesting pictographs are – you have to reserve and join one of the pictograph, birding or hiking **tours** (☑915-857-1135; per person $2; ⊙call for schedule).

Guadalupe Mountains National Park

We won't go so far as to call it Texas' best-kept secret, but the fact is that a lot of Texans aren't even aware of the **Guadalupe Mountains National Park** (☑915-828-3251; www.nps.gov/gumo; US Hwy 62/180; 7-day pass adult/child under 16yr $5/free). It's just this side of the Texas–New Mexico state line and a long drive from practically everywhere in the state.

Despite its low profile, it is a Texas high spot, both literally and figuratively. At 8749ft, **Guadalupe Peak** is the highest point in the Lone Star State. The fall foliage in **McKittrick Canyon** is the best in west Texas, and more than half the park is a federally designated wilderness area.

The National Park Service has deliberately curbed development to keep the park wild. There are no restaurants or indoor accommodations and only a smattering of services and programs. There are also no paved roads within the park, so whatever you want to see, you're going to have to work for it. But if you're looking for some of the best hiking and high-country splendor Texas can muster, you should put this park on your itinerary.

MARK NEWMAN / GETTY IMAGES ©

USA's National Parks

National parks are America's big backyards. Every cross-country road trip rolls through the USA's big-shouldered cities, but many visitors skip these remarkable parks, rich in unspoiled wilderness, rare wildlife and history. There's no better time to go than now, as the National Park Service (NPS) celebrates its upcoming centennial in 2016.

Above Glacier National Park (p793)

Contents

Evolution of the Parks

Many parks look much the same as they did centuries ago, when this nation was just starting out. From craggy islands off the Atlantic Coast, to prairie grasslands and buffalo herds across the Great Plains, to the Rocky Mountains raising their jagged teeth along the Continental Divide, and onward to the tallest trees on earth – coast redwoods – standing sentinel on Pacific shores, you'll be amazed by the USA's natural bounty.

Go West!

Historically speaking, the nation's voracious appetite for land and material riches drove not only the false doctrine of Manifest Destiny, but also a bonanza of building – pioneer homesteads, farms, livestock fences, great dams, roadways and train tracks from sea to shining

sea. This artificial infrastructure quickly swallowed up vast wilderness tracts from the Appalachian Mountains to the mighty Mississippi River and far into the West. That is, until the creation of a web of federally protected public lands, starting with the national parks.

Voices in the Wilderness

During a trip to the Dakotas in 1831, artist George Catlin had a dream. As he watched the USA's rapid westward expansion harm both the wilderness and Native American tribes, Catlin penned a call to action for 'a nation's park, containing man and beast, in all the wild and freshness of their nature's beauty!' Four decades later, Congress created Yellowstone National Park, the nation's first.

The late 19th century saw a rush of new parks – including Yosemite, Sequoia

1. The Fly Geyser, Great Basin National Park (p824)
2. Canyonlands National Park (p870)
3. Bison, Badlands National Park (p641)

and Mount Rainier – as a nascent conservation movement fired up public enthusiasm. The poetic herald of the Sierra Nevada, naturalist John Muir, galvanized the public while campaigning for a national park system, delivering open-air lectures and writing about the spiritual value of wilderness above its economic opportunities.

Growing the Parks

Inspired by a visit to Yosemite with Muir in 1903, President Theodore Roosevelt, a big-game hunter and rancher, worked to establish more wildlife preserves, national forests and national parks and monuments. The Antiquities Act of 1906 preserved a priceless trove of archaeological sites from Native American cultures, including Mesa Verde, and two years later the Grand Canyon itself.

The National Park Service (NPS) was created in 1916, with self-made millionaire and tireless parks promoter Stephen Mather as its first director. In the 1930s, President Franklin D Roosevelt added 50 more historic sites and monuments to the NPS portfolio and hired Depression-era Civilian Conservation Corps (CCC) workers to build scenic byways and create recreational opportunities in the parks.

After WWII, the NPS kept growing. First lady during the 1960s, 'Lady Bird' Johnson contributed to the groundbreaking report *With Heritage So Rich*, which led to the National Historic Preservation Act of 1966 expanding the NPS system. Her parks advocacy also influenced her husband, President Lyndon Johnson, who enacted more environmental-protection legislation than any administration since FDR.

The Parks Today

Today the NPS protects over 400 parklands and more than 80 million acres of land from coast to coast. Recent additions designated by President Barack Obama include noteworthy historical sites: Ohio's Charles Young Buffalo Soldiers National Monument, Maryland's Harriet Tubman Underground Railroad National Monument and First State National Monument in Delaware and Pennsylvania. Thousands more natural areas are overseen by other federal land-management agencies, including the US Forest Service (USFS; www.fs.fed.us), US Fish & Wildlife Service (USFWS; www.fws. gov) and Bureau of Land Management (BLM; www.blm.gov).

Not all national parks growth has been free of controversy, for example, when local residents protest restrictions on public land use, or when agency goals conflict with the self-determination rights of Native Americans. Federal budget cuts and the enormous pressures of 280 million visitors every year have also taken huge tolls on the parks, as has global warming, leading to habitat loss and species extinction. Recent media spotlights that have helped sway public opinion about the vital importance of parks include Ken Burns' documentary film *The National Parks: America's Best Idea* (www.pbs.org/nationalparks).

Practical Tips for Park Visitors

Park entrance fees vary from nothing at all to $25 per vehicle. The **'America the Beautiful' annual pass** ($80; http://store. usgs.gov/pass), which admits four adults and all children under 16 years old free to all federal recreational lands for 12

1. The Subway, Zion National Park (p874)
2. Glacier National Park (p793)
3. Grand Canyon National Park (p840)

calendar months, is sold at park entrances and visitor centers. Lifetime senior-citizen passes ($10) and access passes for those with disabilities (free) are also available. ATMs are scarce in parks, so bring cash for campsites, permits, tours and activities.

Park lodges and campgrounds book up far in advance; for summer vacations, reserve six months to one year ahead. Some parks offer first-come, first-served campgrounds – if so, try to arrive between 10am and noon, when other campers may be checking out. For overnight backpacking and some day hikes, you'll need a wilderness permit; the number of permits is often subject to quotas, so apply far in advance (up to six months before your trip). Some park stores sell basic camping and outdoor supplies, but prices are usually inflated and some items may be out of stock – try to bring your own gear if you can.

ECO-TRAVEL IN THE PARKS

Do your utmost to preserve the parks' wild and beautiful natural environments. Follow the principles of the Leave No Trace (www.lnt.org) outdoor ethics. To help kids learn about conservation and how they can help protect the parks, inquire at visitor centers about free (or low-cost) junior ranger activity programs (www.nps.gov/learn/juniorranger.cfm).

Park policies and regulations may seem restrictive, but they're intended to keep you safe and to protect both natural and cultural resources. Pets are not allowed outside of the parks' developed areas, where they must be leashed and attended to at all times.

Flora & Fauna

Along winding scenic drives and forested hiking trails, from mountain wildflower meadows to arid deserts and deep river-cut canyons, the USA's national parks present prime-time opportunities for wildlife watching. They're also biodiverse havens for endangered and threatened species that you may not be able to spot anywhere else.

1. Grizzly bear
Prowling from the Rocky Mountains up into Alaska, these fierce, omnivorous predators can grow up to 8ft tall and weigh 800lb.

2. Black bear
Smaller than their grizzly cousins, these skilled tree climbers range almost continent-wide. Their fur shows a variety of colors, even cinnamon and blond.

3. Moose
The biggest of all deer species, this forest-dwelling grazer's giant antlers spread up to 6ft across. Although sedentary, moose can surprisingly sprint up to 35mph.

4. Gray wolf
These howling pack hunters were nearly extirpated from the lower 48 states, but controversial conservation projects have reintroduced them to the Rocky Mountains.

5. Bison
Few animals evoke the spirit of the West more than the American bison, also known as the buffalo, which 19th-century hunters drove almost to extinction.

6. Beaver
Busy builders of river dams, canals and lodges with underwater entrances, North America's largest rodent has soft fur historically prized for hat-making.

7. Alligator
Native only to the US and China, these prehistoric lizard-like amphibians inhabit freshwater swamps, marshlands, ponds, rivers and lakes in southeastern USA.

8. Bighorn sheep
Identified by their curved horns, these sure-footed mountain climbers range from the Sierra Nevada and Rocky Mountains to lowland deserts in California and the Southwest.

9. Desert tortoise
Long-lived natives of the Mojave and Sonoran Deserts, slow-moving tortoises can go long periods without food or water. Habitat loss now threatens the species.

10. Bald eagle
The white-headed national bird has soared off the endangered species list. Feeding mostly on fish, these birds of prey build the world's largest tree nests.

11. Coast redwood
Holding the world's record for the tallest tree, coast redwoods thrive in forests along the foggy Pacific shores of Northern California and southern Oregon.

12. Saguaro
Symbols of the desert Southwest, these tree-sized cacti can grow over 60ft tall and live for up to 150 years.

Eastern USA

Roam from New England's rocky, wild and weather-beaten shores to Florida's sugar-sand beaches shaded by palm trees. Or immerse yourself in the USA's wealth of historic sites starting in the nation's capital, Washington DC, then roll through the pastoral hills of old-timey Appalachia on the scenic Blue Ridge Parkway.

Great Smoky Mountains National Park

Receiving more visitors than any other US national park, this southern Appalachian woodland pocket protects thickly forested ridges where black bears, white-tailed deer, antlered elk, wild turkeys and more than 1500 kinds of flowering plants find sanctuary.

Acadia National Park

Catch the first sunrise of the new year atop Cadillac Mountain, the highest point on the USA's eastern seaboard. Or come in summer to play on end-of-the-world islands tossed along this craggy, wind-whipped North Atlantic coastline.

Shenandoah National Park

Drive from the Great Smoky Mountains north along the historic Blue Ridge Parkway past Appalachian hillside hamlets to Shenandoah, a pastoral preserve where waterfall and woodland paths await, just 75 miles from the nation's capital.

Everglades National Park

Home to snaggle-toothed crocodiles, stealthy panthers, pink flamingos and mellow manatees, South Florida's Caribbean bays and 'rivers of grass' attract wildlife watchers, especially to unique flood-plain islands called hammocks.

Mammoth Cave National Park

With hidden underground rivers and more than 400 miles of explored terrain, the world's longest cave system shows off sci-fi-looking stalactites and stalagmites up close.

1. Appalachian Trail (p327) **2.** Great Smoky Mountains National Park (p349) **3.** Acadia National Park (p249)

EMILY RIDDELL / GETTY IMAGES ©

St Mary's Lake, Glacier National Park (p793) **2.** Grand Prismatic Spring (p777), Yellowstone National Park **3.** Elk, Rocky Mountain National Park (p751)

Great Plains & Rocky Mountains

Wildflower-strewn meadows, saw-toothed peaks and placid lakes along the spine of the Continental Divide are among America's most prized national parks. Equally rich in wildlife, Native American culture and Old West history, the Rocky Mountains and Great Plains embody the American frontier.

Yellowstone National Park

The country's oldest national park is full of geysers, hot springs and a wealth of megafauna – grizzly bears, bison, elk and more – that range across North America's largest intact natural ecosystem.

Rocky Mountain National Park

Atop the Continental Divide, jagged mountain peaks are only the start of adventures at this park, speckled with more than 150 lakes and 450 miles of streams running through aromatic pine forests.

Glacier National Park

Fly along the high-altitude Going-to-the-Sun Rd, which appears to defy gravity as it winds for 50 miles through the mountainous landscape that some Native Americans call 'The Backbone of the World.'

Badlands National Park

Amid native prairie grasslands, where bison and bighorn sheep roam, this alarmingly named park is a captivating outdoor museum of geology, with fossil beds revealing traces of North America's prehistoric past.

Mesa Verde National Park

Clamber onto the edge of the Colorado Plateau to visit the well-preserved Native American cliff dwellings of Ancestral Puebloans who inhabited the remote Four Corners area for many generations.

JOHN ELK III / GETTY IMAGES ©

Grand Canyon National Park (p840) **2.** Double Arch, Arches
ional Park (p869) **3.** Saguaro National Park (p851)

3

Southwest

It takes time to explore the Southwest's meandering canyon country, arid deserts and Native American archaeological ruins. An ancient, colorful chasm carved by one of the USA's most powerful rivers is just the beginning. Meander down backcountry byways to discover ancient sand dunes, twisting slot canyons and giant cacti.

Grand Canyon National Park

Arguably the USA's best-known natural attraction, the Grand Canyon is an incredible spectacle of colored rock strata, carved by the irresistible flow of the Colorado River. Its buttes and peaks spire into a landscape that's always changing with the weather.

Zion National Park

Pioneers almost believed they'd reached the promised land at this desert oasis, run through by a life-giving river. Get a thrill by rappelling down a slot canyon or pulling yourself up the cables to aerial Angels Landing viewpoint.

Bryce Canyon National Park

On the same geological 'Grand Staircase' as the Grand Canyon, Bryce Canyon shows off a whimsical landscape of totem-shaped hoodoo rock formations, some rising as tall as a 10-story building.

Arches National Park

Just outside the four-seasons base camp of Moab, Utah, this iconic landscape of more than 2000 naturally formed sandstone arches is most mesmerizing at sunrise and sunset, when the gorgeously eroded desert rocks seem to glow.

Saguaro National Park

An icon of the American West, spiky saguaro cacti stretch toward the sky in this Arizona desert park, where coyotes howl, spotted owls hoot and desert tortoises slowly crawl through the sere landscape.

West Coast

Thunderous waterfalls, the sirens' call of glacier-carved peaks and the world's tallest, biggest *and* oldest trees are just some of the natural wonders that California offers. Meet smoking volcanic mountains, misty rainforests and untamed beaches in the Pacific Northwest.

Yosemite National Park

Visit glaciated valleys, alpine wildflower meadows, groves of giant sequoia trees and earth-shaking waterfalls that tumble over sheer granite cliffs in the USA's second-oldest national park.

Olympic National Park

Lose yourself in the primeval rainforests, mist-clouded mountains carved by glaciers and lonely, wild Pacific Coast beaches. Watch salmon swim free in the restored Elwha River, site of the world's largest dam removal project.

1. Redwood trees 2. Death Valley National Park (p949)
3. Yosemite Valley (p1009), Yosemite National Park

Death Valley & Joshua Tree National Parks

Slide down sand dunes and stroll across salt flats at Badwater, the USA's lowest elevation spot, in hellishly hot Death Valley. Or hop between boulders, native fan-palm oases and forests of crooked Joshua trees, all in Southern California's deserts.

Mt Rainier National Park

Meet a glacier-covered, rumbling giant that may have last erupted only 120 years ago and still reigns over the Pacific Northwest's volcanic Cascades Range. Day hike among wildflower meadows or tramp across snow fields even in midsummer.

Redwood National Park

Be awed by towering ancient stands of coast redwoods, the tallest trees on earth, along the often foggy Northern California coast. Spot shaggy Roosevelt elk foraging in woodland prairies, then go tide-pooling along rugged beaches.

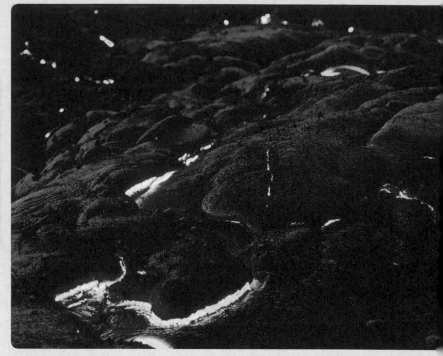

Lava flow, Kilauea Volcano, Hawai'i Volcanoes National Park (p111

Final Frontiers

Officially US states for little more than 50 years, far-flung Alaska and Hawaii offer some unforgettable wilderness experiences you just can't get in the 'Lower 48' or on 'da mainland'. Active volcanoes, icy glaciers, rare and endangered wildlife and a rich vein of historic sites make these parks worth a detour.

Alaska

In 1980, the Alaska National Interest Lands Conservation Act turned more than 47 million acres of wilderness over to the NPS, more than doubling the federal agency's holdings with a single stroke of President Jimmy Carter's pen.

Today Alaska's national parks give visitors a chance to see glacial icebergs calve at Kenai Fjords and Glacier Bay, watch brown bears catch salmon at Katmai or summit the USA's highest peak, Denali (Mt McKinley). Along the aquatic Inside Passage, admire Native Alaskan totem poles in Sitka and retrace the hardy steps of 19th-century Klondike gold-rush pioneers at Skagway.

Hawaii

The USA's remotest archipelago is tailor-made for tropical escapades. On Hawai'i, the Big Island, witness the world's longest continuous volcanic eruption or possibly see lava flow at Hawai'i Volcanoes National Park, then snorkel with sea turtles beside an ancient Hawaiian place of refuge on the Kona coast. On Maui, trek deep inside a volcano and swim in stream-fed pools at mind-bogglingly diverse Haleakalā National Park. Last, pay your respects to O'ahu's WWII-era USS Arizona Memorial.

Rocky Mountains

Includes ➡

Best Places to Eat

➡ Root Down (p744)

➡ Salt (p749)

➡ Rickshaw (p798)

➡ Pine Creek Cookhouse (p761)

➡ Silk Road (p791)

Best Places to Stay

➡ Curtis (p742)

➡ Boise Guest House (p796)

➡ Chautauqua Lodge (p748)

➡ Alpine House (p785)

➡ Old Faithful Inn (p781)

Why Go?

The high backbone of the lower 48, the Rockies are nature on steroids, with rows of snowcapped peaks, rugged canyons and wild rivers running buckshot over the Western states. With its beauty and vitality, it's no wonder that 100 years ago, it beckoned ailing patients with last-ditch hopes for cures.

The healing power of the Rocky Mountains persists. You can choose between tranquility (try Wyoming, the USA's most under-populated state) and adrenaline (measured in vertical drop). Locals love a good frozen, wet or mud-spattered adventure and, with plenty of climbing, skiing and white-water paddling, it's easy to join in. Afterwards, relax by soaking in hot springs under a roof of stars, sipping cold microbrews or feasting farm-to-table style.

Lastly, don't miss the supersized charms of Yellowstone, Rocky Mountain, Grand Teton and Glacier national parks, where the big five (grizzly bears, moose, bison, mountain lions and wolves) still roam wild.

When to Go
Denver

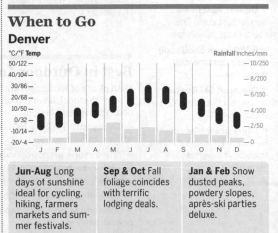

Jun–Aug Long days of sunshine ideal for cycling, hiking, farmers markets and summer festivals.

Sep & Oct Fall foliage coincides with terrific lodging deals.

Jan & Feb Snow dusted peaks, powdery slopes, après-ski parties deluxe.

DON'T MISS

Don a Stetson hat and gallop the sagebrush wilderness of Wyoming or Montana. Guest ranches offer memorable summer rides in the Rockies.

Fast Facts

→ **Hub city** Denver (population 600,000)

→ **Mountains** Colorado has the most summits over 14,000ft in the continental US

→ **Time zone** Mountain (two hours behind NYC)

Did You Know?

Pitch your tent in Yellowstone National Park and you'll be sleeping atop one of the world's largest supervolcanoes. It's active every 640,000 years: an eruption is due soon – give or take 10,000 years.

Resources

→ **Denver Post** (www. denverpost.com) The region's top newspaper

→ **5280** (www.5280.com) Denver's best monthly magazine

→ **Discount Ski Rental** (www.rentskis.com) At major resorts

→ **14ers** (www.14ers.com) Resource for hikers climbing the Rockies' highest summits

Getting There & Around

Denver (DEN) has the only major international airport in the region. Both Denver and Colorado Springs offer flights on smaller planes to Jackson, WY, Boise, ID, Bozeman, MT, Aspen, CO, and other destinations.

Two Amtrak train routes pass through the region. *California Zephyr,* traveling daily between Emeryville, CA and Chicago, IL, has six stops in Colorado, including Denver, Fraser-Winter Park, Glenwood Springs and Grand Junction. *Empire Builder* runs daily from Seattle, WA, or Portland, OR, to Chicago, IL, with 12 stops in Montana (including Whitefish and East and West Glacier) and one stop in Idaho at Sandpoint.

Greyhound travels some parts of the Rocky Mountains. But to really get out and explore you'll need a car.

NATIONAL PARKS

The region is home to some of the USA's biggest national parks. In Colorado, **Rocky Mountain National Park** offers awesome hiking through alpine forests and tundra. There's also the Sahara-like wonder of **Great Sand Dunes National Park** and **Mesa Verde National Park**, an archaeological preserve with elaborate cliff-side dwellings.

Wyoming has **Grand Teton National Park**, with dramatic craggy peaks, and **Yellowstone National Park**, the country's first national park, a true wonderland of volcanic geysers, hot springs and forested mountains. In Montana, **Glacier National Park** features high sedimentary peaks, small glaciers and lots of wildlife, including grizzly bears. Idaho is home to **Hells Canyon National Recreation Area**, where the Snake River carves the deepest canyon in North America. **National Park Service** (NPS; www.nps. gov) also manages over two dozen other historic sites, monuments, nature preserves and recreational areas in Idaho.

Best in Outdoor Instruction

With plenty of wilderness and tough terrain, the Rockies are a natural school for outdoor skills, and a perfect place to observe nature in action.

→ **Chicks with Picks** (p766) Fun ice-climbing clinics for women, by women.

→ **Yellowstone Institute** (www.yellowstoneassociation.org) Study wolves, ecology or arts with experts in the park.

→ **Teton Science Schools Ecology** (p784) Best for kids; both about nature and experiencing it.

→ **Colorado Mountain School** (p753) Climb a peak safely or learn belay skills.

History

Before the late 18th century, when French trappers and Spaniards stepped in, the Rocky Mountain area was a land of many tribes, including the Nez Percé, the Shoshone, the Crow, the Lakota and the Ute.

Meriwether Lewis and William Clark claimed enduring fame after the USA bought almost all of present-day Montana, Wyoming and eastern Colorado in the 1803 Louisiana Purchase. Their epic survey covering 8000 miles in three years. Their success urged on other adventurers, setting migration in motion. Wagon trains voyaged to the Rockies right into the 20th century, only temporarily slowed by the completion of the Transcontinental Railroad across southern Wyoming in the late 1860s.

To accommodate settlers, the US purged the western frontier of the Spanish, British and, in a truly shameful era, most of the Native American population. The government signed endless treaties to defuse Native American objections to increasing settlement, but always reneged and shunted tribes onto smaller reservations. Gold-miners' incursions into Native American territory in Montana and the building of US Army forts along the Bozeman Trail ignited a series of wars with the Lakota, Cheyenne, Arapaho and others.

ROCKY MOUNTAINS IN...

Two Weeks

Start your Rocky Mountain odyssey in the **Denver** area. Go tubing, vintage-clothes shopping or biking in outdoor-mad, boho **Boulder**, then soak up the liberal rays eavesdropping at a sidewalk cafe. Enjoy the vistas of the **Rocky Mountain National Park** before heading west on I-70 to play in the mountains around **Breckenridge**, which also has the best beginner slopes in Colorado. Go to ski and mountain bike mecca **Steamboat Springs** before crossing the border into Wyoming.

Your first stop in the state should be **Lander**, rock-climbing destination extraordinaire. Continue north to chic **Jackson** and the majestic **Grand Teton National Park** before hitting iconic **Yellowstone National Park**. Save at least three days for exploring this geyser-packed wonderland.

Cross the state line into 'big sky country' and slowly make your way northwest through Montana, stopping in funky **Bozeman** and lively **Missoula** before visiting **Flathead Lake**. Wind up your trip in Idaho. If it's summer, you can paddle the wild whitewater of **Hells Canyon National Recreation Area** before continuing to up-and-coming **Boise**. End your trip with a few days skiing **Sun Valley** and partying in **Ketchum**. The town and ski resort, despite being *the* winter playground *du jour* for Hollywood, are refreshingly unpretentious.

One Month

With a month on your hands, you can really delve into the region's off-the-beaten-path treasures. Follow the two-week itinerary, but dip southwest in Colorado – an up-and-coming wine region – before visiting Wyoming. Ride the 4WD trails around **Ouray**. Be sure to visit **Mesa Verde National Park** and its ancient cliff dwellings.

In Montana, you'll want to get lost backpacking in the **Bob Marshall Wilderness Complex** and visit **Glacier National Park** before the glaciers disappear altogether. In Idaho, spend more time playing in **Sun Valley** and be sure to explore the shops, pubs and yummy organic restaurants in delightful little **Ketchum**. With a one-month trip, you also have time to drive along a few of Idaho's fantastically remote scenic byways. Make sure you cruise Hwy 75 from Sun Valley north to **Stanley**. Situated on the wide banks of the Salmon River, this stunning mountain hamlet is completely surrounded by national forest land and wilderness areas. Wild good looks withstanding, Stanley is also blessed with world-class trout fishing and mild to wild rafting. Take Hwy 21 from Stanley to Boise. This scenic drive takes you through miles of dense ponderosa forests, and past some excellent, solitary riverside camping spots – some of which come with their own natural hot springs pools.

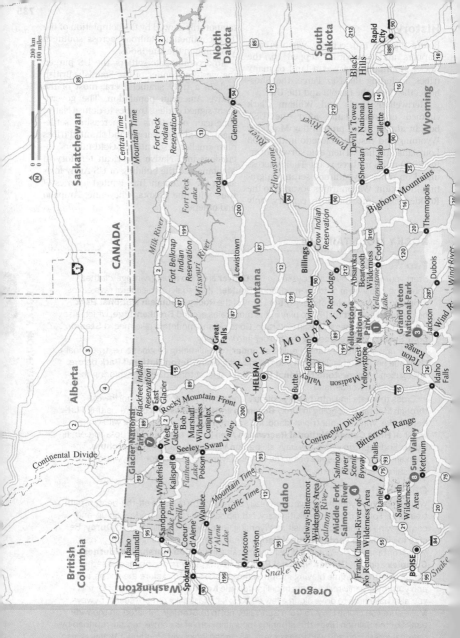

Rocky Mountains Highlights

1 Spotting bears, bison and geysers at **Yellowstone National Park** (p777).

2 Reveling in Hollywood gone cowboy in the party resort of **Aspen** (p759).

3 Hiking and climbing the craggy wilderness of **Grand Teton National Park** (p782).

4 Paddling top-notch white water at the **Middle Fork of the Salmon River** (p799).

5 Getting your groove on in the outdoor mecca of **Boulder** (p747).

6 Roaming the San Juan's picturesque Wild West towns of **Southern Colorado** (p755).

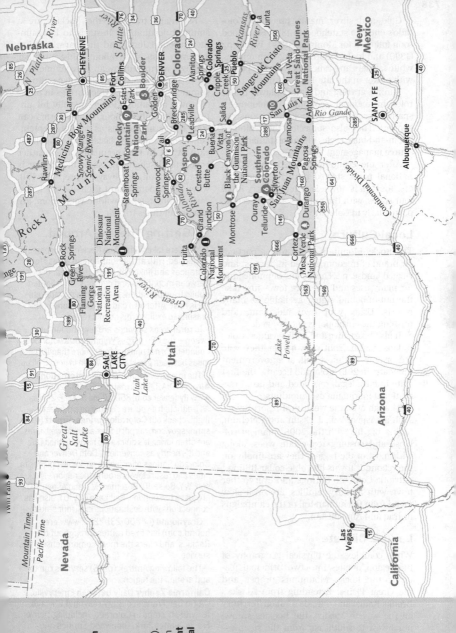

7 Enjoying the untamed splendor of **Glacier National Park** (p793).

8 Powder skiing in the sunshine of classic ski resort **Sun Valley** (p797).

9 Scaling the heights of majestic **Rocky Mountain National Park** (p751).

10 Roaming the high desertscapes of **Great Sand Dunes National Park** (p773).

Gold and silver mania preceded Colorado's entry to statehood in 1876. Statehood soon followed for Montana (1889), Wyoming (1890) and Idaho (1890). Along with miners, white farmers and ranchers were the people with power in the late 19th century.

Mining, grazing and timber played major roles in regional economic development, sparking growth for financial and industrial support. They also subjected the region to boom-and-bust cycles by unsustainable resource management.

After the economy boomed post-WWII, national parks started attracting vacationers. Tourism is now a leading industry in all four states, with the military a close second, particularly in Colorado.

Local Culture

The Rocky Mountain states tout a particular brand of freedom echoed in the vast and rugged landscape. There's lots of public land for many uses and rules are few – just take the out-of-bound skiing available at many resorts. Using your own judgment (and pushing the envelope) is encouraged.

It also boasts live and let live values. Coloradans may be split on whether they vote red or blue, but most balk at a government mandate. In 2013, Colorado became the first state to have legal, regulated and taxed recreational marijuana use for adults.

Though even the wealthiest resort towns, such as Aspen, Vail, Jackson and Ketchum, took a big hit with the 2008 financial collapse and ensuing real-estate woes, along with most of the region, they are finally on the rebound. Towns like blue-collar Billings, patriotic Colorado Springs and every other town with military families, are on a slow mend from the human toll of the campaigns in Iraq and Afghanistan.

Land & Climate

While complex, the physical geography of the region divides into two principal features: the Rocky Mountains proper and the Great Plains. Extending from Alaska's Brooks Range and Canada's Yukon Territory all the way to Mexico, the Rockies sprawl northwest to southeast, from the steep escarpment of Colorado's Front Range westward to Nevada's Great Basin. Their towering peaks and ridges form the Continental Divide: to the west, waters flow to the Pacific, and to the east, toward the Atlantic and the Gulf of Mexico.

For many travelers, the Rockies are a summer destination. It starts to feel summery around June, and the warm weather generally lasts until about mid-September (though warm outerwear is recommended for evenings in mountain towns during summer). The winter, which brings in packs of powder hounds, doesn't usually hit until late November, though snowstorms can start in the mountains as early as September. Winter usually lasts until March or early April. In the mountains, the weather is constantly changing (snow in summer is not uncommon), so always be prepared. Fall, when the aspens flaunt their fall gold, and early summer, when wildflowers bloom, are wonderful times to visit.

ℹ️ Getting There & Around

Travel here takes time. The Rockies are sparsely developed, with attractions spread across long distances and linked by roads that meander between mountains and canyons. With limited public transportation, touring in a private vehicle is best. After all, road-tripping is one of *the* reasons to explore this scenic region.

In rural areas services are few and far between – the I-80 across Wyoming is a notorious offender. It's not unusual to go more than 100 miles between gas stations. When in doubt, fill up.

The main travel hub is **Denver International Airport** (DIA; ☑ information 303-342-2000; www.flydenver.com; 8500 Peña Blvd; ⊙ 24hrs; ☜), although if you are coming on a domestic flight, check out **Colorado Springs Airport** (www.springsgov.com/airportindex.aspx) as well: fares are often lower, it's quicker to navigate than DIA and it's nearly as convenient. Both Denver and Colorado Springs offer flights on smaller planes to cities and resort towns around the region – Jackson, WY, Boise, ID, Bozeman, MT, and Aspen, CO, are just a few options. Salt Lake City, UT, also has connections with destinations in all four states.

Greyhound (☑ 800-231-2222; www.greyhound.com) has fixed routes throughout the Rockies, and offers the most comprehensive bus service.

The following Amtrak (p746) services run to and around the region:

California Zephyr Daily between Emeryville, CA (in San Francisco Bay Area), and Chicago, IL, with six stops in Colorado, including Denver, Fraser-Winter Park, Glenwood Springs and Grand Junction.

Empire Builder Runs daily from Seattle, WA, or Portland, OR, to Chicago, IL, with 12 stops in Montana (including Whitefish and East and West Glacier) and one stop in Idaho at Sandpoint.

ROCKY MOUNTAINS

COLORADO

From double-diamond runs to stiff espressos, Colorado is all about vigor. This is also the state graced with the greatest concentration of high peaks – dubbed 14ers for their height of 14000ft. But it isn't all about the great outdoors. Universities and high-tech show the state's industrious side, though even workaholics might call in sick when snow starts falling.

It's no wonder that the sunny state attracts so many East Coasters and Californians. Latinos also have answered the calling to shore up a huge hospitality industry. And while much of the state is considered conservative, there is common ground in everyone's mad love for the outdoors and a friendly, can-do ethos that inspires.

ⓘ Information

Colorado Road Conditions (☏877-315-7623; www.state.co.us) Highway advisories.
Colorado State Parks (☏303-470-1144; www.parks.state.co.us) Tent and RV sites cost from $10 to $24 per night, depending on facilities. Rustic cabins and yurts are also available in some parks and those with wood-burning stoves may be available year-round. Advance reservations for specific campsites are taken, but subject to a $10 nonrefundable booking fee. Reservation changes cost $6.
Colorado Travel & Tourism Authority (☏800-265-6723; www.colorado.com) State-wide tourism information.
Denver Post (www.denverpost.com) Denver's major daily newspaper.

Denver

Denver's mile-high gravity is growing, pulling all objects in the Rocky Mountain West toward her glistening downtown towers, hopped-up brewpubs, hemped-out cannabis dispensaries, trails, toned-and-tanned mountain warriors, and growing western cosmopolitanism that's fostered a burgeoning arts scene, and brought great restaurants and hip bars to a cow-town gone world-wide crazy.

While most of the tourist action centers on the Downtown and Lower Downtown (LoDo) Districts, travelers in the know are heading out to neighborhoods like Highlands, Washington Park, Cherry Creek, Five Points, South Santa Fe and the River North (RiNo) to dive into the spirited heart of Denver's ever-expanding culture club.

Top that off with back-door service to the Rocky Mountains, one of the best off-road bike trail systems in the USA, and plenty of parks, open spaces, riverfronts and sunshiney perches for a sky-high psychedelic carpet ride.

⊙ Sights & Activities

★ **Denver Art Museum**   MUESUM
(DAM; ☏ticket sales 720-865-5000; www.denverartmuseum.org; 100 W 14th Ave; adult/child/student $13/5/10, 1st Sat of each month free; ⊙10am-5pm Tue-Thurs, 10am-8pm Fri, 10am-5pm Sat-Sun; ℗⛟; ☒9,16,52,83LRTD) ✎ The DAM is home to one of the largest Native American art collections in the USA, and puts on special avant-garde multimedia exhibits. The Western American Art section of the permanent collection is justifiably famous. This isn't your Momma's museum, and the best part of a visit is diving into the interactive exhibits – kids love this place.

COLORADO FACTS

Nickname Centennial State

Population 5 million

Area 104,247 sq miles

Capital city Denver (population 566,974)

Other cities Boulder (population 91,500), Colorado Springs (population 372,400)

Sales tax 2.9% state tax, plus individual city taxes

Birthplace of Ute tribal leader Chief Ouray (1833–80); South Park creator Trey Parker (b 1969); actor Amy Adams (b 1974); climber Tommy Caldwell (b 1978)

Home of Naropa University (founded by Beat poets), powder slopes, boutique beers

Politics Swing state

Famous for Sunny days (300 per year), the highest altitude vineyards and longest ski run in the continental USA

Kitschiest souvenir Deer-hoof bottle openers

Driving distances Denver to Vail 100 miles, Boulder to Rocky Mountain National Park 38 miles

Denver

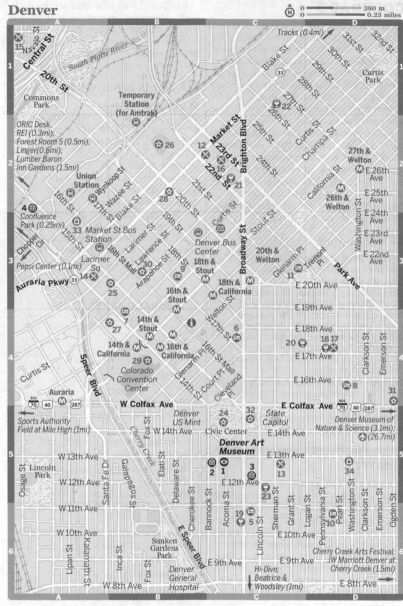

The landmark $110-million Frederic C Hamilton wing, designed by Daniel Libeskind, is quite simply awesome. Whether you see it as expanding crystals, juxtaposed mountains or just architectural indulgence, it's an angular modern masterpiece. If you think the place looks weird from the outside, look inside: shapes shift with each turn thanks to a combination of design and uncanny natural-light tricks.

Denver

Clyfford Still Museum   MUSEUM
(📞 720-354-4880; www.clyffordstillmuseum.org; 1250 Bannock St; adult/child $10/3; ⊙10am-5pm, till 8pm Fri) Dedicated exclusively to the work and legacy of 20th century American Abstract Expressionist, Clyfford Still, this fascinating museum's collection includes over 2400 works by the powerful and narcissistic master of bold. When he died in 1980, in his will Still insisted that his body of work only be exhibited in a singular space. So Denver built him a museum.

History Colorado Center   MUSEUM
(📞 303-447-8679; www.historycoloradocenter.org; 1200 Broadway; adult/student/child $10/8/8; ⊙10am-5pm Mon-Sat, noon-5pm Sun; 🅿) Discover Colorado's frontier roots and high-tech modern triumphs at this sharp, smart and charming museum. There are plenty of interactive exhibits, including a Jules Verne-esque 'Time Machine' that you push across a giant map of Colorado to explore seminal moments in the Centennial State's history.

★ **Confluence Park**   PARK
(2200 15th St; 🚻; 🚌10 RTD) 🚲 **FREE** Where Cherry Creek and Platte River meet is the nexus and plexus of Denver's sunshine loving culture. It's a good place for an afternoon picnic, and there's a short white-water park for kayakers and tubers.

Head south from here along the Cherry Creek trail and you can get all the way to Cherry Creek Shopping Center and beyond to Cherry Creek Reservoir. If you go Southwest along the Platte Trail, you'll eventually ride all the way to Chatfield Reservoir. By heading north, and connecting to the Clear Creek Trail, you can get to Golden.

Museum of Contemporary Art   GALLERY
(📞 303-298-7554; www.mcadenver.org; 1485 Delgany St; adult/student/child/after 5pm $8/5/1/5; ⊙noon-7pm Tue-Thu, noon-8pm Fri, 10am-7pm Sat-Sun; 🅿; 🚌6 RTD) This space was built with interaction and engagement in mind, and Denver's home for contemporary art can be provocative, delightful or a bit disappointing, depending on the show.

**Denver Museum of
Nature & Science**   MUSEUM
(📞 303-370-6000; www.dmns.org; 2001 Colorado Blvd; museum adult/child $13/8, IMAX $10-8, Planitarium $5/4; ⊙9am-5pm; 🅿🚻; 🚌20, 32, 40 RTD) The Denver Museum of Nature & Science is located on the eastern edge of City Park. This classic natural science museum has excellent temporary exhibits, plus those cool panoramas we all loved as kids. The IMAX theater and Gates Planetarium are especially fun.

WORTH A TRIP

BEST MILE HIGH DAY HIKES

There are literally hundreds of day hikes within an hour of Denver. Many people choose to head up to Boulder's Mountain Parks or Colorado Springs for a day.

Jefferson County Open Space Parks (www.jeffco.us/openspace; 🚹) Top picks include Matthews Winters, Mount Falcon, Elk Meadow and Lair o' the Bear.

Golden Gate Canyon State Park (✆303-582-3707; www.parks.state.us/parks; 92 Crawford Gulch Road, Golden; entrance/camping $7/24; ⊙5am-10pm) Located halfway between Denver and Nederland, this massive 12,000-acre state park can be reached in about 45 minutes from downtown Denver.

Staunton State Park (✆303-816-0912; www.parks.state.co.us/parks) Colorado's newest state park sits on a historic ranch site 40 miles west of Denver. It is accessed from Hwy 285 between Conifer and Bailey.

Waterton Canyon (✆303-634-3745; www.denverwater.org/recreation/watertoncanyon; Kassler Center) South of the city, just west of Chatfield Reservoir, this pretty canyon has an easy 6.5-mile trail to the Strontia Springs Dam. From there, the **Colorado Trail** (CTF; ✆303-384-3729; www.coloradotrail.org; PO Box 260876; ⊙9am-5pm Mon-Fri) will take you all the way to Durango!

Buffalo Creek Mountain Bike Area (www.frmbp.org; Pine Valley Ranch Park) If you're into single-track mountain biking, this area has about 40 miles of bike trails.

★ Festivals & Events

Cinco de Mayo　　　　　　　CULTURAL
(www.cincodemayodenver.com; ⊙May; 🚹) `FREE`
Enjoy salsa music and margaritas at one of the country's biggest Cinco de Mayo celebrations, held over two days on the first weekend in May.

Cherry Creek Arts Festival　　　ARTS
(www.cherryarts.org; cnr Clayton St & E 3rd Ave; 🚹) A sprawling celebration of visual, culinary and performing arts where a quarter of a million visitors browse the giant block party.

Taste of Colorado　　　　　　FOOD
(✆303-295-6330; www.atasteofcolorado.com; Civic Center Park; 🚹) Food stalls of over 50 restaurants; there's also booze, live music, and arts-and-crafts vendors at this Labor Day festival.

Great American Beer Festival　　BEER
(✆303-447-0816; www.greatamericanbeerfestival.com; 700 14th St; $75; ⊙early Sept; 🚹; 🚌101 D-Line, 101 H-Line, 🚊1, 8, 30, 30L, 31, 48 RTD) 🚲 Colorado has more microbreweries than any other US state, and this hugely popular event in early September sells out in advance.

⌂ Sleeping

Besides the places mentioned here, there are chain and independent motels throughout the city, with rooms starting at $75. Save big with the online aggregators. Denver's hostels tend to cater more to transients than backpackers.

Denver International Youth Hostel HOSTEL $
(✆303-832-9996; www.youthhostels.com/denver; 630 E 16th Ave; dm $19; 🅿@🤖; 🚊15, 15L, 20 RTD) If cheap really matters then the Denver International Youth Hostel might be the place for you. It's basic and vaguely chaotic, but has a ramshackle charm and a great downtown location. All dorms have attached bathroom facilities and the common area in the basement has a large-screen TV, library and computers for guests to use.

11th Avenue Hotel　　　　　HOTEL $
(✆303-894-0529; www.11thavenuehotel.com; 1112 Broadway; dm $19-22, r with/without bath $45/39; ☺❄🤖) This budget hotel has a good location for art lovers in the Golden Triangle district. The lobby looks vaguely like something from a Jim Jarmusch movie. The upstairs rooms, some with attached bathrooms, are bare but clean. It's safe, secure and a decent place for budget travelers.

★Curtis　　　　　BOUTIQUE HOTEL $$
(✆303-571-0300; www.thecurtis.com; 1405 Curtis St; d $159-279; ☺❄@🤖; 🚊15 RTD) It's like stepping into a doobop Warhol wonderworld at this temple to post-modern pop culture. Attention to detail – be it through the service or the decor in the rooms – is paramount at the Curtis, a one of a kind hotel in Denver.

There are 13 themed floors and each is devoted to a different genre of American pop culture. Rooms are spacious and very mod without being too out there to sleep. The hotel's refreshingly different take on sleeping may seem too kitschy for some – you can get a wake up call from Elvis – but if you're tired of the same old international brands and looking for something different, this joint in the heart of downtown might be your tonic.

★ **Queen Anne Bed & Breakfast Inn**   B&B **$$**
(☏ 303-296-6666; www.queenannebnb.com; 2147 Tremont Pl; r incl breakfast $135-215; P ⊜ ✳ 🛜) ⚑ Soft chamber music wafting through public areas, fresh flowers, manicured gardens and evening wine tastings create a romantic ambience at this ecoconscious B&B in two late-1800s Victorian homes. Featuring period antiques, private hot tubs and exquisite hand-painted murals, each room has its own personality.

Green features include mattresses made from recycled coils and green-tea insulation, organic fabrics (just like the delicious full breakfast), and products and produce purchased from local merchants when possible. They even have free bikes.

Patterson Historic Inn   HISTORIC HOTEL **$$**
(☏ 303-955-5142; www.pattersoninn.com; 420 E 11th Ave; r incl breakfast from $169; ✳ @ 🛜) This 1891 Grande Dame was once a Senator's home. It's now one of the best historic bed-and-breakfasts in town. The gardens are limited, but the Victorian charm, sumptuous breakfast, and well appointed chambers in this nine-room château will delight. Rooms come with modern touches like silk robes, down comforters and flat-screens.

Lumber Baron Inn Gardens   B&B **$$**
(☏ 303-477-8205; www.lumberbaron.com; 2555 W 37th Ave; r $149-239; P ⊜ ✳ 🛜; 🚍 38 RTD) ⚑ Murder mystery dinners and romance-inducing suites make this elegantly quirky B&B in the cooled-out Highlands neighborhood stand out from the pack – even the locals choose to stay here for a weekend mystery getaway! The five suites are all different, although all feature Jacuzzis and giant plasma TVs.

Brown Palace Hotel   HISTORIC HOTEL **$$$**
(☏ 303-297-3111; www.brownpalace.com; 321 17th St; r from $299; P ⊜ ✳ @ 🛜) Standing agape under the stained-glass crowned atrium, it's clear why this palace is shortlisted among the country's elite historic hotels. There's deco artwork, a four-star spa, imported marble, and staff who discretely float down the halls.

The rooms, which have been hosting presidents since Teddy Roosevelt's days, have the unique elegance of a distant era, but can be a bit small by modern standards.

JW Marriott Denver at Cherry Creek   HOTEL **$$$**
(☏ 303-316-2700; www.jwmarriottdenver.com; 150 Clayton Ln; d from $245; P ⊜ ✳ 🛜 ✳; 🚍 1, 2, 3, 46 RTD) Spacious digs come with high-thread count sheets, plump beds and marble bathrooms featuring top class soaps and shampoos. The onsite bar is also quite cool - you might even spot a Denver Bronco... Local artwork and colorful blown glass grace lobbies and rooms.

Hotel Monaco   BOUTIQUE HOTEL **$$$**
(☏ 303-296-1717, 800-990-1303; www.monaco-denver.com; 1717 Champa St; r from $127; P ⊜ ✳ 🛜 ✳; 🚍 0, 6, 30, 30L, 31, 36, 48, 52 RTD) This ultrastylish boutique is a favorite with the celebrity set. Modern rooms blend French and art-deco styles – think bold colors and fabulous European-style feather beds. Don't miss the evening 'Altitude Adjustment Hour,' when guests enjoy free wine and five-minute massages. The place is 100% pet-friendly; staff will even deliver a named goldfish to your room upon request!

✖ Eating

While the downtown restaurants offer the greatest depth and variety in Denver, insiders head to strollable neighborhoods like Highlands, Cherry Creek, South Pearl Street, Uptown, Five Points, Washington Park and Old Town Littleton, where little five-block commercial strips hold some of Denver's best eateries. Check out www.5280.com or www.diningout.com/denver for new eats.

Snooze   BREAKFAST **$**
(☏ 303-297-0700; www.snoozeeatery.com; 2262 Larimer St; mains $6-12; ⊙ 6:30am-2:30pm Mon-Fri, 7am-2:30pm Sat & Sun; ✳ 👶) ⚑ This retro-styled cheery breakfast-and-brunch spot is one of the hottest post-party breakfast joints in town. It dishes up spectacularly crafted breakfast burritos and a smokin' salmon benedict. The coffee's always good, but you have the option of an early-morning Bloody Mary. The wait can be up to an hour on weekends!

City O' City
VEGETARIAN, VEGAN **$**

(☎303-831-6443; www.cityocitydenver.com; 206 E 13th Ave; mains $8-15; ☺7am-2am Mon-Fri, 8am-2am Sat, 8am-midnight Sun; ☑☀; ☐2, 9, 52 RTD) ☞ This popular vegan/vegetarian restaurant mixes stylish decor with an innovative spin on greens, grains, faux meat and granola. The menu offers tapa boards, big salads, some good trans-national noodle dishes and the best vegan pizza pie in D-Town.

Buenos Aires Pizzeria
ARGENTINEAN **$**

(☎303-296-6710; www.bapizza.com; 1307 22nd St; empanadas $2.50, mains $6-10; ☺11:30am-10pm Tues-Sat, noon-8pm Sun) An authentic taste of Argentina in the heart of cow-town Colorado, this wide-angled pizzeria looks and feels like the real-deal Holyfield. You can either pig out on two or three empanadas (stuffed pastries) or dig into yummy sandwiches, above average pizza and pasta. Alas, no steaks.

★ Beatrice & Woodsley
TAPAS **$$**

(☎303-777-3505; www.beatriceandwoodsley.com; 38 S Broadway; small plates $9-13; ☺5-11pm Mon-Fri, 10am-2pm, 5-10pm Sat-Sun; ☐0 RTD) Beatrice and Woodsley is the most artfully designed dining room in Denver. Chainsaws are buried into the wall to support shelves, there's an aspen growing through the back of the dining room and the feel is that of a mountain cabin being elegantly reclaimed by nature. The menu of small plates is whimsical and Continental inspired.

★ Steuben's Food Service
AMERICAN **$$**

(☎303-803-1001; www.steubens.com; 523 E 17th Ave; mains $8-21; ☺11am-11pm Sun-Thu, 11am-midnight Fri & Sat; ☀) ☞ Although styled as a midcentury drive-in, the upscale treatment of comfort food (mac and cheese, fried chicken, lobster rolls) and the solar-powered kitchen demonstrate Steuben's contemporary smarts. In summer, open garage doors lining the street create a breezy atmosphere and after 10pm they have the most unbeatable deal around: a burger, hand-cut fries and beer for $5.

★ Root Down
MODERN AMERICAN **$$$**

(☎303-993-4200; www.rootdowndenver.com; 1600 W 33rd Ave; small plates $7-17, mains $18-28; ☺5-10pm Sun-Thu, 5-11pm Fri & Sat, brunch 10am-2:30pm Sat & Sun; ☑) ☞ In a converted gas station, chef Justin Cucci has undertaken one of the city's most ambitious culinary concepts, marrying sustainable 'field-to-fork' practices, high-concept culinary fusions and a low-impact, energy efficient ethos. The menu changes seasonally, but consider yourself lucky if it includes the sweet-potato falafel or hoisin-duck confit sliders.

★ Rioja
MODERN AMERICAN **$$$**

(☎303-820-2282; www.riojadenver.com; 1431 Larimer St; mains $18-29; ☺11:30am-2:30pm Wed-Fri, 10am-2:30pm Sat & Sun, 5-10pm Mon-Sun; ☀☑; ☐2, 12, 15, 16th St Shuttle) This is one of Denver's most innovative restaurants. Smart, busy and upscale, yet relaxed and casual – just like Colorado – Rioja features modern cuisine inspired by Italian and Spanish traditions and powered by modern culinary flavors.

☙ Drinking

Top nightlife districts include Uptown for gay bars and a young professional crowd, LoDo for loud sports bars, heavy drinking and dancing, River North for hipsters, Lower Highlands for an eclectic mix and sweet decks, Cherry Creek over 35s, and Broadway and Colfax for old school wannabees.

★ Forest Room 5
BAR

(☎303-433-7001; www.forestroom5.com; 2532 15th St; ☺4pm-2am) One of the best damned bars in Denver, this LoHi (that's Lower Highlands) juggernaut has an outdoor patio with fire circles (where you can smoke!), streams and a funked-out Airstream.

Linger
LOUNGE

(☎303-993-3120; www.lingerdenver.com; 2030 W 30th Ave; mains $8-14; ☺11:30am-2:30pm, 4pm-2am Tues-Sat, 10am-2:30pm Sun) This rambling LoHi complex sits in the former Olinger mortuary. Come nighttime, they black out the 'O' and it just becomes Linger. The light-up-the-night rooftop bar has a replica of the RV made famous by the Bill Murray smash *Stripes*.

Bar Standard
CLUB

(☎303-534-0222; www.coclubs.com; 1037 Broadway; ☺8pm-2am Fri & Sat; ☐0 RTD) It's ice cold without the attitude, and when the right DJ is on the tables it can be some of the best dancing in town.

The attached Milk Bar takes a page from Anthony Burgess' classic *A Clockwork Orange*.

Tracks
GAY

(☎303-863-7326; www.tracksdenver.com; 3500 Walnut St; ☺9pm-2am Fri & Sat, hrs vary Sun-Thu) Denver's best gay dance club has an 18-and-up night on Thursdays, Friday drag shows, and lesbian nights (just once a month).

Denver Wrangler   GAY

(☎303-837-1075; www.denverwrangler.com; 1700 Logan St; ⊙11am-2am; ▣101 RTD) Though it attracts an amiable crowd of gay male professionals after work, the central location endows Denver's premiere bear bar.

Great Divide Brewing Company   BREWPUB

(www.greatdivide.com; 2201 Arapahoe St; ⊙2-8pm Mon & Tue, 2-10pm Wed-Sat) This excellent local brewery does well to skip the same old burger menu and the fancy digs to keep its focus on what it does best: crafting exquisite beer.

Ace   BAR

(☎303-800-7705; www.acedenver.com; 501 E 17th Ave; ⊙11am-midnight Mon-Fri, 2pm-midnight Sat-Sun) The best ping-pong bar in Denver - street rules apply.

Matchbox   BAR

(www.matchboxdenver.com; 2625 Larimer St; ⊙4pm-2am Mon-Fri, noon-2am Sat-Sun) Located in the ever-hip RiNo (River North) art district, this hole-in-the-wall appeals to the thick-glasses and blue-jeans crowd.

The Church   CLUB

(www.coclubs.com; 1160 Lincoln St) The Church has three dance floors, acrobats, a couple of lounges and even a sushi bar!

☆ Entertainment

To find out what's happening with music, theater and other performing arts, pick up a free copy of **Westword** (www.westword.com).

★ Denver Performing
Arts Complex   PERFORMING ARTS

(☎720-865-4220; www.artscomplex.com; cnr 14th & Champa St) This massive complex - one of the largest of its kind - occupies four city blocks and houses several major theaters, including the historic Ellie Caulkins Opera House and the Seawell Grand Ballroom. It's also home to the Colorado Ballet, Denver Center for the Performing Arts, Opera Colorado and the Colorado Symphony Orchestra.

★ El Chapultepec   LIVE MUSIC

(☎303-295-9126; www.thepeclodo.com; 1962 Market St; ⊙7am-2am, music from 9pm) This smoky old-school jazz joint attracts a diverse mix of people. Since it opened in 1951 Frank Sinatra, Tony Bennett and Ella Fitzgerald have played here, as have Jagger and Richards.

Red Rocks Amphitheatre   CONCERT VENUE

(☎303-640-2637; www.redrocksonline.com; 18300 W Alameda Pkwy; ⊙5am-11pm; ♿) Red Rocks Amphitheatre is set between 400ft-high red sandstone rocks 15 miles southwest of Denver. Acoustics are so good many artists record live albums here.

Hi-Dive   LIVE MUSIC

(☎303-733-0230; www.hi-dive.com; 7 S Broadway) Local rock heroes and touring indie bands light up the stage at the Hi-Dive, a venue at the heart of Denver's local music scene.

Grizzly Rose   LIVE MUSIC

(☎303-295-1330; www.grizzlyrose.com; 5450 N Valley Hwy; ⊙from 6pm Tue-Sun; ♿) This is one kick-ass honky-tonk - 40,000 sq ft of hot live music - attracting real cowboys from as far as Cheyenne.

Bluebird Theater   LIVE MUSIC

(☎303-377-1666; www.bluebirdtheater.net; 3317 E Colfax Ave; ♿; ▣15, 15L RTD) This medium-sized theater is general admission standing-room, and has terrific sound and clear sight lines from the balcony.

Ogden Theatre   LIVE MUSIC

(☎303-832-1874; www.ogdentheatre.net; 935 E Colfax Ave; ♿; ▣15 RTD) One of Denver's best live-music venues.

Comedy Works   COMEDY

(☎303-595-3637; www.comedyworks.com; 1226 15th St; ▣6, 9, 10, 15L, 20, 28, 32, 44, 44L RTD) Denver's best comedy club occupies a basement space in Larimer Sq (enter down a set of stairs at the corner of Larimer and 15th).

Lannie's Clocktower Cabaret   CABARET

(☎303-293-0075; www.lannies.com; 1601 Arapahoe St; tickets $25-40; ⊙1-5pm Tue, to 11pm Wed-Thu, 1pm-1:30am Fri & Sat; ▣Arapahoe) Bawdy, naughty and strangely romantic, Lannie's Clocktower Cabaret is a wild child standout among LoDo's rather straight-laced (or at least straight) night spots.

Coors Field   BASEBALL

(☎800-388-7625; www.mlb.com/col/ballpark/; 2001 Blake St; ♿) The Colorado Rockies play baseball at the highly rated Coors Field. Tickets for the outfield - The Rockpile - cost $4. Not a bad deal.

Sports Authority Field
at Mile High   STADIUM

(☎720-258-3000; www.sportsauthorityfieldatmile-high.com; 1701 S Bryant St; ♿) The much-lauded

Denver Broncos football team and the Denver Outlaws lacrosse team play at Mile High Stadium, 1 mile west of downtown.

Pepsi Center STADIUM
(303-405-1111; www.pepsicenter.com; 1000 Chopper Circle) The mammoth Pepsi Center hosts the Denver Nuggets basketball team, the Colorado Mammoth of the National Lacrosse League and the Colorado Avalanche hockey team.

🛍 Shopping

Head to the pedestrian mall on 16th Street or LoDo for downtown shopping. Cherry Creek, Highlands Square and South Broadway are other top shopping districts.

★Tattered Cover Bookstore BOOKS
(www.tatteredcover.com; 1628 16th St; ⊙6:30am-9pm Mon-Fri, 9am-9pm Sat, 10am-6pm Sun) There are plenty of places to curl up with a book in Denver's beloved independent bookstore, one of two locations in the Denver area.

★REI OUTDOOR EQUIPMENT
(Recreational Equipment Incorporated; 303-756-3100; www.rei.com; 1416 Platte St; ♿) In addition to top outdoor gear, it has a rental department, maps and a climbing wall.

Wax Trax Records MUSIC
(303-831-7246; www.waxtraxrecords.com; 638 E 13th Ave; ☐2, 10, 15, 15L RTD) Your best spot for vinyl.

ℹ Information

Visitors & Convention Bureau Information Center (303-892-1112; www.denver.org; 1600 California St; ☎♿; ☐California)

ORIC Desk (Outdoor Recreation Information Center; REI main line 303-756-3100; www.oriconline.org; 1416 Platte St; ☎) For outdoor trips, hit this desk inside the REI store.

Police Headquarters (720-913-2000; 1331 Cherokee St)

Post Office (www.usps.com; 951 20th St; ⊙8am-6:30pm Mon-Fri, 9am-6:30pm Sat) Main branch.

University of Colorado Hospital (720-848-0000; www.uch.edu; 12605 E 16th Ave, Aurora; ⊙24hr) Emergency services.

ℹ Getting There & Away

Denver International Airport (p738) is served by around 20 airlines and offers flights to nearly every major US city. Located 24 miles east of downtown, DIA is connected with I-70 exit 238

by 12-mile-long Peña Blvd. Tourist and airport information is available at a **booth** (303-342-2000) in the terminal's central hall.

Greyhound buses stop at **Denver Bus Center** (303-293-6555; 1055 19th St), which runs services to Boise (from $151, 19 hours), Los Angeles (from $125, 22 hours) and other destinations.

The **Colorado Mountain Express** (CME; 800-525-6363; www.coloradomountainexpress.com; ☎) has shuttle service from DIA, downtown Denver or Morrison to Summit County, including Breckenridge and Keystone ($35-$49, 2.5 hours) and Vail ($45-$82, 3 hours).

Amtrak's *California Zephyr* runs daily between Chicago and San Francisco via Denver. Trains arrive and depart from a **Temporary Station** (1800 21st St) behind Coors Field until light-rail renovations at **Union Station** (Amtrak 303-534-2812; www.denverunionstation.org; cnr 17th & Wynkoop Sts; ☐31X, 40X, 80X, 86X, 120X RTD) finish in 2014. **Amtrak** (800-872-7245; www.amtrak.com) can also provide schedule information and train reservations.

ℹ Getting Around

TO/FROM THE AIRPORT

All transportation companies have booths near the baggage-claim area. Public **Regional Transit District** (RTD; 303-299-6000; www.rtd-denver.com) runs a SkyRide service to the airport from downtown Denver hourly ($9 to $13, one hour). RTD also goes to Boulder ($13, 1½ hours) from the **Market Street Bus Station** (cnr 16th & Market Sts). **Shuttle King Limo** (303-363-8000; www.shuttlekinglimo.com) charges $65 for rides from DIA to destinations in and around Denver. **SuperShuttle** (303-370-1300; www.supershuttle.com) offers shared van services (from $22) between the Denver area and the airport.

BICYCLE

BikeDenver.org (www.bikedenver.org) or **City of Denver** (www.denvergov.org) have downloadable bike maps for the city.

Denver B-Cycle (denver.bcycle.com) is the first citywide bicycle-share program in the US. Directions are given at the over 80 stations found throughout the city. Rentals under 30 minutes are free. Helmets are not included, and not required in Denver.

CAR & MOTORCYCLE

Street parking can be a pain, but there are slews of pay garages in downtown and LoDo. Nearly all the major car-rental agencies have counters at DIA, a few have offices in downtown Denver.

PUBLIC TRANSPORTATION

RTD provides public transportation throughout the Denver and Boulder area. Free shuttle buses operate along the 16th St Mall. RTD's light rail line currently has six lines servicing 46 stations. Fares are $2.25 for one to two stops, $4 for three fare zones, and $5 for all zones.

TAXI

For 24-hour cab service:

Metro Taxi (☑ 303-333-3333; www.metrotaxi-denver.com)

Yellow Cab (☑ 303-777-7777; www.denveryellowcab.com)

Boulder

Tucked against the Flatirons' cragged and near-vertical rockface, this idyllic town has a sweet location and a palpable idealism that's a magnet to entrepreneurs, athletes, hippies and hard-bodies. It's also home to the University of Colorado and the Beat-founded, Buddhist-leaning Naropa University.

Boulder's mad love of the outdoors was officially legislated in 1967, when it became the first US city to tax itself specifically to preserve open space. Thanks to such vision, packs of cyclists whip up and down the Boulder Creek corridor, which links city and county parks those taxpayer dollars have purchased. The pedestrian-only Pearl St Mall is lively and perfect for strolling, especially at night, when residents peruse until the wee hours.

In many ways it is Boulder, not Denver, that is the region's tourist hub. The city is about the same distance from Denver International Airport, and staying here puts you closer to local trails in the foothills, as well as the big ski resorts west on I-70 and Rocky Mountain National Park.

◉ Sights & Activities

Boulder's two areas to see and be seen are the downtown Pearl St Mall and the University Hill district (next to campus), both off Broadway, though The Hill is rarely the haunt of anyone over 25. Overlooking the city from the west are the Flatirons, an eye-catching rock formation.

★**Chautauqua Park**   PARK
(www.chautauqua.com; 900 Baseline Rd; admission free; 🚌 HOP 2) **FREE** This historic landmark park is the gateway to Boulder's most magnificent slab of open space (we're talking about the Flatirons), and it also has a wide,

lush lawn that attracts picnickers. It gets copious hikers, climbers and trail runners. World-class musicians perform each summer at the auditorium and there's a quality restaurant at the dining hall.

Boulder Creek Bike Path   CYCLING
(admission free; ⊙ 24 hr; 🚹) **FREE** The most utilized commuter bike path in town, this fabulously smooth and mostly straight creekside concrete path follows Boulder Creek from Foothill Parkway all the way to the split of Boulder Canyon and Four Mile Canyon Rd west of downtown – a total distance of over 5 miles one-way. The path also feeds urban bike lanes that lead all over town.

Eldorado Canyon State Park   OUTDOORS
(☑ 303-494-3943; ⊙ visitor center 9am-5pm) One of the country's most favored rock-climbing areas, offering class 5.5 to 5.12 climbs and some nice hiking trails. The park entrance is on Eldorado Springs Dr, west of Hwy 93. Information is available from Boulder Rock Club.

University Bicycles   CYCLING
(www.ubikes.com; 839 Pearl St; 4hr rental $15; ⊙ 10am-6pm Mon-Sat, 10am-5pm Sun) Plenty of places rent bicycles to cruise around town, but U Bikes has the widest range of rides and the most helpful staff.

Boulder Rock Club   ROCK CLIMBING
(☑ 303-447-2804; http://boulderrockclub.com; 2829 Mapleton Ave; day pass adult/child $17/10; ⊙ 8am-10pm Mon, 6am-11pm Tue-Thu, 8am-11pm Fri, 10am-8pm Sat & Sun; 🚹) Climb indoors at

---

THE THOUSAND-YEAR FLOOD

It came after a drought that followed the worst wildfire in Colorado history. On September 12, 2013, the Front Range woke up to flooding canyons and inundations that isolated mountain communities. Eight people died and thousands lost their homes. A disaster of this magnitude is considered a thousand-year flood, with a 0.1% probability in any given year. The month's 17in of rainfall blasted September's usual 1.7in average. Now cited as the second-largest natural disaster in US history, after Hurricane Katrina, it will take years to recover from. The affected area was roughly the size of Connecticut. Losses were estimated at $2 billion.

ROCKY MOUNTAINS BOULDER

this massive warehouse full of artificial rock faces cragged with ledges and routes. The auto-belay system allows solo climbers an anchor. The staff are a great resource for local climbing routes and tips too.

⚡️ Festivals & Events

Boulder Creek Festival
MUSIC, FOOD

(📞 303-449-3137; www.bceproductions.com; Canyon Blvd, Central Park; ⊗ May; 🚶; 🚌 206, JUMP) **FREE** Billed as the kick-off to summer and capped with the fabulous Bolder Boulder, this massive Memorial Day weekend festival has 10 event areas featuring more than 30 live entertainers and 500 vendors. With food and drink, music and sunshine, what's not to love?

Bolder Boulder
ATHLETICS

(📞 303-444-7223; www.bolderboulder.com; adult from $59; ⊗ May; 🚶) Held in a self-consciously hyper athletic town, this is the biggest foot race within the city limits. It doesn't take itself too seriously – spectators scream, there are runners in costume, and live music plays throughout the course. It's held on Memorial Day.

🛏️ Sleeping

Boulder has dozens of options – drive down Broadway or Hwy 36 to take your pick. Booking online usually scores the best discounts.

Boulder Outlook
HOTEL $

(📞 303-443-3322, 800-542-0304; www.boulderoutlook.com; 800 28th St; d incl breakfast $89-99; 🅿️❄️🛜🏊🐾) 🐾 Boulder's first zero-waste hotel is just off the highway at the south end of town, with easy access from Denver, and has funky colors, a sustainability focus and pet-friendly atmosphere. Strangely, motel-style rooms with outdoor access are less expensive than their main building counterparts. There's a dimly-lit indoor pool and climbing wall.

The onsite restaurant and bar often hosts blues bands.

★ Chautauqua Lodge
HISTORIC HOTEL $$

(📞 303-442-3282; www.chautauqua.com; 900 Baseline Rd; r from $73, cottages $125-183; 🅿️😊❄️🛜; 🚌 HOP 2) Adjoining beautiful hiking trails to the Flatirons, this leafy neighborhood of cottages is our top pick. It has contemporary rooms and one- to three-bedroom cottages with porches and beds with patchwork quilts. It's perfect for families and pets. All have full kitchens, though the wraparound porch of the Chautauqua Dining Hall is a local favorite for breakfast.

Hotel Boulderado
BOUTIQUE HOTEL $$$

(📞 303-442-4344; www.boulderado.com; 2115 13th St; r from $264; 🅿️❄️🛜; 🚌 HOP, SKIP) With over a century of service, the charming Boulderado is a National Registered Landmark and a romantic getaway. Think Victorian elegance and antique-filled rooms. The stained glass atrium and glacial water fountain accent the lobby, usually awash with jazz music.

St Julien Hotel & Spa
HOTEL $$$

(📞 720-406-9696, reservations 877-303-0900; www.stjulien.com; 900 Walnut St; r from $309; 🅿️😊❄️@🛜🏊) In the heart of downtown, Boulder's finest four-star is modern and refined, with photographs of local scenery and cork walls that warm the room ambiance. With fabulous Flatiron views, the back patio hosts live world music, jazz concerts and wild salsa parties. Rooms are plush, and so are the robes.

🍴 Eating

Boulder's dining scene has dozens of great options. Most are centered on the Pearl Street Mall, while bargains are more likely to be found on the Hill. Between 3:30pm and 6:30pm nearly every restaurant in the city features a happy hour with some kind of amazing food and drink special. It's a great way to try fine dining on a budget – check websites for details.

Spruce Confections
BAKERY $

(📞 303-449-6773; 767 Pearl St; cookies from $3.25; ⊗ 6:30am-6pm Mon-Fri, 7am-6pm Sat & Sun; 🚶; 🚌 206) Boulder's go-to bakehouse has sinful scones and breakfast lattes. Come for lunch for good homemade soups and salads.

Dish
SANDWICHES $

(📞 720-565-5933; www.dishgourmet.com; 1918 Pearl St; mains $10; ⊗ 9am-6pm Mon-Fri, 11am-4pm Sat; 🚶; 🚌 204, HOP) Bank lines flank this gourmet deli at lunchtime. At $10, the sandwiches are hardly cheap but they are satisfying. Think roasted turkey carved in chunks, pate, natural beef, slow-cooked brisket and baguettes smothered with butter and top-tier cheeses.

Zoe Ma Ma
CHINESE $

(2010 10th St; mains $5-13; ⊙11am-10pm Sun-Thu, 11am-11pm Fri & Sat; 🚌206, SKIP, HOP) 🅿 At Boulder's hippest noodle bar you can slurp and munch fresh street food at a long outdoor counter. Mama, the Taiwanese matriarch, is on hand, cooking and chatting up customers in her Croc sandals. Organic noodles are made from scratch, as are the garlicky melt-in-your mouth pot stickers.

The Sink
PUB $

(www.thesink.com; 1165 13th St; mains $5-12; ⊙11am-2am, kitchen to 10pm; 🍴; 🚌203, 204, 225, DASH, SKIP) Dim and graffiti-scrawled, the Sink has been a Hill classic since 1923 and once Robert Redford worked here. Colorful characters cover the cavernous space – the scene alone is almost worth a visit. Almost. Once you've washed back the legendary Sink burger with a slug of a local microbrew, you'll be glad you stuck around.

Alfalfa's
SELF-CATERING $

(www.alfalfas.com; 1651 Broadway St; ⊙7:30am-10pm; 🚌AB, B, JUMP, SKIP) A small, community-oriented natural market with a wonderful selection of prepared food ($1 to $16) and an inviting indoor-outdoor dining area to enjoy it in.

Cafe Aion
SPANISH $$

(☎303-993-8131; www.cafeaion.com; 1235 Pennsylvania Ave; tapas $5-13; ⊙11am-10pm Tues-Fri, 9am-3pm Sat-Sun; 🚌203, 204, 225, DASH, SKIP) Original and unpretentious, this side street cafe mimics the relaxed rhythms of Spain with fresh tapas and delectable house-made sangria. Papas bravas have the perfect crisp, and grilled spring onions and dolmas are springtime-fresh. Check out the all-evening happy hour on Tuesday.

Lucile's
CAJUN $$

(☎303-442-4743; www.luciles.com; 2142 14th St; mains $8-14; ⊙7am-2pm Mon-Fri, from 8am Sat & Sun; 🍴; 🚌205, 206, HOP) 🅿 This New Orleans–style diner has perfected breakfast; the Creole egg dishes (served over creamy spinach alongside cheesy grits or perfectly blackened trout) are all-stars. Start with the chicory coffee and an order of beignets. Their homemade jam is perfect on a steaming biscuit.

★ Salt
MODERN AMERICAN $$$

(☎303-444-7258; www.saltboulderbistro.com; 1047 Pearl St; mains $14-28; ⊙11am-10pm Mon-Wed, to 11pm Thu-Sat, 10am-10pm Sun; 🍴; 🚌208, HOP, SKIP) While farm-to-table is

---

FOODIE FINDS IN THE ROCKIES

Start by digging into regional *Edible* (www.ediblecommunities.com) magazines online – a great resource for farmers markets and innovative eats. There are editions for the Front Range and Aspen.

Boulder is worth a stop since being named America's Foodiest Small Town, according to *Bon Appetit*. At Kitchen (p749) Monday is community night, which means shared tables and a homegrown five-course meal served family-style, with 20% of proceeds going to charity. Go behind the scenes with **Local Table Tours** (☎303-909-5747; www.localtabletours.com; tours $25-70), a tour presenting a smattering of great local cuisine and inside knowledge on food and wine or coffee and pastries. The cocktail crawl is a hit.

For fine dining in a warehouse or an airplane hangar, Denver's Hush (www.hushdenver.com) sponsors fun pop-up dinners with top regional chefs, by invitation only – make contact online.

---

ubiquitous in Boulder, this spot surpasses expectations. The sweet pea ravioli with lemon *buerre blanc* and shaved radishes is a feverish delight. But Salt also knows meat: local and grass-fed, basted, braised and slow roasted to utter perfection. When in doubt, ask – the servers really know their stuff.

It also has one of Boulder's best happy hours, with bargain bites. The house mixologist has repeatedly won the competition for Boulder's best.

Kitchen
MODERN AMERICAN $$$

(☎303-544-5973; www.thekitchencafe.com; 1039 Pearl St; mains $18-32; 🍴; 🚌206, HOP) 🅿 Clean lines and fresh farmers-market ingredients provide the building blocks at Boulder's most lauded kitchen. Think tapas of roasted root vegetables, shaved prosciutto and mussels steamed in wine and cream. The pulled-pork sandwich rocks, but save room for the sticky toffee pudding.

A younger crowd gathers at the more casual upstairs bar and the Kitchen Next Door, with cheaper eats (mains $10).

Drinking & Entertainment

Playboy didn't vote CU the best party school for nothing – the blocks around the Pearl St Mall and the Hill churn out fun, with many restaurants doubling as bars or turning into all-out dance clubs come 10pm.

★ **Mountain Sun Pub & Brewery** BREWERY
(1535 Pearl St; ⊙11am-1am; 🌐; 🚌 HOP, 205, 206) Boulder's favorite brewery serves a rainbow of brews from chocolaty to fruity, and packs in an eclectic crowd of yuppies, hippies and everyone in between. Walls are lined with tapestries, there are board games to amuse you and the pub grub (especially the burgers) is delicious. There's usually live music of the bluegrass and jam-band variety on Sunday and Monday nights. Second location 627 S Broadway.

Bitter Bar COCKTAIL BAR
(☎303-442-3050; www.thebitterbar.com; 835 Walnut St; cocktails $9-15; ⊙5pm-12am Mon-Thur, 5pm-2am Fri-Sat; 🚌 HOP) A chic Boulder speakeasy where killer cocktails – such as the scrumptious lavender-infused Blue Velvet – make the evening slip happily out of focus. The patio is great for conversation and their monthly classes buy you the know-how to mix two drinks that would make a Mad Man weep. There's live music at 9pm on Thursday.

WORTH A TRIP

SUSTAINABLE BREWS

New Belgium Brewing Co (☎800-622-4044; www.newbelgium.com; 500 Lined St; ⊙guided tours 10am-6pm, Tue-Sat) FREE satisfies beer connoisseurs with its hearty Fat Tire Amber Ale, and diverse concoctions like 1554, Trippell and Sunshine Wheat. Recognized as one of the world's most environmentally conscious breweries, a 100,000kw turbine keeps it wind-powered. The brewery also sponsors cool events such as bike-in cinema and ski resort scavenger hunts. It's in the college town of Fort Collins (home to Colorado State University), a worthwhile 46-mile drive north of Boulder on I-25 – especially if you're heading to Wyoming. Reserve tickets online – these popular tours include complimentary tasting of the flagship and specialty brews.

Boulder Dushanbe Teahouse TEAHOUSE
(☎303-442-4993; 1770 13th St; mains $8-19; ⊙8am-10pm; 🚌 203, 204, 205, 206, 208, 225, DASH, JUMP, SKIP) Step into this incredible Tajik work of art – a gift from Boulder's sister city (Dushanbe, Tajikistan). Incredible craftsmanship and meticulous painting envelop the vibrant multicolored interior. The international fare is sadly less notable than the setting, but it's perfect for tea.

Boulder Theater CINEMA, MUSIC
(☎303-786-7030; www.bouldertheatre.com; 2032 14th St) This old movie theater-turned-historic venue brings in slightly under-the-radar acts like jazz great Charlie Hunter, the madmen rockers of Gogol Bordello and West African divas, Les Nubians. But it also screens classic films and short-film festivals that can and should be enjoyed with a glass of beer.

Shopping

Boulder has great shopping and galleries. The outdoor 29th St Mall, with a movie theatre, just off 28th St between Canyon and Pearl St, is a more recent addition.

Pearl Street Mall MALL
The main feature of downtown Boulder is the Pearl Street Mall, a vibrant pedestrian zone filled with kids' climbing boulders and splash fountains, bars, galleries and restaurants.

Momentum HANDICRAFTS
(www.ourmomentum.com; 1625 Pearl St; ⊙10am-7pm Tue-Sat, 11am-6pm Sun) 🍃 The kitchen sink of unique global gifts – Zulu wire baskets, fabulous scarves from India, Nepal and Ecuador – all handcrafted and purchased at fair value from disadvantaged artisans. Every item purchased provides a direct economic lifeline to the artists.

Common Threads CLOTHING
(www.commonthreadsboulder.com; 2707 Spruce St; ⊙10am-6pm Mon-Sat, noon-5pm Sun) Vintage shopping at its most haute couture, this fun place is where to go for secondhand Choos and Prada purses. The shop is a pleasure to browse, with clothing organized by color and type on visually aesthetic racks, just like a big-city boutique. Also runs clothes-making courses.

Boulder Bookstore BOOKS
(www.boulderbookstore.indiebound.com; 1107 Pearl St; 🛜🌐) Boulder's favorite indie bookstore has a huge travel section downstairs and hosts readings and workshops.

ℹ Information

Boulder Visitor Center (☑303-442-2911; www.bouldercoloradousa.com; 2440 Pearl St; ⊘8:30am-5pm Mon-Thu, 8:30am-4pm Fri) Offers information and internet access.

ℹ Getting There & Around

Boulder has fabulous public transportation, with services extending as far away as Denver and its airport. Ecofriendly buses are run by **RTD** (☑303-299-6000; www.rtd-denver.com; per ride $2-4.50; ⧆). Maps are available at **Boulder Station** (cnr 14th & Walnut Sts). RTD buses (route B) operate between Boulder Station and Denver's Market St Bus Station ($5, 55 minutes). RTD's SkyRide bus (route AB) heads to Denver International Airport ($13, one hour, hourly). **SuperShuttle** (☑303-444-0808; www.supershuttle.com; one-way around $27) provides hotel ($27) and door-to-door ($34) shuttle service from the airport.

For two-wheel transportation, **Boulder B-Cycle** (boulder.bcycle.com; 24-hr rental $7) is a new citywide program with townie bikes available at strategic locations, but riders must sign up online first.

Northern Mountains

With one foot on either side of the continental divide and behemoths of granite in every direction, Colorado's Northern Mountains offer out-of-this-world alpine adventures, laid-back skiing, kick-butt hiking and biking, and plenty of rivers to raft, fish and float as you stare into the big-blue arching Colorado sky.

Rocky Mountain National Park

Rocky Mountain National Park showcases classic alpine scenery, with wildflower meadows and serene mountain lakes set under snowcapped peaks. There are over 4 million visitors annually, but many stay on the beaten path. Hike an extra mile and enjoy the incredible solitude. Elk are the park's signature mammal – you will even see them grazing on hotel lawns, but also keep an eye out for bighorn sheep, moose, marmots and black bear.

◉ Sights & Activities

With over 300 miles of trail, traversing all aspects of its diverse terrain, the park is suited to every hiking ability.

Those with the kids in tow might consider the easy hikes in the Wild Basin to Calypso Falls or to Gem Lakes in the Lumpy Ridge area, or the trail to Twin Sisters Peak south of Estes Park, while those with unlimited ambition, strong legs and enough trail mix will be lured by the challenge of summiting Longs Peak.

Regardless, it's best to spend at least one night at 7000ft to 8000ft prior to setting out to allow your body to adjust to the elevation. Before July, many trails are snowbound and high water runoff makes passage difficult.

In the winter, avalanches are a hazard.

★**Moraine Park Museum** MUSEUM (☑970-586-1206; Bear Lake Rd; ⊘9am-4:30pm Jun-Oct) Built by the Civilian Conservation Corps in 1923 and once the park's proud visitors lodge, this building has been renovated in recent years to host exhibits on geology, glaciers and wildlife.

🛏 Sleeping & Eating

The only overnight accommodations in the park are at campgrounds. Dining options and the majority of motel or hotel accommodations are around Estes Park or Grand Lake, located on the other side of the Trail Ridge Road Pass (open late May to October).

You will need a backcountry permit to stay outside developed park campgrounds. None of the campgrounds have showers, but they do have flush toilets in summer and outhouse facilities in winter. Sites include a fire ring, picnic table and one parking spot.

Olive Ridge Campground CAMPGROUND $ (☑303-541-2500; campsites $19; ⊘mid-May–Nov) This well-kept USFS campground has access to four trailheads: St Vrain Mountain, Wild Basin, Longs Peak and Twin Sisters. In the summer it can get full, though sites are mostly first come, first served.

Longs Peak Campground CAMPGROUND $ (☑970-586-1206; MM 9, State Hwy 7; campsites $20; ℗) This is the base camp of choice for the early morning ascent of Longs Peak. There are no reservations, but if you're planning to bag Longs Peak after sleeping here, get here early one day before the climb.

Moraine Park Campground CAMPGROUND $ (☑877-444-6777; www.recreation.gov; off Bear Lake Rd; summer campsites $20) In the middle of a stand of ponderosa pine forest off Bear Lake Road, this is the biggest of the park's campgrounds.

Reservations are accepted and recommended from the end of May through to the end of September; other times of the year the campground is first come, first served. At night in the summer, there are numerous ranger-led programs in the ampitheater.

Aspenglen Campground CAMPGROUND $
(☑877-444-6777; www.recreation.gov; State Hwy 34; campsites summer $20) With only 54 sites, this is the smallest of the park's reservable camping. There are many tent-only sites, including some walk-ins.

Timber Creek Campground CAMPGROUND $
(Trail Ridge Rd, US Hwy 34; campsites $20) This campground has 100 sites and remains open through winter. No reservations accepted. The only established campground on the west side of the park, it's 7 miles north of Grand Lake.

Glacier Basin Campground CAMPGROUND $
(☑877-444-6777; www.recreation.gov; off Bear Lake Rd; campsites summer $20) This developed campground has a large area for group camping and accommodates RVs. It is served by the shuttle buses on Bear Lake Rd throughout the summer. Make reservations through the website.

❶ Information

For private vehicles, the park entrance fee is $20, valid for seven days. Individuals entering the park on foot, bicycle, motorcycle or bus pay $10 each. All visitors receive a free copy of the park's information brochure, which contains a good orientation map and is available in English, German, French, Spanish and Japanese.

Backcounty permits ($20 for a group up to 12 people for seven days) are required for overnight stays in the 260 designated backcountry camping sites in the park. They are free between November 1 and April 30. Phone reservations can be made only from March 1 to May 15. Reservations by snail mail or in person are accepted via the **Backcountry Office.** (☑970-586-1242; www.nps.gov/romo).

A bear box to store your food is required if you are staying overnight in the backcountry (established campsites already have them). These can be rented for around $3 to $5 per day from REI (p746) or the **Estes Park Mountain Shop** (☑970-586-6548; www.estesparkmountain-shop.com; 2050 Big Thompson Ave; 2-person tent $10, bear box $3 per night; ⊙8am-9pm).

Alpine Visitor Center (www.nps.gov/romo; Fall River Pass; ⊙10:30am-4:30pm late May–mid-Jun, 9am-5pm late Jun-early Sep, 10:30am-4:30pm early Sep–mid-Oct; ❸) The views from this popular visitors center and souvenir store at 11,796ft, and right in the middle of the park, are extraordinary.

Beaver Meadows Visitor Center (☑970-586-1206; www.nps.gov/romo; US Hwy 36; ⊙8am-9pm late Jun-late Aug, to 4:30pm or 5pm rest of year; ❸) The primary visitors center and best stop for park information if you're approaching from Estes Park.

Kawuneeche Visitor Center (☑970-627-3471; 16018 US Hwy 34; ⊙8am-6pm last week May-Labor Day, 8am-5pm Labor Day-Sep, 8am-4:30pm Oct-May; ❸) This is the main visitors center on the west side of the park, offering a film about the park, ranger-led walks and discussions, backcountry permits and family activities.

❶ Getting There & Away

Trail Ridge Rd (US 34) is the only east–west route through the park and is closed in winter. The most direct route from Boulder follows US 36 through Lyons to the east entrances.

There are two entrance stations on the east side, Fall River (US 34) and Beaver Meadows (US 36). The Grand Lake Station (also US 34) is the only entry on the west side. Year-round access is available through Kawuneeche Valley along the Colorado River headwaters to Timber Creek Campground. The main centers of visitor activity on the park's east side are the Alpine Visitor Center, high on Trail Ridge Rd and Bear Lake Rd, which leads to campgrounds, trailheads and the Moraine Park Museum.

North of Estes Park, Devils Gulch Rd leads to several hiking trails. Further out on Devils Gulch Rd, you pass through the village of Glen Haven to reach the trailhead entry to the park along the North Fork of the Big Thompson River.

❶ Getting Around

In summer a free shuttle bus operates from the Estes Park Visitor Center multiple times daily, bringing hikers to a park-and-ride location where you can pick up other shuttles. The year-round option leaves the Glacier Basin parking area toward Bear Lake, in the parks lower elevations. During the summer peak, a second shuttle operates between Moraine Park campground and the Glacier Basin parking area. Shuttles run on weekends only from mid-August through September.

Estes Park

It's no small irony that becoming a nature-lovers hub has turned the gateway to one of the most pristine outdoor escapes in the US into kind of Great Outdoors Disney. And while there are plenty of T-shirt shops and mountain kitsche, a nice river runs through town, it has cool parks, decent restaurants and a haunted hotel.

🏃 Activities

★ Colorado Mountain School
ROCK CLIMBING

(📞 800-836-4008; www.totalclimbing.com; 341 Moraine Ave; half-day guided climbs per person from $125) There's no better resource for climbers in Colorado. Basic courses, such as Intro to Rock Climbing, are a great way for novices to deeply experience the Rockies, more experienced climbers can hire guides to take them up some of the radical neighboring peaks. It has an stay on-site in dorm lodging.

🛏 Sleeping

Estes Park's dozens of hotels fill up fast in summer. There are some passable budget options but the many lovely area campgrounds are the best-value.

Try the **Estes Park Visitor Center** (📞 970-577-9900; www.estesparkresortcvb.com; 500 Big Thompson Ave; ⏰ 9am-8pm Jun-Aug, 8am-5pm Mon-Fri, 9am-5pm Sat, 10am-4pm Sun Sep-May), just east of the US 36 junction, for help with lodging; note that many places close in winter.

Total Climbing Lodge
HOSTEL $

(📞 303-447-2804; www.totalclimbing.com; 341 Moraine Ave; dm $25; 🅿🍳@📶) A bustling hub of climbers, lodging here is the best dorm option in town. Expect simple pine bunks, a ping-pong table and a laid-back vibe.

Estes Park Hostel
HOSTEL $

(📞 970-237-0152; www.estesparkhostel.com; 211 Cleave St; dm/s/d $26/38/52; 📶) This hostel, with a handful of shared rooms and simple privates, isn't going into history books as the plushest digs ever, but there's a kitchen on site, and Terri, the owner, is helpful. The price is right too.

★ YMCA of the Rockies – Estes Park Center
RESORT $$

(📞 970-586-3341; www.ymcarockies.org; 2515 Tunnel Rd; r & d from $109; cabins from $129; 🅿🍳❄📶🏊) Estes Park Center is not your typical YMCA boarding house. Instead it's a favorite vacation spot. There are upmarket motel-style accommodations and cabins set on hundreds of acres of high alpine terrain. Book ahead.

Riversong
BOUTIQUE HOTEL $$

(📞 970 586 4666; www.romanticriversong.com; 1766 Lower Broadview Dr; d from $165; 🅿🍳) Tucked down a dead-end dirt road overlooking the Big Thompson River, Riversong of-fers nine romantic rooms with private bath in a arts-and-crafts-style mansion. The minimum stay is two nights, and prices vary by amenities. West of town take Moraine Ave, turn onto Mary's Lake Rd and take the first right.

Stanley Hotel
HOTEL $$$

(📞 970-577-4000; www.stanleyhotel.com; 333 Wonderview Ave; r from $199; 🅿📶🏊) The white Georgian Colonial Revival hotel stands in brilliant contrast to the towering peaks of Rocky Mountain National Park framing the skyline. A favorite local retreat, this best-in-class hotel served as the inspiration for Stephen King's famous cult novel *The Shining*. Rooms are decorated to retain some of the Old West feel while still ensuring all the creature comforts.

🍴 Eating

Estes Park Brewery
BREWERY

(www.epbrewery.com; 470 Prospect Village Dr; ⏰ 11am-2am Mon-Sun) The town's brewpub serves pizza, burgers and wings, and at least eight different house beers, in a big, boxy room resembling a cross between a classroom and a country kitchen. Pool tables and outdoor seating keep the place rocking late into the night.

Ed's Cantina & Grill
MEXICAN $$

(📞 970-586-2919; www.edscantina.com; 390 E Elkhorn Ave; mains $9-13; ⏰ 11am-late daily, from 8am-10pm Sat & Sun; 🍽) With an outdoor patio right on the river, Ed's is a great place to kick back with a margarita and one of the daily $3 blue-plate specials (think fried, rolled tortillas) with shredded pork and guacamole). Serving Mexican and American staples, the restaurant is in a retro-mod space with leather booth seating and a bold primary color scheme. The bar is in a separate room with light-wood stools featuring comfortable high backs.

ℹ Getting There & Away

From Denver International Airport, **Estes Park Shuttle** (📞 970-586-5151; www.estesparkshuttle.com) runs four times daily to Estes Park (one-way/return $45/85).

Steamboat Springs

With luxuriant tree-skiing, top-notch trails for mountain-biking and a laid-back Western feel, Steamboat beats out other ski towns in both real ambience and offerings.

Its historic center is cool for rambling, its hot springs top off a hard day of play, and locals couldn't be friendlier.

◉ Sights & Activities

Steamboat Mountain Resort   SNOW SPORTS
(⏰ticket office 970-871-5252; www.steamboat. com; lift ticket adult/child $94/59; ⏰ticket office 8am-5pm) Known for a 3600ft vertical drop, excellent powder and trails for all levels, this is the main draw for winter visitors, offering some of the best skiing in the US. In the ski area there are (overpriced) food and equipment vendors galore.

★Strawberry Park Hot Springs HOT SPRING
(⏰970-870-1517; www.strawberryhotsprings. com; 44200 County Rd; per day adult/child $10/5; ⏰10am-10:30pm Sun-Thu, to midnight Fri & Sat; ⏰) ✐ Steamboat's favorite hot springs are actually outside the city limits, but offer great back-to-basics relaxation. Water is 104°F in these tasteful stone pools formed by cascading drops. To stay over, choose from camping or rustic cabins. There's no electricity (you get gas lanterns) and you'll need your own linens.

Be sure to reserve. Weekend reservations require a two-night stay. Note that the thermal pools are clothing optional after dark.

Orange Peel Bikes   BICYCLE RENTAL
(⏰970-879-2957; www.orangepeelbikes.com; 1136 Yampa St; bike rental per day $20-65; ⏰10am-6pm Mon-Fri, to 5pm Sat; ⏰) Stop by the coolest bike shop in town to pick up a cruiser or top-line mountain bike. They have a great biking map, and plenty of info on the best spots to ride, including Emerald Mountain (just out of town), Spring Creek, Mad Creek and Red Dirt. Families can rent cruisers and do the 7-mile-trail that follows the Yampa near town.

Bucking Rainbow Outfitters   RAFTING, FISHING
(⏰970-879-8747; www.buckingrainbow.com; 730 Lincoln Ave; inner tubes $17, rafting $43-100, fishing $150-340; ⏰daily) This excellent outfitter offers rafting trips on the Yampa, Platte, Eagle and Elk Rivers (Class II-IV), tubes and shuttle services for the relatively flat section of the Yampa in town, fishing year round and plenty more.

Old Town Hot Springs   HOT SPRING
(⏰970-879-1828; www.oldtownhotsprings.org; 136 Lincoln Ave; adult/child $16/9, waterslide $6; ⏰5:30am-10pm Mon-Fri, 7am-9pm Sat, 8am-9pm Sun; ⏰) Right in the center of town, the mineral water here is warmer than most in the area. The springs recently underwent a $5-million renovation and now there's a new pool, a pair of 230ft-long waterslides and, perhaps coolest of all, an aquatic climbing wall! Kids will dig it!

🛏 Sleeping & Eating

There are plenty of places to sleep; contact **Steamboat Central Reservations** (⏰877-783-2628; www.steamboat.com; Mt Werner Circle, off Gondola Sq) for condos and other options near the ski area.

Hotel Bristol   HOTEL $$
(⏰970-879-3083; www.steamboathotelbristol. com; 917 Lincoln Ave; d $129-149; ⏰⏰) The elegant Hotel Bristol has small, but sophisticated, Western digs, with dark-wood and brass furnishings and Pendleton wool blankets on the beds. There's a ski shuttle, a six-person indoor Jacuzzi and a cozy restaurant.

The Boathouse   MODERN AMERICAN $$
(⏰970-879-4797; 609 Yampa; $12-20; ⏰restaurant 11am-10pm, bar to 1am) You can't beat the view from the riverfront deck, and the creative menu takes you across continents with innovative plates such as 'When Pigs Fly,' a piquant pork-chop-wasabi invention. Great for afternoon cloud-watching.

Carl's Tavern   AMERICAN $$
(⏰970-761-2060; www.carlstavern.com; 700 Yampa Ave; $14-31) This local's favorite has great pub grub, a happening patio, live music, cool waitstaff, and a raucous spirit that will get your hear thumping.

ℹ Information

Steamboat Springs Visitor Center (⏰970-879-0880; www.steamboat-chamber.com; 125 Anglers Drive; ⏰8am-5pm Mon-Fri, 10am-3pm Sat)

ℹ Getting There & Away

Buses between Denver and Salt Lake City stop at the **Greyhound Terminal** (⏰800-231-2222; www.greyhound.com; 1505 Lincoln Ave), about half a mile west of town. **Steamboat Springs Transit** (⏰970-879-3717, for pick-up in Mountain Area 970-846-1279; http://steamboatsprings.net) runs free buses between Old Town and the ski resort year-round. Steamboat is 166 miles northwest of Denver via US 40.

Central Colorado

Colorado's central mountains are well known for their plethora of world-class ski resorts, sky-high hikes and snow-melt rivers. To the southeast is Colorado Springs and Pikes Peak, which anchor the southern Front Range.

Winter Park

Less than two hours from Denver, unpretentious Winter Park is a favorite ski resort with Front Rangers, who flock here from as far away as Colorado Springs to ski fresh tracks each weekend. Beginners can frolic on miles of powdery groomers while experts test their skills on Mary Jane's world-class bumps. Most services are along US 40 (the main drag), including the **visitor center** (☑970-726-4118; www.winterpark-info.com; 78841 Hwy 40; ⊙9am-5pm daily).

South of town, **Winter Park Resort** (☑970-726-1564; www.winterparkresort.com; Hwy 40; lift ticket adult/child $104/62; ⬦) covers five mountains and has a vertical drop of more than 2600ft. Experts love it here because more than half of the runs are geared solely for highly skilled skiers. It also has 45 miles of lift-accessible **mountain-biking trails** (www.trestlebikepark.com; day pass adult/child $39/29; ⊙mid-Jun–mid-Sep) connecting to a 600-mile trail system running through the valley.

★**Devil's Thumb Ranch** (☑800-933-4339; www.devilsthumbranch.com; 3530 County Rd 83; bunkhouse $100-180, lodge $240-425, cabins from $365; ❄🗢🐾🐕) 🍴, with a cowboy chic lodge and cabins alongside a 65-mile network of trails, makes an ultra-romantic getaway for the active-minded. Geothermal heat, reclaimed wood and low-emission fireplaces make it green. It's ideal for **cross-country skiing and horseback rides** (☑970-726-5632; www.devilsthumbranch.com; 3530 County Rd 83; trail passes adult/child $20/8, horseback riding $95-175; ⬦) in the high country.

The best deal around is the friendly **Rocky Mountain Chalet** (☑970-726-8256; www.therockymountainchalet.com; 15 Co Rd 72; dm $30, r summer/winter $89/149; 🅿❄🗢), with plush, comfortable doubles, dorm rooms and a sparkling kitchen.

For inspired dining, **Tabernash Tavern** (☑970-726-4430; www.tabernashtavern.com; 72287 US Hwy 40; mains $20-34; ⊙5-9pm Tue-Sat) 🍴 whets the appetite with buffalo rib ragout or venison burgers. Reserve ahead. It's north of town.

Breckenridge & Around

Set at 9600ft, at the foot of a marvelous range of treeless peaks, Breck is a sweetly surviving gold-mining town with a lovely national historic district. With down-to-earth grace, the town boasts family-friendly ski runs that don't disappoint and always draw a giddy crowd. If you should happen to grow restless, there are five great ski resorts and outlet shopping less than an hour away.

🏃 Activities

Breckenridge Ski Area　　SNOW SPORTS
(☑800-789-7669; www.breckenridge.com; lift ticket adult/child $115/68; ⊙8:30am-4pm Nov–mid-Apr; ⬦) Spans five mountains and features some of the best beginner and intermediate terrain in the state (the green runs are

---

THE ROCKIES FOR POWDER HOUNDS

Well worth the five-hour road trip from Denver, **Crested Butte** promises deep powder and lovely open terrain next to a mining outpost re-tooled to be one of Colorado's coolest small towns.

If you're short on travel time, go directly to Summit County. Use lively **Breckenridge** as your base and conquer five areas on one combo lift ticket, including the mastodon resort of **Vail**, our favorite for remote back bowl terrain, and the ultralocal and laid-back Arapahoe Basin Ski Area. A-Basin stays open into June, when spring skiing means tailgating with beer and barbecue in between slush runs.

From Crested Butte, you can head a little further south and ski the slopes at **Telluride**, from Summit County and Vail, **Aspen** is nearby. Both are true old gold towns. Be sure to devote at least a few hours to exploring Aspen's glitzy shops and Telluride's down-to-earth bars for a real local vibe in a historic Wild West setting.

From Aspen, catch a local flight up to **Jackson Hole Mountain Resort** to do some real vertical powder riding in the Grand Tetons.

flatter than most in Colorado), as well as killer steeps and chutes for experts, and a renowned snowboard park.

Arapahoe Basin Ski Area
SNOW SPORTS

(☑970-468-0718; www.arapahoebasin.com; Hwy 6; lift adult/child 6-14yr $79/40; ☺9am-4pm Mon-Fri, from 8:30 Sat & Sun) North America's highest resort, about 12 miles from Breck, is smaller, less commercial and usually open until at least mid-June! Full of steeps, walls and back-country terrain, it's a local favorite because it doesn't draw herds of package tourists.

Peak 8 Fun Park
AMUSEMENT PARK

(☑800-789-7669; www.breckenridge.com; Peak 8; day pass 3-7yr/8yr & up $34/68; ☺9:30am-5:30pm mid-Jun–mid-Sep; 🖾) With a laundry list of made-for-thrills activities, including a big-air trampoline, climbing wall, mountain-bike park (rental half/full day $49/59) and the celebrated SuperSlide – a luge-like course taken on a sled at exhilarating speeds. Get the day pass, do activities à la carte or simply take a scenic ride up the chair lift (without/with bike $10/17).

🎊 Festivals & Events

Ullr Fest
CULTURE

(www.gobreck.com; ☺early to mid-January) The Ullr Fest celebrates the Norse god of winter with a wild parade and four-day festival featuring a twisted version of the Dating Game, an ice-skating party and a bonfire.

International Snow Sculpture Championship
ART

(www.gobreck.com; ☺mid-Jan; 🖾) Sculptors from around the world descend on Breck to create meltable masterpieces. It starts in mid-January and lasts for two weeks on Riverwalk.

🛏 Sleeping

For upscale slope-side rentals, contact **Great Western Lodging** (☑888-453-1001; www.gw-lodging.com; 322 N Main St; condos summer/winter from $125/275; P❄🐾📶). Campers can look for **USFS campgrounds** (☑877-444-6777; www.recreation.gov) outside of town.

Fireside Inn
B&B, HOSTEL $

(☑970-453-6456; www.firesideinn.com; 114 N French St; summer/winter dm $30/41, summer/winter d $101/140; P❄@📶) The best deal for budget travelers in Summit County, this chummy hostel and B&B is a find. All guests can enjoy the chlorine-free barrel hot tub and resident snuggly dog. The English hosts are delight and very helpful with local information. It's a 10-minute walk to the gondola in ski boots.

★ Abbet Placer Inn
B&B $$

(☑970-453-6489; www.abbettplacer.com; 205 S French St; r summer $99-179, winter $119-229; P❄@📶) This violet house has five large rooms decked-out with wood furnishings, iPod docks and fluffy robes. It's very low key. The warm and welcoming hosts cook big breakfasts, and guests can enjoy a lovely outdoor Jacuzzi deck and use of a common kitchenette. The top-floor room has massive views of the peaks from a private terrace. Check-in is from 4pm to 7pm.

🍴 Eating & Drinking

Clint's Bakery & Coffee House
CAFE $

(131 S Main St; sandwiches $4.95-7.25; ☺7am-8pm; 📶🖾) Brainy baristas steam up a chalkboard full of latte and mocha flavors and dozens of loose-leaf teas. If you're hungry, the downstairs bagelry (which closes at 3pm) stacks burly sandwiches and tasty breakfast bagels with egg and ham, lox, sausage and cheese.

WORTH A TRIP

THE VAGABOND RANCH

Moose outnumber people at the remote **Vagabond Ranch** (☑303-242-5338; www.vagabondranch.com; per person $50; 🖾), a fine backcountry spot in Colorado's pristine Never Summer Range. By backcountry we mean a 3-mile dirt access road – it can be driven in summer but you'll need to park the car and ski or snowmobile in for winter fun.

Ringed by high peaks and ponderosa forest, this former stagecoach stop features a smattering of comfortable cabins – ranging from rustic to elegant – at 9000ft. Features include chef-worthy cooking facilities, firewood, a hot tub, solar power and composting toilets. Like any ski hut, lodgings may be shared, but couples or groups can book privates (we recommend the retro-gorgeous Parkview for couples). Dedicated trails are groomed in winter for cross-country skiing or snowmobiling. It also hosts yoga and meditation retreats.

It's 22 miles from Granby (near Winter Park).

CLIMBING YOUR FIRST 14ER

Known as Colorado's 'easiest' 14er, **Quandary Peak** (www.14ers.com; County Rd 851), near Breckenridge, is the state's 15th-highest peak at 14,265ft. Though you will see plenty of dogs and children, easiest may be misleading – the summit remains three grueling miles from the trailhead. Go between June and September.

The trail ascends to the west; after about 10 minutes of moderate climbing, follow the right fork to a trail junction. Head left, avoiding the road, and almost immediately you will snatch some views of Mt Helen and Quandary (although the real summit is still hidden).

Just below timberline you'll meet the trail from Monte Cristo Gulch – note it so you don't take the wrong fork on your way back down. From here it's a steep haul to the top. Start early and aim to turn around by noon, as afternoon lightning is typical during summer. It's a 6-mile round-trip, taking roughly between seven and eight hours. To get here, take Colorado 9 to County Rd 850. Make a right and turn right again onto 851. Drive 1.1 miles to the unmarked trailhead. Park parallel on the fire road.

Hearthstone　　　　MODERN AMERICAN **$$$**
(☑970-453-1148; hearthstonerestaurant.biz; 130 S Ridge St; mains $26-44; ☺4pm-late; ☑) 🅿
One of Breck's favorites, this restored 1886 Victorian churns out creative mountain fare such as blackberry elk and braised buffalo ribs with tomatillos, roasted chiles and polenta. Fresh and delicious, it's worth a splurge, or hit happy hour (4pm to 6pm) for $5 plates paired with wine. Reserve.

Downstairs at Eric's　　　　BAR
(www.downstairsaterics.com; 111 S Main St; ☺11am-midnight; ⊞) Downstairs at Eric's is a Breckenridge institution. Locals flock to this game-room-style basement joint for the brews, burgers and delicious mashed potatoes. There are over 100 beers (20 on tap) to choose from.

🛍 Shopping

Outlets at Silverthorne　　　　CLOTHING
(www.outletsatsilverthorne.com; ☺10am-8pm Mon-Sat, 10am-6pm Sun) Located 15 minutes from Breckenridge, just off I-70, are three shopping villages of designer brand stores with discount prices. Brands include Calvin Klein, Nike, Levi's, Gap and many others.

ℹ Information

Visitor Center (☑877-864-0868; www.go-breck.com; 203 S Main St; ☺9am-9pm; 🛜⊞) Partly set in a 19th-century cabin, with plenty of info and a small but interesting museum.

ℹ Getting There & Around

Breckenridge is about 80 miles from Denver, 9 miles south of I-70 on Hwy 9.

Colorado Mountain Express (☑800-525-6363; www.coloradomountainexpress.com; adult/child $70/36; 🛜) runs shuttles between Breckenridge and Denver International Airport.

Free buses (www.townofbreckenridge.com; ☺8am-11:45pm) run along four routes throughout town.

To get between Breckenridge, Keystone and Frisco, hop on free **Summit Stages buses** (☑970-668-0999; www.summitstage.com; 150 Watson Ave). To get to Vail, take the **Fresh Tracks shuttle** (☑970-453-4052; www.fresh-trackstransportation.com; $20 one-way).

Vail

Darling of the rich and sometime famous, Vail resembles an elaborate adult amusement park, with everything man-made from the golf greens down to the indoor waterfalls. It's compact and highly walkable, but the location (I-70 runs alongside) lacks the natural drama of other Rocky Mountain destinations. That said, no serious skier would dispute its status as the best ski resort in Colorado, with its powdery back bowls, chutes and wickedly fun terrain.

◉ Sights & Activities

Colorado Ski Museum　　　　MUSEUM
(www.skimuseum.net; 3rd fl, ☺10am-5pm; ⊞) **FREE** Humble but informative, this museum takes you from the invention of skiing to the trials of the Tenth Mountain Division, a decorated WWII alpine unit that trained in these mountains. There are also hilarious fashions from the past, as well as the fledgling Colorado Ski and Snowboard Hall of Fame. It's located at the exit of the Vail Village parking garage.

★**Vail Mountain** SNOW SPORTS
(☑970-754-8245; www.vail.com; lift ticket adult/
child $129/89; ⊙9am-4pm Dec–mid-Apr; ⊕)
Vail Mountain is our favorite in the state,
with 5289 skiable acres, 193 trails, three
terrain parks and some of the highest
lift-ticket prices in the country. If you're a
Colorado ski virgin, it's worth paying extra
to start here – especially on a sunny, blue,
fresh-powder day. Multiday tickets are good
at four other resorts. The mountaintop Adventure Ridge has child-friendly winter and
summer sports and is slated to morph into
the much larger Epic Discovery (www.ep-
icdiscovery.com) in summer 2015.

Holy Cross Wilderness HIKING
(☑970-827-5715; www.fs.usda.gov/whiteriver;
24747 US Hwy 24, Minturn; ⊙9am-4pm Mon-Fri)
Consult rangers for hiking tips. The strenuous Notch Mountain Trail affords great
views of Mt of the Holy Cross (14,005ft),
or very experienced hikers can climb the
mountain itself (a class 2 scramble) via Half
Moon Pass Trail.

Vail to Breckenridge Bike Path CYCLING
(www.fs.usda.gov) This paved car-free bike
path stretches 8.7 miles from East Vail to
the top of Vail Pass (elevation gain 1831ft),
before descending 14 miles into Frisco (nine
more if you go all the way to Breckenridge).
If you're only interested in the downhill, hop
on a shuttle from a **bike rental shop** (☑970-
476-5385; www.bikevalet.net; 520 E Lionshead Cir;
bike rental per day from $30; ⊙10am-5pm; ⊕)
and enjoy the ride back to Vail.

🛌 Sleeping

Vail is as expensive as Colorado gets, and
lodging – generally private condo rentals –
is very hit or miss.

Gore Creek Campground CAMPGROUND $
(☑877-444-6777; www.recreation.gov; Bighorn Rd;
campsites $18; ⊙mid-May–Sep; ⊛) At the end
of Bighorn Rd, this campground has 25 first-
come, first-served tent sites with picnic tables and pit toilets nestled in the woods by
Gore Creek. It's 6 miles east of Vail Village
via exit 180 (East Vail) off I-70.

★**Minturn Inn** B&B $$
(☑970-827-9647; www.minturninn.com; 442 Main
St; r summer/winter from $100/150; P ♥; 🖳ECO)
If you don't need to be at the heart of the ac-
tion, the rustic Minturn Inn should be your
pick. Set in a 1915 log-hewn building in Min-
turn (8 miles from Vail), this cozy B&B lays

on the mountain charm with handcrafted
log beds, river-rock fireplaces and antlered
decor. Reserve one of the newer River Lodge
rooms for private Jacuzzi access.

★**The Sebastian** HOTEL $$$
(☑800-354-6908; www.thesebastianvail.com;
16 Vail Rd; r summer/winter from $230/500;
P ❄ ♥ ⊠ ❀) Deluxe and modern, this sophisticated hotel showcases tasteful contemporary art and an impressive list of amenities
from a mountainside ski valet to spectacular
pool area with hot tubs frothing and spilling over like champagne. Given the prices in
Vail, the Sebastian certainly offers the most
bang for your buck, but you'll need to reserve
months in advance for the best rates.

🍴 Eating & Drinking

★**Yellowbelly** SOUTHERN $
(www.yellowbellychicken.com; unit 14, 2161 N. Frontage Rd; $10 plates; ⊙11am-8:30pm; P ♥ ⊕; 🖳Vail
Transit) It may be hidden in a West Vail strip
mall, but man is this chicken good. We could
tout the healthy angle (free-range, no GMOs,
veggie-fed birds), but it's the dynamite gluten-
free batter that earns this place its stars. Spicy,
tender pieces of chicken come with two sides
(brussel slaw, citrus quinoa, mac and cheese)
and a drink; alternatively, order an entire rotisserie bird for the whole gang.

★**bōl** MODERN AMERICAN $$
(☑970-476-5300; www.bolvail.com; 141 E Meadow
Dr; mains $14-28; ⊙5pm-1am, from 2pm in win-
ter ; ♥ ✐ ⊕) Half hip -atery, half space-age
bowling alley, bōl is hands down the funki-
est hangout in Vail. You can take the kids
bowling in the back ($50 per hour), but it's
the surprisingly eclectic menu that's the real
draw: creations range from a filling chicken
paillard salad with gnocchi to shrimp and
grits with grapefruit. Prices are relatively af-
fordable by Vail standards. Reserve.

Matsuhisa JAPANESE $$$
(☑970-476-6628; www.matsuhisavail.com; 141 E
Meadow Dr; mains $29-39, 2 piece sushi $8-12; ⊙6-
10pm) Legendary chef Nobu Matsuhisa has
upped Vail's gastronomic standards with this
modern, airy space, set at the heart of the So-
laris complex. Expect traditional sushi and
tempura alongside his signature new-style
sashimi – Matsuhisa opened his first restaurant in Peru, and continues to incorporate
South American influences into his cuisine.
Star dishes include black cod with miso and
scallops with jalapeño salsa. Reserve.

Los Amigos BAR

(400 Bridge St; ⊙11:30am-9pm) If you want views, tequila, and rock and roll with your après-ski ritual, come to Los Amigos. The Mexican food is decent at best, but the happy hour prices and slope-side seating more than make up for any culinary shortcomings.

ℹ Information

Vail Visitor Center (⎆970-479-1385; www.visitvailvalley.com; 241 S Frontage Rd; ⊙8:30am-5:30pm winter, till 8pm summer; 🛜) A second office is located in Lionshead Village.

ℹ Getting There & Around

Eagle County Airport (⎆970-328-2680; www.flyvail.com; 219 Eldon Wilson Drive), 35 miles west of Vail, has services to destinations across the country (many of which fly through Denver) and rental car counters.

Colorado Mountain Express (⎆800-525-6363; www.coloradomountainexpress.com; 🛜) shuttles run to/from Denver International Airport ($92) and Eagle County Airport ($51). Greyhound buses stop at the **Vail Transportation Center** (⎆970-476-5137; 241 S Frontage Rd) en route to Denver ($33, 2½ hours) or Grand Junction ($28, three hours).

Vail's **free buses** (www.vailgov.com; ⊙6:30am-1:50am) shuttle between West Vail, Lionshead and Vail Village; most have ski/bike racks. **Regional buses** (ECO; www.eaglecounty.us; per ride $4, $7 to Leadville) also run to Beaver Creek, Minturn and Leadville. To get to Breckenridge and other Summit County resorts, take the Fresh Tracks shuttle (p757).

Compact Vail Village, filled with upscale restaurants, bars and boutiques, is traffic free. Motorists must park in the public parking garage ($25 per day in winter, free in summer) before entering the pedestrian mall area near the chairlifts. Lionshead is a secondary base area about half a mile to the west; it also has a parking garage (same rates). It has direct lift access and is usually less crowded.

Aspen

Immodestly posh Aspen is Colorado's glitziest high-octane resort, playing host to some of the wealthiest skiers in the world. The handsome, historic red-brick downtown is as alluring as the glistening slopes, but Aspen's greatest asset is its magnificent scenery. The stunning alpine environment – especially during late September and October, when the aspen trees put on a spectacular display – just adds extra sugar to an already sweet cake.

◉ Sights & Activities

★**Aspen Center for Environmental Studies** WILDLIFE RESERVE

(ACES; ⎆970-925-5756; www.aspennature.org; Hallam Lake, 100 Puppy Smith St; ⊙9am-5pm Mon-Fri; 🅿🚼) FREE The Aspen Center for Environmental Studies is a 22-acre (10-hectare) wildlife sanctuary that hugs the Roaring Fork River. It has three other locations throughout the region and runs guided hikes, birding programs and snowshoe tours year-round. Great for families.

Aspen Art Museum MUSEUM

(⎆970-925-8050; www.aspenartmuseum.org; cnr East Hyman Ave & Spring St; ⊙10am-6pm Tue-Sat, to 7pm Thu, noon-6pm Sun) FREE No permanent collection here, just edgy, innovative contemporary exhibitions. Its brand-new home was under construction at press time; it's expected to open in summer 2014, with gorgeous rooftop views. Art lovers will not leave disappointed.

★**Aspen Mountain** SNOW SPORTS

(⎆800-525-6200; www.aspensnowmass.com; lift ticket adult/child $117/82; ⊙9am-4pm Dec–mid-Apr; 🚼) The Aspen Skiing Company runs the area's four resorts – Aspen (intermediate/expert), Snowmass (longest vertical drop in the US), Buttermilk (beginner/terrain parks) and the Highlands (expert) – which are spread out through the valley and connected by free shuttles. Both Aspen and Snowmass are open in summer (lift ticket adult/child $28/11) for sightseeing, mountain biking and kids activities.

Maroon Bells WILDERNESS AREA

If you have but one day to enjoy a slice of the pristine, you'd be wise to spend it in the shadow of Colorado's most iconic peaks. Hikes

---

DON'T MISS

CYCLING TO MAROON BELLS

According to the Aspen cycling gurus, the most iconic road-bike ride in Aspen is the one to the stunning Maroon Bells. The climb is 11 lung-wrenching miles to the foot of one of the most picturesque wilderness areas in the Rockies. If you crave sweet, beautiful pain, rent two wheelers at **Aspen Bike Tours** (⎆970-925-9169; www.aspenbikerentals.com; 430 S Spring St; half/full day adult from $33/40, child $22/29; ⊙9am-6pm; 🚼).

range from the popular 1.8-mile-long excursion (Crater Lake) to more serious challenges like Buckskin Pass (12,462ft). To get here, you'll need to catch a **shuttle** (Aspen Highlands; adult/child $6/4; ☉9am-4:30pm daily Jun 15-Aug, Fri-Sun Sep-Oct 6) from the Highlands.

The access road is only open to vehicle traffic ($10) from 5pm to 9am and is not plowed in winter. It can get awfully crowded, so if you prefer solitude, check out the Hunter-Fryingpan Wilderness near Basalt.

Ashcroft Ski Touring   SNOW SPORTS
(☏970-925-1971; www.pinecreekcookhouse.com/tours; 11399 Castle Creek Rd; adult/child $15/10; ♿) Twenty miles of groomed Nordic trails through 600 acres of subalpine country with a truly spectacular backdrop. You can rent gear and sign up for various lessons and tours. Shuttles ($35) to/from Aspen are available.

✰ Festivals

Aspen Music Festival   MUSIC
(☏970-925-9042; www.aspenmusicfestival.com; ☉Jul & Aug) Every summer classical musicians from around the world come to play, perform and learn from the masters of their craft.

🛏 Sleeping

Aspen is popular year-round. Reserve well in advance. The **Aspen Ranger District** (☏970-925-3445; www.fs.usda.gov/whiteriver; 806 W Hallam St; ☉8am-4:30pm Mon-Fri) operates some-twenty **campgrounds** (☏877-444-6777; www.recreation.gov; campsites $15-21) in the Maroon Bells, Independence Pass and Hunter-Fryingpan wilderness areas.

WORTH A TRIP

SCENIC DIVE: INDEPENDENCE PASS

Looming at 12,095ft, Independence Pass on **Hwy 82** is one of the more high-profile passes along the Continental Divide. The views along the narrow ribbon of road range from pretty to stunning to downright cinematic, and by the time you glimpse summer snowfields just below knife-edged peaks, you'll be living in your own IMAX film. Stop at the ghost town of **Independence** (www.aspenhistorysociety.com; suggested donation $3; ☉10am-6pm mid-Jun–Aug) FREE on the way up. **Hwy 82** is only open from late May to October.

St Moritz Lodge   HOSTEL $
(☏970-925-3220; www.stmoritzlodge.com; 334 W Hyman Ave; dm summer/winter $60/66, d summer $130-269, winter $155-299; P✷@⊛☎) St Moritz is the best no-frills deal in town. Perks include a heated outdoor pool and grill overlooking Aspen Mountain, and a lobby with games, books and a piano. The European-style lodge offers a wide variety of options, from quiet dorms to two-bedroom condos. The cheapest options share bathrooms. There's a kitchen downstairs.

Annabelle Inn   HOTEL $$
(☏877-266-2466; www.annabelleinn.com; 232 W Main St; r incl breakfast summer/winter from $169/199; P✷@☎) Personable and unpretentious, the cute and quirky Annabelle Inn resembles an old-school European-style ski lodge in a central location. Rooms are cozy and come with flat-screen TVs and warm duvets. You can also enjoy after-dark ski video screenings from the upper-deck hot tub (one of two on the property).

★ Limelight Hotel   HOTEL $$$
(☏800-433-0832; www.limelighthotel.com; 355 S Monarch St; r summer/winter from $245/395; P✷☎⊛☎) Sleek and trendy, the Limelight's brick-and-glass modernism reflects Aspen's effortless alpine chic vibe. Rooms are spacious and have their perks: gas fireplaces, leather furnishings and mountain views from the balconies and rooftop terraces. In addition to the ski valet and shuttle services, you can also catch live music most winter nights in the lobby's Italian kitchen. Breakfast is included.

✕ Eating & Drinking

★ Justice Snow's   PUB $$
(☏970-429-8192; www.justicesnows.com; 328 E Hyman Ave; mains $10-22; ☉11am-2am; ☎♪) ✿ Located in the historic Wheeler Opera House, Justice Snow's is a retro-fitted old saloon that marries antique wooden furnishings with a deft modern touch. Although nominally a bar – the speakeasy cocktails give the place its soul – the affordable and locally sourced menu ($10 gourmet burger! in Aspen!) is what keeps the locals coming back.

The Meatball Shack   ITALIAN $$$
(☏970-925-1349; www.themeatballshack.com; 312 S Mill Rd; lunch $13, dinner $21-28; ☉11:30am-11:30pm; ♿) ✿ Helmed by Florentine chef Eddie Baida and NYC transplant Michael Gurtman, the shack specializes in – you

guessed it – fettuccine and meatballs (*nonna*'s, chicken or veal). It's quite the happening place come evening, but forget about the scene for a minute and concentrate on what's on your plate: this is some of the best Italian fare in the Rockies.

★ **Pine Creek Cookhouse**   AMERICAN $$$
(☎970-925-1044; www.pinecreekcookhouse.com; 12700 Castle Creek Rd; lunch and summer dinner mains $13-41, winter dinner prix-fixe with ski tour/sleigh $90/110; ⊙11:30am-2:30pm daily, 2:30-8:30pm Jun-Sep, seatings at noon & 1:30pm daily, plus 7pm Wed-Sun Dec-Mar; ☑⊕) This log-cabin restaurant, located 1.5 miles past the Ashcroft ghost town at the end of Castle Creek Rd (about 30 minutes from Aspen), boasts the best setting around. In summer you can hike here; in winter it's cross country skis or horse-drawn sleigh in the shadow of glorious white-capped peaks. Sample alpine delicacies like house-smoked trout, buffalo tenderloin and grilled elk brats.

★ **Aspen Brewing Co**   BREWERY
(www.aspenbrewingcompany.com; 304 E Hopkins Ave; ⊙noon-late daily; ☜) With six signature flavors and a sun-soaked balcony facing the mountain, this casual spot is definitely the place to unwind after a hard day's play. Brews range from the flavorful This Year's Blonde and high-altitude Independence Pass Ale (its IPA) to the mellower Conundrum Red Ale and the chocolatey Pyramid Peak Porter.

Woody Creek Tavern   PUB
(☎970-923-4585; www.woodycreektavern.com; 2 Woody Creek Plaza, 2858 Upper River Rd; ⊙11am-10pm) Formerly one of Hunter S Thompson's favorite watering holes, this funky tavern is well worth the 8-mile trek from Aspen. The lunch menu features organic salads, low-fat but juicy burgers and popular Mexican food including some quality guacamole. The dinner menu is less imaginative, but there's plenty of alcohol. Eleven gallons of margaritas a day can't be wrong.

❶ Information

Aspen Visitor Center (☎970-925-1940; www.aspenchamber.org; 425 Rio Grande Pl; ⊙8:30am-5pm Mon-Fri)

❶ Getting There & Around

Four miles north of Aspen on Hwy 82, **Aspen-Pitkin County Airport** (☎970-920-5380; www.aspenairport.com; 233 E Airport Rd; ☜) has direct flights from Denver, Los Angeles, Dallas and Chicago. **Colorado Mountain Express** (☎800-525-6363; www.coloradomountain-express.com; adult/child $118/61; ☜) runs frequent shuttles to/from Denver International Airport ($118, three hours).

Roaring Fork Transit Agency (www.rfta.com) buses connect Aspen with all four ski areas (free) and runs free trips to and from Aspen-Pitkin County Airport.

If you're driving, it's easiest to park in the public garage ($15 per day) next to the Aspen Visitor Center on Rio Grande Pl.

Salida

Blessed with one of the state's largest historic downtowns, Salida is not only a charming spot to explore, it also has an unbeatable location, with the Arkansas River on one side and the intersection of two mighty mountain ranges on the other. The plan of attack here is to raft, bike or hike during the day, then come back to town to refuel with grilled buffalo ribs and a cold IPA at night.

🏃 Activities

Most rafting companies are based just south of Buena Vista (25 miles north of Salida), near where Hwys 24 and 285 diverge.

Buffalo Joe's Whitewater Rafting   RAFTING
(☎866-283-3563; www.buffalojoe.com; 113 N Railroad St; half/full day adult $64/98, child $54/78; ⊙May-Sep; ⊕) One of the top river outfitters, this shop is located in downtown Buena Vista.

River Runners   RAFTING
(☎800-723-8987; www.riverrunnersltd.com; 24070 Co Rd 301; half/full day adult $60/98, child $50/88; ⊙May-Sep; ⊕) Another recommended river outfitter based in both Buena Vista and the Royal Gorge.

Absolute Bikes   BICYCLE RENTAL
(☎719-539-9295; www.absolutebikes.com; 330 W Sackett Rd; bike rental $40-80, tours from $90; ⊙9am-7pm; ⊕) From the Monarch Crest and Rainbow Trails to across-the-river cruising. Maps, gear, advice, guided tours and rentals.

🛏 Sleeping

The Arkansas Headwaters Recreation Area operates six campgrounds (bring your own water) along the river. The nicest is **Hecla Junction** (☎800-678-2267; http://coloradostateparks.reserveamerica.com; Hwy 285, MM135; $16 per site; 🐾), located north of Salida. Reserve in summer.

RAFTING THE ARKANSAS RIVER

The headwaters of the Arkansas is Colorado's most popular stretch of river for rafters and kayakers, with everything from extreme rapids to mellow flatwater. Although most rafting companies cover the river from Leadville to the Royal Gorge, the most popular trips descend Brown's Canyon, a 22-mile stretch that includes class III/IV rapids. If you're with young kids or just looking for something mellower, Bighorn Sheep Canyon is a good bet. Those after more of an adrenaline rush can head upstream to the Numbers or downstream to the Royal Gorge, both of which are class IV/V.

Water flow varies by season, so time your visit for early June for a wilder ride – by the time August rolls around, the water level is usually pretty low. If you're rafting with kids, note that they need to be at least six years old and weigh a minimum 50 pounds.

★ **Simple Lodge & Hostel** HOSTEL **$**
(☑ 719-650-7381; www.simplelodge.com; 224 E 1st St; dm/d/q $24/55/76; [P][🛜][🐾]) If only Colorado had more spots like this. Run by a super-friendly husband-wife team (Jon and Julia), this hostel is simple but stylish, with a fully stocked kitchen and comfy communal area that feels just like home. It's a popular stopover for touring cyclists following the coast-to-coast Hwy 50.

Eating & Drinking

★ **Amícas** PIZZA, MICROBREWERY **$$**
(www.amicassalida.com; 136 E 2nd St; pizzas & paninis $8.10-11.55; ⊙ 11:30am-9pm; [✎][♿]) Thin-crust woodfired pizzas and six microbrews on tap? Amícas can do no wrong. This laid-back, high-ceilinged hangout (formerly a funeral parlor) is the perfect spot to replenish all those calories you burned off during the day. Savor a Michelangelo (pesto, sausage and goat cheese) or Vesuvio (artichoke hearts, sun-dried tomatoes, roasted peppers) alongside a cool glass of Headwaters IPA.

Fritz TAPAS **$$**
(☑ 719-539-0364; http://thefritzdowntown.com; 113 East Sackett St; tapas $4-8, mains $9-14; ⊙ 11am-2am; [🛜]) This fun and funky riverside watering hole serves up clever American-style tapas. Think Mac and three-cheese with bacon, fries with truffle aioli, shrimp curry and even bone marrow with red onion jam. It also does a mean grass-fed beef burger and other sandwiches at lunch. Good selection of beers on tap.

ℹ Information

USFS Ranger Office (☑ 719-539-3591; www.fs.usda.gov; 5575 Cleora Rd; ⊙ 8am-4:30pm Mon-Fri) Located east of town off Hwy 50, with info on hiking and camping in the Collegiates and northern Sangre de Cristo ranges.

ℹ Getting There & Away

Salida is located at the intersection of Hwys 285 and 50, west of Cañon City and south of Leadville. You'll need your own car to get here.

Colorado Springs

The site of one of the country's first destination resorts, Colorado Springs sits at the foot of majestic Pikes Peak. Pinned down with four military bases and recently beset by a series of devastating summer wildfires, the city has evolved into a strange and sprawling quilt of neighborhoods – visitors can best come to grips with the layout by dividing it in three. From east to west along Hwy 24 is the downtown district, an odd mix of fine art, Olympic dreams and downbeat desperation; Old Colorado City, whose Old West brothels and saloons now host restaurants and shops; and new agey Manitou Springs, whose mountainside location makes it the most visitor-friendly part of town.

◉ Sights & Activities

★ **Pikes Peak** MOUNTAIN
(☑ 719-385-7325; www.springsgov.com; highway per adult/child $12/5; ⊙ 7:30am-8pm Jun-Aug, 7:30am-5pm Sep, 9am-3pm Oct-May; [♿]) Originally known as the Mountain of the Sun by the Ute, Pikes Peak (14,110ft) may not be the tallest of Colorado's 54 14ers, but it's certainly the most famous. Maybe because it's the only one with a train to the top? Or perhaps because the views from the summit inspired Katherine Bates to write the lyrics for *America the Beautiful* in 1893?

In all likelihood, its location as the easternmost 14er – rising 7400ft straight up from the plains – has contributed significantly to its renown. Today, over half a million visitors ascend its summit every year. The **cog rail-**

way (☑719-685-5401; www.cograilway.com; 515 Ruxton Ave; round-trip adult/child $35/19; ☉8am-5:20pm May-Oct, reduced hours rest of year; ⓓ) leaves from Manitou Springs (about three hours 10 minutes round-trip), while the Pikes Peak Highway (about five hours round trip) climbs 19 miles to the top from Hwy 24 west of town. For an entirely different experience, consider hiking up (p763) instead.

Garden of the Gods   PARK
(www.gardenofgods.com; 1805 N 30th St; ☉5am-11pm May-Oct, 5am-9pm Nov-Apr; ⓟⓓ) FREE This gorgeous vein of red sandstone (about 290 million years old) appears elsewhere along Colorado's Front Range, but the exquisitely thin cathedral spires and mountain backdrop of the Garden of the Gods are particularly striking. Explore the network of paved and unpaved trails, enjoy a picnic and watch climbers test their nerve on the sometimes flaky rock.

In the summer, **Rock Ledge Ranch** (www.rockledgeranch.com; adult/child $8/4; ☉10am-5pm Wed-Sat Jun–mid-Aug; ⓓ), a living history museum near the park entrance, is worth a visit for those interested in the lives of Native Americans and 19th-century homesteaders in the region.

★ **Colorado Springs**
Fine Arts Center   MUSEUM
(FAC; ☑719-634-5583; www.csfineartscenter.org; 30 W Dale St; adult/student $10/8.50; ☉10am-5pm Tue-Sun; ⓟ) A sophisticated collection with terrific Latin American art, Mexican clay figures, Native American basketry and quilts, wood-cut prints and abstract work from local artists. One of Colorado's best fine arts museums.

US Air Force Academy   MILITARY ACADEMY
(☑719-333-2025; www.usafa.af.mil; I-25 exit 156B; ☉visitor center 9am-5pm; ⓟ) FREE One of the highest-profile military academies in the country, a visit to this campus offers a limited but nonetheless fascinating look into the lives of an elite group of cadets. The visitor center provides general background on the academy; from here you can walk over to the dramatic chapel (1963) or embark on a driving tour of the grounds. The entrance is via the North Gate, 14 miles north of Colorado Springs.

Barr Trail   HIKING
(www.barrcamp.com; Hydro Dr) The tough 12.5-mile Barr Trail ascends Pikes Peak with a substantial 7400ft of elevation gain. Most hikers split the trip into two days, stop-

ping to overnight at Barr Camp, the halfway point. If you're interested in doing it as a day hike, you can buy a one-way ticket up to Barr Camp ($22; first or last departure only) from the Cog Railway. The trailhead is just above the Manitou Springs cog railway depot; parking is $5.

🎪 Festivals & Events

Colorado Balloon Classic   BALLOONING
(www.balloonclassic.com; 1605 E Pikes Peak Ave; ☉Labor Day weekend; ⓓ) For nearly 40 years running, hot-air ballooners, both amateur and pro, have been launching Technicolor balloons just after sunrise for three straight days over the Labor Day weekend. You'll have to wake with the roosters to see it all, but it's definitely worth your while.

🛏 Sleeping

Barr Camp   CAMPGROUND $
(www.barrcamp.com; tent sites $12, lean-tos $17, cabin dm $28; ⓓ) At the halfway point on the Barr Trail, about 6.5 miles from the Pikes Peak summit, you can pitch a tent, shelter in a lean-to or reserve a bare-bones cabin. There's drinking water and showers; dinner ($8) is available Wednesday to Sunday. Reservations are essential and must be made online in advance. It's open year-round.

Mining Exchange   HOTEL $$
(☑719-323-2000; www.wyndham.com; 8 S Nevada Ave; r $135-200; ⓟ❋☎) Opened in 2012 and set in the turn-of-the-century bank where Cripple Creek prospectors once traded in their gold for cash (check out the vault door in the lobby), the Mining Exchange takes the prize for Colorado Spring's most stylish hotel. Twelve-foot-high ceilings, exposed brick walls and leather furnishings make for an inviting, contemporary feel, though its downtown location lacks the charm of Manitou Springs. Excellent-value rates.

Two Sisters Inn   B&B $$
(☑719-685-9684; www.twosisinn.com; 10 Otoe Pl, Manitou Springs; r without bath $79-94, with bath $135-155; ⓟ❋☎) A longtime favorite among B&B aficionados, this place has five rooms (including the honeymoon cottage out back) set in a rose-colored Victorian home, built in 1919 by two sisters. It was originally a boarding house for schoolteachers and has been an inn since 1990. There's a magnificent stained-glass front door and an 1896 piano in the parlor; it has won awards for its breakfast recipes.

WORTH A TRIP

CRIPPLE CREEK CASINOS

Just an hour from Colorado Springs yet worlds away, Cripple Creek hurls you back into the Wild West of lore. This once lucky lady produced a staggering $413 million in gold by 1952.

The booze still flows and gambling still thrives, but yesteryear's saloons and brothels are now modern casinos. If you're more interested in the regional history or simply need a break from the slots, check out the **Heritage Center** (www.visitcripplecreek.com; 9283 Hwy 67; ⊗8am-7pm; 🖪), the popular **gold mine tour** (www.goldminetours.com; 9388 Hwy 67; adult/child $18/10; ⊗8:45am-6pm mid May–Oct; 🖪) and the **narrow gauge railroad** (http://cripplecreekrailroad.com; Bennet Ave; adult/child $13/8; ⊗10am-5pm mid-May–mid-Oct; 🖪🖪) to historic Victor.

Cripple Creek is 50 miles southwest of Colorado Springs on scenic Hwy 67. For an even more impressive drive, check out the old Gold Camp Rd (Hwy 336) out of Victor on the way home. It's unpaved and narrow, but provides spectacular views. It takes about 90 minutes down to the Springs. Alternatively, catch the **Ramblin' Express** (☎719-590-8687; www.ramblinexpress.com; round-trip tickets $25; ⊗departures 7am-midnight Wed-Sun) from Colorado Springs' 8th St Depot.

Broadmoor   RESORT $$$
(☎855-634-7711; www.broadmoor.com; 1 Lake Ave; r from $280-500; 🅿❄🛜🏊🖪) One of the top five-star resorts in the US, the 744-room Broadmoor sits in a picture-perfect location against the blue-green slopes of Cheyenne Mountain. Everything here is exquisite: acres of lush grounds and a lake, a glimmering pool, world-class golf, myriad bars and restaurants, an incredible spa and ubercomfortable guest rooms (which, it must be said, are of the 'grandmother' school of design).

There's a reason that hundreds of Hollywood stars, A-list pro athletes and nearly every president since FDR have made it a point to visit.

🍴 Eating & Drinking

Shuga's   CAFE $
(www.shugas.com; 702 S Cascade St; dishes $8-9; ⊗11am-midnight; 🛜🖪) If you thought Colorado Springs couldn't be hip, stroll to Shuga's, a southern-style cafe with a knack for knockout espresso drinks and hot cocktails. Cuter than buttons, this little white house is decked out in paper cranes and red vinyl chairs. There's also patio seating. The food – brie BLT on rosemary toast, Brazilian coconut shrimp soup – comforts and delights. Don't miss vintage-movie Saturdays.

⭐**Marigold**   FRENCH $$
(☎719-599-4776; www.marigoldcafeandbakery. com; 4605 Centennial Blvd; lunch $8.25-11, dinner $9-19; ⊗11am-2:30pm & 5pm-9pm Mon-Sat, bakery 8am-9pm) Way out by the Garden of the Gods is this buzzy French bistro and bakery that's easy on both the palate and the wallet. Feast on delicacies such as snapper Marseillaise, garlic and rosemary rotisserie chicken, and gourmet salads and pizzas, and be sure to leave room for the double (and triple!) chocolate mousse cake and lemon tarts.

Adam's Mountain Cafe   MODERN AMERICAN $$
(☎719-685-1430; www.adamsmountain.com; 934 Manitou Ave; mains $9-19; ⊗8am-3pm daily, 5-9pm Tue-Sat; 🛜🍴🖪) In Manitou Springs, this slow-food cafe makes a lovely stop. Breakfast includes orange-almond French toast and huevos rancheros (eggs and beans on a tortilla). Lunch and dinner are more eclectic with offerings such as Moroccan chicken, pasta gremolata and grilled watermelon salad. The interior is airy and attractive with marble floors and exposed rafters, and there's patio dining and occasional live music too.

Jake & Telly's   GREEK $$
(☎719-633-0406; www.greekdining.com; 2616 W Colorado Ave; lunch $9-12, dinner $16-24.50; ⊗11:30am-9pm daily; 🛜🖪) One of the best choices in Old Colorado City, this eatery looks slightly touristy – lots of Greek monument murals on the walls and themed music on the stereo – but the food is absolutely delicious. It does a nice Greek-dip sandwich as well as traditional dishes such as souvlaki, dolmadas and spanakopita. It's set on a 2nd-story terrace above a magic wand shop.

⭐**Swirl**   WINE BAR
(www.swirlwineemporium.com; 717 Manitou Ave; ⊗noon-10pm Sun-Thu, to midnight Fri & Sat) Behind a stylish bottle shop in Manitou Springs, this nook bar is intimate and cool.

The garden patio has dangling lights and vines while inside are antique armchairs and a fireplace. If you're feeling peckish, sample the tapas and homemade pasta.

Bristol Brewing Co BREWERY
(www.bristolbrewing.com; 1604 S Cascade Ave; ◷11am-10pm; ◉) Although a bit out of the way in south Colorado Springs, this brewery – which in 2013 spearheaded a community center in the shuttered Ivywild Elementary School – is worth seeking out for its Laughing Lab ale and Blue Star–inspired pub grub. Other back-to-school tenants include a bakery, deli, cafe, art gallery and movie theater in the former gym.

ℹ Information

Colorado Springs Convention and Visitors Bureau (☑719-635-7506; www.visitcos.com; 515 S Cascade Ave; ◷8:30am-5pm; ◉)

ℹ Getting There & Around

Colorado Springs Municipal Airport (☑719-550-1900; www.springsgov.com; 7770 Milton E Proby Parkway; ◉) is a viable alternative to Denver. The **Yellow Cab** (☑719-777-7777) fare from the airport to the city center is $30.

Buses between Cheyenne, WY, and Pueblo, CO, stop daily at **Greyhound** (☑719-635-1505; 120 S Weber St). **Mountain Metropolitan Transit** (www.springsgov.com; per trip $1.75, day pass $4) offers schedule information and route maps for all local buses; find information online.

All street parking is meter only; if you have your own wheels, bring lots of quarters.

Southern Colorado

Home to the dramatic San Juan and Sangre de Cristo mountain ranges, Colorado's bottom half is just as pretty as its top, has fewer people and is filled with stuff to see and do.

Crested Butte

Powder-bound Crested Butte has retained its rural character better than most Colorado ski resorts. Remote, and ringed by three wilderness areas, this former mining village is counted among Colorado's best ski resorts (some say it's *the* best). The old town center features beautifully preserved Victorian-era buildings refitted with shops and businesses. Strolling two-wheel traffic matches its laidback, happy attitude.

Most everything in town is on Elk Ave, including the **visitor center** (☑970-349-

6438; www.crestedbuttechamber.com; 601 Elk Ave; ◷9am-5pm).

★**Crested Butte Mountain Resort** (☑970-349-2222; www.skicb.com; 12 Snowmass Rd; lift ticket adult/child $98/54; ⊞) sits 2 miles north of the town at the base of the impressive mountain of the same name, surrounded by forests, rugged mountain peaks and the West Elk, Raggeds and Maroon Bells-Snowmass Wilderness Areas. The scenery is breathtakingly beautiful. It caters mostly to intermediate and expert riders.

Crested Butte is also a **mountain-biking** mecca, full of excellent high-altitude singletrack trails. For maps, information and mountain-bike rentals, visit the **Alpineer** (☑970-349-5210; www.alpineer.com; 419 6th St; bike rental per day $20-55; ⊞).

Crested Butte International Hostel (☑970-349-0588, toll-free 888-389-0588; www.crestedbuttehostel.com; 615 Teocalli Ave; dm $35, d shared bath $89, r $99-109; ◉) is one of Colorado's nicest hostels. The best private rooms have their own baths. Dorm bunks come with reading lamps and lockable drawers. The communal area is mountain rustic with a stone fireplace and comfortable couches. Rates vary dramatically by season, with fall being cheapest.

With phenomenal food, the funky-casual **Secret Stash** (☑970-349-6245; www.thesecretstash.com; 303 Elk Ave; mains $8-20; ◷8am-late; ☑⊞) is adored by locals, who also dig the original cocktails. The house specialty is pizza; its Notorious Fig (with prosciutto, fresh figs and truffle oil) won the World Pizza Championship. Breakfast is best enjoyed at **Izzy's** (218 Maroon Ave; mains $7-9; ◷7am-1pm Wed-Mon), where fresh bagels, eggs and latkes are served at crowded picnic tables.

The original **Montanya** (130 Elk; snacks $3-12; ◷11am-9pm) distillery has moved here, with wide acclaim. Its basiltini, made with basil-infused rum, fresh grapefruit and lime, will have you levitating. For music, lively **Eldo Brewpub** (☑970-349-6125; www.eldobrewpub.com; 215 Elk Ave; cover charge varies; ◷3pm-late, music from 10:30pm; ⊞) is one of the town's most popular microbreweries, it also hosts the most out-of-town bands. Check out the great deck.

Crested Butte's air link to the outside world is **Gunnison County Airport** (☑970-641-2304), 28 miles south of the town. Shuttle **Alpine Express** (☑970-641-5074; www.alpineexpressshuttle.com; per person $34) goes to Crested Butte; reserve ahead in summer.

The free **Mountain Express** (970-349-7318; www.mtnexp.org) connects Crested Butte with Mt Crested Butte every 15 minutes in winter, less often in other seasons; check times at bus stops.

Ouray

With gorgeous ice falls draping the box canyon and soothing hot springs that dot the valley floor, Ouray is a privileged place for nature, even for Colorado. For ice-climbers it's a world-class destination, but hikers and 4WD fans can also appreciate its rugged (and sometimes stunning) charms. The town is a well-preserved quarter-mile mining village sandwiched between imposing peaks.

Between Silverton and Ouray, US 550 is one of the state's most memorable drives and is paved, but the road is scary in rain or snow, so take extra care.

Activities

The visitor center is at the hot-springs pool. Check out their leaflet on an excellent walking tour that takes in two-dozen buildings and houses constructed between 1880 and 1904.

Ouray Ice Park ICE CLIMBING
(970-325-4061; www.ourayicepark.com; Hwy 361; 7am-5pm mid-Dec–March;) FREE Enthusiasts from around the globe come to ice climb at the world's first public ice park, spanning a 2-mile stretch of the Uncompahgre Gorge. The sublime (if chilly) experience offers something for all skill levels.

★**Chicks with Picks** COURSE, CLIMBING
(970-316-1403, office 970-626-4424; www.chickswithpicks.net; 163 County Rd 12) Arming women with ice tools and crampons, this group of renowned women athletes gives excellent instruction for all-comers (beginners included) in rock climbing, bouldering and ice climbing. Programs are fun and change frequently, with multiday excursions or town-based courses. The climbing clinics also go on the road all over the US.

Ouray Hot Springs HOT SPRINGS
(970-325-7073; www.ourayhotsprings.com; 1220 Main St; adult/child $12/8; 10am-10pm Jun-Aug, noon-9pm Mon-Fri & 11am-9pm Sat & Sun Sep-May;) For a healing soak, try the historic Ouray Hot Springs. The natural spring water is free of the sulfur smells plaguing other hot springs around here, and the pool features a variety of soaking areas at temperatures ranging from 96° to 106°F (35.5° to 41°C). The complex also offers a gym and massage service.

San Juan Mountain Guides ROCK CLIMBING, SKIING
(800-642-5389, 970-325-4925; www.ourayclimbing.com; 725 Main St;) Ouray's own professional guiding and climbing group is certified with the International Federation of Mountain Guides Association (IFMGA). It specializes in ice and rock climbing and wilderness backcountry skiing.

DON'T MISS

SCENIC DRIVE: SAN JUAN MOUNTAIN PASSES

With rugged peaks and deep canyon drops, the scenery of the San Juan mountain range is hard to beat. Suitable for all vehicles, the **Million Dollar Highway** (US 550) takes its name from the valuable ore in the roadbed. But the scenery is also golden – the paved road clings to crumbly mountains, passing old mine-head frames and big alpine scenery.

A demanding but fantastic drive, the 65-mile **Alpine Loop Backcountry Byway** (www.alpineloop.com) begins in **Ouray** and travels east to **Lake City** – a wonderful mountain hamlet worth a visit – before looping back to its starting point. Along the way you'll cross two 12,000ft mountain passes and swap pavement and people for solitude, spectacular views and abandoned mining haunts. You'll need a high-clearance 4WD vehicle and some off-road driving skills to conquer this drive; allow six hours.

Spectacular during autumn for the splendor of its yellow aspens, **Ophir Pass** connects Ouray to Telluride via a former wagon road. The moderate 4WD route passes former mines, with a gradual ascent to 11,789ft. To get there, drive south of Ouray on Hwy 550 for 18.1 miles to the right-hand turnoff for National Forest Access, Ophir Pass.

As with all 4WD routes and mountain passes, check for road closures before going. The road is scary in rain or snow, so take extra care.

✖✦ Festivals & Events

Ouray Ice Festival
ICE CLIMBING

(📞 970-325-4288; www.ourayicefestival.com; donation for evening events; ⊗ Jan; 🐾) The Ouray Ice Festival features four days of climbing competitions, dinners, slide shows and clinics in January. There's even a climbing wall set up for kids. You can watch the competitions for free, but to check out the various evening events you will need to make a donation to the ice park. Once inside you'll get free brews from popular Colorado microbrewer New Belgium.

🛏 Sleeping & Eating

Amphitheater Forest Service Campground
CAMPGROUND $

(📞 877-444-6777; http://www.recreation.gov; US Hwy 550; tent sites $16; ⊗ Jun-Aug) With great tent sites under the trees, this high-altitude campground is a score. On holiday weekends a three-night minimum applies. South of town on Hwy 550, take a signposted left-hand turn.

★ Wiesbaden
HOTEL $$

(📞 970-325-4347; www.wiesbadenhotsprings.com; 625 5th St; r $132-347; ⊗ 🐾 🛏) Few hotels can boast their own natural indoor vapor cave (long ago used by Chief Ouray). This quirky New Age inn charms with quilted bedcovers, free organic coffee and a spacious outdoor hot-spring pool. Guests can use the Aveda salon or book a private, clothing-optional soaking tub with a waterfall ($35 per hour).

Box Canyon Lodge & Hot Springs
LODGE $$

(📞 970-325-4981, 800-327-5080; www.boxcanyonouray.com; 45 3rd Ave; r $110-165, apt $278-319; 🛏) 🐾 With geothermal heat, these pine-board rooms are toasty and spacious. A set of outdoor spring-fed barrel hot tubs are perfect for a romantic stargazing soak. Book well ahead.

Buen Tiempo Mexican Restaurant & Cantina
MEXICAN $$

(📞 970-325-4544; 515 Main St; mains $7-20; ⊗ 6-10pm; 🐾) From the chili-rubbed sirloin to the *posole* (hearty hominy soup) served with warm tortillas, Buen Tiempo delivers. Start with one of its signature margaritas, served with chips and spicy homemade salsa.

ℹ Information

Visitor Center (📞 970-325-4746; www.ouray-colorado.com; 1220 Main St; ⊗ 9am-5pm)

ℹ Getting There & Away

Ouray is 24 miles north of Silverton along US 550 and best reached by private vehicle.

Telluride

Surrounded on three sides by mastodon peaks, exclusive Telluride feels cut off from the hubbub of the outside world, and it often is. Once a rough mining town, today it's dirtbag-meets-diva – mixing the few who can afford the real estate with those scratching out a slope-side living for the sport of it. The town center still has palpable old-time charm and the surroundings are simply gorgeous.

Colorado Ave, also known as Main St, is where you'll find most businesses. From downtown you can reach the ski mountain via two lifts and the gondola. The latter also links Telluride with Mountain Village, the true base for the Telluride Ski Area. Located 7 miles from town along Hwy 145, Mountain Village is a 20-minute drive east, but is only 12 minutes away by gondola (free for foot passengers).

✦ Activities

Telluride Ski Resort
SNOW SPORTS

(📞 970-728-7533, 888-288-7360; www.telluride skiresort.com; 565 Mountain Village Blvd; lift tickets $98) Covering three distinct areas, Telluride Ski Resort is served by 16 lifts. Much of the terrain is for advanced and intermediate skiers, but there's still ample choice for beginners.

✖✦ Festivals & Events

★ Mountainfilm
FILM

(www.mountainfilm.org; ⊗ Memorial Day weekend, May) A four-day screening of outdoor adventure and environmental films on Memorial Day weekend.

Telluride Bluegrass Festival
MUSIC

(📞 800-624-2422; www.planetbluegrass.com; 4-day pass $195; ⊗ late Jun) A wild frolic held in June, with all-day and evening music, food stalls and local microbrews. Camping is popular during the festival. Check out the website for info on sites, shuttle services and combo ticket-and-camping packages – it's all very organized!

Telluride Film Festival
FILM

(📞 603-433-9202; www.telluridefilmfestival.com) National and international films are premiered throughout town in early September, and the event attracts big-name stars. For more information on the relatively complicated pricing scheme, visit the film festival website.

🛏 Sleeping

Telluride's lodgings can fill quickly, and for the best rates it's best to book online. Unless you're planning to camp, however, don't expect budget deals. Telluride's activities and festivals keep it busy year-round. For vacation rentals, the most reputable agency is **Telluride Alpine Lodging** (☑888-893-0158; www.telluridelodging.com; 324 W Colorado Ave).

Telluride Town Park Campground
CAMPGROUND $

(☑970-728-2173; 500 E Colorado Ave; campsite with/without vehicle space $23/15; ⊙mid-May–mid-Oct; ☎) Right in the center of town, these 20 sites have access to showers, swimming and tennis. It fills up quickly in the high season. For other campgrounds within 10 miles of town, check with the visitor center. 'Walkin' camping spots don't have space for a car, but you can park your car in an adjacent lot.

Victorian Inn
LODGE $$

(☑970-728-6601; www.victorianinntelluride.com; 401 W Pacific Ave; r incl breakfast from $124; ⊛❄☎) The smell of fresh cinnamon rolls greets visitors at one of Telluride's better deals, offering comfortable rooms (some with kitchenettes), and a hot tub and dry sauna in a nice garden area. Staff are friend-

---

WORTH A TRIP

COLORADO HUT TO HUT

An exceptional way to enjoy hundreds of miles of single-track in summer or virgin powder slopes in winter, **San Juan Hut Systems** (☑970-626-3033; www.sanjuanhuts.com; per person $30) continues the European tradition of hut-to-hut adventures with five backcountry mountain huts. Bring just your food, flashlight (torch) and sleeping bag: amenities include padded bunks, propane stoves, wood stoves for heating and firewood.

Mountain-biking routes go from Durango or Telluride to Moab, winding through high alpine and desert regions. Or pick one hut as your base for a few days of backcountry skiing or riding. There's terrain for all levels, though skiers should have knowledge of snow and avalanche conditions. If not, go with a guide.

The website has helpful tips and information on rental skis, bikes and (optional) guides based in Ridgway or Ouray.

---

ly and guests get lift-ticket discounts. Kids aged 12 and under stay free, and you can't beat the downtown location.

Hotel Columbia
HOTEL $$$

(☑970-728-0660, toll-free 800-201-9505; www.columbiatelluride.com; 300 W San Juan Ave; d/ste from $175/305; ℗⊛❄☎⛤) Locally owned and operated, this stylish hotel pampers guests. The gondola is across the street, so leave your gear in the ski and boot storage and head directly to a room with espresso maker, fireplace and heated tile floors. With shampoo dispensers and recycling, it's also pretty ecofriendly. Other highlights include a rooftop hot tub and fitness room.

🍴 Eating & Drinking

For the best deals, look for food carts serving Mediterranean food, hot dogs, tacos and coffee on Colorado Ave.

★ La Cocina de Luz
MEXICAN, ORGANIC $$

(www.lacocinatelluride.com; 123 E Colorado Ave; mains $9-19; ⊙9am-9pm; ⊿) 🍃 As they lovingly serve two Colorado favorites (organic and Mexican), it's no wonder that the lunch line runs deep at this healthy taqueria. Delicious details include a salsa and chip bar, handmade tortillas and margaritas with organic lime and agave nectar. Vegan, gluten-free options too.

The Butcher & The Baker
CAFE $$

(☑970-728-3334; 217 E Colorado Ave; mains $10-14; ⊙7am-7pm Mon-Sat, 8am-2pm Sun; 👪) 🍃 Two veterans of upscale local catering started this heartbreakingly cute cafe, and no one beats it for breakfast. Organic ingredients and locally sourced meats make it a cut above. The to-go sandwiches are the best bet for a gourmet meal on the trail.

Brown Dog Pizza
PIZZA $$

(☑970-728-8046; www.browndogpizza.net; 10 E Colorado Ave; pizzas $10-22; ⊙11am-10pm) The pizza? It's thin crust and fair enough, but the crowd makes the place interesting. Ten minutes after you belly up to the bar for a slice and a cheap pint of Pabst, you'll be privy to all the local dirt. Among the most affordable meals on the strip.

New Sheridan Bar
BAR

(☑970-728-3911; www.newsheridan.com; 231 W Colorado Ave; ⊙5pm-2am) Mixes real local flavor with the see-and-be-seen crowd. Most of this historic bar survived the waning mining fortunes even as the adjoining hotel sold off chandeliers to pay the bills. Look for the bullet holes in the wall.

There COCKTAIL BAR

(970-728-1213; http://therebars.com; 627 W Pacific Ave; appetizers from $4; ⊙ 5pm-12am Mon-Fri, 10am-3pm Sat-Sun) A hip social alcove for cocktails and nibbling, plus weekend brunch. For those with a bigger appetite, there's shareable entrees. East-meets-West in yummy lettuce wraps, duck ramen and sashimi tostadas, paired with original hand-shaken drinks. We liked the jalapeño kiss.

☆ Entertainment

Fly Me to the Moon Saloon LIVE MUSIC

(970-728-6666; 132 E Colorado Ave; ⊙ 3pm-2am) Let your hair down and kick up your heels to the tunes of live bands at this saloon, the best place in Telluride to groove to live music.

Sheridan Opera House THEATER

(970-728-4539; www.sheridanoperahouse.com; 110 N Oak St; ⽥) This historic venue has a burlesque charm and is always the center of Telluride's cultural life.

ⓘ Information

Visitor Center (888-353-5473, 970-728-3041; www.telluride.com; 398 W Colorado Ave; ⊙9am-5pm)

ⓘ Getting There & Around

Commuter aircraft serve the mesa-top **Telluride Airport** (970-778-5051; www.tellurideairport.com; Last Dollar Rd) 5 miles east of town on Hwy 145. If the weather is poor, flights may be diverted to Montrose, 65 miles north. For car rental, National and Budget both have airport locations.

In ski season Montrose Regional Airport, 66 miles north, has direct flights to and from Denver (on United), Houston, Phoenix and limited cities on the East Coast.

Shared shuttles by **Telluride Express** (970-728-6000; www.tellurideexpress.com) go from the Telluride Airport to town or Mountain Village for $15. Shuttles between the Montrose Airport and Telluride cost $50.

Mesa Verde National Park

Shrouded in mystery, Mesa Verde, with its cliff dwellings and verdant valley walls, is a fascinating, if slightly eerie, national park to explore. It is here that a civilization of Ancestral Puebloans appears to have vanished in AD 1300, leaving behind a complex civilization

---

DON'T MISS

TELLURIDE'S GREAT OUTDOORS

Sure, the festivals are great, but there's much more to a Telluride summer.

Mountain biking
Follow the River Trail from Town Park to Hwy 145 for 2 miles. Join **Mill Creek Trail** west of the Texaco gas station; it climbs and follows the contour of the mountain and ends at the Jud Wiebe Trail (hikers only).

Hiking
Just over 2 miles, **Bear Creek Trail** ascends 1040ft to a beautiful cascading waterfall. From here you can access the strenuous **Wasatch Trail**, a 12-mile loop that heads west across the mountains to **Bridal Veil Falls** – Telluride's most impressive waterfalls. The Bear Creek trailhead is at the south end of Pine St, across the San Miguel River.

Cycling
A 31-mile (one-way) trip, **Lizard Head Pass** features amazing mountain panoramas.

---

of cliff dwellings, some accessed by sheer climbs. Mesa Verde is unique among parks for its focus on preserving this civilization's cultural relics so that future generations may continue to interpret the puzzling settlement, and subsequent abandonment, of the area.

Mesa Verde rewards travelers who set aside a day or more to take the ranger-led tours of Cliff Palace and Balcony House, explore Wetherill Mesa or participate in one of the campfire programs. But if you only have time for a short visit, check out the Chapin Mesa Museum and walk through the Spruce Tree House, where you can climb down a wooden ladder into the cool chamber of a kiva (ceremonial structure, usually partly underground).

◉ Sights & Activities

Chapin Mesa Museum MUSEUM

(970-529-4475; www.nps.gov/meve; Chapin Mesa Rd; admission included with park entry; ⊙ 8am-6:30pm Apr–mid-Oct, 8am-5pm mid-Oct–Apr; ⽧⽥) A good first stop, with detailed dioramas and exhibits pertaining to the park. When park headquarters are closed on weekends, staff at the museum provide information.

Chapin Mesa
ARCHEOLOGICAL SITE

The largest concentration of Ancestral Puebloan sites is at Chapin Mesa, where you'll see the densely clustered **Far View Site** and the large **Spruce Tree House**, the most accessible of sites, with a paved half-mile round-trip path.

If you want to see **Cliff Palace** or **Balcony House**, the only way is through an hour-long ranger-led tour booked in advance at the visitor center ($3). These tours are extremely popular; go early in the morning or a day in advance to book. Balcony House requires climbing a 32ft and 60ft ladder – those with medical problems should skip it.

Wetherill Mesa
ARCHEOLOGICAL SITE

This is the second-largest concentration. Visitors may enter stabilized surface sites and two cliff dwellings, including the **Long House**, open late May to August. South from Park Headquarters, the 6-mile **Mesa Top Road** connects excavated mesa-top sites, accessible cliff dwellings and vantage points to view inaccessible dwellings from the mesa rim.

★ Aramark Mesa Verde
HIKING

(☑970-529-4421; www.visitmesaverde.com; adult $42-48) Highly recommended, these backcountry ranger tours are run through the park concessionaire. Backcountry hikes sell out fast, since they provide exclusive access to **Square House** (via an exposed one-mile hike) and **Spring House** (an eight-hour, 8-mile hike), but make very personalized trips to excavated pit homes, cliff dwellings and the **Spruce Tree House** daily from May to mid-October. Tickets available only online.

🛏 Sleeping & Eating

The nearby towns of Cortez and Mancos have plenty of midrange places to stay; inside the park there's camping and a lodge.

Morefield Campground
CAMPGROUND $

(☑970-529-4465; www.visitmesaverde.com; North Rim Rd; tent/RV site $29/37; ⊙May–early-Oct; 🐾) 🐾 Deluxe campers will dig the big canvas tents kitted out with two cots and a lantern. The park's camping option, located 4 miles from the entrance gate, also has 445 regular tent sites on grassy grounds conveniently located near Morefield Village. The village has a general store, gas station, restaurant, free showers and laundry. Free evening campfire programs take place nightly from Memorial Day (May) to Labor Day (September) at the Morefield Campground Amphitheater.

Far View Lodge
LODGE $$

(☑970-529-4421, toll-free 800-449-2288; www.visitmesaverde.com; North Rim Rd; r $115-184; ⊙mid-Apr–Oct; 🅿☺❄) Perched on a mesa top 15 miles inside the park entrance, this tasteful Pueblo-style lodge has 150 rooms, some with kiva fireplaces. Standard rooms don't have air con (or TV) and summer daytimes can be hot. The Southwestern-style kiva rooms are a worthwhile upgrade, with balconies, pounded copper sinks and bright patterned blankets. You can even bring your dog for an extra $10 per night.

Far View Terrace Café
CAFE $

(☑970-529-4421, toll-free 800-449-2288; www.visitmesaverde.com; North Rim Rd; dishes from $5; ⊙7-10am, 11am-3pm & 5-8pm May–mid-Oct; ☑🐾) Housed in Far View Lodge, this self-service place offers reasonably priced meals. Don't miss the house special – the Navajo Taco.

Metate Room
MODERN AMERICAN $$$

(☑800-449-2288; www.visitmesaverde.com; North Rim Rd; mains $15-28; ⊙5-7:30pm year-round, & 7-10am Apr–mid-Oct; ☑🐾) 🐾 Featuring lovely views, this innovative restaurant in the Far View Lodge offers regional flavors with some innovation, serving dishes such as cinnamon chili pork, elk shepherd's pie and trout crusted in pine nuts. You can also get local Colorado beers.

ℹ Information

The park entrance is off US 160, midway between Cortez and Mancos. New in 2012, the **Mesa Verde Visitor and Research Center** (☑800-305-6053, 970-529-5034; www.nps.gov/meve; North Rim Rd; ⊙8am-7pm daily Jun–early Sep, 8am-5pm early Sep–mid-Oct, closed mid-Oct–May; 🐾), located near the entrance, has information and news on park closures (many areas are closed in winter). It also sells tickets for **tours** ($3) of the magnificent Cliff Palace or Balcony House.

Durango

An archetypal old Colorado mining-town, Durango is a regional darling that is nothing short of delightful. Its graceful hotels, Victorian-era saloons and tree-lined streets of sleepy bungalows invite you to pedal around soaking up all the good vibes. There is plenty to do outdoors. Style-wise, Durango is torn between its ragtime past and a cool, cutting-edge future where townie bikes, caffeine and farmers markets rule.

The town's historic central precinct is home to boutiques, bars, restaurants and theater halls. Foodies will revel in the innovative organic and locavore fare that is making it the best place to eat in the state. But the interesting galleries and live music, combined with a relaxed and congenial local populace, also make it a great place to visit.

🏃 Activities

Mountain Biking
CYCLING

From steep single-track to scenic road rides, Durango is a national hub for mountain biking. The easy **Old Railroad Grade Trail** is a 12.2-mile loop that uses both US Hwy 160 and a dirt road following the old railway tracks. From Durango take Hwy 160 west through the town of Hesperus. Turn right into the Cherry Creek Picnic Area, where the trail starts. For something a bit more technical, try **Dry Fork Loop**, accessible from Lightner Creek just west of town. It has some great drops, blind corners and vegetation. Cycling shops on Main or Second Ave rent out mountain bikes.

★ Durango & Silverton Narrow Gauge Railroad
RAILWAY

(☎970-247-2733, toll-free 877-872-4607; www.durangotrain.com; 479 Main Ave; adult/child return from $85/51; ⊙ departure at 8am, 8:45am, 9:30am; 👶) Riding the Durango Silverton Narrow Gauge Railroad is a Durango must. These vintage steam locomotives have been making the scenic 45-mile trip north to Silverton (3½ hours each way) for over 125 years. The dazzling journey allows two hours for exploring Silverton. This trip operates only from May through October. Check online for different winter options.

Durango Mountain Resort
SNOW SPORTS

(☎970-247-9000; www.durangomountainresort.com; 1 Skier Pl; lift tickets adult/child from $75/45; ⊙ mid-Nov–Mar; 👶) Also known as Purgatory, this resort, 25 miles north on US 550, offers 1200 skiable acres of varying difficulty and boasts 260in of snow per year. Two terrain parks offer plenty of opportunities for snowboarders to catch big air. Check local grocery stores and newspapers for promotions and two-for-one lift tickets.

🛏 Sleeping

Hometown Hostel
HOSTEL $

(☎970-385-4115; www.durangohometownhostel.com; 736 Goeglein Gulch Rd; dm $28; ⊙ reception 3:30-8pm; P@🛜) The bee's knees of hostels, this suburban-style house sits on the winding road up to the college, next to a convenient bike path. A better class of backpackers, it's all-inclusive, with linen, towels, lockers and wi-fi. There are two single-sex dorms and a larger mixed dorm, and a great common kitchen and lounge area. Room rates fall with extended stays.

Adobe Inn
MOTEL $

(☎970-247-2743; www.durangohotels.com; 2178 Main Ave; d $84; ❄☀@🛜) Locally voted the best value lodging, this friendly motel gets the job done with clean, decent rooms and friendly service. You might even be able to talk them into giving their best rate if you arrive late night. Check out their Durango tip sheet.

★ Rochester House
HOTEL $$

(☎970-385-1920, toll-free 800-664-1920; www.rochesterhotel.com; 721 E 2nd Ave; d $169-229; ❄☀🛜) Influenced by old Westerns (movie posters and marquee lights adorn the hallways), the Rochester is a little bit of old Hollywood in the new West. It's linked to smaller accommodations, Leland House, across the street, where all guests check in. Rooms in both are spacious but slightly worn, some with kitchenettes. Still, you can't beat the cool townie bikes, available for guests to take spins around town. Pet rooms come with direct access outside.

Strater Hotel
HOTEL $$$

(☎970-247-4431; www.strater.com; 699 Main Ave; d $197-257; ❄☀@🛜) The past lives large in this historical Durango hotel with walnut antiques, hand-stenciled wallpapers and relics ranging from a Stradivarius violin to a gold-plated Winchester. But we can boast about the friendly staff, who go out of their way to resolve guests' queries. Rooms lean toward the romantic, with comfortable beds amid antiques, crystal and lace. The hot tub is a romantic plus (reserved by the hour) as is the summertime melodrama (theater) the hotel runs. In winter, rates drop by more than 50%, making it a virtual steal. Look online.

🍴 Eating & Drinking

Durango has a fantastic dining scene, especially strong on organic and locally sourced foods. Get a local dining guide (available in most hostels and at the visitors center) for all the options. It's also home to a slew of breweries.

Homeslice   PIZZERIA **$**
(☑970-259-5551; http://homeslicedelivers.com;
441 E College Ave; slice $4; ☺11am-10pm) Locals
pile into this no-frills pizza place for thick
pies with bubbly crust, sriracha sauce on the
side. There's patio seating, gluten-free crust
options and salads too.

Durango Diner   DINER **$$**
(☑970-247-9889; www.durangodiner.com; 957
Main Ave; mains $7-18; ☺6am-2pm Mon-Sat, 6am-
1pm Sun; ☑☻) Enjoy the open view of the
griddle at this lovable greasy spoon with
monstrous plates of eggs, smothered burri-
tos or French toast. It's a local institution.

Jean Pierre Bakery   FRENCH, BAKERY **$$**
(☑970-247-7700; www.jeanpierrebakery.com; 601
Main Ave; mains $9-22; ☺8am-9pm; ☑☻) This
French patisserie has tempting delicacies
made from scratch. Prices are dear, but the
soup-and-sandwich lunch special, with a
sumptuous French pastry (we recommend
the sticky pecan roll), is a good deal.

East by Southwest   FUSION, SUSHI **$$**
(☑970-247-5533; http://eastbysouthwest.com; 160
E College Dr; sushi $4-13, mains $12-24; ☺11:30am-
3pm, 5-10pm Mon-Sat, 5-10pm Sun; ☑☻) ☙
Low-lit but vibrant, this is a worthy local
favorite. Skip the standards for goosebump-
good house favorites like sashimi with
jalapeño and rolls with mango and wasabi
honey. Fish is fresh and sustainably sourced.
An extensive fusion menu also offers Thai,
Vietnamese and Indonesian, well matched
with creative martinis and sake cocktails.
For a deal, hit the happy-hour food specials
(5pm to 6:30pm).

Steamworks Brewing   BREWERY
(☑970-259-9200; www.steamworksbrewing.com;
801 E 2nd Ave; mains $10-15; ☺11am-midnight
Mon-Thur, 11am-2am Fri-Sun) DJs and live mu-
sic pump up the volume at this industrial
micro-brewery with high sloping rafters and
metal pipes. College kids fill the large bar
area, but there's also a separate dining room
with a Cajun-influenced menu.

Diamond Belle Saloon   BAR
(☑970-376-7150; www.strater.com; 699 Main Ave;
☺11am-late; ☻) A rowdy corner of the his-
toric Strater Hotel, this elegant old-time bar
has waitresses dressed in vintage Victorian
garb and flashing fishnets, and live ragtime
that keeps out-of-town visitors packed in –
standing room only at happy hour (4pm to
6pm daily). The food is below average.

ℹ Information

Visitor Center (☑800-525-8855; www.du-
rango.org; 111 S Camino del Rio) South of town
at the Santa Rita exit from US 550.

ℹ Getting There & Around

Durango-La Plata County Airport (DRO;
☑970-247-8143; www.flydurango.com; 1000
Airport Rd) is 18 miles southwest of Durango
via US 160 and Hwy 172. Greyhound buses run
daily from the **Durango Bus Center** (☑970 259
2755; 275 E 8th Ave), north to Grand Junction
and south to Albuquerque, NM.

Check **Durango Transit** (☑970-259-5438;
www.getarounddurango.com) for local transit
information. Durango buses are fitted with bi-
cycle racks. It's free to ride the red T shuttle bus
that circulates Main St.

Durango is at the junction of US 160 and US
550, 42 miles east of Cortez, 49 miles west of
Pagosa Springs and 190 miles north of
Albuquerque.

Silverton

Ringed by snowy peaks and steeped in sooty
tales of a tawdry mining town, Silverton
seems more at home in Alaska than the
lower 48. But here it is. Whether you're into
snowmobiling, powder skiing, fly-fishing,
beer on tap or just basking in some very
high-altitude sunshine, Silverton delivers.

It's a two-street town, but only one is
paved. The main drag, Greene St, is where
you'll find most businesses. Notorious Blair
St, still unpaved, runs parallel to Greene and
is a blast from the past. During the silver
rush, Blair St was home to thriving brothels
and boozing establishments.

⚐ Activities

In summer, Silverton has some of the west's
best 4WD trails. Traveling in modified Chevy
Suburbans without the top, **San Juan Back-
country** (☑970-387-5565; toll-free 800-494-
8687; www.sanjuanbackcountry.com; 1119 Greene
St; 2hr tours adult/child $60/40; ☺May-Oct; ☻)
☙ offers both tours and rental jeeps.

⮒ Sleeping & Eating

**Red Mountain Motel
& RV Park**   MOTEL, CAMPGROUND **$$**
(☑970-382-5512, toll-free 800-970-5512; www.
redmtmotelrvpk.com; 664 Greene St; motel r from
$110, cabins from $120, tent/RV sites $22/38;
☺year-round; Ⓟ☻☎) Campers can try Red
Mountain Motel & RV Park, a pet-friendly
place that stays open year-round.

Inn of the Rockies at the
Historic Alma House
B&B $$

(📞970-387-5336, toll-free 800-267-5336; www.innoftherockies.com; 220 E 10th St; r incl breakfast $109-173; 🅿️😊❄️) Splurge for romance here with an outdoor hot tub and New Orleans–inspired breakfast.

Stellar
ITALIAN $$

(📞970-387-9940; 1260 Blair St; mains $8-20; ☺4pm-9:30pm; 🚻) Your best bet for a sit-down meal is Stellar, an atmospheric pizzeria with full bar and beer on tap. Go for the lasagna if it isn't sold out.

🍷 Drinking

★Montanya Distillers
BAR

(www.montanyadistillers.com; 1309 Greene St; mains $6-13; ☺12pm-10pm) The town has its share of Western-style saloons, but for something original seek out Montanya Distillers, a smart bar with rooftop summer seating and exotic cocktails crafted with homemade syrups and award-winning rum. Organic tamales and other yummy edibles are served.

ℹ️ Getting There & Away

Silverton is 50 miles north of Durango and 24 miles south of Ouray off US 550.

Great Sand Dunes National Park

Landscapes collide in a shifting sea of sand at **Great Sand Dunes National Park** (📞719-378-6399; www.nps.gov/grsa; 11999 Hwy 150; adult/child $3/free; ☺visitor center 8:30am-6:30pm summer, shorter hours rest of year), making you wonder whether a spaceship has whisked you to another planet. The 55-sq-mile dune park – the tallest sand peak rises 700ft above the valley floor – is squeezed between the jagged 14,000ft peaks of the Sangre de Cristo and San Juan Mountains and flat, arid scrub-brush of the San Luis Valley.

Plan a visit to this excellent-value national park ($3 admission is a steal) around a full moon. Stock up on supplies, stop by the visitor center for your free backcountry camping permit and hike into the surreal landscape to set up camp in the middle of nowhere (bring plenty of water). You won't be disappointed.

There are numerous **hiking trails**, like the half-mile **Zapata Falls** (BLM road 5415), reached through a fun slot canyon (wear grippy shoes, you may be in standing water). And there's always **sandboarding**, where you ride a snowboard down the dunes, though it's best left to those who already snowboard.

The most popular month to visit is June, when Medano Creek is flowing and kids get a natural refreshment by wading in. Be sure to bring lots of water. Walking in loose sand is difficult, and summer temperatures on the dunes can exceed 130°F (54°C).

🛏️ Sleeping

Pinyon Flats Campground
CAMPGROUND $

(📞888-448-1474; www.recreation.gov; Great Sand Dunes National Park; campsites $20; 🚻) In the national park, Pinyon Flats has 88 sites and year-round water.

Zapata Falls Campground
CAMPGROUND $

(www.fs.usda.gov; BLM road 5415; campsites $11; ☺year-round; 🚻) With awesome valley panoramas, the more secluded Zapata Falls lies seven miles south via a steep 3.6-mile dirt access road. Bring your own water.

Zapata Ranch
RANCH $$$

(📞719-378-2356; www.zranch.org; 5303 Hwy 150; d with full board $300) Ideal for horse-riding enthusiasts, the exclusive Zapata Ranch is a working cattle and bison ranch set amid groves of cottonwood trees. Owned and operated by the Nature Conservancy, the main inn is a refurbished 19th-century log structure, with distant views of the sand dunes.

ℹ️ Getting There & Away

The national park is about 35 miles northeast of Alamosa and 250 miles south of Denver. From Denver, take I-25 south to Hwy 160 west and turn onto Hwy 150 north. There is no public transportation.

WYOMING

With wind, restless grasses and wide blue skies, the most sparsely populated state offers solitude to spare. Called the 'Bunchgrass edge of the World' by writer Annie Proulx, Wyoming may be nuzzled in the bosom of America, but it's emptiness that defines it.

Though steeped in ranching culture – just see the line of Stetsons at the local credit union – Wyoming is the number-one coal producer in the US, and is also big in natural gas, crude oil and diamonds. Deeply conservative, its propensity toward industry has sometimes made it an uneasy steward of the land.

But wilderness may be Wyoming's greatest bounty. Its northwestern corner is home to the magnificent national parks of Yellowstone and Grand Teton. Chic Jackson and

WYOMING FACTS

Nickname Equality State

Population 576,000

Area 97,100 sq miles

Capital city Cheyenne (population 60,100)

Sales tax 4%

Birthplace of Artist Jackson Pollock (1912-1956)

Home of Women's suffrage, coal mining, geysers, wolves

Politics Conservative to the core

Famous for Rodeo, ranches, former Vice President Dick Cheney

Kitschiest souvenir Fur jock strap from a Jackson boutique

Driving distances Cheyenne to Jackson 440 miles

progressive Lander make great bases for epic hiking, climbing and skiing. For a truer taste of Western life, check out the plain prairie towns of Laramie and Cheyenne.

ℹ️ Information

Even on highways, distances are long, with gas stations few and far between. Driving hazards include frequent high gusty winds and fast-moving snow squalls that can create whiteout blizzard conditions. If the weather gets too rough, the highway patrol will shut the entire interstate until it clears.

Wyoming Road Conditions (☎307-772-0824, 888-996-7623; www.wyoroad.info)

Wyoming State Parks & Historic Sites (☎307-777-6323; www.wyo-park.com; admission $6, historic site $4, campsite per person $17) Wyoming has 12 state parks. Camping reservations are taken online or over the phone.

Wyoming Travel & Tourism (☎800-225-5996; www.wyomingtourism.org; 1520 Etchepare Circle)

Cheyenne

Many a country tune has been penned about Wyoming's state capital and largest city, though Cheyenne is more like the Hollywood Western *before* the shooting begins – that is, until Frontier Days festival, a raucous July celebration of cowboy fun. At the junction of I-25 and I-80, it's an obvious pit stop.

👁 Sights & Activities

Cheyenne Gunslingers   WILD WEST SHOW
(☎800-426-5009; www.cheyennegunslingers.com; cnr W 15th at Pioneer Ave; ⊗noon Sat & 6pm Thu-Fri Jun, 6pm Mon-Fri, 12pm Sat Jul; 🚻) **FREE** A non-profit group of actors who puts on a lively, if not exactly accurate Old West show – from near hangings to slippery jailbreaks. Stars include corrupt judges, smiling good guys and, of course, the bad-ass villains.

Frontier Days Old West Museum   MUSEUM
(☎307-778-7290; www.oldwestmuseum.org; 4601 N Carey Ave; adult/child $10/5; ⊗8am-6pm Mon-Fri, 9am-5pm Sat & Sun summer, 9am-5pm Mon-Fri, 10am-5pm Sat & Sun winter) For a peek into the pioneer past, visit the lively Frontier Days Old West Museum at I-25 exit 12. It is chock-full of rodeo memorabilia – from saddles to trophies. For the audio tour, call ☎307-316-0071.

🎊 Festivals & Events

⭐ **Cheyenne Frontier Days**   RODEO
(☎1-800-227-6336; www.cfdrodeo.com; 4501 N Carey Ave; admission free-$32; ⊗July; 🚻) If you've never seen a steer wrestler leap into action, this very Western event is bound to brand an impression. Beginning in late July, Wyoming's largest celebration features 10 days of rodeos, concerts, dances, air shows, and chili cook-offs. Free events include morning 'slack' rodeos, pancake breakfasts and parades. There's also an art sale and 'Indian village.'

🛌 Sleeping & Eating

Reservations are a must during Frontier Days, when rates double and everything within 50 miles is booked; see www.cheyenne.org/availability for bookings. The cheapest motels line noisy Lincolnway (I-25 exit 9).

Nagle Warren Mansion Bed & Breakfast   B&B $$
(☎307-637-3333; www.naglewarrenmansion.com; 222 E 17th St; r incl breakfast from $155; ❄🎧🐾) This lavish spread is a fabulous find. In a quickly-going-hip neighborhood, this historic 1888 house is decked out with late-19th-century regional antiques. Spacious and elegant, the mansion boasts a hot tub, a reading room tucked into a turret and classic 1954 Schwinn bikes for cruising. Jim, the owner, entertains with his deep knowledge of local history.

It's worth stopping at the excellent art gallery next door.

Tortilla Factory
MEXICAN $

(715 S Greeley Hwy; mains $3-10; ☺ 6am-8pm Mon-Sat, 8am-5pm Sun) A delicious Mexican dive serving homemade tamales for $1.50, and authentic classics such as shredded-beef tacos and huevos rancheros.

Shadows Pub & Grill
BREWERY $

(Depot Station; mains $8-15; ☺ 11am-11pm Mon-Thur, 11am-1am Fri-Sat, 11am-9pm Sun) It's hard to beat the ambience at this handsome brick brewpub at the 1860s Union Pacific depot. The pub fare is standard, but there's ample patio seating for sunny days and good microbrews on tap.

🛍 Shopping

Boot Barn
CLOTHING, SOUVENIRS

(1518 Capitol Ave; ☺ 9am-9pm Mon-Sat, 9am-6pm Sun) If you are hankering after a Stetson hat, rhinestone belt-buckle or authentic cowboy boots, look no further. This hub of Western wear is full of gems.

ℹ Information

Cheyenne Visitor Center (☎ 307-778-3133; www.cheyenne.org; 1 Depot Sq; ☺ 8am-7pm Mon-Fri, 9am-5pm Sat, 11am-5pm Sun, closed weekends in winter) A great resource.

ℹ Getting There & Around

Cheyenne Airport (CYS; ☎ 307-634-7071; www.cheyenneairport.com; 200 E 8th Ave) has daily flights to Denver. Greyhound buses depart from the **Black Hills Stage Lines** (☎ 307-635-1327; www.blackhillsstagelines.com; 5401 Walker Rd) daily for Billings, MT, ($84, 9½ hours) and Denver, CO ($31, 2¾ hours), among other destinations.

On weekdays, the **Cheyenne Transit Program** (☎ 307-637-6253; adult $1, 6-18yr 75¢; ☺ service 6am-7pm Mon-Fri, 10am-5pm Sat) operates six local bus routes. Also, **Cheyenne Street Railway Trolley** (☎ 800-426-5009; 121 W 15th St; adult/child $10/5; ☺ May-Sep) takes visitors on tours through downtown.

Laramie

Home to the state's only four-year university, Laramie can be both hip and boisterous, a vibe missing from most Wyoming prairie towns. Worth exploring is the small historic downtown, a lively five-block grid of attractive two-story brick buildings with hand-painted signs and murals pushed up against the railroad tracks.

For an infusion of culture, check out one of the museums on the University of Wyoming (UW) campus, the newly refurbished **Geological Museum** (☎ 307-766-2646; www.uwyo.edu/geomuseum; Hwy 287 at I-80; ☺ 10am-4pm Tues-Fri, 10am-3pm Sat-Sun) **FREE** features an impressive collection of dinosaur remains, including those of a Tyrannosaurus rex. If you're traveling with the kids (or just feel like one), stop by the **Wyoming Frontier Prison** (☎ 307-745-616; www.wyomingfrontierprison.org; 975 Snowy Range Rd; adult/child $7/6; ☺ 8am-5pm; ♿), a curious restoration of an early prison and frontier town.

There are numerous cheap sleeps off I-80 at exit 313. With landscaped gardens, lauded homemade granola and three snug rooms, **Mad Carpenter Inn** (☎ 307-742-0870; madcarpenter.com; 353 N 8th St; r incl breakfast $95-125; 🛜) has warmth to spare. A serious game room features billiards and table tennis. In town, the **Gas Lite Motel** (☎ 307-742-6616; 960 N 3rd St; r $61; ❄🐾🛜🐴) relies on an outrageously kitsch setup (think cowboy cutouts and plastic horses) to sell its well-priced and pet-friendly digs.

With superlative brews, **Coal Creek Coffee Co** (110 E Grand Ave; mains $3-6; ☺ 6am-10pm; 🛜) is modern and stylish, with Fair Trade roasts and tasty sandwiches (eg bluecheese and portobello panini). Doubtless the healthiest food for miles, **Sweet Melissa's** (213 S 1st St; mains $8-10; ☺ 11am-9pm Mon-Sat; 🍴) does good down-home vegetarian. It's packed at lunchtime.

For live country music and beer, favorite dive **Old Buckhorn Bar** (☎ 307-742-3554; 114 Ivinson St; ☺ 9am-12am Sun-Wed, 9am-2am Thur-Sat) is Laramie's oldest standing bar. Check out the hand-scratched graffiti and old condom dispenser in the bathroom.

Located 4 miles west of town via I-80 exit 311, **Laramie Regional Airport** (☎ 307-742-4164) has daily flights to Denver ($98 one-way). **Greyhound** (☎ 307-742-5188) buses stop at the **Diamond Shamrock gas station** (1952 Banner Road). Fill up your tank (and tummy) in Laramie; heading west on I-80, the next services aren't for 75 miles.

Lander

Lander just might be the coolest little one-street town in Wyoming – and there are many of those. Just a stone's throw from the Wind River Reservation, it's a rock-climbing and mountaineering mecca in a friendly and unpretentious foothills setting. It is also home to NOLS (www.nols.edu; 284 Lincoln St.), the National Outdoor Leadership School, a renowned outdoor school that leads trips around the world and locally into the Wind River Range.

The **Lander Visitor Center** (☑307-332-3892; www.landerchamber.org; 160 N 1st St; ☺9am-5pm Mon-Fri) is a good source of general information. If you've come to hike, camp or climb, you're best popping into **Wild Iris Mountain Sports** (☑307-332-4541; 166 Main St), a gear shop offering good advice and rental climbing or snow shoes. Pick up their cheat sheet with local tips. If you want to check out the single-track trails outside town, head to **Gannett Peak Sports** (351B Main Street; ☺10am-6pm Mon-Fri, 9am-5pm Sat).

The beautiful **Sinks Canyon State Park** (☑307-332-3077; 3079 Sinks Canyon Rd; admission $6; ☺visitor center 9am-6pm Jun-Aug), 6 miles south of Lander, features a curious underground river. Flowing through a narrow canyon, the Middle Fork of the Popo Agie River disappears into the soluble Madison limestone called the Sinks and returns warmer a quarter-mile downstream in a pool called the Rise. The scenic **campgrounds** (campsites $17) come highly recommended by locals.

Chain hotels line Main St, but for a deal try the locally owned **Holiday Lodge** (☑307-332-2511; www.holidaylodgelander.com; 210 McFarlane Dr; camping $10 per person, r incl breakfast from $50; ❄☎). The look might say 1961, but it's scrubbed shiny and friendly, with thoughtful extras like an iron, makeup remover and sewing kits. Recommended riverside camping includes breakfast and showers.

Decompress from long hours of travel or adventure at the backyard patio of **Gannett Grill** (☑307-332-8227; 128 Main St; mains $6-9; ☺11am-9pm), a local institution, where you take a microbrew from the **Lander Bar** (☑307-332-8228; 126 Main St; mains $6-9; ☺11am-late) next door and wander back to your shady picnic table to dine on local beef burgers, crisp waffle fries and stone-oven pizzas. If you're feeling fancy, try the adjoining **Cowfish**, a more upscale dinner offering from the same folks. There's live music many nights.

Grab your coffee at chic **Old Town Coffee** (300 Main St; ☺7am-7pm; ☎) where each cup is brewed to order, as stiff as you like it.

Wind River Transportation Authority (☑307-856-7118; www.wrtabuslines.com) provides bus service to Jackson ($160) and other destinations; check the website for schedules.

Cody

Raucous Cody revels in its Wild West image (it's named after legendary showman William 'Buffalo Bill' Cody). With a staged streak of yeehaw, the town happily relays yarns (not always the whole story, mind you) about its past. Summer is high season, and Cody puts on quite an Old West show for the throngs of visitors making their way to Yellowstone National Park, 52 miles to the west. From Cody, the approach to geyserland through the Wapiti Valley is dramatic to say the least. President Teddy Roosevelt once said this stretch of pavement was 'the most scenic 50 miles in the world.'

The **visitor center** (☑307-587-2777; www.codychamber.org; 836 Sheridan Ave; ☺8am-6pm Mon-Sat, 10am-3pm Sun Jun-Aug, 8am-5pm Mon-Fri Sep-May) is the logical starting point.

Cody's major tourist attraction is the superb **Buffalo Bill Historical Center** (www.bbhc.org; 720 Sheridan Ave; adult/child $18/10; ☺8am-6pm May-Oct, 10am-5pm Nov, Mar & Apr, 10am-5pm Thu-Sun Dec-Feb). A sprawling complex of five museums, it showcases everything Western: from posters, grainy films and other lore pertaining to Buffalo Bill's world-famous Wild West shows, to galleries showcasing frontier artwork and a museum dedicated to Native Americans. Its Draper Museum of Natural History is a great primer for the Yellowstone ecosystem, with information on everything from wolves to grizzlies.

Also popular is the **Cody Nite Rodeo** (www.codystampederodeo.com; 519 West Yellowstone Ave; adult/child 7-12 yr $18/8), which giddy-ups nightly from June to August.

The lovely **Chamberlin Inn** (☑307-587-0202; 1032 12th St.; d/ste $185/325) offers an elegant downtown retreat. Built by ol' Bill himself in 1902, **Irma Hotel** (☑307-587-4221; www.irmahotel.com; 1192 Sheridan Ave; mains $8-23; ❄) is now better known for its restaurant – the ornate cherrywood was a gift from Queen Victoria. Gunfights break out nightly at 6pm in front of the hotel from June through September.

The **Silver Dollar Bar** (1313 Sheridan Ave; mains $7-12; ☺11am-12pm) is a historic watering hole with live music nightly on the outdoor deck. It serves epic burgers and has pool tables.

Yellowstone Regional Airport (COD; www.flyyra.com) is 1 mile east of Cody and runs daily flights to Salt Lake City and Denver.

Yellowstone National Park

They grow their critters and geysers big up in Yellowstone, America's first national park and Wyoming's flagship attraction. From shaggy grizzlies to oversized bison and magnificent packs of wolves, this park boasts the lower 48's most enigmatic concentration of wildlife. Throw in half the world's geysers, the country's largest high-altitude lake and a plethora of blue-ribbon rivers and waterfalls, all sitting pretty atop a giant supervolcano, and you'll quickly realize you've stumbled across one of Mother Nature's most fabulous creations.

When John Colter became the first white man to visit the area in 1807, the only inhabitants were Tukadikas (aka Sheepeaters), a Shoshone Bannock people who hunted bighorn sheep. Colter's reports of exploding geysers and boiling mud holes (at first dismissed as tall tales) brought in expeditions and tourism interest eagerly funded by the railroads. The park was established in 1872 (as the world's first) to preserve Yellowstone's spectacular geography: the geothermal phenomena, the fossil forests and Yellowstone Lake.

The 3472-sq-mile park is divided into five distinct regions (clockwise from the north): Mammoth, Roosevelt, Canyon, Lake and Geyser Countries.

Of the park's five entrance stations, only the North Entrance, near Gardiner, MT, is open year-round. The others, typically open May to October, offer access from the northeast (Cooke City, MT), east (Cody, WY), south (Grand Teton National Park) and west (West Yellowstone, MT). The park's main road is the 142-mile Grand Loop Rd scenic drive.

⊙ Sights & Activities

Just sitting on the porch of the Old Faithful Inn with a cocktail in hand waiting for Old Faithful geyser to erupt could be considered enough activity by itself but there's plenty else to keep you busy here, from hiking and backpacking to kayaking and fly-fishing. Most park trails are not groomed, but unplowed roads and trails are open for cross-country skiing.

Yellowstone is split into five distinct regions, each with unique attractions. Upon entering the national park you'll be given a basic map and a park newspaper detailing the excellent ranger-led talks and walks (well worth attending). All the visitor centers have information desks staffed by park rangers who can help you tailor a hike to your tastes, from great photo spots to best chance of spotting a bear.

Geyser Country   GEYSER, HIKING

With the densest collection of geothermal features in the park, Upper Geyser Basin contains 180 of the park's 250-odd geysers. The most famous is **Old Faithful**, which spews from 3700 to 8400 gallons of water 100ft to 180ft into the air every 1½ hours or so. For an easy walk, check out the predicted eruption times at the brand new visitor center and then follow the easy boardwalk trail around the Upper Geyser Loop. The park's most beautiful thermal feature is **Grand Prismatic Spring** in the Midway Geyser Basin. The Firehole and Madison Rivers offer superb fly-fishing and wildlife viewing.

Mammoth Country   GEYSER, HIKING

Known for the geothermal terraces and elk herds of historic **Mammoth** and the hot springs of **Norris Geyser Basin**, Mammoth Country is North America's most volatile and oldest-known continuously active thermal area. The peaks of the Gallatin Range rise to the northwest, towering above the area's lakes, creeks and numerous hiking trails.

Roosevelt Country   HIKING

Fossil forests, the commanding **Lamar River Valley** and its tributary trout streams, **Tower Falls** and the Absaroka Mountains'

ⓘ BEAT THE CROWDS
....

Yellowstone's wonderland attracts up to 30,000 visitors daily in July and August and over three million gatecrashers annually. Avoid the worst of the crowds with the following advice:

➡ Visit in May, September or October for decent weather and few people; or even in winter.

➡ Ditch 95% of the crowds by hiking a backcountry trail. Lose 99% by camping in a backcountry site (permit required).

➡ Mimic the wildlife and be most active in the golden hours after dawn and before dusk.

➡ Pack lunch for one of the park's many scenic picnic areas and eat lodge dinners late (after 9pm).

➡ Make reservations for park lodging months in advance and book concession campgrounds *at least* the day before.

Yellowstone & Grand Teton National Parks

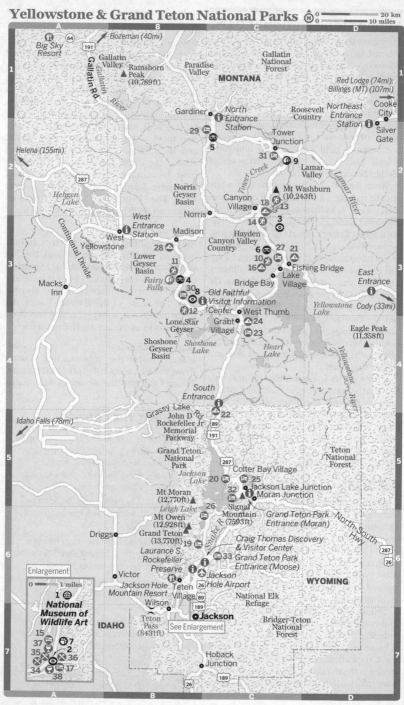

Yellowstone & Grand Teton National Parks

ROCKY MOUNTAINS YELLOWSTONE NATIONAL PARK

craggy peaks are the highlights of Roosevelt Country, the park's most remote, scenic and undeveloped region. Several good hikes begin near **Tower Junction**.

Canyon Country
LOOKOUT, HIKING

A series of scenic overlooks linked by hiking trails highlight the colorful beauty and grandeur of the Grand Canyon of the Yellowstone and its impressive **Lower Falls**. South Rim Dr leads to the canyon's most spectacular overlook, at **Artist Point**. **Mud Volcano** is Canyon Country's primary geothermal area.

Lake Country
LAKE, BOATING

Yellowstone Lake, the centerpiece of Lake Country and one of the world's largest alpine lakes, is a watery wilderness lined with volcanic beaches and best explored by boat or sea kayak. Rising east and southeast of the lakes, the wild and snowcapped Absaroka Range hides the wildest lands in the lower 48, perfect for epic backpacking or horseback trips.

Hiking Trails
HIKING

Hikers can explore Yellowstone's backcountry from more than 92 trailheads that give access to 1100 miles of hiking trails. A free backcountry-use permit, which is available at visitor centers and ranger stations, is required for overnight trips. Backcountry camping is allowed in 300 designated sites, 60% of which can be reserved in advance by mail; a $25 fee applies to all bookings that are more than three days in advance.

After much heated debate and a narrowly avoided fistfight, we have settled on the following as our favorite five-day hikes in the park.

➡ **Lone Star Geyser Trail**

A good family hike or bike ride along an old service road to a geyser that erupts every three hours. Start at the Kepler Cascades parking area, southeast of the Old Faithful area (5 miles, easy).

➡ **South Rim Trail**

A web of interconnected trails that follows the spectacular Yellowstone Canyon rim past the Lower Falls to scenic Artists Point then Lily Pad Lake, returning to Uncle Tom's trailhead via thermal areas and Clear Lake (3.5 miles, easy).

➡ Mt Washburn

A fairly strenuous uphill hike from Dunraven Pass trailhead to a mountaintop fire tower, for 360-degree views over the park and nearby bighorn sheep (6.4 miles, moderate).

➡ Elephant Back Mountain

An 800ft climb from near Lake Hotel to a panoramic viewpoint over Yellowstone Lake (3.5 miles, moderate).

➡ Fairy Falls

Climb off-trail to a viewpoint over spectacular Grand Prismatic Spring and then hike through lodgepole forest to the falls, before continuing on to beautiful Imperial Geyser (6 miles, easy).

Cycling   CYCLING

Cyclists can ride on public roads and a few designated service roads, but not on the backcountry trails. The best season is April to October, when the roads are usually snow-free. From mid-March to mid-April the Mammoth–West Yellowstone park road is closed to cars but open to cyclists, offering a long but stress-free ride.

Yellowstone Raft Company   ADVENTURE TOUR
(☑ 800-858-7781; www.yellowstoneraft.com; halfday adult/child $40/30) There is exhilarating white water through Yankee Jim Canyon on the Yellowstone River just north of the park boundary in Montana. This company offers a range of guided adventures out of Gardiner starting in late May.

🛏 Sleeping

NPS and private campgrounds, along with cabins, lodges and hotels, are all available in the park. Reservations are essential in summer. Contact the park concessionaire **Xanterra** (☑ 307-344-5395; www.yellowstonenationalparklodges.com) to reserve a spot at its campsites, cabins or lodges.

Plentiful accommodations can also be found in the gateway towns of Cody, Gardiner and West Yellowstone.

The best budget options are the seven NPS–run campgrounds (campsites from $15-20) in **Mammoth** (campsites $14; ☺ year-round), **Tower Fall**, **Indian Creek**, **Pebble Creek**, **Slough Creek**, **Norris** and **Lewis Lake**, which are first-come, first-served. Xanterra runs five more campgrounds (listed below; reservations accepted, $20 to $45 per night), all with cold-water bathrooms, flush toilets and drinking water. RV sites with hookups are available at Fishing Bridge.

Xanterra-run cabins, hotels and lodges are spread around the park and are open from May or June to October. Mammoth Hot Springs Hotel and Old Faithful Snow Lodge are the exceptions; these are also open mid-December through March. All places are nonsmoking and none have air con or TV. Where wi-fi is available, it costs extra.

Bridge Bay Campground   CAMPGROUND $
(campsite $21) Near the west shore of Yellowstone Lake, popular with boaters, and with 425 sites for tents and RVs.

WHERE THE BEARS & BISON ROAM...

Along with the big mammals – grizzly, black bear, moose and bison – Yellowstone is home to elk, pronghorn antelope and bighorn sheep. Wolves have been part of the national park since reintroduction in 1996, though they are now legally hunted outside park boundaries. Native to the area, both wolves and bison nearly met extinction by the end of the last century because of hunting and human encroachment. While their numbers have resurged, taking them off the endangered species list means they may yet be hunted out of the park.

In Yellowstone's heart between Yellowstone Lake and Canyon Village, **Hayden Valley** is your best all-round bet for wildlife viewing. For the best chances of seeing wildlife, head out at dawn or dusk and stakeout a turnout anywhere off the Grand Loop Rd. Bring patience and binoculars, a grizzly just might wander into your viewfinder, or perhaps you'll spy a rutting elk or hear the bugle of a solitary moose reaching the river for a drink.

Lamar Valley, in the northeast, is where wolves were first reintroduced and ground zero for spotting them. Ask rangers where packs are most active or attend a wolf-watching (or other) excursion with the recommended **Yellowstone Institute** (www.yellowstoneassociation.org). Hearing howls echo across the valley at dusk is a magical, primeval experience.

Canyon Campground CAMPGROUND $
(campsite $25.50) Centrally located, with pay showers and coin laundry nearby. There are 250 sites for tents and RVs.

Fishing Bridge RV Park CAMPGROUND $
(campsite $45) Full hook-ups for hard-shell RVs only ($37). Pay showers and coin laundry. There are 325 sites.

Grant Village Campground CAMPGROUND $
(campsite $25.50) On Yellowstone Lake's southwest shore, it has 400 sites for tents and RVs. Pay showers and coin laundry nearby.

Madison Campground CAMPGROUND $
(✆307-344-7311; www.yellowstonenationalpark-lodges.com; campsite $21; ⊘early May-late Oct) The closest campground to Old Faithful, with 250 sites for tents and RVs.

Old Faithful Lodge Cabins CABIN $
(cabins $69-115) Views of Old Faithful; simple, rustic cabins.

Roosevelt Lodge Cabins CABIN $$
(✆866-439-7375; www.yellowstonenationalpark-lodges.com; cabins $69-115; 🐾) These cabins are good for families. With a cowboy vibe, the place offers nightly 'Old West dinner cookouts,' during which guests travel by horse or wagon to a large meadow 3 miles from the lodge for open-air buffets (book ahead).

Lake Lodge Cabins CABIN $$
(cabins $75-188) The main lodge boasts a large porch with lakeside mountain views and a cozy room with two fireplaces. Choose from rustic 1920s wooden cabins or more modern motel-style modules.

Old Faithful Snow Lodge HOTEL $$
(cabins $99-155, r from $229; 🛜) A stylish modern option that combines timber-lodge style with modern fittings and park motifs.

⭐**Old Faithful Inn** HOTEL $$
(✆866-439-7375; www.yellowstonenationalpark-lodges.com; old house d with shared/private bath from $103/140, standard from $164; ⊘early May-early Oct) Next to the signature geyser, this grand inn is the most requested lodging in the park. A national historic landmark, it features an immense timber lobby, with huge stone fireplaces and sky-high knotted-pine ceilings. Rooms come in all price ranges, and many of the most interesting historic rooms share baths. Public areas offer plenty of allure.

It's worth staying two nights to soak up the atmosphere.

Lake Yellowstone Hotel HOTEL $$
(✆866-439-7375; www.yellowstonenationalpark-lodges.com; cabins $130, r $149-299; ⊘mid-May-Sep) Oozing grand 1920s Western ambience, this romantic, historic hotel is a classy option. It has Yellowstone's most divine lounge, which was made for daydreaming, with big picture windows overlooking the lake, ample natural light and a live string quartet playing in the background. Rooms are well appointed, cabins more rustic.

Canyon Lodge & Cabins CABIN $$
(cabins $99-188, r $185) Clean and tidy in a central locale.

Mammoth Hot Springs Hotel & Cabins HOTEL $$
(cabins $86-229, r with/without bath $123/87; 🛜) Wide variety of sleeping options; elk are often seen grazing on the front lawn.

Grant Village HOTEL $$
(r $155) Near the southern edge of the park, it offers comfortable but dull motel-style rooms. Two nearby restaurants have fabulous lake views.

🍴 Eating

Snack bars, delis, burger counters and grocery stores are scattered around the park. In addition, most of the lodges offer breakfast buffets, salad bars, and lunch and dinner in formal dining rooms. Food, while not always exceptional, is quite good considering how many people the chef is cooking for, and not too overpriced for the exceptional views.

⭐**Lake Yellowstone Hotel Dining Room** AMERICAN $$$
(✆307-344-7311; mains $13-33; ⊘6:30-10am, 11:30am-2:30pm, 5-10pm; 🍴) Keep one unwrinkled outfit to dine in style at the dining room of the Lake Yellowstone Hotel, the best in the park. Lunch options include Montana lamb sliders, lovely salads and bison burgers. Local and gluten-free options. Dinner consists of heavier fare, with reservations highly recommended.

Old Faithful Inn Dining Room AMERICAN $$$
(✆307-545-4999; dinner mains $13-29; ⊘6:30-10:30am, 11:30am-2:30pm, 5-10pm; 🍴) The buffets here will maximize your time spent geyser gazing but the à la carte options are more innovative, think elk burgers, bison pot roast and the ever-popular pork osso bucco. With gluten-free options. Reservations recommended.

ROCKY MOUNTAINS YELLOWSTONE NATIONAL PARK

SCENIC DRIVE: THE ROOF OF THE ROCKIES

The most scenic route into Yellowstone Park, **Beartooth Highway** (www. beartoothhighway.com; US 212; ⊙ Jun–mid-Oct) connects Red Lodge to Cooke City and Yellowstone's north entrance by an incredible 68-mile journey alongside 11,000ft peaks and wildflower-sprinkled alpine tundra. It's been called both American's most scenic drive and its premier motorcycle ride. There are a dozen USFS campgrounds (reservations for some accepted at www. recreation.gov) along the highway, four within 12 miles of Red Lodge.

ℹ Information

The park is open year-round, but most roads close in winter. Park entrance permits (hiker/vehicle $12/25) are valid for seven days for entry into both Yellowstone and Grand Teton National Parks. Summer-only visitor centers are evenly spaced every 20 to 30 miles along Grand Loop Rd.

Albright Visitors Center (☑307-344-2263; www.nps.gov/yell; ⊙8am-7pm Jun-Sep, 9am-5pm Oct-May) Serves as park headquarters. The park website is a fantastic resource.

ℹ Getting There & Away

The closest year-round airports are: Yellowstone Regional Airport (COD) in Cody (52 miles); Jackson Hole Airport (JAC) in Jackson (56 miles); Gallatin Field Airport (BZN) in Bozeman, MT (65 miles); and Idaho Falls Regional Airport (IDA) in Idaho Falls, ID (107 miles). The airport (WYS) in West Yellowstone, MT, is usually open June to September. It's often more affordable to fly into Billings, MT (170 miles), Salt Lake City, UT (390 miles) or Denver, CO (563 miles) and rent a car.

There is no public transportation to or within Yellowstone National Park.

Grand Teton National Park

With its jagged, rocky peaks, cool alpine lakes and fragrant forests, the Tetons rank among the finest scenery in America. Directly south of Yellowstone, Grand Teton National Park has 12 glacier-carved summits, which frame the singular Grand Teton (13,770ft). For mountain enthusiasts, this sublime and crazy terrain is thrilling. Less crowded than Yellowstone, the Tetons also have plenty of

tranquility, along with wildlife such as bear, moose, grouse and marmot.

The park has two entrance stations: Moose (south), on Teton Park Rd west of Moose Junction; and Moran (east), on US 89/191/287 north of Moran Junction. The park is open year-round, although some roads and entrances close from around November to May 1, including part of Moose-Wilson Rd, restricting access to the park from Teton Village.

🏃 Activities

With 200 miles of **hiking trails** you can't really go wrong. Consult at the visitor center where you can grab a hiking map. A free backcountry-use permit, also available here, is required for overnight trips. The Tetons are also known for excellent short-route **rock climbs** as well as classic longer routes to summits like Grant Teton, Mt Moran and Mt Owen.

Fishing is another draw, with several species of whitefish and cutthroat, lake and brown trout thriving in local rivers and lakes. Get a license at the Moose Village store, Signal Mountain Lodge or Colter Bay Marina.

Cross-country skiing and **snowshoeing** are the best ways to take advantage of park winters. Pick up a brochure detailing routes at Craig Thomas Discovery & Visitor Center.

Jenny Lake Ranger Station ROCK CLIMBING (☑307-739-3343; ⊙8am-6pm Jun-Aug) For climbing information.

Exum Mountain Guides ROCK CLIMBING (☑307-733-2297; www.exumguides.com) For instruction and guided climbs.

🛏 Sleeping

Three different concessionaires run the park's six campgrounds. Demand is high from early July to Labor Day. Most campgrounds fill by 11am (Jenny Lake fills much earlier; Gros Ventre rarely fills up). Colter Bay and Jenny Lake have tent-only sites reserved for backpackers and cyclists.

Climbers' Ranch CABIN $ (☑307-733-7271; www.americanalpineclub.org; Teton Park Rd; dm $25; ⊙Jun-Sep) Started as a refuge for serious climbers, these rustic log cabins run by the American Alpine Club are now available to hikers who can take advantage of the spectacular in-park location. There is a bathhouse with showers and a sheltered cook station with locking bins for coolers. Bring your own sleeping bag and pad (bunks are bare, but still a steal).

Flagg Ranch Resorts CAMPGROUND $
(www.flaggranch.com; 2-person campsites $35)
Accepts online reservations for Flagg Ranch
campground, and also has cabins. Forever
Resorts manages Signal Mountain and Liz-
ard Creek campgrounds in the park.

Grand Teton Lodge
Company ACCOMMODATIONS SERVICES $
(🗐307-543-2811; www.gtlc.com; campsites $21)
Runs most of the park's private lodges,
cabins and the campgrounds of Colter Bay,
Jenny Lake and Gros Ventre. Call for last-
minute cancellations, though it's best to
reserve ahead, as nearly everything is completely booked by early June. Each lodge has
an activity desk.

Colter Bay Village CABIN $$
(🗐307-543-2811; www.gtlc.com; tent cabins $57,
cabins with bath $135-239, without bath $73; ☺ Jun-
Sep) Half a mile west of Colter Bay Junction,
the village has two types of accommoda-
tions. Tent cabins (June to early September)
are very basic structures with bare bunks
and shared bathrooms in a separate build-
ing. At these prices, you're better off camp-
ing. The log cabins, some original, are much
more comfortable and a better deal; they're
available late May to late September.

Signal Mountain Lodge CAMPGROUND, LODGE $$
(🗐307-543-2831; www.signalmtnlodge.com; camp-
sites $21, r $194-230, cabins $156-185; ☺ May–mid-
Oct) This spectacularly located place at the
edge of Jackson Lake offers cozy, well-appointed cabins and rather posh rooms with
stunning lake and mountain views.

★ **Jenny Lake Lodge** LODGE $$$
(🗐307-733-4647; www.gtlc.com; Jenny Lake; cabins
incl half board $655; ☺ Jun-Sep) Worn timbers,
down comforters and colorful quilts imbue
this elegant lodging off Teton Park Rd with a
cozy atmosphere. It doesn't come cheap, but
includes breakfast, a five-course dinner, bi-
cycle use and guided horseback riding. Rainy
days are for hunkering down at the fireplace
in the main lodge with a game or book from
the stacks. The log cabins sport a deck but no
TVs or radios (phones on request).

Jackson Lake Lodge LODGE $$$
(🗐307-543-2811; www.gtlc.com; r & cabins $249-
335; ☺ Jun-Sep; 🐾🖥🕎) With soft sheets,
meandering trails for long walks and enormous picture windows framing the luminous peaks, this lodge is the perfect place to
woo. Yet, you may find the 348 cinder-block

cottages generally overpriced. Has a heated
pool and pets are OK.

Spur Ranch Log Cabins CABIN $$$
(🗐307-733-2522; www.dornans.com; cabins $185-
265; ☺year-round) Gravel paths running
through a broad wildflower meadow link
these tranquil duplex cabins on the Snake
River in Moose. Lodgepole-pine furniture,
Western styling and down bedding create a
homey feel, but the views are what make it.

✕ Eating

Colter Bay Village, Jackson Lake Lodge,
Signal Mountain and Moose Junction have
several reasonably priced cafes for breakfast
and fast meals.

Pioneer Grill DINER $$
(🗐307-543-1911; Jackson Lake Lodge; mains $9-
23; ☺6am-10:30pm; 🖼) A casual classic with
leatherette stools lined up in a maze, the
Pioneer serves up wraps, burgers and salads.
Kids adore the hot fudge sundaes. A takeout
window serves boxed lunches (order a day
ahead) and room-service pizza for pooped
hikers (5pm to 9pm).

Mural Room MODERN AMERICAN $$$
(🗐307-543-1911; Jackson Lake Lodge; mains $22-
40; ☺7am-9pm) With stirring views of the
Tetons, gourmet selections include game
dishes and imaginative creations like trout
wrapped in sushi rice with sesame seeds.
Breakfasts are very good; dinner reserva-
tions are recommended.

Peaks AMERICAN $$$
(🗐307-543-2831; Signal Mountain Lodge; meals
$18-31) Dine on selections of cheese and fruit,
local free-range beef, and organic polenta
cakes. Small plates, like wild game sliders,
are also available. While the indoor ambience
is rather drab, the patio seating, starring sunsets over Jackson Lake and top-notch huckleberry margaritas, gets snapped up early.

Jenny Lake Lodge
Dining Room MODERN AMERICAN $$$
(🗐307-543-3352; breakfast $24, lunch mains
$12-15, dinner prix-fixe $85; ☺7am-9pm) A real
splurge, this may be the only five-course wil-
derness meal of your life, but it's well worth
it. For breakfast, crab-cake eggs benedict is
prepared to perfection. Trout with polenta
and crispy spinach satisfies hungry hikers,
and you can't beat the warm atmosphere
snuggled in the Tetons. Dress up in the
evening, when reservations are a must.

ⓘ Information

Park permits (hiker/vehicle $12/25) are valid for seven days for entry into both Yellowstone and Grand Teton National Parks. It's easy to stay in one park and explore the other in the same day.

Craig Thomas Discovery & Visitor Center
(☑307-739-3399, backcountry permits 307-739-3309; Teton Park Rd; ⊙8am-7pm Jun-Aug, 8am-5pm rest of year) Located in Moose.

Laurance S Rockefeller Preserve Center
(☑307-739-3654; Moose-Wilson Rd; ⊙8am-6pm Jun-Aug, 9am-5pm rest of year) This recent addition gives information about the new and highly recommended Rockefeller Preserve, a less crowded option for hiking, located 4 miles south of Moose.

Park Headquarters (☑307-739-3600; www. nps.gov/grte; ⊙8am-7pm Jun-Aug, 8am-5pm rest of year) Shares a building with the Craig Thomas center.

Jackson

Technically this is Wyoming, but you'll have a hard time believing it. With a median age of 32, this Western town has evolved into a mecca for mountain lovers, hard-core climbers and skiers, easily recognizable as sun-burned baristas. The upswing of being posh and popular? Jackson is abuzz with life: trails and outdoor opportunities abound. Fresh sushi is flown in daily and generous purse-strings support a vigorous cultural life. Skip the souvenirs and remember why you came to Jackson in the first place: to visit its glorious backyard, Grand Teton National Park.

⊙ Sights

Downtown Jackson has a handful of historic buildings.

★ National Museum of Wildlife Art
MUSEUM
(☑307-733-5771; www.wildlifeart.org; 2820 Rungius Rd; adult/child $12/6; ⊙9am-5pm) If you visit one area museum, make it this one. Major works by Bierstadt, Rungius, Remington and Russell that will make your skin prickle. The discovery gallery has a kids' studio for drawing and print rubbing that adults plainly envy. Check the website for summer film series and art-class schedules.

Center for the Arts
ARTS CENTER
(☑307-733-4900; www.jhcenterforthearts.org; 240 S Glenwood S) One-stop shopping for culture, attracting big-name concert acts and featuring theater performances, classes, art exhibits and events. Check the calendar of events online.

National Elk Refuge
WILDLIFE RESERVE
(☑307-733-9212; www.fws.gov/nationalelkrefuge; Hwy 89; horse-drawn sleigh ride adult/child $18/14; ⊙8am-5pm Sep-May, 8am-7pm Jun-Aug, horse-drawn sleigh ride 10am-4pm mid-Dec–Mar) **FREE** Protects thousands of migrating wapiti from November to March. A 45-minute **horse-drawn sleigh ride** is a highlight of a winter visit.

Town Square Shoot-out
WILD WEST SHOW
(⊙6.15pm Mon-Sat summer; ⊕) **FREE** In summer this hokey tourist draw takes place at 6:15pm Monday to Saturday.

🏃 Activities

★ Jackson Hole Mountain Resort
SNOW SPORTS
(☑307-733-2292; www.jacksonhole.com; lift ticket adult/child $99/59) One of the country's top ski destinations, Jackson Hole Mountain Resort boasts the USA's greatest continuous vertical rise – from the 6311ft base at Teton Village to the 10,450ft summit of Rendezvous Mountain. Terrain is mostly advanced, boasting lots of fluffy powder and rocky ledges made for jumping. Tickets are slightly discounted online.

When the snow melts, the resort runs a plethora of summertime activities; check the website for details.

🕭 Courses

Teton Science Schools Ecology
SCIENCE SCHOOL
(☑307-733-1313; www.tetonscience.org) No one beats this nonprofit for fun experiential education, with programs ranging from GPS scavenger hunts to ecology expeditions. Make inquiries through the website.

🛏 Sleeping

Jackson has plenty of lodging options, both in town and around the ski hill. Reservations are essential in summer and winter.

Hostel
HOSTEL $
(☑307-733-3415; www.thehostel.us; 3315 Village Dr; dm/d $34/99; ⊙closed fall & spring shoulder seasons; ⊛) Teton Village's only budget option, this old ski lodge offers private doubles and bunk-bed rooms with renovated showers for up to four. The spacious lounge with fireplace is ideal for movies or Scrabble tournaments and there's a playroom for tots. Guests can use a microwave and outdoor grill, coin laundry and a ski-waxing area.

Buckrail Lodge   MOTEL **$**
(☑ 307-733-2079; www.buckraillodge.com; 110 E Karnes Ave; r from $93; ❄ 🛜) Spacious and charming log-cabin-style rooms, this steal is centrally located, with ample grounds and an outdoor Jacuzzi.

Golden Eagle Motor Inn   MOTEL **$$**
(☑ 307-733-2042; 325 E Broadway; r $148; ≋) Super-friendly and just far enough out of the fray, this refurbished motel with friendly hosts is a reliable choice in the center.

Alpine House   B&B **$$$**
(☑ 307-739-1570; www.alpinehouse.com; 285 N Glenwood St; d $250, cottage $450; ◉) Two former Olympic skiers have infused this downtown home with sunny Scandinavian style and personal touches like great service and a cozy mountaineering library. Amenities include plush robes, down comforters, a shared Finnish sauna and an outdoor Jacuzzi. Save your appetite for the creative breakfast options such as poached eggs over ricotta with asparagus or multigrain French toast.

✕ Eating & Drinking

Jackson is home to Wyoming's most sophisticated and exotic food. Many restaurants double as bars, with the real deals dished out for happy hour.

★ Coco Love   DESSERT **$**
(☑ 307-733-3253; 55 N Glenwood Dr; desserts $5-8; ☺ 9am-8pm) Master dessert chef Oscar Ortega shows off his French training with a pastry case of exquisite object d'art desserts and handmade chocolates that make you quiver in delight. Do it.

Pica's Mexican Taqueria   MEXICAN **$$**
(1160 Alpine Lane; mains $7-15; ☺ 11:30am-9pm Mon-Fri, 11am-4pm Sat & Sun; 🍴) Cheap and supremely satisfying, with Baja tacos wrapped in homemade corn tortillas or *cochinita pibil* (chili-marinated pork), served with Mexican sodas. Locals love this place; it's the best value around.

Pizzeria Caldera   PIZZERIA **$$**
(☑ 307-201-1472; 20 West Broadway; pizzas $12-16; ☺ 11am-9:30pm; 🍴) 🌱 Fresh and unpretentious, this upstairs pizzeria serves their pies on the thinner side. Try topping yours with briny kalamata olives or fragrant bison sausage with sage, which begs one of the beers on tap. Salads use locally-grown arugula and beets.

Bubba's Bar-B-Que   BARBECUE **$$**
(☑ 307-733-2288; 100 Flat Creek Dr; mains $6-20; ☺ 7am-10pm; 🍴) Get the biggest, fluffiest breakfast biscuits for miles at this friendly and energetic bring-your-own-bottle (BYOB) eatery. Later on, it's got a decent salad bar, and serves up a ranch of ribs and racks.

★ Snake River Grill   MODERN AMERICAN **$$$**
(☑ 307-733-0557; 84 E Broadway; mains $21-52; ☺ from 5:30pm) With a roaring stone fireplace, an extensive wine list and snappy

---

IF YOU HAVE A FEW MORE DAYS

Wyoming is full of great places to get lost, sadly there are too many for us to elaborate on in this guide, but we'll prime you with a taster.

With vast grassy meadows, seas of wildflowers and peaceful conifer forests, the **Bighorn Mountains** in north-central Wyoming are truly awe-inspiring. Factor in gushing waterfalls and abundant wildlife and you've got a stupendous natural playground with hundreds of miles of marked trails.

Rising a dramatic 1267ft above the Belle Fourche River, the nearly vertical monolith of **Devil's Tower National Monument** is an awesome site. Known as Bears Lodge by some of the 20-plus Native American tribes who consider it sacred, it's a must-see if you are traveling between the Black Hills (on the Wyoming–South Dakota border) and the Tetons or Yellowstone.

West of Laramie, the lofty national forest stretching across **Medicine Bow Mountains** and **Snowy Range** is a wild and rugged place, perfect for multiday hiking and camping trips.

Nestled in the shadow of the Bighorn Mountains, **Sheridan** boasts century-old buildings once home to Wyoming cattle barons. It's popular with adventure fanatics who come to play in the Bighorns.

white linens, this grill creates notable American haute cuisine. Start with tempura string beans with spicy sriracha dipping sauce. The crispy pork falls off the bone and grilled elk chops show earthy goodness. Splurge-desserts like crème brulée or homemade ice cream easily satisfy two.

★ Stagecoach Bar
BAR

(☑307-733-4407; 5755 W Hwy 22, Wilson) Wyoming has no better place to shake your booty. 'Mon-day' means reggae, Thursday is disco night and every Sunday the house band croons country-and-western favorites until 10pm. Worth the short drive to Wilson (just past the Teton Village turnoff).

Snake River Brewing Co
BREWPUB

(☑307-739-2337; 265 S Millward St; ☺11:30am-midnight) With an arsenal of 22 microbrews crafted on the spot, some award-winning, it's no wonder that this is a favorite rendezvous spot. Food includes wood-fired pizzas and pasta (mains $6 to $18). Happy hour is from 4pm to 6pm.

Million Dollar Cowboy Bar
BAR

(25 N Cache Dr) Touristy to the gills, but tempting nonetheless. Plunk your hind quarters on a saddle stool in this dark chop house, an obligatory stop on the Western tour. On weekends the dance floor sparks up and karaoke drones.

ℹ Information

Jackson Hole Wyoming (www.jacksonholenet.com) A good website for information on the area.

Valley Bookstore (125 N Cache St) Sells regional maps.

Visitor Center (☑307-733-3316; www.jacksonholechamber.com; 532 N Cache Dr; ☺9am-5pm)

ℹ Getting There & Around

Jackson Hole Airport (JAC; ☑307-733-7682) is 7 miles north of Jackson off US 26/89/189/191 within Grand Teton National Park. Daily flights serve Denver, Salt Lake City, Dallas and Houston, while weekend flights connect Jackson with Chicago.

Alltrans' Jackson Hole Express (☑307-733-3135; www.jacksonholebus.com) buses provide a shuttle to Grand Teton National Park ($14 per day) and the airport ($16). It also departs at 6:30am daily from Maverik County Store (cnr Hwy 89 S and S Park Loop Rd) for Salt Lake City ($70, 5½ hours).

MONTANA

Maybe it's the independent frontier spirit, wild and free and oh-so American, that earned Montana its 'live and let live' state motto. The sky seems bigger and bluer. The air is crisp and pine-scented. From its mountains that drop into undulating ranchlands to brick brewhouses and the shaggy grizzly found lapping at an ice-blue glacier lake, Montana brings you to that euphoric place, naturally. And then it remains with you long after you've left its beautiful spaces behind.

ℹ Information

Montana Fish, Wildlife & Parks (☑406-444-2535; http://fwp.mt.gov) Camping in Montana's 24 state parks costs around $15/23 per night for residents/nonresidents, while RV hookup sites (where available) cost an additional $5. Make reservations at ☑1-855-922-6768 or http://montanastateparks.reserveamerica.com.

Montana Road Conditions (☑800-226-7623, within Montana 511; www.mdt.mt.gov/travinfo)

Travel Montana (☑800-847-4868; www.visitmt.com)

Bozeman

In a gorgeous locale, surrounded by rolling green hills, pine forests and snowcapped peaks, Bozeman is the defending title holder of Coolest Town in Montana. Brick buildings with brewpubs and boutiques line historic Main St, mashing bohemian style up against cowboy cool and triathlete verve. A prime location up against the Bridger and Gallatin mountains makes it one of the very best outdoor towns in the West.

◉ Sights & Activities

Museum of the Rockies
MUSEUM

(☑406-994-2251; www.museumoftherockies.org; 600 W Kagy Blvd; adult/child $14/10; ☺8am-8pm; 👪) Montana State University's (MSU) museum is the most entertaining in Montana and shouldn't be missed, with stellar dinosaur exhibits, early Native American art and laser planetarium shows.

★ Bridger Bowl Ski Area
SNOW SPORTS

(☑406-587-2111; www.bridgerbowl.com; 15795 Bridger Canyon Rd; day lift ticket adult/child under 12yr $49/16; ☺mid-Dec–Mar) Only in Bozeman would you find a nonprofit ski resort. But this excellent community-owned facility, 16 miles north of Bozeman, is just that. It's known for its fluffy, light powder and unbeatable prices – especially for children under 12.

🛏 Sleeping

The full gamut of chain motels lies north of downtown on 7th Ave, near I-90. There are more budget motels east of downtown on Main St, with rooms starting at around $50, depending on the season.

Bear Canyon Campground CAMPGROUND $
(☑ 800-438-1575; www.bearcanyoncampground. com; tent sites $20, RV sites $28-33; ☉ May–mid-Oct; 🛜🏊) Three miles east of Bozeman off I-90 exit 313, Bear Canyon Campground is on top of a hill with great views of the surrounding valley. There's even a pool.

Howlers Inn B&B $$
(☑ 406-586-0304; www.howlersinn.com; 3185 Jackson Creek Rd; d incl breakfast $110-150, 2-person cabin $195; 🛜) Wolf-watchers will love this beautiful sanctuary 15 minutes outside of Bozeman. Rescued captive-born wolves live in an enclosed 4-acre area, supported by profits of the B&B. There's three spacious Western-style rooms in the main lodge and a two-bedroom cabin. With luck, you will drift off to sleep serenaded by howls. Take exit 319 off I-90.

Lewis & Clark Motel MOTEL $$
(☑ 800-332-7666; www.lewisandclarkmotelboze-man.com; 824 W Main St; r weekend/weekday $159/99; 🅿🛜) For a drop of Vegas in your Montana, stay at this flashy, locally owned motel. The large rooms have floor-to-ceiling front windows and the piped 1950s music adds to the retro Rat Pack vibe. With hot tub and steam room.

🍴 Eating & Drinking

As a college town, Bozeman has no shortage of student-oriented cheap eats and enough watering holes to quench a college football team's thirst. Nearly everything is located on Main St.

La Tinga MEXICAN $
(12 E Main St; mains $1.50-7; ☉ 8:30am-2:30pm) Simple, cheap and authentic, La Tinga is no-frills dining at its tastiest. The tiny order-at-the-counter taco joint makes a delicious version of the Mexican pork dish it is named after, and lots of freshly made tacos starting at just $1.50, or choose the daily lunch combo deal for less than $7.

Community Co-Op SUPERMARKET $
(www.bozo.coop; 908 W Main; mains $5-10; ☉ 7am-10pm Mon-Sat, 8am-10pm Sun; 🛜🍴) 🍃 This beloved local is the best place to stock up on organic and bulk foods, as well as hot meals, salads and soups to eat in or take away. The W Main branch has a great organic coffee-house upstairs.

Plonk WINE BAR $$
(www.plonkwine.com; 29 E Main St; dinner mains $13-32; ☉ 11:30am-midnight) Where to go for a drawn-out three-martini, gossipy lunch? Plonk serves a wide-ranging menu from light snacks to full meals, mostly made from local organic products. In summer the entire front opens up and cool breezes enter the long building, which also has a shotgun bar and pressed-tin ceilings.

John Bozeman's Bistro AMERICAN $$
(☑ 406-587-4100; www.johnbozemansbistro. com; 125 W Main St; mains $14-34; ☉ 11:30am-2:30pm, 5-9:30pm Tues-Sat; 🍴) Bozeman's best

---

MONTANA FACTS

Nickname Treasure State, Big Sky Country

Population 1,005,000

Area 145,552 sq miles

Capital city Helena (population 28,600)

Other cities Billings (population 105,600), Missoula (67,300), Bozeman (38,000)

Sales tax No state sales tax

Birthplace of Movie star Gary Cooper (1901–61), motorcycle daredevil Evel Knievel (1938–2007), actress Michelle Williams (1980)

Home of Crow, Blackfeet and Salish Native Americans

Politics Republican ranchers and oilmen generally edge out the Democratic students and progressives of left-leaning Bozeman and Missoula

Famous for Fly-fishing, cowboys and grizzly bears

Random fact Some Montana highways didn't have a speed limit until the 1990s!

Driving distances Bozeman to Denver 695 miles, Missoula to Whitefish 136 miles

FLY-FISHING IN BIG SKY

Ever since Robert Redford and Brad Pitt made it look sexy in the 1992 classic, *A River Runs Through It,* Montana has been closely tied to fly-fishing cool. Whether you are just learning or a world-class trout wrangler, the wide, fast rivers are always spectacularly beautiful and filled with fish. Although the film – and book it is based on – is set in Missoula and the nearby Blackfoot River, the movie was actually shot around Livingston and the Yellowstone and Gallatin Rivers.

For DIY trout fishing, the Gallatin River, 8 miles southwest of Bozeman along Hwy 191, has the most accessible, consistent angling spots, closely followed by the beautiful Yellowstone River, 25 miles east of Bozeman in the Paradise Valley.

For the scoop on differences between rainbow, brown and cutthroat trout – as well as flies, rods and a Montana fishing license – visit **Bozeman Angler** (☑ 406-587-9111; www.bozemanangler.com; 23 E Main St; ☺ 9:30am-5:30pm Mon-Sat, 10am-3pm Sun). Owned by a local couple for nearly two decades, the downtown shop runs a great introduction-to-fly-fishing class ($125 per person, casting lessons $40 per hour) on the second Saturday of the month between May and September.

restaurant offers Thai, Creole and pan-Asian slants on the cowboy dinner steak, plus starters like lobster chowder and a weekly 'superfood' special, featuring especially nutritious seasonal vegetarian fare.

Molly Brown BAR
(www.mollybrownbozeman.com; 703 W Babcock) Popular with local MSU students, this noisy dive bar offers 20 beers on tap and eight pool tables for getting your game on.

Zebra Cocktail Lounge LOUNGE
(☑ 406-585-8851; 15 N Rouse St; ☺ 8pm-2am) Inside the Bozeman Hotel, this place is the epicenter of the local live music scene, strong on club and hip-hop.

ℹ️ Information

Visitor Center (☑ 406-586-5421; www.bozemanchamber.com; 1003 N 7th Ave; ☺ 8am-5pm Mon-Fri) Information on lodging and area attractions.

ℹ️ Getting There & Away

Gallatin Field Airport (BZN; ☑ 406-388-8321; www.bozemanairport.com) is 8 miles northwest of downtown. **Karst Stage** (☑ 406-556-3540; www.karststage.com) runs buses daily, December to April, from the airport to Big Sky ($51, one hour) and West Yellowstone ($102, two hours); summer service is by reservation only.

Rimrock Stages buses depart from the **bus depot** (☑ 406-587-3110; www.rimrocktrailways.com; 1205 E Main St), half a mile from downtown, and service all Montana towns along I-90.

Gallatin & Paradise Valleys

Outdoor enthusiasts could explore the expansive beauty around the Gallatin and Paradise Valleys for days. **Big Sky Resort** (☑ 800-548-4486; www.bigskyresort.com; lift ticket adult $89), with multiple mountains, 400in of annual powder and Montana's longest vertical drop (4350ft), is one of the nation's premier downhill and cross-country ski destinations, especially now it has merged with neighboring Moonlight Basin. Lift lines are the shortest in the Rockies, and if you are traveling with kids then Big Sky is too good a deal to pass up – children under 10 ski free, while even your teenager saves $20 off the adult ticket price. In summer it offers gondola-served hiking and mountain biking.

For backpacking and backcountry skiing, head to the Spanish Peaks section of the **Lee Metcalf Wilderness**. It covers 389 sq miles of Gallatin and Beaverhead National Forest land west of US 191. Numerous scenic USFS campgrounds snuggle up to the Gallatin Range on the east side of US 191.

Twenty miles south of Livingston, off US 89 en route to Yellowstone, unpretentious **Chico Hot Springs** (☑ 406-333-4933; www.chicohotsprings.com; 2-person cabin $225, main lodge r $55-93; ☺ 8am-11pm; 🐾) has garnered quite a following in the last few years, even attracting celebrity residents from Hollywood. Some come to soak in the swimming-pool-sized open-air hot pools (admission for nonguests $7.50), others come for the lively bar hosting swinging country-and-western dance bands on weekends. The on-site restaurant (mains $20 to $32) is known for fine steak and seafood. You can stay here overnight, too. It's not called Paradise Valley for nothing.

Absaroka Beartooth Wilderness

The fabulous, vista-packed Absaroka Beartooth Wilderness covers more than 943,377 acres and is perfect for a solitary adventure. Thick forests, jagged peaks and marvelous, empty stretches of alpine tundra are all found in this wilderness, saddled between Paradise Valley in the west and Yellowstone National Park in the south. The thickly forested Absaroka Range dominates the area's west half and is most easily reached from Paradise Valley or the Boulder River Corridor. The Beartooth Range's high plateau and alpine lakes are best reached from the Beartooth Hwy south of Red Lodge. Because of its proximity to Yellowstone, the Beartooth portion gets two-thirds of the area's traffic.

A picturesque old mining town with fun bars and restaurants and a good range of places to stay, **Red Lodge** offers great day hikes, backpacking and, in winter, skiing right near town. The **Red Lodge Visitor Center** (☎406-446-1718; www.redlodge.com; 601 N Broadway Ave; ⏰8am-6pm Mon-Fri, 9am-5pm Sat & Sun) has information on accommodations.

Billings

It's hard to believe laid-back little Billings is Montana's largest city. The friendly oil and ranching center is not a must-see but makes for a decent overnight pit stop. The historic downtown is hardly cosmopolitan, but has its own unpolished charm.

Road-weary travelers will appreciate the downtown **Dude Rancher Lodge** (☎800-221-3302; www.duderancherlodge.com; 415 N 29th St; d from $89; @📶), a fine and friendly motel with groovy oak furniture dating back to the 1940s, Western-styling, flat-screen TVs and in-room coffee.

With a hefty dose of Martha Stewart, plush **Harper & Madison** (☎406-281-8550; 3115 10th Av N; mains $4-10; ⏰7am-6pm Mon-Fri, 7am-1pm Sat) does some brisk business. It's no wonder with the excellent coffee, homemade quiches and gourmet pressed sandwiches. If you're rushing to hit the road, grab some French pastries to go.

The upscale **Walkers Grill** (www.walkers-grill.com; 2700 1st Ave N; tapas $8-14, mains $17-33; ⏰5-10pm) offers good grill items and fine tapas at the bar, with sophisticated Western decor. For classic dive ambience, check out **Angry Hank's** (☎(406) 252-3370; 2405 1st Ave N; ⏰4-8pm Mon-Sat), a former auto repair shop turned popular tap room and brewery.

Logan International Airport (BIL; www.flybillings.com), 2 miles north of downtown, has direct flights to Salt Lake City, Denver, Minneapolis, Seattle, Phoenix and destinations within Montana. The **bus depot** (☎406-245-5116; 2502 1st Ave N; ⏰24hr) has services to Bozeman ($30, three hours) and Missoula ($61, eight hours).

Helena

With one foot in cowboy legend (Gary Cooper was born here) and the other in the more hip, less stereotypical lotus land of present-day Montana, diminutive Helena is one of the nation's smallest state capitals (population 28,000), a place where white-collared politicians draft legislation, while white-knuckle

WORTH A TRIP

CUSTER'S LAST STAND

The best detour from Billings is to the **Little Bighorn Battlefield National Monument** (☎406-638-3224; www.nps.gov/libi; admission per car $10; ⏰8am-9pm), 65 miles outside town in the arid plains of the Crow (Apsaalooke) Indian Reservation. Home to one of the USA's best-known Native American battlefields, this is where General George Custer made his famous 'last stand.'

Custer, and 272 soldiers, messed one too many times with Native Americans (including Crazy Horse of the Lakota Sioux), who overwhelmed the force in a (frequently painted) massacre. A visitor center tells the tale or, better, take one of the five daily tours with a Crow guide through **Apsalooke Tours** (☎406-638-3897; apsaalooketourism@gmail.com; ⏰Memorial Day-Labor Day). The entrance is a mile east of I-90 on US 212. If you're here for the last weekend of June, the **Custer's Last Stand Reenactment** (www.custerslaststand.org; adult/child $20/10) is an annual hoot, 6 miles west of Hardin.

adventurers race into the foothills to indulge in that other Montana passion.

Back in town, half hidden among the Gore-tex and outdoor outfitters, you will find an unexpected Gallic-inspired neo-Gothic cathedral. Another pleasant surprise is the artsy pedestrian-only shopping quarter.

Sights & Activities

Many of Helena's sites are free, including the elegant old buildings along Last Chance Gulch (Helena's pedestrian shopping district), and the sights covered here.

State Capitol   LANDMARK
(cnr Montana Ave & 6th St; ⊙8am-6pm Mon-Fri) This grand neoclassical building was completed in 1902 and is known for its beacon-like dome, richly decorated with gold-rimmed paintings inside.

Cathedral of St Helena   CHURCH
(530 N Ewing St) Rising like an apparition from old Europe over the town is this neo-Gothic cathedral completed in 1914. Highlights include the baptistry, organ and intricate stained-glass windows.

Holter Museum of Art   MUSEUM
(www.holtermuseum.org; 12 E Lawrence St; ⊙10am-5.30pm Tue-Sat, noon-4pm Sun) FREE Exhibits modern pieces by Montana artists.

Mt Helena City Park   OUTDOORS
Nine hiking and mountain-biking trails wind through Mt Helena City Park, including one that takes you to the 5460ft-high summit of Mt Helena.

Sleeping & Eating

East of downtown near I-15 is a predictable string of chain motels. Most rooms are $70 to $95, and come with free continental breakfast, pool and Jacuzzi.

Sanders   B&B $$
(☎406-442-3309; www.sandersbb.com; 328 N Ewing St; r incl breakfast $130-145; ❋) A historic B&B with seven elegant guest rooms, a wonderful old parlor and a breezy front porch. Each bedroom is unique and thoughtfully decorated, it's run by a relative of the Ringling Brothers Circus family, with appropriate memorabilia.

Fire Tower Coffee House   CAFE, BREAKFAST $
(www.firetowercoffee.com; 422 Last Chance Gulch; breakfast $4-9; ⊙6.30am-6pm Mon-Fri, 8am-3pm Sat; 🛜) The hub for coffee, light meals and live music on Friday evening. The breakfast menu features granola and breakfast burritos, while lunch has a wholesome and interesting sandwich selection.

🛈 Information

Helena Visitor Center (☎406-442-4120; www.helenachamber.com; 225 Cruse Ave; ⊙8am-5pm Mon-Fri)

🛈 Getting There & Around

Two miles north of downtown, **Helena Regional Airport** (HNL; www.helenaairport.com) operates flights to most other airports in Montana, as well as to Salt Lake City, Seattle and Minneapolis. Rimrock Trailways leave from Helena's **Transit Center** (630 N Last Chance Gulch; ⊙2-4pm, 8-9pm) where at least daily buses go to Missoula ($25, 2¼ hours), Billings ($52, 4¾ hours) and Bozeman ($22, two hours).

Missoula

Outsiders in Missoula usually spend the first 30 minutes wondering where they took a wrong turn; Austin, Texas? Portland, Oregon? Canada, perhaps? The confusion is understandable given the city's lack of standard Montana stereotypes. There's no Wild West saloons here and even fewer errant cowboys. Instead, Missoula is a refined university city with ample green space and abundant home pride.

Not surprisingly, its metro-west bounty is contagious. Though among the fastest growing cities in the US, sensible planning means that Missoula rarely feels clamorous. The small traffic-calmed downtown core broadcasts an interesting array of historic buildings, and bicycle transportation is ever hip.

Sights

Missoula is a great city for walking, especially in the spring and summer, when enough people emerge onto the streets to give it a definable metro personality.

Smokejumper Visitor Center   MUSEUM
(W Broadway; ⊙10am-4pm Jun-Aug) FREE Located seven miles west of downtown is this active base for the heroic men and women who parachute into forests to combat raging wildfires. Its visitor center has thought-provoking audio and visual displays that do a great job illustrating the life of the Western firefighter.

Missoula Art Museum
MUSEUM

(www.missoulaartmuseum.org; 335 North Pattee; ⊙10am-5pm Mon-Thu, 10am-3pm Fri-Sun) **FREE**
All hail a city that encourages free-thinking art and then displays it in a plush new building that seamlessly grafts a sleek contemporary addition onto a 100-year-old library.

Activities

Clark Fork River Trail System
CYCLING, HIKING

Sitting astride the Clark Fork River, Missoula has been bequeathed with an attractive riverside trail system punctuated by numerous parks. **Caras Park** is the most central and active green space with over a dozen annual festivals and a unique hard-carved **carousel**.

Mount Sentinel
HIKING

A steep switchback trail from behind the football stadium leads up to a concrete whitewashed 'M' (visible for miles around) on 5158ft Mt Sentinel. Tackle it on a warm summer's evening for glistening views of this much-loved city and its spectacular environs.

★ Adventure Cycling HQ
CYCLING

(www.adventurecycling.org; 150 E Pine St; ⊙8am-5pm Mon-Fri, open Sat Jun-Aug) ◢ The HQ for America's premier nonprofit bicycle travel organization is something of a pilgrimage site for cross-continental cyclists, many of whom plan their route to pass through Missoula. Staff offer a warm welcome and plenty of cycling information.

Fly-fishing
FISHING

A River Runs Through It was set here (although it was filmed outside Bozeman) and fly-fishers will find some of the best angling in the state. **Rock Creek**, 21 miles east, is a designated blue-ribbon trout stream and the best year-round fishing spot.

Sleeping

Mountain Valley Inn
MOTEL $

(☑800-249-9174; www.mountainvalleyinnmissoula.com; 420 W Broadway; d from $79; P ❉ 🛜) Offering a good deal for the downtown location, the Mountain Valley pulls few surprises, but delivers where it matters – clean rooms and a polite welcome.

Goldsmith's Bed & Breakfast
B&B $$

(☑406-728-1585; www.missoulabedandbreakfast.com; 809 E Front St; r $124-169; ❉ @) A delightful riverside B&B. The wraparound deck is the perfect place to kick back with other guests or a good novel. Comfy Victorian-style rooms are simply lovely. Some come with private decks, river views, fireplaces and reading nooks.

Eating & Drinking

Liquid Planet
CAFE $

(www.liquidplanet.com; 223 N Higgins; mains $4-9) ◢ Started by a university professor in 2003, this sustainable coffeehouse and wine outlet proffers handwritten recommendations for every bottle. Coffee beans are also thoughtfully deconstructed. For smoothies, teas and pastries, you're on your own.

★ Silk Road
INTERNATIONAL $$

(www.silkroadcatering.com; 515 S Higgins; tapas $4-12; ⊙5-10pm) Spanning global dishes from the Ivory Coast to Piedmont, Silk Road takes on lesser-known world cuisine and, more often than not, nails it. Dishes are tapas-sized, allowing you to mix and match. A warm welcome and an ambience of cushions and candlelit tapestries set the scene.

Caffe Dolce
MODERN AMERICAN $$

(☑406-830-3055; www.caffedolcemissoula.com; cnr Brooks & Beckwith; mains $11-30; ⊙7am-9pm Mon-Thur, 7am-10pm Fri, 8am-9pm Sat, 8am-3pm Sun) In a stately stone building, this chic newcomer is abuzz with well-clad Missoulans getting their fix of gelato, pastries, wine and gorgeous salads. Dinner can be pricey but exotic pizzas like the salty fig and proscuitto offer a lighter, cheaper option. Coffee is a serious business here, and it deals in the best Montana roasters. With patio seating. It's located after the bridge going north of downtown.

Iron Horse Brewpub
BREWERY

(www.ironhorsebrewpub.com; 501 N Higgins St; ⊙11:30am-late) Rather swanky for a brewpub, the Iron Horse includes a plush upstairs bar complete with a saltwater aquarium. It's popular with students for its microbrews and traditional American pub grub.

❶ Information

Visitor Center (☑406-532-3250; www.missoulacvb.org; 101 E Main St; ⊙8am-5pm Mon-Fri)

❶ Getting There & Around

Missoula County International Airport (MSO; www.flymissoula.com) is 5 miles west of Missoula on US 12 W.

Greyhound buses serve most of the state and stop at the **depot** (1660 W Broadway), 1 mile west of town. **Rimrock Trailways** (www.rimrock-trailways.com) buses, connecting to Kalispell, Whitefish, Helena and Bozeman, also stop here.

Flathead Lake

The largest natural freshwater lake west of the Mississippi, sitting not an hour's drive from Glacier National Park, completes western Montana's embarrassment of natural lures. The lake's north shore is dominated by the nothing-to-write-home-about city of Kalispell; far more interesting is the southern end embellished by the small polished settlement of **Polson**, which sits on the Flathead Indian Reservation. There's a **visitor center** (www.polsonchamber.com; 418 Main St; ⊗9am-5pm Mon-Fri) and a handful of accommodations here including the lakeside **Kwataqnuk Resort** (☑406-883-3636; www.kwataqnuk.com; 49708 US 93; r from $130; ▣❋☎☀), an above-average Best Western with a boat dock, indoor and outdoor pools and a relatively innocuous game room. Directly opposite, the lurid pink **Betty's Diner** (49779 US 93; meals $10-15) delivers salt-of-the-earth American food with customary Montana charm. From town you can walk 2 miles south along a trail starting on 7th Ave E to the mind-boggling **Miracle of America Museum** (www.miracleofamericamuseum.org; 58176 Hwy 93; admission $5; ⊗8am-8pm). At turns random and fascinating, it consists of 5 acres cluttered with the leftovers of American history. Wander past weird artifacts including the biggest buffalo (now stuffed) ever recorded in Montana.

Flathead Lake's eastern shore is kissed by the mysterious Mission Mountains while the west is a more pastoral land of apple orchards and grassy hills. To get the best all-round view, hit the water. Soloists can kayak or canoe the conceptual **Flathead Lake Marine Trail**, which links various state parks and **campsites** (☑406-751-4577; tent sites from $10) around the lake. The nearest site to Polson is Finley Point 5.5 miles away by water.

Lake cruises (www.kwataqnuk.com) are run out of the Kwataqnuk Resort in Polson. The 1½ hour Bay Cruise leaves daily at 10:30am and costs $15. Summer dining cruises leave at 4pm on Wednesdays and Saturdays (cost per person is $30).

Bob Marshall Wilderness Complex

Away from the Pacific coast, America's northwest harbors some of the most lightly populated areas in the lower 48. Point in question: the Bob Marshall Wilderness Complex, an astounding 2344 sq miles of land strafed with 3200 miles of trails including sections that are a 40-mile slog from the nearest road. And you thought the US was car-obsessed.

Running roughly from the southern boundary of Glacier National Park in the north to Rogers Pass (on Hwy 200) in the south, there are actually three designated wilderness areas within the complex: Great Bear, Bob Marshall and Scapegoat. On the periphery the complex is buffered with national-forest lands offering campgrounds, road access to trailheads and quieter country when 'the Bob' (as locals and park rangers call it) hosts hunters in fall.

The main access point to the Bob from the south is from Hwy 200 via the **Monture Guard Station Cabin** (cabins $60), on the wilderness perimeter. To reach it you'll need to drive 7 miles north of Ovando and snowshoe or hike the last mile to your private abodes at the edge of the gorgeous Lewis and Clark Range. Contact the USFS about reservations.

Other Bob access points include the Seeley-Swan Valley in the west, Hungry Horse Reservoir in the north and the Rocky Mountain Front in the east. The easiest (and busiest) access routes are from the Benchmark and Gibson Reservoir trailheads in the Rocky Mountain Front.

Trails generally start steep, reaching the wilderness boundary after around 7 miles. It takes another 10 miles or so to really get into the Bob's heart. Good day-hikes run from all sides. Two USFS districts tend to the Bob, **Flathead National Forest Headquarters** (☑406-758-5208; www.fs.fed.us/r1/flathead; 650 Wolfpack Way; ⊗8am-4:30pm Mon-Fri) and **Lewis & Clark National Forest Supervisors** (☑406-791-7700; www.fs.fed.us/r1/lewisclark; 1101 15th St N; ⊗8am-4:30pm Mon-Fri).

Whitefish

One square mile of rustic Western chic, tiny Whitefish (population 8000) easily charms. Once sold as the main gateway to Glacier National Park, this charismatic and caffeinated New West town would merit a long-distance trip itself. Aside from grandiose Glacier (an easy day's cycling distance), Whitefish is home to an attractive stash of restaurants, a historic railway station that doubles up as a **museum** (www.stumptownhistoricalsociety.org; 500 Depot St; ⊗10am-4pm Mon-Sat) **FREE** and underrated **Whitefish Mountain Resort** (📞406-862-2900; www.bigmtn.com), known as Big Mountain until 2008, guards 3000 acres of varied ski terrain and offers night skiing on weekends. In the summer there's lift-assisted mountain biking and zip lines.

Check with the **Whitefish Visitor Center** (www.whitefishvisit.com; 307 Spokane Ave; ⊙9am-5pm Mon-Fri) for more info on activities.

A string of chain motels lines US 93 south of Whitefish, but the savvy dock in town at the cheerful **Downtowner Inn** (📞406-862-2535; www.downtownermotel.cc; 224 Spokane Ave; d $123; ❉❄) with a gym, a Jacuzzi and a morning bagel bar. The more upmarket **Pine Lodge** (📞406-862-7600; www.thepinelodge.com; 920 Spokane Ave; d from $145; P❉❄≋), offers deep discounts outside the peak seasons. Decent restaurants and bars abound, though most locals will point you in the direction of the **Buffalo Café** (www.buffalocafewhitefish.com; 514 3rd St E; breakfast $7-10), a breakfast and lunch hot spot. Later check out **The Great Northern Brewing Co** (📞406-863-1000; www.greatnorthernbrewing.com; 2 Central Ave; ⊙tours 1pm & 3pm Mon-Thu), with factory tours and sampling.

Amtrak stops daily at Whitefish's **railroad depot** (📞406-862-2268; 500 Depot St; ⊙6am-1:30pm, 4:30pm-midnight) en route to West Glacier ($7, 30 minutes) and East Glacier ($15, two hours). **Rimrock Trailways** (www.rimrocktrailways.com) runs daily buses to Kalispell and Missoula from the same location.

Glacier National Park

Few of the world's parks of great natural wonders can emulate the US national park system, and few national parks are as magnificent and pristine as Glacier. Created in 1910 during the first flowering of the American conservationist movement, Glacier ranks with Yellowstone, Yosemite and the Grand Canyon.

It is renowned for its historic 'parkitecture' lodges, spectacular arterial road (the Going-to-the-Sun Road), and intact pre-Columbian ecosystem. This is the only place in the lower 48 states where grizzly bears still roam in abundance and smart park management has kept the place accessible yet, at the same time, authentically wild (there is no populated town site à la Banff or Jasper). Among a slew of outdoor attractions, the park is particularly noted for its hiking, wildlife-spotting, and sparkling lakes, ideal for boating and fishing.

Although Glacier's tourist numbers are relatively high (two million a year), few visitors stray far from the Going-to-the-Sun Road and almost all visit between June and September. Choose your moment and splendid isolation is yours for the taking. The park remains open year-round; however, most services are open only from mid-May to September.

Glacier's 1562 sq miles are divided into five regions, each centered on a ranger station: Polebridge (northwest); Lake McDonald (southwest), including the West Entrance and Apgar village; Two Medicine (southeast); St Mary (east); and Many Glacier (northeast). The 50-mile Going-to-the-Sun Road is the only paved road that traverses the park.

◉ Sights & Activities

Going-to-the-Sun Road   OUTDOORS
(⊙mid-Jun–late Sep) A strong contender for the most spectacular road in America, the 53-mile Going-to-the-Sun Road is a national historic landmark, flanked by hiking trails and a mountain pass, served by a free shuttle.

The road skirts near shimmering Lake McDonald before angling sharply to the Garden Wall – the main dividing line between the west and east sides of the park. At Logan Pass you can stroll 1.5 miles to Hidden Lake Overlook; heartier hikers can try the 7.5-mile Highline Trail. The shuttle stops on the western side of the road at the trailhead for Avalanche Lake, an easy 4-mile return hike to a stunning alpine lake in a cirque beautified with numerous weeping waterfalls.

Many Glacier   HIKING
Anchored by the historic 1915 Many Glacier Lodge and sprinkled with more lakes than glaciers, this picturesque valley on the park's east side has some tremendous hikes, some of which link to the Going-to-the-Sun Road. A favorite is the 9.4-mile (return) **Iceberg Lake Trail**, a steep but rewarding jaunt through flower meadows and pine forest to an iceberg infested lake.

Glacier Park Boat Co   BOATING, HIKING
(📞406-257-2426; www.glacierparkboats.com; St Mary Lake cruise adult/child $25/12) Rents out kayaks and canoes, and runs popular lake cruises from five locations in Glacier National Park. Also offers guided hikes.

🛏 Sleeping

There are 13 **NPS campgrounds** (📞406-888-7800; http://reservations.nps.gov; tent & RV sites $10-23) and seven historic lodges in the park, which operate between mid-May and the end of September. Of the sites, only Fish Creek and St Mary can be reserved in advance (up to five months). Sites fill by mid-morning, particularly in July and August.

Glacier also has seven historic lodges dating from the early 1900s.

★Many Glacier Hotel HOTEL $$

(📞406-732-4411; www.glacierparkinc.com; r $163-250; ⊙mid-Jun–mid-Sep; 🐾) Modeled after a Swiss chalet, this national historic landmark on Swiftcurrent Lake is the park's largest hotel, with 208 rooms featuring panoramic views. Evening entertainment, a lounge and fine-dining restaurant specializing in fondue all add to the appeal.

Lake McDonald Lodge HOTEL $$

(📞406-888-5431; www.glacierparkinc.com; cabin/lodge r from $137/79; ⊙May-Sep; 🐾) 🦮 Built in 1913, this old hunting lodge is adorned with stuffed-animal trophies and exudes relaxation. The 100 rooms are lodge, chalet or motel style. Nightly park-ranger talks and lake cruises add a rustic ambience. There's a restaurant and pizzeria.

Glacier Park Lodge HOTEL $$

(📞406-226-5600; www.glacierparkinc.com; r $152-235; ⊙late May-Sep) 🦮 The park's flagship lodge is a graceful, elegant place featuring interior balconies supported by Douglas fir timbers and a massive stone fireplace in the lobby. It's an aesthetically appealing, historically charming and very comfortable place to stay. Pluses include nine holes of golf and cozy reading nooks.

Rising Sun Motor Inn MOTEL $$

(📞406-732-5523; www.glacierparkinc.com; r $134-142; ⊙late May-early Sep) One of two classic 1940s-era wooden motels, the Rising Sun lies on the north shore of St Mary Lake in a small complex that includes a store, restaurant and boat launch. The rustic rooms and cabins offer everything an exhausted hiker could hope for.

🍴 Eating

In summer there are grocery stores with limited camping supplies in Apgar, Lake McDonald Lodge, Rising Sun and at the Swiftcurrent Motor Inn. Most lodges have on-site restaurants. Dining options in West Glacier and St Mary offer mainly hearty hiking fare.

Polebridge Mercantile BAKERY, SUPERMARKET $

(Polebridge Loop Rd, North Fork Valley; snacks $4; ⊙8am-6pm May-Nov; 🐾) Come here for the cinnamon buns, known to pump a good couple of hours into tired hiking legs.

Park Café AMERICAN $

(www.parkcafe.us; US 89, St. Mary; breakfast $7-12; ⊙7am-10pm Jun-Sep) Offers hearty breakfasts and comes recommended for the homemade pies topped in whipped cream or ice cream.

Ptarmigan Dining Room INTERNATIONAL $$$

(Many Glacier Lodge; mains $15-32; ⊙6:30am-9:30pm, mid-Jun–early Sep) With its lakeside views, this is the most refined of the lodge restaurants, also serving wine and microbrews.

ℹ Information

Visitor centers and ranger stations in the park sell field guides and hand out hiking maps. Those at Apgar and St Mary are open daily May to October; the visitor center at Logan Pass is open when the Going-to-the-Sun Road is open. The Many Glacier, Two Medicine and Polebridge Ranger Stations close at the end of September. **Park headquarters** (📞406-888-7800; www.nps.gov/glac; ⊙8am-4:30pm Mon-Fri), in West Glacier between US 2 and Apgar, is open year-round.

Entry to the park (hiker/vehicle $12/25) is valid for seven days. Day-hikers don't need permits, but overnight backpackers do (May to October only). Half of the permits are available on a first-come, first-served basis from the **Apgar Backcountry Permit Center** (permits per person per day $4; ⊙May 1-Oct 31), St Mary Visitor Center, and the Many Glacier, Two Medicine and Polebridge ranger stations.

The other half can be reserved at the Apgar Backcountry Permit Center, St Mary and Many Glacier visitor centers and Two Medicine and Polebridge ranger stations.

ℹ Getting There & Around

Amtrak's Empire Builder train stops daily at West Glacier (year-round) and East Glacier Park (April to October) on its route between Seattle and Chicago. **Glacier National Park** (www.nps.gov/glac) runs shuttles (adult/child $10/5) from Apgar Village to St Mary over Going-to-the-Sun Road from July 1 to Labor Day. **Glacier Park, Inc** (www.glacierparkinc.com) offers the East Side Shuttle (adult/child $10/5) on the eastern side of the park with daily links to Waterton (Canada), Many Glacier, St Mary, Two Medicine and East Glacier.

IDAHO

Famous for not being particularly famous, the nation's 43rd state is a pristine wilderness of Alaskan proportions, rudely ignored by passing traffic heading west to Seattle or east to Montana. In truth, much of this lightly trodden land is little changed since the days of Lewis and Clark, including a vast 15,000-sq-km 'hole' in the middle of the state which is bereft of roads, settlements, or any other form of human interference.

Flatter, dryer southern Idaho is dominated by the Snake River, deployed as a transportation artery by early settlers on the Oregon Trail and tracked today by busy Hwy 84. But, outside of this narrow populated strip, the Idaho landscape is refreshingly free of the soulless strip-mall, fast-food infestations so ubiquitous elsewhere in the US.

Boise

Understated, underrated and underappreciated, Idaho's state capital (and largest city) gets little name recognition from people outside the northwest. The affable downtown surprises blinkered outsiders with the modest spirit of an underdog. Cool surprises include Basque culture, a grandiose Idaho capitol building and a fair number of well-heeled bars and Parisian-style bistros. With a university campus to boot and a 'city of trees' moniker, it's not just a marketing ploy. Boise leaves a poignant and lasting impression – primarily because it's not supposed to.

◉ Sights & Activities

Delve into the main business district, bounded by State, Grove, 4th and 9th Sts.

★ Basque Block   NEIGHBORHOOD

(www.thebasqueblock.com) Unbeknownst to many, Boise harbors one of the largest Basque populations outside Spain. European émigrés first arrived in the 1910s to work as Idaho shepherds. Elements of their distinct culture can be glimpsed along Grove St between 6th St and Capitol Blvd.

Sandwiched between the ethnic taverns, restaurants and bars is the **Basque Museum & Cultural Center** (www.basquemuseum.com; 611 Grove St; adult/senior & student $5/4; ⊙10am-4pm Tue-Fri, 11am-3pm Sat), a commendable effort to unveil the intricacies of Basque culture and how it was transposed

6000 miles west to Idaho. Language lessons in Euskara, Europe's oldest language, are held here, while next door in the **Anduiza Fronton Building** (619 Grove St) there's a Basque handball court where aficionados play the traditional sport of *pelota*.

Idaho State Capitol   LANDMARK

The joy of US state capitol buildings is that visitors can admire some of the nation's best architecture for free. The Boise building, constructed from native sandstone, celebrates the neoclassical style in vogue when it was built in 1920. It was extensively refurbished in 2010 and is now heated with geothermal hot water.

Boise River & Greenbelt   PARK, MUSEUM

⚑ Laid out in the 1960s, the tree-lined riverbanks of the Boise River protect 30 miles of vehicle-free trails. It personifies Boise's 'city of trees' credentials, with parks, museums and river fun.

The river is insanely popular for its floating and tubing. The put-in point is **Barber Park** (Eckert Rd; tube rental $12) 6 miles east of downtown. It's a 5-mile float to the take-out

---

IDAHO FACTS

Nickname Gem State

Population 1,596,000

Area 83,570 sq miles

Capital city Boise (population 210,100)

Other cities Idaho Falls (population 57,600)

Sales tax 6%

Birthplace of Lewis and Clark guide Sacagawea (1788–1812); politician Sarah Palin (b 1964); poet Ezra Pound (1885–1972)

Home of Star garnet, Sun Valley ski resort

Politics Reliably Republican with small pockets of Democrats, eg Sun Valley

Famous for Potatoes, wilderness, the world's first chairlift

North America's deepest river gorge Idaho's Hells Canyon (7,900 ft deep)

Driving distances Boise to Idaho Falls 280 miles, Lewiston to Coeur d'Alene 116 miles

point at Ann Morrison Park. There are four rest-stops en route and a shuttle bus ($3) runs from the take-out point.

The most central and action-packed space on the Greenbelt, 90-acre Julia Davis Park contains the **Idaho State Historical Museum** (610 N Julia Davis Dr; adult/child $5/3; ⊙9am-5pm Tue-Fri, 11am-5pm Sat) with well thought-out exhibits on Lewis and Clark; and the **Boise Art Museum** (www.boiseart-museum.org; 670 N Julia Davis Dr; adult/senior & student $6/3; ⊙10am-5pm Tue-Sat, noon-5pm Sun). There's also a pretty outdoor rose garden.

Ridge to Rivers Trail System   HIKING
(www.ridgetorivers.org) ✐ More rugged than the greenbelt are the scrub- and brush-covered foothills above town offering 75 miles of scenic, sometimes strenuous hiking and mountain-biking routes. The most immediate access from downtown is via Fort Boise Park on E Fort St, five blocks southeast of the state capitol building.

🛏 Sleeping

Here are three true gems.

Leku Ona   HOTEL $
(☑208-345-6665; www.lekuonaid.com; 117 S 6th St; r $65-85; 🛜) Run by a Basque-born immigrant, this central boarding house has seen some wear. The downtown location can be noisy on weekends, but it certainly is economical. The restaurant next door serves delicious *pintxos* (Basque tapas).

★ **Boise Guest House**   GUESTHOUSE $$
(☑208-761-6798; boiseguesthouse.com; 614 North 5th St; suites $89-119; 🛜🐾) The dearest home away from home, this artist-owned guesthouse has a handful of stylin' suites with kitchens and living areas. Whimsical and well thought-out, it's decked out in lovely decor with good books on the shelf and appealing local art. The free cruiser bikes (with handlebar streamers – hello!) encourage further exploration.

Modern Hotel   BOUTIQUE MOTEL $$
(☑208-424-8244; www.themodernhotel.com; 1314 W Grove St; d incl breakfast from $99; 🅿🐾🛜) Making an oxymoron (a boutique motel!?) into a fashion statement, the Modern Hotel offers retro-trendy minimalist rooms and a slavishly hip bar slap-bang in the middle of downtown. The power showers are huge and the service is five-star.

🍴 Eating & Drinking

Restaurants and nightspots are found downtown in the brick-lined pedestrian plaza of the Grove, and the gentrified former warehouse district between 8th St and Idaho Ave. Count on some exciting Basque specialties, authentic bistros and exceptional bars.

★ **Fork**   MODERN AMERICAN $$
(☑207-287-1700; www.boisefork.com; 199 North 8th St; mains $8-29; ⊙11am-10pm; ✐) ✐ Twenty years ago, this kind of upscale green-boosted menu would have been Idaho heresy. No more. Down-home starts with cast-iron-fried chicken with waffles and balsamic maple syrup. But there's also heaping salads and braised greens in addition to local meat and many regionally-sourced ingredients. Don't even think of skipping the rosemary parmesean fries. So popular, service can be slow.

Vietnam Pho Nouveau   VIETNAMESE $$
(☑208-367-1111; www.phonouveau.com; 780 West Idaho St; mains $9-15; ⊙11am-9:30pm Mon-Thur, 11am-10:30pm Sat, 12-8:30pm Sun) A small, smart cafe oozing understated cool, it's Boise's happy destination for Asian comfort food. Dig into *bun* (a big bowl of noodles with grilled meat and plenty of greens), lily blossom salad with tender shredded pork, or Saigon crepes.

Grape Escape   WINE BAR $$
(800 W Idaho St; appetizers $7-11, mains $11-18; ⊙11am-close) Sit alfresco and enjoy your Pinot Noir with light supper fare (bruschetta, salads and highly creative pizzas) while logging the ubiquity of downtown cyclists, closet intellectuals and bright young things out for an early evening aperitif. The wine menu is almost as good as the people-watching. With jazz Sundays.

Bittercreek Ale House & Red Feather Lounge   MODERN AMERICAN $$
(www.justeatlocal.com; 246 N 8th St; mains $7-15; ⊙11:30am-late) ✐ These adjoining restaurants offer lively, intimate environs and lots of personality. They also serve wholesome, usually locally produced food with an emphasis on sustainable growth. The nouveau-American menu features a good selection of vegetarian options. The more polished Red Feather does delicious wood-oven pizza.

Order one of the whiskey cocktails that are made using an old-fashioned pre-Prohibition-era recipe.

Bar Gernika   PUB

(www.bargernkia.com; 202 S Capitol Blvd; lunch $8-10; ⊘11am-midnight Mon-Thu till 1am Fri & Sat) *Ongi etorri* (welcome) to the Basque block's most accessible pub-tavern with a menu that leans heavily on old-country favorites such as lamb kebab, chorizo and beef tongue (Saturdays only). Pair your meal with a 20oz Guinness or regional microbrew. It's a true only-in-Boise kind of place.

Bardenay   PUB

(www.bardenay.com; 610 Grove St; mains $8-18; ⊘11am-late) Bardenay was the USA's very first 'distillery-pub,' and remains a one-of-a-kind watering hole. Today it serves its own home-brewed vodka, rum and gin in casual, airy environs. It gets consistently good reviews.

ℹ Information

Visitor Center (☑208-344-7777; www.boise. org; 250 S. 5th St, Ste. 300; ⊘10am-5pm Mon-Fri, 10am-2pm Sat Jun-Aug, 9am-4pm Mon-Fri Sep-May) Stop by the visitor center.

ℹ Getting There & Around

Boise Municipal Airport (BOI; I-84 exit 53) has daily flights to Denver, Las Vegas, Phoenix, Portland, Salt Lake City, Seattle and Spokane. Greyhound services depart from the **bus station** (1212 W Bannock St) with routes fanning out to Spokane, Pendleton and Portland, and Twin Falls and Salt Lake City.

Ketchum & Sun Valley

In one of Idaho's most stunning natural locations sits a piece of ski history. Sun Valley was the first purpose-built ski resort in the US, hand-picked by Union Pacific Railroad scion William Averell Harriman (after an exhaustive search) in the 1930s and publicized by glitterati Ernest Hemingway, Clark Gable and Gary Cooper. When Sun Valley opened in 1936 it sported the world's first chairlift and a showcase 'parkitecture' lodge that remains its premier resort.

Sun Valley has kept its swanky Hollywood clientele and extended its facilities to include the legendary Bald Mountain, yet it remains a refined and pretty place (no fast-food joints or condo sprawl here). Highly rated nationwide, the resort is revered for its reliably good snow, big elevation drop and almost windless weather. The adjacent village of Ketchum, 1 mile away, holds a rustic beauty despite the skiing deluge. Heming-

way made it prime territory for fishing and hunting, though these days fat tires are the summer rage.

⭧ Activities

Main St between 1st and 5th Sts is where you'll find nearly all the businesses. Sun Valley and its lodge is 1 mile to the north and easily walkable. Twelve miles south of Ketchum, also on Hwy 75, is Hailey, another delightful small town with a bar scene.

Wood River Trail   HIKING, CYCLING

There are numerous hiking and mountain biking trails around Ketchum and Sun Valley, as well as excellent fishing spots. The Wood River Trail is the all-connecting artery linking Sun Valley with Ketchum and continuing 32 bucolic miles south down to Bellevue via Hailey. Bikes can be hired from **Pete Lane's** (bikes per day $35) in the mall next to the Sun Valley Lodge.

Sun Valley Resort   SNOW SPORTS

(www.sunvalley.com; adult/child Bald Mountain $95/54, Dollar Mountain $54/39) Famous for its light, fluffy powder and celebrity guests, the dual-sited resort comprises advanced-terrain **Bald Mountain** and easier-on-the-nerves **Dollar Mountain**, which also has a tubing hill. In summer, take the chairlift to the top of either mountain (adult/child ride $15/10), and hike or cycle down. Facilities are predictably plush.

🛏 Sleeping

In summer, there is free camping on Bureau of Land Management (BLM) land very close to town, see the visitor center for details.

Lift Tower Lodge   MOTEL $

(☑208-726-5163; 703 S Main St; r $89-109; [P][🐾]) Lifelong members of the hoi polloi can hobnob with millionaires and decamp afterwards to this friendly and economical small motel on the cusp of Ketchum with firm quilted beds. A landmark exhibition chairlift (c 1939) is lit up after dark.

Tamarack Lodge   HOTEL $$

(☑208-726-3344; www.tamaracksunvalley.com; 500 E Sun Valley Rd; r $149-169; [❄][🐾][🏊]) Tasteful rooms complete with fireplace, balcony and many amenities are offered at this well-maintained lodge. Sterling service, a Jacuzzi and indoor pool are definite assets. Discounts are often available midweek and off-season.

HEMINGWAY: THE FINAL DAYS

Although Sun Valley and Ketchum never featured explicitly in the work of Ernest Miller Hemingway, the globe-trotting author had a deep affection for the area. He became a frequent visitor following its development as a ski resort in the late 1930s. Legend has it that he completed his Spanish Civil War masterpiece *For Whom the Bell Tolls* in room 206 of the Sun Valley Lodge in between undertaking fishing and hunting excursions with friends such as Gary Cooper and Clark Gable.

In the 1940s and '50s, Hemingway migrated south to Key West and Cuba. After the Cuban revolution in 1959, Hemingway's Havana house was expropriated and the author moved permanently to Idaho. Increasingly paranoid and in declining physical and mental health, on July 2, 1961, Hemingway took his favorite gun, walked out onto the porch of his home off Warm Springs Rd and blew his brains out at age 61.

There is a surprising (and refreshing) lack of hullabaloo surrounding Hemingway in Ketchum. You'll have to look hard to find the small, pretty **cemetery** half a mile north of the center on Hwy 75, where he is buried alongside his granddaughter Margaux. Pennies, cigars and the odd bottle of liquor furnish his simple grave. Hemingway's house is out of bounds to the public but a **monument** honors him near Trail Creek, 1 mile beyond the Sun Valley Lodge. In Ketchum, his favorite drinking holes were the Casino Club (p798) and the Alpine Club, now known as **Whiskey Jacques** (☑208-726-5297; 251 Main St; cover up to $5; ☺4pm-2am).

Sun Valley Lodge HOTEL $$$

(☑208-622-2001; www.sunvalley.com; 1 Sun Valley Rd; r $287-405; ✳@🛜🏊) Hemingway completed *For Whom the Bell Tolls* in this swank 1930s-era beauty and the place has lost little of its luxurious pre-war sheen. Old-fashioned elegance is the lure in comfortable rooms that sometimes feel a little small by today's standards. Amenities include a fitness facility, game room, bowling alley and sauna. There's also a ski shuttle and children's program.

✖ Eating & Drinking

Despo's MEXICAN $

(☑208-726-3068; 211 4th St; mains $7-14; ☺11:30am-10pm Mon-Sat) Locals dig this healthy Mexican joint, even if it isn't the most authentic. Everything is fresh, salads huge, and homemade salsas (warm, hot and smokin') are worthy.

★Rickshaw ASIAN $$

(www.eat-at-rickshaw.com; 460 Washington Ave N; small plates & mains $4-15; ☺5:30-10.30pm Tue-Sat, 5:30-9.30pm Sun) Small and crooked as an actual rickshaw, welcoming and with the vitality of a busy thoroughfare, this red-hot fusion restaurant turns out A-plus versions of street food from Vietnam, Thailand, Korea and Indonesia. Tender short ribs with a jalapeno-cilantro glaze are maddeningly wonderful. From green curry to cashew stir fry, the default here is spicy. A must.

Glow VEGAN $$

(380 Washington #105; mains $7-12; ☺10am-6pm Mon-Fri, 10am-5pm Sat; 🌿) A pleasure palace for raw and vegan dining. With a laundry list of smoothies, chia pudding for breakfast, organic salads, blended soups and (thank God) handmade raw chocolates, you too might glow. The crowd: perfect, Sun Valley types in yoga pants.

Pioneer Saloon STEAKHOUSE $$$

(www.pioneersaloon.com; 320 N Main St; mains $9-29; ☺5:30-10pm) Around since the 1950s and originally an illicit gambling hall, the Pio is an unashamedly Western den decorated with deer heads, antique guns, bullet boards and – oh yes – good food too, as long as you like beef and trout. All dinners are guaranteed.

Casino Club BAR

(220 N Main St) In a ski resort less than 75 years old, this dive bar is the oldest thing still standing from days of yore. It has witnessed everything from gambling fist fights, to psychedelic hippies, to the rise and fall of Ernest Hemingway, to tattooed men on Harleys riding through the front door.

ⓘ Information

Sun Valley/Ketchum Visitors Center (☑208-726-3423; www.visitsunvalley.com; 491 Sun Valley Rd; ☺6am-7pm) Staffed only from 9am-6pm, you can still come in and get maps and brochures before and after hours as it smartly doubles as a Starbucks cafe.

ℹ Getting There & Around

The region's airport, **Friedman Memorial Airport** (www.flyfma.com) in Hailey is 12 miles south of Ketchum. **A-1 Taxi** (☑208-726-9351; www.a1sunvalley.com) offers transportation. **Sun Valley Express** (www.sunvalleyexpress. com) operates a daily shuttle between Sun Valley and Boise Airport in both directions ($65 one-way).

Stanley

Backed by the ragged Sawtooths, Stanley (population 100), with its gravel roads, log homes and rusted iron sheds might be the most scenic small town in America. Surrounded by protected wilderness and national-forest land, the remote outpost sits in the crook of the Salmon River, miles from anywhere. Here the high summer twilight stretches past 10pm and the roaring creek lulls you to sleep.

🏃 Activities

Middle Fork of the Salmon   RAFTING
Stanley is the jumping-off point for rafting the legendary Middle Fork of the Salmon. Billed as the 'last wild river,' it's part of the longest undammed river system outside Alaska. Full trips last six days and allow you to float for 106 miles through the 300 or so rapids (class I to IV) of the 2.4-million-acre Frank Church–River of No Return Wilderness, miles from any form of civilization.

Main Fork of the Salmon   RAFTING
(🚣) For more affordable, albeit slightly less dramatic, white-water action than Middle Fork, do a DIY float trip down the Main Fork of the Salmon in a raft or inflatable kayak. There are 8 miles of quiet water, starting in Stanley, with views of the Sawtooth Mountains you can't see from the road. Bring fishing gear.

DON'T MISS

CENTRAL IDAHO'S SCENIC BYWAYS

Goodbye suburban strip malls, hello unblemished wilderness. All three roads into the remote Idahoan outpost of Stanley are designated National Scenic Byways (it's the only place in the US where this happens). Considering there are only 125 such roads in the country, it means 2.4% of American's prettiest pavement runs through bucolic Stanley.

Sawtooth Scenic Byway

Following the Salmon River along Hwy 75 north from Ketchum to Stanley this 60-mile drive is gorgeous, winding through a misty, thick ponderosa pine forest – where the air is crisp and fresh and smells like rain and nuts – before ascending the 8701ft **Galena Summit**. From the overlook at the top, there are views of the glacially carved Sawtooth Mountains.

Ponderosa Pine Scenic Byway

Hwy 21, between Stanley and Boise, is so beautiful it will be hard to reach your destination because you'll want to stop so much. From Stanley the trees increase in density, until you find yourself cloaked in pine – more Pacific Northwest than classic Rockies. With frequent bursts of rain, the roadway can feel dangerous. Even in late May the snowfields stretch right down to the highway.

   Two of the road's many highlights are **Kikham Creek Hot Springs** (parking $6; ☺6am-10pm), 6 miles east of Lowman, a primitive campground and natural hot springs boiling out of the creek; and the old restored gold rush town of **Idaho Falls**.

Salmon River Scenic Byway

Northeast of Stanley, Hwy 75 and US 93 make up another scenic road that runs beside the Salmon River for 161 miles to historic **Lost Trail Pass** on the Montana border, the point where Lewis and Clark first crossed the continental divide in 1805. Much of the surrounding scenery has changed little in over 200 years.

Fly Fishing
FISHING

(⊙Mar-Nov) The Salmon and surrounding mountain lakes have epic trout fishing from March until November, with late June to early October best for dry fly-fishing. The eight species of local trout include the mythical steelhead, which measure up to 40in. These fish travel 900 miles from the Pacific Ocean at winter's end, arriving near Stanley in March and April.

Tours

White Otter
RAFTING

(📞208-788-5005; www.whiteotter.com; 100 Yankee Fork Road and Hwy 75, Sunbeam, ID; half-day adult/child $75/55) The sole rafting outfit that's locally run, White Otter is recommended for fun class III day trips. It also arranges float trips in inflatable kayaks.

Solitude River Trips
RAFTING

(📞800-396-1776; www.rivertrips.com; 6-day trip $2185; ⊙Jun-Aug) Offers top-notch multiday trips on the famed Middle Fork of the Salmon. Camping is riverside and guides cook excellent food.

Silver Creek Outfitters
FISHING

(📞207-622-5282; www.silver-creek.com; 1 Sun Valley Rd) Run out of Sun Valley, Silver Creek does custom trips to the Salmon and remote river spots, only accessible via drift boat or float tube.

Sleeping & Eating

There are about half a dozen hotels in Stanley, all done in traditional pioneer log-cabin style. During the short summer season a couple of restaurants open up.

Sawtooth Hotel
HOTEL $

(📞208-721-2459; www.sawtoothhotel.com; 755 Ace of Diamonds St; d with/without bath $100/70; 📶) Set in a nostalgic 1931 log motel, the Sawtooth updates the slim comforts of yesteryear, but keeps the hospitality effusively Stanley-esque. Six rooms are furnished old-country style, two with private bathrooms. Room No 9 is the fave. Don't expect TVs or room phones, but count on home-spun dining that is exquisite.

★Stanley Baking Co
BAKERY, BREAKFAST $

(www.stanleybakingco.com; 250 Wall St; breakfast & lunch $3-10; ⊙7am-2pm May-Oct) After having lumbered the world with unhealthy delights, this middle-of-nowhere bakery and brunch spot is a godsend. Operating for five months of the year out of a small log cabin, Stanley Baking Co is the only place in town where you're likely to see a queue. The reason: off-the-ratings-scale homemade baked goods and oatmeal pancakes.

Idaho Panhandle

Idaho grabbed the long, skinny spoon-handle that brushes up against Canada in an 1880's land dispute with Montana. Yet in both looks and attitude, the area has more in common with the Pacific Northwest than the Rockies. Spokane, a few miles west in Washington, acts as the regional hub and most of the panhandle observes Pacific Standard Time.

Near the Washington border, fast-growing **Coeur d'Alene** (population 44,000) is an extension of the Spokane metro area and the panhandle's largest town. There's a rather tacky boardwalk waterfront and one of those Anywhere USA–type golf and spa resorts. The adjacent lake is ideal for water-based activities like standup paddling. The **Coeur d'Alene Visitors Bureau** (📞877-782-9232; www.coeurdalene.org; 105 N 1st; ⊙10am-5pm Tue-Sat) has further information. Lodgers can count on the quirky pink-door **Flamingo Motel** (📞208-664-2159; www.flamingomotel-idaho.com; 718 Sherman Ave; d/ste $100/170; 📶), a retro 1950s throwback with themed rooms like English Garden and Americana. The best coffee is at **Java on Sherman** (324 Sherman, Coeur d'Alene; mains $4-9; ⊙6am-7pm), also serving good breakfasts and sandwiches.

Sandpoint, on Lake Pend Oreille, is the nicest panhandle town. Set in a gorgeous wilderness locale surrounded by mountains, it also sports Idaho's only serviceable Amtrak **train station**, an attractive historic building dating from 1916. The *Empire Builder,* running daily between Seattle/Portland and Chicago, stops here.

You can soak up Idaho's largest lake from the **Pend Oreille Scenic Byway** (US 200), which hugs the north shore. Eleven miles northwest of town is highly rated **Schweitzer Mountain Resort** (www.schweitzer. com; ski tickets adult/child $68/50), lauded for its tree-skiing, with mountain biking in summer.

The best accommodation bargain for miles around is the clean, friendly mom-and-pop-run **Country Inn** (📞208-263-3333; www.countryinnsandpoint.com; 470700 Hwy 95; s/d $64/80; 📶📶), 3 miles south of Sandpoint.

Southwest

Includes →

Best Places to Eat

→ Elote Cafe (p839)

→ Hell's Backbone (p872)

→ Love Apple (p892)

→ Cafe Roka (p856)

→ Raku (p815)

Best Places to Stay

→ Ellis Store Country Inn (p899)

→ El Tovar Hotel (p844)

→ Motor Lodge (p840)

→ St Regis Deer Valley (p864)

→ Vdara (p812)

Why Go?

The Southwest is America's untamed backyard, where life plays out before a stunning backdrop of red rocks, lofty peaks, shimmering lakes and deserts dotted with saguaros (cacti). Reminders of the region's multicultural beginnings and hardscrabble past dot the landscape, from curious pictographs and abandoned cliff dwellings to crumbling missions and rusty mining towns. Today, history-making continues, with astronomers and rocket builders peering into star-filled skies while artists and entrepreneurs flock to urban centers and quirky mountain towns, energizing the region.

The best part for travelers? A splendid network of scenic drives linking the most beautiful and iconic sites. But remember: It's not just iconic, larger-than-life landscapes that make a trip through the Southwest memorable. Study that saguaro up close. Ask a Hopi artist about his craft. Savor some green-chile stew. It's the tap-you-on-the-shoulder moments you may just cherish the most.

When to Go

Las Vegas

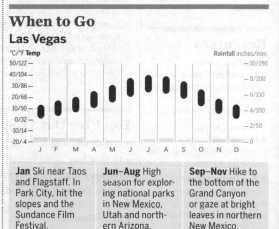

Jan Ski near Taos and Flagstaff. In Park City, hit the slopes and the Sundance Film Festival.

Jun–Aug High season for exploring national parks in New Mexico, Utah and northern Arizona.

Sep–Nov Hike to the bottom of the Grand Canyon or gaze at bright leaves in northern New Mexico.

> **DON'T MISS**
>
> A hike in the desert. Your choices? The Sonoran, Chihuahuan and Great Basin.

Fast Facts

➡ **Hub cities** Las Vegas (population 596,400), Phoenix (population 1.4 million), Salt Lake City (population 189,314)

➡ **Las Vegas to Grand Canyon National Park South Rim** 280 miles

➡ **Los Angeles to Albuquerque** 670 miles

➡ **Time zones** Nevada (Pacific), Arizona (Mountain, does not observe DST), Utah (Mountain), New Mexico (Mountain)

Did You Know?

Flash floods can occur from mid-July to early September. Avoid camping on sandy washes and canyon bottoms; don't drive across flooded roads. If hiking, move quickly to higher ground.

Resources

➡ **Public Lands Information Center** (www.publiclands.org) Descriptions, maps and book recommendations.

➡ **Grand Canyon Association** (www.grandcanyon.org) Extensive online bookstore.

➡ **Recreation.gov** (www.recreation.gov) Reservations for camping and activities at nationally run outdoor areas.

Getting There & Around

Las Vegas' McCarran International Airport and Phoenix' Sky Harbor International Airport are the region's busiest airports, followed by the airports serving Salt Lake City, Albuquerque and Tucson.

Greyhound stops at major points within the region but doesn't serve all national parks or off-the-beaten-path towns such as Moab. In larger cities, bus terminals can be in less-safe areas of town. Private vehicles are often the only means to reach out-of-the-way towns, trailheads and swimming spots.

Amtrak train service is much more limited than the bus system, although it does link many major cities and offers bus connections to others (including Santa Fe and Phoenix). The *California Zephyr* crosses Utah and Nevada; the *Southwest Chief* stops in Arizona and New Mexico; and the *Sunset Limited* traverses southern Arizona and New Mexico.

NATIONAL & STATE PARKS

Containing 50 national parks and monuments, the Southwest is a scenic and cultural jackpot. Add several stunning state parks, and, well, you might need to extend your trip.

One of the most deservedly popular national parks is Arizona's Grand Canyon National Park (p840). Other Arizona parks include Monument Valley Navajo Tribal Park (p849), a desert basin with towering sandstone pillars and buttes; Canyon de Chelly National Monument (p848), with ancient cliff dwellings; Petrified Forest National Park (p849), with its odd mix of Painted Desert and fossilized logs; and Saguaro National Park (p851), with pristine desert and giant cacti.

The southern red-rock Canyon Country in Utah includes five national parks: Arches (p869), Canyonlands (p870), Zion (p874), Bryce Canyon (p873) and Capitol Reef (p871), which offers exceptional wilderness solitude. Grand Staircase-Escalante National Monument (p872) is a mighty region of undeveloped desert. New Mexico boasts Carlsbad Caverns National Park (p899) and the mysterious Chaco Culture National Historic Park (p893). In Nevada, Great Basin National Park (p824) is a rugged, remote mountain oasis. For more information, check out the National Park Service website (www.nps.gov).

Top Five Day Hikes

➡ **Angels Landing** Zion National Park, UT

➡ **Winsor Trail** Santa Fe, NM

➡ **Navajo Loop** Bryce Canyon National Park, UT

➡ **South Kaibab Trail to Cedar Ridge** (p841) South Rim, Grand Canyon, AZ

➡ **Cape Final** North Rim, Grand Canyon, AZ

History

By about AD 100, three dominant cultures had emerged in the Southwest: the Hohokam, the Mogollon and the Ancestral Puebloans (formerly known as the Anasazi).

The Hohokam lived in the Arizona deserts from 300 BC to AD 1450, and created an incredible canal irrigation system, earthen pyramids and a rich heritage of pottery. Archaeological studies suggest that a cataclysmic event in the mid-15th century caused a dramatic decrease in the Hohokam's population, most notably in larger villages. Though it's not entirely clear what happened or where they went, the oral traditions of local tribes suggest that some Hohokam remained in the area and that members of these tribes are their descendants. From 200 BC to AD 1450 the Mogollon lived in the central mountains and valleys of the Southwest, and left behind what are now called the Gila Cliff Dwellings.

The Ancestral Puebloans left the richest heritage of archaeological sites, such as that at Chaco Culture National Historic Park. Today descendants of the Ancestral Puebloans are found in the Pueblo groups throughout New Mexico. The Hopi are descendants, too, and their village Old Oraibi may be the oldest continuously inhabited settlement in North America.

In 1540 Francisco Vásquez de Coronado led an expedition from Mexico City to the Southwest. Instead of riches, his party found Native Americans, many of whom were then killed or displaced. More than 50 years later, Juan de Oñate established the first capital of New Mexico at San Gabriel. Great bloodshed resulted from Oñate's attempts to control Native American pueblos, and he left in failure in 1608. Santa Fe was established as the new capital around 1610.

Development in the Southwest expanded rapidly during the 19th century, mainly due to railroad and geological surveys. As the US pushed west, the army forcibly removed whole tribes of Native Americans in often horrifyingly brutal Indian Wars. Gold and silver mines drew fortune seekers, and practically overnight the lawless mining towns of the Wild West mushroomed. Capitalizing on the development, the Santa Fe Railroad lured an ocean of tourists to the West.

Modern settlement is closely linked to water use. Following the Reclamation Act of 1902, huge federally funded dams were built to control rivers, irrigate the desert and encourage development. Rancorous debates and disagreements over water rights are ongoing, especially with the phenomenal boom in residential development. Other big issues today are illegal immigration and fiscal solvency.

Local Culture

The Southwest is one of the most multicultural regions of the country, encompassing a rich mix of Native American, Hispanic and Anglo populations. These groups have all influenced the area's cuisine, architecture and arts, and the Southwest's vast Native American reservations offer exceptional opportunities to learn about Native American culture and history. Visual arts are a strong force as well, from the art colonies dotting New Mexico to the roadside kitsch on view in small towns everywhere.

NEVADA

Nevada has a devil-may-care exuberance that's dangerously intoxicating – and sometimes a little bit wacky. Here, dazzling replicas of the Eiffel Tower, the Statue of Liberty and an Egyptian pyramid rise from the desert. Cowboys gather to recite poetry. Artists build a temporary city on a windswept playa. An Air Force base inspires alien conspiracies. And smack in the middle of it all is a lonely tree, its branches draped in sneakers tossed by mischievous road trippers.

On the map, the state is a vast and mostly empty stretch of desert, dotted with former mining towns that have traded pickaxes for slot machines. The mother lode is Las Vegas, an over-the-top place where people still catch gold fever. In the west, adventure outfitters are staking their claims on new treasures: gorgeous scenery and outdoor fun, which beckon from the Sierra Nevada mountains.

The first state to legalize gambling, Nevada is loud with the chime of slot machines singing out from gas stations, supermarkets and hotel lobbies. There's no legally mandated closing time for bars, and in rural areas, legalized brothels and hole-in-the-wall casinos sit side by side with Mormon and cowboy culture.

Our advice? Never ask 'Why?' Just embrace the state's go-for-broke joie de vivre.

Southwest Highlights

❶ Stroll the Rim Trail at **Grand Canyon National Park** (p840).

❷ Live your own John Wayne Western in northeastern Arizona's **Monument Valley** (p849).

❸ Practice your fast draw in dusty **Tombstone** (p855).

❹ Gallery-hop and jewelry-shop on the stylish streets of **Santa Fe** (p882).

❺ Sled down a shimmering sand dune at **White Sands National Monument** (p897).

❻ Wander a wonderland of stalactites at **Carlsbad Caverns National Park** (p899).

❼ Live the high life on Las Vegas' **Strip** (p809).

❽ Drive through flaming-red sandstone formations in **Valley of Fire State Park** (p819).

❾ Ski incredible terrain and enjoy chichi nightlife in **Park City** (p862).

❿ Explore a majestic canyon and climb Angels Landing at **Zion National Park** (p874).

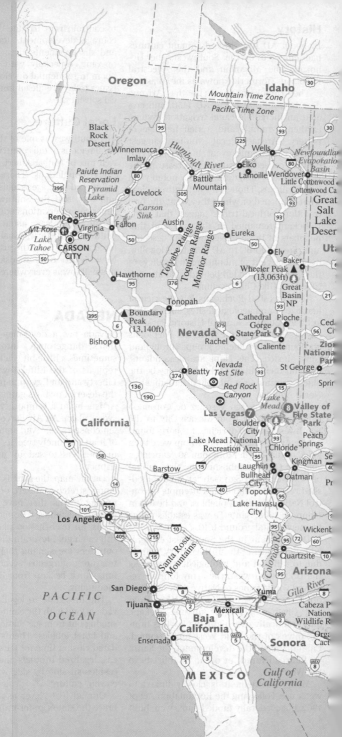

SOUTHWEST IN...

One Week

Museums and a burgeoning arts scene set an inspirational tone in **Phoenix**, an optimal springboard for exploring. In the morning, follow Camelback Rd into **Scottsdale** for top-notch shopping and gallery-hopping in Old Town. Drive north to **Sedona** for spiritual recharging before pondering the immensity of the **Grand Canyon**. From here, choose either bling or buttes. For bling, detour onto **Route 66**, cross the new bridge beside **Hoover Dam** then indulge your fantasies in **Las Vegas**. For buttes, drive east from the Grand Canyon into the Navajo country, cruising beneath the giant rock formations in **Monument Valley Navajo Tribal Park**, then stepping back in time at stunning **Canyon de Chelly National Monument**.

Two Weeks

Start in glitzy **Las Vegas** before kicking back in funky **Flagstaff** and peering into the abyss at **Grand Canyon National Park**. Check out collegiate **Tucson** or frolic among cacti at **Saguaro National Park**. Watch the gunslingers in **Tombstone** before settling into Victorian **Bisbee**.

Secure your sunglasses for the blinding dunes of **White Sands National Monument** in nearby New Mexico then sink into **Santa Fe**, a magnet for art-lovers. Explore a pueblo in **Taos** and watch the sunrise at awesome **Monument Valley Navajo Tribal Park**. Head into Utah for the red-rock national parks, **Canyonlands** and **Arches**. Do the hoodoos at **Bryce Canyon** then pay your respects at glorious **Zion**.

ⓘ Information

Prostitution is illegal in Clark County (which includes Las Vegas) and Washoe County (which includes Reno), although there are legal brothels in many of the smaller counties.

Nevada is on Pacific Standard Time and has two areas codes: Las Vegas and vicinity is ☑702, while the rest of the state is ☑775.

Nevada Commission on Tourism (☑800-638-2328; www.travelnevada.com) Sends free books, maps and information on accommodations, campgrounds and events.

Nevada Department of Transportation (☑in-state 511, 877-687-6237; www.nvroads.com) For up-to-date road conditions.

Nevada Division of State Parks (☑775-684-2770; www.parks.nv.gov; 901 S Stewart St, 5th fl, Carson City; ⊘8am-5pm Mon-Fri) Camping in state parks ($10 to $15 per night) is first-come, first-served. You can pick up maps and brochures at this office.

Las Vegas

Ah, Vegas. A dazzling rhinestone of a city where you can sip champagne inside a three-story chandelier. You can also travel the world in a day, gliding through the canals of Venice, climbing the Eiffel Tower and crossing the Brooklyn Bridge. It's a slice of desert that's transformed itself into one of the most lavish places on earth, nothing is halfway – even the illusions.

A city of multiple personalities, Las Vegas has been reinventing itself since the days of the Rat Pack. To grab your attention, not to mention your cash, the old is constantly torn down for the new. Once-famous signs collect dust in a neon boneyard while the clang of construction echoes over the Strip. The horizon is ever-evolving. But it's a different story inside the casinos, where time seems to stand still. There are no clocks, just fresh-pumped air, endless buffets and ever-flowing drinks.

Sin City's reach is all-inclusive. Hollywood bigwigs gyrate at A-list ultralounges, while college kids seek cheap debauchery and grandparents whoop it up at the penny slots. You can sip designer martinis as you sample the apex of world-class cuisine or wander the casino floor with a 3ft-high cocktail tied around your neck.

History

Contrary to popular legend, there was much more at the dusty crossroads than a gambling parlor and some tumbleweeds the day mobster Ben 'Bugsy' Siegel rolled in and erected a glamorous tropical-themed casino, the Flamingo, under the searing sun.

Speared into the modern era by the completion of a railroad that linked up Salt Lake City to Los Angeles in 1902, Las Vegas boomed in the 1920s thank to federally sponsored construction projects. The legalization of gambling in 1931 carried Vegas through the Great Depression, WWII brought a huge air-force base and aerospace bucks, plus a paved highway to Los Angeles. Soon after, the Cold War justified the Nevada Test Site. It proved to be a textbook case of 'any publicity is good publicity': monthly aboveground atomic blasts shattered casino windows downtown while the city's official Miss Mushroom Cloud mascot promoted atomic everything in tourism campaigns.

A building spree sparked by the Flamingo in 1946 led to mob-backed tycoons upping the glitz ante at every turn. Big-name entertainers like Frank Sinatra, Liberace and Sammy Davis Jr arrived on stage at the same time as topless French showgirls.

The high-profile purchase of the Desert Inn in 1966 by eccentric billionaire Howard Hughes gave the gambling industry a much-needed patina of legitimacy. The debut of the MGM Grand in 1993 signaled the dawn of the corporate mega-resort era.

An oasis in the middle of a final frontier, Sin City continues to exist chiefly to satisfy the desires of visitors. Hosting 39.7 million people a year, until recently Las Vegas was the engine of North America's fastest-growing metropolitan area. The housing crisis hit residents here especially hard, but construction has picked up on the Strip and the Downtown Project is revitalizing the Fremont area.

◉ Sights

Roughly 4 miles long, the Strip, aka Las Vegas Blvd, is the center of gravity in Sin City. Circus Circus Las Vegas caps the north end and Mandalay Bay is at the south end, near the airport. Whether you're walking or driving, distances on the Strip are deceiving; a walk to what looks like a nearby casino usually takes longer than expected.

Downtown Las Vegas is the original town center and home to the city's oldest hotels and casinos: expect a retro feel, cheaper drinks and lower table limits. Its main drag is fun-loving Fremont St, a four-block stretch of casinos and restaurants covered by a dazzling canopy that runs a groovy light show every evening.

Major tourist areas are safe. However, Las Vegas Blvd between downtown and the Strip gets shabby, and Fremont St east of downtown is rather unsavory, although that's beginning to change, with new bars and restaurants opening their doors.

At press time, the $550 million LINQ shopping and entertainment district on the central Strip planned to open soon. LINQ's calling card is the 550ft-tall High Roller, billed as the world's tallest Ferris wheel. Projections aren't as certain for Skyvue, a 500ft-tall Ferris wheel (and electronic billboard) at the south end of the Strip across from Mandalay Bay. Construction has stagnated, and there are rumors of financial problems.

Openings are ongoing in the Fremont East neighborhood, where the online retailing giant Zappos is moving its headquarters. Zappos CEO Tony Hsieh, through

NEVADA FACTS

Nickname Silver State

Population 2.76 million

Area 109,800 sq miles

Capital city Carson City (population 54,800)

Other cities Las Vegas (population 596,400), Reno (population 227,000)

Sales tax 6.85%

Birthplace of Patricia Nixon (b 1912), Andre Agassi (b 1970), Greg LeMond (b 1961)

Home of The slot machine, Burning Man

Politics Nevada has six electoral votes – the state went for Obama in the 2012 presidential election, but it is split evenly in sending elected officials to Washington; US Senate Majority Leader Harry Reid (D) is Nevada's best-known politician

Famous for The 1859 Comstock Lode (the country's richest known silver deposit), legalized gambling and prostitution (outlawed in certain counties), and liberal alcohol laws allowing 24-hour bars

Best Las Vegas T-Shirt "I saw nothing at the Mob Museum."

Driving distances Las Vegas to Reno: 452 miles, Great Basin National Park to Las Vegas: 313 miles

SOUTHWEST LAS VEGAS

Las Vegas

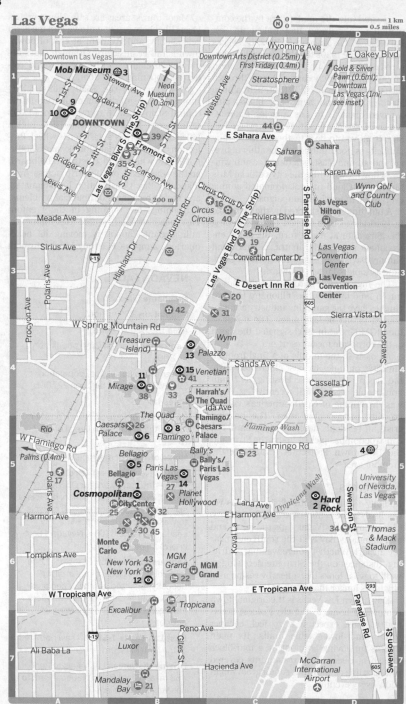

N

0 ___ 1 km
0 ___ 0.5 miles

Downtown Las Vegas

Mob Museum 🏛3

Stewart Ave

Ogden Ave

S 1st St

9

10

DOWNTOWN

Neon Museum (0.3mi)

Fremont St 7

39

37

35

Bridger Ave

Carson Ave

S 3rd St

S 4th St

S 5th St

S 6th St

Lewis Ave

Las Vegas Blvd S (The Strip)

0 ___ 200 m

Wyoming Ave

Downtown Arts District (0.25mi)
First Friday (0.4mi)

Stratosphere

E Oakey Blvd

Gold & Silver Pawn (0.6mi);
Downtown Las Vegas (1mi; see inset)

18

44

E Sahara Ave

Sahara

Sahara

Karen Ave

S Paradise Rd

Wynn Golf and Country Club

Las Vegas Hilton

Western Ave

Circus Circus Dr

16

Circus Circus

40

Riviera Blvd

Riviera

36

19

Convention Center Dr

Las Vegas Convention Center

Meade Ave

Sirius Ave

Polaris Ave

Highland Dr

Industrial Rd

I-15

E Desert Inn Rd

Las Vegas Convention Center

Sierra Vista Dr

Swenson St

W Spring Mountain Rd

42

20

31

Wynn

TI (Treasure Island)

13 Palazzo

Sands Ave

Cassella Dr

28

Procyon Ave

15 Venetian

41

Mirage

11

38

33

Harrah's/The Quad

Ida Ave

Flamingo/Caesars Palace

Flamingo Wash

The Quad

Caesars Palace

26

6

8

Flamingo

E Flamingo Rd

4

Rio

Palms (0.4mi)

W Flamingo Rd

Bellagio

5

Bellagio

Paris Las Vegas

Bally's

Bally's/Paris Las Vegas

23

Polaris Ave

17

Cosmopolitan 1

CityCenter

25

14

27

Planet Hollywood

Lana Ave

Tropicana Wash

University of Nevada, Las Vegas

2 **Hard Rock**

Harmon Ave

32

29

30 45

Monte Carlo

New York New York

43

12

MGM Grand

22

E Harmon Ave

Koval La

34

Swenson St

Thomas & Mack Stadium

Tompkins Ave

MGM Grand

E Tropicana Ave

593

W Tropicana Ave

Excalibur

24

Tropicana

Reno Ave

Giles St

Paradise Rd

Swenson St

Ali Baba La

I-15

Luxor

Hacienda Ave

McCarran International Airport

605

Mandalay Bay

21

SOUTHWEST LAS VEGAS

Las Vegas

his Downtown Project initiative, has injected hundreds of millions of dollars into community-based projects to revitalize the neighborhood.

◉ The Strip

★Cosmopolitan
CASINO

(www.cosmopolitanlasvegas.com; 3708 Las Vegas Blvd S; ⊙24hr) The twinkling three-story chandelier inside this sleek addition to the Strip isn't a piece of contemporary art only to be ogled. It's a step-inside, sip-a-swanky-cocktail and survey-your-domain kind of place, worthy of your wildest fairy tale. And

Cinderellas, you simply must step into the Roark Gourley–designed giant slipper for an Instagrammy moment. A bit much? Not really. It's all pure fun, and the Cosmopolitan manages to avoid utter pretension, despite the near-constant wink-wink moments, from the Art-o-Matics (vintage cigarette machines hawking local art not nicotine) to the hidden pizza joint.

★Hard Rock
CASINO

(www.hardrockhotel.com; 4455 Paradise Rd; ⊙24hr) This casino hotel has got the moves like Jagger – getting older, but still strutting across the stage like a pouty-lipped bad boy.

Fresh off a $750 million expansion that added two new towers, the tres-hip Hard Rock is still luring them in with concerts, attitude and a very impressive collection of rock and roll memorabilia. Highlights include Jim Morrison's handwritten lyrics to one of the Doors' greatest hits and leather jackets from a who's who of famous rock stars. The Joint concert hall, Vanity Nightclub and 'Rehab' summer pool parties at Paradise Beach attract a pimped-out, sex-charged crowd flush with celebrities.

Bellagio
CASINO

(www.bellagio.com; 3600 Las Vegas Blvd S; ☉24hr) The Bellagio dazzles with Tuscan architecture and an 8.5-acre artificial lake, complete with don't-miss choreographed dancing fountains. Look up as you enter the lobby: the stunning ceiling is adorned with a backlit glass sculpture composed of 2000 handblown flowers by renowned artist Dale Chihuly. The **Bellagio Gallery of Fine Art** (adult/student/child $16/11/free; ☉10am-8pm) showcases temporary exhibits by top-notch artists. The **Bellagio Conservatory & Botanical Gardens** (☉24hr) **FREE** features changing exhibits throughout the year.

Caesars Palace
CASINO

(www.caesarspalace.com; 3570 Las Vegas Blvd S; ☉24hr) Forget Caesar. It's King Minos who springs to mind at this sprawling, labyrinth-like Greco-Roman fantasyland where maps are few (and not oriented to the outside). The interior is captivating, however, with marble reproductions of classical statuary, including a not-to-be-missed 4-ton Brahma

shrine near the front entrance. Towering fountains, goddess-costumed cocktail waitresses and the swanky haute-couture **Forum Shops** all up the glitz. And the minotaur? It's the new **Bacchanal Buffet**. But it can never be slayed.

Venetian
CASINO

(www.venetian.com; 3355 Las Vegas Blvd S; gondola ride adult/private $19/76; ☉24hr) Hand-painted ceiling frescoes, roaming mimes, gondola rides and full-scale reproductions of famous Venice landmarks are found at the romantic Venetian. Next door, the **Palazzo** (www.palazzo.com; 3325 Las Vegas Blvd S) exploits a variation on the Italian theme with a luxurious but less interesting effect.

Mirage
CASINO

(www.mirage.com; 3400 Las Vegas Blvd S; ☉24hr) A domed atrium filled with jungle foliage and soothing cascades captures the imagination at this tropically themed wonderland. Circling the atrium is a vast Polynesian-themed casino, which places gaming areas under separate roofs to evoke intimacy, including a popular high-limit poker room. Pause by the front desk for the 20,000-gallon saltwater aquarium, with 60 species of critters hailing from Fiji to the Red Sea. Out front in the lagoon, a fiery faux volcano erupts hourly after dark until midnight.

Paris-Las Vegas
CASINO

(www.parislv.com; 3655 Las Vegas Blvd S; ☉24hr) Evoking the gaiety of the City of Light, Paris Las Vegas strives to capture the essence of the grand dame by re-creating her land-

---

LAS VEGAS FOR CHILDREN

With its recent focus on adult-oriented fun – marked by the now-iconic slogan 'What happens in Vegas stays in Vegas' – the city isn't a great choice for families. People under 21 can walk through most casinos on their way to shops, shows and restaurants but they cannot stop. Policies vary on whether under-21s must be accompanied by an adult, but younger children should always be with an adult for safety reason. Some casinos prohibit strollers.

If you do land in Sin City with the kids, don't abandon all hope. The **Circus Circus** (www.circuscircus.com; 2880 Las Vegas Blvd S; ☉24hr; 🚼) hotel complex is all about kiddie fun, and its **Adventuredome** (www.adventuredome.com; day pass over/under 48in tall $28/17, per ride $5-8; ☉hour vary; 🚼) is a 5-acre indoor theme park with rock climbing, bumper cars and a new 70mph roller coaster, the El Loco, which is set to open by the end of 2013. The **Midway** (☉11am-midnight; 🚼) **FREE** features animals, acrobats and magicians performing on center stage.

If your kids are literally bouncing off the walls, take them to the trampoline-filled **Skyzone** (www.skyzone.com/LasVegas; 4915 Steptoe St; 30 min/60 min $9/12; ☉2-8pm Mon-Thu, 2-10pm Fri, 10am-9pm Sat, 11am-8pm Sun) where such behavior is encouraged.

marks. Fine likenesses of the Opéra, the Arc de Triomphe, the Champs-Élysées, the soaring Eiffel Tower and even the Seine frame the property.

Flamingo
CASINO

(www.flamingolasvegas.com; 3555 Las Vegas Blvd S; ☺24hr) The Flamingo is quintessential vintage Vegas. Weave through the slot machines to the **Wildlife Habitat** (3555 S Las Vegas Blvd; ☺8am-dusk) **FREE** to see the flock of Chilean flamingos that call these 15 tropical acres home.

New York-New York
CASINO

(www.newyorknewyork.com; 3790 Las Vegas Blvd S; ☺24hr) A mini metropolis featuring scaled-down replicas of the Empire State Building, the Statue of Liberty, a September 11 memorial, and the Brooklyn Bridge. There's also a classic roller coaster with a drop of 144ft (tickets $14).

◉ Downtown & Off the Strip

★Mob Museum
MUSEUM

(☑702-229-2734; www.themobmuseum.org; 300 Stewart Ave; adult/child $20/14; ☺10am-7pm Sun-Thu, to 8pm Fri & Sat) Bugs. Lucky. Whitey. Yeah goombah, all the boys are hanging out at downtown's new mob museum, which fills three floors in the old federal building. The fascinating, often lurid, exhibits trace the development of organized crime in America and look at the mob's connection to Las Vegas. Learn how money is laundered, listen in on a wiretap, get your mug shot taken and catch your breath in front of the bullet-and-blood-ridden wall that backed the victims of the 1929 St Valentine's Day Massacre.

Plan to spend several hours here. The museum is not appropriate for children.

★Neon Museum
MUSEUM

(☑702-387-6366; www.neonmuseum.org; 770 Las Vegas Blvd N; day tour adult/child $18/12, night tour $25/22; ☺9-10am & 7:30-9pm Jun-Aug, extended daytime hours beginning at 10am rest of the year) A tour of the neon boneyard here is a fun stroll through Sin City's 'electrifying' past. Guides share stories about the city's former bigwigs as you walk past the gaudy signs that fronted their casinos, from Binion's to the Stardust. The new visitor center is housed in the lobby of the La Concha Motel, a striking mid-city modern structure that was saved from demolition in 2005 and moved here. All tours are guided, and they sell out quickly, so reserve beforehand online. At press time, the museum was offering evening tours on a trial basis, when a few of the signs are illuminated. There are no afternoon tours in the summer due to the heat. Call ahead to confirm tour times, which change seasonally.

The museum also has a public-art component, with a series of restored vintage signs scattered across downtown. This 'urban gallery' is best viewed at night when the neon blazes. Most of these signs are on Las Vegas Blvd between Fremont St and Washington Ave.

Atomic Testing Museum
MUSEUM

(www.atomictestingmuseum.org; 755 E Flamingo Rd; adult/child $14/11; ☺10am-5pm Mon-Sat, noon-5pm Sun) Recalling an era when the word 'atomic' conjured modernity and mystery, the Smithsonian-run Atomic Testing Museum remains an intriguing testament to the period when the fantastical – and destructive – power of nuclear energy was tested just outside Las Vegas. Don't skip the deafening Ground Zero Theater, which mimics a concrete test bunker.

Fremont Street Experience
PLAZA

(www.vegasexperience.com; Fremont St, btwn Main St & Las Vegas Blvd; ☺hourly 7pm-midnight) A four-block pedestrian mall topped by an arched steel canopy and filled with computer-controlled lights, the multi-sensory Fremont Street Experience, between Main St and Las Vegas Blvd, has re-energized downtown. Every evening, the canopy transforms into a six-minute light-and-sound show enhanced by 550,000 watts of wraparound sound. Bands play on several stages and zipliners whizz past overhead after stepping off Slotzilla, a 12-story slot machine scheduled to open soon.

Golden Nugget
CASINO

(www.goldennugget.com; 129 E Fremont St; ☺24hr) This casino hotel has set the downtown benchmark for extravagance since opening in 1946. It's currently earning wows for its three-story waterslide, which drops through a 200,000-gallon shark tank. No brass or cut glass was spared inside the swanky but lovely casino, known for its nonsmoking poker room and the RUSH Lounge, where live local bands play. The gigantic 61lb Hand of Faith, the world's largest gold nugget, is around the corner from the hotel lobby.

SOUTHWEST LAS VEGAS

SOUTHWEST LAS VEGAS

Downtown Arts District   ARTS

On the **First Friday** (www.firstfridaylasvegas.com; ⊙5-11pm) of each month, 10,000 art-lovers, hipsters, indie musicians and hangers-on descend on Las Vegas' downtown arts district for gallery openings, performance art, live bands and tattoo artists. The action revolves around S Casino Center Blvd between Colorado Ave and California Ave, northwest of the Stratosphere. Activities have also extended to Fremont East.

🏃 Activities

For area hiking and biking trails, check out the Neon to Nature listings on www.gethealthyclarkcountry.org.

Qua Baths & Spa   SPA

(☑866-782-0655; www.harrahs.com/qua-caesars-palace; 3570 Las Vegas Blvd S, Caesars Palace; ⊙6am-8pm) Social spa-going is encouraged in the tea lounge, herbal steam room and arctic ice room, where dry-ice snowflakes fall.

Desert Adventures   KAYAKING, HIKING

(☑702-293-5026; www.kayaklasvegas.com; 1647 Nevada Hwy, Suite A, Boulder City; trips from $149) With Lake Mead and Hoover Dam just 30 minutes away, would-be river rats should check out Desert Adventures for guided half-, full- and multiday kayaking adventures. Hiking and horseback-riding trips, too.

Escape Adventures   MOUNTAIN BIKING

(☑800-596-2953; www.escapeadventures.com; 10575 Discovery Dr; trips incl bike from $129) The source for guided mountain-bike tours of Red Rock Canyon State Park.

🛏 Sleeping

Rates rise and fall dramatically. Some hotel websites feature calendars listing day-by-day room rates. Most of the hotels on the Strip are now adding a daily resort fee. These daily fees are noted below.

🛏 The Strip

★ Vdara   HOTEL $$

(☑702-590-2767; www.vdara.com; 2600 W Harmon Ave; r $159-196; ℗ 🛜 🏊) Cool sophistication and warm hospitality merge easily at Vdara, a no-gaming, all-suites hotel in the new CityCenter complex. With earth-toned walls, chocolate-brown furniture and riparian green pillows, the suites have a soothing 'woodland' appeal, apropos for a LEED-certified property. If you're nice, you might score a room with a view of Bellagio's dancing waters. The hotel is near the Bellagio monorail stop. Resort fee is $28.

Tropicana   CASINO HOTEL $$

(☑702-739-2222; www.troplv.com; 3801 Las Vegas Blvd S; r from $129, ste from $229; ℗ ❄ @ 🛜 🏊) After a multi-million-dollar renovation this

---

LAS VEGAS: HIGH-OCTANE THRILLS

Driving Hop into a race car at **Richard Petty Driving Experience** (☑800-237-3889; www.drivepetty.com; 6975 Speedway Blvd, Las Vegas Motor Speedway, off I-15 exit 54; ride-alongs from $99; drives from $449; ⊙hour vary) or careen around the track in a souped-up go-kart at **Fast Lap** (☑702-736-8113; www.fastlaplv.com; 4288 S Polaris; per race $25; ⊙10am-11pm Mon-Sat, 10am-10pm Sun).

Indoor Skydiving No time to jump from a plane? Enjoy the thrill without the altitude at **Vegas Indoor Skydiving** (☑702-731-4768; www.vegasindoorskydiving; 200 Convention Center Dr; single flight $85; ⊙9.45am-8pm).

Shooting If you're dying to fire a sub-machine gun or feel the heft of a Glock in your hot little hands, visit the high-powered **Gun Store** (☑702-454-1110; www.thegunstorelasvegas.com; 2900 E Tropicana Ave; from $99; ⊙9am-6:30pm; 🖵201), with an indoor video training range.

Stratosphere Atop this 110-story **casino** (☑702-380-7777; www.stratospherehotel.com; Stratosphere, 2000 Las Vegas Blvd S; elevator adult/concession $18/15, incl 3 thrill rides $33, all-day pass $34, SkyJump from $110; underground rail Sahara) you can ride a roller coaster, drop 16 stories on the Big Shot, spin above thin air, or plummet 108ft over the edge.

Ziplining Whoosh over Bootleg Canyon on four separate ziplines with **Flightlinez** (☑702-293-6885; www.flightlinezbootleg.com; 1152 Industrial Rd, Boulder City; adult/child $159/99; ⊙7am-5pm). You'll drop 11 stories over throngs of tourists from the 12-story Slotzilla, set to open on Fremont St.

retro property, which has kept the Strip's tropical love going since 1953, just got cool again. The vibe is finger-snappin' hip, but still inviting, with a bright, monochromatic color scheme, lush, relaxing gardens and earth-toned, breezy rooms and bi-level suites. Resort fee is $20.

MGM Grand
CASINO HOTEL **$$**

(📞702-891-7777, 800-929-1111; www.mgmgrand. com; 3799 Las Vegas Blvd S; r from $122, ste from $150; 🅿✳@🛜🏊) With more than 5000 rooms, this green leviathan is one of the world's largest hotels, but is bigger better? That depends, but top-drawer restaurants, a sprawling pool complex and a monorail station always make it a good bet – if you can find your room. Standard rooms have blah decor, so stay in the minimalist-modern West Wing instead. Try the Signature Suites for more space, high thread counts and a kitchenette. Resort fee is $28.

Caesars Palace
CASINO HOTEL **$$**

(📞866-227-5938; www.caesarspalace.com; 3570 Las Vegas Blvd S; r from $197; 🅿✳@🏊) Send away the centurions and decamp in style – Caesars' standard rooms are some of the most luxurious in town. Resort fee is $25.

Cosmopolitan
CASINO HOTEL **$$$**

(📞702-698-7000; www.cosmopolitanlasvegas. com; 3708 Las Vegas Blvd S; r/ste from $320/470; 🅿✳@🛜🏊) This place is like Hogwarts for hipsters, an uber-trendy warren tantalizing guests with magically impressive details and fun surprises. The wonder starts in the lobby where digitally enhanced columns display eye-catching backdrops. Rooms preen with mod designs, but the real delight is to stumble from your room at 1am to play pool in the upper lobbies before going on a mission to find the 'secret' pizza joint. Resort fee is $25.

Mandalay Bay
CASINO HOTEL **$$$**

(📞702-632-7777, 877-632-7800; www.mandalaybay.com; 3950 Las Vegas Blvd S; r $141-291; 🅿✳@🛜🏊) The ornately appointed rooms here have a South Seas theme, and the amenities include floor-to-ceiling windows and luxurious bathrooms. Swimmers will swoon over the pool complex, with a sand-and-surf beach. Resort fee is $28.

Encore
CASINO HOTEL **$$$**

(📞702-770-8000; www.encorelasvegas.com; 3121 Las Vegas Blvd S; r/ste from $303/449; 🅿✳@🛜🏊) Classy and playful rather than overblown and opulent – even people cheering

at the roulette table clap with more elegance. The rooms are studies in subdued luxury. Resort fee is $28.

🛏 Downtown & Off The Strip

Downtown hotels are generally less expensive than those on the Strip.

Main Street Station
CASINO HOTEL **$**

(📞800-713-8933, 702-387-1896; www.mainstreetcasino.com; 200 N Main St; r from $50; 🅿✳🛜) For one of the best deals out there, try this 17-floor downtown hotel with marble-tiled foyers and Victorian sconces in the hallways. The classically styled rooms lack 'oomph,' but they do come with plantation shutters and comfy beds. The Mob Museum and Fremont St are within walking distance, and there's a microbrewery on-site.

Golden Nugget
CASINO HOTEL **$$**

(📞800-846-5336, 702-385-7111; www.goldennugget.com; 129 E Fremont St; r $99-239, ste $179-269; 🅿✳@🛜🏊) Rooms feel swankier in the Gold and Rush Towers, but the vibe is still nice in the more traditionally decored Carson Tower. Outside, enjoy the lavish pool area, or brave the three-story water slide, which plunges through a shark tank.

Platinum Hotel
BOUTIQUE HOTEL **$$**

(📞702-365-5000, 877-211-9211; www.theplatinumhotel.com; 211 E Flamingo Rd; r from $152; 🅿✳@🛜🏊🏊) Just off the Strip, the coolly modern rooms at this non-gaming property are comfortable, spacious and full of nice touches – many have fireplaces and all have kitchens and Jacuzzi tubs. The Strip is a 10 to 15-minute walk. One-time pet fee of $75.

Hard Rock
CASINO HOTEL **$$$**

(📞800-473-7625, 702-693-5000; www.hardrockhotel.com; 4455 Paradise Rd; r $122-399; 🅿✳@🛜🏊) Everything about this boutique hotel spells stardom. French doors reveal skyline and palm tree views, and brightly colored Euro-minimalist rooms feature souped-up stereos and plasma TVs. While we dig the jukeboxes in the HRH All-Suite Tower, the standard rooms are nearly as cool. The hottest action revolves around the lush Beach Club.

Red Rock Resort
RESORT **$$$**

(📞702-797-7777; www.redrock.sclv.com; 11011 W Charleston Blvd; r $140-380; 🅿✳@🛜🏊) If you're planning to hike in Red Rock Canyon, this oasis-like resort 15 miles west of the Strip is a stylish place to rest beforehand.

Rooms are comfy, spacious and well-appointed, with forest greens, deep browns and lots of pillows. On-site you'll find a bowling alley and a movie theater. There's free transportation to and from the Strip and the airport.

✖ Eating

Sin City is an unmatched eating adventure. Reservations are a must for fancier restaurants.

✖ The Strip

On the Strip itself, cheap eats beyond fast-food joints are hard to find.

Secret Pizza   PIZZA $
(3708 Las Vegas Blvd S, Cosmopolitan; slice $5, pizza $25; ⊙11:30am-3am) There's an unmarked pizza joint hidden deep within Cosmopolitan. We're not going to reveal its exact location because, well, where's the fun in that? But if you're craving a late-night slice of New York pizza, go to the third level and look for the narrow hallway between the other eateries. Or just join the queue of over-imbibers already waiting.

Earl of Sandwich   SANDWICHES $
(www.earlofsandwichusa.com; 3667 Las Vegas Blvd S, Planet Hollywood; mains under $7; ⊙24hr) Yes, calm down, we know it's a chain. But you know what? The sandwiches are tasty, the prices are easy on the wallet and it's in a convenient central Strip location. And everybody seems to like it.

WORTHY INDULGENCES: BEST BUFFETS

Extravagant all-you-can-eat buffets are a Sin City tradition. Three of the best include:

Bacchanal Buffet (www.caesars-palace.com; 3570 Las Vegas Blvd S, Caesars Palace; breakfast $20, lunch $30, dinner $40)

Wicked Spoon Buffet (www.cosmopolitanlasvegas.com; 2708 Las Vegas Blvd S, Cosmopolitan; brunch $33, dinner $41)

Buffet Bellagio (⌨702-693-7111; www.bellagio.com; Bellagio, 3600 Las Vegas Blvd S; breakfast $18, lunch $22, dinner $33)

Todd English PUB   PUB $$
(www.toddenglishpub.com; 3720 Las Vegas Blvd S, Crystals; mains $16-24; ⊙11am-2am Mon-Fri, 9:30am-2am Sat & Sun) A rollicking City Center venture from Bostonian chef Todd English, PUB is a strangely fun cross between a British pub and a frat party, with creative sliders, an 80+ beer list that includes English pub classics, and an interesting promotion: if you drink your beer in less than seven seconds, it's on the house.

Society Café   CAFE $$
(www.wynnlasvegas.com; 3121 Las Vegas Blvd S, Encore; breakfast $14-22, lunch $14-24, dinner $15-39; ⊙7am-11pm Sun-Thu, 7am-11:30pm Fri & Sat; ⌨) A slice of reasonably priced culinary heaven amid Encore's loveliness. The basic cafe here is equal to fine dining at other joints. There's a short list of vegan options on all menus.

Social House   JAPANESE $$
(⌨702-736-1122; www.socialhouselv.com; 3720 Las Vegas Blvd S, Crystals Mall, CityCenter; lunch prix fixe $20, sushi $6-24, mains $22-38; ⊙5-10pm Mon-Thu, noon-11pm Fri & Sat, noon-10pm Sun) Nibble on creative dishes inspired by Japanese street food in one of the Strip's most serene yet sultry dining rooms. Watermarked scrolls, wooden screens, and loads of dramatic red and black conjure visions of Imperial Japan, while the sushi and steaks are totally contemporary.

Joël Robuchon   FRENCH $$$
(⌨702-891-7925; www.mgmgrand.com; 3799 Las Vegas Blvd S, MGM Grand; mains $135-175, menu per person $120-420; ⊙5:30-10pm Sun-Thu, to 10:30pm Fri & Sat) A once-in-a-lifetime culinary experience; block off a solid three hours and get ready to eat your way through the multicourse seasonal menu of traditional French fare. Next door at **L'Atelier de Joël Robuchon** (⌨702-891-7358; www.mgmgrand.com; 3799 Las Vegas Blvd S, MGM Grand; mains $41-97; ⊙5-11pm), you can belly up to the counter for a slightly more economical but still delicious meal.

Picasso   FRENCH $$$
(⌨702-693-8865; www.bellagio.com; 3600 Las Vegas Blvd S, Bellagio; prix-fixe menu $115; ⊙5:30-9:30pm Wed-Mon) Why yes, I would like to dine with Picasso tonight – or a least one of his paintings. But the art isn't just on the wall at chef Julian Serrano's swanky French restaurant, where dishes on the four-course prix-fixe menu are masterworks themselves. Servings are small, but you should leave

satisfied after several courses. Desserts are spectacular.

Gordon Ramsay Steak
STEAKHOUSE **$$$**

(☑877-346-4642; www.parislasvegas.com; 3655 Las Vegas Blvd S, Paris; mains $32-63; ⊘4:30-10:30pm, bar to midnight Fri & Sat) For a top-notch steak, leave Paris and the Eiffel Tower behind and stroll through 'the chunnel' to Gordon Ramsay's new steakhouse. Rib-boned in red and domed by a jaunty Union Jack, this is one of the top seats in town. No reservation? Sit at the bar, where the knowledgable bartenders will explain the cuts and their preparations. And definitely say yes to the side of bread. Fish, chops and one lonely chicken dish round out the a la carte menu.

Sage
AMERICAN **$$$**

(☑702-590-8690; www.arialasvegas.com; 3730 Las Vegas Blvd S, Aria; mains $35-54; ⊘5-11pm Mon-Sat) Acclaimed chef Shawn McClain meditates on the seasonally sublime with global inspiration and artisanal, farm-to-table ingredients in one of Vegas' most drop-dead gorgeous dining rooms. Don't miss the inspired seasonal cocktails doctored with housemade liqueurs, French absinthe and fruit purees.

DOCG Enoteca
ITALIAN **$$$**

(☑877-893-2003; www.cosmopolitanlasvegas.com; 3708 Las Vegas Blvd S, Cosmopolitan; mains $22-45; ⊘6-11pm) Order to-die-for fresh pasta or a wood-fired pizza in the stylish *enoteca* (wine shop)–inspired room that feels like you've joined a festive dinner party. Or head next door to sexy **Scarpetta** (☑877-893-2003; www.cosmopolitalasvegas.com; 3708 Las Vegas Blvd S; mains $24-55; ⊘6-11pm), which offers a more intimate, upscale experience by the same fantastic chef, Scott Conant.

✕ Downtown & Off The Strip

For gourmands, off the Strip is where dining gets really interesting. Downtown's restaurants offer better value than those on the Strip, and new eateries are popping up in the E Fremont St neighborhood.

The Asian restaurants on Spring Mountain Rd in Chinatown are also good budget options, with lots of vegetarian choices.

★ Raku
JAPANESE **$$**

(☑702-367-3511; www.raku-grill.com; 5030 W Spring Mountain Rd; small plates $2-18, mains $8-19; ⊘6pm-3am Mon-Sat) Japanese owner-chef Mitsuo Edo crafts small plate dishes that simmer with delicate, exquisite flavors. You'll find yourself ordering just one more thing – again and again – from the menu of grilled meats, homemade tofu and seasoned vegetables. Try one of the tofus and the kobe beef with wasabi. Raku is a 15-minute cab ride from the Strip. Make reservations or angle for a seat at the small bar.

★ Lotus of Siam
THAI **$$**

(☑702-735-3033; www.saipinchutima.com; 953 E Sahara Ave; mains $9-30; ⊘11:30am-2:30pm Mon-Fri, buffet to 2pm, 5:30-10pm daily) The top Thai restaurant in the US? According to *Gourmet Magazine,* this is it. One bite of simple pad Thai – or any of the exotic northern Thai dishes – nearly proves it.

Firefly
TAPAS **$$**

(www.fireflylv.com; 3824 Paradise Rd; small dishes $4-10, large dishes $12-20; ⊘11:30am-2am Sun-Thu) A meal at Firefly can be twice as fun as an overdone Strip restaurant, and half the price. Is that why it's always hopping? Nosh on traditional Spanish tapas, while the bartender pours sangria and flavor-infused *mojitos.*

Eat
BREAKFAST, AMERICAN **$$**

(☑702-534-1515; www.facebook.com/eatdown-townlv; 707 Carson Ave; breakfast $8-20, lunch $9-25; ⊘8am-3pm Mon-Fri, to 2pm Sat & Sun) What makes newcomer Eat so special? Community spirit and down-home cooking are what first leap to mind. Trust us, you'll feel compelled to share 'ooohs' and 'aahhs' with fellow diners when a humongous serving of chicken-fried steak lands at the adjacent table. With a concrete floor and spare decor, it can get loud, but that just adds to the fun as folks chow down on beignets, truffled egg sandwiches, and shrimp and grits.

The restaurant is a collaboration between chef Natalie Young, a veteran of Las Vegas kitchens, and the Downtown Project, led by Zappo's CEO Tony Hsieh.

Pink Taco
MEXICAN **$$**

(www.hardrockhotel.com; 4455 Paradise Rd, Hard Rock; mains $14-21; ⊘11am-10pm Sun-Thu, to late Fri & Sat) Whether it's the $5 margarita happy hour, the leafy poolside patio, or the friendly rock and roll clientele, Pink Taco always feels like a worthwhile party.

Hugo's Cellar
STEAK, SEAFOOD **$$$**

(Four Queens; ☑702-385-4011; www.hugoscel-lar.com; 702 Fremont St; mains $37-60; ⊘5:30-

EMERGENCY ARTS

A coffee shop, an art gallery, studios, and a de facto community center of sorts, all under one roof and right smack downtown? The **Emergency Arts** (www.emergencyartslv.com; 520 Fremont St) building, also home to **Beat Coffeehouse** (www.thebeatlasvegas.com; sandwiches $6-8; ⊙7am-midnight Mon-Fri, 9am-midnight Sat, 9am-5pm Sun; ☎) is a friendly bastion of laid-back cool and strong coffee where vintage vinyl spins on old turntables. If you're aching to meet some savvy locals who know their way around town, this is your hangout spot.

10:30pm) This is old-school Vegas, but in a good way. In a dark and clubby space beneath the Four Queens, Hugo's Cellar is a return to the days when service was king. Ladies are given a rose, salads are tossed beside the table and the service is attentive but not intrusive. Party like it's 1959 with veal Oscar, beef Wellington and cherries jubilee.

♀ Drinking

Loads of new and interesting bars are opening on E Fremont St. Zip down Slotzilla then walk over. Definitely worth a wander.

♟ The Strip

★Chandelier Bar   BAR
(www.cosmopolitanlasvegas.com; 3708 Las Vegas Blvd S, Cosmopolitan; ⊙varies by floor, 24hr for 1st fl) In a city full of lavish hotel lobby bars, this one pulls out all the stops. Kick back with the Cosmopolitan hipsters and enjoy the curiously thrilling feeling that you're tipsy inside a giant crystal chandelier.

Mix   LOUNGE
(www.mandalaybay.com; 3950 Las Vegas Blvd S, 64th fl, THEhotel at Mandalay Bay; cover after 10pm $20-25; ⊙5pm-1am Sun-Wed, to 2am Thu, to 3am Fri & Sat) The place to grab sunset cocktails. The glassed-in elevator has amazing views, and that's before you even glimpse the mod interior design and soaring balcony.

Rhumbar   COCKTAIL BAR
(☎702 792-7615; www.mirage.com; 3400 Las Vegas Blvd S, Mirage; ⊙1pm-midnight Sun-Thu, 1pm-2am Fri & Sat) Minty mojitos and frozen daiquiris

are pure mixology magic at this Caribbean-flavored bar and cigar lounge. Rhumbar is handy to the Mirage's south entrance. Chill at breezy, beachy open-air lounge tables on the chic Strip-view patio.

Parasol Up – Parasol Down   BAR, CAFE
(www.wynnlasvegas.com; 3131 Las Vegas Blvd S, Wynn; ⊙11am-2am, to 4am Fri & Sat at Parasol Up) Unwind with a fresh fruit *mojito* by the soothing waterfall at the Wynn to experience one of Vegas' most successful versions of paradise.

Carnaval Court   BAR
(☎702-369-5000; www.harrahslasvegas.com; 3475 Las Vegas Blvd S, outside Harrah's; cover varies; ⊙11am-3am) Bartenders juggle fire for raucous crowds at this outdoor bar. Live pop and rock cover bands tear up the stage at night, but all eyes are on the hot bods at the bar. Party on, dudes.

♟ Downtown & Off the Strip

Want to chill out with the locals? Head to one of their go-to favorites. New bars and cafes are opening along E Fremont St, making it the number one alternative to the Strip.

Griffin   BAR
(☎702-382-0577; 511 E Fremont St; cover $5-10; ⊙5pm-3am Mon-Fri, 7pm-3am Sat, 8pm-2am Sun) Escape from the casinos' clutch and imbibe at this indie joint, a short walk along the less illuminated side of Fremont St. Crackling fireplaces, leather booths and an almost unbearably cool jukebox make this dark and cozy spot popular with rebels, hipster sweethearts and surely an in-the-know vampire or two.

Commonwealth   COCKTAIL BAR
(www.commonwealthlv.com; 525 E Fremont St; ⊙6pm-2am Wed-Fri, 8pm-2am Sat & Sun) This new cocktail bar might be a little too hip for laid-back E Fremont St, but whoa, its Steampunk interior is worth a look. Softly glowing chandeliers. Saloon-style bar. Victorian-era bric-a-brac. Enjoy your tipple. It also has a rooftop bar and, we hear, a secret bar within the bar.

Downtown Cocktail Room   LOUNGE
(☎702-880-3696; www.downtownlv.net; 111 Las Vegas Blvd S; cover free-$10; ⊙4pm-2am Mon-Fri, 7pm-2am Sat) With a retro cocktail list you must take seriously, this speakeasy with sateen pillows and suede-covered couches

feels decades removed from the old-school carpet joints on Fremont St. In true Prohibition-era style, the entrance is disguised.

Fireside Lounge
COCKTAIL BAR

(www.peppermilllasvegas.com; 2985 Las Vegas Blvd S, Peppermill; ☺24hr) The Strip's most unlikely romantic hideaway is inside a retro coffee shop. Courting couples flock here for the low lighting, sunken fire pit and cozy nooks built for supping on multistrawed tiki drinks.

Double Down Saloon
BAR

(www.doubledownsaloon.com; 4640 Paradise Rd; no cover; ☺24hr) You can't get more punk rock than a dive whose tangy, blood-red house drink is named 'Ass Juice' and where the noon to 5pm happy hour means everything in the bar is two bucks. Killer jukebox, cash only.

☆ Entertainment

Las Vegas has no shortage of entertainment on any given night, and **Ticketmaster** (☏800-745-3000; www.ticketmaster.com) sells tickets for pretty much everything. **Tix 4 Tonight** (☏877-849-4868; www.tix4tonight.com; 3200 Las Vegas Blvd S, Fashion Show; ☺10am-8pm) offers half-price tickets for a limited lineup of same-day shows and small discounts on 'always sold-out' shows.

Nightclubs & Live Music

In 2012, seven of the 10 highest-earning nightclubs in the US were in Vegas, with both XS and Marquee earning more than $80 million each. Admission prices to nightclubs vary wildly based on the mood of door staff, male-to-female ratio, and how crowded the club is that night. Avoid waiting in line by booking ahead with the club VIP host. Most bigger clubs have someone working the door in the late afternoon and early evening. Your hotel concierge will also typically have free passes for clubs, or be able to make reservations. Also consider bottle service. It usually waives cover charges and waiting in line.

XS
CLUB

(www.xslasvegas.com; 3131 Las Vegas Blvd S, Encore; cover $20-50; ☺9:30pm-4am Fri & Sat, 10:30pm-4am Sun & Mon) The only club where we've seen club-goers jump in the pool to dance (and not be thrown out by the bouncers), XS is a Vegas favorite with a more diverse crowd (read: you won't feel outta place if you're over 30) than most. Dress up or you won't get in.

Marquee
CLUB

(www.cosmopolitanlasvegas.com; 3708 Las Vegas Blvd, Cosmopolitan) When someone asks what the coolest club in Vegas is, Marquee is the undisputed answer. Celebrities (we spotted Macy Gray as we danced through the crowd), an outdoor beach club, hot DJs and that certain *je ne sais quoi* that makes a club worth the line.

Tao
CLUB

(www.taolasvegas.com; 3355 Las Vegas Blvd S, Venetian; ☺lounge 5pm-midnight Sun-Thu, to 1am Thu-Sat, nightclub 10pm-5am) Some Vegas clubbing aficionados claim that Tao has reached a been-there-done-that saturation point. Newbies, however, still gush at the decadent details and libidinous vibe: from the giant gold Buddha to the near-naked go-go girls languidly caressing themselves in rose petal-strewn bathtubs.

Stoney's Rockin' Country
LIVE MUSIC

(www.stoneysrockincountry.com; 6611 Las Vegas Blvd S; cover free-$20; ☺7pm-2am Sun-Wed, to 3am Thu-Sat) This fun-lovin' country-western bar recently moved closer to the Strip. Dance lessons are offered every night of the week, with two-stepping on Tuesdays at 7:30pm. On Fridays, chicks wearing Daisy Dukes and cowboy boots get in free. On Saturdays, come for the $15 all-you-can-drink drafts.

Production Shows

There are hundreds of shows to choose from in Vegas. Any Cirque du Soleil show tends to be an unforgettable experience.

★LOVE
PERFORMING ARTS

(☏800-963-9634, 702-792-7777; www.cirquedusoleil.com; tickets $99-150; ☺7pm & 9:30pm Thu-Mon; ⊞) This show at the Mirage is a popular addition to the Cirque du Soleil lineup; locals who have seen many Cirque productions come and go say it's the best.

Zumanity
PERFORMING ARTS

(☏702-740-6815; www.cirquedusoleil.com; tickets $76-138) A sensual and sexy adult-only show at New York-New York.

La Rêve
LIVE PERFORMANCE

(☏888-320-7110; www.wynnlasvegas.com; 3131 Las Vegas Blvd S, Wynn; tickets from $105; ☺7pm & 9:30pm Fri-Tue) Aquatic acrobatic feats are the centerpiece of La Rêve, which means 'The Dream' in French. The theater holds a one-million-gallon swimming pool and performers must be scuba-certified. Note that cheaper seats are in the 'splash zone.'

House of Blues
LIVE MUSIC

(☑702-632-7600; www.hob.com; 3950 Las Vegas Blvd S, Mandalay Bay) Blues is the tip of the hog at this Mississippi Delta juke joint, showcasing modern rock, pop and soul.

🛍 Shopping

Bonanza Gift Shop
SOUVENIRS

(www.worldslargestgiftshop.com; 2440 Las Vegas Blvd S; ⊘8am-midnight) More than 40,000 sq ft of...stuff! The best place for only-in-Vegas kitsch souvenirs.

Gold & Silver Pawn
JEWELRY

(☑702-385-7912; http://gspawn.com; 713 Las Vegas Blvd S; ⊘shop 9am-9pm, night window 9pm-9am) As seen on the reality-TV hit series *Pawn Stars*, this humble-looking storefront has untold treasures inside, from Wild West shotguns and restored 1950s classic cars to vintage Vegas casino and autographed star memorabilia. Line up outside by the red-velvet rope.

Fashion Show Mall
MALL

(www.thefashionshow.com; 3200 Las Vegas Blvd S; ⊘10am-9pm Mon-Sat, 11am-7pm Sun) Nevada's biggest and flashiest mall.

Forum Shops
MALL

(www.caesarspalace.com; 3570 Las Vegas Blvd S, Caesars Palace; ⊘10am-11pm Sun-Thu, to midnight Fri & Sat) Upscale stores in an air-conditioned version of Ancient Rome.

The Shops at Crystals
MALL

(www.crystalsatcitycenter.com; 3720 Las Vegas Blvd S; ⊘10am-11pm Sun-Thu, to midnight Fri & Sat) From Assouline to Versace, this posh new mall beside Aria preens with more than 40 luxury shops.

Grand Canal Shoppes
MALL

(www.thegrandcanalshoppes.com; 3355 Las Vegas Blvd S, Venetian; ⊘10am-11pm) Italianate indoor luxury mall with gondolas.

Shoppes at the Palazzo
MALL

(www.theshoppesatthepalazzo.com; 3327 Las Vegas Blvd S, Palazzo; ⊘10am-11pm Sun-Thu, to midnight Fri & Sat) Sixty international designers flaunt their goodies.

ℹ Information

EMERGENCY & MEDICAL SERVICES

Gamblers Anonymous (☑855-222-5542; www.gamblersanonymous.com) Assistance with gambling concerns.

Police (☑702-828-3111; www.lvmpd.com)

Sunrise Hospital & Medical Center (☑702-731-8000; www.sunrisehospital.com; 3186 S Maryland Pkwy) Children's hospital and 24-hour emergency room.

University Medical Center (☑702-383-2000, emergency 702-383-2661; www.umcsn.com; 1800 W Charleston Blvd; ⊘24hr) Nevada's most advanced trauma center, and 24-hour emergency department.

INTERNET ACCESS & MEDIA

Wi-fi is available in most hotel rooms (about $10 to $25 per day, sometimes included in the 'resort fee') and there are internet kiosks with attached printers in most hotel lobbies.

Eater Vegas (www.vegas.eater.com) News about Sin City's chefs and new restaurants, with a regularly updated list of the city's top 38 eateries.

Las Vegas Review-Journal (www.lvrj.com) Daily paper with a weekend guide, *Neon,* on Friday.

Las Vegas Weekly (www.lasvegasweekly.com) Free weekly with good entertainment and restaurant listings.

Vegas Chatter (www.vegaschatter.com) The latest on what's happening in Vegas, from restaurant openings to the hottest pools.

MONEY

Every hotel-casino and bank and most convenience stores have an ATM. The ATM fee at most casinos is around $5. Best to stop at off-Strip banks if possible.

Travelex Currency Services (☑702-369-2219; 3200 Las Vegas Blvd S, Fashion Show; ⊘10am-9pm Mon-Sat, 11am-7pm Sun) Changes currencies at Fashion Show Mall.

POST

Post office (www.usps.com; 201 Las Vegas Blvd S; ⊘9am-5pm Mon-Fri) Downtown.

TOURIST INFORMATION

Las Vegas Tourism (www.onlyinvegas.com) Official tourism website.

Las Vegas Visitor Information Center (LVCVA | Las Vegas Convention & Visitors Authority; ☑702-892-7575, 877-847-4858; www.visitlasvegas.com; 3150 Paradise Rd; ⊘8am-5:30pm Mon-Fri) Free local calls, internet access and maps galore.

Las Vegas.com (www.lasvegas.com) Travel services.

Vegas.com (www.vegas.com) Travel information with booking service. Also lists kid-friendly attractions.

ℹ Getting There & Around

Just south of the major Strip casinos and easily accessible from I-15, **McCarran International**

Airport (LAS; ☑702-261-5211; www.mccarran. com; 5757 Wayne Newton Blvd; 🛜) has direct flights from many US cities, and some from Canada and Europe. Most domestic flights arrive in Terminal 1. International flights arrive in the new Terminal 3. **Bell Trans** (☑702-739-7990; www.bell-trans.com) offers a shuttle service ($7) between the airport and the Strip. Fares to downtown destinations are slightly higher. At the airport, exit at door 9 near baggage claim to find the Bell Trans booth.

Most of the attractions in Vegas have free self-parking and valet parking available (tip $2). Fast, fun and fully wheelchair accessible, the **monorail** (www.lvmonorail.com; 1 ride $5, 24/72hr pass $12/28, child under 6yr free; ⊙7am-midnight Mon, to 2am Tue-Thu, to 3am Fri-Sun) connects the Sahara Station (closest to Circus Circus) to the MGM Grand, stopping at major Strip megaresorts along the way. The **Deuce** (☑702-228-7433; www.rtcsouthernnevada. com; 2/24hr pass $6/8), a local double-decker bus, runs frequently 24 hours daily between the Strip and downtown.

Around Las Vegas

Red Rock Canyon
National Conservation Area   PARK
(☑702-515-5350;   www.redrockcanyonlv.org; day-use per car/bicycle $7/3; ⊙scenic loop 6am-8pm Apr-Sep, earlier Oct-Mar, visitor center 8am-4:30pm) This dramatic park is the perfect antidote to Vegas' artificial brightness. A 23-mile drive west of the Strip, the canyon is actually more like a valley, with the steep, rugged red-rock escarpment rising 3000ft on its western edge. There's a 13-mile scenic loop with access to hiking trails and first-come, first-served **camping** (September to May) 2 miles east of the visitor center. The 2.5-mile round-trip hike to Calico Tanks climbs through the red rocks and ends with a lofty view of Las Vegas.

Lake Mead & Hoover Dam   LAKE, HISTORIC SITE
Lake Mead and Hoover Dam are the most-visited sites within the **Lake Mead National Recreation Area** (☑park information desk 702-293-8906, visitor center 702-293-8990; www.nps. gov/lake; car/bicycle $10/5; ⊙24hr, visitor center 9am-4:30pm Wed-Sun), which encompasses 110-mile-long Lake Mead, 67-mile-long Lake Mohave and many miles of desert around the lakes. The excellent **Alan Bible Visitor Center** (☑702-293-8990; www.nps.gov/ lake; Lakeshore Scenic Dr, off US Hwy 93; ⊙9am-4:30pm), on Hwy 93 halfway between Boulder City and Hoover Dam, has information

on recreation and desert life. Here, hikers and cyclists can pick up a map of the River Mountains Loop Trail (www.rivermountain-strail.com), which offers 32-miles of hiking and biking around the lake. From the visitor center, North Shore Rd and Lakeshore Rd wind around the lake and make a great scenic drive. Lakeshore Rd stretches all the way to Valley of Fire Hwy, which leads to the stunning Valley of Fire State Park.

Straddling the Arizona–Nevada border, the graceful curve and art-deco style of the 726ft **Hoover Dam** (☑866-730-9097, 702-494-2517; www.usbr.gov/lc/hooverdam; Hwy 93; visitor center $8, incl power-plant tour adult/child $11/9, all-inclusive tour $30; ⊙9am-6pm, last ticket sold 5:15pm) contrasts superbly with the stark landscape. Don't miss a stroll over the new **Mike O'Callaghan-Pat Tillman Memorial Bridge**, which features a pedestrian walkway with perfect views upstream of Hoover Dam. Not recommended for anyone with vertigo. Parking for access to the bridge is off Hwy 172/Hoover Dam Access Rd. Visitors can either take the 30-minute **power plant tour** (adult/child $11/9) or the more in-depth, one-hour **Hoover Dam tour** (no children under 8yr; tours $30). If you're interested in history and construction, spring for the longer tour.

Tickets for both tours are sold at the **visitor center**. Tickets for the power plant tour only can be purchased online.

Nearby Boulder City was home to the men and women who built the dam. Today, the inviting downtown is a nice place to grab a meal or spend the night. Center-of-the-action **Milo's** (www.miloswinebar.com; 538 Nevada Hwy; mains $9-13; ⊙11am-10pm Sun-Thu, to midnight Fri & Sat) serves fresh sandwiches, salads and gourmet cheese plates at sidewalk tables outside its wine bar. Around the corner is the pleasant **Boulder Dam Hotel**

VALLEY OF FIRE STATE PARK

A masterpiece of desert scenery filled with psychedelically shaped sandstone outcroppings, this **park** (☑702-397-2088; www.parks.nv.gov/parks/valley-of-fire-state-park; per vehicle $10; ⊙visitor center 8:30am-4:30pm) is a great escape 55 miles from Vegas. Hwy 169 runs right past the visitor center, which has hiking and **camping** (tent/RV sites $20/30) information and excellent desert-life exhibits.

WORTH A TRIP

BURNING MAN

For one week at the end of August, **Burning Man** (www.burningman.com; admission $380) explodes onto the sunbaked Black Rock Desert, and Nevada sprouts a third major population center – Black Rock City. An experiential art party (and alternative universe) that climaxes in the immolation of a towering stick figure, Burning Man is a whirlwind of outlandish theme camps, dust-caked bicycles, bizarre bartering, costume-enhanced nudity and a general relinquishment of inhibitions.

(☑702-293-3510; www.boulderdamhotel.com; 1305 Arizona St; r incl breakfast $72-89, ste $99; ❋ @ ☎), where the rate includes made-to-order breakfasts and admission to the onsite Boulder City/Hoover Dam museum.

Western Nevada

A vast and mostly undeveloped sagebrush steppe, the western corner of the state is carved by mountain ranges and parched valleys. It's the place where modern Nevada began with the discovery of the famous Comstock silver lode in and around Virginia City. This part of the state lures visitors today with outdoor adventure in the form of hiking, biking, and skiing on its many mountains. Contrasts here are as extreme as the weather: one moment you're driving through a quaint historic town full of grand homes built by silver barons, and the next you spot a tumbleweed blowing by a homely little bar that turns out to be the local (and legal) brothel.

Reno

In downtown Reno you can gamble at one of two-dozen casinos in the morning then walk down the street and shoot rapids at the Truckee River Whitewater Park. These contrasts are what makes 'The Biggest Little City in the World' so interesting – it's holding tight to its gambling roots but also earning kudos as a top-notch basecamp for outdoor adventure. The Sierra Nevada Mountains and Lake Tahoe are less than an hour's drive away, and the region is teaming with lakes, trails and ski resorts.

◉ Sights

The downtown Riverwalk District (www.renoriver.org) hugs the Truckee River. Kayakers and inner tubers ride the rapids in the whitewater park that stretches east from Wingfield Park to Virginia St.

National Automobile Museum   MUSEUM
(☑775-333-9300; www.automuseum.org; 10 S Lake St; adult/child $10/4; ☺ 9:30am-5:30pm Mon-Sat, 10am-4pm Sun; ♿) Stylized street scenes illustrate a century's worth of automobile history at this engaging car museum. The collection is enormous and impressive, with one-of-a-kind vehicles, including a 1928 Model A Ford given to Mary Pickford by Douglas Fairbanks and a 1935 Dusenburg owned by Sammy Davis Jr. Rotating exhibits bring in all kinds of souped-up or fabulously retro rides.

Nevada Museum of Art   MUSEUM
(☑775-329-3333; www.nevadaart.org; 160 W Liberty St; adult/child $10/1; ☺10am-5pm Wed-Sun, 10am-8pm Thu) In a sparkling building inspired by the geological formations of the Black Rock Desert north of town, a floating staircase leads to galleries showcasing temporary exhibits and images related to the American West. Climb to the roof for a view of the Sierras. Great cafe for postcultural refueling.

Virginia Street
Wedged between the I-80 and the Truckee River, downtown's N Virginia St is casino central. South of the river it continues as S Virginia St. All of the following hotel-casinos are open 24 hours.

Circus Circus   CASINO
(www.circusreno.com; 500 N Sierra St; ♿) The most family-friendly of the bunch, it has free circus acts to entertain kids beneath a giant, candy-striped big top, which also harbors a gazillion carnival and video games.

Silver Legacy   CASINO
(www.silverlegacyreno.com; 407 N Virginia St) A Victorian-themed place, it's easily recognized by its white landmark dome, where a giant mock mining rig periodically erupts into a tame sound-and-light show.

Eldorado
CASINO

(www.eldoradoreno.com; 345 N Virginia St) The Eldorado has a kitschy Fountain of Fortune that probably has Italian sculptor Bernini spinning in his grave.

Harrah's
CASINO

(www.harrahsreno.com; 219 N Center St) Founded by Nevada gambling pioneer William Harrah in 1946, it's still one of the biggest and most popular casinos in town.

🏃 Activities

Reno is a 30- to 60-minute drive from Tahoe ski resorts, and many hotels and casinos offer special stay and ski packages.

Truckee River
Whitewater Park
WATER SPORTS

(www.reno.gov) Mere steps from the casinos, the park's Class II and III rapids are gentle enough for kids riding inner tubes, yet sufficiently challenging for professional freestyle kayakers. Two courses wrap around Wingfield Park, a small river island that hosts free concerts. **Tahoe Whitewater Tours** (📞775-787-5000; www.gowhitewater.com) and **Wild Sierra Adventures** (📞866-323-8928; www.wildsierra.com) offer kayak trips and lessons.

Historic Reno
Preservation Society
WALKING TOUR

(📞775-747-4478; www.historicreno.org; tours $10) Dig deeper with a walking or cycling tour highlighting subjects including architecture, politics and literary history.

🛏 Sleeping

Lodging rates vary widely depending on the day of the week and local events. Sunday through Thursday are generally the best; Friday is more expensive and Saturday can be as much as triple the midweek rate.

In summer, there's gorgeous high-altitude camping at **Mt Rose** (📞877-444-6777; www.recreation.gov; Hwy 431; RV & tent sites $17-50).

Sands Regency
CASINO HOTEL $

(📞775-348-2200; www.sandsregency.com; 345 N Arlington Ave; r Sun-Thu from $29, Fri & Sat $69; P ❄ 🛜 ≋ 🐾) The exterior is a little tired, but rooms are fine, decked out in a cheerful tropical palette of upbeat blues, reds and greens. Empress Tower rooms are best. A good deal.

Wildflower Village
MOTEL, B&B $

(📞775-747-8848; www.wildflowervillage.com; 4395 W 4th St; hostel $30, motel $55, B&B $125;

P ❄ @ 🛜) This welcoming artists' colony on the west edge of town has a tumbledown yet creative vibe. Murals decorate the facade of each room, and you can hear the freight trains rumble on by. Has three types of rooms: hostel, motel and B&B.

★ Peppermill
CASINO HOTEL $$

(📞866-821-9996, 775-826-2121; www.peppermillreno.com; 2707 S Virginia St; r/ste Sun-Thu from $70/130, Fri & Sat from $170/200; P ❄ @ 🛜 ≋) Now awash in Vegas-style opulence, the popular Peppermill boasts Tuscan-themed rooms in its newest 600-room tower, and has almost completed a plush remodel of its older rooms. The three sparkling pools (one indoor) are dreamy, with a full spa on hand. Geothermal energy powers the resort's hot water and heat.

🍴 Eating

Reno's dining scene goes far beyond the casino buffets.

Peg's Glorified Ham & Eggs
DINER $

(www.eatatpegs.com; 420 S Sierra St; breakfast $9-14, lunch $8-12; ⏰6:30am-2pm; 🔸) Locally regarded as the best breakfast in town, Peg's offers tasty grill food that's not too greasy. Look for the mint-and-white striped awning.

★ Old Granite Street Eatery
AMERICAN $$

(📞775-622-3222; www.oldgranitestreeteatery.com; 243 S Sierra St; lunch $9-14, dinner $11-26; ⏰11am-11pm Mon-Thu, 11am-midnight Fri, 10am-midnight Sat, 10am-4pm Sun) A lovely place for organic and local comfort food, old-school artisanal cocktails and seasonal craft beers, this antique-strewn hot spot enchants diners with its stately wooden bar, water served in old liquor bottles and its lengthy seasonal menu.

ℹ RENO AREA TRAIL INFORMATION

For extensive information on regional hiking and biking trails, including the Mt Rose summit trail and the Tahoe-Pyramid Bikeway, download the **Truckee Meadows Trails Guide** (www.reno.gov/Index.aspx?page=291). You can pick up a copy of the guide at the **Galena Creek Visitor Center** (www.galenacreekvisitorcenter.org; 18250 Mt Rose Hwy; ⏰9am-6pm Tue-Sun) at Galena Creek Regional Park, where you'll find three of the trails that are included in the guide.

No reservation? Check out the iconic rooster and pig murals and wait for seats at a 'community table' fashioned from a barn door.

Silver Peak Restaurant & Brewery PUB $$
(124 Wonder St; mains lunch $8.25-11, dinner $9.25-22; ⊘ restaurant 11am-10pm Sun-Thu, to 11pm Sat & Sun, pub open 1hour later) Casual and pretense-free, this place hums with the chatter of happy locals settling in for a night of micro-brews and great eats, from pizza with pesto shrimp to spinach and ricotta ravioli to filet mignon. In the heart of the downtown Riverwalk District.

🍷 Drinking

Great Basin Brewing Co BREWERY $$
(www.greatbasinbrewingco.com; 5525 S Virginia St; mains $8-19; ⊘ 11am-midnight Sun-Thu, 11am-1:30am Fri & Sat) There's a debate in town over who brews the best beer, Great Basin or Silver Peak. We're not picking sides, but we give extra points to Great Basin for its outdoorsy ambience, which includes a mountain scene splashed across the wall. Serves five flagship beers with 13 seasonal brews. Also has a nice selection of Belgian ales. It's 3 miles south of downtown on Virginia St.

Imperial Bar & Lounge BAR
(150 N Arlington Ave; ⊘ 11am-2am Fri & Sat, to 10pm Sun-Thu) A classy bar inhabiting a relic of the past, this building was once an old bank, and in the middle of the wood floor you can see cement where the vault once stood. Sandwiches and pizzas go with 16 beers on tap and a buzzing weekend scene.

Jungle Java & Jungle Vino CAFE, WINE BAR
(www.javajunglevino.com; 246 W 1st St; ⊘ coffee 6am-midnight, wine 3pm-midnight Mon-Fri, noon-midnight Sat & Sun; 🐾) A side-by-side coffee shop and wine bar with a cool mosaic floor and an internet cafe all rolled into one.

☆ Entertainment

The free weekly **Reno News & Review** (www.newsreview.com) is your best source for listings.

Edge CLUB
(www.edgeofreno.com; 2707 S Virginia St, Peppermill; admission $10-20; ⊘ from 9pm Thu & Sat, from 7pm Fri) The Peppermill reels in the night-hounds with a big glitzy dance club, where go-go dancers, smoke machines and laser lights may cause sensory overload. If so, step outside to the patio and relax in front of cozy fire pits.

Knitting Factory LIVE MUSIC
(☑ 775-323-5648; http://re.knittingfactory.com; 211 N Virginia St) This mid-sized venue opened in 2010, filling a gap in Reno's music scene with mainstream and indie favorites.

ℹ Information

An information center sits near the baggage claim at Reno-Tahoe International Airport, which also has free wi-fi.

Reno-Sparks Convention & Visitors Authority Visitor Center (☑ 775-682-3800; www.visitrenotahoe.com; 135 N Sierra St; ⊘ 9am-6pm) Inside the RENO eNVy store (get it?) in the Riverwalk District. Has brochures and maps and free parking with validation. Also has an airport desk.

ℹ Getting There & Away

About 5 miles southeast of downtown, **Reno-Tahoe International Airport** (RNO; www.renoairport.com; 🐾) is served by most major airlines.

The **North Lake Tahoe Express** (☑ 866-216-5222; www.northlaketahoeexpress.com) operates a shuttle ($45 one-way, about six to eight daily, 3:30am to midnight) to and from the airport to multiple North Shore Lake Tahoe locations including Truckee, Squaw Valley and Incline Village. Reserve in advance.

To reach South Lake Tahoe (weekdays only), take the wi-fi-equipped **RTC Intercity bus** (www.rtcwashoe.com) to the Nevada DOT stop in Carson City ($4, one hour, six per weekday) and then the **BlueGo** (www.bluego.org) 21X bus ($2 with RTC Intercity transfer, one hour, five to six daily) to the Stateline Transit Center.

Greyhound (☑ 775-322-2970; www.greyhound.com; 155 Stevenson St) buses run daily service to Truckee, Sacramento and San Francisco ($11 to $41, five to seven hours), as does the once-daily westbound *California Zephyr* train route operated by **Amtrak** (☑ 800-872-7245, 775-329-8638; 280 N Center St). The train is slower and more expensive, but also more scenic and comfortable, with a bus connection from Emeryville for passengers to San Francisco ($60, eight hours).

ℹ Getting Around

The casino hotels offer frequent free airport shuttles for their guests.

Local **RTC Ride buses** (☑ 775-348-7433; www.rtcwashoe.com; per ride $2, daily pass pre-paid/on-board $4/5) blanket the city, and most routes converge at the RTC 4th St Station downtown. Useful routes include the RTC Rapid line for Center St and S Virginia St, 11 for Sparks and 19 for the airport. The free Sierra Spirit bus, which has wi-fi, loops around all major downtown landmarks – including the casinos and the university – every 15 minutes from 7am to 7pm.

Carson City

This underrated town is an easy drive from Reno or Lake Tahoe, and it's a perfect stop for lunch and a stroll around the quiet, old-fashioned downtown.

The **Kit Carson Blue Line Trail** passes pretty historic buildings on pleasant tree-lined streets. Pick up a copy of the trail map at the **visitor center** (☑800-638-2321, 775-687-7410; www.visitcarsoncity.com; 1900 S Carson St; ☉8am-5pm Mon-Fri, 9am-5pm Sat & Sun), a mile south of downtown, or download it from the visitor center website.

Anchoring downtown is the **1870 Nevada State Capitol** (cnr Musser & Carson; ☉8am-5pm Mon-Fri) **FREE**, where you might spot the governor himself chatting with one of his constituents. There's a small museum with state-related paraphernalia on the 2nd floor – check out that elk-antler chair. Ouch! Train buffs shouldn't miss the **Nevada State Railroad Museum** (☑775-687-6953; www.museums.nevadaculture.org; 2180 S Carson St; adult/child $6/free; ☉9am-5pm Fri-Mon), which displays some 65 train cars and locomotives from the 1800s to the early 1900s.

Grab lunch at fetching **Comma Coffee** (www.commacoffee.com; 312 S Carson St; breakfast $6-8, lunch $8-10; ☉7am-8pm Mon & Wed-Thu, to 10pm Tue, Fri & Sat; ⬤🖉▣) and eavesdrop on the politicians. Or spend the evening at the locally owned microbrewery, **High Sierra Brewing Company** (www.highsierrabrewco. com; 302 N Carson St; mains $9-17; ☉11am-10pm Sun-Thu, to 2am Fri & Sat), for great beer and burgers.

Hwy 395/Carson St is the main drag. For hiking and camping information in the area, stop by the United States Forest Service (USFS) **Carson Ranger District Office** (☑775-882-2766; 1536 S Carson St; ☉8am-4:30pm Mon-Fri).

Virginia City

The discovery of the legendary Comstock Lode in 1859 sparked a silver bonanza in the mountains 25 miles south of Reno. During the 1860s gold rush, Virginia City was a high-flying, rip-roaring Wild West boomtown. Newspaperman Samuel Clemens, alias Mark Twain, spent some time in this raucous place during its heyday; years later his eyewitness descriptions of mining life were published in a book called *Roughing It*.

The high-elevation town is a National Historic Landmark, with a main street of Victorian buildings, wooden sidewalks and some hokey but fun museums. To see how the mining elite lived, stop by the **Mackay Mansion** (☑775-847-0173; 129 South D St; adult/child $5/free; ☉10am-5pm in summer, vary in winter) and the **Castle** (B St). Mark Twain's desk and, er, toilet, are among a haphazard collection of artifacts in the **Mark Twain Museum at The Territorial Enterprise** (53 South C St; adult/child $4/3; ☉10am-5pm) in the old newspaper press room. The basement level space survived the devastating 1878 town fire.

Locals agree that the best food in Virginia City is probably at **Cafe del Rio** (www.cafedelriovc.com; 394 S C St; dinner $19-15, brunch $9.25-14; ☉11am-8pm Wed-Sat, 10am-7pm Sun), serving a nice blend of *nuevo* Mexican and good cafe food, including breakfast. Wet your whistle at the longtime family-run **Bucket of Blood Saloon** (www.bucketofbloodsaloonvc. com; 1 S C St; ☉9am-7pm Sun-Thu, to 9pm Fri & Sat), which serves up beer and 'bar rules' at its antique wooden bar ('If the bartender doesn't laugh, you are not funny').

The main drag is C St, where you'll find the **visitor center** (☑800-718-7587, 775-847-7500; www.visitvirginiacitynv.com; 86 S C St; ☉10am-5pm).

Nevada Great Basin

A trip across Nevada's Great Basin is a serene, almost haunting experience. But those on the quest for the 'Great American Road Trip' will relish the fascinating historic towns and quirky diversions tucked away along lonely desert highways.

Along I-80

Heading east from Reno, **Winnemucca**, 150 miles to the northeast, is the first worthwhile stop. It boasts a vintage downtown and a number of Basque restaurants, along with a yearly Basque festival. For information, stop by the **Winnemucca Visitor Center** (☑775-623-5071, 800 962 2638; www.winnemucca.com; 30 W Winnemucca Blvd; ☉8am-5pm Mon Fri). Check out the displays here, like a buckaroo (cowboy) hall of fame and big-game museum. Don't miss the **Griddle** (www.thegriddlecom; 460 W Winnemucca Blvd; mains $10-15; ☉6am-2pm), one of Nevada's

CATHEDRAL GORGE STATE PARK

Awe, then *ahhh*. **Cathedral Gorge State Park** (☑775-728-4460; www.parks.nv.gov/parks/cathedral-gorge; Hwy 93; entry $7, tent & RV sites $17; ☉ visitor center 9am-4:30pm) really does feel like you've stepped into a magnificent, many-spired cathedral, albeit one whose dome is a view of the sky. Sleep under the stars at the first-come, first-served tent & RV sites ($17) set amid badlands-style cliffs.

best retro cafes, serving up fantastic breakfasts, diner classics and homemade desserts since 1948.

The culture of the American West is most diligently cultivated in **Elko**. Aspiring cowboys and cowgirls should visit the **Western Folklife Center** (www.westernfolklife.org; 501 Railroad St; adult/child $5/1; ☉ 10am-5:30pm Mon-Fri, 10am-5pm Sat), which offers art and history exhibits, musical jams, dance nights and also hosts the popular **Cowboy Poetry Gathering** each January. Elko also holds a **National Basque Festival** every July 4, with games, traditional dancing and a 'Running of the Bulls' event. If you've never sampled Basque food, the best place in town for your inaugural experience is the **Star Hotel** (www.elkostarhotel.com; 246 Silver St; lunch $6-12, dinner $15-32; ☉ 11am-2pm & 5-9pm Mon-Fri, 4:30-9:30pm Sat), a family-style supper club located in a circa-1910 boardinghouse for Basque sheepherders.

Along Highway 50

In Nevada, the transcontinental Hwy 50 is better known by its nickname, 'The Loneliest Road in America.' It cuts across the heart of the state, connecting Carson City in the west to Great Basin National Park in the east. It was once part of the Lincoln Hwy and follows the route of the Overland Stagecoach, the Pony Express and the first transcontinental telegraph line. Towns are few, and the only sounds are the hum of the engine or the whisper of wind.

About 25 miles southeast of Fallon, the **Sand Mountain Recreation Area** (☑775-885-6000; www.blm.gov/nv; admission free for brief, non-motorized use; ☉ 24hr) **FREE** is worth a stop for a look at its 600ft sand dune and

the ruins of a Pony Express station. Just east, enjoy a juicy burger at an old stagecoach stop, **Middlegate Station** (42500 Austin Hwy) then toss your sneakers onto the new **Shoe Tree** on the north side of Hwy 50 just ahead (the old one was cut down).

A fitting reward for surviving Hwy 50 is the awesome, uncrowded **Great Basin National Park** (☑775-234-7331; www.nps.gov/grba; ☉ 24hr) **FREE**. Near the Nevada–Utah border, it's home to 13,063ft Wheeler Peak, which rises abruptly from the desert. Hiking trails near the summit take in superb country with glacial lakes, ancient bristlecone pines and even a permanent ice field. In summer, the **Great Basin Visitor Center** (☑775-234-7331; www.nps.gov/grba; ☉ 8am-4:30pm Jun-Aug), just north of the town of **Baker**, is the place to get oriented.

For a 60- or 90-minute guided tour of the caves here, which are richly decorated with rare limestone formations, head to the year-round **Lehman Caves Visitor Center** (☑775-234-7331, tour reservations 775-234-7517; www.nps.gov/grba; adult $8-10, child $4-5; ☉ 8am-4:30 pm, tours 8:30am-4pm) five miles outside of Baker. Reservations recommended. In warmer months, drive 12 scenic miles to the Wheeler Peak summit. There are five first-come, first-served developed **campgrounds** (☑775-234-7331; www.nps.gove/grba; primitive camping free, tent & RV sites $12) in the park.

Along Highway 95

Hwy 95 runs roughly north–south through the western part of the state; the southern section is starkly scenic as it passes the Nevada Test Site (where more than 720 nuclear weapons were exploded in the 1950s).

Along Highways 375 & 93

Hwy 375 is dubbed the 'Extraterrestrial Hwy' because of the huge number of UFO sightings along this stretch and because it intersects Hwy 93 near top-secret **Area 51**, part of Nellis Air Force Base and a supposed holding area for captured UFOs. Some people may find Hwy 375 more unnerving than the Loneliest Road; it's a desolate stretch of pavement and cars are few and far between. In the tiny town of **Rachel**, on Hwy 375, **Little A'Le'Inn** (☑775-729-2515; www.littlealeinn.com; 1 Old Mill Rd, Alamo; RV sites with hookups $15, r $35-150; ☉ restaurant 8am-9pm; ❋ 🛜 🐾) accommodates earthlings and aliens alike, and sells extraterrestrial souvenirs. Probings not included.

ARIZONA

The nation's 6th-largest state is dotted with stunning works of nature: the Grand Canyon, Monument Valley, the Chiricahua Mountains, and the red rocks of Sedona, to name a few. In the shadows of these icons, a compelling cast of settlers and explorers tried to tame Arizona's wilds, building prehistoric irrigation canals through desert scrub, mapping the labyrinth of canyons and mining the state's underground riches. Gorgeous backroads link these natural and historic sites, making Arizona a prime destination for roadtrippers.

Greater Phoenix, ringed by mountains, is one of the biggest metro areas in the Southwest. It has the eateries, sights and glorious spas you'd expect in a spot that stakes its claim on rest and renewal. Tucson is the funky, artsy gateway to southern Arizona's astronomical and historical sights. Only 60 miles from the Mexican border, it embraces its cross-border heritage.

History

Arizona was the last territory in the Lower 48 to become a state, and it celebrated its centennial in 2012. Why did it take so long for a territory filled with copper and ranchland to join the Union? Arizonans were seen as troublemakers by the federal government, and for years acquiring their riches wasn't worth the potential trouble.

Cynics might say that Arizonans are still making trouble. In 2010, Arizona's legislature passed the most restrictive anti-immigration law in the nation, known as SB 1070. The controversial bill was passed soon after the mysterious shooting death of a popular rancher near the Mexican border.

The US Supreme Court recently struck down several sections of the hot-button law but retained the provision stating that an officer can try to determine the immigration status of a person who as been stopped, as long as the officer has a reasonable suspicion that the person is here illegally. At press time, implementation of the provision is facing legal challenge.

The state was shaken in 2011 by the shooting of Democratic Congresswoman Gabrielle Giffords during a public appearance. She was critically injured and six bystanders and staff members were killed.

An ongoing statewide fiscal crisis led to deep cuts for the state park system, forcing many parks to join forces with nonprofit groups and local governments for funding.

ℹ️ Information

Arizona is on Mountain Standard Time but is the only western state that does not observe daylight saving time from spring to early fall. The exception is the Navajo Reservation, which *does* observe daylight saving time.

Generally speaking, lodging rates in southern Arizona (including Phoenix, Tucson and Yuma) are much higher in winter and spring, which are considered the 'high season.' Great deals are to be had in the hot areas at the height of summer.

Arizona Department of Transportation (☑ in-state 511, 888-411-7623; www.az511.com) Updates on road conditions and traffic statewide, with links to weather and safety information.

Arizona Office of Tourism (☑ 602-364-3700; www.arizonaguide.com) Free state information.

Arizona Public Lands Information Center (☑ 602-417-9200; www.publiclands.org) Information about USFS, NPS, Bureau of Land Management (BLM) and state lands and parks.

Arizona State Parks (☑ 602-542-4174; www.azstateparks.com) Fifteen state parks have

---

ARIZONA FACTS

Nickname Grand Canyon State

Population 6.5 million

Area 113,637 sq miles

Capital city Phoenix (population 1.48 million)

Other cities Tucson (population 524,000), Flagstaff (population 67,400), Sedona (population 10,000)

Sales tax 6.6%

Birthplace of Apache chief Geronimo (1829–1909), political activist Cesar Chavez (1927–93), singer Linda Ronstadt (b 1946)

Home of Sedona New Age movement, mining towns turned art colonies

Politics Majority vote Republican

Famous for Grand Canyon, saguaro cacti

Best souvenir Pink cactus-shaped neon lamp from roadside stall

Driving distances Phoenix to Grand Canyon Village: 235 miles, Tucson to Sedona: 230 miles

campgrounds. Online reservations are available for all of them, with a $5 reservation fee. (campsites $15 to $50, cabins and yurts $35 to $75).

Phoenix

Despite the heat, Phoenix has a bit of spring in its step. The city, which is hosting the 2015 Super Bowl, is welcoming guests these days to its new downtown dining-and-entertainment district, Cityscape. And the city-to-airport rail line, the SkyTrain, opened ahead of schedule.

Several 'towns' make up the region known as Greater Phoenix, which is the largest urban area in the Southwest. The City of Phoenix, with its downtown high-rises and top-notch museums, is the patriarch of the bunch. Scottsdale is the stylish big sister who married up, Tempe the good-natured but occasionally rowdy college kid, and Mesa is the brother who wants a quiet life in the suburbs. And mom? She left for Flagstaff in June because it's just too darn hot.

How hot? In summer temperatures reach above 110°F (43°C). Resort rates drop dramatically, which is great for travelers on a budget, but the most popular time to visit is winter and spring, when pleasant days prevail.

◎ Sights

Greater Phoenix, also known as the Valley of the Sun, is ringed by mountains that range from 2500ft to more than 7000ft in elevation. Central Ave runs north–south through Phoenix, dividing west addresses from east addresses; Washington St runs west–east, dividing north addresses from south addresses.

Scottsdale, Tempe and Mesa are east of the airport. Scottsdale Rd runs north–south between Scottsdale and Tempe. The airport is 3 miles southeast of downtown.

◉ Phoenix

★ **Heard Museum**   MUSEUM
(☏ 602-252-8848; www.heard.org; 2301 N Central Ave; adult/child 6-12 yr & student/senior $18/7.50/13.50; ☺ 9:30am-5pm Mon-Sat, 11am-5pm Sun; ⊕) This private museum opened in 1929 when Dwight and Maie Bartlett Heard decided to share their extensive collection of Native American artifacts. Today, across 10 galleries, the museum displays Native American art, textiles, and ceramics, and spotlights Native American history and traditions. The focus is Southwestern tribes.

Check out the kachina (Hopi spirit doll) collection as well as the 'Boarding School Experience' gallery, a moving look at the controversial federal policy of removing Native American children from their families and sending them to remote boarding schools to Americanize them.

Musical Instrument Museum   MUSEUM
(☏ 480-478-6000; www.themim.org; 4725 E Mayo Blvd; adult $18, teen 13-19 yr $14, child $10; ☺ 9am-5pm Mon-Sat, 10am-5pm Sun, to 9pm first Fri of the month) From Ugandan thumb pianos to Hawaiian ukuleles to an Indonesian gong, the ears have it at this new museum that celebrates the world's musical instruments. More than 200 countries and territories are represented within five regional galleries, where music and video performances automatically start as you stop beside individual displays.

The free-to-use wireless headsets are a necessity, but they are very easy to operate. Just don't walk too quickly between the Alice Cooper exhibit and the Fife & Drums display in the United States gallery – your head will spin! To get to the museum from downtown, follow Hwy 51 north to Hwy 101 east. From 101, take exit 31. Turn right onto N Tatum Blvd and then turn right just ahead and you're there.

★ **Desert Botanical Garden**   GARDENS
(☏ 480-941-1225; www.dbg.org; 1201 N Galvin Pkwy; adult/child/student/senior $18/8/10/15; ☺ 8am-8pm Oct-Apr, 7am-8pm May-Sep) On 145 acres, this inspirational garden is a refresh-

---

CACTUS LEAGUE SPRING TRAINING

Before the start of the major league baseball season, teams spend March in Arizona (Cactus League) and Florida (Grapefruit League) auditioning new players, practicing and playing games. Tickets are cheaper (from about $8 to $10 depending on venue), the seats better, the lines shorter and the games more relaxed. Check www.cactus-league.com for schedules and links for purchasing tickets, or www.visitphoenix.com for a summary of team and ticket information.

ing place to reconnect with nature and offers a great introduction to desert plant life. Looping trails lead past an astonishing variety of desert denizens arranged by theme, including a desert wildflower loop and a Sonoran Desert nature loop. Check for special seasonal events like the summer flashlight tours (7pm Tuesday and Saturday June to August).

★ **Phoenix Art Museum**   MUSEUM
(☑602-257-1222; www.phxart.org; 1625 N Central Ave; adult/child 6-17yr/student/senior $15/6/10/12, free 3-9pm Wed & 1st Fri of the month 6-10pm; ☺10am-9pm Wed, 10am-5pm Thu-Sat, noon-5pm Sun; ♿) The Phoenix Art Museum is Arizona's premier repository of fine art. Galleries include works by Claude Monet, Diego Rivera and Georgia O'Keeffe. Landscapes in the Western American gallery set the tone for adventure.

◉ Scottsdale

Scottsdale's main draw is its popular shopping districts, which include Old Town, known for its early-20th-century buildings (and others built to look old), and the adjacent Arts District. The neighborhoods are stuffed with art galleries, clothing stores for the modern cowgirl, and some of the best eating and drinking in the Valley of the Sun.

Taliesin West   ARCHITECTURE
(☑480-860-2700; www.frankloydwright.org; 12621 Frank Lloyd Wright Blvd; ☺9am-4pm, closed Tue & Wed Jul & Aug) Taliesin West was Frank Lloyd Wright's desert home and studio, built between 1938 and 1940. Still home to an architecture school and open to the public for guided tours, it's a prime example of organic architecture with buildings incorporating elements and structures found in surrounding nature. To see the house and grounds, you must take a tour. The 90-minute **Insights Tour** (adult/4-12yr/student & senior $32/17/28; ☺half-hourly 9am-4pm Nov–mid-Apr, hourly 9am-4pm mid-Apr–Oct) is both informative and quick-moving. Shorter and longer tours are also available; see website for prices and times.

◉ Tempe

Founded in 1885 and home to around 58,000 students, **Arizona State University** (ASU; www.asu.edu) is the heart and soul of Tempe. The **Gammage Auditorium** (☑box

---

SCENIC DRIVES: ARIZONA'S BEST

Oak Creek Canyon A thrilling plunge past swimming holes, rockslides and crimson canyon walls on Hwy 89A between Flagstaff and Sedona.

Hwy 89/89A Wickenburg to Sedona The Old West meets the New West on this lazy drive past dude ranches, mining towns, art galleries and stylish wineries.

Patagonia–Sonoita Scenic Road This one's for the birds, and those who like to track them, in Arizona's southern wine country on Hwys 82 and 83.

Kayenta–Monument Valley Become the star of your own Western on an iconic loop past cinematic red rocks in Navajo country just off Hwy 163.

Vermilion Cliffs Scenic Road A solitary drive on Hwy 89A through the Arizona Strip linking condor country, the North Rim and Mormon hideaways.

---

office 480-965-3434, tours 480-965-6912; www.as-ugammage.com; cnr Mill Ave & Apache Blvd; tickets from $20; ☺1-4pm Mon-Fri Oct-May) was Frank Lloyd Wright's last major building.

Easily accessible by light-rail from downtown Phoenix, **Mill Avenue**, Tempe's main drag, is packed with chain restaurants, themed bars and other collegiate hangouts. While visiting, it's worth checking out **Tempe Town Lake** (www.tempe.gov/lake), an artificial lake with boat rides and paths perfect for strolling or biking its fringes. At **Cox Splash Playground** (☺10am-7pm Apr-Sep; ♿) at the beach park, kids love to frolic under the oversized sprinklers.

◉ Mesa

Founded by Mormons in 1877, low-key Mesa is one of the fastest-growing cities in the nation and is the third-largest city in Arizona, with a population of 452,000.

Arizona Museum of Natural History   MUSEUM
(☑480-644-2230; www.azmnh.org; 53 N Mac-Donald St; adult/child 3-12yr/student/senior $10/6/8/9; ☺10am-5pm Tue-Fri, 11am-5pm Sat, 1-5pm Sun; ♿) Worth a trip if your kids are into dinosaurs (aren't they all?). In addition

Phoenix

to the multilevel Dinosaur Mountain, there are loads of life-sized casts of the giant beasts plus a touchable Apatosaurus thighbone. Other exhibits highlight Arizona's colorful past, from a prehistoric Hohokam village to an eight-cell territorial jail.

🏃 Activities

Find trail information for Piestewa Peak, South Mountain Park, Camelback Park and others at http://phoenix.gov/recreation/rec/parks/preserves/index.html.

Piestewa Peak/Dreamy Draw Recreation Area   HIKING
(☎602-261-8318; www.phoenix.gov/parks; Squaw Peak Dr, Phoenix; ☉trails 5am-11pm, last entry 6:59pm) Previously known as Squaw Peak, this easy-to-access viewpoint was renamed for local Native American soldier Lori Piestewa, killed in Iraq in 2003. The trek to the 2608ft summit is hugely popular and

the saguaro-dotted park can get jammed on winter weekends. Dogs are allowed on some trails.

South Mountain Park   HIKING
(☎602-262-7393; 10919 S Central Ave, Phoenix; ☉5am-11pm, last entry 6:59pm) The 51-mile trail network (leashed dogs allowed) dips through canyons, over grassy hills and past granite walls, offering city views and access to Native American petroglyphs.

Cactus Adventures   BIKING
(☎480-688-4743; www.cactusadventures.com; half-day rental from $45; ☉hours vary) Cactus Adventures rents bikes and offers guided hiking and biking tours. Will deliver bikes to South Mountain trailhead or Arizona Grand Resort; flexible with pick-up times for bikes.

Ponderosa Stables   HORSEBACK RIDING
(☎602-268-1261; www.arizona-horses.com; 10215 S Central Ave, Phoenix; 1/2hr rides $33/55;

⊙6am-5pm Jun-Sep, 8am-5pm rest of year) This outfitter leads rides through South Mountain Park. Reservations required for most trips.

☞ Tours

Arizona Detours   SIGHTSEEING
(☏866-438-6877; www.detoursaz.com) Leads day tours to far-flung locations such as Tombstone (adult/child $145/75) and the Grand Canyon (adult/child $155/90), and a half-day Phoenix/Scottsdale tour (adult/child $80/45).

Arizona Outback Adventures   HIKING
(☏480-945-2881; www.aoa-adventures.com; 16447 N 91st St, Scottsdale) Offers half-day trips for hiking ($95, minimum two people), mountain biking ($115, minimum two people), and Salt River kayaking ($150, minimum two people).

★☆ Festivals & Events

Tostitos Fiesta Bowl   SPORTS
(☏480-350-0911; www.fiestabowl.org) Held in early January at the University of Phoenix Stadium in Glendale, this football game is preceded by massive celebrations and parades.

⎸═ Sleeping

Greater Phoenix is well stocked with hotels and resorts, but you won't find many B&Bs or cozy inns. Prices plummet in the scorching summer, a time when Valley residents take advantage of super-low prices at their favorite resorts.

⎸═ Phoenix

HI Phoenix Hostel   HOSTEL **$**
(☏602-254-9803; www.phxhostel.org; 1026 N 9th St; dm from $20, s/d $37/47; ❄@🛜) This inviting 14-bed hostel sits in a working-class residential neighborhood and has relaxing garden nooks. The owners are fun, and they know Phoenix. Check-in is from 8am to 10am (until noon Friday and Saturday) and 5pm to 10pm. Closed July and August. No credit cards.

Budget Lodge Downtown   MOTEL **$**
(☏602-254-7247; www.blphx.com; 402 W Van Buren St; r incl breakfast $60-67; P❄🛜) In the heart of downtown, this simple, two-story motel is a clean, low-cost place to lay your head, and it provides the most important amenities: a microwave and fridge in every room, and complimentary breakfast.

Aloft Phoenix-Airport   HOTEL **$$**
(☏602-275-6300; www.aloftphoenixairport.com; 4450 E Washington St; r $109-149; P@🛜🏊❄) Rooms blend a pop-art sensibility with the cleanest edges of modern design. The hotel is near Tempe and across the street from the Pueblo Grand Museum. No extra fee for pets.

Palomar Phoenix   HOTEL **$$$**
(☏877-488-1908, 602-253-6633; www.hotelpalomar-phoenix.com; 2 E Jefferson St; r $349-359; P❄🛜🏊❄) Shaggy pillows, antler-shaped lamps and portraits of blue cows. Yep, whimsy takes a stand at the new, 242-room Palomar, and we like it. Rooms, which are larger than average, pop with modern style and come with a yoga mat and animal-print robes. You can relax in style at the

Phoenix

3rd-floor outdoor pool and lounge, with nice views of downtown. The hotel anchors the new CityScape dining and entertainment district. Rates are slightly lower on weekends.

Royal Palms Resort & Spa   RESORT $$$
(☑ 602-840-3610; www.royalpalmsresortandspa.com; 5200 E Camelback Rd; r $333-423, ste from $342-519; P ❋ @ ≋ ☀) This posh boutique resort at the base of Camelback Mountain is a hushed and elegant place, dotted with Spanish Colonial villas, flower-lined walkways, and palms imported from Egypt. Pets are pampered with soft beds, personalized biscuits and walking services. There's a $34 daily resort fee.

⊨ Scottsdale

Sleep Inn   HOTEL $$
(☑ 480-998-9211; www.sleepinnscottsdale.com; 16630 N Scottsdale Rd; r incl breakfast $139-159; P ❋ @ ≋ ☀) This outpost of the national chain in North Scottsdale wins points for its extensive breakfast, friendly staff and proximity to Taliesin West. Rooms have microwaves and refrigerators.

Saguaro Inn   HOTEL $$
(☑ 480-308-1100; www.jdvhotels.com; 4000 N Drinkwater Blvd; r $189; P ❋ ≋ ☀ ☀) Embrace your inner hipster at this candy-bright hideaway beside Old Town. The vibe skews young and attention to detail may sometimes be lacking, but the location is great, palm trees surround the pool and the rate is lower than neighborhood competitors.

★ **Hotel Valley Ho**   BOUTIQUE HOTEL $$$
(☑ 480-248-2000; www.hotelvalleyho.com; 6850 E Main St; r $249-299, ste $399-509; P ❋ @ ≋ ☀ ☀) Everything's swell at the Valley Ho, a jazzy joint that once bedded Bing Crosby, Natalie Wood and Janet Leigh. Today, bebop music, upbeat front staff and the 'ice fireplace' recapture the Rat Pack–era vibe, and the theme travels well to the balconied rooms. Pets stay free; wi-fi is complimentary for 12 hours per day.

Bespoke Inn, Cafe & Bicycles   B&B $$$
(☑ 480-664-0730; www.bespokeinn.com; 3701 N Marshall Way; r from $299; P ❋ ≋ ☀ ☀) Ooh la la. Are we in the French countryside or downtown Scottsdale? At this breezy new B&B guests can sip coffee in the chic cafe, loll in the infinity edge pool, or pedal

the neighborhood on Pashley city bikes. Rooms are plush with handsome touches like handcrafted furniture and nickel bath fixtures. Gourmet breakfasts are served around a communal farm table. From $199 in summer.

Boulders RESORT $$$
(☑ 480-488-9009; www.theboulders.com; 34631 N Tom Darlington Dr, Carefree; casitas $319-369, villas $599-1149; P ❉ @ 🛜 ☒) Blending nearly imperceptibly into a landscape of natural rock formations, this escape-the-city retreat is simultaneously sumptuous and laid-back. Everything here is calculated to take the edge off travel. Extra stressed? Enjoy a session at the ultraposh on-site spa. Daily resort fee is $30. Weekend rates can drop as low as $125 in summer.

🛏 Tempe

Best Western Inn of Tempe HOTEL $
(☑ 480-784-2233; www.innoftempe.com; 670 N Scottsdale Rd; r incl breakfast $89-99; P ❉ @ 🛜 ☒) This well-kept, helpful hotel is within walking distance of Tempe Town Lake and close to ASU and lively Mill Ave. Has 24-hour airport shuttle.

★ Sheraton Wild Horse Pass Resort & Spa RESORT $$$
(☑ 602-225-0100; www.wildhorsepassresort.com; 5594 W Wild Horse Pass Blvd, Chandler; r $209-279, ste $284-520, mains $44-54; P ❉ @ 🛜 ☒) Scan the horizon for the namesake wild horses at this striking property, designed by the Gila River tribe as a luxurious place to soak up the best of Native American healing and wisdom. This oasis has comfortable rooms, spacious common areas, fine dining, two 18-hole golf courses, an equestrian center, tennis courts, a spa and a water slide modeled after Hohokam ruins.

✗ Eating

The Phoenix-Scottsdale area has the largest selection of restaurants in the Southwest. To sample a variety of Arizona's finest foods, stop by **Food Truck Friday** (www.phxstreet-food.org; 721 N Central Ave, Phoenix Public Market, downtown; ⊙ 11am-1:30pm Fri) at the Phoenix Public Market downtown.

★ Matt's Big Breakfast BREAKFAST $
(☑ 602-254-1074; www.mattsbigbreakfast.com; 825 N 1st St, at Garfield St; breakfast $5-10, lunch $7-10; ⊙ 6:30am-2:30pm) Matt re-opened his legendary breakfast joint in a bigger location down the block from its old digs, but folks still cluster on the sidewalk to wait for a table. Regular menu items are great, but daily specials, such as eggs scrambled with peppers and chorizo into fluffy-spicy-ohmygoodness on a bed of mouth-watering crispy homefries, are supremely yummy.

Tee Pee Mexican Food MEXICAN $
(☑ 602-956-0178; www.teepeemexicanfood.com; 4144 E Indian School Rd; mains $5-14; ⊙ 11am-10pm Mon-Sat, to 9pm Sun) If you like piping-hot plates piled high with cheesy, messy American-style Mexican fare then grab a booth at this 40-year-old fave. When George W Bush ate here in 2004, he ordered two cheese and onion enchiladas, rice and beans – now called the Presidential Special.

La Grande Orange Grocery CAFE $
(www.lagrandeorangegrocery.com; 4410 N 40th St; breakfast under $8, lunch $7-9, pizza $12-15; ⊙ cafe 6:30am-10pm, pizzeria from 4pm Mon-Thu, from 11am Fri & Sat) Take away a muffin and coffee for breakfast, pop in for a guacamole BLT at lunch or nibble margherita pizza at dinner. This bustling gourmet market, bakery, cafe and pizzeria sits at the corner of 40th St and and E Campbell Ave.

★ Dick's Hideaway NEW MEXICAN $$
(☑ 602-241-1881; http://richardsonsnm.com; 6008 N 16th St; breakfast $5-20, lunch $12-16, dinner $12-35; ⊙ 7am-midnight Sun-Wed, to 1am Thu-Sat) Grab a table beside the bar or join the communal table in the side room and settle in for hearty servings of savory, chile-slathered enchiladas, tamales and other New Mexican cuisine. We especially like the Hideaway for breakfast, when the Bloody Marys arrive with a shot of beer. The unmarked entrance is between the towering shrubs.

Pizzeria Bianco PIZZERIA $$
(☑ 602-258-8300; www.pizzeriabianco.com; 623 E Adams St; pizza $12-16; ⊙ 11am-9pm Mon, 11am-10pm Tue-Sat) The dining room is small and the menu short, but flavors are big and savory at this famed eatery run by James Beard winner Chris Bianco. The thin crust, wood-fired pies include the Rosa, with red onion, parmesan, rosemary and Arizona pistachios, and the Wiseguy with wood-roasted onions, house-smoked mozzarella and fennel sausage.

SOUTHWEST PHOENIX

Beckett's Table NEW AMERICAN $$
(☑ 602-954-1700; www.beckettstable.com; 3717 E
Indian School Rd; mains $13-21; ⊙ 5-10pm Tue-Sat,
5-9pm Sun) Enjoy a country supper in the
village's most stylish barn, complete with
concrete floor, trussed beams and wooden
accents. The urban farm concept really
shines as you savor chef Justin Beckett's lo-
cally sourced dishes, from tender pork *osso
bucco* to short ribs with mashed potatoes.
Don't miss the bacon cheddar biscuit with
candied jalapeno apple butter. Dining solo?
Join the conversation at the black-walnut
communal table.

Durant's STEAKHOUSE $$$
(☑ 602-264-5967; 2611 N Central Ave; lunch $10-
30, dinner $20-50; ⊙ 11am-4pm Mon-Fri, dinner
daily) This dark and manly place is a gloriously old-school steakhouse. You will get
steak. It will be big and juicy. There will
be a potato. The ambience is awesome
too: cozy red-velvet booths and the sense
the Rat Pack is going to waltz in at any
minute.

PHOENIX FOR CHILDREN

Wet 'n' Wild Phoenix (☑ 623-201-
2000; www.wetnwildphoenix.com; 4243
W Pinnacle Peak Rd, Glendale; over/under
42in tall $39/30, senior $30; ⊙ 10am-6pm
Sun-Wed, 10am-10pm Thu-Sat, varies May,
Aug & Sep; ⊛) water park has pools,
tube slides, wave pools, waterfalls and
floating rivers. It's in Glendale, 2 miles
west of I-17 at exit 217.

At the re-created 1880s frontier
town **Rawhide Western Town &
Steakhouse** (☑ 480-502-5600; www.
rawhide.com; 5700 W N Loop Rd, Chandler;
admission free, per attraction or show $5,
unlimited day pass $15; ⊙ 5-10pm Wed-
Sun, varies seasonally; ⊛), about 20
miles south of Mesa, kids can enjoy all
sorts of hokey-but-fun shenanigans.
The steakhouse has rattlesnake for
adventurous eaters.

Arizona Science Center (☑ 602-
716-2000; www.azscience.org; 600 E
Washington St; adult/child 3-17 yr/senior
$15/11/13; ⊙ 10am-5pm; ⊛) is a high-
tech temple of discovery; there are
more than 300 hands-on exhibits and a
planetarium.

Scottsdale

Sugar Bowl ICE CREAM $
(☑ 480-946-0051; www.sugarbowlscottsdale.com;
4005 N Scottsdale Rd; ice cream $2.25-9, mains $6-
12; ⊙ 11am-10pm Sun-Thu, 11am-midnight Fri & Sat;
⊛) This pink-and-white Valley institution
has been working its ice-cream magic since
the '50s. For more substantial fare, there's a
whole menu of sandwiches and salads.

The Mission MEXICAN $$
(☑ 480-636-5005; www.themissionaz.com; 3815
N Brown Ave; lunch $9-12, dinner $12-32; ⊙ 11am-
3pm & 5-10pm Sun-Thu, to 11pm Fri & Sat) With
its dark interior, glowing votives and reli-
gious icons, this *nuevo* Latin spot looks very
15th-century, but sunny patios with orange
umbrellas keep the vibe light. For a satisfy-
ing lunch, try the steak taco with green chile
salsa, avocado and tecate-marinated beef.
The guacamole is made table-side. Margari-
tas and mojitos round out the fun.

Herb Box AMERICAN $$
(☑ 480-289-6160; www.theherbbox.com; 7134 E
Stetson Dr; lunch $10-19, dinner $15-28; ⊙ lunch
daily, dinner Tue-Sat) It's not just about sparkle and air kisses at this chichi bistro. It's
also about fresh, regional ingredients, artful
presentation and attentive service.

Tempe

★**Essence** CAFE $
(☑ 480-966-2745; 825 W University Dr; breakfast
$5-9, lunch $7.25-9; ⊙ 7am-3pm Mon-Sat; ☑) This
breezy box of deliciousness serves egg dishes
and French toast at breakfast, and salads,
gourmet sandwiches and a few Mediterranean specialties at lunch. The iced caramel
coffee and the macaroons make a nice mid-
afternoon reward.

★**Kai Restaurant** NATIVE AMERICAN $$$
(☑ 602-225-0100; www.wildhorsepassresort.com;
5594 W Wild Horse Pass Blvd, Chandler; mains $44-
54, tasting menus $135-$225; ⊙ 5-9pm Tue-Thu,
to 9:30pm-Fri & Sat) Simple ingredients from
mainly Native American farms and ranches
are turned into something extraordinary.
Dinners are like fine tapestries with dishes –
such as the pecan-crusted Colorado lamb
with native seeds mole – striking just the
right balance between adventure and com-
fort. Dress nicely (no shorts or hats). It's at
the Sheraton Wild Horse Pass Resort & Spa
on the Gila River Indian Reservation. Kai
closes for one month in August.

SOUTHWEST PHOENIX

🍸 Drinking

Scottsdale has the greatest concentration of trendy bars and clubs; Tempe attracts the student crowd.

⭐ Postino Winecafé Arcadia   WINE BAR

(www.postinowinecafe.com; 3939 E Campbell Ave, at 40th St, Phoenix; ⊙ 11am-11pm Mon-Thu, 11am-midnight Fri, 9am-midnight Sat, 9am-10pm Sun) This convivial, indoor-outdoor wine bar is a perfect gathering spot for a few friends ready to enjoy the good life, but solos will do fine too. Highlights include the misting patio, rave-inducing bruschetta and $5 wines by the glass from 11am to 5pm.

Edge Bar   BAR

(5700 E McDonald Dr, Sanctuary on Camelback Mountain, Paradise Valley) Enjoy a sunset 'on the edge' at this stylish cocktail bar perched on the side of Camelback Mountain at the Sanctuary resort. No room outside? The equally posh, big-windowed Jade Bar should do just fine. Complimentary valet.

Four Peaks Brewing Company   BREWERY

(☑ 480-303-9967; www.fourpeaks.com; 1340 E 8th St, Tempe; ⊙ 11am-2am Mon-Sat, 10am-2am Sun) So this is where everybody is. Beer-lovers are in for a treat at this quintessential neighborhood brewpub in a cool Mission Revival-style building.

Rusty Spur Saloon   BAR

(☑ 480-425-7787;   www.rustyspursaloon.com; 7245 E Main St, Scottsdale; ⊙ 10am-1am Sun-Thu, to 2am Fri & Sat) Nobody's putting on airs at this fun-lovin', pack-'em-in-tight country bar where the grizzled Budweiser crowd gathers for cheap drinks and twangy country bands; check the website to see who's playing. It's in an old bank building that closed during the Depression.

☆ Entertainment

The **Phoenix Symphony Orchestra** (☑ administration 602-495-1117, box office 602-495-1999; www.phoenixsymphony.org; 75 N 2nd St, box offices 1 N 1st St, 75 N 2nd St) performs at **Symphony Hall** (75 N 2nd St). In 2013, the **Arizona Opera** (☑ 602-266-7464; www.azopera.com; 1636 N Central Ave) moved into a new opera hall across the street from the Phoenix Art Museum

The men's basketball team, the **Phoenix Suns** (☑ 602 379 7900; www.nba.com/suns; 201 E Jefferson St, Phoenix), and the women's team, the **Phoenix Mercury** (☑ 602-252-9622; www.

wnba.com/mercury; 201 E Jefferson St, Phoenix), play at the US Airways Center. The **Arizona Cardinals** (☑ 602-379-0101; www.azcardinals.com; 1 Cardinals Dr, Glendale) football team plays in Glendale at the new University of Phoenix Stadium, which will host the Super Bowl in 2015. The **Arizona Diamondbacks** (☑ 602-462-6500; www.arizona.diamondbacks.mlb.com; 401 E Jefferson St, Phoenix) play baseball at Chase Field.

Rhythm Room   LIVE MUSIC

(☑ 602-265-4842; www.rhythmroom.com; 1019 E Indian School Rd, Phoenix; ⊙ doors usually open 7:30pm) Some of the Valley's best live acts take the stage at this small venue, where you pretty much feel like you're in the front row of every gig. It tends to attract more local and regional talent than the big names, which suits us just fine.

Char's Has the Blues   BLUES

(☑ 602-230-0205;   www.charshastheblues.com; 4631 N 7th Ave, Phoenix; Mon-Wed no cover, Thu & Sun $3, Fri & Sat $7; ⊙ 8pm-1am Sun-Wed, 7:30pm-1am Thu-Sat) Dark and intimate, but very welcoming, this blues and R & B cottage packs 'em in with solid acts most nights of the week, but somehow still manages to feel like a well-kept secret.

BS West   GAY

(☑ 480-945-9028; www.bswest.com; 7125 E 5th Ave, Scottsdale; ⊙ 2pm-2am) A high-energy gay video bar and dance club in the Old Town Scottsdale area. This place has go-go dancers and hosts karaoke on Sundays.

🛍 Shopping

The valley has several notable shopping malls. For more upscale shopping, visit the **Scottsdale Fashion Square** (www.fashion-square.com; 7014 E Camelback, at Scottsdale Rd, Scottsdale; ⊙ 10am-9pm Mon-Sat, 11am-6pm Sun) and the even more exclusive **Biltmore Fashion Park** (www.shopbiltmore.com; 2502 E Camelback Rd, at 24th St, Phoenix; ⊙ 10am-8pm Mon-Sat, noon-6pm Sun). In northern Scottsdale, the outdoor **Kierland Commons** (www.kierlandcommons.com; 15205 N Kierland Blvd, Scottsdale; ⊙ 10am-8pm Mon-Thu, 10am-9pm Sat, noon-6pm Sun) pulls in the crowds.

Heard Museum Shop & Bookstore   ARTS & CRAFTS

(www.heardmuseumshop.com; 2301 N Central Ave, Phoenix; ⊙ shop 9:30am-5pm, from 11am Sun, bookstore 9:30am-5:30pm Mon-Sat, to 5pm Sun) Has a range of books about Native Americans, and a reliable and expansive selection of Native American arts and crafts, including jewelry and kachina dolls.

❶ Information

EMERGENCY & MEDICAL SERVICES

Banner Good Samaritan Medical Center (⌨602-839-2000; www.bannerhealth.com; 1111 E McDowell Rd, Phoenix) Has a 24-hour emergency room.

Police (⌨602-262-6151; http://phoenix.gov/police; 620 W Washington St, Phoenix)

INTERNET RESOURCES & MEDIA

Arizona Republic (www.azcentral.com) Arizona's largest newspaper; publishes a free entertainment guide, *Calendar*, every Thursday.

Burton Barr Central Library (⌨602-262-4636; www.phoenixpubliclibrary.org; 1221 N Central Ave, Phoenix; ◷9am-5pm Mon, Fri & Sat, 9am-9pm Tue-Thu, 1-5pm Sun; 🖥) Free internet access.

KJZZ 91.5 FM (http://kjzz.org) National Public Radio (NPR).

Phoenix New Times (www.phoenixnewtimes.com) The major free weekly; lots of event and restaurant listings.

POST

Downtown Post Office (⌨602-253-9648; 522 N Central Ave, Phoenix; ◷9am-5pm Mon-Fri)

TOURIST INFORMATION

Downtown Phoenix Visitor Information Center (⌨877-225-5749; www.visitphoenix.com; 125 N 2nd St, Suite 120; ◷8am-5pm Mon-Fri) The Valley's most complete source of tourist information.

Mesa Convention & Visitors Bureau (⌨800-283-6372, 480-827-4700; www.visitmesa.com; 120 N Center St, Mesa; ◷8am-5pm Mon-Fri)

Scottsdale Convention & Visitors Bureau (⌨800-782-1117, 480-421-1004; www.experiencescottsdale.com; 4343 N Scottsdale Rd, Suite 170; ◷8am-5pm Mon-Fri) Inside the Galleria Corporate Center. Very helpful staff. Pick up the free Desert Discovery Guide for a good list of area trails.

Tempe Convention & Visitors Bureau (⌨866-914-1052, 480-894-8158; www.tempetourism.com; 51 W 3rd St, Suite 105; ◷8:30am-5pm Mon-Fri)

❶ Getting There & Around

Sky Harbor International Airport (⌨602-273-3300; http://skyharbor.com; 3400 E Sky Harbor Blvd; 🖥) is 3 miles southeast of downtown Phoenix and served by 17 airlines, including United, American, Delta and British Airways. Its three terminals (Terminals 2, 3 and 4; Terminal 1 was demolished in 1990) and the parking lots are linked by the free 24-hour Airport Shuttle Bus. The free **Phoenix Sky Train**, which began operating in 2013, currently runs between the economy parking lot, Terminal 4 and the METRO light-rail station at 44th St and E Washington St.

  Greyhound (⌨602-389-4200; www.greyhound.com; 2115 E Buckeye Rd) runs buses to Tucson ($21 to $23, two hours, eight daily), Flagstaff ($38, three hours, five daily), Albuquerque

---

VERDE VALLEY WINE TRAIL

Vineyards, wineries and tasting rooms have opened their doors along Hwy 89A and I-17, bringing a dash of style and energy to Cottonwood, Jerome and Cornville.

In Cottonwood, you can float to Verde River–adjacent **Alcantara Vineyards** (www.alcantaravineyard.com; 3445 S Grapevine Way) then stroll through Old Town where two new tasting rooms, **Arizona Stronghold** (www.azstronghold.com; 1023 N Main St; tastings $9; ◷noon-7pm Sun-Thu, to 9pm Fri & Sat) and **Pillsbury Wine Company** (www.pillsburywine.com; 1012 N Main St; ◷11am-6pm Sun-Thu, 11am-8pm Fri), sit across from each other on Main St. Art, views and wine-sipping converge in Jerome, where there's a tasting room on every level of town, starting with **Cellar 433** (www.bittercreekwinery.com; 240 Hull Ave; ◷11am-5pm Mon-Wed, 11am-6pm Thu-Sun) near the chamber of commerce visitor center. From there, stroll up to **Caduceus Cellars** (www.caduceus.org; 158 Main St; ◷11am-6pm Sun-Thu, to 8pm Sun) then end with a final climb to **Jerome Winery** (⌨928-639-9067; 403 Clark St; ◷11am-5pm Mon-Thu, 11am-8pm Sat, 11am-4pm Sun Jun-Aug, shorter hours Sep-May) with its inviting patio.

Three wineries with tasting rooms hug a short stretch of Page Springs Rd east of Cornville: bistro-housing **Page Springs Cellars** (www.pagespringscellars.com; 1500 N Page Springs Rd; wine tasting $10; ◷11am-7pm Mon-Wed, to 9pm Thu-Sun), welcoming **Oak Creek Vineyards** (www.oakcreekvineyards.net; 1555 N Page Springs Rd; wine tasting $5; ◷10am-6pm) and mellow-rock-playing **Javelina Leap Vineyard** (www.javelinaleapwinery.com; 1565 Page Springs Rd; wine tasting $8; ◷11am-5pm).

($78 to $85, 10 to 12½ hours, seven daily) and Los Angeles ($38, seven to eight hours, eight daily). Valley Metro's No 13 buses link the airport and the Greyhound station.

Valley Metro (☑ 602-253-5000; www.valley-metro.org; tickets $2) operates buses all over the Valley and a 20-mile light-rail line linking north Phoenix with downtown Phoenix, Tempe/ ASU and downtown Mesa. Fares for light-rail and bus are $2 per ride (no transfers) or $4 for a day pass. Buses run daily at intermittent times. **FLASH buses** (www.tempe.gov) operate daily around ASU and downtown Tempe, while the **Scottsdale Trolley** (www.scottsdaleaz.gov/ trolley; ⊗11am-6pm Fri-Wed, to 9pm Thu during Artwalk) loops around downtown Scottsdale, both at no charge.

Flagstaff

Flagstaff's laid-back charms are myriad, from its pedestrian-friendly historic downtown crammed with eclectic vernacular architecture and vintage neon to its high-altitude pursuits such as skiing and hiking. Locals are generally a happy, athletic bunch, skewing more toward granola than gunslinger. Northern Arizona University (NAU) gives Flagstaff its college-town flavor, while its railroad history still figures firmly in the town's identity. Throw in a healthy appreciation for craft beer, freshly roasted coffee beans and an all-round good time and you have the makings of a town you want to slow down and savor.

◉ Sights

With its cultural sites, historic downtown and access to outdoorsy pursuits, it's easy to fall for Flagstaff. Pick up walking-tour maps for Route 66 and haunted buildings at the visitor center.

Museum of Northern Arizona   MUSEUM
(☑ 928-774-5213; www.musnaz.org; 3101 N Fort Valley Rd; adult/child/senior $10/6/9; ⊗9am-5pm) For a helpful primer about the region, stop here. Three miles north of downtown, the museum spotlights local geology, biology and arts as well as Native American anthropolopogy, with exhibits spotlighting archaeology, history and customs of local tribes.

Lowell Observatory   OBSERVATORY
(☑ 928-233-3212; www.lowell.edu; 1400 W Mars Hill Rd; adult/child $12/5; ⊗9am-10pm Jun-Aug, shorter hour Sep-May) This observatory witnessed the first sighting of Pluto in 1920. Weather permitting, there's nightly stargazing, helped by the fact that Flagstaff is the first International Dark Sky city in the world. Day tours are offered from 1pm to 4pm.

Walnut Canyon National Monument   CANYON
(☑ 928-526-3367; www.nps.gov/waca; 7-day admission adult/child $5/free; ⊗8am-5pm May-Oct, 9am-5pm Nov-Apr) Sinagua cliff dwellings are set in the nearly vertical walls of a small limestone butte amid a forested canyon at this worth-a-trip monument. A short hiking trail descends past many cliff-dwelling rooms. The monument is 11 miles southeast of Flagstaff, off I-40 exit 204.

✳ Activities

Alpine Pedaler   CYCLING
(☑ 928-213-9233; www.alpinepedaler.com; per person $25) Hop on the bus – or should we say communal bicycle – to pedal to downtown bars. This 15-seater makes pub crawling a whole lot easier. Tours are two hours.

Humphreys Peak   HIKING
The state's highest mountain (12,663ft) is a reasonably straightforward, though strenuous, hike in summer. The trail, which begins in the Arizona Snowbowl, winds through forest, eventually coming out above the beautifully barren tree line. The distance is 4.5 miles one-way; allow six to eight hours round-trip.

Arizona Snowbowl   SKIING
(☑ 928-779-1951; www.arizonasnowbowl.com; Hwy 180 & Snowbowl Rd; lift ticket adult/child $55/15; ⊗9am-4pm) Six lifts service 40 runs and a snowboarding park at elevations between 9200ft and 11,500ft. You can ride the chairlift (adult/child $15/10) in summer.

⊨ Sleeping

Flagstaff provides the widest variety of lodging choices in the region. Unlike in southern Arizona, summer is high season here.

Grand Canyon International Hostel   HOSTEL $
(☑ 928-779-9421; www.grandcanyonhostel.com; 19½ S San Francisco St; dm $22-24, r without bath room $44-56, both incl breakfast; ✳@🛜) A site along Flagstaff's Route 66 walking tour, this historic property now holds a hostel. Run by friendly people, dorms are clean and small. There's a kitchen, laundry facilities and tours to the Grand Canyon and Sedona. It's one block from the Amtrak station, and guests are fetched from the Greyhound bus

for free. This hostel gets more traffic than sister-property Dubeau Hostel.

Dubeau Hostel
HOSTEL $

(☑ 928-774-6731; www.grandcanyonhostel.com; 19 W Phoenix St; dm $22-24, r $48-68, both incl breakfast; P ❄ @ 🛜) Run by the Grand Canyon International Hostel folks. The private rooms are like basic hotel rooms, with refrigerators and bathrooms with showers, but at half the price. The quieter of the two hostels.

Hotel Monte Vista
HOTEL $$

(☑ 928-779-6971; www.hotelmontevista.com; 100 N San Francisco St; d $65-110, ste $120-140; 🛜) Feather lampshades, vintage furniture, bold colors and old-fashioned layouts – things are historically frisky in the 50 rooms and suites here, which are named for the film stars who slept in them. Ask for a quiet room if you're opposed to the live music that may drift up from Monte Vista Lounge. For the supernaturally curious, there's a ghost information sheet at the front desk.

Drury Inn & Suites
HOTEL $$

(☑ 928-773-4900; www.druryhotels.com; 300 S Milton Rd; r incl breakfast $155-165, ste $200; P ❄ @ 🛜 ☲ 🏊) The stone columns in the lobby set an adventurous mood at this six-story, LEED-certified property, but the deal clincher is the hearty Kickback happy hour which serves up complimentary beer and wine (with a limit) and a hearty spread of appetizers. The free breakfast is also filling. All rooms have a microwave and refrigerator. Pets are $10 per day.

✖ Eating

Wander around downtown and you'll stumble on plenty of eating options.

Diablo Burger
BURGERS $

(www.diabloburger.com; 120 N Leroux St; mains $10-13.25; ⏱ 11am-9pm Mon-Wed, 11am-10pm Thu-Sat) The cheddar-topped Blake at this gourmet burger joint gives a nod to New Mexico with Hatch chile mayo and roasted green chilies. Diablo uses locally sourced, antibiotic-free beef and fresh cut, deep-fried frites with dipping sauce. The place is tiny, four tables inside and a few bar seats (serves wine and beer), so come early.

Beaver Street Brewery
BREWPUB $$

(www.beaverstreetbrewery.com; 11 S Beaver St; lunch $8-13, dinner $10-20; ⏱ 11am-11pm Sun-Thu, to midnight Fri & Sat; 🍴) This bustling brewpub does bar food right, offering delicious pizzas, burgers and salads. It usually has five handmade beers on tap and some seasonal brews. Surprisingly, it's very family friendly.

Criollo Latin Kitchen
FUSION $$

(☑ 928-774-0541; www.criollolatinkitchen.com; 16 N San Francisco St; lunch $8-17, dinner $10-22, brunch $8-10; ⏱ 11am-9pm Mon-Thu, 11am-10pm Fri, 9am-10pm Sat, 9am-9pm Sun) This Latin fusion spot has a romantic, industrial setting for cozy cocktail dates and delectable late-night small plates. The blue-corn blueberry pancakes make a strong argument for showing up for Sunday brunch. Food is sourced locally and sustainable when possible.

🍷 Drinking & Entertainment

Follow the 1-mile Flagstaff Ale Trail (www.flagstaffaletrail.com) to sample craft beer at downtown breweries and a pub or two.

★ Museum Club
BAR

(☑ 928-526-9434; www.themuseumclub.com; 3404 E Rte 66; ⏱ 11am-2am) This honky-tonk roadhouse has been kickin' up its boot heels since 1936. Inside what looks like a huge log cabin you'll find a large wooden dance floor, animals mounted on the walls and a sumptuous elixir-filled mahogany bar. The origins of its name? In 1931 it housed a taxidermy museum.

Macy's
CAFE

(www.macyscoffee.net; 14 S Beaver St; mains under $8; ⏱ 6am-8pm; 🛜) Macy's delicious house-roasted coffee has kept Flagstaff buzzing for over 30 years. Tasty vegetarian menu includes many vegan choices, with traditional cafe grub.

Cuvee 928
WINE BAR

(☑ 928-214-9463; www.cuvee928winebar.com; 6 E Aspen Ave; ⏱ 11:30am-9pm Mon-Thu, to 10pm Fri & Sat, 10am-3pm Sun) With a central location on Heritage Sq, and patio seating, this wine bar is a pleasant venue for people-watching.

Charly's Pub & Grill
LIVE MUSIC

(☑ 928-779-1919; www.weatherfordhotel.com; 23 N Leroux St; ⏱ 8am-10pm) This restaurant at the Weatherford Hotel has live music on the weekends. Its fireplace and brick walls provide a cozy setting for the blues, jazz and folk played here. Upstairs, stroll the wraparound verandah outside the popular 3rd-floor Zane Grey Ballroom.

ℹ Information

Visitor Center (☑ 800-842-7293, 928-774-9541; www.flagstaffarizona.org; 1 E Rte 66; ⊘8am-5pm Mon-Sat, 9am-4pm Sun) Inside the historic Amtrak train station.

ℹ Getting There & Around

Flagstaff Pulliam Airport is 4 miles south of town off I-17. **US Airways** (☑ 800-428-4322; www.usairways.com) offers several daily flights between Pulliam Airport and Phoenix Sky Harbor International Airport. **Greyhound** (☑ 800-231-2222, 928-774-4573; www.greyhound.com; 880 E Butler Ave) stops in Flagstaff en route to/from Albuquerque, Las Vegas, Los Angeles and Phoenix. **Arizona Shuttle** (☑ 800-888-2749, 928-226-8060; www.arizonashuttle.com) has shuttles that run to the park (one-way $29), Sedona (one-way $25) and Phoenix Sky Harbor Airport (one-way $45).

Operated by **Amtrak** (☑ 800-872-7245, 928-774-8679; www.amtrak.com; 1 E Rte 66; ⊘3am-10:45pm), the Southwest Chief stops at Flagstaff on its daily run between Chicago and Los Angeles.

Central Arizona

This part of Arizona draws people year-round for outdoor fun and is an oasis for summer visitors searching for cooler climes. After Phoenix, the land gains elevation, turning from high rolling desert to jagged hills covered in scrubby trees. Farther north still, mountains punctuate thick stands of pine.

Williams

Affable Williams, 60 miles south of Grand Canyon Village and 35 miles west of Flagstaff, is a gateway town with character. Classic motels and diners line Route 66, and the old-school homes and train station give a nod to simpler times.

Most tourists visit to ride the turn-of-the-19th-century **Grand Canyon Railway** (☑ 800-843-8724, 928-635-4253; www.thetrain.com; Railway Depot, 233 N Grand Canyon Blvd; round trip adult/child from $75/45; 🚻) to the South Rim; departs Williams 9:30am, returns at 5:45pm. Even if you're not a train buff, a trip is a scenic stress-free way to visit the Grand Canyon. Characters in period costumes provide historical and regional narration, and banjo folk music sets the tone. There's also a wildly popular Polar Express service (adult/child from $32/18) from November through early January, ferrying pajama-clad kids to

the 'North Pole' to visit Santa. Kids and pre-teens will most enjoy **Bearizona** (☑ 928-635-2289; www.bearizona.com; 1500 E Rte 66; adult/child/under 4yr $20/10/free; ⊘8am-6pm Jun–mid-Aug, hours vary rest of year), an awesomely named drive-through wildlife park where visitors drive themselves past gray wolves, bison, bighorn sheep and black bears. Stop by the Fort Bearizona walking area for an up-close look at younger bears.

The **Red Garter Bed & Bakery** (☑ 928-635-1484; www.redgarter.com; 137 W Railroad Ave; d $135-160; ❋ 🛜) is an 1897 bordello turned B&B where the ladies used to hang out the windows to flag down customers. The four rooms have nice period touches and the downstairs bakery has good coffee. The funky little **Grand Canyon Hotel** (☑ 928-635-1419; www.thegrandcanyonhotel.com; 145 W Rte 66; dm $40, r without bathroom $67, r with bathroom $74-125; ⊘Mar-Nov; ❋ @ 🛜) has small themed rooms and a six-bed dorm room; no TVs. You can sleep inside a 1929 Santa Fe train caboose or a Pullman railcar at the **Canyon Motel & RV Park** (☑ 928-635-9371; www.thecanyonmotel.com; 1900 E Rodeo Rd, Williams; RV sites $35-38, cottages $74-78, train cars $78-160; ❋ 🛜 🏊), just east of downtown.

Sedona

Nestled amid majestic red sandstone formations at the southern end of Oak Creek Canyon, Sedona attracts artists, spiritual seekers, hikers and cyclists, and day-trippers from Phoenix fleeing the oppressive heat. Many New Age types believe that this area is the center of vortexes that radiate the earth's power, and Sedona's combination of scenic beauty and mysticism draws throngs of tourists year-round. New Age businesses dot downtown, along with galleries and gourmet restaurants, while the surrounding canyons offer excellent hiking and mountain biking.

In the middle of town, the 'Y' is the landmark junction of Hwys 89A and 179. Businesses are spread along both roads.

◉ Sights & Activities

New Agers believe Sedona's rocks, cliffs and rivers radiate Mother Earth's mojo. The world's four best-known vortexes are here: **Bell Rock** near Village of Oak Creek east of Hwy 179, **Cathedral Rock** near Red Rock Crossing, **Airport Mesa** along Airport Rd, and **Boynton Canyon**. Airport Rd is also a great location for watching the Technicolor sunsets.

Coconino National Forest   PARK
(Red Rock Visitor Contact Center; ☏ 928-203-7500; www.redrockcountry.org/recreation; 8375 Hwy 179; ⊙8am-5pm) The best way to explore the area is by hiking, biking or horseback riding in the surrounding forest. Many day-use and parking areas require a Red Rock Pass ($5/15 per day/week), which can be purchased at most area stores and lodgings, and self-serve kiosks at popular sites.

For a map of local trails, download the Red Rock Country map (www.redrockcountry.org/maps/index.shtml) or pick up a free copy at the helpful USFS visitor center just south of the Village of Oak Creek.

The most scenic spots are along Hwy 89A north of Sedona, which snakes alongside Oak Creek through the heavily visited **Oak Creek Canyon**, and the drive between Sedona and the Village of Oak Creek to the south.

Chapel of the Holy Cross   CHURCH
(☏ 928-282-4069; www.chapeloftheholycross.com; 780 Chapel Rd; ⊙9am-5pm Mon-Sat, 10am-5pm Sun) **FREE** Situated between spectacular, statuesque red-rock columns 3 miles south of town, this modern, nondenominational chapel was built in 1956 by Marguerite Brunwig Staude in the tradition of Frank Lloyd Wright.

Slide Rock State Park   PARK
(☏928-282-3034; www.azstateparks.com/Parks/SLRO; 6871 N Hwy 89A; per car Memorial Day-Labor Day $20, Sep-May $10; ⊙8am-7pm Memorial Day-Labor Day, 8am-5pm Sep-May) Swoosh down big rocks into cool creek water at Oak Creek Canyon's star attraction, or walk the hiking trails.

Pink Jeep Tours   DRIVING TOUR
(☏928-282-5000; www.pinkjeeptours.com; 204 N Hwy 89A) Many companies offer 4WD tours,

ROADSIDE ATTRACTIONS ON ROUTE 66

Route 66 enthusiasts will find 400 miles of pavement stretching across Arizona, including the longest uninterrupted portion of old road left in the country, between Seligman and Topock. The **Mother Road** (www.azrt66.com) connects the dots between gun-slinging Oatman, Kingman's mining settlements, Williams' 1940s-vintage downtown, and Winslow's windblown streets, with plenty of kitschy sights, listed here from west to east, along the way.

Wild Burros of Oatman Mules beg for treats in the middle of the road.

Grand Canyon Caverns & Inn (☏928-422-3223; www.gccaverns.com; Route 66, Mile 115; 1hr tour adult/child $19/13, r $85, campsites $15-30; ⊙8am-6pm May-Sep, 10am-4pm Oct-Apr) A guided tour 21 stories underground loops past mummified bobcats, civil-defense supplies and a $800 motel room.

Burma Shave signs Red-and-white ads from a bygone era between Grand Canyon Caverns and Seligman.

Seligman's Snow-Cap Drive In Prankish burger and ice-cream joint open since 1953.

Meteor Crater (☏928-289-5898; www.meteorcrater.com; adult/child/senior $16/8/15; ⊙7am-7pm Jun–mid-Sep, 8am-5pm mid-Sep–May) A 550ft-deep pockmark that's nearly 1 mile across, near Flagstaff.

Wigwam Motel (☏928-524-3048; www.galerie-kokopelli.com/wigwam; 811 W Hopi Dr, Holbrook; r $56-62; ❋) Concrete wigwams with hickory logpole furniture in Holbrook.

but Pink Jeep Tours has a great reputation and a vast variety of outings.

Sedona Bike & Bean
MOUNTAIN BIKING
(☑ 928-284-0210; www.bike-bean.com; 75 Bell Rock Plaza; 2hr/half-/full day from $30/40/50) A mountain-bike rental place near trails for hiking, biking and vortex-gazing. Also serves coffee.

🛌 Sleeping

Sedona hosts many beautiful B&Bs, creek-side cabins, motels and full-service resorts.

Dispersed camping is not permitted in Red Rock Canyon. The USFS (☑ 877-444-6777; www.recreation.gov; campsites $18) runs campgrounds, none with hookups, along Hwy Alt 89 in Oak Creek Canyon. All are nestled in the woods just off the road. It costs $18 to camp, and you don't need a Red Rock Pass. Reservations are accepted for all campgrounds except Pine Flat East. Six miles north of town, Manzanita has 19 sites, showers and is open year-round; 11.5 miles north, Cave Springs has 78 sites, and showers; Pine Flat East and Pine Flat West, 12.5 miles north, together have 58 sites, with 18 reservable.

Star Motel
MOTEL $
(☑ 928-282-3641; www.starmotelsedona.com; 295 Jordan Rd; r $80-100) Low rates, warm hospitality and a prime uptown location are the big draw at the retro Star Motel. You won't find candy on your pillow, but the bed is clean, the shower strong and the refrigerator handy for chilling those sunset beers.

Cozy Cactus
B&B $$$
(☑ 928-284-0082; www.cozycactus.com; 80 Canyon Circle Dr; r incl breakfast $190-290; ❋ @ 🛜) This five-room, recently revamped B&B is particularly well suited to adventure-loving types ready to enjoy the great outdoors. The Southwest-style abode bumps up against a National Forest trail and is just around the bend from cyclist-friendly Bell Rock Pathway.

🍴 Eating & Drinking

Coffee Pot Restaurant
BREAKFAST $
(☑ 928-282-6626; www.coffeepotsedona.com; 2050 W Hwy Alt 89; mains $6-14; ⊗ 6am-2pm; 👶) The go-to breakfast and lunch joint for decades, it's always busy. Meals are reasonably priced and the selection is huge – 101 types of omelet, for a start.

Sedona Memories
DELI $
(☑ 928-282-0032; 321 Jordan Rd; sandwiches under $7; ⊗ 10am-2pm Mon-Fri) This tiny local spot assembles gigantic sandwiches on slabs of homemade bread, with several vegetarian options. Cash only.

★ Elote Cafe
MEXICAN $$$
(☑ 928-203-0105; www.elotecafe.com; 771 Hwy 179, King's Ransom Hotel; mains $17-26; ⊗ 5pm-late Tue-Sat) Arrive early for some of the best, most authentic Mexican food you'll find in the region, with unusual traditional dishes you won't find elsewhere, such as the fire-roasted corn with lime and cotija cheese, or tender, smoky pork cheeks. No reservations.

Oak Creek Brewery & Grill
PUB
(☑ 928-282-3300; www.oakcreekpub.com; 336 Hwy 179; beers $5.75; ⊗ 11:30am-8:30pm; 🛜) For an outdoor town, Sedona is surprisingly short on microbreweries. Fortunately, this spacious brewpub at Tlaquepaque Village will satisfy your post-hike drinking needs. The menu includes upmarket pub-style dishes. Oak Creek also runs a low-frills brewery (☑ 928-204-1300; www.oakcreekbrew.com; 2050 Yavapai Dr; ⊗ 4-10pm Mon-Thu, noon-midnight Fri-Sun) in West Sedona; it's open later than the brewpub and has live music regularly.

ℹ Information

Sedona Chamber of Commerce Visitor Center
(☑ 800-288-7336, 928-282-7722; www.visitsedona.com; 331 Forest Rd, Uptown Sedona; ⊗ 8:30am-5pm Mon-Sat, 9am-3pm Sun) Has tourist information and last-minute hotel bookings.

ℹ Getting There & Around

The Sedona-Phoenix Shuttle (☑ 800-448-7988, 928-282-2066; www.sedona-phoenix-shuttle.com; one-way/return $50/90) runs between Phoenix Sky Harbor International Airport and Sedona eight times daily. For Jeep rentals, try Barlow Jeep Rentals (☑ 800-928-5337, 928-282-8700; www.barlowjeeprentals.com; 3009 W Hwy 89A; ⊗ 8am-6pm summer, 9am-5pm winter).

Jerome

The childhood game Chutes and Ladders comes to mind on a stroll up and down the stairways of Jerome, a historic mining town clinging to the side of Cleopatra Hill – not always successfully as evidenced by the crumbling Sliding Jail. Shabbily chic, this resurrected ghost town was known as the 'Wickedest Town in the West' during its late-1800s mining heyday, but today its historic buildings have been lovingly restored and turned into galleries, restaurants, B&Bs and wine-tasting rooms.

Feeling brave? Stand on the glass platform covering the 1910ft mining shaft at **Audrey Headframe Park** (55 Douglas Rd; ☺8am-5pm) **FREE** – it's longer than the Empire State Building by 650ft! Just ahead is the excellent **Jerome State Historic Park** (☑928-634-5381; www.azstateparks.com; adult/child $5/2; ☺8:30am-5pm), which preserves the 1916 mansion of mining mogul Jimmy 'Rawhide' Douglas and spotlights the town's mining past.

A community hospital during the town's mining years, the **Jerome Grand Hotel** (☑928-634-8200; www.jeromegrandhotel.com; 200 Hill St; r $120-205, ste $270-460; ❀ ❂) plays up its past with hospital relics in the hallways and an entertaining ghost tour that kids will enjoy. Wi-fi is available in the lobby only. The adjoining **Asylum Restaurant** (☑928-639-3197; www.theasylum.biz; 200 Hill St; lunch $10-16, dinner $20-32; ☺11am-9pm), with its valley and red-rock views, is a breathtaking spot for a fine meal and glass of wine. Downtown, the popular **Spirit Room Bar** (☑928-634-8809; www.spiritroom.com; 166 Main St; ☺10:30am-1am) is the town's liveliest watering hole. For wine drinkers, there are three tasting rooms just a few steps away.

Step into the **Flatiron Café** (☑928-634-2733; www.theflatironjerome.com; 416 Main St; breakfast $3-11, lunch $8-10; ☺8am-4pm Wed-Mon) at the Y intersection for a savory gourmet breakfast or lunch. Its specialty coffees are delicious.

The **chamber of commerce** (☑928-634-2900; www.jeromechamber.com; Hull Ave, Hwy 89A north after the Flatiron Café split; ☺10am-3pm), inside a small trailer, offers tourist information on the local attractions and art scene.

Prescott

With a historic Victorian-era downtown and a colorful Wild West history, Prescott feels like the Midwest meets cowboy country. Residents are a diverse mix of retirees, artists and families looking for a taste of yesteryear's wholesomeness. The town boasts more than 500 buildings on the National Register of Historic Places and is the home of the world's oldest rodeo. Along the plaza is **Whiskey Row**, an infamous strip of old saloons that still serve up their fair share of booze.

Just south of downtown, the fun-loving **Motor Lodge** (☑928-717-0157; www.themotorlodge.com; 503 S Montezuma St; r $99-119, ste $149, apt $159; ❀ ❂) welcomes guests with 12 snazzy bungalows arranged around a central driveway – it's indie lodging at its best.

For breakfast, mosey into the friendly **Lone Spur Café** (☑928-445-8202; www.thelonespur.com; 106 W Gurley St; breakfast & lunch $8-17, dinner $14-24; ☺8am-2pm daily, 4:30-8pm Fri), where you always order your breakfast with a biscuit and a side of sausage gravy. Portions are huge, and there are three bottles of hot sauce on every table. Cajun and Southwest specialties spice up the menu at welcoming **Iron Springs Cafe** (☑928-443-8848; www.ironspringscafe.com; 1501 Iron Springs Rd; brunch $10-13, lunch $10-15, dinner $10-21; ☺8am-8pm Wed-Sat, 9am-2pm Sun), which sits inside an old train station 3 miles northwest of downtown.

On Whiskey Row, the **Palace** (☑928-541-1996; www.historicpalace.com; 120 S Montezuma St; lunch $9-12, dinner $16-27; ☺lunch & dinner, bar opens at 11am) is an atmospheric place to drink; you enter through swinging saloon doors into a big room anchored by a Brunswick bar (saved during a 1900 fire).

The **chamber of commerce** (☑800-266-7534, 928-445-2000; www.visit-prescott.com; 117 W Goodwin St; ☺9am-5pm Mon-Fri, 10am-2pm Sat & Sun) has tourist information, including a handy walking tour pamphlet ($1) of historical Prescott.

Prescott Transit Authority (☑928-445-5470; www.prescotttransit.com; 820 E Sheldon St) runs buses to/from Phoenix airport (one-way adult/child $30/17, two hours, eight daily). Also offers a local taxi service.

Grand Canyon National Park

Mather Point, near the park's southern entrance, is usually packed elbow-to-elbow with a global array of photo-snapping tourists. But even with the crowds, there's a sense of communal wonder that keeps the scene polite. The sheer immensity of the canyon grabs you first, followed by the dramatic layers of rock, which pull you in for a closer look. Next up are the artistic details – rugged plateaus, crumbly spires, maroon ridges – that flirt and catch your eye as shadows flicker across the rock.

Snaking along its floor are 277 miles of the Colorado River, which has carved the canyon over the past six million years and exposed rocks up to two billion years old – half the age of the earth.

The two rims of the Grand Canyon offer quite different experiences; they lie more than 200 miles apart by road and are rarely visited on the same trip. Most visitors choose the South Rim with its easy access, wealth of services and vistas that don't disappoint. The quieter North Rim has its own charms; at 8200ft elevation (1000ft higher than the South Rim), its cooler temperatures support wildflower meadows and tall, thick stands of aspen and spruce.

June is the driest month, July and August the wettest. January has average overnight lows of 13°F (-11°C) to 20°F (-7°C) and daytime highs around 40°F (4°C). Summer temperatures inside the canyon regularly soar above 100°F (38°C). While the South Rim is open year-round, most visitors come between late May and early September. The North Rim is open from mid-May to mid-October.

ℹ Information

The most developed area in the **Grand Canyon National Park** (☎ 928-638-7888; www.nps. gov/grca; entrance ticket vehicles/cyclists & pedestrians $25/12) is Grand Canyon Village, 6 miles north of the South Rim Entrance Station. The North Rim has one entrance, which is 30 miles south of Jacob Lake on Hwy 67; continue another 14 miles south to the actual rim. The North Rim and South Rim are 215 miles apart by car, 21 miles on foot through the canyon, or 10 miles as the condor flies.

The park entrance ticket is valid for seven days and can be used at both rims.

All overnight hikes and backcountry camping in the park require a permit. The **Backcountry Information Center** (☎ fax 928-638-2125 928-638-7875; ☉ 8am-noon & 1-5pm, phone staffed 1-5pm Mon-Fri) accepts applications for backpacking permits ($10, plus $5 per person per night) starting four months before the proposed month. Your chances are decent if you apply early (four months in advance for spring and fall) and provide alternative hiking itineraries. Reservations are accepted in person or by mail or fax. For more information see www.nps.gov/grca/planyourvisit/backcountry-permit.htm.

If you arrive without a permit, head to the backcountry office, by Maswik Lodge, to join the waiting list.

As a conservation measure, note that the park no longer sells bottled water. Instead, fill your thermos at water filling stations along the rim or at Canyon View Marketplace. Water bottles constituted 20% of the waste generated in the park.

VISITOR CENTERS

In addition to the visitor centers listed below, information is available inside the park at **Yavapai Museum of Geology** (☉ 8am-7pm Mar-Nov, to 6pm Dec-Feb), **Verkamp's Visitor Center** (☉ 8am-7pm Mar-Nov, to 6pm Dec-Feb), **Kolb Studio** (☎ 928-638-2771; Grand Canyon Village; ☉ 8am-7pm Mar-Nov, to 6pm Dec-Feb), **Tusayan Ruin & Museum** (☎ 928-638-2305; ☉ 9am-5pm) and **Desert View Information Center** (☎ 928-638-7893; ☉ 9am-5pm).

Grand Canyon Visitor Center (www.nps. gov/grca; South Rim; ☉ 8am-5pm Mar-Nov, from 9am Dec-Feb) Three hundred yards behind Mather Point, a large plaza holds the visitor center and the Books & More Store. Outdoor bulletin boards display information about trails, tours, ranger programs and the weather. The center's bright, spacious interior includes a ranger-staffed information desk, a theater and a lecture hall, where rangers offer daily talks.

National Geographic Visitor Center (☎ 928-638-2468; www.explorethecanyon.com; 450 Hwy 64, Tusayan; adult/child $14/11; ☉ 8am-10pm Mar-Oct, 10am-8pm Nov-Feb) In Tusayan, 7 miles south of Grand Canyon Village; pay your $25 vehicle entrance fee here and spare yourself a potentially long wait at the park entrance, especially in summer. The IMAX theater screens the terrific 34-minute film *Grand Canyon – The Hidden Secrets*.

The North Rim Visitor Center (p846) is adjacent to the Grand Canyon Lodge, with maps, books, trail guides and current conditions.

South Rim

To escape the throngs, visit during fall or winter, especially on weekdays. You'll also gain some solitude by walking a short distance away from the viewpoints on the Rim Trail or by heading into the canyon itself.

◉ Sights & Activities

Driving & Hiking

A **scenic route** follows the rim on the west side of Grand Canyon Village along Hermit Rd. Closed to private vehicles March through November, the 7-mile road is serviced by the free park shuttle bus; cycling is encouraged because of the relatively light traffic. Stops offer spectacular views, and interpretive signs explain canyon features.

Hiking along the South Rim is among park visitors' favorite pastimes, with options

SOUTHWEST GRAND CANYON NATIONAL PARK

Grand Canyon National Park

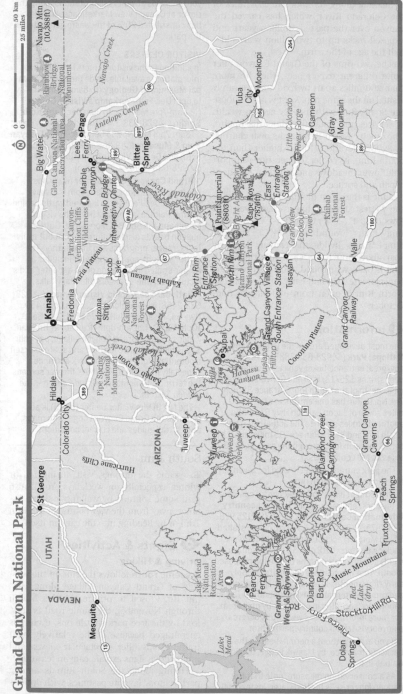

for every skill level. The **Rim Trail** is the most popular, and easiest, walk in the park. It dips in and out of the scrubby pines of Kaibab National Forest and connects a series of scenic points and historical sights over 13 miles. Portions are paved, and every viewpoint is accessed by one of the three shuttle routes. The new **Trail of Time** exhibit borders the Rim Trail just west of Yavapai Geology Museum. Here, every meter along the trail represents one million years of geologic history, with exhibits providing the details.

Desert View Drive starts to the east of Grand Canyon Village and follows the canyon rim for 26 miles to Desert View, the east entrance of the park. Pullouts offer spectacular views, and interpretive signs explain canyon features and geology.

The most popular of the corridor trails is the beautiful **Bright Angel Trail**. The steep and scenic 8-mile descent to the Colorado River is punctuated with four logical turnaround spots. Summer heat can be crippling; day hikers should either turn around at one of the two resthouses (a 3- to 6-mile round-trip) or hit the trail at dawn to safely make the longer hikes to Indian Garden and Plateau Point (9.2 and 12.2 miles round-trip respectively). Hiking to the river in one day should not be attempted. In 2013 the park spruced up the Bright Angel Trailhead by adding a shaded plaza, new restrooms and a stone trailhead marker. These improvements are just west of Bright Angel Lodge.

The **South Kaibab** is arguably one of the park's prettiest trails, combining stunning scenery and unobstructed 360-degree views with every step. Steep, rough and wholly exposed, summer ascents can be dangerous, and during this season rangers discourage all but the shortest day hikes – otherwise it's a grueling 12.6-mile round-trip to the river and back. Turn around at **Cedar Ridge**, (about 3 miles round-trip), perhaps the park's finest short day hike.

Individuals and groups who prefer a more in-depth experience while giving something back can apply for various programs with **Grand Canyon Volunteers** (☏928-774-7488; www.gcvolunteers.org). Multiday regional programs include habitat assessments, wildlife monitoring and botany training.

Cycling

Bright Angel Bicycles   BICYCLE RENTAL
(☏928-638-3055; www.bikegrandcanyon.com; 10 S Entrance Rd, Grand Canyon Visitor Center; full-day adult/child $40/30; ⊙8am-6pm May-Oct, 10am-4pm Nov, Mar-Apr & Oct) Renting 'comfort cruiser' bikes, the friendly folks here custom-fit each bike to the individual. Rate includes helmet. Also rents wheelchairs ($10 per day).

☞ Tours

Xanterra
(☏303-297-2757, 888-297-2757; www.grandcanyonlodges.com) Park tours are run by Xanterra, which has information desks at Bright Angel (p844), Maswik (p844) and Yavapai (p844) lodges. Various daily bus tours (tickets from $22) are offered.

Due to erosion concerns, half-day mule rides into the canyon from the South Rim are not offered and the NP has limited inner-canyon mule rides to those traveling all the way to Phantom Ranch. Rather than going below the rim, three-hour day trips ($123) now take riders along the rim, through the ponderosa, piñon and juniper forest to the Abyss overlook. Overnight trips (one/two people $507/895, year-round) and two-night trips (one/two people $714/1192, November to March) follow the Bright Angel Trail to the river, travel east on the River Trail and cross the river on the Kaibab Suspension Bridge. Riders spend the night at Phantom Ranch.

If you arrive at the park and want to join a mule trip the following day, ask about availability at the transportation desk at Bright Angel Lodge.

⫇ Sleeping

Advance or same-day reservations are required for the South Rim's six lodges, which are operated by **Xanterra** (☏888-297-2757, 303-297-2757; www.grandcanyonlodges.com). Use this phone number to make advance reservations (highly recommended) at any of the places (although its best to call Phantom Ranch directly) listed here. For same-day reservations or to reach a guest, call the **South Rim switchboard** (☏928-638-2631). If you can't find accommodations in the national park, try Tusayan (at South Rim Entrance Station), Valle (31 miles south), Cameron (53 miles east) or Williams (about 60 miles south).

All campgrounds and lodges are open year-round except Desert View.

Phantom Ranch   CABIN $
(☏reservations 888-297-2727; dm $46, cabin $148; ⊙year-round; ❋) It's not the Four Seasons, but this summer-campy complex has

undeniable charm. Perched beside Phantom Creek at the bottom of the canyon, the ranch has basic cabins sleeping four to 10 people and segregated dorms. Call at the first of the month for reservations 13 months ahead. The canteen serves family-style meals (breakfast from $21, dinner $29 to $44). No overnight reservation? Stop by the Bright Angel Lodge transportation desk to get on the waiting list, then show up at the desk at 6:30am the following morning to try to snag any canceled bunks.

Desert View Campground   CAMPGROUND $

(campsites $12; ☺May–mid-Oct) Near the East Entrance Station, 26 miles east of Grand Canyon Village, this first-come, first-served campground is a quieter alternative to Mather. A small cafeteria/snack shop serves meals.

Mather Campground   CAMPGROUND $

(☑877-444-6777; www.recreation.gov; Grand Canyon Village; campsites $18; ☺year-round) Well-dispersed, relatively peaceful sites amid pine and juniper trees. There are pay showers and laundry facilities nearby, drinking water, toilets, grills and a small general store. First-come, first-served during winter months.

Trailer Village   CAMPGROUND $

(☑888-297-2757, same-day reservations 928-638-2631; www.xanterra.com; Grand Canyon Village; campsites $35; ☺year-round) Camp here if everywhere else is full. You can reserve well in advance or same day. Managed by Xanterra.

Bright Angel Lodge   LODGE $$

(www.grandcanyonlodges.com; Grand Canyon Village; r without/with bathroom $83/94, suites $185-362, cabins $120-340; ☺year-round; 🌐@🛜) The log-and-stone Bright Angel offers historic charm and refurbished rooms, the cheapest of which have shared bathrooms. Don't expect a TV in these very basic rooms (think university dorm room), but rim cabins have better views than TV.

Maswik Lodge   LODGE $$

(Grand Canyon Village; r South/North $92/176, cabins $94; ☺year-round; 🌐@🛜) Set away from the rim, Maswik is comprised of 16 modern, two-story buildings. Rooms at Maswik North have private patios, air-con, cable TV and forest views; those at Maswik South are smaller with fewer amenities and more forgettable views. Cabins are available in summer only.

Kachina & Thunderbird Lodges   LODGE $$

(Grand Canyon Village; r streetside/rimside $180/191; ☺year-round; 🌐) Decent motel-style rooms in a central location. Some have canyon views.

Yavapai Lodge   LODGE $$

(Grand Canyon Village; r West/East $125/166; ☺Apr-Oct; 🌐🛜) Basic lodging amid peaceful piñon and juniper forest. No air-conditioning in Yavapai West.

★El Tovar Hotel   LODGE $$$

(Grand Canyon Village; r $183-281, ste $348-440; 🌐🛜) Open since 1905, this dark-timbered lodge encourages lingering, even if you're not a guest. Inviting porches wrap around the rambling structure and the lobby has plenty of comfy seats – better for gazing at the impressive collection of animal mounts. These public spaces show the lodgelike, genteel elegance of the park's heyday. The standard rooms are small but first-class. Suites are fantastic.

🍴 Eating & Drinking

Maswik Cafeteria   CAFETERIA $

(Maswik Lodge; mains $7-15; ☺6am-10pm) A cafeteria-style place.

Yavapai Cafeteria   CAFETERIA $

(Yavapai Lodge; breakfast $6-10, lunch & dinner $5-11; ☺6:30am-8pm) Cafeteria food, service and seating.

Canyon Village Marketplace   MARKET $

(Market Plaza; ☺8am-7pm) Stock up on groceries or hit the deli (8am to 6pm).

★El Tovar Dining Room   INTERNATIONAL $$$

(El Tovar; ☑928-638-2631, ext 6432; breakfast $9-13, lunch $10.25-16, dinner $17.25-33; ☺6:30-10:45am, 11:15am-2pm & 4:30-10pm) A stone's throw from the canyon's edge, it has the best views of any restaurant in the state, if not the country. The grand stone and dark-oak dining room warms the soul like an upscale lodge of yore, and the food, especially the steaks, makes the trip worthwhile. If you're not seated near a window, head to the verandah of the El Tovar Lounge afterward for a guaranteed Grand Canyon vista.

Arizona Room   AMERICAN $$$

(Bright Angel Lodge; lunch $8-12, dinner $8-28; ☺11:30am-3pm Mar-Oct & 4:30-10pm Mar-Dec) 🍴 Antler chandeliers hang from the ceiling and picture windows overlook the canyon. Mains include steak, chicken and fish dishes. No reservations; there's often a wait.

Bright Angel Bar BAR
(Bright Angel Lodge; mains $4-9; ⊙ 11:30am-10pm)
Come here for your post-hike beer and burger. It's a fun place to relax at night when the lack of windows and dark decor aren't such a big deal. Some evenings there might be musical entertainment. The bar is beside the charmless Bright Angel Restaurant.

❶ Getting There & Around

Most people arrive at the canyon in private vehicles or on a tour. Parking can be a chore in Grand Canyon Village. Under the Park-n-Ride program, summer visitors can buy a park ticket at the National Geographic Visitor Center, park their vehicle at a designated lot, then hop aboard a free **park shuttle** (⊙ 8am-9:30pm mid-May–early Sep) that follows the Tusayan Route to the Grand Canyon Visitor Center inside the park. Park passes are also OK for this option. The trip takes 20 minutes, and the first bus departs from Tusayan at 8am. The last bus from the park leaves at 9:30pm.

Inside the park, free park shuttles operate along three routes: around Grand Canyon Village, west along Hermits Rest Route and east along Kaibab Trail Route. Buses typically run at least twice per hour, from one hour before sunset to one hour afterward.

A free shuttle from Bright Angel Lodge during the summer months, the **Hiker's Express** (⊙ 4am, 5am & 6am Jun-Aug. 5am, 6am & 7am May & Sep) has pickups at the Backcountry Information Center and Grand Canyon Visitor Center, and then heads to the South Kaibab trailhead.

North Rim

Head here for blessed solitude; of the park's 4.4 million annual visitors, only 400,000 make the trek to the North Rim. Meadows are thick with wildflowers and dense clusters of willowy aspen and spruce trees, and the air is often crisp, the skies big and blue.

Facilities on the North Rim are closed from mid-October to mid-May, although you can drive into the park and stay at the campground until the first snow closes the road from Jacob Lake.

Call the **North Rim Switchboard** (☑ 928-638-2612) to reach facilities on the North Rim.

◉ Sights & Activities

The short and easy paved trail (0.5 miles) to **Bright Angel Point** is a canyon must. Beginning from the back porch of Grand Canyon Lodge, it goes to a narrow finger of an overlook with fabulous views.

The **North Kaibab Trail** is the North Rim's only maintained rim-to-river trail and connects with trails to the South Rim. The first 4.7 miles are the steepest, dropping 3050ft to **Roaring Springs** – a popular all-day hike. If you prefer a shorter day hike below the rim, walk just 0.75 miles down to **Coconino Overlook** or 2 miles to the **Supai Tunnel** to get a taste of steep inner-canyon hiking. The 28-mile round-trip to the Colorado River is a multiday affair. For a ranger-recommended short hike that works well for families, try the 4-mile round-trip **Cape Final** trail, which leads through ponderosa pines to sweeping views of the eastern Grand Canyon area.

SOUTHWEST GRAND CANYON NATIONAL PARK

RAFTING THE COLORADO RIVER

A boat trip down the Colorado is an epic, adrenaline-pumping adventure. The biggest single drop at Lava Falls plummets 37ft in just 300yd. But the true highlight is experiencing the Grand Canyon by looking at, not down from the rim. Its human history comes alive in ruins, wrecks and rock art. Commercial trips run from three days to three weeks and vary in the type of watercraft used. At night you camp under stars on sandy beaches (gear provided). It takes about two or three weeks to run the entire 279 miles of river through the canyon. Shorter sections of around 100 miles take four to nine days. Space is limited and the trips are popular, so book as far in advance as possible – although you might luck out and find a last-minute bargain on a rafting company Facebook page.

Arizona Raft Adventures (☑ 800-786-7238, 928-526-8200; www.azraft.com; 6-day Upper Canyon hybrid trips/paddle trips $2025/2125, 10-day Full Canyon motor trips $2965)

Arizona River Runners (☑ 800-477-7238, 602-867-4866; www.raftarizona.com; 6-day Upper Canyon oar trip $1925, 8-day Full Canyon motor trip $2650)

Canyon Trail Rides (☑ 435-679-8665; www.canyonrides.com; ☻ mid-May–mid-Oct) offers one-hour ($40) and half-day ($80, minimum age 10 years) mule trips. Of the half-day trips, one is along the rim and the other drops into the Canyon on the North Kaibab Trail.

🛏 Sleeping

Accommodations are limited to one lodge and one campground. If these are booked, try your luck 80 miles north in Kanab, UT, or 84 miles northeast in Lees Ferry. There are also campgrounds in the Kaibab National Forest north of the park.

North Rim Campground CAMPGROUND $
(☑ 928-638-7814, 877-444-6777; www.recreation.gov; tent sites $6-18, RV sites $18-25; ☻ mid-May–Oct; 🐾) This campground, 1.5 miles north of Grand Canyon Lodge, offers pleasant sites on level ground blanketed in pine needles. There is water, a store, a snack bar and coin-operated showers and laundry facilities, but no hookups. Hikers and cross-country skiers can use the campground during winter months if they have a backcountry permit. Reservations accepted.

Grand Canyon Lodge LODGE $$
(☑ advance reservations 877-386-4383, reservations outside USA 480-337-1320, same-day reservations 928-638-2611; www.grandcanyonlodgenorth.com; r $124, 2-person cabins $124-192, extra guest over 15yr $10; ☻ mid-May–mid-Oct; 🐕) Made of wood, stone and glass, the lodge enjoys a lofty perch beside the rim. Rustic yet modern cabins make up the majority of accommodations. The most expensive cabins offer two rooms, a porch and beautiful rim views. The canyon views from the Sun Room are stunning, the lobby regal. Reserve far in advance.

🍴 Eating & Drinking

The lodge will prepare sack lunches ($12), ready for pickup as early as 5:30am, for those wanting to picnic on the trail. Place your order the day before. For sandwiches, pizza and breakfast burritos, try **Deli in the Pines** (mains $4-8; ☻ 7am-9pm mid-May–mid-Oct), also at the Lodge.

★ Grand Canyon Lodge Dining Room AMERICAN $$
(☑ 928-638-2611, 928-645-6865 call Jan 1-Apr 15 for next season; www.grandcanyonlodgenorth.com; breakfast $7-12, lunch & dinner $12-30; ☻ 6:30-

10am, 11:30am-2:30pm & 4:45-9:45pm mid-May–mid-Oct) The windows are so huge that you can sit anywhere and get a good view. The menu includes rainbow trout, bison flank steak, several vegetarian dishes and Arizona-crafted mircrobrews. Dinner reservations are required. Next door is the atmospheric **Rough Rider Saloon** (snacks $2-5; ☻ breakfast 5:30am-10:30am, drinks & snacks 11:30am-10:30pm), full of memorabilia from the country's most adventurous president. Come here for coffee, pastries and breakfast burritos in the morning and saloon drinks later in the day.

Grand Canyon Cookout Experience AMERICAN $$
(adult/child/child under 6yr $30/15/free; ☻ 6:15pm Jun-Sep; 🐾) This chuck-wagon-style cookout featuring barbecue and cornbread is more of an event than a meal. Kids love it. Make arrangements at the Grand Canyon Lodge.

ℹ️ Information

North Rim Visitor Center (☑ 928-638-7864; www.nps.gov/grca; North Rim; ☻ 8am-6pm mid-May–mid-Oct, 9am-4pm Oct 16-31) Sitting beside Grand Canyon Lodge, this is the place to get information about the park. It's also the starting point for ranger-led nature walks and evening programs.

ℹ️ Getting There & Around

The **Transcanyon Shuttle** (☑ 877-638-2820, 928-638-2820; www.trans-canyonshuttle.com; one-way/return $85/160; ☻ May 15-Oct 31) departs daily from Grand Canyon Lodge for the South Rim (five hours) and is perfect for rim-to-rim hikers. Reserve at least one or two weeks in advance. A complimentary hikers' shuttle to the North Kaibab Trail departs at both 5:45am and 7:10am from Grand Canyon Lodge. You must sign up for it at the front desk 24 hours ahead; if no one signs up, it will not run.

Around the Grand Canyon

Havasu Canyon

In a hidden valley with stunning, spring-fed waterfalls and azure swimming holes, this is one of the most beautiful spots in the region. It's also hard to reach, but the hike down and back up is what makes the trip unique – and a bit of an adventure.

Located on the Havasupai Indian Reservation, Havasu Canyon is about 195 miles west of the South Rim. The four falls lie 10 miles below the rim, accessed via a moderately challenging hiking trail, and trips require an overnight stay in the nearby village of Supai.

Supai offers two sleeping options and reservations must be secured before starting out. There's a $35 entrance fee for all overnight guests. The **Havasupai Campground** (☑928-448-2180, 928-448-2141, 928-448-2121; www.havasupai.nsn.gov.tourism.html; Havasupai Tourist Enterprise, PO Box 160, Supai, AZ 86435; per night per person $17), 2 miles north of Supai, has primitive campsites along a creek. In addition, every camper must pay a $5 environmental fee. The **Havasupai Lodge** (☑928-448-2111; www.havasupai-nsn.gov/tourism.html; PO Box 159, Supai, AZ 86435; r $145; ❋) has motel rooms with canyon views but no phones or TVs. Check in by 5pm, when the lobby closes. A village cafe serves meals and accepts credit cards.

Continue through Havasu Canyon to the waterfalls and blue-green swimming holes. If you don't want to hike to Supai, call the lodge or campground to arrange for a mule or horse (round-trip to lodge/campground $135/197) to carry you there. Rides depart from Hualapai Hilltop, where the hiking trail begins. The road to Hualapai Hilltop is 7 miles east of Peach Springs off Route 66. Look for the marked turnoff and follow the road for 62 miles.

Grand Canyon West

Grand Canyon West is not part of Grand Canyon National Park, which is about 215 driving miles to the east. Run by the Hualapai Nation, the remote site is 70 miles northeast of Kingman, and the last 9 miles are unpaved and unsuitable for RVs.

Grand Canyon Skywalk   PARK
(☑928-769-2636; www.grandcanyonwest.com; per person $88; ☺7am-7pm Apr-Sep, 8am-5pm Oct-Mar) A slender see-through glass horseshoe levitates over a 4000ft chasm of the Grand Canyon. The only way to visit is to purchase a package tour. A hop-on, hop-off shuttle travels the loop road to scenic points along the rim. Tours can include lunch, horse-drawn wagon rides from an ersatz Western town, and informal Native American performances.

Northeastern Arizona

Between the brooding buttes of Monument Valley, the blue waters of Lake Powell and the fossilized logs of the Petrified Forest National Park are photogenic lands locked in ancient history. Inhabited by Native Americans for centuries, this region is largely made up of reservation land called Navajo Nation, which spills into surrounding states. The Hopi reservation is here as well, completely surrounded by Navajo land.

Lake Powell

The country's second-largest artificial reservoir and part of the **Glen Canyon National Recreation Area** (☑928-608-6200; www.nps.gov/glca; 7-day pass per vehicle $15), Lake Powell stretches between Utah and Arizona. Set amid striking red-rock formations, sharply cut canyon and dramatic desert scenery, it's water-sports heaven.

South of the lake and looking out over a pleasant stretch of the Colorado River is **Lee's Ferry** (www.nps.gov/glca; tent & RV sites $12), a very scenic stopover with first-come, first served camping.

HOPI NATION

Descendants of the Ancestral Puebloans, the Hopi are one of the most untouched tribes in the United States. Their village of **Old Oraibi** may be the oldest continuously inhabited settlement in North America.

Hopi land is surrounded by the Navajo Nation. Hwy 264 runs past the three mesas (First, Second and Third Mesa) that form the heart of the Hopi reservation. On Second Mesa, some 10 miles west of First Mesa, the **Hopi Cultural Center Restaurant & Inn** (☑928-734-2401; www.hopiculturalcenter.com; Hwy 264; r $95-110, breakfast $5-15, lunch $8-20, dinner $13-20; ☺breakfast, lunch, dinner) is as visitor-oriented as things get on the Hopi reservation. It provides food and lodging, and there's the small **Hopi Museum** (☑928-734-6650; adult/child $3/1; ☺8am-5pm Mon-Fri, 9am-3pm Sat), filled with historic photographs and introductory cultural exhibits.

Photographs, sketching and recording are not allowed.

The region's central town is **Page**, and Hwy 89 forms the main strip. The **Carl Hayden Visitor Center** (☎928-608-6404; www.nps.gov/glca; Hwy 89; ☺8am-6pm Jun-Aug, shorter hours rest of year) is located at Glen Canyon Dam, 2.5 miles north of Page. **Tours** (☎928-608-6072; www.glencanyonnha. org; adult/child $5/2.50) run by the Glen Canyon Natural History Association take you inside the dam.

To visit photogenic **Antelope Canyon** (www.navajonationparks.org/htm/antelopecanyon. htm), a stunning sandstone slot canyon with two main parts, you must join a tour. **Upper Antelope Canyon** is easier to navigate and more touristed. Several tour companies offer trips into Upper Antelope Canyon; expect a bumpy ride and a bit of a cattle call; try **Roger Ekis's Antelope Canyon Tours** (☎928-645-9102; www.antelopecanyon.com; 22 S Lake Powell Blvd; adult/child 5-12yr from $35/25). The more strenuous **Lower Antelope Canyon** sees much smaller crowds.

A deservedly popular hike is the 1.5 mile roundtrip trek to **Horseshoe Bend**, where the river wraps around a dramatic stone outcropping to form a perfect U. The trailhead is south of Page off Hwy 89, across from mile marker 541.

Chain hotels line Hwy 89 in Page and a number of independent places line 8th Ave. The revamped **Lake Powell Motel** (☎928-645-3919; www.powellmotel.com; 750 S Navajo Dr; r $69-159; ☺Apr-Oct; ✱☎), formerly Bashful Bob's, was originally constructed to house Glen Canyon Dam builders. Four units here have kitchens, and book up quickly. A fifth, smaller room is typically held for walk-ups.

For breakfast in Page, the **Ranch House Grille** (www.ranchhousegrille.com; 819 N Navajo Dr; mains $7-16; ☺6am-3pm) has good food, huge portions and fast service. The murals of local landcapes are impressive inside **Bonkers** (www.bonkerspagaz.com; 810 N Navajo

---

> ### ⓘ HIGHWAY 89
>
> Travelers should note that the 24-mile stretch of Hwy 89 between Page and Bitter Springs, which is just south of Lees Ferry, closed in February 2013 after a landslide buckled the road. Beginning in August 2013, drivers will be rerouted to Navajo Route 20, which has been paved and renamed 89T. It is the most direct route until 89A re-opens.

Dr; mains $9-22; ☺from 4pm Mon-Sat), which serves satisfying steaks, seafood, pasta and a few burgers and sandwiches.

Navajo Nation

The wounds are healing but the scars remain on Arizona's Navajo lands, a testament to the forced relocation of thousands of Native Americans to reservations.

Amid the isolation is some of North America's most spectacular scenery, including Monument Valley and Canyon de Chelly. Cultural pride remains strong and many still speak Navajo as their first language. The Navajo rely heavily on tourism; visitors can help keep their heritage alive by staying on reservation land or purchasing their renowned crafts. Stopping at roadside stalls is a nice way for personal interaction and making sure money goes straight into the artisan's pocket.

Unlike Arizona, the Navajo Nation observes Mountain daylight saving time. During summer, the reservation is one hour ahead of Arizona.

For details about hiking and camping, and required permits, visit www.navajo-nationparks.org.

CAMERON

Cameron is the gateway to the east entrance of the Grand Canyon's South Rim, but the other reason people come here is for **Cameron Trading Post** (www.camerontradingpost. com), just north of the Hwy 64 turnoff to the Grand Canyon. Food, lodging, a gift shop and a post office are in this historic settlement. It's one of the few worthwhile stops on Hwy 89 between Flagstaff and Page.

CANYON DE CHELLY NATIONAL MONUMENT

This many-fingered canyon (pronounced *duh-shay*) contains several beautiful Ancestral Puebloan sites important to Navajo history, including ancient cliff dwellings. Families still farm the land, wintering on the rims then moving to hogans on the canyon floor in spring and summer. The canyon is private Navajo property administered by the NPS. Enter hogans only with a guide and don't photograph people without their permission.

The only lodging in the park is **Sacred Canyon Lodge** (☎800-679-2473; www.sacred-canyonlodge.com; r $122-129, ste $178, cafeteria mains $5-17; breakfast, lunch & dinner; ✱@☎✱), formerly Thunderbird Lodge. It has comfortable rooms and an inexpensive cafeteria serving Navajo and American meals. The nearby Navajo-run campground has about 90 sites on a first-come, first-served basis ($10), with water but no showers.

The Canyon de Chelly **visitor center** (✆ 928-674-5500; www.nps.gov/cach; ⊙ 8am-5pm) is 3 miles from Rte 191 in the small village of Chinle. Two scenic drives follow the canyon's rim. For travel within the canyon, stop by the visitor center for a list of tour companies; this list is also on the park website.

FOUR CORNERS NAVAJO TRIBAL PARK

Don't be shy: do a spread eagle at the **four corners marker** (✆ 928-871-6647; www.navajonationparks.org; admission $3; ⊙ 8am-7pm May-Sep, 8am-5pm Oct-Apr), the middle-of-nowhere landmark that's looking spiffy after a 2010 renovation of the central plaza. The only spot in the US where you can straddle four states – Arizona, New Mexico, Colorado, and Utah – it makes a good photograph, even if it's not 100% accurate. According to government surveyors, the marker is almost 2000ft east of where it should be (but it is the legally recognized border point, regardless).

MONUMENT VALLEY NAVAJO TRIBAL PARK

With flaming-red buttes and impossibly slender spires bursting to the heavens, the Monument Valley landscape off Hwy 163 has starred in countless Hollywood Westerns and looms large in many a road-trip daydream.

For up-close views of the towering formations, you'll need to visit the **Monument Valley Navajo Tribal Park** (✆ 435-727-5874; www.navajonationparks.org/htm/monumentvalley.htm; adult/child $5/free; ⊙ drive 6am-8:30pm May-Sep, 8am-4:30pm Oct-Apr, visitor center 6am-8pm May-Sep, 8am-5pm Oct-Apr), where a rough and unpaved scenic driving loop covers 17 miles of stunning valley views. You can drive it in your own vehicle or take a tour (1½ hours $75, 2½ hours $95) through one of the kiosks in the parking lot (tours enter areas private vehicles can't).

Inside the tribal park is the **View Hotel at Monument Valley** (✆ 435-727-5555; www.monumentvalleyview.com; Hwy 163; r $209-265, ste $299-329; 🅿 @ 🛜). Built in harmony with the landscape, the sandstone-colored hotel blends naturally with its surroundings,

and most of the 96 rooms have private balconies facing the monuments. The Navajo-based specialties at the adjoining restaurant (mains $10 to $30, no alcohol) are mediocre, but the red-rock panorama is stunning. Wi-fi is available in the lobby. A gift shop and small museum are within the hotel complex. At press time the campground was closed for construction.

The historic **Goulding's Lodge** (✆ 435-727-3231; www.gouldings.com; r $205-242, tent sites $26, RV sites $5, cabins $92; 🅿 🛜 ♨ 🐕), just across the border in Utah, offers lodge rooms, camping and small cabins. Book early for summer. In Kayenta, 20 miles south, there are a handful of okay hotels. Try the **Wetherill Inn** (✆ 928-697-3231; www.wetherillinn.com; 1000 Main St/Hwy 63; r incl breakfast $136; 🅿 @ 🛜 ♨) if everything in Monument Valley is booked.

Winslow

'Standing on a corner in Winslow, Arizona, such a fine sight to see...' Sound familiar? Thanks to the Eagles' twangy 1970s tune 'Take It Easy,' otherwise nondescript Winslow has earned its wings in pop-culture heaven. A small **park** (www.standinonthecorner.com; 2nd St) on Route 66 at Kinsley Ave pays homage to the band.

Just 50 miles east of Petrified Forest National Park, Winslow is a good regional base. Old motels border Route 66, and eateries sprinkle the downtown. The inviting 1929 **La Posada** (✆ 928-289-4366; www.laposada.org; 303 E 2nd St; r $119-169; 🅿 🛜 ♨) is a restored hacienda designed by star architect du jour Mary Jane Colter. Elaborate tilework, glass-and-tin chandeliers, Navajo rugs and other details accent its palatial Western-style elegance. The on-site restaurant, the much-lauded **Turquoise Room** (www.theturquoiseroom.net; La Posada; breakfast $8-12, lunch $9-13, dinner $19-40; ⊙ 7am-9pm), serves the best meals between Flagstaff and Albuquerque; dishes have a neo-Southwestern flair.

Petrified Forest National Park

The multicolored Painted Desert here is strewn with fossilized logs predating the dinosaurs. This **national park** (✆ 928-524-6228; www.nps.gov/pefo; vehicle/walk in, bicycle & motorcycle $10/5; ⊙ 7am-8pm Jun & Jul, shorter hour Aug-May) is an extraordinary site. The hard-to-miss **visitor center** is just half a mile north of I-40 and has maps and information on guided tours and science lectures.

The park straddles I-40 at exit 311, 25 miles east of Holbrook. From this exit, a 28-mile paved park road offers a splendid **scenic drive**. There are no campsites, but a number of short trails, ranging from less than a mile to 2 miles, pass through the best stands of petrified rock and ancient Native American dwellings in the park. Those prepared for rugged backcountry camping need to pick up a free permit at the visitor center.

Western Arizona

The Colorado River is alive with sun worshippers at Lake Havasu City, while Route 66 offers well-preserved stretches of classic highway near Kingman. South of the I-10, the wild, empty landscape is among the most barren in the West. If you're already here, there are some worthwhile sites, but there's nothing worth planning an itinerary around unless you're a Route 66 or boating fanatic.

Kingman & Around

Faded motels and gas stations galore grace Kingman's main drag, but several turn-of-the-19th-century buildings remain. If you're following the Route 66 trail (aka Andy Devine Ave here) or looking for cheap lodging, it's worth a stroll.

Pick up maps and brochures at the historic **Powerhouse Visitor Center** (☑866-427-7866, 928-753-6106; www.gokingman.com; 120 W Andy Devine Ave; ⊙8am-5pm), which has a small but engaging **Route 66 museum** (☑928-753-9889; www.kingmantourism.org; 120 W Andy Devine Ave; adult/child/senior $4/free/3; ⊙9am-5pm).

A cool neon sign draws road-trippers to the **Hilltop Motel** (☑928-753-2198; www.hilltopmotelaz.com; 1901 E Andy Devine Ave; r $44; ❋@🛜❋🐾) on Route 66. Rooms are a bit of a throwback, but are well kept, and the views are superb. Pets (dogs only) stay for $5. As rednecks, we can confirm that the pork at **Redneck's Southern Pit BBQ** (www.redneckssouthernpitbbq.com; 420 E Beale St; mains $5-22; ⊙11am-8pm Tue-Sat; 🖼) is tasty, but Southerners rarely use the word 'sammich,' as displayed on the menu. 'Big ole tater,' however, is fine.

Lake Havasu City

When the city of London auctioned off its 1831 bridge in the late 1960s, developer Robert McCulloch bought it, took it apart, shipped it, and then reassembled it at Lake Havasu City, which sits along a dammed-up portion of the Colorado River. The place attracts hordes of young spring-breakers and weekend warriors who come to play in the water and party hard. An 'English Village' of pseudo-British pubs and tourist gift shops surrounds the bridge and houses the **visitor center** (☑928-855-5655; www.golakehavasu.com; 422 English Village; ⊙9am-5pm; 🛜) where you can pick up tourist information and access the internet.

The hippest hotel in town is **Heat** (☑928-854-2833; www.heathotel.com; 1420 N McCulloch Blvd; r $209-299, ste $249-439; ❋❋), a slick boutique property where the front desk doubles as a bar. Rooms are contemporary and most have private patios with views of London Bridge. For a hearty, open-air breakfast, rise and shine at the **Red Onion** (☑928-505-0302; www.redonionhavasu.com; 2013 N McCulloch Blvd; mains $7-12; ⊙7am-2pm), a popular eatery where the menu is loaded with omelets and diet-busting fare. For microbrews and good pub grub, try the **Barley Brothers** (☑928-505-7837; www.barleybrothers.com; 1425 N McCulloch Blvd; mains $9-24; ⊙11am-9pm Sun-Thu, to 10pm Fri & Sat), which has great views of the lake.

Tucson

Arizona's second-largest city is set in the Sonoran Desert, full of rolling, sandy hills and crowds of cacti. The vibe here is ramshackle-cool and cozy compared with the shiny vastness of Phoenix. A college town, Tucson (the 'c' is silent) is home turf to the 40,000-strong University of Arizona (U of A) and was an artsy, dress-down kind of place before that was the cool thing to be. Eclectic shops and scores of funky restaurants and bars flourish in this arid ground. Tucsonans are proud of the city's geographic and cultural proximity to Mexico (65 highway miles south); more than 35% of the population is of Mexican or Central American descent.

◉ Sights & Activities

Downtown Tucson and the historic district are east of I-10 exit 258. About a mile northeast of downtown is the U of A campus; 4th Ave is the main drag here, packed with cafes, bars and interesting shops. For downtown's historic highlights, pick up a Presidio Trail walking tour map at the visitor center (p854).

Saguaro National Park
PARK

(⌨ Tucson Mountain District 520-733-5158, headquarters 520-733-5100; www.nps.gov/sagu; 2700 N Kinney Rd, western district; 7-day pass per vehicle/bicycle $10/5; ⊘ vehicles sunrise-sunset, walkers & cyclists 24hr) This prickly canvas of green cacti and desert scrub is split in half by 30 miles of freeway and farms. Both sections sit at the edges of Tucson, but are still officially within the city.

You'll have a nice time exploring in either section, but if you want to make a day of it, head to **Saguaro West** (Tucson Mountain District), where you'll find several fun activities in and around the park. For maps and ranger-led programs, stop at the **Red Hills Visitor Center** (⌨ 520-733-5158; 2700 N Kinney Rd; ⊘ 9am-5pm), which is also the starting point for the **Cactus Garden Trail**, a short, wheelchair-accessible path with interpretive signs for many of the park's cacti. The **Bajada Loop Drive**, an unpaved 6-mile loop that begins 1.5 miles west of the visitor center, provides fine views of cactus forests, several picnic spots and access to trailheads.

Saguaro East is 15 miles east of downtown. The **visitor center** (⌨ 520-733-5153; 3693 S Old Spanish Trail; ⊘ 9am-5pm) has information about day hikes, horseback riding and backcountry camping. Backcountry camping requires a permit ($6 per site per day) and must be obtained by noon on the day of your hike. This section of the park has about 130 miles of hiking and 5.3 miles of mountain biking. The meandering 8-mile **Cactus Forest Scenic Loop Drive**, a paved road open to cars and bicycles, provides access to picnic areas, trailheads and viewpoints.

★ **Arizona-Sonora Desert Museum**
MUSEUM

(⌨ 520-883-2702; www.desertmuseum.org; 2021 N Kinney Rd; adult/child Sep-May $14.50/5, Jun-Aug $12/4; ⊘ 8:30am-5pm Oct-Feb) This tribute to the Sonoran Desert is one part zoo, one part botanical garden and one part museum – a trifecta that'll keep young and old entertained for easily half a day. All sorts of desert denizens, from precocious coatis to playful prairie dogs, make their home in natural enclosures hemmed in by invisible fences. The grounds are thick with desert plants,

MINI TIME MACHINE MUSEUM OF MINIATURES

'Meddle ye not in the affairs of Dragons, for ye are crunchy and tasteth good with condiments,' reads the sign beside the Pocket Dragons, one of several magical creatures inhabiting the Enchanted Realm gallery at this gobsmackingly fun **museum** (www.theminitimemachine.org; 4455 E Camp Lowell Rd; adult/child $9/6; ⊘ 9am-4pm Tue-Sat, noon-4pm Sun; ♿). Here you can walk over a snowglobe-y Christmas village, peer into intricate mini-homes built in the 1700s and 1800s, and search for the tiny inhabitants of a magical tree. This is a great museum for families and for adults who still have a sense of fun.

To get here from downtown, follow E Broadway Blvd east 3.5 miles. Turn left onto N Alvernon Way and drive 3 miles to E Fort Lowell Rd, which turns into Camp Lowell. Turn right and continue almost 1 mile.

and docents are on hand to answer questions and give demonstrations. Strollers and wheelchairs are available, and there's a gift shop, art gallery, restaurant and cafe. Hours vary seasonally.

Old Tucson Studios
FILM LOCATION

(⌨ 520-883-0100; www.oldtucson.com; 201 S Kinney Rd; adult/child $17/11; ⊘ hours vary; ♿) A few miles southeast of the Arizona-Sonora Desert Museum, Old Tucson Studios was an actual Western film set. Today it's a Western theme park with shootouts and stagecoach rides. Call or check website for opening hours.

Pima Air & Space Museum
MUSEUM

(⌨ 520-574-0462; www.pimaair.org; 6000 E Valencia Rd; adult/child/senior & military $16/9/13; ⊘ 9am-5pm, last admission 4pm; ♿) An SR-71 Blackbird spy plane and JFK's Air Force One are among the stars at this private aircraft museum, home to 300 'birds.' Hard-core plane-spotters should book ahead for the 90-minute bus tour of the nearby 309th **Aerospace Maintenance & Regeneration Center** (AMARG; adult/child $7/4; ⊘ Mon-Fri, departure times vary seasonally) – aka the 'boneyard' – where almost 4000 aircraft are mothballed. Book through the Pima Air & Space Museum.

SOUTHWEST TUCSON

✦ Festivals & Events

Fiesta de los Vaqueros RODEO
(Rodeo Week; ☑ 520-741-2233; www.tucsonrodeo.com; ☺ last week of Feb) This huge nonmotorized parade with Western-themed floats is a locally famous spectacle.

⬛ Sleeping

Lodging prices vary considerably, with lower rates in summer and fall. To sleep under stars and saguaros, try **Gilbert Ray Campground** (☑ 520-877-6000; www.pima.gov/nrpr/camping; Kinney Rd; tent/RV sites $10/20) near the western district of Saguaro National Park.

Roadrunner Hostel & Inn HOSTEL $
(☑ 520-940-7280; www.roadrunnerhostelinn.com; 346 E 12th St; dm/r incl breakfast $22/45; ✴ @ ⬠) This comfortable hostel within walking distance of the arts district has a large kitchen, free coffee and waffles in the morning, and a big-screen TV for watching movies. Dorms close between noon and 3pm for cleaning. Takes cash and traveler's checks only.

Quality Inn Flamingo Hotel MOTEL $
(☑ 520-770-1910; www.flamingohoteltucson.com; 1300 N Stone Ave; r incl breakfast $65-80; ✴ @ ⬠ ⬛ ☕) Though not as spiffy as it used to be, this motel retains its great 1950s Rat Pack vibe. And the fact that Elvis slept here doesn't hurt. Rooms have stylish striped bedding, comfy beds and flat-screen plasma TVs. Pets stay for $20 per day.

★ Catalina Park Inn B&B $$
(☑ 520-792-4541; www.catalinaparkinn.com; 309 E 1st St; r $140-170; ☺ closed Jul & Aug; ✴ @ ⬠) Style, hospitality and comfort merge seamlessly at this inviting B&B just west of the University of Arizona. Hosts Mark Hall and Paul Richard have poured their hearts into restoring this 1927 Med-style villa, and their efforts are on display in the six guest rooms, from the oversized and over-the-top peacock-blue-and-gold Catalina Room to the white and uncluttered East Room with an iron canopy bed.

Hotel Congress HISTORIC HOTEL $$
(☑ 520-622-8848; www.hotelcongress.com; 311 E Congress St; r $89-129; ⓟ ✴ @ ⬠ ☕) A little bit hip, a little bit historic and whole lotta fun, the Congress is a nonstop buzz of activity, mostly because of its popular bar, restaurant and nightclub. Infamous bank robber John Dillinger and his gang were captured here in

1934 – check out the wall of photos and articles beside the lobby. Many rooms have period furnishings, rotary phones and wooden radios – but no TVs. Ask for a room at the far end of the hotel if you're noise-sensitive. Pets stay for $10 per night.

Windmill Inn at St Philips Plaza HOTEL $$
(☑ 520-577-0007; www.windmillinns.com; 4250 N Campbell Ave; r incl breakfast $120-134; ✴ @ ⬠ ⬛ ☕) This modern, friendly place wins kudos for spacious two-room suites (no charge for kids under 18 years of age), free continental breakfast, a lending library, a heated pool and free bike rentals. Pets stay free.

Arizona Inn RESORT $$$
(☑ 800-933-1093, 520-325-1541; www.arizonainn.com; 2200 E Elm St; r $329-399, ste $459-579; ✴ @ ⬠ ⬛) The mature gardens and old Arizona grace provide a respite not only from city life but also from the 21st century. Sip coffee on the porch, take high tea in the library, lounge by the small pool or join a game of croquet, then retire to rooms furnished with antiques. The on-site spa is our favorite in town.

✖ Eating

Your best bet for great food at good prices is 4th Ave; we've listed some of Tucson's standouts.

Mi Nidito MEXICAN $
(☑ 520-622-5081; www.minidito.net; 1813 S 4th Ave; mains $6-13; ☺ lunch & dinner Wed-Sun) The wait is worth it at this bustling spot (My Little Nest), where Bill Clinton's order has become the signature president's plate: a heaping mound of tacos, tostadas, burritos, enchiladas etc – groaning under melted cheese. Also give the prickly pear cactus chile or the *birria* (spicy, shredded beef) a whirl.

★ Cafe Poca Cosa SOUTH AMERICAN $$
(☑ 520-622-6400; www.cafepocacosatucson.com; 110 E Pennington St; lunch $12-15, dinner $18-26; ☺ 11am-9pm Tue-Thu, to 10pm Fri & Sat) At this award-winning Nuevo-Mexican bistro, a chalkboard menu circulates between tables because dishes change twice daily. It's all freshly prepared, innovative and beautifully presented. The undecided can't go wrong by ordering the Plato Poca Cosa and letting chef Suzana D'avila decide. Great margaritas, too.

Cup Cafe   AMERICAN, GLOBAL **$$**
(📞 520-798-1618; www.hotelcongress.com/food;
311 E Congress St; breakfast $7-12, lunch $10-12,
dinner $13-23; ⊙ 7am-10pm Sun-Thu, to 11pm Fri
& Sat; 🍷) Wine-bottle chandeliers above.
Penny-tiled floor below. And 'Up on Crippled
Creek' on the speakers. Yep, we're gonna like
it here. In the morning, choices include a
Creole dish with andouille sausage, eggs
and potatoes, as well as cast-iron baked eggs
with Gruyere cheese. There's a global mix of
dishes for lunch and dinner, with a decent
selection of vegetarian entrees. The coffee is
excellent.

Lovin' Spoonfuls   VEGAN **$$**
(📞 520-325-7766; 2990 N Campbell Ave; breakfast
$7-9, lunch $6-8, dinner $8-12; ⊙ 9:30am-9pm
Mon-Sat, 10am-3pm Sun; 🍷) Burgers, country-
fried chicken, a BLT, salads... The menu here
reads like a typical cafe, but there's one big
difference: no animal products find their
way into this vegan haven.

Hub Restaurant & Creamery   AMERICAN **$$**
(📞 520-207-8201; www.hubdowntown.com; 266 E
Congress Ave; lunch $9-16, dinner $10-21; ⊙ 11am-
midnight Sun-Wed, to 2am Thu-Sat) Upscale com-
fort food is the name of the game here, plus
a few sandwiches and salads. If you don't
want a meal, pop in for a scoop of flavor-
packed gourmet ice cream – bacon scotch
anyone?

El Charro Café   MEXICAN **$$**
(📞 520-622-1922; www.elcharrocafe.om; 311 N
Court Ave; lunch $6-10, dinner $7-18; ⊙ lunch &
dinner) The Flin family has been making innovative Mexican food at this busy hacienda
since 1922. It's famous for the *carne seca*,
sundried lean beef that's been reconstituted,
shredded and grilled with green chile and
onions.

🍷 **Drinking & Entertainment**

Downtown 4th Ave, near 6th St, is the happening bar-hop spot, and there are a number
of nightclubs on downtown Congress St.

Che's Lounge   BAR
(📞 520-623-2088; 350 N 4th Ave; ⊙ noon-2am) A
slightly skanky but hugely popular watering hole that rocks with live music Saturday
nights. And it never charges a cover.

Thunder Canyon Brewery   MICROBREWERY
(www.thundercanyonbrewery.com; 220 E Broadway
Blvd; ⊙ 11am-11pm Sun-Wed, to 2am Thu-Sat) This
cavernous new microbrewery, within walk-

ing distance of Hotel Congress, serves its
own brews as well as beer from other breweries. Forty beers on tap.

Chocolate Iguana   COFFEE SHOP
(www.chocolateiguanaon4th.com; 500 N 4th Ave;
⊙ 7am-8pm Mon-Thu, 7am-10pm Fri, 8am-10pm
Sat, 9am-6pm Sun) For coffee-lovers and choc-
oholics, this is the place.

Club Congress   LIVE MUSIC
(📞 520-622-8848; www.hotelcongress.com; 311 E
Congress St; cover free-$24) Live and DJ music
are found at this very popular place that's
sometimes a rock hangout and sometimes a
dance club. The crowd depends on the night,
but it's almost always a happening place.

ℹ️ **Information**

EMERGENCY & MEDICAL SERVICES
Police (📞 520-791-4444; http://cms3.
tucsonaz.gov; 270 S Stone Ave)
Tucson Medical Center (📞 520-327-5461;
www.tmcaz.com/TucsonMedicalCenter; 5301 E
Grant Rd) Has 24-hour emergency services.

INTERNET ACCESS
Joel D Valdez Main Library (📞 520-594-5500;
101 N Stone Ave; ⊙ 9am-8pm Mon-Wed, 9am-
6pm Thu, 9am-5pm Fri, 10am-5pm Sat, 1-5pm
Sun; 📶) Free internet, including wi-fi.

MEDIA
Arizona Daily Star (http://azstarnet.com) The
Tucson region's daily newspaper.
Tucson Weekly (www.tucsonweekly.com) A
free weekly full of entertainment and restau-
rant listings.

POST
Post office (📞 520-629-9268; 825 E University Blvd, Suite 111; ⊙ 8am-5pm Mon-Fri,
9am-12:30pm Sat)

SOUTHWEST TUCSON

TOURIST INFORMATION

Tucson Convention & Visitors Bureau
(☑800-638-8350, 520-624-1817; www.visit-tucson.org; 100 S Church Ave; ⊙9am-5pm Mon-Fri, to 4pm Sat & Sun) Ask for its free *Official Destination Guide*.

❶ Getting There & Around

Tucson International Airport (☑520-573-8100; www.flytucson.com; 7250 S Tucson Blvd) is 15 miles south of downtown. **Arizona Stagecoach** (☑520-889-1000; www.azstagecoach.com) runs shared van service with fares for about $25 between downtown and the airport. **Greyhound** (☑520-792-3475; www.greyhound.com; 471 W Congress St) runs buses to Phoenix ($21 to $23, two hours, daily) and other destinations. The station is on the western end of Congress St, 3 miles from downtown. **Amtrak** (☑800-872-7245, 520-623-4442; www.amtrak.com; 400 E Toole Ave) is across from Hotel Congress and has train services to Los Angeles (from $56, 10 hours, three weekly) on the Sunset Limited.

The **Ronstadt Transit Center** (215 E Congress St, cnr Congress St & 6th Ave) is the major downtown transit hub. From here **Sun Tran** (☑520-792-9222; www.suntran.com) buses serve metropolitan Tucson (day pass $3.50).

Around Tucson

The places listed here are less than 1½ hours' drive from town and make great day trips.

West of Tucson

You want wide solitude? Follow Hwy 86 west from Tuscon into some of the emptiest parts of the Sonoran Desert – except for the ubiquitous green-and-white border patrol trucks.

The lofty **Kitt Peak National Observatory** (☑520-318-8726; www.noao.edu/kpno; Hwy 86; visitor center by donation; ⊙9am-4pm) west of Sells features the largest collection of optical telescopes in the world. Guided tours (adult/child $9.75/4.25 November to May, $7.75/3.25 June to October, at 10am, 11:30am and 1:30pm) last about an hour. Book two to four weeks in advance for the worthwhile nightly observing program (adult/child $49/45; no programs from mid-July through August because of monsoon season). Clear, dry skies equal an awe-inspiring glimpse of the cosmos. Dress warmly, buy gas in Tucson (the nearest gas station is 30 miles from the observatory) and note that children under eight years of age are not allowed at the evening program for safety reasons. The picnic area

draws amateur astronomers at night. It's about a 75-minute drive from Tucson.

If you truly want to get away from it all, you can't get much further off the grid than the huge and exotic **Organ Pipe Cactus National Monument** (☑520-387-6849; www.nps.gov/orpi; Hwy 85; per vehicle $8; ⊙visitor center 8:30am-4:30pm) along the Mexican border. It's a gorgeous, forbidding land that supports an astonishing number of animals and plants, including 28 species of cacti, first and foremost its namesake organ-pipe. A giant columnar cactus, it differs from the more prevalent saguaro in that its branches radiate from the base. The 21-mile **Ajo Mountain Drive** takes you through a spectacular landscape of steep-sided, jagged cliffs and rock tinged a faintly hellish red. There are 208 first-come, first-served sites at **Twin Peaks Campground** (www.nps.gov/orpi; tent/RV sites $12) by the visitor center.

South of Tucson

South of Tucson, I-19 is the main route to Nogales and Mexico. Along the way are several interesting stops.

The striking **Mission San Xavier del Bac** (☑520-294-2624; www.patronatosanxavier.org; 1950 W San Xavier Rd; donations appreciated; ⊙museum 8:30am-5pm, church 7am-5pm), 9 miles south of downtown Tucson, is Arizona's oldest European building still in use. It's a graceful blend of Moorish, Byzantine and late Mexican Renaissance architecture with an unexpectedly ornate interior.

At exit 69, 16 miles south of the mission, the **Titan Missile Museum** (☑520-625-7736; www.titanmissilemuseum.org; 1580 W Duval Mine Rd, Sahuarita; adult/child/senior $9.50/6/8.50; ⊙8:45am-5pm) features an underground launch site for Cold War–era intercontinental ballistic missiles. Tours are chilling and informative.

If history or shopping for crafts interest you, head 48 miles south of Tucson to the small village of **Tubac** (www.tubacaz.com), with more than 100 galleries, studios and shops.

Patagonia & the Mountain Empire

This lovely riparian region, sandwiched between the Mexican border and the Santa Rita and Patagonia Mountains, is one of the shiniest gems in the Arizona jewel box. It's a tranquil destination for bird-watching and wine tasting.

Bird-watchers and nature-lovers wander the gentle trails at the **Patagonia-Sonoita Creek Preserve** (☑ 520-394-2400; www.nature.org/arizona; 150 Blue Heaven Rd; admission $6; ☉ 6:30am-4pm Wed-Sun Apr-Sep, 7:30am-4pm Wed-Sun Oct-Mar), an enchanting creekside willow and cottonwood forest managed by the Nature Conservancy. The peak migratory seasons are April through May, and late August to September. For a leisurely afternoon of wine tasting, head to the villages of Sonoita and Elgin north of Patagonia (see www.arizonavinesandwines.com). The big-sky views are terrific.

If you stick around for dinner, try the fantastic gourmet pizzas at **Velvet Elvis** (☑ 520-394-2102; www.velvetelvispizza.com; 292 Naugle Ave, Patagonia; mains $10-26; ☉ 11:30am-8:30pm Thu-Sat, to 7:30pm Sun). Salute the old West and its simple charms at the **Stage Stop Inn** (☑ 520-394-2211; www.stagestophotelpatagonia.com; 303 McKeown, Patagonia; s $79, d $89-99, ste $109; 🖥🖢🏠), where rooms surround a central courtyard and pool. The stage coach did indeed stop here on the Butterfield Trail.

A small **visitor center** (☑ 888-794-0060; www.patagoniaaz.com; 307 McKeown Ave, Patagonia; ☉ 10am-5pm Mon-Thu & Sat, 11am-4pm Fri) is tucked inside Mariposa Books & More in Patagonia.

Southeastern Arizona

Chockablock with places that loom large in the history of the Wild West, southern Arizona is home to the wonderfully preserved mining town of Bisbee, the OK Corral in Tombstone, and a wonderland of stone spires at Chiricahua National Monument.

Kartchner Caverns State Park

The emphasis is on education at **Kartchner Caverns State Park** (☑ information 520-586-4100, reservations 520-586-2283; http://azstateparks.com; Hwy 90; park entrance per vehicle/bicycle $6/3, Rotunda Tour adult/child $23/13, Big Room Tour mid-Oct–mid-Apr $23/13; ☉ 8am-5pm Jun-Sep, 7am-6pm Oct-May), a 2.5-mile wet limestone fantasia of rocks. Two guided tours explore different areas of the caverns, which were 'discovered' in 1974. The Rotunda/Throne Room Tour is open year-round; the Big Room Tour closes in mid-April for five months to protect the migratory bats

that roost here. The park is 9 miles south of Benson, off I-10 at exit 302. The $6 entrance fee is waived for reserved tour tickets.

Chiricahua National Monument

The towering rock spires at remote but mesmerizing **Chiricahua National Monument** (☑ 520-824-3560; www.nps.gov/chir; Hwy 181; adult/child $5/free) in the Chiricahua Mountains sometimes rise hundreds of feet high and often look like they're on the verge of tipping over. The **Bonita Canyon Scenic Drive** takes you 8 miles to Massai Point (6870ft) where you'll see thousands of spires positioned on the slopes like some petrified army. There are numerous hiking trails, but if you're short on time, hike the **Echo Canyon Trail** at least half a mile to the Grottoes, an amazing 'cathedral' of giant boulders where you can lie still and enjoy the wind-caressed silence. The monument is 36 miles southeast of Willcox off Hwy 186/181.

Tombstone

In Tombstone's 19th-century heyday as a booming mining town the whiskey flowed and six-shooters blazed over disputes large and small, most famously at the OK Corral. Now a National Historic Landmark, it attracts hordes of tourists to its old Western buildings, stagecoach rides and gunfight reenactments.

And yes, you must visit the **OK Corral** (☑ 520-457-3456; www.ok-corral.com; Allen St btwn 3rd & 4th Sts; admission $10, without gunfight $6; ☉ 9am-5pm), site of the legendary gunfight where the Earps and Doc Holliday took on the McLaurys and Billy Clanton on October 26, 1881. The McClaurys and Clanton now rest at the **The Boot Hill Graveyard** on Hwy 80 north of town. Also make time for the dusty **Bird Cage Theater** (☑ 520-457-3421; 517 E Allen St; adult/child/senior $10/8/9; ☉ 9am-6pm), a one-time dance hall and saloon now crammed with historic odds and ends. And a merman.

The **Visitor & Information Center** (☑ 520-457-3929; www.tombstonechamber.com; cnr 395 E Allen & 4th Sts; ☉ 9am-5pm) has walking maps and local recommendations.

Bisbee

Oozing old-fashioned ambience, Bisbee is a former copper-mining town that's now a delightful mix of aging Bohemians, elegant buildings, sumptuous restaurants and charming hotels. Most businesses are found in the Historic District (Old Bisbee), along Subway and Main Sts.

To burrow under the earth in a tour led by the retired miners who worked here, take the **Queen Mine Tour** (☑ 520-432-2071; www.queenminetour.com; 478 Dart Rd, off Hwy 80; adult/child $13/5.50; ☺ tours 9am-3:30pm; ☒). Right outside of town, check out the **Lavender Pit**, an ugly yet impressive testament to strip mining.

Rest your head at **Shady Dell RV Park** (☑ 520-432-3567; www.theshadydell.com; 1 Douglas Rd; rates $87-145, closed early Jul–mid-Sep; ☒), a kitschy trailer park extraordinaire. Everything's done up with fun, retro furnishings. Swamp coolers provide cold air. You can sleep in a covered wagon at the quirky but fun **Bisbee Grand Hotel** (☑ 520-432-5900; www.bisbeegrandhotel.com; 61 Main St, Bisbee; r incl breakfast $89-175; ☒ ☎), which brings the Old West to life (or maybe it never died) with Victorian-era decor and a kick-up-your-spurs saloon.

For good eats, stroll up Main St and pick a restaurant – you can't go wrong. For fine American food, try stylish **Cafe Roka** (☑ 520-432-5153; www.caferoka.com; 35 Main St; dinner $17-24; ☺ 5-9pm Thu-Sat), where four-course dinners include salad, soup, sorbet and a rotating choice of crowd-pleasing mains. Continue up Main St for wood-fired pizzas and punk-rock style at **Screaming Banshee Pizza** (☑ 520-432-1300; 200 Tombstone Canyon Rd; pizzas $7-15; ☺ 4-9pm Tue & Wed, 11am-10pm Thu-Sat, 11am-9pm Sun). Bars cluster in Brewery Gulch, at the south end of Main St.

The **visitor center** (☑ 520-432-3554; www.discoverbisbee.com; 478 Dart Rd; ☺ 8am-5pm Mon-Fri, 10am-4pm Sat & Sun), in the Queen Mine Tour Building just south of downtown, is a good place to start.

UTAH

Shhhhh, don't tell. We wouldn't want word to get out that this oft-overlooked state is really one of nature's most perfect playgrounds. Utah's rugged terrain comes ready-made for hiking, biking, rafting, rappelling, rock climbing, skiing, snowboarding, snow riding, horseback riding, four-wheel driving... Need we go on?

More than 65% of the state's lands are public, including 12 national parks and monuments – a dazzling display of geology that leaves many awestruck. Southern Utah is a seemingly endless expanse of sculpted sandstone desert, its red-rock country defined by soaring Technicolor cliffs, spindles and spires. The 11,000ft-high forest- and snow-covered peaks of the Wasatch and other mountains and valleys dominate northeastern Utah.

Across the state you'll find well-organized towns with pioneer-era buildings dating to when the first Mormon settlers arrived; still today, church members make up more than 50% of the wonderfully polite population. Rural towns may be quiet and conservative, but the rugged beauty has attracted many outdoorsy, independent thinkers as well. Salt Lake and Park cities especially have vibrant nightlife and foodie scenes.

So come wonder at the roadside geologic kaleidoscope, hike out into the vast expanses or enjoy a great craftworks micro-brew. Just don't tell your friends: we'd like to keep this secret to ourselves.

History

Traces of the Ancestral Puebloan (or Anasazi) and Fremont people, this land's earliest human inhabitants, can today be seen in the rock art and ruins they left behind. But it was the modern Ute, Paiute and Navajo tribes who were living here when settlers of European heritage arrived in large numbers. Led by second church president, Brigham Young, Mormons fled to this territory to escape religious persecution starting in the late 1840s. They set about attempting to settle every inch of their new land, no matter how inhospitable, which resulted in skirmishes with Native Americans – and more than one abandoned ghost town.

For nearly 50 years after the United States acquired the Utah Territory from Mexico, petitions for statehood were rejected as a result of the Mormon practice of polygamy (taking multiple wives), which was illegal in the US. Tension and prosecutions grew until 1890, when Mormon leader Wilford Woodruff had a divine revelation and the church officially discontinued the practice. Utah became the 45th state in 1896. The modern Mormon church, now called the Church of Jesus Christ of Latter-Day Saints (LDS) continues to exert a strong influence here.

ⓘ Information

Note that it can be difficult to change currency outside Salt Lake City, but ATMs are widespread.

Utah Office of Tourism (☑800-200-1160; www.utah.com) Publishes the free *Utah Travel Guide*; runs several visitor centers statewide.

Utah State Parks & Recreation Department (☑801-538-7220; www.stateparks.utah.gov) Produces comprehensive guide to the 40-plus state parks; available online and at visitor centers.

ⓘ Getting There & Away

Salt Lake City (SLC) has the state's only international airport. It may be cheaper to fly into Las Vegas (425 miles south) and rent a car.

ⓘ Getting Around

You will need a private vehicle to get around anywhere besides SLC and Park City. Utah towns are typically laid out in a grid with streets aligned north–south or east–west. There's a zero point in the town center at the intersection of two major streets (often called Main St and Center St). Addresses and numerical street names radiate out from this point, rising by 100 with each city block. Thus, 500 South 400 East will be five blocks south and four blocks east of the zero point. The system is complicated to explain, but thankfully it's quite easy to use.

Salt Lake City

Snuggled up against the soaring peaks of the Wasatch Mountains, Salt Lake City is a small town with just enough edge to satisfy city slickers. Yes, it is the Mormon equivalent of Vatican City, but Utah's capital city is quite modern. A redeveloped downtown and local foodie scene balance out the city's charming anachronisms.

⊙ Sights & Activities

Top church-related sights cluster near downtown's zero point: the corner of S Temple (east–west) and Main St (north–south). See those 132ft-wide streets? They were originally built so that four oxen pulling a wagon could turn around.

Don't forget that just 45 minutes away, world-class hiking, climbing and snow sports await in the Wasatch Mountains (p862).

UTAH FACTS
....

Nickname Beehive State

Population 2.85 million

Area 82,169 sq miles

Capital city Salt Lake City (population 189,314), metro area (1.2 million)

Other cities St George (population 75,561)

Sales tax 5.95%

Birthplace of Entertainers Donny (b 1957) and Marie (b 1959) Osmond, beloved bandit Butch Cassidy (1866–1908)

Home of 2002 Winter Olympic Games

Politics Mostly conservative

Famous for Mormons, red-rock canyons, polygamy

Best souvenir Wasatch Brewery T-shirt: 'Polygamy Porter – Why Have Just One?'

⊙ Temple Square Area

Temple Square PLAZA
(www.visittemplesquare.com; cnr S Temple & N State Sts; ⊙grounds 24hr, visitor centers 9am-9pm) 🅿🆓 The city's most famous sight, a 10 acre square filled with stunning LDS architecture, flower gardens and fountains, is certainly awe-inspiring. Disarmingly nice LDS-member 'sister' and 'brother' volunteers answer questions and lead free 30-minute grounds tours from the visitor centers, just inside the two entrances (on S and N Temple).

Lording over the square, the 210ft-tall **Salt Lake Temple** is at its most ethereal when lit up at night. Atop the tallest spire stands a statue of the angel Moroni, who appeared to first LDS prophet, Joseph Smith, and led him to the Book of Mormon. The Temple and its ceremonies are private, open only to LDS members. In addition to the sights listed, the square also contains a church history museum, Joseph Smith theater and restaurants.

Tabernacle RELIGIOUS
(http://mormontabernaclechoir.org; Temple Sq; ⊙9am-9pm) 🆓 This domed, 1867 auditorium – with a massive 11,000-pipe organ –

SALT LAKE CITY FOR CHILDREN

Young and old alike appreciate the attractions in the University-Foothill District, but there are also a couple of kid-specific sights to see.

Discovery Gateway (www.childmuseum.org; 444 W 100 South; admission $8.50; ⏰10am-6pm Mon-Thu, 10am-8pm Fri & Sat, noon-6pm Sun; 📶) is an enthusiastic, hands-on children's museum. The mock network-news desk in the media zone is particularly cool for budding journos.

More than 800 animals inhabit zones like the Asian Highlands on the landscaped 42-acre grounds of **Hogle Zoo** (www.hoglezoo.org; 2600 E Sunnyside Ave; adult/child $13/10; ⏰9am-5pm; 📶). Daily animal-encounter programs help kids learn more about their favorite species.

has incredible acoustics. A pin dropped in the front can be heard in the back, almost 200ft away. Free organ recitals are held here at noon Monday through Saturday. For more on the famous choir performances, see Entertainment.

Beehive House HOUSE
(☑801-240-2671; www.visittemplesquare.com; 67 E South Temple St; ⏰9am-8:30pm Mon-Sat) FREE
The Beehive House was Brigham Young's main home during his tenure as governor and church president in Utah. The required tours begin on your arrival and vary in the amount of historic house detail versus religious education offered.

Family History Library LIBRARY
(www.churchhistory.org; 35 N West Temple St; ⏰8am-5pm Mon, 8am-9pm Tue-Fri, 9am-5pm Sat) FREE Investigating your ancestors? This incredible library contains more than 3.5 million genealogy-related microfilms, microfiches, books and other records gathered from more than 110 countries.

◉ Greater Downtown

Utah State Capitol HISTORIC BUILDING
(www.utahstatecapitol.utah.gov; 350 N State St; ⏰building 7am-8pm Mon-Fri, 8am-6pm Sat & Sun, visitor center 8:30am-5pm Mon-Fri) FREE Inside the 1916 State Capitol, colorful Works Progress Administration (WPA) murals of pioneers, trappers and missionaries adorn the dome. Free, hourly guided tours (9am to 5pm, Monday to Friday) start at the 1st-floor visitor center; self-guided tours are also available.

City Creek PLAZA
(www.shopcitycreekcenter.com; Social Hall Ave, btwn Regent & Richards Sts) Smack dab in the middle of the city you'll find this 20-acre

pedestrian plaza fraught with pleasant fountains and outdoor fireplaces, plus a whole host of restaurants and an indoor-outdoor mall.

◉ University-Foothill District & Beyond

★**Natural History Museum of Utah** MUSEUM
(http://umnh.utah.edu; 301 Wakara Way; adult/child $11/6; ⏰10am-5pm Thu-Tue, 10am-8pm Wed) The stunning architecture of the Rio Tinto Center forms a multistory indoor 'canyon' that showcases exhibits to great effect. Walk up through the layers as you explore both indigenous peoples' and natural history.

The Past Worlds paleontological displays are the most impressive. You get an incredible perspective from beneath, next to, and above a vast collection of dinosaur fossils – one that represents the full breadth of pre-history.

This Is the Place Heritage Park HISTORIC SITE
(www.thisistheplace.org; 2601 E Sunnyside Ave; adult/child $10/7; ⏰9am-5pm Mon-Fri, 10am-5pm Sat; 📶) A 450-acre park marks the spot where Brigham Young uttered the fateful words, 'This is the place.' The centerpiece is a living-history village where, June through August, costumed docents depict mid-19th-century life. Admission includes a tourist train ride and activities. During the off-season guests can wander the village at reduced rates.

Red Butte Garden GARDEN
(www.redbuttegarden.org; 300 Wakara Way; adult/child $10/6; ⏰9am-7:30pm) Both landscaped and natural gardens cover the lovely 150, trail-accessible acres of Red Butte Gardens in the Wasatch foothills. Check online to see

who's playing at the popular, outdoor summer concert series also held here.

Church Fork Trail
HIKING

(Millcreek Canyon, off Wasatch Blvd; day-use $3) Looking for the nearest workout with big views? Hike the 6-mile round-trip, pet-friendly trail up to Grandeur Peak (8299ft). Millcreek Canyon is 13.5 miles southwest of downtown.

Tours

Utah Heritage Foundation
WALKING TOURS

(☎801-533-0858; www.utahheritagefoundation. com; tours per person $5-20) The local heritage society offers walking tours of different neighborhoods, as well as 'Thirst Fursday' pub crawls. For do-it-yourselfers, detailed self-guided walking-tour brochures are available online (or at the city visitor center).

Sleeping

Downtown, rates vary greatly depending on local events and daily occupancy. Cheaper chain motels cluster off I-80: near the airport and south in suburban Midvale. Outside ski season, prices plunge at Wasatch Mountain resorts, about 45 minutes from downtown.

Crystal Inn & Suites
MOTEL $

(☎800-366-4466, 801-328-4466; www.crystal-innsaltlake.com; 230 W 500 South; r incl breakfast $78-120; P ❈ @ ❄ ☒) Utah-owned, multi-story motel with a super-friendly staff and loads of free amenities (including a huge, hot breakfast buffet).

Avenues Hostel
HOSTEL $

(☎801-539-8888, 801-359-3855; www.saltlake-hostel.com; 107 F St; dm $18, s/d without bathroom $40/46, with bathroom $56/60; ❈ @ ❄) Well-worn hostel, a bit halfway house–like with long-term residents. But it has a convenient location.

★ Inn on the Hill
INN $$

(☎801-328-1466; www.inn-on-the-hill.com; 225 N State St; r incl breakfast $135-220; P ❈ @ ❄) Exquisite woodwork and Maxfield Parrish Tiffany glass are just some of the adornments in this sprawling 1906 Renaissance Revival mansion turned inn. Guest rooms are classically comfortable, not at all stuffy, and you have the run of two patios, a billiard room, a library and a dining room. High above Temple Sq, expect great views – and an uphill hike back from town.

Peery Hotel
HOTEL $$

(☎801-521-4300, 800-331-0073; www.peeryhotel. com; 110 W 300 South; r $90-130; P ❈ @ ❄) This stately historic hotel (1910) has a great location in the Broadway Ave entertainment district, within walking distance of restaurants, bars and theaters. Expect upscale conveniences such as Egyptian-cotton robes, iPod docking stations and Tempurpedic mattresses.

SVEA
B&B $$

(☎801-832-0970; www.svea.us; 720 Ashton Ave; r incl breakfast $155-165; P ❈ ❄) Both elegant and eclectic, the 1890s Victorian house that contains this B&B has a few odd angles and room configurations. Continental breakfast arrives in a basket at your door daily.

Grand America
HOTEL $$$

(☎800-621-4505; www.grandamerica.com; 555 S Main St; r $199-289; P ❈ @ ❄ ☒) Italian marble bathrooms, English wool carpeting, tasseled damask draperies and other cushy details decorate SLC's most luxurious hotel. If that's not enough to spoil you, there's always afternoon high tea or the lavish Sunday brunch.

Eating

Many of Salt Lake City's bountiful assortment of ethnic and organically minded restaurants are within the downtown core. There's also a good collection (Middle Eastern, a noodle house, upscale new American, a cafe...) at 9th and 9th (cnr 900 East and 900 South Sts).

POLYGAMY TODAY

Though the Mormon church eschewed plural marriage in 1890, there are unaffiliated offshoot sects that still believe it is a divinely decreed practice. Most of the roughly 7000 residents in Hilldale-Colorado City on the Utah–Arizona border are polygamy-practicing members of the Fundamentalist Church of Jesus Christ of Latter-Day Saints (FLDS). Walk into a Walmart in Washington or Hurricane and the shoppers you see in pastel-colored, prairie-style dresses – with lengthy braids or elaborate updos – are likely sister wives. Other, less-conspicuous polygamy-practicing sects are active in the southern parts of the state as well.

Lion House Pantry Restaurant AMERICAN $
(www.templesquarehospitality.com; 63 E South
Temple St; meals $7-13; ⏰11am-8pm Mon-Sat)
Down-home, carb-rich cafeteria cookin' just
like your Mormon grandmother made. Several
of Brigham Young's wives used to live in
this historic house (including this author's
great-great-great grandmother).

Ekamai Thai THAI $
(http://ekamaithai.com/; 336 W 300 South; dishes
$6-9; ⏰11am-9pm Mon-Sat) In nice weather
you can enjoy this tasty Thai curry takeaway at the patio tables outside.

★ **Tin Angel** MODERN AMERICAN $$
(http://thetinangel.com; 365 W 400 South; small
plates & sandwiches $10-16, dinner mains $19-25;
⏰11am-3pm & 5-10pm Mon-Sat) Using ingre-
dients from local growers, the chef melds
different cuisines to create fresh, new Amer-
ican flavors. Think wild boar ribs with gor-
gonzola gnocchi. Vintage china and local art
lining the walls give this great little place an
even more eclectic vibe.

Red Iguana MEXICAN $$
(www.rediguana.com; 736 W North Temple; mains
$8-16; ⏰11am-10pm) Ask for a sample plate of
mole if you can't decide which of the seven
chile- and chocolate-based sauces sounds
best. Really, you can't go wrong with any of
the thoughtfully flavored Mexican food at
this always-packed, family-run restaurant.

Squatters Pub Brewery AMERICAN $$
(www.squatters.com; 147 W Broadway; dishes $10-
22; ⏰11am-midnight Sun-Thu, to 1am Fri & Sat)
Come for an Emigration Pale Ale, stay for

the blackened tilapia salad. The lively pub
atmosphere here is always fun.

Copper Onion INTERNATIONAL $$$
(✆801-355-3282; www.thecopperonion.com; 111
E Broadway Ave; brunch & small plates $7-15, din-
ner mains $22-29; ⏰11am-3pm & 5-10pm) Locals
keep the Copper Onion bustling at lunch, at
dinner, at weekend brunch, at happy hour
in the bar... And for good reason: small
plates like wagyu beef tartare and pasta car-
bonara call out to be shared. Design-driven
rustic decor provides a convivial place to
enjoy it all.

Takashi JAPANESE $$$
(✆801-519-9595; 18 W Market St; rolls $10-18,
mains $18-30; ⏰11:30am-2pm & 5:30-10pm Mon-
Sat) The best of a number of surprisingly
good sushi restaurants in landlocked Salt
Lake; even LA restaurant snobs rave about
the excellent rolls at oh-so-chic Takashi.

🍷 Drinking & Nightlife

Epic Brewing Company CAFE
(www.epicbrewing.com; 825 S State St; ⏰11am-
9pm Mon-Thu, 10am-11pm Fri & Sat, 11am-7pm
Sun) Utah's first full-strength beer brewery.
You have to order something small to eat
(Utah law) at this small tasting counter, but
then staff pour samples ($0.40 to $1) and
full glasses of their 30 ales, IPAs, lagers and
stouts.

Gracie's BAR
(326 S West Temple; ⏰11am-2am) Even with two
levels and four bars, this upscale hang-out
still gets crowded. The two sprawling patios

CAN I GET A DRINK IN UTAH?

Absolutely. Although there are still a few unusual liquor laws on the books, regulations
have relaxed somewhat in recent years. Private club memberships are no more: a 'bar'
is now a bar (no minors allowed), and you don't have to order food to consume alco-
hol in one of them. These are few and far between though. Most establishments, even
brewpubs, are 'restaurants', where you have to order something small to imbibe alcohol.
Also note that not all restaurants have full liquor licenses; many sell only wine and beer.

Remaining rules to remember:

➡ You must be actually dining at a fully licensed restaurant to order any alcoholic
drink there.

➡ Mixed drinks and wine are available only after noon. In bars and restaurants, beer can
be served from 10am.

➡ Packaged liquor can only be sold at state-run liquor stores (closed on Sundays), some
beer is sold in convenience stores.

➡ Most beer you get here does not exceed 3.2% alcohol content by weight (a typical
Budweiser is 5%).

are the best place to kick back. Live music or DJs most nights.

Beerhive Pub PUB
(128 S Main St; ⊙noon-1am) More than 200 beer choices, including many Utah-local microbrews, are wedged into this small downtown bar.

Coffee Garden CAFE
(895 E 900 South; ⊙ 6am-11pm Sun-Thu, 6am-midnight Fri & Sat; 🛜) Amazing baked goods and great coffee in one of SLC's most character-filled neighborhood coffeehouses.

☆ Entertainment

Music
A complete list of local music is available online at www.cityweekly.net. Orchestra, organ, choir and other LDS-linked performances are listed at www.mormontabernaclechoir.org.

Mormon Tabernacle Choir LIVE MUSIC
(🖉801-570-0080; www.mormontabernaclechoir.org) FREE Hearing the world-renown Mormon Tabernacle choir is a must-do during any SLC visit. A live, half-hour choir broadcast goes out every Sunday at 9:30am. Doors open at 8:30am and tickets are free, but guests must be seated by 9:15am.

September through November and January through May, attend the broadcast in person at the Tabernacle. From June to August and in December, to accommodate larger crowds, the choir performs at the 21,000-seat LDS Conference Center. Public rehearsals are held at the Tabernacle year round from 8pm to 9pm on Thursdays.

Theater
The Salt Lake City Arts Council provides a complete cultural events calendar on its website (www.slcgov.com/city-life/ec). Local venues include **Abravanel Hall** (www.slcfa.org; 123 W South Temple St), **Capitol Theater** (http://theatresaltlakecity.com; 50 W 200 South) and the **Rose Wagner Performing Arts Center** (www.slccfa.org; 138 W 300 South). You can reserve through **ArtTix** (🖉888-451-2787, 801-355-2787; www.arttix.org).

Sports
Energy Solutions Arena STADIUM
(🖉801-355-7328; www.energysolutionsarena.com; 301 W South Temple St) Utah Jazz, the men's professional basketball team, play at this downtown stadium – as does the indoor soccer league. Concerts are held here, too.

THE BOOK OF MORMON, THE MUSICAL
Singing and dancing Mormon missionaries have been lighting up Broadway since 2011. But rumor has it that *The Book of Mormon*, the musical, may actually open in Salt Lake City before the 10-years-down-the-road date originally forecast. This light-hearted satire about brothers and sisters on their mission trip in Uganda came out of the comic minds that created the *Avenue Q* musical and the animated TV series *South Park*. No wonder people laughed them all the way to nine Tony Awards. The LDS church's official response? Actually quite measured, though it was made clear that their belief is that while the *Book*, the musical, can entertain you, the Book, the scripture, can change your life.

Maverik Center STADIUM
(🖉tickets 800-745-3000; www.maverikcenter.com; 3200 S Decker Lake Dr, West Valley City) The International Hockey League's Utah Grizzlies play 8.5 miles outside town.

🛍 Shopping
City Creek (p858) is the indoor-outdoor mall of choice for big-name-brand shopping downtown. A small but interesting array of boutiques line up along **Broadway Avenue** (300 South), between 100 and 300 East. A few crafty shops can be found on the 300 block of **W Pierpont Avenue**.

ℹ Information

EMERGENCY & MEDICAL SERVICES
Salt Lake Regional Medical Center (🖉801-350-4111; www.saltlakeregional.com; 1050 E South Temple; ⊙ emergency24hr)

INTERNET ACCESS
Main Library (www.slcpl.org; 210 E 400 South; ⊙9am-9pm Mon-Thu, 9am-6pm Fri & Sat, 1-5pm Sun; 🛜) Free wi-fi and computer internet access.

MEDIA
City Weekly (www.cityweekly.net) Free alternative weekly with restaurant and entertainment listings.
Salt Lake Tribune (www.sltrib.com) Utah's largest-circulation paper; entertainment section lists eateries and events.

WORTH A TRIP

GREAT SALT LAKE

Once part of prehistoric Lake Bonneville, Great Salt Lake today covers 2000 sq miles and is far saltier than the ocean; you can easily float on its surface. The pretty, 15-mile-long **Antelope Island State Park** (☑801-773-2941; http://stateparks.utah.gov; Antelope Dr; day use per vehicle $9, tent & RV sites without hookups $13; ⊙7am-10pm Jul-Sep, 7am-7pm Oct-Jun), 40 miles northwest of SLC, has nice hiking and the best beaches for lake swimming (though at low levels they're occasionally smelly). It's also home to one of the largest bison herds in the country. A basic campground operates year-round. Six of the 26 sites are available first-come, first-served, the rest by reservation.

MONEY

Wells Fargo (www.wellsfargo.com; 79 S Main St; ⊙9am-6pm Mon-Fri, 9am-3pm Sat) Currency-exchange services.

TOURIST INFORMATION

Public Lands Information Center (☑801-466-6411; www.publiclands.org; REI Store, 3285 E 3300 South; ⊙10:30am-5:30pm Mon-Fri, 9am-1pm Sat) Recreation information for the Wasatch-Cache National Forest; located inside the REI store.

Visit Salt Lake (☑801-534-4900; www.visitsaltlake.com; visitor center 90 S West Temple, Salt Palace Convention Center; ⊙9am-6pm Mon-Fri, 9am-5pm Sat & Sun) Large office with lots of brochures and gift shop.

WEBSITES

Downtown SLC (www.downtownslc.org) Arts, entertainment and business information about the downtown core.

❶ Getting There & Away

AIR

A new terminal is in the planning stages, but for now the **Salt Lake City International Airport** (SLC; www.slcairport.com; 776 N Terminal Dr), 5 miles northwest of downtown, has mostly domestic flights except for a few jaunts to Canada and Mexico. **Delta** (☑800-221-1212; www.delta.com) is the main SLC carrier.

BUS

Greyhound (☑800-231-2222; www.greyhound.com; 300 S 600 West) connects SLC with Southwestern towns such as Las Vegas, NV ($86, eight hours), and Denver, CO ($114, 10 hours).

TRAIN

Traveling between Chicago and Oakland/Emeryville, the *California Zephyr* from **Amtrak** (☑800-872-7245; www.amtrak.com) stops daily at **Union Pacific Rail Depot** (340 S 600 West). Scheduled delays can be substantial, and trains depart at odd hours, but you can connect with destinations such as Denver ($150, 15 hours) and Reno, NV ($68, 10 hours).

❶ Getting Around

TO/FROM THE AIRPORT

In 2013 the **Utah Transit Authority** (UTA; www.rideuta.com; one-way $2) completed a 6-mile TRAX light-rail extension that connects the airport with the Energy Solutions Arena stop (green line). Bus 453 also connects the airport with downtown.

Express Shuttle (☑800-397-0773; www.xpressshuttleutah.com) shared van service costs about $16 to downtown; a taxi will run you roughly $25

PUBLIC TRANSPORTATION

Utah Transit Authority (p862) continues to expand its TRAX light-rail system. The seven stops in the center of downtown SLC are a fare-free zone and are on all three, color-coded lines. During ski season UTA buses serve the local ski resorts (one-way $4.50).

Park City & the Wasatch Mountains

Utah has awesome skiing, some of the best anywhere in North America. Its fabulous low-density, low-moisture snow – between 300in and 500in annually – and thousands of acres of high-altitude terrain helped earn Utah the honor of hosting the 2002 Winter Olympics. The Wasatch Mountain Range, which towers over SLC, is home to numerous ski resorts, abundant hiking, camping and mountain biking – not to mention chichi Park City with its upscale amenities and famous film festival.

Salt Lake City Resorts

On the western side of the Wasatch mountain range, the four impressive snow-sport resorts in Little Cottonwood and Big Cottonwood Canyons lie within 40 minutes' drive of downtown SLC. All have lodging and dining facilities. A one- to 10-day **Super**

Pass (www.visitsaltlakecity.com/ski/superpass; 3-day pass adult/child $219/114) offers ski access to all resorts (one per day) plus round-trip transportation from SLC.

For a full list of summer hiking and biking trails, see www.utah.com/saltlake/hiking.htm.

BIG COTTONWOOD CANYON

Solitude SNOW SPORTS
(801-534-1400; www.skisolitude.com; 12000 Big Cottonwood Canyon Rd; day lift ticket adult/child $72/46) Exclusive, European-style village surrounded by excellent snow-sport terrain. The Nordic Center has cross-country skiing in winter and nature and mountain-biking trails in summer.

Brighton Resort SNOW SPORTS
(800-873-5512; www.brightonresort.com; 12601 Big Cottonwood Canyon Rd; day lift ticket adult/child $57/31) Small but stellar slopes where all of SLC learned to ski and snowboard. Brighton is still an old-school, family and first-timer favorite.

LITTLE COTTONWOOD CANYON

Snowbird SNOW SPORTS
(800-232-9542; www.snowbird.com; Hwy 210, Little Cottonwood Canyon; day lift ticket adult/child $65/42) Biggest and busiest of SLC's snow-sport resorts, Snowbird has all-round great snow riding – think steep and deep. Numerous lift-assist summer hiking trails; aerial tramway runs year-round.

Alta Ski Area SKIING
(800-258-2716; www.alta.com; Highway 210, Little Cottonwood Canyon; day lift ticket adult/child $65/42) A laid-back choice exclusive to skiers. No snowboarders affecting snow cover here. Enjoy summer hiking among the hundreds of wildflowers in Albion Basin.

Park City

A mere 35 miles east of SLC via I-80, Park City (elevation 6900ft) first skyrocketed to international fame when it hosted the downhill, jumping and sledding events at the 2002 Winter Olympics. The Southwest's most popular ski destination is still home to the US ski team. Come summer, residents (population 7873) gear up for hiking and mountain biking among the nearby peaks.

The town itself – a silver-mining community during the 19th century – has an attractive main street lined with upscale galleries, shops, hotels, restaurants and bars. Despite the spread of prefab condos across the valley, the setting remains relatively charming. Winter (roughly late December through March) is high season. In other months, businesses may close various days and resorts operate limited facilities.

◉ Sights

Park City Museum MUSEUM
(www.parkcityhistory.org; 528 Main St; adult/child $10/4; ⊙10am-7pm Mon-Sat, noon-6pm Sun) A well-staged, interactive museum touches on the highlights of the town's history as a mining boomtown, hippie hang-out and premier ski resort.

Utah Olympic Park ADVENTURE SPORTS
(435-658-4200; http://utaholympiclegacy.com; 3419 Olympic Pkwy; tours adult/child $10/7; ⊙10am-6pm, tours 11am-4pm) FREE Tour the 2002 Olympic ski-jumping, bobsledding, skeleton, Nordic combined and luge facilities, check out the free ski museum, and if you're lucky, watch the pros practice during a freestyle show (summer and winter; $10). Activities (rates $15 to $200 per ride) include a winter/summer bobsled, an alpine slide, zip lines and a chair lift.

🏃 Activities

In addition to snow sports, each area resort has posh lodging close to the slopes, abundant eateries and various summer activities, including mountain-bike rental and lift-assist hiking. More than 300 miles of interconnecting hiking/biking trails crisscross area mountains; maps are available from the visitor center or online at http://mountaintrails.org. Two of the newer trails to open, **Armstrong** (4 miles; Park City Mountain Resort

---

SCENIC DRIVE: MIRROR LAKE HIGHWAY

This alpine route, also known as Hwy 150, begins about 12 miles east of Park City in Kamas and climbs to elevations of more than 10,000ft as it winds the 65 miles into Wyoming. The highway provides breathtaking mountain vistas, passing scores of lakes, campgrounds and trailheads in the **Uinta-Wasatch-Cache National Forest** (www.fs.usda.gov/uwcnf). Note that sections may be closed to traffic into late spring due to heavy snowfall; check online.

trailhead) and **Pinecone Ridge** (4 miles) combine for excellent mountain biking.

Park City
Mountain Resort   ADVENTURE SPORTS
(☏435-649-8111; www.parkcitymountainresort.com; 1310 Lowell Ave; day lift ticket adult/child $80/50) Family-friendly, super-central Park City Mountain Resort has activities galore: more than 3300 acres of skiable terrain, snow-tubing, an alpine coaster, year-round in-town lift, summer trails, a zip line...

Deer Valley   ADVENTURE SPORTS
(☏800-424-3337; www.deervalley.com; Deer Valley Dr; day lift ticket adult/child $100/64) The area's most exclusive resort is known as much for its superb dining and luxury hilltop hotels, such as the St Regis, as it is for the meticulously groomed, capacity-controlled slopes and ski valets. No snowboarding.

Canyons   ADVENTURE SPORTS
(☏888-226-9667; www.thecanyons.com; 4000 Canyons Resort Dr; day lift ticket adult/child $80/60) The largest resort in Utah, with a year-round gondola, encompasses nine mountain peaks, five bowls and three terrain parks. In summer there are guided hiking and mountain biking in addition to zip-line tours.

✹✷ Festivals & Events

Sundance Film Festival   FILM
(☏888-285-7790; www.sundance.org/festival) Independent films, their makers, movie stars and fans fill the town to bursting for 10 days in late January. Passes, ticket packages and the few individual tickets sell out well in advance; plan ahead.

🛏 Sleeping

More than 100 condos, hotels and resorts rent rooms in Park City; none are dirt cheap. For complete listings, check www.visitparkcity.com. High-season winter rates are quoted below (minimum stays may be required); prices drop by half or more out of peak season. Better deals are to be found at chain motels at the intersection of I-40 and Hwy 248, and in SLC.

Chateau Apres Lodge   HOSTEL $
(☏800-357-3556, 435-649-9372; www.chateauapres.com; 1299 Norfolk Ave; dm $40, d/q $125/175; ☎) The only budget-ish accommodation in town is this very basic, 1963 lodge – with a 1st-floor dorm – near the town ski lift. Reserve ahead.

★ Old Town Guest House   B&B $$
(☏800-290-6423, 435-649-2642; www.old-townguesthouse.com; 1011 Empire Ave; r incl breakfast $169-199; ✲ @ 🖥 ☎) Grab the flannel robe, pick a paperback off the shelf and snuggle under a quilt on your lodgepole-pine bed or relax in the hot tub on the large deck at this comfy in-town B&B. The host will gladly provide space for your gear and give you the lowdown on the area's great outdoors.

Park City Peaks   HOTEL $$
(☏800-333-3333, 435-649-5000; www.parkcitypeaks.com; 2121 Park Ave; r $149-249; ✲ @ 🖥 ☎) Hobnob with junior bobsledders and other US team hopefuls who stay at this hotel between downtown and Olympic Park. December through April, breakfast is included with the cushy contemporary rooms.

Sky Lodge   LUXURY HOTEL $$$
(☏888-876-2525, 435-658-2500; www.theskylodge.com; 201 Heber Ave; ste $400-1000; ✲ @ 🖥 🖥) The urban-loft-like architecture containing the chic Sky Lodge suites both complements and contrasts with the three historic buildings that house the property's stellar restaurants. You can't be more stylish, or more central, if you stay here.

St Regis Deer Valley   LUXURY HOTEL $$$
(☏866-932-7059, 435-940-5700; www.stregisdeervalley.com; 2300 Deer Valley Dr E; r $700-1300; ✲ @ 🖥 ☎) You have to ride a private funicular just to get up to the St Regis. So whether you're lounging by the outdoor fire pits, dining on an expansive terrace or peering out over your room's balcony rail, the views are sublime. The studied elegant rusticity here is the height of Deer Valley's luxury lodging.

✕ Eating

Park City is not known for cheap eats, but it does have exceptional upscale dining; Deer Valley (p864) has some of the best resort restaurants. Pick up the menu guide put out by Park City Magazine (www.parkcitymagazine.com) for more. Note that from April through November restaurants reduce hours and may take extended breaks. Reservations are required for all top end ($$$) e stablishments.

Java Cow Coffee & Ice Cream   CAFE $
(402 Main St; dishes $3-8; ⏱7am-10pm; ☎) Enjoy a scoop of site-made ice cream like Mooana (with organic banana chunks) along with your Ibis coffee at this always lively cafe. Sandwiches and crepes, too.

Uptown Fare   CAFE $
(227 Main St; sandwiches $6-11; ⊙11am-3pm) Comforting house-roasted turkey sandwiches and homemade soups are served at this cozy cafe hidden below Treasure Mountain Inn.

★**Silver Star Cafe**   NEW AMERICAN $$
(www.thesilverstarcafe.com; 1825 Three Kings Dr; breakfast & small plates $9-14, dinner mains $15-20; ⊙8am-9pm) We can't decide if it's the inventive, hearty Western dishes or the perfect, out-of-the-way mountain-base location that first hooked us. Either way, we love kicking back on the sunny patio aprés ski or enjoying the singer-songwriter showcases.

Good Karma   FUSION $$
(www.goodkarmarestaurants.com; 1782 Prospector Ave; breakfast $7-12, mains $12-22; ⊙7am-10pm) ∥ Whenever possible, local and organic ingredients are used in the Indo-Persian meals, with an Asian accent. You'll recognize the place by the Tibetan prayer flags flapping out front.

Vinto   ITALIAN $$
(www.vinto.com; 900 Main St, Summit Watch Plaza; dishes $8-17; ⊙11am-10pm Mon-Sat, 4-9pm Sun) Minimalist surrounds are suitably stylish for Main St. But the wood-fired pizzas and light, fresh Italian dishes, surprisingly, won't break your bank.

Riverhorse on Main   NEW AMERICAN $$$
(☏435-649-3536; http://riverhorseparkcity.com; 540 Main St; brunch $25-35, dinner mains $35-45; ⊙5-10pm Mon-Thu, 5-11pm Fri & Sat, 11am-2:30pm & 5-10pm Sun) Consistently one of the town's top performers, garnering numerous awards for its upscale American dishes such as pistachio-covered Utah trout. Live music nightly in winter.

Wahso   ASIAN $$$
(☏435-615-0300; www.billwhiterestaurantgroup. com/wahso.html; 577 Main St; mains $30-50; ⊙5:30-10pm Wed-Sun) Engagingly exotic. A see-and-be-seen crowd frequents this sophisticated Indochine fusion restaurant.

🍷 Drinking & Nightlife

Main St is where it's at, with half a dozen or more bars, clubs and pubs. In winter, there's action nightly – even restaurants have music. Outside peak season, the scene is weekends-only. For listings, see www.thisweekinparkcity.com.

ROBERT REDFORD'S SUNDANCE RESORT

Wind your way up narrow and twisting Hwy 92, for a truly special experience at Robert Redford's **Sundance Resort** (☏800-892-1600, 801-225-4107; www.sundanceresort.com; 9521 Alpine Loop Rd, Provo; r $199-500; ⊛). ∥ Even if a night's stay at this elegantly rustic, ecoconscious wilderness getaway is out of reach, you can have a stellar meal at the Treehouse Restaurant or deli, attend an outdoor performance at the amphitheater or watch pottery being made (and sold) at the art shack. Skiing, hiking and spa services are also on site. Just walking the grounds is an experience. The resort is 30 miles south of Park City and 50 miles southeast of SLC.

High West Distillery & Saloon   BAR
(703 Park St; ⊙11am-10pm, tours 3pm & 4pm) A former livery and Model A–era garage is home to Park City's own microdistillery. Take a tour, sample some rye, order a whiskey lemonade and stay for supper.

No Name Saloon & Grill   BAR
(447 Main St; ⊙11am-1am) There's a motorcycle hanging from the ceiling, Johnny Cash's 'Jackson' playing on the stereo and a waitress who may or may not be lying about the history of this memorabilia-filled bar.

ℹ Information

Library (☏435-615-5600; http://parkcity-library.org; 1255 Park Ave; ⊙10am-9pm Mon-Thu, 10am-6pm Fri & Sat, 1-5pm Sun; ⊛) Free wi-fi and internet stations for use.

Main Street Visitor Center (☏435-649-7457; 528 Main St; ⊙10am-7pm Mon-Sat, noon-6pm Sun) Small desk inside the busy Park City Museum.

Visitor Information Center (☏800-453-1360, 435-649-6100; www.visitparkcity.com; 1794 Olympic Pkwy; ⊙9am-6pm; ⊛) Vast visitor center with a coffee bar, terrace and incredible views of the mountains near Olympic Park. Visitor guides available online.

ℹ Getting There & Around

Park City Transportation (☏800-637-3803, 435-649-8567; www.parkcitytransportation. com) and **Canyon Transportation** (☏800-255-1841; www.canyontransport.com) both run shared-van service ($40 one-way) and private-charter vans (from $100 for one to three people) to/from Salt Lake City airport. The latter also has ski transfers (from $50) that will take you from Park City to Salt Lake City resorts.

PC-SLC Connect (bus 902) takes you from central Salt Lake to the **Park City Transit Center** (www.parkcity.org; 558 Swede Alley). No need for a car once you get to Park City. The excellent transit system covers the town: accessing the historic district, Kimbell Junction and all three ski resorts. The free buses run one to six times an hour from 8am to 11pm (reduced frequency in summer). There's a downloadable route map online.

Northeastern Utah

Most people head northeast to explore Dinosaur National Monument, but this rural, oil-rich area also has some captivating wilderness terrain. All towns are a mile above sea level.

Vernal

As the closest town to Dinosaur National Monument, it's not surprising that Vernal welcomes you with a large pink dino-buddy. Since oil and gas production in the region has expanded, and the monument is fully operational after many dormant years, new things are popping up in town all the time.

The informative film at the **Utah Field House of Natural History State Park Museum** (http://stateparks.utah.gov; 496 E Main St; ☺9am-5pm Mon-Sat; 🐾) is a great all-round introduction to Utah's dinosaurs. Interactive exhibits, video clips and, of course, giant fossils are wonderfully relevant to the area.

Don Hatch River Expeditions (☑435-789-4316, 800-342-8243; www.donhatchrivertrips.com; 221 N 400 East; 1 day adult/child $99/76) offers rapid-riding and gentler float trips on the nearby Green and Yampa Rivers.

Chain motels are numerous along Main St, but they book up with local workers – so don't expect a price break. **Holiday Inn Express & Suites** (☑435-789-4654; www.vernal-hotel.com; 1515 W Hwy 40; r incl breakfast $100-170, ste $130-200; ❄🐾🔆🏊) has the most amenities, and **Econo Lodge** (☑435-789-2000; www.econolodge.com; 311 E Main St; r $69-99) will do in a bargain pinch. For something different, try **Landmark Inn & Suites** (☑888-738-1800, 435-781-1800; www.landmark-inn.com; 301 E 100 S; motel r incl breakfast $129-169, B&B $80-100; 🔆),

which has both an upscale motel and an off-site inn.

Backdoor Grille (87 W Main St; mains $5-8; ☺11am-6pm Mon-Sat) makes fresh sandwiches and cookies, which are great to take on a picnic; you can also pick up a hiking guide at the associated bookshop. For dinner, the **Porch** (www.facebook.com/theporchvernal; 251 E Main St; lunch $8-12, dinner $14-22; ☺11am-2pm & 5-9pm Mon-Fri, 5-9pm Sat) is the place to go for Southern US favorites. **Don Pedro's Mexican Family Restaurant** (http://klcyads.com/don-pedros; 3340 N Vernal Ave; dishes $8-15; ☺11am-2pm & 5-10pm), north of town, serves festive meals from south of the border.

Vernal Chamber of Commerce (☑800-477-5558; www.dinoland.com; 134 W Main; ☺9am-5pm Mon-Fri) provides information on the entire region, including numerous driving-tour brochures for area rock art and dino tracks.

Dinosaur National Monument

Straddling the Utah–Colorado state line, **Dinosaur National Monument** (www.nps.gov/dino; off Hwy 40; 7-day per vehicle $10; ☺24hr) protects one of North America's largest dinosaur fossil beds, discovered here in 1909. Though both state's sections are beautiful, Utah has the bones. Don't miss the **Quarry Exhibit** (9am to 4pm), which is an enclosed, partially excavated wall of rock with more than 1600 bones protruding – quite the sight to see.

In summer, you will have to take a shuttle to see the quarry and hours may be extended a little; out of season you may be required to wait until a ranger-led caravan of cars is scheduled to drive up. From below the quarry parking lot, follow the Fossil Discovery Trail (2.2 miles round-trip) to see a few more giant femurs and such sticking out of the rock. The rangers' interpretive hikes are highly recommended. Plus there's easily-accessible Native American rock art to see on the Utah side.

In Colorado, the Canyon Area is at a higher elevation – with some stunning overlooks – but is closed to snow until late spring. Both sections have numerous hiking trails, interpretive driving tours (brochures for sale), Green or Yampa river access and campgrounds ($8 to $15 per tent and RV site). The Quarry portion of the park is 15 miles northeast of Vernal, UT, on Hwy 149. The Canyon Area is roughly 30 miles farther east, outside Dinosaur, CO.

There are two visitor centers: the **Quarry Visitor Center** (☉8am-6pm mid-May–late Sep, 9am-5pm late Sep–mid-May) and, in Colorado, the **Canyon Area Visitor Center** (☑970-374-3000; www.nps.gov/dino; Dinosaur, CO; ☉9am-5pm Jun-early Sep, 10am-4pm Sat & Sun only mid-April–May).

Flaming Gorge National Recreation Area

Named for its fiery red sandstone, this gorge-ous park has 375 miles of reservoir shoreline, part of the Green River system. Area resort activities at **Red Canyon Lodge** (☑435-889-3759; www.redcanyonlodge.com; 790 Red Canyon Rd, Dutch John; cabins $115-145) include fly-fishing, rowing, rafting and horseback riding, among others. Its pleasantly rustic cabins have no TVs. **Flaming Gorge Resort** (☑435-889-3773; www.flaminggorgeresort.com; 155 Greendale/Hwy 191, Dutch John; r $90-120, ste $120-160) has similar water-based offerings and rents motel rooms and suites. Both have decent restaurants.

Get general information at www.flaminggorgecountry.com and contact the **USFS Flaming Gorge Headquarters** (☑435-784-3445; www.fs.fed.us/r4/ashley; 25 W Hwy 43, Manila; ☉8am-5pm Mon-Fri) for the public camping lowdown. The area's 6040ft elevation ensures pleasant summers – daytime highs average about 80°F.

Moab & Southeastern Utah

Snow-blanketed peaks in the distance provide stark contrast to the red-rock canyons that define this rugged corner of the Colorado Plateau. For 65 million years water has carved serpentine, sheer-walled gorges along the course of the Colorado and Green Rivers. Today these define the borders of expansive Canyonlands National Park (p870). At nearby Arches National Park (p869), erosion sculpted thousands of arches and fin rock formations. Base yourself between the parks in Moab, aka activity central – a town built for mountain biking, river running and four-wheel driving. In the far southeastern corner of the state, Ancestral Puebloan sites are scattered among remote and rocky wilderness areas and parks. Most notable is Monument Valley, which extends into Arizona.

Green River

The 'World's Watermelon Capital,' the town of Green River offers a good base for river running on the Green and Colorado Rivers. The legendary one-armed Civil War veteran, geologist and ethnologist John Wesley Powell first explored these rivers in 1869 and 1871. Learn about his amazing travels at the extensive **John Wesley Powell River History Museum** (www.jwprhm.com; 885 E Main St; adult/child $3/1; ☉8am-7pm Apr-Oct, 8am-4pm Nov-Mar), which also has exhibits on the Fremont Indians, geology and local history. The museum serves as the local visitor center.

Outfitters **Holiday Expeditions** (☑800-624-6323, 435-564-3273; www.holidayexpeditions.com; 10 Holiday River St; day trip adult/child $195/175) and **Moki Mac River Expeditions** (☑800-284-7280, 435-564-3361; www.mokimac.com; day trip $160) run one-day rafting trips in Westwater Canyon, as well as multiday excursions.

Family-owned, clean and cheerful, **Robbers Roost Motel** (☑435-564-3452; www.rrmotel.com; 325 W Main St; s $35, d $45; ❋☞✿) is a motorcourt budget-motel gem. Otherwise, there are numerous chain motels where W Main St (Business 70) connects with I-70. Residents and rafters alike flock to **Ray's Tavern** (25 S Broadway; dishes $8-26; ☉11am-10pm), the local beer joint, for the best hamburgers and fresh-cut French fries in Southeastern Utah.

Green River is the only stop in the area on the daily *California Zephyr* train run by **Amtrak** (☑800-872-7245; www.amtrak.com; 250 S Broadway) to Denver, CO ($90, 10¾ hours). Green River is 182 miles southeast of Salt Lake City and 52 miles northwest of Moab.

Moab

Southeastern Utah's largest community (population 5093) bills itself as the state's recreation capital, and... oh man, does it deliver. Scads of rafting and riding (mountain bike, horse, 4WD...) outfitters here make forays into surrounding public lands. Make this your base, too, and you can hike Arches or Canyonlands National Parks during the day, then come back to a comfy bed, a hot tub and your selection of surprisingly good restaurants at night. Do note that this alfresco adventure gateway is not a secret: the town is mobbed, especially during spring and fall events. If the traffic irritates you, remember that you can disappear into the vast surrounding desert in no time.

Activities

The Moab visitor center puts out several brochures on near-town rock art, hiking trails, driving tours, etc. It also keeps a list of the numerous area outfitters that offer half-day to multiday adventures (from $60 for a sunset 4WD tour to $170 for a white-water day on the river) that include transport, the activity and, sometimes, meals. Book ahead.

Outfitters

Sheri Griffith Expeditions RAFTING
(800-332-2439; www.griffithexp.com; 2231 S Hwy 191; day trip $170) Highly rated rafting outfitter; some multisport adventures.

Poison Spider Bicycles MOUNTAIN BIKING
(800-635-1792, 435-259-7882; www.poison-spiderbicycles.com; 497 N Main St; per day rental $45-70) Mountain- and road-bike rentals and tours; superior advice and service.

Farabee's Jeep Rental & Outlaw Tours ADVENTURE SPORTS
(877-970-5337; www.farabeesjeeprentals.com; 1125 S Highway 191; per day Jeep rental $150-225) Four-wheel-drive rentals, self-drive and fully guided off-road Jeep tours.

Moab Desert Adventures ADVENTURE SPORTS
(877-765-6622, 435-260-2404; www.moabdesertadventures.com; 415 N Main St; half-/full-day $165/285) Top-notch climbing tours scale area towers and walls; canyoneering and multisport packages available.

Red Cliffs Lodge HORSEBACK RIDING
(866-812-2002, 435-259-2002; www.redcliffslodge.com; Mile 14, Hwy 128; half-day $80) Daily half-day trail rides offered; advanced, open-range rides also available.

Sleeping

Most lodgings in town have bike storage facilities and hot tubs to soothe sore muscles. Despite having an incredible number of motels, the town does fill up; reservations are highly recommended March through October. Rates drop significantly in the off-season.

Individual **BLM campsites** (www.blm.gov/utah/moab; tent & RV sites $10-12; year-round) in the area are first-come, first-served. In peak season, check with the Moab Information Center to see which sites are full.

Adventure Inn MOTEL $
(866-662-2466, 435-259-6122; www.adventureinnmoab.com; 512 N Main St; r incl breakfast $80-105; Mar-Oct) A great little indie motel, the Adventure Inn has spotless rooms (some with refrigerators) and decent linens, as well as laundry facilities.

Cali Cochitta B&B $$
(888-429-8112, 435-259-4961; www.moabdreaminn.com; 110 S 200 East; cottages incl breakfast $135-170;) Make yourself at home in one of the charming brick cottages a short walk from downtown. A long wooden table on the patio provides a welcome setting for community breakfasts.

Sunflower Hill INN $$
(800-662-2786, 435-259-2974; www.sunflowerhill.com; 185 N 300 East; r incl breakfast $165-225;) Relax amid the manicured gardens of a rambling 100-year-old farmhouse and an early-20th-century home. All 12 guest quarters have a sophisticated country sensibility.

Gonzo Inn MOTEL $$
(800-791-4044, 435-259-2515; www.gonzoinn.com; 100 W 200 South; r incl breakfast Apr-Oct $160-180;) Brushed metal-and-wood headboards, concrete shower stalls and colorful retro patio furniture spruce up this desert-colored adobe motel.

Sorrel River Ranch LODGE $$$
(877-359-2715, 435-259-4642; www.sorrelriver.com; Mile 17, Hwy 128; r $420-530;) Southeast Utah's full-service luxury lodge, set on 240 acres along the banks of the Colorado River, was originally an 1803 homestead. Horseback riding, spa services and gourmet restaurant on site.

Eating

There's no shortage of places at which to fuel up in Moab, from backpacker coffeehouses to gourmet dining rooms. Pick up the *Moab Menu Guide* (www.moabmenuguide.com) at area lodgings. Some restaurants close earlier, or on variable days, from December through March.

Love Muffin CAFE $
(www.lovemuffincafe.com; 139 N Main St; dishes $6-8; 7am-2pm;) The largely organic menu at this vibrant cafe includes imaginative sandwiches, breakfast burritos and egg dishes such as 'Verde,' with brisket and slow-roasted salsa.

Milt's   BURGERS $
(356 Mill Creek Dr; dishes $5-10; ⊙11am-8pm Mon-Sat) A classic 1954 burger stand with fresh-cut fries and oh-so-thick milkshakes.

Miguel's Baja Grill   MEXICAN $$
(www.miguelsbajagrill.com; 51 N Main St; mains $14-24; ⊙5-10pm) Dine on fish tacos or fajitas, and sip margaritas, in the sky-lit breezeway patio lined with brightly painted walls.

Cowboy Grill   AMERICAN $$
(☑435-259-2002; http://redcliffslodge.com; Mile 14, Hwy 128, Red Cliffs Lodge; breakfast & lunch $10-16, dinner $14-28; ⊙6:30-10am, 11:30am-2pm & 5-10pm) Incredible Colorado River sunset views are to be had from the patio or behind the huge picture windows here. The hearty meat and seafood dishes aren't bad either.

★**Sabuku Sushi**   FUSION $$$
(☑435-259-4455; http://sabakusushi.com; 90 E Center St; rolls $12-18, small plates $14-19; ⊙5-10pm Tue-Sun) Such impossibly fresh sushi is especially impressive this far into the desert. Try inventive rolls and small plates such as elk *tataki* (like carpaccio, with an Asian twist).

Desert Bistro   SOUTHWESTERN $$$
(☑435-259-0756; http://desertbistro.com; 36 S 100 West; mains $20-50; ⊙5:30-10pm Mar-Nov) Stylized preparations of game and seafood are the specialty at this welcoming white-tablecloth restaurant. Great wine list, too

🛍 Shopping

Look for art and photography galleries – along with T-shirt and Native American knickknacks – near the intersection of Center and Main Sts.

Arches Book Company &
Back of Beyond   BOOKS
(83 N Main St; ⊙9am-8pm; 🔊) Excellent, adjacent indie bookstores with extensive regional selection, including guides and maps.

ℹ Information

Most businesses and services, including fuel and ATMs, are along Hwy 191, also called Main St in the center of town.

BLM (Bureau of Land Management; ☑435-259-2100; www.blm.gov/utah/moab) Public-land phone and internet assistance only.

Grand County Public Library (www.moabli-brary.org; 257 E Center St; per hr free; ⊙9am-

8pm Mon-Fri, to 5pm Sat) Easy 15-minute internet; register for longer access.

Moab Information Center (www.discover-moab.com; cnr Main & Center Sts; ⊙8am-7pm Mon-Sat, 9am-6pm Sun) Excellent source of information on area parks, trails, activities, camping and weather; big bookstore, too. Free brochures also available online.

ℹ Getting There & Around

Great Lakes Airlines (☑800-554-5111; www.fly-greatlakes.com) has regularly scheduled flights from **Canyonlands Airport** (CNY; www.moabair-port.com; off Hwy 191), 16 miles north of town via Hwy 191, to Denver, CO, and Prescott, AZ.

Moab Luxury Coach (☑435-940-4212; www.moabluxurycoach.com) operates van service to and from SLC ($160 one-way, 4¾ hour) and Grand Junction ($90 one-way, 3¾ hour).

Roadrunner Shuttle (☑435-259-9402; www.roadrunnershuttle.com) and **Coyote Shuttle** (☑435-260-2097; www.coyoteshuttle.com) offer on-demand Canyonlands Airport, hiker-biker and river shuttles.

Moab is 235 miles southeast of Salt Lake City, 150 miles northeast of Capital Reef National Park.

Arches National Park

One of the Southwest's most gorgeous parks, **Arches** (☑435-719-2299; www.nps.gov/arch; Hwy 191; 7-day per vehicle $10; ⊙24hr, visitor center 7:30am-6:30pm Mar-Oct, 9am-4pm Nov-Feb) boasts the world's greatest concentration of sandstone arches – more than 2000, ranging from 3ft to 300ft wide at last count. Nearly one million visitors make the pilgrimage here, just 5 miles north of Moab, every year. Many noteworthy arches are easily reached by paved roads and relatively short hiking trails; much of the park can be covered in a day. To avoid crowds, consider a moonlight exploration, when it's cooler and the rocks feel ghostly.

Highlights include **Balanced Rock**, oft-photographed **Delicate Arch** (best captured in the late afternoon), spectacularly elongated **Landscape Arch** and popular **Windows Arches**. Reservations are necessary for the twice-daily ranger-led hikes into the maze-like fins of the **Fiery Furnace**; book at least a few days in advance – in person or online at www.recreation.gov.

Because of water scarcity and heat, few visitors backpack, though it is allowed with free permits (available from the visitor center). Advance reservations are a must for the

DON'T MISS

NEWSPAPER ROCK RECREATION AREA

This tiny, free recreation area showcases a single large sandstone rock panel packed with more than 300 **petroglyphs** attributed to Ute and Ancestral Puebloan groups during a 2000-year period. It's about 12 miles along Hwy 211 from Hwy 191, en route to the Needles section of Canyonlands National Park (8 miles further).

scenic **Devils Garden Campground** (☑877-444-6777; www.recreation.gov; tent & RV sites $20), 18 miles from the visitor center. Dates book up far in advance for stays from March to October. No showers, no hook-ups.

Canyonlands National Park

Red-rock fins, bridges, needles, spires, craters, mesas, buttes – **Canyonlands** (www.nps.gov/cany; 7-day per vehicle $10, tent & RV sites without hookups $10-15; ☉24hr) is a crumbling, decaying beauty, a vision of ancient earth. Roads and rivers make inroads into this high-desert wilderness stretching 527 sq miles, but much of it is still untamed. You can hike, raft and 4WD here but be sure that you have plenty of gas, food and water. **Cataract Canyon** offers some of the wildest white water in the West (find outfitters in Moab and Green River).

The canyons of the Colorado and Green Rivers divide the park into separate districts. The **Island in the Sky** district offers amazing overlooks. The **visitor center** (☑435-259-4712; Hwy 313, Canyonlands National Park; ☉visitor center 8am-6pm Mar-Oct, 9am-4pm Nov-Feb) is 32 miles northwest of Moab. Our favorite short hike there is the half-mile loop to oft-photographed **Mesa Arch**, a slender, cliff-hugging span framing a picturesque view of Washer Woman Arch and Buck Canyon. Drive a bit further to reach the **Grand View Overlook** trail; the path follows the canyon's edge and ends at a praise-your-maker precipice. Wilder and more far-flung, the **Needles** section is ideal for backpacking and off-roading. To reach the **visitor center** (☑435-259-4711; Hwy 211; ☉8am-6pm Mar-Oct, 9am-4:30pm Nov-Feb), follow Hwy 191 south and Hwy 211 west, 40 miles from Moab. Both sections have small, basic campgrounds (no

showers) that are available first-come, first served.

In addition to normal entrance fees, advance-reservation permits ($10 to $30) are required for backcountry camping, 4WD trips and river trips. For more, contact the **Backcountry Reservations Office** (☑435-259-4351; http://www.nps.gov/cany/planyourvisit/backcountrypermits.htm; Canyonlands National Park).

Dead Horse Point State Park

Tiny but stunning **Dead Horse Point State Park** (www.stateparks.utah.gov; Hwy 313; park day-use per vehicle $10, tent & RV sites $20; ☉park 6am-10pm, visitor center 8am-6pm Mar-Oct, 9am-4pm Nov-Feb) has been the setting for numerous movies, including scenes from *Mission Impossible II* and *Thelma & Louise*. Located en route to the Needles Section of Canyonlands NP, the park is an easy stop off Hwy 313. Mesmerizing views are worth the detour: look out at red-rock canyons rimmed with white cliffs, the Colorado River, Canyonlands and the distant La Sal Mountains. The 21-site campground has limited water (bringing your own is highly recommended); no showers, no hookups. Reserve ahead.

Bluff

One hundred miles south of Moab, this tiny tot town (population 258) makes a comfortable, laid-back base for exploring the desolately beautiful southeastern corner of Utah. Bluff sits surrounded by redrock and public lands near the junction of Hwys 191 and 162, along the San Juan River. The settlement was founded by Mormon pioneers in 1880. Other than a trading post and a couple of places to eat or sleep, there's not much town.

For backcountry tours that access rock art and ruins, hire **Far Out Expeditions** (☑435-672-2294; www.faroutexpeditions.com; half-day from $125) to lead a day or multiday hike into the remote region. A rafting trip with **Wild Rivers Expeditions** (☑800-422-7654; www.riversandruins.com; 101 Main St; day trip adult/child $175/133), a history and geology-minded outfitter, also includes ancient site visits.

The hospitable **Recapture Lodge** (☑435-672-2281; www.recapturelodge.com; Hwy 191; r incl breakfast $70-90; ❋@🛜❋) is a rustic, cozy place to stay. Owners sell maps and know the region inside and out; you can follow trails from here to the river. Also nice are the spacious log rooms at the **Desert Rose Inn** (✆888-475-7673, 435-672-2303; www.desertroseinn.com; Hwy 191; r $105-119, cabins $139-179; ✳@🖙).

Artsy **Comb Ridge Coffee** (www.combridgecoffee.com; 680 S Hwy 191; dishes $3-7; ◷7am-5pm Tue-Sun, varies Nov-Feb; ☏) serves espresso, muffins and sandwiches inside a timber and adobe cafe. For lunch and dinner, the organic-minded **San Juan River Kitchen** (www.sanjuanriverkitchen.com; 75 E Main St; mains $14-20; ◷5:30-10pm Tue-Sat) offers regionally sourced, inspired Mexican American dishes.

Hovenweep National Monument

Beautiful, little-visited **Hovenweep** (www.nps.gov/hove; Hwy 262; park 7-day per vehicle $6, tent & RV sites $10; ◷park dusk-dawn, visitor center 8am-6pm Jun-Sep, 9am-5pm Oct-May), meaning 'deserted valley' in the Ute language, contains impressive towers and granaries that are part of prehistoric Ancestral Puebloan sites. The Square Tower Group is accessed near the visitor center; other sites require long hikes. The campground has 31 basic, first-come, first-served sites (no showers, no hookups). The main access is east of Hwy 191 on Hwy 262 via Hatch Trading Post, more than 40 miles northeast of Bluff.

Monument Valley

Twenty-five miles west from Bluff, after the village of **Mexican Hat** (named for an easy-to-spot sombrero-shaped rock), Hwy 163 winds southwest and enters the Navajo Indian reservation. Thirty miles south, the incredible mesas and buttes of **Monument Valley** rise up. Most of the area, including the tribal park with a 17-mile unpaved driving loop circling the massive formations, is in Arizona (p849).

Natural Bridges National Monument

Fifty-five miles northwest of Bluff, this really remote **monument** (www.nps.gov/nabr; Hwy 275; park 7-day per vehicle $6, tent & RV sites $10; ◷24hr, visitor center 8am-6pm May-Sep, 9am-5pm Oct-Apr) protects a white sandstone canyon (it's not red!) containing three impressive and easily accessible natural bridges. The oldest, the Owachomo Bridge, spans 180ft but is only 9ft thick. The flat 9-mile Scenic Drive loop is ideal for overlooking. The

campground has 13 basic sites (no showers, no hookups) that are available on a first-come, first-served basis. There is some primitive overflow camping space, but be aware that there are no services before Blanding (40 miles east).

Zion & Southwestern Utah

Local tourist boards call it 'color country,' but the cutesy label hardly does justice to the eye-popping hues that saturate the landscape. The deep-crimson canyons of Zion, the delicate pink-and-orange minarets at Bryce Canyon, the swirling yellow-white domes of Capitol Reef – the land is so spectacular that located here are three national parks and the gigantic Grand Staircase-Escalante National Monument (GSENM).

Capitol Reef National Park

Not as crowded as its fellow parks but equally scenic, **Capitol Reef** (✆435-425-3791, ext 4111; www.nps.gov/care; cnr Hwy 24 & Scenic Dr; admission free, 7-day scenic drive per vehicle $5, tent & RV sites $10; ◷24hr, visitor center & scenic drive 8am-6pm Apr-Oct, to 4:30pm Nov-Mar) contains much of the 100-mile Waterpocket Fold, created 65 million years ago when the earth's surface buckled up and folded, exposing a cross-section of geologic history that is downright painterly in its colorful intensity. Hwy 24 cuts grandly through the park, but

ⓘ ELEVATION MATTERS

As elsewhere, southern Utah is generally warmer than northern Utah. But before you go making any assumptions about weather, check the elevation of your destination. Places less than an hour apart may have several thousand feet of elevation – and 20°F temperature – difference.

➡ St George (3000ft)

➡ Zion National Park – Springdale entrance (3900ft)

➡ Cedar Breaks National Monument (10,000ft)

➡ Bryce National Park Lodge (8100ft)

➡ Moab (4026ft)

➡ Salt Lake City (4226ft)

➡ Park City (7100ft)

make sure to take the **scenic drive** south, which passes through orchards – a legacy of Mormon settlement. In season, you can freely pick cherries, peaches and apples, as well as stop by the historic **Gifford Farmhouse** to see an old homestead and buy fruit-filled minipies. The shady, green campground (no showers, no hookups) is first-come, first-served; it fills early spring through fall.

Torrey

Just 15 miles west of Capital Reef, the small pioneer town of Torrey serves as the base for most national park visitors. In addition to a few Old West–era buildings, there are a dozen or so restaurants and motels.

Western-themed on the outside, **Austin's Chuckwagon Motel** (☎435-425-3335; www.austinschuckwagonmotel.com; 12 W Main St; r $75-85, cabins $135; ☺Mar-Oct; ✴☎✳✳) has nice, clean, slightly characterless guest rooms on the inside. Note that budget digs are over the general store, where you can grab supplies or sandwiches.

Dressed with country elegance, each airy room at the 1914 **Torrey Schoolhouse B&B** (☎435-633-4643; www.torreyschoolhouse.com; 150 N Center St; r incl breakfast $118-148; ☺Apr-Oct; ✴☎) has a story to tell. (Butch Cassidy may have attended a town dance here.) After consuming the full gourmet breakfast, laze in the garden or the huge 1st-floor lounge before you head out hiking.

Whenever possible, **Capitol Reef Cafe** (☎435-425-3271; www.capitolreefinn.com; 360 W Main St; breakfast & lunch $6-12, dinner $16-22; ☺7am-9pm Apr-Oct) uses local and organic ingredients in its meals. Homemade pies are a hit, but so are healthier dishes like trout. At this writing, the renowned local restaurant, **Cafe Diablo** (☎435-425-3070; http://cafediablo.net; 599 W Main St; lunch $10-14, dinner $22-40; ☺11:30am-10pm mid-Apr–Oct; ✎) was undergoing an ownership change.

If you want to explore further or find local outfitters, contact the **Wayne County Travel Council** (☎800-858-7951, 435-425-3365; www.capitolreef.org; cnr Hwys 24 & 12; ☺noon-7pm Mon-Sat Apr-Oct).

Boulder

Though the tiny outpost of **Boulder** (www.boulderutah.com), population 227, is just 32 miles south of Torrey on Hwy 12, you have to cross over Boulder Mountain to get there. The area is so rugged and isolated that a paved Hwy 12 didn't connect through until 1985. From here, the attractive **Burr Trail Rd** heads east across the northeastern corner of the Grand Staircase-Escalante National Monument, eventually winding up on a gravel road that leads either up to Capital Reef or down to Bullfrog Marina on Lake Powell.

To explore area canyons and rock art, consider a one-day (pet-friendly) trek with knowledgeable **Earth Tours** (☎435-691-1241; www.earth-tours.com; trips per person from $150; ☺Mar-Oct; ✴). The small but excellent **Anasazi State Park Museum** (www.stateparks.utah.gov; Main St/Hwy 12; admission $5; ☺8am-6pm Mar-Oct, 9am-5pm Nov-Apr) curates artifacts and a Native American site inhabited from AD 1130 to 1175. Get information on area public lands inside the museum, at the GSENM Interagency Desk.

Rooms at **Boulder Mountain Lodge** (☎435-335-7460; www.boulder-utah.com; 20 N Hwy 12; r $110-175; ✴@☎) are plush, but it's the 15-acre wildlife sanctuary setting that's unsurpassed. An outdoor hot tub with mountain views is a particularly soothing spot to bird-watch. The lodge's destination restaurant, **Hell's Backbone Grill** (☎435-335-7464; http://hellsbackbonegrill.com; 20 N Hwy 12, Boulder Mountain Lodge; breakfast $8-12, lunch $12-18, dinner $18-27; ☺7:30-11:30am & 5-9:30pm Mar-Oct) serves soulful, earthy preparations of regionally inspired and sourced cuisine. Book ahead.

Organic vegetable tarts, eclectic burgers and scrumptious homemade desserts at **Burr Trail Grill & Outpost** (http://burrtrailgrill.com; cnr Hwy 12 & Burr Trail Rd; dishes $8-18; ☺grill 11am-2:30pm & 5-9:30pm, outpost 7:30am-8pm Mar-Oct; ☎) rival dishes at the more famous Hell's Backbone Grill nearby. You'll also find a coffee shop and a gallery.

Grand Staircase-Escalante National Monument

The 2656-sq-mile **Grand Staircase-Escalante National Monument** (GSENM; www.ut.blm.gov/monument; ☺24hr) **FREE** covers more territory than Delaware and Rhode Island combined. It sprawls between Capitol Reef National Park, Glen Canyon National Recreation Area and Bryce Canyon National Park. The nearest services, and GSENM visitor centers, are in Boulder and Escalante on Hwy 12 in the north, and Kanab on US 89 in the south. Otherwise, infrastructure is minimal, leaving a vast, uninhabited canyonland full of 4WD roads that call to adventurous travelers who have the time, equipment and knowledge to explore. Be warned: this waterless region was so inhospitable that it was the last to be mapped in the continental US.

A 6-mile round-trip to the falls at **Lower Calf Creek** (Mile 75, Hwy 12; day use $2, tent & RV sites $7; ⊙ day use dawn-dusk), between Boulder and Escalante, is the most accessible and most used trail in the park. The 13 popular creekside campsites (no showers, no hookups) fill fast; no reservations taken.

Escalante

This national monument gateway town of 792 people is the closest thing to a metropolis for miles and miles. It's a good place to base yourself – or to stock up and map it out – before venturing into the adjacent GSENM. The **Escalante Interagency Office** (☑ 435-826-5499; www.ut.blm.gov/monument; 775 W Main St; ⊙ 8am-4:30pm daily Apr-Sep, Mon-Fri Oct-Mar) is a superb resource center with complete information on all monument and forest service lands in the area. Escalante is 30 slow and windy miles from Boulder and 65 from Torrey, near Capital Reef National Park.

Escalante Outfitters & Cafe (☑ 435-826-4266; www.escalanteoutfitters.com; 310 W Main St; ⊙ 8am-9pm) is a traveler's oasis: the bookstore sells maps, guides, camping supplies – and liquor(!). The pleasant cafe is the place for homemade breakfast, pizzas and salads. It also rents out tiny, rustic cabins ($45) and mountain bikes (from $35 per day). Long-time area outfitter **Excursions of Escalante** (☑ 800-839-7567; www.excursionsofescalante.com; 125 E Main St; full-day from $145; ⊙ 8am-6pm) leads canyoneering, climbing and photo hikes; it, too, has a cafe on site.

There are a number of decent lodgings in town, including **Canyons Bed & Breakfast** (☑ 866-526-9667, 435-826-4747; www.canyonsbnb.com; 120 E Main St; r incl breakfast $135-165; ❋ 🕯) with upscale cabin-rooms that surround a shady courtyard, and the **Circle D Motel** (☑ 435-826-4297; www.escalantecircledmotel.com; 475 W Main St; r $65-75; ❋ 🕯 🐾), an older-but-updated budget motel with a friendly proprietor and a full-service restaurant.

Kodachrome Basin State Park

Dozens of red, pink and white sandstone chimneys highlight this colorful **state park** (☑ 435-679-8562; www.stateparks.utah.gov; off

Cottonwood Canyon Rd; day-use per vehicle $6, tent & RV sites with/without hookups $25/16; ⊙ day use 6am-10pm), named for its photogenic landscape by the National Geographic Society. Some of the developed campsites (showers available) at the campground can be reserved online. Horseback riding and cabin concessions also on-site.

Bryce Canyon National Park

The Grand Staircase, a series of steplike uplifted rock layers elevating north from the Grand Canyon, culminates at this rightly popular **national park** (☑ 435-834-5322; www.stateparks.utah.gov; Hwy 63; 7-day vehicle pass $25, tent & RV sites without hookups $15; ⊙ 24hr; visitor center 8am-8pm May-Sep, to 4:30pm Oct-Apr) in the Pink Cliffs formation. It's full of wondrous sorbet-colored pinnacles and points, steeples and spires, and totem-pole-shaped 'hoodoo' formations. The 'canyon' is actually an amphitheater eroded from the cliffs. From Hwy 12, turn south on Hwy 63; the park is 50 miles southwest of Escalante.

Rim Road Scenic Drive (8000ft) travels 18 miles, roughly following the canyon rim past the visitor center, the lodge, incredible overlooks (don't miss **Inspiration Point**) and trailheads, ending at **Rainbow Point** (9115ft). From early May through early October, a free shuttle bus runs (8am until at least 5:30pm) from a staging area just north of the park to as far south as **Bryce Amphitheater**.

The park has two camping areas, both of which accept some reservations through the park website. **Sunset Campground** is bit more wooded, but is not open year round. Coin-op laundry and showers are available at the general store near **North Campground**. During summer, remaining first-come sites fill before noon.

The 1920s **Bryce Canyon Lodge** (☑877-386-4383, 435-834-8700; www.brycecanyonforever.com; Hwy 63, Bryce Canyon National Park; r & cabins $175-200; ☺Apr-Oct; @) exudes rustic mountain charm. Rooms are in modern hotel-style units, with up-to-date furnishings, and thin-walled duplex cabins with gas fireplaces and front porches. No TVs. The lodge **restaurant** (☑435-834-8700; Bryce Canyon National Park; breakfasts $6-12, lunch & dinner $18-40; ☺7-10:30am, 11:30am-3pm & 5:30-10pm Apr-Oct) is excellent, if expensive.

Just north of the park boundaries, **Ruby's Inn** (☑435-834-5341; www.rubysinn.com; 1000 S Hwy 63; r $115-170, tent sites $26-55, RV sites with hookups $35-60; ✻@✿✖) is a town as much as it is a resort complex. Choose from several motel lodging options, plus a campground, before you take a helicopter ride, watch a rodeo, admire Western art, wash laundry, shop for groceries, fill up with gas, dine at one of several restaurants and then post a letter about it all.

Eleven miles east of the park on Hwy 12, the small town of **Tropic** (www.brycecanyoncountry.com/tropic.html) has additional food and lodging.

Kanab

At the southern edge of Grand Staircase-Escalante National Monument, vast expanses of rugged desert surround remote Kanab (population 3564). Western filmmakers made dozens of films here from the 1920s to the 1970s, and the town still has an Old West movie-set feel to it.

The **Kanab GSENM Visitor Center** (☑435-644-1300; www.ut.blm.gov/monument; 745 E Hwy 89; ☺8am-4:30pm) provides monument information; **Kane County Office of Tourism** (☑800-733-5263, 435-644-5033; www.kaneutah.com; 78 S 100 East; ☺9am-7pm Mon-Fri, to 5pm Sat) focuses on town and movie sites. John Wayne, Maureen O'Hara and Gregory Peck are a few Hollywood notables who slumbered at the somewhat-dated **Parry Lodge** (☑888-289-1722, 435-644-2601; www.parrylodge.com; 89 E Center St; r 70-125; ✻✿✖✿).

A colorful, retro-cool style pervades all 13 rooms at **Quail Park Lodge** (☑435-215-1447; www.quailparklodge.com; 125 N 300 W; r $115-159; ✻@✿✖✿), a refurbished 1963 motorcourt motel. Stay there, then eat downtown at **Rocking V Cafe** (www.rockingvcafe.com; 97 W Center St; lunch $9-14, dinner $15-29; ☺11:30am-10pm; ☑), where fresh ingredients star in

dishes such as buffalo tenderloin and curried quinoa.

Zion National Park

Entering **Zion National Park** (www.nps.gov/zion; Hwy 9; 7-day per vehicle $25; ☺24hr; Zion Canyon visitor center 8am-7:30pm Jun-Aug, closes earlier rest of year) from the east along Hwy 9, the route rolls past yellow sandstone and **Checkerboard Mesa** before reaching an impressive gallery-dotted tunnel and 3.5 miles of switchbacks going down in red-rock splendor. More than 100 miles of park trails here offer everything from leisurely strolls to wilderness backpacking and camping.

If you've time for only one activity, the 6-mile **Scenic Drive**, which pierces the heart of Zion Canyon, is it. From April through October, taking a free shuttle from the visitor center is required, but you can hop off and on at any of the scenic stops and trailheads along the way. The famous **Angels Landing Trail** is a strenuous, 5.4-mile vertigo-inducer (1400ft elevation gain, with sheer drop-offs), but the views of Zion Canyon are phenomenal. Allow four hours round-trip.

For the 16-mile backpacking trip down through the **Narrows** (June to September only), you need a hiker shuttle (book through Zion Adventure Company (p875) and a backcountry permit from the visitor center, which in season requires advance reservations available on the park website. You can get part of the experience by walking up from **Riverside Walk** 5 miles to **Big Springs**, where the canyon walls narrow and day trips end. Remember, in either direction, you're hiking *in* the Virgin River for most of the time.

Reserve far ahead and request a riverside site in the cottonwood-shaded **Watchman Campground** (☑for reservations 877-444-6777; www.recreation.gov; Hwy 9, Zion National Park; tent sites $16, RV sites with hookups $18-20) by the canyon. Adjacent **South Campground** (Hwy 9, Zion National Park; tent & RV sites without hookups $16; ☺early Mar-Oct) is first-come, first-served only. Together these two campgrounds have almost 300 sites.

Smack in the middle of the scenic drive, rustic **Zion Lodge** (☑435-772-7700, 888-297-2757; www.zionlodge.com; Zion Canyon Scenic Dr; r $185, cabins $195, ste $225; ✻@✿) has 81 well-appointed motel rooms and 40 cabins with gas fireplaces. All have wooden porches with stellar red-rock cliff views, but no TVs. The lodge's full-service dining room, **Red Rock Grill** (☑435-772-7760; Zion Canyon Scenic Dr, Zion Lodge; breakfast & sandwiches $8-14, dinner $18-30; ⊙6:30-10:30am, 11:30am-3pm & 5-10pm Mar-Oct, hours vary Nov-Feb), has similarly amazing views. Just outside the park, the town of Springdale offers many more services.

Note that you must pay an entrance fee to drive on public Hwy 9 through the park, even if you are just passing through. Motorhome drivers are also required to pay a $15 escort fee to cross through the 1.1-mile Zion-Mt Carmel tunnel at the east entrance.

Springdale

Positioned at the main south, entrance to Zion National Park, Springdale is a perfect little park town. Stunning red cliffs form the backdrop to eclectic cafes, restaurants are big on organic ingredients, and artist galleries are interspersed with indie motels and B&Bs.

In addition to hiking trails in the national park, you can take outfitter-led climbing, canyoneering, mountain biking and 4WD trips (from $140 per person, per half-day) on adjacent BLM lands. All the excellent excursions from **Zion Rock & Mountain Guides** (⊡435-772-3303; www.zionrockguides.com; 1458 Zion Park Blvd; ⊙8am-8pm Mar-Oct, hours vary Nov-Feb), including family trips, are private; solo travelers may be able to save money by joining an existing group through **Zion Adventure Company** (⊡435-772-1001; www. zionadventures.com; 36 Lion Blvd; ⊙8am-8pm Mar-Oct, 9am-noon & 4-7pm Nov-Feb). Both offer Narrows outfitting and have hiker/biker shuttles; the latter also offers river tubing in summer.

Springdale has an abundance of good restaurants and nice lodging options. The updated motorcourt rooms at **Canyon Ranch Motel** (⊡866-946-6276, 435-772-3357; www. canyonranchmotel.com; 668 Zion Park Blvd; r $99-119, apt $120-140; ❉ 🛜 ⚫) ring a shady lawn with picnic tables and swings. Five flower-filled acres spill down to the Virgin River bank at **Cliffrose Lodge** (⊡800-243-8824, 435-772-3234; www.cliffroselodge.com; 281 Zion Park Blvd; r $159-189; ❉ 🛜 ⚫).

Of the area B&Bs, **Zion Canyon B&B** (⊡435-772-9466; www.zioncanyonbandb.com; 101 Kokopelli Circle; r incl breakfast $135-185; ❉ 🛜) is the most traditional, serving a full, sit-down repast. We like the **Red Rock Inn** (⊡435-772-3139; www.redrockinn.com; 998 Zion Park Blvd; cottages incl breakfast $127-132; ❉ 🛜) for its individual, upscale cottages and pastry-chef-quality goodies delivered to your door. The owners' creative collections of art and artifact enliven the 1930s bungalow that is **Under the Eaves Inn** (⊡435-772-3457; www. undertheeaves.com; 980 Zion Park Blvd; r incl breakfast $110-160, ste $185; ❉ 🛜); the morning meal is a gift certificate to a local restaurant.

For a coffee and *trés bonnes* crêpes – both sweet and savory – make **Meme's Cafe** (www.facebook.com/memescafezion#!; 975 Zion Park Blvd; dishes $6-10; ⊙7am-9pm) your first stop of the day. It also serves paninis and waffles, and in season has live music and barbecues on the patio. In the evening, the Mexican-tiled patio with twinkly lights at **Oscar's Cafe** (www.cafeoscars.com; 948 Zion Park Blvd; breakfast & burgers $10-15, dinner mains $16-30; ⊙8am-10pm) and the rustic **Bit & Spur Restaurant & Saloon** (www.bitandspur. com; 1212 Zion Park Blvd; mains $16-28; ⊙5-10pm daily Mar-Oct, 5-10pm Thu-Sat Nov-Feb) are local-favored places to hang out, eat and drink.

Zion Canyon Visitors Bureau (⊡888-518-7070; www.zionpark.com) does not have a physical office; research or request a town guide online. A free Springdale menu magazine, available at local lodgings, comes out every spring.

St George

Nicknamed 'Dixie' for its warm weather and southern location, St George (population 75,561) is popular with retirees. This spacious Mormon town, with an eye-catching temple and pioneer buildings, is a possible stop between Las Vegas (120 miles) and Salt

---

IF YOU HAVE A FEW MORE DAYS: CEDAR CITY & BREAKS

At 10,000ft, the summer-only road to **Cedar Breaks National Monument** (⊡435-586-0787; www.nps.gov/cebr; Hwy 148; 7-day per person $4; ⊙24hr, visitor center 9am-6pm mid-Jun–mid-Oct) is one of the last to open after winter snow. But it's worth the wait for the amazing amphitheater overlooks that rival those of Bryce Canyon. Nearby **Cedar City** (www.scenicsouthernutah.com) is known for its four-month-long Shakespeare Festival and an abundance of B&Bs. The town is on I-15, 52 miles north of St George and 90 miles west of Bryce Canyon; the national monument is 22 miles northeast of the town.

Lake City (304 miles) – or en route to Zion National Park. The 15,000-sq-ft collection of in-situ dino tracks and exhibits at **Dinosaur Discovery Site** (www.dinotrax.com; 2200 E Riverside Dr; adult/child $6/3; ⊘10am-6pm Mon-Sat) are worth a detour.

Nearly every chain motel known to man is represented somewhere in St George; they're your best bet if you're looking for lodging cheaper than what's available 40 miles (one hour) east in Springdale. **Best Western Coral Hills** (☑800-542-7733, 435-673-4844; www.coralhills.com; 125 E St George Blvd; r incl breakfast $80-139; ✿@☎☒) is walking distance from downtown restaurants and historic buildings. Two lovely, late-1800 houses contain **Seven Wives Inn** (☑800-600-3737, 435-628-3737; www.sevenwivesinn.com; 217 N 100 West; r & ste incl breakfast $99-185; ✿@☎☒), a B&B with a small, central swimming pool.

The **Utah Welcome Center** (☑435-673-4542; http://travel.utah.gov; 1835 S Convention Center Dr, Dixie Convention Center; ⊘8:30am-5:30pm), off I-15, addresses statewide queries.

NEW MEXICO

It's called the Land of Enchantment for a reason. The play of sunlight on juniper-speckled hills that roll to infinity; the traditional Hispanic mountain villages with pitched tin roofs atop old adobe homes; the gentle magnificence of the 13,000ft Sangre de Cristo Mountains; plus volcanoes, river canyons and vast high desert plains beneath an even vaster sky – the beauty sneaks up on you, then casts a powerful spell. The culture, too, is alluring, with silhouetted crosses topping historic mud-brick churches, ancient and living Indian pueblos, chili-smothered enchiladas, real-life cowboys and a vibe of otherness that makes the state feel like it might be a foreign country.

The legend of Billy the Kid lurks around every corner. Miracle healings bring flocks of faithful pilgrims to Chimayo. Bats plumb the ethereal corners of Carlsbad Caverns. Something crashed near Roswell...

Maybe New Mexico's indescribable charm is best expressed in the captivating paintings of Georgia O'Keeffe, the state's patron artist. She herself exclaimed, on her very first visit: 'Well! Well! Well!...This is wonderful! No one told me it was like this.'

But seriously, how could they?

History

People roamed the land here as far back as 10,500 BC, but by Coronado's arrival in the 16th century, pueblos (Native American villages) were the dominant communities. Santa Fe was crowned the colonial capital in 1610, after which Spanish settlers and farmers fanned out across northern New Mexico, and missionaries began their often violent efforts to convert the area's Puebloans to Catholicism. Following a successful revolt in 1680, Native Americans occupied Santa Fe until 1692, when Diego de Vargas recaptured the city.

In 1851 New Mexico became US territory. Native American wars, settlement by cowboys and miners and trade along the Santa Fe Trail further transformed the region, and the arrival of the railroad in the 1870s created an economic boom.

Painters and writers set up art colonies in Santa Fe and Taos in the early 20th century. In 1943 a scientific community descended on Los Alamos and developed the atomic bomb. For the past few years, New Mexico has been hit hard by drought.

❶ Information

Where opening hours are listed by season (not month), readers should call first, as hours can fluctuate based on weather, budgets or for no reason at all.

New Mexico Route 66 Association (www.rt66nm.org) Information on the famous path through the state.

New Mexico State Parks Division (☑888-667-2757; www.emnrd.state.nm.us/SPD) Info on state parks, with a link to camping reservations.

Public Lands Information Center (☑877-851-8946; www.publiclands.org) Camping and recreation information.

Albuquerque

This bustling crossroads has a sneaky charm, one based more on its locals than big-city sparkle. The citizens here are proud of their city, and folks are more than happy to share history, highlights and must-try restaurants – which makes the state's most populous city much more than a dot on the Route 66 map.

Centuries-old adobes line the lively Old Town area, and the shops, restaurants and bars in the hip Nob Hill zone are all within easy walking distance of each other. Ancient petroglyphs cover rocks just outside town while modern museums explore space and nuclear energy. There's a distinctive and vibrant mix of university students, Native Americans, Hispanics, gays and lesbians. You'll find square dances and yoga classes flyered with equal enthusiasm, and ranch hands and real-estate brokers chowing down at hole-in-the-wall taquerias and retro cafes.

Albuquerque's major boundaries are Paseo del Norte Dr to the north, Central Ave to the south, Rio Grande Blvd to the west and Tramway Blvd to the east. Central Ave is the main artery (aka old Route 66) – it passes through Old Town, Downtown, the university and Nob Hill. The city is divided into four quadrants (NW, NE, SW and SE), and the intersection of Central Ave and the railroad tracks just east of Downtown serves as the center point of the city.

◉ Sights

◉ Old Town

From its foundation in 1706 until the arrival of the railroad in 1880, the plaza was the hub of Albuquerque; today Old Town is the city's most popular tourist area.

Also in the Old Town are **San Felipe de Neri Church** (www.sanfelipedeneri.org; Old Town Plaza; ⊙7am-5:30pm daily, museum 9:30am-4:30pm Mon-Sat), built in 1793, ¡Explora! (p878) and the **New Mexico Museum of Natural History & Science** (www.nmnaturalhistory.org; 1801 Mountain Rd NW; adult/child $7/4; ⊙9am-5pm; ♿).

★ **American International Rattlesnake Museum** MUSEUM
(www.rattlesnakes.com; 202 San Felipe St NW; adult/child $5/3; ⊙10am-6pm Mon-Sat, 1-5pm Sun May-Sep, 11:30am-5:30pm Mon-Fri, 10am-6pm Sat, 1-5pm Sun, Sep-May) From eastern diamondback to rare tiger rattlers, you won't find more types of live rattlesnakes anywhere else in the world. Once you get over the freak-out factor, you'll be amazed not just by the variety of vipers but by the intricate beauty of their colors and patterns. Hopefully you'll never see them this close in the wild! Weekday hours are a little longer in summer.

Albuquerque Museum of Art & History MUSEUM
(www.cabq.gov/museum; 2000 Mountain Rd NW; adult/child $4/1; ⊙9am-5pm Tue-Sun) Conquistador armor and weaponry are highlights at the Albuquerque Museum of Art & History, where visitors can study the city's tricultural Native American, Hispanic and Anglo past. Works by New Mexico artists also featured.

◉ Around Town

The University of New Mexico (UNM) area has loads of good restaurants, casual bars, offbeat shops and hip college hangouts. The main drag is Central Ave between University and Carlisle Blvds. Just east is trendy Nob Hill, a pedestrian-friendly neighborhood lined with indie coffee shops, stylish boutiques and patio-wrapped restaurants.

★ **Indian Pueblo Cultural Center** MUSEUM
(IPCC; ☎505-843-7270; www.indianpueblo.org; 2401 12th St NW; adult/child $6/3; ⊙9am-5pm) Operated by New Mexico's 19 pueblos, the Indian Pueblo Cultural Center is a must for contextualizing the history of northern

---

NEW MEXICO FACTS

Nickname Land of Enchantment

Population 2 million

Area 121,599 sq miles

Capital city Santa Fe (population 68,700)

Other cities Albuquerque (population 553,000), Las Cruces (population 99,700)

Sales tax 5% to 8%

Birthplace of John Denver (1943–97), Smokey Bear (1950–76)

Home of International UFO Museum & Research Center (Roswell), Julia Roberts

Politics A 'purple' state, with a more liberal north and conservative south

Famous for Ancient pueblos, the first atomic bomb (1945), where Bugs Bunny should have turned left

State question 'Red or green?' (chili sauce, that is)

Highest/Lowest points Wheeler Peak (13,161ft)/Red Bluff Reservior (2842ft)

Driving distances Albuquerque to Santa Fe 50 miles, Santa Fe to Taos 71 miles

SOUTHWEST ALBUQUERQUE

New Mexico. Appealing displays trace the development of Pueblo cultures, exhibit customs and crafts, and feature changing exhibits.

National Museum of
Nuclear Science & History   MUSEUM
(www.nuclearmuseum.org; 601 Eubank Blvd SE; adult/child & senior $8/7; ⊙9am-5pm; ⊛) Exhibits examine the Manhattan Project, the history of arms control and the use of nuclear energy as an alternative energy source. Docents here are retired military, and they're very knowledgeable.

Petroglyph National
Monument   ARCHAEOLOGICAL SITE
(www.nps.gov/petr; ⊙visitor center 8am-5pm) 🖉 More than 20,000 rock etchings are found inside the Petroglyph National Monument northwest of town. Stop by the visitor center (on Western Trail at Unser Blvd) to determine which of three viewing trails – in different sections of the park – best suits your interests. For a hike with great views but no rock art, hit the Volcanoes trail. Note: smash-and-grab thefts have been reported at some trailhead parking lots, so don't leave valuables in your vehicle. Head west on I-40 across the Rio Grande and take exit 154 north.

Sandia Peak Tramway   CABLE CAR
(www.sandiapeak.com; Tramway Blvd; vehicles $1, adult/youth 13-20yr/child $20/17/12; ⊙9am-8pm Wed-Mon, from 5pm Tue Sep-May, 9am-9pm Jun-Aug) The 2.7-mile Sandia Peak Tramway starts in the desert realm of cholla cactus and soars to the pines atop 10,378ft Sandia Peak in about 15 minutes. The views are huge and that's what you're paying for at the restaurant at the top.

🏃 Activities

The omnipresent Sandia Mountains and the less-crowded Manzano Mountains offer outdoor activities, including hiking, skiing (downhill and cross-country), mountain biking, rock climbing and camping. For information and maps, head to the Cibola National Forest office (☑505-346-3900; 2113 Osuna Rd NE; ⊙8am-4:45pm Mon-Fri) or the Sandia Ranger Station (☑505-281-3304; 11776 Hwy 337, Tijeras; ⊙8am-4:30pm Mon-Fri), off I-40 exit 175 south, about 15 miles east of Albuquerque.

Sandia Crest National
Scenic Byway   DRIVING, HIKING
(I-40 exit 175 north) Reach the top of the Sandias via the eastern slope along the lovely Sandia Crest National Scenic Byway, which passes numerous hiking trailheads. Alternatively, take the Sandia Peak Tramway or Hwy 165 from Placitas (I-25 exit 242), a dirt road through Las Huertas Canyon that passes the prehistoric dwelling of Sandia Man Cave.

Sandia Peak Ski Park   SKIING/CYCLING
(☑505-242-9052; www.sandiapeak.com; lift tickets adult/child $50/40; ⊙9am-4pm Dec-Mar & Jun-Sep) Sometimes the snow here is great, other times it's lame, so check before heading up. The ski area opens on summer weekends and holidays (June to September) for mountain bikers. You can rent a bike at the base facility ($58 with $650 deposit) or ride the chairlift to the top of the peak with your own bike ($14). Drive here via Scenic Byway 536, or take the Sandia Peak Tramway (skis are allowed on the tram, but not bikes).

Discover Balloons   BALLOONING
(☑505-842-1111; www.discoverballoons.com; 205c San Felipe NW; adult/under 12yr $160/125) Sev-

---

ALBUQUERQUE FOR CHILDREN

The gung-ho ¡Explora! (www.explora.us; 1701 Mountain Rd NW; adult/child $8/4; ⊙10am-6pm Mon-Sat, noon-6pm Sun; ⊛) will captivate your kiddies for hours. From the lofty high-wire bike to the leaping waters to the arts-and-crafts workshop, there's a hands-on exhibit for every type of child (don't miss the elevator). Not traveling with kids? Check the website to see if you're in town for the popular 'Adult Night.' Typically hosted by an acclaimed local scientist, it's become one of the hottest tickets in town.

The teen-friendly New Mexico Museum of Natural History & Science (p877) features an Evolator (evolution elevator), which transports visitors through 38 million years of New Mexico's geologic and evolutionary history. The new Space Frontiers exhibit highlights the state's contribution to space exploration, from ancient Chaco observatories to an impressive, full-scale replica of the Mars Rover. The museum also contains a Planetarium (adult/child $7/4) and the 3-D IMAX-screened DynaTheater (adult/child $10/6).

eral companies will float you over the city and the Rio Grande, including Discover Balloons. Flights last about an hour, and many are offered early in the morning to catch optimal winds and the sunrise.

👉 Tours

From mid-March to mid-December, the Albuquerque Museum of Art & History (p877) offers informative, guided **Old Town walking tours** (⊙11am Tue-Sun, Mar-Dec). They last 45 minutes to an hour and are free with museum admission.

⚜ Festivals & Events

Gathering of Nations Powwow   CULTURAL
(www.gatheringofnations.com; ⊙April) The biggest Native American powwow in the world, with traditional music, dance, food, crafts and the crowning of Miss Indian World.

International Balloon Fiesta   FIESTA
(www.balloonfiesta.com; ⊙early Oct) Some 800,000 spectators are drawn to this weeklong event. The highlight is the mass ascension, when more than 500 hot-air balloons launch nearly simultaneously.

🛏 Sleeping

Route 66 Hostel   HOSTEL $
(☑505-247-1813; www.rt66hostel.com; 1012 Central Ave SW; dm $20, r from $25; P ❋ 🛜) Clean, fun and inexpensive, this place is simple and has a good travelers' vibe. A kitchen, library and outdoor patio are available for its guests to use.

Hotel Blue   HOTEL $
(☑877-878-4868; www.thehotelblue.com; 717 Central Ave NW; r incl breakfast $60-99; P ❋ @ 🛜 ≋) Well positioned beside a park and Downtown, the art-deco 134-room Hotel Blue has Tempurpedic beds and a free airport shuttle. Bonus points awarded for the good-sized pool and 40in flat-screen TVs.

★ Andaluz   BOUTIQUE HOTEL $$
(☑505-242-9090; www.hotelandaluz.com; 125 2nd St NW; r $160-290; P ❋ @ 🛜) Albuquerque's best hotel will wow you with style and attention to detail, from the dazzling lobby – where six arched nooks with tables and couches offer alluring spaces to talk and drink in public-privacy, to the Italian-made hypoallergenic bedding. The restaurant is one of the best in town, and there's a beautiful guest library and a rooftop bar. The hotel is so 'green' you can tour its solar water-

heating system – the largest in the state. You'll get big discounts if you book online.

Mauger Estate B&B   B&B $$
(☑800-719-9189, 505-242-8755; www.maugerbb. com; 701 Roma Ave NW, cnr 7th St NW; r incl breakfast $99-195, ste $160-205, townhouse $129-195; P 🛜 🐾) This restored Queen Anne mansion (Mauger is pronounced 'major') has comfortable rooms with down comforters, stocked fridges and freshly cut flowers. Kids are welcome and there's one dog-friendly room complete with Wild West decor and a small yard ($20 extra).

Böttger Mansion   B&B $$
(☑505-243-3639, 800-758-3639; www.bottger. com; 110 San Felipe St NW; r incl breakfast $104-179; P ❋ @ 🛜) A friendly and informative proprietor gives this well-appointed Victorian-era B&B an edge over some tough competition. The eight-bedroom mansion, built in 1912, is close to Old Town Plaza, top-notch museums and several in-the-know New Mexican restaurants. The honeysuckle-lined courtyard is a favorite with bird-watchers. Famous past guests include Elvis, Janis Joplin and Machine Gun Kelly.

🍴 Eating

★ Frontier   NEW MEXICAN $
(www.frontierrestaurant.com; 2400 Central Ave SE; mains $3-11; ⊙5am-1am; 🅿 🚸) An Albuquerque tradition, the Frontier boasts enormous cinnamon rolls, addictive green-chili stew, and the best huevos rancheros ever. The food and people-watching are outstanding, and students love the low prices on breakfast, burgers and Mexican food.

Flying Star Café   AMERICAN $
(www.flyingstarcafe.com; 3416 Central Ave SE; mains $6-12; ⊙6am-11pm Sun-Thu, to midnight Fri &Sat; 🛜 🅿 🚸) With seven constantly packed locations, including a branch at **Juan Tabo Blvd** (4501 Juan Tabo Blvd NE; ⊙6am-10pm Sun-Thu, 6am-11pm Fri & Sat; 🛜), this is the place to go for creative diner food made with regional ingredients, including homemade soups, main dishes from sandwiches to stir-fries, and yummy desserts. There's something here for everyone.

Golden Crown Panaderia   BAKERY $
(☑505-243-2424; www.goldencrown.biz; 1103 Mountain Rd NW; mains $5-20; ⊙7am-8pm Tue-Sat, 10am-8pm Sun) Who doesn't love a friendly neighborhood bakery? Especially one with gracious staff, fresh-from-the-oven

bread and pizza, fruit-filled empanadas, smooth coffee and the frequent free cookie. Call ahead to reserve a loaf of quick-selling green-chili bread. Go to the website to check out the 'bread cam.'

Annapurna INDIAN $
(www.chaishoppe.com; 2201 Silver Ave SE; mains $7-12; ⊘7am-9pm Mon-Fri, 8am-9pm Sat, 10am-8pm Sun; 🛜🍴) For some of the freshest, tastiest health food in town, grab a seat within the bright, mural-covered walls of Annapurna. The delicately spiced ayurvedic dishes are all vegetarian or vegan, but they're so delicious that even carnivores will find something to love.

Artichoke Café MODERN AMERICAN $$$
(☑505-243-0200; www.artichokecafe.com; 424 Central Ave SE; lunch mains $10-16, dinner mains $19-30; ⊘11am-2:30pm Mon-Fri, 5-9pm daily, to 10pm Fri & Sat) Voted an Albuquerque favorite many times over, this place takes the best from Italian, French and American cuisine and serves it with a touch of class.

🍷 Drinking & Entertainment

Popejoy Hall (www.popejoypresents.com; Central Ave, at Cornell St SE) and the historic **KiMo Theatre** (www.cabq.gov/kimo; 423 Central Ave NW, downtown) are the primary venues for big-name national acts, local opera, symphony and theater. To find out what's happening in town, grab a free copy of the weekly *Alibi* or visit www.alibi.com. Most of Albuquerque's trendy cafes and bars are found in the Nob Hill/UNM districts, though a few good ones are downtown.

Satellite Coffee CAFE
(2300 Central Ave SE; ⊘6am-11pm; 🛜) Don't be put off by the hip, space-age appearance. The staff are welcoming and seats are filled with all manner of laptop-viewing, java-swilling locals. There are eight locations scattered across town; also try the one in **Nob Hill** (3513 Central Ave NE, Nob Hill).

Anodyne BAR
(409 Central Ave NW; ⊘4pm-1:30am Mon-Fri, 7pm-1:30am Sat, 7-11:30pm Sun) Anodyne is a huge but cozy space with 10 red pool tables, wood ceilings, plenty of overstuffed chairs, more than 100 bottled beers. You'll find a diverse crowd where everyone belongs.

Kelly's Brewery BREWERY
(www.kellysbrewpub.com; 3222 Central Ave SE; ⊘8am-10:30pm Sun-Thu, to midnight Fri & Sat)

Grab a seat at a communal table then settle in for a convivial night of people-watching and house-brewed pints at this former Ford dealership and gas station. On warm spring nights, it seems everyone in town is chilling on the sprawling patio.

Launch Pad LIVE MUSIC
(www.launchpadrocks.com; 618 Central Ave SW, downtown) Indie, reggae, punk and country bands rock the house most nights (though not at the same time). Look for the spaceship on Central Ave. Right next door is the **El Rey Theater** (www.elreytheater.com; 620 Central Ave SW, downtown), another longtime favorite for live music.

🛍 Shopping

For eclectic gifts, head to Nob Hill, east of the university. Park on Central Ave SE or one of the college-named side streets, then take a stroll past the inviting boutiques and specialty stores.

Palms Trading Post ARTS & CRAFTS
(1504 Lomas Blvd NW; ⊘9am-5:30pm Mon-Fri, 10am-5:30pm Sat) If you're looking for Native American crafts and informed salespeople who can give you advice, come here.

Silver Sun JEWELRY
(116 San Felipe St NW; ⊘10am-4:30pm) Just south of the plaza, Silver Sun is a reputable spot for turquoise and silver, where you can sometimes see the smiths at work.

Mariposa Gallery ART & CRAFTS
(www.mariposa-gallery.com; 3500 Central Ave SE, Nob Hill) Beautiful and funky arts, crafts and jewelry, mostly by regional artists.

ℹ Information

EMERGENCY & MEDICAL SERVICES

Police (☑505-764-1600; 400 Roma Ave NW)

Presbyterian Hospital (☑505-841-1234, emergency 505-841-1111; 1100 Central Ave SE; ⊘emergency 24hr)

UNM Hospital (☑505-272-2411; 2211 Lomas Blvd NE; ⊘emergency 24hr) Head here if you don't have insurance.

INTERNET ACCESS

Lots of restaurants and cafes have wi-fi.

Main Library (☑505-768-5141; 501 Copper Ave NW; ⊘10am-6pm Mon & Thu-Sat, 10am-7pm Tue & Wed; 🛜) Free internet access after purchasing a $3 SmartCard. Wi-fi available for free but must obtain access card.

POST

Post Office (201 5th St SW; ☺9am-4:30pm Mon-Fri)

TOURIST INFORMATION

Albuquerque Convention & Visitors Bureau (www.itsatrip.org; Albuquerque International Airport; ☺9:30am-8pm Sun-Fri, to 4:30pm Sat) At the lower-level baggage claim.
Old Town Information Center (☑505-243-3215; www.itsatrip.org; 303 Romero Ave NW; ☺10am-5pm Oct-May, to 6pm Jun-Sep)

USEFUL WEBSITES

Albuquerque.com (www.albuquerque.com) Attractions, hotels and restaurants.
City of Albuquerque (www.cabq.gov) Information on public transportation, area attractions and more.

❶ Getting There & Around

AIR

Albuquerque International Sunport (☑505-244-7700; www.cabq.gov/airport; 2200 Sunport Blvd SE) is New Mexico's main airport and most major US airlines fly here. Cabs to Downtown cost $20 to $25; try **Albuquerque Cab** (☑505-883-4888; www.albuquerquecab.com).

BUS

The **Alvarado Transportation Center** (100 1st St SW, cnr Central Ave) houses **ABQ RIDE** (☑505-243-7433; www.cabq.gov/transit; 100 1st St SW; adult/child $1/35, day pass $2), the public bus system. It covers most of Albuquerque from Monday to Friday and hits the major tourist spots daily. Most lines run until 6pm. ABQ RIDE Route 50 connects the airport with downtown (last bus at 8pm Monday to Friday, limited service Saturday). Check the website for maps and exact schedules. Route 36 stops near Old Town and the Indian Pueblo Cultural Center.

Greyhound (☑800-231-2222, 505-243-4435; www.greyhound.com; 320 1st St SW) serves destinations throughout New Mexico. **Sandia Shuttle** (☑888-775-5696; www.sandiashuttle. com; one-way/return $28/48; ☺8:45am-11:45pm) runs daily shuttles from the airport to many Santa Fe hotels, while **Twin Hearts Express** (☑575-751-1201; www.twinhearts-expresstransportation.com) runs a shuttle service from the airport to northern New Mexico destinations, including Taos and surrounding communities.

TRAIN

The *Southwest Chief* stops daily at Albuquerque's **Amtrak station** (☑800-872-7245, 505-842-9650; 320 1st St SW; ☺10am-5pm), heading east to Chicago ($173, 26 hours) or west through Flagstaff, AZ ($91, five hours), to Los Angeles, CA (from $114, 16½ hours).

A commuter line, the **New Mexico Rail Runner Express** (www.nmrailrunner.com), shares the station, with eight departures for Santa Fe weekdays (one-way/day pass $8/9), four on Saturday and three on Sunday, though weekend service may be discontinued. The trip takes about 1½ hours.

Along I-40

Although you can zip between Albuquerque and Flagstaff, AZ, in less than five hours, the national monuments and pueblos along the way are well worth a visit. For a scenic loop, take Hwy 53 southwest from Grants, which leads to all the following sights except Acoma. Hwy 602 brings you north to Gallup.

SCENIC DRIVES: NEW MEXICO'S BEST

Billy the Kid National Scenic Byway This mountain-and-valley loop (www.billyby-way.com) in southeastern New Mexico swoops past Billy the Kid's stomping grounds, Smokey Bear's gravesite and the orchard-lined Hondo Valley. From Roswell, take Hwy 380 west.

High Road to Taos The back road between Santa Fe and Taos passes through sculpted sandstone desert, fresh pine forests and rural villages with historic adobe churches and horse-filled pastures. The 13,000ft Truchas Peaks soar above. From Santa Fe, take Hwy 84/285 to Hwy 513 then follow the signs.

NM Highway 96 From Abiquiu to Cuba, this little road wends through the heart of Georgia O'Keeffe country, beneath the distinct profile of Cerro Pedernal, then passing Martian red buttes and sandstone cliffs striped purple, yellow and ivory.

NM Highway 52 Head west from Truth or Consequences into the dramatic foothills of the Black Range, through the old mining towns of Winston and Chloride. Continue north, passing the Monticello Box – where Geronimo finally surrendered – and emerging onto the sweeping Plains of San Augustin before reaching the bizarre Very Large Array.

Acoma Pueblo

The dramatic mesa-top 'Sky City' sits 7000ft above sea level and 367ft above the surrounding plateau. One of the oldest continuously inhabited settlements in North America, this place has been home to pottery-making people since the later part of the 11th century. Guided **tours** (adult/senior/child $23/20/15; ⊙ hourly 9:30am-3:30pm Apr-early Nov, check online or call for winter schedule) leave from the **visitor center** (☑ 800-747-0181; www.acomaskycity.org; ⊙ 9am-5pm Apr-early Nov; check online or call for winter opening hours) at the bottom of the mesa and take two hours, or one hour just to tour the historic mission. From I-40, take exit 102, which is about 60 miles west of Albuquerque, then drive 12 miles south. Call ahead to make sure it's not closed for ceremonial or other reasons.

El Morro National Monument

The 200ft sandstone outcropping at this **monument** (www.nps.gov/elmo; admission free; ⊙ 9am-5pm, last trail entry 4pm) **FREE**, also known as 'Inscription Rock,' has been a travelers' oasis for millennia. Thousands of carvings – from petroglyphs in the pueblo at the top (c 1275) to elaborate inscriptions by the Spanish conquistadors and the Anglo pioneers – offer a unique means of tracing history. It's about 38 miles southwest of Grants via Hwy 53.

Zuni Pueblo

The Zuni are known worldwide for their delicately inlaid silverwork, which is sold in stores lining Hwy 53. Check in at the **visitor center** (☑ 505-782-7238; www.zunitourism.com; 1239 Hwy 53; tours $10; ⊙ 8:30am-5:30pm Mon-Fri, 10:30am-4pm Sat, noon-4pm Sun) for information, photo permits and tours of the pueblo, which lead you among stone houses and beehive-shaped adobe ovens to the massive **Our Lady of Guadalupe Mission**, featuring impressive kachina murals. The **Ashiwi Awan Museum & Heritage Center** (www.ashiwi-museum.org; Ojo Caliente Rd; admission by donation; ⊙ 9am-5pm Mon-Fri) displays early photos and other tribal artifacts.

The friendly, eight-room **Inn at Halona** (☑ 800-752-3278, 505-782-4547; www.halona.com; Halona Plaza; r from $79; P 🛜), decorated with local Zuni arts and crafts, is the only place to stay on the pueblo. Its breakfasts rank with the best of any B&B in the state.

Gallup

Not just a classic Route 66 town, Gallup also serves as the Navajo and Zuni peoples' major trading center, making it one of the best places in New Mexico to buy top-quality Native American art and crafts at fair prices. You'll find many trading posts, pawnshops, jewelry stores and crafts galleries in the historic district.

The town's lodging jewel is **El Rancho** (☑ 505-863-9311; www.elranchohotel.com; 1000 E Hwy 66; r from $85; P ✳ 🛜 🌊). Many of the great actors of the 1940s and '50s stayed here. El Rancho features a superb Southwestern lobby, a restaurant, a bar and an eclectic selection of simple rooms. There's wifi in the lobby. Most chain hotels are found along Route 66, west of the town center.

Santa Fe

Walking among the historic adobe neighborhoods or even around the tourist-filled plaza, there's no denying that Santa Fe has a timeless, earthy soul. Founded around 1610, Santa Fe is the second-oldest city and oldest state capital in the USA. It's got the oldest public building and throws the oldest annual party in the country (Fiesta). Yet the city is synonymous with contemporary chic, and boasts the second-largest art market in the nation, gourmet restaurants, great museums, spas and a world-class opera.

At 7000ft, it's also the highest state capital in the US, sitting at the base of the Sangre de Cristo range, a conveniently fantastic place to hike, mountain bike, backpack and ski.

Cerrillos Rd (I-25 exit 278), a 6-mile strip of hotels and fast-food restaurants, enters town from the south; Paseo de Peralta circles the center of town; St Francis Dr (I-25 exit 282) forms the western border of downtown and turns into Hwy 285, which heads north toward Los Alamos and Taos. Most downtown restaurants, galleries, museums and sights are within walking distance of the plaza, the historic center of town.

⊙ Sights

Art enthusiasts coming for the weekend may want to arrive early on Friday to take advantage of the evening's free admission policies at many museums.

MUSEUM OF NEW MEXICO

The Museum of New Mexico administers four (or five, depending on how you count them) unique and excellent museums around town. Admission is free for children 16 and under. Adults can buy a four-day pass with entry into all four (or five) museums for $20. Two (or three) are at the plaza, two are on Museum Hill.

Museum of International Folk Art (www.internationalfolkart.org; 706 Camino Lejo; adult/child $9/free, free 5-8pm Fri summer; ☺10am-5pm, closed Mon Sep-May) The galleries here, on Museum Hill, are at once whimsical and mind-blowing – featuring the world's largest collection of traditional folk art. Try to hit the incredible folk-art market, held each July.

Museum of Indian Arts & Culture (www.indianartsandculture.org; 710 Camino Lejo; adult/child $9/free, free Fri 5-8pm in summer; ☺10am-5pm, closed Mon Sep-May) On Museum Hill, this is one of the most complete collections of Native American arts and crafts – and a perfect companion to the nearby Wheelwright Museum.

Palace of the Governors (☎505-476-5100; www.palaceofthegovernors.org; 105 W Palace Ave; adult/child $9/free; ☺10am-5pm, closed Mon Oct-May) On the plaza, this 400-year-old abode was once the seat of the Spanish colonial government. It displays a handful of regional relics, but most of its holdings are now shown in an adjacent exhibit space called the **New Mexico History Museum** (113 Lincoln Ave), a glossy, 96,000-sq-ft expansion. One ticket works for both.

New Mexico Museum of Art (www.nmartmuseum.org; 107 W Palace Ave; adult/child $9/free; ☺10am-5pm, closed Mon Sep-May) Just off the plaza, there are more than 20,000 pieces of fine art here, mostly by Southwestern artists.

★**Georgia O'Keeffe Museum** MUSEUM
(☎505-946-1000; www.okeeffemuseum.org; 217 Johnson St; adult/child $12/free; ☺10am-5pm, to 7pm Fri) Possessing the world's largest collection of her work, the Georgia O'Keeffe Museum features the artist's paintings of flowers, bleached skulls and adobe architecture. Tours of O'Keeffe's house in Abiquiu require advance reservations.

Canyon Rd GALLERIES
(www.canyonroadarts.com) The epicenter of the city's upscale art scene, more than 100 galleries, studios, shops and restaurants line this narrow historic road. Look for Santa Fe School masterpieces, rare Native American antiquities and wild contemporary work. The area positively buzzes with activity during the early-evening art openings on Fridays, and especially on Christmas Eve.

Wheelwright Museum of the American Indian MUSEUM
(www.wheelwright.org; 704 Camino Lejo; ☺10am-5pm Mon-Sat, 1-5pm Sun) FREE In 1937, Mary Cabot established the Wheelwright Museum of the American Indian, part of Museum Hill, to showcase Navajo ceremonial art. While its strength continues to be Navajo exhibits, it now includes contemporary Native American art and historical artifacts as well.

St Francis Cathedral CHURCH
(www.cbsfa.org; 131 Cathedral Pl; ☺8:30am-5pm) Houses the oldest Madonna statue in North America.

Shidoni Foundry GARDENS, GALLERY
(www.shidoni.com; 1508 Bishop's Lodge Rd, Tesuque; ☺9am-5pm Mon-Sat; 🚻) Five miles north of the plaza; outdoor sculpture garden (open dawn to 5pm), indoor gallery and an on-site glass-blowing studio (open 9am to 5pm). On Saturdays, watch the artisans do huge bronze pours in the workshop ($5).

Loretto Chapel CHURCH
(www.lorettochapel.com; 207 Old Santa Fe Trail; admission $3; ☺9am-5pm Mon-Sat, 10:30am-5pm Sun) Famous for its 'miraculous' spiral staircase that appears to be supported by thin air.

🏃 Activities

The **Pecos Wilderness** and **Santa Fe National Forest**, east of town, have more than 1000 miles of hiking trails, several of which lead to 12,000ft peaks. The popular and scenic **Winsor Trail** starts at the Santa Fe Ski Basin. Summer storms are frequent, so prepare for hikes by checking weather reports. For maps and details, contact the Public Lands Information Center. If mountain

Santa Fe

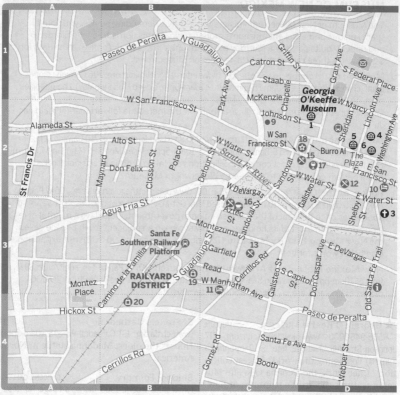

biking is your thing, drop into **Mellow Velo** (☑505-995-8356; www.mellowvelo.com; 132 E Marcy St; rentals per day from $35; ◷9am-5:30pm Mon-Sat), which rents bikes and has loads of information about regional trails.

Busloads of people head up to the Rio Grande and Rio Chama for white-water river running on day and overnight adventures. Contact **Santa Fe Rafting Co** (☑505-988-4914; www.santaferafting.com; ◷Apr-Sep) and stay cool on trips through the Rio Grande Gorge (half-day/full day $65/99), the wild Taos Box (full day $110) or the Rio Chama Wilderness (three days $595).

Ski Santa Fe

SKIING

(☑505-982-4429, snow report 505-983-9155; www.skisantafe.com; lift ticket adult/child $66/46; ◷9am-4pm late Nov-Apr) A half-hour drive from the plaza up Hwy 475, you'll find the second-highest ski area in the USA. When the powder is fresh and the sun is shining, it's as good as it gets.

Ten Thousand Waves

SPA

(☑505-982-9304; www.tenthousandwaves.com; 3451 Hyde Park Rd; communal tubs $24, private tubs per person $31-51; ◷noon-10:30pm Tue, 9am-10:30pm Wed-Mon Jul-Oct, reduced hours Nov-Jun) The Japanese-style 10,000 Waves, with landscaped grounds concealing eight attractive tubs in a smooth Zen design, offers waterfalls, cold plunges, massage and hot and dry saunas. Call to reserve private tubs.

🍴 Courses

Santa Fe School of Cooking

COOKING

(☑505-983-4511; www.santafeschoolofcooking .com; 125 N Guadalupe St; classes $75-98; ◷9:30am-5:30pm Mon-Fri, 9:30am-5pm Sat, noon-4pm Sun) If you develop a love for New Mexican cuisine, try cooking lessons here. Classes, including hands-on green and red chili workshops, are typically between two and three hours long.

Geronimo (0.1mi);
El Farol (0.25mi)

✨ Festivals & Events

★ Spanish Market   CULTURAL
(www.spanishcolonial.org; ☉ late Jul) Traditional Spanish colonial arts, from *retablos* (paintings on wooden panels) and *bultos* (wooden carvings of religious figures) to handcrafted furniture and metalwork, make this juried show an artistic extravaganza.

★ Santa Fe Indian Market   CULTURAL
(www.swaia.org) Typically held the weekend after the third Thursday in August, this event draws the country's finest Native American artisans to the plaza – and tens of thousands of visitors.

★ Santa Fe Fiesta   CULTURAL
(www.santafefiesta.org; ☉ early Sep) Two weeks of events, including concerts, dances, parades and the burning of Zozobra (Old Man Gloom).

🛏 Sleeping

Cerrillos Rd is lined with chains and independent motels. There's camping in developed sites in Santa Fe National Forest and Hyde State Park on Hwy 475, the road to the ski basin; for more information, go to the Public Lands Information Center (p876).

Silver Saddle Motel   MOTEL **$**
(🖉 505-471-7663; www.santafesilversaddlemotel. com; 2810 Cerrillos Rd; r winter/summer from $45/62; P❋@🛜🐾) Shady wooden arcades outside and rustic cowboy-inspired decor inside, including some rooms with attractively tiled kitchenettes. For a bit of kitsch, request the Kenny Rogers or Wyatt Earp room. Probably the best value in town.

Rancheros de Santa Fe Campground   CAMPGROUND **$**
(🖉 505-466-3482; www.rancheros.com; 736 Old Las Vegas Hwy; tent/RV sites/cabins $25/41/49; ☉ Mar-Oct; 🛜🐾🐾) Super-friendly, this wooded campground is 7 miles southeast of town. Enjoy hot showers, cheap morning coffee and evening movies.

Santa Fe Motel & Inn   HOTEL **$$**
(🖉 505-982-1039; www.santafemotel.com; 510 Cerrillos Rd; r $89-155, casitas $129-169; P❋@🛜🐾) It's the aesthetic and technological attention to detail that make this downtown-adjacent motel a great pick. Bright tiles, clay sunbursts, LCD TVs and a welcoming chili pepper carefully placed atop your towels are just a few memorable pluses. Savor hot breakfasts on the kiva-anchored patio.

El Rey Inn   HOTEL **$$**
(🖉 505-982-1931; www.elreyinnsantafe.com; 1862 Cerrillos Rd; r incl breakfast $105-165, ste from $150; P❋@🛜🐾) A highly recommended classic courtyard hotel, with super rooms, a great pool and hot tub, and even a kids' playground scattered around 5 acres of greenery. The inn recycles and takes a lot of green-friendly steps to conserve resources. Most rooms have air con.

★ La Fonda   HISTORIC HOTEL **$$$**
(🖉 800-523-5002; www.lafondasantafe.com; 100 E San Francisco St; r/ste from $140/260; P❋@🛜🐾) Claiming to be the original 'Inn at the end of the Santa Fe Trail,' here in one form or another since perhaps 1610, La Fonda has always offered some of the best lodging in town. Freshly renovated in 2013, the hotel blends modern luxury with folk-art touches; it's authentic, top-shelf Santa Fe style.

Santa Fe

✗ Eating

★ San Marcos Café NEW MEXICAN $
(☎ 505-471-9298; www.sanmarcosfeed.com; 3877 Hwy 14; mains $7-10; ⊗ 8am-2pm; 🖼) About 10 minutes' drive south on Hwy 14, this spot is well worth the trip. San Marcos has a down-home feeling and the best red chili you'll ever taste. The whole place is connected to a feed store, giving it some genuine Western soul – and turkeys and peacocks strut and squabble outside. The pastries and desserts – especially the bourbon apple pie – sate any sweet tooth. Make reservations on weekends.

Horseman's Haven NEW MEXICAN $
(4354 Cerrillos Rd; mains $8-12; ⊗ 8am-8pm Mon-Sat, 8:30am-2pm Sun; 🖼) Hands down the hottest green chili in town! (The timid should order it on the side). Service is friendly and fast, and the enormous 3-D burrito might be the only thing you need to eat all day.

Cleopatra's Cafe MIDDLE EASTERN $
(www.cleopatrasantafe.com; 418 Cerrillos Rd, Design Center; mains $6-14; ⊗ 11am-8pm Mon-Sat; 🛜) Makes up for lack of ambience with taste and value – big platters of delicious kebabs, hummus, falafel and other Middle Eastern favorites. It's inside the Design Center.

Tia Sophia's NEW MEXICAN $
(210 W San Francisco St; mains $7-10; ⊗ 7am-2pm Mon-Sat, 8am-1pm Sun; 🍴🖼) Arguably the best New Mexican food downtown.

Tune-Up Café INTERNATIONAL $$
(www.tuneupsantafe.com; 1115 Hickox St; mains $7-14; ⊗ 7am-10pm Mon-Fri, from 8am Sat & Sun; 🖼) This local favorite is casual, busy and does food right. The chef, from El Salvador, adds a few twists to classic New Mexican and American dishes, while also serving Salvadoran *pupusas* (stuffed corn tortillas), huevos and other specialties. The fish tacos and the *mole colorado enchiladas* (flavored with red chili and a hint of chocolate) are especially tasty. Enjoy the patio when the weather allows.

Cowgirl Hall of Fame BARBECUE $$
(www.cowgirlsantafe.com; 319 S Guadalupe St; mains $8-18; ⊗ 11am-11pm Sun-Thu, to midnight Fri & Sat; 🖼) Two-step up to the cobblestoned courtyard and try the salmon tacos, butternut-squash casserole or the BBQ platter – all served with Western-style feminist flair. Youngsters are welcomed, with an outdoor play yard and buckets of coloring crayons to draw on the lengthy kids' menu. It also has a perennially popular bar with live music and attached pool hall.

★ Cafe Pasqual's INTERNATIONAL $$$
(☎ 505-983-9340; www.pasquals.com; 121 Don Gaspar Ave; breakfast & lunch mains $9-17, dinner mains $16-30; ⊗ 7am-3pm & 5:30-9pm; 🍴🖼) Sante Fe's most famous breakfast, for good reason.

Geronimo MODERN AMERICAN $$$
(☎ 505-982-1500; www.geronimorestaurant.com; 724 Canyon Rd; mains $30-45; ⊗ 5:45-10pm Mon-Thu, to 11pm Fri & Sat) Housed in a 1756 adobe, Geronimo is among the finest and most romantic restaurants in town. The short but diverse menu includes fiery sweet chili and honey-grilled prawns and peppery elk tenderloin with applewood-smoked bacon.

🍸 Drinking & Entertainment

You'll also find live music and good drinking most nights at the Cowgirl Hall of Fame (p886).

★ 317 Aztec   CAFE
(317 Aztec St; ⊙ 8am-10pm Mon-Sat; 🛜) Even with new owners, the former Aztec Cafe remains our pick for best local coffeehouse and juice/smoothy bar, with its colorful indoor art space and outdoor patio. The food is great (and healthy) too!

Evangelo's   BAR
(200 W San Francisco St; ⊙ midday-1:30am Mon-Sat, to midnight Sun) There's foot-stompin' live music nightly at Evangelo's. The sounds of rock, blues, jazz and Latin combos spill into the street.

Bell Tower Bar   BAR
(100 E San Francisco St; ⊙ 3pm-sunset Mon-Thu, 2pm-sunset Fri-Sun May-Oct, closed rest of yr) At La Fonda hotel, ascend five floors to the newly renovated Bell Tower and watch one of those patented New Mexico sunsets.

★ El Farol   TRADITIONAL DANCE, LIVE MUSIC
(www.elfarolsf.com; 808 Canyon Rd; ⊙ 11am-midnight Mon-Sat, 11am-11pm Sun) As much a restaurant as a bar, El Farol specializes in tapas ($8), live music, world-class flamenco and the ambience of Santa Fe's oldest cantina.

★ Santa Fe Opera   OPERA
(☎ 505-986-5900; www.santafeopera.org; Hwy 84/285, Tesuque; backstage tours adult/child $5/free; ⊙ late Jun-late Aug, backstage tours 9am Mon-Fri Jun-Aug) You can be a decked-out socialite or show up in cowboy boots and jeans; it doesn't matter. Opera fans (and those who've never attended an opera in their lives) come to Santa Fe for this alone: an architectural marvel, with views of wind-carved sandstone wilderness crowned with sunsets and moonrises, and at center stage internationally renowned vocal talent performing masterworks of aria and romance.

Lensic Performing Arts
Theater   PERFORMING ARTS
(☎ 505-984-1370; www.lensic.com; 211 W San Francisco St) For live performances and movies, see what's doing at the Lensic Performing Arts Center. This beautifully renovated 1930s movie house is the city's premier venue for performing arts. Continuing its film history, it also holds $5 classic-movie screenings.

🛍 Shopping

Offering carved howling coyotes, turquoise jewelry and fine art, Santa Fe attracts shoppers of all budgets. Head to the sidewalk outside the Palace of the Governors to buy Indian jewelry direct from the craftspeople who make it.

★ Santa Fe Farmers Market   MARKET
(☎ 505-983-4098; 55yd west of Guadalupe St, Paseo de Peralta; ⊙ 7am-noon Sat & Tue Apr-Nov; ♿) Don't miss this market at the redeveloped rail yard. Free samples and a festive mood make for a very pleasant morning.

Pueblo of Tesuque Flea Market   MARKET
(Hwy 84/285; ⊙ 8am-4pm Fri-Sun Mar-Nov) This outdoor market a few minutes' drive north of Santa Fe at Tesuque Pueblo offers deals on high-quality rugs, jewelry, art and clothing.

Kowboyz   CLOTHING
(www.kowboyz.com; 345 W Manhattan Ave) This secondhand shop has everything you need to cowboy up. Shirts are a great deal at $10 each; the amazing selection of boots, however, demands top dollar. Movie costumers looking for authentic Western wear often come in here.

Travel Bug   MAPS
(www.mapsofnewmexico.com; 839 Paseo de Peralta; ⊙ 7:30am-5:30pm Mon-Sat, 11am-4pm Sun; 🛜) A huge selection of guidebooks, maps and travel gear, plus travel slide shows on Saturdays.

ℹ Information

EMERGENCY & MEDICAL SERVICES
Police (☎ 505-955-5000; 2515 Camino Entrada)
St Vincent's Hospital (☎ 505-983-3361; 455 St Michael's Dr) Has 24-hour emergency care.

INTERNET ACCESS
Santa Fe Public Library (☎ 505-955-6781; 145 Washington Ave) Reserve up to an hour of free access.
Travel Bug (☎ 505-992-0418; 839 Paseo de Peralta; 🛜) Free wi-fi and internet access from on-site terminals.

POST
Post office (120 S Federal Pl)

TOURIST INFORMATION
New Mexico Tourism Bureau (☎ 505-827-7440; www.newmexico.org; 491 Old Santa Fe Trail; ⊙ 8am-5pm) Has brochures, a hotel

DON'T MISS

CHIMAYO

Twenty-eight miles north of Santa Fe is the so-called 'Lourdes of America' – **El Santuario de Chimayo** (www.elsantuariodechimayo.us; ⏲9am-5pm Oct-Apr, to 6pm May-Sep), one of the most important cultural sites in New Mexico. In 1816, this two-towered adobe chapel was built where the earth was said to have miraculous healing properties – even today, the faithful come to rub the *tierra bendita* – holy dirt – from a small pit inside the church on whatever hurts; some mix it with water and drink it. During holy week, about 30,000 pilgrims walk to Chimayo from Santa Fe, Albuquerque and beyond, in the largest Catholic pilgrimage in the USA. The artwork in the *santuario* is worth a trip on its own. Stop at **Rancho de Chimayo** (☎505-984-2100; www.ranchodechimayo.com; County Rd 98; mains $8-18; ⏲8:30-10:30am Sat & Sun, 11:30am-9pm daily, closed Mon Nov-Apr) afterward for lunch or dinner.

reservation line, free coffee and free internet access.

Public Lands Information Center (☎505-438-7542; www.publiclands.org; 301 Dinosaur Trail; ⏲8:30am-4pm Mon-Fri) Tons of maps and information on exploring New Mexico's National Forests, Parks and Monuments, wilderness areas, and other public lands. Just south of the intersection of Cerillos Rd and I-25.

Useful Websites

New Mexican (www.santafenewmexican.com) Daily paper with breaking news.

SantaFe.com (www.santafe.com) Listings for upcoming concerts, readings and openings in northern New Mexico.

Santa Fe Information (www.santafe.org) Official online visitors' guide.

Santa Fe Reporter (www.sfreporter.com) Free alternative weekly; culture section has thorough listings of what's going on.

Getting There & Around

A few commercial airlines fly daily between **Santa Fe Municipal Airport** (SAF; ☎505-955-2900; wwwsantafenm.gov; 121 Aviation Dr) and Dallas, Denver, Los Angeles, and Phoenix; historically, these routes have been added and cut with surprising frequency, so check to make sure they are all still active. Many more flights arrive at and depart from Albuquerque (one-hour drive south of Santa Fe).

Sandia Shuttle Express (☎888-775-5696; www.sandiashuttle.com) runs between Santa Fe and the Albuquerque Sunport ($28). **North Central Regional Transit** (www.ncrtd.org) provides free shuttle bus service to Espanola, where you can transfer to shuttles to Taos, Los Alamos, Ojo Caliente and other northern destinations. Downtown pickup/drop-off is on Sheridan St, a block northwest of the plaza.

The **Rail Runner** (www.nmrailrunner.com) commuter train has multiple daily departures for Albuquerque – with connections to the airport and the zoo. The trip takes about 1½ hours. Weekend service may be discontinued. **Amtrak** (☎800-872-7245; www.amtrak.com) stops at Lamy; buses continue 17 miles to Santa Fe.

Santa Fe Trails (☎505-955-2001; www.santafenm.gov; one-way adult/child $1/free, day pass $2) provides local bus services. If you need a taxi, call **Capital City Cab** (☎505-438-0000; www.capitalcitycab.com).

If driving between Santa Fe and Albuquerque, try to take Hwy 14 – the Turquoise Trail – which passes through the old mining town (now art-gallery town) of Madrid, 28 miles south of Santa Fe.

Around Santa Fe

Pueblos

North of Santa Fe is the heart of Puebloan lands. **Eight Northern Indian Pueblos** (www.enipc.org) publishes the excellent and free *Eight Northern Indian Pueblos Visitors Guide,* available at area visitor centers. Its annual arts-and-crafts show is held in July; check the ENIPC website for exact dates and location.

Eight miles west of Pojoaque along Hwy 502, the ancient **San Ildefonso Pueblo** (☎505-455-3549; per vehicle $10, camera/video/sketching permits $10/20/25; ⏲8am-5pm) was the home of Maria Martinez, who in 1919 revived a distinctive traditional black-on-black pottery style. Stop at the **Maria Poveka Martinez Museum** (⏲8am-4pm Mon-Fri) FREE and browse the shops of the exceptional potters (including Maria's direct descendants) who work in the pueblo today.

Just north of San Ildefonso, on Hwy 30, **Santa Clara Pueblo** is home to the **Puye Cliff Dwellings** (☎888-320-5008; www.puyecliffs.com; tours adult/child $20/18; ⏲hourly 9am-

5pm May-Sep, 10am-2pm Oct-Apr), where you can visit Ancestral Puebloan cliffside and mesa-top ruins.

Las Vegas

Not to be confused with the glittery city to the west in Nevada, this Vegas is one of the loveliest towns in New Mexico and one of the largest and oldest towns east of the Sangre de Cristo Mountains. Its eminently strollable downtown has a pretty Old Town Plaza and some 900 historic buildings listed in the National Register of Historic Places. Its architecture is a mix of Southwestern and Victorian.

Built in 1882 and carefully remodeled a century later, the elegant **Plaza Hotel** (☑800-328-1882, 505-425-3591; www.plazahotel-nm.com; 230 Old Town Plaza; r incl breakfast from $89; P✲@☎☀) is Las Vegas' most celebrated and historic lodging. Choose between Victorian-style, antique-filled rooms in the original building or bright, modern rooms in a newer adjoining wing.

Right on the plaza, you can get your chili fix at **El Encanto Restaurant** (1816 Plaza; mains $5-9; ☺6am-2pm), your caffeine fix at **World Treasures Travelers Cafe** (1814 Plaza St; snacks $3-6; ☺7:30am-4:30pm Mon-Sat; ☎), and your ice cream fix at the soda fountain at **Plaza Drug** (178 Bridge St; ☺8am-6pm Mon-Sat).

From the plaza, Hot Springs Blvd leads 5 miles north to Gallinas Canyon and the massive **Montezuma Castle**; once a hotel, it's now the United World College of the West. Along the road there, you can soak in a series of natural **hot-spring pools**. Bring a swimsuit and test the water – some are scalding hot! Don't miss the **Dwan Light Sanctuary** (admission free; ☺6am-10pm) **FREE** on the school campus, a meditation chamber where prisms in the walls cast rainbows inside.

Ask for a walking-tour brochure from the **visitor center** (☑800-832-5947; www.lasvegas-newmexico.com; 500 Railroad Ave; ☺9am-5pm).

Los Alamos

The top-secret Manhattan Project sprang to life in Los Alamos in 1943, turning a sleepy mesa-top village into a busy laboratory of secluded brainiacs. Here, in the 'town that didn't exist,' the first atomic bomb was developed in almost total secrecy. Today you'll encounter a fascinating dynamic in which souvenir T-shirts emblazoned with atomic explosions and 'La Bomba' wine are sold next to books on pueblo history and wilderness hiking.

You can't actually visit the **Los Alamos National Laboratory**, where lots of classified cutting-edge research still takes place, but you can visit the well-designed, interactive **Bradbury Science Museum** (www.lanl.gov/museum; 1350 Central Ave; ☺10am-5pm Tue-Sat, 1-5pm Sun & Mon) **FREE**, which covers atomic history and includes new exhibits on security technology. A short film traces the community's wartime history and reveals a few fascinating secrets. The small but interesting **Los Alamos Historical Museum** (www.losalamoshistory.org; 1050 Bathtub Row; ☺10am-4pm Mon-Fri, from 11am Sat, from 1pm Sun) **FREE** is on the nearby grounds of the former Los Alamos Ranch School – an outdoorsy school for boys that closed when the scientists arrived.

Grab a bite with local braniacs at the **Coffee House Cafe** (www.thecoffeebooth.com; 723 Central Ave; mains $6-12, pizzas $21-30; ☺6am-8pm Tue-Fri, 7am-3pm Sat, 8am-3pm Sun, 6am-3pm Mon), opposite Smith's supermarket.

Bandelier National Monument

Ancestral Puebloans dwelt in the cliffsides of beautiful Frijoles Canyon, now preserved within **Bandelier** (www.nps.gov/band; per vehicle $12; ☺visitor center 9am-4:30pm, park to dusk; ▦). The adventurous can climb ladders to reach ancient caves and kivas used until the mid-1500s. There are also almost 50 sq miles of canyon and mesalands offering scenic backpacking trails, plus camping at **Juniper Campground** (campsites $12), set among the pines near the monument entrance. Note that between 9am and 3pm, from the end of May to mid-October, you need to take a shuttle bus to Bandelier from the White Rock Visitor Center, along Hwy 4.

Abiquiu

The tiny community of Abiquiu (sounds like 'barbecue'), on Hwy 84 about 45 minutes' drive northwest of Santa Fe, is famous because the renowned artist Georgia O'Keeffe lived and painted here from 1949 until her death in 1986. With the Chama River flowing through farmland and spectacular rock landscape, the ethereal setting continues to attract artists, and many live and work in

Abiquiu. O'Keeffe's adobe house is open for limited visits, with one-hour **tours** (✒505-685-4539; www.okeeffemuseum.org; tours $35-45) offered on Tuesday, Thursday and Friday from March to November, and Tuesday through Saturday from June to October, often booked months in advance.

A retreat center on 21,000 Technicolor acres that obviously inspired O'Keeffe's work (and was a shooting location for the movie *City Slickers*), **Ghost Ranch** (✒505-685-4333; www.ghostranch.org; US Hwy 84; suggested donation $3; ⊞) has hiking trails, a **dinosaur museum** (suggested donation $2; ◷9am-5pm Mon-Sat, 1-5pm Sun) and offers horseback rides (from $50), including instruction for kids four and up ($30). Basic **lodging** (tent sites $19, RV sites $22-29, dm incl breakfast $50, r without/with bathroom incl breakfast from $70/80) is available, too.

The lovely **Abiquiú Inn** (✒888-735-2902, 505-685-4378; www.abiquiuinn.com; US Hwy 84; RV sites $18, r $110-150, casitas from $179; P⊚) is a sprawling collection of shaded faux-adobes. Its spacious casitas have kitchenettes, and wi-fi is available in the lobby and the on-site restaurant, **Cafe Abiquiú** (breakfast mains under $10, lunch & dinner mains $10-20; ◷7am-9pm). The lunch and dinner menu includes numerous fish dishes, from chipotle honey-glazed salmon to trout tacos.

Ojo Caliente

At 140 years old, **Ojo Caliente Mineral Springs Resort & Spa** (✒800-222-9162, 505-583-2233; www.ojospa.com; 50 Los Baños Rd; r $139-169, cottages $179-209, ste $229-349; ⊞⊚) is one of the country's oldest health resorts – and Pueblo Indians were using the springs long before then! Fifty miles north of Santa Fe on Hwy 285, the newly renovated resort offers 10 soaking pools with several combinations of minerals (shared/private pools from $18/40). In addition to the pleasant, if nothing special, historic hotel rooms, the resort has added 12 plush, boldly colored suites with kiva fireplaces and private soaking tubs, and 11 New Mexican–style cottages. Wi-fi is available in the lobby. The on-site **Artesian Restaurant** (breakfast mains $5-10, lunch mains $9-12, dinner mains $16-28; ◷7:30am-11am, 11:30am-2:30pm & 5-8:30pm Sun-Thu, to 9pm Fri & Sat) prepares organic and local ingredients with aplomb.

Taos

Taos is a place undeniably dominated by the power of its landscape: 12,300ft snow-capped peaks rise behind town; a sage-speckled plateau unrolls to the west before plunging 800ft straight down into the Rio Grande Gorge; the sky can be a searing sapphire blue or an ominous parade of rumbling thunderheads so big they dwarf the mountains. And then there are the sunsets...

Taos Pueblo, believed to be the oldest continuously inhabited community in the United States, roots the town in a long history with a rich cultural legacy – including conquistadors, Catholicism and cowboys. In the 20th century, Taos became a magnet for artists, writers and creative thinkers, from DH Lawrence to Dennis Hopper. It remains a relaxed and eccentric place, with classic adobe architecture, fine-art galleries, quirky cafes and excellent restaurants. Its 5000 residents include Bohemians, alternative-energy aficionados and old-time Hispanic families. It's rural and worldly, and a little bit otherworldly.

◉ Sights

The Museum Association of Taos offers a pass for $25 to five museums: Harwood Museum of Art, Taos Historic Museums, Millicent Rogers Museum and Taos Art Museum & Fechin Institute.

★**Millicent Rogers Museum**   MUSEUM
(www.millicentrogers.org; 1504 Millicent Rogers Rd; adult/child $10/2; ◷10am-5pm, closed Mon Nov-Mar) Filled with pottery, jewelry, baskets and textiles, this has one of the best collections of Native American and Spanish Colonial art in the US.

Harwood Foundation Museum   MUSEUM
(www.harwoodmuseum.org; 238 Ledoux St; adult/child $10/free; ◷10am-5pm Tue-Sat, noon-5pm Sun) Housed in a historic mid-19th-century adobe compound, the Harwood Museum of Art features paintings, drawings, prints, sculpture and photography by northern New Mexico artists, both historical and contemporary.

Taos Historic Museums   MUSEUM
(www.taoshistoricmuseums.org; each museum adult/child $8/4; ◷10am-5pm Mon-Sat, midday-5pm Sun) Taos Historic Museum runs two houses: **Blumenschein Home** (www.taoshis-

toricmuseums.org; 222 Ledoux St; adult/child $8/4), a trove of art from the 1920s by the Taos Society of Artists, and **Martínez Hacienda** (708 Hacienda Way, off Lower Ranchitos Rd), a 21-room colonial trader's former home from 1804.

Taos Art Museum & Fechin Institute
MUSEUM

(www.taosartmuseum.org; 227 Paseo del Pueblo Norte; adult/child $8/free; ⊙10am-5pm Tue-Sun, shorter hours in winter) The home of Russian-born artist Nicolai Fechin, the house itself is worth just as much of a look as the collection of paintings, drawings and sculptures.

San Francisco de Asís Church
CHURCH

(St Francis Plaza; ⊙9am-4pm Mon-Fri) Four miles south of Taos in Ranchos de Taos, the San Francisco de Asís Church, famed for the angles and curves of its adobe walls, was built in the mid-18th century but didn't open until 1815. It's been memorialized in Georgia O'Keeffe paintings and Ansel Adams photographs. Hours are not really fixed, and the church may be open on Saturday. Mass is held three times on Sunday morning, once in Spanish.

Rio Grande Gorge Bridge
BRIDGE, CANYON

At 650ft above the Rio Grande, the steel Rio Grande Gorge Bridge is the second-highest suspension bridge in the US; the view down is eye-popping. For the best pictures of the bridge itself, park at the rest area on the western end of the span.

Earthships
ARCHITECTURE

(www.earthship.com; US Hwy 64; self-guided tours $7; ⊙10am-4pm) 🌿 Just 1.5 miles west of the bridge is the fascinating community of Earthships, with self-sustaining, environmentally savvy houses built with recycled materials that are completely off the grid. You can also stay overnight in one.

🏃 Activities

During summer, **white-water rafting** is popular in the **Taos Box**, the steep-sided cliffs that frame the Rio Grande. Day-long trips begin at around $100 per person; contact the visitor center for local outfitters, where there's also good info about **hiking** and **mountain-biking** trails.

Taos Ski Valley
SKIING

(www.skitaos.org; half-/full-day lift ticket $64/77) With a peak elevation of 11,819ft and a 2612ft vertical drop, Taos Ski Valley offers some of the most challenging skiing in the US and

TAOS PUEBLO

Built around AD 1450 and continuously inhabited ever since, the streamside **Taos Pueblo** (☎505-758-1028; www.taospueblo.com; Taos Pueblo Rd; adult/child $10/free, photo or video permit $6; ⊙8am-4:30pm) is the largest existing multistoried pueblo structure in the US and one of the best surviving examples of traditional adobe construction. Dances held at the pueblo during the Pow-Wow (in July) and San Geronimo Day (September) are open to the public; call or check the website for exact dates. The pueblo closes for 10 weeks around February to March.

yet remains low-key and relaxed. The resort now allows snowboarders on its slopes.

🛏 Sleeping

Sun God Lodge
MOTEL $

(☎575-758-3162; www.sungodlodge.com; 919 Paseo del Pueblo Sur; r from $55; P❄🐾📶) The hospitable folks at this well-run two-story motel can fill you in on local history as well as the craziest bar in town. Rooms are clean – if a bit dark – and decorated with low-key Southwestern flair. Located 1.5 miles south of the plaza, it's one of the better budget choices in town.

Abominable Snowmansion
HOSTEL $

(☎575-776-8298; www.snowmansion.com; 476 Hwy 150, Arroyo Seco; tent sites $22, dm $27, r without/with bathroom $50/55, tepee $55; P@📶🐾) About 9 miles northeast of Taos, this well-worn and welcoming hostel is a cozy mountainside alternative to central Taos. A big, round fireplace warms guests in winter, and kitschy tepees are available in summer.

★ Earthship Rentals
BOUTIQUE HOTEL $$

(☎505-751-0462; www.earthship.com; US Hwy 64; earthship $145-305; 📶🐾) Experience an off-grid overnight in a boutique-chic, solar-powered dwelling. A cross between organic Gaudí architecture and space-age fantasy, these sustainable dwellings are put together using recycled tires, aluminum cans and sand, with rain catchment and gray-water systems to minimize their footprint. Half-buried in a valley surrounded by mountains, they *could* be hastily camouflaged alien vessels – you never know.

Historic Taos Inn
HISTORIC HOTEL $$

(☎ 575-758-2233; www.taosinn.com; 125 Paseo del Pueblo Norte; r $75-275; P ✳ 🤶) Even though it's not the plushest place in town, it's still fabulous, with a cozy lobby, a top-notch restaurant, heavy wooden furniture, a sunken fireplace and lots of live local music at its famed Adobe Bar. Parts of this landmark date to the 1800s – the older rooms are actually the nicest.

🍴 Eating

Michael's Kitchen
NEW MEXICAN $

(www.michaelskitchen.com; 304c Paseo del Pueblo Norte; mains $7-16; ⊘ 7am-2:30pm Mon-Thu, to 8pm Fri-Sun; 🖭) Great breakfasts, freshly made pastries and tasty New Mexican fare. Go for the stuffed sopapilla! Then try to walk...

El Gamal
MIDDLE EASTERN $

(www.elgamaltaos.com; 12 Doña Luz St; mains $7-12; ⊘ 9am-5pm Sun-Wed, to 9pm Thu-Sat; 🤶 🖋 🖭) Vegetarians rejoice! Here's a fabulous meatless Middle Eastern menu. There's a big kids' playroom in back, plus a pool table and free wi-fi.

Taos Pizza Out Back
PIZZA $

(www.taospizzaoutback.com; 712 Paseo del Pueblo Norte; slices $4-8, whole pies $13-29; ⊘ 11am-10pm May-Sep, to 9pm Oct-Apr; 🖋 🖭) Warning: these pizza pies may be cruelly habit-forming. This place uses organic ingredients and serves epicurean combos such as a Portabella Pie with sun-dried tomatoes and gorgonzola. Slices are the size of a small country.

Taos Diner
DINER $

(www.taosdiner.com; 908 Paseo del Pueblo Norte; mains $4-14; ⊘ 7am-2:30pm; 🖭) It's with some reluctance that we share the existence of this marvelous place, a mountain-town diner with wood-paneled walls, tattooed waitresses, fresh-baked biscuits and coffee cups that are never less than half-full. This is diner grub at its finest, prepared with a Southwestern, organic spin. Mountain men, scruffy jocks, solo diners and happy tourists – everyone's welcome here. We like the Copper John's eggs with a side of green chili sauce. There's another branch south of the plaza.

★ Love Apple
ORGANIC $$

(☎ 575-751-0050; www.theloveapple.net; 803 Paseo del Pueblo Norte; mains $13-22; ⊘ 5-9pm Tue-Sun) Housed in the 19th-century-adobe Placitas Chapel, the understated rustic-sacred atmosphere is as much a part of this only-in-New-Mexico restaurant as the food is. From the veggie lasagne to the grilled antelope with couscous, every dish is made from organic or free-range regional foods. Make reservations!

★ Trading Post Cafe
INTERNATIONAL $$$

(☎ 575-758-5089; www.tradingpostcafe.com; Hwy 68, Ranchos de Taos; lunch mains $8-14, dinner mains $15-32; ⊘ 11am-9pm Tue-Sat) A longtime favorite, the Trading Post is a perfect blend of relaxed and refined. The food, from paella to pork chops, is always great. Portions of some dishes are so big you should think about splitting a main course – or if you want to eat cheap but well, get a small salad and small soup. It'll be plenty!

🍷 Drinking & Entertainment

Adobe Bar
BAR

(125 Paseo del Pueblo Norte, Historic Taos Inn; ⊘ 11am-11pm) Everybody's welcome in 'the living room of Taos.' And there's something about it: the chairs, the Taos Inn's history, the casualness, the tequila. There's a streetside patio in summer, an indoor kiva fireplace in winter, plus top-notch margaritas and an eclectic lineup of live music all year round.

KTAO Solar Center
LIVE MUSIC

(www.ktao.com; 9 Ski Valley Rd; ⊘ bar from 4pm) Watch the DJs at the 'world's most powerful solar radio station' while hitting happy hour at the solar center bar. It's also a happenin' live-music venue for grooving local or big-name bands. There's even a play area for kids on the grassy lawn.

Alley Cantina
LIVE MUSIC

(121 Terracina Lane; ⊘ 11:30am-11pm) It's a bit-cooler-than-thou, but maybe 'tude happens when you inhabit the oldest building in town. Catch live rock, blues, hip-hop or jazz almost nightly.

🔒 Shopping

Taos has historically been a mecca for artists, demonstrated by the huge number of galleries and studios in and around town. Indie stores and galleries line the **John Dunn Shops** (www.johndunnshops.com) pedestrian walkway linking Bent St to Taos Plaza. Here you'll find the well-stocked **Moby Dickens Bookshop** (www.mobydickens.com; 124A Bent Street; ⊘ 10am-6pm) and the tiny but intriguing **G Robinson Old Prints & Maps**

(124D Bent St; ⊙11am-5pm), a treat for cartography geeks.

Just east of the Plaza, pop into **El Rincón Trading Post** (114 Kit Carson Rd; ⊙10am-5pm) and **Horse Feathers** (109 Kit Carson Rd; ⊙10:30am-5:30pm) for classic Western memorabilia.

❶ Information

Taos.org (www.taos.org) Great resource for visitors, with easy-to-navigate links.

Taos Visitor Center (☑575-758-3873; Paseo del Pueblo Sur, Paseo del Cañon; ⊙9am-5pm; ☜)

Wired? (705 Felicidad Lane; ⊙8am-6pm Mon-Fri, 8:30am-6pm Sat & Sun, shorter hours weekends in winter) Funky coffee shop with computers ($7 per hour). Free wi-fi for customers.

❶ Getting There & Away

From Santa Fe, take either the scenic 'high road' along Hwys 76 and 518, with galleries, villages and sites worth exploring, or follow the lovely unfolding Rio Grande landscape on Hwy 68.

North Central Regional Transit (www.ncrtd.org) provides free shuttle-bus service to Espanola, where you can transfer to Santa Fe and other destinations. **Twin Hearts Express** (☑800-654-9456; www.twinhearts-expresstransportation.com) will get you to Santa Fe ($40) and the Albuquerque airport ($50).

Northwestern New Mexico

Dubbed 'Indian Country' for good reason – huge swaths of land fall under the aegis of the Navajo, Pueblo, Zuni, Apache and Laguna tribes – this quadrant of New Mexico showcases remarkable ancient Indian sites alongside solitary Native American settlements and colorful geological badlands.

Farmington & Around

The largest town in New Mexico's northwestern region, Farmington makes a convenient base from which to explore the Four Corners area. The **visitors bureau** (☑505-326-7602; www.farmingtonnm.org; 3041 E Main St, Farmington Museum at Gateway Park; ⊙8am-5pm Mon-Fri) has more information.

Shiprock, a 1700ft-high volcanic plug that rises eerily over the landscape to the west, was a landmark for the Anglo pioneers and is a sacred site to the Navajo.

An ancient pueblo, **Salmon Ruin & Heritage Park** (www.salmonruins.com; adult/child $3/1; ⊙8am-5pm Mon-Fri, 9am-5pm Sat & Sun; from noon Sun Nov-Apr) features a large village built by the Chaco people in the early 1100s. Abandoned, resettled by people from Mesa Verde and again abandoned before 1300, the site also includes the remains of a homestead, petroglyphs, a Navajo hogan and a wickiup (a rough brushwood shelter). Take Hwy 64 east 11 miles toward Bloomfield.

Fourteen miles northeast of Farmington, the 27-acre **Aztec Ruins National Monument** (www.nps.gov/azru; adult/child $5/free; ⊙8am-5pm Sep-May, to 6pm Jun-Aug) features the largest reconstructed kiva in the country, with an internal diameter of almost 50ft. A few steps away, let your imagination wander as you stoop through low doorways and dark rooms inside the West Ruin. In summer, rangers give early-afternoon talks about ancient architecture, trade routes and astronomy.

About 35 miles south of Farmington along Hwy 371, the undeveloped **Bisti Badlands & De-Na-Zin Wilderness** is a trippy, surreal landscape of strange, colorful rock formations, especially spectacular in the hours before sunset; desert enthusiasts shouldn't miss it. The Farmington **BLM office** (☑505-564-7600; www.nm.blm.gov; 6251 College Blvd; ⊙7:45am-4:30pm Mon-Fri) has information.

The lovely, three-room **Silver River Adobe Inn B&B** (☑800-382-9251, 575-325-8219; www.silveradobe.com; 3151 W Main St, Farmington; r $115-175; ✳☜) offers a peaceful respite among the trees along the San Juan River.

Managing to be both trendy *and* kid-friendly, the hippish **Three Rivers Eatery & Brewhouse** (www.threeriversbrewery.com; 101 E Main St, Farmington; mains $8-26; ⊙11am-9pm; ☖) has good steaks, pub grub, and its own microbrews. It's the best restaurant in town by a mile.

Chaco Culture National Historic Park

Featuring massive Ancestral Puebloan buildings set in an isolated high-desert environment, intriguing **Chaco** (www.nps.gov/chcu; per vehicle/bike $8/4; ⊙7am-sunset) contains evidence of 5000 years of human occupation. In its prime, the community at Chaco Canyon was a major trading and ceremonial hub for the region – and the city the Puebloan people created here was masterly in its layout and design. Pueblo Bonito is four stories tall and may have had 600 to 800 rooms and kivas. As well as taking the self-guided loop tour, you can hike various **backcountry trails**. For stargazers, there's the **Night Skies** program offered Tuesday, Friday and Saturday evenings April through October.

The park is in a remote area approximately 80 miles south of Farmington. **Gallo Campground** (campsites $10) is 1 mile east of the visitor center. No RV hook-ups.

Chama

Nine miles south of the Colorado border, Chama's **Cumbres & Toltec Scenic Railway** (☑575-756-2151; www.cumbrestoltec.com; adult/child from $89/49; ◷ late May–mid-Oct) is the longest (64 miles) and highest (over the 10,015ft-high Cumbres Pass) authentic narrow-gauge steam railroad in the US. It's a beautiful trip, particularly in September and October during the fall foliage, through mountains, canyons and high desert. Lunch is included and on many trips kids ride free. See the website for details on trip options.

Northeastern New Mexico

East of Santa Fe, the lush Sangre de Cristo Mountains give way to vast rolling plains. Dusty grasslands stretch to infinity and further – to Texas. Cattle and dinosaur prints dot a landscape punctuated with volcanic cones. Ranching is an economic mainstay, and on many roads you'll see more cows than cars.

The Santa Fe Trail, along which pioneer settlers rolled in wagon trains, ran from New Mexico to Missouri. You can still see the wagon ruts in some places off I-25 between Santa Fe and Raton. For a bit of the Old West without a patina of consumer hype, this is the place.

Cimarron

Cimarron once ranked among the rowdiest of Wild West towns; it's name even means 'wild' in Spanish. According to local lore, murder was such an everyday occurrence in the 1870s that peace-and-quiet was newsworthy, one paper going so far as to report:

'Everything is quiet in Cimarron. Nobody has been killed in three days.'

Today, the town is quiet, luring nature-minded travelers who want to enjoy the great outdoors. Driving here to or from Taos, you'll pass through gorgeous **Cimarron Canyon State Park**, a steep-walled canyon with several hiking trails, excellent trout fishing and camping.

You can stay or dine (restaurant mains $7 to $20) at what's reputed to be one of the most haunted hotels in the USA, the 1872 **St James** (☑888-376-2664; www.exstjames.com; 617 Collison St; r $85-135; ❈🐾) – one room is so spook-filled that it's never rented out! Many legends of the West stayed here, including Buffalo Bill, Annie Oakley, Wyatt Earp and Jesse James, and the front desk has a long list of who shot whom in the now-renovated hotel bar. The authentic period rooms make this one of the most historic-feeling hotels in New Mexico.

Capulin Volcano National Monument

Rising 1300ft above the surrounding plains, **Capulin** (www.nps.gov/cavo; admission per vehicle $5; ◷8am-4pm) is the most accessible of several volcanoes in the area. From the visitor center, a 2-mile road spirals up the mountain to a parking lot at the crater rim (8182ft), where trails lead around and into the crater. The entrance is 3 miles north of Capulin village, which itself is 30 miles east of Raton on Hwy 87.

Southwestern New Mexico

The Rio Grande Valley unfurls from Albuquerque down to the bubbling hot springs of funky Truth or Consequences and beyond. Before the river hits the Texas line, it feeds one of New Mexico's agricultural treasures: Hatch, the so-called 'chili capital of the world.' The first atomic device was detonated at the Trinity Site, in the bone-dry desert east of the Rio Grande known since Spanish times as the Jornada del Muerto – Journey of Death.

To the west, the rugged Gila National Forest is wild with backpacking and fishing adventures. The mountains' southern slopes descend into the Chihuahuan Desert that surrounds Las Cruces, the state's second-largest city.

Truth or Consequences & Around

An offbeat joie de vivre permeates the funky little town of Truth or Consequences, which was built on the site of natural hot springs in the 1880s. A bit of the quirkiness stems from the fact that the town changed its name from Hot Springs to Truth or Consequences (or 'T or C') in 1950, after a popular radio game show of the same name. Publicity these days comes courtesy of Virgin Galactic CEO Richard Branson and other space-travel visionaries driving the development of nearby **Spaceport America**, where wealthy tourists will launch into orbit sometime soon. **Spaceport tours** (☑575-740-6894; www.ftstours.com; adult/under 12yr $59/29; ☺9am & 1pm Fri & Sat, 9am Sun) include a look at the launch site and mission control.

About 60 miles north of town, sandhill cranes and Arctic geese winter in the 90 sq miles of fields and marshes at **Bosque del Apache National Wildlife Refuge** (www.fws.gov/southwest/refuges/newmex/bosque; per vehicle $5; ☺dawn-dusk). There's a visitor center and driving tour. The Festival of the Cranes is held in mid-November.

🛏 Sleeping & Eating

Many local motels double as spas.

★**Blackstone Hotsprings** BOUTIQUE HOTEL $
(☑575-894-0894; www.blackstonehotsprings.com; 410 Austin St; r $75-135; P☀☎) Blackstone embraces the T or C spirit with an upscale wink, decorating each of its seven rooms in the style of a classic TV show, from the *Jetsons* to the *Golden Girls* to *I Love Lucy*. Best part? Each room comes with its own hot-spring tub or waterfall. Worst part? If you like sleeping in darkness, quite a bit of courtyard light seeps into some rooms at night.

Riverbend Hot Springs BOUTIQUE HOTEL $
(☑575-894-7625; www.riverbendhotsprings.com; 100 Austin St; r from $70; ☀☎) Former hostel Riverbend Hot Springs now offers more traditional motel-style accommodations – no more tepees – from its fantastic perch beside the Rio Grande. Rooms exude a bright, quirky charm, and several units work well for groups. Private hot-spring tubs are available by the hour (guest/nonguest $10/15), as is a public hot-spring pool (guest/nonguest free/$10).

Happy Belly Deli DELI $
(313 N Broadway; mains $2-8; ☺7am-3pm Mon-Fri, 8am-3pm Sat, 8am-noon Sun) Draws the morning crowd with fresh and filling breakfast combos.

★**Café Bellaluca** ITALIAN $$
(www.cafebellaluca.com; 303 Jones St; lunch mains $8-15, dinner mains $13-38; ☺11am-9pm Mon, Wed & Thu, to 10pm Fri & Sat, to 8pm Sun) Earns raves for its Italian specialties; pizzas are amazing.

Las Cruces & Around

The second-largest city in New Mexico, Las Cruces is home to New Mexico State University (NMSU), but there's surprisingly little of real interest for visitors.

⊙ Sights

For many, a visit to neighboring **Mesilla** (aka Old Mesilla) is the highlight of their time in Las Cruces. Wander a few blocks off Old Mesilla's plaza to gather the essence of a mid-19th-century Southwestern town of Hispanic heritage.

★**New Mexico Farm & Ranch Heritage Museum** MUSEUM
(www.nmfarmandranchmuseum.org; 4100 Dripping Springs Rd; adult/child $5/2; ☺9am-5pm Mon-Sat, noon-5pm Sun; ⊞) This terrific museum in Las Cruces has more than just engaging displays about the agricultural history of the state – it's got livestock! There are daily milking demonstrations and an occasional 'parade of breeds' of beef cattle, along with stalls of horses, donkeys, sheep and goats. Other demonstrations include blacksmithing (Friday to Sunday), spinning and weaving (Wednesday), and heritage cooking (call for schedule).

White Sands Missile Test Center Museum MUSEUM
(www.wsmr-history.org; Bldg 200, Headquarters Ave; ☺8am-4pm Mon-Fri, 10am-3pm Sat) FREE About 25 miles east of Las Cruces along Hwy 70 (look for the White Sands Missile Range Headquarters sign), White Sands has been a major military testing site since 1945, and it still serves as an alternative landing site for the space shuttle. Look for the crazy outdoor missile park. Since it's on an army base, everyone entering over the age of 18 years must show ID, and the driver might have to present car registration and proof of insurance.

WORTH A TRIP

EAVESDROPPING ON OUTER SPACE

Past the town of Magdalena on Hwy 60 is the **Very Large Array** (VLA; www. nrao.edu; off Hwy 52; ⊘ 8:30am-sunset) **FREE** radio telescope facility, a complex of 27 huge antenna dishes sprouting like giant mushrooms in the high plains. At the visitor center, watch a short film about the facility and take a self-guided walking tour with a window peek into the control building. It's 4 miles south of Hwy 60 off Hwy 52.

🛏 Sleeping

★ **Lundeen Inn of the Arts** B&B $$
(☑ 505-526-3326; www.innofthearts.com; 618 S Alameda Blvd, Las Cruces; r incl breakfast $80-125, ste $99-155; P ❋ 🐾 🛜) In Las Cruces, Lundeen Inn of the Arts, a large turn-of-the-19th-century Mexican territorial-style inn, has seven guest rooms (all unique), genteel hosts, an airy living room with soaring ceilings (made of pressed tin) and impressive freshly made breakfasts.

🍴 Eating

Nellie's Café NEW MEXICAN $
(1226 W Hadley Ave; mains $5-8; ⊘ 8am-2pm Tue-Sun) A favored local New Mexican restaurant, great for breakfast and lunch. Cash only.

La Posta NEW MEXICAN $$
(www.laposta-de-mesilla.com; 2410 Calle de San Albino; mains $8-15; ⊘ 11am-9pm) The most famous restaurant in Old Mesilla, in a 200-year-old adobe, may at first raise your doubts with its fiesta-like decor and touristy feel. But the New Mexican dishes are consistently good, portions are huge and service is prompt.

ℹ Information

Las Cruces Visitors Bureau (☑ 575-541-2444; www.lascrucescvb.org; 211 N Water St; ⊘ 8am-5pm Mon-Fri)

ℹ Getting There & Away

Greyhound (☑ 575-524-8518; www.greyhound.com; 800 E Thorpe Rd, Chucky's Convenience Store) buses traverse the two interstate corridors (I-10 and I-25). Daily destinations include Albuquerque ($29, 3½ hours), Roswell ($52, four hours) and El Paso ($12.60, one hour).

Silver City & Around

The spirit of the Wild West still hangs in the air here, as if Billy the Kid himself – a former resident – might amble past at any moment. But things are changing, as the mountain-man/cowboy vibe succumbs to the charms of art galleries, coffeehouses and gelato. (One word of caution when strolling through downtown Silver City – look carefully before you step off the sidewalk. Because of monsoonal summer rains, curbs are higher than average, built to keep the Victorian and the brick and cast-iron buildings safe from quick-rising waters.)

Silver City is also the gateway to outdoor activities in the **Gila National Forest**, which is rugged country suitable for remote cross-country skiing, backpacking, camping, fishing and other activities.

Two hours north of Silver City, up a winding 42-mile road, is **Gila Cliff Dwellings National Monument** (www.nps.gov/gicl; admission $3; ⊘ trail 9am-4pm, visitor center to 4:30pm), occupied in the 13th century by Mogollons. Mysterious and relatively isolated, these remarkable cliff dwellings are easily accessed from a 1-mile loop trail and look very much as they would have at the turn of the first millennium. For **pictographs**, stop by the Lower Scorpion Campground and walk a short distance along the marked trail.

Weird rounded monoliths make the **City of Rocks State Park** (www.nmparks.com; Hwy 61; day-use $5, tent/RV sites $8/10) an intriguing playground, with great camping among the formations; there are tables and fire pits. For a rock-lined gem of a spot, check out campsite 43, the Lynx. Head 24 miles northwest of Deming along Hwy 180, then 3 miles northeast on Hwy 61.

For a smattering of Silver City's architectural history, overnight in the 22-room **Palace Hotel** (☑ 575-388-1811; www.silvercitypalacehotel.com; 106 W Broadway; r from $51; ❋ 🛜). Exuding a low-key, turn-of-the-19th-century charm (no air con, older fixtures), the Palace is a great choice for those tired of cookie-cutter chains. On the corner, the lofty **Javalina** (201 N Bullard St; pastries from $2; ⊘ 6am-9pm Mon-Thu, to 10pm Fri & Sat, to 7pm Sun; 🛜) offers coffee, snacks and wi-fi in a comfy, come-as-you-are space.

Downtown offers a variety of eateries, including the deservedly popular **Diane's Restaurant & Bakery** (☑ 575-538-8722; www.dianesrestaurant.com; 510 N Bullard St; lunch $8-10, dinner $15-30; ⊙11am-2pm & 5:30-9pm Tue-Sat, 11am-2pm Sun) and the Peace Meal Cooperative (www.peacemealcoop.com; 601 N Bullard St; mains $6-10; ⊙11am-7pm Wed-Mon; ✍) build-your-own burrito bar. For a real taste of local culture, head 7 miles north to Pinos Altos and the Buckhorn Saloon (☑575-538-9911; www.buckhornsaloonandoperahouse.com; Main St, Pinos Altos; mains $10-39; ⊙5-9pm Mon-Sat), where the specialty is steak and there's live music most nights. Call for reservations.

ℹ Information

The visitor center (☑575-538-3785; www.silvercity.org; 201 N Hudson St; ⊙9am-5pm Mon-Fri, 10am-2pm Sat & Sun) and the Gila National Forest Ranger Station (☑575-388-8201; www.fs.fed.us/r3/gila; 3005 E Camino Del Bosque; ⊙8am-4:30pm Mon-Fri) have area information. To learn about the town's contentious mining history, watch the blacklisted 1954 movie *Salt of the Earth*.

Southeastern New Mexico

Two of New Mexico's greatest natural wonders are tucked down here in the arid southeast – mesmerizing White Sands National Monument and magnificent Carlsbad Caverns National Park. This region is also home to some of the state's most enduring legends: aliens in Roswell, Billy the Kid in Lincoln and Smokey Bear in Capitan. Most of the lowlands are covered by hot, rugged Chihuahuan Desert, but you can escape to cooler climes by driving up to higher altitudes around the popular forested resort towns such as Cloudcroft and Ruidoso.

White Sands National Monument

Slide, roll and slither through brilliant, towering sand hills. Sixteen miles southwest of Alamogordo (15 miles southwest of Hwy 82/70), gypsum covers 275 sq miles to create a dazzling white landscape at this crisp, stark monument (www.nps.gov/whsa; adult/under 16yr $3/free; ⊙7am-9pm Jun-Aug, to sunset Sep-May). These captivating windswept dunes are a highlight of any trip to New Mexico. Don't forget your sunglasses – the sand is as bright as snow!

Spring for a $17 plastic saucer at the visitor center gift store then sled one of the back dunes. It's fun, and you can sell the disc back for $5 at day's end (no rentals to avoid liability). Check the park calendar for sunset strolls and occasional full-moon bike rides (adult/under 16 years $5/2.50), the latter best reserved far in advance. Backcountry campsites, with no water or toilet facilities, are a mile from the scenic drive. Pick up one of the limited permits ($3, issued first-come, first-served) in person at the visitor center at least one hour before sunset.

Alamogordo & Around

Alamogordo is the center of one of the most historically important space- and atomic-research programs in the country. The four-story New Mexico Museum of Space History (www.nmspacemuseum.org; Hwy 2001; adult/child $6/4; ⊙9am-5pm; ♿) has excellent exhibits on space research and flight. Its Tombaugh IMAX Theater & Planetarium (adult/child $6/4.50; ♿) shows outstanding science-themed films on a huge wraparound screen.

Numerous motels stretch along White Sands Blvd, including Best Western Desert Aire Hotel (☑575-437-2110; www.bestwestern.com; 1021 S White Sands Blvd; r from $78; ❄❀@🖥🏊), with standard-issue rooms and suites (some with kitchenettes), along with a sauna. If you'd rather camp, hit Oliver Lee State Park (www.nmparks.com; 409 Dog Canyon Rd; tent/RV sites $8/14), 12 miles south of Alamogordo. Grab some grub at the friendly Pizza Patio & Pub (2203 E 1st St; mains $7-15; ⊙11am-8pm Mon-Thu & Sat, to 9pm Fri; ♿), which has pizzas, pastas, big salads and pitchers or pints of beer on tap.

Cloudcroft

Pleasant Cloudcroft, with turn-of-the-19th-century buildings, offers lots of outdoor recreation, a good base for exploration and a low-key feel. Situated high in the mountains, it provides welcome relief from the lowlands heat to the east. For good information on hiking trails, free maps of forest roads, and topo maps for sale, go to the Lincoln National Forest Ranger Station (4 Lost Lodge Rd; ⊙7:30am-4:30pm Mon-Fri). High Altitude (☑575-682-1229; www.highaltitude.org; 310 Burro Ave; ⊙10am-5:30pm Mon-Thu, to 6pm Fri & Sat, to 5pm Sun) rents mountain bikes and has maps of local fat-tire routes.

The Lodge Resort & Spa (☑888-395-6343; www.thelodgeresort.com; 601 Corona Pl; r from $125; @🖥🏊) is one of the Southwest's best historic hotels. Rooms in the main Bavarian-style hotel are furnished with period and Victorian pieces. Within the lodge, Rebecca's (575-682-3131; Lodge Resort & Spa, 601 Corona Pl; mains $8-36; 7-10am, 11:30am-2pm & 5:30-9pm), named after the resident ghost, offers by far the best food in town.

Ruidoso

Downright bustling in summer and big with racetrack bettors, resorty Ruidoso (it means 'noisy' in Spanish) has an utterly pleasant climate thanks to its lofty and forested perch near Sierra Blanca (12,000ft). It's spread out along Hwy 48 (known as Mechem Dr or Sudderth Dr), the main drag.

◉ Sights & Activities

To stretch your legs, try the easily accessible forest trails on Cedar Creek Rd just west of Smokey Bear Ranger Station (575-257-4095; 901 Mechem Dr; 7:30am-4:30pm Mon-Fri year-round, plus Sat in summer). Choose from the USFS Fitness Trail or the meandering paths at the Cedar Creek Picnic Area. Longer day hikes and backpacking routes abound in the White Mountain Wilderness, north of town. Always check fire restrictions around here – it's not unusual for the forest to close during dry spells.

Ski Apache SKIING
(www.skiapache.com; lift ticket adult/child $51/33) The best ski area south of Albuquerque. It's 18 miles northwest of Ruidoso on the slopes of beautiful Sierra Blanca Peak (about 12,000ft). To get there, take exit 532 off Hwy 48.

Ruidoso Downs Racetrack HORSE RACING
(www.raceruidoso.com; Hwy 70; grandstand seats free; Fri-Mon late May-early Sep) Serious horse racing happens here.

Hubbard Museum of the American West MUSEUM
(www.hubbardmuseum.org; 26301 Hwy 70; adult/child $6/2; 10am-4:30pm;) Displays Western-related items, with an emphasis on Old West stagecoaches, Native American artifacts and, well, all things horse.

⛏ Sleeping & Eating

Numerous motels, hotels and cute little cabin complexes line the streets. There's plenty of primitive camping along forest roads on the way to the ski area.

Sitzmark Chalet HOTEL $
(800-658-9694; www.sitzmark-chalet.com; 627 Sudderth Dr; r from $60; ✳ ☎) This ski-themed chalet offers 17 simple but nice rooms. Picnic tables, grills and an eight-person hot tub are welcome perks.

Upper Canyon Inn LODGE $$
(575-257-3005; www.uppercanyoninn.com; 215 Main Rd; r/cabins from $79/119; ☎) Rooms and cabins range from simple good values to rustic-chic luxury.

Cornerstone Bakery BREAKFAST $
(www.cornerstonebakerycafe.com; 359 Sudderth Dr; mains under $10; 7am-2pm;) Stay around long enough and this eatery may become your touchstone. Everything on the menu, from the omelets to croissant sandwiches, is worthy, and the piñon-flavored coffee is wonderful.

Café Rio PIZZA $
(2547 Sudderth Dr; mains $8-25, cash only; 11:30am-8pm, closed Wed off-season;) Friendly service isn't the first description that leaps to mind at this scruffy pizza joint, but oh…take one bite of a pillowy slice and all will be forgiven.

☆ Entertainment

Flying J Ranch VARIETY
(888-458-3595; www.flyingjranch.com; 1028 Hwy 48; adult/child $27/15; from 5:30pm Mon-Sat late May-early Sep, Sat only to mid-Oct;) Circle the wagons and ride over about 1.5 miles north of Alto for a meal. This 'Western village' stages gunfights and offers pony rides with its cowboy-style chuckwagon.

❶ Information

The **chamber of commerce** (575-257-7395; www.ruidoso.net; 720 Sudderth Dr; 8am-4:30pm Mon-Fri, 9am-3pm Sat) has visitor information.

Lincoln & Capitan

Fans of Western history won't want to miss little Lincoln. Twelve miles east of Capitan along the Billy the Kid National Scenic Byway (www.billybyway.com), this is where the gun battle that turned Billy the Kid into a legend took place. The whole town is beautifully preserved in close to original form and the main street has been designated the Lincoln State Monument (www.nmmonuments.org/lincoln; adult/child $5/free; 8:30am-4:30pm); modern influences (such as neon-

SOUTHWEST SOUTHEASTERN NEW MEXICO

DON'T MISS

CARLSBAD CAVERNS NATIONAL PARK

Scores of wondrous caves hide under the hills at this unique **national park** (☑575-785-2232, bat info 505-785-3012; www.nps.gov/cave; 3225 National Parks Hwy; adult/child $6/free; ☉caves 8:30am-5pm late May-early Sep, 8:30am-3:30pm early Sep-late May; ▦), which covers 73 sq miles. The cavern formations are an ethereal wonderland of stalactites and fantastical geological features. From the **visitor center** (☉8am-5pm, to 7pm late May-early Sep) you can ride an elevator, which descends the length of the Empire State Building in under a minute, or take a 2-mile subterranean walk from the cave mouth to the Big Room, an underground chamber 1800ft long, 255ft high and more than 800ft below the surface. If you've got kids (or are just feeling goofy), plastic caving helmets with headlamps are sold in the gift shop.

Guided tours (☑877-444-6777; www.recreation.gov; adult $7-20, child $3.50-10) of additional caves are available, and should be reserved well in advance. Wear long sleeves and closed shoes; it gets chilly.

The cave's other claim to fame is the 300,000-plus Mexican free-tailed bat colony that roosts here from mid-May to mid-October. Be here by sunset, when they cyclone out for an all-evening insect feast.

lit motel signs, souvenir stands, fast-food joints) are not allowed.

Buy tickcts to the historic town buildings at the **Anderson-Freeman Museum**, where you'll also find exhibits on Buffalo soldiers, Apaches and the Lincoln County War. Make the fascinating **Courthouse Museum** your last stop; this is the well-marked site of Billy's most daring – and violent – escape. There's a plaque where one of his bullets slammed into the wall.

For overnighters, the **Ellis Store Country Inn** (☑800-653-6460; www.ellisstore.com; Hwy 380; r incl breakfast $89-129) offers three antique-filled rooms (complete with wood stove) in the main house; five additional rooms are located in a historic mill on the property. From Wednesday to Saturday the host offers an amazing six-course dinner ($75 per person), served in the lovely dining room. Perfect for special occasions; reservations recommended.

A few miles west on the road to Capitan, **Laughing Sheep Farm and Ranch** (☑575-653-4041; www.laughingsheepfarm.com; Hwy 380; mains $10-35; ☉5-9pm Thu-Sat; ▦) raises sheep, cows and bison – along with vegetables and fruit – then serves them up for dinner. The dining room is comfortable and casual, with a play-dough table and an easel for kids and live music each night it's open. Comfortable cabins with hot tubs are rented by the night from $130.

Like Lincoln, cozy Capitan is surrounded by the beautiful mountains of **Lincoln National Forest**. The main reason to come is

so the kids can visit **Smokey Bear Historical State Park** (118 W Smokey Bear Blvd; adult/child $2/1; ☉9am-5pm), where Smokey (yes, there actually was a real Smokey Bear) is buried.

Roswell

If you believe 'The Truth Is Out There', then the Roswell Incident is already filed away in your memory banks. In 1947 a mysterious object crashed at a nearby ranch. No one would have skipped any sleep over it, but the military made a big to-do of hushing it up, and for a lot of folks, that sealed it: the aliens had landed! International curiosity and local ingenuity have transformed the city into a quirky extraterrestrial-wannabe zone. Bulbous white heads glow atop the downtown streetlamps and busloads of tourists come to find good souvenirs.

Believers and kitsch-seekers must check out the **International UFO Museum & Research Center** (www.roswellufomuseum.com; 114 N Main St; adult/child $5/$2; ☉9am-5pm), displaying documents supporting the cover-up as well as lots of far-out art and exhibitions. The annual **Roswell UFO Festival** (www.roswellufofestival.com) beams down in early July, with an otherworldly costume parade, guest speakers, workshops and concerts.

Ho-hum chain motels line N Main St. About 36 miles south of Roswell, the **Heritage Inn** (☑575-748-2552; www.artesiaheritage-inn.com; 209 W Main St, Artesia; r incl breakfast from $119; ❋ @ 🛜 ❋) in Artesia offers 11 Old West–style rooms and is the nicest lodging in the area.

For simple, dependable New Mexican fare, try **Martin's Capitol Cafe** (110 W 4th St; mains $7-15; ⊙6am-8:30pm Mon-Sat); for American eats, **Big D's Downtown Dive** (www.bigdsdowntowndive.com; 505 N Main St; mains $7-10; ⊙11am-9pm) has the best salads, sandwiches and burgers in town.

Pick up local information and have your picture snapped with an alien at the **visitors bureau** (🖉575-624-6860; www.seeroswell. com; 912 N Main St; ⊙8:30am-5:30pm Mon-Fri, 10am-3pm Sat & Sun; 🛜).

The **Greyhound Bus Depot** (🖉575-622-2510; www.greyhound.com; 1100 N Virginia Ave) has buses to Carlsbad ($30, 1½ hours) and El Paso, TX, via Las Cruces ($52, four hours).

Carlsbad

Travelers use Carlsbad as a base for visits to nearby Carlsbad Caverns National Park and the Guadalupe Mountains. The **Park Service office** (🖉575-885-8884; 3225 National Parks Hwy; ⊙8am-4:30pm Mon-Fri) on the south edge of town has information on both.

On the northwestern outskirts of town, off Hwy 285, **Living Desert State Park** (www.nmparks.com; 1504 Miehls Dr, off Hwy 285; adult/child $5/3; ⊙8am-5pm Jun-Aug, 9am-5pm Sep-May) is a great place to see and learn about desert plants and wildlife. There's a good 1.3-mile trail that showcases different

habitats of the Chihuahuan Desert, with live antelopes, wolves, roadrunners and more.

Most of Carlsbad lodging consists of chain motels on S Canal St or National Parks Hwy. The top value is the **Stagecoach Inn** (🖉575-887-1148; 1819 S Canal St; r from $50; ❋🛜❋), with clean rooms, a pool, and a good on-site playground for kids. The best accommodation in town is the new, luxurious **Trinity Hotel** (🖉575-234-9891; www.thetrinityhotel.com; 201 S Canal St; r from $169-219; ❋🛜), a historic building that was originally the First National Bank; the sitting room of one suite is inside the old vault! The restaurant here is Carlsbad's classiest.

The perky **Blue House Bakery & Cafe** (609 N Canyon St; mains $4-8; ⊙6am-noon Mon-Sat) brews the best coffee in this quadrant of New Mexico and specializes in breakfasts and pastries. For country-style dinner, hit the lip-smackin' good **Red Chimney Pit Barbecue** (www.redchimneypitbarbecue. com; 817 N Canal St; mains $7-15; ⊙11am-2pm & 4:30-8:30pm Mon-Fri), where you're sure to get your fill.

For other in-the-know advice, visit the **chamber of commerce** (🖉575-887-6516; www.carlsbadchamber.com; 302 S Canal St; ⊙9am-5pm Mon, 8am-5pm Tue-Fri).

Greyhound (🖉575-628-0768; www.greyhound.com; 3102 National Parks Hwy) buses depart from the Shamrock gas station inside Food Jet South, heading only to El Paso ($52, three hours) and Lubbock, TX ($52, four hours).

California

Includes ➡

Best Places to Eat

➡ Benu (p982)

➡ Chez Panisse (p993)

➡ French Laundry (p996)

➡ George's at the Cove (p942)

➡ Bazaar (p924)

Best Places to Hike

➡ Yosemite National Park (p1009)

➡ Sequoia & Kings Canyon National Parks (p1013)

➡ Marin County (p991)

➡ Redwood National & State Parks (p1001)

Why Go?

With bohemian spirit and high-tech savvy, not to mention a die-hard passion for the good life – whether that means cracking open a bottle of old-vine Zinfandel, climbing a 14,000ft peak or surfing the Pacific – California soars beyond any expectations sold on Hollywood's silver screens.

More than anything, California is iconic. It was here that the hurly-burly gold rush kicked off in the mid-19th century, poet-naturalist John Muir rhapsodized about the Sierra Nevada's 'range of light,' and Jack Kerouac and the Beat Generation defined what it really means to hit the road.

California's multicultural melting pot has been cookin' since this bountiful promised land was first staked out by Spain and Mexico. Today, waves of immigrants from around the world still look to find their own American dream on these palm-tree-studded Pacific shores.

Come see the future in the making in California. Then stay for the beaches.

When to Go
Los Angeles

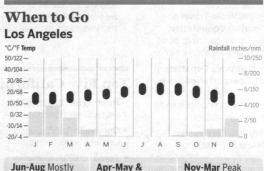

Jun-Aug Mostly sunny weather, some coastal fog; summer vacation crowds.

Apr-May & Sep-Oct Cooler nights, mostly cloudless days; travel bargains.

Nov-Mar Peak tourism at mountain ski resorts and in SoCal's warm deserts.

DON'T MISS

You can't leave California without hugging a tree! We suggest a coast redwood, which can live for 2000 years and grow to 379ft tall.

Fast Facts

➡ **Hub cities** Los Angeles (population 3,819,702), San Francisco (population 812,826)

➡ **Driving time** LA to San Francisco (5½ hours via inland I-5 & I-580 Fwys, 8½ hours via coastal Hwys 101 & 1)

➡ **Time zone** Pacific Standard

Did You Know?

Just a few of California's inventions: the internet and the iPad, power yoga and reality TV, the space shuttle and Mickey Mouse, the Cobb salad and the fortune cookie.

Resources

➡ **California Travel & Tourism Commission** (www.visitcalifornia.com) Official state tourism info.

➡ **California Department of Transportation** (www.dot.ca.gov/cgi-bin/roads.cgi) Road conditions and highway closures.

➡ **USGS Earthquake Hazards** (http://quake.usgs.gov/recenteqs/latest.htm) Real-time earthquake maps.

Getting There & Around

Los Angeles (LAX) and San Francisco (SFO) are major international airports. Small airports in San Diego, Orange County, Oakland, San Jose, Sacramento, Burbank, Long Beach and Santa Barbara handle primarily domestic flights.

Four long-distance Amtrak routes connect California with the rest of the USA: *California Zephyr* (Chicago–San Francisco Bay Area), *Coast Starlight* (Seattle–Los Angeles), *Southwest Chief* (Chicago–LA) and *Sunset Limited* (New Orleans–LA). Amtrak's intrastate routes include the *Pacific Surfliner* (San Diego–LA–Santa Barbara–San Luis Obispo), the *Capitol Corridor* (San Jose–Oakland–Berkeley–Sacramento) and the *San Joaquin* (Bakersfield to Oakland or Sacramento, with Yosemite Valley buses from Merced).

Greyhound buses travel to many corners of the state. But to really get out and explore, especially away from the coast, you'll need a car.

CALIFORNIA'S NATIONAL & STATE PARKS

Yosemite and Sequoia became California's first national parks in 1890, and today there are seven more: Kings Canyon, Death Valley, Joshua Tree, Channel Islands, Redwood, Lassen Volcanic and Pinnacles. The **National Park Service** (www.nps.gov) manages two dozen other historic sites, monuments, nature preserves and recreational areas statewide. Entry fees vary from nothing up to $25 per vehicle for a seven-day pass; campsites cost up to $20 nightly. **Recreation.gov** (☎877-444-6777, 518-885-3639; www.recreation.gov) handles camping reservations for all federal lands.

California's 280 **state parks** (☎800-777-0369, 916-653-6995; www.parks.ca.gov) are a diverse bunch – everything from marine preserves to redwood forests – protecting a third of the coastline and offering 3000 miles of hiking, biking and equestrian trails. Some state parks may be closed or have reduced opening hours due to budget cutbacks (call ahead or check the website). Day-use parking fees are $4 to $15, campsites $5 to $75 nightly. **ReserveAmerica** (☎800-444-7275; www.reserveamerica.com) handles state-park camping reservations.

Top Five California Beaches

➡ **Huntington Beach** (p932) Bonfires, beach volleyball and rolling waves in 'Surf City USA.'

➡ **Coronado** (p935) Sun yourself along San Diego's boundless Silver Strand.

➡ **Zuma** (p917) Aquamarine waters, frothy surf and tawny sand near Malibu.

➡ **Santa Cruz** (p961) Surf's up! And the beach boardwalk's carnival fun never stops.

➡ **Point Reyes** (p992) Wild, windy, walkable beaches for sunsets and wildlife watching.

History

By the time European explorers arrived in the 16th century, as many as 300,000 indigenous people called this land home. Spanish conquistadors combed through what they called Alta (Upper) California in search of a fabled 'city of gold,' but they left the territory virtually alone after failing to find it. Not until the Mission Period (1769–1833) did Spain make a serious attempt to settle the land; it established 21 Catholic missions – many founded by Franciscan priest Junípero Serra – and presidios (military forts) to deter the British and Russians.

After winning independence from Spain in 1821 Mexico briefly ruled California, but then was trounced by the fledgling United States in the Mexican War (1846–48). The discovery of gold just 10 days before the Treaty of Guadalupe Hidalgo was signed soon saw the territory's nonindigenous population quintuple to 92,000 by 1850, when California became the 31st US state. Thousands of imported Chinese laborers helped complete the transcontinental railroad in 1869, which opened up markets and further spurred migration to the Golden State.

The 1906 San Francisco earthquake was barely a hiccup as California continued to grow exponentially in size, diversity and importance. Mexican immigrants streamed in during the 1910–20 Mexican Revolution, and again during WWII, to fill labor shortages. Military-driven industries developed during wartime, while anti-Asian sentiments led to the unjust internment of many Japanese Americans, including at Manzanar in the Eastern Sierra.

California has long been a social pioneer thanks to its size, confluence of wealth, a diversity of immigration and technological innovation. Since the early 20th century, Hollywood has mesmerized the world with its cinematic dreams. Meanwhile, San Francisco reacted against the banal complacency of post-WWII suburbia with Beat poetry in the 1950s, hippie free love in the '60s and gay pride in the '70s. The internet revolution, initially spurred by high-tech visionaries in Silicon Valley, rewired the nation and led to a 1990s boom in overspeculated stocks.

When that tech bubble burst, plunging the state's economy into chaos, Californians blamed their Democratic governor, Gray Davis, and, in a controversial recall election, voted to give actor-turned-Republican Arnold Schwarzenegger (aka 'The Governator') a shot at fixing things. During the US recession that started in 2008, California's budget shortfalls caused another staggering

---

CALIFORNIA FACTS

Nickname Golden State

State motto Eureka ('I Have Found It')

Population 38 million

Area 155,779 sq miles

Capital city Sacramento (population 472,178)

Other cities Los Angeles (population 3,819,702), San Diego (population 1,326,179), San Francisco (population 812,826)

Sales tax 7.5%

Birthplace of Author John Steinbeck (1902–68), photographer Ansel Adams (1902–84), US president Richard Nixon (1913–94), pop-culture icon Marilyn Monroe (1926–62)

Home of The highest and lowest points in the contiguous US (Mt Whitney, Death Valley), world's oldest, tallest and biggest living trees (ancient bristlecone pines, coast redwoods and giant sequoias, respectively)

Politics Majority Democrat (multiethnic), minority Republican (mostly white), one in five Californians votes independent

Famous for Disneyland, earthquakes, Hollywood, hippies, Silicon Valley, surfing

Kitschiest souvenir 'Mystery Spot' bumper sticker

Driving distances Los Angeles to San Francisco 380 miles, San Francisco to Yosemite Valley 200 miles

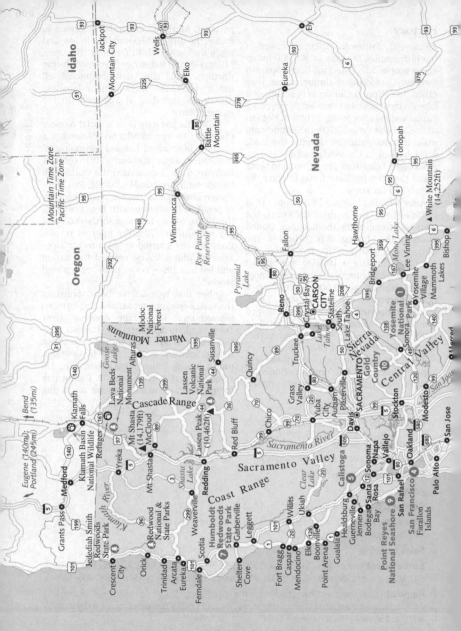

California Highlights

❶ Chasing waterfalls and climbing granite domes in **Yosemite National Park** (p1009).

❷ Making the most of multicultural neighborhoods and Hollywood's red-carpet nightlife in **Los Angeles** (p906).

❸ Cruising Hwy 1 above sculpted sea cliffs along the rocky coast of **Big Sur** (p957).

❹ Tasting farm-fresh bounty at the Ferry Building in **San Francisco** (p964).

❺ Wallowing in mud baths near famous Napa Valley vineyards in **Calistoga** (p994).

❻ Chowing on fish tacos and surfing perfect waves off sunny **San Diego** (p933) beaches.

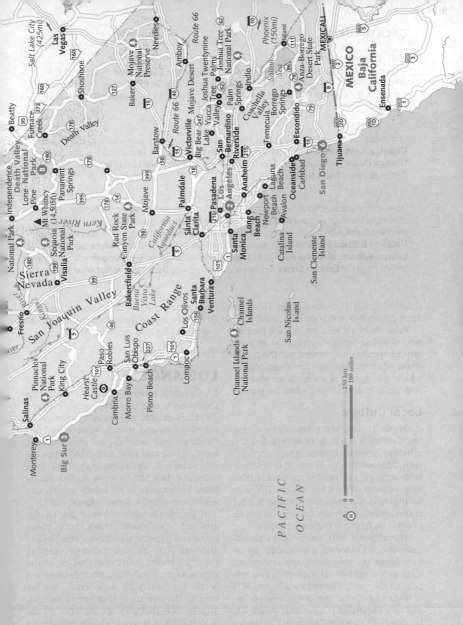

⑦ Craning your neck at the world's tallest trees along Avenue of the Giants in the **Humboldt Redwoods State Park** (p1001).

⑧ Trekking across sand dunes and ambling Old West ghost towns in **Death Valley** (p949).

⑨ Spotting whales, seals and tule elk at **Point Reyes National Seashore** (p992).

⑩ Dipping into swimming holes and panning like a 49er in **Gold Country** (p1005).

CALIFORNIA IN...

One Week

California in a nutshell: start in **Los Angeles**, detouring to **Disneyland**. Head up the breezy Central Coast, stopping in **Santa Barbara** and **Big Sur**, before getting a dose of big-city culture in **San Francisco**. Head inland to nature's temple, **Yosemite National Park**, then zip back to LA.

Two Weeks

Follow the one-week itinerary above, but at a saner pace. Add jaunts to NorCal's **Wine Country**; **Lake Tahoe**, perched high in the Sierra Nevada; the bodacious beaches of **Orange County** and laid-back **San Diego**; or **Joshua Tree National Park**, near the chic desert resort of **Palm Springs**.

One Month

Do everything described above, and more. From San Francisco, head up the North Coast, starting in Marin County at **Point Reyes National Seashore**. Stroll Victorian-era **Mendocino** and **Eureka**, find yourself on the **Lost Coast** and ramble through fern-filled **Redwood National & State Parks**. Inland, snap a postcard-perfect photo of **Mt Shasta**, detour to **Lassen Volcanic National Park** and ramble California's historic **Gold Country**. Trace the backbone of the **Eastern Sierra** before winding down into **Death Valley National Park**.

financial crisis that once-again Governor Jerry Brown has now begun to resolve.

Meanwhile, the need for public education reform builds, prisons overflow, state parks are chronically underfunded and the conundrum of illegal immigration from Mexico, which fills a critical cheap labor shortage (especially in agriculture), vexes the state.

Local Culture

Currently the world's ninth-largest economy, California is a state of extremes, where grinding poverty shares urban corridors with fabulous wealth. Waves of immigrants keep arriving, and neighborhoods are often mini versions of their homelands. Tolerance for others is the social norm, but so is intolerance, which you'll encounter if you smoke, or drive on freeways during rush hour.

Untraditional and unconventional attitudes define California, a trendsetter by nature. Image is an obsession, appearances are stridently youthful and outdoorsy, and self-help all the rage. Whether it's a luxury SUV or Nissan Leaf, a car may define who you are and how important you consider yourself to be, especially in SoCal (Southern California).

Think of California as the USA's most futuristic social laboratory. If technology identifies a new useful gadget, Silicon Valley will build it at light speed. If postmodern celebrities, bizarrely famous for the mere fact of being famous, make a fashion statement or get thrown in jail, the nation pays attention. No other state's pop culture has as big an effect on how the rest of Americans work, play, eat, love, consume and, yes, recycle.

LOS ANGELES

LA County – America's largest – represents the nation in extremes. Its people are among America's richest and poorest, most established and newest arrivals, most refined and roughest, most beautiful and most botoxed, most erudite and most airheaded. Even the landscape is a microcosm of the USA, from cinematic beaches to snow-dusted mountains, skyscrapers to suburban sprawl, and wilderness where mountain lions prowl.

If you think you've already got LA figured out – celebutants, smog, traffic, bikini babes and pop-star wannabes – think again. Although it's an entertainment capital, the city's truths aren't delivered on movie screens or reality shows; rather, in bite-sized portions of everyday experiences on the streets. The one thing that brings together Angelenos is that they are seekers – or the descendants of seekers – drawn by a dream of fame, fortune or rebirth.

Now is an especially exciting time to visit LA: Hollywood and Downtown are undergoing an urban renaissance, and the art, music, food and fashion scenes are all in high gear. Chances are, the more you explore, the more you'll love 'La-La Land.'

History

The hunter-gatherer existence of the Gabrieleño and Chumash peoples ended with the arrival of Spanish missionaries and colonial pioneers in the late 18th century. Spain's first civilian settlement, El Pueblo de Nuestra Señora la Reina de Los Ángeles, remained an isolated farming outpost for decades after its founding in 1781. The city wasn't officially incorporated until 1850.

LA's population repeatedly swelled after the collapse of the California gold rush, the arrival of the transcontinental railroad, the growth of the citrus industry, the discovery of oil, the launch of the port of LA, the birth of the movie industry and the opening of the California Aqueduct. After WWII, the city's population doubled from nearly two million in 1950 to almost four million today.

LA's growth has caused problems, including suburban sprawl and air pollution – though, with aggressive enforcement, smog levels have fallen every year since records have been kept. Traffic, a fluctuating real-estate market and the occasional earthquake or wildfire remain nagging concerns but, with a diverse economy and decreasing crime rate, all things considered, LA's a survivor.

Sights

A dozen miles inland from the Pacific, Downtown LA combines history and highbrow arts and culture. Hip-again Hollywood awaits northwest of Downtown, while urban-designer chic and lesbi-gays rule West Hollywood. South of WeHo, Museum Row is Mid-City's main draw. Further west are ritzy Beverly Hills, Westwood near the UCLA campus and West LA. Beach towns include kid-friendly Santa Monica, boho Venice, star-powered Malibu and busy Long Beach. Upscale Pasadena lies northeast of Downtown.

Downtown

For decades, LA's historic core and main business and government district emptied out on nights and weekends. No more. Crowds fill performance and entertainment venues, and young professionals and artists have moved into new lofts, bringing bars, restaurants and art galleries. Don't expect Manhattan just yet; still, adventurous urbanites won't want to miss Downtown.

Downtown is most easily explored on foot combined with short subway and DASH minibus rides. Parking is cheapest (from $6 all day) around Little Tokyo and Chinatown.

EL PUEBLO DE LOS ANGELES & AROUND

Compact, colorful and car-free, this historic district is an immersion in LA's Spanish-Mexican roots. Its spine is Olvera St, a festive kitsch-o-rama where you can snap up handmade folkloric trinkets, then chomp on tacos or sugar-sprinkled churros.

'New' Chinatown is about a half-mile north along Broadway and Hill St, crammed with dim-sum parlors, herbal apothecaries, curio shops and Chung King Rd's edgy art galleries.

La Plaza de Cultura y Artes MUSEUM
(Map p910; ☎ 213-542-6200; www.lapca.org; 501 N Main St; ⊙ noon-7pm Wed-Mon) **FREE** Open

---

LOS ANGELES IN...

Distances are ginormous in LA, so allow extra time for traffic and don't try to pack too much into a day.

One Day

Fuel up for the day at the **Griddle Cafe** and then go star-searching on the **Hollywood Walk of Fame** along Hollywood Blvd. Up your chances of spotting actual celebs by hitting the fashion-forward boutiques on paparazzi-infested **Robertston Blvd**, or get a dose of nature at **Griffith Park**. Then drive west to the lofty **Getty Center** or head out to the **Venice Boardwalk** to see the seaside sideshow. Catch a Pacific sunset in **Santa Monica**.

Two Days

Explore rapidly evolving Downtown LA. Dig up its roots at **El Pueblo de Los Angeles**, then catapult to the future at dramatic **Walt Disney Concert Hall** topping the **Cultural Corridor**. Walk off lunch ambling between Downtown's historic buildings and nouveau art galleries nearby **Little Tokyo**. At South Park's glitzy **LA Live** entertainment center, romp through the multimedia **Grammy Museum**, then join real-life celebs cheering on the LA Lakers next door at **Staples Center**.

since 2010, La Plaza chronicles the Mexican-American experience in LA with exhibits about the city's history from the Zoot Suit Riots to the Chicana movement and Latino art. It adjoins 1822 **La Placita** (Map p910; www.laplacita.org; 535 N Main St) church.

Avila Adobe   MUSEUM
(Map p910; ☎213-628-1274; http://elpueblo.lacity.org; Olvera St; ⊙9am-4pm) **FREE** Claiming to be LA's oldest building, this 1818 ranch home is decorated with period furniture. A video gives history and highlights of the neighborhood.

Greater Los Angeles

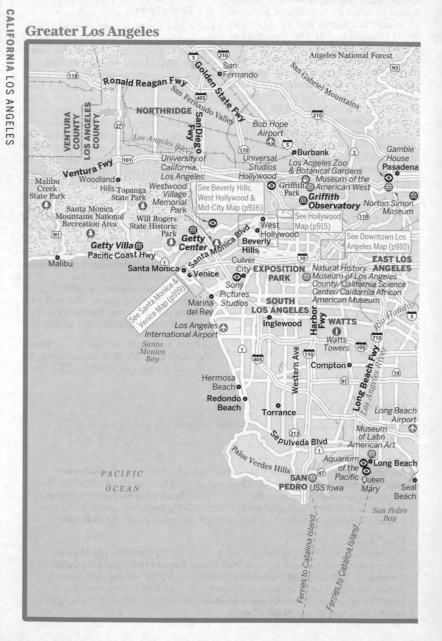

Union Station
LANDMARK

(Map p910; 800 N Alameda St; P) The last of America's grand rail stations (1939), Union Station's glamorous art-deco interior appears in *Blade Runner, 24, Speed* and many other films and TV shows. Parking costs from $2 for 20 minutes, $6 all day.

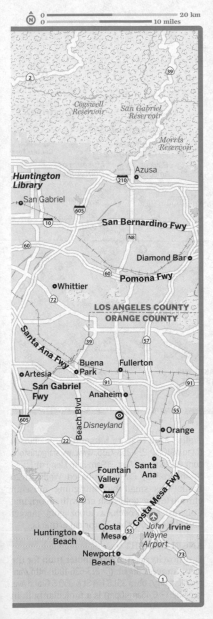

Chinese American Museum
MUSEUM

(Map p910; ☎ 213-485-8567; www.camla.org; Garnier Bldg, 425 N Los Angeles St; adult/child $3/2; ☺ 10am-3pm Tue-Sun) Small but smart, this museum inhabits a 19th-century Chinese merchant's building and community center, built before LA's Chinatown moved north.

CIVIC CENTER & CULTURAL CORRIDOR

North Grand Ave's 'Cultural Corridor' is anchored by the **Music Center** (Map p910; ☎ 213-972-7211; www.musiccenter.org; 135 N Grand Ave), where performing arts fill the Dorothy Chandler Pavilion, Mark Taper Forum and Ahmanson Theater.

★ Museum of Contemporary Art
MUSEUM

(MOCA; Map p910; ☎ 213-626-6222; www.moca. org; 250 S Grand Ave; adult/child $12/free, 5-8pm Thu free; ☺ 11am-5pm Mon & Fri, to 8pm Thu, to 6pm Sat & Sun) Housed in a building designed by Arata Isozaki, MOCA Grand Ave stages headline-grabbing special exhibits. Its permanent collection presents heavy hitters from the 1940s to the present. Parking at Walt Disney Concert Hall costs from $9 (cash only). MOCA has two other branches: the Geffen Contemporary in Little Tokyo and at West Hollywood's Pacific Design Center.

★ Walt Disney Concert Hall
CULTURAL BUILDING

(Map p910; ☎ info 213-972-7211, tickets 323-850-2000; www.laphil.org; 111 S Grand Ave; ☺ guided tours usually 10:30am & 12:30pm Tue-Sat; P) **FREE** Architect Frank Gehry's now-iconic 2003 building is a gravity-defying sculpture of curving and billowing stainless-steel walls that's home base for the Los Angeles Philharmonic (p926). Free tours are available subject to concert schedules, and walkways encircle the mazelike roof and exterior. Parking from $9 (cash only). Self-guided audio tours usually run between 10am and 2pm daily. Reservations are required for all tours.

Cathedral of Our Lady of the Angels
CHURCH

(Map p910; ☎ 213-680-5200; www.olacathedral. org; 555 W Temple St; ☺ 6:30am-6pm Mon-Fri, from 9am Sat, from 7am Sun; P) **FREE** Architect José Rafael Moneo mixed Gothic proportions with bold contemporary design for the main church of LA's Catholic Archdiocese. Built in 2002 it teems with art, and soft light through alabaster panes lends serenity. Tours (1pm Monday to Friday) and organ recitals (12:45pm Wednesday) are both free and popular.

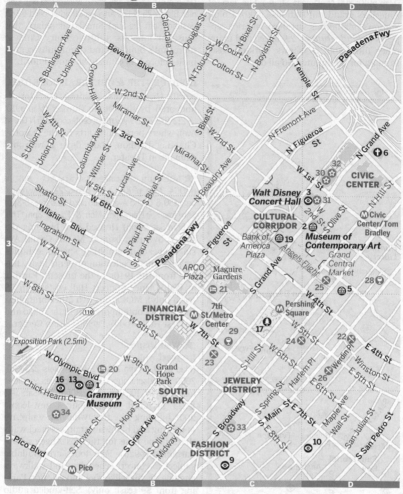

Weekday parking costs from $4 per 15 minutes (daily maximum $18) until 4pm, $5 flat-rate on weekends and holidays.

City Hall
LANDMARK

(Map p910; ☎213-978-1995; www.lacity.org; 200 N Spring St; ☺9am-5pm Mon-Fri) **FREE** Until the mid-1960s, no LA building stood taller than City Hall. This 1928 building, with its ziggurat-shaped top, cameoed in the *Superman* and *Dragnet* TV series and the 1953 sci-fi thriller *War of the Worlds*. Soak up views of the city and mountains from the observation deck. Weekday morning tours are free (reservations required).

Wells Fargo History Museum
MUSEUM

(Map p910; ☎213-253-7166; www.wellsfargohistory. com; 333 S Grand Ave; ☺9am-5pm Mon-Fri) **FREE** Sponsored by California-based Wells Fargo Bank, this small but intriguing museum chronicles the gold-rush era with an original Concord stagecoach, a 100oz gold nugget and all sorts of other historical artifacts.

ANGELS FLIGHT

Part novelty act, part commuter train for the lazy, **Angels Flight** (☎213-626-1901; http://angelsflight.org/; btwn 351 S Hill St & 350 S Grand Ave; fare 50¢; ☺6:45am-10pm) is a funicular built in

Downtown Los Angeles

◎ Top Sights

◎ Sights

◎ Sleeping

◎ Eating

◎ Drinking & Nightlife

◎ Entertainment

1901 and billed as the 'shortest railway in the world' (298ft). The adorable cars chug up and down Bunker Hill's steep incline between Hill St and California Watercourt Plaza.

LITTLE TOKYO

Little Tokyo swirls with shopping arcades, Buddhist temples, public art, traditional gardens, authentic sushi bars and noodle shops and a branch of **MOCA** (Map p910; ☑213-626-6222; www.moca.org; 152 N Central Ave; adult/child $12/free; ☉11am-5pm Mon & Fri, to 8pm Thu, to 6pm Sat & Sun).

Japanese American National Museum MUSEUM
(Map p910; ☑213-625-0414; www.janm.org; 100 N Central Ave; adult/child $9/5; ☉11am-5pm Tue-Wed & Fri-Sun, noon-8pm Thu) Get an in-depth look at the Japanese immigrant experience, including the painful chapter of WWII internment camps. Traveling exhibitions focus on Asian American art and civil rights. Check the online calendar for neighborhood

HISTORIC DOWNTOWN LA

At the center of Downtown's historic district, **Pershing Square** (Map p910; www.laparks. org/pershingsquare; 532 S Olive St) was LA's first public park (1866) and has been modernized many times since. Now encircled by high-rises, the park exhibits public art and hosts summer concerts and outdoor movie nights.

Nearby, some of LA's turn-of-the-last century architecture remains as it once was. Pop into the 1893 **Bradbury Building** (Map p910; www.laconservancy.org; 304 S Broadway; ⊙ lobby usually 9am-5pm), whose dazzling galleried atrium cameoed in several hit movies, including *Blade Runner*, *(500) Days of Summer* and *The Artist*.

In the early 20th century, Broadway was a glamorous shopping and theater strip, where megastars such as Charlie Chaplin leapt from limos to attend premieres at lavish movie palaces. Some of these – such as the 1926 **Orpheum Theater** (Map p910; www. laorpheum.com; 842 S Broadway) – have been restored and once again host film screenings and events. Otherwise, the best way to get inside is with Los Angeles Conservancy (p920) on a weekend walking tour (reservations advised).

walking tours, film screenings, Japanese cooking classes and folkcraft workshops.

SOUTH PARK

South Park isn't actually a park but an emerging Downtown LA neighborhood around **LA Live** (Map p910; www.lalive.com; 800 W Olympic Blvd), a dining and entertainment hub where you'll find the Staples Center (p926) and the **Nokia Theatre** (Map p910; ☎ 213-763-6030; www.nokiatheatrelive.com; 777 Chick Hearn Court), home of the MTV Music Awards and *American Idol* finals. Parking at LA Live or in nearby private lots is expensive (flat-rate from $10 to $30).

★ **Grammy Museum**   MUSEUM
(Map p910; www.grammymuseum.org; 800 W Olympic Blvd; adult/child $13/11, after 6pm $8; ⊙ 11:30am-7:30pm Mon-Fri, from 10am Sat & Sun; ♿) Music fans of all stripes will get lost in these mind-expanding interactive displays about the history of American music, where interactive sound booths let you and your entourage try mixing and remixing pop and rock hits, and singing and rapping with the stars.

EXPOSITION PARK & AROUND

Just south of the University of Southern California (USC) campus, this park has a full day's worth of kid-friendly museums. Outdoor landmarks include the **Rose Garden** (www. laparks.org; 701 State Dr; admission free; ⊙ 9am-sunset Mar 15–Dec 31) and the 1923 **Los Angeles Memorial Coliseum**, site of the 1932 and 1984 Summer Olympic Games. Parking costs from $8. From Downtown, take the Metro Expo Line or DASH minibus F.

★ **Natural History Museum of Los Angeles**   MUSEUM
(☎ 213-763-3466; www.nhm.org; 900 Exposition Blvd; adult/child $12/5; ⊙ 9:30am-5pm; ♿) Dinos to diamonds, bears to beetles, even an ultra-rare megamouth shark: this science museum will take you around the world and back millions of years in time. Great activities for kids include digging for fossils in the Discovery Center and gaping at gigantic skeletons in the recently reopened **Dinosaur Hall**.

California Science Center   MUSEUM
(☎ film schedule 213-744-2109, info 323-724-3623; www.californiasciencecenter.org; 700 Exposition Park Dr; ⊙ 10am-5pm; ♿) **FREE** A simulated earthquake, hatching baby chicks and a giant techno-doll named Tess bring out the kid in everyone at this great hands-on science museum. It's the new home of the retired Space Shuttle *Endeavour* (reservations are required for viewing). IMAX movies (adult/child $8.25/5) cap off an action-filled day.

California African American Museum   MUSEUM
(☎ 213-744-7432; www.caamuseum.org; 600 State Dr; ⊙ 10am-5pm Tue-Sat, from 11am Sun) **FREE** Browse a handsome showcase of African American art, culture and history, focusing on California and the western US.

Watts Towers   MONUMENT
(www.wattstowers.org; 1727 E 107th St; adult/child $7/free; ⊙ art center 10am-4pm Wed-Sat, from noon Sun; Ⓟ) South LA's beacon of pride, the world-famous Watts Towers are a huge

and fantastical free-form sculpture cobbled together from found objects – from 7-Up bottles to seashells and pottery shards – by folk artist Simon Rodia. Entry by guided tour only. Tours every 30 minutes; 10:30am to 3pm Thursday, Friday and Saturday, from 12:30pm Sunday.

👁 Hollywood

Just as aging movie stars get the occasional facelift, so has Hollywood. While it still hasn't recaptured its mid-20th century 'Golden Age' glamour, its modern seediness is disappearing. The **Hollywood Walk of Fame** (Map p915; www.walkoffame.com; Hollywood Blvd) honors over 2000 celebrities with stars embedded in the sidewalk.

The Metro Red Line stops beneath **Hollywood & Highland** (Map p915; ☑323-467-6412; www.hollywoodandhighland.com; 6801 Hollywood Blvd), a multistory mall with nicely framed views of the hillside **Hollywood Sign**, erected in 1923 as an advertisement for a land development called Hollywoodland. Validated mall parking costs $2 for two hours (daily maximum $13).

TCL Chinese Theatre   CINEMA
(Map p915; ☑tour info 323-461-3331; 6925 Hollywood Blvd) Even the most jaded visitor may feel a thrill in Grauman's famous forecourt, where generations of screen legends have left their imprints in cement: feet, hands, dreadlocks (Whoopi Goldberg), and even magic wands (young stars of *Harry Potter* films). Actors dressed as Superman, Marilyn Monroe and the like pose for photos (for tips), and you may be offered free tickets to TV shows.

Dolby Theatre   THEATER
(Map p915; ☑323-308-6300; www.dolbytheatre.com; tour adult/child $17/12; ⊙tours usually 10:30am-4pm) Real-life celebs sashay along this theater's red carpet for the Academy Awards – columns with names of Oscar-winning films line the entryway. Pricey 30-minute tours take you inside the auditorium, VIP room and past an actual Oscar statuette.

Hollywood Forever Cemetery   CEMETERY
(☑323-469-1181; www.hollywoodforever.com; 6000 Santa Monica Blvd; ⊙8am-5pm; ℗) Rock-and-roll faithful flock to the monument of Johnny Ramone at this historical boneyard, whose other famous residents include Rudolph Valentino, Cecil B DeMille and Bugsy Siegel. Check the online calendar of movie screenings and concerts (yes, really).

Hollywood Museum   MUSEUM
(Map p915; www.thehollywoodmuseum.com; 1660 N Highland Ave; adult/child $15/5; ⊙10am-5pm Wed-Sun) Inside the art-deco Max Factor Building, this slightly musty 35,000-sq-ft shrine to the stars is crammed with kitsch, costumes, knickknacks and props from Marilyn Monroe to *Glee*.

👁 Griffith Park

America's largest urban **park** (☑323-913-4688; www.laparks.org/dos/parks/griffithpk; 4730 Crystal Springs Dr; ⊙5am-10:30pm, trails sunrise-sunset; ℗🐕) **FREE** is five times the size of New York's Central Park, with an outdoor theater, zoo, observatory, museum, merry-go-round, antique and miniature trains, children's playgrounds, golf, tennis and over 50 miles of hiking paths, including to the original *Batman* TV series cave.

WORTH A TRIP

TOURING MOVIE & TV STUDIOS

Half the fun of visiting Hollywood is hoping you'll see stars. Up the odds by joining the studio audience of a sitcom or game show, which usually tape between August and March. For free tickets, contact **Audiences Unlimited** (☑818-260-0041; www.tvtickets.com).

For an authentic behind-the-scenes look, take a small-group shuttle tour at **Warner Bros Studios** (☑877-492-8687, 818-972-8687; www.wbstudiotour.com; 3400 W Riverside Dr, Burbank; tours from $49; ⊙8:15am-4pm Mon-Sat, hours vary Sun) or **Paramount Pictures** (☑323-956-1777; www.paramount.com; 5555 Melrose Ave; tours from $48; ⊙tours 9:30am-2pm Mon-Fri, hours vary Sat & Sun), or a walking tour of **Sony Pictures Studios** (☑310-244-8687; www.sonypicturesstudiostours.com; 10202 W Washington Blvd; tour $35; ⊙tours usually 9:30am-2:30pm Mon-Fri). All of these tours show you around sound stages and backlots (outdoor sets), and inside wardrobe and make-up departments. Reservations are required (minimum-age restrictions apply); bring photo ID.

★ **Griffith Observatory** MUSEUM
(☑213-473-0800; www.griffithobservatory.org;
2800 E Observatory Rd; admission free, planetarium
shows adult/child $7/3; ⊙noon-10pm Tue-Fri, from
10am Sat & Sun; P❋) FREE Inside the iconic
triple domes of this 1935 observatory are a
state-of-the-art planetarium and the Leonard
Nimoy Event Horizon multimedia theater. If
nighttime skies are clear, you can often peer
through public telescopes at heavenly bodies.

Los Angeles Zoo & Botanical Gardens ZOO
(☑323-644-4200; www.lazoo.org; 5333 Zoo Dr;
adult/child $17/12; ⊙10am-5pm; P❋) Make
friends with 1100 finned, feathered and
furry creatures at this conservation-oriented
zoo, including in the Campo Gorilla Reserve
and the Sea Life Cliffs, which replicate the
California coast complete with harbor seals.

Museum of the American West MUSEUM
(☑323-667-2000; www.autrynationalcenter.org;
4700 Western Heritage Way; adult/child $10/4, 2nd
Tue of month free; ⊙10am-4pm Tue-Fri, to 5pm Sat
& Sun; P) Exhibits on the good, the bad and
the ugly of America's westward expansion
rope in even the most reluctant of cowpokes
(lazy cowboys). Gems include a Colt firearms collection, an ornate saloon and Native
American and California gold-rush relics.

⊙ **West Hollywood**

Welcome to the city of WeHo, where rainbow flags fly proudly over Santa Monica
Blvd and celebs keep gossip rags happy by
misbehaving at clubs on the fabled **Sunset
Strip**. Boutiques along Robertson Blvd and
Melrose Ave purvey sassy and ultrachic
fashions for Hollywood royalty and celebutants. WeHo's also a hotbed of cutting-edge
interior design, particularly along the **Avenues of Art, Fashion & Design** (www.av-
enueswh.com).

Pacific Design Center BUILDING
(PDC; Map p916; www.pacificdesigncenter.com; 8687
Melrose Ave; ⊙9am-5pm Mon-Fri) Some 120
galleries and showrooms fill the monolith-
ic blue, green and red 'whales' of this Cesar
Pelli–designed building, which houses a
branch of **MOCA** (Map p916; ☑213-621-1741;
www.moca.org; ⊙11am-5pm Tue-Fri, to 6pm Sat
& Sun) FREE. Visitors can window-shop,
though most sales are to the trade. Hourly
parking from $6 (daily maximum $13).

⊙ **Mid-City**

Some of LA's best museums line 'Museum
Row,' a short stretch of Wilshire Blvd east of
Fairfax Ave.

★ **Los Angeles County
Museum of Art** MUSEUM
(LACMA; Map p916; ☑323-857-6000; www.lacma.
org; 5905 Wilshire Blvd; adult/child $15/free;
⊙11am-5pm Mon-Tue & Thu, to 9pm Fri, 10am-7pm
Sat & Sun; P) One of the country's top art museums (and the largest in the western US),
LACMA's seven buildings brim with paintings, sculpture and decorative arts: European
masters such as Rembrandt, Cézanne and
Magritte; ancient pottery from China, Turkey

DON'T MISS

UNIVERSAL STUDIOS HOLLYWOOD

Universal Studios Hollywood (www.universalstudioshollywood.com; 100 Universal City
Plaza; admission from $80, child under 3yr free; ⊙ daily, hours vary; P❋) first opened to
the public in 1915, when studio head Carl Laemmle invited visitors at a quaint 25¢ each
(including a boxed lunch) to watch silent films being made. Nearly a century later, Universal remains one of the world's largest movie studios.

Your chances of seeing an actual movie shoot are approximately nil at Universal's
current theme park incarnation, yet generations of visitors have had a ball here. Start
with the 45-minute narrated **studio tour** aboard a giant multicar tram that takes you
past working soundstages, outdoor sets and **King Kong 360**, the planet's biggest 3D
experience. Also prepare to survive a shark attack à la *Jaws*. It's cheesy but fun.

Among dozens of other attractions, take a motion-simulated romp on the **Simpsons
Ride**, splash down among **Jurassic Park** dinosaurs or fight off Decepticons in **Trans-
formers: The Ride 3-D**. The **Special Effects Stage** illuminates the craft of movie-
making. **WaterWorld** may have bombed as a movie, but the live action show based on
it is a runaway hit, with stunts including giant fireballs and a crash-landing seaplane.

Self-parking is $15 (after 3pm $10), or arrive via the Metro Red Line.

Hollywood

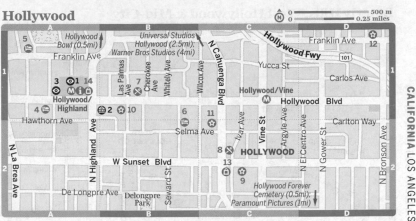

and Iran; photographs by Ansel Adams; and a jewel-box of Japanese screen paintings and sculpture. Parking is $10.

Inside the Renzo Piano–designed **Broad Contemporary Art Museum** at LACMA are seminal pieces by Jasper Johns, Cindy Sherman and Ed Ruscha, and two gigantic works in rusted steel by Richard Serra. LACMA often has headline-grabbing touring exhibits too.

La Brea Tar Pits ARCHAEOLOGICAL SITE
(Map p916) Between 11,000 and 40,000 years ago, tarlike bubbling crude oil trapped saber-toothed cats, mammoths and other extinct ice-age critters, which are still being excavated here. Check out their fossilized remains at the **Page Museum** (Map p916; ☑ 323-934-7243; www.tarpits.org; 5801 Wilshire Blvd; adult/child $12/5, 1st Tue of month Sep-Jun free; ☺ 9:30am-5pm; P 🖐). New fossils are being discovered all the time, and an active staff of archaeologists works behind glass. Parking is $7 to $9 (cash only).

Petersen Automotive Museum MUSEUM
(Map p916; www.petersen.org; 6060 Wilshire Blvd; adult/child $12/3; ☺ 10am-6pm Tue-Sun; P) A four-story ode to the auto, Petersen's exhibits shiny vintage cars galore, plus a fun LA streetscape showing how the city's growth has been shaped by traffic. Parking costs from $2 (maximum $12).

◉ Beverly Hills & Around

The mere mention of Beverly Hills conjures images of Maseratis, manicured mansions and megarich moguls. It's a stylish, sophisticated haven for the well-heeled and famous.

Hollywood

◉ Sights

⏝ Sleeping

⊗ Eating

✪ Entertainment

ⓐ Shopping

Stargazers could take a guided bus tour to scout for stars' homes.

No trip to LA would be complete without a saunter along pricey, pretentious **Rodeo Drive**, a three-block ribbon where sample-size fembots browse for fashions from international houses – from Armani to Zegna – in couture-design stores. If the prices make you gasp, Beverly Dr, one block east, has more down-to-earth boutiques.

Several central municipal lots and garages offer two hours of free parking.

Beverly Hills, West Hollywood & Mid-City

Paley Center for Media   MUSEUM

(Map p916; ☎310-786-1000; www.paleycenter.
org; 465 N Beverly Dr; suggested donation adult/
child $10/5; ☺noon-5pm Wed-Sun; ℗) TV and
radio addicts can indulge their passion at
this mind-boggling archive of TV and radio
broadcasts from 1918 through the internet
age. Pick your faves, grab a seat at a private
console and enjoy. Public programs include
lectures and screenings.

Annenberg Space for Photography   MUSEUM

(www.annenbergspaceforphotography.org; 2000
Ave of the Stars; ☺11am-6pm Wed-Fri, 11am-7:30pm
Sat & 11am-6pm Sun; ℗) FREE See thought-
provoking rotating exhibitions inside the
camera-shaped interior of this museum just
west of Beverly Hills, among the skyscrapers
of Century City. Validated self-parking is
$3.50 from Wednesday to Friday ($1 after
4:30pm), $1 on weekends.

◉ West LA

★ Getty Center   MUSEUM

(☎310-440-7300; www.getty.edu; 1200 Getty
Center Dr, off I-405 Fwy; ☺10am-5:30pm Tue-Sun,
to 9pm Sat; ℗) FREE Triple delights: a stellar art collection from Renaissance masters

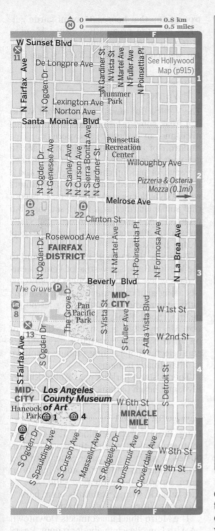

Beverly Hills, West Hollywood & Mid-City

edu; 10899 Wilshire Blvd; adult/child $10/free, Thu free; ⊙11am-8pm Tue-Fri, to 5pm Sat & Sun) has cutting-edge contemporary art exhibits; validated parking is $3.

Westwood Village Memorial Park CEMETERY (www.dignitymemorial.com; 1218 Glendon Ave; ⊙8am-dusk) Tucked among Westwood's high-rises, this postage-stamp-sized graveyard is packed with such famous 6ft-under residents as Marilyn Monroe and Dean Martin. The gate is south of Wilshire Blvd, one block east of Westwood Blvd.

◎ Malibu

Hugging 27 spectacular miles of the Pacific Coast Hwy, Malibu has long been synonymous with surfing and Hollywood stars, but

to David Hockney, with Richard Meier's fabulous architecture and Robert Irwin's ever-changing gardens. On clear days, add breathtaking views of the city and ocean to the list. Crowds thin in the late afternoon. Parking is $15 (after 5pm $10).

**University of California,
Los Angeles** UNIVERSITY
(UCLA; www.ucla.edu; P) Westwood is dominated by the vast campus of prestigious UCLA, with its impressive botanical and sculpture gardens. The university's excellent **Hammer Museum** (http://hammer.ucla.

it actually looks far less posh than glossy tabloids make it sound. Still, it has been celebrity central since the 1930s. Steven Spielberg, Barbra Streisand, Dustin Hoffman and other A-listers have homes here, and can sometimes be spotted shopping at the villagelike **Malibu Country Mart** (www.malibucountrymart.com; 3835 Cross Creek Rd) or more utilitarian **Malibu Colony Plaza** (www.malibucolonyplaza.com; 23841 W Malibu Rd).

One of Malibu's twin natural treasures is mountainous **Malibu Creek State Park** (☎818-880-0367; www.malibucreekstatepark.org; ⊙dawn-dusk), a popular movie- and TV-filming location with hiking trails galore (parking $12). The other is a string of beaches, including aptly named **Surfrider** west of Malibu Pier, wilder **Point Dume State Park** and family fave **Zuma Beach** (beach parking $10).

★ **Getty Villa**   MUSEUM
(☎310-430-7300; www.getty.edu; 17985 Pacific Coast Hwy; ⊙10am-5pm Wed-Mon; P) FREE Malibu's cultural star, this replica Roman villa is a fantastic showcase of Greek, Roman and Etruscan antiquities, embraced by peristyle and herb gardens. Admission is by timed ticket (no walk-ins, reservations required). Parking is $15.

⊙ Santa Monica

The belle by the beach mixes urban cool with a laid-back vibe. Tourists, teens and street performers make car-free, chain-store-lined **Third Street Promenade** the most action-packed zone. For more local flavor, shop celeb-favored **Montana Avenue** or eclectic **Main Street**, backbone of the neighborhood once nicknamed 'Dogtown,' the birthplace of skateboard culture.

There's free 90-minute parking in most public garages downtown.

Santa Monica Pier   AMUSEMENT PARK
(Map p919; http://santamonicapier.org; all-day ride pass $13-20; P ⟐) FREE Kids love the venerable pier, where attractions include a quaint carousel and a solar-powered Ferris wheel. Peer under the pier at the tiny **aquarium** (Map p919; ☎310-393-6149; www.healthebay.org; 1600 Ocean Front Walk; adult/child $5/free; ⊙2-5pm Tue-Fri, 12:30-5pm Sat & Sun; ⟐). Parking rates vary seasonally.

Bergamot Station Arts Center   ARTS CENTER
(www.bergamotstation.com; 2525 Michigan Ave; ⊙10am-6pm Tue-Fri, 11am-5:30pm Sat; P) Art fans gravitate inland toward this former trolley stop that houses 35 avant-garde galleries and the progressive **Santa Monica Museum of Art** (www.smmoa.org; 2525 Michigan Ave; donation adult/child $5/3; ⊙11am-6pm Tue-Sat).

⊙ Venice

The **Venice Boardwalk** (Ocean Front Walk) is a freak show, a human zoo, a wacky carnival and an essential LA experience. This cauldron of counterculture is the place to get your hair braided and a *qi gong* back massage, or pick up cheap sunglasses and a Rastafarian-colored-knit beret. Encounters with bodybuilders, hoop dreamers, a Speedo-clad snake charmer or a roller-skating Sikh minstrel are almost guaranteed, especially on sunny afternoons. Alas, the vibe gets creepy after dark.

To escape the hubbub, meander inland to the **Venice Canals**, a vestige of Venice's early days when Italian gondoliers poled tourists along artificial waterways. Today locals lollygag in rowboats in this flower-festooned neighborhood. Funky, hipper-than-ever **Abbot Kinney Blvd** is a palm-lined mile of restaurants, cafes, yoga studios, art galleries and eclectic shops selling vintage furniture and handmade fashions.

There's street parking near Abbot Kinney Blvd, and beach parking lots ($5 to $15).

⊙ Long Beach

Long Beach stretches along LA County's southern flank, heralding the world's third-busiest container port after Singapore and Hong Kong. Its industrial edge has been worn smooth downtown – **Pine Ave** is chockablock with restaurants and bars – and along the restyled waterfront.

The Metro Blue Line connects Downtown LA with Long Beach in about an hour. **Passport** (www.lbtransit.com) minibuses shuttle around major tourist sights for free ($1.25 elsewhere in town).

Queen Mary   BOAT
(www.queenmary.com; 1126 Queens Hwy; tours adult/child from $14/7; ⊙10am-6:30pm; P) Long Beach's 'flagship' is the grand (and supposedly haunted!) British ocean liner, which is permanently moored here. Larger and fancier than the *Titanic,* it transported royals, dignitaries, immigrants and troops during its 1001 Atlantic crossings between 1936 and 1964. Parking is $12.

Santa Monica & Venice

and take a self-guided audio tour of this re-tired Pacific battleship, which transported FDR and General MacArthur during WWII and saw action in the Cold War. Parking from $1.

Museum of Latin American Art MUSEUM
(www.molaa.org; 628 Alamitos Ave; adult/child $9/free, Sun free; ⊙11am-5pm Wed-Sun, to 9pm Thu; ℗) Although small, it's the only western US museum specializing in contemporary art from south of the border. The permanent collection highlights spirituality and land-scapes, with colorful temporary exhibits and a sculpture garden out back.

⊙ Pasadena

Below the lofty San Gabriel Mountains, this city drips with wealth and gentility, feeling a world apart from urban LA. It's known for its early 20th-century arts-and-crafts archi-tecture and the Tournament of Roses Parade on New Year's Day.

Amble on foot around the shops, cafes, bars and restaurants of **Old Town Pasade-na**, along Colorado Blvd east of Pasadena Ave. Metro Gold Line trains connect Pasade-na and Downtown LA (30 minutes).

Aquarium of the Pacific AQUARIUM
(☑ tickets 562-590-3100; www.aquariumofpacific.org; 100 Aquarium Way; adult/child $26/15; ⊙9am-6pm; ⊕) Let kids take a high-tech adventure through an underwater world where sharks dart, jellyfish dance and sea lions frolic. Vali-dated parking is $8 to $15. *Queen Mary* or LA Zoo combination tickets are discounted for even less online.

USS Iowa MUSEUM, MEMORIAL
(☑ 877-446-9261; www.pacificbattleship.com; 250 S Harbor Blvd, Berth 87; adult/child $18/10; ⊙10am-5pm, from 9am Jun-Aug; ℗) Near the port in San Pedro, step onto the gangway

★ Huntington Library MUSEUM, GARDEN
(☑ 626-405-2100; www.huntington.org; 1151 Ox-ford Rd, San Marino; adult weekday/weekend & hol $20/23, child $8, 1st Thu of month free; ⊙10:30am-4:30pm Wed-Mon Jun-Aug, noon-4:30pm Mon &

Wed-Fri, from 10:30am Sat, Sun & hol Sep-May; Ⓟ)
Its name is LA's biggest understatement.
While the Huntington does have a library of
rare books, including a Gutenberg Bible, it's
the masterful collection of European art and
exquisite gardens that make it a destination.
The Rose Garden blooms with over 1200 varieties and the Desert Garden has Seussian-
shaped succulents. Free admission on first
Thursdays requires advance ticketing.

Gamble House   ARCHITECTURE
(🅙info 626-793-3334, tickets 800-979-3370; www.
gamblehouse.org; 4 Westmoreland Pl; tours adult/
child from $12.50/free; ⊙tours noon-3pm Thu-Sun,
gift shop 10am-5pm Tue-Sat, 11:30am-5pm Sun;
Ⓟ) A masterpiece of California arts-and-
crafts architecture, the 1908 Gamble House
designed by architects Charles and Henry
Greene was Doc Brown's home in the movie
Back to the Future. Admission is only by
guided tour (reservations recommended).

Norton Simon Museum   MUSEUM
(www.nortonsimon.org; 411 W Colorado Blvd; adult/
child $10/free; ⊙noon-6pm Wed-Mon, to 9pm Fri;
Ⓟ) Stroll west of Old Town to visit Rodin's
The Thinker, a mere overture to the symphony of European, Asian, modern and contemporary art – even priceless prints and
photography – at this modest museum.

🏃 Activities

Cycling & In-line Skating
Get scenic exercise in-line skating or riding
along the paved **South Bay Bicycle Trail**,
which parallels the beach for most of the 22
miles between Santa Monica and Pacific Palisades. Rental outfits are plentiful in beach
towns. Warning: it's crowded on weekends.

Hiking
Turn on your celeb radar while strutting it
with the hot bods along **Runyon Canyon
Park** above Hollywood. **Griffith Park** is
also laced with trails. For longer rambles,
head to the Santa Monica Mountains, where
Will Rogers State Historic Park, **Topanga
State Park** and **Malibu Creek State Park**
are all excellent gateways to beautiful terrain (parking $8 to $12).

Swimming & Surfing
Top beaches for swimming are Malibu's
Zuma Beach, **Santa Monica State Beach**
and the South Bay's **Hermosa Beach**. Malibu's **Surfrider Beach** is a legendary surfing
spot. Parking rates vary seasonally.

'Endless Summer' is, sorry to report, a
myth, so much of the year you'll want to
wear a wet suit in the Pacific. Water temperatures become tolerable by June and peak
at about 70°F (21°C) in August and September. Water quality varies; check the 'Beach
Report Card' at www.healthebay.org.

👉 Tours

★ Esotouric   BUS TOUR
(🅙 323-223-2767; www.esotouric.com; tours $58)
Hip, offbeat, insightful and entertaining
tours themed around famous crime sites
(Black Dahlia), literary lions (Chandler to
Bukowski) and LA's historic neighborhoods.

Los Angeles Conservancy   WALKING TOUR
(🅙info 213-430-4219, reservations 213-623-2489;
www.laconservancy.org; tours adult/child $10/5)
Thematic guided tours, mostly of Downtown LA, focusing on architecture and history. Check the website for self-guided audio
tours.

Museum of Neon Art   BUS TOUR
(🅙213-489-9918; http://neonmona.org; tours $55;
⊙Sat Jun-Sep) Nighttime guided bus tours
that cruise the city's neon jungle, starting
from Downtown LA.

Melting Pot Tours   WALKING TOUR
(🅙800-979-3370; www.meltingpottours.com; tours
adult/child from $53/28) Eat your way through
the Original Farmers Market, Thai Town or
East LA's Latin flavors.

Dearly Departed   BUS TOUR
(🅙800-979-3370; www.dearlydepartedtours.com;
tours $45-75) Occasionally creepy, hilarious
'tragical' history tours of where famous stars
kicked the bucket.

🎉 Festivals & Events

Monthly street fairs for art-gallery hopping,
shopping and food-truck meet-ups include
Downtown LA Art Walk (www.downtownart-
walk.com; ⊙2nd Thu of month) and **First Fridays in Venice** (⊙1st Fri of month).

Tournament of Roses   PARADE, SPORTS
(www.tournamentofroses.com) New Year's Day
cavalcade of flower-festooned floats along
Pasadena's Colorado Blvd, followed by the
Rose Bowl college football game.

Fiesta Broadway   STREET FAIR
(http://fiestabroadway.la) Mexican-themed market in Downtown LA, with performances by
Latino stars, on the last Sunday in April.

Watts Towers Day of the Drum & Jazz Festivals
ART, MUSIC

(http://wattstowers.org) Two days of drums circles, jazz jams and an arts-and-crafts fair in South LA during late September.

West Hollywood Halloween Carnaval
STREET FAIR

(www.visitwesthollywood.com) Eccentric, often NC17-rated costumes, live bands and DJs along Santa Monica Blvd on October 31.

🛌 Sleeping

For seaside life, base yourself in Santa Monica, Venice or Long Beach. Cool-hunters and party people will be happiest in Hollywood or WeHo; culture-vultures, in Downtown LA. Expect a lodging tax of 12% to 14%.

🛏 Downtown

Figueroa Hotel HISTORIC HOTEL $$
(Map p910; ☏ 213-627-8971, 800-421-9092; www.figueroahotel.com; 939 S Figueroa St; r $148-194, ste $225-265; P ❋ @ 🛜 ☀ 🐾) A rambling 1920s oasis across from LA Live welcomes travelers with a richly tiled Spanish-style lobby that segues to a sparkling pool. Rooms are furnished in a global mash-up of styles (Morocco, Mexico, Zen), varying in size and configuration. Parking is $12.

Standard Downtown LA BOUTIQUE HOTEL $$$
(Map p910; ☏ 213-892-8080; http://standardhotels.com/downtown-la; 550 S Flower St; r $245-525; ste $1150-1300; P ❋ @ 🛜 ☀ 🐾) This design-savvy hotel in a former office building goes for a young, hip and shag-happy crowd – the rooftop bar fairly pulses – so don't come here to get a solid night's sleep. Mod, minimalist rooms have platform beds and peekthrough showers. Parking from $33.

🛏 Hollywood & West Hollywood

USA Hostels Hollywood HOSTEL $
(Map p915; ☏ 800-524-6783, 323-462-3777; www.usahostels.com; 1624 Schrader Blvd; dm $28-41, r without bath $81-104; ❋ @ 🛜) Not for introverts, this energetic hostel puts you within steps of Hollywood's party circuit. Make new friends during BBQ and comedy nights, city tours or fruit-and-pancake breakfasts in the common kitchen.

★ Magic Castle Hotel HOTEL $$
(Map p915; ☏ 323-851-0800; http://magiccastlehotel.com; 7025 Franklin Ave; r incl breakfast from $175; P ❋ @ 🛜 ☀ 🐾) Walls are thin, but renovated

apartments in this courtyard building come with contemporary furniture and attractive art, and suites have a separate living room. Complimentary snacks and access to a private club for magicians. Parking is $10.

Hollywood Roosevelt Hotel BOUTIQUE HOTEL $$$
(Map p915; ☏ 323-466-7000, 800-950-7667; www.hollywoodroosevelt.com; 7000 Hollywood Blvd; r from $330; P ❋ @ 🛜 ☀) Venerable historic hotel has hosted elite players since the first Academy Awards were held here in 1929. It pairs a palatial Spanish lobby with sleek Asian contemporary rooms, a glam pool scene and rockin' restos and lounges. Parking is $33.

London West Hollywood LUXURY HOTEL $$$
(Map p916; ☏ 866-282-4560; www.thelondonwesthollywood.com; 1020 N San Vicente Blvd; ste incl breakfast from $279; P ❋ @ 🛜 ☀ 🐾) Gleaming like Harry Winston diamonds, just south of the Sunset Strip, the London dazzles with slick design, a swish restaurant by *Hell's Kitchen* chef Gordon Ramsay and a rooftop pool sporting panoramic views of the Hollywood Hills. Parking is $30.

🛏 Mid-City & Beverly Hills

StayOn Beverly HOSTEL $
(www.stayonbeverly.com; 4619 Beverly Blvd; r without bath $50-55; P ❋ 🛜) In Koreatown, this Danish photographer's stripped-down

hostel is a tidy, secure base camp for backpackers and flashpackers. Ten basic rooms each have a mini fridge, with a shared microwave in the common coffee corner. Limited free self-parking.

Farmer's Daughter Hotel MOTEL $$
(Map p916; ☑ 323-937-3930, 800-334-1658; www.farmersdaughterhotel.com; 115 S Fairfax Ave; r from $185; P✳@☎❄) Opposite the Original Farmers Market and CBS Studios, this perennial pleaser gets high marks for its sleek 'urban cowboy' look. Adventurous lovebirds, ask about the No Tell Room. Parking is $18.

Avalon Hotel HOTEL $$$
(Map p916; ☑ 310-277-5221, 800-670-6183; www.viceroyhotelgroup.com/avalon; 9400 W Olympic Blvd; r from $210; ✳@☎❄☀) Mid-century modern gets a 21st-century spin at this fashion-crowd fave, formerly Marilyn Monroe's pad in its apartment-building days. Today the beautiful, moneyed and metrosexual vamp it up in the buzzy resto-bar overlooking an hourglass-shaped pool. Parking is $30.

🛏 Santa Monica

★**HI Los Angeles-Santa Monica** HOSTEL $
(Map p919; ☑ 310-393-9913; www.hilosangeles.org; 1436 2nd St; dm $38-49, r without bath $99-159; ✳@☎) Near the beach and Third Street Promenade, the location is the envy of much fancier places. Its 260 beds in single-sex dorms and bed-in-a-box doubles are clean and safe, and there are plenty of groovy public spaces to lounge or surf the web. All accommodation with shared bath.

Sea Shore Motel MOTEL $$
(Map p919; ☑ 310-392-2787; www.seashoremotel.com; 2637 Main St; r from $110; P✳☎) Clean, friendly, family-owned lodgings are two blocks from the beach and right on happening Main St (expect ambient noise). Spanish-tiled rooms are basic but attractive, and kitchen suites are roomy enough for families.

★**Viceroy** BOUTIQUE HOTEL $$$
(Map p919; ☑ 310-260-7500, 800-622-8711; www.viceroysantamonica.com; 1819 Ocean Ave; r from $350; P✳@☎❄☀) Ignore the high-rise eyesore exterior to plunge headlong into *Top Design* judge Kelly Wearstler's campy 'Hollywood Regency' decor and color palette of dolphin gray to lime green. Lounge in poolside cabanas, Italian designer linens and a chic resto-bar. Parking is $35.

🛏 Long Beach

Hotel Varden BOUTIQUE HOTEL $$
(☑ 562-432-8950, 877-382-7336; www.thevardenhotel.com; 335 Pacific Ave; r incl continental breakfast from $119; P✳@☎❄) Interior designers clearly had a modernist field day renovating the 35 diminutive rooms at this 1929 hotel: tiny desks, tiny sinks, lots of right angles, cushy beds, white, white and more white. It's two blocks west of hoppin' Pine Ave. Parking is $11.

🛏 Pasadena

Saga Motor Hotel MOTEL $
(☑ 626-795-0431, 800-793-7242; www.thesagamotorhotel.com; 1633 E Colorado Blvd; r incl breakfast $79-99; P✳@☎♿) On historic Route 66, this midcentury modern 1950s motel has rooms that are spotless, even if they don't set new style standards. A heated pool ringed by chaises lets you soak up SoCal sunshine.

✖ Eating

LA's culinary scene is California's most vibrant and eclectic, from celebrity chefs whipping up farmers-market menus to down-home authentic global cuisine. With some 140 nationalities living in LA, ethnic neighborhoods for foodies to explore abound, including downtown's **Little Tokyo** and **Chinatown**, Mid-City's **Koreatown**, **Thai Town** east of Hollywood, East LA's **Boyle Heights** for Mexican flavors, the South Bay's **Torrance** for Japanese kitchens, and **Monterey Park** and **Alhambra**, east of Pasadena, for dim sum and regional Chinese cooking.

✖ Downtown

For cheap, fast meals-on-the-go, graze the international food stalls of the historic **Grand Central Market** (Map p910; www.grandcentralsquare.com; 317 S Broadway; ◷9am-6pm).

Philippe the Original DINER $
(Map p910; ☑ 213-628-3781; www.philippes.com; 1001 N Alameda St; mains $4-10; ◷6am-10pm; P♿) LAPD hunks, stressed-out attorneys and Midwestern vacationers chow down at this legendary 'home of the French dip sandwich,' dating back to 1908. Order your choice of meat on a crusty roll dipped in *jus,* and hunker down at community tables on the sawdust-covered floor. Cash only.

Gorbals
EASTERN EUROPEAN **$$**

(Map p910; ☑213-488-3408; www.thegorbalsla. com; 501 S Spring St; dishes $6-43; ☺lunch & dinner) *Top Chef* winner Ilan Hall tweaks traditional Jewish comfort food: bacon-wrapped matzo balls, potato latkes with smoked apple sauce, *gribenes* (chicken-skin cracklings) served BLT style. It's hidden at the back of the Alexandria Hotel lobby.

Nickel Diner
DINER **$$**

(Map p910; ☑213-623-8301; http://nickeldiner. com; 524 S Main St; mains $7-14; ☺ 8am-3:30pm Tue-Sun, 6-10:30pm Tue-Sat) In Downtown's historic theater district, this red-vinyl joint feels like a 1920s throwback. Ingredients are 21st-century, though: avocados stuffed with quinoa salad, 'lowrider' chili burgers and must-try doughnuts. Expect long waits.

Bäco Mercat
TAPAS **$$$**

(Map p910; ☑213-687-8808; http://bacomercat.com; 408 S Main St; small plates $8-19; ☺ 11:30am-2pm & 5:30-11pm Mon-Thu, 11:30-3pm & 5:30pm-midnight Fri & Sat, 11:30am-3pm & 5-10pm Sun) Daringly creative pan-Asian and Californian twists on traditional Spanish tapas flow out to outdoor patio tables at this elegant downtown kitchen. Specialty *bäco* (flatbread sandwiches) comes happily stuffed with anything from oxtail hash to pork carnitas.

Bottega Louie
ITALIAN **$$$**

(Map p910; ☑213-802-1470; www.bottegalouie. com; 700 S Grand Ave; mains $8-35; ☺8am-11pm Mon-Thu, 8am-midnight Fri, 9am-midnight Sat, 9am-11pm Sun) Louie's wide marble bar has become a magnet for the artsy loft set and office workers alike. The open-kitchen crew, in chef's whites, grills housemade sausage and wood-fired thin-crust pizzas in the white-on-white dining room. Always busy, always buzzy.

✕ Hollywood

Griddle Café
BREAKFAST **$$**

(Map p916; ☑323-874-0377; www.thegriddlecafe. com; 7916 W Sunset Blvd; mains $10-18; ☺7am-4pm Mon-Fri, from 8am Sat & Sun) Whimsically named sugar-bomb pancakes, giant-sized egg scrambles and French-press coffee pots keep the wooden tables and U-shaped counter full all day long at this pit-stop favored by Hollywood's young and tousled. Hungover hordes huddle outside on weekends.

Umami Urban
BURGERS **$$**

(Map p915; ☑323-469-3100; www.umami.com; 1520 N Cahuenga Blvd; mains $10-15; ☺11am-11pm Sun-Thu, to midnight Fri & Sat) Inside hip Space 15 Twenty shopping plaza, Umami elevates gourmet burgers with green Hatch chilies, smoked-salt onion strings and more. Order poutine fries, craft beers or peppermint lemonade on the side. Also in Los Feliz, Santa Monica, Westwood and Mid-City.

★Pizzeria & Osteria Mozza
ITALIAN **$$$**

(☑323-297-0100; www.mozza-la.com; 6602 Melrose Ave; pizzas $11-20, dinner mains $27-38; ☺pizzeria noon-midnight daily, osteria 5:30-11pm Mon-Fri, 5-11pm Sat, 5-10pm Sun) Reserve weeks ahead for LA's hottest Italian eatery, run by celebrity chefs Mario Batali and Nancy Silverton. Two restaurants share the same building, with a wide-ranging traditional Italian menu at the osteria, and precision-made pizzas and savory antipasti inside the pizzeria.

Musso & Frank Grill
AMERICAN **$$$**

(Map p915; ☑323-467-7788; www.mussoandfrank. com; 6667 Hollywood Blvd; mains $9-45; ☺ 11am-11pm Tue-Sat) Hollywood history hangs thickly in the air at the boulevard's oldest eatery. Waiters balance platters of steaks, chops and other heart-attack dishes harking back to the days when cholesterol wasn't part of our vocabulary. Service is smooth, and so are the martinis.

✕ West Hollywood, Mid-City & Beverly Hills

Veggie Grill
VEGETARIAN **$**

(Map p916; ☑323-822-7575; www.veggiegrill.com; 8000 W Sunset Blvd; mains $7-10; ☺11am-11pm; ☑⬛) If crispy chickin' wings or a carne asada sandwich don't sound vegetarian, know that this darn tasty local chain uses seasoned vegetable proteins (mostly tempeh). Gluten-free and nut-free options are offered too. Also in Hollywood, Mid-City, Westwood, Santa Monica and Long Beach.

Original Farmers Market
MARKET **$**

(Map p916; www.farmersmarketla.com; 6333 W 3rd St; most mains $6-12; ☺9am-9pm Mon-Fri, to 8pm Sat, 10am-7pm Sun; ⬛⬛) Although now heavily commercialized, the market still has a few worthy, budget-friendly eateries, most alfresco. Try Du-Par's classic diner, Cajun-style cooking at the Gumbo Pot or ¡Loteria! Mexican grill. Free two-hour validated parking.

★ **Night + Market**   THAI $$

(Map p916; ☑ 310-275-9724; www.nightmarketla. com; 9041 W Sunset Blvd; mains $10-19; ☺ 6-10:30pm Tue-Sun, last order 9:45pm) Dying for spicy-hot Thai food? Good, because that's the only way you're going to get it at this tiny Sunset Strip kitchen dishing up street food like salt-crusted fish, duck larb and 'startled' grilled pork. Enter through Talesai restaurant and duck behind the red curtain by the bar.

★ **Bazaar**   SPANISH $$$

(Map p916; ☑ 310-246-5555; www.thebazaar.com; SLS Hotel, 465 S La Cienega Blvd; small plates $8-42; ☺ 6-10:30pm Sun-Wed, to 11:30pm Thu-Sat) Bazaar dazzles with over-the-top interior design by Philippe Starck and 'molecular gastronomic' tapas by José Andrés. Stuffed piquillo peppers and sea-urchin sandwiches explode with flavor in your mouth, or bite into cotton-candy foie gras and Wagyu-beef Philly cheese-steaks on 'air bread.'

✖ Malibu

Malibu Seafood   SEAFOOD $$

(☑ 310-456-3430; www.malibuseafood.com; 25653 Pacific Coast Hwy; most mains $8-15; ☺ 11am-8pm; ℗ ☢) Beloved by locals, this roadside seafood market grills tasty, simply prepared fish fillets, baskets of fried seafood, sandwiches and salads. Homemade tartar sauce and clam chowder are both winners.

Paradise Cove Beach Cafe   AMERICAN $$$

(☑ 310-457-2503; www.paradisecovemalibu.com; 28128 Pacific Coast Hwy; mains $11-36; ☺ 8am-10pm; ℗ ☢) It's your movie-perfect image of SoCal: stick your feet in the sand and knock back piña coladas and fish tacos at this California-casual institution on a private beach where *Beach Blanket Bingo* was filmed. Four-hour validated parking $6.

✖ Santa Monica & Venice

★ **Santa Monica**

Farmers Markets   MARKET $

(Map p919; www.smgov.net/portals/farmersmarket; Arizona Ave, btwn 2nd & 3rd Sts; ☺ 8:30am-1:30pm Wed, to 1pm Sat; ☢) ✐ Downtown Santa Monica's twice-weekly farmers market brings out even star chefs to peruse a cornucopia of fresh, often organic produce, while local restaurants set up stalls in the food tent. Main St's Saturday morning market is more of a community street fair.

Lemonade   CALIFORNIAN $$

(http://lemonadela.com; 1661 Abbot Kinney Blvd; small dishes $5-11; ☺ 11am-9pm) Look for an imaginative seasonal line-up of deli salads, such as butter lettuce with pink grapefruit; seafood plates like seared tuna with watermelon radish; jerk pineapple chicken; custom-made sourdough sandwiches; and lotsa flavored lemonades – blueberry-mint! Also in Downtown LA, Mid-City, Pasadena and at LAX airport.

Santa Monica Place   SHOPPING CENTER $$

(Map p919; www.santamonicaplace.com; 395 Santa Monica Pl; ☺ restaurants daily, hours vary; ☢) We wouldn't normally eat at a mall, but this one gets high marks for Latin-Asian fusion at Zengo, Antica's wood-oven-fired pizzas and M.A.K.E. raw vegan cuisine. Most 3rd-floor restaurants have seating with views across rooftops – some to the ocean – while market stalls do everything from *salumi* to soufflés. Ground floor True Food Kitchen trends healthy, vegetarian-friendly and gluten-free.

Father's Office   PUB $$

(☑ 310-736-2224; www.fathersoffice.com; 1018 Montana Ave; dishes $5-15; ☺ 5-10pm Mon-Wed, 5-11pm Thu, 4-11pm Fri, noon-11pm Sat, noon-10pm Sun) Everybody knows your name, or they soon will, at this loud, elbow-to-elbow watering hole where barkeeps skillfully explain dozens of beers on tap. Just don't ask for substitutions on their decadent burgers. Bar open till midnight or later daily. Second location in Culver City.

✖ Long Beach

George's Greek Café   GREEK $$

(☑ 562-437-1184; www.georgesgreekcafe.com; 135 Pine Ave; mains $9-26; ☺ 10am-10pm Sun-Thu, to 11pm Fri & Sat) George himself may greet you at the entrance by the airy patio, in the heart of Pine Ave's restaurant row. Locals are addicted to the flaming *saganaki* (fried cheese), fresh pita bread and lamb chops.

✖ Pasadena

Ración   SPANISH $$

(☑ 626-396-3090; http://racionrestaurant.com; 119 W Green St; shared plates $5-27; ☺ 6-10pm Tue-Thu, 6-11pm Fri, 11am-2pm & 5:30-11pm Sat, 11am-2pm & 5:30-10pm Sun) Two blocks south of Old Town Pasadena, this warm, streetfront tapas bar lets you sample Basque-inspired dishes, including house-cured charcuterie, imported cheeses and seasonal smoked vegetables.

🍷 Drinking

Hollywood has been legendary sipping territory since before the Rat Pack days, and the rockin' Sunset Strip is almost as much of a party zone as it was in the 1960s. Creative cocktails are the order of the day at the reinvented watering holes in Downtown LA and edgier neighborhoods. Beachside bars run the gamut from surfer dives and Irishesque pubs to candlelit cocktail lounges.

★ Edison
BAR

(Map p910; ☎ 213-613-0000; www.edisondowntown.com; 108 W 2nd St, off Harlem Pl; ⊘ 5pm-2am Wed-Fri, from 7pm Sat) *Metropolis* meets *Blade Runner* at this industrial-chic basement boîte, where you'll be sipping hand-crafted cocktails surrounded by turbines and other machinery back from its days as a power plant. It's all tarted up with cocoa leather couches, three cavernous bars and a hoity-toity dress code.

Copa d'Oro
BAR

(Map p919; www.copadoro.com; 217 Broadway, Santa Monica; ⊘ 5:30pm-midnight Mon-Wed, to 2am Thu-Sat) A smooth, lamplit ambience will woo your sweetheart at this Santa Monica sanctuary. Artisanal cocktails draw from a well of top-end liquors and a farmers market's basket of fresh herbs, fruit and even veggies. Teetotaler? Ask for a fresh-pressed organic juice or homemade soda.

Seven Grand
BAR

(Map p910; ☎ 213-614-0737; http://sevengrand-bars.com; 2nd fl, 515 W 7th St; ⊘ 5pm-2am Mon-Wed, from 4pm Thu & Fri, from 7pm Sat) At Seven Grand, hipsters have invaded Mummy and Daddy's hunt club, amid tartan-patterned carpeting and deer heads on the walls. Whiskey is the drink of choice: choose from over 100 brands from Tennessee, Scotland, Ireland and Japan. There's an enforced dress code.

El Carmen
BAR

(Map p916; 8138 W 3rd St; ⊘ 5pm-2am Mon-Fri, from 7pm Sat & Sun) Mounted bull heads and *lucha libre* (Mexican wrestling) masks create an over-the-top 'Tijuana North' look that pulls in an entertainment-industry-heavy crowd. Swig happy-hour margaritas or peruse the 100-strong tequila and mezcal menu.

Intelligentsia Coffeebar
CAFE

(Map p919; www.intelligentsiacoffee.com; 1331 Abbot Kinney Blvd; ⊘ 6am-8pm Mon-Wed, to 11pm Thu & Fri, 7am-11pm Sat, 7am-8pm Sun; 🛜) In Venice's hip, architecturally minimalist monument to coffee, perfectionistic baristas never short you on foam or caffeine, and direct-trade beans are artfully roasted. Also in Silver Lake and Pasadena.

GAY & LESBIAN LA

'Boystown,' along Santa Monica Blvd in West Hollywood (WeHo), is gay ground zero, where dozens of high-energy bars, cafes, restaurants, gyms and clubs mostly cater to men. Silver Lake, LA's original gay enclave, has evolved from largely leather-and-Levi's to encompass multiethnic, metrosexual hipsters. Long Beach has a more laid-back gay community.

Out & About (www.outandabout-tours.com) Leads weekend walking tours of the city's lesbi-gay cultural landmarks. **LA Pride** (www.lapride.org) celebrations in mid-June attract hundreds of thousands of LGBT locals and out-of-town visitors for nonstop partying and a parade down Santa Monica Boulevard.

Abbey (Map p916; www.abbeyfoodandbar.com; 692 N Robertson Blvd; mains $9-13; ⊘ 8am-2am) At WeHo's essential gay bar and restaurant, take your pick of preening on a leafy patio, in a slick lounge or on a dance floor, and enjoy flavored martinis and upscale pub grub. A dozen other bars and nightclubs are within walking distance.

Akbar (www.akbarsilverlake.com; 4356 W Sunset Blvd) Killer jukebox and a Los Feliz crowd that's been known to change from hour to hour – gay, straight or just hip, but not too-hip-for-you. Some nights the back room becomes a dance floor.

Roosterfish (Map p919; www.roosterfishbar.com; 1302 Abbot Kinney Blvd; ⊘ 11am-2am) Venice's oldest gay bar has been serving men for over three decades. It's dark and divey yet chill, with a pool table and back patio.

☆ Entertainment

LA Weekly (www.laweekly.com) and the *Los Angeles Times* (www.latimes.com) have extensive entertainment listings. Buy tickets online, at the box office or through **Ticketmaster** (☎213-480-3232; www.ticketmaster.com). For discounted and half-price tickets, check **Goldstar** (www.goldstar.com) and **ScoreBig** (www.scorebig.com) for stage, concert, comedy and sports events, or **LA Stage Alliance** (www.lastagealliance.com) and **Plays 411** (www.plays411.com) strictly for theater.

To confirm all your pre-conceived prejudices about LA, look no further than a velvet-roped nightclub in Hollywood. Come armed with a hot bod or a fat wallet to impress the goonish bouncers. Clubs are generally open from 9:30pm to 2am Thursdays to Sundays; cover charges average $20 (bring photo ID).

★ **Hollywood Bowl**   LIVE MUSIC
(☎323-850-2000; www.hollywoodbowl.com; 2301 N Highland Ave; ☉Jun-Sep; 🚻) This historic outdoor amphitheater is the LA Phil's summer home and a stellar place to catch big-name rock, jazz, blues and pop acts. Come early for a preshow picnic (alcohol allowed).

Staples Center   SPECTATOR SPORTS, LIVE MUSIC
(Map p910; ☎213-742-7340; www.staplescenter.com; 1111 S Figueroa St; 🚻) Fans fill this flying-saucer-shaped home of the LA Lakers, Clippers and Sparks basketball teams, and Kings ice-hockey team. Headliners – Brunos Mars to Justin Bieber – also perform.

Los Angeles Philharmonic   ORCHESTRA
(Map p910; ☎323-850-2000; www.laphil.org; 111 S Grand Ave) The world-class LA Phil performs classics and cutting-edge works at Walt Disney Concert Hall (p909) under the baton of Venezuelan phenom Gustavo Dudamel.

★ **Upright Citizens**
Brigade Theatre   COMEDY
(Map p915; ☎323-908-8702; http://losangeles.ucbtheatre.com; 5919 Franklin Ave; tickets $5-10) Founded in NYC by *Saturday Night Live* alum Amy Poehler and others, this sketch-comedy and improv club is frequented by Hollywood screenwriters and young TV stars.

★ **Egyptian Theater**   CINEMA
(Map p915; ☎323-466-3456; www.americancinematheque.com; 6712 Hollywood Blvd) Exotic 1922 movie house, home to the American Cinematheque, which presents arty retrospectives and Q&As with directors, writers and actors.

Actors' Gang Theater   THEATER
(www.theactorsgang.com; 9070 Venice Blvd, Culver City) Co-created by Tim Robbins, this socially mindful troupe wins awards for its bold reinterpretations of classic plays and new works pulled from ensemble workshops.

Arclight Cinemas   CINEMA
(Map p915; ☎323-464-1478; www.arclightcinemas.com; 6360 W Sunset Blvd; tickets $14-16) Star-sighting potential is exceptionally high at this state-of-the-art cineplex that has all-reserved seating (no late admission), at Hollywood's landmark Cinerama Dome.

House of Blues   LIVE MUSIC
(Map p916; ☎323-848-5100; www.hob.com; 8430 W Sunset Blvd) Despite a Disneyfied 'Mississippi blues shack' exterior, this Sunset Strip music hall books quality, and sometimes quirky, rock, hip-hop, jazz and blues acts.

Center Theatre Group   THEATER
(☎213-628-2772; www.centertheatregroup.org) Contemporary and classic plays and musicals, including Broadway touring productions, perform on three stages in Downtown LA and Culver City.

Largo at the
Coronet   LIVE MUSIC, PERFORMING ARTS
(Map p916; ☎310-855-0530; www.largo-la.com; 366 N La Cienega Blvd) Pop-culture lab brings edgy comedy (Sarah Silverman), nouveau radio plays (*Thrilling Adventure Hour*) and indie bands to Mid-City's historic theatre.

Hotel Cafe   LIVE MUSIC
(Map p915; ☎323-461-2040; www.hotelcafe.com; 1623½ N Cahuenga Blvd; tickets $10-20) The 'it' place for handmade music is a social stepping stone for message-minded newbie balladeers. Get there early and enter from the alley.

Troubadour   LIVE MUSIC
(Map p916; ☎tickets 877-435-8949; www.troubadour.com; 9081 Santa Monica Blvd) Decades after catapulting Joni Mitchell and Tom Waits to stardom, this music hall is still great for catching tomorrow's headliners.

Los Angeles Opera   OPERA
(Map p910; ☎213-972-8001; www.laopera.com; 135 N Grand Ave, Dorothy Chandler Pavilion) Helmed by Plácido Domingo, this renowned ensemble plays it safe with crowd-pleasers like *Tosca*.

Will Geer's Theatricum Botanicum THEATER
(☎310-455-3723; www.theatricum.com; 1419 N Topanga Canyon Blvd, Topanga; 🚻) Enchanting summer repertory in the woods for Shakespearean classics and family-friendly plays.

Dodger Stadium   BASEBALL
(☏ 866-363-4377; www.dodgers.com; 1000 Elysian Park Ave; ⊙ Apr-Sep) LA's Major League Baseball team plays within tobacco-spitting distance of downtown.

🔒 Shopping

Although Rodeo Drive is the most iconic strip in LA, the city abounds with other options for retail therapy. Besides those listed below, chain-free strips include **Main Street** (Map p919; btwn Bay & Marine Sts) in Santa Monica, **Abbot Kinney Boulevard** (Map p919) in Venice and **Vermont Avenue** (btwn Franklin & Prospect Aves) in Los Feliz.

Rodeo Drive   SHOPPING AREA
(Map p916; btwn Wilshire & Santa Monica Blvds) LA's most famous shopping street, in Beverly Hills.

Robertson Boulevard   SHOPPING AREA
(Map p916; btwn Beverly Blvd & 3rd St) Where fashionistas, and their paparazzi piranhas, flock to in Mid-City.

Montana Avenue   SHOPPING AREA
(btwn Lincoln Blvd & 20th St) Santa Monica's poshest shopping promenade.

Melrose Avenue   SHOPPING AREA
(Map p916; btwn San Vicente Blvd & La Brea Ave) In West Hollywood, Melrose Ave is still a fave of Gen-Y hipsters, including at **Melrose Trading Post** (Map p916; http://melrose-tradingpost.org; Fairfax High School, 7850 Melrose Ave; admission $2; ⊙ 9am-5pm Sun), a weekly flea market. Celebs are frequently sighted at **Book Soup** (Map p916; ☏ 310-659-3110; www.booksoup.com; 8818 W Sunset Blvd; ⊙ 9am-10pm Mon-Sat, to 7pm Sun) on the Sunset Strip.

Amoeba Music   MUSIC
(Map p915; ☏ 323-245-6400; www.amoeba.com; 6400 W Sunset Blvd; ⊙ 10:30am-11pm Mon-Sat, 11am-9pm Sun) Hollywood is ground zero for groovy tunes at this import from San Fran's Bay Area.

Sunset Junction   SHOPPING AREA
(Sunset Blvd, btwn Santa Monica & Griffith Park Blvds) Silver Lake, to the east of Hollywood, has cool kitsch, collectibles and emerging LA designers, especially around Sunset Junction.

Retro Row   SHOPPING AREA
(E 4th St, btwn Cherry & Junipero Aves) Long Beach's Retro Row brims with shops selling vintage clothing and mid-century furniture at prices from 'how much?' to '*how* much?'

DON'T MISS

IT'S A WRAP

Dress just like a movie star – in their actual clothes! Packed to the rafters, Mid-City's **It's a Wrap** (Map p916; ☏ 310-246-9727; www.itsawraphollywood.com; 1164 S Robertson Blvd; ⊙ 10am-8pm Mon-Fri, 11am-6pm Sat & Sun) sells wardrobe castoffs – tank tops to tuxedos – worn by actors and extras working on TV or movie shoots. Tags are coded, so you'll be able to brag with the knowledge of which studio or show's clothing you're wearing. Original location in Burbank.

Distant Lands   BOOKS
(☏ 626-449-3220; www.distantlands.com; 20 S Raymond Ave; ⊙ 10:30am-8pm Mon-Thu, to 9pm Fri & Sat, 11am-6pm Sun) Pasadena's Distant Lands bookshop is a treasure chest of travel guides and gadgets.

Rose Bowl Flea Market   MARKET
(www.rgcshows.com; 1001 Rose Bowl Dr, Pasadena; admission from $8; ⊙ 9am-4:30pm 2nd Sun of month, last entry 3pm) There are more than 2500 vendors and 15,000 buyers here every month.

Fashion District   FASHION
(Map p910; www.fashiondistrict.org) Bargain hunters with couture taste head to Downtown LA's markets. The 100-block Fashion District is a head-spinning selection of samples, knockoffs and original designs at cut-rate prices; haggling is ubiquitous. Nearby, gold and diamonds are the main currency in the **Jewelry District** along Hill St.

Flower Market   MARKET
(Map p910; www.laflowerdistrict.com; Wall St; admission Mon-Fri $2, Sat $1; ⊙ 8am-noon Mon, Wed & Fri, 6am-noon Tue, Thu & Sat) Downtown LA's flower market is the USA's largest, dating from 1919.

ℹ Information

DANGERS & ANNOYANCES
Crime rates are lowest in West LA, Beverly Hills, beach towns (except Venice and Long Beach) and Pasadena. Avoid walking alone and after dark around Downtown's 'Skid Row', roughly bounded by 3rd, Alameda, 7th and Main Sts.

INTERNET ACCESS
Coffee shops offer wi-fi with purchase (sometimes for free).

Los Angeles Public Library (☑213-228-7000; www.lapl.org; 630 W 5th St; ◷10am-8pm Mon-Thu, to 5:30pm Fri & Sat; @ 🛜) Free wi-fi and public internet terminals. Call or check the website for branch locations and hours.

Santa Monica Public Library (☑310-458-8600; www.smpl.org; 601 Santa Monica Blvd, Santa Monica; ◷10am-9pm Mon-Thu, to 5:30pm Fri & Sat, 1-5pm Sun; @ 🛜) Free wi-fi and public internet terminals.

MEDIA

KCRW 89.9 FM (www.kcrw.org) National Public Radio (NPR) station for cutting-edge music, news and public-affairs shows.

KPCC 89.3 FM (www.kpcc.org) NPR station airs BBC programming and intelligent SoCal talk shows.

LA Weekly (www.laweekly.com) Free alternative news, arts and entertainment weekly with a current-events calendar.

Los Angeles Magazine (www.lamag.com) Glossy lifestyle monthly has a useful restaurant guide.

Los Angeles Times (www.latimes.com) Pulitzer Prize–winning daily newspaper and info-packed website.

MEDICAL SERVICES

Cedars-Sinai Medical Center (☑310-423-3277; http://cedars-sinai.edu; 8700 Beverly Blvd, West Hollywood) Has a 24-hour emergency room.

MONEY

TravelEx (☑310-659-6093; www.travelex.com; US Bank, 8901 Santa Monica Blvd, West Hollywood; ◷9:30am-5pm Mon-Thu, 9am-6pm Fri, 9am-1pm Sat) Additional branches in Hollywood, Mid-City and Santa Monica open weekdays only.

TELEPHONE

LA County is covered by multiple area codes. Dial ☑1 +(area code) before all local seven-digit numbers.

TOURIST INFORMATION

Beverly Hills Visitor Center (Map p916; ☑310-248-1015; www.lovebeverlyhills.com; 9400 S Santa Monica Blvd, Beverly Hills; ◷9am-5pm Mon-Fri, from 10am Sat & Sun)

Downtown LA Visitor Information Center (Map p910; http://discoverlosangeles.com; 800 N Alameda St, Union Station; ◷9am-5pm Mon-Fri)

Hollywood Visitor Information Center (Map p915; ☑323-467-6412; http://discoverlosangeles.com; Hollywood & Highland complex, 6801 Hollywood Blvd; ◷10am-10pm Mon-Sat, to 7pm Sun)

Santa Monica Visitor Center (Map p919; ☑800-544-5319, 310-393-7593; www.santamonica.com; 1920 Main St, Santa Monica; ◷9am-5:30pm Mon-Fri, to 5pm Sat & Sun) Additional info kiosks at Santa Monica Pier, Palisades Park and Third St Promenade.

WEBSITES

Daily Candy LA (www.dailycandy.com/los-angeles/) Little bites of LA style.

Discover Los Angeles (http://discover-losangeles.com) Official tourist info site.

Experience LA (www.experiencela.com) Comprehensive cultural events calendar.

LAist (http://laist.com) Arts, entertainment, food, events and pop-culture gossip.

LA Observed (www.laobserved.com) News blog that often scoops mainstream media.

❶ Getting There & Away

AIR

LA's gateway hub is **Los Angeles International Airport** (LAX; ☑310-646-5252; www.lawa.org/lax; 1 World Way; 🛜), the USA's second busiest. The nine terminals are linked on the lower (arrivals) level by free shuttle bus A. Hotel and car-rental shuttles stop there as well.

Smaller **Long Beach Airport** and Burbank's **Bob Hope Airport** (BUR; ☑818-840-8840; www.burbankairport.com; 2627 N Hollywood Way) handle mostly domestic flights.

BUS

Greyhound's main **bus terminal** (☑213-629-8401; www.greyhound.com; 1716 E 7th St) is in an unsavory part of Downtown LA, so avoid arriving after dark. If you absolutely must, call a taxi from inside the bus terminal.

CAR

The usual international car-rental agencies have branches at LAX airport and throughout LA.

TRAIN

Long-distance Amtrak trains roll into Downtown LA's historic **Union Station** (☑800-872-7245; www.amtrak.com; 800 N Alameda St). *Pacific Surfliner* regional trains run southwards to San Diego ($37, 2¾ hours) and northwards to Santa Barbara ($25 to $30, three hours) and San Luis Obispo ($40, 5½ hours).

❶ Getting Around

TO/FROM THE AIRPORT

Door-to-door shared-ride vans operated by **Prime Time** (☑800-733-8267; www.primetimeshuttle.com) and **Super Shuttle** (☑800-258-3826; www.supershuttle.com) leave from the lower level of LAX terminals; typical destinations include Santa Monica ($19), Hollywood ($25) and Downtown LA ($16). **Disneyland Express** (☎714-978-8855; http://graylineanaheim. com; one way/round-trip $22/32; ⊙7:30am-10:30pm) travels at least hourly between LAX and Disneyland-area hotels; a round-trip family pass costs $99.

Curbside dispatchers summon **taxis** at LAX. A flat fare applies to Downtown LA ($46.50) or Santa Monica ($30 to $35). Otherwise, metered fares (including $4 airport surcharge) average $45 to $55 for Hollywood and up to $95 to Disneyland, excluding tip.

LAX FlyAway Buses (☎866-435-9529; www. lawa.org; one way $7) depart LAX terminals every 30 minutes for Westwood ($10, 25 to 45 minutes) between 6am and 11pm daily, and 24 hours to Downtown LA's Union Station ($7, 30 to 50 minutes).

Other public transportation is slower and less convenient but cheaper. From the lower level outside any LAX terminal, catch a free shuttle bus C to the Metro Bus Center, a hub for buses serving all of LA; or take shuttle bus G to Aviation Station on the Metro Green Line light rail, then transfer at Willowbrook Station to the Blue Line, which connects Downtown LA and Long Beach.

CAR & MOTORCYCLE

Driving in LA doesn't need to be a hassle (a GPS device helps), but be prepared for some of the worst traffic in the country during weekday rush hours (roughly 7:30am to 9am and 4pm to 6:30pm).

Self-parking at motels is usually free; most hotels charge anywhere from $10 to $35. Valet parking at restaurants, hotels and nightspots is commonplace, with rates averaging $3 to $10.

PUBLIC TRANSPORTATION

If you're not in a hurry, public transportation suffices around – but not necessarily between – LA's most-touristed neighborhoods.

Local **DASH minibuses** (☎323-808-2273, 213-808-2273; www.ladottransit.com; fare 50¢; ⊙6am-7pm) run around Downtown LA, Hollywood and Los Feliz. Santa Monica–based **Big Blue Bus** (☎310-451-5444; www.bigbluebus. com; fares from $1) covers much of West LA, including Westwood, Venice and LAX; its Rapid 10 Freeway Express connects Santa Monica with Downtown LA ($2, one hour).

Trip-planning help is available via LA's **Metro** (☎323-466-3876; www.metro.net), which operates 200 bus lines and the following six subway and light-rail lines:

Blue Line Downtown (7th St/Metro Center) to Long Beach

Expo Line Downtown (7th St/Metro Center) to Culver City, via Exposition Park

Gold Line Union Station to Pasadena and east LA

Green Line Norwalk to Redondo Beach

Purple Line Downtown to Koreatown

Red Line Downtown (Union Station) to North Hollywood, via Hollywood and Universal City

Metro train or bus fares are $1.50. On buses, bring exact change and ask the driver when boarding for a transfer. Note there are no free transfers between trains and buses. Metro 'TAP card' unlimited ride passes cost $5/20/75 per day/week/month. Purchase train tickets and TAP cards at vending machines inside train stations, or check www.metro.net for other locations.

TAXI

Except for taxis lined up outside airports, train and bus stations and major hotels, it's best to phone for a cab. Metered taxis charge $2.85 at flagfall, then $2.70 per mile. Taxis accept major credit cards, though sometimes grudgingly.

Checker (☎800-300-5007; http://ineed taxi.com)

Independent (☎800-521-8294; http://taxi 4u.com)

LOCAL KNOWLEDGE

CAR-FREE LA

'Nobody walks in LA,' the '80s band Missing Persons famously sang. That was then. Fed up with traffic, smog and high gas prices, the city that defined car culture is slowly developing an alt-transportation culture. Angelenos are moving into more densely populated neighborhoods where walking, cycling and taking public transit makes more sense.

The Metro Red Line subway connects Downtown LA with Koreatown, Hollywood and Universal Studios. Base yourself near one of its art-filled stations and you may not even need a car. Unlimited-ride tickets (per day $5) are a bargain; plus, given LA's legendary traffic, it's often faster to travel below ground than above.

While eventual plans call for a 'Subway to the Sea,' for now you'll be bussing it to Mid-City, Beverly Hills, Westwood and Santa Monica. From the Red Line (Wilshire/Vermont station) or Purple Line (Wilshire/Western station), transfer to Metro's Rapid 720 bus, making limited stops along Wilshire Blvd. For more information visit www.metro.net.

SOUTHERN CALIFORNIA COAST

Disneyland & Anaheim

The mother of all West Coast theme parks, aka the 'Happiest Place on Earth,' Disneyland is a parallel world that's squeaky clean, enchanting and wacky all at once. Smaller and somewhat more modest than Florida's Disney World, this was Walt Disney's original theme park. He famously dreamt of a 'magical park' where children and their parents could have fun together. For all his visions of waterfalls, castles and gigantic teacups, Disney was also a practical businessman, choosing to construct his fantasy land within easy reach of metropolitan LA.

Disneyland opened to great fanfare in 1955 and the workaday city of Anaheim grew up around it. Today the Disneyland Resort comprises the original theme park and newer California Adventure Park. Anaheim itself doesn't have much in the way of attractions outside the Disney juggernaut.

◉ Sights & Activities

You can see either **theme park** (☎714-781-4636; www.disneyland.com; 1313 Harbor Blvd; adult/child 3-9yr 1-day pass $92/86, 2-day park-hopper pass $210/197; ◷ daily, seasonal hours vary) in a day, but going on all the rides requires at least two days, as waits for top attractions can be an hour or more. To minimize wait times, especially in summer, arrive midweek before the gates open, buy print-at-home tickets online and use the parks' Fastpass system, which pre-assigns boarding times at some rides and attractions. Check online for seasonal park hours and schedules of parades, shows and fireworks. Admission prices, contact information and opening hours are the same for both theme parks, although you'll need to buy a higher-priced park-hopper ticket to visit both parks rather than just one.

Disneyland Park   THEME PARK
(🖑) Spotless, wholesome Disneyland is still laid out according to Walt's original plans. **Main Street USA**, a pedestrian thoroughfare lined with old-fashioned ice-cream parlors and shops, is the gateway. At its far end is **Sleeping Beauty Castle**, an obligatory photo op and a central landmark worth noting – its towering blue turrets are visible from many areas.

The park's themed sections stuffed with rides and attractions radiate out from Sleeping Beauty Castle like spokes on a wheel. Although kids will make a beeline for the rides, adults may enjoy the antique photos and history exhibit just inside the main entrance at the **Disneyland Story**.

Your best bet for meeting princesses and other characters in costume is **Fantasyland**, home to the spinning teacups of Mad Tea Party, It's a Small World cruise and Peter Pan's Flight. For something a bit more fast-paced, head to the exhilarating Space Mountain roller coaster in **Tomorrowland**, where the Finding Nemo Submarine Voyage and Star Wars' Jedi Training Academy await.

The ever-popular Indiana Jones Adventure ride awaits in **Adventureland**. Nearby **New Orleans Square** offers several worthwhile attractions – the Haunted Mansion (not too scary for older kids) and Pirates of the Caribbean cruise, where cannons shoot

KNOTT'S BERRY FARM

What, Disney's not enough for you? Find even more thrill rides and cotton candy at **Knott's Berry Farm** (☎714-220-5200; www.knotts.com; 8039 Beach Blvd, Buena Park; adult/child $60/31; ◷ from 10am daily, closing time varies seasonally 6-11pm; 🖑). This Old West–themed amusement park teems with packs of speed-crazed adolescents testing their mettle on a line-up of rides. Gut-wrenchers include the Boomerang 'scream machine,' wooden GhostRider and 1950s-themed Xcelerator, while the single-digit-aged find tamer action at Camp Snoopy. From late September through October, the park transforms into Halloween-themed 'Knott's Scary Farm.'

When summer heat waves hit, jump next door to **Soak City OC** (☎714-220-5200; www.soakcityoc.com; 8039 Beach Blvd, Buena Park; adult/child 3-11yr $35/25; ◷10am-5pm, 6pm or 7pm mid-May–mid-Sep) water park. Save time and money by buying print-at-home tickets for both parks online. Parking is $15.

across the water, wenches are up for auction and the mechanical Jack Sparrow character is creepily lifelike. Big Thunder Mountain Railroad, another popular roller coaster, is in cowboy-themed Frontierland.

If you've got little ones in tow, you'll likely spend time at **Mickey's Toontown** and in **Critter Country**, where families can cool off on Splash Mountain's log-flume ride.

Disney's California Adventure   THEME PARK
(DCA; 🖰) Disneyland resort's larger but less crowded park, DCA celebrates the natural and pop-cultural glories of the Golden State but lacks the density of attractions and depth of imagination. The best rides are Soarin' Over California, a virtual hang-glide; the famous Twilight Zone Tower of Terror, which drops you down an elevator chute; and Grizzly River Run, a white-water rafting ride.

Smaller children will love A Bug's Land and the Radiator Springs Racers, a slot-car roller coaster mimicking the Route 66 scenery of the *Cars* movie. Hang around Paradise Bay after dark to gawk at the World of Color light, sound and special-effects spectacular.

🛏 Sleeping

Chain motels and hotels are a dime a dozen in the surrounding city of Anaheim.

HI Fullerton   HOSTEL $
(🖰714-738-3721; www.hiusa.org; 1700 N Harbor Blvd, Fullerton; dm $24-27; ⊘mid-Jun—early Sep; 🖰@🖰) About 6 miles north of Disneyland on an old dairy farm, this two-story hacienda houses 20 beds in mixed and single-sex dorms. Rates include continental breakfast. Public buses stop nearby.

Hotel Menage   HOTEL $$
(🖰714-758-0900; www.hotelmenage.com; 1221 S Harbor Blvd; r $100-200; @🖰🖰🖰🖰) Off the I-5 Fwy, this stylish modern hotel pulls off an urbane atmopshere with leather headboards, plasma TVs and some sofa beds. The poolside tiki bar makes a relaxing respite after a day of running around Disney's 'Mouse House.'

Alpine Inn   MOTEL $$
(🖰714-772-4422; www.alpineinnanaheim.com; 715 W Katella Ave; r incl breakfast $79-149; 🖰@🖰🖰🖰) Connoisseurs of kitsch will delight in this alpine chalet covered to the tippy-top of its A-framed rafters with artificial snow and icicles. Compact rooms have mod cons, but it's all about the convenient location outside Disneyland Resort's main gate.

Paradise Pier Hotel   HOTEL $$$
(🖰info 714-999-0990, reservations 714-956-6425; http://disneyland.disney.go.com/paradise-pier-hotel; 1717 S Disneyland Dr; d from $240; 🖰🖰@🖰🖰🖰) It's one big surfin' safari at the sun-dappled Paradise Pier Hotel, the brightest, happy-go-luckiest of the Disneyland Resort hotel trio, with splashy colors, Beach Boys tunes, upbeat staff and a rooftop pool deck with a waterslide and after-dark fireworks viewing. It's a 10-minute walk to Downtown Disney.

🍴 Eating & Drinking

There are dozens of dining options inside the theme parks; it's part of the fun to hit the walk-up food stands for treats like giant turkey legs and sugar-dusted churros.

For reservations or information on Disneyland Resort restaurants, call **Disney Dining** (🖰714-781-3463; http://disneyland.disney.go.com/dining). No alcohol is allowed inside Disneyland Park; it's sold at DCA and Downtown Disney. Budget-conscious visitors and families with kids can store their own food and drinks (no glass) in the lockers ($7 to $15) along Disneyland's Main Street USA, DCA's Buena Vista Street and outside both parks' main entrance.

An open-air pedestrian mall adjacent to the parks, **Downtown Disney** (http://disneyland.disney.go.com/downtown-disney/; ⊘open daily, seasonal hours vary) has generic but family-friendly chain restaurants. The same is true of **Anaheim GardenWalk** (www.anaheimgardenwalk.com; 321 W Katella Ave; ⊘11am-9pm, some restaurants open later), an outdoor mall just east of the parks. If you want to steer clear of Mickey Mouse food, drive to retro-flavored **Old Towne Orange** (7 miles southeast), **Little Arabia** (3 miles west) or **Little Saigon** (12 miles southwest).

Earl of Sandwich   DELI $
(www.earlofsandwichusa.com; Downtown Disney; dishes $2-8; ⊘8am-11pm Sun-Thu, to 12am Fri & Sat; 🖰) Lines are long, but worth it for Downtown Disney's best budget eats: hot and cold sandwiches, wraps, salads and soups that won't break the bank, and warm, oven-fresh cookies.

Café Orleans   CAJUN, CREOLE $$
(Disneyland Park; mains $15-20; ⊘seasonal hours vary; 🖰) In Disneyland's New Orleans Sq, this cafeteria-style Southern restaurant dishes up bowls of jambalaya and gumbo, serves pan-fried Monte Cristo sandwiches and will shake up virgin mint-julep cocktails for customers. Reservations accepted.

Napa Rose
CALIFORNIAN $$$

(Grand Californian Hotel; mains $38-45, 4-course prix-fixe dinner from $90; ⊙ 5:30-10pm; ⚑) Inside a soaring Craftsman-style dining room with colorful leaded-glass windows, Napa Rose is Disney's top-drawer restaurant. The chef's tasting menu exquisitely pairs seasonal ingredients with California-grown wines. Reservations essential.

Catal Restaurant & Uva Bar
MEDITERRANEAN $$$

(☑714-774-4442; www.patinagroup.com/catal; Downtown Disney; mains breakfast $10-15, dinner $23-41; ⊙8am-10pm; ⚑) Looking for something sophisticated yet unfussy? Share Mediterranean-inspired tapas and grill plates as you sip cocktails and craft beer in Downtown Disney. Book ahead, especially for balcony seating.

❶ Information

Stroller rentals ($15 per day) and drop-off pet kennels ($20 per day) are available outside the parks' main entrance.

Anaheim/Orange County Visitor & Convention Bureau (www.anaheimoc.org) Free travel-planning website and smartphone mobile app.

Disneyland City Hall (☑714-781-4565; Main Street USA) One of several theme-park guest information centers, it offers foreign-currency exchange.

MousePlanet (www.mouseplanet.com) One-stop online resource for news, updates, trip planning and discussion boards.

MouseWait (www.mousewait.com) Free phone app with up-to-the-minute wait times and what's happening in the parks.

Touring Plans (http://touringplans.com) Online crowd calendar and free phone app with theme-park itineraries, wait times and restaurant menus.

❶ Getting There & Around

The Disneyland Resort is just off I-5 (Santa Ana Fwy), about 30 miles southeast of Downtown LA. As you approach the area, freeway signs indicate which exit ramps to take for Disney's theme parks, hotels or Anaheim's streets.

Amtrak trains between LA's Union Station ($14, 40 minutes) and San Diego ($28, two hours) stop almost hourly in Anaheim. The **train station** (☑714-385-1448; 2150 E Katella Ave), next to Angel Stadium, is a quick bus or taxi ride east of Disneyland. **Metrolink** (☑800-371-5465; www.metrolinktrains.com) commuter trains from LA's Union Station ($8.75, 45 minutes) stop at the same station.

Anaheim Resort Transit (ART; ☑714-563-5287; www.rideart.org; day pass adult/child $5/2) provides frequent bus service between Disneyland Resort and many area hotels and motels.

A free tram connects Disneyland Resort's main parking garage (per day $15 to $20) and Downtown Disney, a short walk from the theme parks.

Orange County Beaches

If you've seen *The OC* or *Real Housewives*, you'll think that you already know what to expect from this giant quilt of suburbia connecting LA and San Diego, which lolls beside 42 miles of glorious coastline. In reality, Hummer-driving hunks and Botoxed beauties mix it up with hang-loose surfers and beatnik artists to give each of Orange County's beach towns a distinct vibe.

Just across the LA–OC county line, old-fashioned **Seal Beach** is refreshingly non-commercial, with a quaint walkable downtown. Nine miles further south along the Pacific Coast Hwy (Hwy 1), **Huntington Beach** – aka 'Surf City, USA' – epitomizes SoCal's surfing lifestyle. Fish tacos and happy-hour specials abound at bars and cafes along downtown HB's Main St, not far from a shortboard-sized **surfing museum** (☑714-960-3483; www.surfingmuseum.org; 411 Olive Ave; admission by donation; ⊙noon-5pm Sun & Mon, to 9pm Tue, to 7pm Wed-Fri, 11am-7pm Sat).

Next up is the ritziest of the OC's beach communities: yacht-filled **Newport Beach**. Families and teens steer toward Balboa Peninsula for its beaches, vintage wooden pier and quaint amusement center. From nearby the 1906 Balboa Pavilion, **Balboa Island Ferry** (www.balboaislandferry.com; 410 S Bay Front; adult/child $1/50¢, car incl driver $2; ⊙6:30am-midnight Sun-Thu, to 2am Fri & Sat) shuttles across the bay to Balboa Island for strolls past historic beach cottages and boutiques along Marine Ave.

Continuing south, Hwy 1 zooms past the wild beaches of **Crystal Cove State Park** (☑949-494-3539; www.parks.ca.gov; 8471 N Coast Hwy; per car $15, campsites $25-75) before winding downhill into **Laguna Beach**, the OC's most cultured and charming seaside community, where secluded beaches, glassy waves and eucalyptus-covered hillsides create a Riviera-like feel. Art galleries dot the narrow streets of the 'village' and the coastal highway, where the clifftop **Laguna Art Museum** (☑949-494-8971; www.lagunaartmuseum.org; 307

Cliff Dr; adult/child $7/free; ☉usually 11am-5pm Fri-Tue, to 9pm Thu) exhibits modern and contemporary Californian artworks. Soak up the natural beauty right in the center of town at **Main Beach**.

Another 10 miles south, detour inland to **Mission San Juan Capistrano** (☎949-234-1300; www.missionsjc.com; 26801 Ortega Hwy, San Juan Capistrano; adult/child $9/6; ☉9am-5pm), one of California's most beautifully restored missions, with flowering gardens, a fountain courtyard and the charming 1778 Serra Chapel.

🛏 Sleeping & Eating

Oceanside motels and hotels along PCH (Hwy 1) charge surprisingly steep rates, especially on summer weekends. Dive inland near the freeways for better bargains.

★**Crystal Cove Beach Cottages** CABIN $$
(☎reservations 800-444-7275; www.crystalcove beachcottages.com; 35 Crystal Cove, Newport Beach; r without bath $42-127, cottages $162-249; ☉check-in 4-9pm; ▣) To snag one of these historic mid-20th-century oceanfront cottages at Crystal Cove State Park, book on the first day of the month, seven months before your intended stay – or pray for last-minute cancellations.

Shorebreak Hotel BOUTIQUE HOTEL $$$
(☎714-861-4470; www.shorebreakhotel.com; 500 Pacific Coast Hwy, Huntington Beach; r $189-495; ▣@☎▣) Fashionably hip hotel livens things up with a surf concierge, beanbag chairs in the lobby and geometric-patterned rooms. Knock back sunset cocktails on the upstairs deck. Parking is $27.

Zinc Cafe & Market HEALTHY $
(www.zinccafe.com; 350 Ocean Ave, Laguna Beach; mains $6-11; ☉market 7am-6pm, cafe until 4pm; ▣) Maybe it's the happy-making tomato-colored walls or the open-air patio that draws the young and beautiful here. An all-vegetarian cafe menu ranges from breakfast quiche to pizzettes, garden-fresh salads and deli sandwiches for lunch.

Bear Flag Fish Company SEAFOOD $$
(☎949-673-3434; www.bearflagfishco.com; 407 31st St, Newport Beach; dishes $8-15; ☉11am-9pm Tue-Sat, to 8pm Mon & Sun; ▣) Seafood market dishes up spankin' fresh oysters, fish tacos, Hawaiian-style *poke* and more. Pick exactly what you want from the ice-cold display cases. Expect long lines. Cash only.

DON'T MISS

LAGUNA'S FESTIVAL OF ARTS

Hey, did that painting just move? Welcome to the **Pageant of the Masters** (☎800-487-3378; tickets from $15; ☉8:30pm daily mid-Jul-Aug), in which elaborately costumed humans step into painstaking recreations of famous paintings on an outdoor stage. The pageant began in 1933 as a sideshow to Laguna Beach's **Festival of Arts** (www.foapom.com; admission $7-10; ☉usually 10am-11:30pm Jul & Aug) and has been a prime attraction ever since. Our favorite part: watching the paintings deconstruct.

San Diego

San Diegans shamelessly promote their hometown as 'America's Finest City.' Smug? Maybe, but it's easy to see why: the weather is practically perfect, with coastal high temperatures hovering around 68°F (20°C) all year, and beaches are rarely more than a quick drive away. San Diego's population (1.3 million) makes it America's eighth-largest city and California's second-largest after LA, yet we're hard-pressed to think of a more laid-back metropolis anywhere.

The city grew by leaps and bounds during WWII, when the Japanese attack on Pearl Harbor prompted the US Navy to relocate the US Pacific Fleet from Hawaii to San Diego's natural harbor. The military, tourism, education and scientific research industries (especially medicine and oceanography), as well as high-tech ventures cropping up in inland valleys, have helped to shape the city. It all makes SD seem quintessentially all-American – its Mexico borderlands notwithstanding.

◉ Sights

San Diego's compact downtown hinges on the historic Gaslamp Quarter, a beehive after dark. Coronado is reached via a stunning bridge to the southwest, while museum-rich Balboa Park (home of the San Diego Zoo) is north of downtown. Neighboring the park to the northwest is Hillcrest, the city's lesbigay hub, where everyone's welcome in the restaurants, cafes, bars and shops. Heading west is touristy Old Town and Mission Bay's aquatic playground.

Greater San Diego

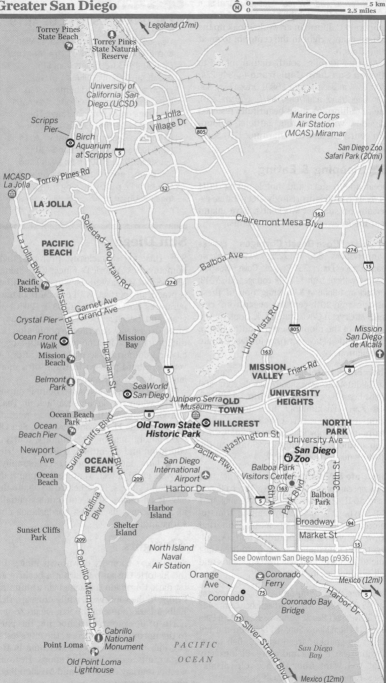

N

0 ___ 5 km
0 ___ 2.5 miles

Legoland (17mi)

Torrey Pines State Beach

Torrey Pines State Natural Reserve

University of California, San Diego (UCSD)

Scripps Pier

Birch Aquarium at Scripps

La Jolla Village Dr

805

Marine Corps Air Station (MCAS) Miramar

San Diego Zoo Safari Park (20mi)

MCASD La Jolla

Torrey Pines Rd

5

LA JOLLA

52

Clairemont Mesa Blvd

163

274

15

PACIFIC BEACH

Soledad Mountain Rd

La Jolla Blvd

Pacific Beach

274

Balboa Ave

Mission Blvd

Garnet Ave
Grand Ave

Crystal Pier

Ocean Front Walk

Mission Beach

Mission Bay

Linda Vista Rd

805

163

Mission San Diego de Alcalá

Ingraham St

5

MISSION VALLEY

Friars Rd

8

Belmont Park

SeaWorld San Diego

Junipero Serra Museum

OLD TOWN

UNIVERSITY HEIGHTS

NORTH PARK

Ocean Beach Park

8

Old Town State Historic Park

HILLCREST

Washington St

University Ave

San Diego Zoo

Ocean Beach Pier

Sunset Cliffs Blvd

Nimitz Blvd

209

OCEAN BEACH

San Diego International Airport

Pacific Hwy

Balboa Park Visitors Center

6th Ave

163

Park Blvd

30th St

Balboa Park

Newport Ave

Ocean Beach

Harbor Dr

5

Broadway

94

Sunset Cliffs Park

Catalina Blvd

209

Harbor Island

Shelter Island

Market St

15

North Island Naval Air Station

See Downtown San Diego Map (p936)

Mexico (12mi)

Cabrillo Memorial Dr

Orange Ave

Coronado Ferry

75

Coronado

Harbor Dr

5

Coronado Bay Bridge

Cabrillo National Monument

Point Loma

Old Point Loma Lighthouse

PACIFIC OCEAN

75

Silver Strand Blvd

San Diego Bay

Mexico (12mi)

Cruising up the coast, Ocean Beach, Mission Beach and Pacific Beach live the laid-back SoCal dream, while La Jolla sits pretty and privileged. Further north, line up North County's eclectic beach towns: ritzy Del Mar, design-savvy Solana Beach, new-agey Encinitas and flowery Carlsbad, home of Legoland. The I-5 Fwy cuts through the region north–south.

Downtown & Embarcadero

In the 1860s, real-estate wrangling by developer Alonzo Horton created so-called 'New Town', which is Downtown San Diego today. The main street, 5th Ave, was once a notorious strip of saloons, gambling joints and bordellos known as Stingaree. These days, Stingaree has been beautifully restored and rechristened the **Gaslamp Quarter**, a heart-thumping playground of restaurants, bars, clubs, boutiques and galleries.

At downtown's northern edge, **Little Italy** (www.littleitalysd.com) has evolved into one of the city's hippest places to live, eat and shop. **India St** is the neighborhood's main drag.

★USS Midway Museum   MUSEUM
(Map p936; ☑619-544-9600; www.midway.org; 910 N Harbor Dr; adult/child $19/10; ☺10am-5pm, last entry 4pm; 🅿 ♿) Step aboard the US Navy's longest-serving 20th-century aircraft carrier (1945–91). Self-guided audio tours take in berthing spaces, the galley, sick bay and the killer flight deck with its restored aircraft, including an F-14 Tomcat. Flight simulator experiences cost extra. Parking is $5 to $20.

★Maritime Museum   MUSEUM
(Map p936; ☑619-234-9153; www.sdmaritime.org; 1492 N Harbor Dr; adult/child $16/8; ☺9am-9pm late May-early Sep, to 8pm rest of year; ♿) The 1863 *Star of India* is one of seven historic sailing vessels open to the public at this museum. Don't miss clambering down inside the B-39 Soviet attack submarine. A 45-minute historical bay cruise costs just $5 extra.

Museum of Contemporary Art   MUSEUM
(MCASD Downtown; Map p936; ☑858-454-3541; www.mcasd.org; 1001 Kettner Blvd; adult/child $10/free, 5-7pm 3rd Thu of month free; ☺11am-5pm Thu-Tue, to 7pm 3rd Thu of month) MCASD emphasizes minimalist and pop art, plus conceptual and cross-border works. The 1100 Kettner Bldg is at the historic Santa Fe Depot. There's another branch in La Jolla (p939). Same ticket valid for seven-day admission to all.

Gaslamp Museum   MUSEUM
(Map p936; ☑619-233-4692; www.gaslampquarter.org; 410 Island Ave; adult/child $5/4; ☺10am-5pm Tue-Sat, noon-4pm Sun) Peruse the period exhibits inside this Victorian-era saltbox house that was the one-time home of William Heath Davis, the man credited with founding 'New Town.' Guided historical walking tours of the quarter usually depart at 11am Saturday (adult/child $15/free).

Petco Park   STADIUM
(Map p936; ☑619-795-5011; www.padres.com; 100 Park Blvd; tours adult/child/senior $11/7/8) In the Gaslamp Quarter's southeast corner stands the home of the San Diego Padres Major League Baseball (MLB) team. You can take a behind-the-scenes tour year-round. Call for tour schedules.

Coronado

Technically a peninsula, Coronado Island is joined to the mainland by a soaring boomerang-shaped bridge. The main draw here is the Hotel del Coronado (p940), known for its seaside Victorian architecture and illustrious guest book, which includes Thomas Edison, Brad Pitt and Marilyn Monroe (its exterior stood in for a Miami hotel in the classic flick *Some Like it Hot*).

The hourly **Coronado Ferry** (Map p936; ☑619-234-4111; www.sdhe.com; fare $4.25; ☺9am-10pm) departs from the Embarcadero's Broadway Pier (990 N Harbor Dr) and from Downtown's San Diego Convention Center. All ferries arrive on Coronado at the foot of 1st St, where **Bikes & Beyond** (☑619-435-7180; http://hollandsbicycles.com; 1201 1st St, Coronado; rental per hr/day from $7/25; ☺9am-sunset) rents cruisers and tandems, perfect for pedaling past Coronado's beaches sprawled south along the **Silver Strand**.

Balboa Park

Balboa Park is an urban oasis brimming with more than a dozen museums, gorgeous gardens and architecture, performance spaces and a zoo. Early 20th-century beaux arts and Spanish-Colonial buildings (the legacy of world's fairs) are grouped around plazas along east–west El Prado promenade.

Stop by the Balboa Park Visitors Center (p943) for maps, events information and discount attraction passes. Free parking lots off Park Blvd fill quickly on weekends.

Downtown San Diego

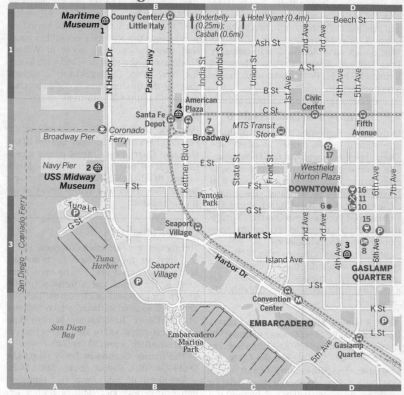

From downtown, take MTS bus 7 ($2.25, 20 minutes). A free tram shuttles visitors around the park, but it's more enjoyable to stroll around the botanical gardens, past the **Spreckels Organ Pavilion**, the shops and galleries of the **Spanish Village Art Center** and the international-themed exhibitions cottages by the **United Nations Building**.

★ **San Diego Zoo**   ZOO
(☑ 619-231-1515; www.sandiegozoo.org; 2920 Zoo Dr; adult/child $44/34; ☺ 9am-9pm mid-Jun–early Sep, to 5pm or 6pm rest of year; ℗ ⊞) 🅿 If it slithers, crawls, stomps, swims, leaps or flies, chances are you'll find it in this world-famous zoo. It's home to more than 4000 animals representing 800-plus species in a beautifully landscaped setting, including the Australian Outback and Panda Canyon. Admission includes a narrated 35-minute double-decker-bus tour. For a wildlife viewing experience that's closer to the real thing,

get a combo ticket to Escondido's San Diego Zoo Safari Park (p943).

Museum of Man   MUSEUM
(☑ 619-239-2001; www.museumofman.org; Plaza de California, 1350 El Prado; adult/child $12.50/5; ☺ 10am-4:30pm) Topped by a dazzling blue-and-yellow-tiled tower, the churrigueresque **California Building** houses the Museum of Man, exhibiting world-class pottery, jewelry, baskets and anthropological artifacts from all around the Americas. Behind are the **Old Globe** theaters, an historic three-stage venue hosting a summer Shakespeare festival.

San Diego Air & Space Museum   MUSEUM
(☑ 619-234-8291; www.sandiegoairandspace.org; 2001 Pan American Plaza; adult/child $18/7; ☺ 10am-5:30pm Jun-Aug, to 4:30pm Sep-May; ⊞) Highlights include the original Apollo 9 command module and a replica of Charles Lindbergh's *Spirit of St Louis*. Flight simulators entail a surcharge.

Downtown San Diego

San Diego Natural History Museum   MUSEUM

(☏619-232-3821; www.sdnhm.org; 1788 El Prado; adult/child $17/11; ☺10am-5pm; 🚼) Dinosaur skeletons, glow-in-the-dark scorpions, ice-age fossils and nature-themed movies in a giant 3D cinema bring family crowds to 'The Nat.'

Timken Museum of Art   MUSEUM

(☏619-239-5548; www.timkenmuseum.org; 1500 El Prado; ☺10am-4:30pm Tue-Sat, from 1:30pm Sun) **FREE** Small but exquisite museum showcases European and American heavyweights, from Rembrandt to Cézanne, and Western landscape painters.

San Diego Museum of Art   MUSEUM

(☏619-232-7931; www.sdmart.org; 1450 El Prado; adult/child $12/4.50; ☺10am-5pm Mon-Tue & Thu-Sat, from noon Sun, also 5-9pm Thu Jun-Sep) SDMA gets accolades for its European old masters and curated collections of American and Asian art.

Mingei International Museum   MUSEUM

(☏619-239-0003; www.mingei.org; 1439 El Prado; adult/child $8/5; ☺10am-4pm Tue-Sun; 🚼) This museum exhibits stunning folk art, craft and design from around the globe, along with a colorful gift shop.

Reuben H Fleet Science Center   MUSEUM

(☏619-238-1233; www.rhfleet.org; 1875 El Prado; adult/child $12/10, incl IMAX movie $16/13; ☺10am-5pm Mon-Thu, to 8pm Fri, to 7pm Sat, to 6pm Sun; 🚼) Family-oriented hands-on science museum and IMAX movie theater near the fountain.

San Diego Model Railroad Museum MUSEUM

(☏619-696-0199; www.sdmrm.org; Casa de Balboa, 1649 El Prado; adult/child $8/free; ☺11am-4pm Tue-Fri, to 5pm Sat & Sun; 🚼) The world's largest of its kind, with evocatively landscaped train sets.

◉ Old Town & Mission Valley

In 1769 a band of Spanish soldiers and missionaries, led by Franciscan friar Junípero Serra, founded the first of California's 21 historic mission churches on San Diego's

Presidio Hill. A small pueblo (village) grew up around it, but the spot turned out to be less than ideal for a mission. In 1774 the mission moved upriver, closer to a steady water supply and fertile land.

★ Old Town State Historic Park
HISTORIC SITE

(☑ 619-220-5422; www.parks.ca.gov; 4002 Wallace St; ☺ visitor center & museums 10am-4pm Oct-Apr, to 5pm May-Sep; P) FREE This open-air park preserves five original adobe buildings and several recreated structures from the first pueblo, including a schoolhouse and newspaper office. Most buildings now contain museums, shops or restaurants. The visitor center offers free guided walking tours at 11am and 2pm daily.

Mission Basilica San Diego de Alcalá
CHURCH

(☑ 619-281-8449; www.missionsandiego.com; 10818 San Diego Mission Rd; adult/child $3/1; ☺ 9am-4:45pm; P) Secluded in a corner of what's now called Mission Valley, California's 'Mother of the Missions' hides beautifully restored buildings in bougainvillea gardens with views over the valley to the ocean.

Junípero Serra Museum
MUSEUM

(☑ 619-232-6203; www.sandiegohistory.org; 2727 Presidio Dr; adult/child $6/3; ☺ 10am-4pm Sat & Sun mid-Sep–May, 10am-5pm Fri-Sun Jun–mid-Sep; P ♿) Atop Presidio Hill, in a handsome 1920s Spanish Revival building, multicultural historical exhibits highlight life during the city's rough-and-tumble early days.

◉ Point Loma

This pretty peninsula wraps around the entrance to crescent-shaped San Diego Bay.

Cabrillo National Monument
MONUMENT

(☑ 619-557-5450; www.nps.gov/cabr; 1800 Cabrillo Memorial Dr; per car $5; ☺ 9am-5pm, last entry 4:30pm; P) Soak up bay panoramas or go hiking and tide pooling at this monument, which honors the leader of the first Spanish exploration of the West Coast in 1542. The Old Point Loma Lighthouse (1854) here is now a tiny historical museum.

◉ Mission Bay & Beaches

San Diego's big three beach towns all have ribbons of hedonism where armies of tanned, taut bodies frolic in the sand.

West of amoeba-shaped Mission Bay, surf-friendly **Mission Beach** and its northern neighbor, **Pacific Beach** (aka 'PB'), are connected by car-free **Ocean Front Walk**, which swarms with skaters, joggers and cyclists year-round. Mission Beach's pint-sized **Belmont Park** (☑ 858-458-1549; www.belmontpark.com; 3146 Mission Blvd; per ride $2-6, all-day pass adult/child $27/16; ☺ from 11am daily, closing time varies; P) beckons with a historic wooden roller coaster, wave simulators and an indoor pool.

South of Mission Bay, bohemian **Ocean Beach** ('OB') has a fishing pier, beach volleyball and good surf. Its main drag, **Newport Ave**, is chockablock with scruffy bars, flip-flop eateries and shops selling surf gear, tattoos, vintage clothing and antiques.

SeaWorld San Diego
THEME PARK

(☑ 800-257-4268; www.seaworld.com/seaworld/ ca; 500 SeaWorld Dr; adult/child 3-9yr $70/62; ☺ 9am-10pm Sun-Thu, to 11pm Fri-Sat mid-Jun– mid-Aug, shorter hours rest of year; P ♿) It's easy to spend a day at Mission Bay's four-star attraction. The biggest draws are live animal shows, but there are also zoolike animal exhibits and a few amusement-park rides. Recent controversy about SeaWorld's safety policies after the death of a trainer, along with questions about the ethics of keeping killer whales and dolphins in captivity, have arisen. Parking is $15.

◉ La Jolla

Facing one of SoCal's loveliest sweeps of coastline, wealthy La Jolla (la-*hoy*-ah ; Spanish for 'the jewel') possesses shimmering beaches and an upscale downtown filled with boutiques. Oceanfront diiversions include the **Children's Pool** (no longer for swimming, it's now home to barking sea lions), kayaking and exploring sea caves at **La Jolla Cove** and snorkeling at **San Diego-La Jolla Underwater Park**.

Torrey Pines State Natural Reserve
PARK

(☑ 858-755-2063; www.torreypine.org; 12600 N Torrey Pines Rd, La Jolla; per car $10; ☺ 7:15am-dusk, visitor center 10am-4pm Oct-Apr, 9am-6pm May-Sep; P) ✿ Up the coast near Del Mar, this wildlife reserve protects endangered Torrey pine trees and is perfect for ocean-view hikes and bird-watching.

Birch Aquarium at Scripps AQUARIUM
(☏858-534-3474; http://aquarium.ucsd.edu;
2300 Exhibition Way, La Jolla; adult/child $14/9.50;
☺9am-5pm; P♿) ⚓ University-run ocean-
front aquarium for kids uncovers tide-pool
and kelp-forest displays, floating seahorses
and a shark reef.

MCASD La Jolla MUSEUM
(☏858-454-3541; www.mcasd.org; 700 Prospect
St, La Jolla; adult/child $10/free, 5-7pm 3rd Thu of
month free; ☺11am-5pm Thu-Tue, to 7pm 3rd Thu of
month) Sister venue of Downtown's contemporary art museum (same ticket valid for
seven-day entry to both).

🏃 Activities

Surfing and windsurfing are both excellent,
although in some areas territorial locals
are a major irritation. For surf reports, call
☏619-221-8824.

Pacific Beach Surf School SURFING
(☏858-373-1138; www.pbsurfshop.com; 4150 Mission Blvd; ☺store 9am-7pm, lessons hourly until
4pm) Learn to hang 10 (private lesson $85)
or just rent a board and wet suit (half-day
from $35) at SD's oldest surf shop.

Surf Diva SURFING
(☏858-454-8273; www.surfdiva.com; 2160 Avenida
de la Playa; ☺store 9am-5:30pm) In La Jolla,
women board riders teach newbies how to
shred with private lessons (from $75) and
weekend clinics.

OEX Dive & Kayak WATER SPORTS
(☏858-454-6195; www.oexcalifornia.com; 2243
Avenida de la Playa; ☺9am-6pm Mon-Fri, from 8am
Sat & Sun) For kayak, snorkel, scuba-diving
and stand-up paddleboarding (SUP) rentals
and guided tours, talk to La Jolla's one-stop
resource. There is a second location at **Mission Bay** (☏619-866-6129; www.oexcalifornia.
com; 1010 Santa Clara Pl; ☺8am-6pm Mon-Fri,
9am-5pm Sat & Sun).

**Hike, Bike, Kayak
San Diego** ADVENTURE SPORTS
(☏858-551-9510; www.hikebikekayak.com; 2216
Avenida de la Playa) Just what it says: hiking,
cycling and kayaking tours, plus stand-up
paddleboarding lessons and water-sports
gear and bicycle rentals. Based in La Jolla.

👉 Tours

Another Side of San Diego GUIDED TOUR
(Map p936; ☏619-239-2111; www.anotherside-
ofsandiegotours.com; 308 G St; tours from $30)

Gaslamp Quarter food and history walking
tours and Segway tours all over town.

Old Town Trolley Tours TOUR
(☏888-910-8687; www.trolleytours.com; adult/
child $36/18) Hop-on, hop-off narrated loop
around the city's main tourist attractions.

🛏 Sleeping

Rates skyrocket in summer, especially by the
beaches. Chain hotels and motels cluster inland off major freeways and in Mission Valley. Expect a 10.5% lodging tax.

🛏 Downtown

HI San Diego Downtown Hostel HOSTEL $
(Map p936; ☏619-525-1531; www.sandiegohos-
tels.org; 521 Market St; dm/d with shared bath incl
breakfast from $31/75; ❋@🛜) At this well-run
hostel inside a 19th-century hotel, there's
loads of space to socialize. Dorms lack
pizazz, but they're clean. Rates include a
pancake breakfast. Quieter second location
at **Point Loma** (☏619-223-4778; www.sandiego-
hostels.org; 3790 Udall St; dm/r with shared bath
incl breakfast $25/54; P@🛜).

★USA Hostels San Diego HOSTEL $
(Map p936; ☏800-438-8622, 619-232-3100; www.
usahostels.com; 726 5th Ave; dm/r with shared bath
incl breakfast from $30/71; @🛜) In a converted
Victorian-era brothel, this Gaslamp hostel
sports cheerful rooms, a shared kitchen and
a lounge for chilling. Rates include a pancake
breakfast. Taco dinners and Tijuana tours
are cheap.

500 West Hotel HOSTEL $
(Map p936; ☏info 619-234-5252, reservations
619-231-4092; www.500westhotelsd.com; 500
W Broadway; s/d with shared bath from $59/79;
@🛜) Rooms are shoebox-sized and baths
are down the hallway in this renovated
1920s YMCA, but hipsters on a budget love
the bright decor, communal kitchen and fitness gym ($5).

★Hotel Indigo BOUTIQUE HOTEL $$
(Map p936; ☏619-727-4000; www.hotelinsd.
com; 509 9th Ave; r from $149; P❋@🛜🐾)
⚓ San Diego's first hotel to be certified by
Leadership in Energy & Environmental De-
sign (LEED), this Gaslamp boutique hotel
is smartly designed. Popping with vibrant
color, room decor is contempo-chic, with
huge floor-to-ceiling windows, rain showers
and hardwood floors. Parking is $38. Second
location in coastal Del Mar.

Hotel Vyant
B&B $$

(📞800-518-9930; www.hotelvyant.com; 505 W Grape St; r with/without bath from $149/109; 🌐🏠) This pretty Little Italy B&B is a charming place to hang your hat. Two dozen rooms all have inviting beds and bathrobes; deluxe rooms come with a whirlpool tub or kitchenette. Upgrade to an urban-chic apartment for a full kitchen.

🛏 Beaches

Pearl
MOTEL $$

(📞619-226-6100, 877-732-7574; www.thepearlsd.com; 1410 Rosecrans St; r from $130; P🌐🏠🏊) A mash-up of a boutique hotel and a 1960s motel, this swingin' crash-pad pulls in cool cats. Every sassy room comes with its own pet goldfish, and the tiniest digs have mirrored ceilings. Poolside movie nights and a cocktail bar keep things buzzing. Limited self-parking $10.

Best Western Island Palms
MOTEL $$

(📞800-922-2336, 619-222-0561; www.islandpalms.com; 2051 Shelter Island Dr; r from $149; P🌐@🏠🏊🍴) Gaze out over the bobbing boats of the marina at this tiki-inspired motor lodge on Shelter Island, right across the bay from Downtown. Say aloha to tropical-island style in crisp rooms with balconies swathed by sea breezes.

Ocean Beach Hotel
HOTEL $$

(📞619-223-7191; www.obhotel.com; 5080 Newport Ave; r from $100; 🌐🏠🏊) In surf-shabby OB, this remodeled courtyard hotel is across the street from the beach. Spotless guest rooms with mini fridges and microwaves are small and the French-provincial look is a tad dated.

★ Hotel del Coronado
LUXURY HOTEL $$$

(📞619-435-6611, 800-468-3533; www.hoteldel.com; 1500 Orange Ave; r from $325; P🌐@🏠🏊) San Diego's iconic hotel, the Del provides more than a century of star-spangled history, plus tennis courts, a spa, shops, splashy restaurants, manicured grounds and a white-sand beach. The original Victorian building lacks ocean views. Parking is $30.

Crystal Pier Hotel & Cottages
COTTAGE $$$

(📞800-748-5894, 619-483-6983; www.crystalpier.com; 4500 Ocean Blvd; d from $175; P🏠🍴) White clapboard, blue-shuttered cottages with kitchenettes – some built in the 1930s – sit right atop Pacific Beach's oceanfront Crystal Pier, offering one-of-a-kind sea views from private decks. Book up to 11 months in advance.

Tower23
BOUTIQUE HOTEL $$$

(📞866-869-3723; www.t23hotel.com; 723 Felspar St; r from $249; 🌐@🏠🏊) A mod and modernist showplace for an ubercool beach stay, this boxy, bold white hotel is splashed with lots of teals and mint blues – and a sense of humor. Catch sunset from the rooftop deck and cocktail bar. Parking is $20.

Inn at Sunset Cliffs
HOTEL $$$

(📞866-786-2453, 619-222-7901; www.innatsunsetcliffs.com; 1370 Sunset Cliffs Blvd; r/ste from $175/289; P🌐@🏠🏊🍴) Hear the surf crashing onto the rocky shore at this breezy 1960s oceanfront charmer wrapped around a flower-bedecked courtyard. Recently renovated rooms are light-filled but on the small side; some suites have a kitchen.

🍴 Eating

San Diego's dynamic dining scene caters to all tastes and budgets. Generally speaking, you'll find fine steakhouses and seafood institutions near Downtown's waterfront, boisterous gastropubs in the Gaslamp Quarter, casual seafood and burgers by the beach, hip kitchens in neighborhoods around Balboa Park, and tacos and margaritas, well, everywhere.

🍴 Downtown & Embarcadero

Neighborhood
PUB $$

(Map p936; www.neighborhoodsd.com; 777 G St; mains $7-14; ☺noon-midnight) More down-to-earth than other trendy gastropubs, this corner joint churns out crowd-pleasers like smoky chipotle burgers, kicky jalapeno mac 'n' cheese and hot dogs with braised pork and fried egg. Order a pint of microbrewed beer that's hoppy, fruity, malty or sour.

Underbelly
ASIAN, FUSION $$

(📞619-269-4626; 750 W Fir St; dishes $5-12; ☺11:30am-midnight) Off Little Italy's bustling strip of pizzerias and wine bars, this sleek noodle shop loads up steaming bowls of ramen with oxtail dumplings, hoisin-glazed short ribs and smoked brisket and bacon (vegetarian versions available). Two dozen craft beers on tap.

Cafe 21
BREAKFAST $$

(Map p936; 📞619-795-0721; www.cafe-21.com; 750 5th Ave; breakfast mains $9-15; ☺8am-10pm Sun-Thu, to 11pm Fri & Sat; 🍴) The Gaslamp's favorite brunch stop slings stuffed French toast with agave cream cheese, fruit-topped pancakes and farm-fresh egg frittatas served in mini iron skillets. Housemade sangria rocks.

Island Prime SEAFOOD, STEAKHOUSE **$$$**
(☑619-298-6802; www.islandprime.com; 880 Harbor Island Dr; mains restaurant $25-52, lounge $15-30; ☺restaurant 5-9pm Sun-Thu, to 10pm Fri & Sat, lounge from 11:30am daily) The bay views are panoramic at this elegant seafood restaurant on Harbor Island, west of Downtown. Ever-popular dishes include the lobster BLT sandwich, seared tuna stack and shrimp with grits. Weekday happy hour in C Level lounge offers $5 'bites, brews and libations.'

🍴 Balboa Park & Around

⭐**Carnitas' Snack Shack** CALIFORNIAN, MEXICAN **$**
(http://carnitassnackshack.com; 2632 University Ave; mains $7-9; ☺noon-midnight Wed-Mon; ♿) Like a food truck that has rolled to a stop in happening North Park, this dressed-down shack has a daily-changing menu of all things porky: carnitas tacos, pork burgers with bacon jam, pork schnitzel sandwiches, pulled pork poutine with bacon crumble etc.

Bread & Cie BAKERY, CAFE **$**
(www.breadandcie.com; 350 University Ave; mains $5-11; ☺7am-7pm Mon-Fri, to 6pm Sat, 8am-6pm Sun; ℗) Crusty sandwiches, salads, French quiche and decadent pastries (try a ridiculously oversized *pain au chocolat*) make this busy bakery-cafe a Hillcrest institution. Free parking in rear lot.

⭐**Buona Forchetta** ITALIAN **$$**
(www.buonaforchettasd.com; 3001 Beech St; pizzas $7-15, small plates $5-13; ☺5-10pm Sun & Tue-Thu, to 11pm Fri & Sat; 🧒) A gold-painted brick wood-fired oven custom-built in Italy delivers authentic Neapolitan pizzas straight to merrily jammed-together tables at this South Park trattoria with a dog-friendly patio. Leafy salads, handmade pasta and sweet *dolci* (desserts) are just as satisfying. No reservations.

Hash House a Go Go AMERICAN **$$**
(☑619-298-4646; www.hashhouseagogo.com; 3628 5th Ave; mains breakfast $9-18, dinner $15-29; ☺7.30am-2pm Mon-Fri, to 2:30pm Sat & Sun,

dinner 5:30-9pm Tue-Thu, to 9:30pm Fri-Sun; ♿) This Hillcrest bungalow makes towering plates of 'twisted farm food': sausage-gravy pot pie, gianormous meatloaf sandwiches, tractor-wheel-sized pancakes and potato hash seven different ways. Come hungry for brunch.

⭐**Prado** CALIFORNIAN **$$$**
(☑619-557-9441; www.pradobalboa.com; House of Hospitality, 1549 El Prado; mains lunch $12-21, dinner $22-35; ☺11:30am-3pm Mon-Fri, from 11am Sat & Sun, 5-9pm Sun & Tue-Thu, to 10pm Fri & Sat) This sought-after Balboa Park spot spices up fresh Cal-Mediterranean cuisine with Latin and Asian touches, from the seafood paella and chorizo pork burgers to chopped salads. Breezy outdoor seating and a colorfully tiled interior are equally inviting. Happy-hour food and drinks are a steal.

🍴 Beaches

South Beach Bar & Grille SEAFOOD, MEXICAN **$**
(www.southbeachob.com; 5059 Newport Ave, Ocean Beach; most dishes $3-12; ☺11am-2am) Maybe it's the lightly fried mahi and wahoo fish. Or the zippy white sauce. Or layered fresh cabbage and peppery tomato salsa. Whatever the secret, the fish tacos (discounted on Tuesdays) at this raucous beachside bar really stand out.

Hodad's BURGERS **$**
(www.hodadies.com; 5010 Newport Ave, Ocean Beach; dishes $3-10; ☺11am-9pm Sun-Thu, to 10pm Fri & Sat) OB's legendary burger joint serves great shakes, massive baskets of onion rings and paper-wrapped hamburgers. The walls are covered in license plates and your bearded, tattooed server might sidle right into your booth to take your order. Also has a branch in **Downtown** (Map p936; 945 Broadway Ave; ☺11am-9pm Sun-Thu, to 10pm Fri & Sat).

Point Loma Seafoods SEAFOOD **$$**
(http://pointlomaseafoods.com; 2805 Emerson St; dishes $3-16, mains $9-13; ☺9am-7pm Mon-Sat, from 10am Sun; ℗♿) Stroll up and order right at the counter inside this fish market, grill and deli with a sushi bar, where almost everything is fresh off the boat. It's a briny San Diego institution, with picnic tables outside.

★ **George's at the Cove** CALIFORNIAN $$$
(☎858-454-4244; www.georgesatthecove.com; 1250 Prospect St, La Jolla; mains $18-50; ⏰11am-10pm Mon-Thu, to 11pm Fri-Sun) George's has graced just about every list of top restaurants in California, and chef Trey Foshee's Euro-Cal cuisine is as dramatic as the oceanfront location. Three venues allow you to enjoy it at stratospherically ascending price points: **George's Bar** (lunch mains $10-18), **Ocean Terrace** (dinner mains $18-35) and **California Modern** (dinner mains $30-50). Walk-ins welcome at the bar (hit happy hour from 3:30pm to 6:30pm weekdays).

🍷 Drinking & Entertainment

Downtown's Gaslamp Quarter has the rowdiest bars and hottest nightclubs. Check the *San Diego Reader* (www.sandiegoreader. com) or *U-T San Diego* (www.utsandiego. com) for the latest happenings around town. **Arts Tix** (Map p936; ☎858-381-5595; www.sdarts tix.com; Lyceum Theatre, 79 Horton Plaza; ⏰hours vary) sells half-price and discounted tickets to performing arts events, including plays, comedy shows, music concerts and more.

Prohibition LOUNGE
(Map p936; www.prohibitionsd.com; 548 5th Ave; ⏰7pm-2am Wed-Sat) Sophisticated 1930s-style bar takes music and cocktails seriously. The house rules aren't a joke either: no cell phones at the bar and a strict dress code. Live jazz, blues, soul sounds or tiki tunes after 9pm.

Noble Experiment BAR
(Map p936; ☎619-888-4713; http://nobleex-perimentsd.com; 777 G St; ⏰7pm-2am Tue-Sun) Knock on the hidden door of this contempo speakeasy with gold skulls adorning the walls and a 400-strong cocktail list. Text a week ahead for a reservation and cryptic directions.

Hamilton's Tavern BAR
(http://hamiltonstavern.com; 1521 30th St; ⏰3pm-2am Mon-Fri, from 1pm Sat & Sun; 🐾) Detour to the South Park 'hood and squeeze yourself onto a barstool at this low-key hangout with shuffleboard, pool, A+ pub grub and and a head-spinning menu of craft beers.

Tipsy Crow BAR
(Map p936; ☎619-338-9300; http://thetipsycrow. com; 770 5th Ave; ⏰3pm-2am Mon-Fri, from noon Sat & Sun) In a historic Gaslamp building, this atmospheric watering hole has a loungelike 'Nest' (rumored to have been a brothel) and brick-walled 'Underground' dance floor with rockin' live bands and comedy acts.

Casbah LIVE MUSIC
(☎619-232-4355; www.casbahmusic.com; 2501 Kettner Blvd; tickets $5-45) MGMT, Liz Phair and the Smashing Pumpkins all rocked the funky Casbah on their way up the charts. Catch local bands and indie-rock headliners here and at the legendary **Belly Up** (☎858-481-8140; www.bellyup.com; 143 S Cedros Ave, Solana Beach; tickets $10-45) in Solana Beach.

DON'T MISS

SAN DIEGO'S MICROBREWERIES

San Diegans take their craft beers seriously – even at a dive bar, you might overhear local beer geeks debating the merits of 'hoppiness' and cask conditioning. Gargantuan to garage-sized microbreweries around the city specialize in all kinds of brews. Check out the following:

Stone Brewing Company (☎760-471-4999; www.stonebrew.com; 1999 Citracado Pkwy, Escondido; ⏰tours noon-6pm daily) Take a tour ($3) before tasting the Oaked Arrogant Bastard Ale and Old Guardian Barley Wine.

Lost Abbey (☎800-918-6816; www.lostabbey.com; Suite 104, 155 Mata Way, San Marcos; ⏰1-6pm Mon-Tue, to 9pm Wed & Fri, to 8pm Thu, 11:30am-8pm Sat, noon-7pm Sun) More than 20 brews ($1 per taste) are on tap in the tasting room, including the Belgian-style ales Judgment Day and Red Barn.

Green Flash (☎858-622-0085; www.greenflashbrew.com; 6550 Mira Mesa Blvd; ⏰3-9pm Tue-Thu, to 10pm Fri, noon-9pm Sat, noon-6pm Sun) Sip American and Belgian ales ($1 per taste) in an outdoor beer garden; book ahead online for tours ($5).

AleSmith (☎858-549-9888; www.alesmith.com; 9366 Cabot Dr; ⏰2-8pm Tue-Thu, to 9pm Fri, 11am-8pm Sat, 11am-6pm Sun) The Scotch ale Wee Heavy, citrusy Horny Devil and Speedway Stout ($1 to $2 per taste) are addictive.

La Jolla Playhouse THEATER
(☑858-550-1010; www.lajollaplayhouse.org; 2910 La Jolla Village Dr; tickets $15-70) Award-winning plays and world-premiere musicals that sometimes go on to shine brightly on Broadway take over multiple stages inside this coastal performing arts center.

❶ Information

INTERNET ACCESS

Coffee shops offer wi-fi with purchase (sometimes for free).

San Diego Public Library (☑619-236-5800; www.sandiego.gov/public-library; 820 E St; ⊙noon-8pm Mon & Wed, 9:30am-5:30pm Tue & Thu-Fri, 9:30am-2:30pm Sat, 1-5pm Sun; @ 🛜) Free wi-fi and public internet terminals. Call or check the website for branch locations.

MEDIA

San Diego Magazine (www.sandiegomagazine. com) Glossy monthly lifestyle magazine.
San Diego Reader (www.sandiegoreader.com) Free alternative weekly tabloid.
U-T San Diego (www.utsandiego.com) The city's major daily newspaper.

MEDICAL SERVICES

Scripps Mercy Hospital (☑619-294-8111; www.scripps.org; 4077 5th Ave) Has a 24-hour emergency room.

MONEY

TravelEx (www.travelex.com) Foreign currency-exchange services are at the airport (p943), Downtown (☑619-235-0901; www.travelex. com; 177 Horton Plaza; ⊙10am-7pm Mon-Fri, to 6pm Sat, 11am-4pm Sun), Fashion Valley (☑619-542-1173; www.travelex.com; 7007 Friars Rd; ⊙10am-9pm Mon-Sat, 11am-7pm Sun) and La Jolla (☑858-457-2412; www. travelex.com; University Town Centre, 4417 La Jolla Village Dr; ⊙10am-7pm Mon-Fri, to 6pm Sat, 11am-4pm Sun).

TOURIST INFORMATION

Balboa Park Visitors Center (☑619-239-0512; www.balboapark.org; House of Hospitality, 1549 El Prado; ⊙9:30am-4:30pm) Buy discounted one-day ($39) and seven-day (adult/child $39/27, including zoo $85/49) passports to park museums.
San Diego Visitor Information Centers (☑619-236-1212; www.sandiego.org) Downtown (Map p936; 1140 N Harbor Dr; ⊙9am-5pm Jun-Sep, to 4pm Oct-May) La Jolla (☑858-454-5718; www.sandiego.org; 7966 Herschel Ave; ⊙11am-6pm Jun-Sep, to 4pm Oct-May) Downtown's waterfront location sells discounted attraction and tour tickets.

WEBSITES

Gaslamp Quarter Association (http:// gaslamp.org) Everything about the bustling Gaslamp Quarter, including parking tips.
San Diego Convention & Visitors Bureau (www.sandiego.org) Official tourist info site.

❶ Getting There & Away

Served mainly by domestic US and Mexico flights, **San Diego International Airport** (SAN; ☑619-400-2404; www.san.org; 3325 N Harbor Dr) sits 3 miles northwest of downtown.

Greyhound (Map p936; ☑619-515-1100; www.greyhound.com; 1313 National Ave) has hourly direct buses to Los Angeles ($19, two to three hours).

Amtrak (☑800-872-7245; www.amtrak.com) runs the *Pacific Surfliner* several times daily to Los Angeles ($37, 2¾ hours) and Santa Barbara ($41, 5¾ hours) from downtown's historic **Santa Fe Depot** (1055 Kettner Blvd).

Major international car-rental companies have desks at the airport. Smaller, independent **West Coast Rent a Car** (☑619-544-0606; http:// sandiegoautos.org; 834 W Grape St; ⊙9am-6pm Mon-Sat, to 5pm Sun) rents to under-25s, with free airport pick-ups.

❶ Getting Around

City buses ($2.25 to $2.50) and trolleys ($2.25), including south to the Mexico border, are operated by **Metropolitan Transit System** (MTS; ☑619-557-4555; www.sdmts.com). MTS's **Transit Store** (Map p936; ☑619-234-1060; 102 Broadway; ⊙9am-5pm Mon-Fri) sells regional passes ($5/9/12/15 for one/two/three/four days); purchase one-day passes on-board buses.

MTS bus 992 ($2.25) runs every 15 to 30 minutes between the airport and downtown from 5am to 11pm daily. Airport shuttles such as the **Super Shuttle** (☑800-258-3826; www.supershuttle. com) charge $8 to $10 to downtown. An airport taxi to downtown averages $10 to $15, plus tip.

Metered taxis charge $2.80 at flag fall, then $3 per mile.

Around San Diego

San Diego Zoo Safari Park

Take a walk on the 'wild' side at this 1800-acre open-range zoo (☑760-747-8702; www. sdzsafaripark.org; 15500 San Pasqual Valley Rd; adult/child from $44/34, 2-day ticket incl San Diego Zoo $79/61; ⊙9am-7pm late Jun–mid-Aug, to 5pm or 6pm rest of year; 🅿 ♿). Giraffes graze, lions lounge and rhinos roam more or less freely on the valley floor. For that instant safari feel, board the Africa tram ride, which tours you around the second-largest continent in just 25 minutes.

The park is in Escondido, about 35 miles northeast of Downtown San Diego. Take the I-15 Fwy to the Via Rancho Pkwy exit, then follow the signs. Parking is $10.

Legoland

This fun fantasy theme park (☑760-918-5346; http://california.legoland.com; 1 Legoland Dr, Carlsbad; adult/child from $78/68; ⊙daily mid-Mar–Aug, Wed-Sun only Sep–mid-Mar, seasonal hours vary; ℗) of rides, shows and attractions is mostly suited to the elementary-school set. Tots can dig for dinosaur bones, pilot helicopters and earn their driver's license. Families with young children can overnight in the brand-new, colorful Lego-themed hotel. From Downtown San Diego (about 33 miles), take the I-5 Fwy north to Carlsbad's Cannon Rd exit. Parking is $15.

PALM SPRINGS & THE DESERTS

From swanky Palm Springs to desolate Death Valley, Southern California's desert region swallows 25% of the entire state. At first what seems harrowingly barren may eventually be transformed in your mind's eye to perfect beauty: weathered volcanic peaks, booming sand dunes, purple-tinged mountains, cactus gardens, tiny wildflowers pushing up from hard-baked soil in spring, lizards scurrying beside colossal boulders, and in the night sky uncountable stars. California's deserts are serenely spiritual, surprisingly chic and ultimately irresistible, whether you're a bohemian artist, movie star, rock climber or 4WD adventurer.

Palm Springs

The Rat Pack is back, baby – or, at least, its hangout is. In the 1950 and '60s, Palm Springs (population 45,573), some 100 miles east of LA, was the swinging getaway of Sinatra, Elvis and other stars. Once the Rat Pack packed it in, however, Palm Springs surrendered to retirees in golf clothing. Recently a new generation has rediscovered the city's retro-chic charms: kidney-shaped pools, 'starchitect' bungalows, midcentury-modern boutique hotels and bars serving perfect martinis. Today retirees mix comfortably with hipsters and a significant lesbigay community.

⊙ Sights & Activities

Palm Springs is the hub of the Coachella Valley, a string of desert towns along Hwy 111. In PS' compact downtown, one-way southbound Palm Canyon Dr is paralleled by northbound Indian Canyon Dr.

★ Palm Springs Aerial Tramway   CABLE CAR
(☑888-515-8726; www.pstramway.com; 1 Tram Way; adult/child $24/17; ⊙10am-8pm Mon-Fri, from 8am Sat & Sun, last tram down 9:45pm) Enjoy dizzying views as you're whisked 2.5 miles from sunbaked desert to a pine-scented alpine wonderland atop Mt San Jacinto. It gets chilly up here, so bring a jacket. Hiking trails wind through the adjacent wilderness, or rent snowshoes and cross-country skis at the Mountain Station's Winter Adventure Center (snowshoe/skis rental per day $18/21; ⊙10am-4pm Thu-Fri & Mon, from 9am Sat & Sun, last rentals 2:30pm).

Living Desert Zoo & Gardens   ZOO
(☑760-346-5694; www.livingdesert.org; 47900 Portola Ave, Palm Desert, off Hwy 111; adult/child $17.25/8.75; ⊙9am-5pm Oct-May, 8am-1:30pm Jun-Sep) 🐾 At this engaging zoo off Hwy 111, kids can spy on North American and African wildlife, take a spin on the endangered species carousel and walk through a wildlife hospital. It's worth the 30-minute drive down-valley.

Palm Springs Art Museum   MUSEUM
(☑760-322-4800; www.psmuseum.org; 101 Museum Dr; adult/child $12.50/free, 4-8pm Thu free; ⊙10am-5pm Tue-Wed & Fri-Sun, noon-8pm Thu) Downtown's art beacon views the evolution of American painting, sculpture, photography and architecture over the past century or so. Second location in Palm Desert.

Palm Springs Air Museum   MUSEUM
(☑760-778-6262; www.air-museum.org; 745 N Gene Autry Trail; adult/child $15/8; ⊙10am-5pm) An exceptional collection of WWII aircraft, flight memorabilia and photos near the airport.

Tahquitz Canyon   HIKING
(☑760-416-7044; www.tahquitzcanyon.com; 500 W Mesquite Ave; adult/child $12.50/6; ⊙7:30am-5pm Oct-Jun, Fri-Sun only Jul-Sep) Featured in Frank Capra's 1937 movie Lost Horizon, this canyon is famous for its seasonal waterfall and ancient rock art. Explore on your own or join a ranger-guided hike.

Indian Canyons   HIKING
(☑760-323-6018; www.indian-canyons.com; off S
Palm Canyon Dr; adult/child $9/5, 90min guided
hike $3/2; ☺8am-5pm Oct-Jun, Fri-Sun only Jul-
Sep) Shaded by fan palms and flanked by
soaring cliffs, these ancestral lands of the
Cahuilla people are a desert hiker's delight,
especially during spring wildflower blooms.

Knott's Soak City   SWIMMING
(☑760-327-0499; www.soakcityps.com; 1500 S
Gene Autry Trail; adult/child $35/25; ☺hours vary,
mid-Apr–early Oct) Keep cool on hot days with
Knott's massive wave pool, towering water
slides and tube rides. Buy discount tickets
online. Parking is $12.

🛏 Sleeping

High-season winter rates are quoted below; rates drop midweek and during summer. Chain motels hug Hwy 111 southeast of
downtown. Book ahead.

Caliente Tropics   MOTEL $
(☑800-658-6034, 760-327-1391; www.caliente-
tropics.com; 411 E Palm Canyon Dr; r from $60;
🕸☀♨🐕) Tiki-style motor lodge, where
Elvis once frolicked poolside, shelters surprisingly spacious rooms with comfy beds.

★Orbit In   BOUTIQUE HOTEL $$
(☑877-966-7248, 760-323-3585; www.orbitin.
com; 562 W Arenas Rd; r incl breakfast from $149;
🕸☀♨) Swing back to the Rat Pack era at
this quintessential mid-century modern
property set around a saline pool and hot
tub. Rooms sport designer furniture (Eames,
Noguchi et al), while freebies include cocktail hour, daytime sodas and snacks, and
cruiser bicycles to borrow.

Del Marcos Hotel   BOUTIQUE HOTEL $$
(☑800-676-1214, 760-325-6902; www.delmar-
coshotel.com; 225 W Baristo Rd; r incl breakfast
$139-189; 🕸☀♨🐕) At this 1947 gem de-
signed by William F Cody, groovy tunes ush-
er you toward a saltwater pool and ineffably
chic rooms (some have kitchenettes) named
for mid-century modern architectural luminaries. Complimentary beach cruisers for
guests. No kids allowed.

Ace Hotel & Swim Club   HOTEL $$
(☑760-325-9900; www.acehotel.com/palm-
springs; 701 E Palm Canyon Dr; r from $100;
🕸@♨☀🐕) Get all the sass *sans* attitude
at this hipster hangout. Rooms (many with
patios) sport a glorified cabana-shack look
and are crammed with digerati lifestyle es-

sentials. Laughable karaoke, trivia and bingo nights, with DJs and live bands to boot.

El Morocco Inn & Spa   BOUTIQUE HOTEL $$$
(☑760-288-2527, 888-288-9905; www.elmoroc-
coinn.com; 66814 4th St, Desert Hot Springs; r incl
breakfast $179-219; 🕸☀♨) Heed the call of
the kasbah at this exotic adult-only hideaway whose 10 rooms wrap around a pool
deck. Perks include a spa, natural-springs
pool and homemade mint tea and 'Morocco-
tinis.' It's a 20-minute drive north of PS.

🍴 Eating

Some restaurants keep shorter hours and
close for a few weeks in summer.

Tyler's Burgers   BURGERS $
(http://tylersburgers.com; 149 S Indian Canyon Dr;
dishes $2-9; ☺11am-4pm Mon-Sat; 🐕) The best
burgers in town. 'Nuff said. Expect a line.

Native Foods   VEGAN $
(☑760-416-0070; www.nativefoods.com; Smoke
Tree Village, 1775 E Palm Canyon Dr; mains $8-
11; ☺11am-9:30pm Mon-Sat; 🍴🐕) Organic,
meatless and made-from-scratch salads,
wraps and bowls that don't sacrifice a lick
of taste.

★Cheeky's   CALIFORNIAN $$
(☑760-327-7595; www.cheekysps.com; 622 N
Palm Canyon Dr; mains $8-13; ☺8am-2pm Wed-
Mon, last seating 1:30pm) 🍃 Waits can be oh-
so long, but the seasonal and often organic
farm-to-table menu dazzles with its witty

inventiveness. Actual dishes change weekly, but tomatillo chilaquile plates, bacon 'flights' and pomegranate mimosas keep making appearances.

Sherman's
DELI, BAKERY $$

(☑760-325-1199; www.shermansdeli.com; 401 E Tahquitz Canyon Way; mains $8-18; ⊙7am-9pm; 🖪) With a breezy sidewalk patio, this 1950s kosher-style deli pulls in an all-ages crowd with its 40 sandwich varieties (great hot pastrami!), finger-lickin' rotisserie chicken and to-die-for pies. Also in **Palm Desert** (☑760-568-1350; www.shermansdeli.com; 73-161 County Club Dr; mains $8-18; ⊙7am-9pm; 🖪).

Trio
CALIFORNIAN $$$

(☑760-864-8746; www.triopalmsprings.com; 707 N Palm Canyon Dr; mains $13-29; ⊙11am-10pm) The winning formula at this 1960s modernist space equals updated American comfort food (Yankee pot roast and mac 'n' cheese), eye-catching artwork and picture windows. Three-course prix-fixe dinner ($19) before 6pm.

Copley's
AMERICAN $$$

(☑760-327-9555; www.copleyspalmsprings.com; 621 N Palm Canyon Dr; mains $19-39; ⊙from 5:30pm daily late Aug–mid-Jun, Tue-Sun only mid-Jun–early Jul, closed early Jul-Aug) Swoon-worthy American fare on the former Cary Grant estate. The 'Oh My Lobster Pot Pie' is unlikely to ever go out of style. Bring your sweetie and your platinum AmEx card.

🍷 Drinking & Entertainment

Arenas Rd, east of Indian Canyon Dr, is lesbi-gay nightlife central.

Koffi
CAFE

(www.kofficoffee.com; 1700 S Camino Real; ⊙5:30am-7pm) Minimalist coffee shop for gourmet baked goods, organic coffee and handcrafted espresso drinks. Also downtown at 515 N Palm Canyon Dr.

Birba
BAR

(www.birbaps.com; 622 N Palm Canyon Dr; ⊙5-11pm Sun & Wed-Thu, to midnight Fri & Sat) At this seductive cocktail lounge, floor-to-ceiling glass doors open onto a hedge-fringed patio with sunken fire pits.

Shanghai Red's
BAR

(www.fishermans.com; 235 S Indian Canyon Dr; ⊙4pm-late Mon-Sat, from noon Sun) Behind a seafood shack, this courtyard watering hole has happy-hour drink specials and live blues music on Friday and Saturday nights.

🛍 Shopping

For art galleries, modern design stores and fashion boutiques, including fabulous **Trina Turk** (☑760-416-2856; www.trinaturk.com; 891 N Palm Canyon Dr; ⊙10am-5pm Mon-Fri, to 6pm Sat, noon-5pm Sun), head 'Uptown' to North Palm Canyon Dr. If you're riding the retro wave, uncover treasures in thrift, vintage and consignment shops scattered around downtown and along Hwy 111. For a local version of Rodeo Dr, drive down-valley to Palm Desert's **El Paseo**.

ℹ Information

Desert Regional Medical Center (☑760-323-6511; www.desertregional.com; 1150 N Indian Canyon Dr) Has a 24-hour emergency room.

Palm Springs Library (www.palmspringsca.gov; 300 S Sunrise Way; ⊙10am-5pm Wed-Sat, to 7pm Tue; @ 🛜) Free wi-fi and public internet terminals.

Palm Springs Official Visitors Center (☑760-778-8418; www.visitpalmsprings.com; 2901 N Palm Canyon Dr; ⊙9am-5pm) Inside a 1965 Albert Frey–designed gas station at the tramway turnoff, 3 miles northwest of downtown.

ℹ Getting There & Around

About 3 miles east of downtown, **Palm Springs International Airport** (PSP; ☑760-323-8299; www.palmspringsairport.com; 3400 E Tahquitz Canyon Way) is served by US and Canadian airlines; major car-rental agencies are on-site.

Thrice-weekly Amtrak trains to/from LA ($40, 2¾ hours) stop at the unstaffed, kinda-creepy North Palm Springs station, 6 miles north of downtown, as do several daily Greyhound buses to/from LA ($26, three hours).

SunLine (www.sunline.org; fare/day pass $1/3) runs slow-moving local buses throughout the valley.

Joshua Tree National Park

Like figments from a Dr Seuss book, whimsical-looking Joshua trees (actually tree-sized yuccas) welcome visitors to this wilderness park where the Sonora and Mojave Deserts converge. You'll find most of the main attractions, including all of the Joshua trees, in the park's northern half. 'J-Tree' is perennially popular with rock climbers and day hikers, especially in spring when the trees bloom with cream-colored flowers. The mystical quality of this stark, boulder-strewn landscape has inspired countless artists, most famously the rock band U2.

⊙ Sights & Activities

Dominating the north side of the **park** (☎760-367-5500; www.nps.gov/jotr; 7-day entry per car $15), the epic **Wonderland of Rocks** calls to climbers. Sunset-worthy **Keys View** overlooks the San Andreas Fault and, on clear days, as far as Mexico. For pioneer history, tour **Keys Ranch** (☎reservations 760-367-5555; www.nps.gov/jotr; adult/child $5/2.50; ⊙10am & 1pm late Sep-early Apr). Hikers seek out native desert fan-palm oases like **49 Palms Oasis** (3-mile round-trip) and **Lost Palms Oasis** (7.2-mile round-trip). Kid-friendly nature trails include **Barker Dam** (1.3-mile loop), which passes Native American petroglyphs; **Skull Rock** (1.5-mile loop); and **Cholla Cactus Garden** (0.25-mile loop). For a scenic 4WD route, tackle bumpy 18-mile **Geology Tour Road**, which is also open to mountain bikers.

🛌 Sleeping

The park itself only has camping. Bunches of independent and chain motels line Hwy 62.

**Joshua Tree National
Park Campgrounds**   CAMPGROUND $
(www.nps.gov/jotr; camping & RV sites $10-15; 🌐🐾🚻) Of the park's nine campgrounds, only Cottonwood and Black Rock have potable water and flush toilets. Indian Cove and Black Rock accept **reservations** (☎518-885-3639, 877-444-6777; www.recreation.gov) from October to May. Other campgrounds are first-come, first-served, often filling by 10am in spring. **Joshua Tree Outfitters** (☎760-366-1848; www.joshuatreeoutfitters.com; 61707 Hwy 62) rents camping gear.

Harmony Motel   MOTEL $
(☎760-367-3351; www.harmonymotel.com; 71161 Hwy 62; r $65-90; 🌐@🚻🏊) Where U2 wrote its album *The Joshua Tree*, this minimalist motel is a bit designy, with oversized rooms and cabin decorated in a jumble of styles. There's a communal kitchenette and library.

★ Kate's Lazy Desert   INN $$
(☎845-688-7200; www.lazymeadow.com; 58380 Botkin Rd, Landers; d $175-200; 🌐🚻🏊🐾) Owned by Kate Pierson of the B-52s, this desert camp surrounds a petite pool. Six Airstream trailers are kitted out with a kitchenette and fanasta-pop design, from groovy tiki to woodsy lodge kitsch. It's a 30-minute drive north of Yucca Valley, near the wacky **Integratron** (☎760-364-3126; www.integratron.com; 2477 Belfield Boulevard, Landers; sound baths $20-80).

WORTH A TRIP

PIONEERTOWN

About 4.5 miles northwest of Yucca Valley, **Pioneertown** was built as a Hollywood movie set in 1946, and it hasn't changed much since. On Mane St, witness mock gunfights at 2:30pm on Saturdays from April to October. Enjoy BBQ, cheap beer and live music at honky-tonk **Pappy & Harriet's Pioneertown Palace** (☎760-365-5956; www.pappyandharriets.com; 53688 Pioneertown Rd; mains $8-29; ⊙11am-2am Thu-Sun, from 5pm Mon). Snooze at the **Pioneertown Motel** (☎760-365-7001; www.pioneertownmotel.com; 5040 Curtis Rd; r $70-120; 🌐🚻🏊), where old-time movie stars once slept. Simple rooms are crammed with Western-themed memorabilia.

Spin & Margie's Desert Hide-a-Way   INN $$
(☎760-366-9124; www.deserthideaway.com; 64491 Hwy 62; ste $135-175; 🌐🚻) Not far from the park, this hacienda-style inn encloses five boldly colored kitchenette suites with striking design using corrugated tin, old license plates and cartoon art. Two-night minimum stay required.

✕ Eating & Drinking

Natural Sisters Cafe   VEGETARIAN $
(☎760-366-3600; 61695 Hwy 62, Joshua Tree; dishes $4-8; ⊙7am-7pm; 🚻🐾) Fill up on fruit smoothies, garden-fresh salads, tofu wraps, vegan curries and homemade kombucha at this much-adored J-Tree cafe.

★ Palm Kabob House   MIDDLE EASTERN $$
(☎760-362-8583; 6341 Adobe Rd, Twentynine Palms; mains $6-14; ⊙11am-9pm; 🐾🚻) Hustle over to near Twentynine Palms' marine base for home-baked pita bread, lamb or chicken shwarma, refreshingly cool eggplant dip and vegetable salads.

Pie for the People   PIZZERIA $$
(http://pieforthepeople.com; 61740 Hwy 62, Joshua Tree; pizzas $13-25; ⊙11am-9pm Mon-Thu, to 10pm Fri & Sat, to 8pm Sun; 🚻) Chew thin-crust NYC-style pizzas, calzones and other stuff-your-face Italian-American fare, just outside the park.

Ma Rouge   CAFE
(www.marouge.net; 55844 Hwy 62, Yucca Valley; ⊙7am-6pm) Swing by this community coffee house for organic coffee, espresso and baked goods.

ℹ Information

Pick up park information at NPS visitor centers at **Joshua Tree** (6554 Park Blvd; ☉8am-5pm), **Oasis** (74485 National Park Dr; ☉8am-5pm) and **Cottonwood** (Cottonwood Springs, 8 miles north of I-10 Fwy; ☉9am-3pm) and at **Black Rock Nature Center** (9800 Black Rock Canyon Rd; ☉8am-4pm Sat-Thu, noon-8pm Fri Oct-May ; 🖭). There are no park facilities aside from restrooms. Get gas and stock up in the three desert communities linked by the Twentynine Palms Hwy (Hwy 62) along the park's northern boundary: down-to-earth Yucca Valley, which has the most services (banks, supermarkets, post office, public library with free wi-fi and internet terminals etc); beatnik Joshua Tree, where outdoor outfitters cluster; and Twentynine Palms, home of the USA's largest marine base.

Anza-Borrego Desert State Park

Shaped by an ancient sea and tectonic forces, Anza-Borrego is the largest state park in the USA outside Alaska. Cradling the park's only commercial hub – tiny Borrego Springs (pop 3429) – are 600,000 acres of mountains, canyons and badlands; a fabulous variety of plants and wildlife; and intriguing historical relics of Native American tribes, Spanish explorers and gold-rush pioneers. Wildflower blooms (usually from late February through April – call ☏760-767-4684 for updates) bring the biggest crowds, right before Hades-like heat makes daytime exploring dangerous.

◉ Sights & Activities

Two miles west of Borrego Springs, the park **visitor center** (☏760-767-4205; www.parks.ca.gov; 200 Palm Canyon Dr; ☉9am-5pm Oct-May, Sat & Sun only Jun-Sep) has natural-history exhibits, informational handouts and updates on road conditions. Driving through the park is free, but if you camp, hike or picnic, a day-use parking fee (per car $5 to $8) applies. You'll need 4WD to tackle the 500 miles of backcountry dirt roads. If you'll be hiking or mountain biking, pack extra water.

Park highlights include: **Fonts Point** desert lookout; **Clark Dry Lake** for birding; **Elephant Tree Discovery Trail** near Split Mountain's wind caves; and **Blair Valley**, with its Native American pictographs and *morteros* (grinding stones). Further south, soak in hot-springs pools at **Agua Caliente County Park** (☏760-765-1188; www.sdcounty.ca.gov/parks/; 39555 Rte S2; entry per car $5; ☉9:30am-5pm Sep-May).

🛏 Sleeping & Eating

Free backcountry camping without a permit is permitted anywhere in the park, as long as you're at least 100ft from water or roads (no campfires or gathering of vegetation).

For country-style B&Bs and famous apple pie, the gold-mining town of **Julian** (www.julianca.com) is a 30-mile drive southwest of Borrego Springs.

Anza-Borrego Desert State Park Campgrounds CAMPGROUND $ (☏reservations 800-444-7275; www.reserveamerica.com; tent/RV sites $25/35; 🖭🐾) Book ahead for campsites at busy Borrego Palm Canyon Campground, 3 miles northwest of Borrego Springs, or smaller but shadier Tamarisk Grove (nonpotable water only), 12 miles south near Hwy 78.

Borrego Springs Motel MOTEL $ (☏760-767-4339; www.borregospringsmotel.com; 2376 Borrego Springs Rd; r $75-95; ☉late Sep-early Jun; ❄🛜🐾) 🏊 Just north of in-town Christmas Circle, this refurbished 1940s motel (now solar-powered) has eight spic-and-span, spartan rooms with deluxe mattresses. Go stargazing by the outdoor fire pit.

SALTON SEA & SALVATION MOUNTAIN

East of Anza-Borrego and south of Joshua Tree awaits a most unexpected sight: the **Salton Sea** (http://saltonsea.ca.gov), California's largest lake, which sits in the middle of its biggest desert. After the Colorado River flooded in 1905, it took 1500 workers and half a million tons of rock to put it back on course. With no natural outlet, the artificial lake's surface is 220ft below sea level and its waters 30% saltier than the Pacific – an environmental nightmare that's yet to be cleaned up.

An even stranger sight near the lake's eastern shore is **Salvation Mountain** (www.salvationmountain.us), a 50ft-high hill of hand-mixed clay blanketed in colorful acrylic paint and found objects, and inscribed with Christian messages. It's the vision of folk artist Leonard Knight. It's in Niland, about 3 miles east of Hwy 111, via Main St and Beal Rd.

Borrego Valley Inn   INN $$$
(☑ 800-333-5810, 760-767-0311; www.borregoval-leyinn.com; 405 Palm Canyon Dr; r incl breakfast $180-280; ❄❂❃) An intimate adults-only spa resort sports 15 elegant adobe-style rooms (some with kitchenettes) accented with Southwestern decor, plus two pools (one clothing-optional) and an outdoor hot tub.

Carlee's Place   AMERICAN $$
(660 Palm Canyon Dr; mains lunch $7-14, dinner $12-23; ◷ 11am-9pm) Join locals for OK bar-and-grill food, pool tables and crazy karaoke.

❶ Information

Borrego Springs has banks with ATMs, gas stations, a post office, supermarket and public library with free wi-fi and internet terminals, all on Palm Canyon Dr.

Mojave National Preserve

If you're on a quest for the 'middle of nowhere,' you may find it in **Mojave National Preserve** (☑ 760-252-6100; www.nps.gov/moja) **FREE** a 1.4-million-acre jumble of sand dunes, Joshua trees, volcanic cinder cones and habitats for desert tortoises, jack rabbits and coyotes. No gas is available here.

Southeast of Baker and the I-15 Fwy, Kelbaker Rd crosses a ghostly landscape of cinder cones before arriving at **Kelso Depot**, a 1920s Mission Revival-style railroad station. It now houses the park's main **visitor center** (☑ 760-252-6108; ◷ 9am-5pm Fri-Tue), which has excellent natural and cultural history exhibits, and an old-fashioned lunch counter. It's another 11 miles southwest to 'singing' **Kelso Dunes**. When wind conditions are right, they emanate low-pitched vibrations caused by shifting sands – running downhill can jump-start the effect.

From Kelso Depot, the Kelso–Cima Rd takes off northeast. After 19 miles, Cima Rd slingshots northwest toward I-15 around **Cima Dome**, a 1500ft-high hunk of granite with crusty lava outcroppings, whose slopes are home to the world's largest **Joshua tree forest**. For close-ups, summit **Teutonia Peak** (3 miles round-trip); the trailhead is 6 miles northwest of Cima.

Further east, Mojave Rd is a scenic backdoor route to first-come, first-served **campgrounds** (tent sites $12) with potable water at Mid Hills (no RVs) and Hole-in-the-Wall. The campgrounds bookend a rugged 12-mile scenic drive along **Wild Horse Canyon**

Rd, ending near Hole-in-the-Wall's **visitor center** (☑ 760-252-6104; ◷ 9am-4pm Wed-Sun Oct-Apr, 10am-4pm Sat May-Sep) and the slot-canyon **Rings Loop Trail**. Both of these dirt roads usually don't require 4WD.

🛏 Sleeping & Eating

Free backcountry and roadside camping is permitted throughout the preserve in already impacted areas; ask at the visitor center or consult the free park newspaper.

For historical ambience, **Hotel Nipton** (☑ 760-856-2335; http://nipton.com; 107355 Nipton Rd; cabins/r with shared bath from $65/80; ◷ reception 8am-6pm; ❂) encompasses a century-old adobe villa with rustic rooms and tent cabins in a remote railway outpost, northwest of the preserve. Check in at the trading post next to Mexican American **Oasis** (dishes $7-10; ◷ usually 11am-6pm Sun-Fri, to 8pm Sat) cafe.

Off I-15, Baker (35 miles northwest of Kelso) is the nearest town with bare-bones motels and fast food, while state-line Primm, NV (50 miles northeast) has well-worn casino hotels and restaurants by an outlet mall.

Death Valley National Park

The name itself evokes all that is harsh and hellish – a punishing, barren and lifeless place of Old Testament severity. Yet closer inspection reveals nature puts on a spectacular show here, with water-sculpted canyons, windswept sand dunes, palm-shaded oases, jagged mountains and wildlife aplenty. It's also a land of superlatives, holding the US records for the hottest temperature ($134°F/57°C$), lowest point (Badwater, 282ft below sea level) and largest national park outside Alaska (more than 5000 sq miles). Peak tourist season is when spring wildflowers bloom.

⊙ Sights & Activities

From **Furnace Creek**, the central hub of the **park** (☑ 760-786-3200; www.nps.gov/deva; 7-day entry per car $20), drive southeast up to **Zabriskie Point** for spectacular sunset views across the valley and golden badlands eroded into waves, pleats and gullies. Twenty miles southeast at **Dante's View**, you can simultaneously spot the highest (Mt Whitney, 14,505ft) and lowest (Badwater) points in the contiguous USA.

Badwater itself, a timeless landscape of crinkly salt flats, is 17 miles south of Furnace Creek. Along the way, **Golden Canyon** and **Natural Bridge** are easily explored on short hikes from roadside parking lots. A 9-mile detour along **Artists Drive** through a narrow canyon is best in late afternoon when the eroded hillsides erupt in fireworks of color.

Northwest of Furnace Creek, near Stovepipe Wells Village, trek across the Saharanesque **Mesquite Flat sand dunes** – magical during a full moon – and scramble along the smooth marble walls of **Mosaic Canyon**.

About 35 miles north of Furnace Creek is whimsical **Scotty's Castle** (✍reservations 877-444-6777; www.recreation.gov; ☺grounds 7am-5:30pm, tour times vary), where tour guides in historical character dress bring to life the Old West tales of con-man 'Death Valley Scotty' (reservations advised). Five miles west of Grapevine junction, circumambulate volcanic **Ubehebe Crater** and its younger sibling.

In summer, stick to paved roads (dirt roads can quickly overheat vehicles), limit your exertions and visit higher-elevation areas: for example, the scenic drive up **Emigrant Canyon**, starting 8 miles west of Stovepipe Wells, passing turnoffs to ghost towns and ending with a 3-mile unpaved stretch up to the historic beehive-shaped **Charcoal Kilns**. Nearby is the trailhead for the 8.4-mile round-trip hike up **Wildrose Peak** (9064ft). At the park's western edge, utterly remote **Panamint Springs** offers panoramic vistas and a 2-mile round-trip hike to tiny Darwin Falls.

RHYOLITE

Four miles west of Beatty, NV, look for the turnoff to the ghost town of **Rhyolite** (www.rhyolitesite.com; off Hwy 374; ☺sunrise-sunset) FREE, which epitomizes the hurly-burly, boom-and-bust story of so many Western gold-rush mining towns. Don't miss the 1906 'bottle house' or the skeletal remains of a three-story bank. Next door is the bizarre **Goldwell Open Air Museum** (www.goldwellmuseum.org; off Hwy 374; ☺24hr) FREE of trippy art installations begun by Belgian artist Albert Szukalski in 1984.

Activities offered at the Ranch at Furnace Creek include horseback riding, golf, mountain biking and hot-springs pool swimming.

🛏 Sleeping & Eating

In-park lodging is often booked solid in springtime when campgrounds fill by mid-morning, especially on weekends. Backcountry camping (no campfires) is allowed in previously impacted sites 2 miles away from any paved road and developed or day-use area, and 100yd from water sources; pick up free permits at the visitor center.

The closest town with cheaper lodging is Beatty, NV (40 miles northeast of Furnace Creek); accommodations are more plentiful in Las Vegas, NV (120 miles southeast) and Ridgecrest, CA (120 miles southwest).

Death Valley National Park Campgrounds ⠀⠀⠀CAMPGROUND $ (www.nps.gov/deva; campsites free-$30; 🚻🐾) Of the park's nine campgrounds, only Furnace Creek accepts **reservations** (✍518-885-3639, 877-444-6777; www.recreation.gov) and only from mid-October to mid-April. In summer, Furnace Creek is first-come, first-served, and the only other campgrounds open are Mesquite Spring, near Scotty's Castle, and those along Emigrant Canyon Rd (high-clearance 4WD may be required). Other valley-floor campgrounds – including RV-oriented Stovepipe Wells and Sunset, and shadier tent-friendly Texas Springs – are open October to April.

Ranch at Furnace Creek ⠀⠀⠀MOTEL, CABINS $$ (✍760-786-2345, 800-236-7916; www.furnacecreekresort.com; Hwy 190; d $139-219; 🚻🐾🏊🛏) Tailor-made for families, this rambling resort offers lodge rooms awash in desert colors, with French doors opening onto porches or patios, as well as duplex cabins. The ranch encompasses a natural spring-fed pool, golf course and tennis courts. The **49'er Cafe** (mains $10-25) cooks up decent American standards, or grab beers and pizza at **Corkscrew Saloon**.

Cynthia's ⠀⠀⠀HOSTEL, INN $$ (✍760-852-4580; www.discovercynthias.com; 2001 Old Spanish Trail Hwy, Tecopa; dm $22-25, r $75-140, tipi $165; ☺check-in 3-8pm; 🛜) Match your budget to your bed: eclectic-looking private rooms and dorm beds come in vintage trailers with common kitchens, or camp out at China Ranch in a Native American-style tipi with thick rugs, a fire pit and king-sized bed. Reservations essential. It's in the hot-springs town of Tecopa, 70 miles southeast of Furnace Creek.

Stovepipe Wells Village   MOTEL $$
(☑760-786-2387; www.escapetodeathvalley.com; Hwy 190; RV sites $33, r $95-160; ✳@ 🛜✳🛏🐕) Spruced-up rooms lay out quality linens beneath cheerful Native American bedspreads. The small pool is cool, while a cowboy-style saloon and restaurant deliver three square yet unmemorable meals a day (mains $6 to $23).

Inn at Furnace Creek   HOTEL $$$
(☑800-236-7916, 760-786-2345; www.furnacecreekresort.com; Hwy 190; r/ste from $345/450; ⊗mid-Oct–mid-May; ✳🛜✳) Enjoy languid valley views while lounging by the spring-fed pool or when you roll out of bed and pull back the curtains at this minimalist 1927 mission-style hotel. The upscale restaurant (dress code at dinner) is only recommended for its Sunday brunch buffet ($25). Come for sunset cocktails on the terrace.

❶ Information

Purchase a seven-day entry pass ($20 per car) at self-service pay stations throughout the park. For a free map and newspaper, show your receipt at the **visitor center** (☑760-786-3200; www.nps.gov/deva; ⊗8am-5pm) in Furnace Creek, where you'll also find a general store, gas station, post office, ATM, laundromat and showers. Stovepipe Wells Village, a 30-minute drive northwest, has a general store, gas station, ATM and showers. Panamint Springs, on the park's western edge, has an ATM, gas, wi-fi, snacks and drinks. Cell-phone reception is spotty to nonexistent in the park.

CENTRAL COAST

No trip to California would be worth its salt without a jaunt along the surreally scenic Central Coast. Among California's most iconic roads, Hwy 1 skirts past posh Santa Barbara, retro Pismo Beach, collegiate San Luis Obispo, fantastical Hearst Castle, soulstirring Big Sur, cutesy Carmel, down-to-earth Monterey and hippie Santa Cruz, often within view of the Pacific. Slow down – this idyllic coast deserves to be savored, not gulped. Incidentally, that same advice goes for award-winning locally grown wines too.

Santa Barbara

Life is sweet in Santa Barbara, a coastal Shangri-La where the air is redolent of citrus and jasmine, flowery bougainvillea drapes whitewashed buildings with Spanish red-tiled roofs, and it's all cradled by pearly beaches – just ignore those pesky oil derricks out to sea. Downtown's main drag, **State St**, abounds with bars, cafes, theaters and boutiques.

◉ Sights

Mission Santa Barbara   CHURCH
(www.santabarbaramission.org; 2201 Laguna St; adult/child $5/1; ⊗9am-4:15pm) Established in 1786, California's hilltop 'Queen of the Missions' was the only one to escape secularization under Mexican rule. Look for Chumash artwork inside the vaulted church, unusually topped by twin bell towers, and a moody cemetery out back.

Santa Barbara Museum of Art   MUSEUM
(www.sbma.net; 1130 State St; adult/child $10/6, 5-8pm Thu free; ⊗11am-5pm Tue-Wed & Fri-Sun, to 8pm Thu) Downtown galleries house an impressive, tightly edited collection of contemporary California artists, modern masters including Matisse and Chagall, 20th-century photography and Asian art, plus provocative special exhibits.

County Courthouse   HISTORIC BUILDING
(☑805-962-6464; www.sbcourts.org; 1100 Anacapa St; ⊗8am-4:45pm Mon-Fri, from 10am Sat & Sun) FREE Built in Spanish-Moorish revival style, it's an absurdly beautiful place to stand trial. Marvel at hand-painted ceilings and intricate murals, then climb the *Vertigo*-esque clock tower for panoramic views. Free tours given daily (call for schedules).

Santa Barbara Historical Museum   MUSEUM
(www.santabarbaramuseum.com; 136 E De La Guerra St; donations welcome; ⊗10am-5pm Tue-Sat, from noon Sun) FREE Around a romantic cloistered adobe courtyard, peruse a fascinating mishmash of memorabilia, including Chumash woven baskets. Learn about odd historical footnotes, like the city's involvement in toppling the last Chinese monarchy.

Santa Barbara Maritime Museum   MUSEUM
(www.sbmm.org; 113 Harbor Way; adult/child $7/4, 3rd Thu of month free; ⊗10am-5pm, to 6pm late May-early Sep; 🛟) Set by the harbor, this

OFF THE BEATEN TRACK

IF YOU HAVE A FEW MORE DAYS

Remote, rugged **Channel Islands National Park** (www.nps.gov/chis) earns the nickname 'California's Galápagos' for its unique wildlife. These islands offer superb snorkeling, scuba diving and sea kayaking. Spring, when wildflowers bloom, is a gorgeous time to visit; summer and fall can be bone-dry, and winter stormy.

Anacapa, an hour's boat ride from the mainland, is the best island for day-tripping, with easy hikes and unforgettable views. Santa Cruz, the biggest island, is for overnight camping excursions, kayaking and hiking. Other islands require longer channel crossings and multiday trips. San Miguel is often shrouded in fog. Tiny Santa Barbara supports seabird and seal colonies. So does Santa Rosa, which also protects Torrey pines and Chumash archaeological sites.

Boats leave from Ventura Harbor, off Hwy 101, where the park's **visitor center** (☑ 805-658-5730; 1901 Spinnaker Dr, Ventura; ☺ 8:30am-5pm) has info and maps. The main tour-boat operator is **Island Packers** (☑ 805-642-1393; www.islandpackers.com; 1691 Spinnaker Dr; cruises adult/child from $36/26); book ahead. Primitive island campgrounds require reservations; book through Recreation.gov (p902) and bring food and water.

two-story exhibition hall celebrates the town's briny history with yesteryear artifacts, documentary videos and hands-on and virtual-reality exhibits.

Santa Barbara Botanic Garden   GARDEN (www.sbbg.org; 1212 Mission Canyon Rd; adult/child $8/4; ☺ 9am-6pm, to 5pm Nov-Feb; ⊞) Uphill from the mission, this garden devoted to California's native flora meanders beside rolling trails past cacti and wildflowers. Nearby is a natural-history museum for kids.

🏃 Activities

Overlooking busy municipal beaches, 1872 **Stearns Wharf** is the West's oldest continuously operating wooden pier, strung with touristy shops and restaurants. Outside town off Hwy 101, bigger palm-fringed **state beaches** (www.parks.ca.gov; entry per car $10; ☺ 8am-sunset) await at Carpinteria, 12 miles east, and El Capitan and Refugio, over 20 miles west of town.

Santa Barbara Sailing Center   WATER SPORTS (☑ 800-350-9090, 805-962-2826; www.sbsail. com; off Harbor Way; kayak/SUP rentals from $10/15, cruises/tours from $25/50) Rent kayaks or join a paddling tour, sign up for sailing classes or take a whale-watching or sunset cocktail cruise.

Channel Islands Outfitters   WATER SPORTS (☑ rentals 805-617-3425, tours 805-899-4925; www.channelislandso.com; 117b Harbor Way; surfboard/kayak/SUP rentals from $10/25/40) Friendly kayaking, surfing and stand-up

paddle boarding (SUP) outfitter also leads coastal kayaking tours.

Wheel Fun   CYCLING (www.wheelfunrentalssb.com; 22 State St & 23 E Cabrillo Blvd; 1hr/half-day bicycle rentals from $9/24; ☺ 8am-8pm, to 6pm Nov-Feb) Pedal along the paved recreational trail connecting miles of beautiful beaches.

Santa Barbara Adventure Co   WATER SPORTS, CYCLING (☑ 877-885-9283, 805-884-9283; www.sbadventureco.com; 720 Bond Ave; tours/lessons from $49/109) Take a kayak or cycling tour or a traditional board-surfing or SUP lesson.

🛏 Sleeping

Hello, sticker shock: even basic motel rooms can command over $200 in summer. Less expensive motels line upper State St, north of downtown, and Hwy 101. Make **reservations** (☑ 800-444-7275; www.reserveamerica. com; campsites $10-70; ⊞🐾) for state-park campgrounds outside town.

Santa Barbara Auto Camp   CAMPGROUND $$ (☑ 888-405-7553; http://sbautocamp.com; 2717 De La Vina St; trailer q $139-199; ❄🐾⊞🐾) 🐾 Slumber inside a vintage Airstream trailer decked out with minimalist mod decor, sustainable design features, a full kitchen, redwood deck and outdoor BBQ grill. Book far ahead (two-night minimum stay).

Agave Inn   MOTEL $$ (☑ 805-687-6009; http://agaveinnsb.com; 3222 State St; r from $119; ❄🐾) This affordable gem has arty panache and personality, with its

'Mexican pop meets modern' motif. Family-sized rooms have kitchenettes. Thin walls and limited parking.

Marina Beach Motel MOTEL **$$**
(☑877-627-4621, 805-963-9311; www.marina-beachmotel.com; 21 Bath St; r incl breakfast $150-210; ✴☎🖥) Old-fashioned one-story motor lodge, a short walk from the beach, has been all done up inside with crisp linens and plantation shutters. Some rooms have kitchenettes. Free bikes to borrow.

El Capitan Canyon CABINS, CAMPGROUND **$$$**
(☑866-352-2729, 805-685-3887; www.elcapitancanyon.com; 11560 Calle Real, off Hwy 101; safari tents $155, cabins from $225; ☎🖥✴) 🔊
Go 'glamping' in this car-free zone near El Capitan State Beach, a 30-minute drive west of town via Hwy 101. Safari tents are rustic, while creekside cedar cabins come with dreamy beds and outdoor fire pits.

Spanish Garden Inn BOUTIQUE HOTEL **$$$**
(☑805-564-4700; www.spanishgardeninn.com; 915 Garden St; d incl breakfast from $319; ✴@☎🖥) Elegant Spanish Revival–style hotel downtown harbors two dozen romantic luxury rooms and suites facing a gracious fountain courtyard. Concierge services are top-notch.

✖ Eating

Silvergreens CALIFORNIAN **$**
(www.silvergreens.com; 791 Chapala St; dishes $4-10; ⊙7am-10pm Mon-Fri, from 8am Sat & Sun; 🖥) 🔊 Who says fast food can't be fresh and tasty? With the tag line 'Eat smart, live well,' this sun-drenched cafe makes nutritionally sound salads, soups, sandwiches, burgers, breakfast burritos and much more.

Lilly's Taqueria MEXICAN **$**
(http://lillystacos.com; 310 Chapala St; items from $1.75; ⊙10:30am-9pm Sun-Mon & Wed-Thu, to 10pm Fri & Sat) There's almost always a line out the door, so be snappy with your order – locals will fight for these authentic street tacos, especially with *adobada* (marinated pork) or *lengua* (beef tongue).

Olio Pizzeria ITALIAN **$$**
(☑805-899-2699; www.oliopizzeria.com; 11 W Victoria St; mains $9-18; ⊙11:30am-9pm Sun-Thu, to 10pm Fri & Sat) Convivial, high-ceilinged pizzeria with a happening wine bar sets out a tempting selection of crispy pizzas, imported cheeses and meats, traditional antipasti and *dolci* (desserts).

Santa Barbara Shellfish Company SEAFOOD **$$**
(www.sbfishhouse.com; 230 Stearns Wharf; dishes $3-16; ⊙11am-9pm) 'From sea to skillet to plate' best describes this end-of-the-wharf crab shack that's more of a counter joint. Great crab cakes, ocean views and the same location for 30 years.

🍷 Drinking & Entertainment

Nightlife orbits lower State St. You can ramble between a dozen wine-tasting rooms along the city's **Urban Wine Trail** (www.urbanwinetrailsb.com). The free alt-weekly *Santa Barbara Independent* (www.independent.com) has an entertainment calendar.

Brewhouse BREWERY
(www.brewhousesb.com; 229 W Montecito St; ⊙11am-11pm Sun-Thu, to midnight Fri & Sat; ☎) Rowdy dive down by the railroad tracks crafts its own unique small-batch beers and has rockin' live music from Wednesday to Saturday nights.

Soho LIVE MUSIC
(☑805-962-7776; www.sohosb.com; Suite 205, 1221 State St; tickets $5-30) Unpretentious brick room located upstairs behind a McDonald's has live bands almost nightly, from indie rock, folk and world beats to jazz and blues.

ℹ Information

Santa Barbara Car Free (www.santabarbaracarfree.org) Eco-travel tips and discounts.
Santa Barbara Visitors Center (☑805-965-3021; www.santabarbaraca.com; 1 Garden St; ⊙9am-5pm Mon-Sat, from 10am Sun, to 4pm Nov-Jan) Maps and self-guided tour brochures by the waterfront.

ℹ Getting There & Around

From the **train station** (209 State St) south of downtown, Amtrak trains roll toward LA ($25 to $30, three hours) and San Luis Obispo ($28 to $34, 2¾ hours). From a downtown **bus station** (☑805-965-7551; 224 Chapala St), Greyhound has a few daily buses to LA ($19, two to three hours) and via San Luis Obispo ($28, two hours) to Santa Cruz ($53, six hours) and San Francisco ($57, nine hours).

Metropolitan Transit District (MTD; ☑805-963-3366; www.sbmtd.gov) runs city-wide buses ($1.75) and electric shuttles (50¢) between downtown's State St and Stearns Wharf and along beachfront Cabrillo Blvd.

Santa Barbara to San Luis Obispo

You can speed up to San Luis Obispo in less than two hours along Hwy 101, or take all day detouring to wineries, historical missions and hidden beaches.

A scenic backcountry drive north of Santa Barbara follows Hwy 154, where you can go for the grape in the **wine country** (www.sbcountywines.com) of the Santa Ynez and Santa Maria Valleys. For eco-conscious vineyard tours, ride along with **Sustainable Vine** (☑805-698-3911; www.sustainablevine.com; tour $125) ✦, or just follow the pastoral **Foxen Canyon Wine Trail** (www.foxencanyonwinetrail.com) north to cult winemakers' vineyards. In the town of **Los Olivos**, where two dozen more wine-tasting rooms await, **Los Olivos Cafe & Wine Merchant** (☑805-688-7265; www.losolivoscafe.com; 2879 Grand Ave; mains $12-29; ⊙11:30am-8:30pm) ✦ is a charming Cal-Mediterranean bistro with a wine bar.

Further south, the Danish-immigrant village of **Solvang** (www.solvangusa.com) is aflutter with kitschy windmills and fairytale-esque bakeries. Fuel up on buffalo chicken breakfast biscuits, cinnamon-cumin pork-belly sandos and organic Thai salads at **Succulent Cafe & Trading Company** (☑805-691-9235; www.succulentcafe.com; 1555 Mission Dr; breakfast & lunch mains $8-12; ⊙9am-1pm & 11am-3pm Wed-Sun, 5:30-9pm Thu-Sat) ✦. For a picnic lunch or BBQ takeout, swing into **El Rancho Marketplace** (www.elranchomarket.com; 2886 Mission Dr; ⊙6am-10pm), east of Solvang's 19th-century Spanish **mission** (☑805-688-4815; www.missionsantaines.org; 1760 Mission Dr; adult/child $5/free; ⊙9am-4:30pm). West of Hwy 101 in Buellton, **Avant** (www.avantwines.com; 35 Industrial Way; ⊙11am-9pm) wine bar and **Figueroa Mountain Brewing Co** (www.figmtnbrew.com; 45 Industrial Way; ⊙4-9pm Mon-Thu, from 11am Fri-Sun) are side-street locals' hangouts.

Follow Hwy 246 about 15 miles west of Hwy 101 to **La Purísima Mission State Historic Park** (www.lapurisimamission.org; 2295 Purisima Rd; entry per car $6; ⊙9am-5pm, guided tour 1pm). Exquisitely restored, it's one of California's most evocative Spanish Colonial missions, with flowering gardens, livestock pens and adobe buildings. South of Lompoc off Hwy 1, Jalama Rd travels 14 twisting miles to windswept **Jalama Beach County Park** (☑805-736-3616; www.sbparks.org; 9999 Jalama Rd; per car $10). Book ahead for its crazy-popular **campground** (http://sbparks.org/reservations; tent/RV sites $28/43, cabins $110-210), where newly built, simple wooden cabins have kitchenettes.

Heading north on Hwy 1, rough-and-tumble **Guadalupe** is the gateway to North America's largest coastal dunes, where the **Lost City of DeMille** (www.lostcitydemille.com), a movie set from *The Ten Commandments* (1923), lies buried beneath the sands. Scenes from *Hidalgo* (2004) and *Pirates of the Caribbean: At World's End* (2007) were also filmed here. The best dunes access is west of town via Hwy 166.

Where Hwy 1 rejoins Hwy 101, **Pismo Beach** has a long, lazy stretch of sand and a **butterfly grove** (www.monarchbutterfly.org; Hwy 1) FREE, where migratory monarchs perch in eucalyptus trees from late October to February. Adjacent **North Beach Campground** (☑800-444-7275; www.reserveamerica.com; Hwy 1; campsites $35; ☏) offers beach access and hot showers. Dozens of motels and hotels stand by the ocean and along Hwy 101, but rooms fill quickly, especially on weekends. **Pismo Lighthouse Suites** (☑805-773-2411, 800-245-2411; www.pismolighthousesuites.com; 2411 Price St; ste incl breakfast from $219; P❄@☏❄♿) has everything vacationing families need, from kitchenette suites to a life-sized outdoor chessboard; ask about off-season discounts. Nearby Pismo's seaside pier, **Old West Cinnamon Rolls** (www.oldwestcinnamon.com; 861 Dolliver St; items $3-5; ⊙6:30am-5:30pm) is gooey goodness. Uphill at the **Cracked Crab** (www.crackedcrab.com; 751 Price St; mains $9-53; ⊙11am-9pm Sun-Thu, to 10pm Fri & Sat; ♿), make sure you don a plastic bib before a fresh bucket o' seafood gets dumped on your butcher-paper-covered table.

The nearby town of **Avila Beach** has a sunny waterfront promenade, an atmospherically creaky old wooden fishing pier and a historical **lighthouse** (☑hiking info 805-541-8735, trolley tour 855-533-7843; www.sanluislighthouse.org; entry per hiker $5, trolley tour $20; ⊙Sat only, reservations required). Back toward Hwy 101, pick juicy berries or apples and feed the goats at **Avila Valley Barn** (http://avilavalleybarn.com; 560 Avila Beach Dr; ⊙9am-6pm; ♿) farmstand, then do some stargazing from a private redwood hot tub at **Sycamore Mineral Springs** (☑805-595-7302; www.sycamoresprings.com; 1215 Avila Beach Dr; 1hr per person $13.50-17.50; ⊙8am-midnight, last reservation 10:45pm).

San Luis Obispo

Halfway between LA and San Francisco, San Luis Obispo is a low-key place. But CalPoly university students inject a healthy dose of hubbub into the streets, pubs and cafes, especially during the weekly **farmers market** (⊙6-9pm Thu; ♿) ✐, which turns downtown's Higuera St into a carnival with live music and sidewalk BBQs. Like several other California towns, SLO grew up around a Spanish Catholic **mission** (☑805-543-6850; www.missionsanluisobispo.org; 751 Palm St; donation $2; ⊙9am-5pm, to 4pm early Nov–mid-Mar), founded in 1772 by Junípero Serra. These days, SLO is just a grape's throw from thriving **Edna Valley wineries** (www.slowine.com), known for crisp Chardonnay and smooth Pinot Noir.

🛏 Sleeping

SLO's motel row is north of downtown along Monterey St. Chain motels line Hwy 101.

HI Hostel Obispo　　　　　　　　HOSTEL $
(☑805-544-4678; www.hostelobispo.com; 1617 Santa Rosa St; dm $25-28, r from $55; ⊙check-in 4:30-10pm; @🛜) ✐ Solar-powered hostel inhabits a cozy Victorian near the train station. Amenities include a common kitchen and bike rentals (from $10 per day). No credit cards or curfew; BYOT (bring your own towel). All accommodation with shared bath.

Peach Tree Inn　　　　　　　　MOTEL $$
(☑805-543-3170,　　800-227-6396;　www.peachtreeinn.com; 2001 Monterey St; r incl breakfast $70-175; ❄@🛜♿) Folksy, nothing-fancy motel rooms are relaxing, especially those set creekside or with rocking chairs overlooking a rose garden. Hearty continental breakfasts include homemade breads.

Madonna Inn　　　　　　　　HOTEL $$$
(☑805-543-3000; www.madonnainn.com; 100 Madonna Rd; r $189-309; ❄@🛜♨) Fantastically campy, this garish confection is visible from Hwy 101. Overseas tourists, vacationing Midwesterners and irony-loving hipsters adore the 110 themed rooms – including the rock-walled Caveman and hot-pink Floral Fantasy (gawk at photos online).

🍴 Eating & Drinking

Downtown abounds with cafes, restaurants, wine bars, brewpubs and the USA's first solar-powered cinema, **Palm Theatre** (☑805-541-5161; www.thepalmtheatre.com; 817 Palm St; tickets $5-8) ✐, screening indie flicks.

Firestone Grill　　　　　　　BARBECUE $
(www.firestonegrill.com; 1001 Higuera St; dishes $4-10; ⊙11am-10pm Sun-Wed, to 11pm Thu-Sat; ♿) Sink your teeth into an authentic Santa Maria–style tri-tip BBQ sandwich on a toasted garlic roll, or a chopped Cobb steak salad.

Sidecar　　　　　　　　CALIFORNIAN $$
(☑805-540-5340;　http://sidecarslo.com; 1127 Broad St; mains $7-22; ⊙11am-11pm Mon-Fri, from 10am Sat & Sun) ✐ Pull out a chair around a 1950s dinette table and feast on a creative chef's seasonal menu of local farm and ranch goodness. Weekend brunch is sociable, and so is the regional wine list.

Big Sky Café　　　　　　　CALIFORNIAN $$
(www.bigskycafe.com; 1121 Broad St; mains $9-20; ⊙7am-9pm Mon-Thu, to 10pm Fri, 8am-10pm Sat, 8am-9pm Sun; ✐) ✐ With the tagline 'analog food for a digital world,' this airy, sustainable-minded cafe gets top marks for market-fresh breakfasts (served until 1pm daily), healthy big-plate dinners and homemade soups and baskets of cornbread.

ℹ Information

San Luis Obispo Car Free (http://slocarfree.org) Eco-travel tips and discounts.

Visitor Center (☑805-781-2777; www.visitslo.com; 895 Monterey St; ⊙10am-5pm Sun-Wed, to 7pm Thu-Sat) Downtown near Higuera St.

WORTH A TRIP

PINNACLES NATIONAL PARK

Named for the towering spires that rise abruptly out of the chapparal-covered hills, **Pinnacles National Park** (☑831-389-4485; www.nps.gov/pinn; 5000 Hwy 146, Paicines; per car $5) is a study in geologic drama, with craggy monoliths, sheer-walled canyons and ancient volcanic remnants. Besides hiking and rock climbing, the park's biggest attractions are talus caves and endangered California condors. Visit during spring or fall – summer heat and humidity are extreme. A family **campground** (☑877-444-6777; www.recreation.gov; tent/RV sites $23/36; ❄♿♨) is situated near the park's east entrance, off Hwy 25 northwest of King City, a two-hour drive north of San Luis Obispo.

❶ Getting There & Around

Amtrak trains from Santa Barbara ($28 to $34, 2¾ hours) and LA ($40, 5½ hours) arrive at SLO's **train station** (1011 Railroad Ave), 0.6 miles southeast of downtown. Inconveniently stopping 2.5 miles southwest of downtown off Hwy 101, **Greyhound** (1460 Calle Joaquin) has a few daily buses to Santa Barbara ($28, two hours), LA ($40, five hours), Santa Cruz ($42, four hours) and San Francisco ($53, seven hours).

Operated by **SLO Regional Transit Authority** (☑ 805-541-2228; www.slorta.org; fares $1.50-3, day pass $5), county-wide buses with limited weekend services converge on downtown's **transit center** (cnr Palm & Osos Sts).

Morro Bay to Hearst Castle

A dozen miles northwest of SLO via Hwy 1, **Morro Bay** is a sea-sprayed fishing town where **Morro Rock**, a volcanic peak jutting up from the ocean floor, is your first hint of the coast's upcoming drama. (Never mind those powerplant smokestacks obscuring the views.) Hop aboard a cruise or rent kayaks along the Embarcadero, packed with touristy shops, cafes and bars. A classic seafood shack, **Giovanni's** (www.giovannisfishmarket.com; 1001 Front St; mains $6-17; ⊙ 11am-6pm; 🖲) cooks killer garlic fries and fish-and-chips. Midrange motels cluster uphill off Harbor and Main Sts and along Hwy 1.

Nearby are fantastic state parks for coastal hikes and **camping** (☑ 800-444-7275; www.reserveamerica.com; campsites $5-50; 🖲🏵). South of the Embarcadero, **Morro Bay State Park** (☑ 805-772-2694; www.parks.ca.gov; admission free, museum entry adult/child $2/free) has a natural-history museum and heron rookery. Further south in Los Osos, west of Hwy 1, wilder **Montaña de Oro State Park** (www.parks.ca.gov; Pecho Valley Rd) FREE features coastal bluffs, tide pools, sand dunes, peak hiking and mountain-biking trails. Its Spanish name ('mountain of gold') comes from native California poppies that blanket the hillsides in spring.

Heading north of downtown Morro Bay along Hwy 1, surfers love the Cal-Mexican **Taco Temple** (2680 Main St; mains $8-15; ⊙ 11am-9pm Mon & Wed-Sat, to 8:30pm Sun), a cash-only joint, and **Ruddell's Smokehouse** (www.smokerjim.com; 101 D St; dishes $4-16; ⊙ 11am-6pm), serving smoked-fish tacos by the beach in Cayucos. Vintage motels line Cayucos' Ocean Ave, including the cute, family-run **Seaside Motel** (☑ 805-995-3809; www.seasidemotel.com; 42 S Ocean Ave; d $80-160; 🖘), offering kitchenettes. Inhabiting a historic sea captain's home, **Cass House Inn** (☑ 805-995-3669; http://casshouseinn.com; 222 N Ocean Ave; r incl breakfast $175-365; 🖘) has plush rooms, some with soaking tubs and antique fireplaces to ward off chilly coastal fog, and an elegant, seasonally inspired French-Californian **restaurant** (4-course prix-fixe menu $68; ⊙ 5:30pm-7:30pm Thu-Mon) downstairs.

North of Harmony (population: just 18 souls), Hwy 46 leads east into the vineyards of **Paso Robles wine country** (www.pasowine.com). Further north along Hwy 1, quaint **Cambria** has lodgings along unearthly pretty Moonstone Beach, where the **Blue Dolphin Inn** (☑ 805-927-3300, 800-222-9157; www.cambriainns.com; 6470 Moonstone Beach Dr; r incl breakfast from $179; 🖘🏵) offers crisp, modern rooms with romantic fireplaces. Inland, **HI Cambria Bridge Street Inn** (☑ 805-927-7653; www.bridgestreetinncambria.com; 4314 Bridge St; dm $25-28, r $49-75, all with shared bath; ⊙ check-in 5pm-9pm; 🖘) sleeps like a hostel but feels like a grandmotherly B&B, while the retro **Cambria Pines Motel** (☑ 866-489-4485, 805-927-4485; www.cambriapalmsmotel.com; 2662 Main St; r $89-139; ⊙ check-in 3pm-9pm; 🖘🖲🏵) has clean-lined rooms, some with kitchenettes. An artisan cheese and wine shop, **Indigo Moon** (☑ 805-927-2911; www.indigomooncafe.com; 1980 Main St; mains lunch $9-14, dinner $14-35; ⊙ 10am-9pm) has breezy bistro tables and market-fresh salads and sandwiches at lunch. With a sunny patio and take-out counter, **Linn's Easy as Pie Cafe** (www.linnsfruitbin.com; 4251 Bridge St; mains $7-12; ⊙ 10am-6pm; 🖲) is famous for its ollalieberry pie.

About 10 miles north of Cambria, hilltop **Hearst Castle** (☑ reservations 800-444-4445; www.hearstcastle.org; 750 Hearst Castle Rd; tours adult/child from $25/12; ⊙ usually 9am-sunset) is California's most famous monument to wealth and ambition. William Randolph Hearst, the newspaper magnate, entertained Hollywood stars and royalty at this fantasy estate dripping with European antiques, accented by shimmering pools and surrounded by flowering gardens. Try to make tour reservations in advance, especially for Christmas holiday evening living-history programs.

Across Hwy 1, overlooking a historic whaling pier, **Sebastian's Store** (442 Slo San Simeon Rd; mains $6-12; ⊙ 11am-5pm Wed-Sun, deli closes 4pm) sells Hearst Ranch beef burgers and giant sandwiches for impromptu beach picnics. Five miles back south along Hwy 1, past a forgettable row of budget and mid-range motels in San Simeon, **Hearst San Simeon State Park** (☑800-444-7275; www. reserveamerica.com; campsites $5-35; 🚻🐾) has primitive and developed creekside campsites.

Heading north, Point Piedras Blancas is home to an enormous **elephant seal colony** that breeds, molts, sleeps, frolics and, occasionally, goes aggro on the beach. Keep your distance from these wild animals, who move faster on the sand than you can. The signposted vista point, 4.5 miles north of Hearst Castle, has interpretive panels. Seals haul out year-round, but the frenzied birthing and mating season runs from January through March, aptly peaking on Valentine's Day. Nearby, the 1875 **Piedras Blancas Light Station** (☑805-927-7361; www.piedrasblancas. org; tours adult/child $10/5; ☉ tours usually 9:45am Mon-Sat mid-Jun–Aug, Tue, Thu & Sat Sep–mid-Jun) is an outstandingly scenic spot; call ahead to check tour schedules and meeting points.

Big Sur

Much ink has been spilled extolling the raw beauty and energy of this 100-mile stretch of craggy coastline sprawling south of Monterey Bay. More a state of mind than a place you can pinpoint on a map, Big Sur has no traffic lights, banks or strip malls. When the sun goes down, the moon and stars are the only illumination – if summer fog hasn't extinguished them, that is.

Lodging, food and gas are all scarce and pricey in Big Sur. Demand for rooms is high year-round, especially on weekends, so book ahead. The free *Big Sur Guide* (www.bigsur-california.org), an info-packed newspaper, is available everywhere along the way. Note the day-use parking fee ($10) charged at Big Sur's state parks is valid for same-day entry to all.

It's about 25 miles from Hearst Castle to blink-and-you-miss-it Gorda, home of **Tree-bones Resort** (☑877-424-4787, 805-927-2390; www.treebonesresort.com; 71895 Hwy 1; d with shared bath incl breakfast from $199; 🛜🐾🚻), which offers back-to-nature clifftop yurts and a small locavarian **restaurant** (dinner mains $24-33; ☉noon-2pm & 5:30pm-8pm) and sushi bar. Basic **USFS campgrounds** (☑877-444-6777, 518-885-3639; www.recreation. gov; campsites $22; 🐾) are just off Hwy 1 at Plaskett Creek and Kirk Creek.

Ten miles north of Lucia is the new-agey **Esalen Institute** (☑831-667-3047; www. esalen.org; 55000 Hwy 1), famous for its esoteric workshops and ocean-view hot-springs baths. By reservation, you can frolic nekkid in the latter from 1am to 3am nightly ($25, credit cards only). It's surreal.

Another 3 miles north, **Julia Pfeiffer Burns State Park** hides one of California's only coastal waterfalls, 80ft-high Mc-Way Falls; the viewpoint is reached via a quarter-mile stroll. Two more miles north, a steep dirt trail descends from a hairpin turn on Hwy 1 to **Partington Cove**, a raw and breathtaking spot where crashing surf salts your skin – but swimming isn't safe, sorry.

Seven miles further north, nestled among redwoods and wisteria, quaint **Deetjen's Restaurant** (☑831-667-2378; www.deetjens. com; Deetjen's Big Sur Inn, 48865 Hwy 1; dinner mains $24-38; ☉8am-noon Mon-Fri, to 12:30pm Sat & Sun, 6-9pm daily) serves country-style comfort fare. Just north, the beatnik **Henry Miller Memorial Library** (☑831-667-2574; www.henrymiller.org; 48603 Hwy 1; ☉11am-6pm Wed-Mon) is the heart and soul of Big Sur bohemia, with a jam-packed bookstore, live-music concerts and DJs, open-mike nights and outdoor film screenings. Opposite, food takes a back seat to dramatic ocean views at clifftop **Nepenthe** (☑831-667-2345; www. nepenthebigsur.com; 48510 Hwy 1; mains $15-42; ☉11:30am-4:30pm & 5-10pm), meaning 'island of no sorrow.' Its Ambrosia burger is mighty.

Heading north, **Big Sur Station** (☑831-667-2315; www.fs.usda.gov/lpnf/; ☉8am-4pm, closed Mon & Tue Oct-Apr) can clue you in about hiking trails and camping options. Rangers issue overnight parking ($5) and campfire permits (free) for backpacking trips into Ventana Wilderness, including the popular 10-mile one-way hike to Sykes Hot Springs.

---

❶ DRIVING HWY 1

Navigating the narrow two-lane highway through Big Sur can be slow going. Allow at least 2½ hours to drive nonstop between Hearst Castle and Monterey Bay, much more if you stop to explore. Driving after dark can be risky and, more to the point, it's futile because you'll miss all the scenery. Watch out for cyclists and use signposted roadside pullouts to let faster-moving traffic pass. For updates on road conditions, call ☑800-427-7623.

On the opposite side of Hwy 1 just south, turn onto obscurely marked Sycamore Canyon Rd, which drops two narrow, twisting miles to crescent-shaped **Pfeiffer Beach** (per car $5; ⊙9am-8pm), with a towering offshore sea arch and strong currents too dangerous for swimming. Dig down into the sand – it's purple!

Next up, **Pfeiffer Big Sur State Park** is crisscrossed by sun-dappled trails through redwood forests, including the 1.4-mile round-trip to seasonal Pfeiffer Falls. Make **campground** (⊙800-444-7275; www.reserveamerica.com; campsites $35-50; ⊕⊛) reservations or stay at the rambling, old-fashioned **Big Sur Lodge** (⊙800-424-4787, 831-667-3100; www.bigsurlodge.com; 47225 Hwy 1; d $205-365; ⊛⊕), which has rustic duplex cottages (some with kitchens and wood-burning fireplaces), a simple **restaurant** (mains $10-27; ⊙8-11:30am & noon-10pm) and a well-stocked general store.

Most of Big Sur's commercial activity is concentrated just north along Hwy 1, including private campgrounds with rustic cabins, motels, restaurants, gas stations and shops. **Glen Oaks Motel** (⊙831-667-2105; www.glenoaksbigsur.com; 47080 Hwy 1; d from $225; ⊛), a redesigned 1950s redwood-and-adobe motor lodge, rents snug rooms and cabins with gas fireplaces. Nearby, the Big Sur River Inn's **general store** (http://bigsurriverinn.com; 46840 Hwy 1; mains $6-9; ⊙11am-7pm) hides a burrito and fruit-smoothie bar at the back, while **Maiden Publick House** (⊙831-667-2355; Hwy 1; ⊙3pm-2am Mon-Fri, from noon Sat & Sun) pulls off an encyclopedic beer menu and live-music jams. Back south, near the post office, grab a sandwich from **Big Sur Deli** (http://bigsurdeli.com; 47520 Hwy 1; dishes $1.50-7; ⊙7am-8pm), attached to the laid-back **Big Sur Taphouse** (www.bigsurtaphouse.com; 47520 Hwy 1; ⊙noon-10pm Mon-Thu, to midnight Fri & Sat, 10am-10pm Sun; ⊛), a craft beer bar with pub grub, board games and sports TVs.

Heading north again, don't skip **Andrew Molera State Park**, a gorgeous trail-laced pastiche of grassy meadows, waterfalls, ocean bluffs and rugged beaches. Learn all about endangered California condors at the park's **Discovery Center** (⊙831-624-1202; www.ventanaws.org; ⊙10am-4pm Sat & Sun late May-early Sep; ⊕) (**FREE**); book ahead for popular bird-tracking tours ($50). From the dirt parking lot, a 0.4-mile trail leads to a first-come, first-served primitive **campground** (www.parks.ca.gov; tent sites $25).

Six miles before landmark Bixby Creek Bridge, you can tour 1889 **Point Sur Lightstation** (⊙831-625-4419; www.pointsur.org; adult/child from $12/5). Check online or call for tour schedules, including seasonal moonlight walks, and directions to the meeting point. Arrive early because space is limited (no reservations).

Carmel

Once a bohemian artists' seaside resort, quaint Carmel-by-the-Sea now has the well-manicured feel of a country club. Simply plop down in any cafe and watch the parade of behatted ladies toting fancy-label shopping bags and dapper gents driving top-down convertibles along Ocean Ave, the village's slow-mo main drag.

◉ Sights & Activities

Often foggy, municipal **Carmel Beach** is a gorgeous white-sand crescent, where pampered pups excitedly run off-leash.

★Point Lobos State Natural Reserve   PARK
(www.pointlobos.org; Hwy 1; per car $10; ⊙8am-7pm, closes 30min after sunset early Nov–mid-Mar) They bark, they bray, they bathe and they're fun to watch – sea lions are the stars here, 4 miles south of town, where a dramatically rocky coastline offers excellent tide-pooling. The full perimeter hike is 6 miles, but shorter walks take in Bird Island, Piney Woods and the Whalers Cabin. Show up early on weekends since parking is limited.

San Carlos Borroméo de Carmelo Mission   CHURCH
(www.carmelmission.org; 3080 Rio Rd; adult/child $6.50/2; ⊙9:30am-5pm Mon-Sat, from 10:30am Sun) A mile south of downtown, this gorgeous mission is an oasis of calm and solemnity, ensconced in flowering gardens. Its stone basilica is filled with original art, while a separate chapel holds the memorial tomb of California's peripatetic mission founder Junípero Serra.

Tor House   HISTORIC BUILDING
(⊙831-624-1813; www.torhouse.org; 26304 Ocean View Ave; adult/child $10/5; ⊙10am-3pm Fri & Sat) Even if you've never heard of 20th-century poet Robinson Jeffers, a pilgrimage to his handbuilt house with its Celtic-inspired Hawk Tower offers fascinating insights into bohemian Old Carmel. Admission only by guided tour (reservations essential).

✕ Eating & Drinking

Bruno's Market & Deli   DELI, MARKET $
(www.brunosmarket.com; cnr 6th & Junípero Aves;
sandwiches $6-9; ⊙7am-8pm) Pick up a saucy
tri-trip beef sandwich and all the other ac-
coutrements for a beach picnic.

Mundaka   SPANISH $$
(☑831-624-7400; www.mundakacarmel.com; San
Carlos St, btwn Ocean & 7th Aves; small plates $7-
20; ⊙5:30-10pm Sun-Wed, to 11pm Thu-Sat) This
courtyard hideaway is a svelte escape from
Carmel's stuffy 'newly wed and nearly dead'
crowd. Take Spanish tapas plates for a spin
and sip housemade sangria while DJs spin
or flamenco guitarists play.

Katy's Place   AMERICAN $$
(http://katysplacecarmel.com; Mission St, btwn 5th
& 6th Aves; mains $11-21; ⊙7am-2pm; ⊕) In a
cutesy cottage, this popular breakfast kitch-
en cooks 16 different kinds of eggs Benedict,
from crab-meat to spicy Cajun, along with
equally filling omelettes, fruit-topped pancakes, chef's salads and club sandwiches.

Monterey

Working-class Monterey is all about the sea.
It lures visitors with a top-notch aquarium
that's a veritable temple to Monterey Bay's
underwater universe. A National Marine
Sanctuary since 1992, the bay begs for exploration by kayak, boat, scuba or snorkel. Meanwhile, downtown's historic quarter preserves
California's Spanish and Mexican roots. Don't
waste too much time on touristy Fisherman's
Wharf or Cannery Row. The latter was immortalized by novelist John Steinbeck back
when it was the hectic, smelly epicenter of
the sardine-canning industry, which was
Monterey's lifeblood until the 1950s.

◉ Sights

★ Monterey Bay Aquarium   AQUARIUM
(☑info 831-648-4800, tickets 866-963-9645;
www.montereybayaquarium.org; 886 Cannery Row;
adult/child $35/22; ⊙9:30am-6pm Mon-Fri, to
8pm Sat & Sun Jun-Aug, 10am-5pm or 6pm daily
Sep-May; ⊕) ⊘ Give yourself at least half a
day to see sharks and sardines play hide-
and-seek in kelp forests, observe the antics
of frisky otters, meditate upon psychedelic
jellyfish and get touchy-feely with sea cu-
cumbers, bat rays and other tide-pool creatures. Feeding times are the most fun. To
avoid the biggest crowds, get tickets in advance and arrive when the doors open.

Monterey State Historic Park   HISTORIC SITE
(☑audio tour 831-998-9458; www.parks.ca.gov)
Downtown, Old Monterey boasts a cluster
of lovingly restored 19th-century brick-and-
adobe buildings, including novelist Robert Louis Stevenson's one-time boarding
house and the Cooper-Molera Adobe, a sea
captain's home. Admission to the gardens
is free, but individual buildings' opening
hours, admission fees and tour schedules
vary. Pick up walking-tour maps and check
current schedules at the **Pacific House**
(☑831-649-7118; www.parks.ca.gov; 20 Custom
House Plaza; admission $3, incl walking tour $5;
⊙10am-4pm Fri-Mon), a multicultural historical museum.

Museum of Monterey   MUSEUM
(☑831-372-2608; http://museumofmonterey.org;
5 Custom House Plaza; admission $5; ⊙10am-7pm
Tue-Sat & noon-5pm Sun late May-early Sep, 10am-
5pm Wed-Sat & noon-5pm Sun early Sep-late May)
Near the waterfront, this voluminous modern exhibition hall illuminates Monterey's
helter-skelter past, from its Spanish colonial
mission days to the roller-coaster rise and fall
of the local sardine industry. Gems include
the ship-in-a-bottle collection and historic
Fresnel lens from Point Sur Lightstation.

Point Pinos Lighthouse   LIGHTHOUSE
(☑831-648-3176; www.pointpinos.org; 90 Asilomar
Ave, Pacific Grove; adult/child $2/1; ⊙1-4pm Thu-
Mon) The West Coast's oldest continuously
operating lighthouse has been warning
ships off this peninsula's hazardous point
since 1855. Inside are exhibits on its history
and its failures: local shipwrecks.

Monarch Grove Sanctuary Park   PARK
(www.ci.pg.ca.us; off Ridge Rd, Pacific Grove;
⊙dawn-dusk) FREE Between October and
February, over 25,000 migratory monarch
butterflies cluster in a thicket of eucalyptus
trees off Lighthouse Ave.

⚡ Activities

Diving and snorkeling reign supreme, although the water is rather frigid, even in
summer. Year-round, Fisherman's Wharf is
a launchpad for whale-watching trips. Rent
a bicycle or walk the paved **Monterey Peninsula Recreation Trail**, which edges the
coast past Cannery Row, ending at Lovers
Point in Pacific Grove. The overhyped **17-
Mile Drive** (www.pebblebeach.com; per car/bicy-
cle $10/free) toll road connects Monterey and
Pacific Grove with Carmel-by-the-Sea.

Adventures by the Sea   WATER SPORTS, CYCLING
(☑ 831-372-1807; http://adventuresbythesea.com; 299 Cannery Row; rental per day kayak or bicycle $30, SUP set $50) Stop by for bicycle and water-sports gear rentals, SUP lessons ($60) and kayaking tours (from $60). Also downtown at 210 Alvarado St.

Monterey Bay Kayaks   KAYAKING
(☑ 800-649-5357; www.montereybaykayaks.com; 693 Del Monte Ave; rental per day kayak or SUP set from $30) Kayak and SUP rentals, paddling lessons (from $50) and tours (from $50) of Monterey Bay and Elkhorn Slough, including sunrise and full-moon trips.

Sanctuary Cruises   WHALE-WATCHING
(☑ 831-917-1042; www.sanctuarycruises.com; adult/child $50/40) 🐋 Departing from Moss Landing, over 20 miles north of Monterey, this biodiesel boat runs whale-watching tours year-round (reservations essential).

Seven Seas Scuba   SCUBA DIVING
(☑ 831-717-4546; http://sevenseasscuba.com; 225 Cannery Row; snorkel/scuba rental package per day $35/65) Call ahead for scuba equipment rental and guided bayshore dives ($50 to $100), including at Point Lobos.

🛏 Sleeping

Skip the frills and save a bunch of dough at motels along Munras Ave south of downtown, or on N Fremont St east of Hwy 1. For camping, drive south to Big Sur.

HI Monterey Hostel   HOSTEL $
(☑ 831-649-0375; www.montereyhostel.org; 778 Hawthorne St; dm $27-35, r from $99,; ☺ check-in 4-10pm; @☎) Four blocks from Cannery Row, this simple, clean hostel is just the ticket for backpackers on a budget (reservations strongly recommended). Take MST bus 1 from downtown's Transit Plaza. All accommodation with shared bath.

Asilomar Conference Grounds   LODGE $$
(☑ 888-635-5310, 831-372-8016; www.visitasilomar.com; 800 Asilomar Ave; r incl breakfast $115-175; @☎☀🐾) This coastal state-park lodge preserves buildings designed by architect Julia Morgan, of Hearst Castle fame. Historic rooms are small and thin-walled, but charming nonetheless. The lodge's fireside rec room has pool tables and bicycle rentals.

Monterey Hotel   HISTORIC HOTEL $$
(☑ 800-966-6490, 831-375-3184; www.montereyhotel.com; 406 Alvarado St; r $80-195; ☎) Right downtown, this quaint 1904 edifice harbors small, somewhat noisy renovated rooms sporting reproduction Victorian furniture. No elevator. Parking is $17.

InterContinental–Clement   HOTEL $$$
(☑ 866-781-2406, 831-375-4500; www.ictheclementmonterey.com; 750 Cannery Row; r from $220; ❋@☎☀🐾) Like an upscale version of a millionaire's seaside clapboard house, this resort presides over Cannery Row. For utmost luxury, book an ocean-view suite with a private balcony and fireplace. Parking is $21.

🍴 Eating & Drinking

Restaurants, bars and live-music venues line Cannery Row and downtown's Alvarado St.

First Awakenings   DINER $$
(www.firstawakenings.net; American Tin Cannery, 125 Oceanview Blvd; mains $6-13; ☺ 7am-2pm Mon-Fri, to 2:30pm Sat & Sun; 🖼) Sweet and savory creative breakfasts and lunches, bottomless pitchers of coffee and an outdoor patio make this hideaway cafe in a mall near the aquarium worth finding.

Cannery Row Brewing Co   PUB $$
(☑ 831-643-2722; www.canneryrowbrewingcompany.com; 95 Prescott Ave; mains $8-18; ☺ 11:30am-11pm, bar till midnight Sun-Thu, 2am Fri & Sat) Dozens of craft beers from around the world pull raucous crowds into this bar-and-grill, with roaring fire pits on the back deck. Decent burgers, barbecue, salads and garlic fries.

★Passionfish   SEAFOOD $$$
(☑ 831-655-3311; www.passionfish.net; 701 Lighthouse Ave; mains $16-26; ☺ 5-9pm Sun-Thu, to 10pm Fri & Sat) Eureka! Finally, a perfect, chef-owned seafood restaurant where the sustainable fish is dock-fresh, every preparation fully flavored and the wine list affordable. Reservations strongly recommended.

East Village Coffee Lounge   CAFE
(www.eastvillagecoffeelounge.com; 498 Washington St; ☺ 6am-late Mon-Fri, from 7am Sat & Sun) Sleek coffeehouse with a liquor license and live-music, DJ and open-mike nights.

ℹ Information

Monterey Visitors Center (☑ 877-666-8373, 831-657-6400; www.seemonterey.com; 401 Camino El Estero; ☺ 9am-6pm Mon-Sat, to 5pm Sun, closes 1hr earlier Nov-Mar) Ask for a free *Monterey County Literary & Film Map*.

❶ Getting There & Around

Regional and local **Monterey-Salinas Transit** (MST; ☑ 888-678-2871; www.mst.org; fares $1.50-3, day pass $10) buses converge on downtown's **Transit Plaza** (cnr Pearl & Alvarado Sts), including routes to Pacific Grove, Carmel, Big Sur (summer only) and Salinas (for Greyhound bus and Amtrak train connections). In summer, free trolleys shuttle between downtown Monterey and Cannery Row and around Pacific Grove.

Santa Cruz

SoCal beach culture meets NorCal counterculture in Santa Cruz. The university student population makes this old-school radical town youthful, hip and lefty-political. Some worry that Santa Cruz's weirdness quotient is dropping, but you'll disagree when you witness the freak show (and we say that with love, man) along Pacific Ave downtown.

◉ Sights & Activities

Most of the action takes place by **Main Beach**, a mile south of downtown. Locals favor less-trampled beaches off E Cliff Dr.

Santa Cruz

Beach Boardwalk AMUSEMENT PARK
(☑ 831-423-5590; www.beachboardwalk.com; 400 Beach St; rides $3-6, all-day pass $32; ☺ daily late May-early Sep, off-season hours vary; 🖈) A short walk from the municipal wharf, this slice of Americana is the West Coast's oldest beachfront amusement park, boasting the 1924 Giant Dipper roller coaster and 1911 Looff carousel. Show up in summer for free concerts and outdoor movies.

Santa Cruz State Parks PARK
(www.thatsmypark.org; per car $8-10; ☺ sunrise-sunset) Streamside trails through coast redwood forests await at Henry Cowell Redwoods and Big Basin Redwoods State Parks, off Hwy 9 north of town in the Santa Cruz Mountains, and the Forest of Nisene Marks State Park, off Hwy 1 south near Aptos. For mountain biking, explore Wilder Ranch State Park, off Hwy 1 northbound.

Santa Cruz Surfing Museum MUSEUM
(www.santacruzsurfingmuseum.org; 701 W Cliff Dr; admission by donation; ☺ 10am-5pm Wed-Mon Jul 4-early Sep, noon-4pm Thu-Mon early Sep-Jul 3) About a mile southwest of the wharf, the old lighthouse is packed with memorabilia, including vintage redwood boards. It overlooks experts-only **Steamers Lane** and beginners' **Cowells**, both popular surf breaks.

Natural Bridges State Beach BEACH
(www.parks.ca.gov; 2531 W Cliff Dr; per car $10; ☺ 8am-sunset) This pretty beach bookends a scenic coastal cycling path about 3 miles southwest of the wharf. There are tide pools to explore and leafy trees where monarch butterflies roost from October to February.

Seymour Marine Discovery Center MUSEUM
(☑ 831-459-3800; http://seymourcenter.ucsc.edu; end of Delaware Ave; adult/child $6/4; ☺ 10am-5pm Tue-Sat, from noon Sun; 🖈) ⚲ University-run Long Marine Lab has cool interactive science exhibits for kids, including touch tanks. Look for the world's largest blue-whale skeleton outside.

Sanctuary Exploration Center MUSEUM
(☑ 831-421-9993; http://montereybay.noaa.gov; 35 Pacific St; ☺ 10am-5pm Wed-Sun; 🖈) ⚲ **FREE** Virtually journey into the kelp forests and submarine canyons of Monterey Bay National Marine Sanctuary at this educational mini museum down by the wharf.

Venture Quest KAYAKING
(☑ 831-425-8445, 831-427-2267; www.kayaksantacruz.com; Municipal Wharf; kayak rentals from $30) Experience the craggy coastline on sea-cave and wildlife-watching kayak tours (adult/child from $60/35), including moonlight paddles and excursions to Elkhorn Slough.

Roaring Camp Railroads TRAIN RIDES
(☑ 831-335-4484; www.roaringcamp.com; adult/child from $26/19; 🖈) For family fun, hop aboard a narrow-gauge steam train up into the redwoods or a standard-gauge train leaving from the beach boardwalk.

O'Neill Surf Shop SURFING
(☑ 831-475-4151; www.oneill.com; 1115 41st Ave; wetsuit/surfboard rental $10/20; ☺ 9am-8pm Mon-Fri, from 8am Sat & Sun) Head east to Capitola to this internationally renowned surfboard maker's mothership store. There's a smaller downtown branch at 110 Cooper St.

Santa Cruz Surf School SURFING
(☑ 831-426-7072; www.santacruzsurfschool.com; 131 Center St; group/private lesson from $90/120; 🖈) Friendly folks can teach you how to get out there on the waves (surfboard and wetsuit rental included with lessons).

🛏 Sleeping

Motels border Ocean St near downtown, Mission St by the university campus and Hwy 1 heading south. Make reservations for state-park **campgrounds** (☎800-444-7275; www.reserveamerica.com; campsites $35-65; 🚗🐾) at beaches off Hwy 1 and in forests off Hwy 9.

HI Santa Cruz Hostel HOSTEL $
(☎831-423-8304; www.hi-santacruz.org; 321 Main St; dm $26-29, r $60-110; ⊙check-in 5pm-10pm; 📧) Budget overnighters dig this cute hostel at the Carmelita Cottages in a flowery garden setting, two blocks from the beach. All accommodations come with shared bath. Make reservations. Parking is $2.

Adobe on Green B&B B&B $$
(☎831-469-9866; www.adobeongreen.com; 103 Green St; r incl breakfast $149-219; 🛜) 🌿 Peace and quiet are the mantras here. Your hosts are practically invisible, but their thoughtful touches are everywhere: from boutique amenities inside airy solar-powered rooms to breakfast spreads from organic gardens.

Pelican Point Inn INN $$
(☎831-475-3381; www.pelicanpointinn-santacruz. com; 21345 E Cliff Dr; ste $109-199; 🛜🚗🐾) Ideal for families, these roomy apartment-style lodgings near kid-friendly Twin Lakes Beach are equipped with everything you'll need for a lazy beach vacation, including kitchenettes. Expect some noise.

Dream Inn HOTEL $$$
(☎866-774-7735, 831-426-4330; www. dreaminnsantacruz.com; 175 W Cliff Dr; r $200-380; ❄📧🛜🐾) Overlooking the wharf from its hillside perch, this retro-chic boutique hotel is as stylish as Santa Cruz gets. Rooms have all mod cons, while the beach is just steps away. Hit happy hour at the bar inside oceanview Aquarius Restaurant. Parking is $24.

🍴 Eating

Downtown is chockablock with just-OK cafes. Cruise Mission St near the university campus and 41st Ave in neighboring Capitola for cheaper takeout and international eats.

Picnic Basket DELI, BAKERY $
(http://thepicnicbasketsc.com; 125 Beach St; items $3-8; ⊙7am-9pm, shorter hours off-season; 🚗) Locavores' kitchen across the street from the beach boardwalk makes creative sandwiches, soups, fruit sodas and baked goodies from scratch.

Penny Ice Creamery DESSERT $
(http://thepennyicecreamery.com; 913 Cedar St; items $2-4; ⊙noon-11pm) 🌿 Artisanal ice-cream shop dreams up zany flavors using local, often organic ingredients like avocado, Meyer lemon and wildflower honey.

Hula's Island Grill FUSION $$
(☎831-426-4852; www.hulastiki.com; 221 Cathcart St; dinner mains $11-20; ⊙11:30am-9:30pm Sun & Tue-Thu, to 11pm Fri & Sat, 4:30pm-9:30pm Mon) Sip a tropical cocktail at the tiki bar inside this faux lil' grass shack with glowing lanterns. Fish tacos, macadamia-nut-encrusted ahi (tuna) and luau pork plates will sate big kahunas.

Laili AFGHAN $$$
(☎831-423-4545; www.lailirestaurant.com; 101 Cooper St; dinner mains $13-26; ⊙11:30am-3pm & 5-10pm) Taste the flavors of the Silk Road at this chic, high-ceilinged dining room: pomegranate eggplant, lamb kabobs, lentil-yogurt soup and savory flatbreads are all delish.

Soif BISTRO $$$
(☎831-423-2020; www.soifwine.com; 105 Walnut Ave; small plates $5-17, mains $19-26; ⊙5-9pm Sun-Thu, to 10pm Fri & Sat) Downtown wine shop caters to bon vivants with a heady selection of 45 international wines by the glass paired with a sophisticated, seasonally driven Euro-Cal menu.

🍷 Drinking & Entertainment

Downtown is jam-packed with bars, live-music lounges, low-key nightclubs and coffeehouses. Check the free *Santa Cruz Weekly* (www.santacruzweekly.com) tabloid for more venues and current events.

Santa Cruz Mountain Brewing BREWERY
(www.scmbrew.com; 402 Ingalls St; ⊙noon-10pm) Bold, organic brews are poured west of downtown off Mission St, squeezed between Santa Cruz Mountains winery tasting rooms.

Caffe Pergolesi CAFE
(www.theperg.com; 418 Cedar St; ⊙7am-11pm; 🛜) On a leafy sidewalk verandah, discuss art and conspiracy theories over strong coffee, organic juices or beer.

Surf City Billiards & Café BAR
(http://surfcitybilliardscafe.com; 931 Pacific Ave; ⊙5pm-midnight Sun-Thu, to 2am Fri & Sat) For shooting stick, dartboards, big-screen TVs and darn good pub grub.

Catalyst LIVE MUSIC
(☑831-423-1338; www.catalystclub.com; 1011 Pacific Ave) Over the years, this landmark concert venue downtown has put cutting-edge national acts up on stage, from Nirvana to the Cold War Kids.

❶ Information

KPIG 107.5 FM Plays the classic Santa Cruz soundtrack – think Bob Marley, Janis Joplin and Willie Nelson.

Santa Cruz Visitor Center (☎800-833-3494, 831-425-1234; www.santacruzca.org; 303 Water St; ⊙9am-4pm Mon-Fri, 10am-3pm Sat & Sun; 🛜)

❶ Getting There & Away

Regional **Santa Cruz Metro** (☎831-425-8600; www.scmtd.com; fare/day pass $2/6) buses converge on downtown's **Metro Center** (920 Pacific Ave). From there, Greyhound operates a few daily buses to San Francisco ($16, three hours), San Luis Obispo ($42, four hours), Santa Barbara ($53, six hours) and LA ($59, nine hours). Daily during summer and on weekends in fall, a trolley (25¢) shuttles between downtown and the wharf.

Santa Cruz to San Francisco

Far more scenic than any freeway, this curvaceous 70-mile stretch of coastal Hwy 1 is bordered by wild beaches, organic farm stands and sea-salted villages, all scattered like loose diamonds in the rough.

About 20 miles northwest of Santa Cruz, **Año Nuevo State Park** (☑tour reservations 800-444-4445; www.parks.ca.gov; entry per car $10, tour per person $7; ⊙8:30am-5pm, last entry 3:30pm Apr-Aug, to 4pm, last entry 3pm Sep-Nov, tours only mid-Dec–Mar) is home base for the world's largest mainland breeding colony of northern elephant seals. Call ahead to reserve a 2½-hour, 3-mile guided walking tour, given during the cacophonous winter birthing and mating season.

On a quiet windswept coastal perch further north, green-business-certified **HI Pigeon Point Lighthouse Hostel** (☑650-879-0633; www.norcalhostels.org/pigeon; 210 Pigeon Point Rd; dm $26-30, r $75-180, all with shared bath; ⊙check-in 3:30pm-10:30pm; @🛜🎖) 🏄 inhabits the historic lightkeepers' quarters; it's popular, so book ahead. For more creature comforts, sleep in a tent bungalow or cozy fireplace cabin at **Costanoa** (☑877-262-7848, 650-879-1100; www.costanoa.com; 2001 Rossi Rd; tent/cabin with shared bath from $89/179; 🛜🎖).

Five miles north of Pigeon Point, **Pescadero State Beach** (www.parks.ca.gov; per car $8; ⊙8am-sunset) attracts beachcombers and birders to its marshy nature preserve nearby. For picnic supplies, head a few miles inland to Pescadero village and the bakery-deli at **Arcangeli Grocery Co** (www.normsmarket.com; 287 Stage Rd; ⊙10am-6pm). Nearby family-owned **Harley Farms Cheese Shop** (☑650-879-0480; www.harleyfarms.com; 250 North St; ⊙10am-5pm Thu-Sun; 🎖) 🏄 offers goat-dairy farm tours by reservation.

Another 15 miles north, busy Half Moon Bay is bordered by 4-mile-long **Half Moon Bay State Beach** (www.parks.ca.gov; per car $10; 🎖) and scenic **campsites** (☑800-444-7275; www.reserveamerica.com; campsites $35-50). Get out on the water with **Half Moon Bay Kayak** (☑650-773-6101; www.hmbkayak.com; Pillar Point Harbor; kayak rentals/tours from $25/75). For oceanfront luxury, the **Inn at Mavericks** (☑650-728-1572; www.innatmavericks.com; 364 Princeton Ave; r from $209; 🛜🎖) has spacious, romantic roosts. It overlooks Pillar Point Harbor, which has a decent brewpub with a sunset-view patio. In Half Moon Bay's quaint downtown, homey cafes, restaurants and eclectic shops line Main St, just inland from Hwy 1. **Flying Fish Grill** (☑650-712-1125; www.flyingfishgrill.net; 211 San Mateo Rd; dishes $5-17; ⊙11am-8:30pm Wed-Mon; 🎖) is the tastiest seafood shack around.

North of the harbor off Hwy 1, follow the signs to **Moss Beach Distillery** (www.mossbeachdistillery.com; 140 Beach Way; ⊙noon-8:30pm Sun-Thu, to 9pm Fri & Sat), a historic bootleggers' joint with a dog-friendly oceanview deck for sunset drinks. Just north, **Fitzgerald Marine Reserve** (www.fitzgeraldreserve.org; end of California Ave; ⊙8am-sunset; 🎖) **FREE** protects tide pools teeming with colorful sea life; time your visit for low tide. Another mile north, ecofriendly **HI Point Montara Lighthouse Hostel** (☑650-728-7177; www.norcalhostels.org/montara; 16th St & Hwy 1; dm $27-30, r $74-110, all with shared bath; ⊙check-in 3:30pm-10:30pm; @🛜🎖) 🏄 fronts a small private beach (reservations essential). From there, it's less than 20 miles to San Francisco via Pacifica and the Devil's Slide Tunnels.

SAN FRANCISCO & THE BAY AREA

San Francisco

If you've ever wondered where the envelope goes when it's pushed, here's your answer. Psychedelic drugs, newfangled technology, gay liberation, green ventures, free speech and culinary experimentation all became mainstream long ago in San Francisco. After 160 years of booms and busts, losing your shirt has become a favorite local pastime at the clothing-optional Bay to Breakers race, Pride Parade and hot Sundays on Baker Beach. So long, inhibitions; hello, San Francisco.

History

Before gold changed everything, San Francisco was a hapless Spanish mission built by conscripts from the Native American Ohlone and Miwok communities. Without immunity to European diseases, some 5000 of these native builders fell sick and died; they are buried beside the aptly named 18th-century Mission Dolores, 'Mission of Sorrows'.

In 1849 the gold rush turned a 800-person village into a port city of 100,000 prospectors, con artists, prostitutes and honest folk. Panic struck when Australian gold flooded the market in 1854. Frustrated miners rioted against San Francisco's Chinese community, who from 1877 to 1943 were restricted to living and working in Chinatown by anti-Chinese laws. Chinese laborers were left with few options in the 1860s to '90s besides dangerous work building railroads for San Francisco's robber barons, who dynamited, mined and clear-cut across the Golden West, and built grand Nob Hill mansions.

The city's lofty ambitions came crashing down in 1906, when earthquake and fire reduced the city to rubble. San Franciscans rebuilt an astounding 15 buildings per day. By 1915, the rebuilt city hosted the Panama-Pacific International Expo in grand style.

During WWII, soldiers accused of homosexuality and insubordination were dismissed in San Francisco, cementing the city's counterculture reputation. The Summer of Love brought free food, love and music to the hippie Haight, and enterprising gay activists founded an out-and-proud community in the Castro.

San Francisco's unconventional thinking spawned the web in the mid-1990s, and is behind today's boom in social media, mobile apps and biotech. Congratulations: you're just in time for San Francisco's next wild ride.

◉ Sights

Let San Francisco's 43 hills and more than 80 arts venues stretch your legs and your imagination, and deliver breathtaking views. Downtown sights are within walking distance of Market St, but keep your city smarts and wits about you, especially around South of Market (SoMa) and the Tenderloin (5th to 9th Sts).

SAN FRANCISCO IN...

One Day

Since the Gold Rush, San Francisco adventures have started in **Chinatown**, where you can still find hidden fortunes – in cookies, that is. Beat it to **City Lights Bookstore** to revel in Beat poetry, then pass **Transamerica Pyramid** en route to dumplings at **City View**. Hit downtown **galleries**, then head to the **Asian Art Museum**, where art transports you across centuries and oceans within an hour. Take a spooky night tour of **Alcatraz**, then make your escape from the island prison in time for dinner at the **Ferry Building** before you hit the dance floor in **SoMa** clubs.

Two Days

Start your day amid mural-covered garage doors lining **Balmy Alley**, then window-shop to **826 Valencia** for pirate supplies and ichthyoid antics in the Fish Theater. Break for burritos, then hoof it to the Haight for flashbacks at vintage boutiques and the Summer of Love site: **Golden Gate Park**. Glimpse Golden Gate Bridge views atop **MH de Young Museum**, take a walk on the wild side inside **California Academy of Sciences**, then dig into organic Cal-Moroccan feasts at **Aziza**.

San Francisco & the Bay Area

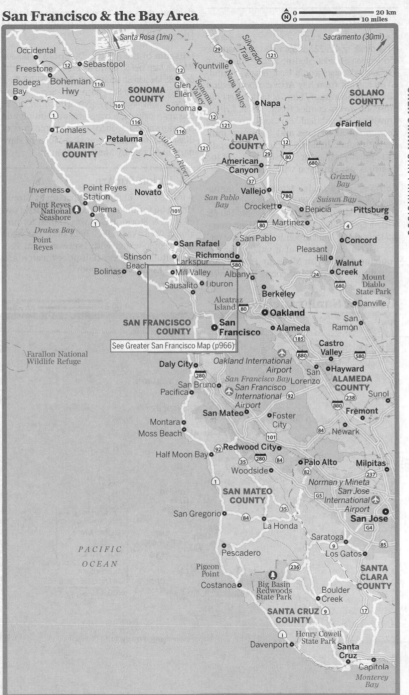

See Greater San Francisco Map (p966)

◉ SoMa

Cartoon Art Museum   MUSEUM
(Map p968; ☏ 415-227-8666; www.cartoonart.org; 655 Mission St; adult/student $7/5; ⊙ 11am-5pm Tue-Sun; Ⓜ Montgomery, Ⓑ Montgomery) Founded on a grant from Bay Area cartoon legend Charles M Schultz of *Peanuts* fame, this bold museum covers comics from '70s R Crumb drawings to political cartoons from the *Economist*. At lectures and openings, mingle with comic legends, Pixar studio heads, and obsessive collectors. First Tuesday of the month is 'pay what you wish' entry.

Contemporary Jewish Museum   MUSEUM
(Map p968; ☏ 415-344-8800; www.thecjm.org; 736 Mission St; adult/child $10/free, after 5pm Thu $5; ⊙ 11am-5pm Fri-Tue, 1-8pm Thu; Ⓜ Montgomery, Ⓑ Montgomery) That upended brushed-steel box isn't a sculpture, but a gallery for the Contemporary Jewish Museum. Exhibits are thoughtfully curated and compelling, investigating ideas and ideals through artists as diverse as Andy Warhol, Gertrude Stein and Harry Houdini.

Museum of the African Diaspora   MUSEUM
(MoAD; Map p968; ☏ 415-358-7200; www.moadsf.org; 685 Mission St; adult/student/child $10/5/free; ⊙ 11am-6pm Wed-Sat, noon-5pm Sun; Ⓜ Montgomery, Ⓑ Montgomery) Exploring four main themes – origins, movement, adaptation and transformation – MoAD tells the epic story of diaspora, including a moving video of slave narratives, told by Maya Angelou.

◉ Union Square

Bordered by high-end department stores, Union Sq (at the intersection of Geary, Powell, Post & Stockton Sts) was named for pro-Union Civil War rallies held here 150 years ago. People-watch with espresso from Emporio Rulli, and score half-price theater tickets at TIX Bay Area's booth.

Greater San Francisco

Powell St Cable Car Turnaround LANDMARK
(Map p968; cnr Powell & Market Sts; ⓜPowell, ⒷPowell) Cable cars can't go backwards, so cable-car operators turn them by hand on a revolving platform at the terminus of Powell St lines. Powell-Mason cars are quickest to the Wharf, but Powell-Hyde cars traverse more terrain and hills.

👁 Civic Center

Asian Art Museum MUSEUM
(Map p968; 🕾415-581-3500; www.asianart.org; 200 Larkin St; adult/student/child $12/8/free, 1st Sun of month free; ⏱10am-5pm Tue-Sun, to 9pm Thu Feb-Sep; ⓜCivic Center, ⒷCivic Center) Imaginations race from ancient Persian miniatures to cutting-edge Japanese fashion through three floors spanning 6000 years of Asian arts. Besides the largest collection outside Asia – 18,000 works – the museum offers excellent programs, from shadow-puppet shows to mixers with cross-cultural DJ mash-ups.

City Hall HISTORICAL BUILDING
(Map p968; 🕾art exhibit info 415-554-6080, tour info 415-554-6023; www.ci.sf.ca.us/cityhall; 400 Van Ness Ave; ⏱8am-8pm Mon-Fri, tours 10am, noon & 2pm; ♿; ⓜCivic Center, ⒷCivic Center) 𝐅𝐑𝐄𝐄 That mighty beaux-arts dome covers San Francisco's grandest ambitions and swinging tendencies. Designed in 1915 to outclass Paris and outsize Washington, DC's capitol dome, San Francisco's Rotunda remained unsteady until its retrofit after the city's 1989 earthquake, which enabled the dome to swing on its base.

👁 Financial District

Suits abound, but the 'FiDi' has redeeming quirks such as a redwood grove sprouted from whaling ships below rocket-shaped **Transamerica Pyramid** (Map p968; www. thepyramidcenter.com; 600 Montgomery St; ⏱9am-6pm Mon-Fri; ⓜEmbarcadero, ⒷEmbarcadero). Eccentric art collectors descend from hilltop mansions for First Thursday gallery openings at **14 Geary**, **49 Geary** and **77 Geary**, which are all run by the **San Francisco Art Dealers Association** (SFADA; www.sfada.com; ⏱gallery openings 10:30am-5:30pm Tue-Fri, 11am-5pm Sat).

Ferry Building LANDMARK
(Map p968; 🕾415-983-8000; www.ferrybuilding-marketplace.com; Market St & the Embarcadero; ⏱10am-6pm Mon-Fri, 9am-6pm Sat, 11am-5pm Sun; ⛴2, 6, 9, 14, 21, 31, ⓜF, J, K, L, M, N, T) Hedonism thrives at this transit hub turned gourmet emporium, where foodies happily miss their ferries while slurping local oysters and bubbly. Star chefs are spotted at the Tuesday, Thursday and Saturday farmers market (p982) year-round.

👁 Chinatown

Since 1848 this community has survived riots, earthquakes, bootlegging gangsters and politicians' attempts to relocate it down the coast.

**Chinese Historical
Society of America** MUSEUM
(CHSA; Map p968; 🕾415-391-1188; www.chsa.org; 965 Clay St; adult/child $5/2, 1st Thu of month free; ⏱noon-5pm Tue-Fri, 11am-4pm Sat; ⛲1, 30, 45, ⛴California St) Picture what it was like to be

CALIFORNIA SAN FRANCISCO

Greater San Francisco

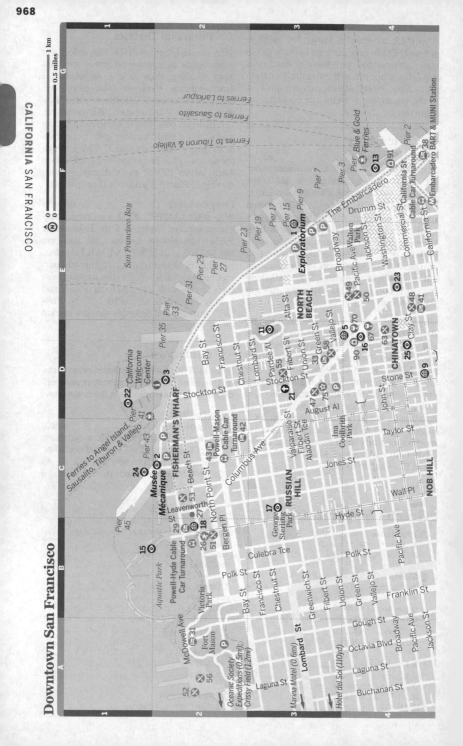

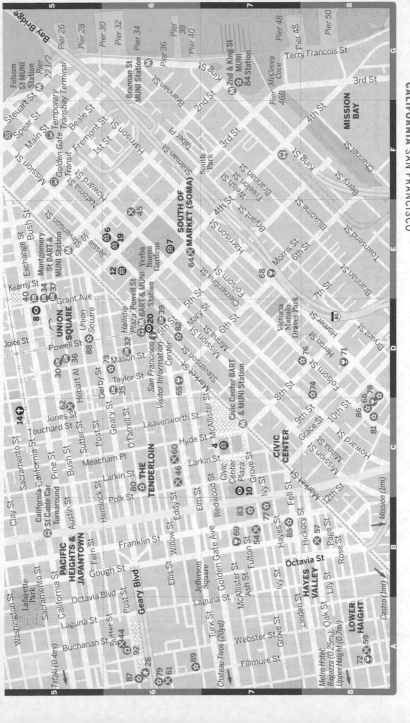

Downtown San Francisco

Chinese in America during the gold rush, the transcontinental railroad construction or San Francisco's Beat heyday in this 1932 landmark, built as Chinatown's YWCA by Julia Morgan (also chief architect of Hearst Castle).

Waverly Place STREET
(Map p968; 🚌30, 🚋California St, Powell-Mason) At Waverly Place's flag-festooned historic temples, services have been held since 1852 – even in 1906, while altars were smoldering after San Francisco's earthquake and fire. Due to 19th-century race-based restrictions, temples were built atop barber shops, laundries and restaurants lining Waverly Place.

◉ North Beach

Beat Museum MUSEUM
(Map p968; 📞1-800-537-6822; www.kerouac.com; 540 Broadway; admission adult/student $8/5; ◷10am-7pm Tue-Sun; 🖳; 🚌10, 12, 30, 41, 45, 🚋Powell-Hyde, Powell-Mason) The Beat goes on at this obsessive collection of San Francisco literary-scene ephemera c 1950–69. The banned edition of Allen Ginsberg's *Howl* is the ultimate free-speech trophy, but those Jack Kerouac bobble-head dolls are real head-shakers.

Jack Kerouac Alley STREET
(Map p968; btwn Grant & Columbus Aves; 🚌1, 10, 12, 30, 45, 🚋Powell-Hyde, Powell-Mason) 'The air was soft, the stars so fine, the promise of every cobbled alley so great...' This ode by *On the Road* author Jack Kerouac is embedded in his namesake alley, a fittingly poetic and slightly seedy shortcut between Chinatown bars and North Beach via City Lights.

◉ Russian Hill & Nob Hill

Grace Cathedral CHURCH
(Map p968; 📞415-749-6300; www.gracecathedral. org; 1100 California St; suggested donation adult/ child $3/2, Sun services free; ◷8am-6pm, services 8:30am & 11am Sun; 🚌1, 🚋California St) This Episcopal church has been rebuilt three times since the gold rush, and the current concrete Gothic cathedral features stained-glass windows honoring human endeavor, including a depiction of Albert Einstein uplifted in swirling nuclear particles.

Lombard St STREET

(Map p968; 900 block of Lombard St; 🚋Powell-Hyde) You've probably already seen Lombard Street's flower-lined switchbacks, made famous by Hitchcock's Vertigo and notorious in Tony Hawk's Pro Skater video game. In the 1920s, Lombard St's natural 27% grade was too steep for automobiles to ascend – so local property owners added eight turns to this redbrick street.

◉ Fisherman's Wharf

★**Exploratorium** MUSEUM

(Map p968; ☑415-528-4444; www.exploratorium.edu; Pier 15; adult/child $25/19, Thu evening $15; ☉10am-5pm Tue-Sun, to 10pm Wed, adults over-18yr only Thu 6pm-10pm; 👶; Ⓜ F) ✐ Hear salt sing, stimulate your appetite with color, and find out what cows see, through hands-on exhibits by MacArthur Genius grant-winners. Manhattan Project nuclear physicist Frank Oppenheimer founded the Exploratorium in 1969 to explore science and human perception, and you might experience '60s flashbacks as you grope through the Tactile Dome.

★**Musée Mécanique** AMUSEMENT PARK

(Map p968; www.museemechanique.org; Pier 45, Shed A; ☉10am-7pm; 👶; 🚌47, 🚋Powell-Mason, Powell-Hyde, Ⓜ F) Where else can you guillotine a man for a quarter? Here, creepy 19th-century arcade games such as macabre French Execution compete for your spare change with the diabolical Ms Pac-Man.

Maritime Museum MUSEUM

(Aquatic Park Bathhouse; Map p968; www.maritime.org; 900 Beach St; ☉10am-4pm; 👶; 🚌19, 30, 47, 🚋Powell-Hyde) **FREE** A monumental hint to sailors needing a scrub, the ship-shape 1939 streamline moderne Aquatic Park Bathhouse is decked out with a playful seal sculpture by Beniamino Bufano, Hilaire Hiler's underwater murals, Richard Ayer's reliefs, and veranda mosaics and a carved slate doorway by pioneering African American artist Sargent Johnson.

USS Pampanito HISTORIC SITE

(Map p968; ☑415-775-1943; www.maritime.org/pamphome.htm; Pier 45; adult/child $12/6; ☉9am-8pm Thu-Tue, to 6pm Wed; 👶; 🚌19, 30, 47, 🚋Powell-Hyde, Ⓜ F) Explore a restored WWII submarine that survived six tours of duty, while you listen to

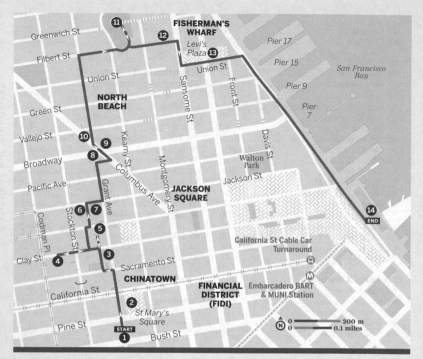

🏃 City Walk
Chinatown to the Waterfront

START CHINATOWN'S DRAGON GATE
FINISH FERRY BUILDING
LENGTH 1.8 MILES; 4½ HOURS

Discover revolutionary plots, find hidden fortunes, see controversial art and go gourmet with Gandhi. Starting at ❶ **Chinatown's Dragon Gate**, head past Grant St's gilded dragon lamps to ❷ **Old St Mary's Square**, site of a brothel leveled in the 1906 fire. Today, renegade skateboarders turn different kinds of tricks under the watchful eye of Beniamino Bufano's 1929 statue of Chinese revolutionary Sun Yat-Sen. Pass flag-festooned temple balconies along ❸ **Waverly Place**, then head to the ❹ **Chinese Historical Society of America** (p967) museum, in the majestic Chinatown YWCA built by Julia Morgan.

Enter ❺ **Spofford Alley**, where mahjong tiles click, Chinese orchestras play and beauticians gossip over blow-dryers – hard to believe this is where Prohibition bootleggers fought turf wars, and Sun Yat-Sen plotted the 1911 overthrow of China's last dynasty at No

36. Once packed with brothels, ❻ **Ross Alley** turned movie star as a location for *Karate Kid II* and *Indiana Jones and the Temple of Doom*. At No 56, make a fortune and watch it get folded into a warm cookie at ❼ **Golden Gate Fortune Cookie Factory**.

Back on Grant, take a shortcut through ❽ **Jack Kerouac Alley** (p970), where the binge-prone author often wound up *On the Road*. Stop by ❾ **City Lights** (p989) bookstore on Columbus Ave, champion of Beat poetry and free speech, and savor free verse with espresso at ❿ **Caffe Trieste** at 601 Vallejo St, under the Sicilian mural where Francis Ford Coppola wrote *The Godfather* script.

Climb to ⓫ **Coit Tower** (p973) for viewing-platform panoramas and 1930s lobby murals. Take ⓬ **Filbert St Steps** downhill past wild parrots and hidden cottages to ⓭ **Levi's Plaza**, named for the denim inventor. Head right on Embarcadero to the ⓮ **Ferry Building** (p967) for lunch Bayside, with a gaunt bronze Gandhi peeking over your shoulder.

sub-mariners' tales of stealth mode and sudden attacks in a riveting audio tour ($2) that makes surfacing afterwards a relief.

Hyde Street Pier Historic Ships HISTORIC SITE
(Map p968; ☑415-447-5000; www.nps.gov/safr; 499 Jefferson St, at Hyde St; adult/child $5/free; ☺9am-5pm; ⓜF, ☗Powell-Hyde) Tour 19th-century ships moored here as part of the Maritime National Historical Park, including triple-masted 1886 **Balclutha** and 1890 steamboat **Eureka**; summer sailing trips are available aboard elegant 1891 schooner **Alma** (☺Jun-Nov; adult/child $40/20).

Sea Lions at Pier 39 OUTDOORS
(Map p968; ☑981-1280; www.pier39.com; Beach St & the Embarcadero, Pier 39; ☺Jan-Jul; ☐15, 37, 49, F) Since California law requires boats to make way for marine mammals, yacht owners relinquish valuable slips to hundreds of sea lions who 'haul out' onto the docks from January to July, and whenever else they feel like sunbathing.

⊙ The Marina & Presidio

★Crissy Field PARK
(www.crissyfield.org; 1199 East Beach; Ⓟ; ☐30, PresidioGo Shuttle) The Presidio's army airstrip has been stripped of asphalt and reinvented as a haven for coastal birds, kite fliers and windsurfers enjoying sweeping views of Golden Gate Bridge.

★Baker Beach BEACH
(Map p966; ☺sunrise-sunset; Ⓟ; ☐29, PresidioGo Shuttle) Unswimmable waters but unbeatable views of the Golden Gate make this former Army beachhead San Francisco's tanning location of choice, especially the clothing-optional north end – at least until the afternoon fog rolls in.

⊙ The Mission

★Balmy Alley STREET ART
(☑415-285-2287; www.precitaeyes.org; btwn 24th & 25th Sts; ☐10, 12, 27, 33, 48, Ⓑ 24th St Mission) Inspired by Diego Rivera's 1930s San Francisco murals and outraged by US foreign policy in Central America, Mission artists set out in the 1970s to transform the political landscape, one mural-covered garage door at a time.

Dolores Park PARK
(www.doloresparkworks.org; Dolores St, btwn 18th & 20th Sts; ⛹⛹; ☐14, 33, 49, Ⓑ16th St Mission, ⓜJ) Semiprofessional tanning, taco picnics

and a Hunky Jesus Contest every Easter: welcome to San Francisco's sunny side. Dolores Park has something for everyone, from tennis and political protests to the Mayan pyramid playground.

★826 Valencia CULTURAL SITE
(☑415-642-5905; www.826valencia.org; 826 Valencia St; ☺noon-6pm; ⛹; ☐14, 33, 49, Ⓑ16th St Mission, ⓜJ) The eccentric Pirate Supply Store sells eye patches, scoops from an actual tub o' lard, and McSweeney's literary magazines to support a teen-writing nonprofit organization and the Fish Theater. It's a shop, but really it's much more than that. There's even a vat of sand where kids can rummage for buried pirates' booty.

Mission Dolores CHURCH
(Misión San Francisco de Asís; ☑415-621-8203; www.missiondolores.org; 3321 16th St; adult/child $5/3; ☺9am-4pm Nov-Apr, to 4:30pm May-Oct; ☐22, 33, Ⓑ16th St Mission, ⓜJ) The city's oldest building and its namesake, whitewashed adobe Misión San Francisco de Asís was founded in 1776 and rebuilt in 1782 with conscripted Ohlone and Miwok labor – note the ceiling patterned after native baskets.

⊙ The Castro

GLBT History Museum MUSEUM
(☑415-777-5455; www.glbthistory.org/museum; 4127 18th St; admission $5; ☺11am-7pm Mon-Sat, noon-5pm Sun; ⓜCastro) America's first gay-history museum showcases Harvey Milk's

---

COIT TOWER

Adding an exclamation mark to San Francisco's landscape, **Coit Tower** (Map p968; ☑415-362-0808; http://sfrecpark.org/destination/telegraph-hill-pioneer-park/coit-tower; Telegraph Hill Blvd; elevator entry (nonresident) adult/child $7/5; ☺10am-5:30pm Mar-Sep, 9am-4:30pm Oct-Feb; ☐39) offers views worth shouting about – especially after you climb the giddy, steep **Filbert St steps** to get here. Check out 360-degree views of downtown from the viewing platform, and wrap-around 1930s lobby murals glorifying San Francisco workers – once denounced as communist but now a beloved landmark. To glimpse murals hidden inside Coit Tower's stairwell, take free docent-led tours at 11am Saturdays.

SAN FRANCISCO NEIGHBORHOODS IN A NUTSHELL

North Beach Poetry and parrots, sidewalk cafes, Italian restaurants.

Fisherman's Wharf Sea-lion antics, vintage video games, and getaways to and from Alcatraz.

Downtown & the Financial District Glossy flagship stores and top-chef bistros, gallery openings and clearance sales.

Chinatown Pagoda roofs, dim sum, and fortunes made and lost in historic alleyways.

Hayes Valley & Civic Center Grand buildings and great performances, foodie finds and local designs.

Tenderloin Theater district, Skid Row, dive bars and noodle shops.

SoMa Where high technology meets higher art, and everyone gets down and dirty on the dance floor.

Mission A book in one hand, a burrito in the other, murals all around.

Castro Out and proud with samba whistles, rainbow flags and policy platforms.

Haight Sixties flashbacks, alternative fashion, free music and pricey skateboards.

Japantown & the Fillmore Sushi, shopping and rock at the Fillmore.

Marina & the Presidio Boutiques, organic dining, nature and nudity at a former army base.

Golden Gate Park & Around San Francisco's mile-wide wild streak, surrounded by gourmet surfer hangouts.

---

campaign literature, matchbooks from long-gone bathhouses, audiovisual interviews with Gore Vidal and pages of the 1950s penal code banning homosexuality.

The Haight

Alamo Square Park PARK
(Hayes & Scott Sts; 🎟; ☐5, 21, 22, 24) **FREE** Summit Alamo Sq to see downtown framed by gabled Victorian rooflines and wind-sculpted pines. Pastel 'Painted Lady' Victorian mansions along eastside **Postcard Row** pale in comparison to colorful neighbors, including gilded green 1889 Westerfield House, which survived tenancies by czarist bootleggers, hippie communes, even tower rituals by Church of Satan founder Anton LaVey.

Haight & Ashbury LANDMARK
(☐6, 33, 37, 43, 71) The legendary psychedelic '60s intersection remains a counterculture magnet, where you can sign Green Party petitions, commission poems, hear Hare Krishna on keyboards and Bob Dylan on banjo. The clock overhead always reads 4:20 – better known in herbal circles as International Bong-Hit Time.

Golden Gate Park & Around

San Francisco was way ahead of its time in 1865, when the city voted to turn 1017 acres of sand dunes into the world's largest city stretch of green, **Golden Gate Park**. Tenacious park architect William Hammond Hall ousted hotels and casinos for this nature preserve. The park ends at **Ocean Beach** (Map p966; ☑415-561-4323; www.park-sconservancy.org; Great Hwy; ☺sunrise-sunset; ☐5, 18, 31, ⓂN), where **Cliff House** restaurant overlooks the splendid ruin of **Sutro Baths** (Map p966; www.nps.gov/goga/historycul-ture/sutro-baths.htm; Point Lobos Ave; ☺sunrise-sunset; visitor center hours 9am-5pm; Ⓟ; ☐5, 31, 38) **FREE**. Follow the partly paved trail around **Lands End** for shipwreck sightings and Golden Gate Bridge views.

California Academy of Sciences MUSEUM
(☑415-379-8000; www.calacademy.org; 55 Music Concourse Dr; adult/child $35/25, discount with Muni ticket $3; ☺9:30am-5pm Mon-Sat, 11am-5pm Sun; 🎟; ☐5, 6, 31, 33, 44, 71, ⓂN) Architect Renzo Piano's LEED-certified green building houses 38,000 weird and wonderful animals, with a four-story rainforest and aquarium under a 'living roof' of California wildflowers. After the penguins nod off to

sleep, the wild rumpus starts at kids-only Academy Sleepovers and over-21 NightLife Thursdays.

MH de Young Museum   MUSEUM

(☑ 415-750-3600; www.famsf.org/deyoung; 50 Hagiwara Tea Garden Dr; adult/child $10/6, discount with Muni ticket $2, 1st Tue of month free, online booking fee $1 per ticket; ⊙ 9:30am-5:15pm Tue-Sun, to 8:45pm Fri mid-Jan–Nov; ☐ 5, 44, 71, Ⓜ N) Follow sculptor Andy Goldsworthy's sidewalk fault line into Herzog & de Meuron's sleek copper-clad building, and broaden your artistic horizons with Oceanic ceremonial masks and sculptor Al Farrow's cathedrals built from bullets.

Legion of Honor   MUSEUM

(Map p966; ☑ 415-750-3600; http://legionofhonor. famsf.org; 100 34th Ave; adult/child $10/6, discount with Muni ticket $2, 1st Tue of month free; ⊙ 9:30am-5:15pm Tue-Sun; ☒; ☐ 1, 18, 38) A museum as eccentric and illuminating as San Francisco itself, the Legion showcases a wildly eclectic collection, ranging from Monet water lilies to John Cage soundscapes, ancient Iraqi ivories and R Crumb comics.

Conservatory of Flowers   NATURAL SITE

(☑ info 415-831-2090; www.conservatoryofflowers.org; 100 John F Kennedy Dr; adult/child $7/5; ⊙ 10am-4:30pm Tue-Sun; ☐ 71, Ⓜ N) This recently restored 1878 Victorian greenhouse is home to outer-space orchids, contemplative floating lilies and creepy carnivorous plants that reek of insect belches.

Japanese Tea Garden   GARDEN

(☑ tea ceremony reservations 415-752-1171; www. japaneseteagardensf.com; 75 Hagiwara Tea Garden Dr; adult/child $7/5, before 10am Mon, Wed & Fri free; ⊙ 9am-6pm Mar-Oct, to 4:45pm Nov-Feb; ☐ 5, 44, 71, Ⓜ N) Since 1894, this picturesque 5-acre garden and bonsai grove has blushed with cherry blossoms in spring and turned flaming red with maple leaves in fall. Lose all track of time in the meditative Zen Garden.

San Francisco Botanical Garden   GARDEN

(Strybing Arboretum; ☑ 415-661-1316; www.strybing.org; 1199 9th Ave; adult/child $7/5, 2nd Tue of month free; ⊙ 9am-6pm Apr-Oct, to 5pm Nov-Mar, bookstore 10am-4pm; ☒; ☐ 6, 43, 44, 71, Ⓜ N) ✿ Sniff your way around the world inside this 55-acre garden. Almost anything grows in the peculiar microclimates of this corner of Golden Gate Park, from South African savannah grasses to Japanese magnolias.

◉ San Francisco Bay

★ Golden Gate Bridge   BRIDGE

(Map p966; www.goldengatebridge.org/visitors; off Lincoln Blvd; northbound free, southbound toll $6; ☐ 28, all Golden Gate Transit buses) San Francisco's 1937 suspension bridge was almost nixed by the navy in favor of yellow-striped concrete pylons. Instead, engineer Joseph B Strauss, architects Gertrude and Irving Murrow and daredevil workers created an International Orange deco icon. The southbound toll is billed electronically to your vehicle's license plate; for details, see www.goldengate.org/tolls.

🏃 Activities

★ Kabuki Springs & Spa   SPA

(Map p968; ☑ 415-922-6000; www.kabukisprings.com; 1750 Geary Blvd; admission $25; ⊙ 10am-9:45pm, co-ed Tue, women-only Wed, Fri & Sun, men-only Mon, Thu & Sat; ☐ 22, 38) Scrub down with salt in the communal steam room, soak in the hot pool, take the cold plunge and reheat in the sauna. Silence sets a meditative mood – if you hear the gong, it means shhhh!

DON'T MISS

ALCATRAZ

Over 150 years, **Alcatraz** (Map p966; ☑ Alcatraz Cruises 415-981-7625; www. alcatrazcruises.com; day tours adult/child/ family $30/18/92, night tours adult/child $37/22; ⊙ call center 8am-7pm, ferries depart Pier 33 half-hourly 9am-3:55pm, night tours 6:10pm & 6:45pm) has been the nation's first military prison, a maximum-security penitentiary housing A-list criminals including Al Capone, and hotly disputed Native American territory. No prisoners escaped Alcatraz alive, but since importing guards and supplies cost more than putting up prisoners at the Ritz, the prison was closed in 1963.

Day visits include the cruise to and from the penitentiary and captivating audio tours with prisoners and guards recalling life on 'the Rock,' while night tours are led by a park ranger; reserve tickets at least two weeks ahead.

Alcatraz

Book a ferry from Pier 33 and ride 1.5 miles across the bay to explore America's most notorious former prison. The trip itself is worth the money, providing stunning views of the city skyline. Once you've landed at the **Ferry Dock & Pier** **1**, you begin the 580-yard walk to the top of the island and prison; if you're out of shape, there's a twice-hourly tram.

As you climb toward the **Guardhouse** **2**, notice the island's steep slope; before it was a prison, Alcatraz was a fort. In the 1850s, the military quarried the rocky shores into near-vertical cliffs. Ships could then only dock at a single port, separated from the main buildings by a sally port (a drawbridge and moat in what became the guardhouse). Inside, peer through floor grates to see Alcatraz' original prison.

Volunteers tend the brilliant **Officer's Row Gardens** **3** – an orderly counterpoint to the overgrown rose bushes surrounding the burned-out shell of the **Warden's House** **4**. At the top of the hill, by the front door of the **Main Cellhouse** **5**, beauty shots unfurl all around, including a **view of the Golden Gate Bridge** **6**. Above the main door of the administration building, notice the **historic signs & graffiti** **7**, before you step inside the dank, cold prison to find the **Frank Morris cell** **8**, former home to Alcatraz' most notorious jail-breaker.

TOP TIPS

➡ Book at least two weeks prior for self-guided daytime visits, longer for ranger-led night tours. For info on garden tours, see www.alcatraz gardens.org.

➡ Be prepared to hike; a steep path ascends from the ferry landing to the cell block. Most people spend two to three hours on the island. You need only reserve for the outbound ferry; take any ferry back.

➡ There's no food (just water) but you can bring your own; picnicking is allowed at the ferry dock only. Dress in layers as weather changes fast and it's usually windy.

JOHN A VLAHIDES ©

Historic Signs & Graffiti
During their 1969–71 occupation, Native Americans graffitied the water tower: 'Home of the Free Indian Land.' Above the cellhouse door, examine the eagle-and-flag crest to see how the red-and-white stripes were changed to spell 'Free.'

Warden's House
Fires destroyed the warden's house and other structures during the Indian Occupation. The government blamed the Native Americans; the Native Americans blamed agents provocateurs acting on behalf of the Nixon Administration to undermine public sympathy.

Parade Grounds

DAVID CLAPP / GETTY IMAGES ©

Ferry Dock & Pier
A giant wall map helps you get your bearings. Inside nearby Bldg 64, short films and exhibits provide historical perspective on the prison and details about the Indian Occupation.

View of Golden Gate Bridge

The Golden Gate Bridge stretches wide on the horizon. Best views are from atop the island at Eagle Plaza, near the cellhouse entrance, and at water level along the Agave Trail (September to January only).

Main Cellhouse

During the mid-20th century, the maximum-security prison housed the day's most notorious troublemakers, including Al Capone and Robert Stroud, the 'Birdman of Alcatraz' (who actually conducted his ornithology studies at Leavenworth).

Power House

Recreation Yard

Water Tower

6

5

8

Officers' Club

7

Lighthouse

3

4

Guard Tower

2

Frank Morris Cell

Peer into cell 138 on B-Block to see a re-creation of the dummy's head that Frank Morris left in his bed as a decoy to aid his notorious – and successful – 1962 escape from Alcatraz.

Guardhouse

Alcatraz' oldest building dates to 1857 and retains remnants of the original drawbridge and moat. During the Civil War the basement was transformed into a military dungeon – the genesis of Alcatraz as prison.

Officer's Row Gardens

In the 19th century soldiers imported topsoil to beautify the island with gardens. Well-trusted prisoners later gardened – Elliott Michener said it kept him sane. Historians, ornithologists and archaeologists choose today's plants.

1

JAPANTOWN & PACIFIC HEIGHTS

Atop every Japantown sushi counter perches a *maneki neko,* the porcelain cat with one paw raised in permanent welcome: you are invited for shopping at New People (p989), shiatsu massages at Kabuki Springs & Spa (p975), eco-entertainment at Sundance Kabuki Cinema (p988), world-class jazz at Yoshi's (p987) or mind-blowing rock at the Fillmore (p987).

★18 Reasons   COOKING

(☑415-568-2710; www.18reasons.org; 3674 18th St; classes & events $5-35; ⊘varies by event; ●; 🖵22, 33, Ⓜ J) 🖉 Deliciously educational events: shochu tastings, knife-skills and cheese-making workshops, and California cuisine classes. Mingle at family-friendly Wednesday soup suppers and Thursday happy hours.

Blazing Saddles   CYCLING

(Map p968; ☑415-202-8888; www.blazingsaddles. com; 2715 Hyde St; bike rental per hour $8-15, per day $32-88; electric bikes per day $48-88; ⊘8am-7:30pm; ●; 🚋Powell-Hyde) Convenient for biking the Embarcadero or to the Golden Gate Bridge, this outfit offers electric bikes, rentals with packs and bungee cords, and 24-hour return service.

👉 Tours

★Precita Eyes Mission Mural Tours   TOUR

(☑415-285-2287; www.precitaeyes.org; adult $15-20, child $5; ⊘see website calendar for tour dates; ●) Muralists lead two-hour tours on foot or bicycle covering 60 to 70 murals in a six-to-10-block radius of mural-bedecked Balmy Alley; proceeds fund mural upkeep at this community arts nonprofit.

Chinatown Alleyway Tours   TOUR

(☑415-984-1478; www.chinatownalleywaytours. org; adult/student $18/12; ⊘11am Sat & Sun; ●) Neighborhood teens lead two-hour community nonprofit tours for up-close-and-personal peeks into Chinatown's past (weather permitting). Book five days ahead or pay double for Saturday walk-ins; cash only.

Oceanic Society Expeditions   TOUR

(☑415-474-3385; www.oceanicsociety.org; 3950 Scott St; whale-watching trips per person $120-125; ⊘office 8:30am-5pm Mon-Fri, trips Sat & Sun; 🖵30) Naturalist-led weekend boating daytrips depart from Yacht Harbor. Kids must be 10 years or older. Reservations required.

Public Library City Guides   TOUR

(www.sfcityguides.org; donations/tips welcome) FREE Volunteer local historians lead non-profit tours organized by neighborhood and theme: Gold Rush Downtown, Secrets of Fisherman's Wharf, Telegraph Hill Stairway Hike and more.

⭐ Festivals & Events

Chinese New Year Parade   CULTURE

(www.chineseparade.com; ⊘Feb) Chase the 200ft dragon, and see lion dancers and toddler kung-fu classes parade through Chinatown.

SF International Film Festival   FILM

(www.sffs.org; ⊘Apr) Stars align and directors launch premieres at the nation's oldest film festival.

Bay to Breakers   SPORT

(www.baytobreakers.com; race registration $58-90; ⊘May) Run costumed from Embarcadero to Ocean Beach on the third Sunday in May, while joggers dressed as salmon run upstream.

Carnaval   CULTURE

(www.carnavalsf.com; ⊘May) Brazilian, or just faking it with a wax and a tan? Shake your tail feathers in the Mission on the last weekend of May.

SF Pride Celebration   CULTURE

(⊘Jun) A day isn't enough to do San Francisco proud: June begins with **International LGBT Film Festival** (www.frameline.org), and goes out in style the last weekend with Pink Saturday's **Dyke March** (www.dykemarch.org) and the frisky, million-strong **Pride Parade** (www.sfpride.org).

Folsom Street Fair   STREET FAIR

(www.folsomstreetfair.com; ⊘Sep) Work that leather look and enjoy public spankings for local charities at this adults-only bondage festival. Runs the last weekend of September.

Hardly Strictly Bluegrass   MUSIC

(www.strictlybluegrass.com; ⊘Oct) San Francisco celebrates Western roots with three days of free Golden Gate Park concerts and headliners ranging from Elvis Costello to Gillian Welch in early October.

Litquake LITERATURE
(www.litquake.com; ⊙Sep) Score signed books and grab drinks with authors afterwards.

Green Festival CULTURE
(www.greenfestivals.org; ⊙mid-Nov) Energy-saving spotlights are turned on green cuisine, technology, fashion and booze for three days in mid-November.

🛏 Sleeping

San Francisco is the birthplace of the boutique hotel, which offers stylish rooms for a price: $120 to $200 midrange, plus 15.5% hotel tax (hostels exempt) and $35 to $50 for overnight parking. For vacancies and deals, check San Francisco Visitor Information Center's reservation line (p990), **Bed & Breakfast San Francisco** (☑415-899-0060; www.bbsf.com) and **Lonely Planet** (http://hotels.lonelyplanet.com).

🛏 Union Square & Civic Center

★**Orchard Garden Hotel** BOUTIQUE HOTEL $$
(Map p968; ☑888-717-2881, 415-399-9807; www.theorchardgardenhotel.com; 466 Bush St; r $189-259; ❊@🛜; 🚊2, 3, 30, 45, Ⓑ Montgomery) 🌱 San Francisco's first all-green-practices hotel uses sustainably grown wood, chemical-free cleaning products and luxe recycled fabrics in its soothingly quiet rooms. Don't miss the sunny rooftop terrace.

Hotel Rex BOUTIQUE HOTEL $$
(Map p968; ☑415-433-4434, 800-433-4434; www.jdvhotels.com; 562 Sutter St; r $159-229; ❊@🛜🐾; 🚋Powell-Hyde, Powell-Mason, ⓂPowell) 🌱 French gramophone lobby music conjures New York's Algonquin in the 1920s, and handsome guest rooms feature hand-painted lampshades, local art and plush beds with crisp linens and down pillows. Street-facing rooms are bright but noisy; request air-con.

Hotel Triton BOUTIQUE HOTEL $$
(Map p968; ☑800-800-1299, 415-394-0500; www.hoteltriton.com; 342 Grant Ave; r $175-275, ste $350; ❊@🛜🐾🐕; ⓂMontgomery, Ⓑ Montgomery) 🌱 Beyond the colorful, comic-bookish lobby are hip rooms with San Francisco–centric details – such as wallpaper of Kerouac's *On the Road* – plus ecofriendly amenities, shagworthy beds and unlimited ice cream. Don't miss tarot-card readings and chair massages during nightly wine hour.

Hotel Zetta HOTEL $$
(Map p968; ☑855-212-4187, 415-543-8555; www.hotelzetta.com; 55 5th St; r $189-249; ❊@🛜🐾; ⒷPowell St, ⓂPowell St) 🌱 Opened in 2013, this eco-conscious downtowner caters to play-hard techies; there's billiards, shuffleboard and a Plinko wall above the art-filled lobby. Bigger-than-average rooms have padded black-leather headboards, low-slung platform beds and web-enabled flat-screen TVs.

Golden Gate Hotel HOTEL $$
(Map p968; ☑800-835-1118, 415-392-3702; www.goldengatehotel.com; 775 Bush St; r with/without bath $175/115; @🛜; 🚊2, 3, 🚋Powell-Hyde, Powell-Mason) Like an old-fashioned pension, this 1913 Edwardian hotel has kindly owners and homey mismatched furniture.

SAN FRANCISCO FOR CHILDREN

Although it has the least kids per capita of any US city – according to recent San Francisco SPCA data, there are 32,000 more dogs than children in town – San Francisco is packed with attractions for kids, including Golden Gate Park, Exploratorium, California Academy of Sciences, Cartoon Art Museum and Musée Mécanique. For babysitting, **American Child Care** (☑415-285-2300; www.americanchildcare.com; 580 California St, Suite 1600) charges $20 per hour plus gratuity; four-hour minimum.

The **Children's Creativity Museum** (Map p968; ☑415-820-3320; www.zeum.org; 221 4th St; admission $11; ⊙10am-4pm Wed-Sun Sep-May, Tue-Sun Jun-Aug; 🐾; ⓂPowell, Ⓑ Powell) has technology that's too cool for school: robots, live-action video games, DIY music videos and 3D animation workshops with Silicon Valley innovators.

At **Aquarium of the Bay** (Map p968; www.aquariumofthebay.com; Pier 39; adult/child/family $18/10/50; ⊙9am-8pm summer, 10am 6pm winter; 🐾; 🚊49, 🚋Powell-Mason, ⓂF), glide through glass tubes underwater on conveyer belts as sharks circle overhead.

Fire Engine Tours (Map p968; ☑415-333-7077; www.fireenginetours.com; departs Beach St, at the Cannery; adult/child $50/30; ⊙tours depart 9am, 11am, 1pm, 3pm) are hot stuff: take a 75-minute, open-air vintage fire-engine ride over Golden Gate Bridge.

Rooms are small but comfortable; most have private baths. Homemade cookies and a resident kitty-cat provide comfort after sightseeing.

Hotel Abri

HOTEL $$

(Map p968; ☑415-392-8800, 888-229-0677; www.hotelabrisf.com; 127 Ellis St; r $169-249; ❊ @ ❢ ❧; Ⓜ Powell, Ⓑ Powell) Contemporary chic, with bold black-and-tan motifs, pillow-top beds with feather pillows, iPod docks, flat-screen TVs and big workstations. Few bathrooms have tubs, but rainfall showerheads compensate.

Hotel des Arts

ART HOTEL $$

(Map p968; ☑800-956-4322, 415-956-3232; www.sfhoteldesarts.com; 447 Bush St; r with bath $119-159, without bath $79-99; ❢; Ⓜ Montgomery, Ⓑ Montgomery) A budget hotel for art freaks, with jaw-dropping murals by underground artists. Downsides: thin linens, earplugs possibly needed, and rooms with private bath require seven-night stays.

★ Hotel Monaco

BOUTIQUE HOTEL $$

(Map p968; ☑415-292-0100, 866-622-5284; www.monaco-sf.com; 501 Geary St; r $179-269; ❊ @ ❢ ❧; ☐38, ☐ Powell-Hyde, Powell-Mason) ✎ Snazzy Monaco gets the details right: colorful guest rooms offer high-thread-count sheets, ergonomic workspaces and ample closet space. Extras include spa with Jacuzzi, gym, evening wine and bicycles.

☐ Financial District & North Beach

San Remo Hotel

HOTEL $

(Map p968; ☑800-352-7366, 415-776-8688; www.sanremohotel.com; 2237 Mason St; d with shared bath $79-129; @ ❢ ❧; ☐30, 47, ☐ Powell-Mason) One of the city's best-value spots, this 1906 inn is an old-fashioned charmer with vintage furnishings. Bargain rooms face the corridor; family suites accommodate up to five. No elevator.

Pacific Tradewinds Hostel

HOSTEL $

(Map p968; ☑888-734-6783, 415-433-7970; www.sanfranciscohostel.org; 680 Sacramento St; dm $30; @ ❢; ☐1, ☐ California St, Ⓑ Montgomery) San Francisco's smartest-looking all-dorm hostel has a blue-and-white nautical theme, fully equipped kitchen, spotless glass-brick showers, no lockout time and great service. No elevator means hauling bags up three flights.

★ Hotel Bohème

BOUTIQUE HOTEL $$

(Map p968; ☑415-433-9111; www.hotelboheme.com; 444 Columbus Ave; r $174-224; @ ❢; ☐10, 12, 30, 41, 45) A love letter to the Beat era, with moody orange, black and sage-green color schemes nodding to the 1950s, parasol lights and vintage photos. Rooms are smallish and some face noisy Columbus Ave, but you're in the heart of vibrant North Beach.

Hotel Vitale

BOUTIQUE HOTEL $$$

(Map p968; ☑888-890-8688, 415-278-3700; www.hotelvitale.com; 8 Mission St; r from $255; ❊ @ ❢ ❧; Ⓜ Embarcadero, Ⓑ Embarcadero) Tinted glass disguises a fashion-forward hotel, with up-to-the-minute luxuries: 450-thread-count sheets, on-site spa with rooftop hot tubs, and some rooms that offer spectacular bridge views.

☐ Fisherman's Wharf & The Marina

★ HI San Francisco Fisherman's Wharf

HOSTEL $

(Map p968; ☑415-771-7277; www.sfhostels.com; Bldg 240, Fort Mason; dm incl breakfast $30-40, r $65-100; Ⓟ @ ❢; ☐28, 30, 47, 49) A former army hospital building offers bargain-priced private rooms and dorms (some co-ed) with four to 22 beds and a huge kitchen. No curfew, but no heat during the day: bring warm clothes. Limited free parking.

Hotel del Sol

MOTEL $$

(☑415-921-5520, 877-433-5765; www.thehoteldelsol.com; 3100 Webster St; d $189-269; Ⓟ ❊ @ ❢ ❧ ❧ ❧; ☐22, 28, 30, 43) ✎ A spiffy, kid-friendly, tropical-themed 1950s motor lodge, with palm-lined central courtyard and heated outdoor pool. Family suites have trundle beds and board games. Free parking.

Tuscan Inn

BOUTIQUE HOTEL $$

(Map p968; ☑800-648-4626, 415-561-1100; www.tuscaninn.com; 425 North Point St; r $169-299; ❊ @ ❢ ❧ ❧; ☐47, ☐ Powell-Mason, Ⓜ F) ✎ Managed by fashion-forward Kimpton, the Tuscan's spacious jewel-toned rooms have more character than most chain-hotel digs. Kids love in-room Nintendo; parents love afternoon wine hours.

Marina Motel

MOTEL $$

(☑800-346-6118, 415-921-9406; www.marinamotel.com; 2576 Lombard St; r $139-199; Ⓟ ❢ ❧; ☐28, 30, 41, 43, 45) The vintage 1939 Marina has a Spanish-Mediterranean look, with a bougainvillea-lined courtyard. Rooms are homey and well maintained, and some have full kitchens (extra $10 to $20).

★ **Argonaut Hotel** BOUTIQUE HOTEL **$$$**
(Map p968; ☎866-415-0704, 415-563-0800; www.argonauthotel.com; 495 Jefferson St; r $205-325, with view $305-550; ❄☎♨☎; ☎19, 47, 49, ☎Powell-Hyde) ✦ Built as a cannery in 1908, Fisherman's Wharf's best inn has wooden beams, exposed brick walls, and an over-the-top nautical theme that includes porthole-shaped mirrors. Ultracomfy beds and iPod docks are standard, though some rooms are tiny, with limited sunlight – pay extra for a mesmerizing bay view.

🛏 **The Mission**

Inn San Francisco B&B **$$**
(☎415-641-0188, 800-359-0913; www.innsf.com; 943 S Van Ness Ave; r incl breakfast $185-295, with shared bath $135-185, cottage $325-385; ℗@☎; ☎14, 49) ✦ An impeccably maintained 1872 Italianate-Victorian mansion, this inn has period antiques, fresh-cut flowers and fluffy feather beds; some have Jacuzzi tubs. Outside there's an English garden and a redwood hot tub. Limited parking: reserve ahead. No elevator.

🛏 **The Castro**

Parker Guest House B&B **$$**
(☎888-520-7275, 415-621-3222; www.parkerguesthouse.com; 520 Church St; r incl breakfast $159-269; @☎; ☎33, Ⓜ J) The Castro's stateliest gay digs occupy two side-by-side Edwardian mansions sharing a garden and steam room. Rooms have supercomfortable beds and down duvets; bath fixtures gleam. No elevator.

🛏 **The Haight**

Metro Hotel HOTEL **$**
(☎415-861-5364; www.metrohotelsf.com; 319 Divisadero St; r $88-138; @☎; ☎6, 24, 71) A central Haight hotel providing cheap, clean rooms with private bath and garden patio. Ragazza pizzeria (p984) is downstairs. No elevator.

Red Victorian Bed, Breakfast & Art B&B **$**
(☎415-864-1978; www.redvic.net; 1665 Haight St; r incl breakfast $159-189, without bath $99-139; ☎; ☎33, 43, 71) ✦ The trippy '60s live at this 1904 Victorian, with room themes that include Sunshine, Flower Children and Summer of Love. Only four of the 18 rooms have private baths; but all include breakfast in organic Peace Café downstairs.

Chateau Tivoli B&B **$$**
(☎800-228-1647, 415-776-5462; www.chateautivoli.com; 1057 Steiner St; r incl breakfast $170-215, without bath $115-135, ste $275-300; ☎; ☎5, 22) This glorious chateau off Alamo Sq once hosted Isadora Duncan and Mark Twain, and shows character with turrets, cornices, woodwork and, rumor has it, the ghost of a Victorian opera diva. No elevator; no TVs.

✕ **Eating**

Hope you're hungry – there are 10 times more restaurants per capita in San Francisco than in any other US city. Most of San Francisco's top restaurants are quite small, so reserve ahead. For bargain eats, hit Mission taquerias, Chinatown dim-sum joints and North Beach delis.

✕ **SOMA, Union Square & Civic Center**

Saigon Sandwich Shop VIETNAMESE **$**
(Map p968; ☎415-474-5698; saigon-sandwich.com; 560 Larkin St; sandwiches $3.50; ☺7am-5pm; ☎19, 31) Wait on a sketchy sidewalk for baguettes piled high with your choice of roast pork, chicken, pâté, meatballs and/or tofu, plus pickled carrots, cilantro, jalapeño and onion.

Brenda's French Soul Food CREOLE, SOUTHERN **$$**
(Map p968; ☎415-345-8100; www.frenchsoulfood.com; 652 Polk St; mains lunch $9-13, dinner $11-17; ☺8am-3pm Mon & Tue, to 10pm Wed-Sat, to 8pm Sun; ☎19, 31, 38, 47, 49) Chef–owner Brenda Buenviaje serves Cal-Creole classics, including Hangtown fry (eggs with bacon and fried oysters), shrimp-stuffed po' boys, fried chicken with collard greens, hot-pepper jelly and watermelon sweet tea.

★ **Rich Table** CALIFORNIAN **$$$**
(Map p968; ☎415-355-9085; http://richtablesf.com; 199 Gough St; meals $30-40; ☺5:30-10pm Sun-Thu, to 10:30pm Fri-Sat; ☎5, 6, 21, 47, 49, 71, Ⓜ Van Ness) ✦ Licking plates is the obvious move after finishing apricot soup with pancetta and rabbit canneloni with nasturtium cream. Co-chefs/co-owners/spouses Sarah and Evan Rich invent playful Californian food such as the Dirty Hippie: silky

goat-buttermilk panna cotta topped with nutty hemp. Book two to four weeks ahead (call the restaurant directly).

Sweet Woodruff CAFE, CALIFORNIAN $$
(Map p968; ☑ 415-292-9090; www.sweetwood-ruffsf.com; 798 Sutter St; dishes $8-13; ⊙11am–9:45pm; ☐2, 3, 27) ✐ Little sister to Michelin-starred Sons & Daughters, this storefront cafe uses seasonal-regional ingredients for small plates such as roasted padron peppers with fromage blanc and sea-urchin baked potatoes with bacon. There's no waiter service and no stove – just an oven, hot plate and imagination.

Zero Zero PIZZA $$
(Map p968; ☑ 415-348-8800; www.zerozerosf.com; 826 Folsom St; pizzas $10-19; ⊙11:30am-2:30pm & 5:30-10pm Mon-Thu, to 11pm Fri, 11:30am-11pm Sat, 11:30am-10pm Sun; Ⓜ Powell, Ⓑ Powell) Neapolitan pizza credentials – '00' flour is used for Naples' famous puffy-edged crust – with inspired San Francisco–themed toppings. The cross-town, cross-cultural Geary includes Manila clams, bacon and chilies, and the crowd-pleasing Castro comes turbo-loaded with housemade sausage.

★**Benu** CALIFORNIAN, FUSION $$$
(Map p968; ☑ 415-685-4860; www.benusf.com; 22 Hawthorne St; mains $26-42; ⊙5:30-10pm Tue-Sat; ☐10, 12, 14, 30, 45) San Francisco has refined fusion cuisine over 150 years, but no one rocks it quite like chef-owner Corey Lee (formerly of Napa's French Laundry), who remixes local, sustainable fine-dining staples and Pacific Rim flavors with a SoMa DJ's finesse. Dungeness crab and black-truffle custard bring such outsize flavor to faux-shark's-fin soup, you'll swear there's Jaws in there.

★**Jardinière** CALIFORNIAN $$$
(Map p968; ☑ 415-861-5555; www.jardiniere.com; 300 Grove St; mains $19-37; ⊙5-10:30pm Tue-Sat, to 10pm Sun & Mon; ☐5, 21, 47, 49, Ⓜ Van Ness) ✐ Iron Chef, Top Chef Master and James Beard Award winner Traci des Jardins has a particular flair with California's organic vegetables, free-range meats and sustainably caught seafood. Housemade tagliatelle is lavished with bone marrow and velvety scallops are topped with satiny sea urchin. On Mondays $49 scores you three decadent courses with wine pairings.

Financial District, Chinatown & North Beach

★**Liguria Bakery** BAKERY $
(Map p968; ☑ 415-421-3786; 1700 Stockton St; focaccia $4-5; ⊙8am-1pm Mon-Fri, from 7am Sat; ✐ ; ☐8X, 30, 39, 41, 45, ☐ Powell-Mason) Bleary-eyed art students and Italian grandmothers line up by 8am for cinnamon-raisin focaccia hot from the 100-year-old oven, leaving 9am dawdlers a choice of tomato or classic rosemary/garlic and 11am stragglers out of luck. Cash only.

FIVE TASTY REASONS TO MISS THAT FERRY

When it comes to California dining, you'll be missing the boat unless you stop for local specialties at the Ferry Building:

➡ Today's catch at **Hog Island Oyster Company** (Map p968; ☑ 415-391-7117; www. hogislandoysters.com; 1 Ferry Bldg; 6 oysters $16-20; ⊙11:30am-8pm Mon-Fri, 11am-6pm Sat & Sun; Ⓜ Embarcadero, Ⓑ Embarcadero) ✐ , including $1 oysters at happy hour.

➡ Gourmet picnic supplies from the **farmers market** (Map p968; ☑ 415-291-3276; www. cuesa.org; ⊙10am-2pm Tue & Thu, from 8am Sat) – especially 4505 artisan meats, Donna's tamales and Namu Gaji's Korean tacos.

➡ Iron Chef Traci des Jardins' *nuevo* Mexican street eats at **Mijita** (Map p968; ☑ 415-399-0814; www.mijitasf.com; 1 Ferry Bldg; dishes $4-8; ⊙10am-7pm Mon-Thu, to 8pm Fri-Sat, 8:30am-3pm Sun; ✐ ; Ⓜ Embarcadero, Ⓑ Embarcadero).

➡ Free-range beef burgers and sweet-potato fries at **Gott's Roadside** (Map p968; www. gotts.com; 1 Ferry Bldg; burgers $8-11; ⊙10:30am-10pm; ; Ⓜ Embarcadero, Ⓑ Embarcadero) ✐

➡ Cal-Vietnamese Dungeness crab over cellophane noodles at Charles Phan's family-operated **Slanted Door** (Map p968; ☑ 415-861-8032; www.slanteddoor.com; 1 Ferry Bldg; lunch $15-28, dinner $19-42; ⊙11am-2:30pm & 5:30-10pm Mon-Sat, 11:30-3pm & 5:30-10pm Sun; Ⓜ Embarcadero, Ⓑ Embarcadero).

City View
CHINESE $

(Map p968; ☑415-398-2838; 662 Commercial St; dishes $3-8; ◷11am-2:30pm Mon-Fri, from 10am Sat & Sun; ◻8X, 10, 12, 30, 45, ◪California St) Take your seat in the sunny dining room and take your pick from carts loaded with delicate shrimp and leek dumplings, garlicky Chinese broccoli, tangy spare ribs, coconut-dusted custard tarts and other tantalizing dim sum.

Cinecittà
PIZZA $

(Map p968; ☑415-291-8830; www.cinecittarestau-rant.com; 663 Union St; pizza $12-15; ◷noon-10pm Sun-Thu, to 11pm Fri & Sat; ✍◨; ◻8X, 30, 39, 41, 45, ◪Powell-Mason) Follow tantalizing aromas into this 22-seat eatery for thin-crust Roman pizza, including the classic Travestere (fresh mozzarella, arugula and prosciutto) and Neapolitan O Sole Mio (capers, olives, mozzarella and anchovies). Local brews are on tap, house wine is $5 from 3pm to 7pm, and house-made tiramisu is SF's best.

★Cotogna
ITALIAN $$

(Map p968; ☑415-775-8508; www.cotognasf.com; 470 Pacific Ave; mains $14-26; ◷11:30am-11:30pm Mon-Sat, 11:30am-2:30pm & 5-9pm Sun; ✍; ◻10, 12) Since chef-owner Michael Tusk won the James Beard Award for best chef, bookings are coveted at rustic Italian Cotogna (and fancier sister-restaurant Quince) for pristine pastas, toothsome wood-fired pizzas and rotisserie-caramelized meats.

Z & Y
CHINESE $$

(Map p968; ☑415-981-8988; www.zandyrestaurant.com; 655 Jackson St; mains $9-18; ◷11am-10pm Mon-Thu, to 11pm Fri-Sun; ◻8X, ◪Powell-Mason, Powell-Hyde) Sensational Szechuan dishes that go down in a blaze of glory: spicy pork dumplings, heat-blistered string beans, housemade tantan noodles with peanut-chili sauce, and fish poached in flaming chili oil and buried under red Szechuan chili-peppers. Go early; expect a wait.

Ristorante Ideale
ITALIAN $$

(Map p968; ☑415-391-4129; www.idealerestaurant.com; 1315 Grant Ave; pasta $15-18; ◷5:30-10:30pm Mon-Thu, to 11pm Fri-Sat, 5-10pm Sun; ◻8X, 10, 12, 30, 41, 45, ◪Powell-Mason) Roman chef Maurizio Bruschi serves authentic *bucatini ammatriciana* (tube pasta with tomato-pecorino sauce and house-cured pancetta), and ravioli and gnocchi that are both handmade and housemade ('of course!'). Ask the Tuscan staff to recommend well-priced wine, and everyone goes home happy.

★Coi
CALIFORNIAN $$$

(Map p968; ☑415-393-9000; www.coirestaurant.com; 373 Broadway; set menu $175; ◷5:30-10pm Wed-Sat; ℗; ◻8X, 30, 41, 45, ◪Powell-Mason) ✐ Chef-owner Daniel Patterson's imaginative eight-course tasting menu is like licking the California coastline: purple ice-plant petals are strewn atop warm duck's tongue, and wild-caught Monterey Bay abalone appears in a tidepool of pea shoots, inducing a uniquely Golden State of bliss.

Fisherman's Wharf & the Marina

Off the Grid
FOOD TRUCK $

(Map p968; www.offthegridsf.com; dishes $5-10; ◷5-10pm Fri; ◻22, 28) Thirty food trucks circle their wagons at Fort Mason for mobile gourmet feasts. Arrive before 6:30pm or expect 20-minute waits for Chairman Bao's clam-shell buns with duck and mango, Roli Roti's free-range herbed roast chicken, and dessert from the Crème Brûlée Man. Cash only.

In-N-Out Burger
BURGERS $

(Map p968; ☑800-786-1000; www.in-n-out.com; 333 Jefferson St; meals under $10; ◷10:30am-1am Sun-Thu, to 1:30am Fri & Sat; ◨; ◻30, 47, ◪Powell-Hyde) Prime chuck beef processed on site, plus fries and shakes made with ingredients you can pronounce, all served by employees paid a living wage. Order yours off the menu 'animal style' – cooked in mustard with grilled onions.

★Greens
VEGETARIAN, CALIFORNIAN $$

(Map p968; ☑415-771-6222; www.greensres-taurant.com; Bldg A, Fort Mason Center, cnr Marina Blvd & Laguna St; lunch $15-17, dinner $17-24; ◷11:45am-2:30pm & 5:30-9pm Tue-Fri, from 11am Sat, 10:30am-2pm & 5:30-9pm Sun, 5:30-9pm Mon; ✍; ◻28) ✐ Career carnivores won't realize there's zero meat in the hearty black-bean chili with crème fraîche and pickled jalapeños or in the roasted eggplant panini packed with ingredients mostly grown on a Zen organic farm. Enjoy takeout on a wharfside bench; reserve ahead for weekend dinners or Sunday brunch.

★Gary Danko
CALIFORNIAN $$$

(Map p968; ☑415-749-2060; www.garydanko.com; 800 North Point St; 3-/5-course menu $73/107; ◷5:30-10pm; ◻19, 30, 47, ◪Powell-Hyde) Smoked-glass windows prevent passersby from tripping over their tongues at the sight of James Beard Award–winning feasts: roasted lobster with trumpet mushrooms, blushing duck breast and rhubarb compote, lavish cheeses and trios of crèmes brûlées. Reservations required.

✗ The Mission

★ **La Taqueria** MEXICAN $
(☑415-285-7117; 2889 Mission St; burritos $6-8; ⊙11am-9pm Mon-Sat, to 8pm Sun; 🖉; 🚇12, 14, 48, 49, Ⓑ24th St Mission) The definitive burrito at La Taqueria has no debatable saffron rice, spinach tortilla or mango salsa, just perfectly grilled meats, slow-cooked beans and classic *tomatillo* or *mesquite* salsa wrapped in a flour tortilla. Spicy pickles and *crema* (Mexican sour cream) complete the burrito bliss.

★ **Namu Gaji** KOREAN, CALIFORNIAN $$
(☑415-431-6268; www.namusf.com; 499 Dolores St; small plates $8-22; ⊙11:30am-10pm Tue-Thu, to 11pm Fri & Sat; 🚇22, 33, ⓂJ, Ⓑ16th St Mission) 🖉 San Francisco's unfair culinary advantages – organic local ingredients, Silicon Valley inventiveness and Pacific Rim roots – are showcased in Namu's Korean-inspired soul food. Menu standouts include ultrasavory shiitake-mushroom dumplings, tender marinated beef tongue, and Marin Sun Farms grass-fed steak atop sizzling rice served in a stone pot.

★ **Commonwealth** CALIFORNIAN $$$
(☑415-355-1500; www.commonwealthsf.com; 2224 Mission St; small plates $11-16; ⊙5:30-10pm Sun-Thu, to 11pm Fri & Sat; 🖉; 🚇14, 22, 33, 49, Ⓑ16th St Mission) California's most imaginative farm-to-table dining isn't in some quaint barn but in a converted cinderblock Mission dive. Here chef Jason Fox serves green strawberries and black radishes with fennel pollen,

GOURMET TO GO

Bi-Rite (☑415-241-9760; www.biritemarket.com; 3639 18th St; sandwiches $7-10; ⊙9am-9pm; 🖢; 🚇14, 22, 33, 49, Ⓑ16th St Mission) Nemesis of grocery budgets and ally of foodies best at reheating, the Bi-Rite store in the Mission area displays artisan chocolates, sustainable cured meats and organic fruit like jewels, with dazzling California wine-and-cheese selections. Get deli sandwiches to go to Dolores Park.

and poached oysters atop foraged succulents and rhubarb ice. Savor the $75 prix-fixe knowing $10 is donated to charity.

✗ The Castro

Chilango MEXICAN $$
(☑415-552-5700; www.chilangorestaurantsf.com; 235 Church St; dishes $8-12; ⊙11am-10pm; ⓂChurch) 🖉 Upgrade from taqueria to sit-down restaurant at this casual Mexican spot that uses all-organic ingredients in filet-mignon tacos, chicken *mole* (cocoa-based sauce) and succulent carnitas (roast pork).

Starbelly CALIFORNIAN, PIZZA $$
(☑415-252-7500; www.starbellysf.com; 3583 16th St; dishes $6-19; ⊙11:30am-11pm Sun-Thu, to midnight Fri & Sat; ⓂCastro) 🖉 Nab a spot on the heated garden patio for *salumi* (Italian cured meat), market-fresh salads, scrumptious pâté, roasted mussels with housemade sausage and thin-crust pizzas.

★ **Frances** CALIFORNIAN $$$
(☑415-621-3870; www.frances-sf.com; 3870 17th St; mains $27-28; ⊙5-10.30pm Tue-Sun; ⓂCastro) Chef-owner Melissa Perello's daily menus showcase bright, seasonal flavors and luxurious textures: cloudlike sheep's milk ricotta gnocchi with crunchy breadcrumbs and broccolini, grilled calamari with preserved Meyer lemon, and Sonoma artisan wine on tap.

✗ The Haight

★ **Rosamunde Sausage Grill** FAST FOOD $
(Map p968; ☑415-437-6851; http://rosamundesausagegrill.com; 545 Haight St; sausages $4-6; ⊙11:30am-10pm; 🚇6, 22, 71, ⓂN) Impress a dinner date on the cheap: load up classic Brats or duck-fig links with complimentary roasted peppers, grilled onions, wholegrain mustard and mango chutney. Enjoy with your choice from 100 beers at Toronado, next door.

Ragazza PIZZA $$
(☑415-255-1133; www.ragazzasf.com; 311 Divisadero St; pizza $13-18; ⊙5-10pm Mon-Thu, to 10:30 Fri & Sat; 🖢; 🚇6, 21, 24, 71) 'Girl' is what the name means, as in, 'Oooh, *girl*, did you try the potato-leek pizza?!' Artisan *salumi* is the star of many Ragazza pies, from the Amatriciana with pecorino, bacon and egg to the pork belly with Calabrian chili and beet greens. Arrive early to nab garden patio tables.

Magnolia Brewpub CALIFORNIAN, AMERICAN **$$**
(✆415-864-7468; www.magnoliapub.com; 1398 Haight St; mains $11-20; ⊘11am-midnight Mon-Thu, to 1am Fri, 10am-1am Sat, to midnight Sun; ☐6, 33, 43, 71) ✐ Organic pub grub and home-brew samplers keep conversation flowing at communal tables, while grass-fed Prather Ranch burgers satisfy stoner appetites in the booths – it's like the Summer of Love all over again, only with better food.

⚔ Japantown & Pacific Heights

Benkyodo JAPANESE **$**
(Map p968; ✆415-922-1244; www.benkyodocompany.com; 1747 Buchanan St; dishes $1-10; ⊘8am-5pm Mon-Sat; ☐2, 3, 22, 38) The perfect retro lunch counter cheerfully serves an old-school egg-salad sandwich or pastrami for $5, but the real draw is the $1.25 *mochi* (Japanese filled rice cake) made in-house daily – come early for popular flavors including green tea and chocolate-filled strawberry. Cash only.

Tataki JAPANESE, SUSHI **$$**
(✆415-931-1182; www.tatakisushibar.com; 2815 California St; dishes $12-20; ⊘11:30am-2pm & 5:30-10:30pm Mon-Thu, to 11:30pm Fri, 5-11:30pm Sat, 5-9:30pm Sun; ☐1, 24) ✐ Pioneering sushi chefs Kin Lui and Raymond Ho rescue dinner and the oceans with sustainable delicacies: silky Arctic char drizzled with yuzu-citrus replaces at-risk wild salmon; and the Golden State Roll features spicy, line-caught scallop, Pacific tuna, organic-apple slivers and edible 24-carat gold.

State Bird Provisions CALIFORNIAN **$$**
(Map p968; ✆415-795-1272; statebirdsf.com; 1529 Fillmore St; ⊘5:30pm-10pm Mon-Thu, to 11pm Fri-Sat; ☐22, 38) Forget Kentucky-fried: San Francisco prefers its poultry creative, locally sourced and dim-sum-sized. Pumpkin seeds and baguette crumbs are secrets to the golden state bird (quail), the signature of this high-concept, low-key California cuisine hot spot, which was the 2013 James Beard Award winner for best new restaurant in America. Reserve ahead or join the 5pm bar-seat line.

⚔ The Richmond

★Outerlands CALIFORNIAN **$$**
(Map p966; ✆415-661-6140; www.outerlandssf.com; 4001 Judah St; sandwiches & small plates $8-9, mains $12-27; ⊘11am-3pm & 6-10pm Tue-Fri, 10am-3pm & 5:30-10pm Sat & Sun; ♿; ☐18, Ⓜ N) ✐ When windy Ocean Beach leaves you feeling shipwrecked, drift into this beach-shack bistro for organic California comfort food. Brunch demands Dutch pancakes in iron skillets with housemade ricotta, lunch brings $12 grilled artisan cheese combos with farm-inspired soup, and slow-cooked lamb shoulder slouches on flatbread at dinner. Reserve ahead.

★Aziza MOROCCAN, CALIFORNIAN **$$$**
(Map p966; ✆415-752-2222; www.aziza-sf.com; 5800 Geary Blvd; mains $16-29; ⊘5:30-10:30pm Wed-Mon; ☐1, 29, 31, 38) Chef Mourad Lahlou's inspiration is Moroccan, his ingredients organic Californian, and his flavors out of this world: Sonoma duck confit melts into caramelized onion inside flaky pastry *basteeya*, while saffron infuses slow-cooked local lamb atop barley.

🍷 Drinking & Nightlife

For a pub crawl, your best bets are North Beach saloons or Mission bars around Valencia and 16th St. Top chefs serve craft cocktails downtown, Hayes Valley has wine bars and the Tenderloin mixes dives with speakeasies. The Castro has historic gay bars and SoMa has leather bars, while Marina bars are preppy and straight, and Haight bars draw mixed alterna-crowds.

★Bar Agricole BAR
(Map p968; ✆415-355-9400; www.baragricole.com; 355 11th St; ⊘6-10pm Sun-Wed, to late Thu-Sat; ☐9, 12, 27, 47) Drink your way to a history degree with well-researched cocktails: Bellamy Scotch Sour with egg whites passes the test, but Tequila Fix with lime, pineapple gum and hellfire bitters earns honors. For its modern design with natural materials and a sleek deck, Agricole won a James Beard Award.

★Smuggler's Cove BAR
(Map p968; ✆415-869-1900; www.smugglerscovesf.com; 650 Gough St; ⊘5pm-1:15am; ☐5, 21, 49, Ⓜ Van Ness) Yo-ho-ho and a bottle of rum...or perhaps you'll try a Dead Reckoning with Angostura bitters, Nicaraguan rum, tawny port and vanilla liqueur, unless someone will share the flaming Scorpion Bowl? With 400 rums and 70 cocktails gleaned from rum-running around the world, you won't be dry-docked long.

★ **Comstock Saloon**   BAR

(Map p968; ☑415-617-0071; www.comstocksaloon. com; 155 Columbus Ave; ☺4pm-2am Sat-Thu, from noon Fri; ☐8X, 10, 12, 30, 45, ☐Powell-Mason) Welcome to the Barbary Coast, where cocktails at this Victorian saloon remain period-perfect: Pisco Punch is made with pineapple gum, and martini-precursor Martinez features gin, vermouth, bitters and maraschino liqueur. Call ahead to claim booths or tufted-velvet parlour seating.

★ **Toronado**   PUB

(Map p968; ☑415-863-2276; www.toronado.com; 547 Haight St; ☺11:30am-2am; ☐6, 22, 71, ☐N) Glory hallelujah, beer-lovers: your prayers have been heard with 50-plus beers on tap and hundreds more bottled, including spectacular seasonal microbrews. Bring cash. Order sausages from Rosamunde next door to accompany ale made by Trappist monks.

★ **Specs Museum Cafe**   BAR

(Map p968; ☑415-421-4112; 12 William Saroyan Pl; ☺5pm-2am; ☐8X, 10, 12, 30, 41, 45, ☐Powell-Mason) What do you do with a drunken sailor? Here's your answer. The walls are plastered with Merchant Marine mementos, and you'll be plastered too if you try to keep up with the salty old-timers holding court in back. Your order is obvious: pitcher of Anchor Steam, coming right up.

★ **Elixir**   BAR

(☑415-522-1633; www.elixirsf.com; 3200 16th St; ☺3pm-2am Mon-Fri, noon-2am Sat & Sun; ☐16th St Mission) ✍ Do the planet a favor and have a drink at San Francisco's first certified-green bar in an actual 1858 Wild West saloon. Elixir serves knock-out cocktails made with farm-fresh organic mixers and small-batch spirits that will get you air-guitar-rocking to the killer jukebox.

GAY/LES/BI/TRANS SAN FRANCISCO

Doesn't matter where you're from, who you love or who's your daddy: if you're here, and queer, welcome home. The Castro is the heart of the gay cruising scene, but South of Market (SoMa) has thump-thump clubs. The Mission is the preferred 'hood of alt-chicks, trans FTMs (female-to-males) and flirty femmes. *Bay Area Reporter* (aka BAR; www.ebar.com) covers community news and listings; *San Francisco Bay Times* (www. sfbaytimes.com) also has good resources for transsexuals; free mag *Gloss Magazine* (www.glossmagazine.net) covers nightlife. For roving dance parties, check **Honey Soundsystem** (Map p968; www.honeysoundsystem.com); **Juanita More** (www.juanita-more.com); and **Sisters of Perpetual Indulgence** (www.thesisters.org). San Francisco is home to some top GLBT venues.

Stud (Map p968; ☑415-252-7883; www.studsf.com; 399 9th St; admission $5-8; ☺5pm-3am; ☐12, 19, 27, 47) Join parties in-progress since 1966: Meow Mix Tuesday drag variety shows; Wednesday raunchy comedy; and Friday 'Some-thing' parties with midnight drag, pool-table crafts and dance beats.

Aunt Charlie's (Map p968; ☑415-441-2922; www.auntcharlieslounge.com; 133 Turk St; admission $5; ☐Powell, ☐Powell) Divey Aunt Charlie's brings vintage pulp-fiction covers to life with drag Hot Boxxx Girls Friday and Saturday nights (call for reservations) and Thursday's Tubesteak Connection ($5), featuring vintage porn and '80s disco.

EndUp (Map p968; www.theendup.com; 401 6th St; admission $5-20; ☺10pm-4am Mon-Thu, 11pm-11am Fri, 10pm Sat-4am Mon; ☐12, 27, 47) Anyone on the streets after 2am weekends is subject to the magnetic pull of the EndUp's marathon dance sessions and gay Sunday tea dances, in full force since 1973.

Lexington Club (☑415-863-2052; www.lexingtonclub.com; 3464 19th St; ☺3pm-2am; ☐14, 33, 49, ☐16th St Mission) San Francisco's all-grrrrl bar can be cliquish, so compliment someone on her skirt (she designed it herself) or tattoo (ditto) and mention you're undefeated at pinball, pool or thumb-wrestling. When she wins (because she's no stranger to the Lex), pout and maybe she'll buy you a $4 beer.

Cafe Flore (☑415-621-8579; www.cafeflore.com; 2298 Market St; ☺7am-midnight Sun-Thu, to 2am Fri & Sat; ☎; ☐Castro) You haven't done the Castro till you've unwound on Flore's sunny patio. Great happy-hour drink specials, such as two-for-one margaritas. Wi-fi weekdays only, no electrical outlets.

Zeitgeist BAR

(☑415-255-7505; www.zeitgeistsf.com; 199 Valencia St; ⊘9am-2am; 🚌22, 49, 🅱16th St Mission) You've got two seconds flat to order one of 40 beers on draft from tough-gal barkeeps used to putting macho bikers in their place. Regulars head straight to the bar's huge graveled beer garden to sit at long picnic tables to smoke. Bring cash for the bar and for late-night food vendors who circulate.

Trick Dog BAR

(☑415-471-2999; www.trickdogbar.com; 3010 20th St; ⊘3pm-2am; 🚌12, 14, 49) Choose your drink by Pantone-paint-swatch color: Razzle Dazzle Red gets you local Hangar One vodka with house cordials, strawberries and lime, while Gypsy Tan means Rittenhouse rye with Fernet, lemon-ginger and nutmeg.

El Rio CLUB

(☑415-282-3325; www.elriosf.com; 3158 Mission St; admission $3 8; ⊘1pm-2am; 🚌12, 14, 27, 49, 🅱24th St Mission) The DJ mix at El Rio takes its cue from the patrons: eclectic, fearless, funky and sexy, no matter your orientation. Powerful margaritas will get you bopping to disco-post-punk mashups and flirting shamelessly in the back garden. Cash only.

☆ Entertainment

TIX Bay Area (Map p968; www.tixbayarea.org) sells last-minute theater tickets half-price. Other event listings are covered in *7x7 magazine* (www.7x7.com), *SF Bay Guardian* (www.sfbg.com) newspaper, *SF Weekly* (www.sfweekly.com) newspaper and **Squid List** (www.squidlist.com/events) blog.

Live Music

★ SFJAZZ Center JAZZ

(Map p968; ☑866-920-5299; www.sfjazz.org; 201 Franklin St; ⊘showtimes vary; 🚌5, 7, 21, 🅼Van Ness) Jazz greats coast-to-coast and further afield from Argentina to Yemen are showcased at America's newest, largest, LEED-certified green jazz center. The San Francisco Jazz Festival takes place here in July, but year-round the calendar features such legends as McCoy Tyner, Regina Carter, Bela Flek and Tony Bennett (who left his heart here, after all). Upper-tier cheap seats are more like stools, but offer clear stage views.

Fillmore Auditorium LIVE MUSIC

(Map p968; ☑415-346-6000; http://thefillmore. com; 1805 Geary Blvd; admission $15-50; ⊘box office 10am-4pm Sun, 7:30-10pm show nights; 🚌22, 38) Jimi Hendrix, Janis Joplin, the

Doors – they all played the Fillmore. Now you might catch the Indigo Girls, Duran Duran or Tracy Chapman in the historic 1250-capacity standing-room theater; don't miss the '60s psychedelic posters in the upstairs gallery.

Slim's LIVE MUSIC

(Map p968; ☑415-255-0333; www.slims-sf.com; 333 11th St; tickets $12-30; ⊘5pm-2am; 🚌9, 12, 27, 47) Guaranteed good times by Gogol Bordello, Tenacious D and the Expendables fit the bill at this midsized club, owned by R&B star Boz Skaggs. Shows are all-ages, though shorties may have a hard time seeing once the floor starts bouncing. Reserve dinner for $25, and score seats on the small balcony.

Mezzanine LIVE MUSIC

(Map p968; ☑415-625-8880; www.mezzaninesf. com; 444 Jessie St; admission $10-40; 🅼Powell, 🅱Powell) Big nights come with bragging rights at the Mezzanine, which has one of the city's best sound systems. Crowds are hyped for alt-bands, breakthrough hip-hop and R&B shows by Wyclef Jean, Quest Love, Method Man, Nas and Snoop Dogg.

Great American Music Hall LIVE MUSIC

(Map p968; ☑415-885-0750; www.gamh.com; 859 O'Farrell St; admission $12-35; ⊘box office 10:30am-6pm Mon-Fri & on show nights; 🚌19, 38, 47, 49) Once a bordello, the rococo Great American Music Hall has a balcony with table seating, a top-notch sound system, and reasonable food and drinks. Music ranges from alt-rock and metal to jazz and bluegrass.

Yoshi's JAZZ, LIVE MUSIC

(Map p968; ☑415-655-5600; www.yoshis.com; 1300 Fillmore St; ⊘shows 8pm and/or 10pm Tue-Sun, dinner Tue-Sun; 🚌22, 31) San Francisco's definitive jazz club draws the world's top talent, and hosts appearances by the likes of Leon Redbone and Nancy Wilson, along with occasional classical and gospel acts. Students: ask about half-priced tickets.

Cafe du Nord/Swedish American Hall LIVE MUSIC

(☑415-861-5016; www.cafedunord.com; 2170 Market St; cover varies; 🅼Church) Rockers, chanteuses, comedians, raconteurs and burlesque acts perform nightly at this former basement speakeasy with bar and showroom, and the joint still looks like it did in the '30s.

Drag

Cat Club
DRAG

(Map p968; www.catclubsf.com; 1190 Folsom St; admission after 10pm $5; ⊙ 9pm-3am Tue-Sun; Ⓜ Civic Center, Ⓑ Civic Center) You never really know your friends till you've seen them belt out A-ha's 'Take on Me' at 1984, Cat Club's Thursday-night retro dance party. Tuesdays it's karaoke, Wednesdays Bondage-a-Go-Go, Fridays Goth, and Saturdays '90s power pop – but confirm online, lest you dress the wrong part.

DNA Lounge
DRAG

(Map p968; www.dnalounge.com; 375 11th St; admission $3-25; ⊙ 9pm-3am Fri & Sat, other nights vary; ⏘ 12, 27, 47) One of San Francisco's last megaclubs hosts live bands, mash-up dance party Bootie, epic drag at Trannyshack, and Monday's 18-and-over Goth Death Guild. Early arrivals may hear crickets.

AsiaSF
DRAG CABARET

(Map p968; ☑ 415-255-2742; www.asiasf.com; 201 9th St; per person from $39; ⊙ 7-11pm Wed & Thu, 7pm-2am Fri, 5pm-2am Sat, 7-10pm Sun, reservation line 1-8pm; Ⓜ Civic Center, Ⓑ Civic Center) Cocktails and Asian-inspired dishes are served with sass and a secret: your servers are drag stars. Every hour, they dance atop the bar, while gaggles of girlfriends squeal and straight blushing businessmen play along. Once inspiration and drinks kick in, everyone mixes it up on the downstairs dance floor.

Classical Music & Opera

★ Davies Symphony Hall
CLASSICAL MUSIC

(Map p968; ☑ 415-864-6000; www.sfsymphony.org; 201 Van Ness Ave; Ⓜ Van Ness, Ⓑ Civic Center) Home of nine-time Grammy-winning San Francisco Symphony, conducted with verve by Michael Tilson Thomas. The season runs September to July.

★ San Francisco Opera
OPERA

(Map p968; ☑ 415-864-3330; www.sfopera.com; War Memorial Opera House, 301 Van Ness Ave; tickets $10-350; Ⓑ Civic Center, Ⓜ Van Ness) San Francisco has been obsessed with opera since the gold rush, and it remains a staple from July to December. Tuesdays attract local socialites, when you can spot fabulous gowns and tuxedos. After 10am, the box office sells 150 standing-room spots ($10; cash only); snag empty seats after intermission.

San Francisco Ballet
DANCE

(Map p968; ☑ 415-861-5600, tickets 415-865-2000; www.sfballet.org; War Memorial Opera House, 301 Van Ness Ave; tickets $10-120; Ⓜ Van Ness) The San Francisco Ballet is America's oldest ballet company and the first to premier the *Nutcracker*. The company regularly performs at War Memorial Opera House.

Theater

★ American Conservatory Theater
THEATER

(ACT; Map p968; ☑ 415-749-2228; www.act-sf.org; 415 Geary St; ⏘ 38, ⏘ Powell-Mason, Powell-Hyde) Breakthrough shows begin at ACT's turn-of-the-century Geary Theater, which has launched Tony Kushner's *Angels in America* and Robert Wilson's *Black Rider*, with a libretto by William S Burroughs and music by the Bay Area's own Tom Waits. ACT's **Strand Theater** (1127 Market St) is scheduled to open late 2014.

Beach Blanket Babylon
CABARET

(BBB; Map p968; ☑ 415-421-4222; www.beachblanketbabylon.com; 678 Green St; admission $25-100; ⊙ shows 8pm Wed, Thu & Fri, 6:30pm & 9:30pm Sat, 2pm & 5pm Sun; ⏘ 8X, ⏘ Powell-Mason) Snow White searches for Prince Charming in San Francisco: what could possibly go wrong? The Disney-gone-drag musical-comedy cabaret has been running since 1974, but topical jokes keep it outrageous and wigs as big as parade floats are gasp-worthy.

Cinemas

★ Castro Theatre
CINEMA

(☑ 415-621-6120; www.thecastrotheatre.com; 429 Castro St; adult/child $11/8.50; ⊙ Tue-Sun; Ⓜ Castro) The Mighty Wurlitzer organ rises from the deco movie palace's orchestra pit before evening shows, ending with (sing along, now): 'San Francisco open your Golden Gate/ You let no stranger wait outside your door...'

★ Roxie Cinema
CINEMA

(☑ 415-863-1087; www.roxie.com; 3117 16th St; regular screening/matinee $10/7; ⏘ 14, 22, 33, 49, Ⓑ 16th St Mission) A little neighborhood nonprofit cinema with major international clout for indie premieres, controversial films and documentaries banned elsewhere. No ads; personal introductions to every film.

Sundance Kabuki Cinema
CINEMA

(Map p968; ☑ 415-929-4650; www.sundancecinemas.com; 1881 Post St; adult $9.50-15, child $9; ⏘ 2, 3, 22, 38) ✿ A multiplex initiative by Robert Redford's Sundance Institute,

Kabuki features big-name flicks and festivals, served with local chocolates and booze. And it's green, with recycled-fiber seating.

Sports

San Francisco Giants
BASEBALL

(Map p968; http://sanfrancisco.giants.mlb.com; AT&T Park; tickets $5-135) Watch and learn how the World Series is won – bushy beards, women's underwear and all.

San Francisco 49ers
FOOTBALL

(Map p966; ☑415-656-4900; www.sf49ers.com; Levi's Stadium from 2014; tickets $25-100 at www. ticketmaster.com; Ⓜ T) The 49ers were the National Football League dream team from 1981 to 1994, claiming five Superbowl championships. After decades shivering through games and a fumbled bid for the 2012 Superbowl, the 49ers have a new home in 2014: Santa Clara's brand-new Levi's Stadium.

🔒 Shopping

★City Lights
BOOKS

(Map p968; ☑415-362-8193; www.citylights.com; 261 Columbus Ave; ☉10am-midnight; 🚌8X, 10, 12, 30, 41, 45, 🚋Powell-Mason, Powell-Hyde) 🖉 'Abandon all despair, all ye who enter,' orders the sign by the door to City Lights bookstore by founder and San Francisco poet laureate Lawrence Ferlinghetti. This commandment is easy to follow when you're upstairs in the sunny **Poetry Room**, with freshly published verse, designated **Poet's Chair** and views over Jack Kerouac Alley.

★New People
CLOTHING, GIFTS

(Map p968; www.newpeopleworld.com; 1746 Post St; ☉noon-7pm Mon-Sat, to 6pm Sun; 🚌2, 3, 22, 38) Wall-to-wall *kawaii* (cuteness): Japanimation T-shirts; *Alice in Wonderland*-inspired Lolita fashions at 2nd-floor **Baby the Stars Shine Bright**; ninja shoes with contemporary graphics at **Sou-Sou**; contemporary art at **Superfrog Gallery**; and tea cakes at **Crown & Crumpet**.

★Betabrand
CLOTHING

(☑800-694-9491; www.betabrand.com; 780 Valencia St; ☉11am-6pm Mon-Thu, to 7pm Fri-Sat, noon-6pm Sun; 🚌14, 22, 33, 49, Ⓑ16th St Mission) Crowd-source fashion decisions at Betabrand, where experimental designs are put to an online vote, and winners are produced in limited editions: lunch-meat-patterned socks, reversible smoking jackets, disco-ball windbreakers and bike-to-work pants with reflective-strip cuffs.

ℹ️ Information

EMERGENCY & MEDICAL SERVICES

American College of Traditional Chinese Medicine (☑415-282-9603; www.actcm.edu; 450 Connecticut St; ☉8:30am-9pm Mon-Thu, 9am-5:30pm Fri & Sat; 🚌10, 19, 22) Acupuncture, herbal remedies and other traditional Chinese medical treatments provided at low cost.

Haight Ashbury Free Clinic (☑415-762-3700; www.healthright360.org; 558 Clayton St; ☉by appointment; 🚌6, 33, 37, 43, 71, Ⓜ N) Clinic whose services are offered by appointment only; provides substance abuse and mental-health services.

Police, Fire & Ambulance (☑911, nonemergency 311)

San Francisco General Hospital (☑emergency 415-206-8111, main hospital 415-206-8000; www.sfdph.org; 1001 Potrero Ave; ☉24hr; 🚌9, 10, 33, 48) Provides care to uninsured patients, including psychiatric care; no documentation required beyond ID.

Trauma Recovery & Rape Treatment Center (☑415-437-3000; www.traumarecoverycenter. org) A 24-hour hotline.

Walgreens (☑415-861-3136; www.walgreens. com; 498 Castro St, cnr 18th St; ☉24hr; 🚌24, 33, 35, Ⓜ F, K, L, M) Pharmacy and over-the-counter meds; dozens of locations citywide.

BEST SHOPPING AREAS

All those rustic-chic dens, well-stocked cupboards and fabulous outfits don't just pull themselves together – San Franciscans scoured their city for it all. Here's where to find what:

Hayes Valley Local and independent designers, home design, sweets, shoes.

Valencia St Bookstores, local design collectives, art galleries, vintage whatever.

Haight St Head shops, music, vintage, skate, snow and surf gear.

Upper Fillmore & Union Sts Date outfits, girly accessories, wine and design.

Powell & Market Sts Department stores, megabrands, discount retail, Apple store.

Grant St From Chinatown souvenirs to eccentric North Beach boutiques.

Ferry Building Local food, wine and kitchenware.

INTERNET ACCESS

San Francisco has free wi-fi hot spots citywide – locate one nearby with www.openwifispots.com. Connect for free in Union Sq, most cafes and hotel lobbies.

Apple Store (www.apple.com/retail/sanfrancisco; 1 Stockton St; ☉9am-9pm Mon-Sat, 10am-8pm Sun; @ ☎; ⓜPowell St) Free wi-fi and internet terminal usage.

San Francisco Main Library (www.sfpl.org; 100 Larkin St; ☉10am-6pm Mon & Sat, 9am-8pm Tue-Thu, noon-5pm Fri & Sun; @ ☎; ⓜCivic Center) Free 15-minute internet terminal usage; spotty wi-fi access.

MEDIA

KALW 91.7 FM (www.kalw.org) National Public Radio (NPR) affiliate.

KPFA 94.1 FM (www.kpfa.org) Alternative news and music.

KPOO 89.5 FM (www.kpoo.com) Community radio with jazz, R & B, blues and reggae.

KQED 88.5 FM (www.kqed.org) NPR and Public Broadcasting (PBS) affiliate offering podcasts and streaming video.

San Francisco Bay Guardian (www.sfbg.com) San Francisco's free, alternative weekly covers politics, theater, music, art and movie listings.

San Francisco Chronicle (www.sfgate.com) Main daily newspaper with news, entertainment and event listings.

MONEY

Bank of America (www.bankamerica.com; 1 Market Plaza; ☉9am-6pm Mon-Fri)

POST

Rincon Center Post Office (Map p968; ☎800-275-8777; www.usps.gov; 180 Steuart St; ☉8am-6pm Mon-Fri, 9am-2pm Sat; ⓜEmbarcadero, Ⓑ Embarcadero) Postal services, plus historic murals in historic wing.

TOURIST INFORMATION

San Francisco Visitor Information Center (Map p968; ☎415-391-2000, events hotline 415-391-2001; www.onlyinsanfrancisco.com; Market & Powell Sts, lower level, Hallidie Plaza; ☉9am-5pm Mon-Fri, to 3pm Sat & Sun; 🚋Powell-Mason, Powell-Hyde, ⓜPowell St, Ⓑ Powell St) Provides practical information for tourists, publishes glossy tourist-oriented booklets and runs a 24-hour events hotline.

WEBSITES

The global social media platforms **Craigslist** (http://sfbay.craigslist.org), **Twitter** (www.twitter.com) and **Yelp** (www.yelp.com) were all invented in San Francisco and are city institutions; check them out for news on pop-up shops, free shows, bar and restaurant reviews and the like.

❶ Getting There & Away

AIR

San Francisco International Airport (SFO; www.flysfo.com) is 14 miles south of downtown off Hwy 101 and accessible by Bay Area Rapid Transit (BART). **Oakland International Airport** (OAK; ☎510-563-3300; www.oaklandairport.com) serves primarily domestic destinations and is located about a 50-minute drive or BART ride across the Bay from San Francisco.

BUS

Until 2017, San Francisco's intercity hub remains the **Temporary Transbay Terminal** (Map p968; Howard & Main Sts), where you can catch buses on **AC Transit** (☎511; www.actransit.org) to the East Bay, **Golden Gate Transit** (Map p968; www.goldengatetransit.org) north to Marin and Sonoma Counties, and SamTrans south to Palo Alto and the Pacific coast. **Greyhound** (☎800-231-2222; www.greyhound.com) buses leave daily for Los Angeles ($59, eight to 12 hours), Truckee near Lake Tahoe ($31, 5½ hours) and other destinations.

TRAIN

Amtrak (☎800-872-7245; www.amtrakcalifornia.com) offers rail passes that are good for seven days of travel in California within a 21-day period (from $159). *Coast Starlight's* spectacular 35-hour run from Los Angeles to Seattle stops in Oakland, and *California Zephyr* takes its sweet time (51 hours) from Chicago to Oakland. Both have sleeping cars and dining/lounge cars with panoramic windows. Amtrak runs free shuttle buses to San Francisco's Ferry Building and CalTrain station.

CalTrain (www.caltrain.com; cnr 4th & King Sts) connects San Francisco with Silicon Valley hubs and San Jose.

❶ Getting Around

For Bay Area transit options, departures and arrivals, call ☎511 or check www.511.org.

TO/FROM SAN FRANCISCO INTERNATIONAL AIRPORT

A taxi to downtown San Francisco costs $35 to $50.

BART (Bay Area Rapid Transit; www.bart.gov; one way $8.25) Fast 30-minute ride to/from downtown San Francisco from/to SFO BART station of the International Terminal.

SamTrans (www.samtrans.com; one way $5) Express bus KX takes about 30 minutes to reach Temporary Transbay Terminal.

SuperShuttle (☎800-258-3826; www.supershuttle.com) Shared van rides to downtown San Francisco for $17.

TO/FROM OAKLAND INTERNATIONAL AIRPORT

From Oakland International Airport, take the AirBART shuttle ($3) to Coliseum station to catch BART to downtown San Francisco ($3.85); take a shared van to downtown for $27 to $35 with SuperShuttle; or or pay $55 to $70 for a taxi to San Francisco destinations.

BOAT

Blue & Gold Ferries (Map p968; www.blueand-goldfleet.com) operates the Alameda–Oakland ferry from Pier 41 and the Ferry Building. **Golden Gate Ferry** (www.goldengateferry.org) runs from the Ferry Building to Sausalito and Lark-spur in Marin County.

CAR

Avoid driving in San Francisco if possible: street parking is elusive and meter readers are ruthless. Downtown parking lots are at Embarcadero Center, 5th and Mission Sts, Union Sq, and Sutter and Stockton Sts. National car-rental agencies have airport and downtown offices.

PUBLIC TRANSPORTATION

MUNI (Municipal Transit Agency; ☑ 511; www.sfmta.com) operates bus, streetcar and cable-car lines; *MUNI Street & Transit Map* is available free online. Standard fare for buses or street-cars is $2; cable-car fare is $6. **MUNI Passport** (1/3/7 days $14/22/28) allows unlimited travel on all MUNI transportation, including cable cars; it's sold at San Francisco Visitor Information Center and Union Sq's TIX Bay Area kiosk. **City Pass** (www.citypass.com; adult/child $84/59) covers Muni and admission to four attractions.

BART links San Francisco with the East Bay and runs beneath Market St, down Mission St, south to SFO and Millbrae, where it connects with CalTrain.

TAXI

Fares run about $2.75 per mile; meters start at $3.50.

DeSoto Cab (☑ 415-970-1300)

Green Cab (☑ 415-626-4733; www.626green.com) Fuel-efficient hybrids; worker-owned collective.

Luxor (☑ 415-282-4141)

Yellow Cab (☑ 415-333-3333)

Marin County

Majestic redwoods cling to coastal hills just across the Golden Gate Bridge in wealthy, laid-back **Marin** (www.visitmarin.org). The southernmost town, **Sausalito**, is a tiny bayside destination for bike trips over the bridge (take the ferry back to San Francisco). Near the harbor, the **San Francisco**

Bay-Delta Model (Map p966; ☑ 415-332-3871; www.spn.usace.army.mil; 2100 Bridgeway Blvd, Sausalito; admission by donation; ☺ 9am-4pm Tue-Fri, 10am-5pm Sat & Sun late May-early Sep, 9am-4pm Tue-Sat early Sep-late May; ☻) is a way-cool giant hydraulic recreation of the entire bay and delta.

Marin Headlands

These windswept, rugged headlands are laced with hiking trails, providing panoramic views of the city and bay. To find the **visitor center** (Map p966; ☑ 415-331-1540; www.nps.gov/goga/marin-headlands.htm; Fort Barry, Bldg 948; ☺ 9:30am-4:30pm Sat-Mon Apr-Sep), take the Alexander Ave exit after crossing north over the Golden Gate Bridge, turn left under the freeway onto Bunker Rd then follow the signs.

Nearby attractions include **Point Bonita Lighthouse** (Map p966; www.nps.gov/goga/pobo.htm; off Field Rd; ☺ 12:30-3:30pm Sat-Mon) **FREE**, **Rodeo Beach** and the educational **Marine Mammal Center** (Map p966; ☑ 415-289-7325; www.tmmc.org; 2000 Bunker Rd; admission by donation; ☺ 10am-5pm; ☻) ☞ at Fort Cronkite. East of Hwy 101 at Fort Baker, the interactive **Bay Area Discovery Museum** (Map p966; ☑ 415-339-3900; www.baykidsmuseum.org; 557 McReynolds Rd, Sausalito; admission $11, 1st Wed of month free; ☺ 9am-5pm Tue-Sun; ☻) is awesome for kids.

Near the visitor center, eco-conscious **HI Marin Headlands Hostel** (Map p966; ☑ 415-331-2777; www.norcalhostels.org/marin; Fort Barry, Bldg 941; dm $26-30, r withouth bath $72-92; ☻) ☞ occupies two historic 1907 buildings on a forested hill, with private rooms in a former officer's house. For historical luxury, book a fireplace room with bay views at Fort Baker's LEED-certified **Cavallo Point** (Map p966; ☑ 415-339-4700, 888-651-2003; www.cavallopoint.com; 601 Murray Circle; r from $379; ☀ ☂ ☲ ☻ ☙) ☞ lodge.

Mt Tamalpais State Park

Majestic Mt Tam (2571ft) is a woodsy playground for hikers and mountain bikers. **Mt Tamalpais State Park** (Map p966; ☑ 415-388-2070; www.friendsofmttam.org; per car $8) encompasses 6300 acres of parklands and over 200 miles of trails; don't miss driving up to East Peak Summit lookout. Panoramic Hwy climbs from Hwy 1 through the park to **Stinson Beach**, a mellow seaside town with a sandy crescent-shaped beach.

Park headquarters are at **Pantoll Station** (Map p966; ✉ 415-388-2070; 801 Panoramic Hwy, Mill Valley; ⊙ 8am-7pm Fri-Sun, shorter hr winter; ☎), the nexus of many trails, with a first-come, first-served **campground** (Map p966; tent sites $25). Book far ahead for a rustic cabin (no electricity or running water) or walk-in campsite at **Steep Ravine** (✉ 800-444-7275; www.reserveamerica.com; tent site $25, cabin $100), off Hwy 1 south of Stinson Beach. Or hike in with food, a sleeping bag and a towel to off-the-grid **West Point Inn** (Map p966; ✉ info 415-388-9955, reservations 415-646-0702; www.westpointinn.com; 100 Old Railroad Grade Fire Rd, Mill Valley; r per adult/child $50/25); reservations required.

Muir Woods National Monument

Wander among an ancient stand of the world's tallest trees at 520-acre **Muir Woods National Monument** (Map p966; ✉ 415-388-2595; www.nps.gov/muwo; Muir Woods Rd, Mill Valley; adult/child $7/free; ⊙ 8am-7:30pm, closes earlier mid-Sep–mid-Mar), 10 miles northwest of the Golden Gate Bridge. Easy hiking trails loop past thousand-year-old redwoods at Cathedral Grove. By the entrance, a **cafe** serves light lunches and drinks. Come midweek to avoid crowds; otherwise arrive early morning or late afternoon. Take Hwy 101 to the Hwy 1 exit, then follow the signs.

The **Muir Woods Shuttle** (Marin Transit Bus 66; ✉ 415-455-2000; www.goldengatetransit.org; round-trip adult/child $5/free) operates weekends and holidays from early May through late October, running every 10 to 20 minutes from Marin City, with limited connections to Sausalito's ferry terminal.

Point Reyes National Seashore

The windswept peninsula of **Point Reyes National Seashore** (www.nps.gov/pore) juts 10 miles out to sea on an entirely different tectonic plate, protecting over 100 sq miles of beaches, lagoons and forested hills. A mile west of Olema, **Bear Valley Visitor Center** (✉ 415-464-5100; www.nps.gov/pore; ⊙ 10am-5pm Mon-Fri, from 9am Sat & Sun) has maps, information and natural-history displays. The 0.6-mile **Earthquake Trail**, which crosses the San Andreas Fault zone, starts nearby.

Crowning the peninsula's westernmost tip, **Point Reyes Lighthouse** (end of Sir Francis Drake Blvd; ⊙ 2:30pm-4pm Thu-Mon, weather permitting) FREE is ideal for winter whale-watching. Off Pierce Point Rd, the 9.5-mile round-trip **Tomales Point Trail** rolls atop blustery bluffs past herds of tule elk to the peninsula's northern tip. Paddling Tomales Bay gets you up close to seabirds and seals; **Blue Waters Kayaking** (✉ 415-669-2600; www.bwkayak.com; rentals/tours from $50/70; ♿) launches from Inverness and Marshall (reserve in advance).

Nature lovers bunk at the only in-park lodging, **HI Point Reyes Hostel** (✉ 415-663-8811; www.norcalhostels.org/reyes; 1390 Limantour Spit Rd; dm $24, r without bath $82-120; ⊙ check-in 2:30pm-10pm; @♿) ✿, 8 miles inland from the visitor center. By marshy wetlands, **Motel Inverness** (✉ 866-453-3839, 415-236-1967; www.motelinverness.com; 12718 Sir Francis Drake Blvd; r $99-190; ☎) sports spiffy rooms and a fireplace lounge with pool tables. The **West Marin Chamber of Commerce** (✉ 415-663-9232; www.pointreyes.org) checks availability at cozy inns, cottages and B&Bs.

Two miles north of Olema, the tiny town of **Point Reyes Station** has heart-warming bakeries, cafes and restaurants. Gather a picnic lunch at **Tomales Bay Foods & Cowgirl Creamery** (www.cowgirlcreamery.com; 80 4th St; sandwiches $6-12; ⊙ 10am-6pm Wed-Sun; ✈) ✿ or revel in handmade, seasonal Cal-Italian cuisine at **Osteria Stellina** (✉ 415-663-9988; http://osteriastellina.com; 11285 Hwy 1; mains $14-24; ⊙ 11:30am-2:30pm & 5-9pm; ✈) ✿.

Berkeley

Not much has changed since the 1960s heyday of anti–Vietnam War protests – except the bumper stickers: 'No Blood for Oil' has supplanted 'Make Love Not War.' You can't walk around nude on campus anymore, but 'Berserkeley' remains the Bay Area's radical hub, crawling with university students, scoffing skateboarders and aging Birkenstock-shod hippies.

⊙ Sights & Activities

Leading to the campus's south gate, **Telegraph Avenue** is as youthful and gritty as San Francisco's Haight St, packed with cafes, cheap eats, bookshops and music stores.

University of California, Berkeley   UNIVERSITY
(www.berkeley.edu) One of the country's top universities, 'Cal' is home to over 35,000 diverse, politically conscious students. The **Visitor Services Center** (✉ 510-642-5215;

http://visitors.berkeley.edu; 101 Sproul Hall; ⊘ tours usually 10am Mon-Sat, 1pm Sun) leads free campus tours (reservations required). Ride the elevator to the top of the landmark 1914 **Campanile** (Sather Tower; adult/child $2/1; ⊘10am-3:45pm Mon-Fri, to 4:45pm Sat, 10am-1:30pm & 3-4:45pm Sun; ♿). The **Bancroft Library** displays the small gold nugget that kicked off California's gold rush in 1848.

UC Berkeley Art Museum　　　MUSEUM
(☑510-642-0808; www.bampfa.berkeley.edu; 2626 Bancroft Way; adult/child $10/7; ⊘11am-5pm Wed-Sun) Eleven galleries showcase a wide range of works, from ancient Chinese to cutting-edge contemporary American art. Across the street, its **Pacific Film Archive** (PFA; ☑510-642-5249; www.bampfa.berkeley.edu; 2575 Bancroft Way; adult/child $9.50/6.50) screens independent and avant-garde films. Both are scheduled to move to a new location on Oxford St, between Center and Addison Sts.

Tilden Regional Park　　　PARK
(www.ebparks.org/parks/tilden) Up in the Berkeley Hills, escape on 40 miles of hiking and biking trails, with botanical gardens, swimming at Lake Anza and a merry-go-round and a steam train for kiddos.

🛌 Sleeping

Motels line University Ave west of campus.

YMCA　　　HOSTEL $
(☑510-848-6800; www.ymca-cba.org/downtown-berkeley; 2001 Allston Way; s/d without bath from $49/81; @ 🛜 🏊) The recently remodeled 100-year-old downtown 'Y' is Berkeley's best budget option. Rates for austere private rooms include pool, fitness center and kitchen access.

Downtown Berkeley Inn　　　MOTEL $$
(☑510-843-4043; www.downtownberkeleyinn.com; 2001 Bancroft Way; r from $109; 🅿 ❄ 🛜) Showing off elements of boutique style, this 27-room motel has good-sized rooms with modern amenities. Free parking.

Hotel Durant　　　BOUTIQUE HOTEL $$$
(☑510-845-8981; www.hoteldurant.com; 2600 Durant Ave; r $195-309; 🅿 @ 🐾) 🐾 A block from campus, the lobby of this 1928 hotel is cheekily adorned with embarrassing yearbook photos, while smallish rooms have bongs repurposed into bedside lamps. Parking is $16 (free for hybrid cars).

🍽 Eating

Cream　　　DESSERTS $
(www.creamnation.com; 2399 Telegraph Ave; items $2-4; ⊘ noon-midnight Mon-Wed, to 2am Thu-Fri, 11am-2am Sat, 11am-11pm Sun) Crazily creative ice-cream sandwiches let you mix and match your own flavors – salted caramel with snickerdoodles, anyone? Cash only.

Cheese Board Pizza　　　PIZZERIA $
(http://cheeseboardcollective.coop; 1512 Shattuck Ave; slice/half pizza $2.50/10; ⊘11:30am-3pm & 4:30-8pm Tue-Sat; 🐾 ♿) Sit down for a slice of crispy one-option-per-day veggie pizza at this worker-owned collective, where live music often plays at night.

Bette's Oceanview Diner　　　DINER $$
(www.bettesdiner.com; 1807 4th St; mains $6-13; ⊘6:30am-2:30pm Mon-Fri, to 4pm Sat & Sun) At this buzzing breakfast spot near the I-80 Fwy, table waits can be long, but it's worth it for baked souffle pancake perfection.

★Chez Panisse　　　CALIFORNIAN $$$
(☑cafe 510-548-5049, restaurant 510-548-5525; 1517 Shattuck Ave; cafe dinner mains $18-29, restaurant prix-fixe dinner $65-100; ⊘cafe 11:30am-2:45pm & 5-10:30pm Mon-Thu, to 3pm & to 11:30pm Fri & Sat; restaurant seatings 6-6:30pm & 8:30-9:15pm Mon-Sat) 🐾 Genuflect at the culinary temple of Alice Waters: the birthplace of California cuisine remains at the pinnacle of Bay Area dining. Book one month ahead for its seasonally inspired prix-fixe restaurant menu (no substitutions) or upstairs at the à la carte cafe.

🍷 Drinking & Entertainment

Caffe Strada　　　CAFE
(2300 College Ave; ⊘6am-midnight; 🛜) Caffeine-wired students mob the outdoor patio to study, ardently talk philosophy or flirt.

Freight & Salvage Coffeehouse　　　LIVE MUSIC
(☑510-644-2020; http://thefreight.org; 2020 Addison St; tickets $5-30) Originating in the radical '60s era, this legendary club stages all-ages shows of traditional folk and world music.

Berkeley Repertory Theatre　　　THEATER
(☑510-647-2949; www.berkeleyrep.org; 2025 Addison St; tickets $35-100) Highly respected company has produced bold versions of classical and contemporary plays since 1968.

ⓘ Getting There & Around

AC Transit (p990) runs local buses around Berkeley ($2.10) and to Oakland ($2.10) and San Francisco ($4.20). **BART** (⚡511, 510-465-2278; www.bart.gov) trains connect downtown Berkeley, a short walk from campus, with Oakland ($1.75) and SF ($3.70).

NORTHERN CALIFORNIA

The Golden State goes wild in Northern California, with coast redwoods swirled in fog and Wine Country vineyards and mud-bath wallows. Befitting this dramatic meeting of land and water is an unlikely melange of local residents: timber barons and hippie tree huggers, dreadlocked Rastafarians and biodynamic ranchers, pot farmers and political radicals of every stripe. Come for the scenery, but stay for the top-notch wine and farm-to-fork restaurants, along with misty hikes among the world's tallest trees, a nekkid hot-springs soak and rambling conversations that begin with 'Hey, dude!' and end hours later.

Wine Country

A patchwork of vineyards stretches from sunny inland Napa to windy coastal Sonoma – California's premier wine-growing region. Napa has art-filled tasting rooms by big-name architects, with prices to match. In down-to-earth Sonoma, you may drink in a shed and meet the vintner's dog. Wine Country is at least an hour's drive north of San Francisco via Hwy 101 or I-80.

Napa Valley

Over 200 wineries crowd 30-mile-long Napa Valley along three main routes. Traffic-jammed on weekends, Hwy 29 is lined with blockbuster wineries. Running parallel, Silverado Trail moves faster, passing boutique winemakers, bizarre architecture and cult-hit Cabernet Sauvignon. West toward Sonoma, Hwy 121 (Carneros Hwy) has landmark vineyards specializing in sparkling wines and Pinot Noir.

At the southern end of the valley, **Napa** – the valley's workaday hub – lacks rusticity, but has trendy restaurants and tasting rooms downtown. Stop by the **Napa Valley Welcome Center** (⚡855-333-6272, 707-251-5895; www.visitnapavalley.com; 600 Main St;

⊙9am-5pm Sep-Apr, 9am-5pm Mon-Thu, to 6pm Fri-Sun May-Oct) for wine-tasting passes and winery maps.

Heading north on Hwy 29, the former stagecoach stop of tiny **Yountville** has more Michelin-starred eateries per capita than anywhere else in the USA. Another 10 miles north, traffic rolls to a stop in charming **St Helena** – the Beverly Hills of Napa – where there's genteel strolling and shopping, if you can find parking, that is.

At the valley's northern end, folksy **Calistoga** – Napa's least-gentrified town – is home to hot-spring spas and mud-bath emporiums using volcanic ash from nearby Mt St Helena.

◉ Sights & Activities

Most Napa wineries require reservations. Book one appointment, then build your day around it. Plan to visit no more than a few tasting rooms each day.

★**Hess Collection**   WINERY, GALLERY
(⚡707-255-8584; www.hesscollection.com; 4411 Redwood Rd, Napa; tasting $10; ⊙10am-5pm) ⚐ Northwest of downtown Napa, this sustainable winery pairs monster Cabernet with blue-chip modern art by Robert Rauschenberg and others. Reservations suggested.

★**di Rosa Art +
Nature Preserve**   GALLERY, GARDEN
(⚡707-226-5991; www.dirosaart.org; 5200 Hwy 121, Napa; admission $5, tours $12-15; ⊙10am-4pm Wed-Sun, to 6pm Wed-Sun Apr-Oct) When you notice scrap-metal sheep grazing Carneros vineyards, you've spotted one of the best collections of modern NorCal art anywhere. Reservations advised for tours.

Frog's Leap   WINERY
(⚡707-963-4704; www.frogsleap.com; 8815 Conn Creek Rd, Rutherford; tasting $15, incl tour $20; ⊙10am-4pm; ⚐⚐) ⚐ Meandering paths wind through gardens surrounding an 1884 barn at this LEED-certified winery, pouring stand-out Sauvignon Blanc and Cabernet. Book tours in advance.

Pride Mountain   WINERY
(⚡707-963-4949; www.pridewines.com; 3000 Summit Trail, St Helena; tasting $10, incl tour $15-75; ⊙by appointment) Cult-favorite Pride straddles the Sonoma–Napa border and makes stellar Cabernet, Merlot, Chardonnay and Viognier at an unfussy hilltop estate with spectacular picnicking.

Casa Nuestra WINERY
(☑866-844-9463; www.casanuestra.com; 3451 Silverado Trail, St Helena; tasting $10; ☺ by appointment) ✦ A peace flag and portrait of Elvis greet you at this tiny solar-powered winery, known for growing unusual varietals. Goats frolic beside the picnic area.

Castello di Amorosa WINERY, CASTLE
(☑707-967-6272; www.castellodiamorosa.com; 4045 Hwy 29, Calistoga; admission & tasting $18-28, incl guided tour $33-69; ☺ 9:30am-6pm, to 5pm Nov-Feb) Tour a recreated 13th-century Tuscan castle, complete with a dungeon tasting room stocked with Italian varietals.

Indian Springs Spa SPA
(☑707-942-4913; www.indianspringscalistoga. com; 1712 Lincoln Ave, Calistoga; ☺ by appointment 9am-8pm) Book ahead for a volcanic-mud bath at Calistoga's original 19th-century mineral-springs resort. Treatments include access to spring-fed pools.

🛌 Sleeping

The valley's best values are midweek at Napa's less-than-exciting motels.

Bothe-Napa Valley
State Park Campground CAMPGROUND $
(☑800-444-7275; www.reserveamerica.com; 3801 Hwy 128, Calistoga; camping & RV sites $35; ☀☂☀) Hillside campsites with a summertime swimming pool, coin-op hot showers and hiking trails beneath moss-covered oaks await.

Chablis Inn MOTEL $$
(☑707-257-1944; www.chablisinn.com; 3360 Solano Ave, Napa; r $105-179; ✴@☂☀) On Napa's suburban strip, these crisp, modern rooms are spacious and don't cut corners – some even have jetted tubs for couples.

EuroSpa & Inn MOTEL $$
(☑707-942-6829; www.eurospa.com; 1202 Pine St, Calistoga; r incl breakfast $145-195; ✴☂☀) Immaculate single-story motel on a quiet side street has just 13 rooms with two-person whirlpool tubs and gas fireplaces. Skip the on-site spa, though.

★ Indian Springs Resort RESORT $$$
(☑707-942-4913; www.indianspringscalistoga. com; 1712 Lincoln Ave, Calistoga; r/cottage from $199/229; ✴@☂☀☂) At Calistoga's most harmonious hot-springs resort, charming bungalows (some with kitchens) face a broad lawn with rustling palm trees, shuffleboard and bocce courts, hammocks and BBQ grills. Bicycles are free for pampered guests to borrow.

🍴 Eating

Many Wine Country restaurants keep shorter hours in winter and spring.

Oxbow Public Market MARKET $
(☑707-226-6529; www.oxbowpublicmarket.com; 644 1st St, Napa; dishes from $3; ☺9am-7pm Mon-Sat, 10am-5pm Sun) ✦ Oxbow showcases sustainably produced artisanal foods by 20-plus vendors. Feast on Hog Island oysters, Model Bakery muffins, Ca' Momi's crispy pizzas or Three Twins organic ice cream.

Gott's Roadside AMERICAN $$
(☑707-963-3486; http://gotts.com; 933 Main St, St Helena; dishes $3-14; ☺7am-9pm, to 10pm May-Sep; ✦) A 1950s drive-in diner with 21st-century sensibilities: burgers are all-natural beef, organic chicken or sushi-grade tuna, with sides like chili-dusted sweet-potato fries and handmade milkshakes.

Oakville Grocery DELI, MARKET $$
(☑707-944-8802; www.oakvillegrocery.com; 7856 Hwy 29, Oakville; sandwiches $9-14; ☺6:30am-5pm) Pick up picnic staples or grab a gourmet meal on the go, with specialty sandwiches crafted from locally made artisanal ingredients and decadent desserts. Second location in downtown Healdsburg.

Wine Spectator
Greystone Restaurant CALIFORNIAN $$$
(☑707-967-1010; www.ciarestaurants.com; 2555 Main St, St Helena; dinner mains $22-34; ☺11:30am-2:30pm & 5-9pm Mon-Fri, 11:30am-9pm Sat, noon-7:15pm Sun; ☂) An 1889 stone chateau houses the Culinary Institute of America's fine-dining restaurant, bakery-cafe and gadget-filled shop. Book ahead for weekend cooking demos and wine-tasting classes.

Ad Hoc CALIFORNIAN $$$
(☑707-944-2487; www.adhocrestaurant.com; 6476 Washington St, Yountville; prix-fixe dinner from $52; ☺5-10pm Wed-Sun, plus 10am-1pm Sun) Don't ask for a menu at chef Thomas Keller's dressed-down 'experimental' kitchen. Changing daily, a four-course family-style dinner allows no substitutions (except for dietary restrictions), but none are

needed – every dish is comforting, fresh and spot-on.

★**French Laundry** CALIFORNIAN $$$
(☑707-944-2380; www.frenchlaundry.com; 6640 Washington St, Yountville; prix-fixe dinner $270; ☺seatings 11am-1pm Fri-Sun & 5:30pm-9:15pm daily) Sparkling with three Michelin stars, the French Laundry is a high-wattage culinary experience, full of whimsy and wit. Book exactly two months ahead: call at 10am (or try OpenTable.com at midnight). If you can't score a reservation, console yourself at chef Thomas Keller's nearby note-perfect French brasserie **Bouchon** or with pastries from **Bouchon Bakery**.

Sonoma Valley

More laid-back, less commercial than Napa, Sonoma Valley enfolds over 70 wineries off Hwy 12 – and, unlike in Napa, most welcome picnicking. Note there are actually three Sonomas: the town, the valley and the county.

◉ Sights & Activities

Downtown Sonoma was once the capital of the short-lived Bear Flag Republic. Today **Sonoma Plaza** – the state's largest town square – is bordered by chic boutiques, historical buildings and a **visitor center** (☑866-996-1090, 707-996-1090; www.sonomavalley.com; 453 1st St E; ☺9am-5pm Mon-Sat, from 10am Sun).

Jack London State Historic Park PARK
(☑707-938-5216; www.jacklondonpark.com; 2400 London Ranch Rd, Glen Ellen; per car $8, tour adult/child $4/2; ☺9:30am-5pm Thu-Mon) Obey the call of the wild where adventurer-novelist Jack London built his dream house – it burned on the eve of completion in 1913. Tour the writer's original cottage or browse memorabilia inside the small museum standing in a redwood grove. Twenty miles of hiking and mountain-biking trails weave through the park's 1400 hilltop acres.

★**Bartholomew Park Winery** WINERY
(☑707-939-3024; www.bartpark.com; 1000 Vineyard Lane, Sonoma; tasting $10, incl tour $20; ☺11am-4:30pm) ✐ In a 400-acre nature preserve that's perfect for picnicking, the family-owned vineyards originally cultivated in 1857 are now organic-certified, yielding citrus-sunshine Sauvignon Blanc and smoky-midnight Merlot.

Gundlach-Bundschu Winery WINERY
(☑707-939-3015; www.gunbun.com; 2000 Denmark St, Sonoma; tasting $10, incl tour $20-50; ☺11am-4:30pm, to 5:30pm Jun–mid-Oct) ✐ West of downtown, this sustainable winery dating from 1858 looks like a storybook castle. Winemakers craft legendary Tempranillo and signature Gewürztraminer.

Kunde WINERY
(☑707-833-5501; www.kunde.com; 9825 Hwy 12, Kenwood; tasting & tour $10-40; ☺10:30am-5pm) ✐ Make reservations for a sustainable vineyard tour, guided hike or mountain-top tasting of estate-grown Cabernet, Zinfandel and Sauvignon Blanc.

Kaz Winery WINERY
(☑707-833-2536; www.kazwinery.com; 233 Adobe Canyon Rd, Kenwood; tasting $5; ☺11am-5pm Fri-Mon, by appointment Tue-Thu; ✈☺) ✐ Veer off Hwy 12 for offbeat, organically grown, cult-favorite wines, poured at a wooden barrel-top bar inside a barn.

Ravenswood Winery WINERY
(☑707-933-2332; www.ravenswoodwinery.com; 18701 Gehricke Rd, Sonoma; tasting $10, incl tour $15; ☺10am-4:30pm) With the slogan 'no wimpy wines,' this buzzing tasting room pours a full slate of Zinfandels. Novices welcome.

Cornerstone Sonoma GARDENS
(☑707-933-3010; www.corenerstonegardens.com; 23570 Arnold Dr, Sonoma; ☺10am-4pm) FREE There's nothing traditional about this avante-garde tapestry of landscaped gardens, 5 miles south of downtown Sonoma.

☋ Sleeping

At the valley's north end, Santa Rosa has more budget-saving motels and hotels.

Sugarloaf Ridge State Park CAMPGROUND $
(☑800-444-7275; www.reserveamerica.com; 2605 Adobe Canyon Rd, Kenwood; camping & RV sites $35; ✈☺) Near mid-valley wineries, campsites laze in a stream-fed hillside meadow by forested hiking trails. Coin-op hot showers available.

Sonoma Hotel HISTORIC HOTEL $$
(☑800-468-6016, 707-996-2996; www.sonomahotel.com; 110 W Spain St, Sonoma; r incl breakfast

$115-240) Old-fashioned rooms squeeze inside this 19th-century plaza landmark. No elevator or parking lot. Two-night minimum stay most weekends

Beltane Ranch   B&B $$$
(☑707-996-6501; www.beltaneranch.com; 11775 Hwy 12, Glen Ellen; d incl breakfast $150-265; �) Wide porches are dotted with swings and white wicker chairs at this cheerful lemon-yellow 1890 ranch house and cottage surrounded by pasturelands. No phones or TVs.

Gaige House Inn   B&B $$$
(☑800-935-0237, 707-935-0237; www.gaige.com; 13540 Arnold Dr, Glen Ellen; d incl breakfast from $275; ☎☀☃) Near vineyards, Asian-chic rooms and fireplace suites adorn a historic home, with pebbled meditation courtyards out by the pool. Sister inns in Sonoma, Healdsburg and Yountville.

✕ Eating

Fremont Diner   AMERICAN $$
(☑707-938-7370; http://thefremontdiner.com; 2698 Fremont Dr, Sonoma; breakfast & lunch mains $6-14; ☉8am-3pm Mon-Wed, to 9pm Thu-Sun; ☒) ⬤ Feast on Southern-inspired, farm-to-table cooking at this down-home diner with picnic tables outside. Arrive early to avoid long waits.

Fig Cafe & Winebar   FRENCH $$
(☑707-938-2130; www.thefigcafe.com; 13690 Arnold Dr, Glen Ellen; mains $10-20; ☉10am-3pm Sat & Sun, 5:30pm-9pm daily) Imagine French-inspired comfort food like steamed mussels and duck cassoulet in a convivial room with vaulted wooden ceilings. Even better: no reservations or corkage fee.

Red Grape   ITALIAN $$
(☑707-996-4103; http://theredgrape.com; 529 1st St W, Sonoma; mains $10-20; ☉11:30am-10pm; ☒) At this sunlight-filled pizzeria, thin-crust pies topped with locally made cheeses, panini sandwiches and pasta shake hands with small-production Sonoma wines.

★Cafe La Haye   CALIFORNIAN $$$
(☑707-935-5994; www.cafelahaye.com; 140 E Napa St, Sonoma; mains $20-30; ☉5:30pm-9pm Tue-Sat) ⬤ This tiny bistro with an open kitchen creates earthy New American dishes from ingredients all sourced within 60 miles. Tables are squeezed together elbow-to-elbow. Book ahead.

Russian River Valley

Redwood trees tower over small wineries in the Russian River Valley, about 75 miles northwest of San Francisco (via Hwys 101 and 116), in western **Sonoma County**.

Famous for its apple orchards and farm-tour trails, **Sebastopol** has a New Age spiritual aura, with downtown bookshops, art galleries and boutiques and antiques stores further south. Have a pint and pub grub in the beer garden at **Hopmonk Tavern** (☑707-829-9300; www.hopmonk.com; 230 Petaluma Ave; mains $12-23; ☉11:30am-9pm Sun-Wed, to 9:30pm Thu-Sat, bar till 1:30am; ☎), shaking with world beats at night. Four miles northwest, **Willow Wood Market Cafe** (☑707-823-0233; www.willowwoodgraton.com; 9020 Graton Rd, Graton; most mains $7-17; ☉8am-9pm Mon-Sat, to 3pm Sun; ☒) cooks comfort-food breakfasts and hot, haute sandwiches at lunch.

Guerneville is the main river beach town, buzzing with Harleys and gay-friendly honky-tonks. Explore old-growth redwoods at **Armstrong Redwoods State Reserve** (☑707-869-2015; www.parks.ca.gov; 17000 Armstrong Woods Rd; per car $8; ☉8am-sunset; ☒), next to no-reservations **Bullfrog Pond Campground** (www.stewardsofthecoastandredwoods.org; campsites $25; ☒☃). Paddle downriver, past herons and otters, with **Burke's Canoe Trips** (☑707-887-1222; www.burkescanoetrips.com; 8600 River Rd, Forestville; canoe rental incl shuttle $60). Head southeast to sip bubbly at the outdoor hilltop tasting bar at **Iron Horse Vineyards** (☑707-887-1507; www.ironhorsevineyards.com; 9786 Ross Station Rd, Sebastopol; tasting $15, incl tour $20; ☉10am-4:30pm). Other excellent wineries are scattered along rural Westside Rd, which follows the river to Healdsburg. Guerneville's **visitor center** (☑877-644-9001, 707-869-9000; www.russianriver.com; 16209 1st St; ☉10am-5pm) offers winery maps and lodging info. The town's best eats are at California-smart **Boon Eat + Drink** (☑707-869-0780; http://eatatboon.com; 16248 Main St; dinner mains $15-26; ☉11am-3pm Mon-Tue & Thu-Fri, 5-9pm Mon-Fri, 10am-3pm & 5-10pm Sat & Sun), which manages the boutique **Boon Hotel + Spa** (☑707-869-2721; www.boonhotels.com; 14711 Armstrong Woods Rd; r $165-275; ☎☀☃) ⬤, a minimalist green oasis with a saline pool.

The aptly named 10-mile Bohemian Hwy winds south of the river to tiny **Occidental**, where **Howard Station Cafe** (www.

howardstationcafe.com; 3811 Bohemian Hwy; mains $6-11; ⊙7am-2:30pm Mon-Fri, to 3pm Sat & Sun; 👫🐕) serves hearty breakfasts like blueberry cornmeal pancakes (cash only) and **Barley & Hops Tavern** (☏707-874-9037; www.barleynhops.com; 3688 Bohemian Hwy; ⊙4-9:30pm Mon-Wed, 11am-9:30pm Thu & Sun, to 10pm Fri & Sat) pours craft beers. It's another three miles south to **Freestone**, home of the phenomenal bakery **Wild Flour Bread** (www.wildflourbread.com; 140 Bohemian Hwy; items from $3; ⊙8:30am-6pm Fri-Mon) and invigorating cedar-enzyme baths at **Osmosis** (☏707-823-8231; www.osmosis.com; 209 Bohemian Hwy; ⊙by appointment) spa.

Healdsburg to Boonville

More than 100 wineries dot the valleys within a 20-mile radius of **Healdsburg**, where upscale eateries, wine-tasting rooms and stylish hotels surround a Spanish-style plaza. For tasting passes and maps, drop by the **visitor center** (☏800-648-9922, 707-433-6935; www.healdsburg.org; 217 Healdsburg Ave; ⊙9am-5pm Mon-Fri, to 3pm Sat, 10am-2pm Sun). Dine with California-chic locavores on the leafy patio at **Barndiva** (☏707-431-0100; www.barndiva.com; 231 Center St; dinner mains $25-36; ⊙noon-2pm Wed-Sat, 11am-2pm Sun & 5:30pm-9:30pm Wed-Sun, to 10pm Fri & Sat), or grab lunch near the Alexander Valley's vineyards at country-style **Jimtown Store** (☏707-433-1212; www.jimtown.com; 6706 Hwy 128; sandwiches $6-14; ⊙7:30am-4pm Mon-Thu, to 5pm Fri-Sun). Afterward bed down at old-fashioned **L&M Motel** (☏707-433-6528; www.landmmotel.com; 70 Healdsburg Ave; r $85-165; 🌂🐕) or retro-romantic **Healdsburg Modern Cottages** (☏866-964-0110; www.healdsburgcottages.com; 425 Foss St; d from $250; 🌂).

Picture-perfect farmstead wineries await discovery in **Dry Creek Valley**, west of Hwy 101 from Healdsburg. Pedal a bicycle out to taste Zinfandel at **Truett Hurst Vineyards** (☏707-433-9545; www.truetthurst.com; 5610 Dry Creek Rd; tastings $5-10; ⊙10am-5pm) 🍷 and **Bella Vineyards & Wine Caves** (☏707-473-9171; www.bellawinery.com; 9711 West Dry Creek Rd; tasting $10; ⊙11am-4:30pm), or motor toward the Russian River and biodynamic **Porter Creek Vineyards** (☏707-433-6321; www.portercreekvineyards.com; 8735 Westside Rd; tasting $10; ⊙10:30am-4:30pm) 🍷 for Pinot Noir and Viognier poured at a bar made from a bowling-alley lane.

North of Healdsburg, follow Hwy 128 through the **Anderson Valley**, known for

its fruit orchards and stand-out winemakers like **Navarro** (☏707-895-3686; www.navarrowine.com; 5601 Hwy 128, Philo; ⊙9am-5pm, to 6pm May-Sep) and **Husch** (☏800-554-8724; www.huschvineyards.com; 4400 Hwy 128, Philo; ⊙10am-5pm). Outside **Boonville**, which has roadside cafes, bakeries, delis and ice-cream shops, brake for disc-golf and beer at solar-powered **Anderson Valley Brewing Company** (☏707-895-2337; www.avbc.com; 17700 Hwy 253; ⊙11am-6pm Sat-Thu, to 7pm Fri, tours 1:30pm & 3:30pm daily, closed Tue & Wed Jan-Mar) 🍷.

🛈 Getting There & Around

Getting to and around Wine Country by public transportation is slow, but just possible.

For Napa, take **Vallejo Baylink Ferry** (☏877-643-3779; www.baylinkferry.com) from San Francisco's Ferry Building ($13, one hour). In Vallejo, connect with Napa Valley's **Vine Transit** (☏707-251-2800; www.ridethevine.com) buses to Napa ($1.50 to $3.25, 40 to 55 minutes), with limited onward connections to Yountville, St Helena and Calistoga. Alternatively, take BART to El Cerrito del Norte station, then connect on weekdays with Vine Transit bus 29 to Napa ($3.25, 1¼ hours); on weekends, transfer to **SolTrans** (☏707-648-4666; www.soltransride.com) bus 80 to Vallejo ($1.75, 25 minutes), then catch Vine Transit bus 11 to Napa ($1.50, 55 minutes).

For Sonoma, **Greyhound** (☏800-231-2222; www.greyhound.com) buses connect San Francisco and Santa Rosa ($24, 1¾ hours). **Golden Gate Transit** (☏415-455-2000, 511; http://goldengate.org) also links San Francisco to Santa Rosa ($10.75, two to three hours). From Santa Rosa, **Sonoma County Transit** (☏800-345-7433, 707-576-7433; www.sctransit.com) buses connect to Sonoma ($3.05, 70 minutes) via Sonoma Valley towns.

Rent bicycles (per day $30 to $85) from **Napa River Vélo** (☏707-258-8729; www.naparivervelo.com; 680 Main St, Napa), **Wine Country Cyclery** (☏707-966-6800; www.winecountry-cyclery.com; 262 W Napa St, Sonoma), **Calistoga Bike Shop** (☏707-942-9687; www.calistogabikeshop.com; 1318 Lincoln Ave, Calistoga) or **Spoke Folk Cyclery** (☏707-433-7171; www.spokefolk.com; 201 Center St, Healdsburg).

North Coast

Metropolitan San Francisco, only a few hours behind in the rearview mirror, feel eons away from the frothing, frigid crash of Pacific tide and two-stoplight towns on this jagged edge of the continent. Valleys of redwoods brush up against the moody ocean waves and rural farms here on California's North Coast, home to hippies, hoppy microbrews and, most famously, the tallest trees on earth. The winding coastal drive gets more rewarding with every gorgeous, white-knuckled mile of narrow highway.

Bodega Bay to Fort Bragg

Compared with the famous Big Sur coast, the serpentine stretch of Hwy 1 up the North Coast is more challenging, remote and *real*: it passes farms, fishing towns and hidden beaches. Drivers use roadside pull-outs to scan the hazy Pacific horizon for migrating whales and to amble the coastline dotted with rock formations and relentlessly pounded by the surf. The 110-mile stretch from Bodega Bay to Fort Bragg takes at least three hours of nonstop driving; at night in the fog, it takes steely nerves and much, much longer.

Bodega Bay, the first pearl in a string of sleepy fishing towns, was the setting for Hitchcock's terrifying 1963 psycho-horror flick *The Birds*. Today the skies are free from bloodthirsty gulls, but you'd best keep an eye on that picnic basket as you explore the arched rocks, secret coves and wildflower-covered bluffs of **Sonoma Coast State Park** (www.parks.ca.gov; per car $8), with beaches rolling even beyond Jenner, 10 miles north. **Bodega Bay Charters** (☏707-875-3495; http://bodegacharters.com; Eastshore Rd) runs winter whale-watching trips (adult/child $50/35). **Bodega Bay Surf Shack** (☏707-875-3944; http://bodegabaysurf.com; 1400 N Hwy 1; surfboard/wet-suit/kayak rentals from $17/17/45) rents surfboards, wet-suits and kayaks. Landlubbers hike Bodega Head or saddle up horses at **Chanslor Riding Stables** (☏707-785-8849; www.chanslorranch.com; 2660 N Hwy 1; rides from $40).

Where the wide, lazy Russian River meets the Pacific, there isn't much to **Jenner**, a cluster of shops and restaurants dotting coastal hills. Informative volunteers protect the resident colony of harbor seals at the river's mouth during pupping season, between March and August.

Twelve miles north of Jenner, the salt-weathered structures of **Fort Ross State Historic Park** (☏707-847-3286; www.fortrossstatepark.org; 19005 Hwy 1; per car $8; ◔10am-4pm Sat & Sun, also 10am-4pm Fri late May-early Sep) preserve an 1812 trading post and Russian Orthodox church. It's a quiet place, but the history is riveting: this was once the southernmost extent of Tsarist Russia's North American trading expeditions. The small, wood-scented museum offers historical exhibits and respite from the windswept cliffs.

Seven miles further north, **Salt Point State Park** (☏707-847-3321; per car $8; ◔visitor center 10am-3pm Sat & Sun Apr-Oct) abounds with hiking trails and tide pools and has two **campgrounds** (☏800-444-7275; www.reserveamerica.com; campsites $35, walk-in tent sites $25; ♿🐾). At neighboring **Kruse Rhododendron State Reserve**, pink blooms spot the misty green woods in springtime. Cows graze the surrounding rock-strewn fields on the bluffs heading north to **Sea Ranch**, where public-access hiking trails lead from roadside parking lots downhill to pocket beaches.

Two miles north of Point Arena town, detour to wind-battered **Point Arena Lighthouse** (☏707-882-2777; www.pointarenalighthouse.com; 45500 Lighthouse Rd; adult/child $7.50/1; ◔10am-3:30pm, to 4:30pm late May-early Sep), built in 1908. Ascend 145 steps to inspect the flashing Fresnel lens and get jaw-dropping coastal views. Eight miles north of the Little River crossing at Hwy 128 is **Van Damme State Park** (☏707-937-5804; www.parks.ca.gov; per car $8), where the popular 5-mile round-trip **Fern Canyon Trail** passes through a lush river canyon with young redwoods, continuing another mile each way to a pygmy forest. The park's **campground** (☏800-444-7275; www.reserveamerica.com; walk-up/drive-in sites $25/35; ♿🐾) has coin-op hot showers.

In **Mendocino**, a historical village perched on a gorgeous headland, baby boomers stroll around New England saltbox and water-tower B&Bs, quaint shops and art galleries. Wilder paths pass berry brambles, wildflowers and cypress trees standing guard over rocky cliffs and raging surf at **Mendocino Headlands State Park** (www.parks.ca.gov) FREE. Ask at the **Ford House Museum & Visitor Center** (☏707-537-5397; http://mendoparks.org; 735 Main St; ◔11am-4pm) about guided weekend wildlife-watching walks. Just south of town, paddle your way up the Big River tidal estuary with **Catch a Canoe & Bicycles Too!** (☏707-937-0273; www.catchacanoe.com; Stanford Inn, 44850 Comptche-Ukiah Rd; kayak & canoe rental adult/child from $28/14; ◔9am-5pm).

Medocino's scrappy sister city, **Fort Bragg** is trying to lure some of the well-heeled weekenders 10 miles further north, but it still has a way to go. You'll find cheap gas here and the historic **Skunk Train** (☑707-964-6371; www.skunktrain.com; foot of Laurel St; adult/child from $20/10; ⛟🚂), whose diesel and steam engines make diverting half-day excursions through the woods.

🛏 Sleeping

Every other building in Mendocino seems to be a B&B; there are dozens to choose from, but always book ahead. Fort Bragg, just 10 miles north, has plenty of motels.

Gualala Point Regional Park　　CAMPGROUND $
(http://parks.sonomacounty.ca.gov; 42401 Highway 1, Gualala; camp sites & RV sites $30-45; ⛟) Shaded by redwoods and fragrant California bay laurel trees, a short trail connects this creekside campground to the windswept beach. Choose a drive-up campsite or secluded hike-in tent site. Coin-op hot showers available.

Andiorn　　CABIN $$
(☑800-955-6478, 707-937-1543; http://theandiorn.com; 6051 N Hwy 1, Little River; most cabins $109-199; 🛜⛟🚂) 🅿 This cluster of 1950s roadside cottages is a refreshingly playful after the cabbage-rose and lace aesthetic of Mendocino. Duplex cabins come with complementary whimsical themes; some have kitchenettes and fireplaces.

★Mar Vista Cottages　　CABIN $$$
(☑877-855-3522, 707-884-3522; www.marvistamendocino.com; 35101 S Hwy 1, Gualala; cottages $175-295; 🛜⛟🚂) 🅿These renovated 1930s cottages with kitchens are a simply restful seaside escape at Anchor Bay. Linens are line-dried over lavender, guests harvest their own dinner from the organic vegetable garden and chickens cluck around the grounds, laying the next morning's breakfast. Two-night minimum.

Brewery Gulch Inn　　B&B $$$
(☑800-578-4454, 707-937-4752; www.brewerygulchinn.com; 9401 N Hwy 1, Mendocino; d incl breakfast $245-495; 🛜) 🅿 Just south of Mendocino, this serene, eco-conscious inn wins hearts that crave luxury, with modern fireplace rooms and hosts who pour heavily at wine hour and leave sweets for midnight snacking. Cooked-to-order breakfasts are served in a small dining room overlooking the distant sea.

🍴 Eating & Drinking

Even small coastal towns usually have a bakery, deli, natural-foods market and a few roadside cafes and restaurants.

Spud Point Crab Company　　SEAFOOD $
(www.spudpointcrab.com; 1910 Westshore Rd, Bodega Bay; dishes $4-11; ⊙9am-5pm; ⛟) Classic dockside seafood shack makes salty-sweet crab sandwiches and *real* clam chowder to eat at picnic tables overlooking the marina.

Franny's Cup & Saucer　　BAKERY $
(www.frannyscupandsaucer.com; 213 Main St, Point Arena; items from $2; ⊙8am-4pm Wed-Sat) Fairytale patisserie pops colorful fresh berry tarts, handmade cookies and rich chocolate confections into petite shopfront windows.

GoodLife Cafe　　CAFE $
(http://goodlifecafemendo.com; 10485 Lansing St, Mendocino; items $3-10; ⊙8am-4pm) 🅿 Strong organic espresso, buttery baked goods, savory empandas, from-scratch soups and fresh salads and juices will wake you up.

Piaci Pub & Pizzeria　　ITALIAN $$
(www.piacipizza.com; 120 W Redwood Ave, Fort Bragg; mains $8-18; ⊙11am-9:30pm Mon-Thu, to 10pm Fri & Sat, 4-9:30pm Sun) Chat up locals while downing microbrews and wood-fired brick-oven pizzas, calzones and focaccia topped with 'adult' flavors like pesto-chevre and proscuitto-potato. It's tiny, loud and fun.

Café Beaujolais　　CALIFORNIAN $$$
(☑707-937-5614; www.cafebeaujolais.com; 961 Ukiah St, Mendocino; dinner mains $23-35; ⊙11:30am-2:30pm Wed-Sun, dinner from 5:30pm daily) 🅿 Mendocino's iconic, beloved country Cal-French restaurant occupies an 1893 farmhouse restyled into a chic dining room, perfect for holding hands by candlelight. Refined and inspired, the locally sourced menu merrily changes with the seasons.

North Coast Brewing Co　　BREWERY
(☑707-964-3400; www.northcoastbrewing.com; 444 N Main St, Fort Bragg; ⊙4-9:30pm Wed-Thu & Sun, to 10pm Fri & Sat) Overpriced fish-and-chips and garlicky waffle fries are not up to the same standard as the stellar handcrafted brews like Red Seal Ale and Belgian-style 'Brother Thelonious' poured in the taproom.

❶ Getting There & Around

Neither Greyhound nor Amtrak serves towns along Hwy 1. **Mendocino Transit Authority** (MTA; ☑800-696-4682; www.mendocinotransit.org) bus 65 travels daily between Fort Bragg and Santa Rosa ($21, 2½ hours) via Ukiah; from Santa Rosa, catch hourly **Golden Gate Transit** (☑415-455-2000; http://goldengate.org) bus 101 to San Francisco ($10.75, 2¾ hours). On weekdays, MTA bus 60 shuttles several times between Fort Bragg and Mendocino ($1.25, one hour), with one onward connection to Point Arena and Gualala.

Ukiah to Garberville

While the coastal Hwy 1 route is ideal for dawdling, much of the traffic on inland Hwy 101 is rushing toward remote regions beyond the 'Redwood Curtain.' Diversions along the way include the down-home vineyards around Ukiah, bounteous redwood forests north of Leggett and the abandoned wilds of the Lost Coast.

Although **Ukiah** is mostly a place to gas up or get a bite, nearby **Vichy Springs Resort** (☑707-462-9515; www.vichysprings.com; 2605 Vichy Springs Rd; 2hr/day pass $30/50) offers North America's only naturally carbonated mineral baths (swimwear required).

Just north of tiny **Leggett** on Hwy 101, you can take a dip or fish in the Eel River at **Standish-Hickey State Recreation Area** (☑707-925-6482; www.parks.ca.gov; 69350 Hwy 101; per car $8; ☼), where 9 miles of hiking trails traipse through virgin and second-growth redwoods; look for the 225ft-tall Miles Standish tree. Seven miles south of **Garberville** on Hwy 101, **Richardson Grove State Park** (☑707-247-3318; www.parks.ca.gov; per car $8) protects 2000 acres of old-growth redwood forest. Both parks have developed **campgrounds** (☑800-444-7275; www.reserveamerica.com; campsites $35-45; ☼☀).

The **Lost Coast** tops any dedicated hiker's itinerary, offering the most rugged coastal backpacking in California. It became 'lost' when the highway bypassed the mountains of the King Range, which rise 4000ft within several miles of the ocean, leaving the region largely undeveloped. From Garberville, it's 23 miles along a rough road to **Shelter Cove**, the main supply point but little more than a seaside subdivision with a general store, cafes and motels. Heed 'no trespassing' signs before wandering off-trail, lest you encounter extremely territorial farmers of the region's illicit cash crop, marijuana.

Along Hwy 101, 82-sq-mile **Humboldt Redwoods State Park** (www.humboldtredwoods.org) FREE protects some of the world's oldest redwoods and has 80% of the world's tallest 137 trees. Magnificent groves rival those in Redwood National Park, a long drive further north. Even if you don't have time to hike, at least drive the awe-inspiring **Avenue of the Giants**, a 32-mile, two-lane road parallel to Hwy 101. Book ahead for **campsites** (☑800-444-7275; www.reserveamerica.com; campsites $20-35; ☼). Get hiking info and maps at the **visitor center** (☑707-946-2263; ◷9am-5pm Apr-Oct, 10am-4pm Nov-Mar).

🛏 Sleeping & Eating

Campgrounds and RV parks are plentiful along Hwy 101, where every one-horse town guarantees at least a natural-foods store with a deli, a drive-thru espresso stand, a hippie-owned cafe and a handful of motels. Woodsy cabin resorts and aging motels along Avenue of the Giants are mostly mediocre at best.

Benbow Inn   HISTORIC HOTEL **$$$**
(☑707-923-2124, 800-355-3301; www.benbowinn.com; 445 Lake Benbow Dr, Garberville; r/cottage from $180/230; ✿☀☎☼) With almost comically highbrow decor, this 1926 Tudor-style manor is nevertheless a memorable getaway. There's complimentary afternoon tea service and decanted sherry in each room. The white-tablecloth restaurant and wood-paneled bar are inviting on foggy evenings.

Ardella's   DINER **$**
(77 S Main St, Willits; mains $6-11; ◷7am-2:45pm Wed-Sat, 8am-2pm Sun; ☼) On Hwy 101, hippie hitchhikers, truckers and tourists all pat their bellies after gobbling giant omelets, potato hashes, gourmet salads and homemade soups like curried carrot-ginger. Cash only.

❶ Getting There & Around

Daily Greyhound buses connect San Francisco with Ukiah ($43, three hours), Willitts ($43, 3½ hours) and Garberville ($58, 5½ hours). **Redwood Transit System** (☑707-443-0826; www.hta.org; ☎) operates infrequent weekday buses between Garberville and Eureka ($5, 1¾ hours).

Eureka to Crescent City

Past the strip malls that sprawl from its edges, the heart of **Eureka** is Old Town, abounding with fine Victorians buildings, antique shops and restaurants. Cruise the

CALIFORNIA NORTH COAST

harbor aboard the blue-and-white 1910 Madaket (☑707-445-1910; www.humboldtbay-maritimemuseum.com; tour from $10; ☺Jun-early Oct), departing from the foot of C St; sunset cocktail cruises serve from the state's smallest licensed bar. The visitor center (☑800-356-6381, 707-442-3738; www.eurekachamber.com; 2112 Broadway; ☺8:30am-5pm Mon-Fri; @ 🛜) is on Hwy 101, south of downtown.

On the north side of Humboldt Bay, Arcata is a patchouli-dipped hippie haven of radical politics. Biodiesel-fueled trucks drive in for the weekly farmers market (www.humfarm.org; Arcata Plaza; ☺9am-2pm mid-Apr–mid-Oct; ♿) 🚲 on the central plaza, surrounded by art galleries, shops, cafes and bars. Make reservations to soak at Finnish Country Sauna & Tubs (☑707-822-2228; http://cafemokkaarcata.com; cnr 5th & J Sts; 30min per adult/child $10/2; ☺noon-11pm Sun-Thu, to 1am Fri & Sat). Northeast of downtown is the Humboldt State University (www.humboldt.edu) campus.

A working fishing town 16 miles north of Arcata, Trinidad sits on a bluff overlooking a breathtakingly beautiful harbor. Stroll sandy beaches or take short hikes around Trinidad Head after meeting tide-pool critters at the HSU Telonicher Marine Laboratory (☑707-826-3671; www.humboldt.edu/marinelab; 570 Ewing St; donation $1; ☺9am-4:30pm Mon-Fri, plus noon-4pm Sat & Sun mid-Sep–mid-May; ♿). Heading north of town, Patrick's Point Dr is dotted with forested campgrounds, cabins and lodges. Patrick's Point State Park (☑707-677-3570; www.parks.ca.gov; 4150 Patrick's Point Dr; per car $8) has stunning rocky headlands, beachcombing, wildlife-watching and an authentic reproduction of a Yurok village. The park's campgrounds (☑800-444-7275; www.reserveamerica.com; campsites $35-45; ♿🛁) offer coin-op hot showers.

Heading north, Hwy 101 passes Redwood National Park's Thomas H Kuchel Visitor Center (☑707-465-7765; www.nps.gov/redw; Hwy 101, Orick; ☺9am-5pm, to 4pm Nov-Mar; ♿). Together, the national park and three state parks – Prairie Creek, Del Norte and Jedediah Smith – are a World Heritage site containing over 40% of all remaining old-growth redwood forests. The national park is free, while some state-park areas have an $8 day-use parking fee and also developed campgrounds (☑800-444-7275; www.reserveamerica.com; campsites $35; ♿🛁).

This patchwork of state and federally managed land stretches all the way north to the Oregon border, interspersed with several towns. Furthest south, you'll first encounter Redwood National Park, where a 1-mile nature trail winds through Lady Bird Johnson Grove. Pick up a first-come, first-served permit (free) back at the Thomas H Kuchel Visitor Center to visit Tall Trees Grove, home to some of the world's tallest trees.

Six miles north of Orick, the 10-mile Newton B Drury Scenic Parkway runs parallel to Hwy 101 through Prairie Creek Redwoods State Park. Roosevelt elk graze in the pastoral meadow outside the visitor center (☑707-488-2039; www.parks.ca.gov; ☺9am-5pm May-Oct, 10am-4pm Nov-Apr), where several sunlight-dappled hiking trails begin. Three miles back south, unpaved Davison Rd heads northwest to Gold Bluffs Beach, dead-ending at lush Fern Canyon, which cameoed in the *Lost World: Jurassic Park*.

North of tiny Klamath, Hwy 101 passes the Trees of Mystery (☑800-638-3389; www.treesofmystery.net; 15500 Hwy 101; adult/child $15/8; ☺8am-6:30pm Jun-Aug, 9:30am-4:30pm Sep-May; ♿🛁), a kitschy roadside attraction with aerial tram rides. Next up, Del Norte Coast Redwoods State Park preserves virgin redwood groves and 8 miles of unspoiled coastline. The 5-mile round-trip Damnation Creek Trail careens over 1000ft downhill past skyscraping redwoods to a hidden rocky beach, best visited at low tide. The trailhead is at a parking turn-out on Hwy 101 near Mile 16.

Sprawling over a crescent-shaped bay, Crescent City is a drab little town, but it's the only sizable coastal settlement north of Arcata. More than half the town was destroyed by a tidal wave in 1964 and rebuilt with utilitarian architecture. When the tide's out, you can walk across to the 1856 Battery Point Lighthouse (☑707-467-3089; www.delnortehistory.org; adult/child $3/1; ☺10am-4pm Wed-Sun Apr-Oct) from the south end of A St.

Jedediah Smith Redwoods State Park is the northernmost park in the system, 5 miles beyond Crescent City. The redwood stands here are so dense that there are few trails, but a couple of easy hikes start near riverside swimming holes along Hwy 199 and rough, unpaved Howland Hill Rd, an 11-mile scenic drive. The park visitor center (☑707-458-3496; www.parks.ca.gov; Hwy 199, Hiouchi; ☺9am-5pm mid-May-mid-Sep) has maps and information.

🛏 Sleeping & Eating

A mixed bag of motels are scattered along Hwy 101, including in Eureka, Arcata and Crescent City. Arcata has the biggest variety of dining options, from organic juice bars and vegan cafes to Californian and world-fusion bistros.

Requa Inn
B&B $$

(📞 707-482-1425; www.requainn.com; 451 Requa Rd, Klamath; r $119-199; 🛜) Built in 1914, this simple inn caters to outdoorsy types, with a big breakfast and old-fashioned rooms overlooking the river. No TVs or phones.

Carter House Inns
B&B $$$

(📞 800-404-1390, 707-444-8062; http://carterhouse.com; 301 L St, Eureka; r incl breakfast $189-385; 🛜🐾) The cushiest option near Eureka's Old Town are these lovingly tended Victorians. Many of the rooms and suites have romantic fireplaces. Evening wine and hors d'oeuvres and milk with cookies are complimentary. Seasonal Cal-French cuisine at the hotel's **Restaurant 301** (dinner mains $20-30; ⊘6-9pm) is the most haute dining around.

Wildberries Marketplace
MARKET, DELI $

(www.wildberries.com; 747 13th St, Arcata; sandwiches $4-10; ⊘6am-midnight; 🅿) Step inside the North Coast's best natural-foods grocery store, with a healthy-minded deli and fruit-smoothie bar. Stock up on snacks and drinks for beach picnics and trailside lunches.

Samoa Cookhouse
AMERICAN $$

(📞707-442-1659; www.samoacookhouse.net; 908 Vance Ave, Samoa; all-you-can-eat meals $11-16; ⊘7am-9pm; 🅿) On Humboldt Bay's Samoa Peninsula, this popular dining hall was originally built for an 1890s lumber camp. Today road-trippers and hippies stuff themselves at long red-checked oilcloth-covered tables. Kids eat for half-price.

Lost Coast Brewery
BREWERY $$

(📞707-445-4480; www.lostcoast.com; 617 4th St, Eureka; mains $9-15; ⊘11am-10pm Sun-Thu, to 11pm Fri & Sat; 🛜🅿) At this legendary North Coast brewery, the Downtown Brown and Great White beers are worth stopping for, but the kitchen turns out only so-so wings, nachos and other pub grub. True beer geeks should also visit Fortuna's organic Eel River Brewing, Arcata's Redwood Curtain Brewing, McKinleyville's Six Rivers Brewery and Blue Lake's Mad River Brewing Company.

ℹ Getting There & Around

Arcata's **Greyhound depot** (925 E St) has daily buses to San Francisco ($57, seven hours) via Eureka, Garberville, Willits and Ukiah. Several daily **Redwood Transit System** (📞707-443-0826; www.hta.org) buses stop in Eureka and Arcata on the Trinidad–Scotia route ($2.75, 2½ hours).

Sacramento

California's first nonmission European settlement, the state capital is an anomalous place: the first city to shoot up during the gold-rush era is flat and fairly bland, with shady trees, withering summer heat and jammed highways.

In 1839 eccentric Swiss immigrant John Sutter built a fort here. Once gold was discovered in the nearby Sierra foothills in 1848, the town's population boomed. After much legislative waffling, Sacramento eventually became California's capital in 1854.

Old Sacramento remains a visitor's magnet – a riverside area with raised wooden sidewalks that can feel like a ye olde tourist trap. More interesting food and culture are hidden on the grid of streets downtown and in Midtown, where a fledgling arts scene quietly defies the city's reputation as a cow town.

◉ Sights

California Museum
MUSEUM

(www.californiamuseum.org; 1020 O St; adult/child $8.50/6; ⊘10am-5pm Mon-Sat, from noon Sun) This modern museum is home to the California Hall Of Fame – perhaps the only place to simultaneously encounter Amelia Earhart, Cesar Chavez and Mark Zuckerburg. The exhibit 'California Indians: Making A Difference' covers the traditions and culture of indigenous tribes, past and present.

California State Capitol
HISTORIC BUILDING

(📞916-324-0333; http://capitolmuseum.ca.gov; 1315 10th St; ⊘8am-5pm Mon-Fri, from 9am Sat & Sun, tours hourly 9am-4pm) FREE The 19th-century state capitol is a white jewel rising from the manicured Capitol Mall. Inside are California art and history exhibits and period-furnished chambers. The Assembly and Senate rooms are open to the public.

California State Railroad Museum
MUSEUM

(📞916-445 6645; www.californiastaterailroadmuseum.org; 125 I St; adult/child $10/5, incl train ride $20/10; ⊘10am-5pm, train rides hourly Apr-Sep;

⚓) Step aboard dozens of meticulously restored beasts of steam and diesel by the river
in **Old Sacramento** (www.oldsacramento.com),
a walkable district of historical buildings
and tiny museums.

Sutter's Fort State
Historic Park
HISTORIC SITE
(☑916-445-4422; www.parks.ca.gov; 2701 L St;
adult/child $5/3; ☺10am-5pm) Within the walls
of this restored fort, the original cannon and
a working ironsmith are straight out of the
1850s. Next door is the tiny but fascinating
California State Indian Museum (☑916-
324-0971; www.parks.ca.gov; 2618 K St; adult/child
$3/2; ☺10am-5pm Wed-Sun).

Crocker Art Museum
MUSEUM
(☑916-264-5423; www.crockerartmuseum.org; 216
O St; adult/child $10/5; ☺10am-5pm Tue-Wed &
Fri-Sun, to 9pm Thu) Adjoining the handsome
residence of a 19th-century California Supreme Court judge, modern galleries highlight early and contemporary California art.

🛏 Sleeping & Eating

Sacramento's hotels cater to business travelers, so look for weekend bargains. The
freeways and suburbs around the city are
glutted with chain lodgings. For more restaurants and bars, make for Midtown, especially J St east of 16th St.

HI Sacramento Hostel
HOSTEL $
(☑916-443-1691; http://norcalhostels.org/sac; 925
H St; dm $30-36, r with/without bath from $76/58;
☺check-in 2pm-10pm; @☎) A short walk from
the capitol, this restored Victorian mansion
has common areas of nearly B&B quality,
spacious dorms and staff who know about
local nightlife.

Delta King
B&B $$
(☑800-825-5464, 916-444-5464; www.deltak-
ing.com; 100 Front St; d incl breakfast from $139;
✳☎) Snuggle into compact rooms aboard
the *Delta King*, a 1927 paddle-wheeler
docked in Old Sacramento. The boat has a
nautical-themed bar and restaurant. Park-
ing is $18.

Citizen Hotel
BOUTIQUE HOTEL $$$
(☑info 916-447-2700, reservations 916-492-
4460; www.jdvhotels.com; 926 J St; r $139-269;
✳@☎✳) Elegant rooms at this 1920s downtown office building are lovely with luxurious linens, bold-patterned fabrics and iPod
docking stations. Little touches make a big
impression: vintage political cartoons adorn-

ing the walls and political movies to borrow.
On the ground floor, **Grange** (☑916-492-4450;
www.grangesacramento.com; 926 J St; dinner mains
$19-39; ☺6:30-10:30am & 11:30am-2pm Mon-Fri,
8am-2pm Sat & Sun, 5:30pm-10pm Mon-Thu, to 11pm
Fri & Sat, to 10pm Sun; ☎) cooks California farm-
to-table fare. Hotel parking is $25.

La Bonne Soupe Cafe
DELI $
(☑916-492-9506; 920 8th St; items $4-8; ☺11am-
3pm Mon-Fri) Divinely epicurean sandwiches
and scratch soups, all handmade with love
by a chef, bring downtown office workers to
line up out the door.

Tower Cafe
ECLECTIC $$
(☑916-441-0222; www.towercafe.com; 1518 Broad-
way; mains $7-18; ☺8am-10pm Sun-Thu, to 11pm
Fri & Sat) Best bet for big ol' breakfasts –
custardy French toast topped with fruit, or
chorizo sausage with eggs – at a 1938 art-
deco movie theater.

Mulvaney's B & L
CALIFORNIAN $$$
(☑916-441-6022; www.mulvaneysbl.com; 1215
19th St; dinner mains $26-38; ☺11:30am-2:30pm
Tue-Fri, 5-10pm Tue-Sat) Arguably the classiest
restaurant in town, here inside an 1890s fire
house a hyper-seasonal, European-touched
menu changes every single day.

🍷 Drinking & Entertainment

Temple Coffee
CAFE
(www.templecoffee.com; 1010 9th St; ☺6am-11pm;
☎) 🌿 Sip sustainably sourced, locally roasted coffee at communal wooden tables.

Rubicon Brewing Company
BREWERY
(☑916-448-7032; www.rubiconbrewing.com;
2004 Capitol Ave; ☺11am-11:30pm Mon-Thu, to
12:30am Fri & Sat, to 10pm Sun) The place for
award-winning ales, hot wings and brewhouse chili-cheese fries.

Sacramento River Cats
SPORTS
(www.milb.com; Raley Field, 400 Ballpark Dr; tickets
$5-65; ☺Apr-Sep) Minor-league baseball team
plays at Raley Field, with dazzling views of
Tower Bridge.

🛈 Getting There & Around

About 11 miles northwest of downtown off I-5,
Sacramento International Airport (☑919-
929-5411; www.sacairports.org; 6900 Airport
Blvd) is served mainly by domestic flights.

From downtown's **train station** (☑877-974-
3322; www.capitolcorridor.org; 401 I St), Amtrak
runs frequent *Capitol Corridor* trains to/from the
San Francisco Bay Area ($28 to $38, 90 minutes

to three hours); twice-daily *San Joaquin* trains, with onward bus connections to Yosemite Valley ($37, five hours); and daily long-distance *Coast Starlight* and *California Zephyr* trains. **Greyhound** (420 Richards Blvd) has several daily buses to San Francisco ($27, two hours) and Los Angeles ($78, 7½ to nine hours).

Sacramento Regional Transit (www.sacrt. com; fare/day pass $2.25/6) runs a bus and light-rail system around town.

Gold Country

Hard to believe, but this is where it all began – the quiet hill towns and drowsy oak-lined byways of Gold Country belie the wild, chaotic, often violent establishment of California. After a glint caught James Marshall's eye in Sutter's Creek in 1848, the gold rush brought a 300,000-stong stampede of '49ers to these Sierra foothills. The frenzy paid little heed to the starched moral decorum of Victorian society, and traces of its lawless boom towns and environmental havoc remain today.

Traveling here might be a thrill ride for history buffs – the fading historical markers tell tales of bloodlust and banditry – but more tactile pleasures await the traveler willing to plunge into a swimming hole, rattle down a mountain-biking trail or go white-water rafting in the icy currents of the American, Stanislaus and Tuolumne Rivers. Based in the Central Valley, **All-Outdoors California Whitewater Rafting** (☎ 800-247-2387; www.aorafting.com) outfits a variety of day and overnight rafting trips for all skill levels from spring through fall.

Hwy 50 divides the Northern and Southern Mines. Winding Hwy 49, which connects everything, has plenty of pull-outs and vistas of the surrounding hills. **The Gold Country Visitors Association** (www.calgold. org) has many more touring ideas.

Northern Mines

Known as the 'Queen of the Northern Mines,' **Nevada City** has narrow streets gleaming with lovingly restored buildings, tiny theaters, art galleries, cafes and shops. The **visitor center** (☎ 530-265-2692; www. nevadacitychamber.com; 132 Main St; ⊙ 9am-5pm Mon-Fri, 11am-4pm Sat, 11am-3pm Sun) dispenses information and self-guided walking-tour maps. On Hwy 49, **Tahoe National Forest Headquarters** (☎ 530-265-4531; www.fs.usda.

gov/tahoe; 631 Coyote St; ⊙ 8am-4:30pm Mon-Fri) provides camping, hiking and mountain-biking information and wilderness permits.

Four miles south, **Grass Valley** is Nevada City's functional sister, where artists, hippies and ranchers get their trucks' oil changed. Just over a mile east of Hwy 49, **Empire Mine State Historic Park** (☎ 530-273-8522; www.empiremine.org; 10791 E Empire St; adult/child $7/3; ⊙ 10am-5pm) marks the site of one of the richest mines in California. From 1850 to 1956 it produced more than 5.6 million ounces of gold – about $5 billion in today's market.

When it's swelteringly hot outside during summer, if you see a line of cars parked roadside along Hwy 49, that's your signal to discover a swimming hole. One of the best is where the North and South forks of the American River join up, a few miles east of **Auburn**, an I-80 pit stop about 25 miles south of Grass Valley.

Coloma is where California's gold rush started. Riverside **Marshall Gold Discovery State Historic Park** (☎ 530-622-3470; www.parks.ca.gov; per person/car $6/8; ⊙ park 8am-5pm, to 7pm late May-early Sep, museum 10am-3pm, to 4pm Mar-Nov; ▣) pays tribute to James Marshall's riot-inducing discovery, with a replica of Sutter's Mill, restored buildings and gold-panning opportunities. There's a hilltop monument to Marshall himself, who, in one of the many ironic twists of the gold rush, died as a penniless ward of the state.

🛏 Sleeping & Eating

Nevada City boasts the biggest spread of restaurants and historical B&Bs. Motels speckle Hwy 49 in Grass Valley and I-80 in Auburn.

Broad Street Inn INN $$
(☎ 530-265-2239; www.broadstreetinn.com; 517 E Broad St, Nevada City; r $110-120; ❄ 🛜 🅿) Unlike dozens of frilly bed-and-breakfasts in Gold Country, this sun-drenched, six-room inn keeps things refreshingly simple with modern, brightly furnished rooms.

Outside Inn MOTEL, CABIN $$
(☎ 530-265-2233; www.outsideinn.com; 575 E Broad St, Nevada City; r $79-155, cottage $200; ❄ 🛜 ▣ 🅿) More fun than any ho-hum chain are these knotty-pine-walled themed rooms (some with kitchenettes), BBQ grills and friendly owners who are outdoor enthusiasts.

Treats
DESSERT $

(http://treatsnevadacity.com; 110 York St, Nevada City; items $2-5; ⊙noon-9pm Sun-Thu, to 10pm Fri & Sat, shorter hr winter; ♠) Handmade, often organic ice cream, seasonal sorbets and other cool treats.

Ikedas
MARKET $

(www.ikedas.com; 13500 Lincoln Way, Auburn; items from $3; ⊙8am-7pm, to 8pm Sat & Sun) Off I-80 north of downtown Auburn, Tahoe-bound travelers stop for fresh fruit, homemade pies and picnic fixin's.

Ike's Quarter Cafe
CREOLE, CALIFORNIAN $$

(☎530-265-6138; www.ikesquartercafe.com; 401 Commercial St, Nevada City; mains $7-15; ⊙8am-3pm Wed-Mon; ♠) Dig into gut-busting breakfasts like the 'Hangtown Fry,' a gold miners' mess of cornmeal-crusted oysters and bacon, or N'awlins-style fare like muffaletta sandwiches on the fountain patio. Cash only.

Southern Mines

The towns of the Southern Mines – from Placerville to Sonora – receive less traffic and their dusty streets have a whiff of Wild West, today evident in the motley assortment of Harley riders, gold prospectors (still!) and outsider winemakers who populate them. Some, like **Plymouth** (Ole Pokerville) and **Mokelumne Hill**, are virtual ghost towns, slowly crumbling into photogenic oblivion. Others, like **Sutter Creek**, **Murphys** and **Angels Camp**, are gussied-up showpieces of Victorian Americana. Get off the beaten path at family-run vineyards and subterranean caverns, where geological wonders reward those willing to navigate the touristy gift shops above ground.

A short detour off Hwy 49 is **Columbia State Historic Park** (☎209-588-9128; www.parks.ca.gov; 11255 Jackson St, Columbia; ⊙museum 9am-4:30pm Apr-Oct, from 10am Nov-Mar; ♠) **FREE**, which preserves four square blocks of authentic 1850s buildings complete with shopkeepers and street musicians in period costumes; it's crazy-busy with school-kids panning for gold. Also near Sonora, **Railtown 1897 State Historic Park** (☎209-984-3953; www.railtown1897.org; 18115 5th Ave, Jamestown; museum adult/child $5/3, incl train ride $15/8; ⊙9:30am-4:30pm Apr-Oct, 10am-3pm Nov-Mar, train rides 11am-3pm Sat & Sun Apr-Oct; ♠) offers excursion trains through the surrounding hills where Hollywood Westerns including *High Noon* were filmed.

🛏 Sleeping & Eating

Lacy B&Bs, cafes and ice-cream parlors are in nearly every town. Busy Sonora, just over an hour's drive from Yosemite National Park, and Placerville have the most motels.

Indian Grinding Rock State Historic Park Campground
CAMPGROUND $

(www.parks.ca.gov; 14881 Pine Grove-Volcano Rd, Pine Grove; camping & RV sites $30; ⊙mid-Mar–Sep; ♠🐾) Around 10 miles northeast of Sutter Creek, this pastoral state-park campground has 22 sites set among trees (no reservations) and coin-op hot showers.

Gunn House Hotel
HISTORIC HOTEL $$

(☎209-532-3421; www.gunnhousehotel.com; 286 S Washington St, Sonora; r incl breakfast $79-115; ❄🐾) For an alternative to cookie-cutter chains, this historic hotel hits the sweet spot. B&B-esque rooms feature period decor. On summer evenings, sink back into rocking chairs on the front porch.

City & Fallon Hotels
HISTORIC HOTEL $$

(☎800-532-1479; www.briggshospitalityllc.com; 22768 Main St, Columbia; r incl breakfast without bath $105-175; ❄🐾) Twin restored period hotels in historic Columbia town are decked out with museum-quality pieces. After dark, shoot whiskey at What Cheer Saloon or watch plays at the Fallon's repertory theater.

Volcano Union Inn
HISTORIC HOTEL $$

(☎209-296-7711; www.volcanounion.com; 21375 Consolation St, Volcano; r incl breakfast $119-149; ❄🐾) Of a quartet of lovingly updated rooms with crooked floors, two have street-facing balconies. Downstairs, **Union Pub** (mains $10-19; ⊙5-8pm Thu & Mon, 3-9pm Fri, noon-9pm Sat, 10am-8pm Sun) has billiards, shuffleboard, darts and gourmet pub grub.

Cozmic Café & Pub
HEALTHY $

(www.ourcoz.com; 594 Main St, Placerville; items $4-10; ⊙7am-6pm Tue & Wed, to 8pm Thu-Sun; 🐾🍴) Grab tables *inside* a historic mining tunnel at Placerville's funky organic, health-conscious cafe. There are microbrews on tap and live music on weekends.

Magnolia Cafe
CAFE $$

(☎209-728-2186; www.magnoliacafemurphys.com; 64 Mitchler St, Murphys; mains $7-13; ⊙8am-3pm Wed-Sun) Breakfast on chef Devon's chorizo-egg tortas and vanilla-bean French toast, or Asian-spiced pulled-pork burritos and classic steak sandwiches with mustard aioli at lunch.

★ **Taste**   CALIFORNIAN **$$$**
(☎209-245-3463; www.restauranttaste.com; 9402 Main St, Plymouth; dinner mains $27-43; ☺11:30am-2pm Sat & Sun, dinner from 5pm Thu & Fri, 4:30pm Sat & Sun) The antidote to Gold Country's dependence on burgers, Taste plates artful, fresh, seasonal dishes with European influences that pair well with wines from Amador County's vineyards.

ⓘ Getting There & Around

A patchwork of public buses sporadically serves some towns. For the Northern Mines, **Gold Country Stage** (☎888-660-7433, 530-477-0103; www.mynevadacounty.com; fares $1.50-3) buses link Nevada City, Grass Valley and Auburn, while **Placer County Transit** (☎530-885-2877; www.placer.ca.gov/transit; fare $1.25) buses connect Auburn with Sacramento. Among the Southern Mines, weekday-only **Amador Transit** (☎209-267-9395; http://amadortransit.com; fares $1-2) runs buses between Sutter Creek and Sacramento, Jackson and Plymouth. **Calaveras Transit** (☎209-754-4450; http://transit.calaverasgov.us; fare $2) buses serve Angels Camp, Jackson and Murphys. **Tuolumne County Transit** (☎209-532-0404; www.tuolumnecountytransit.com; fare $1.50) buses and trolleys loop between Sonora, Columbia and Jamestown.

Northern Mountains

Remote, empty and eerily beautiful, these are some of California's least-visited wild lands, an endless show of geological wonders, alpine lakes, rushing rivers and high desert. The major peaks – Lassen, Shasta and the Trinity Alps – have few geological features in common, but all offer backcountry camping under starry skies. Isolated towns dotting the region aren't attractions, but are handy resupply points for wilderness adventures.

Redding to Yreka

Much of the drive north of Redding is dominated by **Mt Shasta**, a 14,179ft snow-capped goliath at the southern end of the volcanic Cascades Range. It rises dramatically, fueling the anticipation felt by outdoor enthusiasts who seek to climb its slopes. A helpful pit stop just off I-5 is the **California Welcome Center** (☎800-474-2784, 530-365-1180; www.shastacascade.com; 1699 Hwy 273, Anderson; ☺9am-5pm Mon-Sat, 10am-4pm Sun),

12 miles south of Redding at the Shasta Outlets mall.

Don't believe the tourist brochures; **Redding**, the region's largest city, is a snooze. The best reason to detour off I-5 is the **Sundial Bridge**, a glass-bottomed pedestrian marvel designed by Spanish architect Santiago Calatrava. It spans the Sacramento River at **Turtle Bay Exploration Park** (☎800-887-8532; www.turtlebay.org; 844 Sundial Bridge Dr; adult/child $14/10, after 3:30pm $9/5; ☺9am-5pm Mon-Sat & 10am-5pm Sun, closes 1hr earlier Oct-Mar; ♿), a kid-friendly science center with botanical gardens.

About 6 miles west of Redding along Hwy 299, explore a genuine gold-rush town at **Shasta State Historical Park** (☎520-243-8194; www.parks.ca.gov; museum adult/child $3/2; ☺10am-5pm Fri-Sun). Two miles further west, **Whiskeytown National Recreation Area** (☎530-246-1225; www.nps.gov/whis; per car $5; ☺visitor center 9am-5pm late May-early Sep, 10am-4pm early Sep-late May) **FREE** is home to Whiskeytown Lake, with sandy beaches, waterfall hikes and water-sports and camping opportunities.

At **Weaverville**, another 35 miles west of Whiskeytown, **Joss House State Historic Park** (☎530-623-5284; www.parks.ca.gov; cnr Hwy 299 & Oregon St; tour adult/child $4/2; ☺10am-5pm Thu-Sun, hourly tours until 4pm) preserves an 1874 Chinese immigrant temple. **Weaverville Ranger Station** (☎530-623-2121; www.fs.usda.gov/stnf; 360 Main St; ☺8am-4:30pm Mon-Fri) issues backcountry permits for the near-pristine wilderness of the surrounding **Trinity Alps**.

North of Redding, I-5 crosses deep-blue **Shasta Lake**, California's biggest reservoir, formed by towering **Shasta Dam** (☎530-275-4463; www.usbr.gov/mp/ncao/shasta/; 16349 Shasta Dam Blvd; ☺visitor center 8am-5pm, tours 9am-3pm) **FREE** and surrounded by shoreline hiking trails and RV campgrounds. High in the limestone megaliths at the lake's northern end are the prehistoric caves of **Lake Shasta Caverns** (☎800-795-2283, 530-238-2341; http://lakeshastacaverns.com; 20359 Shasta Caverns Rd; adult/child $24/14; ☺tours 9am-4pm late May-early Sep, to 3pm Apr-late May & Sep, 10am-2pm Oct-Mar; ♿), where guided tours include a catamaran ride.

Another 35 miles north on I-5, **Dunsmuir** is a teeny historic railroad town with vibrant cafes and art galleries in its quaint downtown. If for no other reason, stop to fill your bottle from the public fountains:

Dunsmuir claims to have the best H_2O on earth. Just south off I-5, **Castle Crags State Park** (✆530-235-2684; www.parks.ca.gov; per car $8) shelters forested **campsites** (✆800-444-7275; www.reserveamerica.com; campsites $15-30; 🚻 🐾). Be awed by stunning views of Mt Shasta from the summit of the 5.4-mile round-trip **Crags Trail**.

Ten miles north of Dunsmuir, **Mt Shasta town** lures climbers, New Age hippies and back-to-nature types, all of whom revere the majestic mountain looming overhead. The **Everitt Memorial Hwy** ascends the mountain to a perfect sunset-watching perch at almost 8000ft; simply head east from town on Lake St and keep going 14 more miles. For experienced mountaineers only, climbing the peak above 10,000ft requires a Summit Pass ($20), available from **Mt Shasta Ranger Station** (✆530-926-4511; www.fs.usda. gov/stnf; 204 W Alma St; ⊘8am-4:30pm Mon-Fri), which has weather reports and sells topographic maps. Stop by downtown's **Fifth Season** (✆530-926-3606; http://thefifthseason. com; 300 N Mt Shasta Blvd) outdoor-gear shop for equipment rentals. **Shasta Mountain Guides** (✆530-926-3117; http://shastaguides. com) offers multiday mountaineering trips (from $500).

🛏 Sleeping & Eating

Roadside motels are abundant in all parts but the remote northeast. Redding has the most chain motels and hotels, clustered near major highways. Campgrounds are abundant, especially on public lands.

McCloud River Mercantile Hotel   INN $$
(✆530-964-2330; www.mccloudmercantile.com; 241 Main St, McCloud; r $139-250; 🛜) Guests are greeted with fresh flowers and can drift to sleep on feather beds after soaking in clawfoot tubs. Exposed brick and antique accents are a perfect marriage of preservationist class and modern panache. The 1930s soda fountain downstairs cooks country-style breakfasts and lunches (mains $6 to $10). It's about 10 miles east of Mt Shasta town off Hwy 89.

Railroad Park Resort   INN, CAMPGROUND $$
(✆530-235-4440, 800-974-7245; www.rrpark. com; 100 Railroad Park Rd, Dunsmuir; tent/RV sites from $29/37, d $115-150; ❄🛜🏊🚻🐾) The most memorable overnight stay is inside a wood-paneled caboose, off I-5 just south of town.

Sengthongs   THAI, VIETNAMESE $$
(✆530-235-4770; http://sengthongs.com; 5855 Dunsmuir Ave, Dunsmuir; mains $11-20; ⊘usually 5-8:30pm Thu-Sun) Beloved long-running Southeast Asian restaurant hosts live music a few doors down in its Blue Sky Room.

Café Maddalena   BISTRO $$$
(✆530-235-2725; www.cafemaddalena.com; 5801 Sacramento Ave, Dunsmuir; mains $14-25; ⊘5-10pm Thu-Sun Feb-Nov) Chef-owner Bret LaMott maintains this cozy riverfront restaurant's stellar reputation with Mediterranean specialties and a well-stocked wine bar. Reservations recommended.

ℹ Getting There & Around

Amtrak's *Coast Starlight* trains stop in Redding and Dunsmuir, incovneniently in the middle of the night. Greyhound buses serve Redding and Weed. **Siskiyou County STAGE** (✆800-247-8243, 530-842-8295; www.co.siskiyou.ca.us/GS/stage.aspx; fares $2.50-4) buses run up and down I-5 several times daily, connecting Dunsmuir, Mt Shasta and Weed.

Northeast Corner

Site of California's last major Native American conflict and a half-million years of volcanic destruction, **Lava Beds National Monument** (✆530-667-8113; www.nps.gov/labe; 7-day entry per car $10) is a peaceful monument to centuries of turmoil. This park's got it all: lava flows, craters, cinder and spatter cones, and more than 500 lava tubes. It was the site of the Modoc War, and Native American petroglyphs are etched into cave walls. Pick up info, maps and flashlights for spelunking at the **visitor center** (✆530-667-8113; 1 Indian Well, Tulelake; ⊘8am-6pm late May-early Sep, 8:30am-5pm mid-Sep–mid-May). Nearby is the park's **campground** (campsites $10), where basic sites accommodate tents and small RVs; drinking water is available.

Just north, the **Klamath Basin National Wildlife Refuge Complex** (www.fws.gov/klamathbasinrefuges) comprises six separate refuges. This is a prime stopover on the Pacific Flyway and an important wintering site for bald eagles. The **visitor center** (✆530-667-2231; 4009 Hill Rd, Tulelake; ⊘8am-4:30pm Mon-Fri, 9am-4pm Sat & Sun) is off Hwy 161, about 4 miles south of the Oregon border. Self-guided 10-mile auto tours of the Lower Klamath and Tule Lake reserves provide excellent birding opportunities. For gas, food and lodging, drive into Klamath Falls, OR.

The **Modoc National Forest** (☑530-233-5811; www.fs.usda.gov/modoc) blankets over 3000 sq miles of northeastern California. Camping is free and reservations are not accepted, although campfire permits are required. **Medicine Lake**, about an hour's drive southwest of Lava Beds National Monument, is a pristine, gleaming blue crater lake surrounded by pine forest, hulking volcanic formations and cool, secluded campgrounds. Further east is landmark **Glass Mountain**, where Native Americans quarried jet-black obsidian. East of Cedarville via Hwy 299, near the Nevada border, the high desert of **Surprise Valley** is a gateway to the wild **Warner Mountains** – possibly California's least-visited range.

Quietly impressive **Lassen Volcanic National Park** (☑530-595-4444; www.nps.gov/lavo; 7-day entry per car $10) has hydrothermal sulfur pools, boiling mud pots and steaming pools, as glimpsed from the **Bumpass Hell** boardwalk. At 10,462ft, **Lassen Peak** is the world's largest plug-dome volcano. The park has two entrances: an hour's drive east of Redding off Hwy 44, near popular **Manzanita Lake Campground** (☑877-444-6777; www.recreation.gov; campsites $10-18, cabins $59-84); and northwest of Lake Almanor off Hwy 89, by the **Kohm Yah-ma-nee Visitor Center** (☑530-595-4480; www.nps.gov/lavo; ◉9am-5pm, closed Tue & Wed Nov-Mar). Hwy 89 through the park is typically snow-free and open to cars from May or June through October or November (snowshoes and cross-country skis permitted in winter).

SIERRA NEVADA

The mighty Sierra Nevada – baptized the 'Range of Light' by naturalist John Muir – is California's backbone. This 400-mile phalanx of craggy peaks, chiseled and gouged by glaciers and erosion, both welcomes and challenges outdoor-sports enthusiasts. Cradling three national parks (Yosemite, Sequoia and Kings Canyon), the Sierra is a spellbinding wonderland of superlative wilderness, embracing the contiguous USA's highest peak (Mt Whitney), North America's tallest waterfall (Yosemite Falls) and the world's oldest and biggest trees (ancient bristlecone pines and giant sequoias, respecctively).

Yosemite National Park

There's a reason why everybody's heard of it: the granite-peak heights are dizzying, the mist from thunderous waterfalls drenching, the Technicolor wildflower meadows amazing and the majestic silhouettes of El Capitan and Half Dome almost shocking against a crisp blue sky. It's a landscape of dreams, surrounding oh-so-small people on all sides.

Then, alas, the hiss and belch of another tour bus, disgorging dozens, rudely breaks the spell. While staggering crowds can't be ignored, these rules will shake most of 'em:

➡ Avoid summer in the valley. Spring's best, especially when waterfalls gush in May. Autumn is blissfully peaceful, and snowy winter days can be magical too.

➡ Park your car and leave it – simply by hiking a short distance up almost any trail, you'll lose the car-dependent hordes.

➡ Forget jet lag. Get up early, or go for moonlit hikes with stargazing.

◉ Sights

The main entrances to the **park** (☑209-372-0200; www.nps.gov/yose; 7-day entry per car $20) are at Arch Rock (Hwy 140), Wawona (Hwy 41) and Big Oak Flat (Hwy 120 west). Tioga Pass (Hwy 120 east) is open only seasonally.

◉ Yosemite Valley

From the ground up, this dramatic valley cut by the meandering Merced River is song-inspiring: rippling green meadow-grass; stately pines; cool, impassive pools reflecting the looming granite monoliths; and cascading

---

ℹ IMPASSABLE TIOGA PASS

Hwy 120 is the only road connecting Yosemite National Park with the Eastern Sierra, climbing through Tioga Pass (9945ft). Most maps mark this road 'closed in winter,' which, while literally true, is also misleading. Tioga Rd is usually closed from the first heavy snowfall in October or November, not reopening until May or June. If you are planning a trip through Tioga Pass in spring, you'll likely be out of luck. Call ☑209-372-0200 or check www.nps.gov/yose/planyourvisit/conditions.htm for current road conditions.

ribbons of glacially cold white-water. Often overrun and traffic-choked, **Yosemite Village** is home to the park's main visitor center (p1012), museum, photography gallery, general store and many more services. **Curry Village** is another valley hub, offering public showers and outdoor equipment rental and sales, including for camping.

Spring snowmelt turns the valley's famous waterfalls into thunderous cataracts; most are reduced to a mere trickle by late summer. **Yosemite Falls** is North America's tallest, dropping 2425ft in three tiers. A wheelchair-accessible trail leads to the bottom of this cascade or, for solitude and different perspectives, you can trek the grueling switchback trail to the top (7.2 miles round-trip). No less impressive are other waterfalls around the valley. A strenuous granite staircase beside **Vernal Fall** leads you, gasping, right to the waterfall's edge for a vertical view – look for rainbows in the clouds of mist.

You can't ignore the valley's monumental **El Capitan** (7569ft), an El Dorado for rock climbers. Toothed **Half Dome** (8842ft) soars above the valley as Yosemite's spiritual centerpiece. The classic panoramic photo op is at **Tunnel View** on Hwy 41 as you drive into the valley. Early or late in the day during spring or early summer, hike 2 miles round-trip from the eastern

valley floor out to **Mirror Lake** to catch the ever-shifting reflection of Half Dome in the still waters.

Glacier Point

Rising 3200ft above the valley floor, dramatic **Glacier Point** (7214ft) practically puts you at eye level with Half Dome. It's about an hour's drive from Yosemite Valley up Glacier Point Rd (usually open from late May into November) off Hwy 41, or a strenuous hike along the **Four Mile Trail** (actually, 4.8 miles one way) or the less-crowded, waterfall-strewn **Panorama Trail** (8.5 miles one way). To hike one-way downhill from Glacier Point, reserve a seat on the hikers' shuttle bus (p1013).

Wawona

At **Wawona**, almost an hour's drive south of Yosemite Valley, drop by the **Pioneer Yosemite History Center**, with its covered bridge, pioneer cabins and historic Wells Fargo office. Further south, wander giddily around towering **Mariposa Grove**, home of the Grizzly Giant and other giant sequoias. Free shuttle buses run to the grove from Wawona from spring through fall; in winter, the access road is usually closed to vehicles, but you can snowshoe along it.

Tuolumne Meadows

A 90-minute drive from Yosemite Valley, high-altitude **Tuolumne Meadows** (pronounced *twol*-uh-mee) draws hikers, backpackers and climbers to the park's northern wilderness. The Sierra Nevada's largest subalpine meadow (8600ft), it's a vivid contrast to the valley, with wildflower fields, azure lakes, ragged granite peaks and polished domes, and cooler temperatures. Hikers and climbers have a paradise of options; swimming and picnicking by lakes are also popular. Access is via scenic Tioga Rd (Hwy 120), which is only open seasonally (see p1009), following a 19th-century wagon road and older Native American trading route. West of Tuolumne Meadows and **Tenaya Lake**, stop at **Olmsted Point** for epic vistas of Half Dome.

Hetch Hetchy

It's the site of perhaps the most controversial dam in US history. Despite not existing

---

DON'T MISS

SUPERSIZED FORESTS

In California you can stand under the world's oldest trees (ancient bristlecone pines) and its tallest (coast redwoods), but the record for biggest in terms of volume belongs to giant sequoias (*Sequoiadendron giganteum*). They grow only on the western slope of the Sierra Nevada range and are most abundant in Sequoia, Kings Canyon and Yosemite National Parks. John Muir called them 'Nature's forest masterpiece,' and anyone who's ever craned their neck to take in their soaring vastness has probably done so with the same awe. These trees can grow to over 300ft tall and 100ft in circumference, protected by bark up to 2ft thick. The Giant Forest Museum (p1013) in Sequoia National Park has exhibits about the trees' unusual ecology.

in its natural state, Hetch Hetchy Valley remains pretty and mostly crowd-free. It's a 40-mile drive northwest of Yosemite Valley. A 5.4-mile round-trip hike across the dam and through a tunnel to the base of **Wapama Falls** lets you get thrillingly close to an avalanche of water crashing down into the sparkling reservoir. In spring, you'll get drenched.

Activities

With over 800 miles of varied hiking trails, you're spoiled for choice. Easy valley-floor routes can get jammed; escape the teeming masses by heading up. The ultimate hike summits **Half Dome** (14 miles round-trip), but be warned: it's very strenuous, and advance **permits** (www.nps.gov/yose/planyourvisit/hdpermits.htm; from $12.50) are required even for day hikes. It's rewarding to hike just as far as the top of Vernal Fall (3 miles round-trip) or Nevada Fall (5.8 miles round-trip) via the **Mist Trail**. A longer, alternate route to Half Dome follows a more gently graded section of the long-distance **John Muir Trail**.

For overnight backpacking trips, **wilderness permits** (209-372-0826; www.nps.gov/yose/planyourvisit/wildpermits.htm; from $10) are required year-round. A quota system limits the number of hikers leaving from each trailhead. Make reservations up to 24 weeks in advance, or try your luck at the Yosemite Valley Wilderness Center or another permit-issuing station, starting at 11am on the day before you want to hike.

Yosemite Mountaineering School
ROCK CLIMBING
(209-372-8344; www.yosemitemountaineering.com; Curry Village; ⊙Apr-Oct) With sheer spires, polished domes and soaring monoliths, Yosemite is rock-climbing nirvana. YMS offers topflight instruction for novice to advanced climbers, plus guided climbs and equipment rental. During summer, it also operates at Tuolumne Meadows.

Badger Pass
SKIING, SNOWBOARDING
(209-372-8430; www.badgerpass.com; lift ticket adult/child $42/23; ⊙9am-4pm mid-Dec–Mar) Gentle slopes are perfect for beginner skiers and snowboarders. Cross-country skiers can glide along 25 miles of groomed tracks and 90 miles of marked trails, which are also open to snowshoers. Equipment rental and lessons available for all ages.

Sleeping & Eating

Concessionaire **DNC** (801-559-4884; www.yosemitepark.com) has a monopoly on park lodging and eating establishments, including ho-hum food courts and snack bars. Lodging reservations (up to 366 days in advance) are essential during peak season (May through September). During summer, DNC sets up simple canvas-tent cabins at riverside **Housekeeping Camp** (d from $95) in Yosemite Valley; busy **Tuolumne Meadows Lodge** (d from $120), a 90-minute drive from the valley; and quieter **White Wolf Lodge** (d from $120) off Tioga Rd, an hour away from the valley.

Curry Village CABINS $$
(d without bath from $95;) With a nostalgic summer-camp atmosphere, Curry Village has hundreds of helter-skelter cabins scattered beneath towering evergreens in Yosemite Valley. Soft-sided tent cabins resemble Civil War army barracks with scratchy wool blankets. Solid-wood cabins are smaller but cozy.

Wawona Hotel HISTORIC HOTEL $$
(r with/without bath incl breakfast from $225/155;) Filled with character, this Victorian-era throwback has wide porches, manicured lawns, tennis courts and a golf course. Half the thin-walled rooms share baths. The dining room serves three just-OK meals a day (dinner mains $19 to $34). Wawona is about a 45-minute drive south of the valley.

Ahwahnee Hotel HISTORIC HOTEL $$$
(r from $470;) Sleep where Steve Jobs, Eleanor Roosevelt and JFK bedded down at this national historic landmark, built in 1927. Sit a spell by the roaring fireplace beneath soaring sugar-pine timbers. Skip the formal dining room, serving overpriced California fare (dinner mains $26 to $46), for cocktails at the lobby bar instead.

Yosemite Lodge at the Falls LODGE $$$
(r from $220;) Spacious motel rooms come with ecofriendly upgrades and patios or balconies overlooking Yosemite Falls, meadows or the parking lot. Fork into sustainably caught river trout and organic veggies at the lodge's Mountain Room (dinner mains $18 to $35), open nightly (no reservations). For a beer and small bites, the next-door lounge has a convivial fireplace.

Degnan's Deli & Loft DELI, PIZZERIA $$
(mains $8-12; ☺ deli 7am-5pm year-round, pizzeria usually 5-9pm Apr-Sep; ⊞) Grab a deli sandwich and bag of chips downstairs before hitting the trail. After dark, head upstairs for cold brewskies and crispy pizzas.

⌸ Outside Yosemite National Park

Gateway towns that have a mixed bag of motels, hotels, lodges and B&Bs include Fish Camp, Oakhurst, El Portal, Midpines, Mariposa, Groveland and Lee Vining.

★**Yosemite Bug**
Rustic Mountain Resort HOSTEL, CABINS $
(☎866-826-7108, 209-966-6666; www.yosemite-bug.com; 6979 Hwy 140, Midpines; dm $23-26, tent cabins $45-75, r with/without bath from $75/65; ☺cafe 7am-4pm & 6-8:30pm; @🛜⊞) ✍ Tucked into the forest about 30 miles west of Yosemite Valley, this mountain hostelry hosts globetrotters who dig the clean rooms, low-key spa, shared kitchen access and laundry. The cafe's fresh, organic and vegetarian-friendly meals (mains $5 to $18) get raves.

★**Evergreen**
Lodge Resort CABINS, CAMPGROUND $$$
(☎209-379-2606; www.evergreenlodge.com; 33160 Evergreen Rd, Groveland; tents $80-120, cabins $210-380; @🛜🏊⊞) ✍ Near Hetch Hetchy, this woodsy 1920s resort welcomes families and couples with its prefurnished tents and comfy mountain cabins. Outdoor recreational activities abound, with equipment rentals and nightly s'mores in the rec room. There's a general store, a tavern with a pool table and a country restaurant (dinner mains $18 to $30) serving three hearty meals a day.

❶ Information

Yosemite Village, Curry Village and Wawona stores all have ATMs. Drivers should fill up before entering the park. High-priced gas is sold at Wawona and Crane Flat year-round and at Tuolumne Meadows in summer. Cell-phone service is spotty throughout the park. Unreliable pay-as-you-go internet kiosks are available next to Degnan's Deli and at Yosemite Lodge, which offers slow fee-based wi-fi.

Wawona Branch Library (www.mariposalibrary.org; Chilnualna Falls Rd; ☺1-6pm Mon-Fri, 10am-3pm Sat late May-early Sep, noon-5pm Mon, Wed & Fri, 10am-3pm Sat early Sep-late May; @) Free public internet terminals.

Yosemite Medical Clinic (☎209-372-4637; 9000 Ahwahnee Dr; ☺9am-7pm daily late May-late Sep, 9am-5pm Mon-Fri late Sep-late May) Urgent-care clinic in Yosemite Valley.

Yosemite Valley Branch Library (www.mariposalibrary.org; Girls Club Bldg, 9000 Cedar Ct; ☺9am-noon Mon, 8:30am-12:30pm Tue, 3-7pm Wed & 4-7pm Thu; @) Free public internet terminals.

Yosemite Valley Visitor Center (☎209-372-0200; www.nps.gov/yose; ☺9am-6pm, to 5pm

---

CAMPING IN YOSEMITE

From March through October, many park campgrounds require **reservations** (☎518-885-3639, 877-444-6777; www.recreation.gov), which are available starting five months in advance. Campsites routinely sell out online within *minutes*. All campgrounds have bearproof lockers and campfire rings; most have potable water.

In summer, most campgrounds are noisy and booked to bulging, especially **North Pines** (campsites $20; ☺Apr-Oct; ⊞🏊), **Lower Pines** (campsites $20; ☺Apr-Oct; ⊞🏊) and year-round **Upper Pines** (campsites $20; ⊞🏊) in Yosemite Valley; **Tuolumne Meadows** (campsites $20; ☺mid-Jul-late Sep; ⊞🏊) off Tioga Rd, a 90-minute drive from the valley; and riverside **Wawona** (campsites $20; ⊞🏊), under an hour's drive from the valley.

Year-round **Camp 4** (shared tent sites per person $5), a rock-climber's hangout in the valley; **Bridalveil Creek** (campsites $14; ☺mid-Jul-early Sep), a 45-minute drive from the valley off Glacier Point Rd; and **White Wolf** (campsites $14; ☺Jul-mid-Sep; 🏊), an hour's drive from the valley off Tioga Rd, are all first-come, first-served and often full before noon, especially on weekends.

Looking for a quieter, more rugged experience? Try the primitive campgrounds (no potable water) at **Tamarack Flat** (tent sites $10; ☺Jul-Sep), **Yosemite Creek** (tent sites $10; ☺Jul-mid-Sep; 🏊) and **Porcupine Flat** (campsites $10; ☺Jul-Sep; 🏊) off Tioga Rd. They're all first-come, first-served.

in winter) Smaller visitor centers at Wawona, Tuolumne Meadows and Big Oak Flat are open seasonally.

Yosemite Valley Wilderness Center (☑209-372-0826; www.nps.gov/yose; ☺8am-5pm May-Oct, 7:30am-5pm Jul & Aug) Backcountry permits and bear-canister rentals also available seasonally at Wawona, Tuolumne Meadows and Big Oak Flat.

❶ Getting There & Around

The nearest Greyhound and Amtrak stations are in Merced. **YARTS** (☑877-989-2787; www.yarts.com) buses travel year-round from Merced to Yosemite Valley via Hwy 140, stopping at towns along the way. In summer, YARTS buses run from Yosemite Valley to Mammoth Lakes via Tuolumne Meadows along Hwy 120. One-way fares (including park entry fee) are $12.50 from Merced, $18 from Mammoth Lakes.

Free shuttle buses loop around Yosemite Valley and, in summer, the Tuolumne Meadows and Wawona/Mariposa Grove areas. **DNC** (☑209-372-4386; www.yosemitepark.com) runs hikers' buses from the valley to Tuolumne Meadows (one way/round-trip $15/23) and Glacier Point (one way/round-trip $25/41). Valley bike rentals (per hour/day $11/32) are available seasonally at Yosemite Lodge and Curry Village.

In winter, highways to the parks are kept open (except Tioga Rd/Hwy 120, see p1009), although snow chains may be required at any time. During ski season, a free twice-daily shuttle bus connects Yosemite Valley with Badger Pass.

Sequoia & Kings Canyon National Parks

In these neighboring parks, giant sequoia trees are bigger – up to 30 stories high! – and more numerous than anywhere else in the Sierra Nevada. Tough and fire-charred, they'd easily swallow two freeway lanes each. Giant, too, are the mountains – including Mt Whitney (14,505ft), the tallest peak in the lower 48 states. Finally, there is the deep Kings Canyon, carved out of granite by ancient glaciers and a powerful river. For quiet, solitude and close-up sightings of wildlife, including black bears, hit the trail and lose yourself in peaceful wilderness.

◉ Sights

Sequoia was designated a national park in 1890; Kings Canyon, in 1940. Though distinct, the two **parks** (☑559-565-3341; www.nps.gov/seki; 7-day entry per car $20) operate as one unit with a single admission fee. From the south, Hwy 198 enters Sequoia National Park beyond the town of Three Rivers at Ash Mountain, then ascends the zigzagging Generals Hwy to Giant Forest. From the west, Hwy 180 enters Kings Canyon National Park near Grant Grove, then plunges down into the canyon to Cedar Grove.

◉ Sequoia National Park

We dare you to try hugging the trees in **Giant Forest**, a 3-sq-mile grove that protects the park's most gargantuan specimens – the world's largest is the **General Sherman Tree**. With sore arms and sticky sap fingers, lose the crowds by venturing onto the network of forested hiking trails (bring a map).

Giant Forest Museum   MUSEUM
(☑559-565-4480; Generals Hwy; ☺9am-4:30pm or 6pm mid-May–mid-Oct; ⊕) A short drive or shuttle ride south of Lodgepole Village, this tiny museum has exhibits on giant sequoia ecology and wildlife conservation. For 360° panoramic mountain views, climb the steep quarter-mile staircase up **Moro Rock** off Crescent Meadow Rd nearby.

Crystal Cave   CAVE
(☑info 559-565-3759; www.sequoiahistory.org; Crystal Cave Rd; tours adult/child from $15/8; ☺mid-May–Nov; ⊕) Discovered in 1918, this cave protects marble formations estimated to be 10,000 years old. First-come, first-served tickets for the 45-minute introductory tour are only available in person at the Lodgepole and Foothills visitor centers, *not* at the cave. Bring a jacket.

Mineral King   HISTORIC SITE
(Mineral King Rd) Take a detour to Mineral King Valley (7500ft), a late-19th-century mining and logging camp ringed by craggy peaks and alpine lakes. The 25-mile one-way scenic drive – navigating almost 700 hairraising hairpin turns – is usually open from mid-May to late October.

◉ Kings Canyon National Park & Scenic Byway

Just north of Grant Grove Village, **General Grant Grove** brims with majestic giants. Beyond, Hwy 180 begins its 30-mile descent into **Kings Canyon**, serpenting past chiseled rock walls laced with waterfalls. The road meets the Kings River, its roar ricocheting off granite cliffs soaring over 8000ft high, making this one of North America's deepest canyons. The scenic byway past Hume Lake to Cedar Grove Village is usually closed from mid-November through mid-April.

Cedar Grove
OUTDOORS

Cedar Grove Village is the last outpost of civilization before the rugged grandeur of the Sierra Nevada backcountry begins. Hike from **Roads End**, with its river beach and summertime swimming holes, to roaring **Mist Falls** (8.4 miles round-trip). Popular with birders, an easy 1.5-mile nature trail loops around **Zumwalt Meadow**, just west of Roads End.

Boyden Cavern
CAVE

(www.boydencavern.com; Hwy 180; tours adult/child from $13/8; ⊙ May–mid-Nov; 🐾) While its smaller and less impressive than Sequoia National Park's Crystal Cave, tours of the beautiful and whimsical formations here require no advance tickets.

🏃 Activities

Hiking is why people come here – with over 850 miles of marked trails to prove it. Cedar Grove and Mineral King offer the best backcountry access. Trails usually begin to open by early summer, though there's hiking year-round in the Foothills area. Overnight backcountry trips require **wilderness permits** (📞 559-565-3766; www.nps.gov/seki/planyourvisit/backpacking.htm; per trip $15), subject to a quota system from late May through late September, so reserve in advance.

In summer, cool off by swimming in **Hume Lake**, on national forest land off Hwy 180, and at riverside swimming holes in

TOP SIERRA NEVADA SCENIC DRIVES

Tioga Road (Hwy 120) Yosemite's rooftop of the world

Generals Highway (Hwy 198) Historic byway past giant sequoias

Kings Canyon Scenic Byway (Hwy 180) Drop into one of North America's deepest canyons

Mineral King Rd Wind up into a high Sierra valley

Eastern Sierra Scenic Byway (US 395) Where snowy mountains overshadow the desert

both parks. In winter, you can cross-country ski or snowshoe among giant sequoias; equipment rental is available at Grant Grove Village and Wuksachi Lodge. For groomed cross-country ski trails and other winter sports, visit old-fashioned **Montecito Sequoia Lodge**, off the Generals Hwy between the two parks.

🛏 Sleeping & Eating

Camping **reservations** (📞 518-885-3639, 877-477-6777; www.recreation.gov) are accepted only during summer at Lodgepole and Dorst Campgrounds in Sequoia National Park. The parks' dozen other developed campgrounds (campsites $10 to $20) are first-come, first-served. Lodgepole, Azalea, Potwisha and South Fork are open year-round. Overflow camping is available in the surrounding Sequoia National Forest.

The markets in Grant Grove, Lodgepole and Cedar Grove have limited groceries. Lodgepole and Cedar Grove also have snack bars serving basic, budget-friendly meals; Grant Grove has a simple restaurant, seasonal pizzeria and espresso cart.

Outside Sequoia's southern entrance, mostly well-worn independent and chain motels, rustic cabins and down-home eateries line Hwy 198 through Three Rivers town.

John Muir Lodge & Grant Grove Cabins
LODGE, CABINS $$

(📞 559-335-5500, 866-522-6966; www.sequoia-kingscanyon.com; Hwy 180; cabins without bath $65-95, r $120-190; 🕸🐾) In Grant Grove Village, this woodsy lodge has amply sized, if generic-looking, rooms and a fireplace lobby with board games. Oddly assorted cabin types range from thin-walled canvas tents to historical cabins.

Cedar Grove Lodge
LODGE $$

(📞 559-335-5500, 866-522-6966; www.sequoia-kingscanyon.com; Hwy 180; r $129-135; ⊙ mid-May–early Oct; ❄🐾) The almost two dozen motel-style rooms with shared porches overlooking the Kings River are simple and worn, but they're your best option down canyon.

Montecito Sequoia Lodge
LODGE $$

(📞 559-565-3388, 800-227-9900; www.mslodge.com; 63410 Generals Hwy; cabins with/without bath from $159/79, r $99-249; 🕸🐾) Family camps keep things raucous all summer long. In winter, go ice-skating and snow tubing. Basic lodge rooms and rustic cabins are midway between the parks. Rates include meals.

Wuksachi Lodge LODGE $$$
(☑559-565-4070, 866-807-3598; www.visitsequoia.
com; 64740 Wuksachi Way, off Generals Hwy; r from
$225; ☎) Don't be misled by the grand lobby
because oversized motel-style rooms here are
nothing to brag about. The upscale **Peaks
Restaurant** (☑559-565-4070; www.visitsequoia.
com; dinner mains $17-32; ⊙breakfast, lunch & din-
ner daily, seasonal hr vary) is hit-or-miss (dinner
reservations required). If you've got stamina,
hike 11.5 miles each way to the lodge's **Bear-
paw High Sierra Camp** (☑866-807-3598, 801-
559-4930; www.visitsequoia.com; tent cabin incl all
meals s/d $175/225; ⊙mid-Jun–mid-Sep), which
books up far in advance.

❶ Information

Lodgepole Village and Grant Grove Village are
the parks' main commerical hubs. Both have
visitor centers, post offices, markets, ATMs,
coin-op laundry and public showers (summer
only).

Lodgepole Visitor Center (☑559-565-4436;
⊙9am-4:30pm or 6pm daily, shorter winter hr)
in Lodgepole Village, **Foothills Visitor Center**
(☑559-565-4212; ⊙8am-4:30pm) at Ash
Mountain and **Kings Canyon Visitor Center**
(☑559-565-4307; ⊙8am or 9am to 4:30pm
or 5pm, shorter winter hr) in Grant Grove stay
open year-round. **Cedar Grove Visitor Center**
(☑559-565-4307; ⊙8am or 9am to 4:30pm
or 5pm late May-early Sep) in Kings Canyon
and **Mineral King Ranger Station** (☑559-565-
3768; ⊙8am-4pm late May-early Sep) in Se-
quoia are open seasonally. Check the free park
newspaper for other visitor services.

Expensive gas is available at Hume Lake (year-
round) and Stony Creek (summer only) outside
the park boundaries on national forest land.

❶ Getting There & Around

From late May to early September, free buses
loop around the Giant Forest and Lodgepole
Village areas of Sequoia National Park, while the
Sequoia Shuttle (☑877-287-4453; www.se-
quoiashuttle.com) links the park to Three Rivers
and Visalia (round-trip fare including park entry
fee $15, reservations required), with onward
connections to Amtrak from Visalia. Kings Can-
yon National Park has no public transportation.

Eastern Sierra

Vast, empty and majestic, here jagged peaks
plummet down into the Great Basin desert,
a dramatic juxtaposition that creates a po-
tent scenery cocktail. Hwy 395 runs the
entire length of the Sierra Nevada, with
turnoffs leading to pine forests, wildflower-
strewn meadows, placid lakes, hot springs
and glacier-gouged canyons. Hikers, back-
packers, mountain bikers, fishers and skiers
all escape here. The main visitor hubs are
Mammoth Lakes and Bishop.

At **Bodie State Historic Park** (☑760-647-
6445; www.bodiefoundation.org; Hwy 270; adult/
child $7/5; ⊙9am-6pm mid-May–Oct, to 3pm
Nov–mid-May), a gold-rush ghost town is pre-
served in a state of 'arrested decay.' Weath-
ered buildings sit frozen in time on a dusty,
windswept plain. To get there, head east for
13 miles (the last three unpaved) on Hwy
270, about 7 miles south of Bridgeport. The
access road is closed by snow during winter.

Further south at **Mono Lake** (www.mon-
olake.org), unearthly tufa towers rise from
the alkaline water like drip sandcastles. Off
Hwy 395, **Mono Basin Scenic Area Visi-
tor Center** (☑760-647-3044; ⊙8am-5pm Apr–
Nov) has excellent exhibits and schedules of
guided walks and talks. The best photo ops
are from the south shore's **South Tufa Area**
(adult/child $3/free). From the nearby town
of Lee Vining, Hwy 120 heads west into
Yosemite National Park via seasonal Tioga
Pass (p1009).

Continuing south on Hwy 395, detour
along the scenic 16-mile **June Lake Loop**
or push on to **Mammoth Lakes**, a popu-
lar four-seasons resort guarded by 11,053ft
Mammoth Mountain (☑800-626-6684;
www.mammothmountain.com; 10001 Minaret
Rd), a top-notch skiing area. The slopes
morph into a mountain-bike park in sum-
mer, when there's also camping, fishing and
day hiking around Mammoth Lakes Basin
and Reds Meadow. Nearby are the 60ft-
high basalt columns of **Devils Postpile
National Monument** (☑760-934-2289; www.
nps.gov/depo; shuttle day pass adult/child $7/4;
⊙late May-Oct), formed by volcanic activ-
ity. Hot-springs fans can soak in primitive
pools off Benton Crossing Rd or view the
geysering water at **Hot Creek Geological
Site** (www.fs.usda.gov/inyo; Hot Creek Hatchery
Rd; ⊙sunrise-sunset) **FREE**, both off Hwy 395
southeast of town. The in-town **Mammoth
Lakes Welcome Center & Ranger Station**
(☑866-466-2666; www.visitmammoth.com; 2510
Main St; ⊙8am-5pm) has helpful maps and
information.

Further south, Hwy 395 descends into
the Owens Valley, soon arriving in frontier-
flavored **Bishop**, whose minor attractions
include art galleries and a historical **railroad**

museum ([📞]760-873-5950; www.lawsmuseum.org; Silver Canyon Rd; donation $5; ⊙10am-4pm; [♿]). Bishop is the main gateway for pack-horse trips and access to the best fishing and rock climbing in the entire Eastern Sierra.

Budget a half-day for the thrilling drive up to the **Ancient Bristlecone Pine Forest** ([📞]760-873-2500; www.fs.usda.gov/inyo; per car $6; ⊙usually mid-May–Nov). These gnarled, otherworldly looking trees are found above 10,000ft on the slopes of the White Mountains, where you'd think nothing could grow. The oldest tree – called Methuselah – is estimated to be over 4700 years old. The road (closed by snow in winter and spring) is paved to the visitor center at Schulman Grove, where hiking trails await. From Hwy 395 in Big Pine, take Hwy 168 east for 13 miles, then head upll another 10 miles on White Mountain Rd.

Hwy 395 barrels south to Independence and **Manzanar National Historic Site** ([📞]760-878-2194; www.nps.gov/manz; 5001 Hwy 395, Independence; ⊙dawn-dusk, visitor center 9am-4:30pm) [FREE], which memorializes the war relocation camp where some 10,000 Japanese Americans were unjustly interned during WWII following the attack on Pearl Harbor. Interpretive exhibits and a short film vividly chronicle life at the camp, marked by a short self-guided auto tour route.

Further south in Lone Pine, you will finally catch a glimpse of 14,505ft **Mt Whitney** (www.fs.usda.gov/inyo), the highest mountain in the lower 48 states. The heart-stopping, 12-mile scenic drive up **Whitney Portal Road** (closed in winter) is spectacular. Climbing the peak is hugely popular, but requires a **permit** (www.recreation.gov; per person

$15) issued on a lottery basis. West of Lone Pine, the bizarrely shaped boulders of the **Alabama Hills** have enchanted the makers of Hollywood Westerns. Peruse vintage memorabilia and movie posters at the **Museum of Lone Pine Film History** ([📞]760-876-9909; www.lonepinefilmhistorymuseum.org; 701 S Main St; adult/child $5/free; ⊙10am-6pm Mon-Wed, to 7pm Thu-Sat, to 4pm Sun). South of town, the **Eastern Sierra InterAgency Visitor Center** ([📞]760-876-6222; www.fs.fed.us/r5/inyo; Hwys 395 & 136; ⊙8am-5pm) issues wilderness permits, dispenses outdoor-recreation information and sells books and maps.

🛏 Sleeping

The Eastern Sierra is freckled with campgrounds; backcountry camping requires a wilderness permit, reservable in advance and available at ranger stations. Bishop, Lone Pine and Bridgeport have the most motels. Mammoth Lakes has a few motels and dozens of inns, B&Bs and condo and vacation rentals. Reservations are essential everywhere in summer.

El Mono Motel   MOTEL $
([📞]760-647-6310; www.elmonomotel.com; 51 Hwy 395, Lee Vining; r with/without bath from $89/69; ⊙mid-May–Oct; [📶]) Neighboring a coffee shop, snug motel rooms nearby Mono Lake are a short drive from Yosemite National Park's Tioga Pass entrance.

Whitney Portal Hostel   HOSTEL $
([📞]760-876-0030; www.whitneyportalstore.com; 238 S Main St, Lone Pine; dm/q $25/84; [❄][📶][🐕]) Carpeted bunk-bed rooms at this ultrabasic hostel are popular launchpads for Whitney summit hikes. Public showers ($5) available.

★**Tamarack Lodge**   LODGE, CABINS $$
([📞]800-626-6684, 760-934-2442; www.tamaracklodge.com; 163 Twin Lakes Rd, Mammoth Lakes; r with/without bath from $149/99, cabins from $169; [@][📶][♿]) 🛥 Since 1924, this heart-warming lakeside resort has rented lodge rooms and cabins with kitchens, ranging from rustic to deluxe – some have wood-burning fireplaces.

Dow Hotel & Dow Villa Motel   HOTEL, MOTEL $$
([📞]800-824-9317, 760-876-5521; www.dowvillamotel.com; 310 S Main St, Lone Pine; r $85-150, without bath $70; [❄][@][📶][♿][🐕]) John Wayne and Errol Flynn are among the movie stars who have slept at this 1922 hotel, restored with rustic charm. Modern motel rooms are a mite more comfortable.

DON'T MISS

TOP EASTERN SIERRA OUTDOOR SPOTS

Bodie State Historic Park (p1015) An eerie gold-rush ghost town.

Mono Lake (p1015) Unearthly, mysterious-looking mineral formations.

Mammoth Mountain (p1015) Lofty winter sports and mountain biking.

Ancient Bristlecone Pine Forest (p1016) Earth's oldest living trees.

Manzanar National Historic Site (p1016) Uncensored history of WWII-era internment camps.

✗ Eating & Drinking

Good Life Café AMERICAN $
(http://mammothgoodlifecafe.com; 126 Old Mammoth Rd, Mammoth Lakes; mains $7-10; ⊗6:30am-3pm) Stomach-stuffing breakfasts, brawny burgers and Cal-Mexican burritos, healthy veggie wraps and big salad bowls keep this spot with a sunny patio packed.

Raymond's Deli DELI $
(http://raymondsdeli.com; 206 N Main St, Bishop; items $5-9; ⊗10am-5:30pm; 🖉) A brash den of kitsch and pinball, Raymond's makes overstuffed sandwiches with names like 'When Pigs Fly' and 'Flaming Farm.' Kick back with California craft beers.

★Whoa Nellie Deli CALIFORNIAN $$
(☑760-647-1088; Tioga Gas Mart, 22 Vista Point Rd, off Hwy 120, Lee Vining; mains $7-20; ⊗7am-9pm late Apr–early Nov; 🖬) Great food in a gas station? Really, you gotta try chef Matt Toomey's amazing roadside kitchen, dishing up fish tacos, wild buffalo meatloaf and barbecue ribs.

Skadi EUROPEAN $$$
(☑760-934-3902; http://skadirestaurant.com; 587 Old Mammoth Rd, Mammoth Lakes; mains $24-32; ⊗5:30-9:30pm) As you gaze out at dreamy mountain vistas, feast on Scandinavian 'alpine cuisine' – like roasted crispy-skin salmon and juniper-spiced duck breast with lingonberries – with stellar wines.

**Mammoth Brewing
Company Tasting Room** BREWERY
(www.mammothbrewingco.com; 94 Berner St, Mammoth Lakes; ⊗10am-6pm) Sample a dozen brews on tap for free, then buy take-home bottles of IPA 395 or Double Nut Brown.

Looney Bean Coffee CAFE
(www.looneybean.com; 399 N Main St, Bishop; ⊗6am-6pm Mon-Sat, 7am-5pm Sun; 🖘) Local hangout for freshly roasted brews, fruit smoothies and baked goods. Also in Mammoth Lakes.

Lake Tahoe

Shimmering in myriad blues and greens, Lake Tahoe is the nation's second-deepest lake. Driving around its spellbinding 72-mile scenic shoreline gives you quite a workout behind the wheel. The north shore is quiet and upscale; the west shore, rugged and old-timey; the east shore, undeveloped; and the south shore, busy with families and flashy casinos. The horned peaks surrounding the lake (elevation 6225ft), which straddles the California–Nevada state line, are year-round outdoor playgrounds.

Tahoe gets packed in summer, on winter weekends and over holidays, when reservations are essential. **Lake Tahoe Visitors Authority** (☑800-288-2463; www.tahoesouth.com) and **North Lake Tahoe Visitors' Bureau** (☑888-434-1262; www.gotahoenorth.com) run multiple visitor information centers. There's camping in **state parks** (☑800-444-7275; www.reserveamerica.com; campsites $35-50; 🖬🖼) and on **USFS lands** (☑877-444-6777, 518-885-3639; www.recreation.gov; campsites $20-40; 🖬🖼).

South Lake Tahoe & West Shore

With retro motels and eateries lining busy Hwy 50, South Lake Tahoe gets crowded. Gambling at Stateline's casino hotels, just across the Nevada border, attracts thousands, as does the world-class ski resort of **Heavenly** (☑775-586-7000; www.skiheavenly.com; 3860 Saddle Rd; 🖬). In summer, a trip up Heavenly's **gondola** (adult/child $38/20) guarantees fabulous views of the lake and **Desolation Wilderness**, a starkly beautiful landscape of raw granite peaks, glacier-carved valleys and alpine lakes that's a favorite of hikers. Get maps, information and **wilderness permits** (☑877-444-6777; www.recreation.gov; per adult $5-10) from the **USFS Taylor Creek Visitor Center** (☑530-543-2674; www.fs.usda.gov/ltbmu; Hwy 89; ⊗daily late May–Oct, hr vary). It's 3 miles north of the 'Y' intersection of Hwys 50/89, at **Tallac Historic Site** (Tallac Rd; entry free, tour adult/child $5/3; ⊗10am-4:30pm mid-Jun-Sep, Fri & Sat only late May–mid-Jun; 🖼), preserving early-20th-century vacation estates.

From sandy, swimmable **Zephyr Cove** across the Nevada border or the in-town Ski Run Marina, **Lake Tahoe Cruises** (☑800-238-2463; www.zephyrcove.com; adult/child from $47/10) ply the 'Big Blue' year-round. Back on shore, boutique-chic motels include the **Alder Inn** (☑530-544-4485; www.thealderinn.com; 1072 Ski Run Blvd; r $85-229; 🖘🖳) and the hip **Basecamp Hotel** (☑530-208-0180; http://basecamphotels.com; 4143 Cedar Ave; r incl breakfast $115-239; 🖘🖼), which has a rooftop hot tub and communal fire pits. Fuel up at vegetarian-friendly **Sprouts** (3123 Harrison Ave; mains $6-10; ⊗8am-9pm; 🖉), a natural-foods cafe, or with a peanut-butter-topped burger and garlic fries at the **Burger Lounge** (☑530-542-2010; www.burgerloung-eintahoe.com; 717 Emerald Bay Rd; items $4-9; ⊙10am-8pm, shorter hr Oct-May; ☑).

Hwy 89 threads northwest along the thickly forested west shore to **Emerald Bay State Park** (☑530-541-6498; www.parks.ca.gov; per car $8-10; ⊙daily late May-Sep), where granite cliffs and pine trees frame a sparkling fjordlike inlet. A 1-mile trail leads steeply downhill to **Vikingsholm Castle** (tours adult/child $10/8; ⊙10:30am or 11am-4pm daily late May-Sep). From this 1920s Scandinavian-style mansion, the **Rubicon Trail** ribbons 4.5 miles north along the lakeshore past petite coves to **DL Bliss State Park** (☑530-525-7277; www.parks.ca.gov; per car $10; ⊙usually late May-Sep; ☑), offering sandy beaches. Further north, **Tahoma Meadows B&B Cottages** (☑866-525-1533, 530-525-1553; www.tahomamea-dows.com; 6821 W Lake Blvd, Homewood; cottages incl breakfast $109-199; 🛜☑🐾) rents darling country cabins.

North & East Shores

The north shore's commercial hub, **Tahoe City** is great for grabbing supplies and renting outdoor gear. It's not far from **Squaw Valley USA** (☑800-403-0206; www.squaw.com; 1960 Squaw Valley Rd, Olympic Valley; ☑), a megasized ski resort that hosted the 1960 Winter Olympics. Après-ski crowds gather at woodsy **Bridgetender Tavern** (www.tahoe-bridgetender.com; 65 W Lake Blvd; mains $8-12; ⊙11am-11pm, to midnight Fri & Sat) back in town. In the morning, gobble eggs Benedict with house-smoked salmon at down-home **Fire Sign Cafe** (www.firesigncafe.com; 1785 W Lake Blvd, Sunnyside; mains $7-11; ⊙7am-3pm; ☑), 2 miles south along the lakeshore.

In summer, swim or kayak at **Tahoe Vista** or **Kings Beach**. Overnight at **Franciscan Lakeside Lodge** (☑800-564-6754, 530-546-6300; http://franciscanlodge.com; 6944 N Lake Blvd, Tahoe Vista; d $95-285; 🛜🏊☑), where simple cabins, cottages and suites have kitchenettes, or at well-kept, compact **Hostel Tahoe** (☑530-546-3266; http://hostel-tahoe.com; 8931 N Lake Blvd, Kings Beach; dm $32, r $65-80; ⊙check-in 4-7pm; @🛜). East of Kings Beach's casual lakeside eateries, Hwy 28 barrels into Nevada. You can catch a live-music show at **Crystal Bay Club Casino** (☑775-833-6333; www.crystalbaycasino.com; 14 Hwy 28, Crystal Bay), but, for more happening bars and bistros, drive further to **Incline Village**.

With pristine beaches, lakes and miles of multi-use trails, **Lake Tahoe-Nevada State Park** (http://parks.nv.gov; per car $7-12) is the east shore's biggest draw. Summer crowds splash in the turquoise waters of **Sand Harbor**. The 13.5-mile **Flume Trail**, a mountain biker's holy grail, ends further south at **Spooner Lake**. Back in Incline Village, **Flume Trail Bikes** (☑775-298-2501; www.flume-trailtahoe.com; 1115 Tunnel Creek Rd; bike rental per day $35-90, shuttle $10-15) offers bicycle rentals and trailhead shuttles.

Truckee & Around

North of Lake Tahoe off I-80, Truckee is not in fact a truck stop but a thriving mountain town, with coffee shops, trendy boutiques and dining in downtown's historical district. Ski bums have several area resorts to pick from, including glam **Northstar-at-Tahoe** (☑800-466-6784; www.northstarat-tahoe.com; 5001 Northstar Dr; ☑); kid-friendly **Sugar Bowl** (☑530-426-9000; www.sugarbowl.com; 629 Sugar Bowl Rd, Norden; ☑), cofounded by Walt Disney; and **Royal Gorge** (☑530-426-3871; www.royalgorge.com; 9411 Pahatsi Rd, Soda Springs; ☑), paradise for cross-country skiers.

West of Hwy 89, Donner Summit is where the infamous Donner Party became trapped during the fierce winter of 1846–47. Fewer than half survived – some by cannibalizing their dead friends. The grisly tale is chronicled at the museum inside **Donner Memorial State Park** (www.parks.ca.gov; Donner Pass Rd; per car $8; ⊙museum 10am-5pm, closed Tue & Wed Sep-May; ☑), where **Donner Lake** is popular with swimmers and paddlers.

Do-it-yourself hikers and skiers who don't mind doing small chores stay at the Sierra Club's rough-hewn **Clair Tappan Lodge** (☑800-679-6775, 530-426-3632; www.sierraclub.org/outings/lodges/ctl; 19940 Donner Pass Rd, Norden; dm incl meals adult/child from $60/30; ☑) 🍴 outside town. On the outskirts of Truckee, green-certified **Cedar House Sport Hotel** (☑866-582-5655, 530-582-5655; www.cedarhousesporthotel.com; 10918 Brockway Rd; r incl breakfast $170-290; 🛜🐾) 🍴 offers stylish boutique rooms and an outdoor hot tub. Down pints of 'Donner Party Porter' at **Fifty Fifty Brewing Co** (www.fifty-fiftybrewing.com; 11197 Brockway Rd; ⊙11am-9pm, to 9:30pm Fri & Sat) 🍴.

❶ Getting There & Around

South Tahoe Express (☑ 866-898-2463, 775-325-8944; www.southtahoeexpress.com; one way/round-trip $30/53) runs several daily shuttles from Nevada's Reno-Tahoe International Airport to Stateline. **North Lake Tahoe Express** (☑ 866-216-5222, 775-786-3706; www.north-laketahoeexpress.com; one way/round-trip $45/85) connects Reno's airport with Truckee, Northstar, Squaw Valley and north-shore towns.

Truckee's **Amtrak depot** (10065 Donner Pass Rd) has daily trains to Sacramento ($50, 4½ hours) and Reno ($16, 1½ hours), and twice-daily Greyhound buses to Reno ($18, one hour), Sacramento ($45, 2½ hours) and San Francisco ($41, six hours). Amtrak buses connect Sacramento with South Lake Tahoe ($34, 2½ hours).

Tahoe Area Regional Transit (TART; ☑ 800-736-6365, 530-550-1212; www.placer.ca.gov/tart; fare/day pass $1.75/3.50) operates local buses from Truckee around the north and west shores. South Lake Tahoe is served by **BlueGO** (☑ 530-541-7149; www.bluego.org; fare/day pass from $2/5) buses. BlueGO's summer-only Nifty 50 trolley heads up the west shore to Tahoma, connecting with TART.

If you're driving, tire chains are often required in winter on I-80, US 50 and other mountain highways, which may close temporarily due to heavy snow.

Pacific Northwest

Best Places to Eat

➡ Cascina Spinasse (p1036)

➡ Saffron Mediterranean Kitchen (p1053)

➡ Ox (p1060)

➡ New Sammy's Cowboy Bistro (p1074)

Best Places to Stay

➡ Sun Mountain Lodge (p1048)

➡ Kennedy School (p1059)

➡ Oxford Hotel (p1071)

➡ Hotel Five (p1033)

Why Go?

As much a state of mind as a geographical region, the US's northwest corner is a land of subcultures and new trends, where evergreen trees frame snow-dusted volcanoes, and inspired ideas scribbled on the back of napkins become tomorrow's business start-ups. You can't peel off the history in layers here, but you *can* gaze wistfully into the future in fast-moving, innovative cities such as Seattle and Portland, which are sprinkled with food carts, streetcars, microbreweries, green belts, coffee connoisseurs and weird urban sculpture.

Ever since the days of the Oregon Trail, the Northwest has had a hypnotic lure for risk takers and dreamers, and the metaphoric carrot still dangles. There's the air, so clean they ought to bottle it; the trees, older than many of Rome's Renaissance palaces; and the end-of-the-continent coastline, holding back the force of the world's largest ocean. Cowboys take note; it doesn't get much more 'wild' or 'west' than this.

When to Go
Seattle

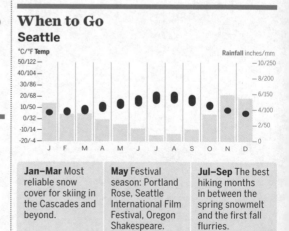

Jan–Mar Most reliable snow cover for skiing in the Cascades and beyond.

May Festival season: Portland Rose, Seattle International Film Festival, Oregon Shakespeare.

Jul–Sep The best hiking months in between the spring snowmelt and the first fall flurries.

Grunge & Other Subcultures

Synthesizing Generation X angst with a questionable approach to personal hygiene, grunge first dive-bombed onto Seattle's music scene in the early 1990s like a clap of thunder on an otherwise dry and sunny afternoon. The anger had been fermenting for years. Hardcore punk originated in Portland in the late 1970s, led by resident contrarians the Wipers, whose antifashion followers congregated in legendary dive bars such as Satyricon. Another musical blossoming occurred in Olympia, where DIY-merchants Beat Happening invented 'lo-fi' and coyly mocked the corporate establishment. Scooping up the fallout of a disparate youth culture, Seattle quickly became grunge's pulpit, spawning bands such as Pearl Jam, Soundgarden and Alice in Chains. The genre went global in 1991 when Nirvana's *Nevermind* album knocked Michael Jackson off the number-one spot, but the movement was never meant to be successful and the kudos quickly killed it. Since the mid '90s the Pacific Northwest has kept its subcultures largely to itself, though the music's no less potent or relevant.

MICROBREWERIES

'Beer connoisseurship' is a nationwide phenomenon these days, but the campaign to put a dash of flavor into commercially brewed beer was first ignited in the Pacific Northwest in the 1980s.

One of America's first microbreweries was the mercurial Cartwright Brewing Company, set up in Portland in 1980. The nation's first official brewpub was the now defunct Grant's, which opened in the Washington city of Yakima in 1982. The trend went viral in 1984 with the inauguration of Bridgeport Brewing Company in Portland, followed a year later by Beervana's old-school brewing brothers Mike and Brian McMenamin, whose quirky beer empire still acts as a kind of personification of the craft-brewing business in the region.

Today, Washington and Oregon operate nearly 300 microbreweries (Portland alone has more than 50). These take classic, natural ingredients – malt, hops and yeast – to produce high-quality beer in small batches.

Best State Parks

→ **Moran State Park** Orcas Island

→ **Ecola State Park** Cannon Beach

→ **Deception Pass State Park** Whidbey Island

→ **Fort Worden State Park** Port Townsend

→ **Lime Kiln Point State Park** San Juan Island

→ **Cape Perpetua State Park** Near Yachats

→ **Smith Rock State Park** Near Bend

DON'T MISS

Between them, the states of Washington and Oregon harbor four of the US's most spectacular national parks: Mt Rainier (established 1899), Crater Lake (1902), Olympic (1938) and North Cascades (1968).

PACIFIC NORTHWEST

Fast Facts

→ **Hub cities** Seattle (621,000), Portland (594,000)

→ **Distances from Seattle** Portland (172 miles), Vancouver BC (140 miles)

→ **Time zone** Pacific Standard

Did You Know?

Over the winter of 1998–99, the Mt Baker ski resort in northwest Washington received 1140in of snow in a single season, the largest annual snowfall ever recorded.

Resources

→ **Washington State Parks & Recreation Commission** (www.parks.wa.gov)

→ **Oregon State Parks & Recreation Dept** (www.oregonstateparks.org)

→ **Washington State Tourism Office** (www.tourism.wa.gov)

→ **Oregon Tourism Commission** (www.traveloregon.com)

Pacific Northwest Highlights

1 Cycling and kayaking around the quieter corners of the **San Juan Islands** (p1045).

2 Exploring the gorgeous **Oregon Coast** (p1077), from scenic Astoria to balmy Port Orford.

3 Admiring trees older than Europe's Renaissance castles in Washington's **Olympic National Park** (p1041).

4 Watching the greatest outdoor show in the Pacific Northwest in Seattle's theatrical **Pike Place Market** (p1026).

5 Walking the green and serene neighborhoods of **Portland** (p1053), energized by beer, coffee and food-cart treats.

6 Witnessing the impossibly deep blue waters and scenic panoramas of **Crater Lake National Park** (p1072).

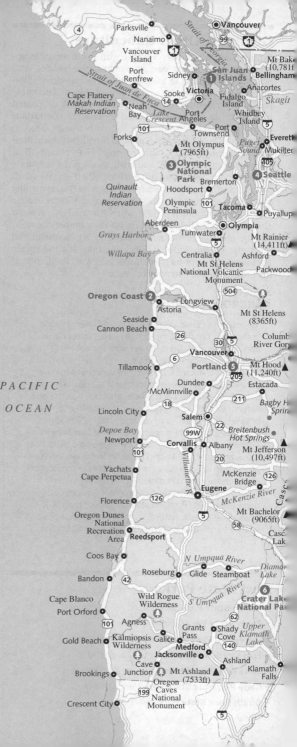

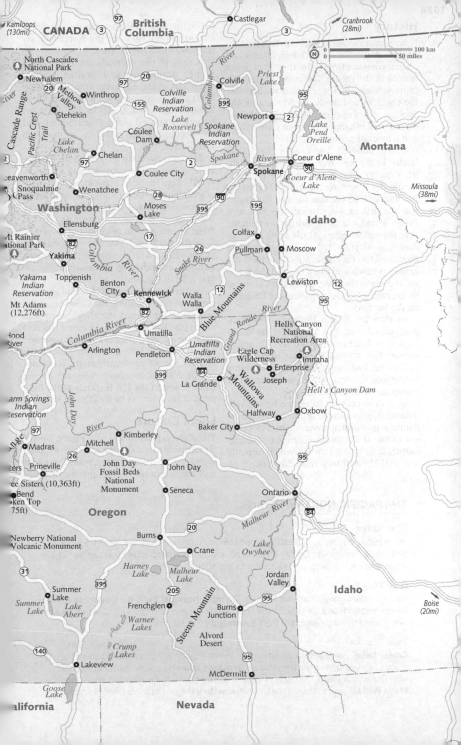

History

Native American societies, including the Chinook and the Salish, had long-established coastal communities by the time Europeans arrived in the Pacific Northwest in the 18th century. Inland, on the arid plateaus between the Cascades and the Rocky Mountains, the Spokane, Nez Percé and other tribes thrived on seasonal migration between river valleys and temperate uplands.

Three hundred years after Columbus landed in the New World, Spanish and British explorers began probing the northern Pacific coast, seeking the fabled Northwest Passage. In 1792 Captain George Vancouver was the first explorer to sail the waters of Puget Sound, claiming British sovereignty over the entire region. At the same time, an American, Captain Robert Gray, found the mouth of the Columbia River. In 1805 the explorers Lewis and Clark crossed the Rockies and made their way down the Columbia to the Pacific Ocean, extending the US claim on the territory.

In 1824 the British Hudson's Bay Company established Fort Vancouver in Washington as headquarters for the Columbia region. This opened the door to waves of settlers but had a devastating impact on the indigenous cultures, which were assailed by European diseases and alcohol.

In 1843 settlers at Champoeg, on the Willamette River south of Portland, voted to organize a provisional government independent of the Hudson's Bay Company, thereby casting their lot with the US, which formally acquired the territory from the British by treaty in 1846. Over the next decade, some 53,000 settlers came to the Northwest via the 2000-mile Oregon Trail.

Arrival of the railroads set the region's future. Agriculture and lumber became the pillars of the economy until 1914, when WWI and the opening of the Panama Canal brought increased trade to Pacific ports. Shipyards opened along Puget Sound, and the Boeing aircraft company set up shop near Seattle.

Big dam projects in the 1930s and '40s provided cheap hydroelectricity and irrigation. WWII offered another boost for aircraft manufacturing and shipbuilding, and agriculture continued to thrive. In the postwar period, Washington's population, especially around Puget Sound, grew to twice that of Oregon.

In the 1980s and '90s, the economic emphasis shifted with the rise of the high-tech industry, embodied by Microsoft in Seattle and Intel in Portland.

Hydroelectricity production and massive irrigation projects along the Columbia, however, have threatened the river's ecosystem in the past few decades and logging has also left its scars. But the region has reinvigorated its eco credentials by attracting some of the country's most environmentally conscious companies and its major cities are among the greenest in the US. It stands at the forefront of US efforts to tackle climate issues.

Local Culture

The stereotypical image of a Pacific Northwesterner is a casually dressed, latte-supping urbanite who drives a Prius, votes Democrat and walks around with an unwavering diet

---

THE PACIFIC NORTHWEST IN...

Four Days

Hit the ground running in **Seattle** to see the main sights, including Pike Place Market and the Seattle Center. On day three, head down to **Portland**, where you can be like the locals and cycle to bars, cafes, food carts and shops.

One Week

Add a couple highlights like **Mt Rainier**, **Olympic National Park**, the **Columbia River Gorge** and **Mt Hood**. Or explore the spectacular Oregon Coast (try the **Cannon Beach** area) or the historic seaport of **Port Townsend** on the Olympic Peninsula.

Two Weeks

Crater Lake is unforgettable, and can be combined with a trip to **Ashland** and its Shakespeare Festival. Don't miss the ethereal **San Juan Islands** up near the watery border with Canada, or **Bend**, the region's biggest outdoor draw. If you like wine, Washington's **Walla Walla** is your mecca, while the **Willamette Valley** is Oregon's Pinot Noir paradise.

of Nirvana-derived indie rock programmed into their iPod. But, as with most fleeting regional generalizations, the reality is far more complex.

Noted for their sophisticated cafe culture and copious microbrew pubs, the urban hubs of Seattle and Portland are the Northwest's most emblematic cities. But head east into the region's drier and less verdant interior, and the cultural affiliations become increasingly more traditional. Here, strung out along the Columbia River Valley or nestled amid the arid steppes of southeastern Washington, small towns host raucous rodeos, tourist centers promote cowboy culture, and a cup of coffee is served 'straight up' with none of the chai lattes and frappés that are par for the course in Seattle.

In contrast to the USA's hardworking eastern seaboard, life out West is more casual and less frenetic than in New York or Boston. Idealistically, Westerners would rather work to live than live to work. Indeed, with so much winter rain, the citizens of the Pacific Northwest will dredge up any excuse to shun the nine-to-five treadmill and hit the great outdoors a couple of hours (or even days) early. Witness the scene in late May and early June, when the first bright days of summer prompt a mass exodus of hikers and cyclists making enthusiastically for the national parks and wilderness areas for which the region is justly famous.

Creativity is another strong Northwestern trait, be it redefining the course of modern rock music or reconfiguring the latest Microsoft computer program. No longer content to live in the shadow of California or Hong Kong, the Pacific Northwest has redefined itself internationally in recent decades through celebrated TV shows (*Frasier* and *Portlandia*, for example), iconic global personalities (Bill Gates) and a groundbreaking music scene that has spawned everything from grunge rock to riot grrrl feminism.

Tolerance is widespread in Pacific Northwestern society, from recreational drug use to gay rights to physician-assisted suicide. Commonly voting Democrat in presidential elections, the population has also enthusiastically embraced the push for 'greener' lifestyles in the form of extensive recycling programs, 'sustainable' restaurants and biodiesel whale-watching tours. An early exponent of ecofriendly practices, former Seattle mayor Greg Nickels has become a leading spokesperson on climate change, while progressive Portland regularly features at the top of America's most sustainable and bike-friendly cities.

❶ Getting There & Around

AIR
Seattle-Tacoma International Airport (p1039), aka 'Sea-Tac' and Portland International Airport (p1064) are the main airports for the region, serving many North American and a few international destinations.

BOAT
Washington State Ferries (WSF; p1039) links Seattle with Bainbridge and Vashon Islands. Other WSF routes cross from Whidbey Island to Port Townsend on the Olympic Peninsula, and from Anacortes through the San Juan Islands to Sidney, BC. Victoria Clipper (p1039) operates services from Seattle to Victoria, BC, and ferries to Victoria also operate from Port Angeles. **Alaska Marine Highway** (AMHS; ☎ 800-642-0066; www.ferryalaska.com) ferries go from Bellingham, WA, to Alaska.

BUS
Greyhound (www.greyhound.com) provides service along the I-5 corridor from Bellingham in northern Washington down to Medford in southern Oregon, with connecting services across the US and Canada. East–west routes fan out toward Spokane, Yakima, the Tri-Cities (Kennewick, Pasco and Richland in Washington), Walla Walla and Pullman in Washington, and Hood River and Pendleton in Oregon. Private bus companies service most of the smaller towns and cities across the region, often connecting to Greyhound or Amtrak.

CAR
Driving your own vehicle is by far the most convenient way of touring the Pacific Northwest. Major and minor rental agencies are commonplace throughout the region. The I-5 is the major north–south artery. In Washington I-90 heads east from Seattle to Spokane and into Idaho. In Oregon I-84 branches east from Portland along the Columbia River Gorge to link up with Boise in Idaho.

TRAIN
Amtrak (www.amtrak.com) runs train services north (to Vancouver, Canada) and south (to California) linking Seattle, Portland and other major urban centers with the Cascades and Coast Starlight routes. The famous Empire Builder heads east to Chicago from Seattle and Portland (joining up in Spokane).

WASHINGTON

Divided in two by the spinal Cascade Mountains, Washington isn't so much a land of contrasts as a land of polar opposites. Centered on Seattle, the western coastal zone is wet, urban, liberal and famous for its fecund evergreen forests; splayed to the east between the less celebrated cities of Spokane and Yakima, the inland plains are arid, rural, conservative and covered by mile after mile of scrublike steppe.

Of the two halves it's the west that harbors most of the quintessential Washington sights, while the more remote east is less heralded, understated and full of surprises.

WASHINGTON FACTS

Nickname Evergreen State

Population 6,897,000

Area 71,342 sq miles

Capital city Olympia (population 47,266)

Other cities Seattle (population 620,778), Spokane (population 210,103), Yakima (population 92,512), Bellingham (population 81,862), Walla Walla (population 32,148)

Sales tax 6.5%

Birthplace of Singer and actor Bing Crosby (1903–77), guitarist Jimi Hendrix (1942–70), computer geek Bill Gates (b 1955), political commentator Glen Beck (b 1964), musical icon Kurt Cobain (1967–94)

Home of Mt St Helens, Microsoft, Starbucks, Nordstrom, Evergreen State College

Politics Democrat governor, Democrat senators, Democrat in presidential elections since 1988

Famous for Grunge rock, coffee, *Grey's Anatomy*, *Twilight*, volcanoes, apples, wine, precipitation

State vegetable Walla Walla sweet onion

Driving distances Seattle to Portland 174 miles, Spokane to Port Angeles 365 miles

Seattle

Combine the brains of Portland, OR, with the beauty of Vancouver, BC, and you'll get something approximating Seattle. It's hard to believe that the Pacific Northwest's largest metropolis was considered a 'secondary' US city until the 1980s, when a combination of bold innovation and unabashed individualism turned it into one of the dot-com era's biggest trendsetters, spearheaded by an unlikely alliance of coffee-supping computer geeks and navel-gazing musicians. Reinvention is the buzzword these days in a city where grunge belongs to the history books and Starbucks now competes among a cavalcade of precocious indie coffee providers eking out their market position.

Surprisingly elegant in places and coolly edgy in others, Seattle is notable for its strong neighborhoods, top-rated university, monstrous traffic jams and proactive city mayors who harbor green credentials. Although it has fermented its own pop culture in recent times, it has yet to create an urban mythology befitting Paris or New York, but it does have 'the Mountain.' Better known as Rainier to its friends, Seattle's unifying symbol is a 14,411ft mass of rock and ice, which acts as a perennial reminder to the city's huddled masses that raw wilderness and potential volcanic catastrophe are never far away.

⊙ Sights

◎ Downtown

★ **Pike Place Market** MARKET
(www.pikeplacemarket.org; btwn Virginia St & Union St & 1st Ave & Western Ave; ⊙9am-6pm Mon-Sat, to 5pm Sun; ⓡWestlake) ✦ Take a bunch of small-time businesses and sprinkle them liberally around a spatially challenged waterside strip amid crowds of old-school bohemians, new-wave restaurateurs, tree-huggers, bolshie students, artists, urban buskers and artisans. The result: Pike Place Market, a cavalcade of noise, smells, personalities, banter and urban theater that's almost London-like in its cosmopolitanism. In operation since 1907, Pike Place is Seattle in a bottle, a wonderfully 'local' experience that highlights the city for what it really is: all-embracing, eclectic and proudly singular.

WORTH A TRIP

PIONEER SQUARE

Pioneer Sq is Seattle's oldest quarter, which isn't saying much if you're visiting from Rome or London. Most of the buildings here date from just after the 1889 fire (a devastating inferno that destroyed 25 city blocks, including the entire central business district), and are referred to architecturally as Richardsonian Romanesque, a red-brick revivalist style in vogue at the time. In the early years, the neighborhood's boom-bust fortunes turned its arterial road, Yesler Way, into the original 'skid row' – an allusion to the skidding logs that were pulled downhill to Henry Yesler's pier-side mill. When the timber industry fell on hard times, the road became a haven for the homeless and its name subsequently became a byword for poverty-stricken urban enclaves countrywide.

Thanks to a concerted public effort, the neighborhood avoided being laid to waste by the demolition squads in the 1960s and is now protected in the Pioneer Sq–Skid Rd Historic District.

The quarter today mixes the historic with the seedy, while harboring art galleries, cafes and nightlife. Its most iconic building is the 42-story **Smith Tower** (cnr 2nd Ave S & Yesler Way; observation deck adult/child $7.50/5; ☉10am-dusk), completed in 1914 and, until 1931, it was the tallest building west of the Mississippi. Other highlights include the 1909 **Pergola**, a decorative iron shelter reminiscent of a Parisian Metro station, and **Occidental Park**, containing totem poles carved by Chinook artist Duane Pasco.

Klondike Gold Rush National Historical Park (www.nps.gov/klse; 117 S Main St; ☉9am-5pm; ☐International District/Chinatown) is a shockingly good museum eloquently run by the US National Park Service. It's full of exhibits, photos and news clippings from the 1897 Klondike gold rush, when a Seattle-on-steroids acted as a fueling depot for prospectors bound for the Yukon in Canada. It would cost $10 anywhere else; in Seattle it's free!

Seattle Art Museum   MUSEUM
(SAM; www.seattleartmuseum.org; 1300 1st Ave; adult/child $17/11; ☉10am-5pm Tue, Wed, Sat & Sun, to 9pm Thu & Fri; ☐University St) While it can't be compared with the big guns in New York and Chicago, Seattle Art Museum is no slouch and is constantly updating. Over the last decade, it has added more than 100,000 sq ft to its gallery space and acquired about $1 billion worth of new art, including works by Zurbarán and Murillo. The museum is known for its extensive Native American artifacts and work from the local Northwest school, in particular by Mark Tobey (1890-1976). Modern American art is also well represented.

Belltown   NEIGHBORHOOD
Where industry once fumed, glassy condos now rise in the thin walkable strip of Belltown. The neighborhood gained a reputation for trend-setting nightlife in the 1990s and two of its bar-clubs, the Crocodile (p1037) and Shorty's (p1036), can still claim legendary status. Then there are the restaurants – more than 100 of them – and not all are prohibitively expensive. Belltown covers an area of roughly 10 blocks by six blocks, sandwiched in between downtown and the Seattle Center.

Olympic Sculpture Park   PARK, SCULPTURE
(2901 Western Ave; ☉sunrise-sunset; ☐13) **FREE**
Hovering above train tracks, in an unlikely oasis between the water and busy Elliott Ave, is the 8.5-acre, $85-million Olympic Sculpture Park. Worth a visit just for its views of the Olympic Mountains over Elliott Bay, the park has begun to grow into its long-range plan by filling a former brownfield industrial site with vibrant art and plant life.

◉ **International District**

For 'international' read Asian. East of Pioneer Sq, the shops and businesses are primarily Chinese, Vietnamese and Filipino.

Wing Luke Asian Museum   MUSEUM
(www.wingluke.org; 719 S King St; adult/child $12.95/8.95; ☉10am-5pm Tue-Sun; ☐Chinatown/International District E) Relocated and refurbished in 2008, the Wing Luke examines Asian and Pacific American culture, focusing on prickly issues such as Chinese settlement in the 1880s and Japanese internment camps in WWII. There are also art exhibits and a preserved immigrant apartment. Guided tours are available and recommended.

Seattle

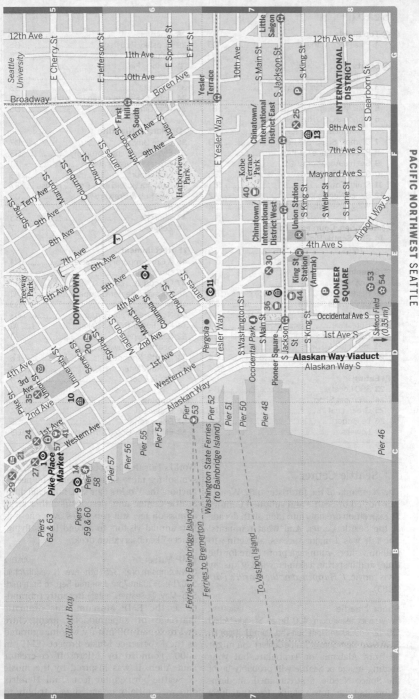

PACIFIC NORTHWEST SEATTLE

Seattle

◉ Seattle Center

The remnants of the futuristic 1962 World's Fair hosted by Seattle and subtitled Century 21 Exposition are now into their sixth decade at the Seattle Center. And what remnants! The fair was a major success, attracting 10 million visitors, running a profit (rare for the time) and inspiring a skin-crawlingly kitschy Elvis movie, *It Happened at the World's Fair* (1963).

Space Needle   LANDMARK
(www.spaceneedle.com; 400 Broad St; adult/child $19/12; ☉9:30am-11pm Sun-Thu, 9am-11:30pm Fri & Sat, 9am-11pm Sun; Ⓜ Seattle Center) You might be from Alabama or Timbuktu, but your abiding image of Seattle will probably be of the Space Needle, a streamlined, modern-before-its-time tower built for the 1962

World's Fair that has been the city's defining symbol for more than 50 years. The needle anchors the World's Fair site, now called the Seattle Center, and, despite its rather steep admission fee, still persuades over one million annual visitors to ascend to its flying-saucer-like observation deck.

EMP Museum   MUSEUM
(www.empsfm.org; 325 5th Ave N; adult/child $20/14; ☉10am-7pm Jun–mid-Sep, to 5pm mid-Sep–May; Ⓜ Seattle Center) Recently rebranded as the EMP Museum, this dramatic marriage of supermodern architecture and rock-and-roll history was inaugurated as the Experience Music Project (EMP) in 2000. Founded by Microsoft co-creator Paul Allen, it was inspired by the music of Seattle-born guitar icon Jimi Hendrix and was initially intended as a tribute to

Hendrix alone, although the collection has since expanded to include other local musicians.

Chihuly Garden & Glass   MUSEUM
(📞206-753-3527; www.chihulygardenandglass.com; 305 W Harrison St; adult/child $19/12; ⊙11am-7pm Sun-Thu, to 8pm Fri & Sat; Ⓜ Seattle Center) It's not every year that a city of Seattle's size adds a museum of such high quality to its list of urban attractions. Reinforcing the metropolis's position as the Venice of North America, this exquisite expose of the life and work of dynamic local glass sculptor Dale Chihuly requires a sharp intake of breath on first viewing. It opened in May 2012, and has quickly become a top city icon to rival the Space Needle.

◉ Capitol Hill

Millionaires mingle with goth musicians in irreverent Capitol Hill, a well-heeled but liberal neighborhood rightly renowned for its fringe theater, alternative music scene, indie coffee bars, and vital gay and lesbian culture. You can take your dog for a herbal bath here, go shopping for ethnic crafts on Broadway, or blend in (or not) with the young punks and the old hippies on the eclectic Pike-Pine Corridor. The junction of Broadway and E John St is the nexus from which to navigate the quarter's various restaurants, brewpubs, boutiques and dingy, but not dirty, dive bars.

◉ Fremont

Fremont pitches young hipsters among old hippies in an unlikely urban alliance, and vies with Capitol Hill as Seattle's most irreverent neighborhood. It's full of junk shops, urban sculpture and a healthy sense of its own ludicrousness.

Public Sculpture   MONUMENT
Public art has never been as provocative as it is in Fremont. Look out for **Waiting for the Interurban** (cnr N 34th St & Fremont Ave N), a cast-aluminum statue of people awaiting a train that never comes: the Interurban linking Seattle and Everett stopped running in the 1930s (it started up again in 2001 but the line no longer passes this way). Check out the human face on the dog; it's Armen Stepanian, once Fremont's honorary mayor, who made the mistake of objecting to the sculpture. Equally eye-catching is the **Fremont Troll** (cnr N 36th St & Troll Ave), a scary-

HIGHER THAN THE SPACE NEEDLE

Everyone makes a rush for the iconic Space Needle, but it's neither the tallest nor the cheapest of Seattle's glittering viewpoints. That honor goes to the sleek, tinted-windowed **Columbia Center** (701 5th Ave; adult/concession $9/6; ⊙8:30am-4:30pm Mon-Fri), built in 1985. At 932ft high it's the loftiest building in the Pacific Northwest. From the plush observation deck on the 73rd floor you can look down on ferries, cars, islands, roofs and – ha, ha – the Space Needle!

looking 18ft troll crushing a Volkswagen Beetle in its left hand. The **Fremont Rocket** (cnr Evanston Ave & N 35th St) is a rocket that was found lying around in Belltown in 1993 and that now sticks out of a building – mmm, interesting. Fremont's most controversial art is the **statue of Lenin** (cnr N 36th St & Fremont Pl N) salvaged from Slovakia after it was toppled during the 1989 revolution. Even if you hate the politics, you have to admire the art – and the audacity!

◉ The U District

U-dub, a neighborhood of young, studious out-of-towners, places the beautiful, leafy University of Washington campus next to the shabbier 'Ave,' an eclectic strip of cheap boutiques, dive bars and ethnic restaurants.

University of Washington   UNIVERSITY
(www.washington.edu; 🚌70) Founded in 1861, Seattle's university is almost as old as the city itself and is ranked highly worldwide (the prestigious *Times Higher Education* magazine listed it 24th in the world in 2013). The present-day 700-acre campus that sits at the edge of Lake Union, about 3 miles northeast of downtown, is flecked with stately trees and beautiful architecture, and affords wondrous views of Mt Rainier framed by fountains and foliage.

Burke Museum   MUSEUM
(www.burkemuseum.org; cnr 17th Ave NE & NE 45th St; adult/child $10/7.50; ⊙10am-5pm; 🚌70) Of the University of Washington's two on-site museums, the Burke is the best. The main collection has an impressive stash of fossils

including a 20,000-year-old sabre-toothed cat. Equally compelling is the focus on 17 different Native American cultures.

◉ Ballard

A former seafaring community with a strong Scandinavian heritage, Ballard still feels like a small town engulfed by a bigger city. Traditionally gritty, no-nonsense and uncommercial, it's slowly being condo-ized, but remains a good place to down a microbrew or see a live band.

Hiram M Chittenden Locks GARDENS
(3015 NW 54th St; ⊘ locks 24hr, ladder & gardens 7am-9pm, visitor center 10am-6pm May-Sep; 🖳62) Seattle shimmers like an impressionist painting on sunny days at the Hiram M Chittenden Locks. Here, the fresh waters of Lake Washington and Lake Union that flow through the 8-mile-long Lake Washington Ship Canal drop 22 feet into salt-water Puget Sound. On the southern side of the locks you can view a fish ladder from underwater glass-sided tanks. Flanking Carl English Jr Botanical Gardens on the northern side is a small museum and a visitors center documenting the history of the locks.

DON'T MISS

DISCOVERY PARK

A former military installation that has been transformed into a wild coastal park, **Discovery Park** (www.seattle. gov/parks/environment/discovery.htm; 🖳33) is a relatively recent addition to the city landscape – it wasn't officially inaugurated until 1973 and the American military finally left in 2012. Comprising the largest green space in the city, the park's 534 acres are laced with cliffs, meadows, sand dunes, forest and beaches, all of which provide a welcome breathing space for hemmed-in Seattleites and a vital corridor for wildlife. For a map of the park's trail and road system, stop by the **Discovery Park Environmental Learning Center** (📞206-386-4236; 3801 W Government Way; ⊘8:30am-5pm) near the Government Way entrance. The park is located five miles northwest of downtown Seattle in the neighborhood of Magnolia. To get there, catch bus 33 from 3rd Ave & Union St downtown.

🏃 Activities

Cycling

A cycling favorite, the 16.5-mile **Burke-Gilman Trail** winds from Ballard to Log Boom Park in Kenmore on Seattle's Eastside. There, it connects with the 11-mile **Sammamish River Trail**, which winds past the Chateau Ste Michelle winery in Woodinville before terminating at Redmond's Marymoor Park.

More cyclists pedal the popular loop around **Green Lake**, situated just north of Fremont and 5 miles north of the downtown core. From Belltown, the 2.5-mile **Elliott Bay Trail** runs along the Waterfront to Smith Cove.

Get a copy of the *Seattle Bicycling Guide Map*, published by the City of Seattle's **Transportation Bicycle & Pedestrian Program** (www.cityofseattle.net/transportation/bikemaps. htm) online or at bike shops.

For bicycle rentals and tours, try **Recycled Cycles** (www.recycledcycles.com; 1007 NE Boat St; rentals per 6/24hr $20/40; ⊘10am-8pm Mon-Fri, to 6pm Sat & Sun; 🚲; 🖳66), a friendly U District shop that also rents out chariots and trail-a-bike attachments for kids, or **SBR Seattle Bicycle Rental & Tours** (📞800-349-0343; www.seattlebicyclerentals.com; Pier 58; rental per hr/ day $10/40; ⊘11am-7pm Wed-Mon; 🚇University St), which offers reasonable rates and daily tours (book online).

Water Sports

Seattle is not just on a network of cycling trails. With Venice-like proportions of downtown water, it is also strafed with kayak-friendly marine trails. The **Lakes to Locks Water Trail** links Lake Sammamish with Lake Washington, Lake Union and – via the Hiram M Chittenden Locks – Puget Sound. For launching sites and maps, check the website of the **Washington Water Trails Association** (www.wwta.org).

Northwest Outdoor Center Inc (www. nwoc.com; 2100 Westlake Ave N; kayaks per hr $14-22; 🖳62) on Lake Union rents kayaks, and offers tours and instruction in sea and white-water kayaking.

👉 Tours

Seattle Free Walking Tours WALKING TOUR
(www.seattlefreewalkingtours.org) A nonprofit set up by a couple of world travelers and Seattle residents in 2012. These intimate two-hour tours meet daily at 11am on the corner of Western Ave and Virginia St. If

SEATTLE FOR CHILDREN

Make a beeline for the Seattle Center, preferably on the monorail, where food carts, street entertainers, fountains and green space will make the day fly by. One essential stop is the **Pacific Science Center** (www.pacsci.org; 200 2nd Ave N; adult/child exhibits-only $18/13, with IMAX $22/17; ☺10am-5pm Mon-Fri, to 6pm Sat & Sun; Ⓜ Seattle Center), which entertains and educates with virtual-reality exhibits, laser shows, holograms, an IMAX theater and a planetarium – parents won't be bored either.

Downtown on Pier 59, **Seattle Aquarium** (www.seattleaquarium.org; 1483 Alaskan Way, Pier 59; adult/child $19/12; ☺9:30am-5pm; ⚑; ⓡ University St) is a fun way to learn about the natural world of the Pacific Northwest. Even better is **Woodland Park Zoo** (Ⓙ20 6-684-4800; www.zoo.org; 5500 Phinney Ave N; adult/child Oct-Apr $12.50/8.75, May-Sep $18.75/11.75; ☺9:30am-4pm Oct-Apr, to 6pm May-Sep; ⚑; ⓡ5) in the Green Lake neighborhood, one of Seattle's greatest tourist attractions and consistently rated as one of the top 10 zoos in the country.

you have a rip-roaring time (highly likely), there's a suggested $15 donation.

Seattle by Foot   WALKING TOUR

(Ⓙ206-508-7017; www.seattlebyfoot.com; tours $20-25) This company runs a handful of tours including the practically essential Coffee Crawl, which will ply you liberally with caffeine while explaining the nuances of latte art and dishing the inside story on the rise of Starbucks. It costs $25 including samples. Registration starts at 9.50am from Thursday to Sunday outside Seattle Art Museum.

Savor Seattle   FOOD TOUR

(Ⓙ206-209-5485; www.savorseattletours.com; tours $59.99) These guys lead a handful of gastronomic tours, the standout being the two-hour Booze-n-Bites that runs daily at 4pm from the corner of Western Ave & Virginia St.

✲ Festivals & Events

Seattle International Film Festival   FILM

(SIFF; www.siff.net; tickets $13-30; ☺mid-May) The city's biggest film festival uses a half-dozen cinemas around town but also has its own dedicated cinema in McCaw Hall's Nesholm Family Lecture Hall.

Seafair   WATER

(www.seafair.com; ☺Jul/Aug) Huge crowds attend this festival held on the water, which includes hydroplane races, a torchlight parade, an air show, music and a carnival.

Bumbershoot   MUSIC, LITERATURE

(www.bumbershoot.com; ☺Sep) A major arts and cultural event at Seattle Center on the Labor Day weekend in September, with live music, author readings and lots of unclassifiable fun.

🛏 Sleeping

From mid-November through to the end of March, most downtown hotels offer Seattle Super Saver Packages – generally 50% off rack rates, with a coupon book for savings on dining, shopping and attractions. Make reservations online at www.seattlesuper-saver.com.

★ Moore Hotel   HOTEL $

(Ⓙ206-448-4851; www.moorehotel.com; 1926 2nd Ave; s/d with shared bath $68/80, with private bath $85/97; ☎; ⓡ Westlake) Old-world and allegedly haunted, the Moore nonetheless has a friendly front desk and a prime location. If that doesn't swing you, the price should. There's a cute little cafe on the premises and the divey Nitelite Lounge next door. You can practically hold your breath and walk to Pike Place Market from here.

City Hostel Seattle   HOSTEL $

(Ⓙ206-706-3255; www.hostelseattle.com; 2327 2nd Ave; 6-/4-bed dm $28/32, d $73, all incl breakfast; @☎; ⓡ Rapid Ride D-Line) ✎ Sleep in an art gallery for peanuts – in Belltown, no less. That's the reality in this new 'art hostel', which will make your parent's hostelling days seem positively spartan by comparison. Aside from arty dorms, expect a common room, hot tub, in-house movie theater (with free DVDs) and all-you-can-eat breakfast.

★ Hotel Five   BOUTIQUE HOTEL $$

(Ⓙ206-441-9785; www.hotelfiveseattle.com; 2200 5th Ave; r from $165; Ⓟ✳☎; ⓡ13) This wonderful reincarnation of the old Ramada Inn on Fifth Ave in Belltown mixes retro '70s furniture with sharp color accents to produce something that is dazzlingly modern. And it's functional, too. The ultracomfortable beds could be nominated as a valid cure for insomnia, while the large reception area invites lingering, especially when they lay out the complimentary cupcakes and coffee in the late afternoon.

★ Maxwell Hotel
BOUTIQUE HOTEL $$

(☑206-286-0629; www.themaxwellhotel.com; 300 Roy St; r from $179; P❀@🔊🏊; 🚃 Rapid Ride D-Line) A gorgeous boutique hotel that graces the Lower Queen Anne neighborhood, the Maxwell's huge designer-chic lobby is enough to make anyone dust off their credit card. Look out for periodic offers online.

Ace Hotel
HOTEL $$

(☑206-448-4721; www.acehotel.com; 2423 1st Ave; r with shared/private bath $109/199; P🔊; 🖥13) Emulating (almost) its hip Portland cousin, the Ace sports minimal, futuristic decor (everything's white or stainless steel, even the TV), antique French army blankets, condoms instead of pillow mints and a copy of the *Kama Sutra* instead of the Bible. Parking costs $15.

Belltown Inn
HOTEL $$

(☑206-529-3700; www.belltown-inn.com; 2301 3rd Ave; s/d $159/164; P❀@🔊; 🚃Rapid Ride D-Line) Can it be true? The Belltown is such a bargain and in such a prime location that it's hard to believe it hasn't accidentally floated over from a smaller, infinitely cheaper city. But no: clean functional rooms, handy kitchenettes, roof terrace, free bikes and – vitally important – borrow-and-return umbrellas are all yours for the price of a posh dinner.

Mediterranean Inn
HOTEL $$

(☑206-428-4700; www.mediterranean-inn,com; 425 Queen Anne Ave N; r from $159; P❀@; 🚃Rapid Ride D-Line) There's something about the surprisingly un-Mediterranean Med Inn that just clicks. Maybe it's the handy cusp-of-Belltown location, or the genuinely friendly staff, or the kitchenettes in every room, or the small downstairs gym or the surgical cleanliness. Don't try to define it – just go there and soak it up.

★ Edgewater
HOTEL $$$

(☑206-728-7000; www.edgewaterhotel.com; Pier 67, 2411 Alaskan Way; r 420-750; P❀@🔊; 🖥13) Fame and notoriety has stalked the Edgewater. Perched over the water on a pier, it was once the hotel of choice for every rock band that mattered, including the Beatles, the Rolling Stones and, most infamously,

Led Zeppelin, who took the 'you can fish from the hotel window' advertising jingle a little too seriously and filled their suite with sharks.

Hotel Monaco
BOUTIQUE HOTEL $$$

(☑206-621-1770; www.monaco-seattle.com; 1101 4th Ave; d/ste $339/399; P❀@🔊🏊; 🚃University St) 🐾 Whimsical, with dashes of European elegance, the downtown Hotel Monaco is worthy of all four of its illustrious stars. Bed down amid the stripy wallpaper and heavy drapes.

Inn at the Market
BOUTIQUE HOTEL $$$

(☑206-443-3600; www.innatthemarket.com; 86 Pine St; r with/without water view $370/255; P❀🔊; 🚃Westlake) The only hotel lodging in venerable Pike Place Market, this elegant 70-room boutique hotel has large rooms, many of which enjoy views onto market activity and Puget Sound. Parking costs $20.

✕ Eating

The best budget meals are to be found in Pike Place Market. Take your pick from fresh produce, baked goods, deli items and takeout ethnic foods.

★ Top Pot Hand-Forged Doughnuts
CAFE $

(www.toppotdoughnuts.com; 2124 5th Ave; doughnuts from $1.50; ⏰6am-7pm; 🖥13) Top Pot is to doughnuts what champagne is to wine – a different class. And its cafes – especially this one in an old car showroom with floor-to-ceiling library shelves and art-deco signage – are equally legendary. The coffee's pretty potent, too.

★ Piroshky Piroshky
BAKERY $

(www.piroshkybakery.com; 1908 Pike Pl; snacks $2-7; ⏰8am-6:30pm Oct-Apr, from 7:30am May-Sep; 🚃Westlake) Proof that not all insanely popular Pike Place holes-in-the-wall go global (à la Starbucks), Piroshky is still knocking out its delectable mix of sweet and savory Russian pies and pastries in a space barely big enough to swing a small kitten. Join the melee and order one 'to go.'

★ Salumi
SANDWICHES $

(www.salumicuredmeats.com; 309 3rd Ave S; sandwiches $7-10; ⏰11am-4pm Tue-Fri; 🚃International District/Chinatown) The queue outside Salumi has long been part of the sidewalk furniture. This place has even formed its own community of chatterers, food bloggers, Twitter posters and gourmet-sandwich aficionados who compare notes. The fact that it's owned by the father of celebrity chef Mario Batali probably helps.

★**Pie**   PIES **$**

(☎206-436-8590; www.sweetandsavorypie.com; 3515 Fremont Ave N; pies $5.95; ☺9am-9pm Mon-Thu, to 2am Fri & Sat, 10am-6pm Sun; ☐26) ✦ It's as simple as P-I-E. Bake fresh pies daily on-site, stuff them with homemade fillings (sweet and savory) and serve them in a cool, bold-colored Fremont cafe. The pies are ideal for a snack lunch, or you can double up and get a sweet one for desert, too.

★**Green Leaf**   VIETNAMESE **$**

(☎206-340-1388; www.greenleaftaste.com; 418 8th Ave S; pho $7.95, specials $11.95; ☺11am-10pm; ☐Chinatown/International District E) As narrow as a railway carriage and as crowded as a pub full of Sounders supporters, Green Leaf shoots out rapid-fire dishes from its tiny kitchen to its shiny black tables. People shout about the huge bowls of traditional or vegetarian pho (noodle soup) and a swoon-inducing version of *bahn xeo* – a sort of cross between a pancake and an omelet.

Crumpet Shop   CRUMPETS **$**

(1503 1st Ave; crumpets $3-6; ☺7am-5pm; ☐Westlake) Take a treasured British culinary invention (the crumpet) and give it a distinct American twist (ridiculously lavish toppings) and you've got another reason to have your breakfast or lunch in Pike Place Market.

Macrina   BAKERY **$**

(☎206-448-4032; 2408 1st Ave; pastries $2-3.75; ☺7am-7pm; ☐13) That snaking queue is there for a reason – damned good artisan bread (you can watch through the window as the experts roll out the dough). There are two options and two lines at Macrina. One for the fantastic takeout bakery (possibly the best in Seattle); the other for the sit-down cafe with its so-good-it-could-be-Paris sandwiches, soups and other such snacks. Join the pilgrimage.

Lowells   DINER **$**

(www.eatatlowells.com; 1519 Pike Pl; mains $6-9; ☺7am-6pm; ☐Westlake) Fish and chips is a simple meal often done badly – but not here. Slam down your order for Alaskan cod at the front entry and take it up to the top floor for delicious views over Puget Sound. Lowells also serves corned-beef hash and an excellent clam chowder.

★**Serious Pie**   PIZZA **$$**

(www.tomdouglas.com; 316 Virginia St; pizzas $16-18; ☺11am-11pm; ☐Westlake) It's an audacious move to take the down-to-earth Italian pizza and give it a gourmet spin, but local culinary phenomenon Tom Douglas pulls off the trick with casual aplomb. In the crowded confines of Serious Pie, you can enjoy beautifully blistered pizza bases topped by such unconventional ingredients as clams, kale, potato, apples, pistachio and more. It's seriously good!

★**Wild Ginger**   ASIAN **$$**

(www.wildginger.net; 1401 3rd Ave; mains $15-28; ☺11am-3pm & 5-11pm Mon-Sat, 4-9pm Sun; ☐University St) Food from around the Pacific Rim – via China, Indonesia, Malaysia, Vietnam and Seattle, of course – is the wide-ranging theme at this highly popular downtown fusion restaurant. The signature fragrant duck goes down nicely with a glass of Riesling. The restaurant also provides food for the swanky **Triple Door** (☎206-838-4333; www.thetripledoor.net; 216 Union St; ☐University St) club downstairs.

★**Toulouse Petit**   CAJUN **$$**

(☎206-432-9069; 601 Queen Anne Ave N; mains $13-17; ☺8am-2am; ☐13) Something of a Seattle phenomenon, Toulouse Petit is hailed for its generous happy hours, cheap brunches and rollicking atmosphere – it's perennially (and boisterously) busy. Somewhere underneath all this cacophony is the specialty food, which pays more than a passing nod to the 'Big Easy' (aka New Orleans).

360 Local   NORTHWEST **$$**

(☎206-441-9360; www.local360.org; cnr 1st Ave & Bell St; mains $16-26; ☺11am-late Mon-Fri, 8am-late Sat & Sun; ☐13) ✦ Snaring 90% of its ingredients from within a 360-mile radius, this new restaurant follows it ambitious 'locavore' manifesto pretty rigidly. The farms where your meat was reared are displayed on the daily blackboard menu and the restaurant's wood-finish interior looks like a rustic barn. With such a fertile hinterland to draw upon the food is pretty special; try the rabbit, the oysters or the chickpea cake.

Le Pichet   FRENCH **$$**

(www.lepichetseattle.com; 1933 1st Ave; lunch/mains $9/18; ☺8am-midnight; ☐Westlake) Say *bienvenue* to Le Pichet just up from Pike Place Market, a very French bistro with pâtés, cheeses, wine, chocolate and a refined Parisian feel. An economical way to impress a date.

★ **Cascina Spinasse**   ITALIAN $$$
(☑ 206-251-7673; www.spinasse.com; 1531 14th Ave; 2-course meal $40; ◷ 5-10pm Sun-Thu, to 11pm Fri & Sat; ▣ 11) Behind the rather fussy lace curtains hides what is possibly the finest new restaurant in Seattle. Spinasse special-izes in cuisine of the Piedmont region of northern Italy. This means delicately pre-pared ravioli, buttery risottos (enhanced with stinging nettles, no less), rabbit meat-balls and roasted artichokes.

★ **Sitka & Spruce**   NORTHWEST $$$
(☑ 206-324-0662; www.sitkaandspruce.com; 1531 Melrose Ave E; small plates $8-24; ◷ 11:30am-2pm & 5:30-10pm; ▣ 10) Now in a new location in the Capitol Hill 'hood, this small-plates fine-diner has won acclaim for its casual vibe, constantly changing menu, good wine selec-tion and involved chef-owner (he'll be the guy who brings bread to your table). All the ingredients are obtained from local produc-ers, and the idea is to assemble a meal out of a bunch of different taster-sized dishes.

Tavolàta   ITALIAN $$$
(☑ 206-838-8008; 2323 2nd Ave; meals $40-75; ◷ 5-11pm; ▣ 13) Eating around a large com-munal table was once something you did re-luctantly in youth hostels, but lately it's been deemed trendy, which is why it's become a feature in cool restaurants in Belltown such as Tavolàta, owned by top Seattle chef Ethan Stowell. Decor is industrial Belltown, but the menu is more Italian trattoria (homemade pasta) with some Northwestern inflections (nettles).

🍷 **Drinking & Nightlife**

Starbucks is the tip of the iceberg when it comes to coffee culture in Seattle; the city has spawned plenty of smaller indie chains, many with their own roasting rooms. Look out for Uptown Espresso, Caffe Ladro and Espresso Vivace.

You'll find cocktail bars, dance clubs and live music on Capitol Hill. The main drag in Ballard has brick taverns both old and new, filled with the hard-drinking older set in daylight hours and indie rockers at night. Belltown has gone from grungy to shabby chic, and has the advantage of many drink-ing holes neatly lined up in rows.

Zeitgeist   CAFE
(www.zeitgeistcoffee.com; 171 S Jackson St; ◷ 6am-7pm Mon-Fri, from 8am Sat & Sun; 🔊; ▣ Pioneer Sq) Listen. The comforting buzz of conver-sation! People actually talk in the attractive exposed-brick confines of Zeitgeist – they're not all glued to their laptops. Bolstered by tongue-loosening doses of caffeine, you can join them discussing the beautiful smooth-ness of your *doppio macchiato* or the sweet intensity of your to-die-for almond croissant.

★ **Pike Pub & Brewery**   BREWERY
(www.pikebrewing.com; 1415 1st Ave; ◷ 11am-mid-night; ▣ University St) Leading the way in the microbrewery revolution, this brewpub was an early starter, opening in 1989 underneath Pike Place Market. Today it continues to serve sophisticated pub food and hop-heavy beers in a neoindustrial multilevel space that's a beer nerd's heaven. The brewery runs free tours daily at 2pm.

★ **Espresso Vivace at Brix**   CAFE
(www.espressovivace.com; 532 Broadway E; ◷ 6am-11pm; ▣ 60) Loved in equal measure for its no-nonsense walk-up stand on Broadway and this newer cafe (a large retro place with a beautiful streamline moderne counter), Vivace is known to have produced some of the Picassos of latte art. But it doesn't just offer pretty toppings. Many of Seattle's coffee experts rate the espresso shots as the best in the city.

★ **Fremont Brewing**   BREWERY
(www.fremontbrewing.com; 3409 Woodland Park Ave N; ◷ 11am-7pm Mon-Wed, to 8pm Thu-Sat, to 6pm Sun; ▣ 26) No conventional bar (this, after all, is Fremont!), this 2008-inaugurated brewery has what is called an 'Urban Beer Garden'; ie you sit at a couple of communal tables in the brewery and enjoy samples of what are quickly being hailed as some of the finest microbrews in the city.

★ **Shorty's**   BAR
(www.shortydog.com; 2222 2nd Ave; ◷ noon-2am; ▣ 13) Shorty's is all about beer, pinball and music, which is punk and metal mostly. A remnant of Belltown's grungier days that refuses to become an anachronism, it keeps the lights low (to cover the grime?) and the music loud. Pinball machines are built into every table and very basic snacks (hot dogs, nachos) soak up the beer.

★ **Noble Fir**   BAR
(☑ 206-420-7425; www.thenoblefir.com; 5316 Bal-lard Ave NW; ◷ 4-11pm Mon-Wed, to 1am Thu-Sat, noon-11pm Sun; ▣ 17) Possibly the first bar devoted to the theme of wilderness hiking, the Noble Fir is a bright, shiny, new Ballard

spot with an epic beer list that might just make you want to abandon all your plans for outdoor adventure. Should your resolve begin to flag, head to the back corner, where there's a library of activity guides and maps that will reinspire you.

Elysian Brewing Company BREWERY
(www.elysianbrewing.com; 1221 E Pike St; ☉11:30am-2am; ☐Pike-Pine) The Elysian's huge windows are great for people-watching – or being watched. This is one of Seattle's best brewpubs, and is loved in particular for its spicy pumpkin beers. The same folks also run the Tangletown Pub near Green Lake.

Panama Hotel Tea & Coffee House CAFE
(607 S Main St; ☉8am-7pm Mon-Sat, from 9am Sun; ☐Chinatown/International District W) The Panama, a historic 1910 building containing the only remaining Japanese bathhouse in the US, doubles as a memorial to the neighborhood's Japanese residents forced into internment camps during WWII. The beautifully relaxed cafe has a wide selection of teas and is one of the few places in Seattle to sell Lavazza Italian coffee.

Caffè Umbria CAFE
(www.caffeumbria.com; 320 Occidental Ave S; ☉6am-6pm Mon-Fri, from 7am Sat, 8am-5pm Sun; ☐Pioneer Sq) Umbria has a European flavor with its 8oz cappuccinos, chatty clientele, pretty Italianate tiles and baguettes so fresh they must have been teleported over from Milan. Ideal for Italio-philes and Starbucks-phobes.

Blue Moon BAR
(712 NE 45th St; ☉2pm-late; ☐66) A legendary counterculture dive near the university that first opened in 1934 to celebrate the repeal of the prohibition laws, the Blue Moon makes much of its former literary patrons: doyens Dylan Thomas, Allen Ginsberg and Tom Robbins get mentioned a lot.

Re-Bar GAY
(www.rebarseattle.com; 1114 Howell St; ☐70) This storied dance club, where many of Seattle's defining cultural events have happened (such as Nirvana album releases), welcomes gay, straight, bi or undecided revelers to its lively dance floor. It's in the Denny Triangle.

Neighbours GAY
(www.neighboursnightclub.com; 1509 Broadway Ave E; ☐Pike-Pine) Check out the always-packed dance factory for the gay club scene and its attendant glittery straight girls.

☆ Entertainment

Consult the *Stranger, Seattle Weekly* or the daily papers for listings. Tickets for big events are available at **TicketMaster** (www.ticketmaster.com). Tickets can be picked up at branches of Fred Meyer electronics stores. Local addresses are listed on the Ticket-Master website.

Live Music

★Crocodile LIVE MUSIC
(www.thecrocodile.com; 2200 2nd Ave; ☐13) Nearly old enough to be called a Seattle institution, the Crocodile is a clamorous 560-capacity music venue that first opened in 1991, just in time to grab the coattails of the grunge explosion. Everyone who's anyone in Seattle's alt music scene has since played here, including a famous occasion in 1992 when Nirvana appeared unannounced on a bill supporting Mudhoney.

Neumo's LIVE MUSIC
(www.neumos.com; 925 E Pike St; ☐Pike-Pine) A punk, hip-hop and alternative-music venue that counts Radiohead and Bill Clinton (not together) among its former guests, Neumo's (formerly known as Moe's) fills the big shoes of its original namesake. Yes, it can get hot, and yes, mid-show it's a long walk to the toilets; but that's rock and roll.

Tractor Tavern LIVE MUSIC
(☏206-789-3599; www.tractortavern.com; 5213 Ballard Ave NW; ☐17) The premier venue for folk and acoustic music, the elegant Tractor Tavern in Ballard also books local songwriters and regional bands such as Richmond Fontaine, plus touring acts like John Doe and Wayne Hancock. It's a gorgeous room, usually with top-quality sound.

Cinema

Northwest Film Forum CINEMA
(www.nwfilmforum.org; 1515 12th Ave; ☐Pike-Pine) A film arts organization whose two-screen cinema offers impeccable programming, from restored classics to cutting-edge independent and international films. It's in Capitol Hill, of course!

Cinerama CINEMA
(www.cinerama.com; 2100 4th Ave; ☐13) Possibly Seattle's most popular theater, Cinerama is one of only three of its type left in the world (with a giant curved three-panel screen). Regular renovations, the latest in 2010, have kept it up to date. It presents a good mix of new releases and 70mm classics.

PACIFIC NORTHWEST SEATTLE

Performing Arts

★ A Contemporary Theatre
THEATRE

(ACT; www.acttheatre.org; 700 Union St; University St) One of the three big companies in the city, ACT fills its $30-million home at Kreielsheimer Place with performances by Seattle's best thespians and occasional big-name actors. Terraced seating surrounds a central stage and the interior has gorgeous architectural embellishments.

Intiman Theater Company
THEATRE

(206-269-1900; www.intiman.org; 201 Mercer St; ticket office noon-5pm Tue-Sun; Seattle Center) In a shocking move, Seattle's Tony Award-winning Intiman Theater abruptly closed in April 2011, a victim of the financial crisis. But city icons aren't allowed to die. The theater raised the $1 million necessary for a heroic reopening in 2012 and is back doing what it does best: magnificent stagings of Shakespeare and Ibsen. Time for another Tony?

Seattle Opera
CLASSICAL MUSIC

(www.seattleopera.org; Seattle Center) Features a program of four or five full-scale operas every season at Seattle Center's McCaw Hall, including Wagner's *Ring* cycle that draws sellout crowds in summer.

On the Boards
THEATRE

(206-217-9888; www.ontheboards.org; 100 W Roy St; 13) *The* place for avant-garde performance art, the nonprofit On the Boards makes its home at the intimate Behnke Center for Contemporary Performance in the Lower Queen Anne neighborhood. It showcases some innovative and occasionally weird dance and music.

Pacific Northwest Ballet
DANCE

(www.pnb.org; Seattle Center) The foremost dance company in the Northwest puts on more than 100 shows a season September through June at Seattle Center's McCaw Hall.

Sport

Seattle Mariners
BASEBALL

(www.mariners.org; tickets $7-60) Established in 1977 but yet to appear in a World Series, the Mariners make their home at Safeco Field.

Seattle Seahawks
FOOTBALL

(www.seahawks.com; tickets $42-95) Runners up to Pittsburgh Steelers in the 2006 Super Bowl, the Seahawks play at CenturyLink Field.

Seattle Sounders
SOCCER

(206-622-3415; www.seattlesounders.net; tickets from $37) Share CenturyLink with the Sea-hawks. The Sounders are the best supported team in Major League Soccer with average gate attendance of 43,000.

🔒 Shopping

The main big-name shopping area is downtown between 3rd and 6th Aves and University and Stewart Sts. Pike Place Market is a maze of arts-and-crafts stalls, galleries and small shops. Pioneer Sq and Capitol Hill have locally owned gift and thrift shops. There are many only-in-Seattle shops that are worth seeking out.

Elliott Bay Book Company
BOOKS

(www.elliottbaybook.com; 1521 10th Ave; 10am-10pm Mon-Fri, to 11pm Sat, 11am-9pm Sun; Pike-Pine) Perish the day when e-books render bookstores obsolete. What will happen to the Saturday-afternoon joy of Elliott Bay books, where 150,000 titles inspire author readings, discussions, reviews and hours of serendipitous browsing?

★ DeLaurenti's
FOOD

(206-622-0141; cnr 1st Ave & Pike Pl; 9am-6pm Mon-Sat, 10am-5pm Sun; University St) DeLaurenti's is a mandatory market stop for the Italian chef or continental food enthusiast. Not only is there a stunning selection of cheese, sausages, ham and pasta, but there's also the largest selection of capers, olive oil and anchovies that you're likely to find this side of Genoa.

★ Bop Street Records
MUSIC

(www.bopstreetrecords.com; 2220 NW Market St; noon-8pm Tue-Wed, to 10pm Thu-Sat, to 5pm Sun; 17) What is probably the most impressive collection of vinyl you're ever likely to see lines the heavily stacked shelves of Bop Street Records, in the north Seattle neighborhood of Ballard. The collection of half-a-million records covers every genre – there's even old-school 78s.

Babeland
ADULT

(www.babeland.com; 707 E Pike St; 11am-10pm Mon-Sat, noon-7pm Sun; Pike-Pine) Remember those pink furry handcuffs and that glass dildo you needed? Well, look no further.

ℹ Information

EMERGENCY & MEDICAL SERVICES
45th St Community Clinic (206-633-3350; 1629 N 45th St) Medical and dental services.

Harborview Medical Center (☎206-731-3000; 325 9th Ave) Full medical care, with emergency room.

Seattle Police (☎206-625-5011)

Washington State Patrol (☎425-649-4370) The local traffic police.

MEDIA

KEXP 90.3 FM Legendary independent music and community station.

Seattle Times (www.seattletimes.com) The state's largest daily paper.

The Stranger (www.thestranger.com) Irreverent weekly edited by Dan Savage of 'Savage Love' fame.

MONEY

Travelex-Thomas Cook Currency Services Airport (☎6am-8pm); Westlake Center (400 Pine St, Level 3; ☎9:30am-6pm Mon-Sat, 11am-5pm Sun) The booth at the main airport terminal is behind the Delta Airlines counter.

American Express (Amex; 600 Stewart St; ☎8:30am-5:30pm Mon-Fri)

POST

Post Office (301 Union St; ☎8:30am-5:30pm Mon-Fri)

TOURIST INFORMATION

Seattle Visitor Center & Concierge Services (☎206-461-5840; www.visitseattle.org; Washington State Convention Center, E Pike St & 7th Ave; ☎9am-5pm)

❶ Getting There & Away

AIR

Seattle-Tacoma International Airport (Sea-Tac; ☎206-787-5388; www.portseattle.org/sea-tac; 17801 International Blvd), 13 miles south of Seattle on I-5, has daily services to Europe, Asia, Mexico and points throughout the USA and Canada, with frequent flights to and from Portland, OR, and Vancouver, BC.

BOAT

Victoria Clipper (www.clippervacations.com) operates several high-speed passenger ferries to Victoria, BC, and to the San Juan Islands. It also organizes package tours that can be booked in advance through the website. Victoria Clipper runs from Seattle to Victoria up to six times daily (round-trip adult/child $149/74.50).

Washington State Ferries (WSF; www.wsdot. wa.gov/ferries) includes maps, prices, schedules, trip planners and weather updates on its website, plus estimated waiting times for popular routes. Fares depend on the route, vehicle size and trip duration, and are collected either for round-trip or one-way travel depending on the departure terminal.

BUS

Various intercity coaches serve Seattle at different drop-off points.

Greyhound (www.greyhound.com; 811 Stewart St; ☎6am-midnight) connects Seattle with cities all over the country, including Chicago ($228 one way, two days, two daily), Spokane ($51, eight hours, three daily), San Francisco ($129, 20 hours, three daily) and Vancouver, BC ($32, four hours, five daily). The company has its own terminal in the Denny Triangle within easy walking distance to downtown.

Fast and efficient **Quick Shuttle** (www. quickcoach.com; ☎) has 5 to 6 daily buses to Vancouver ($43). Pickup is at the Best Western Executive Inn in Taylor Ave N near the Seattle Center. Grab the monorail or walk to downtown. Free on-board wi-fi.

Bellair Airporter Shuttle (www.airporter. com) runs buses to Yakima, Bellingham and Anacortes and stops at King Street station (for Yakima) and the downtown Convention Center (for Bellingham and Anacortes).

TRAIN

Amtrak (www.amtrak.com) serves Seattle's **King Street Station** (303 S Jackson St; ☎6am-10:30pm, ticket counter 6:15am-8pm). Three main routes run through town: the Amtrak Cascades (connecting Vancouver, Seattle, Portland and Eugene); the very scenic Coast Starlight (connecting Seattle, Oakland and Los Angeles) and the Empire Builder (a cross-continental roller coaster to Chicago).

Chicago, IL (from $227, 46 hours, daily)

Oakland, CA ($131, 23 hours, daily)

Portland, OR ($25, three to four hours, five daily)

Vancouver, BC ($30, three to four hours, five daily)

❶ Getting Around

TO/FROM THE AIRPORT

There are a number of options for making the 13-mile trek from the airport to downtown Seattle. The most efficient is via the new light-rail service run by Sound Transit (p1040).

Shuttle Express (☎800-487-7433; www. shuttleexpress.com) has a pickup and drop-off point on the 3rd floor of the airport garage; its charges approximately $18 and is handy if you have a lot of luggage.

Taxis are available at the parking garage on the 3rd floor. The average fare to downtown is $42.

CAR & MOTORCYCLE

Trapped in a narrow corridor between mountains and sea, Seattle is a horrendous traffic bottleneck and its nightmarish jams are famous. I-5 has a high-occupancy vehicle lane for vehicles carrying two or more people. Otherwise, try to work around the elongated 'rush hours.'

PUBLIC TRANSPORTATION

Buses are operated by **Metro Transit** (www. metro.kingcounty.gov), part of the King County Department of Transportation. Fares cost a flat $2.50 (off-peak $2.25).

The **Seattle Street Car** (www.seattlestreet-car.org) runs from the Westlake Center to Lake Union along a 2.6-mile route. There are 11 stops allowing interconnections with numerous bus routes. A second route from Pioneer Square via First Hill to Capitol Hill opens in 2014.

Seattle's Link Light Rail run by **Sound Transit** (www.soundtransit.org), operates between Sea-Tac Airport and downtown (Westlake Center) every 15 minutes between 5am and midnight. The ride takes 36 minutes and costs $3. There are additional stops in Pioneer Sq and the International District.

TAXI

All Seattle taxi cabs operate at the same rate, set by King County; $2.50 at meter drop, then $2.70 per mile.

Orange Cab Co (☑206-444-0409; www. orangecab.net)

Yellow Cab (☑206-622-6500; www.yellowtaxi. net)

Around Seattle

Olympia

Small in size but big in clout, state capital Olympia is a musical, political and outdoor powerhouse. Look no further than the street-side buskers on 4th Ave belting out acoustic grunge, the smartly attired bureaucrats marching across the lawns of the state legislature, or the Gore-Tex-clad outdoor fiends overnighting before sorties into the Olympic Mountains. Progressive Evergreen State College has long lent the place an artsy turn (creator of the *Simpsons,* Matt Groening studied here), while the dive bars and secondhand guitar shops of downtown provided an original pulpit for riot grrrl music and grunge.

◉ Sights & Activities

Washington State Capitol　　　　LANDMARK
(☺8am-4:30pm) FREE Looking like a huge Grecian temple, the Capitol complex, set in a 30-acre park overlooking Capitol Lake, dominates the town. The campus' crowning glory is the magnificent **Legislative Building** (1927) topped by a 287ft dome that is only slightly smaller than its namesake in Washington, DC. Free guided tours are available.

State Capital Museum　　　　MUSEUM
(211 W 21st Ave; admission $2; ☺10am-4pm Tue-Fri, from noon Sat) Preserves the general history of Washington State, from the Nisqually tribe to the present day.

Olympia Farmers Market　　　　MARKET
(700 Capitol Way N; ☺10am-3pm Thu-Sun Apr-Oct, Sat & Sun Nov-Dec) 🍃 At the north end of Capitol Way, this is one of the state's best markets, with fresh local produce, crafts and live music.

🛏 Sleeping & Eating

Phoenix Inn Suites　　　　HOTEL $$
(☑360-570-0555; www.phoenixinn.com; 415 Capitol Way N; r $139-179; ❋ ﹫ ▣) The town's most upmarket accommodations is slick, efficient and well tuned to dealing with demanding state government officials.

Traditions Cafe & World Folk Art AMERICAN $
(www.traditionsfairtrade.com; 300 5th Ave SW; sandwiches $8.25; ☺9am-6pm Mon-Fri, 10am-5pm Sat & Sun; ☑) Your fair-trade hippy enclave of yummy salads, sandwiches (meat, veggie and vegan), a few Mexican and Italian plates for good measure, coffee and a selection of herbal teas. Also pop into the eclectic folk art store attached.

🍷 Drinking & Nightlife

The city's never-static music scene still makes waves on 4th Ave at the retrofitted **4th Avenue Tavern** (210 4th Ave E) or the graffiti-decorated **Le Voyeur** (404 4th Ave E), an anarchistic, vegan-friendly dive bar with a busker invariably guarding the door. Try the most famous locally roasted coffee at **Batdorf & Bronson** (Capitol Way S; ☺6am-7pm Mon-Fri, 7am-6pm Sat & Sun) 🍃.

Fish Tale Brew Pub　　　　BREWERY
(515 Jefferson St) Fish Brewing has a classic selection of organic beers, hard ciders and India Pale Ales making it one of Washington's best-known microbreweries.

Burial Grounds　　　　CAFE
(406 Washington St SE; specialty lattes $3.50; ☺10am-12am Mon-Sat, to 10pm Sun) Order fantastic coffee drinks such as the Zombie Attacker Latte (two shots with nutmeg and almond), which comes with a skeleton head drawn in the foam. The goth decor looks like a horror-movie-obsessed teenager's bedroom.

ⓘ Information

The **State Capitol Visitor Center** (cnr 14th Ave & Capitol Way; ⊙10am-2pm Oct-Apr, till 4pm May-Sep) offers information on the capitol campus, the Olympia area and Washington State.

Olympic Peninsula

Surrounded on three sides by sea and exhibiting many of the characteristics of a full-blown island, the remote Olympic Peninsula is about as 'wild' and 'west' as America gets. What it lacks in cowboys it makes up for in rare, endangered wildlife and dense primeval forest. The peninsula's roadless interior is largely given over to the notoriously wet Olympic National Park, while the margins are the preserve of loggers, Native American reservations and a smattering of small but interesting settlements, most notably Port Townsend. Equally untamed is the western coastline, America's isolated end point, where the tempestuous ocean and misty old-growth Pacific rainforest meet in aqueous harmony.

Olympic National Park

Declared a national monument in 1909 and a national park in 1938, the 1406-sq-mile **Olympic National Park** (www.nps.gov/olym) shelters one of the world's only temperate rainforests and a 57-mile strip of Pacific coastal wilderness that was added in 1953. Opportunities for independent exploration abound, with activities from hiking and fishing to kayaking and skiing.

EASTERN ENTRANCES

The graveled Dosewallips River Rd follows the river from US 101 (turn off approximately 1km north of Dosewallips State Park) for 15 miles to **Dosewallips Ranger Station**, where hiking trails begin; call ⚡360-565-3130 for road conditions. Even hiking smaller portions of the two long-distance paths, including the 14.9 mile Dosewallips River Trail, with views of glaciated **Mt Anderson**, is reason enough to visit the valley. Another eastern entry for hikers is the **Staircase Ranger Station** (⚡360-877-5569; ⊙May-Sep), just inside the national-park boundary, 15 miles from Hoodsport on US 101. Two state parks along the eastern edge of the national park are popular with campers: **Dosewallips State Park** (⚡888-226-7688; tent/RV sites $23/32) and **Lake Cushman State Park**

(⚡888-226-7688; tent/RV sites $22/28). Both have running water, flush toilets and some RV hookups. Reservations are accepted.

NORTHERN ENTRANCES

The park's easiest – and hence most popular – entry point is at **Hurricane Ridge**, 18 miles south of Port Angeles. At the road's end, an interpretive center gives a stupendous view of Mt Olympus (7965ft) and dozens of other peaks. The 5200ft altitude can mean you'll hit inclement weather and the winds here (as the name suggests) can be ferocious. Aside from various summer trekking opportunities, the area maintains one of only two US national-park-based ski runs, operated by the small, family-friendly **Hurricane Ridge Ski & Snowboard Area** (www.hurricaneridge.com; 🛝).

Popular for boating and fishing is **Lake Crescent**, the site of the park's oldest and most reasonably priced **lodge** (⚡360-928-3211; www.olympicnationalparks.com; 416 Lake Crescent Rd; lodge r $153, cottages $162-300; ⊙May-Oct; 🅿❄🛜). Delicious sustainable food is served in the lodge's ecofriendly restaurant. From **Storm King Information Station** (⚡360-928-3380; ⊙May-Sep) on the lake's south shore, a 1-mile hike climbs through old-growth forest to Marymere Falls.

Along the Sol Duc River, the **Sol Duc Hot Springs Resort** (⚡360-327-3583; www.northolympic.com/solduc; 12076 Sol Duc Hot Springs Rd, Port Angeles; RV sites $36, r $172-210; ⊙late Mar-Oct; ❄🈂) 📶 has lodging, dining, massage and, of course, hot-spring pools (adult/child $10/7.50), as well as great day hikes.

WESTERN ENTRANCES

Isolated by distance and home of one of the country's rainiest microclimates, the Pacific

> ## ⓘ WASHINGTON STATE DISCOVER PASS
>
> For parking access to millions of acres of Washington State's recreational lands from State Parks to trail heads, you'll need to buy a Discover Pass (one day/annual $10/30). Passes are available from vending machines at many of the larger parking lots they serve and at state-park headquarters 'when staff is available,' or with a 10% service fee online (www.fishhunt.dfw.wa.gov).

side of the Olympics remains the wildest. Only US 101 offers access to its noted temperate rainforests and untamed coastline. The **Hoh River Rainforest**, at the end of the 19-mile Hoh River Rd, is a Tolkienesque maze of dripping ferns and moss-draped trees. The **Hoh Visitor Center and Campground** (☑ 360-374-6925; campsites $12; ⊙ 9am-6pm Jul & Aug, to 4:30pm Sep-Jun) has information on guided walks and longer backcountry hikes. There are no hookups or showers; first come, first served.

A little to the south lies **Lake Quinault**, a beautiful glacial lake surrounded by forested peaks. It's popular for fishing, boating and swimming, and is punctuated by some of the nation's oldest trees. **Lake Quinault Lodge** (☑ 360-288-2900; www.olympicnational-parks.com; 345 S Shore Rd; r $202-305; ❋ ⌨ ▧), a luxury classic of 1920s 'parkitecture,' has a heated pool and sauna, a crackling fireplace and a memorable dining room. For a cheaper sleep nearby, try the ultrafriendly **Quinault River Inn** (☑ 360-288-2237; www.quinaultriverinn.com; 8 River Dr; r $79-119; ❋ ⌨) in Amanda Park, a favorite with anglers.

A number of short hikes begin just outside the Lake Quinault Lodge, or you can try the longer **Enchanted Valley Trail**, a medium-grade 13-miler that begins from the Graves Creek Ranger station at the end of South Shore Rd and climbs up to a large meadow resplendent with wildflowers and copses of alder trees.

ℹ Information

The park entry fee is per person/vehicle $5/15, valid for one week, payable at park entrances. Many park visitor centers double as United States Forestry Service (USFS) ranger stations, where you can pick up permits for wilderness camping (per group $5, valid up to 14 days, plus $2 per person per night).

Forks Visitor Information Center (1411 S Forks Ave; ⊙ 10am-4pm) Suggested itineraries and seasonal information.

Olympic National Park Visitor Center (3002 Mt Angeles Rd, Port Angeles; ⊙ 9am-5pm) The best overall center is situated at the Hurricane Ridge gateway, a mile off Hwy 101 in Port Angeles.

Wilderness Information Center (3002 Mt Angeles Rd, Port Angeles; ⊙ 7:30am-6pm Sun-Thu, to 8pm Fri & Sat May-Sep, 8am-4:30pm daily Oct-Apr) Directly behind the Olympic National Park Visitor Center; you'll find maps, permits and trail information.

Port Townsend

Historical relics are rare in the Pacific Northwest, which makes time-warped Port Townsend all the more fascinating. Small, nostalgic and culturally vibrant, this showcase of 1890s Victorian architecture is the 'New York of the West that never was,' a one-time boomtown that went bust at the turn of the 20th century, only to be rescued 70 years later by a group of farsighted locals. Port Townsend today is a buoyant blend of inventive eateries, elegant fin de siècle hotels and quirky annual festivals.

◉ Sights

Jefferson County Historical Society Museum   MUSEUM
(210 Madison St; adult/12yr & under $4/1; ⊙ 11am-4pm Mar-Dec) The local historic society runs this well-maintained exhibition area that includes mock-ups of an old courtroom and jail cell, along with the full lowdown on the rise, fall and second coming of this captivating port town.

Fort Worden State Park   PARK
(www.parks.wa.gov/fortworden; 200 Battery Way) This attractive park located within Port Townsend's city limits is the remains of a large fortification system constructed in the 1890s. The extensive grounds and array of historic buildings have been refurbished in recent years into a lodging, nature and historical park. The **Commanding Officer's Quarters** (admission $4; ⊙ 10am-5pm daily Jun-Aug, 1-4pm Sat & Sun Mar-May & Sep-Oct), a 12-bedroom mansion, is open for tours, and part of one of the barracks is now the **Puget Sound Coast Artillery Museum** (admission $2; ⊙ 11am-4pm Tue-Sun), which tells the story of early Pacific coastal fortifications.

Hikes lead along the headland to **Point Wilson Lighthouse Station** and some wonderful windswept beaches.

🛏 Sleeping

Palace Hotel   HISTORIC HOTEL $
(☑ 360-385-0773; www.palacehotelpt.com; 1004 Water St; r $59-109; ❋ ⌨) Built in 1889, this beautiful Victorian building is a former brothel that was once run by the locally notorious Madame Marie, who managed her business from the 2nd-floor corner suite. It's been reincarnated as an attractive

period hotel with antique furnishings and claw-foot baths.

Waterstreet Hotel
HOTEL $

(☑ 360-385-5467; www.waterstreethotelport-townsend.com; 635 Water St; r $60-160; ☺❀☏) Of Port Townsend's old dockside hotels, the easy-on-the-wallet Waterstreet has to be the best bargain in town. A multitude of rooms can accommodate between two and six people. Some have shared bathrooms.

✗ Eating

Waterfront Pizza
PIZZERIA $$

(951 Water St; large pizzas $11-21) This buy-by-the-slice outlet inspires huge local loyalty and will satisfy even the most querulous of Chicago-honed palates. The secret: crisp sourdough crusts, or creative but not over-stacked toppings? Who knows.

★ Sweet Laurette Cafe & Bistro
FRENCH $$

(1029 Lawrence St; mains $12-28; ☺ 8am-5pm Wed & Thu, to 9pm Fri & Sat, to 3pm Sun) This adorable French shabby-chic cafe serves breakfast, lunch & dinner in the bistro, and delicious coffee and pastries between meal times.

❶ Information

To get the lowdown on the city's roller-coaster boom-bust history, call in at the **visitor center** (www.ptchamber.org; 2437 E Sims Way; ☺ 9am-5pm Mon-Fri, to 4pm Sat & Sun).

❶ Getting There & Away

Port Townsend can be reached from Seattle by a ferry-bus connection; from Colman Dock in Seattle take the ferry across to Bainbridge Island. From here, catch bus 90 to Poulsbo and then bus 7 to Port Townsend. **Washington State Ferries** (☑ 206-464-6400; www.wsdot.wa.gov/ferries) goes to and from Coupeville on Whidbey Island (car and driver $10.25/foot passenger $3.10, 35 minutes).

Port Angeles

Despite the name, there's nothing Spanish or particularly angelic about Port Angeles, propped up by the lumber industry and backed by the steep-sided Olympic Mountains. Rather than visiting to see the town per se, people come here to catch a ferry for Victoria, BC, or plot an outdoor excursion into the nearby Olympic National Park. The **visitor center** (www.portangeles.org; 121 E Railroad Ave; ☺ 8am-8pm mid-May–mid-Oct, 10am-4pm mid-Oct–mid-May) is adjacent to the ferry terminal. For information on the national park, the Olympic National Park Visitor Center (p1042) is just outside town.

The **Olympic Discovery Trail** (www.olympicdiscoverytrail.com) 🚴 is a 30-mile off-road hiking and cycling trail between Port Angeles and Sequim, starting at the end of **Ediz Hook**, the sand spit that loops around the bay. Bikes can be rented at **Sound Bikes & Kayaks** (www.soundbikekayaks.com; 120 Front St; bike rental per hr/day $9/30)

Port Angeles' most comfortable accommodations is the **Olympic Lodge** (☑ 360-452-2993; www.olympiclodge.com; 140 Del Guzzi Drive; r from $119; ❀@☏☎), which offers a swimming pool, on-site bistro, so-clean-they-seem-new rooms and complimentary cookies and milk. Backpackers will find their happiness at the new, well run and social **Toadlily House** (☑ 360-797-3797; www.toadlilyhouse.com; 105 E 5th St; per person $25; ☏).

★**Bella Italia** (118 E 1st St; mains $12-20; ☺ from 4pm) has been around a lot longer than Bella, the heroine of the *Twilight* saga, but its mention in the book as the place where Bella and Edward Cullen go for their first date has turned an already popular restaurant into an icon. Try the clam linguine, chicken marsala or smoked duck breast.

The **Coho Vehicle Ferry** (www.cohoferry.com; passenger/car $15.50/55) runs to/from Victoria, BC, and the crossing takes 1½ hours. **Olympic Bus Lines** (www.olympicbuslines.com) runs twice daily to Seattle ($39) from the public transit center at the corner of Oak and Front Sts. **Clallam Transit** (www.clallamtransit.com) buses go to Forks and Sequim, where they link up with other transit buses, enabling you to circumnavigate the whole Olympic Peninsula.

Northwest Peninsula

Several Native American reservations cling to the extreme northwest corner of the continent, and are welcoming to visitors. The small weather-beaten settlement of **Neah Bay** on Hwy 112 is home to the Makah Indian Reservation, whose **Makah Museum** (www.makah.com; 1880 Bayview Ave; admission $5; ☺ 10am-5pm) displays artifacts from one of North America's most significant archaeological finds from the 500-year-old Makah village of Ozette. Several miles beyond the museum, a short boardwalk trail leads to stunning **Cape Flattery**, a 300ft promontory that marks the most northwesterly point in the lower 48 states.

THE TWILIGHT ZONE

A small lumber town on Hwy 101, Forks was little more than a speck on the map when Stephenie Meyer set her now famous *Twilight* vampire novels here in 2003. Once the *Twilight* film franchise began around 2008, Forks apparently saw a 600% rise in tourism, although now that the book and movie series are complete those numbers are falling. Many of the visitors are wide-eyed under 15 year olds who are more than a little surprised to find out what Forks really is: chillingly ordinary (and wet).

Vampire fans can get into fantasy-Forks at a few *Twilight* merchandise shops or on daily **Twilight Tours** (adult/child $39/25; ⊗8am, 11:30am, 3pm & 6pm) that visit most of the places mentioned in Meyer's books.

Other areas to pick up the Twilight trail include film and book locations such as Port Angeles, Ecola State Park, Silver Falls State Park and the werewolf lair of La Push (actually a Quileute Indian Reservation where in real local legend the people were changed into humans from wolves).

Convenient to the Hoh River Rainforest and the Olympic coastline is **Forks**, a one-horse lumber town that's now more famous for its *Twilight* paraphernalia. It's a central town for exploring Olympic National Park. A good accommodation choice is the **Miller Tree Inn** (⏰360-374-6806; www.millertreeinn.com; 654 E Division St; r $115-230; 🅿️🐾).

Northwest Washington

Wedged between Seattle, the Cascades and Canada, northwest Washington draws influences from three sides. Its urban hub is collegiate Bellingham, while its outdoor highlight is the pastoral San Juan Islands, an extensive archipelago that glimmers like a sepia-toned snapshot from another era. Anacortes is the main hub for ferries to the San Juan Islands and Victoria, BC.

Whidbey Island

While not as detached (there's a bridge connecting it to adjacent Fidalgo Island at its northernmost point) or nonconformist as the San Juans, life is almost as slow, quiet and pastoral on Whidbey Island. Having six state parks is a bonus, along with a plethora of B&Bs, two historic fishing villages (Langley and Coupeville), famously good clams and a thriving artist's community.

Deception Pass State Park (⏰360-675-2417; 41229 N State Hwy 20) straddles the eponymous steep-sided water chasm that flows between Whidbey and Fidalgo Islands, and incorporates lakes, islands, campsites and 27 miles of hiking trails.

Ebey's Landing National Historical Reserve (www.nps.gov/ebla; ⊗8am-5pm mid-Oct–Mar, 6:30am-10pm Apr–mid-Oct) **FREE** comprises 17,400 acres encompassing working farms, sheltered beaches, two state parks and the town of **Coupeville**. This small settlement is one of Washington's oldest towns and has an attractive seafront, antique stores and a number of old inns, including the **Coupville Inn** (⏰800-247-6162; www.thecoupevilleinn.com; 200 Coveland St; r with/without balcony incl breakfast $150/110; ❄️📶), which bills itself as a French-style motel (if that's not an oxymoron), with fancy furnishings and a substantial breakfast. For the famous fresh local clams, head to **Christopher's** (⏰360-678-5480; www.christophersonwhidbey.com; 103 NW Coveland St; mains $15-23; ⊗11:30am-2pm Mon-Fri, 12-2:30pm Sat & Sun, nightly from 5pm).

Washington State Ferries (WSF; www.wsdot.wa.gov/ferries) link Clinton to Mukilteo (car and driver $8, foot passenger free, 20 minutes, every 30 minutes) and Coupeville to Port Townsend (car and driver $10.25, foot passenger $3.10, 35 minutes, every 45 minutes). Free **Island Transit buses** (www.islandtransit.org) 🚲 run the length of Whidbey every hour daily, except Sundays, from the Clinton ferry dock.

Bellingham

Welcome to a green, liberal and famously livable settlement that has taken the libertine, nothing-is-too-weird ethos of Oregon's 'City of Roses' and given it a peculiarly Washingtonian twist. Mild in both manners and weather, the 'city of subdued excitement,' as a local mayor once dubbed it, is an unlikely alliance of espresso-supping students, venerable retirees, all-weather triathletes and placard-waving peaceniks. Publications such as *Out-*

side Magazine have consistently lauded it for its abundant outdoor opportunities.

🏃 Activities

Bellingham offers outdoor activities by the truckload. **Whatcom Falls Park** is a natural wild region that bisects Bellingham's eastern suburbs. The change in elevation is marked by four sets of waterfalls, including **Whirlpool Falls**, a popular summer swimming hole. The substantial intra-urban trails extend south as far as Larabee State Park, with a popular 2.5-mile section tracking Bellingham's postindustrial waterfront. **Fairhaven Bike & Mountain Sports** (www.fairhavenbike.com; 1103 11th St) rents bikes from $40 a day and has all the info (and maps) on local routes.

Victoria/San Juan Cruises (www.whales.com; 355 Harris Ave) has whale-watching trips to the San Juan Islands. Boats leave from the Bellingham Cruise Terminal in Fairhaven.

🛏 Sleeping

Guesthouse Inn MOTEL $
(☑360-671-9600; www.bellinghamvaluinn.com; 805 Lakeway Dr; r from $95; ❀ ⚙) The clean, personable Guesthouse Inn is just off I-5 and an easy 15-minute walk from downtown Bellingham. The Vancouver–Seattle Bellair Airporter Shuttle (p1039) stops here, making it an ideal base for overnighters who want to explore the Bellingham area.

★ **Hotel Bellwether** BOUTIQUE HOTEL $$$
(☑360-392-3100; www.hotelbellwether.com; 1 Bellwether Way; r $165-284, lighthouse from $398; ❀ ⚙ 🐕) Bellingham's finest and most charismatic hotel is positioned on the waterfront and offers views of the whale-like hump of Lummi Island. Its crowning glory is the celebrated 900-sq-ft lighthouse condominium, a converted three-story lighthouse with a wonderful private lookout.

🍴 Eating

Old Town Cafe CAFE $
(316 W Holly St; mains $6-9; ⊙6.30am-3pm) This is a classic bohemian breakfast haunt where you can get to know the locals over fresh pastries, espresso and an excellent huevos rancheros. Wandering musicians sometimes drop by to enhance the happy-go-lucky atmosphere.

★ **Pepper Sisters** MODERN AMERICAN $$
(www.peppersisters.com; 1055 N State St; mains $9-16; ⊙from 5pm Tue-Sun; 🐾) People travel from far and wide to visit this cult restaurant with

its bright turquoise booths. Try the cilantro-and-pesto quesadillas, blue-corn *rellenos* (stuffed peppers) and potato-garlic burritos.

ℹ Information

The best downtown tourist information can be procured at the **Visitor Info Station** (www.downtownbellingham.com; 1304 Cornwall St; ⊙9am-6pm).

ℹ Getting There & Away

Alaska Marine Highway (AMHS; www.dot.state.ak.us/amhs; 355 Harris Ave) ferries go to Juneau (60 hours) and other southeast Alaskan ports (from $326 without car). The Bellair Airporter Shuttle (p1039) runs to Sea-Tac Airport ($34), with connections en route to Anacortes and Whidbey Island.

San Juan Islands

Take the ferry west out of Anacortes and you'll feel like you've dropped off the edge of the continent. A thousand metaphoric miles from the urban inquietude of Puget Sound, the nebulous San Juan archipelago conjures up Proustian flashbacks from another era and often feels about as American as – er – Canada (which surrounds it on two sides).

There are 172 landfalls in this expansive archipelago but unless you're rich enough to charter your own yacht or seaplane, you'll be restricted to seeing the big four – San Juan, Orcas, Shaw and Lopez Islands – all served daily by Washington State Ferries. Communally, the islands are famous for their tranquility, whale-watching opportunities, sea kayaking and seditious nonconformity.

A great way to explore the San Juans is by sea kayak or bicycle. Expect a guided half-day trip to cost from $45 to $65. Cycling-wise, Lopez is flat and pastoral and San Juan is worthy of an easy day loop, while Orcas offers the challenge of undulating terrain and a steep 5-mile ride to the top of Mt Constitution.

ℹ Getting There & Around

Airlines serving the San Juan Islands include **San Juan Airlines** (www.sanjuanairlines.com) and **Kenmore Air** (www.kenmoreair.com).

Washington State Ferries (WSF; www.wsdot.wa.gov/ferries) leave Anacortes for the San Juans; some continue to Sidney, BC, near Victoria. Ferries run to Lopez Island (45 minutes), Orcas Landing (60 minutes) and Friday Harbor on San Juan Island (75 minutes). Fares vary by season; the cost of the entire round-trip is collected on westbound journeys only (except those returning from Sidney, BC). To visit all the islands, it's cheapest to go to Friday Harbor first and work your way back through the other islands.

Shuttle buses ply Orcas and San Juan Island in the summer months.

San Juan Island

San Juan Island is the archipelago's unofficial capital, a harmonious mix of low forested hills and small rural farms that resonate with a dramatic and unusual 19th-century history. The only real settlement is Friday Harbor, where the **chamber of commerce** (www.sanjuanisland.org; 135 Spring St; ⏰10am-5pm Mon-Fri, to 4pm Sat & Sun), home to the visitor center, sits inside a small mall off the main street.

◉ Sights & Activities

San Juan Island
National Historical Park   HISTORIC SITE
(www.nps.gov/sajh; ⏰8:30am-4pm, visitor center 8:30am-4:30pm Thu-Sun, daily Jun-Sep) ✔FREE San Juan Island hides one of the 19th-century's oddest political confrontations, the so-called 'Pig War' between the USA and Britain. This curious 19th-century cold war standoff is showcased in two historical parks on either end of the island that once housed opposing American and English military encampments. On the island's southern flank, the **American Camp** hosts the small **visitor center**, the remnants of a fort, desolate beaches and a series of interpretive trails. At the opposite end of the island, **English Camp**, 9 miles northwest of Friday Harbor, contains the remains of the 1860s-era British military facilities.

Lime Kiln Point State Park   PARK
(⏰8am-5pm mid-Oct–Mar, 6:30am-10pm Apr–mid-Oct) ✔ Clinging to San Juan Island's rocky west coast, this beautiful park overlooks the deep Haro Strait and is, reputedly, one of the best places in the world to view whales from the shoreline.

🛏 Sleeping & Eating

There are hotels, B&Bs and resorts scattered around the island, but Friday Harbor has the highest concentration.

Wayfarer's Rest   HOSTEL $
(☏360-378-6428; 35 Malcolm St; dm $35, r $65-80; 🗐) The island's only backpacker hostel is a short hike from the ferry terminal. Budget travelers will love its comfortable dorms and cheap private rooms, but beware – it gets busy.

Roche Harbor Resort   RESORT $$
(☏800-451-8910; www.rocheharbor.com; Roche Harbor; r with shared bath $149, 1- to 3-bedroom condos $275-450, 2-bedroom townhouses $499; ❄🗐≋) Located on the site of the former lime kiln and estate of limestone king John McMillin, this seaside 'village' is a great getaway. The centerpiece is the old Hotel de Haro, where the pokey rooms are enlivened by the fact that John Wayne once brushed his teeth here.

Juniper Lane Guest House   INN $$
(☏360-378-7761; www.juniperlaneguesthouse.com; 1312 Beaverton Valley Rd; r $85-135; 🗐) ✔ The handful of wood-paneled rooms here are decorated with a colorful and eclectic assortment of refurbished or recycled art and furnishings. The result is a sublimely cozy and livable hybrid of an upscale backpackers and an inn.

Market Chef   DELI $
(225 A St; ⏰10am-6pm) ✔ Several hundred locals can't be wrong, can they? The 'Chef's' specialty is deli sandwiches, and very original ones at that. Join the queue and watch staff prepare the goods with fresh, local ingredients.

Orcas Island

Precipitous, unspoiled and ruggedly beautiful, Orcas Island is the San Juans' emerald icon, excellent for hiking and, more recently, gourmet food. The ferry terminal is at Orcas Landing, 8 miles south of the main village, Eastsound.

On the island's eastern lobe is **Moran State Park** (⏰6:30am-dusk Apr-Sep, from 8am Oct-Mar), dominated by Mt Constitution (2409ft), with 40 miles of trails and an amazing 360-degree mountaintop view.

Kayaking in the calm island waters is a real joy here. **Shearwater** (www.shearwaterkayaks.com; 138 North Beach Rd, Eastsound) has the equipment and know-how. Three-hour guided trips start at $75.

🛏 Sleeping

Doe Bay Village Resort
& Retreat   HOSTEL, RESORT $
(☏360-376-2291; www.doebay.com; dm $55, cabin d from $90, yurts from $120; 🗐) ✔ Doe Bay has the atmosphere of an artists' com-

mune cum hippie retreat. Accommodations include sea-view campsites, a small hostel with dormitory and private rooms, and various cabins and yurts, most with views of the water.

Golden Tree Hostel   HOSTEL $
(☑360-317-8693; www.goldentreehostel.com; 1159 North Beach Rd, Eastsound; dm/d with shared bath $38/88; @ 🛜) An 1890s-era heritage mansion with a hip remodel, and a hot tub and sauna out back. Immaculate six-bed single-sex dorms and bright private rooms.

Outlook Inn   HOTEL $
(☑360-376-2200; www.outlookinn.com; 171 Main St, Eastsound; r with shared/private bath from $79/119; 🛜) The Outlook Inn (1888) is an island institution that has kept up with the times by expanding into a majestic white (but still quite small) bayside complex. Also on-site is the fancy New Leaf Cafe.

✖ Eating & Drinking

★ **Mijita's**   MEXICAN $$
(310 A St, Eastsound; mains $13-22; ⊙4-9pm Wed-Sun) Ooh and aah over the Mexican native chef's family recipes, such as slow-braised short ribs with blackberry mole or the vegetarian quinoa cakes with mushrooms, chevre, almonds and *pipian* (Mexican piquant sauce).

Island Hoppin' Brewery   BREWERY
(www.islandhoppinbrewery.com; 33 Hope Lane, Eastsound; ⊙4-9pm Tue-Sun) This is *the* place to go to enjoy six changeable brews on tap while making friends with those islanders who enjoy beer. There's often live music on weekends.

Lopez Island

If you're going to Lopez – or 'Slow-pez,' as locals prefer to call it – take a bike. With its undulating terrain and salutation-offering locals (who are famous for their three-fingered 'Lopezian wave'), this is the ideal cycling isle. A leisurely pastoral spin can be tackled in a day, with good overnight digs available next to the marina in the **Lopez Islander Resort** (☑800-736-3434; www.lopezfun.com; Fisherman Bay Rd; r from $139; 🛜▨), which has a restaurant, gym and pool and offers free parking in Anacortes (another incentive to dump the car). If you arrive cycleless, call up **Village Cycles** (☑360-468-4013; www.villagecycles.net; 9 Old Post Rd; rentals per hour/day from $7/30;

⊙10am-4pm Wed-Sun), which can deliver a bicycle to the ferry terminal for you.

North Cascades

Geologically different from their southern counterparts, the North Cascade Mountains are peppered with sharp, jagged peaks, copious glaciers and a preponderance of complex metamorphic rock. Thanks to their virtual impregnability, the North Cascades were an unsolved mystery to humans until relatively recently. The first road was built across the region in 1972 and, even today, it remains one of the Northwest's most isolated outposts.

Mt Baker

Rising like a ghostly sentinel above the sparkling waters of upper Puget Sound, Mt Baker has been mesmerizing visitors to the Northwest for centuries. A dormant volcano that last belched smoke in the 1850s, this haunting 10,781ft peak shelters 12 glaciers, and in 1999 registered a record-breaking 95ft of snow in one season.

Well-paved Hwy 542, known as the Mt Baker Scenic Byway, climbs 5100ft to **Artist Point**, 56 miles from Bellingham. Near here you'll find the **Heather Meadows Visitor Center** (Mile 56 Mt Baker Hwy; ⊙8am-4:30pm May-Sep) and a plethora of varied hikes including the 7.5-mile Chain Lakes Loop that leads you around a half-dozen lakes surrounded by huckleberry meadows.

Receiving more annual snow than any ski area in North America, the **Mt Baker Ski Area** (www.mtbakerskiarea.com) has 38 runs, eight lifts and a vertical rise of 1500ft. The resort has gained something of a cult status among snowboarders, who have been coming here for the Legendary Baker Banked Slalom every January since 1985.

On the 100 or so days a year when Baker breaks through the clouds, the views from the deck at the **Inn at Mt Baker** (☑360-599-1359; www.theinnatmtbaker.com; 8174 Mt Baker Hwy; r $155-165; 🛜), seven miles east of Maple Falls, are stunning. On your way up the mountain, stop for a bite at authentic honky-tonk bar and restaurant **Graham's** (9989 Mt Baker Hwy; mains $4-14; ⊙dinner Mon-Sun, breakfast & lunch Sat & Sun; hours vary) and grab trail munchies at **Wake & Bakery** (6903 Forest St, Glacier; munchies from $4; ⊙7:30am-5pm), both in the town of Glacier.

Leavenworth

Blink hard and rub your eyes. This isn't some strange Germanic hallucination. This is Leavenworth, a former lumber town that underwent a Bavarian makeover back in the 1960s after the rerouting of the cross-continental railway threatened to put it permanently out of business. Swapping wood for tourists, Leavenworth today has successfully reinvented itself as a traditional Romantische Strasse village, right down to the beer, sausages and the lederhosen-loving locals (25% of whom are German). The classic *Sound of Music* mountain setting helps, as does the fact that Leavenworth serves as the main activity center for sorties into the nearby Alpine Lakes Wilderness.

The **Leavenworth Ranger Station** (600 Sherbourne St; ⏰7:30am-4:30pm daily mid-Jun–mid-Oct, from 7:45am Mon-Fri mid-Oct–mid-Jun) can advise on the local outdoor activities. Highlights include the best climbing in the state at **Castle Rock** in Tumwater Canyon, about 3 miles northwest of town off US 2.

The Devil's Gulch is a popular off-road mountain bike trail (25 miles, four to six hours). Local outfitters **Der Sportsmann** (☑509-548-5623; www.dersportsmann.com; 837 Front St; One-day bike/cross-country ski rentals from $25/14; ⏰9am-6pm) rents mountain bikes from $25 a day.

🛏 Sleeping & Eating

Hotel Pension Anna   HOTEL **$$**
(☑509-548-6273; www.pensionanna.com; 926 Commercial St; r incl breakfast $155-250, chapel ste $240-360) The most authentic Bavarian hotel in town; each room is decorated in imported Austrian decor and the European-inspired breakfasts may induce joyful yodels. The adjacent St Joseph's chapel (which the owners rescued and moved here in 1992) is perfect for families.

Enzian Inn   HOTEL **$$**
(☑509-548-5269; www.enzianinn.com; 590 Hwy 2; d $110-205, ste $215-375; 📶🏊) Taking the German theme up a notch, the Enzian goes way beyond the call of duty with an 18-hole putting green, a racquetball court, a sunny breakfast room and a lederhosen-clad owner who entertains guests with an early morning blast on the alphorn.

★München Haus   GERMAN **$**
(www.munchenhaus.com; 709 Front St; snacks from $6; ⏰11am-11pm May-Oct, closed Mon-Fri Nov-Apr;

☑) An alfresco beer garden that serves the best charbroiled Bavarian sausages this side of Bavaria.

Lake Chelan

Long, slender Lake Chelan is central Washington's water playground. **Lake Chelan State Park** (☑509-687-3710; S Lakeshore Rd; tent/RV sites $23/32) has 144 campsites; a number of lakeshore campgrounds are accessible only by boat. If you'd rather sleep in a real bed, try the great-value **Midtowner Motel** (☑509-682-4051; www.midtowner.com; 721 E Woodin Ave; r $65-120; 📶@🛜🏊) in town. The town of **Chelan**, at the lake's southeastern tip, is the primary base for accommodations and services, and has a **USFS ranger station** (428 Woodin Ave). Several wineries have also opened in the area and many have excellent restaurants. Try **Tsillan Cellars** (www.tsillancellars.com; 3875 Hwy 97A; ⏰noon-5pm Sun-Thu, to 6pm Fri & Sat).

Link Transit (www.linktransit.com) buses connect Chelan with Wenatchee and Leavenworth ($1).

Beautiful **Stehekin**, on the northern tip of Lake Chelan, is accessible only by **boat** (www.ladyofthelake.com; round-trip from Chelan $39), **seaplane** (www.chelanairways.com; round-trip from Chelan $159) or a long hike across Cascade Pass, 28 miles from the lake. You'll find lots of information about hiking, campgrounds and cabin rentals at www.stehekin.com. Most facilities are open from mid-June to mid-September.

Methow Valley

The Methow's combination of powdery winter snow and abundant summer sunshine has transformed the valley into one of Washington's primary recreation areas. You can bike, hike and fish in summer, and cross-country ski on the second-biggest snow trail network in the US in winter.

The 200km of trails are maintained by the nonprofit organization **Methow Valley Sport Trails Association** (MVSTA; www.mvsta. com; 209 Castle Ave, Winthrop) 🎿, which, in the winter, provides the most comprehensive network of hut-to-hut (and hotel-to-hotel) skiing in North America. An extra blessing is that few people seem to know about it. For classic accommodations and easy access to the skiing, hiking and cycling trails, decamp at the exquisite **Sun Mountain Lodge** (☑509-996-2211; www.sunmountainlodge.com;

Box 1000, Winthrop; r $175-375, cabins $150-750; ⊙closed 21 Oct-7 Dec; ❈ 🛜 ☒), 10 miles west of the town of Winthrop. While the rooms and facilities are cozy cabin-style (including a lot of taxidermy), it's the views from up here and the endless choice of hiking and cross-country skiing trails surrounding the resort that make it so special.

North Cascades National Park

Even the names of the lightly trodden and dramatic mountains in **North Cascades National Park** (www.nps.gov/noca) sound wild and untamed: Desolation Peak, Jagged Ridge, Mt Despair and Mt Terror. Not surprisingly, the region offers some of the best backcountry adventures outside of Alaska.

The **North Cascades Visitor Center** (502 Newhalem St; ⊙ 9am-4:30pm mid-Apr–Oct, closed Mon-Fri Nov-Mar) 🖉, in the small settlement of Newhalem on Hwy 20, is the best orientation point for visitors and is staffed by expert rangers who can enlighten you on the park's highlights.

Built in the 1930s for loggers working in the valley that was soon to be flooded by Ross Dam, the floating cabins at the **Ross Lake Resort** (✆ 206-386-4437; www.rosslakeresort.com; cabins $155-315; ⊙ mid-Jun–Oct) on the eponymous lake's west side are the state's most unique accommodations. There's no road in – guests can either hike the 2-mile trail from Hwy 20 or take the resort's tugboat-taxi-and-truck shuttle from the parking area near Diablo Dam.

Northeastern Washington

Spokane

Washington's second-biggest population center is one of the state's latent surprises and a welcome break after the treeless monotony of the eastern scablands. Situated at the nexus of the Pacific Northwest's so-called 'Inland Empire,' this understated yet confident city sits clustered on the banks of the Spokane River, close to where British fur traders founded a short-lived trading post in 1810.

Though rarely touted in national tourist blurbs, Spokane hosts the world's largest mass participation running event (May's annual Bloomsday).

⊙ Sights & Activities

Riverfront Park   PARK
(www.spokaneriverfrontpark.com; 🚻) On the former site of Spokane's 1974 World's Fair, park highlights include a 17-point **sculpture walk**, plenty of bridges and trails to satisfy the city's plethora of amateur runners and **Spokane Falls**, a gushing combination of scenic waterfalls and rapids. There are various viewing points over the river, including a short **gondola ride** (⊙ 11am-6pm Sun-Thu, to 10pm Fri & Sat Apr-Sep) that takes you directly above the falls. Walkers and joggers crowd the interurban **Spokane River Centennial Trail** (www.spokanecentennialtrail.org), which extends for 37 miles to the Idaho border and beyond. The park also includes an ice-skating rink, IMAX theater and carousel; check the website for details.

Northwest Museum of Arts & Culture   MUSEUM
(www.northwestmuseum.org; 2316 W 1st Ave; adult/child $7/5; ⊙ 10am-5pm Wed-Sun) Encased in a striking state-of-the-art building in the posh Browne's Addition neighborhood, the museum has – arguably – one of the finest collections of indigenous artifacts in the Northwest.

🛏 Sleeping & Eating

Hotel Ruby   BOUTIQUE MOTEL $
(✆ 509-747-1041; www.hotelrubyspokane.com; 901 W 1st Ave; r $68-110; ❈ 🛜 🐾) This basic motel with a hip red-and-black color scheme has an unbeatable downtown location opposite the Davenport.

★**Davenport Hotel**   HISTORIC HOTEL $$
(✆ 509-455-8888; www.thedavenporthotel.com; 10 S Post St; Davenport Hotel/Davenport Tower r from $130/120; ❈ 🛜 🐾) A historic Spokane landmark (opened in 1914) that is considered one of best hotels in the US. If you can't afford a room, linger in the exquisite lobby. The adjacent Davenport Tower is the modern version of all this glam with a surprisingly sophisticated safari theme.

★**Mizuna**   FUSION $$
(✆ 509-747-2004; 214 N Howard St; mains lunch/dinner $10/28; ⊙ 11am-10pm Mon-Sat, 4-10pm Sun; 🖉) A well-lit, antique brick building, with simple wood furniture, and tables topped with fresh flowers. Dishes such as lemongrass green curry with scallops and clams or equally good vegetarian specialties are washed down with exquisite wines. Heaven.

WORTH A TRIP

GRAND COULEE DAM

While the more famous Hoover Dam (conveniently located between Las Vegas and the Grand Canyon) gets around 1.6 million visitors per year, the much larger (four times) and arguably more significant Grand Coulee Dam (inconveniently located far from everything) gets only a trickle of tourism. It's the largest concrete structure in the US and also the largest producer of electricity in the US.

The **Grand Coulee Visitor Arrival Center** (☎509-633-9265; ⊙9am-5pm) details the history of the dam and surrounding area with movies, photos and interactive exhibits, while free guided **tours** of the facility run on the hour from 10am until 5pm (from May to September) and involve taking a glass-walled elevator 465ft down an incline into the Third Power Plant, where you can view the tops of the generators from an observation deck.

Similarly spectacular is the nightly **laser show** (⊙May-Sep after dark) – purportedly the world's largest – which illustrates the history of the Columbia River and its various dams against a gloriously vivid backdrop.

🍸 Drinking & Entertainment

With a vibrant student population based at Gonzaga University, Spokane has a happening nighttime scene.

Northern Lights Brewing Company   BREWERY
(www.northernlightsbrewing.com; 1003 E Trent Ave) You can sample the locally handcrafted ales at Spokane's best microbrewery, near the university campus.

Bing Crosby Theater   THEATRE
(www.mettheater.com; 901 W Sprague Ave) The former Met, now named after local hero Bing, presents concerts, plays, film festivals and the Spokane Opera in a fairly intimate setting.

ℹ Information

Spokane Area Visitor Information Center (www.visitspokane.com; 201 W Main Ave at Browne St; ⊙8:30am-5pm Mon-Fri, 9am-6pm Sat & Sun) keeps a raft of information.

ℹ Getting There & Away

Buses and trains depart from the **Spokane Intermodal Transportation Station** (221 W 1st Ave). **Amtrak** (www.amtrak.com) has a daily service on the esteemed Empire Builder route to Seattle ($53, 7½ hours), Portland ($53, 9½ hours) and Chicago ($163, 45 hours).

South Cascades

The South Cascades are taller but less clustered than their northern counterparts, extending from Snoqualmie Pass east of Seattle down to the mighty Columbia River on the border with Oregon. The highpoint in more ways than one is 14,411ft Mt Rainier. Equally compelling for different reasons is Mt St Helens (8365ft), still recovering from a devastating 1980 volcanic eruption. Lesser-known Mt Adams (12,276ft) is notable for the huckleberries and wildflowers that fill its grassy alpine meadows during the short but intense summer season.

Mt Rainier National Park

The USA's fourth-highest peak (outside Alaska), majestic Mt Rainier is also one of its most beguiling. Encased in a 368-sq-mile national park (the world's fifth national park when it was inaugurated in 1899), the mountain's snowcapped summit and forest-covered foothills harbor numerous hiking trails, huge swaths of flower-carpeted meadows and an alluring conical peak that presents a formidable challenge for aspiring climbers.

Mt Rainier National Park (www.nps.gov/mora; entry per pedestrian/car $5/15) has four entrances. Call ☎800-695-7623 for road conditions. The National Park Service (NPS) website includes downloadable maps and descriptions of 50 park trails. The most famous trail is the hardcore, 93-mile-long Wonderland Trail that completely circumnavigates Mt Rainier and takes around 10 to 12 days to tackle.

For overnight trips, you'll need a wilderness camping permit (free) from ranger stations or visitor centers. The six campgrounds in the park have running water and toilets, but no RV hookups. Reservations at **park campsites** (☎800-365-2267; www.mount.rainier.national-park.com/camping.htm; reserved campsites $12-15) are strongly advised during summer months and can be made up to two months in advance by phone or online.

Evergreen Escapes (www.evergreenescapes.com; 10hr tour $195) runs deluxe and eco-minded guided bus tours from Seattle.

NISQUALLY ENTRANCE

The busiest and most convenient gate to Mt Rainier National Park, Nisqually lies on Hwy 706 via Ashford, near the park's southwest corner. It's open year-round. Longmire, 7 miles inside the Nisqually entrance, has a **museum and information center** (⊘ 9am-6pm Jun-Sep, to 5pm Oct-May) `FREE`, a number of important trailheads, and the rustic **National Park Inn** (☑ 360-569-2275; www.guestservices.com/rainier; r with shared/private bath $116/164, units $244; P ❄) complete with an excellent restaurant. More hikes and interpretive walks can be found 12 miles further east at loftier Paradise, which is served by the informative **Henry M Jackson Visitor Center** (☑ 360-569-2211, ext 2328; Paradise; ⊘ 10am-7pm daily Jun-Oct, 10am-5pm Sat & Sun Oct-Dec), and the vintage **Paradise Inn** (☑ 360-569-2275; www.mtrainierguestservices.com; r with shared/private bath from $69/114; ⊘ May-Oct), a historic 'parkitecture' inn constructed in 1916 and long part of the national park's fabric. Climbs to the top of Rainier leave from the inn; excellent four-day guided ascents are led by **Rainier Mountaineering Inc** (www.rmiguides.com; 30027 SR706 E, Ashford; 4-day ascent $991).

OTHER ENTRANCES

The three other entrances to Mt Rainier National Park are **Ohanapecosh**, via Hwy 123 and accessed via the town of Packwood, where lodging is available; **White River**, off Hwy 410, which literally takes the high road (6400ft) to the beautiful viewpoint at the **Sunrise Lodge Cafeteria** (☑ 360-569-2425; snacks $5-7; ⊘ 10am-7pm Jun 30-Sep 16); and remote **Carbon River** in the northwest corner, which gives access to the park's inland rainforest.

Mt St Helens National Volcanic Monument

What it lacks in height, Mt St Helens makes up for in fiery infamy – 57 people perished on the mountain when it erupted with a force of 1500 atomic bombs on May 18, 1980. The cataclysm began with an earthquake measuring 5.1 on the Richter scale, which sparked the biggest landslide in human history and buried 230 sq miles of forest under millions of tons of volcanic rock and ash. Today it's a fascinating landscape of recovering forests, new river valleys and ash-covered slopes. There's an $8 fee to enter the monument.

For those without a car, Mt St Helens can be seen on a day trip by bus from Portland with **Eco Tours of Oregon** (www.ecotours-oforgeon.com; 3127 SE 23rd Ave, Portland; $59.50). If traveling independently, there are three entrances to the mountain, and plenty of short and long hikes along the way. From around mid-June through September, Hwy 25 opens up and links the Eastside and Southeastern entrances.

NORTHEAST ENTRANCE

From the main northeast entrance on Hwy 504, your first stop should be the **Silver Lake Visitor Center** (3029 Spirit Lake Hwy; admission $3; ⊘ 9am-5pm), which has films, exhibits and free information about the mountain (including trail maps). For a closer view of the destructive power of nature, venture to the **Johnston Ridge Observatory** (⊘ 10am-6pm mid-May–late Oct), situated at the end of Hwy 504, which looks directly into the mouth of the crater.

A welcome stop in an accommodations-lite area, the **Eco Park Resort** (☑ 360-274-6542; www.ecoparkresort.com; 14000 Spirit Lake Hwy; campsites $20, yurts $75, cabins $100-110) offers seven rooms in a large house opposite the Silver Lake Visitor Center.

SOUTHEASTERN & EASTSIDE ENTRANCES

The southeastern entrance via the town of **Cougar** on Hwy 503 holds some serious lava terrain, including the two-mile-long **Ape Cave** lava tube, which you can explore year-round but be prepared for chill as it remains a constant 41°F (5°C). Bring two light sources per adult or rent lanterns at **Apes' Headquarters** (8303 Forest Rd; ⊘ 10:30am-5pm Jun-Sep) for $5 each.

The eastside entrance is the most remote but the harder-to-reach **Windy Ridge** viewpoint on this side gives you a palpable, if eerie, sense of the destruction from the blast – it's often closed until June. A few miles down the road you can descend 600ft on the 1-mile-long **Harmony Trail** (hike 224) to Spirit Lake.

Central & Southeastern Washington

The sunny, dry near-California-looking central and southeastern parts of Washington harbor one not-so-secret weapon: wine. The fertile land that borders the Nile-like Yakima and Columbia River valleys is awash with enterprising new wineries producing quality grapes that now vie with the Napa and Sonoma Valleys for national recognition. Yakima and its more attractive cousin Ellensburg once held the edge, but nowadays the real star is Walla Walla, where talented restaurateurs and a proactive local council are crafting a wine destination par excellence.

Yakima & Ellensburg

Situated in its eponymous river valley, the city of Yakima is a rather bleak trading center that doesn't really live up to its 'Palm Springs of Washington' tourist label. The main reason to stop here is to visit one of the numerous wineries that lie between Yakima and Benton City; pick up a map at the **Yakima Valley Visitors & Convention Bureau** (www.visityakima.com; 10 N 8th St; ⊙9am-5pm Mon-Sat, 10am-4pm Sun).

A better layover is Ellensburg, a diminutive settlement 36 miles to the northwest that juxtaposes the state's largest rodeo (each Labor Day) with a town center that has more coffee bars per head than anywhere else in the world (allegedly). Grab your latte at local roaster **D&M Coffee** (www.dmcoffee.com; 301 N Pine St; ⊙7am-5pm) and overnight at centrally located and charming

Victorian **Guesthouse Ellensburg** (☏509-962-3706; www.guesthouseellensburg.com; 606 Main St; r $145), which also runs the excellent **Yellow Church Cafe** (www.yellowchurchcafe.com; 111 S Pearl St; brunch $8-10, dinner $13-23; ⊙11am-8pm Mon-Fri, 8am-8pm Sat & Sun).

Greyhound (www.greyhound.com) services both cities with buses to Seattle, Spokane and points in between.

Walla Walla

Over the last decade, Walla Walla has converted itself from an obscure agricultural backwater, famous for its sweet onions and large state penitentiary, into the hottest wine-growing region outside of California. While venerable Marcus Whitman College is the town's most obvious cultural attribute, you'll also find zany coffee bars here, along with cool wine-tasting rooms, fine Queen Anne architecture, and one of the state's freshest and most vibrant farmers markets.

⊙ Sights

You don't need to be sloshed on wine to appreciate Walla Walla's historical and cultural heritage. Its Main St has won countless historical awards, and to bring the settlement to life, the local **chamber of commerce** (www.wallawalla.org; 29 E Sumach St; ⊙8:30am-5pm Mon-Fri, 9am-4pm Sat & Sun May-Sep) has concocted some interesting walking tours, complete with leaflets and maps. For information on the region's wine culture, check out **Walla Walla Wine News** (www.wallawallawinenews.com).

DON'T MISS

YAKIMA VALLEY WINE TOUR

If you find yourself driving between Ellensburg and Walla Walla, do yourself a favor along the way and do some swish-and-spit wine tasting; it sounds unappealing but this is the way the pros do it and it will keep you legal. The Yakima Valley AVA (American Viticultural Area) is the oldest, largest and most diverse in the state. You'll find www.wineyakimavalley.org is a top resource for finding great wineries.

Bonair Winery (www.bonairwine.com; 500 S Bonair Rd, Zillah; ⊙10am-5pm) In the Rattlesnake Hills near Zillah; has lovely gardens and is a laid-back place to sample luscious reds.

Terra Blanca (www.terrablanca.com; 34715 N DeMoss Rd , Benton City; ⊙11am-6pm) Majestically located up on Red Mountain with views over the valley, this is one of the fanciest vineyards in the region, and perfect for sipping sweet dessert wines on the patio.

Maison Bleue (☏509-378-6527; www.mbwines.com; 357 Port Ave, Studio D, Prosser; ⊙by appointment) By appointment only, these lauded Rhone-style wines can be tasted in Vinter's Village in Prosser. The village isn't a scenic stop, but the wines are great.

Fort Walla Walla Museum   MUSEUM
(755 Myra Rd; adult/child $7/3; ⊙10am-5pm; ⊕)
A pioneer village of 17 historic buildings,
with the museum housed in the old cavalry
stables. There are collections of farm implements, ranching tools and what could be
the world's largest plastic replica of a mule
team.

Waterbrook Wine   WINERY
(www.waterbrook.com; 10518 W US 12; ⊙11am-6pm
Mon-Thu, till 8pm Fri & Sat) The pondside patio
of this large winery situated about 10 miles
west of town is a great place to imbibe a
long selection of wines on a sunny day. Outrageously good tacos (two for $6) are served
on Fridays and Saturdays.

Amavi Cellars   WINERY
(3796 Peppers Bridge Rd; ⊙10am-4pm) South of
Walla Walla amid a scenic spread of grape
and apple orchards, you can sample some
of the most talked-about wines in the valley (try the Syrah and Cabernet Sauvignon).
The classy yet comfortable outdoor patio has
views of the Blue Mountains.

🛏 Sleeping & Eating

Colonial Motel   MOTEL $
(📞509-529-1220; www.colonial-motel.com; 2279
Isaacs Ave; r from $70; ▣🖤) A simple family-
run motel halfway to the airport, the Colonial is welcoming and bike-friendly, with
safe cycle storage and plenty of local maps.

Marcus Whitman Hotel   HOTEL $$
(📞509-525-2200; www.marcuswhitmanhotel.com;
6 W Rose St; r $119-325; ▣🖤🐾) In keeping
with the settlement's well-preserved image,
this red-bricked 1928 beauty has been ele-
gantly renovated with ample rooms kitted
out in rusts and browns, and embellished
with Italian-crafted furniture.

Graze   CAFE $
(5 S Colville St; sandwiches from $8; ⊙10am-
7:30pm Mon-Sat, to 3:30pm Sun; 🍴) Have your
amazing sandwiches packed for your pic-
nic or eat them at the simple cafe. Try the
butternut squash panini with mozzarella,
roasted garlic, sage and provolone or the
flank steak torta with pickled jalapenos, avo-
cado, tomato, cilantro and chipotle dressing.

**★Saffron
Mediterranean Kitchen**   MEDITERRANEAN $$$
(📞509-525-2112; www.saffronmediterraneankitchen.
com; 125 W Alder St; mains $15-27; ⊙2-10pm, to 9pm
in winter) Saffron takes seasonal, local ingredi-

ents and turns them into pure gold. The Med-
inspired menu lists dishes such as pheasant,
ricotta gnocchi, amazing flatbreads and weird
yogurt-cucumber combo soups that could
stand up against anything in Seattle.

❶ Getting There & Away

Alaska Airlines services **Walla Walla Regional
Airport** (www.wallawallaairport.com) with four
daily flights to Seattle.
   Greyhound (www.greyhound.com) buses
run once daily to Seattle via Yakima and Ellensburg; change buses in Pasco for buses east to
Spokane and beyond.

OREGON

It's hard to slap a single characterization
onto Oregon's geography and people. Its
landscape ranges from rugged coastline
and thick evergreen forests to barren, fossil-
strewn deserts, volcanoes and glaciers. As
for its denizens, you name it – Oregonians
run the gamut from pro-logging conserva-
tives to tree-hugging liberals, and everything
in between. What they all have in common is
an independent spirit, a love of the outdoors
and a fierce devotion to where they live.

Portland

Call it what you want – PDX, Stumptown,
City of Roses, Bridge City, Beervana or Portlandia – Portland positively rocks. It's a city
with a vibrant downtown, pretty residential neighborhoods, ultragreen ambitions
and zany characters. Here, liberal idealists
outnumber conservative stogies, Gore-Tex
jackets are acceptable in fine restaurants
and everyone supports countless brewpubs,
coffeehouses, knitting circles, lesbian pot-
lucks and eclectic book clubs. Portland is an
up-and-coming destination that has finally
arrived, and makes for an appealing, can't-
miss stop on your adventures in the Pacific
Northwest.

◉ Sights

◎ Downtown

★Tom McCall Waterfront Park   PARK
This sinuous, 2-mile-long park flanks the
west bank of the Willamette River and is
both an unofficial training ground for lunchtime runners and a commuter path for the

OREGON FACTS

Nickname Beaver State

Population 3,900,000

Area 95,998 sq miles

Capital city Salem (population 157,000)

Other cities Portland (population 594,000), Eugene (population 157,000), Bend (population 78,000)

Sales tax Oregon has no sales tax

Birthplace of President Herbert Hoover (1874–1964), writer and merry prankster Ken Kesey (1935–2001), actor and dancer Ginger Rogers (1911–95), *The Simpsons* creator Matt Groening (b 1954), filmmaker Gus Van Sant (b 1952)

Home of Oregon Shakespeare Festival, Nike, Crater Lake

Politics Democratic governor, Democrat majorities in Congress, Democrat in Presidential elections since 1984

Famous for Forests, rain, microbrew, coffee, Death with Dignity Act

State beverage Milk (dairy's big here)

Driving You can't pump your own gas in Oregon; Portland to Eugene 110 miles, Portland to Astoria 96 miles

city's avid army of cyclists. It's also a great spot for picnics, and hosts large summertime festivals.

★ **Pioneer Courthouse Square** LANDMARK
Portland's downtown hub, this people-friendly brick plaza attracts tourists, sunbathers, lunching office workers, buskers and the odd political activist. Formerly a parking lot, and before that a posh hotel, the square today hosts concerts, festivals, rallies and farmers markets. Across 6th Ave is the muscular **Pioneer Courthouse**, the oldest federal building in the Pacific Northwest.

Portland Building LANDMARK
(cnr SW 5th Ave & SW Main St) In a downtown devoid of big skyscrapers, the city's signature structure is the Portland Building, designed in 1980 by Michael Graves. A triumph of postmodernism to some, but a mine of user-unfriendliness to others, the 15-story block

is embellished by the **Portlandia** statue, representing the Goddess of Commerce (and the second-largest hammered-copper statue in the US – after the Statue of Liberty).

Oregon Historical Society MUSEUM
(☑ 503-222-1741; www.ohs.org; 1200 SW Park Ave; adult/child 6-18yr $11/5; ⊙ 10am-5pm Mon-Sat, noon-5pm Sun) Along the tree-shaded South Park Blocks sits the state's primary history museum, which dedicates most of its space to the story of Oregon and the pioneers who made it. There are interesting sections on Native American tribes and the travails of the Oregon Trail.

Portland Art Museum MUSEUM
(☑ 503-226-2811; www.portlandartmuseum.org; 1219 SW Park Ave; adult/child $15/free; ⊙ 10am-5pm Tue, Wed & Sat, to 8pm Thu & Fri, noon-5pm Sun) Right on the South Park Blocks, the art museum's excellent exhibits include Native American carvings, Asian and American art, and English silver. The museum also houses the Whitsell Auditorium, a first-rate theater that frequently screens rare or international films.

Aerial Tram CABLE CAR
(www.gobytram.com; 3303 SW Bond Ave; round-trip $4; ⊙ 5:30am-9:30pm Mon-Fri, 9am-5pm Sat) Portland's aerial tram runs from the south Waterfront (there's a streetcar stop) to Marquam Hill. The tram runs along a 3300ft line up a vertical ascent of 500ft. The ride takes three minutes. The tram opened in 2007, smashing its budget predictions and causing much public controversy.

◉ Old Town & Chinatown

The core of rambunctious 1890s Portland, the once-notorious Old Town used to be the lurking grounds of unsavory characters, but today disco queens outnumber drug dealers. It's one of the livelier places in town after dark, when nightclubs and bars open their doors and hipsters start showing up.

Shanghai Tunnels HISTORIC SITE
(www.shanghaitunnels.info; adult/child $13/8) Running beneath Old Town's streets is this series of underground corridors through which, in the 1850s, unscrupulous people would kidnap or 'shanghai' drunken men and sell them to sea captains looking for indentured workers. Tours run Fridays and Saturdays at 6:30pm and 8pm. Book online.

Chinatown
NEIGHBORHOOD

The ornate **Chinatown Gates** (cnr W Burnside St & NW 4th Ave) defines the southern edge of Portland's Chinatown, which has a few token Chinese restaurants (most are on 82nd Ave over to the east). The main attraction here is the **Classical Chinese Garden** (☑503-228-8131; www.lansugarden.org; 239 NW Everett St; adult/child $8/7; ⊙10am-6pm), a wonderfully tranquil block of reflecting ponds and manicured greenery.

Saturday Market
MARKET

(☑503-222-6072; www.portlandsaturdaymarket. com; SW Ankeny St & Naito Pkwy; ⊙10am-5pm Sat, 11am-4:30pm Sun Mar-Dec) The best time to hit the river for a walk is on a weekend to catch this famous market, which showcases handicrafts, street entertainers and food booths.

Skidmore Fountain
FOUNTAIN

(SW 1st Ave & Ankeny St) Located beneath the Burnside Bridge, the Victorian-era Skidmore Fountain (1888) was idealistically designed with three 'drinking' tiers; the top for humans, the middle for horses and the lowest for dogs.

◉ The Pearl District & Northwest

The Pearl District
NEIGHBORHOOD

(www.explorethepearl.com) Northwest of downtown, the Pearl District is an old industrial quarter that has transformed its once grotty warehouses into expensive lofts, upscale boutiques and creative restaurants. On the first Thursday of every month, the zone's abundant **art galleries** extend their evening hours and the area turns into a fancy street party of sorts. The **Jamison Square Fountain** (810 NW 11th Ave) is one of its prettier urban spaces, and don't miss the **Museum of Contemporary Craft** (☑503-223-2654; www. museumofcontemporarycraft.org; 724 NW Davis St; admission $4; ⊙11am-6pm Tue-Sat, to 8pm 1st Thu of every month), which has many fine ceramics.

Northwest 23rd Ave
NEIGHBORHOOD

NW 23rd Ave ('Trendy-third') is an upscale shopping street, near the West Hills area, that brims with clothing boutiques, home decor shops and cafes. The restaurants here – including some of Portland's finest lie along parallel NW 21st Ave. This is a great neighborhood for strolling, window-shopping, coffee breaks and looking at lovely arts-and-crafts houses.

◉ West Hills

Behind downtown Portland is the West Hills area, known for its exclusive homes, huge parks and – if you're lucky – peek-a-boo views of up to five Cascade volcanoes.

★ Forest Park
PARK

(www.forestparkconservancy.org) Not many cities have more than 5000 acres of temperate rainforest within their limits, but then not many cities are like Portland. Abutting the more manicured Washington Park to the west is the far wilder Forest Park, whose dense foliage harbors plants, animals and an avid hiking fraternity. The **Portland Audubon Society** (☑503-292-6855; www.audubonportland.org; 5151 NW Cornell Rd; ⊙9am-5pm, nature store 10am-6pm Mon-Sat, till 5pm Sun) maintains a bookstore, wildlife rehabilitation center and 4 miles of trails within its Forest Park sanctuary.

The main sight in the park is the **Pittock Mansion** (☑503-823-3623; www.pittockmansion.org; 3229 NW Pittock Dr; adult/child 6-18yr $8.50/5.50, grounds free; ⊙11am-4pm), a mansion built in 1914 by Henry Pittock, who revitalized the Portland-based Oregonian newspaper. It's worth visiting the grounds just to check out the spectacular views – bring a picnic.

Washington Park
PARK

(www.washingtonparkpdx.org) West of Forest Park, extensive Washington Park contains several attractions within its 400 acres of greenery. **Hoyt Arboretum** (☑503-865-8733; www.hoytarboretum.org; 4000 Fairview Blvd; ⊙trails 6am-10pm, visitor center 9am-4pm Mon-Fri, 11am-3pm Sat & Sun) **FREE** showcases more than 1000 species of native and exotic trees and has 12 miles of walking trails. It's prettiest in the fall. The **International Rose Test Gardens** (☑503-823-3636; www.rosegardenstore.org/rose-gardens.cfm; 400 SW Kingston Ave; ⊙7:30am-9pm) **FREE** has fine city views and is the centerpiece of Portland's famous rose blooms; there are more 500 types on show here. Further uphill is the **Japanese Garden** (☑503-223-1321; www.japanesegarden.com; 611 SW Kingston Ave; adult/child 6-17yr $9.50/6.75; ⊙noon-7pm Mon, 9am-7pm Tue-Fri & Sun, 9am-9pm Sat), another oasis of tranquility.

◉ Northeast & Southeast

Across the Willamette River from downtown is the **Lloyd Center**, Oregon's largest shopping mall and where notorious ice-queen Tonya Harding first learned to skate in the rink here. A few blocks to the southwest are the unmissable glass towers of the **Oregon Convention Center**, and nearby is **Moda Center** (previously called the Rose Garden Arena) – home of professional basketball team the Trailblazers.

Further up the Willamette, **N Mississippi Avenue** used to be full of run-down buildings but is now a hot spot of trendy shops and eateries. Northeast is artsy **NE Alberta Street**, a long ribbon of art galleries, boutiques and cafes (don't miss Last Thursday street-art event here, taking place

Portland

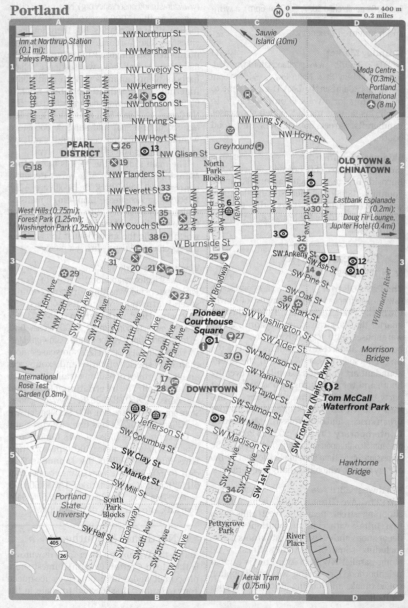

on the last Thursday of each month). **SE Hawthorne Boulevard** (near SE 39th Ave) is affluent hippy territory, with gift stores, cafes, coffeeshops and two branches of Powell's bookstores. One leafy mile to the south, **SE Division Street** has become a foodie destination, with plenty of excellent restaurants, bars and pubs. The same is true of **E Burnside at NE 28th Avenue**, though it has a more concentrated and upscale feel.

🏃 Activities

Hiking

The best hiking is found in Forest Park (p1055), which harbors an unbelievable 80 miles of trails and often feels more like Mt Hood's foothills than Portland's city limits. The park's **Wildwood Trail** starts at the Hoyt Arboretum and winds through 30 miles of forest, with many spur trails that allow for loop hikes. Other trailheads into Forest Park are located at the western ends of NW Thurman and NW Upshur Sts.

Cycling

Portland has been voted the 'most bike-friendly city in the US' several times in the media by the likes of CNN Travel, NBC News and *Bicycling Magazine*. There are many streets that cater to bicycles, and drivers are used to watching out for cyclists. Riding along downtown riverside paths is a great way to see the city.

To the east the **Springwater Corridor** starts near the Oregon Museum of Science & Industry (as an extension of the Eastbank Esplanade) and goes all the way to the suburb of Boring – 21 miles away. In the northwest, **Leif Erikson Drive** is an old logging road leading 11 miles into Forest Park and offering occasional peeks over the city.

For scenic farm country, head to **Sauvie Island**, 10 miles northwest of downtown Portland. This island is prime cycling land – it's flat, has relatively little traffic and much of it is wildlife refuge.

For bike rental, try **Waterfront Bicycle Rentals** (✆503-227-1719; www.waterfrontbikes. com; 10 SW Ash St; per day $40). Good cycling maps can be found at the tourist office and any bike store.

Kayaking

Situated close to the confluence of the Columbia and Willamette Rivers, Portland has miles of navigable waterways. **Portland**

Portland

◎ Top Sights
1	Pioneer Courthouse Square	C4
2	Tom McCall Waterfront Park	D4

◎ Sights
3	Chinatown Gates	C3
4	Classical Chinese Gardens	D2
5	Jamison Square Fountain	B1
6	Museum of Contemporary Craft	C2
7	Oregon Historical Society	B5
8	Portland Art Museum	B5
9	Portland Building	C5
10	Saturday Market	D3
11	Shanghai Tunnels	D3
12	Skidmore Fountain	D3
13	The Pearl District	B2

◎ Activities, Courses & Tours
14	Pedal Bike Tours	D3

◎ Sleeping
15	Ace Hotel	B3
16	Crystal Hotel	B3
17	Heathman Hotel	B4
18	Northwest Portland Hostel	A2

◎ Eating
19	Andina	B2
20	Jake's Famous Crawfish	B3
21	Kenny & Zuke's	B3
22	Little Big Burger	B3
23	Nong's Khao Man Gai	B3
24	Piazza Italia	B1

◎ Drinking & Nightlife
25	Bailey's Taproom	C3
26	Barista	B2
27	Departure Lounge	C4

◎ Entertainment
28	Arlene Schnitzer Concert Hall	B4
29	Artists Repertory Theatre	A3
30	CC Slaughters	D2
31	Crystal Ballroom	B3
32	Dante's	C3
	Darcelle XV	(see 30)
33	Jimmy Mak's	B2
34	Keller Auditorium	C5
35	Portland Center Stage	B3
36	Silverado	C3

◎ Shopping
37	Pioneer Place	C4
38	Powell's City of Books	B3

Kayak Company (☎503-459-4050; www.portlandkayak.com; 6600 SW Macadam Ave) offers kayaking rentals, instruction and tours including a three-hour circumnavigation of Ross Island on the Willamette River. For rentals, instruction and wildlife-based tours around Sauvie Island, try **Scappoose Bay Kayaking** (☎503-397-2161; www.scappoosebaykayaking.com; 57420 Old Portland Rd), located in Scappoose, which is 20 miles northwest of Portland.

☞ Tours

Pedal Bike Tours
BICYCLE TOUR

(☎503-243-2453; www.pedalbiketours.com; 133 SW 2nd Ave) Bike tours with all sorts of themes – history, food carts, beer– and options to head to the coast or gorge.

Portland Walking Tours
WALKING TOUR

(☎503-774-4522; www.portlandwalkingtours.com) Food, chocolate, underground and even ghost-oriented tours.

Forktown
FOOD TOUR

(☎503-234-3663; www.forktown.com) Experience Stumptown's neighborhood eateries from the point of view of your tastebuds.

Pubs of Portland Tours
BEER TOUR

(☎512-917-2464; www.pubsofportlandtours.com) Visit several breweries and brewpubs with guides who will educate you on the beer-brewing process, various styles of beer and, essentially, how to taste the stuff.

✷ Festivals & Events

Portland Rose Festival
ROSE FESTIVAL

(www.rosefestival.org; ☉late May–mid-Jun) Rose-covered floats, dragon-boat races, fireworks, roaming packs of sailors and the crowning of a Rose Queen combine to make this Portland's biggest celebration.

Oregon Brewers Festival
BEER FESTIVAL

(www.oregonbrewfest.com; ☉Jul & Dec) Quaff microbrews during the summer (late July) in Tom McCall Waterfront Park and during the winter (early December) at Pioneer Courthouse Sq.

Bite of Oregon
FOOD FESTIVAL

(www.biteoforegon.com; ☉early Aug) All the food (and beer) you could think of consuming, much of it from great local restaurants – and some of it from Portland's now-famous food carts. Good microbrews, too. Bite of Oregon benefits Special Olympics Oregon.

Art in the Pearl
ART FESTIVAL

(www.artinthepearl.com; ☉first Mon in Sep & weekend prior) On Labor Day weekend, more than 100 carefully selected artists come together to show and sell their fine works. Plenty of food and live music.

🛏 Sleeping

Reserve ahead in summer.

Hawthorne Portland Hostel
HOSTEL $

(☎503-236-3380; www.portlandhostel.org; 3031 SE Hawthorne Blvd; dm $28, d with shared bath $60; ☺@☎) ✐ This ecofriendly hostel has good vibes and a great Hawthorne location. Private rooms are decent and dorms spacious. There are summertime open-mic nights in the grassy backyard, and bike rentals available. The Hawthorne is very environmentally conscious; it composts and recycles, uses rainwater to flush toilets and has a nice eco-roof. Discounts are available to those bike touring; non-HI members pay $3 extra.

Northwest Portland Hostel
HOSTEL $

(☎503-241-2783; www.nwportlandhostel.com; 425 NW 18th Ave; dm $20-29, d with shared bath $65; ☺✳@☎) Perfectly located between the Pearl District and NW 21st and 23rd Aves, this friendly and clean hostel takes up four old buildings and features plenty of common areas (including a small deck) and bike rentals. Dorms are spacious and private rooms can be as nice as in hotels, though all share outside bathrooms. Non-HI members pay $3 extra.

★ Ace Hotel
BOUTIQUE HOTEL $$

(☎503-228-2277; www.acehotel.com; 1022 SW Stark St; d with shared/private bath from $135/185; ☺✳@✿) Portland's trendiest place to sleep is this unique hotel fusing classic, industrial, minimalist and retro styles. From the photo booth and sofa lounge in its lobby to the recycled fabrics and furniture in its rooms, the Ace makes the warehouse-feel work. A Stumptown coffee shop on the premises adds even more comfort. Parking costs $25.

Crystal Hotel
HOTEL $$

(☎503-972-2670; www.mcmenamins.com/CrystalHotel; 303 SW 12th Ave; r $85-165; ✳☎) Room furnishings that blend Grateful Dead–inspired psychedelia with the interior of a Victorian boudoir can only mean one thing. Welcome to the latest McMenamins hotel, filled with 51 guestrooms (the cheapest with bathrooms down the hall), each 'inspired' by a song. A wondrous saltwater soaking pool lies in the basement.

Jupiter Hotel   BOUTIQUE MOTEL $$
(☑ 503-230-9200; www.jupiterhotel.com; 800 E Burnside; d from $159; ✆❄🛜🐾) The hippest hotel in town, this slick, remodeled motel is within walking distance of downtown and right next to Doug Fir Lounge (p1062), a top-notch live-music venue. Standard rooms are tiny – go for the Metropolitan instead, and ask for a pad away from the bamboo patio if you're more into sleeping than staying up late. Kitchenettes and bike rentals available; walk-ins after midnight get a discount.

Clinton St Guesthouse   GUESTHOUSE $$
(☑ 503-234-8752; www.clintonstreetguesthouse. com; 4220 SE Clinton St; d $100-145; ✆❄🛜) Four simple but beautiful rooms (two with shared bathroom) are on offer in this lovely arts-and-crafts house in a residential neighborhood. Furnishings are elegant, the linens luxurious and your hosts gracious. Located in a great residential neighborhood with many restaurants within walking distance.

★ McMenamins Edgefield   HOTEL $$
(☑ 503-669-8610; www.mcmenamins.com/54-edgefield-home; 2126 SW Halsey St, Troutdale; dm $30, d with shared bath $70-115, with private bath $120-155; ✆❄🛜) This former county poor farm, restored by the McMenamin brothers, is now a one-of-a-kind 38-acre hotel complex with a dizzying variety of services. Taste wine and homemade beer, play golf, watch movies, shop at the gift store, listen to live music, walk the extensive gardens and eat at one of its restaurants. It's about a 20-minute drive east from downtown.

★ Kennedy School   HOTEL $$
(☑ 503-249-3983; www.mcmenamins.com; 5736 NE 33rd Ave; d $115-155; ✆🛜) This Portland institution, a former elementary school, is now home to a hotel (yes, the bedrooms are converted classrooms), a restaurant, several bars, a microbrewery and a movie theater. There's a soaking pool, and the whole school is decorated with mosaics, fantasy paintings and historical photographs.

Inn at Northrup Station   BOUTIQUE HOTEL $$
(☑ 503-224-0543; www.northrupstation.com; 2025 NW Northrup St; d from $174; ✆❄@) Almost over the top with its bright color scheme and funky decor, this supertrendy hotel boasts huge artsy suites, many with patio or balcony, and all with kitchenettes or full kitchens. There's a cool rooftop patio with plants, and complimentary streetcar tickets are included (the streetcar runs just outside).

Heathman Hotel   LUXURY HOTEL $$$
(☑ 503-241-4100; www.heathmanhotel.com; 1001 SW Broadway; d from $249; ❄@🛜🐾) A Portland institution, the Heathman has top-notch services and one of the best restaurants in the city. Rooms are elegant, stylish and luxurious, and the location is very central. It also hosts high tea in the afternoons, jazz in the evenings and has a library stocked with signed books by authors who have stayed here. Parking costs $32.

✖ Eating

Portland's rapidly evolving food scene tore up the rule book years ago and has branched out into countless genres and subgenres. Vegetarianism is well represented, as is brunch, Asian fusion and the rather loose concept known as 'Pacific Northwest.' Then there are the city's famous food carts, representing dozens of cuisines and quirky food niches.

Little Big Burger   BURGERS $
(☑ 503-274-9008; www.littlebigburger.com; 122 NW 10th Ave; burgers $4; ⏱11am-10pm) A simple six-item menu takes fast food to the next level with mini-burgers made from prime ingredients. Try a beef burger topped with cheddar, Swiss, chevre or blue cheese, served with a side of truffled fries, and wash it down with a gourmet root-beer float. There are several locations; check the website.

Pok Pok   THAI $$
(☑ 503-232-1387; www.pokpokpdx.com; 3226 SE Division St; mains $11-16; ⏱11:30am-10pm) Spicy Thai street food with a twist draws crowds of flavor-seekers to this famous eatery; don't miss the renowned chicken wings. To endure the inevitably long wait, try a tastier-than-it-sounds drinking vinegar at the restaurant's nearby bar, Whiskey Soda Lounge. There's a second location at 1469 NE Prescott St.

Navarre   EUROPEAN $$
(☑ 503-232-3555; www.navarreportland.blogspot. com; 10 NE 28th Ave; small plates $4-8, large plates $10-18; ⏱4:30-10:30pm Mon-Thu, till 11:30pm Fri, 9:30am-11:30pm Sat, till 10:30pm Sun) The paper menu at this industrial-elegant restaurant lists various small plates (don't call them tapas), which rotate daily – though a few popular dishes are fixed commodities. Expect

a simple and truly delicious approach to crab cakes, lamb and roasted veggies. Weekend brunch is just as good.

Piazza Italia   ITALIAN $$
(☎ 503-478-0619; www.piazzaportland.com; 1129 NW Johnson St; pasta $13-17; ⊙ 11:30am-3pm & 5-9pm Mon-Thu, till 10pm Fri-Sun) Remember that great *ragù* (meat sauce) you last had in Bologna or those memorable *vongole* (clams) you once polished off in Sicily? Well, you'll find them here in this highly authentic restaurant that succeeds where so many fail: replicating the true essence of Italian food in North America.

Pambiche   CUBAN $$
(☎ 503-233-0511; www.pambiche.com; 2811 NE Glisan St; mains $12-17; ⊙ 11am-10pm Mon-Thu, to midnight Fri, 9am-midnight Sat, to 10pm Sun) Portland's best Cuban food served in a riotously colorful atmosphere. All your regular favorites including *ropa vieja* (shredded beef in a tomato sauce) are available, and leave room for dessert. Happy hour is a good deal (2pm to 6pm Monday to Friday, 10pm to midnight Friday and Saturday). Be prepared to wait for dinner.

Kenny & Zuke's   DELI $$
(☎ 503-222-3354; www.kennyandzukes.com; 1038 SW Stark St; sandwiches $10-15; ⊙ 7am-8pm Mon-Thu, till 10pm Fri, 8am-10pm Sat, till 8pm Sun) The only place in the city for real Jewish deli food: bagels, pickled herring, homemade pickles and latkes. But the real draw is the house pastrami, cut to order and gently sandwiched in one of the best Reubens you'll ever eat. Bustles for breakfast, too. Also in North Portland.

★ Ox   STEAKHOUSE $$$
(☎ 503-284-3366; www.oxpdx.com; 2225 Martin Luther King Jr Blvd; mains $19-38; ⊙ 5-10pm Tue-Sun) Currently Portland's most popular restaurant, this is an upscale Argentine-inspired steakhouse (who said Portland is all vegetarian?). Go for the 'Gusto' (grass-fed beef rib-eye for $38) or, if there are two of you, the *asado* is a good choice for trying many different cuts ($60). Reserve ahead and bring your wallet.

Paley's Place   FRENCH, FUSION $$$
(☎ 503-243-2403; www.paleysplace.net; 1204 NW 21st Ave; mains $23-36; ⊙ 5:30-10pm Mon-Thu, till 11pm Fri & Sat, 5-10pm Sun) ✐ Established by Vitaly and Kimberly Paley, this is one of Portland's premier restaurants, offering a creative blend of French and Pacific Northwest cuisines. Whether you're enjoying seared Alaskan halibut or crispy sweetbreads with fava-bean puree, you can count on fresh ingredients and excellent service.

Andina   PERUVIAN $$$
(☎ 503-228-9535; www.andinarestaurant.com; 1314 NW Glisan St; lunch mains $14-17, dinner mains $22-30; ⊙ 11:30am-2:30pm & 5-9:30pm Sun-Thu, till

---

PORTLAND'S FOOD CARTS

One of the most fun ways to explore Portland's cuisine is to eat at a food cart. These semipermanent kitchens-on-wheels inhabit parking lots around town and are usually clustered together in 'pods,' often with their own communal tables, ATMs and portaloos. As many of the owners are immigrants (who can't afford a hefty restaurant start-up), the carts are akin to an international potluck.

Food-cart locations vary, but the most significant cluster is on the corners of SW Alder St and SW 9th Ave. For a current list and some background information, see www.foodcartsportland.com. Highlights in a highly competitive field:

Nong's Khao Man Gai (☎ 971-255-3480; www.khaomangai.com; SW 10th & SW Alder St; mains $7; ⊙ 10am-4pm Mon-Fri) Tender poached chicken with rice. That's it – and enough. Also at 411 SW College St and 609 SE Ankeny St.

Viking Soul Food (www.vikingsoulfood.com; 4262 SE Belmont Ave; mains $5-6; ⊙ noon-8pm Tue-Thu, 11:30am-9:30pm Fri & Sat, 11:30am-8:30pm Sun) Delicious sweet and savory wraps.

Rip City Grill (www.ripcitygrill.com; cnr SW Moody & Abernathy, south waterfront; sandwiches $5-7; ⊙ 10am-2pm Mon-Fri) The tri-tip steak sandwich is not to be missed.

Thrive Pacific NW (www.thrivepacificnw.com; mains $5-8) Organic, free-range and gluten-free exotic food bowls. See the website for changing location and hours.

Pepper Box (www.pepperboxpdx.com; 2737 NE Martin Luther King Jr Blvd; tacos & quesadillas $3.50-4; ⊙ 9am-2pm Tue-Fri, till 1pm Sat) Awesome breakfast tacos and fancy quesadillas.

10:30pm Fri & Sat) A modern take on traditional Peruvian food produces delicious mains such as quinoa-crusted scallops on a bed of wilted spinach, or slow-cooked lamb shank in cilantro-and-black-beer sauce. For lighter fare, hit the bar for tapas, great cocktails and Latin-inspired live music.

Jake's Famous Crawfish SEAFOOD $$$
(☎503-226-1419; 401 SW 12th Ave; lunch mains $10-16, dinner mains $19-39; ☺11:30am-10pm Mon-Thu, till midnight Fri & Sat, 3-10pm Sun) Some of Portland's best seafood can be found here within an elegant old-time atmosphere. The oysters are divine, the crab cakes a revelation and the macadamia-crusted wild halibut your ticket to heaven. Come at happy hour for more-affordable treats.

♟ Drinking & Nightlife

Portland is famous for its coffee, and boasts more than 50 breweries within its borders – more than any other city on earth. It also offers a wide range of excellent bars, from dive bars to hipster joints to pubs and ultra-modern lounges. You'll never get thirsty in these parts.

★ Barista CAFE
(☎503-274-1211; www.baristapdx.com; 539 NW 13th Ave; ☺6am-6pm Mon-Fri, 7am-6pm Sat & Sun) One of Portland's best coffee shops is owned by award-winning barista Billy Wilson and known for its lattes. It sources its beans from specialty roasters. Also at 529 SW 3rd Ave and 1725 NE Alberta St.

Amnesia Brewing BREWERY
(☎503-281-7708; www.amnesiabrews.com; 832 N Beech St; ☺3pm-midnight Mon, noon-midnight Tue-Sun) This brewery, located on hip Mississippi Street (though its official address is Beech St), has picnic tables out front and a very casual feel. For excellent (and despite the name, memorable) beer, try the Desolation IPA, Amnesia Brown or Wonka Porter. An outdoor grill offers burgers and sausages, and there's live music on weekends.

Horse Brass Pub PUB
(☎503-232-2202; www.horsebrass.com; 4534 SE Belmont St; ☺11am-2:30am) Portland's most authentic English pub, cherished for its dark-wood atmosphere, excellent fish and chips, and about four dozen beers on tap. Play some darts, watch soccer on TV and just take it all in.

Coava Coffee CAFE
(☎503-894-8134; www.coavacoffee.com; 1300 SE Grand Ave; ☺6am-6pm Mon-Fri, 7am-6pm Sat, 8am-6pm Sun) The decor takes the concept of 'neo-industrial' to extremes, but most people love that – and Coava delivers where it matters. Their pour-over makes for a fantastic cup of java, and their espressos are exceptional, too.

Bailey's Taproom BREWERY
(☎503-295-1004; www.baileystaproom.com; 213 SW Broadway; ☺2pm-midnight) Unique and popular beer bar offering a rotation selection of 20 eclectic beers from Oregon and beyond. Cool digital menu board lets you know all about the beers, and how much of each is left. No food served, but you can bring something in from outside.

Belmont Station BREWERY
(☎503-232-8538; www.belmont-station.com; 4500 SE Stark St; ☺noon-11pm) More than 20 excellent rotating taps in a simple 'biercafé' with sidewalk seating. Attached to one of the city's best bottle shops, which sells more than 1200 beers and offers a small discount if customers pay in cash.

Departure Lounge BAR
(☎503-802-5370; www.departureportland.com; 525 SW Morrison St; ☺4pm-midnight Sun-Thu, to 1am Fri & Sat) This rooftop restaurant-bar (atop the 15th floor of the Nines Hotel) fills a deep downtown void: a cool bar with unforgettable views. The vibe is distinctly spaceship LA, with mod couches and sleek lighting. For something different, try the spicy tasho macho cocktail.

Ristretto Roasters CAFE
(☎503-288-8667; www.ristrettoroasters.com; 3808 N Williams Ave; ☺6:30am-6pm Mon-Sat, 7am-6pm Sun) Medium-roast, small-batch and single-origin coffee beans that result in a mellow, subtle cup of java. Free cuppings (tasting sessions) Fridays at 1pm. Also at 555 NE Couch St and 2181 NW Nicolai St (in a cool Schoolhouse Electric building).

Breakside Brewery BREWERY
(☎503-719-6475; www.breakside.com; 820 NE Dekum St; ☺3-10pm Mon-Thu, noon-11pm Fri & Sat, noon-10pm Sun) More than 20 taps of some of the most experimental, tasty beer you'll ever drink, laced with fruits, vegetables and spices. Past beers have included a Meyer lemon kolsch, mango IPA and a beet beer with ginger. For dessert, pray they have the

GAY & LESBIAN PORTLAND

For current listings, see *Just Out,* Portland's free gay biweekly. Stark St, around SW 10th St, has several edgy gay bars.

CC Slaughters (☎503-248-9135; www.ccslaughterspdx.com; 219 NW Davis St) Popular and long-running nightclub with big, loud dance floor, laser light show and DJs. There's a Sunday night drag show and fun themed nights. The relaxed lounge is good for conversation.

Darcelle XV (☎503-222-5338; www.darcellexv.com; 208 NW 3rd Ave; ⊙shows Wed-Sat) Portland's Vegas-style cabaret show, featuring glitzy drag queens in big wigs, fake jewelry and over-stuffed bras. Male strippers perform at midnight on Friday and Saturday.

Silverado (☎503-224-4493; www.silveradopdx.com; 318 SW 3rd Ave) Almost nightly stripper shows (Monday is karaoke) catering to men. Mixed crowd, cheap drinks, potential groping and muscled dancers, so bring plenty of dollar bills and expect a wild time.

salted-caramel milk stout. Good food and nice outdoor seating, too.

Stumptown Coffee Roasters   CAFE
(☎503-230-7702; www.stumptowncoffee.com; 4525 SE Division St; ⊙6am-7pm Mon-Fri, 7am-7pm Sat & Sun) The first microroaster to put Portland on the coffee map, and still its most famous coffee shop. Stumptown is proud to deal directly with coffee farmers to ensure quality beans. See the website for other Portland (and US) locations.

Green Dragon   BREWERY
(☎503-517-0660; www.pdxgreendragon.com; 928 SE 9th Ave; ⊙11am-11pm Sun-Wed, to 1am Thu-Sat) Although it is owned by Rogue Breweries, Green Dragon serves a whopping 62 guest taps – and it's an eclectic mix to boot. It has decent pub-fare food, too. Located in an echoey eastside warehouse space; sit on the patio on warm days.

Rontoms   BAR
(☎503-236-4536; 600 E Burnside St; ⊙4:30pm-2:30am) First the downside of this trendy-industrial bar – the food's just ok, the service can be mediocre, and if you're not a hipster you might feel out of place. But if it's a nice

day, the large patio in back is the place to be. It's at the corner of E Burnside and 6th (too cool for a sign).

Hopworks Urban Brewery   BREWERY
(☎503-232-4677; www.hopworksbeer.com; 2944 SE Powell Blvd; ⊙11am-11pm Sun-Thu, till midnight Fri & Sat) ✿ Organic beers made with local ingredients, served in an ecobuilding with bicycle frames above the bar. Good selection of food in a family-friendly atmosphere; the back deck can't be beat on a warm day. Also at 3947 N Williams Ave.

Sterling Coffee Roasters   CAFE
(www.sterlingcoffeeroasters.com; 417 NW 21st Ave; ⊙7am-4pm Mon-Fri, 8am-4pm Sat & Sun) Very small but elegant coffee shop that roasts complex, flavorful beans. Simple menu, great cappuccino and espresso, and knowledgeable baristas. Also at 1951 W Burnside (where it's called Coffeehouse Northwest).

☆ Entertainment

The best guide to local entertainment is the free *Willamette Week* (www.wweek.com), which comes out on Wednesday and lists theater, music, clubs, cinema and events in the metro area. Also, try the *Portland Mercury* (www.portlandmercury.com).

For summer outdoor concerts, check what's happening at the Oregon Zoo.

Live Music

Doug Fir Lounge   LIVE MUSIC
(☎503-231-9663; www.dougfirlounge.com; 830 E Burnside St) Paul Bunyan meets the Jetsons at this ultratrendy venue. Doug Fir books edgy, hard-to-get talent, drawing crowds from tattooed youth to suburban yuppies. Their decent restaurant has long hours; located next to the rock-star quality Jupiter Hotel.

Dante's   LIVE MUSIC
(☎503-345-7892; www.danteslive.com; 350 W Burnside St) This steamy red bar books vaudeville shows along with national acts such as the Dandy Warhols and Concrete Blonde. Drop in on Sunday night for the eclectic Sinferno Cabaret.

Crystal Ballroom   LIVE MUSIC
(☎503-225-0047; www.mcmenamins.com; 1332 W Burnside St) Major acts have played at this large and historic ballroom, including the Grateful Dead, James Brown and Jimi Hendrix. The 'floating' dance floor makes dancing a balancing act. If you like '80s music, head to Lola's Room downstairs on Friday nights.

Mississippi Studios LIVE MUSIC
(☑ 503-288-3895; www.mississippistudios.com; 3939 N Mississippi Ave) Intimate venue good for checking out budding acoustic talent, along with more established alternative musical groups. Excellent sound system. There's a good restaurant-bar with patio next door.

Jimmy Mak's LIVE MUSIC
(☑ 503-295-6542; www.jimmymaks.com; 221 NW 10th Ave; ⊙ music from 8pm) Stumptown's premier jazz venue, which also serves excellent Mediterranean food in their fancy dining room. There's a casual bar with pool tables and darts in the basement.

Cinema

Kennedy School CINEMA
(☑ 503-249-3983; www.mcmenamins.com; 5736 NE 33rd Ave) McMenamins' premier Portland venue; watch $3 movies in the old school gym.

Bagdad Theater CINEMA
(☑ 503-249-7474; www.mcmenamins.com; 3702 SE Hawthorne Blvd) An awesome McMenamins venue that shows bargain flicks.

Laurelhurst Theater CINEMA
(☑ 503-232-5511; www.laurelhursttheater.com; 2735 E Burnside St) Great gourmet pizza-and-microbrew theater with nearby nightlife.

Cinema 21 CINEMA
(www.cinema21.com; 616 NW 21st Ave) This is Portland's premier art-house and foreign-film theater.

Performing Arts

Portland Center Stage THEATER
(☑ 503-445-3700; www.pcs.org; 128 NW 11th Ave) The city's main theater company now performs in the Portland Armory – a newly renovated Pearl District landmark with state-of-the-art features.

Arlene Schnitzer Concert Hall CLASSICAL MUSIC
(☑ 503-228-1353; www.pcpa.com/schnitzer; 1037 SW Broadway) The Oregon Symphony performs in this beautiful, if not acoustically brilliant, downtown venue.

Artists Repertory Theatre THEATER
(☑ 503-241-1278; www.artistsrep.org; 1515 SW Morrison St) Some of Portland's best plays, including regional premiers, are performed in two intimate theaters.

Keller Auditorium THEATER
(☑ 503-248-4335; www.pcpa.com/keller; 222 SW Clay St) The Portland Opera and Oregon Ballet Theatre stage performances here, and it's also home to some Broadway productions.

Sports

Portland's Trailblazers play at **Moda Center** (☑ 503-235-8771; www.rosequarter.com; 300 N Winning Way). The city's A-League soccer teams are the **Timbers** (www.portlandtimbers.com), who play at Jeld-Wen Field along with their female counterparts, the **Thorns** (www.portlandtimbers.com/thornsfc), who won their leagues' inaugural championship in 2013. Other major sports teams include the **Winter Hawks** (www.winterhawks.com), who play ice-hockey at Moda Center, and **Rose City Rollers** (www.rosecityrollers.com), a roller-derby team who play at The Hanger in Oaks Amusement Park.

🔒 Shopping

Portland's downtown shopping district extends in a two-block radius from Pioneer Courthouse Sq and hosts all of the usual suspects. **Pioneer Place** (☑ 503-228-5800; www.pioneerplace.com; 700 SW 5th Ave; ⊙ 10am-8pm Mon-Sat, 11am-6pm Sun), a fancy mall, is east of the square. The Pearl District is dotted with high-end galleries, boutiques and home-decor shops. On weekends, you can visit the quintessential Saturday Market (p1055) by the Skidmore Fountain. For a pleasant, upscale shopping street, head to NW 23rd Ave.

> **DON'T MISS**
>
> ### POWELL'S CITY OF BOOKS
>
> You remember bookstores, don't you? Well they haven't all disappeared. Enter **Powell's City of Books** (☑ 503-228-4651; www.powells.com; 1005 W Burnside St; ⊙ 9am-11pm), an empire of reading that takes up a whole city block on multiple stories, and once claimed to be 'the largest independent bookstore in the world.' Don't miss it during your Portland tenure; it's a local institution, tourist attraction and a worthy place to hang out for a few hours (it'll take you that long to get through it). There are other branches around town and at the airport, but none as large.

Eastside has lots of trendy shopping streets that also host restaurants and cafes. SE Hawthorne Blvd is the biggest, N Mississippi Ave is the most recent and NE Alberta St is the most artsy and funky. Down south, Sellwood is known for its antique shops.

ⓘ Information

EMERGENCY & MEDICAL SERVICES

Legacy Good Samaritan Medical Center (☑503-413-7711; www.legacyhealth.org; 1015 NW 22nd Ave)

Portland Police (☑503-823-0000; www.portlandoregon.gov/police; 1111 SW 2nd Ave)

INTERNET ACCESS

Backspace (☑503-248-2900; www.backspace.bz; 115 NW 5th Ave; ☺7am-midnight Mon-Fri, 10am-midnight Sat & Sun) Youth-oriented hangout with arcade games, coffee, long hours and even live music.

Central Library (☑503-988-5123; www.multcolib.org; 801 SW 10th Ave) Downtown; for other branches check the website.

MEDIA

KBOO 90.7 FM (www.kboo.fm) Progressive local station run by volunteers; alternative news and views.

Portland Mercury (www.portlandmercury.com) Free local sibling of Seattle's the *Stranger*.

Willamette Week (www.wweek.com) Free weekly covering local news and culture.

MONEY

Travelex (☺5:30am-4:30pm) Downtown (900 SW 6th Ave); Portland International Airport (☑503-281-3045; ☺5:30am-4:30pm) Foreign-currency exchange.

POST

Post Office (☑503-525-5398; www.usps.com; 715 NW Hoyt St; ☺8am-6:30pm Mon-Fri, 8:30am-5pm Sat) This is the main branch, but there are many others around Portland.

TOURIST INFORMATION

Portland Oregon Visitors Association (www.travelportland.com; 701 SW 6th Ave; ☺8:30am-5:30pm Mon-Fri, 10am-4pm Sat, till 2pm Sun) In Pioneer Courthouse Sq. There's a small theater with a 12-minute film about the city, and Tri-Met bus and light-rail offices inside.

USEFUL WEBSITES

Oregon Live (www.oregonlive.com) *The Oregonian's* website, with news, sports and entertainment.

Portland Food & Drink (www.portlandfoodanddrink.com) Unbiased reviews of Portland's restaurants, along with specialty articles.

Portland Monthly (www.portlandmonthlymag.com) *Portland Monthly* magazine's website features interesting local content.

Travel Portland (www.travelportland.com) What to do, where to go, how to save.

ⓘ Getting There & Away

AIR

Portland International Airport (PDX; ☑503-460-4234; www.flypdx.com; 7000 NE Airport Way) Portland International Airport has daily flights all over the US, as well as to several international destinations. It's situated just east of I-5 on the banks of the Columbia River (a 20-minute drive from downtown heading northeast via the Steel Bridge). Amenities include money changers, restaurants, bookstores (including three Powell's branches) and business services such as free wi-fi.

BUS

Greyhound (☑503-243-2361; www.greyhound.com; 550 NW 6th Ave) Greyhound connects Portland with cities along I-5 and I-84. Destinations include Chicago, Boise, Denver, San Francisco, Seattle and Vancouver, BC.

Bolt Bus (☑877-265-8287; www.boltbus.com) If you're traveling between Portland, Seattle and Vancouver, BC, try Bolt Bus, which provides service in large buses with wi-fi and power outlets.

TRAIN

Amtrak (☑503-273-4865; www.amtrak.com; 800 NW 6th Ave) Amtrak offers services up and down the West Coast. The *Empire Builder* travels to Chicago, the *Cascades* goes to Vancouver, BC, and the *Coast Starlight* runs between Seattle and LA.

ⓘ Getting Around

TO/FROM THE AIRPORT

Portland International Airport (PDX) is about 10 miles northeast of downtown, next to the Columbia River. Tri-Met's light-rail MAX line takes about 40 minutes to get from downtown to the airport. If you prefer a bus, **Blue Star** (☑503-249-1837; www.bluestarbus.com) offers shuttle services between PDX and several downtown stops.

Taxis charge around $34 from the airport to downtown (not including tip).

BICYCLE

It's easy riding a bicycle around Portland, often voted 'the most bike-friendly city in America.'

Rental companies include **Clever Cycles** (☑503-334-1560; www.clevercycles.com/rentals; 900 SE Hawthorne Blvd) and Waterfront Bicycle Rentals (p1057).

PUBLIC TRANSPORTATION

Portland has a good public-transportation system, which consists of local buses, streetcars and the MAX light-rail. All are run by **TriMet** (☑503-238-7433; www.trimet.org; 701 SW 6th Ave), which has an information center at Pioneer Courthouse Sq.

Tickets for the transportation systems are completely transferable within two hours of the time of purchase. Buy tickets for local buses from the fare machines as you enter; for streetcars, you can buy tickets either at streetcar stations or on the streetcar itself. Tickets for the MAX must be bought from ticket machines at MAX stations (before you board); there is no conductor or ticket seller on board (but there are enforcers).

If you're a night owl, be aware that there are fewer services at night, and only a few run past 1am; check the website for details on specific lines.

CAR

Most major car-rental agencies have outlets both downtown and at Portland International Airport (PDX). Many of these agencies have added hybrid vehicles to their fleets. **Zipcar** (www.zipcar.com) is a popular car-sharing option, but there are many. For cheap parking downtown, see www.portlandoregon.gov/transportation/35272.

CHARTER SERVICE

For custom bus or van charters and tours, try **EcoShuttle** (☑503-548-4480; www.ecoshuttle.net). Vehicles are run on 100% biodiesel.

PEDICAB

For an ecofriendly option, there are several pedicab operators in town, including **PDX Pedicab.** (☑503-828-9888; www.pdxpedicab.com) Bicycle pedicabs come with 'drivers' that pedal you around downtown.

TAXI

Cabs are available 24 hours by phone. Downtown, you can often just flag them down. Try **Broadway Cab** (☑503-333-3333; www.broadwaycab.com) or **Radio Cab** (☑503-227-1212; www.radiocab.net).

Willamette Valley

The Willamette Valley, a fertile 60-mile-wide agricultural basin, was the Holy Grail for Oregon Trail pioneers who headed west more than 150 years ago. Today it's the state's breadbasket, producing more than 100 kinds of crops – including renowned Pinot Noir grapes (see p1065). Salem, Oregon's capital, is about an hour's drive from Portland at the northern end of the Willamette

---

WILLAMETTE VALLEY WINE COUNTRY

Just a hour's drive from Portland is the Willamette Valley, home to hundreds of wineries producing world-class tipples, especially Pinot Noir. McMinnville, Newberg and Dundee provide many of this region's services, which include some very fine restaurants, shops, B&Bs and wine-tasting rooms. Check out www.willamettewines.com for more information on the region's wineries.

Meandering through plush green hills on winding country roads from one wine-tasting room to another is a delightful way to spend an afternoon (just make sure you designate a driver). If you'd rather go on a tour, **Grape Escape** (☑503-283-3380; www.grapeescapetours.com) offers some good ones. If you like to bicycle, Portland-based Pedal Bike Tours (p1058) runs five-hour bike tours.

For something more cerebral, head to McMinnville's **Evergreen Aviation Museum** (☑503-434-4180; www.evergreenmuseum.org; 500 NE Captain Michael King Smith Way; adult/child 5-16yr $25/23 (incl 3-D movie); ☺9am-5pm; ⊞) and check out Howard Hughes' **Spruce Goose**, the world's largest wood-framed airplane. There's also a replica of the Wright brothers' *Flyer,* along with a 3-D theater and – oddly enough – an excellent water park.

For an interesting place to stay, head to **McMenamins Hotel Oregon** (☑503-472-8427; www.mcmenamins.com; 310 NE Evans St, McMinnville; d $75-145; ⊜⊞⊗⊞), an older building renovated into a charming hotel. It has a wonderful rooftop bar. And for a spectacular restaurant experience, consider **Joel Palmer House** (☑503-864-2995; www.joelpalmerhouse.com; 600 Ferry St, McMinnville; prix fixe $49-80; ☺4:30-9:30pm Tue-Sat) ☞; its dishes are peppered with wild mushrooms collected locally by the chefs.

Valley, and most of the other attractions in the area make easy day trips as well. Toward the south is Eugene, a dynamic college town worth a few days of exploration.

Salem

Oregon's legislative center (not the Salem associated with witches, which is in Massachusetts) is renowned for its cherry trees, art-deco capitol building and Willamette University.

Willamette University's **Hallie Ford Museum of Art** (900 State St; admission adult/under 12yr $3/free; ⊘10am-5pm Tue-Sat, from 1pm Sun) showcases the state's best collection of Pacific Northwest art, including an impressive Native American gallery.

The **Oregon State Capitol** (900 Court St NE; FREE, built in 1938, looks like a background prop from a lavish Cecil B DeMille movie; free tours are offered. Rambling 19th-century **Bush House** (☑503-363-4714; www.salemart.org; 600 Mission St SE; adult/child 6-15yr $6/3; ⊘1-4pm Wed-Sun, closed Jan & Feb) is an Italianate mansion now preserved as a museum with historic accents, including original wallpapers and marble fireplaces.

You can get oriented at the **Visitors Information Center** (www.travelsalem.com; 181 High St NE; ⊘8:30am-5pm Mon-Fri, 10am-4pm Sat).

Salem is served daily by **Greyhound** (☑503-362-2428; www.greyhound.com; 500 13th St SE) buses and **Amtrak** (☑503-588-1551; www.amtrak.com; 500 13th St SE) trains.

Eugene

Eclectic Eugene – also known as 'Tracktown' – is full of youthful energy and liberal politics, and famous for its track-and-field champions (Nike was born here, after all). And while the city maintains a working-class base in timber and manufacturing, some unconventional citizens live here as well, from ex-hippie activists to eco-green anarchists to upscale entrepreneurs to high-tech heads.

Eugene offers a great art scene, exceptionally fine restaurants, boisterous festivals, miles of riverside paths and several lovely parks. It's an awesome place to be, for both energetic visitors and those lucky enough to settle here.

⊙ Sights

Alton Baker Park   PARK
(100 Day Island Rd) This popular 400-acre riverside park is heaven for cyclists and joggers. It provides access to the **Ruth Bascom Riverbank Trail System**, a 12-mile cycleway that flanks both sides of the Willamette. The park is divided roughly in half, demarcating wild and manicured areas. Abutting the Willamette River, it connects to the city's wider trail network via three footbridges. Just northwest of Alton Baker Park and on the opposite side of the river, **Skinner Butte** (682ft) is a landmark hill replete with lawns, hiking trails and a prime city view.

WORTH A TRIP

HOT SPRINGS

Oregon has an abundance of hot springs and there some not far from Salem. A couple of hours' drive east of the city is **Bagby Hot Springs** (www.bagbyhotsprings.org; per person $5), a rustic hot spring with various wood tubs in semiprivate bathhouses. It's reachable via a 1.5 mile lovely hiking trail. From Estacada, head 26 miles south on Hwy 224. This road turns into Forest Rd 46; keep going straight for 3.5 more miles, then turn right onto Forest Rd 63 and go 3.6 miles to USFS Rd 70. Turn right again and go about 6 miles to the parking area.

There's another good soak at **Terwilliger Hot Springs** (aka Cougar Hot Springs), a beautiful cluster of terraced outdoor pools framed by large rocks ($6 per person fee). They're rustic but well maintained, with the hottest on top. From the parking lot, you'll have to walk 0.25 miles to the springs. To get here, turn south onto Aufderheide Scenic Byway from Hwy 126 and drive 7.5 miles.

For something more developed, check out **Breitenbush Hot Springs** (☑503-854-7174; www.breitenbush.com), a fancier spa with massages, yoga and vegetarian food. Breitenbush is east of Salem on Hwy 46, just past the town of Detroit.

University of Oregon UNIVERSITY
([✏]541-346-1000; www.uoregon.edu) Established in 1872, the University of Oregon is the state's foremost institution of higher learning, with a focus on the arts, sciences and law. The campus is filled with historic ivy-covered buildings and includes a **Pioneer Cemetery**, with tombstones that give vivid insight into life and death in the early settlement. A campus highlight is the **Jordan Schnitzer Museum of Art** ([✏]541-346-3027; www.jsma.uoregon.edu; 1430 Johnson Lane; admission adult/child $5/free; ⏰11am-5pm Tue-Sun, till 8pm Wed), which offers a rotating permanent collection of world-class art from Korean scrolls to Rembrandt paintings. The **Museum of Natural and Cultural History** ([✏]541-346-3024; http://natural-history.uoregon. edu; 1680 E 15th Ave; adult/3-18yr $3/2, free Wed; ⏰11am-5pm Wed-Sun) is also worth a visit for its Native American exhibits.

🛌 Sleeping

Eugene has all the regular chain hotels and motels. Prices rise sharply during key football games and graduation.

Campus Inn MOTEL $
([✏]541-343-3376; www.campus-inn.com; 390 E Broadway; d $70-80; ✷❄@🛜🐾) Very pleasant motel with spacious business-style rooms and simple yet stylish decor. Get the $10 upgrade for a bigger bed and more space. Small gym, communal Jacuzzi and upstairs outside patio available.

Eugene Whiteaker Hostel HOSTEL $
([✏]541-343-3335; www.eugenehostels.com; 970 W 3rd Ave; dm incl breakfast $25, r incl breakfast $40-70; ✷@🛜) Casual hostel in an old rambling house. Artsy vibe, nice front and back patios to hang out in, and a free simple breakfast. Campsites are available ($15 per person), and there's an annex down the street.

★C'est La Vie Inn B&B $$
([✏]541-302-3014; www.cestlavieinn.com; 1006 Taylor St; d $150-170; ✷❄@🛜) This gorgeous Victorian house, run by a friendly French woman and her American husband, is a neighborhood show-stopper. Beautiful antique furniture fills the living and dining areas, while the three tastefully appointed rooms offer comfort and luxury. Also available is an amazing suite with kitchenette ($260).

🍴 Eating

Sweet Life Patisserie CAFE, BAKERY $
([✏]541-683-5676; www.sweetlifedesserts.com; 755 Monroe St; pastries $2-5; ⏰7am-11pm Mon-Fri, from 8am Sat & Sun) 🥐 Eugene's best dessert shop; think pecan sticky buns, savory croissants and *pain au chocolat*. Even the day-old pastries it often sells off half-price are delicious. Organic coffee, too.

Belly Taquería MEXICAN $
([✏]541-687-8226; www.eatbelly.com; 291 E 5th Ave; tacos $3-4, tostadas $5-6; ⏰5-9pm Mon-Thu, till 10pm Fri & Sat) Corn tortilla tacos are on tap here – order the *carnitas* (slow-cooked pork), *camarones* (shrimp), scallops (beer-battered and fried) or *lengua* (tongue – don't knock it 'till you try it).

★Beppe & Gianni's Trattoria ITALIAN $$
([✏]541-683-6661; www.beppeandgiannis.net; 1646 E 19th Ave; mains $15-25; ⏰5-9pm Sun-Thu, to 10pm Fri & Sat) One of Eugene's most beloved restaurants and certainly its favorite for Italian food. Homemade pastas are the real deal here, and the desserts are excellent. Expect a wait.

McMenamins North Bank AMERICAN $$
([✏]541-343-5622; www.mcmenamins.com; 22 Club Rd; mains $9-20; ⏰11am-11pm Sun-Thu, to midnight Fri & Sat) Gloriously located on the banks of the mighty Willamette, this pub-restaurant boasts some of the best views in Eugene. Grab a riverside patio table on a warm, sunny day and order a cheeseburger with the Hammerhead ale – you can't get more stylin'.

ℹ️ Information

For information, try the **Visitor Center** (www. eugenecascadecoast.org; 754 Olive St; ⏰8am-5pm Mon-Fri).

ℹ️ Getting There & Around

Eugene's **Amtrak station** ([✏]541-687-1383; www.amtrak.com; cnr E 4th Ave & Willamette St) runs daily trains to Vancouver, BC, and LA, and everywhere in between on its *Cascade* and *Coast Starlight* lines. **Greyhound** ([✏]541-344-6265; www.greyhound.com; 987 Pearl St) runs north to Salem and Portland, and south to Grants Pass and Medford. **Porter Stage Lines** (www. kokkola-bus.com) runs a daily bus from outside the train station to the coast.

Local bus service is provided by **Lane Transit District** ([✏]541-682-6100; www.ltd.org; 3500

E 17th Ave). For bike rentals, try **Paul's Bicycle Way of Life** (152 W 5th St; ☉ 9am-7pm Mon-Fri, 10am-5pm Sat & Sun).

Columbia River Gorge

The fourth-largest river in the US by volume, the mighty Columbia runs 1243 miles from Alberta, Canada, into the Pacific Ocean just west of Astoria. For the final 309 miles of its course, the heavily dammed waterway delineates the border between Washington and Oregon and cuts though the Cascade Mountains via the spectacular Columbia River Gorge. Showcasing numerous ecosystems, waterfalls and magnificent vistas, the land bordering the river is protected as a National Scenic Area and is a popular sporting nexus for windsurfers, cyclists, anglers and hikers.

Not far from Portland, **Multnomah Falls** is a huge tourist draw, while **Vista House** offers stupendous gorge views. And if you want to stretch your legs, the **Eagle Creek Trail** is the area's premier tromp – provided you don't get vertigo!

Hood River & Around

Famous for its surrounding fruit orchards and wineries, the small town of Hood River – 63 miles east of Portland on I-84 – is also a huge mecca for windsurfing and kiteboarding. Strong river currents, prevailing westerly winds and the vast Columbia River provide the perfect conditions for these wind sports.

⊙ Sights & Activities

In operation since 1906, the 22-mile **Mount Hood Railroad** (☑ 800-872-4661; www.mthoodrr.com; 110 Railroad Ave) was built to transport lumber to the Columbia River. Today, it transports tourists beneath Mt Hood's snowy peak and past fragrant orchards on summer excusions. Reserve in advance.

Want to go wine tasting? Not far away is **Cathedral Ridge Winery** (☑ 800-516-8710; www.cathedralridgewinery.com; 4200 Post Canyon Dr).

To partake in Hood River's wind sports, contact **Hood River Waterplay** (☑ 541-386-9463; www.hoodriverwaterplay.com; Port of Hood River Marina) for rentals and classes. There's also great **mountain biking** in the area; head to **Discover Bicycles** (☑ 541-386-4820; www.discoverbicycles.com; 210 State St; ☉ 10am-

6pm Mon-Sat, till 5pm Sun) for information and rentals.

🛏 Sleeping & Eating

Inn of the White Salmon   INN, HOSTEL **$$**
(☑ 509-493-2335; www.innofthewhitesalmon.com; 172 West Jewett Blvd; d $129-189; ✆❋🎧) Over in White Salmon, Washington is this very pleasant and contemporary 18-room inn with comfortable rooms and a lovely patio-garden out back. There's also a very nice eight-bed dorm room available (single bunk $29, queen bunk for two $40), along with a common-use kitchenette area.

Hood River Hotel   HISTORIC HOTEL **$$**
(☑ 541-386-1900; www.hoodriverhotel.com; 102 Oak St; d $99-179; ✆❋🎧🐾) Located in downtown Hood River, this fine 1913 hotel offers comfortable old-fashioned rooms with tiny baths. The suites have the best amenities and views. Kitchenettes available.

Double Mountain Brewery   BREWPUB **$**
(☑ 541-387-0042; www.doublemountainbrewery.com; 8 4th St; sandwiches $7.50-10, pizzas $16-22; ☉ 11:30am-11pm Sun-Thu, till midnight Fri & Sat) This popular Hood River brewpub-restaurant is great for a tasty sandwich, excellent brick-oven pizza and home-brewed beer. Live music on weekends.

❶ Information

For information head to the **chamber of commerce** (☑ 541-386-2000; www.hoodriver.org; 720 E Port Marina Dr; ☉ 9am-5pm Mon-Fri year-round, 10am-5pm Sat & Sun Apr-Oct).

❶ Getting There & Away

Hood River is connected to Portland by daily **Greyhound** (☑ 541-386-1212; www.greyhound.com; 110 Railroad Ave) buses. **Amtrak** (www.amtrak.com) runs on the Washington side.

Oregon Cascades

The Oregon Cascades offer plenty of dramatic volcanoes that dominate the skyline for miles around. Mt Hood, overlooking the Columbia River Gorge, is the state's highest peak, and has year-round skiing plus a relatively straightforward summit ascent. Tracking south you'll pass Mt Jefferson and the Three Sisters before reaching Crater Lake, the ghost of erstwhile Mt Mazama that collapsed in on itself after blowing its top approximately 7000 years ago.

Mt Hood

The state's highest peak, Mt Hood (11,240ft) pops into view over much of northern Oregon whenever there's a sunny day, exerting an almost magnetic tug on skiers, hikers and sightseers. In summer, wildflowers bloom on the mountainsides and hidden ponds shimmer blue, making for some unforgettable hikes; in winter, downhill and cross-country skiing dominates people's minds and bodies.

Mt Hood is accessible year-round from Portland on US 26 and from Hood River on Hwy 35. Together with the Columbia River Hwy, these routes comprise the Mt Hood Loop, a popular scenic drive. Government Camp is at the pass over Mt Hood, and is the center of business on the mountain.

🏃 Activities

Skiing

Hood is rightly revered for its skiing. There are six ski areas on the mountain, including **Timberline** (📞503-272-3158; www.timberlinelodge.com; lift ticket adult/child 15-17/child 7-14 $68/56/42), which lures snow-lovers with the only year-round skiing in the US. Closer to Portland, **Mt Hood SkiBowl** (📞503-272-3206; www.skibowl.com; lift ticket adult/child 7-12 $49/30) is no slacker either. It's the nation's largest night-ski area and popular with city slickers who ride up for an evening of powder play from the metro zone. The largest ski area on the mountain is **Mt Hood Meadows** (📞503-337-2222; www.skihood.com; lift ticket adult/child 7-14 $74/39) and the best conditions usually prevail here.

Hiking

The Mt Hood National Forest protects an astounding 1200 miles of trails. A Northwest Forest Pass ($5) is required at most trailheads.

One popular trail loops 7 miles from near the village of Zigzag to beautiful **Ramona Falls**, which tumbles down mossy columnar basalt. Another heads 1.5 miles up from US 26 to **Mirror Lake**, continues 0.5 miles around the lake, then tracks 2 miles beyond to a ridge.

The 41-mile **Timberline Trail** circumnavigates Mt Hood through scenic wilderness. Noteworthy portions include the hike to McNeil Point and the short climb to Bald Mountain. From Timberline Lodge, Zigzag Canyon Overlook is a 4.5-mile round-trip. At research time, however, part of the trail was washed out, with no timetable for when it would be repaired.

Climbing Mt Hood should be taken seriously, as deaths do occur. Dog-owners are able to bring their dogs along. The climb can be done in a long day. Contact **Timberline Mountain Guides** (📞541-312-9242; www.timberlinemtguides.com) for guided climbs.

🛏 Sleeping & Eating

Reserve **campsites** (📞877-444-6777; www.reserveusa.com; campsites $12-18) in summer. Streamside campgrounds Tollgate and Camp Creek are on US 26. Large and popular Trillium Lake has great views of Mt Hood.

Huckleberry Inn INN $
(📞503-272-3325; www.huckleberry-inn.com; 88611 E Government Camp Loop; r $85-180; 😊📶) You'll find simple and comfortably rustic rooms here, including a bunk room that sleeps up to 14. The inn is in a great central location in Government Camp, and has a casual restaurant (which doubles as the hotel's reception). Holiday rates go up by 20%.

★**Timberline Lodge** LODGE $$
(📞800-547-1406; www.timberlinelodge.com; d $115-290; 😊📶🏊) More a community treasure than a hotel, this gorgeous historic wood gem from the 1930s offers a variety of rooms, from bunk rooms that sleep up to 10 to deluxe fireplace rooms. Huge wooden beams tower over multiple fireplaces, there's a year-round heated outdoor pool, and the ski lifts are close by. Enjoy awesome views of Mt Hood, access to nearby hiking trails, and the use of two bars and a good dining room. Not to be missed.

★**Rendezvous Grill & Tap Room** AMERICAN $$
(📞503-622-6837; www.rendezvousgrill.net; 67149 E US 26, Welches; lunch mains $9-16, dinner mains $13-22; ⏱11:30am-9pm) This excellent restaurant is in a league of its own. Outstanding dishes include citrus-curry wild salmon and char-grilled pork chop with apple-fennel chutney. Lunch means gourmet sandwiches, burgers and salads on the outdoor patio.

Ice Axe Grill BREWPUB $$
(📞503-272-3172; www.iceaxegrill.com; 87304 E Government Camp Loop, Government Camp; mains $12-18; ⏱11am-10pm) Government Camp's only brewery-restaurant, the Ice Axe offers a friendly, family-style atmosphere and pub

fare including good pizzas, shepherd's pie and upscale burgers. There are veggie chili and lentil burgers, too.

ⓘ Information

If you're approaching from Hood River, visit the **Hood River Ranger Station** (☑541-352-6002; 6780 Hwy 35, Parkdale; ☺8am-4:30pm Mon-Fri). The **Zigzag Ranger Station** (☑503-622-3191; 70220 E Hwy 26; ☺7:45am-4:30pm Mon-Sat) is more handy for Portland arrivals. **Mt Hood Information Center** (☑503-272-3301; 88900 E US 26; ☺9am-5pm) is in Government Camp. The weather changes quickly here; carry chains in winter.

ⓘ Getting There & Away

From Portland, Mt Hood is one hour (56 miles) by car along Hwy 26. Alternatively, you can take the prettier and longer approach via Hwy 84 to Hood River, then Hwy 35 south (1¾ hours, 95 miles). The **Central Oregon Breeze** (☑800-847-0157; www.cobreeze.com) shuttle between Bend and Portland stops briefly at Government Camp, 6 miles from the Timberline Lodge. There are regular **shuttles** (www.skihood.com) from Portland to the ski areas during the winter.

Sisters

Straddling the Cascades and high desert, where mountain pine forests mingle with desert sage and juniper, is the darling town of Sisters. Once a stagecoach stop and a trade town for loggers and ranchers, today Sisters is a bustling tourist destination whose main street is lined with boutiques, art galleries and eateries housed in Western-facade buildings. Visitors come for the mountain scenery, spectacular hiking, fine cultural events and awesome climate – there's plenty of sun and little precipitation here. And while the town's atmosphere is a bit upscale, people are still friendly and the back streets are still undeveloped enough that deer are often seen nibbling in neighborhood garden plots.

At the southern end of Sisters, the city park has **camp sites** ($15) but no showers. For ultracomfort, bag a room in the luxurious **Five Pine Lodge** (☑866-974-5900; www.fivepinelodge.com; 1021 Desperado Trail; d $170-257, cabins $179-317; ☺✳@☎☀). On the quieter and cheaper side is **Sisters Motor Lodge** (☑541-549-2551; www.sistersmotorlodge.com; 511 W Cascade St; r $119-225; ☺✳☎☀), offering 11 cozy rooms with homey decor (and some with kitchenettes).

For great gourmet treats head to **Porch** (☑541-549-3287; www.theporch-sisters.com; 243 N Elm St; small plates $6-12, mains $15-17; ☺5-9pm Tue-Sat), which offers morsels such as truffle fries and creamy butternut-squash risotto. **Three Creeks Brewing** (☑541-549-1963; www.threecreeksbrewing.com; 721 Desperado Ct; ☺11:30am-10pm Sun-Thu, till 11pm Fri & Sat) is the place to go for home brew and pub grub.

For local orientation, see the **chamber of commerce** (☑541-549-0251; www.sisterscountry.com; 291 Main St; ☺10am-4pm Mon-Sat).

Valley Retriever (www.kokkola-bus.com/VRBSchedule.html) buses connect Sisters with Bend, Newport, Corvallis, Salem, McMinnville and Portland; they stop at the corner of Cascade and Spruce Sts.

Bend

Bend is where all outdoor-lovers should live – it's an absolute paradise. You can ski fine powder in the morning, paddle a kayak in the afternoon and take in a game of golf into the evening. Or would you rather go mountain biking, hiking, mountaineering, stand-up paddleboarding, fly-fishing or rock climbing? It's all close by, and top-drawer. Plus, you'll probably be enjoying it all in great weather, as the area gets nearly 300 days of sunshine each year.

With the lovely Deschutes River carving its way through the heart of the city, Bend also offers a vibrant and attractive downtown area full of shops, galleries and upscale dining. South of downtown, the Old Mill District has been renovated into a large shopping area full of brand-name stores, fancy eateries and modern movie theaters. Bend has also become a beer-lover's dream; it has more than a dozen breweries and per capita more than any other city in Oregon.

◉ Sights

★**High Desert Museum**   MUSEUM
(☑541-382-4754; www.highdesertmuseum.org; 59800 S US 97; adult/child 5-12yr May-Oct $15/9, Nov-Apr $12/7; ☺9am-5pm; ☒) Don't miss this excellent museum about 3 miles south of Bend on US 97. It charts the exploration and settlement of the West, using re-enactments of a Native American camp, a hard-rock mine and an old Western town. The region's natural history is also explored; kids love the live snake, tortoise and trout exhibits, and watching the birds of prey and otters is always fun.

🏃 Activities

Cycling

Bend is a mountain-biking paradise, with hundreds of miles of awesome bike trails to explore. For a good bike-trails map, get the *Bend, Central Oregon Mountain Biking and XC Skiing* map ($12), available at the Visit Bend tourist office and elsewhere.

The king of Bend's mountain-biking trails is **Phil's Trail** network, which offers a variety of excellent fast single-track forest trails just minutes from town. If you want to catch air, don't miss the **Whoops Trail**.

Cog Wild (www.cogwild.com; 255 SW Century Dr) offers bike rentals, along with organized tours and shuttles out to the best trailheads.

Rock Climbing

About 25 miles northeast of Bend lies **Smith Rock State Park** (☑800-551-6949; www.oregonstateparks.org; 9241 NE Crooked River Dr; day use $5), where 800ft cliffs over the Crooked River offer gorgeous lead and trad climbing. The park's 1800-plus routes are among the best in the nation. Guides can be procured through **Smith Rock Climbing Guides Inc** (www.smithrockclimbingguides.com).

Skiing

Bend hosts Oregon's best skiing 22 miles southwest of the town at the glorious **Mount Bachelor Ski Resort** (☑800-829-2442; www.mtbachelor.com; lift tickets adult/child 6-12yr/child 13-18yr $59/36/49), famous for its 'dry' powdery snow, long season (until late May) and ample terrain (it's the largest ski area in the Pacific Northwest). The mountain has long advocated cross-country skiing in tandem with downhill, and maintains 35 miles of groomed trails.

🛏 Sleeping

Mill Inn   INN **$**
(☑877-748-1200, 541-389-9198; www.millinn.com; 642 NW Colorado Ave; dm $35, d incl breakfast $90-130; ☺🖧🛜) A 10-room boutique hotel with small, classy rooms decked out in velvet drapes and comforters; four share outside bathrooms. Full breakfast and hot tub use is included, and there's a nice back patio and basement recreation room. Budget travelers should go for the one (tight) dorm room.

★McMenamins Old St Francis School   HOTEL **$$**
(☑541-382-5174; www.mcmenamins.com; 700 NW Bond St; d $135-175, cottages $185-395; ☺🖧🛜) One of McMenamins' best venues, this old schoolhouse has been remodeled into a classy 19-room hotel. Two rooms have side-by-side clawfoot tubs, and the fabulous tiled saltwater Turkish bath is worth the stay alone, though nonguests can soak for $5. A restaurant-pub, three other bars, a cinema and creative artwork complete the picture.

★Oxford Hotel   BOUTIQUE HOTEL **$$$**
(☑877-440-8436; www.oxfordhotelbend.com; 10 NW Minnesota Ave; d $289-549; ☺🖧🛜🐾) 🐾 Bend's premier and very popular boutique hotel. The smallest rooms are huge (470 sq ft) and decked out with eco-features including soy-foam mattresses and cork flooring. High-tech aficionados will love the iPod docks and smart-panel work desk. Suites with kitchen and steam shower are available, and the basement restaurant is slick.

🍴 Eating & Drinking

★Chow   AMERICAN **$$**
(☑541-728-0256; www.chowbend.com; 1110 NW Newport Ave; mains $8-14; ⊙7am-2pm) 🐾 The signature poached-egg dishes here are spectacular and beautifully presented, served with sides such as crab cakes, house-cured ham and corn-meal-crusted tomatoes (don't miss their homemade hot sauces). Or try the caramelized banana French toast, or bacon biscuits with thyme. Gourmet sandwiches and salads are available for lunch, with many vegetables grown in the garden. Good cocktails, too.

Jackson's Corner   AMERICAN **$$**
(☑541-647-2198; www.jacksonscornerbend.com; 845 NW Delaware Ave; mains $10-26; ⊙7am-9pm; 🖐) This homey corner restaurant has a market-like feel and is very popular with families. Homemade pizzas and pastas are always tasty, as are the organic salads (add on chicken, steak or prawns). There's a kids menu, and outside seating for sunny days; just remember to order at the counter first.

Deschutes Brewery & Public House   BREWERY
(☑541-382-9242; www.deschutesbrewery.com; 1044 NW Bond St; ⊙11am-11pm Mon-Thu, till midnight Fri & Sat, till 10pm Sun) Bend's first microbrewery serves up handcrafted beers, including Mirror Pond Pale Ale, Black Butte Porter and Obsidian Stout, and plenty of food at their beautiful huge two-story restaurant with balcony seating. Free daily tours run every hour from 1pm tp 4pm at the plant, located at 901 SW Simpson Ave.

PACIFIC NORTHWEST OREGON CASCADES

Crux BREWERY

(☑ 541-385-3333; www.cruxfermentation.com; 50 SW Division St; ⊙ 11:30am-10pm Tue-Sun) Bend's latest brewpub darling, located in an industrial neighborhood (don't let the 'private road' signs put you off). It has an awesome casual atmosphere. Fermentation tanks behind glass windows house the unique, experimental beers. There's outdoor seating, it's family-friendly and has a good range of foods made with beer.

❶ Information

For local information, see the **Visit Bend** (☑ 800-949-6086; www.visitbend.com; 750 NW Lava Rd; ⊙ 9am-5pm Mon-Fri, 10am-4pm Sat) tourist office.

❶ Getting There & Away

Central Oregon Breeze (p1070) offers transport to Portland two or more times daily. Connect to Sisters, Willamette Valley destinations and the coast with Valley Retriever (p1070) and **Porter Stage Lines** (www.kokkola-bus.com/PSLSchedule.html).

High Desert Point (www.highdesert-point.com) buses link Bend with Chemult, where the nearest train station is located (65 miles south). High Desert Point also has bus services to Eugene, Ontario and Burns.

Cascades East Transit (www.cascadeseast-transit.com) is the regional bus company in Bend, covering La Pine, Mt Bachelor, Sisters, Prineville and Madras. It also provides bus transport within Bend.

Newberry National Volcanic Monument

Newberry National Volcanic Monument (day use $5) showcases 400,000 years of dramatic seismic activity. Start your visit at the **Lava Lands Visitor Center** (☑ 541-593-2421; 58201 S Hwy 97; ⊙ 9am-5pm mid-June to Labor Day weekend, limited hours off-season), 13 miles south of Bend. Nearby attractions include **Lava Butte**, a perfect cone rising 500ft, and **Lava River Cave**, Oregon's longest lava tube. Four miles west of the visitor center is **Benham Falls**, a good picnic spot on the Deschutes River.

Newberry Crater was once one of the most active volcanoes in North America, but after a large eruption a caldera was born. Close by are **Paulina Lake** and **East Lake**, deep lakes rich with trout, while looming above is 7985ft **Paulina Peak**.

Crater Lake National Park

It's no exaggeration: Crater Lake is so blue, you'll catch your breath. And if you get to see it on a calm day, the surrounding cliffs are reflected in those deep waters like a mirror. It's a stunningly beautiful sight. Crater Lake is Oregon's only national park (entry costs $10 per vehicle).

The secret lies in the water's purity. No rivers or streams feed the lake, meaning its content is made up entirely of rain and melted snow. It is also exceptionally deep – at 1949ft, it's the deepest lake in the US. The classic tour is the 33-mile rim drive (open from approximately June to mid-October), but there are also exceptional hiking and cross-country skiing opportunities. Note that because the area receives some of the highest snowfalls in North America, the rim drive and north entrance are sometimes closed up until early July.

You can stay from late May to mid-October at the **Cabins at Mazama Village** (☑ 541-830-8700; www.craterlakelodges.com; d $140; ❀) or the majestic and historic **Crater Lake Lodge** (☑ 888-774-2728; www.craterlakelodges.com; d $165-292; ❀ ☎), opened in 1915. Campers head to **Mazama Campground** (☑ 888-774-2728; www.craterlakelodges.com; tent/RV sites from $21/29; ☎ ❀).

For more information, head to **Steel Visitor Center** (☑ 541-594-3100; ⊙ 9am-5pm May-Oct, 10am-4pm Nov-Apr).

Southern Oregon

With a warm and sunny climate that belongs in nearby California, southern Oregon is the state's banana belt. Rugged landscapes, scenic rivers and a couple of attractive towns top the highlights list.

Ashland

Oregon was unknown territory to the Elizabethan explorers of William Shakespeare's day, so it might seem a little strange to find that the pretty settlement of Ashland in southern Oregon has established itself as the English playwright's second home. The irony probably wouldn't have been lost on Shakespeare himself. 'All the world's a stage,' the great Bard once opined, and fittingly people come from all over to see Ashland's famous Shakespeare Festival, which has been held here under various guises since

OREGON SHAKESPEARE FESTIVAL

One of southern Oregon's highlights is Ashland's wildly popular Oregon Shakespeare Festival (OSF). Despite being deeply rooted in Shakespearean and Elizabethan drama, the festival also features plenty of revivals and contemporary theater from around the world.

Productions run from February to October in three theaters near Main and Pioneer Sts: the outdoor **Elizabethan Theatre** (open from June to October), the **Angus Bowmer Theatre** and the intimate **Thomas Theatre**. Children under six are not allowed. There are no performances on Mondays.

Performances sell out quickly; obtain tickets at www.osfashland.org. The **box office** (541-482-4331; 15 S Pioneer St; tickets $25-95) also has last minute tickets. Be sure to book backstage **tours** (adult/child 6-17yr $15/11) well in advance.

Check the **OSF Welcome Center** (76 N Main St; ⊘10am-6pm Tue-Sun) for other events, which may include scholarly lectures, play readings, concerts and preshow talks.

the 1930s. The 'festival' moniker is misleading; the shows here are a semipermanent fixture occupying nine months of the annual town calendar and attracting up to 400,000 theater-goers per season.

Even without the shows, Ashland is an attractive town, propped up by various wineries, upscale B&Bs and fine restaurants.

◉ Sights & Activities

Lithia Park   PARK
(59 Winburn Way) Adjacent to Ashland's three splendid theaters (one of which is outdoors) lies one of the loveliest city parks in Oregon, whose 93 acres wind along Ashland Creek above the center of town. Unusually, the park is in the National Register of Historic Places and is embellished with fountains, flowers, gazebos and an ice-skating rink (winter only).

Schneider Museum of Art   MUSEUM
(541-552-6245; www.sou.edu/sma; 1250 Siskiyou Blvd; suggested donation $5; ⊘10am-4pm Mon-Sat) Like all good Oregonian art museums, this one's on the local university campus and displays a fine collection of paintings, sculptures and artifacts.

Jackson Wellsprings   SPA
(541-482-3776; www.jacksonwellsprings.com; 2253 Hwy 99; ⊘8am-midnight, shorter hours winter) For a good soak, try this casual New Age-style place, which maintains an 85°F (29°C) mineral-fed swimming pool and 103°F (39°C) private soaking tubs. It's about a mile north of town.

Mt Ashland Ski Resort   SKI RESORT
(541-482-2897; www.mtashland.com; lift pass adult/child 7-12yr $43/33) Powdery snow is surprisingly abundant at this resort 18 miles southwest of Ashland on Mt Ashland (7533ft), which has some excellent advanced terrain.

Siskiyou Cyclery   BICYCLE RENTAL
(541-482-1997; www.siskiyoucyclery.com; 1729 Siskiyou Blvd; ⊘10am-6pm Mon-Sat, 11am-4pm Sun) Pedal-pushers can rent a bike here and explore the countryside on the semi-completed Bear Creek Greenway, a 21-mile bike path between Ashland and the town of Central Point.

⊨ Sleeping

Reserve ahead in summer when the thespians descend in droves.

Manor Motel   MOTEL $
(541-482-2246; www.manormotel.net; 476 N Main St; d $87-129; ⊛✳⊚☎) Cute motel with 12 pleasant rooms and one- and two-bedroom units near downtown; kitchenettes available. The Garden Suite has its own private garden.

Ashland Hostel   HOSTEL $
(541-482-9217; www.theashlandhostel.com; 150 N Main St; dm $28, d $45-94; ⊛✳☎) Central and somewhat upscale hostel (shoes-off inside!). Most private rooms share bathrooms; some are connected to dorms. Hangout spaces include the cozy basement living room and shady front porch. No alcohol or smoking on premises; call ahead as reception times are limited.

Ashland Commons   APARTMENTS, HOSTEL $
(541-482-6753; www.ashlandcommons.com; 437 Williamson Way; dm $26, s $45-65, d $60-80; ⊛✳☎) Interesting dorm or private-room accommodations, provided within three large apartments. All vary in atmosphere, and are either two- or four-bedroom, with

kitchen and living areas. Great for large groups, as entire apartments can be rented.

The Palm
BOUTIQUE HOTEL $$

(☑541-482-2636; www.palmcottages.com; 1065 Siskiyou Blvd; d $98-239; ☻❀🛜🏊🐾) Fabulous small motel remodeled into 16 charming garden cottage rooms and suites (some with kitchens). It's an oasis of green on a busy avenue, complete with grassy lawns and a saltwater pool. A house harbors three large suites ($299).

Columbia Hotel
HOTEL $$

(☑541-482-3726; www.columbiahotel.com; 262 1/2 E Main St; d $89-179; ☻❀🛜) Awesomely located 'European-style' hotel – which means most rooms share outside bathrooms. It's the best deal in downtown Ashland, with 24 quaint vintage rooms (no TVs), a nice lobby and a thick historic feel. The rooms are on the 2nd floor and there's no elevator.

✖ Eating & Drinking

There are plenty of great eating choices in Ashland, which levies a 5% restaurant tax. Dinner reservations in summer are a good idea at the fancier spots.

★ Morning Glory
CAFE $

(☑541-488-8636; www.morninggloryrestaurant.com; 1149 Siskiyou Blvd; mains $11-13; ☻8am-1:30pm) This colorful, casual cafe is one of Ashland's best breakfast joints. Creative dishes include the Alaskan crab omelet, vegetarian hash with roasted chilis and shrimp cakes with poached eggs. For lunch there's gourmet salad and sandwiches. Go early or late to avoid a long wait.

Ashland Food Cooperative
SELF-CATERING $

(☑541-482-2237; www.ashlandfood.coop; 237 N 1st St; ☻7am-9pm) Head to this awesome food co-op if you've scored a kitchenette in your hotel room. All the typical healthy foods are available, and there's a small cafe-deli and to-go food bar.

★ New Sammy's
Cowboy Bistro
FRENCH, AMERICAN $$$

(☑541-535-2779; 2210 S Pacific Hwy, Talent; mains $25-28, prix fixe $45; ☻noon-1:30 & 5-9pm Wed-Sun) 🍃 One of Oregon's best restaurants has only a handful of tables and a spectacular wine selection. Mains are few but the flavor combinations can be incredible; many vegetables come from the garden outside. Located in Talent, about 2 miles north of Ashland. Reserve a week in advance for dinner.

Caldera Tap House
BREWPUB

(☑541-482-4677; www.calderabrewing.com; 31 Water St; ☻2pm-close) Popular, casual brewpub with outdoor decks under a street overpass. Typical pub grub accompanied by award-winning ales and lagers; live music two to three times per week. Also has a fancier restaurant at 590 Clover St.

❶ Information

For information, visit the **Chamber of Commerce** (☑541-482-3486; www.ashlandchamber.com; 110 E Main St; ☻9am-5pm Mon-Fri).

Jacksonville

This small but endearing former gold-prospecting town is the oldest settlement in southern Oregon and a National Historic Landmark. The main drag is lined with well-preserved buildings dating from the 1880s, now converted into boutiques and galleries. Music-lovers shouldn't miss the September **Britt Festival** (www.brittfest.org; ☻Jun-Sep), a world-class musical experience with top-name performers. Seek more enlightenment at the **Chamber of Commerce** (☑541-899-8118; www.jacksonvilleoregon.org; 185 N Oregon St; ☻10am-5pm Mon-Fri, till 3pm Sat & Sun).

Jacksonville is full of fancy B&Bs; for budget motels head 6 miles east to Medford. The **Jacksonville Inn** (☑541-899-1900; www.jacksonvilleinn.com; 175 E California St; d $159-199; ☻❀🛜🏊) is the most pleasant abode, shoe-horned downtown in an 1863 building with regal antique-stuffed rooms. There's a fine restaurant on-site.

Wild Rogue Wilderness

Situated between the town of Grants Pass on I-5 and Gold Beach on the Oregon coast, the aptly named Wild Rogue Wilderness is anchored by the turbulent Rogue River, which cuts through 40 miles of untamed, roadless canyon. The area is known for challenging white-water rafting (classes III and IV) and long-distance hikes.

The humble city of **Grants Pass** is the gateway to adventures along the Rogue. For information, the **chamber of commerce** (☑541-450-6180; www.visitgrantspass.org; 1995 NW Vine St; ☻8am-5pm Mon-Fri) is right off I-5, exit 58. For raft permits and backpacking advice, contact the Bureau of Land Management's **Smullin Visitors Center** (☑541-479-3735; www.blm.gov/or/resources/recreation/rogue;

14335 Galice Rd, Galice; ☉ 7am-3pm) in Galice, 16 miles northwest of Grants Pass.

Rafting the Rogue is legendary, but not for the faint of heart; a typical trip takes three days and costs upward of $780. A good outfitter is **Rogue Wilderness Adventures** (☑ 800-336-1647; www.wildrogue.com; 325 Galice Rd, Merlin). Kayaking the river is equally exhilarating; for instruction and guidance, contact **Sundance Kayak** (☑ 541-386-1725; www.sundancekayak.com).

Another highlight of the region is the 42-mile **Rogue River Trail**, once a supply route from Gold Beach. The full trek takes four to five days; day hikers might aim for Whiskey Creek Cabin, a 6-mile round-trip from the Grave Creek trailhead. The trail is dotted with rustic lodges ($110 to $160 per person including meals; reservations required) – try **Black Bar** (☑ 541-479-6507; www.blackbarlodge. com; Merlin). There are also primitive campgrounds along the way.

North Umpqua River

This 'Wild and Scenic' river boasts world-class fly-fishing, fine hiking and serene camping. The 79-mile **North Umpqua Trail** begins near Idleyld Park, three miles east of Glide, and passes through Steamboat en route to the Pacific Crest Trail. A popular sideline is pretty **Umpqua Hot Springs**, east of Steamboat near Toketee Lake. Not far away, stunning, two-tiered **Toketee Falls** (113ft) flows over columnar basalt, while **Watson Falls** (272ft) is one of the highest waterfalls in Oregon. For information, stop by Glide's **Colliding Rivers Information Center** (☑ 541-496-0157; 18782 N Umpqua Hwy, Glide; ☉ 9am-5pm May-Sep). Adjacent is the **North Umpqua Ranger District** (☑ 541-496-3532; 18782 N Umpqua Hwy; ☉ 8am-4:30pm Mon-Fri).

Between Idleyld Park and Diamond Lake are dozens of riverside campgrounds; these include lovely **Susan Creek** and primitive **Boulder Flat** (no water). Area accommodations fill up quickly in summer; try the log-cabin-like rooms at **Dogwood Motel** (☑ 541-496-3403; www.dogwoodmotel.com; 28866 N Umpqua Hwy; d $70-75; ☉ ❋ 🛜 🐾).

Oregon Caves National Monument

This very popular cave (there's only one) lies 19 miles east of Cave Junction on Hwy 46. Three miles of passages are explored via

90-minute cave tours that include 520 rocky steps and dripping chambers running along the River Styx. Dress warmly, wear shoes with good traction and be prepared to get dripped on.

Cave Junction, 28 miles south of Grants Pass on US 199 (Redwood Hwy), provides the region's services – though the best area sleeps are at the **Holiday Motel** (☑ 541-592-3003; 24810 Redwood Hwy; d $68-78; ☉ ❋ 🛜), two miles north in Kerby. For fancy lodgings right at the cave there's the impressive **Oregon Caves Chateau** (☑ 541-592-3400; www.oregoncaveschateau.com; 20000 Caves Hwy; r $109-199; ☉ mid-May to late Sep; ☉); grab a milkshake at the old-fashioned soda fountain here. Campers should head to **Cave Creek Campground** (☑ 541-592-4000; campsites $10), 14 miles up Hwy 46, about 4 miles from the cave.

Eastern Oregon

Oregon east of the Cascades bears little resemblance to its wetter western cohort, either physically or culturally. Few people live here – the biggest town, Pendleton, numbers only 20,000 – and the region hoards high plateaus, painted hills, alkali lake beds and the country's deepest river gorge.

John Day Fossil Beds National Monument

Within the soft rocks and crumbly soils of John Day country lies one of the world's greatest fossil collections, laid down between six and 50 million years ago. Roaming the forests at the time were nimravids (false saber-toothed cats), pint-sized horses, bear-dogs and other early mammals.

The national monument includes 22 sq miles at three different units: Sheep Rock Unit, Painted Hills Unit and Clarno Unit. Each has hiking trails and interpretive displays. To visit all of the units in one day requires quite a bit of driving, as more than 100 slow miles of curvy roads separate the fossil beds – it's best to take it easy and spend the night somewhere.

Visit the excellent **Thomas Condon Paleontology Center** (☑ 541-987-2333; www.nps.gov/joda; 32651 Hwy 19, Kimberly; ☉ 10am-5pm, occasionally closed due to short staffing), 2 miles north of US 26 at the **Sheep Rock Unit**. Displays include a three-toed horse and petrified dung-beetle balls, along with many other fossils and geologic history exhibits. If you feel like walking, take the short hike up the Blue Basin Trail.

The **Painted Hills Unit**, near the town of Mitchell, consists of low-slung, colorfully banded hills formed about 30 million years ago. Ten million years older is the **Clarno Unit**, which exposes mud flows that washed over an Eocene-era forest and eroded into distinctive, sheer white cliffs topped with spires and turrets of stone.

Rafting is popular on the John Day River, the longest free-flowing river in the state. **Oregon River Experiences** (☑800-827-1358; www.oregonriver.com) offers trips of up to five days. There's also good fishing for smallmouth bass and rainbow trout; find out more at the **Oregon Department of Fish & Wildlife** (www.dfw.state.or.us).

Most towns in the area have at least one hotel; these include the atmospheric **Historic Oregon Hotel** (☑541-462-3027; 104 E Main St; dm $20, d $45-69; ☎) in Mitchell and economical **Dreamers Lodge** (☑800-654-2849; 144 N Canyon Blvd; d from $63; ☯❋☎☯) in the town of John Day (which has most of the area's services). There are several public campgrounds in the area, including Lone Pine and Big Bend (camp sites $5) on Hwy 402.

Wallowa Mountains Area

The Wallowa Mountains, with their glacier-hewn peaks and crystalline lakes, are among the most beautiful natural areas in Oregon. The only drawback is the large number of visitors who flock here in summer, especially to the pretty Wallowa Lake area. Escape them all on one of several long hikes into the nearby **Eagle Cap Wilderness** area, such as the 6-mile one-way jaunt to **Aneroid Lake** or the 8-mile trek on the **Ice Lake Trail**.

Just north of the mountains, in the Wallowa Valley, **Enterprise** is a homely backcountry town with several motels such as the **Ponderosa** (☑541-426-3186; 102 E Greenwood St; d $70-80; ❋☎☯). If you like beer and good food, don't miss the town's microbrewery, **Terminal Gravity Brewing** (☑541-426-3000; www.terminalgravitybrewing.com; 803 SE School St; mains $9-12; ☯11am-9pm Sun-Tue, till 10pm Wed-Sat). Just 6 miles south is Enterprise's fancy cousin, the upscale town of **Joseph**. Expensive bronze galleries and artsy boutiques line the main strip, along with some good eateries.

Hells Canyon

North America's deepest river gorge (yes – even deeper than the Grand Canyon when measured from the highest mountain peak) provides visitors with some wild and scenic vistas. The mighty Snake River has taken 13 million years to carve its path through the high plateaus of eastern Oregon to its present depth of 8000ft. The canyon itself is a true wilderness bereft of roads but open to the curious and the brave.

For perspective, drive 30 miles northeast from Joseph to Imnaha, where a slow-going 24-mile gravel road leads up to the excellent lookout at **Hat Point**. From here you can see the Wallowa Mountains, Idaho's Seven Devils, the Imnaha River and the wilds of the canyon itself. This road is open from late May until snowfall; give yourself two hours each way for the drive.

For white-water action and spectacular scenery, head down to **Hells Canyon Dam**, 25 miles north of the small community of Oxbow. A few miles past the dam, the road ends at the **Hells Canyon Visitor Center** (☑541-785-3395; ☯8am-4pm May-Sep), which has good advice on the area's campgrounds and hiking trails. Beyond here, the Snake River drops 1300ft in elevation through wild rapids accessible only by jet boat or raft. **Hells Canyon Adventures** (☑800-422-3568; www.hellscanyonadventures.com) is the main operator running raft trips and jet-boat tours from May through September (reservations required).

The area has many campgrounds. Just outside Imnaha is the huntsman-style **Imnaha River Inn** (☑866-601-9214; www.imnahariverinn.com; 73946 Rimrock Rd; s/d from $70/130), a B&B replete with Hemingway-esque animal trophies, while Oxbow has the good-value **Hells Canyon B&B** (☑541-785-3373; www.hcbb.us; 49922 Homestead Rd; d $80; ☯❋☎). For more services, head to the towns of Enterprise, Joseph and Halfway.

Steens Mountain & Alvord Desert

The highest peak in southeastern Oregon, Steens Mountain (9773ft) is part of a massive, 30-mile-long fault-block range that was formed about 15 million years ago. On the western slope of the range, Ice Age glaciers bulldozed trenches that formed massive U-shaped gorges and hanging valleys. To the east, 'the Steens' – as the range is usually referred to as – drop off to the Alvord Desert, 5000ft below.

Beginning in Frenchglen (population 12), the gravel 56-mile **Steens Mountain Loop Rd** is Oregon's highest road and offers the range's best sights with its awesome overlooks, and also has access to camping and hiking trails. You'll see sagebrush, bands of junipers and aspen forests, and finally fragile rocky tundra at the top. **Kiger Gorge viewpoint** is especially stunning; it's 25 miles up from Frenchglen. It takes about two hours all the way around if you're just driving through, but you'll want to see the sights so give yourself much more time. You can also see the eastern side of the Steens via the Fields-Denio road, which goes through the **Alvord Desert** between Hwys 205 and 78. Take a full tank of gas and plenty of water, and be prepared for weather changes at any time of year.

Frenchglen has the charming **Frenchglen Hotel** (☑541-493-2825; fghotel@yahoo.com; 39184 Hwy 205, Frenchglen; d $75-115; ☺mid-Mar–Oct; ☻❋☗), with its small dining room (reserve for dinners), a small store with seasonal gas pump and not much else. There are camping options on the Steens Mountain Loop Rd, such as the BLM's pretty **Page Springs**, open year-round. A few other campgrounds (sites $6 to $8), further into the loop, are very pleasant but accessible in summer only. Water is available at all of these campgrounds. Free backcountry camping is also allowed in the Steens.

Oregon Coast

Thanks to a farsighted government in the 1910s, Oregon's 363-mile Pacific Coast was set aside as public land. This magnificent littoral is paralleled by US 101, a scenic highway that winds its way through towns, resorts, state parks (more than 70 of them) and wilderness areas. Everyone from campers to gourmet-lovers will find a plethora of ways to enjoy this exceptional region.

Astoria

Astoria sits at the 5-mile-wide mouth of the Columbia River and was the first US settlement west of the Mississippi. The city has a long seafaring history and has seen its old harbor, once home to poor artists and writers, attract fancy hotels and restaurants in recent years. Inland are many historical houses, including lovingly restored Victorians – a few converted into romantic B&Bs.

◉ Sights

Adding to the city's scenery is the 4.1-mile Astoria-Megler Bridge, the longest continuous truss bridge in North America, which crosses the Columbia River into Washington State. See it from the Astoria Riverwalk, which follows the trolley route. Pier 39 is an interesting covered wharf with an informal cannery museum and a couple places to eat.

★ Columbia River Maritime Museum   MUSEUM
(☑503-325-2323; www.crmm.org; 1792 Marine Dr; adult/child 6-17yr $12/5; ☺9:30am-5pm) Astoria's seafaring heritage is well interpreted at this wave-shaped museum. It's hard to miss the Coast Guard boat, frozen in action, through the huge outside window. Other exhibits highlight the salmon-packing industry, local lighthouses and the river's commercial history; also check out the Columbia River Bar exhibit and 3-D theater.

Flavel House   HISTORIC BUILDING
(www.cumtux.org; 441 8th St; adult/child 6-17yr $5/4; ☺10am-5pm) The Queen Anne Flavel House was built by Captain George Flavel, one of Astoria's leading citizens during the 1880s.

Astoria Column   LANDMARK
(☑503-325-2963; www.astoriacolumn.org; Coxcomb Hill; parking $1) Rising high on Coxcomb Hill, the Astoria Column (1926) is a 125ft tower painted with scenes from the westward sweep of US exploration and settlement. The top of the column (up 164 steps) offers excellent views over the area.

Fort Stevens State Park   PARK
(☑503-861-1671; www.oregonstateparks.org; 100 Peter Iredale Rd, Hammond; day use $5) Ten miles west of Astoria, this park holds the historic military installation that guarded the mouth of the Columbia River. Near the **Military Museum** (☑503-861-2000; ☺10am-6pm May-Sep, to 4pm Oct-Apr) **FREE** are gun batteries dug into sand dunes – interesting remnants of the fort's mostly demolished military buildings. There's a popular beach at the small Peter Iredale 1906 shipwreck, plus camping and 12 miles of paved bike trails.

LEWIS & CLARK: JOURNEY'S END

In November 1805 William Clark and his fellow explorer Meriwether Lewis of the Corps of Discovery staggered, with three dozen others, into a sheltered cove on the Columbia River, 2 miles west of the present-day Astoria-Megler Bridge, completing what was indisputably the greatest overland trek in American history.

After the first truly democratic ballot in US history (in which a woman and a black slave both voted), the party elected to make their bivouac 5 miles south of Astoria at Fort Clatsop, where the Corps spent a miserable winter in 1805–06. Today this site is called the **Lewis and Clark National & State Historical Parks** (www.nps. gov/lewi), where you'll find a reconstructed Fort Clatsop, along with a visitor's center and historical reenactments in summer.

🛏 Sleeping & Eating

Norblad Hotel & Hostel   HOTEL, HOSTEL $
(☑ 503-325-6989; www.norbladhotel.com; 443 14th St; dm $30, d $59-89; ☺🛜🐾) This central option offers six simple but elegant private rooms, most with shared bathroom and one with en-suite ($74). There are also several dorm rooms and a communal kitchen. Some have flat-screen TVs and glimpses of the river.

★Commodore Hotel   BOUTIQUE HOTEL $$
(☑ 503-325-4747; www.commodoreastoria.com; 258 14th St; d with shared/private bath from $89/149; ☺🛜) Hip travelers should beeline to this slick and trendy hotel, which offers small, chic, minimalist rooms. Choose either private bathrooms or go euro-style (sinks in rooms but baths down the hall; 'deluxe' rooms have better views). Great living room–style lobby with attached cafe. Room 309 has the best river view.

Blue Scorcher Bakery Café   CAFE $
(☑ 503-338-7473; www.bluescorcher.com; 1493 Duane St; mains $7-13; ☺8am-5pm; 📶🍴) 🍃 Artsy, organic co-op coffeehouse and bakery. Tasty salads, sandwiches, pizza and egg dishes for breakfast. Vegetarian and vegan friendly; doughnut-free.

Fort George Brewery   BREWPUB $$
(☑ 503-325-7468; www.fortgeorgebrewery.com; 1483 Duane St; mains $9-14; ☺11am-11pm Mon-Thu, till midnight Fri & Sat, noon-11pm Sun) Atmospheric brewery-restaurant in a historic building – this was the original settlement site of Astoria. Today you can get gourmet burgers, homemade sausages, organic salads and a few eclectic dishes. Afternoon brewery tours on weekends.

ℹ Information

Find local information head to the **visitor center** (www.oldoregon.com; 111 W Marine Dr; ☺9am-5pm).

ℹ Getting There & Away

Twice-daily **Northwest Point** (☑ 503-484-4100; www.northwest-point.com) buses head to Seaside, Cannon Beach and Portland. **Sunset Empire Transit** (☑ 503-861-7433; www.ridethebus. org; 900 Marine Dr) provides local transport; buses also head to Warrenton, Cannon Beach and Seaside.

Cannon Beach

Charming Cannon Beach is one of the most popular and upscale beach resorts on the Oregon coast. The streets are full of boutiques and art galleries, and lined with colorful flowers. Lodging is expensive, and the streets are jammed; on a warm sunny Saturday, you'll spend a good chunk of time just finding a parking spot.

◎ Sights & Activities

Photogenic **Haystack Rock**, a 295ft sea stack, is the most spectacular landmark on the Oregon coast and accessible from the beach at low tide. Birds cling to its ballast cliffs and tide pools ring its base.

The coast to the north, protected inside **Ecola State Park** (☑ 503-436-2844; day use $5), is the Oregon you may have already visited in your dreams: sea stacks, crashing surf, hidden beaches and gorgeous pristine forest. The park is 1.5 miles from town and is crisscrossed by paths, including part of the Oregon Coast Trail, which leads over Tillamook Head to the town of Seaside.

The Cannon Beach area is good for surfing, though not the beach itself. The best spots are Indian Beach in Ecola State Park, 3 miles to the north, and Oswald West State Park, 10 miles south. **Cleanline Surf Shop** (www.cleanlinesurf.com; 171 Sunset Blvd) is a friendly local shop that rents out boards and mandatory wetsuits.

Sleeping & Eating

Cannon Beach Hotel   HISTORIC HOTEL **$$**
(☑ 503-436-1392; www.cannonbeachhotellodgings.com; 1116 S Hemlock St; d incl breakfast $139-269; ☺☜) A classy, centrally located hotel with just 10 rooms. Standards are lovely but very small; even the regular suites are tight. A good breakfast at the cafe on the premises is included.

Blue Gull Inn Motel   MOTEL **$$**
(☑ 800-507-2714; www.haystacklodgings.com; 487 S Hemlock St; d $119-219; ☺☜☷) Some of the more affordable rooms in town, with comfortable atmosphere and toned-down decor. Kitchenette and Jacuzzi units available. Run by Haystack Lodgings.

Sleepy Monk Coffee   CAFE **$**
(☑ 503-436-2796; www.sleepymonkcoffee.com; 1235 S Hemlock St; ☺ 8am-2pm Mon & Tue, till 4pm Fri-Sun) ☕ For organic, certified fair-trade coffee, try this little coffee shop on the main street. It also runs the **Irish Table**, an excellent restaurant in the same building.

★ **Newman's at 988**   FRENCH, ITALIAN **$$$**
(☑ 503-436-1151; www.newmansat988.com; 988 S Hemlock St; mains $22-36; ☺ 5:30-9pm daily Jul 1-Oct 15, Tue-Sun Oct 16-Jun 30) Small but quality restaurant on the main drag. Award-winning chef John Newman comes up with a fusion of French and Italian dishes. Desserts are sublime.

ⓘ Information

For information try the **Chamber of Commerce** (☑ 503-436-2623; www.cannonbeach.org; 207 N Spruce St; ☺ 10am-5pm).

ⓘ Getting There & Away

Northwest Point (www.northwest-point.com) buses head from Astoria to Portland (and vice versa) every morning, stopping at Cannon Beach; buy tickets at the Beach Store, next to Cannon Beach Surf.

The **Cannon Beach Shuttle** (☑ 503-861-7433; www.ridethebus.org), also known as 'The Bus,' runs the length of Hemlock St to the end of Tolovana Beach; the schedule varies seasonally. Both buses go to Seaside and Astoria, too.

The **Wave** buses (www.tillamookbus.com) go south towards Manzanita and Lincoln City several times daily.

Newport

Home to Oregon's largest commercial fishing fleet, Newport is a lively tourist city with several fine beaches and a world-class aquarium. In 2011 it became the host of NOAA, the National Oceanic and Atmospheric Administration. Good restaurants – along with some tacky attractions, gift shops

PACIFIC NORTHWEST OREGON COAST

WORTH A TRIP

SCENIC DRIVE: THREE CAPES

Cape Meares, Cape Lookout and Cape Kiwanda, about halfway between Cannon Beach and Newport, are some of the coast's most stunning headlands, strung together on a slow, winding and sometimes bumpy 40-mile alternative to US 101. It's a worthwhile drive, though in March 2013 a section of road north of Cape Meares began sinking and was closed. Repairs are ongoing, so you might have to drive to Cape Meares via Netarts and Oceanside, then backtrack.

The forested headland at **Cape Meares** offers good views from its lighthouse, which is 38ft tall (Oregon's shortest). Short trails lead to Oregon's largest Sitka spruce and the 'Octopus Tree,' another Sitka shaped like a candelabra.

A panoramic vista atop sheer cliffs that rise 800ft above the Pacific makes **Cape Lookout State Park** a highlight. In winter, the end of the cape, which juts out nearly a mile, is thronged with whale-watchers. There are wide sandy beaches, hiking trails and a popular campground near the water.

Finally there's **Cape Kiwanda**, a sandstone bluff that rises just north of the little town of Pacific City. You can hike up tall dunes, or drive your truck onto the beach. It's the most developed of the three capes, with plenty of services nearby. Don't miss **Pelican Brewpub** (Cape Kiwanda; mains $12-32; ☺ 8am-10pm Sun-Thu, till 11pm Sat & Sun) if you like beer. Watch the dory fleet launch their craft or, after a day's fishing, land as far up the beach as possible.

and barking sea lions – abound in the historic bay-front area, while bohemian Nye Beach offers art galleries and a friendly village atmosphere. The area was first explored in the 1860s by fishing crews who found oyster beds at the upper end of Yaquina Bay.

The world-class **Oregon Coast Aquarium** (✆541-867-3474; www.aquarium.org; 2820 SE Ferry Slip Rd; adult/child 13-17yr/child 3-12yr $18.95/16.95/11.95; ⊙9am-6pm; ⊕) is an unmissable attraction, featuring a sea-otter pool, surreal jellyfish tanks and Plexiglas tunnels through a shark tank. Nearby, the **Hatfield Marine Science Center** (✆541-867-0100; www.hmsc.oregonstate.edu; 2030 SE Marine Science Dr; ⊙10am-5pm; ⊕) **FREE** is much smaller but still worthwhile. For awesome tide-pooling and views, don't miss the **Yaquina Head Outstanding Area** (✆541-574-3100; 750 NW Lighthouse Dr; admission $7; ⊙sunrise-sunset, interpretive center 10am-6pm), site of the coast's tallest lighthouse and an interesting interpretive center.

Campers can head to large and popular **South Beach State Park** (✆541-867-4715; www.oregonstateparks.org; tent sites/RV sites/yurts $21/27/40; ⚑), two miles south on US 101. Book-lovers can stay at the **Sylvia Beach Hotel** (✆541-265-5428; www.sylviabeachhotel.com; 267 NW Cliff St; d incl breakfast $115-220; ⊜), which has simple but comfy rooms, each named after a famous author; reservations are mandatory.

For great seafood, head to **Local Ocean Seafoods** (✆541-574-7959; www.localocean.net; 213 SE Bay Blvd; mains $11-23; ⊙11am-8:30pm Sun-Thu, till 9pm Fri & Sat) ✐ – it's especially great for lunch, when the glass walls open to the port area.

Get information at the **chamber of commerce** (✆541-265-8801; www.newportchamber.org; 555 SW Coast Hwy; ⊙8am-5pm Mon-Fri, 10am-3pm Sat).

Yachats & Around

One of the Oregon coast's best-kept secrets is the neat and friendly little town of Yachats (ya-hots). People come here and to the small remote inns and B&Bs just south of town to get away from it all, which isn't hard to do along this relatively undeveloped coast.

Three miles to the south, lofty **Cape Perpetua** was first sighted by Captain Cook in 1778. Volcanic intrusions have formed a beautifully rugged shoreline, with dramatic features such as the Devil's Churn, where

powerful waves crash through a 30ft inlet. For an easy hike, take the paved **Captain Cook Trail** (a 1.2 mile round trip) down to tide pools near Cooks Chasm, where at high tide the geyser-like spouting horn blasts water out of a sea cave. For information head to the **Cape Perpetua Visitor Center** (✆541-547-3289; www.fs.usda.gov/siuslaw; ⊙10am-4pm daily Mar-May & Sept-Oct, till 5pm daily Jun-Aug, closed Tue Nov-Feb).

Fifteen miles to the south on US 101 is the almost-tourist trap but fun **Sea Lion Caves** (✆541-547-3111; www.sealioncaves.com; 91560 US 101; adult/child 6-12yr $14/8; ⊙9am-6pm), a noisy grotto filled with groaning sea lions, accessed via an elevator.

Camp at **Beachside State Park** (✆800-551-6949; www.oregonstateparks.org; tent sites/RV sites/yurts $21/26/40; ⚑), five miles north of Yachats on US 101. The **Ya'Tel Motel** (✆541-547-3225; www.yatelmotel.com; cnr US 101 & 6th St; d $64-84; ⊜@✈⊛⚑) is a good, inexpensive place to sleep, and for snacks there's the **Green Salmon Coffee House** (✆541-547-4409; www.thegreensalmon.com; 220 US 101; mains $7-11; ⊙7:30am-2pm; ✐).

Oregon Dunes National Recreation Area

Stretching for 50 miles between Florence and Coos Bay, the Oregon Dunes form the largest expanse of coastal dunes in the USA. They tower up to 500ft and undulate inland as far as three miles to meet coastal forests, harboring curious ecosystems that sustain an abundance of wildlife. Hiking trails, bridle paths, and boating and swimming areas are available, but avoid the stretch south of Reedsport as noisy dune buggies dominate. For tourist info, head to the Oregon Dunes National Recreation Area's **headquarters** (✆541-271-3495; www.fs.usda.gov/siuslaw; 855 Highway Ave; ⊙8am-4:30pm Mon-Fri, to 4pm Sat & Sun) in Reedsport.

State parks with camping include popular **Jessie M Honeyman** (✆800-452-5687, 541-997-3641; www.oregonstateparks.org; 84505 US 101 S; tent sites/RV sites/yurts $21/26/39; ⚑), 3 miles south of Florence, and pleasant **Umpqua Lighthouse** (✆800-452-5687, 541-271-4118; www.oregonstateparks.org; 460 Lighthouse Rd; tent sites/RV sites/yurts/cabins/deluxe yurts $19/24/36/39/76; ⚑), 4 miles south of Reedsport. There's plenty of other camping in the area, too.

Port Orford

Occupying a rare natural harbor and guarding plenty of spectacular views, the scenic hamlet of Port Orford sits on a headland wedged between two magnificent state parks. **Cape Blanco State Park**, nine miles to the north, is the second most-westerly point in continental USA, and the promontory is often lashed by fierce 100mph winds. As well as hiking, visitors can tour the **Cape Blanco Lighthouse** (☎ 541-332-2207; www.oregonstateparks.org; US 101; admission $2; ☉ 10am-3:30pm Wed-Mon) built in 1870; it's the oldest and highest operational lighthouse in Oregon.

Six miles south of Port Orford, in **Humbug Mountain State Park**, mountains and sea meet in aqueous disharmony with plenty of angry surf. You can climb the 1750ft peak on a 3-mile trail through old-growth cedar groves.

For an affordable stay try **Castaway-by-the-Sea Motel** (☎ 541-332-4502; www.castawaybythesea.com; 545 W 5th St; d $85-145; ☺ @ 🛜 🐾). Food in this fishing village means a visit to slick **Redfish** (☎ 541-336-2200; www.redfishportorford.com; 517 Jefferson St; mains $21-29; ☉ 11am-9pm Mon-Fri, 9am-9pm Sat & Sun) 🍽 for the freshest seafood in town.

PACIFIC NORTHWEST OREGON COAST

Alaska

Best Places to Eat

➡ Snow City Café (p1097)

➡ Ludvig's Bistro (p1089)

➡ Tracy's King Crab Shack (p1091)

➡ Coastal Cold Storage (p1088)

➡ Sack's Café (p1098)

Best Places to Stay

➡ Copper Whale Inn (p1097)

➡ Black Bear Inn (p1086)

➡ Juneau International Hostel (p1091)

➡ Beach Roadhouse (p1093)

➡ Alaskan Sojourn Hostel (p1094)

Why Go?

Big, beautiful and wildly bountiful. Far away, rurally isolated and very expensive. Alaska is a traveler's dilemma.

There are few places in the world with such grandeur and breathtaking beauty. Mt McKinley, the highest peak in North America, is a stunning sight when you catch its alpenglow in Wonder Lake. Forty bald eagles perched on a single tree is something seen in Haines, not Iowa.

Alaska is also a remote and costly destination for anybody tripping through the rest of the country, a place where accommodations are expensive and transportation options meager. But, from the Northwest, a slice of Alaska can be an affordable side trip, whether it's a few days cruising Southeast Alaska on the state ferry or a 2½-hour flight to Anchorage for the weekend. Once there you'll marvel at the grandeur of the land and begin plotting your ultimate adventure, a summer in Alaska. This chapter focuses on Southeast Alaska and Anchorage.

When to Go
Anchorage

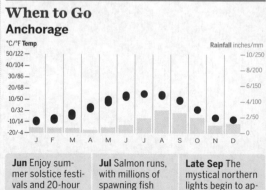

Jun Enjoy summer solstice festivals and 20-hour days. Stay up and play outdoors.

Jul Salmon runs, with millions of spawning fish choking streams, hit their peak.

Late Sep The mystical northern lights begin to appear in the night skies.

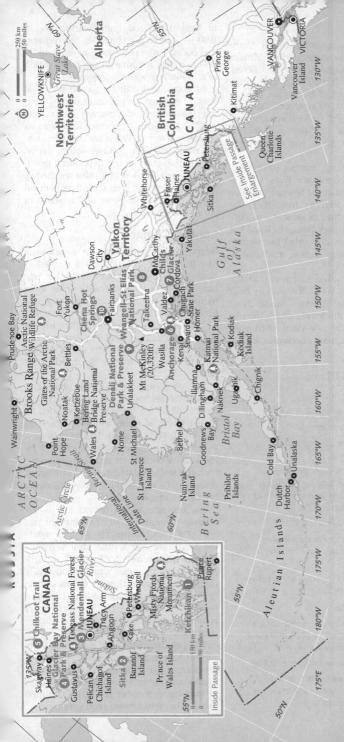

Alaska Highlights

1 Zip-lining down to a stream full of bears feasting on salmon in **Ketchikan** (p1086).

2 Uncovering Russia's history in Alaska at **Sitka National Historical Park** (p1089).

3 Hiking alongside Alaska's most popular river of ice, **Mendenhall Glacier** (p1090).

4 Kayaking with seals at **Glacier Bay National Park & Preserve** (p1091).

5 Following the Klondike stampedes of 1898, hiking the **Chilkoot Trail** (p1094).

6 Exploring Alaska's history and culture at the **Anchorage Museum** (p1095).

History

Indigenous Alaskans – Athabascans, Aleuts and Inuit, and the coastal tribes Tlingits and Haidas – migrated over the Bering Strait land bridge 20,000 years ago. In the 18th century waves of Europeans arrived: first British and French explorers, then Russian whalers and fur traders, naming land formations, taking otter pelts and leaving the cultures of the Alaska Native peoples in disarray.

With the Russians' finances badly overextended by the Napoleonic Wars, US Secretary of State William H Seward was able to purchase the territory from them for $7.2 million – less than 2¢ an acre – in 1867. There was uproar over 'Seward's Folly,' but the land's riches soon revealed themselves: whales initially, then salmon, gold and finally oil.

After Japan bombed and occupied the Aleutian Islands in WWII, the military built the famous Alcan (Alaska–Canada) Hwy, which connected the territory with the rest of the USA. The 1520-mile Alcan contributed greatly to postwar Alaska becoming a state in 1959. The Good Friday earthquake in 1964 left Alaska in a shambles, but recovery was boosted when oil was discovered under Prudhoe Bay, resulting in the construction of a 789-mile pipeline to Valdez.

In 2006 Sarah Palin, a former mayor of Wasilla, stunned the political world by beating the incumbent governor to become Alaska's first female governor as well as its youngest at age 42. Two years later presidential candidate John McCain named her as his running mate on the Republican ticket. Even though they lost and Palin resigned as governor later that year, she offers political commentary to Fox News and is active in conservative politics.

Land & Climate

Simply put, Alaska is huge. Or, as residents love to point out: if Alaska was divided in half, each half would rank as the top two largest states in the country, dropping Texas to third. At latitudes spanning the Arctic Circle, the main body of Alaska is about 800 sq miles, with the arc of the Aleutian Islands chain stretching some 1600 miles south and west, and a 'panhandle' strip running 600 miles southeast down the North American coast.

The coastal regions, such as Southeast and Prince William Sound, have lush coniferous forests, while the Interior is dominated by boreal forest of white spruce, cottonwood and birch. Further north is a taiga zone – a moist, subarctic forest characterized by muskeg, willow thickets and stunted spruce – then the treeless Arctic tundra, with grass, mosses and a variety of tiny flowers thriving briefly in summer.

Alaska's size is the reason for its extremely variable climate. The Interior can top 90°F (32°C) during the summer, while the Southeast and Southcentral maritime regions will average 55°F (13°C) to 70°F (21°C). In the Southeast it rains almost daily from late September through October, while in June you'll experience the longest days of the year. In Anchorage that means 19 hours of sunshine, while in Barrow the sun never sets at all.

The peak tourist season runs from early July to mid-August, when the best-known parks are packed and it's essential to make reservations for ferries and accommodations. In May and September you'll still find mild weather, but fewer crowds and lower prices.

ALASKA FACTS

Nickname Final Frontier

Population 731,449

Area 586,400 sq miles

Capital City Juneau (population 32,556)

Other cites Anchorage (population 291,826), Fairbanks (population 32,213), Ketchikan (population 8250), Kodiak (population 6457)

Sales tax No state sales tax

Birthplace of Singer and poet Jewel (b 1974), cartoonist Virgil F Partch (1916–84)

Home of Iditarod Sled Dog Race, tallest mountain in North America, Sarah Palin

Politics Red state

Famous for Giant veggies, including a 127lb cabbage grown in 2010, and giant king crab

Best souvenir Moose nugget earrings

Driving distances Anchorage to Fairbanks 586 miles, Anchorage to Denali National Park 425 miles

Parks & Activities

Alaska has room to play outdoors and plenty of parks to do it in. Travelers come here for the mountains, the trails, the wildlife, the camping – the adventure. Hiking trails are boundless and are the best way to escape the summer crowds in places like Juneau and the Kenai Peninsula. Mountain biking is allowed on many trails, and bikes can be rented throughout the state. You can also rent kayaks throughout the Southeast, where paddlers enjoy sea kayaking in protective fjords, often within view of glaciers. Other popular outdoor activities are rafting, bear- and whale-watching, fishing, ziplining and just pulling over on the road and admiring the scenery.

The best places to play and see wildlife are Alaska's many parks and preserves. Within the state, the National Park Service administers 54 million acres as national parks, preserves and monuments. The most popular national parks are Klondike Gold Rush National Historical Park (p1094) in Skagway, Denali National Park & Preserve (p1099) in the Interior and **Kenai Fjords National Park** (📞907-224-2125; www.nps.gov/kefj) near Seward. **Tongass National Forest** (📞907-586-8800; www.fs.fed.us/r10/tongass) covers most of Southeast while **Chugach State Park** (📞907-345-5014; dnr.alaska.gov/parks/units/chugach), on the edge of Anchorage, is the country's third-largest state park at 773 sq miles.

ℹ Information

The **Alaska Travel Industry Association** (www.travelalaska.com) is the official tourism marketing arm for the state and publishes a vacation planner with listings of B&Bs, motels, tours and more. An excellent source for tour companies and outfitters committed to responsible tourism is **Alaska Wilderness Recreation and Tourism Association** (📞907-258-3171; www.visitwildalaska.com).

The best place for information on national parks, state parks and all public-land agencies, along with their cabin-rental programs, is one of the four Alaska Public Lands Information Centers (APLICs) scattered around the state. Anchorage has the largest **APLIC** (📞907-644-3661; www.alaskacenters.gov) and the Southeast Alaska Discovery Center (p1087) in Ketchikan is another.

Note that Alaska's smoking laws vary by town and borough; don't assume that all bars and restaurants are smoke-free. For example, Anchorage is but Skagway is not. In towns that do not enforce a smoking ban, it is up to individual business owners whether their premises are smoke-free or not.

ℹ Getting There & Around

AIR

The vast majority of visitors to Alaska fly into **Ted Stevens Anchorage International Airport** (ANC; www.dot.state.ak.us/anc; 📶). Several budget airlines debuted flights in 2013, including **JetBlue** (📞1-800-538-2583; www.jetblue.com), which lowered prices considerably.

Alaska Airlines (📞800-252-7522; www.alaskaair.com) Has direct flights to Anchorage from Seattle, Chicago, Los Angeles and Denver. It also flies between many towns within Alaska, including daily northbound and southbound flights year-round through Southeast Alaska, with stops at all main towns including Ketchikan and Juneau.

Continental (📞800-525-0280; www.continental.com) Flies nonstop from Houston, Chicago, Denver and San Francisco.

Delta (📞800-221-1212; www.delta.com) Direct flights from Minneapolis, Phoenix and Salt Lake City.

BOAT

The **Alaska Marine Highway** (AMHS; 📞800-642-0066; www.ferryalaska.com) ferries connect Bellingham, WA, with 14 towns in Southeast Alaska. The complete trip (Bellingham–Haines, $353, 3½ days) stops at ports along the way and should be scheduled in advance. Trips within the Inside Passage, weaving through the islands of Alaska's panhandle, include Ketchikan–Petersburg ($60, 11 hours), Sitka–Juneau ($45, five hours) and Juneau–Haines ($37, two hours). The ferries are equipped to handle cars (Bellingham–Haines $462), but space must be reserved months ahead. The ferries also service five towns in Southcentral Alaska, and twice a month make a special run across the Gulf of Alaska from Juneau to Whittier ($221).

Cruise ships are another convenient way to tour Alaska, especially Southeast. A smaller boat will afford more flexibility and intimacy, while the larger companies will be more affordable. You can expect to have all meals included and a menu of tour and learning options. Larger cruise companies include **Princess** (www.princess.com) and family-friendly **Celebrity** (www.celebritycruises.com). For smaller boats consider **AdventureSmith Explorations** (📞800-344-2875; www.adventuresmithexplorations.com), which has charters for 12 people or a larger boat that carries 100, and **Discovery Voyages** (📞800-324-7602; www.discoveryvoyages.com). Both offer excellent excursions and are learning-focused.

ALASKA

BUS

From Anchorage bus service is available to many areas of the state.

Alaska/Yukon Trails (☑800-770-7275; www.alaskashuttle.com) Goes to Denali ($75, six hours) and Fairbanks ($99, nine hours).

Seward Bus Line (☑907-563-0800; www.sewardbuslines.net) Goes to Seward ($40, three hours).

Homer Stage Lines (☑907-868-3914; http://stagelineinhomer.com) To Homer ($90, 4½ hours) and points in between.

TRAIN

The **Alaska Railroad** (☑907-265-2494; www.akrr.com) offers service between Seward and Anchorage and between Anchorage and Denali, before ending in Fairbanks. Book seats in advance on this popular train.

SOUTHEAST ALASKA

The Southeast is as close as Alaska comes to the continental USA, but most of it is inaccessible by road. It's possible to fly to the panhandle for a quick visit, but a better option, if you can spare a week, is to cruise the Inside Passage, a waterway made up of thousands of islands, glacier-filled fjords and a mountainous coastline. You can jump on a state ferry and stop at a handful of ports for hiking, kayaking and whale-watching. Cruises (p1085) are also popular, as they offer easy transport and lodging, with meals included.

Ketchikan

Ketchikan, the first stop of the Alaska Marine Highway (p1085) and most cruise ships, is one long, thin town: several miles long, never more than 10 blocks wide and crammed with Alaskan character, adventure and the scenery you came looking for.

◉ Sights & Activities

Dolly's House   MUSEUM
(www.dollyshouse.com; 24 Creek St; adult/child $5/free; ⊙8am-5pm) The star of Ketchikan's former red-light district, Creek St, this place is the parlor of Ketchikan's most famous madam, Dolly Arthur.

Totem Bight State Historical Park   HISTORIC SITE
(N Tongass Hwy; ⊙6am-10pm) FREE Ten miles north of downtown Ketchikan is this seaside park that contains 14 restored totem poles, a colorful community house and viewing deck overlooking Tongass Narrows. Next door to the state park is the equally intriguing **Potlatch Park** (www.potlatchpark.com; 9809 Totem Bight Rd; ⊙7:30am-4pm) FREE, home to another dozen totems and five beautiful tribal houses.

Totem Heritage Center   MUSEUM
(601 Deermont St; adult/child $5/free; ⊙8am-5pm) Features a collection of 19th-century totems in a spiritual setting.

Alaska Canopy Adventures   EXTREME SPORTS
(☑907-225-5503; www.alaskacanopy.com; 116 Wood Rd; per person $190) Fly through the trees! Uses eight zip lines, three suspension bridges and 4WD vehicles so you can zip 4600ft down a mountain. Afterwards you can watch bears feast on a salmon run.

Deer Mountain Trail   HIKING
This 3-mile walking trail begins near the city center and provides access to the alpine world above the timberline and wonderful views of the town.

⌊⌋ Sleeping

Ketchikan Hostel   HOSTEL $
(☑907-225-3319; www.ketchikanhostel.com; 400 Main St; dm $20; ⊙Jun-Aug) A friendly, clean hostel, with separate male and female dorms located in a Methodist church downtown.

New York Hotel   BOUTIQUE HOTEL $$
(☑866-225-0246, 907-225-0246; www.thenewyorkhotel.com; 207 Stedman St; r $149-189, ste $229; @ 🛜) A historic boutique hotel in the heart of town but far enough away to escape the cruise-ship madness. Its rooms and unique suites are filled with antiques and overlook the waterfront or Creek St.

Gilmore Hotel   HISTORIC HOTEL $$
(☑907-225-9423; www.gilmorehotel.com; 326 Front St; d $105-165; @) Built in 1927, the Gilmore has 38 'historically proportioned' (ie small) rooms that include cable TV, coffeemakers and hair dryers.

★ Black Bear Inn   B&B $$$
(☑907-225-4343; www.stayinalaska.com; 5528 N Tongass Hwy; r $160-230; @ 🛜) This incredible B&B, 2.5 miles north of downtown, offers both rooms and small apartments. Among the many amenities is a covered outdoor hot tub where you can soak while watching eagles soaring overhead.

ALASKA KETCHIKAN

✕ Eating & Drinking

Sushi Fever   SUSHI $
(☑907-225-1233; 629 Mission St; lunch specials $9-11, rolls $7-14; ☺11am-9pm) This Japanese restaurant bustles with locals and cruise-ship workers alike. There are almost 40 types of roll on the menu but just a bowl of the udon noodles will fuel you all afternoon.

Burger Queen   BURGERS $
(518 Tongass Ave; burgers $6-9; ☺11am-3pm Mon, to 7pm Tue-Sat) Ketchikan's favorite shake-and-burger joint will deliver your hamburger to the Arctic Bar across the street where you can be sipping a beer.

**★ Bar Harbor
Restaurant**   MODERN AMERICAN $$$
(☑907-225-2813; 2813 Tongass Ave; mains $20-34; ☺5-9pm Mon-Sat) A cozy place with a covered outdoor deck, between downtown and the ferry terminal. Yeah, they serve seafood here – who doesn't in Southeast? – but the signature dish is Ketchikan's best prime rib.

First City Saloon   LOUNGE
(830 Water St; ☎) A sprawling club that rocks with live music during the summer, often impromptu performances when cruise-ship bands are looking to let loose.

❶ Information

Ketchikan Visitor Information & Tour Center
(☑907-225-6166; www.visit-ketchikan.com; 131 Front St; ☺7am-6pm) Helpful staff will book tours and accommodations.

Southeast Alaska Discovery Center (☑907-228-6220; www.fs.fed.us/r10/tongass/districts/discoverycenter; 50 Main St; adult/child $5/free; ☺8am-3pm) Houses an impressive exhibit hall; provides details of outdoor activities.

❶ Getting There & Around

Alaska Airlines (p1085) and Alaska Marine Highway (p1085) ferries service Ketchikan. For wheels, try **Alaska Car Rental** (☑907-225-5123; www.akcarrental.com; 2828 Tongass Ave; compacts $57).

Wrangell

Strategically located near the mouth of the Stikine River, Wrangell is the only town to have been ruled by four nations: Tlingit, Russia, Britain and the USA. Today it is one

MISTY FJORDS NATIONAL MONUMENT

In the wilderness neighborhood that surrounds Ketchikan, this 3750-sq-mile monument is packed with wildlife-watching opportunities and spectacular views of 3000ft sheer granite walls that rise from the ocean. **Allen Marine Tours** (☑877-686-8100, 907-225-8100; www.allenmarinetours.com; adult/child $159/109) runs a four-hour trip around the monument but a more enjoyable adventure is to spend a few days paddling the fjords. **Southeast Sea Kayaks** (☑907-225-1258; www.kayakketchikan.com; 1621 Tongass Ave, Ketchikan; 1-/2-person kayak per day $45/59) can supply rentals and water-taxi service into the heart of this watery wilderness, letting you bypass the long open-water paddle from Ketchikan.

ALASKA WRANGELL

of the few ports in which the state ferries dock downtown, so at the very least jump off the boat for a quick look around town.

◉ Sights

For its size, Wrangell has an impressive collection of totems. Pick up the free *Wrangell Guide* at the visitor center and spend an afternoon locating them all. Make sure you stop at **Chief Shakes Island**, near the boat harbor downtown.

Wrangell Museum   MUSEUM
(296 Campbell Dr; adult/child/family $5/2/12; ☺10am-5pm Mon-Sat) In this museum at the Nolan Center you can learn about gold-rush Wrangell or why Wyatt Earp filled in as the town's deputy marshal for 10 days.

🛏 Sleeping & Eating

Wrangell Hostel   HOSTEL $
(☑907-874-3534; 220 Church St; dm $20) In the Presbyterian church.

Stikine Inn   MOTEL $$
(☑888-874-3388, 907-874-3388; www.stikineinn.com; 107 Stikine Ave; s $146-169, d $163-184; ☎) Wrangell's largest motel is on the waterfront near the ferry dock and includes 34 rooms and a restaurant with tables overlooking the boat traffic on the water.

Alaskan Sourdough Lodge　　LODGE $$

(☑907-874-3613; www.akgetaway.com; 1104 Peninsula St; s/d $114/124; @☎) This family-owned lodge offers 16 rooms, and a front deck full of wicker furniture and a view of the harbor.

Diamond C Café　　CAFE $$

(223 Front St; breakfast $6-12, lunch $8-17; ☉6am-3pm) Eat what the locals eat (eggs, biscuits and deep-fried fish-and-chips) while listening to the conservative pulse of this community.

❶ Information

Wrangell Visitor Center (☑907-874-3901; www.wrangell.com; 293 Campbell Dr; ☉10am-5pm Mon-Sat) At the Nolan Center.

Petersburg

At the north end of the spectacular Wrangell Narrows lies the picturesque community of Petersburg, a town known for its Norwegian roots and home to one of Alaska's largest fishing fleets.

◉ Sights & Activities

The center of Old Petersburg is **Sing Lee Alley**, which winds past weathered homes and boathouses perched on pilings above the water.

Clausen Memorial Museum　　MUSEUM

(www.clausenmuseum.net; 203 Fram St; adult/child $3/free; ☉10am-5pm Mon-Sat) Features local artifacts and fishing relics, and a small but excellent museum store.

Tongass Kayak Adventures　　KAYAKING

(☑907-772-4600; www.tongasskayak.com; single/double kayak $55/65) Offers rentals and drop-off transportation, as well as several guided paddles, including a day-long paddle at LeConte Glacier ($265), North America's southernmost tidewater glacier and often the site of spectacular falling ice and breaching whales.

⌂ Sleeping

Scandia House　　HOTEL $$

(☑907-772-4281; www.scandiahousehotel.com; 110 Nordic Dr; s/d $110/150; ☎) The most impressive place in town, this hotel has 33 modern rooms (some with kitchenettes), a courtesy shuttle service and a main-street location.

Nordic House　　B&B $$

(☑907-772-3620; www.nordichouse.net; 806 S Nordic Dr; r without bathroom $82-149; ☎) Within an easy walk of the ferry terminal, this place offers five large rooms and a common area overlooking the boat harbor.

Tides Inn　　MOTEL $$

(☑907-772-4288; www.tidesinnalaska.com; 307 1st St; s $115-126, d $132-143; @☎) Largest motel in town, with 45 rooms, some with kitchenettes.

✖ Eating & Drinking

★ Coastal Cold Storage　　SEAFOOD $

(306 N Nordic Dr; breakfast $4-8, lunch $8-12; ☉7am-3pm Mon-Sun; ☎) The local specialty is halibut beer bits and this place serves the best ones in this seafood town.

Beachcomber Inn　　AMERICAN $$

(☑907-772-3888; 384 Mitkof Hwy; mains $19-30; ☉5-9pm Tue-Sat) This wonderful restaurant is built on pilings over the sea so every table has a fabulous maritime-and-mountain view.

Harbor Bar　　BAR

(310 Nordic Dr; ☎) The classic place for deck-hands and cannery workers, with pool tables, free popcorn and an excellent beer selection. In that great Alaskan tradition, patrons have started pinning dollar bills to the walls.

❶ Information

Petersburg Chamber of Commerce (☑907-772-4636; www.petersburg.org; cnr Fram & 1st Sts; ☉9am-5pm Mon-Sat, noon-4pm Sun) Has B&B and United States Forest Service information.

Sitka

Russians established Southeast Alaska's first nonindigenous settlement here in 1799, and the town flourished on fur. Today Sitka sees itself as both the cultural center of the Southeast and, because it's the only one facing the Pacific Ocean, the region's most beautiful city.

◉ Sights & Activities

Sitka has superb hiking, and the **Gaven Hill Trail** into the mountains is accessible from the downtown area. There are also many kayaking trips around **Baranof** and **Chichagof Islands**.

Thanks to Sitka's ocean location, marine-wildlife boat tours have mushroomed in the town.

Sitka National Historical Park　HISTORIC SITE
(www.nps.gov/sitk/index.htm; Lincoln St; adult/child $4/free; ☺8am-5pm) Alaska's smallest national park has an intriguing 1-mile trail that winds past 15 totem poles, while inside its visitor center are Russian and indigenous artifacts and traditional carving demonstrations.

Alaska Raptor Center　WILDLIFE RESERVE
(www.alaskaraptor.org; 101 Sawmill Creek Rd; adult/child $12/6; ☺8am-4pm; 🚺) For an eye-to-eye encounter with a bald eagle, head to this center where injured birds relearn to fly.

St Michael's Cathedral　CHURCH
(240 Lincoln St; admission $5; ☺9am-4pm Mon-Fri) A replica of the original 1840s Russian Orthodox cathedral destroyed by fire in 1966 and still the centerpiece of Sitka. The original icons and religious objects were salvaged and are on display. It's only open when cruise ships are in.

Baranof's Castle　MONUMENT
Castle Hill is the site of Baranof's Castle, where Alaska was officially transferred from Russia to the USA.

Russian Bishop's House　HISTORIC BUILDING
(Lincoln St; adult/child $4/free; ☺9am-5pm) Built in 1842, this is Sitka's oldest intact Russian building.

Sheldon Jackson Museum　MUSEUM
(104 College Dr; adult/child $5/free; ☺9am-5pm) Houses an excellent indigenous culture collection.

Sitka Sound Ocean Adventures　KAYAKING
(☑907-752-0660; www.kayaksitka.com; single/double kayak $75/95) Rents kayaks and runs guided trips; its office is a blue bus at the Centennial Building.

Allen Marine Tours　CRUISE
(☑907-747-8100; www.allenmarinetours.com; adult/child $99/69; ☺1:30-4:30pm Sat) Offers three-hour tours, in a fully enclosed catamaran with wraparound windows, that often include spotting otters and whales.

🛏 Sleeping

Ann's Gavan Hill B&B　B&B $
(☑907-747-8023; www.annsgavanhill.com; 415 Arrowhead St; s/d $75/95; @🤖) An easy walk from downtown, this lovely Alaskan home has three guest rooms and a wraparound deck with two hot tubs. Ahhh!

Sitka International Hostel　HOSTEL $
(☑907-747-8661; www.sitkahostel.org; 109 Jeff Davis St; dm $24; @🤖) Sitka's newest – and only – hostel is downtown less than a block from Crescent Harbor and features five single-sex dorm rooms and one private room ($60).

Sitka Hotel　HOTEL $$
(☑907-747-3288; www.sitkahotel.net; 118 Lincoln St; s/d $116/124; @🤖) This venerable hotel is right downtown and its back rooms are large, comfortable and feature views of Sitka Sound.

Shee Atika Totem Square Inn　HOTEL $$$
(☑866-300-1353, 907-747-3693; www.totemsquareinn.com; 201 Katlian St; r $179-249; @🤖) Extensively renovated, this is Sitka's finest hotel, with 68 large, comfortable rooms perched above a harbor that bustles with boats bringing in the day's catch.

🍴 Eating & Drinking

Kenny's Wok & Teriyaki　CHINESE $
(210 Katlian St; lunch $7-10, dinner $9-12; ☺11:30am-9pm Mon-Fri, noon to 9pm Sat & Sun) This Chinese restaurant in the Katlian district seems to be always full. It's partly because it has only nine tables but mostly because the locals love the portions and the prices.

★Ludvig's Bistro　MEDITERRANEAN $$$
(☑907-966-3663; www.ludvigsbistro.com; 256 Katlian St; tapas $14-18, mains $26-36; ☺5-9pm) Sitka's boldest restaurant is also the Southeast's best. The menu is described as 'rustic Mediterranean fare' and almost everything is local, even the sea salt.

Highliner Coffee　CAFE
(www.highlinercoffee.com; 327 Seward St, Seward Sq Mall; light fare under $5; ☺6am-5pm Mon-Sat, 7am-4pm Sun; 🤖) At the Highliner they like their coffee black and their salmon wild. Come here to catch the buzz from a latte and the local issues.

Fly-in Fish Inn Bar BAR
(485 Katlian St) A delightful little six-stool bar on the back side of a inn. On the covered deck outside you can watch deckhands unload the day's catch.

❶ Information

Sitka Convention & Visitors Bureau (☑907-747-5940; www.sitka.org; 330 Harbor Dr; ⊙8am-5pm Mon-Fri) Across the street from Michael's Cathedral, and also at a desk in the Centennial Building.

United States Forest Service Office (USFS; ☑907-747-6671; 204 Siginaka Way; ⊙8am-4:30pm Mon-Fri) Can provide hiking and kayaking information for the area.

❶ Getting There & Away

Sitka Airport (SIT; ☑907-966-2960), on Japonski Island, is served by Alaska Airlines (p1085).

Northstar Rental (☑907-966-2552; www.northstarrentacar.com; Sitka Airport) has midsize cars from $69 per day. **Alaska Marine Highway** (☑907-747-8737; www.ferryalaska.com) ferries stop almost daily at the terminal, which is 7 miles north of town. **Ferry Transit Bus** (☑907-747-5800; one-way/return $6/10) will take you into town.

Juneau

The first town to be founded after Alaska's purchase from the Russians, Juneau became the territorial capital in 1906 and today is the most scenic capital in the country. Its historic downtown clings to the gap between snowcapped mountains and a bustling waterfront. The rest of the city spreads north into the Mendenhall Valley. Juneau is also Alaska's cruise-ship capital and the gateway to many attractions, including Tracy Arm and Glacier Bay National Park.

❍ Sights

Mendenhall Glacier GLACIER
Juneau's famous 'drive-in' glacier is one of the most picturesque attractions in Southeast Alaska. This frozen river and its informative **USFS Visitor Center** (Glacier Spur Rd; adult/child $3/free; ⊙8am-7:30pm) is 12 miles from the city. **Mendenhall Glacier Transport** (☑907-789-5460; round-trip $16) runs buses from downtown.

Last Chance Mining Museum HISTORIC SITE
(☑907-586-5338; 1001 Basin Rd; adult/child $5/free; ⊙9:30am-12:30pm & 3:30-6:30pm) The compressor building of Alaska Juneau Gold Mining Company is now a museum and the only building open to the public from Juneau's Gold Rush era.

Alaska State Museum MUSEUM
(www.museums.state.ak.us; 395 Whittier St; adult/child $7/free; ⊙8:30am-5:30pm; ♿) Has artifacts from Alaska's six major indigenous groups, plus a full-size eagles' nest atop a two-story tree.

Juneau-Douglas City Museum MUSEUM
(www.juneau.org/parkrec/museum; 114 W 4th St; adult/child $6/free; ⊙9am-6pm Mon-Fri, 10am-5pm Sat & Sun) Highlights the area's gold-mining history and offers a **Historic Downtown Walking Tour** (adult/child incl museum $20/15; ⊙1:30pm Tue-Thu).

🏃 Activities

Hiking HIKING
Hiking is the most popular activity in the area, and some trails access USFS cabins. **Juneau Parks & Recreation** (☑907-586-0428; www.juneau.org/parksrec) organizes free hikes. **West Glacier Trail**, which sidles along Mendenhall Glacier, has the most stunning scenery. The **Mt Roberts Trail** is the most popular hike to the alpine country above Juneau.

Taku Glacier Lodge SCENIC FLIGHTS
(☑907-586-6275; www.wingsairways.com; adult/child $297/250) The most popular tours in Juneau are flightseeing, glacier viewing and salmon bakes and a trip to this historic camp combines all three. You reach it via a floatplane that includes flying across a half-dozen glaciers. At the log lodge you enjoy an incredible meal of wild salmon to the view of Taku Glacier.

Mt Roberts Tram CABLE CAR
(www.goldbelttours.com; 490 S Franklin St; adult/child $31/15.50; ⊙11am-9pm Mon, 8am-9pm Tue-Sun; ♿) Takes passengers from the cruise-ship dock to the timberline, where there is a nature center and a restaurant.

Alaska Boat & Kayak Center KAYAKING
(☑907-364-2333; www.juneaukayak.com; 11521 Glacier Hwy; single/double kayak $50/70; ⊙9am-5pm) Rents boats and offers a self-guided Mendenhall Lake paddle ($109).

Orca Enterprises WHALE-WATCHING
(📞888-733-6722, 907-789-6801; www.alaskawhale-watching.com; adult/child $119/59) Uses a 42ft jet boat for three-hour whale-watching tours.

🛏 Sleeping

Juneau International Hostel HOSTEL $
(📞907-586-9559; www.juneauhostel.net; 614 Harris St; dm adult/child $12/5; @🖤) Alaska's best hostel – thanks to its location in a historic home as well as its friendly vibe – is a five-minute walk from the state capitol.

Driftwood Lodge MOTEL $$
(📞907-586-2280; www.driftwoodalaska.com; 435 Willoughby Ave; r $105-145; 🖤) The rooms are no-frills but clean, and many have kitchenettes. There's a courtesy airport and ferry van, a coin laundry and bike rental.

Silverbow Inn BOUTIQUE HOTEL $$$
(📞907-586-4146; www.silverbowinn.com; 120 2nd St; r $189-219; @🖤) A wonderful boutique inn on top of a downtown bagel shop. Along with 11 rooms, there's an outdoor hot tub with a view of the mountains.

Juneau Hotel HOTEL $$$
(📞907-586-5666; www.juneauhotels.net; 1200 W 9th St; ste $179; @🖤) An all-suites hotel located within easy walking distance of the downtown attractions.

🍴 Eating & Drinking

S Franklin St is Juneau's historic and at times colorful drinking sector.

Pel'Meni DUMPLING $
(Merchant's Wharf, Marine Way; ⊙11:30am-1:30pm Sun-Thu, 11:30am-3:30pm Fri & Sat) It serves one thing and one thing only – a bowl of authentic homemade Russian dumplings, filled with either potato or sirloin.

Tracy's King Crab Shack SEAFOOD $$
(www.kingcrabshack.com; 356 S. Franklin St; crab $13-30; ⊙10:30am-8pm) Squeezed between the library parking garage and the cruise ship docks, this little hut serves up crab, from outstanding bisque to mini-cakes. A bucket of king crab pieces ($60) is 2lb of the sweetest seafood you'll ever have.

Island Pub PIZZERIA $$
(www.theislandpub.com; 1102 2nd St; large pizza $13-20; ⊙4-10pm Mon-Thu, to midnight Fri, 1pm-midnight Sat, 1-10pm Sun) Across the channel in Douglas is the capital city's best pizzeria, serving firebrick-oven focaccias and gourmet pizza to a mountainous view.

Twisted Fish SEAFOOD $$
(www.twistedfish.hangaronthewharf.com; 550 S Franklin St; dinner mains $16-40; ⊙11am-10pm) Beef be gone! Located between Taku Smokeries

ALASKA JUNEAU

WORTH A TRIP

GLACIER BAY NATIONAL PARK & PRESERVE

Eleven tidewater glaciers that spill out of the mountains and fill the sea with icebergs of all shapes, sizes and shades of blue have made Glacier Bay National Park and Preserve an icy wilderness renowned worldwide. This can be an expensive side trip from Juneau but, for most people who include it on their itinerary, well worth the extra funds.

Gustavus (www.gustavusak.com) is a weekly stop ($33, 4½ hours) for the Alaska Marine Highway (p1085). Alaska Airlines (p1085) has daily flights between Gustavus and Juneau.

Food, lodging and transportation to Bartlett Cove in the park is available in Gustavus. **Annie Mae Lodge** (📞907-697-2346; www.anniemae.com; Grandpa's Farm Rd; s $160-220, d $170-230; 🖤) has 11 rooms, most with private entrances and bathrooms.

The **park headquarters** (📞907-697-2230; www.nps.gov/glba; 1 Park Rd; ⊙8am-4:30pm Mon-Fri) in Bartlett Cove maintains a free campground and a **visitor center** (📞907-697-2627; ⊙6am-9pm) at the dock, which provides backcountry permits and maps. You can stay at **Glacier Bay Lodge** (📞888-229-8687; www.visitglacierbay.com; 199 Bartlett Cove Rd; r $199-224), the only hotel and restaurant at Bartlett Cove.

To see the glaciers, board the *Fairweather Express* operated by **Glacier Bay Lodge & Tours** (📞90/-264-4600; adult/child $190/95) for an eight-hour cruise up the West Arm of Glacier Bay. The only developed hiking trails are in Bartlett Cove, but there is excellent kayaking, rent equipment from **Glacier Bay Sea Kayaks** (📞907-697-2257; www.glacierbayseakayaks.com; single/double kayak per day $45/60).

GLACIERS OF TRACY ARM

This steep-sided fjord, 50 miles southeast of Juneau, has a pair of tidewater glaciers and a gallery of icebergs floating down its length. Tracy Arm makes an interesting day trip, far less expensive and perhaps even more satisfying than a visit to Glacier Bay. You're almost guaranteed to see seals inside the arm, and you might spot whales on the way there. **Adventure Bound Alaska** (☏907-463-2509; www.adventurebound-alaska.com; adult/child $150/95; 🚢) is the longtime tour operator to Tracy Arm and uses a pair of boats that leave daily from the Juneau waterfront. Reserve a seat in advance if you can (the full-day tour is popular with cruise ships) and pack a lunch along with your binoculars.

and a wharf where commercial fishermen unload their catch, this restaurant is all about local seafood. Half the pizzas on the menu have something from the sea on them.

Red Dog Saloon   BAR
(☏907-463-3658; 278 S Franklin St) The (in)famous Red Dog Saloon has a sawdust floor and relic-covered walls.

Alaskan Hotel   BAR
(☏907-586-1000; 167 S Franklin St) Hidden here is a unique bar with historic ambience and occasional live music.

❶ Information

Juneau Convention & Visitors Bureau
(☏907-586-2201; www.traveljuneau.com; cruise ship terminal; ⊙8am-5pm) Also has locations in Marine Park, and at the airport and the ferry terminal.
Juneau Library (☏907-586-5249; 292 Marine Way; ⊙11am-8pm Mon-Thu, noon-6pm Fri, noon-5pm Sat & Sun; 🖥) Gorgeous views and free internet.
Juneau Ranger Station (☏907-586-8800; 8510 Mendenhall Loop Rd; ⊙8am-5pm Mon-Fri) Head to the Mendenhall Valley for information on cabins, trails and kayaking.

❶ Getting There & Around

AIR
The main airline serving Juneau is Alaska Airlines (p1085). Smaller companies such as

Wings of Alaska (☏907-789-0790; www.wingsofalaska.com) provide services to isolated communities.

BOAT
The terminal for the Alaska Marine Highway (p1085) is 14 miles from downtown; the high-speed M/V *Fairweather* connects to Petersburg ($66, four hours) and Sitka ($45, 4½ hours).

BUS
Juneau's public bus system, **Capital Transit** (☏907-789-6901; www.juneau.org/capital-transit; adult/child $2/1), can take you from the airport to the city center, but not the ferry terminal.

CAR
Numerous car-rental places offer pick-up, drop-off and unlimited mileage.
Rent-A-Wreck (☏888-843-4111, 907-789-4111; 2450c Industrial Blvd)

Haines

Haines is Southeast Alaska's most scenic departure point and a crucial link to the Alcan Hwy for thousands of RVers (recreational vehicle drivers) every summer on their way to Interior Alaska. The Northwest Trading Company arrived here in 1878, followed by gold prospectors and the US Army, which built its first permanent post in Alaska, Fort Seward, in 1903. The perceived threat of a Japanese invasion in WWII resulted in the construction of the Haines and Alcan Hwys, connecting Haines to the rest of the USA. If mammoth cruise ships depress you, Haines is a much better destination choice than Skagway.

❍ Sights & Activities

Sheldon Museum   MUSEUM
(www.sheldonmuseum.org; 11 Main St; adult/child $5/free; ⊙10am-5pm Mon-Fri, 1-4pm Sat & Sun) Features indigenous artifacts upstairs, and gold-rush relics downstairs.

American Bald Eagle Foundation   MUSEUM
(www.baldeagles.org; 113 Haines Hwy; adult/child $10/5; ⊙9am-5pm Mon-Sat; 🚢) Displays almost 180 species of animals, including almost two dozen eagles, in their natural habitat.

Hammer Museum   MUSEUM
(www.hammermuseum.org; 108 Main St; adult/child $3/free; ⊙10am-5pm Mon-Fri) For something

quirky, a 1500-hammer monument to owner Dave Pahl's obsession with the tool.

Hiking
HIKING
Haines offers two major hiking-trail systems – **Mt Riley** and **Mt Ripinsky** – as well as afternoon walking tours of **Fort Seward** (the visitor center has details).

Chilkat Guides
RAFTING
(☑907-766-2491; www.raftalaska.com; adult/child $94/65) Runs a four-hour Chilkat River raft float.

🛏 Sleeping

Fort Seward Lodge
MOTEL $
(☑877-617-3418, 766-2009; 39 Mud Bay Rd; r $110, without bathroom $75; 🐾) The former Post Exchange of Fort Seward offers Haines' best value in accommodations, with updated rooms and a friendly bar.

Bear Creek Cabins & Hostel
HOSTEL $
(☑907-766-2259; www.bearcreekcabinsalaska.com; Small Tract Rd; dm/cabins $20/68) To escape the metropolis of Haines, head a mile out of town to this pleasant hostel on the edge of the woods.

★ Beach Roadhouse
B&B $$
(☑866-741-3060, 907-766-3060; www.beachroadhouse.com; Mile 1, Beach Rd; r/cabins $115/145; 🐾) This large cedar home is perched above Lynn Canal in a tranquil, woodsy setting, offering four rooms with kitchenettes and two lovely cabins.

Alaska Guardhouse Lodging
B&B $$
(☑866-290-7445, 907-766-2566; www.alaskaguardhouse.com; 15 Seward Dr; s/d $115/145; 🐾) A building that was used to jail misbehaving soldiers now houses visitors in four large and comfortable bedrooms.

Captain's Choice Motel
MOTEL $$
(☑907-766-3111; www.capchoice.com; 108 2nd Ave N; s/d US$127/137; @🐾) Haines' largest motel has the best view of the Chilkat Mountains and Lynn Canal and a huge sundeck to enjoy it.

🍴 Eating & Drinking

★ Fireweed Restaurant
BISTRO $$
(37 Blacksmith St; mains $9-20; ⊘11:30am-3pm Wed-Sat & 4:30-9pm Tue-Sat; 🍴) This bright and laid-back bistro looks like it belongs in California with words like 'organic' and 'veggie' on its menu as opposed to 'deep fried' and 'captain's special.'

Mosey's Cantina
MEXICAN $$
(www.moseyscantina.com; 31 Tower Rd; lunch $8-14, dinner $16-24; ⊘11:30am-2:30pm & 5:30-8:30pm Wed-Sat) This may be Haines but Mosey's offers some of the best Mexican fare outside of Anchorage, in a cute and cozy setting.

Klondike
PIZZA $$
(Dalton City; medium pizza $14-18; ⊘5-8pm Mon-Sat) Haines' newest restaurant serves excellent wood-fired pizza, salads and beer that's brewed only two doors down.

Haines Brewing Company
BREWERY
(www.hainesbrewing.com; Dalton City; ⊘1-6pm Mon-Sat) It's well worth the walk to the town's delightful one-room brewery.

ℹ Information
Haines Convention & Visitors Bureau (☑907-766-2234; www.haines.ak.us; 122 2nd Ave; ⊘8am-5pm Mon-Fri, 9am-4pm Sat & Sun)

ℹ Getting There & Away
Several air-charter companies service Haines, the cheapest being **Wings of Alaska** (☑907-983-2442; www.wingsofalaska.com).

VALLEY OF THE EAGLES

The 75-sq-mile **Alaska Chilkat Bald Eagle Preserve** (www.dnr.alaska.gov/parks/units/eagleprv.htm), along the Chilkat River near Haines, protects the world's largest-known gathering of bald eagles. The greatest numbers, up to 4000 birds, are spotted in December and January, but Haines comes alive during its **Alaska Bald Eagle Festival** (www.baldeagles.org/festival; ⊘mid-Nov) in the second week of November, a five-day event that attracts hundreds of birders from around the country to witness the event.

But you can see eagles here any time during summer, albeit not as many. Head north on the Haines Hwy and pull over at the posted lookouts on the Haines between Miles 18 and 22, the best spots to search for eagles. Don't have wheels? During the summer **Alaska Nature Tours** (☑907-766-2876; www.alaskanaturetours.net; adult/child $78/63; 🚶) offers a Valley of the Eagles Nature Tour, a 3½-hour tour up the Chilkat River with a naturalist.

The **Haines–Skagway Fast Ferry** (☑888-766-2103, 907-766-2100; www.hainesskagwayfastferry.com; one-way adult/child $35/18; ⊙ Jun-Sep) will get you to and from Skagway.

Eagle Nest Car Rentals (☑907-766-2891; 1183 Haines Hwy), in the Eagle Nest Motel, has cars available for $57 per day with 100 miles included.

Skagway

The northern terminus of the Alaska Marine Highway (p1085), Skagway was a gold-rush town infamous for its lawlessness. In 1887 the population was two; 10 years later it was Alaska's largest city, with 20,000 residents. Today Skagway survives entirely on tourism and gets packed when a handful of cruise ships pull in and thousands of passengers converge on the town as if the Klondike gold rush was still on.

⊙ Sights & Activities

Klondike Gold Rush
National Historical Park   HISTORIC SITE
(☑983-9223; www.nps.gov/klgo; visitor center Broadway St at 2nd Ave; ⊙8am-6pm, to 7pm Fri) FREE A seven-block corridor along Broadway St that features 17 restored buildings, false fronts and wooden sidewalks from Skagway's golden era as a boom town. Thanks to the cruise ships, it's the most popular national park in Alaska. To best appreciate this amazing moment in Skagway's history, join

---

DON'T MISS

CHILKOOT TRAIL

The Chilkoot is the ultimate Alaska trek, combining great scenery, a historical site and an incredible sense of adventure. It was the route used by the Klondike gold miners in the 1898 gold rush, and walking it is not so much a wilderness adventure as a history lesson. The 33-mile trek takes four days and includes the **Chilkoot Pass** – a steep climb up to 3525ft that has hikers scrambling on all fours. The highlight for many is riding the historic White Pass & Yukon Route Railroad (p1094) back to Skagway.

Interested? Stop at the **Trail Center** (☑907-983-9234; www.nps.gov/klgo; Broadway St at 2nd Ave, Skagway; ⊙8am-5pm) to obtain backpacking permits and set up the hike.

---

a free, ranger-led walking tour, at the visitor center on the hour from 9am to 4pm.

Skagway Museum   MUSEUM
(☑907-983-2420; cnr 7th Ave & Spring St; adult/child $2/1; ⊙9am-5pm Mon-Fri, 10am-5pm Sat, noon-4pm Sun) One of the best museums in the Southeast, and its gold-rush relics are some of the most interesting exhibits in a town filled with museums.

Mascot Saloon   MUSEUM
(290 Broadway St; ⊙8am-6pm) A museum devoted to Skagway's heyday as the 'roughest place in the world.'

★**White Pass &**
Yukon Route Railroad   RAILROAD
(☑800-343-7373; www.wpyr.com; 231 2nd Ave; adult/child from US$115/57.50; ⊙May-Sep) Offers the best tour: the three-hour Summit Excursion climbs the high White Pass in a historic narrow-gauge train.

🛏 Sleeping

Alaskan Sojourn Hostel   HOSTEL $
(☑907-983-2040; www.alaskansojourn.net; 488 8th Ave; dm/r $28/58; 🐾) Skagway's best hostel is open and airy, has dorms, private rooms, free coffee in the morning and a barbecue in a courtyard for the evening.

Sgt Preston's Lodge   MOTEL $$
(☑866-983-2521, 907-983-2521; http://sgt-prestons.eskagway.com; 370 6th Ave; s $97-115, d US$119-151; @🐾) This motel is the best bargain in Skagway and just far enough from Broadway St to escape most of the cruise-ship crush. Prices include taxes.

Skagway Inn   INN $$
(☑888-752-4929, 907-983-2289; www.skagwayinn.com; Broadway St at 7th Ave; r incl breakfast $129-229; @🐾) In a restored 1897 Victorian house that was originally one of the town's brothels – what building still standing in Skagway wasn't? – the inn is downtown and features 10 rooms, four with shared bathrooms. All are small but filled with antique dressers, iron beds and chests. A delicious breakfast is included.

Mile Zero B&B   B&B $$
(☑907-983-3045; www.mile-zero.com; 901 Main St; r $135-145; @) This B&B is like a motel with the comforts of home, the six large rooms have their own bathroom and a private entrance on the wraparound porch.

✖ Eating & Drinking

In 2012, Skagway's restaurants and bars became a smoke-free zone.

★ Stowaway Café   CAJUN $$
(☎ 907-983-3463; www.stowawaycafe.com; 205 Congress Way; mains US$11-24; ☺10am-9pm) Near the Harbor Master's office, this funky cafe serves excellent fish and Cajun-style steak dinners. Make sure you try the wasabi salmon.

Starfire   THAI $$
(☎ 907-983-3663; 4th Ave at Spring St; lunch $12-15, dinner $14-19; ☺11am-10pm; 🖊) Order pad Thai or curry dishes in five colors (purple is 'Fire with Flavor'!) here and then enjoy them with a beer on the outdoor patio.

Skagway Brewing Company   BREWERY
(www.skagwaybrewing.com; cnr 7th Ave & Broadway; burgers $15; ☺10am-10pm Mon-Fri, 11am-10pm Sat & Sun) Skagway's sole brewing company pours at least five home brews, including Prospector Pale, and serves up food that pairs well with them, such as burgers and pizza, in a historic building.

Red Onion Saloon   BAR
(205 Broadway St) This former brothel is now Skagway's liveliest bar. Naturally.

ⓘ Information

Klondike Gold Rush National Historical Park Visitors Center (☎ 907-983-9223; www.nps.gov/klgo; 154 Broadway St; ☺8am-6pm, to 7pm Fri) For everything outdoors: local trails, public campgrounds and National Park Service programs.

Skagway Convention & Visitors Bureau (☎ 907-983-2854; www.skagway.com; cnr Broadway St & 2nd Ave; ☺8am-6pm Mon-Fri, to 5pm Sat & Sun) In the can't-miss Arctic Brotherhood Hall (think driftwood).

ⓘ Getting There & Away

Regularly scheduled flights from Skagway to Juneau, Haines and Glacier Bay are available from Wings of Alaska (p1093).

Alaska Marine Highway (p1085) has ferries departing every day in summer, and Haines–Skagway Fast Ferry (p1094) runs daily to Haines.

Sourdough Car Rentals (☎ 907-983-2523; www.sourdoughrentals.com; 350 6th Ave) has compacts for $80 a day.

White Pass & Yukon Route Railroad (☎ 907-983-2217; www.wpyr.com; 231 2nd Ave; ☺Jun-Aug) goes to Fraser, British Columbia, where there's a bus connection to Whitehorse (adult/child $120/60).

ANCHORAGE

Anchorage offers the comforts of a large US city but is only a 30-minute drive from the Alaskan wilderness. Founded in 1914 as a work camp for the Alaska Railroad, the city was devastated by the 1964 Good Friday earthquake but quickly rebounded as the industry headquarters for the Prudhoe Bay oil boom. Today almost half the state's residents live in or around the city, as Anchorage serves as the economic and political heart of Alaska. Sorry, Juneau.

⊙ Sights & Activities

★ Anchorage Museum   MUSEUM
(www.anchoragemuseum.org; 625 C Street; adult/child $15/7; ☺9am-6pm; 🖼) A $106-million renovation has made this Alaska's best cultural experience. Spend an afternoon viewing paintings by Alaskan masters, including Sydney Laurence, on the 1st floor and then check out the incredible Smithsonian exhibit on the 2nd. There is plenty for kids to love, too.

Alaska Native Heritage Center   CULTURAL BUILDING
(www.alaskanative.net; 8800 Heritage Center Dr; adult/child $25/17; ☺9am-5pm) This cultural center is spread over 26 acres and includes studios with artists carving baleen (the filter-feeder system found inside the mouths of whales) or sewing skin-boats, a small lake and five replica villages. Other than traveling to the Bush, this is the best place to see how humans survived – even thrived – before central heating.

Alaska Heritage Museum   MUSEUM
(301 W Northern Lights Blvd; ☺noon-4pm Mon-Fri) **FREE** This museum-in-a-bank is home to the largest private collection of original paintings

---

ⓘ CULTURE PASS JOINT TICKET

Anchorage's top two attractions, the Alaska Native Heritage Center and Anchorage Museum, can both be enjoyed at a 30% discount with a special joint-admission ticket. The Culture Pass Joint Ticket is $30 per person and includes admission to both museums as well as shuttle transportation between them. You can purchase the joint pass from the ticket offices at either location.

and Alaska Native artifacts in the state. The collection is so large there are displays in the elevator lobbies throughout the bank.

Alaska Aviation Heritage Museum   MUSEUM
(www.alaskaairmuseum.org; 4721 Aircraft Dr; adult/child $10/6; ⊘9am-5pm) Ideally located on Lake Hood, the world's busiest floatplane lake, this museum is a tribute to Alaska's colorful Bush pilots and includes 25 of their faithful planes.

Alaska Zoo   ZOO
(www.alaskazoo.org; 4731 O'Malley Rd; adult/child $12/6; ⊘9am-9pm; ▣) The unique wildlife of the Arctic is on display at the only zoo in North America that specializes in northern animals, ranging from all three species of Alaskan bear to wolverines, moose, caribou and Dall sheep.

Flattop Mountain   HIKING
A three- to five-hour, 3.4-mile round-trip of Alaska's most-climbed peak starts from a trailhead on the outskirts of Anchorage. Maps are available at the Alaska Public Lands Information Center (p1099) and the **Flattop Mountain Shuttle** (☑907-279-3334; www.hike-anchorage-alaska.com; return adult/child $22/15) will run you to the trailhead (and it also runs a hike/bike combo).

Tony Knowles Coastal Trail   HIKING
On the other side of the creek from the Flattop Mountain trail, beginning at the west end of 2nd Ave, this 11-mile trail is the most scenic of the city's 122 miles of paved path.

Downtown Bicycle Rental   CYCLING
(www.alaska-bike-rentals.com; 333 W 4th Ave; 3-/24-hr rental $16/32; ⊘8am-10pm) Anchorage has been called a 'Bike Utopia.' Rent a bike and find out why.

☞ Tours

Rust's Flying Service   SCENIC FLIGHT
(☑907-243-1595; www.flyrusts.com; 4525 Enstrom Circle) Has 30-minute tours ($100), a three-hour flight to view Mt McKinley in Denali National Park ($385) and a 1½-hour tour of Knik Glacier ($245).

Anchorage City Trolley Tours   BUS TOUR
(☑888-917-8687, 907-775-5603; www.alaskatrolley.com; 612 W 4th Ave; adult/child $20/7.50; ⊘tours 9am-5pm) One-hour rides in a bright-red trolley depart on the hour, passing Lake Hood, Earthquake Park and Cook Inlet, among other sights.

🛏 Sleeping

Qupqugiaq Inn   INN $
(☑907-563-5633; www.qupq.com; 640 W 36th Ave; s/d $90/100, without bathroom $75/85; @ 🖘) ✦ This colorful establishment has a continental breakfast that includes French-pressed coffee, roll-your-own-oats, and homemade waffle mix, and the rooms are bright and clean. Plans are under way for 'sleeping pods' ($45) in 2014.

Alaska Backpackers Inn   HOSTEL $
(☑907-277-2770; www.alaskabackpackers.com; 327 Eagle St; dm/s/d $25/60/70; @) A bit east of central downtown, this roomy and comfortable hostel is still within walking distance of restaurants and bars. New annexes offer a chill lobby and deluxe suites ($75).

Spenard Hostel   HOSTEL $
(☑907-248-5036; www.alaskahostel.org; 2845 W 42nd Ave; dm $25; @ 🖘) This friendly, independent hostel is near the airport and has 24-hour check-in (you'll need a reservation if you arrive after 11pm) – great for red-eye arrivals in Alaska. There's free coffee in the morning and bike rentals ($3 per hour) are available. You can pitch a tent in the yard for $20.

Wildflower Inn   B&B $$
(☑907-274-1239; www.alaska-wildflower-inn.com; 1239 I St; r incl breakfast $144-154; @ 🖘) In a historic home just three blocks south of Delaney Park, this B&B offers three large rooms, pleasant sitting areas and a full breakfast in the morning, including caramelized French toast.

Long House Alaskan Hotel   HOTEL $$
(☑888-243-2133, 907-243-2133; www.longhouse-hotel.com; 4335 Wisconsin St; s/d $159/169; 🖘) A block off Spenard Rd, this log hotel has 54 huge rooms and lots of amenities including 24-hour shuttle to the airport.

Puffin Inn   MOTEL $$
(☑907-243-4044; www.puffininn.net; 4400 Spenard Rd; r $125-165; 🖘) Arriving on the red-eye? This motel offers free 24-hour airport shuttle as well as four tiers of fine rooms, from 26 sardine-can economy rooms to full suites.

City Garden B&B   B&B $$
(☑907-276-8686; www.citygarden.biz; 1352 W 10th Ave; r $125-175; 🖘) This open, sunny, gay-and-lesbian-friendly place has three rooms, one with a private bathroom.

★**Copper Whale Inn** INN $$$
(📞866-258-7999, 907-258-7999; www.copperwhale.com; cnr W 5th Ave & L St; r $189-240; @🖥) An ideal downtown location, recently remodeled rooms and a bright and elegant interior make this gay-friendly inn one of the best top-end places in Anchorage. Many rooms and the breakfast lounge give way to views of Cook Inlet. Are those beluga whales out there?

**Anchorage Downtown
Hotel** BOUTIQUE HOTEL $$$
(📞907-258-7669; www.anchoragedowntownhotel.com; 826 K St; r $189-212; 🖥) This boutique hotel is a very pleasant place to stay, with 16 colorful and comfortable rooms that feature private bathrooms, coffeemakers and small refrigerators. In the morning you're handed a newspaper to start the day.

Millennium Alaskan Hotel HOTEL $$$
(📞907-243-2300; www.millenniumhotels.com; 4800 Spenard Rd; r $249-340; @🖥) A large, 248-room resort with a woodsy lodge feel overlooking Lake Spenard, 4 miles from downtown. Kids love the mounted animals and fish.

✖ **Eating**

In Anchorage you'll enjoy great menus, from Polynesian and Mexican to good old burgers, and clean air. All restaurants and bars are smoke-free.

Yak & Yeti ASIAN $
(www.yakandyetialaska.com; 3301 Spenard Rd; mains $7-13; ⊘11am-2:30pm & 5-9pm; 🍴) This small restaurant serves Himalayan food: daal, curries, chai and naan. It's excellent. There's no alcohol served but you can bring your own. It also has a cafe in the same complex as REI.

Arctic Roadrunner BURGERS $
(5300 Old Seward Hwy; burgers $5-7; ⊘10:30am-9pm Mon-Sat) Since 1964 this place has been turning out beefy burgers that can be enjoyed outdoors while watching salmon spawn up Campbell Creek.

Ray's Place VIETNAMESE $
(📞907-279-2932; www.raysplaceak.com; 32412 Spenard Rd; mains $8-15; ⊘10am-3pm & 5-9pm Mon-Fri; 🍴) This Vietnamese restaurant does great cold-noodle salads and stir fries and stocks Vietnamese beer. The pho is heavenly on a rainy day.

New Sagaya's City Market SUPERMARKET $
(www.newsagaya.com; W 13th Ave; ⊘6am-10pm Mon-Sat, 8am-9pm Sun) Eclectic and upscale, this grocery store has a great deli specializing in Asian fare and seating indoors and outdoors.

★**Snow City Café** CAFE $$
(www.snowcitycafe.com; 1034 W 4th Ave; breakfast $8-15, lunch $10-15; ⊘7am-3pm Mon-Fri, to 4pm Sat & Sun; 🖥) This hip and busy cafe serves healthy grub to a mix of clientele that ranges from the tattooed to the up-and-coming. Surrounding all of them are walls adorned with local art. It's worth reserving a table on the weekend.

Moose's Tooth Pub & Pizzeria PIZZERIA $$
(www.moosestooth.net; 3300 Old Seward Hwy; large pizza $16-25; ⊘10:30am-11pm Mon-Thu, to midnight Fri & Sat, 11am-11pm Sun; 🍴) An Anchorage institution serving more than a dozen custom-brewed beers, including monthly specials, and 40 gourmet pizzas including 10 veggie options.

Bear Tooth Grill TEX-MEX $$
(www.beartoothgrill.freshalepubs.com; 1230 W 27th St; burgers $10-16, mains $12-20; ⊘11am-11:30pm Mon-Fri, 10am-11:30pm Sat & Sun) A popular hangout with an adjacent movie theater, the Bear Tooth Grill serves excellent burgers and seafood as well as Tex-Mex dishes. The margaritas are the best in town, and local Broken Tooth beer is on tap.

Middle Way Cafe CAFE $$
(www.middlewaycafe.com; lunch & brunch $8-13; ⊘7am-6pm Mon-Fri, from 8am Sat & Sun; 🖥🍴) One of Anchorage's best brunch spots (try

ℹ **MORE AFFORDABLE CAR RENTALS**

Avoid renting a car at the airport if at all possible as you will be hit with a 34% rental tax. Rental agencies within Anchorage will tack on only 18% tax and generally have cheaper rates. And while they can't pick you up at the airport, if you drop the car off during business hours some rental places will provide you with a ride to the airport.

Finally, if you can rent a vehicle in May or September as opposed to June or August, you will usually save more than 30%.

ALASKA ANCHORAGE

the huevos rancheros), but also perfect for sandwiches, salads, coffee and smoothies. It has many vegetarian and dairy- and gluten-free options.

Spenard Roadhouse FUSION $$
(www.spenardroadhouse.com; 1049 W Northern Lights Bvld; mains $9-14 ; ⊙11am-11pm Mon-Fri, from 9am Sat & Sun; 🖉) Appealing to Anchorage's hipsters with bourbon, beer and bacon. There are inexpensive appetizers including tater tots and TV dinners on Sundays.

Sack's Café FUSION $$$
(🖉907-274-4022; www.sackscafe.com; 328 G St; lunch mains $12-16, dinner $24-34; ⊙11am-2:30pm & 5-9pm Sun-Thu, to 10pm Fri & Sat) A bright, colorful restaurant serving Asian-Mediterranean fusion fare that is consistently creative (reservations recommended).

Glacier Brewhouse BREWERY $$$
(www.glacierbrewhouse.com; 737 W 5th Ave; lunch $12-19, dinner $18-30; ⊙11am-9:30pm Mon, to 10pm Tue-Thu, to 11pm Fri & Sat, noon-9:30pm Sun) Grab a table overlooking the three giant copper brewing tanks and enjoy Alaskan seafood and rotisserie-grilled ribs and chops with a pint of oatmeal stout.

🍷 Drinking & Nightlife

Bernie's Bungalow Lounge LOUNGE
(www.berniesak.com; 626 D St) Pretty people, pretty drinks: this is the place to see and be seen. The outdoor patio, with a water-spewing serpentine, is the city's best and on summer weekends it rocks late into the night with live music.

Crush WINE BAR
(www.crushak.com; 343 W 6th Ave) This swanky club and restaurant is a great place for a glass of wine or the entire bottle – plus small bites.

Snow Goose & Sleeping Lady Brewing Co BREWERY
(717 W 3rd Ave) If the sun is setting over Cook Inlet and the Alaska Range, head to the rooftop deck of this brewpub. Only the beer is better than the view.

Humpy's Great Alaskan Alehouse PUB
(www.humpys.com; 610 W 6th Ave; mains $15-21; 🕾) Anchorage's most beloved beer place, with almost 60 beers on tap. There's also ale-battered halibut, gourmet pizzas, outdoor tables and live music most nights.

☆ Entertainment

Check the *Anchorage Press* for the latest entertainment listings.

★Chilkoot Charlie's LIVE MUSIC
(www.koots.com; 2435 Spenard Rd) 'Koots,' as locals call this beloved landmark, is big and brash, with 10 bars, four dance floors and sawdust everywhere. There's live music every night and $2.50 pints until 10pm.

Tap Root LIVE MUSIC
(www.taprootalaska.com; 3300 Spenard Rd) With the addition of Tap Root, Spenard Rd cemented its reputation as the heart of Anchorage nightlife. The lively bar has 20 microbrews on tap, an impressive list of single-malt Scotch whiskeys and live bands every night of the week.

Cyrano's Theatre Company THEATER
(🖉907-274-2599; www.cyranos.org; 413 D St) This may be the best live theater in town, staging everything from Hamlet to a Mel Brooks' jazz musical, with a strong commitment to local theater artists and Alaskan playwrights.

Mad Myrna's DANCE
(🖉907-276-9762; 530 E 5th Ave) A fun, cruisy bar with drag shows on Friday and dance music most other nights after 9pm.

🛍 Shopping

Oomingmak Musk Ox Producers Co-op CLOTHING
(www.qiviut.com; 604 H St) Handles a variety of very soft, very warm and very expensive garments made of arctic musk-ox wool, hand-knitted in isolated Inupiaq villages.

REI OUTDOOR EQUIPMENT
(1200 W Northern Lights Blvd; ⊙10am-8pm Mon-Fri, to 7pm Sat, to 6pm Sun) The large REI has the city's finest selection of backpacking, kayaking and camping gear.

ANMC Craft Shop ARTS & CRAFTS
(🖉907-729-1122; 4315 Diplomacy Dr; ⊙10am-2pm Mon-Fri, 11am-2pm 1st & 3rd Sat of month) On the 1st floor of the Alaska Native Medical Center; has some of the finest Alaska Native arts and crafts available to the public.

ℹ Information

INTERNET ACCESS
ZJ Loussac Public Library (🖉907-343-2975; www.anchoragelibrary.org; 3600 Denali St;

10am-9pm Mon-Thu, to 6pm Fri & Sat, 1-5pm Sun) Free internet access.

MEDIA

Tourist freebies are available everywhere, including the *Official Anchorage Visitors Guide*.

Anchorage Daily News (www.adn.com) This daily has the largest circulation in the state.

Anchorage Press (www.anchoragepress.com) A fabulous free weekly with events listings and social commentary.

MEDICAL SERVICES

Alaska Regional Hospital (☑907-276-1131; 2801 DeBarr Rd; ⊗24hr) For emergency care.

First Care Medical Center (☑907-248-1122; 3710 Woodland Dr, suite 1100; ⊗7am-11pm) Walk-in clinic in midtown.

Providence Alaska Medical Center (☑907-562-2211; 3200 Providence Dr; ⊗24hr)

MONEY

Key Bank (☑907-257-5502; 601 W 5th Ave) Downtown.

Wells Fargo (☑907-265-2805; 301 W Northern Lights Blvd) The main bank is in midtown.

POST

Post Office (344 W 3rd Ave) Downtown in the Village at Ship Creek Center.

TOURIST INFORMATION

Alaska Public Lands Information Center (☑866-869-6887, 907-644-3661; www.alaskacenters.gov; 605 W 4th Ave, suite 105; ⊗9am-5pm) Has park, trail and cabin information as well as excellent displays.

Log Cabin Visitor Center (☑907-257-2363; www.anchorage.net; 524 W 4th Ave; ⊗8am-7pm) Has pamphlets, maps, bus schedules and city guides.

ⓘ Getting There & Around

TO/FROM THE AIRPORT

Alaska Shuttle (☑907-694-8888, 907-338-8888; www.alaskashuttle.net) offers door-to-door transportation between the airport and downtown and South Anchorage (one to three people $50) and Eagle River ($55). The city's bus service (People Mover) picks up from the South Terminal (bus 7) on a route that heads back downtown.

ALASKA ANCHORAGE

THE BEST OF THE REST OF ALASKA

Came for a quick peek and are so smitten by the grandeur of Alaska you want to linger? Go ahead; skip Nebraska and stay another week or two. Here's more of Alaska that's worth changing your travel plans for:

➡ A breathtaking wilderness, **Denali National Park & Preserve** (☑907-683-2294; www.nps.gov/dena) includes North America's highest peak and an amazing array of wildlife.

➡ At the tip of the Kenai Peninsula, **Homer** (www.homeralaska.org) is a scenic town with good eating, a great art scene and giant halibut offshore.

➡ There's great hiking in **Chena River State Recreation Area** and Mother Nature's own Jacuzzi to soak in afterwards at **Chena Hot Springs** (www.chenahotsprings.com).

➡ To watch giant brown bears snag salmon in mid-air or to hike in the Valley of 10,000 Smokes, come to **Katmai National Park** (www.nps.gov/katm).

➡ Another scenic Kenai Peninsula town, **Seward** (www.sewardak.org) is the place to go for marine wildlife in **Kenia Fjords National Park** or **Alaska SeaLife Center** (☑800-224-2525; www.alaskasealife.org; 301 Railway Ave; adult/child $20/10; ⊗8am-7pm).

➡ Stretching between Seward and Fairbanks, the **Alaska Railroad** (www.akrr.com) is one of the most amazing train rides in the world.

➡ Walk the same streets that Wyatt Earp did in the colorful gold-rush town of **Nome** (www.nomealaska.org) or pan for some color on **Golden Sands Beach**.

➡ At the end of the McCarthy Rd in the heart of **Wrangell–St Elias National Park**, the country's largest, are the twins towns of **Kennecott and McCarthy** (www.nps.gov/wrst), full of history, artifacts and glaciers.

➡ **Childs Glacier** alone makes it worth jumping on the Alaska Marine Highway for the fishing port of **Cordova** (www.cordovachamber.com) in Prince William Sound.

➡ The most amazing ferry trip in the USA is the **Trusty Tusty** (www.ferryalaska.com) run to Unalaska, a four-day cruise from Homer to the Aleutian Islands.

AIR

Ted Stevens Anchorage International Airport (p1085) has frequent inter- and intra-state flights. Terminals are off International Airport Rd. Alaska Airlines (p1085) flies to 19 Alaskan towns, including Fairbanks, Juneau, Nome and Barrow.

Era Aviation (☑907-266-8394, 800-866-8394; www.flyera.com) Flies to Cordova, Valdez, Kodiak and Homer.

Pen Air (☑800-448-4226; www.penair.com) Serves southwest Alaska.

BUS

People Mover (☑907-343-6543; www.peoplemover.org; adult/child $1.75/1) is the local bus service; its main terminal is located at the Downtown Transit Center (cnr W 6th Ave & G St). For more bus options, see p1086.

CAR

Midnight Sun Car & Van Rental (☑888-877-3585, 907-243-8806; www.ineedacarrental.com; 4211 Spenard Rd) rents compacts (per day/week $70/420), as does **Denali Car Rental** (☑907-276-1230; www.akdenalicarrental.com; 1209 Gambell St) for $65/390.

TRAIN

Alaska Railroad (☑907-265-2494; www.akrr.com) chugs its way south to Whittier (adult/child $74/37, 2½ hours) and Seward ($79/40, four hours), and north to Denali ($150/75, eight hours) and then Fairbanks ($216/108, 12 hours).

Hawaii

Includes →

Best Beaches

→ Kailua Beach (p1108)

→ Malaekahana State Recreation Area (p1108)

→ Anaeho'omalu Beach Park (p1111)

→ Kapalua Beach (p1114)

→ Pali Ke Kua (Hideaways) Beach (p1119)

Best Small Towns

→ Hale'iwa (p1109)

→ Hilo (p1112)

→ Pa'ia (p1117)

→ Hanalei (p1119)

→ Hanapepe (p1120)

Why Go?

Truth: this string of emerald islands in the cobalt-blue Pacific, more than 2000 miles from any continent, takes work to get to. And besides, aren't these beaches totally crushed by sun-baked tourists and cooing honeymooners? Cue the galloping *Hawaii Five-0* theme music, Elvis crooning and lei-draped beauties dancing hula beneath wind-rustled palms.

Hawaii, as tourist bureaus and Hollywood constantly remind us, is 'paradise.' Push past the hype and you may find they're not far wrong. Hawaii is diving coral-reef cities in the morning and listening to slack key guitar at sunset. It's biting into juicy *liliko'i* (passion fruit) with hibiscus flowers in your hair. These Polynesian islands are an expression of nature's diversity at its most divine, from fiery volcanoes to lacy rainforest waterfalls to crystal-clear aquamarine bays.

Locals know Hawaii isn't always paradise, but on any given day it can sure feel like it.

When to Go
Honolulu

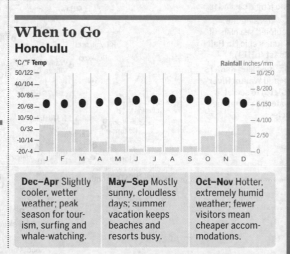

Dec–Apr Slightly cooler, wetter weather; peak season for tourism, surfing and whale-watching.

May–Sep Mostly sunny, cloudless days; summer vacation keeps beaches and resorts busy.

Oct–Nov Hotter, extremely humid weather; fewer visitors mean cheaper accommodations.

Hawaii Highlights

1 Exploring multicultural **Honolulu** (p1104), with its eye-popping museums and ethnic eats.

2 Snorkeling with tropical fish and sea turtles in **Hanauma Bay** (p1108).

3 Watching pros surf the monster winter waves on O'ahu's epic **North Shore** (p1109).

4 Witnessing the eruption of a living volcano inside **Hawai'i Volcanoes National Park** (p1113).

5 Stargazing atop Hawaii's highest mountain, **Mauna Kea** (p1111), on the Big Island.

6 Catching dawn over Maui's 'house of the rising sun' at **Haleakalā National Park** (p1118).

7 Driving Maui's twisting seaside **Hana Highway** (p1117) past black-sand beaches and jungle cascades.

8 Trekking the sculpted sea cliffs of Kaua'i's epic **Na Pali Coast** (p1119).

9 Kayaking Kaua'i's sacred **Wailua River** (p1118) to secret waterfall swimming holes.

History

Little is known about Hawai'i's first Polynesian settlers, who arrived around AD 500. Tahitians had landed by AD 1000 and, for the next three centuries, navigated thousands of miles back and forth across the Pacific Ocean in double-hulled canoes. Ruled by chiefs, ancient Hawaiian society and its religion followed strict laws known as *kapu*.

Beginning in the 1790s, a Big Island chief named Kamehameha conquered and united the main Hawaiian Islands. He is credited with bringing peace and stability to a society that was often in flux due to wars and ruling-class power struggles. After Kamehameha's death in 1819, his son Liholiho inherited the throne, while Kamehameha's favored wife, Ka'ahumanu, became co-regent. In a stunning repudiation of traditional Hawaiian religion, these rulers deliberately violated *kapu*, an act followed up by the destruction of many temples.

Christian missionaries arrived soon after and, amid Hawai'i's social and spiritual chaos, began to 'save souls.' New England whalers also weighed anchor, and by the 1840s Lahaina and Honolulu were the busiest whaling towns in the Pacific. Foreign residents made a grab for Hawai'i's fertile land, turning vast tracts into sugarcane plantations; needing field workers, they encouraged a flood of immigrants from Asia and Europe. This gave rise to Hawai'i's multi-ethnic culture, but also displaced Native Hawaiians, who mostly became landless.

In 1893 a group of American businessmen overthrew the Hawaiian monarchy. The US government was initially reluctant to support the coup, but soon rationalized colonialism by citing the islands' strategic economic, political and military importance, annexing Hawaii in 1898. Hawaii played another pivotal role in history when a surprise attack on Pearl Harbor in 1941 catapulted the US into WWII. Hawaii became the 50th state in 1959.

Local Culture

Compared to 'the mainland' – a blanket term for the rest of the US – Hawaii may as well be another country. Not coincidentally, some Native Hawaiians would like to restore its status as an independent nation. Both geologically and culturally speaking, Hawaii developed in isolation and, like its flora and fauna, island lifestyles are unique.

No ethnicity can claim a majority, but this racial diversity is distinct from typical US multiculturalism: Hawaii has large Asian populations and tiny African American and Latino communities. About 10% of residents identify themselves as Native Hawaiian.

As befits a tropical paradise, Hawaii is decidedly casual. Except in cosmopolitan Honolulu, aloha shirts and sandals or 'rubbah slippah' (flip-flops) are acceptable attire for almost any occasion. Socializing revolves around food and family, and fun means sports and outdoor pursuits. Caring for the land and the community are intertwined.

Then there's aloha. It's a greeting, meaning hello or goodbye. But beyond that, it describes a gentle, everyday practice of openness, hospitality and loving welcome – one that's extended to everyone, including visitors.

Language

Hawaii has two official state languages, English and Hawaiian, and one unofficial language, pidgin. The Hawaiian language has experienced a renaissance but, outside a formal setting (eg classroom, performance), you are unlikely to hear it spoken. All residents speak English, but when locals 'talk story' with each other they may reach for the relaxed, fun-loving cadences of pidgin. Pidgin developed on sugar plantations as a common tongue for immigrant workers.

HAWAII FACTS

Nickname Aloha State

Population 1.4 million

Area 6423 sq miles

Capital city Honolulu (population 337,250)

Sales tax 4% (4.5% on O'ahu)

Birthplace of Olympian Duke Kahanamoku (1890–1968), entertainer Don Ho (1930–2007), President Barack Obama (b 1961), actor Nicole Kidman (b 1967)

Home of Ukulele and the USA's only royal palace

Politics Majority vote Democrat, minority Native Hawaiian separatists

Famous for Surfing, hula, mai tais, the world's longest-erupting volcano

State fish *Humuhumunukunukuapua'a* (reef triggerfish, literally 'fish with a nose like a pig')

O'AHU

O'ahu is the *ali'i* (chief) of Hawaii's main islands – so much so that others are referred to as 'Neighbor Islands.' Honolulu is the center of state government, commerce and culture, while nearby Waikiki's beaches gave birth to the whole tiki-craze fantasia. If you want to take the measure of Hawaii's diversity, O'ahu offers the full buffet in one tidy package: in the blink of an eye you can go from crowded metropolis to turquoise bays teeming with sea life – and surfers.

Getting There & Around

Honolulu International Airport (HNL; ☎808-836-6411; http://hawaii.gov/hnl; 300 Rodgers Blvd, Honolulu) is Hawaii's major air hub. From the US mainland, fares start around $400 from California. **Roberts Hawaii** (☎800-831-5541, 808-441-7800; www.airportwaikikishuttle.com) runs 24-hour airport shuttles to/from Waikiki (one way/return $13/24).

Hawaiian Airlines (☎800-367-5320; www.hawaiianairlines.com) and **go!** (☎888-435-9462; www.iflygo.com) are the main carriers flying between islands. Service is frequent and flight times are short; one-way fares vary wildly from $80 to $180 (book ahead).

O'ahu's public transit system, **TheBus** (☎808-848-5555; www.thebus.org; fare $2.50, 4-day visitor pass $25; ⊙ infoline 5:30am-10pm), covers the entire island, excluding most hiking trailheads and scenic lookouts.

Honolulu & Waikiki

Among its many museums, historical sites and cultural offerings, Honolulu is also a foodie haven dishing up everything from cheap noodles to gourmet Hawaii Regional Cuisine. Saunter over to Waikiki Beach to lounge on the sand, play in the water, hear Hawaiian music and watch hula dancers sway after sunset.

◉ Sights

Neighboring downtown Honolulu, **Chinatown** lends itself to exploring on foot. Bring an appetite – you'll be grazing pan-Asian marketplaces and cafes between antique and lei shops, temples and art galleries.

★**Bishop Museum**   MUSEUM
(☎museum 808-847-3511, planetarium 808-848-4136; www.bishopmuseum.org; 1525 Bernice St; adult/child $20/15; ⊙9am-5pm Wed-Mon; P ♦)
✐ Ranked among the world's best Polynesian anthropological museums, Bishop Museum boasts impressive cultural displays such as the triple-decker Hawaiian Hall. The family-oriented **Science Adventure Center** puts kids virtually inside an erupting volcano.

★**'Iolani Palace**   PALACE
(☎info 808-538-1471, tour reservations 808-522-0832/0823; www.iolanipalace.org; 364 S King St;

HAWAII IN...

Four Days

Anyone on a trans-Pacific stopover will land at **Honolulu**, so spend the few days you have on **O'ahu**. In between surfing and sunning on **Waikiki Beach**, check out Honolulu's museums and wander the city's **Chinatown**, summit **Diamond Head** and snorkel **Hanauma Bay**. In winter, admire monster waves on the **North Shore**.

One Week

With a week, fit in another island – say, **Maui**. Explore the old whaling town of **Lahaina**, head to **Haleakalā National Park** to see the sunrise above the volcano's summit, take a whale-watching cruise, snorkel or dive **Molokini Crater**, drive the serpentine **Hana Highway** and swim in waterfall pools at **Ohe'o Gulch**.

Two Weeks

With two weeks, tack on a third island. On **Hawai'i, the Big Island**, explore ancient Hawaiian ways at Pu'uhonua O Honaunau National Historical Park, lounge on golden beaches in **North Kona and South Kohala**, visit coffee farms in **South Kona** and say aloha to Pele at **Hawai'i Volcanoes National Park**.

If you choose **Kaua'i**, kayak the **Wailua River**, hike **Waimea Canyon and Koke'e State Parks,** hang ten at **Hanalei Bay**, and trek or paddle past towering sea cliffs on the **Na Pali Coast**.

grounds admission free, adult/child basement galleries $7/3, self-guided audio tour $15/6, guided tour $22/6; ⊘9am-5pm Mon-Sat, last entry 4pm) In the heart of downtown Honolulu, this historical site where the monarchy was overthrown offers a glimpse into the Kingdom of Hawai'i's final decades. Reservations recommended for guided tours.

★ **Honolulu Museum of Art** MUSEUM
(☑808-532-8700; www.honolulumuseum.org; 900 S Beretania St; adult/child $10/5, free 1st Wed & 3rd Sun each month; ⊘10am-4:30pm Tue-Sat, 1-5pm Sun, also 6-9pm last Fri each month Jan-Oct; P⊞) Displays must-see collections of Asian, European and Pacific art. Reserve ahead for offsite tours ($25) of Doris Duke's former mansion Shangri La, a trove of Islamic art, near Diamond Head.

Hawai'i State Art Museum MUSEUM
(☑808-586-0900; www.hawaii.gov/sfca; 2nd fl, No 1 Capitol District Bldg, 250 S Hotel St; ⊘10am-4pm Tue-Sat, also 6-9pm 1st Fri each month) ✐ FREE Showcases traditional and modern works by multicultural island artists.

Lyon Arboretum GARDEN
(☑info 808-988-0456, tour reservations 808-988-0461; www.hawaii.edu/lyonarboretum; 3860 Manoa Rd; donation $5, guided tour $5; ⊘8am-4pm Mon-Fri, 9am-3pm Sat, tours usually 10am Mon-Fri; P⊞) ✐ Wander tree-shaded nature trails and a Hawaiian ethnobotanical garden.

Waikiki Aquarium AQUARIUM
(☑808-923-9741; www.waquarium.org; 2777 Kalakaua Ave; adult/child $9/2; ⊘9am-5pm, last entry 4:30pm; ⊞) ✐ Eco-conscious educational exhibits about marine wildlife and hands-on touch tanks.

🏃 Activities

It's all about loooong **Waikiki Beach**. Catamarans and outrigger canoes pull right up onto the sand, while concession stands offer surf lessons and rent boards. For a swim without the tourist crowds, head to mile-long **Ala Moana Beach Park** (1201 Ala Moana Blvd; P⊞), just west of Waikiki.

Several of Honolulu's hiking trails in the verdant upper Manoa and Makiki Valleys offer sweeping city views. A few are just barely accessible by TheBus, including the 1.6-mile-long round-trip to **Manoa Falls**. Consult **Na Ala Hele** (http://hawaiitrails.ehawaii.gov) for trail information and directions.

✽ Festivals & Events

To discover many more celebrations on all islands, browse www.gohawaii.com.

Waikiki Spam Jam FOOD
(www.spamjamhawaii.com; ⊘late April; ⊞) This street festival goes nuts for canned Spam.

Mele Mei MUSIC, ART
(www.melemei.com; ⊘May) May's month-long celebration of Hawaiian music and hula.

Pan-Pacific Festival ART, CULTURE
(www.pan-pacific-festival.com; ⊘early Jun) Three days of Japanese, Hawaiian and South Pacific entertainment.

★ **Aloha Festivals** ART, CULTURE
(www.alohafestivals.com; ⊘September) Statewide cultural festival brings a royal court and block party to Waikiki.

🛏 Sleeping

Waikiki's main beachfront strip is lined with swanky high-rise resort hotels; for better-value hotels, head inland. Overnight hotel parking averages over $20. Partyin' international backpacker hostels line back-alley Lemon Rd.

Hostelling International (HI) Waikiki HOSTEL $
(☑808-926-8313; www.hostelsaloha.com; 2417 Prince Edward St; dm/r from $25/58, all with shared bath; ⊘reception 7am-3am; P@⊕) Inside a converted apartment building, this tidy hostel is set back from the beach. Sex-segregated, fan-cooled dormitories share a kitchen, coin-op laundry and lockers. No curfew, alcohol or smoking. Reservations essential.

Hotel Renew BOUTIQUE HOTEL $$
(☑808-687-7700, 888-485-7639; www.hotelrenew.com; 129 Pa'oakalani Ave; r from $180; P✳@⊕) ✐ Just a block from the beach, this eco-savvy, gay-friendly boutique hotel satisfies sophisticated urbanites and romantic dreamers alike with sleek rooms, attentive staff and loads of little niceties.

Aqua Hospitality HOTELS, RESORTS $$
(☑808-924-6543, 866-406-2782; www.aquahospitality.com; r from $80; P✳@⊕⊞⊠) The O'ahu hotels of this value-priced boutique chain are Lotus, Bamboo, Skyline, Pearl and Palms.

Outrigger & Ohana HOTELS, RESORTS $$
(☑866-956-4262; www.outrigger.com; r/apt from $95/190; P✳@⊕⊠⊞) Best O'ahu beach hotels in this Hawaii-wide chain: Reef

on the Beach, Regency on Beachwalk and Waikiki on the Beach.

Aston
HOTELS, CONDOS $$
(☑808-924-2924, 877-997-6667; www.astonhotels.com; r/apt from $125/140; P✳@☎☒♨) Family-friendly chain's decent value hotels on O'ahu: Waikiki Banyan, Waikiki Circle and Waikiki Beach.

★ Royal Hawaiian
RESORT $$$
(☑808-923-7311, 866-716-8110; www.royal-hawaiian.com; 2259 Kalakaua Ave; r from $400; P✳@☎☒♨) With its Spanish Moorish-style turrets, the aristocratic, oh-so-pink Royal Hawaiian was Waikiki's first true luxury hotel. It's now spiffier than ever, thanks to multi-million-dollar renovations. For old-school ambience, ask for the historic section; for ocean views, stick with the modern tower.

🍴 Eating

Honolulu is a multiethnic chowhound capital, from Chinatown's streetfront kitchens to locals' joints near Ala Moana Center and star chef's kitchens by the beach.

★ Marukame Udon
JAPANESE $
(www.facebook.com/marukameudon; 2310 Kuhio Ave; dishes $2-8; ☺7-9am & 11am-10pm; ♨) Off-duty military personnel, Asian tourists,

budget backpackers and hotel employees all love Waikiki's cafeteria-style Japanese noodle shop. Stack plates of tempura and *musubi* on your self-service tray, washing everything down with iced barley tea. Lines are looooooong.

Me BBQ
LOCAL, KOREAN $
(151 Uluniu Ave; meals $5-12; ☺7am-8:45pm Mon-Sat; ♨) No-nonsense takeout counter dishes up plentiful island-style mixed plates – devour 'em at sidewalk picnic tables or picnic by the beach.

Leonard's
BAKERY $
(www.leonardshawaii.com; 933 Kapahulu Ave; snacks from $1; ☺5:30am-10pm Sun-Thu, to 11pm Fri & Sat; ♨) O'ahu's best hot, oven-fresh *malasadas* (Portuguese doughnuts).

Lucky Belly
ASIAN, FUSION $$
(☑808-531-1888; www.luckybelly.com; 50 N Hotel St; mains $8-14; ☺11am-2pm & 5pm-midnight Mon-Sat) At this eatery in Chinatown's arts district, pop art hangs over bistro tables. Diners pack in elbows-to-shoulders for hot, spicy pan-Asian bites, fatty ramen bowls, knock-out artisanal cocktails and amazingly fresh, almost architectural salads.

Side Street Inn
LOCAL $$
(☑808-591-0253; www.sidestreetinn.com; 1225 Hopaka St; mains $7-20; ☺2pm-2am, takeout only 10am-2pm Mon-Fri) Outside it looks like hell, but Honolulu's top chefs hang out after work at this late-night sports bar near Ala Moana Center. Divinely tender Korean-style *kalbi* short ribs and pork chops are signature dishes. Bring a group. Also in Waikiki.

Haili's Hawaiian Foods
HAWAIIAN $$
(http://hailishawaiianfood.com; 760 Palani Ave; meals $11-16; ☺10am-7pm Tue-Thu, to 8pm Fri & Sat, 11am-3pm Sun) ✐ Locals shoehorn themselves into this storefront for heaping plates of Hawaiian home cooking – *kalua* pig, *lomilomi* salmon and *laulau* wraps – served with scoops of poi or rice.

★ Roy's Waikiki
HAWAII REGIONAL CUISINE $$$
(☑808-923-7697; www.royshawaii.com; 226 Lewers St; mains $30-42, 3-course prix-fixe menu without/with wine pairings $47/67; ☺11am-9:30pm Sun-Thu, to 10pm Fri & Sat) Groundbreaking chef Roy Yamaguchi doesn't actually cook here, but his signature *misoyaki* butterfish, blackened ahi (tuna), macadmadia nut-encrusted mahimahi and deconstructed sushi rolls always appear on the menu. Reservations essential.

🍸 Drinking & Entertainment

Waikiki is bursting with Hawaiian hula and live music. Honolulu's hippest nightlife scene revolves around Hotel St in Chinatown's once notorious red-light district.

Thirtyninehotel
LOUNGE, CLUB

(☎808-599-2552; www.thirtyninehotel.com; 39 N Hotel St; ⊙4pm-2am Tue-Sat) More arty than clubby, this space is a gallery by day, low-key lounge after dark. DJs spin on weekends, while live bands test the acoustics some weeknights.

Hula's Bar & Lei Stand
GAY BAR

(www.hulas.com; 2nd fl, Castle Waikiki Grand, 134 Kapahulu Ave; ⊙10am-2am; 🛜) Breezy oceanview lanai (balcony) gazes at Diamond Head and Queen's Surf Beach, a prime destination for a sun-worshipping LGBTQ crowd.

★House Without a Key
LIVE MUSIC, HULA

(☎808-923-2311; www.halekulani.com; Halekulani, 2199 Kalia Rd; ⊙7am-9pm, live music usually 5:30-8:30pm) At this genteel open-air oceanfront bar beside a century-old kiawe tree, lilting Hawaiian music accompanies hula dancing by former Miss Hawaii pageant winners.

Kuhio Beach Hula Show
LIVE MUSIC, HULA

(☎808-843-8002; www.honolulu.gov/moca; Kuhio Beach Park, off Kalakaua Ave; ⊙usually 6-7pm or 6:30-7:30pm Tue, Thu, Sat & Sun, weather permitting; 👶) 🎫 **FREE** Bask in the warm aloha with performances by local hula troupes and musicians at this city-sponsored show near Waikiki's Duke Kahanamoku statue.

🛍 Shopping

★Native Books/Nā Mea Hawaii
BOOKS, GIFTS

(☎808-597-8967; www.nativebookshawaii.com; Ward Warehouse, 1050 Ala Moana Blvd; ⊙10am-8:30pm Mon-Thu, to 9pm Fri & Sat, to 6pm Sun) Specializes in Hawaiiana books, CDs and artisan crafts; also hosts free cultural workshops in hula dancing, Hawaiian language, lei-making and *lauhala* weaving, ukulele playing etc.

Bailey's Antiques & Aloha Shirts
CLOTHING, ANTIQUES

(http://alohashirts.com; 517 Kapahulu Ave; ⊙10am-6pm) Hawaii's most encyclopedic collection of vintage and contemporary aloha shirts promises thousands of choices, so you're guaranteed to find something memorable.

Tin Can Mailman
ANTIQUES, BOOKS

(http://tincanmailman.net; 1026 Nu'uanu Ave; ⊙11am-5pm Mon-Thu, to 4pm Fri & Sat) If you're a fan of tiki ware and 20th-century books and prints about the Hawaiian Islands, you'll fall in love with this little Chinatown shop.

Island Slipper
SHOES

(www.islandslipper.com; Ward Warehouse, 1050 Ala Moana Blvd; ⊙10am-9pm Mon-Sat, to 8pm Sun) Slip on a comfy pair of island-made 'rubbah slippah' (flip-flops).

Kamaka Hawaii
MUSIC

(☎808-531-3165; www.kamakahawaii.com; 550 South St; ⊙8am-4pm Mon-Fri) 🎵 Handcrafted ukuleles since 1916; call ahead for factory tours.

ℹ Information

At Waikiki and university neighborhood cybercafes, internet costs about $6 to $12 per hour.

Hawaii State Library (☎808-586-3500; www.librarieshawaii.org; 478 S King St; ⊙10am-5pm Mon & Wed, 9am-5pm Tue, Fri & Sat, 9am-8pm Thu; 🛜) Temporary visitor card ($10) allows free internet access at any public library statewide.

Hawaii Visitors & Convention Bureau (☎808-923-1811, 800-464-2924; www.gohawaii.com; suite 801, Waikiki Business Plaza, 2270 Kalakaua Ave; ⊙8am-4:30pm Mon-Fri) Stocks the same tourist brochures as at the airport.

Queen's Medical Center (☎808-538-9011; www.queensmedicalcenter.net; 1301 Punchbowl St; ⊙24hr) Honolulu's biggest hospital and ER.

Pearl Harbor

On December 7, 1941, a Japanese attack on Pearl Harbor took 2500 military and civilian lives, destroyed 20 ships and fatefully pushed the US into WWII. Today about 1.6 million people a year remember 'a date which will live in infamy' by visiting the **USS Arizona Memorial** (☎808-422-3300; www.nps.gov/valr; 1 Arizona Memorial Pl; admission free, boat-tour reservation fee $1.50; ⊙7am-5pm, boat tours 8am-3pm) **FREE**. The memorial sits directly over the sunken USS *Arizona;* visitors look down at the shallow wreck, still a tomb for 1177 sailors. On shore, the NPS visitor center and museum runs 75-minute tours including a documentary film and boat ride to the memorial. Reserve tours in advance online (www.recreation.gov);

① PEARL HARBOR 411

Strict security measures are in place at Pearl Harbor's memorials, museums and visitor center. You may not bring in any items that allow concealment (eg purses, camera bags, fanny packs, backpacks, diaper bags). Wallets and personal-sized cameras and camcorders are allowed. Don't lock valuables in your car – use the storage facility (per bag $3) outside the main entrance.

otherwise, first-come, first-served tickets may all be gone by mid-morning.

Visit the adjacent **USS Bowfin Submarine Museum & Park** (☑ 808-423-1341; www.bowfin.org; 11 Arizona Memorial Dr; museum adult/child $5/3, incl self-guided submarine tour $10/4; ⊙ 7am-5pm, last entry 4:30pm) to clamber down inside the 'Pearl Harbor Avenger' submarine. Shuttle buses head over to the hangar-sized **Pacific Aviation Museum** (☑ 808-441-1000; www.pacificaviationmuseum.org; 319 Lexington Blvd, Ford Island; adult/child $20/10, incl guided tour $30/20; ⊙ 9am-5pm, last entry 4pm) and the **Battleship Missouri Memorial** (☑ 808-455-1600, 877-644-4896; www.ussmissouri.com; 63 Cowpens St, Ford Island; admission incl tour adult/child from $22/11; ⊙ 8am-4pm, to 5pm Jun-Aug) on Ford Island. Interestingly, the 'Mighty Mo' hosted the Japanese surrender ending WWII.

From Waikiki and Honolulu, buses 42 and 20 stop at Pearl Harbor ($2.50, one hour).

Diamond Head & Southeast O'ahu

O'ahu's southeast coast abounds in dramatic scenery and outdoor activities. For windy 360-degree panoramas, make the 0.8-mile climb up **Diamond Head** (www.hawaiistateparks.org; off Diamond Head Rd btwn Makapu'u & 18th Aves; per pedestrian/car $1/5; ⊙ 6am-6pm, last trail entry 4:30pm; ♿), the 760ft extinct volcano tuff cone visible from Waikiki.

Go eyeball-to-mask with tropical fish at **Hanauma Bay** (☑ 808-396-4229; www.honolulu.gov/parks/facility/hanaumabay; Hanauma Bay Rd, off Hwy 72; adult/child $7.50/free; ⊙ 6am-6pm Wed-Mon Nov-Mar, to 7pm Wed-Mon Apr-Oct; ♿), a turquoise bathtub set in a rugged volcanic ring. For the best snorkeling conditions, ar-

rive early. You can rent snorkel gear on-site. Parking costs $1, but when the lot fills, often by mid-morning, all cars are turned away. From Waikiki, take bus 22 ($2.50, 45 minutes, no service Tuesday).

Long and lovely **Sandy Beach Park**, along Hwy 72 northeast of Hanauma Bay, offers very challenging, even life-risking bodysurfing with punishing shorebreaks, making it a favorite of pros – and exhilarating to watch. Bus 22 also stops here.

Kailua & Windward Coast

The snaggletoothed Ko'olau Mountains are scenic backdrop for the entire Windward Coast. From Honolulu, drive the Pali Hwy (Hwy 61) over the mountains, stopping at the windy lookout at **Nu'uanu Pali State Wayside** (www.hawaiistateparks.org; per car $3; ⊙ sunrise-sunset).

Beneath the windswept *pali* (cliffs) sits beautiful **Kailua Beach**, O'ahu's top windsurfing spot, while offshore islands are popular with kayakers. Water-sports gear rental, lessons and tours are available from several outfitters, including **Kailua Sailboards & Kayaks** (☑ 808-262-2555, 888-457-5737; www.kailuasailboards.com; Kailua Beach Center, 130 Kailua Rd; ⊙ 8:30am-5pm Mon-Sat) near the beach. **Kailua** has plenty of sleeping and eating options, and makes a good adventure base camp. For B&Bs, cottages and condos, check with **Affordable Paradise** (☑ 808-261-1693; www.affordable-paradise.com). From Honolulu, take bus 57 ($2.50, 45 minutes).

Other jewel-like Windward Coast beaches include reef-protected **Waimanalo Bay**, cinematic **Kualoa Regional Park** and **Malaekahana State Recreation Area** (www.hawaiistateparks.org; Kamehameha Hwy; ⊙ 7am-7:45pm Apr-early Sep, 7am-6:45pm early Sep-Mar) **FREE**, a dramatic stretch near La'ie for swimming, windsurfing or snorkeling, with Moku'auia (Goat Island), a near-shore bird sanctuary. To see where Hurley built his *Lost* golf course, Godzilla left his footprints and *Jurassic Park* dinosaurs rampaged, tour **Kualoa Ranch** (☑ 808-237-7321, 800-231-7321; www.kualoa.com; 49-560 Kamehameha Hwy; tours adult/child from $26/15; ⊙ tours 9am-3pm; ♿); reservations are advised.

Run by the Mormon church, La'ie's **Polynesian Cultural Center** (PCC; ☑ 800-367-7060; www.polynesia.com; 55-370 Kamehameha Hwy; adult/child from $50/36; ⊙ noon-5pm Mon-

Sat; 🐾) is a tour-bus theme park with villages, performances and luau buffets – only Pearl Harbor draws more visitors. Further northwest in **Kahuku**, roadside food trucks sell plates of fried shrimp for around $15 – expect long lines around lunchtime.

From Honolulu, bus 55 trundles along the Windward Coast via Kaneohe to Hale'iwa ($2.50, 2¼ hours).

Hale'iwa & North Shore

O'ahu's North Shore is legendary for the massive 30ft winter waves that thunder against its beaches. In the 1950s surfers learned to ride these deadly waves, and today the North Shore hosts the world's premier pro contest, the **Triple Crown of Surfing** (http://vanstriplecrownofsurfing.com), every November and December.

The gateway to the North Shore, **Hale'iwa** is the region's only real town – along its main drag you'll spot art galleries, shops selling surf gear and bikinis and rusty pickup trucks with surfboards tied to the roof. When the surf's up, folks drop everything to hit the waves. They don't have to go far: in-town **Hale'iwa Ali'i Beach Park** (66-167 Hale'iwa Rd) gets towering swells.

Outside town, **Waimea Bay Beach Park** (61-031 Kamehameha Hwy) has a split personality. In summer the water can be as calm as a lake and ideal for swimming and snorkeling; in winter it rips with the island's highest waves. **Sunset Beach Park** (59-104 Kamehameha Hwy) is another classic winter surf spot with powerful breaks. At **'Ehukai Beach Park** (59-337 Ke Nui Rd), the famous Banzai Pipeline breaks over a shallow reef, creating a death-defying ride for pro surfers only. Snorkelers, divers and tide-poolers gather at **Pupukea Beach Park** (59-727 Kamehameha Hwy), a marine-life conservation district. For calmer cove swimming, hit resort-backed **Turtle Bay**.

Team Real Estate (☎808-637-3507, 800-982-8602; www.teamrealestate.com; 1br/2br apt from $100/150) rents accommodations, from studio apartments to beachfront luxury homes, along the North Shore; book in advance. **Food trucks** park alongside the Kamehameha Hwy and on the south side of Hale'iwa town. Opposite Sunset Beach, **Ted's Bakery** (www.tedsbakery.com; 59-024 Kamehameha Hwy; meals $7-16; ⊙7am-8pm; 🐾) is renowned for island-style plate lunches and *haupia* (coconut pudding) pie. In Hale'iwa town, find fiery, authentic tastes at **Opal Thai** (☎808-381-8091; Hale'iwa Town Center, 66-460 Kamehameha Hwy; mains $8-13; ⊙11am-3pm & 5-10pm Tue-Sat; 🍴) or good-karma, healthy deli dishes at **Beet Box Cafe** (www.thebeetboxcafe.com; Celestial Natural Foods, 66-443 Kamehameha Hwy; mains $7-10; ⊙9am-5pm Mon-Sat, to 4pm Sun; 🍴) 🌿. Day-trippers queue for shave ice at **Matsumoto's** (www.matsumotoshaveice.com; 66-087 Kamehameha Hwy; snacks $3-5; ⊙9am-6pm; 🐾) tin-roofed 1950s general store.

From Honolulu, bus 52 runs to Hale'iwa ($2.50, 1¾ hours), from where bus 55 continues along the North Shore and Windward Coast.

HAWAI'I, THE BIG ISLAND

Almost twice the size of all the other Hawaiian Islands combined, the Big Island contains a continent's worth of adventures. Even more thrillingly, it's still growing – Hawai'i's most active volcano, Kilauea, has been erupting here almost nonstop for three decades. Along with red-hot lava, the Big Island offers summit stargazing, ancient places of refuge, rugged hikes into forgotten valleys and hypnotizing beaches, from bone-white strands to black sands cratered with lava-rock tide pools.

ℹ️ Getting There & Around

Mainland and inter-island flights arrive at **Kona** (KOA; ☎808-327-9520; http://hawaii.gov/koa; 73-7200 Kupipi St, Kailua-Kona) or **Hilo** (ITO; ☎808-961-9300; http://hawaii.gov/ito; 2450 Kekuanaoa St, Hilo) airports, both of which have taxis and car-rental booths. **Hele-On** (☎808-961-8744; www.heleonbus.org; fare $2) public buses circle the island, but with mostly limited Monday-to-Saturday commuter routes.

Kailua-Kona

It's the sort of tourist town where you sit in open-air cafes and bars and count sunburnt vacationers going by for amusement. With gold-medal beaches heading north and south, and stacks of ocean-centric activities close at hand, this condo-rich area also makes an affordable island base camp for wider explorations.

⊙ Sights & Activities

Near Kailua Pier, **Kamakahonu Beach** was once Kamehameha the Great's royal residence and includes the restored **Ahu'ena Heiau** (www.ahuena.com; 75-5660 Palani Road) **FREE**, the temple where King Kamehameha I died in 1819. Meander southeast on Ali'i Dr to lava-rock **Moku'aikaua Church** (www.mokuaikaua.org; 75-5713 Ali'i Dr; ⊙7:30am-5:30pm) **FREE**, built in 1837 by Hawaii's first Christian missionaries. Across the street, **Hulihe'e Palace** (☑808-329-1877; www.huliheepalace.net; 75-5718 Ali'i Dr; adult/child $6/1; ⊙10am-3pm Tue-Sat) was a retreat for Hawaiian royalty; its museum is packed with memorabilia and historical artifacts.

A few miles south of town via Ali'i Dr, sun yourself at sparkling **White Sands Beach**, but don't swim in winter when the sand disappears. Further south, Keauhou's **Kahalu'u Beach Park** offers surfing and fab snorkeling with sea turtles. Myriad outfitters in Kailua-Kona rent water-sports gear and guide boat tours, including amazing nighttime snorkeling and diving with **manta rays** (www.mantapacific.org).

🛏 Sleeping

For condos, check with **ATR Properties** (☑888-311-6020, 808-329-6020; www.konacondo.com) and **Kona Hawaii Vacation Rentals** (☑800-244-4752, 808-329-3333; www.konahawaii.com).

Koa Wood Hale Inn/Patey's Place HOSTEL $
(☑808-329-9663; 75-184 Ala Ona Ona St; dm/s/d from $30/55/65, all without bathroom; @🕾) A short walk from Ali'i Dr, this crash pad is Kona's best budget deal, with plain, clean dorms and private rooms. Nighttime quiet hours and no-shoes-inside policy.

Kona Tiki Hotel HOTEL $$
(☑808-329-1425; www.konatikihotel.com; 75-5968 Ali'i Dr; r $80-145; P🕾🏊) It's all about the price and the surf crashing right outside your window. Motel-style rooms are straightforward (no TVs or phones); some have kitchenettes.

King Kamehameha's
Kona Beach Hotel HOTEL $$$
(☑808-329-2911, 800-367-2111; www.konabeachhotel.com; 75-5660 Palani Rd; r $170-250; P❄@🕾🏊) Anchoring Ali'i Dr, the mammoth 'King Kam' sports chic renovated rooms, killer views and a classic poolside bar for mai tais. Avoid noisy rooms facing the street.

🍴 Eating & Drinking

Da Poke Shack SEAFOOD $
(76-6246 Ali'i Dr; mains from $5; ⊙10am-6pm) A huge variety of *poke* creations, with picnic tables outside.

Kona Brewing Company AMERICAN $$
(☑808-334-2739; www.konabrewingco.com; 75-5629 Kuakini Hwy; mains $13-18; ⊙11am-9pm Sun-Thu, to 10pm Fri & Sat) 🍴 The Big Island's original microbrewery makes top-notch ales with a tropical touch, along with thin-crust pizzas and juicy burgers. The torch-lit patio packs 'em in nightly. Call for reservations and brewery-tour schedules.

Island Lava Java CAFE $$
(www.islandlavajava.com; Ali'i Sunset Plaza, 75-5799 Ali'i Dr; meals $9-18; ⊙6:30am-9:30pm; 🕾🍴) A favorite gathering spot for sunny breakfasts, this sidewalk cafe offers an irresistible combo of 100% Kona coffee, sea breezes and local seafood, organic farm salads and homemade sandwiches.

Big Island Grill LOCAL $$
(75-5702 Kuakini Hwy; mains $10-19; ⊙7:30am-9pm Mon-Sat; 🍴) Hawaiian-style home cooking draws everyone and their auntie to this beloved institution (aka 'Biggie's'). Look no further than *loco moco* and plate lunches, all with 'two scoop' rice.

Kanaka Kava CAFE
(www.kanakakava.com; Coconut Grove Marketplace, 75-5803 Ali'i Dr; ⊙10am-10pm Sun-Wed, to 11pm Thu-Sat) Join locals for some mildly intoxicating kava (juice of the *'awa* plant) and tasty island-style *pupu* (appetizers) at this tiny, tropical cafe.

South Kona Coast

Linger along the verdant South Kona coast, with its fragrant coffee farms, ancient Hawaiian sites and characterful small towns. For a window on local life, escape up the cool, misty slopes of Mt Hualalai to **Holualoa** village, packed with artist-owned galleries, the community-run **Donkey Mill Art Center** (☑808-322-3362; www.donkeymillartcenter.org; 78-6670 Hwy 180; ⊙10am-4pm Tue-Sat; 🍴) **FREE** and **Kimura Lauhala Shop** (☑808-324-0053; www.holualoahawaii.com/member_sites/kimura.html; cnr Hualalai Rd & Hwy 180; ⊙9am-5pm Mon-Fri, to 4pm Sat) 🍴 selling traditional Hawaiian pandanus-leaf woven goods.

Off Hwy 11, a side road leads to sparkling, mile-wide **Kealakekua Bay**. On its north side is Ka'awaloa Cove (where Captain Cook was killed in 1779), now the Big Island's premier snorkeling destination. You can hike in via a steep 3.6-mile round-trip trail, but it's more fun to kayak – ask local tour and rental outfitters if the moratorium on kayaking and boat tours has been lifted yet.

In the town of **Captain Cook**, the 1917 **Manago Hotel** (☑ 808-323-2642; www.managohotel.com; 82-6151 Mamalahoa Hwy; s $56-75, d $59-78) is a classic experience: stay in the simple, no-frills motel rooms and order the restaurant's signature pork chops. **Ka'awa Loa Plantation** (☑ 808-323-2686; www.kaawaloaplantation.com; 82-5990 Upper Napo'opo'o Rd; r incl breakfast $130-150; @ 🛜), a stylish garden estate with four-poster beds and a sunset-view lanai, is perfect for romantics. Roadside **Super J's** (☑ 808-328-9566; 83-5409 Mamalahoa Hwy; mains under $10; ⊙ 10am-6:30pm Mon-Sat) kitchen does right by Native Hawaiian faves such as *laulau* and *kalua* pork.

South of Kealakekua Bay, **Pu'uhonua o Honaunau National Historical Park** (☑ 808-328-2326, 808-328-2288; www.nps.gov/puho; 7-day entry per car $5; ⊙ park 7am-sunset, visitor center 8:30am-4:30pm) is an ancient place of refuge, a sanctuary where *kapu* breakers could have their lives spared. Walk the evocative grounds and inspect a reconstructed temple. Immediately north of the park is a terrific snorkeling spot called **Two-Step**. Afterward refresh yourself with an organic smoothie from **South Kona Fruit Stand** (☑ 808-328-8547; www.southkonafruitstand.com; 84-4770 Mamalahoa Hwy; items $5-9; ⊙ 9am-6pm Mon-Sat, 10am-4pm Sun).

North Kona & South Kohala Coasts

The lava-blackened coast running north of Kailua-Kona is strung with secluded palm-lined beaches, ancient Hawaiian sites and posh resorts. Stand-out strands, all off Hwy 19, include dreamy sugar-colored **Kekaha Kai State Park** (www.hawaiistateparks.org; ⊙ 9am-7pm), requiring 4WD; black-sand **Kiholo Bay** (⊙ 7am-7pm); windsurfers' **'Anaeho'omalu Beach Park** (Waikoloa Beach Dr; ⊙ 6am-8pm), white-sand **Beach 69** (⊙ 7am-8pm; 🅿) at Waialea Bay; the **Puako Tide Pools**, resort-backed **Mauna Kea Beach** on crescent-shaped Kauna'oa Bay; and swoon-worthy **Mau'umae Beach**.

The Waikaloa resort area is home to an ancient Hawaiian **petroglyph preserve** (Waikoloa Beach Dr; ⊙ dawn-dusk, 1hr tour 9:30am) **FREE** and two shopping malls offering free entertainment. Blurring the line between resort and theme park is **Hilton Waikoloa Village** (☑ 808-886-1234, 800-221-2424; www.hiltonwaikoloavillage.com; 425 Waikoloa Beach Dr; r from $225; 🅿 ❄ @ 🛜 ☰), with pools, lagoons and activities to please all ages, although almost everything entails a surcharge, even parking.

The Mauna Lani resort area also has ancient Hawaiian sites – fishponds, lava tubes and over 3000 petroglyphs – near the ecofriendly **Mauna Lani Bay Hotel & Bungalows** (☑ 808-885-6622, 800-367-2323; www.maunalani.com; 68-1400 Mauna Lani Dr; r from $400; 🅿 ❄ 🛜 ☰) 🍴, a full-service oceanfront resort with lofty palms and aloha spirit.

To boogie under the stars, head north to Kawaihae's **Blue Dragon Musiquarium** (☑ 808-882-7771; www.bluedragonhawaii.com; 61-3616 Kawaihae Rd; mains $18-36; ⊙ 5-10pm Wed-Thu & Sun, to 11pm Fri & Sat), offering eclectic surf-and-turf and engaging island musicians.

Mauna Kea

When measured from its base beneath the sea, this sacred mountain (13,796ft) is the planet's tallest. Its summit is clustered with world-class astronomical observatories.

Partway up the mountain, **Mauna Kea Visitor Information Station** (MKVIS; ☑ 808-961-2180; www.ifa.hawaii.edu/info/vis; ⊙ 9am-10pm) offers educational displays and free stargazing programs almost nightly. Continuing to the summit for sunset is unforgettable, but it requires either a 4WD, a challenging 6-mile, high-altitude hike (eight-plus hours round-trip), or a guided van tour with **Hawaii Forest & Trail** (☑808-331-8505, 800-464-1993; www.hawaii-forest.com; summit tours $200).

To get here, drive Saddle Rd (Hwy 200), connecting the Kona and Hilo coasts; although scenic, it's accident-prone and some car-rental companies prohibit driving on it. From the marked turn-off near mile marker 28, it's another 6 miles uphill along Mauna Kea's paved summit access road to MKVIS.

Hamakua Coast

The Hamakua Coast ranks among the Big Island's most spectacular scenery. It's a *Lost*-worthy show of deep ravines, jungly valleys and cascading waterfalls.

Most scenic of all is **Waipi'o Valley**, the largest of seven magnificent amphitheater valleys on Hawai'i's windward side. Hwy 240 dead-ends at a dramatic overlook: the road down is so steep that only 4WDs can make it. It's worth the mile-long hike down – *and* the return uphill – to meditate on the thunderous black-sand beach, backgrounded by ribbony waterfalls feeding taro patches.

The valley viewpoint is less than 10 miles from the ex-sugar plantation town of **Honoka'a**, abounding with art galleries and shops. **Tex Drive-In** (☑808-775-0598; www.texdriveinhawaii.com; Hwy 19; mains $5-10; ☺6:30am-8pm) is famous for hot *malasadas*. Outside town, a handful of family-run farms (taste vanilla, honey and tea) are open for agri-tours.

Heading southeast along Hwy 19, **'Akaka Falls State Park** (www.hawaiistateparks.org; 'Akaka Falls Rd; entry per car/pedestrian $5/1) has two stunning waterfalls easily accessed along a 0.4-mile rainforest loop trail.

Hilo

The Big Island's capital has been dubbed the 'rainiest city in the USA,' a soggy reputation that keeps some tourists away. It's their loss, however: Hilo, with its working-class waterfront and historical buildings downtown, brims with weather-beaten charm. Ethnically diverse, it's a slice of the 'real Hawaii.'

◉ Sights & Activities

★'Imiloa Astronomy Center of Hawai'i   MUSEUM
(☑808-969-9700; www.imiloahawaii.org; 600 'Imiloa Pl; adult/child $17.50/9.50; ☺9am-5pm Tue-Sun) One of Hawaii's most eye-popping museums explores Native Hawaiian culture, ecology and the environment, with astronomical discoveries filtered through Mauna Kea's lens.

Pacific Tsunami Museum   MUSEUM
(☑808-935-0926; www.tsunami.org; 130 Kamehameha Ave; adult/child $8/4; ☺9am-4:15pm Mon-Sat) Hilo has survived multiple major tsunami and this dramatic museum brings these chilling events to life, with multimedia exhibits including documentary film footage.

★Lyman Museum & Mission House   MUSEUM
(☑808-935-5021; www.lymanmuseum.org; 276 Haili St; adult/child $10/3; ☺10am-4:30pm Mon-Sat) Drop by for a kid-friendly overview of Hawaii's natural and cultural history. Catch a guided tour (usually 11am and 2pm daily) of the 1830s mission house next door.

Mokupapapa Discovery Center   MUSEUM
(☑935-8358; www.papahanaumokuakea.gov/education/center.html; 76 Kamehameha Ave; ☺check website for opening hours) **FREE** Virtually explore the Northwestern Hawaiian Islands, an isolated chain of islets and atolls protecting the USA's healthiest coral reefs.

Farmers Market   MARKET
(www.hilofarmersmarket.com; cnr Mamo St & Kamehameha Ave; ☺8am-4pm Wed & Sat) Time your visit for a big Hilo market day, an event that's equal parts gossip and shopping, both for island-grown foodstuffs and local crafts.

🛏 Sleeping

★Hilo Bay Hostel   HOSTEL $
(☑808-933-2771; www.hawaiihostel.net; 101 Waianuenue Ave; dm without bathroom $27, r with/without bath $77/67; ☞) Perfectly situated in a historic building downtown, this airy, spick-and-span hostel welcomes a diverse all-ages crowd.

★Dolphin Bay Hotel   HOTEL $$
(☑877-935-1466, 808-935-1466; www.dolphinbayhotel.com; 333 Iliahi St; studio/1br/2br apt from $119/169/189; ☞) This modest hotel is a perennial favorite with travelers who like to settle in. Apartment suites aren't snazzy, but they're comfortable enough and have kitchens.

Shipman House B&B   B&B $$$
(☎ 808-934-8002; www.hilo-hawaii.com; 131 Ka'iulani St; r incl breakfast $219-249; ☎) Hilo's most gracious historical B&B occupies a Victorian mansion packed with museum-quality Hawaiiana. Queen Lili'uokalani once entertained on the grand piano.

✖ Eating

★ Farmers Kitchen Cafe   CAFE $
(57 Mamo St; mains $4-6; ☺ 7am-3pm Tue-Sat; ☎) 'Ono (delicious) homemade plate lunches with creative touches right downtown.

Ken's House of Pancakes   DINER $
(1730 Kamehameha Ave; meals $6-12; ☺ 24hr) Mac-nut pancakes and Spam omelets are faves on a mile-long menu.

★ Hilo Bay Cafe   AMERICAN, SUSHI $$$
(☎ 935-4939; www.hilobaycafe.com; 123 Lihiwai St; mains $15-30; ☺ 11am-9pm Mon-Thu, to 9:30pm Fri & Sat, 5-9pm Sun) Unpretentious yet sophisticated dishes whipped up with organic ingredients at this urban-chic cafe – in a strip mall! – will keep your honey's heart warm even when rain is pounding.

☆ Entertainment

Palace Theater   THEATER
(☎ 808-934-7010, box office 934-7777; www.hilopalace.com; 38 Haili St) Eclectic programming includes arthouse and silent films (accompanied by the house organ), music concerts, hula performances and cultural festivals.

Hawai'i Volcanoes National Park

Even among Hawaii's many natural wonders, this **national park** (HAVO; ☎ 808-985-6000; www.nps.gov/havo; 7-day entry per car $10) stands out: its two active volcanoes testify to the ongoing birth of the islands. Majestic Mauna Loa (13,677ft) looms like a sleeping giant, while youthful Kilauea has been erupting continually since 1983. With luck, you'll witness the primal event of molten lava tumbling into the sea. But the park contains much more to see, including sun-baked lava deserts, steaming craters, lava tubes and rainforest oases.

By the main entrance, **Kilauea Visitor Center & Museum** (☎ 808-985-6017; Crater Rim Dr; ☺ 7:45am-5pm) makes a great

---

> ### ℹ WHERE'S THE LAVA?
>
> For lava updates, check the **USGS** (http://hvo.wr.usgs.gov) website. Park visitor-center staff can advise you on how, if it's possible, to hike to the active flow. At the time of research, **Hawai'i County** (☎ 808-961-8093) maintained a lava-viewing site outside the park at Kalapana in the Puna district (call for current conditions and opening hours). Be prepared to hike across recent lava flows to witness the tell-tale steam plume marking the spot where molten lava enters the ocean, then stay after sunset to see the fiery glow. For boat tours, talk to **Lava Ocean Adventures** (☎ 808-966-4200; www.lavaocean.com; tours from adult/child $150/125).

---

introduction, with free movies and rangers providing updates on volcanic activity and guided walks, including in the park's remote Kahuku Unit. The nearby **Volcano Art Center** (☎ 866-967-7565; www.volcanoartcenter.org; ☺ 9am-5pm) 🖼 gallery coordinates special events, Hawaiian cultural performances and craft workshops.

Note that volcanic eruptions can cause unexpected road and trail closures. When open, the 11-mile **Crater Rim Drive** circles Kilauea Caldera, offering almost non-stop views of the goddess Pele's scorched, smoldering home. At the **Jaggar Museum** (☎ 808-985-6051; ☺ 8:30am-7:30pm) **FREE**, see working seismographs and a stupendous vista of fiery **Halema'uma'u Crater**. Don't miss **Thurston Lava Tube**, an enormous cave left by flowing lava, or the 4-mile **Kilauea Iki Trail** across a cratered moonscape. The park's equally scenic 19-mile **Chain of Craters Road** leads down to the coast, ending abruptly where modern lava flows have buried its end.

The park maintains drive-up **Kulanaokuaiki Campground** (www.nps.gov/havo; Hilina Pali Rd) **FREE**; no reservations. Book ahead for a rustic A-frame cabin at **Namakanipaio Campground** (☎ 808-756-9625, 866-536-7972; www.hawaiivolcanohouse.com; campsites $15, cabins $80) or a crater-view room inside the park's historic **Volcano House** (☎ 866-536-7972, 808-756-9625; www.hawaiivolcanohouse.com; 1 Crater Rim Dr; r $285-350), a recently renovated lodge.

The nearby village of **Volcano** has arty, heart-warming B&Bs, rainforest cottages and vacation homes. With country-cozy rooms, rambling **Kilauea Lodge** (808-967-7366; www.kilauealodge.com; 19-3948 Old Volcano Rd; d $180-290, mains $21.50-49;) runs the area's only fine-dining restaurant, serving hearty chophouse staples (antelope filet, anyone?) and, for breakfast, tropically flavored comfort food. **Volcano Country Cottages** (808-967-7960; www.volcanocountrycottages.com; 19-3990 Old Volcano Rd; d $105-135;) is a private rainforest retreat of lovingly restored plantation cottages stocked with DIY breakfast fixings. Simple, ecofriendly **Volcano Inn** (800-628-3876, 808-967-7773; www.volcanoinn-hawaii.com; 19-3820 Old Volcano Rd; r $89-139;) is value-priced.

MAUI

According to some, you can't have it all. Perhaps those folks haven't been to Maui, which consistently lands atop travel-magazine reader polls as one of the world's most romantic islands. And why not? With its sandy beaches, deluxe resorts, gourmet cuisine, fantastic luau, world-class windsurfing, whale-watching, snorkeling, diving and hiking, it leaves most people even a little more in love than when they arrived.

Getting There & Around

US mainland and inter-island flights land at **Kahului** (OGG; 808-872-3830; www.hawaii.gov/ogg; 1 Kahului Airport Rd). From the airport, bio-diesel **Speedi Shuttle** (877-242-5777; www.speedishuttle.com) charges from $30 to Kihei and $50 to Lahaina.

Public **Maui Bus** (808-871-4838; www.maui-county.gov/bus) operates several daily routes that stop at some main towns, but exclude many tourist destinations (eg Haleakalā National Park). To rent your own wheels, consider an ecofriendly car or Jeep from **Bio-Beetle** (808-873-6121; www.bio-beetle.com; 55 Amala Pl, Kahului; per day $50-90, per week $229-359).

Lahaina & West Maui

For the megahotel and resort experience, bunk down in West Maui, with its prime sunset beaches. For historical atmosphere, entertainment and dining out, make time for Lahaina, a 19th-century whaling town rich in old-timey architecture.

Sights & Activities

The focal point of Lahaina is its bustling small-boat harbor, backed by the **Pioneer Inn** and **Banyan Tree Square**, home to the USA's largest banyan tree. Oceanside Front St is chock-a-block with art galleries, shops and restaurants. Within walking distance of the waterfront are a handful of small historical museums, missionary homes, a prison built for rowdy sailors and a Chinese temple. Lahaina's **visitor center** (808-667-9193; www.visitlahaina.com; Old Lahaina Courthouse, 648 Wharf St; 9am-5pm) offers free walking-tour maps.

Further north in Ka'anapali, stop by the little **Whalers Village Museum** (808-661-5992; www.whalersvillage.com/museum.htm; Whalers Village, 2435 Ka'anapali Pkwy; adult/child $3/1; 10am-6pm) to inspect scrimshaw carvings and whistle sea shanties.

For those world-famous beaches, head north and keep going: between Ka'anapali and Kapalua, one impossibly perfect strand follows another. Three top-ranked gems are **Kahekili Beach**, **Kapalua Beach** and **DT Fleming Beach Park**. Nearly all water sports are possible, and gear rental and tour outfitters abound.

Sleeping

Ka'anapali Beach Hotel RESORT $$
(808-661-0011, 800-262-8450; www.kbhmaui.com; 2525 Ka'anapali Pkwy; r from $169;) While not the fanciest, newest or biggest, this low-key Ka'anapali resort hotel has an enviable beach location and, most of all, genuine aloha. Take free kid-friendly lessons in ukulele, hula and Hawaiian crafts.

Plantation Inn B&B $$
(800-433-6815, 808-667-9225; www.theplanta-tioninn.com; 174 Lahainaluna Rd; r/ste incl breakfast from $158/$248;) Forget cookie-cutter resorts – if you want a taste of Old Hawaii, book a romantic if small room at Lahaina's genteel oasis, furnished with antiques and Hawaiian quilts on four-poster beds.

Hale Napili CONDO $$$
(800-245-2266, 808-669-6184; www.halenapili.com; 65 Hui Dr; apt $190-330;) Small, personable complex smack on Napili Bay's crescent-shaped beach is a welcome throwback to an earlier era. Tidy condos have tropical decor and oceanfront lanai.

✕ Eating

Star Noodle ASIAN **$$**
(☎808-667-5400; www.starnoodle.com; 286 Kupuohi St; mains $7-15, shared plates $3-30; ◷10:30am-10pm) From *Top Chef* competitor Sheldon Simeon, Lahaina's sleek noodle shop lets everyone dive into exquisitely flavored noodle dishes and nibble on eclectic Asian tapas.

★Mala Ocean Tavern ECLECTIC **$$$**
(☎808-667-9394; www.malaoceantavern.com; 1307 Front St; mains lunch $12-26, dinner $19-45; ◷11am-9:30pm Mon-Fri, 9am-9:30pm Sat, 9am-9pm Sun) For Lahaina's best waterfront fine dining, stop searching. Mala marries Mediterranean and Pacific Rim influences with organic, farm-fresh ingredients and a bounty of just-caught seafood.

Sansei SUSHI, SEAFOOD **$$$**
(☎808-669-6286; www.sanseihawaii.com; 600 Office Rd; mains $16-45; ◷5:30-10pm Sat-Wed, 5:30pm-1am Thu & Fri) In Kapalua, trendy Sansei is always uber-busy, serving out-of-this-world sushi and Japanese-Hawaiian fusion fare. Food orders placed by 6pm are discounted 25%. Make reservations.

⚑ Drinking & Entertainment

Around sunset, catch the free torch-lighting and cliff-diving ceremony at Pu'u Keka'a (Black Rock) on northern Ka'anapali Beach.

Hula Grill & Barefoot Bar BAR
(www.hulagrillkaanapali.com; Whalers Village, 2435 Ka'anapali Pkwy; ◷11am-11pm) It's your Maui postcard: sunset mai tais, sand beneath your sandals and the lullaby sounds of Hawaiian slack-key guitar. Skip the food, though.

★Old Lahaina Luau LUAU
(☎808-667-1998, 800-248-5828; www.oldlahainaluau.com; 1251 Front St; adult/child $98/68; ◷from 5:15pm or 5:45pm; ⊞) For a night to remember, this beachside luau is unsurpassed for its authenticity and aloha – the hula is first-rate and the feast darn good. Book ahead.

Feast at Lele LUAU
(☎808-667-5353, 866-244-5353; www.feastatlele.com; 505 Front St; adult/child $115/85; ◷from 5:30pm, 6pm or 6:30pm) ✐ No half-hearted buffet, this gourmet luau is a culinary tour of Pacific Island cultures, accompanied by talented music-and-dance performances.

Ma'alaea

Ma'alaea Bay runs along the low isthmus separating West Maui's mountains from Haleakalā volcano. Prevailing tradewinds funnel between the mountain masses, creating strong midday gusts and some of Maui's top **windsurfing** conditions.

The USA's largest tropical aquarium, **Maui Ocean Center** (☎808-270-7000; www.mauioceancenter.com; 192 Ma'alaea Rd; adult/child $26/19; ◷9am-5pm Sep-Jun, to 6pm Jul & Aug; ⊞) is a feast for the eyes (but not your stomach!). Dedicated to Hawaii's marine life, exhibits are as close as you can get to underwater critters without donning scuba gear.

Kihei & South Maui

Sun-kissed beaches run for miles and miles south of Kihei, which is decidedly less ritzy than West Maui. Vacationers frequent this more affordable coast for swimming, snorkeling, kayaking and abundant condos.

DON'T MISS

WHALE-WATCHING

Every winter from late November through mid-May, around 10,000 humpback whales crowd the shallow waters along Maui's western shores to breed, calve and nurse. These truly awesome creatures can be easily spotted from the shore, particularly when they perform their acrobatic breaches. You can eavesdrop on their singing at www.whalesong.net online.

To get a closer look, take a whale-watching cruise with the nonprofit **Pacific Whale Foundation** (☎800-942-5311, 808-667-7477; www.pacificwhale.org; tour adult/child from $25/18), which sails from Lahaina and Ma'alaea harbors. Another place to get acquainted with these majestic mammals is at Kihei's coastal **Hawaiian Islands Humpback Whale National Marine Sanctuary Headquarters** (☎808-879-2818, 800-831-4888; www.hawaiihumpbackwhale.noaa.gov; 726 S Kihei Rd; ◷10am-3pm Mon-Fri, also 10am-1pm Sat Dec-Mar; ⊞) **FREE**, which has educational displays and telescopes for spotting whales from shore.

MOLOKA'I & LANA'I

Sparsely populated by mostly Native Hawaiians and largely undeveloped for tourism, rural Moloka'i is ideal for those seeking the 'other' Hawaii: unpackaged, traditional, still wild and exuding aloha. Its untamed natural beauty appears today much as it did a century or more ago. **Moloka'i Ferry** (☑877-500-6284, 808-667-9266; www.molokaiferry.com; adult/child round-trip $115/55) runs daily return-trips from Lahaina, Maui. Flights connect Molokai's **airport** (MKK; ☑808-567-9660; http://hawaii.gov/mkk; Ho'olehua) with Kahului (Maui) and Honolulu (O'ahu).

Once home to Hawaii's largest pineapple plantation, Lana'i has been refashioned into a playground for the wealthy. Home to elite resorts and pro-worthy golf courses, Lana'i is ideal for a quick day or overnight getaway from Maui. **Expeditions** (☑800-695-2624, 808-661-3756; www.go-lanai.com; adult/child one-way $30/20) runs several daily round-trip ferries from Lahaina, Maui. You can fly to Lana'i's **airport** (LNY; ☑808-565-7942; http://hawaii.gov/lny; Lana'i Ave, Lana'i City) from Kahului or Honolulu.

South Pacific Kayaks (☑808-875-4848; www.southpacifickayaks.com; kayak rental/tour from $45/69; ⊙rentals 6:45-11am, reservations 6am-8pm) leads adventurous coastal paddles and teaches surfing and stand-up paddle boarding (SUP).

South of Kihei, **Wailea** boasts million-dollar resorts and a prized stretch of coastline cradling tawny beaches of dreamy perfection. Further south, **Makena** has knockout, mostly undeveloped beaches – particularly **Malu'aka Beach** (aka 'Turtle Town'), **Big Beach** and secluded **Little Beach** – as well as the **'Ahihi-Kina'u Natural Area Reserve**, which protects hidden coves for snorkeling.

To reach **Molokini**, an underwater volcanic crater favored by snorkelers and divers, climb aboard with **Maui Dreams Dive Co** (☑808-874-5332; www.mauidreamsdiveco.com; 1993 S Kihei Rd, Kihei; shore/boat dives from $69/129) or **Blue Water Rafting** (☑808-879-7238; www.bluewaterrafting.com; tours $50-125).

🛌 Sleeping

Sort through Kihei's condo possibilities with **Bello Realty** (☑800-541-3060; www.bellomaui.com), or browse **VRBO** (VRBO; www.vrbo.com).

Kihei Kai Nani   CONDO $$
(☑800-473-1493, 808-879-9088; www.kiheikai-nani.com; 2495 S Kihei Rd; apt from $140; ✸ 🛜 ♒) Opposite Kihei's beach, this retro low-rise complex has roomy condos (only some have air-con and wi-fi) with decor ranging from dated to stylish. Ask about weekly discounts.

Tutu Mermaids on Maui B&B   B&B $$
(☑800-598-9550, 808-874-8687; www.twomermaids.com; 2840 Umalu Pl; d incl breakfast $140-170; ✸ @ 🛜 ♒ ⋒) For a personal touch, check out the two kitchenette units at this cheerful B&B. The ocean-themed suite has air-con, a private hot tub and a bamboo-shaded lanai.

★Punahoa   CONDO $$$
(☑800-564-4380, 808-879-2720; www.punahoabeach.com; 2142 Ili'ili Rd; apt $189-299; ✸ 🛜) Hidden on a side street, this boutique condo complex fronts a quiet beach frequented by sea turtles. Who needs a pool? All units have oceanview sunset lanai, while penthouses enjoy air-con.

🍴 Eating & Drinking

Some of South Maui's best dining options are branches of other island restaurants, including **Da Kitchen Express** and **Sansei** in Kihei, and **Mala** in Wailea.

Eskimo Candy   SEAFOOD $$
(☑808-891-8898; www.eskimocandy.com; 2665 Wai Wai Place; mains $8-17; ⊙10:30am-7pm Mon-Fri; ⋒) Fresh seafood fanatics should zero in on the *poke*, ahi wraps and fish tacos at Kihei's side-street fish market with a takeout counter and just a few tables.

Joy's Place   CAFE $$
(www.joysplacemaui.com; Island Surf Bldg, 1993 S Kihei Rd; mains breakfast $3-9, lunch $7-13; ⊙8am-4pm Mon-Sat; ✐) 🍃 Little Kihei kitchen for organic, free-range and locally harvested fare, including healthy sandwiches, tropical smoothies and addictive daily specials.

808 Bistro   BISTRO $$$
(☑808-879-8008; www.808bistro.com; 2511a S Kihei Rd; breakfast $7-15, dinner $15-24; ⊙7am-noon & 5-9pm) Creative comfort food like short-rib pot pie, mango-chutney pork chops and

banana-bread French toast gets dished up on an airy lanai. Hit next-door 808 Deli for lunchtime sandwiches.

South Shore Tiki Lounge
BAR
(☏ 808-874-6444; www.southshoretikilounge.com; Kihei Kalama Village, 1913 S Kihei Rd; ⊙ 11am-2am; 🛜) Tropical strip-mall shack has a heart as big as its lanai. Great mai tais, live music, DJs and dancing.

Kahului & Wailuku

Maui's two largest communities flow together into one urban sprawl. Kahului has Maui's windsurfing shops, whose staff give lessons at gusty **Kanaha Beach** near the airport. On the outskirts of Wailuku, **'Iao Valley State Monument** (www.hawaiistateparks.org; 'Iao Valley Rd; entry per car $5; ⊙ 7am-7pm) centers on picturesque 'Iao Needle, a rock pinnacle jutting above the valley floor.

Step back into the 1920s at **Old Wailuku Inn** (☏ 808-244-5897; www.mauiinn.com; 2199 Kaho'okele St; r incl breakfast $165-195; ✳🛜), an elegant period home authentically restored by gracious innkeepers. Spacious rooms are comfy, with Hawaiian quilts warming the beds. Downtown, international backpackers are welcomed at Wailuku's **Northshore Hostel** (☏ 808-986-8095, 866-946-8095; www.northshorehostel.com; 2080 W Vineyard St; dm $29, r from $69, all without bathroom; ✳@🛜).

At **Da Kitchen** (☏ 808-871-7782; www.da-kitchen.com; Triangle Square, 425 Koloa St; mains $10-25; ⊙ 11am-9pm Mon-Sat) unbeatable island-style *'ono grinds* ('good eats') fill plates big enough to feed two, and the *kalua* pork is 'so tender it falls off da bone.' Expect a crowd, but service is pretty fast.

Pa'ia

A former sugar plantation town, Pai'a is Maui's windsurfing and surfing capital. To gawk at all the action, head to **Ho'okipa Beach**. Nearby, **Mama's Fish House** (☏ 808-579-8488; www.mamasfishhouse.com; 799 Poho Pl; mains $35-50; ⊙ 11am-2:30pm & 4:15-9pm) is Maui's most celebrated seafood restaurant, pairing beachside romance with impeccably prepared fish (reservations essential).

Downtown has a burgeoning row of restaurants and boutique shops. **Pa'ia Fish Market** (☏ 808-579-8030; www.paiafishmarket.com; 110 Baldwin Ave; mains $9-19; ⊙ 11am-9:30pm) is the go-to place for fish-and-chips. **Flatbread Company** (☏ 808-579-8989; www.flatbreadcompany.com; 89 Hana Hwy; pizzas $12-22; ⊙ 11am-10pm) 🌱 crafts wood oven-fired pizzas topped with local, often organic ingredients.

Hana

Mainland influences evident everywhere else on Maui are missing in Hana, where many residents are Native Hawaiian, and they treasure the town's sleepy pace and rural isolation. Families splash and swim at **Hana Bay Beach Park**, which has a snack bar, and at gorgeous gray-sand **Hamoa Beach** (Haneo'o Rd), south of town.

The road south from Hana is incredibly beautiful, passing organic farms and fruit stands. **'Ohe'o Gulch** is a breath-taking series of wide pools and waterfalls, each tumbling downstream into the one below. It's inside the coastal section of Haleakalā National Park (p1118), where hiking trails lead through bamboo groves and there's free primitive **camping** (no reservations) – bring water and insect repellent!

Can't pull yourself away? At Hana's boutique luxury hotel, **Travaasa Hana** (☏ 855-868-7282, 808-359-2401; www.travaasa.com; 5031

DON'T MISS

SCENIC DRIVE: ROAD TO HANA

One of Hawaii's most spectacular scenic drives, the **Hana Highway** (Hwy 360) winds its way past jungle valleys and back out above a rugged coastline. The road is a real cliff-hugger with 54 one-lane bridges and head-spinning views. Gas up and buy snacks and drinks in Pa'ia before starting out.

Waterfall swimming holes, heart-stopping vistas and incredible hikes call out almost nonstop along the way. Detour to explore coastal trails and the black-sand beach at **Wai'anapanapa State Park** (www.hawaiistateparks.org; off Hwy 360). For basic tent camping (sites $18) and rustic housekeeping cabins ($90), advance reservations are required. Book online with Hawaii's **Division of State Parks** (www.hawaii-stateparks.org).

Hana Hwy; d from $400; ✉), airy rooms and cottages breathe tranquility. Unwind with a traditional Hawaiian *lomilomi* massage at the hotel's spa.

Haleakalā National Park

No trip to Maui is complete without visiting this sublime **park** (✆ 808-572-4400; www.nps.gov/hale; 3-day entry per car $10). From the towering volcano's rim near the summit, there are dramatic views of a lunarlike surface and multicolored cinder cones. For an unforgettable (and chilly) experience, arrive in time for sunrise – an event Mark Twain called the 'sublimest spectacle' he'd ever seen. Check weather conditions and sunrise times before driving up.

The adventure needn't stop at roadside viewpoints. With hiking boots and warm, waterproof clothing layers, you can walk down into the volcano on the Halemau'u or Sliding Sands Trails. Find free drive-up tent camping (no reservations) at Hosmer Grove, near the main park entrance. For an unforgettable overnight, rent a **wilderness cabin** (✆ 808-572-4400; https://fhnp.org/wcr; per cabin with 1-12 people $75) deep inside the volcano's belly; demand is sky-high, so book online up to 90 days in advance.

KAUA'I

On Hawaii's oldest main island, nature's fingers have had time to dig deep – carving the Na Pali Coast's fluted cliffs and the tremendous depths of Waimea Canyon. Lush Kaua'i is beloved by outdoorsy types, especially hikers and kayakers. It has also been the darling of honeymooners ever since Elvis tied the knot here in *Blue Hawaii*. Everyone comes to the 'Garden Isle' for its heavenly temple – the one you'll find outside, that is. And the price of salvation? Just a pair of boots or a paddle and a little sweat.

❶ Getting There & Around

Limited US mainland and frequent inter-island flights land at **Lihu'e** (LIH; ✆ 808-274-3800; http://hawaii.gov/lih; 3901 Mokulele Loop, Lihu'e), with taxis and major car-rental companies wait. With reduced weekend services, public **Kaua'i Bus** (✆ 808-246-8110; www.kauai.gov; fare $2) reaches many towns, but not all tourist destinations.

Lihu'e

This ex-plantation town is Kaua'i's capital and commercial center. Pick up information at **Kaua'i Visitors Bureau** (✆ 800-262-1400, 808-245-3971; www.kauaidiscovery.com; 4334 Rice St). The insightful **Kaua'i Museum** (✆ 808-245-6931; www.kauaimuseum.org; 4428 Rice St; adult/child $10/2; ◷ 10am-5pm Mon-Sat) traces the island's independent history.

Just minutes from Kalapaki Beach, the **Garden Island Inn** (✆ 800-648-0154, 808-245-7227; www.gardenislandinn.com; 3445 Wilcox Rd; d $100-150; ❋ ☎ ✉) offers modest, cheerful rooms. Seafood and *poke* lovers may find themselves grabbing island-style takeout plates at **Fish Express** (✆ 808-245-9918; 3343 Kuhio Hwy; mains $7-12; ◷ 10am-6pm Mon-Sat, to 5pm Sun, lunch-2pm daily) every day. Hole-in-the-wall **Hamura Saimin** (✆ 808-245-3271; 2956 Kress St; dishes $3-8; ◷ 10am-10:30pm Mon-Thu, to midnight Fri & Sat, to 9:30pm Sun) specializes in homemade *saimin* (noodle soup) and *liliko'i* chiffon pie.

Wailua & Eastside

You wouldn't know it from the strip-mall-lined Kuhio Hwy, but the Wailua area offers great outdoor opportunities. Families head to **Lydgate Beach Park** (www.kamalani.org; 🚶), which has the best kids' playground in Hawaii and safe, protected swimming. The mountains above Wailua are laced with scenic hiking routes, including the **Kuilau Ridge & Moalepe Trails** and **Nounou Mountain Trails**.

However, most people come to kayak the **Wailua River**. To ancient Hawaiians, the Wailua River was among the most sacred places in the archipelago. The river basin, near its mouth, was one of the island's two royal centers and home to high chiefs. The river's easy, bucolic 5-mile paddle – with stops for swimming holes and waterfall hikes – is so popular that it's restricted mostly to guided tours (daily except Sunday). Book ahead with **Wailua Kayak Adventures** (✆ 808-639-6332, 808-822-5795; www.kauaiwailuakayak.com; 4-1596 Kuhio Hwy, Kapa'a; kayak rental/tour from $25/50) or smaller, family-owned **Kayak Wailua** (✆ 808-822-3388; www.kayakwailua.com; 4565 Haleilio Rd, Wailua; tour $50).

Budgeteers will be forever spoiled by **Rosewood Kaua'i** (✆ 808-822-5216; www.rosewoodkauai.com; 872 Kamalu Rd; r without bathroom $65-75; ☎), where tidy private bunkrooms have kitchenettes. The owner rents beach homes, cottages and condos nearby. With a surf-casual deli counter, **Pono Market** (☑ 808-822-4581; 4-1300 Kuhio Hwy, Kapa'a; meals $6-8; ☺ 6am-6pm Mon-Fri, to 4pm Sat) is all local grinds, all the time – savor *laulau* plate lunches, sushi rolls and smoked marlin.

Hanalei & North Shore

Unspoiled and unhurried, Kaua'i's North Shore features otherworldly scenery and outdoor adventures enough for a lifetime.

Stop at **Kilauea Point National Wildlife Refuge** (☑ 808-828-1413; www.fws.gov/kilaueapoint; Lighthouse Rd; adult/child $5/free; ☺ 10am-4pm), a thriving seabird sanctuary with a century-old lighthouse. Gentle **'Anini Beach Park** (⛺) has calm, reef-protected waters, easy snorkeling and Kaua'i's best beginner windsurfing. Camping is allowed nightly (except Tuesday); get advance permits from Kaua'i's **Department of Parks & Recreation** (☑ 808-241-4463; www.kauai.gov; 4444 Rice St, Lihu'e; campsites from $25; ☺ 8:15am-4pm Mon-Fri).

Known for glamorous resort living (golf, tennis, horse riding, spas etc), Princeville provides glorious sunset perches, like at tiny **Pali Ke Kua (Hideaways) Beach** (⛺), accessible through the St Regis resort. Condolike 'ocean villas' at the **Westin Princeville Ocean Resort** (☑ 866-716-8112, 808-827-8700; www.westinprinceville.com; 3838 Wyllie Rd; apt from $275; ✳ @ 🖥 🏊) are equipped with kitchens and whirlpool tubs.

In **Hanalei**, the hippie-surfer vibe is palpable. At magnificent **Hanalei Bay** the surfing is spectacular – it really swells in winter. Take a meditative trip upriver with **Kayak Kaua'i** (☑ 800-437-3507; www.kayakkauai.com; 5-5070 Kuhio Hwy; kayak/SUP set rental from $30/45, tours from $60; ☺ 7am-8pm), which also rents bicycles and camping, snorkeling and surfing gear. Hanalei also makes a good meal stop.

Doubters become converts at **Hanalei Taro & Juice Co** (☑ 808-826-1059; Kuhio Hwy; snacks from $3, meals $8-10; ☺ 11am-3pm Mon-Sat; 🅿 🖉 ⛺), where the taro-based smoothies and Hawaiian plate lunches are yum-yum. Trendy **Bar Acuda Tapas & Wine** (☑ 808-826-7081; www.restaurantbaracuda.com; Hanalei Center, 5-5161 Kuhio Hwy; shared plates $7-16; ☺ 5:30-9pm) 🖉 features local produce like North Shore honeycomb and Kailani Farms greens. After sunset, sport your best vintage aloha shirt at **Tahiti Nui** (☑ 808-826-6277; www.thenui.com;

WORTH A TRIP

NA PALI COAST

Hikers on Kaua'i shouldn't miss the challenging but oh-so-rewarding 11-mile **Kalalau Trail**, which runs along the dizzying Na Pali cliffs and slides through lush valleys inside **Na Pali Coast State Wilderness Park** (www.hawaiistateparks.org; end of Hwy 560) **FREE**. To hike beyond Hanakoa Valley and for backcountry camping, reserve permits ($20 per person, per night) online up to a year in advance with Hawaii's Division of State Parks (p1117).

Hard-core paddlers can admire the same scenery from the sea during a strenuous 17-mile Na Pali Coast kayak. Taking all day (but feeling so much longer), it's only possible between May and September. **Na Pali Kayak** (☑ 808-826-6900; www.napalikayak.com; 5 5075 Kuhio Hwy, Hanalei; tours from $200) is an experienced local outfitter.

5-5134 Kuhio Hwy; ☺ noon-10pm Sun-Thu, to 11pm Fri & Sat), a tiki dive bar with live music and a weekly luau night (make reservations).

Marking the western end of Hwy 560 are **Makua (Tunnels) Beach** and **Ke'e Beach**, where snorkelers swim in summer. Nearby, **Limahuli Garden** (☑ 808-826-1053; www.ntbg.org; 5-8291 Kuhio Hwy; self-guided/guided tour $15/30; ☺ 9:30am-4pm Tue-Sat, guided tour 10am Tue-Fri) conserves Hawaii's native botanical wealth. Back at **Ha'ena Beach Park**, camping is allowed nightly (except Monday); get advance permits from Kaua'i's Department of Parks & Recreation. The **Hanalei Colony Resort** (☑ 800-628-3004, 808-826-6235; www.hcr.com; 5-7130 Kuhio Hwy; apt from $275; ✳ @ 🖥 🏊) may have dated decor, but peaceful condos (no TVs or phones) are in an idyllic waterfront location.

Po'ipu & South Shore

Sunny, family-friendly **Po'ipu** fronts a fabulous run of sandy beaches. It's good for swimming and snorkeling year-round and summer surfing. Tour the stunning **National Tropical Botanical Garden** (☑ 808-742-2623; www.ntbg.org; 4425 Lawa'i Rd; self-guided tour adult/child $15/7.50, guided tour $45/20; ☺ daily, hours vary) or admire windswept cliffs, tide pools and pristine beaches while hiking the 4-mile **Maha'ulepu Heritage Trail** (www.hikemahaulepu.org).

Po'ipu is awash with resorts, condos and vacation rentals for all budgets; browse listings with **Parrish Collection Kaua'i** (☑ 800-325-5701, 808-742-1412; www.parrishkauai.com) and **Po'ipu Connection Realty** (☑ 800-742-2260; www.poipuconnection.com). Get magnificent valley views from **Marjorie's Kaua'i Inn** (☑ 800-717-8838, 808-332-8838; www.marjorieskauaiinn.com; Hailima St, Lawa'i; r incl breakfast $140-195; ☜ ☒), where tropical rooms have kitchenettes.

At dinnertime, head to chef-owned **Josselin's Tapas Bar & Grill** (☑ 808-742-7117; www.josselins.com; Shops at Kukui'ula, 2829 Ala Kalanikaumaka St; shared plates $8-36; ☺ 5-10pm) for Asian fusion cuisine and thirst-slaking *liliko'i* or lychee sangria. Locals line up at **Koloa Fish Market** (☑ 808-742-6199; 5482 Koloa Rd; mains $4-8; ☺ 10am-6pm Mon-Fri, to 5pm Sat) for outstanding *poke*, Japanese-inspired bento boxes and island-style plate lunches to go.

Waimea & Westside

The top destinations here are **Waimea Canyon** – the 'Grand Canyon of the Pacific' with cascading waterfalls – and adjacent **Koke'e State Park** (www.hawaiistateparks.org) `FREE`.

Both feature breathtaking views and a vast network of hiking trails; some, like Koke'e's **Awa'awapuhi & Nu'alolo Trails**, stroll along the knife-edge of precipitously eroded cliffs. Waimea Canyon Dr (Hwy 550) is peppered with scenic lookouts. Pick up trail information at the pint-sized **Koke'e Museum** (☑ 808-335-9975; www.kokee.org; donation $1; ☺ 9am-4:30pm).

Pitch your rainproof tent at the park's campground (campsites $18); for advance permits (required), contact Hawaii's Division of State Parks (p1117). Back downhill by the coast, **Waimea** town makes a civilized base for Westside explorations. Sleep beside rustling palm trees in vintage 1930s and '40s **Waimea Plantation Cottages** (☑ 866-774-2924, 808-338-1625; www.waimea-plantation.com; 9400 Kaumuali'i Hwy; d from $199; ☜ ☒).

Also worth exploring is **Hanapepe**, a quaint town where false-fronted historical buildings hide art galleries, boutique shops and cafes. Outside town, **Salt Pond Beach Park** is perfect for swimming with kids; for camping nightly (except Tuesday), get an advance permit from Kaua'i's Department of Parks & Recreation (p1119). Nearby **Port Allen** offers snorkeling and whale-watching cruises and Zodiac tours of the Na Pali Coast.

Understand
USA

USA Today

Big changes are unfolding across the American landscape when it comes to politics, cultural diversity and civil rights. A second term for Barack Obama has brought moments of self-reflection to both the Democrats, who achieved mixed results during the president's first term, and defeated Republicans, who must evolve or face certain defeat in future elections. Meanwhile same-sex marriage, legalized marijuana, government spying and changing eating habits remain the hot topics of the moment.

Best in Print

On the Road (1957) Jack Kerouac on post-WWII America.
The Great Gatsby (1925) F Scott Fitzgerald's powerful Jazz Age novel.
Beloved (1987) Toni Morrison's searing Pulitzer Prize–winning novel set during the post–Civil War years.
Huckleberry Finn (1884) Mark Twain's moving tale of journey and self-discovery.

Best on Film

Singin' in the Rain (1952) Among the best in the era of musicals, with an exuberant Gene Kelly and a timeless score.
Annie Hall (1977) Woody Allen's brilliant romantic comedy, with New York City playing a starring role.
North by Northwest (1959) Alfred Hitchcock thriller with Cary Grant on the run across America.
Godfather (1972–90) Famed trilogy that looks at American society through immigrants and organized crime.

New Forces in Politics

President Obama won reelection in 2012, aided in large part by assembling the most ethnically and racially diverse coalition in American history. More than 90% of African Americans and nearly 70% of Latinos voted for the man who described himself as a 'mutt.'

The failure of Republicans to attract voters from different ethnic backgrounds has caused some soul searching in the party. Following the 2012 election, Louisiana Governor Bobby Jindal directed harsh criticism toward his own party, saying it should stop being 'the stupid party.' This was likely in reference to bizarre comments among his constituents, such as presidential candidate Mitt Romney, who wanted to encourage illegal immigrants to opt for self-deportation, and Indiana senatorial candidate Richard Mourdock, who said that 'even when life begins in that horrible situation of rape that it is something that God intended to happen.'

Perhaps in answer to this search for a new identity, Republicans have seen the rise of new faces from vastly different backgrounds. The young Florida Senator and Cuban-American Marco Rubio is seen as one of the party's rising stars (not so subtly hailed by *Time* magazine as 'The Republican Savior'). He's become a reasoned voice in the heated discussions over immigration reform, and is as comfortable talking about hip-hop as he is health-care. He's one to watch in the 2016 presidential elections.

Obama 2.0

Although Democrats cheered his victory, Obama returned to office without the same hope and optimism that surrounded him the first time. Times had changed, and America, like much of the world, had struggled through tough years since the global economic crisis erupted in 2007. When Obama took the oath of office in 2013, the unemployment rate, hovering around 8%, was about what it had been during his first inauguration, in 2009, though economic growth seems at last to be on a solid foundation.

On other fronts, Obama has had mixed success. He ended the US involvement in Iraq, but 63,000 troops still remained in Afghanistan, and the US mission there seems increasingly obscure, particularly after the successful operation that finally brought down Osama bin Laden.

His ambitious plan to bring healthcare reform has passed through Congress, becoming the most significant new healthcare expansion since the passage of Medicare and Medicaid in 1965. Despite challenges by Republicans who threatened to repeal it, and a close call by the Supreme Court (which narrowly ruled the new healthcare act constitutional by a vote of 5 to 4), the law was slated to go into effect in 2014. Whether it will be a success or failure is still hotly debated by Democrats and Republicans, though the outcome probably won't be clear for some years.

War Inside America

There have been more than 67 mass shootings in the past 30 years. Devastating incidents include the 2012 Newtown, CT, massacre, where a heavily armed 20-year-old man slaughtered 20 young children and six adults. The following year, a gunman killed 12 and wounded four in a rampage at the Navy Yard in Washington, DC. On average, 32 Americans are murdered by guns every day and another 140 wounded. Add to this accidental shootings and suicides and some 32,000 Americans are killed each year by guns.

Despite evidence (including a 2013 study published in the *American Journal of Medicine*) that more guns equals more murders, and the comparatively low rates of death by firearms in countries with strict gun laws, American legislators have been reluctant to enact even modest gun control laws – in 2013 a ban on assault weapons and Obama's proposals to introduce stricter background checks on gun owners were rejected by Congress. The reason: gun lobbies such as the National Rifle Association (NRA) wield incredible power, contributing over $16 million annually to state and national political campaigns.

Spies Like Us

Another promise of Obama's was to have a more open and transparent government. Transparent indeed it became after the blow-up of the Snowden affair in 2013. Edward Snowden was a former contractor for the National Security Agency (NSA) who leaked classified information about a mass surveillance program conducted by US intelligence.

The revelations were astonishing: the US and UK intelligence communities had been spying not only on foreign nations but on allies as well as American citizens. In a top-secret program called Prism, the NSA had direct access to citizen's emails, file transfers and live chats using Google, Facebook, Apple and other US internet giants. A media storm ensued, costing Obama no small degree of credibility – and an immediate drop of nearly 10% in his approval ratings.

POPULATION: **317 MILLION**

GROSS DOMESTIC PRODUCT: **$15.94 TRILLION**

GROSS DOMESTIC PRODUCT PER CAPITA: **$50,700**

UNEMPLOYMENT: **7.6%**

ANNUAL INFLATION: **2.1%**

if USA were 100 people

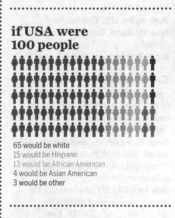

65 would be white
15 would be Hispanic
13 would be African American
4 would be Asian American
3 would be other

belief systems
(% of population)

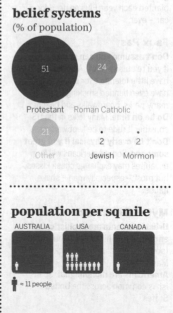

51 — Protestant
24 — Roman Catholic
21 — Other
2 — Jewish
2 — Mormon

population per sq mile

AUSTRALIA   USA   CANADA

= 11 people

Best Road Songs

America Simon & Garfunkel
On the Road Again Willie Nelson
Take It Easy The Eagles
Summer of '69 Bryan Adams
American Pie Don McLean
(Get Your Kicks on) Route 66 Nat King Cole
Me & Bobby McGee Janis Joplin
Goin' Down the Road Feeling Bad Grateful Dead
Midnight Train to Georgia Gladys Knight & the Pips
Walk on the Wild Side Lou Reed
Take Me Home, Country Roads John Denver
Big Yellow Taxi Joni Mitchell

Greenest Cities

Portland, OR Huge parks, 200 miles of bike lanes, a walkable city center and an eco-mad populace.
San Francisco, CA Abundant green markets, organic restaurants and eco-friendly buildings (even the ballpark is solar-powered). Biking, walking and public transit rules.
New York City, NY New bike-sharing programs, waterfront parks and green spaces, with 100,000 trees planted each year. Plus no need for a car – ever.

Faux Pas

Don't assume you can smoke – even if you're outside. Most Americans have little tolerance for smokers and have even banned smoking from many parks, boardwalks and beaches.
Do be on time. Many folks in the US consider it rude to be kept waiting.
Don't be overly physical if you greet someone. Some Americans will hug, urbanites may exchange cheek kisses, but most – especially men – shake hands.

Myths Debunked

Urban residents are sophisticated and rural folk hillbillies... You'll find foodies in Appalachia and hicks in Manhattan.
Americans are monolingual. Spanish is common across the United States.

Going to Pot

In 2012 voters in Colorado and Washington state approved ballot measures to legalize marijuana. This has created tension between these two states and the federal government, which still treats marijuana as an illegal substance. The Obama administration hasn't announced a clear policy on the new laws, stating only that the federal law remains in effect, but that 'it doesn't make sense' for the government to target marijuana users in states that have legalized its use.

Meanwhile, the prevailing attitude across the US is one of relaxing restrictions on cannabis. Some 18 states have supported the legalization of marijuana for medicinal use. A handful have also decriminalized marijuana, making possession of small amounts of the substance a misdemeanor rather than a felony. How Colorado and Washington will handle the taxing and selling of marijuana come 2014 (when the law goes into effect) is the big unknown.

Marriage for All

Another hot topic that some states and the federal government have often failed to see eye-to-eye on is gay marriage. Although Obama declared his public support for same-sex marriage in 2012, the federal government remained tacitly opposed to it. National polls continued to show a majority of Americans supported legalized marriage for all. Meanwhile, some states had set their own rulings about gay marriage, sometimes leaving it up to the voters to decide. By 2013, some 13 states had legalized same-sex marriage.

A breakthrough occurred in June 2013, when the Supreme Court ruled that the discriminatory *Defense of Marriage Act* – the law barring the federal government from recognizing same-sex marriages legalized by the states – was unconstitutional. The ruling, which came just days before scheduled Gay Pride parades nationwide, added to particularly exuberant and well-attended celebrations.

Unhealthy Appetites

In terms of diet, Americans have been doing some soul searching. No one could deny that Americans were obese – shows like *The Biggest Loser* and Eric Schlosser's book and film *Fast Food Nation* shine a spotlight on the nation's deadly eating habits. Fast food, soft drinks and too much television have all been vilified in recent years.

Changes big and small are happening in communities across the country. New York City has helped lead the way, banning the use of trans fats and requiring fast-food restaurants to post the calorie content of all menu items (however, an attempt to ban the sale of sugary beverages over 20oz failed).

Michelle Obama has been one of the nation's most vocal advocates of healthy eating, targeting childhood obesity (an alarming one in three American children is obese) and encouraging parents to make more informed decisions about eating. Apps such as the government's MyPlate – a food diary and calorie counter that's popular on social media sites such as Pinterest – are among an increasing number of tools helping diners make better choices.

History

From its early days as an English colony to its rise to number one on the world stage in the 20th century, the history of America has been anything but dull. War against the British, westward expansion, slavery and its abolishment, Civil War and Reconstruction, the Great Depression, the post-war boom and more recent conflicts in the 21st century – they've all played a part in shaping the nation's complicated identity.

Turtle Island

According to oral traditions and sacred myths, indigenous peoples have always lived on the North American continent, which some called Turtle Island. When Europeans arrived, approximately two to 18 million Native American people occupied the turtle's back north of present-day Mexico and spoke more than 300 languages.

Among North America's most significant prehistoric cultures were the Mound Builders, who inhabited the Ohio and Mississippi River valleys from around 3000 BC to AD 1300. In Illinois, Cahokia was once a metropolis of 20,000 people, the largest in pre-Columbian North America.

In the Southwest, Ancestral Puebloans occupied the Colorado Plateau from around AD 100 to AD 1300, until warfare, drought and scarcity of resources likely drove them out. You can still see their cliff dwellings at Colorado's Mesa Verde National Park and desert adobe pueblos at New Mexico's Chaco Culture National Historic Park.

It was the Great Plains cultures that came to epitomize 'Indians' in the popular American imagination, in part because these tribal peoples put up the longest fight against the USA's westward expansion. Oklahoma is rich in sites that interpret Native American life before Europeans arrived, including at Anadarko and along the Trail of Tears.

In 1502, Italian explorer Amerigo Vespucci used the term Mundus Novus (New World) to describe his discoveries. His reward? In 1507, new maps labeled the western hemisphere 'America.'

Enter the Europeans

In 1492, Italian explorer Christopher Columbus, backed by Spain, voyaged west – looking for the East Indies. He found the Bahamas. With visions of gold, Spanish explorers quickly followed: Cortés conquered much of today's Mexico; Pizarro conquered Peru; Ponce de León wandered through

TIMELINE	20,000–40,000 BC	8000 BC	7000 BC–AD 100
	The first people to reach the Americas arrive from Central Asia by migrating over a wide land bridge between Siberia and Alaska (when sea levels were lower than today).	Widespread extinction of ice-age mammals including the woolly mammoth, due to cooperative hunting by humans and a warming climate. Indigenous peoples begin hunting smaller game and gathering native plants.	'Archaic period' marked by nomadic hunter-gatherer lifestyle. By the end of this period, corn, beans and squash (the agricultural 'three sisters') and permanent settlements are well established.

Florida looking for the fountain of youth. Not to be left out, the French explored Canada and the Midwest, while the Dutch and English cruised North America's eastern seaboard.

European explorers left in their wake diseases to which indigenous peoples had no immunity. More than any other factor – war, slavery or famine – disease epidemics devastated Native populations, reducing numbers by 50% to 90%. By the 17th century, indigenous North Americans numbered only about a million, and many of the continent's once-thriving societies were in turmoil and transition.

In 1607, English noblemen established North America's first permanent European settlement in Jamestown. Earlier settlements had ended badly, and Jamestown almost did too: the English chose a swamp, planted their crops late and many died from disease and starvation. Some despairing colonists ran off to live with the local tribes, who provided the settlement with enough aid to survive.

For Jamestown and America, 1619 proved a pivotal year: the colony established the House of Burgesses, a representative assembly of citizens to decide local laws, and it received its first boatload of 20 African slaves.

The next year was equally momentous, as a group of radically religious Puritans pulled ashore at what would become Plymouth, Massachusetts. The Pilgrims were escaping religious persecution under the 'corrupt' Church of England, and in the New World they saw a divine opportunity to create a new society that would be a religious and moral beacon. The Pilgrims signed a 'Mayflower Compact,' one of the seminal texts of American democracy, to govern themselves by consensus.

Capitalism & Colonialism

For the next two centuries, European powers competed for position and territory in the New World, extending European politics into the Americas. As Britain's Royal Navy came to rule Atlantic seas, England increasingly profited from its colonies and eagerly consumed the fruits of their labors – sweet tobacco from Virginia, sugar and coffee from the Caribbean.

Over the 17th and 18th centuries, slavery in America was slowly legalized into a formal institution to support this plantation economy. By 1800, one out of every five people was a slave.

Meanwhile, Britain mostly left the American colonists to govern themselves. Town meetings and representative assemblies, in which local citizens (that is, white men with property) debated community problems and voted on laws and taxes, became common.

However, by the end of the Seven Years' War in 1763, Britain was feeling the strains of running an empire: it had been fighting France for a

The New World (2005), directed by Terrence Malick, is a brutal but passionate film that retells the tragic story of the Jamestown colony and the pivotal peace-making role of Pocahontas, a Powhatan chief's daughter.

Colonial Sights

Williamsburg, Virginia

Jamestown, Virginia

Plymouth, Massachusetts

North End, Boston

Philadelphia, Pennsylvania

Annapolis, Maryland

Charleston, South Carolina

1492	1607	1620
Italian explorer Christopher Columbus 'discovers' America, making three voyages throughout the Caribbean. He names the indigenous people 'Indians,' mistakenly thinking he has reached the Indies.	The English found the first English colony, the Jamestown settlement on marshland in present-day Virginia. The first few years are hard, with many dying from sickness and starvation.	The *Mayflower* lands at Plymouth with 102 English Pilgrims, who have come to the New World to escape religious persecution. The Wampanoag tribe saves them from starvation.

➡ Memorial, Jamestown

DENNIS JOHNSON / GETTY IMAGES ©

century and had colonies scattered all over the world. It was time to clean up bureaucracies and share financial burdens.

The colonies, however, resented English taxes and policies. Public outrage soon culminated in the 1776 Declaration of Independence. With this document, the American colonists took many of the Enlightenment ideas then circulating worldwide – of individualism, equality and freedom; of John Locke's 'natural rights' of life, liberty and property – and fashioned a new type of government to put them into practice.

Frustrations came to a head with the Boston Tea Party in 1773, after which Britain clamped down hard, shutting Boston's harbor and increasing its military presence. In 1774 representatives from 12 colonies convened the First Continental Congress in Philadelphia's Independence Hall to air complaints and prepare for the inevitable war ahead.

Revolution & the Republic

In April 1775, British troops skirmished with armed colonists in Massachusetts, and the Revolutionary War began. George Washington, a wealthy Virginia farmer, was chosen to lead the American army. Trouble was, Washington lacked gunpowder and money (the colonists resisted taxes even for their own military), and his troops were a motley collection of poorly armed farmers, hunters and merchants, who regularly quit and returned to their farms due to lack of pay. On the other side, the British 'Redcoats' represented the world's most powerful military. The inexperienced General Washington had to improvise constantly, sometimes wisely retreating, sometimes engaging in 'ungentlemanly' sneak attacks. During the winter of 1777–78, the American army nearly starved at Valley Forge.

Meanwhile, the Second Continental Congress tried to articulate what exactly they were fighting for. In January 1776, Thomas Paine published the wildly popular *Common Sense,* which passionately argued for independence from England. Soon, independence seemed not just logical, but noble and necessary, and on July 4, 1776, the Declaration of Independence was finalized and signed. Largely written by Thomas Jefferson, it elevated the 13 colonies' particular gripes against the monarchy into a universal declaration of individual rights and republican government.

However, to succeed on the battlefield, General Washington needed help, not just patriotic sentiment. In 1778, Benjamin Franklin persuaded France (always eager to trouble England) to ally with the revolutionaries, and they provided the troops, material and sea power that helped win the war. The British surrendered at Yorktown, VA, in 1781, and two years later the Treaty of Paris formally recognized the 'United States of America.'

Great Presidential Reads

Washington, Ron Chernow

Thomas Jefferson, RB Bernstein

Lincoln, David Herbert Donald

Mornings on Horseback, David McCullough

The Bridge, David Remnick

1675	1756–63	1773	1775
For decades, the Pilgrims and local tribes live fairly cooperatively, but deadly conflict erupts in 1675. King Philip's War lasts 14 months and kills over 5000 people (mostly Native Americans).	In the Seven Years' War (or the 'French and Indian War'), France loses to England and withdraws from Canada. Britain now controls most territory east of the Mississippi River.	To protest a British tax on tea, Bostonians dress as Mohawks, board East India Company ships and toss their tea overboard during what would be named the Boston Tea Party.	Paul Revere rides from Boston to warn colonial 'Minutemen' that the British are coming. The next day, 'the shot heard round the world' is fired at Lexington, starting the Revolutionary War.

TECUMSEH'S CURSE

According to legend, a curse spanning more than 100 years hung over every president elected in a year ending in zero (every 20 years). It all began with future president William Henry Harrison, who in 1811 led a battle against the Shawnee, which devastated the hopes of Tecumseh (Native American chief of the Shawnee) for a pan-Indian alliance. After the bitter defeat, Tecumseh placed a curse, uttering something along the lines of 'Harrison will die, and after him every great chief chosen 20 years thereafter will also die. And when each dies, let everyone remember the death of my people.'

1840 William Henry Harrison elected president. He died of pneumonia just 32 days in office – the shortest term in presidential history.

1860 Abraham Lincoln elected, then reelected in 1864. He was assassinated after just five days after the end of the Civil War.

1880 James Garfield was shot; he died months later from infection.

1900 William McKinley elected to his second term in office. A year later he was shot and killed by an anarchist.

1920 Warren G Harding elected. He died from a stroke in 1923 while visiting San Francisco.

1940 Franklin Roosevelt, elected to his third term. He died in 1945 from a stroke, just a month before Nazi Germany surrendered.

1960 John F Kennedy elected. He was violently gunned down in 1963.

1980 Reagan elected. He narrowly avoided dying in office following the 1981 assassination attempt by John Hinckley (whose bullet lodged an inch from Reagan's heart). The curse was broken.

According to legend, George Washington was so honest that, after chopping down his father's cherry tree when he was just a child, he admitted, 'I cannot tell a lie. I did it with my little hatchet.'

At first, the nation's loose confederation of fractious, squabbling states was hardly 'united.' So the founders gathered again in Philadelphia, and in 1787 drafted a new-and-improved Constitution: the US government was given a stronger federal center, with checks and balances between its three major branches; and to guard against the abuse of centralized power, a citizen's Bill of Rights was approved in 1791.

With the Constitution, the scope of the American Revolution solidified to a radical change in government, and the preservation of the economic and social status quos. Rich landholders kept their property, which included their slaves; Native Americans were excluded from the nation; and women were excluded from politics. These blatant discrepancies and injustices, which were widely noted, were the results of both pragmatic compromise (eg to get slave-dependent Southern states to agree) and also widespread belief in the essential rightness of things as they were.

1776	1787	1791	1803
On July 4, the colonies sign the Declaration of Independence. Famous figures who helped create this document include John Hancock, Samuel Adams, John Adams, Benjamin Franklin and Thomas Jefferson.	The Constitutional Convention in Philadelphia draws up the US Constitution. Power is balanced between the presidency, Congress and judiciary.	Bill of Rights adopted as constitutional amendments outlining citizens' rights, including free speech, assembly, religion and the press; the right to bear arms; and prohibition of 'cruel and unusual punishments.'	France's Napoleon sells the Louisiana Territory to the US for just $15 million, thereby extending the boundaries of the new nation from the Mississippi River to the Rocky Mountains.

Westward, Ho!

As the 19th century dawned on the young nation, optimism was the mood of the day. With the invention of the cotton gin in 1793 – followed by threshers, reapers, mowers and later combines – agriculture was industrialized, and US commerce surged. The 1803 Louisiana Purchase doubled US territory, and expansion west of the Appalachian Mountains began in earnest.

Relations between the US and Britain – despite lively trade – remained tense and, in 1812, the US declared war on England again. The two-year conflict ended without much gain by either side, although the British abandoned its forts, and the US vowed to avoid Europe's 'entangling alliances.'

In the 1830s and 1840s, with growing nationalist fervor and dreams of continental expansion, many Americans came to believe it was 'Manifest Destiny' that all the land should be theirs. The 1830 Indian Removal Act aimed to clear one obstacle, while the building of the railroads cleared another hurdle, linking Midwestern farmers with East Coast markets.

In 1836 a group of Texans fomented a revolution against Mexico. (Remember the Alamo?) Ten years later, the US annexed the Texas Republic and, when Mexico resisted, the US waged war for it – and while they were at it, took California too. In 1848, Mexico was soundly defeated and ceded this territory to the US. This completed the USA's continental expansion.

By a remarkable coincidence, only days after the 1848 treaty with Mexico was signed, gold was discovered in California. By 1849, surging rivers of wagon trains were creaking west filled with miners, pioneers, entrepreneurs, immigrants, outlaws and prostitutes, all seeking their fortunes. This made for exciting, legendary times, but throughout loomed a troubling question: as new states joined the USA, would they be slave states or free states? The nation's future depended on the answer.

> You can follow the Lewis and Clark expedition on its extraordinary journey west to the Pacific and back again online at www.pbs.org/lewisandclark, which features historical maps, photo albums and journal excerpts.

The Civil War

The US Constitution hadn't ended slavery, but it had given Congress the power to approve (or not) slavery in new states. Public debates raged constantly over the expansion of slavery, particularly since this shaped the balance of power between the industrial North and the agrarian South.

Since the founding, Southern politicians had dominated government and defended slavery as 'natural and normal,' which an 1856 *New York Times* editorial called 'insanity.' The Southern proslavery lobby enraged Northern abolitionists. But even many Northern politicians feared that ending slavery would be ruinous. Limit slavery, they reasoned, and in the

> James McPherson is a pre-eminent Civil War historian, and his Pulitzer Prize–winning *Battle Cry of Freedom* (1988) somehow gets the whole heartbreaking saga between two covers.

1803–06	1812	1823	1849
President Thomas Jefferson sends Meriwether Lewis and William Clark west. Guided by the Shoshone tribeswoman Sacagawea, they trailblaze from St Louis, MO, to the Pacific Ocean and back.	The War of 1812 begins with battles against the British and Native Americans in the Great Lakes region. Even after the 1815 Treaty of Ghent, fighting continues along the Gulf Coast.	President Monroe articulates the Monroe Doctrine, seeking to end European military interventions in America. Roosevelt later extends it to justify US interventions in Latin America.	After the 1848 discovery of gold near Sacramento, an epic cross-country gold rush sees 60,000 'forty-niners' flock to California's Mother Lode. San Francisco's population explodes from 850 to 25,000.

competition with industry and free labor, slavery would wither without inciting a violent slave revolt – a constantly feared possibility. Indeed, in 1859, radical abolitionist John Brown tried unsuccessfully to spark just that at Harpers Ferry.

The economics of slavery were undeniable. In 1860, there were more than four million slaves in the US, most held by Southern planters – who grew 75% of the world's cotton, accounting for more than half of US exports. Thus, the Southern economy supported the nation's economy, and it required slaves. The 1860 presidential election became a referendum on this issue, and the election was won by a young politician who favored limiting slavery: Abraham Lincoln.

In the South, even the threat of federal limits was too onerous to abide, and as President Lincoln took office, 11 states eventually seceded from the union and formed the Confederate States of America. Lincoln faced the nation's greatest moment of crisis. He had a choice: let the Southern states secede and dissolve the union, or wage war to keep the union intact. He chose the latter, and war soon erupted.

It began in April 1861, when the Confederacy attacked Fort Sumter in Charleston, SC, and raged on for the next four years – in the most gruesome combat the world had ever known until that time. By the end, more than 600,000 soldiers, nearly an entire generation of young men, were dead; Southern plantations and cities (most notably Atlanta) lay sacked and burned. The North's industrial might provided an advantage, but its victory was not preordained; it unfolded battle by bloody battle.

As fighting progressed, Lincoln recognized that if the war didn't end slavery outright, victory would be pointless. In 1863 his Emancipation Proclamation expanded the war's aims and freed all slaves. In April 1865 Confederate General Robert E Lee surrendered to Union General Ulysses S Grant in Appomattox, VA. The Union had been preserved, but at a staggering cost.

Great Depression, the New Deal & World War II

In October 1929, investors, worried over a gloomy global economy, started selling stocks and, seeing the selling, everyone panicked until they'd sold everything. The stock market crashed and the US economy collapsed like a house of cards.

Thus began the Great Depression. Frightened banks called in their dodgy loans, people couldn't pay, and the banks folded. Millions lost their homes, farms, businesses and savings, and as much as 50% of the American workforce became unemployed.

This Republic of Suffering (2008), by historian Drew Gilpin Faust, is a poignant look at the Civil War through the eyes of loved ones left behind by fallen soldiers on both sides of the Mason-Dixon line.

Steven Spielberg's *Lincoln* (2012) does a masterful job in conjuring up the final months of America's greatest president (Daniel Day-Lewis won an Academy Award for his portrayal).

1861–65	1870	1880–1920	1882
American Civil War erupts between North and South (delineated by the Mason–Dixon line). The war's end on April 9, 1865, is marred by President Lincoln's assassination five days later.	Freed black men are given the vote, but the South's segregationist 'Jim Crow' laws (which remain until the 1960s) effectively disenfranchise blacks from every meaningful sphere of daily life.	Millions of immigrants flood in from Europe and Asia, fueling the age of cities. New York, Chicago and Philadelphia swell in size, becoming global centers of industry and commerce.	Racist sentiment, particularly in California (where over 50,000 Chinese immigrants have arrived since 1848) leads to the Chinese Exclusion Act, the only US immigration law to exclude a specific race.

In 1932 Democrat Franklin D Roosevelt was elected president on the promise of a 'New Deal' to rescue the US from its crisis, which he did with resounding success. When war once again broke out in Europe in 1939, the isolationist mood in America was as strong as ever. However, the extremely popular President Roosevelt, elected to an unprecedented third term in 1940, understood that the US couldn't sit by and allow victory for fascist, totalitarian regimes. Roosevelt sent aid to Britain and persuaded a skittish Congress to go along with it.

Then, on December 7, 1941, Japan launched a surprise attack on Hawaii's Pearl Harbor, killing more than 2000 Americans and sinking several battleships. As US isolationism transformed overnight into outrage, Roosevelt suddenly had the support he needed. Germany also declared war on the US, and America joined the Allied fight against Hitler and the Axis powers. From that moment, the US put almost its entire will and industrial prowess into the war effort.

Initially, neither the Pacific nor European theaters went well for the US. In the Pacific, fighting didn't turn around until the US unexpectedly routed the Japanese navy at Midway Island in June 1942. Afterward, the US drove Japan back with a series of brutal battles recapturing Pacific islands.

In Europe, the US dealt the fatal blow to Germany with its massive D-Day invasion of France on June 6, 1944: unable to sustain a two-front war (the Soviet Union was savagely fighting on the eastern front), Germany surrendered in May 1945.

Nevertheless, Japan continued fighting. Newly elected President Harry Truman – ostensibly worried that a US invasion of Japan would lead to unprecedented carnage – chose to drop experimental atomic bombs on Hiroshima and Nagasaki in August 1945. Created by the government's top-secret Manhattan Project, the bombs devastated both cities, killing over 200,000 people. Japan surrendered days later. The nuclear age was born.

NATIVE AMERICANS

Authoritative and sobering, *Bury My Heart at Wounded Knee* (1970), by Dee Brown, tells the story of the late-19th-century Indian Wars from the perspective of Native Americans.

The Red Scare, Civil Rights & the Wars in Asia

The US enjoyed unprecedented prosperity in the decades after WWII but little peace.

Formerly wartime allies, the communist Soviet Union and the capitalist USA soon engaged in a running competition to dominate the globe. The superpowers engaged in proxy wars – notably the Korean War (1950–53) and Vietnam War (1954–75) – with only the mutual threat of nuclear annihilation preventing direct war. Founded in 1945, the UN

1896	1898	1906	1908
In Plessy v Ferguson, the US Supreme Court rules that 'separate but equal' public facilities for blacks and whites are legal, arguing that the Constitution addresses only political, not social, equality.	Victory in the Spanish-American War gives US control of the Philippines, Puerto Rico and Guam, and indirect control of Cuba. But the Philippines' bloody war for independence deters future US colonialism.	Upton Sinclair publishes *The Jungle*, an exposé of Chicago's unsavory meatpacking industry. Many workers suffer through poverty and dangerous, even deadly, conditions in choking factories and sweatshops.	The first Model T (aka 'Tin Lizzie') car is built in Detroit, MI. Assembly-line innovator Henry Ford is soon selling one million automobiles annually.

THE AFRICAN AMERICAN EXPERIENCE: THE STRUGGLE FOR EQUALITY

It's impossible to properly grasp American history without taking into account the great struggles and hard-won victories of African Americans who come from all spheres of life.

Slavery

From the early 17th century until the 19th century, an estimated 600,000 slaves were brought from Africa to America. Those who survived the horrific transport on crowded ships (which sometimes had 50% mortality rates) were sold in slave markets (African males cost $27 in 1638). The majority of slaves ended up in Southern plantations where conditions were usually brutal – whipping and branding were commonplace.

All (White) Men are Created Equal

Many of the founding fathers – George Washington, Thomas Jefferson and Benjamin Franklin – owned slaves, though privately expressed condemnation for the abominable practice. The abolition movement, however, wouldn't appear until the 1830s, long after the appearance of the rousing but ultimately hollow words 'all men are created equal' on the Declaration of Independence.

Free at Last

While some revisionist historians describe the Civil War as being about states' rights, most scholars agree that the war was really about slavery. Following the Union victory at Antietam, Lincoln drafted the Emancipation Proclamation, which freed all blacks in occupied territories. African Americans joined the Union effort, with more than 180,000 serving by war's end.

Jim Crow Laws

During Reconstruction (1865–77) federal laws provided civil rights protection for newly freed blacks. Southern bitterness, however, coupled with centuries of prejudice, fueled a backlash. By the 1890s the Jim Crow laws (named after a derogatory character in a minstrel show) appeared. African Americans were effectively disenfranchised, and America became a deeply segregated society.

Civil Rights Movement

Beginning in the 1950s, a movement was under way in African American communities to fight for equality. Rosa Parks, who refused to give up her seat to a white passenger, inspired the Montgomery bus boycott. There were sit-ins at lunch counters where blacks were excluded; massive demonstrations led by Martin Luther King Jr in Washington, DC; and harrowing journeys by 'freedom riders' that aimed to end bus segregation. The work of millions paid off: in 1964, President Johnson signed the Civil Rights Act, which banned discrimination and racial segregation.

1914	1917	1920s	1941–45
Panama Canal opens, linking the Atlantic and Pacific Oceans. US won the right to build and run the canal by inciting a Panamanian revolt over independence from Colombia.	President Woodrow Wilson engages US in WWI. The US mobilizes 4.7 million troops, and suffers around 110,000 of the war's 9 million military deaths.	Spurred by African American migration to northern cities, the Harlem Renaissance inspires an intellectual flowering of literature, art and music. Important figures include WEB Du Bois and Langston Hughes.	WWII: America deploys 16 million troops and suffers 400,000 deaths. Overall, civilian deaths outpace military deaths two to one, and total 50 to 70 million people from over 50 countries.

couldn't overcome this worldwide ideological split and was largely ineffectual in preventing Cold War conflicts.

Meanwhile, with its continent unscarred and its industry bulked up by WWII, the American homeland entered an era of growing affluence. In the 1950s a mass migration left the inner cities for the suburbs, where affordable single-family homes sprang up. Americans drove cheap cars using cheap gas over brand-new interstate highways. They relaxed with the comforts of modern technology, swooned over TV, and got busy, giving birth to a 'baby boom.'

Middle-class whites did, anyway. African Americans remained segregated, poor and generally unwelcome at the party. Echoing 19th-century abolitionist Frederick Douglass, the Southern Christian Leadership Coalition (SCLC), led by African American preacher Martin Luther King Jr, aimed to end segregation and 'save America's soul': to realize color-blind justice, racial equality and fairness of economic opportunity for all.

Beginning in the 1950s, King preached and organized nonviolent resistance in the form of bus boycotts, marches and sit-ins, mainly in the South. White authorities often met these protests with water hoses and batons, and demonstrations sometimes dissolved into riots, but with the 1964 Civil Rights Act, African Americans spurred a wave of legislation that swept away racist laws and laid the groundwork for a more just and equal society.

Meanwhile, the 1960s saw further social upheavals: rock 'n' roll spawned a youth rebellion, and drugs sent Technicolor visions spinning in their heads. President John F Kennedy was assassinated in Dallas in 1963, followed by the assassinations in 1968 of his brother, Senator Robert Kennedy, and of Martin Luther King. Americans' faith in their leaders and government was further shocked by the bombings and brutalities of the Vietnam War, as seen on TV, which led to widespread student protests.

Yet President Richard Nixon, elected in 1968 partly for promising an 'honorable end to the war,' instead escalated US involvement and secretly bombed Laos and Cambodia. Then, in 1972, the Watergate scandal broke: a burglary at Democratic Party offices was, through dogged journalism, tied to 'Tricky Dick,' who, in 1974, became the first US president to resign from office.

The tumultuous 1960s and '70s also witnessed the sexual revolution, women's liberation, struggles for gay rights, energy crises over the supply of crude oil from the Middle East and, with the 1962 publication of Rachel Carson's *Silent Spring,* the realization that the USA's industries had created a polluted, diseased environmental mess.

In *The Souls of Black Folk* (1903), WEB Du Bois, who helped found the National Association for the Advancement of Colored People (NAACP), eloquently describes the racial dilemmas of politics and culture facing early-20th-century America.

HISTORY THE RED SCARE, CIVIL RIGHTS & THE WARS IN ASIA

RACIAL POLITICS

1948–51	1963	1964	1965–75
The US-led Marshall Plan funnels $12 billion in material and financial aid to help Europe recover from WWII. The plan also aims to contain Soviet influence and reignite America's economy.	On November 22, President John F Kennedy is publicly assassinated while riding in a motorcade through Dealey Plaza in Dallas, TX.	Congress passes the Civil Rights Act, outlawing discrimination on basis of race, color, religion, sex or national origin. First proposed by Kennedy, it was one of President Johnson's crowning achievements.	US involvement in the Vietnam War tears the nation apart as 58,000 Americans die, along with four million Vietnamese and 1.5 million Laotians and Cambodians.

Reagan, Clinton & Bush

In 1980, Republican California governor and former actor Ronald Reagan campaigned for president by promising to make Americans feel good about America again. The affable Reagan won easily, and his election marked a pronounced shift to the right in US politics.

Reagan wanted to defeat communism, restore the economy, deregulate business and cut taxes. To tackle the first two, he launched the biggest peacetime military build-up in history, and dared the Soviets to keep up. They went broke trying, and the USSR collapsed.

Military spending and tax cuts created enormous federal deficits, which hampered the presidency of Reagan's successor, George HW Bush. Despite winning the Gulf War – liberating Kuwait in 1991 after an Iraqi invasion – Bush was soundly defeated in the 1992 presidential election by Southern Democrat Bill Clinton. Clinton had the good fortune to catch the 1990s high-tech internet boom, which seemed to augur a 'new economy' based on white-collar telecommunications. The US economy erased its deficits and ran a surplus, and Clinton presided over one of America's longest economic booms.

In 2000 and 2004, George W Bush, the eldest son of George HW Bush, won the presidential elections so narrowly that the divided results seemed to epitomize an increasingly divided nation. 'Dubya' had the misfortune of being president when the high-tech bubble burst in 2000, but he nevertheless enacted tax cuts that returned federal deficits even greater than before. He also championed the right-wing conservative 'backlash' that had been building since Reagan.

On September 11, 2001, Islamic terrorists flew hijacked planes into New York's World Trade Center and the Pentagon in Washington, DC. This catastrophic attack united Americans behind their president as he vowed revenge and declared a 'war on terror.' Bush soon attacked Afghanistan in an unsuccessful hunt for Al-Qaeda terrorist cells, then he attacked Iraq in 2003 and toppled its anti-US dictator, Saddam Hussein. Meanwhile, Iraq descended into civil war.

Following scandals and failures – torture photos from Abu Ghraib, the federal response in the aftermath of Hurricane Katrina and the inability to bring the Iraq War to a close – Bush's approval ratings reached historic lows in the second half of his presidency.

Obama

In 2008, hungry for change, Americans elected political newcomer Barack Obama as America's first African American president. He certainly had his work cut out for him. These were, after all, unprecedented

---

Suspicious of political factoids? Factcheck.org is a nonpartisan, self-described 'consumer advocate' that monitors the accuracy of statements made by US politicians during debates, speeches, interviews and in campaign ads. It's a great resource for parsing truth from bombast and is particularly handy during election cycles.

The People: Indians of the American Southwest (1993), by Stephen Trimble, is a diverse account of indigenous history and contemporary culture as related by Native Americans themselves.

1969

American astronauts land on the moon, fulfilling President Kennedy's unlikely 1961 promise to accomplish this feat within a decade and culminating in the 'space race' between the US and USSR.

➡ US astronaut suit

DENNIS JOHNSON / GETTY IMAGES ©

1973

In Roe v Wade, the Supreme Court legalizes abortion. Today, this decision remains controversial and divisive, pitting 'right to choose' advocates against the 'right to life' anti-abortion lobby.

1980s

New Deal–era financial institutions, deregulized under President Reagan, gamble with their customers' savings and loans, and fail, leaving the government with the bill: $125 billion.

times economically, with the US in the largest financial crisis since the Great Depression. What started as a collapse of the US housing bubble in 2007 spread to the banking sector, with the meltdown of major financial institutions. The shock wave quickly spread across the globe, and by 2008 many industrialized nations were experiencing a recession in one form or another.

The 21st century has certainly been a tumultuous one for the USA. As Americans looked toward the future, many found it difficult to leave the past behind. This was not surprising since wars in Afghanistan and Iraq, launched a decade prior, continued to simmer on the back burner of the ever-changing news cycle, and the 10-year anniversary of September 11 brought back memories of that day when thousands perished in terrorist

FIGHTING FOR CHANGE: FIVE WHO SHAPED HISTORY

American history is littered with larger-than-life figures who brought dramatic change through bold deeds, sometimes at great personal cost. While presidents tend to garner all the attention, there are countless lesser-known visionaries who have made enormous contributions to civic life.

Rachel Carson (1907–64) An eloquent writer with a keen scientific mind, Carson helped spawn the environmental movement. Her pioneering work *Silent Spring* illustrated the ecological catastrophe unleashed by pesticides and unregulated industry. The ensuing grassroots movement spurred the creation of the Environmental Protection Agency.

Cesar Chavez (1927–93) A second-generation Mexican-American who grew up in farm labor camps (where entire families labored for $1 a day), Chavez was a charismatic and inspiring figure – Gandhi and Martin Luther King Jr were among his role models. He gave hope, dignity and a brighter future to thousands of poor migrants by creating the United Farm Workers.

Harvey Milk (1930–78) California's first openly gay public servant was a tireless advocate in the fight against discrimination, encouraging gays and lesbians to 'come out, stand up and let the world know. Only that way will we start to achieve our rights.' Milk, along with San Francisco mayor George Moscone, was assassinated in 1978.

Betty Friedan (1921–2006) Founder of the National Organization of Women (NOW), Friedan was instrumental in leading the feminist movement of the 1960s. Friedan's groundbreaking book *The Feminine Mystique* inspired millions of women to envision a life beyond being a 'homemaker.'

Ralph Nader (1934–) The frequent presidential contender (in 2008, Nader received 738,000 votes) is one of America's staunchest consumer watchdogs. The Harvard-trained lawyer has played a major role in insuring Americans have safer cars, cheaper medicines and cleaner air and water.

1989	1990s	2001	2003
The 1960s-era Berlin Wall is torn down, marking the end of the Cold War between the US and the USSR (now Russia). The USA becomes the world's last remaining superpower.	The World Wide Web debuts in 1991. Silicon Valley, CA, leads a high-tech internet revolution, remaking communications and media, and overvalued tech stocks drive the massive boom (and subsequent bust).	On September 11, Al-Qaeda terrorists hijack four commercial airplanes, flying two into NYC's twin towers, and one into the Pentagon (the fourth crashes in Pennsylvania); nearly 3000 people are killed.	After citing evidence that Iraq possesses weapons of mass destruction, President George W Bush launches a preemptive war that will cost over 4000 American lives and some $3 trillion.

attacks. Earlier in 2011, in a subterfuge operation vetted by President Obama, Navy Seals raided Osama bin Laden's Pakistan hideout, bringing an end to the mastermind behind Al-Qaeda and America's greatest public enemy.

Following his sober announcement describing the raid, President Obama saw his approval ratings jump by 11%. The president, for his part, certainly needed a boost. The economy remained in bad shape, and the ambitious $800-billion stimulus package passed by Congress in 2009 hadn't borne much fruit in the eyes of many Americans – even though economists estimated that the stimulus did soften the blow of the recession, which would have been much worse without it. At the end of his first term, his approval ratings were around 49%, drawn down no doubt by the sluggish economy.

With lost jobs, overvalued mortgages and little relief in sight, millions of Americans found themselves adrift. This was not a recession they could spend their way out of, as Obama's predecessor had suggested. Nor was a little extra thrift going to make a difference. People were upset and gathered in large numbers to voice their anger. This, in turn, gave birth to the Tea Party, a wing of politically conservative Republicans who believed that Obama was leaning too far to the left, and that government handouts would destroy the economy and, thus, America. High federal spending, government bailouts (of the banking and auto industries) and especially Obama's healthcare reform (derisively named 'Obamacare') particularly roused their ire.

If history is a partisan affair, Howard Zinn makes his allegiance clear in *A People's History of the United States* (1980 & 2005), which tells the often-overlooked stories about laborers, minorities, immigrants, women and radicals.

Healthcare for All

For Democrats, however, Obama's healthcare bill, which became law in 2010, was a major victory in bringing healthcare coverage to more Americans, lowering the cost of healthcare and closing loopholes that allowed insurance companies to deny coverage to individuals. Meanwhile, critics from both sides rained blows. From the right: 'This is socialism!' From the left: 'Where's the public option?' (ie a government-backed plan, which would not force consumers to remain at the mercy of insurance companies).

Whether the new program achieves the lofty goals touted by Democrats (new coverage for 30 million uninsured Americans and lower premiums for all) or wreaks havoc as per Republican predictions (busting budgets and causing staggering job losses) remains the great unknown.

2005	2008–09	2012	2013
On August 29, Hurricane Katrina hits the Mississippi and Louisiana coasts, rupturing poorly maintained levees and flooding New Orleans. Over 1800 people die, and cost estimates exceed $110 billion.	Barack Obama becomes the first African American president. The stock market crashes due to mismanagement by major American financial institutions. The crisis spreads worldwide.	Hurricane Sandy devastates the East Coast, becoming the second-costliest hurricane ($65 billion) in American history. Over 80 Americans die (plus 200 more in other countries).	Scandal erupts when former National Security Agency contractor Edward Snowden leaks classified information about a US intelligence program that monitors communication between American citizens and its allies.

The Way of Life

One of the world's great melting pots, America boasts an astonishing variety of cultures and creeds. The country's diversity was shaped by its rich history of immigration, though today, regional differences (East Coast, South, West Coast and Midwest) play an equally prominent role in defining American identity. Religion, sport, politics and, of course, socioeconomic backgrounds are also pivotal in creating the complicated American portrait.

Multiculturalism

From the get-go, America was called a 'melting pot,' which presumed that newcomers came and blended into the existing American fabric. The country hasn't let go of that sentiment completely. On one hand, diversity is celebrated (Cinco de Mayo, Martin Luther King Day and Chinese New Year all get their due) but, on the other hand, many Americans are comfortable with the status quo.

Immigration is at the crux of the matter. Immigrants currently make up a little over 13% of the population. About 480,000 newcomers enter the US legally each year, with the majority from Mexico, followed by Asia and Europe. Another 11 million or so are in the country illegally. This is the issue that makes Americans edgy, especially as it gets politicized.

'Immigration reform' has been a Washington buzzword for more than a decade. Some people believe the nation's current system deals with illegal immigrants too leniently – that walls should be built on the border, immigrants who are here unlawfully should be deported and employers who hire them should be fined. Other Americans think those rules are too harsh – that immigrants who have been here for years working, contributing to society and abiding by the law deserve amnesty; that perhaps they could pay a fine and fill out the paperwork to become citizens while continuing to live here with their families. Despite several attempts, Congress has not been able to pass a comprehensive package addressing illegal immigration, though it has put through various measures to beef up enforcement.

Age has a lot to do with Americans' multicultural tolerance. When asked in a recent survey if immigration strengthens the nation, only about one-third of older Americans said yes, whereas more than half of 18- to 26-year-olds said yes, according to the Pew Research Center. In a similar survey, those aged 60 and older were asked if it's acceptable for whites and African Americans to date each other: 35% said no, but that dropped to 6% when asked of Americans aged 30 and younger.

Many people point to the election of President Barack Obama as proof of America's multicultural achievements. It's not just his personal story (white mother, black father, Muslim name, has lived among the diverse cultures of Hawaii, Indonesia and the Midwest, among others). Or that he's the first African American to hold the nation's highest office (in a country where as recently as the 1960s African Americans couldn't even vote in certain regions). It's that Americans of all races and creeds voted overwhelmingly to elect the self-described 'mutt' and embrace his message of diversity and change.

The US holds the world's second-largest Spanish-speaking population, behind Mexico and just ahead of Spain. Latino people are also the fastest-growing minority group in the nation.

Four million Americans tune in every week to Midwestern raconteur Garrison Keillor's old-timey radio show, *A Prairie Home Companion*; listen to the live music, sketches and storytelling online at http://prairiehome.publicradio.org.

Religion

When the Pilgrims (early settlers to the United States who fled their European homeland to escape religious persecution) came ashore, they were adamant that their new country would be one of religious tolerance. They valued the freedom to practice religion so highly they refused to make their Protestant faith official state policy. What's more, they forbade the government from doing anything that might sanction one religion or belief over another. Separation of church and state became the law of the land.

Today Protestants are on the verge of becoming a minority in the country they founded. According to the Pew Research Center, Protestant numbers have declined steadily to just over 50%. Meanwhile, other faiths have held their own or seen their numbers increase.

The country is also in a period of exceptional religious fluidity. Forty-four percent of American adults have left the denomination of their childhood for another denomination, another faith or no faith at all, according to Pew. A unique era of 'religion shopping' has been ushered in. As for the geographic breakdown: the USA's most Catholic region is shifting from the Northeast to the Southwest; the South is the most evangelical; and the West is the most unaffiliated.

All that said, America's biggest schism isn't between religions or even between faith and skepticism. It's between fundamentalist and progressive interpretations within each faith. Most Americans don't care much if you're Catholic, Episcopalian, Buddhist or atheist. What they do care about are your views on abortion, contraception, gay rights, stem-cell research, teaching of evolution, school prayer and government displays of religious icons. The country's Religious Right (the oft-used term for evangelical Christians) has pushed these issues onto center stage, and the group has been effective at using politics to codify its conservative beliefs into law. This effort has prompted a slew of court cases, testing the nation's principles on separation of church and state. The split remains one of America's biggest culture wars, and it almost always plays a role in politics, especially during elections.

> Americans are increasingly defining their spiritual beliefs outside of organized religion. The proportion of those who say they have 'no religion' is now around 16%. Some in this catch-all category disavow religion altogether (around 4%), but the majority sustain spiritual beliefs that simply fall outside the box.

BELIEFS

Lifestyle

The USA has one of the world's highest standards of living. The median household income is around $51,000, though it varies by region (with higher earnings in the Northeast and West followed by the Midwest and the South). Wages also vary by ethnicity, with African Americans and Latinos earning less than whites and Asians ($33,000 and $39,000 respectively, versus $56,000 and $66,000, according to census data).

STATES & TRAITS

Regional US stereotypes now have solid data behind them, thanks to a study titled *The Geography of Personality*. Researchers processed more than a half-million personality assessments collected from individual US citizens, then looked at where certain traits stacked up on the map. Turns out 'Minnesota nice' is for real – the most 'agreeable' states cluster in the Midwest, Great Plains and South. These places rank highest for friendliness and cooperation. The most neurotic states? They line up in the Northeast. But New York didn't place number one, as you might expect; that honor goes to West Virginia. Many of the most 'open' states lie out West. California, Nevada, Oregon and Washington all rate high for being receptive to new ideas, although they lag behind Washington, DC, and New York. The most dutiful and self-disciplined states sit in the Great Plains and Southwest, led by New Mexico. Go figure.

KNOW YOUR GENERATIONS

American culture is often stratified by age groups. Here's a quick rundown to help you tell Generation X from Z, and then some.

Baby Boomers Those born from 1946 to 1964. After American soldiers came home from WWII the birthrate exploded (hence the term 'baby boom'). Youthful experimentation, self-expression and social activism was often followed by midlife affluence.

Generation X Those born between 1961 and 1981. Characterized by their rejection of Baby Boomer values, skepticism and alienation are X's pop-culture hallmarks.

Generation Y Those born from roughly the early 1980s to mid-1990s (aka Millennials). Known for being brash and self-confident, they were the first to grow up with the internet.

Generation Z Basically applies to those born from the mid-1990s to the present. Weaned on iPods, text messaging, instant messaging and social-networking websites, they are a work in progress. Stay tuned (and check their Facebook page for updates).

Nearly 87% of Americans are high-school graduates, while some 30% go on to graduate from college with a four-year bachelor's degree.

More often than not there are two married parents in an American household, and both of them work. Single parents head 9% of households. Twenty-eight percent of Americans work more than 40 hours per week. Divorce is common – more than 40% of first marriages go kaput – but both divorce and marriage rates have declined over the last three decades. Despite the high divorce rate, Americans spend more than $160 billion annually on weddings. The average number of children in an American family is two.

While many Americans hit the gym or walk, bike or jog regularly, over 50% don't exercise at all during their free time, according to the Centers for Disease Control (CDC). Health researchers speculate this lack of exercise and Americans' fondness for sugary and fatty foods have led to rising obesity and diabetes rates. More than two-thirds of Americans are overweight, with one-third considered obese, the CDC says.

About 26% of Americans volunteer their time to help others or help a cause. This is truer in the Midwest, followed by the West, South and Northeast, according to the Corporation for National and Community Service. Eco-consciousness has entered the mainstream: over 75% of Americans recycle at home, and most big-chain grocery stores – including Walmart – now sell organic foods.

Americans tend to travel close to home. Just over one-third of Americans have passports so most people take vacations within the 50 states. According to the US Department of Commerce's Office of Travel and Tourism Industries, Mexico and Canada are the top countries for international getaways, followed by the UK, Italy, France, Germany and Japan. America's reputation as the 'no-vacation nation,' with many workers having only five to 10 paid annual vacation days, contributes to this stay-at-home scenario.

NPR (National Public Radio) radio host Terry Gross interviews Americans from all walks of life, from rock stars to environmental activists to nuclear scientists. Listen online at www. npr.org/freshair.

Sports

What really draws Americans together, sometimes slathered in blue body paint or with foam-rubber cheese wedges on their heads, is sports. It provides a social glue, so whether a person is conservative or liberal, married or single, Mormon or pagan, chances are come Monday at the office they'll be chatting about the weekend performance of their favorite team.

The fun and games go on all year long. In spring and summer there's baseball nearly every day. In fall and winter, a weekend or Monday night doesn't feel right without a football game on, and through the long days and nights of winter there's plenty of basketball to keep the adrenaline going. Those are the big three sports. Car racing has revved up interest in recent years. Major League Soccer (MLS) is attracting an ever-increasing following. And ice hockey, once favored only in northern climes, is popular nationwide, with four Stanley Cup winners since 2000 hailing from either California or the South.

Baseball

Despite high salaries and its biggest stars being dogged by steroid rumors, baseball remains America's pastime. It may not command the same TV viewership (and subsequent advertising dollars) as football, but baseball has 162 games over a season versus 16 for football.

Besides, baseball isn't about seeing it on TV, it's all about the live version: being at the ballpark on a sunny day, sitting in the bleachers with a beer and hot dog, and indulging in the seventh-inning stretch, when the entire park erupts in a communal singalong of 'Take Me Out to the Ballgame.' The play-offs, held every October, still deliver excitement and unexpected champions. The New York Yankees, Boston Red Sox and Chicago Cubs continue to be America's favorite teams, even when they're abysmal (the Cubs haven't won a World Series in more than 100 years).

Tickets are relatively inexpensive – seats average about $15 at most stadiums – and are easy to get for most games. Minor-league baseball games cost half as much, and can be even more fun, with lots of audience participation, stray chickens and dogs running across the field, and wild throws from the pitcher's mound. For info, click to www.milb.com.

Football

Football is big, physical and rolling in dough. With the shortest season and least number of games of any of the major sports, every match takes on the emotion of an epic battle, where the results matter and an unfortunate injury can deal a lethal blow to a team's play-off chances.

Football's also the toughest because it's played in fall and winter in all manner of rain, sleet and snow. Some of history's most memorable matches have occurred at below-freezing temperatures. Green Bay Packers fans are in a class by themselves when it comes to severe weather. Their stadium in Wisconsin, known as Lambeau Field, was the site of the infamous Ice Bowl, a 1967 championship game against the Dallas Cowboys where the temperature plummeted to –13°F (–25°C) – mind you, that was with a wind-chill factor of –48°F (–44°C).

The rabidly popular Super Bowl is pro football's championship match, held in late January or early February. The bowl games (such as Rose Bowl and Orange Bowl) are college football's title matches, held on and around New Year's Day.

Basketball

The teams bringing in the most fans these days include the Chicago Bulls (thanks to the lingering Michael Jordan effect), Detroit Pistons (a rowdy crowd in which riots have broken out), Cleveland Cavaliers, the San Antonio Spurs and last but not least, the Los Angeles Lakers, which won five championships between 2000 and 2010. Small-market teams like Sacramento and Portland have true-blue fans, and such cities can be great places to take in a game.

College-level basketball also draws millions of fans, especially every spring when March Madness rolls around. This series of college play-off games culminates in the Final Four, when the four remaining teams

---

Key Sports Sites

www.mlb.com – baseball

www.nfl.com – football

www.nba.com – basketball

www.nascar.com – auto-racing

The Super Bowl costs America $800 million dollars in lost workplace productivity as employees gossip about the game, make bets and shop for new TVs online.

SUPER BOWL

compete for a spot in the championship game. The Cinderella stories and unexpected outcomes rival the pro league for excitement. The games are widely televised – and bet on. This is when Las Vegas bookies earn their keep.

Politics

There's nothing quite like a good old-fashioned discussion of politics to throw a bucket of cold water onto a conversation. Many Americans have fairly fixed ideas when it comes to political parties and ideologies, and bridging the Republican-Democratic divide can often seem as insurmountable as leaping over the Grand Canyon. Here's a quick cheat sheet on the dominant American parties and where they stand on the major topics of the day.

Republicans

Known as the GOP (Grand Old Party), Republicans believe in a limited role of federal government. They also prescribe to fiscal conservatism: free markets and lower taxes are the path toward prosperity. Historically, Republicans were strong supporters of the environment: President Theodore Roosevelt was a notable conservationist who helped create the National Parks system, and President Richard Nixon established the Environmental Protection Agency in 1970. More recently, however, Republicans have sided with business over environmental regulation. Climate change remains a hot topic: more than 55% of Congressional Republicans and 65% of Republican Senators deny its basic tenets. There's also a fundamentalist wing in the party that believes in creationism and a literalist interpretation of the bible. Republicans also believe in social conservatism, promoting family and church values, and are often opposed to same-sex marriage and abortion. The Republican Party is most successful in the South and Midwest.

Democrats

The Democratic Party is liberal and progressive. The role model for most Democrats is President Franklin D Roosevelt, whose New Deal policies (namely creating government jobs for the unemployed and regulating Wall Street) are credited with partially ending the Great Depression. Democrats believe government should take an active role in regulating the economy to help keep inflation and unemployment low, and in a progressive tax structure to reduce economic inequality. They also have a strong social agenda, endorsing the government to take an active role in providing poverty relief, maintaining a social safety net, creating a healthcare system for all and ensuring civil and political rights. By and large, Democrats support abortion rights and same-sex marriage, and believe in subsidizing alternative energy sources to help combat climate change, which most party members accept as indisputable. The Democratic Party is strongest in big cities and in the Northeast.

Even college and high-school football games enjoy an intense amount of pomp and circumstance, with cheerleaders, marching bands, mascots, songs and mandatory pre- and post-game rituals, especially the tailgate – a full-blown beer-and-barbecue feast that takes place over portable grills in parking lots where games are played.

THE WAY OF LIFE POLITICS

Native Americans

Although a fraction of its pre-Columbian size, there are more than three million Native Americans from 500 tribes, speaking some 175 languages and residing in every region of the United States. Not surprisingly, North America's indigenous people are an extremely diverse bunch with unique customs and beliefs, molded in part by the landscapes they inhabit – from the Inuit living in the frozen tundra of Alaska, to the many tribes of the arid, mountainous Southwest.

The Tribes

Observe reservation etiquette. Most tribes ban alcohol. Ask before taking pictures or drawing; if granted permission, a tip is polite and often expected. Treat ceremonies like church services; watch respectfully (no photos), and wear modest clothing. Silent listening shows respect.

The Cherokee, Navajo, Chippewa and Sioux are the largest tribal groupings in the lower 48 (ie barring Alaska and Hawaii). Other well-known tribes include the Choctaw (descendants of a great mound-building society originally based in the Mississippi valley), the Apache (a nomadic hunter-gatherer tribe that fiercely resisted forced relocation) and the Hopi (a Pueblo people with Southwest roots dating back 2000 years).

Culturally speaking, America's tribes today grapple with questions about how to prosper in contemporary America while protecting their traditions from erosion and their lands from further exploitation, and how to lift their people from poverty while maintaining their sense of identity and the sacred.

Cherokee

The Cherokee (www.cherokee.org) originally lived in an area of more than 80 million acres, covering a huge swath of the South (including Tennessee, Virginia, the Carolinas and Kentucky). However, in 1830 they were forcibly relocated east of the Mississippi and today reside largely in

---

NATIVE AMERICAN ART & CRAFTS

It would take an encyclopedia to cover the myriad artistic traditions of America's tribal peoples, from pre-Columbian rock art to the contemporary multimedia scene.

What ties such diverse traditions together is that Native American art and crafts are not just functional for everyday life, but can also serve ceremonial purposes and have social and religious significance. The patterns and symbols are woven with meanings that provide a window into the heart of Native American peoples. This is as true of Zuni fetish carvings as it is of patterned Navajo rugs, Southwestern pueblo pottery, Sioux beadwork, Inuit sculptures and Cherokee and Hawaiian woodcarvings, to name just a few examples.

In addition to preserving their culture, contemporary Native American artists have used sculpture, painting, textiles, film, literature and performance art to reflect and critique modernity since the mid-20th century, especially after the civil rights activism of the 1960s and cultural renaissance of the '70s. *Native North American Art*, by Berlo and Phillips, offers an introduction to North America's varied indigenous art.

Many tribes run craft outlets and galleries, usually in the main towns of reservations. The **Indian Arts & Crafts Board** (www.iacb.doi.gov) lists Native American–owned galleries and shops state-by-state online (click on 'Source Directory of Businesses').

Oklahoma (home to more than 200,000 Cherokee). Tahlequah has been the Cherokee capital since 1839.

Cherokee society was originally matrilineal, with bloodlines traced through the mother. Like some other native tribes, the Cherokee recognize seven cardinal directions: north, south, east and west along with up, down and center (or within).

Navajo

The Navajo Reservation (www.discovernavajo.com) is by far the largest and most populous in the US. Also called the Navajo Nation and Navajoland, it covers 17.5 million acres (over 27,000 sq miles) in Arizona and parts of New Mexico and Utah.

The Navajo were feared nomads and warriors who both traded with and raided the Pueblos and who fought settlers and the US military. They also borrowed generously from other traditions: they acquired sheep and horses from the Spanish, learned pottery and weaving from the Pueblos, and picked up silversmithing from Mexico. Today, the Navajo are renowned for their woven rugs, pottery and inlaid silver jewelry, as well as for their intricate sandpainting, which is used in healing ceremonies.

Chippewa

Although Chippewa or Ojibway is the commonly used term for this tribe, members prefer to be called Anishinabe. They are based in Minnesota, Wisconsin and Michigan. According to legend, the Chippewa once lived on the Atlantic coast and gradually migrated west over 500 years. They traditionally survived by fishing, hunting and farming corn and squash. They also harvested (by canoe) wild rice, which remains an essential Chippewa tradition.

Sioux

Like the Iroquois, the Sioux is not one tribe but a consortium of three major tribes (and various subbranches) speaking different dialects but sharing a common subculture. Prior to European arrival they lived in the northeast of present-day North America but slowly migrated to the Great Plains by 1800. The Sioux were fierce defenders of their lands, and fought many battles to preserve them, although the slaughter of the buffalo (on whom they had survived) did more to remove them from their lands than anything else. Today, they live in Minnesota, Nebraska, North Dakota and South Dakota – the latter contains the 2-million-acre Pine Ridge Reservation, the nation's second-largest.

NATIVE AMERICANS THE TRIBES

700–1400
North America's largest ancient city, Cahokia, supports a population of 10,000 to 20,000 at its peak. By 1400 it is abandoned.

750–1300
Ancestral Puebloans living near Chaco Canyon flourish. This advanced desert civilization develops adobe dwellings in enormous complexes.

1831
Following the 1830 *Indian Removal Act*, Cherokee and other tribes are forced to abandon homelands to areas west of the Mississippi. Thousands die on the 1000-mile Trail of Tears.

1876
Lakota chief Sitting Bull defeats Custer at the Battle of Little Big Horn, one of the last military victories by Native Americans in the effort to protect their lands.

1968
The American Indian Movement (AIM) is founded. Through protests, marches and demonstrations, AIM brings attention to marginalized peoples.

1968
Navajo Community College becomes the first college on any reservation founded and run by Native Americans. Later, other tribal community colleges are founded, growing to 30 today.

1975
President Nixon passes the *Indian Self-Determination Act*, empowering Native Americans to control how federal moneys are spent on native matters.

2011
FNX, the first Native American television network, launches in California. It presents Native American films, documentaries, children's programs and more.

American Cuisine

Americans have mixed myriad food cultures to create their own rich cuisine, based on the bounty of the continent: drawing on the seafood of the North Atlantic, Gulf of Mexico and Pacific Ocean, the fertility of Midwest farmlands, and vast western ranchlands. Massive waves of immigrants have added even more variety to American gastronomy by adapting foreign ideas to home soil, from Italian pizza and German hamburgers to Eastern European borscht, Mexican huevos rancheros and Japanese sushi.

Culinary Revolution

Not until the 1960s did food and wine become serious topics for American newspapers, magazines and TV, led by a Californian named Julia Child who taught Americans how to cook French food through black-and-white programs broadcast from Boston's public TV station. By the 1970s, everyday folks (and not just hippies) had started turning their attention to issues of organic, natural foods and sustainable agriculture. In the 1980s and '90s, the 'foodie revolution' encouraged entrepreneurs to open restaurants featuring regional American cuisine, from the South to the Pacific Northwest, that would rank with Europe's best.

Staples & Specialties

Americans have such easy access to regional foods that once-unique specialties are now often readily available everywhere: a Bostonian might just as easily have a taco or barbecue ribs for lunch as a Houstonian might eat Maine lobster for dinner.

Breakfast

Long billed by American nutritionists as 'the most important meal of the day,' morning meals in America are big business – no matter how many folks insist on skipping them. From a giant stack of buttermilk pancakes at a vintage diner to lavish Sunday brunches, Americans love their eggs and bacon, their waffles and hash browns, and their big glasses of fresh-squeezed orange juice. Most of all, they love that seemingly inalienable American right: a steaming cup of morning coffee with unlimited refills. (Try asking for a free refill in other nations, and you'll get anything from an eye-roll to a smirk to downright confusion.)

Lunch

Usually after a midmorning coffee break, an American worker's lunch hour affords only a sandwich, quick burger or hearty salad. The formal 'business lunch' is more common in big cities like New York, where food is not necessarily as important as the conversation.

While you'll spot diners drinking a beer or a glass of wine with their lunch, the days of the socially acceptable 'three martini lunch' are long gone. It was a phenomenon common enough in the mid-20th century to become a catchphrase for indulgent business lunches, usually written off as a corporate, tax-deductible expense. The classic noontime beverage, in fact, is a far cry from a martini: iced tea (almost always with unlimited refills).

Dinner

Usually early in the evening, Americans settle in to a more substantial weeknight dinner, which, given the workload of so many two-career families, might be takeout (eg pizza or Chinese food) or prepackaged meals cooked in a microwave. Desserts tend toward ice cream, pies and cakes. Some families still cook a traditional Sunday night dinner, when relatives and friends gather for a big feast. Traditional dishes might include roast chicken with all the fixings (mashed potatoes, green beans and corn on the cob). In warmer months, many Americans like to fire up the barbecue to grill steaks, burgers and veggies, which are served alongside plenty of cold beer and wine.

Quick Eats

Eating hot dogs or pretzels from city street carts or tacos and barbecue from roadside trucks carries a small risk that you might pick up some nasty bacteria, but generally fast food tends to be safe and vendors are usually supervised by the local health department. At festivals and county fairs, you can take your pick from cotton candy, corn dogs, candy apples, funnel cakes, chocolate-covered frozen bananas and plenty of tasty regional specialties. Farmers markets often have more wholesome, affordable prepared foods.

NYC: Foodie Capital

They say that you could eat at a different restaurant every night of your life in New York City, and not exhaust the possibilities. Considering that there are more than 23,000 restaurants in the five boroughs, with scores of new ones opening each year, it's true. Owing to its huge immigrant population and an influx of over 50 million tourists annually, New York captures the title of America's greatest restaurant city, hands down. Its diverse neighborhoods serve up authentic Italian food and thin-crust pizza, all manner of Asian food, French haute cuisine and classic Jewish deli food, from bagels to piled-high pastrami on rye. More exotic cuisines are found here as well, from Ethiopian to Scandinavian.

Read *New York* magazine (www.nymag.com) or *Time Out* (www.timeout.com/newyork) for the latest restaurant openings, reviews and insight into famed and up-and-coming chefs. Finally, don't let NYC's image as expensive get to you: you can eat well here without breaking the bank, especially if

Top Food TV Shows

Anthony Bourdain: Parts Unknown (Travel Channel)

Man vs Food (Travel Channel)

Top Chef (Bravo)

Iron Chef America (Food Network)

Diners, Drive-ins and Dives (Food Network)

Bizarre Foods with Andrew Zimmern (Travel Channel)

VEG HEAVEN

Some of the most highly regarded American restaurants cater exclusively to vegetarians and vegans. They abound in major US cities, though not always in small towns and rural areas away from the coasts. Eateries that are exclusively vegetarian or vegan are noted throughout this book using the 🖉 symbol. To find more vegetarian and vegan restaurants, browse the online directory at www.happycow.net. Here are a few of our go-to faves for when the veggie cravings hit.

Green Elephant (p246), Portland, ME

Moosewood Restaurant (p127), Ithaca, NY

Café Zenith (p166), Pittsburgh, PA

Green Vegetarian Cuisine (p685), San Antonio, TX

Bouldin Creek Coffee House (p675), Austin, TX

Greens (p984), San Francisco

Angelica Kitchen (p104), NYC

Dandelion Communitea Cafe (p506), Orlando, FL

THE AMERICAN DIET CRAZE

America's almost as well know for its fad diets as it is for its fast food. Some of the most bizarre diets? In the 1920s and 1930s, there was the Cigarette Diet, the Bananas and Skim Milk Diet and the Grapefruit Diet – also called the Hollywood Diet. The 1960s brought the Steak and Martini Diet; the 1980s ushered in the Cabbage Soup Diet. In the 1990s, fat free and high carb was all the rage – until, that is, the Atkins Diet came in with its low-carb mantra. Stars embraced the Master Cleanse, aka the Lemonade Diet, and then just as quickly abandoned it. Today's most popular one? It's called the Paleo diet, and entails eating like a caveman: organ meats, broths, fresh and fermented vegetables – but no grains, refined sugar, pasteurized dairy products or other food items unavailable to prehistoric peoples.

you limit your cocktail intake. There may be no free lunch in New York, but compared to other world cities, eating here can be a bargain.

New England: Clambakes & Lobster Boils

New England's claim to have the nation's best seafood is hard to beat, because the North Atlantic offers up clams, mussels, oysters and huge lobsters, along with shad, bluefish and cod. New Englanders love a good chowder (seafood stew) and a good clambake, an almost ritual meal where the shellfish are buried in a pit fire with corn, chicken, potatoes and sausages. Fried clam fritters and lobster rolls (lobster meat with mayonnaise served in a bread bun) are served throughout the region. There are excellent cheeses made in Vermont, cranberries (a Thanksgiving staple) harvested in Massachusetts and maple syrup tapped from New England's forests. Maine's coast is lined with lobster shacks; baked beans and brown bread are Boston specialties; and Rhode Islanders pour coffee syrup into milk and embrace traditional cornmeal johnnycakes.

Mid-Atlantic: Cheesesteaks, Crab Cakes & Scrapple

From New York down through Maryland and Virginia, the mid-Atlantic states share a long coastline and a cornucopia of apple, pear and berry farms. New Jersey and New York's Long Island are famous for their spuds (potatoes). Chesapeake Bay's blue crabs are the finest anywhere and Virginia salt-cured 'country-style' hams are served with biscuits. In Philadelphia, you can gorge on 'Philly' cheesesteaks, made with thin, sautéed beef and onions and melted cheese on a bun. And in Pennsylvania Dutch Country, stop by a farm restaurant for chicken pot pie, noodles and meatloaf-like scrapple.

The South: BBQ, Biscuits & Gumbo

No region is prouder of its food culture than the South, which has a long history of mingling Anglo, French, African, Spanish and Native American foods in dishes such as slow-cooked barbecue, which has as many meaty and saucy variations as there are towns in the South. Southern fried chicken is crisp outside and moist inside. In Florida, dishes made with alligator, shrimp and conch incorporate hot chili peppers and tropical spices. Breakfasts are as big as can be, and treasured dessert recipes tend to produce big layer cakes or pies made with pecans, bananas and citrus. Light, fluffy hot biscuits are served well buttered, and grits (ground corn cooked to a porridge-like consistency) are a passion among Southerners, as are cool mint-julep cocktails.

Louisiana's legendary cuisine is influenced by colonial French and Spanish cultures, Afro Caribbean cooking and Choctaw traditions. Cajun food is found in the bayou country and marries native spices such as sassafras and

LOUISIANA CUISINE

Louisiana is renowned among epicures for its French-influenced Cajun and Creole cuisine. Famous dishes include gumbo, a roux-based stew of chicken and shellfish, or sausage and often okra; jambalaya, a rice-based dish with tomatoes, sausage and shrimp; and blackened catfish.

chili peppers with provincial French cooking. Creole food is more urban, and centered in New Orleans, where dishes such as shrimp rémoulade, crabmeat ravigote, crawfish étouffée and beignets are ubiquitous.

Midwest: Burgers, Bacon, & Beer
Midwesterners eat big and with plenty of gusto. Portions are huge – this is farm country, where people need sustenance to get their day's work done. So you might start off the day with eggs, bacon and toast; have a double cheeseburger and potato salad for lunch; and fork into steak and baked potatoes for dinner – all washed down with a cold brew, often one of the growing numbers of microbrews. Barbecue is very popular here, especially in Kansas City, St Louis and Chicago. Chicago is also an ethnically diverse culinary center, with some of the country's top restaurants. One of the best places to sample Midwestern foods is at a county fair, which offers everything from bratwurst to fried dough to grilled corn on the cob. Elsewhere at diners and family restaurants, you'll taste the varied influences of Eastern European, Scandinavian, Latino and Asian immigrants, especially in the cities.

The Southwest: Chili, Steak & Smoking-Hot Salsa
Two ethnic groups define Southwestern food culture: the Spanish and Mexicans, who controlled territories from Texas to California until well into the 19th century. While there is little actual Spanish food today, the Spanish brought cattle to Mexico, which the Mexicans adapted to their own corn-and-chili-based gastronomy to make tacos, tortillas, enchiladas, burritos, chimichangas and other dishes made of corn or flour pancakes filled with everything from chopped meat and poultry to beans. Don't leave New Mexico without trying a bowl of spicy green chili stew. Steaks and barbecue are always favorites on Southwestern menus, and beer is the drink of choice for dinner and a night out. Don't miss the fist-sized burritos in San Francisco's Mission District and fish tacos in San Diego.

California: Farm-to-Table Restaurants & Taquerías
Owing to its vastness and variety of microclimates, California is truly America's cornucopia for fruits and vegetables, and a gateway to myriad Asian markets. The state's natural resources are overwhelming, with wild salmon, Dungeness crab and oysters from the ocean; robust produce year-round; and artisanal products such as cheese, bread, olive oil, wine and chocolate. Starting in the 1970s and '80s, star chefs such as Alice Waters and Wolfgang Puck pioneered 'California cuisine' by incorporating the best local ingredients into simple, yet delectable, preparations. The influx of Asian immigrants, especially after the Vietnam War, enriched the state's urban food cultures with Chinatowns, Koreatowns and Japantowns, along with huge enclaves of Mexican Americans who maintain their own culinary traditions across the state. Global fusion restaurants are another hallmark of California's cuisine.

AMERICAN CUISINE STAPLES & SPECIALTIES

FOOD TRUCKS

The hottest dining craze on wheels is food trucks. From crab-cake tacos to red velvet cupcakes, there's no telling what creative, healthy, gourmet, decadent, or downright bizarre twist on 'fast food' you'll discover. To find the best trucks, visit Portland, Austin, Minneapolis, Los Angeles, New York, Las Vegas, San Francisco and Miami.

SLOW, LOCAL, ORGANIC
The Slow Food movement, along with renewed enthusiasm for eating local, organically grown fare, is a leading trend in American restaurants. The movement, which was arguably started in 1971 by chef Alice Waters at Berkeley's Chez Panisse (p994), continues with First Lady Michelle Obama – the First Lady of food if there ever was one – and her daughters, who have planted an organic garden on the White House lawn. Recently, farmers markets have been popping up all across the country and they're a great place to meet locals and take a big bite out of America's cornucopia of foods, from heritage fruit and vegetables to fresh, savory and sweet regional delicacies.

Pacific Northwest: Salmon & Starbucks

The cuisine of the Pacific Northwest region draws on the traditions of the local tribes of Native Americans, whose diets traditionally centered on game, seafood – especially salmon – and foraged mushrooms, fruits and berries. Seattle spawned the modern international coffeehouse craze with Starbucks.

Hawaii: Island Style

In the middle of the Pacific Ocean, Hawaii is rooted in a Polynesian food culture that takes full advantage of locally caught fish such as mahimahi, 'opakapaka, 'ono and 'ahi. Traditional luau celebrations include cooking kalua pig in an underground pit layered with hot stones and ti leaves. Hawaii's contemporary cuisine incorporates fresh, island-grown produce and borrows liberally from the islands' many Asian and European immigrant groups. This also happens to be the only state to grow coffee commercially; 100% Kona beans from the Big Island have the most gourmet cachet.

Habits & Customs

Americans tend to eat early at restaurants and at home, so don't be surprised to find a restaurant half full at noon or 5:30pm. In smaller towns, it may be hard to find anywhere to eat after 8:30pm or 9pm. Dinner parties for adults usually begin around 6:30pm or 7pm with cocktails followed by a buffet or sit-down meal. If invited to dinner, it's polite to be prompt: ideally, you should plan to arrive within 15 minutes of the designated time.

Americans are informal in their dining manners, although they will usually wait until everyone is served before eating. Many foods are eaten with the fingers, and an entire piece of bread may be buttered and eaten all at once. To the surprise of some foreign visitors, the sight of beer bottles on the dinner table is not uncommon.

Dos & Don'ts

Do tip: 15% of the total bill is standard; tip 20% (or more) for excellent service.

It's customary to place your napkin on your lap, even before the meal is served.

Try to avoid putting your elbows on the table.

Wait until everyone is served to begin eating.

In formal situations, diners customarily wait to eat until the host(ess) has lifted their fork.

At home, some Americans say a prayer before meals; it's fine to sit quietly if you prefer not to participate.

Food Glossary

barbecue	a technique of slow-smoking spice-rubbed and basted meat over a grill
beignet	New Orleans square, doughnut-like fritter dusted with powdered sugar
biscuit	flaky yeast-free roll served in the South
blintz	Jewish pancake stuffed with various fillings such as jam, cheese or potatoes
BLT	bacon, lettuce and tomato sandwich
blue plate	special of the day in a diner or luncheonette
Boston baked beans	beans cooked with molasses and bacon in a casserole
Buffalo wings	deep-fried chicken wings glazed with a buttery hot sauce and served with blue cheese dressing; originated in Buffalo, NY
burrito	Mexican American flour tortilla wrapped around beans, meat, salsa and rice
California roll	fusion sushi made with avocado, crabmeat and cucumbers wrapped in vinegared rice and nori (dried seaweed)
chili	hearty meat stew spiced with ground chilies, vegetables and beans; also called chili con carne
clam chowder	potato-based soup full of clams, vegetables and sometimes bacon, thickened with milk
club sandwich	three-layered sandwich with chicken or turkey, bacon, lettuce and tomato
corned beef	salt-cured or brined beef, traditionally served with cabbage on St Patrick's Day (March 17)

crab cake	crabmeat bound with breadcrumbs and eggs then fried
eggs Benedict	poached eggs, ham and hollandaise sauce on top of English muffins
French toast	egg-dipped fried bread served with maple syrup
grits	white cornmeal porridge; a Southern breakfast or side dish
guacamole	mashed avocado dip with lime juice, onions, chilies and cilantro, served with tortilla chips
hash browns	shredded pan-fried potatoes
huevos rancheros	Mexican breakfast of corn tortillas topped with fried eggs and salsa
jambalaya	Louisiana stew of rice, ham, sausage, shrimp and seasonings
lobster roll	lobster meat mixed with mayonnaise and seasonings, and served in a toasted frankfurter bun
lox	Jewish version of brine-cured salmon
nachos	Mexican American fried tortilla chips often topped with cheese, ground beef, jalapeño peppers, salsa and sour cream
pastrami	Jewish American brined beef that is smoked and steamed
pickle	cucumber brined in vinegar
Reuben sandwich	sandwich of corned beef, Swiss cheese and sauerkraut on rye bread
smoothie	cold, blended drink made with pureed fruit, ice, milk and/or yogurt
stone crab	Floribbean crab whose claws are eaten with melted butter or mustard-mayonnaise sauce
surf 'n' turf	combination plate of seafood (often lobster) and steak
wrap	tortilla or pita bread stuffed with a variety of fillings

Wine, Beer & Beyond

Americans have a staggering range of choices when it comes to beverages. A booming microbrewery industry has brought finely crafted beers to every corner of the country. The US wine industry continues to produce first-rate vintages – and it's not just Californian vineyards garnering all the awards. Washington, Oregon, New York, Virginia and many other states create celebrated pinots and rosés. Meanwhile, coffee culture continues to prevail, with cafes and roasteries elevating the once humble cup of coffee to high art.

DUI (driving under the influence) is taken very seriously in the USA. Designating a sober driver who doesn't drink has become a widespread practice among groups of friends consuming alcohol at restaurants, bars, nightclubs and parties.

Beer

It's hard to deny that beer is about as American as Chevrolet, football, and apple pie: just tune in to the Super Bowl commercials (America's most popular yearly televised event, featuring its most expensive advertisements) and you'll see how beer has become intertwined with American cultural values. Just look at the slogans, celebrating individuality ('This Bud's for You'), sociability ('It's Miller Time!'), ruggedness ('Head for the Mountains') and authenticity ('Real Men Drink Bud Light').

Despite their ubiquity, popular brands of American beer have long been the subject of ridicule abroad due to their low alcohol content and 'light' taste. Regardless of what the critics say, sales indicate that American beer is more popular than ever – and now, with the meteoric rise of microbreweries and craft beer, even beer snobs admit that American beer has reinvented itself.

Craft & Local Beer

Today, beer aficionados (otherwise known as beer geeks) sip and savor beer as they would wine, and some urban restaurants even have beer 'programs,' 'sommeliers' and cellars. Many brewpubs and restaurants host beer dinners, a chance to experience just how beers pair with different foods.

Microbrewery and craft-beer production is rising meteorically, generating roughly $12 billion in retail sales in 2012. Today there are more than 1500 craft breweries across the USA. Portland, Oregon, is the current capital of the industry with some 50-plus small breweries – more than in any other city in the world. In recent years, it's become possible to 'drink local' all over the country as microbreweries pop up in urban centers, small towns and unexpected places.

Wine

In the USA, where restaurants and bars often pay the legal minimum wage (or less), servers rely on tips for their livelihood. A good rule: tip at least a dollar per drink, or roughly 15% to 20% of the total bill.

In the seminal 1972 film *The Godfather,* Marlon Brando's Vito Corleone muses, 'I like to drink wine more than I used to.' The country soon followed suit, and nearly four decades later, Americans are still drinking more wine than ever. According to the *Los Angeles Times,* 2010 marked the first year that the US actually consumed more wine than France.

To the raised eyebrows of European winemakers, who used to regard even California wines as second class, many American wines are now even (gulp!) winning prestigious international awards. In fact, the nation is the world's 4th-largest producer of wine, behind Italy, France and Spain.

Wine isn't cheap in the US, as it's considered a luxury rather than a staple – go ahead and blame the Puritans for that. But it's possible to procure a perfectly drinkable bottle of American wine at a liquor or wine shop for around $10 or $12.

Wine Regions

Today almost 90% of US wine comes from California, while other regions are producing wines that have achieved international status. In particular, the wines of New York's Finger Lakes, Hudson Valley and Long Island are well worth sampling, as are the wines from both Washington and Oregon, especially Pinot Noirs and Rieslings.

Without a doubt, the country's hotbed of wine tourism is in Northern California, just outside of the Bay Area in the Napa and Sonoma Valleys. As other regions, from Oregon's Willamette Valley to Texas' Hill Country have evolved as wine regions, they have spawned an entire industry of bed-and-breakfast tourism that seem to go hand and hand with the quest to find the perfect Pinot Noir.

So, what are the best American wines? Amazingly, though it's only been a few decades since many American restaurants served either 'red,' 'white,' or sometimes 'pink' wine, there are many excellent 'New World' wines that have flourished in the rich American soil. The most popular white varietals made in the US are Chardonnay and Sauvignon Blanc; best-selling reds include Cabernet Sauvignon, Merlot, Pinot Noir and Zinfandel.

The Hard Stuff

You might know him by his first name, Jack. (Hint: Daniels is his last name). Good ole Jack Daniels remains the most well-known brand of American whiskey around the world, and is also the oldest continually operating US distillery, going strong since 1870.

While whiskey and bourbon are the most popular American exports, rye, gin and vodka are also crafted in the USA. Bourbon, made from corn, is the only native spirit and traditionally it is made in Kentucky.

Cocktails were invented in America before the Civil War. Born in New Orleans, an appropriately festive city to launch America's contribution to booze history, the first cocktail was the Sazerac – a mix of rye whiskey or brandy, simple syrup, bitters and a dash of absinthe (before it was banned in 1912, that is). American cocktails created at bars in the late 19th and early 20th centuries include such long-standing classics as the martini, the Manhattan, and the old-fashioned.

Blame it on Hollywood: Merlot is just not that cool anymore. Paul Giamatti's Academy Award–winning performance in the film *Sideways* singlehandedly destroyed its sophisticated reputation through the following line: 'If anyone orders Merlot, I'm leaving. I am *not* drinking any f*&%ing Merlot!' In the film, he favors Pinot Noir.

LEGENDARY AMERICANS DISH ABOUT DRINKING

While these Americans are all lauded for their talents in the arts or entertainment, they were undeniably (and often infamously) associated with the boozing life. Here are a few choice words they have on the subject.

➡ Ernest Hemingway: 'Always do sober what you said you'd do drunk. That will teach you to keep your mouth shut.'

➡ Frank Sinatra: 'Alcohol may be man's worst enemy, but the Bible says "love your enemy."'

➡ Dorothy Parker: 'I'd rather have a bottle in front of me than a frontal lobotomy.'

➡ WC Fields: 'A woman drove me to drink, and I never had the courtesy to thank her.'

➡ William Faulkner: 'The tools I need for my work are paper, tobacco, food, and a little whiskey.'

➡ Homer Simpson: 'Beer – the cause of and solution to all of life's problems.'

COCA-COLA

The Vintage Cocktail Craze

Across US cities, it's become decidedly cool to party like it's 1929 by drinking retro cocktails from the days – less than a century ago – that alcohol was illegal to consume across the entire United States. Good old Prohibition, of course, instead of spawning a nation of teetotalers, only solidified a culture in which the forbidden became appealing, it felt good to be bad, flappers carried flasks of gin in their purses, and so-called respectable citizens congregated in secret 'speakeasies' to drink homemade moonshine and dance to hot jazz.

Fast forward to the 21st century. While Prohibition isn't in danger of being reinstated, you'll find plenty of bars where the spirit of the Roaring Twenties and the illicit 1930s lives on. Inspired by vintage recipes featuring spirits and elixirs – remember, back in the day you couldn't just grab a bottle of scotch at the grocery store! – these cocktails, complete with ingredients like small-batch liqueurs, whipped egg whites, hand-chipped ice and fresh fruits, are lovingly concocted by nattily dressed bartenders who regard their profession as something between an art and a science.

Nonalcoholic Drinks

Tap water in the USA is safe to drink, though its taste varies depending on the region and city. Most nonalcoholic drinks are quite sugary and served over ice, from Southern-style iced 'sweet tea' and lemonade to quintessential American soft drinks such as Coca-Cola, Pepsi and Dr Pepper, along with retro and nouveau soft-drinks, often made with cane sugar instead of corn syrup.

Interestingly, carbonated nonalcoholic beverages have different nicknames depending on where you order them. In many parts of the South, a 'coke' means any kind of soda, so you may have to specify which kind you mean, for example, if you say 'I'll have a Coke,' the waiter might ask, 'Which kind?' In the Midwest, soda is called 'pop.' On the East Coast and elsewhere, it's called 'soda.' Go figure...

The Coffee Addiction

While Americans kick back with beer, and unwind with wine, the country runs on caffeine. The coffee craze has only intensified in the last 25 years, ever since cafe culture exploded in urban centers and spread throughout the country.

Blame it on Starbucks – the coffee that America loves (or loathes) above all others. The world's biggest coffee chain was born amid the Northwest's progressive coffee culture in 1971, when Starbucks opened its first location across from Pike Place Market in Seattle. The idea, to offer a variety of roasted beans from around the world in a comfortable cafe, helped start filling the American coffee mug with more refined, complicated (and expensive) drinks compared to the ubiquitous Folgers and diner cups of joe. By the early 1990s, specialty coffeehouses began springing up across the country, everywhere from cities to university towns.

While many coffee chains only have room for a few chairs and a take-out counter, independent coffee shops support a coffeehouse culture that encourages lingering; think free wi-fi, comfortable indoor and outdoor seating and good snacks and light fare. At the most high-level cafes, experienced baristas will happily banter about the origins of any roast (single-origin beans rather than blends are the latest in coffee snobbery) and will share their ideas about bean grinds and more.

The most infamous rumor about Coca-Cola, developed in 1886 at an Atlanta pharmacy, is true: once marketed as a medicine, it did indeed contain trace amounts of cocaine. Having once contained about 9mg per glass, cocaine was eliminated from the product in 1903.

Arts & Architecture

Geography and race together create the varied regionalism that is key to understanding America's arts. And despite a popular affinity for technology, it is nature and wilderness that still inspire the nation's soul and, consequently, much of its art.

Film

Hollywood and American film are virtually inseparable. No less an American icon than the White House itself, Hollywood is increasingly the product of an internationalized cinema and film culture. This evolution is partly pure business: Hollywood studios are the showpieces of multinational corporations, and funding flows to talent that brings the biggest grosses, regardless of nationality.

But this shift is also creative. It's Hollywood's recognition that if the studios don't incorporate the immense filmmaking talent emerging worldwide, they will be made irrelevant by it. Co-option is an old Hollywood strategy, used most recently to subvert the challenge posed by the independent film movement of the 1990s that kicked off with daring homegrown films like *Sex, Lies, and Videotape* and *Reservoir Dogs*, and innovative European imports. That said, for the most part, mainstream American audiences remain steadfastly indifferent to foreign films.

Television

In the 20th century, it could be argued that TV was the defining medium of the modern age. An average American still watches an astonishing 34 hours of TV a week. Americans *love* TV, but they are watching differently: recording or downloading online, viewing according to their schedules (not the networks') and skipping the commercials. As the internet messes with the economics of this corporate-owned, ad-driven entertainment, TV executives shudder.

For many decades, critics sneered that TV was lowbrow, and movie stars wouldn't be caught dead on it. But well-written, thought-provoking shows have existed almost since the beginning. In the 1950s, the original *I Love Lucy* show was groundbreaking: shot on film before a live audience and edited before airing, it pioneered syndication. It established the sitcom ('situation comedy') formula, and showcased a dynamic female comedian, Lucille Ball, in an interethnic marriage.

In its brief history, TV has proved to be one of the most passionately contested cultural battlegrounds in American society, blamed for a whole host of societal ills, from skyrocketing obesity to plummeting attention spans and school test scores. On the other hand, as cable TV has emerged as the frontier for daring and innovative programming, some of the TV shows of the past decade have proved as riveting and memorable as anything Americans viewers (and the scores of people around the world who watch American TV) have ever seen.

Of course, 'good' American TV has been around for a long time, whether through artistic merit or cultural and political importance.

Art in Out-of-the-Way Places

Marfa, TX

Santa Fe, NM

Traverse City, MI

Park City, UT

Bellingham, WA

Beacon, NY

Provincetown, MA

Jhumpa Lahiri won the Pulitzer Prize for her first breathtaking collection of stories, *Interpreter of Maladies*, about the experience of Indian immigrants in the contemporary United States.

The 1970s comedy *All in the Family* aired an unflinching examination of prejudice, as embodied by bigoted patriarch Archie Bunker, played by Carroll O'Connor. Similarly, the sketch-comedy show *Saturday Night Live,* which debuted in 1975, pushed social hot buttons with its subversive, politically charged humor.

In the 1980s, videotapes brought movies into American homes, blurring the distinction between big and small screens, and the stigma Hollywood attached to TV slowly faded. Another turning point in this decade was *The Cosby Show,* starring comedian Bill Cosby. While not the first successful African American show, it became the nation's highest-rated program and spurred more multicultural TV shows.

In the 1990s, TV audiences embraced the unformulaic, no-holds-barred cult show *Twin Peaks,* leading to a slew of provocative idiosyncrasies like *The X-Files.*

Now, YouTube, Hulu, Blip.tv and its ilk are changing the rules again. The networks have responded by creating more edgy, long-narrative serial dramas, as well as cheap-to-produce, 'unscripted' reality TV: what *Survivor* started in 2000, the contestants and 'actors' of *American Idol, Dancing with the Stars, Project Runway* and *The Jersey Shore* keep alive today, for better or for worse.

In the last decade, networks have created some much-loved series, including *The Sopranos, The Wire* and *Curb Your Enthusiasm.* More recent hits include *Mad Men* (which follows the antics of 1960s advertising execs in NYC), *Parks and Recreation* (a mock-documentary-style comedy that revolves around mid-level bureaucrats in a fictional Indiana town), *Portlandia* (a satire of Oregonian subcultures) and *Breaking Bad* (about a terminally ill high school teacher who builds a meth lab to safeguard his family's financial future).

Literature

American Identity through Literature

America first articulated a vision of itself through its literature. Until the American Revolution, the continent's citizens identified largely with England, but after independence, an immediate call went out to develop an American national voice. Not until the 1820s, however, did writers take up the two aspects of American life that had no counterpart in Europe: the untamed wilderness and the frontier experience.

James Fenimore Cooper is credited with creating the first truly American literature with *The Pioneers* (1823). In Cooper's 'everyman' humor and individualism, Americans first recognized themselves.

In his essay *Nature* (1836), Ralph Waldo Emerson articulated similar ideas, but in more philosophical and spiritual terms. Emerson claimed that nature reflected God's instructions for humankind as plainly as the Bible did, and that individuals could understand these through rational thought and self-reliance. Emerson's writings became the core of the transcendentalist movement, which Henry David Thoreau championed in *Walden; or, Life in the Woods* (1854).

Literary highlights of this era include Herman Melville's ambitious *Moby Dick* (1851) and Nathaniel Hawthorne's examination of the dark side of conservative New England in *The Scarlet Letter* (1850). Canonical poet Emily Dickinson wrote haunting, tightly structured poems, which were first published in 1890, four years after her death.

The Civil War & Beyond

The celebration of common humanity and nature reached its apotheosis in Walt Whitman, whose poetry collection *Leaves of Grass* (1855) signaled the arrival of an American literary visionary. In Whitman's informal, intimate, rebellious free verse were songs of individualism, democracy, earthy spirituality, taboo-breaking sexuality and joyous optimism that encapsulated the heart of a throbbing new nation.

But not everything was coming up roses. Abolitionist Harriet Beecher Stowe's controversial novel *Uncle Tom's Cabin* (1852) depicted African American life under slavery with Christian romanticism but also enough realism to inflame passions on both sides of the 'great debate' over slavery, which would shortly plunge the nation into civil war.

After the Civil War (1861–65), two enduring literary trends emerged: realism and regionalism. Regionalism was especially spurred by the rapid late-19th-century settlement of the West; novelist Jack London serialized his adventures for popular magazines such as the *Saturday Evening Post*.

However, it was Samuel Clemens (aka Mark Twain) who came to define American letters. In *Adventures of Huckleberry Finn* (1884), Twain made explicit the quintessential American narrative of an individual journey of self-discovery. The image of Huck and Jim – a poor white teenager and a runaway black slave – standing outside society's norms and floating together toward an uncertain future down the Mississippi River challenges American society still. Twain wrote in the vernacular, loved 'tall tales' and reveled in satirical humor and absurdity, while his folksy, 'anti-intellectual' stance endeared him to everyday readers.

Disillusionment & Diversity

With the dramas of world wars and a newly industrialized society for artistic fodder, American literature came into its own in the 20th century.

Dubbed the 'Lost Generation,' many US writers, most famously Ernest Hemingway, became expats in Europe. His novels exemplified the era, and his spare, stylized realism has often been imitated, yet never bettered. Other notable American figures at Parisian literary salons included modernist writers Gertrude Stein and Ezra Pound, and iconoclast Henry Miller, whose semiautobiographical novels were published in Paris, only to be banned for obscenity and pornography in the USA until the 1960s.

F Scott Fitzgerald eviscerated East Coast society life with his fiction, while John Steinbeck became the great voice of rural working poor in the West, especially during the Great Depression. William Faulkner examined the South's social rifts in dense prose riddled with bullets of black humor.

Between the world wars, the Harlem Renaissance also flourished, as African American intellectuals and artists took pride in their culture and undermined racist stereotypes. Among the most well-known writers were poet Langston Hughes and novelist Zora Neale Hurston.

After WWII, American writers delineated ever-sharper regional and ethnic divides, pursued stylistic experimentation and often caustically repudiated conservative middle-class American values. Writers of the 1950s Beat Generation, such as Jack Kerouac, Allen Ginsburg and Lawrence Ferlinghetti, threw themselves like Molotov cocktails onto the profusion of smug suburban lawns. Meanwhile, novelists JD Salinger, Russian immigrant Vladimir Nabokov, Ken Kesey and poet Sylvia Plath darkly chronicled descents into madness by characters who struggled against stifling social norms.

The South, always ripe with paradox, inspired masterful short-story writers and novelists Flannery O'Connor and Eudora Welty and novelist Dorothy Allison. The mythical romance and modern tragedies of the West have found their champions in Chicano writer Rudolfo Anaya, Larry McMurtry and Cormac McCarthy, whose characters poignantly tackle the rugged realities of Western life.

On the subject of Mark Twain's influence on American letters, Ernest Hemingway once declared, 'All modern American literature comes from one book by Mark Twain called *Huckleberry Finn*. There was nothing before. And there has been nothing as good since.'

African American writers rose in the 20th century, led by Richard Wright (*Black Boy*, 1945) and Ralph Ellison (*Invisible Man*, 1952). James Baldwin became a groundbreaking openly gay writer (*Giovanni's Room*, 1956) while African American women writers were led by Toni Morrison (*The Bluest Eye*, 1970), Maya Angelou (*I Know Why the Caged Bird Sings*, 1971) and Alice Walker (*The Color Purple*, 1982).

As the 20th century ended, American literature became ever more personalized, starting with the 'me' decade of the 1980s. Narcissistic, often nihilistic narratives by writers such as Jay McInerney and Brett Easton Ellis, catapulted the 'Brat Pack' into pop culture.

Since the 1990s, an increasingly diverse, multiethnic panoply of voices reflects the kaleidoscopic society Americans live in. Ethnic identity (especially that of immigrant cultures), regionalism and narratives of self-discovery remain at the forefront of American literature, no matter how experimental. The quarterly journal *McSweeney's*, founded by Dave Eggers (*A Heartbreaking Work of Staggering Genius*, 2000), publishes titans of contemporary literature such as the prolific Joyce Carol Oates and Michael Chabon, both Pulitzer Prize winners. Watch out for the next novel by emerging novelists like Nicole Krauss, Junot Diaz, Gary Shytengart and Jonathan Safran-Foer. For a sweeping, almost panoramic look at American society, read Jonathan Franzen's *The Corrections* or *Freedom*, the 2010 novel that wowed critics at home and abroad, prompting London's *Guardian* to deem it 'the novel of the century.'

More recent literary hits include Kevin Powers' *The Yellow Birds* (2012), a powerfully written tale of young American soldiers on their first tour in Iraq. In 2013, the reclusive award-winning author Thomas Pynchon published *Bleeding Edge*, a bold and labyrinthine novel set in NYC during the terrorist attacks of September 11.

Edgar Allan Poe was the first American writer to achieve international acclaim. His gruesome stories (such as 'The Tell-Tale Heart,' 1843) helped popularize the short-story form, and he is credited with inventing the mystery story, the horror story and science fiction, all extremely popular and enduring genres in America.

Painting & Sculpture

An ocean away from Europe's aristocratic patrons, religious commissions and historic art academies, colonial America was not exactly fertile ground for the visual arts. Since then, thankfully, times have changed: once a swampy Dutch trading post, New York is the red-hot center of the art world, and its make-or-break influence shapes tastes across the nation and around the globe.

Shaping a National Identity

Artists played a pivotal role in the USA's 19th-century expansion, disseminating images of far-flung territories and reinforcing the call to Manifest Destiny. Thomas Cole and his colleagues in the Hudson River School translated European romanticism to the luminous wild landscapes of upstate New York, while Frederic Remington offered idealized, often stereotypical portraits of the Western frontier.

After the Civil War and the advent of industrialization, realism increasingly became prominent. Eastman Johnson painted nostalgic scenes of rural life, as did Winslow Homer, who later became renowned for watercolor seascapes.

Top US
Photo-
graphers

Ansel Adams

Walker Evans

Man Ray

Alfred Stieglitz

Richard Avedon

Robert Frank

Dorothea Lange

Cindy Sherman

Edward Weston

Diane Arbus

Lee Friedlander

An American Avant-Garde

Polite society's objections to Eakins' painting had nothing on the near-riots inspired by New York's Armory Show of 1913. This exhibition introduced the nation to European modernism and changed the face of American art. It showcased impressionism, fauvism and cubism, including the notorious 1912 *Nude Descending a Staircase, No. 2* by Marcel Duchamp, a French artist who later became an American citizen.

New York's 1913 Armory Show was merely the first in a series of exhibitions evangelizing the radical aesthetic shifts of European modernism, and it was inevitable that American artists would begin to grapple with what they had seen. Alexander Calder, Joseph Cornell and Isamu Noguchi produced sculptures inspired by surrealism and constructivism; the precisionist paintings of Charles Demuth, Georgia O'Keeffe and Charles Sheeler combined realism with a touch of cubist geometry.

In the 1930s the Works Progress Administration's (WPA) Federal Art Project, part of President Franklin D Roosevelt's New Deal, commissioned murals, paintings and sculptures for public buildings nationwide. WPA artists borrowed from Soviet social realism and Mexican muralists to forge a socially engaged figurative style with regional flavor.

Abstract Expressionism

In the wake of WWII, American art underwent a sea change at the hands of New York school painters such as Franz Kline, Jackson Pollock and Mark Rothko. Moved by surrealism's celebration of spontaneity and the unconscious, these artists explored abstraction and its psychological potency through imposing scale and the gestural handling of paint. The movement's 'action painter' camp went extreme; Pollock, for example, made his drip paintings by pouring and splattering pigments over large canvases.

Having stood the test of time, abstract expressionism is widely considered to be the first truly original school of American art.

Art + Commodity = Pop

Once established in America, abstract expressionism reigned supreme. However, stylistic revolts had begun much earlier, in the 1950s. Most notably, Jasper Johns came to prominence with thickly painted renditions of ubiquitous symbols, including targets and the American flag, while Robert Rauschenberg assembled artworks from comics, ads and even – à la Duchamp – found objects (a mattress, a tire, a stuffed goat). Both artists helped break down traditional boundaries between painting and sculpture, opening the field for pop art in the 1960s.

America's postwar economic boom also influenced pop. Not only did artists embrace representation, they drew inspiration from consumer images such as billboards, product packaging and media icons. Employing mundane mass-production techniques to silkscreen paintings of movie stars and Coke bottles, Andy Warhol helped topple the myth of the solitary artist laboring heroically in the studio. Roy Lichtenstein combined newsprint's humble Benday dots with the representational conventions of comics. Suddenly, so-called 'serious' art could be political, bizarre, ironic and fun – and all at once.

Minimalism

What became known as minimalism shared pop's interest in mass production, but all similarities ended there. Like the abstract expressionists, artists such as Donald Judd, Agnes Martin and Robert Ryman eschewed representational subject matter; their cool, reductive works of the 1960s and '70s were often arranged in gridded compositions and fabricated from industrial materials.

The '80s & Beyond

By the 1980s, civil rights, feminism and AIDS activism had made inroads in visual culture; artists not only voiced political dissent through their work but embraced a range of once-marginalized media, from textiles and graffiti to video, sound and performance. The decade also ushered in the so-called Culture Wars, which commenced with tumult over photographs by Robert Mapplethorpe and Andres Serrano.

To get the pulse of contemporary art in the US, check out works by artists like Jenny Holzer, Kara Walker, Chuck Close, Martin Puryear and Frank Stella.

ARTS & ARCHITECTURE PAINTING & SCULPTURE

ANDY WARHOL

Pop art icon Andy Warhol turned the art world on its head in the early 1960s with his celebrity portraits of figures such as Marilyn Monroe and Jackie Onassis that at once commented on celebrity and commercial culture while making the American public look at these legendary figures in a startling new light.

Theater

American theater is a three-act play of sentimental entertainment, classic revivals and urgent social commentary. From the beginning, Broadway musicals (www.livebroadway.com) have aspired to be 'don't-miss-this-show!' tourist attractions. And today, they continue to be one of NYC's biggest draws. Broadway shows earn over a billion dollars in revenue from ticket sales each year, with top shows pulling in a cool $2 million a week. The most successful Broadway shows often go on to even greater earnings world-wide. (Gross earnings globally of *The Phantom of the Opera* topped an astounding $5.6 billion.) Meanwhile, long-running classics such as *The Lion King* and *Wicked* continue to play before sold-out houses. Keep an eye out for the much-loved classic, *Les Miserables*, set to return to Broadway in 2014.

Independent theater arrived in the 1920s and '30s, with the Little Theatre Movement, which emulated progressive European theater and developed into today's 'off-Broadway' scene. Always struggling and scraping, and mostly surviving, the country's 1500 nonprofit regional theaters are breeding grounds for new plays and foster new playwrights.

AMERICA DANCES

America fully embraced dance in the 20th century. New York City has always been the epicenter for dance innovation and the home of many premier dance companies, but every major city supports resident and touring troupes, both ballet and modern.

Modern ballet is said to have begun with Russian-born choreographer George Balanchine's *Apollo* (1928) and *Prodigal Son* (1929). With these, Balanchine invented the 'plotless ballet' – in which he choreographed the inner structure of music, not a pantomimed story – and thereby created a new, modern vocabulary of ballet movement. In 1934, Balanchine founded the School of American Ballet; in 1948 he founded the New York City Ballet, turning it into one of the world's foremost ballet companies. Jerome Robbins took over that company in 1983, after achieving fame choreographing huge Broadway musicals, such as *West Side Story* (1957). Broadway remains an important venue for dance today. National companies elsewhere, like San Francisco's Lines Ballet, keep evolving contemporary ballet.

The pioneer of modern dance, Isadora Duncan, didn't find success until she began performing in Europe at the turn of the 20th century. Basing her ideas on ancient Greek myths and concepts of beauty, she challenged the strictures of classical ballet and sought to make dance an intense form of self-expression.

Martha Graham founded the Martha Graham School for Contemporary Dance in 1926 after moving to New York, and many of today's major American choreographers developed under her tutelage. In her long career she choreographed more than 140 works and developed a new dance technique, now taught worldwide, aimed at expressing inner emotion and dramatic narrative. Her most famous work was *Appalachian Spring* (1944).

Merce Cunningham, Paul Taylor and Twyla Tharp succeeded Graham as leading exponents of modern dance; they all have companies that are active today. In the 1960s and '70s, Cunningham explored abstract expressionism in movement, collaborating famously with musician John Cage. Taylor experimented with everyday movements and expressions, while Tharp is known for incorporating pop music, jazz and ballet.

Another student of Martha Graham, Alvin Ailey, was part of the post-WWII flowering of African American culture. He made his name with *Revelations* (1960), two years after he founded the still-lauded Alvin Ailey American Dance Theater in New York City.

Other celebrated postmodern choreographers include Mark Morris and Bill T Jones. Beyond New York, San Francisco, Los Angeles, Chicago, Minneapolis and Philadelphia are noteworthy for modern dance.

Some also develop Broadway-bound productions, while others sponsor festivals dedicated to the Bard himself, William Shakespeare.

Eugene O'Neill – the first major US playwright, and still widely considered the best – put American drama on the map. After WWII, American playwrights joined the nationwide artistic renaissance. Two of the most famous were Arthur Miller, who famously married Marilyn Monroe and wrote about everything from middle-class male disillusionment to the dark psychology of the mob mentality of the Salem witch trials, and the prolific Southerner Tennessee Williams.

As in Europe, absurdism and the avant-garde marked American theater in the 1960s. Few were more scathing than Edward Albee, who started provoking bourgeois sensibilities. Neil Simon arrived at around the same time; his ever-popular comedies kept Broadway humming for 40 years.

Other prominent, active American dramatists emerging in the 1970s include David Mamet, Sam Shephard and innovative 'concept musical' composer Stephen Sondheim. August Wilson created a monumental 10-play 'Pittsburgh Cycle' dissecting 20th-century African American life.

Today, American theater is evolving in its effort to remain a relevant communal experience in an age of ever-isolating media. Shows including *Breakfast with Mugabe* explore the trauma of the past, while *Avenue Q*, with its trash-talking, love-making puppets, presents a hilarious send-up of life on *Sesame Street*. More immersive experiences such as *Sleep No More* put theater-goers inside the play to wander freely among wildly decorated rooms – including a graveyard, stables, psychiatric ward and ballroom – as the drama (loosely based on *Macbeth*) unfolds around them.

Upton Sinclair's *The Jungle* (1906) shocked the public with its harrowing exposé of Chicago's meatpacking industry, and instantly became a modern classic. Nearly a century later, Eric Schlosser's *Fast Food Nation* (2001) similarly alerted America to the dark underside of the fast-food industry.

Architecture

In the 21st century, computer technology and innovations in materials and manufacturing allow for curving, asymmetrical buildings once considered impossible, if not inconceivable. Architects are being challenged to 'go green,' and the creativity unleashed is riveting, transforming skylines and changing the way Americans think about their built environments. The public's architectural taste remains conservative, but never mind: avant-garde 'starchitects' are revising urban landscapes with radical visions that the nation will catch up with – one day.

The Colonial Period

Perhaps the only lasting indigenous influence on American architecture has been the adobe dwellings of the Southwest. In the 17th and 18th centuries, Spanish colonists incorporated elements of what they called the Native American *pueblo* (village). It reappeared in late-19th and early-20th-century architecture in both the Southwest's Pueblo Revival style and Southern California's Mission Revival style.

Elsewhere until the 20th century, immigrant Americans mainly adopted English and continental European styles and followed their trends. For most early colonists in the eastern US, architecture served necessity rather than taste, while the would-be gentry aped grander English homes, a period well preserved in Williamsburg, Virginia.

After the Revolutionary War, the nation's leaders wanted a style befitting the new republic and adopted neoclassicism. Virginia's capitol, designed by Thomas Jefferson, was modeled on an ancient Roman temple, and Jefferson's own private estate, Monticello, sports a Romanesque rotunda.

Professional architect Charles Bulfinch helped develop the more monumental federal style, which paralleled the English Georgian style. The grandest example is the US Capitol in Washington, DC, which became a model for state legislatures nationwide. As they moved into the 19th

Books Once Banned in America

Are You There, God? It's Me, Margaret
Judy Blume

Lord of the Flies
William Golding

1984
George Orwell

The Catcher in the Rye
JD Salinger

Adventures of Huckleberry Finn
Mark Twain

The Color Purple
Alice Walker

ARTS & ARCHITECTURE ARCHITECTURE

century, Americans, mirroring English fashions, gravitated toward the Greek and Gothic Revival styles, still seen today in many churches and college campuses.

Building the Nation

Meanwhile, small-scale architecture was revolutionized by 'balloon-frame' construction: a light frame of standard-milled timber joined with cheap nails. Easy and economical, balloon-frame stores and houses made possible swift settlement of the expanding west and, later, the surreal proliferation of the suburbs. Home-ownership was suddenly within reach of average middle-class families, making real the enduring American Dream.

After the Civil War, influential American architects studied at Paris' École des Beaux-Arts, and American buildings began to show increasing refinement and confidence. Major examples of the beaux-arts style include Richard Morris Hunt's Biltmore Estate in North Carolina and New York's Public Library.

In San Francisco and other cities across America, Victorian architecture appeared as the 19th century progressed. Among well-to-do classes, larger and fancier private houses added ever more adornments: balconies, turret, towers, ornately painted trim and intricate 'gingerbread' wooden millwork.

In a reaction against Victorian opulence, the Arts and Crafts movement arose after 1900 and remained popular until the 1930s. Its modest bungalows, such as the Gamble House in Pasadena, California, featured locally handcrafted wood and glasswork, ceramic tiles and other artisan details.

ART DECO

Remarkable examples of art-deco skyscrapers include New York City's Chrysler Building and Empire State Building. Art deco simultaneously appeared nationwide in the design of movie houses, train stations, and office buildings across the country, and in neighborhoods like Miami's South Beach.

Reaching for the Sky

By the 1850s, internal iron-framed buildings had appeared in Manhattan, and this freed up urban architectural designs, especially after the advent of Otis hydraulic elevators in the 1880s. The Chicago School of architecture transitioned beyond beaux-arts style to produce the skyscraper – considered the first truly 'modern' architecture, and America's most prominent architectural contribution to the world at that time.

In the 1930s, the influence of art deco – which became instantly popular in the US after the Paris Exposition of 1925 – meant that urban high-rises soared, becoming fitting symbols of America's technical achievements, grand aspirations, commerce and affinity for modernism.

Modernism & Beyond

When the Bauhaus school fled the rise of Nazism in Germany, architects such as Walter Gropius and Ludwig Mies van der Rohe brought their pioneering modern designs to American shores. Van der Rohe landed in Chicago, where Louis Sullivan, considered to be the inventor of the modern skyscraper, was already working on a simplified style of architecture in which 'form ever follows function.' This evolved into the International style, which favored glass 'curtain walls' over a steel frame. IM Pei, who designed Cleveland's Rock and Roll Hall of Fame, is considered the last living high-modernist architect in America.

In the mid-20th century, modernism transitioned into America's suburbs, especially in Southern California. Midcentury modern architecture was influenced not only by the organic nature of Frank Lloyd Wright homes but also the spare, geometric, clean-lined designs of Scandinavia. Post-and-beam construction allowed for walls of sheer glass that gave the illusion of merging indoor and outdoor living spaces. Today, a striking collection of midcentury modern homes and public buildings by Albert Frey, Richard Neutra and other luminaries can be found in Palm Springs, CA.

Rejecting modernism's 'ugly boxes' later in the 20th century, post-modernism reintroduced decoration, color, historical references and whimsy. In this, architects like Michael Graves and Philip Johnson took the lead. Another expression of postmodernism is the brash, mimetic architecture of the Las Vegas Strip, which Pritzker Prize–winning architect Robert Venturi held up as the triumphant antithesis of modernism (he sardonically described the latter as 'less is a bore').

Today, aided and abetted by digital tools, architectural design favors the bold and the unique. Leading this plunge into futurama has been Frank Gehry; his Walt Disney Concert Hall in Los Angeles is but one example. Other notable contemporary architects include Richard Meier (Los Angeles' Getty Center), Thom Mayne (San Francisco's Federal Building) and Daniel Libeskind (San Francisco's Contemporary Jewish Museum and the Denver Art Museum's Hamilton Building).

Even as the recession crippled the American economy in 2008 and stalled new construction, several phenomenal new examples of visionary architecture have burst upon the scene in American cities. Notable examples include Jeanne Gang's Acqua building in Chicago, Peter Bohlin's already-iconic glass cube at New York City's Fifth Avenue Apple Store, and Renzo Piano's stunning (and sustainable) California Academy of Sciences in San Francisco, which includes a 2.5-acre living roof made of 1.7 million native plants.

Famous Literary Recluses

Emily Dickinson (1830-1886)

JD Salinger (1919-2010)

Harper Lee (1926-)

Don DeLillo (1936-)

Thomas Pynchon (1937-)

ARTS & ARCHITECTURE ARCHITECTURE

The Music Scene

American popular music is the nation's heartbeat and its unbreakable soul. It's John Lee Hooker's deep growls and John Coltrane's passionate cascades. It's Hank Williams' yodel and Elvis' pout. It's Beyoncé and Bob Dylan, Duke Ellington and Patti Smith. It's a feeling as much as a form – always a foot-stomping, defiant good time, whether folks are boot scooting to bluegrass, sweating to zydeco, jumping to hip-hop or stage-diving to punk rock.

Blues

The South is the mother of American music, most of which has roots in the frisson and interplay of black-white racial relations. The blues developed after the Civil War, out of the work songs, or 'shouts,' of black slaves and out of black spiritual songs and their 'call-and-response' pattern, both of which were adaptations of African music.

Improvisational and intensely personal, the blues remain at heart an immediate expression of individual pain, suffering, hope, desire and pride. Nearly all subsequent American music has tapped this deep well.

At the turn of the 20th century, traveling blues musicians, and particularly female blues singers, gained fame and employment across the South. Early pioneers included Robert Johnson, WC Handy, Ma Rainey, Huddie Ledbetter (aka Lead Belly) and Bessie Smith, who some consider the best blues singer who ever lived. At the same time, African American Christian choral music evolved into gospel, whose greatest singer, Mahalia Jackson, came to prominence in the 1920s.

After WWII, blues from Memphis and the Mississippi Delta dispersed northward, particularly to Chicago, in the hands of a new generation of musicians such as Muddy Waters, Buddy Guy, BB King, John Lee Hooker and Etta James.

Today's generation of blues players include the likes of Bonamassa, Warren Haynes (a longtime player for the Allman Brothers), Seasick Steve, the Tedeschi Trucks Band and the sometimes-blues players The Black Keys.

The country that spawned the world's most successful recording industry also popularized the technology accused of killing it. From the emergence of file sharing to Apple's 2011 unveiling of the iCloud, a music-streaming service, it's no surprise that the American music industry is under stress – though from its ability to evolve, you'd hardly know it.

Jazz

Down in New Orleans, Congo Sq, where slaves gathered to sing and dance from the late 18th century onward, is considered the birthplace of jazz. There ex-slaves adapted the reed, horn and string instruments used by the city's often French-speaking, multiracial Creoles – who themselves preferred formal European music – to play their own African-influenced music. This fertile cross-pollination produced a steady stream of innovative sounds.

The first variation was ragtime, so-called because of its 'ragged,' syncopated African rhythms. Beginning in the 1890s, ragtime was popularized by musicians such as Scott Joplin, and was made widely accessible through sheet music and player-piano rolls.

Dixieland jazz, centered on New Orleans' infamous Storyville red-light district, soon followed. In 1917 Storyville shut down and New Orleans' jazz musicians dispersed. In 1919 bandleader King Oliver moved to Chicago, and his star trumpet player, Louis Armstrong, soon followed. Armstrong's distinctive vocals and talented improvisations led to the solo becoming an integral part of jazz throughout much of the 20th century.

The Jazz Age & Beyond

The 1920s and '30s are known as the Jazz Age, but music was just part of the greater flowering of African American culture during New York's Harlem Renaissance. Swing – an urbane, big-band jazz style – swept the country, led by innovative bandleaders Duke Ellington and Count Basie. Jazz singers Ella Fitzgerald and Billie Holiday combined jazz with its Southern sibling, the blues.

After WWII, bebop (aka bop) arose, reacting against the smooth melodies and confining rhythms of big-band swing. A new crop of musicians came of age, including Charlie Parker, Dizzy Gillespie and Thelonious Monk. Critics at first derided such 1950s and '60s permutations as cool jazz, hard-bop, free or avant-garde jazz, and fusion (which combined jazz and Latin or rock music) – but there was no stopping the postmodernist tide deconstructing the era. Pioneers of this era include Miles Davis, Dave Brubeck, Chet Baker, Charles Mingus, John Coltrane, Melba Liston and Ornette Coleman.

Country

Early Scottish, Irish and English immigrants brought their own instruments and folk music to America, and what emerged over time in the secluded Appalachian Mountains was fiddle-and-banjo hillbilly, or 'country,' music. In the Southwest, steel guitars and larger bands distinguished 'western' music. In the 1920s, these styles merged into 'country-and-western' music and became centered on Nashville, Tennessee, especially once the *Grand Ole Opry* began its radio broadcasts in 1925. Country musicians that are now 'classics' include Hank Williams, Johnny Cash, Willie Nelson, Patsy Cline and Loretta Lynn.

Country music influenced rock and roll in the 1950s, while rock-flavored country was dubbed 'rockabilly.' In the 1980s, country and western achieved new levels of popularity with stars like Garth Brooks. Today, country-music stations dominate other genres. Musicians with record-breaking success include Shania Twain, Dwight Yoakam, Tim McGraw and Taylor Swift. Occupying the eclectic 'alt country' category are Lucinda Williams and Lyle Lovett.

Folk

The tradition of American folk music was crystallized in Woody Guthrie, who traveled the country during the Depression singing politically conscious songs. In the 1940s, Pete Seeger emerged as a tireless preserver of America's folk heritage. Folk music experienced a revival during 1960s protest movements, but then-folkie Bob Dylan ended it almost single-handedly when he plugged in an electric guitar to shouts of 'traitor!'

Folk has seen a resurgence in the last decade, particularly in the Pacific Northwest. Iron and Wine's mournful tunes channel pop, blues and rock, while Joanna Newsom, with her extraordinary voice and unusual instrumentation (she plays the harp) add a new level of complexity to folk. The young sister duo Lily & Madeleine sing ethereal, incredibly rich folk ballads.

Rock & Roll

Most say rock and roll was born in 1954 the day Elvis Presley walked into Sam Phillips' Sun Studio and recorded 'That's All Right.' Initially, radio stations weren't sure why a white country boy was singing black music, or whether they should play it. Two years later Presley scored his first big breakthrough with 'Heartbreak Hotel.'

Musically, rock and roll was a hybrid of guitar-driven blues, black rhythm and blues (R&B), and white country-and-western music. R&B evolved in the 1940s out of swing and the blues and was then known

PRINCE

One of rock music's most phenomenal success stories, Prince, was born Prince Rogers Nelson in 1950s Minneapolis. He originally tried out for the high-school basketball team, but being too short at 5ft 2in, he was cut. His back-up hobby? He took up the guitar.

as 'race music.' With rock and roll, white performers and some African American musicians transformed 'race music' into something that white youths could embrace freely – and oh, did they.

Rock and roll instantly abetted a social revolution even more significant than its musical one: openly sexual as it celebrated both dancing freely across color lines, rock scared the nation. Authorities worked diligently to control 'juvenile delinquents' and to sanitize and suppress rock and roll, which might have withered if not for the early 1960s 'British invasion,' in which the Beatles and the Rolling Stones, emulating Chuck Berry, Little Richard and others, shocked rock and roll back to life.

The 1960s witnessed a full-blown youth rebellion, epitomized by the drug-inspired psychedelic sounds of the Grateful Dead and Jefferson Airplane, and the electric wails of Janis Joplin and Jimi Hendrix. Ever since, rock has been about music *and* lifestyle, alternately torn between hedonism and seriousness, commercialism and authenticity.

Punk arrived in the late 1970s, led by the Ramones and the Dead Kennedys, as did the working-class rock of Bruce Springsteen and Tom Petty. As the counterculture became the culture in the 1980s, critics prematurely pronounced 'rock is dead.' Rock was saved (by the Talking Heads, REM, Nirvana, Sonic Youth, Pavement and Pearl Jam among others) as it always has been: by splintering and evolving, whether it's called new wave, heavy metal, grunge, indie rock, world beat, skate punk, hardcore, goth, emo or electronica.

Even though hip-hop has become today's outlaw sound, rock remains relevant, and it's not going anywhere. Cue up the Killers, the Yeah Yeah Yeahs, Kings of Leon or the Strokes to hear why. Other heavy hitters of the moment include Vampire Weekend, the National and Band of Horses.

Hip-Hop

From the ocean of sounds coming out of the early 1970s – funk, soul, Latin, reggae, and rock and roll – young DJs from the Bronx in NYC began to spin a groundbreaking mixture of records together in an effort to drive dance floors wild.

And so hip-hop was born. Groups such as Grandmaster Flash and the Furious Five were soon taking the party from the streets to the trendy clubs of Manhattan and mingling with punk and new wave bands including the Clash and Blondie. In parallel, break-out graffiti artists Futura 2000, Keith Haring and Jean-Michel Basquiat moved from the subways and the streets to the galleries, and soon to the worlds of fashion and advertising.

As groups like Run-DMC, Public Enemy and the Beastie Boys sold millions, the sounds and styles of the growing hip-hop culture rapidly diversified. The daring 'gangsta rap' sound of Niggaz With Attitude came out of Los Angeles, and the group got both accolades and bad press for its daring sounds and social commentary – which critics called battle cries for violence – on racism, drugs, sex and urban poverty.

Come the turn of the millennium, what started as some raggedy gang kids playing their parents' funk records at illegal block parties had evolved into a multibillion-dollar business. Russell Simmons and P Diddy stood atop media empires, and stars Queen Latifah and Will Smith were Hollywood royalty. A white rapper from Detroit, Eminem, sold millions of records and hip-hop overtook country as America's second-most-popular music behind pop rock.

Today, many view hip-hop as a vapid wasteland of commercial excess – glorifying consumerism, misogyny, homophobia, drug use and a host of other social ills. But just as the hedonistic days of arena rock and roll gave birth to the rebel child of punk, the evolving offspring of hip-hop and DJ culture are constantly breaking the rules to create something new and even more energizing. Major players of the moment include Jay-Z, Kanye West, Nicki Minaj and the more experimental and feel-good hip-hop duo of Macklemore & Ryan Lewis.

One-Hit Wonders in US Charts

'Tell Him,' The Exciters (1962)

'Just One Look,' Doris Troy (1963)

'Cruel to Be Kind,' Nick Lowe (1979)

'Video Killed the Radio Star,' The Buggles (1979)

'Funkytown,' Lipps, Inc. (1980)

'Turning Japanese,' The Vapors (1980)

'Mickey,' Toni Basil (1982)

'Tainted Love,' Soft Cell (1982)

'Come on Eileen,' Dexys Midnight Runners (1983)

'Rock Me Amadeus,' Falco (1985)

'Baby Got Back,' Sir Mix-a-Lot (1992)

'Whoomp...There It Is,' Tag Team (1993)

'Crazy,' Gnarls Barkley (2006)

The Land & Wildlife

The USA is home to creatures both great and small, from the ferocious grizzly to the indus-trious beaver, with colossal bison, snowy owls, soaring eagles, howling coyotes and doe-eyed manatees all part of the great American menagerie. The nation's varied geography – coastlines along two oceans, mountains, deserts, rain forests, and massive bay and river systems – harbor ecosystems where a wide range of plant and animal life can flourish.

Geography

The USA is big, no question. Covering more than 3.5 million sq miles, it's the world's third-largest country, trailing only Russia and Canada, its friendly neighbor to the north. The continental USA is made up of 48 contiguous states ('the lower 48'), while Alaska, its largest state, is northwest of Canada, and the volcanic islands of Hawaii, the 50th state, are 2600 miles southwest of the mainland in the Pacific Ocean.

It's more than just size, though. America feels big because of its in-credibly diverse topography, which began to take shape around 50 to 60 million years ago.

In the contiguous USA, the east is a land of temperate, deciduous for-ests and contains the ancient Appalachian Mountains, a low range that parallels the Atlantic Ocean. Between the mountains and the coast lies the country's most populated, urbanized region, particularly in the cor-ridor between Washington, DC, and Boston, MA.

Wilderness Films

Winged Migration, by Jacques Perrin

Grizzly Man, by Werner Herzog

Into the Wild, by Sean Penn

White Fang, by Randal Kleiser

RETURN OF THE WOLF

The wolf is a potent symbol of America's wilderness. This smart, social predator is the largest species of canine – averaging more than 100lb and reaching nearly 3ft at the shoulder. An estimated 400,000 once roamed the continent from coast to coast, from Alaska to Mexico.

Wolves were not regarded warmly by European settlers. The first wildlife legislation in the British colonies was a wolf bounty. As 19th-century Americans tamed the West, they slaughtered the once-uncountable herds of bison, elk, deer and moose, replacing them with domestic cattle and sheep, which wolves found equally tasty.

To stop wolves from devouring the livestock, the wolf's extermination soon became official government policy. Up until 1965, for $20 to $50 an animal, wolves were shot, poisoned, trapped and dragged from dens until in the lower 48 states only a few hun-dred gray wolves remained in northern Minnesota and Michigan.

In 1944, naturalist Aldo Leopold called for the return of the wolf. His argument was ecology, not nostalgia. His studies showed that wild ecosystems need their top preda-tors to maintain a healthy biodiversity; in complex interdependence, all animals and plants suffered with the wolf gone.

Despite dire predictions from ranchers and hunters, gray wolves were reintroduced to the Greater Yellowstone Region in 1995–96 and red wolves to Arizona in 1998.

Protected and encouraged, wolf populations have made a remarkable recovery, with more than 5500 now counted in the wild.

AMERICA'S WORST NATURAL DISASTERS

Earthquakes, wildfires, tornadoes, hurricanes and blizzards – the US certainly has its share of natural disasters. A few of the more infamous events that have shaped the national conscience:

Galveston Hurricane In 1900 Galveston – then known as 'the jewel of Texas' – was practically obliterated by a category-4 hurricane. Fifteen-foot waves destroyed buildings and at one point the entire island was submerged. More than 8000 perished, making it America's deadliest natural disaster.

1906 San Francisco Earthquake A powerful earthquake (estimated to be around an 8 on the Richter scale) leveled the city, followed by even more devastating fires. The quake was felt as far away as Oregon and Central Nevada. An estimated 3000-plus died, while more than 200,000 people (of a population of 410,000) were left homeless.

Dust Bowl During a prolonged drought of the 1930s, the overworked topsoil of the Great Plains dried up, turned to dust and billowed eastward in massive windstorm-fueled 'black blizzards', reaching all the way to NYC and Washington, DC. Millions of acres of crops were decimated and more than 500,000 people were left homeless. The great exodus westward by stricken farmers and migrants was immortalized in John Steinbeck's *The Grapes of Wrath*.

Hurricane Katrina August 29, 2005, is not a day easily forgotten in New Orleans. A massive category-5 hurricane swept across the Gulf of Mexico and slammed into Louisiana. As levees failed, floods inundated more than 80% of the city. The death toll reached 1836, with more than $100 billion in estimated damages – making it America's costliest natural disaster. Heartbreaking images of the destroyed city, and anger over the government's response, still linger.

Tornado Alley In 2011 the US experienced its largest tornado outbreak in recorded history. More than 300 tornadoes raged across 21 states over three harrowing days. Amazingly, this occurred just weeks after the second-largest tornado outbreak in US history. The storms left more than 300 dead and $10 billion in damages.

Hurricane Sandy In 2012 America suffered its second-costliest hurricane in US history. It affected some 24 states, with New Jersey and New York among the hardest hit. More than 80 died in the USA, and estimated damages amounted to more than $68 billion. It was also the largest Atlantic hurricane ever recorded, with storm winds spanning over 1000 miles.

One of the most fascinating theories about the planet is James Lovelock's Gaia hypothesis, which proposes that the earth is a living, complex, self-regulating organism. Read about Lovelock's mind-blowing ideas in *The Ages of Gaia*.

To the north are the Great Lakes, which the USA shares with Canada. These five lakes, part of the Canadian Shield, are the greatest expanse of fresh water on the planet, constituting nearly 20% of the world's supply.

Going south along the East Coast, things get wetter and warmer till you reach the swamps of southern Florida and make the turn into the Gulf of Mexico, which provides the USA with a southern coastline.

West of the Appalachians are the vast interior plains, which lie flat all the way to the Rocky Mountains. The eastern plains are the nation's breadbasket, roughly divided into the northern 'corn belt' and the southern 'cotton belt.' The plains, an ancient sea bottom, are drained by the mighty Mississippi River, which together with the Missouri River forms the world's fourth-longest river system, surpassed only by the Nile, Amazon and Yangtze Rivers. Going west, farmland slowly gives way to cowboys and ranches in the semiarid, big-sky Great Plains.

The young, jagged Rocky Mountains are a complex set of tall ranges that run all the way from Mexico to Canada, providing excellent skiing. West of these mountains are the Southwestern deserts, an arid region of extremes that has been cut to dramatic effect by the Colorado River system. This land of eroded canyons leads to the unforgiving Great Basin as you go across Nevada. Also an ancient sea bottom, the Great Basin is where the military practices and where the USA plans to bury its nuclear waste.

Then you reach America's third major mountain system: the southern, granite Sierra Nevada and the northern, volcanic Cascades, which both parallel the Pacific Coast. California's Central Valley is one of the most fertile places on earth, and the coastline from San Diego to Seattle is celebrated in folk songs and Native American legends – a stretch of sandy beaches and old-growth forests, including coast redwoods.

But wait, there's more. Northwest of Canada, Alaska reaches the Arctic Ocean and contains tundra, glaciers, an interior rainforest and the lion's share of federally protected wilderness. Hawaii, in the Pacific Ocean, is a string of tropical island idylls.

Land Mammals

Nineteenth-century Americans did not willingly suffer competing predators, and federal eradication programs nearly wiped out every single wolf and big cat and many of the bears in continental US. Almost all share the same story of abundance, precipitous loss and, today, partial recovery.

The grizzly bear, a subspecies of brown bear, is one of North America's largest land mammals. Male grizzlies can stand 7ft tall, weigh up to 850lb and consider 500 sq miles home. At one time, perhaps 50,000 grizzlies roamed the West, but by 1975 fewer than 300 remained. Conservation efforts, particularly in the Greater Yellowstone Region, have increased the population in the lower 48 states to around 1300. By contrast, Alaska remains chock-full of grizzlies, with upwards of 30,000. Despite a decline in numbers, black bears survive nearly everywhere. Smaller than grizzlies, these opportunistic, adaptable and curious animals can survive on very small home ranges.

Another extremely adaptable creature is the coyote, which looks similar to a wolf but is about half the size, ranging from 15lb to 45lb. An icon of the Southwest, coyotes are found all over, even in cities. The USA has one primary big-cat species, which goes by several names: mountain lion, cougar, puma and panther. In the east, a remnant population of panthers

Unusual Wildlife Reads

Rats, by Robert Sullivan

Pigeons, by Andrew Blechman

Cod, by Mark Kurlansky

Ants, by Bert Hölldobler & EO Wilson

Secret Life of Lobsters, by Trevor Corson

WILDLIFE WATCHING: USA'S ENDANGERED SPECIES

Currently, more than 1300 plants and animals are listed in the USA as either endangered or threatened. Although all endangered species are vital to the ecosystem, if it's brag-worthy animals that you're keen to see (and photograph), here are places to spot them before (gulp) it's too late:

Bighorn sheep Anza-Borrego Desert State Park, CA, and Zion National Park, UT

California condor Big Sur, CA, and Grand Canyon National Park, AZ

Desert tortoise Mojave National Preserve, CA

Florida panther Everglades National Park, FL

Gray wolf Yellowstone National Park, WY

Hawaiian goose Haleakalā National Park, HI

Hawaiian monk seal Waikiki Aquarium, HI

Manatee Everglades National Park, FL

Mexican long-nosed bat Big Bend National Park, TX

Whooping cranes Arkansas National Wildlife Refuge, TX, and Bosque del Apache National Wildlife Refuge, NM

is defended within Everglades National Park. In the west, mountain lions are common enough for human encounters to be on the increase. These powerful cats are about 150lb of pure muscle, with short tawny fur, long tails and a secretive nature.

The story of the great American buffalo is a tragic one. These massive herbivores numbered as many as 65 million in 1800 – in herds so thick they 'darkened the whole plains,' as explorers Lewis and Clark wrote. They were killed for food, hides, sport and to impoverish Native Americans, who depended on them for survival. By the 20th century, only a few hundred bison remained. Overcoming near extinction, new herds arose from these last survivors, so that one of America's noblest animals can again be admired in its gruff majesty – among other places, in Yellowstone, Grand Teton and Badlands National Parks.

Marine Mammals & Fish

Perhaps no native fish gets more attention than salmon, whose spawning runs up Pacific Coast rivers provide famous spectacles. However, both Pacific and Atlantic salmon are considered endangered; hatcheries release millions of young every year, but there is debate about whether this practice hurts or helps wild populations.

As for marine life, gray, humpback and blue whales migrate annually along the Pacific Coast, making whale-watching very popular. Alaska and Hawaii are important breeding grounds for whales and marine mammals, and Washington State's San Juan Islands are visited by orcas. The Pacific Coast is also home to ponderous elephant seals, playful sea lions and endangered sea otters.

In California, Channel Islands National Park and Monterey Bay preserve unique, highly diverse marine worlds. For coral reefs and tropical fish, Hawaii and the Florida Keys are the prime destinations. The coast of Florida is also home to the unusual, gentle manatee, which moves between freshwater rivers and the ocean. Around 10ft long and weighing on average 1000lb, these agile, expressive creatures number around 3800 today, and may once have been mistaken for mermaids.

The Gulf of Mexico is another vital marine habitat, perhaps most famously for endangered sea turtles, which nest on coastal beaches.

Birds

Birding is the most popular wildlife-watching activity in the US, and little wonder – all the hemisphere's migratory songbirds and shorebirds rest here at some point, and the USA consequently claims some 800 native avian species.

The bald eagle was adopted as the nation's symbol in 1782. It's the only eagle unique to North America, and perhaps half a million once ruled the continent's skies. By 1963, habitat destruction and, in particular, poisoning from DDT had caused the population to plummet to 487 breeding pairs in the lower 48. By 2006, however, bald eagles had recovered so well, increasing to almost 9800 breeding pairs across the continent (plus 50,000 in Alaska), that they've now been removed from the endangered species list.

Another impressive bird is the endangered California condor, a prehistoric, carrion-eating bird that weighs about 20lb and has a wingspan over 9ft. Condors were virtually extinct by the 1980s (reduced to just 22 birds), but they have been successfully bred and reintroduced in California and northern Arizona, where they can sometimes be spotted soaring above the Grand Canyon.

High in the White Mountains (east of California's Sierra Nevada) stand the oldest single living plant species on earth. Known as bristlecone pines, these bare and dramatically twisted trees date back more than 4000 years and have long mystified scientists for their extraordinary longevity.

The fastest bird in North America is believed to be the peregrine falcon, which has been clocked diving for prey at speeds of up to 175mph.

The Environmental Movement

The USA is well known for its political and social revolutions, but it also birthed environmentalism. The USA was the first nation to make significant efforts to preserve its wilderness, and US environmentalists often spearhead preservation efforts worldwide.

America's Protestant settlers believed that civilization's Christian mandate was to bend nature to its will. Not only was wilderness deadly and difficult, but it was a potent symbol of humanity's godless impulses, and the Pilgrims set about subduing both with gusto.

Then, in the mid-19th century, taking their cue from European Romantics, the USA's transcendentalists claimed that nature was not fallen, but holy. In *Walden; or, Life in the Woods* (1854), iconoclast Henry David Thoreau (1817–62) described living for two years in the woods, blissfully free of civilization's comforts. He persuasively argued that human society was harmfully distant from nature's essential truths. This view marked a profound shift toward believing that nature, the soul and God were one.

The Sierra Club (www.sierraclub.org) was the USA's first conservation group and it remains the nation's most active, with educational programs, organized trips and tons of information.

IT'S NOT EASY BEING GREEN

The USA has long been one of the world's greatest consumers of energy, accounting for a quarter of the world's greenhouse gases. Sustainability, however, seems to be on everyone's lips these days, and interest in renewable energy is at an all-time high.

Though enormous obstacles lie ahead, the US has made marked advances in lowering its carbon footprint.

Winds of change Although wind energy generates about 3.8% of the nation's electricity, the US is the world's second-largest producer of wind energy (after China), and shows enormous potential for growth. The US Department of Energy envisions 20% of the nation's power supplied by this clean energy by 2030.

Solar power Interest in solar power is high – with solar power growing at a rate of 40% per year. The US currently generates roughly half of the world's solar energy. Ambitions are grand for solar plants (including three massive 500MW plants under construction in the west), though private citizens and small businesses are also contributing, adding solar panels to help meet energy needs.

Biofuels The USA is now the world's largest producer of ethanol (fuel made from corn and other common crops). As of 2013, it accounted for roughly 10% of the nation's total domestic fuel consumption – a big jump from 2001 when it was only 1%.

Electric cars American automobile manufacturers, once wedded to gas-guzzling SUVs and trucks, have responded to consumer demand for more fuel-efficient cars. More than 18,000 plug-in electric vehicles are sold annually, with growing numbers on the horizon. More than 5000 charging stations are scattered across the country. The US government has also pledged over $2 billion in federal grants to support the development of next-generation electric cars as well as expanding electric vehicle charging infrastructure.

Ecofriendly architecture Green buildings have arrived and are garnering much attention at home and abroad. Energy-efficient windows, more ecofriendly building materials and water conservation features (such as greywater systems that utilize rainwater) are just a few features of LEED-certified buildings emerging nationwide.

Greenways Back in the 1980s, the notion of riding a bicycle down Broadway in New York City seemed pure suicide. Today, NYC – along with Chicago, Boston, Washington, DC, and other cities – has added hundreds of miles of bike lanes, and urbanites are finding greener (and sometimes faster) ways of getting around town.

John Muir & National Parks

The continent's natural wonders – vividly captured by America's 19th-century landscape painters – had a way of selling themselves, and rampant nationalism led to a desire to promote them. In the late 1800s, US presidents began setting aside land for state and national parks.

Scottish naturalist John Muir (1838–1914) soon emerged to champion wilderness for its own sake. Muir considered nature superior to civilization, and he spent much of his life wandering the Sierra Nevada mountain range and passionately advocating on its behalf. Muir was the driving force behind the USA's emerging conservation movement, which had its first big victory in 1890 when Yosemite National Park was established. Muir founded the Sierra Club in 1892 and slowly gained national attention.

Reading Climate Change

Field Notes from a Catastrophe, Elizabeth Kolbert

The Weather Makers, Tim Flannery

Eaarth, Bill McKibben

The Great Disruption, Paul Gilding

Environmental Laws & Climate Change

Over the following decades, the USA passed a series of landmark environmental and wildlife laws that resulted in significant improvements in the nation's water and air quality, and the partial recovery of many near-extinct plants and animals. The movement's focus steadily broadened – to preserving entire ecosystems, not just establishing parks – as it confronted devastation wrought by pollution, overkill of species, habitat destruction through human impact and the introduction of non-native species.

Today, environmentalism is a worldwide movement, one that understands that each nation's local problems also contribute to a global threat: climate change. In the USA, the dangers of global warming are inspiring an environmental awareness as widespread as at any time in US history. Whether or not average Americans believe God speaks through nature, they're increasingly disturbed by the messages they are hearing.

Survival Guide

Directory A–Z

Accommodations

For all but the cheapest places and the slowest seasons, reservations are advised. In high-season tourist hot spots, hotels can book up months ahead. In general, many hotels offer specials on their websites, but low-end chains sometimes give a slightly better rate over the phone. Chain hotels also increasingly offer frequent-flyer mileage deals and other rewards programs; ask when booking. Online travel booking, bidding and comparison websites are another good way to find discounted hotel rates – but are usually limited to chain hotels; also check out **Hotels.com**

SLEEPING PRICE RANGES

Accommodations rates are based on double occupancy for high season (generally May to September), and don't include taxes, which can add 10% to 15%. When booking, ask for the rate including taxes.

$ less than $100

$$ $100 to $200

$$$ more than $200

(www.hotels.com), **Hotwire** (www.hotwire.com) and **Booking.com** (www.booking.com).

House & Apartment Rentals

To rent a house or apartment from locals, visit **Airbnb** (www.airbnb.com), which has thousands of listings across the country. Budget travelers can also rent a room; a great way to connect with locals if you don't mind sharing facilities.

B&Bs

In the USA, many B&Bs are high-end romantic retreats in restored historic homes that are run by personable, independent innkeepers who serve gourmet breakfasts. These B&Bs often take pains to evoke a theme – Victorian, rustic, Cape Cod and so on – and amenities range from merely comfortable to indulgent. Rates normally top $100, and the best run are from $200 to $300. Some B&Bs have minimum-stay requirements, and most exclude young children.

European-style B&Bs also exist: these may be rooms in someone's home, with plainer furnishings, simpler breakfasts, shared baths and cheaper rates. These often welcome families.

B&Bs can close out of season and reservations are essential, especially for top-end places. To avoid surprises, always ask about bathrooms (whether shared or private).

B&B agencies are sprinkled throughout this guide. Also check listings online:

Bed & Breakfast Inns Online (www.bbonline.com)

BedandBreakfast.com (www.bedandbreakfast.com)

BnB Finder (www.bnbfinder.com)

Select Registry (www.selectregistry.com)

Hostels

Hostels are mainly found in urban areas, in the northeast, the Pacific Northwest, California and the Southwest.

Hostelling International USA (📞240-650-2100; www.hiusa.org) runs more than 50 hostels in the US. Most have gender-segregated dorms, a few private rooms, shared baths and a communal kitchen. Overnight fees for dorm beds range from $23 to $54 (NYC being the priciest). HI-USA members are entitled to small discounts. Reservations are accepted (you can book online) and advised during high season, when there may be a three-night maximum stay.

The USA has many independent hostels not affiliated with HI-USA. For online listings, check the following:

Hostels.com (www.hostels.com)

Hostelworld.com (www.hostelworld.com)

Hostelz.com (www.hostelz.com)

Camping

Most federally managed public lands and many state parks offer camping. First-come, first-served 'primitive' campsites offer no facilities; overnight fees range from free to less than $10. 'Basic' sites usually provide toilets (flush or pit), drinking water, fire pits and picnic tables; they cost $5 to $15 a night, and some or all may be reserved in advance. 'Developed' campsites, usually in national or state parks, have nicer facilities and more amenities: showers, barbecue grills, RV sites with hookups etc. These are $15 to $45 a night, and many can be reserved in advance.

Camping on most federal lands – including national parks, national forests and Bureau of Land Management land – can be reserved through **Recreation.gov** (✆877-444-6777, international 518-885-3639; www.recreation. gov). Camping is limited to 14 days and can be reserved up to six months in advance. For some state park campgrounds, you can book through **ReserveAmerica** (✆California State Park Reservations 800-444-7275, Colorado State Park Reservations 800-678-2267, NRRS Federal Campground Reservations 877-444-6777; www.reserveamerica. com). Both websites let you search for campground locations and amenities, check availability, reserve a site, view maps and get driving directions.

Private campgrounds tend to cater to RVs and families (tent sites may be few and lack atmosphere). Facilities may include playgrounds, convenience stores, wi-fi access, swimming pools and other activities. Some rent camping cabins, ranging from canvas-sided wooden platforms to log-frame structures with real beds, heating and private baths. **Kampgrounds of America** (KOA; ✆406-248-7444; www.koa. com) is a national network of private campgrounds with a full range of facilities. You can order KOA's free annual directory (shipping fees apply) or browse its comprehensive campground listings and make bookings online.

Hotels

Hotels in all categories typically include in-room phones, cable TV, private baths and a simple continental breakfast. Many midrange properties provide minibars, microwaves, hairdryers, internet access, air-conditioning and/or heating, swimming pools and writing desks, while top-end hotels add concierge services, fitness and business centers, spas, restaurants, bars and higher-end furnishings.

Even if hotels advertise that children 'sleep free,' cots or rollaway beds may cost extra. Always ask about the hotel's policy for telephone calls; all charge an exorbitant amount for long-distance and international calls, but some also charge for dialing local and toll-free numbers.

Motels

Motels – distinguishable from hotels by having rooms that open onto a parking lot – tend to cluster around interstate exits and on main routes into town. Some remain smaller, less-expensive 'mom-and-pop' operations; breakfast is rarely included, and amenities might be a phone and TV (maybe with cable). Motels often have a few rooms with simple kitchenettes.

Although many motels are of the bland, cookie-cutter variety, these can be good for discount lodging or when other options fall through.

Don't judge a motel solely on looks. Facades may be faded and tired, but the proprietor may keep rooms spotlessly clean. Of course, the reverse could also be true. Try to see your room before you commit.

BOOK YOUR STAY ONLINE

For more accommodations reviews by Lonely Planet authors, check out http://lonelyplanet.com/hotels/ usa. You'll find independent reviews, as well as recommendations on the best places to stay. Best of all, you can book online.

Customs Regulations

For a complete list of US customs regulations, visit the official portal for **US Customs & Border Protection** (www. cbp.gov). Duty-free allowance per person is as follows:

➡ 1L of liquor (provided you are at least 21 years old)

➡ 100 cigars and 200 cigarettes (18 years and up)

➡ $200 worth of gifts and purchases ($800 if you're a returning US citizen)

If you arrive with $10,000 in US or foreign currency, it must be declared.

There are heavy penalties for attempting to import illegal drugs. Forbidden items include drug paraphernalia, lottery tickets, items with fake brand names, and most goods made in Cuba, Iran, North Korea, Myanmar (Burma) and Sudan. Fruit, vegetables or other food or plant material must be declared or left in the arrival area bins.

Discount Cards

Save on museums, accommodations and some transport (including Amtrak):

International Student Identity Card (ISIC: www.isic.org) For international nonstudents under 26.

Student Advantage Card (www.studentadvantage.com) For US and foreign travelers.

American Association of Retired Persons (AARP; www.aarp.org) For US travelers age 50 and older.

Members in the **American Automobile Association** (AAA; www.aaa.com) and reciprocal clubs can also earn discounts.

Electricity

120V/60Hz

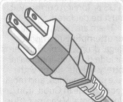

120V/60Hz

Embassies & Consulates

In addition to the following foreign embassies in Washington, DC (see www.embassy.org for a complete list), most countries have an embassy for the UN in New York City.

Some countries have consulates in other large cities; go online, look under 'Consulates' in the yellow pages, or call local directory assistance.

Australian Embassy (☎20 2-797-3000; www.usa.embassy.gov.au; 1601 Massachusetts Ave NW)

Canadian Embassy (☎20 2-682-1740; www.canadainternational.gc.ca; 501 Pennsylvania Ave NW)

French Embassy (☎20 2-644-6000; www.info-france-usa.org; 4101 Reservoir Rd NW)

German Embassy (☎20 2-298-4000; www.germany.info; 2300 M St NW)

Irish Embassy (☎202-462-3939; www.embassyofireland.org; 2234 Massachusetts Ave NW)

Mexican Embassy (☎20 2-728-1600; http://embamex.sre.gob.mx/eua; 1911 Pennsylvania Ave NW)

Netherlands Embassy (☎877-388-2443; http://dc.the-netherlands.org; 4200 Linnean Ave NW)

New Zealand Embassy (☎202-328-4800; www.nzembassy.com/usa; 37 Observatory Circle NW)

UK Embassy (☎20 2-588-6500; www.gov.uk/government/world/usa; 3100 Massachusetts Ave NW)

Food

See p1144 for everything you need to know about food culture in the USA.

FOOD PRICES

Rates for main meals in Eating sections are:

$ less than $10

$$ $10 to $20

$$$ more than $20

Gay & Lesbian Travelers

It's never been a better time to be gay in the USA. GLBT travelers will find lots of places where they can be themselves without thinking twice. Beaches and big cities typically are the most gay-friendly destinations.

In this guide, many cities have a boxed text or section that describes the best offerings for GBLT travelers.

Hot Spots

Manhattan has loads of great gay bars and clubs, especially in Hells Kitchen, Chelsea and the West Village. A few hours away (by train and ferry) is Fire Island, the sandy gay mecca on Long Island. Other East Coast cities that flaunt it are Boston, Philadelphia, Washington, DC, Massachusetts' Provincetown on Cape Cod and Delaware's Rehoboth Beach. Even Maine brags a gay beach destination: Ogunquit.

In the South, there's always steamy 'Hotlanta' and Texas gets darn-right gay-friendly in Austin and parts of Houston. In Florida, Miami and the 'Conch Republic' of Key West support thriving gay communities, though Fort Lauderdale attracts bronzed boys and girls too. Of course, everyone gets their freak on in New Orleans.

In the Midwest, seek out Chicago and Minneapolis. Further west, you'll find San Francisco, probably the happiest gay city in America. There's also Los Angeles and Las Vegas, where pretty much anything goes. When LA or Vegas gets to be too much, flee to the desert resorts of Palm Springs.

Lastly, for an island idyll, Hawaii is generally gay-friendly, especially in Waikiki.

Attitudes

Most major US cities have a visible and open GLBT community that is easy to connect with.

The level of acceptance varies nationwide. In some places, there is absolutely no tolerance whatsoever, and in others acceptance is predicated on GLBT people not 'flaunting' their sexual preference or identity. Bigotry still exists. In rural areas and conservative enclaves, it's unwise to be openly out, as violence and verbal abuse can sometimes occur. When in doubt, assume locals follow a 'don't ask, don't tell' policy. Following a Supreme Court ruling in 2013, same-sex marriage is now legally recognized, and 13 states have same-sex marriages.

Resources

The Queerest Places: A Guide to Gay and Lesbian Historic Sites, by Paula Martinac, is full of juicy details and history, and covers the country. Visit her blog at queerestplaces. wordpress.com.

Advocate (www.advocate. com) Gay-oriented news website reports on business, politics, arts, entertainment and travel.

Damron (www.damron.com) Publishes classic gay travel guides; useful online event calendar.

Gay & Lesbian National Help Center (☑888-843-4564; www.glnh.org; ◷1-9pm Mon-Fri, 9am-2pm Sat, Pacific Standard Time) A national hotline for counseling, information and referrals.

Gay Travel (www.gaytravel. com) Online guides to dozens of US destinations.

Gay Yellow Network (www. glyp.com) Yellow-page listings for more than 30 US cities.

National Gay & Lesbian Task Force (www.thetask-force.org) National activist group's website covers news, politics and current issues.

Out Traveler (www.out-traveler.com) Gay-oriented Hawaii travel articles free online.

Purple Roofs (www.purpleroofs.com) Lists gay-owned and gay-friendly B&Bs and hotels.

Health

The USA offers excellent health care. The problem is that, unless you have good insurance, it can be prohibitively expensive. It's essential to purchase travel health insurance if your regular policy doesn't cover you when you're abroad.

Bring any medications you may need in their original containers, clearly labeled. A signed, dated letter from your physician that describes all medical conditions and medications, including generic names, is also a good idea.

If your health insurance does not cover you for medical expenses abroad, consider supplemental insurance. Check the Travel Services section of the **Lonely Planet** (www.lonelyplanet. com/usa) website for more information. Find out in advance if your insurance plan will make payments directly to providers or reimburse you later for overseas health expenditures.

Medical Checklist

Recommended items for a medical kit:

➡ acetaminophen (Tylenol) or aspirin

➡ antibacterial ointment (eg Bactroban) for cuts and abrasions

➡ antihistamines (for hay fever and allergic reactions)

➡ anti-inflammatory drugs (eg ibuprofen)

➡ bandages, gauze, gauze rolls

➡ sunblock

➡ insect repellent for the skin

Resources

The World Health Organization publishes a superb book, called *International Travel and Health,* which is revised annually and is available free online at www.who.int/ith/en. **MD Travel Health** (www. mdtravelhealth.com) provides travel health recommendations for every country, updated regularly.

It's usually a good idea to consult your government's travel health website before departure:

Australia (www.smarttraveller.gov.au)

Canada (www.hc-sc.gc.ca/index-eng.php)

UK (www.nhs.uk/nhsengland/Healthcareabroad)

Availability & Cost of Health Care

In general, if you have a medical emergency the best bet is for you to find the nearest hospital and go to its emergency room. If the problem isn't urgent, you can call a nearby hospital and ask for a referral to a local physician, which is usually cheaper than a trip to the emergency room. Stand-alone, for-profit urgent-care centers can be convenient, but may perform large numbers of expensive tests, even for minor illnesses.

Pharmacies are abundantly supplied, but you may find that some medications that are available over the counter in your home country (such as Ventolin, for asthma) require a prescription in the USA and, as always, if you don't have insurance to cover the cost of prescriptions, they can be shockingly expensive.

Insurance

No matter how long or short your trip, make sure you have adequate travel insurance, purchased before departure. At a minimum, you need coverage for medical emergencies and treatment, including hospital stays and an emergency flight home if necessary. Medical treatment in the USA is of the highest caliber, but the expense could bankrupt you.

You should also consider getting coverage for luggage theft or loss and trip cancellation. If you already have a home-owner's or renter's policy, see what it will cover and consider getting supplemental insurance to cover the rest. If you have prepaid a large portion of your trip, cancellation insurance is a worthwhile expense. A comprehensive travel insurance policy that covers all these things can cost up to 10% of the total cost of your trip.

If you will be driving, it's essential that you have liability insurance. Car rental agencies offer insurance that covers damage to the rental vehicle and separate liability insurance, which covers damage to people and other vehicles.

Worldwide travel insurance is available at http://www.lonelyplanet.com/travel-insurance. You can buy, extend and claim online anytime – even if you're already on the road.

Internet Access

Travelers will have few problems staying connected in the tech-savvy USA.

This guide uses an internet icon @ when a place has a net-connected computer for public use and the wi-fi icon when it offers wireless internet access, whether free or fee-based. These days, most hotels and some motels have either a public computer terminal or wi-fi (sometimes free, sometimes for a surcharge of $10 or more per day); ask when reserving.

Big cities have a few internet cafes and even wi-fi connected parks and plazas, but in smaller towns, you may have to head to the public library or a copy center to get online if you're not packing a laptop or other web-accessible device. Most libraries have public terminals (though they have time limits) and often wi-fi. Occasionally out-of-state residents are charged a small fee.

If you're not from the US, remember that you will need an AC adapter for your laptop, plus a plug adapter for US sockets; both are available at larger electronics shops, such as Best Buy.

Legal Matters

In everyday matters, if you are stopped by the police, bear in mind that there is no system of paying traffic or other fines on the spot. Attempting to pay a fine to an officer is frowned upon at best and may result in a charge of bribery. For traffic offenses, the police officer or highway patroller will explain the options to you. There is usually a 30-day period to pay a fine. Most matters can be handled by mail.

If you are arrested, you have a legal right to an attorney, and you are allowed to remain silent. There is no legal reason to speak to a police officer if you don't wish to, but never walk away from an officer until given permission to do so. Anyone who is arrested is legally allowed to make one phone call. If you can't afford a lawyer, a public defender will be appointed to you free of charge. Foreign visitors who don't have a lawyer, friend or family member to help should call their embassy; the police will provide the number upon request.

As a matter of principle, the US legal system presumes a person innocent until proven guilty. Each state has its own civil and criminal laws, and what is legal in one state may be illegal in others.

Drinking

Bars and stores often ask for photo ID to prove you are of legal drinking age (ie 21 or over). Being 'carded' is standard practice; don't take it personally. The sale of liquor is subject to local government regulations; some counties prohibit liquor sales on Sunday, after midnight or before breakfast. In 'dry' counties, liquor sales are banned altogether.

Driving

In all states, driving under the influence of alcohol or drugs is a serious offense, subject to stiff fines and even imprisonment.

WI-FI

Wi-fi hot spots don't entirely cover the USA yet, but wireless internet access is common. Most cities and college towns have neighborhood hot spots, and even the smallest towns usually have at least one coffee shop, internet cafe or hotel with wi-fi. You can even connect in the woods: private campgrounds (like KOA) increasingly offer it, and so do some state parks (for example, in California, Michigan, Kentucky and Texas).

The following websites provide lists of free and fee-based wi-fi hot spots nationwide:

➡ www.hotspot-locations.com

➡ http://v4.jiwire.com

➡ www.wififreespot.com

Drugs

Fifteen states treat possession of small amounts of marijuana as a misdemeanor (generally punishable with a fine of around $100 or $200 for the first offense). In addition, Colorado and Washington State have legalized marijuana – but it is still illegal to smoke in public in either state. The legal sale of marijuana is expected to happen in these two states in 2014.

Aside from marijuana, recreational drugs are prohibited by federal and state laws. Possession of any illicit drug, including cocaine, ecstasy, LSD, heroin, hashish or more than an ounce of marijuana, is a felony potentially punishable by a lengthy jail sentence. For foreigners, conviction of any drug offense is grounds for deportation. The exception is first convictions for possession of 30 grams or less of marijuana for your own use.

Maps

For a good road atlas or driving maps, try **Rand McNally** (www.randmcnally.com), available at many bookstores and some gas stations. It also has a road atlas iPad app, which requires no internet connection after it's downloaded. Members of automobile associations may be able to get free high-quality maps from regional offices; AAA has reciprocal agreements with some international auto clubs. For online driving directions and free downloadable maps, visit **Google Maps** (http://maps.google.com)

If you're heading into the backcountry, don't venture out on the trail without a good topographic map, often sold at park visitor centers, outdoor outfitters and supply stores. The most detailed topo maps are published by the **US Geological Survey** (USGS; ☎888-275-8747; www.store.usgs.gov), which offers online downloads and orders; the website has a comprehensive list of retailers. You can pay

to create custom, downloadable topo maps at **Trails.com** (www.trails.com) or buy personalized topo-map creation software from **National Geographic** (www.nationalgeographic.com); its online store has all the mapping products you'd ever want.

For on- and off-road driving and outdoor adventures on foot and bicycle, GPS gear and mapping software are available from **Garmin** (www.garmin.com) and **Magellan** (Map p919; www.magellangps.com). Of course, GPS units can sometimes fail and may not work in all areas of the country, such as in thick forests or deep canyons.

Money

Most locals do not carry large amounts of cash for everyday use, relying instead

on credit cards, ATMs and debit cards. Smaller businesses may refuse to accept bills larger than $20. Prices quoted in this book are in US dollars and exclude taxes, unless otherwise noted.

ATMs

ATMs are available 24/7 at most banks, and in shopping centers, airports, grocery stores and convenience shops. Most ATMs charge a service fee of $2.50 or more per transaction and your home bank may impose additional charges. Withdrawing cash from an ATM using a credit card usually incurs a hefty fee; check with your credit-card company first.

For foreign visitors, ask your bank or credit-card company for exact information about using cards in stateside ATMs. If you will be relying on ATMs (not a bad strategy), bring more than one card and carry them separately. The exchange rate on ATM transactions is usually as good as you'll get anywhere. Before leaving home, notify your bank and credit-card providers of your upcoming travel plans. Otherwise, you may trigger fraud alerts with atypical spending patterns, which may result in your accounts being temporarily frozen.

Credit Cards

Major credit cards are almost universally accepted. In fact, it's almost impossible to rent a car or make phone reservations without one (some airlines require a US credit-card billing address – a hassle if you're booking domestic flights once there). It's highly recommended that you carry at least one credit card, if only for emergencies. Visa and MasterCard are the most widely accepted.

If your credit cards are lost or stolen, contact the issuing company immediately:

American Express (☑800-528-4800; www.americanexpress.com)

Diners Club (☑800-234-6377; www.dinersclub.com)

Discover (☑800-347-2683; www.discover.com)

MasterCard (☑800-627-8372; www.mastercard.com)

SMOKING

As of 2013, 28 states, the District of Columbia and many municipalities across the US were entirely smoke-free in restaurants, bars and workplaces. You may still encounter smoky lobbies in chain hotels and budget-minded inns, but most other accommodations are smoke-free. For more on smoking, see www.cdc.gov.

Visa (☑800-847-2911; www.visa.com)

Currency Exchange

Banks are usually the best places to exchange foreign currencies. Most large city banks offer currency exchange, but banks in rural areas may not. Currency-exchange counters at the airport and in tourist centers typically have the worst rates; ask about fees and surcharges first. **Travelex** (☑877-414-6359; www.travelex.com) is a major currency-exchange company, but **American Express** (☑800-528-4800; www.americanexpress.com) travel offices may offer better rates.

Taxes

Sales tax varies by state and county, and ranges from 5% to 9%. Hotel taxes vary by city from about 10% to over 18% (in NYC).

Tipping

Tipping is *not* optional; only withhold tips in cases of outrageously bad service.

Airport & hotel porters $2 per bag, minimum per cart $5.

Bartenders 10% to 15% per round, minimum per drink $1.

Hotel maids $2 to $4 per night, left under the card provided.

Restaurant servers 15% to 20%, unless a gratuity is already charged on the bill.

Taxi drivers 10% to 15%, rounded up to the next dollar.

Valet parking attendants At least $2 when handed back the keys.

Traveler's Checks

Since the advent of ATMs, traveler's checks are becoming obsolete, except as a trustworthy backup. If you carry them, buy them in US dollars; local businesses may not cash them in a foreign currency. Keep a separate record of their numbers in case they are lost or stolen. American Express and Visa traveler's checks are the most widely accepted.

Opening Hours

Typical opening times are as follows:

Bars 5pm to midnight Sunday to Thursday, to 2am Friday and Saturday.

Banks 8:30am to 4:30pm Monday to Thursday, to 5:30pm Friday (and possibly 9am to noon Saturday).

Nightclubs 10pm to 2am or 4am Thursday to Saturday.

Post offices 9am to 5pm Monday to Friday.

Shopping Malls 9am to 9pm; stores 10am to 6pm Mon-Sat, noon to 5pm Sunday; supermarkets 8am to 8pm, some open 24 hours.

Photography & Video

Print film can be found in a few specialty camera shops. Digital camera memory cards are widely available at chain retailers such as Best Buy and Target.

Some Native American tribal lands prohibit photography and video completely; when it's allowed, you may be required to purchase a permit. Always ask permission if you want to photograph someone close up; anyone who then agrees to be photographed may expect a small tip.

For more advice on picture-taking, consult Lonely Planet's *Travel Photography* book.

Post

For 24-hour postal information, including post office locations and hours, contact the **US Postal Service** (☑800-275-8777; www.usps.gov), which is reliable and inexpensive.

For urgent or important letters and packages domestically or internationally, **Federal Express** (FedEx; ☑800-463-3339; www.fedex.com) and **United Parcel Service** (UPS; ☑800-742-5877; www.ups.com) offer more-expensive door-to-door delivery services.

Postal Rates

The postal rates for 1st-class mail within the USA are 46¢ for letters weighing up to 1oz (20¢ for each additional ounce) and 33¢ for postcards. First-class mail goes up to 13oz, and then priority-mail rates apply.

International airmail rates are $1.10 for a 1oz letter or a postcard.

Sending & Receiving Mail

If you have the correct postage, you can drop mail weighing less than 13oz into any blue mailbox. To send a package weighing 13oz or more, you must go to a post office.

Public Holidays

On the following national public holidays, banks, schools and government offices (including post offices) are closed, and transportation, museums and other services operate on a Sunday schedule. Holidays falling on a weekend are usually observed the following Monday.

New Year's Day January 1

Martin Luther King Jr Day Third Monday in January

Presidents' Day Third Monday in February

Memorial Day Last Monday in May

Independence Day July 4

Labor Day First Monday in September

Columbus Day Second Monday in October

Veterans Day November 11

Thanksgiving Fourth Thursday in November

Christmas Day December 25

During spring break, high school and college students get a week off from school so they can overrun beach towns and resorts. This occurs throughout March and April. For students of all ages, summer vacation runs from June to August.

Safe Travel

Despite its seemingly apocalyptic list of dangers – violent crime, riots, earthquakes, tornadoes – the USA is actually a pretty safe country to visit. The greatest danger for travelers is posed by car accidents (buckle up – it's the law).

Crime

For the traveler it's not violent crime but petty theft that is the biggest concern. When possible, withdraw money from ATMs during the day, or at night in well-lit, busy areas. When driving, don't pick up hitchhikers, and lock valuables in the trunk of your car before arriving at your destination. In hotels, you can secure valuables in room or hotel safes.

Scams

Pack your street smarts. In big cities, don't forget that three-card-monte card games are always rigged, and that expensive electronics, watches and designer items sold on the cheap from sidewalk tables are either fakes or stolen. Those truly fascinated by all the myriad ways small-time American hucksters make a living today (usually with credit card, real estate and investment frauds) can browse the 'Consumer Guides' on the government's website, www.usa.gov.

Natural Disasters

Most areas with predictable natural disturbances – tornadoes in the Midwest, tsunamis in Hawaii, hurricanes in the South, earthquakes in California – have an emergency siren system to alert communities to imminent danger. These sirens are tested periodically at noon, but if you hear one and suspect trouble, turn on a local TV or radio station, which will be broadcasting safety warnings and advice.

The **US Department of Health & Human Services** (www.phe.gov) has preparedness advice, news and information on all the ways your vacation could go horribly wrong. But relax: it probably won't.

Telephone

The US phone system comprises regional service providers, competing long-distance carriers and several mobile-phone and pay-phone companies. Overall, the system is very efficient, but it can be expensive. Avoid making long-distance calls on a hotel phone or on a pay phone. It's usually cheaper to use a regular landline or cell phone. Most hotels allow guests to make free local calls.

Telephone books can be handy resources: some list community services, public transportation and things to see and do as well as phone and business listings. Online phone directories include www.411.com and www.yellowpages.com.

Cell Phones

In the USA cell phones use GSM 1900 or CDMA 800, operating on different frequencies from other systems around the world. The only foreign phones that will work in the USA are GSM tri- or quad-band models. If you have one of these phones, check with your service provider about using it in the USA. Ask if roaming charges apply, as these will turn even local US calls into pricey international calls.

It might be cheaper to buy a compatible prepaid SIM card for the USA, like those sold by AT&T, which you can insert into your international mobile phone to get a local phone number and voicemail. **Planet Omni** (www.planetomni.com) and **Telestial** (www.telestial.com) offer these services, as well as cell-phone rentals.

If you don't have a compatible phone, you can buy inexpensive, no-contract (prepaid) phones with a local number and a set number of minutes, which can be topped up at will. Virgin Mobile, T-Mobile, AT&T and other providers offer phones starting at US$10, with a package of minutes starting around $40 for 400 minutes. Electronics stores such as Radio Shack and Best Buy sell these phones.

Huge swathes of rural America, including many national parks and recreation areas, don't pick up a signal. Check your provider's coverage map.

Dialing Codes

All phone numbers within the USA consist of a three-digit area code followed by a seven-digit local number. In most places, you will need to dial the entire 10-digit number even for a local call.

If you are calling long distance, dial 1 plus the area code plus the phone number. If you're not sure whether the number is local or long distance (new area codes are added all the time, confusing even residents), try one way, and if it's wrong, usually a recorded voice will correct you. Toll-free numbers begin with ☑800, ☑888, ☑877 and ☑866 and when dialing, are preceded by ☑1. Most can only be used within the USA, some only within the state, and some only from outside the state. You won't know until you try dialing. The ☑900-series of area codes

and a few other prefixes are for calls charged at a premium per-minute rate – phone sex, horoscopes, jokes etc.

➡ ☑1 is the international country code for the USA if calling from abroad (the same as Canada, but international rates apply between the two countries).

➡ Dial ☑011 to make an international call from the USA (followed by country code, area code and phone number)

➡ Dial ☑00 for assistance making international calls

➡ Dial ☑411 for directory assistance nationwide

➡ ☑800-555-1212 is directory assistance for toll-free numbers

Pay Phones

Pay phones are an endangered species in an ever-expanding mobile-phone world. Local calls at pay phones that work (listen for a dial tone before inserting coins) cost 35¢ to 50¢ for the first few minutes; talking longer costs more. Only put in the exact amount because pay phones don't give change. Some pay phones (eg in national parks) only accept credit cards or prepaid phone cards. Local calls from pay phones get expensive quickly, while long-distance calls can be prohibitive, especially if you use the operator (0) to facilitate long-distance or collect (reverse-charge) calls. It's usually cheaper to use a prepaid phone card or the access line of a major carrier like **AT&T** (☑800-321-0288).

Phone Cards

A prepaid phone card is a good solution for travelers on a budget. Phone cards are easy to find in larger towns and cities, where they are sold at newsstands, convenience stores, supermarkets and major retailers. Be sure to read the fine print, as many cards contain hidden charges such as 'activation fees' or per-call 'connection

fees' in addition to the rates. AT&T sells a reliable phone card that is widely available in the USA.

Time

The USA uses Daylight Saving Time (DST). On the second Sunday in March, clocks are set one hour ahead ('spring forward'). Then, on the first Sunday of November, clocks are turned back one hour ('fall back'). Just to keep you on your toes, Arizona (except the Navajo Nation), Hawaii and much of Indiana don't follow DST.

The US date system is written as month/day/year. Thus, 8 June 2015 becomes 6/8/15.

Tourist Information

The official tourism website of the USA is www.discoveramerica.com. It has links to every US state and territory tourism office and website, plus loads of ideas for itinerary planning.

Any tourist office worth contacting has a website, where you can download free travel e-guides. They also field phone calls; some local offices maintain daily lists of hotel room availability, but few offer reservation services. All tourist offices have self-service racks of brochures and discount coupons; some also sell maps and books.

State-run 'welcome centers,' usually placed along interstate highways, tend to have materials that cover wider territories, and offices are usually open longer hours, including weekends and holidays.

Many cities have an official convention and visitors bureau (CVB); these sometimes double as tourist bureaus, but since their main focus is drawing the business trade, CVBs can be less useful for independent travelers.

Keep in mind that in smaller towns, when the local chamber of commerce runs the tourist bureau, its lists of hotels, restaurants and services usually mention only chamber members; the town's cheapest options may be missing.

Similarly, in prime tourist destinations, some private 'tourist bureaus' are really agents who book hotel rooms and tours on commission. They may offer excellent service and deals, but you'll get what they're selling and nothing else.

Travelers with Disabilities

If you have a physical disability, the USA can be an accommodating place. The Americans with Disabilities Act (ADA) requires that all public buildings, private buildings built after 1993 (including hotels, restaurants, theaters and museums) and public transit be wheelchair accessible. However, call ahead to confirm what is available. Some local tourist offices publish detailed accessibility guides.

Telephone companies offer relay operators, available via teletypewriter (TTY) numbers, for the hearing impaired. Most banks provide ATM instructions in Braille and via earphone jacks for hearing-impaired customers. All major airlines, Greyhound buses and Amtrak trains will assist travelers with disabilities; just describe your needs when making reservations at least 48 hours in advance. Service animals (guide dogs) are allowed to accompany passengers, but bring documentation.

Some car-rental agencies, such as Budget and Hertz, offer hand-controlled vehicles and vans with wheelchair lifts at no extra charge, but you must reserve them well in advance. **Wheelchair Getaways** (☑800-642-2042; www.wheelchairgetaways.com) rents

accessible vans throughout the USA. In many cities and towns, public buses are accessible to wheelchair riders and will 'kneel' if you are unable to use the steps; just let the driver know that you need the lift or ramp.

Most cities have taxi companies with at least one accessible van, though you'll have to call ahead. Cities with underground transport have elevators for passengers needing assistance; DC has the best network (every station has an elevator); NYC's elevators are few and far between.

Many national and some state parks and recreation areas have wheelchair-accessible paved, graded dirt or boardwalk trails. US citizens and permanent residents with permanent disabilities are entitled to a free 'America the Beautiful' Access Pass. Go online (www.nps.gov/findapark/passes.htm) for details.

Some helpful resources for travelers with disabilities:

Disabled Sports USA (☑301-217-0960; www.disabledsportsusa.org) Offers sports and recreation programs for those with disabilities and publishes *Challenge* magazine.

Flying Wheels Travel (☑877-451-5006, 507-451-5005; www.flyingwheelstravel.com) A full-service travel agency, highly recommended for those with mobility issues or chronic illness.

Mobility International USA (☑541-343-1284; www.miusa.org) Advises disabled travelers on mobility issues and runs educational international exchange programs.

Visas

Be warned that all of the following information is highly subject to change. US entry requirements keep evolving as national security regulations change. All travelers should double-check current

visa and passport regulations *before* coming to the USA.

The **US State Department** (www.travel.state.gov/visa) maintains the most comprehensive visa information, providing downloadable forms, lists of US consulates abroad and even visa wait times calculated by country.

Visa Applications

Apart from most Canadian citizens and those entering under the Visa Waiver Program (p1182), all foreign visitors will need to obtain a visa from a US consulate or embassy abroad. Most applicants must schedule a personal interview, to which you must bring all your documentation and proof of fee payment. Wait times for interviews vary, but afterward, barring problems, visa issuance takes from a few days to a few weeks.

➡ Your passport must be valid for at least six months after the end of your intended stay in the USA. You'll need a recent photo (2in by 2in), and you must pay a nonrefundable $160 processing fee, plus in a few cases an additional visa issuance reciprocity fee. You'll also need to fill out the online DS-160 nonimmigrant visa electronic application.

➡ Visa applicants are required to show documents of financial stability (or evidence that a US resident will provide financial support), a round-trip or onward ticket and 'binding obligations' that will ensure their return home, such as family ties, a home or a job. Because of these requirements, those planning to travel through other countries before arriving in the USA are generally better off applying for a US visa while they are still in their home country, rather than while on the road.

➡ The most common visa is a nonimmigrant visitor's visa, type B-1 for business purposes, B-2 for tourism or

VISA WAIVER PROGRAM

Currently under the Visa Waiver Program (VWP), citizens of the following countries may enter the USA without a visa for stays of 90 days or fewer: Andorra, Australia, Austria, Belgium, Brunei, Chile, Czech Republic, Denmark, Estonia, Finland, France, Germany, Greece, Hungary, Iceland, Ireland, Italy, Japan, Latvia, Liechtenstein, Lithuania, Luxembourg, Malta, Monaco, the Netherlands, New Zealand, Norway, Portugal, San Marino, Singapore, Slovakia, Slovenia, South Korea, Spain, Sweden, Switzerland, Taiwan and the UK.

If you are a citizen of a VWP country, you do not need a visa *only if* you have a passport that meets current US standards *and* you have gotten approval from the Electronic System for Travel Authorization (ESTA) in advance. Register online with the Department of Homeland Security at https://esta.cbp.dhs.gov/esta at least 72 hours before arrival; once travel authorization is approved, your registration is valid for two years. The fee is $14.

Visitors from VWP countries must still produce all the same evidence as for a nonimmigrant visa application at the port of entry. They must demonstrate that their trip is for 90 days or less, and that they have a round-trip or onward ticket, adequate funds to cover the trip and binding obligations abroad.

In addition, the same 'grounds for exclusion and deportation' apply, except that you will have no opportunity to appeal or apply for an exemption. If you are denied under the VWP at a US point of entry, you will have to use your onward or return ticket on the next available flight.

---

visiting friends and relatives. A visitor's visa is good for multiple entries over one or five years, and specifically prohibits the visitor from taking paid employment in the USA. The validity period depends on what country you are from. The actual length of time you'll be allowed to stay in the USA is determined by US immigration at the port of entry.

➡ If you're coming to the USA to work or study, you will need a different type of visa, and the company or institution to which you are going should make the arrangements.

➡ Other categories of nonimmigrant visas include an F-1 visa for students attending a course at a recognized institution; a H-1, H-2 or H-3 visa for temporary employment; and a J-1 visa for exchange visitors in approved programs.

Grounds for Exclusion & Deportation

If on your visa application form you admit to being a subversive, smuggler, prostitute, drug addict, terrorist or an ex-Nazi, you may be excluded. You can also be refused a visa or entry to the USA if you have a 'communicable disease of public health significance' or a criminal record, or if you've ever made a false statement in connection with a US visa application. However, if these last three apply, you are still able to request an exemption; many people are granted them and then given visas.

Communicable diseases include tuberculosis, the Ebola virus, SARS and most particularly HIV. US immigration doesn't test for disease, but officials at the point of entry may question anyone about his or her health. They can exclude anyone whom they believe has a communicable disease, perhaps because they are carrying medical documents, prescriptions or AIDS/HIV medicine. Being gay is not grounds for exclusion; being an IV drug user is. Visitors may be deported if US immigration finds out they have HIV but did not declare it. Being HIV-positive is not grounds for deportation, but failing to provide accurate information on the visa application is.

The US immigration department has a very broad definition of a criminal record. If you've ever been arrested or charged with an offense, that's a criminal record, even if you were acquitted or discharged without conviction. Don't attempt to enter through the VWP if you have a criminal record of any kind; assume US authorities will find out about it.

Often USCIS (United States Citizenship & Immigration Services) will grant an exemption (a 'waiver of ineligibility') to a person who would normally be subject to exclusion, but this requires referral to a regional immigration office and can take some time (allow at least two months). If you're tempted to conceal something, remember that US immigration is strictest of all about false statements. It will often view favorably an applicant who admits to an old criminal charge or a communicable disease, but it is extremely harsh on anyone who has ever attempted to mislead it, even on minor points. After you're admitted to the USA, any evidence of a false statement to US immigration is grounds for deportation.

Prospective visitors to whom grounds of exclusion may apply should consider their options *before* applying for a visa.

Entering the USA

➜ As of 2013, the arrival/departure record (form I-94) that was once required of all foreign visitors, is no longer used. Instead, you'll be asked to fill out only the US customs declaration, which is usually handed out on the plane. Have it completed before you approach the immigration desk. For the question, 'US Street Address,' give the address where you will spend the first night (a hotel address is fine).

➜ No matter what your visa says, US immigration officers have an absolute authority to refuse admission to the USA or to impose conditions on admission. They may ask about your plans and whether you have sufficient funds; it's a good idea to list an itinerary, produce an onward or round-trip ticket and have at least one major credit card.

➜ The Department of Homeland Security's registration program, called Office of Biometric Identity Management includes every port of entry and nearly every foreign visitor to the USA. For most visitors (excluding, for now, most Canadian and some Mexican citizens), registration consists of having a digital photo and electronic (inkless) fingerprints taken; the process takes less than a minute.

Visa Extensions

To stay in the USA longer than the date stamped on your passport, go to a local **USCIS** (☎800-375-5283; www.uscis.gov) office to apply for an extension well *before* the stamped date. If the date has passed, your best chance will be to bring a US citizen with you to vouch for your character, and to produce lots of other verification that you are not trying to work illegally and have enough money to support yourself. However, if you've overstayed, the most likely scenario is that you will be deported. Travelers who enter the USA under the VWP are ineligible for visa extensions.

Short-Term Departures & Re-entry

➜ It's temptingly easy to make trips across the border to Canada or Mexico, but upon return to the USA, non-Americans will be subject to the full immigration procedure.

➜ Always take your passport when you cross the border.

➜ If your immigration card still has plenty of time on it, you will probably be able to re-enter using the same one, but if it has nearly expired, you will have to apply for a new card, and border control may want to see your onward air ticket, sufficient funds and so on.

➜ Traditionally, a quick trip across the border has been a way to extend your stay in the USA without applying for an extension at a USCIS office. Don't assume this still works. First, make sure you hand in your old immigration card to the immigration authorities when you leave the USA, and when you return make sure you have all the necessary application documentation from when you first entered the country. US immigration will be very suspicious of anyone who leaves for a few days and returns immediately hoping for a new six-month stay; expect to be questioned closely.

➜ Citizens of most Western countries will not need a visa to visit Canada, so it's really not a problem at all to cross to the Canadian side of Niagara Falls, detour up to Québec or pass through on the way to Alaska.

➜ Travelers entering the USA by bus from Canada may be closely scrutinized. A round-trip ticket that takes you back to Canada will most likely make US immigration feel less suspicious.

➜ Mexico has a visa-free zone along most of its border with the USA, including the Baja Peninsula and most of the border towns, such as Tijuana and Ciudad Juárez; note that the latter, with over 5000 murders since 2009, is not a safe place to visit. You'll need a Mexican visa or tourist card if you want to go beyond the border zone.

Volunteering

Volunteer opportunities abound in the USA, and they can be a great way to break up a long trip. They can also provide truly memorable experiences: you'll get to interact with people, society and the land in ways you never would by just passing through.

Casual, drop-in volunteer opportunities are plentiful in big cities, where you can socialize with locals while helping out. Check weekly alternative newspapers for calendar listings, or browse the free classified ads online at **Craigslist** (www.craigslist.org). The public website **Serve.gov** (www.serve.gov) and private websites **Idealist.org** (www.idealist.org) and **VolunteerMatch** (www.volunteermatch.org) offer free searchable databases of short- and long-term volunteer opportunities nationwide.

More formal volunteer programs, especially those designed for international travelers, typically charge a fee of $250 to $1000, depending on the length of the program and what amenities are included (eg housing, meals). None cover travel to the USA.

Green Project (☎504-945-0240; www.thegreenproject.org) Working to improve battered communities in New Orleans in sustainable, green ways.

Habitat for Humanity
(☑800-422-4828; www.habitat.org) Focuses on building affordable housing for those in need.

Sierra Club (☑415-977-5522; www.sierraclub.org) 'Volunteer vacations' restore wilderness areas and maintain trails, including in national parks and nature preserves.

Volunteers for Peace
(☑802-540-3060; www.vfp.org) Grassroots, multiweek volunteer projects emphasize manual labor and international exchange.

Wilderness Volunteers
(☑801-949-3099; www.wildernessvolunteers.org) Week-long trips helping maintain national parklands and outdoor recreation areas.

World Wide Opportunities on Organic Farms USA (☑415-621-3276; www.wwoofusa.org) Represents more than 1500 organic farms in all 50 states that host volunteer workers in exchange for meals and accommodation, with opportunities for both short- and long-term stays.

Women Travelers

Women traveling alone or in groups should not expect to encounter any particular problems in the USA. The community website www.journeywoman.com facilitates women exchanging travel tips, and has links to other helpful resources. The booklet *Her Own Way*, published by the Canadian government, is filled with general travel advice, useful for any woman; click to http://travel.gc.ca/travelling/publications to download the PDF or read it online.

When first meeting someone, don't advertise where you are staying, or even that you are traveling alone. Americans can be eager to help and even take in solo travelers, but don't take all offers of help at face value. If someone who seems trustworthy invites you to his or her home, let someone (eg hostel or hotel manager) know where you're going. This advice also applies if you go for a hike by yourself. If something happens and you don't return as expected, you want to know that someone will notice and know where to begin looking for you.

Some women carry a whistle, mace or cayenne-pepper spray in case of assault. If you purchase a spray, contact a police station to find out about local regulations. Laws regarding sprays vary from state to state; federal law prohibits them being carried on planes.

If you are assaulted, consider calling a rape-crisis hotline before calling the police, unless you are in immediate danger, in which case you should call 911. But be aware that not all police have as much sensitivity training or experience assisting sexual assault survivors, whereas staff at rape crisis centers will tirelessly advocate on your behalf and act as a link to other community services, including hospitals and the police. Telephone books have listings of local rape-crisis centers, or contact the 24-hour **National Sexual Assault Hotline** (☑800-656-4673; www.rainn.org). Alternatively, go straight to a hospital emergency room.

National advocacy groups that may be useful:

National Organization for Women (NOW; ☑202-628-8669; www.now.org)

Planned Parenthood (☑800-230-7526; www.plannedparenthood.org) Offers referrals to women's health clinics throughout the country.

Work

If you are a foreigner in the USA with a standard non-immigrant visitor's visa, you are forbidden to partake in paid work in the USA and will be deported if you're caught working illegally. Employers are required to establish the bona fides of their employees or face fines, making it much tougher for a foreigner to get work than it once was.

To work legally, foreigners need to apply for a work visa before leaving home. A J-1 visa, for exchange visitors, is issued to young people (age limits vary) for study, student vacation employment, work in summer camps, and short-term traineeships with a specific employer. One organization that can help arrange international student exchanges, work placements and J-1 visas is **International Exchange Programs** (IEP), which operates in **Australia** (☑03-9329-3866; www.iep.com.au) and **New Zealand.** (☑0800-443-769; www.iep.org.nz).

For nonstudent jobs, temporary or permanent, you need to be sponsored by a US employer who will have to arrange a H-category visa. These are not easy to obtain, since the employer has to prove that no US citizen or permanent resident is available to do the job.

Seasonal work is possible in national parks and at tourist attractions and ski resorts. Contact park concessionaire businesses, local chambers of commerce and ski-resort management. Lonely Planet's *Gap Year Book* has more ideas on how best to combine work and travel.

American Institute for Foreign Study (☑866-906-2437; www.aifs.com)

Au Pair in America (☑800-928-7247; www.aupairinamerica.com)

BUNAC (☑020-7870-9570; www.bunac.org)

Camp America (☑in the UK 020-7581-7373; www.campamerica.co.uk)

Council on International Educational Exchange (☑207-553-4000; www.ciee.org)

InterExchange (☑212-924-0446; www.interexchange.org) Camp and au-pair programs.

Driving in the USA

For maximum flexibility and convenience, and to explore rural America and its wide-open spaces, a car is essential. Although petrol prices are high, you can often score fairly inexpensive rentals (NYC excluded), with rates as low as $20 per day. For more about transport in the USA, see p1189.

Automobile Associations

The **American Automobile Association** (AAA; www.aaa. com) has reciprocal membership agreements with several international auto clubs (check with AAA and bring your membership card from home). For its members, AAA offers travel insurance, tour books, diagnostic centers for used-car buyers and a wide-ranging network of regional offices. AAA advocates politically for the auto industry.

A more ecofriendly alternative, the **Better World Club** (☑866-238-1137; www. betterworldclub.com) donates 1% of revenue to assist environmental cleanup, offers ecologically sensitive choices for every service it provides and advocates politically for environmental causes.

With organizations, the primary member benefit is 24-hour emergency roadside assistance anywhere in the USA. Both also offer trip planning, free travel maps, travel-agency services, car in-surance and a range of travel discounts (eg on hotels, car rentals, attractions).

Bring Your Own Vehicle

For details on driving your own car over the border from Canada or from Mexico, see p1190. Unless you're moving to the USA, don't even think about freighting your car.

Drive-Away Cars

'Drive-away cars' refers to the business of driving cars across the country for people who are moving or otherwise can't transport their cars themselves. For flexible travelers, they can be a dream come true: you can cover the long distances between A and B for the price of gas. Timing and availability are key.

To be a driver you must be at least 23 years old with a valid driver's license (non-US citizens should have an International Driving Permit); you'll also need to provide a $350 deposit – sometimes requested in cash – which is refunded upon safe delivery of the car, a printout of your 'clean' driving record from home, a major credit card and/or three forms of identification (or a passport).

The drive-away company provides insurance; you pay for gas. The stipulation is that you must deliver the car to its destination within a specified time and mileage, which usually requires that you drive no more than eight hours and about 400 miles a day along the shortest route (ie no sightseeing). Availability depends on demand.

One major company is **Auto Driveaway** (☑800-346-2277; www.autodriveaway. com), which has more than 40 offices nationwide.

Driver's License

Foreign visitors can legally drive a car in the USA for up to 12 months using their home driver's license. However, an International Driving Permit will have more credibility with US traffic police, especially if your home license doesn't have a photo or isn't in English. Your automobile association at home can issue an IDP, valid for one year, for a small fee. Always carry your home license together with the IDP.

To ride a motorcycle in the USA, you will need either a valid US state motorcycle license or an IDP specially endorsed for motorcycles.

Insurance

Don't put the key into the ignition if you don't have insurance, which is legally required. You risk financial ruin and legal consequences if there's an accident. If you

Driving Distances & Times

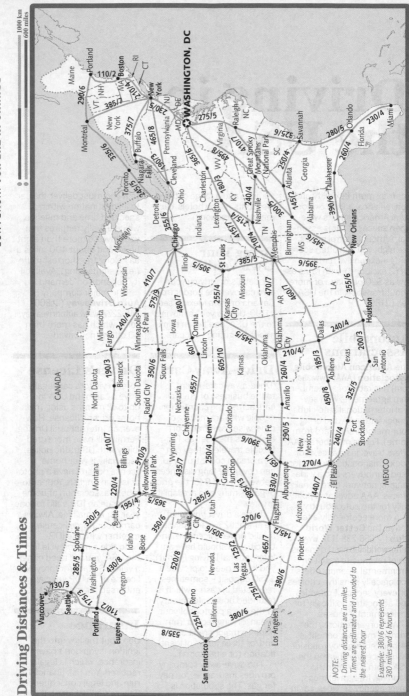

NOTE:
- Driving distances are in miles
- Times are estimated and rounded to the nearest hour

Example: 380/6 represents 380 miles and 6 hours

already have auto insurance, or if you buy travel insurance that covers car rentals, make sure your policy has adequate liability coverage for where you will be driving; it probably does, but beware that states specify different minimum levels of coverage.

Rental-car companies will provide liability insurance, but most charge extra. Rental companies almost never include collision-damage insurance for the vehicle. Instead, they offer an optional Collision Damage Waiver (CDW) or Loss Damage Waiver (LDW), usually with an initial deductible cost of between $100 and $500. For an extra premium, you can usually get this deductible covered as well. Paying extra for some or all of this insurance increases the cost of a rental car by as much as $30 a day.

Many credit cards offer free collision damage coverage for rental cars, if you rent for 15 days or less and charge the total rental to your card. This is a good way to avoid paying extra fees to the rental company, but note that if there's an accident, sometimes you must pay the rental car company first and then seek reimbursement from the credit-card company. There may be exceptions that are not covered, too, such as 'exotic' rentals (eg 4WD Jeeps, convertibles). Check your credit-card policy.

Purchase

Buying a car is usually much more hassle than it's worth, particularly for foreign visitors and for trips of less than four months. Foreigners will have the easiest time arranging this if they have stateside friends or relatives who can provide a fixed address for registration, licensing and insurance.

Once purchased, the car's transfer of ownership papers must be registered with the state's Department of Motor Vehicles (DMV) within 10 days; you'll need the bill of sale, the title (or 'pink slip') and proof of insurance. Some states also require a 'smog certificate.' This is the seller's responsibility, so don't buy a car without a current certificate. A dealer will submit all necessary paperwork to the DMV for you.

For foreigners, independent liability insurance is difficult to virtually impossible to arrange without a US driver's license. A car dealer or AAA may be able to suggest an insurer who will do this. Even with a local license, insurance can be expensive and difficult to obtain if you don't have evidence of a good driving record. Bring copies of your home auto-insurance policy if it helps establish that you are a good risk. All drivers under 25 will have problems getting insurance.

Finally, selling a car can become a desperate business. Selling to dealers gets you the worst price but involves a minimum of paperwork. Otherwise, fellow travelers and college students are the best bets – but be sure the DMV is properly notified about the sale, or you may be on the hook for someone else's traffic tickets later on.

Adventures on Wheels (☎800-943-3579; www.adventuresonwheels.com) offers a six-month buy-back program: you buy one of their cars, they register and insure it, and when your trip's done, they buy it back for a preestablished price.

Rental

Car

Car rental is a competitive business in the USA. Most rental companies require that you have a major credit card, be at least 25 years old and have a valid driver's license. Some major national companies may rent to drivers between the ages of 21 and 24 for an additional charge of around $25 per day. Those under 21 are usually not permitted to rent at all.

Good independent agencies are listed in this guide.

Car-rental prices vary wildly so shop around.The average daily rate for a small car ranges from around $30 to $75, or $200 to $500 per week. If you belong to an auto club or frequent-flier program, you may get a discount (or earn rewards points or miles).

Some other things to keep in mind: most national agencies make 'unlimited mileage' standard on all cars, but independents might charge extra for this. Tax on car rental varies by state and agency location; always ask for the total cost *including* all taxes and fees. Most agencies charge more if you pick the car up in one place and drop it off in another; usually only national agencies even offer this option. Be careful about adding extra days or turning in a car early; extra days may be charged at a premium rate, or an early return may jeopardize any

---

FUELING UP

Many gas stations in the USA have fuel pumps with automated credit card pay screens. Most machines ask for your ZIP code after you swipe your card. For foreign travelers – or those with cards issued outside the US – you'll have to pay inside before fueling up. Just indicate how much you'd like to put on the card. If there's still credit left over after you fuel up, just pop back inside, and the attendant will put the difference back on your card.

weekly or monthly discounts you originally arranged.

Some major national companies, including Avis, Budget and Hertz, offer 'green' fleets of hybrid rental cars (eg Toyota Priuses, Honda Civics), although you'll usually have to pay quite a bit more to rent a hybrid. Some independent local agencies, especially on the West Coast, also offer hybrid-vehicle rentals. Try Southern California's **Simply Hybrid** (www.simplyhybrid.com) and Hawaii's **Bio-Beetle** (www.bio-beetle.com).

Motorcycle & Recreational Vehicle

If you dream of cruising across America on a Harley, **EagleRider** (☏888-900-9901; www.eaglerider.com) has offices in major cities nationwide and rents other kinds of adventure vehicles, too. Beware that motorcycle rental and insurance are expensive.

Road Conditions & Hazards

America's highways are thought of as legendary ribbons of unblemished asphalt, but not always. Road hazards include potholes, city commuter traffic, wandering wildlife and, of course, cell-phone-wielding, kid-distracted and enraged drivers. Caution, foresight, courtesy and luck usually gets you past them. For nationwide traffic and

road-closure information, click to www.fhwa.dot.gov/trafficinfo/index.htm.

In places where winter driving is an issue, many cars are fitted with steel-studded snow tires; snow chains can sometimes be required in mountain areas. Driving off-road, or on dirt roads, is often forbidden by rental-car companies, and it can be very dangerous in wet weather.

In deserts and range country, livestock sometimes graze next to unfenced roads. These areas are signed as 'Open Range' or with the silhouette of a steer. Where deer and other wild animals frequently appear roadside, you'll see signs with the silhouette of a leaping deer. Take these signs seriously, particularly at dusk and dawn.

Road Rules

In the USA, cars drive on the right-hand side of the road. The use of seat belts and child safety seats is required in every state. Most car rental agencies rent child safety seats for around $13 per day, but you must reserve them when booking. In some states, motorcyclists are required to wear helmets.

On interstate highways, the speed limit is sometimes raised to 75mph. Unless otherwise posted, the speed limit is generally 55mph or 65mph on highways, 25mph to 35mph in cities and towns and as low as 15mph in school zones (strictly

enforced during school hours). It's forbidden to pass a school bus when its lights are flashing.

Unless signs prohibit it, you may turn right at a red light after first coming to a full stop – note that turning right on red is illegal in NYC. At four-way stop signs, cars should proceed in order of arrival; when two cars arrive simultaneously, the one on the right has the right of way. When in doubt, just politely wave the other driver ahead. When emergency vehicles (ie police, fire or ambulance) approach from either direction, pull over safely and get out of the way.

In an increasing number of states, it is illegal to talk on a handheld cell (mobile) phone while driving; use a hands-free device instead.

The maximum legal blood-alcohol concentration for drivers is 0.08%. Penalties are very severe for DUI – driving under the influence of alcohol and/or drugs. Police can give roadside sobriety checks to assess if you've been drinking or using drugs. If you fail, they'll require you to take a breath test, urine test or blood test to determine the level of alcohol or drugs in your body. Refusing to be tested is treated the same as if you'd taken the test and failed.

In some states it is illegal to carry 'open containers' of alcohol in a vehicle, even if they are empty.

Transportation

GETTING THERE & AWAY

Flights and tours can be booked online at www.lonely-planet.com/booking.

Entering the USA

If you are flying to the US, the first airport that you land in is where you must go through immigration and customs, even if you are continuing on the flight to another destination. Upon arrival, all international visitors must register with the Department of Homeland Security's Office of Biometric Identity Management program, which entails having your fingerprints scanned and a digital photo taken.

Once you go through immigration, you collect your baggage and pass through customs. If you have nothing to declare, you'll probably clear customs without a baggage search, but don't assume

this. If you are continuing on the same plane or connecting to another one, it is your responsibility to get your bags to the right place. There are usually airline representatives just outside the customs area who can help you.

If you are a single parent, grandparent or guardian traveling with anyone under 18, carry proof of legal custody or a notarized letter from the nonaccompanying parent(s) authorizing the trip. This isn't required, but the USA is concerned with thwarting child abduction, and not having authorizing papers could cause delays or even result in being denied admittance to the country.

Passports

Every visitor entering the USA from abroad needs a passport. Your passport must be valid for at least six months longer than your intended stay in the USA. Also, if your passport does not meet current US standards, you'll be

turned back at the border. If it was issued on or after October 26, 2006, it must be an e-passport with a digital photo and an integrated RFID chip containing biometric data.

Air

Airports

The USA has more than 375 domestic airports, but only a baker's dozen are the main international gateways. Many other airports are called 'international' but may have only a few flights from other countries – typically Mexico or Canada. Even travel to an international gateway sometimes requires a connection in another gateway city (eg London–Los Angeles flights may involve transferring in Houston).

International gateway airports in the USA:

Hartsfield-Jackson International Airport (ATL; Atlanta; www.atlanta-airport.com)

CLIMATE CHANGE & TRAVEL

Every form of transport that relies on carbon-based fuel generates CO_2, the main cause of human-induced climate change. Modern travel is dependent on airplanes, which might use less fuel per mile per person than most cars but travel much greater distances. The altitude at which aircraft emit gases (including CO_2) and particles also contributes to their climate change impact. Many websites offer 'carbon calculators' that allow people to estimate the carbon emissions generated by their journey and, for those who wish to do so, to offset the impact of the greenhouse gases emitted with contributions to portfolios of climate-friendly initiatives throughout the world. Lonely Planet offsets the carbon footprint of all staff and author travel.

Logan International Airport (Boston; www.massport. com/logan)

O'Hare International Airport (Chicago; www.ohare. com)

Dallas-Fort Worth International Airport (DFW; www. dfwairport.com)

Honolulu International Airport (HNL; ☑808-836-6411; http://hawaii.gov/hnl; 300 Rodgers Blvd, Honolulu)

Houston George Bush Intercontinental Airport (IAH; www.fly2houston.com/ iah; Will Clayton Parkway or JFK Blvd, off I-59, Beltway 8 or I-45)

Los Angeles (LAX; www.lawa. org/lax)

Miami International Airport (MIA; www.miami-airport. com)

John F Kennedy (JFK; New York; www.panynj.gov)

Liberty International (EWR; Newark; www.panynj. gov)

San Francisco International Airport (SFO; www. flysfo.com)

Seattle-Tacoma International Airport (SEA; www. portseattle.org/Sea-Tac)

Dulles International Airport (Washington, DC; www. metwashairports.com/dulles)

Tickets

Flying midweek and in the off-season (usually fall to spring, excluding holidays) is always less expensive, but fare wars can start any time. To ensure you've found the cheapest possible ticket for the flight you want, check every angle: compare several online travel booking sites with the airline's own website. Engage a living, breathing travel agent if your itinerary is complex.

Keep in mind your entire itinerary. Some deals for travel within the USA can only be purchased overseas in conjunction with an international air ticket, or you may get discounts for booking air and car rental together. Or

you may find domestic flights within the USA are less expensive when added on to your international airfare.

The big three US travel-booking websites are **Travelocity** (www.travelocity.com), **Orbitz** (www.orbitz.com) and **Expedia** (www.expedia.com). Similar to these and worth trying are **Cheap Tickets** (www.cheaptickets.com) and **Lowest Fare** (www.lowestfare. com). Typically, these sites don't include budget airlines such as Southwest.

Meta sites like **Kayak** (www.kayak.com) and **Hipmunk** (www.hipmunk.com) are good for price comparisons, as they gather from many sources (but don't provide direct booking).

Bidding for travel can be very successful, but read the fine print carefully before bidding. Try **Hotwire** (www. hotwire.com), **Skyauction** (www.skyauction.com) and **Priceline** (www.priceline.com).

Land
Border Crossings

The USA has more than 20 official border crossings with Canada in the north and almost 40 with Mexico in the south. It is relatively easy crossing from the USA into either country; it's crossing *into* the USA that can pose problems if you haven't brought all your documents. Some borders are open 24 hours, but most are not.

Busy entry points with Canada include those at Detroit, MI–Windsor; Buffalo, NY–Niagara Falls; Blaine, WA–British Columbia.

The main USA–Mexico posts are, San Diego, CA–Tijuana; Nogales West, AZ–Nogales East; El Paso, TX–Ciudad Juárez and Brownsville, TX–Matamoros. As always, have your papers in order, be polite and don't make jokes or casual conversation with US border officials.

At research time, cartel violence and crime were

serious dangers along the US–Mexico border. Before heading out, check the latest warnings of the **US State Department** (www.travel. state.gov/visa).

Canada
BUS

Greyhound has direct connections between main cities in Canada and the northern USA, but you may have to transfer to a different bus at the border. Book through **Greyhound USA** (☑800-231-2222, international customer service 214-849-8100; www. greyhound.com) or **Greyhound Canada** (☑in Canada 800-661-8747; www.greyhound. ca). Greyhound's Discovery Pass allows unlimited travel in both the USA and Canada.

CAR & MOTORCYCLE

If you're driving into the USA from Canada, bring the vehicle's registration papers, proof of liability insurance and your home driver's license. Canadian auto insurance is typically valid in the USA, and vice versa. Canadian driver's licenses are also valid, but an International Driving Permit (IDP) is a good supplement.

If your papers are in order, taking your own car across the US–Canadian border is usually fast and easy, but occasionally the authorities of either country decide to search a car *thoroughly*. On weekends and holidays, especially in summer, traffic at the main border crossings can be heavy and waits long.

TRAIN

Amtrak (☑toll-free 800 872 7245; www.amtrak.com) and **VIA Rail Canada** (☑888-842-7245; www.viarail. ca) operate daily services between Montreal and New York, Toronto and New York via Niagara Falls, Toronto and Chicago via Detroit, and Vancouver and Seattle. Customs inspections occur at the border.

Mexico

BUS

Greyhound US (☎800-231-2222, international customer service 214-849-8100; www.greyhound.com) and **Greyhound México** (☎in Mexico 800-710-8819; www.greyhound.com.mx) operate direct bus routes between main towns in Mexico and the USA.

For connections to smaller destinations south of the border, there are numerous domestic Mexican bus companies; **Ticketbus** (☎800-009-9090, in Mexico 5133-5133; www.ticketbus.com.mx) is an alliance of several.

CAR & MOTORCYCLE

As with Canada, if you're driving into the USA from Mexico, bring the vehicle's registration papers, proof of liability insurance and your driver's license from your home country. Mexican driver's licenses are valid, but it's worth having an IDP.

Very few car-rental companies will let you take a car from the US into Mexico. US auto insurance is not valid in Mexico, so even a short trip into Mexico's border region requires you to buy Mexican car insurance, available for around $25 per day at most border crossings, as well as from **AAA** (☎800-874-7532; www.aaa.com).

For a longer driving trip into Mexico beyond the border zone or Baja California, you'll need a Mexican *permiso de importación temporal de vehículos* (temporary vehicle import permit). You can call Mexico's tourist information number in the USA on ☎800-446-3942.

Sea

If you're interested in taking a cruise ship to America – as well as to other interesting ports of call – a good specialized travel agency is **Cruise Web** (☎800-377-9383; www.cruiseweb.com).

You can also travel to and from the USA on a freighter, though it will be much slower and less cushy than a cruise. Nevertheless, freighters aren't spartan (some advertise cruise ship–level amenities), and they are much cheaper (sometimes by half). Trips range from a week to two months; stops at interim ports are usually quick.

For more information:

Cruise & Freighter Travel Association (☎800-872-8584; www.travltips.com)

Tours

Group travel can be an enjoyable way to get to and tour the USA.

Reputable tour companies:

American Holidays (☎01-673-3840; www.americanholidays.com) Ireland-based company specializes in tours to North America.

Contiki (☎866-266-8454; www.contiki.com) Party-hardy sightseeing tour-bus vacations for 18- to 35-year-olds.

North America Travel Service (☎020-7499-7299; www.northamericatravelservice.co.uk) UK-based tour operator arranges luxury US trips.

Trek America (☎in North America 800-873-5872, in the UK 0844-576-1400; www.trekamerica.com) For active outdoor adventures; group sizes are kept small.

GETTING AROUND

Air

When time is tight, book a flight. The domestic air system is extensive and reliable, with dozens of competing airlines, hundreds of airports and thousands of flights daily. Flying is usually more expensive than traveling by bus, train or car, but it's the way to go when you're in a hurry.

Main 'hub' airports in the USA include all international gateways plus many other large cities. Most cities and towns have a local or county airport, but you usually have to travel via a hub airport to reach them.

Airlines in the USA

Overall, air travel in the USA is very safe (much safer than driving out on the nation's highways); for comprehensive details by carrier, check out **Airsafe.com** (www.airsafe.com).

The main domestic carriers:

AirTran Airways (☎800-247-8726; www.airtran.com) Atlanta-based airline; primarily serves the South, Midwest and eastern US.

Alaska Airlines (☎800-252-7522; www.alaskaair.com) Has direct flights to Anchorage from Seattle, Chicago, Los Angeles and Denver. It also flies between many towns within Alaska, including daily northbound and southbound flights year-round through Southeast Alaska, with stops at all main towns including Ketchikan and Juneau.

American Airlines (☎800-433-7300; www.aa.com) Nationwide service.

Delta Air Lines (☎800-221-1212; www.delta.com) Nationwide service.

Frontier Airlines (☎800-432-1359; www.flyfrontier.com) Denver-based airline with nationwide service, including to Alaska.

Hawaiian Airlines (☎800-367-5320; www.hawaiianair.com)

JetBlue Airways (☎800-538-2583; www.jetblue.com) Nonstop connections between eastern and western US cities, plus Florida, New Orleans and Texas.

Southwest Airlines (SWA; ☎800-435-9792; www.southwest.com) Service across the continental USA.

Spirit Airlines (☎801-401-2200; www.spiritair.com) Florida-based airline; serves many US gateway cities.

United Airlines (☎800-864-8331; www.united.com) Nationwide service.

US Airways (☎800-428-4322; www.usairways.com) Flies between Flagstaff, AZ, and Sky Harbor International Airport in Phoenix.

Virgin America (☎877-359-8474; www.virginamerica.com) Flights between East and West Coast cities and Las Vegas.

Air Passes

International travelers who plan on doing a lot of flying might consider buying a North American air pass. Passes are normally available only to non-North American citizens, and they must be purchased in conjunction with an international ticket. Conditions and cost structures can be complicated, but all passes include a certain number of domestic flights (from two to 10) that typically must be used within a 60-day period. Often you must plan your itinerary in advance, but sometimes dates (and even destinations) can be left open. Talk with a travel agent to determine if an air pass will save you money. Two of the biggest airline networks offering air passes are **Star Alliance** (www.staralliance.com) and **One World** (www.oneworld.com).

Bicycle

Regional bicycle touring is popular. It means coasting winding backroads (bicycles are often not permitted on freeways), and calculating progress in miles per day, not miles per hour. Cyclists must follow the same rules of the road as automobiles, but don't expect drivers to respect your right of way. **Better World Club** (www.betterworldclub.com) offers a bicycle roadside assistance program.

For epic cross-country journeys, get the support of a tour operator; it's about two months of dedicated pedaling coast to coast.

For advice, and lists of local bike clubs and repair shops, browse the website of the League of American Bicyclists (www.bikeleague.org). If you're bringing your own bike to the USA, be sure to call around to check oversize luggage prices and restrictions. Amtrak trains and Greyhound buses will transport bikes within the USA, sometimes charging extra.

It's not hard to buy a bike once you're here and resell it before you leave. Every city and town has bike shops; if you prefer a cheaper, used bicycle, try garage sales, bulletin boards at hostels and colleges, or the free classified ads at **Craigslist** (www.craigslist.org). These are also the best places to sell your bike, though stores selling used bikes may also buy from you.

Long-term bike rentals are also easy to find; recommended rental places are listed throughout this guide. Rates run from $100 per week and up, and a credit-card authorization for several hundred dollars is usually necessary as a security deposit.

Boat

There is no river or canal public transportation system in the USA, but there are many smaller, often state-run, coastal ferry services, which provide efficient, scenic links to the many islands off both coasts. Most larger ferries will transport private cars, motorcycles and bicycles.

The most spectacular coastal ferry runs are on the southeastern coast of Alaska and along the Inside Passage. The Great Lakes have several islands that can be visited only by boat, such as Mackinac Island, MI; the Apostle Islands, off Wisconsin; and remote Isle Royale National Park, MN. Off the coast of Washington State, ferries reach the scenic San Juan Islands.

Bus

To save money, travel by bus, particularly between major towns and cities. Gotta-go middle-class Americans prefer to fly or drive, but buses let you see the countryside and meet folks along the way. As a rule, buses are reliable, cleanish and comfortable, with air-conditioning, barely reclining seats, lavatories and no smoking.

Greyhound (☎800-231-2222; www.greyhound.com) is the major long-distance bus company, with routes throughout the USA and Canada. To improve efficiency and profitability, Greyhound has recently stopped service to many small towns; routes generally trace major highways and stop at larger population centers. To reach country towns on rural roads, you may need to transfer to local or county bus systems; Greyhound can usually provide their contact information. Greyhound often has excellent online fares – web-only deals will net you substantial discounts over buying at a ticket counter.

Competing with Greyhound are the 75-plus franchises of **Trailways** (☎703-691-3052; www.trailways.com). Trailways may not be as useful as Greyhound for long trips, but fares can be competitive. Long-distance bus lines that offer decent fares and free wi-fi (that doesn't always work) include **Megabus** (☎877-462-6342; www.megabus.com) and **BoltBus** (www.boltbus.com); both operate routes primarily in the Northeast and Midwest.

Most baggage has to be checked in; label it loudly and clearly to avoid it getting lost. Larger items, including skis, surfboards and bicycles, can be transported, but there may be an extra charge. Call to check.

The frequency of bus services varies widely, depending on the route. Despite the elimination of many tiny destinations, nonexpress Greyhound buses still stop every 50 to 100 miles to pick up passengers – long-distance buses will stop for meal breaks and driver changes.

Many bus stations are clean and safe, but some are in dodgy areas; if you arrive in the evening, it's worth spending the money on a taxi. Some towns have just a flag stop. If you are boarding at one of these, pay the driver with exact change.

Costs

For lower fares on Greyhound, purchase tickets at least seven days in advance (purchasing 14 days in advance will save even more). Round trips are also cheaper than two one-way fares. Special promotional fares are regularly offered on Greyhound's website, especially for online bookings. If you're traveling with family or friends, Greyhound's companion fares let up to two additional travelers get 50% off with a minimum three-day advance purchase.

As for other Greyhound discounts: tickets for children aged two to 11 get 25% off; seniors over 62 get 5% off; and students get 20% off if they have purchased the $20 **Student Advantage Discount Card** (www.studentadvantage.com).

Reservations

Tickets for some Trailways and other buses can only be purchased immediately prior to departure. Greyhound, Megabus and BoltBus tickets can be bought online. You can print all tickets at home or in the case of Megabus or BoltBus, simply show ticket receipts through an email on a smartphone. Greyhound also allows customers to pick up tickets at the terminal using 'Will Call' service.

Seating is normally first come, first served. Greyhound recommends arriving an hour before departure to get a seat.

Car & Motorcycle

For information about driving, see the Driving in the USA chapter (p1185) and the Road Trips & Scenic Drives chapter (p38).

Local Transportation

Except in large US cities, public transportation is rarely the most convenient option for travelers, and coverage can be sparse to outlying towns and suburbs. However, it is usually cheap, safe and reliable. In addition, more than half the states in the nation have adopted 🖉511 as an all-purpose local-transportation help line.

Airport Shuttles

Shuttle buses provide inexpensive and convenient transport to/from airports in most cities. Most are 12-seat vans; some have regular routes and stops (which include the main hotels) and some pick up and deliver passengers 'door to door' in their service area. Costs range from $15 to $30 per person.

Bicycle

Some cities are more amenable to bicycles than others, but most have at least a few dedicated bike lanes and paths, and bikes can usually be carried on public transportation.

BUS FARES

Bus

Most cities and larger towns have dependable local bus systems, though they are often designed for commuters and provide limited service in the evening and on weekends. Costs range from free to between $1 and $3 per ride.

Subway & Train

The largest systems are in New York, Chicago, Boston, Philadelphia, Washington, DC, Chicago, Los Angeles and the San Francisco Bay Area. Other cities may have small, one- or two-line rail systems that mainly serve downtown.

Taxi

Taxis are metered, with flag-fall charges of around $2.50 to start, plus $2 to $3 per mile. They charge extra for waiting and handling baggage, and drivers expect a 10% to 15% tip. Taxis cruise the busiest areas in large cities; otherwise, it's easiest to phone and order one.

Tours

Hundreds of companies offer all kinds of organized tours of the USA; most focus on either cities or regions.

Backroads (🖉800-462-2848, 510-527-1555; www.backroads.com) Designs a range of active, multisport and outdoor-oriented trips for all abilities and budgets.

Here are some sample standard one-way adult fares and trip times on Greyhound:

SERVICE	PRICE ($)	DURATION (HR)
Boston–Philadelphia	57	7
Chicago–New Orleans	149	24
Los Angeles–San Francisco	59	8
New York–Chicago	119	18
New York–San Francisco	269	72
Washington, DC–Miami	155	25

Gray Line (☎800-472-9546; www.grayline.com) For those short on time, Gray Line offers a comprehensive range of standard sightseeing tours across the country.

Green Tortoise (☎800-867-8647, 415-956-7500; www.greentortoise.com) Offering budget adventures for independent travelers, Green Tortoise is famous for its sleeping-bunk buses. Most trips leave from San Francisco, traipsing through the West and nationwide.

Road Scholar (☎800-454-5768; www.roadscholar.org) For those aged 55 and older, this venerable nonprofit offers 'learning adventures' in all 50 states.

Train

Amtrak (☎800-872-7245; www.amtrak.com) has an extensive rail system throughout the USA, with Amtrak's Thruway buses providing connections to and from the rail network to some smaller centers and national parks. Compared with other modes of travel, trains are rarely the quickest, cheapest, timeliest or most convenient option, but they turn the journey into a relaxing, social and scenic all-American experience.

Amtrak has several long-distance lines traversing the nation east to west, and even more running north to south. These connect all of America's biggest cities and many of its smaller ones. Long-distance services (on named

trains) mostly operate daily on these routes, but some run only three to five days per week. See Amtrak's website for detailed route maps, as well as the Getting There & Around sections in this guide's regional chapters.

Commuter trains provide faster, more frequent services on shorter routes, especially the northeast corridor from Boston, MA, to Washington, DC. Amtrak's high-speed Acela Express trains are the most expensive, and rail passes are not valid on these trains. Other commuter rail lines include those serving the Lake Michigan shoreline near Chicago, IL, major cities on the West Coast and the Miami, FL, area.

CLASSES & COSTS

Amtrak fares vary according to the type of train and seating; on long-distance lines, you can travel in coach seats (reserved or unreserved), business class, or 1st class, which includes all sleeping compartments. Sleeping cars include simple bunks (called 'roomettes'), bedrooms with en-suite facilities and suites sleeping four with two bathrooms. Sleeping-car rates include meals in the dining car, which offers everyone sit-down meal service (pricey if not included). Food service on commuter lines, when it exists, consists of sandwich and snack bars. Bringing your own food and drink is recommended on all trains.

Various one-way, round-trip and touring fares are available from Amtrak, with discounts of 15% for seniors aged 62 and over and for students with a 'Student Advantage' card ($20) or an International Student Identity Card (ISIC), and 50% discounts for children aged two to 15 when accompanied by a paying adult. AAA members get 10% off. Web-only 'Weekly Specials' offer deep discounts on certain undersold routes.

Generally, the earlier you book, the lower the price. To get many of the standard discounts, you need to reserve at least three days in advance. If you want to take an Acela Express or Metroliner train, avoid peak commute times and aim for weekends.

Amtrak Vacations (☎800-268-7252; www.amtrak-vacations.com) offers vacation packages that include rental cars, hotels, tours and attractions. Air-Rail packages let you travel by train in one direction, then return by plane the other way.

RESERVATIONS

Reservations can be made any time from 11 months in advance up to the day of departure. Space on most trains is limited, and certain routes can be crowded, especially during summer and holiday periods, so it's a good idea to book as far in advance as you can; this also gives you the best chance of fare discounts.

TRAIN PASSES

Amtrak's USA Rail Pass offers coach-class travel for 15 ($439), 30 ($669) or 45 ($859) days, with travel limited to eight, 12 or 18 one-way 'segments,' respectively. A segment is *not* the same as a one-way trip. If reaching your destination requires riding more than one train (for example, getting from New York to Miami with a transfer in Washington, DC)

TRAIN FARES

Sample standard, one-way, adult coach-class fares and trip times on Amtrak's long-distance routes:

SERVICE	PRICE ($)	DURATION (HR)
Chicago–New Orleans	127	20
Los Angeles–San Antonio	182	29
New York–Chicago	101	19
New York–Los Angeles	248	68
Seattle–Oakland	163	23
Washington, DC–Miami	179	23

ALL ABOARD!

Who doesn't enjoy the steamy puff and whistle of a mighty locomotive as glorious scenery streams by? Dozens of historic narrow-gauge railroads still operate today as attractions, rather than as transportation. Most trains only run in the warmer months, and they can be extremely popular – so book ahead.

Here are some of the best:

1880 Train (☑866 367 1880; www.1880train.com; 103 Winter St; adult/child round trip US$21/US$12 Oct) Classic steam train running through rugged Black Hills country.

Cass Scenic Railroad (www.cassrailroad.com) Nestled in the Appalachian Mountains in West Virginia.

Cumbres & Toltec Scenic Railroad Depot (☑888-286-2737; www.cumbrestoltec.com; 5234 Hwy 285; adult/child from $89/49; ☒) Living, moving museum from Chama, NM, into Colorado's Rocky Mountains.

Durango & Silverton Narrow Gauge Railroad (☑970-247-2733, toll-free 877-872-4607; www.durangotrain.com; 479 Main Ave; adult/child return from $85/51; ☺departure at 8am, 8:45am, 9:30am; ☒) Ends at historic mining town Silverton in Colorado's Rocky Mountains.

Great Smoky Mountain Railroad (☑800-872-4681; www.gsmr.com; 226 Everett St, Bryson City; Nantahala Gorge trip adult/child 2-12yr from $55/31 ; ☺Mar-Dec) Rides from Bryson City, NC, through the Great Smoky Mountains.

Mount Hood Railroad (☑800-872-4661; www.mthoodrr.com; 110 Railroad Ave) Winds through the scenic Columbia River Gorge outside Portland, OR.

Skunk Train (☑707-964-6371; www.skunktrain.com; foot of Laurel St; adult/child from $20/10; ☒☒) Runs between Fort Bragg, CA, on the coast and Willits farther inland, passing through redwoods.

White Pass & Yukon Route Railroad (☑800-343-7373; www.wpyr.com; 231 2nd Ave; adult/child from US$115/57.50; ☺May-Sep) Klondike Gold Rush–era railroad has departures from Skagway, AK, and Fraser (British Columbia) and Carcross and Whitehorse (Yukon) in Canada.

Also worth riding are the vintage steam and diesel locomotives of Arizona's **Grand Canyon Railway** (☑800-843-8724, 928-635-4253; www.thetrain.com; Railway Depot, 233 N Grand Canyon Blvd; round trip adult/child from $75/45; ☒), New York State's **Delaware & Ulster Rail Line** (☑845-586-3877; www.durr.org; Hwy 28; adult/child $12/7; ☺11am & 2pm, Sat & Sun Jun-Nov, additional trips Thu & Fri Jul-Sep; ☒) and Colorado's **Pikes Peak Cog Railway**.

that one-way trip will actually use two segments of your pass.

Present your pass at an Amtrak office to pick up your ticket(s) for each trip. Reservations should be made by phone (call ☑800-872-7245, or ☑215-856-7953 from outside the USA) as far in advance as possible. Each

segment of the journey must be booked. At some rural stations, trains will only stop if there's a reservation. Tickets are not for specific seats, but a conductor on board may allocate you a seat. Business-class, 1st-class and sleeper accommodations cost extra and must be reserved separately.

All travel must be completed within 180 days of purchase. Passes are not valid on the Acela Express, Auto Train, Thruway motorcoach connections or the Canadian portion of Amtrak routes operated jointly with Via Rail Canada. Fares can double if you don't buy them at least three or four days in advance.

Behind the Scenes

SEND US YOUR FEEDBACK

We love to hear from travelers – your comments keep us on our toes and help make our books better. Our well-traveled team reads every word on what you loved or loathed about this book. Although we cannot reply individually to postal submissions, we always guarantee that your feedback goes straight to the appropriate authors, in time for the next edition. Each person who sends us information is thanked in the next edition – the most useful submissions are rewarded with a selection of digital PDF chapters.

Visit **lonelyplanet.com/contact** to submit your updates and suggestions or to ask for help. Our award-winning website also features inspirational travel stories, news and discussions.

Note: We may edit, reproduce and incorporate your comments in Lonely Planet products such as guidebooks, websites and digital products, so let us know if you don't want your comments reproduced or your name acknowledged. For a copy of our privacy policy visit lonelyplanet.com/privacy.

OUR READERS

Many thanks to the travelers who used the last edition and wrote to us with helpful hints, useful advice and interesting anecdotes:

Alexander Farrill, Alison Wolf, Berna Collier, Deborah Taylor, Diane Antonich, Dennis Klein, Eric Young, Evgeny Knyazev, Jamie McBride, Jeremy Crowley, Jeremy Lock, Julia Kimmerly, Lucinda Steer, Marla Black, Martin Aristia, Neal Salan, Nick Shchetko, Sonja Heuscher and Stefan Hey.

AUTHOR THANKS

Regis St Louis

This book is dedicated to the many talented editors I've worked with at Lonely Planet during the past 11 years. Special thanks to Suki Gear and Kathleen Munnelly, who have helped create many world-class guidebooks over the years. I consider myself blessed to have known you. Your dedication, creativity and good humor will be sorely missed. Wishing you all the best in future endeavours and a lifetime of rewarding adventures.

Amy C Balfour

Big thanks to my friends and experts in the Carolinas: Mike Stokes, Jay Bender, Dan Oden, Lori Bauswell, Jeff Otto, Paul Stephen, Josh Lucas, Barry Radcliffe, Patricia Robison, Lacy Davidson, Deborah Wright, Amy Marks, Paige Abbitt Schoenauer, Barbara Blue, Anna Schleunes, David Kimball, Noell and Jack Kimball and Jennifer Pharr Davis. In the Southwest, kudos to BLM maestro Chris Rose for his invaluable Nevada insights and Elvis knowledge; Justin Shephard, Tracer Finn, Jim Christian, Alex Amato, Mike Roe, Catrien van Assendelft, Lewis Pipkin, Sara Benson, Dan Westermeyer; fellow adventurers Sandee McGlaun, Lisa McGlaun, Paul Hanstedt; and Grand Canyon power-walker Karen Schneider.

Sandra Bao

Thanks to my husband Ben Greensfelder, who kept our home (mostly) intact while I was off researching. Kudos to my top-notch coordinating authors on the *Pacific Northwest* (whose information I adapted for this book), Celeste Brash and Brendan Sainsbury. A big hug to commissioning editor Suki Gear – thanks for the gig and best of luck in your coming life adventures. And finally, I could not have done this book without the support of my parents and brother.

Michael Benanav

Big thanks to Suki for convincing me to drive to all the little corners of New Mexico, a state that I love – and for her pitch-perfect blend of professionalism and humor. Also to Kelly and Luke, who always let me go, and always let me come back.

Greg Benchwick

Special thanks to my friend and commissioning editor Suki, my coordinating author and the rest of the Lonely Planet team.

Sara Benson

Thanks to Suki Gear, Sasha Baskett, Alison Lyall, Regis St Louis and everyone at Lonely Planet for making this book happen. I'm grateful to everyone I met on the road, from park rangers to beer geeks and foodies, who generously shared their local expertise. Big thanks to my Golden State friends and family, especially the Picketts, Starbins and Boyles. Jonathan, you kept on driving, even when you didn't know exactly where we'd end up – thank you.

Alison Bing

Heartfelt thanks to Lonely Planet guidebook mastermind Suki Gear, managing editor Sasha Baskett, and coauthor and fellow adventurer John Vlahides; to intrepid research companions Sahai Burrowes, Haemin Cho, Lisa Park, Yosh Han, Rebecca Bing, Tony Cockrell and Akua Parker; but above all to Marco Flavio Marinucci, who made a Muni bus ride into the trip of a lifetime.

Catherine Bodry

Thanks to Suki Gear for commissioning me, Celeste Brash for frantic last-minute help, and the gang at Lonely Planet for all their work.

Celeste Brash

Thanks to my family for helping me research beaches and mountains some days, and getting on at home without me on others. To old friends who I found scattered across Washington: Oliver Irwin, Kati Halmos Jones, Dan Jones, the Forster family and Jackie Capalan-Auerbach. And to new friends I made: too many to mention!

Gregor Clark

Thanks to all the generous fellow Vermonters who helped with this project, especially John McCright, Sarah Pope, Namik Sevlic, Saba Rizvi, Sarah Shepherd, Sue Heim and David Alles. Love and thanks as well to Gaen, for sharing my excitement about exploring that next side road, to Meigan for giving me hugs at deadline time and to Chloe, whose infectious love of climbing Mt Mansfield barefoot always makes me smile.

Lisa Dunford

So many kindred spirits on the Utah road – thanks to all, including Karla Player for the beautiful craftsmanship. Karen and John, it was great having a chat. And I'm so glad I got to reconnect with my friend Trista Kelin Rayner; wishing her and daughter Mechelle all the best.

Ned Friary

Thanks to all the people I met along the way who shared their tips, including the helpful folks staffing the counters at the local tourist offices. A special thanks to the rangers at the Cape Cod National Seashore and to Bob Prescott of the Massachusetts Audubon Society for sharing their one-of-a-kind insights.

Michael Grosberg

Special thanks to Carly Neidorf, my sometime trip and otherwise companion; my parents, Sheldon and Judy for advice; to Kristin Mitchell and Claire Shubik on Pittsburgh; Darrah Feldman on Milford; Rebbecca Steffan for Adirondacks help; Gregory Henderson in the Catskills; Julie Donovan in the Laurel Highlands; Nina Kelly in the Brandywine Valley; and Terri Dennison for Route 6 insight.

Paula Hardy

I'd like to thank the following for sharing the best of Connecticut and Rhode Island: Anne McAndrews, Dave Fairty, Pat and Wayne Brubaker, Rick Walker, Sanjeev Seereeram, Cinta Burgos, David King, Dave Helgerson, Harry Schwartz, Elizabeth MacAlister and the Preservation Society of Newport. Thanks also to the super Jennye Garibaldi and Mara Vorhees. Finally, thanks to Rob Smith for the laughs and letting me bring home Baggo.

Adam Karlin

Thank you to the Lonely Planet crew: Regis St Louis, for coordinating this beast; Michael Grosberg, the understanding, gracious and ever helpful coordinating author of *New York & the Mid-Atlantic's Best Trips*; the fabulous in-house team of Suki Gear, Bruce Evans, Alison Lyall, Emily Wolman and Jennye Garibaldi. Thanks to Mom and Dad for raising me the way they did, and to Rachel Houge, my wife, greatest fan and best friend. And finally, thank you Lonely Planet. You let me wander the world and write about it. That's a blessedly exciting and rewarding way to make a living.

Mariella Krause

Thanks to Suki Gear for an amazing year full of Lonely Planet goodness, and to Jay Cooke for getting me involved in the first place. And thanks to all the amazing people I met on the road who served as a constant reminder of what traveling is all about.

Carolyn McCarthy

I'm indebted to the good people of the Rocky Mountains. Special thanks to Lance and his Ouray friends for the bed and BBQ, Melissa and Steve for the Billings grand tour, the amazing Jones in Steamboat and Jennifer in Crested Butte. Richard and Rachel were the best drivers and companions. Thanks to Coraline, for steadfast motoring, and the generous Conan Bliss. Virtual beers go out to Regis St Louis, Greg Benchwick and Chris Pitts for being great to work with.

Brendan Sainsbury

Thanks to all the untold bus drivers, tourist info volunteers, restaurateurs, coffee baristas and indie punk rockers who helped me during my research. Special thanks to my wife Liz and seven-year-old son Kieran for their company on the road.

Caroline Sieg

Thanks to everyone who shared their tips with me and for the friendly conversations at lobster shacks, ski resorts and brewpubs. A very special thank you to the Schmidt family who keep me coming back to New England year after year.

Adam Skolnick

Thanks to Stephanie Greene, Dana McMahan, Carla Carlton, Phoebe Lipkis, Kristin Schofield and Louisville Basketball in Louisville; Jennifer Bohler and Shanna Henderson in Nashville; Nealy Dozier, Walter Thompson, Chloe Friedman, Lydia Hardy and Chi Bui in Atlanta; and Keith, Peggy and Melissa in Natchez. My love and appreciation go out to best Savannah buds Alicia Magee, Anna Cypris Jaubert, and (by proxy) Joe Bush. Thanks also to Suki Gear, Regis St Louis and the whole Lonely Planet team. It's a joy and privilege to work with and know you all!

Ryan Ver Berkmoes

Serious thanks to my parents, who believed in the value of road trips, and my sister, who always sided with demanding that the motel pool have a slide. In South Dakota I saw high-school winter formal date Sue Hegland (who's followed the unworn path out of Santa Cruz, CA, to the Plains). At Lonely Planet, wide open thanks to Suki and Regis for their hard work. And more special thanks go to unnamed Plains cooks and bartenders everywhere.

Mara Vorhees

My heart goes out to all the victims of the Boston Marathon bombings, all of the runners and the city as a whole. Patriots Day has always been about facing challenges with courage – it's now true more than ever. Bostonians love their city. Love will prevail.

Karla Zimmerman

Many thanks to Carrie Biolo, Lisa DiChiera, Lea Dooley, Jim DuFresne, Ruggero Fatica, Mark Fornek, Jonathan Hayes, April Ingle, Julie Lange, Kari Lydersen, Melissa McCarville, Betsy Riley and Neil Anderson, Susan Hayes Stephan, Andrea and Greg Thomson, Sara Zimmerman and Karen and Don Zimmerman. Thanks most to Eric Markowitz, the world's best partner-for-life, who indulges all my harebrained, pie-filled road trips. Sorry about the bug bites.

ACKNOWLEDGMENTS

Climate map data adapted from Peel MC, Finlayson BL & McMahon TA (2007) 'Updated World Map of the Köppen-Geiger Climate Classification', Hydrology and Earth System Sciences, 11, 1633-44.

Illustrations pp84-5, pp264-5 by Javier Martinez Zarracina; pp976-7 by Michael Weldon.

Cover photograph: Statue of Liberty, New York City, Travelpix.

THIS BOOK

This 8th edition of Lonely Planet's *USA* guidebook was researched and written by a stellar author team (see Our Writers), commissioned in Lonely Planet's Oakland office, and produced by the following:

Commissioning Editor
Suki Gear

Coordinating Editors
Briohny Hooper, Lorna Parkes

Senior Cartographer
Alison Lyall

Book Designer Jessica Rose

Managing Editors Sasha Baskett, Bruce Evans, Angela Tinson

Assisting Editors Alison Barber, Michelle Bennett, Elin Berglund, Janice Bird, Carolyn Boicos, Penny Cordner, Kate Daly, Samantha Forge, Carly Hall, Kate James, Kate Mathews, Alan Murphy, Susan Paterson, Monique Perrin, Alison Ridgway, Jeanette Wall, Simon Williamson

Assisting Cartographer
Rachel Imeson

Cover Research Naomi Parker

Thanks to Anita Banh, Ryan Evans, Larissa Frost, Genesys India, Jouve India, Trent Paton, Mazzy Prinsep, Gerard Walker

Index

Map Pages **000**
Photo Pages **000**

Map Pages **000**
Photo Pages **000**

Map Legend

Sights
- Beach
- Bird Sanctuary
- Buddhist
- Castle/Palace
- Christian
- Confucian
- Hindu
- Islamic
- Jain
- Jewish
- Monument
- Museum/Gallery/Historic Building
- Ruin
- Sento Hot Baths/Onsen
- Shinto
- Sikh
- Taoist
- Winery/Vineyard
- Zoo/Wildlife Sanctuary
- Other Sight

Activities, Courses & Tours
- Bodysurfing
- Diving
- Canoeing/Kayaking
- Course/Tour
- Skiing
- Snorkeling
- Surfing
- Swimming/Pool
- Walking
- Windsurfing
- Other Activity

Sleeping
- Sleeping
- Camping

Eating
- Eating

Drinking & Nightlife
- Drinking & Nightlife
- Cafe

Entertainment
- Entertainment

Shopping
- Shopping

Information
- Bank
- Embassy/Consulate
- Hospital/Medical
- Internet
- Police
- Post Office
- Telephone
- Toilet
- Tourist Information
- Other Information

Geographic
- Beach
- Hut/Shelter
- Lighthouse
- Lookout
- Mountain/Volcano
- Oasis
- Park
- Pass
- Picnic Area
- Waterfall

Population
- Capital (National)
- Capital (State/Province)
- City/Large Town
- Town/Village

Transport
- Airport
- BART station
- Border crossing
- Boston T station
- Bus
- Cable car/Funicular
- Cycling
- Ferry
- Metro/Muni station
- Monorail
- Parking
- Petrol station
- Subway/SkyTrain station
- Taxi
- Train station/Railway
- Tram
- Underground station
- Other Transport

Note: Not all symbols displayed above appear on the maps in this book

Routes
- Tollway
- Freeway
- Primary
- Secondary
- Tertiary
- Lane
- Unsealed road
- Road under construction
- Plaza/Mall
- Steps
- Tunnel
- Pedestrian overpass
- Walking Tour
- Walking Tour detour
- Path/Walking Trail

Boundaries
- International
- State/Province
- Disputed
- Regional/Suburb
- Marine Park
- Cliff
- Wall

Hydrography
- River, Creek
- Intermittent River
- Canal
- Water
- Dry/Salt/Intermittent Lake
- Reef

Areas

- Airport/Runway
- Beach/Desert
- Cemetery (Christian)
- Cemetery (Other)
- Glacier
- Mudflat
- Park/Forest
- Sight (Building)
- Sportsground
- Swamp/Mangrove

Brendan Sainsbury

Pacific Northwest An expat Brit from Hampshire, England, now living near Vancouver, Canada, Brendan is a Nirvana-loving, craft-beer-appreciating, outdoors-embracing, art-admiring, bus-utilizing coffee addict who had no problem finding like-minded souls in Seattle. He's been writing Lonely Planet guides for the last nine years and collecting notes on Seattle since 2009. He is the author of Lonely Planet's current guide to Seattle, and has contributed to the last three editions of this book.

Caroline Sieg

New England Caroline Sieg is a half-Swiss, half-American writer. Her relationship with New England began when she first lived in Boston and she began heading up to Maine for foodie treats and windswept coastal walks. She was delighted to return to the land of lobster and blueberry pies for Lonely Planet.

Read more about Caroline at:
lonelyplanet.com/members/carolinesieg

Adam Skolnick

The South Adam writes about travel, culture, health, and politics for Lonely Planet, *Outside, Men's Health*, and *Travel & Leisure*. He has coauthored over 20 Lonely Planet guidebooks to destinations in Europe, the US, Central America and Asia. He drove 5990 miles during his research trip for this guide, and will from here on blame the state of Kentucky for his growing bourbon dependency. Read more of his work at www.adamskolnick.com. Find him on Twitter and Instagram (@adamskolnick).

Ryan Ver Berkmoes

Great Plains Ryan first drove across the Great Plains with his family in the 1960s. Among his treasured memories are a pair of Wild West six-shooters he got at Wall Drugs in South Dakota and which he still has (in a box someplace, not under his pillow). Through the years he has never passed up a chance to wander the backroads of America's heartland, finding beauty and intrigue where you'd least expect it. Find more at www.ryanverberkmoes.com; @ryanvb.

Mara Vorhees

New England Born and raised in St Clair Shores, Michigan, Mara traveled the world (if not the universe) before finally settling in the Hub. She now lives in a pink house in Somerville, MA, with her husband, two kiddies and two kitties. She is the author of Lonely Planet guides *New England* and *Boston*, among others. Follow her adventures online at www.havetwinswilltravel.com.

Karla Zimmerman

Great Lakes A life-long Midwesterner, Karla is well-versed in the region's bea ballparks, breweries and pie shops. When she's not home in Chicago watc Cubs (or writing for magazines, websites and books), she's exploring. For this gig, she curled in Minnesota, caught a wave in Michigan, heard the curds squeak in Wisconsin and drank an embarrassing number of milkshakes in Ohio. Karla has written for several Lonely Planet guides to the USA, Canada, the Caribbean and Europe.

Ned Friary

New England Ned's college days were spent in Amherst, and traveling around his old stomping grounds always feels like a homecoming of sorts. He now lives on Cape Cod and has explored the region from one end to the other, searching out the best lobster roll, canoeing the marshes, and hiking and cycling the trails. His favorite moment while researching this book was catching the sunset over the Connecticut River valley from the summit at Skinner State Park.

Michael Grosberg

New York, New Jersey & Pennsylvania Thanks to an uncle and aunt's house upstate on the Delaware River in the southern Catskills, Michael has had a base to explore the region for two decades – when not home in Brooklyn, NYC, that is. No matter his love for the city, getaways are necessary and he has taken every opportunity to range far and wide in New York, New Jersey and Pennsylvania, from cross-country skiing in the Adirondacks or pitching a tent on an island in the St Lawrence to chowing down on ballpark food at a Pirates game in Pittsburgh and finding a classic diner in Jersey's Pine Barrens.

Paula Hardy

New England The British half of an American-British couple, Paula spends a lot of time hopping across the pond, torn between the bright lights of London town and Boston, where weekending in the New England countryside is a near-weekly activity. Research for this book though took her way off the beaten path into Connecticut's dairy barns, lobster shacks (yum!) and wine-tasting rooms, and to Rhode Island's tiny East Bay villages and breezy Block Island cycling trails, where lasting memories of Baggo defeats and Mudslide sundowners aren't easily forgotten.

Adam Karlin

Washington, DC & the Capital Region, The South Adam was born in Washington, DC, raised in rural Maryland and lives in New Orleans – a city he discovered on assignment for Lonely Planet. His love of travel stems from a love of place that was engendered by the tidal wetlands of the Mid-Atlantic. That need for wandering has pushed him overseas and across the world, and in the process he has written some 40 guidebooks for Lonely Planet, from the Andaman Islands to the Zimbabwe border.

Mariella Krause

Florida, Texas This is Mariella's fourth go-round with the USA guide, but her first time taking on two whole states. Having written both the Florida and Texas chapters, she now considers herself an expert on places with panhandles. Mariella will always consider Texas home, and she still sprinkles her language with Texanisms whenever possible, much to the amusement of those who don't consider 'y'all' a legitimate pronoun.

Carolyn McCarthy

Rocky Mountains Carolyn fell for the Rockies as an undergraduate at Colorado College, where she spent her first break camping in a blizzard in the Sangre de Christo Range. For this title she sampled the craft beers of four states, tracked wolves and heard even more Old West ghost stories. Carolyn has contributed to over 20 Lonely Planet titles, specializing in the American west and Latin America, and has written for *National Geographic, Outside, Lonely Planet Magazine* and other publications.

Christopher Pitts

Rocky Mountains Chris first drove west on a family road trip across the US and instantly fell in love with Colorado's star-studded nights. After four years at Colorado College, he decided to move up to Boulder for grad school – but only after mastering Chinese. Fifteen years, several continents and two kids later, he finally made it to the end of what is normally a 90-minute drive. Chris currently divides his time between writing, dad-dom and exploring Colorado's wilder corners. Visit him online at www.christopherpitts.net.

Greg Benchwick

Rocky Mountains A Colorado native, Greg's been all over the Centennial State. He has taught skiing in Vail, walked through fire pits in campsites across the state and attended journalism school in Boulder. He calls Denver's Highlands home.

Read more about Greg at:
lonelyplanet.com/members/gbenchwick

Sara Benson

California, Hawaii After graduating from college in Chicago, Sara jumped on a plane to San Francisco with just one suitcase and $100 in her pocket. She has bounced around California ever since, in between stints living in Asia and Hawaii and working as a national park ranger. The author of 55 travel and nonfiction books, Sara summited Sierra Nevada peaks, uncovered the Lost Coast and survived Death Valley while researching this guide. Follow her adventures online at www.indietraveler.blogspot.com and @indie_traveler on Twitter. Sara also wrote the USA's National Parks chapter.

Read more about Sara at:
lonelyplanet.com/members/sara_benson

Alison Bing

California During over 15 years in San Francisco, Alison has done everything you're supposed to do in the city and many things you're not, including falling in love on the Haight St bus and quitting a Silicon Valley day job to write 43 Lonely Planet guidebooks and commentary for magazines, mobile guides and other media. Join further adventures as they unfold on Twitter @AlisonBing.

Catherine Bodry

Alaska Catherine has spent the bulk of her life escaping her suburban upbringing and after 13 years considers Alaska home. She loves mountains and road trips, and spends a lot of time running the trails in the Chugach Range. Catherine has contributed to several Lonely Planet guides including *Alaska, Thailand, Canada* and *Pacific Northwest's Best Trips*.

Celeste Brash

Pacific Northwest Locals have a hard time believing it, but the beauty of the Pacific Northwest is what coaxed Celeste back to the US after 15 years in Tahiti. She was thrilled to explore and imbibe the treasures of her new backyard for this book, hike snowy peaks, look for orcas and get in touch with her cowboy and Indian roots. Find out more about Celeste and her award-winning writing at www.celestebrash.com.

Gregor Clark

New England Gregor fell in love with Vermont at age 16, while working as a summer conservation volunteer in the state's southwestern corner. He's made his home there since 1997, during which time he's explored the state from top to bottom. A lifelong polyglot with a degree in Romance languages, Gregor has written regularly for Lonely Planet since 2000, focusing on Europe and Latin America. He lives with his wife, two daughters, five cats and two chickens in Middlebury, VT.

Lisa Dunford

Southwest As one of Brigham Young's (possibly thousands of) great-great-granddaughters, Lisa was first drawn to Utah by ancestry. But it's the incredible red rocks that have kept her coming back for 10 years. She feels at home hiking through pinkish sand around Zion or Arches until her shoes are permanently stained, rounding a bend and being accosted by purple-crimson- and rose-colored cliffs, or witnessing brilliant wildflowers among the hardened dunes of the Grand Staircase-Escalante National Monument (GSENM). Lisa coauthored Lonely Planet's *Zion & Bryce Canyon National Parks*.

OUR STORY

A beat-up old car, a few dollars in the pocket and a sense of adventure. In 1972 that's all Tony and Maureen Wheeler needed for the trip of a lifetime – across Europe and Asia overland to Australia. It took several months, and at the end – broke but inspired – they sat at their kitchen table writing and stapling together their first travel guide, *Across Asia on the Cheap*. Within a week they'd sold 1500 copies. Lonely Planet was born.

Today, Lonely Planet has offices in Melbourne, London and Oakland, with more than 600 staff and writers. We share Tony's belief that 'a great guidebook should do three things: inform, educate and amuse'.

OUR WRITERS

Regis St Louis

Coordinating Author A Hoosier by birth, Regis grew up in a sleepy riverside town where he dreamed of big-city intrigue. In 2001 he settled in New York, which had all that and more. He has also lived in San Francisco and Los Angeles. Regis has crossed the country by train, bus and car, while visiting its remote corners. Favorite memories from his most recent trip include village hopping and fruit picking in eastern Long Island, mountainside rambles in the Catskills and crab feasting on the Chesapeake Bay. Regis has contributed to more than 40 Lonely Planet titles, including *New York City* and *Washington, DC*. For this guide, Regis wrote the Plan Your Trip and Understand sections.

Amy C Balfour

The South, Southwest A southerner of Scots-Irish descent, Amy has hiked, biked, paddled and gambled her way across the US. She's been visiting the Outer Banks since she was a child and never tires of running down Jockey's Ridge. In Arizona she enjoyed a return trip to Phantom Ranch, hiking down the South Kaibab Trail and up the Bright Angel. Amy has authored or coauthored more than 15 books for Lonely Planet and has written for *Backpacker, Every Day with Rachael Ray, Redbook, Southern Living* and *Women's Health*.

Sandra Bao

Pacific Northwest Sandra has lived in Buenos Aires, New York and California, but Oregon has become her final stop. Researching the Beaver state has been a highlight of Sandra's 14-year-long authoring career with Lonely Planet, which has covered four continents and dozens of guidebooks. She's come to appreciate the wondrous beauty of her home state, how much it has to offer both travelers and locals and how friendly people can be in tiny towns in the middle of nowhere.

Michael Benanav

Southwest Michael came to New Mexico in 1992, fell under its spell, and moved to a village in the Sangre de Cristo foothills, where he still lives. Since then he's spent years exploring the state's mountains, deserts and rivers as a wilderness instructor. Aside from his work for Lonely Planet, he's authored two nonfiction books and writes and photographs for magazines and newspapers. Check out his work at www.michaelbenanav.com.

OVER PAGE MORE WRITERS

Published by Lonely Planet Publications Pty Ltd
ABN 36 005 607 983
8th edition – March 2014
ISBN 978 1 74220 741 4
© Lonely Planet 2014   Photographs © as indicated 2014
10 9 8 7 6 5 4 3 2 1
Printed in Singapore